The Encyclopedia of Southern History

FLAGS
of the
CONFEDERATE STATES OF AMERICA

The Battle Flag

The Stars and Bars

The First Official Flag

The Second Official Flag

The Battle Flag and Naval Jack

THE
Encyclopedia of
SOUTHERN
HISTORY

Edited by

DAVID C. ROLLER and ROBERT W. TWYMAN

Avery O. Craven
Dewey W. Grantham, Jr.
GENERAL CONSULTANTS

Paul V. Crawford
CONSULTING CARTOGRAPHER

LOUISIANA STATE UNIVERSITY PRESS
Baton Rouge and London

Copyright © 1979 by Louisiana State University Press
All rights reserved
Manufactured in the United States of America
All state maps copyright by Rand McNally & Company,
R.L. No. 73–S–73

Designer: Dwight Agner
Type face: VIP Caledonia
Typesetter: Graphic Composition, Inc.
Printer and binder: Kingsport Press, Inc.

LIBRARY OF CONGRESS CATALOGING IN PUBLICATION
DATA

Main entry under title:

Encyclopedia of Southern history.

Includes index.
1. Southern States—History—Dictionaries.   I. Roller,
David C., 1937–   II. Twyman, Robert W., 1919–
F207.7.E52   975′.003   79–12666
ISBN 0–8071–0575–9

CONTENTS

MAPS

TABLES

PREFACE

PREPARATION of an encyclopedia of the South requires no justification. In a nation in which regionalism has played so crucial a historical role, no region's history has been studied more widely or researched more deeply. Yet there has been no authoritative and comprehensive reference work devoted to the subject. We hope that this volume will meet that need.

After examining numerous historical encyclopedias and dictionaries, we envisioned this encyclopedia as a single-volumed desk reference of roughly one million words chosen to answer those questions about the South most frequently asked by scholars, teachers, students, and laymen. We knew entries would have to be brief, very brief. For those users desiring additional information, each entry would have to include a reasonably complete bibliography. Collectively, the subjects selected for individual articles would have to encompass the history of the region from earliest times to the present. During the past twelve years, *The Encyclopedia of Southern History* has mushroomed beyond its anticipated length. A few topics have been dropped because of a reappraisal of their significance, but additional subjects worthy of inclusion continue to be identified; and time after time the coverage of a given subject has been expanded because it could not adequately be discussed within the word lengths initially assigned to it. Nevertheless, the finished volume remains very much as we first envisioned it and very visibly shaped by the parameters we first assigned to it.

There are several competing definitions of the territory known as "the South," but we have defined it as encompassing the District of Columbia and those states that accepted the practice of slavery in 1860. Thus we have included within this volume materials relating to Delaware, Kentucky, Maryland, and Missouri as well as Alabama, Arkansas, Florida, Georgia, Louisiana, Mississippi, North and South Carolina, Tennessee, Texas, Virginia, and West Virginia. To the regret of some, we have not included Oklahoma. We understand that some scholars will quarrel with this definition, but no definition of the South enjoys a consensus (see the article **"South, boundaries of"**).

Because of the immense diversity of historical experience within the South, we reserved at the outset of this project a fifth of the volume's space for articles on each of the region's sixteen states. The state histories no longer fill quite that proportion of the volume, but they remain one of its principal features and attractions. After reading a general article on such subjects as the American Revolution, slavery, Reconstruction, populism, or World War II, readers will find additional information on each of these subjects in the state histories. Thus, in addition to being able to trace the unique character of each southern state from its initial settlement to the present, users of the *Encyclopedia* will be able to study the way in which general historical phenomena were experienced by people in different states.

Against the advice of several consultants, we have included biographical articles on hundreds of southerners. We could not have an article on every person our research uncovered unless we gave the bulk of the volume over to biographies. To conserve space we have therefore omitted biographical articles of some persons whose importance stems solely from an event or an achievement covered separately within the *Encyclopedia*. We have, however, made an effort to include many other significant figures about whom little has been written or about whom information is difficult to obtain. This category includes many southern women and blacks. To provide the necessary space for such persons, articles dealing with such famous and well-known figures as Robert E. Lee and Woodrow Wilson are often deliberately brief, tend to be interpretative in nature, and emphasize bibliographic materials. Although some governors are discussed in separate articles, for easy reference a complete list of governors is found at the conclusion of each state's history along with terms of office and party affiliations.

We believed short biographical entries that discussed the work and achievements of major scholars of the South would be useful in answering the historiographical questions of our readers, but deciding which historians to include proved especially difficult. Ulrich B. Phillips was, for example, an automatic selection, but where should a limit be established for the many hundreds of individuals who have contributed to our knowledge and understanding of the South? With our apologies to anyone who takes exception to our list of notable scholars, we arbitrarily decided to admit only historians who had completed their academic careers. Our reasoning here was that, though many of these are living historians who may well continue to make significant contributions to the field, we at least had a sufficient body of their work to attempt an appraisal of its character and importance.

Several hundred towns and cities have been noted as separate entries on the basis of either their past significance or their present importance as centers of cultural, political, or economic activity. No consistent population figure could be used across the South to gauge the present importance of an urban center. A city of 25,000 people might be a relatively major center in Virginia, but in a more urbanized state like Texas it often made little sense to include every such city. Thus a floating standard has been used in an effort to measure a city's importance relative to its locale. All city articles list population figures from the 1970 census and mention the city's major newspapers. The region's principal newspapers, both past and present, receive additional coverage in separate articles.

Of particular interest to amateur and professional historians alike should be the articles on numerous state and regional associations devoted to the study of the South. These range from the Filson Club to the Southern Speech Communication Association and from the Association for the Study of Afro-American Life and History to the Daughters of the Republic of Texas. These articles deal not only with the history of each group, but also give its address and deal with its awards, activities, journals, and other publications. Indeed, users of the *Encyclopedia* should note that coverage of the *Journal of Southern History*, for example, will be found in the text under the entry for its sponsoring organization, the Southern Historical Association. Similarly, the articles on major libraries, manuscript collections, and universities have been designed primarily to aid the practicing historian to locate primary research materials.

Teachers, students, and history buffs, on the other hand, may find more useful the topical articles, for instance, those on colloquial expressions and economic and geographical terms. We have allotted additional coverage to such varied topics as literature, reptiles, and geology of the South and to individual industries and agricultural crops. We hope our volume will serve to encourage a user's interest in the South and to guide him or her toward additional reading.

Cross-references within the text identify other articles with additional information on the same or a related topic. These cross-referenced topics appear in small capitals and without other designation.

For readers with questions that go beyond the scope of this volume, we trust that our bibliographic notes will make *The Encyclopedia of Southern History* a valuable research guide. We have sought to indicate at the end of most articles a reasonably complete list of references. Although they cannot displace more exhaustive and more specialized bibliographies, manuscript guides, and indexes, we hope that our bibliographic notes may save many a scholar yet another visit to a library reference shelf.

During the dozen years we have spent planning and preparing this volume, by far the most pleasant reward has been the privilege of working and corresponding with so many helpful and warm-hearted people in the profession. We have in the process acquired a heavy burden of indebtedness. At the very top of the list must be the contributors, some 1,130 in all, representing educational institutions from every section of the United States and several foreign countries, who gave of their time and expertise just for the satisfaction of seeing a useful volume completed. Their words of encouragement and sense of humor helped to brighten many a difficult period. The contributor's name is at the end of each of the articles that he or she wrote. (All articles to which no name is attached were written by the editors.) We feel an extra degree of gratitude toward those contributors who expressed their faith by donating their time and energies in the earliest days of the project, when there was still no assurance that the volume would even see completion. Fine scholars like Edgar T. Thompson (Duke), Joseph G. E. Hopkins (Scribner's), David Skaggs (Bowling Green), Holman Hamilton (Kentucky), Sanford W. Higginbotham (Rice), and of course our two outstanding consultants, Avery O. Craven (Chicago) and Dewey W. Grantham (Vanderbilt), fall in this category, and there are no words to express adequately our appreciation.

Other scholars who, in addition to writing one or more articles, contributed advice in their areas of expertise were Steven A. Channing, Thomas D. Clark, Richard N. Current, Robert F. Durden, Clement Eaton, Willard Gatewood, R. Don Higginbotham, Robert W. Johannsen, Joseph H. Parks, Louis Rubin, James I. Robertson, Jr., Theodore Saloutos, Lewis Simpson, Kenneth M. Stampp, John F. Stover, Emory M. Thomas, Frank E. Vandiver, Bell I. Wiley, and T. Harry Williams.

A special word also should be said for Bowling

Green State University, which paid for some of the maps, provided some of the student assistants and secretarial help, and permitted us to use our faculty franking privileges for the project, a not inconsiderable financial assist. We are likewise especially grateful to the Louisiana State University Press (including its former director Charles East), which agreed to put its considerable reputation in southern history behind the project. Leslie Phillabaum, Dwight Agner, Beverly Jarrett, and Martha L. Hall gave invaluable advice throughout; and Marie Carmichael, who read the entire manuscript, proved to be little short of a genius in catching errors undetected by us. It is a far better volume because of her.

Others who aided in ways "above and beyond" were Pat Bogni Farrand, Nedra Bradley, Connie Montgomery, Cindy Smith, Judy Gilbert, Jo Mahoney, Phyllis Wulff, and Kathy Bachman, who together typed the thousands of letters and countless pages of manuscript that the project demanded. Edmund Danziger, Ray Yeager, Ron Seavoy, Robert Keefe, Alvar Carlson, all fine scholars on our own campus at Bowling Green, gave expert advice in their respective fields.

The individual state maps are reproduced by a purchase agreement with Rand McNally & Company. Except for these maps, the Landforms of the Southern States (by E. Raisz), and the cross-sectional diagram of the black belt (by Sam Hilliard), all maps were prepared by graduate student cartographers Jeffrey C. Patton, William R. Doslak, and Mark Nixon under the guidance of the highly capable Paul V. Crawford, Bowling Green State University cartographer. Since these maps and most tables were prepared under our direction and from information and statistics provided by us, we assume responsibility for any errors found therein. Patty Wise (Mrs. David G.), Toledo, Ohio, prepared the colorplate for the Confederate flags.

Student and graduate assistants who at different times over the twelve-year period worked loyally for the project include John Allton, Marie Apidone, Marie Arps, Mark Arizmendi, Jean Ashburn, Rod Bauer, Richard Beebe, Cathy Brady, Mary Bustamante, Cheryl Clausen, Peter Alan Cowie, Joyce Anraku Culek, Susan Deshler, Dennis J. Doughty, Harry Edwards, Kathy Ernsthausen, Anne Eshleman, Chris Geist, Linda Grugel, Joy Hillis, Royal Jackson, Carol Jacobson, Lauri Jones, Kenneth Kreuger, Rick Ketzenbarger, Ann Marie Kosten, Kristen C. Lantz, Joyce Niehaus, Teri McAlpin, Toni Moore, Brian Pavlac, Fred Pepple, Gary Piper, Greg Patterson, Carole S. Pierce, Kamila Plesmid, Gail Lewellan, Jo Sheets, Larry Snavley, John Sobczak, Nancy Suhr, Ruth Tisher, Jeffrey Welsh, Pat Wilderman, Kathleen Williams, Stephen Wise, and Wendy Zimpfer. The devotion and enthusiasm of these young people for the project were an inspiration.

Finally, the monumental task of keeping up to date the file records on every article and every contributor, of keeping track of deadlines, of sending reminders, and of channeling the staggering volume of mail was performed by Betty Jane Twyman with a competence and loyalty that could have been inspired only by true love.

DAVID C. ROLLER
ROBERT W. TWYMAN

The Encyclopedia of Southern History

A

ABBEVILLE, S.C. (pop. 5,515), produces textiles and serves as a market for Piedmont grain and cotton growers. It was founded by HUGUENOT settlers in the eighteenth century and named after a town in France. A very early secessionist meeting (November 22, 1860) and the last meeting of the Confederate cabinet (May 2, 1865) both assembled here. Consequently, the town is sometimes called "the cradle and grave of the Confederacy."

ABBOTT, ROBERT SENGSTACKE (1868–1940), was born in the Georgia SEA ISLANDS, the son of slaves, and became, in the estimate of Gunnar Myrdal, "the greatest single force in [modern] Negro journalism." Under the telling influence of elitist, house-servant ancestry and a Hampton Institute education, Abbott went forward in the tradition of BOOKER T. WASHINGTON, driven with a petit bourgeois zeal to make good and to uplift his people. In 1905 he founded the Chicago *Defender*, which by 1920 stood as the most influential black newspaper in the United States. Abbott emerged as one of the most militant critics of American race relations; and the *Defender*, circulated from hand to hand like abolitionist literature, became a seditious item in the South, its shipments confiscated and its readers persecuted. Abbott was forced to travel in disguise when he visited his Georgia relatives. Abbott not only denounced the South, but he heralded the North, especially Chicago, as the promised land. However exaggerated such an assessment, there can be no doubt that the *Defender*'s "Great Northern Drive," as Abbott proclaimed it, often worked as a catalyst in sponsoring the momentous NEGRO MIGRATION. With the disappointment of the "black metropolis" and the despair of the Great Depression, Abbott became more introspective and less sanguine about a northern solution to the race problem. By the time he died, he had long since counseled blacks to remain in the South and once again to embrace self-help.

See R. Ottley, *The Lonely Warrior* (1955); F. G. Detweiler, *The Negro Press* (1922); G. S. Schuyler, *Fifty Years of Progress in Negro Journalism* (1950); H. R. Cayton and S. C. Drake, *Black Metropolis* (1945); A. H.

Spear, *Black Chicago* (1967); and M. P. T. Lochard, *Phylon* (Summer, 1947).

WALTER B. WEARE
University of Wisconsin, Milwaukee

ABERDEEN, MD. (pop. 12,375), named for the city in Scotland, was founded in 1800 and incorporated in 1892. Located approximately 30 miles east of Baltimore on the upper Chesapeake Bay, it was the birthplace of both Edwin Booth and JOHN WILKES BOOTH. It remained a small farming and cannery village until World War II. The location there of the U.S. Army's Aberdeen Proving Grounds and the postwar suburban growth of Baltimore combined to triple the city's population during the 1950s.

ABERNATHY, RALPH (1926–). MARTIN LUTHER KING's alter ego or "right hand," he played a supportive role in the CIVIL RIGHTS MOVEMENT from 1955 until 1968. The son of a middle-class farmer, Abernathy grew up in rural Alabama, served in World War II, and went to college, graduating in 1951 with a master's degree in sociology. Preaching, however, was his first love, and he accepted a call to Montgomery's largest black church, First Baptist. In December, 1954, he received the first notification of Rosa Parks's arrest (MONTGOMERY BUS BOYCOTT), but recognizing King's potential for leadership Abernathy stepped aside. He helped found the SOUTHERN CHRISTIAN LEADERSHIP CONFERENCE, served as King's perennial jail partner in the 1960s, and organized both Operation Breadbasket and the Poor People's Campaign. King chose Abernathy as his successor; following the assassination, Abernathy's first task was establishing his leadership while holding the SCLC together. Lacking both the charismatic personality and oratorical talents of King, Abernathy took over during a period of declining interest in civil rights due in part to increasing concern for law and order. As a result he failed to raise sufficient funds, nearly resigned in 1972, and has generally slipped from public view.

See C. C. Douglas, *Ebony* (Jan., 1970); P. Good, *New York Times Magazine* (May 26, 1968); and B. Carter, *Reporter* (Sept. 28, 1961).

DUNCAN R. JAMIESON
University of Alabama

ABERNETHY, THOMAS PERKINS (1890–1975), a historian, was born in Lowndes County, Ala., and received his A.B. degree (1912) from the College of Charleston and M.A. (1915) and Ph.D. (1922) from Harvard. He taught at Vanderbilt (1921–1922), Chattanooga (1922–1928), Alabama (1928–1930), Virginia (1930–1961), Texas (1961–1962), and Arizona (1962–1964). Abernethy began his writing career against the background of World War I and postwar disillusionment. C. A. Beard's *Economic Interpretation of the Constitution* was new (1913), and J. F. Jameson's *American Revolution Considered as a Social Movement* was soon to come (1925). Throughout his career, Abernethy evinced similar interests in democracy's origins, meaning, and operation. Studying under Frederick Jackson Turner, Abernethy dissented from his mentor's "frontier thesis." Turner, reared on the frontier, believed American democracy originated there; Abernethy, with a different background, strongly questioned this. In three case studies—*Formative Period in Alabama* (1922), *From Frontier to Plantation in Tennessee* (1932), and *Three Virginia Frontiers* (1940)—Abernethy scrutinized the role of wealthy speculators (whom Turner neglected) and the frontier's reputedly democratic nature. Abernethy concluded that, in the South, elements of democracy and aristocracy arose simultaneously. In over a dozen articles and in *Western Lands in the American Revolution* (1937), *The Burr Conspiracy* (1954), and *The South in the New Nation* (1961), he reiterated and amplified his basic tenet of the beneficial effects of an aristocratic element produced by early speculators.

RAY GRANADE
Ouachita Baptist University

ABLEMAN V. BOOTH (21 Howard 506 [1858]), a major assertion of the supremacy of the federal judiciary over the judicial power of the states, arose from the controversies over slavery. Sherman Booth, an abolitionist newspaper editor, was convicted in a federal court in Wisconsin of violating the Fugitive Slave Act of 1850 (FUGITIVE SLAVE LAWS). A Wisconsin state judge intervened, issuing a writ of habeas corpus to free Booth. In the ensuing jurisdictional struggles, the supreme court of Wisconsin not only issued a writ of habeas corpus to thwart the authority of the federal district court, but also attempted to circumvent the Supreme Court of the United States. Thus, when the highest federal court issued a writ of error, the supreme court of Wisconsin ordered its clerk to ignore it. In an unprecedented action, the attorney general of the United States provided an unofficial copy of the record of the action of the Wisconsin supreme court to the U.S. Supreme Court, which entered this unofficial copy on its docket and acted upon it as if it had been officially returned by the clerk of the Wisconsin supreme court. In 1858, the U.S. Supreme Court held the Wisconsin attempts at thwarting its jurisdictional authority to be unconstitutional. Paradoxically, the Wisconsin legislature, in adopting resolutions condemning the decision, invoked states' rights doctrines that were similar to the antinationalist arguments of southern leaders who were considering secession.

See C. G. Haines, *Role of Supreme Court* (1944); and H. V. Ames (ed.), *State Documents on Federal Relations* (1900).

JOHN R. SCHMIDHAUSER
University of Southern California

ABRAHAM LINCOLN QUARTERLY (1940–1952) was the first regular publication of the Abraham Lincoln Association in Springfield, Ill. Published between March, 1940, and December, 1952, the *Quarterly* succeeded the *Bulletin of the Abraham Lincoln Association*, which was published irregularly between 1923 and 1939. Contributors to the *Quarterly*, in addition to many well-known Lincoln specialists, included the three editors, who also served successively as executive directors of the Abraham Lincoln Association: Paul Angle (1940–1945), William Barringer (1945–1947), and Roy E. Basler (1947–1952). The appearance of articles in the *Quarterly* often served to announce the imminent publication of a new biography of Abraham Lincoln or some other major work in which Lincoln was a prominent figure. The *Quarterly* also published the texts of previously unknown Lincoln documents and contained news of interest to collectors of Lincolniana. Financial hardship, plus the publication of the multivolumed *Collected Works of Abraham Lincoln* (sponsored by the association), ended the need for its publication program in 1952. The Abraham Lincoln Association was reactivated in 1961, but did not revive a regular publication program.

WILLIAM K. ALDERFER
Illinois State Historical Library

ABSENTEE BALLOTS permit a qualified voter away from his legal residence or confined for some reason on election day to vote by mail or in person prior to the election. The first extensive use originated during the Civil War to permit voting by Confederate and Union military personnel. All but four Confederate states (Arkansas, Louisiana, Mississippi, and Texas) provided for voting in the field. Extension to civilians occurred mainly after 1900. All states and the District of Columbia authorize absentee voting by civilian and military personnel in general elections, but two southern states, Alabama and South Carolina, permit only certain groups of civilians to vote absentee. Alabama limits absentee voting to the physically disabled, seamen, and persons away on business; South Carolina allows only students away at school to vote absentee.

A 1970 act of Congress modified the restrictions of Alabama and South Carolina in presidential elections. In voting for president, all states must provide absentee ballots to persons who apply as late as the seventh day before the election and must accept them until the polls close on election day. The states must provide for absentee registration. A voter who moves within 30 days of the election must be permitted to vote in person or by absentee ballot from his former residence.

Voting irregularities have often been associated with absentee ballots. In 1949, V. O. KEY found that absentee voting did not create difficulty in the South except in two states. In western North Carolina and southwestern Virginia, where Democrats and Republicans competed on approximately equal terms, control of the election machinery by Democrats enabled them to use absentee ballots to their advantage. Following the 1938 election the North Carolina state board of elections recommended drastic revision of the law because of corrupt election practices. The legislature retained absentee voting only for general elections, because Democrats were hard pressed by Republicans in the western counties and needed "a little leeway." Abuses continued, and in 1947 the board unsuccessfully recommended complete repeal of the civilian absentee ballot law. Virginia took no action to correct abuses.

See J. H. Benton, *Voting in Field* (1915); V. O. Key, Jr., *Politics, Parties, and Pressure Groups* (1964) and *Southern Politics* (1949); Council of State Governments, *Book of States* (1970–1971, 1972–1973, & 1974–1975) and *Modernizing Electoral Systems* (1973); Congressional Research Service, Library of Congress, *Absentee Registration and Voting* (1973).

FREDERIC D. OGDEN
Eastern Kentucky University

ACADEMIC FREEDOM is the right of members of educational institutions to engage in the activities necessary to the accumulation, maintenance, and communication of ideas and the results of research. The phrase refers most directly to the actions of members of the faculty in higher education while working within their own disciplines. Generally regarded as involved more tangentially are the rights of professors outside their own area of expertise or their academic roles. One of the most serious, continuing questions for education in the South has been whether academic freedom upholds or denies to an institution the right of holding and advocating views, especially religious ones.

Colonial colleges, created by denominations, came to be viewed as arms of the ecclesiastical bodies, although religious character and control were frequently weak. Power was in the hands of boards of absentee laymen, which exercised rigid control over the schools and the lives of teachers and students. Because ideological controversies were not prevalent and the concept of academic freedom was still embryonic, the major cause for controversy was the attempt of faculties to gain more control over internal governance and more freedom in personal affairs.

During the early nineteenth century it was assumed, even by faculty members, that a teacher at an institution should support the position of its administration. Men applied for, and were awarded, positions on the basis of agreement on the important questions. If they later came into conflict, professors naturally moved to a more congenial climate of opinion. The almost universal opposition to abolitionism of southern faculty members was thus dependent more upon their sincere convictions than upon university pressure or the legal limitations upon civil liberties. In the proliferating denominational colleges the professors, mostly ministers, were dedicated rather than coerced supporters of the creed and practice that the schools inculcated. The new state universities were usually staffed and controlled by Northern-trained champions of the Enlightenment, heavily Federalist and Unitarian. Few instances of overt infringement of teachers' rights emerged because the presidents held autocratic powers, because the faculties were largely loyal, and because intellectual objectivity of the institutions was not considered desirable.

The rise of Darwinism brought new troubles, however (EVOLUTION CONTROVERSY). As professors at the sectarian colleges and seminaries attempted to reconcile Christian teachings to the discoveries of science, some of them moved far from the traditional interpretations. Conservative denominational leaders insisted that the purpose of the schools was violated if its teachers, particularly those who treated religious topics, did not remain within the bounds of sectarian orthodoxy. Liberals contended that the creedal measurement was too strict and that teachers should be required only to remain "Christian." In a few cases (*i.e.*, JAMES WOODROW at the Presbyterian Seminary in Columbia, S.C.) the question of doctrinal agreement and of how much latitude could be allowed was determined at a "trial" by a denominational court. In the struggle some institutions increasingly resisted denominational control and even broke all ties (Vanderbilt); others, however, followed the opposite extreme and limited faculty freedom and dismissed heterodox teachers.

As the scientific spirit spread into philosophy, ethics, and sociology, the tendency was to evaluate dogmas and religion critically, and even to create substitutionary religious systems. By the early 1920s, conservative religious leaders began to insist that a few professors were using tax-supported institutions to attack traditional creeds and inculcate alternative religions in violation of the First Amendment. Extreme fundamentalists wanted laws to prohibit any teaching of evolution, but moderates asked only for official recognition that the separation of church and state required that state institutions neither support nor attack religion. The author of Tennessee's evolution law may have favored the fundamentalist plan, but the measure was probably passed as the moderates' statement of legislative opinion. The SCOPES TRIAL hopelessly confused the issue, but the state supreme court decision left the law on the books only as a warning against direct attacks on religion by public schools. In 1968 the U.S. Supreme Court (*Epperson* v. *Arkansas*) ruled a similar Arkansas law unconstitutional and removed this restriction upon teaching. The controversy has served to further discredit religion in academia.

Social, intellectual, and scientific developments had broken down the control of single philosophies over both state and private institutions. Faculty members began to challenge regional and institutional positions on race, politics, and ethics and maintained their position by appeals to academic freedom and by the support of intellectual and educational hierarchies. Even when an individual lost his job in such a contest, he frequently was rewarded with a better position at a more prestigious institution—usually outside the South. Academic freedom, tenure, and due process stands taken by professional and accreditation associa-

tions and, more recently, the courts have extended the teachers' protection. The increased size of institutions and the changed role of administrators have reduced the ability of college presidents to set the intellectual tone on campus. Limits on freedom, where they exist, are enforced mainly through selective hiring and promotion practices of middle administrators, and confrontations take on the appearance of due process disputes.

See C. Eaton, *Freedom of Thought* (1964); W. Gatewood, *Controversy in the Twenties: Fundamentalism* (1969); R. Hofstadter and W. P. Metzger, *Development of Academic Freedom* (1955); and G. Kennedy (ed.), *Evolution and Religion* (1957).

CHARLES F. OGILVIE
University of Tennessee, Martin

ACADIANS, anglicized as CAJUNS, now inhabitants of southern Louisiana, were originally early seventeenth-century French colonists in Acadia, an area encompassing modern Nova Scotia. The British capture of Nova Scotia in 1713 ultimately resulted in the expulsion of the Acadians in 1755. Well over 6,000 of them were exiled, their homes destroyed, and their families ruthlessly separated. Fully half of them were sent to southern colonies, where they were met with suspicion and open hostility. The Acadians generally emigrated from the southern British colonies rapidly, and by 1760 few traces of them remained along the seaboard. Many drifted to Louisiana, welcomed there as important increments to that sparsely populated region. By 1790 some 4,000 Acadians were settled along the lower Mississippi River. Gradually, many moved to the bayous and grasslands of south-central Louisiana, remote from New Orleans and difficult of access until recently, and still the heart of Acadian country. Although under first Spanish and then American control, Acadians long resisted assimilation. Fishermen, farmers, and cattle herders, their rural isolation, their distinctive language, and their large but closely knit families functioned to preserve an extraordinary degree of cultural integrity, rich in tradition and folklore, which successfully absorbed elements of other cultures. Although modern forces have modified their patterns of living, the Acadians yet retain much of their traditional cohesiveness today.

See A. G. Doughty, *Acadian Exile* (1916); E. Lauvrière, *Tragedie d'un Peuple* (1923); E. McCrady, *History of South Carolina* (1899); J. T. Scharf, *History of Maryland* (1879); C. Gayarré, *History of Louisiana* (1903); C. J. Milling, *Exile Without End* (1943); O. W. Winzerling, *Acadian Odyssey* (1955); A. H. Clark, *Geography of Early Nova Scotia* (1968); J. A. Robertson, *Louisiana Under Spain, France, and the U.S.* (1911); L. C. Post, *Cajun*

Country (1962); C. Ramsey, *Cajuns on Bayous* (1957); C. Millard, *Virginia Magazine of History and Biography* (July, 1932); M. B. Hamer, *Journal of Southern History* (May, 1938); A. Begnaud, *Louisiana History* (Winter, 1964); C. L. Saucier, *Louisiana Historical Quarterly* (April, 1951); and F. S. Costa, *Southwestern Louisiana Journal* (Winter, 1958).

WILLIAM H. LONGTON
University of Toledo

ADAIR, JAMES (1709?–1783?), best known for his *History of the American Indians* (London, 1775), was a Scotch-Irish immigrant who established himself as a trader among the CHICKASAW INDIANS in the 1740s and 1750s. At the request of Governor James Glen of South Carolina, he helped instigate a revolt of the powerful CHOCTAW INDIANS from their alliance with the French, but the opportunity to win them over to the English side was bungled, to Adair's great disgust. Despite his alienation from the colonial authorities, Adair periodically came to their assistance, as in 1760, when he led a body of Chickasaws during the Cherokee War. An acute observer, Adair preferred life among the Indians to life with his countrymen, and his book is an important ethnographic source for the Indians of the Southeast.

See J. Adair, *History of American Indians* (1775); and E. Washburn, in L. H. Leder (ed.), *Colonial Legacy* (1973), III, for primary and secondary sources.

WILCOMB E. WASHBURN
Smithsonian Institution

ADAMS, HERBERT BAXTER (1850–1901), was one of the pioneer academic historians in the United States. After doing graduate work in Germany, he spent his career at Johns Hopkins University (1876–1901). There he propounded his "germ theory" of the European origins of American institutions and, illustrating the theory, introduced the German seminar system into American graduate studies. More important than his scholarship were such professional activities as his teaching; building up collections of manuscripts and other historical materials; establishing (1883) and editing the Johns Hopkins University Studies in Historical and Political Science; and helping found the American Historical Association (1884).

Adams had a pronounced impact on southern higher education and on the study of the history of the South. Many of his students were southerners; some produced the first academic studies of the region's history. Subsequently teaching at southern institutions, several (*e.g.*, JOHN S. BASSETT, William P. Trent, and George Petrie) spread the new gospel of a relatively disciplined, dispassionate study of history to a new generation of southern historians. After Adams' death, leadership in advanced study of southern history passed to WILLIAM ARCHIBALD DUNNING at Columbia University.

See W. H. Stephenson, *Southern History* (1964); W. S. Holt (ed.), *Historical Scholarship* (1938); *Herbert B. Adams* (1902); J. J. Mathews, *Journal of Southern History* (Feb., 1965); B. D. Saunders, "Herbert Baxter Adams" (Ph.D. dissertation, University of Texas, 1975).

PETER WALLENSTEIN
University of Toronto

ADAMS, JOHN, ADMINISTRATION (1797–1801). John Adams was never truly popular in the South. In both 1796 and 1800 he received only a dozen southern electoral votes, representing 25 to 30 percent of the region's electorate. As president, however, Adams enjoyed a substantial temporary rise in public esteem during the quasi war with France. As the French crisis unfolded after 1796, three southern attitudes toward Adams were apparent. Most numerous were the "pure" Republicans, denying any real French threat and opposing military preparations, the Alien and Sedition Acts, and war taxes. They considered the administration anti-French, gave Adams no credit for maintaining peace, and supported Thomas Jefferson eagerly in 1800. The "High" Federalists, far the weakest group, thought Adams too mild toward France and favored every war measure without exception. Horrified by Adams' peace overtures, they preferred CHARLES COTESWORTH PINCKNEY for president in 1800. The moderates, comprising most Federalists and some Republicans, hoped for an honorable peace with France but felt it only prudent to prepare for an unwanted war; most of them also supported the Alien and Sedition Acts. Their national pride aroused, voters rebuked the anti-Adams Republicans by electing 22 Federalist congressmen (a gain of seven) in 1798–1799. This was an expression of nationalism rather than an embrace of the Federalist party, however, and as peace returned in 1800 many moderates drifted back to the Jeffersonian ranks.

See L. A. Rose, *Prologue to Democracy* (1968); M. J. Dauer, *Adams Federalists* (1953); H. M. Ammon, "Republican Party in Virginia" (Ph.D. dissertation, University of Virginia, 1948); N. E. Cunningham, *Jeffersonian Republicans* (1957); D. H. Gilpatrick, *Jeffersonian Democracy in North Carolina* (1931); G. R. Lamplugh, "Politics on the Periphery" (Ph.D. dissertation, University of Georgia, 1973); L. M. Renzulli, *Maryland: Federalist Years* (1972); and J. H. Wolfe, *Jeffersonian Democracy in South Carolina* (1940).

JAMES H. BROUSSARD
Southwest Texas State University

ADAMS, JOHN QUINCY, ADMINISTRATION (1825–1829).

With three strong candidates from the South—HENRY CLAY, WILLIAM CRAWFORD, AND ANDREW JACKSON—running for the presidency in 1824, there was much optimism in the South that the next administration would support conservative, states' rights principles. But with the election of John Quincy Adams by the House, the South faced four difficult years of bitter sectional strife with the North. Although there were three southerners in the new cabinet, only Clay had any influence over Adams, and many southerners distrusted Clay because of his suspected "corrupt bargain" with Adams in acquiring the presidency.

Animosity between the South and Adams began with his first annual message to Congress, in which he advocated a nationalistic program, financed partly from tariff revenues. He proposed federally financed internal improvements, a national university, a national astronomical observatory, new scientific expeditions, a stronger navy, and participation in the Panama Congress. Fortunately for the South, Congress rejected most of these proposals. Two other issues during the Adams administration greatly angered the South. Supported by the West and all of the South, Georgia attempted to force the Indians west in order to secure more valuable land. President Adams refused to accept this strategy; his opponents accused him of interfering with states' rights. The most serious breach occurred over the politically inspired Tariff Act of 1828, which the South bitterly opposed. The policies of the Adams administration completely united the South in support of the candidacy of Andrew Jackson.

See J. Richardson (ed.), *Messages* (1897), II; F. Simkins, *History of South* (1963); C. Sydnor, *Southern Sectionalism* (1948); G. Dangerfield, *American Nationalism* (1965); E. Roseboom, *Presidential Elections* (1970); S. Bemis, *Adams and Union* (1956); and P. Nagel, *Journal of Southern History* (Aug., 1960).

ROBERT C. HARRIS
University of West Florida

ADAMSON, WILLIAM CHARLES (1854–1929),

was born and educated in Bowdon, a north Georgia town near the Alabama border. Admitted to the bar in 1876, he practiced law at Carrollton until his election to the U.S. House of Representatives in 1897. During his early years in Congress he was active in behalf of public health, water power, and labor measures. When the Democrats came to power in 1913 under WOODROW WILSON, Adamson became chairman of the House Interstate and Foreign Commerce Committee. Adamson is best known for the railroad law that bears his name. In 1916, during a dispute between railroad brotherhoods and the railroads, he pressed for federal legislation. Among its provisions, the Adamson Act gave railroad workers an eight-hour day at the previous ten hours' pay with time and a half for overtime. It was the first federal legislative intervention in wage bargaining in a private industry. Adamson resigned from Congress in December, 1917, to accept a position on the Board of U.S. General Appraisers, a seat he held until retiring in 1928.

See T. W. Loyless, *Georgia's Public Men* (1905); W. J. Northen, *Men of Mark in Georgia* (1908); and E. W. Sigmund, "Federal Laws Concerning Railroad Labor Disputes" (Ph.D. dissertation, University of Illinois, 1961).

JOHN DITTMER
Tougaloo College

ADDRESS OF THE SOUTHERN DELEGATES

(1848) was intended by JOHN C. CALHOUN to be the culmination of his long struggle for southern unity. Its immediate provocation was a northern Whig suggestion to abolish the slave trade and ultimately slavery itself in the District of Columbia. To repel this attack Calhoun called a caucus of the southerners in Congress in December, 1848. Sixty-nine members assembled and chose a committee of five (two Democrats, two Whigs, and Calhoun) to prepare the address. Calhoun seems to have been its chief if not sole author. His strongly worded manifesto created such a furor that it was returned to the committee of five. John M. Berrien prepared a milder, alternative statement, but after an angry debate the caucus rejected Berrien's work. Calhoun's draft was accepted with one clause stricken, but only a third of the southern representatives in the House agreed to sign the statement. Calhoun's movement was thus a failure.

See A. Nevins, *Ordeal of Union* (1947); C. Wiltse, *J. C. Calhoun, Sectionalist* (1951); and R. B. Draughon, Jr., *Alabama Digest* (July, 1966).

RALPH DRAUGHON, JR.
University of Georgia

AFFLECK, THOMAS DUNBAR (1812–1868).

As monograph author, publisher, prolific correspondent and editor of the *Southern Rural Almanac*, Affleck was an effective advocate of southern antebellum agricultural reform. He urged conservation, soil analysis, selected stock breeding, scientific control of insects and plant diseases, and government-subsidized research. Journal account books of his design were a model for plantation management, stressing the usually neglected factors of capital depreciation and cost accounting. He was born in Scotland, farmed and operated commercial nurseries in Mississippi and Texas, and died in Texas.

See R. W. Williams, *Agricultural History* (June, 1957) and "Affleck" (Ph.D. dissertation, Tulane University, 1954); F. C. Cole, "Affleck: Texas Career" (Ph.D. dissertation, Louisiana State University, 1941); and manuscript collection, Louisiana State University Library.

ROBERT W. WILLIAMS
University of North Carolina

AFRICAN METHODIST EPISCOPAL CHURCH

had its earliest beginnings in late eighteenth-century Philadelphia in Richard Allen's quest for a separate place of worship for black Methodists, which culminated in the dedication of Bethel Church in 1794. After years of controversy over their autonomy, church property, and ordination, these dissident Methodists and several sister congregations united in 1816 with another small group from Baltimore, led by Daniel Coker, to form the first independent black denomination, with Allen as the first bishop. Shortly thereafter, with similar motivations and difficulties in separating from the parent white congregation and after rejecting union with the Allenites, the African Methodist Episcopal Zion church was formed in New York under the leadership of James Varick and Christopher Rush. Both churches essentially accepted the Methodist discipline, though the AMEZ had superintendents rather than bishops until the 1860s. Both were resolutely antislavery, though the AME General Conference was reluctant to take a militant stand even on the issue of those black members who remained slaveholders. The AMEZ in particular had ties with some of the best-known black abolitionists.

Before the Civil War the major activity of both churches was effectively confined to the North and a few border states. Under Morris Brown, a large AME church grew in Charleston, S.C., before 1820, but suspected involvement of the church in the VESEY PLOT in 1822 and the general repression of free blacks that followed its exposure scattered the church and drove Brown north. By 1863, however, both churches had begun their sweep into the South, winning many unconverted freedmen as well as numerous Methodists who had previously been under the religious domination of white southerners.

During the 1840s, under the prodding of Bishop Daniel Payne, the AME church had committed itself to providing centers of education for its clergy. As the independent black Methodists moved into the South, they quickly became involved in educating the freedmen, and the AME church in particular launched an ambitious program for building schools and colleges, which for decades were among the best available to black people. The goal of an educated clergy, however, was not fully realized.

For as long as elective office was open to blacks, preachers of both denominations were active in politics. In post-Reconstruction years some activist ministers fought JIM CROW, and others, such as Bishop HENRY TURNER, championed immigration to Africa. But the clergy, particularly in the South, became an increasingly accommodationist force within the black community.

The history of the African Methodists becomes more difficult to trace during the twentieth century. The black church has frequently been charged with gradually losing touch with the needs and aspirations of its members during these years. The denominations as a whole have failed to attack the social and economic problems of their members, especially in the South, at least partly because of poverty, overchurching, and an undereducated clergy. Attempts to unify the black Methodists and thus eliminate some of these impediments to action have failed. Although the general conferences passed resolutions supporting the nonviolent civil rights efforts of the early 1960s, little concrete aid was forthcoming, and these denominations were sparsely represented in the SOUTHERN CHRISTIAN LEADERSHIP CONFERENCE. The African Methodists have not regained the positions of moral and political leadership that they occupied prior to World War I.

See G. S. Wilmore, *Black Religion and Black Radicalism* (1972); G. A. Singleton, *Romance of African Methodism* (1952); D. H. Bradley, *History of AME Zion Church* (1956–70); W. J. Gaines, *African Methodism in the South* (1890); J. M. Batten, *Church History* (Sept., 1938); and M. C. Sernett, *Black Religion and American Evangelism* (1975).

ANNE KUSENER NELSEN
Forecasting International, Ltd., Arlington, Va.

AGEE, JAMES RUFUS

AGEE, JAMES RUFUS (1909–1955). Following graduation from Harvard in 1932, Agee moved to *Fortune* magazine, the first of several magazines for which he would work. While there, Agee published his first work, a slim volume of poetry entitled *Permit Me Voyage* (1934). On assignment to cover sharecroppers (SHARECROPPING) in the South, he and photographer Walker Evans became intensely involved in a collaborative effort published as *Let Us Now Praise Famous Men* (1941). A study of three tenant families in photographs and prose, it evoked the pride of the people it covered as well as their miserable living conditions. The book was a critical success but a commercial failure; only after Agee's death was it, in a sense, rediscovered.

During the 1940s, Agee worked as film critic for both *Time* and the *Nation*. He also worked in the industry itself, writing screenplays for, among others, *The Quiet One* (1948), *The African Queen* (1951), and *The Night of the Hunter* (1954). Most of Agee's work, film and nonfilm, has certain cinematic qualities, especially the use of scene and a consistent flow of action.

When not working in films, Agee was engaged in several other projects. In 1945 he finished *The Morning Watch* (1951), an autobiographical novella about his prep school days, and in 1948 he began work on *A Death in the Family* (1957), his major work. Because Agee was a furious worker, his health began to decline while he was engaged on this novel. Fortunately, he had virtually completed his writing (the exact order of some sections of the novel remains a question) at the time of his death, and it was published posthumously. More than anything else he wrote, *A Death in the Family* captures familial love, a city (Knoxville), and the gradual understanding a child must gain about death.

See Kenneth Seib, *James Agee* (1968).

WILLIAM H. YOUNG
Lynchburg College

AGNES SCOTT COLLEGE (Decatur, Ga. 30030) was founded in 1899 as Decatur Female Seminary, a Presbyterian school offering grammar school work. In 1900 it was renamed Agnes Scott Institute in honor of the mother of the founder, Colonel G. W. Scott, and in 1906 it was chartered as Agnes Scott College (WOMEN'S COLLEGES). The first Georgia college to be accredited by the Southern Association of Colleges and Schools (1906) and the second institution in Georgia to be granted a Phi Beta Kappa chapter, it continues as a small liberal arts college with a nominal Presbyterian affiliation and an enrollment of approximately 750 students.

AGNEW, SPIRO THEODORE (1918–). Son of a Greek immigrant, he grew up in Baltimore and its environs. He completed his legal studies (interrupted by World War II) at the University of Baltimore in 1947. After a decade of varied law and business endeavors of modest success, he plunged into Republican politics. In 1957 he was named to the Baltimore County Zoning Appeals Board; he won election as county executive in 1962. Four years later, he was elected governor of Maryland after a campaign that contrasted his moderate liberalism on civil rights to his rival's racist appeals. His near-liberal image endured until his stern reaction to the racial unrest of 1968. Though confessedly "not a household word" when chosen to run with presidential candidate Richard M. Nixon in 1968, Agnew became noted for his conservative rhetoric. As vice-president, he endeared himself to conservatives by assailing such foes as TV commentators guilty of "instant analysis" and the "effete corps of impudent snobs" who condoned antiwar activism. Reelected in 1972, Agnew was soon beset by federal prosecutors, who unearthed evidence that he had taken kickbacks while serving as county executive, governor, and vice-president. He resigned his office on October 10, 1973, pleaded *nolo contendere* to one count of tax evasion, and was fined and placed on probation.

See R. Cohen and J. Witcover, *Heartbeat Away* (1974); T. Lippman, *Spiro Agnew's America* (1972), and J. Albright, *What Makes Spiro Run?* (1972), both critical; J. Coyne, *Impudent Snobs* (1972), laudatory; and S. Agnew, *Frankly Speaking* (1970), speeches.

RICHARD FRIED
University of Illinois, Chicago

AGRICULTURAL ADJUSTMENT ADMINISTRATION, established by the Agricultural Adjustment Act of 1933, represented the attempt by the NEW DEAL to raise farm prices by limiting production. Farm prices were to be brought up to "parity"—that is, on a par with the purchasing power farmers had enjoyed during the period 1909–1914, figured on the basis of the price relationship of farm products to manufactured goods. The secretary of agriculture was empowered to cut production through acreage control of seven basic commodities: wheat, cotton, corn, hogs, rice, tobacco, and milk and dairy products. By cooperatively agreeing to take land out of production, farmers could benefit in two ways: prices presumably would rise, and growers would receive parity payments from the federal government.

Funds for payments were to come from a tax levied on the manufacturers who first processed the basic commodity for the domestic market. The processors would then pass along their increased cost to the consumer in the form of higher prices on consumer goods. It was the processing tax scheme that the Supreme Court declared unconstitutional in *U.S. v. Butler* (1936). A second AAA, established in 1938, was funded directly from the general treasury.

Since many crops were already in the ground

before the first AAA was established in 1933, the agency found it necessary to plow up one-fourth of the cotton crop and to slaughter 6 million baby pigs that threatened to glut the market. Anti–New Deal critics were quick to attack this destruction at a time when people badly needed food and clothing. Despite the criticism, the "economics of scarcity" succeeded in its main goal of raising farm prices.

Although the AAA was also successful in refinancing farm mortgages and reorganizing rural credit banks, recent New Deal historiography has tended to emphasize the agency's shortcomings, pointing out that it conserved much more than it changed, especially in the South, where farm tenancy was highest. In very simple terms, the AAA helped those farmers who needed it least, relatively substantial landowners, and hurt those who needed it most, poor sharecroppers and tenant farmers (SHARECROPPING; TENANT FARMING). AAA parity checks were always made payable to the landowner. The landlord was then supposed to share it with the tenants according to the amount each tenant held in the crop. Many landlords found it easy to evict their sharecroppers, keep the entire check, and work their land with day laborers who had no stake in the crop. Although the 1938 law was supposed to prevent this, the final interpretation was left up to the local county agricultural agent, who was usually a friend of the landowning farmers. Thus, many parity payments never got to the very poor, and the AAA was at least partly responsible for many of the mass tenant evictions in the South during the 1930s.

See G. C. Fite, *George N. Peek and Fight for Farm Parity* (1954); R. Lord, *Wallaces of Iowa* (1947); E. G. Nourse, J. S. Davis, and J. D. Black, *Three Years of Agricultural Adjustment Administration* (1971); H. Wallace, *New Frontiers* (1934); and T. Saloutos, *Journal of American History* (Sept., 1974).

LOUIS CANTOR
Indiana University, Ft. Wayne

AGRICULTURAL EXPERIMENT STATIONS.

Although the nation's first state agricultural experiment (SAE) station was begun in Connecticut in 1875, similar stations were soon opened in North Carolina, Tennessee, Alabama, Louisiana, and Kentucky. After passage of the Hatch Act (1887), the concept of today's modern experimental stations began gradually to emerge; now all southern states have SAE stations. The cooperative research of individual farmers, agribusinessmen, and both federal and SAE station scientists has done much to upgrade agriculture and to improve human existence.

The impact of southern SAE stations on the region's economy and history has been immense. For example, extensive soil studies conducted by SAE stations have resulted in the growth of the citrus industry in Florida and Texas. Southern SAE scientists contributed to the development of fertilizers (FERTILIZER INDUSTRY), chemicals, and hybrids, all of which have increased CORN crops. Simultaneously, they have helped to produce new and better varieties of crops adapted to southern soil and climate, including hybrid sorghum and SOYBEANS. SAE station tests on coastal Bermuda and Kentucky-31 fescue grass (GRASSES) have contributed to the extension of the South's CATTLE INDUSTRY, and tests on new breeds of livestock (*e.g.*, the Brahman and Santa Gertrudis), artificial insemination, and feedlot operations have increased the industry's profitability. The production of POULTRY and HOGS also has increased partly as a result of southern SAE station experiments. In a different vein the mechanical cotton harvester, developed with the aid of the Texas SAE station engineers, has helped to keep COTTON as an important southern crop; in Mississippi and other states, SAE stations have discovered better varieties of and new uses for cotton and cotton meal.

Responsive to the special needs and problems of its own state, each SAE station has made its own contributions to agricultural research and education. Particular concerns of several SAE stations include the following: Virginia—apples, minimum tillage cropping, and bovine hyperkeratosis; North Carolina—control of cotton insects and the development of varieties of grass used to prevent erosion on sand dunes and beaches; South Carolina—mechanical harvesting of peaches; Georgia—coastal Bermuda grass; Florida—vegetables and citrus fruits; Tennessee—forest genetics; Alabama—peanuts and fish; Mississippi—soybeans, grasses, and cotton; Louisiana—sugarcane; Texas—eradication programs for Texas tick fever and the development of hybrid sorghum; Arkansas—rice and cotton insects control programs; Missouri—corn and cooking of meat; Kentucky—dairy marketing programs; West Virginia—wheat; Maryland—commercial fishing and seafood processing; and Delaware—soybeans.

See E. Butler, *Progressive Farmer* (April, 1975); A. C. True, *History of Agricultural Experiment and Research in U.S.* (1937); H. C. Knoblauch *et al.*, *State Agricultural Experiment Station* (1962); I. M. May, Jr., "Historical Research Within College of Agriculture" (Paper, National Agricultural Library Symposium, Sept., 1975); T. Moses, *Agricultural Research in Texas Since 1888* (1956); C. E. Rosenberg, *Agricultural History* (Jan., 1971); USDA,

Yearbook of Agriculture (1975); and H. N. Young, *Virginia Agricultural Experiment Station* (1975).

IRVIN MAY, JR.
Texas Agricultural Experiment Station

AGRICULTURAL HISTORY SOCIETY (U.S. Department of Agriculture, Economic Research Service, Rm. 146, 500-12th St. SW, Washington, D.C. 20250), founded in 1919, had a membership of 1,400 in 1974. It publishes the quarterly *Agricultural History* (University of California Press, 2223 Fulton St., Berkeley, Calif. 94720), which since 1927 has become a leading scholarly journal for research on the development of agriculture. Its articles touch on almost every aspect of southern agricultural history, but are not exclusively on the South. The journal offers an annual award of $50 for the best article by a student.

AGRICULTURAL ORGANIZATIONS first assumed the form of planters' clubs and societies organized to discuss farming problems, to further commerce, and to stimulate agriculture, the arts, and manufacturing. Membership in the South Carolina Agricultural Society, organized in 1785 and for all practical purposes the first society of its kind, was confined largely to the aristocratic planters of the Charleston district. The high mortality rate among the early societies was caused by the lack of enough working members, the high dues, the failure to pay premiums, partisanship, and the passing of the Merino sheep-breeding craze. Eventually, more permanent societies emerged, which were broader in appeal, required lower dues, and allowed women to attend livestock exhibitions.

Societies to promote annual fairs became popular during the 1840s and 1850s in Kentucky, Tennessee, and Missouri. State agricultural societies also were formed, and some legislatures assisted these societies and state fairs. However, the interest of the southern states in the United States Agricultural Society, formed in 1841 and revived in 1852, was dulled by the rising tide of sectionalism. Finally in 1853 the Agricultural Association of the Slaveholding States was organized in Montgomery as part of the larger movement to consolidate the economic interests of the South.

The GRANGE, the first general farmers' organization to appear after the Civil War, had the support first of planters and small farmers in South Carolina and Mississippi and then in other southern states. Efforts to net greater returns for the members on their sales and purchases through cooperative marketing and purchasing associations were nullified by poor management, opposition from the traditional business agencies, and internal dissension. Modest attempts also were made to satisfy the credit needs of the members, eliminate discriminatory railroad rates and services, stress the need for a practical education in agriculture, and improve the social life of the farmer and his family through social gatherings, picnics, barbecues, and comparable activities. Never mustering the support that it gained in the Middle West, the Grange in the South nevertheless helped allay sectional differences and served as a model for other bodies.

The southern FARMERS' ALLIANCE came into formal existence in 1887 with the merger of the Texas Farmers' Alliance, organized in 1874 or 1875, and the Louisiana Farmers' Union and adopted the National Farmers' Alliance and Cooperative Union (NFA CU) as its official name. It appealed to small white farmers and tenants who felt menaced by corporations, bankers, mortgage companies, and public land seizures. In 1888 the NFA CU united with the Agricultural Wheel, which earlier had merged with the Brothers of Freedom, to form the National Farmers' and Laborers' Union (NF LU); then in 1889 the NF LU adopted the name National Farmers' Alliance and Industrial Union (NFAIU). The Colored National Farmers' Alliance got its start as a result of the liberal charter-issuing policies of the Northern Farmers' Alliance and became loosely identified with the southern Alliance owing to geographic and economic considerations. The Farmers' Alliance declined for the same reasons as the Grange; it failed to produce the promised economic benefits, and it suffered from poor leadership and internal dissension.

The short-lived Southern Cotton Association, organized about 1900, was committed to the principle of raising prices through the curtailment of production. The same principle guided the American Society of Equity in Kentucky and Tennessee, which sought to raise the price of tobacco by withholding the crop from market and restricting production. The longest-lived organization that sought the same objective was the Farmers' Educational and Cooperative Union, better known as the FARMERS' UNION. It was founded in Point, Tex., in 1902.

Three organizations emerged after World War I: the American Cotton Association, an educational organization that in a way revived the philosophy of the old Southern Cotton Association; the Farm Labor Union, which seems to have had much in common with the Farmers' Union and the Farmers' Alliance; and the AMERICAN FARM BUREAU FEDERATION, an organization of middle western antecedents, which was slow at first in appealing to southern farmers, who were primarily interested in cotton and tobacco.

The SOUTHERN TENANT FARMERS' UNION (STFU), a product of the depressed thirties, attempted to organize tenants, sharecroppers, and farm laborers. It attracted liberal groups and the press, but internal dissension, an inability to collect dues, the fluid state of its membership, and World War II obscured the efforts of the STFU, which had been absorbed by the United Cannery, Agricultural, Packing, and Allied Workers of America.

In the post–World War II years the AFBF abandoned its parity price goals of the 1930s and campaigned for an open market. Membership in the southern states also soared to its highest levels, in excess of 1.2 million farm families in 1974, not so much because of its open market policy, but owing to a wide variety of services available to its members. It is now the largest organization of its kind in the South.

See L. C. Gray, *History of Agriculture in the Southern States Until 1860* (1933), II; E. Wiest, *Agricultural Organizations* (1923), early years; S. J. Buck, *Granger Movement* (1913), excellent on 1870s; D. S. Nordin, *Rich Harvest* (1974), Grange to 1900; J. D. Hicks, *Populist Revolt* (1931), standard work; T. Saloutos *Farmer Movements* (1960), major groups; O. M. Kile, *Farm Bureau Through Three Decades* (1948), sympathetic; C. M. Campbell, *Farm Bureau and the New Deal* (1961); D. H. Grubbs, *Cry from the Cotton* (1971), on STFU; and J. R. Crampton, *National Farmers' Union* (1965), sociological.

THEODORE SALOUTOS
University of California, Los Angeles

AGRICULTURE is the dominant factor affecting the historical development of southern life and institutions. Until recent decades the South could best be characterized as a rural, agrarian society, in which most people derived their livelihood from farming and in which most believed the rural life to be the most wholesome, moral, and virtuous. Only since World War II has the urban-industrial orientation become dominant in southern life. Until 1940 a majority of southerners lived in rural areas. In 1970, one-third of the South's population lived in rural areas, but only 3 million southerners (5 percent) lived on farms and derived their livelihood from farming. Cash receipts from southern farm marketings in 1972 were $19.4 billion or 30 percent of the national total. Southern agricultural development, for convenience, can be divided into four major periods: (1) colonial, (2) antebellum, (3) agrarian, and (4) modern.

Colonial agriculture derived in large part from a blend of European and Indian technology applied to native plant varieties. TOBACCO, COTTON, CORN, beans, squash, pumpkins, potatoes, tomatoes, and sweet potatoes were all indigenous to America and composed a major portion of the staple and food crops of the South in colonial and later times. The great bulk of British imports from America came from the southern colonies and included prominently tobacco, INDIGO, and RICE (COMMERCE). Commercial farming, plantations, and slave labor became important after 1700, but colonial agriculture mainly involved self-sufficient family or pioneer farming. Most production, except for tobacco, indigo, and rice, was for domestic consumption.

Of the three cash or export crops, tobacco was most important, although both rice and indigo were strong rivals. John Rolfe shipped the first cargo of tobacco to England in 1613. By 1627, Virginia was exporting over half a million pounds of tobacco. A woman, ELIZA LUCAS PINCKNEY, is credited with introducing indigo cultivation into the Carolinas about 1734. Parliament placed indigo on the free list in 1734 and in 1748 provided a bounty or subsidy, which remained in effect until 1777. Rice cultivation began in South Carolina about 1685. By 1775, the Carolinas and Georgia were exporting in excess of 500 million pounds annually. Cattle, HORSES, and HOGS, introduced into the Americas by Spanish explorers in the early 1500s, provided the nucleus of the southern livestock industry that flourished in the eighteenth century.

The antebellum era is characterized by cotton, slavery, and the plantation system. Cotton dominated the southern economy in the nineteenth century and shaped the whole of American economic development by its impact upon westward EXPANSIONISM, shipping, manufacturing, credit, slavery, and tenancy. Cotton production increased from 3,000 bales in 1790, valued at about $500,000, to almost 4.5 million bales in 1860, valued at $270 million. The growth of slavery appeared to match the growth and westward expansion of the cotton industry. In 1790 there were about 750,000 slaves in the southern states, and in 1860 about 4 million. Throughout the antebellum period slaves composed about one-third of the total population of the South.

Although the plantation-slave system dominated the economic and social structure of the antebellum South, most southerners before 1860 were small, independent, nonslaveholding YEOMEN FARMERS. Of the 1 million white families in the slave states in 1860, about 384,000 owned slaves.

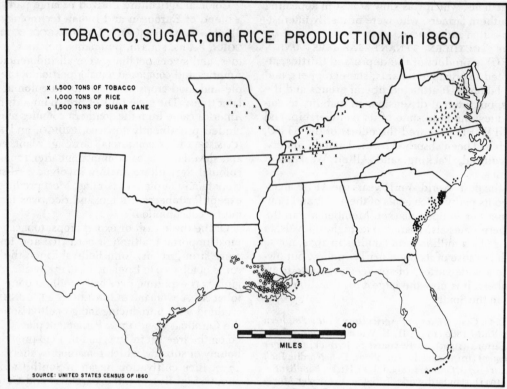

TOBACCO, SUGAR, and RICE PRODUCTION in 1860

x 1,500 TONS OF TOBACCO
• 1,000 TONS OF RICE
o 1,500 TONS OF SUGAR CANE

0   400
MILES

SOURCE: UNITED STATES CENSUS OF 1860

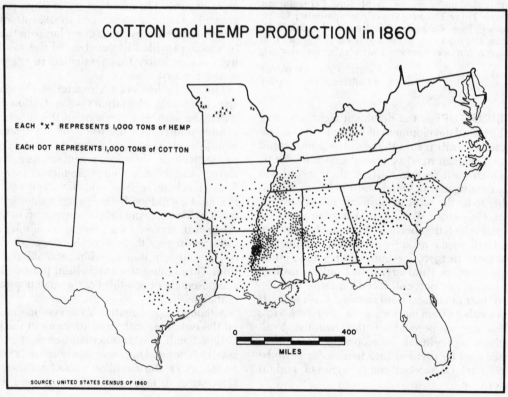

COTTON and HEMP PRODUCTION in 1860

EACH "x" REPRESENTS 1,000 TONS of HEMP

EACH DOT REPRESENTS 1,000 TONS of COTTON

0   400
MILES

SOURCE: UNITED STATES CENSUS OF 1860

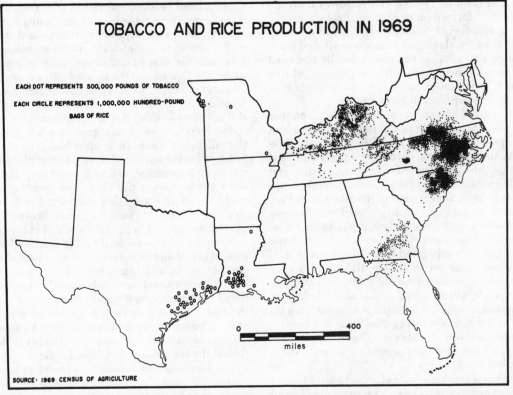

TOBACCO AND RICE PRODUCTION IN 1969

EACH DOT REPRESENTS 500,000 POUNDS OF TOBACCO

EACH CIRCLE REPRESENTS 1,000,000 HUNDRED-POUND
BAGS OF RICE

0   400
miles

SOURCE: 1969 CENSUS OF AGRICULTURE

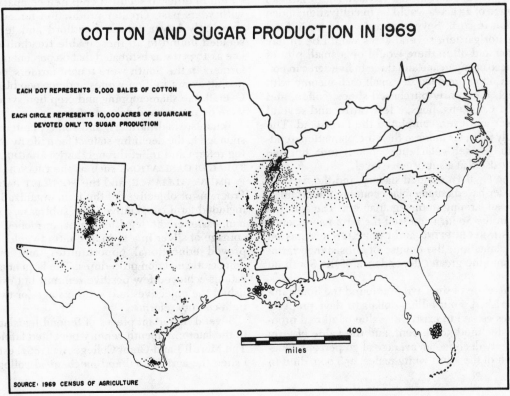

COTTON AND SUGAR PRODUCTION IN 1969

EACH DOT REPRESENTS 5,000 BALES OF COTTON

EACH CIRCLE REPRESENTS 10,000 ACRES OF SUGARCANE
DEVOTED ONLY TO SUGAR PRODUCTION

0   400
miles

SOURCE: 1969 CENSUS OF AGRICULTURE

Of these, almost 275,000 owned fewer than ten slaves and farmed on or near subsistence levels. Of the approximately 100,000 farmers who owned more than ten slaves, only 10,000 possessed more than 50 slaves. A planter was generally regarded as one who owned more than 30 slaves. At this level a slaveholder could hire an OVERSEER or manager to supervise the labor force.

The typical labor organization on the plantation included the overseer in the role of manager and field gangs variously styled as the plow gang, hoe gang, and trash gang, each gang supervised by a DRIVER, who was himself a slave. Domestics and skilled artisans or craftsmen usually worked under the direct supervision of the planter and his wife. Working conditions for field hands were most severe on the rice and sugar plantations. The severity of the slave system is believed to have been partially mitigated by the capital value of the slave, since mistreatment, illness, injury, or runaways depreciated the owner's capital. Slavery and the plantation system represented the center of capital accumulation in the antebellum South, just as the manufacturing plant was the central form of northern capital; yet, in both sections before the Civil War, most people were small, independent, family farmers.

A typical southern farm of 1850 ranged in size from 50 to 210 acres. On a 120-acre family farm an average of 25 acres would be in cultivation, much of that in corn. Several acres would be in food crops or garden; several acres would be in hay crops; and often there would be a small plot of tobacco or sugarcane and three to five acres in cotton. Cotton provided the small cash income with which the family purchased shoes, coffee, and tools. Chickens, hogs, a few cattle, and several horses and oxen completed the farmstead. The family farm, far more so than the plantation, tended to be a self-sufficient economic unit, but one that existed at a subsistence level.

The Civil War ended slavery, and the rise of a broader-based commercial economy undermined yeoman farming in the agrarian era. The agrarian age in the South witnessed the farm movements, the SHARECROPPING and CROP LIEN systems on the plantation, the demise of subsistence farming, and the greater dependence of the South on cotton.

The close of the Civil War found the South impoverished. Four billion dollars in slave property values ceased to exist. The value of all real property declined 50 percent, and the value of farm property declined an average of 70 percent. One-fourth of the adult white males, 258,000, died in war. Railroad mileage was reduced by two-thirds, and steamship tonnage by an equal amount. Specie was gone, currency was worthless, and stocks and bonds were valueless. Farm prices collapsed and, as in the case of cotton, generally continued to decline throughout the nineteenth century, and nonfarm prices, especially the cost of credit, rose. The scarcity of cash and credit contributed to the rise of tenant farming and the crop lien.

The crop lien was a mortgage on a future crop, the only asset southern farmers had. The cotton factor or broker advanced money to the planter in return for a mortgage on an expected crop and for the right to market the crop. The planter, who could not afford wage labor, contracted with farm workers or tenants to farm on shares. Shares were usually recognized in thirds: one-third of the crop was due for labor, one-third for the land, and one-third for seed and equipment. The average sharecropper, white and black, farmed 17 acres, from which he received variously one-third or two-thirds of the crop receipts, deducting from those the cost of living expenses charged to his account at the plantation store or commissary. Croppers frequently ended a crop year more deeply in debt than at the beginning, as did the landlord.

The landlord was forced to respond to falling commodity prices by increasing acreages in cultivation in order to secure a crop lien comparable with years past. Greater production forced increasingly lower prices. Landlord and tenant seemed bound to an inescapable treadmill. As late as 1935 it was estimated that 60 percent of the farmers in the South were tenant farmers, comprising over 1 million whites and 700,000 blacks. Overall, the sharecropping and crop lien systems were pernicious and dehumanizing.

Tenants, small farmers, and some planters responded to the declining state of farm life by seeking reform and relief through national AGRICULTURAL ORGANIZATIONS such as the GRANGE, the FARMERS' ALLIANCE, and the POPULIST PARTY. Programs or objectives of the farm organizations included farm cooperatives, the subtreasury system, easier credit, legal tender paper money, the coinage of silver in a favorable ratio to gold, improved educational opportunities, and more democratic election procedures. The farm organizations achieved few positive reforms, but established the objectives and set the stage for twentieth-century reform.

Several important pieces of federal legislation in the later nineteenth century benefited farmers. The Morrill Land-Grant College Act (1862) established the agricultural and mechanical colleges, which were generally organized in the South during Reconstruction. The Hatch Act (1887) established agricultural experiment stations, and the Interstate Commerce Act (1887) provided a more equitable rate structure for railroads. In the twentieth century, farmers obtained beneficial legislation through the auspices of lobby groups such as the Farm Bureau, the FARMERS' UNION, and the Farm Bloc.

The modern age of southern agriculture brought with it almost revolutionary developments: (1) the mechanization of agriculture; (2) the massive exodus of whites and blacks from farms; (3) increasing specialization in crop production and marketing; (4) an increase in the size of the productive unit; (5) higher yields; (6) improved varieties and new commercial crops, such as peanuts, grain sorghums, and SOYBEANS; (7) the advent of federal farm programs ranging from the Smith-Lever Act, which established the agricultural extension service, and the AGRICULTURAL ADJUSTMENT ADMINISTRATION of the NEW DEAL, to the soil bank program and agricultural acts and Public Law 480 programs after World War II. The great impact of this revolution in agriculture has been that far fewer southern farmers are producing far greater crops on less acreage.

The GREAT DEPRESSION traumatically affected southern farm life. Farmers entered their depression fully a decade before the rest of the nation. The agricultural price index dropped from 170 to 80 between April and December of 1920 and remained distressingly low. Cotton prices on the New Orleans exchange dropped from 41.4 cents per pound to 14.6 cents per pound in the same period. By 1929, when the market crashed, southern farmers were heavily mortgaged. Farm investments in buildings and equipment were nominal throughout the decades 1920–1940.

Mechanization on southern farms was mostly a post–World War II development. Mechanization was delayed because: (1) the South's earlier dependence upon slave labor, subsistence farming, and tenant farming discouraged investment in capital equipment; (2) crops such as tobacco and cotton discouraged mechanical harvesting; (3) farm labor and management were unskilled and untrained; and (4) capital for investment was lacking. The rice industry began to mechanize in the late 1880s, employing harvesters, combines, and steam tractors. Steam tractors were generally unsuited for cotton, sugar, or tobacco farms, and mechanization awaited the internal combustion engine. Although some tractors appeared on southern farms before World War I, substantial

mechanization did not occur until the 1940s, when tractors, combines, mechanical cotton pickers, airplanes, binders, balers, and sophisticated machinery largely replaced men and MULES.

The modern southern CATTLE INDUSTRY essentially had twentieth-century origins. The range cattle industry, established in the Carolinas in colonial days, included all the accouterments and nomenclature of the later western frontier. For a short time before the Civil War the cattle frontier had shifted to Louisiana and southeast Texas, then moved northward and westward. Texas fever (and its control), hard winters and droughts in the 1880s, barbed wire, the railroad, and scientific breeding and husbandry ended the open-range cattle industry. In its place a highly specialized modern industry developed. Hogs, chickens, turkeys (POULTRY INDUSTRY), and other livestock are similarly raised under scientifically controlled, high intensity conditions.

Where depression and hard times failed to displace inefficient, marginal farmers, New Deal programs succeeded in displacing them and facilitated the transition of labor from the farm to the city. Programs such as the Agricultural Adjustment Act reduced acreages, making it impossible for the small or inefficient farmer to survive. The more efficient producer was rewarded by placing a premium on yields. The New Deal forced American farmers to be better farmers and eased the transition from agricultural to agribusiness and industrial employment. The technological-industrial revolution, which struck the South so forcefully only after World War II, provided jobs for displaced farm families and created a new life-style for the southerner.

Southern traditions and culture are still shaped by the viable rural-agrarian heritage. Southern politics and legislatures have a rural orientation. Southern FOODS, CLOTHING, and MUSIC draw upon the farm and ranch heritage. Southern people continue to be outdoorsmen, hunters, fishermen, and gardeners. Although they have gone to the city, most southerners continue to be engaged in farm-related industries, such as food processing and marketing. The southern life-style has changed, but so far the South's basic commitment to agriculture and the agrarian heritage is unchanged.

See L. C. Gray, *Agriculture in the South to 1860* (2 vols.; 1932); U. B. Phillips, *American Negro Slavery* (1918), and *Life and Labor* (1929); F. L. Olmsted, *Cotton Kingdom* (1953); F. L. Owsley, *Plain Folk* (1949); T. Saloutos, *Farmer Movements* (1960); R. P. Vance, *Human Factors* (1929); C. V. Woodward, *Tom Watson* (1938); H. D. Woodman, *King Cotton* (1968), finance and marketing;

J. H. Street, *New Revolution* (1957), mechanization;
D. E. Conrad, *Forgotten Farmers* (1965), tenancy; and
H. H. Edwards, *Agriculture in Southern U.S.* (1971),
bibliography.

HENRY C. DETHLOFF
Texas A. & M. University

AIR TRANSPORT has been a prominent feature
of the region since the early twentieth century,
when the Wright brothers inaugurated heavier-
than-air flight at Kitty Hawk, N.C. The first scheduled air passenger service in the world was provided across Tampa Bay by the St. Petersburg–
Tampa Airboat Line in 1914, and a pioneer airmail
route was begun between Key West and Havana
by Florida West Indies Airways in 1920–1921.
The popularity of the South as a winter vacation-
land, the lure of the Bahamas and Caribbean islands, and the desire of thirsty Americans to escape the reach of Prohibition all stimulated the
development in the early 1920s of commercial
routes from northern cities to such places as Miami
and Key West and thence to Nassau, Bimini, and
Havana. In 1927 Pan American Airways, the first
permanent American international airline, began
operating from Key West to Cuba.

Motivated by the experiments of entomologist
B. R. Coad, the South spawned a unique agribusiness in the 1920s: aerial crop-dusting. The first
commercial crop-dusting company, Huff-Daland,
had grown by 1928 into an enterprise called Delta, which in 1929 under the leadership of C. E.
Woolman (1889–1966) also began carrying passengers from its Monroe, La., base. Other airlines,
however, had already commenced in the South,
led by Florida Airways, which operated an airmail
route between Atlanta and Miami from 1926 to
1927. The Gulf–St. Tammany line, inspired in
part by Charles A. Lindbergh's flights of the latter
year, began in 1928 to fly mail over the New Orleans–Mobile–Birmingham–Atlanta route. It was
absorbed by American Airlines, which also outbid
Delta in 1930 for a key airmail contract on a southern transcontinental route, which the latter firm
had in part pioneered. Meanwhile another carrier,
Eastern, won a north-south airmail contract and
thrived on the Florida tourist trade.

Following a U.S. Senate committee's exposure
in 1933 of serious improprieties in the awarding
of previous airmail contracts, Delta won certification for the airmail route between Ft. Worth–Dallas and Charleston, S.C., via Birmingham, Atlanta,
and other intermediate points. Delta began mail
and passenger service on this run in mid-1934 and
transferred its headquarters from Monroe to Atlanta in 1941. Its position as a regional carrier was
strengthened by its acquisition of a route between
Atlanta and Cincinnati in 1941, the awarding of a
popular vacation route from Chicago to Miami in
1945, and by the establishment of cooperative interchange services to the Great Lakes and the Pacific Coast with Trans World Airlines and American Airlines. Ultimately Delta won access to
northern and western cities in the 1950s. In 1953
it absorbed Chicago & Southern Airlines, a Mem-
phis-based enterprise connecting the cities of the
Mississippi Valley and operating various important Caribbean routes. It cemented its status as a
giant of the industry by acquiring Northeast Airlines in 1971. It was the first American carrier to
inaugurate service with the Douglas DC-8 in 1959
and the Douglas DC-9 in 1965.

Meanwhile, American expanded its southern
services by adding to its basic Ft. Worth–Memphis–Nashville–Washington trunk route, and
Eastern continued its lucrative New York-to-Miami
route while serving such major regional centers as
Atlanta, New Orleans, and Richmond. An important southern-born enterprise, National Airlines,
began in the 1930s by serving various points in
Florida, won a route from New York to Miami, and
ultimately became both a transcontinental and
transatlantic carrier. Under government policies
encouraging the growth of feeder lines after 1944,
Southern Airways established a variety of local
routes centered on its main offices in Atlanta, providing service to such cities as Charlotte and Mobile; eventually it won certification to Chicago,
Washington, and New York. Piedmont Airlines,
another feeder, began service in 1948 to points in
North Carolina, Virginia, and Kentucky and gained
access to major eastern and midwestern centers in
the following decades.

Commercial airports in the South, like those
elsewhere in the nation, evolved from primitive
origins to the giant fields at such places as Atlanta,
Miami, and Dallas–Ft. Worth. A case example, the
Atlanta airport, dates to 1926, when horse-drawn
machines began grading swampland within the
oval of an old racetrack. By the end of 1927 it had
two landing strips, each 1,500 feet long. From un-
lighted dirt runways to the massive complexes
where jets land and take off in darkness and light,
southern airports have grown with southern economic and demographic expansion.

See R. E. G. Davies, *Airlines Since 1914* (1972), encyclopedic but poorly written; R. Miller and D. Sawers,
Technical Development of Aviation (1968); C. Putnam,
High Journey (1943), account of Chicago & Southern by
founder; E. Rickenbacker, *Rickenbacker* (1967), autobiography of president of Eastern; H. L. Smith, *Airways*
(1942), old but superior; J. F. Taylor, *High Horizons*

(1955); E. W. Downes and G. F. Lemmer, *Agricultural History* (July, 1965); and W. P. Newton, *Alabama Review* (April, 1973). Source materials include *Aircraft Year Book* (1919–); annual reports of Delta, Eastern, National, Southern, etc.; and C. E. Woolman Historical Papers, Delta Airlines offices, Atlanta.

W. DAVID LEWIS and
WESLEY PHILLIPS NEWTON
Auburn University

ALABAMA is a Deep South state whose name comes from an Indian word meaning "thicket clearers." Alabamians are a homogeneous people. White settlers came largely from Georgia and the Upper South and were mainly Anglo-Saxon. The slaves they brought with them, however, quickly became an increasing and significant minority. Developing a plantation system based on cotton production, the planters, both Democrats and Whigs, dominated the state's antebellum economic, political, and social history. Leanings toward aristocracy were tempered by the large number of YEOMEN FARMERS and the influences of Jacksonian Democracy, the frontier, and evangelical Protestantism. After the Civil War and the political battles of Reconstruction, the Republicans were defeated, and the state became solidly Democratic. Except for sporadic challenges, the one-party situation held until the 1960s. Agriculture remained the state's major source of wealth until the middle of the twentieth century. From 1865 to the present, Alabamians, both black and white, have contended with economic impoverishment, the complexities accompanying the shift from the agrarian to an industrial economy, and profound problems of race.

Geography. Lying north-south, Alabama contains 51,609 square miles and ranks twenty-ninth among the states in size. Its elevation ranges from 2,407 feet to sea level. The mean annual temperature ranges from 60 to 70 degrees and the mean annual rainfall from 53 to 65 inches. Overall, the climate is temperate with hot summers and mild winters. There are five physiographic provinces: the highland rim (containing the Tennessee River valley); the Cumberland Plateau; the Appalachian Ridge and Valley; the Piedmont; and the coastal plain (containing the BLACK BELT). Alabama has an exceptional system of navigable rivers, the major ones being the Tennessee, Coosa, Tallapoosa, Alabama, Black Warrior, Tombigbee, and Chattahoochee.

From exploration to statehood. The first Alabamians were Indians. In the prehistoric period they developed villages, had systems of religion and government, and, as reminders of their civilization, left behind numerous earthen mounds. By the early sixteenth century the Mound Builders with their ceremonial structures had long since disappeared. In Alabama the Europeans encountered four major groups of Indians: the CHOCTAWS of the southwest, the CHICKASAWS of the northwest, the CHEROKEES of the north and northeast, and the most numerous and powerful of all, the CREEKS of the east and southeast. Within these classifications were numerous subtribes.

The land "Alabama" appeared on European maps by the early 1500s. Alonzo de Piñeda, a Spanish explorer, probably made the first European contact when he came ashore at Mobile Bay in 1519. In 1528 the ill-fated expedition of Pánfilo de Narváez stopped briefly at Mobile Bay. The first significant land exploration was that of HERNANDO DE SOTO in the summer of 1540. That fall de Soto's Spaniards defeated the Indians led by Chief Tuscaloosa at the battle of MAUVILLA, an Indian town near the junction of the Alabama and Tombigbee rivers. Favorable reports from the explorer Guido de los Bazares stimulated Spain in 1559 to attempt a settlement, led by Tristán de Luna, in the Mobile Bay area. The experiment was Spain's only serious attempt to plant a colony in Alabama, and it was abandoned in 1561 because of supply difficulties and the failure to find gold.

France laid claim to the Mississippi Valley in the late seventeenth century. French expansion moved eastward along the Gulf coast in 1699, when a small fleet under PIERRE LE MOYNE D'IBERVILLE anchored at Mobile Bay. In January, 1702, JEAN BAPTISTE LE MOYNE DE BIENVILLE founded Mobile—Ft. Louis de la Mobile, named in honor of Louis XIV—the first French settlement in Alabama. Although Spain's Indian allies made sporadic moves against Mobile, Spanish and French claims were momentarily fixed at the Perdido River. In the next decades, the French colony of Louisiana was under private, corporate, and finally, from 1732 to 1763, royal control. As the southeastern end of France's North American empire, Mobile was important. In 1717 Ft. Toulouse was constructed at the confluence of the Coosa and Tallapoosa rivers and became the second French settlement in Alabama. A military and diplomatic outpost, the fort served as a deterrent to English fur traders and trappers from the Carolinas. Meanwhile, Mobile prospered. Slaves were brought in (1719), and the Alabama settlements numbered almost a thousand persons.

England had tentative claims to Alabama based on two sweeping geographical grants by the crown

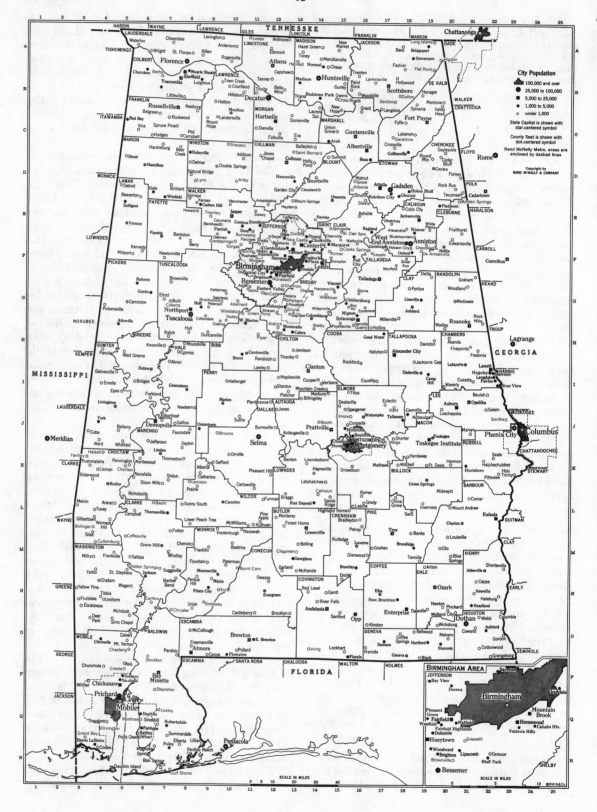

City Population

- 100,000 and over
- 25,000 to 100,000
- 5,000 to 25,000
- 1,000 to 5,000
- under 1,000

State Capital is shown with star-centered symbol

County Seat is shown with dot-centered symbol

Rand McNally Metro. areas are enclosed by dashed lines

Copyright by
RAND McNALLY & COMPANY

BIRMINGHAM AREA

SCALE IN MILES

to Carolina proprietors early in the seventeenth century. When George I granted Georgia to JAMES OGLETHORPE in 1732, a new threat was raised to both Spanish and French colonial claims. In 1735 the French erected Ft. Tombeckbee on the Tombigbee River to counter the aggressive English. By making a treaty with the Creeks, Oglethorpe secured the British flank in Alabama and confined French settlements to coastal and river areas.

In the sixteenth and seventeenth centuries, England, France, and Spain fought a series of wars (COLONIAL WARS). Queen Anne's War, involving border fighting in the South and the North, ended with the Treaty of Utrecht (1713) and was the only one of importance to the New World. The Seven Years' War or FRENCH AND INDIAN WAR that followed spread from the interior of North America to Europe. It culminated in British victory and the Peace of Paris in 1763. France ceded to Great Britain possessions in India and the West Indies, Canada, and all territory east of the Mississippi except New Orleans; France yielded New Orleans and its claims west of the Mississippi to its ally Spain to compensate for that country's loss of Florida to the British. Thus the area of Alabama—explored by the Spanish and settled by the French—became briefly part of British Florida.

In 1763 George III issued a proclamation separating East and West Florida at the Apalachicola-Chattahoochee River. West Florida therefore encompassed the southern portions of Alabama, Mississippi, and, except for New Orleans, Louisiana east of the Mississippi. Although Pensacola was the capital, Mobile remained important. Encouraged by the British, settlers came into West Florida and soon outnumbered the Spanish and French population. During the Revolutionary War, both East and West Florida became havens for British refugees. After Spain and France entered the war, Spain seized Mobile and Pensacola in 1781 and, by the Treaty of Paris of 1783, Great Britain granted the American colonies their independence and returned the Floridas to Spain. Florida's northern boundary, however, became an issue between Spain and the United States until Pinckney's Treaty (1795) established the thirty-first parallel as the Florida demarcation. After the Florida boundary was surveyed, St. Stephens was yielded to the Americans, although Mobile remained Spanish. The development of the cotton gin made the cultivation of short-staple cotton both feasible and profitable. Included in the influx of settlers were squatters without valid claims. Additional impetus came following the LOUISIANA PURCHASE in 1803—Spain had retroceded the territory to France. More immigrants poured in, and Spain's possession of Florida increasingly became tenuous.

Meanwhile, the central and northern portions of the future state of Alabama gradually were taking form. The Georgia-Alabama boundary was generally defined in 1787 after negotiations between American officials and the Creeks. That same year South Carolina ceded its western lands. This completed Georgia's northern borders and created the strip along Tennessee's southern border that in 1798 became the Mississippi Territory. In the mid-1790s the YAZOO LAND FRAUD, involving land sold by the Georgia legislature in Alabama and Mississippi, cast doubt on the legitimacy of titles. In 1802 Georgia ceded its western lands to the government for a cash settlement. As the Indians gave up their lands piecemeal, the territory of Mississippi grew. The rapid expansion was aided by the construction of the Federal Road cutting southwest out of Georgia. Congress recognized the claims of squatters but required future entry on public lands to be accomplished legally through land offices.

The territory's first elected legislative assembly of 1800 created Washington County, the first county in what is now Alabama. The new entity made national news in 1807, when Aaron Burr was arrested there on charges of treason. By 1810 new counties and towns had been created, and Alabamians, claiming that Natchez—the territorial capital—was too remote, were pressuring Congress to divide the Mississippi Territory.

In 1810, American frontiersmen captured Baton Rouge and proclaimed West Florida an independent republic. President James Madison approved, believing that West Florida to the Perdido River had been included in the Louisiana Purchase. Congress confirmed the annexation in 1811 and added it to the Mississippi Territory. During the WAR OF 1812, because Spain was Great Britain's ally, General JAMES WILKINSON led American soldiers in a bloodless occupation of Mobile. Alabama Indians, stirred by the Shawnee chief Tecumseh and also by Spanish authorities, fought battles at Burnt Corn and the Holy Ground. Led by the half-breed William Weatherford, Indians massacred almost 500 persons at Ft. Mims. In 1814, General Andrew Jackson's militiamen overwhelmed the Indians at the battle of Horseshoe Bend. The defeated Creeks signed the Treaty of Ft. Jackson ceding lands in Georgia and nearly half of present-day Alabama.

Despite frontier conflict, the territory continued to expand, and in 1817 Mississippi was admitted as a slave state. Alabama became a separate territory with St. Stephens as its temporary capital.

President James Monroe appointed William Wyatt Bibb, former U.S. senator from Georgia, as governor. Early territorial politics were dominated by what was called the "Georgia party." The pattern of growth continued, as did cessions of Indian land. One unique settlement was that of the French Vine & Olive Company at Demopolis by Napoleonic refugees. Although given a grant of land by Congress, the settlers ultimately were unsuccessful.

Agriculture boomed, and Mobile became an important port for cotton planters. In 1819 Alabama became the twenty-second state. A democratic constitution, modeled on that of Mississippi, was drafted at Huntsville, the temporary capital. There the territorial legislature elected United States senators and incorporated a new town, Cahaba, as the state capital. Bibb was chosen as the first governor. The senators were selected from north and south Alabama, a geographical rivalry that would be important throughout the state's history. In 1820 Alabama had a population in its first census of 127,901 persons.

Antebellum period. Bringing their institutions and traditions with them from other areas, the citizens of the new state experienced a melding of the past with the demands of the frontier. What emerged were patterns and characteristics recognizable from their former lives but possessing new and unique qualities.

Their religious heritage plus their isolated, rural lives made churchgoing profoundly important to Alabamians. They responded to several revival movements, including the emotional preaching of the Methodist minister Lorenzo Dow. CAMP MEETINGS were common throughout the state. Most numerous among the majority Protestant sects were the BAPTISTS, followed by the METHODISTS and PRESBYTERIANS (in 1860 Alabama had nine Catholic churches).

Few citizens were inclined toward creative literature. Still, JOSEPH G. BALDWIN's *Flush Times of Alabama and Mississippi* and JOHNSON JONES HOOPER's writings about the picaresque frontiersman Simon Suggs were important. In 1851 Albert J. Pickett published his brilliant *History of Alabama*. The people were avid newspaper readers. Edited by learned and outspoken editors, the journals were intensely political. The state had 96 newspapers on the eve of the Civil War.

Antebellum Alabama never achieved educational excellence, but progress was made. A Jesuit priest taught at the first school established shortly after Mobile was founded in 1702. A log cabin housed the first nonsectarian school set up in 1799,

and the territorial legislature chartered Washington Academy at St. Stephens in 1811. By 1860 the state legislature had chartered over 250 private academies, including the famous Greene Springs Academy established in 1847 by Dr. Henry Tutwiler. Many planters engaged private tutors to instruct their children. When statehood was achieved, the sixteenth section of every township was reserved for public schools. Federal revenue for public schools came with the division of the surplus in 1836, but a public school system was not established until 1854. William F. Perry, elected by the legislature, was the first superintendent of education. The state constitution granted two entire townships for an institution of higher learning, and the University of Alabama was incorporated in 1819. It opened its doors at Tuscaloosa in 1831, but, throughout the period, church schools were larger and more popular than the university. A state medical college was founded at Mobile in 1859.

Beginning in the 1820s, steamboating became important on Alabama's extensive river system. On land, stagecoaches made their slow way over badly kept roads. The first highways were military roads. Later they were maintained by the counties, and there were several privately controlled turnpikes that charged tolls. The Tuscumbia Railroad Company, chartered in 1830 and two miles long, was the state's first railroad. The Mobile & Ohio Railroad was one of two lines in the nation to first receive a federal land grant, but state aid bills in the 1850s were vetoed on the ground that the state should not engage in internal improvements. In 1860 there were 743 miles of track, but the mountain regions were unpenetrated, and the northern and southern portions were not linked. Furthermore, there was no standard gauge.

Industrial development before 1860 was limited. Profits from agriculture meant that mineral deposits were barely touched, although there were some iron foundries. In 1860 the state had 14 textile mills. Daniel Pratt, a New Englander, developed the town of Prattville into the world's largest manufacturer of cotton gins. Yet Alabama's cities existed largely as strategic points of trade and commerce, not as industrial centers. Manufactured goods were obtained through factors at Mobile and elsewhere. Because the factors were in turn indebted to northerners, Alabama became largely an economic colony of the North. Late in the 1850s there was a belated effort to industrialize.

Agriculture dominated, and Alabama became a cotton state. Mobile was second only to New Orleans as a cotton port. Cotton planters brought their slaves with them, and the state entered the Union with an established plantation slavery system. Yet never more than 25 percent of white Alabamians owned slaves. Waves of immigrants meant that Alabama's population more than doubled in the 1820s and almost doubled again in the next decade. Blacks made up 38.48 percent of the population in 1820 and 45.48 percent in 1860. The black belt, the Tennessee Valley, and other river valleys became the cotton kingdom and the centers of population. In 1860, 791,964 bales of cotton were produced. Dependent on agriculture and selling their cotton on an open market, most Alabamians supported free trade and opposed a protective tariff. A few Whigs supported the tariff, hoping that it would enable the state to industrialize.

By the 1830s most white Alabamians looked on slavery as both an economic necessity and a positive good. Alabama's slave population grew by natural increase, but it was also a slave-buying state with Mobile as the biggest market. In 1860 there were 437,770 slaves in the state. The state's slave code was patterned on the harsh code of South Carolina. The 2,690 free Negroes were anachronisms, discriminated against and mistrusted by the whites.

North and south Alabama rivalry was established when William Bibb, the Georgia party candidate, became governor. The capital was moved to Cahaba (north Alabamians wanted Tuscaloosa). Bibb, in office only a few months when he died, was succeeded by his brother, president of the state senate. Thomas Bibb did not seek reelection, and Israel Pickens became the new governor. Charging the Georgia party with enriching itself through private banks, Pickens was easily reelected. The PANIC OF 1819 forced many of Alabama's private banks to suspend specie payments and paved the way for a state-owned and state-operated bank. Established with Pickens' backing in 1824, the State Bank was prosperous and at one time paid most of the expenses of state government. But legislators became heavily indebted to it, and the PANIC OF 1837 triggered the conditions that carried it into bankruptcy.

Senate seats continued to be divided between north and south Alabama. Among the powerful senators who emerged were WILLIAM RUFUS KING, John W. Walker, CLEMENT C. CLAY, Gabriel Moore, and Arthur P. Bagby. When Cahaba proved unsatisfactory because of frequent flooding, the upcountry river valleys exerted their political power to get the capital removed to Tuscaloosa in 1826, where it remained until 1846.

Andrew Jackson, a military hero in Alabama. was popular with small farmers and the rank and file. Planters feared him and the democracy that he represented. Led by Dixon H. Lewis, Alabamians voted for Jackson in the presidential elections of 1824 and 1828. The old DEMOCRATIC-REPUBLICAN PARTY evolved by the late 1820s into the DEMOCRATIC PARTY. Its adherents stood for states' rights and opposed the second Bank of the United States and federal aid for internal improvements. Sharing opposite views were members of the WHIG PARTY. In general, the Democrats comprised the mass of the small farmers, plus some planters and merchants. The Whigs, representing merchants and planters in the black belt and the river valleys, tended toward aristocracy rather than egalitarianism. They were powerful in only two congressional districts and were never able to elect a governor or carry the state for a Whig presidential candidate.

Andrew Jackson's battle with South Carolina over the tariff and NULLIFICATION cost him the support of Dixon Lewis, but he remained popular with most Alabamians. Various governors opposed the tariff but would not go so far as nullification. Jackson lost support, however, when federal authorities delayed the occupation of lands previously owned by the Creeks. Governor John Gayle broke with Old Hickory over the issue and later drifted into the Whig party. Still, Jackson was responsible for the final removal to the West of the Indians remaining in Alabama.

Limited Whig successes in the late 1830s provoked a Democratic attempt to hold congressional elections on a statewide or general rather than a district basis. When the plan was voted down in a referendum, the legislature redrew the congressional district boundaries, basing them solely on the white population. Despite Whig protests, the system remained in effect until 1854, when the Whigs were no longer a threat.

As the State Bank floundered in the 1840s, Governors Arthur P. Bagby and BENJAMIN FITZPATRICK instituted reforms. Sharing their views were JOHN A. CAMPBELL and the newly emerging leader WILLIAM LOWNDES YANCEY. As governor, Fitzpatrick got branch banks liquidated, and the State Bank's charter was not renewed when it expired in 1845. Some Whigs favored the bank as did a wing of the Democrats headed by Nathaniel Terry. In 1845 Terry was defeated by Joshua L. Martin, an Independent Democrat who ran as a reformer. A commission headed by Francis S. Lyons completed liquidation of the State Bank in 1847. The year before, south Alabama and the black belt had demonstrated their power by winning a bitter fight to remove the state capital from Tuscaloosa to Montgomery.

The banking crisis hurt the Democrats, and pro-bank Democrats, still angry at Martin's victory as an Independent Democrat, refused to grant him renomination in 1847. Reuben Chapman was nominated instead, and he defeated his Whig opponent.

Yancey gained notoriety in 1848 with his ALABAMA PLATFORM. It was devised as an answer to the WILMOT PROVISO and the questions raised regarding territory acquired as a result of the Mexican War. The Alabama Platform stated that the federal government could not abolish slavery in the territories and, in fact, should protect its existence there. Alabama's delegates to the Democratic National Convention in Baltimore deserted Yancey as the Democrats nominated Lewis Cass, who endorsed the idea of POPULAR SOVEREIGNTY. Yancey bolted, and, without his support, Cass carried Alabama by only a narrow margin.

In 1849 Henry W. Collier won the governorship without opposition. Henry Clay's COMPROMISE OF 1850, supported in Congress by William Rufus King, touched off the NASHVILLE CONVENTION, to which southern states sent delegates to decide what action to take. John Campbell, an Alabama delegate, spoke for the compromise, and Collier won reelection in 1851 on the issue of accepting Clay's plan. During the campaign, Henry W. Hilliard, a leading Whig, debated the compromise's merits with Yancey, who strongly opposed it.

John A. Winston became the first native-born governor in 1853. Both Winston and his successor, John B. Moore, faced growing problems as national events swung support toward Yancey's idea of secession. Opposed to the stand of northern Whigs, especially regarding the Kansas situation, southern Whigs, Alabamians among them, lost their identity. In 1855 the American or KNOW-NOTHING PARTY reached the state. Alabamians who joined were attracted by the party's doctrine—nativism, anti-Catholicism, ritualism—and the organization also filled a political vacuum left by the shattered Whigs. The Democrats, moving toward a final confrontation, were able to defeat the Know-Nothing challenge.

Civil War and Reconstruction. Few Alabamians were content that in 1860 their state was enjoying unprecedented economic prosperity. Like other southerners, they believed the right to take slave property into the territories would be determined by the coming presidential election. John Brown's HARPERS FERRY RAID galvanized their feelings.

In January, 1860, the Democratic state convention split over what to do when the national convention met at Charleston, S.C. Yancey's advocates dominated, but separate factions organized to pledge support to compromise candidates. In February, the legislature instructed Governor Moore to call a convention if a president advocating the principles of the Republican party were elected.

At the CHARLESTON CONVENTION, the Democrats adjourned after failing to nominate a candidate. Yancey and other southerners, who had insisted that Stephen A. Douglas and northern Democrats support their position on slavery in the territories, walked out. In June, the convention reconvened at Baltimore, Md., and, when no agreement could be reached, the two wings met separately. Northern Democrats nominated Douglas (Benjamin Fitzpatrick declined nomination as Douglas' running mate), and the southern Democrats named JOHN C. BRECKINRIDGE of Kentucky. Meeting later at Chicago, the Republicans nominated Abraham Lincoln on a broad platform specifically opposing the introduction of slavery into the territories. A few days later the CONSTITUTIONAL UNION PARTY was formed, and it nominated JOHN BELL of Tennessee. In Alabama the new party comprised former Whigs and Know-Nothings.

In the election Alabama gave Breckinridge 48,000 votes, Bell 27,000, and Douglas 13,000; Lincoln carried the northern and western states, however, and his electoral total made him the clear winner. Early in December, Governor Moore—in accordance with the legislative resolution of February—called for the election of delegates to discuss secession at a special convention. Voting on Christmas Eve, Alabamians elected 100 men, 54 "straight outs," or advocates of immediate secession, who largely represented the black belt and south Alabama. The remaining 46, coming mainly from north Alabama, favored "cooperation" with other southern states in taking appropriate action. In the hill counties a small and unorganized minority of "unconditional Unionists" rejected the idea of secession.

When the convention opened on January 7, Alabama soldiers already had seized federal military installations in the state. Yancey controlled the meeting, and on January 11 the ordinance of secession passed by a vote of 61 to 39. Alabama became the fourth state to secede, although the vote was closer than in any other state of the Lower South.

At South Carolina's suggestion, Alabama invited the other southern states to meet at Montgomery on February 4 to decide upon joint action. The MONTGOMERY CONVENTION quickly adopted a constitution, elected JEFFERSON DAVIS and ALEXANDER H. STEPHENS as president and vice-president, and turned itself into a provisional congress to function until an election could be held. After Confederate forces fired on FT. SUMTER and Lincoln's call for volunteers, the Upper South joined the Confederacy. In May the capital was removed from Montgomery to Richmond, Va. That November, John Gill Shorter, an ardent secessionist, defeated THOMAS HILL WATTS in the gubernatorial election, demonstrating the state's support of the new government.

During the Civil War, Alabama was the scene of over 300 "military events," at nearly 200 different places. Yet no major battles were fought in the state. Alabama furnished 63 infantry regiments, 12 cavalry regiments, and 18 batteries of artillery. The exact number of military personnel is uncertain, but at least 75,000 Alabamians served in the Confederate armed forces. Of the 425 men who became Confederate general officers, Alabama provided 45, including JOSEPH ("FIGHTING JOE") WHEELER. Alabama units were engaged in every major battle east of the Mississippi. On the high seas, the state furnished RAPHAEL SEMMES, commander of the cruiser *Alabama*. JOSIAH GORGAS was Confederate chief of ordnance. Also, an estimated 3,000 white Alabamians and 10,000 blacks served in the Union army.

Besides furnishing men and agricultural products, Alabama was an important source of Confederate war matériel. Iron furnaces were located in several counties, and the city of Selma had one of the South's largest manufacturing complexes. Alabama maintained a military prison at Cahaba named Castle Morgan (CAHABA PRISON).

Spared in the early fighting, Alabama suffered in the spring of 1862, when a Union division captured Huntsville. During the occupation a federal brigade sacked the town of Athens, and for the remainder of the war the Tennessee Valley was controlled by Union armies, which systematically swept across the region. Penetrating the interior were three major raids: those of Colonel Abel D. Streight in the spring of 1863; General Lovell H. Rousseau in July, 1864; and General James H. Wilson in 1865. Coming late, WILSON'S RAID was the most extensive and was coordinated with Union operations against Mobile.

Mobile was blockaded early, but runners always managed to slip through. After New Orleans and Pensacola fell in 1862, Mobile became the Confederacy's only major port on the Gulf. On August 5, 1864, Commodore DAVID G. FARRAGUT passed the guns of Ft. Morgan and Ft. Gaines and won the battle of MOBILE BAY. Later, the two forts fell to Union land forces. The following spring the Union generals Edward R. S. Canby and Frederick Steele converged on Mobile's eastern shore defenses, capturing Spanish Fort and Ft. Blakely. Confederate General DABNEY H. MAURY evacuated Mobile, and Canby occupied the city on April 13 (MOBILE CAMPAIGN).

During the Mobile campaign, General Wilson moved south with 13,500 cavalrymen. He divided his command, sending General John T. Croxton to Tuscaloosa, where he captured the city and burned the buildings of the University of Alabama. Wilson continued south destroying the ironworks at Montevallo. On April 2, he defeated General NATHAN B. FORREST's badly outnumbered command and captured Selma. The manufacturing complex and much of the city were burned. Turning east, Wilson took and spared the undefended city of Montgomery on April 12. He then divided his force, which won simultaneous engagements at West Point and Girard, the last battles fought in Alabama. Wilson's forces then swept eastward into Georgia.

The home front was a story of shortages, widespread poverty, hunger, and a growing disenchantment with the war. "Tories" in the hill counties offered physical resistance to Confederate authorities. Political alienation came in 1863, when most of Alabama's secessionists in the Confederate Congress were replaced by peace advocates (PEACE MOVEMENT). Yancey, who had been on a fruitless diplomatic mission to Europe before serving as a Confederate senator, died in 1863. Watts, who had been defeated by Shorter in 1861, carried the state by a four-to-one margin over the incumbent in the governor's election of 1863. Watts' brief administration was divided between defending the state and resisting Confederate attempts to conscript materials. On May 5, 1865, General RICHARD TAYLOR surrendered the remaining Confederate forces to General Canby at Citronell, Ala. Taylor's capitulation ended the war. Shortly afterward, martial law was declared, and civil government in Alabama ceased to operate until a provisional government could be set up.

President ANDREW JOHNSON on June 21 named Lewis E. Parsons, an old-line Whig, as provisional governor. Parsons began the process of setting up a civil government, and he called a constitutional convention, but fewer than 30,000 voters elected the 100-member convention that drafted the constitution of 1865. The document nullified the ordinance of secession, ratified the Thirteenth

Amendment, and redundantly reiterated the abolition of slavery. The war debt was repudiated, and provision was made for the election of civil officers. In November, former Whig ROBERT M. PATTON was elected governor.

President Johnson proclaimed an official end to the insurrection on April 2, 1866. General Wager Swayne was placed in command of the Alabama FREEDMEN'S BUREAU. Throughout the year new counties were created, fiscal problems mounted, and most white Alabamians took Johnson's side in his struggles with Congress. On the advice of Governor Patton, the legislature refused to ratify the FOURTEENTH AMENDMENT.

In the spring of 1867 the Radicals passed the RECONSTRUCTION ACTS, which put the South under military control, over Johnson's veto. General officers were appointed to supervise the drafting of new constitutions and the establishing of new state governments. Alabama was placed in the Third District under General John Pope. By early summer in 1867, the REPUBLICAN PARTY—comprising local whites called SCALAWAGS, recently arrived northerners known as CARPETBAGGERS, and blacks—had been organized.

In October, 1867, Alabama voters, a majority of whom were blacks, mandated the calling of a constitutional convention and elected 100 delegates. Out of these, 96 Republicans, including 17 blacks and 28 northerners, framed the new carpetbagger constitution. It modernized the state by guaranteeing public education, providing for the development of industry and internal improvements, abolishing property qualifications for voting, and promoting equal rights. The votes on the constitution and for civil officers occurred simultaneously in February, 1868. The Conservative Democratic party, a name adopted to attract prewar Whigs, attempted to boycott the election. But Congress passed a resolution in June declaring the constitution ratified and civil officers elected, including WILLIAM H. SMITH as governor. Smith, who had organized Union cavalry in north Alabama during the war, was inaugurated in July. Two northerners, George E. Spencer and WILLARD WARNER, were elected U.S. senators. They and the congressmen-elect, all Republicans, were permitted to take their seats. Alabama was again one of the United States.

In the black belt and the Tennessee Valley, white Alabamians organized the KU KLUX KLAN to use terror and violence to intimidate the Republicans. They accused the Radicals of corruption, especially regarding state support for railroad construction. The Republicans warred among themselves, and as a result the Democrats gained seats in the legislature, defeated Senator Warner, and recaptured the governorship in 1870.

ROBERT B. LINDSAY, the new Democratic governor, was unable to cope with a stalemated legislature, political rivalries within and between the two parties, and financial crises. He was plagued by the difficulties of the Alabama & Chattanooga Railroad, which defaulted on the interest on its bonds. In the complex election of 1872, Republican DAVID P. LEWIS won the governorship, and Spencer was returned to the Senate. After much dispute the Democrats were awarded control of the state legislature.

Only in its early stages was the Republican party directed by carpetbaggers, whose power came from their control of the UNION LEAGUE. When that organization declined by 1868, the influence of black Republicans was limited largely to the black belt, and the power of the state's carpetbaggers was severely curtailed. Although some carpetbaggers were corrupt, some were quite capable, and on balance they did not suffer in comparison with their Democratic contemporaries. The majority of Republican officeholders, however, were native white Alabamians, or scalawags. They tended to be small farmers, indifferently educated, without political experience, and Unionist in their sentiments. Most came from the hill counties of the north and had resented the affluent slaveholders of the black belt and southern Alabama. Yet, a number of scalawags were men of wealth and education who lived in the black belt, a few of whom had fought for the Confederacy. In any case, scalawags became Republicans for reasons that included an acceptance of reality and an ideological commitment to the universal rights of man, as well as political and economic opportunism.

The greatest proportion of Alabama Republicans, however, were black. Some 500,000 slaves had been freed as a consequence of the war, and in 1867 more than 100,000 blacks were registered as voters. Yet the political equality of Reconstruction did not mean social and economic equality, and, even in politics, blacks never received rewards commensurate with their contributions. Between 1867 and 1876, 76 freedmen served in the legislature; 17 were delegates to the convention of 1867; no black served as a U.S. senator; and only three were elected to Congress. Indeed, Radical Reconstruction in Alabama was notable for its lack of radicalism. There was no confiscation of property, no redistribution of land, no mass arrest of Confederate leaders, and no extended period of political discrimination. Moreover, despite the turmoil of the period, positive achievements were

made, especially in education. The University of
Alabama was reopened. The agricultural and mechanical college at Auburn was begun in 1872 under the terms of the Morrill Act, and in 1873 a normal and industrial school for Negroes was started
at Huntsville.

By 1874, however, the excesses of the GRANT
ADMINISTRATION, national weariness with southern problems, and an interest in business expansion created the atmosphere in which Reconstruction ended. The Conservative Democrats, a
coalition of former Whigs and wartime Democrats, were determined to "redeem" Alabama.
Known in the state as BOURBONS, they ran on a
program of strict economy and honesty in government. More important, however, was their shib-
boleth of white supremacy. They accused the Republicans of using illiterate black voters to
bankrupt the state, both economically and morally, and of forcing equality of the two races. Campaigning on this platform, the Bourbons elected
George Smith Houston, a former Unionist, governor in 1874. The election shattered the Republican party, ended Reconstruction in Alabama, and
established a political pattern that would hold far
into the twentieth century.

Bourbons, Populists, and Progressives. Led by the
Bourbons of the black belt, the Democrats drafted
a new constitution in 1875, which abolished the
disability provisions, eliminated state aid for railroads, and segregated public education. The new
constitution retained universal manhood suffrage,
and no formal move was undertaken to disfranchise the state's blacks. Instead, the Bourbons
controlled the effects of the black franchise by
way of the whites' economic dominance over black
sharecroppers and tenant farmers (SHARECROP-
PING; TENANT FARMING) and, when necessary, by
manipulation of the blacks' ballots. Only when
confronted by a formidable combination of economically dispossessed blacks and whites during
the agrarian revolt of the 1890s did the Bourbon
Democrats push for the formal and final DISFRAN-
CHISEMENT of black voters.

While the Democrats solidified their political
position through control of the state's election machinery, the Republicans split into warring factions: the BLACK AND TANS and the LILY-WHITES.
Such leaders as Dr. Robert A. Moseley, Jr., and the
Negro William Stevens tried to keep the party
alive, but the Alabama Republicans were hopelessly crippled after 1875. Despite the Republicans' impotence, political opposition to the dominant Democrats did not entirely disappear. Many

northern Alabamians continued to dislike black
belt politicians and the capital's location at Montgomery. The Democrats worked out a regional rotation of the governor's office, but geographical
conflict between the state's northern and southern
sections lingered. Moreover, although the Bourbons scaled down the public debt (DEBTS OF
SOUTHERN STATES) and brought the state back to
solvency by the early 1880s, fiscal radicals turned
to the INDEPENDENT and the GREENBACKER
movements. In 1878 and 1880, William M. Lowe
won election as a Greenbacker to Congress, and
the party made unsuccessful attempts to capture
the governorship in the 1880s. Both the Greenbackers and the independents lacked organization and leadership. Although they were supported by the Republicans (who did not nominate a
candidate between 1876 and 1886), little effort
was made to attract the support of black voters in
the black belt. The Democrats easily repulsed
these challenges, identifying them as bizarre forms
of hyphenated Republican radicalism. Yet the discontent remained, particularly among the farmers
of northern Alabama, and the Republicans did
succeed at least in keeping their organization intact.

After the Civil War immigration and industry
became interrelated goals. The Republicans had
set up agencies to attract settlers. Although the
Bourbons abandoned all official commissions, they
also encouraged outsiders to move in. Unfortunately, immigrants declined to come South to
compete with black labor and face the uncertainties of political unrest. Newcomers tended to settle in the cities of northern Alabama, which also
attracted impoverished Negroes from south Alabama. Black belt planters resented the loss of their
labor supply. Provincialism and a distrust of foreigners were other factors in a lack of immigration. In 1890 Alabama's native-born population
was 99.02 percent, larger than it had been in 1860.

Northern and southern businessmen interpreted political peace as necessary for economic development. Some citizens preached the NEW
SOUTH concept (industry balanced with agriculture) as a means of freeing Alabama from northern
dominance. As a result, some industrial progress
was made. The TEXTILE INDUSTRY became important. Water power juxtaposed to cotton fields
made possible an increase in textile mills from six
in 1872 to 44 in 1900. The experience of Reconstruction limited state participation in industrial
development; but the Bourbons relented by lowering corporation taxes, permitting local tax exemptions, and continuing the CONVICT LEASE
SYSTEM. Industrialists benefited further when

Congress permitted the purchase of mineral lands at the same rate as agricultural lands.

Financed by local and northern capital, Birmingham became a railroad center and a major producer of iron and steel. Nearby were numerous coal mines. Anniston, Sheffield, Bessemer, and Gadsden were other boom cities of the New South. The Louisville & Nashville emerged as the major railroad and became a powerful political and economic force in Alabama. Railroad companies, despite the creation of a railroad commission in 1881, were neither severely regulated nor heavily taxed. Increasingly, northern know-how and northern capital meant northern control. A mill worker or a miner was only slightly better off than a sharecropper. Voices of protest began to rise. There was little industrial expansion in the black belt or the wire grass or the piney woods, where retrogression rather than progress prevailed. Despite appeals to immigrants and the growth of industry, Alabama's dirt farmers were worse off than ever.

An attempt to revive the prewar state agricultural society had failed, and the depression in the 1870s drove many Alabama farmers into the GRANGE. Offering educational and social benefits, the Grange also engaged in cooperative ventures in marketing and purchasing. In Alabama, as throughout the South, the Grange was nonpolitical. When inexperience, competition, and a lack of capital destroyed the order's economic efforts, farmers deserted. By 1880 the Alabama Grange was impotent, but its program of collective action set the stage for more militant agricultural orders.

The legislature created a state department of agriculture in 1883 and a state agricultural society in 1884. Both agencies became active, especially after REUBEN F. KOLB became commissioner in 1887. An aristocrat, a Confederate veteran, and a scientific agriculturist, Kolb was criticized for using his position to build a political following.

In the late 1880s the Agricultural Wheel and the FARMERS' ALLIANCE moved into Alabama. At first both orders eschewed political activity. In 1888–1889 the more active Farmers' Alliance absorbed the Wheel. When its economic ventures failed, the Alliance turned to politics and moved to seize control of the Democratic party. The maneuver would avoid the threat to white supremacy posed by establishing a third party. The Alliance demanded regulation of monopolies, greater governmental control of railroads, the abolishment of the convict lease system, an equitable tax structure, and monetary inflation. By 1890 Alabama's white Alliance had over 125,000 members. A separate Negro Alliance had enrolled over 50,000 adherents. In that year the Alliance endorsed Kolb

for governor, but a coalition of his opponents gave the Democratic nomination to THOMAS G. JONES, a Bourbon and Confederate veteran, who won the election easily. Kolb's followers promised a day of reckoning.

The third-party movement evolved at a series of national conventions. In 1892 the POPULIST PARTY was officially launched, with James B. Weaver of Iowa and James G. Field of Virginia as its candidates. In Alabama, Kolb resisted, but the Knights of Labor and various local Alliances endorsed the Populists. Joseph C. Manning, a young editor, helped form a statewide People's party in May, 1892.

Alabamians were more interested in state politics than the national campaign. Governor Jones and Kolb were opponents again in 1892. Claiming that the state Democratic convention was rigged, Kolb bolted the party and was nominated by a group calling itself the Jeffersonian Democrats. The Jeffersonians accepted Populist reforms and advocated voting rights for blacks. Endorsed by the Populists, Kolb was supported also by most Republicans (the party did not nominate a candidate), by blacks, and by organized labor (union members in the mineral counties objected to convicts working in the coal mines). Democrats countered by conjuring up Reconstruction horrors and by affirming white supremacy. In the August election Kolb carried the white counties, but the Bourbons illegally manipulated the returns from the black belt, allowing Jones to win by a narrow majority of 11,435 votes. Without a state contest law, Kolb was helpless before Jones's heavy majorities in the black belt. Incongruously, the Democrats had used black voters to uphold white supremacy.

In 1894 economic depression and evidence of foul play were factors favoring Kolb in his third gubernatorial campaign. Despite opposition from free-silver Democrats, the Bourbons secured the nomination of WILLIAM C. OATES, a Confederate veteran and an implacable foe of the agrarians. The Republicans and organized labor again joined Kolb's camp, and Negroes in the black belt attempted to boycott the polls so that their ballots would not be falsely counted. The election was a repetition of 1892. Democrats counted Kolb out again, and Oates's wide black belt margins carried him to a narrow victory. In the congressional elections the Populists absorbed the Jeffersonian Democrats, fused with the Republicans, and won four congressional seats.

In 1896 Kolb stepped aside, to be replaced by Albert T. Goodwyn. Populists fused with the Republicans on the state ticket, and the platform endorsed free silver, fair elections, and voting rights for blacks. The Democrats, abandoning the conservatives, nominated James F. Johnston on a platform of free silver and white supremacy. Goodwyn was able, but many Populists were disillusioned. Johnston was popular and energetic, and, for the first time since 1890, the Democrats won an untainted victory. Populists ran candidates in the next elections, but the party was never again a threat in Alabama. Some Populists quit politics; others joined the Republicans; but most, like Kolb, returned to the Democrats. Despite a conservative reaction, many Populist reforms were later enacted into law.

The Progressive era overlapped the Populist period and continued until World War I. Unlike populism, rural and based on economic discontent, PROGRESSIVISM was the product of middle-class, urban-centered grievances. It was led by professional men: editors, lawyers, educators, ministers, and businessmen. Alabama Progressives wanted to correct abuses and make government serve the interests of society. Yet, Alabama progressivism contained a major paradox: political reforms were preceded by the retrogressive constitution of 1901. The convention, dominated by black belt politicians and BIG MULE industrialists, produced a constitution whose suffrage provisions—a cumulative poll tax, as well as property, residence, and literacy requirements—eliminated most black voters and many POOR WHITES. The requirement for legislative reapportionment every ten years went unfulfilled until the federal courts ordered it in the 1960s. Moreover, the constitution did not provide for a strong railroad commission and failed to reform either child labor or convict leasing. The state was forbidden to engage in internal improvements, and severe tax and debt limits were placed on counties and municipalities.

With the new constitution, Alabamians faced the issues of progressivism. In 1902 the Democratic party held its first primary for state officers, and the next year the legislature passed the first comprehensive primary election law. In 1906 Alabama became the first southern state to use the primary to achieve the direct election of U.S. senators. Progressive Governor BRAXTON B. COMER (1907–1911) persuaded the legislature to pass measures regulating campaign contributions and questionable political maneuvers. In 1914 Charles Henderson defeated Comer, but the 1915 legislature was controlled by Progressives who enacted a new primary law, a corrupt practices act, and a new registration law. The secret ballot was extended to primaries, and there were numerous provisions relating to election procedures. Another law prohibited state, county, and municipal boards and commissions from holding executive or secret sessions.

The problems of Alabama's cities became the concern of Governor Emmett O'Neal (1911–1915). At his urging the 1911 legislature enacted municipality laws that permitted towns and cities to establish commission forms of government, and by 1915 Birmingham and other cities had adopted variations of the GALVESTON PLAN. Despite newspaper campaigns, no initiative or referendum laws were adopted, although four municipal government laws contained recall provisions.

In the drive to gain the vote for women, suffrage clubs and leagues were formed, and in 1912 they joined forces as the Alabama Equal Suffrage Association. The association was unable to persuade the legislature to amend the state constitution to permit women to vote, and in 1919 the legislature defeated the Nineteenth Amendment. When it was ratified nationally, a special legislative session passed a law of implementation. In November, 1920, Alabama women voted for the first time in state and national elections.

During Comer's administration several acts regulating the railroads were passed. In addition, telephone, telegraph, and express companies were placed under the railroad commission. Later, in 1915, all public carriers and utilities were put under the control of a public service commission.

State Superintendent of Education John W. Abercrombie led the way toward improving public education. School terms were extended, a textbook commission was created, and public high schools, one in each county, were established. School districts were allowed to levy taxes for education, compulsory school attendance was ordered, and a state board of education was created.

The convict lease system was reformed but not abolished. By the late 1890s the Reverend EDGAR GARDNER MURPHY, the Alabama Federation of Women's Clubs, and the WOMAN'S CHRISTIAN TEMPERANCE UNION were working for laws regulating CHILD LABOR. They were hampered by attitudes that regarded children as cheap labor and as sources of family income. Bills concerning child labor were either defeated or emasculated, and not until 1919 did Alabama enact a measure that complied with federal guidelines.

The Alabama Federation of Women's Clubs, founded in 1895 and led by Mrs. Robert D. Johnston (18??–1934), was largely responsible for the opening of a state industrial school for boys and for the establishment of juvenile courts. A similar organization of black women operated a farm and school for wayward Negro youths that was later taken over by the state. Under Comer, appropriations for such schools and for a girls' industrial school were increased. A colony for epileptics and a tuberculosis commission were also set up.

For Alabamians the war against liquor was progressivism seen as a moral force. Counties voted "dry," the Anti-Saloon League and other groups were active, and restrictive laws were passed. Most counties exercised local option to defeat the "wets," and in 1909 a statewide prohibition law went into effect. Yet in that same year the voters turned down a proposal to make prohibition a part of the state constitution. Amid much acrimony and debate the issue remained prominent, affected gubernatorial contests, and did not end until the ratification of the Eighteenth Amendment in 1919.

Progressivism was mainly for whites and was seriously flawed, but it did exist. One reform further disfranchised black voters, as the direct primary became the "white" primary. Yet state government became more efficient. If progressivism was never well formulated or wholly successful, it was at least a reform movement that called into question certain concepts of the status quo.

Recent Alabama. The GREAT DEPRESSION began in Alabama much earlier than 1929. As the prosperity of World War I turned sour, the textile industry declined, and the cotton market faced increasing foreign competition. The BOLL WEEVIL, soil erosion, falling farm prices, and mortgage foreclosures became chronic problems. Blacks and whites alike left the countryside, migrating in search of jobs to Alabama's or, frequently, to northern cities. This demographic shift cost small-town merchants and professional men their customers and further aggravated the worsening economic conditions in much of the state.

With the economy declining, the mood of many Alabamians became increasingly emotional. Immigrants, labor unions, Catholics, and Jews became generally suspect. And the Ku Klux Klan (Imperial Wizard William J. Simmons was a native Alabamian) became a powerful force. Although it briefly attracted such prominent persons as HUGO L. BLACK, the Klan's excesses drove decent people out. Exposés of the Klan by Grover C. Hall, Sr., in the Montgomery *Advertiser* won a Pulitzer Prize, however; and, in the late 1920s, the legislature passed an antiflogging act. The presidential ELECTION OF 1928 was yet another instance of the strength of emotional issues in the state. Viewing Al Smith as representative of eastern city politics, immigrant influences, antiprohibition in-

terests, and Catholic intrigues, five southern states voted for Herbert Hoover. In Alabama, U.S. Senator J. THOMAS HEFLIN led the bolt, but the state went Democratic by a narrow margin.

Throughout the 1920s, blacks in Alabama remained second-class citizens. Prominent Negroes such as Robert Russa Moton and GEORGE WASHINGTON CARVER, both of TUSKEGEE INSTITUTE, could do little to mitigate the situation. BOOKER T. WASHINGTON's dream of economic independence seemed very distant indeed, and racial justice appeared to be at least as remote, especially during the SCOTTSBORO CASE of the 1930s.

Politically, however, Alabamians sustained the moderate reform traditions of the Progressive period. In 1918, Thomas E. Kilby was elected governor on his pledge to reorganize the state's budgetary system. He reorganized the public schools, increased appropriations for education and public health, established a state welfare department, signed a workmen's compensation act into law, constructed a new state penitentiary, expanded the port of Mobile, and accelerated the building of roads. Despite his new budgetary system with tax adjusters in each county of the state, most of his programs operated on deficit budgets. Governor William ("Plain Bill") Brandon (1923–1927) further strengthened education, and Bibb Graves, who succeeded Brandon, pushed through an ambitious tax program to fund the state's multiple new services. New revenues were obtained from levies on coal and iron operators, tobacco sales, public utilities, and corporations. His administration (1927–1931) also abolished the convict lease system. During a later second term in office (1935–1939), Graves inaugurated a cameo New Deal for Alabama.

LABOR UNIONS, organized late in the nineteenth century, met spectacular defeat in railroad and mine strikes. Cooperation between state troops and management broke up the strikes and became a twentieth-century practice. A textile strike at Huntsville in 1937 ended in compromise but no real gains for labor. Alabama's lack of an industrial tradition, the individualism of its rural people, and the feeling that unions threatened industrial prosperity slowed the growth of organized labor. Various NEW DEAL measures aided the movement. By the mid-1930s, the Alabama United Mine Workers' membership was over 50 percent black. There was racial discrimination, but both races shared common interests. Pay and promotions became more equalized in the 1950s, largely because of pressure from the federal government. By the late 1960s new inroads were made in the textile industry. In the 1970s the largest union was that of the steelworkers, followed by those of the electrical workers, communications workers, and miners.

Alabama boomed during World War II. Numerous military installations, as well as munitions factories and the shipyards at Mobile, brought unprecedented prosperity. A large number of Alabamians served in the armed forces. Yet the 1940s marked a rise in political conservatism. Alabama had benefited greatly from Franklin D. Roosevelt's New Deal measures, and the president easily carried the state four times. Alabamians JOHN H. BANKHEAD, WILLIAM BANKHEAD, LISTER HILL, Hugo Black, Henry Stegall, and AUBREY WILLIAMS were key New Deal figures. Gradually, conservative southerners became alienated from the New Deal's liberal measures. Wartime demands blunted the drift but also exacerbated the situation. Blacks entering the armed services became less willing to accept compromise. In the cities whites and blacks competing for jobs increased the tensions. Conservative Governor Frank Dixon (1939–1943) opposed federal centralization and social experimentation. Among other programs, he opposed FDR's Fair Employment Practices Committee, which oversaw the awarding of defense contracts. A riot in 1943 at Mobile between white and black shipyard workers resulted in injury and the dispatching of soldiers by Governor Chauncey Sparks. The issue was finally negotiated by the FEPC.

After the Supreme Court declared the white primary unconstitutional (SMITH V. ALLWRIGHT, 1944), southern conservatives attempted other expedients. In Alabama the Boswell amendment, passed in 1946, assigned wide discretionary powers to local registrars in enrolling voters. Yet Alabama blacks registered in significant numbers in the late 1940s.

JAMES E. FOLSOM, a colorful latter-day Populist, was elected governor in 1946. Conservatives opposed his program of legislative reapportionment, poll tax repeal, old-age pensions, farm-to-market roads, and increased teachers' pay. Never a racist, he accepted the Supreme Court's decision on civil rights in 1954. Despite a second term (1955–1959), Folsom was hurt politically by his racial stand and failed in later attempts at a comeback.

The States' Rights or DIXIECRAT PARTY, born of racial and economic discontent, was a combination of urban and rural elements. In 1948 conservative southerners refused to accept the Democratic party's nomination of HARRY S. TRUMAN on a strong civil rights platform. Having bolted the national convention, delegates from several Deep South states met in Birmingham in July, formed the States' Rights party, and nominated J. STROM THURMOND of South Carolina and Fielding Wright of Mississippi. The party fared badly nationally and carried only four southern states. Although Folsom supported Truman, Alabama voted for the Dixiecrats. The election demonstrated opposition to "big government" and to concern by the national party for the interests of northern urban blacks. It was a portent of massive resistance.

Although the state voted Democratic in 1952 (partly because U.S. Senator JOHN SPARKMAN was the vice-presidential nominee) and in 1956, Republican Dwight D. Eisenhower ran well both times, and many Alabamians abandoned traditional party loyalties. Even so, the *Brown* decision, the school crisis at Little Rock, Ark., and the CIVIL RIGHTS ACT OF 1957 all occurred under Eisenhower. In the ELECTION OF 1960, the presence of LYNDON B. JOHNSON on the ticket with John F. Kennedy was insufficient to prevent Alabama from wasting its electoral votes on Senator HARRY F. BYRD of Virginia. Alabamians were no longer loyal to the national Democratic party, and in the ELECTION OF 1964 Alabama was one of five Lower South states to vote for Barry Goldwater. In that same election, the Republicans captured five out of eight seats in the U.S. House of Representatives.

By 1968, GEORGE C. WALLACE had become a national figure. A former legislator and circuit judge, he was defeated for governor in 1958 by John Patterson. In 1962 Wallace swamped the field and at his inauguration made clear his belief in segregation. Opposing school integration, he stood in the door at the University of Alabama until forced to back down by a court order. The confrontation occurred in June, 1963, the same year as the Selma freedom march. Blacks, thwarted by voter registration officials in Dallas County, dramatized their frustration by staging a 60-mile march from Selma to Montgomery. Their trek made international headlines. Black resistance was led by the Reverend MARTIN LUTHER KING, whose Montgomery bus boycott and SOUTHERN CHRISTIAN LEADERSHIP CONFERENCE emphasized massive but peaceful resistance.

In 1966 Wallace, legally unable to succeed himself, handpicked his wife Lurleen, who won easily over a group of male rivals. Wallace himself ran well in several Democratic presidential primaries in 1968. After Hubert Humphrey and Richard Nixon were nominated, Wallace was nominated by the American Independent party. He raised the issue of law and order, opposed big government, and championed middle- and lower-income working people. In the election Wallace carried five southern states, including Alabama. He received 45 electoral votes and almost 10 million popular votes, for 13.5 percent of the national total. His candidacy hurt both parties but was devastating to the Democrats, assuring Nixon's election.

Mrs. Wallace died in 1968 and was succeeded by Lieutenant Governor Albert Brewer. In the governor's race of 1970, Wallace finished second to Brewer in the first primary but won in the runoff. At the national level, Wallace won several Democratic primaries in 1972. His platform denounced forced busing to achieve school integration. Campaigning in Maryland, Wallace was shot and seriously wounded and had to withdraw from the race. In the election Alabama voted for Nixon over George McGovern. Wallace was reelected governor in 1974 and in 1976 campaigned for the presidential nomination again, this time in a wheelchair. His physical condition and the presence of another southerner, former governor JIMMY CARTER of Georgia, as a rival hurt Wallace. He withdrew from the contest and advocated Carter's nomination.

By 1960 Alabama had become an urban state, more dependent on industry than on agriculture. Its citizens had survived a prolonged depression, a world war, and the traumatic postwar decades. In the 1970s Alabama retained a distinctiveness, but it had entered the mainstream of American life.

Manuscripts. The three major depositories for Alabama history are the Alabama Department of Archives and History, Montgomery; University of Alabama; and Auburn University. Other institutions with manuscript holdings for Alabama history are Samford University; University of North Carolina; Duke University; University of Florida; Birmingham Public Library; Library of Congress; and the National Archives.

General works. The best study of early Alabama is A. Pickett, *History of Alabama* (1851). A. Moore, *History of Alabama* (1934), is the standard one-volume work. M. McMillan is currently revising Moore's book; McMillan's own exhaustive *Constitutional Development in Alabama* (1955) is indispensable. Two earlier works are W. Brewer, *Alabama* (1872), and T. Owen, *History of Alabama and Dictionary of Alabama Biography* (4 vols.; 1921). Published every four years is the useful *Alabama Official and Statistical Register*.

Early studies. See P. Hamilton's pioneering *Colonial Mobile* (1910); T. Abernethy, *Formative Period in Alabama* (1922); R. Rea and M. Howard, *Memoire of Monbereaut* (1965); J. Holmes, *Gayosa* (1965); N. Crowe, *Lemoyne d'Iberville* (1954); and A. Royall, *Letters from Alabama* (1969). A sound study of an early political leader is H. Bailey's *John Williams Walker* (1964).

Antebellum period. None is more important or better written than J. Baldwin, *Flush Times of Alabama and Mississippi* (1953). For politics see T. Jack, *Party Politics*

ALABAMA GOVERNORS

Governor	Party	Term
TERRITORY		
William W. Bibb		1817–1819
William W. Bibb		1819–1820
Thomas Bibb		1820–1821
Israel Pickens		1821–1825
STATE		
John Murphy	Dem.	1825–1829
Gabriel Moore	Dem.	1829–1831
Samuel B. Moore	Dem.	1831
John Gayle	Dem.	1831–1835
Clement C. Clay	Dem.	1835–1836
Hugh McVay	Dem.	1837
Arthur P. Bagby	Dem.	1837–1841
Benjamin Fitzpatrick	Dem.	1841–1845
Joshua L. Martin	Ind.-Dem.	1845–1847
Reuben Chapman	Dem.	1847–1849
Henry W. Collier	Dem.	1849–1853
John A. Winston	Dem.	1853–1857
Andrew B. Moore	Dem.	1857–1861
John G. Shorter	Dem.	1861–1863
Thomas H. Watts	Dem.	1863–1865
Lewis E. Parsons (provisional)		1865
Robert M. Patton (provisional)	Rep.	1865–1867
John Pope (military)		1867–1868
William H. Smith	Rep.	1868–1870
Robert B. Lindsay	Dem.	1870–1872
David P. Lewis	Rep.	1872–1874
George S. Houston	Dem.	1874–1878
Rufus W. Cobb	Dem.	1878–1882
Edward A. O'Neal	Dem.	1882–1886
Thomas Seay	Dem.	1886–1890
Thomas G. Jones	Dem.	1890–1894
William C. Oates	Dem.	1894–1896
James F. Johnston	Dem.	1896–1900
William D. Jelks	Dem.	1900–1907
Braxton B. Comer	Dem.	1907–1911
Emmett O'Neal	Dem.	1911–1915
Charles Henderson	Dem.	1915–1919
Thomas E. Kilby	Dem.	1919–1923
William W. Brandon	Dem.	1923–1927
Bibb Graves	Dem.	1927–1931
Benjamin M. Miller	Dem.	1931–1935
Bibb Graves	Dem.	1935–1939
Frank M. Dixon	Dem.	1939–1942
Chauncey Sparks	Dem.	1942–1947
James E. Folsom	Dem.	1947–1951
Gordon Persons	Dem.	1951–1955
James E. Folsom	Dem.	1955–1959
John M. Patterson	Dem.	1959–1963
George C. Wallace	Dem.	1963–1967
Lurleen B. Wallace	Dem.	1967–1968
Albert P. Brewer	Dem.	1968–1971
George C. Wallace	Dem.	1971–1979
Forrest James	Dem.	1979–

in Alabama (1919); C. Denman, *Secession Movement in Alabama* (1933); L. Dorman, *Politics in Alabama* (1935); and J. Du Bose, *William Lowndes Yancey* (1892). Significant recent studies are W. Jackson, *William Rufus King* (1952); R. Nuermberger, *Clays of Alabama* (1958); and W. Barney, *Secessionist Impulse* (1974). For agriculture, slavery, and economic life before the Civil War, see two sound works by W. Jordan, *Hugh Davis* (1948) and

ALABAMA POPULATION, 1820-1970

Year	Total	White	Nonwhite		% Growth	Rank	
			Slave	Free		U.S.	South
1820	127,901	85,451	41,879	571	1,314.0	19	9
1830	309,527	190,406	117,549	1,572	142.0	15	8
1840	590,756	335,185	253,532	2,039	90.9	12	7
1850	771,623	426,514	342,844	2,265	30.6	12	6
1860	964,201	526,271	435,080	2,850	25.0	13	7
1870	996,992	521,384	475,608		3.4	16	7
1880	1,262,505	662,185	600,320		26.6	17	8
1890	1,513,401	833,718	679,683		19.9	17	8
1900	1,828,697	1,001,152	827,545		20.8	18	8
1910	2,138,093	1,228,832	909,261		16.9	18	7
1920	2,348,174	1,447,032	901,142		9.8	18	6
1930	2,646,248	1,700,844	945,404		12.7	15	5
1940	2,832,961	1,849,097	983,868		7.1	17	7
1950	3,061,743	2,079,591	982,152		8.1	17	7
1960	3,266,740	2,283,609	983,131		6.7	10	8
1970	3,444,165	2,533,831	910,334		5.4	21	10

Antebellum Alabama (1957); C. Davis, *Cotton Kingdom of Alabama* (1939); and J. Sellers, *Slavery in Alabama* (1950). Social and intellectual studies are those of M. Boyd, *Alabama in the Fifties* (1931); W. Posey, *British Travelers in Alabama* (1938); W. Hoole, *Alias Simon Suggs* (1952); J. Sulzby, *Historic Alabama Hotels and Resorts* (1960); W. Brantley, *Three Capitals* (1947); and R. Hammond, *Antebellum Mansions in Alabama* (1951).

Civil War and Reconstruction. Dated but comprehensive is W. Fleming, *Civil War and Reconstruction* (1906); less satisfactory is J. Du Bose, *Alabama's Tragic Decade* (1940). H. Bond, *Negro Education in Alabama* (1939), is far broader than its title indicates. See also F. Vandiver, *Ploughshares into Swords* (1952); G. Sterkx, *Alabama Women in the Civil War* (1970); M. McMillan, *Confederate Reader* (1962); B. Martin, *Desertion of Alabama Troops* (1932); P. Kolchin, *First Freedom* (1972); and J. Hunnicutt, *Reconstruction in West Alabama* (1969), a contemporary account.

1874-1920. Alabama history in the last half of the nineteenth and the early decades of the twentieth centuries has received considerable scholarly interest. See A. Going, *Bourbon Democracy in Alabama* (1951); H. Hammett, *Hilary Abner Herbert* (1976); R. Ward and W. Rogers, *Labor Revolt in Alabama* (1965); E. Armes, *Story of Coal and Iron in Alabama* (1910); J. Clark, *Populism in Alabama* (1927); S. Hackney, *Populism to Progressivism* (1969); W. Rogers, *One-Gallused Rebellion* (1970); J. Doster, *Railroads in Alabama Politics* (1951); and L. Harlan, *Booker T. Washington* (1972). Two trenchant contemporary accounts are J. Manning, *Fadeout of Populism* (1928), and W. Skaggs, *The Southern Oligarchy* (1924).

Twentieth century. D. Carter's *Scottsboro* (1969) is excellent. Other works of merit are V. Hamilton, *Hugo Black* (1972); W. Barnard, *Dixiecrats and Democrats* (1974); E. Lawrence, *George Washington Carver* (1966); J. Larson, *Reapportionment in Alabama* (1955); B. Cosman, *Five States for Goldwater* (1966); H. Walters, *Wernher Von Braun* (1964); A. Walker, *Braxton Bragg Comer*; and J. Sellers, *Prohibition Movement in Alabama* (1943). See also P. Hubbard, *Origins of TVA* (1957); H. Bailey, *Edgar Gardner Murphy* (1968); B. Jones, *The Wallace Story* (1966); and C. Lincoln, *Martin Luther King, Jr.* (1969).

More work is needed on religion in Alabama, but see

B. Riley, *Baptists of Alabama* (1923), and A. West, *Methodists in Alabama* (1893). Education has been more fully treated in S. Weeks, *Public Education in Alabama* (1895); J. Sellers, *History of the University of Alabama* (1953); L. Griffith, *Alabama College* (1969); R. Ellison, *Huntingdon College* (1954); J. Parks and O. Weaver, *Birmingham-Southern College* (1957); C. Smith, *Troy State* (1972); and W. Hughes, *Robert R. Moton* (1956).

The *Alabama Review* and the *Alabama Historical Quarterly* regularly publish articles on Alabama history. The *Journal of Southern History* and other quarterlies also contain material on the state. For information on theses and dissertations, see A. Jones, *Alabama Review* (July, 1969). A sampling of excellent dissertations includes W. Cash, "Alabama Republicans During Reconstruction" (University of Alabama, 1973); E. Johnson, "Oscar W. Underwood" (University of North Carolina, 1953); S. Wiggins, "Scalawag in Alabama" (Louisiana State University, 1965); A. Jones, "Direct Primary in Alabama" (University of Alabama, 1964); R. Gilmour, "The Other Emancipation" (Johns Hopkins University, 1972); L. Schweingier, "James Rapier and Reconstruction" (University of Chicago, 1971); and R. Granade, "Higher Education in Antebellum Alabama" (Florida State University, 1968).

WILLIAM WARREN ROGERS
Florida State University

ALABAMA, UNIVERSITY OF (University, Ala.

35486). In 1819 the U.S. Congress donated 46,000 acres of land in Alabama for higher education, but not until 1831 was the university opened. Most of its buildings were destroyed by federal cavalry (April 4, 1865) during the Civil War. Construction of new buildings began in 1867, and the university reopened in 1869. Fifteen years later, the federal government donated 72 sections of public land in recompense for the destroyed buildings. Today, this publicly supported coeducational institution has an enrollment of 13,000. Its library of 750,000 volumes is the repository for numerous manuscript collections relating chiefly to Alabama history, including the papers of HENRY DE LAMAR CLAYTON, JAMES THOMAS HEFLIN, William C. Gorgas, Basil Manly, and JULIA TUTWILER, as well as the Shelby Iron Company Records (1862–1923).

See J. B. Sellers, *History of University of Alabama, 1818–1902* (1953).

ALABAMA DEPARTMENT OF ARCHIVES AND HISTORY

(624 Washington Ave., Montgomery, Ala. 36130) is publisher since 1930 and intermittently of the *Alabama Historical Quarterly*, circulation 1,000, which prints scholarly articles and book reviews limited to the history of the state of Alabama. The department also publishes quadrennially the *Alabama Official and Statistical Register*.

ALABAMA HISTORICAL ASSOCIATION

traces its origins to 1850, when the Alabama Historical Society was organized, with the president of the University of Alabama playing a major role. The society became inactive during the Civil War, when much of its collection was destroyed by southern soldiers. It was reestablished in 1874, but its growth was curtailed when the legislature created the Department of Archives and History, which took over some of the society's prime functions. In 1947 a new organization called the Alabama Historical Association was founded at Montevallo. In cooperation with the University of Alabama Press, it began to publish in 1948 the quarterly *Alabama Review*. The *Review* prints papers read by members of the association at the annual meeting, as well as book reviews and scholarly articles concerning the history of the state. The *Review* in 1976 had a circulation of 1,750. The association also supports a highway historical marker program and encourages the organization of county historical societies.

ALABAMA PLATFORM

was adopted by the Democratic state convention in Montgomery in February, 1848, amid a flurry of WILLIAM LOWNDES YANCEY's oratory. It was Yancey's answer to the WILMOT PROVISO and POPULAR SOVEREIGNTY: declaring that Congress could not abolish slavery in the territories but in fact must protect it, since slaves were property and the federal government must protect the property of all its citizens. It was advanced ground for the times, but ground upon which Yancey stood until majority opinion in the Lower South caught up with him in 1860. The Alabama Platform contained every essential item of many later restatements of southern rights, including the Southern Platform of the CHARLESTON CONVENTION (1860). It helped prepare the climate for the repeal of the MISSOURI COMPROMISE and the issuance of the DRED SCOTT decision. When the Alabama Platform was defeated and Lewis Cass was nominated on a popular sovereignty ticket at Baltimore in 1848, Yancey almost alone among Alabama delegates obeyed instructions to walk out. In the convention held in Charleston 12 years later, he led a majority of southern delegates out of the convention.

See M. C. McMillan, *Alabama Review* (July, 1967); C. P. Denman, *Secession Movement in Alabama* (1933); and J. W. Du Bose, *W. L. Yancey* (2 vols; 1892).

MALCOLM C. MCMILLAN
Auburn University

ALABAMA RIVER

is formed seven miles northeast of Montgomery by the confluence of the Coosa and Tallapoosa rivers. Both tributaries begin in the mountains of western Georgia and flow generally west and southwest to central Alabama. From the head of the Coosa to the mouth of the Alabama, the entire river system measures approximately 720 miles. HERNANDO DE SOTO was the first to explore the river when, in 1540, he and his party followed the Coosa downstream to the Alabama. After the settlement of MOBILE in 1702, French colonists gradually moved upriver, using the rich alluvial land of the lower Alabama to raise rice and indigo. And throughout the eighteenth century both French and British-American fur traders worked the whole length of the river system. Lumbering on the Coosa and steamboat traffic on the lower Alabama made the system vital to the settlement and development of the state prior to the Civil War. RAILROADS virtually displaced river transportation in the decades after the war, but traffic on this inland waterway has been expanding regularly throughout the current century. With a series of dams and canals, the Alabama and Coosa rivers are now navigable as far upstream as Rome, Ga.

ALABAMO, BATTLE OF.

See MAUVILLA, BATTLE OF

ALAMANCE, BATTLE OF

(May 16, 1771), resulted when Governor WILLIAM TRYON of North Carolina attempted to disperse the REGULATORS and force them to submit to provincial and royal authority. One wing of the loyalist force under General Hugh Waddell had been cut off by the insurgents at Salisbury. Tryon was moving to Waddell's aid with 1,100 men when he reached Big Alamance Creek. He was opposed by about 2,000 Regulators, many unarmed, lacking a commanding officer. Expecting the governor to negotiate, the Regulators were mauled by the loyalist artillery but contested the ground stubbornly for two hours. Nine were killed on both sides, but the Regulators were overwhelmingly defeated, suffering far more wounded. One Regulator was hanged immediately after the battle, six others a month later after a trial. Failing to reform the corrupt local government system, many Regulators migrated to the Watauga settlements and helped establish what became the Tennessee frontier (WATAUGA ASSOCIATION).

See J. S. Bassett, "Regulators of North Carolina," *Annual Report of the AHA, 1894* (1895), best; S. A. Ashe, *History of North Carolina* (1908), I, good; W. S. Powell, *War of Regulation* (1949), for bibliography; H. T. Lefler and A. R. Newsome, *History of North Carolina* (1973); G. R. Adams, *North Carolina Historical Review* (Oct., 1972); and W. S. Powell, J. K. Huhta, and T. J. Farnham (eds.), *Documentary History* (1971).

CLYDE R. FERGUSON
Kansas State University

ALAMO, THE. In downtown San Antonio is a shrine to Texas liberty, the chapel of the Alamo mission. Founded in 1718 by Father Antonio Buenaventura Olivares, the mission was first named San Antonio de Padua, then changed to San Antonio de Valero, and finally called simply the Alamo.

During the Texas revolution, after the rebel forces had captured Bexar (San Antonio) from Mexican General Martín Perfecto de Cós on December 10, 1835, fewer than 100 Texans were left behind to hold the town. Governor Henry Smith did send WILLIAM BARRET TRAVIS with 25 men as reinforcements on February 3, 1836; however, General SAM HOUSTON decided to abandon Bexar, and he dispatched JAMES BOWIE and 30 men to the town with orders to destroy the fortifications. Bowie, like Travis, convinced that San Antonio was the key to Texas, instead disobeyed these orders and determined to hold the fort at all costs. Also at the Alamo were James Butler Bonham and DAVID CROCKETT, a former Tennessee congressman. In the meantime, General Antonio López de Santa Anna, leading a large force of Mexicans, arrived in Texas at least a month before he was expected, and on February 23 began a 13-day siege of the Alamo.

In 1836 the roof and towers of the Alamo's chapel had already collapsed, but its four-foot-thick and 22½-foot-high walls were intact; attached to the chapel was a large enclosed area of nearly three acres, including the long barracks, a building 186 feet long and 18 feet wide. Most of the area was surrounded by a wall that had no embrasures. The Texans within these defenses mounted their 21 cannons on high scaffolds or large piles of debris and earth.

On February 24 Travis answered Santa Anna's demand for surrender with a cannon shot and sent out pleas for help. The only aid came on March 1, when Captain Albert Martin led 32 men from Gonzales into the Alamo. Bonham returned March 3 after a fruitless mission for help and rode to certain death inside the Alamo. At 4:00 A.M. Sunday, March 6, Santa Anna ordered a four-column attack. Two attacks were repulsed, but the Mexicans came over the northwest wall on the third try. After hand-to-hand fighting in the courtyard and finally in the chapel, all the defenders were killed except Brigido Guerrero, who escaped death by claiming to be a prisoner of the Texans. Mexican losses consisted of 1,544 men out of an army of 5,000. The Texans lost approximately 180 men, including Gregorio Esparza and seven other Mexican-Texans who died defending the Alamo. There were about 15 women, children, and slaves who survived. The sacrifice of the men at the Alamo gave the disorganized Texans a battle cry and bought time that enabled them to achieve independence at San Jacinto on April 21, 1836.

See Williams, *Southwest Historical Quarterly* (April, July, Oct., 1933; Jan., 1934); T. L. Miller, *Texana* (Spring, 1964); *Journal of Mexican-American History* (Fall, 1971); Lord, *A Time to Stand* (1961); and Tinkle, *Thirteen Days to Glory* (1958). T. L. Connelly, *Journal of Southern History* (Aug., 1960), argues that Crockett and five others survived the battle only to be executed.

THOMAS LLOYD MILLER
Texas A. & M. University

ALBANY, GA. (pop. 72,623), at the navigational head of the Flint River, is a major market and processing point for area agriculture and the seat of a variety of light industries. The town was founded and laid out in 1836 by Alexander Shotwell, a Quaker from New Jersey. He named the town after Albany, N.Y. The first residents, however, were settlers led by Colonel Nelson Tift, who came up the river from Apalachicola, Fla. Growth of the town and development of the surrounding area were retarded by malaria and by a shortage of clean drinking water. The latter problem was eliminated in 1881, when John Porter Fort drilled the state's first artesian well there; the former was brought under control in the twentieth century. Originally a center for cotton culture, the area now supports a diversified agriculture dominated by pecans and peanuts.

See Nelson Tift, *Diary* (3 vols.; 1856, 1871, 1874); M. E. Bacon, *Albany* (1970), juvenile; DAR, *History and*

Reminiscences (1924); and files of the Albany *Patriot* (1846–66) and the Albany *Herald* (1855–).

ALBEMARLE SETTLEMENTS, around ALBE-MARLE SOUND in northeastern North Carolina, first occurred while the area constituted geographically the southern frontier of Virginia and legally the northern fringe of "Carolana" (or Carolina), a grant to Sir Robert Heath in 1629. Nathaniel Batts, an Indian trader from Norfolk and Nansemond counties in Virginia, became the first permanent resident of the Albemarle in 1655, and a large number of Virginia farmers seeking more fertile land followed him into the region between 1658 and 1661. Virginia initiated attempts to govern the area, but the 1663 Carolina charter ended those efforts. At that time the Albemarle contained approximately 500 settlers, and by 1665 the Carolina proprietors had instituted a formal government for the region, which was designated Albemarle County.

See W. S. Powell, *Ye Countie of Albemarle* (1958); H. R. Paschal, "Proprietary North Carolina" (Ph.D. dissertation, University of North Carolina, 1961); E. G. McPherson, *North Carolina Historical Review* (Jan., 1966); L. S. Butler, *Virginia Magazine of History and Biography* (Jan., 1971), excellent summary; and H. T. Lefler and W. S. Powell, *Colonial North Carolina* (1973).

ALAN D. WATSON
University of North Carolina, Wilmington

ALBEMARLE SOUND is an arm of the Atlantic Ocean formed by a barrier beach of the North Carolina OUTER BANKS. It is adjoined by Currituck Sound to the north and by Croatan and Roanoke sounds to the south. ROANOKE ISLAND (located between the two southern sounds) was explored in 1584 and made the location of SIR WALTER RALEIGH's first settlement the following year. Not until almost a century later, however, was the area surrounding the several sounds first permanently settled by colonists from Jamestown, Va. Although used commercially by ships out of EDENTON during the eighteenth century, Albemarle Sound was not much traveled until after completion in 1828 of the DISMAL SWAMP Canal. The canal provided easy transportation between Elizabeth City (on the Pasquotank River) and the Virginia cities of PORTSMOUTH and NORFOLK for a developing antebellum lumber industry. The canal was closed early in the Civil War by the federal blockade, and Confederates sought to reopen it early in 1864 by an attack on PLYMOUTH, N.C. Besides lumbering, truck farming, and pleasure boating, the Albemarle Sound area now hosts a growing number of tourists bound for the Outer Banks and for Ft. Raleigh National Park on Roanoke Island.

ALCORN, JAMES LUSK (1816–1894), migrated to Mississippi from Kentucky in 1844. He settled in the Mississippi Delta, prospered as a planter and rising Whig politician, and became an active promoter of a centralized LEVEE system. A Unionist before the Civil War, he transferred his loyalty to his state when Mississippi seceded and supported neither the occupying Union army nor the Confederate government during the war. Afterward he joined the Republican party, seeing it as the successor to the Whig party, and was elected governor of Mississippi in 1869. He provided constructive leadership for his war-torn state, but encountered increasing difficulty with KU KLUX KLAN–inspired violence. In 1871 he resigned to become U.S. senator, but by then his power was being undermined by a split within the state Republican party between those demanding greater participation and equality for blacks and those supporting his more conservative leadership. Democrats regained control of the state in 1875; because Alcorn, unlike many former Whigs, refused to join them, his political career ended with the expiration of his term as senator in 1877.

See L. A. Pereyra, *James Lusk Alcorn* (1966), extensive bibliography; M. F. Robinson, *Journal of Mississippi History* (1950); C. Swift, Jr., manuscript biography in Mississippi State Archives, based on reminiscences; and Alcorn Papers, in Mississippi State Archives and University of North Carolina Library, Chapel Hill.

LILLIAN A. PEREYRA
University of Portland

ALDEN, JOHN RICHARD (1908–), is a historian. He was born in Grand Rapids, Mich. Educated at the University of Michigan (A.B., 1929; A.M., 1930; Ph.D., 1939), he taught at Bowling Green and Nebraska before joining the faculty of Duke University in 1955. From 1963 to 1976 he was James B. Duke Professor of History. As a writer of American history Alden is well known for his research into the Revolutionary era. His writing is characterized by an eschewing of historiographical fads coupled with a lucid style and impeccable scholarship. Alden's scholarly works are marked by two emphases: the South in the Revolution and military history. They are evident in his first monograph, *John Stuart and the Colonial Frontier* (1944), awarded the Beveridge Prize by the American Historical Association (1945), and in his subsequent *South in the Revolution* (1957), *First South* (1961), and *Robert Dinwiddie* (1973). Alden is best known for his volume in the New American Nation series, *The American Revolution, 1775–1783* (1954). In addition, he is the author of *General Gage in America* (1948), *General Charles Lee* (1951), *The American Revolution* (1969), and three textbooks.

MILES M. MERWIN
University of Santa Clara

ALDERMAN, EDWIN ANDERSON (1861–1931), a native of North Carolina, served as president of the University of North Carolina (1896–1900), Tulane University (1900–1904), and the University of Virginia (1904–1931). In all these positions he vigorously championed education as a function of society, although he acquiesced in the system of racial segregation. His belief that North Carolina lacked a firm financial commitment to public education at least partially motivated his decision to leave his alma mater and to accept the presidency of Tulane University. An invitation in 1904 to become the first president of "Mr. Jefferson's University" terminated his brief administration at Tulane. Alderman's administrative abilities combined with the university's national reputation to account for the success of his tenure at Virginia. As a pioneer member of the SOUTHERN EDUCATION BOARD, Alderman associated with the prominent figures of his time, and in 1911 he and Armistead C. Gordon, rector of the University of Virginia, published a laudatory chronicle of the education apostle J. L. M. CURRY. Plagued by attacks of tuberculosis after 1912, Alderman nevertheless traveled extensively to promote the education campaign and to fulfill speaking engagements. Although not an original scholar, he effectively symbolized the reawakening of learning in the South.

See manuscripts in the Alderman Library, University of Virginia; D. Malone, *E. A. Alderman* (1940); and C. Eaton, *North Carolina Historical Review* (April, 1946).

BETTY J. BRANDON
University of South Alabama

ALEXANDER, EDWARD PORTER (1835–1910), was born on a plantation in Washington, Wilkes County, Ga. He graduated from West Point in 1857, serving in the U.S. Army until April, 1861, when he resigned to accept a captaincy in the Confederate army. During his brief U.S. Army career he helped develop the Wigwag signal system. His Confederate career covered virtually every major eastern battle. He served the Army of Northern Virginia as signal officer, ordnance chief,

secret service officer, reconnaissance officer, and even balloonist until November, 1862, when he was given command of STEPHEN DILL LEE's 26-gun artillery battalion. Here Alexander became the Confederacy's premier artillery officer, displaying a blend of boldness, imagination, dedication, and above all versatility. After acting for a time as de facto chief of artillery for JAMES B. LONGSTREET's corps, he was promoted brigadier and officially tendered the position in February, 1864.

After the war Alexander taught at the University of South Carolina before going into railroading. In short order he rose to become president of the Georgia Railroad, vice-president of the Louisville & Nashville Railroad, and president of the Central of Georgia Railroad. He left railroading in 1892, served as an arbitrator for a Nicaragua–Costa Rica boundary dispute in 1898–1900, and then turned to the writing of his memoirs. His *Military Memoirs of a Confederate* (1907), perhaps the best account of the war by a participant, was in fact a scholarly military history that aroused controversy among Confederate veterans but gained national acclaim.

See E. P. Alexander manuscripts and Alexander-Hillhouse family manuscripts, University of North Carolina Library, Chapel Hill; M. Boggs (ed.), *Alexander Letters* (1910); and M. Klein, *Edward P. Alexander* (1971), complete bibliography.

MAURY KLEIN
University of Rhode Island

ALEXANDER, WILL WINTON (1884–1956), a Methodist minister, eventually left the ministry and rose to prominence as an authority on race relations. Alarmed by racial tensions after World War I, he spearheaded creation of the COMMISSION ON INTERRACIAL COOPERATION in Atlanta, Ga., in 1919 and served as its director until 1944. Concerned with bettering Negro education in the South, Alexander helped establish Dillard University, serving as acting president from 1931 to 1935, and he sat on the boards of trustees of several Negro educational institutions, including Atlanta University. As vice-president of the ROSENWALD FUND, he helped provide fellowships for advanced study to many promising Negroes and southern whites.

During the 1930s, Alexander helped frame New Deal farm tenancy legislation, was assistant administrator of the RESETTLEMENT ADMINISTRATION, and served as administrator of the FARM SECURITY ADMINISTRATION. He was especially interested in giving Negroes a fair share of the

New Deal. He later acted as consultant on racial matters to various government agencies during World War II. In later life he devoted much time and thought to the problem of segregation, the ultimate issue in southern race relations.

See W. Dykeman and J. Stokely, *Seeds of Southern Change* (1962); and W. W. Alexander, "Reminiscences," Columbia University Oral History Project (1952).

HENRY E. BARBER
Virginia Intermont College

ALEXANDRIA, LA. (pop. 41,557), is in the central portion of the state, 95 miles northwest of Baton Rouge and on the Red River. It was founded in 1810 by Alexander Fulton and grew quickly into a shipping and trading center for area cotton growers and lumbermen. During the RED RIVER CAMPAIGN of 1864, the town was held by Union forces and was at the center of numerous fights and skirmishes (May 1–8). Known as the Hub City, it continues to be an important river port and an industrial city, producing railroad equipment, lumber products, naval stores, chemicals, dairy products, and oil drilling supplies.

See files of Alexandria *Towntalk* (1883–), available on microfilm.

ALEXANDRIA, VA. (pop. 110,938), has been an independent city since 1870, when the Virginia legislature granted it a separate civil status from Arlington County (ARLINGTON). The townsite was surveyed and laid out in 1749 by George Washington. As a colonial port city on the Potomac River, it exported not only tobacco but even larger amounts of wheat. Although Alexandria was part of the area ceded by Virginia to create the District of Columbia, the federal government never incorporated it into the federal district and returned the town and its environs to Virginia in 1847. The town continued to prosper as a port until the 1840s, when the Baltimore & Ohio Railroad diverted commerce with the interior to Baltimore. Occupied by federal troops in May, 1861, it was used during the Civil War as an operational base for the Union army in northern Virginia and as the seat of FRANCIS PIERPONT's Unionist state government. Present-day Alexandria is essentially a residential suburb of Washington, D.C., which, with over 450 surviving structures built before 1830, retains much of its historic charm and identity.

See F. L. Brockett and G. W. Rock, *Concise History of Alexandria, 1669–1883* (1883); F. Harrison, *Landmarks of Old Prince William* (1964), early history; G. M. Moore, *Seaport* (1949); M. G. Powell, *History of Old Alexandria, 1749–1861* (1928); and M. D. Somerville, *Washington Walked Here* (1970). The Alexandria Library maintains additional pamphlets, as well as the McKnight Papers (1774–1921), financial and census records, and accounts of early Scottish merchants.

ALEXANDRIA (VA.) GAZETTE began publication in 1800 as the *Advertiser and Intelligencer*. Renamed the *Gazette* in 1808, it was first issued as a daily publication in 1813. Although it was suspended briefly during the British occupation in 1814 and was reduced to triweekly editions during the 1820s, the *Gazette* has been in continuous, daily publication since 1834.

See L. J. Cappon, *Virginia Newspapers, 1821–1935* (1936); and *Gazette* issues, available on microfilm from Library of Congress (1800–).

ALEXANDRIA CONFERENCE (March, 1785) is frequently termed the Mount Vernon Conference. This meeting of delegates from Virginia and Maryland was called to settle the many disagreements between the two states concerning navigation of the Potomac and Pokomoke rivers and the Chesapeake Bay. Daniel of St. Thomas Jenifer, Thomas Stone, and SAMUEL CHASE represented Maryland. The Virginia delegation was to consist of GEORGE MASON, EDMUND RANDOLPH, Alexander Henderson, and JAMES MADISON, but through some bureaucratic oversight they were never notified of their appointments. Mason learned of his appointment "by mere Accident" just a few days before the conference was to convene. He hurried to Alexandria, where he was able to alert Henderson, but it proved impossible to contact either Madison or Randolph in time. The two Virginia delegates, along with the three from Maryland, adjourned to Mount Vernon, where, as guests of General GEORGE WASHINGTON, they drafted a 13-part compact that significantly increased cooperation between the two states on commercial matters of mutual interest. The success of the meeting prompted the subsequent call for the ANNAPOLIS CONVENTION, which in turn led to the proposal for a general convention in Philadelphia in May, 1787.

See R. A. Rutland (ed.), *Papers of George Mason* (1970), most accurate; C. Rossiter, *The Grand Convention* (1966); and H. H. Miller, *George Mason* (1975).

RICHARD R. BEEMAN
University of Pennsylvania

ALGONQUIN INDIANS, by definition, are the members of those tribes that speak a form of the Algonquian language. In historic times such tribes occupied extensive territories in Canada and the present United States, including the Upper South. Many southern Algonquins were to be found along the East Coast from Maryland to North Carolina, some of the best known being the Nanticokes of eastern Maryland, the various groups composing the POWHATAN Confederacy of tidewater Virginia, and the Pamlicos of eastern North Carolina. During the seventeenth century these tribes were greatly reduced by disease and warfare. They survived only by migration or by accepting restriction to reservations. Another Algonquin tribe was the SHAWNEE INDIANS, whose very name is derived from the Algonquian word for *south*. A portion of this tribe once lived along the Cumberland River in what is now middle Tennessee, but migrated beyond the Ohio River during the first half of the eighteenth century and subsequently hunted in Kentucky. Later, under the pressure of white expansionism, many of the Shawnees moved west of the Mississippi River and eventually down into Oklahoma and Texas, where their descendants now live.

See W. C. Sturtevant (ed.), *Handbook of North American Indians* (1976).

DOUGLAS EDWARD LEACH
Vanderbilt University

ALLATOONA PASS, BATTLE OF (October 5, 1864). After the battle of Atlanta, JOHN B. HOOD dispatched Samuel G. French and 5,000 men to the Union depot at Allatoona Pass to capture federal supplies and pull William T. Sherman northward into difficult terrain. In turn, Sherman sent John B. Corse and 2,000 men to the area. Rapidly, the federals moved into a good defensive position on two pieces of high ground separated by a draw. When French arrived, a battle began at dawn. Corse's force maintained its position through numerous and heavy Confederate assaults, incessant artillery pounding, and the loss of communications. Sherman, viewing the brave defense from atop Kennesaw Mountain, sent the heliographic message: "Hold out; relief is coming!" Corse did just that despite a loss of about 700 men. French lost about 800. Realizing he was stymied, French withdrew. Thus, Hood's stratagem failed, and he began his futile march that would end in disaster in Tennessee.

See F. E. Brown, *Civil War History* (Sept., 1960); V. Hicken, *Civil War Times Illustrated* (June, 1968); S. G. French, *Two Wars* (1901); and W. Salter, *Annals of Iowa, 1895–1896*.

JAMES W. POHL
Southwest Texas State University

ALLEGHENY MOUNTAINS, as defined by geomorphologists, occupy a strip of rugged land along the eastern edge of the unglaciated part of the Allegheny Plateau, within the Appalachian Plateaus province. They extend some 300 miles from north-central Pennsylvania southwestward across western Maryland into West Virginia and average 50 miles across. Like the adjoining CUMBERLAND PLATEAU to the south, the Allegheny Plateau is a highland region underlain by roughly horizontal sedimentary rock layers and severely dissected by a dendritic network of stream valleys. The landscape is a maze of hills and valleys with little rolling upland remaining. Within the Allegheny Mountains section, however, erosion acting upon gentle folds in the underlying rock has formed several parallel ridges, oriented northeast-southwest, where more resistant rocks are exposed (for example, Backbone Mountain in Maryland). Separated by strips of more typical dissected plateau, these ridges give the topography a degree of linearity not characteristic of the rest of the Allegheny Plateau. Also, because maximum altitudes, which exceed 4,000 feet in West Virginia, and relief are in general greater than elsewhere in the plateau, the landscape has a more mountainous aspect. The easternmost ridge, developed on upturned resistant rocks at the plateau margin, forms an imposing east-facing escarpment, the Allegheny Front, which stands 1,000 feet or more above the adjacent valleys of the folded Appalachians, or ridge and valley province.

Historically, the term Allegheny Mountains has not always been used in this restricted sense. Into this century, it was applied variously to the entire highland system usually identified today as the APPALACHIAN MOUNTAINS, to the parallel mountains of the ridge and valley province, and to all the hilly land of the Allegheny and Cumberland plateaus from Pennsylvania southward.

See W. D. Thornbury, *Regional Geomorphology of U.S.* (1965); and C. B. Hunt, *Natural Regions of U.S.* (1974).

WALLACE M. ELTON
Middlebury College

ALLEMANDS, CÔTE DES. See CÔTE DES ALLEMANDS

ALLEN, HENRY WATKINS (1820–1866), was born in Farmville, Va., and raised in Missouri. In 1837 he moved to Mississippi, where he taught school until opening a law practice in 1841. He served with SAM HOUSTON's forces in Texas (1842) and in the Mississippi legislature (1845). In 1851 he settled at Allendale, his sugar plantation near

Baton Rouge, La. He served in the Louisiana legislature from 1857 to 1861 and was a mustering officer for the state militia after secession. In 1861 he became a colonel in the Confederate army, commanding the 4th Louisiana Regiment. In 1862 he was wounded at SHILOH and again at the battle of BATON ROUGE. Shortly after becoming a general in 1863, he was elected governor of unoccupied Louisiana and organized in the unoccupied portion an extensive self-help program, establishing state laboratories, factories, dispensaries, and stores. After the war he moved to Mexico City, where he published and edited the *Mexican Times* until his death.

See V. H. Cassidy and A. E. Simpson, *Henry W. Allen* (1964), extensive bibliography; L. E. Chandler, "Career of Allen" (Ph.D. dissertation, Louisiana State University, 1940); and S. A. Dorsey, *Recollections* (1866), eulogistic.

AMOS E. SIMPSON
University of Southwestern Louisiana

ALLEN, WILLIAM WIRT (1835–1894), although born in New York City, moved to Alabama as a small child; and his family became prominent in the Montgomery area. Graduating from Princeton (1854), he read law but never practiced it. Instead, he ran his own plantation. In April, 1861, he entered Confederate service as a first lieutenant of the Montgomery Mounted Rifles. By March, 1862, he was promoted major in the 1st Alabama Cavalry serving under BRAXTON BRAGG. In February, 1864, he was made brigadier general and served under JOSEPH WHEELER. He was nominated by Jefferson Davis to major general in March, 1865, but records show that the Confederate Senate never authorized this rank. During his lengthy war career, he served in campaigns at SHILOH, CORINTH, PERRYVILLE, STONES RIVER, and ATLANTA. While under the command of J. E. JOHNSTON, he surrendered at Salisbury, N.C. In the course of the fighting, he sustained three wounds. Following the war, Allen resumed planting and entered the railroad business. He also enjoyed a public life as adjutant general of Alabama and U.S. marshal.

See W. W. Allen Papers, Department of History and Archives, Montgomery, Ala., small collection; W. B. Jones, *Confederate Veteran* (Nov., 1894); E. J. Warner, *Generals in Gray* (1959); and T. M. Owen, *History of Alabama* (1921).

JAMES W. POHL
Southwest Texas State University

ALMANACS in the South numbered more than a dozen in the eighteenth century, proliferated in number and spread to every southern state in the nineteenth century, and declined in the twentieth century as government information agencies and new media replaced their chief functions. Next to the Bible, they were the most ubiquitous volumes in the rural home. They were, as Moses Coit Tyler said, the "most despised, most prolific, most indispensable of books, which every man uses and no man praises, the very quack, clown, packhorse and pariah of modern literature." Basically, southern almanacs contained the usual astronomical data, relating these data and other events to the weather and to the calendar and to the farmer's work schedule. Charts and guides were presented for planting, cultivating, and gathering crops, along with recipes, household hints, and health advice.

Professional groups, political parties, and religious and moral societies sponsored almanacs to present their views. Commercial promoters, with patent medicine vendors in the majority, used them to advertise their wares. "Puffing," the art of extolling the virtues of some product offered for sale for a share in the profits, was almost a universal practice among almanac editors.

Southern almanacs make available a wealth of information on southern life. The CHEROKEE INDIANS published their own almanac in the Cherokee language. Political almanacs presented the proslavery argument and the southern political position. The Confederate almanacs, which numbered over 150 despite critical paper shortages, reveal much about southern life during the Civil War. Comic almanacs, forerunners of the humor magazine and the joke book, provide an insight into nineteenth-century tastes in humor.

The best almanacs were those edited by leaders in the scientific movement in southern agriculture. These publications, of which THOMAS AFFLECK's *Southern Rural Almanac and Plantation and Garden Calendar* was an excellent example, carried authoritative and well-written articles on such subjects as land conservation, plant diseases, weed and pest control, and farm management. Most southern almanacs were of short life, small circulation, and little lasting influence, but the best provided a real service to the farmer, as well as reading material that occasionally reflected intellectual and literary merit.

See M. C. Tyler, *History of American Literature* (1949); and M. H. Drake, *Almanacs of the United States* (1970), which has the most extensive checklist of almanacs.

ROBERT W. WILLIAMS
University of North Carolina

ALMOND, JAMES LINDSAY, JR. (1898–), governor of Virginia (1958–1962), was an important figure in the school desegregation controversy during the 1950s. The son of a locomotive engineer, Almond was born in Charlottesville. After receiving his law degree from the University of Virginia, he served in various public offices before becoming the commonwealth attorney general in 1948. During the early 1950s, he defended Virginia's public school segregation laws before the U.S. Supreme Court in one of the cases decided by the BROWN V. BOARD OF EDUCATION OF TOPEKA decision of 1954. Almond's speaking ability, his identification with the defense of segregation, and his loyalty to the HARRY F. BYRD organization propelled him into the governor's office. A proponent of "massive resistance" to school desegregation, Almond responded to federal court decisions by closing the nine Virginia schools under court orders to desegregate in the fall of 1958. His actions raised profound constitutional questions, which were ultimately resolved in January, 1959, when he reopened the nine closed schools on a desegregated basis.

See R. L. Gates, *Making of Massive Resistance* (1962); and B. Muse, *Virginia's Massive Resistance* (1961).

NUMAN V. BARTLEY
University of Georgia

ALTAMAHA RIVER, draining much of central Georgia, is formed 137 miles from the Atlantic coast by the confluence of the Ocmulgee and Oconee rivers. The 250-mile-long Ocmulgee is formed southeast of Atlanta and flows through Macon, where the Ocmulgee National Monument preserves and displays the mounds, pyramids, and artifacts of six successive Indian settlements over a span of 10,000 years. The Oconee rises in northeastern Georgia and flows 280 miles past Athens and Milledgeville. First flatboat and then steamboat trade plied the rivers' waters during the early nineteenth century. Although railroads had diminished traffic on these rivers by the time of the Civil War, the Altamaha has been dredged and is once again developing as an inland waterway.

ALUMINUM INDUSTRY. Since domestic reserves of bauxite, the ore most commonly used for the commercial production of aluminum, are limited to three states—Alabama, Arkansas, and Georgia—aluminum and the South have had a close relationship from the industry's inception in 1885. In that year the Cowles Electric Smelting & Aluminum Company of Cleveland, Ohio, produced the first commercial aluminum in the United States. However, technical problems made aluminum relatively expensive to produce. Unit cost in 1886 amounted to $11.13 a pound, too

much to enable the metal to compete for most uses. Further research led to the discovery of an electrolytic process that opened the door to lower costs and volume use and to the formation in 1888 of a second firm, the Pittsburgh Reduction Company. With each firm possessing a patent, litigation followed. Eventually, the Cleveland enterprise sold its patent to the Pittsburgh concern and left the industry. With the cost of production reduced to 57 cents a pound in 1893, demand for aluminum grew.

Pittsburgh began to acquire bauxite deposits in Georgia in 1894 and later extended its acquisitions to Alabama and Arkansas. Since the manufacture (reduction) of aluminum requires large amounts of electricity, the firm sought power sites. Between 1906 and 1912 power rights were acquired, giving the firm, renamed Aluminum Company of America (Alcoa) in 1907, almost exclusive control along a 40-mile stretch of the Little Tennessee River in the Great Smoky Mountains. With rapidly expanding sales in 1911 and 1912, the company continued its development with the erection of a million-dollar reduction plant at a company town called Alcoa, built near Maryville, Tenn. With these moves, the industry became solidly established in the South.

Today, seven firms operate 15 aluminum smelters in the South. Texas has three plants; Alabama, Arkansas, Louisiana, and Tennessee each have two; and Kentucky, Maryland, North Carolina, and West Virginia each have one. All of the plants in the United States that process alumina, the product from which aluminum is obtained, are in the South: three in Louisiana, two each in Arkansas and Texas, and one in Alabama. Bauxite, from which alumina is processed, is relatively scarce in the United States. Only about 14 percent of the necessary supply is mined domestically, with about 95 percent of this amount coming from Arkansas mines and the remainder coming from mines in Alabama and Georgia. The two largest aluminum producers, Alcoa and Reynolds Metals Company, constitute the domestic bauxite industry.

Although 48 percent of the primary aluminum plants and 55 percent of the plant capacity are in the South, the development of facilities to fabricate semifinished and finished aluminum products in the region has not been commensurate. Since aluminum has been sold either on a freight-allowed basis or on a uniform delivered-price basis nationally, aluminum fabricators pay the same price for the product delivered to their places of business, irrespective of location. There is no incentive for fabricators to locate their operations near the reduction plants. A system of pricing aluminum f.o.b. plant, without freight absorption permitted to the seller, would encourage fabricators to locate closer to their sources of supply. It would also promote more effective price competition among the sellers of primary aluminum.

See D. H. Wallace, *Market Control in Aluminum* (1937); J. V. Krutilla, *Southern Economic Journal* (Oct., 1955); B. O. James, "Aluminum Industry" (M.S. thesis, University of Tennessee, 1960); M. J. Peck, *Competition in Aluminum* (1961); and M. S. Brown and J. Butler, *Copper and Aluminum* (1968).

RONALD H. WOLF
University of Tennessee

AMARILLO, TEX. (pop. 123,973), the largest city in the Panhandle, is situated almost 250 miles west of Oklahoma City. Except for buffalo hunters and cattle ranchers, the area remained unsettled until 1887, when Henry B. Sanborn laid out the townsite near the intersections of several railroads. Named for Amarillo ("yellow") Creek, the town almost instantly became the world's largest cattle-shipping market during the next decade. The city continues to be a major cattle-shipping point—the second largest today in Texas—but, since the turn of the century, it also has been the principal market for area wheat farmers. Moreover, the discovery of helium gas 20 miles north of town in 1918 and of petroleum in 1921 has given the city a diversified industrial base for its continuing growth and prosperity.

See S. R. Boaz, "History of Amarillo" (M.A. thesis, University of Texas, 1950); J. W. Crudgington, *Old Town Amarillo* (1957); C. T. Hammond, *Amarillo* (1971); and D. T. Key, *Cattle Country, 1887–1966* (1968). The Amarillo Public Library's William Henry Bush Collection contains books, articles, and scrapbooks relating to local history.

AMELIA ISLAND AFFAIR (1817). Amelia, a small Sea Island off the northeastern coast of Spanish Florida, was invaded and occupied in 1817 by forces led by two different supposed Latin American revolutionaries: Scottish-born Gregor MacGregor in June, followed by French-born Luis Aury in September. Though both claimed to act in the name of revolutionary Latin American republics, their commissions were clearly invalid. Using Amelia as a base, both raided Spanish shipping and smuggled the seized goods, including slaves, into Georgia and South Carolina. Because this invasion threatened pending negotiations for the American purchase of Spanish Florida and because of the smuggling, a U.S. naval force ejected Aury and took possession of Amelia Island in December, 1817.

See R. Lowe, *Florida Historical Quarterly* (July, 1966); T. F. Davis, *Florida Historical Quarterly* (July, 1928); and S. Faye, *Louisiana Historical Quarterly* (July, 1941).

RICHARD LOWE
North Texas State University

AMERICAN ASSOCIATION FOR STATE AND LOCAL HISTORY (1400-8th Ave. S, Nashville, Tenn. 37203) was founded in 1940 as an outgrowth of the earlier American History Association's Conference of State and Local Historical Societies begun in 1904. The AASLH had a membership of 4,700 in 1976. It is interested in the technique of history in the local history field and sponsors seminars and regional conferences. The association also publishes books on historical agency work, bulletins and technical leaflets on programs and problems of historical organizations, a monthly journal *History News* (1941), and a biennial directory of nearly 5,000 historical societies of the United States and Canada. Since 1945 awards of merit have been conferred on individuals, institutions, businesses, and even published books in recognition of their excellence in state and local history and historical preservation.

AMERICAN CIVIL LIBERTIES UNION. During World War I a small group of persons joined informally to ensure that civil liberties at home would not be a casualty in the conflict to make the world safe for democracy. In 1920, these persons formally organized the American Civil Liberties Union. The lack in numbers (fewer than 50) was offset by the dedication of the founders: Jane Addams, Roger Baldwin, Clarence Darrow, John Dewey, Felix Frankfurter, Norman Thomas, and others. Today, there are approximately 150,000 members organized into 50 state affiliates (those in the South were late in coming) and a national executive board, which sets policy between conventions. The policy, unaltered since the beginning, is to protect the constitutional rights of all persons. The ACLU was in Tennessee at the SCOPES TRIAL; in Scottsboro, Ala., insisting that black youths be afforded the assistance of counsel at their trial for rape (SCOTTSBORO CASE); in Texas, protesting the white primary (GROVEY V. TOWNSEND, 1935); in West Virginia, protesting the compelled flag salute; and in Baltimore, protesting school prayer. Throughout the South, the ACLU has argued against the concept of a separate-but-equal school system and the practice of segregated lunch counters; today it is protesting the death penalty, which (according to the ACLU) bears so heavily on the black, the poor, and the uneducated.

See B. Habenstreit, *Eternal Vigilance* (1971); C. L. Markmann, *Noblest Cry* (1965); D. O. Johnson, *Challenge to American Freedoms* (1963); and D. E. Bunting, *Liberty and Learning* (1942).

DANIEL H. POLLITT
University of North Carolina, Chapel Hill

AMERICAN COLONIZATION SOCIETY was

organized in Washington, D.C., in 1817 to establish an African colony for free American blacks. Early officers included such prominent southerners as Henry Clay, William Crawford, John Randolph, Bushrod Washington, James Monroe, James Madison, and Andrew Jackson. The ACS was structured as a national organization with paid professional staff, state societies, and local auxiliaries. By 1838, it had chapters in every southern state except South Carolina and Arkansas; the legislatures of Tennessee, Kentucky, Delaware, Maryland, and Virginia had endorsed colonization; and the latter two had appropriated $100,000 and $90,000 respectively in 1832 and 1833 for colonization activities.

Southerners joined for diverse reasons: to end slavery by solving the race problem, to Christianize Africa, to build a model black republic, to reduce vice attributed to American blacks, to strengthen slavery by removing free blacks whose presence might cause slave unrest, to manumit slaves, or because of social pressure. Some southern opposition to the ACS did emerge, however, primarily in the cotton states. After 1837, the society emphasized individual fund raising in the South because of declining interest in its often short-lived auxiliaries, and northerners dominated the national organization. Individual southerners continued to donate funds and slaves to the ACS; by 1860 over half the 1,057 blacks sent to Liberia by the society were southern slaves freed specifically for colonization.

See P. J. Staudenraus, *African Colonization Movement* (1961), thorough, scholarly, excellent bibliography; E. L. Fox, *American Colonization Society* (1917), emphasizes ACS's antislavery role; *African Repository* (1825–92); and *Annual Report of ACS* (1818–1910).

JOHN M. SHAY
Chicago State University

AMERICAN FARM BUREAU FEDERATION was

organized in Chicago in 1919 at a time when the farmers' interest in the cooperative movement was growing, social and economic unrest was rising, most farmers had no organizational affiliation, and many feared that the tide of radicalism would overtake the bulk of the farmers of the country (AGRICULTURAL ORGANIZATIONS). State farm bureaus were organized in nine states of the South by midsummer, 1921, but these failed to attract farmers in large numbers. Southern farmers were more accustomed to organizations built around cotton and tobacco than grain and livestock, which preoccupied the farmers of the Middle West. Furthermore the southerners were not as interested in the McNary-Haugen plan as were the middle westerners.

Things were to change, however. The election of EDWARD A. O'NEAL, an Alabamian, as president of the AFBF, the passage of the first Agricultural Adjustment Act in 1933, and the emergence of southerners in positions of influence in NEW DEAL farm circles were accompanied by a rise in Farm Bureau membership. Alabama, Mississippi, and Arkansas were prominent in Farm Bureau activities during the New Deal and WORLD WAR II years, and membership soared in most states of the South after the war.

As a region, the South surpassed the Midwest in membership beginning in 1967, and by 1974 it had risen to 1,221,293 farm families. This spectacular growth was attributed to the creation of more county Farm Bureau offices, improved programs, effective legislative action at the state level, expanded marketing facilities, insurance and farm supply services, and the use of a professionally trained staff. The AFBF probably became the largest general farmers' organization ever to appear in the South. This occurred despite the fact that after World War II the Farm Bureau turned against the parity price concept that it had championed during the 1930s and advocated an open market for the farmers.

See O. M. Kile, *Farm Bureau Movement* (1921), useful but official history, and *Three Decades of the Farm Bureau* (1948); T. Saloutos, *Southwestern Social Sciences Quarterly* (May, 1947) and *Current History* (June, 1955), Edward A. O'Neal; *Fortune* (June, 1944); and AFBF manuscripts, AFBF headquarters, Park Ridge, Ill.

THEODORE SALOUTOS
University of California, Los Angeles

AMERICAN KNIGHTS, ORDER OF, was sup-

posedly a prosouthern secret society active in the upper Midwest during the Civil War. Phineas C. Wright, while living in New Orleans, developed the American Knights as an idea during "the winter of 1856–57" to combat egocentric sectionalism, unite "conservative men," and further "friendliness and fellowship." In 1858 Wright moved to St. Louis, Mo., seeking to establish himself (without much success) in law and politics. As opposition to Abraham Lincoln's policies developed in

1863, Wright tried to transform the order into a viable political force by writing an address, taking the title "supreme grand commander," and organizing a half-dozen councils in Missouri, Illinois, and Indiana. Interested Democrats visualized the American Knights as an auxiliary of the party, capable of serving as a mutual protection society, ensuring free and open elections, and counteracting the work of the UNION LEAGUE. Plagued by disorganization as well as distrust of Wright, the national convention of December, 1863, in Chicago was a farce—one prominent Democrat called the order "a palpable humbug." The order disintegrated when its promoter moved to New York in January, 1864. Six months later a politically minded colonel stationed in St. Louis gave publicity to the American Knights when he fabricated an exposé entitled "Conspiracy to Establish a Northwestern Confederacy" as propaganda for the presidential campaign. Republican newspapers made much of little, presenting the order as a prosouthern and treasonable society, contributing to another Civil War myth.

See F. L. Klement, *Civil War History* (March, 1972). The John P. Sanderson Papers, Ohio Historical Society, contain a journal, newspaper clippings, and Sanderson's exposé entitled "Conspiracy to Establish a Northwestern Confederacy" (n.d.).

FRANK L. KLEMENT
Marquette University

AMERICAN LETTER EXPRESS COMPANY. Because the U.S. Post Office would not carry mail from the Confederate states, the Southern Express Company in the first months of the Civil War took letters to Louisville, where they were turned over to the Adams Express Company for delivery, all for a fee of 25 cents. By June, 1861, the American Letter Express Company with headquarters both in Nashville and Louisville had been organized to carry mail across the border from both directions (POSTAL SERVICE).

See E. M. Coulter, *Confederate States of America* (1950); and A. Dietz, *Postal Service of Confederate States of America* (1929).

AMERICAN PARTY. See KNOW-NOTHING PARTY

AMERICAN REVOLUTION. See REVOLUTION, AMERICAN

AMERICAN SOCIETY OF FREE PERSONS OF COLOR was organized at a convention of 26 prominent black delegates from Pennsylvania and

neighboring states in September, 1830, under the leadership of Richard Allen and Austin Steward. This meeting led to a series of sessions, known as the National Negro Convention, which met annually from 1830 to 1835 and then irregularly in 1843, 1847, 1848, 1853, 1855, and 1864. The movement has been accurately characterized as the first "national association for the advancement of colored people." Its principal objective was the liquidation of the slavery system and, pending that goal, the social redemption of all blacks, slave and free, through temperance, morality, education, economy, self-help, and guarantees of equality of justice and opportunity. The movement was divided on the issue of black emigration. In general the majority (headed by FREDERICK DOUGLASS and James McCune Smith) favored the development of a black-directed community; the minority, led by MARTIN ROBINSON DELANY and Henry Hyland Garnet, supported plans for colonization outside the United States.

See H. H. Bell (ed.), *Minutes of Proceedings of National Negro Conventions, 1830–1864* (1969).

RICHARD BARDOLPH
University of North Carolina, Greensboro

AMES, ADELBERT (1835–1933), was born in Maine. Graduating from West Point as the Civil War began, he served with distinction in the Union army and afterward was appointed provisional military governor of Mississippi. There he dedicated himself to protecting the freedmen from harassment by whites and supervised elections in which voters of both races set up a new state government. A son-in-law of Radical Republican Benjamin F. Butler, he joined the Republican party in Mississippi and was elected to the U.S. Senate in 1869. In Washington, D.C., he supported an extension of the KU KLUX KLAN ACTS, and in Mississippi he became leader of the Radical wing of the state Republican party.

Elected governor in 1873, he was one of the state's most incorruptible chief executives, but was frustrated by increasing violence directed toward restoring white supremacy and by a split in his party between his supporters, who wanted equality for blacks, and more conservative Republicans. With the judicious use of terror (MISSISSIPPI PLAN), Democrats regained control of the legislature in 1875 and with trumped-up impeachment charges forced Ames to resign. Disillusioned by the failure of his efforts to help blacks, he left the state permanently.

See B. B. Ames, *Chronicles from the Nineteenth Century* (1957), excellent; B. A. Ames, *Adelbert Ames* (1964), sympathetic; and R. W. Current, *Three Carpetbag Governors* (1967).

LILLIAN A. PEREYRA
University of Portland

AMES, JESSIE DANIEL (1883–1972), was born in Palestine, Tex., the daughter of James Malcolm, a railroad stationmaster, and Laura Leonard Daniel, a rural schoolteacher. After graduating from Southwestern University in Georgetown, she married an army surgeon, Roger Post Ames. Widowed in 1914, she entered public life as the organizer of a county suffrage group and, in 1918, became treasurer of the Texas Equal Suffrage Association. She was elected the first president of the Texas League of Women Voters and, throughout the twenties, sought to mobilize enfranchised Texas women in behalf of Progressive reform. Unlike most suffragists, Ames also attempted to use the political skills forged in the WOMEN'S RIGHTS MOVEMENT in the struggle for racial justice. In 1929, she became director of the woman's committee of the Atlanta-based COMMISSION ON INTERRACIAL COOPERATION. A year later, she formed the ASSOCIATION OF SOUTHERN WOMEN FOR THE PREVENTION OF LYNCHING. The association involved at its height 43,000 women pledged to work in their local communities to destroy the belief that lynching was necessary to protect white womanhood. In 1944, when the interracial commission was replaced by the SOUTHERN REGIONAL COUNCIL, Ames retired to Tryon, N.C., where she continued to work in Democratic party politics.

See J. D. Hall, *Revolt Against Chivalry* (1979); J. S. Reed, *Social Problems* (Fall, 1968); H. E. Barber, *Phylon* (Dec., 1973); Association Papers, Atlanta University; and Ames Papers, University of North Carolina, Chapel Hill.

JACQUELYN DOWD HALL
University of North Carolina, Chapel Hill

AMNESTY, after the Civil War, meant a governmental forgiveness of those who had supported the Confederacy and a waiver of prosecution for this rebellion. General amnesty excludes certain persons from its benefits; universal amnesty makes no exceptions, forgiving all persons. When the treatment of former Confederates is compared with that of other defeated peoples in the nineteenth and twentieth centuries who have been subjected to war crimes trials and executions, southern leaders were obviously treated leniently after the Civil War. Imprisonments were generally few and brief, except for JEFFERSON DAVIS, who was jailed for two years and released while still under indictment for treason. Among civil and military leaders only HENRY WIRZ was executed.

Presidential amnesty was particularly lenient and nonvindictive. Abraham Lincoln's proposal of December, 1863, offered amnesty to those who had participated in the rebellion, except high military and civil officials of the Confederacy, if they would take an oath of loyalty. ANDREW JOHNSON's plan of May, 1865, excluded additional classes. The most significant new category was that of men owning property worth $20,000 or more, reflecting Johnson's belief that the war was the work of slaveholders. Nevertheless, he was generous in granting relief from this disability. Congress early challenged the presidential assumption of power to grant amnesty, and the challenge grew as the struggle for control of Reconstruction intensified. After his first amnesty proposal Johnson subsequently issued two general amnesty statements (September, 1867, and July, 1868) before his final universal amnesty announced on Christmas Day, 1868. This last gave clemency to all who had remained unpardoned for aiding the rebellion, thereby disposing of the case against Jefferson Davis, who was still under indictment on the charge of treason.

Meanwhile, the FOURTEENTH AMENDMENT presented another aspect of the amnesty question. Section 3 of the amendment denied office to anyone who had taken an oath to the federal government and thereafter had broken it by aiding the Confederacy. A vote of two-thirds of Congress was necessary to remove this disability, and thousands of southerners now made applications to Congress. Congress was cautious in removing disabilities, haggling over the mildest offenders, and first consideration was given to those likely to affiliate with the southern Republican party. From June, 1868, through March, 1871, Congress removed disabilities from 4,616 persons. Congressional sternness gradually mellowed, and efforts increased to enact a general or universal amnesty law. In May, 1872, Congress finally passed a general amnesty bill, which excepted only senators and representatives of the Thirty-seventh Congress; judicial, military, and naval officers of the U.S.; heads of departments; and U.S. foreign ministers who had supported the Confederacy. Many of these prominent exceptions applied to Congress for relief, which was granted. Further efforts toward universal amnesty failed in 1876, and not until 1896 did Congress pass universal amnesty to remove the disabilities imposed under the Fourteenth Amendment. An earlier universal amnesty would have been a wiser policy.

See J. T. Dorris, *Pardon and Amnesty* (1953); W. A. Russ, "Congressional Disfranchisement" (Ph.D. dissertation,

University of Chicago, 1936); Presidential Amnesty Papers, RG 94, National Archives; and Fourteenth Amendment Amnesty Papers, RG 233, National Archives.

SARAH WOOLFOLK WIGGINS
University of Alabama

AMPHIBIANS. See REPTILES AND AMPHIBIANS.

ANACONDA POLICY was a newspaper term for what George B. McClellan allegedly called Winfield Scott's "boa constrictor" blockade of the Confederacy. In April, 1861, McClellan proposed an advance on Richmond "up the valley of the Great Kanawha." Scott wrote Abraham Lincoln that such plans were "piece-meal" and wrote McClellan that "a powerful movement down the Mississippi" and "a strict blockade" would "bring them to terms with less bloodshed." But the coastal blockade was never passive. Such a blockade, Gideon Welles later noted, would have created "two hostile nations" by treating southern Unionists as enemies. So United States forces did more than, as the Orpheus C. Kerr Papers put it, "gather in a circle around the doomed rabbit of rebellion." Since the Anaconda policy was no more than some general strategic ideas that were never formally debated, little research has been done on it.

See T. Ropp, *Military Affairs* (Summer, 1963).

THEODORE ROPP
Duke University

ANAHUAC, BATTLE OF (June 29, 1835). Anahuac, Tex., was founded by the Mexican government in 1821 as a port of entry. Trouble developed ten years later over the collection of tariffs. Following an 1832 confrontation, the customhouse was abandoned. However, in January, 1835, Mexican Captain Antonio Tenorio arrived to assist in the reinstitution of tax collections. Local merchants protested. One of them, Andrew Briscoe, was arrested. News of Briscoe's detention reached the Texas town of San Felipe simultaneously with stolen Mexican dispatches detailing the crushing of the Zacatecas and Saltillo uprisings by Antonio López de Santa Anna. Apprehension abounded. On June 21, 1835, the leaders of San Felipe called for the expulsion of Tenorio. On June 29, WILLIAM BARRET TRAVIS, with a force of 25 volunteers and a cannon, demanded the surrender of the 36-man garrison. The following day Tenorio capitulated and abandoned Anahuac without firing a shot.

See E. Barker, *Southwestern Historical Quarterly* (Jan., 1901), and *Mexico and Texas, 1821–1835* (1965); W. C. Binkley, *The Texas Revolution* (1952); A. B. Looscan,

Southwestern Historical Quarterly (July, 1898; Jan., 1915); E. Rowe, *Southwestern Historical Quarterly* (April, 1903); and C. A. True, *Southwestern Historical Quarterly* (Oct., 1943).

KENNETH D. YEILDING
Odessa College

ANDERSON, JOSEPH REID (1813–1892), was a scion of Scotch-Irish and Maryland planter heritage from western Virginia. Fourth in the 1836 West Point class, he sought engineering opportunities. Service at Ft. Pulaski in Georgia and three years (1838–1841) of private turnpike building sharpened his managerial skills. The seven years after 1841 saw him climb from a Tredegar Iron Works agent to lessor in 1843 and to owner of the company in 1848. Government ordnance, southern railroad, and sugar- and rolling-mill orders brought profits. By 1859 Anderson, through a series of partnerships with close associates, had liquidated previous stockholders' claims. As a city councilor, Virginia assemblyman, and commercial conventioneer, he vigorously promoted southern railroads and industry.

When the Civil War began he pledged the Tredegar Iron Works to the secessionist cause and served in a field command as a brigadier general. The necessity of adding blast furnaces and coal mines to the Tredegar works, however, demanded his attention and forced him to resign his commission in 1862. The use of slaves was expanded to make up for the loss of workers to the Confederate draft, but the pig iron shortages remained a problem. At the close of the war he hastily accepted amnesty, and Reconstruction expansion brought recovery to his company. The firm weathered the PANIC OF 1873 and prospered until Anderson's death.

See Anderson Family Manuscripts, Virginia State Library; Francis T. Anderson Manuscripts, Duke University, basic; Archer Manuscripts, Richmond; Tredegar Company Records, company archives, spotty; Tredegar Company Records, Virginia State Library; C. B. Dew, *Joseph R. Anderson* (1966), definitive; K. Bruce, *Virginia Iron Manufacture* (1930), basic; and C. B. Sabine, *Civil War Times Illustrated* (May, 1966).

GEORGE RUBLE WOOLFOLK
Prairie View A. & M. University

ANDERSON, RICHARD HERON (1821–1879), was born at Statesburg, S.C. Graduating from West Point in 1842, he served as lieutenant and then captain, in the 1st and 2nd Dragoons, against Comanches, Mexicans, Kansans, and Mormons. He resigned on March 3, 1861. Commissioned a major, Confederate cavalry; then colonel, 1st South

Carolina Regulars; and finally brigadier general, 1861, he helped besiege Fts. SUMTER and Pickens, but was then transferred to Virginia in some disgrace in February, 1862. However, brilliant service as a brigade and division commander in the PENINSULAR CAMPAIGN redeemed him. Promoted major general on July 14, 1862, he led a division under ROBERT E. LEE until succeeding JAMES B. LONGSTREET temporarily as corps commander, on May 7, 1864 (lieutenant general, May 31, 1864). He sparkled at SPOTSYLVANIA but subsequently—with Lee and also as a detached commander—revealed tactical clumsiness and lack of initiative. Longstreet's return on October 19 relegated him to a division-sized corps at Petersburg. He saw little combat there until March–April, 1865. Routed at SAYLER'S CREEK and left without troops, he was relieved on April 8, 1865. Although South Carolina's ranking Confederate general, he lived in the state after the war obscurely and nearly destitutely as a railroad laborer and state phosphate inspector. An effective brigade and division combat commander—scarred by wounds (October 9, 1861, and September 17, 1862)—Anderson lacked the drive and perception to fill the major executive offices entrusted him.

See D. S. Freeman, *Lee's Lieutenants* (1942–44); and C. I. Walker, *Anderson* (1917).

RICHARD J. SOMMERS
U.S. Army Military History Research Collection

ANDERSON, ROBERT (1805–1871), was born

near Louisville, Ky. After graduating from West Point in 1825, he served in routine assignments except for the Blackhawk, Seminole, and Mexican wars. In 1860 he was appointed to command the army posts in Charleston, S.C., then gripped by a secession crisis. After South Carolina seceded on December 20, Anderson concentrated his few soldiers in the uncompleted FT. SUMTER. Although Anderson, a southerner by birth and marriage, hoped for a peaceful secession, he held his post with quiet resolution until he was overwhelmed April 12–13, 1861, by vastly superior Confederate forces. He was allowed by his captors to evacuate his garrison by sea to New York. Accepting a brigadier generalship, he briefly commanded Union forces in Kentucky; but his health failed after a few months, and he ultimately resigned. His wife's fortune had been dissipated by the war, and in order to maximize his retirement pay he moved abroad, dying in Nice, France.

See W. A. Swanberg, *First Blood: The Story of Fort Sumter* (1958); R. N. Current, *Lincoln and the First Shot* (1963); and R. Anderson Manuscripts, Library of Congress.

RALPH J. ROSKE
University of Nevada, Las Vegas

ANDERSON, S.C. (pop. 27,556), in the old

CHEROKEE INDIAN lands of the PIEDMONT, grew up around the Anderson County Courthouse (1826). Both the town and the county took their name to honor General Robert Anderson, a Revolutionary War hero. The town's early economic support was derived from area-grown cotton, but some textiles were manufactured here. During the Civil War, ammunition was produced for the Confederacy, and it was the site of a branch of the Confederate treasury after 1864. When a hydroelectric plant was constructed on the nearby Seneca River in 1897, Anderson's textile mills expanded rapidly. In addition to a variety of textiles, modern Anderson produces fertilizer, food goods, and metal products.

See Anderson *Daily Mail* (1899–); Anderson *Gazette* (1843–61?); Anderson *Intelligencer* (1860–1916); and Anderson *Peoples Advocate* (1890–1918?), all on microfilm.

ANDERSONVILLE PRISON was the most noto-

rious military prison operated in the Civil War. Confederates built it in remote southwestern Georgia to secure prisoners from invading armies and to conserve Richmond's food supply. From the time the first prisoners came from Richmond to the unfinished installation in February, 1864, until it was closed in April, 1865, prison officials lacked the supplies and perhaps the capacity to alleviate basic problems. Situated on 26½ acres, the prison was divided by a stream and enclosed by closely fitted pine logs to which sentry boxes were attached. The enclosure was restricted by a deadline, a rail placed 15 feet inside the stockade that must not be passed. There were no buildings inside the walls; the inmates, all of whom were enlisted men, built their own huts, scattering them at random. Much has been written about the horrors of Andersonville: the insufficient and unbaked rations; the lack of sanitation, clothing, and shelter; the polluted stream; the inadequate medical system; the stinking swamp with its maggots and mosquitoes; the lawless prisoners who tyrannized their fellows; the ill-trained and brutal guards; the bloodhounds that hunted down escaping yankees; and the crowded conditions (nearly 33,000 men were confined in August, just before the captors, fearing Sherman's army, shifted most). About 13,000 captives died from such causes as dysentery, scurvy, and "hospital gangrene." The terrible conditions were fully exploited in the nineteenth century by former prisoners seeking pensions and fame and by northern politicians seeking votes. They insisted that Confederates had deliberately mistreated captives and that the fiendish Captain HENRY WIRZ, who had command of the inmates, fully deserved hanging in 1865. Modern scholars refute these accusers as well as southern apologists, who blamed the North for prison conditions and whitewashed the jailers. Clearly the tragedy of Andersonville resulted from the strains of unlimited warfare, not from malicious prison keepers.

See O. Futch, *History of Andersonville Prison* (1968), a scholarly study that charges "gross mismanagement"; W. B. Hesseltine, *Civil War Prisons* (1930), best brief survey; B. Catton, *American Heritage* (Aug., 1959); *Civil War History* (June, 1962); E. Forbes, *Diary* (1865); and *Official Records, Armies,* Ser. 2, Vols. VI–VIII.

G. THOMAS EDWARDS
Whitman College

ANDREWS' RAID, also called the Great Locomotive Chase, began at Big Shanty, Ga., April 12, 1862, when James J. Andrews, a civilian, and 19 Union soldiers in disguise stole the locomotive General on the Western & Atlantic Railroad and headed north. Their plan was to burn bridges and cut the Confederate supply line. Conductor William A. Fuller gave chase, first on foot, later aboard three different locomotives. En route, Andrews cut the telegraph line and destroyed track. Eventually Fuller met a southbound freight train pulled by the engine Texas. The chase resumed with the Texas running in reverse. Rain prevented Andrews from setting fire to the bridges; instead, he dropped two boxcars to impede pursuit. Two miles north of Ringgold, Ga., with fuel exhausted, the raiders abandoned the General and fled to the woods, ending the 87-mile, eight-hour chase. All were captured. In June, 1862, eight, including Andrews, were hanged as spies in Atlanta. Eight others escaped; those remaining were exchanged. Each soldier was awarded the congressional Medal of Honor, the first ever issued.

See W. Pittenger, *Locomotive Chase* (1893), eyewitness account; W. G. Kurtz, Sr., *Civil War Times Illustrated* (April, 1966), most accurate; and C. O'Neill, *Wild Train* (1956).

EDISON H. THOMAS
Louisville & Nashville Railroad

ANNAPOLIS, MD. (pop. 29,592), in central Maryland on the Severn River, was first settled in 1648 by a group of Puritans. Known then as Providence, the settlement was a center of Puritan power until the Stuart Restoration in England. Renamed Anne Arundel Town after the wife of the second Lord Baltimore, the community grew and prospered due in part to its central location. When in 1694 the capital was moved here from ST. MARY'S CITY, the town was renamed Annapolis in honor of Princess (later Queen) Anne. Although the PEGGY STEWART ARSON occurred in its harbor, the Revolutionary War did not much affect the city. Between 1783 and 1784, however, Annapolis was the scene of the meetings of the Continental Congress and in 1786 was the site of the ANNAPOLIS CONVENTION. Ft. Severn, constructed in 1808, prevented an attack on the city during the War of 1812 and was given to the navy in 1845 to house what became the U.S. Naval Academy. Residents were predominantly Confederate in their Civil War sympathies, but the town—used as a hospital center by the Union—again escaped the ravages of war. Although it is a port of entry and a shipping center for truck farming and seafood, the Naval Academy and the state government represent the most important bases of the community's economy. It remains a charming residential town with several buildings of architectural interest, including the State House (1772–1774), the Old Treasury (1695), the library (1737), and St. Anne's Episcopal Church (1859).

See E. Riley, *Ancient City, 1649–1887* (1887); J. H. Warfield, *Founders of Anne Arundel* (1905); W. B. Norris, *Annapolis* (1925), charming, popular history; E. M. Jackson, *Annapolis* (1937), anecdotal; and *Maryland Gazette* (1745–1839), on microfilm.

ANNAPOLIS CONVENTION (September 11, 1786) was a conference of delegates from five states, called by Virginia to solve commercial problems arising from the clashes of states' sovereignty. The convention was disappointing. With only half the states represented, it could take no positive actions to remove trade barriers, nor could it offer meaningful suggestions to revise the ARTICLES OF CONFEDERATION. However, Alexander Hamilton and JAMES MADISON salvaged the bleak situation by adopting the New Jersey delegates' thinking. Accordingly, the convention reported to the federal Congress that solutions to commercial problems so greatly entailed large political changes in the Articles of Confederation that another convention with broader powers needed to be called. After considerable delay Congress issued a call to send delegates to the CONSTITUTIONAL CONVENTION of 1787.

See H. C. Syrett, *Papers of Alexander Hamilton* (1962), III; and T. A. Emmet, *Annapolis Convention* (1881).

RICHARD WALSH
Georgetown University

SOUTHERN DELEGATES TO THE ANNAPOLIS CONVENTION

Delaware:	*North Carolina (appointed but did not attend):*	*Virginia:*
John Dickinson		Edmund
Richard Bassett		Randolph
George Read	Abner Nash	James Madison
	Hugh Williamson	St. George
	John Gray Blount	Tucker
	No commissioners were appointed from Maryland, South Carolina, and Georgia.	

ANNISTON, ALA. (pop. 31,533), is 55 miles east of Birmingham in Calhoun County. The area was part of the lands of the CREEK INDIAN Confederacy until 1832. Although a few cotton farmers soon moved into the region, there was little development until 1862, when a rail line was constructed to the foot of Blue Mountain (just north of the present town) and the Oxford Iron Works and a Confederate supply base were erected. Both the rail line and the blast furnace were destroyed, however, in a raid by Union troops in 1865. After the war Samuel Noble, an English-born ironmaster, visited the site and became convinced of the area's industrial potential. With Alfred L. Tyler, Noble established the Woodstock Iron Company and founded the town of Anniston (named for Tyler's wife Annie) in 1872. Noble and Tyler also established a textile mill employing women (1880) and the Alabama Mineral Railroad (1883). They literally owned the town until 1883; even its newspaper, first edited in 1883 by HENRY W. GRADY, was published by Noble. Despite several panics and depressions, the town grew from a village of 942 persons in 1880 to almost 10,000 in 1890. Today the city continues to be an important industrial center, as well as a shipping and trading point for area mines and agriculture.

See Anniston *Star* (1883–), 1900– on microfilm; and papers of Noble, Liston-Crow, and Boozer families, and several typewritten histories of persons, businesses, and churches, in the Anniston Public Library.

ANTEBELLUM, derived from the Latin, means literally "before the war" and can be applied to the period preceding any war. But to many southerners there was only *the* war. In the South, therefore, the word *antebellum* relates to anything in American history from 1607 down to the Civil War, but more commonly it refers to just the two or three decades immediately preceding secession. Its antithesis, postbellum (after the war), is rarely used. Most historians prefer such terms as Reconstruction and New South to describe this later period.

ANTEBELLUM SOUTH, HISTORIOGRAPHY OF, has generally fixed on the following issues: Was the South a capitalistic or precapitalistic society? Was slavery profitable, aggressively expansionistic, a godsend to the slave, a boon to the nonslaveholding white, a source of guilt feelings for the master, the cornerstone of a flourishing and genteel culture, the basis of vast and disruptive political conspiracies that led to civil war? Or was it none of these? Since 1900 historians have developed a wide range of differing explanations for every one of these questions.

More than any other historian, ULRICH B. PHILLIPS set firm boundaries for southern historiography beginning in 1918, an era of disillusionment with war and devotion to white supremacy. Sympathetic to slaveholders and assuming the inferiority of the black race, Phillips pictured the antebellum South as a placid, pleasant place. Slavery was a patriarchal, but unprofitable institution, uplifting to blacks, a burden (but not a source of guilt) to white owners, eventually destined (had it not been for a needless civil war) for a slow, peaceful death once it had filled out its "natural borders." The many state and local studies of plantation society done during the early twentieth century reconfirmed Phillips' views. Moreover, the writings of WILLIAM E. DODD and later FRANK L. OWSLEY seemed to confirm that nonslaveholding whites were not adversely affected by slavery. Chauncey Boucher, JAMES G. RANDALL, and others meanwhile reported that no slave-owning conspiracies could be discerned; planter-politicians showed marked division on most issues. Two small camps of extremists, abolitionists and FIRE-EATERS were pictured as responsible for sending a "blundering generation" into a horribly needless war, ultimately abolishing by violence a benign southern civilization, which was destined otherwise for a slow evolution to newer forms.

By the mid-1950s, politically liberal historians had begun revising nearly all of these conclusions, influenced deeply by a cold war atmosphere congenial to warfare, by scientific confutations of black inferiority, and by the rising CIVIL RIGHTS MOVEMENT. For all their significant differences, Kenneth Stampp, Stanley Elkins, Richard Hofstadter, JOHN HOPE FRANKLIN, and other leading revisionists saw race exploitation, repression, and expansionism as central to antebellum civilization. All granted slavery a basis in capitalism, denied that it provided adequately for the slaves either materially or psychologically, and divided evenly on the question of profitability. The guilt feelings of masters received emphasis, but so did their unremitting disregard for civil liberties and free discussion. In politics the issues of expansionism, repression, and slavery's immorality made war not needless, but necessary, and justified the use of violence to destroy the Old South. Elkins added new methodological dimensions, which others have continued, however, by employing interdisciplinary techniques to compare the antebellum South with other slave societies.

By the mid-1970s, the work of Eugene Genovese, George Rawick, John Blassingame, Herbert Guttman, and others had opened the previously unexplored fields in the study of antebellum black cultures. Morally less secure about racism and warfare than a decade earlier, many historians had also softened their criticisms of the Old South as brutally immoral, and some had begun to consider its people as living in a "precapitalistic" system, unique from the rest of the nation, which had to expand continuously or face extinction. Debate over profitability continued, but research failed to demonstrate the antebellum South's economic superiority over the North.

See W. Stevenson, *South Lives* (1955); T. J. Pressly, *Americans Interpret* (1954); D. Potter, *South and Sectional Conflict* (1968); S. Elkins, *Slavery* (1959); E. Genovese, *Political Economy* (1967); A. Lane, *Debate* (1972); H. Woodman, *Slavery* (1966); R. Hofstadter, *Journal of Negro History* (Jan., 1944); D. B. Davis, in C. V. Woodward, *Comparative Approach* (1968); A. Conrad, *Journal of Economic History* (Dec., 1967); J. G. Randall, *Mississippi Valley Historical Review* (June, 1940); and C. W. Ramsdell, *Mississippi Valley Historical Review* (April, 1929).

JAMES BREWER STEWART
Macalester College

ANTIETAM, BATTLE OF (September 17, 1862). Following his victory at Bull Run on August 29 and 30, 1862 (BULL RUN CAMPAIGN, SECOND), Confederate General Robert E. Lee turned his army northward, crossed the Potomac River at Leesburg, and soon occupied Frederick, Md. The Union feared Lee would attack Washington, Bal-

timore, or Philadelphia. But when the Union failed to evacuate Harpers Ferry and Maryland failed to supply Lee, he was forced to send a portion of his army to take Harpers Ferry and open a supply line south through the Shenandoah Valley. Lee and the remainder of the army then moved on to Hagerstown.

The Union commander General George B. McClellan came into possession of Lee's plans and moved slowly to interpose a large Union army between Lee's divided wings. Lee delayed McClellan at South Mountain, but was engaged in battle along Antietam Creek, near Sharpsburg, on September 17, 1862. Lee reunited his army as the battle progressed and was able to repulse the stiff but uncoordinated attacks of the Union forces. It was the bloodiest engagement in U.S. history up to that time, with over 22,000 casualties.

McClellan failed to follow up with renewed attacks on September 18, and on September 19 Lee's army retired unmolested across the Potomac. Essentially the battle was a draw: Lee's invasion of the North was thwarted, but his army escaped. Antietam's outcome played a role in blunting mediation efforts under way in Britain and Europe and also provided a springboard for President Abraham Lincoln's issuance of the preliminary EMANCIPATION PROCLAMATION on September 23.

See R. U. Johnson and C. C. Buel (eds.), *Battles and Leaders* (1888), II; D. S. Freeman, *R. E. Lee* (1935), II; K. P. Williams, *Lincoln Finds General* (1949), I, II; E. J. Stackpole, *From Cedar Mountain to Antietam* (1959); A. Nevins, *War for Union* (1959), II; and B. Catton, *Mr. Lincoln's Army* (1951).

ROBERT H. JONES
University of Akron

ANTI-FEDERALISTS in the South wished to add amendments guaranteeing personal liberties and limiting the power of the central government prior to ratification of the federal Constitution. There were few critics of the Constitution in Georgia, where the document was ratified unanimously. In Maryland, LUTHER MARTIN, SAMUEL CHASE, WILLIAM PACA, and John Francis Mercer led the opposition to ratification but failed to force acceptance of amendments. The most prominent anti-Federalists in South Carolina were RAWLINS LOWNDES, Aedanus Burke, and THOMAS SUMTER. Here, too, the movement to insert amendments prior to ratification failed, but there was an explicit agreement that the South Carolina delegation to Congress would support subsequent amendments. In Virginia, PATRICK HENRY, GEORGE MA-

SON, WILLIAM GRAYSON, and JAMES MONROE unsuccessfully supported the anti-Federalist cause. Only in North Carolina did anti-Federalists, led by Thomas Person, Willie Jones, Samuel Spencer, Timothy Bloodworth, and David Caldwell, actually prevent ratification of the Constitution until amendments had been introduced in the First Congress.

See J. T. Main, *Antifederalists* (1961); R. A. Rutland, *Ordeal of the Constitution* (1965); F. McDonald, *We the People* (1958); C. Kenyon, *William and Mary Quarterly* (Jan., 1955); and P. A. Crowl, *William and Mary Quarterly* (Oct., 1947).

LINDA GRANT DE PAUW
George Washington University

ANTISLAVERY SENTIMENT was readily encountered in the South almost to the 1830s, when the bold assaults begun by William Lloyd Garrison on slave ownership as being a sin antagonized southern leaders and caused them to condemn all antislavery expression as false or dangerous to public order. Antislavery actions, distinguished from sentiments, were less common, though they included passage by Congress of the Ordinance of 1787, formulated and supported by such southerners as Thomas Jefferson and George Washington. This ordinance closed the old Northwest to the institution of slavery.

The invention of the cotton gin in 1793 made slavery a profitable labor system and slaveholders generally firmer in their resistance to abolitionist views. Efforts by Kentucky antislavery advocates, including HENRY CLAY, to outlaw slavery there during its 1798 constitutional convention failed, as did later efforts to accomplish the same goal in Georgia and Virginia. In these states libertarian rhetoric combined with a distaste for the presence of Negroes was insufficient to marshal moral and political support for abolition.

Nevertheless, individuals and groups in the South expressed dissent from the dominant proslavery code. Zephaniah Kingsley's *Treatise on the Patriarchal or Cooperative System of Society* (1828) was by a former slave trader who did not distinguish blacks from whites—he himself married a Negro—though he did distinguish between free persons and slaves. George Bourne (1780–1845), an English-born Presbyterian minister in Virginia, published *The Book and Slavery Irreconcilable* (1818), but he shortly felt constrained to leave his church and migrate to the North. A more substantial group founded the Manumission Society of Tennessee. ELIHU EMBREE of that state in 1819 established the first abolitionist periodicals

in the United States, the short-lived *Manumission Intelligencer* and the monthly *Emancipator*. The Reverend John Rankin (1793–1886) felt pressured to move from Tennessee to Paris, Ky., and then in 1822 to Ripley, Ohio. In 1826, his pioneer *Letters on Slavery*, though published in Ohio, summed up views that had matured in southern terrain.

The abolitionist BENJAMIN LUNDY in the 1820s assumed that the major drive for abolitionist action would be in the South, where slavery flourished. In 1827 there were about 130 antislavery societies in the country, all moderate in sentiments, of which 106 were in the slave states. Most promising seemed the North Carolina Manumission Society, largely comprised of QUAKERS, who sought to encourage Negro education, to introduce bills in the state legislature easing the terms of slavery or encouraging manumissions, and to further colonization schemes for freeing slaves and transporting them to Liberia as settlers or missionaries. This society found its activities antagonistically viewed after 1828, and its members, including the famous UNDERGROUND RAILROAD "president" LEVI COFFIN, were compelled to move to Indiana.

Another southern antislavery worker was JAMES G. BIRNEY of Kentucky and Alabama, who symbolized for northern abolitionists the inhospitality of southerners to their own antislavery partisans. CASSIUS M. CLAY of Lexington, Ky., excited northern sympathizers because of the courage with which he outfaced aggressive proslavery defenders. Clay did not like Negroes, but he was infuriated by a labor system that he felt kept his section of the country from growth and affluence. The Reverend John G. Fee (1816–1901), founder of BEREA COLLEGE in Kentucky, more modestly sought to nurture antislavery feelings especially among POOR WHITES. None made the impression on the South, even though negative, that HINTON R. HELPER and his *The Impending Crisis* (1857) did. Helper was a poor white who purported to show by means of eloquence and statistics that slavery was detrimental to his people. His book was condemned throughout the South and used by Republicans in the North as a campaign document in 1860. By that year, southern antislavery advocates had been wholly silenced.

See "Abolition in South Before 1828," in W. Birney, *James G. Birney* (1890); J. S. Bassett, *Anti-Slavery Leaders of North Carolina* (1898); C. Eaton, *Freedom of Thought in Old South* (1940); L. Filler, *Crusade Against Slavery, 1830–1860* (1960); and P. J. Staudenraus, *African Colonization Movement, 1816–1865* (1961).

LOUIS FILLER
Antioch College

APALACHEE BAY, in the Gulf of Mexico, is formed by a bend in the coastline between the panhandle and the peninsula of Florida. Due south of present-day Tallahassee, it receives the waters of the Aucilla, St. Mark's, and Ochlockonee rivers. The traditional home of the APALACHEE INDIANS, the most populous of the half-dozen Indian tribes of Florida, was the high plain inland from the bay's marshy shore. Seeking to find the reported riches of the Apalachee Indians, ALVAR NÚÑEZ CABEZA DE VACA (1527) and HERNANDO DE SOTO (1539) both explored the bay and its coast. Spanish Franciscan missionaries established over a dozen missions among the Apalachee Indians during the first decade of the seventeenth century. The missions, like the Indians, were located inland from the shore, and not until after an Indian uprising in 1563 did the Spanish establish a small coastal fort near the mouth of the St. Mark's River. The fort at San Marcos de Apalachee was poorly equipped and garrisoned, however, and was easily captured by pirates in 1682. The Spanish rebuilt the fort in 1718, but it always remained only a minor installation in the system of coastal forts and never rivaled such settlements as ST. AUGUSTINE or PENSACOLA. Seized by Andrew Jackson in 1818, the fort was where he executed ARBUTHNOT AND AMBRISTER. Today much of the bay's marshy coast is maintained as a National Wildlife Refuge.

See M. F. Boyd et al., *Here They Once Stood* (1951), for the Apalachee missions; Federal Writers' Project, *Spanish Missions of Florida* (1940); V. E. Chatelain, *Defenses of Spanish Florida* (1941); and M. V. Gannon, *Cross in Sand* (1965).

APALACHEE INDIANS were a Muskogean-speaking people who lived in northwestern Florida between the Aucilla and Ochlockonee rivers. They were first encountered by Pánfilo de Narváez's expedition in 1528 and HERNANDO DE SOTO's expedition in 1539. Spanish missionaries arrived in 1633, and in time most of the Indians became Catholic converts. Their population declined steadily during the seventeenth century. In 1703–1704 James Moore led a large punitive force that shattered the Apalachees. They abandoned their homeland, most of them moving to South Carolina, with others seeking refuge among the French at Mobile. Those in South Carolina aligned with other Indians in the Yamassee War of 1715 (YAMASSEE INDIANS); the survivors found refuge among the CREEK INDIANS. Some of them later returned to Spanish territory, mostly settling around Pensacola. In the 1760s they moved west of the Mississippi River, where their culture and language soon ceased to exist.

See F. Bandelier, *Cabeza de Vaca* (1905); E. G. Bourne, *Hernando de Soto* (1904); and J. Swanton, *Bureau of American Ethnology Bulletin* (1922).

CHARLES HUDSON
University of Georgia

APALACHICOLA RIVER runs 112 miles from its source, the confluence of the Flint and Chattahoochee rivers in southwestern Georgia near the Florida state line, to its mouth on the Georgia coast. The Flint runs generally south 330 miles from its source near Atlanta, and the Chattahoochee winds 436 miles down from the BLUE RIDGE MOUNTAINS. Although this river network was used widely by the Indians as a transportation route, white people were slow to settle along its upper reaches and made little use of this water route until it was opened to steamboat traffic in 1827. During the next half-century it was a carrier first of cotton and then of lumber. Union forces blockaded the mouth of the river system during the early months of the Civil War, and Confederate forces, anxious to deny their foes access to the interior, placed numerous obstructions in the rivers' upper waters. In 1874 the federal government and the Army Corps of Engineers inaugurated a 20-year project of dredging, channeling, straightening, and clearing. But the costs of maintaining these navigational improvements mounted, and use of the river network declined as shippers increasingly availed themselves of the more efficient railroads. The rivers have been little used as a transportation route in the twentieth century, but all three are today the sites of several hydroelectric dams.

See W. H. Thurston, *Georgia Historical Quarterly* (Summer, 1973); and H. P. Owens, "Apalachicola" (Ph.D. dissertation, Florida State University, 1966).

APPALACHIA, or the southern mountain region, as traditionally defined comprises some 112,000 square miles in the hill and valley sections of Virginia, West Virginia, North and South Carolina, Georgia, Alabama, Tennessee, Kentucky, and Maryland. Its population in 1910 was estimated to be 5.3 million. Since 1962 Appalachia has been redefined (by T. R. Ford and his collaborators) as 80,000 square miles in the above states except Maryland and South Carolina, with a population approaching 5.7 million, although more recent federal legislation and federal practice have extended Appalachia into Ohio, Pennsylvania, and

New York. The social and economic characteristics of the region are not subject to systematic statement, for they are as varied as those of any other region. Despite this diversity, the region has traditionally been viewed as quintessentially rural and, since 1935 at least, as quintessentially poor, but in either case as fundamentally different from the rest of the nation.

In the nineteenth and early twentieth centuries, Appalachian otherness was defined in cultural terms. Discovered in the 1870s and 1880s by local-color writers in search of "interesting" material for their sketches and short stories, Appalachia seemed a little corner of the nation not yet touched by the forces of modernization and homogenization, and hence separate from both America and the South. During the 1880s and 1890s, home missionaries of the northern Protestant denominations viewed Appalachia as a likely foothold for evangelical work in the South, from which they had been excluded by the schisms of the Civil War. At the same time, the supposed backwardness of Appalachia offered the added appeal of need to the area as a field of mission work. Attempts to explain the origins of Appalachian otherness raised the issue of "degenerate origins," and this in turn precipitated a defense of the mountaineers as descendants of the noble frontiersmen. Defenders of Appalachia defined the people as "our contemporary ancestors" and referred to the region as "Appalachian America," a legitimately distinct portion of the nation.

After 1895 the terms "Appalachian America" or the "southern highlands" and later "Appalachia" came to replace the "central South" in discussions of Appalachia, and the legitimation of Appalachian otherness effected by naming and explaining made the mountaineers' "need" seem less pressing. During the 1920s in particular, two parallel tendencies appeared: an increasing self-consciousness by Appalachian Americans, manifested in the establishment of regional institutions and in the emerging search for a distinct regional history and culture; and a concomitant decline of concern by outside agencies for the welfare of the mountaineers. During the 1950s, in an affluent and increasingly urbanized America, the place of Appalachia in America came once again to seem a problem. This time, however, Appalachian otherness seemed not so much a matter of being "behind the times" as the result of economic exploitation; and Appalachia, which had once represented America in its seedbed, now came to seem America's victim. In both cases, however, Appalachia as part of America has taken its sense of self, as it has been defined by outsiders, from the changing conceptions of American civilization since 1870.

See J. C. Campbell, *Southern Highlander* (1921); T. R. Ford, *Southern Appalachian Region* (1962); and H. D. Shapiro, *Appalachia on Our Mind* (1977).

HENRY D. SHAPIRO
University of Cincinnati

APPALACHIAN MOUNTAINS is an imprecise term referring to all or portions of the system of subdued highlands of eastern North America extending from Canada southwestward for 1,500 miles into Alabama. The present topography results from the combined effects of a succession of uplifts—perhaps initiated by a collision between the North American and African continental plates hundreds of millions of years ago, which folded, faulted, and otherwise altered the underlying rock—and the action of erosion on those rocks of differing hardness over a long period of time. In general, the degree of rock deformation decreases westward across the system. Within the South, the Appalachian system can be divided lengthwise, on the basis of geologic structure and topography, into four provinces. From the east, they are the PIEDMONT, BLUE RIDGE, ridge and valley, and Appalachian Plateaus provinces. The northeast-southwest orientation of these provinces and of major features within them is an important characteristic of the system.

The Piedmont, although structurally a part of the Appalachian system, in common usage is not included in the Appalachian Mountains. The Blue Ridge province includes a number of ridges and ranges that often rise abruptly 1,000 to 2,000 feet above the Piedmont. These mountains once extended farther east, and today several remnants of that more extensive range (for example, South Mountain in North Carolina) exist as outliers of the Blue Ridge province in the western Piedmont.

The ridge and valley and the Appalachian Plateaus provinces, unlike the two eastern provinces, are underlain by sedimentary rock layers. In the former, the rocks have been tightly folded, producing a series of anticlines (upfolds) and synclines (downfolds) trending northeast-southwest. Erosion acting on these folds has developed a series of longitudinal ridges and valleys, often called the folded Appalachians, also aligned northeast-southwest. The ridges exist where resistant rocks, frequently sandstones, are exposed, and the valleys exist where weaker limestones or shales reach the surface. In the Appalachian Plateaus province, which consists of the ALLEGHENY (north) and CUMBERLAND (south) plateaus, the rocks are not strongly folded. Consequently, the high-standing plateau surface has been carved by streams into a complex of hills and valleys with little pattern imposed by the structure beneath it.

See W. D. Thornbury, *Regional Geomorphology of U.S.* (1965); P. B. King, *Evolution of North America* (1959); R. S. Dietz, *Scientific American* (March, 1972); and J. L. Rich, *Geographical Review* (Oct., 1939).

WALLACE M. ELTON
Middlebury College

APPALACHIAN REGIONAL JOURNALS. The earliest journal to evidence any interest in APPALACHIA was probably the *Berea Quarterly* (1895–1916), but it was through the efforts of HOWARD W. ODUM at the University of North Carolina in the 1930s that there developed a more lasting interest in and concern with the problems of this mountain region. In 1925 appeared the first journal totally dedicated to the study of the Appalachian scene, *Mountain Life and Work*. Supported by the COUNCIL OF SOUTHERN MOUNTAINS in partnership with certain churches, it had a circulation in 1976 of 8,000. Its original purpose was to educate the outside world about Appalachia and to serve as an organ in which to present the mountain people—their poverty and their social problems. In more recent years the journal has assumed an advocate position in the fight against the sometimes unfavorable inroads of the industrial developers, and it publishes material with emphasis on congressional legislation, health problems, the abuses of strip mining, and labor and mine negotiations. Its 11 issues per year now contain fewer scholarly articles and many more of the popular variety of news notes, as well as an occasional book review.

During this same early period, in addition to the state historical journals that contained occasional articles on Appalachia, there appeared the *Kentucky Folklore and Poetry Magazine* in 1926 and soon numerous other FOLKLORE journals, such as the Tennessee Folklore Society's *Bulletin* (1938), *North Carolina Folklore* (1948), and *West Virginia Folklore* (1951). Somewhat later came periodicals intended to offer outlets for the area's literary talent: for example, *Echoes of West Virginia* (1941–1945); the *Black Mountain Review* (1954–1957); *West Virginia Heritage* (1967); and *Twigs* (1970). The *Appalachian Review* (1966–1969), though largely literary, also presented regular news analyses. Perhaps the best-known literary presentation

and the most successful financially has been *Foxfire*, published beginning in 1969 at Rabun Gap, Ga. It is a high school student venture into oral social and cultural history.

Southern regional NEWSPAPERS have played their role as well in regularly bringing features on Appalachia to the public. Among these are the Knoxville *News-Sentinel*, the Asheville *Citizen*, the Louisville *Courier-Journal*, the Whitesburg (Ky.) *Mountain Eagle* (1907), and the *West Virginia Hillbilly* (1956). Added to this are all the special-interest publications. Among these are *Coal Age* (1911–), the *U.M.W. Journal* (1891–), *People's Appalachia* (1970–), and *Appalachian Lookout* (1968–1970). *Appalachian Advance* (1966–) is published by the Appalachian Regional Education Laboratory to make known its work; the highly regarded *Appalachia* has been published since 1967 by the Appalachian Regional Commission. Among the numerous advocate journals are *Black Lung Bulletin*, *Coal Patrol*, *Jackson-Clay Roadrunner*, *Miner's Voice*, and *Mountain Voice*.

Valuable tools in the pursuit of these Appalachian studies are the *Appalachian Outlook*, a bibliographic service published since 1948 by West Virginia University, and the *Newsletter*, published since 1971 by the Appalachian Center of Berea College to report developments in the teaching and study of Appalachia on the college level.

Finally, there are four late entries in this field. *Appalachian Heritage*, a quarterly published at Alice Lloyd College, contains stories, poems, and interviews with the mountain people. *Appalachian Journal* (Box 536, Appalachian State University, Boone, N.C. 28608) with a circulation of 536 in 1976 is a quarterly founded in 1972 to present the history, folklore, culture, and views of the people of the 11-state Appalachian mountain region. It receives its support from subscriptions and from the Appalachian State University Foundation. This journal includes popular as well as scholarly materials, book reviews, photographic essays, and comment. The third in this group is an interdisciplinary quarterly with a circulation of about 500, *Appalachian Notes*, which since 1973 has devoted itself entirely to scholarly, analytical studies of the entire area of the mountains south of the Catskills. It includes, in addition, book reviews, news and notes, and much bibliographic material. It is published privately and is without foundation or university support. The editors in 1976 were Richard B. Drake of Berea College and Lawrence S. Thompson of the University of Kentucky. Last is *Mountain Review*, begun in 1974 by Appalshop, Inc. (Box 660, Whitesburg, Ky. 41858) with the support of the National Endowment for the Arts. It has become a print outlet for the material the Appalshop community has been unable to place on film, its principal medium.

See R. B. Drake, *Appalachian Notes* (First Quarter, 1973).

RICHARD B. DRAKE
Berea College

APPALACHIAN TRAIL is a footpath some 2,000 miles long from Mount Katahdin in north-central Maine to Springer Mountain in north-central Georgia. It was conceived in the early 1900s by Benton MacKaye, who foresaw the need for preserving wilderness areas in the Appalachian highlands to balance the growing urban areas of the Eastern Seaboard. The development of the trail became the goal of many dedicated individuals and organizations. Work began through the Palisades of New Jersey in 1922. The Appalachian Trail Conference was formed in 1925. It is a private, nationwide organization that represents citizens' interests and coordinates the work of many subsidiary trail-maintaining clubs. Many guidebooks and other publications are issued from its headquarters in Washington, D.C. (1718 N St. NW, 20036).

In 1968 the National Trails System Act established the path as a National Scenic Trail, charging the secretary of the interior, in consultation with the secretary of agriculture, with administration of the trail. This act and subsequent cooperative agreements have helped to strengthen the program of trail maintenance and wilderness preservation against the encroachments of competing land uses.

See J. Hare, *Hiking the Appalachian Trail* (1975); and R. Fisher, *Appalachian Trail* (1972).

RICHARD S. LITTLE
West Virginia University

APPOMATTOX CAMPAIGN. It may have been the confidence of desperation, but ROBERT E. LEE retained in February and March of 1865 a slim hope that victory yet lay within his grasp. Despite his army's having dwindled to about 50,000 effectives during the long and bitter winter (Ulysses S. Grant had twice this number), Lee's pride prevented him from ever completely doubting the invincibility of his men. His March 25 assault (led by General JOHN B. GORDON) on Grant's lines outside Petersburg, Va., at FT. STEDMAN, opened his campaign. A success here would have constricted the Army of the Potomac's enveloping lines and perhaps have created an opportunity for a portion of Lee's command to join General JOSEPH JOHN-

STON's army in North Carolina, while the remainder continued to defend the siege lines. Gordon's failure ensured Grant and his cavalry commander, General Philip H. Sheridan, freedom to operate against Lee's right flank in order to cut the central Virginia railroads and force his surrender. Lee should probably have evacuated Richmond and Petersburg immediately afterward, but placed his faith instead in a detached force commanded by GEORGE PICKETT and FITZHUGH LEE. Their troops were poorly led and were defeated on April 1 at FIVE FORKS on Lee's far right flank. This engagement cost him control of the Southside Railroad, brought on the assault that shattered his Petersburg defenses, and compelled his retreat on April 2.

For the next seven days, the Army of Northern Virginia fought valorously enough to create a thousand legends. Indeed, enough of Lee's noble army remained "of unsurpassed courage and fortitude" as to contribute mightily to the myth of the LOST CAUSE after the war. But the retreat began too late. There was a fatal delay at Amelia Courthouse on April 4 (the responsibility for which rests at least partly with Lee), and the Union armies never lost contact with their enemies, sensing victory throughout. Sheridan's troops, in particular, fought viciously. Weary and underfed, roughly one-third of Lee's army was trapped and put out of commission at SAYLER'S CREEK on the sixth of April. Lee reached deeply into his celebrated reserve of personal dignity and gravity to negotiate the surrender three days later, when the remainder of his army was finally surrounded at Appomattox. He had delayed the unthinkable as long as possible and then managed to extract very honorable terms. Over 25,000 Confederates were paroled, but fewer than one-half of them had weapons when the end came.

See *Official Records, Armies*, Ser. 1, Vol. XLVI; D. S. Freeman, *Lee* (1934–35), a brilliant and vain apologia; T. L. Livermore, *Papers of the Military History Society of Massachusetts* (1907), VI, excellent; and B. Rodick, *Appomattox* (1965), the best of the popular histories.

CRAIG SIMPSON
University of Western Ontario

ARANSAS PASS is an inlet off the coast of Texas that cuts between St. Joseph Island to the north and Mustang Island to the south. Known to the Spanish as Porto de Nuezes and also as Paso de Aranzazu, the pass provides passage from the Gulf of Mexico to both Aransas and Corpus Christi bays. Two early communities founded near the pass as shipping centers are now ghost towns: Aransas City (established in 1837) and Aransas (founded in 1841). The first thrived briefly as a port for contraband munitions prior to being sacked and totally destroyed by the Mexican army in 1841. The second town, situated on St. Joseph Island, suffered from the federal blockade of the Confederate coast and was completely annihilated by a federal raiding party late in the Civil War. Present ports utilizing the pass for access to the Gulf are Port Aransas (on Mustang Island) and the cities of Aransas Pass and CORPUS CHRISTI (both on the mainland). Completion of a 40-foot ship channel through the pass in 1926 and development of the INTRACOASTAL WATERWAY have aided the commercial growth of all three cities.

See W. P. Webb (ed.), *Handbook of Texas* (1952); and Federal Writers' Project, *Texas* (1940).

ARBUTHNOT AND AMBRISTER, CASE OF.

These two were British subjects executed by General ANDREW JACKSON during his foray into Spanish West Florida in 1818. The Scottish Alexander Arbuthnot, a seventy-year-old trader with the Indians and Negroes of the area, was captured during Jackson's unopposed seizure of St. Mark's on April 7. A court-martial found him guilty of inciting and aiding the enemy. He was hanged on his own schooner on April 29. Robert C. Ambrister, wearing his British officer's uniform, had blundered into the American camp on April 18. An articulate, young adventurer, he was tried by the same court, found guilty, and sentenced to be shot. On a second poll of the court, the sentence was reduced to 50 lashes and a year in confinement. Jackson refused the second sentence; Ambrister was executed. Although Jackson's actions enhanced greatly his image as a popular hero, they also caused him subsequent political problems. Possible war between Great Britain and the United States was avoided when the English foreign secretary, Viscount Castlereagh, disavowed the Britishers' actions.

See M. James, *Andrew Jackson* (1933); K. Porter, *Journal of Negro History* (July, 1951); and J. L. Wright, Jr., *Journal of Southern History* (Nov., 1968).

EDWIN M. GAINES
University of Arizona

ARCHEOLOGY.

The history of human occupation of the South began more than a dozen millennia ago when people, who had gradually infiltrated the New World from northeastern Asia, began to settle here. During these millennia people moved about in the region, others moved in, some moved out, and all were constantly changing their ways of life as the processes of cultural evolution relentlessly evolved ever more complex cultural systems. The Paleo-Indian hunters of big game animals, such as mastodon and giant bison, gave way some 10,000 or 9,000 years ago to the Archaic hunting and food-gathering peoples. Rudimentary horticulture was gradually added to the economy along with pottery, the bow and arrow, and semipermanent settlements in the Woodland period about 3,000 to 2,000 years ago. During the next few centuries this developed into a fully agricultural economy supplemented by hunting, fishing, and food gathering. By around A.D. 1100, an elaborate socioreligious system had become dominant throughout much of the South. This, the Mississippian period, evolved extensive sociopolitical community complexes often dominated by ceremonial centers with large temple mounds and a strong priesthood.

By the time of European contact these complexes had begun to break down through internecine conflicts. The European invaders accelerated this cultural deterioration, and once-powerful chiefdoms were split into subgroups that were shifting their locations every few years. By the mid-nineteenth century a majority of the native Americans had been removed to areas west of the Mississippi River, mainly to Indian Territory (Oklahoma).

Throughout these millennia there was a certain cohesiveness and similarity within the region that is, in this volume, defined as the South. Archeologists call this the Southeast, with only slightly altered prehistoric boundaries that include east Texas, eastern Oklahoma, southern Missouri; follow the Ohio River to central West Virginia; and cross the Appalachians to the James River valley. The cultural continuity in this region extends to the present. There is good reason for this, based in an ecological cohesiveness within the area. Except for the Appalachian and Ouachita mountains, this is a low, rolling, uplifted coastal plain with a remarkably uniform topography, climate, vegetation, and soil sequence. There are numerous subareas within this region, and arguments could be made for variations of its boundaries, but basically this culture area has remained both ecologically and culturally unified. The South has been the South for several thousand years.

Archeological research in America began in the South when THOMAS JEFFERSON excavated a burial mound in Virginia in the 1780s and William Blanding excavated a temple mound in South Carolina in the 1820s. For the next century sporadic investigations were conducted throughout the South. These were primarily investigations into the curious prehistoric mounds and other ruins, the collecting of museum-quality artifacts, and the gradual development of scientific inquiry into the cultures of ancient peoples. E. G. Squier and E. H. Davis reported on Mississippian mounds in 1847. C. B. Moore explored sites along the Atlantic and Gulf coasts in the 1890s. W. H. Holmes analyzed the pottery of the region in 1903, and others conducted numerous excavations and studies of prehistoric sites in the South during this speculative-descriptive period of American archeology.

The massive WPA and TVA projects of the 1930s stimulated large-scale excavations throughout the South. In the 1940s and 1950s, the River Basin Surveys Program of the Smithsonian Institution and National Park Service developed archeological projects in Texas, but few elsewhere in the South. The 1930s to 1960s was a golden age of large-scale archeological data collecting when chronology, context, and function were emphasized in a field of study that was rapidly becoming a scientific discipline. During this era the study of the ruins of European-American settlements, called historical archeology, added another "culture period" to the discipline. Still another dimension was added in the late 1960s when underwater archeologists began to examine historic shipwrecks and drowned terrestrial sites in rivers and lakes and on the continental shelf.

Archeological research is being conducted today by at least 29 institutions throughout the South. The major ones are the McClung Museum and the Department of Anthropology, University of Tennessee, sponsored by the TVA; the Institute of Archeology and Anthropology, University of South Carolina; and the Arkansas Archeological Survey, University of Arkansas. Excavations and other studies are being conducted on a smaller scale by university archeologists, by state archeologists and state departments of archives and history, as well as by such private foundations as Colonial Williamsburg in Virginia. Much of the contract archeology in all these states is funded by the National Park Service, the Tennessee Valley Authority, and various agencies responsible for environmental impact statements.

See J. L. Coe, "Formative Cultures," *Transactions of the American Philosophical Society* (Aug., 1964); J. B. Griffin, *Archeology of Eastern U.S.* (1952); C. M. Hudson, "Red, White, and Black," *Papers of the Southern Anthropological Society* (1972); A. L. Kroeber, *Cultural and Natural Areas* (1939); W. D. Lipe, *Kiva* (Dec., 1974); T. M. N. Lewis and M. Kneberg, *Hiwasee Island* (1946); C. R. McGimsey, *Public Archeology* (1972); map, "North America Before Columbus," *National Geographic* (Dec., 1972); P. Phillips, J. A. Ford, and J. B. Griffin, "Survey of Mississippi Valley," *Papers of Peabody Museum* (1951);

W. H. Sears, "Southeastern U.S.," in J. D. Jennings and E. Norbeck (eds.), *Prehistoric Man* (1971); S. South, *Method and Theory* (1976); E. G. Squier and E. H. Davis, *Ancient Monuments* (1848); R. L. Stephenson, "Accokeek," Anthropology Papers, University of Michigan, No. 20 (1963); R. L. Stephenson, *Bulletin of the Texas Archeological Society* (1970); R. L. Stephenson, *Notebook of the Institute of Archeology and Anthropology* (May–June, 1975); J. R. Swanton, *Bulletin of the Bureau of American Ethnology*, No. 137 (1946); L. A. White, *Science of Culture* (1949); S. Williams and J. B. Stoltman, "Southeastern U.S. Prehistory," in H. E. Wright and D. G. Frey, *Quaternary of U.S.* (1965); G. R. Willey, *Introduction to American Archeology* (1966), I; H. M. Wormington, *Ancient Man* (1957); and G. R. Willey and J. A. Sabloff, *History of American Archeology* (1974).

ROBERT L. STEPHENSON
University of South Carolina

ARCHITECTURE. Although there was nothing in the South to compare with the great houses of seventeenth-, eighteenth-, or nineteenth-century England, in upwardly mobile America houses were status symbols and the principal expenditures of most families. Consequently, even the small houses of the South often achieved a symmetry, elegance, and sophistication quite rare in the British Isles. Over time, the climate, ethnic origins, availability of local materials, and changing state of the economy combined to produce southern houses as different from those of England as they were from those of New England.

Among the several strains of settlers to come to the South, the Swedes of DELAWARE are often credited with constructing the first log house. This, however, is questionable, as the earliest of English settlers spoke of building "pallisades," or log walls made of vertical posts driven into the ground. Also, the English often used "logg" buildings as prisons because of the difficulty of escaping from such structures. French architectural influences are visible not only in the buildings of Louisiana (especially in New Orleans), but also in the houses of Charleston, S.C. After the slave uprising in Santo Domingo in 1793, many French planters escaped and settled in Charleston. The two- and three-story galleries, which are so much a part of Charleston's architecture, may have been introduced at this time along with jalousies (exterior blinds, sometimes erroneously called shutters). To take advantage of the ocean breezes, the émigrés raised their homes on high basements, built them one-room thick for direct cross ventilation, and constructed them to face not the street but alternating gardens. Despite the significant regional contributions of the Swedes, the French, the HUGUENOTS (Bath, N.C.), the MORAVIANS (New Bern, N.C.), and the German Lutherans

(South Carolina and Shenandoah Valley), the dominant academic influence upon southern colonial architecture remained English.

The English style that had the greatest impact on early seventeenth-century colonists was Jacobean or Gothic Survival. Although it once was popular to trace the evolution of the southern house from a small single-room dwelling into a large residence, the outstanding feature of the Jacobean style in both New England and the South is the great hall, a survival from medieval times. Indeed, as late as the first quarter of the eighteenth century, the typical American house consisted of a large living-cooking-eating room and a small chamber on the first floor and smaller sleeping chambers on the second floor. Jacobean structures, utilizing the formal letter plans of Elizabethan England with much of the decorative detail of the Italian Renaissance, can be seen today along much of the southeastern seaboard. In Maryland, a choice example is the tiny Secretary's Manor (*ca.* 1720); its superb woodwork (now in the Brooklyn Museum) is an excellent example of the sophistication of many small, early American houses. Bacon's Castle, one of the most complete surviving Jacobean structures, is an excellent Virginia example. Built prior to 1672, when it was used as a refuge by insurgents of BACON'S REBELLION, the original structure had a large, multipurpose room on the first floor with an entrance porch on the front and a stair hall to the rear. The basic floor plan of the original structure formed a T or a cruciform. This notable house also has splendid curvilinear Jacobean gables and Flemish bond brickwork.

As southern colonists prospered, their houses became larger and the rooms more numerous. Bacon's Castle was remodeled and retrimmed about 1740, and its great hall was divided into several smaller, symmetrical rooms. Newer structures also used one of several popular letter plans to increase both the number of rooms and the sense of spaciousness: the H plan, with a large connecting room or hall between parallel wings, survives at Stratford (1726) and at Tuckahoe (*ca.* 1712–1730); the T plan was used at Otwell (*ca.* 1720) in Maryland and at Claremont (*ca.* 1725) in Virginia; and the L plan survives at Holly Hill (*ca.* 1690–1720) in Anne Arundel County, Md. Eighteenth-century structures also frequently began to reflect the influence of England's Georgian style of architecture, especially after the construction in Williamsburg of the first capitol (*ca.* 1710) and the Governor's Palace (1725). Georgian plans were characterized by a center hall and a symmetrical exterior. The heavy balusters and bolection moldings of the Jacobean tradition gave way to plainer raised panels and stair balusters with vases and Doric columns.

The Early Georgian style is best exemplified at Westover (before 1734) on the James River in Virginia. Its front and rear exteriors possess almost identical façades originally flanked by symmetrical, detached dependencies (since attached to the primary structure). The vertical proportions of its windows, its four lofty chimneys, and its high-hipped roof (punctuated with dormer windows) make a bold central mass set off by an extensive forecourt.

High Georgian architecture gradually softened the vertical proportions of the Early Georgian style. Drayton Hall (1740) near Charleston, for example, is set upon a high basement to remove the living quarters from the damp earth and features two-story porticoes on both its front and rear façades. Yet, though retaining the simple symmetry of both Georgian periods, Drayton Hall's lower pitched roof and less vertical chimneys set it apart from Westover. Carter's Grove (1750–1753) on the James River is not set on a high basement, yet its exterior lines are also more horizontal than are Westover's. The interiors of both Drayton Hall and Carter's Grove illustrate yet another development over Early Georgian plans. Instead of the single central staircase found at Westover (and in most Jacobean houses as well), both Drayton and Carter's Grove added a service stair while developing a monumental stairway in the front hall.

Late Georgian houses perpetuated the symmetry of earlier Georgian styles and continued the High Georgian emphasis upon horizontal lines. Instead of a large central structure set off by outbuildings, however, Late Georgian structures were composed of three, five, or seven pavilions or elements connected by hyphens. The spreading nature of these structures limited their use in urban areas, yet the Harwood-Hammond House in Annapolis, Md., survives as one of the superb examples of the Late Georgian style.

As the eighteenth century drew to a close, American architecture in general lost the unity and cohesiveness that had marked the entire Georgian period. With the discovery of Herculaneum and Pompeii, citizens of the young American republic looked first to Rome (Federal period, 1780–1820) and then to Greece (Greek Revival, 1820–1840) for architectural models. The Roman Revival was initiated in Virginia by THOMAS JEFFERSON, who long had been displeased with the Georgian architecture of Williamsburg. At Monticello (1770–1809), the new capitol in Richmond (1785), and the University of Virginia (1817–1826),

Jefferson's use of freestanding pillars for porticoes that protruded from the main structures strongly influenced two generations of both residential and public structures. Appropriately, the best and most famous example of Federal style in a house of the Upper South is the White House in Washington, D.C. The high-pitched roofs and irregular gables of Georgian and Jacobean styles were replaced by low domes and/or triangular pediments. In parts of the Deep South, colonnaded porticoes completely surrounded the house (as at Belle Helene in Louisiana), providing both classical splendor and cooling shade.

Not all early nineteenth-century houses strove to look like ancient temples, however. One early nineteenth-century development in the vernacular architecture of southern houses was the raised cottage. In Augusta, Ga., this style is called the Augusta cottage, and along the Gulf coast it is called the raised Gulf cottage. By whatever name, the raised cottage was built on a high basement in a U plan under a gabled roof. It generally featured a center hall opening into an open porch, which was closed on the ends by a pair of unheated rooms. Unlike most houses in the popular classical styles and earlier colonial styles, the raised cottage usually was of a frame construction. Some of the loveliest of these, which were destroyed by the Santee Dam, had simple Adam trim made in the usual method in America, in which it was interpreted by the chisel rather than by raised plaster decoration. So ingenious did carpenters become with chisel decoration that whole rooms would be finished with the drill and chisel in swags, sunburst designs, and even a series of drills that served to suggest dentils. The Great Hall House (*ca.* 1785) in Warrenton, Ga., and Beauvoir (1852), the Jefferson Davis home in Biloxi, Miss., are excellent examples. Their raised basements helped keep them both cool and dry, and their simple Federal trim reflects the period in which they were built.

Yet even the variety and flexibility of the classical and the raised-cottage styles did not long satisfy the needs and tastes of southerners. With the introduction of the Gothic Revival and the Italianate (or Italian Villa) style in the 1840s, the South rediscovered high and wide windows, asymmetrical plans, and the convenience of rooms opening into each other by means of sliding doors. Houses such as the great octagonal house, Longwood (1860), near Natchez, Miss., signaled a willingness to experiment with design, to use new materials including terra-cotta, and to use new structural methods. In the 1870s and 1880s, there also appeared the Queen Anne style and the Tudor Re-

vival, featuring shingles, towers, balconies, and semicircular porches. In the late 1870s also, some members of the architectural firm of McKim, Meade & White initiated the Colonial Revival, and by 1900 this Georgian style was formally set in the pattern of American homes with pediments, porticoes, and central hall plans.

There is space here for but a few of the most important facets of the great subject of American architecture. Only now are studies being made of vernacular and industrial buildings, of the range and diversity of creative expression, and of the devotion of the architects and owners to the good life. Even many famous buildings and cities are awaiting scholarly monographs. Until these are written, no definitive study is possible, but it is hoped that this brief essay will point others to their golden prey.

See H. C. Foreman, *Architecture of Old South, 1585–1850* (1948); L. Mumford, *South in Architecture* (1941, 1961); W. M. Whitehill, *Palladio in America* (1976); W. R. Ware, *Georgian Period* (1923); F. Kimball, *Domestic Architecture in American Colonies* (1922), and *American Architecture* (1928); H. R. Shurtleff, *Log Cabin Myth* (1939); W. Andrews, *Social History of American Architecture* (1947, 1964); R. Newcomb, *Colonial and Federal Houses* (1933), and *Architecture of Old Kentucky* (1953); T. A. Glenn, *Some Colonial Mansions* (1898); R. A. Lancaster, *Historic Virginia Homes and Churches* (1915); H. K. Leiding, *Historic Houses of South Carolina* (1921); E. T. Sale, *Interiors of Virginia Houses* (1927); S. G. Stoney, *Plantations of Carolina Low Country* (1938); T. T. Waterman, *Dwellings of Colonial America* (1950), *Early Architecture of North Carolina* (1941), and *Mansions of Virginia, 1706–1776* (1946); T. F. Hamlin, *Greek Revival Architecture in America* (1944); G. A. Cochran, *Grandeur in Tennessee* (1946); N. C. Curtis, *New Orleans* (1933); R. C. Hammond, *Ante-bellum Mansions of Alabama* (1951); J. F. Smith, *White Pillars* (1941); and guides and histories of individual homes, towns, and locales.

FREDERICK D. NICHOLS
University of Virginia

ARCHIVES OF SOUTHERN HISTORY comprise essentially two types of unpublished materials: the public records of governments, and the private papers of individuals, families, organizations, institutions, and businesses. Laws generally control the maintenance and preservation of the former; individual initiative determines the fate of the latter.

Through the nineteenth century the care of public records was lax at best. Although most states had general laws relating to records, few placed effective control in particular offices. Traditionally the secretary of the colony (and later of the state) was the chief recording officer, but as government expanded even he had less and less control over the steadily proliferating bodies of records. Each state made, with varying degrees of success, sporadic statutory efforts to clarify responsibility. In the case of county records, legislation usually resulted from specific crises, such as the burning of a courthouse. And in the case of both state and county records, millions of documents were destroyed through overzealous housecleanings and through inadequate care leading to mutilation or deterioration from overuse, vermin, water, light, polluted atmosphere, or chemical ingredients of the paper. Theft, too, was not uncommon, and wars took their toll. Still, the marvel is that so many records of southern governments survived, thus attesting to their care by custodians. During the Revolution, for instance, many Georgia records escaped the British by being carted northward to Maryland; and a significant portion of North Carolina's state records was wagoned through Virginia into the tramontane area, now Tennessee.

Influenced by the new breed of "professional" historians inspired by HERBERT BAXTER ADAMS' "seminary method," southern states gave birth to a new type of agency around the turn of the century. In 1901 the ALABAMA DEPARTMENT OF ARCHIVES AND HISTORY, the first of a succession of state archival agencies in the nation, was created. This development shifted to the region the national leadership in documentary preservation and brought into prominence archivists such as Thomas M. Owen of Alabama, Dunbar Rowland of Mississippi, and ROBERT D. W. CONNOR of North Carolina.

For several decades emphasis was upon transferring records to state repositories, but by the 1930s attention was given equally to the passage and enforcement of laws governing the creation, maintenance, preservation, and use of the records in the various public offices. North Carolina's Public Records Act of 1935, written by Albert Ray Newsome, served as a model for other states. And, following World War II, archivists, realizing that the rapid proliferation of records threatened to inundate them, joined in establishing records management programs designed to provide for orderly disposition of nonpermanent records so that the valuable documents could be identified and cared for more easily. The southern states have continued to provide national leadership in archival administration, and almost all of them now support substantial programs in modern facilities.

Private papers, too, suffered until the twentieth century. There was not yet a single good collecting program in the South. The immense appeal of southern history early in the present century, however, brought new urgency to the preservation of private manuscripts and institutional archives, particularly at universities offering graduate work. A number of history professors and librarians added collecting to their duties, and the dean of the pack was JOSEPH GRÉGOIRE DE ROULHAC HAMILTON, who by 1920 conceived the Southern Historical Collection at the UNIVERSITY OF NORTH CAROLINA. Ten years later he gave up his teaching to devote full time to a remarkable second career—that of establishing the first outstanding repository of southern historical manuscripts. On hundreds of trips through the South, Hamilton's carpetbags were filled with source materials and hauled off to Chapel Hill. His contribution was twofold: the preservation of millions of manuscripts and the stimulation of competition.

This competition helped provide the impetus for the establishment of manuscript repositories in every state in the South. Each of the major universities offering graduate work in history is now in the collecting field, and some—notably the UNIVERSITY OF ALABAMA, DUKE UNIVERSITY, LOUISIANA STATE UNIVERSITY, the University of North Carolina, the UNIVERSITY OF SOUTH CAROLINA, the UNIVERSITY OF TEXAS, and the UNIVERSITY OF VIRGINIA—number their manuscripts in the millions.

Specialized collections have been established for church records, such as in the Historical Foundation of the Presbyterian and Reformed Churches at Montreat, N.C.; Negro history, such as in FISK UNIVERSITY and TUSKEGEE INSTITUTE; business records, such as in the Eleutherian Mills Historical Library, Greenville, Del.; labor records, such as in the Southern Labor Archives at Georgia State University, Atlanta; and military records, such as in Air University in Alabama. Among the leading historical society collections are those in the VIRGINIA HISTORICAL SOCIETY, Richmond; MARYLAND HISTORICAL SOCIETY, Baltimore; and ATLANTA HISTORICAL SOCIETY. Considerable quantities of southern records have found their way outside the region. The records of the Confederacy, for instance, are in the National Archives in Washington, D.C.

See copies of addresses by E. M. Coulter, P. M. Hamer, and J. G. de R. Hamilton in G. B. Tindall (ed.), *Pursuit of Southern History* (1964); J. G. de R. Hamilton, *North Carolina Historical Review* (April, 1954); H. G. Jones, *For History's Sake* (1966); E. Posner, *American State Archives* (1964); P. M. Hamer (ed.), *Guide to Archives and Manuscripts* (1961); and published guides of individual repositories, although there is no satisfactory study of the archives of southern history.

H. G. JONES
University of North Carolina

STATE ARCHIVAL AGENCIES

Alabama:	Department of Archives and History, Montgomery, 36130: territorial, state, and local records since 1818; private papers (*e.g.*, papers of John H. Bankhead, Jr. and Sr., Jefferson Davis, Andrew Jackson, William Rufus King, Oscar W. Underwood, Leroy Pope Walker, William L. Yancey).
Arkansas:	History Commission, Little Rock, 72201: territorial, state, and local records since 1790; census and military records; newspaper files; church records; and private papers (*e.g.*, Civil War diaries, business papers 1830–1960, steamboat accounts, letters and papers of William E. Woodruff, William S. Fulton, Homer M. Adkins).
Delaware:	Division of Historical and Cultural Affairs, Hall of Records, Dover, 19901: colonial, state, and local records since 1674; extensive military records and private papers (*e.g.*, papers of John Middleton Clayton, John Dickinson, Henry M. Ridgely, Caesar Augustus Rodney, business papers, shipping accounts 1790–1815, church records 1708–1940).
Florida:	Division of Archives, History, and Records Management, Tallahassee, 32304: territorial, state, and local records since 1822; private papers (*e.g.*, business records, including Florida Coast Line Canal & Transportation Company, Civil War letters, and extensive transcripts and photocopies of manuscripts on Florida that are located elsewhere).
Georgia:	Department of Archives and History, Atlanta, 30334; colonial, state, and local records since 1732; Civil War service records; land-grant records; and private papers (*e.g.*, nineteenth-century business records, family papers 1800–1900, women's clubs, and church records 1789–).
Kentucky:	Department of Library and Archives, Frankfort, 40601: state and local records since 1792, Civil War records, and private papers (*e.g.*, papers of Orlando Brown, Henry Clay, William Henry Harrison,

Samuel Hopkins, Valentine Peers, D. Howard Smith, Zachary Taylor, James Wilkinson).

Louisiana:	Archives and Records Service, Department of State, Baton Rouge, 70804: territorial, state, and local records since 1700; private papers. Some official records also in Department of Archives and Manuscripts, Louisiana State University, Baton Rouge.
Maryland:	Hall of Records, Annapolis, 21404: colonial, state, and local records since 1635; private papers (*e.g.*, church and business records, including those of colonial period, family papers from 1641, and rare maps).
Mississippi:	Department of Archives and History, Jackson, 39205: territorial, state, and local records since 1699, including land titles and French, Spanish, and British records; private papers (*e.g.*, papers of William C. C. Claiborne, Jefferson Davis, Lucius Q. C. Lamar, Robert J. Walker); and extensive business, plantation, and Civil War records.
Missouri:	Records Management and Archives Service, Office of Secretary of State, Jefferson City, 65101: French and Spanish colonial land grants and deeds; territorial, state, and local records since 1821; private papers; and records of Missouri's Confederate state government. Some official state records in Missouri Historical Society, Columbia.
North Carolina:	Division of Archives and History, Department of Cultural Resources, Raleigh, 27611: colonial, state, and local records since 1535, including land survey records; private papers (*e.g.*, papers of John Gray and William Blount, James Iredell, Reginald A. Fessenden, Zebulon Baird Vance); and church, business, and war records.
South Carolina:	Department of Archives and History, Columbia, 29217: colonial, state, and local records since 1670, including land and military records; microfilm of federal records relating to South Carolina; and schedules of the U.S. census. See also M. C. Chandler and E. T. Wade, *The South Carolina Archives: A Temporary Summary Guide* (1976).
Tennessee:	State Library and Archives, Nashville, 37219: territorial, state, and local records since 1777;

	legislative recordings since 1955; private papers (*e.g.*, papers of Richard S. Ewell, George Pearson Buell, Andrew Jackson); many military diaries; turnpike records; and school and church records.
Texas:	State Library and Archives, Austin, 78711: Spanish, Mexican, republic, state, and local records since 1800; private papers (*e.g.*, papers of Anthony Butler, Sam Houston, Walter P. Webb, Mirabeau Buonaparte Lamar, John H. Reagan); and church and business records.
Virginia:	State Library, Richmond, 23219: colonial, state, and local records since 1607; private papers (*e.g.*, papers of Daniel H. Hill, Thomas Jonathan Jackson, Zachariah Johnston, the Lee family, Daniel Morgan), church records; business records; and rare maps.
West Virginia:	Department of Archives and History, Charleston, 25305: state and local records since 1863, private papers (*e.g.*, papers of Arthur I. Boreman, Henry Mason Mathews, Francis Harrison Pierpont, William E. Stevenson), and some church records.

ARISTOCRACY has long served as the focus of historical debate, its very existence often being questioned. The southern version of aristocracy differed in many respects from its European counterpart. From its earliest years Anglo-American aristocracy more frequently exhibited a power based on deference than intimidation. Southern aristocracy evolved through varying stages as it followed the frontier, entered newly flourishing commercial centers, and reflected dissemination of successive staple crops. No matter what the period under study, land, as in Europe, usually underpinned the basically precapitalistic economic structure of this society.

Self-made men always figured large in social eminence, and those of English ancestry, high or low, contended for place with Irish, Scotch-Irish, Scots, and Germans in the British colonies and with French and Spaniards in lands ceded by the LOUISIANA PURCHASE. Market fluctuations, especially in commodities, always remained the primary factor in determining social as well as political and economic status. At various times a military, legal, political, or medical background served to identify individuals as members of an upper caste, but in these cases a symbiotic relationship existed among those specific roles and changing power

loci, deferential acceptance by the populace, and subsequent status in that society.

Race figured largely in creating an aristocratic mystique, thanks to the existence of a large, permanently servile population in antebellum southern black slaves. Emancipation did little to improve materially the economic plight of POOR WHITES or freedmen, in many cases expanding the deprived lower orders while further thinning the ruling class, thus sharpening societal division. Racial amalgams within ruling structures thrived in various localities. Miscegenation between prospective white gentry and members of princely Indian families produced aristocratic elements in seventeenth-century Virginia, the late eighteenth-century old Southwest, and nineteenth-century Oklahoma, Arkansas, and Texas.

In colonial times a combination of self-made men and transplanted gentry patterned their lifestyles after their ideal of the English country gentleman. Lack of any sizable influx of true British gentry and rapid American social mobility necessitated class intermarriages unimaginable in England. An "aristocracy of merit" rather than one of birth subsequently arose in seventeenth- and eighteenth-century Virginia and South Carolina, and it spread its standards with westward and southward emigration.

Although merit and financial acumen counted foremost in developing this caste, family breeding and descent continued to exert real influence, especially throughout the early years of the Republic, when the phrase "white pillars do not a gentleman make" became stock. Lord Thomas Fairfax, the only peer resident in North America, owned the baronial Northern Neck between the Potomac and Rappahannock rivers until his death at the Revolution's close. During his life and for a generation thereafter the most notable families of northern and western Virginia—including the Washingtons, Nevilles, Madisons, Jeffersons, Marshalls, and Morgans—partially based their authority on connections of kinship or policy with him. Virginia's electorate apparently demanded such a condition of authority through inheritance. Revolution hardly diminished family and good breeding as prerequisites to political power. Because British-style free schools were lacking in the South, knowledge disseminated slowly, necessitating reliance on an educated minority limited in number by family ability to hire domestic tutors or propinquity to sparse urban communities.

The gradual decline of southern aristocracy resulted from a juxtaposition of financial and political phenomena. Intermittent fiscal panics and depressions, especially in the antebellum South, more likely served to replenish the power structure with new blood than to democratize it. Leveling society stage by stage, no events so tellingly destroyed aristocratic pretense and control of politics and society as the Revolutionary War, Civil War, Populist movement, and Great Depression.

See F. B. Simkins and C. P. Roland, *History of South* (1972); G. B. Tindall, *Pursuit of Southern History* (1964); and P. Gerster and N. Cords, *Myth and Southern History* (1974).

JAMES T. BANNON
St. Louis University

ARKANSAS is a border state. The presence of slavery and the fact that the state joined the Confederacy in 1861 clearly indicate its affinity with the South. The overwhelming majority of its white settlers migrated from states in the Upper South, yet its early isolation and physiographical setting influenced its people to develop a culture similar to that in the Midwest and the Southwest.

The state can be divided physiographically and historically into two major regions. The eastern and southern half of the state consists of the Mississippi alluvial and western Gulf coastal plains. Here, in the lowlands of Arkansas, one finds most of the characteristics of the South deeply rooted. It is the region of cotton, slavery, and segregation. The plantation economy developed here before the Civil War, and a one-crop, sharecropping, or tenant-farming system evolved after the war. White Arkansans were almost all native southerners, homogeneous in national origin and politics, Protestant in whatever religion they preferred, rural, and frustrated in their quest for economic abundance. In the other half of the state, the highlands, one finds a slightly different set of conditions. First, and most obvious, the highlands are hilly and mountainous. North of the ARKANSAS RIVER one finds the OZARK PLATEAU, which is itself divided into the Salem and Springfield plateaus and the Boston Mountains. The latter are not actually mountains, but an eroded plateau. South of the Arkansas River rise the OUACHITA MOUNTAINS. The Ozarks were settled early in the state's history. The region was dotted with small diversified farmers. Flour mills, gristmills, tanneries, and sawmills, the earliest manufacturing establishments, developed here. The people of the Ozarks had a more diversified political outlook, unionism in 1861–1865 was widespread, and the Republican party persisted in the region through the years. In the late nineteenth century the agrarian revolt was most at home in the Arkansas Valley, which divides the Ozarks from the Ouachita Mountains.

Sitting astride the boundary between the highlands and lowlands is the capital, Little Rock. Much of the state's history can be seen and understood in terms of the clash of interests between the highlands and lowlands, with Little Rock and central Arkansas serving as the countervailing power determining which area's interest predominates. It is and always has been the state's principal urban center, and its importance as the political capital is unchallenged. It also exerts great influence on the state through its newspaper, the ARKANSAS GAZETTE, founded in 1819 at Arkansas Post and moved to Little Rock in 1821 with the capital. Economically, Little Rock influences most of the state, but it has less influence on eastern Arkansas, which looks to Memphis or New Orleans rather than to Little Rock.

Arkansas got its name from one of the three native tribes, the QUAPAW INDIANS. Father Jacques Marquette called them Arkansea, and from this the name Arkansas was derived. In 1824 the surviving Quapaw were moved west into what is now Oklahoma. The following year the remaining OSAGE INDIANS were moved west, and the boundary between Arkansas and the Osage was established by a line running due north from Ft. Smith to the southwest corner of Missouri. The remainder of the western boundary from Ft. Smith to the Red River was created by the Choctaw Treaty of 1825.

Modern Arkansas has an area of 53,104 square miles and is twenty-seventh in size in the United States. The climate is moderate. In the winter the mean Fahrenheit temperature varies from 36 degrees in the northwest to 48 degrees in the south. In the summer the mean temperature ranges from 78 degrees in the northwest to 82 degrees in the southwest. The growing season in the northwest is about 200 days, and in the south and southwest it is 30 days longer. The mean annual precipitation ranges from about 40 inches in the western Arkansas River valley to about 60 inches in the western Ouachita Mountains. Most of the state receives an average of between 46 and 50 inches of rain a year.

Arkansas is both blessed and cursed by numerous rivers. The most important are the MISSISSIPPI, Arkansas, WHITE, St. Francis, RED, and the Ouachita rivers. Their frequent flooding has often taken a heavy toll in property damage and human misery. Modern LEVEES, drainage districts, and dams have reduced flood damage, but these rivers continue to do great property damage. In early Arkansas history and in the second half of the twentieth century, these rivers served as a major means of transportation. Steamboats, modern river tugs, and barges use the streams as highways. The com-

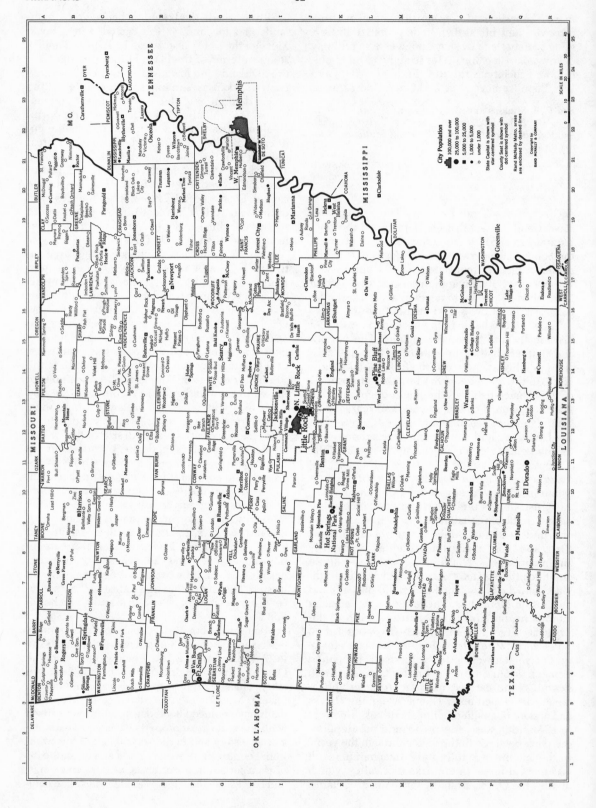

pletion of the Arkansas River Navigation Project in 1970 made the state's most important interior river navigable from the Mississippi in the east to Catoosa, Okla. (near Tulsa), in the west. The project is gradually producing an economic growth in the Arkansas River valley that may become the most significant event in the state's economic history.

French and Spanish periods. In 1541 the Spanish explorer HERNANDO DE SOTO crossed the Mississippi River near Sunflower Landing, about 20 miles south of Helena in Phillips County. There he encountered the Quapaw Indians living in numerous villages. Since the Quapaw had no gold or other portable wealth, de Soto moved west up the Arkansas River. Near present Little Rock he turned south and probably visited the hot springs. Continuing in a southwesterly direction he was defeated by the CADDO INDIANS at Caddo Gap (Montgomery County), and he turned back to the east. He wintered somewhere between Arkadelphia and El Dorado on the Ouachita River and in the spring of 1542 continued his journey down the river into northern Louisiana. The only lasting consequence of the expedition is the tradition that the original Arkansas razorback was the descendant of some of de Soto's hogs.

Having found no wealth of consequence in Arkansas, the Spaniards turned their interests to other and more promising lands. It was 132 years before another European of record visited Arkansas. In 1673, while exploring the Mississippi River, Father Marquette and Louis Jolliet visited the Quapaw. Later RENÉ ROBERT CAVELIER DE LA SALLE led an expedition down the Mississippi River in 1682, claimed all the land drained by its tributaries for his king, Louis XIV, and named the empire Louisiana.

La Salle left his friend Henri de Tonty in command and returned to France to secure additional backing and colonists. On the return voyage La Salle intended to sail into the Gulf and up the Mississippi River, where he would rendezvous with Tonty and establish his colony. He missed the mouth of the river and landed in Texas, where he eventually was murdered by one of his men. After a long wait, Tonty went in search of La Salle. Sometime after Easter Sunday, 1686, Tonty established Arkansas Post, a fort and trading establishment on the lower Arkansas River. The first European settlement in Arkansas, this post was moved several times before it was finally abandoned in the early nineteenth century.

French interest in the Mississippi Valley continued to ebb and flow. JEAN BAPTISTE LE MOYNE DE BIENVILLE made good France's claim to Louisiana in the early eighteenth century. Arkansas Post continued to struggle for existence and almost became a thriving colony when John Law attempted to settle the area with German immigrants and slaves in 1719. When Law's MISSISSIPPI BUBBLE burst, however, the 1,000 settlers, 700 Europeans and 300 slaves, abandoned the Arkansas colony. Bernard de La Harpe explored the Arkansas Valley in 1722 and revitalized Arkansas Post, but, when France lost the French and Indian War, Louisiana was ceded to Spain in 1763. France's chief legacy to Arkansas is the many French place-names.

Spain held Louisiana until Napoleon reacquired the territory in 1800. The most memorable event of this period for Arkansas occurred during the American Revolution. A small British-led force, consisting mainly of Indians, attempted but failed to take Arkansas Post in 1783.

In 1797 Sylvanus Phillips, an American, squatted on Spanish land near present Helena and established a river trading post. He represented the steady encroachment on Spanish Louisiana by Americans that so disturbed officials like FRANCISCO DE CARONDELET. Hoping to forestall the westward march of the American frontier, Spain tried to stir discontent among frontiersmen in an effort to persuade them to secede from the United States and either join Spanish Louisiana or establish a Spanish-backed buffer state.

Territorial Arkansas. The LOUISIANA PURCHASE in 1803 was welcomed by most Americans, but the princely domain that President Thomas Jefferson had bought was of unknown value. Jefferson sent several expeditions into the new territory in an effort to discover just what he had acquired. ZEBULON PIKE explored the middle regions of the purchase in 1806 and, when his party reached the great bend of the Arkansas River, he dispatched Lieutenant James B. Wilkinson (son of JAMES WILKINSON) and three men to descend the river to its mouth. Wilkinson found no white settlements until he reached Arkansas Post. Arkansas was still virtually unsettled. Numerous explorers and travelers scouted the area in the years that followed, but few settlers came.

One reason for the slow development was the great New Madrid earthquake of 1811, which left eastern Arkansas from Helena northward a seemingly impenetrable swamp. To reach habitable land in Arkansas, it was necessary to go down the Mississippi to the mouth of the Arkansas, then up that river, and the Arkansas was very difficult to navigate. Beyond Arkansas lay either foreign territory (Texas) or Indian country. So, in the first two decades of the nineteenth century, pioneers preferred to settle in Missouri or Louisiana, both of which were more accessible and more civilized.

Originally a district in the territory of Orleans (Louisiana), Arkansas became a district of the new Missouri Territory in 1812, when Louisiana achieved statehood. The Missouri territorial legislature in 1813 created Arkansas County and in 1815 divided that county into Arkansas and Lawrence counties. In 1818 three more counties were created, but the population of these five most southern Missouri counties was still sparse. Missouri's petition for statehood and Arkansas' petition for territorial status triggered a thorough debate in Congress on the feasibility of allowing slavery to expand into the Louisiana Purchase. The advocates of excluding slavery from Arkansas almost succeeded when they temporarily secured a provision that called for freeing the children of Arkansas slaves after 25 years. They also tried to secure a provision that would not allow a slave to remain in the territory for longer than nine months at a time, but this too was rejected. The debate and the MISSOURI COMPROMISE of 1820 ushered in a new era of sectionalism, with slavery occupying the center of attention.

The other external influence on Arkansas' development was Jacksonian politics. Arkansas' growth in the 1820s was slow because of the lingering effects of the PANIC OF 1819 and the presence of more attractive lands in Mississippi and Alabama. Only one of the appointments that Presidents James Monroe and John Quincy Adams made in Arkansas made any lasting impact on the territory's politics. Monroe appointed Robert Crittenden of Kentucky as territorial secretary, and this remarkable young man built a sizable political following. Because neither of the first two territorial governors wanted the job and both lacked enthusiasm, Crittenden was left free to act as governor for half of the first ten years of the territory's history.

After ANDREW JACKSON's victory over Adams in 1828, this changed. Governor George Izard died in office in 1828, and the U.S. Senate refused to confirm Adams' appointment of a replacement so that Jackson would have the opportunity to nominate the new governor. He chose John Pope of Kentucky and also replaced Crittenden with William Savin Fulton, one of the numerous old friends and associates the president sent to Arkansas in the next eight years.

The president's men formed an alliance with a local group of leaders whose loyalty outside the territory was firmly Jacksonian and within the territory was built around a remarkable family. The Conways, the JOHNSON FAMILY, the Seviers, the Ashleys, the Rectors, and the powerful editor of the *Arkansas Gazette*, William E. Woodruff, were either related through marriage or interest and dominated the politics of the state for 40 years. The family founders were Henry Wharton Conway (1793–1827) and his brother James Sevier Conway (1798–1855). The Conways were from Tennessee and came to Arkansas by way of Missouri as land surveyors. In 1823 Henry Conway was elected territorial representative to Congress and was reelected in 1825 and 1827.

In the 1827 election Conway was opposed by Robert C. Oden, a Crittenden man. The campaign was ugly, with both sides swapping charges of favoritism and corruption. Crittenden actively supported Oden, and, when Oden lost by a landslide, an anonymous writer in the *Gazette* gloated over Oden's defeat and attributed it to Crittenden's friendship. During the election Conway strongly implied that Crittenden was a liar, and after the election this goaded Crittenden into challenging Conway to a duel (DUELING). When the two men met on a sandbar in the Mississippi River, Crittenden mortally wounded Conway. Outsiders interpreted the duel as an Arkansas means of eradicating political opponents who could not be defeated at the polls. Crittenden escaped prosecution on a legal technicality. In the subsequent special election Ambrose Hundley Sevier (a Conway relative) won election to Congress.

Governor Pope, who arrived in Arkansas shortly after the duel, tried to maintain friendly relations with both factions. His nephew, however, soon became involved in a quarrel with a Crittenden man and was himself killed in a duel. Pope's effort to maintain impartiality soon alienated the family, and the governor found himself to be an enemy of both factions. Fulton disliked Pope and undermined him in private letters to President Jackson. This combination of jealousy and ambition proved to be Pope's undoing. It was difficult enough to ward off the attacks of both factions in Arkansas and impossible to counter the backbiting of the secretary. Fulton accused Pope of being friendly with HENRY CLAY, of having criticized Jackson's bank policy, and of plotting against Jackson. When Pope's second term expired in 1835, Jackson nominated Fulton to replace him. Yet Pope gave Arkansas the best leadership it had in the territorial period. Among his contributions was his supervision of the design and construction of the first capitol, which served the state in that capacity until the twentieth century. Since 1951 the building has housed the state archives and museum.

In the 1830s Arkansas grew and prospered. By 1834 its growth indicated statehood would soon be possible. Although almost everyone desired statehood at the earliest possible date, there was little popular enthusiasm for action. In fact, the central concern of the early thirties was over who would be the dominant political influence in the territory, the Conway family or the Crittenden faction. After the election of 1833 in which Sevier, the family's candidate, soundly beat Crittenden in a head-on contest for the delegate's seat in Congress, that issue was resolved.

In 1833 and again in 1834 Sevier pushed for statehood. A group of citizens appeared in Washington with a petition for Michigan statehood. Sevier feared that if Michigan succeeded in gaining admission alone, the balance between free and slave states would be broken and Arkansas might have difficulty entering the Union as a slave state. Bills were introduced authorizing the admissions of both Michigan and Arkansas, but the bills were tabled before the session ended.

Efforts for statehood for the two territories were renewed in Congress in 1834–1835, but they were again stymied. Abolitionism had entered the halls of Congress, and the slavery question was gaining public attention. Politics also were contributing to the delay. Jackson's opponents Henry Clay, Daniel Webster, and JOHN C. CALHOUN all wanted to stall the addition of any new frontier (and Jacksonian) states until after the coming presidential canvass of 1836.

In Arkansas the prevailing attitude was one of expectant apathy, until Sevier and Woodruff inserted the slavery question into public consideration. In separate articles in the *Gazette* they tried to rally Arkansans in support of statehood. Woodruff wrote that he believed that Arkansas could secure admission unless statehood was delayed beyond the next session of Congress, when the growing antislavery movement might succeed in blocking its admission. Sevier echoed Woodruff's remarks and added a comment characterizing abolitionists as "fanatics."

At that point Sevier and Woodruff discovered that some ANTISLAVERY SENTIMENT had infected Arkansas. The Reverend Thomas H. Tennant, a Methodist preacher living in Washington County in northwest Arkansas, took both men to task for calling antislavery people fanatics. He asked in a letter to the *Gazette*, "Do you not know sir . . . that slavery is wrong? morally, religiously, politically, wrong; and the only argument now to be offered in its justification, is expediency." Both Woodruff and Sevier quickly replied that they meant the term to apply to the abolitionists like the Tappans and William Lloyd Garrison, not to Arkansas constituents. This exchange shows that there was a small but vocal opposition to slavery in Arkansas and that its leaders did not want to risk alienating them. In Arkansas and the rest of the South in the 1830s, there was no unanimity on the question of slavery. Later events would silence even the mildest criticism of the South's peculiar institution, but in the mid-1830s even proslavery men found it necessary to treat the opposition with deference.

Raising the slavery issue did, however, stir Arkansans to action. In the spring and summer of 1835 town meetings were held all over the territory to promote statehood, and Sevier publicly urged Governor Fulton to call a special session of the legislature to authorize an election of delegates to a constitutional convention. Fulton, who said he supported statehood, steadfastly refused to summon the special session. It is impossible to fathom his reasoning at this distant time. He wrote confidentially to his old friend President Jackson that he feared the statehood movement was somehow connected with "Bankism as well as Whiteism" (HUGH LAWSON WHITE). His messages to the secretary of state suggest that he believed some sort of rebellion was taking place! Late in 1835 the territorial legislature convened for its regular session and promptly authorized the election of delegates for a constitutional convention to be held in January, 1836.

The only local controversy was over the division of the delegates to the convention between the generally proslavery eastern and southern counties and the nonslaveholding northwest. The solution was to split the convention equally between the two sections. In the constitution the same split occurred. The slaveholding section received a small majority in the senate and the nonslaveholding section was given a small majority in the house of representatives of the state general assembly. Thus, even in Arkansas a sectional compromise based on slavery was necessary. In Congress a brief but unsuccessful attempt to block Arkansas' admission as a slave state failed. On June 15, 1836, President Jackson signed the bill admitting Arkansas as the twenty-fifth state.

Antebellum period. The pro-Democratic Conway family dominated the first state election as it was to do for the rest of the antebellum period. In November, Arkansas proclaimed its loyalty to Jacksonian Democracy by giving Martin Van Buren a two-to-one majority in the presidential ELECTION OF 1836. James Sevier Conway was elected governor, and Archibald Yell was sent to the U.S. House of Representatives. Sevier and Fulton were elected U.S. senators.

Yet, statehood did not prove to be as salutary as most had expected. Governor Conway appealed to the first general assembly to provide for an adequate educational system and internal improvements. The assembly responded by ignoring the schools and appropriating pitifully little money for roads, bridges, and levees. It did charter two banks, the State Bank and the Real Estate Bank, and pledged the state's credit in support of them. Mismanagement and the PANIC OF 1837 ruined both banks, however, before the first regular state elections were held. The family, though deeply involved in the Real Estate Bank, managed so as not to be either embarrassed or economically ruined by the bank's failure and depression that followed. The state's support of the bank's debt became a persistent issue in Arkansas politics until 1884, when the state repudiated most of its debt, including the unpaid obligations of the bank.

Arkansas' population doubled or tripled every ten years during the antebellum period. The panic of 1837 slowed growth for a while, but the interest of many Americans in the new Republic of Texas drew many settlers through Arkansas on their way to Texas, and many of them stayed in Arkansas. Washington, in Hempstead County in southwest Arkansas, was the jumping-off place for pioneers headed for Texas, and the town's growth and importance reflected the fortunes of the Texans. A few adventurers used Van Buren in western Arkansas as the terminal for one leg of the SANTA FE TRADE. When gold was discovered in California, a steady stream of wagons and forty-niners crossed the state on their way west, and again many dropped out of the western migration to take up homes and farms in the state. Arkansas' rivers, especially the Arkansas and the Mississippi, became important arteries of trade as the shallow-draft steamboats carried commerce and passengers up and down the rivers.

Although the state was not a significant beef producer in the antebellum period, numerous enterprising Arkansas cattlemen drove herds to California in the 1850s to take advantage of the high prices being offered in the goldfields. As late as 1857 their herds left Dover in Pope County and reached California. One herd of 700 cattle, accompanied by 137 travelers from Arkansas and Missouri, was ambushed and slaughtered by disgruntled MORMONS at Mountain Meadow in 1857.

Until 1850 most of the land sold in Arkansas was bought by small farmers. In 1849 the state produced only 65,344 bales of cotton, 2.5 percent of the southern total. During the 1850s the plantation system took root in eastern and southern Arkansas, and by 1859 the state produced 7 per-

cent of the cotton grown in the South. Yet one should be cautious in generalizing the presence of a widespread plantation system. Only one man, Elisha Worthington of Chicot County, owned more than 500 slaves in 1860. Only 66 slaveholders owned as many as 100 on the eve of the Civil War. Most farmers worked the land not as a business but as a way of life. Arkansas farms did not produce over 4 percent of any of the traditional southern farm crops and possessed only 5.5 percent of the horses and mules (2.7 percent of the U.S. total), 4.4 percent of the cattle, and 4 percent of the swine in the South.

Arkansas had almost no manufacturing establishments in 1860. The entire capital employed in manufacturing consisted of only .13 percent of the national total. The small investment devoted to manufacturing was in flour and meal mills, sawmills, and blacksmith shops. One local blacksmith to earn a place of distinction of sorts was James Black of Hempstead County, who fashioned the famous Bowie knife.

Arkansas' antebellum cultural achievements were made by the local-color writers. Charles Fenton Mercer Noland, a Virginian who settled in Batesville, produced a series of yarns and stories about Pete Whetstone of Devil's Fork that foreshadowed the frontier tales of fighting, bear hunting, and politicking. Sandford C. Faulkner created the humorous "Arkansas Traveller" story, and Edward Payson Washburn painted the two pictures depicting the story. Most famous of all, however, was the short story written by Thomas Bangs Thorpe, "The Big Bear of Arkansas," which combined frontier humor, dialect, and tall-tale boasting (HUMOR).

In 1860 Arkansas was more southern than it had ever been in the previous 40 years. During the fifties the state grew in every way. It seemed on the verge of an economic takeoff that would bring genuine prosperity for its people. It still lacked capital, however, and it had only 38 miles of railroad. Politically Arkansas was still dominated by the Conway family, which embraced the Jeffersonian model of the less government the better. But new leaders like THOMAS CARMICHAEL HINDMAN began to challenge the family's domination and to hold out the prospect of meaningful change. Then came the Civil War.

Civil War and Reconstruction. Arkansas voters gave JOHN C. BRECKINRIDGE 28,730 votes in 1860, 20,094 voted for JOHN BELL, and Stephen A. Douglas received 5,227 votes. Not a single vote was counted for Abraham Lincoln. Henry Massie Rector defeated the Conway family candidate for the governorship and in his inaugural address urged Arkansans to secede with the other slave states. A special convention to consider Arkansas' future met in Little Rock in early March, 1861.

The slave counties supported secession, but the rest of the state had a wait-and-see attitude. By a vote of 39 to 35 the convention decided not to withdraw from the Union at that time and recessed until fall, hoping that the border states convention called to meet in May in Kentucky might formulate a workable compromise to preserve the Union. After the firing on FT. SUMTER and Lincoln's call for volunteers, however, the mood changed. David Walker, Arkansas' most respected Whig and president of the convention, reconvened the delegates. After little ceremony they voted 65 to five to secede and join the Confederacy. A motion to make the proposition unanimous failed by one vote, when ISAAC MURPHY of Batesville refused to cast his vote for disruption of the Union.

Arkansas was even more ill prepared for war than was the South in general. The state could not provide all its volunteers with arms. There was not a single operating lead mine (for bullets) in the state. There was no iron foundry and only one small clothing factory. And a large minority living in northern and northwestern Arkansas refused to fight to save the slaveholders' property. Before the war was over, 15,000 Arkansans fought on the Union side. This was one-fifth of the total number of Arkansans who served in the war.

During the war only three other Confederate states witnessed more battles and engagements than Arkansas. The major battles and campaigns began with PEA RIDGE (March 6–9, 1862) in northwest Arkansas, where a federal victory left Missouri firmly attached to the Union. When EARL VAN DORN's Confederate army was transferred to Memphis to help defend the Mississippi River line, Arkansas was virtually defenseless. Thomas C. Hindman raised a new army and attempted to drive the yankees out of northwest Arkansas, but he failed at PRAIRIE GROVE on December 7, 1862. In the battle of HELENA, that town fell to General Samuel R. Curtis on July 12, 1862.

As part of the VICKSBURG CAMPAIGN, General John McClernand seized Arkansas Post January 11, 1863. As Ulysses S. Grant closed in on Vicksburg, Miss., the Confederate command tried to relieve the pressure by a counteroffensive against Helena, Ark. On July 4, 1863, General Theophelus Hunter Holmes attacked the Union garrison at Helena and was driven off by General Frederick Steele. Steele pursued Holmes and in the process seized Little Rock (September 10, 1863).

The RED RIVER CAMPAIGN was the last major struggle of the war in Arkansas. In the spring of 1864 Steele moved south from Little Rock to join Nathaniel P. Banks, who was moving up the Red River in Louisiana. A series of battles and skirmishes occurred, with Steele taking Camden (April 15, 1864) on the Ouachita River in south-central Arkansas. By that time Banks had been repulsed in Louisiana, so Steele withdrew to Little Rock. The last engagement of that campaign was the battle of Jenkins' Ferry on the Saline River (April 29–30, 1864). The concluding chapter of the war in which Arkansas was involved was the heroic but futile cavalry raid into Missouri (PRICE'S RAID ON MISSOURI) led by STERLING PRICE in the fall of 1864.

As the fighting waned, Arkansas' Confederate war governor, Harris Flanigan, sent AUGUSTUS HILL GARLAND to negotiate the conclusion of the war in Arkansas. The federal government would not meet with Garland, so Flanigan packed his belongings, abandoned the Confederate state capital at Washington, and went home to Arkadelphia. Thus the Confederate state government died without fanfare.

When Little Rock fell to General Steele in 1863, Union sentiment in the occupied northern half of Arkansas grew bold enough to suggest forming a loyalist government. Town meetings selected delegates to a constitutional convention, which met in Little Rock in January, 1864. A slightly revised version of the constitution of 1836 was adopted, and Isaac Murphy was named provisional governor. In March, 1864, the loyalist voters approved the constitution by an overwhelming margin (12,177 for, 226 against) and elected Murphy to a five-year term as governor. The constitution abolished slavery but made no provision for safeguarding the civil liberties of the freedmen. Nothing was done about this until after the election of 1866, when former Confederates and old-line Democrats won a majority of the seats in the general assembly. They adopted the state's old BLACK CODE. It denied blacks the franchise, prohibited them from serving on juries, and required segregated public schools. The representatives and senators elected to Congress in 1864 were denied recognition by a suspicious national legislature, which quite naturally had doubts about the loyalty of such southerners. In Arkansas the Union army cooperated with the Murphy regime, and trouble was kept to a minimum.

When the South refused to adopt voluntarily the FOURTEENTH AMENDMENT, Congress imposed tighter controls over the formerly rebellious states. The RECONSTRUCTION ACTS of 1867 required Arkansas and the rest of the South to try again to reconstruct governments that would recognize the citizenship of the freedmen and afford Republicans the opportunity to enlist black voters in the South. Elections in Arkansas in the fall of 1867 authorized another constitutional convention. This time male blacks were included as voters; by a vote of 27,576 for a new convention to 13,558 against, they set in motion the congressional plan of Reconstruction. The convention wrote a new constitution, which required the establishment of a public school system and included numerous other popular reforms. Old-line Democrats and Whigs adopted a policy of noncooperation, and David Walker urged Arkansans to boycott the elections in March, 1868, as a protest. Many followed Walker's advice and voluntarily disfranchised themselves. The ratifying election was close; the new document won approval by a vote of 27,913 for and 26,597 against. Had the Walker Whigs and Democrats voted, they would likely have momentarily stalled the Reconstruction process. The simultaneous election for officials chose POWELL CLAYTON, a Republican, the new governor. On June 22, 1868, Arkansas became the first southern state readmitted under the Reconstruction Acts of 1867.

Clayton had come to Arkansas from Kansas as a Union officer. After the war he settled on a plantation near Pine Bluff, made Arkansas his new home, and served as a delegate to the constitutional convention of 1868. As Arkansas' carpetbag governor, Clayton built a solid but not unanimous following among state Republicans and influenced the political history of Arkansas far beyond his own involvement in it. By the twentieth century the tradition that Clayton and the Republicans misruled Arkansas had taken so firm a hold on the minds of Arkansans as to be unquestioned. Yet mid-century revisionists have raised new or different questions, and the Clayton years no longer appear as villainous as they once did. Clayton Republicans funded the state debt, created a railroad commission with power to help construct much needed rail facilities for the state, established the Arkansas Deaf Mute Institute, revitalized the school for the blind, chartered the UNIVERSITY OF ARKANSAS, and provided for a genuine public educational system. This is an impressive list of achievements. The new and improved services provided by the state were welcomed by most Arkansans whether they were black or white.

In 1871 Clayton moved on to the U.S. Senate, leaving his handpicked successor Ozra A. Hadley to complete his term as governor. The ELECTION OF 1872 produced a visible split in the Republican party that opened the door for the return of the Democratic party to power in Arkansas. The Clayton wing, which identified with the national Republican party, nominated ELISHA BAXTER, a Batesville Republican who had lived in Arkansas since 1852. The brindle-tail faction, led by the Reverend JOSEPH BROOKS, identified with the national Liberal Republicans. After the election both sides claimed victory, but it appeared that Baxter won with 52 percent of the 80,096 votes cast in the gubernatorial election. U. S. Grant also won the presidential election in Arkansas by an almost identical margin, 52.1 percent of the votes, over Horace Greeley.

Brooks accused the Clayton-Baxter faction of stealing the election and tried to rally support to deny Baxter his seat in the statehouse. Brooks also appealed to the state supreme court for help, but the court refused to be drawn into the squabble. On January 3, 1873, Baxter was inaugurated. As governor, he pursued a rather independent course. He appointed a few Democrats to office, was more cautious about approving the use of state credit for railroad building, and did not yield to Clayton's every wish. By the spring of 1873 Clayton, who had become disenchanted with Baxter, began courting Brooks. A general realignment of political factions took place, with Clayton and Brooks now cooperating against Baxter, who more and more found his most trustworthy friends to be Democrats.

In the spring of 1874, the Pulaski County Circuit Court nullified Baxter's election and declared Brooks the rightful governor. Brooks, surprising Baxter in his office, evicted him. Baxter then set up a temporary headquarters in downtown Little Rock and declared martial law. Supporters of both sides poured into Little Rock. Baxter and Brooks solicited support from President Grant. Under the circumstances there was surprisingly little actual violence, and on May 15, 1874, Grant recognized Baxter as governor. The famous BROOKS-BAXTER WAR was over.

During the "war" the general assembly authorized an election for a new constitutional convention. In June, 1874, the voters overwhelmingly approved the convention call and elected delegates, who convened in Little Rock in July. They wrote a new and more conservative constitution, one more in keeping with the negative governmental philosophy of pre–Civil War Democrats, and submitted it to the voters. The constitution was ratified by a vote of 78,697 for and 24,807 votes against. The Democratic candidate Augustus Garland was elected governor under the new constitution. Democrats also won a majority of the seats in the general assembly. Clayton Republicans ignored the Democrats and refused to recognize the new regime. When Democratic congressmen appeared in Washington, D.C., Clayton tried to muster opposition to their acceptance. A special congressional investigation headed by Luke P. Poland of Vermont decided in favor of the new constitution, and Congress seated the representatives elected in 1874. This officially ended Reconstruction in Arkansas.

Redeemers and the agrarian revolt. During the late 1870s and early 1880s TENANT FARMING and SHARECROPPING grew to dominate the agricultural economy. Former slaves worked the land as family units on a share basis. Due to the hard times that followed the PANIC OF 1873, numerous small independent farmers found debts rising faster than their ability to pay. More and more land fell into the hands of merchants and banks, who became absentee landlords. The growth of railroads aggravated farmers' problems even more. Farming had been a way of life for most Arkansans; but railroads were transforming farming into a business, and few agrarians understood the complex forces that were altering their lives. What they did understand was the reality of climbing debts, falling prices, and a government both on the local and national levels that seemed to ignore their needs while catering to such special interests as the railroads.

Redeemer governments were less interested in the numerous people-oriented services that had been provided by the Republicans. They quickly reduced the state's biennial budget from $1,889,229 in 1873–1874 to $740,847 in 1875–1876. The reduction stirred protests from people who missed the services, and in subsequent budgets the amount steadily rose again. The REDEEMERS starved the public school system and begrudgingly supported a few public health programs (*e.g.*, a state board of health, created during Governor THOMAS JAMES CHURCHILL's administration, 1881–1883). Moreover, as the post-Reconstruction Democratic party contained many pre–Civil War Whigs, aid to businesses like railroads had to be worked into the party program. In a sense, the Redeemers continued the Republican program of aid to businesses but on a much reduced level. Distressed farmers could not understand why it was proper for the state government to help railroads but improper for that government to come to the aid of its voting and tax-paying citizens. Furthermore, one of the most cherished advantages Democrats claimed over Republicans was their example of scandal-free, honest government.

This advantage disappeared during Churchill's term, when considerable petty corruption was exposed.

Yet it took a decade or more to convince some farmers that their interests would be served by political action outside the Democratic party. The process of change began with the Patrons of Husbandry, the GRANGE, which came to Arkansas in 1872. John Thompson Jones of Helena organized the first chapter in Arkansas, and the movement grew rapidly across the state. The Grange brought together farmers, who then discovered that their individual problems were shared by their neighbors. In the late 1870s the GREENBACKER MOVEMENT spread to Arkansas, and in 1878 the party attempted to persuade a prominent Democrat, Henry M. Rector, to carry the party's banner in the state election. Rector declined the nomination because of his loyalty to the Democratic party, but the corruption of the Churchill administration and continuing hard times prepared the way for a genuine political revolt.

In 1882 seven rural men met in a log schoolhouse eight miles southwest of Des Arc and started the Arkansas Agricultural Wheel. It was, like the Brothers of Freedom (a companion order that sprang up almost simultaneously in the western Arkansas River valley), a dirt farmer, rural, agrarian organization. Among the specific demands of the Wheel and the Brothers were: (1) better crop reporting facilities; (2) liberalization of the harsh debt law; (3) honest elections; (4) control of big business, especially of the railroads, insurance companies, and fertilizer and seed distributors; and (5) organization of buying and selling cooperatives. By 1885 the two agrarian organizations combined into one order, the Agricultural Wheel, and claimed almost 100,000 members in Arkansas. By 1887 the Wheel had rolled into three other states (AGRICULTURAL ORGANIZATIONS).

Although the Wheelers had at first tried to stay out of politics, they soon discovered they could not avoid it if they hoped to succeed. Arkansas Republicans capitalized as best they could on the growing disenchantment of the voters with the Democratic party. The Republican percentage of the total vote cast in Arkansas elections rose from 27 percent in 1880 to 33 percent in 1882 and 36 percent in 1884. The Democrats countered by emphasizing party loyalty and vigorously denouncing Republicans as corrupt vagabonds who neither knew nor cared about the needs of Arkansans. Discontent among voters fell off in 1886, but that proved to be the calm before the storm.

In 1888 many agrarians threw caution to the wind and supported a one-legged Confederate veteran, C. M. Norwood, for governor. Norwood ran under the Union Labor party banner. The state Republicans decided to throw their support to him in an all-out effort to unseat the Democrats. The official results indicated that the Democratic candidate, James Philip Eagle, defeated Norwood by a vote of 99,214 to 84,213, but the agrarians felt they had been counted out. Ample surviving evidence suggests they probably were correct.

The election was a turning point in Arkansas history. The Democrats only narrowly had averted political disaster. If something was not done soon the prospects were good that the combined agrarian-Republican opposition would succeed. The Democrats rededicated themselves to denouncing the evils of Reconstruction Republicans and made some effort to satisfy the demands of the agrarians. They also discovered that the race issue could be exploited to drive a wedge between the disgruntled agrarians and the Republicans.

In 1891 the general assembly adopted the state's first significant SEGREGATION measure. The separate coach law required the segregation of the races on railroads. This was followed by what purported to be an election reform, but in fact was a major step toward the DISFRANCHISEMENT of blacks. In 1893, the poll tax amendment was adopted, which reduced the number of eligible voters by almost 50 percent. The introduction of the WHITE PRIMARY in the early part of the twentieth century completed the electorate-control program. Blacks were not totally disfranchised in Arkansas, but, along with numerous poor and ignorant whites, their numbers as voters were significantly lowered. From the end of Reconstruction until 1892, when the election reform began, 27 blacks served in the Arkansas general assembly. In 1891, while the separate coach law was being debated, there was one black in the state senate, George W. Bell from Chicot and Desha counties in southeastern Arkansas, and seven blacks in the house of representatives, all from eastern and southern Arkansas. After the reform bill and poll tax amendment were adopted, however, blacks were eliminated from the general assembly until the 1960s.

Judge Isaac Charles Parker of Ft. Smith is one of the most colorful figures in Arkansas history. A Republican from Missouri, he was appointed judge of the federal district court at Ft. Smith in 1875. He had jurisdiction over western Arkansas and the Indian Territory, where frontier conditions lingered and criminals of every description abounded. Parker pursued an individualistic approach to the law and became known as the Hanging Judge. In his 21 years on the bench at Ft. Smith (1875–1896) he sentenced 160 men to the gallows and actually hanged 79 of them. He sent out a corps of federal marshals whose methods of apprehending outlaws were as questionable as some of Parker's courtroom methods.

Progressive era. In the early twentieth century the reform impulse known in American history as PROGRESSIVISM swept over the South and Arkansas. Progressives were interested in some of the reforms that the agrarians had fought to win, but they were more concerned with the problems of a growing urban industrial society than those of an outmoded rural agricultural system.

Arkansas was still rural and agrarian, but it faced some of the modern challenges of its neighbors. For Arkansas in the early twentieth century, industry meant the railroads and large insurance companies. In 1870 the state had only 270 miles of railroad track. By 1890 the mileage had increased to 2,262, which made significant contributions to the economic growth of the state. Among the most obvious changes was to the LUMBER INDUSTRY. Railroads brought loggers deep into the virgin forest and tourists to the beautiful Ozarks. Railroads enabled cotton farming to expand from the river bottoms to the upland counties. Railroads also facilitated a small influx of non-English and non-African immigrants. Germans settled the Grand Prairie and up and down the Arkansas Valley; a Polish settlement grew up near Little Rock; Bohemians settled around Dardanelle; Italians began the wine industry in northwestern Arkansas; and there was a scattering of Greeks, Syrians, Swiss, and Chinese settling in the state.

Progressivism in Arkansas began with JEFF DAVIS, a fiery politician who relished a good quarrel. He began his statewide career as attorney general (1899–1901) and took up the struggle against "the interests": the trusts, the monopolies, and big business. In Arkansas his dragons were insurance companies and cotton seed businesses. When the interests blocked his trust-busting efforts by persuading the state supreme court to nullify the antitrust law, Davis ran for governor. Throughout the campaign he railed at the trusts, railroads, yankees, and his perennial bogeyman, the *Arkansas Gazette*. Davis won in 1900 and became the first Arkansan to be reelected governor for a second and a third term. Davis' actual achievements were sparse. He did eventually secure an antitrust law (1905) tailored to his needs, and he closed down two-thirds of the insurance companies in the state. That victory was undone in 1907, when "the interests" succeeded in amending the law to permit the companies that had been driven out of the state to return. Davis succeeded in raising taxes on the railroads, modernized the state hospital for the mentally ill, lowered passenger fares, and stopped work on the new state capitol because he regarded it as a waste of money.

Davis' successor, John S. Little, had a "nervous collapse" shortly after his inaugural in 1907 and was unable to serve out his term. It was a Conway building contractor, George Washington Donaghey (1909–1913), who gave the state a taste of genuine reform. Donaghey helped complete the new state capitol and made a manful attempt to reform the state penitentiary. He pardoned 361 convicts in an effort to break the cruel and bestial CONVICT LEASE SYSTEM. He began a juvenile court system in 1911, supported the Rockefeller Sanitary Commission campaign to stamp out HOOKWORM, oversaw the beginning of a state health department, supported the campaign against illiteracy, and did more for public education than had been done in the previous 30 years.

JOSEPH TAYLOR ROBINSON followed Donaghey into the statehouse, but did almost nothing except maneuver his election to the U.S. Senate in less than two months after his inauguration. Arkansas' last Progressive governor, CHARLES HILLMAN BROUGH, was a former college professor. Elected in 1916 and reelected in 1918, Brough gave the state good leadership. He put the operation of the state government on a cash basis, but he failed— as others before him had—to persuade the general assembly to accept a budget system. Brough renewed the effort to find a solution to one of the state's most persistent problems, the prison system. He backed women's rights, created a state commission of charities and correction in 1917, launched a girls' industrial school and separate prison farm for women in 1919, and supported an unsuccessful attempt to revise the state's constitution in 1917. A tragic incident occurring during his term was the ELAINE RACE RIOT of 1919. At least 25 whites and as many as 100 blacks were killed before Governor Brough sent the state militia to enforce order. Arrested were 143 blacks and two whites; 122 blacks were convicted of crimes ranging from night-riding to murder. Of those convicted 12 were sentenced to be hanged, but Scipio A. Jones, a black Little Rock lawyer, secured reverses of the death penalties.

The twenties and the Great Depression. The twenties opened with the discovery of oil near El Dorado, and oil replaced coal as the state's most valuable mineral resource. Although bauxite was commercially mined as early as 1899, the boom in this industry was produced by the abnormal demand for aluminum during World War II (ALUMINUM INDUSTRY). Arkansas' only unique mineral resource is diamonds. John M. Huddleston, a farmer, discovered diamonds in his fields in 1906 near Murfreesboro in Pike County, and diamonds are still being found in small quantities.

The violence of the Elaine race riot seemed to be a prelude to widespread lawlessness. A combination of PROHIBITION and depressed economic conditions in agriculture made the twenties both memorable and lamentable for the South. The crime wave of the post–World War I period was aggravated by racial tension and the rowdiness of the oil boomtowns. Furthermore, the country was changing faster than Arkansas. The census of 1920 indicated that for the first time most Americans lived in towns and earned their living in nonagricultural jobs. Arkansas, in 1920, was still overwhelmingly rural and agrarian. The automobile, another source of change, was fast making inroads into traditional customs and mores.

Against such a background, many Arkansans found solace in the revival of the KU KLUX KLAN. In the summer of 1921 the Klan came to Arkansas and spread rapidly over the state. James A. Comer, a former Republican and an attorney, became head of Little Rock Klavern No. 1. He attempted and nearly succeeded in converting the Little Rock Klan into his personal political weapon in 1922. The KKK's strength is difficult to assess. Reports of floggings, beatings, lynchings, and an assortment of extralegal activities came from all parts of the state. The Klan meddled heavily in gubernatorial politics in 1924, and, although its candidate lost, he lost to a Klan member who was not on friendly terms with local Klan leadership. In central Arkansas the Klan dominated Pulaski County politics. Elsewhere in the state the Klan's influence waned after 1924.

The campaign against the teaching of evolution in the public schools was part of the hysteria of the twenties (EVOLUTION CONTROVERSY). The Arkansas general assembly rejected a bill in 1927 that would have made it a crime to teach that man had evolved from lower species. But the defenders of the faith were not discouraged, and in 1928 they won the adoption of an amendment to the state's constitution that outlawed the teaching of evolution. That there was a spark of liberalism or progressivism in Arkansas, however, is indicated by the fact that the state was the first to ratify the proposed CHILD LABOR amendment to the U.S. Constitution in 1924.

Of only passing interest to outsiders, but of long-range significance locally, was the rise to power of

Leo P. McLaughlin in Hot Springs. The spa city had long been the state's gambling and vice center, but the ebb and flow of corruption and reform had prevented the institutionalization of vice. After McLaughlin's victory in the mayor's election in 1927, Hot Springs was thrown wide open to gambling and accompanying vices. Occasional spurts of piety would temporarily slow the city down, but not until the 1960s would open casino gambling be halted. Hot Springs gambling interests reached the general assembly in 1935, when the legislature legalized pari-mutuel betting at Oaklawn Racetrack.

Three other developments of the twenties warrant mentioning. The first took place on February 18, 1922, when Arkansas' first radio station WOK began operating in Pine Bluff. The second was the coming of the automobile age, and the last was the great flood of 1927.

Arkansas struggled for years to find a solution to the problems created by the automobile. The first important effort was the Harrellson Road Act of 1923, which shifted the cost of building and maintaining highways from landowners to road users. Arkansas' roads remained inadequate until after World War II, when a massive highway construction program was launched by Governor Sid McMath and carried on by subsequent administrations.

The people of Arkansas also suffered from the ravages of nature. The flood of 1927 inundated one-fifth of the entire state, destroying crops and homes and taking a death toll of 127 people. Levee construction after the flood helped reduce the losses when the 1937 flood struck (FLOOD CONTROL).

Arkansas' history in the 1930s was dominated by the GREAT DEPRESSION and the NEW DEAL's attempts to restore prosperity. For most Arkansans the thirties meant simply a worsening of the hard times that had begun in the twenties. In 1940 the value of Arkansas' farms had fallen 43 percent since 1920. In 1930 almost two-thirds of farm workers were tenant farmers and sharecroppers, and life for them became almost unendurable.

New Deal agricultural programs added to the misery of farm tenants because landowners expelled surplus agricultural workers without any compensation (AGRICULTURAL ADJUSTMENT ADMINISTRATION). Two sensitive and courageous small businessmen in Tyronza, in east Arkansas, organized the SOUTHERN TENANT FARMERS' UNION in 1934 to protect the tenants' rights. The STFU succeeded in calling attention to the plight of farm workers and is credited with inspiring creation of the FARM SECURITY ADMINISTRATION.

The New Deal benefited the state in countless ways. The WORKS PROGRESS ADMINISTRATION, the CIVILIAN CONSERVATION CORPS, and a plethora of alphabet agencies brought jobs and resources to a needy people. The U.S. government spent over $137 million in impoverished Arkansas. This vast governmental effort also had a strong impact on Arkansas politics.

The death of Senator Joseph T. Robinson in 1937 precipitated a local power struggle that colored the state policies for decades. The Democratic party monopolized officeholding in the state, and Robinson's death left factions led by Carl E. Bailey and Homer Adkins to fight for domination. Adkins emerged the winner until he in turn was defeated by J. WILLIAM FULBRIGHT in a spirited contest for HATTIE CARAWAY's U.S. Senate seat in 1944.

World War II completed the economic revival of Arkansas as it did the nation. Defense and war plants and military installations provided jobs and capital and helped drain off the surplus farm labor left after the exodus of the Arkies, during the thirties. The famous GI bill continued benefiting the state in the postwar years.

Arkansas after the war. Arkansas suffers and has suffered a critical shortage of capital throughout its history. The oil production of the twenties did not generate an economic boom, and the rich bauxite deposits did not benefit the state until World War II, when two large aluminum reduction plants were constructed at Hurricane Creek and Jones Mill. Even after the war the federal government continued to be the largest single investor in the state. The Arkansas River Navigation Project, completed in 1970, cost $1.2 billion and opened the Arkansas River to year-round navigation.

Postwar politics continued to be influenced by national events. Governor Benjamin Travis Laney, a self-made businessman, farmer, and oilman, secured the adoption of the Revenue Stabilization Act in 1945 that put the state on a tight pay-as-you-go budget. Laney also became identified with the DIXIECRAT PARTY revolt of 1948. Arkansas was momentarily distracted from the civil rights crusade by the progressive leadership of Sid McMath (1949–1953), who pursued a moderate course on civil rights and emphasized highway construction. In 1954, however, the U.S. Supreme Court desegregation decision (BROWN V. BOARD OF EDUCATION) catapulted the civil rights movement back into the political arena. Arkansas accepted the decision with considerable grace even if the majority of whites disliked it. Racial discrimination there was already in orderly retreat, for the University of Arkansas previously had admitted blacks to its professional schools and other vestiges of JIM CROW were slowly disappearing.

McMath was succeeded by a moderately progressive east Arkansas judge, Francis Cherry, in 1953. Cherry lacked administrative skills and alienated the political leaders in the state. He was challenged in his reelection bid in 1954 by a former McMath highway commissioner from the Ozarks, ORVAL EUGENE FAUBUS. In spite of the revelation during the campaign that as a youth he had briefly attended a Communist college at Mena, Ark., Faubus won. During his first term as governor (1955–1957), Faubus gave mildly progressive leadership. He demonstrated acute administrative skill. He balanced conflicting interests, raised taxes, and increased aid for the public schools and old-age pensions. He appointed Winthrop Rockefeller to the Arkansas Industrial Development Commission in a renewed drive for economic diversification. He was challenged in his 1956 campaign by a staunch segregationist, Jim Johnson, who denounced Faubus for being too liberal on the race question. Faubus won reelection with little difficulty. Arkansas did not appear to be a likely place for the first national showdown over school desegregation, but then came the Little Rock Central High School tragedy.

The city's school board worked casually on a plan for the token desegregation of Central High. The school superintendent, Virgil Blossom, appeared before civic clubs and organizations in the spring and summer of 1957 explaining the plan. The school board's strategy was to play down the integration plan so as not to stir a protest. Neither the city nor the state government paid any attention to the plan. In August, 1957, the Capital Citizens' Council (CITIZENS' COUNCILS) launched a last-minute campaign to stop the integration of Central High. Rallies, speeches, leaflets, and a media campaign against integration succeeded in bringing the school's desegregation plan into the limelight. Both sides appealed to Faubus to intervene. Although he had vaguely promised not to impose forced integration on anyone, he had also rejected the suggestion that he interpose the state's sovereignty to prevent the carrying out of the Court's plan. The truth seems to be that Faubus did not at first want to be drawn into the dispute. He even appealed to the national government to intervene, but Washington then was no more anxious to be drawn into the dispute than was Faubus.

As the September opening of school approached, rumors of impending violence increased. On the appointed day, Faubus yielded and, calling up the Arkansas National Guard, blocked the entry of the nine black students. He steadfastly maintained that he sent the troops to Central High to prevent violence, not to prevent integration. The subtlety of his reasoning escaped most observers, however. Segregationists were delighted; integrationists were dismayed. When the federal district court ordered Faubus to stop interfering, he withdrew the guard. Then the ugliest phase of the tragedy took place, with the nation witnessing it all on television. When city police were not equipped to handle the mob that gathered at the school, President Dwight D. Eisenhower finally responded by sending the 101st Airborne Division to Little Rock. Arkansas had become the symbol of southern racist reaction. The soldiers maintained order around the school, and integration proceeded. But the state legislature enacted measures authorizing the closing of Central High, and Faubus used this authority to close the school for the academic year 1958–1959.

The crisis made Faubus an international figure. He enjoyed the solid support of adamant Arkansas segregationists, and with it he won election to six consecutive terms (1955–1967). The 1874 constitution had been designed to limit the role of state government and throw up checks and balances to block any official from exercising too much power. Faubus' long tenure in the governor's office made a shambles of that principle, however. By the end of his last term he had appointed a controlling majority to most of the boards and agencies that establish governmental policy. Faubus had become the epitome of what he and his most loyal supporters claimed to fear and hate most: the wielder of nearly absolute political power in the state. However, Arkansas slowly changed in ways that numbered his days, and he sensed it. In 1966 he announced that he would not seek a seventh term.

In 1966 the Democrats showed no indication that they had learned anything from the Faubus era; they nominated Jim Johnson, a former state supreme court justice. The Republicans, or more accurately Winthrop Rockefeller, offered the voters a genuine alternative to the old politics. Rockefeller had moved to Arkansas in 1953 and had become one of the state's most respected and admired citizens. Win, as he was affectionately called, worked hard to convert Arkansas Republicans into a real political party. He gathered a group of bright, conscientious young men and women around him and accomplished what seemed to many to be a miracle. He won the gubernatorial election of 1966 and carried on his coattails a young Republican businessman, John Paul Hammerschmidt, from north Arkansas, into the U.S. House of Representatives. Rockefeller had four turbulent years as governor. The Democrat-dominated general assembly did little to make life even bearable for the Republican, but his two terms were salutary for the state.

His election was made possible by the wholesale temporary desertion of moderate to liberal Democrats from their party. During his terms genuine effort was made to humanize the Arkansas prison system; the Republican administration brought new faces and fresh ideas into state government; blacks were encouraged to vote; state jobs and other benefits were made available to blacks and women; and the governor supported the growing demand for a constitutional convention. Constitutional revision was the most promising reform supported by the Rockefeller administration. The 1874 document reflected the negative philosophy of government in vogue when it was written and prevented action on many twentieth-century needs. Fifty-two amendments had created a confusing legal tangle that perplexed judges, attorneys, and most of all ordinary citizens. In the election of 1968 the voters approved the calling of a convention to prepare a new charter. The convention met in 1969–1970 and submitted a moderately progressive constitution, which the voters rejected in the 1970 general election. The defeat was engineered by a small but well-financed group, which attacked the new document on the basis that the old constitution had stood the test of time and that the proposed constitution made it too easy for the general assembly to raise taxes.

In 1970 the Democrats turned to a fresh face, Dale Bumpers. Television already played a significant part in shaping political fortunes, and Bumpers was blessed with an excellent media adviser and that indispensable TV presence that some called charisma. Rockefeller made the mistake of running for a third term. His opposition to Faubus and his appeal to the voters had been based in part upon the simple proposition that two terms were enough. Furthermore, and most important, Bumpers gave thousands of Democrats who had abandoned their party an attractive reason for coming back.

Bumpers' victory seemed to be the dawning of a new political era for Arkansas. In 1972 a young Camden Democratic businessman, David Pryor, came within a flicker of upsetting venerable John L. McClellan for the Senate seat. Two years later, Pryor was elected governor, and Bumpers ended the long and distinguished Senate career of J. William Fulbright. By 1976 another fixture in Arkansas politics, Congressman Wilbur Mills, stepped down after an escapade with a Washington, D.C., stripper revealed that he was an alcoholic. When Mills decided not to seek reelection, Arkansans found that their senior representative in the House was the Republican Hammerschmidt.

In economics the most noteworthy developments of the 1960s and 1970s were (1) the decline of cotton to fourth from first as the state's most valuable agricultural crop; (2) the rise of soybeans to the top from second in the value of the crops; (3) the growth of the rice industry to second from fourth in value; (4) the remaining of the broiler industry in third place in value; (5) the fact that in 1972 the value added by manufacturing was more than double the value of cash receipts from agriculture; and (6) the expanding TOURISM. In spite of the progress measured in absolute terms, Arkansas ranks near the bottom of the states in per capita income. In 1962 the state ranked forty-ninth; that figure was constant until it rose to forty-eighth in 1970 and forty-sixth in 1974. Whether these figures suggest a trend or turn out to be another fleeting note of encouragement will not be known for years.

Certainly if this is a trend, it suggests that Arkansas is changing in those characteristics that have made it a part of the South. Agriculture is still important to the economy, but its importance has fallen to second place. Most of the state's citizens now live in an urban setting. Arkansans are apparently gathering a larger share of the gross national product than ever before. Blacks have found an unprecedented place in the cultural, social, political, and economic spheres of the state's life. Much still remains to be done to eradicate the race barriers that so hindered the state in the past, but so much progress has been made that a modern Rip Van Winkle awakening from a 20-year snooze would scarcely recognize the state. Yet, as C. VANN WOODWARD has pointed out, Arkansas still has its history. That history shares much with the South and will continue to occupy an important place in the makeup of southerners, as long as the distinction continues to have meaning.

Manuscripts. Principal depositories are the State Archives, 300 W. Markham, Little Rock; and the University of Arkansas, Fayetteville. There are no recent catalogs for either. Other depositories are Duke University, the University of North Carolina at Chapel Hill, the University of Virginia, and the University of Texas, including the best collection of Arkansas newspapers.

Contemporary accounts. First eyewitness accounts of Arkansas were by men of de Soto's expedition. E. G. Bourne (ed.), *Narratives* (2 vols.; 1922), includes accounts by Gentleman of Elvas, Biedma the factor, and Ranjel, de Soto's secretary. A fourth account is an imaginative story told by Garcilaro de La Vega, *Florida of the Inca*, trans. and ed. J. G. Varner and J. J. Varner (1951). For La Salle, see I. J. Cox, *Journeys* (2 vols.; 1905). First general accounts of Americans in Arkansas are H. R. Schoolcraft, *Schoolcraft in Ozarks*, ed. H. Parks (1955); T. Nuttall, *Journal* (1905); G. W. Featherstonhaugh, *Excursion Through Slave States* (2 vols.; 1844), vivid and highly critical; C. F. M. Noland, *Pete Whetstone*, ed. T. R. Worley and E. A. Nolte (1957); W. F. Pope, *Early Days in Arkansas* (1895), exaggerates the good; W. J. Lemke (ed.), *Life and Letters of Judge David Walker* (1957); C. Washburn, *Reminiscences of Indians* (1955), by a missionary to the Cherokee; P. Clayton, *Aftermath of the Civil War in Arkansas* (1915), by carpetbag governor; J. M. Harrell, *Brooks-Baxter War* (1893), with much contemporary information; and W. S. Morgan, *History of Wheel and Alliance* (1889), a basic work by an agrarian. M. W. Gibbs, *Shadow and Light* (1902); W. Pickens, *Bursting Bonds* (1923); and J. R. Riley, *Philosophy of Negro Suffrage* (1894), are blacks' accounts of the late nineteenth century. G. W. Donaghey left his *Autobiography* (1939) and *Building a State Capitol* (1937). See also J. Q. Wolf, *Life in Leatherwoods* (1974); and H. L. Mitchell, *Arkansas Historical Quarterly* (Winter, 1973), for the Southern Tenant Farmers' Union. Mitchell also has a long oral history interview at Columbia University. See V. T. Blossom, *It Has Happened Here* (1959), by participant in Little Rock crisis; B. Hays, *A Southern Moderate Speaks* (1959); D. Bates, *Long Shadow of Little Rock: A Memoir* (1962); O. E. Faubus, *In This Faraway Land* (1971), mostly about World War II; M. Angelou, *I Know Why Caged Bird Sings* (1971), story of a black child growing up in Arkansas; and W. G. Still, *Arkansas Historical Quarterly* (Autumn, 1967), by the noted composer-conductor.

Other primary printed or microfilmed sources. *American State Papers* (38 vols.; 1822–61) contains much information on early Arkansas. Best source on territorial period is C. W. Carter (ed.), *Territorial Papers of U.S.* (1953–54), XIX–XXI. The *Arkansas Gazette* (1819–) is an indispensable newspaper source. Microfilm (60 reels) of STFU Papers (1934–70) is at UNC at Chapel Hill.

Guides. See R. H. Allen (ed.), *Arkansas Imprints, 1821–1872* (1947); V. L. Jones and G. H. Clark, *Arkansas Books and Writers* (mimeographed pamphlet, University of Arkansas, 1952); Arkansas Library Commission, *Compilation of Arkansas Shelf Lists of Public Libraries of Arkansas* (1967).

Histories of the state. See J. L. Ferguson and J. H. Atkinson, *Historic Arkansas* (1966), best overall coverage; W. L. Brown, *Our Arkansas* (1963); O. E. McKnight *et al.*, *Living in Arkansas* (1963); W. W. Moore, *Arkansas* (1975); H. Presson, *Story of Arkansas* (1963); and J. G. Fletcher, *Arkansas* (1947), readable but incomplete. Among old works still of use, see D. T. Herndon, *Centennial History of Arkansas* (3 vols.; 1922); D. Y. Thomas (ed.), *Arkansas and Its People* (4 vols.; 1930); J. H. Reynolds, *Makers of Arkansas History* (1911); and WPA, *Arkansas Guide to the State* (1941), usable. L. Duvall (ed.), *Arkansas: Colony and State* (1973), is heavy on economic history.

Topics. For prehistoric times, see C. R. McGimsey III, *Bulletin of Arkansas Archeological Society* (Spring, Summer, Fall, 1969), and *Indians of Arkansas* (1969). On the age of exploration, see N. W. Caldwell, *French in*

Mississippi Valley (1941); J. A. Caruso, *Mississippi Valley Frontier* (1966); and F. Parkman, *La Salle and Discovery of Great West* (1869). Most authoritative account of de Soto's expedition was done in 1939, *The De Soto Expedition Commission Final Report*, House Document No. 71, 76th Cong., 1st Sess. On territorial period, see L. J. White, *Politics on Southwestern Frontier* (1964); W. W. Moore, "Territorial Arkansas, 1819–1836" (Ph.D. dissertation, University of North Carolina, 1963); J. L. Ferguson, "William E. Woodruff" (Ph.D. dissertation, Tulane University, 1960); and B. W. Johnson, *Arkansas Frontier* (1957).

On antebellum Arkansas, see D. A. Stokes, "Public Affairs in Arkansas, 1836–1850" (Ph.D. dissertation, University of Texas, 1966); R. B. Walz, "Migration into Arkansas, 1834–1880" (Ph.D. dissertation, University of Texas, 1958); M. Dougan, *Arkansas Historical Quarter-*

ARKANSAS GOVERNORS

Governor	Party	Term
TERRITORIAL		
James Miller	Dem.	1819–1825
George Izard	Dem.	1825–1828
John Pope	Dem.	1829–1835
William S. Fulton	Dem.	1835–1836
STATE		
James S. Conway	Dem.	1836–1840
Archibald Yell	Dem.	1840–1844
Thomas S. Drew	Dem.	1844–1849
John S. Roane	Dem.	1849–1852
Elias N. Conway	Dem.	1852–1860
Henry M. Rector	Dem.	1860–1862
Harris Flanigan	Dem.	1862–1865
Isaac Murphy	Union-Dem.	1864–1868
Powell Clayton	Rep.	1868–1871
Ozra A. Hadley	Rep.	1871–1873
Elisha Baxter	Rep.	1873–1874
Augustus H. Garland	Dem.	1874–1877
William R. Miller	Dem.	1877–1881
Thomas J. Churchill	Dem.	1881–1883
James H. Berry	Dem.	1883–1885
Simon P. Hughes	Dem.	1885–1889
James P. Eagle	Dem.	1889–1893
William M. Fishback	Dem.	1893–1895
James P. Clarke	Dem.	1895–1897
Daniel W. Jones	Dem.	1897–1901
Jeff Davis	Dem.	1901–1907
John S. Little	Dem.	1907–1909
George W. Donaghey	Dem.	1909–1913
Joseph T. Robinson	Dem.	1913
George W. Hays	Dem.	1913–1917
Charles H. Brough	Dem.	1917–1921
Thomas C. McRae	Dem.	1921–1925
Thomas J. Terral	Dem.	1925–1927
John E. Martineau	Dem.	1927–1928
Harvey Parnell	Dem.	1928–1933
Junas M. Futrell	Dem.	1933–1937
Carl E. Bailey	Dem.	1937–1941
Homer M. Adkins	Dem.	1941–1945
Benjamin T. Laney	Dem.	1945–1949
Sidney S. McMath	Dem.	1949–1953
Francis Cherry	Dem.	1953–1955
Orval E. Faubus	Dem.	1955–1967
Winthrop Rockefeller	Rep.	1967–1971
Dale Bumpers	Dem.	1971–1975
David Pryor	Dem.	1975–1979
William Clinton	Dem.	1979–

ARKANSAS POPULATION, 1810–1970

Year	Total	White	Nonwhite		% Growth	Rank U.S.	Rank South
			Slave	Free			
1810	1,062	924	136	2			
1820	14,255	12,579	1,617	59	1,244.0	26	14
1830	30,388	25,671	4,576	141	112.9	28	15
1840	97,574	77,174	19,935	465	221.1	25	12
1850	209,897	162,189	47,100	708	115.1	26	13
1860	435,450	324,143	111,115	192	107.5	25	13
1870	484,471	362,115	122,356		11.3	26	13
1880	802,525	591,531	210,994		65.6	25	13
1890	1,128,179	818,752	309,427		40.6	24	11
1900	1,311,564	944,580	366,984		16.3	25	12
1910	1,574,449	1,131,026	443,423		20.0	25	11
1920	1,752,204	1,279,757	472,447		11.3	25	11
1930	1,854,482	1,375,315	479,167		5.8	25	11
1940	1,949,387	1,466,084	483,303		5.1	24	11
1950	1,909,511	1,481,507	428,004		-2.0	30	15
1960	1,786,272	1,395,703	390,569		-6.5	31	15
1970	1,923,295	1,565,915	357,380		7.7	32	14

ly (Summer, 1970); and O. W. Taylor, *Negro Slavery in Arkansas* (1958). For the Civil War, see T. A. Belser, Jr., "Military Operations in Missouri and Arkansas, 1861–1865" (Ph.D. dissertation, Vanderbilt University, 1958); D. Y. Thomas, *Arkansas in War and Reconstruction* (1926); and *Arkansas Historical Quarterly*, for numerous articles on battles, campaigns, and other aspects of war.

For Reconstruction, see M. A. Ellenburg, "Reconstruction in Arkansas" (Ph.D. dissertation, University of Missouri, 1967); T. S. Staples, *Reconstruction in Arkansas, 1862–1874* (1923); and G. H. Thompson, "Leadership in Arkansas Reconstruction" (Ph.D. dissertation, Columbia University, 1968).

On the agrarian revolt and Gilded Age, see S. R. Crawford, "Poll Tax" (M.A. thesis, University of Arkansas, 1944); G. D. Davis, *Arkansas Historical Quarterly* (Winter, 1945); F. C. Elkins, *Arkansas Historical Quarterly* (Autumn, 1954; Summer, 1970); C. Parsley, *Arkansas Historical Quarterly* (Spring, 1966); T. Saloutos, *Arkansas Historical Quarterly* (June, 1943); G. Shirley, *Law West of Fort Smith* (1968); F. H. Harrington, *Hanging Judge* (1951); G. W. Graves, *Arkansas Historical Quarterly* (Summer, 1973; Autumn, 1967); A. E. Taylor *Arkansas Historical Quarterly* (Spring, 1956); J. H. Fair, "Political Disfranchisement of Negroes in Arkansas" (M.A. thesis, University of Arkansas, 1961); and W. B. Gatewood, *Arkansas Historical Quarterly* (Autumn, 1972).

For the Progressive period, see T. L. Baxley, *Arkansas Historical Quarterly* (Spring, 1963), the Donaghey administration; C. R. Ledbetter, *Arkansas Historical Quarterly* (Spring, 1974), Jeff Davis; S. Towns, *Arkansas Historical Quarterly* (Winter, 1965), Joseph T. Robinson; H. C. Dethloff, *Arkansas Historical Quarterly* (Spring, 1971), rice industry; O. A. Rogers, Jr., *Arkansas Historical Quarterly* (Summer, 1960), Elaine tragedy from black viewpoint; and J. W. Butts and D. James, *Arkansas Historical Quarterly* (Spring, 1961), unreconstructed white version of Elaine riot.

C. C. Alexander, *Ku Klux Klan in Southwest* (1965), is excellent, but even better are his three articles in *Arkansas Historical Quarterly* (Spring, Fall, Winter, 1963). See also R. Halliburton, Jr., *Arkansas Historical Quarterly* (Autumn, 1964), antievolution law; A. R. and R. B.

Buckalew, *Arkansas Historical Quarterly* (Autumn, 1974), discovery of oil; and G. S. Brewer, *Southern Lumberman* (Dec., 1956), lumber industry.

For the depression and war years, see H. Adams, "Thaddeus Caraway in U.S. Senate" (Ph.D. dissertation, George Peabody College, 1935); T. Coffin, *Senator Fulbright* (1966); B. Drummond, "Arkansas Politics: A One-Party System" (Ph.D. dissertation, University of Chicago, 1957); D. H. Grubbs, *Cry from Cotton* (1971), on STFU and New Deal; D. Holley, *Uncle Sam's Farmers* (1975); N. E. Neal, "Biography of J. T. Robinson" (Ph.D. dissertation, University of Oklahoma, 1957); S. Towns, *Arkansas Historical Quarterly* (Summer, 1966), on Hattie Caraway; and R. P. Vickers, *Arkansas Historical Quarterly* (Summer, 1951), Japanese-American relocation.

For the postwar years, see J. E. P. Griner, "Growth of Manufacturing in Arkansas, 1900–1950" (Ph.D. dissertation, George Peabody College, 1957); A. B. Ader, *Dixiecrat Movement* (1955); H. S. Ashmore, *Epitaph for Dixie* (1958); N. V. Bartley, *Rise of Massive Resistance* (1969); J. Ranchino, *From Faubus to Bumpers, 1960–1970* (1972); C. R. Ledbetter *et al.*, *Politics in Arkansas: Constructive Experience* (1972); T. Murton, *Accomplices to Crime* (1969); W. Nunn and K. G. Collett, *Political Paradox: Constructive Revision in Arkansas* (1973); N. Pierce, *Deep South States* (1974); C. R. Roland, *Impossible Era* (1975); A. J. Sawkow, *From Race Riot to Sit-in* (1966); and R. Yates, "Arkansas," in W. C. Havard, *Changing Politics of the South* (1972).

WADDY WILLIAM MOORE
University of Central Arkansas

ARKANSAS, UNIVERSITY OF (Fayetteville, 72701). In 1860, although the state had several private academies, it had not a single public high school, much less a university. Interest in creating a state institution of higher learning was at least as old as the state itself, but the costs of such an undertaking and the politics of the antebellum period combined to defeat every serious proposal. In 1864, however, the state's Unionist government accepted the federal government's land-grant offer under the Morrill Act of 1862. Complying with the terms of the federal statute, the legislature in 1868 established the machinery of a state university but little else. A board of trustees was not appointed until 1871, and not until the following year did the board agree on the school's name and location.

Known until 1899 as Arkansas Industrial University, the school originally comprised primary, preparatory, and normal schools of instruction as well as college-level offerings. Although its location in the small town of FAYETTEVILLE (pop. 1,500) in the mountains of northwestern Arkansas may seem somewhat anomalous, the area's Unionist Republicans and its active support of education help to explain the board's choice. Indeed, in 1860, one-fifth of the state's public schools had been located in Fayetteville's Washington County. Functioning as a university since 1899, the institution has approximately 12,000 students enrolled in a wide range of curricula at its main campus. Additional programs of instruction are offered at the university's branch campus in Little Rock. Library holdings at Fayetteville include the papers of several state governors (C. H. BROUGH, T. C. McRae, H. Parnell), records of the state's PRESBYTERIAN CHURCH, and an outstanding collection of Ozark Mountains FOLKLORE.

See R. A. Leflar, *First 100 Years* (1972); H. Harrison, *University of Arkansas, 1871–1948* (1948); T. Rothrock, *Arkansas Historical Quarterly* (Spring, 1971); and W. Gatewood, *Arkansas Historical Quarterly* (Summer, 1971).

ARKANSAS DEMOCRAT, the second newspaper to bear this name, began publication in Little Rock in 1871. Seven years later it was purchased by James Mitchell (1832–1902), a former professor at the University of Arkansas and a past editor of the ARKANSAS GAZETTE. Throughout the late nineteenth century, the *Democrat*'s advocacy of an inflated currency and support of expanded public education made it the principal organ for reform elements within the state Democratic party. Still formally affiliated with the Democratic party, the paper has a daily circulation of over 60,000 copies.

See F. W. Allsopp, *History of Arkansas Press* (1922); bound copies at Library of Congress and at Little Rock Public Library; and microfilm from Bell & Howell.

ARKANSAS GAZETTE, known as the "Old Lady" of state journalism, began publication in 1819 at Arkansas Post. Its founder and first editor, William E. Woodruff, moved the paper to Little Rock in 1921 and published it until 1836 as a Democratic weekly. Subsequent sales of the property and changes in editors resulted in numerous shifts in the paper's political views. In 1843, with assistance from ALBERT PIKE, the paper was purchased by a group of Whigs and took the unpopular position of opposing the annexation of Texas. In 1850, the *Gazette* was reacquired by Woodruff. He had been publishing a weekly, the *Democrat*, which he merged with the *Gazette* to form the *Gazette and Democrat*. Under Woodruff's direction, the paper again supported Democratic candidates and espoused Democratic principles. In 1853, however, the paper was purchased by advocates of the KNOW-NOTHING PARTY, who in 1860 supported the candidacy of JOHN BELL. Although the *Gazette* denied the legitimacy of secession, it expressed sentiments of southern nationalism and ultimately justified separation from the Union on the basis of man's natural right to rebel against tyranny.

Since the Civil War the *Arkansas Gazette* has enjoyed both greater stability in its ownership and greater editorial consistency. Generally it has held to conservative positions, though HARRY ASHMORE, a recent editor, received a Pulitzer Prize in 1957 for his opposition to Governor ORVAL FAUBUS and for his support for court-ordered DESEGREGATION of the Little Rock schools. Presently an independent Democratic daily, the *Arkansas Gazette* is the most widely distributed paper in the state, with a circulation in excess of 100,000 copies.

See M. Ross, *Arkansas Gazette, 1819–1866* (1969), and *Arkansas Historical Quarterly* (Spring, 1969); F. W. Allsopp, *History of Arkansas Press* (1922); bound copies at Library of Congress, Historical Society of Wisconsin, and University of Arkansas Library; and microfilm from Arkansas Historical Commission (1846–) and from Bell & Howell (1891–).

ARKANSAS HISTORICAL ASSOCIATION (University of Arkansas, Fayetteville, 72703), founded in 1941, meets annually to hear scholarly papers and addresses by local as well as nationally known historians. It has a membership of about 1,500. It began issuing the *Arkansas Historical Quarterly* in 1942, which prints scholarly articles, book reviews, and an occasional reminiscence or essay related to the history of the state. In 1975 the association offered its first awards for excellence in a variety of categories to county historical society publications.

ARKANSAS INDIANS. See QUAPAW INDIANS

ARKANSAS POST, BATTLE OF (January 10–11, 1863). Confederate authorities in the Trans-Mississippi Department, alarmed by Union activities on the Mississippi, in September, 1862, commenced construction of a four-bastioned earthen fort at Arkansas Post. This fort, on the north bank of the Arkansas 25 miles above its mouth, guarded the river approach to Little Rock, Ark., and provided a base from which Confederates could attack Union shipping on the Mississippi.

Capture of the unarmed steamer *Blue Wing* in December, 1862, focused Union attention on Arkansas Post. Contrary to statements in their memoirs by General William T. Sherman and Admiral David D. Porter that the proposal to attack the post was theirs, it was also advocated by General John A. McClernand, the army commander.

The expedition (32,000 soldiers convoyed by numerous gunboats) sailed from Milliken's Bend, La., January 5, 1863, ascended the Arkansas River, and landed below the post on the tenth. General Thomas J. Churchill and his 4,900 Confederates engaged McClernand's advance. Outflanked, the southerners retired into the rifle pits extending from the fort to Post Bayou. On January 11, while Union infantry assailed the rifle pits, Porter's gunboats bombarded the fort. Outnumbered, the Confederates surrendered. Union forces were recalled from the Arkansas after accomplishing their mission. Capture of Arkansas Post eliminated a danger to U. S. Grant's Mississippi River supply line during his VICKSBURG CAMPAIGN.

See *Official Records, Armies*, Ser. 1, Vol. XVII; *Official Records, Navies*, Ser. 1, Vol. XXIV; W. T. Sherman, *Memoirs* (1875); D. D. Porter, *Incidents and Anecdotes* (1885); A. T. Mahan, *Gulf and Inland Waters* (1883); R. S. Huffstot, *Civil War Times Illustrated* (Jan., 1969); and E. C. Bearss, *Arkansas Historical Quarterly* (Autumn, 1959).

EDWIN C. BEARSS
National Park Service

ARKANSAS RIVER. Discovered by HERNANDO DE SOTO in 1541, the lower Arkansas Valley was not again visited by Europeans until Louis Jolliet in 1673. Then in 1686 Henri de Tonty founded Arkansas Post, which later became the first capital of Arkansas Territory. Bernard de La Harpe mapped the lower river in 1721. Acquisition by the United States in 1803, plus the coming of the steamboat by 1820, hastened change. The army post of Ft. Smith was opened in 1817, Arkansas became a territory, and the ARKANSAS GAZETTE began publishing in 1819. The capital was moved to Little Rock in 1821. Because the navigable stream was the best means of access to central Arkansas until the 1870s, much of the early activity in the state focused on the river. Agriculture, commerce, and immigration depended on it, and even

some of the Indian removals of the 1830s were by water. The town of Ft. Smith, near the head of deepwater navigation, was a center for trade and justice in the Indian Territory. Control of the river influenced Civil War strategy, and many of the Confederate Indians were residents of the middle Arkansas Valley.

Cotton was the major cash crop before 1860, but by 1870 the upriver region became increasingly economically diversified, with the LUMBER INDUSTRY, COAL MINING, orcharding, PETROLEUM production, and especially since 1945 light manufacturing. The McClellan-Kerr Arkansas River Navigation System, completed during 1959–1969, has made the river navigable nearly to Tulsa, Okla., and has helped control the floods that once periodically devastated the valley (FLOOD CONTROL).

See U.S. Army Engineers, *The Arkansas* (1969); M. Ross, *Arkansas Gazette* (Nov. 30, 1958); R. A. Smith, *Arkansas Historical Quarterly* (Winter, 1951); T. Nuttall, *Travels in Arkansas Territory* (1966); and I. D. Richards, *Story of a Rivertown* (1969).

ROBERT B. WALZ
Southern Arkansas University

ARLINGTON, VA. (pop. 174,284), is an urban county, governed as a unit without civil subdivisions. Situated on the southwest bank of the POTOMAC RIVER opposite the District of Columbia, the area was visited in 1608 by Captain John Smith. Effective settlement did not begin, however, until after the Iroquois Indians ceded the land to Virginia in 1722. John Alexander, a tobacco planter, in 1740 constructed Abingdon, the first mansion within the present limits of Arlington; its ruins are on the grounds of Washington, D.C., National Airport. John Parke Custis, stepson of GEORGE WASHINGTON, purchased the plantation and its residence from Alexander's heirs in 1778, and his son Washington Custis began construction of a new mansion in 1802. This home, Arlington, was completed in 1817 and willed in 1857 by Custis to his daughter, MARY CUSTIS LEE, wife of ROBERT E. LEE. Over the 400 acres of the original plantation have been the grounds since 1864 of Arlington National Cemetery.

The general area of present-day Arlington County and the city of ALEXANDRIA constitute the portion of Virginia ceded to the federal government to form the District of Columbia. Awaiting formal incorporation of the land into the federal district, the Virginia legislature in 1801 organized it as the temporary county of Alexandria. The capital city was slow to grow, and the general belief was that the federal government never would need the Virginia portion of the district. So, in 1847, after residents had voted for retrocession, Congress surrendered federal claims to the territory. The Virginia legislature granted the town of Alexandria status as an independent city separate from the rest of the county in 1870, and the county changed its name to Arlington in 1920 to end confusion between the town and the county. Recent Arlington has grown along with the federal government. Besides being the suburban residence of many Washingtonians, it is the site of an increasing number of federal offices and installations, including the Pentagon and Ft. Meyer.

See F. Harrison, *Landmarks of Old Prince William* (1924, 1964), early history of area; E. L. Templeman, *Arlington Heritage* (1959); and annual issues of *Arlington Historical Magazine* (1957–). Arlington Public Library maintains the Virginiana Collection of books, documents, maps, and oral history tapes relating to the area.

ARMING OF SLAVES (by the Confederacy).

General PATRICK CLEBURNE advocated the enlistment of black soldiers as early as 1863, but his fellow officers rejected the notion. Several military units from Alabama and Mississippi as well voiced their willingness to serve with blacks and sought appropriate legislation from the Confederate Congress. Yet, President JEFFERSON DAVIS ignored suggestions to recruit Negroes, free or slave, because he knew the idea was generally unpopular.

As Confederate commanders grew desperate for men in late 1864, he changed his mind and asked Congress to authorize the enlistment of slaves as cooks and teamsters in the army to free white men for combat. Expanding on Davis' plan, Secretary of War JAMES A. SEDDON suggested that slaves be permitted to serve as soldiers in return for their freedom at the end of the war. Gradually other prominent southerners came to accept the idea. In late 1864 under prodding from Governor WILLIAM ("EXTRA BILLY") SMITH, the Virginia legislature authorized the enlistment of slaves in state units but failed to provide for their emancipation. ROBERT E. LEE in January, 1865, foresaw defeat and encouraged the arming of slaves in order to prevent a Union victory. Over continued opposition, Congress in March, 1865, did finally endorse a law permitting masters to volunteer their slaves for military service. Still, Confederate legislators made no provision to free those slaves who served. To stimulate enlistment, officials recruited one black unit and paraded it in Richmond but to no effect. Few blacks appeared interested, and masters were unwilling to release their slaves for military duty. Evidently the law came too late to be of

value, and none of the blacks recruited for the Confederate army ever served in combat.

See T. R. Hay, *Mississippi Valley Historical Review* (June, 1919); N. W. Stephenson, *American Historical Review* (Jan., 1913); and R. F. Durden, *Gray and Black* (1972).

EUGENE H. BERWANGER
Colorado State University

ARMISTEAD, LEWIS ADDISON (1817–1863),

was born at New Bern, N.C., into a family with a strong military tradition. He briefly attended West Point, entered the army in 1839 as a second lieutenant in the 6th Infantry, and eventually became captain of that unit. During the MEXICAN WAR he was twice brevetted for gallantry. When Virginia seceded he resigned his commission and entered the Confederate service, first as a major and then as colonel of the 57th Virginia. Promoted brigadier general in April, 1862, he served capably from the PENINSULAR CAMPAIGN to Gettysburg with Benjamin Huger's and then GEORGE PICKETT's division. During Pickett's charge at the battle of GETTYSBURG, he conspicuously led his men forward. A remnant of his brigade pierced the Union position but was quickly overwhelmed by federal reinforcements, and Armistead fell mortally wounded.

See F. B. Heitman, *Historical Register* (1903); C. A. Evans, *Confederate Military History* (1899), III; J. E. Poindexter, *Southern Historical Society Papers* (1909); and R. Martin, *Southern Historical Society Papers* (1904).

PETER MASLOWSKI
University of Nebraska, Lincoln

ARMSTRONG, SAMUEL CHAPMAN (1839–

1893), was born and received his early education in Hawaii. Later his missionary parents sent him to Williams College, Massachusetts. Upon graduation in 1862, Armstrong became a Union army captain. In 1863 he unenthusiastically accepted a colonelcy in the 9th Regiment, U.S. Colored Troops. This wartime experience gave him a lifelong interest in black Americans. In 1866 Armstrong became FREEDMEN'S BUREAU agent for eastern Virginia. Impressed with the need for black education, he urged the American Missionary Association to purchase a plantation and establish an industrial school. In 1868 the AMA founded HAMPTON INSTITUTE with Armstrong as principal. Hampton became the first outstanding Negro agricultural and industrial school. Armstrong took to Hampton a blatant racial prejudice and a belief that industrial education would benefit backward, slothful blacks. They were inferior to whites, he thought, and should emphasize moral and economic progress rather than full citizenship. Armstrong, the most influential person in BOOKER T. WASHINGTON's life, clearly foreshadowed Washington's economic and educational views.

See S. Carson [Lowitt], "Armstrong" (Ph.D. dissertation, Johns Hopkins University, 1953), the best; E. A. Talbot, *Armstrong* (1904); *Southern Workman* (1872–93), on microfilm; and S. C. Armstrong, *Ideas on Education* (1940).

JOE M. RICHARDSON
Florida State University

ART. In the South, where painting was more widely appreciated than sculpture, anyone with family pride graced the walls of his home with portraits of his family and ancestors. Although the South contributed its share of indigenous painters, there were also other artists who at times worked in the South, particularly portrait painters, who were not native southerners. John Singleton Copley of Boston received commissions for portraits from the wealthy Carolina planters. Henrietta Johnston and Jeremiah Theus, who worked in South Carolina, were natives of Great Britain and Switzerland, respectively.

One of the most gifted and recognized painters of the South was Ralph E. W. Earl (1788?–1838), who worked in Tennessee during the early part of the nineteenth century. He studied in England with John Trumbull and Benjamin West for a time before returning to the United States to practice his art in the South as a portrait painter. A great many of the artist's portraits are of ANDREW JACKSON, a subject for which Earl received numerous requests. His best portrait of Jackson may be seen in the Brooks Memorial Art Gallery in Memphis, Tenn.

During the middle decades of the nineteenth century, two native Tennesseans—Samuel M. Shaver (1816?–1878) and Washington B. Cooper (1802–1889), whose skill as painters is characterized by simplicity and directness—garnered for themselves most of the portrait commissions in eastern and central Tennessee. A transplanted Philadelphia artist, James Cameron (1817–1882), made a significant contribution to southern art while residing in Chattanooga from 1850 to 1860. His work reflected a primary interest in landscape painting, though economic need required that he seek portrait commissions as well. The work of these three men is identified with the state of Tennessee in the period of its greatest early expansion and reflects vividly the taste and pride of the builders of this region.

William James Hubard (1807–1862) established himself in Richmond, Va., in 1841 after exhibiting in Boston and Philadelphia and gaining a reputation for his small full-length portraits of celebrated leaders. Examples of his fine paintings may be seen in Richmond's famed Valentine Museum.

Another distinguished painter of the South was Francis Blackwell Mayer (1827–1899) of Baltimore. He studied at the Pennsylvania Academy of the Fine Arts and in 1847 with some of his friends and fellow artists helped found the Maryland Art Association. He worked both in Baltimore and Annapolis, devoting his time and skill to meticulously realistic genre and historical paintings. Also from Maryland came one of America's greatest artists, the multitalented Charles Willson Peale (1741–1827). His enduring fame rests upon his brilliant representations of colonial life and his many portraits of GEORGE WASHINGTON.

Louisiana's first and most distinguished painter of landscapes in the nineteenth century was Richard Clague (1816–1873). Born of a wealthy family, he received a classical education and early artistic training at an academy in Geneva, Switzerland, and later at the École des Beaux-Arts in Paris. He returned to New Orleans to teach and paint, demonstrating an accomplished hand both with portraits and landscapes. Because of his training his work is reminiscent of the Barbizon painter, Theodore Rousseau; yet his paintings still exhibit his affinity with the natural environment of Louisiana and the Deep South.

Another eminent southern painter was George Cooke (1793–1849), who was born in St. Mary's County, Md. In the 1820s he opened a studio in Richmond and soon developed an impressive career as a portrait painter. He later studied in Italy and France for five years, returning thereafter to the United States. Although he was a skilled landscape artist, evidenced by his fine views of Richmond, Washington, Charleston, Monticello, and Mount Vernon, his true forte was portraiture. His splendid portraits of HENRY CLAY and JOHN C. CALHOUN testify to his exceptional ability in this medium.

John Gadsby Chapman (1808–1889) of Alexandria, Va., was a prominent southern painter. After studying in Rome, Italy, for three years he returned to America and gained national fame for his giant mural *The Baptism of Pocahontas*, now in the rotunda of the Capitol in Washington, D.C. Because so many of his historical and genre paintings have been preserved in engravings, his landscapes and portraits are not as well known. In the field of portraiture, however, he was one of the most capable artists in the United States during the 1830s and 1840s. He did outstanding portraits of the elderly JAMES MADISON, Chief Justice Salmon P. Chase, DAVID CROCKETT, and others.

Although the well-to-do of the city of Savannah, Ga., chiefly patronized painters from Philadelphia, New York, and Boston, mention should be made of Jeremiah Theus (1719?–1774) and his successor Henry Benbridge (1744–1812), who spent most of their lives in Charleston doing portraits of the Tidewater gentry. The New England miniaturist Edward Greene Malbone (1777–1807) had a studio in Charleston from 1801 to 1804. Charles Fraser (1782–1860) lived and worked there, and for a short time Samuel F. B. Morse also painted in Charleston. The first woman artist in America and a pioneer in pastel painting was Henrietta Johnston of Charleston, who worked there from at least 1705 until her death in 1729.

The commonwealth of Kentucky produced three native-born artists, each of whom won national recognition during the nineteenth century. They were Matthew Harris Jouett (1787–1827), William Edward West (1788–1857), and Joseph H. Bush (1793–1865). Jouett, the best of the three, worked under Gilbert Stuart in Boston in 1816. His early portraits show the influence of Stuart, and his later works reflect the style of Thomas Sully, the latter having taught both West and Bush.

Missouri can boast of the popular and famous genre painter George Caleb Bingham (1811–1879). Born in Virginia, he spent most of his life in Missouri, where his faithful renditions of fur traders, flatboatmen, and local political scenes made him one of the nation's most beloved artists.

The best-known artist of genre paintings dealing with the life of the black people in the South was William Aiken Walker (1838–1921), born in Charleston. His meticulous renderings of the cotton fields and portraits of the workers are documentary records of that era.

Painting, like most other southern cultural activities, waned during the several decades following the Civil War. By the early 1930s, however, interest had revived to the extent that the section was supporting several dozen schools of art and numerous outstanding art museums. Although its regional artists were not usually recognized as in the front rank of the world, the South did produce a number of talented painters, including Hugh Henry Breckenridge (1870–1937), born in Virginia, and Alexandre Hogue (1898–), born in Missouri, who both have works in numerous museums throughout the nation.

Leading collections of paintings in the South include the Ringling Art Museum at Sarasota, Fla., J. B. Speed Art Museum in Louisville, Delgado Museum of Art in New Orleans, Houston Museum of Fine Arts, Baltimore Museum of Art, High Museum of Art in Atlanta, St. Louis Art Museum, Gibbes Art Gallery in Charleston, Valentine Museum and Virginia Museum of Fine Arts in Richmond, and, of course, the Corcoran Gallery of Art, Joseph H. Hirshhorn Museum, National Collection of Fine Arts, National Portrait Gallery, and National Gallery of Art, all in Washington, D.C.

See U. M. Gregory, "Fine Arts," in W. T. Couch, *Culture in the South* (1935); M. M. Swan, *Antiques* (Oct., 1931); W. B. Floyd, *Antiques* (April, 1974); B. H. Bishop, *Antiques* (Sept., 1971); W. N. Banks, *Antiques* (Sept., 1972); and Federal Writers' Project, WPA, American Guide series (various dates).

WILLIAM D. ALEXANDER
Bowling Green State University

ARTHUR, CHESTER A., ADMINISTRATION

(1881–1885). As had his immediate predecessors, Arthur sought to augment Republican strength in the South. Because he came to the White House with the reputation of a spoilsman and stalwart, old-line Republicans expected a return to Reconstruction days. But as Arthur saw it, the only salvation for the Republican party in the South was through a policy of cooperation with the INDEPENDENT MOVEMENTS, now appearing in nearly every southern state. With his chief advisers, such as William E. Chandler of New Hampshire, urging full recognition and support of the independents, Arthur embraced these political figures as the new leaders of the REPUBLICAN PARTY in the South.

He hoped to unite Republicans, those in the READJUSTER and GREENBACKER movements, independents, and "liberals" in the South for the overthrow of the southern Democrats and for the political and material regeneration of the NEW SOUTH. In pursuing this goal, Arthur was at variance with orthodox Republicans, because he courted the favor of a number of independent economic radicals in the South. And he even favored the idea of Republicans in the South giving up their identity and interests and merging under the leadership of the independents. To Arthur this development presented the best opportunity the Republicans had had for redeeming the South since the federal troops were removed.

Arthur's stance was a novel and radical one for a Republican president to take in the South, but the election results showed that he achieved no substantial success with it. And Arthur was no more successful than Rutherford B. Hayes in producing a formula to break up the Democratic South.

See V. P. De Santis, *Republicans Face the Southern Question* (1959) and *Journal of Southern History* (Aug., 1953), the fullest account; S. P. Hirshon, *Farewell to Bloody Shirt* (1962); and T. C. Reeves, *Gentleman Boss* (1975).

VINCENT P. DE SANTIS
University of Notre Dame

ARTICLES OF CONFEDERATION (1776–1788). On June 7, 1776, RICHARD HENRY LEE of Virginia proposed that the Continental Congress declare its independence from Great Britain and create a plan for the confederation of the states. A committee consisting of one delegate from each of the 13 states was created to draft articles of confederation on June 12, 1776. Creating "a firm league of friendship" among the states, the Articles were finally sent to the states for ratification in November, 1777. Not included were those powers requisite to a real national government. Even then, Maryland refused to ratify the Articles of Confederation until Virginia agreed to cede to the confederation its claims to the territory north and west of the Ohio River; thus the official adoption was delayed until March 1, 1781. Despite the delay in unanimous ratification by the states, the Continental Congress began operating according to the provisions of the Articles in 1778. From 1779 to 1781, when Georgia and South Carolina were occupied by the British, southern delegates generally supported efforts to strengthen the Articles in order to make Congress more effective in prosecuting the war.

Southern delegates felt a kinship in Congress because their states shared a common agricultural economy and feared dominance of the confederation by mercantile New England. Sectional politics thus required that congressional appointments include a southern representative. But within the South there was also a conscious distinction between the upper and lower southern states. It was for this reason, for example, that Congress was compelled to appoint both THOMAS JEFFERSON of Virginia and HENRY LAURENS of South Carolina to the peace commission so that they might protect the special interests of their respective sections of the South.

In 1786 Virginia convened the ANNAPOLIS CONVENTION to establish unified commercial regulations among the states after Congress had failed to amend the Articles to that end; this gathering in turn issued the call for a convention in May, 1787,

to strengthen the Articles generally, leading to the writing of the Constitution.

The southern members of the committee to draft the Articles of Confederation were Thomas McKean, Delaware; Thomas Stone, Maryland; THOMAS NELSON, Virginia; Joseph Hewes, North Carolina; EDWARD RUTLEDGE, South Carolina; and Button Gwinnett, Georgia.

See E. C. Burnett, *Articles of Confederation* (1941); M. Jensen, *Articles of Confederation* (1940), and *New Nation* (1950); F. McDonald, *E Pluribus Unum* (1965); E. C. Burnett (ed.), *Letters of Members of the Continental Congress* (8 vols.; 1921–36); G. Hunt (ed.), *Journals of the Continental Congress* (34 vols.; 1904–37); and Papers of the Continental Congress, National Archives.

GARY D. OLSON
Augustana College, Sioux Falls, S.D.

ASHBY, HARRISON STERLING PRICE (1848–1923). A colorful Populist leader in Texas, Stump Ashby was born in Missouri. After serving in the Confederate army and acting in amateur theatricals, he drifted to Texas, where he became a cowboy, teacher, and Methodist circuit rider. Initially, he was successful in the ministry, but a reputed weakness for whiskey caused his superiors to shift him from one post to another, each less desirable, until he resigned in 1887. Becoming a farmer, he turned his talents to the FARMERS' ALLIANCE and POPULIST PARTY. His magnetic personality and ability as an orator gave him a place of leadership. He served as chairman of the Populist state executive committee in 1894 and as delegate to the Populist National Convention in 1896. Because the Populist party in Texas included strong prohibitionist elements, his drinking habits eventually proved an embarrassment. He withdrew from party affairs in the late 1890s and by 1902 had moved to Oklahoma, where he entered politics.

See R. C. Martin, *People's Party in Texas* (1933); J. D. Hicks, *Populist Revolt* (1931); and *Handbook of Texas* (1952).

MARILYN M. SIBLEY
Houston Baptist University

ASHEVILLE, N.C. (pop. 57,681). On a plateau between the BLUE RIDGE and the GREAT SMOKY mountains, the area was part of the CHEROKEE INDIANS' hunting grounds prior to the American Revolution. Called Morristown when founded in 1794, the settlement was renamed in 1797 to honor Governor Samuel Ashe. Antebellum Asheville prospered as a mountain trade center at the junction of the FRENCH BROAD RIVER and a plank road. In the 1850s, the town gained the added distinction of being a health resort of international renown. The Asheville Rifles, the first company of Confederate troops organized in the western section of the state, represented only part of the city's contribution to the Civil War; its Enfield Rifle Factory produced weapons and made the town a minor Confederate military center. The postwar development of railroads reinforced Asheville's position as a commercial center, and the increased demand for bright leaf TOBACCO gave area farmers a new cash crop. Today Asheville continues to be a resort and tourist city, and a diversity of light industry and annual folkcraft and folk music festivals give it a blend of tradition and modernity.

See Federal Writers' Project, *Asheville* (1941); and F. A. Sondley, *Asheville and Buncombe* (1922). Pack Memorial Public Library houses the state's third largest collection of local history materials as well as extensive holdings of state poetry and fiction, including the Thomas Wolfe Collection. See also files of Asheville *Citizen* (1870–), Asheville *Gazette-News* (1904–15), and Asheville *Times* (1896–), all available on microfilm.

ASHLAND, KY. (pop. 22,245). The area was largely unsettled until after the War of 1812 effectively broke the power of the Ohio Valley Indians. In 1815, however, the Poage family of Virginia pioneered the site and began the first of several scattered lumbering settlements. After the discovery of coal and iron in nearby hills and the construction of an iron furnace in 1826, Poague's Settlement grew and prospered as an iron and mining center on the Ohio River. It was renamed Ashland in 1850 in honor of HENRY CLAY's home near Lexington. After completion of the area's first railroad in 1857 and during the Civil War, Ashland consolidated its industrial position. The post–Civil War development of nearby oil and natural gas made Ashland a major refinery, and during the 1880s the use of native clays in bricks and tiles added yet additional industries to the city's list. Today it remains a center of heavy industry. Although local iron deposits are no longer worked, Ashland boasts one of the Western world's largest steel blast furnaces (IRON AND STEEL INDUSTRY), and its industries produce PETROLEUM, chemicals, shoes, prepared foods, bricks, and tiles, as well as steel.

See Ashland Centennial Commission, *Ashland, 1786–1954* (1954); and files of Ashland *Independent* (1896–). The Ashland Public Library and its Boyd County Historical Collection includes several manuscript histories and a growing genealogical collection.

ASHMORE, HARRY (1916–), executive editor of the ARKANSAS GAZETTE, in 1957 received the first double Pulitzer Prize in history for distinguished service in the Little Rock school integration controversy. A moderate, he described Little Rock as the result of a default of leadership that silenced reasonable compromise, threatened economic growth, and challenged fundamental concepts of morality, of social change, and of law. Born in Greenville, S.C., he has called himself an unabashed individualist, a partisan Democrat, and a journalist. His writings reveal a loyal critic who reluctantly accepts the passing of *noblesse oblige* for the necessary but often crass growth of his native South. He has favored a free press, democracy, the two-party system, a diversified economy, as well as education and health reforms and responsible local government planning. In 1959 Ashmore joined the Center for the Study of Democratic Institutions. Presently he is vice-chairman of the American Civil Liberties Union's National Advisory Council and a member of the board of the National Committee for an Effective Congress.

See Greenville *Piedmont* (1937–39) and *News* (1939–41); Charlotte *News* (1945–47); *Arkansas Gazette* (1947–59); and H. Ashmore, *Epitaph for Dixie* (1958) and *Negro and the Schools* (1954).

DOROTHY C. KINSELLA
NETWORK, Washington, D.C.

ASSOCIATION, or Continental Association, was the name given to a set of economic sanctions against Britain, adopted by the Continental Congress in October, 1774, and designed to force a redress of colonial grievances. The name and form were copied from earlier provincial associations in the South. Delegates from Maryland, Virginia, and North Carolina played a principal part in persuading Congress to adopt the Association and to agree not to import or consume British goods and not to export colonial products until Parliament repealed various objectionable measures taken since 1763. The success of the Association, which was well supported in all portions of the South except the interior of North Carolina and Georgia, gave striking evidence that Congress was becoming the central government for many North Americans. After fighting began, Congress relaxed the Association in order to prosecute the war.

See A. M. Schlesinger, *Colonial Merchants* (1918), the fullest and best study.

IRA D. GRUBER
Rice University

ASSOCIATION FOR THE PRESERVATION OF VIRGINIA ANTIQUITIES (2705 Park Ave., Richmond, Va. 23220) was founded in 1889 through the efforts of Cynthia Beverly Tucker Coleman of Williamsburg and Mary Jeffrey Galt of Norfolk initially to effect repairs to Bruton Parish Church in Williamsburg. Later, with the donation of 22.5 acres of land at Jamestown, it began the restoration of that historic site. The association, aided by dues, grants, endowments, and income from Jamestown National Park, acquires legal title to or maintains properties that are historically significant or architecturally unique and approves all restoration work at 37 sites. Additional preservation or perpetuation includes monuments, tombs, and graveyards and active support for restoration of complete urban districts and the encouragement of private ownership or adaptive use of historic properties. The APVA maintains a small research library limited to use by members (about 7,200 in 1976) and a staff to do basic research in archeology, history, architecture, decorative arts, and other fields related to historical preservation. In the journal *Discovery* it publishes articles describing APVA preservation accomplishments in Virginia. It gives two preservation awards annually, and it also has an advisory service for restoring and preserving old structures.

ASSOCIATION FOR THE STUDY OF AFRO-AMERICAN LIFE AND HISTORY (1407-14th St. NW, Washington, D.C. 20005) was founded in 1915 and has a present membership of 25,000. Supported by foundation aid, funds from memberships, subscriptions, and book sales, the association publishes the highly respected *Journal of Negro History*, a quarterly, and the *Negro History Bulletin*, as well as books and papers. The association holds the CARTER WOODSON Collection of papers and offers a limited number of awards and grants. The purpose of the organization is to encourage understanding; therefore it accepts a wide variety of articles related to Negro history, race relations, slavery and antislavery, changing historical traditions, education, politics, and religion.

See W. M. Brewer, *Journal of Negro History* (April, 1966).

ASSOCIATION OF SOUTHEASTERN RESEARCH LIBRARIES is an organization of representatives of 29 research libraries in ten southeastern states. Meetings are usually held during the annual and midwinter conferences of the

American Library Association and during the biennial conferences of the Southeastern Library Association. Organized on June 21, 1956, in Miami Beach, ASERL's stated purpose was "to improve the resources and services of research libraries in the Southeast Region of the United States through cooperative effort." The steering committee that recommended its organization was headed by Benjamin Powell, Duke University librarian. Its first chairman was A. Frederick Kuhlman, director of the Joint University Libraries in Tennessee.

The association has sponsored such bibliographical publications as *A Southeastern Supplement to the Union Lists of Serials* (1959), *Foreign Newspapers in Southeastern Libraries* (1963), and *Major Microform Holdings of ASERL Members* (1965). It also compiles statistical data of member libraries.

Probably ASERL's most far-reaching project has been the sponsorship of a computerized library network to serve the libraries of the Southeast. After a speech at the 1972 Chicago meeting describing the purposes and accomplishments of the Ohio College Library Center, ASERL appointed a committee comprised of John Gribbin (Tulane), Kenneth Toombs (University of South Caroline), and John Kennedy (Georgia Institute of Technology) to study the feasibility of such a network. Their report indicated that a southeastern network of the type in Ohio was both technically and economically feasible, and in the fall of 1972 ASERL became the sponsor, collection agency, and grant seeker for the proposed SOUTHEASTERN LIBRARY NETWORK.

See A. F. Kuhlman, *Southeastern Librarian* (Fall, 1956); *Southeastern Librarian* (Fall, 1965); J. H. Gribbin, *Southeastern Librarian* (Fall, 1974); and *College and Research Libraries* (Nov., 1956).

ELAINE VON OESEN
North Carolina Department of Cultural Resources

ASSOCIATION OF SOUTHERN WOMEN FOR THE PREVENTION OF LYNCHING, founded November 1, 1930, in Atlanta, Ga., by JESSIE DANIEL AMES and sponsored by the COMMISSION ON INTERRACIAL COOPERATION, was a movement of southern white women to end lynching in the South for any reason, especially "in defense of white women." Its goal was to educate public opinion against the crime and to prevent possible lynchings. The association itself comprised only a few women who served as a steering force, and the actual work was carried on by already existing women's church and civic groups that associated themselves with the cause.

The ASWPL dissolved in 1942 because of the decline in lynchings and World War II. Tactics included antilynching resolutions, speeches before women's and men's organizations, publication and distribution of antilynching literature, investigation of lynchings and attempted lynchings, and visits and letters to sheriffs, governors, and other public officials. The association did not support federal antilynching legislation.

See H. E. Barber, *Phylon* (Dec., 1973); J. S. Reed, *Social Problems* (Fall, 1968); and H. E. Barber, "Association" (M.A. thesis, University of Georgia, 1967).

HENRY E. BARBER
Virginia Intermont College

ATCHISON, DAVID RICE (1807–1886). A leading figure in the southern rights movement of the 1850s, Atchison graduated from TRANSYLVANIA UNIVERSITY in 1825, where his classmates included five men who would later serve with him in the U.S. Senate. Moving to Liberty on the Missouri frontier in 1830 to practice law, he quickly became active in local political and militia affairs. He served two terms in the Missouri legislature and one as circuit judge before accepting an appointment to the U.S. Senate in October, 1843, in place of the recently deceased Lewis F. Linn.

A gregarious man, Atchison quickly became popular among his fellow senators, who elected him president pro tem 16 times between August, 1846, and November, 1854. He became particularly interested in extending United States aid and protection to the Oregon settlers, a work begun by his predecessor, and helped lead the unsuccessful 54° 40′ movement in 1846. The WILMOT PROVISO and the events leading to the COMPROMISE OF 1850 brought him under the influence of JOHN C. CALHOUN, and after the South Carolinian's death Atchison became one of the most prominent southern ultras in the Senate. When the Missouri Democrats split over the issue of slavery extension in the territories, he took the lead in defeating the bid of THOMAS HART BENTON, the state party's long-time chieftain, for reelection to the Senate in 1850.

Although an ardent champion of territorial expansion, Atchison opposed the organization of Nebraska Territory until he was able to secure free access for slave owners through the repeal of the MISSOURI COMPROMISE in the KANSAS-NEBRASKA ACT. Thereafter he worked ardently at the head of the BORDER RUFFIANS to encourage proslavery settlement of Kansas while actively harassing the Free-Soilers who also sought to move there. When the latter finally carried the day, he retired in 1857 to manage farming interests in Clinton County, Mo.

When the Civil War broke out, Atchison actively supported the Confederate cause and intervened with Jefferson Davis in behalf of southern recognition for the Missouri state government of CLAIBORNE F. JACKSON. He moved to Grayson County, Tex., following the battle of PEA RIDGE, where he remained until 1867, when he returned to his Clinton County farm. Although making occasional public appearances, he did not again actively pursue a political or legal career.

See W. E. Parrish, *David Rice Atchison of Missouri* (1961); and P. O. Ray, *Repeal of the Missouri Compromise* (1909).

WILLIAM E. PARRISH
Westminster College, Fulton, Mo.

ATHENS, GA. (pop. 44,342), was founded as the home of the UNIVERSITY OF GEORGIA. In 1785, after the state legislature had chartered and made provisions for a university, Governor JOHN MILLEDGE purchased and donated to the state 633 acres of land overlooking the Oconee River in northeast-central Georgia. Although deep in CHEROKEE INDIAN territory, the hillside site possessed an excellent spring, suffered from no "harmful vapors," and protected students from the supposed evils of town life. Construction of both the school and the town did not begin, however, until 16 years later. When the town was incorporated in 1806, it boasted "538 free people, 26 four-wheeled carriages, and 26 widows." There was little change or growth in Athens until, in the 1850s, construction of the Georgia Railroad provoked an unprecedented upsurge in economic activity. Although there was no actual fighting in Athens, the Civil War arrested the growth and prosperity of what citizens had come to call the Manchester of the South. Not until the opening of the new cotton mills in the 1880s and the national prosperity of the pre–World War I era did Athenians again witness a growth comparable with that of the pre–Civil War decade. Present-day Athens, served by five railroads and seven truck lines, derives its economic support from the university, from cotton and textile mills, and from poultry processing.

See Athens *Banner-Herald* (1832–); and E. C. Hynds, *Antebellum Athens* (1973).

ATHENS BANNER-HERALD dates back at least to the formation in 1828 of the Athens, Ga., *Athenian*. Reorganized in 1832 as the *Southern Banner*, it was a low tariff, states' rights organ of the

Democratic party, which opposed the doctrine of NULLIFICATION. It supported the COMPROMISE OF 1850 but, during the ELECTION OF 1860, it endorsed the candidacy of JOHN C. BRECKINRIDGE. After changing its name to the *Northeast Georgian* (1872–1875) and then to the Athens *Georgian* (1875–1877), it readopted the title *Southern Banner* in 1878. Antebellum political divisions and journalistic institutions made less and less sense after the Civil War and Reconstruction, so in 1882 the *Banner* merged with its long-standing foe, a Whig paper known as the *Southern Watchman* (1854–1882). Seven years later it adopted a simplified name and was known until 1921 as the *Banner*. Since its merger in that year, however, with the Athens *Herald*, it has used its present hyphenated name.

See L. T. Griffith and J. E. Talmadge, *Georgia Journalism* (1951); and bound copies of papers at American Antiquarian Society, Library of Congress, county clerk's office in Athens, and University of Georgia Library (1927–).

ATLANTA, GA. (pop. 1,390,164), variously styled as the Railroad City and the Gate City of the South, was officially founded in 1847 on the site of earlier towns known as Marthasville and Terminus. RAILROADS were the dominant factor in the city's growth during the nineteenth century, which saw Atlanta's population jump from 2,572 in 1850 to 89,872 in 1900. The city originated as the meeting point of four railroads, the most significant being the state-owned Western & Atlantic, which linked Chattanooga and Atlanta. Until 1872, when the South & North Railroad was completed, the Western & Atlantic was the principal conduit of foodstuffs from the Ohio and Mississippi valleys into the Southeast. These foodstuffs, together with produce from the surrounding area and northern manufacturers, were the principal items of trade in nineteenth-century Atlanta; all these goods were transported to the city chiefly by the railroads.

Perhaps the most outstanding feature of Atlanta's history has been its record of booster activities. To many observers, Atlantans' urban boosterism has always seemed out of place in a region dominated by agrarian ideals. Especially after 1865, this booster spirit found expression in striking forms. The industrial fairs held in nineteenth-century Atlanta (COMMERCIAL EXPOSITIONS), beginning with the International Cotton Exposition of 1881 and ending with the Cotton States and International Exposition of 1895 (at which BOOKER T. WASHINGTON delivered his ATLANTA COMPRO-

MISE speech), constituted early attempts by local promoters to broadcast the city's potential. These fairs had modern descendants in the well-known Forward Atlanta campaigns of the 1920s and 1960s. HENRY GRADY, CLARK HOWELL, and RALPH MCGILL—three prominent editors of the Atlanta *Constitution* whose careers bridged the nineteenth and twentieth centuries—had much to do with engineering several of these ventures. One common theme of booster spokesmen like Grady, Howell, and to a lesser extent McGill was the allegedly harmonious race relations of Atlanta in comparison with those of other southern cities. Although the city both successfully avoided the excesses of Little Rock and New Orleans during the school desegregation crises of the 1950s and 1960s and also tolerated the sometime presence of MARTIN LUTHER KING, JR., the ATLANTA RACE RIOT of 1906 reminded historically oriented observers that the city had not always been "too busy to hate." Nevertheless, Atlanta by 1970 had become the commercial, financial, and transportation center of the Southeast.

See F. M. Garett, *Atlanta* (1954); J. M. Russell, "Atlanta" (Ph.D. dissertation, Princeton University, 1972); P. Miller, *Atlanta* (1949); W. P. Reed, *History of Atlanta* (1889); and D. F. White and T. J. Crimmins, *Journal of Urban History* (Feb., 1976).

JAMES M. RUSSELL
University of Tennessee, Chattanooga

ATLANTA CAMPAIGN (May–September, 1864) was a decisive campaign in which federal armies under William T. Sherman advanced from Chattanooga into Georgia against a Confederate force led first by JOSEPH E. JOHNSTON and, after July 17, by JOHN BELL HOOD. Sherman's forces numbered about 110,000 men; the Confederate army, about 70,000. Sherman's capture of Atlanta deprived the Confederacy of one of its more important transportation and manufacturing centers, inflicted a heavy blow to southern morale, and played a major role in the reelection of Abraham Lincoln.

The northern objective was to capture Atlanta and destroy the southern army defending the city. The Confederates were never able to agree on their strategy for the campaign. The civilian authorities wanted Johnston to launch an offensive movement to regain control of Tennessee. Johnston believed that he was not strong enough to undertake such an offensive and preferred to defeat Sherman in Georgia before attempting to invade Tennessee. As the campaign progressed, Sherman continually moved his larger force around Johnston's flanks, forcing the Confederates back from one line to another. Always the southern commander hoped to find a position from which he could not be driven. Major battles of the first part of the campaign were RESACA (May 13–15), NEW HOPE CHURCH (May 25–June 2), and KEN-NESAW MOUNTAIN (June 10–July 2). On July 9, Johnston retreated across the Chattahoochee River and fell back almost to the outskirts of Atlanta.

In mid-July the Confederate government, displeased with Johnston's constant pattern of retreat and alarmed that he might abandon Atlanta, removed him from command and replaced him with Hood. Unlike Johnston, Hood believed that the Confederates must undertake an offensive against the northerners. At PEACH TREE CREEK (July 20), Atlanta (July 22), and Ezra Church (July 28), Hood sent his columns out from Atlanta to fight the federals. In these battles victory rested with the northerners, although Hood's boldness curtailed some of Sherman's activities and led many southerners to believe that he had stymied the federal threat.

In August Hood sent most of his cavalry on what turned out to be a totally unsuccessful raid against Sherman's line of supply. With the cavalry gone, Hood was deprived of his best means of obtaining information about Sherman's activities. This fatal mistake enabled the federal commander to move almost all of his army around Hood's left flank to Jonesboro, some 30 miles south of Atlanta. From this position Sherman controlled the last railroad that supplied the Confederates in Atlanta. A Confederate attempt to drive the northerners away from Jonesboro (August 31) was unsuccessful. On September 1, Confederate forces there fought a delaying action while the remaining southerners evacuated Atlanta.

Historians have often faulted Sherman for concentrating too much on the capture of Atlanta rather than the destruction of the Confederate army. Otherwise, they have generally approved his strategy, tactics, and logistics. Johnston has traditionally been regarded as a master of Fabian warfare whose timely retreats saved his army from destruction. Recently, however, writers have taken Johnston to task for abandoning rich areas of north Georgia and retreating into the Confederacy's industrial heartland. They have expressed doubt that he could have held Atlanta. Hood has been regarded as an incompetent and unlucky general, who was promoted far above the position to which his limited abilities would have carried him.

See S. Carter, *Siege of Atlanta, 1864* (1973); T. L. Connelly, *Autumn of Glory* (1971); J. D. Cox, *Atlanta* (1882);

R. M. McMurry, *Civil War History* (March, 1976); and *Official Records, Armies*, Ser. 1, Vol. XXXVIII.

RICHARD M. MCMURRY
Valdosta State College

ATLANTA COMPROMISE refers to the speech made by BOOKER T. WASHINGTON at the Cotton States and International Exposition at Atlanta, Ga., in September, 1895. Washington's speech pleaded for consideration of his people in the economic development of the South, pointed out the importance of their labor to southern prosperity, and asked blacks to cooperate with white southerners in "every manly way" to bring about harmonious race relations there. He played down the race's grievances and left the impression among many whites that blacks should not agitate and protest for the enforcement of their constitutional rights, saying that "progress in the enjoyment of all privileges" would come to them as a result of "severe and constant struggle rather than artificial forcing." The speech helped to divide black opinion over the methods of achieving their constitutional rights for the next two decades. Opposition to Washington's philosophy, however, did not crystallize until 1903, when W. E. B. DU BOIS of Atlanta University published a collection of essays, *The Souls of Black Folk*, one of which popularized the speech as the "Atlanta Compromise." Du Bois believed that the white South interpreted the speech as a surrender of the race's demand for civil and political equality and for a working basis for mutual understanding on the race question.

See B. T. Washington, *Up from Slavery* (1901); W. E. B. Du Bois, *Souls of Black Folk* (1903); and A. Meier, *Negro Thought* (1963).

JAMES E. HANEY
Tennessee State University

ATLANTA CONSTITUTION, long one of the South's most influential daily newspapers, was first published on June 16, 1868, by Carey W. Styles, who intended that it strongly oppose Radical Reconstruction. One of its contemporaries observed that the new paper treated Radicals "with its gloves off." Later, Styles sold the paper to G. H. Anderson and William A. Hemphill, wrongly identified by Frank Luther Mott as its founder. Evan P. Howell purchased an interest in the *Constitution* in 1876, beginning an extended Howell family association with the journal. Besides Howell, who was largely responsible for the *Constitution*'s growth in reputation, the major figure in its earlier years was HENRY WOODFIN GRADY. Grady joined the staff in 1876. In 1880, using money borrowed from New York financier Cyrus Field, he bought a quarter interest in the paper and became managing editor, a position he retained until his death in 1889. JOSEPH E. BROWN, JOHN B. GORDON, and ALFRED COLQUITT overtly dominated state politics in the 1880s, but they owed their offices to campaigns that Grady managed and publicized in the *Constitution*.

CLARK HOWELL succeeded Grady as editor, and under his leadership the publication, which had occasionally indulged in sensationalism earlier, became sensationalized on a regular basis. It also carried on a bitter political and editorial warfare with the ATLANTA JOURNAL from the 1890s until well into the twentieth century, this centering on the conflicting political ambitions of Howell and HOKE SMITH, the *Journal*'s owner from 1887 to 1900. More recently, RALPH MCGILL, as editor and publisher, was the *Constitution*'s strongest voice, calling in editorials for racial justice and moderation. In 1950 the *Constitution* merged with its long-time rival, the *Journal*, the two forming Atlanta Newspapers, Inc. Each has continued to be published separately, the *Constitution* in the mornings, except for Sunday editions.

See L. T. Griffith and J. E. Talmadge, *Georgia Journalism* (1951); R. Nixon, *Henry W. Grady* (1943); and issues of the paper from Microfilm Corporation of America.

JOSEPH A. TOMBERLIN
Valdosta State College

ATLANTA DAILY WORLD, the first daily black newspaper in the United States, was established as a weekly in August, 1928, becoming a daily four years later. The founder William A. Scott II, murdered in 1934, was succeeded as editor by his younger brother Cornelius A. Scott, who retains the position. The paper is a family-owned and -operated enterprise. In the 1930s and 1940s, the Scotts headed a syndicate of more than 50 black newspapers and founded the Birmingham *World* (1930) and the Memphis *World* (1931). Democratic in the 1930s but Republican more recently, the paper has grown more conservative, opposing the radicalism of the 1960s and suffering some decline in circulation (25,000 in 1970). Since 1969 it has been published four times a week.

See copies on microfilm at Atlanta University Library, Kent State University Library, and Library of Congress; master copies from Bell & Howell; and G. Blackwell, "Black Control of Media in Atlanta" (Ph.D. dissertation, Emory University, 1973).

JOHN M. MATTHEWS
Georgia State University

ATLANTA HISTORICAL SOCIETY (Box 12423, Atlanta, Ga. 30305), founded in 1926, is largely supported by an endowment fund established by one of the founders, Walter McElreath, and by dues and donations. The society maintains a museum and an archive, which houses significant holdings of Civil War manuscripts and pictures, the Atlanta City Council minutes from 1848 to 1900, and some 30,000 photographs, architectural drawings, and maps. In 1927 the society began publishing, in addition to an occasional newsletter, the *Atlanta Historical Bulletin*, a journal that for many years appeared only intermittently but that has since 1975 become a quarterly. With a circulation of about 2,000, the *Bulletin* accepts only scholarly articles on the history of Atlanta or Georgia or the South and on urban history, in that order of preference. The *Bulletin* also includes an occasional review article and a limited number of book reviews. In 1976 the society published a guide to its manuscript collection. It also maintains the Tully Smith House, an upland Georgia farmhouse of 1840, and the Swan House, a 1920s mansion of architectural significance.

ATLANTA JOURNAL, originally the Atlanta *Evening Journal*, first appeared on February 24, 1883. It was founded by E. F. Hoge, eminent Atlanta attorney. The new publication initially struggled for survival, but its management sensibly chose to concentrate on local affairs rather than trying to compete with the established ATLANTA CONSTITUTION in reporting national and international news. This was a sagacious course, for by 1887 the *Journal* had surpassed the *Constitution*'s circulation. In 1887, HOKE SMITH, a politically ambitious young lawyer, purchased the *Journal*. During his tenure and beyond, the paper dueled politically and editorially with the *Constitution*. Throughout the nineties, the *Journal*'s hallmark was sensationalism, and it was jingoistic in the crisis surrounding the SPANISH-AMERICAN WAR, milking the situation of all its news value, as did its competitor. Smith sold his interest to James R. Gray in 1900, but the sniping between the *Journal* and the *Constitution* abated only at the end of Smith's political career. The Gray family controlled the publication until 1939, when former Ohio governor and 1920 presidential candidate James M. Cox bought it and the Atlanta *Georgian*, merging the two staffs, which appreciably increased the *Journal*'s size.

Although the *Journal* has not enjoyed the renown of its older rival, it has enjoyed its own triumphs. For example, *Journal* reporter George Godwin won a Pulitzer Prize for his exposure of fraud in the 1946 state elections. In 1950, the *Journal* merged with the *Constitution* into Atlanta Newspapers, Inc. It continues to be published separately each afternoon, except Sunday.

See L. T. Griffith and J. E. Talmadge, *Georgia Journalism* (1951); and D. Grantham, *Hoke Smith* (1958). Microfilm is available from Microfilm Corporation of America.

JOSEPH A. TOMBERLIN
Valdosta State College

ATLANTA RACE RIOT. On Saturday, September 22, 1906, mounting racial tensions in Atlanta, Ga., erupted into violence. That afternoon, Atlanta newspapers circulated extra editions that carried headlines about assaults by Negro men on white women. That night crowds of people, gathered in the Five Points intersection at the center of the city and in the adjacent saloon and entertainment districts, were incited to mob action. On Monday night the main scene of the disturbance moved to Brownsville, a Negro community on the outskirts of Atlanta. Toward the end of the week the violence subsided. According to the report of the relief committee organized to assist victims of the riot, 12 persons were killed (two whites and ten Negroes) and 70 were injured (ten whites and 60 Negroes). The Fulton County Grand Jury placed major responsibility for the riot on the afternoon newspapers, particularly the Atlanta *News*, condemning the sensational manner in which these papers had been reporting and publicizing criminal news. Other events had also intensified racial antagonisms in the city. In the state Democratic primary on August 22, 1906, HOKE SMITH had won the gubernatorial nomination after a long and bitterly fought campaign, in which the candidates had appealed to racial prejudices. In the fall of 1905, the play *The Clansman* had attracted large audiences in Atlanta. This drama was based on THOMAS DIXON's novel of the same name, published earlier that year. The Atlanta riot, in the extent of its destruction of life and property and its disruption of the life of the city, was one of the most serious disturbances of its kind in the South during the first decade of the twentieth century.

See C. Crowe, *Journal of Negro History* (April, 1969; July, 1968); W. G. Cooper, *Official History of Fulton County* (1934); R. S. Baker, *Following the Color Line* (1908); T. Gibson, *Harper's Weekly* (Oct. 13, 1906); and J. M. Barber, *Voice* (Nov., 1906).

PENELOPE L. BULLOCK
Atlanta University

ATLANTA UNIVERSITY (Atlanta, Ga. 30314). Founded in 1865 and chartered in 1867 to provide black youths with a "liberal and Christian education," this privately supported institution opened in 1869, offering primarily grammar school and some high school instruction. It graduated its first normal school class in 1873 and its first college class in 1876. Between 1894 and 1928, however, Atlanta phased out all of its precollege levels of instruction. Since 1930 it has been exclusively a graduate and professional college affiliated with four other black institutions in Atlanta: Clark College (Methodist, 1869); Morehouse College (Baptist, 1867); Morris Brown College (AME, 1881); and Spelman College (1881). Atlanta University's library holdings include especially notable collections on slavery (Slaughter Collection), twentieth-century Atlanta (Towns Collection), and Negro history. Among the latter group are the manuscripts of John Brown (1826–1859); the papers of the SOUTHERN REGIONAL COUNCIL; the records of the COMMISSION ON INTERRACIAL COOPERATION; the records of the ASSOCIATION OF SOUTHERN WOMEN FOR THE PREVENTION OF LYNCHING; and the files of the SOUTHERN CONFERENCE FOR HUMAN WELFARE.

See C. A. Bacote, *History of Atlanta University* (1969).

AUBURN UNIVERSITY (Auburn, Ala. 36830) was chartered in 1856 by the Methodist church and opened in 1859 as East Alabama Male College. The Civil War forced a suspension of classes, and the Methodists' postwar financial problems caused them to turn the college over to the state of Alabama in 1872. The college became coeducational in 1892. In 1899 the legislature changed the name to Alabama Polytechnic Institute and in 1960 to Auburn University. Traditionally strong programs in engineering and technical subjects have been augmented by growing support for the humanities and social sciences. Of especial interest to historians are the library's holdings of the manuscripts of WILLIAM L. YANCEY and the records of the Atomic Energy Commission.

AUDUBON, JOHN JAMES (1785–1851), born in Haiti, arrived in America in 1804 and settled near Philadelphia. Between 1805 and 1806 he studied painting with Jacques Louis David in Paris. Back in America (1807), Audubon ran a dry goods store in Louisville, Ky., but went bankrupt. Moving to New Orleans, he opened a portrait studio and gave drawing lessons. Unable to obtain subscribers to have his 400 watercolor and pastel drawings of birds engraved, he set sail in 1824 for England and succeeded in having the folio *Birds of America* (1827–1838) published. The work was later supplemented by the *Ornithological Biography* (1831–1839), written by Audubon and the naturalist William MacGillivray. In 1834 Audubon began work on *Viviparous Quadrupeds of North America*, which was completed in 1854 by his sons John, Jr., and Victor. The final years of his life were passed in seclusion in northern Manhattan on the Hudson River.

A recorder of feather, claw, and fur, Audubon preserved for future generations studies of birds and animals, some of which are extinct today. His manner in rendering scientific data and capturing the species' physical animation reveals his importance as a contributor to wildlife resources and American art.

See M. R. Audubon, *Audubon and His Journals* (1960), most definitive; A. Ford, *Audubon's Animals* (1951), and *John James Audubon* (1964), best; D. C. A. Peattie, *Audubon's America* (1940); R. H. Pough, *Audubon Land Bird Guide* (1949); *M. & M. Karolik Collection of American Water Colors and Drawings, 1800–1875* (1962), I,II, well documented; R. P. Warren, *Audubon* (1969); and D. A. Shelly, *Magazine of Art* (May, 1946), good observations.

GEORGE M. COHEN
Hofstra University

AUGUSTA, CONGRESS OF, was a conference held at Augusta, Ga., November 5–10, 1763, to iron out problems of Indian-white relations in the southern colonies following the French and Indian War. Some 700 CATAWBA, CHEROKEE, CHICKASAW, CHOCTAW, and CREEK Indians attended. Their leaders, including Attakullakulla of the Cherokee, conferred with Governors James Wright of Georgia, Thomas Boone of South Carolina, Arthur Dobbs of North Carolina, and Francis Fauquier of Virginia and John Stuart, superintendent of Indian affairs for the Southern District. On November 10, all parties agreed to a treaty providing for perpetual peace, good trade relations, and mutual justice. The Creek Indians accepted a readjustment of the line of white settlement in Georgia, making available nearly 2.5 million additional acres for pioneer expansion, a significant factor in the future growth of that colony.

See *Journal of the Congress at Augusta, 1763* (1764), Evans No. 9706; W. Clark (ed.), *State Records of North Carolina* (1895), XI; and W. C. Sturtevant (ed.), *Handbook of North American Indians* (1976).

DOUGLAS EDWARD LEACH
Vanderbilt University

AUGUSTA, GA. (pop. 59,864), was laid out as a trading post in 1735 by JAMES OGLETHORPE. Located at the FALL LINE on the Savannah River, the town flourished as a center of the colonial FUR TRADE. By 1745, it had five warehouses but until 1751 no schools and no churches. During the American Revolution, control of the town shifted numerous times until finally taken on June 5, 1781, and held by ANDREW PICKENS and LIGHT-HORSE HARRY LEE. The war left Augusta ravaged and destitute, but the location here of the state's temporary capital (1786–1796) and the introduction into the area of TOBACCO culture rejuvenated the town's economy. Besides being a major market for tobacco and cotton, antebellum Augusta was the site of a U.S. Army arsenal (1819) and a terminus of the Georgia Railroad (1837), a canal (1845), and a plank road (1850).

The city's central location and excellent transportation facilities made it ideal for a Confederate powder works, which at peak operation produced 75,000 cartridges a day. In the summer of 1864, after the fall of Atlanta, Confederate leaders expected an attack on the city by General William T. Sherman. The arsenal was fortified and cotton stores were readied for burning, but Union forces bypassed Augusta, sparing the city from certain destruction and preserving for posterity many old Roman and Greek Revival homes. The rapid growth during the 1870s and 1880s of the town's industries, especially the TEXTILE INDUSTRY, cemented Augusta's position as the principal economic center for the 18 counties of the central Savannah River area in Georgia and South Carolina.

See F. F. Corley, *Confederate City* (1960); M. G. Cumming, *Two Centuries of Augusta* (1926); Federal Writers' Project, *Augusta* (1941); F. Fleming, *Autobiography of Colony* (1957), first 50 years; R. H. H. German, *Queen City of Savannah, 1890–1917* (1971); C. C. Jones and S. Dutcher, *Memorial History of Augusta* (1890, 1966); A. R. Walden, "History of Richmond County" (1946 manuscript in public library); and files of Augusta *Chronicle* (1783–) and Augusta *Herald* (1890–). Richmond County Historical Society maintains a collection of local history materials.

AUGUSTA, TREATY OF, or New Purchase of June 3, 1773, followed pressure by white traders regarding debts of the CHEROKEE and CREEK Indians. After cessions in 1763 and 1768 John Stuart, southern superintendent of Indian affairs, feared borders would not be maintained as Governor James Wright of Georgia, lacking respect for lines he had helped to draw, authorized settlement 40 miles beyond the limit. Private persons sought grants, and the Cherokee ceded areas claimed by Creeks. To regularize the illegal private transfers and to appease the Creeks, Stuart arranged the 1773 treaty with lands going to the crown and payments being made to the traders from sales. Over

2.1 million acres were ceded along the Altamaha, Ogeechee, and Savannah rivers but more Creek land was coveted. When incidents soon occurred, General Frederick Haldimand did not respond to Wright's pleas for troops. Creek leaders, harassed by CHOCTAWS, accepted the peace Stuart arranged in October, 1774, at Savannah. Debt payment, characterized by chicanery from its inception, long remained disputed for British and American traders; heirs of George Galphin finally received substantial payment from the United States Congress in 1850 (GALPHIN CLAIM).

See J. R. Alden, *John Stuart* (1944), details for 1754–1775; C. C. Jones, *Georgia* (1883), treaty text; W. Bartram, *Travels* (1791), naturalist on boundary survey; L. DeVorsey, *Indian Boundary* (1961), maps; R. S. Cotterill, *Southern Indians* (1954); and D. H. Corkran, *Creek Frontier* (1967).

ELIZABETH C. DURAN
Niagara University

AUGUSTA CHRONICLE, in publication in Augusta, Ga., since 1785, has absorbed during its career several of its competitors including the *Georgia Gazette* (1786–1789), the *States-Rights Sentinel* (1834–1836), and the Augusta *Constitutionalist* (1823–1877). A Whig paper in its editorial viewpoint, the *Chronicle* opposed extreme states' rights positions. During the 1850s, after the demise of the Whig party, it supported the KNOW-NOTHING PARTY, chastised southern FIRE-EATERS, and blamed much of the agitation over slavery on such northern "demagogues" as Stephen A. Douglas. It supported the candidacy of JOHN BELL and the CONSTITUTIONAL UNION PARTY ticket in the election of 1860 as the best possible hope for avoiding disunion. Continuing its tradition of moderate conservatism, the *Chronicle* regularly criticized both the FARMERS' ALLIANCE and the POPULIST PARTY. Its reputation as a regional oracle has declined markedly since the Civil War as the political, intellectual, and population center of Georgia has shifted away from Augusta. Presently it is an independent Democratic paper with a daily circulation of over 50,000 copies.

See E. L. Bell and K. C. Crabbe, *Augusta Chronicle, 1785–1960* (1960); bound copies at libraries of Duke, Georgia, Georgia Southern, Atlanta, Yale, Rice, and Texas universities and at Library of Congress; and microfilm from Bell & Howell.

AUSTIN, MOSES (1761–1821), was born in Durham, Conn. In the mercantile business in Philadelphia, he there married Maria Brown before moving to Richmond, Va., and then to Wythe County, Va., where his company owned several lead mines. In 1796–1797 he explored upper Louisiana (Missouri), obtained a grant of land, and the next year moved his family to Missouri to operate Mine A. Burton. When the Bank of St. Louis, of which he was a stockholder, failed in 1818, he conceived the idea of settling a colony in Texas. In the fall of 1820 he went to Bexar (San Antonio) to get permission for the colony from the Spanish governor, Antonio Martinez. At first Martinez refused his request and ordered him to leave, but Austin met an old friend, Baron de Bastrop, who interceded for him, and his request was forwarded to Mexican officials in Monterrey. This request to settle 300 Americans in Texas was finally authorized. On the return journey Austin was taken ill with a fever and died after making his way back to Missouri. The task of actually beginning the American settlement in Texas was thus left to his son, STEPHEN F. AUSTIN.

See G. P. Garrison (ed.), *American Historical Review* (April, 1900); E. C. Barker, *Life of Stephen F. Austin* (1925); and Austin Papers, University of Texas Archives and Texas State Archives, Austin.

THOMAS LLOYD MILLER
Texas A. & M. University

AUSTIN, STEPHEN FULLER (1793–1836). Eldest son of Maria Brown and MOSES AUSTIN, he was born in Virginia, reared in Missouri, and educated in Connecticut and Kentucky. He joined his father in a lead-mining venture and served in the Missouri territorial legislature, 1814–1820. Upon Moses' death (1821), Austin took control of his father's contract to colonize 300 Anglo-American families in Mexican Texas. He began the settlement, then journeyed to Mexico City to obtain final approval of the contract. He strongly influenced the Imperial Colonization Law of 1823 and received the sole empresario contract granted under it. This was the only empresario contract in Texas to be fulfilled completely. Until 1828 Austin was personally responsible for the good conduct, government, and land system of the colonists in his four grants. His success as empresario rested on his patience and ability to mediate between American settlers and Mexican officials.

Setting an example of loyalty to Mexico, Austin remained aloof from Mexican politics until he presided over the convention in 1832 that protested the antiimmigration provisions of the Mexican law of April 6, 1830, and sought separate Mexican statehood for Texas. The 1833 convention reaffirmed the protests and drafted a constitution. Although Austin opposed the actions, he was delegated to present the petitions to the Mexican government. He obtained repeal of the law but not separation. In despair he wrote a letter recommending that Texas establish itself as a separate state, which led to his arrest in 1834 and an 18-month confinement. He returned to Texas in 1835, advocating revolutionary separation from Mexico.

In October, 1835, after war began, he was elected commander-in-chief of the army. The provisional government, organized soon afterward, sent him to the United States seeking aid. Defeated for the presidency of the Republic of Texas, Austin was named secretary of state but died two months later.

See E. C. Barker, *Life of Stephen F. Austin* (1925), best but dated; E. C. Barker (ed.), *Austin Papers* (3 vols.; 1924–28); and Austin Papers, University of Texas Archives.

DAVID B. GRACY II
Georgia State University

AUSTIN, TEX. (pop. 251,808), is the state's capital and a major commercial and educational center astride the Colorado River. First settled and laid out in 1838 as the town of Waterloo, it became the new capital of the Republic of Texas in 1839 and was renamed in honor of STEPHEN AUSTIN. Although it was chosen in part because its elevation kept it free of coastal fevers, Indian attacks hampered construction and necessitated erection of a stockade around the Hall of Congress. Continuing harassment by the Indians and fears of a Mexican attack caused SAM HOUSTON to move the capital in 1842 to WASHINGTON-ON-THE-BRAZOS. The residents of Austin, being anxious to ensure the eventual return of the capital, refused to surrender the government's archival records. In 1845, Austin again became the seat of Texas government, a location made permanent by act of the legislature in 1872. The uncertainties of the Civil War and Reconstruction stymied growth of the town in the 1860s. During the following decade, however, traffic on the nearby Chisholm Trail and construction of two railroads caused the population to jump from 4,428 to over 11,000. The opening of the UNIVERSITY OF TEXAS (1883) and the damming of the Colorado River in the 1880s furthered the city's growth and helped establish the modern character of present-day Austin.

See W. P. Webb (ed.), *Handbook of Texas* (1952). In addition to materials in the Lyndon Baines Johnson and University of Texas libraries, Austin Public Library maintains the Austin–Travis County Collection of yearbooks, maps, scrapbooks, journals, taped interviews, and manuscripts (75,000 items) relating to local history.

AUTTOSE, BATTLE OF. During the CREEK WAR at dawn on November 29, 1813, 950 Georgia militiamen under Brigadier General John Floyd, aided by several hundred friendly Indians, attacked two Creek towns on the Tallapoosa River. The Creeks were overwhelmed by a ruthless American attack, the towns were burned, and Floyd estimated Indian losses at 200 killed. The Americans had 11 killed and 54 wounded, and the friendly Indians also suffered several casualties.

See H. S. Halbert and T. H. Ball, *Creek War* (1895); J. Brannan, *Official Letters* (1823); and B. J. Lossing, *Pictorial Field Book of War of 1812* (1868).

REGINALD HORSMAN
University of Wisconsin, Milwaukee

AVERY'S TRACE, authorized by the North Carolina legislature in 1787, was one of several routes from the backcountry of that state that opened Tennessee to settlement in the late eighteenth century. It began near the site of Knoxville at the southern end of Clinch Mountain and passed through the Cumberland Mountains at Emory's Gap to the so-called Cumberland Settlement on the route to Nashville. The road, wide enough for wagons, was financed by local taxes. It was marked out by Peter Avery, a hunter familiar with the area, and was cut from the wilderness by the North Carolina militia in 1788. A dispute with the CHEROKEE INDIANS, however, restricted traffic on the road and made military escorts of emigrants essential. The controversy was not satisfactorily resolved until the Tennessee legislature obtained authorization from the federal government to mark out a new road in 1795. Walton Road, as it was known, intersected and followed sections of Avery's Trace; since the new route provided a more direct way to Nashville, it lessened the importance of the earlier road.

See W. E. M'Elwee, *American Historical Magazine* (1903); and laws of North Carolina (1787).

RICHARD T. FARRELL
University of Maryland

AYCOCK, CHARLES BRANTLEY (1859–1912), was born in Wayne County, N.C., as the last of ten children in a slave-owning family of the black belt. With financial assistance from an uncle, he was educated in private academies and was graduated from the University of North Carolina (B.A., 1880). After being admitted to the state bar in 1881, he practiced law in Goldsboro and worked as a popular and effective orator in behalf of local Democratic candidates. He was a partisan, laissez faire Democrat, an ardent defender of white supremacy, and an advocate of improved public education. While state Democrats were losing elections to the fusion slates of Republican and Populist candidates, Aycock served the second Grover Cleveland administration as U.S. district attorney for eastern North Carolina. In 1898, however, he collaborated with FURNIFOLD SIMMONS and JOSEPHUS DANIELS in an inflammatory and racist campaign in defense of white supremacy, which returned the Democrats to control of the state legislature. A disfranchisement amendment to the state constitution followed the Democratic victory, but so did Aycock's renewal of his campaign for universal public education. During his term as governor (1901–1905), increased revenues from corporation property taxes were used to establish 877 libraries, to build schools (599 white schools and 91 black schools were constructed in 1903–1904), and to raise school enrollments (from 61.5 percent of white school-age children to 72.4 percent, and from 49.6 percent to 61 percent of black school-age children).

See O. H. Orr, Jr., *C. B. Aycock* (1961); and L. R. Harlan, *Separate and Unequal* (1958).

AYUBALE, BATTLE OF. Ayubale, or Ayaville, was one of several APALACHEE INDIAN villages in northern Florida served by the Franciscans. Spanish policy aimed to protect Florida from English expansion from the north. In the fall of 1702 the English under Governor James Moore of South Carolina failed to capture St. Augustine and St. Mark's. Undaunted, the governor got some 50 Carolinians and 1,500 YAMASSEE INDIANS to support another invasion. Late in 1703 this army brought terror and destruction to Apalachee country. On January 14, 1704, they attacked Ayubale and met stout resistance from the Apalachee, who repulsed the invaders twice. The defenders, near exhaustion and with no arrows or powder, sought a truce. Their spokesman, Friar Angel de Miranda, appealed to the mercy of Moore. There was no mercy. The Yamassee murdered the friar, destroyed Ayubale, and tortured and killed the Apalachee.

See J. R. Swanton, *Bureau of American Ethnology Bulletin* (1922); V. W. Crane, *Southern Frontier* (1929); and J. J. Tepaske, *Spanish Florida* (1964).

RUSSELL S. NELSON, JR.
University of Wisconsin, Stevens Point

AZILIA, MARGRAVATE OF. To provide a buffer zone against the Spanish for the southern boundary of the colony of South Carolina, Sir Robert Montgomery in 1717 secured a grant from the proprietors to establish what he envisioned to be a utopia between the Altamaha and Savannah rivers. It was to be known as the Margravate of Azilia, with himself as the first marquis of Azilia enthroned in his palace behind his battlements. With cultivation by white labor only, there would be a rich harvest of coffee, tea, rice, fruits, and nuts. Fear of the Spanish by potential colonists apparently doomed the scheme.

See J. A. Caruso, *Southern Frontier* (1963).

B

BACON, AUGUSTUS OCTAVIUS (1839–1914), was born in Bryan County, Ga. He received an A.B. degree from the University of Georgia in 1859 and briefly practiced law in Atlanta before entering Confederate service as a junior officer. After the war Bacon settled in Macon and served in various political positions, including 14 years in the state legislature. In 1894 he was elected to the U.S. Senate and served there until his death. He was deeply involved in the debates on the Dingley and Payne-Aldrich tariff bills and was an ardent antiimperialist. In 1899 he sponsored an amendment to the treaty with Spain whereby the Philippine Islands would be guaranteed their future independence; the Bacon amendment was defeated by the vote of Vice-President Garret A. Hobart. Bacon served as president pro tem of the Senate and chairman of the Foreign Relations Committee. He enjoyed foreign travel and was a trustee of the University of Georgia and a regent for the Smithsonian Institution.

See L. C. Steelman, "A. O. Bacon" (Ph.D. dissertation, University of North Carolina, 1950); Bacon Papers, University of North Carolina; J. T. Boifeuillet, *Georgia Historical Quarterly* (June, 1921); R. L. Jones, *Georgia Historical Quarterly* (Sept., 1930); and D. W. Grantham, *Hoke Smith* (1958).

C. CHARLTON MOSELEY
Georgia Southern College

BACON'S REBELLION (1676) was an uprising led by Nathaniel Bacon against the royal government of Virginia. Bacon, an impetuous young planter who had arrived in the colony two years earlier, assumed leadership of Virginians dissatisfied with the administration of Governor William Berkeley, who had served in Virginia since 1641. The governor had developed a tightly knit political organization; however, the colony's population became more diverse, and other elements also demanded recognition of their political, economic, and social ambitions. The recently enacted Navigation Acts and large grants of land made by the king to his friends complicated economic activity, and some planters charged they deepened the widening chasm between the rich and the poor. Adding to the prevalent unrest was the increasingly hostile activity of nearby Indians. Governor Berkeley, possibly torn between those wanting to maintain friendly relations with the Indians partially in order to trade with them and those eager to attack partially in order to obtain their lands, failed to take effective action.

Nathaniel Bacon seized the initiative and in May, 1676, began popular but unauthorized punitive expeditions against the Indians. The governor recognized Bacon's activity as a challenge to his own authority and, after attempts at reconciliation collapsed, declared Bacon a rebel. When Bacon learned that the governor was trying to organize a military force against him, he drove the governor from the capital at JAMESTOWN across Chesapeake Bay to Virginia's Eastern Shore. Bacon then returned to the interior to fight Indians. Governor Berkeley subsequently returned to the mainland to take control of the capital. Again, in September, Bacon interrupted his campaign against the Indians to deal with Berkeley and this time burned the capital. While the majority of the colonists assumed a neutral stance, forces of "the governor and the rebel" contended for control of the colony. Their strife ended when Bacon's sudden death in October rendered ineffective the forces he had led and unnecessary the warship, troops, and commission that arrived late in 1676 to suppress the uprising. Because the governor quickly executed many of Bacon's followers, he was recalled to England by the king, where he died July 9, 1677.

This crisis did not lead directly to any profound, long-range changes in Virginia. Its significance lies more in what it reveals about the internal and external problems facing this English colony. Although Bacon's Rebellion offered a propitious opportunity for attempts at solution, the moment passed unrecognized.

See W. F. Craven, *Southern Colonies* (1949), balanced; W. E. Washburn, *Bacon's Rebellion* (1957), favorable to Berkeley, and *National Museum Bulletin*, No. 225 (1963), informative on results; T. J. Wertenbaker, *Bacon's Rebellion* (1940), favorable to Bacon; R. Middlehauf, *Bacon's Rebellion* (1964), with excerpts from primary sources; C. M. Andrews, *Insurrections* (1915), with several important primary sources in entirety; and E. G. Swem, *Virginia Historical Index* (1934–36), with references to other materials.

JOHN B. FRANTZ
Pennsylvania State University

BAILEY, ANNE (1742–1825), was a messenger and scout on the Virginia frontier. Born in England, she married Richard Trotter of near Staunton four years after her arrival in 1761. The trauma of Trotter's death at POINT PLEASANT in 1774 apparently caused her to assume a role on the frontier usually reserved for men. Her marriage in 1785 to John Bailey, a frontier commandant, thrust her into the settler-Indian conflict in the Kanawha Valley. Many settlers owed their lives to this tobacco-chewing woman in man's attire who rode to warn them of approaching danger. Subject to dispute is the claim that she saved the occupants of Ft. Lee, the present Charleston, by riding alone to Lewisburg to procure vital ammunition. She spent her last years in Gallipolis, Ohio.

See R. B. Cook, *West Virginia Review* (July, 1934); V. A. Lewis, *Bailey* (1891); M. P. Shawkey, *West Virginia* (1928); and R. W. Dayton, *Pioneers* (1947).

EDWARD L. HENSON, JR.
Clinch Valley College

BAILEY, JOSEPH WELDON (1863–1929), was born in Crystal Springs, Miss. He attended five universities without ever graduating. Admitted to the bar, he began practicing law in Hazlehurst, Miss. After the presidential ELECTION OF 1884, he was implicated by a U.S. Senate investigation in the leadership of a group that, through murder and intimidation, ensured a Democratic victory in Copiah County. Shortly thereafter in 1885, Bailey moved to Gainesville, Tex. In 1890 he was elected to Congress, and in 1897 he was elected minority leader of the Democratic party. In the 1900 senatorial primary, charges were made that Bailey illegally represented Waters Pierce Oil Company, expelled from Texas for violating the antitrust laws because of its connection with the Standard Oil trust. After an investigation, the legislature elected him to the U.S. Senate. Early promise as a potential leader of the Democrats in the Senate was dissipated in 1902, when after a heated debate he physically assaulted Senator Albert Beveridge. In 1906, his reelection secured, new evidence emerged that Bailey had served Waters Pierce and other companies as their attorney. The legislature exonerated him by electing him to the Senate and then conducting another investigation. Facing a stern challenge in the 1912 election, Bailey resigned from the Senate and established a lucrative law practice in Washington, D.C. (1913–1920), and later in Dallas (1920–1929).

See J. W. Bailey Papers, Dallas Historical Society; *Proceedings and Reports of Bailey Investigation Committee* (1907); S. H. Acheson, *Joe Bailey* (1932); and B. C. Holcomb, "Joe Bailey" (Ph.D. dissertation, Texas Tech, 1968).

BOB C. HOLCOMB
Angelo State University

BAILEY, JOSIAH WILLIAM (1873–1946), was born in Warrenton, N.C. As a progressive leader in North Carolina between 1893 and 1931, he fought for direct state aid for public education, for measures facilitating direct democracy, for reform of revenue and taxation systems, for local and state options on prohibition, for reduction of taxes on farmers and small homeowners, and for public ownership of utilities. Yet as U.S. senator (1931–1946) he fought against NEW DEAL programs that he believed would give special privileges to special interests, violate trusted constitutional principles, encourage unsound financial and economic practices, and tend toward centralization of power and collectivistic regimentation. His preference for local and state rule instead of federal rule prevailed until he was confronted with the exigencies of the Second World War. Then he accepted an authoritarianism that would have been unthinkable in peacetime. Bailey brought to consideration of state and national problems an eighteenth- and nineteenth-century liberal theory of economics and politics that served well during the prosperous first three decades of the twentieth century but that limited his vision and response during the successive crises of the Great Depression and the Second World War.

See J. R. Moore, *Senator J. W. Bailey* (1968); and J. W. Bailey Papers, Duke University Library.

JOHN R. MOORE
University of Southwestern Louisiana

BAILEY, THOMAS PEARCE (1868–1949), a psychologist and educator, was born in Georgetown, S.C. He graduated from South Carolina College in 1887 and received his M.A. degree in 1889 and his Ph.D. degree in 1891 from the University of South Carolina. He served on the faculties of the universities of South Carolina, California, Chicago, and Mississippi and at the University of the South. In addition he was superintendent of public schools in Memphis in 1909–1910 and dean of All Saints' Episcopal College in Vicksburg. He accepted an appointment as professor of philosophy, psychology, and ethnology at Rollins College in 1926 and retired in 1938. His publications were generally on educational topics, but his major work was *Race Orthodoxy in the South and Other Aspects of the Negro Question* (1914). It argued that "the real problem is not the Negro but the white man's attitude toward the negro," a rather advanced opinion for its time. He also served as consulting psychologist at the Mississippi State Hospital for the Insane.

See New York *Times* (Feb. 9, 1949).

DONALD K. PICKENS
North Texas State University

BAILEY V. ALABAMA (219 U.S. 219 [1911]) tested an Alabama contract labor law (Alabama Code, 1886, Sec. 3812) that forced agricultural laborers into PEONAGE. Alonzo Bailey, a black agricultural worker, had taken an advance in wages to work for a year, but after just over a month's labor he left and was arrested for "false pretenses." Several Alabama jurists, including William H. Thomas and THOMAS G. JONES, seized the opportunity to test the law and got secret support from BOOKER T. WASHINGTON and from northern liberals. The case was actually handled by lawyers Edward Watts and Fred Ball. After appeals through the state courts, the U.S. Supreme Court ruled that the case was brought before the Court "prematurely" and sent it back for jury trial. According to the Alabama law, Bailey's leaving his job was prima facie evidence of his intent to defraud, and another law prohibited him from testifying in his own behalf. The lower courts held Bailey guilty, and his sponsors, including the U.S. Justice Department, appealed the case again. In 1911 the U.S. Supreme Court ruled that the Alabama law was an unconstitutional violation of the THIRTEENTH AMENDMENT. Other southern states enforced similar contract labor laws until the 1940s, however, when the U.S. Supreme Court finally struck them down.

See P. Daniel, *Shadow of Slavery* (1972).

PETE DANIEL
University of Tennessee, Knoxville

BAKER'S CREEK, BATTLE OF. See CHAMPION HILL, BATTLE OF

BAKER V. CARR (369 U.S. 186 [1962]), a decision of the U.S. Supreme Court, established the jurisdiction of the federal courts to entertain suits challenging state legislative apportionment systems. The case was initiated by a coalition of individuals and groups in Tennessee to challenge the apportionment of seats in the state legislature, unchanged since 1901. Such legislative malapportionment, it was alleged, denied the equal right to vote in violation of the equal protection clause of the FOURTEENTH AMENDMENT. In reversing the district court's dismissal of the case as raising a political or nonjusticiable issue, the Supreme Court held that suits challenging apportionment systems were justiciable and that the federal courts had jurisdiction. The result of this holding was a flood of litigation challenging the apportionment systems in almost every southern state.

The Supreme Court did not indicate in *Baker* v. *Carr* what standard was applicable to state legislative apportionment systems. In *Reynolds* v. *Sims* (1964), however, a case challenging the Alabama apportionment system, the Court held that both houses of a state legislature must be apportioned substantially upon the basis of population. As a result a "reapportionment revolution" occurred, in which the legislatures of all but one of the southern states were reapportioned. The precedent established in *Baker* v. *Carr* also led to the invalidation of the Georgia COUNTY UNIT SYSTEM in *Gray* v. *Sanders* (1963). And in another Georgia case, *Wesberry* v. *Sanders* (1964), the Supreme Court held that congressional districts were required to be as nearly as practicable equal in population. The ultimate result of *Baker* v. *Carr* was, therefore, a significant shift of political power to metropolitan areas in both state legislatures and the Congress.

See R. B. McKay, *Reapportionment* (1965); R. C. Cortner, *Apportionment Cases* (1970); G. Schubert, *Reapportionment* (1965); A. Hacker, *Congressional Districting* (1964); G. E. Baker, *Rural Versus Urban Political Power* (1963); P. T. David and R. Eisenberg, *Devaluation of the Urban and Suburban Vote* (1961–62), with analysis of situation prior to *Baker* v. *Carr*; W. D. Boyd and R. C. Silva, *Selected Bibliography on Legislative Apportionment and Districting* (1963); and Library of Congress Legislative Reference Service, *Congressional Districting and Legislative Apportionment* (1965).

RICHARD C. CORTNER
University of Arizona

BALDWIN, ABRAHAM (1754–1807), was born in North Guilford, Conn., and received his education at Yale. He moved to Georgia in 1783 with the encouragement of Governor LYMAN HALL to devise an educational system for the state. In 1785 he drafted a charter for public-supported academies and a university. Delayed in implementing his plans for a college by frontier conditions, he accepted appointment to the CONSTITUTIONAL CONVENTION, where he purposely split Georgia's vote on the representation issue to permit the Connecticut Compromise. He served in the Congress of the confederation (1785) and later in the U.S. House (1790–1799) and Senate (1799–1807) as a moderate Jeffersonian. At the same time, he prepared a curriculum for the University of Georgia, which began classes in 1801. He died in Washington, D.C., after attending the Ninth Congress. Baldwin never married, never accumulated a vast fortune, and left only meager private papers. His fame lies in the university and in the Constitution.

See H. C. White, *Abraham Baldwin* (1926); E. M. Coulter, *College Life* (1928); R. P. Brooks, *University of Georgia* (1956); and Savannah *Ledger* (March, 1807).

W. CALVIN SMITH
University of South Carolina, Aiken

BALDWIN, JOSEPH GLOVER (1815–1864). Remembered as author of *The Flush Times of Alabama and Mississippi* (1853), a collection of humorous essays, Baldwin also wrote *Party Leaders* (1855), sketches of Thomas Jefferson, John Randolph, Andrew Jackson, Henry Clay, and others, and the incomplete, posthumously published *Flush Times of California*. He savored and ridiculed the ignorance, incompetence, greed, speculative fever, and high spirits of the old southwestern frontier. He expressed his Whiggish, gentlemanly perspective in a mannered style, employing foreign phrases, abundant literary allusions, and complicated sentences. Born near Winchester, Va., educated at Staunton Academy, he was a licensed attorney at twenty-one. After migrating to De Kalb, Miss., and then to Gainesville, Ala., he was elected to the Alabama house of representatives in 1843, served as a Whig delegate to the national convention in 1848, but was defeated by his Democratic opponent in his bid for Congress. Nineteen of his sketches were published in the SOUTHERN LITERARY MESSENGER in the early 1850s. In 1854 he migrated to San Francisco, where he practiced law, became a Democrat, and was elected associate justice of the state supreme court in 1858.

See R. E. Amacher and G. W. Polhemus (eds.), "Biographical Sketch," in J. G. Baldwin, *Flush Times of California* (1966); W. Blair, *Native American Humor* (1960); and N. W. Yates, "Joseph Glover Baldwin," in L. D. Rubin (ed.), *Bibliographical Guide* (1969).

MILTON RICKELS
University of Southwestern Louisiana

BALL, WILLIAM WATTS (1868–1952), was born in Laurens County, S.C., educated at South Carolina College (A.B., 1887; LL.D., 1889), and was admitted to the South Carolina bar in 1890. He

became a newspaperman, however, first as editor of the *Laurens Advertizer* and then of four principal newspapers in South Carolina, as well as a reporter for the Philadelphia *Press* and city editor of the *Florida Times-Union*. Ball was editor of the Columbia (S.C.) *State* (1913–1923), the first dean of the journalism school at the University of South Carolina (1923–1927), and editor of the CHARLESTON NEWS AND COURIER (1927–1951). His editorial policy was the crusading type, and he believed in daily repetition to hammer his point into the consciousness of his readers. He strongly favored the protection of states' rights, opposed the policies of the NEW DEAL, and maintained that the problems of the state could only be solved through government by the "enlightened." He believed the doctrine of equality to be a fallacy because of differences in background, intelligence, and education.

See H. R. Sass, *150 Years of News and Courier* (1953); J. D. Stark, *William W. Ball* (1969); and T. R. Waring, Jr., *Editor and Publisher* (Nov. 29, 1930).

FRANK LOGAN
Wofford College

BALL'S BLUFF, BATTLE OF (October 21, 1861). In a reconnaissance toward Leesburg, Union forces under Brigadier General Charles P. Stone crossed the Potomac River at Edward's Ferry and Ball's Bluff, Va. At the latter, Colonel Edward D. Baker's brigade crossed and met Confederate troops of Colonel Nathan G. ("Shanks") Evans' command. Each force numbered about 1,700. Baker was driven back to the steep wooded bluff, where the recrossing of the swollen river was disastrous. The poorly managed operation, of little strategic importance, cost the federals 921 casualties, many of them drowned. Baker was killed, and Stone's military reputation was seriously marred. Confederate losses were 155. Evans won a vote of thanks from the Confederate Congress and a gold medal from South Carolina.

See J. D. Patch, *Ball's Bluff* (1958); R. W. Hunter, *Southern Historical Society Papers* (1906); J. G. D. Hamilton, *Papers of Randolph A. Shotwell* (1929), I; E. Hunton, *Autobiography* (1933); and G. E. Govan and J. W. Livingood, *Haskell Memoirs* (1960).

LEE A. WALLACE, JR.
National Park Service

BALTIMORE, BATTLE OF (September 12–14, 1814), was marked by an ineffectual bombardment of Ft. McHenry by the British fleet, a standoff engagement at North Point between Baltimore militiamen and twice their number of British veterans, and the repulse of a night amphibious assault on the fort. In the latter two engagements, British casualties were heavy. Historians generally are aware that FRANCIS SCOTT KEY, an observer of the bombardment of Ft. McHenry, wrote the "Star-Spangled Banner," but seem oblivious to the importance of the battle to the WAR OF 1812. News of the repulse was a deciding factor in causing Britain to ameliorate its unacceptable demands for a peace treaty, resulting in the agreement signed December 24, 1814, at Ghent, Holland, that ended the war.

See N. H. Swanson, *Perilous Fight* (1945), on the battle as a whole; and P. W. Filby and E. G. Howard, *Star-Spangled Books* (1972), for Key and "Star-Spangled Banner." Both list additional references.

HUGH BENET, JR.
Star-Spangled Banner Flag House Association

BALTIMORE, MD. (pop. 905,787), the country's seventh largest city and the South's second largest, began as one of the several TOBACCO ports the colony chartered in 1729. During its early years, Annapolis to the south outdistanced Baltimore's tobacco trade, but by the mid-eighteenth century, local farmers discovered the foreign market for flour as lucrative as that for tobacco. With merchants dominating the city's economic life, the tobacco aristocracy continued to contribute an élan to its social life, which retained a reputation for graciousness, charm, conservatism, and cuisine throughout the nineteenth century. Although still a small town of 6,000 at the time of the Revolutionary War, Baltimore served as temporary seat of the CONTINENTAL CONGRESS after that body fled from Philadelphia to escape British capture.

Emerging as a Revolutionary boomtown, the city extended its trade to Europe, the Caribbean, and the Mediterranean. Many of its citizens became hardy seafarers, and the more thoughtful among them developed the distinctive Baltimore clipper, a sailing vessel of immense sheet and hold, well suited to the bulky wheat and tobacco trade (COMMERCE). In the War of 1812, Baltimore privateers put to sea to harass the British, while defenders of the city at Ft. McHenry repulsed British forces sailing up the Chesapeake after the burning of Washington, D.C., and inspired FRANCIS SCOTT KEY to pen the "Star-Spangled Banner."

After the state legislature granted the city a charter in 1797, businessmen continued to guide the city's growth and expansion, extending its piers, developing its Patapsco River waterfront, and dredging its channel to the Chesapeake Bay. Local businessmen also provided the inspiration and the capital for the formation of the first RAILROAD line in the country, the Baltimore & Ohio, which was to become a dominant force in the city's economic and political history throughout the nineteenth century. Merchants established regular transatlantic ties with Bremen, Germany, and other Hanseatic cities, making foreign trade an important element in the city's economy.

The Civil War divided Baltimoreans as it divided the residents of no other American city. With strong emotional and commercial attachments to the South (BALTIMORE RIOT), Baltimore remained a divided city in a border state throughout the war. After the war, the city recovered from economic paralysis, diversified its economic interests, multiplied "rapid" transit facilities, and greatly expanded its physical borders through the annexation of surrounding territory. Physical aspects of the city—its miles of single-family row houses with their white marble steps—remained largely unchanged throughout the nineteenth century. So, too, did its business life, which remained largely individual and commercial. Its chief business was jobbing; its chief customer, the South.

If not typically southern, the postwar city was Bourbon in its politics, its business, its society, and its mental outlook (BOURBONS). Many of the things for which the city was famous were perhaps not to its advantage, including the ubiquitous cobblestones, the lack of sewers and sanitation, the smoky railroad tunnels, antebellum journalism, horsecars, narrow and crooked streets, a rather shabby business district, ring politics, and political turbulence. A western humorist once referred to Baltimore as that place between New York and Washington where they hitched on the dining car. An 1892 study characterized the city as the "most typical southern business city in the Union."

The major catalyst of change in Baltimore was not the disruptive American Civil War, but the much more destructive great fire of 1904, which leveled most of the central business district and seemingly drew Baltimoreans out of their lethargy over public and civic problems. World War I gave impetus to trade in coal and wheat, and the steel and oil industries changed the economic basis of the city to heavy industry (PETROLEUM; IRON AND STEEL INDUSTRY). During both wars, black and white southern emigrants from Appalachia and from the Deep South poured into the city to man the aircraft assembly lines at the Martin Company, the open hearths of the huge Bethlehem Steel works, and the shipyards.

At the eastern terminus of one of the principal and historic trade routes between the East Coast and the Middle West through the Appalachian mountain passes, Baltimore has remained throughout much of its history one of the busiest ports in America. Throughout its history, too, it has retained much of its small-town and slowly paced character, although, like other American cities, Baltimore is facing the end of the twentieth century with tremendous urban problems and a vital urban renewal program. Baltimoreans continue to follow national trends in a movement to nearby suburban counties (the metropolitan area population is 2,070,670) and in an increasing concentration of nonwhites in the central city (46.4 percent black in the 1970 census). Although never housing a majority of immigrants like many other American cities, Baltimore continues to retain small and tightly knit ethnic neighborhoods.

See H. Owens, *Baltimore on Chesapeake* (1941); J. T. Scharf, *Chronicles of Baltimore* (1874); C. C. Hall, *Baltimore* (1912); J. F. Waescher, *Baltimore Today* (1969); C. Hirshfeld, *Baltimore* (1941); C. C. Rhines, "City and Its Social Problems" (Ph.D. dissertation, University of Maryland, 1975); B. Suska, *Catholic Historical Review* (July, 1925); C. D. Wright, *Slums of Baltimore* (1894); W. T. Howard, *Public Health* (1924); M. Janvier, *Baltimore Yesterdays* (1937); J. B. Crooks, *Politics and Progress* (1968); and M. L. Calcott, *Negro in Maryland* (1969).

CHARLOTTE CANNON RHINES
Essex Community College

BALTIMORE AMERICAN began publication in 1799 as the *American and Daily Advertizer*. It was the first newspaper to publish stenographic copies of congressional debates after the nation's capital was moved to nearby Washington, D.C. Yet another of the paper's firsts was its printing of FRANCIS SCOTT KEY's "Star-Spangled Banner." Vitally interested in commercial news and in the economic development of Baltimore, the *American* became a Whig paper in the 1830s and later identified itself with the policies of the Republican party. During the Civil War it was the city's principal journalistic defender of the Abraham Lincoln administration and its war policies. As a Republican newspaper in a Democratic city and state, the *American* was not especially influential after the Civil War. It did play a role, however, in defeating in 1905 a proposed DISFRANCHISEMENT amendment to the state constitution. In 1964 it was merged with the Baltimore *News* (1872–1964) to form the *News-American*, a paper with a circulation of approximately 22,000 copies daily.

See G. W. Johnson *et al.*, *Sunpapers of Baltimore* (1937); bound copies at Enoch Pratt Free Public Library (1823–1924, 1926–64), Peabody Institute (1821–1928), and Maryland Historical Society, Baltimore (1821–1964); and microfilm from Bell & Howell (1799–1920, 1964–).

BALTIMORE CONVENTION (June 18–23, 1860) followed the Democratic party's failure to nominate at its regular CHARLESTON CONVENTION a presidential candidate acceptable to its northwestern and southern wings. Senator Stephen A. Douglas of Illinois had secured the support of a majority of the Charleston delegates both for his nomination and for a platform reaffirming his doctrine of congressional noninterference with slavery in the western territories. Although his platform was adopted, his nomination was thwarted when most southern delegates bolted the convention.

Thus, the Baltimore Convention met in a spirit of heightened party and sectional rancor that boded ill for the Democratic party and the Union. Since his managers were determined that Douglas would win the nomination, they sought to replace the bolting Charleston delegates with Douglas men. The bolters, guided by Alabama's WILLIAM L. YANCEY, were equally intent on crushing Douglas and fought hard for their readmission before the credentials committee. As a compromise, the committee's majority report recommended that some of the bolting delegates be seated and others be refused. The convention endorsed most of the report. Since it rejected the well-reasoned claims of the key Alabama and Louisiana bolters, Yancey's remaining followers withdrew from the convention. This walkout left less than half of the states originally represented to nominate Douglas and Alabama's BENJAMIN FITZPATRICK (later replaced by HERSCHEL V. JOHNSON of Georgia) for the ticket on a slightly revised platform of congressional noninterference with slavery in the territories.

See W. B. Hesseltine (ed.), *Three Against Lincoln* (1960); A. Nevins, *Emergence of Lincoln* (1950); and R. F. Nichols, *Disruption of Democracy* (1948). Apologetic but useful is R. W. Johannsen, *Stephen A. Douglas* (1973).

PHILIP D. SWENSON
University of Massachusetts, Amherst

BALTIMORE REPUBLICAN was a newspaper published between 1827 and 1863. Despite its title, the paper regularly espoused the candidates and the programs of the Democratic party.

See bound copies at Library of Congress (1827–63).

BALTIMORE RIOT (April 19, 1861) resulted from an attempt by southern sympathizers to deny passage through the city to northern troops en route to Washington, D.C. A train of 35 cars, carrying 2,200 Massachusetts and Pennsylvania troops, arrived at the President Street Station to await the horse teams that would draw the cars, one by one, through the streets to the Camden Street Station of the Baltimore & Ohio Railroad, where they would be reconstituted into a train to carry the men to Washington. One car was attacked by a mob and forced back to the President Street Station. Soldiers from the remaining 25 cars were then ordered to march to the Camden Street Station. Pelted by rocks and paving stones, the soldiers opened fire on the mob, and 12 civilians and four soldiers were killed.

See J. T. Scharf, *Chronicles of Baltimore* (1874); and G. W. Brown, *Baltimore and the 19th of April, 1861* (1887).

DAVID S. SPARKS
University of Maryland, College Park

BALTIMORE SUN was founded in 1837 by A. S. Abell (1806–1888) as a penny tabloid modeled after the New York *Sun*. Both its price and its content were intended to appeal to a mass readership. Although nominally a Democratic paper, the *Sun* throughout most of the nineteenth century ignored national politics and emphasized instead municipal politics, local brawls, and fires. Wars, however, were regarded as exceptionally newsworthy, and the *Sun* first gained a national reputation for its detailed and up-to-date coverage of the Mexican War. Throughout the Civil War its news stories and its editorials reflected a distinctly prosouthern bias.

First breaking from its mold of aloof disdain for partisan politics in the 1880s, the *Sun* became a critic of Maryland's Democratic party machine and of its leader, ARTHUR P. GORMAN. Nationally, the *Sun* endorsed Grover Cleveland and defended the policies of his administrations with great warmth and vigor (CLEVELAND ADMINISTRATIONS). Although the paper endorsed William McKinley in 1896 and William Howard Taft in 1908, it did so without any visible enthusiasm and with the argument that William Jennings Bryan's policies departed from the principles of the Democratic party. Yet not until after the Abell family sold the *Sun* in 1910 to Charles H. Grasty did it become regularly partisan. Grasty edited the paper for only four years, but under him it became a leading supporter of WOODROW WILSON's nomination and election. Also during Grasty's tenure the *Sun* began publishing an afternoon as well as a morning edition. Today, under the ownership of A. S. Abell Company, the two editions of the paper have a combined daily circulation in excess of 400,000 copies.

See G. W. Johnson *et al.*, *Sunpapers of Baltimore* (1937); bound copies at Maryland Historical Society and Enoch Pratt Free Public Library, Baltimore (1837–); and microfilm from Library of Congress and Bell & Howell (1837–).

BANDANNA TURBAN was a large handkerchief of brilliant-hued cotton or silk usually worn by the Negro slave women (and sometimes even by the men) as a headdress, rather than the bonnet commonly used by most white women of the antebellum South.

See F. L. Olmsted, *Cotton Kingdom* (1953); W. A. Craige and J. R. Hulbert, *Dictionary of American English* (1938); and M. M. Mathews (ed.), *Dictionary of Americanisms* (1951).

BANKHEAD FAMILY was a closely knit Alabama political dynasty, four members of which served in the U.S. Congress almost continuously from 1887 to 1946. John Hollis Bankhead, Sr. (1842–1920), founder of the dynasty, born near Sulligent, Ala., had little formal education. He was a member of the KU KLUX KLAN and served in the Alabama house of representatives and senate. He was warden of the state penitentiary at Wetumpka (1881–1885). Having moved to Jasper, which became the Bankhead political base, he served in the U.S. House of Representatives (1887–1907) until defeated for reelection, but was then appointed to the U.S. Senate in 1907. In 1912 Bankhead managed OSCAR W. UNDERWOOD's unsuccessful campaign for the Democratic presidential nomination. Although he was noted for his interest in inland waterways and the post office, his most enduring legislative monument is the Federal Highways Act of 1913.

His son, John Hollis Bankhead, Jr. (1872–1946), graduated from the University of Alabama and received his law degree from Georgetown University. In the Alabama house of representatives in 1904–1905, he wrote the election law designed to disfranchise the Negroes (DISFRANCHISEMENT). He served as president of the Bankhead Coal Company (1911–1925). Although defeated for the Democratic senatorial nomination in 1926, he won election to the U.S. Senate in 1930. An authority on cotton legislation and author of much NEW DEAL farm legislation, he sponsored the Bankhead Cotton Control Act of 1934 and the Bankhead-Jones Farm Tenancy Act of 1937. He broke with the Franklin D. Roosevelt administration in the Supreme Court fight of 1937. He died after denying columnist Drew Pearson's charges that he had bought cotton futures prior to speeches urging the removal of wartime price controls from cotton.

William Brockman Bankhead (1874–1940),

younger son of John Bankhead, Sr., achieved political prominence earlier than his brother, who was his political manager. Bill graduated from the University of Alabama and received a law degree from Georgetown University. After serving as city attorney, as circuit solicitor, and one term in the Alabama house of representatives in which he favored the highly conservative constitution of 1901, he was elected to the U.S. House of Representatives in 1916. A frustrated actor, Bill, unlike his older brother and his father, was a skilled orator. A party regular, he favored Woodrow Wilson's war measures, opposed Herbert Hoover's farm policies, and favored most New Deal legislation. He became Speaker of the House on June 3, 1936, although handicapped by serious heart trouble. Bill's name was not attached to any important legislation except for the Bankhead Cotton Control Act, cosponsored by his more able but less genial brother. His presidential ambitions frustrated by Roosevelt's decision to seek a third term, he unsuccessfully sought the vice-presidential nomination in 1940, despite discouragement from Roosevelt.

The Bankhead brothers differed from their father in being party regulars and in favoring progressive legislation. Neither was associated with the Ku Klux Klan, and they were not regarded as antilabor. Other members of the family were: Thomas M. Owen (1866–1920), son-in-law of John H. Bankhead, Sr., and founder of the ALABAMA DEPARTMENT OF ARCHIVES AND HISTORY; Marie Bankhead Owen (1869–1958), wife of Thomas and his successor as director of the Department of Archives and History; Walter Will Bankhead (1897–), son of William B. Bankhead, served one month in the U.S. House of Representatives, 1941; and Tallulah Bankhead (1903–1968), actress, daughter of William B. Bankhead.

See M. S. Koster, "John Hollis Bankhead" (M.A. thesis, University of Alabama, 1931); N. Hamner, "John H. Bankhead, Jr." (M.A. thesis, University of Alabama, 1957); T. M. Owen, *History of Alabama* (1921); W. J. Heacock, "William Brockman Bankhead" (Ph.D. dissertation, University of Wisconsin, 1952); and Bankhead Papers, Alabama Department of Archives and History, Montgomery.

EVANS C. JOHNSON
Stetson University

BANKING. Commercial banking first became important in the South during the early national period. The first Bank of the United States (1791–1811) had branches at Baltimore, Charleston, New Orleans, Norfolk, Savannah, and Washington, D.C.; the second Bank of the United States (1816–1836) had branches at Baltimore, Charleston, Fayette-ville, Lexington, Louisville, Mobile, Nashville, Natchez, New Orleans, Norfolk, Richmond, Savannah, and Washington, D.C. The second bank initially followed the principle that each branch should honor notes issued by all other branches (CURRENCY). This policy encouraged certain branches in the South and West, particularly the one at Baltimore, to issue excessive amounts of notes, a tendency that contributed to the early difficulties of the bank. For the most part the influence of the second Bank of the United States in the South ended when its federal charter expired, although using a charter from Pennsylvania it did engage in speculation in cotton.

During the antebellum period, numerous banks were chartered by southern states. A number were financed in whole or in part by state governments. Among this class there were failures, such as the Bank of the State of Alabama, but the Bank of the State of South Carolina was successful. Several southern states adopted the free-banking system, which provided for free entry and a bond-secured note issue. The free-banking law of Louisiana (1853) was widely praised for its conservative reserve requirements (LOUISIANA SPECIE RESERVE SYSTEM). One measure of banking development, bank money per capita, indicates that in 1860, though the South lagged behind New England and the Middle Atlantic states, it led the north-central region.

The Civil War brought tremendous changes to the southern banking system. Few banks in the South survived the physical and financial devastation wrought by the war, though the other regions emerged with their banking resources enhanced. It has been forcefully argued that the National Banking Act adopted in the North during the Civil War inhibited the rebuilding of the southern banking system and restricted southern economic development during Reconstruction and subsequent periods. The minimum capital requirements of the act were so large that many southern towns could support only one (if any) national bank. The established banks held monopoly positions that could not be challenged. They used their monopoly power to restrict the supply of credit with obvious consequences for the southern economy. To be sure, laws regulating state banks were less restrictive. But state banks were prevented from issuing bank notes, which were important to southern banks. Students of SHARECROPPING have assigned an important role to the lack of banking facilities in fixing this system in the South. The sharecropper's dependence on the local merchant for credit may have been aggravated by the restriction on mortgage lending in the National Banking Act. This prohibition may have lessened the total flow of credit into agriculture, or at least channeled credit through the local store owner (COUNTRY STORE), thus strengthening his position vis-à-vis the sharecropper. Legal barriers to entry in banking may not be the whole explanation of the South's backwardness in banking after the Civil War, but they were surely a contributing factor. One effect was clear: short-term interest rates in the rural South were among the highest in the country during the second half of the nineteenth century.

Between 1900 and 1914 the South's banking structure made noticeable gains. The rate of bank failure declined, and short-term interest rates converged on the national average. The formation of the Federal Reserve System in 1913 and the high agricultural prices of the prewar period presaged a favorable era for southern banking. The Federal Reserve System, after all, was designed to give some weight to regional concerns. Federal Reserve banks were established at Atlanta, Dallas, and Richmond. The twenties and thirties, however, were extremely difficult for southern banking. The failure rate was higher than the national average, and the Federal Reserve did little to stem the tide. Perhaps the initiating factor was the agricultural depression in the South. But surely the impact on the region would have been less had the Federal Reserve pumped new funds into the region rather than allowing loanable funds to be extinguished through bank failure.

The coming of the Federal Deposit Insurance Corporation and agricultural price support programs in the 1930s dramatically reduced bank failures after WORLD WAR II. Indeed it seems reasonable to suppose that the greater soundness of the banking system contributed to, as well as was influenced by, the dramatic economic expansion of the South in the postwar years. These years also witnessed a modernization of the banking structure in the South. The proportion of small, independent, and sometimes nonpar banks declined, and chain and group banking became more important.

See E. Q. Hawk, *Economic History of the South* (1934); L. E. Davis, *Journal of Economic History* (Sept., 1965); F. Redlich, *The Molding of American Banking* (1951), a mine of information; B. Hammond, *Banks and Politics in America* (1957), classic; G. D. Green, *Finance and Economic Development in the Old South* (1972); E. M. Lerner, *Journal of Political Economics* (Dec., 1954); R. Sylla, *Journal of Economic History* (Dec., 1969); R. L. Ransom and R. Sutch, *Journal of Economic History* (Sept., 1972); C. B. Hoover and B. U. Ratchford, *Economic Resources and Policies of the South* (1951); and P. L. Foster, *Bank Expansion in Virginia* (1971).

HUGH ROCKOFF
Rutgers University

BANNEKER, BENJAMIN (1731–1806), was born a free Negro in Baltimore County, Md., the son and grandson of freed Negro slaves; his maternal grandmother was a white English indentured servant. Except for attendance at a country school for several winters, he was entirely self-taught. In his early twenties he constructed a successful wooden striking clock without ever having seen one. He worked as a tobacco planter on his father's 100-acre farm, which he inherited after the latter's death. In about 1789 George Ellicott, a young neighbor, lent him several instruments and texts on astronomy, with which Banneker taught himself in the subject. Shortly thereafter he was employed for four months by Major ANDREW ELLICOTT to assist in the survey of the territory of Columbia, on which the new national capital was to be built. He completed the calculations for an almanac bearing his name first published for the year 1792, with the support of the abolition societies of Maryland and Pennsylvania. Five more issues followed before the series was discontinued. The almanacs were widely distributed, and more than 29 editions of the six issues were published. Because of poor health and his new scientific interests, Banneker abandoned tobacco farming in his final years and lived on income derived from the sale of segments of his farm.

See J. H. B. Latrobe, *Maryland Colonization Journal* (May, 1845); [M. E. Tyson], "Sketch of B. Banneker," read by J. S. Norris before Maryland Historical Society (Oct., 1854); and S. A. Bedini, *Life of Benjamin Banneker* (1972).

SILVIO A. BEDINI
Smithsonian Institution

BAPTIST CHURCHES are more numerous in the South than those of any other religious denomination. The latest figures released by the Census Bureau indicate that nearly 40 percent of all southerners who are affiliated with any church are members of one of the several Baptist bodies in the region.

Baptists of the South trace their origin to the religious upheavals in Europe in the sixteenth and seventeenth centuries. Borrowing their theological, ecclesiastical, and social views from the left-wing elements of the Reformation and the Puritan movement in England, Baptists began organizing churches in England in about 1611. Although these churches lacked uniformity in beliefs and practices, they generally adhered to what have come to be identified as historical Baptist principles: namely, the Bible as the final authority on matters of faith and practice, freedom of conscience, individual responsibility to God, personal salvation by faith alone, the autonomy of the local church, and separation of church and state. Their ordinances, symbolic only, came to be the Lord's Supper and baptism by immersion.

Roger Williams was the first American Baptist of note, although he was an Anglican when he immigrated in 1631 and he remained a Baptist only a few months after embracing the faith and assisting in establishing the first Baptist church in the New World in Providence, R.I., in 1639. From this beginning, Baptists grew slowly in colonial America until the GREAT AWAKENING of the eighteenth century. By the time of the American Revolution, Baptists were the third or fourth largest denomination in the English mainland colonies, and the wave of emotional revivalism around 1800 (GREAT AWAKENING, SECOND) further augmented their numbers and established Baptists in the mainstream of American Protestantism.

Their beliefs in individual freedom of conscience and congregationalism doomed Baptists to continual internal dissension and fragmentation. Controversies over predestination, the display of emotion, the nature of the church, methods of evangelism, foreign missions, slavery, and many other issues divided Baptists into over 20 distinct denominations and numerous smaller groups. The following principal bodies of Baptists have continued into the twentieth century: American Baptist Association (955,900 members), American Baptist Churches in the U.S.A., Inc. (1,484,393 members), Baptist Missionary Association of America (199,640 members), Conservative Baptist Association of America (300,000 members), Freewill Baptists (203,000 members), General Association of Regular Baptist Churches (214,000 members), National Baptist Convention of America (2,668,799 members), National Baptist Convention, U.S.A., Inc. (5,500,000 members), National Primitive Baptist Convention, Inc. (1,645,000 members), Progressive National Baptist Convention, Inc. (521,692 members), and Southern Baptist Convention (12,065,333 members).

The congregational system of church government prevented Baptists from developing a strong ecclesiastical structure. Always zealous for the independence of the local congregation, Baptists attained unity only through voluntary cooperation, not hierarchical pressure. The General Missionary Convention of the Baptist Denomination in the United States or Triennial Convention, organized in 1814, was the closest that the Baptists came to national unity. This harmony was shattered in 1845, however, when the churches of the South withdrew and organized the Southern Baptist Convention in Augusta, Ga. At issue was the refusal of the foreign mission board of the Triennial Convention to appoint slaveholding missionaries. Since the split, Southern Baptists have continually surpassed their northern counterparts in membership, wealth, and activities.

Negro Baptists constitute a major portion of the total number of Baptists in the South today. Prior to the Civil War, slaves shared membership in the same churches with their masters, and, after emancipation, white Baptists attempted to keep the blacks in their churches as a means of social control. But Negro Baptists chose to withdraw and organize their own churches, and the whites assisted them in the process once separation became inevitable. Black Baptists eventually organized two major conventions: the National Baptist Convention of America and the National Baptist Convention of the U.S.A., Inc., with a combined membership of over 8 million.

Southern Baptists—those who support the program of the Southern Baptist Convention—constitute the largest body of Baptists in the United States and, in fact, the largest Protestant denomination in the nation. Of their more than 12 million members, over 10.6 million are found in the South. In the South alone, Southern Baptists maintain over 29,250 churches, six seminaries, 40 senior colleges, ten junior colleges, seven academies, four Bible schools, 25 hospitals, 17 homes for the aged, and 22 children's homes. They also aid in supporting over 2,500 missionaries in 76 countries around the world. To support these and other causes, Southern Baptists contributed over $1 billion in 1973.

Although Southern Baptists have been moving slowly toward centralization in the twentieth century, the focus of activity is still the local church, where pastors are "called" by the membership and where an elected board of deacons leads but with constant reminders that final authority resides in the whole congregation. Most Baptist churches still promote the annual revival, a vestige of the frontier CAMP MEETING or "protracted" meeting. Many of the larger urban churches are modifying the traditional ways by adding kindergartens and grade schools, gymnasiums, study groups, pastoral counseling, involvement in community welfare projects, and other programs in an attempt to meet the needs of a changing society. Although Baptists have been influenced in recent years by the Social Gospel, they remain loyal to their historical commitment to "make disciples of all men." The emphasis on evangelism is apparent in the entire program of the churches and the denomination.

If the South has a folk religion, it is evangelical Protestantism of which Southern Baptists are the major element. Brought into being in defense of the South's peculiar institution, they have over the years defended the "southern way of life." They have supported slavery and the Confederacy, states' rights, segregation of the races, and countless other distinctive facets of southern culture. Only occasionally have they taken stands contrary to the prevailing southern ways, and then only on matters pertaining to a rather narrow view of personal conduct and morality. To the extent that any religious group is responsible for shaping and supporting the culture in which it flourishes, Southern Baptists, because of their numbers, wealth, and influence, must share the praise and the blame for the fortunes and misfortunes of the South.

See the Historical Commission of Southern Baptist Convention, Nashville, for the richest collection of sources, much on microfilm. See also R. G. Torbet, *History of the Baptists* (1963); *Encyclopedia of Southern Baptists* (3 vols.; 1958, 1971); R. A. Baker, *Southern Baptist Convention* (1974); R. B. Spain, *At Ease in Zion* (1967); J. L. Eighmy, *Churches in Cultural Captivity* (1972); C. G. Woodson, *History of the Negro Church* (1921); J. R. Washington, Jr., *Black Religion* (1964); *Yearbook of American and Canadian Churches* (1974); *Southern Baptist Handbook* (1974); and U.S. Bureau of the Census, *Religious Bodies, 1936* (1941). Research on the history of Negro Baptists and the minor Baptist bodies remains to be done.

RUFUS B. SPAIN
Baylor University

BARATARIA BAY, an estuary lying south of New Orleans, La., was once a main channel of the Mississippi before the river moved eastward. The fertile, riparian lands produce much sugar. Varied plant material feeds abundant fish, fur-bearing animals, and wildfowl, making this a sportsman's paradise. An inland arm of the Gulf of Mexico, the bay is rimmed by a series of islands. The only land approach is a two-lane highway from the west. Through a matrix of bayous and canals it connects by boat with New Orleans. This area abounds in deep-seated salt domes, and sulfur is mined by forced hot water from the caprock above. Recently spectacular oil discoveries have been made in the

bay, in the marshes, and out into the Gulf. Drilling is done primarily from barges and giant seaworthy rigs. Pipelines carry the oil to New Orleans and the Mississippi River. Grand Isle, the only inhabited island, is the habitat of commercial fishermen, tourists, and sportsmen. It is noted for its beautiful subtropical plants, natural beach, and deep-sea marina. Grand Terre is a lonely, windswept abandoned island covered with grasses and mangroves. It once served as headquarters for pirates and smugglers, the most famous being JEAN LAFFITE.

See F. Kniffen, *Louisiana* (1968); J. Laffite, *Journal* (1958); A. Fortier, *History of Louisiana* (1904); B. Swanson, *Historic Jefferson* (1975); and S. Lockett, *Louisiana* (1873).

JOHN D. WINTERS
Louisiana Tech University

BARBEE'S CROSSROADS, VA., southeast of Manassas Gap in the Blue Ridge Mountains, was the site of three unrelated cavalry actions during the Civil War. The largest took place on November 5, 1862, when WADE HAMPTON's Confederate cavalry brigade of about 3,000 was attacked by Alfred Pleasonton's cavalry of approximately 1,500. The Confederates withdrew after a brief skirmish, ending the battle. Casualties on both sides were light. The next action was on July 25, 1863, and (according to an official report filed by General George A. Custer) was a very minor cavalry skirmish involving a portion of the 1st Michigan Cavalry. The third occurred September 1, 1863, when a detachment of about 150 of J. E. B. STUART's cavalry ambushed about 50 men from the 6th Ohio Cavalry on the road 1.5 miles southeast of Barbee's Crossroads. The federals fought their way out, suffering 31 casualties and a loss of 30 horses.

See *Official Records, Armies*, Ser. 1, Vols. XIX, XXVII, XXIX, best for details. W. Reid, *Ohio in the War* (1868), and H. B. McClellan, *J. E. B. Stuart* (1885), cover related campaigns.

GERALD C. BROWN
U.S. Military Academy

BARBOUR, JAMES (1775–1842), was born in Barboursville, Va. A lawyer, he was primarily interested in politics. Elected to the Virginia house of delegates in 1798, he supported James Madison's resolutions against the Alien and Sedition Acts. He was Speaker of the house of delegates (1809–1812) and was elected governor in 1812. A states' rights man, he was chosen U.S. senator in 1814, was active during the Missouri controversy, and served until March, 1825, when he became secretary of war. He helped renegotiate the Creek treaty in 1826 concerning their land in Georgia and then recommended that all Indians be relocated in the West. He also urged aid for starving Florida Indians who had already been moved. In 1828 he was appointed ambassador to England. Following his one year there, his political fortunes waned, but in 1839 he did preside over the Whig National Convention. Throughout his career he advocated public education.

See S. F. Bemis, *John Quincy Adams* (1956); M. Hecht, *John Quincy Adams* (1972); G. Moore, *Missouri Controversy* (1966); A. Nevins (ed.), *Diary of John Quincy Adams* (1951); G. Tyler (ed.), *William and Mary Quarterly* (July, 1901); *Annals of Congress*, 13th–18th Cong., esp. 16th Cong., 1st and 2nd Sess.; *Journal of Virginia House of Delegates* (1798–1815); and W. W. Scott, *History of Orange County, Va.* (1907).

ELLIOTT ROBERT BARKAN
California State College, San Bernardino

BARBOUR, PHILIP PENDLETON (1783–1841), was elected to the Virginia house of delegates in 1812 and to the U.S. House of Representatives in 1814. He served there, except for a two-year interim on a state court, until 1830, when Andrew Jackson appointed him to the Federal District Court for Eastern Virginia. He served as Speaker of the House (1821–1823) and played a prominent role at the Virginia constitutional convention (1829–1830). Jackson elevated Barbour to the U.S. Supreme Court in 1836. Although many southerners preceded him there, he was, as befit a member of the RICHMOND JUNTO, the first strict states' rights adherent appointed to the Court. Barbour's short tenure on the Court indicates, however, a moderation in the rigidity of his states' rights position.

See F. Gatell, L. Friedman, and F. Israel, *Justices of the Supreme Court* (1969), the only modern study. No private papers are available.

DONALD ROPER
State University of New York, New Paltz

BARDSTOWN, KY. (pop. 5,816), 36 miles southeast of Louisville, was first settled in 1778 and known as Salem. Later it was renamed for William Baird (or Bard), one of the owners of the land on which the town was situated. With Salem Academy (1788) and Nazareth College for Women (1814), early Bardstown rivaled Louisville and Lexington as an educational center. The Cathedral of St. Joseph (1816–1819) displays paintings that allegedly were gifts from King Louis Philippe of France. The city is a market for area dairy, grain, and tobacco farmers as well as being a producer of distilled whiskey (BOURBON) and hardwood lumber.

Nearby are Wickland (1813), the home of three of Kentucky's governors, and Federal Hill (1795–1818), where STEPHEN FOSTER wrote "My Old Kentucky Home."

BARKLEY, ALBEN WILLIAM (1877–1956). "My entrance into politics was inevitable," Barkley once explained. "I was a Kentuckian and a lawyer and I had a natural inclination to stop whatever I was doing and start making a speech anytime I saw as many as six persons assembled together." During his long career, he supported PROHIBITION, railroad labor laws, farm relief programs, social security, and FLOOD CONTROL projects vital to his native state.

Born in a log cabin near the town of Lowes in western Kentucky, Barkley attended college in Clinton, Ky., read law as a clerk in Paducah, and gained admittance to the bar in 1901. In 1912 he won the first of seven successive elections to the U.S. House of Representatives. In 1923 he campaigned unsuccessfully for the Kentucky gubernatorial nomination, but his defeat (the only one he ever suffered) made him a statewide figure and led to his election in 1926 to the U.S. Senate. Barkley remained a senator until 1949, when he became vice-president of the United States, but Kentucky voters returned him to the Senate in 1955.

Perhaps Barkley's most important contribution to his country came while he was majority leader of the Senate (1937–1947). Although often caught between anti–New Dealers and pro-Roosevelt factions, he maintained good rapport with both sides. His parliamentary skill, common sense, and good humor contributed significantly to passage of relief, labor, and national security legislation.

See the Barkley Collection, University of Kentucky Library, Lexington, the most important source. See also A. W. Barkley, *That Reminds Me* (1954); P. A. Davis, "Barkley" (Ph.D. dissertation, University of Kentucky, 1963); and G. W. Robinson, *Filson Club History Quarterly* (April, 1966), and *Register of Kentucky Historical Society* (July, 1969).

GEORGE W. ROBINSON
Eastern Kentucky University

BARKSDALE, ETHELBERT (1824–1893), one of Mississippi's ablest journalists, had gained a wide reputation by the Civil War. He served in the CONFEDERATE CONGRESS (1861–1865) and later played a major role in overthrowing Republican control in the "revolution of 1875" (MISSISSIPPI PLAN). During this time his Jackson *Clarion* was the most influential Democratic paper in the state. Serious dissension soon erupted within the triumphant Democratic party as Barksdale and others challenged the dominant Bourbon faction led by L. Q. C. LAMAR. In contests over the U.S. Senate seat and the governor's chair, lengthy deadlocks developed in Democratic caucuses in 1880 and 1881 between the Barksdale and Lamar forces. Compromise candidates were eventually chosen, but the animosity lingered. The schism was temporarily healed, and Barksdale served two terms in Congress (1883–1887). But as agrarian distress deepened in Mississippi, Barksdale's differences with the BOURBONS resurfaced. When Senator J. Z. GEORGE opposed the SUBTREASURY PLAN in 1892, the FARMERS' ALLIANCE endorsed Barksdale. In the most bitterly fought campaign since 1875, George won. Less than a year later, Barksdale died. Although he never achieved high state office, he was a force to be reckoned with in the turbulent years following Reconstruction in Mississippi.

See A. D. Kirwan, *Rednecks* (1951); W. D. Halsell, *Journal of Mississippi History* (1942); and O. Peterson, *Journal of Mississippi History* (1952).

CHARLES SALLIS
Millsaps College

BARNEY, JOSHUA (1759–1818), a native of Baltimore, was an American naval hero in both the Revolution and the War of 1812. Although captured three times during the War for Independence, he performed brilliantly against enemy vessels. His victory over the *General Monk* in 1782 marked him as a master tactician. After the war Barney engaged in commercial enterprises. In 1794 he captained the ship carrying James Monroe to his post as minister to France. Barney impressed government officials in Paris, who appointed him a commodore in the French navy. After serving successfully against the British in the West Indies, he returned to Baltimore in 1802 and failed twice to win election to Congress. During the War of 1812 Barney was named commander of a barge flotilla in Chesapeake Bay. Trapped in 1814 by the British squadron carrying troops for the raid on Washington, D.C., he blew up his vessels to avoid capture. He and his men later fought with courage at the battle of BLADENSBURG. Barney himself was wounded and captured but later exchanged.

See H. Footner, *Sailor of Fortune* (1940); R. D. Paine, *Joshua Barney* (1924); W. Lord, *Dawn's Early Light* (1972); and G. W. Allen, *Naval History* (2 vols.; 1913).

FRANK A. CASSELL
University of Wisconsin, Milwaukee

BARNWELL, ROBERT WOODWARD (1801–1882), educator, U.S. senator, and Confederate statesman, was related to many prominent Carolina families. He was born in Beaufort, S.C. Barnwell graduated from Harvard with highest honors in 1821, returned home to study law, was admitted to the bar in 1824, and commenced practice in Beaufort. Chosen for the state legislature in 1826, he was then elected to Congress in 1829 and served there for two terms. In 1835 Barnwell was named president of South Carolina College, where he gained great distinction for his work. Retiring because of ill health in 1841, he remained upon his plantation until chosen to fill the U.S. Senate seat of the deceased Franklin H. Elmore in June, 1850. During his short term he was an active supporter of the southern position and was a leading member of the "cooperative secessionist" movement at the NASHVILLE CONVENTION. Following his state's secession in December, 1860, Barnwell was one of three commissioners appointed to negotiate with President James Buchanan, was selected as a delegate to the MONTGOMERY CONVENTION, and served in the Confederate Senate. In later years he was chairman of the faculty of South Carolina College and was serving as librarian when he died.

See S. B. Barnwell, *Story of an American Family* (1969); E. L. Green, *History of University of South Carolina* (1916); Y. Snowden, *History of South Carolina* (1920), II; and N. W. Stephenson, *American Historical Review* (Jan., 1931).

J. MICHAEL QUILL
Viterbo College

BARRETT, KATE HARWOOD WALLER (1857–1925), was best known for her work with the National Florence Crittenton Mission for unwed mothers. She was born in Falmouth, Va., and educated largely at home. In 1876 she married the Reverend Robert South Barrett. They had seven children. In 1892, after receiving an M.D. degree from the Women's Medical College of Georgia, Mrs. Barrett founded a home for unwed mothers in Atlanta. This began her association with Charles N. Crittenton, a millionaire evangelist dedicated to the rescue of "fallen women." After her husband's death (1896) Mrs. Barrett began actively to direct the more than 50 Florence Crittenton homes. In 1911 she became president of the National Florence Crittenton Mission, a position she held until her death. In 1909 Mrs. Barrett was a delegate to the White House Conference for Dependent Children, in 1914 a special representative to the Labor Department, and in 1924 a delegate to the Democratic National Convention. She was vice-president of the Virginia Equal Suffrage League (1909–1920) and president of several national women's groups.

See O. Wilson, *Fifty Years' Work* (1933); E. O. Lundberg, *Unto the Least of These* (1947); K. H. W. Barrett, *Some Practical Suggestions* (1903?); and National Florence Crittenton Mission, *Fourteen Years' Work* (1897).

DARA DEHAVEN
Emory University

BARUCH, BERNARD MANNES (1870–1965). His Prussian-born father, Simon Baruch, a surgeon with Robert E. Lee, was the first physician to remove successfully a ruptured appendix and was president of the South Carolina Medical Association. In 1881, fleeing the turmoil of Reconstruction, Simon removed the family to New York City, where he joined the faculty of the Columbia College of Physicians and Surgeons. Bernard was graduated from City College in 1889 and by 1896 was a partner in the Wall Street firm of A. A. Housman & Company and held a seat on the New York Stock Exchange. By 1902, Baruch's financial wizardry and probing knowledge of raw materials—gold, copper, sulfur—had brought him a fortune of over $3 million, his own firm, and a huge South Carolina plantation, his garden of Eden, Hobcaw Barony. There the great of the world came to rest, hunt, or recuperate, as Franklin Roosevelt did in 1944.

Wearied of simply making money, this self-styled "speculator" joined the Woodrow Wilson administration, becoming in 1917 chairman of the War Industries Board, with power second only to Wilson's and authority to mobilize all American industry for the war effort. At the Versailles peace conference in 1919, Baruch appeared as a member of the Supreme Economic Council and as Wilson's personal economic adviser. As the nation's "elder statesman," he was consulted by every president from Wilson through John F. Kennedy, but his real power was with the southern bloc on Capitol Hill. Perhaps his supreme moment came in 1946, when he presented the Baruch Plan for the inspection and control of all forms of atomic power, before the United Nations General Assembly.

See J. R. Marcus (ed.), *Memoirs of American Jews* (1956), III; H. Simonhoff, *Saga of American Jewry* (1959); M. L. Coit, in *Encyclopaedia Judaica* (1974); C. Field, *Park Bench Statesman* (1944); and M. L. Coit, *Mr. Baruch* (1957), bibliography. See also Baruch's four books: *Making of Economics and Reparations Section of Peace Treaty* (1920); *American Industry in War* (1941); *My Own Story* (1957); and *Public Years* (1960).

MARGARET L. COIT
Rutherford, N.J.

BASSETT, JOHN SPENCER (1867–1928), was born in Tarboro, N.C. He received his B.A. degree from Trinity College (now Duke University) in 1888 and his Ph.D. degree in history from Johns Hopkins in 1894. He taught at both Trinity (1889–1891, 1894–1906) and Smith College (1906–1928). In 1902 he established and became the first editor of the SOUTH ATLANTIC QUARTERLY; he began the excellent collection of southern Americana in the Duke University Library. In 1903 his editorial in the *South Atlantic Quarterly*, "Stirring Up the Fires of Race Antipathy," a study of the progress of southern black people, became the first triumphant milestone in the battle for ACADEMIC FREEDOM in the South. Despite the demand of JOSEPHUS DANIELS, editor of the Raleigh *News and Observer*, that he be forced to resign, Bassett won the support of his colleagues and of the president and board of trustees of Trinity College. A prolific scholar, he wrote five books on the history of North Carolina and nine other books about American history or historians. In addition, his *A Short History of the United States* (1913) was for a generation the most widely used text in American history. His two-volume *Life of Andrew Jackson* (1911) was the first comprehensive biography of Jackson to draw largely upon manuscript sources. He edited five volumes of primary historical sources and three volumes of the *Correspondence of Andrew Jackson*.

See E. W. Porter, *Trinity and Duke* (1964), for the "Bassett affair"; and Bassett Papers, Duke Archives, a small collection.

E. STANLY GODBOLD, JR.
Valdosta State College

BATE, WILLIAM BRIMAGE (1826–1905), was born in Sumner County, Tenn. He served in the Mexican War and afterward edited a newspaper at Gallatin, Tenn. Elected to the state legislature in 1849, he was licensed to practice law three years later. A Democrat and proponent of secession, Bate enlisted as a private in the Confederate army when the Civil War began. During the war he was wounded three times, had six horses shot from under him, and rose to the rank of major general while seeing action at Shiloh and in the Chattanooga and the Atlanta campaigns. Bate was governor of Tennessee from 1882 to 1886. During his first term he led the legislature to enact a measure settling the state's bonded debt, ending a period of over a dozen years of political controversy over the issue. In 1887 he was elected to the U.S. Senate, where he served continuously until his death. While in the Senate he defended states' rights, opposed federal aid to education and federal supervision of elections, and strongly backed free coinage of silver.

See Governors Papers, Tennessee State Library and Archives; W. N. Chesney, "Career of Bate" (M.A. thesis, University of Tennessee, 1951); P. Marshall, *Life of Bate* (1908); and K. McKellar, *Tennessee Senators* (1942).

ROBERT B. JONES
Middle Tennessee State University

BATES, EDWARD (1793–1869), was born in Virginia and migrated to Missouri in 1814. Admitted to the Missouri bar, he practiced law in St. Louis and was a delegate to Missouri's constitutional convention in 1820. After serving one term in Congress (1827–1829), Bates organized and led Missouri's Whigs in the 1830s and 1840s. He was a delegate to a national 1847 internal improvements convention, and he declined a post in Millard Fillmore's cabinet in 1850. Nominated for president at the 1860 Republican National Convention, he was defeated by Abraham Lincoln, who later named him attorney general. Bates wrote the executive opinion in *ex parte* MERRYMAN (1861) and represented the government in the prize cases (1863). He gained equal status for blacks in the Union army. Bates generally exercised a conservative influence in Lincoln's cabinet. He resigned in November, 1864, but opposed Missouri's Radical Republicans until his death.

See M. R. Cain, *Lincoln's Attorney General* (1965); H. K. Beale (ed.), *Diary of E. Bates* (1933); C. Gibson, *Missouri Historical Society Collection* (1900); Edward Bates Diary and Papers, Missouri Historical Society, St. Louis; and Edward Bates Papers, State Historical Society of Missouri.

M. R. CAIN
University of Missouri, Rolla

BATH, N.C., the oldest settlement in the state, was founded in 1690 by French HUGUENOTS and named in honor of the earl of Bath, one of the Carolinas' lords proprietors. The site faces onto the Pamlico River and had previously been the location of an Indian village called Pamtical (or Pamticough). Despite serving briefly as the provincial capital, the village never has been much developed. It is today as it long has been: a town of several hundred residents who make a living as commercial fishermen or in servicing area agriculture.

BATON ROUGE, BATTLE OF (August 5–6, 1862), was fought in the streets of the northeastern section of the Louisiana capital following the city's capture by federal troops in May. The engagement pitted Confederate General JOHN C. BRECKINRIDGE against Union General Thomas Williams. Although the Confederates enjoyed success at first, their attack lost momentum; and news that the Confederate gunboat *Arkansas* (on which Breckinridge had counted for help) had gone aground and been scuttled by its crew persuaded the Confederate commander to order a withdrawal. From New Orleans, Williams' superior, General Benjamin F. Butler, also ordered Union troops to leave. As they moved out, the soldiers sacked the city and carried off what was left of the state library. The two sides suffered roughly the same number of casualties.

See E. C. Bearss, *Louisiana History* (Spring, 1962), most extensive; and J. D. Winters, *Civil War in Louisiana* (1963).

ELISABETH JOAN DOYLE
St. John's University, Jamaica, N.Y.

BATON ROUGE, LA. (pop. 165,963), is on the east bank of the Mississippi River approximately 70 miles northwest of New Orleans. The city takes its name from a French account, which described a red post (*baton rouge*) used on this site to mark the boundary of two Indian nations. The French built a fort here in 1719, but in 1763 it and its surrounding community were ceded to Great Britain as part of West Florida. Spain seized West Florida in 1779, and, although the east bank of the Mississippi here was not part of the LOUISIANA PURCHASE (1803), Baton Rouge and its environs were annexed by the United States in 1810. The town was the capital of Louisiana from 1849 until federal forces occupied it in May, 1862, when the government moved to Opelousas and later to Alexandria and to Shreveport. A Confederate effort to retake the city in August, 1862, was thwarted (BATON ROUGE, BATTLE OF).

The seat of the state's government returned permanently to the city in 1882, and the gradual growth of LOUISIANA STATE UNIVERSITY (1860) added an educational dimension to the town. The major source of Baton Rouge's post–Civil War growth and prosperity, however, has been its development as a commercial and industrial center. Railroad connections completed in the 1870s and 1880s reinvigorated the old river town's economy, and dredging of the Mississippi (especially during the twentieth century) has made the city one of the nation's most important inland ocean ports of entry. It is a major shipping point for rice, cotton, lumber, petroleum, chemicals, sulfur, and bauxite, and its factories manufacture synthetic rubber, aluminum, optical glass, and machine tools.

See A. C. Albrecht, *Louisiana Historical Quarterly* (Jan., 1945), early settlement; R. M. Meyers, *History of Baton Rouge* (1976); Baton Rouge Foundation, *Baton Rouge Story* (1967); P. H. Howard *et al.*, *Social Forces* (Sept., 1971), for recent voting patterns; and files of *State-Times* (1905–), *Advocate* (1842–1903), both on microfilm, and *Gazette and Comet* (1819–74).

BATON ROUGE DAILY GAZETTE AND COMET

was created by the merger in 1856 of the *Daily Comet* (1850–1856) and the weekly Baton Rouge *Gazette* (1819–1856). The paper ceased daily publication in 1861, though a weekly edition was published as late as 1874.

See bound copies of *Gazette* (1819–56), LSU and University of Kentucky libraries; and bound copies of *Daily Comet* (1850–61), LSU Library.

BAUXITE. See ALUMINUM INDUSTRY

BAXTER, ELISHA (1827–1899), Arkansas' tenth governor, was born in Rutherford County, N.C. In 1852 he moved to Batesville, in north-central Arkansas. He briefly operated a general store, studied law, and was elected a state representative in 1854 and 1858. A slave owner, Baxter opposed secession, but he briefly acted as prosecuting attorney for the Confederacy. Although a supporter of the Union army after it came to Batesville, he rejected a commission. He fled to Missouri, where the Confederates captured him. They returned him to Little Rock and charged him with treason. After escaping, he accepted a Union commission and assumed command at Batesville. He resigned in 1864 to serve on the state supreme court. He held that post only until his election later in the year to the U.S. Senate, but Congress refused to seat him.

He served as circuit judge in the Arkansas Third District from 1868 until Republicans nominated him for governor in 1872. A dissident Republican faction chose JOSEPH BROOKS to oppose him. Baxter won the election, but both sides charged fraud; the controversy culminated in 1874 in the BROOKS-BAXTER WAR. Growing disenchantment with his policies as governor caused many Republicans to switch their support from Baxter to Brooks during the prolonged conflict, but President U. S. Grant's recognition of Baxter as governor settled the issue.

Arkansas' new 1874 constitution vacated all state offices, and Baxter stepped down as governor two years before his term officially ended. Fearing charges of betraying his party, he declined to become the Democratic candidate for governor in 1874. He returned to his farm near Batesville, where, except for an unsuccessful bid for the U.S. Senate in 1878, he remained in private life.

See *Arkansas Gazette* (June 2, 1899); M. A. Ellenburg, "Reconstruction in Arkansas" (Ph.D. dissertation, University of Missouri, 1967); and T. S. Staples, *Reconstruction in Arkansas* (1923).

MARTHA ELLENBURG FOLEY
Warrensburg, Mo.

BAXTER, NATHANIEL, JR. (1844–1913), born near Columbia, Tenn., was a soldier, lawyer, banker, and industrialist, long associated with Nashville. Enlisting in the Confederate army at the age of fifteen, he served under General NATHAN B. FORREST. He took part in the battles of Fishing Creek, Shiloh, Missionary Ridge, Chickamauga, Knoxville, Franklin, Atlanta, and Savannah, was twice wounded, was captured at the battle of Franklin, and then was imprisoned at Ft. Delaware. Baxter entered law practice after the war and in 1877 became president of the First National Bank of Nashville. His most important industrial leadership was in the coal and iron enterprises of Tennessee and Alabama. He was president of the Tennessee Coal, Iron & Railroad Company most of the time from 1888 to 1901. This company was a leader in the development of COAL MINING and iron manufacture (IRON AND STEEL INDUSTRY) in the Sewanee and Chattanooga area, and in the 1890s, after invading the Birmingham district, it grew into the largest industrial enterprise in Alabama. It survives as the T. C. & I. division of United States Steel Corporation.

JAMES F. DOSTER
University of Alabama

BAYARD FAMILY. Descendants of HUGUENOTS who left France for Holland during the religious wars of the sixteenth century and then immigrated to the American colonies in 1647, the Bayards gradually spread throughout the United States and Canada. Substantial numbers settled in the Upper South, particularly in the Bohemia Manor section of Cecil County, Md., and in Delaware. The progenitor of Delaware's most famous political family, which produced five U.S. senators, was James Asheton (also spelled Ashton) Bayard (1767–1815). Raised in Philadelphia, he attended Princeton, studied law with Joseph Reed, and then decided in 1787 to practice his profession in Wilmington. His marriage to Ann Bassett, the daughter of one of Delaware's prominent leaders, certainly helped his career. By 1797 Bayard became the sole representative of his state in the U.S. House of Representatives, was elected senator, and then participated as a member of the bipartisan mission that signed the peace treaty at Ghent ending the War of 1812. A moderate Federalist, respected by members of both parties, Bayard had a power base in Delaware that permitted him to pursue an independent course on national issues.

Two of Bayard's sons rose to national prominence. The eldest, Richard Henry Bayard (1796–1868), became a senator in 1836, was reelected in 1841, and served as chargé d'affaires in Belgium. The second son, James Asheton Bayard (1799–1880), began his political career as a Jacksonian Democrat and was thrice elected to the Senate. A supporter of Abraham Lincoln and the Union, he joined the Republican party but opposed the antislavery measures of 1861–1864, protested the IRONCLAD OATH, took it nevertheless, and then resigned his seat. He was never comfortable in the Republican party after Lincoln's death. His son, Thomas Francis Bayard (1828–1898), was a leading Democrat, remaining in the U.S. Senate from 1869 to 1885, a consistent opponent of Republican Reconstruction policies. A supporter of Grover Cleveland, he was appointed secretary of state and later ambassador to Great Britain. In 1880 and 1884 he received considerable endorsement for the Democratic presidential nomination. Thomas' son, Thomas Francis Bayard (1868–1942), became a senator in 1922. The Bayards, who have intermarried with the Du Ponts, remain a significant influence in Delaware politics. Alexis Irénée Du Pont Bayard (1918–) was lieutenant governor of the state from 1949 to 1953.

See M. Borden, *James A. Bayard* (1955); H. Conrad, *History of Delaware* (1908); C. Mallery, *Ancient Families of Bohemia Manor* (1888); E. Spencer, *Thomas F. Bayard* (1880); C. Tansill, *Thomas F. Bayard* (1940); and J. G. Wilson, *Colonel John Bayard and the Bayard Family* (1885). The largest collection of Bayard Papers is in the Library of Congress.

MORTON BORDEN
University of California, Santa Barbara

BAYLOR, JOHN ROBERT (1822–1894), a veteran Texas Indian fighter and politician, with a small force led the Confederate invasion of New Mexico. After victories over federal forces at Mesilla and San Augustine Pass, he held the Mesilla Valley until the arrival of a larger Confederate force. Baylor's attempted extermination of Apache Indians led to his removal as governor of the territory of Arizona and resignation from the Confederate army. Later elected to the Confederate Congress, Baylor spent the remainder of the war in Richmond, where he tried in vain to persuade Jefferson Davis of the validity of a conquest of the Far Southwest. In 1873 he was unsuccessful in securing the Democratic nomination for governor of Texas and settled at Montell on the Nueces River, where he died.

See J. D. Thompson, *John Robert Baylor* (1971); G. W. Baylor, *John Robert Baylor* (1966); and M. H. Hall, "Planter vs Frontiersman," in *Essays on the Civil War* (1968).

JERRY D. THOMPSON
Laredo Junior College

BAYLOR UNIVERSITY (Waco, Tex. 76703). Chartered in 1845, this Baptist university was first located in Independence, Tex., and offered college preparatory and college level instruction. The school was named for one of its founders, Robert Emmet Bledsoe Baylor (1793?–1873), a native Kentuckian and a prominent Baptist layman in Texas. Although it was originally coeducational, its female department became a separate institution in 1866. In 1886, it consolidated with Waco University to become Baylor University at Waco. Between 1903 and 1931 Baylor added seven professional colleges (including schools of nursing, dentistry, business, law, and music). Today the institution is again coeducational, with an enrollment of almost 9,000 students. Its library of 340,000 volumes has a rich manuscript collection on early Texas, Baptist church history, and Baptist laymen.

See J. D. Bragg, *Southwestern Historical Quarterly* (1945, 1948).

BAYOU. The term has traveled farther than is usually realized. Probably coined in Biloxi in 1699 out of an Indian term *bayuk*, which identified a sluggish or stagnant stream, it spread with the French as *bayouc* or *bayouque*, thence in its present form into Louisiana, from which it went northward and westward until it reached as far north as western Michigan and as far west as the Rocky Mountains. The word is still used in Arkansas, Texas, Kansas, Nebraska, Illinois, and nearby areas to identify clear and swift-running streams, small oxbow lakes, and low wet spots in fields and along some parts of the Gulf coast to denote channels, bays, and inlets affected by tides.

The appellation, however, is used mostly to identify the multitude of sluggish channels that empty into the Gulf of Mexico, with the greatest concentration of streams and the use of the word in southern Louisiana. Some are tributaries of rivers; others are part of the vast expanses of water that are present from the Mississippi westward. A few are famous, like BAYOU TECHE, where Henry Wadsworth Longfellow's Evangeline came as a refugee from Acadia, and BARATARIA BAY, in whose area flourished the pirate JEAN LAFFITE. None was more important than the Lafourche, an arm of the Mississippi, which served once as the "longest street in America," providing the residents along its banks with their only thoroughfare for the exchange of goods among themselves and with the outside world.

See R. C. West, *Association of American Geographers Annals* (1954); E. A. Davis, *Rivers and Bayous of Louisiana* (1968); C. C. Robin, *Voyages dans l'Interieur de la Louisiane* (1807); S. O. Landry, Jr. (trans.), *Voyage to Louisiana* (1966); J. B. Bossu, *Nouveaux Voyages aux Indes Occidentales* (1768); and S. Feiler (trans.), *Travels in Interior of North America, 1751–1762* (1962).

A. L. DIKET
Nicholls State University

BAYOU TECHE, one of Louisiana's beautiful streams, meanders southeasterly along an alluvial ridge from near Port Barre to its terminus near Morgan City, where it joins the Atchafalaya River. The fertile alluvium, during the nineteenth century, produced Louisiana's largest SUGAR and consequential COTTON crops. The lower Teche is still sugar country; cotton, CORN, and CATTLE prevail in the northern region. Early Louisianians used the line settlement pattern to take advantage of the high land along the stream. Later, small holdings were consolidated into plantations. Before railroads, Bayou Teche served as a transportation avenue for the region, but it is not just a stream flowing through Acadiana, the home of the ACADIANS and their descendants. The bayou, its environs, and its people have produced a way of life. The people play and work hard and strive to perpetuate the best of their heritage. Joining agriculture with developing industry, the area has prospered.

See E. A. Davis, *Rivers and Bayous of Louisiana* (1968); F. Kniffen, *Louisiana* (1968); P. Feibleman, *Bayous* (1973); J. deGrummond, "St. Mary Parish" (M.A. thesis, Louisiana State University, 1948); *Teche-Vermilion Basins*, House Document No. 524-89/28 (1966); and M. Reed, *New Orleans and the Railroad* (1966).

RALEIGH A. SUAREZ
McNeese State University

BEALE, HOWARD KENNEDY (1899–1959), was born in Illinois, attended the University of Chicago (1917–1921), and pursued graduate studies at Harvard University (1921–1924). Following a teaching apprenticeship, he accepted a position at the University of North Carolina, where for 13 years he was active in teaching, research, and the direction of graduate studies. In 1948 he joined the faculty at the University of Wisconsin, where he spent his remaining years.

Beale was a prolific author and editor with a multiplicity of interests, but his first major work remains his most significant contribution to southern history: *The Critical Year: A Study of Andrew Johnson and Reconstruction* (1930). In Beale's view the Reconstruction policies of the Republican party were the expression of northern economic interests, intent on controlling the national government by destroying the old agrarian power base of the South and West. President Johnson, in his challenge and opposition to Radical Republicans, attempted to protect the interests of the common man from the narrow and selfish ambitions of eastern capitalism. Beale's interpretation of Reconstruction influenced a generation of students to regard the Radicals as manipulative politicians, devoid of sincerity in their support of Negro rights and aspirations. His premises are under attack, but his work remains a major step in the efforts to understand our past (RECONSTRUCTION, HISTORIOGRAPHY OF).

See H. K. Beale, in *Theory and Practice in Historical Study* (1946), and *American Historical Review* (July, 1940); T. H. Williams, *Journal of Southern History* (Nov., 1946), with explanation of Beale thesis; and L. Kincaid, *Journal of American History* (June, 1970), for rebuttal.

ROBERT DAVID WARD
Georgia Southern College

BEAUFORT, S.C. (pop. 9,434), is on Port Royal Island approximately 50 miles southwest of Charleston. The island and its fine natural harbor were visited in 1521 by Spanish rovers, who called it Punta de Santa Elena. In 1562 French explorers named the island and its sound Port Royal. Not until 1710, however, was the present town laid out; five years later it was almost totally destroyed in an uprising of the YAMASSEE INDIANS. Although it never rivaled Charleston as a port city, it developed as a commercial center and market for Sea Island COTTON. After falling to federal troops on November 7, 1861 (PORT ROYAL SOUND, CAPTURE OF), it became both a base for federal operations along the South Atlantic coast and a haven for runaway slaves (CONTRABAND) seeking protection behind Union lines. By June, 1862, more than 10,000 blacks were on the four principal islands of the Port Royal area. General Rufus Saxon, the military governor in Beaufort, put the slaves to work on the Sea Island plantations for wages; furthermore, he sought to sell the lands of absentee Confederate owners to these workers. Treasury Department interest in collecting back taxes from South Carolina, as well as federal reservations concerning such a policy of land redistribution, stymied Saxon's efforts. After the war's end, this Port Royal experiment was nullified with SHERMAN'S LAND GRANTS during Andrew Johnson's administration. Beaufort's declining position as a port in the late nineteenth century was partially offset by the development of area PHOSPHATE mines and during the post–World War II era by the development of the SEA ISLANDS as a major resort area and center of TOURISM.

See K. M. Jones, *Port Royal Under Six Flags* (1960); M. K. Hilton, *Old Homes of Beaufort County* (1970); G. G. Johnson, *Social History of Sea Islands* (1930); R. Carse, *Department of South: Hilton Head in Civil War* (1961); V. C. Holmgren, *Hilton Head Chronicle* (1959); W. L. Rose, *Rehearsal for Reconstruction* (1964); and files of Beaufort *Gazette* (1897–), on microfilm. Beaufort County Library maintains a collection of published local history and of manuscripts prepared for Beaufort Historical Society.

BEAUMONT, TEX.

BEAUMONT, TEX. (pop. 115,716), an important industrial city and port of entry on the Neches River, is approximately 80 miles east of Houston. A settlement known as Texis Bluff had grown up around the home of Noah and Nancy Texis by 1835, when the site was acquired by a development group. The developers laid out a town in 1837, taking the name from the French for "beautiful hill." Although Beaumont developed initially as a market town for rice, sugar, cattle, and cotton, the post–Civil War demand for lumber, peaking in the 1880s and 1890s, soon displaced these crops as the basis of the city's livelihood. The lumber industry had begun to decline by 1901, but the discovery during that year of petroleum at SPINDLETOP created yet another wave of growth and prosperity. Named a port of entry in 1908, the city gained excellent access to the Gulf of Mexico with the completion in 1916 of a deepwater channel in the Neches River. Then in 1925 the discovery of a second and deeper series of oil wells ensured the city's position as a major producer of petroleum to the present time. Modern Beaumont produces a variety of petroleum-related products, including refined oil, synthetic rubber, and chemicals. It also is a shipping point for area rice, cotton, and lumber and the seat of Lamar State University (1923).

See Federal Writers' Project, *Beaumont* (1939); A. K. English, *Builders of Beaumont* (1929); and files of Beaumont *Enterprise* (1880–) and *Journal* (1889–).

BEAUREGARD, PIERRE GUSTAVE TOUTANT

BEAUREGARD, PIERRE GUSTAVE TOUTANT (1818–1893), was one of the eight full generals of the Confederacy and an important command figure in almost every phase of the South's war for independence. He was born at Contreras plantation in St. Bernard Parish, just south of New Orleans, into a well-to-do and aristocratic Creole family. Beauregard entered the United States Military Academy and was graduated second in the class of 1838. As befitted his high ranking, he received a commission in the elite engineering corps and was eventually assigned to construct coastal defenses on the Louisiana coast. In the Mexican War he was one of the engineer officers assigned to General WINFIELD SCOTT's staff and served ably in every engagement from the siege of Veracruz to the capture of Mexico City.

Again assigned to Louisiana after the war, he resumed his work with the coastal defenses. His most important assignment during the 1850s was as superintending engineer of the federal customhouse in New Orleans. In January, 1861, he assumed the position of superintendent of the military academy at West Point, but because he had announced his support of secession he was almost immediately removed.

In February he was made a brigadier general in the Confederate army and ordered to take command of the forces watching the federal garrison in FT. SUMTER in Charleston harbor. In April, 1861, acting at the direction of the government, he forced the reduction of Sumter and became an instant Confederate hero. He was then ordered to Virginia to command an army being gathered at Manassas Junction. On July 21, supported by troops from JOSEPH E. JOHNSTON's Shenandoah Valley army, he defeated a federal force at the first battle of Manassas or BULL RUN. Promoted full general after the engagement, he became embroiled in controversy with President Jefferson Davis and the War Department over supplies and other matters. Early in 1862 the government, perhaps wanting to get him out of the capital area, sent him to Kentucky as second in command to ALBERT SIDNEY JOHNSTON, commander in the western theater.

After the fall of Fts. Henry and Donelson, Johnston and Beauregard laid plans to strike the federal army under U. S. Grant, which had advanced to Pittsburg Landing on the Tennessee River. Beauregard drew up the plan for the advance that brought on the battle of SHILOH on April 6–7. When Johnston was killed on the sixth, Beauregard succeeded to the command; on the following day, confronted by a reinforced enemy army, he withdrew to Corinth. Criticized for throwing away a chance for victory at Shiloh, he came under more criticism when he evacuated Corinth before an advancing and superior federal army, and President Davis in June relieved him of command of the western army. Davis had become convinced that Beauregard was unfit for field command and exiled him to a comparatively minor command post, directing the defense of the South Carolina and Georgia coasts with headquarters in Charleston. Beauregard served in Charleston until the spring of 1864, conducting a skilled and tenacious defense against almost constant federal attacks by sea and land.

In April he was called back to Virginia to take command of the southern approaches to Richmond. Here he had his finest hour of the war, saving Petersburg from capture. Later he was assigned to command the Military Division of the West, an empty administrative position with no direct command power. At the end of the war he was with J. E. Johnston in North Carolina trying vainly to stem the onward march of W. T. Sherman.

After the war Beauregard resided in New Orleans. He became president of the New Orleans, Jackson & Great Northern Railroad and of the New Orleans & Carrollton Railroad, the latter a part of the city's street railway system. He also served as a supervisor of the drawings of the LOUISIANA STATE LOTTERY Company. Although he suffered some business reverses, he finally amassed a modest fortune.

See T. H. Williams, *P. G. T. Beauregard* (1955); D. S. Freeman, *Lee's Lieutenants* (3 vols.; 1942–44), valuable but uniformly critical of Beauregard; A. Roman, *Military Operations of Beauregard* (2 vols.; 1884), prejudiced but contains valuable documents; and H. Basso, *Beauregard* (1933), interesting, but neglects important episodes. Largest collections of Beauregard Papers are in Library of Congress and Louisiana State University Library.

T. HARRY WILLIAMS
Louisiana State University

BECKLEY, W.VA. (pop. 19,884), is about 35 miles north of Bluefield in the center of the state's bituminous COAL fields. Sometimes called the Smokeless Coal Capital of the World, the modern town also has foundries and machine shops. It was first settled in 1838 by General Alfred Beckley and had become a small town by the Civil War. Although the existence of the coal was known as early as 1774, its mining and shipment did not begin until the 1890s, when newly constructed rail lines made shipment feasible.

See H. Warren, *Beckley, U.S.A.* (4 vols.; 1955–75); C. Hodel, *Brief History of Beckley* (1943); P. Conley, *History of West Virginia Coal Industry* (1960); R. N. Martin, *John Beckley* (1948); and files of Raleigh *Register* (1880–) and *Post-Herald* (1900–), both on microfilm.

BELL, JOHN (1796–1869), political leader, son of Samuel and Margaret Edmiston Bell, was born on Mill Creek near Nashville, Tenn. He graduated from Cumberland College in 1814. Two years later he began the practice of law in Franklin. The following year he was elected to the state senate, but served only one term. In 1818 he married Sally Dickinson and moved to Murfreesboro but soon relocated in Nashville. His wife died in 1832, leaving five children, and Bell subsequently married Jane Erwin Yeatman.

In 1827 he was elected to represent the Nashville district in the U.S. House of Representatives, defeating the distinguished "War Hawk," FELIX GRUNDY. Although Andrew Jackson supported Grundy, Bell entered Congress as a Jacksonian Democrat and gave strong support to administration measures during Jackson's first term. In June, 1834, he was chosen Speaker of the House, a position he held until March, 1835, by which time he was no longer a Jackson man. His break with the administration was largely a result of the controversy over the second Bank of the United States. He led the Tennessee delegation in support of HUGH LAWSON WHITE for president in 1836 and soon joined the ranks of the Whig party. As a reward for his leadership on the national level and in carrying Tennessee for the Whigs in 1840, he was made secretary of war in President William Henry Harrison's cabinet, a position he resigned shortly after John Tyler became president.

From 1841 to 1847 Bell devoted his time to private affairs, supervising his coal and iron mines in Kentucky and Tennessee and practicing law. Upon election to the U.S. Senate in 1847, he became a vigorous opponent of President James K. Polk's Mexican War policy. Subsequently he opposed portions of the COMPROMISE OF 1850, the KANSAS-NEBRASKA ACT, and the effort to admit Kansas under the LECOMPTON CONSTITUTION. Following the disintegration of the Whig party, Bell did not rejoin the Democrats. His opposition to measures designed to extend slavery endeared him to many Republicans, but he had no intention of joining their ranks. For a brief period he cooperated with, but never joined, the KNOW-NOTHINGS. He continued to consider himself as a member of the "opposition."

His conservatism and defense of law and the Constitution brought him the nomination for president on the Constitutional Union ticket in 1860. There was much goodwill between his supporters and those of Stephen A. Douglas, but unlike Douglas he did little campaigning. He carried only Virginia, Kentucky, and Tennessee. Bell opposed secession, insisting that Abraham Lincoln's policy would be moderate. But, following Lincoln's call for troops, humiliation and anger drove him to advocate resistance. Henceforth he classed himself as a "rebel." The war years were spent in retirement among friends at Cedartown, Ga. After the war he made his home near Dover, Tenn., where he died.

See A. V. Goodpasture, *Tennessee History* (Dec., 1916); J. W. Caldwell, *American Historical Review* (July, 1899); and J. H. Parks, *John Bell of Tennessee* (1950). No substantial collection of Bell's papers exists. There are small collections or scattered letters in the Library of Congress; in the Polk-Yeatman Collection, University of North Carolina; in the David Campbell and John J. Crittenden papers, Duke University; and in the Thomas A. R. Nelson Papers, Lawson McGhee Library, Knoxville.

JOSEPH H. PARKS
University of Georgia

BELLE ISLE, Confederate prison camp, was on an island in the James River at Richmond, Va. Opened in the summer of 1861, the prison served as a detention center for enlisted prisoners throughout the war. Facilities at Belle Isle were often desperate; most of the men lived in tents and complained of inadequate rations. Although the population varied considerably, at one point in late 1863 the camp housed 10,000 federal soldiers. The large number of prisoners so near the Confederate capital was one factor that motivated Union raids on Richmond. Raiders could expect to find allies at Belle Isle with whom to exploit an initial success. Overcrowding, poor facilities, and the danger of mass escapes moved the Confederate government to construct more prison camps farther south. Despite the opening of new camps at SALISBURY, N.C., and ANDERSONVILLE, Ga., Belle Isle remained in operation and continued to be a source of concern for the Confederate military and a drain on Richmond's supplies of food and fuel.

See E. M. Thomas, *Confederate State of Richmond* (1971); W. Hesseltine, *Civil War Prisons* (1930); and *Official Records, Armies,* Ser. 2, Vol. VI.

EMORY M. THOMAS
University of Georgia

BELMONT, BATTLE OF (November 7, 1861). Belmont, Mo., on the Mississippi River, was the site of a Confederate fortified camp opposite the major southern position at Columbus, Ky. The immediate Union opposition was based at Cairo, Ill., under Ulysses S. Grant. In early November, 1861, Grant was ordered to undertake a complex series of movements, in which he was to expel Confederate Jeff Thompson's force from southeastern Missouri and prevent LEONIDAS POLK, commanding at Columbus, from reinforcing STERLING PRICE in western Missouri.

Grant executed both movements and, using the navy, landed five regiments (3,114 men) above Belmont on the morning of November 7. As the federals approached, Confederate Colonel J. Tappan left his camp and formed his regiment in line of battle. GIDEON J. PILLOW arrived shortly afterward and deployed his four regiments on Tappan's line. The southerners were forced back through their camp to the riverbank. The federals looted the camp, allowing the Confederates to reorganize and reinforce with five regiments. The northerners conducted a fighting retreat to their transports and successfully reembarked. Union losses were 80 killed, 322 wounded, 54 missing. Confederate casualties were 105 killed, 419 wounded, 117 missing and prisoners. Belmont brought national prominence to Grant and provided combat experience for both sides.

See B. Catton, *Grant Moves South* (1960); U. S. Grant, *Memoirs* (1885), I; J. H. Parks, *General Leonidas Polk* (1962); *Official Records, Armies,* Ser. 1, Vol. III; J. Y. Simon, *Papers of Grant* (1970); and K. P. Williams, *Lincoln Finds a General* (1952).

ROY P. STONESIFER, JR.
Edinboro State College

BENJAMIN, JUDAH PHILIP (1811–1884), was the most powerful member of the CONFEDERATE CABINET and the chief adviser to President Jefferson Davis. He was, except for Davis, the most complex and controversial Confederate leader. Born in St. Croix, British West Indies, he was reared in the Carolinas and went to New Orleans in 1828. He became a distinguished lawyer, a sugar planter, a promoter of commercial schemes, and a successful politician. He was elected to the Louisiana legislature in 1842 and to the U.S. Senate in 1852 and 1859.

While serving as the first attorney general of the Confederacy (February–September, 1861), Benjamin came to be Davis' most trusted adviser. On September 17, 1861, Davis appointed him secretary of war, a position he held until March 18, 1862. His tenure in that office began auspiciously and ended stormily. He imposed order on a chaotic department; he angered touchy generals and vain congressmen; and he inspired jealousy by his closeness to the president. Benjamin was a target who attracted criticism partly because he was in office before problems of war supplies were solved and after illusions of easy victory had died. The loss of Roanoke Island was blamed on him. In the face of a hostile Congress and press, Davis elevated Benjamin to head the State Department.

Benjamin was well suited for this post, and he remained secretary of state until the collapse of the Confederacy. His duties ranged beyond that office, however, as Davis sought his advice on many problems. Benjamin was less provincial and more detached than many Confederates; his advice was practical and realistic. He was bound neither to the past nor to past solutions, as demonstrated when he helped to change cotton policy and when he shifted diplomatic emphasis from Britain to France. He came to advocate ARMING OF SLAVES and freeing those who fought. By 1864 he questioned even the institution of slavery, proposing to Britain and France emancipation in return for recognition. At the end of the war he escaped to England. There he became an eminent lawyer, specializing in appeal cases before the House of Lords and the Privy Council.

See R. D. Meade, *Benjamin* (1943), best biography; P. Butler, *Benjamin* (1907); R. W. Patrick, *Davis and Cabinet* (1944); F. L. and H. C. Owsley, *King Cotton Diplomacy* (1931); *Official Records, Armies*, Ser. 1, Vols. IV, V, VII; J. D. Richardson (ed.), *Messages and Papers of Confederacy* (1905); Confederate Records, National Archives; and Pickett Papers, Library of Congress.

SHARON E. HANNUM
Ball State University

BENTON, THOMAS HART (1782–1858), was born near Hillsboro, N.C. At nineteen he moved with his family to a barely settled tract on the frontier south of Nashville, Tenn., after a traumatic early disgrace when he was expelled from the University of North Carolina for stealing. During the War of 1812, he served under ANDREW JACKSON as a colonel of volunteers in Indian skirmishes on the southern front. The two men became enemies when Jackson acted as a second in a duel that involved Benton's younger brother Jesse, although the general and Benton were reconciled a decade later. Meanwhile Benton practiced law and served in the Tennessee senate in 1809. In 1815 he settled in the village of St. Louis, Mo.

As editor of the St. Louis *Enquirer* (1818–1820), he spoke vehemently for western interests. He espoused Henry Clay's "American system" of economic development and insisted on Missouri's "right" to admission as a slave state. When Missouri won statehood in 1820–1821, Benton be-

came one of its first U.S. senators and served for 30 years—the first senator to do so. In his time he was deemed the peer of Clay, John C. Calhoun, and Daniel Webster. After Jackson lost the presidency in the four-man ELECTION OF 1824, Benton went all out for his former foe in 1828 and remained a staunch Democrat. He advocated an easy land policy for farmer settlers and identified himself with agrarian interests against land speculators. Proclaiming that the fluctuating values of paper money spawned by the Bank of the United States and most state banks were the bane of yeomen farmers and urban workers, Benton advocated "hard money": hence his popular nickname, Old Bullion.

As a small slaveholder and son of the South, Benton sanctioned slavery, but he opposed its further extension. He insisted that the areas won in the 1840s from Mexico were free soil by Mexican law. Meanwhile, he urged the acquisition of Oregon. He opposed the WILMOT PROVISO to contain slavery on the one hand and Calhoun's proslavery resolutions of 1847 on the other. He also condemned Clay's complex COMPROMISE OF 1850 as leaning too far toward the South. Ultimately, Benton came to oppose slavery as an institution, although he was never an abolitionist.

Such views were anathema in a slave state; and in 1851 the Missouri legislature denied him a sixth term in the Senate. Elected to the U.S. House of Representatives from the St. Louis district in 1852, he opposed Stephen Douglas' KANSAS-NEBRASKA ACT of 1854 as a ruse to "smuggle" slavery into the territory. But he also rejected the Republican candidate for president in 1856—his own son-in-law, John Charles Frémont. He also had no use for the Democratic presidents Franklin Pierce and James Buchanan, deeming them weak and vacillating.

In retirement, Benton wrote a two-volumed memoir mixed with the history of his Senate years, *Thirty Years View* (1854, 1856), and the polemical *Examination* of the proslavery DRED SCOTT decision of 1857. Virtually on his deathbed, he completed the multivolumed *Abridgement* of the debates of Congress to 1858, no longer a southerner but a national man.

See W. N. Chambers, *Old Bullion Benton* (1956), with full bibliography, including primary sources.

WILLIAM NISBET CHAMBERS
Washington University, St. Louis, Mo.

BENTON BARRACKS, MO., was a Union military complex during the Civil War. Established by General John Charles Frémont in 1861, it served as a training camp and point of rendezvous for troops of the Middle West and was capable of accommodating 30,000 soldiers. Located just west of the St. Louis fairgrounds on what were then the outskirts of the city, it contained a mile of barracks, warehouses, cavalry stables, parade grounds, and military hospitals. It was abandoned when the war ended.

See J. T. Scharf, *History of St. Louis* (1883), I; and N. Tilley (ed.), *Federals on the Frontier* (1963).

STEPHEN G. CARROLL
Missouri Western State College

BENTONVILLE, BATTLE OF (March 19–21, 1865), was the last attempt to block W. T. Sherman's northward march through the Carolinas. Sherman's immediate objective was Goldsboro, N.C., where he hoped to find supplies and reinforcements. His army, 60,000 strong, was divided into two permanent columns or wings. JOSEPH E. JOHNSTON led a makeshift force of some 20,000. His only hope was to isolate and defeat one of Sherman's wings before the other could come to its assistance, and at Bentonville Union General H. W. Slocum's left wing was reportedly a full day's march from the rest of the army.

At daybreak on March 19, Johnston took up his position. His entrenched line resembled a sickle, with BRAXTON BRAGG's command astride the Goldsboro Road the handle and the divisions of W. J. HARDEE and A. P. Stewart, stretching forward in the fields north of the road, the cutting edge. Slocum's leading division advanced into this unexpected hornets' nest and recoiled to a nearby ravine to entrench. At 3:00 P.M. the Confederates attacked, driving Union troops north of the road back upon the breastwork of the XX Corps, a mile to the rear. Five Confederate attacks against the XX Corps late that afternoon failed.

That night the right wing made a forced march to the battlefield, and on March 21 two Union brigades penetrated the Confederate left, to threaten Johnston's only line of retreat. That night he withdrew to Smithfield. Johnston's plan was sound, but he lacked the numbers necessary to produce a victory. Union casualties were 1,527; Confederate casualties numbered 2,606.

See J. Luvaas, *North Carolina Historical Review* (July, 1956); J. G. Barrett, *Sherman's March* (1956); and *Official Records, Armies,* Ser. 1, Vol. XLVII, Pt. 2.

JAY LUVAAS
Allegheny College

BEREA COLLEGE (Berea, Ky. 40404), 40 miles southeast of Lexington, is a unique institution dedicated to serving the educational needs of southern Appalachia. Founded in 1855 by the Reverend John Fee in cooperation with CASSIUS CLAY, the school was dedicated to the principles of antislavery and an integrated student body. Briefly disrupted by proslavery mobs and the Civil War, the school in 1866 resumed its program of educating students, both black and white, male and female, at all levels from elementary through college. Receiving sustained support from the American Missionary Association, Berea's distinctive program attracted the support of a few northern donors.

After Kentucky's Day Act (1904) ended biracial education for several decades in the state, Berea established Lincoln Institute for the blacks. Recruiting its students almost exclusively from southern Appalachia, Berea financed their education through a special student labor program, eliminating the tuition fee, and training students in a variety of skills as they progressed toward the college degree. Berea served the entire region by supplying teachers and extension programs including traveling libraries, adult education, agricultural guidance, and a rural newspaper. Although recent government programs have replaced some of these pioneer services, Berea College continues its tradition of service to this region in such programs as the rural school improvement project.

See E. Peck, *Berea's First Century* (1955); John Fee Manuscripts, Fisk University Archives; and J. Fee, *Autobiography* (1891). Berea College Library houses papers of Council of Southern Manufacturers and material on Appalachia.

JOHN D. WRIGHT, JR.
Transylvania University

BERMUDA HUNDRED, VA., was a portion of land halfway between Richmond and Petersburg, formed into a peninsula with a narrow neck by the winding James and Appomattox rivers. In U. S. Grant's 1864 campaign against Richmond, General B. F. Butler was ordered to move from Fortress Monroe to CITY POINT, establish a supply base there for Grant's army, build protective entrenchments across the Bermuda Hundred neck, and be prepared to move north against Richmond when Grant approached. On May 5, 35,000 soldiers arrived at City Point and Bermuda Hundred without difficulty. Butler built impressive defense lines and awaited orders from Grant. Not hearing from Grant, he attacked Confederate lines at DREWRY'S BLUFF on May 12. Confederate General P. G. T. BEAUREGARD counterattacked successfully, driving Butler back to his defense line. When Grant moved toward Petersburg in June, Confederates bottled Butler in along his own trenches, and he could not assist in the Petersburg siege. He attempted to build a canal at Dutch Gap, where a large portion of the James River could have been bypassed, but the attempt failed, and his Army of the James remained immobilized during the Petersburg campaign.

See W. H. Smith, *From Chattanooga to Petersburg* (1893); U. S. Grant, *Personal Memoirs* (1885); B. F. Butler, *Butler's Book* (1892); D. S. Freeman, *Lee's Lieutenants* (1944), III; R. U. Johnson and C. C. Buel (eds.), *Battles and Leaders* (1888), IV: Shelby Foote, *Civil War* (1974), III; and *Official Records, Armies*, Ser. 1, Vol. XXXVI, Pt. 2.

BERRY, MARTHA MCCHESNEY (1866–1942),
educator, was born near Rome, Ga., to affluent parents. Against the wishes of her family, she devoted herself to teaching the mountain people of north Georgia. Her work began by teaching Bible stories in a log cabin and expanded to the establishment of a school for boys in 1902 and one for girls in 1909. The schools flourished, and Berry College was added in 1926. These schools emphasized the teaching of agricultural, vocational, and domestic skills. Since the students had little cash, she established a system by which tuition was paid in manual labor. The schools were run on authoritarian lines and stressed a nondenominational religious atmosphere. Berry used her inheritance to establish the schools, but later relied on private donors. Henry Ford eventually contributed nearly $4 million.

See H. T. Kane, *Miracle in Mountains* (1956); M. M. Berry, *Outlook* (Aug. 6, 1904); H. Basso *New Republic* (April 4, 1934); and H. Roberts, *Georgia Review* (Summer, 1955).

MARY MARTHA THOMAS
Jacksonville State University

BETHUNE, MARY MCLEOD (1875–1955), was
an educator and leader for civil rights and women's rights. She was born in Mayesville, S.C., the fifteenth of 17 children. Her parents were born slaves, as were the older children. The McLeod children all worked in the rice and cotton fields. When the Presbyterian mission school opened in Mayesville in 1882, Mary was the only child who could be spared to attend. This was the beginning of her long career in education. With the financial help of a Colorado dressmaker, she was able to attend Scotia Seminary in Concord, N.C. (1887–1894), and Moody Bible Institute in Chicago (1894–1895). When the Presbyterian board of missions refused to send Mary to Africa, she decided

to dedicate herself to teaching children of her own race. She taught in southern mission schools until 1903. In 1898 she met and married Albert Bethune.

In 1904 Mrs. Bethune founded Daytona Normal and Industrial Institute for Girls, at Daytona Beach, Fla. The institute merged with Cookman Institute in 1923 to form BETHUNE-COOKMAN COLLEGE. She was president of the college until 1942. Mary Bethune was the founder-president of the National Council of Negro Women; special adviser to President Franklin Roosevelt on minority affairs; director of the Division of Negro Affairs of the NATIONAL YOUTH ADMINISTRATION; vice-president of the NATIONAL ASSOCIATION FOR THE ADVANCEMENT OF COLORED PEOPLE; and vice-president of the URBAN LEAGUE. In recognition of her public service she received honorary degrees from 11 universities and numerous medals and awards. Throughout her life Mary Bethune was recognized for her powerful presence, her extraordinary speaking ability, and her uncompromising stand on racial equality.

See R. Holt, *Mary McLeod Bethune* (1964); E. Sterne, *Mary McLeod Bethune* (1957); R. Logan, *What the Negro Wants* (1944); and Bethune Manuscripts, Dillard University, partial and incomplete.

DARA DEHAVEN
Emory University

BETHUNE-COOKMAN COLLEGE (Daytona
Beach, Fla. 32015) is the result of a merger in 1923 of Daytona Normal and Industrial Institute for Girls (founded in 1904 by MARY MCLEOD BETHUNE) and Cookman Institute (a Methodist school for young black men). This Methodist-related institution operated as a two-year junior college until 1941, when its teacher education curriculum was expanded to four years.

BEVERLEY, ROBERT (1673?–1722), was a native
Virginian. An apprenticeship under the provincial secretary led by 1696 to three important clerkships of the general court, the council, and the general assembly. A resident of Jamestown, he served as burgess between 1699 and 1706. A large speculator in land, Beverley went to London in 1703 to press an appeal before the Privy Council. Asked while there to correct the manuscript for the Virginia section of John Oldmixon's *British Empire in America* (1708), he declared it "too imperfect to be mended." Instead he wrote his own *History and Present State of Virginia* (1705), which displays a ready and exact knowledge of Virginia, the government, the trade, and particularly the

Indians. Witty and pungent, it is a literary classic. A revised edition (1722) is inferior. While abroad Beverley indiscreetly criticized Governor FRANCIS NICHOLSON and other high officials. Persona non grata on his return to Virginia, he lost his lucrative offices and retired to sylvan Beverley Park in King and Queen County, where he speculated in land and died wealthy.

See R. Beverley, *History and Present State of Virginia*, ed. with intro. L. B. Wright (1947).

WILLIAM M. E. RACHAL
Virginia Historical Society

BIBLE BELT is a term coined by H. L. Mencken in the *American Mercury* in 1924. It was used by him in a derogatory sense to refer to the predominantly rural areas of the South and Midwest in which Low Church Protestantism held sway and in which the white inhabitants subscribed to a puritanical moral code and a literal interpretation of the Bible and had an antiintellectual bias. The phrase has retained this connotation in general usage. The EVOLUTION CONTROVERSY, which agitated the South in particular in the 1920s and culminated in 1925 in the SCOPES TRIAL in Dayton, Tenn., reinforced the connection of the term specifically with the South. The term is ill-defined geographically, though it is usually assumed to refer to the more backwoods, interior portions of those states of the border and Deep South in which the BAPTIST and METHODIST churches and the CHURCHES OF CHRIST predominate; namely, Virginia, West Virginia, the Carolinas, Georgia, Kentucky, Tennessee, Alabama, Mississippi, Arkansas, and portions of Louisiana, Texas, Missouri, and Florida.

See M. E. Barrick, *American Notes & Queries* (Dec., 1970); F. C. Hobson, Jr., *Serpent in Eden* (1974); E. S. Gaustad, in S. S. Hill, Jr. (ed.), *Religion and Solid South* (1972); and K. K. Bailey, *Southern White Protestantism* (1964).

ANNE KUSENER NELSEN
Forecasting International, Ltd., Arlington, Va.

BIENVILLE, JEAN BAPTISTE LE MOYNE, SIEUR DE (1680–1767), founder of New Orleans and "Father of Louisiana," was mostly reared by his brother PIERRE LE MOYNE, SIEUR D'IBERVILLE. Iberville was commissioned to reclaim the Mississippi Valley for France and establish that country's presence on the Gulf of Mexico. Assisting his brother with the establishment of Biloxi and Mobile, Bienville became governor of Louisiana fol-

lowing his brother's death (1706). He maintained the struggling colony despite the motherland's neglect. Nevertheless, the accusations of jealous associates resulted in his dismissal (1707). After Antoine Crozat became proprietor of Louisiana in 1712 (CROZAT GRANT), Bienville was named military commander of the colony (1714); when the regent transferred Louisiana to the Company of the West in 1717 (MISSISSIPPI BUBBLE), Bienville was appointed commandant general in charge of military matters. Seeking to establish a more strategic defense position and a more functional base of operations for the company, he founded New Orleans in 1718, but a simmering quarrel with company officials resulted in his recall (1725). The 1729 Natchez massacre and declining profits forced the company to abandon Louisiana in 1731, however, and the king appointed Bienville governor of the royal colony. He returned to Louisiana in 1733 and continued as governor until his retirement and return to France in 1743.

See G. King, *Jean-Baptiste Le Moyne* (1892), romanticized account; D. Rowland and A. Sanders (eds.), *Mississippi Provincial Architect* (1927–1932), translations of Bienville's correspondence; and *Louisiana Historical Quarterly* (Jan., 1918).

GLENN R. CONRAD
University of Southwestern Louisiana

BIG BETHEL, BATTLE OF (June 10, 1861), was a skirmish near Big Bethel Church, Va., 12 miles northwest of Fortress Monroe, and is often called the first battle of the Civil War. Union General B. F. Butler, learning of Confederate forces blocking the Yorktown Road, ordered 4,400 troops under E. W. Pierce to leave from Fortress Monroe and Newport News at night to meet at Little Bethel Church and join forces for a morning attack at Big Bethel. Union regiments met in the dark and, mistaking each other for the enemy, exchanged fire, alerting the Confederate camp. Southern troops under JOHN B. MAGRUDER were D. H. HILL's 1st North Carolina and some Virginia artillery, totaling about 1,400, in strong positions behind earthworks, with artillery guarding a road and bridge. General Pierce ordered flanking movements, but heavy artillery and fortifications forced his retreat. Union losses were 18 killed, 76 wounded; Confederate losses were one killed, seven wounded.

See *Official Records, Armies*, Ser. 1, Vol. II; B. F. Butler, *Butler's Book* (1892), biased; Richmond *Dispatch* (June 12, 13, 15, 1861); and F. Moore, *Rebellion Record* (1861), I.

FREDERIC SHRIVER KLEIN
Franklin and Marshall College

BIG CYPRESS SWAMP occupies 2,400 square miles of southwestern Florida, mostly in Collier County. It is bounded by the EVERGLADES (east), Gulf of Mexico (west), Tamiami Canal and Trail (south), and Immokalee Island (north). Although sometimes considered part of Florida's Everglades, Big Cypress is higher in elevation and was never in the water course between Lake OKEE-CHOBEE and the sea. A northwestern extension of Big Cypress is called Corkscrew Swamp, where a sanctuary maintained by the Audubon Society contains the largest remaining stand of virgin baldcypress on earth. The Big Cypress region is virtually uninhabited, and few signs of human activity may be observed along the 78-mile highway (Alligator Alley) that bisects it. Most of Big Cypress resembles a prairie, dominated by grasses and sedges. Stands ("domes") of trees occupy small lakes. Domes should not be confused with the "hammocks" of the Everglades: hammocks are forested islands. Besides cypress, other woody species are represented by bay, gum, oak, palm, palmetto, and even pine trees.

See A. Carr, *Everglades* (1973); and U.S. Senate, Committee on Interior and Insular Affairs, *Big Cypress*, 93rd Cong., 2nd Sess.

ROBERT H. FUSON
University of South Florida

BIG HOUSE was the central building and home of the owner of a southern plantation. Although by tradition it was built in the grand style and approached through a beautiful alley of trees, by no means was this always the case. Most were fairly commonplace and utilitarian, but to slaves and POOR WHITES living in an isolated, rural world it was still an impressive structure.

BIG MULE is a term used in the 1940s by Alabama populist candidates to describe powerful industrial groups opposed to NEW DEAL reforms. State newspapers used this term to describe the business leaders of Birmingham and Mobile who joined the conservative agricultural leaders of the BLACK BELT in an attempt to defeat populist candidates for governor and the legislature. More recently, historians and political scientists have adopted big mule as a general term to describe urban business leaders.

See W. D. Barnard, *Dixiecrats and Democrats* (1974); V. O. Key, *Southern Politics* (1950); S. Hackney, *Populism and Progressivism in Alabama* (1969); Birmingham *News* (1942–46); and Huntsville *Times* (1942–46).

FRANCES C. ROBERTS
University of Alabama, Huntsville

BILBO, THEODORE GILMORE (1877–1947), possibly America's most hated bigot when he died, had been a reform governor and liberal New Deal senator. Born in Mississippi's piney woods near Poplarville, an area influenced by Baptist preachers and populism, this youngest child in a large and comparatively prosperous family was educated for the law at Vanderbilt. After a brief teaching career, he entered politics on the side of the reform faction of the Democratic party, which ousted the conservative Delta politicians. He was elected state senator, lieutenant governor, governor twice (1916–1920, 1928–1932), and U.S. senator three times (1934–1940, 1940–1946, 1946–1947). As a Progressive governor, according to G. B. Tindall, "no other leader of the plebeian masses in the teens had either a program or a record to equal his." And during the 1930s few senators gave more loyal support to Franklin Roosevelt's New Deal.

Noted for his vitriolic and vulgar language and for scandals involving both money and women, Bilbo never used race as a political issue prior to World War II. He favored posing as his poor white constituents' defender from exploiting corporations, a practice he stopped in the 1940s, allegedly when big business gave him large contributions. More important, the chairmanship of the District of Columbia Committee brought his first close association with Negroes not in menial positions at the very time of their increased militancy for equality. The title of his book, *Take Your Choice: Separation or Mongrelization* (1947), reflects his conclusions. Soon after the 1946 election, the Senate investigated his financial gains from war contractors and his advocacy of violence to prevent blacks from voting. It refused him the oath of office, but in an unprecedented action it did not expel him; it paid his and his staff's salaries until his death later in 1947.

See B. W. Saucier, "T. G. Bilbo" (Ph.D. dissertation, Tulane University, 1971); L. T. Balsamo, "Bilbo, 1877–1932" (Ph.D. dissertation, University of Missouri, 1967); A. W. Green, *The Man Bilbo* (1963), based on newspapers; and Bilbo Manuscripts, University of Southern Mississippi.

BOBBY W. SAUCIER
Dillard University

BILL OF RIGHTS. To ratification of the federal CONSTITUTION the southern states presented varied reactions, ranging from unanimous votes with little concern for the lack of a bill of rights to refusal because of that lack. Delaware ratified with words of joy, and Georgia, having already in its state constitution some items usually found in a bill of rights, was satisfied. Maryland, having a bill of rights in its state constitution and expecting a series of amendments to the federal Constitution to protect individual liberties, voted six to one. There were, however, strong dissenting factions. South Carolina seemed more interested in states' rights than a bill of rights. The South Carolinians voted better than two to one for ratification but called for amendments to the Constitution to help strengthen it.

The most important debates concerning a bill of rights were carried on in Virginia and North Carolina, although in both cases this probably was not the major issue. Virginia, proud of its own bill of rights, after much heated discussion ratified 89 to 79, with the proposal that a complete bill of rights be attached to the Constitution. ANTI-FEDERALISTS in majority in North Carolina were not so much opposed to the new union as afraid of the threats to local government and to individual liberties. After debating 11 days, they voted neither to reject nor to ratify and asked for amendments to the Constitution and for the calling of a second federal convention. Public opinion began to change, however, and, when it became clear that Congress would propose a bill of rights, North Carolina voted 194 to 77 for ratification.

It is interesting to note that it did not take Maryland, Delaware, South Carolina, and North Carolina long to ratify the Bill of Rights. Virginia did so only after a majority of the others showed their willingness. Georgia did not ratify until 1941, and then as a gesture commemorating the 150th anniversary of the Bill of Rights.

See J. Elliot, *Debates* (1836); R. A. Rutland, *Birth of the Bill of Rights* (1955); and B. Schwartz, *Bill of Rights* (1971).

WILLIAM H. WROTEN, JR.
Salisbury State College

BILOXI, MISS. (pop. 46,497). Founded in 1699 by PIERRE LE MOYNE, SIEUR D'IBERVILLE on the northeastern shore of Biloxi Bay, Old Biloxi (present-day Ocean Springs) was the first permanent French settlement in the lower Mississippi Valley. In 1719 the settlement was moved to its present site on the peninsula that separates the bay from the Mississippi Sound. Biloxi remained a small, coastal fishing and trading village. It had only six landowning families in 1790 and only ten as late as 1836. Meanwhile, its residents retained their French language and Catholic faith. Indian removals of the 1830s and immigration into the surrounding area raised Biloxi's population to 921 by

1850. Antebellum planters and the prevalence of yellow fever in New Orleans and Mobile established Biloxi as a large seaside resort, its population quadrupling each summer. In 1870 a railroad connected the town to the markets of Mobile and New Orleans, triggering a boom for the city's seafood and lumber, which in turn attracted numbers of Slovenian immigrants. In the 1920s construction of a seawall for hurricane protection and highways and bridges to span the area's bays and rivers established tourism. Today, Biloxi remains a fishing and resort city with Keesler Air Force Base as its largest employer.

See R. A. McLemore, *History of Mississippi* (1973); D. Rowland, *History of Mississippi* (1925); J. K. Bettersworth, *Mississippi* (1959); and D. Greenwell, *Twelve Flags* (1968).

M. JAMES STEVENS
Mississippi Coast Historical Society

BILOXI INDIANS are part of the Hokan-Siouan Indian group. They were first encountered by the French in 1699 on the Pascagoula River in Mississippi. During the English occupation of that area, the Biloxi migrated to the Red River region. By 1817 some Biloxi joined the CHOCTAW, but the rest were near Biloxi Bayou in Angelina County, Tex. Little is known of them from 1820 to 1886, when in that year Albert Gatschet rediscovered a small band living in Lecompte, La. Today a few descendants are found in east Texas, Louisiana, and northern Mexico.

See F. Hodge, *Handbook* (1912); J. Dorsey and J. Swanton, *Dictionary of the Biloxi*, Bureau of American Ethnology Bulletin (1912); J. Swanton, *Indian Tribes* (1911); J. Dorsey, *Proceedings of American Association for the Advancement of Science* (1893); and James Owen Dorsey Papers, Bureau of American Ethnology Archives.

EDWARD A. LUKES
Hillsborough College

BINNS, JOHN ALEXANDER (1761–1813), born in Virginia, was a farmer and one of several southern agricultural reformers. Frequently his name and experiments were linked with those of Israel Janney and JOHN TAYLOR of Caroline. Beginning in 1784 Binns experimented with deep plowing. He also experimented with plaster of paris (gypsum) and clover as a preparation for wheat lands. Binns published the results of his experiments in 1803 in a pamphlet entitled *A Treatise on Practical Farming*. The reforms recommended by Binns were popularized as the Loudoun system. Ultimately, the Loudoun system was employed widely in northern Virginia, the upper valley of Virginia, and western Maryland. L. C. Gray credits the experiments of Binns, along with those of Janney, Taylor, and others, with the general transformation of agriculture in Virginia and the continuation of wheat cultivation in Virginia.

See A. O. Craven, *Soil Exhaustion as a Factor in the History of Virginia and Maryland* (1925); L. C. Gray, *History of Agriculture in Southern U.S. to 1860* (1933); and R. M. Brown, *William and Mary Quarterly* (April, 1939).

D. HARLAND HAGLER
North Texas State University

BIRDS. See MAMMALS AND BIRDS

BIRMINGHAM, ALA. (pop. 300,910), was founded in 1871 at a confluence of minerals and railroads in the north-central part of the state. Rich deposits of coal, limestone, and iron ore in the immediate vicinity attracted an influx of northern capital in the 1880s and destined Birmingham from the beginning as a steel center (IRON AND STEEL INDUSTRY). The Elyton Land Company and dozens of other real estate ventures not only carved out the city's space, but also etched its streets and transportation lines and provided its public areas and utilities.

From a population of 38,415 in 1900 the city grew dramatically to 178,806 residents in 1920 and 326,037 in 1950. Birmingham's population growth rate of 749 percent in the first half of the twentieth century was almost three times that of Atlanta. Much of this expansion was due to annexations early in the century, most notably the Greater Birmingham consolidation that joined nine outlying suburbs with the city in 1910, quadrupling Birmingham's land area and more than tripling its population. This expansion imposed severe burdens on city services and finances and constituted the major challenge for municipal leaders over the next two decades. Birmingham's political and social life was often characterized by moral fervor, religious intolerance, and racial bigotry, though control of the city's affairs generally rested with a local commercial-civic elite, which preached a NEW SOUTH gospel of growth and efficiency, and a handful of powerful absentee industrial interests. Municipal policies posed minimal interference with private business activities and were often oriented to the social control of blacks, who composed a large segment of the city's population and labor force.

Birmingham was stricken severely by the GREAT DEPRESSION in the 1930s, and a proliferation of autonomous suburbs and jurisdictions blunted its expansion. The racial violence of the early 1960s was followed by a loss of population in the city proper, though growth continued in the metropolitan area.

See M. C. Mitchell, "Birmingham" (Ph.D. dissertation, University of Chicago, 1946); C. V. Harris, "Economic Power and Politics" (Ph.D. dissertation, University of Wisconsin, 1970); B. A. Brownell, *Journal of Southern History* (Feb., 1972), and *Urban Ethos* (1975); P. B. Worthman, in T. K. Hareven (ed.), *Anonymous Americans* (1971); C. V. Harris, *Journal of Southern History* (Nov., 1972); B. A. Brownell and David R. Goldfield, *City in Southern History* (1976); E. Armes, *Coal and Iron* (1910); and Southern History Collection, Birmingham Public Library.

BLAINE A. BROWNELL
University of Alabama, Birmingham

BIRMINGHAM DIFFERENTIAL in steel pricing was established by the United States Steel Corporation in the early 1920s to replace the PITTSBURGH PLUS system of pricing. The price of important articles of rolled steel, not including rails, was made $3 per ton higher in Birmingham than in Pittsburgh. Competitors followed the practice of pricing their steel delivered in Birmingham at the same figures. The differential was intended to be high enough to encourage the corporation to expand steel-making facilities in Birmingham but low enough to discourage price undercutting by competitors who had to absorb the freight costs from northern mills, *e.g.*, $10 to $12 per ton from Pittsburgh. To encourage the location of steel-fabricating plants in the Birmingham district, the corporation entered into specific contracts to waive the differential. Under the competitive conditions of the depression, the differential substantially broke down in 1932, and it was abolished in June, 1938, when Birmingham mill prices were equalized with those of Pittsburgh.

See U.S. Senate, *Hearings before Temporary National Economic Committee*, 76th Cong., 2nd Sess., Pt. 19.

JAMES F. DOSTER
University of Alabama

BIRMINGHAM NEWS began publication in 1888, and two years later it absorbed the Birmingham *Chronicle* (1883–1890). In 1920 it absorbed yet another of its daily competitors, the Birmingham *Ledger* (1896–1920). Presently published as an independent paper, it is the city's most widely circulated journal, with 180,000 daily copies.

See bound copies at Alabama Department of Archives and Library of Congress (1890–); and microfilm from Bell & Howell (1889–1946) and Microfilm Corporation of America (1947–).

BIRMINGHAM POST-HERALD was formed in 1950 by the merger of the *Post* (1921–1950) and the *Age-Herald* (1888–1950), the latter being itself the product of the merger in 1888 of the *Iron Age* (1874–1888) and the *Herald* (1887–1888). The *Age-Herald* traditionally was associated with the city's business and industrial leaders. During the turbulent decade of the 1890s, the paper applauded mobilization of the state militia to suppress coal miners' strikes, opposed the gubernatorial candidacies of REUBEN KOLB, and called for reapportionment of representation in Democratic state conventions on the sole basis of a county's total white population. The paper currently is politically independent with a daily circulation of approximately 75,000 copies.

See bound copies at Alabama Department of Archives and at Library of Congress; and microfilm from Bell & Howell for *Age* (1886–87), *Age-Herald* (1889–1946), and *Post-Herald* (1950–).

BIRNEY, DAVID BELL (1825–1864), a Union general, was the son of antislavery leader JAMES G. BIRNEY. Born in Huntsville, Ala., he lived in the South until 1838. He graduated from Andover and in 1856 became a lawyer in Philadelphia. Birney inherited his father's antislavery convictions and was an early member of the Republican party. When the Civil War began, he became a colonel in the 23rd Pennsylvania Volunteers, was promoted brigadier general in the Army of the Potomac in 1862, and the following year was elevated to major general and given command of the X Corps. Birney participated in the major campaigns of the eastern theater; twice he faced accusations of dereliction of duty, but the charges were never substantiated. In October, 1864, he died of malaria.

See O. W. Davis, *David Bell Birney* (1867); and James G. Birney Manuscripts, University of Michigan Library.

RICHARD H. ABBOTT
Eastern Michigan University

BIRNEY, JAMES GILLESPIE (1792–1857), abolitionist and Liberty party candidate for president, was born in Danville, Ky., into a wealthy, slaveholding family. He attended Transylvania University and the College of New Jersey (now Princeton) and became a lawyer. In 1817 he moved to Alabama, where he experienced religious conversion and expanded his already established interest in justice for Indians and Negroes.

In 1832 he became an agent for the AMERICAN COLONIZATION SOCIETY and sought to enlist other slaveholders in its program. Disappointed in their response, he returned to Kentucky, where he was also coldly received. In 1835 Birney moved to Cincinnati, Ohio, where he published the *Philanthropist* and suffered threats and riots. Birney was now famous among emancipationists. His *The American Churches, the Bulwarks of American Slavery* (1835) became a standard abolitionist tract. In 1837 Birney moved to New York to become secretary of the American Anti-Slavery Society. He became persuaded of the need for a national political antislavery party, and in 1840 a convention declared him the Liberty party candidate for president. His 7,100 votes that year seemed to refute its expectations. Birney's followers, however, persisted, so he ran again in the ELECTION OF 1844. That year he attracted 15,812 votes in New York State, which would otherwise have gone to Henry Clay and given that moderate on the slavery issue the state and the presidency. Instead, both the state's electoral vote and the presidency went to the proslavery defender James K. Polk. Thereafter, political abolitionism became a factor in party politics and elections.

In 1845 a severe accident, which left him partially paralyzed, caused Birney to retire from active politics. His son WILLIAM BIRNEY's *James G. Birney and His Times* (1890) tried to demonstrate the superiority of his father's antislavery services to those of William Lloyd Garrison.

See D. L. Dumond (ed.), *Letters of J. G. Birney, 1831–1857* (1938); and B. Fladeland, *J. G. Birney* (1955).

LOUIS FILLER
Antioch College

BIRNEY, WILLIAM (1819–1907), was born in Madison County, Ala., but received his education in the North and abroad. He is best known as the author of *James G. Birney and His Times*, a biography of his father, though William was recognized as a reformer in his own right. In the 1840s he served as an officer in the Sons of Temperance of Ohio. While a graduate student at the Paris Ecole de Droit, he commanded at the barricades during the revolution of 1848. In 1863 Birney was appointed one of the superintendents for the enlistment of Negro soldiers, and he organized seven regiments. As a commander of black troops he took part in a number of important engagements that restored Florida to the Union. After the war, as president of the school board of Washington, D.C., he reorganized the district school system.

See W. Birney, *James G. Birney* (1890); W. Birney (ed.), *Constitution of Sons of Temperance* (1846); F. B. Heitman, *Historical Register* (1903); Miami University, *Centennial Catalogue* (1909); *Official Records, Armies*, index; Washington *Post* (Aug. 15, 1907); and Washington *Evening Star* (Aug. 15, 1907).

VICTOR B. HOWARD
Morehead State University

BLACK, HUGO LAFAYETTE (1886–1971), was born in Clay County, Ala., the eighth child of William LaFayette and Martha Ardelluh Black. After receiving his law degree from the University of Alabama in 1906, Black established a law practice in Birmingham. After army service from 1917 to 1919, he resumed his law practice, joining the KU KLUX KLAN in 1923. He was elected to the U.S. Senate with strong Klan support in 1926, although he had resigned from the Klan prior to his election. In the Senate, Black was an ardent New Dealer and received national attention as a relentless investigator, especially of the utilities lobby. He became Franklin Roosevelt's first appointee to the U.S. Supreme Court in August, 1937.

Although the revelation of his association with the Klan prompted demands for his resignation from the Court, during his 34 years of service on the bench Black proved to be one of the most forceful champions of civil liberties in the history of the Court. His most important contribution was his insistence that the FOURTEENTH AMENDMENT was intended to make all of the Bill of Rights applicable to the states. Although this "total incorporation" of the Bill of Rights into the Fourteenth Amendment was never accepted by a majority of the Court, Black did live to see almost all of the Bill of Rights made applicable to the states. He additionally believed the First Amendment's guarantees of free expression and religious freedom were "absolutes" and thus beyond even minimal governmental interference. A supporter of the Supreme Court's desegregation decisions, he was also a leader in enforcing the principles of equality in legislative apportionment and political districting. At his death, Justice Black had served on the Court longer than all of his predecessors except JOHN MARSHALL, Stephen J. Field, and William O. Douglas.

See V. V. de V. Hamilton, *Hugo Black* (1972), excellent on Alabama political career; J. P. Frank, *Mr. Justice Black* (1949); S. P. Strickland (ed.), *Hugo Black and the Supreme Court* (1967); H. L. Black, *Constitutional Faith* (1969); Symposium, *Yale Law Journal* (1956); and H. L. Black, Jr., *My Father* (1975).

RICHARD C. CORTNER
University of Arizona

BLACK AND TANS was the nickname given southern Republicans whose conventions were interracial. From Reconstruction onward they were often a minority, dependent on presidential patronage for strength, although one of them, GEORGE H. WHITE, survived in Congress until 1901. They included B. K. BRUCE, N. W. CUNEY, J. C. Dancy (collector, Wilmington, N.C., and recorder of deeds, Washington, D.C.), R. B. SMALLS, and J. R. LYNCH. After the DISFRANCHISEMENT of southern Negroes between 1890 and 1908, many lost their constituencies. Thenceforth their opponents characterized them as representatives of "rotten boroughs" and seekers after political plums. In state and national conventions they contested the seating of LILY-WHITE Republicans. Some of them—such as Walter Cohen of Louisiana, H. L. Johnson of Georgia, POWELL CLAYTON of Arkansas, and Perry Howard of Mississippi—remained powerful in state organizations until the Republican National Convention of 1928, which recognized chiefly lily-white delegations from the South.

See T. R. Cripps, "Lily-White Republicans" (Ph.D. dissertation, University of Maryland, 1967), good bibliography.

THOMAS CRIPPS
Morgan State University

BLACKBEARD (?–1718), whose real name was possibly Edward Teach, emerged in 1716 as a pirate leader from a largely unknown past (PIRACY). For two years his band robbed scores of merchant vessels while sailing the Caribbean and off the Virginia-Carolina coast. In 1718 an expedition personally sponsored by Governor Alexander Spotswood of Virginia cornered Blackbeard in North Carolina at Ocracoke Inlet and killed him. His colorful contemporary reputation, self-created and publicized to influence quick surrenders from his victims, survives to make his name synonymous with ferocity. Long beard, gaudy clothes, many side arms, lit fuses in his ears, volatile temper, insatiable appetite for wives (supposedly 12 or 14), his alleged buried treasure—all are part of his legend. Yet his career suggests that he may have been no more violent than most pirates.

See R. E. Lee, *Blackbeard* (1974), a detailed revisionist interpretation.

CONVERSE D. CLOWSE
University of North Carolina, Greensboro

BLACK BELT is a crescent-shaped physical region extending some 300 miles across central Alabama and northeastern Mississippi and into Tennessee. Part of the Gulf coastal plain, it is a relatively flat, fertile plain ranging in width from 20 to 25 miles throughout most of its length. The name derives from the dark color of its calcareous soils, which

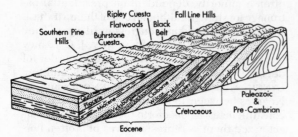

Southern Pine Hills | Ripley Cuesta | Flatwoods | Buhrstone Cuesta | Black Belt | Fall Line Hills | Paleozoic & Pre-Cambrian | Cretaceous | Eocene

See N. M. Fenneman, *Physiography of Eastern U.S.* (1938); W. D. Thornbury, *Regional Geomorphology of U.S.* (1965); E. Rostlund, *Annals of the Association of American Geographers* (Dec., 1957), deals with prairie controversy; and H. F. Cleland, *Geographical Review* (Dec., 1920). The following treat the black belt as an economic or ethnic entity: H. W. Odum, *Southern Regions* (1936); U. B. Phillips, *American Historical Review* (July, 1906); and A. F. Raper, *Tenants of Almighty* (1943).

SAM B. HILLIARD
Louisiana State University

were formed from a geologic formation of Cretaceous age known as the Selma Chalk. The inland boundary of the black belt is formed by the older Eutaw formation, whose surficial manifestation is known as the Fall Line Hills. The Selma Chalk dips southward and westward to disappear beneath the more resistant Ripley formation, which forms asymmetrical ridges known as the Ripley Cuesta in Alabama and Pontotoc Ridge in Mississippi, both of which rise some 200 to 300 feet above the black belt to form its seaward boundary.

Most of the black belt is drained by the Alabama and Tombigbee river systems, with the major streams flowing some 50 to 60 feet below the generally flat black belt surface. Early settlers reported poor drainage with some problems of soil stickiness that inhibited cultivation. There has been debate over its original vegetation cover, with the black soil encouraging a belief that it was originally a grassland (sometimes referred to as the Black Prairie). Early travel accounts, however, do not support this interpretation.

Unfortunately, the term black belt has more than one meaning. Some social scientists have used it in a much looser sense, usually referring to that part of the South dominated by plantations with a consequent high proportion of blacks in the population. H. W. ODUM shows the black belt extending into Georgia and the Carolinas with an outlier in western Mississippi (part of the Mississippi River floodplain). Apparently, some use the term indiscriminately to refer to any part of the South heavily populated by blacks.

High in organic matter, the inherently fertile black belt soils attracted cotton growers quite early, and by the 1820s the area had emerged as one of the most productive agricultural regions in the South. Cotton and corn were the dominant crops during the antebellum period, and the black belt ranked second only to the Mississippi River valley as the most productive part of the cotton belt. Cotton maintained itself as the cash crop until the ravages of the boll weevil early in the twentieth century encouraged agricultural diversification with a strong emphasis on cattle.

BLACK CODES were laws passed by southern legislatures in 1865–1866 to regulate the life and labor of the Negro population. Believing that blacks would work only under compulsion and that white society must be protected from them, white southerners devised these laws to replace the obsolete SLAVE CODES. Postwar black codes generally regulated education, labor, vagrancy, and legal rights and evolved from precedents established in antebellum laws governing slaves and free blacks. The codes ranged from mild to vindictive, and the earlier in Reconstruction they were written, the more severe they were. States with a substantial antebellum free black population were the least panicked about how to regulate the freedmen. The great alarm in 1865 developed because of black reluctance to sign labor contracts for 1866 in the face of the rumored gift of FORTY ACRES AND A MULE.

After Christmas, 1865, more blacks signed contracts, and subsequent contract and vagrancy laws were less discriminatory. But even the most severe of the black codes were less harsh than prewar codes. Reconstruction laws improved the status of blacks who had been free before 1860 and gave the former slaves approximately the place of the antebellum free blacks, a status white southerners considered to be a generous concession. Later Republican state governments repealed or substantially modified the codes. Meanwhile, northerners sternly criticized the South for enacting the black codes, despite the existence of antiblack laws in the North. They interpreted the codes as evidence of the South's lack of penitence for the rebellion and as a southern effort to circumvent the THIRTEENTH AMENDMENT and to reenslave the freedmen (RECONSTRUCTION, CONGRESSIONAL).

See T. B. Wilson, *Black Codes* (1965); W. L. Fleming, *Documentary History of Reconstruction* (1966); and R. N. Current, *Reconstruction* (1965).

SARAH WOOLFOLK WIGGINS
University of Alabama

BLACK HORSE CAVALRY was one of several secret terrorist groups that sprang up in the South after the Civil War. Like the others, such as the Jayhawkers, REGULATORS, and Knights of the White Camellia, it had its roots in the armed slave patrols of the antebellum period. The Black Horse Cavalry was founded in Tallapoosa, Ala., in 1865. It operated in rural areas and spread to neighboring states, especially Georgia. Members murdered freedmen, drove them from plantations to avoid paying wages due, and often practiced simple brigandage. They also attacked and sometimes killed Republican leaders, both black and white. These activities helped motivate Congress to authorize the FREEDMEN'S BUREAU to extend military protection to the freedmen and to override President Andrew Johnson's veto of the 1866 extension of the bureau. The Black Horse Cavalry merged with the KU KLUX KLAN in 1869.

See A. E. Trelease, *White Terror* (1971); and J. G. Randall and D. Donald, *Civil War and Reconstruction* (1969).

DONALD L. GRANT
Ft. Valley State College

BLACK MUSLIMS are members of the black nationalist religious sect, the Nation of Islam, founded by W. D. Fard in Detroit in 1930. When Fard disappeared in 1934, leadership was assumed by Elijah Muhammad, formerly Elijah Poole of Sandersville, Ga. Muhammad shaped the Muslims into a moralistic federation of congregations centered on local mosques, which encouraged black capitalism and education. The weekly newspaper, *Bilalian News* (formerly *Muhammad Speaks*), grew to a circulation of 600,000. Muslim teachings include dietary laws, monogamy, abstinence from alcohol and tobacco, and a call for a portion of the South to be set aside as a black state where white surveillance and domination could be avoided. Wallace Muhammad succeeded to the leadership on his father's death in 1975. Since then the organization has moved from its position that "all whites are devils" to one of accepting nonracist whites and to a growing interest in Third World problems.

In the South, mosques were founded in the larger cities, such as Atlanta. Farms established in Alabama and Georgia met considerable racist opposition. One farm near Pell City, Ala., had its cattle herd partially destroyed by snipers and poisoners in 1970. These Klan-like attacks subsided as white apprehensions proved baseless and when the Alabama law requiring Muslims to register was declared unconstitutional. Nevertheless, southern police attacks on Muslims continued. In a 1972 incident, two policemen and two Muslims died when young Muslim militants, who were touring the South seeking support for their position that the Muslim hierarchy was elitist, were attacked by the police in Baton Rouge, La.

See E. U. Essien-Udom, *Black Nationalism* (1962); and G. Samuels, *New York Times Magazine* (March 22, 1964).

DONALD L. GRANT
Ft. Valley State College

BLACK PATCH WAR (1906–1910), named for the dark leaf tobacco region of western Kentucky, erupted during a sustained effort by tobacco producers to break the monopoly of the "tobacco trust." Producers' cooperatives were formed in western and central Kentucky to gain control of the tobacco supply and to force a rise in prices. In western Kentucky, tobacco growers were first urged, then coerced by threats, whippings, destruction of tobacco beds and barns, and shootings by NIGHT-RIDING groups of masked and armed men, to sell their tobacco through the cooperatives. In late 1907 and early 1908, large groups of heavily armed men (masked and acting on signals with military precision) seized whole towns to burn factories and warehouses and whipped leading officials. Governor A. E. Willson sent the Kentucky National Guard into 23 counties throughout the state. Hundreds of armed citizens joined in to guard threatened towns, patrol rural districts, and search out the identities of the masked riders. As order was restored, dissension surfaced among the night riders themselves, and some turned against their comrades after a federal court in Paducah awarded damages against known members. For a time prices paid for tobacco did rise, but at the end the issue became one of law and order.

See U.S. *Senate Document No. 372*, 59th Cong., 2nd Sess.; C. N. Mayfield, *History of Christian County, Ky.* (1930); J. G. Miller, *Black Patch War* (1936); W. F. Axton, *Tobacco and Kentucky* (1975); and M. Taylor, *Register of Kentucky History* (Oct., 1963; Jan., 1964). Margaret I. King Library of the University of Kentucky has microfilmed copies of most Kentucky county and metropolitan newspapers, which provide a valuable source.

JUDGE WATSON
Florida Southern College

BLACK RECONSTRUCTION is a term used by white southerners to describe the period after the Civil War when, embittered by military defeat, confused by a fumbling national policy, and forced to accept enfranchisement of the former slaves, they felt themselves helpless in the face of a powerful Republican party supported by black voters and the U.S. Army. The term is a misnomer since blacks were never in a majority anywhere except for a two-year period in the South Carolina house of representatives. Using violence and economic intimidation, white Democrats regained control of their states by the late 1870s, but continued to use the term for its political effect on party dissidents to prevent a split of the white vote.

See W. E. B. Du Bois, *Black Reconstruction* (1935); J. H. Franklin, *Reconstruction* (1961); W. A. Dunning, *Reconstruction, Political and Economic* (1907); and A. O. Craven, *Reconstruction* (1969).

JERRELL H. SHOFNER
Florida Technological University

BLACK REPUBLICANS were members of the REPUBLICAN PARTY following its formation in 1854. Northern Democrats such as Stephen A. Douglas used the epithet to identify Republicans as advocates of Negro equality. Southern Democrats used the term, most notably during the 1860 presidential campaign, to suggest that the election of ABRAHAM LINCOLN would lead to slave rebellions and racial mixing in the South.

See R. W. Johannsen (ed.), *Lincoln-Douglas Debates* (1965); B. A. Williams (ed.), *Diary from Dixie* (1949); and D. L. Dumond (ed.), *Southern Editorials* (1931).

RICHARD L. HUME
Washington State University

BLADENSBURG, BATTLE OF (August 24, 1814). In 1814 the British dispatched ships and troops to Chesapeake Bay in an effort to divert American troops from the Canadian border. On August 19, after forcing Captain JOSHUA BARNEY to destroy his barge flotilla in the upper Patuxent River, the British landed 4,000 soldiers at Benedict, Md. By August 24, the British force, commanded by General Robert Ross, had reached Bladensburg, Md., and found 7,000 Americans, mostly ill-trained militiamen, hastily arranged in three lines on high ground. The British soon scattered the first two lines of defenders, but their advance was temporarily checked at the third line by Barney and his flotilla sailors, whose big naval guns took a heavy toll of the attacking enemy. At this critical moment General William Winder, the incompetent American commander, directed the remaining militia troops to retreat, thus permitting the British to flank Barney's position. Barney ordered his men to flee but was himself wounded and captured. American losses amounted to 26 killed and 51 wounded; British casualties were 64 killed and 185 wounded. Following the battle, Ross and his men marched to the national capital. The speedy

rout of Winder's troops was popularly dubbed the "Bladensburg races."

See R. Horsman, *War of 1812* (1969); W. Lord, *Dawn's Early Light* (1972); J. K. Mahon, *War of 1812* (1972); *American State Papers, Military Affairs* (1832–60), I, for official American version of the battle; W. M. Marine, *Invasion of Maryland* (1913); and G. R. Glieg, *Narrative of the Campaigns* (1821), good first-hand account by a British officer.

FRANK A. CASSELL
University of Wisconsin, Milwaukee

BLAIR, JAMES (1655–1743), dominated the politics of Virginia almost from the time he arrived as minister to Henrico Parish in 1685 until his death. He advanced rapidly through the patronage of Henry Compton, bishop of London, who designated him commissary for Virginia in 1689 and secured his appointment to the provincial council in 1694. He soon forged a majority on the council through his wife's relatives, the HARRISON FAMILY, and their intermarriage with other leading families. Blair's connections on both sides of the Atlantic made him the terror of Virginia governors. He secured the dismissal of Edmund Andros and the appointment and removal of FRANCIS NICHOLSON and influenced the fall of Alexander Spotswood. Blair's relations with Virginia's Anglican clergy were turbulent due in part to his Scottish ordination, his efforts to discipline them, and his long neglect of the College of William and Mary, which he founded and of which he was president for life.

See P. Rouse, *James Blair* (1971), which supersedes D. E. Motley, *Commissary James Blair* (1901). See also P. G. Scott, *William and Mary Quarterly* (April, 1976).

GEORGE F. FRICK
University of Delaware

BLAIR, JOHN (1732–1800), was born in Williamsburg, Va., and educated at the College of William and Mary and the Middle Temple, London (1755). Blair served in the HOUSE OF BURGESSES (1766–1770), as clerk of the council of Virginia (1770–1775), and as a signer of the nonimportation agreements of 1770 and 1774. He was a delegate to the Virginia constitutional convention of 1776, a member of the privy council, and a judge of the general court (1778) and chief justice (1780). Blair was a delegate to the Philadelphia Convention in 1787, and he voted in favor of ratification at the Virginia Convention of 1788. President George Washington appointed him associate justice of the U.S. Supreme Court in 1789, where he served until his resignation in 1796.

See *Journal of House of Burgesses* (1766–70); *Journal of Convention of 1776*; and Minutes of Council, Manuscripts, Virginia State Library, all for details of career. For Blair's opinions in key cases, see *Hepburn's Case*, 2 Dallas 409; *State of Georgia* v. *Brailsford*, 2 Dallas 415; *Chisholm* v. *Georgia*, 2 Dallas 419; and *Penhallow* v. *Doane's Administration*, 3 Dallas 54. See also H. B. Grigsby, *Convention of 1776* (1855); and F. Horner, *History of Blair, Banister, and Braxton Families* (1898).

W. ALLAN WILBUR
State University of New York, Albany

BLAIR BILL, an early attempt to provide federal aid to public education, was introduced in the U.S. Senate five times between 1882 and 1890 by Henry W. Blair of New Hampshire. It passed three times, only to be killed in House committees. Based on illiteracy rates, the bill called for distributing $77 million to the states over a period of years. To participate, states were to have free common schools, to match the money equally, and to dispense it without racial bias, though segregated schools were permitted. Although Blair primarily intended to aid the South, reactions never strictly followed sectional or party lines. Some supporters saw an opportunity to advance literacy, and others sought to help the Negro. Opposition came from northerners who continued to seek punishment of the South and from southerners who feared an effort to establish racially mixed schools. Others disapproved of federal aid to states on constitutional grounds. After the bill's failure in 1890, pressure for federal aid to education subsided for several years.

See G. C. Lee, *Federal Aid for Schools* (1949), the best; C. W. Dabney, *Universal Education in South* (1936); and *Congressional Record*, 49th Cong., 1st Sess., Vol. VII, Pt. 2, original version of bill.

GEORGE A. DILLINGHAM
Western Kentucky University

BLAIR FAMILY. Francis P. Blair, Sr. (1791–1876), was born at Abingdon, Va., and reared in Frankfort, Ky. After studying law at Transylvania University, he was circuit court clerk at Frankfort (1814–1831). A radical in Kentucky's old court–new court struggle, he became president of the Commonwealth Bank and wrote newspaper articles supporting the 1828 presidential campaign of ANDREW JACKSON. From 1831 to 1845 he edited the Washington *Globe*, the official Democratic party newspaper, and was highly influential with Presidents Jackson and Martin Van Buren. Forced to resign by President JAMES K. POLK for his opposition to immediate annexation of Texas, Blair became a Free-Soiler in 1848 and presided over the Republican party's first national convention in 1856. He became a close friend and adviser to ABRAHAM LINCOLN and demanded the reinforcement of Ft. Sumter and military action against secession. Although he supported Lincoln, he opposed Radical Reconstruction and eventually rejoined the Democratic party.

Montgomery Blair (1813–1883), oldest son of Francis P. Blair, was born at Frankfort, Ky. After graduation from West Point and service in the Seminole War, he studied law at Transylvania and established a lucrative practice in St. Louis. Moving to Washington, D.C., in 1851, he became solicitor of the court of claims. Representing Dred Scott, he delivered the most significant legal brief for the northern position on territorial slavery (DRED SCOTT V. SANDFORD). As postmaster general under Lincoln, he reformed the service with innovations still in practice. After attacking the Radicals, he resigned in 1864 to regain their support for Lincoln's reelection. He opposed Radical Reconstruction and was an advocate for Samuel J. Tilden in the contested 1876 election.

Francis P. Blair, Jr. (1822–1875), youngest son of Francis P. Blair, was born at Frankfort, Ky. After graduating from Princeton, he studied law at Transylvania, served as judge advocate in New Mexico during the Mexican War, and practiced law in St. Louis. In 1856 he was the first Free-Soiler to be elected to Congress from a slave state. He advocated emancipation and colonization. In 1861 Blair led mobilization efforts in Congress and organized the political and military forces that kept Missouri in the Union. As a general, he fought at Vicksburg, Chattanooga, and Atlanta and was W. T. Sherman's second-in-command in Georgia. Nominated by the Democrats for vice-president in 1868, he demanded a presidential reversal of congressional Reconstruction. Elected senator from Missouri in 1870, he suffered an ultimately fatal stroke in 1872.

The Blairs were strong, aggressive, outspoken men who usually ignored political advantage to support their sometimes paradoxical convictions. They were slaveholders who hated slavery, southern sympathizers who loved the Union above everything, and idealistic democrats who feared the participation of black Americans in politics.

See W. E. Smith, *Blair Family* (1933), occasionally inaccurate; E. B. Smith, *Register* (Oct., 1959); Blair, Andrew Jackson, and Van Buren papers, Library of Congress; and Blair-Lee Papers, Princeton University.

ELBERT B. SMITH
University of Maryland

BLAKELY, BATTLE OF (April 9, 1865), was the final infantry battle in the Civil War. Ft. Blakely and Spanish Fort guarded Mobile's eastern approaches when Union General EDWARD CANBY began his campaign in March, 1865. General DABNEY H. MAURY was the overall Confederate commander. At Blakely, a village on the Tensaw River's eastern bank, Confederate General St. John R. Lidell deployed his 3,500 men along a semicircular line of fortifications. Below Blakely on the eastern bank of the Apalachee River lay Spanish Fort, a Confederate post manned by 3,000 men. As Canby moved 32,000 troops up Mobile Bay's eastern shore, General Frederick Steele marched north from Pensacola, Fla., with 13,000 federal soldiers. On March 27 Canby laid siege to Spanish Fort, which was evacuated on the night of April 8. The next afternoon, several hours after Robert E. Lee had surrendered at Appomattox, federal forces successfully assaulted Blakely. Northern losses were 113 killed, 516 wounded; southern casualties were unknown but slight. Mobile was abandoned, and the city surrendered on April 12.

See R. P. Buchanan, "Military Campaign for Mobile" (Ph.D. dissertation, Auburn University, 1963); and C. C. Andrews, *Campaign of Mobile* (1867).

WILLIAM WARREN ROGERS
Florida State University

BLAND, RICHARD (1710–1776). His life illustrates the best qualities of the eighteenth-century Virginia aristocracy. Educated at William and Mary and admitted to the bar in 1746, he served Prince George County as parish vestryman, justice of the peace, colonel of the militia, and in the House of Burgesses for 33 years (1742–1775). Thomas Jefferson acknowledged him as "one of the oldest, ablest and most respected members" of the legislature. Bland's cautious opposition to British policy in the Revolutionary crises was anchored in a firm conviction in natural rights and natural law. A skillful polemicist, he opposed Governor Robert Dinwiddie's demand for a pistole fee (a payment charged by the governor for affixing his official seal to a patent for land) and defended the legislature against the clergy in the PARSONS' CAUSE controversy (1764). His *An Inquiry into the Rights of the British Colonies* (1766) was the first comprehensive statement attacking British taxation. He attended the First and Second Continental Congress.

See C. Rossiter, *Seedtime of the Republic* (1953); B. Bailyn (ed.), *Pamphlets of the American Revolution* (1965).

PETER M. MITCHELL
Seton Hall University

BLEASE, COLEMAN LIVINGSTON (1868–1942), for 50 years after the political revolution brought about by BENJAMIN TILLMAN was an important factor and a significant figure in South Carolina politics. He ran continually for a state or national office from 1890 to 1938. Although he gained election on only three occasions (in 1910 and 1912 as governor; in 1924 as U.S. senator), he built a loyal following as the spokesman for the state's previously ignored mill workers. More a demagogue than a reformer, Blease held his supporters by appeals to emotional themes, the most important being crude expressions of racism. Other themes were protection of southern womanhood, religious sentiment, individualism, and antagonism toward corporations and the aristocracy.

Blease was one of the most controversial governors ever to hold that office. His four-year term covered one of the most turbulent periods in the state's history. His policy of rewarding his friends and bitterly denouncing his enemies resulted in intense factionalism, and his relations with the legislature and judiciary were tempestuous. Throughout his administration, controversy centered on education, enforcement of the liquor laws, and conditions in the state penitentiary, but little improvement was made in any of these areas. Blease effectively used the nearly universal opposition of the state press to strengthen his political support by depicting himself as a persecuted champion of the people. Five days before the end of his second term, he resigned from office. Following an undistinguished term in the U.S. Senate, Blease was defeated for reelection in 1930 by JAMES BYRNES.

See W. D. Cash, *Mind of the South* (1941); F. B. Simkins, *Pitchfork Ben Tillman* (1944); D. D. Wallace, *History of South Carolina* (1934); and R. D. Burnside, "Governorship of Blease" (Ph.D. dissertation, Indiana University, 1963).

RONALD D. BURNSIDE
Presbyterian College

BLEEDING KANSAS. From 1854 through 1858, the Kansas crisis created a northern antislavery party, brought forward Abraham Lincoln, provided the major national political issue, split the Democratic party, and contributed to the coming of the Civil War. At the end of the crisis the South was an embattled minority faced with a hostile sectional party and deprived of its usual northern Democratic support. Yet the term is a misnomer, for few persons bled or died in Kansas.

Prior to 1854 the South did not initiate or strongly urge repeal of the ban on slavery in the Louisiana Territory. By blocking organization of a free Nebraska Territory, however, southern congressmen had indirectly contributed to the fateful decision to discard the prohibition agreed upon in 1820. Congressional voting on the KANSAS-NEBRASKA ACT, which became national law May 30, 1854, revealed a house dividing. In the slave states Whigs joined with Democrats to form a nearly solid South; in the free states Whigs and many Democrats united in opposition to the Democratic measure sponsored by Senator Stephen A. Douglas and President Franklin Pierce.

Proslavery elements promptly took charge of Kansas Territory, electing a territorial delegate to Congress and, abetted by BORDER RUFFIANS from adjacent Missouri, the territorial legislature. This "bogus legislature" enacted a slave code for the territory, provoking free-state settlers to draft a constitution that prohibited slavery and an ordinance that prohibited entry of Negroes. After adopting the constitution, free-state voters elected a governor and a "state" legislature. By January 15, 1856, Kansas had two governments: the lawfully recognized territorial government and the self-constituted free-soil "state" government.

Violence was normal on the frontier, as pioneers competed for land, townsites, and public offices. Between 1854 and 1857, not above 200 persons were killed in "Bleeding Kansas," but brawling and shooting along the Wakarusa River near Lawrence, Kan., participated in by Border Ruffians, won the exaggerated name of the Wakarusa War. As northern emigrant aid societies encouraged free-state settlers, the South grew apprehensive of "northern aggression." "We should not allow abolitionists to colonize Kansas by emigrant Societies without making an effort to counteract by throwing in a Southern population," Jefferson Davis advised, but assisted emigration merely aggravated sectionalism. Although President Pierce issued a proclamation calling on unruly persons to disperse, civil war erupted in Kansas, lasting from May 21 to September 15, 1856. Proslavery men ravaged Lawrence (the Sack of Lawrence), and the antislavery zealot John Brown with others murdered five proslavery pioneers (the POTTAWATOMIE MASSACRE).

Senator Robert Toombs offered a statesmanlike solution to the problem of dual government in Kansas, proposing a free election to a constitutional convention, which failed of enactment. In the 1856 presidential election, with the Republican candidate winning less than 1,200 votes in the slave states on an antiextension platform, the South increasingly identified itself with the Democratic party. The Kansas controversy, under the blows of the DRED SCOTT decision and James Buchanan's

mismanagement of the LECOMPTON CONSTITUTION, fatefully split the Democratic party. By the end of 1858 it had been determined that Kansas would not become a slave state; but in 1860 the continuing issue of slavery in the territories divided the party and the nation. Bleeding Kansas formed a background for the American Civil War.

See J. A. Rawley, *Race and Politics* (1969); W. F. Zornow, *Kansas* (1957); and *Congressional Globe* (1854–58).

JAMES A. RAWLEY
University of Nebraska, Lincoln

BLENNERHASSETT ISLAND is 1.7 miles south of Parkersburg, W.Va., in the Ohio River. Initially owned by Samuel MacDowell, it was purchased by Elijah Backus of Marietta, Ohio, in 1792. Backus sold the island in 1798 to Harman Blennerhassett and Joseph S. Lewis. Blennerhassett purchased 170 of the island's 509 acres for $4,500 and called it Isle de Beau Pre. He and his wife Margaret completed a ten-room mansion in 1800. The island became famous as the site of the planning of the Aaron BURR CONSPIRACY. In 1972, the West Virginia legislature created a commission to develop restoration plans. The island is owned by E. I. Du Pont de Nemours & Company. It has also been known as Long Island, Belpre Island, and Backus Island.

See T. P. Abernethy, *Burr Conspiracy* (1954); and C. R. Rector, *West Virginia Review* (Sept., 1932).

THOMAS H. SMITH
Ohio Historical Society

BLOCKADE. At the outbreak of the Civil War, the Union navy had only eight ships to blockade more than 3,500 miles of Confederate shoreline. But as the Abraham Lincoln administration increased the purchase and construction of steam gunboats—it was evident that sailing vessels were useless as blockaders—the blockade was materially strengthened. Two blockading squadrons increased to four: the North and South Atlantic, the East and West Gulf. In May, 1861, only two ships guarded the entire coast of North Carolina; a year later, 58 craft policed this sector; and, at the end of the war, the total had reached 142. With additional vessels the character of the blockade changed. To halt BLOCKADE-RUNNING by the swift and agile enemy ships, Union commanders realized that the traditional idea of a blockade—frigates moving up and down before a port at a distance—was inadequate. This practice gave way to stationing large numbers of fast steamers directly at the harbor's entrance.

Despite these changes, the blockade of Charleston was inadequate in terms of safe entrances and clearances until the last months of 1863; and, from the beginning of the third quarter of 1864 until the evacuation of Charleston in 1865, a fairly large and steadily increasing number of safe runs were made into and out of the harbor. The traffic to and from Wilmington continued in considerable volume though with increasing hazard until the fall of FT. FISHER in January, 1865. The illicit trade of the two ports was never completely cut off. In fact, in 1863, 84 percent of all known attempts to sneak through the blockade off the Carolina ports were successful, and this figure decreased only 1 percent in 1864. Despite the best efforts of the Union navy, 1,735 out of 2,054 known attempts to enter or clear the Carolina ports between April 19, 1861, and February 17, 1865, were successful.

The blockade of the Gulf ports was even more thoroughly tested. During the war no less than 2,960 attempts were made to penetrate the blockaders. This was a daily average of two attempted violations. The average for the Carolina ports was 1.5.

At first glance these figures relating to effectiveness seem to contradict the statement that "it was the blockade rather than the ravages of the army that sapped the industrial strength of the Confederacy." In reality the blockade was the North's most potent weapon. Its effectiveness lay not so much in the ships and cargoes captured as in the ships and cargoes its mere existence kept away from southern ports. The decrease in the number of vessels known to have engaged in the trade is significant. There were 274 in 1861, 190 in 1862, 128 in 1863, 112 in 1864, and 29 between January and February, 1865.

See B. Anderson, *By River and by Sea* (1962); V. C. Jones, *Civil War at Sea* (1961–62); E. S. Maclay, *Reminiscences of Old Navy* (1898); J. M. Merrill, *Rebel Shore* (1958); F. L. Owsley, *King Cotton Diplomacy* (1931); *Official Records, Navies*, 30 vols.; I. E. Vail, *Three Years on Blockade* (1902); R. E. Johnson, *American Neptune* (Jan., 1972); and M. W. Price, *American Neptune* (July, 1948; Jan., 1949; Oct., 1951).

JAMES M. MERRILL
University of Delaware

BLOCKADE-RUNNING. An inevitable result of the U.S. Navy's BLOCKADE of southern ports during the Civil War was blockade-running by private persons, the Confederate government, and certain states. Profits were immense and, by 1862, Britishers became convinced that the blockade was ineffective. They saw an opportunity to turn a profit with little risk and enthusiastically entered into the business. Southerners and Britishers adopted a plan of transshipment, and four principal ports—Nassau, Bermuda, Havana, and Matamoros—served as intermediaries in the trade with the Confederacy. Nassau, only 500 to 600 miles from Savannah, Charleston, and Wilmington, became the most important neutral port.

During the early stages of the war, all sorts of vessels—sailboats, schooners, and coasting steamers—carrying Confederate pilots easily eluded the undermanned and inexperienced federal blockaders. But as the Union navy began commissioning a large number of steamships and sending them into southern waters and as Abraham Lincoln's squadrons gained experience, the cordon around the South grew tauter.

As the character of the blockade changed so did the character of the vessels employed to run it. The speed and light draft of the additions to the blockading squadrons made it essential that persons interested in running the blockade purchase ships especially designed for the purpose. Since the Confederates had no adequate local source of supply, they turned to Great Britain. Money was lavished on the construction of sleek, swift steamers. Built on the Clyde River, these long, low sidewheelers of 400 to 600 tons burned a coal that emitted no visible smoke and were equipped with one or two telescopic, rakish funnels. Their hulls, painted a full, neutral color for camouflage, rose only a few feet out of the water. With these short-voyage runners in operation, stockholders, agents, and sea captains reduced blockade-running to a system.

Federal blockaders never completely cut off this trade with the West Indies. In fact, in 1864, 84 percent of all known attempts to penetrate the blockade of the Carolina ports were successful. Such voyages to southern ports immeasurably helped the Confederate armies in carrying on the war against the North.

See B. Anderson, *By River and by Sea* (1962); F. B. C. Bradlee, *Blockade Running* (1925); H. Cochran, *Blockade Runners of Confederacy* (1958); V. C. Jones, *Civil War at Sea* (1961–62); J. M. Merrill, *Rebel Shore* (1958); T. E. Taylor, *Running Blockade* (1896); F. E. Vandiver (ed.), *Confederate Blockade* (1947); W. Watson, *Adventures of Blockade Runner* (1892); J. Wilkinson, *Narrative of Blockade Runner* (1877); *Official Records, Navies*, 30 vols.; R. I. Lester, *Mariner's Mirror* (Aug., 1975); and M. W. Price, *American Neptune* (July, 1948; Jan., 1949; Oct., 1951).

JAMES M. MERRILL
University of Delaware

BLOODY SHIRT. The term grew out of the debate in Congress in 1868 over the impeachment of President ANDREW JOHNSON. Congressman Benjamin F. Butler showed his colleagues the bloodstained shirt of an Ohioan who had been beaten two years earlier in Mississippi to argue that southerners would not accept the results of the Civil War and should be dealt with sternly. For some years thereafter, in an effort to secure northern support for a program of greater federal control over the South and to distract northern voters from the important issues of the day, Republican campaign orators would "wave the bloody shirt." Gradually this practice stopped when even the wavers themselves realized it no longer had any appeal.

See S. P. Hirshson, *Farewell to the Bloody Shirt* (1962).

VINCENT P. DE SANTIS
University of Notre Dame

BLOUNT, JOHN GRAY (1752–1833), was born in Bertie County, N.C. He avoided the political prominence of his brothers Thomas, Willie, and WILLIAM BLOUNT to direct the family mercantile firm of John Gray & Thomas Blount. He was active in statewide civic and educational affairs and helped establish the town of Washington, N.C., where he lived near his principal store. Blount became prosperous through international and coastal shipping, naval stores production, merchandising and credit operations, paper money speculation, slave trading, scientific farming, and various kinds of milling. His enormous land speculations in Carolina and Tennessee dated from an early expedition with DANIEL BOONE and association with RICHARD HENDERSON'S TRANSYLVANIA COMPANY. A Federalist turned Republican, Blount occasionally served in political bodies and constantly maneuvered behind the state's political scenes with a powerful influence deriving from his resources and reputation.

See J. G. Blount Collection, North Carolina State Archives; A. B. Keith and W. H. Masterson (eds.), *J. G. Blount Papers* (3 vols.; 1952–), selections from State Archives collection; A. B. Keith, "Three North Carolina Brothers" (Ph.D. dissertation, University of North Carolina, 1940); and W. H. Masterson, *William Blount* (1954).

W. H. MASTERSON
University of Tennessee, Chattanooga

BLOUNT, WILLIAM (1749–1800), eldest brother of JOHN G. BLOUNT, was born in Bertie County, N.C. A silent partner in the firm of John Gray & Thomas Blount, he combined shipping and mercantile interests with immense land speculations in North Carolina and the Tennessee country. He served in the Continental army, the CONTINENTAL CONGRESS (1782, 1783, 1786, 1787), and often in the state assembly; however, public office attracted him primarily for its opportunities to advance his business interests. For these he was a delegate to the CONSTITUTIONAL CONVENTION and advocated North Carolina's ratification and its cession of the Tennessee country.

Appointed governor of the Southwest Territory by George Washington in 1790, Blount allied politically and economically with JOHN SEVIER and James Robertson. His patronage began important political careers, including that of ANDREW JACKSON. His able administration, however, balanced with difficulty local anti-Indian animosity and Washington's pacific Southwest policy, and Blount was an anti-Federalist by 1796, when elected one of the state's first U.S. senators (1796–1797).

Involved with Robert Morris and many others in immense, precariously financed western land schemes, Blount feared revolutionary France's acquisition of Louisiana and in 1796 adopted a subordinate's plan for a British-assisted frontier filibuster against Louisiana, New Orleans, and the Floridas. This "Blount conspiracy" was doomed by London's refusal to participate, and Blount's part became known through a henchman's betrayal. He was expelled by the Senate and impeached by the House, but the Senate refused to convict, holding that, aside from his expulsion, a senator was not an impeachable civil officer. Blount meanwhile fled to Tennessee for a political comeback but died suddenly.

See W. H. Masterson, *William Blount* (1954); and F. J. Turner, *American Historical Review* (April, 1905).

W. H. MASTERSON
University of Tennessee, Chattanooga

BLOXHAM, WILLIAM DUNNINGTON (1835–1911), was born in Leon County, Fla. After a successful career as a planter, he entered politics in 1861. He served as state comptroller, U.S. surveyor general for Florida, lieutenant governor, and secretary of state (1877–1881). In 1880 he became the first native Floridian elected to the governorship (1881–1885). His blueprint for state development was consistent with REDEEMER GOVERNMENTS throughout the South. Taxes, expenditures, and government services were minimal, and business and industry received government encouragement but never restraint. For example, Bloxham persuaded Hamilton Disston, a Philadelphia industrialist, to purchase 4 million acres of land at

25 cents an acre, thus providing funds to pay off state creditors and clearing title to undeveloped land. Critics correctly charged that the price was too low and that the rights of homesteaders were ignored. Regardless of the cost, Bloxham's decision paved the way for a new era of land development and alleviated the state's financial crisis.

During his first term Bloxham pushed for a voluntary military, a state board of health, increased appropriations for the mentally ill, and educational reforms. Most reforms, however, were given lip service rather than substance. Finally, he supported a new constitution that when adopted ensured governmental efficiency and economy and negated black political participation. In 1896, Bloxham was elected to a second term as governor (1897–1901) backed by a Populist-Democratic coalition. During this term the coalition established a permanent railroad commission, without the governor's signature. In 1897, the establishment of the direct primary for local officials, expanded to include state officials in 1901, democratized the election process for whites but eliminated blacks (DISFRANCHISEMENT).

See R. L. Carson, "Bloxham" (M.A. thesis, University of Florida, 1948); R. K. Johnson, "Bloxham" (M.S. thesis, Florida State University, 1959); and Governors Letter Books, Florida State Library, Tallahassee, and P. K. Yonge Library, Gainesville.

N. GORDON CARPER
Berry College

BLUE COCKADES were rosettes of ribbon worn in their hats by many South Carolinians in 1860 to express their support of secession.

BLUEFIELD, VA. (pop. 5,286), and **BLUEFIELD, W.VA.** (pop. 15,921), are politically separate entities on either side of the state line. Socially and economically, however, they are a single city, approximately 70 miles west of Roanoke. The town was settled in 1777, but real growth was not realized until the construction of rail lines permitted the shipment of coal in the 1880s. In 1921 the Virginia community dropped the original name of Graham, thus achieving a nominal reunion with its sister city in West Virginia. Located in the center of the Pocahontas coalfield, Bluefield is a market and shipping point for area mines, limestone quarries, and lumber mills. Its factories produce electrical coils, explosives, and clothing. Bluefield State College, founded in 1895 as a black normal school, is in the West Virginia sector of the town.

See W. C. Pendleton, *History of Tazewell County* (ca. 1920); and files of Bluefield *Telegraph* (1896–), a Republican daily.

BLUEGRASS (*Poa pratensis*), a rhizogenic meadow GRASS, has lent its popular name to the north-central Kentucky limestone plain. The exact etymology of the word as a generic regional term is unclear. The first recorded observation of *Poa pratensis* west of the Alleghenies was by CHRISTOPHER GIST in Miami County, Ohio, in 1751, and the fact that he recognized it indicates that he was familiar with it from earlier explorations in the east. JOHN FILSON's book *Life of Boone* notes its presence in Kentucky in 1784. It also is thought to have been in early French settlements at Kaskaskia in 1672 and at Vincennes in 1702. It is thought to have come into Kentucky before Daniel Boone arrived. Bluegrass has had many names, such as English grass, meadow grass, or spear grass. The name Kentucky bluegrass probably was not in common usage until after 1833.

See J. S. Johnson, *First Explorations of Kentucky* (1898).

KARL B. RAITZ
University of Kentucky

BLUE LAWS regulate Sabbath behavior. The first such law in British America was enacted in Virginia in 1610, compelling attendance at divine services Sunday morning and afternoon. The term comes from the blue paper that bound seventeenth-century Puritan laws governing morals in Massachusetts. All southern colonies passed blue laws early in their existence, and by 1775 Sabbath laws, fashioned after the law of Charles II, existed in all colonies. Throughout the nineteenth century, states no longer required church attendance, but limited most activities except those of necessity and charity. Enforcement was lax in some larger cities, but most rural communities and medium-sized cities observed them faithfully.

In the twentieth century, recreational restrictions were relaxed, but laws limiting business activities were still in force in all southern states by the 1960s. In 1961, the U.S. Supreme Court upheld a Maryland statute, declaring that a state had the "power to provide a weekly respite from all labor . . . a day of rest, repose, recreation, and tranquillity." All southern states, except North Carolina and Florida, have statewide blue laws, and all allow communities to pass their own. Vigorous controversy over the laws in the 1960s seems to have died down in the 1970s. Enforcement depends largely on the attitudes of a community's dominant businessmen.

See A. W. Johnson and F. H. Yost, *Separation of Church and State* (1948); and W. L. Johns, *Dateline Sunday* (1967).

GERALD E. CRITOPH
Stetson University

BLUE LICKS, BATTLE OF (August 19, 1782). A force of Indians and Loyalist rangers, led by William Caldwell, attacked Bryant's Station near Lexington, Ky., on August 15 seeking prisoners for intelligence concerning GEORGE ROGERS CLARK's plans. Failing in this, Caldwell withdrew his force slowly toward the Ohio on August 18. A mounted Kentucky militia force, numbering 182 and commanded by John Todd, Stephen Trigg, and DANIEL BOONE, pursued the raiders. Major Hugh McGary led a disorganized rush across the Lower Blue Licks ford of Licking River. Awaiting such a move, Caldwell's small detachment of rangers and 200 Indians, directed by Alexander McKee, fell upon the undisciplined militiamen and routed them. The Kentucky force lost 70 killed and 20 captured, and Caldwell's losses were 11 killed and 14 wounded.

See Haldimand Papers, Public Archives of Canada; *Virginia Calendar of State Papers* (1875–93); O. Rice, *Frontier Kentucky* (1975); C. Ward, *War of the Revolution* (1952); and B. Young, *Battle of Blue Licks* (1897).

JONATHAN G. ROSSIE
St. Lawrence University

BLUE RIDGE MOUNTAINS, as well as the Blue Ridge physiographic province in which they lie, extend from southern Pennsylvania southwestward into northern Georgia. Underlain primarily by ancient resistant igneous and metamorphic rocks, the mountains of this province are remnants of a more extensive range initially formed over 225 million years ago.

The province is divided into two topographically distinct segments by the Roanoke River, the southernmost stream that crosses it. To the north it is narrow, five to 15 miles across, and generally consists of several closely spaced ridges with projecting spurs. Here the Blue Ridge Mountains, or simply the Blue Ridge, are essentially coextensive with the physiographic province. Ridgetops, mostly between 1,500 and 3,000 feet in altitude but with some peaks exceeding 4,000 feet, rise 1,000 to 2,000 feet above the adjacent Piedmont and western valleys. Like the Roanoke, the James and Potomac rivers flow eastward through gaps in the Blue Ridge, and most of the mountains are drained by tributaries to these three streams.

South of the Roanoke, the province widens, becoming 75 miles across in North Carolina and Tennessee, and the mountains, including the highest and most majestic in the APPALACHIAN MOUNTAINS system, are more sprawling and less ridgelike in character. Several summits exceed 6,000 feet in altitude. The eastern province boundary is marked by a prominent escarpment, the Blue Ridge Front, along which the mountains rise as much as 2,500 feet above the Piedmont, and in this segment the name Blue Ridge Mountains usually encompasses only the easternmost range along this escarpment. Many of the ranges farther west, including the GREAT SMOKY MOUNTAINS, are collectively designated the Unakas. No streams cross the province here, and drainage is mostly westward by tributaries to the New and Tennessee rivers.

See W. D. Thornbury, *Regional Geomorphology of U.S.* (1965); and N. M. Fenneman, *Physiography of Eastern U.S.* (1938).

WALLACE M. ELTON
Middlebury College

BLUFFTON MOVEMENT. In opposition to the Tariff Act of 1842, ROBERT BARNWELL RHETT launched this movement at Bluffton, S.C., on July 31, 1844. He called for a state convention to nullify the tariff or if necessary to secede from the Union. Secretary of State JOHN C. CALHOUN, who considered the annexation of Texas primarily important, opposed radical action and counseled a reliance on JAMES K. POLK's election as president. Calhoun dispatched FRANCIS PICKENS to Tennessee to get a pledge from Polk on the tariff. A meeting in Charleston, August 19, which expressed confidence in Calhoun, and his return to the state in October silenced the movement. Sympathetic with the insurgents, Governor JAMES HAMMOND nevertheless called for state action on the tariff. But, when the legislature refused to support him and when the Bluffton candidate for governor, Whitemarsh B. Seabrook, suffered defeat, the movement ended.

See L. A. White, *Rhett* (1931); C. M. Wiltse, *Calhoun: Sectionalist* (1951); and Charleston *Mercury* (1844).

THELMA JENNINGS
Middle Tennessee State University

BLYTHEVILLE, ARK. (pop. 24,752), in northeast Arkansas 55 miles north of MEMPHIS, Tenn., was not settled until 1853. An area of dense forests and impenetrable underbrush, it was frequently flooded by the Mississippi River. On a relatively high piece of land, however, the Reverend Henry J. Blythe built a home and a small chapel. The surrounding community grew very slowly and remained unincorporated until 1891. The forests ultimately attracted lumber companies, and the resulting cleared land proved rich for cotton cultivation. Today it is the major shipping and trading market for the surrounding agricultural area of cotton and soybean cultivation and also an industrial center producing textiles, lumber, and dairy products.

See Blytheville *Courier-News* (1903–).

BOGALUSA, LA.

BOGALUSA, LA. (pop. 18,412), 60 miles northeast of New Orleans, was founded in 1906 as a lumber town. Located in the midst of a dense woods of yellow pine, the city grew up around the Great Southern Lumber Mill. Today its economy continues to be based upon lumber-related products: pine nurseries, naval stores, creosoted wood, paper, and turpentine.

See A. Quick, *Louisiana Historical Quarterly* (Jan., 1946); and Washington Parish Library, which maintains a pamphlet collection, cemetery records, family histories, and Civil War documents on town and area.

BOLL WEEVIL

BOLL WEEVIL (*Anthonomus grandis*) was originally described by the Swedish coleopterist C. H. Boheman in 1843 from a specimen collected in Mexico. The presence of the pest in the United States first came to the attention of entomologists in 1894, when many COTTON fields near Brownsville, Tex., were infested. The pest then spread through southern cotton at a rate of 40 to 160 miles annually, reaching the Atlantic coast in about 20 years.

The boll weevil invasion had great economic and social impact on the South and initiated a westward migration of some farmers to noninfested regions, where they planted cotton. A trend toward diversification of southern agriculture, the introduction of entomological studies and research in southern universities, and the formation of the Cooperative Extension Service were all directly related to the depredation of this pest (AGRICULTURAL EXPERIMENT STATIONS). The oft-quoted claim that the boll weevil was actually beneficial, bringing needed change to the South, is at best only partly true. Even with modern technology, the boll weevil is still agriculture's most costly pest. Cotton producers suffer losses in excess of $200 million and spend over $75 million more for control annually. Approximately one-third of all insecticides applied to crops in the United States are used for boll weevil control.

In recent years entomologists have greatly expanded their knowledge of the pest and are developing promising new control techniques. Effective, economical, and less environmentally harsh insecticidal programs directed against the diapausing or potentially overwintering weevil population have been developed. The use of parasites, pathogens, resistant cottons, growth regulator chemicals, and trapping and population manipulation with synthetic pheromones, as well as the release of sexually sterile male weevils, are some of the control techniques being developed. Current control concepts envision large-scale, coordinated suppression programs employing several control techniques. Currently, studies are being conducted to determine the feasibility of employing these new techniques in a nationwide, integrated program to eliminate the pest completely from the United States.

See W. H. Cross, *Annual Review of Entomology* (1973); J. D. Helms, "Boll Weevil in Texas and Louisiana, 1892–1907" (M.A. thesis, Florida State University, 1970); W. D. Hunter and W. D. Pierce, *U.S. Senate Document No. 305* (1912); V. C. Loftin, Smithsonian Report No. 3827 (1945); and D. R. Rummel, *Bulletin of Entomology Society of America* (March, 1975).

DON R. RUMMEL
Texas A. & M. University

BONAPARTE FAMILY

BONAPARTE FAMILY of Baltimore, Md., owed its origins to a visit of Jérôme Bonaparte, Napoleon's youngest brother, to the city in 1803. Following a whirlwind courtship he married Elizabeth Patterson (1785–1879), a reputed belle of the city. Napoleon's refusal to recognize the union and the lure of honors abroad induced the young Jérôme to desert his bride, leaving her to bear a son after his departure. After her desertion, Mme Bonaparte grew into a parsimonious and eccentric old lady. Nearly 20 years of European travels in search of titles for her son so disgusted her wealthy father that she lost most of her inheritance. Nonetheless, skillful speculation netted her a fortune considerably over $1 million. In her later years, she lived in a boardinghouse and spent but 2 percent of her large yearly income. Outliving her son, Jerome Napoleon Bonaparte (1805–1870), she divided her entire fortune between his two children.

The first of the grandsons, Jerome Napoleon Bonaparte (1830–1893), chose a military career, graduated from West Point, and served in the U.S. Army. With the outbreak of the Crimean War, however, he began European adventures that were to last until his proscription during the days of the Paris Commune. After serving with distinction in the Crimean War, he settled permanently into a career as a French army officer, likely with hopes of being well placed to receive possible family honors. He spent his last 20 years in Washington, D.C., and in Newport while traveling extensively in Europe.

His younger brother, Charles Joseph Bonaparte (1851–1921), gained fame not in Europe but in his own country as a lawyer, municipal and civil service reformer, and attorney general of the United States. A brilliant scholar, he attended both Harvard and its law school, graduating in 1874. With ample inherited wealth of his own, his law practice served only litigants whose causes appealed to his sense of justice. Founder and chairman of both the Baltimore Reform League and the National Civil Service Reform League, he also actively supported and contributed to the *Civil Service Reformer*, a Maryland reform journal. His civil service record attracted the attention of young Theodore Roosevelt, then civil service commissioner, and during Roosevelt's presidency he appointed Bonaparte secretary of the navy and, in 1906, attorney general. Bonaparte's interest in the dissolution of huge business combinations led to more than 50 appearances before the Supreme Court and to the institution of 20 antitrust suits.

See J. B. Bishop, *Charles Joseph Bonaparte* (1922); E. L. Didier, *Life and Letters of Mme Bonaparte* (1879); E. F. Goldman, *Charles J. Bonaparte* (1943); Bonaparte Manuscripts, Library of Congress; Baltimore *Sun* (June 29, 1921); Baltimore *American* (June 29, 1921); and Baltimore *News* (June 28, 1921).

CHARLOTTE CANNON RHINES
Essex Community College

BOND, HORACE MANN (1904–1972), although most noted as an educational administrator, made significant contributions to the fields of sociology and history through his books and numerous articles about the American Negro. Born in Nashville, Tenn., he received his A.B. degree from Pennsylvania's Lincoln University (1923) and his A.M. and Ph.D. degrees from the University of Chicago (1926 and 1936). From 1924 to 1928 he was an administrator at Langston University, Oklahoma, and Alabama State College, then joined the social science faculty of Fisk University. In 1934 he resigned to become dean of Dillard University, published *The Education of the Negro in*

the American Social Order, and secured a Rosenwald grant that enabled him to complete his doctorate. His prize-winning dissertation was the basis of his provocative *Negro Education in Alabama: A Study in Cotton and Steel* (1939), in which his revisionist chapters on Reconstruction challenged WALTER L. FLEMING's interpretations. After two years as head of Fisk's education department (1937–1939), he served as president of Ft. Valley State College (1939–1945), president of Lincoln University (1945–1966), and director of that institution's Bureau of Educational and Social Research until his death.

See Atlanta *Constitution* (Dec. 22, 1972); and Atlanta *Journal* (Dec. 22, 1972).

THOMAS A. BELSER, JR.
Auburn University

BONNIE BLUE FLAG was both a lively song that rallied the Confederate cause and "the first flag of the new republic" (*i.e.*, the Confederacy). Both were born amid the excitement and fervor of Mississippi's secession convention in January, 1861. The words to the song were written by a young Irish actor, Harry McCarthy, and were sung to "The Irish Jaunting Car." The flag was made by a group of Mississippi ladies and contained a magnolia tree on a white background with a blue field in the upper left-hand corner on which was imposed a single, white star.

See M. W. Wellman, *They Took Their Stand* (1959).

CATHERINE M. TARRANT
Houston, Tex.

BOONE, DANIEL (1734–1820). Biographers have often failed to distinguish between two Daniel Boones—the historical and the mythological. Attempts to make the distinction have enhanced Boone's historical image. Born in what is now Berks County, Pa., Boone moved with his family to the Shenandoah Valley and hence to the Yadkin Valley in North Carolina. In 1755 he was with General Edward Braddock, and in 1769 he explored Kentucky. As warrior and wilderness scout he blazed the WILDERNESS ROAD and helped RICHARD HENDERSON establish the TRANSYLVANIA COMPANY at BOONESBORO; after his capture by the Shawnee, who proudly introduced him to the British at Detroit, he commanded the epic defense of the fort at Boonesboro in 1778. His last great battle was fought at BLUE LICKS in 1782, where the Kentuckians suffered a severe defeat in what is frequently called the "last battle of the Revolution." Ironically, he had in his time been suspected of Tory sympathies and tried for treason. Long before Boone died in Missouri, his heroic qualities were familiar to Europeans as well as to Americans, thanks to his biographer JOHN FILSON. He is also remembered in the records for traits characteristic of his English Quaker ancestors: kindness, modesty, and good manners.

See J. Bakeless, *Daniel Boone* (1939), excellent; C. W. Alvord, *Journal of the Illinois State Historical Society* (April–July, 1926); R. Slotkin, *Regeneration Through Violence* (1973), on frontier mythology; and L. Elliott, *Long Hunter* (1976).

JOHN WALTON
Johns Hopkins University

BOONESBORO (Boonesborough) was the most important and one of the earliest settlements in Kentucky. In April, 1775, DANIEL BOONE, working for RICHARD HENDERSON's TRANSYLVANIA COMPANY, built a fort on the Kentucky River at the end of the WILDERNESS ROAD. The fort was the capital of the Transylvania colony and in May, 1775, Henderson convened delegates from the three other Kentucky settlements to establish a new government. This was the first legislative body to meet west of the Alleghenies. In April, 1777, Boonesboro suffered its first SHAWNEE attack. Other attacks followed until September, 1778, when the last and greatest siege began and lasted ten days. The town of Boonesboro was established in 1779, and for a time it was a thriving trade center. By the early nineteenth century it had become a ghost town.

See L. Elliott, *Long Hunter* (1976), best biography of Boone; J. Bakeless, *Daniel Boone* (1939); G. W. Ranck, *Boonesborough* (1901); and O. K. Rice, *Frontier Kentucky* (1975).

RICHARD A. VAN ORMAN
Purdue University, Calumet

BOONEVILLE, BATTLE OF (July 1, 1862). After the Confederate evacuation of Corinth, Miss., the southerners concentrated at Tupelo. To protect the movement of some Confederate infantry, Brigadier General JAMES R. CHALMERS with 1,400 cavalrymen made a feint toward Rienzi and clashed with two federal cavalry regiments under Colonel Philip H. Sheridan a few miles west of Booneville in an all-day struggle. After stubborn but indecisive fighting, Sheridan was reinforced, and Chalmers retired unmolested. Sheridan wrote a report that made him look masterly. Brigadier General William S. Rosecrans recommended that Sheridan be made a brigadier, and Brigadier General Alexander S. Asboth telegraphed to Washington that

"he is worth his weight in gold." The federals reported 41 killed, wounded, or missing and no less than 65 dead rebels. Confederate veterans later claimed that no southerners had been killed. After the war Chalmers became a Republican politician and allegedly for that reason never contested Sheridan's account.

See R. U. Johnson and C. C. Buel (eds.), *Battles and Leaders* (1888), II; E. T. Sykes, *Confederate Veteran*, (Sept., 1916); *Official Records, Armies*, Ser. 1, Vol. XVII, Pt. 1.

HERMAN HATTAWAY
University of Missouri, Kansas City

BOONVILLE, BATTLE OF (June 17, 1861). With Missouri's capital at Jefferson City in federal hands, Brigadier General Nathaniel Lyon opened pursuit of the members of the secessionist state administration on June 16, 1861. Governor CLAIBORNE F. JACKSON, summoning the Missouri State Guard to halt Lyon, waited at Boonville on the south bank of the Missouri River some 40 miles northwest. Lyon debarked 2,000 regulars and volunteers below Boonville early on June 17. The guardsmen under Colonel JOHN S. MARMADUKE, with about twice the strength of Lyon's force, deployed four miles from Boonville where the bluff approaches the river. After a two-hour fight, during which Lyon's infantry fired effectively from prone positions while his artillery raked the Confederates with impunity, Marmaduke's forces bolted before a bayonet charge. Lyon reported four fatalities, the guardsmen ten. The morally depressing effect of Lyon's victory, together with his consequent closure of the Missouri River, hamstrung southern recruitment north of that stream and obliged the secessionists to retire southward beyond the Osage.

See *Official Records, Armies*, III; J. B. Barnes, *Infantry Journal* (Dec., 1929); T. L. Snead, *Fight for Missouri* (1886); and Jay Monaghan, *Civil War on the Western Border* (1955).

LESLIE ANDERS
Central Missouri State University

BOOTH, JOHN WILKES (1838–1865), born on a farm near Bel Air, Md., was the son of the famous actor Junius Brutus Booth and brother of the more famous tragedian, Edwin Booth. He began his acting career in Baltimore in 1855 and became a favorite of audiences in the North and South. As a southern sympathizer, Booth was a member of a Richmond militia company in 1859 that participated in the capture and execution of John Brown. During the Civil War he assembled a group of conspirators he hoped to lead in a plan to kidnap President Abraham Lincoln and offer him in exchange for Confederate prisoners of war. Booth later changed his plan from kidnaping to murder. On April 14, 1865, at Ford's Theatre, Booth entered the president's box and shot him (LINCOLN ASSASSINATION). He made good his escape from Washington, but federal soldiers located him on April 26 hiding in a tobacco barn near Bowling Green, Va. The troops set the barn on fire to force him to come out. Instead, he was shot while still inside, either by his own hand or by a soldier who disobeyed orders and fired. Booth died a few hours later.

See A. B. Clarke, *Elder and Younger Booth* (1882), and *Unlocked Book* (1938), both by Booth's sister Asia; S. Kimmel, *Mad Booths of Maryland* (1940); E. Ruggles, *Edwin Booth* (1953); T. A. Jones, *J. W. Booth* (1893); and G. S. Bryan, *Great American Myth* (1940), excellent bibliography.

JOSEPH GEORGE, JR.
Villanova University

BORDER RUFFIANS was a term applied by northerners to Missourians who interfered in Kansas affairs in 1854–1856. Residents of western Missouri, where a substantial slave force worked hemp and tobacco farms, were apprehensive about the creation of a free state in newly organized Kansas Territory. They feared an influx of yankee abolitionists and formed vigilance committees and secret lodges. DAVID ATCHISON of Missouri exhorted them to vote in Kansas elections, and many Missourians crossed the border into Kansas and helped elect a proslavery territorial delegate in November, 1854, and a proslavery legislature in March, 1855. These fraudulent elections inflamed northern sentiment and inspired a free-state movement in Kansas. Besides voting, Missourians also participated in sporadic violence in Kansas, including the Wakarusa War and the Sack of Lawrence (BLEEDING KANSAS).

See J. A. Rawley, *Race and Politics* (1969); W. F. Zornow, *Kansas* (1957); and *House Report No. 200, 34th Cong., 2nd Sess.*

JAMES A. RAWLEY
University of Nebraska, Lincoln

BORDER SLAVE STATES is a term traditionally applied to Maryland, Kentucky, Missouri, and often Delaware. West Virginia is also included at times. In the decades immediately preceding the Civil War, slavery had become less important economically and socially in Maryland, Kentucky, and Missouri and particularly in Delaware. A larger percentage of their growing populations came from northern states and abroad, and their economies became more interwoven with the North. With the secession crisis of 1860–1861, these people found their sympathies and loyalties tragically split in a way incomprehensible to residents of the North or the Deep South. Bound to the South by ties of tradition and blood and often by strong economic relationships, they were also generally intensely attached to the Union. They felt equal resentment toward southern secession and northern abolition, which most blamed for the crisis.

Delaware remained solidly pro-Union, although a number of its men served in Confederate military units. Maryland never seceded, partly due to federal occupation and the arrest of several members of the legislature. That body adopted resolutions deploring war and federal coercion and urging recognition of the Confederacy. Marylanders furnished several Confederate units, and many served in Confederate regiments from other states.

After Kentucky's governor BERIAH MAGOFFIN refused Abraham Lincoln's call for troops in April, 1861, that state attempted a policy of neutrality, although Kentuckians were recruiting companies for each army during the summer. Both sides respected this impossible neutrality until September, because each saw Kentucky as a buffer zone. When Confederates occupied Columbus on September 3, and despite U. S. Grant's seizure of Paducah two days later, the legislature demanded Confederate withdrawal, requested federal aid, and officially endorsed the Union. A provisional government in Russellville soon proclaimed secession, and Kentucky was admitted to the Confederacy in December. The state furnished many soldiers to both armies.

In Missouri the executive officers were secessionists, and a majority of the legislature agreed, authorizing a state convention. The convention, meeting in February, 1861, refused secession. Missouri also attempted neutrality, but federal capture of a militia encampment in May, along with the occupation of Jefferson City and hostilities with state forces in June, converted many wavering Unionists into active Confederates. These included former governor and convention president STERLING PRICE. A session of the convention declared the executive and legislative offices vacant in July and created a pro-Union provisional government. In October a session of the legislature called by the exiled governor, CLAIBORNE F. JACKSON, voted secession and ratified the Confederate constitution. Missouri became the twelfth Confederate state in November. It, like Kentucky, was represented in both governments throughout the war. Approximately 30,000 Missourians served in the Confederate armies.

West Virginia was created through the extraconstitutional separation of the trans-Allegheny Virginia counties. This area had for years been more closely oriented toward Pennsylvania and Ohio than toward Virginia. For political reasons many additional counties were joined to the new state against the will of their citizens.

See F. C. Smith, *Borderland in the Civil War* (1927); C. B. Clark, *Maryland Historical Magazine* (Sept., 1941; June, 1942; Dec., 1942; Dec., 1944; Sept., 1945; Dec., 1945; June, 1946), good, but incomplete account; R. O. Curry, *House Divided* (1964), scholarly analysis of West Virginia statehood; E. M. Coulter, *Civil War and Readjustment in Kentucky* (1926); W. P. Shortridge, *Mississippi Valley Historical Review* (March, 1923); W. E. Parrish, *Turbulent Partnership* (1963); and A. R. Kirkpatrick, "Missouri, the Twelfth Confederate State" (Ph.D. dissertation, University of Missouri, 1954).

A. ROY KIRKPATRICK
Bethany College

BORDLEY FAMILY. In 1794 two Yorkshire brothers immigrated to Maryland and became the progenitors of the two branches of this distinguished family. The elder, Stephen (1674–1709), like his father a Cambridge-educated Anglican clergyman, was appointed rector in Kent County. Of the three children born to Stephen and Ann Hynson, the most prominent was Stephen Bordley, Jr. (1709–1771), who as a lawyer, landowner, and legislator laid the foundation for solid respectability among the gentry of Maryland's Eastern Shore.

Of more prominence was the Annapolis branch founded by the younger immigrant, Thomas (1682–1726). Positions of profit and political importance marked his advance as an attorney. As legislator, commissary general, attorney general, and councilor, Thomas ably upheld the proprietor's prerogative until his dismissal in 1721 for giving "counsel of pernicious Consequence." Thereafter until his death in London he served in the assembly as an antiproprietary leader.

The second Annapolis Bordley of note was Stephen (1709–1764). Educated in England and a member of the Inner Temple, he rose to first rank as a legal practitioner. Following in his father Thomas' footsteps, he served as an assemblyman, attorney general, commissary general, and councilor. Along with his sister Elizabeth (1717–1789), the unmarried Stephen maintained the ancestral home, now known as Bordley-Randall House, until his death.

The third Annapolis Bordley, John Beale (1727–1804), followed the political and legal path blazed by his father Thomas and half-brother as a councilor and judge. As a benefactor of the celebrated artist Charles Willson Peale, as an elected member of the American Philosophical Society, and as a founder and first vice-president of the Philadelphia Society for Promoting Agriculture, Beale achieved fame as an early patron of the arts and a promoter of scientific agriculture.

See E. B. Gibson, *Biographical Sketches of the Bordley Family* (1865), highly subjective but useful; J. Bordley, Jr., *Hollyday and Related Families* (1962); and J. C. Morton, "Stephen Bordley" (Ph.D. dissertation, University of Maryland, 1964).

JOSEPH C. MORTON
Northeastern Illinois University

BOREMAN, ARTHUR INGRAM (1823–1896), son of a Waynesburg, Pa., merchant, read law under his lawyer brother William, a member of the Virginia legislature. Moving to Parkersburg in 1846, he entered politics as a representative to the Virginia legislature (1855–1861). He worked diligently to block secession, serving as a member of the famous extra session of the 1861 Virginia legislature. Following passage of the secession ordinance, he actively supported the movement to maintain western Virginia in the Union and, as president of the Second Wheeling Convention, was instrumental in establishing the "restored" government of Virginia. When West Virginia became a state, Boreman served as governor (1863–1869), in the U.S. Senate (1869–1875), and as circuit court judge (1888–1896).

See G. W. Atkinson and A. F. Gibbens, *Prominent Men of West Virginia* (1890); V. A. Lewis, *How West Virginia Was Made* (1909); J. C. McGregor, *Disruption of Virginia* (1922); A. I. Boreman Papers, State Archives, Charleston; and West Virginia Collection, West Virginia University Library.

F. VAL HUSLEY
West Virginia Institute of Technology

BOSOMWORTH, THOMAS (17?–17?), was one of the most colorful figures in the early history of Georgia. Appointed agent of Indian affairs by JAMES OGLETHORPE, he became acquainted with Mary Musgrove, a mixed-breed woman of the Uchee tribe, who had been educated in Charleston. In 1742 Bosomworth, an Anglican, secured holy orders, and in 1744 he married Mary, by now twice a widow. Very quickly he became involved in a series of adventures in which he asserted the claim of his wife to three islands and a large land grant near Savannah. Successful in getting the CREEKS to choose Mary as their queen, he led a menacing army of Indians to Savannah in 1749. When this show of force failed, the Bosomworths continued their fight in England and Georgia for nearly a decade and kept the colony in a constant state of tension. They finally accepted St. Catherine's Island and a payment of £2,100 in settlement of their claim.

See E. M. Coulter, *Georgia* (1933); M. E. Sirmons, *Colonial South Carolina* (1966); H. T. Malone, *Episcopal Church in Georgia* (1960); E. M. Coulter, *Georgia Historical Quarterly* (March, 1927); and N. W. Caldwell, *Journal of Southern History* (Feb., 1941).

GERALD E. HARTDAGEN
Concordia College, Moorhead, Minn.

BOSTON MOUNTAINS constitute the southern extremity of the OZARK PLATEAU and include the highest land area of the Ozark region. Elevations generally range between 1,500 and 2,200 feet. Stream dissection has created steep-sided mountains and deep, narrow valleys. The major portion of the Boston Mountains is in Arkansas. They extend westward from Independence County in northeast-central Arkansas into Sequoyah County in northeastern Oklahoma. The Boston Mountains are primarily flat-topped ridges representing the original erosion surface of the plateaus. Relatively level land is confined to ridgetops, which are remnants of the old plateau surface and the valley floors. Most of the Boston Mountains area is covered with forests, consisting chiefly of deciduous trees, with shortleaf pine appearing in the eastern and southern parts. The Ozark National Forest covers a large portion of the area. The soils are primarily medium-textured loams, utilized as woodland and pasture, with some general farming.

JAMES E. GRINER
Arkansas State University

BOTTOM RAIL ON TOP, referring to a reversal in rank and circumstances, was a phrase used in the South during Reconstruction to describe postwar conditions and the alleged aims of Republicans. It was used with particular reference to the rise in status of the former slaves and to the humiliation of their former owners. It appeared in Albion W. Tourgée's *A Fool's Errand* (1879) and since has been employed to describe actual or desired alterations in existing relationships of both social and racial groups.

BOURBON (or bourbon whiskey) originally referred to any whiskey produced in old Bourbon County, Va., a district that covered most of the eastern half of present-day Kentucky. Gradually the appellation was restricted to a special kind of whiskey, made from a mixture of corn, rye, and barley, distilled and aged according to specifications that evolved by taste and tradition. Since 1964, by act of Congress, true bourbon whiskey must be distilled from a fermented mash made of at least 51 percent but no more than 79 percent corn, distilled to no more than 160-proof alcohol, and aged a minimum of two years in previously unused, charred barrels made from staves of white oak.

Whiskey, known to the Celts as *uisge beatha* or "water of life," was made at Jamestown perhaps as early as 1617. Exactly how the early Virginians distilled their whiskey is unknown, but a variety of techniques used by later American pioneers included several that required no elaborate equipment. One of the crudest used no more than a mash or beer of fermented grain, a fire, a kettle, and an absorbent cloth stretched to absorb evaporating alcohol. The resulting whiskey was admittedly a raw beverage, less potent but not unlike much "white lightning" manufactured in parts of the South today. The first commercial distillery to operate anywhere in the South was in Charleston, S.C., in 1682.

Despite the early origins of whiskey making in America, most colonists, when they had a choice, elected spirits distilled from either fermented molasses (rum) or fermented fruit (brandy). Imported brandy appears to have been the preference of most seventeenth-century colonists; though, when this was unavailable, domestic brandy, distilled from the wines of either wild or cultivated fruits, was quite acceptable. Early in the eighteenth century, rum replaced brandy as the favorite liquor of American colonials. Rum distilleries became an important industry in colonial New England, and trading in rum, molasses, and slaves was a significant link in the British imperial economy.

It was pioneer farmers of the ever westward-moving frontier who were fondest of whiskey and made it as commonly as they prepared soap, tanned hides, or ground grain. These settlers lacked easy access to eastern sources of rum, and an orchard or vineyard required several years of growth before producing a surplus of fruit for brandy. Corn, rye, wheat, and barley, however, required only a single growing season to produce an abundance of grain for whiskey. Besides being a frontier beverage, whiskey was used by many pioneering families as a principal ingredient in their

FOLK MEDICINES and as a cash crop, which was more easily transported to market than bulky, untreated grain. Kegs and barrels of whiskey also frequently served in frontier regions as a medium of exchange. Specie was scarce; bank notes were suspect; but a barrel of whiskey was a popular commodity with a known and stable value. When Abraham Lincoln's family moved in 1816 from Kentucky to Indiana, his father is supposed to have sold his 30-acre Knob Creek farm for $20 cash and 400 gallons of whiskey valued at $640.

As settlers moved across the Allegheny Mountains and into the Ohio River valley, many brought with them both their distilling skills and their equipment. Copper stills with a 40- or 50-gallon capacity were a customary item among the household utensils of an eighteenth-century farming family. When Kentucky's first newspaper was published in 1787, the frequent advertisement of stills attests to both their availability and their commercial popularity. By 1791, the production of whiskey in Kentucky had grown to sufficient proportions to warrant vigorous opposition to the new excise tax (often called the "whiskey tax") levied on all spirits distilled "from any article of the growth and produce of the United States." Besides the exemption thus given rum distillers, the government's inability to open Spanish New Orleans—the biggest market for western whiskey—helped to arouse anti-Federalist feelings among Kentuckians. But the so-called whiskey tax was not without beneficent side effects for the American whiskey industry.

The original 1791 act levied duties ranging from nine to 25 cents per gallon on six classifications of proof or alcoholic content. Aside from the practice of considering whiskey to be either "good" or "indifferent," distillers and buyers had given little attention to a whiskey's alcoholic content. They might taste the whiskey and make a subjective assessment of its strength; or they might mix the liquor with gunpowder and then touch a flame to it. If the mixture exploded, it was too strong; if it failed to burn, it was too weak; but, if it burned with a steady blue flame, it was "proved perfect" and might be marked as "bearing proof of gunpowder." Clearly, such crude approximations of proof could never satisfactorily categorize whiskeys by different, federally established scales of alcoholic content. Accordingly, each revenue collector was equipped with a gauge and hydrometer, and these instruments signaled both a greater tendency to measure a whiskey's value in terms of its proof and a greater standardization of a distiller's product.

The new federal government was responsible for yet another policy, one promoting large-scale whiskey production. By act of Congress in 1790, all noncommissioned army and navy personnel received a daily ration of one-half gill (an eighth of a pint) of rum, brandy, or whiskey. In 1802 the daily ration was doubled. Although the army discontinued its liquor ration in 1830 and the navy did in 1862, government purchases of whiskey at times exceeded 120,000 gallons annually. While American pioneers continued their westward trek and settled much of the area east of the Mississippi River, foreign difficulties contributed to a further increase in the production and popularity of whiskey. British restrictions on American trade in the West Indies and the almost continuous state of war between Great Britain and France at the end of the eighteenth century seriously curtailed American imports of molasses. In 1800 American distillers were producing only 42 percent of the rum they had made in 1790. The Embargo Act of 1807 and the War of 1812 further limited importations of molasses and the manufacture of rum. Unable to obtain the nation's traditionally favorite liquor, rum drinkers were forced to discover the fine taste of whiskey, particularly Kentucky or bourbon whiskey.

Great numbers of investigators have been intrigued with the question of who was the first person to distill bourbon, a whiskey distilled from a mixture of at least 51 percent corn with a smaller amount of rye grain. They usually have assumed that the creator of bourbon was a Kentuckian, and most have credited the Reverend Elijah Craig (1743–180?) of Georgetown, Ky. Federal tax records identify him as a farmer, schoolteacher, Baptist minister, and operator of a commercial distillery. Craig made whiskey from a mixture of corn and rye, but, well before he journeyed to Kentucky, practicality and economy of production already had established the practice of mixing the two grains, usually in whatever quantities were available. George Washington's Mount Vernon operations, for example, included the distillation of whiskey from a mixture of corn and rye. And, because an acre of land devoted to the cultivation of corn yields a greater harvest than an acre of any other grain, it is reasonable to assume that many individual distillers separately developed what became the classic proportions of bourbon mash.

Perhaps the most apparent characteristic of modern whiskey, including bourbon, is its distinctive amber-red color. This color and much of the flavor of today's bourbon are derived from being aged in barrels of charred white oak. Charring the barrel produces a layer of carmelized wood sugars under the inner surface of the barrel's staves. The charred wood and the carmelized sugar absorb some of the harsher impurities found in freshly distilled whiskey, transform others, and give bourbon its deep and distinctive coloration. Because reuse of these barrels diminishes their capacity to work these functions, today true bourbon whiskey must be aged in previously unused barrels. Although there are numerous stories as to the origin of aging bourbon in such barrels, the practice does not seem to have become standardized until relatively late in the nineteenth century. Oak barrels, whether new or previously used, were the preferred container for aging whiskey—when it was to be aged—at least as early as the War of 1812. Because most available barrels had served already as containers for dried fish, salt pork, vinegar, or flour, shaving or charring their interiors was an essential cleansing process. But only charred and previously unused barrels give to whiskey the distinctive, rich color of bourbon. As no pre–Civil War description of bourbon comments on its having any particular color whatsoever, most antebellum distillers of bourbon probably reused their barrels, whether shaved or charred, many times over.

With the Civil War came the restoration of the excise tax on liquor and of some federal supervision. The so-called whiskey tax, repealed in 1802 and briefly reimposed between 1814 and 1817, was reestablished as a war tax in 1862. To collect it, the government established the Bureau of Internal Revenue. During the war, the initial duty of 20 cents per 100-proof gallon was raised in 1864 to $1.50 and, during the final weeks of the war, to $2.00 per 100-proof gallon. In 1868 the rate was reduced to 50 cents, but the war tax remained and the bureau became a permanent office of the government.

Taxes can be added to a distiller's costs and passed on to the consumer, but PROHIBITION left the whiskey manufacturers with no such alternative. After ratification of the Eighteenth Amendment, some companies switched to the production of chemicals; some distillers, under close federal regulation, produced industrial and medicinal alcohol. Others, however, simply closed down. In 1933 when Prohibition was repealed, many small but once well-established, family-operated distilleries failed to resume operations. Twelve years of inactivity, the economic obstacles posed by the depression, and managerial staffs inadequate for the complex problems of a nationwide market combined to handicap small distillers. Whiskey was again a big business, and big corporations were better suited for its conduct. By merger, by purchase, and by expansion, four corporations—Schenley, Seagrams, National Distillers, and Heublein—came to dominate the distilling industry. Old brands and names traditionally associated with the history of whiskey are still carried on the lists of these companies, but few distilleries are family owned and operated.

The post-Prohibition years witnessed not only changes in the business structure of the whiskey industry, but also a change in its locale. During the late nineteenth century, Illinois had outdistanced Kentucky and Tennessee in the distillation of whiskey. Since 1933, however, the revived industry has returned to the South, notably to Kentucky, where over 55 percent of all American whiskey is now made.

Repeal of the Eighteenth Amendment proved that people still liked to drink, but the distillers' warehouses were empty; and aged whiskey—especially bourbon—was, when it became available, in short supply. During World War II, government rationing of grain and greatly increased needs for industrial alcohol further compounded the shortage of good whiskey. But scarcity of any item usually results in the development of a substitute. As oleomargarine gradually filled much of the market previously served by butter, distillers, aided by a new chemistry of artificial flavors and colorings, expanded their production of inexpensive blends. A single gallon of straight whiskey—diluted with grain spirits and water and doctored with laboratory chemicals—was transformed into three or more gallons of blended whiskey. Necessity, which once had forced rum drinkers to discover straight whiskey, now forced whiskey and bourbon drinkers to discover the blends. In 1948 grain spirit blends accounted for 87 percent of all whiskey produced in the United States.

Since 1948, however, bourbon gradually has rebounded. Distilleries increased the proportion of corn in their mash to produce a lighter bodied potion, and an intensive advertising campaign stressed the "smoothness" and "mildness" of bourbon. By 1963, the production of straight whiskey had surpassed that of the blends for the first time since Pearl Harbor. Today, straight American whiskey represents over three-fifths of the distilled spirits consumed in the U.S., and bourbon fills over half of the demand for domestic whiskey. If bourbon is no longer king of distilled spirits in America, it is at least chairman of the board.

See H. G. Crowgey, *Kentucky Bourbon* (1971), most scholarly study available, though limited to one state and to early nineteenth century. G. Carson, *Social History of Bourbon* (1963), and H. H. Kroll, *Bluegrass, Belles, and Bourbon* (1967), are fragmentary and anecdotal. See also W. H. Perrin, *History of Bourbon* (1882); J. M. Atherton, *Whiskey Industry in Kentucky* (1885); W. R. Jillson, *Early Kentucky Distillers* (1940); H. F. Wilkie and J. A. Prochaska, *Fundamentals of Distillery Practice* (1943); C. B. Garrison, *Impact of Distilled Spirits Tax on Kentucky's Economy* (1965); and J. E. Dabney, *Mountain Spirits* (1974). Archival records of U.S. Treasury Department and local census materials are largely unused sources for post–Civil War period.

BOURBONS were the leaders of the conservative white Democrats who opposed Radical Reconstruction and took power after its defeat. They claimed to represent the old slaveholding class and to have restored most of the traditional policies and social institutions of the slave era. In particular they have been seen as the inveterate foes of Negro participation in politics. More recently C. VANN WOODWARD has shown that the Bourbons were not the old slave-ruling class, but rather a new elite, and that they were not agents of restoration, but rather of adaptation to yankee institutions and ideas, particularly industrial capitalism. Far from opposing Negro voting, the Bourbons controlled a captive Negro vote in their own BLACK BELT counties and made it the basis of their own electoral strength. Finally, though the Bourbons claimed to represent political virtue that distinguished them from supposedly corrupt CARPETBAGGERS and SCALAWAG politicians, they have been shown to have engaged in considerable corruption themselves, usually involving railroad development (REDEEMER GOVERNMENTS).

See C. V. Woodward, *Origins of New South* (1951), definitive; D. W. Grantham, *South Atlantic Quarterly* (Summer, 1961); J. P. Maddex, *Virginia Conservatives* (1970); H. M. Bond, *Journal of Negro History* (July, 1938); A. Going, *Bourbon Democracy in Alabama* (1951); and W. J. Cooper, *Conservative Regime* (1968).

JONATHAN M. WIENER
University of California, Irvine

BOWERS, CLAUDE GERNADE (1878–1958), through most of his life was a newspaper reporter and editorial writer (first in his native Indiana, then for the New York *World* in the 1920s) or diplomat (serving successively as ambassador to Spain and Chile between 1933 and 1953). Always he was an active Democrat. He is best known for his books on American history, particularly his best-selling *Jefferson and Hamilton* (1925), in which he celebrated Thomas Jefferson as the triumphant representative of white democracy and agrarian America, and *The Tragic Era* (1929), in which he championed Andrew Johnson's struggle during Reconstruction against the Republicans and Congress. The latter work, which one historian has termed a "zestful work of imagination," further popularized traditional attitudes toward Reconstruction and the post–Civil War South, much as did Margaret Mitchell's GONE WITH THE WIND (1936). Bowers' volumes reflect his political commitments, his research in newspaper sources, and a novelist's attempt to "recreate the atmosphere" of the times he chronicled. Bowers merits study both as a diplomat and as a popular historian.

See his Oral History Memoir (1954), in the Columbia University Collection, and *My Life* (1962).

PETER WALLENSTEIN
University of Toronto

BOWIE, JAMES (1796–1836), was a legend in his time and has become even more of one in later years. Like most legendary figures, little of what has been written about him is true. A Louisiana planter and entrepreneur, Bowie was neither a brawler nor a duelist. He did not invent or even design the knife that bears his name. The development of the knife was primarily by his brother Resin, and the first Bowie knife was not, as legend has it, made from a meteor. Immigrating to Texas about 1828, Bowie was later active in forming the government of the Republic of Texas, serving as a colonel of volunteers. While so doing he died in the defense of the ALAMO, thereby enshrining himself in Texas history just as he had previously enshrined himself in American history with the "invention" of the Bowie knife. The knife's distinguishing characteristics, although there is some disagreement over the shape, are a very heavy blade, triangular in cross section, extremely thick at the top, approximately eight inches long, with a small guard.

See *American Arms Collector* (1957), I. For primary materials, see Texas Historical Society and Pennsylvania Historical Society.

HUGH BENET, JR.
Star-Spangled Banner Flag House Association

BOWLING GREEN, KY. (pop. 36,253), 65 miles northeast of Nashville, Tenn., was first settled in 1780 by a group of Virginians. The location in the midst of a treeless plain was chosen because of the presence of an excellent spring and the navigability up to this point of the Barren River. By the time of the Civil War, the city had become an important market town serving both rail and river commerce. The city was abandoned by General SIMON BUCKNER's Confederates during Union advances on FTS. HENRY AND DONELSON in February, 1862. Although held by federal forces throughout the remainder of the war, General JOHN HUNT MORGAN briefly hid in nearby Lost River Cave. Modern Bowling Green continues to be the principal market for farmers in this part of southern Kentucky. Its factories produce construction materials, dairy products, processed meats and poultry, and automobile parts. Western Kentucky State University (1906) maintains the Kentucky Library of Folklore and Kentuckiana, the records of the South Union Shaker Colony (1807–1922), and the Lewis-Starling Papers (late eighteenth-century Kentucky).

See files of Bowling Green *Park News* (1882–), available on microfilm; and extensive collection of diaries, newspapers, wills, deeds, and court records at Kentucky Library of the university.

BOYD, JULIAN P. (1903–), was born in Converse, S.C., and educated at Duke University (A.B., M.A.). Although best known as a Thomas Jefferson scholar and editor of *The Papers of Thomas Jefferson*, Boyd has had varied experiences: editor of *The Susquehannah Company Papers* (1928–1932); director of the New York State Historical Association (1932–1934); director of the Historical Society of Pennsylvania (1934–1940); and Princeton University librarian (1940–1952). He is currently professor emeritus of history at Princeton.

Boyd, in his 1943 proposal to publish Jefferson's papers, sought to bring into print all of Jefferson's writings as well as everything that bears on his "recorded actions." Merrill D. Peterson has observed that the series "is a work of historical analysis and interpretation rather than a work of editing as the term is generally understood." Boyd's other eighteenth-century publications include: *Indian Treaties Printed by Benjamin Franklin* (1938); *Anglo-American Union: Joseph Galloway's Plans to Preserve the British Empire, 1774–1788* (1941); *The Declaration of Independence: Evolution of the Text* (1943, 1945); and *Fundamental Laws and Constitutions of New Jersey* (1964).

See B. Bailyn, *New England Quarterly* (Sept., 1960); L. H. Butterfield and J. P. Boyd, *Proceedings of the American Antiquarian Society* (Oct., 1962); and M. D. Peterson, *William and Mary Quarterly* (Oct., 1975), a review of Vols. XVIII and XIX of *Papers of Thomas Jefferson*.

JOAN JACOBS BRUMBERG
Eisenhower College

BOYD, WILLIAM KENNETH (1879–1938), was a historian, a collector of historical source materials, and an educator. He was born in Curryville. Mo., and reared in Weaverville, N.C. He was educated at Trinity College in Durham (A.B., 1897; M.A., 1898) and at Columbia University (Ph.D., 1906), where he studied early church history but was influenced by WILLIAM A. DUNNING. Returning to Durham in 1906 to succeed JOHN SPENCER BASSETT, Boyd spent the remainder of his life at Trinity College and its successor, Duke University. Lacking research materials in early church history, he returned to his earlier interest in southern history. He was a prolific writer; his bibliography comprises 17 pages. His best-known book, *The Story of Durham, City of the New South* (1925), emphasized social and economic factors. But Boyd's greatest contributions were as a collector of source materials and the developer of Duke into a major center for the study of southern history. At his death the Duke collections were preeminent in the region, having grown rapidly after 1930, when the endowed Flowers Collection was founded through his efforts. Boyd was an inspiring teacher, and many of his graduate students also became prominent historians.

See *In Memoriam: W. K. Boyd* (1938); and Boyd Papers, Duke University Archives.

ORVILLE W. TAYLOR
Georgia College

BRADFORD, AUGUSTUS W. (1806–1881), a Baltimore lawyer, was notable as war governor of Maryland in 1862–1866. A Whig in his youth, he was relatively inactive in politics between 1850 and the turbulent election of 1861, when the state's new Union party called upon him to be its candidate. Bradford's election was tainted by charges of federal military intimidation at the polls, but these charges are disputed by recent studies. Bradford was a Maryland delegate to the WASHINGTON PEACE CONFERENCE of February, 1861. As governor he was a strong Unionist and a moderate emancipationist; he promoted the revised Maryland constitution of 1864, which ended slavery in the state.

See H. E. Buchholz, *Governors of Maryland* (1908); J. H. Baker, *Politics of Continuity* (1973); *Biographical Cyclopedia of Representative Men of Maryland and the District of Columbia* (1879); C. Wagandt, *Mighty Revolution* (1964); and Governor's Correspondence, Hall of Records, Annapolis. Some private papers are at Maryland Historical Society, Baltimore.

WILLIAM J. EVITTS
Hollins College

BRADFORD, JOHN (1749–1830), was born in Prince William County, Va. In 1785 he settled in

Lexington, Ky. On August 11, 1787, he published the KENTUCKY GAZETTE, the first newspaper west of Pittsburgh. The self-taught Bradford, called the "Franklin of the West," was not only a printer, publisher, surveyor, and mathematician but was also one of the first historians of Kentucky. His community involvement included the post of secretary of Lexington's Emigration Society, chairman of the town board, chairman of the board of trustees of TRANSYLVANIA UNIVERSITY, and founder of the Lexington library. A supporter of Thomas Jefferson, he organized the Democratic Society of Kentucky and served in the state house of representatives. At his death Bradford was sheriff of Fayette County.

See J. W. Coleman, *John Bradford* (1950); D. C. McMurtrie, *John Bradford* (1931); J. Bradford, *Notes on Kentucky* (1932); and R. M. Hadsell, *Register of the Kentucky Historical Society* (Oct., 1964).

RICHARD A. VAN ORMAN
Purdue University, Calumet

BRAGG, BRAXTON (1817–1876), grew up in wealthy plantation country around Warrenton, N.C. Son of a moderately successful contractor, he graduated from an excellent local academy and West Point (1837). The young artillery officer distinguished himself at Buena Vista in the Mexican War but, disliking routine duty, resigned a lieutenant colonelcy in 1856 to become a Louisiana planter.

One of the most promising soldiers to join the Confederacy, Bragg rose quickly to full general by 1862. First he organized coast defenses from Pensacola to Mobile. In early 1862 he helped gather forces to repel a Union invasion of Tennessee, gallantly leading a corps at SHILOH. Esteemed by Jefferson Davis, he next commanded the Confederacy's chief western army, the Army of Tennessee, in four major campaigns (June, 1862–November, 1863). His daring invasion of Kentucky (July–October, 1862) was aborted after the drawn battle at PERRYVILLE. Next he withdrew before General William S. Rosecrans following the indecisive battle at STONES RIVER, Tenn. (January, 1863). Months of maneuvering in north Georgia's mountains culminated in victory over Rosecrans at CHICKAMAUGA (September, 1863), sending the federals retreating into Chattanooga. Nonetheless, Bragg's cautious siege tactics ended disastrously (November, 1863) when U. S. Grant defeated and drove him to Dalton, Ga. At last the discredited general relinquished field command and served a while as President Davis' military adviser and finally in minor positions. After the war he became a civil engineer in Alabama and later in Texas.

Bragg never quite delivered according to his abilities. An unrivaled organizer and a bold strategist, he would have been an excellent corps commander or a competent second-in-command. Many of his talents, however, were negated by personality faults and slowness in perceiving how warfare had changed. Tall, stooped, and haggard, he suffered from illnesses, some psychosomatic, that made him moody and quarrelsome. His authoritarian manner and contentiousness antagonized subordinates. Although he planned carefully, full responsibility numbed his nerve, and, fearing to make a mistake, he lost several victories by hesitating. Bragg continually called for bayonet assaults, apparently unaware that his older chivalrous tactics had been outmoded by the deadly long-range accuracy of rifled muzzle-loaders.

See G. McWhiney, *Braxton Bragg* (1969); D. C. Seitz, *Braxton Bragg* (1924); and T. L. Connelly, *Army of Heartland* (1967).

JAMES R. CHUMNEY
Memphis State University

BRAGG, THOMAS (1810–1872), the older brother of BRAXTON BRAGG, was a lawyer and politician who moved on the periphery of the North Carolina and national scenes in the Civil War era. An austere and aloof Democrat, Bragg was barely elected governor in 1854 but was reelected by a wider margin two years later. He was elected to the U.S. Senate in 1859, where his posture was largely negative, opposing such measures as homestead legislation. A reluctant secessionist, Bragg resigned his seat and helped prepare the defense of the state in 1861, before serving as attorney general of the Confederacy for a few months in late 1861 and early 1862. He also acted as a representative of Jefferson Davis to keep truculent Governor ZEBULON VANCE in line. Bragg's last public act was as counsel in the impeachment of Governor WILLIAM W. HOLDEN, and his performance lent an aura of legitimacy to the proceedings.

See North Carolina Department of Archives and History for a few papers. University of North Carolina Library has his recently discovered diary, but there is no scholarly study of Bragg.

DONALD ROPER
State University of New York, New Paltz

BRANDEIS, LOUIS DEMBITZ (1856–1941). Although Brandeis was born in Louisville, Ky., a city for which he maintained a lifelong attachment, his career brought him into little contact with southern problems or politics. After establishing a highly successful law practice in Boston, he became one of the best known and most effective reform leaders in the Progressive movement. He consistently attacked monopolies, which he declared were economically inefficient and destructive of political freedom. A firm proponent of Jeffersonian Democracy, he advocated the regulation of competition, which he believed would help maintain a system of individual initiative and enterprise essential to a democratic society. He became the intellectual architect of WOODROW WILSON's New Freedom, and from 1913 through 1915 was an intimate adviser to the president on such matters as antitrust legislation and banking and currency reform. In 1916 Wilson nominated Brandeis to the U.S. Supreme Court.

Together with Oliver Wendell Holmes, Jr., Brandeis became a staunch defender of a liberal interpretation of the law, an approach suggested by Holmes in *The Common Law* (1881), and which Brandeis had put into practical effect in his famous sociological briefs in support of Progressive wages and hours legislation. Many scholars consider him the greatest legal craftsman ever to sit on the Court, and his many dissenting opinions in the 1920s were adopted as correct constitutional interpretation in the late 1930s and 1940s. Off the bench, Brandeis continued to be the informal leader of American Zionism and took a leading role in the expansion and upgrading of the University of Louisville.

See A. T. Mason, *Brandeis* (1946); S. J. Konefsky, *Holmes and Brandeis* (1956); M. I. Urofsky, *Mind of One Piece* (1971); and M. I. Urofsky and D. W. Levy, *Letters of Louis D. Brandeis* (1971–).

MELVIN I. UROFSKY
Virginia Commonwealth University

BRANDY STATION, BATTLE OF (June 9, 1863), is sometimes called the battle of Fleetwood. Following CHANCELLORSVILLE, Robert E. Lee camped near Culpeper and Brandy Station in Virginia on the Orange & Alexandria Railroad preparatory to an invasion of the North to relieve pressure on the deteriorating western front. Joseph Hooker ordered Alfred Pleasonton with the Union cavalry supported by two infantry brigades to cross the Rappahannock, march to Culpeper, destroy Lee's supplies, and ascertain his intentions. Union General John Buford surprised W. E. ("Grumble") Jones at Beverly Ford, but the Union cavalry divisions of David M. Gregg and Alfred N. Duffié were late crossing Kelly's Ford to the south. Bitter fighting occurred north of Brandy Station on Fleetwood Heights, which changed hands several times. Pleasonton finally withdrew in good order despite over 900 casualties, nearly double the Confederate losses. Perhaps the greatest cavalry battle of the Civil War involving approximately 10,000 men on each side, Brandy Station proved that the Union cavalry was now a match for the Confederates. J. E. B. STUART, stung by criticisms in the press, determined to redeem himself in the northern campaign, with disastrous results for the southern cause at GETTYSBURG.

See F. Downey, *Clash of Cavalry* (1959), most thorough study; *Annals of the War* (1879); R. U. Johnson and C. C. Buel (eds.), *Battles and Leaders* (1884–87), III; B. Davis, *Last Cavalier* (1957); and J. W. Thomason, *Jeb Stuart* (1930).

CAREY W. BRUSH
State University of New York, Oneonta

BRAZOS RIVER flows southeasterly across Texas to the Gulf of Mexico. Many pivotal events in Texas history occurred near its banks, and diverse ethnic groups have been associated with it. The Spaniards named it Brazos de Dios, "arms of God." Austin's Colony, the first organized Anglo settlement in Texas, was centered on the lower Brazos, and Texan independence was declared at WASHINGTON-ON-THE-BRAZOS. The Brazos lands became a microcosm of the South. Plantations served by river steamboats lined its lower course, and southern mountaineers settled the hilly lands along its middle course, creating a Texas "Appalachia." Much of the Anglo-Comanche war was fought on the middle and upper Brazos. Additional cultural diversity was added to the Brazos Valley by colonies of Germans, Czechs, Norwegians, Sicilians, Poles, and other groups.

See J. Graves, *Goodbye to a River* (1960); Mrs. J. L. Wallis and L. L. Hill, *Sixty Years on Brazos* (1930); and "Brazos River," *Handbook of Texas* (1952).

TERRY G. JORDAN
North Texas State University

BREAD RIOT is the name given to an "unfortunate disturbance" that occurred in Richmond, Va., on April 2, 1863. A crowd of nearly 1,000, mostly women and children, marched along Cary and Main streets toward the bakeries from which each of the "rioters" was to "take a loaf of bread." President Jefferson Davis confronted the crowd, led by Mary Jackson, and, satisfied that they were looting generally, he warned them that their lawlessness must stop or they would be fired upon; they dispersed. Despite an appeal from the assistant adjutant general, accounts of the "riot" appeared in the press. By April 13, all the parties arrested had either been discharged or sent on for trial before the higher courts.

See *Official Records, Armies*, Ser. 1, Vol. XVIII; V. H. Davis, *Jefferson Davis* (1890); Richmond *Examiner* (April 4, 1863); S. A. B. Putnam, *Richmond During War* (1867); and W. J. Kimball, *Civil War History* (June, 1961).

WILLIAM J. KIMBALL
Converse College

BRECKINRIDGE, JOHN (1760–1806), born near Staunton, Va., of Scotch-Irish descent, attended the College of William and Mary, served in the state legislature, farmed, and practiced law. After moving to Kentucky in 1793, he established a successful bluegrass horse farm and plantation, speculated in land and salt and ironworks, and conducted a lucrative legal practice. State attorney general in 1793–1797, he then served in the legislature, where he sponsored the Kentucky Resolutions of 1798 and 1799 (VIRGINIA AND KENTUCKY RESOLUTIONS) and helped secure penal reform and constitutional revision. Elected to the U.S. Senate in 1801, he was a floor leader in Thomas Jefferson's first term. He became attorney general in 1805 but contributed little to that office before his death at his Cabell's Dale home. Breckinridge was a good example of the natural aristocrats who had an important role in Jeffersonian Democracy.

See L. H. Harrison, *John Breckinridge* (1969); Breckinridge Family Papers, Library of Congress; and E. C. Warfield, *Kentucky Resolutions of 1798* (1887).

LOWELL H. HARRISON
Western Kentucky University

BRECKINRIDGE, JOHN CABELL (1821–1875), was born in Lexington into one of Kentucky's first families. He was educated at Centre, Princeton, and Transylvania colleges. He practiced law briefly in Iowa but returned home after marrying Mary Burch of Georgetown. His oratorical skills attracted attention, and in 1849 he was elected to the legislature as a Democrat. Two years later he upset Leslie Coombs for election to Congress, and in 1853 he held his seat against the formidable challenge of Robert P. Letcher. On the issue of slavery expansion, Breckinridge maintained that Congress should not interfere in any manner.

He resumed his legal practice, but in 1856 he was elected vice-president with James Buchanan. Nominated for president by the southern Democrats in 1860, he won 11 states but failed to carry Kentucky. He believed in states' rights but hoped to avoid secession, and he supported Kentucky's unique neutrality policy in 1861. Breckinridge defended the South in the Senate after March 4, 1861, and in early fall he fled to Richmond to avoid arrest. Commissioned brigadier general, he commanded the Kentucky Brigade in SIMON B. BUCKNER's division. After a creditable performance at SHILOH, he was promoted major general. He failed to capture BATON ROUGE during the summer and was unable to join BRAXTON BRAGG in his invasion of Kentucky. Breckinridge later fought at STONES RIVER, outside VICKSBURG, at CHICKAMAUGA, and at Missionary Ridge. After his line was shattered at Missionary Ridge, Bragg removed him from command.

But in February, 1864, Breckinridge was assigned to the Department of Southwestern Virginia, where he won his finest victory at NEW MARKET. After joining the Army of Northern Virginia before COLD HARBOR, he went on EARLY'S WASHINGTON RAID and fought at WINCHESTER and Marion. Appointed secretary of war on February 4, 1865, he accomplished little in that position. Breckinridge accompanied Davis for a time after Richmond fell, then escaped to Cuba. Fearing arrest, he lived in Europe and Canada until the spring of 1869. Disqualified for public office, Breckinridge devoted his last years to law and railroad promotion. He died in Lexington.

See W. C. Davis, *John C. Breckinridge* (1974), definitive; Lucille Stillwell, *John Cabell Breckinridge* (1936), inadequate; and L. H. Harrison, *Filson Club History Quarterly* (April, 1973).

LOWELL H. HARRISON
Western Kentucky University

BRECKINRIDGE, MADELINE MCDOWELL (1872–1920), exemplified a significant aspect of the Progressive impulse. She was educated at women's academies and studied sporadically at Kentucky State College. Her childless marriage to Desha Breckinridge, editor of the Lexington *Herald*, allowed her scope for a variety of reform activities. She helped establish the Lexington Associated Charities (becoming its director in 1907) and the Lexington Civic League. Her reform efforts produced state legislation concerning CHILD LABOR and juvenile justice, a public health clinic in Lexington (HEALTH, PUBLIC), city beautification, and female prison reform. A victim of TUBERCULOSIS, she worked for its eradication and promoted the establishment of the Lexington Bluegrass Sanitorium. Her weekly women's page in the Lexington *Herald* focused on developing social and political consciousness; and she campaigned for women's suffrage as president of the Kentucky Equal Rights Association and vice-president of the National American Woman Suffrage Association (WOMEN'S RIGHTS MOVEMENT).

See S. P. Breckinridge, *Madeline M. Breckinridge* (1921); M. M. Breckinridge Manuscripts, Library of Congress; I. H. Harper, *History of Woman Suffrage* (1922), V, VI; and M. D. Porter, *Register of the Kentucky Historical Society* (Oct., 1974).

SUSAN M. HARTMANN
University of Missouri, St. Louis

BRENTWOOD, BATTLE OF (March 25, 1863). Toward the end of March, 1863, with William S. Rosecrans preparing to leave his winter base at Nashville and move on to Chattanooga, the ever alert N. B. FORREST fell upon an outlying Union post at Brentwood, Tenn., a few miles south of Nashville. After a swift and well-planned march, Forrest surprised, surrounded, and captured the federal garrison of over 510 men commanded by Lieutenant Colonel Edward Bloodgood. Rosecrans sent G. C. Smith's cavalry to Bloodgood's aid, and he succeeded in recapturing some wagons, arms, and accouterments. Forrest brought up reinforcements and drove the Union forces from the field. The Confederates claimed to capture 759, but Rosecrans claimed the detachment did not number that many.

See A. Lytle, *Forrest and Critter Company* (1931); G. J. Fieberger, *Campaigns* (1941); E. L. Drake, *Chronological Summary of Battles* (1879); *Union Army* (1908); and S. F. Horn, *Army of Tennessee* (1939).

J. H. DEBERRY
Memphis State University

BRIAN, HARDY LEE (1865–1949), was state chairman of the People's or POPULIST PARTY in Louisiana, a newspaper editor, and a legislator. His futile career as a reformer illustrates the difficulties of opposing the state's Democratic oligarchy during the period between Reconstruction and HUEY LONG. The son of a Baptist minister, Brian was born near Pollock, in what is now Grant Parish. His father, the Reverend Benjamin Brian, led an INDEPENDENT MOVEMENT among poor whites and Negroes in Grant and Winn parishes during the 1870s and 1880s. Along with his father, Hardy Brian took the lead in founding the Louisiana People's party in 1890–1891. He edited the Winnfield *Comrade* as a third-party organ (1890–1894); represented Winn Parish in the legislature (1892–1896); was state chairman of the People's party (1896–1898); and published the Natchitoches *Louisiana Populist* (1894–1899) until local Democrats forced him to close the paper. During the early twentieth century, Brian farmed near Verda, in Grant Parish. Never again politically prominent, he continued to crusade locally for

various causes: better schools, Prohibition, and improved roads.

See L. E. Daniel, "Louisiana People's Party" (M.A. thesis, Louisiana State University, 1942); H. C. Dethloff, "Populism and Reform" (Ph.D. dissertation, University of Missouri, 1964); and W. I. Hair, *Bourbonism and Agrarian Protest* (1969).

WILLIAM I. HAIR
Georgia College

BRICE'S CROSSROADS, BATTLE OF (June 10, 1864), is sometimes called the battle of Tishomingo Creek. In late spring, 1864, William T. Sherman's army drove toward Atlanta. To help prevent supply line attacks and reinforcements from reaching JOSEPH E. JOHNSTON, Sherman sent General Samuel D. Sturgis with 8,500 men toward Tupelo, Miss., on June 1, 1864, to destroy or divert NATHAN B. FORREST's cavalry. June 9 found Sturgis' expedition encamped south of Ripley, Miss., just nine miles north of Brice's Crossroads.

Meanwhile, Forrest, who had just been ordered by STEPHEN D. LEE to raid Sherman's supply line, was recalled to meet the new Mississippi invaders. On an extremely hot June 10, Forrest's 3,500 soldiers and Sturgis' 8,000 fought gallantly at Brice's Crossroads. The day ended with Union troops in a disorganized retreat toward Memphis, defeated by poor northern leadership, superior southern generalship, and southern weather. The Union army lost nearly 30 percent of its men. Immediate southern battle losses were slight, but the long-term cost was great because the Confederate units ordered to defend the Mississippi-Alabama region were unavailable to disrupt Sherman's supply line or reinforce Johnston's army. The South's territorial defensive strategy contributed to Sherman's victory at Atlanta.

See *Official Records, Armies*, Ser. 1, Vols. XXXVIII and XXXIX; W. G. Leftwich, Jr., *West Tennessee Historical Society Papers* (1966), best-documented article; D. A. Brown, *Civil War Times Illustrated* (April, 1968), undocumented but well researched; S. D. Lee, *Publications of Mississippi Historical Society* (1902), VI; R. U. Johnson and C. C. Buel (eds.), *Battles and Leaders* (1888), Ser. 1, Vol. IV, Pt. 1; S. D. Sturgis, *The Other Side* (1882), defense of his campaign; and T. L. Connelly, *Autumn of Glory* (1971).

JOHN S. PAINTER
Northern State College

BRIDGES. In the colonial South, pile and beam bridges with braced bents were standard. Constructed of hewn logs, spans were generally no more than 20 feet long. Truss framing, wholly timber until 1840, was used after the turn of the nineteenth century for vehicular traffic and, after about 1830, also for railroad bridges. Commonly used were the Burr system, with parallel chord truss and arch (patent, 1817); the Town lattice truss, with parallel chord latticed web (patent, 1820); and the Howe truss, with a panel system with wrought-iron verticals (patent, 1841). These bridge designs were copied in the South by builders who paid for patent rights. Architect Ithiel Town constructed bridges in North Carolina. Over 100 nineteenth-century covered bridges remain in the South, mostly king-post, queen-post, and Town truss types. Two additional types built were Louis Wernwag's Palladian arched truss (over the Kentucky River at Camp Nelson, Ky., 1838) and Colonel Long's K truss (Jackson Bridge over Baltimore & Ohio Railroad, probably at Baltimore, 1830).

Another classification of bridges is by material. The first masonry bridge with dressed stone is the Carrollton Viaduct (B & O Railroad, 1829), still in use at Baltimore. The first multispan masonry bridge for railroad use was the Thomas Viaduct over the Patapsco River at Relay, Md. (1835).

Another construction type is the arch. The first long-span segmental arch bridge in the United States was an aqueduct over Cabin John Creek, Washington, D.C., built by M. C. Meigs (1864). He also built the nation's second iron arch bridge over Rock Creek, also in Washington, the arches of which (hollow cast-iron tubes) carried water.

Between 1845 and 1861, metal bridge superstructures for railroads and viaducts were used to accommodate greater moving loads over spans more than 100 feet. Pratt truss bridges, with a single-diagonal system (patent, 1844), were built in iron for railroad traffic. East of the Ohio River, Bollman trusses (patent, 1852) were used by the B & O Railroad at Harpers Ferry, W.Va. (1868), and at Benwood over the Ohio River (1871). The only known surviving Bollman truss in the United States is in Savage, Md., over the Little Patuxent River (1869). Also designed for B & O bridges was the Fink truss (patent, 1854). The first iron bridge of this design appeared in Fairmount, W.Va. (1852). Another bridge by Albert Fink was constructed for the Louisville & Nashville Railroad over the Green River near Mammoth Cave, Ky. (1859).

After 1865 bridges greater than 400 feet posed new engineering problems. In use for long-span bridges from 1865 to 1885 was the metal Whipple truss (patent, 1847), and the Warren truss (English patent, 1848) became popular near the end of the nineteenth century. The Whipple truss was in greatest use for Ohio River crossings. Steel Whipple trusses were used by W. S. Smith for the Chicago & Alton Railroad's Missouri River bridge at Glasgow, Mo. (1879). Fink modified the Warren truss by half-length diagonals in his railroad bridge at Louisville (1870). The first steel arch bridge, now used for both vehicular and rail traffic over the Mississippi at St. Louis, Mo., was built by James Eads in 1874.

A variation in bridge construction is the cantilever truss span also built in combinations of continuous trusses with hinged chords and suspended spans. The first railroad cantilever bridge was built by the Cincinnati Southern Railway over the Kentucky River at Dixville, Ky. (1877), using continuous Whipple trusses. A railroad cantilever truss span of 791 feet held the record in clear length when constructed by G. S. Morison and A. Noble over the Mississippi River at Memphis, Tenn., in 1892.

Since 1900 steel truss bridges have used Pratt and Warren truss types with a web system of posts and single diagonals. Most construction was for railroad traffic until the 1920s, when vehicular bridges were built in greater numbers to handle the rapid growth of automobile travel. The Huey P. Long Bridge at New Orleans (1936) has both a rail line and a highway carried by subdivided steel Warren trusses. Reappearing in the early twentieth century, the K truss achieved its greatest length with a highway bridge over the Atchafalaya River at Morgan City, La. (1933).

Concrete bridge construction in the early 1900s was characterized by arch designs built of plain concrete. Examples are the Connecticut Avenue bridge over Rock Creek in Washington, D.C. (1904), and the two-mile Long Key Viaduct in Key West, Fla. (1912), for railroad traffic. Reinforced concrete bridge design evolved steadily throughout the century, using the flattened parabolic arch for highway bridges.

See History of American Engineering Records, National Park Service, Washington, D.C., the major repository. HAER truss posters contain bibliographies; write M. C. Meigs Chapter, Society for Industrial Archeology, c/o HAER. See also R. S. Allen, *Covered Bridges of South* (1970), detailed; American Society of Civil Engineers, *American Wooden Bridges* (1976), good bibliography; D. Plowden, *Bridges* (1968), annotated bibliography, comprehensive text; L. N. Edwards, *Records of Early American Bridges* (1959), good, but not readily available; and D. G. Diebler, *Survey of Metal Bridges in Virginia* (1975).

EMMA JANE NEELLEY
University of Vermont

BRISTOE STATION, BATTLE OF (October 14, 1863). In the course of Robert E. Lee's turning movement against George Meade's Army of the

Potomac, A. P. HILL, commanding the III Corps of the Army of Northern Virginia, learned that the Union forces in their retreat northward were fording a stream near Bristoe Station, Va. Hoping to catch the enemy off balance, Hill ordered HENRY HETH, the commander of his leading division, to attack immediately without allowing time for reconnaissance or proper deployment of the assaulting units. As John R. Cooke's and William W. Kirkland's brigades of Heth's division approached the ford, they came under enfilading fire from G. K. Warren's federals, hidden in a railroad cut on the Confederate right. In order to extricate themselves, Heth's brigades had to wheel about and charge the enemy force in the cut. In the ensuing disaster the Confederates took some 1,300 casualties. Heth, having merely complied with orders, was not blamed for his part in the affair, but Hill was subjected to bitter and widespread criticism for bungling.

See D. S. Freeman, *Lee's Lieutenants* (1946), III; J. L. Morrison, Jr., *Memoirs of Heth* (1974); S. Foote, *Civil War: A Narrative* (1963), II; and *Official Records, Armies*, Vol. XXIX, Pt. 1.

JAMES L. MORRISON, JR.
York College of Pennsylvania

BRISTOL, TENN. (pop. 20,064), and **BRISTOL, VA.** (pop. 14,857), on the state line approximately 20 miles northeast of Johnson City, Tenn., were settled in 1749 as Sapling Grove. In 1771 Colonel Evan Shelby constructed a stockade and trading post on the site of the modern city. Frequented by DANIEL BOONE and JOHN SEVIER, the post was a center of activity for the WATAUGA ASSOCIATION and a supply base for area patriots prior to the battle of KINGS MOUNTAIN (1780). The first territorial capital of Tennessee (1790–1792) was at Rocky Mount, just south of Bristol. When incorporated in 1856, the Virginia community opted for the name Goodson, and the Tennesseans chose Bristol, for the town of the same name in England. In 1890 the Virginians made the change to Bristol. From its origins as a trading center, the city grew into a rail center and a shipping point for area coal and lumber. The modern city is the home of King College, a Presbyterian liberal arts college founded in 1867.

See files of Bristol *Herald-Courier* (1870–); L. P. Summers, *History of Southwest Virginia, 1746–1786* (1903), and *Annals of Southwest Virginia, 1769–1800* (1929); T. W. Preston, *Historical Sketches of Holston Valleys* (1926); D. Sullins, *Recollections of an Old Man, 1827–1897* (1910); R. S. Loving, *Double Destiny* (1955); and files of Bristol Public and Washington County libraries.

BRISTOW, BENJAMIN HELM (1832–1896), was born at Elkton, Ky. When the Civil War erupted, he recruited two regiments for the Union army and fought at Ft. Donelson (FTS. HENRY AND DONELSON CAMPAIGN) and SHILOH. Elected to the Kentucky senate in 1863, he supported the Abraham Lincoln administration and developed a "moderate" Republican party. He was appointed U.S. district attorney in 1865 and actively reimposed federal law upon Kentucky. As first solicitor general of the United States (1870–1872), Bristow argued many Reconstruction cases before the U.S. Supreme Court. After a brief presidency of the California & Texas Construction Company, President U. S. Grant named him secretary of the treasury (1874–1876). Bristow insisted upon the resumption of specie payments, broke foreign control over American finances, cracked the Whiskey Ring, and disclosed the Delano and Belknap scandals. His efforts at reform brought national attention, but lost him the Republican presidential nomination in 1876. He moved to New York in 1878, where he became a prominent corporation lawyer and founder and second president of the American Bar Association.

See Bristow Papers, Library of Congress; W. D. Gilliam, Jr., "Political Career of Benjamin Helm Bristow" (M.A. thesis, Indiana University, 1930); E. B. Thompson, "Bristow, Symbol of Reform" (Ph.D. dissertation, University of Wisconsin, 1940); *Mississippi Valley Historical Review* (June, 1945); and R. A. Webb, *Benjamin Helm Bristow* (1969), and *Civil War History* (March, 1964; March, 1969).

ROSS A. WEBB
Winthrop College

BROOKE, JOHN MERCER (1826–1906), one of an unusual group of southern military scientists and inventors, was born at an army base near Tampa, Fla., and graduated from the U.S. Naval Academy in 1847. Before the Civil War he had distinguished himself in oceanography and navigation and had won the acclaim of several foreign governments. He resigned from the U.S. Navy early in the war, and as a commander in the Confederate navy he helped design and construct the ironclad *Virginia* on the hull of the *Merrimack*. He invented the Brooke gun, a powerful, banded cast-iron rifle, many of which were used in the coast defenses. Brooke ended the war as chief of the Bureau of Ordnance and Hydrography. Until his death, he taught physics and astronomy at Virginia Military Institute, sharing these duties with MATTHEW FONTAINE MAURY. Brooke's achievements mark him as a significant contributor to

southern and national prominence in naval ordnance and the ocean sciences.

See V. C. Jones, *Civil War at Sea* (1965); R. U. Johnson
and C. C. Buel (eds.), *Battles and Leaders* (1888); S. R.
Bright, "Confederate Coast Defense" (Ph.D. dissertation, Duke University, 1961); and *Official Records, Navies*, Ser. 1, Vol. X, Ser. 2, Vols. I, II.

SAMUEL R. BRIGHT
Davidson County Community College

BROOKS, JOSEPH (1821–1877), was a native of
Kentucky and a Methodist minister. He lived in
Ohio and Iowa before moving to Missouri, where
in 1856 he became editor of the antislavery St.
Louis *Central Christian Advocate*. During the
Civil War, he served as a Union army chaplain. He
eventually settled at Helena, Ark., and participated in the 1868 state constitutional convention as
an advocate of black rights. Later that year Ku
Klux Klan members wounded him in an assassination attempt. Noted for his oratorical skills, the
flamboyant Brooks moved to Little Rock in 1868,
where he led opposition within the Republican
party to POWELL CLAYTON. In 1872, he opposed
Republican ELISHA BAXTER for governor. Both
sides charged fraud, but Baxter was declared the
winner. Brooks's efforts to reverse the outcome
culminated in the BROOKS-BAXTER WAR, during
which Brooks forcibly occupied the statehouse.
President U. S. Grant eventually recognized Baxter, and Brooks withdrew. From 1875 until his
death, Brooks was postmaster at Little Rock.

See *Arkansas Gazette* (May 2, 1877); and M. A. Ellenburg, "Reconstruction in Arkansas" (Ph.D. dissertation,
University of Missouri, 1967).

MARTHA ELLENBURG FOLEY
Warrensburg, Mo.

BROOKS, PRESTON SMITH (1819–1857), was
born on the family plantation at Edgefield, S.C.,
graduated from South Carolina College in 1839,
practiced law, and served in the Mexican War.
Handsome, courteous, loyal to his family and state,
he was elected in 1852 as a Democrat to represent
the Fourth Congressional District in western South
Carolina. No fire-eater, he followed JAMES L. ORR
in urging state Democrats to affiliate with the national party. During the sectional turmoil of the
mid-1850s, Brooks was sufficiently conciliatory
that some constituents found him "a little too national." On May 19–20, 1856, Senator Charles
Sumner of Massachusetts in describing the "crime
against Kansas" (BLEEDING KANSAS) made several
tasteless references to Senator Andrew Butler,
Brooks's uncle. Infuriated because of what he

thought were personal affronts, Brooks on May 22,
1856, assaulted Sumner with a cane. After efforts
at expulsion from the House of Representatives
failed, Brooks resigned, won unanimous reelection, and in his last months displayed mounting
hostility against unionism.

See H. Schultz, *Nationalism and Sectionalism in South
Carolina* (1950), valuable; D. Donald, *Charles Sumner*
(1961); P. Brooks, *Massachusetts Historical Society Proceedings* (1928); and *Alleged Assault upon Senator Sumner*, 34th Cong., 1st Sess., House Report 182, Ser. 868,
Vol. I.

MICHAEL W. WHALON
University of Tulsa

BROOKS-BAXTER WAR (1874) marked the climax of factional disputes that had divided Arkansas Republicans since 1868. The regular Republicans led by POWELL CLAYTON were known as the
"minstrels" because one of their members had
been associated with a minstrel show. The reform
Republicans were called "brindle-tails" after
someone remarked that their leader JOSEPH
BROOKS reminded him of a brindle-tail bull. This
split in Republican ranks widened during the
1872 gubernatorial election. Brooks's brindle-tails,
who had abandoned the party charging fraud and
racism, formed a shaky alliance with Democrats,
promising to end the disfranchisement of those
who still could not vote under the Reconstruction
constitution. They nominated Brooks as their candidate. Hoping also to appeal to natives, the minstrels chose southerner ELISHA BAXTER. After
a heated campaign dominated by Brooks and
Clayton with Baxter in the background, the min-
strel-controlled legislature proclaimed Baxter
governor.

Brooks unsuccessfully sought to overturn this
decision in the federal district court, state legislature, U.S. Congress, and state supreme court. As a
last resort in 1874, he appealed to the Pulaski
County circuit court, which declared him elected.
Armed with this decision, Brooks occupied the
statehouse in April, 1874, forcing Baxter to take
up quarters across the street in the Anthony House.
While sporadic fighting occurred throughout the
state for the next four months, both factions appealed to President U. S. Grant for aid. Both sides
sustained casualties, with the most serious fighting occurring in Little Rock, where the statehouse
was described as bristling with bayonets and
muskets.

During the conflict many of the minstrels became disenchanted with Baxter because he enfranchised the Democrats and appointed them to
state offices. He also refused to support a bill giv-

ing further aid to railroads. With the minstrels switching their allegiance to Brooks, Brooks's Democratic allies and some Liberal Republicans transferred their support to Baxter. The conflict ended in July, when Grant recognized Baxter as governor. Brooks acquiesced, paving the way for the constitution of 1874 and the end of Reconstruction in Arkansas.

See J. M. Harrell, *Brooks-Baxter War* (1893); E. F. Woodward, *Arkansas Historical Quarterly* (Winter, 1971); and M. A. Ellenburg, "Reconstruction in Arkansas" (Ph.D. dissertation, University of Missouri, 1967).

MARTHA ELLENBURG FOLEY
Warrensburg, Mo.

BROUGH, CHARLES HILLMAN (1876–1935), an Arkansas educator and politician, was born in Clinton, Miss. He was a graduate of Mississippi College and received a Ph.D. degree from Johns Hopkins and a law degree from the University of Mississippi. He taught for a short time at Mississippi College and Hillman College in Mississippi, before moving to the University of Arkansas in 1903. He taught both political science and sociology and quickly became a popular lecturer.

In 1915 Brough resigned to enter the Democratic primary for governor. Picturing himself as a Progressive in the mold of Woodrow Wilson, Brough defeated his two primary opponents and easily won in the general election. As governor, he supported a constitutional convention to modernize Arkansas' frame of government, only to see the voters reject its proposed constitution in 1918. He worked to increase appropriations for education. Considered a moderate on the racial issue, Brough was a leader in the SOUTHERN SOCIOLOGICAL CONGRESS, although he had declared that Negroes should not be allowed to vote.

During his second administration (1919–1921), unrest among tenant farmers around the community of Elaine led to shootings that left at least 25 and perhaps as many as 100 blacks dead. Brough publicly blamed the ELAINE RACE RIOT on northern "agitators." After leaving office in 1921, he worked as a CHAUTAUQUA speaker and publicist for the Arkansas Advancement Association. A prominent Baptist layman, he accepted the presidency of Central College in Conway, Ark., in 1928. Because he supported the Alfred E. Smith ticket in 1928 and because of his stand against a proposed bill to prohibit the teaching of evolution in Arkansas, Brough resigned this position in 1929. He reentered politics in 1932, but was defeated by HATTIE CARAWAY in the Democratic senatorial primary. It was remarked that he seemed out of touch with the new political realities. In 1934 he

was appointed chairman of a federal commission arbitrating a border dispute between Virginia and the District of Columbia. He died in Washington.

See R. W. Widener, Jr., *Arkansas Historical Quarterly* (Summer, 1975); and Brough Papers, University of Arkansas Library.

DAVID E. RISON
Baptist College at Charleston

BROWARD, NAPOLEON BONAPARTE (1857–1910), son of a prominent planter family, was born in Duval County, Fla. He operated a riverboat on the St. John's River during the 1880s, was elected sheriff, and worked with the liberal Democratic faction that was wresting control from the BOURBONS. In the period before the SPANISH-AMERICAN WAR, he became tremendously popular as a filibuster transporting guns and men aboard his tug, the *Three Friends*, to Cuba. After a term in the state legislature in 1901, he successfully ran for governor in a bitterly fought campaign in which he challenged the railroad and corporate interests. Broward's support came from the farmers and laborers. He emerged as Florida's great Progressive governor (1905–1909), strongly supporting child labor legislation, railroad and utility regulation, as well as election, educational, and tax reform (PROGRESSIVISM). He envisioned draining the Everglades in south Florida by digging canals and making land available for citrus and TRUCK FARMING. "Water Will Run Down Hill" became his slogan during the gubernatorial campaign. Although elected to the U.S. Senate in 1910, he died before taking his oath of office.

See S. Proctor, *Napoleon Bonaparte Broward* (1950), definitive; N. B. Broward, *N. B. Broward* (1904), campaign autobiography; W. Flynt, *D. U. Fletcher* (1971); R. L. Carson, "W. D. Bloxham" (M.A. thesis, University of Florida, 1945); J. E. Dovell, "Everglades" (Ph.D. dissertation, University of North Carolina, 1947); R. V. Rickenbach, "Filibustering" (M.A. thesis, University of Florida, 1948); F. A. Rhodes, "Legal Development of State Supported Higher Education" (Ph.D. dissertation, University of Florida, 1948); W. J. Schellings, "Role of Florida in Spanish-American War" (Ph.D. dissertation, University of Florida, 1958); and N. B. Broward Papers, P. K. Yonge Library, University of Florida, excellent.

SAMUEL PROCTOR
University of Florida

BROWN, ALBERT GALLATIN (1813–1880), the leader of the radical southern nationalists and fire-eating secessionists in the Democratic party in Mississippi in the decade preceding the Civil War, was born in the frontier Chester district of South

Carolina, the son of a poor farmer. The family moved to Copiah County, Miss., in 1823.

From 1832 to 1865, depending upon the poor farmers of eastern and southern Mississippi, Brown continuously held an elective military, legislative, executive, or judicial office: in Mississippi, this included being governor during the Mexican War; in the federal government, filling terms in the House and in the Senate (1854–1861); and in the Confederacy, serving as an army captain and as senator (1862–1865).

In the four years before the war, the two Mississippi senators, plebeian Brown and patrician JEFFERSON DAVIS, were often adversaries. During the war, however, as a southern nationalist, Brown defended President Davis against the powerful states' righters. Near the end Brown sponsored an act which became law calling for the induction of slaves into the Confederate army. After the war, surprisingly, Brown favored reconciliation with the North. He died at his farm near Terry, Miss.

See J. B. Ranck, *A. G. Brown* (1937, 1974); S. P. McCutchen, "Political Career of Albert Gallatin Brown" (Ph.D. dissertation, University of Chicago, 1930); M. W. Cluskey (ed.), *Speeches, Messages, and Writings of Brown* (1859); and letters, documents, and newspapers in Library of Congress and Department of Archives and History of Mississippi.

JAMES B. RANCK
Hood College

BROWN, ALEXANDER (1764–1834), was a successful linen merchant in Belfast prior to his migration to Baltimore before 1800. There he founded the firm that survives until this day. Originally an export-import house, the firm gradually assumed the more specialized function of financing international trade to the exclusion of its earlier activities, with branches in New York, Philadelphia, and Liverpool. Brown & Sons, by 1830, was the foremost firm of its kind in Anglo-American trade. To Brown, according to J. H. Latrobe, "everything was a matter of business." He preached specialization, avoidance of speculation, careful attention to details, and hard work. By the eve of the depression of 1837, three years after the death of the founder, the firm's capital was estimated at $5.5 million, much of it derived from involvement in the southern cotton trade.

See E. J. Perkins, *Financing Anglo-American Trade* (1975), most recent and complete. The bulk of Brown's business papers is in Library of Congress. See also J. C. Brown, *Hundred Years of Merchant Banking* (1925); G. L. Browne, *Maryland Historical Magazine* (Fall, 1974); J. Killick, *Business History* (Jan., 1974); J. A. Kouwenho-

ven, *Partners in Banking* (1968); and E. J. Perkins, *Business History Review* (Winter, 1971).

NATHAN MILLER
University of Wisconsin, Milwaukee

BROWN, BENJAMIN GRATZ (1826–1885), grandson of Kentucky's first U.S. senator, John Brown (1757–1837), was born in Lexington, Ky., graduated from Yale College, studied law, and in 1849 established a law practice in St. Louis. For over 20 years (1852–1873) Brown served Missouri in the general assembly, as U.S. senator, and as governor. From 1854 to 1859 he was editor of the MISSOURI DEMOCRAT. Originally a Henry Clay Whig, Brown, probably due to the influence of his cousin Frank Blair (BLAIR FAMILY), became a Democrat and an ardent supporter of THOMAS HART BENTON; but, with the eclipse of Benton, the Blair-Brown allegiance was transferred to the Republican party.

In 1857, as an advocate of the Free White Labor movement, Brown urged the emancipation of slaves in Missouri and, eventually, throughout the entire Mississippi Valley. Initially a moderate, condemning abolitionists and FIRE-EATERS alike, Brown early in the 1860s became a Radical Republican and as such was elected to the U.S. Senate. Following the collapse of the Confederacy, Brown rejected what he considered to be Radical vindictiveness and became a key figure in the Missouri Liberal Republican movement. As governor (1871–1873) he attempted to alleviate the bitterness of the war years. In 1872 Brown was the vice-presidential candidate of the Liberal Republican party. His call for universal suffrage included women as well as blacks. After the disintegration of the Liberal Republican movement he returned to the Democratic party.

See N. L. Peterson, *Freedom and Franchise* (1965), the only biography, has extensive bibliography, and *Missouri Historical Review* (Oct., 1956); T. S. Barclay, *Liberal Republican Movement in Missouri* (1926); and W. E. Parrish, *Missouri and the Union* (1963), and *Missouri Under Radical Rule* (1965).

NORMA LOIS PETERSON
Adams State College

BROWN, JOHN CALVIN (1827–1889), was born in Giles County, Tenn., read law, and was licensed to practice in 1848. He was a Whig and initially opposed secession, but he enlisted in the Confederate army as a private when the Civil War began, rising to the rank of major general. After the war, in 1870, he was elected governor as a Democrat and reelected in 1872. A strong proponent of economic diversification, Governor Brown successfully urged the legislature to establish bureaus of immigration and of agriculture, to commission a survey of the mineral resources of the state, and to pass a law pledging payment of all the state's bonded debt. After his second term, he became vice-president of the Texas & Pacific Railroad in 1876 and five years later was named general solicitor of all Jay Gould's lines west of the Mississippi. He became president of the Texas & Pacific in 1888 and at his death was president of the powerful Tennessee Coal, Iron & Railroad Company (TENNESSEE COAL & IRON COMPANY).

See Governors Papers, Tennessee State Library and Archives; M. Butler, "Life of Brown" (M.A. thesis, University of Tennessee, 1936); and W. B. Hesseltine, *Confederate Leaders* (1949).

ROBERT B. JONES
Middle Tennessee State University

BROWN, JOHN YOUNG (1835–1904), was born in Elizabethtown, Ky. Upon graduation from Centre College (1885) he studied law and was admitted to the bar. As a fledgling congressman in 1860, he supported Stephen A. Douglas' bid for the presidency. Brown opposed secession and advocated a position of neutrality for Kentucky. He was subsequently denied a seat (1867) by the Fortieth Congress for alleged disloyalty to the Union. He served two successive terms in Congress (1873–1877), returning to his law practice in Henderson, Ky., after the inauguration of President Rutherford B. Hayes, whom he had supported (ELECTION OF 1876) in return for anticipated concessions to the South. He reentered politics, becoming governor of Kentucky (1891–1895) at a time when his special legal abilities were needed for the framing and codifying of laws under a new state constitution. His unsuccessful independent candidacy for governor in 1899 deprived WILLIAM GOEBEL of a clear-cut victory over William S. Taylor, a Republican. As a result, the election was thrown into the legislature. Shortly thereafter, Goebel was assassinated. In the sensational trial that followed, Brown assisted in the defense of the accused.

See Louisville *Courier-Journal* (Jan. 12, 1904); Lexington *Herald* (Jan. 12, 1904); G. L. Willis, *Kentucky Democrats* (1935); and uncataloged records of Brown's administration as governor in Library of Kentucky Historical Society, Frankfort.

JUDGE WATSON
Florida Southern College

BROWN, JOSEPH EMERSON (1821–1894), was educated at Calhoun Academy in South Carolina

and the Yale law school. After being elected state senator (1849), presidential elector (1852), and superior court judge (1855), he served as Democratic governor of Georgia (1857–1865). While governor, he led the establishment of public schools and the expansion of women's rights and advocated secession with ROBERT TOOMBS and HOWELL COBB. As the state's war governor, he came into conflict with Confederate officials over conscription and the tax system. Briefly imprisoned in 1865, he returned to Georgia, advocated support for President Andrew Johnson's plan of Reconstruction, and later counseled acquiescence to congressional Reconstruction. He soon joined the Republican party and became chief justice of the Georgia supreme court. In 1876, he supported ALFRED COLQUITT for governor and became a Democrat again. As a member of the GEORGIA TRIUMVIRATE, he served in the U.S. Senate (1880–1890). During Reconstruction he amassed a fortune, including agricultural property. From 1870 to 1891 he was president of a company leasing the Western & Atlantic Railroad. He also developed coal and iron mines with convict labor.

See L. B. Hill, *Brown and the Confederacy* (1959); D. C. Roberts, *Brown and Reconstruction* (1973); and J. E. Brown manuscripts and scrapbooks, University of Georgia.

DERRELL C. ROBERTS
Dalton Junior College

BROWN, WILLIAM GARROTT (1868–1914), was born in Marion, Ala., and attended Harvard University (B.A., 1891; M.A., 1892). He stayed on as a librarian and part-time instructor in history until 1901, when he left to devote his time to writing. His most important book, *The Lower South in American History* (1902), probed the past and the present in a lively, vivid style that made "dry-as-dust" historians envious and readers delighted. In his historical works and magazine articles, the most notable being "The White Peril" (1904) and "The South in National Politics" (1910), Brown measured his words and insisted, as the celebrated historian U. B. PHILLIPS would later, that race was the basic and most debilitating concern of the white South. A conservative himself and a Democrat, Brown championed the ideal of a two-party South, even to the point of actively cooperating with reform-minded Republicans in North Carolina, where he lived off and on from 1908 to 1913. During that time he wrote regularly for *Harper's Weekly* and hammered away in editorials and signed essays at the need for American ideals of political democracy and racial paternalism in the South.

See B. Clayton, *South Atlantic Quarterly* (Winter, 1963), and *Savage Ideal, 1890–1914* (1972); and W. H. Stephenson, *Southern History in the Making* (1964).

BRUCE CLAYTON
Allegheny College

BROWNLOW, WILLIAM GANNAWAY "PARSON"

(1805–1877), was born in Wythe County, Va., and moved with his parents to eastern Tennessee. Despite little formal education, he became an itinerant Methodist preacher in 1826 and later the editor of three area newspapers: the *Tennessee Whig* (1839) in Elizabethton; the Jonesboro *Whig and Independent Journal* (1840–1849); and the Knoxville *Whig* (1849–1861), the most influential newspaper in eastern Tennessee. During the secession crisis and early war years, he voiced contempt for secessionists and urged Tennesseans to stick by the Union. Facing certain arrest, he fled Knoxville to hide in the Smoky Mountains in November, 1861, but he was found by Confederate scouts, arrested, and charged with treason. On orders from the Confederate secretary of war, Brownlow was transported inside federal lines in March, 1862. While in the North he wrote *Sketches of the Rise, Progress, and Decline of Secession* (1862), an antirebel pamphlet and his most widely heralded publication.

Brownlow returned to eastern Tennessee with the federal army in the fall of 1863 and resumed leadership among local Unionists. Elected governor in 1865 and reelected in 1867, he was determined to disfranchise all who took up arms against the Union. He was elected to the U.S. Senate before the close of his second term, but his health failed him and he lost his capacity to speak.

As an editor, a politician, and a racial theorist, Brownlow reflected the abhorrence held by many east Tennessee whites of interracial contacts; he advocated the removal of those blacks who defied white direction. But he departed from many area whites by demanding the retention of subservient slavelike Negroes.

See O. P. Temple, *Notable Men of Tennessee* (1912); J. W. Patton, *Unionism and Reconstruction in Tennessee* (1934); E. M. Coulter, *Brownlow* (1937); T. B. Alexander, *Political Reconstruction in Tennessee* (1950); and T. A. R. Nelson Manuscripts, Library of Congress.

LAWRENCE J. FRIEDMAN
Bowling Green State University

BROWNSVILLE, TEX.

(pop. 51,080), opposite Matamoros, Mexico, faces onto the Rio Grande approximately 30 miles from the Gulf of Mexico. It is a major market for area cotton and citrus fruit growers, a supply base for offshore drilling rigs, a refiner of petroleum, and an increasingly popular all-year resort. Although the surrounding area had been settled by ranchers since at least 1771, a town was not developed on this side of the river until after construction in 1846 of Ft. Taylor (renamed Ft. Brown during the MEXICAN WAR to honor the fort's slain commander). Two years later, the town of Brownsville was laid out, just in time to accommodate the influx of settlers who came with the California gold rush. During the 1850s the town was at the center of political and armed conflict resulting from contested land claims of Mexican and American ranchers.

With the outbreak of the Civil War, Ft. Brown was evacuated and burned by its Union garrison, and a federal BLOCKADE was imposed at the river's mouth. Goods being shipped to the Mexican port of Matamoros, however, were not subject to blockade and once unloaded could be transported across the river to Brownsville and from there to various points throughout the Confederacy. In part to close this "back door to the Confederacy," a 3,500-man federal military force with naval support was landed at the river mouth on November 2, 1863. Four days later it successfully assaulted Brownsville and closed the city to all commerce for the next three months. The final skirmish of the Civil War was fought nearby at Palmito Hill (May 12–13, 1865), but military activity in the area continued for two years after the war. General Philip H. Sheridan used Brownsville during that period as the base for his 50,000-man army, placed here by Andrew Johnson's administration to force France to withdraw its support from Emperor Maximilian of Mexico.

See L. P. Graf, "Economic History of Lower Rio Grande, 1820–1875" (M.A. thesis, Harvard University, 1942); J. C. Sides, *Fort Brown* (1942); W. H. Chatfield, *Twin Cities of Border* (1893); and files of Brownsville *Herald* (1892–), on microfilm.

BROWNSVILLE AFFAIR

is one of the darker chapters in the annals of American military justice. On August 13, 1906, about 14 black soldiers of the 25th Infantry Regiment allegedly killed a white bartender and wounded a policeman in a midnight raid on Brownsville, Tex. None of the soldiers were ever identified; nor was anyone ever tried in a court of law, military or civil. Yet President Theodore Roosevelt ordered 167 black members of three companies to be discharged "without honor" on the presumption that they had "conspired" to refuse to disclose the names of the participants. Not until 1970, when John D. Weaver published a resourceful reconstruction of events that pointed to white civilians as the actual culprits, was the innocence of the alleged black assailants fairly established. Two years later the secretary of the army directed that the soldiers, most of whom were dead, be given "honorable" discharges.

Roosevelt based his action on the findings of two superficially persuasive military investigations. In a hearing before the Committee on Military Affairs in the spring of 1908, Senator Joseph B. Foraker raised more than reasonable doubt that any black soldiers had been involved. But partly because the Republican administration's prestige was by then an issue and partly because of the blatant racism of southern Democrats, a majority of the committee affirmed the soldiers' guilt. Roosevelt's only concession to Foraker's evidence was the signing of a face-saving bill, which authorized a high military review. The review proved as superficial as the original investigations.

See J. D. Weaver, *Brownsville Raid* (1970), superb; *Affray at Brownsville*, 60th Cong., 1st Sess., Senate Document 402 (1908); E. Morison (ed.), *Letters of T. Roosevelt* (1951–54), VI; J. A. Tinsley, *Journal of Negro History* (Jan., 1956); E. Walters, *Joseph B. Foraker* (1948); E. L. Thornbrough, *Mississippi Valley Historical Review* (Dec., 1957); A. Lane, *Brownsville Affair* (1971); W. H. Harbaugh, *T. Roosevelt* (1963); and H. Pringle, *W. H. Taft* (1939).

WILLIAM H. HARBAUGH
University of Virginia

BROWN V. BOARD OF EDUCATION OF TOPEKA (347 U.S. 483; 74 S.Ct. 686; 98 L.Ed. 873 [1954]).

By 1954, the societal conditions that made separate but equal (PLESSY V. FERGUSON) so attractive a racial doctrine had been radically changed by subsequent events. Constitutionally condoned separation of the races with its explicit laws and its implicit badge of black inferiority had become as great an embarrassment for the country as it was a burden for blacks (SEGREGATION). Change was already in order, and *Brown* v. *Board of Education* became the legal vehicle for that change.

Civil rights lawyers, including the outstanding black legal strategists THURGOOD MARSHALL, Charles Hamilton Houston, and Robert L. Carter, had anticipated the new day. For years they had chipped away at the outer layers of forced segregation. The early cases sought equalization of public school facilities and teachers' salaries. Later, civil rights litigation won desegregation of graduate schools, exposing in the process how thoroughly the separate but equal standard victimized blacks and made hypocrites of whites (*McLaurin* v. *Oklahoma*; SHELLY V. KRAEMER; SIPUEL V. OKLAHOMA BOARD OF REGENTS; and SWEATT V. PAINTER).

The five cases consolidated in the *Brown* decision covered a wide geographical range and varying forms of segregation laws. The Kansas law made school segregation a matter of local option. Cases from South Carolina, Virginia, and Delaware challenged state constitutional and statutory provisions mandating segregation. In the Delaware case, state courts had ordered school desegregation because the separate schools violated the separate but equal standard. In *Bolling* v. *Sharpe* (347 U.S. 497; 74 S.Ct. 693; 98 L.Ed. 884 [1954]), the Supreme Court held that the due process clause of the Fifth Amendment barred segregation of the public schools in the District of Columbia.

By the time the Supreme Court was ready to address the question—Does segregation of children in public schools solely on the basis of race, even though the physical facilities and other "tangible" factors may be equal, deprive the children of the minority group of equal educational opportunities?—its affirmative response was almost predictable. Chief Justice Earl Warren, speaking for a unanimous Court, found the rejection of separate but equal to be required by the importance of public education in a modern society. In addition, the Court recognized that separation of black children "solely because of their race generates a feeling of inferiority as to their status in the community that may affect their hearts and minds in a way unlikely ever to be undone." But it was also true that the Court's rejection of separate educational facilities as "inherently unequal" vastly improved America's image with emerging Third World nations abroad and increasingly restless blacks at home.

The Supreme Court's refusal to require immediate implementation of its decision in *Brown* and its adoption of the "all deliberate speed" standard the following year, provided notice that the struggle to gain the promised right to equal educational opportunity would be long and difficult. The *Brown* decision led to the dismantling of the overt policies of racial segregation that marked every important public function in much of the country. As would be learned later, the decision that removed Colored and White signs had considerably less effect on the more fundamental aspects of racial discrimination that continue to burden blacks and frustrate the equal protection commitments made them in the Constitution.

The *Brown* decision, perhaps the most famous the Supreme Court has ever issued, became the symbol of racial equality. It sparked major reform in racial laws, policies, and even patterns of thought and behavior. Resistance to its full implementation, as well as political and economic factors that may have encouraged its birth, cannot lessen its value or dim the achievement by those whose faith in the Constitution enabled them to be ready when the time finally came for a hopeful change in America's long struggle with race.

DERRICK BELL
Harvard University

BRUCE, BLANCHE KELSO (1841–1898), was born in southern Virginia. The light-skinned Bruce (who may have been the natural son of his owner) knew few of the hardships of slavery. Prior to the Civil War, his master moved to Missouri, where Bruce learned to read while apprenticed to a printer. In 1861 he ran away to Kansas. After opening schools for blacks in Kansas and Missouri, he attended Oberlin College (1865–1867), but he left in 1867, lured by tales of wealth allegedly awaiting qualified freedmen in the Deep South. In Mississippi, with JAMES LUSK ALCORN as his sponsor, Bruce quickly rose through the ranks of appointive and elective offices, serving as sergeant-at-arms in the state senate, assessor, sheriff, and tax collector for Bolivar County, superintendent of schools, and a levee commissioner. Other Negro politicians, such as James Hill and P. B. S. PINCHBACK, as well as white Republican leaders in Mississippi, began to talk of running Bruce for a national office, and their three-year campaign culminated in 1874 in his election to a full term in the U.S. Senate.

In the Senate (1875–1881), Bruce recognized that he would be judged both by his colleagues and by the public as a Negro, and he worked carefully to avoid damaging incidents or unfavorable publicity. He allied himself with Roscoe Conkling, the powerful New York senator, who saw to it that Bruce received favorable committee assignments as well as a generous share of the party's patronage. In turn, Bruce proved to be a reliable member of the "stalwart" faction in the Senate. He introduced very few measures in his six years, nearly all private bills to benefit constituents. The high point of his Senate career came on April 11, 1878, when, rising from a sickbed, Bruce eloquently supported a bill that would have allowed Negroes to serve in integrated units in the army.

Upon his leaving the Senate, his allies in the Republican party as well as Senator L. Q. C. LAMAR endorsed him for a federal appointment, and

President James Garfield offered Bruce several positions before they finally agreed on the registrar of the treasury. In his remaining years he held other minor offices whenever the Republicans were in power, and during Democratic administrations he toured the country as a popular speaker on the "race problem."

See S. D. St. Clair, "National Career of Blanche K. Bruce" (Ph.D. dissertation, New York University, 1947); and M. I. Urofsky, *Journal of Mississippi History* (May, 1967).

MELVIN I. UROFSKY
Virginia Commonwealth University

BRUCE, PHILIP ALEXANDER (1856–1933), was a descendant of one of Virginia's important older families. Growing up on a 5,000-acre tobacco plantation in Charlotte County, he early absorbed the romantic notions and visions of a grandiose age. He received his education at Norwood Academy (Virginia), the University of Virginia, and Harvard Law School. An experienced lawyer, businessman, and newspaper editorial writer, he eventually chose the life of the quiet scholar and penned over 2 million words on the history of Virginia and the South. Today he is primarily remembered for his trilogy dealing with the economic (1895), social (1907), and institutional (1910) history of seventeenth-century Virginia.

With the exception of this trilogy, most of Bruce's work has become extremely dated. He was convinced that free blacks would impede southern progress. Consequently, his first published writings, such as *The Plantation Negro as a Freeman* (1889), dealt with southern blacks. Among his writings about the NEW SOUTH, Bruce's *The Rise of the New South* (1905) did achieve a twofold distinction as the first major work on the subject and as the "capstone of the New South crusade." In his later works, particularly in *Brave Deeds of Confederate Soldiers* (1916), he helped popularize the "moonlight and magnolias" version of the Old South, a literary image that is still firmly entrenched in the mind of the American public.

See L. M. Simms, Jr., "Philip A. Bruce" (Ph.D. dissertation, University of Virginia, 1966), *Virginia Cavalcade* (Autumn, 1966), *Mississippi Quarterly* (Fall, 1966), *Virginia Magazine of History and Biography* (July, 1967), and *McNeese Review* (1967).

L. MOODY SIMMS, JR.
Illinois State University

BRUIN, PETER BRYAN (1756–1826), born in Winchester, Va., attended the College of Philadelphia (1769). During the American Revolution he three times served with DANIEL MORGAN and spent two years as General John Sullivan's aide. As a lieutenant colonel, he fought at Quebec, Brandywine, Germantown, Newport, and Tioga, was twice wounded, and was once captured. Bruin in 1788 migrated to Spanish West Florida. There as a colonel he commanded the Natchez Spanish militia and was an alcalde and syndic for Bayou Pierre. Appointed to the Mississippi territorial supreme court, he participated in the Philip Nolan hearing (1800) and the Mason gang trial (1804) and argued for Aaron Burr's release in 1807 (BURR CONSPIRACY). Threatened with impeachment for drunkenness, he resigned in 1808. Bruinsburg, Miss., and Lake Bruin State Park, La., are named for him.

See W. S. Coker, Natchez *Democrat* (Jan., 1968); *West Virginia History* (July, 1969); and "Bruins," in J. F. McDermott, *Spanish in Mississippi Valley* (1974).

WILLIAM S. COKER
University of West Florida

BRUNSWICK, GA. (pop. 19,585), situated 65 miles down the coast from Savannah on St. Simon's Sound, has been a fishing and port city since it was founded early in the 1770s. The town wasn't incorporated until 1856, and its growth has been slow and dependent upon development of surrounding areas. Today it is a port of entry with shrimp- and crabmeat-processing plants. Local industry produces pulp and plywood, naval stores, plastics, and steam boilers. As the SEA ISLANDS, just offshore, become increasingly popular with vacationers, tourism adds another dimension to the city's economy.

See D. N. Gayner, *Brunswick, 1771–1971* (1971); M. D. Cate, *Story of Brunswick and Coastal Isles* (1926), and *Early Days of Coastal Georgia* (1955); B. Vanstory, *Georgia's Land of Golden Isles* (1956); J. W. Smith, *Visits to Brunswick* (1907), 1853 journal; and files of Brunswick *News* (1902–). Brunswick Junior College Library maintains files of M. D. Cate manuscripts.

BUCHANAN, FRANKLIN (1800–1874), Maryland born, began as a midshipman in 1815 and 30 years later became the first superintendent of the U.S. Naval Academy. Buchanan captained a sloop in the Mexican War, accompanied Matthew Perry to Japan in 1854, and at the outbreak of the Civil War commanded the Washington navy yard. As a captain in the Confederate navy he commanded the *Virginia* in Hampton Roads on March 8, 1862, and sank the *Columbus*, the sloop *Cumberland*, and three small steamers. A serious wound prevented him from taking the *Virginia* into action the next day against the *Monitor*. Buchanan next

saw action at the command of the ram *Tennessee* in Mobile Bay, where he single-handedly took on Admiral David Farragut's fleet and surrendered only after the *Tennessee*'s steering gear had jammed and he had once again been wounded. Before his death he served as a Maryland college president and a Mobile insurance executive.

See V. C. Jones, *Civil War at Sea* (1965); R. U. Johnson and C. C. Buel (eds.), *Battles and Leaders* (1888); *Official Records, Armies*, Ser. 1, Vol. XXXIX, Pt. 1; and *Official Records, Navies*, Ser. 1, Vols. VII, XXI.

SAMUEL R. BRIGHT
Davidson County Community College

BUCHANAN, JAMES, ADMINISTRATION (1857–1861) was incapable of coping with the problems of the divided Democratic party or the dividing nation. In December, 1856, the president-elect announced that the object of his administration was to "arrest, if possible, the agitation of the slavery question at the North, and to destroy sectional parties." Actually, Buchanan's support of the LECOMPTON CONSTITUTION, written by a proslavery minority in Kansas, added to the growing hostility of the northerners within his party and cabinet. Torn between these North-South factions, the politically sensitive president adopted delay as his initial tactic for dealing with the threat of disunification.

Buchanan, a Pennsylvanian, though personally opposed to slavery, was strongly influenced by the persuasive voices of his southern cabinet members: Secretary of the Treasury HOWELL COBB of Georgia, Secretary of War JOHN FLOYD of Virginia, and Secretary of the Interior JACOB THOMPSON of Mississippi. The strong Unionist voice of Attorney General Jeremiah Black and the weaknesses of Secretary of State Lewis Cass added to the dissension among the president's advisers. This dissension was manifested by weak and confusing responses to the threat of secession. Although Buchanan's fourth message to the Congress on December 3, 1860, denied the constitutionality of secession, it denied as well the constitutionality of the use of federal force to put down such insurrection. This ambivalence further infuriated the northern Democrats and offered the southern secessionists tacit guarantees against federal intervention in their plans. At the same time Buchanan unsuccessfully recommended to the Congress the passage of an "explanatory" constitutional amendment that would have protected the institution of slavery. Powerful members of the cabinet, particularly during the administration's lame-duck period, actively urged the South to secede and looked away as southern forces took control of federal property. Observers have generally considered Buchanan to have been the captive of his advisers during the greater part of the administration. He did, however, attempt to replace the southern cabinet members with northern Unionists at the time of secession.

See P. S. Klein, *President James Buchanan* (1962), detailed, objective; F. J. Klingberg, *Journal of Southern History* (Nov., 1943), careful study; T. J. Pressly, *Americans Interpret Their Civil War* (1954), presents conflicting theories; and R. F. Nichols, *Disruption of American Democracy* (1948), well documented.

HELEN GROSS BRUDNER
Fairleigh Dickinson University

BUCHANAN, JOHN P. (1772–1844), was one of Maryland's greatest jurists. He was born in Prince George's County, Md., in 1772. He attended Charlotte Hill Academy in St. Mary's County and studied law under Judges Robert White of Winchester, Va., and Thompson Mason of Hagerstown, Md. In 1797 Buchanan entered the lower house of the state legislature, where he remained until 1806, when he was appointed chief judge of the Fifth Judicial District of Maryland. From 1824 to 1837 he was justice of the appellate court. In 1837 he was sent to London, England, as one of the commissioners to negotiate a sale of $8 million worth of Maryland's railroad and canal stocks. When he returned to Maryland he resumed his seat as chief judge of the Fifth Judicial District, where he remained until his death. Buchanan's most important decision was that in the case of *Chesapeake & Ohio Canal Company* v. *Baltimore & Ohio Railroad Company* (Gill and Johnson 1 [1832]), which determined the validity and privileges of a corporation's charter as conferred by the state legislature.

See W. McSherry, *Maryland Bar Association Report* (1904); T. J. C. Williams, *History of Washington County, Maryland* (1906), I; and A. W. P. Buchanan, *Buchanan Book* (1911).

JAMES E. HANEY
Tennessee State University

BUCK, PAUL HERMAN (1899–), was born in Columbus, Ohio. He attended Ohio State University and completed his graduate studies at Harvard, where he joined the history faculty in 1926, nine years before receiving his Ph.D. degree. Except for fellowships and visiting professorships, Buck remained at Harvard throughout his career, serving as both teacher and administrator. Among his publications in the field of education are *The Role of Education in American History* (1957) and *Libraries and Universities* (1964).

Buck's contribution to southern historiography is *The Road to Reunion* (1937), a study of the struggle for national reconciliation following the Civil War. According to Dr. Buck, the industrial revolution in the South created a class who shared the economic concerns of their northern counterparts. Southern writers created a romanticized vision of the Old South, which helped the North accept the NEW SOUTH. Authors employed such literary devices as the marriage of a northern hero to a southern heroine to dissipate sectional feeling. Memoirs by military figures of both sides celebrated the valor of Confederate and Union troops and made the war, in retrospect, a part of national heritage. Dr. Buck viewed politicians, who used sectional animosities to gather votes, as deterrents to reunification.

See P. M. Gaston, in A. S. Link and R. W. Patrick (eds.), *Writing Southern History* (1965); and Buck Manuscripts, Harvard University Archives.

MELTON A. MCLAURIN
University of South Alabama

BUCKNER, SIMON BOLIVAR (1823–1914), was born in Hart County, Ky. He graduated from West Point in 1844 and served in the Mexican War, but resigned from the army in 1855 to engage in business. Returning to Kentucky, Buckner commanded the Home Guard during Kentucky's unsuccessful effort to stay neutral early in the Civil War. In September, 1861, he joined the Confederate army as brigadier general. Early in 1862 at Ft. Donelson, after two senior commanders escaped through Union siege lines, Buckner was left to preside at the first surrender of a major southern army. After his exchange, Buckner spent the rest of the war in the western theater. He fought at PERRYVILLE and CHICKAMAUGA and later served under EDMUND KIRBY-SMITH in the Trans-Mississippi Department of the Confederacy. After the war, Buckner worked as a newspaper editor in New Orleans and Louisville and acquired considerable wealth through a variety of business interests. Entering politics as a conservative Democrat, he served as governor of Kentucky from 1887 to 1891. In 1896 he ran as the candidate of the Gold Democrats for vice-president.

See A. M. Stickles, *Buckner* (1940); E. M. Coulter, *Civil War and Reconstruction in Kentucky* (1926); and *Official Records, Armies*, Ser. 1, Vols. IV, VII, XXX, XLI, XLVIII.

WILLIAM B. SKELTON
University of Wisconsin, Stevens Point

BUFORD, JOHN (1826–1863), was born in Kentucky, but his family moved to Illinois in the early 1840s. Appointed to West Point from that state, he graduated in 1848 and then served on the frontier, rising to captain. During the Civil War Buford, nicknamed "Old Steadfast," became one of the Union's outstanding cavalry officers and eventually commanded the 1st Cavalry Division of the Army of the Potomac. Among other places, he fought at the second battle of BULL RUN and FREDERICKSBURG. The zenith of his career was the first day at GETTYSBURG, when his badly outnumbered men contained the Confederate advance and preserved the Union position until John F. Reynolds' I Corps arrived. While on his deathbed in December, 1863, Buford received a major general's commission appropriately dating from July 1, 1863.

See G. W. Buford and M. B. Minter, *Genealogy of Buford Family* (1924); F. B. Heitman, *Historical Register* (1903); *Official Records, Armies*, Ser. 1, Vol. XXVII, Pt. 1; and W. W. Hassler, Jr., *Crisis at Crossroads* (1970).

PETER MASLOWSKI
University of Nebraska, Lincoln

BUFORD EXPEDITION (1856). While the destiny of the Kansas Territory was causing excitement in both North and South, each section exhorted settlers to go there. The Buford expedition was the most serious attempt made in the South to send immigrants into Kansas. In November, 1855, Major Jefferson Buford of Alabama began to organize an expedition to counter northern influence. He called for volunteers and contributions, personally pledging $20,000. Buford promised each man 20 acres of land and support for a year. Between 300 and 400 men responded, left Montgomery in April, 1856, and arrived in Kansas a month later. They then scattered to seek homesteads, but reassembled to take part in the attack on Lawrence in May and were caught up in other conflicts between northern and southern factions. Eventually, the party disbanded for good, and Buford left Kansas in January, 1857, returning to Alabama.

See W. C. Fleming, *American Historical Review* (Oct., 1900); A. Nevins, *Ordeal of Union* (1947), II; T. C. Smith, *Parties and Slavery* (1907); J. F. Rhodes, *History of U.S.* (1893); and W. F. Zornow, *Kansas* (1957).

STEPHEN G. CARROLL
Missouri Western State College

BULLDOZING is a term applied during and after Reconstruction to the tactics employed by secret white terrorist organizations that sought to overthrow Republican governments in the South and to maintain white supremacy. With the KU KLUX KLAN apparently broken up by the federal government in 1871, local units of the Klan and similar organizations continued the work initiated by the Klan. Blacks actively sympathetic to the Republican governments were intimidated, maimed, flogged, and killed, as were some whites identified with Republican policies. The term bulldozing appears to have originated in Louisiana in 1875, where the struggle between Republicans and Democratic conservatives was especially bitter. Thereafter the expression spread throughout the South. The tactics denoted by the term played a considerable role in nullifying the black vote and bringing down the Reconstruction governments in Mississippi and South Carolina.

See R. Cruden, *Negro in Reconstruction* (1969); J. Williamson, *After Slavery* (1965); and V. L. Wharton, *Negro in Mississippi* (1947).

ROBERT CRUDEN
Lewis and Clark College

BULL DURHAM TOBACCO COMPANY produced smoking tobacco that was the first manufactured item from North Carolina to become internationally famous (TOBACCO MANUFACTURES). It also put the village of Durham on the map as a tobacco center rivaling the much older Virginia cities. The small tobacco business that John Ruffin Green purchased in 1862 utilized the bright leaf tobacco that had been developed in the region before the Civil War. Green found enthusiastic customers among the soldiers of both armies when General Joseph E. Johnston surrendered to General W. T. Sherman just outside Durham in April, 1865. Inspired by a picture of a bull that appeared on a then-popular brand of mustard made in Durham, England, Green adopted a trademark that soon became famous. In 1867 he took William T. Blackwell as a partner. Upon Green's death two years later, Blackwell purchased the entire business.

Advertising campaigns unprecedented in scope soon made Bull Durham smoking tobacco a household word. Shifting from primitive methods of manufacture, Blackwell turned to machines both for shredding and grinding the tobacco and for making the small cloth bags in which it was packaged and sold. By 1880 the Bull Durham plant, the largest smoking-tobacco factory in the world at one time, had grown to be one of the great showplaces of the New South. Blackwell and his partner Julian S. Carr sold out in 1883 to a Philadelphia firm, E. M. McDowell & Company, which secured a charter from the North Carolina legislature to incorporate as Blackwell's Durham Tobacco Company. In 1899 the DUKE FAMILY's American Tobacco Company purchased the old Blackwell company, and Bull Durham became the property of the Duke-led trust. In the twentieth century the old Bull Durham factory became part of the post-1911 American Tobacco Company's plant in Durham.

See W. K. Boyd, *Story of Durham* (1925); N. M. Tilley, *Bright-Tobacco Industry, 1860–1929* (1948); H. V. Paul, *History of Durham* (1884); and R. F. Durden, *Dukes of Durham, 1865–1929* (1975).

ROBERT F. DURDEN
Duke University

BULLOCK, RUFUS BROWN (1834–1907), Republican governor of Georgia during Reconstruction, was born in Albion, N.Y., attended Albion College, and became a telegrapher and a builder of telegraph lines to the South. Moving to Augusta in the late 1850s, he worked for an express company, then volunteered for the Confederate army. In 1865 Bullock entered business as a banker and railroad official in Augusta and in 1867 joined the Republican party. He was a delegate to the constitutional convention of 1867–1868 and won nomination and election as governor in April, 1868.

In office, Bullock secured state aid to railroads and debtor relief legislation, but his commitment to the freedmen proved shaky; eventually he could control neither the Republican legislature nor the divided Republican party. Evidence of fraud, bribery, and mismanagement turned many Republicans against him. In 1869 he lobbied successfully before Congress to have Georgia remanded to military rule for a third Reconstruction. Later schemes to prolong his power failed, however, and he resigned his office in October, 1871, to avoid impeachment. Bullock returned to Georgia in 1876, stood trial for embezzlement, and was acquitted of all charges. He subsequently became a prominent citizen of Atlanta; he was president of a textile mill and of the Atlanta Chamber of Commerce, a trustee of Atlanta University, and a director of the Cotton States and International Exposition of 1895. A big, handsome, and likable man, Bullock was a poor politician who outlived his reputation for corruption.

See E. S. Nathans, *Losing the Peace* (1968), critical; A. Conway, *Reconstruction of Georgia* (1966); and R. B. Bullock, Atlanta *Independent* (March 19, 1903).

JOHN M. MATTHEWS
Georgia State University

BULL RUN CAMPAIGN, FIRST (July 18–21, 1861). At Manassas Junction, Va., the Orange & Alexandria Railroad was joined by a line that ran 50 miles westward through Manassas Gap to Strasburg in the Shenandoah Valley. The strategic importance of the junction was apparent by May 6, 1861, when troops were ordered there for its defense. On June 3, P. G. T. BEAUREGARD took command at Manassas, and by the end of the month his army numbered about 15,000. JOSEPH E. JOHNSTON with 12,000 men was near Winchester facing 18,000 federals under Robert Patterson.

Assured that Patterson would prevent Johnston from reinforcing Beauregard, Irvin McDowell marched his army of 35,000 from Alexandria and reached Centreville on July 18. That afternoon, Israel B. Richardson's brigade of Daniel Tyler's division was repulsed in a reconnaissance of the Confederate line at Blackburn's Ford on the Bull Run River. McDowell delayed for two days while he formulated his battle plan, unaware that Johnston had eluded Patterson and was moving his troops over the Manassas Gap Railroad to join Beauregard. Johnston arrived on July 20, and as senior officer he was soon in command of 35,000 soldiers positioned along Bull Run.

At daybreak, July 21, McDowell's attack opened with a feint against the Confederate left held by Nathan G. ("Shanks") Evans' brigade at the Stone Bridge on Warrenton Turnpike. McDowell's main column moved around by Sudley Ford to strike the Confederate rear. From Signal Hill, EDWARD P. ALEXANDER detected the movement and warned Evans that his left was turned. Evans shifted his brigade to meet the federals at Matthew's Hill, where he was joined by the composite brigade of Brigadier General Barnard E. Bee and Colonel F. S. Bartow. Overwhelmed, they were driven back to Henry Hill, where THOMAS J. JACKSON's brigade was in position. Bee, rallying his men, pointed and shouted something like, "Look! There is Jackson standing like a stone wall! Rally behind the Virginians!" This was the origin of the sobriquet "Stonewall" soon applied to Jackson and his brigade. The fighting raged in much confusion until late afternoon, when the arrival of fresh troops turned the tide of battle for the Confederates. McDowell's forces left the field in fair order, but their retreat soon became a rout. Federal losses were 2,708 killed, wounded, and missing, and the Confederates lost 1,982.

See R. U. Johnson and C. C. Buel (eds.), *Battles and Leaders* (1888); E. P. Alexander, *Memoirs* (1907); R. M.

Johnston, *Bull Run* (1913); J. M. Hanson, *Bull Run Remembers* (1953); and T. H. Williams, *Beauregard* (1954).

LEE A. WALLACE, JR.
National Park Service

BULL RUN CAMPAIGN, SECOND (August 20–September 1, 1862), resulted from a concentration of Union forces in northern Virginia under General John Pope. While remaining near Richmond to watch George B. McClellan, ROBERT E. LEE transferred STONEWALL JACKSON's command to Gordonsville. When it became apparent that McClellan was withdrawing to join Pope, Lee hurried the bulk of his army to the Rapidan River. Lee's attempt to trap Pope between the Rapidan and Rappahannock rivers failed. He then sent Jackson in a flanking movement to cut Pope's supply line. While JAMES LONGSTREET held the enemy's attention, Jackson marched on August 25. Jackson was able to reach Pope's rear on the following night without opposition. After damaging the railroad, Jackson sent JEB STUART to Manassas Junction, the Union supply depot. This was captured and a Union brigade repulsed when it tried to recapture the depot. The Confederates looted everything that could be carried away and burned the rest.

Pope knew that Jackson had left Lee's army, but did not know his whereabouts until Manassas fell. He concentrated his forces to destroy Jackson before Lee's army could arrive. Jackson withdrew from Manassas to a position at Groveton. Pope again lost track of Jackson and believed the Confederates were retreating. He ordered his units to concentrate at Centreville. Jackson realized the Union forces would be in a position to withdraw into the defenses of Washington, D.C. He attacked late in the afternoon to pin Pope's attention until Lee arrived. During August 29, Pope repeatedly attacked Jackson's position. While Pope was thus occupied, Longstreet arrived and took a position on Jackson's right flank. Pope apparently was unaware of Longstreet's arrival despite some probing attacks late that afternoon.

Pope still believed that the Confederates were retreating. On the afternoon of August 30, he ordered an attack on Jackson. The assault nearly crushed Jackson's right flank, but at the crucial moment Longstreet's massed artillery firing into the flank of the Union attack broke the enemy. Jackson counterattacked while Longstreet's men swept into the Union flank. Pope was driven across Bull Run River and rallied at Centreville. Jackson was sent on another flank march. On September

1, he struck the Union army at Chantilly, and a sharp engagement took place in a thunderstorm. Pope then retreated into the defenses of Washington.

See *Official Records, Armies*, Ser. 1, Vol. XII; D. S. Freeman, *R. E. Lee* (1934), II, and *Lee's Lieutenants* (1943), II; and F. Vandiver, *Mighty Stonewall* (1957).

RICHARD P. WEINERT, JR.
U.S. Army

BUMMERS. During William T. Sherman's famous march through Georgia and the Carolinas, brigade commanders were authorized to establish a company of foragers, usually 30 to 50 men led by an officer, to forage on the flanks of the marching columns. These "bummers" were under orders not to enter occupied houses, engage in abusive language, or burn buildings. The traditional interpretation has been that bummers were the undisciplined scum of Sherman's force and responsible for robbery, pillage, and burnings. Although many bummers engaged in wanton destruction, modern scholarship tends to diminish their responsibility for the amount of devastation claimed, pointing out the activities of stragglers, the Confederate scorched-earth policy, and the tendency of those involved to exaggerate.

See W. T. Sherman, *Memoirs* (1875); J. G. Barrett, *Sherman's March* (1956); R. U. Johnson and C. C. Buel (eds.), *Battles and Leaders* (1888); and L. Lewis, *Sherman* (1932).

MARION B. LUCAS
Western Kentucky University

BUNKUM. Congressman Felix Walker (1753–1828) once delivered an especially long, fatuous, and tiresome speech before the U.S. House of Representatives. Although his colleagues objected, Walker persisted and allegedly explained that his remarks were intended for the benefit of his constituents in Buncombe County, N.C. The term has since been used variously to derogate lengthy speeches and dramas, to disparage conversations that seemingly lack point, and to describe orations, proclamations, and even legislative actions intended for a parochial audience not actually present at the event. In an abbreviated form, the term has passed into contemporary slang as a synonym for nonsense or "bunk."

BURGESS, JOHN WILLIAM (1844–1931), was a university professor, dean, and author. Born in Tennessee of slaveholding but Unionist parents

and educated at Cumberland University, he served in the Union army in 1862–1864. After graduating from Amherst College and teaching at Knox College, he pursued graduate study in Germany (1871–1873). Following three years of teaching at Amherst, he moved to Columbia University, where he persuaded the trustees to create a university giving emphasis to research and graduate study. In 1880 he organized a faculty and school of political science, then unique in America. A few years later he founded the *Political Science Quarterly*. Before retiring in 1913, he trained a generation of graduate students, including historians WILLIAM A. DUNNING and ULRICH B. PHILLIPS, and lectured at universities in Germany and Austria. Among his 13 books, the best known are *The Middle Period, 1817–1858* (1897); *The Civil War and the Constitution* (2 vols.; 1901); *Reconstruction and the Constitution* (1902); and *Political Science and Comparative Constitutional Law* (2 vols.; 1890–91).

DAVID LINDSEY
California State University, Los Angeles

BURGESSES, HOUSE OF. See HOUSE OF BURGESSES

BURKE, EDWARD A. (1840?–1928), an audacious politician-businessman who helped negotiate the Compromise of 1877, which ended Reconstruction, dominated Louisiana's politics during the 1880s. The Man of Iron arrived in Louisiana, penniless, during Reconstruction. He claimed to be an ex-Confederate major born in Kentucky, but his origins were probably northern and his actual war record remains a puzzle. Quickly rising in New Orleans politics, Burke managed the 1876 Democratic state campaign. Following the disputed election of that year, he represented Louisiana's whites in the bargaining sessions at Washington, D.C., where northern Republicans agreed to recognize the state Democratic government.

Associated with the corrupt LOUISIANA STATE LOTTERY, Burke was elected state treasurer in 1878. Presently he branched out into journalism, becoming publisher of the daily New Orleans *Times-Democrat*. Reelected state treasurer and indeed more powerful than the governor, Burke was finally ousted from office by a quasi-reform movement within the Louisiana Democratic party in 1888. The next year he was indicted for embezzlements in state bonds amounting to over $1 million. He never stood trial; leaving for Honduras, where he had purchased mining concessions, he lived there comfortably until his death.

See C. V. Woodward, *Origins of New South* (1951); W. I. Hair, *Bourbonism and Agrarian Protest* (1969); and J. F. Vivian, *Louisiana History* (Spring, 1974).

WILLIAM I. HAIR
Georgia College

BURKITT, FRANK (1843–1914), was a leader of the "common man" in Mississippi in the decades before the emergence of JAMES K. VARDAMAN and THEODORE G. BILBO. Nicknamed the Man in the Wool Hat, he was active in the GRANGE movement of the 1870s, was elected to the Mississippi legislature, and became the chief spokesman of the FARMERS' ALLIANCE in the next decade. Through his newspaper, the Okolona *Chickasaw Messenger*, he attacked oligarchic Bourbon leaders of the Democratic party, who seemed more concerned with industrial development than with the needs of the small farmer. He demanded the regulation of railroads, banks, and corporations, which he charged supported "corrupt political rings." He called for a constitutional convention to provide for reapportionment that would favor the "white" counties. As a member of the 1890 constitutional convention, Burkitt opposed the new constitution because he felt its suffrage requirements, aimed at blacks, would disqualify many whites (DISFRANCHISEMENT). Burkitt left the Democratic party and ran unsuccessfully as a Populist candidate for Congress in 1892 and for governor in 1895. When populism collapsed, he returned to the Democratic fold and served in the Mississippi legislature (1907–1914).

See A. D. Kirwan, *Revolt of Rednecks* (1951); and J. S. Ferguson, "Agrarianism in Mississippi" (Ph.D. dissertation, University of North Carolina, 1952).

CHARLES SALLIS
Millsaps College

BURLESON, ALBERT SIDNEY (1863–1937), was born in San Marcos, Tex. He graduated from the University of Texas Law School, practiced law, and held several local offices before his election to Congress (1899–1913) and his appointment as postmaster general (1913–1921) in the WOODROW WILSON administration. Burleson was quite conservative; however, the influence of his agrarian background and constituency and his dedication to the Democratic party led to his support of some Progressive reform measures during his tenure in Congress and in the Post Office.

Although Burleson was one of Wilson's more active advisers, his primary role in the administration was on Capitol Hill, where he attempted to influence legislation in behalf of the president. He relied on his understanding of the legislative process, on persuasion, and often on the coercion of patronage. Burleson was rather successful in this role in Wilson's first term, but his effectiveness declined in the second. He was an efficient administrator of the Post Office but often a controversial one. His insistence on less pay to the railroads for hauling the mail and on higher postage rates for publishers angered the business community. His adamant opposition to LABOR UNIONS, his SEGREGATION of black postal workers, and his censorship of the mails during World War I alienated others. Possibly the least controversial of the achievements of his administration was the inauguration of airmail service in 1918.

See A. N. Anderson, "A. S. Burleson" (Ph.D. dissertation, Texas Tech University, 1967); A. S. Link, *Wilson* (1947, 1956, 1960, 1964, 1965); and R. N. Richardson, *Colonel House* (1964).

ADRIAN N. ANDERSON
Lamar University

BURNET, DAVID GOUVERNEUR (1788–1870), served as a delegate to the Texas convention of 1833 and the consultation (1835), as president of the temporary Texas government established after the declaration of independence (1836), as vice-president of the republic (1838–1841), and as secretary of state following annexation (1846–1848). Additionally, he ran unsuccessfully for president (1841) and was elected, but never seated, as U.S. senator (1866). Burnet first visited Texas in 1813, then settled there near Harrisburg in 1826, seeking the success that had eluded him in his native New Jersey, in Venezuela, and in Ohio and Louisiana. He never attained financial security; an empresario grant and several business ventures failed, and even the modest livelihood of a public official, lawyer, and farmer gave way to virtual poverty after about 1855. His public career was largely shaped by intense animosity toward SAM HOUSTON, whom he vigorously criticized. Both opposed secession. Burnet's finest hours came during his eight months as president, when he held a divided and bankrupt government together and successfully resisted serious threats by a portion of the army to seize power.

See D. L. Fields, *Southwestern Historical Quarterly* (Oct., 1945), unanalytical; B. Chambless, "First President of Texas" (Ph.D. dissertation, Rice University, 1954), most definitive; S. W. Geiser, *Southwestern Historical Quarterly* (July, 1944); and Burnet materials in papers of Houston, Lamar, and Austin, in published papers of Tex-

as revolution and republic, and in manuscript collections at University of Texas, Austin, and Texas State Archives.

JAMES V. REESE
Texas Tech University

BURNS FUGITIVE SLAVE CASE. Anthony Burns, a fugitive slave claimed by Charles Suttle of Alexandria, Va., was arrested in Boston May 24, 1854, under terms of the Fugitive Slave Act of 1850 (FUGITIVE SLAVE LAWS). To harass the claimant, Lewis Hayden, a Negro abolitionist, filed a $10,000 damage suit, and the court of common pleas directed the United States marshal to produce Burns for a hearing. Thomas Wentworth Higginson launched an unsuccessful attempt to rescue Burns on the eve of the trial. During the melee, one of the guards was killed. Unintimidated, on June 2, Commissioner Edward G. Loring remanded Burns to federal marshals for rendition. Because of hostile public demonstrations, an armed guard escorted the fugitive to a revenue cutter, which sailed for Norfolk, Va. Suttle sold Burns to a North Carolina trader. His freedom was then purchased with funds raised largely by Boston's black community. The Burns case exasperated northern antislavery leaders and inflamed southern opinion. It also tested the will of the PIERCE ADMINISTRATION to enforce the Fugitive Slave Act.

See S. W. Campbell, *Slave Catchers* (1970); J. H. and W. H. Pease, *Fugitive Slave Law and Anthony Burns* (1975); and C. E. Stevens, *Anthony Burns* (1856).

STANLEY W. CAMPBELL
Baylor University

BURNSIDE'S NORTH CAROLINA EXPEDITION (February–July, 1862). Ambrose Burnside obtained approval in October, 1861, to organize a division of men and a flotilla of light-draft amphibious landing craft for conducting operations along the eastern coast of the Confederacy. The purpose was to disrupt lines of transportation on land and sea and to force the diversion of a large number of Confederate troops to protect vital supply lines and sources.

Because of its strategic location dominating both PAMLICO SOUND and ALBEMARLE SOUND along the North Carolina coast, the initial objective of the expedition was to capture and hold ROANOKE ISLAND. Encountering considerable difficulty because of the unanticipated shallowness of the water, 65 vessels and a protective naval force of 20 boats entered Pamlico Sound through Hatteras Inlet. On February 7, 1862, the expeditionary troops came ashore unopposed at Ashby's Harbor on

Roanoke Island and, during the following day, achieved a decisive victory over 2,500 Confederate defenders under the command of HENRY WISE. The defenders suffered 150 casualties, and the Union attackers lost 280, but in addition the entire Confederate force was captured.

Utilizing Roanoke Island as headquarters and staging area, Burnside's troops undertook a number of operations against Confederate strongholds. The greatest Confederate resistance occurred around NEW BERN, which was taken by Union troops on March 14. Excursions and assaults were also mounted against Elizabeth City, Edenton, Winton, Beaufort, Ft. Macon, and Plymouth from February to June, 1862. On July 3, Burnside was ordered to join George B. McClellan at Fortress Monroe.

See R. U. Johnson and C. C. Buel (eds.), *Battles and Leaders* (1888), I; J. G. Barrett, *Civil War in North Carolina* (1963); and J. I. Robertson (ed.), *Civil War History* (Dec., 1966).

JOHN Q. IMHOLTE
University of Minnesota, Morris

BURR CONSPIRACY (1805–1807) was a scheme for the separation from the Union of New Orleans and the Louisiana Territory as well as Spanish-held lands west of the Mississippi. The affair involved personal, regional, and political aspects of Thomas Jefferson's administration.

With General JAMES WILKINSON, the governor of the Louisiana Territory who had earlier led the "Spanish conspiracy" and had been a secret pensioner of the Spanish government, Aaron Burr proposed the separation of the West and the establishment of an independent nation. After overtures for funds from Spain and England proved unsuccessful, much of the financing depended on Harman Blennerhassett, whose island in the Ohio River became a staging area for the little expedition that ultimately descended the river en route to New Orleans (BLENNERHASSETT ISLAND). Aided by his suggestions that the American government supported the plan, Burr enlisted a band of adventurers, his "host of choice spirits."

Personality conflicts and politics contributed materially both to Burr's capture and to his acquittal. Wilkinson, hearing that details of their plans had been revealed, turned against his ally and, posing as both the defender of New Orleans and as a guardian of Spain's interests, alerted Jefferson. The president, having minimized earlier warnings as Federalist attempts to implicate Republicans, chose to use the general to check the equally untrustworthy Burr. Once arrested, the former vice-president was tried in Richmond, where Chief Justice JOHN MARSHALL, Jefferson's political opponent, expeditiously countered the president by holding that there was insufficient evidence for conviction on the charge of treason.

See T. P. Abernethy, *Burr Conspiracy* (1954); H. S. Parmet and M. B. Hecht, *Aaron Burr* (1967); D. Malone, *Jefferson: Second Term* (1974); N. Schachner, *Aaron Burr* (1937); Letters in Relation to Burr's Conspiracy (1806–09) and Innes Papers, Library of Congress; Simon Gratz Collection, Historical Society of Pennsylvania; and Wilkinson Papers, Historical Society of Chicago.

HERBERT S. PARMET
Queensborough Community College

BURTON, WILLIAM (1789–1866), was born in Sussex County, Del. He received an M.D. degree from the University of Pennsylvania and subsequently established a lifelong medical practice in Milford, Del. Active in state politics as a Whig, Burton became a Democrat in 1848 and, in 1854, was defeated as his party's gubernatorial candidate by Peter F. Causey, a Know-Nothing. Renominated in 1858, he was elected governor and served a full four-year term, during which Delaware's attitude toward the South, secession, and the Civil War were central concerns.

Although Delaware remained in the Union, Abraham Lincoln ran third there in 1860, and sentiment within the state was deeply divided. Burton, a Peace Democrat, openly sympathized with the South and consistently opposed the Lincoln administration. He received emissaries from seceded states, gave only grudging compliance to Lincoln's call for volunteers, and supported antiadministration protest meetings. Federal troops twice entered Delaware during Burton's administration to disarm southern sympathizers and to maintain order during state elections. In his last annual message, Burton denounced these intrusions and declared his opposition to the EMANCIPATION PROCLAMATION.

See Burton-Wootten Letters, Delaware State Archives; H. B. Hancock, *Delaware during the Civil War* (1961); J. S. Spruance, *Delaware Stays in the Union* (1955); and H. C. R. Reed, *Delaware* (3 vols.; 1947).

JOHN F. COLEMAN
St. Francis College, Loretto, Pa.

BUTLER, MARION (1863–1938), grew up on his family's farm in Sampson County, N.C., and was graduated from the University of North Carolina in 1885. After becoming president of his county Alliance (FARMERS' ALLIANCE), he bought a Democratic newspaper in the county seat, the Clinton *Caucasian*, which he subsequently moved to Goldsboro and then Raleigh. Elected to the "farmers' legislature" of 1891, he became president of the North Carolina Alliance in 1891 and then president of the National Farmers' Alliance in 1893.

Even after the POPULIST PARTY appeared in other states, Butler was reluctant to leave the Democratic party. But the Democrats' renomination of Grover Cleveland in 1892, plus the state Democratic party's strict ban on ticket splitting, forced Butler and thousands of other Alliance men to leave the "white man's party" and become Populists in 1892. Overrun by the Democrats in that year, the North Carolina Populists in 1894 cooperated with the Republicans and, for the first time since Reconstruction, took control of the legislature away from the Democrats. The "fusionists," as their opponents labeled them, sent Marion Butler to the U.S. Senate in 1895. There Butler, among other things, played an important role in the launching of the rural free delivery of mail.

Butler's greatest national prominence came in 1896, beginning with the keynote address he gave at the Populist National Convention in St. Louis. An ardent supporter of free silver, he helped achieve a compromise that prevented the complete disruption of the national Populist organization: after nominating THOMAS E. WATSON of Georgia as their own vice-presidential candidate, the Populists named the Democratic presidential nominee, William Jennings Bryan, as their presidential candidate. In the ensuing campaign, Butler served as the national chairman of the Populists and, unlike Watson, worked harmoniously with Bryan and the Democratic leaders in the unsuccessful campaign. Butler, losing his seat in the Senate in 1901 after North Carolina Democrats regained control of the state through their massive "white supremacy" campaigns of 1898 and 1900, became and remained a Republican.

See Marion Butler Manuscripts, University of North Carolina, Chapel Hill; R. F. Durden, *Climax of Populism* (1965), and *Reconstruction Bonds* (1962); L, Goodwyn, *American Populism* (1976); and S. L. Jones, *Presidential Election of 1896* (1964).

ROBERT F. DURDEN
Duke University

BUTLER, MATTHEW CALBRAITH (1836–1909),

was born in South Carolina, attended South Carolina College, and was admitted to the bar in 1857. Captain of a cavalry company at the outbreak of the Civil War, he was later colonel of the 2nd South Carolina Regiment. At the age of twenty-seven he was promoted brigadier general and in 1864 major general. Resuming law practice after the war, he also served in the state legislature. At first he led the Union Reform movement, a fusion of honest whites and blacks, in the early 1870s. When convinced that salvation lay in Democratic control of the state, he embraced that party wholeheartedly. While actively campaigning for the election of native whites, he was implicated in race riots in his hometown of Edgefield and in HAMBURG. With the return of political control to the native whites, he was elected to the U.S. Senate by the Democratic legislature, and he served three terms before being defeated by "Pitchfork" BEN TILLMAN. He continued to practice law in Washington, D.C., and served as a major general in the Spanish-American War. Despite his stand in Reconstruction, he was free from inflammatory speech and did much to reconcile the North and South.

See U. R. Brooks, *Butler and Cavalry* (1909), good coverage of military career; J. S. Reynolds, *Reconstruction* (1905), and H. T. Thompson, *Ousting Carpetbaggers* (1927), both sympathetic to Butler; Record Group 109, National Archives, for manuscripts on military phase; and Butler Collection, South Caroliniana Library, University of South Carolina.

WILLARD E. WIGHT
Georgia Institute of Technology

BUTLER, WILLIAM ORLANDO (1791–1880), of

Carrollton, Ky., was a lawyer, farmer, and minor poet but achieved greatest prominence as a soldier and politician. His military career encompassed the War of 1812 and the Mexican War, culminating with his elevation near the end of the latter conflict to command of the army in Mexico. Butler was a favorite of Kentucky Democrats, who twice elected him to Congress (1839–1843) but failed in 1844 to elect him governor. Seeking to add military luster and sectional balance to their ticket, the national Democrats in 1848 nominated Butler for the vice-presidency. In 1852 he had factional support within the party for the presidential nomination. Butler's last public service was as a Kentucky delegate to the 1861 WASHINGTON PEACE CONFERENCE.

See G. F. Roberts, "William O. Butler" (M.A. thesis, University of Kentucky, 1962), best; F. P. Blair, *William O. Butler* (1848); L. Collins, *History of Kentucky* (1874); and "Popular Portraits," *Democratic Review* (Oct., 1848).

JAMES W. HAMMACK, JR.
Murray State University

BYRD, HARRY FLOOD, SR. (1887–1966), was

born in Martinsburg, W.Va. He matured in Winchester, Va., leaving school in 1903 to assume responsibility for various family enterprises, becoming publisher of the Winchester *Evening Star* and manager of the Winchester Telephone Company. In 1906, aided by his uncle, Congressman HENRY D. FLOOD, he leased apple orchards so that by 1914 he was a primary grower, warehouseman, and exporter of apples and peaches. Byrd entered politics; was elected in 1906 to the Winchester city council, in 1915 to the state senate, in 1923 to the Democratic state chairmanship, and in 1925 to the governorship; and in 1933 was appointed to the U.S. Senate, where he remained until his retirement in 1965.

Byrd made "pay as you go" a slogan for business efficiency and economy in government. Aided by the eagerness of Senator CLAUDE A. SWANSON to incorporate his youth in the aging dominant political organization, he won the governorship, simplified state government, delegated more appointive power to courthouses, curtailed state expenditures at the expense of social services and education, and secured national recognition as a progressive business governor.

In 1932 Byrd unsuccessfully combined with Franklin Roosevelt's rivals in an attempt to secure the Democratic presidential nomination. His persistent opposition to the NEW DEAL, though ideological, held political undertones, as Byrd stood available should Rooseveltian liberalism falter. Inheriting the ruling Virginia oligarchy upon the elevation of the estranged Swanson to secretary of navy, Byrd fashioned a cadre of diligent lieutenants and presided for a generation as Virginia's coachman over the BYRD MACHINE. In the Senate, he proposed alternative diminished federal budgets, opposed the growth of civil branches of government, proclaimed massive resistance to desegregation, and served as Finance Committee chairman. His public policies against executive excess echoed the eighteenth-century legislative solution of control and reduction of expenditures.

See H. C. Ferrell, Jr., *Essays in Southern Biography* (1965); articles by J. A. Fry, A. L. Hall, R. T. Hawkes, Jr., P. R. Henriques, J. R. Sweeney, and B. Tarter, in *Virginia Magazine of History and Biography* (June, 1974); R. T. Hawkes, Jr., "The Career of Harry Flood Byrd, Sr., to 1933" (Ph.D. dissertation, University of Virginia, 1975); J. T. Patterson, *Congressional Conservatism* (1967); A. L. Shifflett, "Good Roads in Virginia" (M.A. thesis, East Carolina University, 1971); and J. H. Wilkinson III, *Harry Byrd* (1968).

HENRY C. FERRELL, JR.
East Carolina University

BYRD FAMILY of Virginia has played a leading role in the colony and state since before 1671, when young William Byrd I (1652–1704) arrived from London. He inherited from his maternal uncle Thomas Stegge a large estate, including a lu-crative fur trade and store. Knowledgeable about the Indians and the backcountry, he was a colonel of militia guarding the frontier at the falls of the James River. He was also a member of the governor's council and deputy auditor and receiver general. He added greatly to his land holdings, including Westover plantation on the James.

William Byrd II (1674–1744) was educated in England, attended the Middle Temple, and was admitted to the bar. After his father's death he returned to a considerable Virginia estate and a position as one of the ruling class. He was at once made receiver general and in 1708 a member of the council. Three times he represented the colony as official agent in London. In 1726 he returned to Virginia to busy himself with raising tobacco on his many plantations. He built a handsome, richly furnished house at Westover and acquired a library unequaled in the colony. In 1728 as a commissioner to run the dividing line between North Carolina and Virginia, he spent many weeks in the woods with a party of surveyors and hunters and afterward wrote the charming "History of the Dividing Line," first published in *The Westover Manuscripts* (1841), which gave him a permanent place in American literature. During his adult life he kept a secret shorthand journal, full of minute details of life in England and on the plantation. He died owning some 179,000 acres of rich backcountry. He founded the city of Richmond.

William Byrd III (1728–1777) was educated at home; only sixteen at his father's death, he lived the spendthrift life of a wealthy young aristocrat, racing horses and gambling. He also served as a burgess and after 1754 a councilor. In 1756, suddenly tired of this life, he went to join the English fighting the French in Canada under Lord Loudoun. Five years in the field, he eventually became commander-in-chief of the Virginia forces in Pennsylvania, Virginia, and the Carolinas. Inattentive to business, ignorant of agriculture, and overtrusting, he returned to plantation life to find his fortune tottering. He was one of the few in the council who tried to avoid the Revolution. On January 1, 1777, overwhelmed by financial troubles, mistrusted by his associates, with one son in the Revolutionary forces and one in the British army, he shot himself.

His two oldest sons (from a family of 15) died without children. The third, Thomas Taylor Byrd, had a large family. Noted Virginians descended from this son include Admiral Richard Evelyn Byrd, explorer and aviator, first to fly over the North Pole; and Senator HARRY FLOOD BYRD, SR., architect of the BYRD MACHINE, whose son, Harry Flood Byrd, Jr., carries on the family reputation.

See P. Marambaud, *Virginia Magazine of History and Biography* (April, 1973; Oct., 1974); R. C. Beatty, *William Byrd* (1932), somewhat outdated; P. Marambaud, *William Byrd* (1971), full bibliography; W. Byrd, *Prose Works* (1966), *Secret Diary, 1709–12* (1941), *London Diary, 1717–21* (1958), and *Another Secret Diary, 1739–41* (1942); W. H. Gaines, *Virginia Cavalcade* (Winter, 1951); A. Hatch, *Byrds of Virginia* (1969), and *Virginia Magazine of History and Biography* (July, 1974); and M. Tinling (ed.), *Correspondence of Three William Byrds, 1684–1776* (1977).

MARION TINLING
National Historical Publications Committee

BYRD MACHINE (1922–1965) had its origins in the turmoil of post-Reconstruction politics and in the efforts of Democratic party leaders to gain ascendancy in Virginia. During the 1890s a powerful Democratic organization was constructed under the hand of Senator THOMAS S. MARTIN. Deriving power from a network of loyal officeholders, a controlled electorate made possible by DISFRANCHISEMENT, and the party primary, Martin's group dominated Virginia politics for two decades. Upon Martin's death in 1919, party leadership devolved upon HARRY FLOOD BYRD, SR.

The Byrd machine existed to defend states' rights, to achieve economy in government, and to maintain white supremacy. Professing to despise public indebtedness, Byrd and his followers adopted "pay-as-you-go" programs to provide necessary public services such as highways and schools. An admirer of business, Byrd modeled state government after corporate management techniques, and the state's administration became a closely knit organization based upon efficient operation and loyalty to Byrd.

During the 1930s the Byrd machine became alienated from the platform and policies of the national Democratic party. The machine asserted its independence by refusing to give its wholehearted endorsement to Harry Truman and Adlai Stevenson, and the Republicans won the electoral votes of the Old Dominion in 1952, 1956, and 1960.

The Byrd machine consistently opposed expanding the civil and political rights of black Virginians. After BROWN V. BOARD OF EDUCATION (1954), Governors Thomas B. Stanley and J. LINDSAY ALMOND mounted a "massive resistance" campaign to prohibit integration of the public schools. Massive resistance proved to be the first substantial reversal suffered by the machine, and it was abandoned as a result of federal court pressure and adverse public opinion. The rapid urbanization of northern and eastern Virginia after World War II had diminished the influence of machine loyalists in rural areas and small towns. Even though Harry Flood Byrd, Jr., followed his father to the U.S. Senate when the elder Byrd retired in 1965, the long hegemony of the machine was at an end.

See Harry Flood Byrd, Sr., Papers, University of Virginia Library; J. H. Wilkinson, *Harry Byrd* (1968); J. R. Sweeney, "Byrd and Anti-Byrd" (Ph.D. dissertation, University of Notre Dame, 1973); *Virginia Magazine of History and Biography* (July, 1974); V. Dabney, *Virginia* (1971); B. Muse, *Virginia's Massive Resistance* (1961); F. M. Wilhoit, *Massive Resistance* (1973); and R. H. Pulley, *Old Virginia Restored* (1968).

RAYMOND H. PULLEY
Appalachian State University

BYRNES, JAMES FRANCIS (1879–1972), was born to Irish immigrants in Charleston, S.C. At fourteen he began working in a law office, moving to Aiken seven years later, where he became a court stenographer. He opened his own firm, became circuit solicitor in 1908, and then won election to Congress in 1910. A man of cordiality, humor, and grace, Byrnes won respect for reconciling conflicts. Elected to the U.S. Senate in 1930, he adopted a pragmatic approach to the economic emergency and strongly backed NEW DEAL programs.

Franklin D. Roosevelt valued Byrnes's talents and nominated him to the U.S. Supreme Court in 1941. Soon his administrative abilities were needed, and Byrnes spent most of the war as director of war mobilization, wielding enormous power over resource procurement and allocation. Losing a vice-presidential bid in 1944, Byrnes found himself nominated by Harry Truman to be secretary of state in 1945. Byrnes's inexperience in foreign affairs was exceeded only by Truman's, and he discovered that achieving agreements at the conference table was far more difficult than were compromises in the Senate. His concessions to the Russians at the Moscow Conference (1945) brought presidential censure; and, although he ably represented his country at the Paris Peace Conference (1946), ill health and policy differences led to his resignation in early 1947. After the war, Byrnes opposed the growth of federal power. As governor of South Carolina (1951–1955) he joined other southern politicians to oppose desegregation.

See J. F. Byrnes, *Speaking Frankly* (1947), and *All in One Lifetime* (1958); N. A. Graebner (ed.), *Uncertain Tradition* (1961); R. H. Ferrell (ed.), *American Secretaries of State* (1965), XIV; and Byrnes Papers, Clemson University Library.

T. M. CAMPBELL
Florida State University

C

CABELL, JAMES BRANCH (1879–1958), was born in Richmond of an aristocratic Virginia family. After graduating with honors from William and Mary, he worked for a few years on family genealogy; later he was a newspaperman and then a mining company employee. Most of his life, however, he was a professional man of letters, who lived quietly with his family in Richmond. Extremely prolific, Cabell published over 50 volumes, including his magnum opus, the 18-volumed *Biography of Manuel*, as well as other novels and many volumes in a variety of genres: genealogy, short story, essay, autobiography, history, poetry, and drama.

Cabell's great literary reputation was sparked by the suppression in New York of his fifteenth novel, *Jurgen* (1919). This event made him instantly well known and brought to his defense major writers of the period. Although his reputation in later years never compared with his great notoriety during the twenties, Cabell continued to publish. A critical reappraisal by Edmund Wilson in 1956 (*New Yorker*, April) was the first of a series of serious studies that have initiated a growing revival of interest in Cabell. He was a satirist, whose ironical romances set in the faraway land of Poictesme reflected his wide reading and clothed his biting observations of contemporary Virginia, and a humanist, whose popular reputation as a sly creator of slight, erotic tales indicated how little the general public comprehended his deep seriousness.

See E. Wagenknecht, *Cavalcade . . . American Novel* (1952); F. J. Brewer, *Bibliography* (1957); and J. L. Davis, *Cabell* (1962).

DOROTHY SCURA
Virginia Commonwealth University

CABEZA DE VACA, ÁLVAR NÚÑEZ (1490?–1560?), was an explorer whose stories about the New World spurred Spanish exploration of the American Southwest. A lieutenant in the Spanish army, he joined the expedition of Pánfilo de Narváez to explore in 1528 the Florida peninsula. A large party under Narváez, while exploring the area around Tampa Bay, became separated from the expedition's ships. The group embarked for Mexico on crudely constructed rafts, but a hurri-

cane wrecked most of the craft and killed all but about 80 men. Washed ashore on a sandy island off the Texas coast, only a few, including Cabeza de Vaca, survived disease and privation long enough to be captured by coastal Indians. Cabeza de Vaca became a medicine man with a band of trading Indians in eastern Texas. He broke away from his captors in 1532, however, and was eventually reunited with three of his former crewmen, including Steven, a Moorish slave. In October, 1534, the four set out for Mexico, reaching the Pacific coast of that Spanish colony in March, 1536, seven and one-half years after their shipwreck. Their stories of wealthy lands to the north, which they had not seen, precipitated Francisco Vásquez de Coronado's famous expedition into the Southwest in search of El Dorado. *Los Naufrigios* (1592), an account of their adventure, was written years later by Cabeza de Vaca.

See F. Bandelier, *Cabeza de Vaca* (1922), best translation; C. Hallenbeck, *Cabeza de Vaca* (1940), best general account; and A. Krieger, "De la ruta sequida por Cabeza de Vaca" (Ph.D. dissertation, University of Mexico, 1955), best study of route.

SEYMOUR V. CONNOR
Texas Tech University

CABILDO refers to the municipal council in the Spanish colonial empire of the eighteenth century or to the town hall. The council, unrepresentative and undemocratic, usually consisted of six *regidores*, or aldermen, who purchased or inherited their offices, and two *alcaldes*, or mayor-justices, elected annually by the *regidores*. With the governor's approval, the cabildo could issue ordinances affecting many aspects of civic economic and social life, including price regulation. The *alcalde* presided over a municipal court with limited civil and criminal jurisdiction. The best example in the Spanish-held territory of the South was the cabildo of New Orleans. It offered little to the development of its successor, the American city council.

See C. Gayarré, *History of Louisiana* (1965); J. Clark, J. D. L. Holmes, and S. Wilson, Jr., in *Spain in the Mississippi Valley* (1974); and Books of the Cabildo (minutes of sessions), in New Orleans Public Library.

J. PRESTON MOORE
Louisiana State University

CABLE, GEORGE WASHINGTON (1844–1925), a novelist and reformer, was born in New Orleans. He published in 1873 his first story and in 1879 a collection of seven stories, *Old Creole Days*, followed by the novelette *Madame Delphine* (1881), the novels *The Grandissimes* (1880) and *Dr. Sevier* (1884), and a historical volume, *The Creoles of Louisiana* (1884). These works gained popular and critical praise and established him as portrayer of Creole New Orleans. Acquainted from childhood with French and Spanish residents of New Orleans, a thoughtful student of history, and endowed with an acute ear for speech, he was admirably prepared to record the Creole civilization in both fact and spirit. Recognizing the value of dialect for realistic character portrayal and for humorous effects, he learned to suggest the varieties of dialect spoken by his various characters, including the patois of the French-speaking Negro, without burdening his readers with literal transcription.

Cable's parents had owned slaves, and he had been wounded twice while serving in the Confederate cavalry; but soon after the war he began to question the attitudes on race commonly held by his associates. He introduced the question of Negro rights into some of his early fiction, and beginning in 1885 he used every means available, including lectures and essays, to urge extending full civil rights to the freedmen. Soon after 1890, when southern laws and public opinion in both the North and the South had decreed for the Negro something less than full rights, Cable's editors would no longer accept his controversial essays. Before leaving the debate, he published *John March, Southerner* (1894), a novel in which he dealt with the main elements in the current southern problem.

In 1885 Cable had settled in Northampton, Mass., but he traveled to the South regularly and continued to set his fiction mostly in the region. His later works include three collections of stories—*Bonaventure* (1888), *Strong Hearts* (1899), and *The Flower of the Chapdelaines* (1918)—and five novels—*The Cavalier* (1901), *Bylow Hill* (1902), *Kincaid's Battery* (1908), *Gideon's Band* (1914), and *Lovers of Louisiana* (1918). These books show mastery of fictional techniques, but they lack the sturdy realism that made his early writings memorable.

See biographies by A. Turner (1956) and L. D. Rubin (1969); a book on Cable's years in Northampton by P. Butcher (1959); and Cable Papers, Tulane University.

ARLIN TURNER
Duke University

CADDO INDIANS, living on the lower Red River, now Louisiana and Arkansas, were called Kadohadacho, "real chiefs." The name also applies to the Caddoan linguistic family, a significant group. When La Salle met the Caddo in 1686, 25 tribes were united in confederations, including the Kadohadacho, Hasinai (Hainai of Texas), and Natchitoches. A Woodland people known for earth houses, they acquired much Plains culture. Human sacrifice among the Pawnee was ended by Petalasharo about 1870. Today, related Arikara live in North Dakota. The Caddo proper lost ancestral lands in 1835 and moved to Texas. Threats by Texans forced them to join Wichita kinsmen in Oklahoma Indian Territory by 1858. The Indian Claims Commission in 1960 held that the Caddo tribe was entitled to awards for some 618,000 acres of land in Arkansas and Louisiana taken in 1835; other areas were disputed, and in 1975 the case remained on appeal with the U.S. Court of Claims.

See J. R. Swanton, *Source Material, Caddo* (1942), details with bibliography; Indian Claims Commission, Docket No. 226, Caddo land claims; M. Wright, *Guide to Indian Tribes of Oklahoma* (1968), concise; E. C. Parsons, *Notes on Caddo* (1941); G. W. McGintly, *Louisiana Studies* (Summer, 1963), valuating 1835 cession; and S. Williams, in W. Goodenough, *Explorations in Cultural Anthropology* (1964), aboriginal location maps and bibliography.

ELIZABETH C. DURAN
Niagara University

CAHABA PRISON (sometimes called Castle Morgan), a Confederate prison in Dallas County, Ala., was on the Alabama River, ten miles south of Selma, in the village of Cahaba. Beginning in the fall of 1863 it was used as a temporary way station for Union captives en route to larger Confederate prisons. During the fall of 1864, however, from 2,000 to 3,000 federal prisoners were crowded into the little stronghold (meant to hold 500), and many of them were kept there until shortly before peace came.

The 116-by-193-foot brick prison building, surrounded by a wooden stockade, was originally a cotton warehouse. It had no floor and was only partially roofed. Prisoners had little protection from the elements; and an impoverished Confederate government was unable to provide either adequate clothing or sufficient fuel for fires. The small stream of artesian well water, which was diverted through the building, was highly sulfurous and had already been partially polluted before it reached the prison. In the late winter of 1864–1865, the majority of the prisoners was forced to stand helplessly for several days in cold flood waters. The amount and quality of food, at first reasonably satisfactory, deteriorated with the passage of time. Other aspects of life at Cahaba—the filth, the rats, the lice, the festering sores, the thievery of fellow prisoners—were similar to those in most other Confederate prisons.

Just before the war ended, the weakened inmates of Cahaba were paroled, and several hundred were loaded onto the large river steamer *Sultana* to be shipped to hospitals in the North, only to have the ship destroyed by an explosion, killing possibly a third of those who had just been released (SULTANA DISASTER).

See P. A. Brannon, *Alabama Review* (July, 1950); J. Hawes, *Cahaba* (1888), biased, but highly useful; W. M. Armstrong, *Civil War History* (June, 1962); Report of R. M. Whitefield, *Congressional Report on Prisoners of War*, H.R. 45, 40th Cong., 3rd Sess.; M. Grigsby, *Smoked Yank* (1888); and J. L. Walker, *Cahaba Prison* (1910).

CAJUNS is a term most often used interchangeably with the more formal term ACADIANS and usually refers to those French people driven from Acadia (Nova Scotia) by the British in 1755 who settled in Louisiana. Some located north of New Orleans in St. James Parish, and a much larger number moved westward and made St. Martinville and Opelousas the centers of settlement. Into the nineteenth century fishing, trapping, and large sugar planting were important pursuits, but most Cajuns settled small farms or became ranchers on the prairies to the west. Relative isolation and remarkable growth in numbers enabled this conservative people to develop a distinctive culture and draw others into it. Compulsory education and other modern changes have broken down this isolation, yet much remains in language, customs, music, and food to attest a rich historical experience stretching from the exile, commemorated in Henry Wadsworth Longfellow's *Evangeline*, to the Evangeline Oak in St. Martinville today.

The term has also been used less frequently to refer to people of apparent mixed white, Indian, and possibly Negro ancestry living in southwest Alabama and nearby eastern Mississippi. Usually they are referred to as Cajans or Cajons, and their origin is steeped in folklore. These Cajans were variously reported to be descendants of Gulf Coast pirates who adopted their name from the Louisiana Cajuns; or heirs of a Captain Red Byrd, a Mexican Indian who married a Louisiana Cajun; or even simply as creatures spawned by "coons and foxes" on the sand flats. There is little doubt that at least some of their ancestors included members of the original migrants from Acadia or other early French settlers. By the second quarter of the twentieth century they were depicted as a suspicious, unsophisticated rural people, victims of prejudice and their own lack of education. Although somewhat proud of their partial French and Indian heritage, they were unwilling to acknowledge any Negro ancestry. At present they are still an identifiable group, but, like the Cajuns of Louisiana, they no longer remain quite so secluded from the world about them as formerly.

See A. Fortier, *Louisiana Studies* (1894); C. Gayarré, *History of Louisiana* (1903); M. A. Johnston, *In Acadia* (1893); D. LeBlanc, *True Story* (1932); L. C. Post, *Cajun Sketches* (1962); C. Ramsey, *Cajuns on Bayous* (1957); J. Uhler, *Cajun Country Cookin'* (1966); and C. Carmer, *Stars Fell on Alabama* (1934).

MAJOR L. WILSON
Memphis State University

CALDWELL, ERSKINE (1903–). In an introduction to Ben Field's *The Cock's Funeral* (1937), Caldwell made a statement that explains the background of his writing: "These are the beaten, the uneducated, the writhing mass of people who can be driven no further down in life. They have reached the limits of human endurance and, at last, are fighting for their lives. Because of their subjection, they are born into the world vulgar, unwashed, and ignorant. If their language and habits offend, it is not their shame, but America's." He was born in Coweta County, Ga., and has lived in most of the states of the South, as well as California, Connecticut, Maine, New York, and Pennsylvania. He was educated at Erskine College, the University of Virginia, and the University of Pennsylvania. He worked in a variety of menial jobs before becoming a reporter for the Atlanta *Journal*. As a foreign correspondent he worked in China, Czechoslovakia, Mexico, Spain, and Russia.

Caldwell is a craftsman, an excellent storyteller, and deft at characterization. He has been compared, favorably and unfavorably, with WILLIAM FAULKNER, Ernest Hemingway, and John Steinbeck. If he does not match them in critical acclaim, he has outproduced as well as outlived them. He has published over 60 volumes in more than 325 editions, and his world sales are estimated at over 70 million books. With a body of work so large, it is hardly surprising that he is accused of being repetitious. He is at his best in the short story, *Complete Stories* (1953), and in his short novels, *Tobacco Road* (1932) and *God's Little Acre* (1933). He has been excoriated as pornographic and as a literary traitor to the South, but his reputation grows in reconsideration of him as a proletarian pioneer.

See K. Burke, *New Republic* (April 10, 1934); M. Cowley, *New Republic* (Nov. 6, 1944); and E. Caldwell, *Call It Experience* (1951), and *Deep South* (1968).

RICHARD B. HARWELL
Georgia Southern College

CALHOUN, JOHN CALDWELL (1782–1850), was born near Abbeville in the South Carolina upcountry. Both of his parents were of Scotch-Irish ancestry, and his father was a prosperous planter, who by 1790 owned 31 slaves. Calhoun was educated in a log cabin academy, Yale College, and the Litchfield, Conn., law school of Judge Tapping Reeve. In 1810 he was elected to Congress, and the next year he married his cousin's daughter Floride Calhoun, who was to bear him four daughters and five sons.

As a congressman (1811–1817), Calhoun was a strong nationalist. He used his influence as chairman of the House Committee on Foreign Affairs to help bring about the 1812 declaration of war against Great Britain. After the war he advocated a new national bank, protective tariffs, and federal spending for internal improvements. As secretary of war (1817–1825), he brought vigor and efficiency to the small military establishment. During his first term as vice-president (1825–1829), however, he began to retreat from his nationalistic stand in response to rising antitariff sentiment in the South.

When South Carolina cotton planters, outraged by the tariff of 1828, threatened revolutionary action, Calhoun looked for a legal and constitutional alternative. He thought he found it in his theory of NULLIFICATION, according to which the people of a state could declare a federal law unconstitutional and therefore inoperative within the state. Reelected vice-president, this time on Andrew Jackson's ticket, he soon quarreled with the president. When the tariff of 1832 failed to appease the Carolina planters, he resigned the vice-presidency, took the lead in putting nullification into practice, and was sent to the U.S. Senate to defend his state's position. He claimed a victory for nullification when Congress agreed to a gradual tariff reduction (1833). Actually, the principle had not worked the way he had intended, and no other state had come officially to South Carolina's support. While continuing to elaborate his theory of states' rights, he therefore began also to develop a sense of unity throughout the South.

In the Senate (1832–1842) Calhoun cooperated with the Whig leaders Daniel Webster and HENRY CLAY in opposing Jackson's bank policies, but he maintained his independence of both parties. He contributed to the development of the proslavery argument, characterizing slavery as a "positive good" and as a means of checking the revolutionary tendencies of class conflict. During the MARTIN VAN BUREN ADMINISTRATION he began to work with the Democrats, and early in the JOHN TYLER administration he led the fight against the Whig program in Congress.

Calhoun withdrew from the Senate to seek the Democratic nomination for the presidential campaign of 1844, but gave up before the convention met. As secretary of state (1844–1845), he negotiated a treaty for the annexation of Texas and justified it as a measure essential for the protection of slavery. This caused many northerners to suspect that annexation was a proslavery plot, and the Senate voted down the treaty.

Again a senator (1845–1850), Calhoun opposed war with Mexico, fearing that the acquisition of new territories would intensify both sectional and class conflict. After the war he made himself the foremost spokesman for the extreme southern view that Congress must permit and protect slavery in all the territories. He denounced the proposed COMPROMISE OF 1850 on the grounds that it would not provide adequate guarantees for the slavery interest of the South. He had concluded that the only adequate guarantee would be a dual presidency, with a northern and a southern president, each having an absolute veto.

After his death a collection of Calhoun's works was published (1851–1856), including his "Disquisition on Government" and his "Discourse on the Constitution and Government of the United States." His views greatly influenced the secessionists of 1860–1861, who accepted his doctrine that secession, like nullification, was a perfectly legal remedy for an aggrieved state.

See biographies by C. M. Wiltse (3 vols.; 1944–51), most comprehensive and thorough; M. L. Coit (1950), human-interest approach; and G. M. Capers (1960), brief but realistically critical. See also studies of Calhoun's thought by A. O. Spain (1951) and R. N. Current (1963).

RICHARD N. CURRENT
University of North Carolina, Greensboro

CALHOUN, JOHN CALDWELL (1843–19?), was born in Demopolis, Ala., the son of Andrew Pickens Calhoun and grandson of the South Carolina statesman, JOHN CALDWELL CALHOUN. After attending South Carolina College he joined a cavalry troop and served the Confederacy until the surrender. After the war he prospered as a large-scale cotton planter in Mississippi and Arkansas by employing the freedmen on a cooperative basis. In 1884 he moved to New York and quickly became a Wall Street financier. He soon became involved in the notorious financial manipulations of the Richmond Terminal Company, a holding company that brought under a unified control most of the railroads that were in 1894 organized into the Southern Railway System by J. P. Morgan. He and his brother PATRICK CALHOUN were sometimes referred to as southern carpetbaggers in Wall Street.

JAMES F. DOSTER
University of Alabama

CALHOUN, PATRICK (1856–1943), a son of Andrew Pickens Calhoun and grandson of JOHN CALDWELL CALHOUN, the South Carolina statesman, was born at his grandfather's place at Ft. Hill, S.C. He was admitted to the bar in South Carolina in 1875 and entered law practice in St. Louis, Mo., in 1876. In 1878 he went into the practice of corporation law in Atlanta and soon had a lucrative practice. Calhoun was a director and general counsel of the notorious Richmond Terminal Company, which manipulated railroad accounts, deluded investors, and brought together the greatest conglomeration of railroad lines in the South. After the bankruptcy, a part of the combination's assets were reorganized in 1894 by J. P. Morgan as the Southern Railway System. Calhoun was instrumental in the organization of many business enterprises in the South. In 1897 he moved to Cleveland, Ohio, where he organized real estate development. In 1906 he moved to San Francisco, where he was associated with street railroads and oil field developments.

JAMES F. DOSTER
University of Alabama

CALL, RICHARD KEITH (1792–1862), soldier, lawyer, politician, and planter, is closely identified with the early development of Florida. Although born near Petersburg, Va., he spent his formative years in Kentucky. He received little formal education. Coming first to the Spanish Floridas in 1814 as an officer with Andrew Jackson's punitive expedition against Pensacola, Call began a law practice in that city shortly after the transfer of the territory to the United States in 1821. With Jackson's political support, Call then proceeded to hold a variety of territorial offices, from membership in the legislative council to governor. In addition, President James Monroe appointed him brigadier general of militia in 1823. At all times, he was an advocate of internal improvements and a relentless foe of the SEMINOLE INDIANS. In later years Call devoted himself to his extensive plantation holdings near Tallahassee and to fighting the growing anti-Union sentiment in the state.

See H. J. Doherty, Jr., *Richard Keith Call* (1961); Call Papers, University of Florida and University of North Carolina; and Andrew Jackson Papers, Library of Congress.

JOHN F. REIGER
University of Miami

CALVERT FAMILY founded Maryland, a colony remarkable for the degree to which religious liberty flourished. Sir George Calvert (1580?–1632), secretary of state and privy councilor to King James I, an avowed Catholic after 1624, and the first Lord Baltimore, was the progenitor of this distinguished family. Attempting to replenish the family fortune exhausted in unsuccessfully colonizing Newfoundland, his son Cecilius, or Cecil (1606–1675), the second Lord Baltimore, founded a Catholic colony in Maryland in 1634. Having absolute power to govern and allocate land, the Calverts attempted to create a hierarchical society based on a manorial system.

Forced to remain in England, Cecil ruled his colony through a coalition of friends, coreligionists, and family members. Until 1647 his brother, Governor Leonard Calvert (1610?–1647), guided the fortunes of the struggling colony. After Leonard's death, Cecil instituted far-reaching changes designed to give the Protestant majority greater control in the colony's governance. His policy of granting religious toleration to all Christians was too advanced for an age emphasizing religious differences, and a Puritan uprising in 1654 deprived the Calverts of their colony.

After his restoration as lord proprietor in 1658, Cecil controlled provincial politics through a small cadre dominated by Calverts who had intermarried into prominent Protestant families. His son Charles (1637–1715), governor from 1661 until he succeeded to his father's title in 1675, continued the policy. Between 1666 and 1689 over half the council was related by blood or marriage to the Calvert family. In 1689 a Protestant association, in part responding to the family monopoly in officeholding, overthrew the proprietary government, bringing an end to the Calverts' unique experiment in religious toleration. When the proprietary family was restored in 1715, the Calverts were still politically prominent, but government was no longer a family affair. With independence, the state of Maryland severed all ties with the Calvert family and terminated what was undoubtedly the most successful family enterprise in early American history.

See W. H. Browne, *George and Cecilius Calvert* (1890); C. C. Hall, *Lords Baltimore* (1904), both outdated (Calverts lack modern biographies); J. W. Foster, *Maryland Historical Magazine* (Dec., 1960); J. D. Krugler, *Maryland Historical Magazine* (Fall, 1973); T. M. Coakley, *Maryland Historical Magazine* (Spring, 1976); J. D. Krugler, *Catholic Historical Review* (forthcoming); E. F. O'Gorman, *Descendants of Virginia Calverts* (1947); J. B. C. Nicklin, *Maryland Historical Magazine* (March, June, Sept., Dec., 1921; March, 1929; March, 1930; Sept., Dec., 1931; Dec., 1932); W. H. Browne *et al.*, *Maryland Archives* (1883–1947), and *Calvert Papers* (1889–99); and Calvert Papers, Maryland Historical Society.

JOHN D. KRUGLER
Marquette University

CAMDEN, ARK. (pop. 15,147), is on a bluff that overlooks the navigational head of the Ouachita River 40 miles north of the Louisiana line. The site may have been visited in 1541 by HERNANDO DE SOTO. The first permanent white settlement was established in 1783 by Don Juan Fihiol and named Écore á Fabre (Fabre's Bluff) after a French trader who had settled here earlier. American pioneers began arriving after the LOUISIANA PURCHASE. As steamboats replaced canoes, barks, and rafts, the city became a major river port. It was renamed Camden when the town was incorporated in 1844. During the Civil War, Ft. Lookout was constructed north of the town to protect it from a federal attack. On April 18, 1864, west of the town at Poison Spring, a force of Confederates under J. S. MARMADUKE routed a federal forage train attached to Frederick Steele's command. With 122 federal soldiers killed (117 of whom were black) and only 16 dead Confederates, the battle was the first setback in Steele's RED RIVER CAMPAIGN of 1864. Camden is still an important shipping and trading center for area agriculture, and its principal products are lumber, wood pulp, and paper.

See D. Hernden (ed.), *Annals of Arkansas* (1947); *Ouachita County Historical Quarterly* (1960–); and Camden *Evening News* (1920–). The Camden Public Library maintains numerous scrapbooks and manuscript histories of the city, residents, and river trade, some on microfilm.

CAMDEN, BATTLE OF (August 16, 1780). HORATIO GATES, upon taking command of the remnants of the Southern Department of the American army after the fall of Charleston, immediately ordered an advance from Deep Run in North Carolina to Camden, S.C., where a British post had been established under Lord Rawdon. Near Camden, Gates was reinforced by North Carolina militia but, unwilling to attack Rawdon, who occu-

pied a highly defensible position, he turned away. With the arrival of Virginia militia, Gates felt strong enough to transfer 400 men and two of his eight field pieces to THOMAS SUMTER for a side raid on a British wagon train. Meanwhile, Charles Cornwallis had brought reinforcements from Charleston and assumed the British command. The two armies unexpectedly met at night in a pine clearing seven miles north of Camden. At dawn the British with fixed bayonets advanced against the American left. The Virginia and North Carolina militiamen posted there panicked and fled the field. The Maryland and DELAWARE CONTINENTALS fought bravely but, surrounded and suffering heavy casualties, they were overwhelmed. Gates, who left with the first panic-stricken militia, arrived in Charlotte on a fast charger, his military glory won at Saratoga undone. Camden was the nadir for the American cause in the South.

See H. L. Landers, *Battle of Camden* (1929); W. M. Wallace, *Appeal to Arms* (1951); H. H. Peckham, *War for Independence* (1958); E. McCrady, *South Carolina in the Revolution* (1901); and F. and M. Wickwire, *Cornwallis* (1970).

CHARLES L. ANGER
The Citadel

CAMDEN, S.C. (pop. 8,532), in the sandhills of the north-central portion of the state, is approximately 30 miles northeast of Columbia. The modern city is a popular winter resort, a trade center for area lumber and agriculture, and a manufacturer of textiles. English colonists who settled the area in the 1730s were joined in 1750 by a group of Irish QUAKERS. Both groups made livings by farming and by shipping clay to English potters. Prior to being named in 1768 in honor of the earl of Camden, the settlement was known as Friends' Neck (1750) and as Pine Tree Hill (1758). In June, 1780, after a successful British assault on Charleston, Lord Charles Cornwallis garrisoned his troops at Camden, where on August 16, 1780, he shattered an American counterattack led by HORATIO GATES (CAMDEN, BATTLE OF). The town was burned by evacuating British soldiers on May 8, 1781. In 1816 a second series of fires, coupled with an epidemic of MALARIA, forced the abandonment of the original townsite and its relocation on new and somewhat higher ground. Although Camden prospered prior to the Civil War as a cotton market and rail terminus, it was burned out yet a third time by W. T. Sherman's forces on February 24, 1865 (CAROLINAS CAMPAIGN).

See R. Kennedy, *Historical Camden* (2 vols.; 1905, 1926); and files of Camden *Chronicle* (1888–), on microfilm.

CAMEL CORPS. The need to identify a route through the desert to California following the Mexican War (1846–1848) led to the government's experiment with the use of a unique animal to transport army supplies. The initial idea of using camels in the army was suggested in 1843, but no action was taken. In 1848, Major Henry C. Wayne (1815–1883) of Georgia recommended to the War Department the formation of a camel corps in the army. In 1854, JEFFERSON DAVIS, the secretary of war, strongly urged Congress to approve his proposal to test the adaptation of camels to the United States. The experiment was launched in 1855 under the leadership of Major Wayne.

Lieutenant David D. Porter commanded the first expedition to the Middle East to purchase the camels, returning in 1856 with a cargo of 34 animals. A permanent camp was established at Val Verde, Tex. (about 60 miles northwest of San Antonio), where buildings were erected to shelter the animals. A second expedition resulted in the importation of 41 additional camels.

The first test of the camels' adaptability came under Edward Fitzgerald Beale (1822–1903), who was in charge of a survey of a wagon road from Ft. Defiance, N.Mex., to the Colorado River, along the thirty-fifth parallel. A topographical reconnaissance between the Pecos River and the Rio Grande in Texas was made later by Lieutenant Edward L. Hartz.

The camels proved to be remarkably adaptable but were never used extensively. The animals at Camp Verde fell into the hands of the Confederacy when the camp surrendered, February 28, 1861. Most of the animals ended in the possession of private owners after the army disposed of them in 1865. Many roamed the deserts for years, and numerous lurid tales were told about the "red beasts."

See C. Emmett, *Texas Camel Tales* (1932); L. B. Lesley (ed.), *Uncle Sam's Camels* (1929); O. B. Faulk, *U.S. Camel Corps* (1976); D. DeQuille, *New Mexico Historical Review* (Jan., 1949); L. E. Mahoney, "Camel Corps" (M.S. thesis, University of Texas, 1927); E. W. Fornell, *Southwestern Historical Quarterly* (July, 1955); A. H. Greenly, *Papers of Bibliographical Society of America* (1952), XLVI; L. B. Lesley, *Southwestern Historical Quarterly* (July, 1929); W. S. Lewis, *Washington Historical Quarterly* (Oct., 1928); J. W. Palmer, *Harper's* (Oct., 1857); F. B. Lammons, *Southwestern Historical Quarterly* (July, 1957); and F. S. Perrine, *New Mexico Historical Review* (Oct., 1926).

HOLLIS A. MOORE
Bowling Green State University

CAMPBELL, JOHN ARCHIBALD (1811–1889), an Alabamian and an associate justice of the U.S. Supreme Court, enjoyed a paradoxical life and career. A first-rate attorney but a third-rate politician, Campbell, who served on the Roger B. Taney Court between 1853 and 1861, was a conservative with a progressive streak. A precursor of legal positivism, he championed broad state regulation of corporations. Noted for his dissents, Campbell did not significantly influence the votes of his colleagues, but his approach was nonetheless thoughtful and prophetic in using a pragmatic yardstick: modern and progressive in spirit if anachronistic and parochial in object. A defender of slavery, yet he advocated gradual emancipation. A strong sectionalist, he attempted to moderate its force and fury. A tardy secessionist, who yet was the only slave-state justice to resign from the Court, he attempted to prevent, then to end the war. A reluctant rebel, ostracized by fanatical secessionists, he served in the Confederate War Department, where he helped to fumble conscription. Imprisoned, disfranchised, debarred in 1865, Campbell subsequently became a prominent corporation attorney by representing the very interests and employing the very arguments before the Court that he had previously fought while sitting on its bench.

See W. Gillette, in L. Friedman and F. L. Israel (eds.), *Justices of U.S. Supreme Court* (1969).

WILLIAM GILLETTE
Rutgers University

CAMPBELL, WILLIAM (1745–1781), was born in Augusta County, Va. When his father died in 1767, he moved his mother and sisters to the frontier community of Holston (now Abingdon) in Washington County. Campbell was appointed justice of the peace in 1773 and militia captain the following year, when he served in DUNMORE'S WAR. When the Revolution started, he raised a company in southwestern Virginia that joined Patrick Henry's 1st Virginia Regiment. Campbell married Henry's sister Elizabeth, but resigned to return home when he heard about Indian attacks on frontier settlements. He led 400 Washington County men and became a hero at the battle of KINGS MOUNTAIN and at the battle of GUILFORD COURTHOUSE. Believing, however, that his men were unappreciated and upset by the actions of Colonel LIGHT-HORSE HARRY LEE, Campbell resigned. He later joined the marquis de Lafayette's army as a brigadier general. While trying to trap Charles Cornwallis, Campbell suddenly was taken ill and died in Hanover County.

See L. C. Draper, *King's Mountain and Its Heroes* (1929); and J. L. Peyton, *History of Augusta County, Virginia* (1882).

ROBERT F. OAKS
University of Texas, Arlington

CAMPBELL, WILLIAM BOWEN (1807–1867),

was born near Hendersonville, Tenn. Beginning law practice in Carthage in 1829, he moved to Sparta when elected by the legislature as district attorney general November 11, 1831. He returned to Carthage by 1835 and was elected August 8, 1835, to the Tennessee legislature. Captain in the SEMINOLE WARS in 1836, he served as a Whig in Congress (1837–1843) and was the commander of the "Bloody 1st" of Tennessee in the Mexican War. Campbell served as circuit judge (1847–1850) and governor of Tennessee (1851–1853). Unwilling to run for reelection, he moved to Lebanon, Tenn., in 1853 to become president of the Bank of Middle Tennessee. A staunch Unionist in 1860, he supported the John Bell–Edward Everett ticket. He accepted appointment as brigadier general in the Union army; but he soon resigned his commission. He was elected to Congress in 1865 and was a supporter of Andrew Johnson.

See Papers of David R. Campbell, Duke University Library; M. C. Pilcher, *Historical Sketches of Campbell, Pilcher, and Kindred Families* (1911); St. George L. Sioussat (ed.), *Tennessee Historical Magazine* (June, 1915); and J. W. Caldwell, *Sketches of Bench and Bar of Tennessee* (1898).

J. MILTON HENRY
Austin Peay State University

CAMP FORD and CAMP GROCE, Confederate

prisons in the sandhills of east Texas, were the largest west of the Mississippi River; yet in 1863 Camp Ford (near Tyler), which was used for both officers and men, comprised only one guardhouse and a creek. According to one source the prisoners built log cabins, but others claim that the best they were able to provide for themselves were "shebangs" (caves or foxholes protected from the weather by rough boards). In the beginning, with a benign commandant, Colonel R. T. P. Allen, security was lax, partly because in this remote region there was no place for escapees to go. As the complement of prisoners increased in 1864 after the RED RIVER CAMPAIGN, however, an 18-foot-high log fence was built to encompass a ten-acre area, and a pack of bloodhounds buttressed the new security measures in anticipation of the influx of bluecoats. Shelter arrangements remained the same for the 6,000 inmates, however, and the

press of numbers resulted in the spread of disease. Still, reports from prisoners indicate that most conditions here were superior to those in such infamous camps as ANDERSONVILLE. Not much is known about Camp Groce (near Hempstead) except that apparently it consisted only of an open camp encircled by guards.

See R. L. Kerby, *Kirby-Smith's Confederacy* (1972); W. B. Hesseltine, *Civil War Prisons* (1930); E. B. Long, *Civil War Day by Day* (1971); and E. M. Coulter, *Confederate States of America* (1950).

CAMP JACKSON, a state militia encampment,

was in St. Louis, Mo., near Grand and Olive streets. General Daniel M. Frost established it on May 6, 1861, after Governor CLAIBORNE F. JACKSON, a southern sympathizer for whom the camp was named, ordered militia units to assemble throughout the state for six-day drills to counter recent pro-Union activities. On May 10, Captain Nathaniel Lyon commanded a federal force that demanded the 700-man camp's surrender on the grounds that it threatened the United States government. Greatly outnumbered, Frost capitulated without resistance. However, as Union soldiers marched the militiamen from the camp, a crowd protesting the action exchanged shots with the federal troops. Twenty-eight persons died in the clash. Camp Jackson's seizure and the ensuing melee brought the war to Missouri. The incident exacerbated tensions and caused many moderates to adopt more extreme positions.

See T. L. Snead, *Fight for Missouri* (1888); J. Peckham, *Lyon and Missouri* (1866); and W. E. Parrish, *Turbulent Partnership* (1963), and *History of Missouri* (1973), III.

WILLIAM E. FOLEY
Central Missouri State University

CAMP LAWTON, Confederate prison near Mil-

len, Ga., received its first Union prisoners in October, 1864. Originally planned to reduce overcrowding elsewhere, it was actually built to remove prisoners from threatening Union forces. Ironically, the prison was in the path of SHERMAN'S MARCH TO THE SEA and thus was abandoned after two months. Only in design was Lawton similar to ANDERSONVILLE: a stockade pen enclosed by upright logs. Situated in a well-drained pine forest, the square (1,398 feet by 1,329 feet) 42-acre prison was never overcrowded. Its 10,000 prisoners attested to its excellent water, sanitary facilities, and adequacy of food. Fuel was abundant for cooking and heat, and many prisoners built shelters from timbers left over from the stockade construction.

The one event that nearly every prisoner account of Camp Lawton included was their 1864 presidential "election." Prisoner John Ransom wrote: "Had this election occurred while we were at Andersonville, four-fifths would have voted for [George B.] McClellan." But at the much better Millen prison, Abraham Lincoln won easily.

See *John Ransom's Diary* (1963); W. B. Hesseltine, *Civil War Prisons* (1930); J. McElroy, *Andersonville* (1879); *Official Records, Armies*, Ser. 2, Vols. VII, VIII; L. Long, *Twelve Months in Andersonville* (1886); and W. H. Lightcap, *Horrors of Southern Prisons* (1902).

J. DAVID GRIFFIN
West Georgia College

CAMP MEETINGS

CAMP MEETINGS were a socioreligious institution by which thousands of Americans living on the nineteenth-century frontier were converted to Christianity. Begun by METHODISTS, PRESBYTERIANS, BAPTISTS, and Stonites (later DISCIPLES OF CHRIST) in Kentucky and Tennessee about 1800, this phenomenon was a feature of the out-of-door and warm-weather season. Hundreds of rural folk would gather at a clearing designated, and soon designed, for this type of religious service. Typically they were scheduled for a weekend, or a one-week or two-week period. Attendants would arrive by cart or boat, bringing provisions of food and sleeping equipment. Families slept in tents or in the carts and prepared meals, usually on a sharing basis. Preaching, singing, and testifying went on all day and all night, with laymen as free to testify and exhort as clergymen. Common features were a speaker's stand or two, roughhewn benches or stubs, a mourner's bench, and a communion table. At times extreme emotionalism prevailed, with various strange physical motions resulting.

After its beginnings in the frontier South, the camp meeting acquired some popularity in the old Northwest and old Southwest territories. The Methodist denomination both contributed the most to this development and profited greatest by it. Negroes often attended, but were confined to certain areas of the encampment. By the 1840s its popularity had diminished, though sporadic instances are not unknown even today. Under frontier conditions, the camp meeting enabled many people who lived lonely, isolated lives to enjoy a time of fellowship with friends old and new from miles around. It also provided the churches with a device for converting the lost, reclaiming the backsliders, and intensifying piety.

See D. D. Bruce, *They All Sang Hallelujah* (1974); C. A. Johnson, *Frontier Camp Meeting* (1955); and J. B. Finley, *Autobiography* (1853).

SAMUEL S. HILL, JR.
University of Florida

CAMP OGLETHORPE. See MACON PRISON

CANALS

CANALS. The canal age in the United States extended throughout the antebellum period, with some of the first and last of the towpath and barge waterways being constructed in the South. Most building took place after 1815 and before 1850. In all, more than 4,000 miles of canal were constructed, of which over 500 were in southern states. Several factors, including abundant natural waterways in the coastal areas and difficult terrain in both the deep valleyed upland and the marshy lowland, contributed to the relatively low mileage. Nevertheless, a number of important canals were projected and built, thereby improving the existing transportation network.

Functionally, there were two basic types of southern canals: tidewater and connecting. A third type, two major intersectional canals, stretching from the Chesapeake Basin to the Ohio Valley, was attempted by Maryland and Virginia, but neither the Chesapeake & Ohio nor the James River & Kanawha reached its goal. The primary tidewater projects, which reached inland from coastal ports, include the Susquehanna & Tidewater (1840), Santee & Cooper (1800), and Savannah & Ogeechee (1831) canals. Excepting the former, these waterways and countless other similar projects to improve existing river navigation, especially in the Carolinas and Louisiana, were of limited success. Only the connecting canals have had a continuing significance. These include the Chesapeake & Delaware (1829) and the Dismal Swamp (1805; enlarged and reopened, 1829) canals, the latter augmented by the Chesapeake & Albemarle Canal (1860) and both now a part of the increasingly significant Atlantic INTRACOASTAL WATERWAY, as well as the Carondelet Canal (1794) at New Orleans and the enormously valuable Louisville & Portland Canal (1829) around the falls in the Ohio River. Most southern canals were under 16 miles long. Construction costs averaged above $40,000 per mile, ranging downward from the extremely high figure of $161,000 per mile for the short Chesapeake & Delaware Canal and $80,000 per mile for the heavily traveled Susquehanna & Tidewater Canal.

Much early canal construction in America occurred in southern states. The Dismal Swamp,

Santee, and Chesapeake & Delaware canals, as well as the Potomac and James rivers improvements, were all projected in the 1790s, with the two former being completed by 1805. Although extremely small until its enlargement in the 1820s, the Dismal Swamp Canal proved useful in giving northeastern North Carolina access to the Chesapeake, and the Santee Canal connected Charleston, via the Cooper River and then a 22-mile artificial channel, with the Santee River. The Chesapeake & Delaware Canal, an obvious connection that required a cut of less than 14 miles to link the two bays and first surveyed in the 1760s, had an abortive beginning in 1799–1805; but, following refinancing (partly with state and, for the first time anywhere, federal aid) and relocation, it was completed in 1829. Like most waterways in the North and South, unprofitable to its owners but an economic asset overall, it survived into the twentieth century and was taken over (1919) by the federal government and twice enlarged. Now a lock-free ship canal capable of accommodating continuous two-way traffic, it symbolizes the revival of waterway transportation in this century.

Canals were clearly unsuited to many areas of the South; until the triumph of the RAILROADS, southern commerce relied chiefly upon roadways and natural waterways. Given the convenient access to market via the South's many rivers and coastal waters and its feared impact upon tariff policy, the area opposed federal financing of internal improvements. With four major exceptions, all coming in the 1820s, the southern canals were built by private companies usually supported by the state. The mule and towpath canal era quickly passed, and only the strategically located connecting canals, now transformed into barge or ship canals, remain as legacies of the past and as links in the expanding, 26,000-mile inland waterway system of the present.

See G. R. Taylor, *Transportation Revolution* (1951), best general introduction; B. H. Meyer (ed.), *History of Transportation* (1917); A. F. Harlow, *Old Towpaths* (1926), popular but valuable; U. B. Phillips, *Transportation in Eastern Cotton Belt* (1918); C. Goodrich (ed.), *Canals and American Economic Development* (1960); W. F. Dunaway, *James River and Kanawha Company* (1922); W. S. Sanderlin, *Great National Project* (1946), Chesapeake & Ohio Canal; A. C. Brown, *Dismal Swamp Canal* (1967); J. W. Livingood, *Philadelphia-Baltimore Trade Rivalry* (1947), Susquehanna & Tidewater Canal; R. D. Gray, *National Waterway* (1967), Chesapeake & Delaware Canal; U.S. Census Bureau, *Report on Agencies of Transportation* (1883); *Mitchell's Compendium of Internal Improvements* (1835); P. B. Trescott, *Mississippi Valley Historical Review* (March, 1958), Louisville & Port-

land Canal; J. H. Harrison, "Internal Improvement Issue" (Ph.D. dissertation, University of Virginia, 1954); and American Waterway Operators, *Big Load Afloat* (1965), biased but useful, especially map.

RALPH D. GRAY
Indiana University–Purdue University, Indianapolis

CANBY, EDWARD RICHARD SPRIGG (1817–1873), was born at East Bend, Ky., and reared in Crawfordsville, Ind. Upon graduation from West Point (1839), he chased Indians in Florida until 1842. As assistant adjutant general acting as inspector general, Canby in 1854 toured the military installations in the Indian Territory, Arkansas, Louisiana, and Florida.

By the end of 1861, Colonel Canby was in command of the Department of New Mexico, where he helped to repel the Confederate invasion of that territory. Following defeat at Val Verde (February 21, 1862), he combined forces with the Colorado Volunteers, which stemmed in the engagement of Glorieta Pass (March 28, 1862) the advance of H. H. SIBLEY's Texas troops. Recalled to Washington, General Canby served as assistant to the secretary of war and participated in quelling the draft riots in New York City. In May, 1864, he was assigned to command the Military Division of West Mississippi. In this capacity, he sought to prevent troops west of the river from succoring southern forces farther east. He cooperated with Admiral DAVID G. FARRAGUT at Mobile Bay and accepted the surrender in May, 1865, of the last two Confederate armies—those of RICHARD TAYLOR and E. KIRBY-SMITH.

Shortly after congressional Reconstruction was instituted, Canby was placed in charge of the Second Military District (North and South Carolina). The "Great Reconstructor" also commanded the Fifth (Texas) and First (Virginia) districts. While under his supervision, all four states completed congressional requirements for "readmission" to the Union. Canby was vilified by some southern diehards for administering the Reconstruction Acts, but the states while under his jurisdiction fared rather well. Canby was assassinated during a peace conference with the Modoc Indians.

See M. L. Heyman, *Prudent Soldier: Canby* (1959).

MAX L. HEYMAN, JR.
Los Angeles Valley College

CANDLER, ASA GRIGGS (1851–1929), a Georgia druggist, purchased the formula for Coca-Cola in 1887 from Dr. J. S. Pemberton. Although it was previously marketed as a patent medicine, Candler sold it as a nonalcoholic, carbonated soft drink. The popularity of the beverage led him to expand its sales regionally, nationally, and then internationally. Prior to selling the company in 1917, Candler amassed a huge fortune both from the sale of Coca-Cola and from Atlanta real estate holdings. Like many New South entrepreneurs, he was an advocate of child labor and a generous philanthropist. His gift of $1 million to EMORY UNIVERSITY, where his brother Bishop Warren A. Candler was president, was the first of several gifts made to that institution by the Candler family.

See C. H. Candler, *A. G. Candler* (1950), and *A. G. Candler, Coca-Cola and Emory College* (1953); and W. A. Candler Manuscripts, Emory University Library.

CANNON, JAMES, JR. (1864–1944), churchman and temperance reformer, was born in Salisbury, Md., educated at Randolph-Macon College and Princeton Theological Seminary, and in 1888 entered the Virginia Conference, Methodist Episcopal Church, South. Endowed with great ability, prodigious energy, and a combative temperament, Cannon achieved prominence as principal of Blackstone (Va.) Female Institute, editor of the Baltimore and Richmond *Christian Advocate*, superintendent of the Southern Methodist Assembly at Lake Junaluska, and leader of the Virginia and national antisaloon leagues. Elected a bishop in 1918, he supervised missions in Mexico, Brazil, and the Congo, promoted Methodist unification, and actively participated in the Federal Council of Churches.

Cannon led Virginia drys to victory in 1914, was instrumental during the Woodrow Wilson administration in securing national temperance legislation, and in 1928 organized a successful southern revolt against the presidential candidacy of Alfred E. Smith. Beginning in 1929, however, Cannon's enemies charged him with various misdeeds, including stock market gambling, hoarding, misuse of campaign funds, and adultery. After five years of congressional hearings, church investigations, and legal battles, the bishop was officially exonerated. The scandals discredited him, however, and he retired in 1938, after three decades of relentless crusading for prohibition and the church.

See R. L. Watson, Jr., introduction, *Bishop Cannon's Own Story* (1955), the best account. See also V. Dabney, *Dry Messiah* (1949), hostile; J. T. Kirby, *Westmoreland Davis* (1968); R. A. Hohner, *Virginia Magazine of History and Biography* (Jan., 1966; Oct., 1967), and *Journal of Southern History* (Feb., 1968); M. S. Patterson, *Journal of Southern History* (Nov., 1973); and Cannon Papers, Duke University.

ROBERT A. HOHNER
University of Western Ontario

CAPE CANAVERAL, off the east coast of central Florida, is one of the oldest mapped landmarks on the South Atlantic coast. A barrier island and shoal near the mouth of the Indian River, the cape was explored in 1511 by JUAN PONCE DE LEÓN, who named it Cabo de las Corrientes ("cape of the currents") because of the strength of the waters' currents. Spanish explorers and cartographers soon substituted the name Canaveral from the Spanish word *cañavera* for reed grass. While Spain and France contested control of Florida in the 1750s, the French built a fort on the cape, but it was destroyed by a Spanish force commanded by PEDRO MENÉNDEZ DE AVILÉS. Its principal use prior to the twentieth century was as the site of a lighthouse constructed in the 1820s on the advice of Lieutenant Commander M. C. Perry. During World War II the cape was made the site of the U.S. Navy's Banana River Air Station, an installation that later became Patrick Air Force Base. Real development of the cape, however, began in 1948, when, because of a 5,000-mile range of open sea, it was chosen as the site of this nation's long-range missile center. Throughout the 1950s and 1960s, all of this country's missile tests, earth orbits, and space shots took off from this set of launching pads. Originally constructed at a cost of almost $500 million, the Cape Canaveral Missile Center is now an unused facility. Both the missile center and the cape were renamed in 1963 to honor President John F. Kennedy, but Canaveral is once again the official designation of the cape, now largely a tourist attraction.

See J. L. Williams, *Territory of Florida* (1837, 1962); and M. Douglas, *Florida, Long Frontier* (1967).

CAPE FEAR RIVER is formed in the North Carolina Piedmont by the confluence of the Deep and the Haw rivers at a point approximately 25 miles west of Raleigh. Two hundred miles in length, it flows in a generally southeasterly direction over the FALL LINE near Fayetteville and past Wilmington to the Atlantic Ocean.

See M. Ross, *Cape Fear* (1965); J. A. Oates, *Fayetteville and Upper Cape Fear* (1972); and E. L. Lee, *Lower Cape Fear* (1965).

CAPE GIRARDEAU, MO. (pop. 31,282), is on the Mississippi River approximately 100 miles south of St. Louis. The bend in the river was named Cape Girardeau, supposedly after a French ensign named Girardot, who is said to have settled here about 1720. In 1792 Louis Lorimar, a French Canadian who was a Spanish Indian agent, gained title to the land and established a trading post the following year. Located at the confluence of the Ohio and Mississippi rivers, the post and its surrounding community thrived as a river port during the 1840s and 1850s. River traffic ceased during the Civil War, but the city functioned as an important federal communications center. Modern Cape Girardeau is the home of Southeast Missouri State College (1873). Its factories produce shoes, cement products, and lumber.

See G. A. Naeter, *Old Cape Girardeau* (1946); F. E. Snider, *Cape Girardeau* (1956); R. S. Douglass, *History of Southeast Missouri* (1912); C. Hayden, *Sounds and Pictures of Yesterday* (1933, 1971); A. Hinchey, *Stories of Southeast Missouri* (1932); and files of Cape Girardeau *Eagle* (1849–62), *Democrat* (1891–1909), *Republican* (1904–18), and *Southeast Missourian* (1904–), all on microfilm.

CAPES. The term cape is generally applied to a coastal area exhibiting a sharp change in direction, although it may not be a cape in the geologic sense. On the southern coasts several capes have resulted from the combined action of shore processes upon sands in the shallow waters over the continental shelf. Many take the form of barrier islands and serve to protect HARBORS and sounds, but the waters leading into these may be treacherous. The region near Cape Hatteras has been called the "graveyard of the Atlantic." The land of most southern capes is low, windswept, often marshy and unproductive. Navigation in adjacent waters is made more dangerous by the high frequency of storms, especially hurricanes.

Most historically significant southern capes are on the Atlantic. The first landfall of early European explorers and colonists was usually a cape. In the 1580s, SIR WALTER RALEIGH's two unsuccessful efforts at settlement were on ROANOKE ISLAND in PAMLICO SOUND protected by Cape Hatteras. The first permanent English colonists landed at Cape Henry at the entrance to Chesapeake Bay. Finding the land too marshy, they continued upstream to the Jamestown site.

For the reasons that early settlers found the southern capes inhospitable, pirates often preferred them. BLACKBEARD made his headquarters at Bath, protected by Cape Hatteras, and Stede Bonnet ruled Cape Fear in the early 1700s. JEAN LAFFITE made similar use of Louisiana and Texas capes a century later. Storms and shifting sands and currents helped make ships easy prey for pirates. These same areas were also favored by Confederate blockade-runners. The capture of FT. FISHER, guarding Cape Fear, led directly to Robert E. Lee's surrender. After the war the United States continued to fortify key southern capes, recognizing their value in defending against invasion.

Today most southern capes are occupied only by small fishing villages and beach resorts. Noteworthy exceptions are CAPE CANAVERAL and Cape Florida. The latter is the southern end of the sandy barrier protecting Biscayne Bay at Miami.

See D. Stick, *Graveyard of Atlantic* (1952); D. B. Quinn (ed.), *Roanoke Voyages, 1584–1590* (1955); E. E. Lee, *Lower Cape Fear in Colonial Days* (1965); H. F. Rankin, *Golden Age of Piracy* (1969); J. G. Barrett, *Civil War in North Carolina* (1963); R. H. Brown, *Historical Geography of the United States* (1948); and O. P. Starkey and J. L. Robinson, *Anglo-American Realm* (1969).

DUNCAN P. RANDALL
University of North Carolina, Wilmington

CARAWAY, HATTIE OPHELIA WYATT (1878–1950), U.S. senator from Arkansas, was born in Tennessee. She graduated from Dickson Normal College in that state in 1896 and married Thaddeus H. Caraway, a fellow student, in 1902. The couple settled in Jonesboro, Ark., where Thaddeus entered politics. He was elected to the U.S. House in 1912, to the Senate in 1920 and 1926. After his death in 1931, Governor Harvey Parnell appointed Hattie to her husband's seat; and in January, 1932, Mrs. Caraway ran unopposed in the special election held to fill the final year of her husband's unexpired term. She thus became the first woman elected to the Senate and only the second to serve in that body. She soon announced her candidacy for a full six-year term, catching many Arkansas politicians by surprise. Hattie was the underdog, but she swept the Democratic primary and won the general election with the help of HUEY P. LONG, who campaigned for "the little woman." Senator Caraway broke with Long and generally supported Franklin D. Roosevelt and the New Deal. With Roosevelt's support, she won reelection in 1938; however, she was defeated in 1944 by Congressman JAMES WILLIAM FULBRIGHT. After leaving office she was appointed to the Federal Employees Compensation Commission and to the Employees Compensation Appeals Board.

See New York *Times* (Oct. 22, 1950); H. B. Deutsch, *Saturday Evening Post* (Oct. 15, 1932); D. E. Rison, "Arkansas During Great Depression" (Ph.D. dissertation, UCLA, 1974); and T. M. Adams, "Arkansas Congressional Delegation During New Deal" (M.A. thesis, Vanderbilt University, 1962).

DAVID E. RISON
Baptist College at Charleston

CARDOZO, FRANCIS LOUIS (1837–1903), a leading figure in South Carolina during Reconstruction, was born in Charleston, the son of a free Negro mother and a Jewish father. With savings accumulated while a carpenter, he entered Scotland's University of Glasgow in 1858, winning prizes in humanities and Greek. After completing his studies at seminaries in Edinburgh and London, he returned to the United States to pastor Temple Street Congregational Church in New Haven, Conn. In August, 1865, he established and administered a normal school for black youth in Charleston for the American Missionary Association.

While an influential and respected member of the state constitutional convention of 1868, he was chairman of the important committee on education, which outlined the basis for a universal, tax-supported public school system. He was the first secretary of state (1868–1872) under the new Republican regime, and his most significant accomplishment was the uncovering of fraud in the state's purchase and disposal of land. His eloquent defense of Republican policies and tax programs, while president of the state Union League, made him the logical choice for state treasurer in 1872. During his eight-year tenure in that office, he demonstrated a passion for economy in government. His firm stand against graft led to unsuccessful attempts to impeach him during the legislative session of 1874–1875.

After the Democratic victory of 1876, Cardozo was forced out of state politics. The Democratic legislature sought to discredit him and other selected Republicans, but prosecution efforts were dropped and Cardozo was pardoned by the governor. In 1877 he moved to Washington, D.C., where he was employed by the Post Office Department and, from 1884 to 1903, he served as a principal of public schools.

See W. J. Simmons, *Men of Mark* (1887); *American Missionary* (1866), on his educational activities; F. L. Cardozo, *Address Before Union Leagues of South Carolina* (1870), at University of South Carolina Library; E. F.

Sweat, *Journal of Negro History* (Oct., 1961), and *Phylon* (Summer, 1961); and J. Williamson, *After Slavery* (1965).

EDWARD F. SWEAT
Clark College

CARDOZO, JACOB NEWTON (1786–1873), was editor of Charleston's influential *Southern Patriot* (1817–1845), wrote on a variety of topics for literary journals, including the *Southern Review* (which he helped to found in 1828), and made original contributions to economic theory. He was the first American economist to attack Ricardian rent theory, presented an original view of the relationship between profits and wages in an expansionary economy, and devised a theory of business cycles markedly different from the position of England's classical economists. A member of Charleston's Sephardic Jewish community, Cardozo had little formal education, but played an active role in the city's religious, cultural, and political life. He was less narrowly sectional than other Charleston leaders in confronting the protective tariff and took a minority position in advocating manufactures for South Carolina, but he espoused conventional social attitudes, defended slavery, and favored secession while making a grim assessment of its economic costs.

See M. M. Leiman, *Jacob N. Cardozo* (1966), thorough bibliography; J. Dorfman, *Economic Mind in American Civilization* (1946), II; J. N. Cardozo, *Notes on Political Economy* (1826), his sole theoretical book, and *Reminiscences of Charleston* (1866); and A. C. Flora, Jr., "Jacob N. Cardozo" (M.A. thesis, University of South Carolina, 1949).

DONALD B. MARTI
Indiana University, South Bend

CARMACK, EDWARD WARD (1858–1908), rose from poverty to edit such leading dailies as the Memphis *Commercial Appeal* (1892–1896), where he skillfully expounded views similar to those of William Jennings Bryan. Next he became U.S. congressman from Memphis (1897–1901) and U.S. senator (1901–1907). He was a formidable debater and opponent of monopolies and imperialism. Although one of Tennessee's more powerful politicians, he lost the Democratic senatorial primary after one term. Attributing his defeat to liquor interests and machine politics, he assumed leadership of prohibitionists and challenged Governor M. R. PATTERSON in the 1908 Democratic primary. Farmers, church groups, and independents supported Carmack, who called for total abolition of intoxicants, and the cities and party regulars backed the incumbent, who wanted local option.

Defeated, the bitter Carmack used the Nashville *Tennessean* to denounce Patterson and his advisers. Shortly afterward one of these advisers killed Carmack. The editor's martyrdom brought statewide PROHIBITION in 1909.

See P. E. Isaac, *Prohibition* (1965); S. J. Folmsbee *et al.*, *Tennessee* (1969); and W. D. Smith, "Carmack-Patterson Campaign" (M.A. thesis, Vanderbilt University, 1939).

JAMES R. CHUMNEY
Memphis State University

CAROLANA-FLORIDA was a term used to denote a projected colonial scheme on the southern frontier. Dr. Daniel Coxe, an English promoter, secured the transfer of the 1629 Heath patent to himself in the 1690s. He envisioned a huge western empire by establishing a stock venture named the Florida Company. The result of his maneuverings was to cause the French and Spanish to engage in a race with Britain over the Gulf Coast and Mississippi Valley. Spain occupied Pensacola Bay (November, 1698), and PIERRE LE MOYNE, SIEUR D'IBERVILLE entered the Mississippi the following March. Carolana-Florida underlined the value of the American interior and spotlighted the danger of French encirclement of the English seaboard colonies.

See D. Coxe, Jr., *Description of Carolana* (1722); R. K. Turner, Jr., *Studies in Bibliography* (1957); G. D. Scull, *Pennsylvania Magazine of History and Biography* (1883); F. E. Melvin, *Mississippi Valley Historical Review* (Sept., 1914); and V. W. Crane, *Southern Frontier* (1929).

B. PHINIZY SPALDING
University of Georgia

CAROLINA, FUNDAMENTAL CONSTITUTIONS OF. First drafted in 1669 and several times revised, they were intended by the lords proprietors as the "Grand Model" for the government and society of Carolina. Attempts to implement the arrangement were abandoned about 1702, leaving a legacy consisting mainly of several dozen titles of nobility and strong influence upon later patterns of landholding. Traditionally ascribed to John Locke but possibly by Lord Ashley, the constitutions were influenced by James Harrington's writings. Political power was grounded firmly in property. Two-fifths of the land was allotted to nobles (proprietors, landgraves, caciques) and the remainder to commoners (freeholders and manorial lords with their leet men). Each proprietor received control of some aspect of the colony, and ultimate authority was in the Palatine's Court, consisting of all the proprietors. Within Carolina, legislative power was vested in the governor (a proprietor or landgrave), proprietors' deputies, landgraves, caciques, and freemen's deputies. Although the Anglican church was established, any church was recognized if it had at least seven members. Voters had to profess belief in God and hold 50 acres, and officeholders had to be church members and hold 500 acres. The secret ballot was used in voting.

See C. M. Andrews, *Colonial Period* (1937); and M. E. Sirmans, *Colonial South Carolina* (1966).

MAURICE A. CROUSE
Memphis State University

CAROLINAS CAMPAIGN was the sequel of W. T. SHERMAN'S MARCH TO THE SEA. Sherman's army was essentially that which had marched through Georgia—60,000 men formed into two wings, the Army of Georgia and the Army of the Tennessee, commanded by H. W. Slocum and O. O. Howard, plus a cavalry division under J. H. Kilpatrick.

This force departed the Savannah-Beaufort area toward Columbia on February 1, 1865, marching overland to the direct support of U. S. Grant in Virginia. During the march Sherman sought to destroy the will and capability of the Carolinas to support the dying Confederacy by ruining the railroad systems of those states and their ability to provide men and supplies for the Confederate armies. He accomplished this by advancing on a broad front for a distance of over 400 miles first to Columbia and then to Goldsboro via Cheraw and Fayetteville. As in Georgia, he cut loose from his supply base, and the army subsisted by foraging until it reached Goldsboro. There, on March 23, he met J. M. Schofield's Army of the Ohio and the supplies shipped to him there from New Bern.

The Confederate force in South Carolina, including JOSEPH WHEELER'S cavalry, was less than half Sherman's strength. Although commanded by P. G. T. BEAUREGARD, the Confederate forces were scattered and lacked field organization, cohesion, and logistical support, and Beauregard was unable to concentrate them to oppose Sherman's advance. Although Sherman bypassed Charleston, W. J. HARDEE had to evacuate it on February 17, and on the twentieth Columbia fell. Schofield occupied Wilmington on February 22.

Sherman's forces efficiently executed his policy to destroy South Carolina's will and ability to support the war. Their stragglers and foragers (BUMMERS) increased the devastation manyfold by wanton destruction originating from a desire to wreak special vengeance on South Carolina and lawlessness. Retreating Confederates also destroyed property in Sherman's path and often pillaged their own people. The burning of Columbia on February 17 symbolized South Carolina's fate, though the origin of the fire can never be known. Sherman and his commanders did not order the excessive destruction visited on South Carolina but did little to curb it. North Carolina, not so odious in federal eyes, was spared the widespread destruction visited on the Palmetto State.

General J. E. JOHNSTON succeeded Beauregard to the command of the "southern army" on February 25, and North Carolina's forces came under his command on March 6. Like Beauregard he strove to unite his forces against Sherman, but with only 25,000 men he could only hope to attack successfully one of the federal columns. He fought Sherman's left wing at BENTONVILLE on March 19–21, but only delayed it. In fact, Sherman's march was impeded principally by the Carolinas' broad rivers, heavy rains, and bottomless roads, not by the Confederate forces opposing him.

Raleigh fell on April 13. Robert E. Lee's surrender at APPOMATTOX and his own lack of success convinced Johnston that further resistance was hopeless. With President Jefferson Davis' permission he requested an armistice and a discussion of surrender terms. The two generals first met at Bennett House near Durham on April 17. President Andrew Johnson rejected the first terms agreed upon because of their political content and implications. On April 26 General Johnston surrendered his command on the terms accepted by Lee at Appomattox, effectively ending the war in the east.

See W. T. Sherman, *Memoirs* (1957); J. E. Johnston, *Narrative of Military Operations* (1874); J. G. Barrett, *Civil War in North Carolina* (1963), and *Sherman's March* (1956), excellent accounts and bibliographies; *Official Records, Armies*, Ser. 1, Vol. XLVII; and N. C. Hughes, *Hardee* (1965).

HARRY W. PFANZ
National Park Service

CARONDELET, FRANCISCO LUIS HÉCTOR DE (1747–1807),

was born in Cambrai, France, son of a prominent Burgundian family. He served Spain from 1761, participated in the conquest of Pensacola in 1781, was governor of San Salvador (1789–1791) and of Louisiana and West Florida (1791–1797), and died at his next post as president of the Quito audiencia.

As governor of Louisiana he was industrious, intrepid, a strategist of wide views, and an indefatigable writer of numerous reports. He was ignorant, however, of local conditions when he arrived in New Orleans and fell victim to wild rumors. He pleaded constantly for greater royal expenditures to improve the colony's defenses. Many problems confronted him as governor: threatened invasions by the British, French, and Americans; restlessness among the French Creoles, Jacobins, and slaves; lack of interest in Spain to defend Louisiana adequately; and sluggish growth in Louisiana. Nevertheless, Carondelet built a fleet of river galleys, revived the intrigue with Kentucky separatists, made treaties with the Indians, built new forts and strengthened old ones, and carried on trade despite contrary royal regulations. When his efforts to defend Louisiana were undermined by the Treaty of San Lorenzo (1795), he delayed its implementation until the court supported him. Against insurmountable problems, Carondelet worked diligently if not always wisely to preserve Louisiana for Spain.

See A. P. Whitaker, *Spanish American Frontier* (1927); A. P. Nasatir, *Spanish War Vessels* (1968); and E. Beerman, "Baron de Carondelet" (unpublished article).

GILBERT C. DIN
Ft. Lewis College

CARPETBAGGERS

were white northerners who moved to the South after the beginning of the Civil War and sooner or later became active in southern politics as Republicans. During the Reconstruction period, from 1867 to 1877, they held offices of practically every kind. Hundreds served as constitutional convention delegates, legislators, judges, sheriffs, and other state and local officials. A total of at least 45 sat, at one time or another, in the U.S. House of Representatives, and 17 sat in the U.S. Senate. Ten were governors. These ten included several of the most conspicuous and important of the northern Republicans in the postwar South: in Arkansas, POWELL CLAYTON, from Kansas; in Florida, HARRISON REED, from Wisconsin; in South Carolina, DANIEL H. CHAMBERLAIN, from Massachusetts; in Mississippi, ADELBERT AMES, from Maine; and in Louisiana, HENRY C. WARMOTH and WILLIAM P. KELLOGG, both from Illinois. Another outstanding one was ALBION W. TOURGÉE, from Ohio, not a governor but a judge in North Carolina.

Men such as these were deprecated as "carpetbaggers" by their political opponents, including northern as well as southern Democrats and also Liberal Republicans such as Horace Greeley. The derogatory term (which earlier had been applied occasionally to wildcat bankers on the western frontier) was intended to give the impression that the Republicans from the North were rootless and penniless adventurers who had no real stake in the South and brought no more wealth to it than each of them could carry in a carpetbag, a then common kind of valise covered with carpeting material. The term also implied that they were ruthless exploiters who had gone to the South for the purpose of taking advantage of the Negro vote in order to gain power and pelf.

In fact, the so-called carpetbaggers were a diverse lot, and few if any of them completely fit the stereotype. Most were veterans of the Union army who had decided to remain in or return to the South and who had done so before 1867, that is, before the Reconstruction Acts had imposed Negro suffrage and opened state politics to outsiders. Although some served for a time in the postwar occupation army, the Freedmen's Bureau, or other federal agencies, a much larger number were attracted originally by opportunities in agriculture, business, and the professions—opportunities that seemed to make the late Confederacy a new frontier. By no means impecunious, these investors brought savings and borrowings and thus provided capital that the impoverished section desperately needed. Some prospered but many failed. Those who were to be known as carpetbaggers joined, in 1867 and after, with blacks and with some southern whites (the SCALAWAGS) to form the Republican party of the South. Of the three elements of the party, the carpetbaggers were much the fewest, but they exerted an influence out of proportion to their numbers.

See R. N. Current, in D. Pinckney and T. Ropp (eds.), *Festschrift* (1964), and *Three Carpetbag Governors* (1967), for Ames, Reed, Warmoth; D. H. Overy, Jr., *Wisconsin Magazine of History* (Autumn, 1960); O. H. Olsen, *Carpetbagger's Crusade* (1965), on Tourgée; and B. A. Ames, *Adelbert Ames* (1964).

RICHARD N. CURRENT
University of North Carolina, Greensboro

CARRINGTON, EDWARD (1749–1810), was born in Goochland County, Va. During the Revolution, he was commissioned lieutenant colonel of artillery and became quartermaster general under Nathanael Greene. In 1785–1786, he represented Virginia in the CONTINENTAL CONGRESS. A proponent of federalism in 1787–1788, he later became a close political ally of JAMES MADISON and THOMAS JEFFERSON. With them he opposed assumption and the national bank. Shortly thereafter, however, he was successfully wooed by Alexander Hamilton and became one of Virginia's staunchest Federalists. His elitist philosophy, close association with Richmond commercial and banking interests, and appointment in 1791 as federal supervisor of revenue for Virginia, cemented his

Federalist connections. He spoke out against Edmond Genêt and supported Jay's Treaty and John Adams' provisional army. Carrington served as mayor of Richmond for a period and died there.

See D. A. Fisher, *Revolution* (1965); L. A. Rose, *Prologue* (1968); E. G. Swem, *Virginia Historical Index* (1927); and R. Beeman, *Old Dominion* (1972), useful for state context.

JOHN HOWE
University of Minnesota

CARROLL, CHARLES, OF CARROLLTON (1737–1832), last surviving signer of the DECLARATION OF INDEPENDENCE, led the American Revolution in Maryland and held important offices in the CONTINENTAL CONGRESS. In a 1773 newspaper debate with Daniel Dulany (DULANY FAMILY), he established the authority of the assembly over fees and taxes, denying the governor's claims to this power. He was appointed commissioner to Canada (March, 1776) with Benjamin Franklin and SAMUEL CHASE. Returning to Maryland's convention, he made the motion that declared for independence (June 27); was named a Congress delegate to sign the Declaration of Independence; and was appointed to the committee to draft a state constitution. This document called for election to the state senate by an electoral college process. It forbade privation of civil rights because of personal beliefs, from which he as a Catholic benefited. He served in the Maryland senate (1777–1800), in the U.S. Senate (1789–1792), and on the Board of War for the Continental Congress. He failed in his efforts to eliminate the slave trade by constitutional provision and to initiate emancipation by law in the 1780s; he was president of the AMERICAN COLONIZATION SOCIETY.

He was educated in Jesuit colleges in France and studied law in London. A successful planter, he was a merchant, financier, and entrepreneur, the wealthiest in America at the time of the war, later serving as director of the Baltimore & Ohio Railroad in 1828.

See T. O. Hanley, *Charles Carroll of Carrollton* (1970), and *Charles Carroll Papers* (microfilm ed.; 1971); and E. H. Smith, *Charles Carroll of Carrollton* (1942).

THOMAS O'BRIEN HANLEY
Loyola College

CARROLL FAMILY is best known for CHARLES CARROLL OF CARROLLTON (1737–1832), last surviving signer of the Declaration of Independence, and John Carroll (1735–1815), first Catholic bishop of the United States. Of two distinct lines stemming from Ireland, they are more famous than Charles Carroll, the barrister (1723–1783), also a Marylander descended from Ireland but of a remote relationship.

The progenitor of the Carrollton branch was Charles Carroll (1660–1720), attorney general of Maryland in 1688. By his proprietary patronage his son Charles, of Annapolis (1702–1782), a founder of the Baltimore Iron Works, enlarged the fortune, which came to Charles of Carrollton. The first two Carrolls were noted for their public effort to win freedom for Catholics after 1700. John Lee Carroll (1830–1911), of Doughoregan Manor, was the great-grandson of the signer, governor of Maryland (1874–1880), and state senator (1867–1874).

The grandfather of Bishop Carroll, Keane Carroll of Ireland, is said to have been the brother of the attorney general. The bishop's father Daniel, of Upper Marlboro, probably came to Maryland in the 1720s and married into the Darnall family, into which Carrollton's grandfather and he himself married. Similar relationships existed with the Brooke family. Both John and Carrollton began their education together at Jesuit St. Omer in French Flanders, the former joining the order until its suppression, when he returned to America. He soon served with Carrollton on the commission to Canada for the Continental Congress in 1776. In 1783 he drafted and implemented the first constitution for an American church, being elected its bishop in 1790 and appointed archbishop in 1808.

The bishop's brother Daniel (1730–1796), of Rock Creek, was a prosperous planter and prominent in politics. He was a delegate to the Continental Congress (1780–1784), state senator and council member (1777–1780), and representative of Maryland at the Constitutional Convention. He also served in the U.S. House of Representatives (1789–1791) and was commissioner for the District of Columbia (1791–1795).

Charles the barrister's father came from Ireland about 1715 and was known as Charles the physician (?–1755). After legal studies at the Inner Temple, London, the barrister served with distinction on Revolutionary committees, in the conventions, and as a drafter with Carrollton of the state constitution.

See T. O. Hanley, *Charles Carroll of Carrollton* (1970), *American Revolution and Religion* (1974), and *John Carroll Papers* (3 vols.; 1976); M. V. Geiger, *Daniel Carroll* (1943); and W. S. Holt, *Maryland Historical Magazine* (June, 1936).

THOMAS O'BRIEN HANLEY
Loyola College

CARTER, HODDING (1907–1972), was born in Hammond, La. As editor and publisher of the award-winning Greenville, Miss., *Delta Democrat-Times* (1938–1972), he received national recognition as a southern liberal who urged tolerance with moderate and gradual change. His philosophy was based on Christianity and reliance on the power of education, democracy, and human dignity. Prior to 1954 he crusaded for reform within a "separate but equal" framework. He encouraged numerous civic reforms, especially those that fostered socioeconomic growth through diversified farming and southern-based industry. He opposed T. G. BILBO's inflammatory politics and Dixiecrat sectionalism. Although Carter recognized the moral imperative motivating public school desegregation and the campaigns to outlaw the POLL TAX and LYNCHING, he preferred to seek justice through persuasion rather than federal edict. He refused, however, to sanction southern extremism, and his denunciation of Mississippi's White CITIZENS' COUNCIL outraged the state legislature. He considered Greenville an oasis in a changing South. His battle against the LONG MACHINE in his first newspaper, the Hammond *Daily Courier*, precipitated the invitation to establish a challenging newspaper in the Delta. He achieved this goal.

See H. Carter, *Where Main Street Meets River* (1953), biography; Hammond *Daily Courier* (1932–36), in Louisiana State University Library; *Delta Democrat-Times* (1938–), in Mississippi Department of Archives and History and Bell & Howell; and D. C. Kinsella, "Southern Apologists" (Ph.D. dissertation, St. Louis University, 1971).

DOROTHY C. KINSELLA
NETWORK, Washington, D.C.

CARTER, JAMES EARL "JIMMY," JR. (1924–), was born and reared near Plains, Ga. He briefly attended both Georgia Southwestern College (1941–1942) and Georgia Tech (1942–1943) before entering the U.S. Naval Academy, from which he graduated with distinction in 1947. While in the navy, he pursued postgraduate work in nuclear physics at Union College in New York and worked on the nation's nuclear submarine program. He resigned from the navy as a lieutenant commander after his father's death in 1954 and returned to Georgia to manage the family's businesses: a 2,500-acre farm and a peanut warehouse. After two terms in the state senate (1963–1967), Carter waged an unsuccessful "businessman's" campaign for the gubernatorial nomination in 1966. In his second bid for the nomination, he adopted a populistic, "country boy" style of campaigning. He referred to his opponent as "Cuff Links Carl" and to the Democratic party's leadership (most of whom opposed Carter) as "establishment power brokers." He won both the nomination and the election. As governor (1971–1975), he restructured Georgia's numerous administrative agencies, expanded state services in such areas as education and mental health, and—after proclaiming an end to racial discrimination—hung a portrait of MARTIN LUTHER KING, JR., in the Georgia statehouse. Campaigning for the presidency in 1976, he presented himself as a moderate, NEW SOUTH alternative to GEORGE WALLACE. As he had done in his earlier campaign for governor, he openly solicited the support of black voters and denounced as demagogues those who sought to raise race as an issue. In winning both the nomination and the ELECTION OF 1976, Carter became the first resident of a southern state to gain the presidency by election since ZACHARY TAYLOR.

CARTER, SAMUEL POWHATAN (1819–1891), a staunch east Tennessean, graduate of both Princeton and Annapolis (1846), was a naval lieutenant, detached from his service, who returned home in 1861 to organize, train, and command for the Union a brigade of east Tennessee volunteers. From then until 1865, Carter's participation in the war was inexorably linked to this region. He provided weapons to Union sympathizers; led an important cavalry raid into the area coinciding with the battle of STONES RIVER; commanded the XXIII Corps' cavalry division during Ambrose Burnside's east Tennessee campaign (August–October, 1863); and with "the utmost skill and justice" performed the duties of provost marshal general for the region. In 1865 Carter again served in the XXIII Corps, commanding a division and finally the corps itself, as that unit marched north through the Carolinas. Mustered out as a brevet major general, he returned to the navy, retiring as a commodore in 1881.

See *Official Records, Armies*, Ser. 1, Vols. XIX, XX, XXX, XXXI, XLVI, and XLVII.

JOHN A. COPE, JR.
U.S. Military Academy

CARTER FAMILY was one of the most wealthy and powerful families in early Virginia. At least four Carters settled in Virginia around the mid-seventeenth century: Thomas, John, and Edward in Lancaster County along the Corotoman River; and Giles in Henrico County. Descendants of Thomas were men of substance but not of tremendous wealth. Thomas Carter II (1672–1735) engaged in mercantile business and assisted Robert ("King") Carter in increasing his fortune.

John (1620–1669) was the founder of the most important Carter line. He served in the House of Burgesses and the council. John II died young and without issue. The younger son of the elder John, Robert ("King") Carter (1663–1732) of Corotoman amassed immense wealth (over 300,000 acres) and served in various political offices, including treasurer, president of the council, Speaker of the House of Burgesses, and acting governor (1726). He was an agent for Lord Thomas Fairfax's Northern Neck proprietary. His descendants include two signers of the Declaration of Independence, two presidents, two chief justices, a number of Virginia governors, and ROBERT E. LEE. Daughters of King Carter married into the Burwell, NICHOLAS, HARRISON, Braxton, and Fitzhugh families.

King Carter's five sons were: John Carter of Corotoman and Shirley (1690–1742), secretary of state for Virginia; Robert Carter II (1705–1732), who set up residence at Nomini Hall; Charles Carter of Cleve (1707–1764), who served 28 years in the House of Burgesses; Landon Carter (1710–1778) of Sabine Hall, diarist and pamphleteer, who was a strong advocate of constitutional liberties in the era of the Revolution; and George Carter (1709–1741). Charles Carter married into the Walker, Byrd, and Taliaferro families. Landon Carter married (three times) into the Wormeley, BYRD, and Beale families; he had three sons: Robert Wormeley (1734–1797); Landon (?–?); and John (?–1789). Robert Carter III (1728–1804) of Nomini Hall in Westmoreland County was engaged in diverse manufacturing pursuits and also was a merchant and a factor. He manumitted his slaves and became a religious radical, joining the New church. In 1793, partially to escape social ostracism because of his religion and to attend his mercantile interests, he moved to Baltimore, where he lived the rest of his life. John Carter (1737–1782), grandson of King Carter, was one of the first settlers in western Carolina and became a wealthy landowner; his sons Landon and John fought at KINGS MOUNTAIN. Landon was a member of the Tennessee constitutional convention. A prominent member of this Tennessee line of Carters was SAMUEL P. CARTER (1819–1891), a Union major general and rear admiral.

See the number of books and articles (principally in the *Virginia Magazine of History and Biography* and the *William and Mary Quarterly*), which attest to the great influence of Carters. Consult J. L. Miller, *Descendants of Thomas Carter* (1912); C. Dowdey, *Virginia Dynasties* (1969); C. M. Lynn, "Shirley Plantation" (M.A. thesis, University of Delaware, 1967); and M. A. Stephenson, *Carter's Grove Plantation* (1964). A delightful account of life at Nomini Hall, 1773–1774, is H. D. Farish (ed.), *Journal and Letters of P. V. Fithian* (1957). For three leading members of family, see L. B. Wright (ed.), *Letters of Robert Carter, 1720–27* (1940); J. P. Greene (ed.), *Diary of Landon Carter* (2 vols.; 1965); and L. Morton, *Robert Carter of Nomini Hall* (1945). Old but useful is M. D. Conway, *Barons of Potomack and Rappahannock* (1892). Manuscript collections include Robert Carter Letterbooks, University of Virginia; Robert Carter III Papers, Duke University and Library of Congress; Robert Wormeley Carter of Sabine Hall Papers and Carter Papers (various members of the family), College of William and Mary; and Records, Shirley Plantation.

HARRY M. WARD
University of Richmond

CARUTHERS, ROBERT LOONEY (1800–1882), was born in Smith County, Tenn. He attended Greeneville College and studied law with Judge Samuel Powell. Caruthers was licensed to practice law in 1823 and soon settled in Lebanon. Here he served as circuit judge for five years and represented the area in the general assembly for one term. Caruthers' legal career was distinguished by his work with A. O. P. Nicholson in compiling the statutes of the state in 1836. After serving in the U.S. Congress (1841–1843), he was appointed to the Tennessee supreme court in 1853 and served until 1861. Caruthers helped found Cumberland University in 1842 and became president of its first board of trustees. Five years later, in 1847, he helped to create the university's law school. From 1865 onward, Caruthers devoted most of his life to the school, continuing as president of the board of trustees until his death in 1882.

See A. B. Martin, *Robert L. Caruthers* (1883), best; J. W. Caldwell, *Bench and Bar* (1898); J. W. Green, *Supreme Court* (1947); A. D. Marks, *Green Bag* (1893); H. Phillips, *Tennessee Bar Journal* (Aug., 1967); and manuscripts at Tennessee State Library and Archives.

SAM B. SMITH
University of Tennessee, Nashville

CARVER, GEORGE WASHINGTON (1861–1943), was born in slavery on the Ozark Plateau near Diamond Grove, Mo. While yet a small child, he, his mother, and his older sister were kidnaped by night riders. Moses Carver, their owner, hired John Bentley to find the slaves, but Bentley returned with only the frail, sickly baby George. Mrs. Carver cared for George, and after emancipation he remained on the farm with the benevolent Carvers. At age fourteen, he left Diamond Grove to attend school in Neosho, Mo. Later, he went from town to town in search of knowledge. He traded his labor for lessons wherever he could find a school willing to admit him. He was admitted to Simpson College in Indianola, Iowa, and Iowa State in Ames, from which he graduated in 1894. He became assistant botanist and head of the greenhouse at Iowa State, earning his master's degree in agriculture and bacterial botany in 1896.

Carver joined the faculty of TUSKEGEE INSTITUTE in 1896 and remained there until his death, in spite of attractive outside offers. He developed more than 100 different products from the sweet potato and more than 300 different products from the peanut. To reach the distant farmer, he built a demonstration wagon characterized as the movable school, which was to become a worldwide institution. He also pioneered in the development of dehydrated foods. In 1916, he was named a Fellow of the Royal Academy of England. In 1923, he was awarded the distinguished Spingarn Medal by the NAACP. An unusually pious man, Carver donated his discoveries to mankind, without seeking any monetary gains.

See L. Elliott, *George W. Carver* (1966); R. Holt, *G. W. Carver* (1963); A. D. Smith, *G. W. Carver* (1961); and G. W. Carver Manuscripts, Tuskegee Institute.

AL-TONY GILMORE
University of Maryland

CARY REBELLION (1711) is named for Thomas Cary, chief executive of North Carolina from March, 1705, to October, 1707, and from October, 1708, until January, 1711. During his first term Cary allied with the largely Anglican elite in the Albemarle region; in his second term, with religious dissenters and new settlers in Bath County. When Edward Hyde succeeded him as governor early in 1711, Cary withdrew to Bath. However, in March, Hyde called for legislation against dissenters as well as for the arrest of Cary and his political associate John Porter. With a force of 150 men, Hyde marched on Bath County in May, 1711, to seize Cary but was repulsed. Cary then outfitted a brigantine and sailed for Albemarle Sound in mid-June to seize the government. On June 30, he first engaged Hyde's forces and, by July 17, was defeated with the help of Virginia troops. Fleeing with his lieutenants (all Bath County men) into Virginia, Cary was captured and sent to London to stand trial, but no one ever pressed charges. In 1713, he returned to Bath County and lived tranquilly.

See introductions in W. S. Price, Jr. (ed.), *North Carolina Higher-Court Records, 1702–1708* (1974) and *North Car-*

olina Higher-Court Minutes, 1709–1723 (forthcoming). Best primary sources are W. L. Saunders (ed.), *Colonial Records of North Carolina* (1886–90), I; and V. H. Todd (ed.), *Christoph Von Graffenried's Account of New Bern* (1920).

WILLIAM S. PRICE, JR.
North Carolina Division of Archives and History

CASH, WILBUR JOSEPH (1900–1941), wrote only one book, *The Mind of the South* (1941). A prime example of the regional self-scrutiny of the 1930s, it remains, however, the single most compelling analysis of southern consciousness and culture. Cash was born in Gaffney, S.C., and attended college at Wake Forest in North Carolina. From early on, he planned a study of the southern "mind," the basic lineaments of which were set forth in his "The Mind of the South" essay in *American Mercury* (1929). Although the essay betrayed a heavy Menckenian influence, the mature and complete *Mind* was a deeply felt and exquisitely executed nonfiction narrative, matching in stylistic richness and technical virtuosity the best American historical writing and, indeed, the best American fiction.

Cash's central though controversial thesis was that the South had displayed a unity of thought and feeling throughout its history, despite the wrenching changes wrought by the Civil War, Reconstruction, and the emergence of cities and industries. At the core of southern consciousness Cash saw a tendency toward romanticism and unreality, violence and rhetorical excess, and an individualism that was hostile to institutional restraints. Behind these characteristics lay the influence of the frontier, the lack of urban sophistication, the harsh ambivalences of Protestantism, and the presence of the Negro. Lacking an analytical capability, the masses jumped to the tune of the classes when the region was threatened from without or within or by suspect ideas.

Cash did not deal with the mind of the black southerner, and he underplayed diversity and conflict within the southern mind and politics. But he was no champion of this "savage ideal." He rued the South's tendency to revert to its habitual patterns of thought and action in emergencies. He was guardedly optimistic about the emergence of a labor movement and a critical intelligentsia in the 1920s and 1930s, but ended his book on a rather pessimistic note. Despite his fears, *Mind* was generally well received. Just after publication Cash and his new bride set out for a year in Mexico financed by a Guggenheim grant to write a novel. Once in Mexico City, Cash experienced difficulties in writing. He became ill, began hearing

threatening voices, and on July 1 hanged himself with his own necktie.

See J. L. Morrison's *W. J. Cash* (1967), which includes some of Cash's essays and newspaper articles; for a critique of Cash, see C. V. Woodward, *American Counterpoint* (1971); for a defense, see R. H. King, *New South* (Winter, 1972).

RICHARD H. KING
Federal City College

CASH-SHANNON DUEL (July 5, 1880), in which Colonel Ellerbe B. C. Cash shot and killed Colonel William M. Shannon in Darlington County, S.C., was probably the last fatal duel fought in the South (DUELING). The duel resulted from Cash's belief that Shannon, an attorney, had accused Mrs. Cash of fraud. At first accepting Shannon's denial, Cash became convinced that the alleged aspersions upon her character had contributed to his wife's death in April, 1880. Goaded by Cash and his son Boggan, who circulated some insulting "Camden Soliloquies," Shannon on June 11 wrote to Cash, holding him responsible for the vilification. A series of letters led to the July 5 encounter. Before a crowd of approximately 100 persons, Shannon fired first, but missed. Cash then shot Shannon through the heart. Arrested and tried for murder and dueling, Cash was acquitted in June, 1881, after an earlier trial resulted in a hung jury. Even before he came to trial, an aroused public opinion, led by the Charleston *News and Courier*'s FRANCIS W. DAWSON, had caused the legislature to strengthen the state's antidueling statutes. Furthermore, negative reaction to this affair contributed significantly to the growing unpopularity of dueling in South Carolina and in the South generally.

See H. H. Mullen, *Cash-Shannon Duel* (1963); E. B. C. Cash, *Cash-Shannon Duel* (1881); and H. T. Kane, *Gentlemen, Swords and Pistols* (1951).

JERRY L. BUTCHER
Shippensburg State College

CASKET GIRLS (1721; 1727–1728), young French women sent by John Law's Company of the Indies (MISSISSIPPI BUBBLE) to marry New Orleans settlers, were so called because of the small trunk of clothing provided each woman by the company. They are distinguished from the "correction girls," who were culled from prisons and hospitals and sent to Louisiana periodically after 1704 and in large numbers in 1719–1720. The 1721 casket girls were orphans from the Salpêtrière. Louisiana historians occasionally claim that a second group of poor but thoroughly respectable women was sent in 1727–1728.

See W. H. Blumenthal, *Brides from Bridewell* (1962); J. D. Hardy, Jr., *Louisiana History* (Summer, 1966), best on deportations; M. Giraud, *Histoire de la Louisiane Française* (1953–74), best to 1723; C. E. O'Neill, *Church and State in French Colonial Louisiana* (1966), best bibliography; and unexplored primary materials in Louisiana State Museum and Louisiana Historical Society.

JULIA ANNE SZABO MEARS
University of Iowa

CASTLE MORGAN. See CAHABA PRISON

CASTLE THUNDER, a Confederate prison in Richmond, Va., became known as the South's major political prison. It is doubtful, however, that political prisoners, which included a few women, constituted a majority of its inmates. Other types were Confederate and Union deserters, hardened criminal elements from the Confederate army, civilians and soldiers accused of crimes ranging from counterfeiting to murder, lesser civil and military offenders, and captured blacks. Established in August, 1862, Castle Thunder occupied the three-story Greanor tobacco factory on Cary Street. Eventually two more buildings and a hospital section composed the prison complex. Usually no more than 700 prisoners were housed there, since turnover was rapid and continuous. A Confederate congressional investigating committee refuted charges of cruelty levied against the prison commander in 1863. But hearings revealed that severe restraints were sometimes used to discipline the toughest of the prisoners, often called the dregs of the Confederacy. Confederate military needs in mid-1864 resulted in recruitment of four infantry companies from inmate ranks. Castle Thunder was evacuated April 2, 1865. Robert E. Lee's surrender ended the flight of its prisoners and guards to points farther south.

See *Official Records, Armies*, Ser. 2, Vols. IV–VIII; W. M. Robinson, *Justice in Grey* (1941); and E. M. Thomas, *Confederate State of Richmond* (1971).

HUBERT H. WUBBEN
Oregon State University

CASWELL, RICHARD (1726–1788), North Carolina planter, statesman, and soldier, was born in Maryland, but moved to North Carolina at seventeen. He was elected a member of the assembly from Johnston County in 1754. A spokesman for that body against Governor Arthur Dobbs, he also rose to eminence as an officer of the militia, serving against REGULATORS at ALAMANCE in 1771. He was delegate from the province at the First and Second CONTINENTAL CONGRESS, took part in provincial congresses, and commanded patriots in the defeat of Loyalists at MOORE'S CREEK BRIDGE. As governor (1777–1780) he met the threats of Indians, Loyalist insurrections, and British raids. His reputation was tarnished when militiamen under his command were routed at the battle of CAMDEN (1780), but he returned to prominence as Speaker of the state senate in 1782 and as elected governor in 1784. Ill, he declined to serve as delegate to the Constitutional Convention in 1787.

See personal papers in North Carolina State Archives; and C. B. Alexander, *North Carolina Historical Review* (Jan., April, July, 1946).

KENNETH B. WEST
University of Michigan, Flint

CATAWBA INDIANS, the most important of several Indian groups categorized as eastern Siouans, are one of the few eastern Indian people to have survived through the twentieth century on their ancient tribal lands near Rock Hill, S.C. Because of the constant trafficking in Indian slaves, intertribal wars, devastating smallpox epidemics (1738 and 1759), and land grabbing by the Europeans, few full-blooded Catawba survived the nineteenth century. By 1750 the Catawba were little more than a confederacy of several small Indian nations that lived along the river valleys of the eastern Carolinas. The Catawba became a valuable ally of South Carolina and an important cog in the Indian trade system of the Carolinas and Virginia because of their location in the South Carolina Piedmont. Except for the Yamassee War (1715–1716), they served the South Carolinians faithfully in several Indian wars and emerged as a "colonial satellite." They survived the federal removal efforts and the efforts of South Carolina to extinguish their landholdings. They came under control of the Bureau of Indian Affairs in 1943, but in 1959 the Catawba voted to terminate their ties with the federal government.

See D. S. Brown, *Catawba Indians* (1966); C. M. Hudson, *Catawba Nation* (1970); C. J. Milling, *Red Carolinians* (1940); and J. Mooney, *Siouan Tribes* (1895).

JAMES P. PATE
Livingston University

CATESBY, MARK (1679?–1749), a natural historian, was probably born in London, England, and died there. His third visit to the American colonies (1722–1726) resulted in the elaborate two-volumed *Natural History of Carolina, Florida,* *and the Bahama Islands* (1729, 1747). This popular discussion of the plants and animals he saw included the first detailed description of American mammals of the Southeast. The many illustrations, though somewhat flat and uninspired, made sufficiently clear the structure of the species depicted. This work (recently reprinted) represented the peak of development of natural history in prerevolutionary America.

See G. F. Frick and R. P. Stearns, *Mark Catesby* (1961), only modern study; and E. Allen, *Transactions of American Philosophical Society* (Oct., 1951).

KEIR B. STERLING
Pace University

CAT HAULING, a rare and unusual type of punishment inflicted upon Negro slaves in the Old South, was extremely painful and inhumane. The slave was forced to lie on the ground; his arms and legs were then tied with rope, which was secured to stakes driven into the ground. The person inflicting the punishment then held a large tomcat by his tail, forcing the cat to crawl backwards along the bare back of the slave. The cat, clawing and scratching as he struggled down the slave's back, gouged and lacerated the skin of the slave, causing much bleeding and suffering for the victim.

See A. Singleton, *Letters from South and West* (1824); and N. R. Yetman (ed.), *Life Under the "Peculiar Institution"* (1970).

JULIA F. SMITH
Georgia Southern College

CATHOLIC CHURCH in the United States began in the South, where it was established by Spanish secular clergy at St. Augustine, Fla., in 1565. Franciscan missionaries entered the region soon afterward to introduce Christianity among the aboriginal inhabitants of Florida, Georgia, and South Carolina. Similar Spanish missionary work was undertaken later in the borderlands of Texas, and the French regular clergy, notably Jesuits, first introduced this religion to the Mississippi Valley in the seventeenth and eighteenth centuries. Although Catholics in the English colonies along the Atlantic seaboard were never numerous, they were disenfranchised and otherwise penalized because of their alleged foreign ties to the bishop of Rome (pope). Yet Catholics wholeheartedly supported the patriot cause after 1776.

The first native bishop, John Carroll (CARROLL FAMILY) was consecrated for the premier American diocese, Baltimore, in 1790. Emigration, principally from Ireland and Germany, rapidly increased membership rolls in the new century, and by 1860 Catholics formed the country's largest single religious denomination. That commanding position could not be discerned in the South, however, where, with the exception of Louisiana, Catholics were distinctly in the minority, heavily outnumbered by BAPTISTS, METHODISTS, and other Protestants. The first southern dioceses apart from Baltimore were New Orleans and the Floridas (1793), established by Spain under the *patronato real*; Bardstown (1808), removed later to Louisville; Charleston and Richmond (1820); Mobile (1829); Nashville and Natchez (1837); Little Rock (1843); and Savannah (1850). By 1870 the Catholic population in the eleven former Confederate states was only 438,700 out of a national total of 4,504,000.

Catholics in both the North and South generally took no stand on slavery; those opposed to the institution were mindful that abolitionist leaders were in many instances also anti-Catholic. With the outbreak of the Civil War, Catholics chose sides according to their sections, and thousands fought in the conflict. Of the most prominent southern churchmen in this denomination, three served in the antebellum and war periods. Bishop JOHN ENGLAND, of Charleston, founded the first American Catholic weekly newspaper, the *United States Catholic Miscellany*. Bishop Patrick N. Lynch (1817–1882), of Savannah, was commissioned by the Confederacy in 1864 to represent the southern cause before Pope Pius IX in Rome. Bishop AUGUSTE VEROT, of Savannah, later of St. Augustine, earned the sobriquet "Rebel Bishop" for his outspoken defense of the Confederacy.

Between 1870 and 1900 the Catholic population increased nationally to 12 million. Irish and Germans continued to predominate among Catholic immigrants. Often Irish laborers who came south to work on the railroads lost their identfication with the Catholic religion, in great part because of the lack of priests, and many of those who stayed joined Protestant churches in their new locales. Most immigrants settled in the large industrial centers of the East and Middle West, giving U.S. Catholicism a pronounced urban character, which it has retained.

In the South, Catholics continued to be found widely scattered in rural areas as well as cities. Louisiana would account for about 50 percent of the southern Catholic population until 1960, when new concentrations at Louisville, Richmond, Miami, and other urban centers produced a slightly wider distribution. On the whole Catholicism has existed on the margins of southern culture in

Maryland, Florida, Louisiana, and parts of Texas. No doubt, however, Catholics have become accepted and respected members of southern society. Underground suspicion of Catholicism still runs deep in some sections. But overt prejudice, as exemplified by the post–World War I KU KLUX KLAN, has been discredited, and the election of Catholic John F. Kennedy to the presidency in 1960 suggests that the nativist movement is no longer a significant force in either southern or national affairs.

See M. V. Gannon, *Rebel Bishop* (1964), and *Cross in Sand* (1965); J. H. Schauinger, *Cathedrals in Wilderness* (1952); P. Guilday, *John England* (1927); R. Baudier, *Church in Louisiana* (1939); and J. T. Ellis, *Cardinal Gibbons* (1952).

MICHAEL V. GANNON
University of Florida

CATTLE INDUSTRY. The southern cattle industry might be dated from the earliest English settlement in Virginia. Although cattle were brought on the first ships to Jamestown, the first permanent establishment was after the second shipment in 1611. Black Spanish cattle were taken into Florida and Texas and provided much of the sources for the romantic eras of the cattle industry. By the 1630s settlers had formed a large range in the lower James River area, and numbers were sufficiently great that the Virginians were selling live cattle to New England. By 1647 it was estimated that Virginia had some 20,000 head.

The cattle industry became a frontier or border county occupation as the raisers tended to settle between the hunters and the cultivators. As settlers from Pennsylvania and Virginia moved into the western region of the Carolinas, they found large herds of wild, black Spanish cattle. Although colonial leaders "wanted planters not graziers," South Carolina became the great cow country of the American colonies. In the early 1700s the settlers rounded up herds of wild cattle and branded or marked them much as ranchers on the western plains did in the nineteenth century. Quickly "cow pens"—reminiscent of the cow towns of the plains—developed as gathering and holding places. On a regular basis cattle were driven to such coastal population centers as Charleston, Norfolk, Baltimore, and Philadelphia. They met the same kind of agrarian opposition, even legislative action, as the cattle drives of the western plains.

Relatively mild winters and lack of feed encouraged southerners to let their cattle fend for themselves. Without care or breed improvement, southern cattle were notorious for their poor quality. Before the Revolution, Virginia cattle were worth less than half those of the northern colonies. Shortly before the Civil War, travelers in the South described the cattle as "objects of pity"; in Mississippi "their ribs and hip bones were about as prominent as their horns, and so run down in flesh that a hydraulic press would not be able to extract either milk or fat from them." With the spread of the cotton kingdom, the livestock industry declined in the Deep South, but border states such as Kentucky and Tennessee continued to produce and trail cattle to New Orleans. Kentucky joined northern states in importing blooded stock from England as shorthorns were brought in 1817 and Henry Clay imported some Herefords. Although North and South were about equal in cattle numbers at the time of the Civil War, seven cotton states suffered an actual decline in the 1850s, with only Texas and Arkansas expanding.

The last half of the nineteenth century was the glamour era of cattle raising on the open range, the cowboy and the cattle drive all reminiscent of the colonial era for the South. Texas with its millions of longhorns played a prominent role in that period. The rest of the South had virtually no part in the open-range period or in the development of the modern beef industry with its fenced ranges, its emphasis upon blooded cattle, and its feeder lots to finish the calves for market.

The South remained an area of poor-quality livestock existing on poor pasturage and receiving little care through the first third of the twentieth century. As late as the great federal drought purchase program of 1934, it was hoped that some of the better-quality cattle purchased in the West could be distributed in the South. Although this was not done, the 1930s were a turning point for the South. Texas had always been a major cattle area, but now the old cotton South and Florida became a new center for the industry. The control of Texas tick fever and other diseases facilitated southern expansion, as did the federal programs limiting cotton acreage. Millions of acres of improved pasture were planted, providing winter grazing for the first time. As a result the South expanded its cattle industry more rapidly than the rest of the nation. The gains were both in quantity and quality with an emphasis on blooded cattle. In the last 25 years there has been much experimentation with new and exotic breeds to find cattle able to flourish under the southern conditions. Such breeds as Simmental, Limousin, Chianina, Charolais, and others have been used. The Brahman has had a longer and greater influence. It has played a particularly important role in the increas-

NONDAIRY CATTLE IN THE SOUTH, 1850-1969
(thousands of heads)

	1850	1860	1870	1880	1890	1900	1910	1920	1930	1940	1950	1959	1969	% of U.S. total
Ala.	500	543	316	480	584	547	578	693	467	523	1,124	1,319	1,671	1.7
Ark.	199	397	229	458	662	606	631	693	473	526	1,036	1,077	1,454	1.5
Del.	34	36	26	26	19	22	20	8	24	15	56	26	15	.015
Fla.	188	295	329	425	370	681	747	584	356	617	1,080	1,320	1,801	1.87
Ga.	763	706	466	595	586	640	701	799	481	466	888	1,158	1,593	1.6
Ky.	505	567	451	542	702	732	618	667	612	583	1,486	1,481	2,286	2.3
La.	470	387	234	324	414	502	557	669	506	722	1,205	1,450	1,279	1.3
Md.	143	154	120	139	125	149	125	125	154	114	409	278	324	.3
Miss.	519	523	327	449	607	595	623	861	590	617	1,415	1,671	1,782	1.85
Mo.	561	824	755	1,420	2,209	2,248	1,727	2,161	1,963	1,571	3,101	3,220	4,507	4.7
N. C.	471	466	324	425	408	399	401	371	267	207	544	590	715	.75
S. C.	585	343	151	224	161	222	215	261	135	115	302	397	459	.48
Tenn.	500	515	401	479	620	611	618	774	645	559	1,396	1,286	1,969	2
Tex.	112	2,934	3,066	3,479	5,198	8,671	6,023	5,419	5,526	4,932	7,601	8,010	12,153	12.76
Va.	759	714	323	441	474	552	512	564	498	429	1,094	1,008	1,232	1.29
W. Va.	incl. in Va.		187	302	377	438	388	419	373	308	529	394	405	.4

ingly valuable crossbreeding and developing of new breeds such as the Santa Gertrudis.

The newly active southern cattle industry emphasized production for the feedlots of Texas and the Midwest until the end of the sixties. By 1975 the South held almost half the over 50 million beef cows in the country and appeared as "the most promising beef-producing area of the nation."

See J. W. Thompson, *History of Livestock Raising in U.S., 1607-1860* (1942); P. C. Henlein, *Cattle Kingdom in Ohio Valley, 1783-1860* (1959); E. E. Dale, *Range Cattle Industry* (1929); D. W. Williams, *Beef Cattle Production in South* (1955); and W. A. Emerson, *Collier's* (April 5, 1952).

C. ROGER LAMBERT
Arkansas State University

CATTON, BRUCE (1899–1978), journalist and Pulitzer Prize historian, was distinguished for the high degree of literary skill, the careful research, and the gift for synthesis that he brought to the writing of Civil War history. Born in Michigan, he entered Oberlin College in 1916, which he left to enlist in the navy during World War I. Between wars, he served as newspaper correspondent and editor; and, during World War II, he acted as director of information for the War Production Board, an experience that provided background for his book *The War Lords of Washington* (1948). Since the war, turning avocation to vocation, Catton chiefly wrote Civil War history. So searching was his trilogy, *Mr. Lincoln's Army* (1951), *Glory Road* (1952), and *A Stillness at Appomattox* (1953), the last of which won for him both the Pulitzer Prize and the National Book Award, that David Donald

wrote, "There is very little left that is fresh or important to say about the everyday life of the Northern soldier." Catton viewed the Civil War as positive in achievement, a widening of the area of freedom. The result, moreover, he attributed not alone to a few military leaders but to the efforts of countless individual soldiers. In more than a dozen books since, he continued to write superb military history, most notably in his studies of Ulysses S. Grant and his three-volumed *Centennial History of the Civil War* (1961–1965).

DONALD R. RAICHLE
Kean College of New Jersey

CATTS, SIDNEY JOHNSTON (1863–1936), born into a Dallas County, Ala., plantation family, attended Auburn, Howard College, and Cumberland Law School. Following a brief legal career, he experienced a dramatic conversion and entered the Baptist ministry. His uncontrollable temper kept his churches in turmoil, and he resigned from the ministry in 1911 over a salary dispute. After working as an insurance salesman, he entered the Florida gubernatorial primary race in 1916, attaching his candidacy to the emotional issue of anti-Catholicism. Democratic party officials appealed his narrow victory to the state supreme court, which overturned it in favor of the runner-up. Catts then bolted the party, received the Prohibitionist party's nomination, and easily defeated the Democratic nominee in the November elections.

As governor of Florida, Catts soft-pedaled demagogic religious issues, concentrating instead on a broad reform program. He advocated PROHIBITION, reforms in labor conditions and penology, equitable taxation, and woman suffrage. A conservative legislature defeated many of these and conducted constant warfare with the maverick chief executive. Catts sought to create his own political organization within the Democratic party, but his temperament made him incapable of working effectively with allies. Despite formal charges of bribery and PEONAGE by party regulars, he was acquitted and narrowly lost gubernatorial races in 1924 and 1928. His last years were cynical and embittered. He drank, advocated legalized gambling, and lost the populistic, evangelical constituency that brought his early triumphs.

See J. W. Flynt, *Cracker Messiah* (1977); J. R. Deal, "Sidney J. Catts" (M.A. thesis, University of Florida, 1949); and Catts Sermons Notebook, Samford University.

WAYNE FLYNT
Samford University

CAVES in the South comprise more than three-fourths of all caverns in the United States. Most occur in the Appalachian regions and the interior plateaus. States with the greatest numbers are Kentucky, Tennessee, Missouri, and Virginia, each having 1,000 to 2,000 discovered caves.

Underground voids are most often found in limestone terranes, where they are associated with solution-controlled landscape features termed karst. Limestone (calcium carbonate) is readily dissolved in acidic groundwater moving through interstices toward lower levels. Network patterning in certain caves reflects the influence of earlier hydrogeologic environments. Subsequent erosion may result in conventional caves of horizontal development as well as pits and domes along vertical vectors. Precipitated minerals from dripping water form speleothems such as stalactites, stalagmites, helictites, and travertines.

Limestone in the South occurs at or near the surface in Tertiary sediments of the coastal plains and Paleozoic rocks of the Appalachian Ridge and Valley, Appalachian Plateaus, interior low plateaus, Ozark Plateau, and Edwards Plateau. The largest and greatest number of caves are in the inland "cave country" regions of thick-bedded, essentially flat-lying limestone. At least 130 southern caves have been measured as having more than 3,000 feet of passageways and thus are termed "long caves." Mammoth Cave–Flint Ridge system in Kentucky is the longest in the world (144 miles).

Bones and artifacts are excavated for study by paleontologists and anthropologists from cave sites where surface material has collected in catchment pockets, perhaps washed in through sinkholes. Imbedded fossils are available to historical geologists in residual rock walls; they are conveniently accessible because of the cavern's existence. Unusually good preservation of cave fauna is afforded by stable microclimate where constantly cool temperature approximates the annual mean of the local surface environs (40 to 60 degrees Fahrenheit in the South). Relative humidity is usually near 100 percent.

A significant economic use for over 300 southern caves has been the past mining of saltpeter for gunpowder needed from the time of the Revolutionary War through the Civil War. Niter (sodium nitrate) is found as guano from bats that have inhabited some southern caves in huge numbers for many thousands of years. Onyx (ornamental quartz) is mined principally from Missouri caves but may be found in other states of the plateaus.

In addition, southern caves have been used for shelter by Indians, hunters, pioneers, and soldiers; for clandestine operations by counterfeiters and robbers; for water supply and sewage disposal; for food and drink production; for medical experimentation; for partying and tourism; for behavioral research on cyclic rhythms; for bat study; and even for protection from bombs and fallout. Speleologists and amateur spelunkers continue the search of the subterranean with keen interest and intellectual curiosity.

See National Speleological Society publications (1940–); M. Herak and V. T. Stringfield, *Important Karst Regions of the Northern Hemisphere* (1972), chapter by W. E. Davies and H. LeGrand is excellent; H. N. Sloane and R. H. Gurnee, *Visiting American Caves* (1966); C. E. Mohr and H. N. Sloane (eds.), *Celebrated American Caves* (1955); and F. Folsom, *Exploring American Caves* (1956).

ELIZABETH F. ABBOTT
University of Florida

CEDAR CREEK, BATTLE OF (October 19, 1864), also called the battle of Belle Grove, was the last major clash between federal and Confederate forces in the Shenandoah. The valley had been so devastated by Philip Sheridan that JUBAL A. EARLY was compelled to retreat or attack. Although outnumbered more than two to one, Early with about 15,000 Confederates advanced at night on Sheridan's left flank. His surprise attack in early morning fog sent the VIII and XIX Corps reeling to the rear, but he failed to rout the VI Corps from its withdrawn position near Middletown, Va. Early's infantry—unassisted by cavalry, somewhat disorganized through lack of officers, and exhausted from the overnight march—was unable to clinch its initial success. Meanwhile, Sheridan, at Winchester, Va., rushed to the front, rallied his shaken and scattered troops, and directed a late afternoon counterattack that swept the Confederates from the field. Although he took 25 enemy guns and considerable matériel, his reported losses were much heavier than Early's: 5,665 compared with 2,910.

See *Official Records, Armies*, Ser. 1, Vol. XLIII; P. H. Sheridan, *Memoirs* (1891), II; J. B. Early, *Autobiographical Sketch* (1912, 1960); J. B. Gordon, *Reminiscences* (1904), at odds with Early; D. S. Freeman, *Lee's Lieutenants* (1944), III; B. Catton, *Stillness at Appomattox* (1953); E. J. Stackpole, *Sheridan in Shenandoah* (1961); and R. S. Naroll, "Cedar Creek," in *Military Analysis of Civil War* (1977), critical of Sheridan.

JOHN M. HOFFMANN
Southern Illinois University

CENTENARY COLLEGE OF LOUISIANA (Shreveport, 71104) was founded in 1839 at Clinton, La., in honor of the centennial of Methodism. In 1844, however, the state gave up to Centenary its College of Louisiana (1825) at Jackson, making Centenary the oldest liberal arts college west of the Mississippi River. After Jackson had been bypassed by major railroad connections, the Atkins family of Shreveport offered land in that city, and the college moved to its present campus in 1908. The Methodist, coeducational college has fewer than 800 students; its library houses the minutes of the annual Louisiana Conference of the Methodist Church, South (1847–1950).

See W. H. Nelson, *A Burning Torch* (1931).

CENTRAL THEME. In the study of southern history the central theme has been the quest for the central theme. A past that included a separation from and a war for independence from the United States, the persistence of slavery well into the nineteenth century and legal racial segregation far into the twentieth, along with peculiar folkways and a pronounced individualism, demanded explanations. Why there should have developed a South with a patriotic allegiance of its own has been the subject of the search for a central theme or determining factor, characteristic, or seminal event.

The effort to express the essence of the South in a central theme has taken one of two related streams of thought. One has been to emphasize the effects of environment; the other, the presence of certain acquired characteristics (the inheritance theory) that have determined southern actions and life-style.

The environmental view is much the older. In 1787 William Henry Drayton of South Carolina expressed it: "From the nature of the climate, soil, and produce of the several states, a northern and a southern interest naturally and unavoidably arise." Thus, according to the environmental theory, climate and rainfall produced staple crops in great demand; these in turn required the plantation and slavery for their efficient cultivation; and these institutions provided the basis for a social elite, which then went to war to preserve its property and rank. The cruel sun, in that view, was also to blame for regional oddities such as an exotic diet, rural values, the blood feud, architectural preferences, laziness, and lassitude in speech (DIALECTS) and movement. ULRICH B. PHILLIPS described the climatological theory as a "house that Jack built"— climate determined activity, activity determined the nature of society and the status of the labor force, society determined political platforms, and the labor force created a racial outlook. Clarence Cason defined the South as a hot land whose people lived under the dictates of the tyrant sun. Other environmentalists have argued that the industrial revolution, with its hunger for raw cotton to turn into textiles, inevitably called the South into being. H. J. ECKENRODE and F. B. SIMKINS have defined the South as the result of an adjustment of Anglo-Saxon peoples to a warm subtropical climate.

On the other hand the inheritance theory expressed southern distinctives as results of acquired characteristics all but universally present in the South and all but universally absent in other sections. The list of suggested traits is a long one. Southern apologists have held their people to be superior and have praised the courage, honor, and independence of descendants of English cavaliers, "tropicized Nordics." CHARLES S. SYDNOR cataloged the distinctively southern culture patterns as a way of life modeled after English gentry and including SLAVERY, MALARIA, HOOKWORM, LYNCHING, TENANT FARMING, STATES' RIGHTS, and mockingbirds. Other seekers after inherited behavior patterns have gone farther: some to define the South as a land of one-party politics, one-horse plowing, and one-crop agriculture; some to declare it the land of white racial supremacy. "The cardinal test of a Southerner and the central theme of Southern history," said U. B. Phillips, was the universal resolve that the region should remain a "white man's country." In addition, the South has been defined in one or more of the following terms: the persistence of ancient folkways; militancy and hot tempers; BIBLE BELT fundamentalism; an overromantic world view; laziness; psychological guilt feelings created by MISCEGENATION; even a preference for mules over horses as draft animals.

Another line of argument holds that the South

is the product of its history and came into being only in response to outside attacks. Abolitionists caused a unity of interests among white southerners that cemented a disparate people into a sense of oneness. A corollary to that thesis was that the South was created by a conscious effort at unity directed by those who had something to lose in a rapidly changing nation. Still other students have decided that there can be no central theme because there has never been a unified South, and they argue that southerners and their past are integral parts of the national story. As DAVID POTTER declared, the entity known as the South is an enigma challenging comprehension, "a kind of Sphinx on the American land." And J. G. RANDALL noted the difficulties in summing up many people and events in a single sentence: "Poets," he said, "have done better in expressing this oneness of the South than historians in explaining it."

See D. L. Smiley, *South Atlantic Quarterly* (Summer, 1972), brief discussion of central themes; U. B. Phillips, *Life and Labor* (1929), and *American Historical Review* (Oct., 1928); F. B. Simkins, *Journal of Southern History* (Aug., 1947); C. S. Sydnor, *Journal of Southern History* (Nov., 1945); T. P. Govan, *Journal of Southern History* (Nov., 1955); and D. M. Potter, *Yale Review* (Autumn, 1961).

DAVID LESLIE SMILEY
Wake Forest University

CENTRE COLLEGE OF KENTUCKY (Danville, 40422).

After the Presbyterian church withdrew its support in 1818 from TRANSYLVANIA UNIVERSITY, Centre College was founded as a joint effort by the church and the state of Kentucky. Cooperation proved difficult, however, and after five years of conflict over the school's administration and finances Centre broke all ties with the state government in 1824. The institution remains independent of but affiliated with the Presbyterian church. It has a current enrollment of approximately 800 students in essentially an arts and sciences program.

See R. G. McMurty, *Filson Club History Quarterly* (April, 1959); and N. L. Snider, *Register of the Kentucky Historical Society* (April, 1969).

CHALMERS, JAMES RONALD (1831–1898),

was born near Lynchburg, Va., and moved to Holly Springs, Miss., in 1839. He graduated from South Carolina College and practiced law in Mississippi in the 1850s. He entered politics as a Democrat and was a member of the secessionist convention in 1861. At the start of the war, he was commissioned a captain and later a colonel and brigadier general in the Confederate forces. He fought at Santa Rosa Island, led a brigade at SHILOH, fought at MUNFORDVILLE, was wounded at STONES RIVER, and was with Nathan Bedford Forrest at the FT. PILLOW MASSACRE. In April, 1863, he was put in command of the District of Mississippi and Eastern Arkansas, and in the last months of the war he commanded all the cavalry of Mississippi and western Tennessee.

As a leader in the overthrow of Mississippi's CARPETBAGGER government in 1875, he was elected to Congress as a Democrat in 1876 and reelected in 1878 and 1880. After the latter contest, however, his election was successfully challenged by JOHN R. LYNCH, a Negro Republican, on grounds of fraud. Believing that L. Q. C. LAMAR had not given him adequate support when the "Lamar legislature" of 1880 gerrymandered his district, Chalmers joined the Republicans. From 1882 he challenged both the Democratic party and black Republicans for control of the state. Running as an INDEPENDENT in 1882 with disaffected agrarian, white Republican, and Greenbacker support, he received a majority of the votes, but there were charges of fraud, and he was not seated by the U.S. House until June 25, 1884. He ran again in 1884 and 1886 but was defeated by a fusion of black Republicans and Democrats. His challenge to the Democratic party was largely that of an individual who had been unwilling to accept the dictates of the party.

See A. D. Kirwan, *Revolt of Rednecks* (1951), balanced; C. V. Woodward, *Origins of New South* (1951); V. L. Wharton, *Negro in Mississippi, 1865–1890* (1971), good; and W. D. Hadwell, *Journal of Southern History* (Feb., 1944).

GLENN M. LINDEN
Southern Methodist University

CHAMBERLAIN, DANIEL HENRY (1835–1907),

was born in Massachusetts. He was graduated from Yale in 1862 and attended Harvard Law School before being commissioned lieutenant in the 5th Massachusetts Regiment. After the Civil War, Chamberlain visited South Carolina in the interest of a deceased classmate, and he decided to practice law in Charleston, where he was later elected attorney general in 1868 and 1872. Opinion is divided over his specific acts of corruption. Yet his unsavory relations with the corrupt "legislative ring" should not obfuscate his forthright public condemnation of corruption and admirable career as governor after 1874. As governor, Chamberlain used his veto wisely, and his administration corrected the abusive pardoning system, reduced the public debt, and equalized tax laws. His unpopular advocacy of integration in higher education and his stern handling of the HAMBURG RACE RIOT alienated some supporters. He lost the governorship to WADE HAMPTON in 1876. Chamberlain later practiced law in New York. He became an independent and supported Grover Cleveland for president; he also changed his attitude toward blacks, whom he now regarded as physically repulsive and incapable of achieving social and political equality.

See W. Allen, *Governor Chamberlain* (1969), sympathetic; J. Green, *Personal Recollections* (1908); F. B. Simkins and R. H. Woody, *South Carolina* (1932), balanced; D. D. Wallace, *History of South Carolina* (1943), III; H. T. Thompson, *Ousting Carpetbaggers* (1969); A. B. Williams, *Hampton* (1935); and W. Allen (ed.), *Political Letters* (1883).

DAVID W. BISHOP
North Carolina Central University

CHAMPION HILL, BATTLE OF (May 16, 1863), was a decisive engagement in the Union effort to capture Vicksburg in the summer of 1863. This battle, about 20 miles west of Jackson, pitted the forces of U. S. Grant against those of JOHN C. PEMBERTON. Grant, having successfully outmaneuvered the Confederates as he crossed the Mississippi River south of Vicksburg, felt compelled to crush the forces of Pemberton and JOSEPH E. JOHNSTON west of Vicksburg before an effective siege of that city could take place. During the bloody holocaust of battle that morning, the crest of Champion Hill (often called Baker's Creek battle by the Confederate forces) changed hands no less than three times. By sundown, the Confederates had been outmaneuvered despite valiant fighting and fled across Baker's Creek. This disarrayed flight forced the abandonment of 27 cannons and hundreds of prisoners. Union losses at Champion Hill were 410 killed, 1,844 wounded, and 187 missing. Incomplete Confederate records listed 381 killed, 1,018 wounded, and 2,441 missing. Had the Confederates held at Champion Hill, Johnston and Pemberton would have been able to deploy their forces more effectively for a decisive showdown against the vulnerable Grant. The following day, May 17, Grant resumed his relentless march against the disorganized Confederates.

See R. A. McLemore, *History of Mississippi* (1973); W. C. Everhart, *Vicksburg* (1954); E. C. Bearss, *Decision in Mississippi* (1962); and *Official Records, Armies*, Ser. 1, Vol. XXIV, Pts. 1–3.

EDWARD MCMILLAN
Mississippi College

CHANCELLORSVILLE, BATTLE OF (May 1–4, 1863), was fought in the Wilderness of Spotsylvania. Joseph Hooker launched the campaign by leading a sizable portion of his 130,000-man federal army up the Rappahannock River to cross behind ROBERT E. LEE and jeopardize the positions of the southerners near Fredericksburg, Va. On May 1, the battle was joined west of Fredericksburg as General T. J. ("STONEWALL") JACKSON directed attacks toward Chancellorsville. Early on May 2, Jackson marched west with nearly 30,000 men across the front of the northern army, leaving Lee with only 15,000 troops to face Hooker's main threat. Another 10,000 Confederates had been left behind at Fredericksburg to guard Lee's rear. By late afternoon Jackson had his entire force behind the right flank of Hooker's army, and he was able to launch an overwhelming surprise attack, which caved in the federal line for two and one-half miles, but Jackson, while reconnoitering, was fatally wounded by his own men.

J. E. B. STUART was called to take Jackson's place. On the morning of May 3 he threw his troops against the fortified federal lines one mile west of Chancellorsville. After a violent and costly struggle in the woods, Confederate infantrymen were able to join their comrades to the east and drive Hooker back to a new position a mile north of Chancellorsville. Meanwhile, federals under General John Sedgwick pushed their way past the Confederates who were left to guard Fredericksburg. Lee was forced to send back substantial reinforcements. After extensive fighting near Salem Church on May 3 and 4, Sedgwick was driven back across the Rappahannock River. Hooker returned to the north bank with the main portion of his army on May 6. Federal losses for the campaign totaled more than 17,000; Confederate casualties were about 12,000. Chancellorsville opened the way for the invasion of northern territory, which culminated in the battle of GETTYSBURG.

See J. Bigelow, *Chancellorsville Campaign* (1910), monumental study concentrating on federal operations; A. C. Hamlin, *Eleventh Corps and Chancellorsville* (1895); and C. E. Dornbusch, *Military Bibliography of Civil War* (1973), III. There is need for detailed study of Confederate operations at Chancellorsville.

ROBERT K. KRICK
Fredericksburg National Military Park

CHARLES, ROBERT (1865–1900), was born to a black sharecropper family in Mississippi. He moved to Louisiana in 1894 and promoted "back-to-Africa" movements among New Orleans Negroes. He worked in obscurity until the last week of his life (July 23–27, 1900), when he gained national notoriety by shooting an estimated 27 New Orleans whites, including seven policemen, before he was killed in a gun battle on Saratoga Street. A race riot erupted in the city while Charles was hunted down. Resentment against increased LYNCHING and DISFRANCHISEMENT during the 1890s, together with personal difficulties in Mississippi, led him into black nationalism. He was associated with the International Migration Society and peddled a back-to-Africa magazine, *Voice of Missions*. Charles did not advocate violence against whites except in self-defense, and New Orleans police reports clearly indicate that he acted in self-defense during the trouble that led to his death.

See W. I. Hair, *Carnival of Fury* (1976); and Ida Wells-Barnett, *On Lynchings* (1969).

WILLIAM I. HAIR
Georgia College

CHARLESTON, FEDERAL OPERATIONS AGAINST (1861–1865).

On January 9, 1861, the unarmed *Star of the West*, sent by President James Buchanan and carrying reinforcements and supplies for FT. SUMTER, was turned back by Confederate batteries. A second expedition sent by Abraham Lincoln, arriving April 12–13, found Ft. Sumter under bombardment and never attempted to relieve it. In an effort to close off the harbor, two stone fleets were sunk on December 19–20, 1861, and January 25–26, 1862. In June, 1862, Union troops landed on James Island, and on June 16 an attack under General H. W. Benham was launched on Ft. Lamar at Secessionville. The assault was repulsed, and federal forces soon withdrew. Rear Admiral S. F. Du Pont (DU PONT FAMILY) attempted to take Charleston with nine ironclads on April 7, 1863. Turned back by obstructions, the vessels were driven off by the harbor forts. A combined naval and land assault led by General Q. A. Gillmore and Rear Admiral J. A. Dahlgren on July 10 attacked Morris Island. Stopped on July 11 and 18 from taking Battery Wagner, Gillmore carried out a siege, forcing the evacuation on September 7 of Morris Island. During this time bombardments of Ft. Sumter and Charleston were started and continued throughout the war. A small boat attack on Ft. Sumter, attempting to capture it by surprise, failed on September 9. In February, 1864, an advance on John's Island under General A. Schimmelfennig failed. Early in July, 1864, attacks under General J. P. Hatch in the Charleston area were turned back. On February 11–17, 1865, troops were landed north of the city; however, Charleston was evacuated on February 17.

See *Official Records, Armies*, Ser. 1, Vols. I, VI, XIV, XXVIII, XXXV, XLVII; *Official Records, Navies*, Ser. 1, Vols. I, XII–XVI; E. M. Burton, *Siege of Charleston* (1970); J. Johnson, *Defense of Charleston* (1890); and S. Jones, *Siege of Charleston* (1911).

STEPHEN R. WISE
Columbia, S.C.

CHARLESTON, S.C. (pop. 66,945), chief port and until 1790 the capital of South Carolina, was founded in 1670 under a grant from the lords proprietors. Its position during its first 50 years as the southernmost bastion of the British American empire left it exposed to Indian, French, and Spanish attack. With the frontier secured in 1740, Charleston became an important trading city exporting rice, indigo, and later cotton. The concentration of social, cultural, political, and commercial life in Charleston made it the dominant city of the South between 1730 and 1820. Merchants built great fortunes, and newly rich planters built grand homes. Their combined wealth supported a vigorous cultural life that included a library society and one of two newspapers published in the South. Some felt that it surpassed in grandeur any city in America. The city's population was predominantly English and black, but a polyglot immigration of Barbadians, Germans, French HUGUENOTS, ACADIANS and Dominicans, Scots, Ulster and Catholic Irish, Sephardic Jews, and Italians gave it a cosmopolitan flavor.

British mercantile policy and efforts to displace the local oligarchs forced the merchants, planters, and mechanics into a common cause. "Mob" defiance of authority caused concern even among radical patriots, but the alliance held and Charleston joined the revolt against Britain. The Revolution, two successful defenses of the city (1776 and 1779), and eventual British occupation (1780–1782) interrupted but did not destroy the city's prosperity.

At the beginning of the nineteenth century, younger aristocratic planters wrested control from the older Federalists who had participated in the Revolution. Worsening economic conditions, antislavery agitation, and fear of Negro insurrection (VESEY PLOT) influenced the majority of Charlestonians to lead the South toward nullification (1832) and secession (1860). A Unionist minority existed until the ill-fated Democratic convention of 1860 (CHARLESTON CONVENTION). The "booster" sentiment of this pioneering minority expressed itself in various banking, railroad, and shipping schemes, but politically the planters dominated and imposed an intolerant monolithic political system obsessed with and dedicated to slavery. The Civil War, which began in Charleston harbor (FT. SUMTER), proved disastrous to the city and its commerce. A major part of the city burned in 1861, and the Union navy besieged and blockaded the port. Union forces occupied the city in 1865.

Charleston never recovered its prominence after 1865. Although there was a brief period of prosperity during Reconstruction, the city declined into genteel poverty by the end of the century. A catastrophic earthquake (1886), the flight of capital to the developing up-country, and the discriminatory practices of the railroads destroyed its commerce. After 1890, the agrarians successfully challenged its dominance in state politics. Locally, a bitter political struggle resulted as the "plebeian" whites asserted their right to share political power with the "boni." A protracted struggle over liquor laws between the wet Charlestonians and the dry up-country men colored Carolina politics for most of the twentieth century. A modicum of prosperity returned in World War I because of the development of the navy yard and the docks north of the city. World War II and its aftermath made Charleston once again a major port and one of the most important military bases in the country. In recent years, Charlestonians have capitalized on their eighteenth-century heritage through preservation and restoration.

See G. C. Rogers, Jr., *Charleston in Age of Pinckneys* (1969); R. G. Rhett, *Charleston* (1940); R. Walsh, *Charleston's Sons of Liberty* (1968); *Charleston Year Books* (1881–1940); and primary sources in Charleston Library Society and South Caroliniana Library.

JOHN J. DUFFY
University of South Carolina

CHARLESTON (S.C.) MERCURY was founded in 1822 as a daily newspaper called the *Mercury and Morning Advertiser*. Henry Laurens Pinckney purchased the paper in 1823 and converted it into the organ of the free trade and states' rights wing of the state Democratic party. It was John Stewart (1794–1853) who edited the paper after 1832 and earned for it its reputation as one of the most influential dailies in the Deep South. Under Stewart's editorship, the *Mercury* ardently defended extreme states' rights positions and advocated both nullification and secession. In discussions on slavery Stewart pressed for reforms of the institution so that virtually every white could afford to own at least one slave. In 1857 the editorship passed to R. B. Rhett, Jr., son of South Carolina's famous FIRE-EATER, R. B. RHETT. Rhett's editorials applauded the disintegration of the

Democratic party at the CHARLESTON CONVENTION of 1860, led the move toward secession after Abraham Lincoln's election, and predicted a peaceful separation from the Union until after the firing upon Ft. Sumter. Throughout the Civil War Rhett and his *Mercury* supported the Confederacy, but did so by regularly attacking Jefferson Davis for his military strategy and for his centralization of authority.

See J. S. Coussons, "Charleston *Mercury*" (Ph.D. dissertation, Louisiana State University, 1971); W. L. King, *Newspaper Press of Charleston* (1872, 1970); and Charleston *Mercury*, complete bound volumes at Duke Library and at University of California, Berkeley, and microfilm from Bell & Howell (1822–68).

CHARLESTON (S.C.) NEWS AND COURIER, the South's oldest newspaper, is the result of the consolidation in 1873 of the Charleston *Daily Courier* and the Charleston *Daily News*. The *Courier* had been a Union paper, opposed to nullification and secession, though it supported the Confederacy when the war broke out. For its day and time, the *Courier* was progressive. It used mounted messengers during the Mexican War to get the news a day ahead of the stagecoach. It lent its support to the building of America's first steam railroad from Charleston to Hamburg, S.C.

The Charleston *Daily News* was founded in 1865 while the *Courier* was in the hands of Union authorities. In 1866, B. R. Riordan and Captain FRANCIS WARRINGTON DAWSON became coeditors of the *News*. Then in April, 1873, to settle the estates of the owners, the *Courier* was sold at auction. Riordan and Dawson bought it and combined it with the *News* to form the *News and Courier*.

W. W. BALL, editor of the *News and Courier* (1927–1951), described the paper as "an old-fashioned democratic newspaper and rather aggressive in its political opinion. It believes in the Jefferson idea of strict construction of the Constitution and as little government as possible. It is a low tariff newspaper. It is out of sympathy with most of the policies of the New Deal." The *News and Courier* vehemently opposed the politics of BEN TILLMAN and COLE BLEASE. It advocated diversification of agriculture and led in bringing about interest in the cultivation of tobacco as a South Carolina money crop. It opposed Prohibition. To this day, it continues to be a leading newspaper in South Carolina with a daily circulation of over 60,000.

See H. R. Sass, *150 Years of News & Courier* (1953).

S. FRANK LOGAN
Wofford College

CHARLESTON, W.VA. (pop. 71,505), is situated in the Kanawha River valley. The Virginia House of Burgesses established it as a town (1794) to serve as county seat for Kanawha County and distribution center for the nearby salt licks. Throughout the antebellum era it remained a frontier outpost, culturally an extension of Virginia, but economically a part of the Ohio Valley. Shut off by the Appalachian Mountains to the east, SALT producers shipped salines on barges to points south and west, especially after 1820, when steamboats provided dependable transportation. Peaking in the 1850s, salt production thereafter declined, but not before it nurtured a COAL MINING and LUMBER business. During the Civil War the Kanawha Valley was a strategic buffer zone, besides being a potential salt supplier for the Confederacy. After four Union regiments overwhelmed Confederates stationed at Charleston (July, 1861), the North controlled the valley. The city's postwar economy was sluggish until the 1870s, when the Chesapeake & Ohio Railroad provided access to eastern markets and the federal government undertook improvement of the Kanawha River for navigation. Thereafter, a slow but steady growth was sustained by the opening of the Kanawha–New River coalfields, and the city's new status in West Virginia became apparent when the capital was permanently relocated there in 1885. The early twentieth century saw the beginning of the phenomenal CHEMICAL, primary metals, and electrical power industries in the valley, all of which by 1970 put Charleston at the center of West Virginia's largest metropolitan area.

See J. W. Hess, *Guide to Manuscripts and Archives in West Virginia Collection* (1974); C. H. Ambler, *West Virginia* (1940); J. M. Callahan, *History of West Virginia* (1913); W. S. Laidley, *History of Charleston* (1911); J. E. Stealey, "Salt Industry of Kanawha Valley" (Ph.D. dissertation, West Virginia University, 1970); J. W. Matheney, "History of Charleston" (Ph.D. dissertation, West Virginia University, 1928); C. R. Goodall, "History of Municipal Government at Charleston" (M.A. thesis, West Virginia University, 1936); and E. J. Goodall, "History of Charleston" (M.A. thesis, West Virginia University, 1937).

GEORGE PARKINSON
West Virginia University

CHARLESTON (W.VA.) DAILY MAIL began publication in 1893. After merging in 1897 with the *Star Tribune*, it was known as the *Mail-Tribune*. Since 1901, however, this independent Republican daily has been known simply as the *Daily Mail*; it currently has a circulation of approximately 60,000 copies.

See microfilm from Bell & Howell (1897–1905, 1914–).

CHARLESTON (W.VA.) GAZETTE is an independent Democratic newspaper with a current circulation of approximately 60,000 copies daily. It has been in continuous publication since its founding in 1887.

See bound copies at Library of Congress (1898–); and microfilm from Bell & Howell (1891–1905, 1924–).

CHARLESTON CONVENTION (April, 1860) witnessed an irreparable schism in the Democratic party. Central to the conflict was southern opposition to Stephen A. Douglas of Illinois. He had long been associated with the idea of POPULAR SOVEREIGNTY, regarded by southerners as no better than outright congressional exclusion of slavery from the western territories. The cutting edge of the southern movement was the Alabama Platform, passed in that state's Democratic convention in January, 1860. Alabama delegates at Charleston would walk out should a slave code for the territories not be accepted by the national party. Other southern delegations gave evidence of support for the Alabama initiative.

Faced by a determined and disciplined Douglas majority and without a candidate of their own, southerners concentrated on writing a slave code into the platform. Murat Halstead reported: "Here, then, is the 'irrepressible conflict'—a conflict between enduring forces." The resolutions committee, unable to agree on a single platform, reported three. One incorporated the slave code; the second, supported by the Douglas men, would refer questions of slavery in the territories to the courts; and the third endorsed the Cincinnati platform of 1856. Speaking for the southern position, WILLIAM LOWNDES YANCEY bitterly attacked Douglas and popular sovereignty. As the South could no longer trust Douglas and, by implication, his followers, it must receive guarantees in the form of party support for the slave code. The northern men replied in kind; their message, no compromise.

On April 30, the delegates voted on the platform. As a final gesture to the South, Douglas Democrats offered the Cincinnati platform without any reference to the slavery protection question. Southerners refused to accept this ambiguous document, and, to the applause of the partisan crowd, delegates from seven southern states left the convention. After considerable wrangling among those remaining, the convention adjourned, to reconvene in Baltimore (BALTIMORE CONVENTION). There the fissure was made complete, with disastrous results for the party and the nation.

See R. F. Nichols, *Disruption of American Democracy* (1948); R. W. Johannsen, *Stephen A. Douglas* (1973); and W. B. Hesseltine (ed.), *Three Against Lincoln* (1960).

JOHN T. HUBBELL
Kent State University

CHARLESTON EXPEDITION OF CLINTON

(1776) originated from reports by southern governors indicating that LOYALIST support existed for a British invasion. Acting on instructions, General William Howe put Henry Clinton in command of a force of five infantry regiments and two artillery companies. Clinton intended to invade North Carolina, but decided to attack Charleston, S.C., after a Loyalist defeat at MOORE'S CREEK BRIDGE on February 27. Clinton met Commodore Sir Peter Parker's fleet off the Virginia Capes in April. In May the fleet's last vessels arrived, and on June 4 the force reached Charleston. In January the Continental Congress ordered CHARLES LEE to direct Charleston's defense. By mid-June 6,000 American soldiers under Lee, Colonels WILLIAM MOULTRIE and CHRISTOPHER GADSDEN, and Governor JOHN RUTLEDGE were in position. On Sullivan's Island the Americans had a sizable but unfinished post, later named Ft. Moultrie. Ships entering the harbor were subject to its guns.

On June 9, Clinton's army disembarked on Long Island. Intelligence reports suggested that his troops could march to Sullivan's via a ford, which proved to be seven feet deep. Without boats the army could not move. Favorable winds allowed Parker to launch his attack on June 28. Six of his principal vessels were damaged. During the 12-hour battle the British suffered 200 casualties; the Americans, 32. On June 29, the British sailed back to New York. Loyalist support failed to materialize, notice from London canceling the expedition arrived too late, and the Indians failed to interrupt American defense preparations. Defeat delayed British invasion of the South for two years.

See W. M. Wallace, *Appeal to Arms* (1951); K. Nebenzahl and D. Higginbotham, *Atlas of American Revolution* (1975); W. B. Willcox, *American Rebellion* (1954); and D. Ramsay, *History of Revolution of South-Carolina* (1785).

FRANK C. MEVERS
New Hampshire Historical Society

CHARLESTON LIBRARY SOCIETY was found-

ed in 1748 and incorporated in 1754 as a subscription library based on the model developed in Philadelphia by Benjamin Franklin. It obtained an impressive collection of English periodicals and volumes of art, literature, and science; of par-

ticular importance were the extensive historical and political writings that expressed the republican political ideology of the day. Leading members of the Charleston community supported the society, and it played an important role in the cultural life of the city, founding the Charleston Museum in 1773. CHARLES COTESWORTH PINCKNEY was an active member and a president of the society. It continues to exist and is well known today for a fine collection of eighteenth-century books and newspapers.

See F. P. Bowes, *Culture of Early Charleston* (1942); A. K. Gregorie, *Proceedings of the South Carolina Historical Association* (1935); G. C. Rogers, Jr., *Charleston in Age of Pinckneys* (1969); and M. R. Zahniser, *Charles C. Pinckney* (1967).

SIDNEY CHARLES BOLTON
University of Arkansas, Little Rock

CHARLOTTE, N.C. (pop. 241,178), is near the

South Carolina state line and the Catawba River in the Piedmont. The town was laid out in 1765 to be the political seat of Mecklenburg County and was named for the wife of George III. Despite the town's royal name, its residents' sympathies were distinctly revolutionary (MECKLENBURG RESOLUTIONS). Antebellum Charlotte developed primarily as an agricultural market and a center for area gold mining. Indeed, except during the Civil War, a branch office of the U.S. Mint operated here from 1836 to 1913. After the Civil War, utilizing hydroelectric power generated on the Catawba River, the city became increasingly industrialized, and many of its residents became prominent in advocacy of the NEW SOUTH. Modern Charlotte is the largest city in the state. It is the headquarters of numerous financial and textile firms and the home of three major educational institutions: Queens College (1857), the University of North Carolina at Charlotte, and Central Piedmont Community College.

See D. A. Tompkins, *History of Mecklenburg County* (2 vols.; 1903); L. Blythe and C. R. Brockmann, *Hornets' Nest* (1961), updates Tompkins; J. B. Alexander, *History of Mecklenburg County* (1902), folksy; J. Alexander, *Charlotte in Picture and Prose* (1906); K. and B. Marsh, *Charlotte* (1967), pictorial; D. R. Reynolds, *Charlotte Remembers* (1972), nostalgic; and files of Charlotte *News* (1888–) and *Observer* (1886–), both on microfilm.

CHARLOTTE OBSERVER began publication in

1886 as the *Daily Chronicle*, but since 1892 it has been called either the *Daily Observer* or simply the *Observer*. During the 1890s and the early years of the twentieth century it was owned by industrialist Daniel A. Tompkins and was edited by J. P. Caldwell. Reflecting the NEW SOUTH philosophies of these men, the *Observer* encouraged industrialization and defended the gold standard. In general the paper functioned as the conservative Democratic counterpart to JOSEPHUS DANIELS' reform-oriented Raleigh *News and Observer* on such issues as railroad rates and public regulation of private corporations. Today the paper is politically independent, and its daily circulation of over 175,000 copies is the largest in North Carolina.

See nearly complete bound copies (1887–1928) and complete (1928–) in Duke University Library; and microfilm from Bell & Howell (1886–), Chicago Center for Research Libraries (1892–), and Library of Congress (1955–).

CHARLOTTESVILLE, VA. (pop. 38,880), is in the central portion of the state, approximately 70 miles west of Richmond. The settlement that grew up here in the 1730s was named in 1762 for the wife of George III. It was primarily a small market town of little strategic or economic importance, and it generally was bypassed by the major events of both the Revolutionary and Civil wars. The patriots quartered General John Burgoyne's captured British troops here (1779–1780), and the state chose the site for the new UNIVERSITY OF VIRGINIA. In the twentieth century the town's growth has paralleled that of the university. The development of area apple and peach orchards, slate and soapstone quarries, and lumbering has made the town a shipping point for these products. Moreover, the city's proximity to Thomas Jefferson's Monticello, James Monroe's Ash Lawn, and the birthplaces of George Rogers Clark and Meriwether Lewis has made it a center of area tourism.

See M. Alexander, *Early Charlottesville* (1942); E. Woods, *Albemarle County* (1901), good for family names; J. H. Moore, *History of Albemarle County* (1976); *Magazine of Albemarle County History* (1940–); and files of Charlottesville *Progress* (1892–).

CHASE, SAMUEL (1741–1811), one of the most consistently controversial figures in American history, was born in Somerset County, Md. Soon after he was admitted to the bar in 1761, he entered politics and served in the Maryland general assembly and the CONTINENTAL CONGRESS. He helped persuade Maryland to change its position on independence and later signed the enrolled Declaration of Independence. In 1786 he moved from Annapolis to Baltimore and became chief judge of the general court in 1791. In spite of his opposition to the Constitution in 1788, George Washington nominated him to the U.S. Supreme Court on January 26, 1796. As a justice there he wrote three noteworthy opinions: *Hylton* v. *U.S.*, *Ware* v. *Hylton* (both 1796), and *Calder* v. *Bull* (1798). It was while sitting as a circuit court judge, however, that Chase antagonized the bar. Supporting the Alien and Sedition Acts, he became a "hanging judge." His intemperate and perhaps improper conduct of the Callender and Fries trials, and especially his charge to the Baltimore grand jury in 1803, brought about his impeachment in 1804. The U.S. Senate failed to convict Chase, and his remaining years were quiet and uncontroversial.

See I. Dilliard, in L. Friedman and F. L. Israel (eds.), *Justices of U.S. Supreme Court, 1789–1969* (1969), I. Chase's papers are widely scattered, making an adequate biography difficult.

CHARLES T. CULLEN
Institute of Early American History and Culture

CHATTAHOOCHEE RIVER. See APALACHICOLA RIVER

CHATTANOOGA, TENN. (pop. 119,082), is located on a bend of the Tennessee River east of the Cumberland Mountains and approximately 100 miles north of Atlanta, Ga. Although both French and English trading posts had been established in the vicinity during the eighteenth century, the present city dates only from the opening in 1815 of Ross' Landing, a trading post deep within the CHEROKEE INDIAN Nation. A U.S. Army post was established near Ross' Landing in 1835, and two years later, after the removal of the Cherokee, a town was laid out and christened with the Creek name for Lookout Mountain, meaning "rock rising to a point." Developing initially as a river port, Chattanooga also became an important cotton market after the completion in 1849 of the Western & Atlantic Railroad. Additional rail lines soon followed and, by the time of the Civil War, the city had become a major rail center. Because of its strategic position as a communications link between Confederate armies in the west and the east, the town became a primary objective of the Union army. General BRAXTON BRAGG evacuated the city early in September, 1863, but federal occupation was not secure until after the battles of Lookout Mountain and Missionary Ridge in November, 1863 (CHATTANOOGA CAMPAIGN). It was used thereafter as a Union supply and transportation depot.

With an enhanced reputation for its importance

as a transportation center and with nearby deposits of coal and iron ore, the postwar city developed rapidly into a manufacturer of IRON AND STEEL. During the 1870s, the first plow factory constructed anywhere in the South went into production. The inauguration of the TENNESSEE VALLEY AUTHORITY in the 1930s further revolutionized the economy of this trade and manufacturing center. The availability of abundant supplies of electricity served as a magnet attracting yet additional industries. Besides manufacturing a variety of sheet metal products, pumps, boilers, stoves, and farm machinery, the modern city's factories produce electronic equipment, electrical appliances, glass, ceramics, cellulose, furniture, and textiles. The University of Chattanooga, Union and Confederate cemeteries, and several national military parks are all located here.

See G. E. Govan and J. W. Livingood, *Chattanooga Country* (1952, 1963); Z. Armstrong, *History of Hamilton County* (2 vols.; 1931); P. Heiner, *Chattanooga* (4 vols.; 1951–64), illustrated; C. D. McGuffey, *Standard History of Chattanooga* (1911); and files of *Hamilton County Herald* (1913–), Chattanooga *Times* (1869–), and *News-Free Press* (1888–).

CHATTANOOGA CAMPAIGN (September 21–November 25, 1863). Following his defeat at the battle of CHICKAMAUGA, General W. S. Rosecrans consolidated the Army of the Cumberland in Chattanooga, while Confederate General BRAXTON BRAGG occupied Lookout Mountain and Missionary Ridge commanding the city, cutting all railroads and the Tennessee River. Shaken by Chickamauga, Rosecrans procrastinated while Bragg so effectively invested Chattanooga that food and forage dwindled. Bragg sent cavalry under JOSEPH WHEELER to cut remaining U.S. supply and communication lines. The Army of the Cumberland became more destitute and demoralized, but Bragg failed to strike.

Ulysses S. Grant was sent to Chattanooga with overall command in the West and promptly replaced Rosecrans with General G. H. THOMAS. Two corps of the Army of the Potomac under Joseph Hooker reinforced Chattanooga, as did four divisions of the Army of the Tennessee under W. T. Sherman. In the meantime, President Jefferson Davis went west to settle persistent quarrels among the generals of the Army of Tennessee. Strongly supporting Bragg by scattering his critics, Davis authorized the removal of DANIEL H. HILL, reassigned LEONIDAS POLK to Mississippi, and, later, encouraged Bragg to send JAMES LONGSTREET with 15,000 troops to attack Knoxville. Quarrels among Confederate commanders, however, may have contributed as much as U.S. reinforcements to the final outcome.

After arriving at Chattanooga (October 23), Grant immediately opened a new supply line via a pontoon bridge at Brown's Ferry on the Tennessee River. A Confederate night attack at Wauhatchie (October 28–29) failed to break this "cracker line."

The battle of Chattanooga began November 23 as Thomas sent divisions under Philip H. Sheridan and Thomas J. Wood to capture Orchard Knob, east of Chattanooga at the foot of Missionary Ridge. That night, Sherman moved to the north end of Missionary Ridge. The next day, three divisions under Hooker attacked Lookout Mountain, meeting resistance at the base but none at the crest. Nonetheless, the "battle above the clouds" became part of Civil War legend. At the same time, Sherman occupied the north end of Missionary Ridge, belatedly discovering a deep ravine that separated him from the main Confederate force on Tunnel Hill.

On November 25, Grant's forces launched a three-pronged attack on Missionary Ridge. On the north, Sherman made little progress against PATRICK CLEBURNE's troops. On the south, Hooker's men arrived at the ridge late after a delay in bridging Chattanooga Creek. Thomas' four divisions, ordered to take emplacements at the foot of the ridge in the center, but feeling dangerously exposed there, continued to the crest with relative ease since Confederates there could hardly fire without risk of hitting their retreating comrades. Whether U.S. troops charged spontaneously or under orders remains in dispute. Bragg withdrew toward Dalton, Ga.

During the three-day battle, about 56,000 Union soldiers fought 46,000 Confederates, losing 5,475 killed and wounded to 2,521 Confederates. Over 4,000 missing Confederates (mostly prisoners) balanced by 350 federals, however, conveyed better the message of Confederate defeat. Unable to capitalize on his victory at Chickamauga, Bragg lost all credibility as a commander. Asked later if Bragg had believed his position at Chattanooga impregnable, Grant replied, "Well, it *was* impregnable." The battle of Chattanooga, coming a few months after the battle of GETTYSBURG and the fall of VICKSBURG, completed a pattern of southern defeat in each major theater of war and seemingly doomed the Confederacy.

See *Official Records, Armies*, Ser. 1, Vols. XXX, XXXI; B. Catton, *Grant Takes Command* (1969); and T. L. Connelly, *Autumn of Glory* (1971).

JOHN Y. SIMON
Southern Illinois University, Carbondale

CHATTANOOGA DAILY TIMES, founded in 1868, was the springboard for the journalistic career of Adolph Simon Ochs (1858–1935). Ochs was born in Cincinnati and was the son of a Jewish veteran of the Union army. His family moved to Knoxville after the Civil War, where young Ochs worked as a carrier and as a printer's devil for the Knoxville *Chronicle*. He moved to Chattanooga, and in 1878, at the age of twenty, he purchased the *Times*, a failing Democratic daily. Although Ochs never changed the political viewpoint of the *Times*, its coverage of the news was both detailed and nonpartisan, serving in many ways as a model for twentieth-century journalism. The *Times*'s circulation expanded; Chattanooga grew in population; and Ochs prospered. In 1896, with profits earned from the paper, Ochs purchased the New York *Times* and edited it in the image of the Chattanooga *Times*. The daily continues to be an independent Democratic publication with a circulation in excess of 60,000 copies.

See bound copies at Library of Congress, Chattanooga Public Library, Alabama Department of Archives, Montgomery, and Tennessee State Library, Nashville; and microfilm from Microfilm Corporation of America (1873–).

CHAUTAUQUA MOVEMENT, which began in 1874 at a Lake Chautauqua, N.Y., Methodist Sunday school assembly, spread rapidly southward, propagating a popular gospel of culture and self-improvement. A cofounder, John Heyl Vincent, the future Methodist bishop, was born in Tuscaloosa, Ala. He took great pride in his southern birth and envisioned Chautauqua, in the years following the Civil War, as a means to "mitigate sectional antipathies." There were two offspring of the original Chautauqua: the independents, which were annually convened on the same site; and the circuit or tent Chautauquas. The programs in each type were similar, with something for everyone: inspirational lectures by famous preachers and politicians, martial and symphonic bands, dramatic groups, readings in costume by great authors, light operas, lectures on science and travel, and even magic shows and fireworks. The earliest independent Chautauquas in the South were founded at Hillsboro, Va., 1877; Purcell, Va., 1878; Mountain Lake Park, Md., 1883; Monteagle, Tenn., 1883; DeFuniak Springs, Fla., 1884; Siloam Springs, Ark., 1886; Lexington, Ky., 1887; and the Piedmont Chautauqua at Lithia Springs, Ga., 1888.

The Piedmont, conceived and realized by HENRY W. GRADY, was more grandiose than the other summer assemblies. Supported by Marion C. Kiser and other Atlanta businessmen, construction began on an 8,000-seat, roofed tabernacle, two Italian-style hotels, and a summer college building. This cultural center, which Grady called the "Saratoga of the South," was completed in approximately 30 days. The summer college had a distinguished faculty, headed by Dr. W. R. Harper, dean at Yale College, with professors from Johns Hopkins, Harvard, and the University of Virginia. At the college's closing exercises, Grady paid $2,500 due in faculty salaries from his personal funds.

The tent circuits, which would both exalt and destroy Chautauqua, began in 1903 in the Middle West. Two systems, Alkahest of Atlanta and Radcliffe Attractions of Washington, D.C., controlled most bookings in the South. Alkahest, which claimed to "cover Dixie like the dew," had a main seven-day circuit that traveled to 40 southern towns. Radcliffe ran three circuits through the southern states, covering well over 200 towns. Although the tent circuits were to expire with the advent of the automobile and the radio, many southerners will remember them fondly for first bringing "culture" to hitherto inaccessible areas.

See T. Morrison, *Chautauqua* (1974); V. and R. Case, *We Called It Culture* (1948); H. A. Orchard, *Fifty Years of Chautauqua* (1923); and B. W. Griffith, *Georgia Review* (Spring, 1972).

BENJAMIN W. GRIFFITH
West Georgia College

CHAVIS, JOHN (1763?–1838), a free Negro of uncertain origins, received a classical education at Washington Academy (now Washington and Lee University). After serving as a "riding missionary" in Virginia's Hanover Presbytery, Chavis settled in North Carolina about 1805. Admitted to the Orange Presbytery in 1809, he ministered to whites, free blacks, and slaves in at least three counties. He also conducted a classical school for both races, on a segregated basis. Among his pupils were North Carolinians who became prominent in the professions and in politics. His work among free blacks was particularly significant; he gave his fellows the rudiments of a literary education and, by example, demonstrated good and constructive living, even in difficult times. Conservative by nature, Chavis was actively interested in and knowledgeable about public affairs. Unhesitatingly he advised or chastised U.S. Senator WILLIE P. MANGUM (an intimate friend characterized fondly as "my son") regarding his political course. Although deploring slavery, he opposed immediate emancipation as unwise and denounced abolitionism. Ironically, Chavis was victimized by racial tensions engendered by Nat TURNER'S REBELLION.

North Carolina law forbade the teaching of blacks; and, in 1832, he was forced to resign from the Orange Presbytery (which did provide a modest subsistence for the Chavises). John Chavis' life poignantly reveals the promise and tragedy of antebellum race relations.

See J. H. Franklin, *Free Negro in North Carolina* (1943), highly useful; E. W. Knight, *North Carolina Historical Review* (July, 1930); M. B. Des Champs, *North Carolina Historical Review* (April, 1955); and H. T. Shanks, *Mangum Papers* (1950–56), revealing.

MAX R. WILLIAMS
Western Carolina University

CHEATHAM, BENJAMIN FRANKLIN (1820–1886), was born near Nashville, Tenn. When war with Mexico broke out, he promptly raised a company of volunteers and left for Mexico. As a consequence of his distinguished service at Monterrey and at Cerro Gordo, he was promoted colonel. After returning to Tennessee he resumed farming, although he remained active in state military affairs, holding the position of major general of the Tennessee militia. When the Civil War broke out, Cheatham again promptly volunteered for service. He was commissioned a brigadier general and served the Confederacy valiantly at the battles of BELMONT and SHILOH. He was promoted major general in October, 1862. He commanded a division under BRAXTON BRAGG at PERRYVILLE and STONES RIVER. He took part in campaigns at CHICKAMAUGA, CHATTANOOGA, ATLANTA, and NASHVILLE. After the war he declined an appointment from his friend from the Mexican War, U. S. Grant, and returned to his Tennessee farm. He served as Tennessee superintendent of prisons for four years. In 1885, as a result of Grover Cleveland's election, he was appointed postmaster of Nashville.

See *Official Records, Armies*, Ser. 1, Vols. III, X, XVII, XXX, XXXI, XXXVIII–XL, XLVII, XLIX; R. U. Johnson and C. C. Buel (eds.), *Battles and Leaders* (1888), IV; and C. A. Evans (ed.), *Confederate Military History* (1899), VIII.

RICHARD SONDEREGGER
Northern Michigan University

CHEAT MOUNTAIN, BATTLE OF (September 11–13, 1861). By late summer, 1861, Union troops under General J. J. Reynolds assumed strong defensive positions on and near Cheat Mountain, which overlooked the Staunton-Parkersburg Turnpike, 15 miles west of the crest of the Allegheny Mountains in western Virginia. Robert E. Lee, the Confederate commander, had to deal with constant rainfall, poor communications, intimidating terrain, inexperienced troops, prideful subordinate officers, and his own reluctance to issue firm orders. He devised an overly complicated plan involving five separate columns, three converging on Cheat Mountain and two moving into Tygart's Valley toward Elkwater. After Confederate movements were detected on September 12, Lee's attempt to capture Cheat Mountain was doomed. Although few southern soldiers died, failure at Cheat Mountain led to separate statehood for West Virginia.

See D. Freeman, *Lee* (1934), I, sound and extensive account; G. Moore, *Banner in Hills* (1963); and B. Stutler, *West Virginia in the Civil War* (1963).

MICHAEL W. WHALON
University of Tulsa

CHEMICAL INDUSTRY. The role of the chemical industry within the larger context of twentieth-century American industry is difficult both to exaggerate and appraise. Although its origins can be traced well back into the colonial era, the chemical industry did not begin to achieve major proportions relative to other manufacturing activities until after 1900. In 1899, for example, the production of chemicals stood at one-third the level of output in 1919, a quarter of production in 1925, and only one-seventh of the industry's total production in 1937. The industry is generally defined to include firms producing basic chemicals as well as establishments manufacturing by predominantly chemical processes. Thus, in determining aggregate output to the production of basic chemicals (acids, alkalies, and salts), one must add the chemical products destined for use in further manufacture (synthetic fibers, plastic materials, and pigments) as well as finished chemical products to be used for ultimate consumption (soap, cosmetics, and drugs). Also subsumed in industry-wide compilations are finished chemical products that serve as supplies in other industries: chemical products earmarked for fertilizer, paint, and explosives.

The growth of the chemical industry in the South closely paralleled the development of the region's industrial base after the Civil War (INDUSTRIALIZATION). From the earliest exploitation of the region's chemical resources until roughly World War I, the industry focused on the production of a very limited range of specialty chemicals to meet local demand and the processing of a small variety of products from the region's abundant natural endowment for outside markets. As manufacturing activity in the South expanded, the chemical industry grew apace, exploiting an ever-widening range of the area's raw materials for local consumption as well as entry into interregional and international trade. Historically the American chemical industry followed the migration of consuming industries, and expansion in the South during the early twentieth century was largely a continuation and extension of this basic pattern.

The production of NAVAL STORES, one of the oldest branches of the southern chemical industry, owes its existence, as do a number of other segments of the industry below the Mason-Dixon Line, to the large stands of native pine trees found in the region. During the eighteenth century the industry centered in New England. Soon after the Revolutionary War, however, it migrated to the South, which quickly came to supply the needs of the United States as well as to provide the country with valuable export commodities (COMMERCE). Buoyed by new and expanded uses during the modern industrial era, output rose steadily until setbacks were experienced after the first third of the twentieth century as a result of the introduction of synthetic replacements.

The other major branch of the southern chemical industry whose origins predate the twentieth century is the production of FERTILIZERS. Southern COTTON and TOBACCO crops were the first and largest consumers of chemical plant foods in the United States, and the industry, spawned by regional markets, grew rapidly after the Civil War. From the rich deposits of PHOSPHATES found in South Carolina, Florida, and Tennessee, superphosphate, an essential ingredient in chemical fertilizers, was produced. This process required substantial quantities of sulfuric acid, and hence the production of this commodity also advanced rapidly after the war.

With a few relatively minor exceptions, the rest of the industry did not develop to major proportions until well after the turn of the twentieth century. With the heightened interest in the region's resources and other advantages for manufacturing, chemicals became an increasingly important part of the total mixture of economic endeavors in the South. Growth in the production of wood PULP AND PAPER, cotton textiles, glass, and ceramics created strong demand for a broad spectrum of chemicals, which increasingly came to be produced in the South. Also important was the production of rayon fiber, which centered in the South due to the proximity of raw materials and the migration of the TEXTILE INDUSTRY out of New England. Rounding out the list of major new developments in chemicals in the South after World War I was rapid growth in the production

of alkalies, chlorines, and electrochemical operations. The emergence of these activities, and many others too numerous for mention, was closely tied to a conjunction of factors, the most important of which were resources, climate, and general economic development at both the regional and national levels.

See W. Haynes, *American Chemical Industry* (1948), the best basic reference work. Also useful are National Research Council, *Chemical Progress in South* (1930); L. F. Haber, *Chemical Industry During Nineteenth Century* (1958), and *Chemical Industry, 1900–1930* (1971); and A. Ihde, *Development of Modern Chemistry* (1964).

RICHARD L. EHRLICH
University of Delaware

CHEROKEE INDIANS can be traced only vaguely to their origins. Linguistically they are Iroquoian, probably living in the Great Lakes region before settling in the southern Alleghenies, principally in North Carolina, Georgia, Alabama, and Tennessee. The tribe's name may be a Choctaw corruption of *Tsalagi*, interpreted as "cave people" or "ancient tobacco people." Cherokees seem to have favored *AniKituHwagi*, "people of Kituwha" (the mother settlement in North Carolina) or *AniYunWiya*, "principal people." The census of 1835 gives the best estimate of Cherokee numbers, reporting 16,542 living east of the Mississippi and another 2,000 living in what is now Arkansas. By 1860 the tribe counted about 23,000 members, mostly living in Indian Territory, but including a small contingent in North Carolina.

The Cherokee before their removal to Indian Territory were blessed with a country of bold mountains and fertile valleys laced with Cherokee corn, potatoes, and beans. This happy people enjoyed annual dances, stickball games, and easy camaraderie, but nonetheless were vigorous warriors who defended their country against the SHAWNEE, CATAWBA, CHICKASAW, and CREEK Indians. White encounters began with Hernando de Soto in 1540, but more crucial intercourse came in the next century with English and American colonials. In 1721 the Cherokee made their first land cession and agreed to fixed boundaries in a telling treaty with South Carolina. A treaty with the United States in 1785 at Hopewell, S.C., placed them under federal protection and yielded additional lands. By 1902 the tribe had signed 25 such agreements.

Cherokee advances in white civilization increased with these encounters. An illiterate genius, Sequoya, developed a written system of 85 characters, which Cherokees easily mastered. With

Sequoya's method, laws were published, a national press (*Cherokee Phoenix*) was created, and missionary efforts were expanded. The Cherokee constructed a constitutional government in 1827 after years of political experience. An energetic mixed-blooded leadership, including John Ross, Major Ridge, John Ridge, and Elias Boudinot, arose to challenge white encroachments and to lead the tribe through the dramatic years ahead. Forces congealed by 1832 to push the Cherokee from their homelands. The Georgia legislature extended state laws to remaining portions of Cherokee territory, and invasions of Cherokee lands intensified when gold was discovered within state-chartered limits. Also, President Andrew Jackson pursued a policy of Indian removal and disrupted the Cherokee by curtailing payments for tribal land cessions. U.S. Supreme Court cases proved equally dismaying, especially WORCESTER V. GEORGIA, which placed responsibility on the government to protect the tribe, but which Jackson easily sidestepped. Likewise, internal dissensions dissipated Cherokee strength. The Ridges and Boudinot now doubted the wisdom of resisting removal and influenced others. This faction believed hope lay in moving beyond white influence. Thus tribal factionalism, state sovereignty, and federal executive power eroded the once solid Cherokee foundation.

In December, 1835, the Ridge faction signed the New Echota Treaty, yielding all eastern lands for $5 million and for guarantees to western lands. Despite Chief Ross' efforts, Congress approved the treaty and set removal for May, 1838. Two years of futile negotiations followed before Major General Winfield Scott took charge of removal. He sent off about 2,800 persons, not counting Ridge supporters who left earlier, before Ross agreed to conduct emigration himself to lessen Cherokee losses and military harassment. The tragedy of the Trail of Tears was completed by March, 1839, after nearly a quarter of the tribe was lost. Paradoxically, after removal a veritable reign of terror accompanied a period of renewed social cohesion. Antitreaty assassins murdered the Ridges and Boudinot. Although apparently not sanctioned by Ross, these acts precipitated a half dozen years of bloodshed suffered by both sides. Yet this period also saw a public school system established, male and female seminaries erected, a national press (*Cherokee Advocate*) reinvigorated, and stable government accomplished. The Treaty of 1846 settled major political differences and gave the Cherokee a decade and a half of peace.

Such tranquillity was short-lived. The American Civil War reawakened factionalism within the tribe. Ross, leading full bloods and nonslaveholders, called for neutrality, while STAND WATIE and his cohorts formed a Confederate militia. Pressure of events forced a premature decision. By April, 1861, federal troops had withdrawn from Indian Territory, and Confederate forces controlled surrounding areas. Moreover, promises of a liberal treaty and Confederate military victories convinced the Cherokee to conclude a treaty with the South. The treaty gave them rights they had sought since 1835, but the Confederacy could not fulfill its promises. Federal forces invaded the country in June, 1862, carried off a compliant Ross, and plunged a divided nation into civil strife. During the war, Cherokees suffered greatly as they were shuffled between Kansas and Indian Territory. Watie, the only Indian brigadier general, carried on guerrilla activities and was the last southern general to surrender. Other Cherokees sided with the North and maintained contact with Ross, who worked in Washington, D.C., to convince the government of Cherokee loyalty. At the war's end, the two factions vied for political dominance. The Ross party succeeded in signing the Reconstruction Treaty of 1866, which provided for continuation of Cherokee government, though altering the tribe's physical extent and society. Final dissolution of the Cherokee occurred in 1907 with Oklahoma statehood, despite struggles to maintain independence.

See G. S. Woodard, *The Cherokees* (1963); H. T. Malone, *Cherokees of the Old South* (1956); T. Wilkins, *Cherokee Tragedy* (1970); G. Foreman, *Indian Removal* (1953); M. L. Wardell, *Political History of Cherokee Nation* (1938); and G. E. Moulton, "John Ross" (Ph.D. dissertation, Oklahoma State University, 1973).

GARY E. MOULTON
Southwestern Oklahoma State University

CHEROKEE NATION V. GEORGIA (5 Peters [1831]) was technically a mere denial of jurisdiction by the United States Supreme Court; but the case represented one major episode in a struggle by the CHEROKEE INDIANS to retain their land and relative independence. The historic setting of this formal legal effort at survival by the Cherokee was particularly grim in 1831 because powerful political opponents of the Indians were in firm control of not only the state of Georgia but the legislative and executive branches of the federal government as well. President ANDREW JACKSON had earned a reputation as an Indian fighter and, moreover, was strongly critical of those who aided the cause of the Indians. Jackson and a majority in Congress had approved legislation in 1830 providing for the involuntary removal of the Indians to territory

west of the Mississippi River. Despite such federal approval, governmental leaders of Georgia were not willing to move slowly on its state Indian policies, nor were they willing to acknowledge the jurisdiction of the federal courts on issues involving the Cherokee. The execution of a Cherokee (George Tassel) by a Georgia court for murder committed in the Cherokee Nation was done in the face of a federal writ of error issued by Chief Justice John Marshall.

The cause of the Indians was espoused by groups of religious leaders, by many Whig political leaders, and by several jurists and outstanding lawyers, including former attorney general WILLIAM WIRT. The latter devised the legal strategy utilized in all of the Cherokee cases. A countervailing political attack on the pro-Cherokee legal efforts took the form of states' rights efforts to repeal the provision of the Judiciary Act of 1789, which might have provided a jurisdictional basis for preventing the removal of the Indians or for asserting some measure of Indian independence. Some historians have argued that the issue pitted those who had deep ethical convictions about the fate of the Cherokee against aggressive territorial expansionists. Conversely, others suggest that the legal elite that masterminded the Cherokee litigation also fought Jackson on the bank and other issues. Whichever interpretation ultimately gains acceptance, the pro-Cherokee legal effort was continued after the jurisdictional setback in *Cherokee Nation* v. *Georgia*, when Wirt devised the legal strategy in WORCESTER V. GEORGIA.

See J. C. Burke, *Stanford Law Review* (Feb., 1969); K. Newmyer, *Stanford Law Review* (Feb., 1969); U. B. Phillips, *Annual Report of the American Historical Association* (1901); and C. Warren, *American Law Review* (Jan.–Feb., 1913).

JOHN R. SCHMIDHAUSER
University of Southern California

CHESAPEAKE BAY, the largest inlet on the Atlantic coastal plain, encompasses a 200-mile length, a width of from four to 30 miles, and a total shoreline of 8,100 miles about equally divided between Maryland and Virginia. The bay was created within the past 15,000 years by the flooding of the lower valley of the Susquehanna River. Exploration of the bay began in the early sixteenth century, but the first permanent settlement was not until 1607 under Captain John Smith at JAMESTOWN. The first map of the region was published in a 1590 volume of travels by Théodore de Bry under the name "Chesepioc sinus," named after the Indians who lived on the Elizabeth River near the bay's mouth; *Chesapeake* is believed to have meant "mother of waters" or "country on a great water." After Jamestown, settlement spread northward onto Virginia's Eastern Shore, Kent Island, and Maryland in 1634.

The immense shoreline and many navigable rivers provided an excellent transportation facility and encouraged the dominance of TOBACCO in the colonial economy. By the eve of the Revolution, Virginia and Maryland—with 30 percent of the population—produced 60 percent of the colonies' exports to England and Scotland; tobacco accounted for 90 percent of these exports in value. This staple retarded urban development; not until settlement moved westward and the economy diversified with crops such as wheat and corn and some manufacturing did towns like Baltimore and Richmond appear. During the Revolutionary War, Chesapeake Bay was the scene of a number of naval engagements and campaigns, most notably the 1781 YORKTOWN CAMPAIGN. During both this war and the War of 1812 the bay was a privateering center; a sailing vessel native to its waters, the Baltimore clipper, was largely responsible. In the later war the British blockaded the bay from the end of 1812 and burned Washington, D.C., and attacked Baltimore in 1814.

Although shipbuilding had been important since the seventeenth century, the War of 1812 created a boom, and by the 1830s ship production was at its peak. The completion of the Chesapeake & Ohio and Chesapeake & Delaware CANALS in the 1820s and the serious commencement of RAILROAD construction in the 1830s also laid a solid foundation for economic expansion for the rest of the century. Although temporarily disrupted by the Civil War, by the 1880s the industrialization of the Atlantic seaboard states was well under way, and the bay with ports like Norfolk, Baltimore, Hampton Roads, and others took on new significance as a center of national and international trade, a role it has played increasingly since then.

Throughout its history, the bay has served as a source of food. The growth of the SEAFOOD INDUSTRY peaked in the 1880s and in recent years has experienced new growth. Since 1950 over 50 species of finfish and shellfish, principally oysters and crabs, have been marketed. The 1970 harvest, for example, totaled over 660 million pounds valued at $45 million.

The last 25 years have brought tremendous changes to the bay region. In the 1950s some major bridges were constructed, and in 1964 the Chesapeake Bay Bridge-Tunnel was opened linking Norfolk to the DELMARVA PENINSULA. Stimulated by the easier access to major population centers, industry, URBANIZATION, TOURISM, and other RECREATION-oriented activities have all dramatically increased. Consequently, most of the recent research done about the bay has been about ecological and environmental dangers. Chesapeake Bay supports over 8 million people now, and by the year 2000 the population is projected to be between 10 and 12 million.

See A. P. Middleton, *Tobacco Coast* (1953); M. V. Brewington, *Chesapeake Bay* (1956); L. D. Scisco, *Maryland Historical Magazine* (Dec., 1945); L. G. Carr, *Maryland Historical Magazine* (Summer, 1974); J. M. Price, *Journal of Economic History* (Dec., 1964); R. D. Gray, *National Waterway* (1967); W. S. Sanderlin, *Great National Project* (1946); W. L. Paternotte and L. Monnig, *South Atlantic Economy* (1971); and R. H. Pearsall, "Chesapeake Bay Bridge-Tunnel" (M.A. thesis, East Carolina College, 1965).

RICHARD J. COX
Maryland Historical Society

CHESNUT, JAMES, JR. (1815–1885), was admitted to the South Carolina bar in 1837. He married Mary Boykin Miller, who kept the famous *Diary from Dixie*. Chesnut served in the state legislature (1840–1858). Firmly proslavery but uncommitted to immediate secession, he became U.S. senator in 1858. As senator Chesnut became less moderate, advocating a national territorial slave code. In the fall of 1860 he converted to immediate secession and then resigned as senator. He became a member of the committee that wrote the South Carolina ordinance of secession and served in the first Confederate Congress. Chesnut was one of those who presented the surrender demands to Major ROBERT ANDERSON at Ft. Sumter. He served actively in the South Carolina governor's executive council, was a military aide to Jefferson Davis (1862–1864), and commanded the South Carolina reserve forces (1864–1865). After the war, he presided at the 1867 convention opposing military rule and remained active in state Democratic politics.

See C. E. Cauthen, *South Carolina Goes to War* (1950); H. S. Schultz, *Nationalism and Sectionalism in South Carolina* (1950); and D. Rowland, *Jefferson Davis* (1913), correspondence.

RONALD H. RIDGLEY
University of South Dakota, Springfield

CHESNUTT, CHARLES WADDELL (1858–1932), although born in Ohio, called North Carolina home. He lived 17 of his most impressionable years in Fayetteville, where his parents had returned in 1866. His only formal education was acquired in the colored grade school there, he taught

there, and Fayetteville and its environs, its myths, its legends, and its people were the materials of his fiction.

In his twenty-fifth year, he spent a few months in New York, where he taught himself stenography and, passing for white, worked for Dow-Jones, a Wall Street news agency. When he moved to Cleveland, he studied law and was admitted to the bar, but clients were scarce and an old urge to write overwhelmed him. Although he succeeded in publishing several stories and sketches, it was the publication in 1887 of "The Goophered Grapevine" by the *Atlantic Monthly* that first gained him national recognition. It was a southern "folktale," wholly imagined, and a metaphorical narrative of race relations. His stories began to appear regularly in the *Atlantic*, the *Independent*, and the *Overland Monthly*, and in 1899 several of these were collected and published as *The Conjure Woman*. If this collection of stories dealt with the complexities of the race problem so subtly that many of his contemporary readers missed the point, a second collection, *The Wife of His Youth* (1899), revealed in all their dramatic poignancy the problems and the life-styles of Negro people accommodating to the expectations, the demands, and the prejudiced assumptions of the white world.

Chesnutt wrote three novels: *The House Behind the Cedars* (1900), *The Marrow of Tradition* (1901), and *The Colonel's Dream* (1905). After publication of this last novel, he gave up writing and devoted himself to the practice of law until his death. His novels are now forgotten; but the reputation of Chesnutt—as the first Negro whose mastery of short fiction ranks him with Nathaniel Hawthorne, Edgar Allan Poe, Mark Twain, and Bret Harte—endures.

See biographies by H. M. Chesnutt (1952) and W. E. Farrison (1970); and E. S. Miers, introduction, *Wife of His Youth* (1963). Chesnutt's manuscripts are held by H. M. Chesnutt of Cleveland, Ohio.

SAUNDERS REDDING
Cornell University

CHEVES, LANGDON (1776–1857), congressman and public official, represented plantation society although he was born in Abbeville District, S.C. He served in the South Carolina legislature (1802–1810) and became attorney general (1808). Charlestonians weary of economic depression elected him U.S. representative in 1810. Living in Washington with the "war mess" (JOHN C. CALHOUN, WILLIAM LOWNDES, HENRY CLAY), Cheves focused on naval and financial preparedness for the conflict with England. He became Speaker of the House in 1814, but retired in 1816 and was elected justice of the court of appeals of South Carolina. A nationally recognized expert in finance, Cheves became president of the second Bank of the United States in 1819 (he prevented its bankruptcy). He was chief commissioner of claims under the Treaty of Ghent (1823). Thereafter he withdrew from public life to practice law in South Carolina, where he wrote occasional political commentaries. In 1850, he refused a Senate appointment to replace the late John C. Calhoun. Cheves opposed NULLIFICATION in the 1830s, and, as a South Carolina representative to the NASHVILLE CONVENTION (1850), he denounced separate state action, speaking instead for a nonviolent southern alliance.

See Cheves's manuscripts in South Caroliniana Library, Columbia, and South Carolina Historical Society, Charleston; R. J. Turnbull, *Bibliography of South Carolina* (1956), I–III, for Cheves pamphlets; and J. B. O'Neall, *Biographical Sketches of Bench and Bar of South Carolina* (1859), I.

MARGARET K. LATIMER
Auburn University

CHICANO. This term has no known etymological origin, but it was used in the 1920s by native-born Mexican-Americans in the form *chicamo* to describe and to denigrate Mexican immigrants. To the *chicamo* the native born was a *pocho*, a man in cultural limbo who sought to fade into the majority society by boasting of his "Spanish" inheritance. Both group responses and the division between the two Spanish-surnamed groups arose from psychic exploitation by the Anglo-American society. The Chicano movement began as a protest in the 1960s and then commenced to stress cultural nationalism and the radicalization of Mexican-American political activity. Although the ideology varies from region to region, generally speaking the Chicano movement wishes to construct a new image for Mexican-Americans and end the cultural suppression that it claims continues into the present.

See Chicano Coordinating Council on Higher Education, *El Plan de Santa Barbara* (1969), contains good example of division between "Chicanos" and "Mexican-Americans"; M. Gamio, *Mexican Immigration to U.S.* (1930); C. McWilliams, *North from Mexico* (1949); J. W. Moore with A. Cuéllar, *Mexican Americans* (1970), contains excellent brief analysis of Chicano movement; A. B. Rendon, *Chicano Manifesto* (1972); and R. H. Vigil, *New Mexico Historical Review* (July, 1973).

RALPH H. VIGIL
University of Nebraska, Lincoln

CHICKAHOMINY RIVER begins northwest of RICHMOND, Va., and flows parallel to the JAMES RIVER for 40 miles before bending to the south and entering the James eight miles west of WILLIAMSBURG. Through most of its course the Chickahominy is a shallow, sluggish stream, but in its lower reaches it becomes a broad tidal estuary, capable in colonial times of accommodating large merchant vessels.

By the middle 1600s most of the Indians living near the river were driven to the interior by the advance of James River planters. By 1700 life was attuned to tobacco production, slave labor, and the regular arrival of trading vessels. Two shipyards sprawled near the river's mouth. But soil exhaustion, river siltation, and fires stifled economic growth, and after 1840 the Chickahominy Valley stagnated. Its torpor was broken momentarily during the Civil War by George McClellan's and U. S. Grant's assaults toward nearby Richmond and in the 1880s by construction of the Chesapeake & Ohio Railroad through the valley toward Newport News.

Economic dormancy continued into the twentieth century. By the 1920s the movement of Chickahominy country residents to urban areas had become pronounced, the percentage of idle land was rapidly increasing, and the remaining residents, largely Negroes and a few residual clusters of Indians, eked out an impoverished existence by farming, fishing, trapping, and sawmill employment. These patterns have persisted along the middle Chickahominy, but recently the cutting edge of Richmond's suburban sprawl has reached the upper valley, and downstream areas have enjoyed a minor recreational boom stimulated in part by the expansion of tourism in the Williamsburg-Jamestown area.

See T. Stern, *Proceedings of the American Philosophical Society* (April, 1952); J. J. Corson, *Charles City County* (1929); and J. F. Fausz, "Settlement in James Basin" (M.A. thesis, College of William and Mary, 1971).

MARSHALL BOWEN
Mary Washington College

CHICKAMAUGA, BATTLE OF (September 19–21, 1863). The war in Tennessee went badly for the Confederacy in 1863. By September Knoxville had fallen, control of east Tennessee had been lost, and BRAXTON BRAGG's army had to abandon Chattanooga to a federal army under William S. Rosecrans. Bragg sought to strike his enemy as he advanced into the rugged mountains of north Georgia. After being reinforced by elements of

JAMES B. LONGSTREET's corps from Virginia, Bragg decided to swing north of Rosecrans, cut the roads to Chattanooga, and then destroy the federals in a cul-de-sac formed by the mountains.

After a hesitant beginning on September 18, the battle opened in earnest on the nineteenth as the two armies, numbering close to 65,000 each, clashed on the north flank. Both sides fought furiously until darkness ended the inconclusive action. The next day Bragg ordered his right wing again to turn Rosecrans' left beginning at daybreak; thereafter Confederate corps from right to left were to attack as the sound of battle opened on their immediate right. Although starting late, the Confederates managed to slip around the north flank of GEORGE H. THOMAS' corps, threatening the federal rear. As chance would have it, when Longstreet finally attacked farther south, his troops poured through a gap created inadvertently in the federal line. Severing the Union right from Thomas, Longstreet drove those federals south of the gap into a precipitate withdrawal. He then turned against Thomas and joined in a succession of unsuccessful assaults. Under heavy pressure, Thomas withdrew from the field as darkness fell, and the Union army slipped back into Chattanooga. Thereafter, Bragg followed slowly, choosing to besiege the federals in the town rather than to attack. By failing to press the advantage won at Chickamauga, Bragg eventually relinquished the initiative, inviting his defeat two months later on Missionary Ridge (CHATTANOOGA CAMPAIGN).

See *Official Records, Armies*, Ser. 1, Vol. XXX, Pts. 1–4; T. L. Connelly, *Autumn of Glory* (1971), most recent analysis; G. Tucker, *Chickamauga* (1963); S. F. Horn, *Army of Tennessee* (1941), old but good; K. P. Williams, *Lincoln Finds General* (1959), V, federal side; and S. Foote, *Civil War* (1963), II.

ROY K. FLINT
U.S. Military Academy

CHICKAMAUGA INDIANS, a militant CHERO-KEE secessionist group, carried on sporadic border warfare against American expansion into the old Southwest from 1777 to 1795. The militant nationalist, Dragging Canoe (Tsu-gun-Sini), led a secession movement of 1,000 Cherokee militants to Chickamauga Creek north of Chattanooga in 1777. By early 1782, the Chickamauga, as the militants were now called, had established villages known as the Five Lower Towns near present-day Chattanooga along the Tennessee River. The Chickamauga under Dragging Canoe's leadership carried on the resistance with the aid of a loose confederacy of northern and southern Indians and with British and Spanish support. By using small mobile war parties, the Chickamauga inflicted great losses on the white settlements and disrupted travel. Even the death of Dragging Canoe in 1792 did not halt them; under their new leader John Watts, a half blood, the Chickamauga continued their resistance until their towns were invaded by a Kentucky and middle Tennessee force in 1794. The Chickamauga ended their 18 years of resistance to the whites by signing the Treaty of TELLICO BLOCKHOUSE in 1795.

See J. P. Brown, *Old Frontiers* (1938); J. Haywood, *History of Tennessee* (1823); J. P. Pate, "Chickamauga" (Ph.D. dissertation, Mississippi State University, 1969); and Draper Collection, State Historical Society of Wisconsin, Madison, available on microfilm.

JAMES P. PATE
Livingston University

CHICKASAW BAYOU, BATTLE OF (December 27–29, 1862), was the result of an effort by 33,000 men with seven gunboats and 60 transports under William T. Sherman to take Vicksburg, Miss. Originally planned by U. S. Grant as part of a three-pronged attack, the other two never began. JOHN C. PEMBERTON had overall command of Confederate defense, MARTIN L. SMITH had command within the city, and STEPHEN D. LEE actually directed the battle. Ultimately Pemberton concentrated 12,000 men, but initially the Confederates had 2,700 outside the city and 2,400 manning interior fortifications. Sherman claimed "preparations were extremely hasty," as "this was the nature of the plan," but actually Grant and Sherman had learned that President ABRAHAM LINCOLN was sending General John McClernand to supersede them and wished to act before he arrived. The armada steamed down the Mississippi and 12 miles up the Yazoo River to debark on an area about six miles square, bordered by the Yazoo on the north, an old bed of the Mississippi on the west, a long narrow lake on the south, and Chickasaw Bayou on the east. Terrain, more than planning, brought two Union brigades into assault positions at the bayou, where Lee had set a trap. A morass of mud and water slowed the federals and forced funneling over a log bridge. The assault reached within 150 yards of the Confederate main line when the men broke and retreated. Losses were 1,776 Union and 207 Confederate. Sherman planned another attack, but dense fog settled and a torrential rain instilled fear that a flood might drown the entire command, so he withdrew on January 2. One Union corporal aptly observed that "Sherman or Grant or both had made a bad blunder."

See D. A. Brown, *Civil War Times Illustrated* (July, 1970); and H. Hattaway, *Journal of Mississippi History* (Nov., 1970).

HERMAN HATTAWAY
University of Missouri, Kansas City

CHICKASAW INDIANS. On the eve of European contact the Chickasaw resided in northeastern Mississippi. HERNANDO DE SOTO's expedition reached their towns on the TOMBIGBEE RIVER in 1540. In the period of French exploration of the lower Mississippi Valley, ROBERT CAVELIER DE LA SALLE (1682) visited the Chickasaw. Following French settlement on the Gulf at Biloxi in 1699, PIERRE LE MOYNE, SIEUR D'IBERVILLE sought to bring them under French dominion. At the same time, English traders from Charleston arrived in the Chickasaw towns. The Chickasaw favored the English and refused to cooperate with the French. On four occasions between 1720 and 1752, French armies, braced with CHOCTAW mercenaries, attempted to conquer the Chickasaw and force them to expel the English traders. Each invasion ended in French defeat. The Chickasaw assisted the British in the conquest of the lower Mississippi. During the FRENCH AND INDIAN WAR, British-armed Chickasaws closed the Mississippi River to French shipping, sundering contact between the French settlements in the Northwest and the Gulf and contributing to the French defeat in the West.

During the American REVOLUTION, the Chickasaw supported the British cause and served in Tory armies against Americans in the West. Subsequently the Chickasaw accepted the Americans and, except for one small faction in the tribe, supported the successful American effort to dislodge the Spanish from United States territory in the lower Mississippi Valley, culminating in Pinckney's Treaty (1795).

From the earliest days of the British presence in the Chickasaw Nation, white traders married native women. This produced a large community of mixed bloods. Eventually the mixed-blood clique, led by the Colbert family, came to dominate the political, social, and economic life of the Chickasaw Nation. Many mixed bloods emulated the planters living on the rim of their nation, became slaveholders, and developed productive farms and plantations.

Through successive federal treaties, Chickasaw leaders ceded tribal territory in western Kentucky and Tennessee and, by 1830, all that remained of their once vast domain was a residual area in northern Mississippi and a fragment of territory in northwestern Alabama. By the Treaty of Pontotoc (1832) and an amendatory treaty in 1834, the Chickasaw agreed to sell their eastern lands and remove to Indian Territory. During 1861 the Chickasaw Nation joined the Confederacy, and Chickasaw companies fought in several campaigns against Union troops in the Indian Territory. Following the war, the Chickasaw were required to undergo Reconstruction, which included freeing their slaves and altering their constitution to provide civil and social status for freedmen.

Pressed by the Dawes commission during the latter part of the nineteenth century to accept allotment in severalty, the Chickasaw finally submitted through the Atoka Agreement, signed in 1897. The following year the Curtis Act dissolved the government of the Chickasaw Nation, and in 1907 the Chickasaw were absorbed into the new state of Oklahoma.

See R. S. Cotterill, *Southern Indians* (1954); V. W. Crane, *Southern Frontier* (1929); and G. Foreman, *Five Civilized Tribes* (1934). For primary sources, see National Archives; Gilcrease Museum; Mississippi State Archives; Oklahoma Historical Society; and Tennessee State Archives.

ARRELL MORGAN GIBSON
University of Oklahoma

CHICKASAW OLD FIELDS. Tribal history relates that the CHICKASAW, guided by an oracular pole, migrated from the Far West. Their sacred pole led them to the area of Madison County, Ala. There tribal leaders determined that the Chickasaw should settle, and the resultant cluster of settlements became the first Chickasaw Old Fields. Pressure from neighboring tribes, however, forced the Chickasaw to abandon this Alabama settlement, and their oracular pole commanded them to move west. They then settled in the area of Lee County, Miss., and there the tribe restored Chickasaw Old Fields. It remained the focus of tribal settlement until the 1830s, when the Chickasaw were removed to Indian Territory.

See J. H. Malone, *Chickasaw Nation* (1922); J. R. Swanton, *Myths and Tales of Southeastern Indians* (1929); and R. Dunbar, *History of Mississippi* (1925), I.

ARRELL MORGAN GIBSON
University of Oklahoma

CHILD LABOR. Southern control of child labor has been a twentieth-century development. In 1900, 25 percent of the operatives in the cotton mills, the worst offenders, were between ten and sixteen years old, the same percentage they constituted in 1880. In the same period their percentage of the total northern labor force declined from 15.6 to 7.7, although their absolute number was greater than in the South.

Much of the impetus for correction of the southern evil came from the American Federation of Labor. Following the failure of the Alabama legislature to adopt a child labor law in 1898–1899, it dispatched Irene Ashby to make a study showing the extent of child labor in Alabama mills. Realizing that as a union employee she would have little influence, she took her report to EDGAR GARDNER MURPHY, rector of St. John's Episcopal Church in Montgomery, who mobilized support for a bill imposing a twelve-year age limit on workers. In the ensuing contest, a representative of a northern-owned mill appealed to sectional prejudice to defeat the bill. The outraged Murphy organized the Alabama Child Labor Committee and wrote and widely distributed highly effective pamphlets that first exposed the evils of southern child labor. He held that the worst offenders were northern-owned mills and contended that premature labor prevented child development and inhibited economic growth. Largely as a result of his work, Alabama passed the child labor law under consideration in 1903, and Murphy aided in forming the National Child Labor Committee in 1904. Within a year, 17 states and the District of Columbia organized local committees, which worked with the national committee, and 12 states enacted some type of child labor law.

Murphy's pamphlets aroused the concern of ALEXANDER MCKELWAY, editor of the Charlotte, N.C., *Presbyterian Standard*. Enlisting the support of Governor CHARLES B. AYCOCK, he led North Carolina to enact a 1903 law imposing a twelve-year age limit and a 66-hour week for children under sixteen. Similar laws were passed the same year in South Carolina and Virginia. Much of the rest of the nation, however, had gone to a fourteen-year age limit, and the desire to attain this standard in the South led McKelway in October, 1904, to become assistant secretary of the National Child Labor Committee. Although Georgia adopted a twelve-year limit on child labor in 1906, inadequate inspection resulted in many violations, particularly in the four southern textile states—the Carolinas, Georgia, and Alabama. This encouraged the National Child Labor Committee to endorse the Beveridge bill in December, 1906, which would have excluded from interstate commerce the products of factories employing children under fourteen. A number of southern committee members objected, however, including

Murphy, whose arguments seem to have led President Theodore Roosevelt to withhold his support, and the committee soon rescinded its endorsement. However, it was influential in getting Congress in 1907 to appropriate money for the Department of Commerce and Labor to investigate the conditions of working women and children and for the establishment of the Children's Bureau in 1912.

The national committee working with state committees obtained limited results. In 1907, Alabama adopted a twelve-year age limit without exceptions and a 66-hour week for those under fourteen. North Carolina raised the age limit to thirteen and permitted apprenticeship of twelve-year-olds who attended school four months in the year. South Carolina and Tennessee established the ten-hour day for children; and Florida, in its first bill, set a twelve-year age limit, except for those in domestic service and agriculture. McKelway authored a clause in an Oklahoma school bill that provided that dependent parents of children under fourteen should receive a state pension equal to the children's salaries. By 1913 this mothers' pension bill was adopted in 20 states.

Progress continued to be made in the states but was largely limited to the gains that the more progressive industrialists would accept. By 1910 Kentucky, Virginia, Tennessee, Louisiana, and Arkansas had adopted a fourteen-year age limit and restricted hours for child employees. All of these states except Arkansas had inspections. Although a twelve-year age limit prevailed in the four textile states as well as in Florida and Texas, Alabama had only one inspector, and there was none in Georgia and the Carolinas. In 1911, 20 percent of southern mill employees were still under sixteen, but Georgia established the 60-hour week for all cotton mill workers, and North Carolina imposed a 64- instead of a 66-hour week.

Additional impetus came for reform when the first SOUTHERN SOCIOLOGICAL CONGRESS was held in 1912. Like the National Child Labor Committee, it urged adoption of a uniform child labor law with a fourteen-year minimum age. During the year, Maryland and Mississippi accepted versions of the law, and South Carolina employed two inspectors. In 1913, Florida adopted most features of the uniform law, and Georgia and Arkansas followed in 1914. Alabama adopted the fourteen-year age limit in 1916, although it accepted an 11- rather than an eight-hour day, and South Carolina imposed the fourteen-year limit on January 1, 1917.

Inadequate enforcement, however, mitigated many of the gains, and in 1914 the National Child

Labor Committee returned to advocacy of a national law. In 1916, the Keating-Owen bill was passed to become operative September 1, 1917. It excluded from interstate commerce the products of factories where children under fourteen worked or those with laborers under sixteen working more than eight hours a day or at night, as well as products of mines and quarries with workers under sixteen. This measure was invalidated by the U.S. Supreme Court in 1918; a measure levying a tax on profits of employers of children was passed in 1919, but it was invalidated in 1922. Yet many states received an impetus from the temporary national legislation. In the 1930s all southern states prohibited those under sixteen doing night work, and most enforced a minimum age of fourteen for child labor. Permanent national action came under the National Industrial Recovery Act, which ended child labor in some industries, and the Fair Labor Standards Act of 1938, which prohibited labor in industry of children under sixteen and that of those under eighteen in industries found to be hazardous.

See E. H. Davidson, *Child Labor Legislation* (1939); H. Bailey, *Liberalism in New South* (1969); National Child Labor Committee Papers and Alexander McKelway Papers, Library of Congress; and Edgar Gardner Murphy Papers, University of North Carolina.

HUGH C. BAILEY
Francis Marion College

CHINCOTEAGUE ISLAND is part of Accomack County, Va. Impetus for settlement came in the 1670s, when the Virginia general assembly restricted loose livestock (FENCE LAWS); this and the other coastal islands were then used for the raising of hogs, horses, and cattle. For many years the island was owned only by several families. By 1800 the island had a population of 60, and the land was beginning to be broken into smaller parcels. At the outbreak of the Civil War its populace voted 138 to two against joining the Confederacy, probably induced by its isolation and predominant waterborne trade with the North. This isolation continued well into the twentieth century until the Chincoteague Toll Road & Bridge Company was organized in 1919; three years later the road opened, bringing with it a new era for the island. At the end of World War II the Chincoteague National Wildlife Refuge was established. Today the island is a large producer of shellfish and poultry. It is best known for the roundup of miniature horses, remnants of the colonists' animals, held every year in midsummer and widely popularized by Marguerite Henry's *Misty of Chincoteague* (1947), which later was made into a movie.

See N. M. Turman, *Eastern Shore of Virginia* (1964); and R. T. Whitelaw, *Virginia's Eastern Shore* (1951).

RICHARD J. COX
Maryland Historical Society

CHISHOLM V. GEORGIA (2 Dallas 419 [1793]). On October 31, 1777, two commissioners for the state of Georgia agreed to purchase a large amount of clothing, blankets, and other supplies from Robert Farquhar, a merchant of Charleston, for use by American troops. Farquhar delivered the merchandise well before the December 1, 1777, delivery date but was never paid. After his death in 1784, Alexander Chisholm of South Carolina, executor of the Farquhar estate, filed suit in the U.S. circuit court for Georgia; but the court held that a citizen of another state could not bring suit against Georgia in that court.

Chisholm carried the case to the U.S. Supreme Court, where the important issue was whether, under the United States Constitution, a suit could be brought against a state by a citizen of another state. On February 18, 1793, four of five justices gave opinions in favor of Chisholm. The amount of damages to be awarded was never established, although the case remained on the Court docket until 1798.

The *Chisholm* decision and suits against five other states resulted in the ratification of the Eleventh Amendment to the Constitution, prohibiting suits brought against a state by citizens of another state. In 1794 a settlement was reached between Georgia and Peter Trezevant, husband of Robert Farquhar's daughter; however, Georgia refused to honor some of the certificates issued to Trezevant, and a final settlement was not reached until 1847.

See *Chisholm* v. *Georgia* Case File, Dockets of Supreme Court, and Minutes of the Supreme Court, all in National Archives, RG 267; and D. Mathis, *Journal of American History* (June, 1967).

DOYLE MATHIS
Berry College

CHOCTAW INDIANS, linguistically a Muskogean people, were natives of south-central Mississippi. Predominantly agriculturists, they lived in permanent communities, which were grouped into three political units ruled by an autonomous chief. The social structure of the tribe hinged upon a matrilineal clan system, and its spirit life focused upon the sacred mound, *Nanih Waiya*. Wholly unwarlike, the tribe was famous for its dances and recreational activities. Although HERNANDO DE SOTO visited the Choctaw in 1540, the French were the first Europeans to influence them significantly. After 1699 the French depended upon the tribe to protect their interest in the lower Mississippi Valley against encroachments from English-allied tribes. This alliance was best demonstrated in April, 1736, when the Choctaw joined the French in assaulting the CHICKASAW village of Akia. After 1763, the British never fully won the tribe's allegiance; the Spanish were even less successful between 1783 and 1796.

Recognizing the sovereignty of the United States in 1785, the Choctaw remained aloof from American policy until President Thomas Jefferson's administration. In four treaties negotiated before 1805 they relinquished some 7.5 million acres of their domain. Despite these losses, the Choctaw campaigned with Andrew Jackson during the War of 1812, welcomed Protestant missionaries, supported educational efforts, purchased slaves, and in 1826 adopted a written code of laws. This accommodation notwithstanding, the tribe was forced to sign the Treaty of DANCING RABBIT CREEK on September 28, 1830, whereby it ceded its ancestral domain and agreed to remove to lands in southern Oklahoma. By 1834, 10,000 had emigrated, followed by 3,000 more in mid-1840. At least 3,000, however, were never removed.

In Indian Territory the Choctaw quickly reestablished their society, writing a constitution in 1834 and inaugurating a remarkable educational system. Allied with the Confederacy during the Civil War, the Choctaw suffered severe wartime dislocation. After 1866 railroad construction and the exploitation of coal and timber resources brought tens of thousands of white men to the reservation. This intrusion and government pressure forced the 20,620 Choctaws in 1897 to consent to the final allotment of their reservation. Since 1934 tribal affairs have been conducted by a principal chief and council. Barely escaping "termination" in the 1950s, the Choctaw prospered under the Great Society self-help programs of the 1960s.

See A. Debo, *Rise and Fall of Choctaw* (1934), and *And Still the Waters Run* (1940); A. H. DeRosier, Jr., *Removal of Choctaw* (1970); and W. D. Baird, *Peter Pitchlynn* (1972).

W. DAVID BAIRD
University of Arkansas, Fayetteville

CHOPIN, KATE (1851–1904), was born in St. Louis, Mo., as Katherine O'Flaherty and educated in local convent schools. In 1870 she married Oscar Chopin and moved to Louisiana, where she lived and had six children before her husband's death in 1882. Returning to St. Louis, she began to write short stories of Creole and CAJUN life as she had observed it during her residence in the bayou country. Her stories are remembered for their light, sympathetic touch and for their effective use of dialect. Her first novel, *At Fault* (1890), traced the growing affection between a married man from the North and a widowed mistress of a Louisiana plantation. Although containing insights into character, the novel is cumbersomely constructed and is generally judged more interesting than excellent. Her second novel, *The Awakening* (1899), is recognized, however, as the first fictional study frankly to examine the plight of a married American woman and her compulsive desire for emancipation. Largely criticized when published for its boldness, it is now considered to be a landmark in the development of the American novel. It is an original, challenging, and well-structured work of art, which focuses directly on its perhaps misguided protagonist, a Protestant girl from Kentucky married to a Catholic Creole businessman. Not so well known, but equally challenging and perhaps more charming, is *Athenaise* (1896), a novelette that describes the attempts of an attractive Creole girl to measure up to the expectations of her husband.

See *Bayou Folk* (1894) and *Night in Acadie* (1897), Chopin's short stories; Per Seyersted (ed.), *Complete Works of K. Chopin* (2 vols.; 1969), and *Kate Chopin* (1969); and L. Leary, *K. Chopin* (1970), critical commentary.

LEWIS LEARY
University of North Carolina, Chapel Hill

CHRISTY, DAVID (1802–1868), Cincinnati journalist, wrote several books in the 1850s attacking abolitionism and advocating the colonization of U.S. blacks in Africa. Christy became the Ohio agent for the AMERICAN COLONIZATION SOCIETY in 1848 and wrote and traveled extensively on the society's behalf. His most widely circulated book was *Cotton Is King*, published anonymously in 1855 but acknowledged in two later editions. Although antislavery in tone, it argued that abolitionist attacks actually strengthened slavery, which would remain viable until free labor proved more profitable for planters and colonization solved the race issue. The book was well received by moderate opinion, especially southern; DE BOW'S REVIEW called it "cogent, well-informed, and temperate." It inspired Senator JAMES HAMMOND's famous 1855 reply to William Seward: "No, you dare not make war on cotton. . . . Cotton is king."

In other works Christy condemned the injection of the slavery issue into Protestant denominational politics. Christy's travels and scientific interests led him to make geological observations, which he began publishing in 1848. He was employed briefly as geologist by a North Carolina mining firm. At his death he was writing a treatise, "Geology Attesting Christianity."

See D. Christy, *Lecture on African Colonization* (1849), and *Lecture on African Civilization* (1850), pamphlets in University of Illinois Library. See also D. Christy, *Republic of Liberia* (1852), and *Pulpit Politics: Ethiopia* (1857).

JOHN M. SHAY
Chicago State University

CHURCHES OF CHRIST originated on the American frontier in the early 1800s and share a solid century of history with the DISCIPLES OF CHRIST. Key leaders of the first generation were Alexander Campbell (1788–1866) and his father Thomas (1763–1854), Barton W. Stone (1772–1844), and Walter Scott (1796–1861). All four men rebelled against what they took to be the corruptions of Christianity as reflected in Protestant denominations at the time. They aimed to restore primitive Christianity and thereby to unite a divided church so as to "win the world for Christ." Disavowing all creedal statements as unauthorized tests of Christian fellowship, they affirmed "no creed but Christ" and made a slogan of Thomas Campbell's expression: "Where the Scriptures speak, we speak; where the Scriptures are silent, we are silent." After existing as two groups of reformers, both with Presbyterian backgrounds, the Christians in the West, led by Stone, and the Disciples congregations, under the watchful eye of Alexander Campbell, began the process of coming together in 1832. The resulting fellowship grew rapidly, increasing in membership from approximately 22,000 in 1832 to about 192,000 in 1860 and 1,120,000 in 1900.

Intense and sustained controversy marked this period of expansion. The slavery question and the Civil War figured decisively in the mounting unrest within the denomination, for the thinking of most Disciples reflected the sentiment of the section in which they lived. In addition to political and socioeconomic factors, theological issues—principally the doctrine of the church—provoked great tension. Strict restorationists or exclusivists in the movement maintained that church structure and the elements of corporate worship must conform precisely to the explicit commands and precedents in the New Testament. To their mind, the silence of the Scriptures was proscriptive. The progressives or moderate Disciples also advocated a return to primitive Christianity, but they insisted that the silence of the Scriptures was permissive instead of restrictive. They approved the use of instrumental music in worship and supported missionary societies despite heavy opposition from conservatives. Each congregation faced the necessity of siding with one faction or the other. The schism was recognized officially when the federal religious census of 1906 listed Churches of Christ as a religious body separate and distinct from the Disciples. In that year, according to the census, members of Churches of Christ numbered 159,658, nearly two-thirds of whom lived in the 11 former Confederate states.

The growth of Churches of Christ, especially in urban areas, has been striking in recent decades. Precise statistics are not available because no church agency has the authority and the responsibility to compile data from the thousands of autonomous congregations. But all informed estimates of worldwide membership exceed 2 million. Among the major journals in the movement are the *Gospel Advocate*, published in Nashville, Tenn., and *Firm Foundation*, published in Austin, Tex. Except for Pepperdine University in California, the best-known institutions of higher education related to Churches of Christ are in the South: Abilene Christian College in Texas, Harding College in Arkansas, and David Lipscomb College in Tennessee. Contrary to popular understanding, Churches of Christ are by no means in full agreement with respect to faith and practice. Even so, they remain firmly committed to Christian primitivism and do not participate in the cooperative ventures of either mainstream or evangelical Protestantism.

See E. I. West, *Search for Ancient Order* (2 vols.; 1949, 1950), considered by Churches of Christ as standard study of Campbell-Stone movement to 1906; L. G. McAllister and W. E. Tucker, *Journey in Faith* (1975), comprehensive; E. S. Gaustad, in D. R. Cutler (ed.), *Religious Situation, 1969* (1969); D. E. Harrell, Jr., *Journal of Southern History* (Aug., 1964), *Quest for a Christian America* (1966), and *Social Sources of Division in Disciples of Christ, 1865–1900* (1973); A. V. Murrell, "Exclusivism in Separation of Churches of Christ" (Ph.D. dissertation, Vanderbilt University, 1972); E. I. West, *David Lipscomb* (1954); and C. E. Spencer, *Author Catalog of Disciples of Christ* (1946). Most complete collection of source materials is at Disciples of Christ Historical Society, Nashville.

WILLIAM E. TUCKER
Bethany College, Bethany, W.Va.

CHURCHILL, THOMAS JAMES (1824–1905), was born near Louisville, Ky. After finishing St. Mary's College and reading law at Transylvania, he entered the Mexican War as a lieutenant. In 1848 he moved to Little Rock, where he acquired a sizable plantation close-by, married well, and became postmaster (1857). His background prompted participation in the Civil War, first as colonel of the Arkansas Rifles, a Confederate regiment he raised. WILSON'S CREEK and PEA RIDGE earned him promotion, yet his military record was marred at Arkansas Post, where an inadequate force under his command surrendered prematurely (January, 1863). For the remainder of the war, Churchill served well, but without distinction. In 1874, his role in the BROOKS-BAXTER WAR thrust him forward, and election as state treasurer and governor followed. He had agreed, though with reservation, to repudiate the state's Reconstruction debt and permitted the measure to slip through without his signature. Churchill's public career closed unhappily. Charged with malfeasance while treasurer, he accepted a court decree to make restitution of $80,522.

See F. Hempstead, *Arkansas* (1911), best; D. Herndon, *Arkansas* (1922), useful, with caution; and E. Bearss, *Arkansas Historical Quarterly* (Autumn, 1959).

IRA DON RICHARDS
Henderson State University

CITADEL, THE (Charleston, S.C. 29409), was founded in 1842 as the South Carolina Military Academy. The original building from which the school takes its current name was erected as an arsenal after the VESEY PLOT of 1822. Cadets of the academy participated in the shelling of the federal ship *Star of the West* (FT. SUMTER), and many of the institution's alumni served as Confederate officers during the Civil War. Federal troops occupied the school from February, 1865, until April, 1879, and classes were not resumed until 1892. The college moved to a new campus within the city in 1922, and today this state-supported school has an enrollment of almost 3,000 men. Notable library holdings include materials on the history of Charleston since 1800 and the records of the 24th South Carolina Volunteers.

See O. J. Bond, *Story of Citadel* (1936).

CITIZENS' COUNCILS—and such allied organizations as the Virginia Defenders of State Sovereignty and Individual Liberties, the Tennessee Federation for Constitutional Government, the North Carolina Patriots, and the Georgia States' Rights Council—were organized by southern white segregationists to resist the implementation of the U.S. Supreme Court's school desegregation ruling of 1954. Appearing first in Mississippi in July, 1954, this movement of "white-collar" or "country club Klans" spread rapidly into other states of the Lower South. By late summer, 1955, Citizens' Councils or councillike groups—organized loosely into local, county, district, and state associations—were active in each of the 11 former Confederate states. Dedicated to states' rights as well as to white supremacy, the movement, like the Confederacy itself, failed effectively to overcome traditional southern parochialism and thus never forged a truly united front. Yet a semblance of regional unity was provided in 1956 upon the formation of the Citizens' Councils of America, an informal, Mississippi-based confederation of the principal southern organized resistance groups.

Essentially black belt, low country, tidewater phenomena, the councils' natural habitat was the old, large-scale plantation areas of the DEEP SOUTH, where Negro population density was highest and resistance to social change most adamant. With the notable exceptions of Virginia, where the movement enjoyed the blessings of the BYRD MACHINE, and Arkansas, where Governor ORVAL FAUBUS briefly supported it, councils or councillike groups were neither large nor influential in the states of the so-called rim South. In the Deep South, however, particularly in Alabama, Louisiana, Mississippi, and South Carolina, Citizens' Councils enjoyed not only substantial popular support but also the endorsement of governors, congressmen, judges, physicians, lawyers, industrialists, and bankers. Here, where their power and prestige was greatest, council members denounced Klan VIOLENCE and generally avoided the cruder forms of lawlessness, but they succeeded nonetheless in creating a climate of fear and reprisal in which few whites and even fewer blacks dared challenge the racial status quo. And in Alabama and Mississippi, at least, the movement functioned as a shadow government, which initiated legislation, dictated policy, and exercised a virtual veto power over appointments.

Reliable figures are not available, but total membership in the 11 states probably never exceeded 250,000. Having expanded vigorously in the years immediately after the BROWN V. BOARD OF EDUCATION decision, the movement began gradually to wane following the decisive federal-state confrontation at Little Rock in 1957. By 1961, with biracial schools operating in every southern state but Alabama, Mississippi, and South Carolina, grass-roots support even in the Deep South had all but vanished; and in the rim South, councils and allied groups had virtually ceased to operate. A remobilization campaign begun in that year by the Citizens' Councils of America resulted in the temporary reorganization of many local and most state councils, but it failed to restore the organized resistance movement's original vitality. By the mid-1960s, its membership had dwindled to a hard core of a few thousand unyielding segregationists, and its principal functions, even in Mississippi and Alabama, were the operation of private all-white academies and the promotion of the political fortunes of Governor GEORGE C. WALLACE.

See N. V. Bartley, *Rise of Massive Resistance* (1969); H. Carter III, *South Strikes Back* (1959); and N. R. McMillen, *Citizens' Council* (1971).

N. R. MCMILLEN
University of Southern Mississippi

CITY-MANAGER PLAN has grown more rapidly since 1940 than any form of municipal government in the U.S., increasing by 1974 to 2,588 cities. Of these, 759 are among the 1,824 municipalities of the 16 southern states: 529 in cities above 5,000 population; 230 in municipalities of less than 5,000. The plan originated in Staunton, Va., in 1908, when the city council, confronted with serious problems, appointed a general manager. In 1912, Sumter, S.C., became the first true city-manager municipality when it adopted the Lockport Plan, formulated by Richard S. Childs, a businessman and later president of the National Municipal League. The plan gained national attention in 1914, when Dayton, Ohio, adopted it in an effort to resolve problems caused by a flooding of the Miami River.

The city-manager plan assumes that municipal government can be conducted like a business operation. The council, chosen by a nonpartisan election, is vested with political responsibility. The manager, selected by the council, functions with political neutrality and is compensated as a business executive would be. Critics allege that the plan is best suited to homogeneous white-collar municipalities, that it does not necessarily separate politics and management, and that qualified managers are in short supply.

Fifty-two percent (393 municipalities) are in states along the Eastern Seaboard, from Delaware through Florida. The western tier of southern states—Arkansas, Missouri, and Texas—has 34 percent of the South's manager cities. Few manager municipalities are in Alabama, Louisiana, and Mississippi, probably because statutory provisions for the plan are weak. Although the South has more mayor-council municipalities, the city-manager plan is firmly established in the region.

See C. R. Adrian and C. Press, *Governing Urban America* (1974); J. C. Bollens and H. J. Schmandt, *Metropolis: Its People, Politics, and Economic Life* (1970); R. P. Boynton, *Public Management* (Oct., 1974); and *Municipal Year Book, 1974.*

ROBERT B. HIGHSAW
University of Alabama

CITY POINT, VA., was U. S. Grant's headquarters and the principal supply depot for the Union armies besieging Petersburg from June, 1864, to April, 1865. During that time an average of 40 steamboats, 75 sailing vessels, and 100 barges daily unloaded Union supplies at wharves extending for more than a mile along the James and Appomattox rivers, which meet here. The Union forces built storehouses to hold a 30-day supply of subsistence and large reserves of ordnance, clothing, and hospital stores, as well as repair shops, bakeries, kitchens, and 110 hospital buildings. The Southside Railroad connected the depot with a United States military railroad that was gradually extended along the Petersburg lines.

See E. Risch, *Quartermaster Support of Army* (1962); J. A. Huston, *Sinews of War* (1966); T. Weber, *Northern Railroads in the Civil War* (1952); A. J. Johnston, *Virginia Railroads in the Civil War* (1961), II; G. B. Abdill, *Civil War Railroads* (1961), good photos; and R. W. Lykes, *Campaign for Petersburg* (1970), good photos.

RUSSELL F. WEIGLEY
Temple University

CIVILIAN CONSERVATION CORPS (1933–1942) was established in March, 1933, as one of the first acts of President Franklin Roosevelt's new administration. Its twin aims were to alleviate the critical unemployment situation among American youth and to check the destruction of America's natural resources. The CCC worked through four federal departments: Labor, which selected the enrollees; War, whch administered the camps; and Agriculture and the Interior, which supervised the work projects. The enterprise was coordinated by a director and a small central staff. Enrollees could enlist for terms of six months, with a maximum period of two years, and were paid $30 monthly, of which $25 was sent home to their families. They were selected only from families on relief rolls, supposedly without discrimination on either religious or racial grounds. The first CCC director was Robert Fechner, a Georgia-born American Federation of Labor official, who served until his death in 1939. He was succeeded by his assistant director James J. McEntee.

At its peak in 1935, there were more than 2,500 CCC camps in operation, almost all of them in rural areas, and over 30 percent of them in the South. By 1942, when it was discontinued by congressional action, more than 3 million young men had passed through its ranks. The conservation tasks they had undertaken were various; reforestation was always the most important. In the South, however, a far greater proportion of enrollees was engaged in erosion control than in other regions of the country. The camps, or companies, of about 200 men, each commanded by a military officer, were kept strictly segregated, except for those in the northeastern states. Negroes were enrolled in the ratio of one to every ten men. This meant, therefore, that there was effectively a limit on Negro enrollment despite the strictures against racial discrimination. One of the most popular of all the New Deal agencies, it was also one of the most effective. By the time the rapidly escalating reemployment rate rendered it redundant, it had, in the words of Arthur M. Schlesinger, Jr., "left its movements in the preservation and purification of the land, the water, the forests, and the young men of America."

See J. A. Salmond, *Civilian Conservation Corps* (1967); C. L. Wirth, *CCC Program* (1944); G. P. Rawick, "New Deal and Youth" (Ph.D. dissertation, University of Wisconsin, 1957); J. A. Salmond, *Journal of American History* (June, 1965); and CCC Records, National Archives.

JOHN A. SALMOND
La Trobe University, Melbourne, Australia

CIVIL RIGHTS ACT OF 1866, containing the first statutory definition of United States citizenship, established as the keystone of Republican Reconstruction the recognition of southern Negroes as citizens with legal rights of property and person identical to those enjoyed by white citizens. Prompted in part by the enactment of discriminatory BLACK CODES by southern states, the law invalidated the attempt to formulate a legal status for freedmen intermediary between slave and equal citizen. A Republican party consensus had developed during 1865 that Negroes must be guaranteed the basic rights of free men before the secession states were readmitted to full participation in the Union. This purpose clashed with that of President ANDREW JOHNSON, who wished Congress to restore the states without imposing con-

ditions and objected to a federal guarantee of non-discrimination on the basis of race. Passed over the president's veto, the Civil Rights Act was both the occasion and a major cause of the break between Congress and president that eventually led to the latter's impeachment. Voting and office-holding were not among the rights that the law sought to recognize and protect, nor was it intended to remedy economic inequalities except indirectly. To assure the measure's permanence, as much against Democratic repeal as against a challenge in the courts, Republicans reaffirmed its purpose in the first section of the FOURTEENTH AMENDMENT. In 1968, the U.S. Supreme Court resuscitated the first Civil Rights Act in *Jones* v. *Alfred H. Mayer Company* as a basis for prohibiting racial discrimination in the sale of property.

See T. L. Kohl, *Virginia Law Review* (March, 1969); L. and J. H. Cox, *Politics, Principle, Prejudice* (1963), and *Mississippi Valley Historical Review* (Dec., 1961); H. M. Hyman, *More Perfect Union* (1973); and R. A. Webb, *Civil War History* (March, 1969).

LAWANDA COX
Hunter College, City University of New York

CIVIL RIGHTS ACT OF 1875, introduced by Senator Charles Sumner of Massachusetts in May, 1870, proposed equal rights and facilities on railroad cars, steamboats, public conveyances, hotels, theaters and other places of entertainment, churches, cemetery associations licensed by federal or state governments, and public schools. Refusal by private persons to provide such accommodations was to be a misdemeanor, and injured parties were to be given the right to sue for damages. Largely because of southern opposition to the school integration clause, the bill was not passed until February, 1875. By that time, Republican members of the lame-duck Forty-third Congress, eager to enact bills to aid railroads and maintain Radical Republican strength in the South, agreed to delete the school and cemetery provisos. Most of the remaining features of the statute proved virtually unenforceable, although a number of cases were filed under it. In 1883 the act was declared unconstitutional by the U.S. Supreme Court in the CIVIL RIGHTS CASES.

See W. P. Vaughn, *Schools for All* (1974); A. H. Kelly, *American Historical Review* (April, 1959); W. P. Vaughn, *Southwestern Social Science Quarterly* (Sept., 1967); J. M. McPherson, *Journal of American History* (Dec., 1965); L. E. Murphy, *Journal of Negro History* (April, 1927); B. Wyatt-Brown, *Western Political Quarterly* (Dec., 1965); A. Avins, *Columbia Law Review* (May, 1966), and *Western Reserve Law Review* (May, 1967); F. E. Bonar,

"Civil Rights Act" (M.A. thesis, Ohio State University, 1940); and Charles Sumner Papers, Harvard.

WILLIAM P. VAUGHN
North Texas State University

CIVIL RIGHTS ACT OF 1957 was the first federal civil rights law enacted in the twentieth century. Although numerous bills providing for federal enforcement of civil rights had been introduced, because of southern Democratic opposition and absence of Republican support none had passed. By mid-century, however, the Negro vote was seen by politicians in both parties as the potentially determining vote in pivotal states. In the hope of capturing this vote and to ensure re-election of the ailing president, the EISENHOWER ADMINISTRATION in 1956 proposed civil rights legislation. Dwight D. Eisenhower proposed legislation that would create both a commission to study civil rights and a civil rights division in the Justice Department. Attorney General Herbert Brownell, however, arranged to include additional provisions protecting voting rights and authorizing federal institution of civil suits for civil rights enforcement. Southern opponents succeeded in reducing the act's scope to establishment of the Civil Rights Commission and Civil Rights Division, prohibition of interference with voting rights, and authorization for the attorney general to seek injunctions against interference with voting.

See S. F. Lawson, *Black Ballots* (1976); J. W. Anderson, *Eisenhower, Brownell* (1964); Civil Rights Commission, *Report* (1959); and R. C. Wright, "Civil Rights Acts: 1865, 1957" (Ph.D. dissertation, American University, 1968).

RUTH COWART WRIGHT
Texas Tech University

CIVIL RIGHTS ACT OF 1960, the product of a Republican–northern Democratic congressional coalition, survived one of the U.S. Senate's longest southern-staged round-the-clock filibusters to become law. The act provided for a variety of matters: it authorized the Civil Rights Commission to take sworn testimony; it provided for educating military dependents whose schools were closed to avoid integration; and it made obstruction of or interference with court orders crimes. Yet its main focus was on voting. It required a 22-month retention of all records of voting for federal officials and made them available to the attorney general. It authorized the attorney general, after winning a voting suit under the 1957 Civil Rights Act, to ask the federal district court for a separate finding that a pattern or practice of Negro voting right deprivation existed in the area. When such a finding

was made, the court was empowered to order that Negroes whom it found to be properly qualified be allowed to register, vote, and have their votes counted. The court was authorized to appoint referees to assist in this work. Initial enforcement was undertaken in southern states.

See D. M. Berman, *Bill Becomes Law* (1966); Civil Rights Commission, *Report* (1961); and Congressional Quarterly, *Congress and Nation* (1965).

RUTH COWART WRIGHT
Texas Tech University

CIVIL RIGHTS ACT OF 1964 is the most comprehensive of such statutes. In February, 1963, after Negro, labor, education, and church groups had coalesced into a civil rights lobby, the KENNEDY ADMINISTRATION submitted legislation that would extend the Civil Rights Commission, broaden protection of voting rights, and assist areas desegregating schools. In June, the administration asked Congress also to create a service to assist in the solution of racial problems, authorize withholding of funds from any area practicing discrimination, prohibit employment discrimination by government contractors, afford Negroes access to public accommodations, and authorize the attorney general to file school desegregation suits. President LYNDON JOHNSON, in his first address to Congress, urged passage of a civil rights law as a memorial to John Kennedy.

As had been the case with its predecessors, the 1964 act was passed by a northern Democratic–Republican coalition. This coalition was able to break a three-and-a-half-month filibuster in the Senate by, for the first time, adopting a cloture motion on civil rights. Although southern opponents had been successful in reducing the scope of the two previous acts, in 1964 they were unable to do more than effect a short delay in passage.

The law, as finally enacted, went well beyond the Kennedy administration's initiatives. It required fair application of voter registration and literacy requirements; prohibited discrimination on the basis of race, color, religion, or national origin in admission to most public accommodations; authorized the attorney general to sue for the desegregation of all publicly owned facilities, including schools; granted technical assistance in the desegregation of schools; extended the life of the Civil Rights Commission, as well as specifying its procedures and broadening its authority; required the withholding of federal funds from any program or activity in which discrimination was practiced; prohibited discrimination on the basis of race, color, religion, sex, or national origin in employment and created the Equal Opportunity Commission to effect these provisions; required the Census Bureau to assist the Civil Rights Commission by collecting voting statistics; authorized the attorney general to intervene in civil rights suits; and created the Community Relations Service to assist in the solution of civil rights problems. Enforcement was begun in the South and spread slowly to the rest of the country.

See Civil Rights Commission, *Report* (1963), and *Freedom to Free* (1963); *Congressional Record* (1964), most comprehensive; and Congressional Quarterly, *Congress and Nation* (1965).

RUTH COWART WRIGHT
Texas Tech University

CIVIL RIGHTS ACT OF 1965 was originally designed to enable southern Negroes to vote and has been amended (1975) to protect the voting rights of Alaskan natives, American Indians, persons of Asian or Spanish heritage, and illiterates. As amended, the law prohibits literacy tests or devices as qualifications for voting. It provides that, in areas that had either literacy tests and less than 50 percent voter turnout in the 1964 or 1968 presidential elections (all or part of ten states) or a 5 percent single language minority population, election materials in English only, and less than 50 percent voter turnout in the 1972 presidential election (all or part of nine additional states), federal examiners can be appointed to register voters and supervise elections, and proposed changes in election laws must be approved by the attorney general. Bilingual conduct of elections is required wherever 5 percent of the population speaks a single language other than English and the illiteracy rate in English is greater than the national rate (all or part of another 12 states). By 1975 it was estimated that the law had enabled almost a million additional persons to vote. The majority of these resided in southern states, all of which were covered by the act.

See Congressional Quarterly, *Congress and Nation* (1969), and *Weekly Report* (1975); and L. B. Johnson, *Vantage Point* (1971).

RUTH COWART WRIGHT
Texas Tech University

CIVIL RIGHTS ACT OF 1968 is the last of the quintet of twentieth-century civil rights laws. Attempts by the LYNDON JOHNSON administration to obtain passage of this measure in 1966 were frustrated when the Republican–northern Democratic coalition, which had effected the passage of the four previous civil rights laws, fell apart over the bill's housing provisions. Reaction to the slaying of MARTIN LUTHER KING, JR., is credited with its eventual passage. This measure is often termed the open-housing law, as it prohibited (with certain exemptions relating to owner-occupied or -managed units) discrimination in the rental or sale of housing on the basis of race, color, religion, or national origin. It also made interference with such rights as voting, jury service, work, schooling, or participation in federally aided programs federal crimes. Interference with those attempting to aid others in the exercise of such rights was similarly made criminal. Penalties for rioting were increased. In addition, Indian tribal governments were prohibited from making or enforcing laws violating any citizen's constitutional rights.

See Congressional Quarterly, *Congress and Nation* (1969); L. B. Johnson, *Vantage Point* (1971); and President's Council, *Report and Agenda* (1966).

RUTH COWART WRIGHT
Texas Tech University

CIVIL RIGHTS CASES (109 U.S. 3 [1883]). The federal government, acting on authority of the CIVIL RIGHTS ACT OF 1875, attempted in five related cases to convict persons who had denied blacks accommodations in hotels, a railroad car, or admission to a theater. In an eight-to-one decision, however, Justice Joseph P. Bradley, delivering the opinion for the U.S. Supreme Court, stated that the first and second sections of the Civil Rights Act of 1875 (the act's enabling clauses) were unconstitutional because they were not authorized by the THIRTEENTH AMENDMENT. The inability of a black to receive privately owned accommodations was not a badge of slavery, and the amendment could not be expanded to cover the types of social discrimination involved in these cases. Bradley also argued that the Civil Rights Act of 1875 was not authorized by the first section of the FOURTEENTH AMENDMENT. That amendment, according to Bradley, gave Congress the power to prohibit discrimination only if practiced by the states. As the Civil Rights Act of 1875 applied to discrimination by individuals, Congress did not have the power to act.

The lone dissenting opinion was given by Justice JOHN MARSHALL HARLAN, a Kentucky Republican, who declared that the act of 1875 was constitutional on several grounds, among them a guarantee of universal civil freedom by the Thirteenth Amendment, which included equal accommodations. Harlan also argued that the Fourteenth Amendment might serve as a basis for federal statutory restraints upon private persons

In the civil rights cases of 1883 the issue of protection of minority rights unfortunately became involved with the separate issue of limitation of federal power. The decision ended a brief period that had produced the emergence of integrated public facilities in all parts of the nation and gave official sanction to resegregation of blacks and other minorities. It also absolved the Republican party of any further official concern for black civil rights.

See M. Berger, *Equality by Statute* (1968); R. K. Carr, *Federal Protection of Civil Rights* (1947); E. S. Corwin, *Constitution and What It Means Today* (1974); R. J. Tresolini, *These Liberties* (1965); M. J. Horan, *American Journal of Legal History* (Jan., 1972); and A. F. Westin, in J. A. Garraty (ed.), *Quarrels That Have Shaped Constitution* (1966).

WILLIAM P. VAUGHN
North Texas State University

CIVIL RIGHTS MOVEMENT. Efforts to guarantee civil rights denied to some American citizens had been made from time to time throughout the nation's history, but an organized, effective movement for civil rights did not occur until after the Second World War. Many groups and individuals were involved in this postwar drive for basic rights, but the nation's largest racial minority—Negroes—came to be most closely identified with the movement. Since over one-half of all American blacks lived in the South, the civil rights movement was directly related to that region, although it was also national in scope. After the abolition of slavery, blacks had been granted certain legal rights, but in actual practice discrimination was great. BOOKER T. WASHINGTON, W. E. B. DU BOIS, and the NATIONAL ASSOCIATION FOR THE ADVANCEMENT OF COLORED PEOPLE worked in behalf of black rights during the early years of the twentieth century, but they were not notably successful. In the 1930s the NAACP assisted with lawsuits to bring about limited school desegregation, but little other progress was made. Social change, economic reality, and the ideology of the Second World War—with emphasis upon liberty—gave more American blacks courage to demand liberties rightfully theirs. Building upon earlier partial successes, in the 1950s the NAACP instituted lawsuits to desegregate the nation's public schools. In landmark decisions in 1954 (BROWN V. BOARD OF EDUCATION) and 1955 the U.S. Supreme Court ordered the gradual abolition of biracial school systems. This progress gave additional impetus to blacks, who became more outspoken in their demands.

Blacks desired numerous rights, and at the head of their list were the right to vote, school desegregation, equal economic opportunities, nondiscriminatory accommodations in private and public facilities, and fair-housing conditions. By the middle of the 1950s black humility, patience, and forebearance had given out. Black leaders determined to lead their people in campaigns of civil disobedience to win concessions for their people.

A milestone in the civil rights movement was the successful MONTGOMERY BUS BOYCOTT (Alabama) of 1955–1956. It stirred the nation and was largely responsible for the Negro's move toward the use of direct action in the decades to follow. The boycott brought MARTIN LUTHER KING, JR., to the forefront of the civil rights movement; his SOUTHERN CHRISTIAN LEADERSHIP CONFERENCE (SCLC), designed to coordinate nonviolent, direct-action activities, became an important force in the black movement. The STUDENT NONVIOLENT COORDINATING COMMITTEE (SNCC) became associated with sit-in demonstrations, designed to publicize the fact that many public accommodations were unavailable to blacks. Sponsored by the CONGRESS OF RACIAL EQUALITY (CORE), freedom riders who refused to sit in designated sections on interstate buses further emphasized the second-class status accorded black citizens. The confrontations with law enforcement agencies only made the blacks more determined, and street demonstrations for black rights became commonplace.

In 1963 important black leaders staged a mass rally in Washington, D.C., to show the need for federal action to advance black rights. A. PHILIP RANDOLPH, ROY WILKINS, and Martin Luther King, Jr., delivered speeches from the steps of the Lincoln Memorial at this giant rally. The demonstration was orderly and peaceful, it stimulated a deeper concern for the problems of blacks, and it encouraged increased black militancy. By 1965 many of the nation's blacks were coming to believe that legalism and direct-action strategy were not sufficient to attain the goals they desired. Restless young blacks were not satisfied with turtlelike progress. The tendency toward unity of strategy as symbolized by King began to dissipate, and the movement for black rights became fragmented. To broadly generalize, most members of SNCC and many individuals in CORE constituted the militant left wing of the movement; the conservative wing was composed of a large number of members of the NAACP and URBAN LEAGUE officials, including WHITNEY M. YOUNG, JR., whose efforts with the latter organization were primarily directed toward obtaining jobs for blacks; and Martin Luther King represented the middle or moderate position, which included not only members of SCLC but also many blacks active in CORE and the NAACP. Militant young blacks rejected attempts of older members of their race to work within the limitations of the law, talking in terms of "revolutionary" changes in the entire structure of American society. Stokely Carmichael (1941–), who seized control of SNCC, epitomized these new blacks. Carmichael rejected integration as a valid goal for blacks, preaching instead that blacks should hate whites, have pride in their blackness, and fight against the dominant society. Black power became a watchword for the youthful extremists. The logical extension of such thinking was a movement of separation—not physical separation but the full implication of the realization that the races were in fact separate despite their physical proximity. Elijah Muhammad and the BLACK MUSLIMS advocated separation, but in actual fact the separatists were a small minority of the black population. Most blacks viewed the separatist movement as an unrealistic attempt to destroy or dominate a democratic society; the great majority of blacks still desired their race's original goals.

In the late 1960s some blacks vented their frustrations by rioting in the streets of the nation's major cities. "Burn, baby, burn" became the cry of disillusioned blacks as riots in Harlem, Cleveland, Detroit, Chicago, and many other major cities in the North (plus Los Angeles in the West) revealed how explosive and destructive race relations were in the country. Major southern cities were not entirely free from this wave of violence, although widespread property destruction and violence characteristic of the 1965 Watts riots in Los Angeles or the 1967 riots in Detroit did not occur in the South.

As the momentum of the civil rights movement increased, leaders in all three branches of the federal government acted, albeit usually with some reluctance. The Supreme Court played a major role not only in lessening the number of racially imbalanced schools but also in guaranteeing other basic rights to black citizens. In halting and uneven activity, American presidents used the prestige and power of their high office to assist blacks, and Congress began to pass legislation designed for the same purpose. Franklin D. Roosevelt issued an executive order in 1941 declaring racial discrimination in wartime industries to be contrary to the public interest. HARRY S. TRUMAN spoke out directly and repeatedly for black rights,

desegregated the armed forces, and made numerous recommendations to Congress for legislation beneficial to minority groups. Dwight D. Eisenhower also recommended legislation to the Congress, and Congress finally passed the CIVIL RIGHTS ACT OF 1957 and the CIVIL RIGHTS ACT OF 1960. Neither of these laws brought great specific advances, but they gave a significant psychological lift to the black race. John F. Kennedy ordered penalties for businesses with government contracts who engaged in discriminatory employment practices; he directed the Department of Labor to abolish discrimination in training programs under its general supervision; and he asked Congress to approve additional civil rights legislation. Passed during the presidency of LYNDON B. JOHNSON, the CIVIL RIGHTS ACT OF 1964 resulted in significant legal and actual advances for blacks. Its most important provisions related to discrimination in public accommodations. Also passed during the Johnson administration, the CIVIL RIGHTS ACT OF 1965 provided for elaborate and effective federal machinery for registering voters and assuring the right to vote. Resulting in the registration of hundreds of thousands of black voters for the first time, this bill placed real political power at the disposal of blacks. Then the Congress passed the comprehensive CIVIL RIGHTS ACT OF 1968, which included far-reaching provisions dealing with discrimination in housing. President Johnson appointed ROBERT C. WEAVER head of the Department of Housing and Urban Development and THURGOOD MARSHALL to the Supreme Court. Presidents Richard Nixon and Gerald Ford also included blacks in their administrations, and both of them signed laws to extend the life of the 1965 Civil Rights Act.

By 1976 the nation and its leaders had taken all of the major legal steps available to raise blacks from their second-class status; thereafter progress would come as existing statutes were enforced, as court orders were implemented, and as whites altered their actions and attitudes in their daily lives. Although much needed to be done in the area of personal race relations, the civil rights movement of the third quarter of the twentieth century brought about a significant revolution in American life.

See C. E. Silberman, *Crisis in Black and White* (1964); A. Lewis, *Portrait of a Decade* (1964); L. Lomax, *Negro Revolt* (1962); J. P. Roche, *Quest for Dream* (1963); M. R. Konvitz and T. Leskes, *Century of Civil Rights* (1961); O. Handlin, *Fire-Bell in Night* (1964); K. B. Clark, *Negro Protest* (1963); H. Zinn, *SNCC* (1964); D. Wakefield, *Revolt in South* (1960); A. F. Westin, *Freedom*

Now! (1964); M. L. King, Jr., *Stride Toward Freedom* (1958); E. M. Rudwick, *W. E. B. Du Bois* (1960); W. D. St. James, *NAACP* (1958); C. E. Lincoln, *Black Muslims* (1961); M. Little, *Autobiography of Malcolm X* (1965); and S. R. Spencer, *Booker T. Washington* (1955).

MONROE BILLINGTON
New Mexico State University

CIVIL WAR (1861–1865), the nation's greatest internal tragedy, was resolved with frightful losses in manpower, money, and social upheaval. In theory, the Union was severed at 4:30 A.M., April 15, 1861. A signal shot from a Confederate battery in Charleston harbor heralded 34 hours of bombardment, which led to the surrender of the United States garrison at FT. SUMTER. The four years of conflict that ensued were ended supposedly in April, 1865, by the surrender of Confederate armies from Virginia to Texas. Still, partisan warfare would prevail into 1866, and only on November 6, 1865, did the Confederate cruiser *Shenandoah* surrender to British officials at Liverpool. Even then, it was not until August 20, 1865, that President Andrew Johnson declared that "peace, order, tranquility and civil authority now exist in and throughout the whole of the United States of America."

The insurrection had been stifled at an enormous cost in human lives and resources. Official estimates of deaths in the war reached over 623,000, a figure larger than those suffered in all other American wars from the Revolution to the Second World War. Even incomplete statistics of total war casualties in killed and wounded reached over 1 million. At least 384,000 of these soldiers perished from diseases such as typhus, dysentery, and smallpox. How vast was the loss of human talent is understood well by comparison with the casualties of the Second World War. Less than 52,000 Americans were killed in battle during that conflict; in the Civil War, 94,000 Confederates alone perished on the field.

The economic consequences were no less staggering. Total federal expenditures for the war effort exceeded $6 billion. Even this figure is modest, as it excludes vast sums expended for munitions and equipment by individual northern states. Total expenditures of the Confederate government reached $2.1 billion, a statistic that also fails to include millions spent by individual rebel states. Such losses only overlay far deeper economic disaster. The South lost at least $2 billion in slave investments, and by 1865 had lost over 30 percent of its horses, cattle, and swine. Urban areas such as Richmond, Columbia, S.C., and Atlanta had been devastated. Meanwhile much of the South's 9,000 miles of railroad had been destroyed.

Much of this loss in men and resources reflected a new style of American war evident in two respects, mobilization and technology. Manpower mobilization in the Civil War reached near total proportions. Exclusive of sympathizers in Kentucky, Missouri, and Maryland, the Confederacy in 1861 boasted only 1,116,000 men in what was termed the "military age" category of eighteen to forty-five. Conservative estimates place 800,000 such men in rebel ranks. The free-state area, exclusive of Unionists in the three border states, listed 3,778,000 men of military age. Moderate estimates place 2.2 million men in Union service.

Such mobilization came slowly and was achieved only with the adoption of national conscription. In the weeks of the crisis at Ft. Sumter, the regular army's strength consisted of 1,108 officers and 15,259 enlisted men scattered among military posts from Key West to Puget Sound. With Congress not in session to provide legislation for a volunteer army, President Abraham Lincoln resorted on April 15, 1861, to his only alternative. He invoked the 1795 Militia Act and issued calls for 75,000 militiamen to deal with the insurrection. Subsequent military laws enacted during the summer by Congress quickly created a huge volunteer army. By December 31, 1861, over 736,000 men swelled the ranks of the new Union army; less than 25,000 were regulars. Yet further mobilization proved necessary in 1862 and 1863. A decline in the fervor for enlistment, war weariness, and the morale problems created by the substitution and bounty systems produced a dwindling number of recruits. By August, 1862, volunteering was so slow that Lincoln resorted to a semidraft. There was no federal authority for conscription, but Lincoln on August 4 invoked a special militia draft, calling for 300,000 men.

Still, rising war casualties and slack recruiting made more drastic mobilization necessary. On March 3, 1863, Congress passed Senate bill 511, the first U.S. adoption of conscription, whereby all male citizens between twenty and forty-five years of age were liable for three years' service or for the war's duration. Technically this and three subsequent draft calls were failures. In its four drafts, the Union drew 776,829 names for examination. Yet only 46,347 men, less than 2 percent of the Union army, were actually drafted. More important was the continual use of the draft by Lincoln as a stimulus for volunteering. Whether to escape the odium of the draft or to obtain a volunteer's bounty, enough men volunteered to enable the federal army to maintain sufficient strength dur-

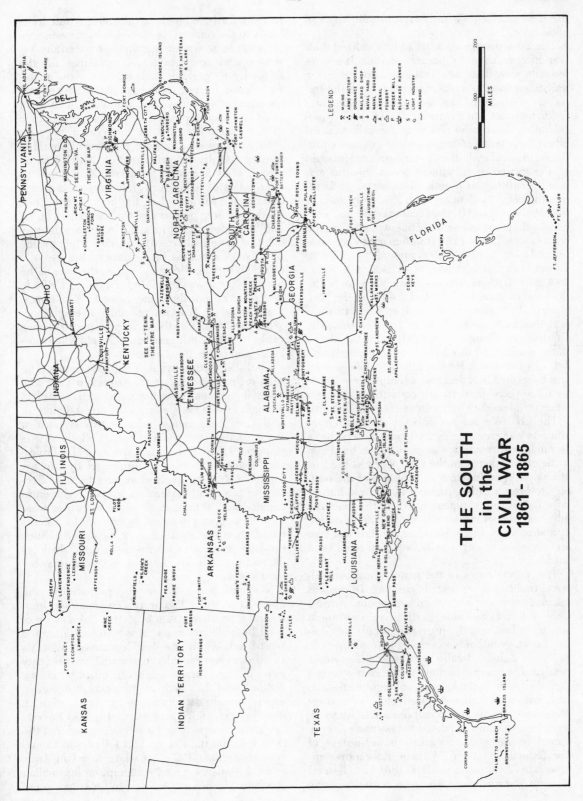

THE SOUTH
in the
CIVIL WAR
1861 - 1865

ing the hard Georgia and Virginia campaigns of 1864.

The Confederates already had nationalized their war effort in 1862. By January of 1862, the Confederate army faced near extinction from expiring enlistments and a dearth of recruits. From the initial creation of the "Provisional Army of the Confederate States" on February 28, 1861, rebel mobilization during the first year was a haphazard affair. Incessant pandering to war govenors produced the dual evils of short-term enlistments and of a potpourri of enlistment terms, such as six-month militia, six-month volunteers, and 12-month men. By January of 1862, fully half of the rebel army, and its most seasoned troops, were 12-month men whose enlistment terms would soon expire. The military disasters of the late winter and early spring of 1862 proved the decisive factor. At FTS. HENRY AND DONELSON and ROANOKE ISLAND alone, 20,000 troops were lost. The debacles of MILL SPRINGS and the fall of the Mississippi River garrisons from Memphis northward cost thousands more. Spurred by the crisis, the Confederate Congress on April 15 nationalized the war effort. In this first national conscription act, all white males between the ages of eighteen and thirty-five, not declared exempt, were liable for three years' duty. In subsequent acts the ages were broadened to between seventeen and fifty.

The Civil War saw not only the American transition to war en masse by a citizen soldiery, but a technological revolution as well. Much has been made of the adage that the Civil War was the first of modern wars in that it saw the use of the military telegraph, submarines, land and sea mines, wire fortifications, repeating rifles, the machine gun, and other innovations. Most of these developments were totally inconsequential. But two technological changes reflected a new mode of warfare.

The 31,000 miles of the nation's railroads altered traditional methods of combat. To possess railroads was not always advantageous. Armies became tied to railroads, flexibility of movement was often lost, and the presence of railroads dictated strategy rather than serving to implement it. Still, the railroad totally revamped the style of combat. Campaigns became far more protracted than the traditional maneuvers of eighteenth-century armies, which were tied closely to their magazines. It was now possible to field huge armies in long campaigns, and to penetrate deeply enemy territory—factors all to the advantage of the federals. General William Rosecrans' approach to Chattanooga in 1862–1863 and General William Sherman's advance upon central Georgia

in 1864 illustrated both the advantages and drawbacks to the new rail technology. Both were able to succor large armies deep in enemy territory, yet were bound closely to the railroad. Ironically, the Confederates perhaps made best use of the mobility offered by rail. General BRAXTON BRAGG's spectacular Kentucky invasion in 1862 could not have been accomplished without a rapid change of front via rail from Mississippi to east Tennessee.

No less important was the adoption of the rifled musket, usually of Springfield or British Enfield design. Only five years before the Ft. Sumter crisis, the United States Army had adopted the principle of the Minie bullet, the heart of the rifled musket's killing power. The conical-shaped bullet had been developed in 1848 by a French army officer, Captain Claude Minie. The Minie principle, that of a hollow base, allowed the use of a conical-shaped bullet smaller than the bore of the barrel. Now it was possible for a military rifle to be loaded as quickly as the musket. More important, range and accuracy were strengthened. Whereas a musket's killing range was scarcely 200 yards, the new Springfield and Enfield rifled muskets could reach 1,000 yards.

Civil War tactical systems were unprepared for such technological change. Armies in 1861 still utilized eighteenth-century linear tactics that had wrought victory for Frederick the Great. Practically all Civil War generals had been exposed at West Point to the strategy and tactics of the Swiss strategist Henri Jomini, as expounded by Professor Dennis Mahan. As interpreted by Mahan, Jominian strategy involved massive tactical offensives. Such training perpetuated the eighteenth-century tactical formations whereby battles were viewed as being decided by open-field assaults based upon the shock effect of the bayonet. Such thinking produced frightful casualties, which indicated that military thought in 1861 ran far behind technology.

Nor were command systems prepared for the new war of 1861. The army's commanding lieutenant general, WINFIELD SCOTT, led a cadre of aged line officers, none of whom had attended West Point. Within the War Department, six of its 11 bureaus were headed by men at least seventy years of age. Abraham Lincoln quickly became disillusioned with such a command arrangement, which wrought disaster at the first battle of BULL RUN (July 21, 1861). Scott was retired on November 1, and the popular former commander of the Ohio state militia, George McClellan, was named general-in-chief. McClellan, who also led the Army of the Potomac, evinced contempt for his civilian chieftain Lincoln and refused to formulate grand

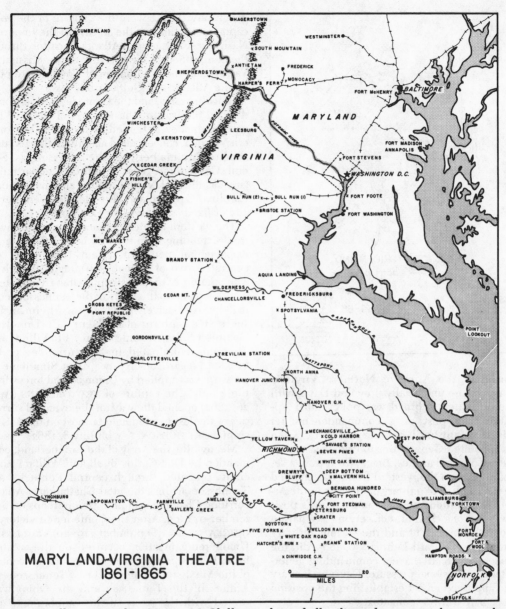

MARYLAND-VIRGINIA THEATRE
1861-1865

strategy. Finally, in March, 1862, as McClellan prepared the Army of the Potomac for a thrust against Richmond, Lincoln removed him as general-in-chief.

In July, 1862, Lincoln named a third general-in-chief, Henry Halleck. It was under Halleck's supervision that Ulysses Grant had won victories at Fts. Henry and Donelson and SHILOH. Halleck's failure to assume responsibility led Lincoln to act as his own general-in-chief until February of 1864, when Grant was given command of Union armies. William T. Sherman was appointed to command the Military Division of the West, which em-

braced all military departments between the Mississippi River and the Appalachians. Halleck was appointed chief of staff, serving as a liaison between Grant and the president.

The Confederates never perfected such a system. Jealous of his constitutional prerogatives and harassed by localism in the South, JEFFERSON DAVIS failed to organize an overall system of military command. For three months in the spring of 1862, ROBERT E. LEE was ordered to Richmond and charged "with the conduct of military operations in the armies of the Confederacy." This ill-defined position ended on June 1, when Lee assumed

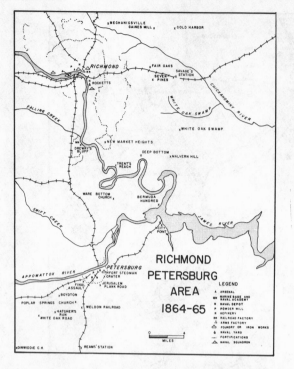

RICHMOND
PETERSBURG
AREA
1864-65

LEGEND

geography. These were the capture of the rebel capital at Richmond; the seizure of the important Nashville-Chattanooga-Atlanta corridor through the central South; the retaking of the Mississippi Valley; and the domination of Confederate ports on the Atlantic and Gulf coasts.

Lincoln's aims, and the Confederates' response, divided the war into basic zones of conflict. The eastern theater, defended by the Army of Northern Virginia, concentrated activity in the 200-mile zone of Virginia between the rival capitals. Several Confederate coastal military departments (such as those of North Carolina and that of South Carolina, Georgia, and east Florida) were generally utilized as reserves for Lee's army.

The western theater embraced a 400-mile-wide front extending from the Mississippi River to the Appalachian mountain system. Here were concentrated two of Lincoln's strategic objectives. The opening of the Mississippi-Ohio river systems was delegated to the Army of the Tennessee, commanded successively by Grant and Sherman. The successive captures of Ft. Henry, Ft. Donelson, Columbus, Ky., Island No. 10, Ft. Pillow, and Memphis culminated in the surrender of the VICKSBURG garrison on July 4, 1863. Simultaneous pressure was applied by Union coastal forces from the South. The capture of NEW ORLEANS (April 26, 1862) opened the way for the eventual surrender of the last Confederate outpost on the Mississippi, PORT HUDSON, LA., on July 8, 1862.

Meanwhile, the Army of the Cumberland, commanded by Don Carlos Buell and William Rosecrans, operated through central Kentucky and Tennessee against the vital Chattanooga-Atlanta corridor. Chattanooga fell to Union troops on September 9, 1863. After the Confederate victory at CHICKAMAUGA (September 19–20), a massive Union reorganization occurred on the western front. Forces previously committed to the capture of the Mississippi Valley and east Tennessee (the Armies of the Tennessee and the Ohio) were united with the Army of the Cumberland in a massive army group, the Military Division of the Mississippi.

Under Grant this new organization opened the way to Atlanta by victories at Lookout Mountain on November 24 and Missionary Ridge on November 25 (CHATTANOOGA CAMPAIGN). After Grant's appointment as general-in-chief, Sherman seized Atlanta after the battles of PEACH TREE CREEK, ATLANTA, and Ezra Church (July–August, 1864). The final elements of resistance by the main Confederate force, the Army of Tennessee, were shattered in the battles of FRANKLIN (November 30) and NASHVILLE (December 15–16).

command of the Army of Northern Virginia.

Although Lee unofficially provided Davis with advice on issues of broad war policy until Appomattox, the post of a commander-in-chief remained vacant until February of 1864, when Davis appointed General Braxton Bragg as general-in-chief of rebel armies. Bragg, fresh from a series of defeats on the western front, was charged "with the conduct of military operations in the Armies of the Confederacy." Actually Bragg's position was that of a chief of staff, serving as a liaison between the president and the various military departments. Not until February 6, 1865, did the Confederacy actually have a commanding general. After congressional pressure, Davis on January 23 had approved an act establishing the position that Lee held until Appomattox.

These command systems grappled over a vast Southland, which stretched literally from the Mexican border to the nation's capital. Georgia alone was larger in area than the combined states of Vermont, Rhode Island, New Jersey, New Hampshire, Massachusetts, Maryland, Connecticut, and Delaware. The Confederate military department of Alabama, Mississippi, and east Louisiana defended an area larger than that of the combined countries of Austria, Hungary, Belgium, and the Netherlands.

From the outset, President Lincoln determined upon four strategic principles vitally affected by

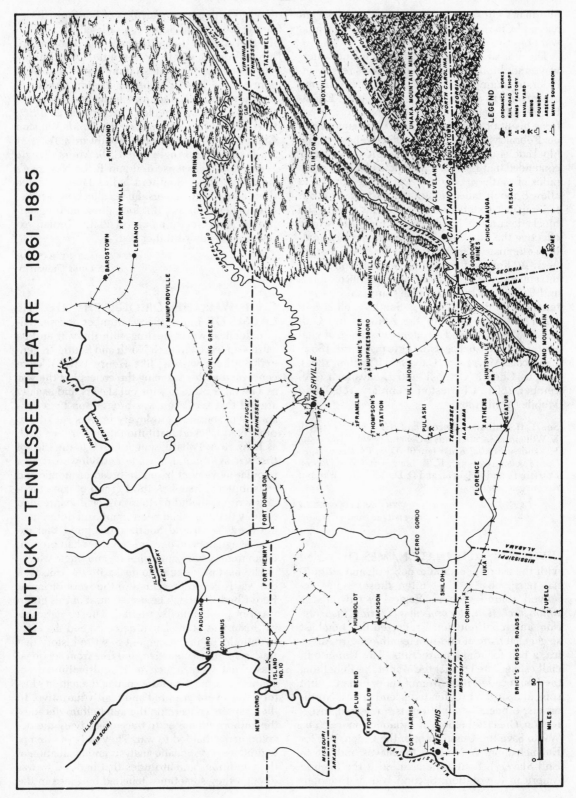

KENTUCKY–TENNESSEE THEATRE   1861–1865

Sherman's subsequent campaign against Savannah and Charleston all but sealed Lincoln's final war objective.

The federal navy dominated both inland waterways and the high seas except in two areas. Confederate commerce raiders such as the *Alabama* destroyed $19 million in federal shipping. Equally pressing was Lincoln's determination to enforce his BLOCKADE of southern ports announced on February 19, 1861. The effectiveness of the blockade is debatable. Historian FRANK OWSLEY contended that Lincoln's attempt to blockade 3,500 miles of southern coastline was feeble enough to allow 8,200 instances of BLOCKADE-RUNNING. But federal naval statistics boasted that over 1,500 blockade-runners had been destroyed. However effective the blockade, Lincoln strove consistently to eliminate potential havens for blockade-runners. By February, 1862, the federals controlled the entranceway to Albemarle and Pamlico sounds and Cape Fear Inlet in North Carolina, Charleston and Port Royal harbors in South Carolina, and other positions on both the Atlantic and Gulf coasts. Then followed a systematic seizure of vital southern ports such as New Orleans (April, 1862), Pensacola (May, 1862), Galveston (October, 1862), Corpus Christi (October, 1863), Savannah (December, 1864), Charleston (February, 1865), and Mobile (April, 1865).

See T. H. Williams, *Lincoln and His Generals* (1952); K. Williams, *Lincoln Finds a General* (5 vols.; 1949–59); F. Vandiver, *Rebel Brass* (1956); D. S. Freeman, *R. E. Lee* (4 vols.; 1934–35); E. B. Long, *Civil War Day by Day* (1971); and J. Randall and D. Donald, *Civil War and Reconstruction* (1969).

THOMAS L. CONNELLY
University of South Carolina

CIVIL WAR, ALTERNATE NAMES OF, varied with the user's geographic, political, and attitudinal perspectives. Most often these names revolved around such ideological catchwords as *union, secession, slavery, emancipation, insurrection,* and *rebellion.* Some reflected that bombast so characteristic of mid-nineteenth-century America, a bait for romantic recruits. The Union officially styled the conflict the War of the Rebellion, the South called it the War of Independence, but song and slogan proliferated pseudonyms. Northerners, especially abolitionists, preferred Insurrection, Great Rebellion, or variations on *war* (*i.e.,* War to Save the Union, War for the Union, War for Emancipation, War to Free the Slaves, and War to End Slavery). Southerners called it the Second American Revolution, Second War of Independ-

ence, Confederate War, War of Southern Independence, War of Secession (a legal impossibility to Unionist theoreticians), War of Northern Aggression, or War to Preserve the Constitution. War Between the States (along with Civil War) expressed a border states or foreign veneer of neutrality. Literary sources furnished evocative variants: Horace Greeley's *American Conflict*; Carl Sandburg's *Storm over the Land*; Winston Churchill's *Crisis*; C. Vann Woodward's *Years of Madness*; P. M. Angle and E. S. Miers' *Tragic Years*; and O. Eisenschiml and R. G. Newman's *American Iliad.* Southern ladies later reflected their gentility in remorseful recollections of "the late unpleasantness." But for pathos, nothing surpassed a succinctly mournful Plains Indian expression: Brother-Brother War.

JAMES T. BANNON
St. Louis University

CIVIL WAR, HISTORIOGRAPHY OF THE CAUSES OF. In the 1860s a number of essentially polemical works dealing with the war and its causes appeared in both North and South. In general northern writers, like Henry Wilson, were concerned with advancing the concept of the war as a moral crusade to wipe out slavery and usually argued that secession was brought on by a conspiracy of southern proslavery leaders seeking to preserve a wicked institution. Southerners, such as Edward A. Pollard, sought to refute the idea of the war as a moral crusade and viewed it as a popular movement based on broad economic and constitutional issues. A third group of contemporary writers, including John Minor Botts, tended to deny that there had been significant differences between North and South and argued that extremist agitators on one or both sides had brought on an unnecessary, undesirable, and tragic war.

The next major effort to deal with the causes of the war is best represented in the work of James Ford Rhodes, though he unlike most of this group was not professionally trained. These "nationalist" historians of the late nineteenth and the early twentieth century attempted to write history that was "scientific," objective, and free from sectional bias. That work, much of it multivolumed accounts covering the entire span of the nation's history, was event oriented and highly narrative. In the chapters concerning the antebellum decades, the authors attempted to trace objectively the developments that led to war. They did not attempt to produce a systematic analysis and evaluation of the conditions and attitudes that had led to war (though they sometimes touched on these in the course of their narratives). Although these historians still saw the war as a conflict between slavery and freedom, they stressed inanimate forces, technology, and conflicting societies as causes of the war and portrayed the motives of southern leaders as honest and secession as a popular movement. In general these nationalist historians tended to view the war as an irreconcilable conflict. For them it was a just and necessary war fought to end slavery and preserve the Union, and they rejoiced in its outcome.

In the early decades of the twentieth century, as economics emerged as a full-fledged academic discipline and as concern for the welfare of the Negro came close to vanishing, the concept of a sectional economic conflict became especially attractive to historians. The morality of slavery scarcely seemed a real issue to historians like Charles and Mary Beard. In their *Rise of American Civilization* (1927) they portrayed the war as a clash between the South's planting society and the North's manufacturing and farming society. Like most of the nationalist historians, they felt the war was irreconcilable, but for economic rather than moral reasons. Somewhat similarly, the neo-Confederate historian FRANK L. OWSLEY saw the war as an irrepressible clash between northern industrialism and southern agrarianism brought on by the aggressive "egocentric sectionalism" of the North.

In the 1930s a number of historians, most of them with southern or border state connections, began to attempt a systematic analysis of the causes of the Civil War. In books and articles devoted solely to that subject, these men—believing, like the compromisers of the Civil War period, that war could and should have been averted—denied that sectional differences had to result in war. CHARLES W. RAMSDELL, AVERY CRAVEN, JAMES G. RANDALL, and others maintained or implied that slavery had reached its zenith by 1860 and would soon have died of its own accord. Like the peace men of the Civil War, they blamed the conflict primarily on individuals rather than on forces—on extremist agitation and on a generation of "blundering" political leadership. For them the war had been a tragic, unnecessary evil. When Allan Nevins' lengthy narrative on the pre–Civil War and wartime years appeared after World War II, he combined nationalist and revisionist arguments and maintained that the war had come about primarily because of slavery and the accompanying problem of racial adjustment—and because of the North's failure to help the South solve its racial problems.

The revisionist concept of the war as an unnecessary conflict was widely accepted by historians until the rise of the neonationalists in the post–World War II period and of the neoabolitionists in the 1960s, both of whom saw war as a perfectly acceptable way of attempting to solve certain dilemmas. These and other postrevisionist historians have been less interested in attempting to weigh and explain all of the principal causes of the war than were their predecessors. Most have decided that the question of whether the war was avoidable is too nebulous to be fruitful, and many have forsaken the old debate of whether the war was a moral crusade. Much of their work has been directed not to the broad question of the causation of the war but to an investigation of specific segments of antebellum history. When they have addressed themselves to the causes of the war, they have asked what factors contributed to the rise of "extremism," to the development of sectional animosity, to the secession of the South, to the northern decision to oppose secession, and so on. They often utilize the tools, theories, methods, and concepts of the social sciences, and their work has become more subtle and sophisticated than ever before. They have become increasingly concerned with the role of images and perceptions in determining action. Intellectual history, once notable for its absence, has been heavily emphasized, and complex and revealing variations have been played on old themes. So many historians are working in the field that even listing their names is impossible: among the more interesting works are those on slavery (SLAVERY, HISTORIOGRAPHY OF), antislavery, and racial attitudes by Stanley Elkins, David Donald, Eugene Genovese, David Davis, John Blassingame, Robert Starobin, Eugene Berwanger, Jacques Voegeli, Eric Foner, Robert Fogel and Stanley Engerman, and Herbert Gutman; on sectionalism by William R. Taylor, DAVID POTTER, Joel R. Silbey, and Thomas B. Alexander; on economic factors by Eugene Genovese and Barrington Moore, Jr.; on constitutional and political factors by Roy Nichols, David Donald, and Arthur Bestor; on the secession crisis by Kenneth Stampp, Richard Current, Steven Channing, and Elbert Smith. And in the mid-1970s several historians, notably John S. Rosenberg, Gerald Gunderson, and Peter Parish, are again attempting to weigh and evaluate the causes of the war.

Although there are few indications that historians have reached a new consensus on the causation of the Civil War, it seems likely that any historian attempting in the mid-1970s a thorough and systematic explanation of the causes of the war would stress the power of ideas, emphasize the role of slavery, and recognize but not dwell on the problem of morality. He would give some recognition to socioeconomic and politico-constitutional factors and would view the war within the context of long-range trends in America and Europe. In addition, he would rely more heavily on statistical data and local studies, make use of a more systematic methodology, and attempt to ask more specific questions than did the revisionists and those who preceded them.

See C. E. Cauthen and L. P. Jones, in A. S. Link and R. W. Patrick (eds.), *Writing Southern History* (1965); T. J. Pressly, *Americans Interpret Their Civil War* (1954); D. M. Potter, *South and Sectional Conflict* (1968); E. Foner, *Civil War History* (Sept., 1974); P. J. Parish, *American Civil War* (1975), Ch. 4; and bibliographies of articles, *Civil War History*, annually.

PATRICIA HICKIN
Richmond, Va.

CIVIL WAR HISTORY (History Department, Kent State University, Kent, Ohio 44242), a quarterly first issued in 1955, when such notables as T. Harry Williams, Douglas Southall Freeman, and Bell I. Wiley interested themselves in its founding, has a circulation of 1,700. Supported by subscriptions, advertising, and Kent State University, the journal publishes book reviews and accepts scholarly articles on the Civil War and "middle period" of American history. One well-appreciated feature is its annual bibliography of journal articles on the Civil War era.

CIVIL WAR MEMOIRS are autobiographical accounts of individuals' wartime experiences. Unlike diaries and journals, they were written largely from memory at a later date. Memoirs differ from autobiographies in an emphasis upon one portion of the author's life and upon public rather than private activities. They range from lengthy discussions of the entire war to accounts of single battles; from elaborate publications to loose manuscript pages. Publication has continued almost yearly since Appomattox, with three major periods of interest: near the end of Reconstruction; following the Spanish-American War; and during the Civil War centennial.

The vast numbers and popularity of Confederate memoirs attest to southerners' recognition of the war as the central event of their lives. Military leaders are of course most prominent, but privates and women wrote with equal enthusiasm of their war efforts.

In their reminiscences, former generals, such as J. B. LONGSTREET, J. A. EARLY, JOSEPH E. JOHN-STON, and J. B. HOOD, debated military strategy, defended their war records, and sought to redeem tarnished reputations. T. J. Jackson, J. E. B. Stuart, and Robert E. Lee left no personal accounts of the war, but their staff officers penned memoirs of these legendary figures: *I Rode with Stonewall*, by Henry Kyd Douglas; *War Years with Jeb Stuart*, by William Blackford; *Four Years with General Lee*, by W. H. Taylor.

The most interesting memoirs convey the immediacy of personal experience within the context of a nation at war. Generals frequently neglected personal details, and privates often lacked the means to place their own experiences in larger perspective. Among the most vivid and engaging books are G. M. Sorrel's *Recollections* (1905); Richard Taylor's *Destruction and Reconstruction* (1879); and Robert Stiles's *Four Years Under Marse Robert* (1903). For a balanced perspective on army life, however, one must include less-polished writings of privates, such as Sam Watkins' *Co. Aytch* (1882) and William A. Fletcher's *Rebel Private Front and Rear* (1954). These books present a less glamorous side of war, where humor and detachment are the only antidotes to horror and suffering.

Women's memoirs are generally more romanticized than the many excellent published diaries and journals. Despite limitations, they contain valuable information about Richmond society, *e.g.*, Mrs. Burton Harrison, *Recollections Grave and Gay* (1911); about hospital administration, *e.g.*, Phoebe Pember, *A Southern Woman's Story* (1879); and about life on the home front, *e.g.*, Parthenia Hague, *A Blockaded Family* (1888), and Mary Gay, *Life in Dixie* (1892).

Lacking the immediacy and frankness of wartime letters and diaries, memoirs reflect changing perceptions of the war during half a century. They reveal the gradual process by which glamour and pride replaced anguish and bitterness, as praise for the gallantry of Confederate men and women softened the memory of defeat.

See D. S. Freeman, *South to Posterity* (1939); A. Nevins, J. I. Robertson, Jr., and B. I. Wiley, *Civil War Books* (1967, 1969), good bibliography in Vol. I, Ch. 3, and Vol. II, Ch. 2 and 7; H. S. Commager, *Blue and Gray* (1950); and C. D. Eby, Jr., *Southwest Review* (Summer, 1962).

RANDALL C. JIMERSON
University of Michigan

CIVIL WAR ROUND TABLES. In the decades immediately following the Civil War, veterans' groups and individuals north and south displayed a lively interest in studying the conflict in which they had played a personal role. Interest continued into this century among such groups as the Battlefield Crackpates of Washington, D.C., and in various state and local historical societies, particularly in the South. However, it was in Chicago, in December of 1940, that the present Civil War round table movement was born. Fifteen men gathered to hear a talk on Stonewall Jackson's valley campaign. One of the leading organizers was Ralph G. Newman, Chicago book dealer and author. The idea took hold, spreading eventually to more than 150 cities in the United States and to Britain and Germany as well. There have been a number of attempts to mold the round tables into a national organization. The groups are independent and autonomous, but maintain an informal, friendly relationship with other round tables.

Civil War round tables flourish almost equally north and south, east and west. The basic pattern has been to hold regular meetings, usually monthly. The speakers are often nationally recognized authorities on their subjects or are local experts on one battle or military leader. The membership is drawn from a wide variety of businesses and professions, with only a relative few being professional historians. There has grown an extraordinary camaraderie among the members. Their depth of study and scholarship varies from the acknowledged expert to those just curious. A universal feature is that the speakers are subjected to questioning, and the arguments thus engendered have been many. Seldom is the discussion on a North-South political basis; more often it is on such matters as the controversial generalship of George B. McClellan of the Union or Joseph E. Johnston of the Confederacy.

Many of the groups take battlefield tours, but they do not, as a rule, engage in battle enactments. The Chicago Round Table since 1951 has had a four-day spring battlefield tour, most frequently to the South. Other round tables publish newsletters and some have undertaken more elaborate publications. Many tape record their programs. The Kansas City Civil War Round Table has established the Harry S. Truman Award, which annually recognizes an outstanding Civil War scholar. Other awards include the Gold Medal of Washington, the Fletcher Pratt Award of New York, and the Allan Nevins–Douglas Southall Freeman Award of Chicago.

See S. Ambrose, *Wisconsin Magazine of History* (Summer, 1959).

E. B. LONG
University of Wyoming

CIVIL WAR TIMES, ILLUSTRATED (Historical Times, Inc., Cameron and Kelker Sts., Harrisburg, Pa. 17105) was launched in 1962 with the help of Bell I. Wiley, E. J. Stackpole, and Glenn Tucker. It is an attractively illustrated monthly. With a present circulation of 105,000, it publishes scholarly and researched popular articles on the Civil War, with an occasional digression into southern history (for which it pays up to $300), plus a limited number of book reviews. The magazine also sponsors the publication of reprints of older classic Civil War books and was recently "involved in re-publication of the 128-volume *Official Records*."

CLAIBORNE, WILLIAM (1587?–1677?), a Virginia colonist, was surveyor of the colony (1621), secretary of state and member of the council (1625–1626), and treasurer of Virginia (1642). He was granted a large tract of land and received (1627–1628) a license from the governor to engage in Indian trade along the Chesapeake. Subsequently he established a trading settlement on Kent Island in Chesapeake Bay, but Lord Baltimore of Maryland claimed proprietary jurisdiction over the "Isle of Kent." Claiborne disputed Baltimore's claim, but the issue was settled in 1638, when the commissioners of plantation in London declared the island to be "wholly within the bounds and limits of Lord Baltimore's patent." Claiborne participated in leading an insurrection that removed Governor Leonard Calvert (CALVERT FAMILY) in 1644, and in 1651 the Puritan Parliament appointed him a member of a commission for the government of "the plantations within the Bay of Chesapeake," which managed Maryland's affairs from 1652 to 1657. One of his last requests was a petition in 1676–1677 to Charles II for Kent Island.

See W. F. Craven, *History of South* (1949); F. B. Simkins, *History of South* (1965); N. C. Hale, *Virginia Ventures: Biography of William Claiborne* (1951); V. De Santis, *Journal of Southern History* (Aug., 1953); J. M. Thornton, *Virginia Magazine of History and Biography* (Jan., 1968); *Maryland Archives* (1883–1947), I, III, IV, V; and *Calvert Papers*, Maryland Historical Society Fund Publications, Nos. 28, 34–35 (1889–99).

GERALD J. GHELFI
Santa Ana College

CLAIBORNE, WILLIAM CHARLES COLE (1775–1817), was born in Virginia, but migrated westward. He participated in the Tennessee statehood convention of 1796 and was appointed to the state supreme court. Almost a year later, he succeeded Andrew Jackson in the U.S. House of Representatives. During his two terms (1797–1801), he opposed American involvement in European affairs, emerged as a vocal Republican stalwart, and supported Thomas Jefferson in the famous Jefferson–Aaron Burr presidential imbroglio in 1800. He became governor of the Mississippi Territory the next year and, with JAMES WILKINSON, served as a commissioner in 1803 to receive the Louisiana Territory. When Louisiana was admitted to statehood in 1812, Claiborne became the state's first elective governor. Some of the more pressing problems confronting him included disputed land titles, smuggling, Spanish-American boundary tensions, the BURR CONSPIRACY, the WEST FLORIDA CONTROVERSY, and British invasion of Louisiana in 1814, followed by General Andrew Jackson's challenge to the local civil authority. However, Claiborne's greatest achievement lay in his advocacy and application of Jeffersonian principles in the Southwest and the peaceful assimilation of Louisiana's largely French populace into the mainstream of American life.

See J. T. Hatfield, *William Claiborne* (1976); T. P. Abernethy, *South* (1961); C. E. Carter (ed.), *Territorial Papers* (1936–40), IV–VI, IX; and D. Rowland, *Official Letter Books* (1917).

JOSEPH T. HATFIELD
Central Missouri State University

CLANTON, JAMES HOLT (1827–1871), a prominent Alabama Democrat during Reconstruction, was born in Georgia and moved to Alabama about 1836. He attended the University of Alabama, served in the Mexican War, and became a wealthy lawyer and legislator, owning $50,000 in property in 1860. A Whig, then a Know-Nothing, he opposed secession and ran as a John Bell–Edward Everett elector. After Alabama seceded, Clanton joined the Confederate army and eventually became a brigadier general. In 1866 he led the organization of the Conservative Union party, later the Democratic and Conservative party. As chairman of its executive committee, Clanton was the most powerful Democrat in Alabama, although he never sought public office. He organized the 1868 boycott of the referendum on the Republican-written constitution, ultimately provoking the March, 1868, Reconstruction Act. His drive to register Democrats as voters after the Alabama legislature relaxed suffrage qualifications helped elect a Democratic governor in 1870. Clanton was fatally shot in September, 1871, in Knoxville, Tenn., while representing Alabama in litigation over the Alabama & Chattanooga Railroad in Tennessee.

His death left Alabama Democrats without his equal in leadership and contributed to the party's defeat in 1872.

See T. M. Owen, *Alabama* (1921); A. J. Going, *East Tennessee Historical Society's Publications* (1955).

SARAH WOOLFOLK WIGGINS
University of Alabama

CLARK, CHARLES (1810–1877), was a Mississippi state legislator, MEXICAN WAR veteran, Confederate brigadier general wounded in the battle of BATON ROUGE, and governor of Mississippi from 1863 to 1865. At the time of his election, he defeated A. M. West, an old-line Whig, and Reuben Davis, a fire-eating Democrat. No enthusiastic secessionist, he nevertheless favored diligent pursuit of the war. Among his achievements was a strong emphasis on strict military discipline, asserting that residents of the state must "repel raids, not make them." He was frequently frustrated by the perplexing problem of reconciling military-civilian political clashes in parts of the state. To shore up the state's economy, he urged that the legislature provide supplies of cotton and wool cards to facilitate production of homespun. He lashed out at excessive railroad rates. Upon effective Union control of Mississippi, he relinquished his executive office to General E. D. Osband on May 25, 1865. After the war Clark practiced law in Bolivar County until 1876, when he was appointed chancellor of the Twenty-fourth District and served in that capacity until his death.

See R. A. McLemore, *History of Mississippi* (1973); D. Rowland, *Mississippi* (1925); and J. K. Bettersworth, *Confederate Mississippi* (1943).

EDWARD MCMILLAN
Mississippi College

CLARK, GEORGE ROGERS (1752–1818), was born near Charlottesville, Va.; he grew up in Caroline County, Va. After limited schooling, he became a surveyor-explorer in the Ohio country, and he served as a militia captain in DUNMORE'S WAR (1774). He was surveying Kentucky River lands for the OHIO COMPANY when the Revolution began. As a delegate from the Kentucky settlements, he negotiated with the Virginia government for defense supplies, and in 1777 he convinced that government to support his plan to seize the British centers of Indian trade and intrigue in the Illinois country.

Leading a force of less than 200 recruits, Clark, without firing a shot, forced the surrender of Kaskaskia, on the Mississippi River (July 4, 1778). Then his "army" occupied nearby Cahokia and Vincennes on the Wabash River. Lieutenant Colonel Henry Hamilton ("the Hair-Buyer") marched with 500 men from British Detroit to recapture Vincennes on December 17. With only 150 men, Clark then set out from Kaskaskia; crossed flooded prairie lands; and, skillfully playing on the fears of Hamilton, his allied Indians, and the French-speaking settlers, regained possession of Vincennes on February 25, 1779.

Although his plans for attacking Detroit never materialized, Clark had ensured Virginia's control of the West during the remaining war years. He was only twenty-seven when he captured the Illinois posts, and his later life was filled with disappointments. He never was able to untangle his accounts with creditors, and various colonizing schemes in Spanish-held lands collapsed. Clark lived for a time at Clarksville in Indiana. Then, after paralysis necessitated amputation of a leg, he resided near Louisville, Ky., until his death.

See J. Bakeless, *Background to Glory* (1957); J. James (ed.), *Clark Papers* (2 vols.; 1912–26); and manuscripts at Virginia State Archives, State Historical Society of Wisconsin (Draper Collection), Filson Club Library, Louisville, and Missouri Historical Society.

CARL UBBELOHDE
Case Western Reserve University

CLARK, JAMES BEAUCHAMP "CHAMP"

(1850–1921), was born in Kentucky and migrated to Pike County, Mo., after graduating from Cincinnati Law School in 1875. He held several local offices and served one term in the Missouri legislature (1889) prior to his election to the U.S. House of Representatives. He served 25 years as Missouri's Ninth District representative (1893–1895, 1897–1921), five years as minority leader (1908–1911, 1919–1921), and eight years as Speaker of the House (1911–1919). Author, CHAUTAUQUA orator, and fierce debater, Champ Clark was a colorful Democratic leader. A Jeffersonian, he reflected a Progressive-agrarian viewpoint and was inclined toward a southern bias. Clark feared the growth of big business and the federal government, favored a direct primary and direct election of senators, and opposed the extension of the civil service. He supported free silver in the 1880s and 1890s, tariff reduction, an income tax, and regulation of business. He opposed lynching and favored equal justice for Negroes, but stated, "I am a Southern man in feeling and thought." Except-

ing Canada and Cuba, Clark opposed imperialism. He believed it undemocratic to include minorities in America who would never be permitted to enjoy full rights of citizenship. He supported the Spanish-American War, but resisted entry into World War I.

Clark enjoyed wide support in the West, Midwest, and South as the presidential election of 1912 approached. His nomination seemed assured, and he led in the voting for 27 ballots, capturing a majority on nine. But his partisanship and "folksy" rhetoric obscured his Progressive tendencies from the urban press, and William Jennings Bryan unexpectedly supported Woodrow Wilson; he thus failed to receive a two-thirds majority.

Clark is far more significant, historically, as a congressional leader than as a presidential contender. As minority leader, he unified the rural and urban factions of the House Democrats, leading them in their opposition to the Payne-Aldrich tariff (1909) and in the removal of Speaker Joseph Cannon from the Rules Committee (1910). As Speaker, he democratized House procedures at the expense of his personal power, restored the caucus, and actively led the Democratic majority in the achievement of New Freedom legislation.

See C. Clark, *My Quarter Century of American Politics* (1920); and G. F. Morrison, "A Political Biography of Champ Clark" (Ph.D. dissertation, St. Louis University, 1972), and *Capitol Studies* (Winter, 1974). Clark's papers are privately held and closed; some manuscripts are at University of Missouri Library, Columbia.

GEOFFREY F. MORRISON
Clayton High School, Clayton, Mo.

CLARK, JOHN

(1766–1832), was the son of Revolutionary War hero and Indian fighter ELIJAH CLARKE. Between 1806 and 1830, the Clark party contended for power against a faction led by George Troup. Support for Clark came from Georgia's western highlands and from settlers from North Carolina. After serving a number of times in the legislature, Clark became governor in 1819 by defeating Troup. Defeating him again in 1821, he lost to Troup in 1825. As governor, Clark made an attack on all private banks in the state and attempted to extinguish all Cherokee rights to land within the state. In 1824 Clark opposed the presidential efforts of his rival WILLIAM H. CRAWFORD, with whom he had once fought a duel (1806), and supported General Andrew Jackson. After 1828 his party became the major element within the Jacksonian Democratic party in Georgia. Clark himself moved to Florida in 1829.

See U. B. Phillips, *Annual Report of American Histori-cal Association* (1901); P. Murray, *Whig Party in Georgia, 1825–1853* (1948); and E. M. Coulter, *Georgia* (1947).

HERBERT ERSHKOWITZ
Temple University

CLARK, THOMAS DIONYSIUS (1903–), historian, was born and reared in rural Mississippi. He earned degrees at the universities of Mississippi and Kentucky and at Duke. While teaching at the University of Kentucky (1931–1968), he contributed greatly to the upgrading of historical scholarship, the improvement of the library, and the establishment of the university press. He was president of the Southern Historical Association (1947), editor of the *Journal of Southern History* (1948–1952), and president of the Organization of American Historians (1957). Clark's publications include *The Beginning of the L & N* (1933), *A Pioneer Southern Railroad* (1936), *A History of Kentucky* (1937), *The Rampaging Frontier* (1939), *The Kentucky* (1942), *Pills, Petticoats, and Plows* (1944), *The Southern Country Editor* (1948), *The Rural Press and the New South* (1948), *Frontier America* (1959), *The Emerging South* (1961), *Three Paths to the Modern South* (1965), (with A. KIRWAN) *The South Since Appomattox* (1967), and *Kentucky: Land of Contrast* (1968). In addition, Clark has edited a six-volumed series on travels in the South. Clark's writing emphasizes the human and colorful aspects of history. His earlier works such as *The Rampaging Frontier* are filled with picturesque personalities and vivid details that evoke the era's special quality. His *History of Kentucky* has remained since 1937 the standard work. Especially significant is *Frontier America*, a comprehensive treatment of the diverse factors involved in frontier development, which balances the Frederick Jackson Turner and European origins perspectives. *The Emerging South*, highly praised for its chapters on the Negro, reveals Clark's profound understanding of the region.

See H. Hamilton's introduction, *Three American Frontiers* (1968); and A. S. Link and R. W. Patrick (eds.), *Writing Southern History* (1965).

JOHN D. WRIGHT, JR.
Transylvania University

CLARK, WALTER (1846–1924), was born in Halifax County, N.C., of an old and well-connected family. After graduating from the University of North Carolina (B.A., 1864) and attending Columbia University Law School, he was admitted to the North Carolina bar at the age of twenty-one. Suc-cessful as an attorney in Halifax County (1867–1873) and Raleigh (1873–1885), he was elected to the post of superior court judge in 1884 and then to the state supreme court in 1888. During his long tenure in the latter post (1889–1924), Clark established his reputation as a liberal, "fighting judge" and as one of the most capable jurists in North Carolina history. His outspoken antipathy toward the American Tobacco Company (DUKE FAMILY) and his general friendliness toward the state's Populists permitted him to retain his seat on the supreme court during the fusion regime of the 1890s. His decisions in support of public education, railroad taxation, women's suffrage, and corporate regulation made him a major force in state and southern PROGRESSIVISM. While sitting on the bench he was a prolific writer, translating W. Constant's *Memoirs of Napoleon* (1895); editing the 16-volumed collection *North Carolina State Records* (1895–1901) and the five-volumed *History of North Carolina Regiments* (1901); and compiling the *Annotated Code of Civil Procedure*, the *Cyclopedia of Law* (1901), and 164 volumes of *U.S. Supreme Court Reports*.

See A. L. Brooks, *Walter Clark* (1944); and W. Clark Papers, North Carolina Archives, Raleigh.

CLARK, WILLIAM (1770–1838), youngest brother of GEORGE ROGERS CLARK, was born in Virginia. He joined the military in 1789, where he probably first met MERIWETHER LEWIS. He resigned in 1796 for personal reasons and eagerly accepted the offer seven years later to join Lewis as coleader of the proposed western expedition to explore the Louisiana Territory. The Corps of Discovery left Wood River, Ill., in May, 1804, and returned from the arduous trek in September, 1806. In addition to his qualities of leadership, Clark contributed great skill in mapmaking. As a reward, he was appointed brigadier general of the Louisiana militia, helping Governor Lewis keep peace with the Indians. In 1813 he was appointed governor of Missouri Territory and superintendent of Indian affairs. He continued as governor until statehood and remained in charge of Indian affairs practically until his death. During this time Clark performed great services to his nation by helping the white man move into Indian lands while he kept the friendship, admiration, and respect of the Indians, who called him the Red Head Chief.

See J. Bakeless, *Lewis and Clark* (1947), closest to a Clark biography; R. G. Thwaites (ed.), *Journals of Lewis and Clark Expedition* (1904–05); D. Jackson (ed.), *Let-*

ters of *Lewis and Clark Expedition* (1962); and E. S. Osgood (ed.), *Field Notes of Captain Clark* (1964).

JOHN A. CAYLOR
Boise State University

CLARKE, ELIJAH (1733–1799), was Georgia's most illustrious partisan-militia leader in the Revolutionary War. Refusing to accept British occupation in 1780, he began the resistance movement on the Georgia–South Carolina frontier. Clarke fought at Alligator Swamp (1778); Kettle Creek (1779); Thickety Fort, Musgrove's Mills, Blackstocks, and Long Canes (1780); Beattie's Mill (1781); and Long Swamp (1782). He participated in both sieges of Augusta and led the exodus of backcountry patriots to Watauga in September-October, 1780. After the Revolution Clarke attempted to expand Georgia's territory at the expense of the CREEK INDIANS. An admirer of JOHN SEVIER and the state of FRANKLIN, Clarke established the TRANS-OCONEE REPUBLIC in 1794 in defiance of Georgia and the United States. He took service with France that same year and attempted to invade East Florida in 1795. He died a broken man, feeling the nation he "had bled for to establish" had betrayed him.

See L. F. Hays, *Hero of Hornet's Nest* (1946), complete but use carefully; W. S. Northen (ed.), *Men of Mark in Georgia* (1907), I, useful; E. M. Coulter, *Proceedings of Mississippi Valley Historical Association* (1919–20); E. A. Bowen, *Wilkes County* (1950); and R. K. Murdoch, *Georgia Historical Quarterly* (Sept., 1951).

CLYDE R. FERGUSON
Kansas State University

CLARKSBURG, W.VA. (pop. 24,869), is on the west fork of the Monongahela River approximately 70 miles east of Parkersburg. It manufactures glass and drilling machinery for wells, but draws its principal livelihood as a market and shipping point for area coal, limestone, oil, gas, and clay. The site was first settled as a trapping camp in 1764, and the town that quickly grew up here was named to honor GEORGE ROGERS CLARK. With roads connecting it to other settlements, the town became a major supply center for travelers and settlers alike. The residents were decidedly Unionist in their sympathies and, after Virginia seceded from the Union, the town became a center of the movement for separate statehood. The area coalfields were developed beginning in the 1870s, and the discovery of oil in 1889 furthered the city's prosperity.

See P. Conley, *History of West Virginia Coal Industry* (1960); and files of *Exponent Telegram* (1910–), *Tribune* (1849–97), *National Telegraph* (1862–68), and *Cooper's Clarksburg Register* (1852–58), all on microfilm.

CLARKSDALE, MISS. (pop. 21,673), is on the Sunflower River in the northwest section of the state. Settled in 1848 on the site of an old Indian village, the town developed very little prior to the Civil War. After the war, the shifting bed of the Mississippi River and completion of rail ties to Clarksdale made it the principal market for area cotton growers. The modern city remains very much a cotton town, with some light industries manufacturing cotton seed and soybean oil, rubber products, mobile homes, and lumber.

See files of Clarksdale *Press-Register* (1865–), *Delta Farm Press* (1944–), and *Banner* (1902–10), all on microfilm.

CLARKSVILLE, TENN. (pop. 31,719), besides manufacturing clothing, air conditioners, and appliance parts, is the home of Austin Peay State University and is one of the nation's larger producers of cowboy boots. Ever since its founding in 1784, however, the city's continuing economic base has been as a market and shipping point for area-grown TOBACCO. Early shipments of fire-cured tobacco were sent by flatboats from this point on the Cumberland River to New Orleans. The city, named for GEORGE ROGERS CLARK, is 40 miles northwest of Nashville and ten miles southeast of U.S. Army Ft. Campbell in Kentucky.

See U. S. Beach, *Along the Warioto* (1964, 1965); W. P. Titus, *Picturesque Clarksville* (1887, 1973); *Montgomery County Genealogical Journal* (1971–); and files of Clarksville *Leaf-Chronicle* (1809–). The public library actively collects and indexes tax lists, census records, city directories, and cemetery records dealing with local history.

CLASSES AND CASTES. The social history of the South is in large part the history of the fluctuations and transformations in its classes and castes. Throughout the colonial period the class structure in the South differed very little from that of the North, except that positions of highest status in the North went to commercial and manufacturing elites as well as to large landowners. Both areas spawned a hierarchical society in which individuals accepted their place and freely deferred to their social and economic superiors. With the Revolution, however, northern and southern societies began to diverge. The South, committed to a plantation economy, remained relatively static. Problems within a society whose social, political, and economic focus remained predominantly rural never became complex enough to overwhelm the leadership of the original landed elite (ARISTOCRACY). Thus, the county court, established by the earliest settlers and dominated by the planter class, continued to hold sway (GOVERNMENT, STATE AND LOCAL). Such planter dominance did not, however, create much class antagonism. The vast majority of southern whites were middle-class YEOMEN whose economic interests coincided with those of the planters and who very likely aspired to become planters themselves. These common interests received strong reinforcement from the caste system. All whites, no matter how lowly, could take pride from a sense of participation in a common brotherhood of white men. Thus, the caste system reinforced the white class structure so that the South throughout the antebellum period remained under a hegemonic consensus that reflected the wishes of the planter class. Self-preservation of that planter class—its most basic demand of all—came to dominate all others by 1860 and pushed the South into secession and civil war.

The Civil War and Reconstruction disrupted both the caste and class structures and created great uncertainties, tensions, and anxieties within southern society. Intervention by the federal government upset traditional race relations, and the class structure suffered disruptions due to wartime devastation and dislocations. By the end of Reconstruction (1877), however, a dominant white class had once again established itself. Consisting of an amalgam of old planters and new commercial men, this class prevailed by means of social sanctions similar to those of the antebellum period. However, new economic conditions fostered class antagonisms in the post-Reconstruction years. The introduction of manufacturing, milling, and railroad enterprises tended to create particular class interests and to place a strain on the traditional harmony among whites. As Populists and conservatives struggled for political dominance, the black man lost his newly gained rights and privileges. Once again the caste system solidified the white class structure. JIM CROW legislation stamped the force of law on the postbellum caste system and provided a workable substitute for the social arrangements of the slave economy. This more rigid caste and class system prevailed until the 1950s. With the U.S. Supreme Court decision of 1954 (BROWN V. BOARD OF EDUCATION), the CIVIL RIGHTS MOVEMENT of the 1960s, and economic changes throughout these years, the South began to undergo an inexorable transformation. Industrial urban cities, with their corporate executives, began to replace rural strongholds as centers of social, economic, and political power. Separate class structures, fostered by a rigid caste system, began to give way to a single class system, comprising both blacks and whites. The South gradually began to lose its distinctive social structure and to become more similar to the larger American society.

See W. Jordan, *White over Black* (1968); D. Bertelson, *Lazy South* (1967); E. Genovese, *Political Economy of Slavery* (1965), and *Roll, Jordan, Roll* (1974); W. Cash, *Mind of South* (1941); F. Owsley, *Plain Folk* (1949); F. Green, *Constitutional Development* (1930); S. Elkins and E. McKitrick, *Political Science Quarterly* (Dec., 1954); R. W. Shugg, *Origins of Class Struggle* (1939); C. V. Woodward, *Origins of New South* (1951), and *Strange Career of Jim Crow* (1955); A. Kirwan, *Revolt of Rednecks* (1951); and G. Tindall, *Emergence of New South* (1967).

ROBERT E. SHALHOPE
University of Oklahoma

CLAY, CASSIUS MARCELLUS (1810–1903), southern emancipationist and diplomat, was born on his father's estate White Hall, in Madison County, Ky. As soon as he was eligible, in 1835, he served several terms in the state legislature, but in 1841 he was defeated on the issue of slave importation into the state. Colorful, ambitious, and able, he made emancipation his primary goal. Unlike most antislavery advocates he felt no religious motivation in what he did. "It is not a matter of conscience with me," he insisted. He declared that slavery was a hindrance to a diversified, manufacturing economy in Kentucky and announced his intention to rid the state of the institution in order to improve conditions among white artisans and laborers. They were in competition with slave labor, which received subsistence rather than wages, and they suffered as a consequence.

In 1845 a mob attacked the *True American*, his Lexington, Ky., newspaper, but in 1851 he ran for governor as an emancipationist. Overwhelmingly defeated in the state, he concentrated upon national politics, working with Free-Soilers and antislavery Whigs. In 1861 Abraham Lincoln appointed him minister to Russia, where he remained, except for a short time in 1862, until 1869. As a diplomat he claimed credit for retaining Russian support of the Union, which had an effect in keeping other European countries neutral in the Civil War. Back in the United States he resumed his quest for political office, changing political parties as opinion shifted. In 1872 he was a Liberal Republican against U. S. Grant and four years later a Democrat opposed to the Radicals; in

1880 he was once again a Republican. His remaining years in retirement were marred by a ready pugnacity and an evident decline in his mental balance.

See C. M. Clay, *Life of C. M. Clay: Memoirs, Writings, and Speeches* (1886), autobiography; H. Greeley (ed.), *Writings of C. M. Clay* (1848); D. L. Smiley, *Lion of White Hall* (1962); files of *True American* in Lexington Public Library; and manuscripts in Library of Congress, Filson Club, Louisville, Lincoln Memorial University, and family collections, Paris, Ky.

DAVID L. SMILEY
Wake Forest University

CLAY, CLEMENT CLAIBORNE (1816–1882), was born near Huntsville, Ala., the son of Governor Clement Comer Clay. After graduating from the University of Alabama (1834) and the University of Virginia law department (1839), Clay became active in Alabama politics and was elected to the U.S. Senate (1853–1861). An eloquent defender of states' rights, he withdrew following Alabama's secession and between 1861 and 1863 represented Alabama in the Confederate Senate. His most notable service during the Civil War was as a secret agent, sent by Jefferson Davis to Canada in April, 1864, with verbal orders to help disrupt the Union war effort by aiding and encouraging northern peace elements and by generating conflicts between Canada and the United States along the border. Clay was active in Horace Greeley's peace effort in mid-1864 and distributed funds to Confederates who staged the St. Alban's raid. Unjustly accused of complicity in the LINCOLN ASSASSINATION, Clay turned himself in and was imprisoned until 1866. He remained politically inactive thereafter.

See E. C. Kirkland, *Peacemakers of 1864* (1927); and R. W. Winks, *Canada and U.S.* (1960), for Clay's activities with Greeley and in Canada.

KINLEY J. BRAUER
University of Minnesota

CLAY, HENRY (1777–1852), was born in Hanover County, Va. In 1792, when his mother and stepfather immigrated to Kentucky, he was left in Richmond as a deputy to the clerk of the Virginia high court of chancery. His intelligence and legible handwriting soon earned for him employment as amanuensis to the chancellor, GEORGE WYTHE. Under the latter's supervision Clay began to read law, and, in late 1796 or early 1797, he embarked on full-time study with the state attorney general. In November, 1797, he was admitted to the bar.

Family ties drew him to Kentucky, where in Lexington he found opportunity and a congenial atmosphere. An ardent Jeffersonian, he became identified with the political and economic interests of central Kentucky and was rewarded with loyal support in his campaigns for office. He was a member of the Kentucky house of representatives (1803–1810), except for brief appointments to the U.S. Senate (1806–1807, 1810–1811). Elected to the Twelfth and Thirteenth Congresses (1811–1814), he was immediately chosen Speaker of the House, an office that he transformed into a position of power and influence and that he held in six Congresses. As leader of the "war hawks" he helped bring on the WAR OF 1812; appointed to the peace commission, he helped negotiate the Treaty of Ghent.

Again in Congress (1815–1821, 1823–1825), he assumed a role of national leadership, urging recognition of the Latin American republics; advocating his "American system" (a protective tariff, internal improvements, and a national bank), which provided a platform for the future; and engineering the MISSOURI COMPROMISE (1820–1821), the first of his successful efforts to prevent the slavery issue from disrupting the Union.

Clay's quest for the presidency began with the ELECTION OF 1824, when he ran last in a field of four. Since the front-runner, ANDREW JACKSON, had only a plurality of the electoral votes, the House of Representatives had the duty of selecting a president. Despite legislative instructions to the Kentucky delegation to vote for Jackson, Clay supported John Quincy Adams as the contender best qualified for the office. When his decision became known, a charge of "bargain" rose from the Jackson camp, and, after Adams became president and appointed Clay to his cabinet, the cry of "bargain and corruption" swelled, never to be completely hushed.

The Kentuckian was an able secretary of state in an administration buffeted by attack, as Jacksonians organized for the victory their leader won over Adams in the ELECTION OF 1828. Out of office in 1829, Clay retired to Ashland, his estate near Lexington, but spoke out strongly in criticism of the new administration. In 1831 he was elected to the U.S. Senate, where he sat until 1842. As leader of the National Republicans (soon called the WHIG PARTY), he struggled unsuccessfully against the economic policies of Jacksonianism and in the ELECTION OF 1832 was soundly defeated in his second bid for the presidency. Nevertheless, when the NULLIFICATION crisis of 1833 threatened the administration and the Union itself, he sponsored compromise legislation that lowered the tariff and removed the immediate danger.

He did not seek the presidency in 1836 and failed to win nomination in 1840, when his party's choice was elected. He was the Whig candidate in the ELECTION OF 1844, but the forthright expansionism of his opponent JAMES K. POLK won the day for the Democrats. After having angled unsuccessfully for a presidential nomination in 1848, Clay returned to the Senate the following year. There, ill and without influence in the administration of Whig President ZACHARY TAYLOR, the old statesman rallied his forces in the face of the sectional crisis that followed the Mexican War. His proposals, though enacted during his absence from Washington, were the foundation of the COMPROMISE OF 1850 and helped earn for him the popular appellation, the Great Pacificator.

Clay was an affectionate husband and father and a public-spirited citizen of his home community. Although a slave owner, he favored emancipation, but only if the Negro could be returned to Africa—hence his long involvement with the AMERICAN COLONIZATION SOCIETY. As a politician he was bold, frank, sometimes imperious, and usually optimistic. In office he served his constituents well, but his economic nationalism was unacceptable to much of the country. He was quick-witted in debate and one of the great orators of his time. Consistent in denouncing both aggressive abolitionists of the North and fire-eating secessionists of the South, he deserves to be remembered for his untiring efforts to preserve the Union.

See C. Eaton, *Henry Clay* (1957); B. Mayo, *Henry Clay* (1937), limited to early period; G. G. Van Deusen, *Life of Henry Clay* (1937); C. Colton (ed.), *Works of Henry Clay* (6 vols.; 1855); and J. F. Hopkins *et al.*, *Papers of Henry Clay* (5 vols. to date; 1959–).

JAMES F. HOPKINS
University of Kentucky

CLAY, LAURA (1849–1941), a daughter of CASSIUS M. CLAY, the noted abolitionist, was born near Richmond, Ky. She graduated from Sayre Female Institute in Lexington in 1865. In 1888 she helped organize the Kentucky Equal Rights Association and was elected its first president. By the mid-1890s, the association had won a number of state legislative and educational victories, including protection of married women's property and wages, coguardianship of minor children, coeducation at several colleges, and a partial school suffrage law for women. Elected auditor of the National American Woman Suffrage Association (NAWSA) in 1896, a post she held for 15 years, she

became a recognized force for moderation and conciliation in association disputes. Clay also served as an unpaid field worker in numerous states and directed campaigns for equal suffrage in Oregon, Oklahoma, and Arizona. She withdrew from NAWSA in 1919, however, believing that the Nineteenth Amendment violated states' rights.

See P. E. Fuller, *Laura Clay* (1975); A. Kraditor, *Ideas of Woman Suffrage Movement* (1965); and Laura Clay Papers, University of Kentucky.

PAUL E. FULLER
Wesleyan College

CLAYBANKS AND CHARCOALS. Following the exile of Missouri's secessionist government, three Unionist factions contended for power: "charcoals," radical immediate emancipationists who drew strength from the St. Louis abolitionist German Home Guards and federal troops; "claybanks," moderately antislavery Unionists with a wide but less cohesive following; and "snowflakes," antiemancipationist Unionists. The claybanks, led by Governor H. R. GAMBLE, early dominated the People's Convention (1861) and the provisional government (1862) but gradually lost control. The charcoals, who had by the fall of 1863 elected the radical B. G. BROWN to the U.S. Senate and pressed for uncompensated immediate emancipation, triumphed.

See W. E. Parrish, *Turbulent Partnership* (1963); E. M. Violette, *Missouri* (1918, 1951); E. C. McReynolds, *Missouri* (1962); E. C. Smith, *Borderland in Civil War* (1927); and B. R. Lee, *Missouri Historical Review* (April, 1952).

JANE H. PEASE and
WILLIAM H. PEASE
University of Maine, Orono

CLAY EATERS. Pica is the practice by some people of consuming unusual substances like dirt, laundry starch, plaster, hair, or clay. Geophagy, a variety of pica, refers specifically to the eating of earth. The "clay eaters" in the South have been a topic of interest to professional historians from the time that scholars first began to research the South; but until recently surprisingly little was known about the subject except what was provided by the occasional comments of early travelers and settlers. Clay or dirt eating was thought by most historians to have been an occasional thing of the past and limited largely to a few degraded POOR WHITES living in remote sections of the southeastern states. Recent studies by sociologists, historians, nutritionists, geographers, and the medical profession, however, reveal that the habit dates back to the colonial era, was prevalent among both whites and blacks (called *cachexia Africana* among the slaves), and is still common today in many parts of the rural South. The amount ingested, though usually small, is sometimes as much as three handfuls at a time, several times a day. It neither results from nor is the main cause of HOOKWORM as was once thought. In fact, the practice often has surprisingly little effect on the victim's health, unless done to excess. Prolonged and large consumption, however, among other things can cause serious intestinal problems, anemia, and, in pregnant women, injury to the unborn. Whether it is caused by hunger pangs, is an acquired social habit that is hard to break, like smoking, or is the result of a dietary deficiency is a matter still under study.

See R. W. Twyman, *Journal of Southern History* (Aug., 1971); F. B. Bradley, *North Carolina Folklore* (Dec., 1964); M. M. Cooper, *Pica* (1957); H. Hertz, *Social Forces* (March, 1947); J. A. Halsted, *American Journal of Clinical Nutrition* (Dec., 1968); and D. E. Vermeer and D. A. Frate, *Annals of Association of American Geographers* (Sept., 1975).

CLAYTON, HENRY DE LAMAR (1827–1889), was born in Pulaski County, Ga., graduated from Emory and Henry College (1848), became a lawyer and planter in Clayton, Ala., and served in the state legislature (1857–1861). A secessionist, he organized forces defending Pensacola (1861–1862), then commanded a regiment under BRAXTON BRAGG in Kentucky and Tennessee. Promoted brigadier general, then major general, he distinguished himself at STONES RIVER, CHICKAMAUGA, and NASHVILLE. Returning to Clayton (1865), he was elected circuit judge and made a widely quoted grand jury charge (September 9, 1866), calling on whites to support freedom, justice, and jobs for blacks. Disqualified under congressional Reconstruction, he was later returned to the bench (1874–1886). He died during an undistinguished administration (1886–1889) as president of the state university.

See Clayton Manuscripts, University of Alabama; A. B. Moore, *History of Alabama* (1927); W. Garrett, *Reminiscences* (1872), grand jury charge; C. A. Evans (ed.), *Confederate Military History* (1899); J. B. Sellers, *History of University of Alabama* (1953); A. J. Going, *Bourbon Democrats* (1951); and W. L. Fleming, *Civil War and Reconstruction* (1905, 1949).

ALDEN B. PEARSON, JR.
University of Alabama, Huntsville

CLAYTON, HENRY DE LAMAR (1857–1929), of Barbour County, Ala., attended the state university (A.B., 1877; LL.B., 1878) and practiced law in Eufaula. He was county registrar (1880–1884), state legislator (1890–1891), district attorney (1893–1896), and congressman (1897–1914). He served as Democratic national committeeman (1888–1908), permanent chairman of the national convention (1908), and chairman of the Democratic House caucus (1907–1909). A prominent Bryanite in the 1896 convention, in 1912 he was a manager of the Underwood group that ensured Woodrow Wilson's nomination. As Judiciary Committee chairman (1911–1914), Clayton was chief prosecutor in the Robert W. Archbald impeachment trial (1912–1913) and primary author of the Antitrust Act of 1914. While district judge in Alabama (1914–1929), he promoted judicial reform and delivered several notable opinions: *Smith v. Jackson* (241 Fed. 747), *U.S. v. Forbes* (259 Fed. 585), and *Alabama Power Company v. Gulf Power Company* (283 Fed. 606).

See Clayton Papers, University of Alabama; U.S. House, Judiciary Committee, *Trust Legislation, Hearings*, 63rd Cong., 2nd Sess. (1914); and *Congressional Record*, 62nd Cong., 3rd Sess., Archbald trial, and 63rd Cong., 2nd Sess., Antitrust Act.

ALDEN B. PEARSON, JR.
University of Alabama, Huntsville

CLAYTON, POWELL (1833–1914), was born in Bethel, Pa., moved to Leavenworth, Kan., in 1855, and entered the Union army as a captain in the 1st Kansas Volunteer Infantry in 1861. After experiencing combat, Clayton, a brigadier general, left the army in 1865 and became a planter near Pine Bluff, Ark. Elected governor of Arkansas as a Republican in 1868, Clayton became a special target of the KU KLUX KLAN, an organization that he, in contrast to other southern Republican governors in the postwar years, was able to repress. He was later elected to the U.S. Senate (1871–1877). He remained active in Republican politics after leaving Washington and was later ambassador to Mexico (1897–1905). Clayton's memoirs, *The Aftermath of the Civil War in Arkansas* (1915), present his side of numerous Reconstruction controversies and rank with those of ALBION TOURGÉE, HENRY CLAY WARMOTH, and Albert Morgan as sources for the carpetbaggers.

See T. S. Staples, *Reconstruction in Arkansas* (1923); A. W. Trelease, *White Terror* (1971); and O. T. Driggs, *Arkansas Historical Quarterly* (Spring, 1941).

RICHARD L. HUME
Washington State University

CLEARWATER, FLA. (pop. 52,074), approximately 18 miles northwest of St. Petersburg, grew up gradually around Ft. Harrison (1841). Incorporated in 1891, it was primarily a shipping point for citrus fruits until into the twentieth century, when it became an increasingly popular winter resort.

See H. Dunn, *Yesterday's Clearwater* (1973); and files of Clearwater *Sun* (1914–), on microfilm.

CLEBURNE, PATRICK RONAYNE (1828–1864), born in Ireland to a prominent Anglo-Irish family, became the Confederacy's most renowned general of foreign birth. He had served as an enlisted man in the British army until discouragement over conditions in Ireland compelled him to emigrate in 1849. Eleven years in Helena, Ark., as a druggist and lawyer forged Cleburne's devotion to southern rights, for which he took up arms in 1861. A superb battle captain and painstaking drillmaster, whose troops were exceptionally dependable, competent, and disciplined, he fought brilliantly at the battles of Richmond, Ky., SHILOH, STONES RIVER, and CHICKAMAUGA and in the CHATTANOOGA and ATLANTA campaigns. Cleburne was promoted major general in 1862 and twice commended by the Confederate Congress. Many considered him the Army of Tennessee's best division commander. Cleburne was, however, denied higher command, possibly because of his foreign birth, his involvement with an officer faction critical of General BRAXTON BRAGG, and his proposal, suppressed by Jefferson Davis, that the Confederacy recruit and emancipate slaves. The "Stonewall Jackson of the West" fell at the battle of FRANKLIN.

See H. and E. Purdue, *Pat Cleburne* (1973); E. Lonn, *Foreigners in Confederacy* (1940); T. L. Connelly, *Autumn of Glory* (1971); I. A. Buck, *Cleburne and His Command* (1908); and W. W. Hassler, *Civil War Times Illustrated* (Oct., 1972).

DAVID H. OVERY
St. Cloud State University

CLEMENS, SAMUEL LANGHORNE (1835–1910), better known as Mark Twain, was born in Florida, Mo., and reared in Hannibal, Mo., on the Mississippi River. Especially before his marriage to Olivia Langdon (1845–1904), a wealthy yet serious-minded and gentle easterner who bore four children, he had an extremely variegated life. He could rightly claim to have resided in every major section of the United States and in several European countries; he worked seriously at a range of jobs, several times dipping close to poverty before bursting into success. He delighted in roughhewn company yet also read tenaciously; he could veer

from raw or even noisome joking into genteel rigidity. Although this pattern of multiple polarities enlarged his range of audiences, it also created a nagging sense of imbalance and even suspicions that reality is more illusory than malleable.

His wavering at the core ran through his attitude toward the South. His Virginia-proud father and his mother, a Kentucky belle, had owned house servants; and, when forced to choose sides in 1861, Clemens spent two lax weeks with Confederate irregulars before decamping to Nevada. After he settled down in Hartford, Conn., in 1870 and joined the northern literary establishment, W. D. Howells eventually judged him a remarkably "desouthernized Southerner." But he turned mugwump in 1884, recanting his Republican fervors, and during his last 15 years could genially call himself a southerner. Beneath his political shiftings lay a rooted ambivalence. His loyalty to his origins, always evident in his drawling accent, reinforced a nostalgic love for the scenes of his childhood. Yet his subconscious bubbled with personal frustrations from the Hannibal years, and doctrinally the postbellum South offended his matured creed of laissez faire economics.

When his fiction set its incidents in Missouri, they suggested mostly a midwestern flavor, as in *The Gilded Age* (1873) and *The Adventures of Tom Sawyer* (1876). The commentary in *Life on the Mississippi* (1883) reproved the South as backward, and *Adventures of Huckleberry Finn* (1885) indicted chattel slavery. However, it stressed more the failings of basic human nature, and though *Pudd'nhead Wilson* (1894) raised gritty doubts about the antebellum myth, it also highlighted the power of environment and training over all men. In any extended work, his overt and covert attitudes often clashed. His final years brought ever-increasing acclaim, which, he purported to believe, would sour if exposed to his frankest ideas.

Psychic indecisions did not impede his preternatural fluency over more than 50 years. His first full-length book, *The Innocents Abroad* (1869), came easily, followed soon enough by *Roughing It* (1872). Likewise, with some padding *A Tramp Abroad* (1880) was ready when he needed a publication, as was *Following the Equator* (1897). Unusual care went into the stilted *Prince and the Pauper* (1882), now less interesting than *A Connecticut Yankee in King Arthur's Court* (1889). *The American Claimant* (1892) was not worth his hasty effort, but neither did *Personal Recollections of Joan of Arc* (1896) repay his reverential care. Many other volumes of mixed grain, his newspaper and magazine pieces, and philosophical dialogues such as *What Is Man?* (1906) fill out a unique gamut. His admirers are equally fascinated with him as a great personality and tortured moralist. He is fixed in the American mind as a culture hero, but the fame of Mark Twain is truly worldwide.

See H. H. Clark, in F. Stovall (ed.), *Eight American Authors* (rev. ed.; 1971); M. Beebe and J. Feaster, *Modern Fiction Studies* (Spring, 1968); and the annual chapters since 1963 in J. Woodress (ed.), *American Literary Scholarship*, all for useful bibliographical guidance. The indispensable collection of primary materials is the Mark Twain Papers, University of California at Berkeley, much of which is slated for publication. The Iowa/California edition, definitive texts of work published during his lifetime, has also begun to appear. For basic biography see A. B. Paine, *Mark Twain* (1912); and D. Wecter, *Sam Clemens of Hannibal* (1952). J. D. Ferguson, *Mark Twain: Man and Legend* (1943); J. Kaplan, *Mr. Clemens and Mark Twain* (1966); and H. Hill, *Mark Twain: God's Fool* (1973), are more interpretive. For literary analysis see first H. N. Smith, *Mark Twain: The Development of a Writer* (1962); and J. M. Cox, *Mark Twain: The Fate of Humor* (1966). For the social and political context start with B. DeVoto, *Mark Twain's America* (1932); and L. Budd, *Mark Twain: Social Philosopher* (1962). For particularly relevant chapters and articles, see J. B. Hubbell, *The South in American Literature, 1607–1900* (1954); A. Turner, *Southern Review* (April, 1968); and L. Rubin, *The Writer in the South* (1972).

LOUIS J. BUDD
Duke University

CLEMENT, FRANK GOAD (1920–1970), was

born at Kyrock, Ky. Elected governor of Tennessee for a two-year term in 1952 and for a four-year term in 1954, he was chosen governor again in 1962, and thus served in that office for a total of ten years. Among the many accomplishments of the Clement era were the establishment of a state department of mental health, expanded highway and educational programs, and free textbooks for students in the lower grades. In 1964, Clement, while governor, unsuccessfully sought the Democratic nomination for senator to fill the unexpired term of ESTES KEFAUVER. Two years later, Democrats nominated him in the primary election, but he was defeated by Howard Baker in the general election.

See Clement Manuscripts, Clement Foundation, Dickson, Tenn., most valuable, and Archives of State Library, Nashville. Consult also S. D. Boyd, "Campaign Speaking of Clement in 1954 Primary" (Ph.D. dissertation, University of Illinois, 1972); and W. L. Davis, "Rhetorical Analysis of Clement, 1952" (M.S. thesis, Wake Forest, 1972).

ROBERT E. CORLEW
Middle Tennessee State University

CLEMSON UNIVERSITY (Clemson, S.C. 29631).

Thomas G. Clemson (mining engineer and agronomist) and his wife (the daughter of JOHN C. CALHOUN) willed most of the land and money for the establishment of this state agricultural college in 1889. The school formally opened in 1893 with a class of 446 and has grown to a current enrollment in excess of 10,000 students. It became a university in 1964. The library has the papers of men such as John C. Calhoun and BENJAMIN TILLMAN, as well as the records of many South Carolina agricultural groups and plantation account books and diaries.

CLEVELAND, BENJAMIN (1738–1806), was born

in Prince William County and reared in Orange County, Va. After a fortunate marriage to Mary Graves, he moved about 1769 with his wife, father-in-law, and others to the foot of the Blue Ridge in the North Carolina backcountry. Although most remembered as a commander at KINGS MOUNTAIN, Cleveland in several ways personified the frontier gentry of his day. With 10,000 acres and a reputation as an Indian fighter, he seemed a natural leader. As such, he was chairman of the Surry County committee of safety from 1775 to 1778. Later in Wilkes County he was simultaneously colonel of the militia, head of the commission of justices, state legislator, and the holder of numerous lesser offices. In politics and on the bench Cleveland supported the positions of his class. Cleveland's last 20 years were in Oconee County, S.C., where he was known as a judge impatient with legal technicalities.

See L. C. Draper, *King's Mountain* (1881), standard; and B. L. Waugh, "Benjamin Cleveland" (Ph.D. dissertation, University of New Mexico, 1971).

E. MILTON WHEELER
William Carey College

CLEVELAND, GROVER, ADMINISTRATIONS

(1885–1889, 1893–1897). When Cleveland's presidency began, the South was very enthusiastic about the first Democratic administration since 1861. Actually Cleveland, a New York conservative, listened mainly to eastern advisers. He did distribute the patronage in a reasonable manner. Among the numerous southerners who received government appointments were two former Confederates, L. Q. C. LAMAR of Mississippi and AUGUSTUS H. GARLAND of Arkansas, who held cabinet positions. Later he appointed Lamar to the U.S. Supreme Court. Cleveland's administration routinely attempted to return all captured Civil

War battle flags, but Union veterans blocked the return of Confederate flags. Although southern benefits from his first term were limited primarily to the symbolic value of the appointments, Cleveland remained popular among white southerners.

When he took office again in 1893, it was the first time since 1861 that the presidency and Congress were controlled by the Democratic party. This led many southern Democrats to expect an expanded role in the federal government. By this time, however, the depression-stricken southern farmers had turned to free silver as a panacea for their problems (POPULIST PARTY). Cleveland and his advisers were strong supporters of the gold standard. In 1893 the president demanded the repeal of the Sherman Silver Purchase Act. Southern Democrats strongly objected, fearing that it would help Populists and Republicans in the South. Cleveland forced repeal anyway by using the patronage as a weapon. This unpopular measure was followed by several bond issues to raise the gold reserve. These actions made many southerners believe that Cleveland had sold them out to eastern business interests. The manner in which he used the patronage caused most southern politicians to desert Cleveland. Populists used the situation to work up even more anti-Cleveland sentiment. The administration's muddled attempts to revise the tariff made matters worse. In 1895 Cleveland tried to rebuild support in the South, but with little success. In the ELECTION OF 1896 most southern state Democratic conventions came out strongly for free silver, clearly demonstrating Cleveland's lack of influence.

See A. Nevins, *Grover Cleveland* (1932); H. S. Merrill, *Bourbon Leader* (1957); and C. V. Woodward, *Origins of New South* (1951). See also P. H. Buck, *Road to Reunion* (1937); J. B. Murphy, *L. Q. C. Lamar* (1937); H. W. Morgan, *Hayes to McKinley* (1969); and A. Nevins (ed.), *Letters of Grover Cleveland* (1933). For additional information on Cleveland's second administration, see H. U. Faulkner, *Politics, Reform, and Expansion* (1959); J. R. Hollingsworth, *Whirligig of Politics* (1938); and F. B. Simkins, *Ben Tillman* (1944).

MARY JANE MCDANIEL
University of North Alabama

CLIMATE of the South, in the absence of a mountain boundary, is not sharply delineated from that of adjoining states. January mean Fahrenheit temperatures range from about 35 degrees along the northern border of the region to 55 at the Gulf coast. In Florida, projecting much farther to the south, January temperatures reach 70 degrees. Outbreaks of Arctic air masses can produce much lower temperatures for short periods of time. Both Kentucky and Missouri have recorded temperatures as low as −20 but Miami, with extreme temperatures ameliorated by its more marine location, has only 27 degrees for its record low temperature. In winter Kentucky, Missouri, and Maryland have recorded temperatures in the upper 70s. Florida has reached the middle 80s and Texas has recorded 90 degrees. Summer temperatures exhibit much less variation with latitude. Mean July temperatures in the border states are usually between 75 and 80 degrees, whereas in the Gulf states they are between 80 and 85. Short-period extreme summer temperatures in the South are in general between 105 and 110 degrees. The higher summer extremes occur in the more northerly states of the region. Marine air from the Gulf and frequent afternoon showers tend to limit extreme temperature in the Gulf and Atlantic states. North Dakota's record high temperatures exceed those of all southern states.

With minor exceptions the South receives 40 inches or more precipitation annually. In the mountains of western North Carolina and north Georgia, the orographic effect helps in producing precipitation in excess of 70 inches annually. Again along the southeast coast of Florida, an area receiving over 60 inches of rainfall appears to be anomalous. Most of the region receives a maximum of precipitation in the summer months. Kentucky, Tennessee, and the northern half of Georgia, Alabama, and Mississippi receive even more in late winter. Except for the Texas coast, the entire South receives the least precipitation in the fall. The combination of rainfall and temperature, the major factors in controlling evapotranspiration, means that soil moisture is minimal in the fall. Likewise, late winter and early spring are the seasons of maximum soil moisture with a surplus available as runoff. Most of the region's precipitation falls in the form of rain. Across the northern tier of states, 18 inches of snowfall would be quite representative. The Gulf states are about bisected by the one-inch snow line. The Appalachian Mountains of West Virginia receive as much as 80 inches of snow. High humidities characterize the South and when combined with temperature result in a climate that is not particularly comfortable in the summer.

The generators of most of the temperature changes and precipitation are typical mid-latitude cyclonic storms. Hurricanes contribute significantly to the precipitation and constitute a real habitational hazard along the entire coastal zone. They are confined for the most part to the latter half of the year. Originating in the South Atlantic, Caribbean, or Gulf, they tend to move westward during their early stages, then curve northward and finally eastward. They usually weaken over land due to the added friction of the rough surface but have maintained their identity in a curved path from the Gulf coast through Kentucky to Virginia.

See U.S. Department of Conservation, *Climatic Atlas of U.S.* (1974); R. D. Ward, *Climates of U.S.* (1925); S. Petterssen, *Introduction to Meteorology* (1958); A. R. Sumner, *Geographical Review* (Jan., 1953); A. Court and R. D. Gerston, *Geographical Review* (Oct., 1966); and H. P. Bailey, *Geographical Review* (Oct., 1964).

JAMES A. SHEAR
University of Georgia

CLINCH RIVER, 300 miles in length, is a major tributary of the TENNESSEE RIVER. It is formed in southwestern Virginia and flows generally southwest into eastern Tennessee. It was first explored and named for an early hunter by DR. THOMAS WALKER in 1750. Norris Dam and Watts Bar Dam, both on the Clinch, are two of the larger installations of the TENNESSEE VALLEY AUTHORITY.

CLINGMAN, THOMAS LANIER (1812–1897), born in Huntsville, N.C., was graduated from the state university in 1832 and admitted to the bar in 1834. He served as a Whig in both houses of the state legislature. Having moved to Asheville, he served in Congress in 1843–1845 and 1847–1858, when he was appointed to the Senate. Acerbic political views provoked a duel with WILLIAM L. YANCEY in 1845 and a defection to the Democrats in 1852. Clingman resigned from the Senate in 1861 to accept a colonelcy in the 25th North Carolina Infantry. He saw action at COLD HARBOR, DREWRY'S BLUFF, and PETERSBURG, and battlefield valor earned him a promotion to brigadier in 1862. Following the war Clingman devoted himself to the practice of law, local politics, geology, and mountain climbing. A major peak of the Appalachians bears his name. He was a delegate to the Democratic National Convention in 1868 and to the state constitutional convention in 1875. Financial difficulty plagued his later years.

See G. Tucker, *North Carolina Historical Review* (April, 1966); J. R. Morrill, *North Carolina Historical Review* (Oct., 1967); E. J. Warner, *Generals in Gray* (1959); and J. P. Kerr, *Trinity Archive* (March, 1899).

MORTON M. ROSENBERG
Ball State University

CLINTON, TENN. (pop. 4,794), 18 miles northwest of Knoxville, has long been a market town for area agriculture and lumber. First settled in 1787, it was named Burrville about the turn of the century in honor of Aaron Burr. After the BURR CONSPIRACY, however, it was renamed by Tennessee's state legislature for New York's governor, De Witt Clinton. This small mountain village has twice written its name in the pages of American history: first in 1943 with the construction here of the Clinton Engineer Works, which produced plutonium for the atomic bomb and other nuclear research; and then in 1956, when the desegregation of its schools produced the first serious civil disturbance of the CIVIL RIGHTS MOVEMENT.

See C. Seeber, *History of Anderson County* (1928); D. J. Brittain, *Case Study of Racial Integration* (1960); S. E. Roberts, *History of Clinton High School* (1971); and files of Clinton *Courier-News* (1887–).

CLOTHING. During the colonial and revolutionary eras, southern dress and costume varied widely, depending in large part upon socioeconomic rank and status. Wealthy ladies and gentlemen most often attired themselves in clothing inspired by British and French styles, with the most sophisticated aristocrats slavishly adhering to the latest fashion dictates from Paris. Upper-class women favored inordinately large hoop skirts of imported silk or satin, whalebone stays or corsets to slim their waistlines, and high-heeled shoes. A southern gentleman's wardrobe might have included a red velvet coat and tight doeskin knee breeches (together with a small sword or sword cane for adornment), ruffled silk shirts, silk stockings, and silver-buckled shoes. Children of southern aristocrats were dressed similarly, with a conscious attempt being made to duplicate adult fashion as much as possible, even to the wearing of uncomfortable stays for young girls.

Nonaristocratic southerners, on the other hand, generally relied on homespun material for their clothing requirements. Some "homespun" was imported from Osnabrück, Germany, in the form of a coarse cloth that was popularly dubbed "Osnibrick," but most southern homespun was indeed homemade, with fustian cloth (a cotton-flax mixture) and linsey-woolsey (flax and wool) being the most popular. The typical small farmer in the South, then, wore a homemade jacket and pants, wool socks, heavy boots, and a linsey-woolsey shirt, and his wife invariably wore a shapeless dress of fustian. Along the frontier, southern men generally opted for deerskin shirts and leather or deerskin moccasins in place of the more "civilized" cloth shirt and heavy boots.

The typical slave was issued a yearly "ration" of clothing by his or her owner: males might receive a suit and pants of coarse wool (in Virginia) or cotton (in the Lower South), two pairs of shoes, several shirts, and a hat; and females generally were given one or two dresses, several shifts or field gowns, and two pairs of shoes. Invariably, the material provided was gray ("Negro gray") in color. Brightly colored handkerchiefs, worn by both sexes, provided a welcome contrast to this sartorial monotony.

A democratic trend in wearing apparel became evident throughout the United States and certainly in the South during the late eighteenth and early nineteenth centuries. Influenced in part by the leveling tendencies of the French Revolution, southern gentlemen began abandoning their aristocratic knee breeches in favor of the full-length pantaloon by 1800. Many Americans also began championing the idea of "republican simplicity" in clothing as a badge of distinction that would highlight American uniqueness. As early as 1783, for example, George Washington wrote that "a plain genteel dress is more admired and obtains more credit than lace and embroidery in the Eyes of the judicious and sensible."

Despite these trends, southern women of means would continue to wear large hoop skirts and stays through the Civil War era. In fact, most upper-class southern "belles" decried that aspect of the northern feminist movement that advocated the replacement of stays and corsets with Amelia Bloomer's new short skirt with loose trousers ("bloomers") gathered around the ankles.

See R. B. Nye, *Cultural Life* (1960); R. R. Davis, *Civil War History* (March, 1969); F. L. Olmsted, *Cotton Kingdom* (1861); C. Eaton, *Old South* (1949); and A. M. Earle, *Two Centuries of Costume* (1903).

ROBERT R. DAVIS, JR.
Ohio Northern University

COAL MINING. After the existence of coal was first noted by explorers and early settlers, coal was mined on a small scale in the South for local use. Large-scale commercial mining developed only when cheap transportation became available. Since coal is of low value by weight, the cost of transportation has always been a vital factor in the mining industry. The first recorded coal mining in the South and in the nation occurred in Virginia. Coal was discovered near the James River above Richmond in 1701, and some commercial mining existed by 1760. Annual production reached 100,000 tons by the 1830s, but did not greatly exceed that figure until well after the Civil War.

Kentucky, Maryland, Missouri, Tennessee, and Virginia were the only southern states to produce a significant amount of coal (100,000 tons or more per year) before the Civil War. Maryland was by far the largest producer. Commercial mining operations developed in Maryland during the first quarter of the nineteenth century, and annual production reached the 800,000-ton level by the 1850s. The Potomac River, canals, and the Baltimore & Ohio Railroad, which reached Cumberland in 1842, provided cheap transportation to eastern markets. Missouri was the next largest producer. The existence of coal was noted by such explorers as Z. M. PIKE, and commercial mining operations began about 1840. By 1860, Missouri was producing approximately 300,000 tons per year. Early settlers in both Kentucky and Tennessee were aware of the rich coal deposits, but poor transportation precluded the rapid development of large-scale mining. Annual production does not appear to have reached the 100,000-ton level until the 1850s.

Coal began to play a truly significant role in the southern economy starting about 1880. The rapid industrialization of the U.S. after the Civil War required a coal supply far exceeding the capacity of the existing fields. Thus capitalists began to develop the long-known but hitherto inaccessible coalfields of the southern Appalachian region. An elaborate network of railroads was established, mines were opened, labor was recruited from as far away as eastern Europe, and new towns were built. The first major new fields opened were in southern West Virginia, when the Chesapeake & Ohio Railroad reached the New River field in 1872. The rich Pocahontas field on the Virginia–West Virginia border was opened by the Norfolk & Western Railroad in 1883. The last of the great coalfields to be opened were those in eastern Kentucky, when an extension of the Louisville & Nashville Railroad reached Harlan County in 1910.

The growth of the southern coal industry was rapid and continuous after 1880. However, the estimated value of coal produced fluctuated considerably, due to the highly erratic nature of the market. The average value (f.o.b. mine) of bituminous coal in the U.S. was $1.12 in 1910, $3.75 in 1920, $1.70 in 1930, and $6.26 in 1970.

Although southern production rose sharply after 1880, there were many significant shifts within the region. By far the most important of these was the increasing domination of West Virginia and Kentucky. By 1970, the two states accounted for approximately 80 percent of the total southern production. Another important change was the growth of surface (strip and auger) mining (STRIP MINING). An insignificant factor as late as 1940, surface mining accounted for approximately 35 percent of southern coal production in 1970.

See H. N. Eavenson, *First Century and a Quarter of American Coal Industry* (1942); H. M. Caudill, *Night Comes to Cumberlands* (1963); K. A. Harvey, *Best-dressed Miners* (1969); R. F. Munn, *Coal Industry in America* (1965); and W. Graebner, *Coal Mining Safety* (1976).

ROBERT F. MUNN
West Virginia University

SOUTHERN COAL PRODUCTION, 1880–1970

Year	Tonnage	% U.S. Total	Estimated Current Value
1880	7,076,000	8.9	$ 8.8 million
1890	23,632,000	14.9	23.3
1900	52,753,000	19.6	54.8
1910	118,159,000	23.6	132.3
1920	173,157,000	26.3	649.3
1930	212,783,000	39.6	361.7
1940	187,545,000	36.6	358.2
1950	264,546,000	42.7	1,280.0
1960	236,617,000	54.5	1,109.7
1970	339,520,000	55.4	2,125.4

COBB, HOWELL (1815–1868), was born into a wealthy middle Georgia planting family and was educated at the University of Georgia. In 1842 he was elected to Congress, where he became known as an ardent defender of the moderate Martin Van Buren wing of the Democratic party. He rose to be House Speaker in 1849 and from the chair deftly guided that body to its endorsement of the COMPROMISE OF 1850. Cobb resigned from Congress in 1851, was elected governor of Georgia by the nationalistic CONSTITUTIONAL UNION PARTY OF GEORGIA, and, after his term expired in 1853, retired briefly from public life. Two years later he returned to Congress and with the election of James Buchanan in 1856 was awarded the secretaryship of the treasury—evidently in payment for his electioneering. Abraham Lincoln's victory four years later, however, revealed the gradual erosion of Cobb's long-held Unionist principles. He resigned from the cabinet in December, 1860, to return to his native state to help carry it out of the Union. The war years saw Cobb serving the Confederacy in several military positions, ultimately achieving the rank of major general. He died shortly after receiving a presidential pardon for his war service.

See J. E. Simpson, *Howell Cobb* (1973); H. E. Montgomery, *Cobb's Confederate Career* (1959); U. B. Phillips (ed.), *Correspondence* (1913); R. P. Brooks (ed.), *Georgia Historical Quarterly* (June–Dec., 1921); and J. E. Simpson, *Georgia Historical Quarterly* (Winter, 1974).

JOHN EDDINS SIMPSON
Savannah State College

COBB, THOMAS READ ROOTS (1823–1862). His life was always overshadowed by that of his elder brother HOWELL COBB, but he gained prominence in his own right. He was born into a wealthy Georgia planting family and he was graduated from the University of Georgia in 1842 and rapidly gained a reputation as an able attorney and legal scholar. He wrote *An Inquiry into the Law of Negro Slavery* (1858) and *A Historical Sketch of Slavery from the Earliest Periods* (1859), but is best remembered for a monumental codification of Georgia laws. In late 1860 he became a foremost advocate of disunion, served as an immediatist delegate to the Georgia secession convention, and finally helped revise the state's constitution after ties with the Union were broken. Formation of the Confederacy found Cobb at the MONTGOMERY CONVENTION representing Georgia. His legal talent was utilized at Montgomery in drawing up the CONFEDERATE CONSTITUTION. Upon returning to Georgia, Cobb received an army commission, raised a regiment (Cobb's Legion), and proceeded to the Virginia front. There he was killed in action at the battle of FREDERICKSBURG.

See W. B. McCash, "Thomas R. R. Cobb" (Ph.D. dissertation, University of Georgia, 1968); T. W. Brown, *Georgia Historical Quarterly* (Winter, 1961); and A. L. Hull (ed.), *Southern History Association Publications* (1907), II.

JOHN EDDINS SIMPSON
Savannah State College

COCKE, JOHN HARTWELL (1780–1866), graduate of the College of William and Mary, planter, brigadier general during the War of 1812, canal promoter, and participant in a variety of reforms, was born into the Virginia aristocracy. Cocke's military service was confined to Virginia, but won him wide recognition. He was associated with THOMAS JEFFERSON in founding the University of Virginia. His plantations, Bremo in Virginia and two in Alabama, were models, not only for humane treatment of slaves, but for scientific agriculture. Cocke was active in encouraging the founding of agricultural societies. He was representative of that southern white minority that condemned slavery. Cocke espoused colonization in

Africa for freed blacks and settled some of his manumitted slaves in Liberia. He was a vice-president of the AMERICAN COLONIZATION SOCIETY. A staunch opponent of tobacco and alcohol, Cocke was president of the American Temperance Union. His religious convictions led him to participate in a number of religious societies, especially the American Board of Commissioners for Foreign Missions.

See C. Eaton, *Mind of Old South* (1967), sympathetic but highly useful; and Cocke Papers, in libraries of University of Virginia, University of North Carolina (microfilm), and College of William and Mary.

LOUIS B. GIMELLI
Eastern Michigan University

COCKRELL, FRANCIS MARION (1834–1915),

was born and reared near Warrensburg, Mo. After being admitted to the bar in 1855, he left his law practice to enlist as a private in the Confederate army and rose through the ranks to brigadier general during the first year of the war. While seeing action at Carthage, VICKSBURG, and MOBILE, he was wounded five times and captured three. He returned to Missouri after the war, entered into a law partnership with T. T. Crittenden, and unsuccessfully sought the Democratic nomination for governor in 1873. Two years later he was named by the state legislature to the U.S. Senate, where he served for the next 30 years distinctively attired in a white linen duster and carrying a corncob pipe. Denied reelection by a Republican legislature, Cockrell was immediately appointed to the U.S. Interstate Commerce Commission (1905–1910).

COFFEE CULTURE. See TEA AND COFFEE

COFFIN, LEVI (1798–1877),

a southern yeoman, became one of the best-known figures in the Atlantic antislavery movement. He was the son of nonslaveholding Quakers, who farmed in New Garden, N.C. Allegedly he became an abolitionist as a child of seven, and as a young man he was already helping slaves escape. In 1826, however, he opened a store at Newport, Ind., in an area heavily settled by southern Quaker migrants. He built up a substantial business in pork and oil processing, but in 1847 took over a free produce store in Cincinnati aimed at undercutting slave merchandise. Coffin became famous as the genius behind the UNDERGROUND RAILROAD. Although its scale and efficiency have been exaggerated, his house was one of its key depots. The wagon he

kept permanently ready for fugitives became part of the Railroad's folklore, and only the Fifteenth Amendment ended his term as its self-styled president. By then Coffin had also become agent for the Western Freedmen's Aid Association. The remainder of his life, during which he wrote his reminiscences, was spent in retirement.

See L. Coffin, *Reminiscences* (1877), broadly reliable; and L. Gara, *Liberty Line* (1965), revisionist on Underground Railroad.

C. DUNCAN RICE
Yale University

COHEE

was a term applied in the late eighteenth century to the inhabitants of the area in Virginia west of the Blue Ridge and is to be contrasted with the TUCKAHOES of the Tidewater-Piedmont region. Generally of Scotch-Irish or German background as opposed to English, these hardy immigrants to the valley and mountains of Virginia had religious commitments and pursued agricultural practices different from the low-country Virginians. They were thought by many Tuckahoes to be socially inferior, a feeling that sometimes led to disagreements and tensions between the two cultures. The exact origin of the term is not really known, though it is said to derive from the Cohees' use of "quo' he" for "quoth he" in their speech.

See W. F. Bliss, *Virginia Magazine of History and Biography* (Oct., 1951).

MICHAEL L. NICHOLLS
Utah State University

COHENS V. VIRGINIA (6 Wheaton 266–448

[1821]) was one of the most notable examples of JOHN MARSHALL's habit of expounding the U.S. Constitution to accord with his own political principles. Marshall's opinion was intended to destroy Virginia's claims, made in the *Fairfax* case in 1815 that Virginia had the right to protect the part of its sovereignty that it had retained at the time of the ratification of the CONSTITUTION and that Section 25 of the Judiciary Act of 1789 was unconstitutional. He rested his opinion on two premises: that the Constitution made a nation, not a league; and that state jealousy was a perpetual threat to unmake the Union, a threat that the national courts must be able to combat whenever the nation was acting to effect objects committed to it by the Constitution. All this amounted to declaring that the U.S. government (speaking through the Supreme Court) had the right to say not only what its own powers were, but also what the limits of state power were.

Marshall's opinion evoked notable counterarguments in Virginia, especially from JOHN TAYLOR of Caroline and Spencer Roane of the Virginia court of appeals.

See C. G. Haines, *Role of Supreme Court, 1789–1835* (1944); and A. J. Beveridge, *Life of Marshall* (1919).

JAMES RABUN
Emory University

COKE, RICHARD (1829–1897), governor of Texas and U.S. senator, was born in Williamsburg, Va., and graduated from the College of William and Mary in 1849. After studying law he went to Texas, settling at Waco in 1851. He favored secession, was elected to the state's secession convention, and served as a Confederate captain. After the war he was appointed a state district judge, and in 1866 he was elected a state supreme court judge on the Conservative ticket. He was removed, however, by the military in 1867. He returned to his Waco law practice until 1873, when he was elected governor. As the state's Redeemer governor he encouraged strict economy (REDEEMER GOVERNMENTS). He was reelected in 1876, but shortly thereafter the legislature elected him to the U.S. Senate. He was reelected senator in 1882 and 1888. During his tenure he favored the free coinage of silver and supported the Interstate Commerce Act, but opposed the BLAIR BILL for education, high protective tariffs, and the FORCE BILL OF 1890. He did not stand for reelection in 1894.

See B. J. Fett, *Texana*, No. 4 (1972); Richard Coke Scrapbook, University of Texas; J. D. Lynch, *Bench and Bar of Texas* (1885); and A. Barr, *Reconstruction to Reform* (1971).

JAMES ALEX BAGGETT
Union University, Jackson, Tenn.

COKER FAMILY. In addition to contributing significantly to the varied economy of the New South, the Cokers of South Carolina are a noteworthy example of family cohesiveness sometimes thought to be peculiar to an agrarian way of life. Caleb Coker, Jr. (1802–1869), and his wife Hannah Lide were the antebellum founders of this exceptional family. Beginning as a bookkeeper in a town store, Caleb became a banker, a railroad investor, and one of the wealthiest planters in Darlington County, S.C. The Civil War halted the growth of the family's fortunes, however, and resulted in the death of one son, the destruction of their home by General W. T. Sherman, and the loss of much of the Cokers' accumulated wealth.

The two oldest sons, James Lide Coker (1837–1918) and William Caleb Coker (1839–1907), sought to recoup the family's losses by managing two small stores in Hartsville and Society Hill, S.C., respectively. The income was sufficient not only to support the family, but to underwrite the experiments of three inventive sons of James. James, Jr. (1863–1931), tested his belief that local pine pulp, if chemically treated, could be made suitable for the manufacture of paper. His successful experiments led directly to construction of the South's first paper mill and to the formation in 1890 of the family-owned Carolina Fiber Company (PULP AND PAPER INDUSTRY). Charles Westfield (1879–1931) experimented with the use of paper cones and tubes in textile mills. His inventions led to the creation of the Southern Novelty Company, also a family-owned enterprise, producing a variety of paper products for the textile industry. A third brother, David (1870–1938), worked with different strains of cotton. His experiments and patents led eventually to the formation of the Pedigreed Seed Company.

The agricultural depression of the 1920s hit the Coker family enterprises especially hard. All were tied directly or indirectly to farm credit and cotton production. Through sound business management and the pooling of the economic assets of the far-flung members of the family, the several Coker family enterprises rode out the depression decades to flourish in the post–World War II prosperity of the South.

See G. L. Simpson, Jr., *Cokers of South Carolina* (1956); and some Coker family manuscripts at University of North Carolina Library, Chapel Hill.

COLD HARBOR, BATTLE OF (June 3, 1864), was U. S. Grant's final effort to capture Richmond and destroy R. E. Lee's army without crossing the James River. Frustrated along the North Anna River, Grant sidled southward to link the Army of the Potomac with reinforcements from the Army of the James. If Grant's forces could swiftly unite at Cold Harbor, they might move up the Richmond Road and compel Lee to fight with his back to one of the several creeks crossing it. Union cavalry captured the crossroads on May 31, but garbled orders and slow marching by tired troops prevented the federals from exploiting this success before most of Lee's army arrived to dig into entrenchments in front of Cold Harbor. Grant's major attack was postponed until the morning of June 3 while he waited for his II Corps to arrive and get into attacking position with the VI and XVIII Corps. No adequate reconnaissance took place; thus, when the attack went forward, the terrain unexpectedly caused the three attacking corps to diverge from each other. They faced flanking as well as frontal fire from the enemy's trenches and met disaster. Its movements constricted by the Totopotomoy swamps to the north and the Chickahominy swamps to the south, Grant's force of 108,000 mounted a frontal assault that cost 7,000 killed and wounded in less than half an hour, against 1,500 Confederate casualties in an army of 59,000.

See A. A. Humphreys, *Virginia Campaign of '64 and '65* (1883), best account by senior participating officer; J. F. C. Fuller, *Generalship of Grant* (1929), analysis by military critic; R. U. Johnson and C. C. Buel (eds.), *Battles and Leaders* (1888), IV; D. S. Freeman, *Lee's Lieutenants* (1944), III; and S. Foote, *Civil War* (1974), III, most recent, detailed.

RUSSELL F. WEIGLEY
Temple University

COLE, ARTHUR C. (1886–1976),

was born in Ann Arbor, Mich., and earned his Ph.D. degree at the University of Pennsylvania (1911). His study *The Whig Party in the South* (1914) was the first to detail the transformation of the southern WHIG coalition from its states' rights, anti-Jackson beginnings to its alignment with the northern wing of the party behind positive federal currency and tariff programs in the early 1840s. Cole detailed the crucial role that southern Whigs played in preserving the Union during the sectional crisis of 1850–1851. Through 1976, no complete new study of southern Whigs had appeared, though recent state studies challenged his view of southern Whigs as exclusively the party of the planter class. Cole's *The Irrepressible Conflict, 1850–1865* (1934) interpreted the South as a society dominated by a handful of slaveholders, who nonetheless retained the loyalty of a subordinated white majority. His book portrayed an economically decaying South tilting against the "spirit of democracy" and humanitarianism represented by the North. Subsequent studies questioned Cole's conclusions, but rarely matched the drama and sweep of his account. Cole taught successively at Ohio State, Western Reserve, and Brooklyn College; he retired in 1956.

See A. C. Cole, *Whig Party in South* (1914), and *Irrepressible Conflict* (1934); C. G. Sellers, *American Historical Review* (Jan., 1954); G. McWhiney, *Journal of Southern History* (Nov., 1957); T. J. Alexander, *Sectional Stress and Party Strength* (1967); and W. L. Barney, *Road to Secession* (1972).

SYDNEY NATHANS
Duke University

COLLEGES AND UNIVERSITIES,

because they preserve and alter culture, have been an integral aspect of southern history since the seventeenth century. Although WILLIAM AND MARY was the South's only college from 1693 until the 1770s, the sons of the South's leadership class often studied in a colonial college or an English university and/or London Inn of Court. After a slow and unpromising beginning, William and Mary survived to train ministers and public officials. Because the Anglican church was established in early Virginia, this colonial college was a state-church institution. The policy of public support for denominationally controlled institutions continued on a limited scale into the nineteenth-century South at TRANSYLVANIA (1780) in Kentucky and at the Colleges of Orleans and Louisiana. The American Revolution, however, tended to divide higher education into public state universities and private denominational colleges.

The republican South led the new nation in founding state universities. Georgia was the first state to charter a public university (1785), and North Carolina's was the first state university to admit students (1795). As state universities multiplied, church fathers resisted the secular spirit of public education by sprinkling Presbyterian, Methodist, Baptist, and other denominational colleges so thickly over the land that by 1860 the section could claim 260 separate institutions of higher learning. This number included military schools like VIRGINIA MILITARY INSTITUTE (1839), women's colleges such as Georgia Female (1836, now Wesleyan College), and professional schools of law and medicine.

Theoretically, state universities trained political leaders; military schools prepared army officers; and church colleges educated clergymen. In reality, the curriculum in each type of institution was similar. Degree requirements usually included Latin, Greek, mathematics, moral philosophy, mental philosophy, political philosophy, natural philosophy, natural history, ethics, general history, English composition, and surveying. Military schools added strategy and tactics. Extracurricular activities usually emphasized literary and debating societies, which were social and intellectual and served as the basis of modern fraternal and scholastic societies, such as Phi Beta Kappa, founded at William and Mary in 1776.

Although the college curriculum of the Old South was designed to serve the leadership class, its expenditure for higher education in 1860 was twice that of the wealthier New England states. It had half the nation's colleges and, including those southerners studying outside the section, as many as two-thirds of the students. The better colleges and universities of the South competed for the nation's most qualified faculty and staff, and Thomas Jefferson's University of VIRGINIA (1819) made an original contribution to American higher education.

There were, however, serious flaws in southern higher education. After the 1820s, the South's defense of slavery and its heightening intolerance alienated and banished some able educators. There were too many colleges for the South's limited income, few qualified students, and a lack of public secondary schools. Yet the nadir of southern higher education, in relation to national standards, awaited the Civil War, Reconstruction, and Redemption periods.

During the 1860s several forces converged to close and hinder the development of southern colleges and universities: the attractions and exigencies of war, which eroded enrollments; the Confederacy's need of college buildings for barracks, hospitals, and refugee depots; the Union army's invasion and destruction; the South's general economic collapse in 1865; the Radicals' racial policies in some state universities; and the Bourbons' conservative economics of retrenchment. Thus after 1860 several institutions of higher learning simply expired. By 1900 the South's former 260 colleges and universities were reduced to 216, despite postwar founding of NEGRO LAND-GRANT COLLEGES and normal schools. Frequently an established university's price for survival was paid by faculties who taught for little or no income.

With college endowments as worthless as their Confederate bonds and with gifts and appropriations slashed, student tuition became the major source of income for southern higher education. The continuing problems posed by too many colleges, too few students, and no public preparatory systems assumed tragic proportions. One result was an uncharitable competition for students. Sectarians denigrated state universities' morality; legislatures taxed church colleges; standards declined; and intolerance increased. The Darwinism of the new sciences was forced to a scholastic accommodation with fundamentalist Christianity. The classical curriculum continued to be dominant in the prestige if not in numbers of graduates. And it was usually impossible to fund the new subjects of history, social sciences, modern languages, and education.

Still the status of higher education in the New South was not totally bleak. The postwar founding of Negro, land-grant, and normal colleges was the South's first significant move toward democratic higher education. By 1900 there were 34 Negro colleges in the section. These provided manual, normal, and some classical education for blacks, consistent with B. T. WASHINGTON's public philosophy. Some notable Negro institutions founded soon after the Civil War were: ATLANTA (1865), FISK (1865), Shaw (1865), HOWARD (1867), Morehouse (1867), St. Augustine's (1867), Storer (1867), HAMPTON (1868), Straight (1868), and TUSKEGEE (1881). By the 1870s southern state governments had availed themselves of the Morrill Act (1862), which provided federal land-grant funds for establishing agricultural and mechanical (or technical) colleges (black and white). These A. & M. colleges sprang up across the section, usually separate from the older state universities. After the 1870s normal schools for both races were multiplying under the leadership of Peabody Normal College (1875) in Nashville.

In addition to Peabody, philanthropists established and endowed the white universities of VANDERBILT (1872), JOHNS HOPKINS (1876), TULANE (1884), RICE (1891), EMORY (1919), and DUKE (1924). Most of these private institutions and the state universities of Virginia and North Carolina became leaders of the South's modern university movement, especially in graduate and professional training. Also, the Southern Association of Colleges and Preparatory Schools (1895) began slowly to raise general college entrance requirements. Between 1902 and 1914, the GENERAL EDUCATION BOARD granted millions of dollars in matching funds to increase local support of all levels of southern education.

The South has experienced considerable growth in higher education since 1900, the year in which the region's 216 colleges had a mere 28,000 students; 1.5 million library volumes; $2.5 million annual income; and only one university in the Lower South (Tulane) that met the Carnegie Foundation's requirements for college rank. Some of the forces that improved southern higher education in the twentieth century were: the Populist and Progressive crusade for universal public education; the able leadership of educators like J. L. M. CURRY, E. A. ALDERMAN, and H. W. ODUM; boards and foundations, such as Carnegie, ROSENWALD, and Ford, which assisted black and white colleges; increased coeducation; community college movements since the 1920s; the growth of Negro enrollments despite the Great Depression, which closed some black colleges and consolidated others; the determination of qualified blacks to attend and thereby desegregate local graduate and professional schools; new sources of federal aid in the form of research grants, the GI bill, student loans, etc.; the Southern Education Board's emphasis since 1948 on interstate cooperation in providing expensive graduate and professional training; the desegregation of higher education since the 1950s (although about 80 percent of Negro students continue in predominantly black colleges); a relatively improved level of academic freedom in the South; nationally recognized university presses and scholarly journals; and, finally, the unprecedented advances of the 1960s based on improved financing, more freedom of expression, increased opportunities for women, and a low level of student radicalism. These factors, largely since 1945, have helped reduce the South's migration of the better-qualified students, faculty, and staff.

Recent advances in southern higher education were modified by continuing problems. In 1974 the region's 860 institutions of higher learning were far too many to emphasize excellence, despite the total enrollment of 2.3 million, a figure that tripled during the 1960s. In that decade graduate enrollments increased 232.6 percent, federal aid more than doubled, and state funding rose 342 percent. But in the 1970s accelerating rates of economic inflation and recession combined to erode the financial strength of all colleges and universities, especially the small private ones with little or no endowment. From 1961 to 1971 the percentage of students enrolled in southern private colleges declined from 33 to 19. As small public colleges sought and achieved university status, there was increasing duplication of services, which seldom improved quality. Only the universities of North Carolina, TEXAS, Virginia, Duke, Vanderbilt, and Tulane belonged to the selective Association of American Universities. In 1971 the region had only nine universities that ranked in the nation's top 39 institutions having more than 1.75 million library volumes. Not one was in the top ten. Thus the South did not have a center for postdoctoral research comparable with the best in the nation. The region's annual salaries ran about $2,000 less than the national average. And the standards of southern black colleges and universities (even Atlanta, Fisk, and Howard) were considerably below their white counterparts. In 1967 the South had 104 traditionally black institutions; 71 were accredited; 21 offered graduate and/or professional degrees; and only one gave the Ph.D. In black colleges, salaries were $1,500 lower than those of comparable white schools. Only 13 to 15 percent of southern blacks (against 44 percent of whites) attended college. Desegregation had the questionable effect of attracting the better-qualified staff and students away from traditional Negro colleges. For both races, the South's greatest needs in higher education were money, leadership, and vision.

See D. G. Tewksbury, *Founding American Colleges* (1932); A. Godbold, *Church College of Old South* (1944); C. Eaton, *Freedom of Thought in Old South* (1940); E. W. Knight, *Public Education in South* (1922); C. W. Dabney, *Universal Education in South* (1936); T. Woody, *Women's Education* (1929); D. O. W. Holmes, *Evolution of Negro College* (1934); E. J. McGrath, *Negro Colleges in Transition* (1965); R. S. Suggs, Jr., *et al.*, *Southern Regional Education Board* (1960); SREB, *Negro and Higher Education in South* (1967); *Fact Book* (1974); S. P. Wiggins, *Higher Education in South* (1968); J. S. Ezell, *South Since 1865* (1975); and C. P. Roland, *South Since World War II* (1975).

RAY MATHIS
Troy State University

COLLINS, LEROY (1909–), the thirty-third governor of Florida (1955–1961), and a Democrat, was born in Tallahassee. He was a lawyer for the Works Progress Administration, a member of the Florida house and senate (1935–1953), and chairman of both the National Governors' Conference and the Southern Governors' Conference (1960). In 1961, he became president of the National Association of Broadcasters, then director of the United States Community Relations Service (1964), and undersecretary of commerce (1965–1967). While governor, he pursued constitutional revision, reapportionment, and the broadening of state social services. Originally a segregationist, Collins became convinced that Florida and the South must follow the mandate of BROWN V. BOARD OF EDUCATION (1954). He refused to acknowledge the legislature's stand in favor of interposition and opposed suggestions that the South adopt a nullification posture. Later, as director of the Community Relations Service, he was responsible for helping to implement the Civil Rights Act of 1964. His stance on civil rights destroyed his political prospects in Florida, and in 1968 he was defeated by Republican Edward Gurney for the U.S. Senate.

See *Administration of Governor Collins* (1961); T. L. Christie, *Apalachee* (1963–67), VI; J. S. Chapman, "Southern Moderate" (M.A. thesis, University of South Florida, 1974); M. Lucoff, "Collins and National Association of Broadcasters" (M.A. thesis, University of South Florida, 1969); and Collins Papers, Florida Historical Society, University of South Florida.

JAMES W. DUNN
Hillsborough Community College

COLLOQUIALISMS AND NICKNAMES. Although every region of the United States has produced its own peculiar set of nicknames and unusual terms, this tendency has been especially true of the South in the past, probably because of its rural nature and relative isolation. With modern improvements in communication and education and changes in southern racial attitudes, some of these terms have fallen into disuse. Others, such as DIXIE, JIM CROW, and BLACK BELT, were considered by the editors to be of sufficient historical importance to be discussed separately under their own individual headings.

Big-benders, a nickname for Tennesseans, seemingly originated from the fact that the Indians referred to the Tennessee River as the "River with the Big Bend." Tennesseans were also sometimes called "mudheads" or "whelps."

Big knives was a term used by the Indians in the colonial period to designate white hunters from either Virginia or Pennsylvania. The Indians were impressed by the large heavy knives carried by these early frontiersmen and by the long swords carried by the colonial militia officers.

Black laws were passed by some northern states and territories before the Civil War regulating the movements of, or placing restrictions on, blacks. Some of these were not repealed until the 1880s. In the South such laws in antebellum times were usually called black codes and dealt with both free Negroes and slaves. Some of the black laws or BLACK CODES passed in the southern states immediately following the Civil War placed severe restrictions on the newly liberated blacks and caused a considerable outcry from northerners. They are usually mentioned as one of the causes of the harsher congressional RECONSTRUCTION policy that followed.

Blacky was one of many colloquialisms used by white people from earliest antebellum times to refer to a Negro.

Blue hen's chickens. Gamecocks in Delaware bred from a particular variety of blue hen won a reputation as especially good fighters in the ring. During the American Revolution, Delaware regiments, proud of their fighting ability, were thus pleased to be called "blue hen's chickens." The nickname was sometimes applied to Delawareans in general.

Boy was used by whites, dating from slavery days, when addressing a black man as an inferior.

Butternuts was a term originally attached during the Civil War to some of the poorer Confederate soldiers from Tennessee whose homemade uniforms were dyed a tan color with the sap taken from the bark, roots, or hulls of butternut trees. The term was later also applied to Confederate soldiers from other parts of the South. In the North it was sometimes used interchangeably with the epithet COPPERHEAD to describe anyone (usually of the Democratic party) accused of a prosouthern or peace-at-any-price attitude toward the war.

Buzzards was once a nickname for Georgians because of a law in their state passed to protect buzzards, or vultures, which were considered to be essential scavengers.

Cavaliers was a term applied to the early Virginia wealthy planters because of their supposedly aristocratic English ancestry.

Corncrackers was a name given to the POOR WHITES in many southern states, but especially in the hillier regions of eastern Kentucky. Its origin probably derives from the poorer classes' heavy dependence on dried corn in their diets, but some insist the nickname is a corruption of corncrake, a bird that commonly frequents cornfields in Kentucky and other parts of the South.

Corn-fed-racy was a not-too-clever name attached to the rebel South during the Civil War by Union soldiers, who were struck by the large role played by corn in the diet of the southerners.

Crackers were the poor whites of Georgia (and sometimes Florida) supposedly so named because of their habit of cracking their whips so sharply when urging on their mules. The nickname may also have come from the common man's heavy dependence on cracked corn in his diet.

Crawthumpers was a nickname for Marylanders and especially for the fishermen of that state, who had long used this name to refer to the lobsters they caught.

Darky was one of the commonest nicknames or colloquialisms for blacks used by white people. It dates from the colonial period.

Fly-up-the-creeks was a nickname for rural Floridians, who were so shy that they fled when strangers appeared. The name was originally applied to a species of heron that inhabits many parts of Florida.

Geechy was a term for Negroes in the low country of the Carolinas and Georgia and for the dialect that these blacks spoke. It was apparently a corruption of Ogeechee, a river in Georgia.

Goober grabbers was a friendly nickname attached to the inhabitants of those parts of the South, Alabama and Georgia in particular, where they raised so many goobers, or PEANUTS.

Graybacks. Just as some northern paper money during the Civil War became known as greenbacks, Confederate paper money was often called graybacks. (Somewhat incongruously it was also at times called bluebacks.) Confederate soldiers themselves were sometimes called graybacks. Union prisoners at Andersonville also referred to the body lice that inhabited their clothing as graybacks, comparing them to their enemies, the southern soldiers.

Johnny Reb was originated by Union forces during the Civil War to apply to Confederate soldiers and was at first thought of as an insult. It became so common, however, that it eventually lost much of its sting, and the southerners themselves often used the term. Sometimes Confederate soldiers were simply referred to as Johnnies.

Minute men. The most familiar use of this term is its application to the colonial militia at the time of the American Revolution. These men were said to be ready to fight the British army with only a minute's notice. In the days immediately preceding the Civil War, however, numerous military groups in several southern states took the same name and vowed to be equally ready to resist any attempt to prevent their states' secession.

Mossbacks were southerners during the Civil War who tried to avoid serving in the Confederate army. Supposedly they hid in the woods for such long periods that moss grew on their backs.

Nigger, dating from the earliest slaveholding era, was perhaps the most common derogatory term used by white people in referring to black people, especially those in a menial position. It may be a corruption of the word *Negro* or, more likely, of *Niger,* referring to the fact that some of the early slaves were brought from the Niger River region of Africa. The term has long been considered to be particularly offensive by black people.

No-man's-land. Much of Kentucky, beginning in the late eighteenth century, was given this title because no one Indian tribe was able to establish a clear claim to it. It was used as a hunting area by many different tribes and was thus the scene of frequent bloody clashes (DARK AND BLOODY GROUND).

Patter-rollers was a corruption by the Negro slaves of the word *patrols.* In some southern states in antebellum days armed white men were appointed to patrol country roads to apprehend and punish any slave caught off the property of his master without a permit. These patrols were much feared by the blacks.

Rebel brigadiers was a northern politician's nickname of derision after the Civil War for those southern congressmen who had been in the Confederate army.

Ricebirds were small birds, usually bobolinks,

that were a serious pest to rice growers in the South and were capable of completely destroying a crop. In time the term came to be a nickname for the rice planters themselves.

Ridge runner was a poor white who lived in the Piedmont or mountainous areas of the South; that is, a hayseed or hillbilly.

Sandhillers were poor whites who lived in the infertile sandy hill regions of such states as Georgia and North and South Carolina. The name usually carried with it the connotation of extreme poverty, ignorance, and shiftlessness.

Sandlappers is a nickname, dating from antebellum times, for poor whites who inhabited the sandy regions or pine barrens of the South, especially the Carolinas. It is sometimes used almost interchangeably with the term CLAY EATERS. At other times it has been used as a nickname for any South Carolinian.

Uncle Tom was originally famous as a faithful old slave in Harriet Beecher Stowe's novel *Uncle Tom's Cabin.* In the twentieth century, however, his name became an uncomplimentary nickname for any black who was thought to be too subservient to white people and unwilling to stand up for his equal rights.

Yellowhammer was a nickname attached to Alabama Confederate soldiers whose uniforms, though meant to be gray, were treated with a homemade dye that gave them a yellowish hue.

See U. B. Phillips, *American Negro Slavery* (1918); B. A. Botkins, *Treasury of Southern Folklore* (1949); W. A. Craigie and J. R. Hulbert, *Dictionary of American English* (1940); G. E. Shankle, *American Nicknames* (1937, 1955); and W. P. Phyfe, *5000 Facts and Fancies* (1966).

COLONIAL ERA. The South in this era encompassed the area between Pennsylvania and the Altamaha River, west to the mountains and beyond. Here, many of the earliest colonization efforts took place including JAMESTOWN, the first permanent English settlement on the continent. During the decades that followed, the proprietary colonies of Maryland and the Carolinas were established. The creation of Georgia (1732), the last of the 13 colonies founded, completed the five provinces that made up the southern complex. Although sharing many geographical and cultural characteristics, southern colonies reflected a wide-ranging diversity in economic, political, and social affairs.

The oldest and most populous of the 13 colonies was Virginia. Founded in 1607, over the next century and a half Virginia produced a succession of political leaders that was virtually unequaled in the colonies. Nurtured in a society in which achievement in politics was greatly prized, Virginians accepted a code of behavior that exacted a high degree of integrity and exalted those who performed at that level. This was especially true of the gentry, a broad group cemented together by the common denominator of wealth. At first no significance was attached to the source of wealth but, by the beginning of the eighteenth century, plantation agriculture—the cultivation of TOBACCO and the ownership of slaves—became the most prestigious economic pursuit. To outsiders, Virginia appeared patently aristocratic, but the gentry never thought of themselves as such. Nor did domination by the small minority produce much antagonism in the colony because of the widespread belief that government was the responsibility of enlightened and capable men.

Maryland, the other half of the "Chesapeake society," was carved out of territory originally belonging to Virginia. Granted to Sir George Calvert (CALVERT FAMILY) in 1632, the colony was launched by Cecilius Calvert two years later with the founding of ST. MARY'S CITY. Although Catholics, the Calverts wisely followed a policy of religious freedom to all Christians. Tobacco, a treasure of enormous importance, did much to fuse the interests of the two Chesapeake neighbors. By mid-eighteenth century, they annually shipped over 70 million pounds of tobacco to Great Britain, a quantity that provided great profits to government and merchant alike. Maryland society was patterned after Virginia, with Negroes, numbering perhaps one-half the population, at the bottom of the hierarchy. Maryland also gained unwanted notoriety for the large number of Englishmen sent to the colony as a penalty for criminal acts.

Settlement of the area south of Virginia came about slowly. Originally assigned to Sir Robert Heath (1629), who failed to settle the area, Carolina was granted by Charles II to eight favorites (1663) with privileges similar to those enjoyed by Lord Baltimore in Maryland. Northern settlements were concentrated on the Chowan and CAPE FEAR rivers. Lacking good ports for large shipping and separated by swamps and rivers from communities in Virginia and Charles Town (Charleston), northern Carolina contrasted sharply with the southern stereotype. The economy of the area was premised upon small farms and the production of NAVAL STORES, subsidized by the British. The plantation system did not develop. The revolt against proprietary rule (1719) and subsequent takeover by the crown (1729) finalized the division between northern and southern Carolina.

South Carolina developed around the important port of Charleston, the only sizable urban center south of Pennsylvania. In addition to shipping, the freshwater swamps were excellent for RICE cultivation, and the better-drained area beyond was well suited to INDIGO production and farming. Farther inland the forests supported a LUMBER INDUSTRY. Added to these activities was the ever profitable Indian trade. Rice and indigo production encouraged the plantation system. Profits from these products were of such magnitude to create the largest, richest group of leisured aristocrats found in eighteenth-century America. Throughout the colonial period South Carolina maintained closer economic ties with the West Indies than any of the other continental colonies.

Georgia, the most southerly of the 13 colonies, resulted from humanitarianism and imperialistic needs for defense on the southern frontier. The new enterprise was directed by JAMES OGLETHORPE and a group of reformers, designated trustees. But Georgia did not flourish. Discontent was reflected in the decision of the trustees to surrender the colony to the crown (1754) two years before required to do so by law. Economically it followed South Carolina's example, adopting both rice and indigo production and the plantation system.

British regulation of American COMMERCE (Navigation Acts) touched the South directly. Tobacco, indigo, naval stores, rice, and other southern products were enumerated. Southern colonies resented instructions to royal officials, which often evidenced little understanding of colonial problems. The disputes between governor and assemblies were symptomatic of a widening division between the commercial empire and the southern colonies.

British efforts to deal with questions of empire after 1763 met with opposition in the South. PATRICK HENRY offered the VIRGINIA RESOLVES OF 1765 in answer to the Stamp Act. The Townshend Acts (1767) elicited written responses from CHARLES C. PINCKNEY and JOHN RUTLEDGE of South Carolina. Reaction to the Tea Act (1772) produced disturbances at Charleston and Annapolis.

Sectionalism, destined to play an influential role in later American history, was not a factor during the colonial period. Yet the southern colonies were bound together by a variety of circumstances. Lacking major cities, southern society was overwhelmingly rural. The plantation system, the institution of slavery, the importance of southern products, gave southern colonies a uniqueness. No other section of the 13 colonies appeared so anxious to preserve English tradition in class distinctions, local government, and religion.

See C. Bridenbaugh, *Myths and Realities* (1952); L. H. Gipson, *British Isles and American Colonies* (1936), II; W. F. Craven, *Southern Colonies in Seventeenth Century* (1949); J. P. Greene, *Quest for Power* (1963); J. R. Alden, *South in Revolution* (1957); C. S. Sydnor, *Gentlemen Freeholders* (1952); W. W. Abbot, *Royal Governors of Georgia* (1959); M. E. Sirmans, *Colonial South Carolina* (1966); R. Hoffman, *Spirit of Dissension* (1973); and H. T. Lefler and W. Powell, *Colonial North Carolina* (1973).

RICHARD M. JELLISON
Miami University

COLONIAL SOUTH, HISTORIOGRAPHY OF.
The historical literature treating the colonial South is best classified in four chronological periods: contemporary histories; writings of the romantic historians; works of the scientific school; and recent studies.

Written before there was a South, the contemporary accounts began the process of creating an image. Only Virginia produced an appreciable number of historians, and even those do not constitute a "school." ROBERT BEVERLEY, in *History and Present State of Virginia* (1705); Henry Hartwell; JAMES BLAIR; Edward Chilton, in *The Present State of Virginia and the College* (*ca.* 1697); and HUGH JONES, in *Present State of Virginia* (1724), all wrote from their personal knowledge or from hearsay. To WILLIAM STITH's *History of the First Discovery and Settlement of Virginia* (1747) belongs the distinction of a work based on research in earlier records. William Byrd (BYRD FAMILY) wrote his *History of the Dividing Line* (*ca.* 1738) for circulation among his friends. Other southern colonies do not approach this record. Georgia had a jointly written production by Patrick Tailfer, Hugh Anderson, and David Douglas, *A True and Historical Narrative of the Colony of Georgia in America* (1741); Maryland had none whatever. North Carolina fared somewhat better: John Lawson, *A New Voyage to Carolina* (1709), with perceptive sketches of the Indians and the natural setting; and Dr. John Brickell, *Natural History of North Carolina* (1737), freely plagiarized from Lawson. South Carolina's Thomas Ashe, in *Carolina; or, A Description of the Present State of That Country and the Natural Excellence Thereof* (1682), precedes all other contemporary southern commentators. Some years later Governor John Archdale published *A New Description of That Fertile and Pleasant Province of Carolina* (1707), in good part a justification of his administration. Best-known of all early books, the Reverend Alexander Hewatt's *An Historical Account of the Rise and Progress of South Carolina and Georgia* (1779) leans heavily on Ashe.

After independence, the nationalist urge sent historians of the romantic school back into the past in search of origins that would establish their identity. They produced a number of state, sectional, and national histories, ranging from trivia up to classics like George Bancroft's *History of the United States*. The writings of PARSON WEEMS, though achieving popularity, illustrate romantic history at its worst. Many of his contemporaries held to sounder standards and produced respectable histories for every southern state. Uneven in literary quality, research, and conceptualization, these numerous titles still must appear in definitive bibliographies, though all have been supplanted. WILLIAM GILMORE SIMMS brought unusual literary gifts to the *History of South Carolina* (1840), but relied heavily on the older works of Hewatt and DAVID RAMSAY for material. Charles C. Jones's *History of Georgia* (1883) devotes the first volume to aboriginal and colonial times. Among Virginia histories, WILLIAM WIRT's *Sketches of the Life and Character of Patrick Henry* (1817) and John Daly Burk's *History of Virginia* (1804–1816) are still useful for suggestions. John V. L. MacMahon's *An Historical View of the Government of Maryland from Its Colonization to the Present Day* (1837) is a constitutional sketch of merit.

The rise of the "scientific" school in the 1880s gave the colonial South a new and richer history. In graduate seminars younger scholars critically scrutinized original sources for political, institutional, social, and occasionally cultural topics on which they produced papers for a new outlet, state historical journals, and theses or dissertations for advanced degrees. Often graceless in literary style, wooden in organization, and burdened with factual detail, hundreds of such works dredged up the colonial past: the land systems, court systems, county and parish institutions, commerce, agriculture, and religious life. Within a few decades major studies had appeared on the southern provinces, as, for example, Newton D. Mereness, *Maryland as a Proprietary Province* (1901), and Edward McCrady, *History of South Carolina Under the Proprietary Government, 1670–1719* (1897), and the succeeding volume on the royal period (1901).

The scientific strain, emphasizing factual accuracy and usually leaning toward a political or institutional framework, has continued until today and has notable exemplification in Richard L. Morton, *Colonial Virginia* (1960). But beginning in the 1930s new tendencies began appearing in such studies as Charles A. Barker, *Background of the Revolution in Maryland* (1940), which touched social structure, intellectual life, and the economy. In the same decade WESLEY FRANK CRAVEN, *Southern Colonies in the Seventeenth Century, 1607–1689* (1949), summed up received doctrine developed in the spate of studies from the scientific school and at the same time faced in new directions.

The "new directions" or the recent tendencies—the latest phase of the historiography of the early South—have made colonial history one of the liveliest American fields of research and writing. Many older views have fallen from currency, new questions have come under study in the application of social science techniques to the reassessment and reinterpretation of the colonial South. Craven's *White, Red, and Black* (1971) and Winthrop D. Jordan's *White over Black* (1968) have put race relations in a new light. Demographic studies and research employing quantitative methods have afforded new insights and offered suggestive hypotheses. Many scholars of the new generation have turned to microanalysis, often county based, to test and refine the sweeping generalities of an earlier day or to build anew from raw data formerly ignored. Two neglected areas, intellectual history and economic history, have their share of investigators. One or two bold spirits have ventured tentatively into psychohistory. In brief, adventuresome work, much of it by younger scholars, is giving a new look to the early South.

See M. Kraus, *Writing of American History* (1953); and H. Wish, *American Historian* (1960).

AUBREY C. LAND
University of Georgia

COLONIAL WARS (1560–1760).

War, a commonplace in colonial North America, was almost a way of life with Indians as well as transplanted Caucasians. Some conflicts were intertribal, some intercolonial, others interracial. Given uncohesive tribal relationships and superior white technology, the aborigines were probably able at no time during the colonial era to expel the European invaders. Nonetheless, Spain, France, and England regularly enlisted the Indian in their respective imperial causes.

A clash among Europeans occurred after Spaniards substituted colonization for exploitation in the Southeast. Challenging this policy by settling in eastern Florida, French Protestants were obliterated by Spanish arms in 1565. HUGUENOTS, un-

welcome in New Spain, would eventually find refuge in British America.

After English settlers successfully colonized Virginia early in the next century, the death of Chief POWHATAN encouraged his half-brother OPECHANCANOUGH to launch hostilities against them in 1622 and again in 1644, when he was killed and the once-powerful Powhatan Confederacy annihilated. Not until 1676, the year of BACON'S REBELLION, was the Virginia frontier disturbed by another major Indian war.

England and France were the principal imperial rivals for control of the valuable fur trade and ultimately for possession of North America. Their competition precipitated four intercolonial wars destined to affect continental politics and culture. The first three Anglo-French wars were European dynastic conflicts, with American counterparts. The fourth war began in the Western Hemisphere as a contest for empire. Although the War of the League of Augsburg (1689–1697), labeled King William's War in British America, was of little consequence in the Southeast, imperial rivalry there became triangular after France planted Louisiana along the lower Mississippi at the turn of the century. During the War of the Spanish Succession (1702–1713), called Queen Anne's War in the colonies, South Carolina was frustrated in its attacks on St. Augustine in 1702 and on Pensacola in 1707. The latter attempt came after the French unsuccessfully invaded Charleston the previous year. During 1711–1712 North Carolina defeated the TUSCARORAS, who thereupon migrated northward to join the Iroquois Confederacy.

The Yamassee War (1715–1716) in South Carolina precipitated a conflict that continued until 1728. During that period CREEK and YAMASSEE Indians, probably provoked by the Spaniards and the French, warred intermittently in the Southeast against the English and their CHEROKEE allies and finally suffered defeat at their hands.

Britain established Georgia in 1733 as a military barrier between South Carolina and Spanish Florida. Commercial rivalry between Spain and England caused the War of Jenkins' Ear (1739–1742), during which colonials fought in the Caribbean alongside army regulars and Georgians with Indian allies attacked St. Augustine. This conflict led into the War of the Austrian Succession (1744–1748), known in America as King George's War. Following an uneasy interlude of sharp Anglo-French competitiveness over the Ohio Valley, the final intercolonial struggle developed on the frontier in 1754. Colonists designated it the FRENCH AND INDIAN WAR, and Europeans called it the Seven Years' War (1756–1763). Concomitantly the

Cherokee War (1758–1761) was waged along the southeastern frontier.

In the South the colonial wars effected numerous changes in politics and society. Raising and financing military forces allowed the lower houses of provincial legislatures to seize some administrative powers from royal governors, thus advancing representative government. Emission of paper money in the South to cover martial expenditures first began during Queen Anne's War in North Carolina. This practice, widely used thereafter, increased the currency in circulation and generally promoted the welfare of debtors. Frontier violence and Indian captivities sowed seeds of a persistent enmity between the races. Toleration and, later, liberty of religion were secured by war-minded dissenters whose contributions to defense could not be ignored. These wars were a nursery for the perfection of Americans in the art of warfare. Such experience stood the patriots in good stead when they rebelled against Britain.

See D. E. Leach, *Arms for Empire* (1973), definitive; H. H. Peckham, *Colonial Wars* (1964); L. H. Gipson, *British Empire* (1936–70); F. Parkman, *France and England* (1865–92), classic; V. W. Crane, *Southern Frontier* (1928); J. P. Greene, *Quest for Power* (1963); D. H. Corkran, *Cherokee Frontier* (1962), and *Creek Frontier* (1967); D. B. Rutman (ed.), *Old Dominion* (1964), Ch. 1–3; and C. R. Young, *West Virginia History* (July, 1966).

CHESTER RAYMOND YOUNG
Cumberland College, Williamsburg, Ky.

COLONIZATION PROPOSALS for resettling blacks away from whites have been voiced since the earliest days of the Republic. Black emigrationists believed they could never achieve full equality among whites and that a black nation was preferable. Most white colonizationists feared race mixture and considered free blacks a threat to slavery. By and large, Afro-Americans have opposed emigration because the United States was their home, because to leave would acknowledge black inferiority, and, before 1860, because leaving would weaken the struggle against slavery.

In the 1780s groups of blacks in Massachusetts and Rhode Island petitioned for help in going to Africa to escape prejudice and to civilize and Christianize the Africans. They were encouraged by the British resettlement of former slaves at Sierra Leone in 1787. But no significant emigration took place until 1816, when Paul Cuffee, a black Quaker ship captain, delivered 38 Afro-American settlers to Sierra Leone.

The AMERICAN COLONIZATION SOCIETY, founded in 1816 by whites, advocated resettlement of Afro-Americans in West Africa. The sponsors acted from motives of racism, benevolence, and protection of the American slavery system. In 1820 the federal government helped the society send 88 settlers to establish Liberia. Auxiliary colonization societies emerged in several states in the North and South. Most free blacks, however, opposed the society and its proslavery patrons, especially through the 1830s and 1840s as the abolitionist crusade hardened ideological lines. But the FUGITIVE SLAVE LAW of 1850 and other losses for free blacks convinced considerable numbers of them to reconsider emigration. Thousands went to Canada, hundreds to Liberia. Chief black spokesman for African immigration was Dr. MARTIN R. DELANY, who opposed the American Colonization Society but urged blacks to settle in Nigeria under the auspices of a black group, the African Civilization Society. The Civil War and emancipation ended Delany's plans, but the colonization society renewed its efforts during Reconstruction among southern freedmen, 3,000 of whom went to Liberia. White efforts to colonize blacks effectively ended as the need for labor increased and as settlement proceeded in the Southwest. After having transported a total of 15,000 blacks to Liberia, the American Colonization Society effectively stopped operations in 1892.

Before and after the Civil War, the black Republic of Haiti attracted interest among Afro-Americans. The first of a small stream of immigrants went there in 1824. In the 1850s James T. Holly, a black Episcopal priest from New Haven, became the most articulate and persistent advocate of immigration to Haiti. James Redpath, a white journalist, helped attract white support to the movement, but emancipation quieted the excitement.

As white support for black emigration faded during Reconstruction, blacks themselves sponsored several schemes. In 1878 a group of South Carolina blacks purchased a ship, the *Azor*, and made one voyage with colonists for Liberia. Chief spokesman for black emigration between 1865 and 1915 was HENRY MCNEAL TURNER, who used nationalist rhetoric to urge settlement in Africa. Collapse of the colonization society, economic troubles in the 1890s, and opposition from other black leaders all kept Turner from sending more than a few hundred people to Liberia. In 1914, Chief Alfred C. Sam created interest among Oklahoma blacks, bought a ship, and took 60 Afro-Americans to Gold Coast, West Africa. Marcus Garvey rekindled the smoldering spark of emigration interest after World War I, but no resettlement took place. Since Garvey's time, there has been little serious interest in emigration. Education about realities in Africa, Haiti, and elsewhere made most Afro-Americans believe that the United States still offered the best chance for advancement, however difficult.

See F. Miller, *Search for Black Nationality* (1975), thorough on pre–Civil War era; P. J. Staudenraus, *African Colonization Movement, 1816–1865* (1961); E. S. Redkey, *Black Exodus* (1969), black-led emigration; W. Bittle and G. Geis, *Longest Way Home* (1964), Oklahoma movement, 1912–1914; and E. D. Cronon, *Black Moses* (1969), best on Garvey.

EDWIN S. REDKEY
State University of New York, Purchase

COLORADO RIVER of Texas rises in the limestone plains of the western portion of the state. It winds generally southeast for 970 miles through the dry and hilly countryside used for grazing cattle and sheep, across the wooded hills of the Edwards Plateau, past AUSTIN, and then down through the coastal plain to its mouth on the Gulf of Mexico. The town of Matagorda, founded in 1825 by MOSES AUSTIN as a port city, is situated near the river's mouth. Three major dams on the main stream provide hydroelectric power and water for irrigation.

COLQUITT, ALFRED HOLT (1824–1894), was born in Walton County, Ga., graduated from Princeton (1844), and admitted to the bar in 1845. In the Mexican War, he rose to the rank of major on the staff of Zachary Taylor. He was elected to the U.S. House of Representatives in 1852 for one term. After supporting JOHN C. BRECKINRIDGE for president in 1860, Colquitt entered the Confederate army as a captain and rose to the rank of major general. He participated in the battle of OLUSTEE in Florida. In 1870, he became president of the Georgia Agricultural Society and president of the state Democratic convention. He served as governor (1876–1882) and with JOSEPH E. BROWN and JOHN B. GORDON was one of the GEORGIA TRIUMVIRATE. These BOURBONS dominated Georgia politics for 20 years. Although charges of corruption were made during his governorship and some state officials were found guilty, no scandal touched Colquitt personally. The constitution of 1877 was written during his governorship. While serving as a U.S. senator (1882–1894), he remained a leader in the southern Methodist church, working as a lay preacher and speaking to religious gatherings of all races, as well as convicts.

See K. Coleman, "Alfred H. Colquitt" (M.A. thesis, University of Georgia, 1940); J. C. Ward, "Bourbon Democrats" (Ph.D. dissertation, University of North Carolina,

1947); A. H. Colquitt Papers, University of Georgia; and Governors Letterbooks, Georgia Department of Archives and History, Atlanta.

DERRELL C. ROBERTS
Dalton Junior College

COLUMBIA, S.C. (pop. 113,542), was founded in 1786 to serve as the state's capital. The site, at the confluence of the Broad and Saluda rivers and the FALL LINE of the Congaree River, was selected as the capital to appease UP-COUNTRY hostility to the influence of the TIDEWATER and Charleston areas in state politics. After the location here of the state legislature in 1790, first stage lines, then steamboats, and eventually railroads began service to the city. With these transportation facilities, Columbia prospered not only as a seat of government but as a major cotton market. Moreover, the presence of the University of South Carolina (1801) and Columbia College for Women (1854) helped make Columbia the cultural and educational center of antebellum South Carolina as well. After its surrender to General W. T. Sherman on February 17, 1865, over half the city was destroyed by fire. WADE HAMPTON, whose cavalry served as a rear guard for retreating Confederate forces, charged Sherman with "deliberately, systematically and atrociously" burning the capital to the ground. Sherman contended that fires begun by Confederates to destroy cotton stores were spread by high winds and that efforts by his troops to contain the fire were responsible for preventing the complete destruction of the city. Whatever the cause of the devastating fire, the city was rebuilt, resumed its role as a cotton market, and gradually was industrialized. Modern Columbia, the largest city in the state, manufactures textiles, fertilizers, steel wire, concrete, and lumber products. More dramatic in its impact on the city than industrialization, however, has been the location here since 1940 of nearby U.S. Army Ft. Jackson.

See H. K. Henning, *Columbia, 1786–1936* (1936); J. F. Williams, *Old and New Columbia* (1929); J. A. Selby, *Memorabilia of Columbia* (1905); J. M. Bateman, *Columbia Scrapbook, 1701–1842* (1915); E. L. Green, *History of Richland County, 1732–1805* (1932); N. S. Graydon, *Tales of Columbia* (1964), illustrated; J. G. Gibbes, *Who Burnt Columbia?* (1902); and files of Columbia *Record* (1897–) and *State* (1891–), on microfilm.

COLUMBIA (S.C.) STATE first came off the press February 18, 1891. It was founded by Ambrose Elliott Gonzales, the first editor, and his brother NARCISO GENER GONZALES. From the outset the *State* was embroiled in political struggles, often on the unpopular side. Among the reform measures supported were compulsory education and complete suffrage for Negroes. The paper also led a bitter fight against BEN TILLMAN and Tillmanism, which climaxed with the fatal shooting of N. G. Gonzales. It continues to this day as a leading newspaper in South Carolina, with a morning circulation of over 100,000.

See L. P. Jones, *Stormy Petrel* (1973).

S. FRANK LOGAN
Wofford College

COLUMBUS, GA.

COLUMBUS, GA. (pop. 154,168), is a major producer of textiles in western Georgia. The city also produces iron, processes meat, and services nearby Lawson Air Force Base and U.S. Army Ft. Benning. Located on the FALL LINE at the Chattahoochee River and the Alabama state line, Columbus was founded in 1828 as a frontier trading post. The first textile mill utilizing the river's water power was constructed ten years later. Also because of its position on the Chattahoochee, Columbus was an important supply point during the Creek Indian War of 1836, the Mexican War, and the Civil War. The town was captured and partially destroyed by federal troops in WILSON'S RAID during April, 1865.

See N. Telfair, *History of Columbus, 1828–1928* (1929); J. H. Martin, *Columbus* (1874, 1972); E. B. Worsley, *Columbus* (1951), illustrated; and files of Columbus *Enquirer* (1828–), *Ledger* (1886–), and *Daily Sun* (1865–73), all on microfilm. Columbus Public Library maintains collections of 4,000 books on Georgia, 2,000 books on genealogy, bound M.A. theses on city history, and all local newspapers on microfilm.

COLUMBUS (GA.) ENQUIRER

COLUMBUS (GA.) ENQUIRER, possessing a complex family tree, is the result of numerous newspaper mergers and purchases. MIRABEAU LAMAR founded the *Enquirer* in 1828 as a states' rights weekly. Gradually moving away from the Democratic party, the *Enquirer* had become a Whig paper by 1840. It supported the COMPROMISE OF 1850, avoided any association with the KNOW-NOTHING movement, and endorsed JOHN BELL in the ELECTION OF 1860.

Four years after the first issue of the *Enquirer*, a journalistic competitor began publication of the Columbus *Sentinel and Herald*. Renamed the *Times and Sentinel* in 1841 and then simply the Columbus *Times* in 1858, it was merged at the end of the Civil War with the *Daily Sun* (1855–1865) to form the *Daily Sun and Times*. With postwar pressure for white solidarity and with limited advertising revenues, the *Enquirer* and the *Sun and Times* were merged in 1874 to form the *En-*

quirer-Sun. A conservative Democratic paper, it supported Grover Cleveland and "goldbug" Democrats during the 1890s against William Jennings Bryan, TOM WATSON, and members of the FARMERS' ALLIANCE.

In 1920, however, Julian Harris became editor of the paper, and under his editorship the *Enquirer-Sun* became one of the more liberal and progressive publications in the state. Harris won a Pulitzer Prize in 1926 for his campaigns against the KU KLUX KLAN, LYNCHING, and antievolution laws (EVOLUTION CONTROVERSY). Since the 1930s the paper has been known simply as the *Enquirer*.

See L. T. Griffith and J. E. Talmadge, *Georgia Journalism, 1763–1950* (1951); and Columbus *Enquirer*, bound copies at Library of Congress and Emory University and microfilm from Bell & Howell (1832–).

COLUMBUS, MISS.

COLUMBUS, MISS. (pop. 25,795), was first settled in 1817 by Thomas Thomas and Spirus Roach. Called Possum Town, the settlement was on the Tombigbee River approximately 80 miles north of Meridian near the Alabama state line. Settlers from Virginia and North Carolina renamed the town in 1821, the same year in which Franklin Academy, the first free school in the state, was founded. Priding itself on being a cultural and educational center, Columbus refused the Mobile & Ohio Railroad a right-of-way and did not gain a rail connection until 1861. During the Civil War, the Mississippi Confederate government moved here after Jackson, the state capital, fell to Union forces in the summer of 1863. Mississippi State College for Women was founded here in 1884, and the town gradually became a transportation center served by three different railroads. A number of fine antebellum homes survive to this day, and the factories of modern Columbus produce bricks, motors, and mobile homes.

See W. L. Lipscomb, *History of Columbus* (1909); Works Progress Administration, *Lowndes County* (1936–38); and Columbus *Commercial-Dispatch* (1902–), on microfilm. Lowndes County Library maintains a collection of *Mississippi Almanacs* (1845–60), on microfilm, and *Pioneer Annals* (1939–), bound copies of papers read at monthly meetings of local historical society.

COLYAR, ARTHUR ST. CLAIR

COLYAR, ARTHUR ST. CLAIR (1818–1907), a Nashville lawyer, industrialist, and newspaper editor, was born near Jonesboro, Tenn. A Whig, he served as a delegate to the Constitutional Unionist convention in Baltimore in 1860. After Tennessee joined the Confederacy in June, 1861, Colyar represented the state in the Confederate Congress (1863–1865). He was also a member of the peace commission that failed to negotiate an end to the war at the HAMPTON ROADS CONFERENCE in February, 1865. After the war Colyar inaugurated a campaign to industrialize Tennessee. He was involved in various industrial enterprises, among the first to employ prison labor on a large scale in Tennessee, and a defender of the CONVICT LEASE SYSTEM. Between 1882 and 1887 he served as editor of the Nashville *American* and Nashville *Union*. After retiring (1888) he wrote a biography of ANDREW JACKSON, contributed to national newspapers and periodicals, and helped establish a Nashville literary magazine, the *Round Table*, in 1890.

See T. W. Davis, "Arthur S. Colyar" (Ph.D. dissertation, University of Missouri, 1963); S. H. M. Howell, "Editorial Career" (M.A. thesis, Vanderbilt University, 1967); and C. L. Ball, *Public Career* (1937).

JAMES E. HANEY
Tennessee State University

COMER, BRAXTON BRAGG (1848–1927), merchant, planter, textile manufacturer, and governor of Alabama, was born at Old Spring Hill, Barbour County, Ala. He attended the University of Alabama and the University of Georgia prior to entering Emory and Henry College in Virginia, where he graduated in 1869. In 1890 he moved to Birmingham, which remained his home for the rest of his life and where he became wealthy as the operator of corn, flour, and textile mills. In 1904, he was elected president of the Alabama railroad commission, but, frustrated in his efforts at reform, he was elected governor on an antirailroad platform that brought denunciation of him as a "radical." He secured legislation strengthening the railroad commission, reforming the tax structure, and expanding social services, especially education. He enacted a tough local option prohibition law. Although regarded as an enemy of child labor legislation, he signed a child labor law that prohibited employment of children under twelve. Comer unsuccessfully sought the Democratic nomination for governor in 1914, a failure caused partially by the opposition of organized labor. In his remaining years, he managed Avondale Mills, which remain in the control of the Comer family. He was appointed in 1920 to the eight-month unexpired term of John H. Bankhead, Sr., in the U.S. Senate.

See O. H. Draper, "Contributions of Comer to Public Education in Alabama" (Ph.D. dissertation, University of Alabama, 1970); and A. J. Going, "Governorship of B. B. Comer" (M.A. thesis, University of Alabama, 1940).

EVANS C. JOHNSON
Stetson University

COMMERCE has played a major part in the South's economy since the founding of the earliest British colonies. From the seventeenth century until well into the modern, post–Civil War era, the South relied heavily upon the export of its staples—particularly tobacco and later cotton—to generate earnings, and the region was highly dependent upon trade to provide it with manufactured goods and many types of foodstuffs.

During the colonial era, each province in the South early developed the production of one or more staples for export. The first to emerge was TOBACCO in the Chesapeake region. By 1637, tobacco shipments from the Chesapeake had risen to 1.5 million pounds annually. A tenfold increase in tobacco exports was achieved during 1637–1669. Then exports rose from 15 to 30 million pounds annually during 1670–1699, following which there was a period of relative stagnation in the trade. By 1740, however, a resumed climb in exports brought the annual total to about 50 million pounds and, by the mid-1770s, 100 million pounds. Not only did tobacco constitute some 90 percent of the exports (by value) of Virginia and Maryland, but it was the source of half of all the American mainland colonies' export trade to Great Britain.

Tobacco exportation became the economic underpinning for population growth in the Chesapeake, from 90,000 in 1700 to nearly 700,000 in 1770 (about a third of the entire population of the 13 colonies at the latter date). Similarly, the vast increase in RICE exports from the Lower South (from 17 million pounds valued at £74,000 in 1730 to 77 million pounds worth £375,000 in 1770) provided the basis for population increase in Georgia and South Carolina, which together had nearly 150,000 persons in 1770. The expansion of the rice trade was greatly aided by Parliament's decision in 1730 to permit direct exportation, bypassing England, from the South to ports in southern Europe; Spain and Portugal took about a fourth of the American crop.

This burgeoning export trade in the staples contributed to a long-term increase in the income and wealth of the South. In terms of average per capita income and consumption by the white population only, the plantation districts were the wealthiest in the colonies in the last half of the eighteenth century. Distinguishing the southern colonies from New England and the middle colonies were the importance of the Atlantic SLAVE TRADE in regional commerce and, of course, the importance of slave labor in production for export. As market opportunities became profitable, for tobacco in the seventeenth century and for rice shortly after

1700 in the Carolinas, planters purchased slaves to provide the labor force for production; and, in the eighteenth century, upwards of 250,000 Africans were transported to the South as a tragic human component of the region's commerce.

Southern trade in the colonial era, although dominated by tobacco and rice, included other important products. In the late seventeenth century and the early eighteenth century, for example, South Carolina maintained an active trade in Indian slaves (sent mainly to the West Indies) and in deerskins (FUR TRADE). Later, exports of NAVAL STORES from the Carolinas generated earnings in the trade with New England and the home country. In the mid-eighteenth century, WHEAT, CORN, and livestock also emerged as important exports, especially from North Carolina, the Piedmont region of Virginia, and Maryland's Eastern Shore. Breadstuffs, meat, LUMBER, and livestock were exported to the West Indies, where about a fourth of the imports of these commodities came from the South. And as the southern forests were cleared, lumber and wood products also left the region in trade with the Indies and coastal ports to the north. The Virginia ironworks also exported large quantities of pig and bar iron to England throughout the eighteenth century. Virginia and Maryland exported grain in rising quantities to the Azores, the Wine Islands, and southern Europe—their most important market for grain by the 1770s—and thereby opened up a direct exchange for wine, salt, and tropical fruit. All the southern colonies were large importers of New England rum, beer, and whaling products (candles and soap).

The South enjoyed a healthy surplus in its balance of trade, but the region relied heavily upon outsiders for shipping services and marketing. Although Virginians, Marylanders, and South Carolinians built and operated ships, they were engaged mainly in the coastwise and West Indies trades. British merchants and ships handled the tobacco trade, and these same outsiders also handled most of the South's imports, although many large planters carried on diversified mercantile businesses in their local neighborhoods.

Planters in the Chesapeake typically loaded and received goods "at the landing" (at their plantations), and this retarded the development of urban centers. Exchange activities were regularized at Williamsburg in the 1770s, but only Norfolk and later Baltimore—both of which handled grain trades rather than principally tobacco—matched the much larger northern port cities in diversity of economic functions or a pattern of urban agglomeration. Localized intracolonial commerce was limited by the relative lack of urban population, but it is well to recall that it did exist in the colonial era as in later days.

The South's importance in national commerce, both foreign and domestic, continued on a similar basis after the American Revolution. Until the Civil War, the South continued to be more heavily dedicated to staple crop production for export than other regions and continued to generate higher export earnings relative to total regional income than was characteristic of other regions. Although tobacco retained its importance as an export staple in the Southeast, it was overshadowed quickly and dramatically by the spread of COTTON culture beginning in the late 1790s. Indeed, by the 1830s cotton dominated the entire national export trade.

The rising foreign demand for cotton from the textile mills of England (and later New England) became the impetus for rapid expansion of the cotton plantation system into the Gulf Coast region. The effects of this expansion, with its pattern of concentration on the plantation-organized production of a single crop, were great for the national economy as a whole. First, it generated a massive commerce for American shipping and mercantile houses. Second, a large area of the lower Mississippi probably became dependent upon the upper Mississippi and Ohio Valley regions for foodstuffs. Third, earnings from the cotton trade helped to sustain a flow of long-term capital investment funds into American banking, state bonds, and canal and railroad securities in the pre-1860 period. Fourth, the cotton trade financed a flow of imports that supplied American households with many items of everyday use. There was, withal, good reason for Friedrich Engels to assert that "England and the United States are bound together by a single thread of cotton, which, weak and fragile as it may appear, is, nevertheless, stronger than an iron cable."

Not least important, the export trade in cotton, complemented by rising consumption of southern cotton in the North's own textile industry, helped fasten upon the South an economic system that fixed the plantation, black slavery, and a lack of diversification on the region. Despite rising southern income in the era of King Cotton, the legacy of that era was one that made long-term economic development difficult.

Like tobacco production in the colonial era, southern specialization in cotton militated against urban growth. Charleston, New Orleans, Mobile, and Galveston emerged as major port cities; but, except for Baltimore, none developed extensive manufacturing. New Orleans was the "hinge" city in the trade that carried not only southern cotton and sugar but also western flour, corn, and meat to the Atlantic coast. New Orleans also became an important entryway for regional imports from the East and Europe. Steamboat arrivals at New Orleans were 250 in 1819–1820 (with $15 million in cargoes); in 1859–1860 they were 3,500 ($200 million in cargoes). Flatboats also remained important in carrying the western exports downriver, late into the 1850s. But as east-west railroad lines supplemented existing canals and the lake trade between the Atlantic seaboard and the West, New Orleans' share of the western trade declined in the pre–Civil War decade. The Crescent City shipped one-fourth of all U.S. exports in 1860, but handled only one-seventh of all imports.

The Civil War brought a northern BLOCKADE of southern ports that strangled the export trade. Union control of the Mississippi from mid-1863 to the war's end cut off the flow of meat from Texas to the eastern part of the Confederacy, a loss only partly made up by shipments from Florida. Successive northern military incursions created often desperate food shortages in southern cities, and farm and plantation production were disrupted by military actions and also by Confederate impressment of food for southern troops. The war ended, too, that unique regional element of commerce, the domestic slave trade.

Post–Civil War southern commerce was vitally affected by intensive new railroad construction. River trade on the smaller inland waterways fell off drastically, and even the volume of Mississippi freight movements fell from 6 million tons in 1889 to 2.5 million in 1906. The railroads served not only the agricultural sector, but also the burgeoning lumber, mining, and iron and steel industries. The export trade of the Gulf Coast ports soared, as New Orleans and Galveston ranked among the top three national ports by the 1890s (HARBORS).

The South was unique among the American regions in its degree of reliance upon foreign markets for farm output. Some 60 percent or more of southern cotton was exported prior to 1920. Although cotton remained the major regional export, tobacco products became increasingly important in interregional trade as the cigarette industry expanded its market in the early decades of the twentieth century. Another major feature of post–Civil War commerce was the cattle trade out of Texas to rail lines and feeder ranges north on the Great Plains, from 1866 to about 1880. After the turn of the century, the rise of PETROLEUM pro-duction in the Southwest inaugurated what later would become the South's most valuable branch of commerce with the Atlantic Coast region. Carried initially by railroads, petroleum was later shipped increasingly by newly built pipelines and by coastwise tanker ships.

Roads and highways, pipelines, and industrial development in the post-1920 era (especially mining, petroleum, CHEMICALS, and TEXTILE manufacturing) have given rise to large-scale urbanization in the South. Cities such as Atlanta and Houston, Dallas and Ft. Worth have become banking and services-industry centers. AIR TRANSPORT has lent additional impetus to urbanization in the region. Natural gas from Louisiana and the Southwest is now sent by pipeline throughout the United States, and the petroleum trade from the southwestern Gulf ports to the Atlantic seaboard is among the largest components of national interregional commerce. Although cotton remains a major item in trade, modern diversified southern agriculture sends citrus and other orchard crops, beef, and TRUCK FARMING products into both regional urban centers and national trade.

The Hampton Roads–Newport News district in Virginia is among the nation's leading ports, specializing in mineral exports. In the last quarter-century, the Mississippi River trade has been transformed by diesel engines and by the introduction of barge fleets, leading to its reemergence as a major commercial route. Moreover, extensive highway construction and the rise of motortruck transportation have brought the region's commerce close to national norms, even as the basic economic structure of the South's economy has shifted, converging more generally with the national pattern.

See A. P. Middleton, *Tobacco Coast* (1953), thorough maritime and commercial history of Chesapeake; J. Price, *Journal of Economic History* (Dec., 1964); J. H. Soltow, *Economic Role of Williamsburg* (1965); C. D. Clowse, *Economic Beginnings of Colonial South Carolina* (1971); T. J. Wertenbaker, *Norfolk* (1931); J. Price, *Perspectives in American History* (1974); J. F. Shepherd and S. H. Williamson, *Journal of Economic History* (Dec., 1972); D. Klingaman, *Virginia Magazine of History and Biography* (Jan., 1969); M. Egnal, *William and Mary Quarterly* (April, 1975); D. Lindstrom, *Agricultural History* (Jan., 1970); A. Fishlow, in R. L. Andreano (ed.), *New Views on American Economic Development* (1965); L. C. Gray, *History of Agriculture in Southern U.S.* (1933); D. C. North, *Economic Growth of U.S., 1790–1860* (1961); H. S. Perloff *et al.*, *Regions, Resources, and Economic Growth* (1960), historical overview of regional economic structures; G. R. Taylor, *Transportation Revolution, 1815–60* (1951); T. D. Clark and A. D. Kirwan, *South Since Appomattox* (1967), excellent summaries of regional economic change by period; E. L. Ullman, *American Commodity Flow* (1957), includes regional analysis; C. B. Hoover and B. U. Ratchford, *Economic Resources and Policies of South* (1951); H. Woodman, *King Cotton and Retainers, 1800–1925* (1968), on middlemen; and H. F. Williamson *et al.; American Petroleum Industry* (1963), II.

HARRY N. SCHEIBER
University of California, San Diego

COMPOSITION OF U.S. EXPORT TRADE,
1800–1860
(millions of dollars, current value)

Year	Total exports	Raw cotton	Leaf tobacco
1800	$ 20		$ 4
1830	59	$ 30	6
1840	112	64	10
1850	135	72	10
1860	317	192	16

COMMERCIAL EXPOSITIONS. The International Cotton Exposition in Atlanta (1881) was the first major southern commercial exposition. It was followed by the Southern Exposition in Louisville (1883), the World's Industrial and Cotton Centennial Exposition (later the American Exposition) in New Orleans (1884–1886), the Cotton States and International Exposition in Atlanta (1895), the Tennessee Centennial Exposition in Nashville (1897), the South Carolina Interstate and West Indian Exposition in Charleston (1901–1902), the Louisiana Purchase Exposition in St. Louis (1904), and the Jamestown Exposition in Virginia (1907).

Organized by local businessmen to boost morale in time of depression and to attract trade and attention to their regions, the expositions were patterned after the great world's fairs of the age. They served as indications that the South desired acceptance as part of the Western world, particularly as a place for capital investment. Rituals of sectional reconciliation at these expositions were commonplace, ranging from joint meetings of Union and Confederate veterans to appearances by the Liberty Bell. Speeches stressed the greatness of the Union and its "free institutions," especially those that facilitated business enterprise. The exhibits were designed to encourage foreign trade (COMMERCE) and to advertise southern resources and advantages to potential investors.

As the "race question" was a major source of intersectional distrust, particular attention was paid to the Negro. The Negro Buildings at Atlanta (1895) and other expositions were as symbolic of the ATLANTA COMPROMISE as was BOOKER T. WASHINGTON's Atlanta exposition address, depicting blacks as able and willing, if subordinate, cogs in the future southern economic machine. Despite some black participation, the Negro exhibits were chiefly white shows, advertising the Negro as an economic asset and assuring northerners that the race problem posed no threat to their investments.

As enterprises the expositions were frequently unsuccessful, falling victim to poor management and overweening ambition. Economically, in the long run they were not important stimulators of healthy cities, nor could they save those in commercial decline. Their chief significance lay in their symbolism; they were pageants in which the NEW SOUTH presented itself to the world and asked for the world's business and acceptance.

See J. Blicksilver, *Cotton History Review* (Oct., 1960); D. C. Hardy, "World's Industrial and Cotton Centennial Exposition" (M.A. thesis, Tulane University, 1964); W. G. Cooper, *Cotton States and International Exposition* (1896); and *Charleston Yearbook, 1902* (1902).

DAVID CARLTON
Yale University

COMMISSION ON INTERRACIAL COOPERATION (1919–1944), a southern organization based in Atlanta, was dedicated to the improvement of race relations in the South. Racial tensions plaguing that region after World War I led WILL W. ALEXANDER, W. D. Weatherford, and several other whites to organize the group. Negro men and black and white women soon were added as members. Initially the commission, which eventually included more than 150 members, worked primarily through state and local interracial committees, churches, and other interested groups. During the 1930s, however, this support waned, and the commission carried on its program through its officers and staff. Alexander served as executive director throughout the commission's lifetime. Financial support came from individuals, churches, and philanthropic foundations.

Its activities focused on two goals: to improve the plight of southern Negroes and correct specific injustices; and to educate southern whites in the problems of Negroes and race relations and thus create a new interracial environment. The issue of segregation per se was avoided, however. Four departments—education, field work, research, and women's work—carried out these aims through the collection and dissemination of information relating to the Negro situation and racial antagonisms. The commission attacked such problems as farm tenancy, the PEONAGE system, unfair treatment before the law, and inadequate provisions for education and social welfare. Concern over LYNCHING led to creation of the Southern Commission on the Study of Lynching and publication of its findings, *The Tragedy of Lynching* (1933), and sponsorship of the ASSOCIATION OF SOUTHERN WOMEN FOR THE PREVENTION OF LYNCHING. The commission published a magazine, the *Southern Frontier*, and several books dealing with specific issues, and it operated a news service, which publicized cases of good race relations. It also encouraged the addition of race relations topics to college and high school curricula. The commission was dissolved in 1944, when its purpose and many of its members were absorbed into the newly created SOUTHERN REGIONAL COUNCIL.

See W. Dykeman and J. Stokely, *Seeds of Southern Change* (1962); E. F. Burrows, "Commission" (Ph.D. dissertation, University of Wisconsin, 1954); R. G. Powell, "Southern Commission" (Ph.D. dissertation, University of South Carolina, 1935); and W. E. Cole, *Social Forces* (May, 1943).

HENRY E. BARBER
Virginia Intermont College

COMMODITY CREDIT CORPORATION was

established by executive order on October 17, 1933, with a charter from the state of Delaware. Its initial purpose was to support CORN and COTTON prices until the NEW DEAL production control programs had time to take effect. The CCC originally operated exclusively through nonrecourse loans, with crops serving as collateral. By 1940, the list of agricultural products eligible for loan supports had expanded substantially. Among the most significant additions were TOBACCO and WHEAT. Between 1933 and 1939, the CCC extended $58.9 million in loans to farmers in the states of the old Confederacy—a sum that amounted to slightly more than half the corporation's total loan disbursements during those years.

Originally organized as an emergency agency, virtually an affiliate of the RECONSTRUCTION FINANCE CORPORATION, the CCC was transferred to the Department of Agriculture in 1939. There, under the Agricultural Act of 1938 and its amendments, the CCC has played an important part in the federal government's production control and price stabilization programs. By law, the prices of certain basic, and some nonbasic, commodities must be supported. Supports for other nonbasic commodities are discretionary.

During World War II the corporation financed foreign and domestic food programs. In the postwar period, it financed purchases for the relief of war-stricken areas and programs for the liquidation of many wartime activities. In 1948, the CCC was reorganized into a federal corporation within the Department of Agriculture by the Commodity Credit Corporation Charter Act. The corporation has a board of directors appointed by the president and a bipartisan advisory board, but it has no operating personnel.

As of June 30, 1975, the CCC had $33.6 million in commodity loans outstanding. The bulk was accounted for by six crops: cotton, tobacco, corn, PEANUTS, SOYBEANS, and wheat. Besides loans, the corporation has authority in some cases to support prices by purchases and direct payments.

See R. Green, *Review of Activities, Functions, and Operation: Commercial Credit Corporation* (1946); and U.S. Department of Agriculture, *Summary of 30 Years' Operation of Commercial Credit Corporation* (1965).

GLADYS L. BAKER
U.S. Department of Agriculture

COMMUNIST PARTY had no strength and only a few, widely scattered members and supporters in the South in the first decade of its existence. Between 1929 and 1936, the party attempted to unionize southern industrial workers (LABOR UNIONS), organize the unemployed into worker councils to demand relief and jobs, and to influence the Negro community. A southern district headquarters was set up in 1930, and a regional newspaper, the *Southern Worker*, was published, but the party did not gain many members. Nor were its organizing efforts in the steel, tobacco, or shipping industries particularly successful.

In its attempt to appeal to American Negroes, the party adopted a position in 1929 called "self-determination in the black belt," alleging that the Negro population in the South, concentrated in a series of contiguous counties stretching from Virginia to Texas, had the essential characteristics of a separate nationality and should be granted political self-sufficiency. The party's greatest success, however, came when the International Labor Defense helped in the legal defense of the SCOTTSBORO CASE. The party's attempts to organize blacks in the South met firm resistance from white southerners and their institutions. The Sharecroppers' Union, an attempt to bring TENANT FARMERS together, triggered mob violence in 1931 and 1932 in Tallapoosa County, Ala. The Communist party gained more notoriety than members in the South during this radical phase of its history. Its strength was never measured at the polls, as election laws effectively kept the party off the ballot. In 1928 the party polled 6,640 votes in eight southern states; in 1940 it received 2,838 votes in only two states.

After 1935, international communism took a new turn in an effort to create a defense against the rise of fascism, a position that was spelled out in its All-Southern Conference in Chattanooga in 1937. The American party cooperated with liberal and labor groups to achieve reforms within the American system, but those liberal and labor organizations that admitted Communists were subjected to intensive Red-baiting by conservatives. Groups such as unions belonging to the Congress of Industrial Organizations, Commonwealth College in Arkansas, Highlander Folk School in Tennessee, and the Southern Conference for Human Welfare were all charged with being front organizations.

Although the party never had a large following in the South (in 1951 only 900 of the party's 31,608 members lived in the 13 states of the Deep South), even this modest strength disappeared during the cold war period. By the 1960s the Communist party had no strength or influence in either the civil rights or student protest movements. Only with the limited resurgence of its strength in the 1970s has the party once again attempted to work in the South.

See F. E. Beal, *Proletarian Journey* (1937); A. Herndon, *Let Me Live* (1937); T. Rosengarten, *All God's Dangers* (1974); D. Carter, *Scottsboro* (1969); T. A. Krueger, *And Promises to Keep* (1967); W. Record, *Race and Radicalism* (1964); T. Draper, *American Communism and Soviet Russia* (1960); and D. Shannon, *Decline of American Communism* (1959).

JOHN SCOTT WILSON
University of South Carolina

COMPENSATED EMANCIPATION. See EMAN-
CIPATION, COMPENSATED

COMPROMISE OF 1850 is one of the most important legislative landmarks in the pre–Civil War period. The major issue confronting Americans was whether slavery should be extended into the 529,017 western and southwestern square miles acquired as a result of the Mexican War. Interest in this question sharpened because of the gold discovery in California and the spectacular gold rush of the forty-niners. With 100,000 fresh arrivals on the West Coast, their need for civil government became acute. The month before the Thirty-first Congress convened in December, 1849, California voters ratified a constitution excluding slavery from their proposed new state. In February, 1850, this constitution reached Congress with the request that California be admitted to the Union.

Numerous southerners opposed California's ad-

mission because they regarded the U.S. Senate as the stoutest remaining bastion of southern security. Since slavery was legal in half the states, the South had nominal Senate equality, in contrast to the House of Representatives' sizable northern majority. Admission of California might give the North a permanent Senate majority. Thus southern interests, respecting the tariff and other matters as well as slavery, would be jeopardized.

Many northerners had a diametrically different point of view. Increasingly they believed in the existence of an insidious "slave power." The prospect of slavery's expansion aroused widespread northern opposition. Support developed for the WILMOT PROVISO, which would keep slavery out of the entire Mexican cession. Although numerous northern politicians hoped for accommodation with the South, others adopted a proviso stand. Clearly, in both northern and southern eyes, free California's admission would be a northern victory.

A complicating factor was the problem of devising some form of governmental structure for the vast, thinly populated region stretching east from California to Texas and the Rocky Mountains. Was slavery to be outlawed there, too? A third complexity concerned both Texas' western boundary (in dispute) and the debt that the state of Texas had inherited from the Texas republic. Moreover, many southerners, unhappy over the unenforceability of the 1793 Fugitive Slave Act, desired stronger legislation to ensure recovery of runaway blacks (FUGITIVE SLAVE LAWS). Finally, much northern sentiment favored abolition of slavery and the slave trade in the District of Columbia.

It is a mistake to assume that Senator HENRY CLAY's resolutions of early 1850 became law. Substantial changes occurred before the compromise was enacted, the size of Texas being one. Clay erred tactically when in the spring, heading a special committee of 13, he advocated combining California statehood and other western "solutions" in a single omnibus bill. President ZACHARY TAYLOR, though a slaveholding southerner, took a basically northern stand opposing the Clay plan. In this, the president was supported by every northern Whig senator except two and by many northern representatives. Even after Taylor's death on July 9 and with procompromise Millard Fillmore in the White House, the omnibus bill went down to defeat. Clay then left Washington for several weeks. Thereupon, Stephen A. Douglas took charge, abandoning the omnibus technique and shepherding the measures through one at a time. Douglas' lieutenants in the House successfully followed similar procedures, and in

September Fillmore signed the five component parts of the "great adjustment." Most of the bills' origin was Democratic, and more of their backing Democratic than Whig.

As a result of the Compromise of 1850, California became the thirty-first state. Territorial governments based on POPULAR SOVEREIGNTY were provided for New Mexico and Utah (comprising future states of Nevada and Utah, most of Arizona and New Mexico, and portions of Colorado and Wyoming). Texas relinquished a large area it had claimed. Concurrently the state obtained approximately 33,000 square miles more than the committee of 13 planned, also getting $5 million, and bondholders received $7.75 million for their Texas securities. A new, stronger, harsher Fugitive Slave Act supplanted the 1793 statute. Congress restricted (but did not abolish) the District slave trade, slavery itself continuing there.

The fugitive slave legislation was the most explosive part of the compromise in operation. The territorial settlements proved generally acceptable to both southerners and northerners. Many southerners viewed California's admission as Exhibit A of their contention that the compromise was a northern triumph. Yet, ironically, the 1851–1860 California senators tended to befriend the South.

The compromise secured temporary tranquillity for the country. It helped postpone the Civil War for a decade, during which the North ran rings around the South in population growth, railroad expansion, and industrial development. In that sense, what was done in 1850 constituted a victory for the North and ultimately for a consolidated nation.

See H. Hamilton, *Prologue to Conflict* (1966), detailed discussion; A. Nevins, *Ordeal of the Union* (1947), I; R. R. Russel, *Journal of Southern History* (Aug., 1956); R. W. Johannsen, *Stephen A. Douglas* (1973); and H. Hamilton, *Zachary Taylor* (1966), II.

HOLMAN HAMILTON
University of Kentucky

CONFEDERACY AT WAR, HISTORIOGRAPHY OF.

With more than 60,000 books, pamphlets, and essays in print on the Civil War, persons interested in Confederate military history have a wide selection from which to choose. Several excellent general histories are available. R. S. Henry, *Story of the Confederacy* (1931), is especially good for the western campaigns; and C. Dowdey, *The Land They Fought For* (1955), concentrates on the eastern theater. S. Foote, *Civil War: A Narrative* (2 vols.; 1958–1963), is an undocumented but dramatically written account

that unfortunately carries the story only through the 1863 engagements. F. E. Vandiver, *Their Tattered Flags* (1970), surveys Confederate history with the armies as focal points. Disappointingly little has been written on the problems of southern strategy and command. A. Jones, *Confederate Strategy from Shiloh to Vicksburg* (1961); F. E. Vandiver, *Confederate Brass* (1956); and T. L. Connelly and A. Jones, *Politics of Command* (1973), stand out as the best works in that area.

D. S. Freeman, *Lee's Lieutenants: A Study in Command* (3 vols.; 1942–1944), is so masterful a history of the Army of Northern Virginia that it has never been seriously challenged. The better studies of generals in that army are Freeman's *R. E. Lee* (4 vols.; 1934–1935), L. Chambers' *Stonewall Jackson* (2 vols.; 1959), and J. Longstreet's *From Manassas to Appomattox* (1896, 1960). For the Confederacy's major force in the western theater, S. F. Horn, *Army of Tennessee* (1941), remains a good summary. T. L. Connelly's *Army of the Heartland* (1967) and *Autumn of Glory* (1971), while providing a fuller command-level history of the same army, are highly critical of all of its generals. Foremost among the few analyses of the trans-Mississippi area are A. E. Castel, *General Sterling Price and the Civil War in the West* (1968); and R. L. Kerby, *Kirby-Smith's Confederacy* (1972). The limited campaigns in the Southwest are sufficiently covered in R. C. Colton, *Civil War in the Western Territories* (1959); M. L. Hall, *Sibley's New Mexico Campaign* (1960); and R. L. Kerby, *Confederate Invasion of New Mexico and Arizona* (1958).

In the area of army logistics and supply, the following works are particularly revealing: R. C. Black III, *Railroads of the Confederacy* (1952); R. D. Goff, *Confederate Supply* (1969); J. L. Nichols, *Confederate Quartermaster in the Trans-Mississippi* (1964); and F. E. Vandiver, *Ploughshares into Swords* (1952).

H. K. Douglas, *I Rode with Stonewall* (1940); M. Howard, *Recollections of a Maryland Confederate Soldier* (1914); A. McDonald (ed.), *Make Me a Map of the Valley* (1973); and G. M. Sorrel, *Recollections of a Confederate Staff Officer* (1905, 1958), are among the best memoirs by men who performed staff duties. The most enlightening introduction to Confederate soldiers in the ranks is B. I. Wiley, *Life of Johnny Reb* (1943); and *Embattled Confederates* (1964), by the same author, presents a vivid and personal account of southern society in wartime. J. I. Robertson, Jr., *Stonewall Brigade* (1963); and H. B. Simpson, *Hood's Texas Brigade* (1970), are recognized as two of the leading Confederate unit histories.

M. M. Boatner III, *Civil War Dictionary* (1959); and E. B. Long, *Civil War Day by Day* (1971), are encyclopedia-style reference works that give brief synopses of both major and minor events. For the most complete listings of Confederate literature, see A. Nevins *et al.*, *Civil War Books: A Critical Bibliography* (2 vols.; 1967–1969); and C. E. Dornbusch, *Military Bibliography of the Civil War* (3 vols.; 1961–1972), II, III.

JAMES I. ROBERTSON, JR.
Virginia Polytechnic Institute and State University

CONFEDERACY ON THE HOME FRONT, HISTORIOGRAPHY OF. Leading bibliographies on this topic are Mary Elizabeth Massey, "The Confederate States of America: The Homefront," in Arthur S. Link and Rembert W. Patrick (eds.), *Writing Southern History* (1966); Ellis Merton Coulter, *Travels in the Confederate States: A Bibliography* (1948, 1961); and Allan Nevins, James I. Robertson, Jr., and Bell I. Wiley (eds.), *Civil War Books: A Critical Bibliography* (2 vols.; 1967–1969), I, II, Ch. 5, 6–8. All general histories of the Confederacy discuss the home front, as do the histories of the individual southern states during the Civil War.

The entire body of writings on the Confederacy, including those on the home front, may be roughly classified as traditional, that is, emphasizing the fortitude and sacrifice of the southern population against overwhelming numbers and material strength; revisionist, emphasizing the weaknesses inherent in the southern society and its unsuccessful efforts to meet the exigencies of total war; or a combination of these two themes. A few selected titles will serve as examples. Among the books stressing the courage and endurance of the Confederate people are such eyewitness accounts as Judith White McGuire, *Diary of a Southern Refugee During the War* (1968); and Robert Manson Myers (ed.), *The Children of Pride: A True Story of Georgia and the Civil War* (1972), Bk. 2, Ch. 1–24. Secondary works along this line include Bell I. Wiley, *The Plain People of the Confederacy* (1944); and Francis B. Simkins and James W. Patton, *The Women of the Confederacy* (1936). The writings of former Confederate leaders—Jefferson Davis, *The Rise and Fall of the Confederate Government* (2 vols.; 1881); and Alexander Stephens, *A Constitutional View of the Late War Between the States: Its Causes, Character, Conduct and Results* (2 vols.; 1870)—are polemical defenses of Confederate means and ends. The most sympathetic scholarly analysis of

Confederate civil and military administration is Rembert W. Patrick, *Jefferson Davis and His Cabinet* (1944).

Works emphasizing the shortcomings and failures of the Confederate population include Charles W. Ramsdell, *Behind the Lines in the Southern Confederacy* (1944); Mary Elizabeth Massey, *Ersatz in the Confederacy* (1952), and *Refugee Life in the Confederacy* (1964); Bell I. Wiley, *Southern Negroes, 1861–1865* (1938); Benjamin Quarles, *The Negro in the Civil War* (1953); and Richard Cecil Todd, *Confederate Finance* (1954). The Confederate government is critically analyzed in Bell I. Wiley, *The Road to Appomattox* (1956); Charles R. Lee, *The Confederate Constitutions* (1963); Wilfred B. Yearns, *The Confederate Congress* (1960); and Thomas B. Alexander and Richard E. Beringer, *The Anatomy of the Confederate Congress* (1972).

Writings combining the themes of strength and weakness include Mary Boykin Chesnut's celebrated journal, *A Diary from Dixie*, ed. Ben Ames Williams (1949); Bell I. Wiley, *Confederate Women* (1975); and James H. Brewer, *The Confederate Negro: Virginia's Craftsmen and Military Laborers, 1861–1865* (1969).

All literature on the Confederate home front conveys a sense of early confidence and enthusiasm gradually turned to despair in the heat of a losing war.

CHARLES P. ROLAND
University of Kentucky

CONFEDERATE ARMY is the term loosely applied to the Confederacy's land forces. Actually these forces consisted of 23 operational organizations known officially and unofficially as armies and named for the states, regions, or military departments with which they were associated. The largest of these were the Army of Northern Virginia (successor to the Confederate Army of the Potomac) and the Army of Tennessee. Normally an army, commanded by a full general, consisted of two or more corps (usually three), led by lieutenant generals; corps comprised two or more divisions, commanded by major generals; divisions consisted of two or more brigades led by brigadier generals; brigades were composed of two or more regiments (usually three or four), led by colonels; infantry regiments had ten companies, commanded by captains; companies consisted of two or more platoons; and platoons sometimes were divided into squads. Infantry battalions, commanded by lieutenant colonels and consisting usually of five to eight companies, were not regimental

components. In the artillery the battalion consisted of four batteries, each containing four or six
guns. The basic cavalry unit was the squadron or
troop, consisting of two or more platoons. Combination of arms normally began with attachment of
artillery and cavalry to an infantry brigade. Engineer, signal, and other supporting elements were
added on the corps or army level.

The Confederacy at first contemplated both a
regular "peacetime" force of professionals, known
as the Confederate States Army (C.S.A.), and a volunteer Provisional Army of the Confederate States
(P.A.C.S.). But, according to Ezra Warner, "the
regular service never progressed beyond the blueprint stage." Corps, divisions, and brigades, instead of being designated by number as on the
federal side, usually were named for their commanders. In the infantry, maximum authorized
strength of the regiment was 49 officers and 1,340
enlisted men and, of the company, four officers
and 135 enlisted men. But after a year or two of
service most units dwindled to less than one-half
their authorized strength. In 1864 companies
sometimes had no more than a score of men, led
by sergeants. Owing to incompleteness of records,
the exact strength of the Confederate army cannot
be ascertained. It probably aggregated about a
million, including 425 generals (eight full generals, 17 lieutenant generals, 72 major generals, and
328 brigadiers), all of whom wore the same rank
insignia on their collars—three stars within a
wreath. Nine-tenths of those who wore the Confederate gray were privates and noncommissioned
officers, widely known as Johnny Rebs (COLLO-
QUIALISMS AND NICKNAMES). About 95 percent
were native Americans, including three brigades
of Indians. Many Negroes served as accessories;
in March, 1865, the Confederate Congress authorized the recruitment of 300,000 blacks, but the
war ended before any got into combat. Of foreigners, the most numerous were the Irish and Germans. A majority of Johnny Rebs were farmers; in
age they ranged from eleven to seventy-three, but
three-fourths were between eighteen and thirty;
about one-fifth were illiterate, and those who could
write usually revealed serious deficiencies in
spelling and grammar. Nearly all were orthodox
Protestant in their religious inclinations, but most
at one time or another fell victim to swearing,
gambling, or other "sins" common to camp. In battle some played the coward, but most were impelled by promptings of pride and duty to acquit
themselves well in battle—so well, indeed, as to
give to Johnny Rebs a very high rating among
combat soldiers of all time.

See W. Amann (ed.), *Personnel of Civil War* (1961), especially I, 173 ff.; M. Boatner, *Civil War Dictionary*
(1959), particularly "Organizations," "Armies," and
"Corps"; E. J. Warner, *Generals in Gray* (1959), especially introduction; and B. I. Wiley, *Life of Johnny Reb*
(1943), and *They Who Fought Here* (1959).

BELL I. WILEY
Emory University

CONFEDERATE CABINET. Although they generally followed federal precedents in developing
a cabinet system, the Confederacy's founders made
several innovations in the administrative power
structure. Disliking the paternalistic tendencies
implicit in the federal government's Interior Department, the Confederate lawmakers deleted that
agency from their organizational setup. This move
abolished the post of secretary of the interior and
reduced the number of cabinet officers from seven
to six. The Confederates also upgraded the status
of the attorney general by establishing the Department of Justice under his direction, a step that
the federal government would later emulate in
1870. Acting in yet another area, the southerners
experimented with the practice (derived from the
English Parliament) of allowing members of Congress to hold seats in the cabinet as well. This
practice was used extensively during the first
months of the new regime but was prohibited
with the ratification of the Confederacy's permanent constitution later in 1861. Even so, traces of
this experiment persisted in a constitutional provision permitting cabinet members to participate
in congressional debates. House or Senate approval was a prerequisite for such participation,
however, and the two houses repeatedly refused
to take the necessary action. Instead, the traditional separation of powers held firm.

The turmoil of the war years found expression
in the Confederate cabinet's rapid personnel turnover. A total of 17 individuals, including three *ad
interim* appointments, held cabinet posts at one
time or another. Disagreements with President
Jefferson Davis figured in several of the resigna-
tions, and other men left because of congressional
hostility, declining health, or ambitions for more
glamorous careers on the battlefield or in the legislative halls. In spite of these pressures, cabinet
members performed their duties competently as a
rule, and several served with distinction. The
South's innovative secretary of the navy, STEPHEN
R. MALLORY, held office throughout the war, as
did efficient Postmaster General JOHN H. REAGAN.
JUDAH P. BENJAMIN, the ablest of Davis' confi-
dants, served successively as attorney general,

CONFEDERATE CABINET MEMBERS

Position	Member	Term
Attorney General	Judah P. Benjamin (La.)	Feb. 25, 1861–Nov. 21, 1861
	Thomas Bragg (N.C.)	Nov. 21, 1861–March 18, 1862
	Thomas H. Watts (Ala.)	March 18, 1862–Oct. 1, 1863
	Wade Keyes (Ala.) *ad int.*	Oct. 1, 1863–Jan. 2, 1864
	George Davis (N.C.)	Jan. 2, 1864–end of war
Secretary of War	Leroy P. Walker (Ala.)	Feb. 21, 1861–Sept. 17, 1861
	Judah P. Benjamin (La.)	Sept. 17, 1861–Nov. 21, 1861 (acting)
		Nov. 21, 1861–March 18, 1862
	George W. Randolph (Va.)	March 18, 1862–Nov. 17, 1862
	Gustavus W. Smith (Ky.) *ad int.*	Nov. 17, 1862–Nov. 21, 1862
	James A. Seddon (Va.)	Nov. 21, 1862–Feb. 6, 1865
	John C. Breckinridge (Ky.)	Feb. 6, 1865–end of war
Secretary of State	Robert Toombs (Ga.)	Feb. 21, 1861–July 25, 1861
	Robert M. T. Hunter (Va.)	July 25, 1861–Feb. 1, 1862
	William M. Browne (Ga.) *ad int.*	Feb. 1, 1862–March 18, 1862
	Judah P. Benjamin (La.)	March 18, 1862–end of war
Secretary of the Treasury	Christopher G. Memminger (S.C.)	Feb. 21, 1861–July 18, 1864
	George A. Trenholm (S.C.)	July 18, 1864–end of war
Secretary of the Navy	Stephen R. Mallory (Fla.)	March 4, 1861–end of war
Postmaster General	John H. Reagan (Tex.)	March 6, 1861–end of war

secretary of war, and secretary of state. Treasury Secretary CHRISTOPHER G. MEMMINGER and War Secretary JAMES A. SEDDON also performed creditably in difficult situations.

Beyond this employment of administrative talents, President Davis utilized his cabinet in other ways as well. Allocating the various posts among the states, for example, he took advantage of the cabinet's patronage opportunities to balance competing geographical and political interests. He successfully blunted criticisms of his administration on several occasions with timely cabinet appointments and dismissals. Perhaps most important, Davis met with his cabinet on a regular basis and frequently followed its advice. Still, these efforts failed to achieve victory, and the question remains of whether a different president, with a different cabinet, could have attained more successful results.

See R. W. Patrick, *Davis and His Cabinet* (1944), authoritative account; B. I. Wiley, *Road to Appomattox* (1956); and B. J. Hendrick, *Statesmen of the Lost Cause* (1939), informative biographical sketches.

JAMES T. MOORE
Virginia Commonwealth University

CONFEDERATE CAVALRY

CONFEDERATE CAVALRY was the most glamorous and successful branch of the Confederate armies. Effectively organized and led by a host of able and colorful leaders, it helped to revolutionize cavalry tactics and dominated its northern counterpart during the early years of the war. With infantry rifle power and lack of cavalry training militating against the effective use of horse soldiers in their classic role as a shock force, the Confederacy emphasized mobility by using its cavalry for screening, reconnaissance, and the novel strategic raid behind enemy lines. Since these tasks often involved dismounted fighting, cavalrymen generally discarded the saber in favor of firearms and were often accompanied by artillery. Such innovations, as well as familiarity with horses and terrain and some exceptional leadership, enabled Confederate cavalry consistently to defeat its poorly led, badly organized, and untrained Union opponents during the first two years of the war.

After mid-1863, however, Union cavalry began to show the results of experience, better organization, and the rise of capable leaders. At the same time, shortages of horses, equipment, and provisions immobilized large portions of the southern mounted forces. Coupled with cavalry's mobility, independent status, and poor discipline, these factors also led to extensive foraging and outright robbery in the countryside. The resultant lowering of civilian morale and cavalry reputation was only reinforced by the depredations of guerrillas and partisan rangers claiming to be cavalry.

Confederate problems were compounded by the death of eastern cavalry leader J. E. B. STUART in 1864 and by strategic and personality conflicts in the West, which led to dispersion and misuse of mounted forces and to occasional refusal by individual cavalry leaders to work with each other or follow orders. Some critics also claim that the colorful raids had little strategic value and actually did more harm than good by depriving the armies of badly needed screening and immediate reconnaissance; others argue, to the contrary, that such screening and reconnaissance should have been further sacrificed in order to launch more raids on overextended enemy lines. Despite the problems, Confederate cavalry continued to score successes throughout the war and to hamper many northern operations. By 1865, however, the combination of superior Union force and southern problems led to its defeat along with the rest of the Confederate armies.

See biographies of specific leaders, battle studies, and the following: T. F. Miller, *Photographic History of the Civil War* (1911), IV; G. C. Evans, *Confederate Military History* (1899); R. U. Johnson and C. C. Buel (eds.), *Battles and Leaders* (1884–87); *Official Records, Armies* (1880–1901); *Southern Historical Society Papers*; D. S. Freeman, *Lee's Lieutenants* (1942–44); E. J. Warner, *Generals in Gray* (1959); T. L. Connelly, *Army of Tennessee* (1967–71); B. I. Wiley, *Life of Johnny Reb* (1943); S. B. Oates, *Confederate Cavalry West of River* (1961); A. Gray, *Cavalry Tactics* (1910); G. F. R. Henderson, *Science of War* (1913); A. G. Brackett, *History of U.S. Cavalry* (1865); J. Wheeler, *Cavalry Tactics* (1863); R. S. Brownlee, *Gray Ghosts* (1958); J. P. Dyer, *Journal of Southern History* (Feb., 1942); C. W. Ramsdell, *American Historical Review* (July, 1930); G. McWhiney, *Civil War History* (March, 1965); S. Z. Starr, *Civil War History* (June, 1965); S. R. Gleaves, *Journal of U.S. Cavalry Association* (1907); and J. Luvaas, *Civil War Times Illustrated* (Jan., 1968). Unfortunately, no comprehensive critical study of Confederate cavalry is available.

MARK A. STOLER
University of Vermont

CONFEDERATE CONGRESS. To have a government operating by the time of Abraham Lincoln's inauguration, the Confederate provisional constitution stipulated that "all legislative powers herein delegated shall be vested in this Congress now assembled." The MONTGOMERY CONVENTION thus became the Provisional Congress. This body consisted of one chamber, with members voting by states. The permanent CONFEDERATE CONSTITUTION established a bicameral Congress almost identical to that of the United States, even retaining the federal ratio. As new states joined, Congress assigned them their proportionate representation.

The Confederate legislative branch contained several innovations. The provisional constitution permitted plural federal officeholding, though its successor limited this to allowing Congress, at its discretion, to let its members also serve as executive department heads. Congress' fiscal powers were restricted in that virtually all appropriations had to be at specific requests by the president, who also had item veto of such bills; and it could not levy a protective tariff or appropriate money for internal improvements. It could now levy an export duty by a two-thirds vote of both houses. The role of Congress in the amending process was somewhat reduced.

Elections to the First Congress were held on November 6, 1861, and generally the states used their old electoral procedures. Campaigning was slight and almost devoid of issues, and even having been a Democrat and/or a secessionist gave a candidate a remarkably slight advantage. The Provisional Congress was chiefly a register of the president's wishes, and the success of its members in securing reelection bespoke widespread satisfaction with the state of affairs.

The legislation of Congress took its nature from the course of the war. At first, moderation was the rule both in finance and military preparation, and the chief attention was on establishing routine procedures of government. After Lincoln's call for volunteers in April, 1861, the army needed increasing amounts of men and equipment, the treasury demanded more money, and the home front had to be mobilized for war. By mid-1863 Congress and the Jefferson Davis administration had geared the Confederacy to gigantic bond issues, taxing agriculture in kind, fiat money and its gradual repudiation, conscription, impressment of military supplies, building railroads, subsidizing manufacturing, and suspending the writ of habeas corpus.

The second elections occurred during the summer of 1863, and now privation and war-weariness provoked heated campaigning on the legislation of Congress and the conduct of the war. The stronger states' rights sentiment in the Second Congress made that body somewhat less compliant, but the solid support of congressmen from occupied and threatened districts enabled the president to continue his dominance of Congress. By 1864, however, the limits of legislation according to nineteenth-century concepts had almost been reached, and Congress was unable to devise any major new program and was almost as hard pressed to extend old ones. Congress' chief controversies with the administration toward the last were over the refusal of Congress to end remaining military exemptions, its attacks on the cabinet, and its insistence that ROBERT E. LEE be made general-in-chief.

See *Journal of Congress of Confederate States* (1904–05); *Southern Historical Society Papers* (1923–59), XLIV–LII; T. B. Alexander and R. E. Beringer, *Anatomy of Confederate Congress* (1972); W. B. Yearns, *Confederate Congress* (1960); J. B. Robbins, "Confederate Nationalism" (Ph.D. dissertation, Rice University, 1964); R. E. Beringer, "Political Factionalism in Confederate Congress" (Ph.D. dissertation, Northwestern University, 1966); and W. B. Yearns and E. J. Warner, *Confederate Congressmen* (1975).

W. BUCK YEARNS
Wake Forest University

CONFEDERATE CONSCRIPTION. At the outbreak of the Civil War, the Confederate government sought to meet its troop needs through voluntary enlistments. It was soon apparent, however, that more drastic methods were needed. On April 16, 1862, a conscription measure calling for three years' service for all able-bodied white males between the ages of eighteen and thirty-five was adopted. In September the age limit was extended to forty-five. A grace period of 30 days was permitted for those eligible for the draft to form volunteer companies, after which they were required to report.

Following enrollment, the men were sent to a "camp of instruction" for physical examinations and, if found acceptable, basic training. When sent to the front, the draftees were usually assigned as replacements in regiments from their own states, rather than formed into new units. No bounties were offered to promote volunteering, but draftees were permitted to hire substitutes to serve in their place. Substitutes had to be ineligible for the draft.

The purpose of substitution was to soften the impact of an unpopular measure and permit those engaged in critical occupations to stay on the job. Abuses occurred, however, and substitution was abolished in December, 1863. But the major flaw in Confederate conscription was an extensive system of occupational exemptions. Five days after adopting the original law, Congress passed a measure exempting government workers, railroad employees, telegraph workers, printers, druggists, and those engaged in many lesser occupations. More categories were added in October, 1862. Abuses were widespread under the law, and, although the list was cut in half in 1864, occupational exemptions continued throughout the war. Slave conscription was approved in March, 1865, but the war ended before any entered combat.

Opposition to the draft was strong. Governors ZEB VANCE of North Carolina and JOE BROWN of Georgia and Vice-President ALEXANDER H. STEPHENS argued that it was unconstitutional, unnecessary, and a violation of the states' rights principle. One device used by state judges hostile to conscription was to free draftees through habeas corpus proceedings. Despite weaknesses, abuses, and opposition, Confederate conscription succeeded in keeping an army in the field, no easy task in the circumstances. Although only 82,000 men were actually drafted, several hundreds of thousands more volunteered under the stimulus of the draft.

See A. B. Moore, *Conscription and Conflict* (1924); M. F. Mitchell, *Legal Aspects of Conscription* (1965), excellent North Carolina study; and *Official Records, Armies*, Ser. 4, Vol. II.

EUGENE C. MURDOCK
Marietta College

CONFEDERATE CONSTITUTION. On February 8, 1861, the Provisional Congress of the Confederacy, representing the seceded states of South Carolina, Georgia, Florida, Alabama, Mississippi, and Louisiana, adopted a provisional constitution. From February 28 to March 11, the delegates of the Provisional Congress conducted the affairs of state by morning and acted as members of the constitutional convention by evening. On March 11, the permanent constitution was adopted after considerable debate by the delegates of the above-mentioned states and Texas. The document was unanimously and speedily ratified by the seven states by April 22, even though approval of only five states was required. Final ratification of all Confederate states occurred when the Upper South state of Tennessee accepted it on August 1. Later in the year unorthodox measures gave it nominal ratification in the border states of Kentucky and Missouri.

The convention's greatest struggle was between the conservatives represented by ALEXANDER H. STEPHENS, who wanted an instrument similar to the U.S. Constitution, and the radicals led by ROBERT BARNWELL RHETT, who favored a stronger states' rights document. The moderating influence was offered by HOWELL COBB, the convention's president. The final document more closely resembled the U.S. Constitution but with some significant departures. Among other things, states were specifically declared to be sovereign, the general welfare clause was omitted, a protective tariff was outlawed, slavery was protected, internal improvement funding was prohibited, and the Confederate president was limited to a single term of six years.

See A. H. Stephens Papers, Library of Congress; R. B. Rhett Papers, University of South Carolina and University of North Carolina; C. R. Lee, Jr., *Confederate Constitutions* (1963); W. B. Yearns, *Confederate Congress* (1960); A. J. Cobb, *Georgia Historical Quarterly* (June, 1921); and W. G. McCabe, *Southern Historical Society Papers* (Sept., 1916).

JAMES W. POHL
Southwest Texas State University

CONFEDERATE CORRUPTION. A brief article can only point to where corruption seems to have existed, for the topic remains largely unexplored. The references listed below contain mostly hints and allusions, not full or even partial treatments. Because of the paucity of information it is impossible to discuss the scale, to be specific about the men or money, or to assess the general influence of what Jefferson Davis termed the "love of lucre."

One partial exception to that generalization does exist. Undoubtedly corruption flourished in the cotton trade of the lower Mississippi Valley. The invading Union forces wanted cotton, and cotton made its way to Union lines despite Confederate regulations outlawing the trade. Private citizens disregarded government policy with impunity; additionally, Confederate officials accepted bribes to let cotton marked for destruction fall into Union hands. But even here precise statements are difficult because some trade had the blessing or the acquiescence of Confederate authorities (CONFEDERATE COTTON).

Other areas that knew corruption are presently enveloped by murkiness. A partial list includes: commodity speculation and hoarding; immense and illegal profits made from BLOCKADE-RUNNING (allegedly even by the Charleston company that provided the last secretary of the treasury); fraud in the commissary and quartermaster departments of the army; embezzlement of government money by government employees; and dishonesty in the criminal justice system.

See C. Eaton, *History of Southern Confederacy* (1954); A. Nevins, *War for Union* (1971), III; and W. M. Robinson, *Justice in Grey* (1941). J. K. Bettersworth, *Confederate Mississippi* (1943); and L. H. Johnson, *Red River Campaign* (1958), have good accounts of cotton trade.

WILLIAM J. COOPER, JR.
Louisiana State University

CONFEDERATE COTTON was potentially a powerful means of securing southern independence, but Confederate cotton policy was a series of miscalculations from first to last. The greatest mistake was the belief that by February, 1862, at the latest, Britain would be forced to break the

Union BLOCKADE to get cotton. Secretary of the Treasury C. G. MEMMINGER, among others, was a victim of this delusion and hence saw no need for the government to acquire cotton. In March, 1862, the Royal Navy not having arrived, Memminger reversed himself and began to buy cotton. To the treasury cotton was valued as a means of supporting government credit, whereas the War and Navy departments wanted to exchange it for urgently needed supplies. All bought cotton in large quantities, often in competition with one another, as well as with the states and private citizens, thus driving up prices. There was also a lack of coordination in transportation and marketing. By November, 1863, the treasury had acquired 417,000 bales but had exported only 574. The principal shipments abroad, about which Memminger knew nothing, were made by the military departments. Memminger raised limited funds abroad by hypothecating cotton that remained in the Confederacy, but his policy did little to prop tottering southern finances.

To facilitate exports, Congress (February 6, 1864) required all ships to reserve 50 percent of their cargo space for government commodities. As the blockade tightened, both Treasury and War departments engaged in trade with the enemy, exchanging cotton for war matériel. By November, 1864, only one-fourth (110,000 bales) of the cotton bought by the Treasury Department had been put to any use. It is not known how much was bought and used by the War and Navy departments, but it surely could not have been more than twice that disposed of by the treasury. Inasmuch as 6.8 million bales were grown in 1861–1864, and about 2 million remained late in 1864, obviously the Confederacy made poor use of its only great natural resource.

See R. Thian (comp.), Confederate Treasury Department Correspondence, and Record Group 56, National Archives; and R. C. Todd, *Confederate Finance* (1954).

LUDWELL H. JOHNSON III
College of William and Mary

CONFEDERATE DEBT. See DEBTS OF SOUTHERN STATES

CONFEDERATE DESERTION was a major problem during the war. The incomplete totals—1,028 officers and 103,400 enlisted men—are shocking by modern standards, but were comparable with Union desertion. Of these, approximately 21,056 were returned to military control, and the remainder were permanently lost to the already outnumbered Confederate army. Desertion became a matter of concern in 1862. The increase in the number of deserters led to harsh measures in 1863 and 1864, which checked the rise. With the decline in Confederate fortunes in 1864, a flood of desertions began in the fall and continued to the end of the war. There were many reasons for this large number of deserters. The inadequate food, clothing, pay, and equipment resulted in low morale. There was homesickness and, as conditions deteriorated, a growing concern by the soldiers for their families. To many the conflict seemed a rich man's war and a poor man's fight. CONFEDERATE CONSCRIPTION brought many men into the army who were ignorant of the causes of the war or who lacked sympathy with secession. In the closing years of the war the declining hope for victory led many to return home without permission. The loss of manpower to the army was serious, but of almost equal impact was the number of men diverted in attempts to recapture deserters. The lawlessness of many deserters resulted in clashes with Confederate troops and added suffering for the civilian population. Large groups of deserters concentrated in the mountains, swamps, and remote areas throughout the South. So common was the crime that it lost much of its stigma, making it more difficult to recapture deserters.

See E. Lonn, *Desertion During Civil War* (1928); *Official Records, Armies*, scattered references; and *House Executive Documents*, 39th Cong., 1st Sess., No. 1, Vol. IV, Pt. 1.

RICHARD P. WEINERT, JR.
U.S. Army Training and Doctrine Command

CONFEDERATE DIPLOMACY was designed to gain foreign recognition of Confederate independence and establish normal trade relations. Following the opening of hostilities, it sought to induce foreign powers to break the federal blockade and furnish war matériel. This policy, conceived and executed by President Jefferson Davis and his three secretaries of state, ROBERT TOOMBS, R. M. T. HUNTER, and JUDAH P. BENJAMIN, was frustrated by poor communications, inept agents abroad, and adverse fortunes of war.

Before hostilities, Toombs announced the Confederacy's adherence to the 1856 Paris Declaration, hoping to forestall a federal blockade. Using the only international leverage he possessed, he offered to Mexico and Spain (Cuba) mutual territorial integrity and friendship based upon common institutions (peonage and slavery) and to England and France, relying on their need for cotton, preferential trade treaties. Benjamin used CON-

FEDERATE COTTON as bait for recognition and as enticement for European powers to force the blockade even at risk of war with the United States. "King Cotton diplomacy" failed because oversupply fed European machines until the winter of 1862–1863. As U. S. Grant stood before Richmond, Benjamin offered the ultimate southern sacrifice: the Kenner mission (January, 1865) would bargain abolition for recognition. Confederate diplomacy had followed the fortunes of southern arms.

Efforts at southern diplomacy failed because of overwhelming odds. England and France could recognize the Confederate States of America only at the risk of war, but even as their cotton shortages became critical, the Polish Insurrection (1863) and the Danish War (1864) made this unthinkable. Having recently abolished slavery in their colonies, the British and French public would not tolerate its support in America. Finally, astute United States diplomacy and intelligence sources effectively countered each southern move. Confederate Commissioners W. L. YANCEY, P. A. ROST, and A. D. MANN managed informal interviews with Lord John Russell in London and Duke Morny in Paris, without result. Although the Confederacy maintained agents in Brussels, Madrid, and Vatican City, Benjamin's efforts centered on London and Paris. JAMES MASON's unsuccessful London mission ended in the fall of 1863. JOHN SLIDELL's more apparent success in Paris resulted in several interviews with Napoleon III and close foreign ministry contacts. Yet his mission also failed.

Several early wartime events encouraged southerners. Anglo-French neutrality proclamations (May and June, 1861) extended belligerent rights to southern ships in their ports. The TRENT AFFAIR (November, 1861) brought England and the United States close to war. The *Florida* and *Alabama* successes further strained English–United States relations. Napoleon III twice (October, 1862, and January, 1863) suggested mediation. In the spring of 1863, William S. Lindsay and John A. Roebuck reported in the House of Commons that Napoleon would recognize the Confederacy if England would, and the United States threatened to break relations with France. But Confederate diplomacy had not created these opportunities; and it failed to exploit them. Slidell accomplished little else than negotiating the ERLANGER LOAN and contracting for construction of six ships in France. Britain never seriously considered intervening in America after Antietam (September, 1862), nor did France after Gettysburg and Vicksburg (July, 1863). Slidell misinterpreted the international implications of Napoleon's intervention in Mexico, expecting closer relations with the Confederacy. Instead, France was forced to exchange mutual neutralities with the United States. Southern diplomacy was hampered by its agents' ineptitude in Europe and defeated by the fortunes of war. Foreign recognition of Confederate independence was lost not in London or Paris, but on the battlefield.

See *Official Records, Navies*, Ser. 2, Vol. III, for documents; F. L. Owsley, *King Cotton Diplomacy* (1959); J. M. Callahan, *Diplomatic History of Southern Confederacy* (1901); E. D. Adams, *Great Britain and American Civil War* (1924); L. M. Case and W. F. Spencer, *U.S. and France: Civil War Diplomacy* (1970); K. A. Hanna, *Journal of Southern History* (Feb., 1954); H. Blumenthal, *Journal of Southern History* (May, 1966); and J. F. Gentry, *Journal of Southern History* (May, 1970).

WARREN F. SPENCER
University of Georgia

CONFEDERATE ECONOMY initially reflected that of the Old South. It primarily produced export staples; and foodstuffs, industry, mining, transportation, import-export business, merchandising, and finance occupied a secondary place. The elements of the economy changed rapidly, however, because of wartime demands and the creeping strangulation of the federal BLOCKADE.

Agricultural conversion was the most successful modification of the Confederate economy. The annual output of cotton dropped from 4.5 million bales in 1861 to 300,000 in 1864, primarily to foster the production of corn, vegetables, and hogs. The tax in kind on these foodstuffs provided extensive rations and was widely credited with keeping the armies in the field. Much of the cotton crop was obtained by the government and used to finance the indispensable importation program (CONFEDERATE COTTON). Nonagricultural production increased also. Iron and textile manufacturing and whiskey distilling, already well established, expanded. Clothing shops, ordnance manufacture, and the mining of such ores as salt and saltpeter (virtually nonexistent industries at the start of the war) burgeoned. Much of this expansion was the result of state socialism.

Transportation disintegrated as the war progressed. Although two crippling gaps in the railroad network were closed, the RAILROADS lost rolling stock and track steadily because industry was unable to replace them and because the Union concentrated on destroying railroads. Steamboat transportation and roads also deteriorated.

Overseas trade management was of vital concern. Although there was considerable interest early in the war in the embargo of cotton in an attempt to force recognition and intervention, the government eventually began to export cotton to buy supplies and blockade-runners. The government also regulated cotton transactions in an attempt to entice foreign shippers to bring in needed articles.

The most ineffective aspect of the economy was CONFEDERATE FINANCE. Cheap money and loans were used in a disproportionate ratio to tax revenues. The government at all levels cranked out paper money at an increasingly reckless rate, and well before the war ended, it was virtually worthless. The funded debt (bonds) rose to an estimated $712 million by 1865. Taxes were imposed by the Confederacy, but Confederate politicians were timid and there were constitutional impediments to tapping the two greatest sources of wealth: land and slaves. When taxes were levied, it was a case of too little and too late, either to curb inflation or to support the government. The effects of scarcity, cheap money, and economic dislocation eroded the Confederacy's social fabric, as inflation, hoarding, and speculation fed on each other, overwhelming such patriotic responses as contributions to the government and the creation of ersatz. Soaring prices outdistanced wages and salaries, causing unrest, particularly in urban areas, where civilian dependents were concentrated. Near the end of the war many areas of the Confederacy had lapsed into a barter economy.

See RG 56, Archives of Confederate Treasury Department, National Archives; RG 109, War Department Collection of Confederate Records, National Archives; R. C. Todd, *Confederate Finance* (1954); J. C. Schwab, *Confederate States of America* (1901); E. M. Coulter, *Confederate States of America* (1950); R. D. Goff, *Confederate Supply* (1969); C. Eaton, *Southern Confederacy* (1954); R. C. Black, *Railroads of Confederacy* (1952); P. Gates, *Agriculture and Civil War* (1965); C. W. Ramsdell, *Behind the Lines* (1944); F. E. Vandiver, *Ploughshares into Swords* (1952); C. H. Wesley, *Collapse of Confederacy* (1937); E. M. Coulter, *Agricultural History* (Jan., 1927); R. W. Donnelly, *Civil War History* (Dec., 1955; Dec., 1959); L. B. Hill, *Southern Sketches* (1936); E. M. Lerner, *Journal of Political Economy* (Dec., 1954; Feb., 1955); C. W. Ramsdell, *Mississippi Valley Historical Review* (Dec., 1921); J. L. Sellers, *American Historical Review* (Jan., 1925), and *Mississippi Valley Historical Review* (Sept., 1927); H. A. Trexler, *Mississippi Valley Historical Review* (Sept., 1940); E. Y. Webb, *North Carolina Historical Review* (April, 1937); and G. Wright, *Journal of Southern History* (May, 1941).

RICHARD D. GOFF
Eastern Michigan University

CONFEDERATE EXPATRIATES. See EXPA-
TRIATES, CONFEDERATE

CONFEDERATE FINANCE. In its extraordinary
straits for money, the Confederate States of America resorted to every expedient known to finance.
Federal specie located in mints and customhouses of the South was confiscated; property of
alien enemies was sequestered and military supplies were impressed; duties were placed on exports and imports; direct taxes were levied; donations were cheerfully accepted; and treasury notes
flooded the market while loans were floated in an
attempt to stabilize the currency and offer a basis
for foreign exchange. Although most of these expedients were used simultaneously, emphasis
originally was placed on loans; later treasury notes
were emphasized, and then, perhaps too late, taxes were stressed. Throughout its existence, the
Confederacy floated 14 loans. These were specie
loans, produce loans, and funding loans and netted $712,046,420.

At an early date, Congress adopted a scheme of
finance based on the issue of treasury notes. According to Secretary of the Treasury CHRISTO-
PHER G. MEMMINGER, change in the financial
policy resulted from three factors: need for a free-
circulating medium of exchange; lack of funds
during the interim incident to setting up machinery for collecting taxes and floating additional
loans; and inability of loans and taxes to meet the
mounting expenditures of a country at war.

Treasury notes were of two classes, interest
bearing and noninterest bearing; the latter became the general circulating currency of the Confederacy, though the government persistently refused to adopt a "legal tender." As treasury notes
increased in volume, the Confederate Congress
took measures to prevent inflation, but the measures were always too little or too late. Evils of an
inflated currency multiplied due to the amount of
notes issued by states, private corporations, and
individuals. Inflation was also aggravated by
counterfeit money and the constant infiltration of
federal "greenbacks." The amount of treasury notes
issued was $1,554,087,354, approximately one-half
the funds raised by the Confederacy.

Memminger assumed from the beginning that
import and export duties would furnish the basis
for a substantial revenue, but in this he erred. Receipts from import duties were less than $3.5 mil-
lion, and export duties on cotton totaled only
$39,068 (CONFEDERATE COTTON).

During the first two years of the Confederacy,
direct taxes, although recommended frequently
by Memminger, were almost completely neglected by Congress, which thought the war would be
of short duration and revenue from duties would
more than supply the government's needs. As it
was, war continued, expenditures mounted, and
the federal blockade greatly diminished income
from duties. As a result, Congress gradually
changed its thinking and placed more emphasis
on taxes in an effort to create a sound foundation
for its financial policy. It came to believe that, by
laying a direct tax, adequate funds would be raised
to pay the principal and interest on loans and, by
making the tax payable in treasury notes, the desirability of notes as a currency would be increased and their redundancy decreased. The tax
legislation of Congress, however, failed to achieve
the desirable objectives expected of it, netting
$203,976,265.

As the financial needs of the government increased, it became necessary to supplement them
by confiscating property of alien enemies, im-
pressing military and naval supplies held by citizens of the Confederacy, and accepting donations
made by numerous individuals, institutions, and
corporations. Receipts from seizures and donations totaled $514,379,376.

By these various means the Confederacy raised
approximately $2,988,028,483 as it vainly endeav-
ored to meet its financial obligations at home and
abroad. That it failed is a well-known fact; whether it could have improved its financial status is a
debatable question. Nevertheless, it appears that
the financial embarrassment of the Confederacy
might have been reduced had Congress adopted
a comprehensive tax plan earlier, instituted a central banking system, proclaimed a legal tender
and at the same time controlled its own issuance
of paper money while forbidding that of public
and private corporations and individuals, and acquired ownership of all cotton at an early date and
immediately shipped it abroad on government account.

These things had all been discussed by Secretary Memminger, by Congress, and by the press;
however, the prevailing "climate of opinion" ruled
against their acceptance. But even had these suggestions been carried out, it is still quite improb-
able that *any* measure short of military victory
would have improved to an appreciable degree
the financial status of the Confederate States of
America.

See R. C. Todd, *Confederate Finance* (1954); J. C.
Schwab, *Financial and Industrial History* (1901); E. M.
Lerner, *Journal of Political Economy* (Dec., 1954); J. L.
Sellers, *American Historical Review* (Jan., 1925); R. C.
Todd, *Georgia Review* (Winter, 1958), and *North Caro-
lina Historical Review* (Jan., 1950); R. P. Thian Collec-

tion, Duke University Library; RG 56, Archives of Confederate Treasury Department, National Archives; and RG 109, War Department Collection of Confederate Records, National Archives.

RICHARD C. TODD
East Carolina University

CONFEDERATE FLAGS. Like other new nations, the Confederacy had difficulty devising its national flag. On February 9, 1861, Congress appointed a committee to select a design. Suggestions began pouring in, and on March 4 Chairman W. P. Miles reported. The report was never adopted, but so great was the desire to have a national flag waving during Abraham Lincoln's inauguration that a model was hastily prepared and on the same day the Stars and Bars flew over the capitol at Montgomery, Ala.

This flag's similarity to the Stars and Stripes, however, brought confusion in battle, notably at first Manassas, and Congress renewed its search. Meanwhile Generals P. G. T. BEAUREGARD, JOSEPH E. JOHNSTON, and Gustavus W. Smith conferred and selected as their battle flag the design that Miles had originally urged on Congress. The War Department endorsed it, and it became the unofficial battle flag. The navy used a rectangular version, which could be flown sideways as a sign of distress.

For a year and a half under the permanent government a joint committee on flag and seal received new models from a populace now committed to radical innovation. After a sharp, final debate, the Congress on May 1, 1863, gave the Confederacy its first official flag. Armies in the field, however, continued to use the battle flag as well.

But in all but the stiffest breeze the long official flag hung limply with little but its white showing. It was also difficult to see, and it soiled easily, so Congress began its search once again. The design adopted on March 4, 1865, differed little from its predecessor; but its squarer shape, the outer red bar, and the enlarged battle flag union probably met the objections to the old flag (see frontispiece).

See E. Coulter, *Georgia Historical Quarterly* (Sept., 1953); W. L. Cabell, *Southern Historical Society Papers* (1903); W. P. Miles Papers, University of North Carolina, Chapel Hill; *Journal of Congress of Confederate States* (1904–05); and J. M. Matthews (ed.), *Statutes at Large of Confederate States of America* (1862–64).

W. BUCK YEARNS
Wake Forest University

CONFEDERATE GUERRILLAS, also known as "bushwackers," were relatively small groups of prosouthern military bands, whose operations were confined almost entirely to the western theater, particularly along the western and northern boundaries between Texas and Missouri. Confederate guerrillas fought and terrorized in this area throughout the Civil War. Many had been involved in the violent border clashes, beginning in 1855, between Kansas and Missouri.

Confederate guerrillas are unique in the military history of the Civil War, both in their tactical methods and in the limited scope of their objectives. Unlike the more organized larger armies, guerrillas often recognized no battle lines, and their method of warfare relied heavily upon ambush, isolated attack, arson, and ravage. Their local reputation for plunder and inspiring terror was immense. The most notorious of the Confederate bushwackers was WILLIAM C. QUANTRILL, whose attack on Lawrence, Kan. (August 21, 1863), with 450 guerrillas, was the largest attack of its kind during the war. Other prominent Confederate raiding leaders included JOHN S. MOSBY (in northern Virginia), William C. Anderson, STERLING PRICE, and George Todd. Frank and Jesse James began their careers as bushwackers.

In many ways, the Confederate guerrilla struck a colorful pose. His uniform—distinguished primarily by the "guerrilla shirt," a low-cut garment ending in ruffles—left a generous capacity for ammunition and as many as eight pistols. Guerrillas were known, however, to wear captured Union uniforms and, dressed as such, were able to fall upon Union soldiers unaware of the deception. Despite their reputation for brutality, especially among Kansans, Confederate guerrillas were generally respected as superb marksmen and horsemen.

See R. S. Brownlee, *Gray Ghosts* (1958), concise background; A. Castel, *American Heritage* (Oct., 1960); W. E. Connelly, *Quantrill* (1910); and J. Viles, *Missouri Historical Review* (Oct., 1907).

KENNETH R. CALLAHAN
John Carroll University

CONFEDERATE IRONCLADS. To combat an established U.S. Navy, the Confederacy built ironclad warships. The prototype was the CSS *Virginia*, featuring an armored casemate with sides inclined to deflect shot. It defeated a squadron of conventional warships in Hampton Roads, Va. (March 8, 1862), then fought a drawn battle with the ironclad USS *Monitor* (MONITOR AND MERRIMACK, BATTLE OF). The *Virginia's* lines, with modification, became the standard of the Confederate ironclad. Builders adapted its model to local conditions in ports like Savannah and Charleston and on rivers like the Yazoo and Tombigbee. Over 30 armored vessels were begun, 22 of which reached completion.

Southerners hoped the ironclads would break the BLOCKADE. But design limitations—low speed, deep draft, and poor maneuverability—forced constructors to plan and build the ships solely for defense. Public pressure for action was continuous, however, and it forced several offensive efforts that ended disastrously. The CSS *Atlanta* sought battle below Savannah, grounded, and was captured. The *Tennessee*, at Mobile, attacked an entire invading fleet, was beaten, and was captured. The *Arkansas* dashed through two U.S. fleets above Vicksburg, then was destroyed when its engines failed above Baton Rouge. Offensive forays off the coasts of North and South Carolina achieved nothing. Because the ironclads did not break the blockade, contemporaries and later students considered them failures. The vessels' designers, however, sought only to defend southern ports and rivers. And the extreme caution the ironclads' presence generated in the minds of Union blockade commanders suggests that they did accomplish their intended purpose.

See J. P. Baxter III, *Introduction of Ironclad Warship* (1933); R. W. Daly, *How Merrimac Won* (1957); V. C. Jones, *Civil War at Sea* (3 vols.; 1960–62); M. Melton, *Confederate Ironclads* (1969); W. N. Still, Jr., *Confederate Shipbuilding* (1969), and *Iron Afloat* (1971); E. W. Fornell, *Civil War History* (Dec., 1956); W. N. Still, *Journal of Southern History* (Aug., 1961), and *Civil War History* (June, 1963); Dabney Scales Diary and L. M. Goldsborough Papers, Duke University Library; Savannah Squadron Papers, Willink Brothers Papers, and William McBlair Papers, Emory University Library; F. Buchanan Letterbooks, S. R. Mallory Diary, and P. E. Smith Papers, University of North Carolina Library; William W. Hunter Papers and J. Roy Diary, Tulane University Library; and J. K. Mitchell Papers and Minor Family Papers, Virginia Historical Society.

MAURICE MELTON
Emory University

CONFEDERATE JUDICIAL SYSTEM, as estab-
lished under both the provisional and permanent Confederate constitutions, provided for a supreme court, a system of district courts, and such inferior courts as Congress might establish. The supreme court was to have had appellate jurisdiction in cases that arose in state courts. Owing probably to the southerners' fear of centralized government, the supreme court was never established. The district courts were the Confederacy's only active tribunals. The district court system was created by the judiciary act of March 16, 1861. The district courts had the jurisdiction that had

been vested in both the district and circuit courts of the United States. Each state (as well as the Confederate territory of Arizona) was divided into two or more districts. Judges held office for good behavior and designated the time and place at which their courts would meet. In most instances the personnel of the U.S. district courts continued to function in their old positions under the Confederacy. Cases in progress at the time of secession were continued. Judgments that had been handed down by U.S. courts (except those in favor of the federal government) were enforced. Antebellum decisions were accepted as precedents. Most of the cases handled by the district courts involved writs of habeas corpus, especially from men seeking release from military service, or the sequestration of enemy alien property. Many cases were dealt with in state courts. These courts claimed concurrent jurisdiction in many cases arising under Confederate law. State courts judged the constitutionality of Confederate laws. For example, state courts upheld Confederate conscription acts.

See W. M. Robinson, Jr., *Justice in Grey* (1941), definitive work; W. Grice, *Georgia Historical Quarterly* (June, 1925); R. R. Havins, *Southwestern Historical Quarterly* (Jan., 1940); and Manuscript Records of the Confederate Courts, Federal Records Center, East Point, Ga.

RICHARD M. MCMURRY
Valdosta State College

CONFEDERATE MEDICINE, despite great diffi-
culties, was outstanding. Southern doctors served the home front and about 1 million military personnel. There was little opportunity to train medical officers. Of 115 trained surgeons in the U.S. regular service, only 24 joined the Confederacy. These men composed the nucleus of the Confederate Medical Department. Assisting Samuel P. Moore, Confederate surgeon general, were about 1,000 "surgeons" (majors), 2,000 "assistant surgeons" (captains), and "contract surgeons" (second lieutenants). Each regiment had a surgeon and assistant surgeon. Moore administered the Medical Department, supervised hospitals, regulated duties of personnel, and issued orders and instructions to all medical personnel. Each army corps and military department had a "medical director" under whom served surgeons and "medical purveyors" (procured and issued medical supplies).

Although many young doctors enlisted at the outbreak of war and medical schools were stripped of instructors, trained personnel were always in short supply. The exigencies of war precluded intensive medical training. Medical books were scarce, and prewar publications were extensively used. In May, 1862, Stonewall Jackson set the precedent of treating captured enemy surgeons as neutrals. Both sides soon followed this practice.

Medical supplies were always scarce. Blockade-runners made enormous profits on medicines; quinine cost $100 an ounce! Patriotic women contributed willow bark, brierroot, sage tea, and other home remedies. Quinine and morphine were smuggled across the lines. Since medicines were contraband, Confederate surgeons developed local substitutes. Medical laboratories effectively conducted extensive research in utilization of indigenous plants and native drugs. Such efforts were surprisingly effective; Confederate service surgeon D. J. Roberts noted that many of his colleagues always had an ample supply of the three most important drugs: quinine, morphine, and chloroform. Bandages were supplied by cotton mills and by civilian donations of old bed sheets and other garments. Surgical instruments were brought from home, imported, and manufactured locally. Ambulances ranged from spring vehicles to springless farm wagons.

Some 90,000 men were killed and 226,000 wounded in the Confederate service. Unit commanders' ignorance of normal sanitary precautions contributed to a high incidence of death by disease. About 60,000 died of such common diseases as chronic diarrhea, dysentery, and measles. Many older men became medical liabilities.

Data on Confederate service hospitals are lacking due to the loss of records at the fall of Richmond. There were major installations like Chimborazo and Winder hospitals in Richmond, but contemporary accounts of improvised hospitals in dwellings, sheds, churches, and tents show conclusively the adaptability of Confederate service medical personnel under severe conditions.

See G. W. Adams, *Doctors in Blue* (1952); *Regulations for Army of Confederate States* (1863); *Regulations, Subsistence Department of Confederate States* (1861); *Official Records, Armies*; J. K. Barnes, *Medical and Surgical History of Rebellion* (1870–88); H. H. Cunningham, *Doctors in Gray* (1958); F. H. Hamilton, *Surgical Memoirs* (1870); C. A. Humphreys, *Field, Camp, Hospital and Prison* (1918); and V. Robinson, *White Caps* (1946).

FRANCIS A. LORD
University of South Carolina

CONFEDERATE MORALE rested upon entrenched southern attitudes and yet was bound inextricably to the various and ever-shifting conditions of the Confederacy. Moreover, each rebel harbored personal interests for himself and the Southland, and, with growing frequency as the war progressed, these personal and national interests clashed, compounding the intricacy of Confederate morale.

The southern intellectual and emotional heritage rendered rebel resistance natural, and FT. SUMTER and first BULL RUN infused southerners with mission. Bonds of group and individual loyalty encouraged and sometimes inspired Confederates to forget personal concerns for the attainment of national goals. Confederate military victories through the spring of 1863 justified and reinforced the socially engendered martial esprit. Nonetheless, the course of the war radically changed the focus of concern for many rebels. With loved ones dead and crippled, some in enemy-held territory, and others experiencing devastation of property and facing tangible need, pursuance of the Confederate goal of independence was superseded by more pressing personal concerns. Turning inward, Confederates withheld the prerequisite moral support to the southern cause. With the enveloping military debacle in the last year of the war, fatigued Confederates encountered an increasing number and growing severity of other wartime impositions. Great contention swirled around the conscription, exemption, confiscation, and habeas corpus issues. Frightening scarcity of basic consumer goods, the pervasive economic insecurity, and the ravaged remains of a transportation and communication system seemed epidemic. Rebel leaders in Richmond, state capitals, and the military appeared to fight one another as much as the federal foe. And, manpower: there just was not enough left for Confederate needs of farm, industry, and war. These crippling conditions inexorably eroded morale.

Confederate morale mercurially ran the gamut in the four years stretching between Ft. Sumter and APPOMATTOX. The extent and rapidity of new developments in a society at war made extraordinary material and spiritual demands, and southerners, who for generations had followed a relatively static and relaxed life-style, found the wartime demands onerous and the necessary accommodations difficult, if not impossible. For most Confederates an irreversible denouement of spirit dawned with the beginning of 1865. For the preceding eight months Generals U. S. Grant and W. T. Sherman had imposed the chronic pain of total war on the Confederacy with a persistence that, when taken in conjunction with the lingering array of Confederate problems, laid bare the results—the collapse of Confederate morale and the southern nation.

See M. E. Massey, in A. S. Link and R. W. Patrick (eds.), *Writing Southern History* (1965), best annotated bibliographical essay; F. E. Vandiver, *Tattered Flags* (1970), poignant assessments of morale; A. Nevins, *War for Union* (1971), III, IV; K. M. Stampp, *Southern Road to Appomattox* (1969), subtle psychohistorical analysis; J. C. Andrews, *South Reports Civil War* (1970), morale reflected in Confederate newspapers; W. J. McNeill, "Stress of War" (Ph.D. dissertation, Rice, 1973), effect of federal invasion of Georgia and Carolinas on morale; and S. S. Blosser and C. N. Wilson, *Southern Historical Collection* (1970), guide to manuscript collection at University of North Carolina.

WILLIAM J. MCNEILL
Lee College

CONFEDERATE NAVY. The Confederate navy's chief assets were about a quarter of the U.S. Navy's officers, including such outstanding ones as MATTHEW F. MAURY, FRANKLIN BUCHANAN, and RAPHAEL SEMMES, and an able secretary, STEPHEN R. MALLORY. Since the naval war was largely a coastal and river one for which the U.S. Navy was almost as unprepared, the Union's eventual superiority was due to its greater industrial and maritime resources. The Confederacy's greatest naval victory was the seizure of Norfolk navy yard with the steam frigate *Merrimack*, 2,000 heavy guns, and other stores. But the South could not build marine engines—the *Merrimack*'s repaired engines could barely move it as the ironclad *Virginia*—and most of the South's 22 improvised ironclads, finished or unfinished, were lost with the ports they defended.

The river and coastal war was fought by ships armored with everything from anchor chains to cotton and was supported by fortifications, barricades, shoals, low water, and torpedoes. These infernal machines sank eight armored and 18 unarmored ships and damaged many others. But the number of Union lives lost in taking all of the major southern ports was once put at 3,090, fewer than those killed on either side at Gettysburg. By failing to break the Union's originally largely symbolic BLOCKADE, the Confederate navy may have lost the Confederate states' best chance for foreign recognition. The blockade's "real" economic and military impact remains hard to determine, because of the early embargo on the export of cotton.

Confederate commerce raiders destroyed about 110,000 tons of American merchant shipping; 800,000 tons were sold to foreign flags. This was almost half the American merchant marine. But the South never unleashed those swarms of privateers that had preyed on British shipping in the Revolutionary and 1812 wars (CONFEDERATE PRIVATEERS). The United States had not signed the 1856 declaration outlawing privateering, but the blockade made it too hard to bring prizes into Confederate ports for prize money, and most captured ships were burned at sea. Most of the captures were made by a dozen ships; none of the five major raiders (two of which, the *Florida* and *Alabama*, were commanded by Semmes) were built in the Confederacy.

All but two of the raiders' 261 captures were sailing ships; the raiders combined the range of sail with the speed of steam. Hunting them in the open sea was hopeless. Gold ships were convoyed from Panama, but the Union would not divert others from blockade to convoy or underwrite war risk insurance. The most successful raiders were bought, partly manned, coaled, and repaired in British ports, violations of international law that cost Britain heavily in the *Alabama* cases. The Confederate admirals never had fleets or a chance to win more than the local command of certain port approaches, as the *Virginia* controlled Hampton Roads until its standoff with the *Monitor* (MONITOR AND MERRIMACK, BATTLE OF). Since the raiders also failed to lift the blockade, most Civil War naval histories are written from the standpoint of the Union. Historians of the Confederate navy have been more likely to stress particular campaigns, ships, or commanders.

See J. T. Scharf, *Confederate States Navy* (1887), still standard; P. V. Stern, *Confederate Navy* (1962), fine pictorial; T. H. Wells, *Confederate Navy: Organization* (1971); F. J. Merli, *Great Britain and Confederate Navy* (1970); W. N. Still, *Confederate Shipbuilding* (1969), and *Iron Afloat* (1971); M. F. Perry, *Infernal Machines* (1965); W. M. Robinson, Jr., *Confederate Privateers* (1928); G. W. Delzell, *Flight from Flag* (1943), effects on U.S. shipping; and J. M. Merrill, *Rebel Shore* (1957), or B. Anderson, *By Sea and by River* (1962), limited, but better general work than V. C. Jones, *Civil War at Sea* (1960–62), or H. P. Nash, Jr., *Naval History* (1972).

THEODORE ROPP
Duke University

CONFEDERATE POST OFFICE is perhaps unique in history; it produced a financial profit. Much of its success was due to the efforts of Postmaster JOHN H. REAGAN. In the formation of his cabinet in 1861 President Jefferson Davis offered the postmastership to Reagan, who commented, "I felt that I was to be condemned by the public for incapacity." His first action was to invite many southerners in the post office in Washington, D.C., to leave, bringing "every form" with them. Reagan also organized a school to train postal officials. By June 1, 1861, the post offices of the Confederacy were open for business.

Throughout the spring of 1861 much administrative work was done although stamps were not available until October, leading to the term "the stampless period." On October 16 Reagan sold the first stamp at the Richmond post office. By February, 1862, stamps and machinery had been brought in by ship from England. The first engraved Confederate stamp, a ten-cent blue, appeared early in 1863. Later in 1863 steel plates were prepared. Toward the close of the war, paper shortages caused letter writers to use a variety of materials as stationery. In early 1865, stamps with gum worn off by handling as small change were frequently affixed on envelopes with molasses. The capture of Richmond resulted in the destruction of many post office records, but many papers were recovered and stored in the Division of Rebel Archives of the Department of National Defense.

See J. H. Reagan, *Memoirs* (1906); A. Dietz, *Postal System of C.S.A.* (1929); P. Brannon, *Organization of Confederate Post Office* (1960); W. A. Mitchell, *Confederate Veteran* (Dec., 1914); S. King, *DAR* (1933); P. Dyson, *American Journal of Legal History* (July, 1975); and J. H. Reagan, *Southern Historical Society Papers* (July, 1902).

SAMUEL A. PLEASANTS
Fairleigh Dickinson University

CONFEDERATE PRISONERS OF WAR were

few in number prior to the surrender of Ft. Donelson. Thereafter the northern prison camps saw their Confederate populations increase gradually until a cartel of exchange was signed in July, 1862. Under this agreement Union and Confederate prisoners were exchanged on a one-for-one basis according to rank. The cartel lasted less than six months, however, as each side accused the other of numerous violations. With the cessation of exchange, prisons quickly became overcrowded, new prisons were opened, and soon they too were filled to capacity. Altogether the total number of Confederates in northern prisons reached nearly 215,000. Almost 26,000 of those prisoners died in Union camps with the highest percentage of the deaths occurring in early 1865, when more than 1,000 died each month.

Union prisons were usually military forts, former camps of instruction, or specially built stockades. The prisoners were housed in barracks, except at POINT LOOKOUT, Md., where they were given tents. Officers and enlisted men were sent to different prisons; and although Johnson's Island (Ohio) was the main prison for Confederate officers, Point Lookout was the most populated Union prison, with 20,000 prisoners at one time.

The next largest camps in descending order were Camp Douglas (Ill.), Elmira (N.Y.), Ft. Delaware (Del.), Camp Chase (Ohio), Rock Island (Ill.), and Camp Morton (Ind.).

Not unexpectedly, prisoners were embittered by their confinement. Their food, consisting primarily of bacon or beef, bread, coffee, and rice or hominy, was frequently of a poor quality and was always less than men in the field received. Prison guards were universally regarded as contemptible, unfit, and sadistic. Health facilities were viewed as inadequate. Prison life seemed so dismal. Prisoners reported for daily roll calls, cooked their own meals, and policed their living quarters. They read, wrote, and played cards to pass the time away, but time seemed to stand still. Many became melancholic. They stared blankly and waited, either for exchange or for death.

See *Official Records, Armies*, Ser. 2, Vols. I–VIII; J. G. Barrett (ed.), *Yankee Rebel* (1966); J. W. Minnich, *Inside of Rock Island Prison* (1908); and R. H. Shuffler (ed.), *Adventures of a Prisoner of War* (1964). For the best secondary accounts, see W. B. Hesseltine, *Civil War Prisons* (1930), and J. F. Rhodes, *History of U.S.* (1904), V.

WILLIAM G. EIDSON
Ball State University

CONFEDERATE PRISONS reflected the character of the Confederate government. Created in a makeshift fashion under stress, the prison system never was able to operate efficiently. In this system, some of the most basic assumptions of the antebellum South received their most severe tests—and largely failed. From the capture of the first prisoners the inadequate southern facilities began a decline that inexorably accelerated during the entire war. Although Confederate prison records are incomplete and, in some cases, inaccurate, most authorities still use the figures of James F. Rhodes: of 211,000 Union soldiers captured, approximately 195,000 spent some time in prisons in the Confederacy.

Although LIBBY and BELLE ISLE in Richmond, Va., along with ANDERSONVILLE in Georgia, were probably best publicized for their execrable conditions, most camps were almost uniformly bad. The poor condition of the prisons and the concomitant suffering were not a conscious policy of the Confederate government. Rather, they indicated the enormous administrative problems for which the Confederacy never discovered a solution. As the government disintegrated, the bleak conditions of the camps intensified.

It is remarkable that there were so few mass "great escapes" during the war. There is, for instance, no evidence that any significant number of prisoners in Richmond sought to exploit the unsuccessful KILPATRICK-DAHLGREN RAID. On the other hand, though individual escapes received widespread press coverage in the North, they did not inspire, apparently, large-scale emulation.

There was one positive aspect to Confederate disorganization. Little was done to "brainwash" Union prisoners. In one camp, however, just before the presidential ELECTION OF 1864, there was an elementary effort at psychological warfare. Guards offered prisoners extra rations if they would vote for George B. McClellan over Abraham Lincoln in an unofficial presidential primary in the camp, but the incumbent defeated his military opponent by a more than two-to-one margin.

The Confederate government was not unaided in creating the enormous misery in the prisons. Much of the evil aspects of the camps could have been avoided if it had not been the policy of the northern government to oppose exchanges. Although this policy seems cruel, it was in harmony with overall strategy of total warfare.

In a war that engendered high emotions, no aspect generated the rancor of prisons. In the postwar era veterans from both sides rallied in their former bloody battlegrounds and embraced in nostalgic friendship. There is no record of large-scale reunions in prison camps.

See W. B. Hesseltine, *Civil War Prisons* (1930), best general survey; W. B. Hesseltine (ed.), *Civil War Prisons* (1962), compilation of journal articles from *Civil War History*; O. L. Futch, *History of Andersonville* (1968), for an outstanding example of an individual prison; and F. T. Lord, *Sandlapper* (Aug., 1975), for Camp Sorghum, an interesting example of an obscure prison.

G. WAYNE KING
Francis Marion College

CONFEDERATE PRIVATEERS were formally authorized on April 17, 1861, when President Jefferson Davis invited southerners to serve "in private-armed vessels on the high seas" operating under "letters of marque and reprisal." Davis' invitation to raid the enemy's commerce met an enthusiastic reception, especially in New Orleans and Charleston. By the middle of the year, at least nine privateers had sailed from those two ports alone. The most illustrious of these vessels was Charleston's *Jefferson Davis*, which harassed northern commerce between New England and the West Indies before grounding on August 18, 1861.

The *Jefferson Davis* was a sailing vessel, as were most Confederate privateers. However, some were steamers, such as the *Gordon*, a fast side-wheeler from Charleston that interdicted north-

ern shipping passing through Hatteras Inlet from July, 1861, until a Union naval expedition closed the sally port of Hatteras in September. Steam also propelled the cigar-shaped ram *Manassas*, built as a privateer in New Orleans but commandeered by the Confederate navy during the attempt to break the Union BLOCKADE of the Mississippi in October, 1861. Even more ingenious was the *Pioneer*, variously described as a "submarine propeller" and a "magazine of powder." Intended for privateering, this predecessor to the South's famous SUBMARINE, the *Hunley*, sank outside New Orleans before it could challenge northern merchantmen in the Gulf.

The threat posed by Confederate privateers diminished sharply after the fall of 1861. Neutral Britain and most other European countries had forbidden the outfitting of privateers and the establishment of prize courts on their soil. Thus Confederate privateers could only operate out of southern ports, where the Union blockade increasingly menaced both the captors and their prizes. Moreover, privateering quickly proved far less profitable than BLOCKADE-RUNNING, to which investors began to turn. For these reasons, commissioned ships of the CONFEDERATE NAVY rather than privateers became the instruments by which the Confederacy inflicted heavy damage upon Union maritime commerce after 1861.

See W. M. Robinson, Jr., *Confederate Privateers* (1928), discursive but definitive; *Official Records, Navies*, Ser. 1, Vols. I, IV–VI, Ser. 2, Vols. I–III; and J. T. Scharf, *History of Confederate Navy* (1886, 1969).

KENNETH J. HAGAN
U.S. Naval Academy

CONFEDERATE PROPAGANDA supported the South's foremost diplomatic objective—obtaining recognition from the leading European nations, particularly Great Britain. But overconfidence in the coercive power of King Cotton to achieve this goal delayed the effective implementation of both diplomatic and propaganda efforts (CONFEDERATE DIPLOMACY).

A belated attempt to influence British action came in November, 1861, when a twenty-seven-year-old naturalized Swiss from Mobile, Ala., Henry Hotze, persuaded a reluctant Secretary of State R. M. T. HUNTER to appoint him as a propaganda agent. From this unpromising beginning, Hotze succeeded by the spring of 1862 in cultivating a corps of English writers who regularly contributed prosouthern articles to such leading British newspapers as the London *Times* and the *Morning Post*. Of much greater long-term significance, however, was his founding of the *Index*, a Confederate paper published in England, which closely copied prevailing English newspaper format and style and pursued a moderate editorial tone. Thus conceived and operated, it served both as an effective propaganda organ and also as a much-needed agency for coordinating and collecting southern news and interpretations. Although Hotze was constantly pressed for funds, the *Index* was published weekly without interruption from May 1, 1862, until August 12, 1865. Hotze's efforts were supplemented by the dedicated work of several sympathetic Englishmen, most notably James Spence, who organized a number of southern independence associations, staged public rallies, and wrote an excellent propaganda tract, *The American Union*, in addition to contributing numerous articles for the British press.

Hotze's success was unknown in Richmond early in 1862. President Jefferson Davis, responding to the urgent pleas of an old friend Edwin De Leon, appointed him chief European propaganda agent. Unlike Hotze, De Leon was given a large contingency fund. After discovering Hotze's thriving operation in England, De Leon went to Paris, where he engaged in numerous propaganda projects but with limited success. He was removed late in 1863, when one of his dispatches containing critical remarks about JOHN SLIDELL, Confederate commissioner to France, was intercepted by the federals and published in northern newspapers.

Hotze's responsibility was then extended to the Continent. During 1864 he managed through the Havas News Agency to get control of most news about the American war published in the French press. He also inserted prosouthern articles in German and Italian journals. In addition to his continental enterprises, Hotze also headed a number of Confederate agents who tried to stem the flow of Irish immigrants to the North, many of whom enlisted in the Union army. Despite weak and inconsistent support from the Richmond government, the southern propaganda program in Europe was surprisingly well organized, coordinated, and imaginative, owing principally to the remarkable genius and untiring efforts of Henry Hotze.

See C. P. Cullop, *Confederate Propaganda* (1969); F. L. Owsley, *King Cotton Diplomacy* (1959); S. B. Oates, *Historian* (Feb., 1965); H. Blumenthal, *Journal of Southern History* (May, 1966); and complete files of the *Index* at University of Virginia and Duke, also available on microfilm.

CHARLES P. CULLOP
East Carolina University

CONFEDERATE REFUGEES included some leaving loyal states to reside in the Confederacy, Unionists leaving the Confederacy, prominent Confederate families leaving war zones and Union-held areas, those removed by military edict, and those displaced by invasion, shelling, or lawless conditions. One scholar estimates that there were between 175,000 and 200,000 refugees over long periods of time. Traveling by railroad, wagon, buggy, or foot, refugees often preferred locating in cities, with Richmond, Atlanta, Columbia, and Wilmington absorbing many. Refugees resided in hotels, rooming houses, tents, caves, stables, railroad cars or with friends and relatives. Most welcome newcomers were physicians, ministers, and teachers. Least accepted were haughty aristocrats, the poor, and draft dodgers. Editors blamed local inflation, shortages, and crime on refugees and urged them to return home. Nevertheless, destitute refugees were aided by individuals, churches, cities, and states.

Generals cared less about the refugees' plight than military objectives. Some preferred that civilians remain at home, but others evicted them. W. T. Sherman's policy varied from removing just enough hostiles at Memphis to ensure community docility, evicting Atlanta's entire population, thereby increasing Confederate food problems, to expelling none at Columbia because of the war's approaching end.

Peace found defeated soldiers joining refugees headed home. Among problems were disrupted transportation, lack of valid currency, limited housing, the numbers involved, and lawless conditions. Military, individual, and organized benevolence helped some. The FREEDMEN'S BUREAU supplied 6.5 million rations to whites along with limited hospital care and housing. Some returning found their property destroyed, cotton confiscated, or homes seized for nonpayment of taxes. Finding conditions at home depressing, some moved westward or to another location in the South.

See M. Massey, *Refugee Life in Confederacy* (1964), most definitive; K. Stone, *Brokenburn*, ed. J. Q. Anderson (1955); J. McGuire, *Diary of Southern Refugee* (1867); A. H. Bill, *Beleaguered City* (1946), Richmond; J. Trowbridge, *Picture of Desolated States* (1868); and H. A. White, *Freedmen's Bureau in Louisiana* (1970).

GEORGE ROBERT LEE
Culver-Stockton College

CONFEDERATE SPIES AND AGENTS. Because of the nature of the Civil War and because it was fought mainly in the South, the Confederate government possessed a distinct advantage in the gathering of military information. The federal government was located in a southern city, and throughout the war it remained full of Confederate sympathizers. Thus, early in the conflict, when the Confederate army needed information on Union troop movements, it was a simple matter to contact sympathizers in Washington, D.C. The Confederates thus began the war with a ready-made espionage system awaiting organization.

During the war several major spy rings were created in Washington. The first was under the direction of a prominent Washington hostess, Rose O'Neal Greenhow. During the first weeks after the outbreak of war, Mrs. Greenhow passed military information on to P. G. T. BEAUREGARD that she had gleaned from high Washington officials. She was partly responsible for keeping Beauregard informed of the movements of the Union army just prior to the first battle of BULL RUN. In August, 1861, she was arrested by the federal government's counterspy, Allan Pinkerton, and exiled to the South. She died in 1863 in a boating accident while returning from an overseas espionage mission.

During the early months of the war Thomas Conrad, a Georgetown schoolmaster, moved back and forth between Richmond and Washington in various disguises, providing J. E. B. STUART with almost daily information concerning the movements of the Union armies. Moreover, Conrad established a spy in the U.S. War Department from whom he gained important information on the movement of Union armies from 1862 through 1864.

Complementing Conrad's ring was another group of spies, headed by Frank Stringfellow, mostly operating behind Union lines. Like Conrad, Stringfellow crossed and recrossed Union-Confederate lines, generally placing himself in Union-held towns and providing Stuart with military information.

An intense and dedicated southerner, the colorful Belle Boyd, became engaged in amateur espionage when her hometown was occupied by Union soldiers shortly after the outbreak of war. She voluntarily gleaned information from admiring Union officers and in the autumn of 1861 was formally appointed by the Confederate government to collect information on the movement of Union troops in the Shenandoah Valley. She was arrested repeatedly and finally banished to the South. A ship taking her on a special mission to England in March, 1864, was captured by the Union blockade ships. She was banished this time to Canada on pain of death.

Perhaps the most famous Confederate agent was Captain Thomas Hines, who was appointed by Jefferson Davis to head a mission into the Northwest aimed at undermining and even overthrowing the state governments in Indiana, Illinois, and Ohio. Although the so-called northwestern conspiracy never materialized, Hines and his group did carry out acts of sabotage (COPPERHEAD).

See J. Bakeless, *Spies of Confederacy* (1970), general discussion; J. Horan, *Confederate Agent* (1954), Northwest conspiracy; I. Ross, *Rebel Rose* (1954), Mrs. Greenhow's exploits; and L. Signaud, *Belle Boyd* (1944).

JACK C. LANE
Rollins College

CONFEDERATE STATES OF AMERICA, the de facto national expression of the Old South, in a strictly legal or literal sense never existed. The would-be nation composed of states that attempted to secede from the United States was founded at Montgomery, Ala. Delegates from the seven states of the Deep South (South Carolina, Mississippi, Alabama, Florida, Louisiana, Georgia, and Texas) met in convention at Montgomery on February 4, 1861. Within five days the delegates had adopted a provisional constitution, elected a president and vice-president, and resolved themselves into the Provisional Congress as well as into a constituent assembly to draft a permanent constitution.

The Confederate founding fathers were fundamentally conservative; they sought no new worlds, but instead sought to perpetuate the world of the Old South as they knew it. The constitution they adopted as permanent in March was quite similar to that of the United States. It sanctified slavery and forbade protective tariffs, but it outlawed the slave trade and created a "permanent" (no more secession?) union. The convention elected Mississippian JEFFERSON DAVIS president and Georgian ALEXANDER H. STEPHENS vice-president. Both men, especially Stephens, were moderate politicians.

The new administration had barely time to organize before the Confederacy faced armed confrontation with the United States. Davis accepted the showdown at FT. SUMTER and ordered General P. G. T. BEAUREGARD to take possession of the installation in Charleston harbor by force if necessary. Accordingly, at 4:30 A.M. on April 12, the Confederates fired on Sumter and three days later raised the Stars and Bars above the fort. Calls for volunteer soldiers went out from Washington, D.C., and Montgomery, and four states of the Upper

South (Virginia, Tennessee, North Carolina, and Arkansas) decided to join rather than fight the Confederacy. Ultimately the Confederate Congress recognized southern governments in exile from Missouri and Kentucky as well, which accounts for the 13 stars in the Confederate flag.

Because the probable front of the Confederacy's war was far from Montgomery, in May the government moved to Richmond. There, within a hundred miles of Washington, the administration believed it could best direct the war and pay proper political homage to Virginia at the same time. On July 22, 1861, this judgment seemed vindicated at the first major battle of the war. First Manassas (BULL RUN) was a spectacular southern victory. To this point the Confederacy had been the incarnation of the Old South, and at Manassas the new nation was the southern apotheosis.

Southerners celebrated the victory for quite some time; they had to do so, because nearly a year passed before they could celebrate another major victory. Meanwhile, the Confederates lost battles and territory. European powers, especially England and France, did not respond to southern pleas for recognition and assistance even when they had provocation (TRENT AFFAIR) and faced a cotton famine (CONFEDERATE COTTON). Thus when Jefferson Davis took the oath as permanent president on February 22, 1862, his administration as well as his nation was in serious trouble.

Driven by wartime necessity, beginning in the spring of 1862 Davis and his Confederates began to create a nation apart from the antebellum norm. Within a year Congress had given the president authority to suspend habeas corpus, to conscript an army (the first draft in North America), to collect income taxes (in kind), to impress food and labor for the army, and (as a by-product of these powers) to construct and operate war industries. Such activity alarmed many southerners, who questioned independence gained by "yankee" methods. Nevertheless, the Confederates eventually adopted foreign trade laws amounting to state socialism and ultimately decided to recruit black troops in the vain hope of victory.

Victories there were. Confederate generals, led by ROBERT E. LEE, adapted Napoleonic strategy and hoped for battles of "annihilation." Content to stand on the defense until a fortuitous moment, the Confederates fought an offensive defensive. Southern armies, however, were unable to win decisively and in the end were victims of the strategy of exhaustion employed by their enemies.

On the home front, privation, inflation, and death did not daunt the Confederate southerners until their resources were exhausted. The double disaster of July, 1863, at VICKSBURG and GETTYSBURG was the turning point for southern morale, which made the transit from confidence to optimism to hope to determination and thence to despair. Southern women, who in the beginning encouraged the men to enlist and bore the burdens of farm, factory, and hospital labor, were perhaps the last to succumb. When Richmond fell on April 2, 1865, the Confederacy lived only a short time thereafter. The Confederates had transformed the Old South and slaughtered many of their sacred cows in the hope of independence. In the end they only salvaged themselves, their land, and their pride in the LOST CAUSE of their nonnation.

See F. E. Vandiver, *Their Tattered Flags* (1970), most readable; C. Eaton, *History of Southern Confederacy* (1954), balanced; E. M. Coulter, *Confederate States of America* (1950), encyclopedic; C. P. Roland, *Confederacy* (1960), best brief work; E. M. Thomas, *Confederacy as Revolutionary Experience* (1971); B. I. Wiley, *Road to Appomattox* (1956); *Official Records, Armies*; *Official Records, Navies*; J. D. Richardson (ed.), *Messages and Papers of Confederacy* (1904); *Journal of Congress of Confederate States* (1904–05); and "Proceedings of Confederate Congress," *Southern Historical Society Papers* (1923–59).

EMORY M. THOMAS
University of Georgia

CONFEDERATE STRATEGY.

To win independence the Confederacy needed only to hold what it had until the Union acquiesced. A defensive strategy implemented this as well as supported the goal of foreign recognition, protected their logistic base, and catered to demands for local defense. Nevertheless, Confederate strategy was not passive. This active defense was implemented by regional departments subjected to effective area and central coordination. President Jefferson Davis supplied coordination by reshaping the departments as the logistical and strategic situation changed and by providing a railroad "pipeline" full of reserves, which he moved from one department to another. The command system and the strategy were basically sound, though change and adaptation were sometimes slow and inept and Davis often too sanguinely relied on spontaneous cooperation of separate department commanders.

Davis' earliest initiative was at the first BULL RUN CAMPAIGN, when Joseph E. Johnston, whom he had ordered to reinforce P. G. T. Beauregard, moved by rail on an interior line and arrived in time to secure a Confederate victory. After the fall of Ft. Donelson in 1862 (FTS. HENRY AND DONELSON CAMPAIGN), Davis again acted to secure a concentration at SHILOH against U. S. Grant before D. C. Buell could join him.

After Braxton Bragg's failure in Kentucky, Davis in 1863 was subjected to much pressure from western generals and politicians to implement a Beauregard-inspired plan for another interdepartmental concentration, this time in middle Tennessee. Robert E. Lee successfully resisted detachment of any troops west. His GETTYSBURG campaign was designed for his logistical relief and as a spoiling maneuver rather than as an aid to VICKSBURG.

Davis failed to save Vicksburg by activating plans to move troops to Mississippi from South Carolina and Tennessee. In August, 1863, however, he acted to apply Beauregard's idea of an interdepartmental offensive concentration. Troops from Virginia and Mississippi were present at CHICKAMAUGA, the high point of Davis' and the Confederacy's use of the railroad to apply on a hitherto unknown scale the strategic practice exemplified in the campaigns of Napoleon, Robert E. Lee, and Stonewall Jackson. These underlying strategic concepts had been explained by Henri Jomini and understood and advocated by Beauregard.

The last year and a half of the war witnessed many offensive campaigns projected by Davis and his advisers but, other than J. B. Hood's desperate gamble in Tennessee, none was attempted. No major interdepartmental concentrations seemed possible against Union offensives that were, at last, well coordinated.

See F. E. Vandiver, *Rebel Brass* (1955) and *American Tragedy* (1959); T. L. Connelly and A. Jones, *Politics of Command* (1973); and R. F. Weigley, *American Way of War* (1973).

ARCHER JONES
North Dakota State University

CONFEDERATE SUPPLY. The resources of the Confederacy suitable for sustaining a prolonged conflict were distinctly inferior to those of the Union. Union successes early in the war denied to the Confederacy most of the grain, meat, mines, and factories of the Upper South. Inefficient leadership was another major impediment. Jefferson Davis and other leaders did not know how to allocate the Confederacy's limited resources. Davis often thwarted innovations advocated by Secretaries of War GEORGE W. RANDOLPH and JAMES A. SEDDON and by the supply officials. With weak central planning, the exigencies of war forced the Confederate administration to exercise numerous coercive controls. The government owned nearly all the mines, ordnance works, and clothing shops; it monopolized horses, wagons, wool, hides, and cotton; it made factories subject to controls on raw materials, labor details, and disposition of products; it subjected crops to tithes and government preemptive sales; and it imposed military direction upon the railroads and shipping.

Other impediments to supplying the Confederate armed forces included obstructionist state governments, feuds between field commanders and supply officials, competition among the supply bureaus, waste by the soldiers, civilian resistance to burdensome supply policies, loss of supply accumulations and key production and transportation centers through military blunders, and a burgeoning mass of civilian dependents. The shortage of manpower for the armed forces and for industrial and agricultural production, the inflationary mode of financing the war, and the steady disintegration of the transportation network created inexorable pressures.

In the face of these problems, the Confederate supply bureaus had commendable records. Isaac M. St. John's Niter and Mining Bureau supplied most of the raw materials for ordnance and iron production until Union advances forced increasing reliance on importation. JOSIAH GORGAS' Ordnance Bureau constructed an impressive industrial complex and was efficient in importing supplies; these operations, supplemented by battlefield captures, assured sufficient arms, ammunition, and artillery.

In accumulating clothing, blankets, tents, and accouterments, the Quartermaster's Department managed to meet most of its obligations. However, it could not accumulate sufficient field transportation and failed to manage railroad transportation efficiently. Most of the reasons for the bureau's failure lay in natural shortages and decisions by superiors, factors outside the control of Quartermaster Generals ABRAHAM C. MYERS and Alexander R. Lawton.

The Subsistence Department, under Commissary General LUCIUS B. NORTHROP, faced virtually insurmountable problems: the loss of the foodstuffs of the Upper South; civilian resistance to impressment of food surpluses; delays by Davis in implementing policies for trading through the lines, controlling railroad transportation, and giving high priority to meat imports.

Imports from Europe were essential to all aspects of the supply effort. An efficient, albeit belated, system of BLOCKADE-RUNNING evolved and was placed under the supervision of the Bureau of Foreign Supply, under Thomas L. Bayne, and of Colin J. McRae in Europe.

Supply efforts and campaigning influenced each other. There were shortages that affected strategy after Manassas. On the other hand, losses in Tennessee and New Orleans in 1862, the loss of the Chattanooga area in 1863, and the siege of Charleston in 1863 severely injured the production, transportation, and importation of supplies.

See War Department Collection of Confederate Records, National Archives; R. D. Goff, *Confederate Supply* (1969); F. E. Vandiver, *Ploughshares into Swords* (1952); R. C. Black, *Railroads of Confederacy* (1952); S. B. Thompson, *Confederate Purchasing Abroad* (1935); F. L. Owsley, *King Cotton Diplomacy* (1959); J. L. Nichols, *Confederate Quartermaster in Trans-Mississippi* (1964); Papers Relating to Subsistence Department, Virginia Historical Society; E. M. Coulter, *Mississippi Valley Historical Review* (March, 1919); W. Diamond, *Journal of Southern History* (Nov., 1940); L. B. Hill, *Southern Sketches* (1936); L. H. Johnson, *Mississippi Valley Historical Review* (March, 1963); and C. W. Ramsdell, *American Historical Review* (July, 1930).

RICHARD D. GOFF
Eastern Michigan University

CONFEDERATE VETERAN MAGAZINE, the unofficial organ of the Confederate veteran, appeared in January, 1893, and continued for 40 years until December, 1932. For 20 years it was under owner-editor Sumner A. Cunningham, who had been a sergeant major in the 41st Tennessee Infantry. The magazine was continued for the last 20 years by Edith Pope. Cunningham, an experienced reporter and editor, covered all events of Confederate life, reunions, and dedications. He is responsible for rescuing from oblivion the hero Sam Davis, executed at Pulaski, Tenn., and Dan Emmett, composer of "Dixie," and was directly responsible for many monuments in the South and for some where Confederate soldiers are buried in the North. Twenty or more libraries have complete runs of this important magazine.

BOB YOUNGER
Dayton, Ohio

CONFEDERATE VETERANS. Southern soldiers and sailors returned from the Civil War conscious of defeat yet proud of their valiant effort. Amid chaotic conditions, these men were ready to accept the results of the war and go to work. At first most turned to agriculture, but in time many entered business and industrial pursuits. Those who were willing to embrace industrialization provided much of the leadership in the NEW SOUTH movement. Examples include Generals JOHN C. BROWN, N. B. FORREST, and WILLIAM MAHONE as railroad developers, Private HENRY F. DE BARDE-

LEBEN in iron and steel, and Washington Duke (DUKE FAMILY) in tobacco. Public esteem for veterans also opened positions for them in education, banking, insurance, and publishing. In politics a grateful people favored Confederate veterans with public office, especially from 1877 to 1900. Veterans led the Democratic party into the SOLID SOUTH, and southern congressional delegations were long dominated by veterans. For example, in the sessions of 1877–1879, 72 percent of the members of the U.S. House and Senate from the former Confederate states were veterans. Southern state governments at all levels were veteran led.

Confederate veterans' organizations began in 1865 on a local scale to bury their dead and care for the indigent veterans. These organizations also emphasized fraternal-social activities, the collection of historical materials about the war, and the building of monuments to memorialize their lost cause. In 1889 unity of organization was attained with the founding of the UNITED CONFEDERATE VETERANS. Overall, Confederate veterans, the living symbol of the Confederacy, were entrusted with leadership in the South well beyond the time span usually allotted to a generation. Building upon this trust they became a powerful influence for southern rebirth and for national reconciliation.

See W. W. White, *Confederate Veteran* (1962), veterans in southern life, bibliography; United Confederate Veterans, *Minutes, Annual Meetings* (1889–1912); *Confederate Veteran* (1893–1932), magazine coverage of veterans' activities; N. K. Burger and J. K. Bettersworth, *South of Appomattox* (1959); and W. B. Hesseltine, *Confederate Leaders of the New South* (1950), good on high-ranking leaders.

WILLIAM W. WHITE
Texas Lutheran College

CONFEDERATE WEAPONS. At the outbreak of war the South was seriously deficient in modern weapons. Captured arsenals and state stockpiles yielded about 500,000 weapons, varying in type and obsolescence. Field artillery consisted almost exclusively of antiquated iron pieces. Some were later reamed out and rifled. A substantial number of heavy seacoast guns were in southern seaports or captured at federal navy yards like Norfolk and Pensacola. Gunpowder stores amounted to a mere 60,000 pounds; and only two powder factories existed in the South. The only cannon foundry was at the Tredegar Iron Works in Richmond.

The Confederate authorities at Montgomery appointed JOSIAH GORGAS head of the Ordnance Bureau. Purchasing officers like RAPHAEL SEMMES got substantial ordnance stores in New York, and Caleb Huse was conspicuously successful in Europe. Gorgas' department was so efficient that Confederate troops were reasonably well supplied with weapons, mainly the .57-caliber Enfield rifled musket, a weapon comparable in efficiency to the federal standard infantry arm, the .58-caliber Springfield. Subordinates like George Washington Rains of the Augusta works were outstanding in providing munitions. Although the Confederates had to avoid lavish expenditures of ammunition, there usually were sufficient quantities. Whenever a scarcity did exist it was due to breakdowns in transportation.

Naval weapons were provided by the Bureau of Ordnance and Hydrography under JOHN MERCER BROOKE. Gabriel J. Rains, brother of G. W. Rains, made brilliant contributions as chief of the torpedo service. Confederate ingenuity produced both land and naval mines and even SUBMARINES. A total of 43 enemy ships were sunk or damaged by mines, and the submarine opened a new era in naval warfare.

Weapons from England and Europe were brought in by BLOCKADE-RUNNERS. Although over 1,500 of these ships were destroyed or captured, they delivered about 600,000 stand of arms. Most weapons were British "Enfields," a basic infantry arm for the Confederate states and so superior that after Vicksburg the federals exchanged their antiquated arms for the British gun. Also imported were a few Whitworth sniper rifles, equipped with telescopic sights and lethal up to 1,800 yards. Artillery imported consisted mainly of Armstrong, Blakely, and Whitworth pieces. A few breech-loading Whitworths were imported. France supplied 12-pounder bronze fieldpieces called "Napoleons." Miscellaneous military stores came from such European ordnance centers as Solingen, Germany, which shipped essentials ranging from edged weapons to canteens.

At home Richmond became the center of arms production. The Tredegar works produced large-caliber cannon, "torpedoes" (mines), submarines, and armor plate. The Richmond Armory produced or repaired over 300,000 weapons and furnished nearly 72 million rounds of small arms ammunition. Other ordnance plants were established in such cities as Fayetteville, N.C., Selma, Ala., and Augusta, Ga. Such essentials as niter and lead were mined, often under severe handicaps of scarcity and inadequate transportation. Patriotic citizens donated bells, lead window weights, and even lead piping. Shotguns and sporting rifles were contributed to the cause, and local blacksmiths furnished crude pikes, swords, Bowie knives, and even lances. Thousands of arms were gleaned from battlefields. About two-thirds of Confederate field artillery pieces were captured from the federals. Despite initial shortages in military and naval weapons, the Confederacy accomplished wonders in providing the essential ordnance stores throughout the war.

See H. L. Abbot, *Siege Artillery* (1867); W. A. Albaugh, *Confederate Handguns* (1951), and *Confederate Edged Weapons* (1960); W. A. Albaugh and R. D. Steuart, *Original Confederate Colt* (1953); W. A. Albaugh and E. N. Simmons, *Confederate Arms* (1957); *Ordnance Manual, CSA* (1863); W. B. Edwards, *Civil War Guns* (1962); C. Fuller and R. D. Steuart, *Firearms of Confederacy* (1944); F. A. Lord, *Civil War Collector's Encyclopedia* (1963), and *North-South Trader* (Jan.–Feb., 1974); M. F. Perry, *Infernal Machines* (1965); H. L. Peterson, *American Knives* (1958); W. Ripley, *Artillery and Ammunition of Civil War* (1970); and F. E. Vandiver, *Ploughshares into Swords* (1952).

FRANCIS A. LORD
University of South Carolina

CONGREGATIONAL CHURCH, the traditional church of New England, is the church of the Pilgrims. It is theologically Calvinistic and takes its name from the form of church government that emphasized the primacy of the local congregation. So loose has church organization been that no national denomination can be said to have existed until "Congregationalists" met first in a national convention at Albany, N.Y., in 1852. Regular meetings of the national council did not begin until 1871.

Despite the New England focus, churches with similar theology and polity appeared in the South. At least ten such churches grew up among southerners, but all except Circular Church in Charleston (1691) and Midway Church in Liberty County, Ga. (1752), merged with other denominations by the time of the Civil War. Other Congregational churches appeared in connection with work supported by Congregationally oriented missionary societies: the American Board of Commissioners for Foreign Missions' work among the Cherokee from 1817 to 1840; the American Home Missionary Society's work in Missouri in the 1840s; and the American Missionary Association's antislavery churches in Kentucky and North Carolina in the 1850s.

On racial matters, Congregationalism has presented a blurred picture. Nationally, it was one of the significant abolitionist denominations by 1850, but both Circular Church and Midway Church reflected local slaveholder attitudes and practices. Probably the major growth of the denomination in the South was between 1865 and 1880 among blacks in association with the educational activities of the American Missionary Association. In the course of the 1880s, several wholly white Congregational churches were formed in southern cities among New England migrants. Also in the 1880s several Congregational Methodist churches, a group originating in south Georgia in the 1850s, joined with the urban white Congregationalists, adding their support to the growing segregation within the denomination. Separate conferences for black and white Congregational churches finally came to be accepted by the national council in 1889.

Through the 1890s and early years of the twentieth century, a substantial effort was made to expand Congregationalism as a white denomination, a tendency strengthened by the merger in 1931 of the Congregational church and the Christian Connection church. The Christian Connection church—a group formed in 1820 uniting Methodist rebels from North Carolina and Virginia, Baptists from Vermont, and former Presbyterians from Kentucky and Alabama—had considerable strength in the South. Most of these southerners held traditional southern views toward blacks. Segregation remained within southern Congregationalism until after the merger between the Congregational-Christian church and the Evangelical and Reformed church, which formed the United Church of Christ in 1956. The reorganization of the United Church of Christ in the 1960s finally abolished the all-black Convention of the South.

Perhaps because of its colonial origins and Congregationalism's early support of education in the founding of Harvard, Yale, and many other colleges, members of Congregational churches have usually been drawn from rather prosperous and well-educated groups. In the twentieth century Congregationalists have usually been liberal in theology, and this church has been one of the great Social Gospel denominations. In the South, however, the denomination has not grown substantially among either blacks or whites. In 1928 Congregationalists in the entire South numbered only 21,329 white and 7,885 black members, but they supported one theological seminary, four senior colleges, and two junior colleges. In addition, the American Missionary Association, largely supported by Congregationalists in the North, supported several black colleges including FISK, Tillotson, Tougaloo, Talladega, DILLARD, and HAMPTON. By 1956 Congregational-Christian membership in the South stood at 62,876 whites and 22,459 blacks. In 1971 United Church membership totaled 162,976 in the entire South, and 9,017 of these were "Continuing Congregationalists," members of Congregational churches that refused to go along with the United Church merger of 1956.

See W. Walker, *History of Congregational Churches* (1894); and G. G. Atkins and F. L. Fagley, *History of American Congregationalism* (1942). For southern story see F. E. Jenkins, *Anglo-Saxon Congregationalism in South* (1908); and R. B. Drake, *Negro History Bulletin* (March, 1958). Information on black churches is in American Missionary Association Papers, Amistad Research Center, Dillard University.

RICHARD B. DRAKE
Berea College

CONGRESSIONAL RECONSTRUCTION. See
RECONSTRUCTION, CONGRESSIONAL

CONGRESS OF RACIAL EQUALITY, founded
in 1942, is the oldest of the nonviolent, direct action, and interracial civil rights organizations. Basing their philosophy on Ghandian pacifism, socialism, and Christian idealism, its young leaders adapted the sit-down strike technique for civil rights demonstrations against segregation in schools, housing, hospitals, and places of public accommodation. Until 1960 most of its activities and members were limited to the North and border states; the one notable exception was the 1947 Journey of Reconciliation, which tested Upper South compliance with court rulings against segregation on interstate commerce. This set the example for CORE's 1961 Freedom Ride from Washington, D.C., to New Orleans. Seven blacks, including CORE leader JAMES FARMER, and six whites, joined by hundreds of others, traveled without incident until reaching Alabama, where a bus was burned outside Anniston. In Alabama and Mississippi, riders were greeted by angry mobs, brutally treated, and jailed. The freedom riders proved the South's refusal to desegregate interstate buses and terminal facilities and won a November ruling in which the Interstate Commerce Commission outlawed segregation on interstate carriers. After this experience CORE spread throughout the South, participating in the 1964 Mississippi summer project, in which the goal was voter registration and freedom schools, and in massive projects in Louisiana, both of which involved sit-ins, protest marches, and the registration of black voters. In both instances the workers were met with violence—at least six people were killed in Mississippi. After 1964 CORE moved toward black power and black nationalism, rejecting its biracial heritage, and by 1968 it had complete-

ly eliminated white participation, an action that seriously hurt its stability.

See I. P. Bell, *CORE* (1968); and J. Farmer, *Freedom—When* (1966).

DUNCAN R. JAMIESON
University of Alabama

CONJURE WOMAN (or conjure man, conjure doctor) was akin to the voodoo doctor of the blacks, the medicine man of the American Indians, and the *traiteur* of the Louisiana French. She employed the magical tactics of the witch doctor but sometimes used herbs and other potions. Although evil deeds were often ascribed to her actions, she was usually considered a healer. Long present in the frontier backwoods, in the southern Appalachians, and in predominantly black areas, she survived into the twentieth century and to some extent still does in the recurring "faith healers" of today.

See N. N. Puckett, *Folk Beliefs of Southern Negro* (1926); V. Randolph, *Ozark Superstitions* (1947); W. D. Steele, *Pictorial Review* (Oct., 1929); *Journal of American Folklore* (Oct., 1899); and annual bibliographies, *Journal of Southern Folklore.*

E. D. JOHNSON
Radford College

CONNALLY, THOMAS TERRY (1877–1963), was born near Hewitt, Tex. After graduation from Baylor (A.B., 1896) and the University of Texas (LL.B., 1889), he plunged into Texas politics and served as a state representative (1901–1904), U.S. representative (1917–1929), and a U.S. senator (1929–1953). During his career in the Senate, Connally served on the Senate Finance, Judiciary, and Privileges and Elections committees as well as chairman of the Public Buildings and Grounds Committee. He sponsored the Jones-Connally Cattle Purchase Act (1934) and the Connally Act (1935) prohibiting the shipment in interstate commerce of oil produced in violation of interstate compacts. Connally led the Senate opposition to Franklin Roosevelt's court-packing plan. Foreign affairs were Connally's primary interests as he served as chairman of the Senate Foreign Relations Committee (1941–1946, 1949–1953). Usually he sanctioned the diplomacy practiced by the Roosevelt-Truman administrations and warned against isolationism.

See F. A. Smyrl, "Tom Connally and New Deal" (Ph.D. dissertation, University of Oklahoma, 1969); D. L. Matheny, "Foreign Policy Speeches of Senator Tom Connally" (Ph.D. dissertation, University of Oklahoma, 1966);

L. V. Patenaude, *Southwestern Historical Quarterly* (July, 1970); and T. Connally, as told to A. Steinberg, *My Name Is Tom Connally* (1954).

IRVIN MAY, JR.
Texas Agricultural Experiment Station

CONNOR, ROBERT DIGGES WIMBERLY (1878–1950), southern historian and first United States archivist, was born in Wilson, N.C.; he received his B.A. degree from the University of North Carolina in 1899 and studied at Columbia University (1920–1921). He was instrumental in establishing the State Historical Commission of North Carolina, a model for the preservation of public archives, which he served as secretary (1907–1921). Appointed by President Franklin D. Roosevelt as first archivist of the United States, Connor served in that post until 1941. He was Kenan Professor of History and Government (1921–1934) and Craige Professor of Jurisprudence and History (1934–1949) at the University of North Carolina. A dedicated teacher, scholar, and archivist, he was known for his progressive, open-minded interpretation of the history of the South. His most important works, all relating to the history of North Carolina, include *Cornelius Harnett* (1909), *Ante-Bellum Builders of North Carolina* (1914), *Revolutionary Leaders of North Carolina* (1916), *Race Elements in the White Population of North Carolina* (1920), and a two-volumed history of North Carolina (1929). He edited documents concerning the history of the University of North Carolina and, with CLARENCE POE, the speeches of North Carolina's education-minded governor, CHARLES B. AYCOCK.

See H. T. Lefler, in C. L. Lord (ed.), *Keepers of the Past* (1965); D. R. McCoy, *American Archivist* (July, 1974); and R. D. W. Connor Papers, University of North Carolina Library, Chapel Hill.

E. STANLY GODBOLD, JR.
Valdosta State College

CONSCIENTIOUS OBJECTORS in the Confederacy were not as numerous as in the North, but they were persecuted more because their pacifism was coupled with opposition to secession and slavery. Still, the Confederate government made special efforts to accommodate the antimilitarist beliefs of religious sects. Both North Carolina and Virginia, which had the largest number of QUAKERS, MENNONITES, and DUNKERS, passed laws prior to the Conscription Act permitting conscientious objectors to avoid service by paying a commutation fee. The Conscription Act of April, 1862, authorized substitution, but made no specific provision for conscientious objectors (CONFEDERATE CONSCRIPTION). In October, 1862, however, the Confederate Congress provided for their exemption through either substitution or the payment of a $500 fee. Despite this law, many uncertainties troubled conscientious objectors. Those who were drafted suffered harassment, and there always existed the prospect that pacifist exemptions might be abolished.

See E. N. Wright, *Conscientious Objectors in Civil War* (1931, 1961), only substantial work.

EUGENE C. MURDOCK
Marietta College

CONSCRIPTION. See CONFEDERATE CONSCRIPTION

CONSERVATION first became a national issue during the Progressive era. Although not directly involved initially, the South was drawn into conservation issues by rising concern over its resources.

The Reclamation Act (1902), providing federal funding for irrigation, stimulated interest in a proposed federal program for draining wetlands. Southerners enthusiastically supported this unsuccessful movement. Extensive drainage occurred, however, under state and private management. State laws facilitated landowner cooperation in drainage projects with Missouri's 1909 drainage law considered exemplary. Drainage interest coincided with agricultural prosperity, declining after 1920. Southerners had a keen interest in Mississippi River FLOOD CONTROL. Some supported plans for LEVEES only; others favored broader proposals including reservoirs to restrain flood waters and reforestation to lessen runoff. After decades of debate this multiple approach became the basis of federal water policy during the NEW DEAL, exemplified by the TENNESSEE VALLEY AUTHORITY's conservation work.

In 1899 citizens in Asheville, N.C., alarmed at the extensive lumbering in the southern mountains, organized the Appalachian National Park Association to urge Congress to preserve part of the forest for its scenic and recreational value. The American Forestry Association assumed leadership of the campaign and linked it to a similar New England effort. Emphasis shifted to the economic benefits of reforestation, which would reduce flooding from runoff and provide sustained-yield FORESTRY. Victory came with the Weeks Act (1911) authorizing purchases for a reserve and federal-state cooperation in forest fire control. Further federal stimulation to southern forestry

came during the 1920s, when the Clarke-McNary Act (1924) and other legislation increased federal-state cooperation in forestry and expanded the acquisition of forest reserve lands. The Great Smoky Mountains Conservation Association, organized in Knoxville, Tenn., in 1923, revived the aesthetic aims of the Asheville group and succeeded in establishing a national park in the southern mountains.

Depletion of the northern white pine forests by 1900 caused the LUMBER INDUSTRY to move south and west. The policy of "cut out and get out" threatened to leave the South with no permanent benefit from its forests. Far-sighted southerners, such as Henry Hardtner (Louisiana), W. Goodrich Jones (Texas), and Charles H. Herty (Georgia), joined representatives of the U.S. Forest Service and the American Forestry Association in generating southern support for forest conservation. They urged reforestation, fire control, and less waste in lumbering and turpentining. A decided NEW SOUTH tone prevailed, with emphasis on wiser resource use to improve the southern economy. The North Carolina Geological Survey, organized in 1891 to develop North Carolina resources, became a major conservation influence in the Lower South under the direction of Joseph A. Holmes. In 1916 Joseph Hyde Pratt organized the Southern Forestry Congress, which effectively publicized the value of forestry and campaigned for state forestry agencies, supported by conservationists, foresters, geologists, and railroad and forest industries. The American Forestry Association organized the Dixie Crusaders to tour Georgia, Florida, and Mississippi (1928–1930) with anti–forest fire programs for schoolchildren. The U.S. Forest Service assisted these pioneering efforts, and its logging engineer in north Florida, Austin Cary, successfully demonstrated the economic value of forestry to southern lumbermen. Southern colleges began adding forestry instruction to their curricula. From 1898 to 1909 Dr. Carl A. Schenck trained foresters at the nation's first scientifically managed forest on Biltmore, the Vanderbilt estate in North Carolina.

By 1900 many species of American wildlife faced extinction from overhunting. After 1901 the National Audubon Society became the leading agency in the South for wildlife conservation, supporting sportsmen's efforts to regulate hunting or, more often, initiating efforts to protect wildlife. The society located areas for inclusion in the federal refuge system, acquired large holdings of its own, and provided wardens for both. T. Gilbert Pearson, secretary of the Audubon Society's southern branch, lobbied to obtain state legislation protecting nongame birds, regulating hunting, and establishing state wildlife agencies. Studies by the U.S. Biological Survey on the role of insectivorous birds in controlling the BOLL WEEVIL aided in obtaining nongame bird protection in the cotton states. In North and South Carolina the state Audubon Society was empowered as the state wildlife agency.

Despite this progress, southern conservation generally fell short of the need until the New Deal brought the region into the mainstream of national conservation. The CIVILIAN CONSERVATION CORPS and other relief measures greatly extended forest conservation on federal, state, and private lands. The Tennessee Valley Authority's total approach touched all phases of conservation in the central South. Wildlife benefited by greater refuge purchases and stimulation to state programs by cooperative funding from the Pittman-Robertson Act (1937). The Soil Conservation Service began its successful programs against soil erosion, a problem that had frustrated southern agricultural reformers since the eighteenth century. By the 1970s the South faced the same host of modern environmental problems as the nation and pursued the same solutions under the impetus of federal legislation and environmentalists' urging.

See F. B. Vinson, "Conservation and South" (Ph.D. dissertation, University of Georgia, 1971), extensive bibliography; C. Callison, *Man and Wildlife in Missouri* (1953); R. Lord, *To Hold This Soil* (1938); W. B. Wilkerson, Jr., *et al.*, *Keepers of Land* (1972); and J. R. Ross, *Forest History* (Jan., 1973).

FRANK BEDINGFIELD VINSON
Georgia College

CONSTITUTION, RATIFICATION OF. Georgia was the first southern state and the fourth in the nation to ratify the Constitution. The vote in the Savannah convention on January 2, 1788, was unanimous (26 to 0). Although evidence is sparse, George Washington's explanation of Georgia's prompt decisive action is usually considered correct: "If a weak State with the Indians on its back and the Spaniards on its flank does not see the necessity of a General Government there must I think be wickedness or insanity in the way." ANTI-FEDERALISTS were strong enough in all the remaining southern states to force some consideration of amendments to the Constitution, but all southern acts of ratification were unconditional.

There was a sharp contest over the Constitution in Maryland since many of the most prominent men in the state favored prior amendment. Maryland Federalists, however, drawing on the support

of George Washington in neighboring Virginia, won an overwhelming majority of the seats at the Annapolis ratifying convention. The amendments proposed by the anti-Federalist minority were tabled in committee, and the Constitution was ratified 63 to 11 on April 26. The Constitution also passed easily in South Carolina, where the Charleston convention voted for ratification 149 to 73 on May 23. Here, however, the Federalists were forced to agree to a list of recommendatory amendments.

Virginia's ratifying convention met in Richmond after eight of the nine states necessary to put the new government into effect had already ratified the Constitution. The Federalists, led by James Madison, worked to prevent the insertion of amendments prior to an act of ratification. They succeeded by the narrow margin of 88 to 80. When the state ratified by a vote of 89 to 79 on June 25, the act was accompanied by a long list of recommended amendments that Virginia representatives to the First Congress would be bound to support.

North Carolina was the only southern state to refuse to accept the Constitution without prior amendment. The Hillsboro convention voted down the unamended Constitution 75 to 193 on August 4. After the introduction of the Bill of Rights in the First Congress, a second convention was called in North Carolina. That body ratified the Constitution 193 to 75 on November 22, 1789, while at the same time recommending eight additional amendments.

See J. Elliot (ed.), *Debates on the Federal Constitution* (1854); W. S. Jenkins and L. A. Hamrick (eds.), *Early State Records on Microfilm* (1950); E. M. Coulter, *Georgia Historical Quarterly* (1926), Georgia; W. W. Abbot, *William and Mary Quarterly* (Jan., 1957); B. C. Steiner, *American Historical Review* (Oct., 1899), Maryland; U. B. Phillips, *American Historical Review* (July, 1909), South Carolina; C. G. Singer, *South Carolina in Confederation* (1941); G. C. Rogers, *South Carolina Historical Association Proceedings* (1961); W. C. Ford, *Massachusetts Historical Society Proceedings* (1903), Virginia; H. B. Grigsby, *Virginia Federal Convention* (1890–91); R. E. Thomas, *Journal of Southern History* (Feb., 1953); L. I. Trenholme, *Ratification in North Carolina* (1932); W. K. Boyd, *Trinity College Historical Society Papers* (1922); A. R. Newsome, *North Carolina Historical Review* (Oct., 1940); and W. C. Pool, *North Carolina Historical Review* (April, 1950).

LINDA GRANT DE PAUW
George Washington University

CONSTITUTIONAL CONVENTION. The South sent an able representation to the federal convention at Philadelphia in 1787. Among the

nationalists who played critical roles were GEORGE WASHINGTON, GEORGE MASON, EDMUND RANDOLPH, and JAMES MADISON of Virginia and JOHN RUTLEDGE and CHARLES COTESWORTH PINCKNEY of South Carolina. They brought with them ideas that provided a broad consensus for a strong government. Some of them also brought a conflict-laden conviction that their export economy and slave labor system must be protected.

The Virginians took the initiative by introducing a plan of government based on Madison's ideas. The Virginia Plan projected a national government radically different from that provided by the ARTICLES OF CONFEDERATION. Although modified by long debates, the plan contained the essential elements of the Constitution.

The arrangement by which slaves were counted for purposes of representation is known as the "three-fifths compromise." Such a rule had been anticipated by the Continental Congress in 1783, and delegates approved it as a minimum southern demand with little debate. For purposes of representation and direct taxation, Article 1, Section 2 established the population of each state by "adding to the whole Number of free Persons, including those bound to Service for a Term of Years, and excluding Indians not taxed, three fifths of all other Persons."

On July 23 the convention appointed a committee of detail to write a constitution. With issues affecting the South yet unresolved, C. C. Pinckney warned its members that no constitution would be acceptable to South Carolina unless it contained a guarantee of slavery and a ban on export taxes. In August, weary members engaged in debate over the special interests of the South. Because southern prosperity was based on exports of tobacco, rice, and indigo, they demanded a ban on export taxes. To the northern argument that such a ban weakened the government by taking away "half the regulation of trade," Mason expressed basic southern fear. The five southern states would be a minority in both houses of Congress and had "good ground for suspicions." The ban entered Article 9, Section 9 of the Constitution: "No tax or Duty shall be laid on Articles exported from any State." Southern members also demanded that taxes on imports be approved by more than a simple majority. They failed to realize this aim.

The committee of detail had recommended that Congress be restrained from barring the immigration or importation of "such persons" as the states chose to admit. These oblique words set off the debate on the slave trade. Some northerners attacked a constitutional recognition of the trade as "inconsistent with the principles of the revolution" and "dishonorable to the American character." The South Carolinians responded that it was not a question of "Religion & humanity" but of "interest alone." "The true question is whether the Southern States shall or shall not be parties to the Union." Since nothing could be clearer, the antislavery members yielded, but were able to limit the restriction to a 20-year period. Later the South Carolinians proposed that "fugitive slaves & servants . . . be delivered up like criminals." In softer language this proposal found its way into the Constitution in Article 4, Section 2 as the fugitive slave clause.

See C. Rossiter, *1787:Grand Convention* (1966); C. D. Bowen, *Miracle at Philadelphia* (1966); and C. Warren, *Making of Constitution* (1928).

BRADLEY CHAPIN
Ohio State University

SOUTHERNERS AT THE CONSTITUTIONAL CONVENTION

Virginia	*Georgia*
*George Washington	*William Few
Dr. James McClurg	*Abraham Baldwin
Edmund Randolph	William Pierce
*John Blair	William Houstoun
*James Madison	*South Carolina*
George Wythe	*John Rutledge
George Mason	*Charles Pinckney
North Carolina	*Charles Cotesworth
Alexander Martin	Pinckney
William R. Davie	*Pierce Butler
*Richard D. Spaight	*Maryland*
*Hugh Williamson	*James McHenry
William Blount	*Daniel of St. Thomas
Delaware	Jenifer
*George Read	*Daniel Carroll
*Gunning Bedford, Jr.	James Francis Mercer
*John Dickinson	Luther Martin
*Richard Bassett	
*Jacob Broom	

*actual signers

CONSTITUTIONAL UNION PARTY (1860) was formed by a Baltimore convention of delegates from 21 states who were principally former supporters of the WHIG PARTY. Leading roles were played by southern moderates including JOHN BELL of Tennessee, JOHN J. CRITTENDEN of Kentucky, John Botts of Virginia, and SAM HOUSTON of Texas. Bell was nominated president, and Edward Everett of Massachusetts was nominated vice-president. The convention adopted a two-paragraph platform, which denounced sectional political parties and endorsed a defense of the

Union and a strict enforcement of all laws of the nation. Leaders of the party hoped that the nomination of Bell, a well-known moderate, and the adoption of a vaguely worded platform would attract voters alarmed by the aggravated sectionalism of the times. During the campaign, party speakers maintained that Congress had no authority to legislate for or against slavery in the territories.

Bell received 588,879 of the 4.6 million popular votes and 39 (Kentucky's 12, Tennessee's 12, Virginia's 15) of the 303 electoral votes (ELECTION OF 1860). In the popular voting he also had substantial support in Alabama, Arkansas, Georgia, Louisiana, Maryland, Massachusetts, Missouri, Mississippi, and North Carolina. The party received its least support in the North and West. In the secession conventions that followed Abraham Lincoln's election, southern Constitutional Unionists usually opposed secession, but after the Civil War began many of them supported the Confederacy.

See E. D. Fite, *Presidential Campaign of 1860* (1911); A. M. Schlesinger, Jr., and F. L. Israel, *History of American Presidential Elections* (1971); O. Crenshaw, *Slave States in Presidential Election of 1860* (1945); D. Y. Thomas, *Political Science Quarterly* (June, 1911); D. A. Arnold, *Journal of Negro History* (April, 1963); J. H. Parks, *John Bell* (1950); P. R. Frothingham, *Edward Everett* (1925); A. C. Cole, *Whig Party in South* (1914); T. B. Alexander, *Journal of Southern History* (Aug., 1961); R. A. Wooster, *Secession Conventions of South* (1962); and D. L. Dumond, *Secession Movement, 1860–1861* (1931).

RICHARD R. WESCOTT
Monmouth College, West Long Branch, N.J.

CONSTITUTIONAL UNION PARTY OF GEORGIA grew out of the bitter struggle in that state over the controversial COMPROMISE OF 1850. Traditional party lines crumbled as conservatives and radicals battled over its acceptance and the larger issue of union or disunion. Georgia's decision was of paramount importance because it was the first southern state to call a convention to consider formal action. Leading a coalition of Unionist Whigs and Democrats in support of the compromise were Whig Congressmen ROBERT TOOMBS and ALEXANDER H. STEPHENS and Democrat HOWELL COBB, recently elected Speaker of the House. Against this powerful GEORGIA TRIUMVIRATE, the opposition southern rightists proved ineffective.

The Unionist-dominated state convention in December, 1850, voted to accept the compromise as a permanent settlement of sectional difficulties, but it warned in its GEORGIA PLATFORM that any further encroachment on southern rights would prompt the state to secede. Georgia's action encouraged other southern states to accept the compromise, and the Union remained intact for another decade. At the state convention, the Constitutional Union party was formally organized by the triumvirate upon the principles of the Georgia Platform. During its brief existence, the party dominated Georgia politics. Cobb sat in the governor's chair; the legislature was heavily Unionist; and six of the state's eight congressional delegates, including Toombs and Stephens, wore the party label. In the spring of 1852, the party began to show signs of an early demise. It was weakened by the basic incompatibility of Whigs and Democrats within its ranks and the failure of its representatives in Washington to launch a nationwide Unionist party. In August the Constitutional Union party was officially dissolved amid the confusion of a presidential election that featured five separate electoral tickets in Georgia. Cobb returned to the Democratic fold, where he was eventually joined by Toombs and Stephens.

See H. Montgomery, *Cracker Parties* (1950), best account; R. H. Shryock, *Georgia and Union in 1850* (1926); W. Y. Thompson, *Robert Toombs* (1966); and Augusta *Chronicle* and Milledgeville *Federal Union*, on microfilm in University of Georgia Library.

WILLIAM Y. THOMPSON
Louisiana Tech University

CONTINENTAL ASSOCIATION. See ASSOCIATION

CONTINENTAL CONGRESS. The call for the First Continental Congress was issued by a southern province, Virginia, and from Delaware to South Carolina there was eager support for the intercolonial gathering. However, the newest colony, Georgia, did not support the meeting, sent no delegates, and was only nominally represented when the Second Continental Congress met. LYMAN HALL, its delegate, was permitted to vote, but he refused, for he thought he could not commit the people of Georgia single-handedly. The other southern colonies not only supported the Congress in 1774, but also sent their leading politicians to Philadelphia. These men spanned the political spectrum from PATRICK HENRY and CHRISTOPHER GADSDEN to GEORGE READ and PEYTON RANDOLPH. At the Congress a South Carolinian, THOMAS LYNCH, dominated the conference, selecting the meeting place, naming the secretary, and, when he refused the chair, nominating Peyton Randolph. Southerners served prominently on all major committees. JOHN RUT-LEDGE's notes were the basis of the Declaration of Rights and Grievances. In the Second Congress, THOMAS JEFFERSON of Virginia wrote the DECLARATION OF INDEPENDENCE.

Interest and support for Congress remained high during war, but, when relative peace returned to America, southern states became lax about keeping delegates in the assembly. The general quality of men who served from Delaware southward after 1783 was also unequal to that of those men who had first voiced opposition to British laws in 1774 and then proclaimed independence in 1776. Recovery from the devastations of war and the concomitant dislocation of the economy demanded that the best talents remain within the states. Maryland was the only southern state to host Congress. In 1776, when the British drove across New Jersey, the delegates moved to Baltimore. The village was small and isolated; but this was beneficial, said Samuel Adams, because they did in three weeks what would have required six months in Philadelphia. The second time Maryland served Congress was 1783, and the location was Annapolis. There was so much entertainment that the delegates accomplished little. Elbridge Gerry said, "The Idea of Business to [the residents] is neither agreeable or reputable."

After the war, many people thought the ARTICLES OF CONFEDERATION insufficient. The impetus for a stronger government to replace the Continental Congress came from the South. Virginia called the first meeting (ALEXANDRIA CONFERENCE), and the second was held in Maryland (ANNAPOLIS CONVENTION). When the Constitution was written, Delaware was the first to ratify, though another southern state, North Carolina, was the last to accede to the charter before the formation of the new government (CONSTITUTION, RATIFICATION OF). From first to last, from 1774 to 1789, the southern states supported unified action and committed their best talents to the Continental Congress.

See *Journals of Congress*; "Papers of Congress," on microfilm; E. C. Burnett, *Congress* (1941) and *Letters of Congress*; published records of Georgia, South Carolina, and North Carolina; C. G. Singer, *South Carolina in Confederation* (1941); F. Ryan, *South Carolina Historical Magazine* (July, 1959); D. T. Morgan and W. J. Schmidt, *North Carolina Historical Review* (July, 1975); C. C. Jones, *Delegates from Georgia* (1891); K. Coleman, *American Revolution in Georgia* (1958); J. T. Main, *William and Mary Quarterly* (Jan., 1955); and E. B. Poythress, "Revolution by Committee" (Ph.D. dissertation, University of North Carolina, 1975).

W. ROBERT HIGGINS
Johns Hopkins University

CONTRABAND, NEGROES AS. According to traditional international law, contraband was military goods destined for the enemy that a belligerent might capture. The classification of slaves, which were used for military purposes, as contraband first occurred when General Benjamin F. Butler arrived at Hampton Roads, Va., from Maryland. On May 22, 1861, his forces secured the area around Ft. Monroe by driving the Confederate troops out of Hampton. Three black men, held as slaves by a Confederate officer, escaped into Union lines. Butler declared them contraband of war and not subject to be returned under the FUGITIVE SLAVE LAW because they had been employed in building fortifications. On May 30, 1861, the matter came before Abraham Lincoln's cabinet, and Secretary of War Simon Cameron was directed to consider such slaves as confiscated from their Confederate owners. Henceforth all slaves coming into Union lines were termed contraband, and the able-bodied were employed as laborers in the Union service. The term contraband ceased to be a legal doctrine after the Confiscation Act of August, 1861, declared that slaves used for war purpose were to be free.

See *Annals of America* (1858–65), IX, 276–78; B. F. Butler, *Autobiography* (1892), and *Correspondence During Civil War* (5 vols.; 1917); F. Moore, *Rebellion Record* (12 vols.; 1862–68), II, Doc. No. 132; J. F. Rhodes, *History of U.S., 1850–1877* (1893–1906), III; and H. L. Trefousse, *Ben Butler* (1957).

VICTOR B. HOWARD
Morehead State University

CONVENTIONS, COMMERCIAL AND POLITICAL. Between 1837 and 1860 the growth of southern nationalism was reflected in meetings of a succession of commercial and political conventions. The PANIC OF 1837 spurred many southern merchants to seek expanded European markets (COMMERCE). In July, 1837, William Dearing, an Athens, Ga., businessman, issued a circular inviting interested merchants to come to an October meeting in Augusta to discuss plans for expanding direct trade with Europe. Only two states were represented, but the convention was widely discussed in newspapers throughout the South and led to a similar gathering in Charleston in April, 1839, representing seven southern states. They, too, urged increased direct southern trade with Europe.

Within a few years, however, many southerners came to feel that RAILROADS and internal improvements were the keys to the region's economic progress and to establishing closer relations with the rapidly growing West. This was the dominant sentiment of a large convention that gathered in Memphis in November, 1845, under the austere gaze of JOHN C. CALHOUN. That meeting enacted resolutions urging the federal government to undertake extensive improvements of navigation in the South and the construction of railway connections between the south Atlantic coast and the Mississippi Valley. Meanwhile, New Orleans merchants, led by the indefatigable J. D. B. De Bow, sponsored a large convention that met in New Orleans on January 5, 1852. More than 600 delegates, representing 11 states, urged economic diversification in the South, which they hoped might result from improvements in transportation.

Between 1852 and 1860, De Bow organized a succession of annual commercial conventions that met in various southern cities to discuss the plight of the region. As Baltimore (1852), Memphis (1853), Charleston (1854), New Orleans (1855), Richmond (1856), Savannah (1857), and Knoxville (1857) hosted such gatherings, however, increasing economic rivalries among major southern cities became as evident on the one hand as a growing spirit of southern economic nationalism on the other. Spirited defenses of slavery became much more common after 1852 than in previous years. Indeed, when delegates met at the Montgomery convention in 1858, the political FIRE-EATERS seized control and used it as a platform for their extreme views. The last southern commercial convention met in Vicksburg in May, 1859, and devoted most of its discussions to slavery expansion.

These antebellum commercial conventions were significant in promoting southern economic nationalism. And it is quite likely that they influenced the minds of many southerners who in the post–Civil War era supported economic diversification and Henry W. Grady's call to build an industrialized NEW SOUTH.

See H. Wender, *Southern Commercial Conventions, 1837–1859* (1930), most useful; and Library of Congress for official reports of particular conventions. For contemporary accounts, see *De Bow's Review*; *Niles' Register* (1828–29, 1837–40, 1842, 1845–46); *Southern Literary Messenger* (1839, 1845, 1846); New York *Times*; New York *Tribune*; Baltimore *American*; Richmond *Enquirer*; and New Orleans *Picayune*.

GERALD D. NASH
University of New Mexico

CONVICT LEASE SYSTEM. Prior to 1860, only Kentucky, Alabama, and Louisiana had resorted to convict hiring or leasing. As slaves, most black offenders had been punished by their masters (SLAVE CODES), and many white felons had been confined in local or county jails (PENAL SYSTEMS). After the Civil War, when both white and black convicts had to be managed by the same judicial process, southern governments began leasing them out to private operators. By 1880, all southern states plus Nebraska and the New Mexico Territory had adopted the convict lease system in one form or another.

Under the "contract" arrangement that prevailed in Virginia, South Carolina, and Texas, inmates continued to be cared for and guarded by state officials; only the convicts' labor was hired (and paid for) by private contractors. A "lease," strictly speaking, however, gave complete control over the entire penal system—convicts, buildings, and guards—to the lessee. This latter version was established in the remaining southern states and was decidedly more brutal because it erased all meaningful vestiges of state control and supervision.

Working under desperate conditions everywhere, southern convicts constructed and repaired levees in Arkansas, Mississippi, and Louisiana; mined coal in Alabama, Georgia, and Tennessee; picked fruit and processed turpentine in Florida; cultivated cotton in the black belt, rice in South Carolina, tobacco in the Upper South, and sugarcane in Louisiana; and built railroads throughout the entire region. During its peak years from 1880 to 1910, thousands of convicts across the South—many of them children and mostly blacks—were worked, starved, or beaten to death, were killed while attempting to escape, or died from untreated diseases. Thousands more were permanently maimed or continually abused. Making money was the sole objective of the lease system. Tennessee, South Carolina, and Louisiana abolished convict leasing in the 1890s, and the last of the lessees had been replaced by state control at the outset of the New Deal.

See H. J. Zimmerman, "Penal Systems in South" (Ph.D. dissertation, University of North Carolina, 1947); D. T. Carter, "Convict Lease" (M.A. thesis, University of Wisconsin, 1964); and M. T. Carleton, *Politics and Punishment* (1971).

MARK T. CARLETON
Public Affairs Research Council of Louisiana, Inc.

COODE'S REBELLION (1689). On July 16, 1689, a small band of south Maryland planters led by the perennial malcontent John Coode (1648–1709) seized the statehouse at St. Mary's City. The ostensible reason for this military coup of the proprietary government was to declare Maryland finally for King William and Queen Mary. Yet deeper reasons for the uprising were present: inadequate defense, economic distress, proprietary favoritism, and a deep anti-Catholicism among the Protestant majority. After the initial violence, further disorder was avoided by the efforts of the local gentry, who maintained control of the county governments. Amid growing charges of opportunism and embezzlement, the rebel regime was replaced by a royal government in 1692. The rebellion had primarily two lasting results: the end of the Baltimore proprietorship for 25 years and the disfranchisement of the Catholic minority.

See L. G. Carr and D. J. Jordan, *Maryland's Revolution* (1974), best account; M. Kammen, *Maryland Historical Magazine* (Dec., 1960); and D. Lovejoy, *Glorious Revolution* (1972).

KEVIN P. KELLY
Bowdoin College

COOKE, JOHN ESTEN (1830–1886). Whether or not the story that John Esten Cooke buried his silver spurs on the surrender field of Appomattox is true is unimportant; it is just the sort of romantic gesture that characterizes him. Born in Winchester, Cooke grew up in Richmond and read for the law, but acceptance of his work by the *Southern Literary Messenger*, a small payment from *Harper's*, and encouragement from William Makepeace Thackeray turned him to a literary career. He gained national recognition for his prewar novels about early Virginia, a period George William Bagby accused him of seeing through rose-colored glasses of hindsight. The *Virginia Comedians* (1854) is the best of his early work. While serving in the Confederate army as Jeb Stuart's ordnance officer, Cooke wrote dispatches to Richmond's *Southern Illustrated News* and published a hastily written *Life of Stonewall Jackson*. After the war he mined his Confederate experiences to produce *Surry of Eagle's Nest* (1866), *Wearing of the Gray* (1867), *Mohun* (1869), *Hammer and Rapier* (1870), and a biography of Robert E. Lee. He later turned to a wider range of subject matter, his best novel of his late years being *My Lady Pokahontas* (1885).

See J. O. Beaty, *John Esten Cooke, Virginian* (1922); R. B. Harwell, *Journal of Southern History* (Nov., 1953); and J. B. Hubbell, *Journal of Southern History* (Nov., 1941).

RICHARD B. HARWELL
Georgia Southern College

COOLIDGE, CALVIN, ADMINISTRATION (1923–1929) initially retained Warren G. Harding's cabinet and continued most of the policies of the HARDING ADMINISTRATION. Following his own election in 1924, however, Coolidge gradually replaced most of the Harding cabinet with less venturesome men. Moreover, Coolidge's personal lassitude and the deep factional divisions among the Republicans in Congress brought embarrassing defeats for the administration. Progressive Republicans, who had opposed Coolidge in 1924, continued to act as an opposition group, forcing him to rely on the presidential veto, or the threat of it, to influence Congress. Evidence of the administration's deteriorating relations with Congress came with the Senate's rejection of Charles Beecher Warren as attorney general—the first cabinet rejection since the administration of Andrew Johnson. Coolidge was largely taken up with the ceremonial aspects of the presidency, providing little direction for his administration. He supported the revival of the Ayer bill in 1927 and opposed the expansion of the Muscle Shoals project (TENNESSEE VALLEY AUTHORITY) at public expense in the same year. He occasionally intervened in Republican party affairs, generally in support of friends in the North and of LILY-WHITE factions in the South.

See D. R. McCoy, *C. Coolidge* (1967); P. R. Moran, *C. Coolidge* (1970); and C. M. Fuess, *C. Coolidge* (1940).

ROGER M. OLIEN
University of Texas, Permian Basin

COOPER, DOUGLAS HANCOCK (1815–1879), the key link between the Confederacy and the Indians of Indian Territory, was a native of Mississippi and a Mexican War veteran. From 1853 to 1861, he was United States agent to the CHOCTAW and CHICKASAW tribes, then became Confederate agent to the two tribes. Commissioned colonel of the 1st Choctaw and Chickasaw Mounted Rifles, he commanded them at the battle of PEA RIDGE, Ark. Cooper later held a brigadier general's commission and commanded all Confederate troops in Indian Territory. He led his forces to defeat at the battle of Honey Springs, the most important engagement of the war in Indian Territory, on July 17, 1863. After the war, Cooper sought payment of Choctaw claims against the federal government. He died in poverty at old Ft. Washita, Indian Territory.

See M. H. Wright, *Chronicles of Oklahoma* (Summer, 1954); *Official Records, Armies*, Ser. 1, Vols. XIII, XXII, XLI; *Annual Reports of Commissioner of Indian Affairs* (1853–61).

LEROY H. FISCHER
Oklahoma State University

COOPER, JOHN SHERMAN (1901–), was born in Pulaski County, Ky. After attending Centre College, Yale University (B.A., 1923), and Harvard Law School, he was admitted to the Kentucky bar and elected to the lower house of the state legislature (1928–1930). He was a county court judge (1930–1938) prior to returning briefly to private practice and to enlisting during World War II in the U.S. Army. He received a special commendation for his work in restructuring the German judicial system in occupied Bavaria. Although he was elected a circuit court judge in 1945 in Kentucky, his future career was as a politician and diplomat. In 1946 he was elected as a Republican to the U.S. Senate. He failed to gain reelection to a full term in 1948, however, and President Harry S. Truman appointed him a delegate to the United Nations (1949–1951). In 1952 he was again elected to a short term in the Senate, but in 1954 he again failed to gain reelection. The Dwight Eisenhower administration named him ambassador to India (1955–1956). The death of ALBEN BARKLEY created yet another short-term vacancy in the Senate, and in 1956 Cooper was elected to that body for a third time. When standing for reelection in 1960, he won his first and only full term of office. The checkered pattern of his success with Kentucky's voters reflected not so much a changing perception of his own ability and integrity, but the steady if irregular growth of Republicanism in this border state.

See R. Schulman, *John Sherman Cooper* (1976).

COOPER, SAMUEL (1798–1876), was the senior general in the Confederate army and one of the few northern-born officers who fought with the South. Born in Hackensack, N.J., he entered the U.S. Military Academy from New York and was commissioned in 1815. Except for brief service in the SEMINOLE WAR, he was almost continuously on staff duty at Washington, where in 1852 he became adjutant general. His marriage to a granddaughter of George Mason and friendship with Jefferson Davis made Cooper thoroughly southern. In March, 1861, he offered his services to the Confederacy and was promptly appointed adjutant general and inspector general with the rank of full general. He did not serve in the field, but his administrative experience proved invaluable to the Confederate army. He fled Richmond with President Davis in April, 1865, but later surrendered. He lived near Alexandria after the war. Hearing of Cooper's hardships, Robert E. Lee sent him $400 raised among former Confederate generals.

See F. Lee *Southern Historical Society Papers* (1877); F. T. Miller, *Photographic History* (1959); E. J. Warner, *Generals in Gray* (1959); G. W. Cullum, *Biographical Register* (1891); F. B. Heitman, *Historical Register* (1903); and C. A. Evans (ed.), *Confederate Military History* (1899).

PALMER H. BOEGER
East Central Oklahoma State University

COOPER, THOMAS (1759–1839), was born in England, educated at Oxford, and became a successful manufacturer and ardent supporter of the abolition movement, the French Revolution, and parliamentary reform. Forced to flee Britain because of his radical views, he settled in Pennsylvania with his friend Joseph Priestly. Cooper's radicalism and his support of Thomas Jefferson brought him a jail term under the Alien and Sedition Acts. Released in 1801, he served as a judge, doctor, scientist, professor, and finally president of South Carolina College. As he grew older he rejected the principles of democracy and substituted a dedication to property and the sovereign state. These later views made him a spokesman for South Carolina during the NULLIFICATION controversy and one of the first southern leaders to advocate secession as a means of preserving states' rights.

See D. Malone, *Thomas Cooper* (1926).

ROBERT T. BROWN
Westfield State College

COOPER V. AARON (358 U.S. 1 [1958]). In February, 1958, the Little Rock, Ark., school board asked permission from the federal courts to delay school integration in that city for two and a half years pending final determination of legal efforts to nullify the U.S. Supreme Court's ruling in BROWN V. BOARD OF EDUCATION. The board based its request upon the "chaos, turmoil, and bedlam" that had accompanied admission of nine black students to Central High School in September, 1957. Governor ORVAL FAUBUS had declared the school off limits to black students and ordered the Arkansas National Guard to block their entrance. The federal government had obtained an injunction against Faubus, enjoining him from preventing the attendance of blacks. When the black students entered Central in September, 1957, a mob had rioted in front of the school. To protect the students, President Dwight D. Eisenhower dispatched federal troops to Little Rock and federalized the National Guard.

The school board's request was granted in district court, but the U.S. Court of Appeals for the

Sixth Circuit reversed the district judge. In September, 1958, the Supreme Court was called into special session to review the case of *Cooper* v. *Aaron*. It unanimously upheld the circuit court's refusal to suspend enforcement, and the black students returned to Central. Chief Justice Earl Warren declared that the school board, as an agency of the state, was restrained by the Fourteenth Amendment from denying to any person equal protection of the laws. He made it plain that the *Brown* decision was the supreme law of the land and would not be reconsidered by the Court. However, Warren left open the possibility that federal district courts, under certain conditions, might permit deferment of desegregation.

See L. Miller, *Petitioners* (1966); D. B. King and C. W. Quick, *Legal Aspects of Civil Rights Movement* (1965); and P. E. Jackson, *Dissent in Supreme Court* (1969).

VIRGINIA V. HAMILTON
University of Alabama, Birmingham

COPPERHEAD was an opprobrious term that Republicans applied to peace Democrats during the Civil War. According to Republican partisans, Copperheads were traitors, "northern tools of the political Brahmins of the South," "blind and venomous enemies of our Government" who did "more to prolong [the] war than all the rebels in the South." Having pinned this label on the peace Democrats during the congressional elections of 1862, Republicans used it indiscriminately during the presidential campaign of 1864 to discredit all opponents of Abraham Lincoln as rebel sympathizers ready to accept "peace at any price." Perhaps *every* Democrat was not a traitor, they said, but certainly every traitor was a Democrat!

Contrary to these politically motivated accusations, the Copperheads as a group were less prosouthern than anti–New England, anti-Republican, and anti-Negro. Although they were numerous in New York and Pennsylvania, their principal strongholds were in the agricultural states of the old Northwest, especially in Ohio, Indiana, and Illinois. There Copperheads professed to represent the interests of western farmers against eastern bankers, railroad operators, and manufacturers. Much of their rhetoric was strikingly similar to that of the Populists of the late nineteenth century. It was also loaded with racial demagoguery. BLACK REPUBLICANS, the Copperheads charged, were tools of the New England abolitionists, waging a war not for the Union but for emancipation, Negro equality, and racial "amalgamation." To advance this unholy cause the Lincoln administration would destroy the liberties of white men by conscription, suppression of free speech, and arbitrary arrests. Copperheads thus stood as defenders of civil liberties against "military despotism."

By 1864, believing the war a failure, Copperheads called for an armistice; to promote peace and resist Lincoln's "tyranny," some joined secret societies, such as the Sons of Liberty (AMERICAN KNIGHTS, ORDER OF; KNIGHTS OF THE GOLDEN CIRCLE). Confederate agents in Canada, encouraged by Republican reports of a Copperhead conspiracy, hoped to enlist Copperhead support for the southern cause. But this hope, like the hope for aid from abroad, was a will-o'-the-wisp. With rare exceptions the peace Democrats were neither conspirators nor believers in peace at any price. Rather, like the celebrated plank that Clement L. Vallandigham wrote for the Democratic national platform of 1864, they favored a negotiated peace on the basis of a restored Union. Unfortunately, some Confederate leaders seemed to take the treason charges of Republican propagandists at face value. The influence of the peace Democrats always fluctuated with the fortunes of war; and the Union military victories in the late summer and fall of 1864 brought the final collapse of copperheadism, as they foretold the ultimate defeat of the Confederacy itself.

See W. Gray, *Hidden Civil War* (1942), a traditional account; F. L. Klement, *Copperheads in Middle West* (1960), best study available; R. O. Curry, *Civil War History* (March, 1967); R. H. Abzug, *Indiana Magazine of History* (March, 1970); and C. H. Coleman, *Mississippi Valley Historical Review* (Sept., 1938).

KENNETH M. STAMPP
University of California, Berkeley

CORINTH, BATTLE OF (October 3 and 4, 1862), took place when EARL VAN DORN's Confederate force attacked the federal garrison in the town commanded by William Rosecrans, Van Dorn's West Point classmate. Van Dorn and STERLING PRICE chose Corinth, Miss., as their objective in conjunction with an advance into Kentucky made by their department commander, BRAXTON BRAGG. The Confederates had occupied Corinth, an important railway junction, earlier, where Van Dorn had been instrumental in constructing the town's fortifications. The first day's assault was in three Confederate waves from north of the town. Although the right and center made little progress against the strong Union position, Price's left cut its way through the outer fortifications and threatened the town. A few hours more of daylight might have turned the tide. During the night Rosecrans regrouped his force and brought up reinforcements from nearby garrisons and halted a new attack with bloody ferocity. Confused Confederate planning and leadership contributed to the repulse, which saw one of the Confederate units under the colorful Texan, Colonel William Rogers, storm into the town before being destroyed. Why Rosecrans did not follow up his victory and annihilate the attackers has never been properly explained. Van Dorn and Price escaped with their survivors into southern Mississippi. Van Dorn later was exonerated of blame for the loss by a court of inquiry. His reputation as a commander suffered, however, and he never held a major command again.

See A. Castel, *Sterling Price* (1968); T. L. Connelly, *Army of Heartland* (1967); M. F. Cockrell (ed.), *Lost Account of Corinth* (1955); and R. Hartje, *Earl Van Dorn* (1967).

ROBERT HARTJE
Wittenberg University

CORN, maize, or Indian corn (*Zea mays*) is a plant of American origin. The modern history of corn begins when white men first set foot on American soil. Later explorers to the New World found corn being grown by the Indians in all parts of America where agriculture was practiced. To the early colonists it became the daily bread by which they were nourished. The first references to corn in the literature appear early in the sixteenth century. According to records of the Spanish in Florida in 1528 and of the French in the Carolinas in 1562, great areas of corn were grown from Tampa Bay to beyond the Mississippi. Early English explorers found corn planted in what is now the area occupied by the states of Virginia, North Carolina, and South Carolina. As agriculture extended westward and to the south, corn moved with the settlers and became the staple diet.

In 1839 Tennessee had a 45 million bushel corn harvest and led all 27 states of the Union. Kentucky produced only 5 million fewer bushels, and Virginia was a close third. The area devoted to corn in the South increased to 37 million acres in 1900 and reached a high of nearly 46 million acres by 1920 (44.6 percent of U.S. total). As additional crops were introduced, the area devoted to corn decreased until at present, when SOYBEANS have replaced much of the corn land, only 12 million acres are grown (16 percent of U.S. total). In 1920 corn occupied 37.6 percent of the total cropland in the South, compared with 13.7 percent now. By 1900 the total production of corn grain in the South was 662 million bushels (31.5 percent of total U.S. production). Production increased to over

1 billion bushels by 1920 (34 percent of U.S. total). At present about 834 million bushels of grain are grown (14.5 percent of total U.S. production). The total dollar value of the corn crop in 1900 was $294 million, and in 1920 it was $1.2 billion, both of which constituted a large portion of the total economy of the South. Average acre yields in 1900 were 17.5 bushels and increased only to 25 bushels by 1950, but this was not much lower than the average for the U.S. With improved cultural practices, greater use of commercial fertilizers, and the growing of hybrids, average yields increased by 1975 to 68 bushels (18 bushels less than U.S. average).

Present-day dent corns arose through crosses between the gourd seed type of Virginia and the eight-rowed flints grown by the Indians. Numerous distinct varieties were developed through mass selection by individual farmers in the years to follow. The first reported case of mass selection, in which the source of the pollen was given consideration, came from Tennessee in 1867, when a farmer selected a variety bearing uniformly two or three ears per plant. Although some self-pollination of lines began prior to 1920, inbreeding of corn began in 1922 in Kentucky, Tennessee, and Louisiana and was soon to follow in 1924 at Tifton, Ga., and in 1927 in Florida. Hybrid seed from these inbreds was first used in 1936. Its use increased slowly, but by 1956 over 90 percent of the corn grown in the South was hybrid. Now practically all corn is hybrid.

Until about 1930 corn was grown mainly for grain, being utilized directly on the farm where grown for human consumption (cornbread, hominy, mush or polenta, griddle cakes, and cereal preparations) and as feed for livestock (HOGS, HORSES, and MULES). White corn was preferred in the South but at present more yellow corn is grown because it is richer in carotene, a precursor of vitamin A. White corn is still preferred for hominy and cereal products. Currently, 56 percent of the corn grain produced is sold from the farms, but much of it finds its way back as processed livestock and poultry feeds. In the middle 1940s, nearly 1 million acres of corn were grown in the South for hogging down, grazing, and forage. Beginning about 1940 the entire plant was harvested and used as ensilage for feeding cattle. About 1.25 million acres are used for this purpose at present. Sweet corn is universally grown in home gardens for immediate table use, and 75,000 acres are grown commercially for the fresh market, principally in Florida during the fall, winter, and spring. Kentucky and Missouri are the only states that grow popcorn for the confectionary trade.

CORN PRODUCTION IN THE SOUTH, 1850–1969
(thousands of bushels)

State	1850	1860	1870	1880	1890	1900	1910	1920	1930	1940	1950	1959	1969	% of U.S. total
Ala.	28,754	33,226	16,978	25,451	30,072	35,053	30,695	43,699	35,684	31,028	40,972	41,819	20,546	.46
Ark.	8,894	17,824	13,382	24,156	33,982	44,144	37,610	34,227	27,388	33,762	21,626	11,345	1,455	.03
Del.	3,146	3,892	3,010	3,894	3,097	4,737	4,840	3,686	3,467	3,598	4,159	7,038	13,506	.3
Fla.	1,997	2,834	2,225	3,174	3,701	5,311	7,024	8,831	6,618	5,191	3,845	7,385	11,105	.25
Ga.	30,080	30,776	17,646	23,202	29,261	34,032	39,375	51,492	39,493	37,604	37,837	49,756	54,195	1.2
Ky.	58,673	64,044	50,091	72,852	78,435	73,974	83,348	71,518	61,008	61,052	71,010	70,153	64,365	1.4
La.	10,266	16,854	7,597	9,890	13,082	22,063	26,010	21,676	18,280	22,444	13,030	11,097	4,077	.09
Md.	10,750	13,445	11,702	15,969	14,928	19,767	17,911	21,083	14,543	15,450	16,761	21,580	37,977	.85
Miss.	22,447	29,058	15,637	21,341	26,148	38,790	28,429	38,095	34,936	36,035	37,934	32,497	7,943	.18
Mo.	36,215	72,892	66,034	202,414	197,000	208,845	191,427	146,342	112,348	124,058	129,968	201,053	169,467	3.8
N.C.	27,941	30,079	18,454	28,020	25,784	34,819	34,064	40,998	35,609	50,797	58,054	70,520	77,788	1.75
S.C.	16,271	15,066	7,614	11,767	13,770	17,430	20,872	27,472	19,326	23,527	23,624	17,525	19,172	.4
Tenn.	52,276	52,090	41,344	62,764	63,635	67,307	67,682	70,639	61,046	54,905	56,100	50,905	28,991	.65
Tex.	6,029	16,501	20,555	29,065	69,112	109,970	75,499	108,377	66,251	69,650	44,077	36,276	25,238	.57
Va.	35,254	38,320	17,649	29,120	27,172	36,748	28,295	42,303	32,773	33,601	33,150	28,312	32,511	.73
W.Va.	incl. in Va.		8,198	14,091	13,731	16,611	17,119	17,010	11,656	12,391	9,650	4,423	3,278	.07

See *USDA Yearbook* (1936), good; H. A. Wallace and E. N. Bressman, *Corn and Corn Growing* (1949); E. V. Komarek, *Florida Corn* (1951); P. Weatherwax, *Indian Corn in Old America* (1954); and *USDA Reports: SCIC* (1939–74).

LEONARD M. JOSEPHSON
University of Tennessee

CORPUS CHRISTI, TEX. (pop. 201,581), is on the south shore of Corpus Christi Bay at the mouth of the Nueces River. Numerous efforts to settle the area after a visit by Spanish explorers in 1519 were thwarted by a combination of the site's relative isolation, the hostility of area Indians, and frequent hurricanes. Between 1817 and 1821, the pirate JEAN LAFFITE ran a commune in the bay area in part because of its remoteness from both Mexican and American settlements. In 1839, however, Colonel Henry Kinney constructed a trading post on the site of the present city, a location contested at that time by both Mexico and the Republic of Texas. Six years later, on August 1, 1845, General ZACHARY TAYLOR's forces arrived at Kinney's trading post to assert American claims to the territory south of the Nueces. From that date on, Corpus Christi has grown as a port of entry and a commercial center.

Publicized as early as 1848 as "the Italy of America," Corpus Christi actively recruited American settlers. As the city grew more populous, tensions between the city's growing Anglo population and the Mexicans of the surrounding backcountry increased. Beginning in 1875, a long and continuing feud between these two groups

erupted in violence. The city's growth as a shipping point for cattle, cotton, wool, and processed meat continued uninterrupted throughout the late nineteenth century. During the 1920s the discovery of nearby petroleum gave the city yet another industry, and the construction here in 1941 of a U.S. naval air station expanded the city's economic base still farther. Del Mar College (1935) and the University of Corpus Christi (1947) are both located here.

See files of Corpus Christi *Caller* (1883–) and *Times* (1909–).

CÔTE DES ALLEMANDS. Partly forming the Louisiana parishes (counties) of St. Charles and St. John, this narrow strip of arable land bordering the Mississippi River between Baton Rouge and New Orleans received its name during the French colonial era. In the 1720s Alsatians, Lorrainers, Swiss, and Germans were settled here as part of the colonizing schemes of the Company of the West (MISSISSIPPI BUBBLE). They were joined in the 1750s by compatriots fleeing religious persecution in Europe. Considering themselves ethnically different from the neighboring French and ACADIANS, these fiercely independent yeomen farmers actively engaged in the rebellion of 1768, marched with BERNARDO DE GALVEZ to besiege Baton Rouge (1779), and stood with Andrew Jackson at the battle of NEW ORLEANS (1815). Their cultural characteristics were gradually gallicized throughout the nineteenth century and then anglicized in the twentieth century. Today, the residents of the German Coast, largely descended from the original colonists, blend a traditional agricultural life-style (mainly sugarcane) with a modern industrial way of life (mainly petrochemicals).

See J. H. Deiler, *German Coast of Louisiana* (1909), only monograph; G. R. Conrad, *Revue d'Histoire de l'Amerique Française* (March, 1975); and R. Le Conte, *Louisiana History* (Winter, 1967).

GLENN R. CONRAD
University of Southwestern Louisiana

COTTEN, SALLIE SIMS SOUTHALL (1846–1929), was born in Brunswick County, Va. She graduated from Greensboro Female College in 1864. After teaching school for two years, she married in 1866 Robert Randolph Cotten, a Confederate veteran, who became a successful merchant and planter in Pitt County, N.C. During the first 30 years of her marriage, Mrs. Cotten gave birth to nine children and was an active worker in the Episcopal church. In 1893 while serving with North Carolina's exhibition committee at the Chicago World's Fair, she became convinced that women's civic spirit should be channeled into an organized effort for community and state improvements. The result was the formation in 1902 of the North Carolina Federation of Women's Clubs. For the next 20 years, under her leadership, this organization played a significant role in local civic reform and in combating adult illiteracy, passing child labor laws, and improving correctional institutions.

See S. S. Cotten, *History of North Carolina Federation of Women's Clubs* (1925); and A. F. Scott, *Notable American Women* (1971).

PAUL E. FULLER
Wesleyan College

COTTERILL, ROBERT SPENCER (1884–1967), was born in Battle Run, Ky. He was educated at Kentucky Wesleyan College (A.B., 1904), University of Virginia (M.A., 1907), University of Wisconsin (Ph.D., 1918)—where he was influenced by Frederick Jackson Turner—and University of Chicago (summers, 1915–1917). Cotterill taught at Kentucky Wesleyan (1910–1914), Western Maryland College (1915–1920), University of Louisville (1920–1928), and Florida State College for Women (Florida State University after 1947) from 1928 until his retirement in 1951. Author of four books, *History of Pioneer Kentucky* (1918), *The Old South* (1936), *A Short History of the Americas* (1939), and *The Southern Indians* (1954),

Cotterill also wrote many articles and book reviews. Although he was one of the first to write a comprehensive single-volumed synthesis of the history of the Old South, he is perhaps most widely known for his sympathetic study of southern Indians' economic, political, and military relations with whites from the colonial period to the Indian removal. Throughout his career Cotterill maintained an interest in Kentucky local history, as well as in the Old South and southern Indians. He also had a special interest in the railroads of the Old South. In 1948 Cotterill was president of the Southern Historical Association.

J. ANTHONY PAREDES
Florida State University

COTTON provided the principal vehicle for the spread of Anglo-Saxon civilization across the southern part of the United States (COTTON BELT) between 1815 and 1845. By 1801 the center of the cotton-growing region had spread from the Georgia and South Carolina coast into the UP-COUNTRY and thence northward into southeastern Virginia. From Georgia its movement was westward into Texas, where it barely reached the hundredth meridian before the Civil War. West of this line cotton was little known until the early decades of the twentieth century, when the BOLL WEEVIL invaded the eastern zone of the cotton belt.

Cotton culture required little skill, and its production provided almost year-round employment. It was relatively nonperishable and possessed a high value per unit of weight. By the Civil War annual American production reached 5,385,000 bales (a bale was 400 pounds), which was more than double that of 1850. This expansion was a result of the growth of demand and the opening of virgin territories in the Southwest. Labor problems were largely solved by shifting slaves from exhausted TOBACCO lands in Virginia and Maryland and by increasing use of tools and improved culture. Before 1860 approximately two-thirds of all American cotton was produced in the area east of the Mississippi River. A century later this area was producing only a third of the nation's total. California began growing cotton in 1916, and by 1960 that state was the second-largest producer, contributing 1,950,000 bales of the nation's total of 14,309,000 bales. The Texas crop of 4,350,000 bales almost equaled that of all states east of the Mississippi.

Beginning as early as 1682, varieties of cotton were introduced into the American colonies from many parts of the world. Nankeen cotton from China was produced before the Revolution in the

COTTON PRODUCTION IN THE SOUTH, 1850–1969
(thousands of running bales)

State	1850[a]	1860[a]	1870[b]	1880[b]	1890[b]	1900[c]	1910	1920	1930	1940	1950	1959	1969	% of U.S. total
Ala.	564	990	429	670	915	1,094	1,130	718	1,313	773	824	683	498	4.8
Ark.	65	367	248	608	617	706	777	869	1,398	1,351	1,584	1,484	1,150	11.0
Del.														
Fla.	45	65	39	55	58	54	65	20	34	11	18	14	10	.1
Ga.	499	702	474	814	1,192	1,233	1,992	1,682	1,344	905	610	521	311	3.0
Ky.	1		1	1	1	1	3	3	9	16	13	11	5	.05
La.	179	778	351	509	659	700	269	307	799	718	607	479	516	5.0
Md.														
Miss.	484	1,203	565	963	1,155	1,287	1,127	958	1,875	1,533	1,497	1,561	1,383	13.4
Mo.		41	1	20	16	26	54	64	225	433	472	482	332	3.2
N.C.	74	146	145	390	336	433	665	858	764	458	472	319	115	1.1
S.C.	301	353	225	523	747	844	1,280	1,477	836	850	544	411	236	2.3
Tenn.	195	296	182	331	191	235	265	307	504	436	617	620	428	4.2
Tex.	58	431	351	805	1,471	2,584	2,455	2,972	3,793	2,724	5,550	4,156	3,041	29.5
Va. & W.Va.	4	13		20	5	10	10	25	52	13	19	12	3	.02

[a] av. 400 lbs.   [b] av. 450 lbs.   [c] av. 500 lbs.

backcountry, where its yellow fiber was put to domestic use. The long-staple, silky, black seed Sea Island cotton (*Gossypium barbadense*), introduced from the West Indies about 1785, was the first to achieve commercial importance. Grown only in a limited area along the seacoast, it had seed that could be separated from the lint by a simple roller gin consisting of two cylinders revolving in opposite directions (COTTON GINNING). The prolific green seed cotton of a much shorter staple was difficult to separate from the seed. This led to Eli Whitney's invention of the gin in 1793. Almost immediately cotton became the commercial crop of the up-country.

Second in importance to Whitney's gin in the development of cotton production was the work of a few Mississippi cotton breeders of the late antebellum period. Despite the disadvantage of its short staple, the green seed variety continued to be grown in the eastern cotton belt until the early 1830s, when it fell prey to disease. In the Mississippi region the black seed or Creole cotton was predominant. It gave a high yield but was difficult to harvest. Mississippi planters therefore early began a search for a more suitable variety and one resistant to rot. Prior to 1820 the Mexican cotton was crossed with the green seed and the Creole to retain some of the better qualities of each. Later Dr. Rush Nutt and others through selective breeding produced a hybrid known as Petit Gulf. Its seed was sold throughout the cotton belt, where it won universal favor. This and several subsequent strains all were descended from Mexican cotton. However, there was little crossbreeding attempt-

ed, and no use was made of botanical knowledge before the Civil War. The most significant advances in agronomy came after 1940; some of these were designed to meet new demands of mechanization and chemical controls of insects and diseases.

Early cultivation of cotton was done with the hoe, but ridge culture developed after 1800. Ridges varied from three to six feet apart depending on fertility. The use of FERTILIZERS began about 1840 with compost, lime, and manure. At the same time contour plowing and primitive terracing techniques were begun. Guano was introduced, but its use spread slowly. The V-shaped harrow came into wide use after 1830 and was used in planting and after culture. Ingenious blacksmiths converted these into cultivators, side harrows, and double shovels. In the early 1840s Martin W. Philips introduced the Mississippi scraper, whose sharp edge ran along the sloping side of the row cutting grass and weeds and loosening the soil. The scraper later was modified to become the Yost plow and scraper, which with additional modifications remained for more than a century the basic plow in cotton cultivation.

The marketing of cotton was done by FACTORS, who also procured planters' supplies and credit. After the Civil War the factorage system was resumed but eventually was replaced by more efficient agencies. The railroads created markets in interior towns, where the local merchant became the principal source of credit and often a landlord in the process. His combined roles of landlord, merchant, and creditor made him the most important economic power in the countryside. He was inseparable from the CROP LIEN on which his credit was extended. The rise of futures sales frequently made him a speculator.

By 1935 fully 60 percent of the South's cotton farms were run by tenants, and the system involved more whites than blacks. The cotton lien encouraged overproduction, and diversification lagged. These problems had become extremely serious and pervasive by the 1930s. At this time were inaugurated federal policies that limited production, supported prices, and provided easier credit. These led to reduced cotton acreages and eventually to the virtual disappearance of the tenant and the small grower.

See L. C. Gray, *History of Agriculture in Southern U.S. to 1860* (2 vols.; 1941); J. C. Bonner, *History of Georgia Agriculture, 1732–1860* (1964); J. H. Moore, *Agriculture in Ante-Bellum Mississippi* (1958); and D. L. Cohn, *Life and Times of King Cotton* (1956).

JAMES C. BONNER
Georgia College

COTTON BELT is the name applied to the region of the United States where COTTON is or was the main agricultural product or where cotton growing created substantial economic and social forces or ideas thought to be peculiar to life in such an area. The belt developed originally in South Carolina and Georgia in the late 1700s, then spread north and west to include part of North Carolina, South Carolina, Georgia, Alabama, northern Florida, Mississippi, western Tennessee, Arkansas, southeastern Missouri, and most of Texas. By 1860 it contained approximately 400,000 square miles. Since the Civil War the belt has moved steadily southwestward, into areas beyond the South. Before the Civil War, slave labor and the plantation system were regarded as the main characteristics of the cotton belt. After the war, plantations were somewhat replaced in the Southeast by small farming units, partly operated by TENANT FARMERS. Perfection of the mechanical cotton picker after 1945 again allowed development of the large farming unit, displacing many tenant farmers.

See W. E. Dodd, *Cotton Kingdom* (1919); and U. B. Phillips, *Life and Labor* (1929). Best depository is University of North Carolina Library, Chapel Hill.

HENRY S. MARKS
Northeast Alabama State Junior College

COTTON GINNING is the process of removing the seed from cotton. A cotton gin is a mechanical device used to extract the seed and is also a processing plant in which ginning is performed. Machines designed to remove seeds from cotton date from antiquity and the terms "gin" and "ginning" used in reference to cotton occur in southern literature at least as early as the 1740s. One of the first devices for separating the lint from the seed of cotton, the *charkha*, originated in India centuries ago. The charkha consisted of a pair of rollers set horizontally on a frame. When the rollers were turned with a hand crank, the seeds were squeezed from the cotton as it passed between them. Machines used in North America early in the eighteenth century employed the roller principle of the charkha.

Although the early roller ginning machines were crudely effective, they possessed certain disadvantages. The major drawback was their failure to work equally well in ginning the two types of cotton known to the early settlers: black seed, or long-staple cotton; and green seed, or short-staple cotton. The seeds of long-staple cotton were smooth and were easily removed by the roller gin, but those of the short-staple variety clung so tightly to the fiber that many were crushed but not removed. By the early 1790s roller-ginned, long-staple cotton was raised commercially along the Georgia-Carolina coast. Although the habitat of long-staple cotton did not extend far inland, short-staple cotton thrived in the Piedmont of Georgia and the Carolinas, where frontier farmers were attempting to grow cotton commercially. They were hindered in their efforts, however, by the failure of the roller gin to remove the seed adequately from the short-staple variety.

Louis Prat (1744), James Marion (1747), Claude Joseph Du Breuil (1752), Baron von Krebs (1774), Joseph Eve (1790), Eli Whitney (1793), Robert Watkins (1796), and William Longstreet (1796) were among those who sought to perfect the cotton gin. Rather than improving upon the roller method, Whitney (1765–1825) invented a new principle. His gin contained a cylinder filled with wire teeth set in annular rows. As the cylinder was turned the teeth drew the cotton into a breastwork of transverse grooves through which the lint but not the seed passed. A major improvement on the Whitney principle came in 1796, when Hodgen Holmes patented a gin in which sawlike teeth were cut into iron disks. This modification gained general acceptance and gave the name "saw gin" to the new machine. The saw gin could easily clean either long-staple or short-staple cotton, but it tended to cut many of the fibers. For this reason it never gained acceptance in the now extinct long-staple (Sea Island) cotton districts of South Carolina, Georgia, and Florida.

Although public gin plants existed from the beginning of commercial cotton culture in the South, before the Civil War ginning was primarily a plantation activity. A planter erected a gin plant by purchasing the gin (or what came to be known as the "gin stand"), the running gear, and the bailing press and erected a structure to house the machinery. The typical ginhouse was a two-story wooden building. The lower floor contained the running gear and the upper one the gin stand. Ginned cotton was discharged into the lint room, which was situated behind or below the gin stand. The fiber was carried from the lint room to the bailing press a few yards from the ginhouse. There, horses hitched to long sweeps turned a screw to compress the lint into bales.

Following the Civil War significant changes occurred in methods of growing and marketing cotton. Small plantation gins declined in importance, and larger, public gin plants began to replace them. Changes in the plantation system were among the most important of the factors that contributed to the rise of the public plants. On prewar plantations, slaves were easily integrated into all phases of cotton production. Cotton was gathered on warm sunny autumn days and was stored; on inclement days the slaves were engaged in operating the cotton gin. Under the post–Civil War tenant farmer system, workers to operate the labor-intensive cotton gin could not be easily convened. As in the 1700s innovators sought to save labor by perfecting a cotton gin, so after the Civil War they sought to save labor by automating the movement of cotton from the wagon to the gin stand and from the gin stand to the press. Robert S. Munger (1854–1923) of Mexia, Tex., made the most important contribution. Between 1883 and 1885 he developed a "ginning system" whereby cotton was moved automatically from the time it left the wagon until a bale was removed from the press. A Munger gin plant with four gin stands easily processed 24 to 30 bales of cotton in the time it took a pre–Civil War gin to process four. Many improvements were later made, but the basic movement of fiber through a gin plant is still that of the Munger ginning system.

Emergence of large, public gin plants had a number of consequences. New buildings were designed to accommodate the ginning system. The number of gin plants decreased. Farming continued to be associated with ginning, but a group of new ancillary activities emerged, including manufacture of fertilizers and processing of cottonseed for oil. Sizes of the new public cotton gins and levels of ancillary businesses varied, but by 1910 cotton ginning was far removed from the simple activity that it had been in 1860.

Widespread adoption of mechanical cotton harvesters after World War II initiated a revolution in cotton ginning that was as sweeping as the one that occurred after the Civil War. The cotton gin of 1945 is as obsolete compared with a plant of the mid-1970s as the pre–Civil War cotton gin was compared with the ginning system of 1910. Machine-harvested cotton has a higher moisture content than hand-harvested fiber. The ginning system could extract a limited amount of trash and could partly dry the cotton, but it was not capable of efficiently ginning fiber gathered by mechanical harvesters. To facilitate removal of trash, additional equipment was installed, and to solve the moisture problem seed cotton driers were developed. Compression of the harvest season was another consequence of mechanical harvesting. The harvest season for hand-picked cotton extended ten to 12 weeks. Because mechanical pickers are not taken into the fields until most of the bolls are open, harvesting is completed in six weeks. Compression of the harvest season resulted in cotton arriving at the gin plant faster than it could be processed. Capacity was increased by considerably enlarging the sizes of gin stands. A modern gin plant can process a bale in three to eight minutes.

Decreases in numbers and substantial increases in costs of gin plants were consequences of the post–World War II revolution in cotton ginning. The number of cotton gin plants in the South reached a peak at the turn of the century. Between 1902 and 1945 the number declined from 31,948 to 8,455 and by 1973 had dropped to 2,880. Because of increases in sizes of plants, ginning capacity remained approximately the same.

See C. S. Aiken, *Proceedings of Association of American Geographers* (1971), and *Geographical Review* (April, 1973); C. A. Bennett, *Roller Cotton Ginning* (1960), and *Cotton Ginning Systems* (1962); and D. H. Thomas, *Journal of Southern History* (May, 1965).

CHARLES S. AIKEN
University of Tennessee, Knoxville

COTTON SNOBS was a derisive term aimed at the new-rich in the late antebellum South. In his 1860 analysis of southern society, Daniel R. Hundley of Alabama described this type as rural, poorly educated, conceited, irreligious, ostentatious, coarse, and debauched. Hundley emphasized that the "Cotton Snob" was the son of the unscrupulous, greedy "Southern Yankee" and was very different from the true "Southern Gentleman," a handsome, dignified fellow of aristocratic lineage. Economically and socially the white antebellum

South was flexible and fluid. Men and families rose or fell according to their abilities in a competitive, capitalistic system that included a small upper class based primarily on wealth, not lineage, a large, diversified middle class, and a smaller lower class (POOR WHITES) clearly above the black slaves.

See D. R. Hundley, *Social Relations* (1860), opinionated but largely accurate; W. R. Taylor, *Cavalier and Yankee* (1957), literary approach; and F. N. Boney, *Midwest Quarterly* (April, 1974).

F. N. BONEY
University of Georgia

COTTON WHIGS, conservative northerners so designated in 1846 to distinguish them from "Conscience Whigs," believed that national unity was necessary because of North-South economic interdependence. Especially numerous among Massachusetts' shipping and textile magnates, the Cotton Whigs found that slavery caused a conflict between their yankee cupidity and their Puritan conscience. On constitutional principle they guaranteed slavery where it existed, denounced abolitionism, but adamantly opposed slavery extension. They supported the COMPROMISE OF 1850 as final but remained faithful to free-soilism when confronted by the KANSAS-NEBRASKA ACT. As a result the national Whig party, already deeply distressed, became defunct.

See A. M. Schlesinger, Jr. (ed.), *U.S. Political Parties* (1973); and T. H. O'Connor, *Lords of Loom* (1968), excellent.

MAX R. WILLIAMS
Western Carolina University

COULTER, ELLIS MERTON (1890-), Regents Professor Emeritus of History, University of Georgia, is widely known as a historian of the South in general and Georgia in particular. Born outside Hickory, N.C., he received his A.B. degree from the University of North Carolina and his A.M. and Ph.D. degrees from the University of Wisconsin. In many ways, Coulter illustrates the scholarly contributions that twentieth-century historians native to the South have made to the history of that section. His findings, favorable to white southern leadership in the Civil War and Reconstruction, emerge clearly in *The South During Reconstruction, 1865–1877* (1947) and *The Confederate States of America, 1861–1865* (1950), both volumes of *A History of the South* of which he was coeditor. His study, *Negro Legislators in Georgia During the Reconstruction Period* (1968), reports similar conclusions. As a prolific historian

of Georgia and a biographer of Georgians and other southerners, Coulter has produced a flood of books and articles. A popular teacher at the University of Georgia, he was also a founder of the Southern Historical Association and was its president (1934–1935), as well as president of the Agricultural History Society (1929–1930) and editor of the *Georgia Historical Quarterly*.

DONALD R. RAICHLE
Kean College of New Jersey

COUNCIL OF SOUTHERN MOUNTAINS, INC. (Drawer 4, Clintwood, Va. 24228), in partnership with certain churches, supports the illustrated *Mountain Life and Work: The Magazine of the Appalachian South* (available on microfilm). With a present circulation of 7,000, it was begun in 1925 to educate the outside world about Appalachia, to call attention to the sometimes unfavorable inroads of the industrial developers, and to serve as an organ in which to present the mountain people—their poverty and their social problems, such as lack of "schools, medical facilities, roads, housing, and communication." In addition, the journal publishes material with emphasis on congressional legislation, health problems, the abuses in the areas of strip mining, and labor and mine negotiations. Its 11 issues per year contain some scholarly but mostly popular articles, news notes, and an occasional book review.

COUNCIL OF SOUTHERN UNIVERSITIES (Suite 484, 795 Peachtree St. NE, Atlanta, Ga. 30308), organized in 1952, and its agency the Southern Fellowships Fund, created in 1966, are supported by Duke, Emory, Louisiana State, North Carolina, Rice, Texas, Tulane, Vanderbilt, and Virginia universities for the purpose of improving higher education in the South and encouraging research and graduate study. In 1966 the Danforth Foundation granted $5 million to be used toward these ends in colleges and universities attended primarily by black students. Subsequently other contributions have been made by CPC International, the Equitable Life Assurance Society, and the Andrew W. Mellon Foundation. Awards are given for both predoctoral and postdoctoral study and research accompanied by stipends in varying amounts. An additional $1 million was granted to the council by the Danforth Foundation in 1972 to continue this program for five more years.

COUNTRY STORE. As the southern frontier pushed westward early in the nineteenth century, country stores—rural mercantile establishments—

were scattered widely over the interior, where they developed as parallel economic institutions to the plantation-factorage system. Just as seaport FACTORS served the planters, who bought and sold in large quantities, country merchants became the economic agents of small farmers, who produced small amounts of diversified farm produce for the market and who bought equally small amounts of goods from the outside world. For the small farmer, the country store became the primary agency supplying him with merchandise, extending him credit, and marketing his crops. Storekeepers were the middlemen linking eastern and southern buyers and wholesalers to small interior farmers. Rural merchants were able to purchase goods on long-term credit and, in turn, to supply farmers with dry goods, groceries, and tools on credit for 12 months. On the basis of this credit, farmers could plant, exist for a year, and harvest their crops, which storekeepers accepted in payment for the goods advanced.

The country store was well rooted in the antebellum South, but its heyday was the 70 years that followed the Civil War. Increased penetration of the rural South by the railroads and the telegraph help explain its growth, but even more important were the end of slavery and the rise of TENANT FARMING. With the decline of large, integrated plantations, the factorage system deteriorated, and cotton selling and buying were removed from large towns to interior crossroads stores. When slaves became tenants, rural merchants became the salesmen, buyers, and suppliers for millions of black freedmen as well as for millions of small white farmers. Planters themselves sometimes opened stores; more often, merchants began extending credit on authority of the landlord and then on the basis of the new lien laws that were passed in every southern state (CROP LIEN). Liens allowed individuals to buy goods on credit, but they also meant that merchants improved their chances of payment and limited their competition. By the end of the 1880s, rural merchants had become powers in the southern countryside.

By providing merchandise and acting as marketing agents, storekeepers had the opportunity to profit on both the goods they sold locally and the crops they marketed elsewhere. Contemporaries often charged that merchants coerced their customers into excessive production of cotton in order to sell them food at inflated prices. Historians have begun to test this old story, but whether storekeepers actually had local monopolies, coerced excessive production of cotton, reaped exaggerated profits from the provisions they sold, or, in general, whether the postwar economic stag-

nation of the South was in part the result of the exploitation of agriculture by country storekeepers is not entirely clear. What is evident, however, is that many tenant farmers escaped slavery only to find that they were in bondage to new masters. Unable to save enough to finance themselves for a full year, tenants became enmeshed in a disastrous credit network. Local merchants demanded liens on the crops, usually cotton, as the only acceptable collateral. Because crop liens took away the farmers' freedom to buy and sell as they wished, the system often resulted in debt PEONAGE.

The country store served rural southerners as a social as well as an economic institution. It provided a place for farmers to congregate, around pot-bellied stoves in winter and on front porches in summer. But the country store was primarily a place to buy and sell, and in the twentieth century those economic functions were gradually removed from it. The rise of towns and industry, the end of liens and farm tenancy, and the changes in agriculture and the credit structure meant that, although country stores did not disappear, they tended to survive to serve the people who had forgotten something at the shopping center.

See, for antebellum South, L. E. Atherton, *Southern Country Store* (1949). For postbellum period, most important are T. D. Clark, *Pills, Petticoats, and Plows* (1944), and H. Woodman, *King Cotton and Retainers* (1968); but see also T. D. Clark, *Journal of Southern History* (Feb., 1946); J. P. Bull, *Journal of Southern History* (Feb., 1952); J. Williamson, *After Slavery* (1965); and J. Wiener, *Past and Present* (Aug., 1975). For conflicting interpretations in new economic studies, see R. L. Ransom and R. Sutch, *Journal of Economic History* (Sept., 1972; March, 1973), and *Agricultural History* (April, 1975); S. J. DeCanio, *Agriculture in Postbellum South* (1974), and *Journal of Economic History* (Sept., 1973); J. D. Reid, Jr., *Journal of Economic History* (March, 1973), and *Agricultural History* (April, 1975); W. W. Brown and M. O. Reynolds, *Journal of Economic History* (Dec., 1973); R. Higgs, *Journal of Economic History* (March, 1973); and J. Rubin *Agricultural History* (April, 1975). For twentieth century, see P. Daniel, *Shadow of Slavery* (1972); and G. B. Tindall, *Emergence of New South* (1967).

JAMES L. ROARK
University of Missouri, St. Louis

COUNTY UNIT SYSTEM. Counties, congressional districts, and other geographic areas constitute the units from which members of legislative bodies are chosen. The county unit system, as it developed in Georgia and Maryland, applied the principle of representation by geographic areas to the election of state officers.

A county unit rule, developed by custom in the

Democratic party, was enacted into law in Georgia by the Neill Primary Act of 1917. The law required that party primaries to nominate candidates for U.S. senator, governor, and other elected state officers be held on a specified date. A candidate who received the largest popular vote in a county in a party primary should be considered to have carried the county and be entitled to its unit votes (that is, two votes for every representative the county had in the lower house of the general assembly) in the party's state convention. Maryland's unit system, similar to that of Georgia, gave to each county and to each legislative district of Baltimore a unit vote equal to the total of its members in the house and senate of the state legislature.

Shifts in population were not adequately recognized by modifications in representation. Rural areas not only dominated the legislatures of Georgia and Maryland, but they also had a heavily weighted vote in the election of state officers. Critics asserted that democratic principle required that each man's vote be counted equally. Supporters of the unit system held "county unit vote" to be the three sweetest words in the English language. In *Gray* v. *Sanders* (1963), however, the U.S. Supreme Court held Georgia's county unit system to be void, as a violation of equal protection. Soon thereafter a federal district court invalidated Maryland's unit system.

See M. E. Jewell, *Politics of Reapportionment* (1962); *Journal of Politics* (Feb., 1950); and A. B. Saye, *Constitutional History of Georgia* (1970).

ALBERT B. SAYE
University of Georgia

COVINGTON, KY. (pop. 52,535), opposite Cincinnati on the Ohio River, was chartered in 1814 and named for a hero of the War of 1812. A ferry and tavern had been in operation here since 1801, but real growth did not occur until the 1830s, when Covington became a market and shipping center for area grain and livestock producers. Periodic flooding has seriously damaged the city on several occasions. Tied to the north bank of the Ohio by six bridges, modern Covington is the largest suburb in metropolitan Cincinnati. Its industries produce machine tools, sheet metals, distilled alcohol, refined petroleum, tobacco products, electrical equipment, and construction materials.

See C. B. Eilerman, *Historic Covington* (1973), excellent bibliography; C. F. Geaslen, *Strolling Along Memory Lane* (2 vols.; 1970–71); files of *Kentucky Post* (1892–), on microfilm; *Licking Valley Register* (1841–47), on microfilm; Covington *Journal* (1848–76), on microfilm; and Kenton County Public Library's collection of city directories, newspapers, and census reports.

COWPENS, BATTLE OF (January 17, 1781), in South Carolina, was an important American victory in the war for American independence, not only because it slowed Lord Cornwallis' advance from the South, but also because it showed that the feared and detested Banastre Tarleton could be defeated by a numerically inferior force. Cornwallis, rolling northward with but few setbacks, was encamped at Winnsboro in upper South Carolina and was concerned to learn that General DANIEL MORGAN was operating to his rear. Accordingly, he detailed Tarleton and the British Legion with almost 1,200 men to move against Morgan and destroy his force.

Morgan had about 600 reliable, seasoned Continental troops; he also commanded 300 militiamen of whose reliability he had doubts. His deployment of these forces was brilliant: they were in three lines, with the Continentals in the third. As Tarleton advanced, his men were fired upon by the militiamen, who thereupon fell back. The overconfident British Legion advanced in disarray and was met with the deadly attack by the Continental troops. The British losses in killed, wounded, and captured were more than ten times those of the Americans. Morgan's victory has been compared with that of Hannibal at Cannae in its design and its effective use of an inferior force. For the British, however, it was only a temporary setback. Within weeks they were in North Carolina and by the early summer had advanced into Virginia in force.

See H. Lee, *Campaign of 1781 in Carolinas* (1824); H. F. Rankin, *North Carolina Historical Review* (July, 1954); and R. F. Weigley, *Partisan War* (1970).

WILLIAM M. DABNEY
University of New Mexico

CRAFTS. All artifacts blend utility with beauty. For analysis, however, they can be arranged along a continuum stretching from the purely utilitarian to the purely aesthetic. Toward one end are the "subsistence crafts." Toward the spectrum's other end are the "arts," which display practical as well as aesthetic dimensions. The artifacts generally termed "crafts" fall near the center of the continuum.

A great pottery tradition flourished in the South and continues still, contracted into a few centers, notably in the North Carolina Piedmont, the Georgia hills, and Texas. Most of the ware produced was basically utilitarian, consisting largely of crocks, jugs, and butter churns. Even this workaday crockery reveals an aesthetic. There was a preference for certain shapes, vertical and modestly contoured when compared with northern work. The northern salt and Albany slip glazes were used, but green and gray ash glazes were also favored and serve to distinguish southern products. The potters—some of them farmers with one-man operations, others full-time specialists in large shops—developed their talents and techniques to support themselves and to supply others with needed tools. But these abilities were also used to create objects in which an aesthetic intent dominated. Continuing in a central European tradition, MORAVIAN potters in North Carolina made slip-decorated plates that were displayed like paintings rather than used for eating. These potters, as well as those working at the Bell pottery in the valley of Virginia, also produced freestanding sculpture after the manner of Staffordshire, England.

Crafts, being tied tightly into both the economic and aesthetic traditions of average southern people, are revealing social historical documents. The dominant basketry technique of the South involves the splitting and weaving of white oak splints. This technique was known widely in western Europe and was surely introduced into the South from northern England. The typical round-bottomed form of the Appalachian and Ozark domains is a common European shape, traceable to the Middle Ages through its appearance in genre paintings. The large cotton basket form of the Deep South represents a New World adaptation of Old World techniques. Oak splint basketry, with its British source, characterizes the South as a whole, but other basketry techniques indicate the presence of other cultures. Twill-woven, split-cane baskets were made widely in the aboriginal South and are still made by CHOCTAW INDIANS in Mississippi. Germans in the valley of Virginia used the Rhenish and Pennsylvanian technique of coiling rye straw. The coiled baskets made by black women in South Carolina, Georgia, and Florida are readily traceable to their source in West Africa.

Craft traditions not only persisted in the movement of black and white southerners across the Atlantic, but they were also elaborated in their new settings. The decorative ironwork gracing the buildings of New Orleans and Charleston has its European antecedents in Spain, England, and Ireland. There was also a great West African blacksmithing tradition; and in the forges of southern black artisans, slave and free, ironwork achieved an ebullience more southern than European.

The variety of southern craftwork is owed to the diversity of the Old World sources of the population, to economic adaptations within a complexly variable physical environment, and to the existence of great centers of innovation in the countrysides surrounding Williamsburg and Staunton in Virginia, Charleston, Nashville, and New Orleans. The result is that crafts, as surely as DIALECTS, separate the South from the North and break the South into subregions: the Chesapeake Bay, the lower southern coast, the Appalachians, the bluegrass, the Ozarks, the Deep South, and the Gulf Coast.

The relation of crafts to history, region, and human need has suggested their revival. Dead crafts have been brought back to life at museums in places like Williamsburg and Old Salem. Dying crafts have been given new life by people attempting to stimulate cash flow to pockets of poverty. Thus revived, old crafts continue, sometimes in vibrant new forms, sometimes as distorted failures. Other old crafts persist because they still serve a practical purpose or because they remain aesthetically satisfying to their practitioners. In loose connection to the craft revival movements, some serious scholarship was devoted to southern crafts in the 1930s, and in the 1970s folklorists and anthropologists are again seeking out and documenting those who make things that bring them pleasure in the midst of labor.

See H. Glassie, *Pattern in Material Folk Culture* (1969), bibliography; R. F. Thompson, in A. L. Robinson, C. C. Foster, and D. H. Ogilvie (eds.), *Black Studies in University* (1969), important; S. Stitt, *Museum of Early Southern Decorative Crafts* (1970); J. W. Chase, *Afro-American Art and Craft* (1971); J. Bivins, *Moravian Potters in North Carolina* (1972); A. H. Eaton, *Handicrafts of Southern Highlands* (1937); R. C. Erskine, *Mountains and Mountain Shop* (1913); E. Wigginton, *Foxfire Book* (1972); E. L. Horwitz, *Mountain People, Mountain Crafts* (1974); *Craft Horizons* (June, 1966); *Arts in Virginia* (Fall, 1971); S. C. Hodges, "Handicrafts" (M.A. thesis, University of Tennessee, 1951); J. R. Vincent, "Two Ozark Woodworking Industries" (M.A. thesis, University of Missouri, 1962); M. O. Jones, "Chairmaking in Appalachia" (Ph.D. dissertation, Indiana University, 1970); and H. W. Marshall, *Mid-South Folklore* (Summer, 1974).

HENRY GLASSIE
University of Pennsylvania

CRAIG V. MISSOURI (4 Peters 410 [1830]) came before the U.S. Supreme Court on a writ of error to the supreme court of Missouri. At issue was the constitutionality of the Missouri act of June, 1821, establishing a loan office with authority to issue certificates secured by personal property and raising the question whether they were "bills of credit," the emission of which was prohibited to states by the Constitution. Chief Justice John Marshall wrote the opinion, construing "bills of credit" broadly to "comprehend any instrument by which a State engages to pay money at a future day" (4 Peters 431), thus striking down the Missouri act. Delivered as it was during the NULLIFICATION crisis and congressional debate over the nature of the Union, Marshall's opinion was a powerful answer to states' rights attacks on the Court. Dissents by Justices Smith Thompson, WILLIAM JOHNSON, and John McLean, however, indicated that states' rights thinking had already touched the Court. Six years later in *Briscoe* v. *Commonwealth Bank of Kentucky* (11 Peters 257) the Jacksonian Court of ROGER TANEY silently overruled *Craig* so far as it applied to state bank notes.

See A. Beveridge, *Life of John Marshall* (1919), IV; and C. G. Haines, *Role of Supreme Court, 1789–1835* (1960), different interpretation.

KENT NEWMYER
University of Connecticut

CRATER, BATTLE OF THE (July 30, 1864). Hoping to break the strong Confederate line outside Petersburg, Va., federal army officers approved a plan developed by former coal miners serving in the 48th Pennsylvania to explode a mine under the Confederate fortifications. The miners dug (June 25–July 23) a tunnel 510 feet long to a point 20 feet under the Confederate line, with 75 feet of branches paralleling Confederate fortifications. At 4:44 A.M., July 30, the explosion of some 8,000 pounds of black powder killed 278 Confederates and created a crater about 170 feet long, 60 to 80 feet wide, and 30 feet deep. Both armies were initially stunned by the magnitude of the explosion. Eventually some 15,000 U.S. troops of Ambrose Burnside advanced into and around the crater, but poor leadership kept them from a decisive breakthrough. Confederate artillery soon found the range of the closely packed troops. Shortly after 8:00 A.M., a brigade under WILLIAM MAHONE drove the federal advance back to the crater, and in the early afternoon, with two additional brigades, Mahone captured the crater. Federal losses were 2,864 killed and wounded, 929 captured; Confederate losses appear to have been around 1,500. Ulysses S. Grant convened a court of inquiry, which established that Burnside had been lackadaisical in preparing for the assault and disobedient in failing to withdraw troops during the morning.

See *Official Records, Armies*, Ser. 1, Vol. XL; *Battle of Petersburg*, Report of Joint Committee on Conduct of War, 38th Cong., 2nd Sess.; N. M. Blake, *Mahone* (1935); and H. Pleasants, Jr., and G. H. Straley, *Inferno at Petersburg* (1961).

JOHN Y. SIMON
Southern Illinois University, Carbondale

CRAVEN, AVERY O. (1886–), in *The Repressible Conflict, 1830–1861* (1939), *The Coming of the Civil War* (1942), *The Growth of Southern Nationalism, 1848–1861* (1953), and *Civil War in the Making, 1815–1860* (1959), contended that causes for the Civil War were emotional, not fundamental, and that the issue of slavery and sectional differences were insufficient to have produced the conflict. Instead, it was caused by a generation of irresponsible leaders. This is the revisionist or "repressible war" view advanced by Craven and certain Civil War historians.

Craven is also identified with the Turner frontier thesis. He studied under Frederick Jackson Turner and in *Democracy in American Life* (1941) advanced the theory that the southern frontier had western elements. The free-range cattle industry, as well as the conditions of lawlessness and disorder, made the character of the southern frontier synonymous with that of the old Southwest, a condition that other frontier historians had failed to consider. Craven's contribution to the history of agricultural reform is seen in his *Soil Exhaustion as a Factor in the Agricultural History of Virginia and Maryland, 1606–1860* (1932). In this study he blamed the agricultural decline of the Chesapeake region on political and economic factors that the planter could not control. In *Edmund Ruffin, Southerner* (1932), he used two nonclimatic factors, the Old World ideal of the country gentleman and the presence of a large slave population, to account for the development of a distinctly southern culture.

Craven's most recent book, *Rachel of Old Louisiana* (1975), tells of the life of a slaveholding widow who managed her cotton plantation and slaves with unusual success. The book is delightfully written and illustrated with Craven's own pencil sketches.

JULIA F. SMITH
Georgia Southern College

CRAVEN, WESLEY FRANK (1905–), a native of Conway, N.C., received his A.B. (1926) and A.M. (1927) degrees at Duke and his Ph.D. degree (1928) at Cornell. He taught (1928–1950) at New York University except for 1943–1946, when he was on leave for historical work with the U.S. Army air forces. From 1950 to his retirement in 1973 he taught at Princeton. He has served on the editorial boards of the *Journal of Modern History* and the *Journal of Southern History* and was coeditor of *The Army Forces in World War II* (7 vols.; 1945–1959). Craven has trained several distinguished historians and has written a number of important books on colonial history, his contributions to the history of seventeenth-century Virginia being especially noteworthy. In such works as *The Southern Colonies in the Seventeenth Century* (1949) he stressed the English background of the colonies without neglecting the determinative contributions of Indians, blacks, and non-English Europeans to a distinctly American colonial culture. Generally his fresh interpretations have merely modified the conclusions of earlier authorities; but their cumulative effect has altered significantly our understanding of colonial history.

See L. J. Ragatz, *Journal of Southern History* (Feb., 1939); O. P. Chitwood, *American Historical Review* (Jan., 1950); and G. W. Mullins, *Journal of American History* (Dec., 1972).

W. CONARD GASS
Campbell College

CRAWFORD, WILLIAM HARRIS (1772–1834), was born in Amherst County, Va. Moving to Georgia as a youth, Crawford became a lawyer (1799) and entered politics as a Jeffersonian Republican. He served in the Georgia legislature before being elected to the U.S. Senate in 1807. There he became one of the leaders of the pro–James Madison wing and an advocate of the Bank of the United States. In 1813 Crawford became minister to France. Returning home in 1815, he was appointed by Madison secretary of war and then secretary of the treasury (1816), a position in which he served until 1825 under President James Monroe. He dealt successfully with many of the fiscal problems that arose from the War of 1812, but toward the end of his administration he came under an investigation for mismanagement. His attempts to cut military appropriations initiated a lifelong dispute with Secretary of War John C. Calhoun.

Before the 1824 presidential election, Crawford received the nomination of the Republican congressional caucus, but it proved ineffective. In a four-way election, he received approximately 14 percent of the popular vote and 41 electoral votes, placing him in third place behind Andrew Jackson and John Quincy Adams and ahead of Henry Clay. In the U.S. House vote that followed, Crawford received the votes of four states to seven for Jackson and 13 for Adams. After the election, Crawford returned to Georgia, serving until his death as a judge of the superior court.

See C. C. Mooney, *William H. Crawford* (1974); A. L. Duckett, *John Forsythe* (1962); U. B. Phillips, *Annual Report of American Historical Association* (1901); and L. D. White, *Jeffersonians* (1951).

HERBERT ERSHKOWITZ
Temple University

CREEK INDIANS (sometimes called Muskogees) lived in what later became northern and central Alabama and most of southern Georgia. They probably migrated from the West by way of the Red River around A.D. 800. They conquered or came to terms with tribes already in Alabama and Georgia, developing a powerful confederacy with some SHAWNEES, plus the Alabama, Koasati, Hitchiti, APALACHEE, Yuchi, YAMASSEE, Natchez, and other tribal groups. Through this rather unusual process small tribes were brought into one integrated Indian nation, known as the Creek Confederacy, which was both powerful and extensive.

They were held together by the ties of language, intermarriage between clans, frequent regional council meetings, and an annual national council. By the eighteenth century the confederacy included approximately 60 towns, 40 of which were located in what was called the Upper Towns on the Coosa and Tallapoosa rivers of Alabama, and 20 in the Lower Towns on the Ocmulgee, Flint, and Chattahoochee rivers of Georgia. Also, the towns were divided into two types: red, or war towns; and white, or peace towns. The capital, during any given year or period of time, was the town in which lived the presiding chief of the confederacy. Okmulgee in the Lower Towns and Okchai in the Upper Towns were the most important white towns, and Coweta and Cussita in the Lower Towns and Okfuskee in the Upper Towns were the most significant red towns.

Creek life was intimately associated with the towns in which individuals lived. Each town contained 25 to 100 houses and was governed by a mico, town king, who was so associated with his town that his given name was forsaken, and he became known as "Coweta Mico" or "Cussita Mico" while he served in office. He presided over the town council and was the leader of the town's civil government. The town's leading warrior was called the *tastanage*, and, though he and other warriors were excluded from official civil functions, he was a person of no little importance. Theoretically, a tastanage was charged with leading the town's military efforts, but he was usually such a powerful figure that he often gained considerable importance in the town and could influence decisions on a wide variety of subjects. Town unity was often weakened by strained relations between the mico and the tastanage and even more by rivalry between clans. Although the tribe may have numbered as many as 18,000 persons in the early 1800s, it had fewer than ten major clans, of which the most important were the Wind, Tiger, Bear, and Eagle clans. Warfare was carried on by clans; punishment for crimes was also handled by clans. To add confusion to chaos, clan loyalty took precedence over town or even tribal loyalty.

Creek Indians were excellent hunters and talented agriculturalists. The bread and hominy they made from corn became an important part of the diet of most white southern frontiersmen and their progeny. They were also fierce warriors, of necessity because they were geographically surrounded by aggressive enemies. They asked no quarter and gave none.

The relentless march of the white frontier from Georgia to the Mississippi River—contested again and again as Creek warriors fought against the white interlopers—cost the Creeks nearly all of their southern homeland. They had surrendered some of their land before the loss of a major part in the disastrous CREEK WAR of 1813–1814; nearly all of the remainder was given up in removal treaties negotiated in 1827 and 1835. Today some Creeks still live east of the Mississippi River, but most keep tribal traditions alive in the Oklahoma homeland to which they were removed in the 1830s.

See A. Debo, *Road to Disappearance* (1941), best account of eastern Creeks; J. W. Caughey, *McGillivray* (1959), excellent; A. H. Abel, *American Historical Association Annual Report* (1906), outstanding; J. R. Swanton, *Early History*, Bulletin No. 73, Bureau of American Ethnology (1922), all listed Swanton publications useful, *Notes on Creeks*, Bulletin No. 123, Bureau of American Ethnology (1939), *Religious Beliefs of Creeks*, 42nd annual report, Bureau of American Ethnology (1928), and *Social Organization of Creeks*, 42nd annual report, Bureau of American Ethnology (1928); D. H. Corkran, *Creek Frontier* (1967), excellent analysis of early history; G. Foreman, *Indian Removal* (1932), old but useful, and *Five Civilized Tribes* (1934); F. P. Prucha, *Indian Policy in Formative Years* (1962), biased but excellent analysis; M. E. Young, *Indian Allotments* (1962); L. DeVorsey, Jr., *Indian Boundary* (1966); J. Adair, *American Indians* (1775); W. Bartram, *Travels* (1792); B. Hawkins, *Hawkins Letters, 1779–1806* (1916); M. B. Pound, *Benjamin Hawkins* (1951); A. Debo, *History of Indians* (1970); J. L. Wright, Jr., *Bowles* (1967); and D. Van Every, *Disinherited* (1966).

ARTHUR H. DEROSIER, JR.
University of Mississippi

CREEK WAR (1813–1814) is sometimes called the Red Sticks War. By 1810 the CREEK INDIANS,

especially a significant minority of upper Creeks, were weary of the continuing demands of whites for more land, and they decided that appeasement must be replaced by a firm military stand against future cessions of land. After all, they reasoned, Creeks had surrendered land in 1796, 1802, and 1805; and still the whites wanted more. Although the Red Sticks, as the war faction was called, were never a majority in the tribe, they were aggressive and agreed to punish by death any mico (town king) who negotiated a land-cession treaty with whites.

The war began when Red Stick Creeks, led by the talented William Weatherford (Red Eagle), attacked Ft. Mims, a few miles north of Mobile, Ala., on August 30, 1813, killing most of the 553 Americans huddled there for protection. There followed other massacres perpetrated by both whites and reds, and finally the dispatching of three American armies to put down the recalcitrant Creeks. Ferdinand Claiborne's army of whites and CHOCTAWS from Mississippi Territory dealt a crippling defeat to the Creeks in the battle of the Holy Ground on December 23, 1813; John Floyd's army of Georgia whites and CHEROKEES was defeated by the Creeks after being lost during most of the campaign; and ANDREW JACKSON with his Tennessee militiamen ended the conflict and became a national hero by defeating the Creeks in brutal hand-to-hand combat at Horseshoe Bend on the Tallapoosa River on March 27, 1814. Of 800 Creeks in the battle, 759 died; and Jackson lost approximately 200 of his 2,000 militiamen. On August 9, 1814, he forced 35 Creek leaders to accept the humbling Treaty of Ft. Jackson requiring the Creeks to surrender 22 million acres of their homeland; it was the largest single cession of land extracted from any southern Indian tribe in history.

See H. S. Halbert and T. H. Ball, *Creek War* (1969), biased but outstanding account; C. C. Royce, *Indian Land Cessions*, 18th annual report, Bureau of American Ethnology (1899), Pt. 2, excellent primary source; A. J. Pickett, *History of Alabama* (1896), old but useful; J. H. O'Donnell III, *Southern Indians* (1973), excellent on prewar period; J. F. H. Claiborne, *Sam Dale* (1860), biased but usable; I. J. Cox, *West Florida Controversy* (1918); O. B. Peake, *Factory System* (1954); A. H. DeRosier, Jr., *Removal* (1970); M. James, *Life of Jackson* (1940), interesting and readable; A. B. Meek, *Red Eagle* (1855); and R. V. Haynes, *Natchez District* (1976).

ARTHUR H. DEROSIER, JR.
University of Mississippi

CREOLE SLAVE CASE (1841). The *Creole* sailed from Richmond, Va., in 1841, bound for New Orleans with a cargo of 135 slaves. Near the Bahamas, the slaves, under the leadership of Madison Washington, seized control of the ship, killing one white crewman, and proceeded to Nassau, where they were freed in accordance with British law, with the exception of 19 who were retained on charges of mutiny and murder. Secretary of State Daniel Webster's demands for the return of the slave cargo were ineffective, and national concern and sectional tension mounted. Congressman Joshua Giddings, an antislavery Whig from Ohio, enraged southern congressmen with his *Creole* resolutions, which stated that slave laws had no effect outside the slave states, while affirming the right of slaves to secure their freedom. Following a vote of censure, Giddings resigned his seat, to be quickly returned by an overwhelming majority of his district. Giddings' immediate reassertion of his *Creole* resolutions in a congressional speech substantially dissipated the effectiveness of the GAG RULE and helped poison the atmosphere during the negotiations for the Webster-Ashburton Treaty (1842).

See S. F. Bemis, *Secretaries of State* (1928); J. R. Spears, *Slave-Trade* (1900); J. B. Stewart, *Joshua Giddings* (1970); and W. B. Jones, *Journal of Southern History* (Jan., 1956).

MARY JO BRATTON
East Carolina University

CRESAP'S WAR. See DUNMORE'S WAR

CRIME. Historical statistics can always be criticized for their lack of accuracy. Indeed, many contemporary scholars of criminology argue with considerable legitimacy that the measurement of crime is an academic impossibility. There is no question but that the *Uniform Crime Reports*, introduced in 1930, leave much to be desired. In light of these statistical limitations, it becomes imperative that southern crime be studied and analyzed systematically within a cultural setting that incorporates the dynamic traditions of both the frontier and slavery.

Crime and punishment in the South during the colonial period generally followed patterns very similar to England's. Drunkards, vagrants, prostitutes, and minor offenders customarily were lodged in jails and workhouses. Lawless and vicious colonists frequently were punished by some form of public disgrace: placed on a pillory, on a dunking stool, or in stocks and/or branded, mutilated, or whipped. As late as 1788, however, capital punishment was used for a variety of crimes including treason, murder, rape, buggery (sodomy), burglary, robbery, arson, malicious maiming, forgery,

counterfeiting, second offenses for lesser felonies, and abetting any of the above crimes.

By the middle of the nineteenth century, the South had acquired a widespread reputation for VIOLENCE. The common use of firearms, the persistence of DUELING, the distrust of legal processes, and the frequent appearance of vigilante groups have been explained by some theorists as results of the South's persistent adherence to its frontier traditions. Others point also to the presence of local militia and to the popularity of military titles and training as both symptomatic of and contributing to the region's toleration of violent action.

SLAVE INSURRECTIONS, either real or perceived, long had been an obsession of white Americans. In the South, where slavery persisted the longest and where approximately one person in three was a black bondsman, these fears were used by whites to justify a variety of repressive actions (SLAVE CODES). The slaves, in turn, responded by displaying overt hostility by breaking tools, committing arson, maltreating livestock, self-mutilation, and, at times, even self-destruction. Moreover, turned inward, these behavioral patterns created a tradition of violence (assault, rape, and homicide) initiated and directed by blacks against other blacks. Thus slavery, like the frontier, functioned to teach and to legitimate violence.

After passage of the THIRTEENTH AMENDMENT and the termination of slavery, a consistent pattern of black pressure and white resistance in many areas of the South contributed to a marked increase in interracial violence. The NEW ORLEANS RIOT and the MEMPHIS RIOT during Reconstruction, the ritualized terror and political violence of the KU KLUX KLAN, and the gradually increasing dependence on LYNCHING to maintain white domination all illustrate the high incidence of violence accepted as a part of interracial behavior in the South. Southern systems of criminal justice functioned with the effect of lowering respect for and enforcement of legal processes. Local law enforcement officers failed to provide equal protection of the law for defendants and frequently left unrecorded both personal and property crimes committed against blacks. Southern courts were conspicuously lax in respecting basic elements of criminal justice: namely, the adversary system, due process, burdens of proof, and the fine points of evidence. Moreover, although Kentucky (1800), Virginia (1800), and Maryland (1812) were among the first in the nation to found state PENAL SYSTEMS, southern prisons were notorious for their brutalization of the keepers and the kept alike. And the CONVICT LEASE SYSTEM, commonplace in the late nineteenth- and early twentieth-century South, furthered aggressive patterns of personal behavior.

Prior to 1921, only eight southern cities (Wheeling, Tampa, Galveston, Austin, Houston, Baltimore, Knoxville, and Memphis) employed Negro policemen. By 1940, although the South had approximately 75 percent of the nation's black population, in the entire region there were not many more than 50 Negro policemen. Without reflecting necessarily on the personal integrity of southern law enforcement officials, the lily-white character of local law enforcement agencies fostered a negative environment of frustration, a sense of powerlessness, and a heightened hostility among the region's black population.

Since World War II there has been considerable improvement in the criminal systems of most southern states. Yet law enforcement has been and will continue to be a pressing problem in the United States. Florida has embraced many of the innovative rules of criminal procedure proposed by the American Bar Association, setting a tone of leadership for all states of the nation. Furthermore, Florida has taken the leadership in combating railroad vandalism. Yet implementation of improved procedures and changes in the personnel of police agencies by themselves are insufficient reforms in and of themselves.

The *Uniform Crime Reports* for 1975 indicate that the South had the lowest total crime rate of the four national regions and the lowest incidence of property crimes, including robberies and auto thefts. Yet the South led the nation in crimes of personal violence. Forty-two percent of all murders in 1975 were committed in the South; 54 of the 129 slain law enforcement officers were killed in the South; and the use of firearms was highest in the South. Only the western states exceeded the South in the incidence of rape and aggravated assault, and only the Northeast exceeds the South in the violent use of knives or other cutting instruments. Thus, although the total crime rate in the South is the lowest in the nation, the traditions of personal violence inherited from the frontier and from the region's history of racial conflict remain an active malignancy that continues to shape the section's patterns of criminal activity.

See M. A. Elliott, *Crime in Modern Society* (1952), and *American Sociological Review* (April, 1944), crime and frontier; B. J. Cohen (ed.), *Crime in America* (1970); H. B. Kerper, *Introduction to Criminal Justice* (1972); H. C. Bearley, *Homicide in U.S.* (1932); J. E. Curry and G. D. King, *Race Tensions and Police* (1962); J. H. Franklin, *Militant South, 1800–1861* (1956); D. Bell, *Antioch Review* (Summer, 1953); E. M. Rudwick, *Journal of Criminal Law* (July, 1960), Negro policemen; R. D. Gas-

til, *American Sociological Review* (June, 1971), homicide and region; U.S. Department of Justice, *Uniform Crime Reports* (annual); and *Report of National Advisory Committee on Civil Disorders* (1968).

JOSEPH BALOGH
Bowling Green State University

CRISP, CHARLES FREDERICK (1845–1896), was born in Sheffield, England. His family moved to the United States when he was nine months old, eventually settling in Ellaville, Ga. In 1861, at the age of seventeen, he joined the 10th Virginia Infantry as a private. Within a year he was promoted lieutenant and served with distinction until his capture in May, 1864. At the end of the war he was admitted to the Georgia bar and moved to Americus, where he served as judge of the superior court from 1877 to 1882. In the latter year he was elected to the U.S. House of Representatives, serving until his death 14 years later. During his tenure in the House, Crisp served as Democratic leader and was twice elected Speaker of the House (1891–1895). He played an important role in the passage of the Interstate Commerce Act, strongly opposed the high protective tariff, and was converted to the cause of free silver. In 1896, Crisp campaigned for a U.S. Senate seat, but he died of a heart attack before the election.

See S. W. Martin, *Georgia Review* (Summer, 1954); *Memorial Addresses* (1897); D. W. Grantham, *Hoke Smith* (1958); C. V. Woodward, *Tom Watson* (1938); and A. M. Arnett, *Populist Movement in Georgia* (1922).

C. CHARLTON MOSELEY
Georgia Southern College

CRITTENDEN, GEORGE BIBB (1812–1880), born in Russellville, Ky., son of Senator JOHN J. CRITTENDEN, graduated from West Point and fought in the Black Hawk War, Texas revolution, and Mexican War. He was a major general in the Confederate army when his defeat in the battle of MILL SPRINGS, Ky. (January 19, 1862), meant the collapse of the right flank of ALBERT SIDNEY JOHNSTON's position at Bowling Green. He resigned and served for the duration in subordinate positions except in 1864, when he temporarily commanded the army in east Tennessee. After the war he was Kentucky state librarian.

See A. D. Kirwan, *John J. Crittenden* (1962); L. F. Johnson, *Franklin County* (1912); L. H. Harrison, *Civil War in Kentucky* (1975); C. P. Roland, *Albert Sidney Johnston* (1964); T. L. Connelly, *Army of Heartland* (1967); and *Official Records, Armies*, Ser. 1, Vols. I, IV, V, VII, XXX, XXXVII, XXXIX, Ser. 2, Vol. I.

JAMES A. RAMAGE
Northern Kentucky State University

CRITTENDEN, JOHN JORDAN (1786–1863), during his efforts in 1861 to conciliate the North and South asserted, "All human life is a compromise." Crittenden's own life and careers were clear expressions of political and legislative compromise rooted in the border state tradition of his native Kentucky, where he was born near Versailles. He was educated in local academies, studied law with George M. Bibb in Lexington, and then attended Washington Academy (now Washington and Lee University) and the College of William and Mary.

After practicing law in Versailles and Russellville, Crittenden was elected to the Kentucky legislature in 1811 and 1813 and served in the U.S. Senate from 1817 to 1819. In the election of 1826 Crittenden returned to the Kentucky house of representatives for one term as an Old Court party legislator from Franklin County. He was elected again in 1829 and was chosen for a full term in the U.S. Senate (1835–1841). He was appointed attorney general under William Henry Harrison and resigned after Harrison's death. In 1842 Crittenden filled Henry Clay's unexpired Senate term and was reelected for a full term from 1842 to 1848. He was governor of Kentucky from 1848 to 1850. Crittenden was appointed attorney general in Millard Fillmore's cabinet in 1850 and, after he pronounced the Fugitive Slave Act constitutional, advised the president to sign Clay's famous COMPROMISE OF 1850. In December, 1855, he returned to the Senate as a defender of the Union and an advocate of compromise.

In 1860 he was one of the founders of the CONSTITUTIONAL UNION PARTY and worked in the Congress from 1860 to 1861 to introduce a series of constitutional amendments designed to prevent secession (CRITTENDEN COMPROMISE). In December, 1860, the special Senate Committee of Thirteen failed to adopt his resolutions, and Crittenden made one more unsuccessful effort at compromise by presenting his plan directly to the Senate on January 3, 1861. He returned to Kentucky in the spring of 1861 to keep his state in the Union and to urge a position of neutrality when war came. With one son fighting for the Confederacy and another for the Union, Crittenden was elected to the U.S. House of Representatives (1861–1863), where he won passage of a resolution declaring the war to be one to preserve the Union and not one dedicated to overthrowing slavery.

See John J. Crittenden Papers, Library of Congress; John J. Crittenden Papers, Duke University Library; Mrs. C. Coleman (ed.), *Life of John J. Crittenden* (1871); A. D. Kirwan, *John J. Crittenden* (1962); and D. W. Zacharias, "John J. Crittenden: Speechmaking" (Ph.D. dissertation, Indiana University, 1963).

DONALD W. ZACHARIAS
University of Texas, Austin

CRITTENDEN, THOMAS LEONIDAS (1819–1893), was born in Russellville, Ky., the son of JOHN J. CRITTENDEN and brother of GEORGE B. CRITTENDEN. He was elected commonwealth district attorney in 1842. During the Mexican War he served as a lieutenant colonel of infantry and later on the staff of ZACHARY TAYLOR. After the war he was consul to Liverpool (1849–1853) and later a lawyer in Frankfort and a merchant in Louisville. A firm Unionist, he rose to major general of U.S. volunteers by July, 1862. He commanded at SHILOH, STONES RIVER, and CHICKAMAUGA. He distinguished himself in the first two engagements, but his career foundered at the last, where his troops broke and fled from the field. Cleared by court of inquiry, he was restored by U. S. Grant to command and served in the operations around Richmond until resigning in December, 1864. After the war he returned to the army as a colonel, serving a number of years in the West.

See R. U. Johnson and C. C. Buel (eds.), *Battles and Leaders* (1888), III. No biography or significant collection of papers is available.

JOSEPH L. HARSH
George Mason University

CRITTENDEN COMPROMISE. In December, 1860, JOHN J. CRITTENDEN, an elderly senator from Kentucky, proposed a series of constitutional amendments to prevent bloodshed between the North and South. A long-time friend and admirer of HENRY CLAY, Crittenden tried to duplicate his fellow Kentuckian's success by modeling his plan after the Compromise of 1850. Crittenden's compromise measures proposed to: (1) prohibit slavery north of the line 36° 30' and to protect slavery south of it in all territory; (2) prevent Congress from abolishing slavery on government property in slave states; (3) apply the same restriction to the District of Columbia as long as slavery existed in Maryland and Virginia; (4) permit interstate slave trade; (5) compensate slaveholders if mob action prevented the recovery of a fugitive slave; and (6) guarantee that no future amendments could apply to the preceding five amendments nor could Congress abolish slavery in the states. He also offered three resolutions declaring the Fugitive Slave Act constitutional and calling for its enforcement and a fourth resolution asking Congress to strengthen and enforce laws prohibiting foreign slave trade. His proposals were rejected by the Senate's Committee of Thirteen on December 20, 1860. Crittenden took his plan directly to the floor of the Senate in a major speech on January 3, 1861, and met defeat through a series of parliamentary maneuvers by Senate Republicans.

See J. J. Auer (ed.), *Antislavery and Disunion, 1858–1861* (1963); R. G. Gunderson, *Old Gentlemen's Convention* (1961); A. D. Kirwan, *John J. Crittenden* (1962); and D. W. Zacharias, "John J. Crittenden: Speechmaking" (Ph.D. dissertation, Indiana University, 1963).

DONALD W. ZACHARIAS
University of Texas, Austin

CROATAN INDIANS, sometimes called Lumbee, live mainly in Robeson County, N.C., and are the largest tribe in the eastern United States (over 30,000). They are believed to be the descendants of SIR WALTER RALEIGH's Lost Colony. The Croatans are a mixed race, but more Indian than white or Negro. The Indians were officially named Croatan in 1885, but they had the word stricken out in 1911 because both whites and Negroes had begun to use it derogatorily. In 1953 the state legislature designated them Lumbee Indians.

See J. Mooney, in F. W. Hodge (ed.), *Handbook of American Indians* (1905); B. Berry, *Almost White* (1963); W. C. Sturtevant and S. Stanley, *Indian Historian* (Summer, 1968); and A. L. Dial and D. K. Eliades, *Only Land I Know* (1975).

YASUHIDE KAWASHIMA
University of Texas, El Paso

CROATAN ISLAND was probably one of several low, barren sand islands between Cape Hatteras on the north and Cape Lookout on the south that form a part of the North Carolina OUTER BANKS. When the settlers of SIR WALTER RALEIGH's Lost Colony abandoned Ft. Raleigh on ROANOKE ISLAND, they left the word *Croatoan* carved on a tree, indicating this as the name of their place of refuge. Croatoan may or may not have been the island already known as Croatan. Some have considered the two places to be identical, and others have argued for separate location on the mainland directly west of Roanoke Island. The relief expedition that reached Roanoke seemed sure of the location, but their account fails to identify the spot. Croatan Island is referred to in the writings of Ralph Lane, governor of the first Raleigh colony, as being 20 miles south of Roanoke Island. The John White map of 1585–1586 shows Croatan as the present-day Ocracoke Island, immediately south of Hatteras. Théodore de Bry's early map of North Carolina seems to confirm this, although

the Nurenberg map of 1661 indicates Core Banks as Croatan. Others have suggested Portsmouth Island or, due to the shifting inlets, possibly a part of several islands.

See R. D. W. Connor, *Beginnings of English America* (1907); J. C. Harrington, *Search for City of Raleigh* (1962); and C. W. Porter, *Adventurers to New World* (1972).

SAMUEL T. EMORY
Mary Washington College

CROATAN SOUND is a shallow, brackish body of water in North Carolina that separates ROANOKE ISLAND, site of Sir Walter Raleigh's Lost Colony, from the low, sandy, swamp-dotted mainland. It serves to connect ALBEMARLE SOUND on the north with PAMLICO SOUND on the south. Never a major artery of traffic, Croatan Sound served Raleigh's colony as a source of finfish and shellfish as well as a defensive barrier against the hostile Indians of the mainland. It was the site of minor activity during the Civil War, and today serves a small group of commercial fishermen and boaters, who use its surface and resources.

See R. D. W. Connor, *Beginnings of English America* (1907); J. C. Harrington, *Search for City of Raleigh* (1962); and C. W. Porter, *Adventurers to New World* (1972).

SAMUEL T. EMORY
Mary Washington College

CROCKETT, DAVID (1786–1836), was born in Greene County, Tenn. Around his seventeenth year he received six months of schooling, the only formal education he had. After an unsuccessful try at farming he fought under Andrew Jackson in the Creek War. Crockett's wife (née Polly Finley) died in 1815, leaving him with two sons and a daughter. The next year he married Elizabeth Patton, a Creek War widow with two children. He served in several minor offices before his election in 1821 and again in 1823 to the state legislature and in 1827, 1829, and 1833 to Congress. While in the legislative bodies, he devoted his attention mainly to public land policies for western Tennessee. As a member of Congress, he generally opposed President Andrew Jackson, a factor that contributed to Crockett's defeat in 1831 and 1835. Following his loss of the election in 1835, Crockett left for Texas for a new start. He swore allegiance to the Texas government in early 1836, then went to San Antonio, where he died in the battle of the ALAMO. Controversy still exists as to whether he was killed while fighting or whether he surrendered and then was shot by order of Antonio López de Santa Anna.

See *Adventures of Davy Crockett* (1955); J. B. Shackford, *David Crockett* (1968); W. Blair, *Southwest Review* (July, 1940); and Constance Rourke, *Southwest Review* (Jan., 1934).

L. TUFFLY ELLIS
University of Texas, Austin

CROP LIEN SYSTEM was the method of providing credit to farmers that was created after the Civil War. Laws passed in all southern states in 1865 and 1866 authorized merchants to provide farmers with supplies necessary for growing the year's crop in return for a portion of the future crop. C. VANN WOODWARD calls it "one of the strangest contractual relationships in the history of finance: the seeker of credit usually pledged an unplanted crop to pay for a loan of unstipulated amount at a rate of interest to be determined by the creditor." Yet the system was necessary because the antebellum slave plantation had been fragmented into small farms operated by poor black and white TENANT FARMERS. Unable to obtain alternative sources of credit, they were forced to pledge their future crops as a lien against credit advanced during the growing season. Local merchants usually held a monopoly position, which they used to prevent farmers from buying supplies or selling crops elsewhere, perhaps on better terms.

Crop lien merchants often were charged with using the system to exploit farmers. The merchants began with high interest rates; their profits were increased by the widespread use of a two-price system, in which the credit price was higher than the cash price, often by 50 percent or more. Merchants also were charged with dishonest weighing and measuring; their customers often were denied the opportunity to check over and challenge the account books in which their debts were recorded.

The crop lien has been blamed for the spread of one-crop agriculture and the decline of food production among southern farms. Lien merchants used their monopoly power to force tenants to plant cotton instead of food crops. The merchant thus acquired a crop that was easily sold and at the same time forced his customers to purchase their food from him instead of raising their own. The result was an excessive production of cotton and a decline in the production of foodstuffs through the cotton South after the Civil War.

The most powerful opponents of the crop lien system in the 25 years after the end of the war were the planters, who saw it as a means by which merchants were threatening the planters' power over land and tenants. The merchant's power to refuse credit determined which tenants remained on the planter's land; as Woodward observes, "The lien system had divorced landownership from its age-old prerogatives." In addition, the crop lien gave the merchant a considerable share of the profit from the crop grown on the planter's land. This permitted some merchants to drive out less efficient planters and acquire the plantations. Planter organizations thus repeatedly called for the abolition of merchants' crop liens.

The merchants replied that they took considerable risks in making loans to marginal farms and that they in turn paid exorbitant interest rates to their own creditors and to northern wholesalers. High rates of business failures among southern merchants in this period support these claims. The South's relative lack of banks and transportation facilities contributed to the problem. The postwar reorganization of agriculture had left a huge number of southerners without land and had forced them into tenancy and into the exploitative credit practices that accompanied it.

See C. V. Woodward, *Origins of New South* (1951); T. D. Clark, *Journal of Southern History* (Feb., 1946); H. D. Woodman, *King Cotton and Retainers* (1968); R. L. Ransom and R. Sutch, *Journal of Economic History* (Sept., 1972); J. D. Reid, *Journal of Economic History* (March, 1973); W. W. Brown and M. O. Reynolds, *Journal of Economic History* (Dec., 1973); and J. M. Wiener, *Past and Present* (Aug., 1975).

JONATHAN M. WIENER
University of California, Irvine

CROSS KEYS, BATTLE OF (June 8, 1862), was a military success for Confederate General STONEWALL JACKSON, during his masterful SHENANDOAH VALLEY CAMPAIGN (May–June, 1862) in the Civil War. After diverting considerable Union forces from George B. McClellan's PENINSULAR CAMPAIGN, Jackson led 15,000 Confederates southwestward through Virginia, pursued by federal divisions under John Charles Frémont and James Shields. Jackson estimated that these columns, separated by a river, could be overwhelmed singly. On June 7 he reached Port Republic, secured the bridge between his pursuers, and stationed 8,500 troops opposite Shields. The remaining Confederates, under RICHARD EWELL, deployed at nearby Cross Keys to challenge Frémont. The next morning, Jackson narrowly escaped capture at Port Republic. Frémont meanwhile attacked Ewell at Cross Keys and advanced to within musket range, but was decisively repulsed by the Confederate right, under Isaac

Trimble. Frémont did not resume battle. Ewell sustained 288 casualties, barely half the federal losses. On June 9, Jackson scattered Shields's force and marched to reinforce Robert E. Lee on the peninsula.

See D. S. Freeman, *Lee's Lieutenants* (1945), fine synthesis; G. F. R. Henderson, *Jackson and War* (1919), flawed but useful; L. Chambers, *Jackson* (1959); *Official Records, Armies*, Vol. XII, Pt. 1; W. Allan, *Southern Historical Society Papers* (Sept., 1920); and A. Tracy, *Virginia Magazine of History and Biography* (July, 1962).

JOHN C. CAVANAGH
Suffolk University

CROWLEY'S RIDGE is a unique geographical formation of the Mississippi alluvial plain of southeastern Missouri and northeastern Arkansas. It extends generally southward from near Cape Girardeau, Mo., to the Mississippi River at Helena, Ark., a distance of approximately 200 miles. It varies in width from about two miles to about 20 miles. Geological evidence indicates an origin of perhaps 100 million years ago. The Missouri portions are known as Bloomfield Ridge and Commerce Bluffs. The ridge was named for the Benjamin Crowley family, which migrated to what is now Greene County, Ark., in the 1820s. A monument in Crowley's Ridge State Park commemorates the settlement.

See J. C. Branner, *Geological Survey of Arkansas* (1891); and R. W. Roberts *et al.*, *Arkansas Natural Resources* (1942).

JAMES E. GRINER
Arkansas State University

CROZAT GRANT (1712–1717) was a 15-year monopoly on trade and manufacturing in the colony of Louisiana granted to Antoine Crozat, French financier, by Louis XIV in 1712. The colony operated under a new policy as a business enterprise rather than as a venture in French imperialism. Governor of the colony during the period was Antoine de la Mothe Cadillac, who erected Ft. Toulouse on the upper Alabama River (1714) and Ft. Rosalie (1716) among the Natchez villages, but failed to achieve the goals of finding gold and silver mines or developing trade with the Spanish in Mexico. Crozat surrendered his grant in 1717.

See D. Rowland and A. Sanders (eds.), *Mississippi Provincial Archives: French Period* (1932), III; H. Fowler, *Franco-Spanish Rivalry in North America, 1524–1763* (1953); and N. Surrey, *Commerce of Louisiana During the French Regime, 1699–1763* (1916).

WALTER G. HOWELL
Mississippi College

CRUM, WILLIAM DEMOS (1859–1912), an Afro-American physician, was the youngest of four brothers and two sisters and the grandson of a German immigrant (née Krum). He grew up on the plantation of his father Darius Crum. After his older brothers put him through Avery Normal Institute, the University of South Carolina, and Howard University Medical School, he became a doctor, a trustee of Avery, and a communicant of the African Methodist Episcopal church. He was a delegate to every Republican National Convention between 1884 and 1904, codirector with BOOKER T. WASHINGTON of the 1901 South Carolina Interstate and West Indian Exposition in Charleston, and candidate for postmaster of Charleston in 1892 and U.S. senator in 1894, while pursuing interests in theater and French literature. He became a cause célèbre in 1902 after President Theodore Roosevelt appointed him customs collector for the port of Charleston as a token of hope for southern Negroes. Fearing further conflict over confirmation, Booker T. Washington in 1909 urged Crum to accept the post of minister to Liberia, which he filled with distinction until a fatal illness struck him in the summer of 1912.

See W. B. Gatewood, *Journal of Negro History* (Oct., 1968); New York *Times* (Dec. 8, 1912); Cleveland *Gazette* (Dec. 14, 1912); T. Cripps, "Lily White Republicans" (Ph.D. dissertation, University of Maryland, 1967); clippings, Hampton Institute; Carter Woodson Collection, Library of Congress; and Booker T. Washington Manuscripts, Library of Congress.

THOMAS CRIPPS
Morgan State University

CRUMP, EDWARD HULL "BOSS" (1874–1954), was born in Holly Springs, Miss. Moving to Memphis at the age of seventeen, he rose from bookkeeper to proprietor of a carriage manufacturing firm by 1903. Supported by a coalition of businessmen, saloon interests, blacks, and rural newcomers, Crump was elected mayor of Memphis in 1909 and reelected overwhelmingly in 1911 and 1915. His administrations focused on improving public services, lowering taxes, and increasing governmental efficiency. Efforts to oust him from office for his refusal to enforce the state PROHIBITION law led to his resignation in 1916, but he was elected soon thereafter as a Shelby County trustee and came to control most local offices and extend his influence into state and national politics. Elected to the U.S. House of Representatives in 1930 and 1932, he enthusiastically supported Franklin D. Roosevelt and NEW DEAL programs, especially the TENNESSEE VALLEY AUTHORITY.

Crump never stooped to racial demagoguery, he was scrupulously honest, and he fashioned a strong and effective political organization. In many respects, he was a political spokesman of the Memphis commercial-civic elite. His long-standing commitment to efficiency was increasingly coupled with a fervent defense of traditional southern morality, and his last years were marked by a florid anticommunism and support for the established order. His unsuccessful proleftist charges against ESTES KEFAUVER in the 1948 U.S. Senate campaign signaled the decline of Crump's political power.

See W. D. Miller, *Mr. Crump* (1964), definitive, and *Memphis* (1957).

BLAINE A. BROWNELL
University of Alabama, Birmingham

CULPEPER'S REBELLION (December, 1677) was an armed uprising of North Carolina colonists against Thomas Miller, who had assumed power as chief executive under questionable authority. Miller had been irregularly commissioned by the recently appointed governor, Thomas Eastchurch, who had stopped in Nevis en route from London, sending Miller to govern temporarily in his stead. After several months of oppressive government under Miller, the colonists ousted him by force. Eastchurch reached Virginia during the upheaval but sickened and died there. A council composed of leaders of the uprising governed North Carolina until legal government was restored in 1679. A tradition that one John Culpeper led the uprising and was made governor by the "rebels" probably accounts for the name given the episode. In fact, Culpeper was not among the chief leaders, and he was never governor.

See M. E. E. Parker (ed.), *North Carolina Higher-Court Records, 1670–96* (1968), and *North Carolina Historical Review* (Spring, 1968); H. F. Rankin, *Upheaval in Albemarle* (1962), different interpretation from Parker's; W. L. Saunders (ed.), *Colonial Records of North Carolina* (1886), I, primary sources; Timothy Biggs, "A Narrative" (1678), Arents Tobacco Collection, New York City Public Library, photocopy in North Carolina State Archives; and Herbert Jeffreys to Henry Covington (Feb. 11, 1678), microfilm in Library of Congress.

MATTIE ERMA E. PARKER
North Carolina Department of Archives and History

CUMBERLAND, MD. (pop. 29,724), on the north branch of the Potomac River in the Appalachian Mountains, grew up around a trading post built by the OHIO COMPANY in 1750. George Washington in 1751 began construction here of Ft. Cumberland, used as an operations' base in 1755 by General Edward Braddock in the FRENCH AND INDIAN WAR. Situated at a natural pass leading to the Ohio River valley, Cumberland became the eastern terminus for the CUMBERLAND ROAD, a switching point for the Baltimore & Ohio Railroad (1842), and the western terminus of the Chesapeake & Ohio Canal (1850). Despite the ravages of periodic floods, excellent transportation facilities have long made the city a prosperous commercial center and shipping point for limestone and bituminous coal. Its factories also produce textiles, railroad equipment, tires, and glassware.

See files of Cumberland *Times* (1869–); J. W. Hunt, *Across the Desk* (1973), collection of 1,134 news articles on area history; W. H. Lowdermilk, *History of Cumberland* (1878); A. B. Hulbert, *Cumberland Road* (1902); J. W. Thomas, *History of Allegany County* (1923); and J. T. Scharf, *History of Western Maryland* (1882).

CUMBERLAND GAP is a natural V-shaped passage through the Cumberland Mountains on the Kentucky-Virginia border near the juncture of Kentucky, Virginia, and Tennessee. It was a significant feature on the WARRIOR'S PATH, the Indian trail that connected the Ohio Valley with the Southeast. Gabriel Arthur was probably the first white man of record to travel through the gap (1674). After DANIEL BOONE blazed the WILDERNESS ROAD through the gap (1775), it became the principal gateway to Kentucky for hunters, traders, land speculators, and settlers. It accounted for three-fourths of Kentucky's rapidly growing population. It also became a passageway for horse and cattle drives and for stagecoaches. The gap had considerable strategic value during the Civil War. When the Confederates evacuated the gap in mid-1862 to strengthen their hold on Chattanooga, it was occupied by Union troops. Later in the summer, the Confederates were in control again and used it as they withdrew following the failure of their Kentucky campaign. In late 1863 it fell again to the federals, who controlled it until the end of the war. Reports of geologists in the 1880s of rich iron and coal deposits in the area triggered a regional boom that lasted until the panic of 1893. Its recreational and scenic value was enhanced in 1959, when the Cumberland Gap National Historical Park was created.

See W. W. Luckett, *Tennessee Historical Quarterly* (Dec., 1964), best; R. L. Kincaid, *Wilderness Road* (1947), useful bibliography; *Official Records, Armies*, Ser. 1, Vol. XVI; and V. J. Esposito, *West Point Atlas* (1959).

DWIGHT L. SMITH
Miami University

CUMBERLAND PLATEAU, the southernmost section of the Appalachian Plateaus province (AP-PALACHIAN MOUNTAINS) and a southwestward continuation of the Allegheny Plateau (ALLEGHE-NY MOUNTAINS), extends from eastern Kentucky across Tennessee into northern Alabama. An elevated region underlain by roughly horizontal sedimentary rock strata, the plateau is cut by deep, steep-sided valleys of tributaries to the Kentucky, Cumberland, and Tennessee rivers. Rolling uplands of varying expanse separate these valleys, and it is this upland characteristic that differentiates the Cumberland from the more dissected Allegheny Plateau. Gentle folds in the strata produce some northeast-southwest trending linear features such as Pine Mountain and Sequatchie Valley, but the landscape lacks the distinct linearity of the ridge and valley province to the east. Altitudes (reaching 4,145 feet at Black Mountain, Ky.) and relief are greatest in the northeastern segment of the plateau along the Kentucky-Virginia border, where folding is more pronounced and thrust faulting has occurred; this segment is often identified as the Cumberland Mountains. Upland elevations generally decrease southward. The Cumberland Front, a prominent east-facing escarpment rising 2,000 feet above the adjacent valleys in places, forms the plateau's eastern margin.

See W. D. Thornbury, *Regional Geomorphology of U.S.* (1965).

WALLACE M. ELTON
Middlebury College

CUMBERLAND RIVER starts its long and winding flow from the Appalachians near Harlan, Ky. It enters the OHIO RIVER some 300 miles to the west. However, due to numerous turns and crooks the Cumberland actually travels well over 600 miles to get to the Ohio. Despite the winding course, the Cumberland was early known as the easiest of the western waters to travel. The Cumberland was used in early America as a major highway to carry produce of all sorts to the Ohio and then down the Mississippi River to New Orleans. In fact, many people in Kentucky had no other means of shipping to a major port.

As far as settlements were concerned, the Cumberland Valley did not fare as well as some other valleys. Few early settlers came from New England or the middle colonies. However, Virginia and North Carolina did provide Cumberland lands as payment to veterans of the Revolution. Until the nineteenth century there were no large settlements more than a few miles south of Nashville, Tenn. As late as the 1970 census, the population

of the entire Cumberland Valley, including its largest city Nashville, was only some 2 million.

During the Civil War the natural path for Union invasion of Tennessee was along the Cumberland and Tennessee rivers. To guard the Cumberland entrance, Ft. Donelson was built near Dover, Tenn. In February, 1862, the fort was hit by both land and water forces. Its loss helped open the heartland of the Confederacy to the Union (FTS. HENRY AND DONELSON CAMPAIGN). In modern times the Cumberland itself has been cut by Wolf Creek Dam. However, both the upper and lower Cumberland now provide thousands of southern tourists with lost causes, lakes, and hydroelectric plants.

See H. S. Arnow, *Seedtime on Cumberland* (1960), and *Flowering Cumberland* (1963); A. Carpenter, *Tennessee* (1968); and C. Eaton, *Southern Confederacy* (1954).

JOE E. PETERS
Calhoun Community College

CUMBERLAND ROAD, or National Road, the great federal highway into the old Northwest, opened from Cumberland, Md., on the Potomac to Vandalia, Ill., between 1811 and 1852. Linked by Maryland, via turnpikes, to Baltimore and Washington on the east and intended to reach St. Louis on the west, it coincided largely with present U.S. Route 40 and Interstate 70 and has been called "one of the great vehicle roads of the world."

By the Ohio Enabling Act of 1802, as amended, Congress pledged 2 percent of receipts from public land sales in the new state for construction of roads to its borders from the headwaters of the rivers flowing to the Atlantic. The act of March 29, 1806, committed the whole of this inadequate fund to a single road from Cumberland, which was completed over the Alleghenies to Wheeling in 1818 via Brownsville, Uniontown, and Washington, Pa., with the consent of the three states traversed. Similar clauses in enabling acts for Indiana (1816), Illinois (1818), and Missouri (1820) promised further projection of the road westward.

Authorized by THOMAS JEFFERSON and begun under JAMES MADISON, the National Road was the great standing precedent for federal internal improvements in the states. Accordingly, after 1816, bills for its survey and location, construction and repair were matter for perennial constitutional debate. President JAMES MONROE vetoed, in 1822, a bill for the erection of toll gates to finance needed repairs but approved the principle of federal appropriation. Responsibility for repairs and eventually full jurisdiction were relinquished piecemeal to the states between 1831 and 1856; but

Congress voted funds for construction and partial macadamization liberally between 1825 and 1838, when strict constructionist arguments were supplemented by depression. Final work was done under authority of Indiana and Illinois, states in which the road was inadequately surfaced and long discontinuous. Along its route were Cambridge, Zanesville, Columbus, and Springfield, Ohio; Richmond, Greenfield, Indianapolis, and Terre Haute, Ind.

See P. D. Jordan, *National Road* (1948); and J. S. Young, *Political and Constitutional Study* (1904).

JOSEPH H. HARRISON, JR.
Auburn University

CUMMINGS V. MISSOURI (4 Wallace 277

[1867]). By 1865, Unionist groups in the border and former Confederate states had developed a systematic loyalty program to assure their domination of state government and economic enterprise. Missouri's constitution, representative in this regard, contained a test oath that identified 86 specific acts disqualifying people from voting, holding office, preaching, teaching, practicing law, engaging in a business or profession, or practicing a trade. Those who could not swear that they had never committed any act of disloyalty to the United States government (IRONCLAD OATH) were excluded from the mentioned activities. In Missouri, a Catholic priest performed his functions without having sworn the oath and was prosecuted. The resultant case, *Cummings* v. *Missouri*, was appealed to the U.S. Supreme Court after the Missouri courts sustained the oath in 1865–1866. When the Court rendered its decision in early 1867, Justice Stephen J. Field ruled for the majority in a five-to-four division that the oath violated the ex post facto and bill of attainder prohibitions in the Constitution.

During the same term, and with the same divisions, the Court also struck down the Federal Test Act of 1865, which prohibited those incapable of swearing to their uninterrupted loyalty to the United States from practicing law in the federal courts. In *ex parte Garland*, Justice Field urged the same grounds advanced in *Cummings* v. *Missouri* to strike the federal oath, but added that since President Andrew Johnson had pardoned Garland, all possible taint had been removed. Despite the Court's rulings, oaths such as those used in Missouri and in the federal courts prevailed for a number of years. Federal and state courts ruled contradictorily concerning their legitimacy and validity, but the unsettled conditions during the Reconstruction period prevented any conclusive answer to the problem until after the more pressing issues had been settled. Nonetheless, Field's rulings remained on the books as precedents and were later used by petitioners seeking to ensure that the rights of free speech, free association, and privacy were not violated by overzealous governmental officials.

See C. Fairman, *Reconstruction* (1971); C. B. Swisher, *Stephen J. Field* (1930); H. Hyman, *To Try Men's Souls* (1959); S. I. Kutler, *Judicial Power* (1968); C. Warren, *Supreme Court* (1926); J. G. Randall, *Constitutional Problems Under Lincoln* (1951); A. Kelly and W. Harbison, *American Constitution* (1970); *ex parte Garland*, 4 Wall. 333 (1867); W. A. Russ, Jr., *Mississippi Law Review* (Dec., 1937); and O. K. Fraenkel, *Iowa Law Review* (Winter, 1952).

GEORGE M. DENNISON
Colorado State University

CUNEY, NORRIS WRIGHT (1846–1898), the

most influential black political leader in Texas, was born at Sunnyside plantation. Colonel Philip Cuney, his father, was of Swiss ancestry, and Adeline Stuart, his mother, then a slave, was of Potomac Indian, Caucasian, and Negro blood. In 1859, Cuney's father sent him to join two brothers at George Vashon's school in Pittsburgh. Young Cuney learned the riverboat trade, which prepared him to build up a profitable stevedoring business in Galveston. In 1869 he supported Republican EDMUND J. DAVIS for governor, and in 1872 he was appointed inspector of customs. As secretary for the Republican state executive committee, he observed party management and by 1883 was ready to assume leadership. Meanwhile, in 1875 he lost a race for mayor of Galveston. He was respected by the businessmen of the city, and they helped him become collector of customs during the Benjamin HARRISON ADMINISTRATION. His control of patronage caused a break with Andrew Jackson Houston, splintering the Republican party. When Governor J. S. HOGG ran successfully for reelection in 1892, Cuney swung the regular Republican vote to Democratic bolter George Clark, who opposed the railroad commission. In 1896 Cuney, despite Mark Hanna's pressures to shift to William McKinley, supported William Allison. Later he turned to E. H. R. Green, son of Hettie, as a way to check Hanna's henchmen. Cuney obtained night schools for whites and blacks in Galveston and championed a college for Negroes at Prairie View. He was grand master of the Prince Hall Masonic Lodge.

See M. C. Hare, *Norris Wright Cuney* (1913, 1968), by his daughter; P. Casdorph, *Republican Party* (1965); C. G. Woodson, *Negro History Bulletin* (March, 1948);

V. N. Hinze, "Norris Wright Cuney" (M.A. thesis, Rice University, 1965); and R. C. Cotner, *J. S. Hogg* (1959).

ROBERT CRAWFORD COTNER
University of Texas

CURRENCY. The South had its beginning as an export economy (COMMERCE), and a resulting nonpecuniary tradition has left southerners the least money minded of Americans. Because of its excess of imports over exports, the South's colonial currency was an erratic mixture of barter, commodity money, tobacco warehouse receipts, specie, paper, and "bills of credit." The use of fiat money in some southern colonies and later during the Revolutionary era led to bankruptcies, inflation, and debtor expropriation. All in all, however, the available currency in every southern state remained inadequate for individual and community needs.

With the framing of the Constitution, the federal government secured exclusive control of coinage, forbidding states to issue bills of credit or any tender for debt payment except bimetallic specie. The new government established a mint in 1792, and its bimetallic currency was supplemented by national bank notes issued by the federally chartered Bank of the United States. A rational currency was thus established in the South as well as in the nation.

After the War of 1812, however, normal growth in the supply of money in both the North and South fell short of what was needed for stable prices. The industrial revolution and the consequent transition to a market economy demanded additional institutions to supply money and to guide domestic savings into capital formation (BANKING). But the South's hard money stance, its antibanking prejudice, and its luxury-oriented factorage system worked to limit the circulation of specie and fiduciary paper. In fact, Virginia was the first state (1837) to require 25 percent specie behind circulating notes; and Louisiana was the first to demand a one-third specie ratio on all note and deposit liabilities. Between 1860 and 1913, the currency circulating throughout the nation grew to a total of approximately $11 billion, but the southern states never had access to their proportionate share. The limited amount of currency that did circulate in the region was inadequate for the expansion of purchasable goods and services and the growth of the population. Prices declined, and further outflow of currency was encouraged by the CROP LIEN SYSTEM with its high interest rates.

The Federal Reserve System, launched in 1914, permanently liberated the South's internal money from its dependence on purely external factors. The system's notes now constitute 85 percent of currency circulation in the South. Richmond, Atlanta, and Dallas—Federal Reserve centers—symbolize the modern South's nascent monetary independence with respect to commercial loan production and exploitation of its own resources.

Increased southern wages, production, per capita INCOME, and demand deposits indicate an increasingly desirable liquidity, a broader currency distribution, and a growth in the middle-income group. Investment capital "inflow" and state bank liaison with northern depositories induce policies, interest rates, and purchasing practices that are now favorable to the South.

See C. P. Nettles, *Money Supply of Colonies* (1939), definitive; C. J. Bullock, *Essays* (1900); A. B. Hepburn, *History of Coinage* (1903), definitive; G. R. Woolfolk, *Cotton Regency* (1958); A. Del Mar, *History of Money* (1968); R. R. Russel, *Southern Sectionalism* (1960); H. D. Woodman, *King Cotton* (1968); C. B. Hoover and B. U. Ratchford, *Economics of the South* (1951); M. L. Greenhut, *Southern States* (1964), definitive; P. Cagan, *Determinants and Effects* (1965), basic; J. V. Sickle, *Planning for South* (1943); A. Leiserson, *American South* (1969); W. E. Laird, *Mid-America* (1966); and L. V. Brock, *Currency in American Colonies* (1975).

GEORGE RUBLE WOOLFOLK
Prairie View A. & M. University

CURRY, JABEZ LAMAR MONROE (1825–1903), was born in Georgia. Trained as a lawyer, he abandoned that profession for politics and education. After he moved to Alabama, Curry, an active Democrat, served in the state legislature (1847, 1853, 1855), the U.S. Congress (1857–1861), and the Confederate Congress (1861–1863, 1864). Elected president of Alabama's Howard College in 1865 and ordained a Baptist minister in 1866, he developed a distinctive career in religion and education. Following 12 years as a professor at Richmond College, he represented the PEABODY EDUCATION FUND from 1881 as a preeminent advocate of public education. After his tenure as U.S. minister to Spain (1885–1888), he resumed his work with the Peabody Fund and in 1890 added the responsibility of administrator for the SLATER FUND. In 1901 he participated in the founding of the SOUTHERN EDUCATION BOARD and in 1903 helped charter the GENERAL EDUCATION BOARD. In the 1880s Curry departed from his states' rights principles to support the BLAIR BILL for federal aid to combat illiteracy. Although a white supremacist, he favored education of blacks. Called the "Father of the Normal Schools in the South," he ardently promoted teacher training and even endorsed coeducation. Curry published a chronicle of the Confederacy and a valuable account of the Peabody Fund, but his reputation has never equaled his accomplishments as a pioneer educator.

See J. P. Rice, *J. L. M. Curry* (1949); E. A. Alderman and A. C. Gordon, *J. L. M. Curry* (1911), life and times; and L. R. Harlan, *Separate and Unequal* (1969).

BETTY J. BRANDON
University of South Alabama

CUSTOMS AND MANNERS. The principal influences that shaped southern customs and manners were the English heritage, the frontier, the climate, slavery, and romantic literature. The English influence was powerful in the colonial period, as the diary of William Byrd II demonstrates, but it also remained strong up to the Reconstruction period. It emphasized class distinctions, provided a pervasive ideal of the country gentleman way of life, and gave to southerners more than to northerners the love of titles, particularly military titles, which the militia system also encouraged. The influence of slavery on manners and customs was subtle and complex, but northern observers noted that the master class developed the habit of command, was impatient of contradiction, and exhibited great personal pride, which led to many duels but also to the practice of *noblesse oblige* and chivalry. Henry Benjamin Whipple (later to become Episcopal bishop of Minnesota) wrote in his travel diary in 1842: "The southerner himself is different from the northerner in many striking particulars. He is more chivalrous, that is to say, he has more of the old English feeling common in the days of the feudal system." Some 25 years later John William De Forest, an officer in the Union army and a Freedmen's Bureau agent in South Carolina, concurred with Whipple's characterization. He observed that "Southerners exhibited more of the antique virtues than the New Englanders; they care less for wealth, art, learning and other delicacies; they care more for individual character and honor."

Visitors to the South were impressed by the greater hospitality of the region in comparison with the North. The reasons for this generous custom were primarily the loneliness of the plantations and semifrontier homes, the profusion of food, and the domestic servants provided by slavery. One important northern visitor, Frederick Law Olmsted, however, believed that the presumed hospitality of southerners was a myth, citing as evidence the fact that during his extensive travels in the region during 1852–1854 he had to pay for meals and lodging in private homes. In addition

to their hospitality, southerners were noted for their politeness. Courtly manners were cultivated by the aristocracy, and even the common people were distinguished by frank and cordial manners. English travelers commented on the great amount of vigorous handshaking, the frequent use in address of "Sir" and "Mam" (for Madam), the extensive chewing of tobacco and of spitting, and the offering to strangers of whiskey before breakfast that they observed below the Mason-Dixon Line.

The manners and customs of the Victorian age held sway in the rural South much longer than in the urbanized North. Divorce, for example, and the use of artificial means of birth control were severely frowned upon, and large families consequently were the rule. Romanticism dominated the attitude of society toward women, and the differences between the sexes were exaggerated. Women were regarded as purer and more refined than men, and sex was a tabooed subject in conversation before ladies. Romantic love was exalted, as illustrated by James Lane Allen's novel *The Kentucky Cardinal* (1894). Letters between the sexes were usually sentimental and formal in tone. Custom dictated that women should not travel except under the protection of a male. The husband became the owner of the property of a woman after they married, and he was supposed to rule the household or be regarded as "henpecked." Mrs. Jefferson Davis, for example, protested against naming one of her babies after the relative of her husband whom she disliked, but she yielded because she said it was her husband's right. There was perhaps little difference between the South and the North in regard to disciplining children, especially the practice of whipping them for offenses. Catherine C. Hopley, a British schoolteacher who served as a tutor on Governor John Milton's plantation in Florida, observed that the children of the master were whipped more often than the slaves.

As in many societies, the customs and manners of the aristocracy and the lower classes differed markedly. DUELING was largely confined to the upper class. The planters were in the habit of traveling in the summer to watering places, such as White Sulphur Springs or Saratoga, and many of them sent their children to northern schools and colleges. In contrast to northerners, they were in the habit of flattering ladies excessively, and the southern belle expected it; also, they staged tournaments in imitation of the days of chivalry, which their favorite author Sir Walter Scott glorified. The distinctive customs of the lower classes included quilting bees, logrolling, cockfights, wrestling, shooting matches, singing old ballads and fiddling lively tunes, dipping snuff and smoking corncob pipes by women, and CLAY EATING by the children of POOR WHITES. The black southerners also had their singular customs, most notable of which were superstitious practices such as carrying amulets, especially a rabbit's foot, a curious marriage ceremony of the couple jumping over a broom, voodoo, dancing the juba and the Congo, and dramatic, emotional funerals.

Political and religious customs were decidedly influenced by the semifrontier conditions of large areas of the South (which also explain the widespread practice of carrying arms). Stump speaking, political barbecues, long and florid orations, treating the electorate with liquor, and attending county court were characteristic customs of the southern region. Southern religion, except for a small class of Episcopalians, had a strong emotional and puritanical quality. Camp meetings at times resulted in mass hysteria. Among the Primitive Baptists the ceremony of foot washing was practiced, and a religious phenomenon often seen in the South was the baptism of converts in rivers and creeks, attended by large crowds.

Following the Civil War many distinctive southern customs gradually became obsolete, and some new ones arose, such as "moonshining." These changes were brought about as a result of greater urbanization, better education of the masses, and the waning of Victorianism. Dueling disappeared, long visits to friends and relatives and to watering resorts decreased, clay eating, gouging, and cockfighting became relics of the past, the practice of chivalry and formal manners went out of fashion, and camp meetings were largely replaced by revivals in the churches. Thus southern customs and manners in general merged into the national pattern, and only in remote regions lingered.

See the following travel accounts, the best contemporary sources for the study of southern manners and customs: F. M. Trollope, *Domestic Manners of the Americans* (1832), biased, but useful; H. Martineau, *Society in America* (1837); J. S. Buckingham, *Slave State of America* (1842); C. Lyell, *A Second Visit to the U.S.* (1849), very judicious; F. Bremer, *America of the Fifties* (1924), a Swedish woman's observations; F. L. Olmsted, *Journey in the Seaboard Slave States* (1856), and *Journey in the Back Country* (1860), both indispensable, yet biased by antislavery and racist preconceptions; W. H. Russell, *My Diary, North and South* (1863), very perceptive; C. Hopley, *Life in South* (1863); A. J. L. Fremantle, *Three Months in the Southern States* (1864); J. R. Dennett, *South as It Is, 1865–1866* (1965); W. Reid, *After the War: A Tour of Southern States, 1865–1866* (1965); E. King, *Great South: A Record of Journeys* (1875), valuable; and G. Campbell, *White and Black: Outcome of a Visit to U.S.* (1879). Perceptive diaries and collections of letters noting manners and customs are: F. A. Kemble, *Journal of a Residence on a Georgian Plantation in 1838–39* (1863), very prejudiced; J. C. Bonner (ed.), *North Carolina Historical Review* (July–Oct., 1956); M. C. S. Oliphant (ed.), *Letters of William Gilmore Simms* (1954); Gertrude Thomas Clanton Diary (1848–89), 13 vols., Duke University Library; Mary Boykin Chesnut, *Diary from Dixie* (1961), exceedingly valuable; and John Berkeley Grimball Diary, University of North Carolina Library. A valuable source for customs and manners are the writings of the southern humorists, particularly the stories of A. B. Longstreet, W. T. Thompson, J. J. Hooper, J. G. Baldwin, and G. W. Harris; also useful is D. R. Hundley, *Social Relations in Our Southern States* (1860). Among modern works are: U. B. Phillips, *Life and Labor in Old South* (1931); F. L. Owsley, *Plain Folk of Old South* (1945); B. I. Wiley, *Plain People of Confederacy* (1944); W. J. Cash, *Mind of South* (1950); W. R. Taylor, *Cavalier and Yankee* (1961); and C. Eaton, *Mind of Old South* (1967), and *Waning of Old South Civilization* (1969).

CLEMENT EATON
University of Kentucky

D

DABNEY, CHARLES WILLIAM (1855–1945), born at Hampden-Sydney, Va., was the son of Stonewall Jackson's chief of staff. After graduating from Hampden-Sydney College (B.A., 1873) and attending the University of Virginia, Dabney earned his Ph.D. degree in chemistry from Göttingen University (1880). He served as the director of the North Carolina Agricultural Experiment Station (1880–1887), but his greatest achievements were as an educator and as a promoter of improved public EDUCATION in the South. While he served as president of the University of Tennessee (1887–1904) and Cincinnati University (1904–1920), his pamphlets, bulletins, speeches, and reports did much to heighten the awareness of the southern public and of northern philanthropists to the needs of southern school-aged children (SOUTHERN EDUCATION BOARD).

See C. W. Dabney, *Universal Education in South* (1936), sketches figures in southern education from T. Jefferson to 1900; and C. W. Dabney Papers, University of North Carolina Library, Chapel Hill.

DABNEY, ROBERT LEWIS (1820–1898). Dabney's life spanned the Old South, Civil War, Reconstruction, and the New South. The son of a Virginia planter, he attended Hampden-Sydney College, University of Virginia, and Union Theological Seminary (1844–1846) before accepting a missionary pastorate in western Virginia. An exceptional scholar and writer, he left there in 1853 to begin a lifelong career of teaching at Hampden-Sydney (1853–1859), Princeton University (1859), Union Theological Seminary (1860–1883), and the University of Texas (1883–1894), where he was cofounder of the Austin Theological Seminary (1884). Throughout his long and vigorous life Dabney carried a vision of the Old South as a Christian, humane, and enlightened civilization. His life, but not his career, achieved its zenith in the Civil War, when he served as chaplain to STONEWALL JACKSON. The South's defeat embittered Dabney, particularly on the issue of race. He opposed Negro education and free education by the state. Still, from 1865 to 1898 in seminaries in Virginia and Texas he trained a generation of Presbyterian ministers, imbuing them with his moral philosophy, ideology of the NEW SOUTH, antimaterialism, and the justice of populism.

See D. H. Overy, Jr., "R. L. Dabney" (Ph.D. dissertation, Wisconsin State University, 1968), best; W. H. Daniel, *Virginia Magazine of History and Biography* (June, 1963), excellent; T. C. Johnson, *Life and Letters of RLD* (1902); R. L. Dabney, *Sign of Temper* (1860), *Life and Campaigns of General T. J. Jackson* (1866), *New South* (1870), *Sensualistic Philosophy* (1875), *Depression of American Farming Interests* (1892), and *Sacred Rhetoric* (1870, 1881, 1902); and Dabney Papers, Duke University and Union Seminary libraries.

JOSEPH P. HARAHAN
U.S. Government Historian

DABNEY, VIRGINIUS (1901–), was born in Charlottesville, where his father was a professor of history at the university. After being graduated Phi Beta Kappa from the University of Virginia (B.A., 1920; M.A., 1921), Dabney opted for a career in journalism. He began as a cub reporter for the Richmond *News-Leader* in 1922. In 1928 he joined the editorial staff of the Richmond *Times-Dispatch*, and eight years later he became that paper's editor-in-chief, a post he held until retiring in 1969. Writing as a liberal Virginia patrician who traced his ancestry from many of the state's most prominent families, he scolded and criticized a wide variety of persons and movements. He was quite impatient with Negro leaders and "outside agitators" who pressed for speedy change in southern race relations. Yet he was equally hostile to religious fundamentalism, prohibition, one-party politics, the poll tax, and segregation. In addition to his regular contributions to the *Times-Dispatch*, he wrote several books: *Liberalism in the South* (1932); *Below the Potomac* (1942); *Virginia: The New Dominion* (1971); and *Dry Messiah* (1949), a critical biography of his *bête noire*, Methodist Bishop JAMES CANNON. He took a leading role at the SOUTHERN CONFERENCE FOR HUMAN WELFARE in 1938 and has served as a director of the SOUTHERN REGIONAL COUNCIL.

DADE MASSACRE (December 28, 1835) resulted from the federal government's attempts to remove the SEMINOLE INDIANS from Florida and is regarded as the first engagement of the Second Seminole War (SEMINOLE WARS). Smarting from the abuse of government officials who had forced the Seminole to accept two removal treaties and from slave traders who were stealing Indians, the

Seminole decided to defend their own interests. On the twenty-eighth a small group murdered Indian agent Wiley Thompson and Lieutenant Constantine Smith near Ft. King. That same day another Indian force of 180 ambushed Major Francis L. Dade's detachment of eight officers and 100 "red-legged" infantrymen on the wagon road between Fts. Brooke and King near the Great Wahoo Swamp. Dade and half the command dropped with the first Indian volley. After the initial shock, however, the soldiers regrouped and dispersed the attackers. During the lull the remaining men built a crude log breastwork, which only delayed the inevitable. By four o'clock not a soldier remained standing. Only three men survived. On January 21, 1836, General WINFIELD SCOTT was ordered to the Florida Territory to command operations, and the Second Seminole War escalated into a major Indian war.

See M. F. Boyd, *Florida Aflame* (1951), best analysis; J. K. Mahon, *Second Seminole War* (1967); W. Potter, *War in Florida* (1836); F. P. Prucha, *Sword of Republic* (1969); and A. F. Roberts, *Florida Historical Quarterly* (Jan., 1927).

EMMETT M. ESSIN
East Tennessee State University

DAHLONEGA, GA. (pop. 2,658), was the center of the nation's first gold rush and the site of a U.S. mint (1838–1861). The area was originally part of the CHEROKEE INDIANS' domain. After the discovery of gold in 1828, however, the state of Georgia claimed title to the territory and distributed 40-acre "gold lots" to would-be miners by way of a lottery. Dahlonega was founded and incorporated in 1833. The discovery of richer gold deposits in California in 1849 and the loss of the federal mint with secession in 1861 ended the town's boom years. Mining activity in the area since the Civil War has been sporadic and expensive. Today it is a small market town for lumber and cotton growers and the home of North Georgia State College. The Georgia Historical Commission supports and maintains the local Gold Museum.

See A. W. Cain, *History of Lumpkin County* (1932); E. M. Coulter, *Auraria* (1956); G. W. Paschal, *94 Years* (1871, 1974); *Harper's* (Sept., 1879); and *Georgia Geological Survey Bulletin*, No. 4-A (1896) and No. 19 (1909).

DAIRY INDUSTRY. In the colonial South, production of milk, butter, and cheese differed very little in manner and extent from the North. But comparatively slower southern urban growth in the first half of the nineteenth century meant that commercial dairy manufacturing and the sale of fluid milk failed to develop there as it did in the North, particularly New York. Although the South contained 40 percent of the total dairy cows in the nation in 1860, the section produced only 19.7 percent of the butter and 1.2 percent of the cheese. Southern farmers produced their own butter supply and only haphazardly supplied milk to urban centers.

Factory manufacture of milk products, originating in the 1850s, did little to change the pattern of the dairy industry in the South from antebellum days until World War II. Southern milk producers continued to lag behind the North in efficiency and production. They produced enough fluid milk to supply all the needs of towns and cities in the region, and farm manufacture of butter continued to supply most of local demand. Cheese, evaporated milk, and all other manufactured dairy products were turned out, however, by northern milk producers and manufacturers to supply a national market. The market for most manufactured dairy products thus became a national one, with production centering in the dairy belt from the Great Lakes to New York, but the market for fluid milk remained Balkanized due to the perishable nature of the product.

In the decade of the 1940s, however, several developments came together to disrupt the pattern of the southern dairy industry. Artificial insemination, begun by an association of New Jersey dairymen in 1938, coupled with steady improvements in dairy husbandry, led to unusually rapid increases in milk production. Bulk handling of milk from farm to the bottler and good interstate highways finally made it feasible to ship midwestern milk, previously reserved for manufacturing, into fluid milk markets in the South. Federal government price support formulas, as well as prices set by state milk stabilization boards, established considerably higher prices for southern than for northern producers. Consequently, fluid milk began moving southward, and price wars developed after the mid-1950s in some areas of the South. Quickly, producers and distributors began trying to stabilize prices.

With the main impetus coming from the South, especially from Texas and Arkansas, giant multimarket milk producers' cooperatives began emerging in the late 1960s; Associated Milk Producers, Inc.; Dairymen, Inc.; and Mid-America Cooperative were the largest. With both southern and northern members, they rationalized the newly enlarged markets for fluid milk. Southern producers still received higher prices, but the differential decreased as milk was marketed over wider areas.

By the 1970s, milk production in the South differed in some important respects from the dairy belt of the North, but resembled dairy farming in far western states like California and Washington. Southern production was more specialized with larger and more highly mechanized farms. For example, Texas farms averaged 20 cows more per dairy than Wisconsin farms in 1967. In contrast to the earlier pattern, by 1970 it was difficult to find meaningful differences in production or efficiency between southern milk producers and those in the remainder of the country. Yet one feature had not changed; dairy manufacturing still took place mostly outside the South.

See L. C. Gray, *History of Agriculture in Southern U.S. to 1860* (2 vols.; 1933); J. T. Schlebecker, *History of American Dairying* (1967), esp. bibliography; and T. R. Pirtle, *History of Dairy Industry* (1926). For statistics and other primary information, see files of *Hoards Dairyman* (1885–); publications of USDA; and files of southern land-grant colleges. Historians of dairying have correctly focused on the northern dairy industry; there is no general history of dairying in the South.

E. DALE ODOM
North Texas State University

DALLAS, TEX. (pop. 844,401). Idealism failed to establish a city near the site of Dallas, but business-oriented boosterism produced the nation's eighth-largest city. John Neely Bryan built a cabin at a crossing on the Trinity River in 1841 and, within five years, Dallas existed. Where neither the Peters Colony nor the utopian La Reunion group succeeded, Bryan's venture became a city. Chartered in 1856, Dallas achieved a solid economic base when it became a Confederate military headquarters as well as a haven for southerners who fled from Union troops during the Civil War.

Through sly legislative maneuvering and cash inducements to railroad leaders, Dallas became a railhead in 1872. Expositions, including the state fair of Texas, attracted business, people, and industry to the city, which already had become the trade center for a blackland cotton-growing region. Industrial growth, augmented by strong banking interests and insurance companies, made Dallas the financial center of the Southwest by 1913.

Business leaders have dominated twentieth-century Dallas. Capitalizing on geographic location and making use of new technology, boosters have expanded the city's economy and brought continual civic improvements. Dallas bankers and entrepreneurs financed the east Texas oil discoveries in the early 1930s, and R. L. Thornton

brought the Texas centennial celebration to Dallas in 1936 despite the superior historical claims of Houston and San Antonio. Although its reputation suffered because of the KENNEDY ASSASSINATION in 1963, dynamic, conservative businessmen in electronics, data processing, banking, and insurance fueled urban growth through 1970, when more than 800,000 people resided in Dallas.

See Works Progress Administration, *Guide and History of Dallas* (1940); A. C. Greene, *Dallas* (1973); P. Lindsley, *Greater Dallas* (1909); S. V. Connor, *Peters Colony* (1959); H. A. Jebsen, *Dallas Park System* (1975); J. W. Rogers, *Lusty Texans* (1965); and R. C. Cotner, *Texas Cities* (1973).

HARRY JEBSEN, JR.
Texas Tech University

DALLAS and GALVESTON NEWS are two daily newspapers that share a common history. Samuel Bang founded the *News* in Galveston, Tex., in 1842. The following year, Willard Richardson (1802–1875), a native of Massachusetts who had become an admirer of JOHN C. CALHOUN, took over as editor. Richardson's *News* was an advocate of the annexation of Texas by the United States, a defender of states' rights and slavery, and the most widely circulated newspaper in the new state. Although the *News* shunned identification with any partisan organization prior to the Civil War, it generally regarded MIRABEAU LAMAR and his political associates with favor and regularly opposed and criticized SAM HOUSTON.

When Confederate authorities ordered civilians to evacuate Galveston in 1862, Richardson loaded the presses, print, and paper of the *News* on a railroad car and moved it to Houston. The experience proved significant. After the paper returned to Galveston in 1866, Richardson determined to improve the delivery and circulation of the statewide edition by a novel use of railroads. Instead of printing the paper in Galveston and shipping it to Houston (and from there to various distribution points throughout the state), he had the statewide edition printed on board the train en route to Houston. The stratagem speeded delivery of the daily and ensured its continued domination of Texas journalism.

Richardson's successor as editor, Alfred H. Belo (1839–1901), made an even bolder use of nineteenth-century technology to extend the sway of the *News*. Although Richardson's rolling print room had permitted the Galveston paper to compete in the Houston market, Belo was convinced that the state's future commercial and population center was in the area around Dallas. Beginning in October, 1885, the *News* was published simultaneously in Galveston and Dallas with the aid of a leased telegraph line. The news copy was telegraphed from Galveston to presses in Dallas, and virtually duplicate editions of the *News* were printed in both cities until 1923, when the Galveston *Daily News* was sold and became a separate enterprise from the Dallas *Morning News*.

Under both Richardson and Belo, the post–Civil War *News* served as the principal press of the state's Conservative Democratic party. Nationally it opposed the Interstate Commerce Act of 1887, and it endorsed William McKinley for president in 1896 and in 1900. On the state level it campaigned for agricultural diversification, resisted legislation regulating corporations, and opposed the programs and policies of Governor JAMES HOGG. In the twentieth century it was an early and an ardent advocate of WOODROW WILSON and a vigorous critic of the KU KLUX KLAN during the 1920s and of governors JAMES AND MIRIAM FERGUSON. Since being inherited in 1946 by E. M. Dealey, the *News* has been one of the state's archconservative dailies with developing ties to the rejuvenated Republican party.

See S. Acheson, *35,000 Days in Texas* (1938); bound copies of Dallas *News* (1910–) and Galveston *News* (1899–), at Library of Congress; and microfilm of Dallas *News* (1885–), from Bell & Howell.

DALTON, GA.

DALTON, GA. (pop. 18,872), 26 miles southeast of Chattanooga, Tenn., was first incorporated in 1847. The town prospered primarily as a market and shipping point for the copper mines at Ducktown, Tenn. In 1863, after the battle of CHATTANOOGA, General BRAXTON BRAGG fell back with his Confederate troops to regroup at Dalton. Here Bragg was relieved of his command and replaced by General JOSEPH E. JOHNSTON. Although Confederate defenders successfully resisted a federal attack (February 22–27, 1864), a second attack by General W. T. Sherman's forces (battle of Rocky Face Ridge, May 5–11) turned Johnston's flank and forced him to withdraw to new positions near Resaca, Ga. During August 14–16, 1864, General JOSEPH WHEELER attempted unsuccessfully to retake the town for the Confederates. Modern Dalton is the site of several cotton and lumber mills and the center of the candlewick bedspread industry.

See Whitfield County Historical Commission, *History of Whitfield County* (1936); R. E. Hamilton, *Reader's Digest* (April, 1941); and J. B. Flemming, *Northwest Georgia Carpet Industry* (1974). University of Georgia Library and Dalton *Citizen-News* maintain microfilm copies of early Dalton newspapers.

DAMS

DAMS have played an important part in the economic and social development of the South. Since BIENVILLE founded New Orleans in 1717, federal FLOOD CONTROL dams have protected crops and urban property from billions of dollars' worth of potential flood destruction. For example, the U.S. Army Corps of Engineers estimates that its flood control projects prevented almost $14 billion worth of damages in the six-state area of Missouri, Arkansas, Kentucky, Tennessee, Mississippi, and Louisiana from the great March, 1973, flood alone. Additionally, dams have linked the South to the Midwest and East in a network of greatly improved navigation systems on Mississippi River tributaries such as the Arkansas, Missouri, Illinois, Ohio, and Tennessee rivers.

The creation of the TENNESSEE VALLEY AUTHORITY (covering seven southern states) in 1933 pioneered the concept of multiple-use dams—*e.g.*, for navigation, power, flood control, and regional resource development. Today all dams, large and small, federal and nonfederal, are built to serve many other needs of the South. These uses include water supply, irrigation, conservation, silt control, waste retention, commercial fish farming, and industrial growth. Nearly all man-made lakes are now used wholly or partly for recreational purposes.

The accumulation of 18,381 dams in the 16 southern states and District of Columbia comprises about three-eighths of the total number of all dams in the United States, according to the U.S. Army Corps of Engineers' 1975 National Dam Inventory Program. This inventory includes only dams that are 25 feet or more in height or have a storage volume of 50 acre-feet (16.3 million gallons) or more. About seven-eighths of these dams are under 50 feet high. Approximately 92 percent of the dams are earthen or rock fill, 7 percent are concrete gravity, and the remaining 1 percent are concrete buttress and arch types. Neglected are tens of thousands of additional small farm ponds and dams that are less than six feet high, regardless of storage volume, or that have storage volumes less than 15 acre-feet (4.9 million gallons), regardless of height.

About 90 percent of all dams in the South are nonfederally owned and operated by numerous state and local governmental agencies, public and private organizations, including power and water utilities, and private individuals. The remaining 10 percent are owned and/or regulated by federal agencies such as TVA; Corps of Engineers; Federal Power Commission; Bureau of Reclamation, Mining Enforcement, and Safety Administration; Forest Service; Bureau of Indian Affairs; Bureau of Land Management; U.S. Geological Survey; and International Boundary and Water Commission. The Soil Conservation Service has provided technical and financial assistance to many individuals and local sponsors for the design and construction of thousands of dams in the South so that farmers and others can more efficiently utilize and manage their land and water resources.

Although fewer major river dams will be constructed in the future because of a reduction of feasible sites, more dams will be a certain trend in the smaller tributaries to quench the South's growing thirst for new water supplies, to satisfy the recreational needs of the entire nation, to ensure resource development and protection, and to promote economic growth. The future construction of dams, however, will be moderated by a growing public demand for economic and environmental accountability, concern for safety to downstream property owners, and resource development alternatives.

See Army Corps of Engineers, *National Program of Inspection of Dams* (1975), App. F, Vols. II–V; ASCE, *Responsibilities and Liabilities of Public and Private Interests on Dams* (1976); ASCE/USCOLD, *Lessons from Dam Incidents* (1975); Army Corps of Engineers, *Flood Control: Lower Mississippi River Valley* (1973); N. R. Moore, *Improvements on Lower Mississippi River and Tributaries, 1931–1972* (1972); *TVA Handbook* (1974); and ASCE, *Safety of Small Dams* (1974).

BRUCE A. TSCHANTZ
University of Tennessee, Knoxville

DANCING RABBIT CREEK, TREATY OF, was

signed on September 27, 1830, between the chiefs of the CHOCTAW INDIAN Nation and commissioners representing the United States. It provided for the removal of most of the Choctaw from their ancient homeland in southern Mississippi to Indian Territory (now Oklahoma). This treaty was the first in a series of such pacts, which were ratified by Congress under an act of May 28, 1830, and which were more or less forced on the southern tribes under ANDREW JACKSON's Indian removal policy. The Choctaw had signed a total of eight earlier treaties with the U.S. government, beginning with the Treaty of Hopewell in 1786. As a result they had seen more and more of their land gradually surrendered to the white man, but until 1830 they had managed to hold onto enough of their original homeland to maintain their position as an Indian "nation," duly recognized by Washington. The situation quickly came to a head in February, 1829, however, when the state of Mississippi enacted the first in a series of laws that declared all Indians and Indian lands in Missis-

sippi subject to state jurisdiction and that prohibited tribal governments. President Jackson and his secretary of war, JOHN EATON, proceeded to bring considerable pressure to bear on the Choctaw to sign a treaty with the federal government and to vacate their remaining lands. The Treaty of Dancing Rabbit Creek provided that the Choctaw were to cede some 7,796,000 acres and agree to emigrate within a period of three years. The treaty acquired a somewhat infamous reputation and became the symbol of the terrible injustices done to all of the eastern Indians during this period in history.

See A. H. DeRosier, *Removal of Choctaw Indians* (1970); M. E. Young, *American Historical Review* (Oct., 1958); G. Foreman, *Indian Removal* (1953); A. Debo, *Rise and Fall of Choctaw Republic* (1934); C. J. Kappler, *Indian Treaties, 1778–1883* (1903); and Choctaw Files, 112, Records of Bureau of Indian Affairs, National Archives.

DANIEL, JOHN WARWICK (1842–1910), a great

believer in southern independence, spent four years in the Confederate army. He was wounded on three separate occasions, but his last injury put him permanently on crutches and earned for him the name "Lame Lion of Lynchburg." Following his graduation from the University of Virginia Law School in 1866, Daniel returned to Lynchburg to practice law with his father, developing a reputation as an excellent legal scholar and attorney. In 1869, he won election to the house of delegates and during the 1870s was elected three times to the state senate. A gifted orator, he became the spokesman of the LOST CAUSE and emerged as Virginia's leader of the Confederate cult. He opposed the READJUSTER MOVEMENT and played an active role in the reorganization of the Conservative party in 1883. Elected to Congress in 1883 and to the U.S. Senate in 1885, he held this latter office until his death. A practical politician, he accepted the New South philosophy and later supported much of the Progressive legislation proposed in Congress; yet in light of his lack of achievement in Congress it would be difficult to call Daniel a statesman.

See R. B. Doss, "J. W. Daniel" (Ph.D. dissertation, University of Virginia, 1955); S. D. Vecellio, "J. W. Daniel" (M.A. thesis, University of Virginia, 1950); A. W. Moger, *Bourbonism to Byrd, 1870–1925* (1968); and J. W. Daniel Papers, Duke University and University of Virginia libraries.

THOMAS E. GAY, JR.
Edinboro State College

DANIEL, PETER VIVIAN (1784–1860), was born

in Stafford County, Va., attended the College of

New Jersey briefly, after which he studied law in Richmond with EDMUND RANDOLPH, whose daughter Lucy he married in 1810. A member of the RICHMOND JUNTO, he championed agrarianism and slavery, limited government generally and states' rights and strict construction in particular. He served on the council of state for 23 years, was lieutenant governor for 17. For his efforts in organizing the Jacksonian Democrats and his loyalty in the war against the second Bank of the United States, he was made federal district judge for the eastern district of Virginia in 1837. President Martin Van Buren appointed him to the U.S. Supreme Court in 1841. As justice he continued his opposition to business corporations, attempting to prevent the surrender of public lands to big speculators. Often in bitter dissents, he resisted the expansion of federal judicial power, rejecting the argument that Congress had exclusive control over commerce and bankruptcy. His "high church agrarianism" was doomed by the onslaught of nationalism and capitalism, however, and he died having left no mark on national law.

See J. P. Frank, *Justice Daniel Dissenting* (1964); and L. Burnette, Jr., *Virginia Magazine of History and Biography* (July, 1954).

KENT NEWMYER
University of Connecticut

DANIELS, JONATHAN (1902–), the son of JOSEPHUS DANIELS, was born in Raleigh, N.C., and was graduated from the University of North Carolina (B.A., 1921; M.A., 1922). After briefly attending Columbia University Law School, he became a reporter working first for the Louisville *Times* and then for his father's Raleigh *News and Observer*. After his father's appointment as Franklin D. Roosevelt's ambassador to Mexico, Jonathan assumed responsibility for editing the family-owned newspaper, a task he carried except while holding a number of federal positions (1942–1948) until 1969. His editorials continued in the same liberal and partisanly Democratic vein associated with his father. Yet Jonathan was also a prolific writer of essays and histories. Among his acclaimed collections of essays are *A Southerner Discovers the South* (1938), *A Southerner Discovers New England* (1938), and *Frontier on the Potomac* (1946). His responsibly researched and easy to read histories range over a variety of subjects and reflect the varied interests of their author. They include *Tar Heels* (1941), a personalized history of North Carolina; *The Prince of Carpetbaggers* (1958), a critical biography of MILTON S. LITTLEFIELD; *Mosby, the Gray Ghost* (1959); *Stonewall Jackson* (1959); *Robert E. Lee* (1960); *The Devil's Back-*

bone (1962), a history of the NATCHEZ TRACE; *Time Between the Wars* (1966), on the 1920s and 1930s; and *The Randolphs of Virginia* (1972).

DANIELS, JOSEPHUS (1862–1948), decided early in his youth to become a newspaperman and at eighteen became editor and general handyman of the Wilson (N.C.) *Advance*. Four years later he was editing three weekly papers, which in 1885 he merged with the Raleigh *News and Observer*, a paper that soon became the most influential in the state. Although a staunch supporter of the Democratic party, Daniels, an innate populist, had no qualms about striking out at the big business interests that stood behind the party and reveled in learning that the corporate magnates called his paper the "Nuisance and Disturber." He first rose to national prominence in his support of William Jennings Bryan, but he was an early admirer of WOODROW WILSON, and in 1912 he played a crucial role in reconciling the differences between Wilson and Bryan.

Daniels' appointment to Wilson's cabinet as secretary of the navy angered the "big navy" advocates as well as the politically powerful Navy League. His prohibitionist sentiments also angered a number of people, who thought that his "grape juice messes" humiliated the navy. During the First World War, however, Daniels confounded his critics. The administrative changes he had introduced enabled the navy to respond quickly and effectively to the challenge of war. After hostilities ended, he again incurred the enmity of the Navy League in his support of disarmament.

In 1920, Daniels returned to his first love, the *News and Observer*, but he kept up his party contacts. He loyally supported Al Smith in 1928, despite his known opposition to Smith's antiprohibitionist attitudes. In 1932 he worked to make his former assistant secretary, Franklin D. Roosevelt, president. Roosevelt soon asked Daniels to become ambassador to Mexico, and again, despite the hostility of the critics, Daniels proved a popular and effective diplomat. He resigned in 1941 and spent the last years of his life editing his newspaper.

See Daniels' autobiography (5 vols.; 1939–47); J. L. Morrison, *Josephus Daniels* (1966), and *Josephus Daniels Says* (1962); and C. Kilpatrick (ed.), *Roosevelt and Daniels* (1953).

MELVIN I. UROFSKY
Virginia Commonwealth University

DANVILLE, KY. (pop. 11,542), 32 miles southwest of Lexington, was founded in 1775. Nine years later, the Virginia supreme court ordered that a permanent court be seated here, and the city served as a center for government west of the Allegheny Mountains until Kentucky was·admitted to the Union. Despite its political eclipse after 1792, it remained an educational center with TRANSYLVANIA UNIVERSITY (1785) and CENTRE COLLEGE (1819). Modern Danville is a market for area tobacco farmers, and its industries manufacture farm machinery, automobile parts, textiles, and furniture. In addition to its many fine antebellum homes, Danville's old courthouse square is maintained as a state shrine.

See M. T. Davies, *History of Mercer and Boyle Counties* (1924); C. M. Fackler, *Early Days in Danville* (*ca.* 1941), and *Historical Homes of Boyle County* (1959); and files of *Advocate-Messenger* (1865–), at Centre College Library and on microfilm.

DANVILLE, VA. (pop. 46,391), was founded in 1793 as a tobacco market and inspection station on the Dan River, approximately 55 miles south of Lynchburg. A canal constructed around the falls in 1820 improved river transportation and encouraged the city's commercial growth. Throughout the Civil War it was an important Confederate supply base, and for seven days (April 3–10, 1865) it served as the capital of the Confederacy. The construction here in 1881 of a yarn mill inaugurated a new era of industrialization. The modern city continues to be a major tobacco market and a manufacturer of textiles; however, its industries also produce truck tires, laminated wood, fertilizers, elevators, and mattresses.

See files of Danville *Register* (1847–) and *Bee* (1899–), both on microfilm.

DARE, VIRGINIA (1587–?), so named because she was the "first Christian born in Virginia," was the daughter of Ananias and Elenor Dare and granddaughter of John White, who had been appointed by SIR WALTER RALEIGH to govern colonists who landed at ROANOKE ISLAND toward the end of July, 1587. On August 27, White departed for England to obtain additional supplies for the colonists. After a three-year delay, he returned in 1590 to find Roanoke Island abandoned. Although Virginia colonists later heard evidence of the existence of survivors from the 1587 effort, none was ever seen.

See D. B. Quinn (ed.), *Roanoke Voyages* (1955), and Hakluyt's *English Voyages* (1965); S. E. Morison, *Northern Voyages* (1971); D. B. Quinn, *England and Discovery of America* (1974); and S. B. Weeks, *American Historical Association Papers* (1891).

GEORGE M. WALLER
Butler University

DARK AND BLOODY GROUND was a term ascribed to Kentucky, probably originally by the Indians because of the deadly struggle between the southern and northern tribes for the hunting grounds there. Later by reason of the continued warfare between the Indians and the first white settlers, the expression continued to be used. This phrase in the past has been taken by some to be the proper translation of the Indian word *kentucky*.

See R. S. Cotterill, *History of Pioneer Kentucky* (1918); A. W. Eckert, *Frontiersmen* (1967); W. P. Phyfe, *5000 Facts and Fancies* (1901); G. E. Shankle, *American Nicknames* (1955).

DAUGHTERS OF THE REPUBLIC OF TEXAS (112 E. 11th St., Capitol Grounds, Austin, Tex. 78701) is a statewide organization of 4,500 members and 64 chapters made up of women descended from Texas pioneers of the colonial and republican periods. Founded in 1891, it was first called Daughters of the Lone Star Republic and had as its first president the widow of ANSON JONES, last president of the Republic of Texas. This society's aims are chiefly patriotic, but it also attempts to encourage historical research and the preservation of relics and documents relative to Texas history. It maintains custody of the Alamo and its library in San Antonio, as well as the Alamo Museum, Long Barrack Museum, the Old Land Office Building Museum in Austin, and the historic French Legation in Austin. The DRT also publishes books and awards scholarships and prizes. It established a junior organization, the Children of the Republic of Texas, and inspired the founding of the Sons of the Republic of Texas in 1922.

DAUPHIN ISLAND. Situated off Mobile Bay in the Gulf of Mexico, this cigar-shaped island was used by Indians for smoking oysters. Named Massacre by Sieur d'IBERVILLE in 1699, it became "the cradle of French Louisiana" and meeting place of the Council of Commerce. Governor Antoine de la Mothe Cadillac built small stockades to defend against pirate raids such as the 1710 one, which spread such havoc. Split into Petit Bois, Pelican, and Dauphin Island during the 1717 hurricane, it saw much action in the Franco-Spanish War (1719–1722), when used as a base to capture Pensacola twice. In the American Revolution it was used as a fortified defense of Mobile after its capture by Spain in 1780. Ft. Gaines, built on Guillory Point (1821–1848), was captured by the Confederates in 1861 but taken by Admiral DAVID FARRAGUT in 1864. Ninety years later lots were developed for residences, and a bridge was completed to the mainland.

See P. J. Hamilton, *Colonial Mobile* (1898); R. G. McWilliams, *Dramatic Dauphin* (1954), popular, but useful chronology; M. Giraud, *French Louisiana* (1974), sound scholarship based on French archives; J. D. L. Holmes, *Alabama Historical Quarterly* (Spring–Summer, 1967), and *Frenchmen and French Ways* (1969), beginnings to 1722, based on archival and published data; T. F. Mulcrone, *Alabama Review* (Jan., 1967), Father Laval at Dauphin in 1720; and D. Rowland and A. G. Sanders, *Mississippi Provincial Archives* (1927–32), collection of French documents.

JACK D. L. HOLMES
University of Alabama, Birmingham

DAVIDSON, DONALD (1893–1968), was a native of middle Tennessee and lived most of his life in Nashville. After a brief period of service in World War I and one year on the faculty of Kentucky Wesleyan College, he joined the department of English at Vanderbilt, where he remained until his retirement in 1964. After 1930 most of his summers were spent as a member of the Bread Loaf School of English of Middlebury College. His literary career covered more than 40 years and brought him distinction as poet, literary and social critic, historian, teacher, and man of letters. A member of the FUGITIVE group of poets, he published five volumes of poetry: *An Outland Piper* (1924), *The Tall Men* (1927), *Lee in the Mountains and Other Poems* (1938), *The Long Street* (1961), and *Poems: 1922–1961* (1966). A leading spokesman for his section, he contributed to both of the Agrarian symposia: I'LL TAKE MY STAND (1930) and *Who Owns America?* (1936). His political, social, and literary views are ably presented in three volumes: *The Attack on Leviathan* (1938), *Still Rebels, Still Yankees and Other Essays* (1957), and *Southern Writers in the Modern World* (1958).

THOMAS DANIEL YOUNG
Vanderbilt University

DAVIDSON COLLEGE (Davidson, N.C. 28036). The first students of this Presbyterian college, founded in 1837, had to work at such chores as chopping wood and harvesting hay as a part of their curricular studies. This practice was soon discontinued, however, giving way to a more traditional program of liberal arts. The Civil War destroyed the college's endowment and left it with only 25 students. By 1890 the school had fully recovered. Traditionally a men's college, Davidson is now coeducational with an enrollment of approximately 1,000 students. In addition to papers, records, and correspondence related to the history of this institution, its library houses the papers of Peter Stuart Ney, reputedly one of Napoleon Bonaparte's marshals.

See W. L. Lingle, *Memories of Davidson* (1947); and C. R. Shaw, *Davidson College* (1923).

DAVIE, WILLIAM RICHARDSON (1756–1820), typified the class of men who vaulted into leadership during the American Revolution. An officer in the North Carolina Line, he fought in the guerrilla conflict in South Carolina in 1780 and then became commissary general for the Continental army in the South and for North Carolina as well. He was a prominent North Carolina legislator from 1784 to 1798, a delegate to the CONSTITUTIONAL CONVENTION, where he helped frame the key compromise on representation, a leader in the state's ratification struggle, governor in 1799, and minister plenipotentiary to France in 1800. A Federalist who despised political tumult, he lost a congressional election in 1803 to the vitriolic Republican, Willis Alston, and thereafter retired from public life and left the state. He was an exemplar and promoter of a new culture for the young republic. As principal founder and early trustee of the UNIVERSITY OF NORTH CAROLINA, he believed in training a natural aristocracy in the values of classical learning and republican virtue.

See B. P. Robinson, *William R. Davie* (1957); D. H. Fischer, *Revolution of American Conservatism* (1965); and C. Rossiter, *1787: Grand Convention* (1966).

ROBERT M. CALHOON
University of North Carolina, Greensboro

DAVIS, EDMUND JACKSON (1827–1883), governor of Texas, was born in St. Augustine, Fla., attended West Point, and was a Mexican War volunteer. In 1848 he moved to south Texas, where he served successively as postal clerk, deputy collector of customs, state district attorney, and district judge. He was defeated as a delegate to the secession convention and refused allegiance to the Confederacy. In May, 1862, he left Texas to organize the 1st Texas Cavalry (Union), and before the war ended he became a brigadier general. After the war he practiced law; was a Radical delegate to the constitutional convention of 1866; served as president of the Reconstruction convention (1868–1869), where he favored disfranchisement of Confederates and division of Texas; and in 1869 with Union League support was elected governor as a Radical Republican. He particularly supported law enforcement, public schools, immigration, and internal improvements. Failing reelection he remained in Austin as a lawyer and state leader of his party. He was defeated for the governorship in 1880 and for Congress in 1882.

See S. S. McKay, "E. J. Davis" (M.S. thesis, University of Texas, 1919); W. C. Nunn, *Texas Under Carpetbaggers* (1962); C. W. Ramsdell, *Reconstruction in Texas* (1910); and F. H. Smyrl, *Southwestern Historical Quarterly* (Oct., 1961).

JAMES ALEX BAGGETT
Union University, Jackson, Tenn.

DAVIS, GARRETT (1801–1872), was born in Mount Sterling, Ky. He began law practice in 1824 in Paris. A Henry Clay Whig, he was a state legislator (1833–1835) and served in the U.S. House of Representatives (1839–1847). In 1848 he declined to run for lieutenant governor on the ticket headed by JOHN J. CRITTENDEN, and in 1855 he declined the KNOW-NOTHING nomination for governor. The following year he was considered for the Know-Nothing nomination for the presidency. A dedicated Unionist, in 1861 he was elected to the U.S. Senate seat vacated by JOHN C. BRECKINRIDGE. He led the unsuccessful fight to expel his Kentucky colleague, Lazarus W. Powell, for disloyalty; however, by January, 1864, he had become so critical of Abraham Lincoln's war policy that he himself narrowly escaped expulsion. An effective debater, he thereafter vigorously opposed the Radical Republicans' Reconstruction measures. In 1867 a Democratic-Conservative coalition reelected him to the Senate; he died during his term.

See E. M. Coulter, *Civil War and Readjustment in Kentucky* (1926); L. and R. H. Collins, *History of Kentucky* (1874), II; and *Official Records, Armies*, Ser. 1, Vols. II, IV.

NORMAN D. BROWN
University of Texas, Austin

DAVIS, GEORGE (1820–1896), the last attorney general of the Confederacy, was for most of his life a lawyer in Wilmington, N.C. A leading Whig in his state and a Unionist through the 1850s, he supported secession after attending the 1861 WASHINGTON PEACE CONFERENCE. Elected to the Provisional Congress and to one term in the Confederate Senate, Davis supported most of the administration's measures. He was appointed attorney general in January, 1864, and served until the end of the Confederacy. He earned the respect of Jefferson Davis, performed his work well, and wrote legal opinions that were competent and conservative but not brilliant. Before and after the war he was chief counsel for railroad companies, most notably the Atlantic Coast Line.

See J. Sprunt, *Davis* (1919); S. A. Ashe, *Davis* (1916); R. W. Patrick, *Davis and Cabinet* (1944); W. M. Robinson, *Justice in Grey* (1941); R. W. Patrick, *Opinions of Confederate Attorneys General* (1950); and North Carolina State Department of Archives and History.

SHARON E. HANNUM
Ball State University

DAVIS, HENRY GASSAWAY (1823–1916), a developer of railroads and coal mining in West Virginia and Maryland, was also a politician active in state and national affairs for over 40 years after the Civil War. His service as a West Virginia legislator (1865–1871) and U.S. senator (1871–1883) was undistinguished, but Davis grew more influential in Democratic party affairs after he left office. One reason was his determined and successful opposition to the tariff reform movement of the Grover Cleveland era. Another was his friendship with many better-known politicians, including President Benjamin Harrison and Senators ARTHUR GORMAN of Maryland and STEPHEN B. ELKINS of West Virginia, the last two of whom were also Davis' relatives and business associates. It was through Gorman's influence that Davis was nominated for the vice-presidency by the Democrats in 1904, and Elkins' ascendancy in West Virginia assured Davis the role of elder statesman until he withdrew from public life at the age of ninety in 1913.

See J. A. Williams, *West Virginia and Captains of Industry* (1976); and C. M. Pepper, *Henry G. Davis* (1920).

JOHN ALEXANDER WILLIAMS
West Virginia University

DAVIS, HENRY WINTER (1817–1865), born in Annapolis, played a significant role in the coming and course of the Civil War as a congressman from Maryland (1855–1861, 1863–1865). His guiding principle was an intense hatred of the Democratic party. First as a Whig, then as a Know-Nothing, and finally as a Republican, he fought fiercely against Democrats and secessionists. Davis became one of Maryland's leading Republicans and part of the Radical bloc. He served on the U.S. House Committee of Thirty-three during the secession crisis and coauthored the Wade-Davis bill (1864). A contentious man, he inspired respect but seldom friendship. Pneumonia brought about his untimely death.

See G. S. Henig, *Davis* (1973), definitive, good bibliography; B. C. Steiner, *Davis* (1916), early chapters autobiographical; H. W. Davis, *Speeches and Addresses* (1867); R. W. Tyson, *Maryland Historical Magazine* (March, 1963); W. L. King, *Lincoln's Manager* (1960);

H. W. Davis Papers, Maryland Historical Society, Baltimore; and S. F. Du Pont Papers, Eleutherian Mills, Del.

WILLIAM J. EVITTS
Hollins College

DAVIS, JAMES HARVEY "CYCLONE" (1854–1940), was born in South Carolina, but his family moved to Texas in 1857. Self-educated, he taught school from 1873 to 1878. In 1878 he was elected county judge of Franklin County. Reelected, he declined to run again in 1882, the year he was admitted to the bar. Davis also served as editor and operator of three newspapers, and he wrote two books. He was an early leader of the Populist movement, and the intensity and fervor of his speeches won him the nickname Cyclone because of the "cyclones" of applause that his speeches received. At the national Populist convention in 1892 he helped in the drafting of the famous Omaha Platform. Davis also played a significant role in the founding of the POPULIST PARTY in Texas. He was the party's candidate for attorney general in 1892 and was easily defeated. In 1894 he ran unsuccessfully for Congress. At the 1896 Populist convention, Davis was a leader of the successful effort to nominate William Jennings Bryan. He campaigned in 27 states for the losing ticket (ELECTION OF 1896). In 1912, he rejoined the Democratic party, supporting Woodrow Wilson for president. In 1914, he was elected congressman-at-large primarily because of his support of PROHIBITION. Two years later he was defeated as interest in Prohibition declined. He ran again for congressman-at-large in 1932, losing in a runoff at the age of seventy-eight.

See M. L. Williams, "Political Career of Cyclone Davis" (M.A. thesis, East Texas University, 1937); J. H. Davis, *Political Revelation* (1894), and *Memoir* (1935); A. Barr, *Texas Politics* (1971); R. C. Cotner, *Hogg* (1959); and M. A. Martin, *People's Party in Texas* (1933).

BOB C. HOLCOMB
Angelo State University

DAVIS, JAMES HOUSTON (1902–). Twice elected governor of Louisiana (1944–1948, 1960–1964), Democrat Jimmie Davis gained early fame as a composer and singer of country and western songs, most notably "You Are My Sunshine." A native of Quitman in the north Louisiana hills, Davis was one of 11 sharecropper children. He attended Louisiana State University, taught school, and entered politics in 1938 as a fire and police commissioner in Shreveport. Like HUEY LONG before him, he first achieved statewide prominence as

public service commissioner for the (northern) third district. But Davis was associated with the conservative anti-Long faction, which preferred low taxes and minimal state services and public regulation. In 1944 he defeated Longite Lewis Morgan in a typical Long versus anti-Long contest, but by 1960 Louisiana was polarized less over economic than over racial, religious, and sectional issues; for the first time since 1924, the Long candidate failed to make the runoff primary, in which Davis defeated New Orleans' mayor, DELESSEPS MORRISON. His second administration witnessed widespread racial turmoil centering on school desegregation in New Orleans; although Governor Davis openly abetted the segregationist defiance in his legislature, his tendency toward indecisiveness, absenteeism, and a bland rhetoric of "peace and harmony" contrasted sharply with the vigorously defiant gubernatorial leadership in Arkansas, Mississippi, and Alabama. His two administrations symbolized Louisiana's transformation from the class conflict of the Long era to a politics dominated by race and the "social issue."

See A. P. Sindler, *Huey Long's Louisiana* (1956); R. L Crain, *School Desegregation* (1968); P. H. Howard, *Political Tendencies* (1971); W. C. Havard, *Changing Politics* (1972); and E. F. Haas, *DeLesseps Morrison* (1974).

HUGH DAVIS GRAHAM
University of Maryland, Baltimore County

DAVIS, JEFF (1862–1913), a three-term Arkansas governor and U.S. senator, was born and reared in the foothills of the Ozark Plateau near the Oklahoma state line. He attended the preparatory department of Arkansas Industrial University and the Vanderbilt University Law School before receiving a law degree from Cumberland University. Elected state attorney general in 1898, he became known for his somewhat Populistic attacks on the "trusts" and on business domination of Arkansas. During his 1900 campaign for governor, he charged that he was opposed by "five hundred and twenty-five insurance agents scattered all over the state, as well as every bank, every railroad, and two-thirds of the lawyers, and most of the politicians." These and similar statements by Davis appealed to the small farmers and mountaineers of the state. He was elected in 1900 and reelected in 1902 and 1904, the first Arkansas governor to win more than two terms. His intemperate attacks on his political enemies resulted in 1903 in a legislative investigation into his administration. When the investigating committee failed to recommend impeachment, Davis announced his intention to run for the U.S. Senate against a conservative in-

cumbent who had occupied the seat since 1885. Despite a bitter campaign, Davis won the Senate seat in 1906 and was reelected in 1912. In·the Senate he was out of his true element, and his fellow senators soon tired of hearing him say that "the only things Arkansas ever had on the free tariff list were possums, sweet potatoes and acorns." When he was governor and senator, his rhetoric proved more radical than his actions. His meteoric career left Arkansas largely unchanged, and the evils he inveighed against lived after him.

See J. G. Fletcher, *Arkansas* (1947); L. S. Dunaway, *Jeff Davis* (1913); Arkansas Writers Project, *Arkansas* (1941); G. B. Tindall, *Emergence of New South* (1967); and D. M. Robinson, *Journal of Southern History* (Aug., 1937).

DAVID E. RISON
Baptist College at Charleston

DAVIS, JEFFERSON FINIS (1808–1889), was born in Fairview, Christian (now Todd) County, Ky., but his family moved to Wilkinson County, Miss., early in his life. Educated locally at St. Thomas College, Ky., Jefferson College, Miss., and Transylvania University, he graduated from West Point in 1828. He served at frontier posts until his resignation from the army in 1835. That same year he married Sarah Knox Taylor, the daughter of Zachary Taylor, but three months later she died of malaria. For a decade Davis lived as a Mississippi planter. In 1845 he married Varina Banks Howell and emerged from relative seclusion at Brierfield, where he had read extensively. Elected to the U.S. House of Representatives in 1845, he left a year later to command a Mississippi regiment in the Mexican War and served ably in that conflict, particularly at Buena Vista. As sectional conflict approached, he firmly advocated his section's cause but did so without rancor or militancy.

His selection as president of the Confederacy surprised him, for he expected and desired military command. At the time of his inauguration (February 18, 1861), Davis seemed admirably qualified by experience, both civil and military, and by personality to provide effective leadership for the new nation. His policies often frustrated die-hard sectionalists, and his humorless manner helped create a host of enemies. His habits were marked by quiet zeal, moral strictness, and firm adherence to what he believed was lawful and ethical. His associates often found him tiresome and unyielding. By the midpoint in the war an increasing number of enemies blamed Davis for Confederate failures and accused him of moving toward despotism in such acts as a general conscription law, legislation that exempted some slave owners from military service, and use of the writ of habeas corpus.

Because of his experience in the army, Davis believed that he was a skilled tactician and strategist. This assumption led him to become in reality the Confederate secretary of war, and thus no one wanted to head that department for long. He was strongly opinionated in his evaluation of commanders, such as in his favorable judgments of BRAXTON BRAGG and negative evaluations of JOSEPH E. JOHNSTON. He often visited the army in the field and obviously enjoyed contact with these units. Although many observers questioned his choice as Confederate president, most scholars agree that no one else could have exceeded his record in that post. Although he was truly dedicated to states' rights, his loyalty was to the entire South, and he threw his full energy into the war effort. Thus he always championed southern nationalism without calling it such and thereby aroused the anger of ardent states' righters. Tall, straight, and formal, Davis failed to personify physically the southerner's ideal of effective leadership; he was perhaps most effective in his relationship with ROBERT E. LEE.

Outwardly he always seemed calm and emotionless, but he suffered quietly as defeat closed in around him. Publicly he seemed optimistic about victory almost until the end of the war. As late as February, 1865, he still refused peace terms unless southern independence was guaranteed. Early in April, he retreated with his cabinet from Richmond and rushed southward, still hoping to continue resistance until the last. Finally, federal cavalry captured him and his escort on May 10 in Irwinville, Ga.

Although arrested by Union officials who planned to try him in court, he was released without trial. Two years of imprisonment at Fortress Monroe gave him an opportunity to display quiet courage and to endear himself to friend and foe alike by his quiet determination. The experience of prison and defeat further impaired his health and shattered him economically. He spent more than two decades fighting for the LOST CAUSE with his voice and his pen, particularly in *The Rise and Fall of the Confederate Government* (1881) and *A Short History of the Confederate States of America* (1890). During these years he resumed work as a planter at Brierfield and also headed an insurance company, which soon failed. Because of his firm dedication to the South and the Confederacy, Davis was a focus for conservatives and all others who sought to justify sectionalism, states' rights, and the Confederacy. He spent a large portion of his later years at Beauvoir, his home on the Mississippi coast, but traveled extensively during this period, particularly to speak at Confederate reunions.

See H. Strode, *Jefferson Davis* (3 vols.; 1955–64), pro-Davis bias; R. McElroy, *Jefferson Davis* (1937), more balanced; A. Tate, *Jefferson Davis* (1929), best brief biography; Mrs. Davis, *Jefferson Davis: Memoir* (1890), highly informative; D. Rowland (ed.), *Jefferson Davis* (10 vols.; 1923), best collection of sources to date; and J. T. McIntosh (ed.), *Papers of Jefferson Davis* (1971–), when all volumes are published, will be most complete collection. Manuscripts are at Mississippi Department of Archives and History, University of Alabama, Library of Congress, National Archives, Duke University, Tulane University, and New York Public Library.

HASKELL MONROE
Texas A. & M. University

DAVIS, JOHN WILLIAM (1873–1955), was born in Clarksburg, W.Va., and was graduated from Washington and Lee. He moved from criminal to corporate law, representing West Virginia railroads and extractive industries. Entering politics reluctantly, he was elected to the West Virginia house (1899–1901) and the U.S. Congress (1910, 1912). He gave up his West Virginia residence permanently to serve ably as WOODROW WILSON's solicitor general (1913–1918). Although the Wilson administration condoned segregation, Davis argued successfully before the U.S. Supreme Court against two Oklahoma attempts to disfranchise blacks and against an Alabama PEONAGE system for black convicts. After an ambassadorship to Great Britain (1918–1921), he built a lucrative practice on Wall Street. A favorite son of West Virginia at the deadlocked Democratic convention, he came to national prominence as the unsuccessful Democratic candidate in the ELECTION OF 1924. His campaign was hampered by Democratic disunity, inept organization, his reserved manner, and an identification with big business, as well as by Calvin Coolidge's popularity. He practiced corporate law from New York and argued 103 cases before the Supreme Court (1913–1954), including an unsuccessful defense of South Carolina's segregated schools in 1952–1953 (BROWN V. BOARD OF EDUCATION). A Jeffersonian democrat, he joined with Al Smith to form the American Liberty League against the NEW DEAL. He never forsook his southern roots. He supported states' rights and the sanctity of private property and condemned the federal regulation of business and the growth and "paternalism" of the federal government. Davis modestly appraised himself: "I seem to have caught at the skirt of great events without really influencing them."

See J. W. Davis Papers, Yale; W. H. Harbaugh, *Lawyer's Lawyer* (1973), definitive and balanced; J. Davis, *Legacy of Love* (1961); J. W. Davis, "Oral Memoir," Columbia (1954); and M. T. Stewart, Jr., "J. W. Davis, Solicitor General" (Ph.D. dissertation, West Virginia University, 1973).

JOSEPH B. CHEPAITIS
University of New Haven

DAVIS, VARINA HOWELL (1826–1906), was born at Marengo plantation, La., to Margaret and William Howell, who later moved to Natchez. She became the second wife of JEFFERSON DAVIS (February 26, 1845), settling at Brierfield near Vicksburg. She bore six children. Well educated and a brilliant hostess, she aided Davis politically and while he was president of the Confederacy. Later sharing the hardships of his prison life and exile abroad on friends' charity, she had a nervous collapse in 1876. When Davis inherited Beauvoir near Biloxi, she recovered and helped with his book on the Confederacy. Upon his death in 1889, she published *Jefferson Davis: A Memoir by His Wife* (1890) and supported herself in New York writing for the *Sunday World* until she died at eighty. She was accorded military burial in Richmond beside her husband.

See E. Rowland, *Varina Howell* (2 vols.; 1931); I. Ross, *First Lady of South* (1958); M. Chesnut, *Diary from Dixie* (1949); H. Strode (ed.), *Jefferson Davis: Letters* (1966); and J. Davis, *Rise and Fall of Confederate Government* (2 vols.; 1881).

MARGARET NEWNAN WAGERS
Southern Methodist University

DAVIS, WESTMORELAND (1859–1942), grew up in Richmond and graduated from the Virginia Military Institute in 1877. He attended Columbia University Law School (1886) and practiced in New York City for 16 years. Davis returned to Virginia as a gentleman farmer in 1903, settling at Morven Park, a plantation near Leesburg. After several apprentice years in "scientific agriculture," he cofounded the Virginia Dairymen's Association (1907), became president of the Virginia State Farmers' Institute (1909), and purchased the prestigious *Southern Planter* (1912). A skillful lobbyist in behalf of farmers, he achieved legislative establishment of the Torrens system of land registration and a state-owned fertilizer plant, among other reforms. Davis won the governorship in 1917 as a result of a three-candidate Democratic primary in which he benefited from a bitter division over prohibition. His administration (1918–1922) is best remembered for its systematizing, businesslike spirit. Davis instituted the executive budget, centralized purchasing, and reformed

prison management. In the 1922 elections Davis challenged U.S. Senator CLAUDE A. SWANSON and lost ignominiously. For the next two decades he engaged sporadically in acrimonious skirmishes with the political organization of HARRY FLOOD BYRD, SR., which finally led him, in the mid-1930s, to propose abolition of the POLL TAX. He was the first significant white Democrat to do so.

See J. T. Kirby, *Westmoreland Davis* (1968); and Davis Papers, University of Virginia Library.

JACK TEMPLE KIRBY
Miami University

DAVIS, WILLIAM WATSON (1884–1960), was a member of W. A. DUNNING's school of Civil War and Reconstruction historians and a professor at the University of Kansas from 1912 until 1954. He was born in Pensacola, Fla., the son of a prosperous lumberman. He graduated from a military academy in Mobile, Ala., and earned bachelor's and master's degrees from Auburn University. In 1913 he won his doctorate at Columbia University. Davis wrote a pioneering monograph on antebellum commercial conventions in the South (1904); a chapter, "The Federal Enforcement Acts," in a book of studies dedicated to Professor Dunning (1914); and articles on the South's yellow pine lumber industry, the rebuilding of Galveston after the flood of 1900, and the commercial implications of Matthew Perry's expedition to Japan. By far his most important work, though, was *The Civil War and Reconstruction in Florida* (1913). This book has been superseded by Edwin E. Johns's work on Florida during the war (1963) and Jerrell H. Shofner's on Florida in the Reconstruction era (1974), but for 50 years and more, Davis' work was the best on its subject. Although it has a distinct southern white, conservative Democrat bias, still it is one of the less prejudiced and most complete of the Dunning school studies.

See F. M. Green, in W. W. Davis, *Civil War and Reconstruction in Florida* (1964).

GEORGE R. BENTLEY
University of Florida

DAWSON, FRANCIS WARRINGTON (1840–1889), was born in London and baptized as Austin John Reeks. He changed his name when he defied British neutrality laws to fight for the Confederacy in the Civil War. At the end of the war, Dawson remained in the South, eventually settling in South Carolina as a working journalist. In 1866 he and two partners bought the Charleston *News*. When, in 1873, B. R. Riordan and Dawson ac-

quired the *Courier*, they combined the two papers. Dawson, not yet thirty-three, became the first editor of the CHARLESTON NEWS AND COURIER. At a time when Reconstruction was about to be overthrown, Dawson opposed the South Carolina hotheads, advocating cooperation with Republicans. He urged acceptance of the Fourteenth Amendment to the Constitution and waged a vigorous campaign against the code duello, even though as a young man he had been involved in numerous "satisfactions" (DUELING). Dawson, the real founder of modern journalism in South Carolina, was one of the ablest journalists America has had.

See H. R. Sass, *150 Years of "News and Courier"* (1953); and Charleston *News and Courier* (Aug. 24, 1958).

S. FRANK LOGAN
Wofford College

DAYTONA BEACH, FLA. (pop. 45,327), is on the Atlantic Ocean, approximately 55 miles southeast of St. Augustine. The area was inhabited originally by Timucua Indians. Although British (later American) settlers had been coming to the Halifax River area since the middle of the eighteenth century, the first town was not laid out until 1870. Founded by Mathias Day of Mansfield, Ohio, Daytona was handicapped by limited transportation until the completion of a rail line in 1890. Developing as a winter resort, Daytona in 1903 also became the site of the well-known annual automobile speed trials. In 1926, Daytona united with two adjacent communities, Seabreeze and Port Orange, under the name Daytona Beach. Noted for its beautiful, white beach, it also is the home of BETHUNE-COOKMAN COLLEGE, and its varied industries produce lumber products, citrus fruit, prepared seafood, electronic supplies, tools and dies, chemicals, and construction materials.

See files of Daytona *Journal* (1904–) and *News* (1904–), both on microfilm.

DE BARDELEBEN, HENRY FAIRCHILD (1840–1910), was instrumental in developing Birmingham, Ala. The first to make competitive pig iron there and the first to build a local coal-hauling railroad, he attracted many investors to the region. De Bardeleben was orphaned at sixteen and became the influential Daniel Pratt's ward. He fought for the Confederacy, and in 1863 he married Pratt's daughter. After the war he managed Pratt's interests around Birmingham. On his own after 1873, De Bardeleben invested widely in coal, coking facilities, and iron furnaces in the area. He formed the De Bardeleben Coal & Iron Company capitalized at $13 million in 1887, which four years later he sold to the TENNESSEE COAL & IRON COMPANY. He lost his fortune in the 1890s attempting to gain control of the Tennessee company.

See S. F. H. Tarrant, *Daniel Pratt* (1894); E. Armes, *Story of Coal and Iron in Alabama* (1910); and G. W. Cruikshank, *History of Birmingham and Its Environs* (1920).

JAMES A. WARD
University of Tennessee, Chattanooga

DEBATABLE LAND, colonial Georgia (1670–1763), was delineated by Antonio de Arredondo in his *Historical Proof of Spain's Title to Georgia* (1742) and named by Herbert E. Bolton. It included the territory between Santa Elena (32° 30′ north latitude) and the entrance of the St. John's River. Spain claimed the northern frontier for Florida following the Treaty of Madrid (1670), and England claimed the southern limit stipulated by Governor JAMES OGLETHORPE of Georgia. Earlier, in 1565, French Huguenots settling the area were slaughtered when PEDRO MENÉNDEZ DE AVILÉS founded Spanish Florida. In 1665, British boundary claims extended south of St. Augustine (29° north latitude) based upon the Carolina Charter. England and Spain later struggled to dominate the "debatable land" in the seventeenth and eighteenth centuries. Following the FRENCH AND INDIAN WAR (1756–1763), Spain ceded Florida to Great Britain and released all rights to Georgia.

See J. T. Lanning, *Diplomatic History of Georgia* (1936); and H. E. Bolton, *Spain's Title to Georgia* (1925).

ROBERT L. GOLD
Southern Illinois University

DE BOW'S REVIEW was a monthly periodical first published in New Orleans during January, 1846. Under the editorship of its founder J. D. B. De Bow, the *Review* was issued in response to the Southern Commercial Convention of 1845 and was intended to direct its attention to the economy of the South and West. During the antebellum years the *Review* was suspended several times due to lack of funds. When De Bow became superintendent of the census the *Review* moved to Washington, D.C., in 1853, returning to New Orleans in 1859. During the prewar era, the *Review* concentrated on agriculture, commerce, industry, urbanization, economic reforms, territorial expansion, and internal improvements. The sectionalistic *Review* also became a showcase for proslavery and secessionist thought.

In 1861, De Bow moved to Richmond, where the *Review* ceased publication in 1862. Except for a single issue published in Columbia, S.C., in 1864, it did not again appear until after the war. In the very few wartime issues, the *Review* defended the Jefferson Davis government. In 1866 the periodical reappeared in Nashville and, after the death of De Bow in 1867, continued publication until 1868 under the direction of R. G. Barnwell. Edited by W. M. Burwell, a poorer-quality *Review* returned to New Orleans, where it was issued 1868–1870 and 1879–1880, when it was forever suspended.

During the postwar years, the new *Review* endorsed presidential Reconstruction and again embraced the idea of advancing the South through the development of agriculture, industry, and commerce. In an age when most magazines were literary and classical in format, the *Review* was a practical and influential departure.

See D. Francis, *Louisiana History* (Spring, 1973); F. Mott, *American Magazines* (1938); H. Nixon, *Sewanee Review* (Jan., 1931); R. Osterweis, *Romanticism and Nationalism* (1949); O. Skipper, *De Bow* (1958); and W. Weatherford, *De Bow* (1935). Complete files of *De Bow's Review* are available on microfilm.

DAVID W. FRANCIS
Chippewa Lake, Ohio

DEBTS OF SOUTHERN STATES. The nineteenth-century indebtedness of southern states arose initially from needs generated by the region's rapid agricultural growth from 1800 to 1840. The COTTON kingdom expanded its sway from the Carolinas to Arkansas during this period, while the lesser domains of TOBACCO and HEMP spread across the Upper South from Kentucky into Missouri. Louisiana's SUGAR INDUSTRY, protected by favorable tariffs, was on the rise as well. Such rapid growth placed inevitable strains on the region's financial and transportation facilities.

Westward expansion also evoked popular cries for turnpikes, CANALS, and (in later decades) RAILROADS to transport the growing volume of staple crops. Lacking private capital for these projects, southerners looked increasingly to political sources for funds. After the War of 1812 such prominent figures as HENRY CLAY of Kentucky and JOHN C. CALHOUN of South Carolina sought to tap the federal government's revenues to finance internal improvements, but the triumph of ANDREW JACKSON's laissez faire creed in the 1830s blocked this approach. Instead, state and local governments would have to underwrite most of the expenses of future economic growth.

North Carolina, Georgia, and Delaware avoided participation in this first round of deficit financing. The rest of the southern states abandoned customary restraints, however, and issued millions of dollars in bonds to aid private banking and transportation companies. Placing their public credit squarely behind these ventures, the states flooded the money markets of the North and Europe with securities during the 1830s. Virginia, Maryland, Kentucky, and South Carolina used their credit primarily to finance canals and other transportation facilities, and the newer states of the Southwest fostered the rise of numerous banking institutions. By 1838, at the peak of this credit boom, Louisiana led the region with a bonded indebtedness of $27 million, and Maryland and Alabama followed with approximately $11 million each. The debts of all the southern states in that year totaled roughly $87 million, a phenomenal increase over the small sums owed in the previous decade. It was the general belief that the banks and transportation projects would pay for themselves in a few years (as New York's Erie Canal had done). Many southerners actually expected the new enterprises to yield such large profits to the states that all direct taxes on the people could be repealed.

These hopes crumbled before the realities of economic collapse in 1837 (PANIC OF 1837). Declining bond sales forced the suspension of work on the internal improvements, and many of the government-financed banks went out of business as well. Anticipated profits failed to materialize, compelling the region to come to grips with the consequences of excessive borrowing. Shouldering their burdens, such states as Alabama and Tennessee increased taxes and kept up their debt payments. Louisiana and Maryland defaulted on interest obligations at the beginning of the 1840s, but the revival of prosperity (together with the imposition of various austerity measures) enabled them to resume payments later in the decade. In Arkansas, Florida, and Mississippi, on the other hand, since it was widely believed that the banks had wasted or mishandled the state bond issues, sentiment developed for punitive action. Exploiting this unrest, the three governments disavowed all responsibility for millions of dollars in bonds and suspended interest payments on additional millions. Repudiation had come to the South.

These events temporarily chilled the region's enthusiasm for public indebtedness. Investors were reluctant to risk additional funds on southern securities, and the states were hesitant to authorize new bond issues. The South's public debts began a prolonged decline, slipping from $87 million in 1838 to only $75 million in 1853. As the 1850s wore on, however, pressures mounted for a resumption of deficit spending. World demand for cotton skyrocketed during the decade. This growth prompted revived enthusiasm for state-financed transportation facilities, especially railroads. Investor confidence gradually recovered, and southerners moved to take advantage of it. A second debt boom soon rivaled the first. Missouri set the pace this time, boosting its public obligations from less than $1 million in 1853 to almost $26 million in 1860. Virginia's debt increased by over $20 million during the same period; Tennessee's, by $17 million; and North Carolina's, by almost $7 million. Reflecting this trend, total indebtedness of the southern states climbed to more than $133 million by the end of the antebellum period.

These expenditures sparked an upsurge in the South's railroad mileage, but at the same time the region's finance structure became more vulnerable to collapse than ever before. This was particularly true of the 11 states that attempted secession during the Civil War. They accounted for slightly more than $87 million of the South's public indebtedness in 1860. Most of them suspended interest payments during the war years, and these overdue obligations boosted their debts to more than $111 million by 1865. Wartime property losses compounded this burden by reducing taxable assets, and the damage inflicted on southern railroads made the situation even worse. Private capital was insufficient to repair the shattered rail network; consequently state bond issues proliferated throughout the Reconstruction years. ANDREW JOHNSON's provisional governments added almost $35 million to the debts of the conquered states between 1865 and 1868, and the Radical Republican regimes of subsequent years kept up the pace. Indeed, the Republicans not only continued the railroad repairs but expanded deficit spending for schools and other social services as well. Waste and fraud undermined investor confidence and drove security prices to record lows. South Carolina marketed bonds for as little as 15 cents on the dollar. Such sales only worsened the region's financial plight, and the debts skyrocketed. By the early 1870s public obligations of the former Confederate states crested at a total of almost a quarter of a billion dollars. Much of this sum was secured by mortgages against railroad property, but interest payments still imposed massive burdens on taxpayers. The South once again faced the threat of economic collapse.

These developments touched off repudiations in the 1870s and 1880s that dwarfed those of previous years. Republican regimes in Louisiana and the Carolinas initiated the debt-scaling process during the last phases of Reconstruction, but elsewhere the drive gained momentum only after retrenchment-oriented Democrats captured control. State after state refused to repay questionable or fraudulent bond issues. By the 1890s the states of the former Confederacy had disavowed responsibility for more than $140 million of their bonds and had slashed the interest rates on much of the remainder. Only Mississippi and Texas (where Reconstruction debts had been small) avoided involvement in this repudiation craze. The South's public credit had suffered yet another blow.

In spite of repudiation the debts continued to influence southern life for years to come. Bondholders brought numerous suits in the federal courts to obtain repayment for their securities, forcing the states into complex legal battles that wore on for decades. Such tactics finally badgered Virginia into compromising with its creditors in 1892, and North Carolina also made partial restitution for claims against it a few years later. Anxious to avoid a recurrence of these problems, moreover, southern state governments adopted an increasingly cautious approach toward fiscal affairs. They made a point of balancing their budgets in the post-Reconstruction years, and several of them amended their constitutions to prohibit future bond issues altogether. Chastened by experience, the New South became financially more conservative than the Old South had been.

See B. U. Ratchford, *American State Debts* (1941), most comprehensive account; W. A. Scott, *Repudiation of State Debts* (1893), excellent on legal aspects; R. C. McGrane, *Foreign Bondholders and State Debts* (1935); R. F. Durden, *Reconstruction Bonds and Politics* (1962); H. S. Hanna, *Financial History of Maryland* (1907); W. L. Coker, *Repudiation and Reaction in Mississippi* (1969); J. T. Moore, *Virginia Debt Controversy* (1974); and B. U. Ratchford, "North Carolina Debt" (Ph.D. dissertation, Duke University, 1932).

JAMES T. MOORE
Virginia Commonwealth University

DECATUR, STEPHEN (1779–1820), the younger, was born at Sinepuxent, Md. He was educated and reared in Philadelphia until 1798, when his father and he accepted appointments, as captain and midshipman respectively, in the newly created U.S. Navy. Advancement came rapidly. Following the daring destruction of the frigate *Philadelphia* (February 16, 1804) during the Tripolitan Wars, he became the navy's youngest captain and was widely acclaimed back home. At first he was assigned gunboat duty in the Norfolk area, but his command responsibilities between March, 1807,

and June, 1812, were enlarged to encompass the defense of the entire southern coast. During the War of 1812 the decisive victory of the *United States* over the *Macedonian* (October 25, 1812) furthered his reputation. The loss of the *President* to a blockading British squadron (January 15, 1815) was overshadowed by a highly successful naval-diplomatic assignment along the Barbary Coast later in 1815. The navy appointed him to the Board of Naval Commissioners at Washington, D.C., but his days as an attentive commissioner and member of Washington society ended March 22, 1820, at Bladensburg, Md., when he was mortally wounded in a duel with suspended commodore James Barron.

See A. S. Mackenzie, *Life of Decatur* (1846), best; *Analectic Magazine and Naval Chronicle* (Jan.–June, 1816); Subject File, 1765–1910, Record Group 45, National Archives; I. Anthony, *Decatur* (1931), good bibliography; and S. P. Waldo, *Life and Character of Stephen Decatur* (1822).

ERNEST H. POST, JR.
Juniata College

DECATUR, ALA. (pop. 38,044), is on a high plateau on the south bank of the Tennessee River some 75 miles north of Birmingham. Originally the site of a CHEROKEE INDIAN river crossing, the town was founded in 1820 and named for Commodore STEPHEN DECATUR at the express wish of President James Monroe. A center for the manufacture of rope and bagging from hemp, the town changed hands several times during the Civil War and was so completely ravaged that only three buildings survived the war intact. Formation of the TENNESSEE VALLEY AUTHORITY during the 1930s greatly stimulated the town's growth. Today, by rail and by river, it is a shipping point for area lumber and cotton and a manufacturer of tire cord fabrics, auto parts, cotton products, fertilizers, and chemicals.

See W. H. Jenkins and J. Knox, *Story of Decatur* (1970), good bibliography; J. Knox, *History of Morgan County* (1967); and T. G. Shelton, Decatur *Daily* (Feb. 26, 1962). Decatur *Daily* (1912–) is available on microfilm (1912–26).

DECLARATION OF INDEPENDENCE was adopted by the Second Continental Congress after North Carolina and Virginia had already authorized their delegates to work for independence. RICHARD HENRY LEE of Virginia offered a resolution for independence on June 7, 1776. Congress, on June 11, appointed a committee with only one southerner, THOMAS JEFFERSON; as chairman he drafted the document. Its ideas, derived chiefly from John Locke's philosophy, included the concepts of natural rights, human equality, consent of the governed, and the right of revolution, ideas so thoroughly accepted that Jefferson later defined them as merely the "common sense of the subject."

Reservations over the issue of slavery, voiced by South Carolina and Georgia, forced the withdrawal of this charge before the declaration was accepted. When slavery became a major political issue in 1820, southern attitudes toward the declaration began to change, and southerners shifted to a legalistic definition excluding blacks. After the NULLIFICATION crisis (1832) this sentiment intensified. Early in the national period the southerner was torn between his economic commitment to slavery and his support of the ideal of freedom as expressed in the Declaration of Independence. Consequently he accepted JOHN C. CALHOUN's view rejecting the doctrine of natural rights as expressed in the declaration, derived from Locke, and reverted to David Hume's more pessimistic view of man. This argument dominated southern thinking in 1860 as the southerner accepted the view of Rufus Choate of Massachusetts denouncing the declaration as merely "glittering generalities" without meaning.

By 1850 the South verged upon support of the right of revolution rather than natural rights, equality, or even consent of the governed, viewed on a national scale. The ultimate results were the ordinances of secession and the Civil War. After 1865 the Declaration of Independence played a decreasing role in southern thinking as the section accepted a doctrine of racism rejected, at least in theory, by the rest of the nation. This attitude was legalized by the 1890s, resulting in the establishment of a thoroughly segregated society. The denial of the declaration's emphasis on the equality of man and the acceptance of the concept of white supremacy endured throughout the first half of the twentieth century and was reversed reluctantly and slowly only after BROWN V. BOARD OF EDUCATION (1954).

See J. Boyd, *Papers of T. Jefferson* (1950–), and *Declaration of Independence* (1943, 1945); D. Malone, *Jefferson the Virginian* (1948); C. Becker, *Declaration of Independence* (1942); M. Peterson, *Jefferson Image in American Mind* (1960); C. Eaton, *Freedom of Thought in Old South* (1940); C. V. Woodward, *Strange Career of Jim Crow* (1957); and U. B. Phillips, *Course of South to Secession* (1939).

CARLOS R. ALLEN, JR.
Widener College

DEEP BOTTOM RUN, BATTLES OF (July 27–29, August 13–20, 1864). Both engagements occurred during the Petersburg, Va., campaign. In July, U. S. Grant launched a diversionary operation designed to draw P. G. T. BEAUREGARD's forces away from the point of the main Union thrust after the intended detonation of the enormous "Petersburg mine" (CRATER, BATTLE OF THE). W. S. Hancock's corps, plus two cavalry divisions and an artillery brigade, crossed to the north bank of the James River in the vicinity of Deep Bottom Run on July 27. Hancock was instructed to attempt a raid on the Virginia Central Railroad or a direct thrust at Richmond. Confederate resistance proved too strong: ROBERT E. LEE rushed five of his eight infantry divisions to counter, forcing Hancock back. Beauregard, however, was seriously weakened, and in this fact the first Deep Bottom operation was a noteworthy success. In August, after the Union failure at the battle of the crater, Grant planned a new Deep Bottom offensive. Believing Confederate forces on that flank to have been weakened by withdrawals to support JUBAL EARLY in the Shenandoah, Grant again launched Hancock from City Point. Departing on the thirteenth, Hancock soon found CHARLES W. FIELD's division in strong entrenchments at Deep Bottom, with CADMUS M. WILCOX within easy supporting distance. Once again, the Union initiative failed, and on the twentieth Hancock withdrew.

See S. Foote, *Civil War* (1974); A. A. Humphreys, *Virginia Campaign of 1864 and 1865* (1883); G. J. Fieberger, *Campaigns of American Civil War* (1914); and *Official Records, Armies*, Ser. 1, Vols. XL, XLII.

PHILIP J. GIOIA
U.S. Army

DEEP SOUTH is a relatively recent term used during the second third of the twentieth century for the area of the states of Mississippi and Louisiana, the southern portions of Georgia and Alabama, and northern Florida. This territory supposedly was the most typically or most extremely "southern" region within the South.

DE GRAFFENRIED, MARY CLARE (1849–1921), was born in Macon, Ga., a descendant of Baron Christopher de Graffenried, the Swiss founder of New Bern, N.C. She combined in her ideas and life-style the unconventional with the traditional. The daughter of a cultured family, Clare graduated from Wesleyan College at the age of sixteen. In 1875 she moved to Washington, D.C., where she taught literature, Latin, and mathematics at Georgetown Female Academy. In 1886 she became a copyist in the federal Patent Office and a few months later an investigator for the Bureau of Labor, a position from which she retired in 1906.

The fruits of her researches were published in 27 articles, mostly on social conditions. She won prizes awarded by the American Economic Association for essays on child labor and wage-earning women, published respectively in the association's *Publications* (1890) and in the March, 1893, issue of the *Forum*. Her most publicized work, "The Georgia Cracker in the Cotton Mills," in *Century* magazine (February, 1891), served to establish the national image of the southern POOR WHITE and aroused considerable controversy. Her writings blended emotion-evoking descriptions, typical of the nineties' protest literature, with statistical and factual information, characteristic of Progressive muckraking. Her publications and lectures to various organizations gave an impetus to social reforms: factory inspection codes, employer liability laws, housing regulations, compulsory education, and especially labor legislation affecting women and children.

See T. P. de Graffenried, *De Graffenried Family* (1925), *De Graffenried Name in Literature* (1950), and *De Graffenried Family Scrap Book* (1958); and L. C. Steelman, in J. F. Steelman *et al.* (eds.), *Studies in History of South* (1966).

LALA C. STEELMAN
East Carolina University

DELANY, MARTIN ROBINSON (1812–1885), known primarily for his pre–Civil War black nationalism, was born free in Charles Town, Va. (now W.Va.). He moved with his family to Pennsylvania, first to Chambersburg and then to Pittsburgh in 1831 for schooling. There he founded in 1843 a weekly, the *Mystery*, which called for abolition of slavery and tried to promote race pride among its black readers. After briefly serving as coeditor with FREDERICK DOUGLASS of the *North Star*, Delany attended Harvard Medical School for one semester (1850–1851), leaving after white students petitioned for his dismissal. Reacting to this experience and to passage of the FUGITIVE SLAVE LAW of 1850, Delany began advocating emigration of Afro-Americans and published an early black nationalist manifesto, *The Condition, Elevation, Emigration, and Destiny of the Colored People of the United States, Politically Considered* (1852). He campaigned widely for emigration and climaxed the decade with a visit to West Africa and publication of *The Official Report of the Niger Valley Exploring Party* (1861). His novel *Blake* was published posthumously in 1970.

When the Civil War erupted, Delany urged Abraham Lincoln to recruit black regiments to conduct guerrilla warfare in the South. Lincoln commissioned him a major, but the war ended before Delany could get into battle. During Reconstruction he served in South Carolina in the FREEDMEN'S BUREAU and became active in Republican politics; he narrowly missed election in 1874 on the Reform ticket as lieutenant governor. In 1876 he endorsed the Democrats, and Governor WADE HAMPTON named him a magistrate in Charleston. Delany's race pride and nationalism again surfaced in 1879, when he published *Principia of Ethnology* and cosponsored a group of immigrants to Liberia.

See V. Ullman, *Delany* (1971), no bibliography; F. J. Miller, *Search for Black Nationality, 1787–1863* (1975); H. H. Bell, *Negro Convention Movement, 1830–1861* (1970); and J. Williamson, *After Slavery* (1965).

EDWIN S. REDKEY
State University of New York, Purchase

DELAWARE, like other border states, has never been sure of its regional identity. The Wilmington-Brandywine area is similar politically, economically, and socially to southeastern Pennsylvania, though Kent and Sussex counties have characteristics similar to those of neighboring counties in Maryland. The division has been clearly visible at times of stress and tension as during the American Revolution and Civil War and has persisted down to the present. Industry first developed before the American Revolution along the Brandywine in the form of flour milling, and Wilmington developed as a center of manufacturing in the nineteenth century, while the lower part of the state remained agricultural and rural. Delaware's population was top-heavy, with the number of inhabitants in New Castle County far exceeding those of the lower counties combined, but political control in the legislature remained in the hands of Kent and Sussex counties until reapportionment took place in 1964. The struggle for domination between Wilmington and the rest of the state is comparable with that between urban Baltimore and rural Maryland. Only in recent years has this division lessened with improved transportation, communication, and the industrialization of the Dover area in Kent County. Today most inhabitants in lower Delaware, especially in Kent County, are inclined to visit Wilmington for special shopping or medical services, though some, especially in Sussex County, still prefer to travel to Baltimore via the Bay Bridge.

The present state of Delaware is 100 miles long

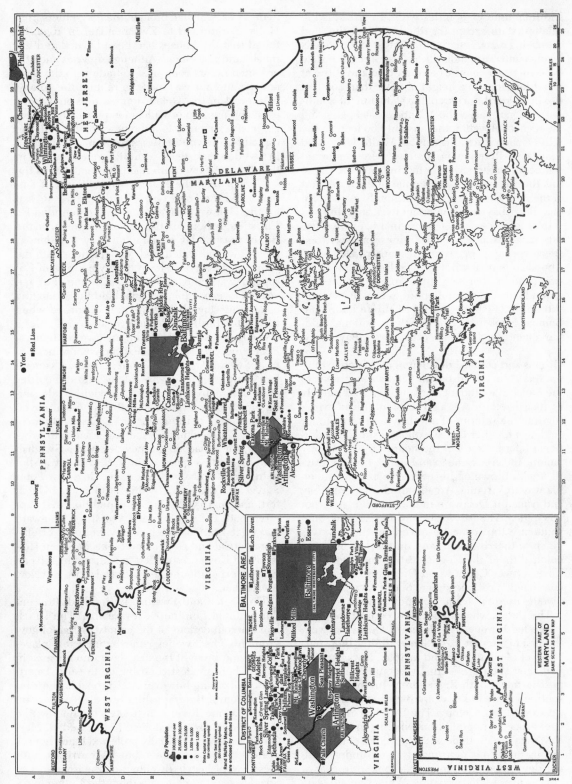

and from nine to 35 miles wide. In size it is the smallest state except for Rhode Island, the land area being 2,400 square miles. Most of the state is level country, a standard jest describing the state as having two counties at high tide and three at low. Elevations to a height of more than 400 feet rise in the northern part of the state, but the southern portion is part of the Atlantic coastal plain, and the highest elevation there is only 60 feet. In the hilly section such streams as White Clay, Red Clay, and Brandywine creeks were important sources of water power for milling; and the Christina River was used for shipping. In the lower part of the state Duck Creek, Mispillion River, and Indian River Bay were important local shipping and shipbuilding centers. The original hardwood forests have disappeared, but pines and softwood species occupy large tracts in southern Delaware. Abundant animal wildlife once frequented Delaware, and its shores continue to provide feeding grounds for large numbers of geese, ducks, and shorebirds. Fishing and shellfish are abundant. Bombay Hook and Prime Hook are national wildlife refuges on the shores of Delaware Bay.

Origins and colonial development. Dutch explorers like Henry Hudson, an English employee of the Dutch East India Company, reported as early as 1609 that there was a great "South River" winding into the interior of a fertile land suitable for settlement. Other Dutch explorers supplied additional information, but the honor of permanently naming the area came to an English captain, David Argall. Blown off his course in 1610 while on his way to Virginia, Argall sailed up a great bay and named it Delaware in honor of the governor of Virginia, Thomas West, Lord De La Warr. Subsequently the name bestowed on the bay was given to the river and land on the left bank. In colonial times the English called the region the Three Lower Counties on Delaware; the Dutch continued to call the stream South River; and the Swedes used the name New South River.

The Dutch, who had been the earliest and most interested European explorers of Delaware, were the first to attempt its settlement. After their purchase of Manhattan Island in 1621, it was natural that they should eventually establish a trading post in the "South River" area. In 1631, on the southern shore of Delaware Bay, they established ZWAANENDAEL Colony. The Dutch at Zwaanendael expected to profit from whaling in Delaware Bay, from the fur trade with the Indians, and from raising tobacco. Unfortunately, a misunderstanding developed after an Indian took a tin coat of arms to use as a tobacco pipe. When Captain David de Vries, who had brought the first settlers from Holland, returned to Zwaanendael in 1632, he found that the houses had been burned and the inhabitants massacred. Although de Vries and other Dutch sailors continued to trade with the Indians, no attempt was made to rebuild the colony.

Interest in the Delaware area persisted, however, and a group of Dutchmen persuaded Swedish businessmen to found a new colony. Half the capital for the venture was raised in Holland, half in Sweden; and Peter Minuit, formerly active in the affairs of New Amsterdam, was engaged as the leader. In 1638 the *Kalmar Nuckel* ("key of Kalmar") and the *Fogel Grip* ("bird griffen") set sail for the Delaware River. The settlers founded Ft. Christina, in honor of their Swedish queen, on the site of present-day Wilmington. New Sweden, as the colony was called, had good relations with the Indians, but it grew slowly, partly because of European wars and difficulties at home. For ten years, Governor Johan Printz held the struggling community together. Printz was disturbed when the Dutch built Ft. Casimir (near New Castle) a few miles downstream from his own settlement. Receiving no aid, guidance, or communication from Sweden, he sailed home. His successor Johan Rising plunged the colony into difficulties even before arriving at New Sweden. While sailing up the Delaware River, Rising was annoyed by the failure of the Dutch at Ft. Casimir to fire a proper salute. The garrison was unable to fire a salute, for it had no gunpowder, and a Swedish landing party captured the fort without a shot being fired. In New Amsterdam, Governor Peter Stuyvesant was upset by this attack upon a Dutch fort, and in 1655 he led an expedition that captured both Fts. Casimir and Christina. Delaware was once again a Dutch colony, but only briefly. Commercial and colonial problems between Holland and England soon led to war, and in 1664 an English expedition seized both Delaware and New Amsterdam.

The Dutch and Swedish period had little enduring impact on the Delaware area. The Dutch laid the foundations of the county system of government. The Swedes contributed a few placenames and brought the first slave into the area in 1639. Their greatest contribution to early American civilization, however, was probably their introduction of the log cabin. Swedish settlers on the Delaware River constructed log homes like those they were accustomed to in Sweden. Most European settlers initially preferred frame houses of heavy sawed timbers, but later arrivals built these Swedish-style dwellings on the frontier. The Swedes also brought with them the Lutheran religion, and one of their churches, Old Swedes, built in 1698, is still in use in Wilmington.

English conquest made little difference to the Dutch and Swedish settlers. Although they took an oath of allegiance to the king of England, they were permitted to retain their lands and continued farming. The duke of York's laws established the English judicial system. Two counties, New Castle in the north and Whorekill in the south, were established. In 1680 a middle county called St. Jones was created out of the northern part of Whorekill County.

King Charles II granted Pennsylvania to William Penn in 1681. Concerned that access to his new possession might be cut off if hostile persons occupied both sides of the Delaware River, Penn persuaded the duke of York in 1682 to grant him the land along the Delaware River south of Pennsylvania. Penn landed at New Castle on October 27, 1682, and the colonists present paid him an oath of allegiance. A short time later he changed the name of St. Jones County to Kent County and Whorekill County to Sussex County. For more than 20 years Pennsylvania and the Three Lower Counties on Delaware participated in the same legislature. Fear by the Lower Counties that they might be completely swallowed up by their larger neighbor led to the creation of a separate assembly for the Lower Counties in 1704. Not until 1776 did this arrangement terminate.

Although little progress was made in government, economic activity, or population growth under the duke of York, great changes occurred under Penn. His liberal policies of religious freedom and cheap land attracted many immigrants. He introduced representative government and continued the county system of government instituted by the Dutch. With his Maryland neighbors he disputed vigorously the boundaries of the Lower Counties. Not until Charles Mason and Jeremiah Dixon came from England in the 1760s to survey the boundaries was the matter settled.

Most of the inhabitants continued to be farmers raising corn, wheat, cattle, hogs, and poultry. Tobacco was a popular crop until about 1750, but probably competition from other southern colonies led to the discontinuance of its cultivation. Land was easy to come by, and in the natural course of events residents anticipated that they would acquire sufficient land to earn a living. In each county from inheritance, milling, commerce, farming, or political preferment, a few people acquired sufficient income to build large brick homes, to patronize Philadelphia merchants, and, in some instances, to send their children out of the colony for an education. In contrast tenants,

former indentured servants, and free blacks without means to buy land sometimes found conditions quite unpleasant.

The Lower Counties, like other Middle Atlantic colonies, were considered to be one of the bread colonies, raising meat, grain, and lumber for export to the West Indies. In return they received sugar, molasses, hardware, rum, silver coins, and slaves. Shipbuilding was important along the Christina and other streams. New Castle was the county seat of New Castle County, but Wilmington, the headquarters of the customs office and the largest town at the beginning of the eighteenth century, surpassed it in economic importance because of flour milling and trade. Christina Bridge, at the head of the stream of that name, and Newport were important towns for the shipment of grain and flour. In lower Delaware only the two county seats, Dover and Lewes, were of much significance.

By the time of the American Revolution most of the inhabitants were English, though there were many Scotch-Irish in New Castle County and a few in Kent and Sussex counties. The three Lower Counties on Delaware were less attractive than southeastern Pennsylvania to Germans, who preferred to be with their kinfolk and friends. The few Dutch and Swedes in Delaware were thus submerged in the waves of English settlers. The total population was estimated to be 37,000, including 2,000 blacks.

Religiously most of the people in the Lower Counties were Anglicans, though the Presbyterian church was strong among the Scotch-Irish in New Castle County. Quakers were strongest in New Castle County and more influential than their scanty numbers indicated. They also had a few meetinghouses in Kent and Sussex counties. The Lutherans had only one church in New Castle County (Old Swedes), and the Catholics established a church at Coffee Run near Wilmington in 1772.

The black inhabitants were almost equally divided among the three counties, and most of them were slaves. Treatment varied according to the master. Usually slaves worked in fields or in domestic services, and wealthy persons might own ten, 15, or 20 slaves of varied ages. As early as 1762 JOHN DICKINSON was concerned that his slaves trained as tanners, carpenters, and tillers of the soil and put up for hire would be kindly treated by their new employers. Efforts to stop the importation of slaves from Africa were not successful prior to the Revolution, but this prohibition was inserted in the state constitution of 1776.

Although William Penn encouraged the establishment of schools, implementation was left in the hands of parents. Subscription schools were common, and clergymen frequently supplemented their earnings by teaching school. The most important secondary school in the colony was Newark Academy, originally founded by a Presbyterian clergyman at New London, Pa., and later moved to New Castle County. Wilmington Academy was also founded prior to the American Revolution. A few Delawareans received part of their education outside the colony. Dr. Charles G. Ridgely (1738–1785) and Dr. James Tilton (1745–1822) of Dover, for example, studied medicine in Philadelphia, and Thomas McKean (1734–1817) and John Dickinson were students in the law courts of London. Dickinson, author of *Letters from a Farmer in Pennsylvania* (1767–1768), presenting American arguments about taxation, was Delaware's best-known literary figure.

Revolutionary ferment, 1775–1815. Delaware cooperated with the other colonies in resistance to British taxation in the decade before the Revolution. Thomas McKean and CAESAR RODNEY represented the colony at the Stamp Act Congress in New York in 1765 and later reported back to the general assembly. The Stamp Act was repealed before the assembly framed its own protest, but these resolutions were sent off to England anyway. The general assembly also protested against the Townshend Act. In a public meeting the residents of New Castle County upheld the Philadelphia agreement against importation of British merchandise in 1769. A committee of inspection was set up in each town in the county to prevent the sale of embargoed goods. In 1774 public meetings in each county passed resolutions against the closing of the port of Boston, and money was collected for the relief of the poor of Boston.

After Congress recommended the formation of new governments, if necessary, the Delaware assembly on June 15, 1776, adopted a resolution in favor of separating from Pennsylvania and Great Britain and calling a constitutional convention. This is the real birthday of the state of Delaware. As a result, a constitutional convention of ten delegates from each county was chosen in the summer and framed a constitution consisting of a bicameral legislature and a president for a three-year term with an advisory privy council of four members. It was approved by the members of the convention on September 20 and went into effect on that day without ratification by the people. Also on June 15, by omitting instructions to its delegates to the Continental Congress, the assem-

bly prepared the way for these three men to approve the Declaration of Independence. One, Thomas McKean, favored independence; the second, GEORGE READ, desired further efforts at reconciliation; the third, Caesar Rodney, made his famous ride from Dover July 1 and 2 in time to break the tie and vote for independence.

During the Revolution New Castle County was the most patriotic county, partly due to its proximity to Philadelphia, its commerce, and its numerous Presbyterian churches. Kent and Sussex counties were more divided. Because of its isolation, strength of the Anglican church, and ties with its neighbors in Maryland counties, Sussex County contained the largest number of LOYALISTS. Kent County contained some Loyalists. Elections in Sussex County were usually riotous and sometimes were not even held. Tory insurrections or disturbances took place in Sussex County in 1776, 1778, and 1781, but no lives were lost. Local grievances—such as destruction of a petition against the change in government, confiscation of weapons, high taxes, and laws discriminating against the poor—were at the bottom of these affairs. In Kent County the most serious disturbance took place in 1778, when Cheney Clow built a fort near the Maryland line and talked of marching with his comrades against the legislature meeting in Dover. Clow and his men fled when Kent County militiamen attacked. Later Clow became a British officer. On a visit home he was captured, accused of shooting to death one of the sheriff's posse sent to bring him in, and finally hanged in 1786. He was the only Tory put to death by Delaware authorities.

The British occupation of New Castle County in the fall of 1777 was brief, but many farmers took advantage of the opportunity to exchange cattle and provisions for British gold or necessities. Delaware's state president, Dr. John McKinly, was taken prisoner to Philadelphia, and many Delaware records were removed, never to be returned. Yet Delaware did not fare badly during the war. The British occupation did not last long and did only minor damage. Delaware farmers could sell all the food they could raise. The paper money situation was not as bad in Delaware as in some states because the state severely limited its own issue of currency. The scarcity of some commodities such as salt and the steady depreciation of Continental currency were more serious problems. The general assembly was often dilatory in dealing with problems and in supplying the needs of soldiers. Following McKinly's capture, for short periods Thomas McKean and George Read were presidents of the state. Caesar Rodney followed in 1778, but his successor John Dickinson was a more forceful executive. The capital was moved permanently to Dover in 1777.

Delaware welcomed the termination of the war, but merchants were concerned at the lack of commercial prosperity. The state sent delegates to the ANNAPOLIS CONVENTION in 1786 and to the CONSTITUTIONAL CONVENTION in Philadelphia in 1787. President Thomas Collins called a special convention of 30 delegates to meet in Dover to consider the work of the latter body on December 3, 1787. Four days later the Constitution was unanimously ratified, Delaware becoming the first state to ratify the new government.

Conservatives were in power in Delaware at the end of the war, and they continued in office to the disgust of radicals, who thought of the officeholders as Tory sympathizers. Such politicians as James A. Bayard (BAYARD FAMILY), Richard Bassett (1745–1815), and George Read became leaders of the Federalist party, and Allen McLane, a revolutionary hero and collector of the port of Wilmington, and Caesar A. Rodney, nephew of the signer of the Declaration of Independence, led the Democratic-Republican party. When the Federalists died out in the rest of the country by 1820, they were still active in Delaware.

Economically in this period Wilmington flourished as a commercial center and began its rise in manufacturing. The water power of the Brandywine, its location on the Christina for shipping, and the proximity to large cities contributed to its progress. In 1790 Wilmington was the center of flour milling in the United States. The inventions of Oliver Evans (1755–1819), a local mechanic, mechanized the industry. The Brandywine also furnished power for a variety of factories such as textile mills, paper mills, and tanneries, but most of these enterprises were short-lived. An exception was the paper mill of Thomas and Joshua Gilpin, started in 1787, which lasted half a century. E. I. Du Pont de Nemours came to America in 1800 and began to produce gunpowder on the Brandywine in 1804 (DU PONT FAMILY). In contrast, Kent and Sussex counties possessed only gristmills, sawmills, and tanneries, depending in part on household manufactures. The War of 1812 had little impact on Delaware. Commodore John P. Beresford, commanding a British squadron off the Delaware Capes, bombarded Lewes on one occasion, but the cannon shells did little damage, and only a number of small boats were seized or burned. E. I. Du Pont feared that a British invasion from Delaware Bay or Chesapeake Bay might destroy his powder mills, but the fear was unfounded.

Religiously the most unusual feature of the period was the growth of the Methodist church. During the Revolution Methodists were often regarded as Tories. At Barratt's Chapel in Kent County, sometimes called the Cradle of Methodism, Bishops Thomas Coke and Francis Asbury discussed the organization of a separate American church in 1784, and this was accomplished at Baltimore. Methodist doctrines and the lively services of the Methodists appealed to the people of Delaware, especially those in Kent and Sussex counties. The first CAMP MEETING in the state was held near Smyrna in 1805. The Anglicans who had organized as a separate American church lost ground, and the Presbyterians did no better. At the time of the Revolution only one Baptist clergyman had been active, but early in the new century that denomination established several churches.

Education continued along the lines established in colonial days. Parents taught children their ABC's at home or sent them to neighborhood subscription schools. The most important secondary schools were in Newark and Wilmington. The first Delaware newspaper, the *Delaware Gazette*, began to be published in Wilmington in 1785.

Slavery reached its high point numerically in the state in 1790, when the census reported 8,887 slaves and 3,899 free blacks. About the time of the Revolution a manumission movement became popular in the state, initiated by the members of the Society of Friends. Warner Mifflin (1745–1798) of Kent County led off in 1775 by freeing 16 slaves. John Dickinson freed 22 slaves in 1777, and others followed. During the period 1775–1792, 600 slaves were freed. Petitions urging the legislature to abolish slavery were frequently submitted. The Quakers founded the African School in Wilmington in 1798 and formed an abolition society in 1801. Humanitarian feeling, Quaker leadership, diversified agriculture, and the wearing out of the soil in southern Delaware contributed to the growth of the movement. Colonization as a scheme was popular in Wilmington, and the legislature in 1827 endorsed such a project, but Wilmington blacks in a meeting in 1831 opposed this solution.

Tug-of-war between North and South, 1815–1865. After the War of 1812 Delaware was undecided as to whether it had more in common with the North or the South. The Wilmington-Brandywine area became increasingly industrialized, found a labor force in Irish and German immigrants, and became the first part of the state to have steamboats and a railroad. Wilmington took on the appearance more and more of an industrial city, noted for the machine shops of Pusey & Jones and of Harlan & Hollingsworth, the cotton goods of Joseph Bancroft & Sons, and the gunpowder produced by the Du Pont company. On the eve of the Civil War, Wilmington boasted that it was the center of carriage manufacturing in the nation, specialized in the production of morocco and patent leather, and built more iron ships than any city in the land. During the Civil War Du Pont became the chief supplier of gunpowder to northern armies.

Southern New Castle County was transformed economically by the construction of the Chesapeake & Delaware Canal in 1829. New Castle County farmers were the most progressive in the state, forming agricultural societies and experimenting with the use of machinery and fertilizers. Peaches were a profitable crop.

Kent and Sussex counties changed more slowly, but transportation improved by the use of steamboats, and the Delaware Railroad was completed to the Maryland line at the southern extremity of the state before the Civil War. Farmers raised corn and wheat by time-honored methods with black labor. The land became worn out, and many inhabitants immigrated to the cities and west. In the 1850s farmers turned to fertilizers and machinery. Peaches became a bonanza crop after the Civil War.

The most important economic factor in the nineteenth century to affect the entire state was the construction of railroads. In 1831 a line was built from New Castle on the Delaware River to Frenchtown on the Chesapeake, which shortened the time for passengers and freight to travel from Philadelphia to Baltimore. In 1837 the Philadelphia, Wilmington & Baltimore Railroad was constructed across northern Delaware. In 1855 began the laying of tracks to the southern border. A score of towns sprang up along the tracks of the Delaware Railroad. Branch lines were built to Chesapeake and Delaware bays, and the main line eventually reached Cape Charles.

Educationally the state was transformed by the passage in 1829 of the first important public school act. As a result public schools appeared in many, but not all, parts of the state. Delaware College was founded in 1833.

Slavery became increasingly an issue in public life in one form or another. Following Nat Turner's insurrection in 1831 and a "play-acted" insurrection by some young men wearing black masks on the southern banks of the Nanticoke River across from Seaford, the assembly in 1832 passed several acts regulating the activities of blacks more carefully. Delaware was an unusual state in that it did not permit either the importation or exportation of slaves except by action of courts or of the legislature in unusual instances. Slave owners were not permitted to take their slaves west or to sell slaves in the South. Of course these regulations were sometimes violated by owners wishing to make money or by kidnapers such as the notorious Patty Cannon (?–1829). On the other hand abolitionists—such as Thomas Garrett, who boasted that by the time of the Civil War he had helped 2,700 slaves escape; HARRIET TUBMAN, a black abolitionist who frequently visited the Eastern Shore of Maryland to aid her countrymen; and John Hunn, another Quaker who was said to be a superintendent of the Underground Railroad—risked life and fortune and worked hard to aid these unfortunates. By 1847 slavery had such a slight hold that an abolitionist proposal was defeated in the legislature by only one vote. By 1860 the number of slaves in the state had decreased to 1,798, and the number of free blacks had risen to 19,829.

Following the disintegration of the Federalist party, most Delawareans preferred the Whig party to the Democratic party, partly because the leader and organizer of the Whigs was John M. Clayton (1796–1856), one of the most popular men in the state. He became a senator and also served as secretary of state under Zachary Taylor. LOUIS MCLANE, the Democratic leader, became secretary of the treasury and minister to England. With the breakup of the Whig party in the early fifties, political life became more complicated. The KNOW-NOTHING PARTY was successful in electing a governor in 1854, and a local party called the People's party appeared. The Republican party had few followers at first. The Democratic party benefited from this fragmentation. The Bayard family was the organizer of the Republicans in New Castle County, and the Saulsbury brothers controlled affairs in Kent and Sussex counties.

As a conservative state, Delaware cast its electoral vote for John C. Breckinridge in 1860. He received more votes than the combined total of all other candidates. When the Civil War began, Delaware was divided. The legislature unanimously rejected a bid from Mississippi in January, 1861, to join the Confederacy. In any case secession was an impossible alternative for Delawareans unless Maryland took the first step. In each town those favoring peace and those wishing to preserve the Union by any means held separate meetings. These gatherings culminated in county meetings and finally in state meetings. Separate militia companies were formed in each community. Delawareans hoped for a peaceful resolution of the crisis through the WASHINGTON PEACE CONFERENCE or the CRITTENDEN COMPROMISE. Instead, with sad hearts, they heard the news of Ft. Sumter.

During the critical winter of 1860–1861, business was poor in Wilmington. A number of textile and leather firms closed, and the slump continued during the summer of 1861. By fall, however, Wilmington manufacturers received orders for ambulances, leather goods, machinery, ships, railroad cars, and gunpowder. Throughout the war Wilmington remained a busy place. In 1864 Henry Du Pont (1812–1889) reported an income of $250,000, and 50 inhabitants, mostly manufacturers, enjoyed incomes of over $10,000. In contrast, in Kent County only five gentlemen reported incomes of over $10,000, and only one man possessed an income of $5,000 in Sussex County.

Of Delawareans who served in the armed forces, the great majority served the Union, but some, perhaps as many as 200 or 300, took the underground railroad in reverse to the Confederacy. A favorite route was by way of the Nanticoke River to the Chesapeake and then via boat on a dark night to Virginia. The Union hero was Admiral S. F. Du Pont, commander of the siege of Charleston.

In 1861 President Abraham Lincoln asked Congressman George P. Fisher (1817–1899) to investigate the possibility of compensated emancipation in the state, but Fisher found that such a proposal could not pass in the legislature. Consequently it was not introduced, but when the Democrats found out about the attempt, they condemned it vigorously in resolutions. Not until ratification of the Thirteenth Amendment in December, 1865, were Delaware and the nation to be free of slavery.

Democrats during the war protested vigorously, but to no avail, against what they considered the misuse of federal power. In 1861 and 1862 federal troops invaded the state and disarmed suspected disloyal militia companies. Beginning in 1862 every election witnessed the use of federal troops at polling places in an effort to bar and discourage Democrats. In spite of this the Democrats usually won control of the state legislature and elected most other officers. The three exceptions are explained by unusual factors: Congressman Fisher was a joint candidate of the People's party and Republicans and received much support from Constitutional Unionists; William Cannon (1809–1865) was a disgruntled Democrat seeking election as governor on the Union ticket; and Congressman

Nathaniel B. Smithers won a short term following a death because the Democrats boycotted the election.

Delaware encounters change, 1865–1945. Despite enactment of the Thirteenth, Fourteenth, and Fifteenth amendments, Delaware's Democratic party continued its prewar dominance of state politics. With the exception of 1872, when they were indifferent toward Horace Greeley, the Democrats won almost every election for some 25 years. Like their counterparts in the Deep South, they campaigned regularly against the potential threat of black political and social dominance. In 1873 they limited the size of the black vote by an assessment act, which required the payment of a poll tax and voter registration many months prior to an election. Fearful of a federal civil rights act, the Democratic legislature passed an act in 1875 that made it possible for the proprietor of a restaurant, hotel, or theater to exclude persons "offensive" to the majority of his patrons. This act remained on the statute books until 1963.

Although Delaware never underwent a Radical Republican Reconstruction and, therefore, owed no Reconstruction debt, retrenchment and low taxes typified Democratic management of the postwar state. Welfare and penal institutions were made the responsibility of the county governments. State appropriations for improvements and for education were minimal, and in 1880 the entire cost of state government in Delaware was less than $200,000. Either James A. Bayard (1799–1880) or his son Thomas F. Bayard (1828–1898) usually occupied one of Delaware's two U.S. Senate seats, the other seat being occupied by one of the Saulsbury brothers from Kent County.

The status of blacks did not improve rapidly during this postwar era. The Assessment Act of 1873 made it difficult for blacks to vote, and JIM CROW laws prevented equal treatment in restaurants, hotels, and theaters. Although some blacks worked in a variety of occupations, especially in Wilmington, most blacks were employed as laborers or as domestic servants. The FREEDMEN'S BUREAU operated briefly in Delaware, mostly assisting in the establishment of schools. It cooperated with the Delaware Association for the Moral Improvement and Education of Colored People, formed for this purpose by a group of Wilmington businessmen. For the most part, the white inhabitants of Kent and Sussex counties were willing to have blacks educated, but in a few instances schoolhouses or churches were burned and several teachers were driven out. One black man near Leipsic in Kent County was lynched in 1867 on suspicion of arson. Another black man accused of a rape-murder was lynched in Wilmington in 1903. Beginning in 1875, blacks were separately taxed for the support of segregated black schools. Delaware State College (NEGRO LAND-GRANT COLLEGES), opened in 1891, provided facilities for secondary education; but until 1952 it and Howard High School in Wilmington were the sole opportunities Delaware blacks had for a secondary education.

Economically, the Wilmington-Brandywine area continued to prosper and to develop its industry. Flour milling ceased to be of great importance, but the Du Pont company became active in the powder trust and by far the most important producer of gunpowder in the nation. Lower Delaware remained agricultural. Corn and wheat continued to be the principal crops, but the production of fruit and vegetables gradually gained in popularity. Indeed, peaches became something of a bonanza crop, and in 1895 the peach blossom became the state flower.

As the nineteenth century came to a close, so also did the era of Democratic political dominance. John Edward Addicks (1841–1919), an outsider from Pennsylvania, came to Delaware in 1889. By 1895 Addicks had formed a vigorous third party, the Union Republican party, and had created a legislative deadlock in the assembly. He was a stock promoter with no real Delaware ties except for his ambition to sit in the U.S. Senate. In 1899 and again in 1901, he was able to prevent the election of a new senator by the legislature, and from 1901 to 1903 Delaware was without representation in the upper house of Congress. In 1903 the deadlock was finally broken with a compromise. One of Addicks' lieutenants was elected to one Senate seat, and the candidate of the regular Republican organization was elected to the other. Addicks' ambition went unfulfilled, but he had jolted the state out of its Democratic complacency, and other Republicans took over and successfully led the machine that he had created. The state remained politically Republican until the Great Depression. The Republicans did eliminate the notorious Assessment Act of 1873 in the new constitution of 1897, but Kent and Sussex counties continued to dominate the assembly, and Republican administration of state affairs proved to be quite as conservative as earlier Democratic administrations had been.

The new century brought with it further expansion of industry in the Wilmington-Brandywine area. In 1902 the Du Pont company was almost sold to outside interests, but three cousins—T. Coleman Du Pont (1863–1930), Alfred I. Du Pont

(1864–1935), and Pierre S. Du Pont (1870–1954)—reorganized the firm and changed its emphasis from gunpowder to chemicals. The company grew like a mushroom during World War I, using some of its profits to purchase an interest in General Motors Company. In the agriculturally oriented lower counties, poultry joined fruits and vegetables as a cash crop during the 1920s. The broiler industry has been the mainstay of Sussex County farmers ever since. The construction of the Du Pont Highway in 1924 also aided farmers and the growing tourist industry as well.

Delaware did not feel the impact of the Great Depression as much as did some areas of the country, partly because so many of its people were still engaged in agriculture. Few banks failed. Alfred I. Du Pont provided pensions for the elderly for two years until the state assumed responsibility for the program, and federal work relief programs aided many people during these hard times. During World War II, both farmers and businessmen profited from the demand for their products. The state's citizens supported bond drives and food conservation measures; and the Du Pont company produced its newly developed fabric rayon in addition to other chemically based products. The establishment of Dover Air Force Base at Dover in 1940 became not only a wartime operation but a continuing factor for change in Kent County to the present.

The challenge of the present and future. Since World War II the state has been transformed in many ways. The Wilmington-Brandywine area is dominated economically by E. I. Du Pont de Nemours & Company and its offspring Atlas and Hercules. Other large employers are the Delmarva Power & Light Company, Diamond State Telephone Company, General Motors, and the Electric Hose & Rubber Company. Wilmington is a major banking center. Although New Castle County has become one of the fastest growing areas in the country in population, the city of Wilmington has declined in size since 1940, and today almost half its population is black. Other large industries, such as Tidewater Oil at Delaware City and the assembly plant of Chrysler at Newark, are important to the economy. More striking changes have occurred in lower Delaware. On the eve of World War II the Du Pont company built a nylon plant in Seaford, and International Latex and the Dover Air Force Base came to Dover. More recently other industries have been attracted to Dover, such as General Foods, and the city grew 140 percent from 1960 to 1970, today having a population of 17,000. The most popular crop in southern Delaware is soybeans, with corn a close second. The broiler industry thrives in Sussex County. Thus far the state has resisted the temptation to permit industrialization of its marsh areas or to permit offshore oil drilling.

Two major changes came with the U.S. Supreme Court decisions about desegregation in 1954 and reapportionment in 1964. Desegregation had already begun at the University of Delaware and in two local schools in 1950. In spite of some resistance in the lower part of the state, desegregation is now well accepted. Since the beginning of representative government in Delaware in 1704, New Castle County had never received the representation to which its population entitled it. Kent and Sussex counties continued to dominate the assembly, even though New Castle County was given slightly increased representation in the constitution of 1897. A major change resulted from the Supreme Court decision of 1964. Today the assembly consists of a senate of 18 members elected for four-year terms and a house of representatives of 35 members chosen for two-year terms.

Politically Delaware has voted Democratic more often than Republican since 1945, though frequently the results are mixed, with the U.S. senators from different parties, the houses of the assembly of different parties, and sometimes even the governor and lieutenant governor of different parties. In 1974 the Democrats were more successful than they had been in many years, though it remains to be seen whether these results will last.

The legislature faces serious problems, mainly the modernization of the structure of government. More funds are needed for increased services in a welfare state, improvements in roads, and education. The assembly turned down a revision of the constitution of 1897, years in the making, and, despite almost 100 amendments, the document creaks and requires attention.

Educational, cultural, and recreational opportunities have greatly increased in recent years. The Wilmington area is filled with attractive museums, such as the Henry Francis Du Pont Winterthur Museum (furniture and the decorative arts of the period before 1840), the Hagley Museum (industrial history), the Delaware Historical Society Museum in Old Town Hall, the Delaware Art Museum, the Brandywine River Museum (art), Longwood Gardens, the Delaware Museum of Natural History, and the Hillendale Museum (geography and geology). In Dover the Delaware State Museum is maintained by the Division of Historical and Cultural Affairs, which also operates a number of historic houses, such as the John Dickinson Mansion. Not only has the public school system expanded but it also offers many opportunities in continuing and extracurricular education. The University of Delaware offers programs in each of the counties, and colleges such as Brandywine College, Wilmington College, Wesley College, and the Delaware Technical & Vocational College also flourish. The state, counties, and towns take more seriously than ever before their responsibilities for recreation, as evidenced by the expanded park system.

Delaware ends the 1970s confident that it is progressing toward better things and with problems that can be solved. Ties with the South have weakened as transportation, communication, and economic ties with Wilmington have strengthened, but some residents of Sussex County still look to Baltimore for many services. Delaware remains a border state facing many of the problems that are prevalent in Maryland.

Manuscript and printed primary sources. Two principal depositories of Delaware records are Hall of Records, Division of Historical and Cultural Affairs, Dover, and Historical Society of Delaware, Old Town Hall, Market St., Wilmington. Guides to holdings and annual accession lists are available at Hall of Records. H. C. Reed has cataloged historical society business manuscripts in *Delaware History* (April, 1964); and a card index of manuscripts is in the library of the society. Researchers would welcome a detailed guide to manuscripts in each depository.

The Eleutherian Mills Historical Library, Greenville, specializes in industrial and technological records of Delaware Valley. Its manuscript holdings are admirably listed in J. B. Riggs, *Guide to Manuscripts in EMHL* (1970), supplement expected soon. For other manuscripts see University of Delaware, Newark, and Henry Francis Du Pont Winterthur Museum, Winterthur, which specializes in furniture and decorative arts but contains some Delaware material, especially before 1840.

Hall of Records printed five volumes of *Military Archives* (1911–16) and occasionally publishes other records, such as minutes of general assembly for 1739–1742, 1762, 1765–1770. Presently it is publishing the minutes of general assembly, 1770–1776, and house of representatives, 1776–1783. Historical Society of Delaware published a series of "papers," 1879–1940, including source material such as minutes of legislative council (senate), 1776–1792 (1886); R. Kirkwood, *Revolutionary Journal* (1910); T. Rodney, *Diary* (1888); and G. Ryden, *Letters to and from Caesar Rodney* (1933). Since 1947 its publishing has been confined to *Delaware History*. EMHL published J. D. Hayes, *S. F. Du Pont: Civil War Letters* (3 vols.; 1969). Independently published were *Records of the Court of New Castle on Delaware* (2 vols.; 1904–35) and L. deValinger, *Court Records of Kent County* (1959). On printed books consult H. C. and M. B. Reed, *Bibliography of Delaware Through 1960* (1966), supplement expected soon.

Contemporary accounts. These include B. B. James and J. F. Jameson (eds.), *Journal of Jasper Danckaerts,*

1679–1680 (1913); A. C. Myers (ed.), *Narratives of Early Pennsylvania, Western New Jersey and Delaware, 1630–1707* (1912); B. Fernow (ed.), *Documents Relating to Dutch and Swedish Settlements on Delaware* (1877); A. Johnson (ed.), *Geographia Americae* (1925); A. B. Benson (ed.), *Peter Kalm's Travels in North America* (2 vols.; 1937); J. F. D. Smyth, *Tour in U.S.* (2 vols.; 1783, repr.); and F. Asbury, *Journal and Letters* (3 vols.; 1958). An interesting political narrative of 1780s is J. A. Munroe (ed.), *Timoleon's Biographical History of Dionysius* (1958), G. Read. On Kent County see *Journal of Nathaniel Luff, M.D.* (1848) and L. deValinger, Jr., and V. E. Shaw (eds.), *Calendar of Ridgely Family Letters* (3 vols.; 1948–61). On Brandywine area consult B. G. Du Pont (ed.), *Life of E. I. Du Pont* (11 vols.; 1923). One of few political memoirs is D. O. Hastings, *Delaware Politics, 1904–1954* (1959).

Histories. J. T. Scharf, *History of Delaware* (2 vols.; 1887), is the best history of the state, though mainly descriptive. H. C. Reed, *Delaware* (4 vols.; 1947), is excellent on welfare, constitutional development, denominational history, and ethnic groups. Other histories are mostly a rewrite and updating of Scharf: H. C. Conrad, *History of Delaware* (3 vols.; 1908); W. A. Powell, *History of Delaware* (1928); and W. L. Bevan and E. M. Williams (eds.), *History of Delaware* (4 vols.; 1929). Also see C. E. Hoffecker, *Delaware* (1977), a bicentennial history.

Excellent studies covering early developments are C. M. Parr, *Voyages of David de Vries* (1969); A. Johnson, *Swedish Settlements* (2 vols.; 1911), a classic; C. Ward, *Dutch and Swedes on Delaware* (1930); R. S. Rodney, *Colonial Finances in Delaware* (1928); and C. A. Weslager, *Dutch Explorers, Traders and Settlers in Delaware* (1961), *English on Delaware, 1610–1682* (1967), and *Log Cabin in America* (1969).

In addition to the Rodney letters mentioned previously, important studies dealing with the Revolution are: J. A. Munroe, *Federalist Delaware, 1775–1815* (1954); C. Ward, *Delaware Continentals* (1941); H. Hancock, *Delaware Loyalists* (1940, 1976); W. T. Read, *G. Read* (1870); W. Hamilton, *T. Rodney* (1956); J. M. Coleman, *Thomas McKean* (1975); and H. Hancock, *Liberty and Independence: Delaware During Revolution* (1976).

In addition to S. F. Du Pont's correspondence, valuable on Civil War are H. Hancock, *Delaware in Civil War* (1962), politics; N. B. Wilkinson, *Brandywine Home Front* (1966); and W. C. Wright, *Secession Movement in Middle Atlantic States* (1973).

Economic histories include B. G. Du Pont, *E. I. Du Pont de Nemours and Company* (1902); D. B. Tyler, *American Clyde: History of Iron and Steel Ships* (1958); R. Gray, *National Waterway* (1967), Chesapeake & Delaware Canal; and A. D. Chandler and S. Salsbury, *Pierre S. Du Pont and Modern Corporation* (1971). Biographies include M. James, *Alfred I. Du Pont* (1941); A. J. Henry, *Life of Alexis I. Du Pont* (2 vols.; 1945) and *F. G. Du Pont* (2 vols.; 1951); J. A. Munroe, *L. McLane* (1973); and C. C. Tansill, *Congressional Career of T. F. Bayard* (1946) and *Foreign Policy of T. F. Bayard* (1940).

Studies of book length on many subjects in Delaware history are often antiquated or inadequate. Histories of Wilmington include A. T. Lincoln, *Wilmington* (1937); and C. E. Hoffecker, *Wilmington, 1830–1910* (1973). For a study of an industrial village, consult C. E. Hoffecker, *Brandywine Village* (1974). Although several dissertations have been written on public and higher education, the standard histories are still L. P. Powell, *Education in Delaware* (1893); and S. B. Weeks, *Public School Education in Delaware* (1917). E. Rink, *Printing in Delaware*, is outstanding. On art consult W. S. Morse and G. Brinckle, *H. Pyle* (1921); D. Allen and D. Allen, Jr., *N. C. Wyeth* (1972); C. D. Abbot, *H. Pyle* (1925); and H. C. Pitz, *Brandywine Tradition* (1969) and *Brandywine Heritage* (1974). On architecture see G. F. Bennett, *Early Aritecture of Delaware* (1932); and H. D. Eberlein and C. V. D. Hubbard, *Historic Houses and Buildings* (1962). Ethnic history is covered only in Reed's four-volumed history and in theses. H. Hancock and J. E. Newton have prepared a historical anthology of black history combin-

DELAWARE POPULATION, 1790–1970

Year	Total	White	Nonwhite Slave	Nonwhite Free	Rank U.S.	Rank South
1790	59,096	46,310	8,887	3,899	12	7
1800	64,273	49,852	6,153	8,268	18	8
1810	72,674	55,361	4,177	13,136	18	9
1820	72,749	55,282	4,509	12,958	21	11
1830	76,748	57,601	3,292	15,855	25	12
1840	78,085	58,561	2,605	16,919	24	13
1850	91,532	71,169	2,290	18,073	32	14
1860	112,216	90,589	1,798	19,829	33	15
1870	125,015	102,221	22,794		38	16
1880	146,602	120,160	26,442		40	16
1890	168,493	140,066	28,386		45	16
1900	184,735	153,977	30,697		45	16
1910	202,322	171,100	31,181		47	16
1920	223,063	192,585	30,335		48	16
1930	238,380	205,694	32,621		48	16
1940	266,505	230,529	35,976		49	16
1950	318,085	273,878	44,207		47	16
1960	446,292	384,327	61,695		47	16
1970	548,104	466,459	81,645		47	16

ing primary and secondary material (1977). Denominational history has fared better than many topics: F. Zebley, *Churches of Delaware* (1947); N. W. Rightmyer, *Anglican Church in Delaware* (1947); E. C. Hallman, *Garden of Methodism* (1953); and T. J. Peterman, *Priests of a Century, 1868–1968* (1971). Recent political history has received attention in P. Dolan, *Government of Delaware* (1956); and C. Liberman, J. M. Rosbrow, and H. B. Rubenstein, *Delaware Citizen* (1967).

Articles. Since 1946 *Delaware History* has published research of scholars on state history. Important articles on the colonial period include: H. C. Reed, "Early New Castle Court" (June, 1951); R. W. Johannsen, "Conflict Between Delaware and Pennsylvania" (Sept., 1952); S. Rodney, "Governor Keith" (March, 1948); and H. Hancock, "Descriptions and Travel Accounts of Delaware, 1700–1740" (Oct., 1962). Studies of facets of the Revolution include J. H. Powell, "J. Dickinson" (Jan., July, 1946); and H. Hancock, "T. Robinson" (March, 1950), loyalist, "Kent County Loyalists" (April, Oct., 1954), and "County Committees and Growth of Independence" (Oct., 1973). Later political history is treated in D. R. Peltier, "Nineteenth Century Voting Patterns" (April, 1969), and "Party Development" (Oct., 1970). Articles on economic history include P. C. Welsh, "Merchants, Millers and Ocean Ships" (Sept., 1957); C. W. Purcell, "Delaware Iron Works" (March, 1959); G. H. Gibson, "Delaware Woolen Industry" (Oct., 1966); and W. F. Holmes, "New Castle and Frenchtown Turnpike and Railroad Company" (April, Oct., 1962; April, 1963). Black history is treated in H. Hancock, "M. A. Shadd" (April, 1973); H. C. Livesay, "Delaware Negroes, 1865–1915" (Oct., 1968); A. M. Hiller, "Disfranchisement of Delaware Negroes" (Oct., 1968); and J. J. Halstead, "Delaware Association for Moral Improvement and Education of Colored People" (April, 1972).

See also H. C. Reed, "Constitution of 1776," *Delaware Notes* (1929) and "Lincoln's Compensated Emancipation Plan," *Delaware Notes* (1931). Other articles of importance are R. O. Bausman and J. A. Munroe, "James Tilton's Notes on Agriculture of Delaware in 1788," *Agricultural History* (1946); and J. A. Munroe, "Negro in Delaware," *South Atlantic Quarterly* (Autumn, 1957) and "Philadelawareans," *Pennsylvania Magazine of History* (April, 1945). On industrial history see H. B. Hancock and N. W. Wilkinson, "Gilpins and Their Endless Papermaking Machine," *Pennsylvania Magazine of History* (Oct., 1957) and "Manufacturer in Wartime: Du Pont, 1860–1865," *Business History Review* (Summer, 1966); and H. C. Livesay, "Lobdell Car Wheel Co., 1830–1867," *Business History Review* (Summer, 1968). On black history see H. Hancock, "Free Negro in 1830's," *Civil War History* (Dec., 1971). On post–Civil War period, see H. Hancock, in R. O. Curry (ed.), *Radicalism, Racism and Party Realignment* (1969). On T. McKean see G. S. Rowe, "T. McKean and Coming of Revolution," *Pennsylvania Magazine of History* (Jan., 1972) and "Valuable Acquisition in Congress: T. McKean," *Pennsylvania History* (July, 1971). *Delaware History* devoted a special issue to the American Revolution in the spring of 1976.

Dissertations and theses. Much excellent research remains buried in university archives unpublished or published only in articles in condensed form. Theses at the University of Delaware include: L. deValinger, Jr., "Local Government, 1638–1682" (1938); H. B. Stewart, "Ne-

gro in Delaware to 1829" (1940); E. D. Hitchens, "Local Government, 1776–1831" (1941); J. A. Munroe, "Continental Congress and Delaware Legislature" (1941); J. Clayton, "Railroad Building in Delaware" (1948); J. F. Abeles, "German Element in Wilmington" (1948); J. M. Herson, "Methodism in Delaware" (1956); P. C. Welsh, "Brandywine Mills" (1956); A. Lindell, "Quakers in Delaware" (1957); C. W. Purcell, "Milling on Red Clay Creek" (1958); E. Chance, "Horse Racing in Delaware" (1959); N. M. Drescher, "Irish in Industrial Wilmington" (1960); J. C. Potter, "Philadelphia, Wilmington and Baltimore Railroad" (1960); S. G. Farris, "Wilmington Merchant" (1960); H. Gibbs, "Delaware Railroad" (1961); F. Holmes, "North Carolina and Frenchtown Turnpike and Railroad Co." (1964); A. M. Hiller, "Disfranchisement of Delaware Negroes" (1965); N. W. Moore, "Anti-Slavery Movement in Delaware" (1965); R. J. Lamden, "Senator W. Saulsbury, 1912–1919" (1966); W. S. Smith, "Senator W. Saulsbury, 1859–1861" (1966); W. G. Johnson, "Political Career of H. A. Du Pont" (1967); G. M. Artner, "Father P. Kenny" (1968); G. D. Wray, "A. T. A. Torbert" (1969); and J. G. Dean, "The Free Negro" (1970).

Dissertations at the University of Delaware include: D. R. Peltier, "Voting in Delaware" (1967); R. L. Mumford, "Constitutional Development" (1968); and L. J. Kempski, "Catholicism" (1965). Dissertations at other universities include: J. H. Peeling, "T. McKean" (University of Chicago, 1929); J. H. Powell, "John Dickinson" (University of Iowa, 1938); G. R. Miller, Jr., "Adolescent Negro Education in Delaware" (New York University, 1944); M. Kane, "Secondary Education in Delaware" (1947); D. Jacobson, "J. Dickinson and J. Galloway" (Princeton, 1959); M. E. Miller, "Oyster Industry in Delaware" (Boston University, 1962); W. J. Satneck, "Delaware State College" (New York University, 1962); G. S. Rowe, "T. McKean" (Stanford, 1969); H. Schwaneger, "Higher Education in Delaware" (University of Pennsylvania, 1969); R. M. Finch, "Secondary Education in Delaware" (Teachers College, Columbia, 1969); D. T. Boughner, "G. Read" (Catholic University, 1970); R. S. Powers, "Wealth and Poverty in Prerevolutionary Pennsylvania, New Jersey, and Delaware" (University of Kansas, 1971); and R. A. Wire, "J. Clayton" (University of Maryland, 1971).

HAROLD B. HANCOCK
Otterbein College

DELAWARE GOVERNORS

Governor	Party	Term
SWEDISH RULE		
Peter Minuit		1638
Peter Hollandaer		1640–1643
Johan Printz		1643–1653
Johan Papegoja		1653–1654
Johan Classon Rising		1654–1655
DUTCH RULE		
Peter Stuyvesant		1655
Dirck Smidt		1655
John Paul Jaquet		1655
Andreas Huddle		1655–1657
Jacob Alrichs		1657
Gregorius Van Dyck		1657–1658

Governor	Party	Term
William Beekman		1658–1659
Alexander D'Hinoyossa		1659–1665
ENGLISH RULE		
Richard Nichola		1664
Robert Needham		1664–1667
Francis Lovelace		1667–1668
John Carr		1668–1673
DUTCH RULE		
Anthony Colve		1673
Peter Alrichs		1673–1674
ENGLISH RULE		
Edmund Andros		1674
Edmund Cantwell		1674–1676
John Collier		1676–1677
Christopher Billop		1677–1681
Anthony Brockholst		1681
William Penn (proprietor)		1681–1718
William Markham (deputy governor)		1681–1684
Thomas Lloyd (president of council)		1684–1688
John Blackwell (deputy governor)		1688–1690
William Markham (deputy governor)		1691–1694
John Goodson (deputy governor)		1694
Samuel Carpenter (deputy governor)		1694–1698
William Markham (deputy governor)		1698–1699
Andrew Hamilton (lieutenant governor)		1699–1702
Edward Shippin (president of council)		1702–1704
John Evans (lieutenant governor)		1704–1709
Charles Gooding (lieutenant governor)		1709–1717
William Keith (deputy governor)		1717–1726
John Penn		
Richard Penn (joint proprietors) Thomas Penn		1718–1746
Patrick Gordon (lieutenant governor)		1726–1736
James Logan (president of council)		1736–1738
George Thomas (lieutenant governor)		1738–1747
Richard Penn (joint proprietors) Thomas Penn		1746–1771
Anthony Palmer (president of council)		1747–1748
James Hamilton (lieutenant governor)		1748–1754
Robert Hunter (lieutenant governor)		1754–1756
William Denny (lieutenant governor)		1756–1759
James Hamilton (lieutenant governor)		1759–1763
John Penn (lieutenant governor)		1763–1771

Governor	Party	Term
Thomas Penn (joint proprietors) John Penn		1771–1776
James Hamilton (president of council)		1771–1775
PRESIDENTS		
John McKinly		1777
Thomas McKean		1777
George Read		1777–1778
Caesar Rodney		1778–1781
John Dickinson		1781–1782
John Cook		1782–1783
Nicholas Van Dyke		1783–1786
Thomas Collins		1786–1789
Jehu Davis		1789
Joshua Clayton		1789–1791
GOVERNORS		
Joshua Clayton	Fed.	1793–1796
Gunning Bedford, Sr.	Fed.	1796–1797
Daniel Rogers	Fed.	1797–1799
Richard Bassett	Fed.	1799–1801
James Sykes	Fed.	1801–1802
David Hall	Dem.-Rep.	1802–1805
Nathaniel Mitchell	Fed.	1805–1808
George Truitt	Fed.	1808–1811
Joseph Haslet	Dem.-Rep.	1811–1814
Daniel Rodney	Fed.	1814–1817
Jacob Stout (acting)		1820–1821
John Collins	Dem.-Rep.	1821–1822
Caleb Rodney	Fed.	1822–1823
Joseph Haslet	Dem.-Rep.	1823
Charles Thomas (acting)		1823–1824
Samuel Paynter	Fed.	1824–1827
Charles Polk	Fed.	1827–1830
David Hazzard	Am.-Rep.	1830–1833
Caleb P. Bennett	Dem.	1833–1836
Charles Polk	Whig	1836–1837
Cornelius P. Comegys	Whig	1837–1841
William B. Cooper	Whig	1841–1845
Thomas Stockton	Whig	1845–1846
Joseph Maull	Whig	1846
William Temple	Whig	1846–1847
William Tharp	Dem.	1847–1851
William H. Ross	Dem.	1851–1855
Peter F. Causey	Am. Know-Nothing	1855–1859
William Burton	Dem.	1859–1863
William Cannon	Union	1863–1865
Gove Saulsbury	Dem.	1865–1871
James Ponder	Dem.	1871–1875
John P. Cochran	Dem.	1875–1879
John W. Hall	Dem.	1879–1883
Charles C. Stockley	Dem.	1883–1887
Benjamin T. Biggs	Dem.	1887–1891
Robert J. Reynolds	Dem.	1891–1895
Joshua H. Marvel	Rep.	1895
William T. Watson	Dem.	1895–1897
Ebe Tunnell	Dem.	1897–1901
John Hunn	Rep.	1901–1905
Preston Lea	Rep.	1905–1909
Simon S. Pennewill	Rep.	1909–1913
Charles R. Miller	Rep.	1913–1917
John G. Townsend, Jr.	Rep.	1917–1921
William D. Denney	Rep.	1921–1925
Robert P. Robinson	Rep.	1925–1929

Governor	Party	Term
C. Douglass Buck	Rep.	1929–1937
Richard C. McMullen	Dem.	1937–1941
Walter W. Bacon	Rep.	1941–1949
Elbert N. Carvel	Dem.	1949–1953
J. Caleb Boggs	Rep.	1953–1961
David Buckson	Rep.	1960–1961
Elbert N. Carvel	Dem.	1961–1965
Charles L. Terry	Dem.	1965–1969
Russell W. Peterson	Rep.	1969–1973
Sherman W. Tribbitt	Dem.	1973–1977
Pierre S. Du Pont	Rep.	1977–1981

DELAWARE, HISTORICAL SOCIETY OF, founded in 1864, had 1,600 members in 1974. Its museum is in the Old Town Hall at 510½ Market St., Wilmington, 19801. The library contains books and manuscript holdings of some 186,000 pieces dating back to 1680 and includes items on the William Penn family, Thomas Garrett, Justice Thomas Rodney, CAESAR RODNEY, the signer of the DECLARATION OF INDEPENDENCE, and Caesar Augustus Rodney, the attorney general. There is also a large collection of documents, deeds, maps, Delaware newspapers, letters of Confederate prisoners at Ft. Delaware, and papers dealing with the West Indian trade. The society has published a semiannual journal, *Delaware History*, since 1946, with a present circulation of 1,600. The journal is limited to articles on Delaware history.

DELAWARE, UNIVERSITY OF (Newark, 19711), began in 1743 as a Presbyterian academy located in New London, Pa. After being moved to Newark in 1765, it remained a primary and preparatory school until 1833, when as Newark College it began offering college-level instruction. Financial and political problems forced the school's closure in 1859. In 1870, however, it was reopened as the state's principal land-grant college, and in 1921 it was merged with the state women's college to form the university. It presently has a combined daytime and evening enrollment of over 18,500 students. Notable library holdings include materials on Delaware history and on the state's Presbyterian, Baptist, and Methodist churches.

See W. G. Cramton and N. W. Moore, *Delaware History* (1966); and G. H. Ryden, *Pennsylvania History* (1935), and *Delaware Notes* (1935).

DELAWARE CONTINENTALS (regiment, battalion), authorized by Congress on December 9, 1775, was distinguished by both valor in combat and an unparalleled length of continuous service. Rarely numbering over 500, the Delawares first gained recognition at Long Island (August 25–28, 1776), met disaster at CAMDEN (August 16, 1780), and formed an important flank detachment for the front line at GUILFORD COURTHOUSE (March 15, 1781), suffering heavy casualties in each engagement. Henry Lee of Virginia stated that no regiment in the army surpassed it in soldiership.

See C. Ward, *Delaware Continentals* (1941), most definitive; F. A. Berg, *Continental Army Units* (1972), short description; H. Lee, *Memoirs* (1870); C. Ward, *War of Revolution* (2 vols.; 1952); military journals of Thomas Anderson, *Historical Magazine* (1867); R. Kirkwood, *Delaware Historical Society Publications* (1910); and W. Seymour, *Pennsylvania Magazine of History and Biography* (1883).

JAMES H. EDMONSON
Union University, Jackson, Tenn.

DELMARVA PENINSULA encompasses the whole state of Delaware and the Eastern Shore of Maryland and Virginia, an area of 6,000 square miles. Exploration and settlement began in the seventeenth century predominantly by the English in Maryland and Virginia and by continental Europeans, such as the Swedes and Dutch, in Delaware. Early boundary disputes between Maryland and Pennsylvania were settled with the MASON-DIXON LINE in 1767, and those between Maryland and Virginia were resolved in 1873. On a number of occasions, starting in the late eighteenth century (with the principal attempt in 1833–1834), efforts were made to create one state out of the peninsula.

From the outset the products of the region reflected in general those of the Chesapeake Bay: tobacco, wheat, corn, oats, lumber, etc. Because of its prosperity, it was a target of British occupation during the Revolutionary War. Economic expansion started with the completion of turnpikes in the early nineteenth century, followed by the opening of the Chesapeake & Delaware Canal in 1829, railroads shortly thereafter, and bridges in the 1950s and 1960s. Today it is undergoing an immense change with many new inhabitants and with industry attracted by the proximity to Philadelphia, Wilmington, Baltimore, and Washington, D.C. However, the basis of the economy is still poultry raising (one of the leading producers in the United States), seafood processing, and tourism.

See E. C. Papenfuse, *Maryland Historical Magazine* (Summer, 1973); W. F. Holmes, *Delaware History* (April,

Oct., 1962; April, 1963); R. D. Gray, *National Waterway* (1967); N. B. Wainwright, *Pennsylvania Magazine of History and Biography* (July, 1963); C. B. Clark (ed.), *Eastern Shore of Maryland and Virginia* (3 vols.; 1950); and *Business Week* (Aug. 18, 1973).

RICHARD J. COX
Maryland Historical Society

DEMAGOGUERY. The demagogue is one of the most spectacular and colorful figures in southern history. Vilified by his enemies and ridiculed by the press, he nonetheless has attracted legions of admirers and usually has been a successful political leader. To date, only a few general studies of the southern demagogue have been published. Therefore, he remains misunderstood and unjustly maligned.

The term *demagogue* is derived from an ancient Greek word meaning leader of the people. Even the early Greeks, however, used it to denote a politician who gains power through unscrupulous appeals to his electorate's emotions, passions, and prejudices. Irresponsible promises, flamboyant campaign methods, and racial and class bigotry are the trademarks of the demagogue. Among the southern political leaders to whom the term has been applied are: Franklin Plummer, ALBERT GALLATIN BROWN, ANDREW JOHNSON, Pitchfork BEN TILLMAN, TOM WATSON, JAMES K. VARDAMAN, THEODORE G. BILBO, EUGENE TALMADGE, MA AND PA FERGUSON, W. LEE ("PAPPY") O'DANIEL, KISSIN' JIM FOLSOM, HUEY and EARL LONG, and GEORGE WALLACE.

The term demagogue is semantically vague, being oversimplified. It also ignores some of the basic realities of American politics. And it is much too broad and general to denote such diverse men as Johnson, Tillman, Long, and Wallace. Each of the demagogues was or is a unique individual. The roots of southern demagoguery, being embedded in the political, social, and economic history of the region, demand serious study, which cannot be accomplished through the use of such a vague epithet as "demagogue."

Since the primary objective of American politicians is not to discuss issues or appeal to the reason of the voters, but to get elected, the methods used to win votes vary according to the composition of the electorate. The electorate of the demagogues was the rural southern poor, and they designed their campaign appeals accordingly, just as urban labor leaders base their appeals on class differences. There is little difference in Eugene Talmadge wearing red galluses in order to appeal to the farmers of rural Georgia and in George Washington distributing rum to the voters of Virginia in order to win a seat in the House of Burgesses.

The often vulgar and crude campaign tactics of the demagogues succeeded in intensifying popular participation in government. They also made good on many of their promises. Under the administrations of such governors as Tillman, Bilbo, the Longs, and Wallace, public spending for roads, hospitals, and schools was increased; welfare benefits were raised; and even Negroes received massive benefits from state government. Some of the demagogues like Talmadge and COLE BLEASE were do-nothing governors, with negative records. Others, like Huey Long, were dangerous usurpers of political power who threatened the checks and balances system. All, however, were or are unique and important contributors to southern history.

See M. Kurtz, "Demagogue Since 1890" (M.A. thesis, University of Tennessee, 1965); R. Luthin, *American Demagogues* (1954), general, and *American Scholar* (Spring, 1951); D. Robinson, *Journal of Southern History* (Aug., 1937); T. H. Williams, *Huey Long* (1969), and *Journal of Southern History* (Feb., 1960); C. V. Woodward, *Tom Watson* (1938); A. W. Green, *Bilbo* (1963); W. Dykeman, *Virginia Quarterly Review* (Summer, 1957); G. W. Johnson, *Virginia Quarterly Review* (Jan., 1936); R. Luthin, *American Historical Review* (Oct., 1951); O. P. Boliam, "James K. Vardaman" (M.A. thesis, Tulane, 1937); S. Lemmon, "Eugene Talmadge" (Ph.D. dissertation, University of North Carolina, 1952); and J. B. Sloane, "Blease" (M.A. thesis, Tulane, 1938).

MICHAEL L. KURTZ
Southeastern Louisiana University

DEMOCRATIC PARTY has been used as a name by so many different political organizations in the South that it is not very useful as a descriptive label without specification of dates and, to some extent, individual states as well. The continuous use of this party name in the South from the Jacksonian period into the 1970s is attributable to the designation of one of the major national parties by that title. Southern political leaders would not have been able to participate effectively in presidential and congressional politics had they not professed allegiance to a national party, even during periods when northern elements of that party were maintaining positions unacceptable to southerners on critical issues. It was the nationwide two-party structure, notwithstanding the disparate nature of the elements within either major party, that compelled the use of the party designation *Democratic* in the South after 1877 as the covering appellation for a variety of state-level arrangements. It should be a proper warning about the varying implications of being a Democrat in the South that in 1872 the party was supported by few black voters but by a large majority of white voters and a century later it encompassed the overwhelming majority of black voters but only a minority of the white.

Major parties in the United States have not had anything approaching the ideological character of parties in twentieth-century multiparty nations, not even of the two major parties in Great Britain. The Democratic party in the South between 1828 and 1976 cannot be described even in terms of consistent issue positions, certainly not in ideological terms. To a greater extent than in the remainder of the United States, *Democratic* has suggested strikingly differing positions on national and local issues during the century and a half that it has been current. It is a surpassing example only that in 1876 the fate of civil rights for black people was in the South the almost exclusive concern of Republicans, but that in 1976 it was far more the concern of Democrats.

The first use of *Democratic party* was in the second two-party system of the country, when Democrats opposed Whigs in the South from 1836 to 1860. Exploratory use of different party labels by southern Whigs in 1856 and 1860 should not be permitted to obscure the fact that a stable voter alignment prevailed, extremely stable in the border South and moderately so in the Lower South. Notwithstanding this stability, the rivalry has not been explained in issue-oriented terms. Repeated efforts to account for the party alignment of individuals or communities by reference to economic or any other definable interests have come to naught. The ethnocultural considerations found useful in analyzing northern party distinctions in the nineteenth century have little relevance to the South. The most revealing distinctions between antebellum southern Democrats and their party opponents appeared in 1860, when most Democrats supported SECESSION and most Whigs were reluctant if not unconditionally opposed. There is some evidence here that, without the disruption of a civil war, the southern two-party system might have evolved into an issue-oriented one insofar as the United States political universe made that possible.

Party names were little used within the Confederacy, but the border South experienced wrenching reorientations of party lines during the Civil War, from which the antebellum Democratic party emerged altered but substantially intact. It was the extending of voting and officeholding privileges to black men during congressional RECONSTRUCTION, however, introducing as it did unprecedented political considerations, that prevented a substantial postwar division of southern white voters between the major parties from outlasting the decade. For almost a century after the ELECTION OF 1876, three-fourths or more of these white voters identified themselves as Democrats for national purposes, although for the first generation the label *Conservative* remained attached to *Democratic* in most southern states as a gesture of comity toward the formerly anti-Democratic element in the omnibus vehicle (REDEEMER GOVERNMENTS).

The South was not altogether a one-party section between 1877 and 1964, but effective practical politics were usually confined to the Democratic ranks at the state and local levels. After 1890 the legal and constitutional DISFRANCHISEMENT of black voters was accomplished in most of the southern states. Subsequently, the advent of the nominating primary election as a national Progressive reform (PROGRESSIVISM) invited the formal institution of a white man's Democratic primary in most though not all of the southern states (WHITE PRIMARY). The exclusion of black southerners from effective participation in politics did not, however, lead to issue-oriented division of southern white voters. Something resembling issue rivalry appeared within some states for brief periods, often described as a Progressive-Conservative dichotomy and sometimes interpreted as a continuation of the 1890s clash between Populists (POPULIST PARTY) and Bourbon Democrats (BOURBONS). Yet, even in these instances, close scrutiny exposed far from either a clear or a persistent pattern. The 1928 one-election southern revolt against Alfred E. Smith, the Catholic Democratic presidential nominee, was a harbinger of a more lasting schism to come (ELECTION OF 1928). Nevertheless, the Democratic party continued for most southern voters and political leaders to be a catchall at the state level that enabled effective participation in national politics.

The NEW DEAL era witnessed the beginning of a radical change in the Democratic party's popular base, as black voters were detached from traditional REPUBLICAN PARTY loyalties. The change was continued as the courts eliminated the Democratic white primary. The companion aspects of civil rights accomplishment during the post–World War II generation not only brought substantial numbers of black voters into the Democratic party's active ranks, but also drove equally substantial numbers of white Democrats into the Republican party. Sporadic third-party activity from the 1948 DIXIECRAT movement to GEORGE WALLACE's efforts of the 1960s eliminated the façade of southern and northern Democratic unity in presidential politics. Simultaneously the voting behavior of southern Democrats exposed a chasm between southern and northern party elements on congressional legislative issues. A plateau of white Republicanism was reached in the South in the ELECTION OF 1964 with Barry Goldwater as the Republican nominee, and eight years later no southern state deviated from the national mode of behavior that gave Richard M. Nixon the electoral votes of every state except Massachusetts.

By 1976, a century after the symbolic end of the Reconstruction era, most of the southern states had a revitalized two-party system at the state and local levels as well as in presidential contests. Whether this voter realignment was a mere episode or whether it reflected an issue-oriented confrontation was difficult to discern from only a decade's experience. If *Democratic* as a party label had come to be meaningful in the South by 1976, the precise contours of the meaning were not clear, and certainly whatever meaning was perceived differed significantly from any associated with that party name in previous southern history.

See treatments of party politics in Vols. V–X of *A History of the South*, written respectively by C. S. Sydnor (1948), A. O. Craven (1953), E. M. Coulter (1950, 1947), C. V. Woodward (1951), and G. B. Tindall (1967); D. W. Grantham, *Democratic South* (1963); J. M. Kousser, *Shaping of Southern Politics, 1880–1910* (1974); V. O. Key, Jr., *Southern Politics* (1950); N. V. Bartley and H. D. Graham, *Southern Politics and Second Reconstruction* (1975); C. P. Roland, *Incredible Era* (1975); R. P. McCormick, *Second American Party System* (1966); R. O. Curry (ed.), *Radicalism, Racism, and Party Realignment* (1969); and C. N. Degler, *Other South* (1974). Useful state studies are cited in the above and in A. S. Link and R. W. Patrick (eds.), *Writing Southern History* (1965).

THOMAS B. ALEXANDER
University of Missouri, Columbia

DEMOCRATIC-REPUBLICAN PARTY. The emergence of political parties in the 1790s was distinctly sectional in nature. Federalists relied mainly on the northern bloc of states for support, and Democratic-Republicans increased their strength in the South throughout this formative decade. The sweeping Beardian thesis that Federalists represented the commercial-shipping-financial interests and Republicans the farmer-planter-slaveholder interests, however, is of limited validity. The planters of the northern neck and Eastern Shore of Virginia, for example, were largely Federalists. The merchants of Wilmington, Del., were overwhelmingly Republicans. No single thesis can explain Republican power in the South, which must be sought in the peculiar local circumstances of each region, in the degree of deferential politics and social control of leaders, in ideological disputes, and in ethnic and religious influences upon party preferences. Jay's Treaty was a pivotal issue that helped swell antiadministration forces in the South as various conservatives abandoned the Federalists to take up the Republican cause. Yet, in South Carolina, Republicanism was not triumphant until 1800, when upcountry voters successfully challenged the pro-Federalist elite of Charleston.

During THOMAS JEFFERSON's two terms, various "old Republicans" became increasingly dissatisfied with what they considered the pragmatic rather than the principled course of the president. Nevertheless, Jefferson's political astuteness kept the Republican party unified despite the defections of a few southerners led by the eccentric JOHN RANDOLPH. After 1815, however, as the Republican party took up Federalist positions on a number of important issues and as Republican presidents failed to exercise effective political controls, sectional pressures were strongly felt. Even Jefferson, in retirement, complained to Albert Gallatin of "many calling themselves Republicans and preaching the rankest doctrines of the old Federalists." The Missouri debates stirred southern Republicans to reaffirm the doctrine of states' rights. Economic issues brought them still closer together. In 1824 Republican representatives from the South voted almost to a man against the tariff. By the close of the 1820s, however, as the Jacksonian tide swept America, the Republican party underwent a metamorphosis, not only changing its name (to Democratic), but altering its character, its policies, and its base of support.

See T. Abernethy, *South in New Nation* (1961); H. Ammon, *Virginia Magazine of History and Biography* (April, 1963); R. Brown, *South Atlantic Quarterly* (Winter, 1966); N. Cunningham, *Jeffersonian Republicans* (1957), and *Jeffersonian Republicans in Power* (1963); and N. Risjord, *Old Republicans* (1965).

MORTON BORDEN
University of California, Santa Barbara

DEPOSIT, RIGHT OF, has its historical background in the United States–Spanish Treaty of

San Lorenzo of 1795 (Pinckney's Treaty), in which the southern states acquired the right to free navigation of the Mississippi River and the privilege of deposit at New Orleans. Flatboats needed a place to store their goods while waiting for the larger vessels to arrive. The treaty provided for a definite limit of three years for the duration of the privilege. Then Spain was to designate a similar site along the Mississippi River.

In the secret Treaty of San Ildefonso (1800), Spain returned Louisiana to France. In 1802 information touching on the abuses of the privilege of deposit by the Americans was received by the Spanish court. Acting on "very secret" orders, Acting Intendant Juan Ventura Morales at New Orleans issued a proclamation dated October 18, 1802, closing the deposit to the Americans. Two rumors now became common throughout the United States: that the French had ordered the closing, as the "secret treaty" of retrocession of the province lost its secrecy; and that the port was actually shut to Americans. Neither was fully true. During the actual time of the closure, October, 1802, to May, 1803, U.S. customs records at the port of Philadelphia offer ample evidence of American vessels using the port. Spain continued to need U.S. foodstuffs at New Orleans. The French never really effectively took over the province before the LOUISIANA PURCHASE (1803).

See A. P. Whitaker, *Mississippi Question* (1934); and C. R. Arena, *Pennsylvania History* (Jan., 1963).

C. RICHARD ARENA
Mary Star of the Sea High School, San Pedro, Calif.

DESEGREGATION OF PUBLIC SCHOOLS.

Following the U.S. Supreme Court's 1954 decision in BROWN V. BOARD OF EDUCATION, each southern state responded individually and somewhat differently to the legal demise of *de jure* segregation of education. Some states and urban areas, labeled the "nows," began desegregation almost immediately. A second group of states, the "nevers," chose to pursue massive legal resistance in an effort to preserve separate school systems.

Among the "nows," cities—notably Washington, D.C.—led the way. The nation's capital desegregated 73 percent of its schools in 1954 and completed its dismantlement of JIM CROW schools by 1955. Arkansas, Delaware, Kentucky, Maryland, Missouri, Tennessee, Texas, and West Virginia also began immediate efforts to desegregate their schools, sometimes peacefully but at other times traumatically, with the first overt resistance

at Milford, Del. By the late 1950s, West Virginia and Missouri had completed statewide desegregation, but in other "now" states total desegregation was not achieved until the early 1970s.

The "nevers" adopted a variety of strategies and devices to fight desegregation: school closures, repeal of compulsory school attendance, public payment of private school tuitions, pupil assignment programs, denial of state aid to desegregated schools, elimination of teacher tenure, so-called freedom of choice options, INTERPOSITION, and NULLIFICATION. The first reaction of Virginia's officials to the *Brown* decision was moderate and restrained. Soon, however, the BYRD MACHINE was utilizing a program of "massive resistance," which included everything from interposition to the closing of desegregated schools. By 1958 school closings proved too unpalatable to continue, and in 1959 the state and federal courts declared Virginia's resistance laws unconstitutional. Other "never" states also saw their massive resistance statutes fail in the courts and turned instead to pupil assignment programs. In 1956, "now" states had desegregated 15 percent of their biracial school districts, and the "nevers" had desegregated none. By 1964 the "nows" had desegregated 50 percent of their school systems; the "nevers," only 20 percent and then only on a token student basis.

After ten years of legislative inaction on the *Brown* decision, Congress passed the CIVIL RIGHTS ACT OF 1964 authorizing the attorney general to instigate desegregation suits and to provide money and counsel for the schools. The Office of Education then issued desegregation guidelines and applied economic pressures (especially under the billion-dollar Elementary and Secondary Education Act of 1965). Since passage of the 1964 act, some 200 southern school districts have been denied federal funding.

In 1968, the Supreme Court added a further impetus to desegregation. During the 14 years since its *Brown* decision, the Court had accepted "good faith" plans designed to produce desegregation at a future date. Moreover, it had upheld nonracial pupil placement programs as constitutional (*Shuttlesworth* v. *Birmingham*, 358 U.S. 101 [1958]). Beginning in 1968, however, the Supreme Court declared it the duty of school boards to desegregate immediately (*Green* v. *Virginia*, 88 S.C. 1689). The next year the Court also required unitary school systems (*Alexander* v. *Holmes*, 90 S.C. 29).

With executive and judicial branches working jointly, desegregation accelerated. New devices were tried, some being educationally controversial: pairing schools, open enrollments, geographic zoning, educational parks and complexes, magnet schools, school mergers, and busing. By 1974 these multiple efforts had accomplished *de jure* desegregation; 92 percent (89 percent nationwide) of the black students in 11 former Confederate states were attending school with whites.

Yet *de jure* school desegregation was not necessarily everything that had been anticipated. By 1970–1971, some 6,900 black educators had been displaced from their jobs by desegregation. Washington, D.C., a leader in desegregation, was also a leader in *de facto* resegregation; as whites moved to the suburbs or sent children to private schools, the capital's black student public school enrollments climbed from 50 percent to 96 percent. Louisville, Ky., a heroine of voluntary desegregation in 1956, was being re-desegregated less heroically in 1975. Recognizing that the process of desegregation could proceed indefinitely in a demographically unstable society, the Supreme Court ruled in 1971 that, once desegregation had occurred, no further federal action would be required unless local authorities interfered to alter demographic patterns (*Swann* v. *Charlotte*, 91 S.C. 1267).

A desegregated school is incompatible with a segregated society. Society needs a consensus on integration; schools need a return to the goal Horace Mann set for them: "to help each child to burgeon forth the best that is within him."

See Southern Education Report Service, *Southern Education News* (1954–65), and *Southern Education Report* (1965–69); U.S. Office of Education, Office of Civil Rights, *Title VI of Civil Rights Act of 1964—Ten Years Later* (1974), and *Official Press Releases* (1967–75); Vanderbilt Law School, *Race Relations Law Reporter* (1956–69), and *Race Relations Law Survey* (1969–72); L. O. Garber (ed.), *Yearbook of School Law* (1953–71); A. P. Blaustein and C. C. Ferguson, Jr., *Desegregation and Law* (1957); and J. W. Peltason, *58 Lonely Men* (1971).

T. L. PATRICK
Tulane University

DE SOTO, HERNANDO (1500?–1542), took a prominent part in the Spanish conquest of Central America and Peru. As a reward for distinguished service, he was made governor of Cuba and adelantado of Florida. De Soto sailed from Havana with 600 persons on May 18, 1539. Tampa Bay, his landing site, was the point of departure for an expedition attempting to repeat the exploits of Hernando Cortes and Francisco Pizarro. Penetrating to the Tallahassee area, de Soto wintered there before exploring the present state of Georgia. Despite discovery of pearls along the Savannah River, he continued northwest to the North Carolina Piedmont. He crossed into Tennessee and descended the Coosa River toward Mobile Bay. He then proceeded northwest to the MISSISSIPPI RIVER near modern Memphis. He journeyed across Arkansas into Oklahoma, thence down the Arkansas River to its mouth, where he died in May, 1542. He was buried in the Mississippi, the river that he is credited with discovering.

See E. G. Bourne, *Narratives of De Soto* (2 vols.; 1904); R. B. C. Graham, *De Soto* (1924); and T. Maynard, *De Soto and Conquistadores* (1930), best.

W. VINCENT DELANEY
Edgecliff College

DEW, THOMAS RODERICK (1802–1846), born in King and Queen County, Va., entered the College of William and Mary in 1817, graduating three years later. After traveling and studying in Europe, he returned to William and Mary to earn his M.A. degree in 1825. In 1826 he was appointed to a chair there requiring him to lecture on metaphysics, natural and national law, political economy, history, and government. Dew's knowledge of history, philosophy, and economics drew him into the political controversies of his day. He attacked isolationism and protectionist tariffs, yet defended slavery as an incentive to economic development. In 1832 Dew vigorously opposed President ANDREW JACKSON's removal of the government deposits from the Bank of the United States. His greatest work was an economic defense of slavery published as *A Review of the Debates in the Virginia Legislature of 1831 and 1832*. In 1836 he was appointed the first layman to become president of the College of William and Mary. Dew was a dedicated teacher, an avid intellectual, an efficient manager, a prolific writer, an outstanding president, and an overwhelming debater—a person who had a tremendous respect and thirst for knowledge.

See H. M. Booker, *Virginia Cavalcade* (Autumn, 1969); W. S. Jenkins, *Pro-Slavery Thought in Old South* (1935), writings of Dew and Chancellor William Harper and others; and J. S. Bryan, *Bulletin of College of William and Mary* (May, 1939).

HENRY MARSHALL BOOKER
Christopher Newport College

DIALECTS. The seventeenth-century English language brought to America by British colonists developed into three principal regional types:

Northern in coastal New England and the lower Hudson Valley; Midland in the Delaware Bay settlements; and Southern in eastern Virginia and the Carolinas. Although speakers of various local and regional British dialects must have mingled in all three of the colonial areas, the leaders and upper-class citizens gave prestige to different varieties of English in the three regions, and the difficulties of communication between the three regions helped prevent homogenization. The Northern and Southern cultural centers kept closer contacts with England than did the Midland settlements and thus shared in changes that took place in Standard British English to a greater extent than did the midlanders, many of whom were Ulster Scots, speaking a variety of Northern British English.

In the western migrations, Midland spread in two branches: North Midland through central Pennsylvania, Ohio, Indiana, and Illinois; and South Midland into the Shenandoah Valley and Appalachia. Southern spread across the cotton belt, where it was spoken alongside and was a model for the creolized English of the slaves. Settlement and migration patterns thus account for the original establishment of two great dialectal subareas of the South: Southern (Coastal Southern) and South Midland (Mountain Southern).

The historical boundary between Southern and South Midland cut across Delaware near Dover and Maryland north of Baltimore, turning south at the Blue Ridge Mountains in northern Virginia; it followed the crest of the Blue Ridge to near Lynchburg, there bending southeastward into North Carolina, then curving southwestward along the FALL LINE across South Carolina and into northern Georgia. One marked distinction between South Midland and Southern was the Midland retention of the consonant /r/ finally and before other consonants, where Southern lost the /r/, making *bore* and *boa* identical, as were such words as *farther* and *father*, *Lear* and *Leah*, *tuner* and *tuna*, *alms* and *arms*. South Midland still makes no distinction between *Rosa's* and *Rosie's*, *Sophie's* and *sofas*, *Mary* and *merry*, and similar words that Southern always has distinguished.

However, Southern and South Midland historically have shared some features not common in North Midland: for example, in vocabulary *light bread* (wheat bread), *branch* (small stream), *pully bone* (wishbone), *snake doctor* (dragonfly), and *you all*, *y'all* (plural you); and in pronunciation distinction between such pairs as *dew* and *do*, *morning* and *mourning*, and *caller* and *collar*. These features, common from the Ohio River to

the Gulf and from Chesapeake Bay to east Texas, have since at least the eighteenth century led northerners, foreign visitors, and southerners to identify a "southern dialect" or a "southern accent" and today lead some dialect geographers to identify a "General Southern," with Coastal Southern and Mountain Southern subareas.

Nineteenth-century migrations carried South Midland (Mountain or Hill Southern) across the northern parts of Georgia, Alabama, and Mississippi and across West Virginia, Kentucky, Tennessee, Arkansas, and east Texas and carried Coastal Southern (sometimes called Plantation Southern) over northern Florida, southern Georgia, Alabama, and Mississippi into Louisiana and east Texas. Both South Midland and Coastal Southern were modified in their westward expansion, primarily as a result of cross migrations that mingled the two dialects in the interior South. The relatively sharp original differences of the Atlantic coast have tended to fade and blend in the westward movement. Coastal Southern picked up some features from Negroes in the slave belt, Muskogean Indians, French speakers in Louisiana, and Mexicans in southeast Texas (who transmitted many Nahuatl Indian words).

Slow growth, social stability, and relative isolation protected distinct dialect subareas on the Atlantic coast such as the DELMARVA PENINSULA, the Virginia Piedmont, eastern North Carolina, the Cape Fear and Peedee River region, and the Charleston area well into the twentieth century. The distinctive vowels in such words as *church*, *bird*, *mouse*, and *about* even today indicate a speaker's Virginia Piedmont provenience, just as unmistakable vowels in such words as *pay*, *late*, *grow*, and *road* identify low-country (historical Charlestonian) origin. In addition to the cross migrations in the inland South, various factors have blurred the historical regional differences: public education, shifts in economy from agriculture to industry, improved transportation, desegregation, in-migration from other parts of the country, urbanization, and national usage in advertising and trade. Systematic investigation of Southern dialect patterns now in progress will delineate the historical and surviving subareas. Preliminary studies indicate that original Southern features are declining in frequency and prestige and that they are being replaced by Midland and Northern features.

There is a persistent urban folk belief that "Elizabethan English" is still spoken in the southern mountains. Undeniably there are some archaisms current in rustic South Midland: for example, *hit* for *it*, *mought* for *might*, and *afeared* for *afraid*, but there are other archaisms in the speech of Boston and Richmond and Atlanta. All varieties of British and American English have changed since the seventeenth century, but in different ways.

The origin, nature, and even existence of Black English are controversial topics. The traditional view is that almost all features of the English of Negroes who do not speak a regional standard were acquired from whites on plantations and preserved in segregated communities. The rival view is that many features of such English are relics of the Plantation Creole, which began as a pidgin merger of English with Hausa, Ibo, Mende, Twi, Wolof, Yoruba, and other West African languages. (GULLAH, spoken on islands off Georgia and South Carolina, is descended from a plantation lingua franca that may have been widespread.) Many features called Negro can be found in the speech of whites, some in POOR WHITE dialects, some in aristocratic dialects. But it is clear that some features, particularly in the verb system and in intonation, had West African or Caribbean origin. What can be said unequivocally is that neither climate nor the shape of speech organs can be differentiating factors.

See H. Kurath, *Word Geography of Eastern U.S.* (1949); H. Kurath and R. I. McDavid, Jr., *Pronunciation of English in Atlantic States* (1961); E. B. Atwood, *Regional Vocabulary of Texas* (1962); G. R. Wood, *Vocabulary Change* (1971); and J. B. McMillan, *Annotated Bibliography of Southern American English* (1971). In progress are three monumental projects: a linguistic atlas of the Middle and South Atlantic states, being prepared under the direction of R. I. McDavid; a linguistic atlas of the Gulf states, under the direction of L. A. Pederson; and a dictionary of regional American English, by F. G. Cassidy.

JAMES B. MCMILLAN
University of Alabama

DICKINSON, JOHN (1732–1808), was born in Talbot County, Md., but his family moved to Dover, Del., in 1740. He abandoned a successful law practice for politics with the advent of the Revolution. Dickinson earned praise as "the penman of the Revolution" for his draft resolutions of the Stamp Act Congress (1765) and his enormously influential *Letters from a Farmer in Pennsylvania* (1767–1768); here he conceded the need for commercial regulation but denied Parliament's right to tax the colonies. His reputation was later shadowed by his seeming reluctance to make the final break from Britain: he is more often remembered for his Olive Branch Petition than his vigorous

Declaration of the Causes and Necessity of Taking Up Arms (1775). He would not support the DECLARATION OF INDEPENDENCE without better assurance of colonial unity and foreign support. And so John Adams sneered at that "certain piddling genius." But Dickinson helped draft the ARTICLES OF CONFEDERATION (1776), bore arms in the war, and served as president of the Delaware executive council (1781) and president of Pennsylvania (1782–1785). A Delaware signer of the Constitution, he successfully urged ratification in his "Fabius" letters. He was a founder of Dickinson College.

See C. J. Stillé, *Life of Dickinson* (1891); J. H. Powell, "Dickinson" (Ph.D. dissertation, University of Iowa, 1938); P. L. Ford (ed.), *Writings* (1891); T. Colbourn, *Pennsylvania Magazine of History and Biography* (July, 1959; July, Oct., 1962); and D. Jacobson, *Dickinson* (1965).

TREVOR COLBOURN
San Diego State University

DIES, MARTIN (1901–1972), congressman from Texas from 1931 to 1945 and 1953 to 1959, is best remembered as the first chairman of the U.S. House Committee on Un-American Activities. As the Second World War approached, he was able to get House approval for the special committee to investigate subversive elements that might endanger governmental principles guaranteed by the Constitution. Despite his original estimate that the investigation would not take more than seven months, the committee's life was extended by each Congress until 1945, the year of Dies's first retirement, when it was unexpectedly made a permanent committee. Under Dies's leadership the committee had a stormy existence, investigating hundreds of organizations, government agencies, and public events such as the Michigan sitdown strikes. As a conservative congressman, Dies fought against immigration, aliens, and minimum wage legislation. In 1952 he was nominated by both the Democratic and Republican parties for a seat as representative-at-large, where he stayed until 1958, when he chose not to seek reelection. Opposition prevented him from returning to a seat on his old committee, a bitter disappointment to him. In 1957 he made an unsuccessful bid for the U.S. Senate.

See G. N. Green, "Far Right Wing" (Ph.D. dissertation, Florida State University, 1967); and A. Alexander, *Antioch Review* (March, 1955).

DONALD W. WHISENHUNT
Eastern New Mexico University

DILLARD UNIVERSITY (New Orleans, La. 70122) enjoys the distinction of being simultaneously among the oldest and the youngest of predominantly black colleges. It was formed in 1935 by the merger of two institutions that dated back to 1869: New Orleans University (Methodist) and Straight College (Congregational). Its present name was taken to honor James Hardy Dillard, the former president of the JEANES FUND. It is a private, coeducational institution with an enrollment of approximately 1,000 students.

See New Orleans University, *70 Years of Service* (1937).

DISCIPLES OF CHRIST. One of the largest native American religious movements, this church traces its origins to early nineteenth-century reform movements led by Barton W. Stone (1772–1844) in Kentucky and Alexander Campbell (1788–1866) and his father Thomas (1763–1854) in Pennsylvania, Ohio, and western Virginia. Drawing members largely from the PRESBYTERIAN and BAPTIST churches, these two reformers united their efforts in 1832 to form a group known both as the Disciples of Christ and the Christian church. Local congregations often were called CHURCHES OF CHRIST.

The central doctrinal plea of the Disciples of Christ was the restoration of New Testament Christianity as a basis of Christian union. Disciples generally believed that this would be possible if all would wear a scriptural name such as "Christian" or "Disciple" and return to the pattern of the first-century church in doctrine, worship, and practice. The church grew rapidly in the nineteenth century, numbering nearly 200,000 by 1860 and reaching a membership of over 1.1 million in the religious census of 1906. It continued to be largely midwestern and southern, with 80 percent of its membership being in the nine states of Illinois, Indiana, Iowa, Kansas, Kentucky, Missouri, Ohio, Tennessee, and Texas.

In the twentieth century the church suffered two major divisions. In 1906 the religious census recognized the separation of the theologically conservative Churches of Christ. The theological issues that defined the rupture were conservative objections to the use of instrumental music in worship, the propriety of missionary and other religious societies, and other "innovations." In fact, the division was rooted in social and economic differences dating back to the slavery controversy and the Civil War. The separation of the more conservative Churches of Christ greatly weakened the Disciples in the Lower South, particularly outside the larger cities.

During the period from 1890 to 1920 a second division took shape, which led to the formation of the evangelical North American Convention of Christian Churches and the more liberal International Convention of the Disciples of Christ. The principal issues in this division were the right of the church to receive unbaptized members from other denominations (open membership) and the growing conflict over Darwinism and higher criticism. Increasingly, the machinery of the church came to be influenced by a group of young liberals associated with the Disciples Divinity House at the University of Chicago and a new journal, the *Christian Century* (1900–), which by the 1920s, still under Disciples leadership, had become the leading interdenominational liberal religious journal in the nation. The *Christian-Evangelist* (later the *Christian*) became the quasi-official paper of the more liberal International Convention, and the *Christian Standard* was the organ of the more conservative North American Convention. By the 1970s each group claimed between 1.5 and 2 million members and were numerous in the states of the Upper South. The North American Convention of Christian Churches remained a loose association of evangelical churches; the liberal group, recently named the General Assembly of the Christian Church (Disciples of Christ), went through a restructuring process in the 1970s that converted it into a representative but centralized denomination.

The various wings of the Disciples maintain many religious, benevolent, and educational organizations in the South. Several southern educational institutions—including Texas Christian University, Transylvania University, and Phillips University—were established by Disciples. Two of the seminaries of the General Assembly of the Christian Church are Brite Theological School, which is associated with TCU, and the College of the Bible in Lexington, Ky. The *Christian* is published in St. Louis, where the Bethany Press, the official publishing house of the General Assembly of Christian Churches, is located.

See L. McAllister and H. Tucker, *Journey in Faith* (1976); W. E. Garrison and A. T. DeGroot, *Disciples of Christ* (1948); J. D. Murch, *Christians Only* (1962); D. E. Harrell, *Social History of Disciples of Christ* (2 vols.; 1966–73); W. Tucker, *J. H. Garrison and Disciples of Christ* (1964); A. L. Ash, "Attitudes Toward Higher Criticism of Old Testament Among Disciples of Christ" (Ph.D. dissertation, University of Southern California, 1966); B. J. Humble, "Missionary Society Controversy, 1823–1875"

(Ph.D. dissertation, State University of Iowa, 1964); and Disciples of Christ Historical Society, Nashville, Tenn.

DAVID EDWIN HARRELL, JR.
University of Alabama, Birmingham

DISFRANCHISEMENT, the erection of barriers to voting high enough to exclude almost all blacks and many poor whites from the southern electorate, did not immediately follow the downfall of the Radical Republican regimes. Instead, in the post-Reconstruction era, fairly stable parties competed for the franchises of an active electorate comprising in most states a majority of the black and up to 90 percent of the white adult males. The South in this period was often the scene of fierce partisan battles between the Democrats and coalitions of blacks with poor hill-country whites, organized under the labels of the Republican, Union Labor, or Populist parties or as INDEPENDENT MOVEMENTS. To insulate the political system from these challenges to their hegemony, white Democratic politicians passed various disfranchisement schemes. The leaders of the disfranchisement movement were virtually all upper-class Democrats, nearly always from heavily Negro areas (the BLACK BELT), usually well-educated men whose socioeconomic profiles bore striking resemblances to social daguerreotypes of the antebellum and Redeemer "patricians." The opponents of disfranchisement were blacks, some white Democrats from the upland areas, and white members of parties opposed to the Democratic party, especially Populists and Republicans.

Democratic violence, intimidation, and chicanery played a large role in stifling opposition parties in the post-Reconstruction South, but the passage of disfranchising laws immediately curtailed political participation and usually decimated parties enemy to the Democrats. For example, of the 75 percent of the adult males (including an estimated 86 percent of the whites and 62 percent of the blacks) who turned out to vote in the Florida gubernatorial election of 1888, 40 percent succeeded in having their votes counted for the GOP candidate. In the next governor's race, after the passage of two disfranchising laws, turnout dropped to 39 percent, estimated black turnout to 11 percent, and the opposition percentage to 21 percent. Instead of directly causing the SOLID SOUTH, force and fraud usually only allowed Democrats to carry enough seats in the state legislatures to pass laws restricting the vote in elections for constitutional conventions delegates or in referenda on more stringent disfranchising laws.

The already-restricted electorate then ratified the harsh legal provisions—in elections often marked by a last orgy of fraud, to be sure—and the poll taxes and literacy tests then finished off all vestiges of a democratically competitive polity. Statewide, Democratic WHITE PRIMARIES succeeded, rather than preceded, disfranchisement and served mainly to channel potential opposition movements into the Democratic party.

Of the often ingenious restrictive statutes, the most effective were the POLL TAX, which inhibited the poor of both races from voting; the literacy test, a measure designed to institute disfranchisement through discriminatory administration by voting registrars; and the secret ballot and multiple-box laws, both of which were de facto literacy tests. Registration laws, though they often had a major short-term disfranchising impact, were employed chiefly just before crucial referenda on more long-lasting restrictive measures to slice off segments of the electorate that might oppose the Democrats' schemes. The potency of each disfranchising device depended on its exact provisions and the manner of its administration. Thus, the most powerful were the cumulative poll tax, which had to be paid for three or more years preceding the election; the Virginia literacy test, which consisted of writing out from memory, on a blank sheet of paper, the answers to a long, complex questionnaire; the EIGHT-BOX LAW, which required the votes for each of eight officers to be deposited in separate ballot boxes; and the strict Australian ballot law, which contained no party designations and arranged the names of all candidates alphabetically by office. Each of these devices hit the poor and illiterate or semiliterate with crushing force.

Southern blacks in this so-called age of accommodation fought back against disfranchisement. They held protest meetings in four states, petitioned or spoke out in state legislatures or constitutional conventions in seven states, organized voters in the referenda on suffrage amendments in six states, and brought suits in Congress and the courts in five states. Although black activism sometimes postponed disfranchisement, the protests, petitions, and campaign activity could not prevail against the overwhelming power of the disfranchisers. And the efforts of black leaders to bring their case before Congress and the courts were ultimately unavailing in these forums as well.

Thus, two cases from Virginia were declared moot and a Louisiana case sponsored by the Afro-American Council never reached the higher courts, though the challenge to the 1901 Alabama constitution, brought in behalf of Jackson W. Giles by a group of Montgomery black Republican activists and funded and directed secretly by BOOKER T. WASHINGTON, elicited one of Justice Oliver Wendell Holmes's craftiest opinions (*Giles* v. *Harris*, 189 U.S. 475 [1901]). His opinion for a six-to-three majority of the U.S. Supreme Court cleverly impaled the blacks on the horns of a false dilemma: how could the Court require Giles to be registered at the same time as it threw out the provisions of the Alabama constitution, which governed registration? Adequate remedy, Holmes concluded, could come only from the state of Alabama or the "legislative and political department of the government of the United States."

Although *Giles* and other court cases are comparatively well known, the efforts of such obscure black men as Cornelius J. Jones to overturn black disfranchisement through congressional action have been largely forgotten. A Greenville lawyer and former Mississippi state legislator, Jones not only challenged his state's racist suffrage provisions in the courts in WILLIAMS V. MISSISSIPPI, but carried his case to Congress in 1896 and 1899, arguing that the whole election procedure in Mississippi was so tainted by the disfranchisement of blacks, contrary to the Fifteenth Amendment, that no Mississippi congressman from a district containing a majority of blacks was entitled to his seat. The House Elections Committee turned Jones down. Although aware of the racially discriminatory intent and impact of suffrage laws enacted by 1902 in nearly all southern states, the semijudicial Elections Committee hesitated to declare the laws unconstitutional, for such action would have eventuated in the unseating of perhaps a third of the congressmen from the South. Probably for the same reason the House defeated the "Crumpacker bill," which proposed to encourage the South to repeal laws restricting the suffrage by invoking the Fourteenth Amendment to reduce the representation of states that had disfranchised large numbers of voters.

The climax of the per se congressional challenges came in a 1904 case brought against South Carolina Congressman ASBURY F. LEVER by a black, Alexander D. Dantzler, and argued by a former treasurer of the Republican National Committee, W. W. Dudley. Refusing to seat Dantzler, the Republican majority on the committee at the same time refrained from declaring Lever legitimately elected. The issue, they piously declared a year after Holmes's decision in the widely noticed *Giles* case, was one for the U.S. Supreme Court.

See J. M. Kousser, *Shaping of Southern Politics* (1974); C. V. Woodward, *Origins of New South* (1971); V. O. Key, *Southern Politics* (1949); J. M. McPherson, *Blacks in America* (1971); and I. A. Newby, *Jim Crow's Defense* (1965), all contain bibliographies. Also see P. Lewinson, *Race, Class and Party* (1965); W. A. Mabry, "Disfranchisement of Negro" (Ph.D. dissertation, Duke, 1933); F. D. Ogden, *Poll Tax in South* (1958); V. P. De Santis, *Republicans Face Southern Question* (1959); S. P. Hirshson, *Farewell to Bloody Shirt* (1962); R. W. Logan, *Betrayal of Negro* (1965); A. Meier, *Negro Thought in America* (1963); and studies of individual states and leaders.

J. MORGAN KOUSSER
California Institute of Technology

DISMAL SWAMP. A densely wooded unique depression—its heart a circular lake draining outward through five streams and innumerable canals—the 6,000-year-old, legend-haunted, 750-square-mile Dismal Swamp, once thrice the size, has been part of southern history since its discovery in 1666 by William Drummond, later the governor of North Carolina. Christened by William Byrd while surveying the Virginia–North Carolina boundary during 1728, the swamp had economic possibilities for the movement of timber and goods that excited George Washington. The resulting Dismal Swamp Canal is America's oldest surviving artificial waterway. Completed in 1828, after 44 years of study, construction, and improvement, the 22-mile, privately owned canal and its feeders flourished for 31 years, regularly trafficked by thousands of freight and passenger vessels, until losing its business to the toll-free Great Bridge Canal. In 1929, the federal government purchased the canal and added it to our free inland waterway system. Meanwhile, the swamp became a focus of interest to military men (vainly hoping the canal would circumvent the blockades of the Napoleonic wars), runaway slaves in search of refuge, poets, writers, journalists, scientists, developers, and naturalists.

The swamp's unequaled wildlife proved its savior. Once home to many now-extinct species, the swamp has over 50 varieties of native birds, 20 species of mammals, 38 types of fish, and 17 kinds of snakes. Among many Orthoptera are 91 kinds of butterflies. There are 3,000 different flora. Overdrainage and fire endanger both the swamp and its inhabitants, and since the 1960s pressure from ecologists and legislators has worked to preserve the swamp. In 1972, Congress authorized a study to determine the feasibility of its protection. This, plus the 50,000-acre gift of the Union Camp Corporation in 1973 "for the preservation of a natural wilderness," may augur a happy ecological future.

See A. C. Brown, *Dismal Swamp Canal* (1946), best description; H. J. Davis, *Great Dismal Swamp* (1962), interesting general account; A. Duke, *Dismal Swamp Wildlife* (1973), excellent on ecology, bibliography; and B. H. Yarborough, *Great Dismal* (1965), succinct, excellent bibliography.

E. GRANT MEADE
Old Dominion University

DIXIE. Although this is almost universally known as a name for the South and as a song popularly associated with the region, considerable uncertainty clouds both the time and place of the term's origin. One version that once enjoyed considerable currency in the North alleged that the word was originally used by former slaves of a Mr. Dix or Dixy of Manhattan Island to describe a paradise on earth for Negroes. A second but equally unsupported version is based upon the bank notes of the Citizens' Bank & Trust Company of New Orleans. All notes issued by this bank were printed in both French and English. Consequently, its ten-dollar notes, alleged to be the most common denomination circulated, bore the French word *dix* on the back. This explanation hypothesizes that people along the Mississippi called these notes "dixes" and spoke of New Orleans as "dixes land" and that through time "dixes" became "dixie" and "Dixie land" came to mean the whole of the South.

The earliest printed record of the term's use was in a play presented in 1850 entitled *The United States Mail and Dixie in Difficulty*, Dixie being the play's principal black character. Like Pompey and Cuffee, Dixie, with its rhythmic sound, may have been a familiar nickname for Negro characters portrayed by blackface minstrels. Daniel D. Emmett (1815–1904), the composer of the song and a native of Mount Vernon, Ohio, was himself one of the foremost minstrel men of the antebellum era. After writing the song as a "walk 'round," Emmett explained that he had used "Dixie's Land" as northern showmen used it to refer to the South. Thus Dixie, both as a term and as a song, probably first emerged from behind the gaslights and the burned cork of minstrelsy.

Whatever the origin of the expression, Emmett's song popularized the term and added it to the national vocabulary. After the song's first performance by Bryant's Minstrel Troupe in New York on April 4, 1859, so popular did it become

that several versions were printed and several writers claimed authorship. Emmett even had difficulty acquiring a copyright. During the Civil War, Frances J. Crosby composed a set of lyrics and retitled her song "Dixie for the Union." Something approximating Emmett's version of the piece had been played at the inauguration of Jefferson Davis, although General Albert Pike later transposed the lyrics to provide a more dignified anthem for the Confederacy:

Southrons hear your country call you
Up! lest worse than death befall you
  To arms! To arms! To arms in Dixie!
Lo! all the beacon fires are lighted,
Let all hearts be now united!
  To arms! To arms! To arms in Dixie!
  Advance the flag of Dixie.

CHORUS
For Dixie's land we'll take our stand
And live and die for Dixie!
  To arms! To arms!
And conquer peace for Dixie
  To arms! To arms!
And conquer peace for Dixie!

Appomattox marked the conclusion of the Civil War, but "Dixie," because of its catchy melody, continued to be under the assault of new lyrics. In 1917, for example, amid America's embarrassing discovery that it lacked a national anthem, one Mary Lowe Woods Orvis suggested that these lyrics, set to "Dixie," be adopted:

There's a Land we Love with a deep devotion
Pilgrim-sought across the ocean
All the way, "U.S.A.,"
Hear us say, "Thine for aye."

There's a Flag we love with a holy madness
Love in Sorrow as in gladness
Everyday, "U.S.A."
Hear us say, "Thine for aye."

CHORUS
'Tis a land of milk and honey, And free to all
From every race they've sought this place
To live and die for freedom—
O' Lord, most high, Keep this the home of freedom!

During these numerous rewritings of Emmett's song, sure knowledge of its original lyrics has in all probability been irretrievably lost. But several versions, all claiming to be the original, are so similar that they can be regarded as reasonably accurate. The following version appeared in the July 26, 1913, issue of *Literary Digest* with the claim that it was printed from a photographic copy of Emmett's original:

I wish I was in de land of cotton
'Simmon seed and sandy bottom
  Look away, look away, away Dixieland!
Dixie land, where I was born in

Early on one frosty mornin'
   Look away, look away, away Dixieland!

Old missus marry Will de Weaber
William way a gay deceaber
   Look away, look away, away Dixieland!
When he put his arm around 'er
He look as fierce as a forty-pounder,
   Look away, look away, away Dixieland!

His face was like a butcher's cleaber
But dat did not seem to greeb 'er,
   Look away, look away, away Dixieland!
Will run away, missus took a decline, o'
Her face was de color of bacon shine, o',
   Look away, look away, away Dixieland!

While missus libbed she libbed in clober,
When she died she died all ober,
   Look away, look away, away Dixieland!
How could she act such a foolish part, o'
And marry a man to break her heart, o',
   Look away, look away, away Dixieland!

Buckwheat cakes an' stony batter,
Makes you fat or a little fatter,
   Look away, look away, away Dixieland!
There's a health to the next al' missus
And de gals dat wants to kiss us,
   Look away, look away, away Dixieland!

Now if you want to drive 'way sorrow,
Come an' hear dis song to-marrow,
   Look away, look away, away Dixieland!
Den hoe it down an' scratch your grabble
To Dixie land I'm bound to trabble,
   Look away, look away, away Dixieland!

CHORUS
Den I wish I was in Dixie
   Hooray! Hooray!
In Dixie land we'll take our stand
   To lib and die in Dixie,
Away, away, away down South in Dixie
Away, away, away down South in Dixie.

See H. Nathan, *Musical Quarterly* (Jan., 1949), an informative study of both song and term; for other versions of Emmett's "original" lyrics, see *Century* (Oct., 1895), and R. Thornton, *American Glossary* (1962).

DIXIECRAT PARTY. Angered by the national Democratic administration's "increasing liberalism," Mississippi's Governor Fielding Wright and other southerners organized a revolt in 1948 to counteract the civil rights program espoused by President HARRY TRUMAN. Influenced by Charles Collins' *Whither Solid South?* (1947), which urged that southerners reassess their affiliation with the national Democratic party, Wright advocated holding a South-wide conclave to discuss the idea's possibilities. In February, 1948, the SOUTHERN GOVERNORS' CONFERENCE rejected Wright's proposal, preferring instead to seek compromises within the national Democratic party. When a meeting with leaders of the Democratic National Committee failed to produce satisfactory assurances, however, the governors or their representatives and delegations from 12 states and Washington, D.C., decided to "demand" a states' rights plank for the Democratic platform and block Truman's nomination at the national convention if possible.

Failing in both efforts at Philadelphia, the "states' righters" reassembled in Birmingham, Ala. They decided to support neither Truman nor Thomas Dewey, the Republican candidate, but to nominate their own men, block a majority vote in the electoral college, and throw the election into the House of Representatives, where they would bargain for concessions. Governor STROM THURMOND of South Carolina and Wright were "recommended" as presidential and vice-presidential nominees, respectively, to the southern states' Democratic conventions, which the "dissidents" anticipated subjugating to themselves. Later a formal convention in Houston, Tex., gave assent to the action taken in Birmingham. Branding themselves States' Rights Democrats, participants in these activities were dubbed "Dixiecrats" by Bill Weisner of the Charlotte *News*, and the name stuck.

Both men campaigned vigorously for states' rights and segregation, maintaining that they were the "true" Democratic party's candidates. Although they exploited the racial issue to appeal to the prejudices of southern whites, their major theme was that individual states should control their own criminal, franchise, social, and work laws. The movement was strong throughout the South, but Truman won the presidency (ELECTION OF 1948), and the Dixiecrats carried only Mississippi, Alabama, South Carolina, and Louisiana, where they had captured the regular Democratic machinery. Once defeated, the movement disintegrated, but its activities heightened southern racial tensions for a time and weakened the grip of the Democratic party on the region, providing the basis for party realignment and some subsequent shifts to the Republican party.

See States' Rights Democrats Papers, Department of Archives and History, Jackson, Miss., excellent; R. C. Ethridge, "Dixiecratic Movement" (Ph.D. dissertation, Mississippi State, 1971); and G. C. Ness, "States' Rights Movement" (Ph.D. dissertation, Duke, 1972).

RICHARD C. ETHRIDGE
East Central Junior College, Decatur, Miss.

DIXON, THOMAS (1864–1946), best known for his fictional accounts of Reconstruction, was born of poor, farming parents near Shelby, N.C. He did not begin a formal education until he was thirteen years old, but, before his twentieth birthday, he had completed his bachelor's and his master's degrees and had begun work on a doctorate in history at Johns Hopkins University. Abandoning history after his first year of study, he pursued in turn careers on the stage, in law, and in politics before settling, in 1877, on the ministry.

The forceful and dramatic eloquence of his sermons earned for him considerable respect among members of his nondenominational Protestant congregations in North Carolina, Boston, and New York City. In 1899, however, he retired from the pulpit to launch a new career as a lecturer and novelist. His first two novels, *The Leopard's Spots* (1902) and *The Clansman* (1905), vividly depicted Reconstruction's alleged horrors of rape, corruption, and unchecked violence. The instant successes of both novels were followed by equally popular productions on the dramatic stage. Dixon tried vainly for two years to produce a film version of *The Clansman* before meeting David Wark Griffith in 1913. Their collaboration produced *The Birth of a Nation*, a movie radically different from the slapstick comedy of the times and the first to capitalize fully on the artistic and dramatic potentialities of the screen.

Commercial release of the film was preceded by private showings in New York and in Washington, D.C.: one for film critics and censors, a second for WOODROW WILSON and his cabinet, and another for members of the U.S. Supreme Court and Congress. Wilson, a friend of Dixon's since meeting him in graduate school at Johns Hopkins, was ecstatic. The historian-turned-president pronounced *Birth of a Nation* "like writing history with lightning. . . . My only regret is that it is all so terribly true." Other viewers, conceding the dramatic force of the film's photography, denounced it as "loathsome" and "indecently foul" for its glorification of the KU KLUX KLAN and its prejudicial portrayal of blacks.

Despite Dixon's admiration for the Klan of Reconstruction, he was an outspoken critic of the twenties' organization of the same name. *Birth of a Nation*, however, was the peak of his career. His popularity declined after World War I. The great crash of 1929 destroyed most of his accumulated wealth; and novels, such as *The Flaming Sword* (1939), warning of the threat posed by international communism, failed to reestablish his reputation. When he died in a Raleigh hotel room, he was penniless and virtually forgotten.

See R. A. Cook, *Fire from the Flint: Careers of T. Dixon* (1968); F. G. Davenport, *Journal of Southern History* (Aug., 1970); and J. Z. Wright, "Dixon: Mind of a Southern Apologist" (Ph.D. dissertation, George Peabody College, 1967).

DODD, WILLIAM EDWARD (1869–1940), was born and reared in North Carolina. Educated at the Virginia Polytechnic Institute and the University of Leipzig, where he received a Ph.D. degree in history in 1899, Dodd taught at Randolph-Macon College (1900–1908) and the University of Chicago (1908–1933). During these years, he established himself as one of America's leading historians of the Old South. His numerous books included biographies of NATHANIEL MACON (1903) and JEFFERSON DAVIS (1907), sketches of THOMAS JEFFERSON and JOHN C. CALHOUN in *Statesmen of the Old South* (1911), *Expansion and Conflict, 1828–1865* (1915), a volume in the *Riverside History of the United States*, *The Cotton Kingdom* (1919), a volume in the Yale Chronicle series, *Woodrow Wilson and His Work* (1920), and *Struggles for Democracy* (1937), the first but only volume in a projected four-volumed history of the Old South. Dodd was elected president of the American Historical Association in 1934. During these years, he was also active in the progressive wing of the Democratic party. In June, 1933, Franklin Roosevelt named him ambassador to Germany, where he served until December, 1937. An early and persistent foe of Adolf Hitler, Dodd provided FDR with perceptive descriptions of Nazi deeds and goals. After returning to the United States in 1938, Dodd became a leading opponent of nazism until his death.

ROBERT DALLEK
University of California, Los Angeles

DONELSON, ANDREW JACKSON (1799–1871), nephew of ANDREW JACKSON, became a member of his uncle's household when orphaned in 1804. He graduated from West Point in 1820 and served as his uncle's aide-de-camp in the Florida campaign of 1820–1821. He resigned from the army in 1822 and was admitted to the bar in 1823. During Jackson's administration, he was the president's private secretary and assisted Jackson in the drafting of several important state papers. His wife Emily served as Jackson's hostess in the White House. After Jackson's retirement he supported JAMES K. POLK and proved instrumental in securing for Polk the Democratic nomination in 1844. President JOHN TYLER appointed Donelson chargé d'affaires to the Republic of Texas in August, 1844; Donelson succeeded in winning Texan acceptance of American annexation in March, 1845. In recognition of his success, in 1846 Polk appointed him minister to Prussia, in which position he served until 1848, when he was named minister to the German Confederation. He was recalled by ZACHARY TAYLOR and returned to the United States in 1850. He counseled moderation when southerners resisted federal restriction of slavery expansion. At the NASHVILLE CONVENTION of 1850, Donelson unsuccessfully proposed resolutions antagonistic to those of the extremists. The KNOW-NOTHING PARTY nominated him for vice-president in 1856. He practiced law in Memphis after 1858 and was a southern Unionist.

See manuscripts, Library of Congress; R. B. Satterfield, "Andrew Jackson Donelson" (Ph.D. dissertation, Johns Hopkins, 1962); and St. G. L. Sioussat (ed.), *Tennessee Historical Magazine* (June, Dec., 1917).

KENNETH W. KELLER
Ohio State University, Marion

DONIPHAN, ALEXANDER WILLIAM (1808–1887),

was born in Mason County, Ky. After graduating from Augusta College, he studied law and then opened an office at Lexington, Mo., in 1830. Three years later he moved to Liberty, Mo., where he rose to prominence because of his ability to sway a jury. Three times he was elected to the state legislature (1836, 1840, 1854) and by 1838 had become a brigadier general in the state militia. That year, on orders of the governor, he drove the Mormons out of Missouri. During the Mexican War Doniphan led the 1st Regiment of Missouri Mounted Volunteers to Santa Fe as part of Stephen Kearny's Army of the West. Afterward he marched his Missourians south to Chihuahua City, then east to link with ZACHARY TAYLOR's forces, winning victories at the battles of El Brazito and Sacramento. After the war he resumed his law practice and served as a commissioner at the WASHINGTON PEACE CONFERENCE in 1861. He refused a general's commission in both the Union and Confederate armies, staying out of the Civil War. He died at Richmond, Mo.

See D. C. Allen, *Doniphan* (1897); and R. W. Settle, *Doniphan* (1947). Excellent personal reminiscences include W. E. Connelley, *Doniphan's Expedition* (1907); F. S. Edwards, *Campaign in New Mexico* (1847); J. T. Hughes, *Doniphan's Expedition* (1847); and A. Wislizenus, *Memoir* (1848).

ODIE B. FAULK
Oklahoma State University

DOTHAN, ALA. (pop. 36,733),

in Houston County in the southeastern part of the state, originally was the site of a campground used by both the Alabama and the CREEK INDIANS. During the 1830s and 1840s, settlers heading toward the Tombigbee began using the clearing and its spring as a campground, and by 1858 nine families had made it their permanent residence. It was named for a biblical quotation (Gen. 37:17, "Let us go to Dothan") and incorporated in 1885. After the Alabama Midland Railway reached the village in 1889, lumbering and turpentining brought its first period of real growth. Today it is the market for area livestock and cotton and peanut growers and a center of varied light industry.

See F. S. Watson, *Hub of Wiregrass, 1903–1972* (1972); K. Baxley, *Some Early Highlights in History of Dothan* (1960); O. L. Tompkins, *Wiregrass Sagas* (1942); and *Dothan Eagle* (Oct. 27, 1953; Aug. 15, 1969).

DOUGHFACE

was a term of derision leveled, mostly in the antebellum period, against northern politicians with prosouthern sympathies. It was first used by the acid-tongued JOHN RANDOLPH of Roanoke, Va., on March 3, 1820, during the congressional debates leading to the passage of the MISSOURI COMPROMISE. Randolph bitterly opposed the compromise, even though it was supported by most other southerners. He used the epithet to deride northern congressmen who supported the South on the measure, especially three members who supposedly did not have the courage to vote but simply absented themselves from Congress to make passage of the bill possible. He was alluding to a custom among young pranksters of wearing masks made of dough to frighten people. It sometimes happened, said Randolph, that the more timid of such "doughfaces," when they looked in a mirror, were shaken with fear by their own repulsiveness. Similarly, these northern congressmen, in voting on the Missouri bill, also lacked courage, feared what they themselves had helped to create, and therefore did not stand faithfully by their antislavery principles.

The term soon became popular in the North, especially with the antislavery Whigs and later the Republicans, who used it effectively as a term of contempt for any northern politician who lent support to southern causes. By the 1830s and 1840s users of the appellation seem to have lost sight of the original derivation of the word but nevertheless continued to feel that it fit the political situation. Any northern politician who failed to oppose slavery had a character like dough—easily molded and without firmness or strong principles. Sometimes the epithet was even spelled "doeface," suggesting that such northerners had the timidity of a female deer. Among the prominent politicians who were often stigmatized as doughfaces were Stephen A. Douglas, Franklin Pierce, Lewis Cass, and James Buchanan. The gibe was used only infrequently after the Civil War.

See G. Moore, *Missouri Controversy* (1953), good discussion of original doughfaces; H. Sperber and J. N. Tidwell, *American Speech* (May, 1950); F. H. Hodder, *Nation* (March 4, 1915); and H. Sperber and T. Trittschuh, *American Political Terms* (1962).

DOUGLASS, FREDERICK (1817–1895), born and reared on a large Maryland plantation, witnessed the peculiar institution from the various perspectives of houseboy, field hand, slave breaker's victim, and urban hireling. In Baltimore he acquired the literacy, consciousness, and contacts that made his escape from slavery all but inevitable. In 1838 he fled to Massachusetts, where he found a mixed reception. White workers in New Bedford refused to work with him, but white abolitionists made him their prize exhibit. By the mid-1840s, Douglass became a power in his own right. Perhaps the finest American orator of the nineteenth century, he gained an international reputation, especially after the publication of his first autobiography in 1845 and his subsequent tour of the British Isles. Such independence ultimately destroyed his relationship with William Lloyd Garrison, who in 1847 advised Douglass against launching the *North Star* and by 1851 condemned him as traitorous for supporting political abolitionism as opposed to Garrison's moral suasion.

Increasingly, during the crises of the 1850s, Douglass acknowledged that abolition would require violence. He refused to accompany John Brown on the HARPERS FERRY RAID, but through the force of his militant rhetoric he nevertheless joined Brown as a symbol of terror in the mind of the Old South. He welcomed the Civil War, and, however unsure others might have been on the issues, Douglass had no doubts. This was a war over slavery and the ultimate place of black people in American society. Along with other radical abolitionists he pressed Abraham Lincoln toward the use of black troops and a redefinition of the war. His zeal for an abolitionist war was surpassed only by his zeal for Radical Reconstruction, and he would spend the rest of his life trying to salvage the promise of emancipation and Reconstruction.

He was a thoroughgoing American liberal who never questioned the American ideal but asked only that it be extended to everyone, women as well as blacks. He had no quarrel with the form of American economic and political institutions, and, once he found himself marginally included, he became a middle-class businessman and a staunch Republican, receiving three federal appointments (U.S. marshal, 1877–1881; recorder of deeds for Washington, D.C., 1881–1885; and minister to Haiti, 1889–1891). His larger legacy remains secure as the progenitor of the twentieth-century civil rights movement, whether it be in his tactics of passive resistance in desegregation or in his call for retaliatory violence in abolition. He also acknowledged, as early as the 1840s, that the race problem was national rather than southern.

See F. Douglass, *Narrative* (1845), *My Bondage and My Freedom* (1855), best on antebellum years, and *Life and Times* (1881); P. Foner, *Life and Writings of F. Douglass* (4 vols.; 1955), most comprehensive, and supplementary Vol. 5 (1975); B. Quarles, *F. Douglass* (1948), best single volume; R. L. Factor, *Black Response to America* (1970), interpretative; and A. Meier, *Negro Thought in America* (1963), analytical.

WALTER B. WEARE
University of Wisconsin, Milwaukee

DOWDEY, CLIFFORD SHIRLEY, JR. (1904–), born in Richmond, Va., received his formal education in the local school system and at Columbia University, which he attended from 1923 to 1925. The author or editor of 11 volumes on southern history, he writes beautifully and is sometimes capable of brilliant hypotheses concerning the motivations of historical figures. Both of these attributes are the result, at least in part, of his earlier experiences as an editor and novelist. (He has been on the editorial staffs of several magazines and published nine novels.) Because Dowdey grew up in the former Confederate capital—where his elderly relatives frequently entertained him with their firsthand tales of "the War"—and had Robert E. Lee's biographer DOUGLAS SOUTHALL FREEMAN as a long-time friend, it is only natural that the bulk of his history volumes would deal with the Confederacy and Lee. But according to some professionally trained historians, Dowdey's work can be criticized for its paucity of direct documentation and its excessive sympathy for what they call "the Southern viewpoint."

See C. S. Dowdey, *Experiment in Rebellion* (1946), *Land They Fought For* (1955), *Death of a Nation* (1958), and *Lee* (1965).

JOHN F. REIGER
University of Miami

DRAKE, CHARLES DANIEL (1811–1892), son of a Cincinnati physician, arrived at St. Louis in 1834. He entered the practice of law but was not a recognized leader of the local bar. Following a brief residence in Cincinnati, he returned in 1850 to St. Louis and shortly became active in politics. By 1859 the Democrats elected him to the Missouri house of representatives. He took an active part against the secession movement and in 1862 was elected to the Unionist state convention. A presidential elector on the Abraham Lincoln ticket in 1864, he was also vice-president of the state's constitutional convention of 1865. Elected to the U.S. Senate in 1867, he actively supported the Radical program of Reconstruction. During his term as senator he caused an amendment to an appropriations bill declaring that no payment for damages sustained in the Civil War should be made unless the claimant had filed an oath that he had never been in rebellion against the federal government. This clause was afterward invalidated by the U.S. Supreme Court. Drake resigned from the Senate to accept the position of chief justice of the U.S. Court of Claims (1870–1885).

See W. R. Jackson, *Missouri Democrats* (1935), I; T. Sharp, *History of St. Louis* (1883); *Congressional Globe*, 40th Cong., 2nd Sess.; Drake Papers, Missouri Historical Society in Columbia and St. Louis; and W. Williams and F. C. Shoemaker, *Missouri* (1930), II.

GOSSIE H. HUDSON
Lincoln University

DRAPETOMANIA, diagnosed in 1851 by a New Orleans physician and derived from the Greek *drapetes* (a runaway), was a mental affliction of slaves desiring freedom. This "mania" for liberty could, Dr. Samuel W. Cartwright asserted, be avoided by master-slave relations neither unbearably harsh nor too bearably soft. His "Goldilocks" theory of slave treatment purported to induce the grateful submissiveness ordained by God for the "sons of Canaan"—an ordination proved, said Cartwright, by the "anatomical conformation" of the black's knee being "more flexed" (and more suited for bending low) "than any other kind." Like his cure for another Negro "disease," acting "like a senseless automaton" (Cartwright prescribed a bath, anointing the body with oil, slapping it in "with a broad leather strap," and weight lifting), the remedy did not stand the test of time. Medical historians' verdict is that Cartwright's stronger suit was imaginative diagnosis, his weaker one, significant societal healing.

See S. W. Cartwright, *De Bow's Review* (Sept., 1851); and K. M. Stampp, *Peculiar Institution* (1956).

A. E. KEIR NASH
University of California, Santa Barbara

DRAW DAY. This was the first Monday of each month, the day that the Confederate government issued rations to feed the destitute families of its soldiers who had not been paid or had died in service. The practice was revived by the federal government during Reconstruction to care for both blacks and whites impoverished as a result of the war. Draw day coincided with "sale day," the regular time for public auctions in the South.

See *Harper's* (May, 1868).

DRAYTON FAMILY of South Carolina was part of a clan of six planter families who were extraordinarily influential in the affairs of the colony and state in the eighteenth century. The members of the family were descended from Thomas Drayton, who came from Barbados in 1679. Two of his grandsons, John and Thomas, married sisters, the daughters of William Bull. John's son was William Henry Drayton (1742–1779); Thomas' son was William Drayton (1732–1790).

William Henry Drayton, a member of the commons house of assembly in the late 1760s, found himself in disagreement with the prevailing denunciation of the British imperial policy. In 1769 he wrote several articles in the *South Carolina Gazette* sharply disagreeing with nonimportation, the weapon used to bring pressure on the British to rescind the Townshend duties. By thus swimming against the tide, Drayton became so unpopular that he and his family sailed for England, and in 1769 he was received at court with gratitude for his loyalty. He had reason to suppose that he would be rewarded for his fidelity by preferment in offices of power and profit upon his return in 1771 to South Carolina, but it was not to be so. Recommended for a judgeship and a postmaster generalship, he was appointed to neither. This disappointment may have been a large factor in his switch from Loyalist to ardent and radical supporter of the American defiance. Drayton was among the first prominent colonists to call for complete separation from Great Britain. He subsequently served the state as chief justice and as delegate to the CONTINENTAL CONGRESS.

William Henry's double first cousin, William Drayton, practiced law for several years in South

Carolina and moved to East Florida soon after the Floridas became British possessions. He served as a member of the council and as chief justice, but repeatedly quarreled with the royal governor and was suspended from his offices. Although suspected of attachment to the patriot cause, he remained loyal to the crown. When Charleston fell to the British, Drayton returned to his home state and remained there for the rest of his life. The prominence of his family and friends was sufficient for him to be forgiven his Toryism, and he held various judicial positions in South Carolina.

The next generation included two notable Draytons: William (1776–1846), son of William, a lawyer, congressman, and antinullifier; and John (1766–1822), son of William Henry, governor of South Carolina at the beginning of the nineteenth century.

See W. M. Dabney and M. Dargan, *W. H. Drayton and American Revolution* (1962); M. E. Sirmans, *Colonial South Carolina* (1966); J. Drayton, *Memoirs of American Revolution* (1821); W. E. Drayton, *Letters of Freeman* (1771); and W. H. Drayton, *Letters from Free-Man of South Carolina* (1774).

WILLIAM M. DABNEY
University of New Mexico

DRED SCOTT V. SANDFORD (19 How. 393 [1857]) involved the status of a Missouri slave taken by his master to reside in a free state (Illinois) and a free territory (Wisconsin) and thence back to Missouri. The U.S. Supreme Court declared Scott still to be a slave. Chief Justice ROGER B. TANEY's opinion, which he and most contemporaries took to be for the Court, held that: (1) no black person descended from slaves was or could be a citizen of the United States and that consequently blacks could not sue in federal courts; and (2) the MISSOURI COMPROMISE (and inferentially any congressional prohibition of slavery in the territories) violated the Fifth Amendment's prohibition of taking property without due process of law. In obiter dicta, Taney claimed that Congress was the "trustee" for the people of the states in the territories, that it could not "authorize" a territorial legislature to exclude slavery, and that it had "the duty of guarding and protecting the [slave] owner in his rights," thus endorsing constitutional theories of JOHN C. CALHOUN, WILLIAM LOWNDES YANCEY, and other southern spokesmen.

Each of the nine justices rendered an opinion; seven concurred in the judgment. Thus there ensued a yet-unresolved professional and scholarly dispute as to exactly what *Dred Scott* held. Justice

Benjamin R. Curtis, in dissent, refuted the faulty historical assumptions that underlay Taney's opinion, and he was echoed in rebuttals by northern lawyers, jurists, and scholars. In defiance of the decision, Congress in 1862 abolished slavery in all American territories. The Fourteenth Amendment (ratified 1868) conferred national and state citizenship on all persons born or naturalized in the United States.

The *Dred Scott* decision was one event of many that precipitated secession and civil war. It encouraged southern political leaders like Senators ALBERT G. BROWN and JEFFERSON DAVIS to demand that Congress affirmatively establish and protect slavery in the territories. But it split the national Democratic party, since it implicitly invalidated Stephen A. Douglas' POPULAR SOVEREIGNTY position and intensified the antagonism between the southern and Douglas factions that produced the 1860 rift. It voided the principal raison d'être of the Republican party as well, and Abraham Lincoln urged that the decision be reversed. Several northern state supreme courts repudiated its premises; Vermont's legislature nullified some of its doctrines by statute. South Carolina justified secession because of this northern defiance in its Declaration of Causes of Secession (1860).

Taney's opinion has been severely criticized by modern authorities, including Edward S. Corwin, Charles Evans Hughes, and Arthur Bestor. It diminished his reputation, but did not greatly weaken the institutional power of the Supreme Court. Taney's Fifth Amendment argument was later seen as a benchmark in the post-Reconstruction emergence of substantive due process.

See Dred Scott Papers, Missouri Historical Society, St. Louis; S. I. Kutler, *Dred Scott Decision* (1967), anthology with good bibliography; V. C. Hopkins, *Dred Scott's Case* (1951); A. Nevins, *Emergence of Lincoln* (1950); W. Ehrlich, "Dred Scott Case" (Ph.D. dissertation, Washington University, 1950); C. B. Swisher, *Roger B. Taney* (1936), defends Taney, and *History of Supreme Court: Taney Period, 1836–64* (1974); E. S. Corwin, *American Historical Review* (Oct., 1911); A. Bestor, *Journal of Illinois State Historical Society* (Summer, 1961); and F. S. Allis, in H. S. Hughes, *Teachers of History* (1954), excellent historiographical survey.

WILLIAM M. WIECEK
University of Missouri

DREW, GEORGE FRANKLIN (1827–1900), although born in New Hampshire, is associated with Florida by political reputation. During the Civil War, he was engaged in the lumber business in Ellaville, Fla., where despite Unionist sympathies he traded extensively with Confederates. In 1876, state Democrats nominated him for governor as an ideal compromise candidate who could unite all white factions against the divided Republicans. His victory in the disputed Florida ELECTION OF 1876 "redeemed" the state from Republican control.

His major accomplishments in office were negative (REDEEMER GOVERNMENTS). He substantially reduced state expenditures by cutting salaries of state officials and by leasing convicts to private employers in order to eliminate the $40,000 annually spent on the state penitentiary. Such economies permitted reductions in the ad valorem tax rate. His proposals for uniform tax assessment, election reforms, and the creation of a state health board died, however, in the state legislature. Although his administration served well the interests of conservative Democrats, they did not renominate him. He had served the purpose for which he was chosen, to unite whites and end Reconstruction rule, and in 1881 Drew returned to his lumber business.

See E. C. Williamson, "Florida Politics, 1877–1893" (Ph.D. dissertation, University of Pennsylvania, 1954), and *Florida Historical Quarterly* (Jan., 1960); J. H. Shofner, *Florida Historical Quarterly* (April, 1970); and Drew Letterbooks, Florida State Library.

WAYNE FLYNT
Samford University

DREWRY'S BLUFF, a major Confederate fort on the James River eight miles below Richmond, Va., is a little less than one mile east of U.S. Route 1 on Chesterfield County Route 609. Federal reports and press frequently called it Ft. Darling; this is thought to have been general usage of a federal code name. Referred to as the "Gibraltar of the Confederacy," it was the anchor of the Richmond-Petersburg defense line. Outlying earthworks were constructed back from the riverbank across the Richmond turnpike with their right resting on the Petersburg & Richmond Railroad. A navy post, it was in effect a unified command, as sailors, a battalion of marines, and an army heavy artillery battalion were the normal garrison. The Confederate naval academy and the school ship *Patrick Henry* were also located here. The Confederate marine section was known as Camp Beall.

A federal naval squadron ascending the James River to Richmond was stopped at this point on May 15, 1862. In May, 1864, the vicinity was the scene of a series of engagements with federal troops under General Benjamin Butler's command, which resulted in his being bottled up near BERMUDA HUNDRED.

In March, 1865, sailors and marines evacuated from Wilmington, N.C., and Charleston, S.C., were assembled at Drewry's Bluff, where they were organized into Flag Officer John R. Tucker's naval brigade. When the post was evacuated on April 2–3, 1865, this unit participated in the APPOMATTOX CAMPAIGN. Most were surrendered at SAYLER'S CREEK on April 6, after fighting a rearguard action that earned them the admiration of their federal opponents.

See W. M. Robinson, Jr., *Civil War History* (June, 1961); R. W. Donnelly, *Virginia Cavalcade* (Autumn, 1966); W. K. Kay, *Virginia Magazine of History and Biography* (April, 1969); F. E. Lutz, *Chesterfield County* (1954); C. T. Mason Papers and S. A. Mann Manuscripts, Virginia Historical Society; *Official Records, Armies,* Ser. 1, Vols. XI, XXXVI, LI; *Official Records, Navies,* Ser. 1 Vols. VII–IX, Ser. 2, Vols. II–III; and R. U. Johnson and C. C. Buel (eds.), *Battles and Leaders* (1888), II, IV.

RALPH W. DONNELLY
U.S. Marine Corps

DRIVERS were black slaves, sometimes termed foremen, superintendents, leaders, or managers, who led slave gangs, usually under the direction of an overseer. Planters used trusted slaves to become part of the plantation hierarchy, because they believed slaves to be more effective in controlling other slaves and because white managers were scarce in the antebellum South. Drivers had many responsibilities, superior privileges, and disciplinary powers. They often held their positions for life. Some had complete control of plantations when a planter or an overseer was absent. Thus, drivers served as agents of accommodation for field hands and helped make plantations self-functioning agricultural units. Their position between owners, overseers, and slaves placed drivers in a difficult situation. Because of functional necessity the black foreman had to be at one and the same time both a driver and a buffer between the slaves and the master and overseer. These roles would vary according to conditions. For example, the roles would vary according to the kind of crop produced on plantations. Some drivers were literate, and reports to their owners exist, suggesting their daily routine and something of the dilemmas the drivers faced.

See S. M. Jackson, "Black Slave Drivers" (M.A. thesis, Purdue University, 1973); R. S. Starobin, *Journal of Social History* (Fall, 1971); W. K. Scarborough, *Overseer*

(1966); and E. D. Genovese, *Roll, Jordan, Roll* (1974). Best archival collections are at the University of North Carolina, Louisiana State University, and Mississippi Department of Archives, Jackson.

SHIRLEY M. JACKSON
Boston College

DU BOIS, WILLIAM EDWARD BURGHARDT

(1868–1963), was born in Great Barrington, Mass., and died in Accra, Ghana. He was the father of the black intelligentsia in the United States, chief founder of the Pan-African movement, a leading inspirer of the modern African liberation movement, a pioneer and outstanding figure in the CIVIL RIGHTS MOVEMENT in the United States, and one of the main organizers of the NAACP. An effective teacher (notably at Wilberforce and Atlanta universities), he also was the author of 18 books and thousands of articles, columns, essays, and pamphlets. His writing covered all forms: plays, pageants, poems, novels, monographs and books in sociology and history. His best-known and most widely circulated volumes were *The Souls of Black Folk* (1903); *Black Reconstruction* (1935); and *The World and Africa* (1947, 1965). Moreover, as a skilled and influential editor, he founded and edited the *Moon* (1905–1906); the *Horizon* (1906–1910); the *Crisis* (1910–1932); the *Brownies' Book* (1920–1921), for children; and PHYLON (1940–1944). The *Crisis* especially had great impact, with a circulation that reached over 90,000 shortly after World War I.

Du Bois resided in the South for 26 years—as a student at Fisk and a teacher in Georgia. He spent long periods in Virginia, Alabama, and Texas, maintained a home in Maryland, and regularly visited other parts of the South from 1885 to the late 1950s. He actively participated in organized efforts to establish equitable educational and transportation systems in the South and in struggles against LYNCHING, DISFRANCHISEMENT, and bad housing. Of Afro-American people, Du Bois was, with FREDERICK DOUGLASS, BOOKER T. WASHINGTON, and Paul Robeson, among the best-known personalities.

He spoke before hundreds of thousands of people in every part of the United States and in every continent, except Australia. And the latter part of his life, via radio and television, he was heard and seen by millions. Indeed, for the three decades from the death of Washington (1915) to the end of the Second World War (1945), he was the single most outstanding black figure. From about 1904 on, he became more and more persuaded of the superiority of socialism over capitalism, a conviction that finally led him to join the COMMUNIST PARTY in 1961.

See W. E. B. Du Bois, *Dusk of Dawn* (1940) and *Soliloquy on Viewing My Life* (1968), autobiographies; H. Aptheker, *Annotated Bibliography of Public Writings of W. E. B. Du Bois* (1973) and *Selected Correspondence* (2 vols.; 1973, 1976; 3rd vol. in prep.); F. L. Broderick, *W. E. B. Du Bois* (1959); and E. M. Rudwick, *W. E. B. Du Bois* (1960).

HERBERT APTHEKER
New York City

DUELING, the custom of personal armed combat governed by formal rules, was practiced infrequently during most of the colonial period. It came into general use among Revolutionary officers, spread to the civilian population, and increased in incidence in the antebellum period. Although widely criticized, it did not wane until the Civil War era, when it transformed into thinly veiled homicide (VIOLENCE).

Although dueling was formal, conditions varied among encounters. The observance of minimal restrictions, especially the principle of fairness, tolerated murderous eccentricities in the choice of weapon, distance, and ground. Pistols at 30 feet or more in the daylight was perhaps the most common practice, but the pistol (Thomas Biddle–Spencer Pettis, 1831) or rifle (Armistead Mason–John McCarty, 1819) at short range, and more bizarre usages, are recorded. Honor was satisfied in accepting apologies, exchanging missed shots (John Randolph–Henry Clay, 1826; Thomas Clingman–William Yancey, 1845), or wounding at least one of the parties (George McDuffie–William Cumming, 1822; Brooks-Reed, 1851). Frequently it was only satisfied by death (Andrew Jackson–Charles Dickinson, 1806; Jonathan Cilley–William Graves, 1838).

In the North, social fluidity early brought dueling into general disuse and the odium attached to the practice grew when its increasing localization in the South associated it with slavery. But it persisted in the slaveholding South as an important feature in the definition of gentlemanly status. That gentlemen dueled on trivial grounds, refused to duel with social inferiors, and published men who refused challenges as cowards (a custom known as "posting") suggest the social function of the practice. It expressed a severe sense of personal honor owing less to traditional ethical authorities than to an idealized female figure who demanded a devotional male role of strenuous effort and the endurance of pain. It is in this sense that dueling was closely related to tournaments and military exercises.

Dueling in the Confederacy became disreputable as misdirected aggression and because the war served honor better. After the war it deteriorated into "shooting on sight," wherein a warning was issued instead of a challenge. By century's end this homicidal custom lay under such public censure that, outside of reckless gunplay, the practice of dueling had virtually ceased to exist (CASH-SHANNON DUEL).

See W. O. Stevens, *Pistols at Ten Paces* (1940); L. Sabine, *Notes on Duels* (1855); B. C. Truman, *Field of Honor* (1884); D. C. Seitz, *Famous American Duels* (1929); H. T. Kane, *Gentlemen, Swords, Pistols* (1951); H. Cochran, *Noted American Duels* (1963); J. L. Wilson, *Code of Honor* (1858); J. A. Quintero, *Code of Honor* (1873); R. B. Rhett, *Code of Honor* (1878); J. Augustin, *Art and Letters* (Aug., 1877); M. T. Adkins, *Magazine of American History* (Jan., 1891); S. B. Weeks, *Magazine of American History* (Dec., 1891); L. Meader, *Century* (June, 1907); M. L. Spaulding, *Records of Columbia Historical Society* (1928); and *Congressional Globe*, 25th Cong., 2nd and 3rd Sess.

WILLIAM H. LONGTON
University of Toledo

DUKE FAMILY of Durham, N.C., became famous in the late nineteenth century in connection with tobacco and later through philanthropy. Washington Duke (1820–1905) was born in Orange County, N.C., and like his father Taylor Duke became a hardworking yeoman farmer. Although an antisecessionist, he was forced to serve in the Confederate armed forces in 1864–1865. Penniless after the war, he decided to manufacture smoking tobacco (TOBACCO MANUFACTURES) for sale rather than growing the new bright leaf tobacco to which an increasing number of farmers in the area were turning. With the children aiding in the manufacturing on the homeplace and Washington Duke "drumming" the trade, the family's tobacco, labeled Pro Bono Publico, achieved a modest success. In 1874, he moved the family a few miles to Durham, and in 1878 the firm of W. Duke, Sons & Company was formally launched.

Both Benjamin Newton Duke (1855–1929) and James Buchanan Duke (1856–1925), Washington Duke's two sons by his second wife, played important roles in the tobacco industry, but it was the latter son who early displayed a native genius for business. At a time when most of the well-established manufacturers of cigarettes insisted that the consumers preferred the hand-rolled variety, it was young James who sold his partners on the idea of gambling on a cigarette machine invented by James A. Bonsack of Virginia. A secret contract in 1885 between the Duke firm and the Bonsack company, plus extensive advertising, entrepreneurial creativeness, and hard work, enabled W. Duke, Sons & Company to forge to the front in cigarette manufacturing in the late 1880s. In 1890, when the five leading cigarette manufacturers combined to form the American Tobacco Company, James B. Duke was elected its president, a position he held through various reorganizations and expansions until the U.S. Supreme Court ordered the giant combination dissolved in 1911.

While James operated out of New York after 1884, Benjamin took the lead in launching the family in the textile business (TEXTILE INDUSTRY) with the establishment of the Erwin Cotton Mill in Durham in 1892. That enterprise, with branches in other communities, eventually became one of North Carolina's major textile producers. The search for economical water power for textile mills led the Dukes into the hydroelectric field, and in 1905 they launched the Southern Power Company. It eventually grew into the Duke Power Company and was a major factor in the economic development of the Piedmont region of the two Carolinas.

A lifelong and devoted Methodist, Washington Duke played the key role in bringing that church's struggling Trinity College to Durham in 1890–1892. From that point on, however, Benjamin N. Duke became most closely identified with the college and served as the family's chief agent in supporting it as well as other charitable causes. After around 1915, James B. Duke began to involve himself more directly in Methodist philanthropies and, with the encouragement of President WILLIAM P. FEW of Trinity College, particularly with that institution. Few sold Duke on the idea of supporting the creation of Duke University around the nucleus of Trinity College. James Duke created the Duke Endowment in December, 1924; though Duke University was the major beneficiary, three other colleges (Davidson, Furman, and Johnson C. Smith), plus numerous other eleemosynary institutions for both races in the two Carolinas, were also included.

See Papers of W. Duke, B. N. Duke, and J. B. Duke, in Manuscripts Department, Duke University; J. W. Jenkins, *James B. Duke* (1927), too reverential; J. K. Winkler, *Tobacco Tycoon* (1942), melodramatic, muckraking; R. F. Durden, *Dukes of Durham* (1975), only documented study; and E. W. Porter, *Trinity and Duke* (1964), solid and first-rate.

ROBERT F. DURDEN
Duke University

DUKE UNIVERSITY

DUKE UNIVERSITY (Durham, N.C. 27706). In 1838, the members of a Randolph, N.C., educational society founded Union Institute to fill a felt need for higher education. The name was changed to Trinity College in 1859, and in 1892 this Methodist men's college moved to Durham. Washington Duke gave the college a small endowment in 1896 contingent upon educating women on "an equal footing with men." Assisted by further gifts from the DUKE FAMILY and from the Duke Endowment, the school was renamed Duke University in 1924 and has grown into one of the South's premier institutions of education and research. Its combined libraries house over 2 million volumes and 4 million manuscripts. In addition to the Trent Collection of medical history and the Duke Archives, the university has the personal papers of numerous persons from the Carolinas, Virginia, and Kentucky: FURNIFOLD SIMMONS, JOSIAH BAILEY, CLYDE R. HOEY (N.C.); JOHN C. CALHOUN, FRANCIS W. PICKENS, CHARLES COTESWORTH PINCKNEY (S.C.); JAMES CANNON, THOMAS NELSON PAGE, WILLIAM MAHONE (Va.); the Clay family (Ala.); and JOHN J. CRITTENDEN (Ky.). Other significant holdings are extensive plantation papers, the records of the Methodist Episcopal Church, South, the files of the Socialist Party of America, and the papers of the Alliance for the Guidance of Rural Youth (1917–1948).

See E. W. Porter, *Trinity and Duke, 1892–1924* (1964); N. C. Chaffin, *Trinity College, 1839–1892* (1950); N. M. Tilley, *Trinity College Historical Society, 1892–1941* (1941); and J. F. Gifford, *Evolution of a Medical Center* (1972).

DULANY FAMILY

DULANY FAMILY. Daniel Dulany the elder (1685–1753) immigrated to Maryland from Ireland in 1703 as an indentured servant, served as a law clerk to a distinguished attorney, and when free entered law practice in southern Maryland. Outstanding success at the bar brought him wealth, local prominence, and social acceptance by the planting gentry into which he married. By 1720, when he moved to the provincial capital Annapolis, he had already acquired plantations, slaves, and indentured servants of his own and had held minor appointive offices.

Dulany's career in the capital was a series of political, social, and economic triumphs that make his life an early example of the American success story. Elected to the assembly, he became a leader of the "country party" and supported its cause with a memorable pamphlet, *The Right of the Inhabitants of Maryland to the Benefit of English Laws* (1728). In 1734 with four wealthy partners he founded the Baltimore Iron Works, which proved even more lucrative. In addition he won appointment to offices of prestige and profit, including the post of councilor. In the last decade of his life Councilor Dulany became immensely wealthy speculating in western lands.

Dulany's sons, reared as gentlemen and well educated, left their mark on the second half of the century. Daniel Dulany the younger (1722–1797) surpassed the brilliant record of his father and became an oracle of Anglo-American law. Walter (1724?–1773), the second son, had an outstanding career as a businessman and public servant. Lloyd (1742–1779), the youngest, a leader in Annapolis society and sporting circles, died in an unseemly duel at thirty-seven.

Daniel the younger, true successor as head of the family, had a meteoric rise. He further expanded the family fortune and mounted to the summit of provincial politics in a single decade. During the STAMP ACT CRISIS of 1765 Dulany wrote *Considerations on the Propriety of Imposing Taxes in the British Colonies*, a pamphlet that carried his reputation as a spokesman for American liberties throughout the empire. Later in the same year a second pamphlet, *The Right to the Tonnage*, took a more conservative position in local politics. During the following decade Dulany stood at the peak of his prestige: an accomplished writer, the leading lawyer in America, a dexterous politician, and a much-quoted statesman in imperial affairs before the final break with England.

Divided between Loyalists and patriots during the Revolution, the family lost power and considerable wealth. Daniel Dulany the younger became a neutral and permanently retired from public affairs.

See A. C. Land, *Dulanys of Maryland* (1968), full discussion; and some papers in Maryland Historical Society, Baltimore.

AUBREY C. LAND
University of Georgia

DUNBAR, WILLIAM

DUNBAR, WILLIAM (1749?–1810), Scottish-born Mississippi planter and scientist, immigrated in 1771 via Philadelphia to the Ohio-Mississippi Valley to trade with the Indians. In 1773 he obtained a land grant near Baton Rouge from the governor of West Florida and bought slaves in Jamaica. His plantation was plundered twice during the American Revolution. Shortly thereafter he moved to "the forest" near Natchez. Barrel staves provided his main income until the 1790s, when he concentrated on cotton. He introduced the square bale and a screw press to form it. Financing the press stimulated Dunbar's discovery of the usefulness of cottonseed oil decades before it became commercially important. Dunbar accepted slavery because it was expedient. He disciplined his slaves firmly, fed them amply, and never understood why some rebelled.

Dunbar corresponded with leading scientists, including Thomas Jefferson, who nominated him to the American Philosophical Society. He wrote in the society's *Transactions* and to Jefferson about Indian sign language, meteorology, longitude, rainbows, hydrology, hot springs, and Louisiana. Dunbar located the 31° latitude for Spain (1798), served in the territorial legislature (1803), and explored the Ouachita River (1804). He married Dinah Clark (?–1821); nine children are recorded.

See Mrs. R. Dunbar, *Life, Letters of Dunbar* (1930); F. L. Riley, *Sir Wm. Dunbar* (1899); A. H. DeRosier, Jr., *Journal of Mississippi History* (Aug., 1966); J. R. Dungan, *Journal of Mississippi History* (Aug., 1961); and Jefferson Papers, Library of Congress.

JOSEPH A. DEVINE, JR.
Stephen F. Austin State University

DUNKERS are a religious group that began with the baptism of eight separatists from the state churches at Schwarzenau, a village in Wittgenstein, Germany, in 1708. Because they baptized by three separate forward actions under the water, called trine immersion, which they believed was the form of baptism used by early Christians, they were sometimes called Tunkers from the German word *tunken*. In America, Tunkers was modified by the English to Dunkers or Dunkards. In addition to the emphasis on following the New Testament as it was interpreted by the early Christians, the Brethren, as they preferred to be known, were influenced by Anabaptism and by Pietism. From the former they received the refusal to participate in military service, and from the latter they received the zeal and enthusiasm that caused them to expand into a number of different areas in Europe.

Wherever they went in Europe, they were persecuted by the religious authorities, and they had difficulty making a living. Consequently, most of the Brethren immigrated to America in two groups in 1719 and in 1729, landing in Philadelphia. Those still in Europe either came to America individually or left the group, thus ending the Brethren as an institution in Europe. From Pennsylvania, the Brethren immigrated by the 1740s into Maryland, Virginia, and the Carolinas. Some of these early settlements were transient, but by the end of the colonial period there were permanent settlements in these four southern colonies, located generally in the western river valleys, such as the Shenandoah River valley of Virginia. By 1800 settlements had been established in Tennessee and in Kentucky; the former became permanent, the latter were eventually lost by becoming associated with other churches.

The Brethren in the South were very active in the late nineteenth and early twentieth centuries in establishing schools of the high school or college level in Maryland, Virginia, Alabama, and Missouri. Virginia had at least three different schools at the same time. Most of these schools closed because of lack of students and other financial pressures. By the 1970s only Bridgewater College, Bridgewater, Va., had survived. It served a large constituency from Maryland to Alabama and Florida.

The Brethren in the South have had a minimum of difficulty with divisions. In the 1880s, however, the Brethren split three ways: the most conservative group was named Old Order German Baptist Brethren; the most liberal group was named Progressive Brethren; and the middle group continued to be called German Baptist Brethren, a name that was changed in 1908 to Church of the Brethren. This latter group was in the 1880s and in the 1970s the largest group. The Progressive Brethren split in the 1930s into Grace Brethren with offices at Winona Lake, Ind., and First Brethren with offices at Ashland, Ohio. All of these groups have churches in the South.

In the nineteenth and twentieth centuries the Brethren have established churches in all of the southern states except Mississippi, although in several states (Arkansas, Georgia, Louisiana, South Carolina) there is only one church. The largest number is found in Virginia; Maryland, West Virginia, Tennessee, Florida, and Missouri also have a number of Brethren churches.

See R. E. Sappington, *Brethren in Virginia* (1973), and *Brethren in Carolinas* (1972); E. S. Moyer, *Brethren in Florida* (1975); P. H. Bowman, *Brethren Education in Southeast* (1955); D. F. Durnbaugh, *Brethren in Colonial America* (1967); R. E. Sappington, *Brethren in New Nation, 1785–1865* (1976); and D. F. Durnbaugh, *Brethren Past and Present* (1971).

ROGER E. SAPPINGTON
Bridgewater College

DUNMORE'S WAR.

DUNMORE'S WAR. In September, 1774, John Murray, earl of Dunmore and the last royal governor of Virginia, led an expedition against the SHAWNEE INDIANS in the Ohio country. On October 10 one wing of his army, led by Colonel Andrew Lewis, was surprised at POINT PLEASANT (located at the confluence of the Ohio and Kanawha rivers) by an army of Indians under Cornstalk. Both sides suffered heavy losses; but Cornstalk eventually retreated, leaving the field to the battered but victorious colonials. Shortly before the clash at Point Pleasant, troops under Dunmore's personal command crossed the Ohio near present-day Parkersburg, W.Va., and marched toward the Shawnee villages located near the mouth of the Scioto. Unaware that Cornstalk had gathered his warriors for an attack on Lewis, Dunmore ordered the colonel to cross the Ohio, march northwest, and join him for a combined attack on the Shawnee towns. But the battle of Point Pleasant ended the fighting. Despite the desire of Lewis' men to wage a war of annihilation, Lord Dunmore negotiated a peace settlement with the Indians at Camp Charlotte. Dunmore's War paved the way for the settlement of Kentucky and quelled the Indians' power so completely that the Virginia frontier remained quiet for nearly three years after the American Revolution began. Land hunger is an important factor in explaining the origins of Dunmore's War. Dunmore championed the "rights" of Virginia despite the refusal of the British government to recognize the colony's western land claims in such laws as the PROCLAMATION OF 1763.

See R. O. Curry, *West Virginia History* (July, 1958; April, 1963); R. G. Thwaites and L. P. Kellogg, *Documentary History of Dunmore's War* (1905); C. W. Alvord, *Mississippi Valley in British Politics* (1917); T. P. Abernethy, *Western Land and American Revolution* (1937); R. C. Downes, *Mississippi Valley Historical Review* (Dec., 1934); J. M. Sosin, *White Hall and Wilderness* (1961); and J. P. Greene, *William and Mary Quarterly* (April, 1962).

RICHARD ORR CURRY
University of Connecticut, Storrs

DUNNING, WILLIAM ARCHIBALD

DUNNING, WILLIAM ARCHIBALD (1857–1922), was one of the most influential historians in the development of the traditional southern apologist interpretation of Reconstruction. His own books and articles were more balanced than the writings of most of those who perpetuated the "Dunning" interpretation but, despite his judicious tone, his works are permeated by the white middle-class assumptions of his day. Believing in the natural superiority of the white race and the necessity of rule by men of quality and property, Dunning judged the Reconstruction experiment to have been a disaster. Radical Republicans were either hopelessly misguided idealists or ruthlessly vindictive partisans. The white South was unnecessarily punished, and its natural leaders were suppressed. Irresponsible outsiders (CARPETBAGGERS), corrupted natives (SCALAWAGS), and inferior natives (freedmen) were placed in control of southern states. This ill-conceived and vindictive plan hindered rather than hastened a spirit of national reunion.

Dunning was born in New Jersey and educated at Columbia University with postgraduate work under Heinrich von Treitschke at the University of Berlin. He was honored as president of the American Historical Association in 1913. Most of his best graduate students at Columbia University (1886–1922) were southerners. They chronicled the story of Reconstruction in the individual southern states and usually were more explicit than their mentor in condemnation of "Carpetbag-Scalawag-Negro misrule." For the first half of the twentieth century, the "Dunning interpretation" remained the conventional, "commonsense" view of RECONSTRUCTION HISTORIOGRAPHY. Since the 1930s, the Dunning school has been challenged by the economic interpretations of the Beard-Beale school and the Marxists and has been virtually demolished by the pro–civil rights interpretations of black, liberal, and radical historians. Dunning stands as an outstanding reminder that even the most judicious and honored of historians are, nevertheless, captives of the ethos of their era.

See W. A. Dunning, *Essays on Civil War and Reconstruction* (1897), and *Reconstruction: Political and Economic* (1907). For discussion of Dunning's scholarly method, see C. E. Miriam, *Social Forces* (Sept., 1926); A. D. Harper, *Civil War History* (March, 1964); W. H. Stephenson, *Southern History in Making* (1964); and P. R. Muller, *Journal of American History* (Sept., 1974).

ROBERT J. MOORE
Columbia College, Columbia, S.C.

DU PONT FAMILY.

DU PONT FAMILY. More than 2,000 Du Ponts who live in the United States trace their origins to the French Physiocrat Pierre Samuel Du Pont de Nemours (1739–1817), who left revolution-torn France in 1799 for a new life in America. Emigrating with Pierre Du Pont were his two sons, Éleuthère Irénée (1771–1834) and Victor Marie (1767–

1827). Éleuthère's decision to enter the powder manufacturing business brought the family in 1802 to a site on the Brandywine Creek, about three miles north of Wilmington, Del. The Du Pont company's major product from 1802 through the end of the nineteenth century was black powder. Indispensable as gunpowder, the Du Pont powder was mostly used for peaceful purposes, such as blasting rocks and stumps from farmers' fields. It became a major factor in mining as well as in the construction of roads, canals, and railways.

On the eve of the Civil War the Du Pont mills produced one-third of the nation's gunpowder. Although located physically in the South, New Castle County, the seat of Du Pont power, was economically and politically tied to southeastern Pennsylvania. The firm's founder, Éleuthère, became a Whig and an ardent supporter of Henry Clay. Henry Du Pont (1812–1889), Éleuthère's second son who headed the company during the Civil War, in common with most Du Ponts, stood by the Union and, as a major general, was placed in command of the state's militia.

Henry's son Henry Algernon (1838–1926), a West Point graduate, fought in Virginia, where he won the congressional Medal of Honor. Rear Admiral Samuel Francis Du Pont (1803–1865), a son of Victor Marie, took a leading part in the naval war against the Confederacy. In September, 1861, Admiral Du Pont assumed command of the South Atlantic Blockading Squadron, and on November 7 he captured PORT ROYAL SOUND, S.C. In April, 1863, with a fleet of ironclads, he failed to capture Charleston and was relieved of command at his own request.

Two Du Ponts, Alfred Victor (1833–1893) and Antoine Biderman (1837–1923), moved to Kentucky in 1854 and, by the 1890s, they owned the Louisville streetcar system and paper mills and coal mines in Central City, Ky. Du Pont money also helped finance HENRY WATTERSON's Louisville Courier-Journal.

In 1902 three great-grandsons of Éleuthère—Thomas Coleman (1863–1930), a son of Antoine Biderman of Louisville; Alfred Irénée (1864–1935); and Pierre Samuel (1870–1954)—took control of the family powder works. The three cousins, just prior to World War I, started to diversify the company's interests out of explosives into such products as paint, artificial silk, and artificial leather. In 1915 T. Coleman sold his interest in the firm to Pierre; Alfred challenged Coleman's sale, and a bitter family fight ensued, which ended with Alfred's separation from the firm. After 1915, under Pierre's leadership, E. I. Du Pont de Nemours & Company completed its transformation from an explosives company into the world's leading chemical enterprise.

In the 1920s Alfred moved to Florida and soon controlled a number of important Florida banks, the Florida East Coast Railway, and large real estate holdings around St. Joseph in west Florida, which became the basis of the St. Joe Paper Company. Upon Alfred's death his property passed into a trust, which is still managed by Edward Ball, the brother of Alfred's third wife.

Despite the passage of time and opportunities elsewhere, the family remains concentrated about Delaware. Although the family ceased to manage the firm in 1967, it retains a large ownership in the company as well as in General Motors. The family also owns Delaware's leading newspapers, the Wilmington Morning News and Evening Journal, the state's largest bank, the Wilmington Trust, and numerous other enterprises. The family has also been active in the cultural life of the state, making large contributions to the endowment of the University of Delaware. Henry Francis Du Pont (1880–1969) founded the Winterthur Museum in Winterthur, Del., which contains the nation's best collection of early American furniture and art.

See J. B. Riggs, *Guide to Manuscripts* (1970). See also A. Saricks, *P. S. Du Pont de Nemours* (1965); W. S. Dutton, *Du Pont* (1942), official company history; A. D. Chandler, Jr., and S. Salsbury, *Pierre S. Du Pont* (1971); J. K. Winkler, *Du Pont Dynasty* (1935); J. D. Hayes (ed.), *S. F. Du Pont Civil War Letters* (4 vols.; 1969); and M. James, *A. I. Du Pont* (1941). The Eleutherian Mills Historical Library in Greenville, Del., houses a massive collection of family papers.

STEPHEN SALSBURY
University of Delaware

DURHAM, N.C. (pop. 95,438), is in the central portion of the state, approximately 50 miles east of Greensboro. The area was settled in the middle of the eighteenth century by English and Scotch-Irish farmers. In 1852, when William Pratt of nearby Prattsburg refused to give a right-of-way to the North Carolina Railway, the rail line, a railway station, and a town were built on the land of Dr. Bartlett Durham. The railroad hamlet was of little importance in the Civil War except that General JOSEPH E. JOHNSTON, on April 18, 1865, surrendered here to General W. T. Sherman. From that date to the present, the story of Durham has been part of the legendary history of TOBACCO MANU-

FACTURES. As headquarters first for the BULL DURHAM TOBACCO COMPANY and then for the DUKE FAMILY tobacco trust, Durham and tobacco, especially cigarettes, became synonymous. The modern city remains a center of tobacco manufactures as well as of textiles. It is the home of DUKE UNIVERSITY and of North Carolina College at Durham (1910).

See W. K. Boyd, *Story of Durham* (1925); N. M. Tilley, *Bright-Tobacco Industry, 1860–1929* (1948); and files of Durham *Sun* (1889–) and *Herald* (1894–).

DURHAM STATEMENT. In October, 1942, 59 prominent southern blacks, summoned at the instigation of JESSIE DANIEL AMES, director of fieldwork of the Atlanta-based COMMISSION ON INTERRACIAL COOPERATION, gathered in Durham, N.C., for what was designated the Southern Conference on Race Relations. A committee appointed by the conference to draft a statement of principles later issued a document entitled "A Basis for Interracial Cooperation and Development in the South: A Statement by Southern Negroes" (December 15, 1942). Known usually as the "Durham statement," the committee report denounced compulsory segregation and urged that steps be taken "now" to end all discriminatory practices against blacks. A conference of white southern liberals sponsored by the Commission on Interracial Cooperation subsequently met in Atlanta (April, 1943) and endorsed the Durham statement. As a direct result of two additional meetings (Richmond, June, 1943; Atlanta, August, 1943) attended by representatives from both the Durham and Atlanta conferences, the SOUTHERN REGIONAL COUNCIL (chartered January, 1944) was founded. Shortly thereafter the Commission on Interracial Cooperation was dissolved and its assets were transferred to the Southern Regional Council.

See G. B. Tindall, *Emergence of New South* (1967); W. Dykeman and J. Stokely, *Seeds of Southern Change* (1962); and *Southern Regional Council* (1944).

NATHANIEL F. MAGRUDER
Converse College

DUTCH FORK is an area in South Carolina about 40 miles long between the Broad and Saluda rivers whose lower portion was settled and developed into small, self-sufficient farms by hardworking conservative Swiss and German people (not Dutch) in the 1740s and 1750s. They were followed later in the upper sections by Scotch-Irish and English from Virginia and Pennsylvania. All of these original settlers have left an imprint on their modern-day descendants of rugged individualism and thrift.

See D. D. Wallace, *South Carolina: Short History* (1961); and Works Progress Administration, *South Carolina, Palmetto State* (1941).

DUVAL, GABRIEL (1752–1844), sixth child of a prominent Maryland family, spanned the nation-forming years with his career. Beginning as clerk to the 1775 Maryland convention, Duval participated in the Revolution in Maryland. His offices from 1781 to 1802 were all state centered: loyalist land commissioner, state councilor, legislative delegate, and supreme court judge. Duval refused appointment to the Philadelphia convention in 1787. Jeffersonian politics pulled him into the national scene, first as congressman (1794–1796) and presidential elector, then as a U.S. comptroller (1802–1811). When James Madison appointed Duval to SAMUEL CHASE's seat on the U.S. Supreme Court, the orthodox Jeffersonian surprised people by supporting John Marshall's nationalism. Duval dissented but three times (*Dartmouth College, Ogden* v. *Saunders*, and *Mima Queen* v. *Hepburn*). His most notable opinions and only written dissent displayed a strong dislike of slavery. In 1836 he acknowledged the handicaps of deafness by retiring from the Court.

See I. Dillard, in *Justices of Supreme Court* (1969). Duval's letters are scattered. Further material is in collections of associates and in federal court records.

JOAN R. GUNDERSEN
St. Olaf College

DUVAL, WILLIAM POPE (1784–1854), was born in Richmond, Va., grew up in the backwoods of Kentucky, made a reputation as a scholar and lawyer, and represented Kentucky for two years in the U.S. Congress (1813–1815). In May, 1822, President James Monroe appointed Duval the first civil governor of the territory of Florida. In 12 years as governor, Duval did much to organize and develop the new territory. Location of the capital in Tallahassee, Indian settlements, conservation of natural resources, and stabilization of the new government were his major contributions. Elected to the Florida constitutional convention in 1839, he opposed statehood, which Florida finally achieved in 1845. He served briefly in the state senate prior to running unsuccessfully for Congress in 1848. Duval moved to Texas in 1849 and died while on a trip to Washington, D.C.

See S. W. Martin, *Florida During Territorial Days* (1944); B. B. Grabowskii, *Duval Family of Virginia* (1931); W. T. Cash, *Tallahassee Historical Society Annual* (1934); and W. D. Barfield, *Jacksonville Historical Society Papers* (1949). Also see P. K. Yonge Collection, University of Florida.

S. WALTER MARTIN
Valdosta State College

E

EARLY, JUBAL ANDERSON (1816–1894), was born in Franklin County, Va. Graduating from West Point (1837) with an inconspicuous record, he served as a second lieutenant in the SEMINOLE WARS until July, 1838, when he returned to Virginia to study law. He sat in the Virginia house of delegates (1841–1842) as a Whig. Until the Civil War, his life as a rural Virginia attorney was interrupted only by brief service in the Mexican War, during which he saw no action. Although opposing secession in the Virginia Convention of 1861, Early offered his military services to the Confederacy. A colonel at Bull Run, he was soon promoted to the rank of brigadier general in the Army of Northern Virginia and by mid-1864 had attained the rank of lieutenant general in command of the II Corps. Early was never popular with his troops or civilian authorities, but his aggressive, tenacious combat manner earned the respect of his military superiors.

After being dispatched to the Shenandoah Valley in the summer of 1864, Early's 14,000-man force threatened Washington and disrupted communication and supply lines in western Maryland and Pennsylvania, causing U. S. Grant to send 48,000 troops under Philip Sheridan to the valley to check the menace. Sheridan defeated Early at the battles of WINCHESTER, FISHER'S HILL, and CEDAR CREEK and on March 2, 1865, completely destroyed Early's decimated army of 1,200 at WAYNESBORO. Following the surrender at Appomattox, Early entered a self-imposed exile in Canada until 1869, when he returned to Virginia. He served as the first president of the Southern Historical Society. He was always the unreconstructed rebel, and his bitterness toward the Union never mellowed.

See M. K. Bushong, *Old Jube* (1955); Early Papers, Library of Congress; J. A. Early, *Autobiographical Sketch* (1912) and *Memoir* (1867); J. W. Daniel, *Southern Historical Society Papers* (1894); and *Official Records, Armies,* Ser. 1.

V. DENNIS GOLLADAY
Pensacola Junior College

EARLY'S WASHINGTON RAID. On June 13, 1864, General JUBAL ANDERSON EARLY led the II Corps of the Army of Northern Virginia toward central Virginia. He was commanding a strategic diversion, one forced on Robert E. Lee by U. S. Grant's circling of Richmond and Petersburg and by secondary threats to the Shenandoah Valley and the huge Confederate depot at Lynchburg. Lee ordered Early to handle federal General David Hunter's move toward Lynchburg, then to march down the Shenandoah, cross the Potomac, and threaten Washington. History proved the sensitivity of northerners to thrusts at that city; Grant might be forced to detach men from Richmond or to attack Lee's entrenchments to protect the federal capital.

Early moved rapidly, defeated Hunter at the battle of LYNCHBURG on June 17 and 18, and pursued him out of the Shenandoah. Swinging down the valley pike, Early's 12,000 fought at WINCHESTER and Harpers Ferry, but crossed the Potomac on July 5 and 6, 1864. Moving east through Catoctin Pass, Early met a federal force under Lew Wallace near Frederick, Md. The battle of Monocacy, July 9, 1864, proved nearly decisive in Early's campaign to threaten Washington. Wallace's troops held Early the full day. When the rebel vanguard reached the capital's defenses on July 11, it was met by garrison troops and by part of a corps Grant had detached from Richmond. Panic in Washington ran for two days and a night; Abraham Lincoln remained calm, even toured threatened Ft. Stevens and heard young Captain Oliver Wendell Holmes yell at him, "Get down, you fool!" Early, outnumbered, decided to retreat to Virginia on the night of the twelfth. The raid had saved the valley and showed what a small, well-led force could accomplish as a strategic diversion.

See F. E. Vandiver, *Jubal's Raid* (1960); *Official Records, Armies,* Ser. 1, Vols. XXXVII, XL; and A. P. McDonald (ed.), *Make Me a Map* (1973).

FRANK E. VANDIVER
Rice University

EATON, CLEMENT (1898–), graduated from the University of North Carolina in 1919. After receiving his doctorate from Harvard in 1929, he taught at Lafayette College for 15 years. In 1946 he moved to the University of Kentucky, where he taught until his retirement in 1968. He was president of the Southern Historical Association (1961) and Pitt Professor at Cambridge (1968–1969). His writing demonstrated that the Old South was not a land of legend, but a society diverse in attitudes and relationships, with peculiar geographic, cultural, and economic aspects. Eaton presented a balanced evaluation of the Old South, investing his books and teaching with an understanding of emotional values that enriched both. *Freedom of Thought in the Old South* (1940) posited that, after the death of Thomas Jefferson, a liberal sentiment that had allowed for debate and dissent gave way to a parochialism in which slavery and religious orthodoxy hindered free intellectual discourse. A popular textbook, *A History of the Old South* (1949, 1975), dealt with this parochialism and the paradoxes it fostered. *The Growth of Southern Civilization, 1790–1860* (1961) analyzed the conflicts of economic progress and social decadence.

See C. Eaton, *History of Southern Confederacy* (1954), *Henry Clay* (1957), *Mind of Old South* (1964), *Waning of Old South Civilization, 1860–1880's* (1968); *Jefferson Davis* (1977); and J. A. Garraty, *Interpreting American History* (1970).

WALTER RUNDELL, JR.
University of Maryland

EATON, JOHN HENRY (1790–1856), born in Halifax County, N.C., moved to middle Tennessee, practiced law, served in the state legislature, and became one of the youngest U.S. senators (1818–1829). He achieved prominence as a mentor and protégé of ANDREW JACKSON—as a mentor whose early biography and encouragement helped make Jackson president and as a protégé whom the president made secretary of war (1829–1831), governor of Florida (1834–1836), and minister to Spain (1836–1840). Above all, the two men were intimate friends. Eaton defended Rachel Jackson's reputation, consoled Jackson when Rachel died, and rode into Washington at the president-elect's side. For his part, Jackson ardently defended Eaton's wife during one of the most famous scandals in history (PEGGY O'NEALE EATON). Although Eaton's endorsement of the Whigs in 1840 deeply strained the Eaton-Jackson relationship, the two were at least partially reconciled shortly before Jackson's death. Peggy at his side, Eaton lived out the remainder of his life as something of a patriarch within Washington's legal community.

See J. Parton, *Jackson* (1860); M. James, *Jackson* (1937); R. V. Remini, *Election of Jackson* (1963); Q. Pollack, *Peggy Eaton* (1931); P. Eaton, *Autobiography* (1932); C. Sellers, *American Historical Review* (April, 1957); and R. P. Hay, *Tennessee Historical Quarterly* (Summer, 1970).

ROBERT P. HAY
Marquette University

EATON, MARGARET "PEGGY" O'NEALE TIMBERLAKE (1796–1879), achieved fame as the center of a major political storm in ANDREW JACKSON's administration. Her father owned and ran a tavern in Washington that was much frequented by political leaders of the day. Peggy's beauty and zest for life made her a great favorite among the guests. At an early age she married John B. Timberlake, a naval purser whose long absences fueled rumors that Peggy was having affairs with other men. Most notable of these was Senator JOHN EATON of Tennessee, a young and wealthy widower who lodged at the tavern and was a leader in the campaign to secure the presidency for his friend Andrew Jackson.

Timberlake died in the Mediterranean in 1828. Four months later, Peggy and John Eaton were married. Shortly thereafter, Eaton was appointed secretary of war in Jackson's cabinet. The cabinet wives, led by Mrs. JOHN C. CALHOUN, snubbed Mrs. Eaton, refusing to receive her. Secretary of State Martin Van Buren, a widower, championed her cause, as did Jackson, whose own recently deceased wife had long been the subject of false imputations of scandal. The "Eaton Malaria" split the cabinet, helped estrange Jackson and Calhoun, and led eventually—although for far more substantive reasons—to a reorganization of the administration that put Van Buren in the ascendancy.

The Eatons returned to Tennessee in 1831. In 1834 he was appointed governor of Florida, and from 1836 to 1840 he was American minister in Madrid, where Peggy reveled in the life at court. The couple returned to Washington, where Eaton died in 1856. Subsequently Peggy married an Italian dancing master, who defrauded her of her property and eloped with her granddaughter.

See *Autobiography of Peggy Eaton* (1932), not reliable; Q. Pollack, *Peggy Eaton* (1931); C. M. Wiltse, *Calhoun, Nullifier* (1949); and other standard works on Jacksonians.

RICHARD H. BROWN
Newberry Library

ECKENRODE, HAMILTON JAMES (1881–), an able and productive southern historian, archivist, biographer, and novelist, took his Ph.D. degree at Johns Hopkins in 1905 under the tutelage of James C. Ballagh. Imbued with the tenets of scientific history, Eckenrode did a factual dissertation, "The Political History of Virginia During the Reconstruction" (1904), one of the more evenhanded of the "Dunning school" studies. As Virginia state archivist from 1907 to 1914, he compiled several calendars and lists on Old Dominion subjects. But Eckenrode's main contribution is in the field of biography: *Nathan B. Forrest* (1918), *Jefferson Davis* (1923), *Rutherford B. Hayes* (1930), *E. H. Harriman* (1933), *James Longstreet* (1936), *George B. McClellan* (1941), *The Randolphs* (1946). The scholarly caution that marked his dissertation and other early works is not always evident in his biographies, which, although carefully researched and exceedingly well written, are highly interpretative and quite judgmental. Eckenrode's works reveal a nostalgic attachment to the Old South, regret over the defeat of the Confederacy, a tendency toward presentism, and pessimism about the future. For years Eckenrode was the historian of the Virginia Conservation Commission. In addition to his some 20 scholarly works, he published one novel, *Bottom Rail on Top*, a story set primarily in the Reconstruction era.

EVERETTE SWINNEY
Southwest Texas State University

EDDIS, WILLIAM (1738–1825), was an Englishman who came to Maryland in 1769 looking for better opportunities through the patronage of the governor Robert Eden. He found them in several lesser offices and finally in his appointment as commissioner of the paper currency office or loan office, a post he held until May, 1777. He is best known for his *Letters from America, Historical and Descriptive, Comprising Occurrences from 1769 to 1777 Inclusive* (1792). This widely quoted work is one of the best contemporary accounts of the coming of the Revolution in Maryland as well as a book that provides insightful descriptions of social life in Annapolis, the Maryland land system, and nonfree labor. The trials of remaining loyal to the crown in the face of growing popularity for the patriot cause are aptly detailed as are the problems facing the Americans in mobilizing for war. After great difficulties Eddis finally returned to England, where he was awarded a small pension and retired into relative obscurity until his death.

See G. H. Williams, *Maryland Historical Magazine* (June, 1965); and W. Eddis, *Letters from America*, ed. A. C. Land (1969).

MICHAEL L. NICHOLLS
Utah State University

EDEN, CHARLES (1673–1722), was governor of North Carolina (1714–1722) and the last person to be created landgrave under the fundamental constitutions of John Locke. Eden came to North Carolina late in the proprietary period. Settlers were already beginning to appeal for royal intervention. Eden was particularly beset by the use of North Carolina's estuaries, creeks, and coves by pirates. He investigated and attempted to control this activity, but the geographical complexity of the Carolina coast and the opportunity for residents to profit by acting as middlemen in traffic with the pirates made eradication impossible. Eden's lenient treatment of the notorious Edward Teach (BLACKBEARD) caused some scandal, but the council cleared him of charges of criminal complicity. Although not an outstanding governor, Eden provided a generally satisfactory administration. After his death Queen Anne's Town was renamed Edenton in his honor.

See *Colonial Records of North Carolina* (1886–90), II; E. McCrady, *History of South Carolina Under Proprietary Government* (1897); and S. A. Ashe, *Biographical History of North Carolina* (1905), I.

CLARENCE J. ATTIG
Westmar College

EDENTON, N.C. (pop. 4,766), a small fishing, lumber, and peanut market town, is on an inlet of Albemarle Sound approximately 30 miles southwest of Elizabeth City. Explored as early as 1622 by John Pory, secretary of the Virginia Colony, the area was first settled in 1658 by colonists from Jamestown. When made the capital of North Carolina in 1710, it was a major port for provincial commerce. It was first called Roanoke, but was rechristened Queen Anne's Town in 1715 and Edenton, after Governor CHARLES EDEN, in 1722. Although it was an important shipbuilding and shipping center throughout the eighteenth century, the town went into a state of economic decline in the nineteenth century. Among several surviving buildings of historic interest are St. Paul's Church (1736) and the courthouse (1767).

See W. C. Boyce, *Chowan County* (1917, repr. 1969); H. T. Lefler and W. S. Powell, *Colonial North Carolina* (1973); and microfilm of Edenton *Gazette and North Carolina Advertiser* (1806–31), from North Carolina Department of Archives and History.

EDUCATION. Three issues are important in viewing the history of public primary and secondary education in the South. The first is why the South has developed public schools at a slower pace than other sections of the country. The traditional answer to this question is found in the works of Edgar W. Knight, who argued that the major reason for southern educational lag, especially in the colonial and antebellum periods, was the region's rural pattern of settlement (URBANI-

ZATION). More specifically, Knight saw sparse population, poor communication among residents, and the plantation system of agriculture as geographical impediments to the development of schools in the South. The second major issue in the educational history of the South is the education of the Negro. This topic assumes special significance in the periods after the Civil War. Racial problems when added to the above-mentioned geographical difficulties provide an almost complete explanation of the South's educational lag. The final factor to be mentioned is the socioeconomic emphasis of the public education that finally did arrive in the late nineteenth-century South. Support for public schools came as part of the New South program for economic development of the region. The economic philosophy of the northern philanthropists and the southern educators and businessmen who shaped the New South programs throughout the late nineteenth and early twentieth centuries pointed the economic and educational development of the region in a direction that maintained the existing social structure and fostered the economic subservience of South to North.

The schools of colonial America were diverse in their patterns of support and control. Yet, within this larger diversity, regional patterns did emerge. Recent histories of colonial education by Bernard Bailyn and Lawrence Cremin follow Knight's traditional interpretation and emphasize the rural character of the South in explaining its slowness to develop schools. In the colonial South as in the other colonies formal schools were usually found in the coastal areas, Virginia and South Carolina in the seventeenth century and Georgia in the eighteenth. Coastal settlements (and hence coastal schools) were less numerous in the South than in New England or the middle colonies, and the backwater areas, always slow to develop schools, were larger and more populous in the South than in other sections. Also contributing to the South's slowness in school development were the indifference of southern Episcopalian clergy to schools (in contrast to the New England Puritans) and the aristocratic social structure that developed with slavery and the plantation system of agriculture. Although most studies in concentrating on regional lag or difference ignore the education of blacks and Indians, those that do mention this topic highlight the missionary activities of the Society for the Propagation of the Gospel among slaves, free blacks, and Indians.

The early national period saw slight changes, north and south, in the pattern of school development. The most notable educational development in this period was the increase in the number of educational plans offered to guide the development of the new nation. The plan drawn by a southerner, THOMAS JEFFERSON, differed from the other plans in calling for a state rather than a national system of schools. Jefferson proposed a statewide system of free schools for Virginia in 1789 and again in 1817; however, it would not be adopted until after the Civil War. Jefferson's energies turned from free schooling toward the University of Virginia, an institution of higher education that the state chose to support in preference to free schools in the early nineteenth century. Similarly, in Georgia, the legislation of 1784 that set up a fund for the implementation of free schools was unsuccessful and the main educational outcome of the early national period was the establishment of Franklin College, later to become the University of Georgia. Thus, in addition to the earlier notion of a lag in the number of schools, we find in the South a preference on the part of state governments for higher education (COLLEGES AND UNIVERSITIES), rather than free schools, and for pauper schools at the lower levels. This is in marked contrast to developments in New England.

The antebellum period was highlighted in the North by a variety of common school crusades, the most notable of which was by Horace Mann in Massachusetts. The South, with the notable exception of Calvin Wiley in North Carolina, witnessed little such activity. In the hands of northern historians, particularly Frank Tracy Carlton, the southern lag in developing common schools is attributed to the entire white population, which was just not interested in education. Recent studies have disputed this interpretation. David Mathews' work on antebellum Georgia and Alabama stresses the role of aristocratic planter whites in preventing the implementation of common schools, which were supported by the up-country whites. Frederick Salzillo cites widespread political support from both up-country and plantation legislators in passing a statewide free school law in Georgia in 1837. The failure to implement this legislation was due to the economic depression of the late 1830s, not because of any lack of support. Don R. Leet, in a comparative study of Mississippi and Illinois, notes that local free school establishment in both states was related to the degree of commercialization in the area. Mississippi, like Illinois, developed schools in its commercialized areas, and Leet further argues that wealthy whites were influential in supporting common schools. These studies, though not identical in interpretation, all question the notion of uniform opposition to free schools among antebellum southern whites. Yet one thing on which almost all southern whites did agree was opposition to the education of Negroes. Recent studies of slavery by Eugene Genovese and of the antebellum free Negro by Ira Berlin show how slaves managed cultural maintenance and free blacks fought for schools in spite of this opposition.

The first widespread legislative interest in statewide public schooling in the South took place during Reconstruction. Reconstruction legislatures gave education an important place in their political programs. In addition, the FREEDMEN'S BUREAU and various northern religious denominations were active in providing schooling for the freedmen. Historians have recently done much research into the causes of the failure of most of these efforts. William Vaughn's recent study of education for blacks during Reconstruction highlights the uniform opposition of southern whites to the various state legislative plans for integrated schooling. However, Vaughn notes the successful implementation of integrated education in New Orleans and at the University of South Carolina. He argues that the successful southern white opposition to integrated education, which finally triumphed in the Tilden-Hayes Compromise of 1877 (ELECTION OF 1876), might have been overcome if southern whites had not had the cooperation of the supposed allies of the freedmen, Congress and other northern whites. Recent studies of the Freedmen's Bureau by William McFeely and of the activities of white liberals by James McPherson have stressed the failure of black schooling and have attributed this failure to the paternalism and lack of fundamental commitment to the cause of the blacks by their white benefactors. Each of these studies implies that it was whites, not just southern whites, who frustrated the education of the freedmen. The recent microfilm publication of the educational records of the Freedmen's Bureau along with further work in the sources of Reconstruction educational legislation, both in Congress and in the southern state legislatures, should bring us a fuller picture of these developments.

The activities of philanthropic northern businessmen in support of schooling in the South began during the later stages of Reconstruction with the work of the PEABODY EDUCATION FUND and continued through the end of the nineteenth and well into the twentieth centuries. The northern philanthropists and their agents, some natives of the South, who oversaw the spending of the educational funds preferred the dual system to integrated schooling and sought for both races public schools that supported a conservative economic philosophy. Historians Merle Curti and HORACE MANN BOND, both writing in the 1930s, stressed the affinity of the white southern educational leader J. L. M. CURRY and the black educational leader BOOKER T. WASHINGTON for a conservative economic and political philosophy that supported northern capital. In contrast to most earlier studies, which saw northern philanthropy and southern educational crusading as part of a political and educational renaissance, recent work has tended to agree with Curti and Bond. Southern educational activity in this period took place in the context of NEW SOUTH rhetoric, which linked developing southern commerce with northern capital and frustrated the economic, political, and educational aspirations of most southerners, black and white alike. James D. Anderson and Martin Carnoy have gone so far in their recent studies as to label southern school developments in this period as a part of northern colonialism. Louis Harlan's recent biography of Booker T. Washington, though not explicitly arguing the colonialist hypothesis, can easily be interpreted as supporting the hypothesis. (Harlan's editing of the Washington papers, a project that has thus far yielded three published volumes, should provide scholars ample opportunity to test the colonialist hypothesis.)

In addition to the theme of economic exploitation, the racial bias of southern public educational efforts in the New South period has been stressed. Allen Going has argued that southern support for federal aid to education (BLAIR BILL) in the 1880s, an unexpected phenomenon in the land of "states' rights," was due to the South's wish for federal assistance in educating the Negroes. C. VANN WOODWARD's classic study of the years 1877–1914 noted the primacy of the racial motive in school reform as well as in other reforms and referred to the southern version of early twentieth-century reform as "Progressivism for Whites Only." Louis Harlan made extensive use of state legislative records and the papers of many of the organizations devoted to the southern educational revival (found mainly in the Southern Historical Collection at the University of North Carolina) to show how white southerners used both philanthropic and public funds to maintain the inequitable dual system of schools. Irving Gershenberg, in a recent quantitative study of school attendance in Alabama, argued that poor whites desirous of education were kept from schooling, like the blacks, by the white ruling groups: planters, industrialists, merchants, and bankers. Patricia A. Graham, in a fascinating "community study" of education in Butler County, Ala., from 1865 to 1918, arrived at a conclusion similar to Gershenberg's. The economic, educational, and racial ideas of poor and rural whites in the late nineteenth and early twentieth centuries are certainly worthy of study to test the hypothesis of class dominance. It is unfortunate that the existing studies of populism, though strong on economic and racial matters, speak little to the attitude of the agrarians toward schooling.

The New South's emphasis on commercial development and schooling fostered commercialization, but not a democratized society. The sponsors of the 1917 legislation providing federal aid to vocational education were both Georgians, HOKE SMITH and Dudley Hughes. The failures of this legislation and other public school programs in the South and in the country at large to provide the democratization and social mobility they promised are typical of the failures of the New South philosophy in its own region. Yet the attack that came on the New South philosophy from within the South was not based on a failure to equalize and democratize the society, but rather on the premise that democratization had somehow succeeded. I'LL TAKE MY STAND, the 1930 manifesto of the southern Agrarian writers, attacked the New South philosophy as a debasement of the authentic southern agrarian life-style (REGIONALISM). This attack did not seek economic or racial justice in schooling or any other aspect of southern life, and its genuinely reactionary wish to return to antebellum ways meant that it could only fail to achieve political support.

The issue of racial justice, which plagued southern society and its schools throughout the twentieth century, became the crucial educational issue after the 1954 Supreme Court decision declaring school segregation illegal. Several studies have been made of the reactions of southerners to both the BROWN V. BOARD OF EDUCATION decision and the CIVIL RIGHTS ACT OF 1964. Notable work on the issue of segregation and integration in southern schools has been done by Margaret Anderson, Numan V. Bartley, Robert Coles, I. A. Newby, and Gary Orfield. Unfortunately, the issue of the economic bias and consequences of southern education is absent from works on the years after World War I. It is hoped that this neglect will be remedied in forthcoming work on southern schools.

In general, the history of southern schooling is an area that has suffered from scholarly neglect. Students of educational history tend to minimize the South, perhaps because of its slow development, and students of southern history seem to prefer the romance of political accounts to the study of schooling. Areas of the most acute neglect are the colonial period, the Confederacy (no study of schooling in the Confederate South could be located), the Populist attitude and that of poor whites in all periods, and the years from 1920 to 1954.

See E. W. Knight, *Education in South* (1922) and *Documentary History* (1949), standard interpretation; H. A. Bullock, *Negro Education* (1967), mostly on post–Civil War Years; H. M. Bond, *Education of Negro in America* (1934), and *Negro Education in Alabama* (1939), bold but excellent; J. D. Anderson, "Education for Servitude" (Ph.D. dissertation, University of Illinois, 1973); R. Coles, *Children of Crisis* (1967), impact of desegregation on schoolchildren; I. Gershenberg, *History of Education Quarterly* (Winter, 1970); P. A. Graham, *Community in American Education* (1974), Ch. 4 on Butler County, Ala.; L. Harlan, *Booker T. Washington* (1972) and *Separate and Unequal* (1958); J. M. McPherson, *American Historical Review* (June, 1970), contentious but convincing; F. D. Mathews, "Education in Alabama and Georgia, 1830–1860" (Ph.D. dissertation, Columbia, 1965); I. A. Newby, *Challenge to Court, 1954–1966* (1967); G. Orfield, *Reconstruction of Southern Education* (1969), 1964 Civil Rights Act; F. E. Salzillo, "Educational Reform in Georgia, 1830–1840" (M.A. thesis, Georgia State, 1973); W. P. Vaughn, *Schools for All* (1974); and J. L. Wagoner, *Thomas Jefferson* (1975).

WAYNE J. URBAN
Georgia State University

EIGHT-BOX LAW, an attempt to disfranchise black voters by subterfuge, was passed by the South Carolina legislature following the 1880 election of a Negro congressman from a black district in Edgefield and Aiken. Congress reversed the reported election results, achieved through fraud and intimidation, and seated the black candidate, ROBERT SMALLS, instead of his opponent, George D. Tillman. The eight-box law, passed in 1882, provided for eight different boxes, each marked for one of eight classes of local, state, and national offices. Votes cast in the wrong box were void, and the measure amounted to a discriminatory literacy test, for box managers helped those voters who they knew would vote "correctly" and foiled others by ignoring them or shifting the boxes during the balloting.

See D. D. Wallace, *South Carolina* (1951); and G. B. Tindall, *South Carolina Negroes* (1952).

PHILIP N. RACINE
Wofford College

EISENHOWER, DWIGHT D., ADMINISTRATION (1953–1961) enjoyed a popularity in the South unmatched by any previous Republican administration. Born in Denison, Tex., Eisenhower had an expressive face, a winning smile, and an impressive record of military leadership. During his long military career, he had never been identified with partisan politics, and even after entering the political fray he continued to project an image of dignity and decency that transcended party divisions. Throughout his tenure in office, Eisenhower was far more popular than was the Republican party, and in the South many avowed Democrats wore "I like Ike" buttons. The Eisenhower campaigns of 1952 and 1956 established the GOP as a respectable alternative for southern voters.

Eisenhower's impact on the solid Democratic South was dramatic. He won the Republican nomination in 1952 after a crucial struggle over contested delegations from Georgia, Louisiana, and Texas. The contests resulted in part from the flood of former Democrats who carried the Eisenhower banner to the normally moribund local GOP conventions, much to the dismay of old guard southern Republicans, most of whom favored the nomination of Senator Robert A. Taft. After winning the nomination, Eisenhower campaigned actively in the South, visiting nine southern states while his Democratic opponent visited only four. In addition to the newly energized Republican effort, prominent southern Democrats, including the governors of Texas, Louisiana, and South Carolina, headed Democrats for Eisenhower campaigns. In the former Confederate states, none of which had voted for a Republican candidate since 1928, Eisenhower carried four states and won almost as many popular votes as the Democratic candidate in the 1952 election and in 1956 won five states and a plurality of the popular vote. The general particularly appealed to southern voters in the burgeoning white-collar urban-suburban neighborhoods and in traditionally Republican mountain counties.

Although Eisenhower helped to undermine the southern one-party system, he followed an equivocal policy toward another peculiar southern institution, de jure racial SEGREGATION. The BROWN V. BOARD OF EDUCATION decision of 1954 confronted the Eisenhower administration with difficult political and moral dilemmas. While some Republican strategists fixed their gaze on black and northern liberal white voters and advocated active support for desegregation, others focused on the deteriorating position of the national Democratic party in the South and favored a cautious approach to race relations that was an early version of what later became known as the "southern strategy." Characteristically, the Eisenhower administration leaned toward the conservative alternative while searching for a middle-of-the-road course. Eisenhower personally seemed to have serious reservations about the Brown decision. Although he was later to state in his memoirs that he fully agreed with the Court's action, his leading biographer noted the president's "serious doubts" about the ruling and points out that never once during his tenure in the White House did Eisenhower offer public support for the Court's position. Eisenhower feared further erosion of the rights of states, and, perhaps more fundamentally, he was a true conservative in viewing social change not as a historic fulfillment of American ideals but as a gradual process that allowed ample time for individual emotional adjustments. Eisenhower did intervene decisively in the Little Rock desegregation crisis when he ordered military forces into the city in September, 1957. The president explained, however, that his purpose was not to promote any given racial policy but only to restore law and order in a situation where mob action had disrupted the normal law enforcement process. The Eisenhower administration also responded to liberal pressure by guiding through Congress the CIVIL RIGHTS ACT OF 1957 and the CIVIL RIGHTS ACT OF 1960, both of which concerned voting rights in the South, lacked adequate enforcement provisions, and were mainly significant as the first civil rights laws since Reconstruction. For the most part, the Eisenhower administration left the problems of race relations to be dealt with by the federal courts. This policy resulted only in the barest token compliance with the Brown decision.

See H. S. Parmet, *Eisenhower and American Crusades* (1972), best biography; and Eisenhower's memoirs, *Mandate for Change* (1963) and *Waging Peace* (1965). See also E. J. Hughes, *Ordeal of Power* (1963); E. F. Morrow, *Black Man in White House* (1963); S. Adams, *Firsthand Report* (1961); J. W. Anderson, *Eisenhower, Brownell and Congress* (1964); N. V. Bartley, *Rise of Massive Resistance* (1960); J. L. Sundquist, *Politics and Policy* (1968); and D. M. Berman, *Bill Becomes a Law* (1962).

NUMAN V. BARTLEY
University of Georgia

ELAINE RACE RIOT. The Elaine, Ark., riot occurred at the end of the "red summer" of 1919, an ugly period of interracial strife when the nation witnessed some 25 race riots, widely regarded as proof of a Bolshevik threat to American society. The Arkansas incident originated in the effort of the Farmers and Laborers Household Union, led by Robert L. Hill, to secure local sharecroppers a fair crop settlement. On October 1 a police officer was killed and another white man wounded outside Hoop Spur Church, a Negro meetinghouse on the outskirts of town. For the next four days whites went on a rampage. Governor CHARLES H. BROUGH ordered in troops and declared martial law, arresting hundreds of blacks and placing them in a stockade. The aura of mystery still hangs over the incident. Who fired the first shot and how many blacks died (probably 20 to 25) will never be known. Authorities accused the "insurrectionists" of plotting the slaughter of white planters, and an all-white jury convicted 12 blacks of murder. In 1923 the Elaine Twelve went free after their death sentences were overturned by the U.S. Supreme Court.

See B. B. McCool, *Union, Reaction, and Riot* (1970); A. I. Waskow, *From Race Riot to Sit-in* (1966); O. A. Rogers, Jr., *Arkansas Historical Quarterly* (Summer, 1960); R. H. Desmarais, *Arkansas Historical Quarterly* (Summer, 1974); C. C. Smith, *Craighead County Historical Quarterly* (Summer, 1974); and L. E. Williams and L. E. Williams, Jr., *Anatomy of Four Race Riots* (1972), inaccurate.

DONALD HOLLEY
University of Arkansas, Monticello

EL DORADO, ARK. (pop. 25,283), 80 miles northeast of Shreveport, La., was settled by a merchant in 1843. It remained a small market village and county seat until the end of the nineteenth century, when railroads reached the town and the lumbering of area forests began. The real wealth and good fortune promised by its name did not come to the city, however, until 1921, when oil was discovered. By the end of its first year as a boomtown, El Dorado had 460 oil-producing wells. It continues to be the headquarters of Arkansas' petroleum industries as well as a shipping and trading center for area farmers and lumbermen.

See files of El Dorado *News-Times* (1921–).

ELECTION, PRESIDENTIAL, OF 1788. In the first election held under the federal Constitution the South had the election secured from the moment that Virginia ratified the new framework of government, for no one other than GEORGE WASHINGTON of Virginia was ever seriously suggested for the presidency. The only questions that lingered during the election were: would Washington accept; and who would win the second largest number of electoral votes and be elected vice-president? Washington received a unanimous vote of the electors (69 votes) and with genuine reluctance did accept the mandate. A more eager John Adams of Massachusetts emerged with 34 votes and the vice-presidency, but only after sharing the electors' second ballots with ten other candidates.

Only five of Adams' votes came from the South. In both the North and South, the people did not have a great deal to do with the election. In many states it was the legislatures that chose the members of the electoral college. In the South, Virginia and Maryland were two of only three states in the Union that permitted the people to vote directly for the electors. North Carolina, on the other hand, had not even ratified the Constitution and thus played no role at all in the election.

See E. H. Roseboom, *History of Presidential Elections* (1970); and D. S. Freeman, *George Washington* (1954), VI.

ELECTION, PRESIDENTIAL, OF 1792. During George Washington's first term the rivalry and disagreements between THOMAS JEFFERSON and Alexander Hamilton became famous, but one thing the two men did agree upon. Both wanted Washington reelected in 1792. When Washington agreed to run a second time the vote was once more unanimous and again interest centered on the vice-presidency. John Adams did win a second term, but the newly emerging Jeffersonian Republicans had labored vigorously against him in favor of George Clinton and were able to deprive the Massachusetts Federalist of the support of Virginia, North Carolina, Georgia, and Kentucky in the South, in addition to New York in the North.

See F. McDonald, *Presidency of Washington* (1974); D. S. Freeman, *George Washington* (1954), VI; and E. H. Roseboom, *History of Presidential Elections* (1970).

ELECTION, PRESIDENTIAL, OF 1796. The South played an important role in the election of 1796, the first partisan presidential contest in American history. With George Washington planning to retire, both parties selected candidates for national office. Two of the four major candidates were southerners: THOMAS JEFFERSON of Virginia, the Republican presidential choice, and THOMAS PINCKNEY of South Carolina, the Federalist vice-presidential nominee. Outside of Maryland, Virginia, and South Carolina, there was relatively little electioneering in the South. The character of the candidates furnished the principal campaign issue. As expected, Jefferson carried the South with 54 electoral votes to Adams' nine. Pinckney and Aaron Burr, the leading Republican vice-presidential candidate, received 14 and 17 southern votes respectively. Nationally Adams won, 71 to 68, over Jefferson, who became the new vice-president. The single votes Adams obtained in Virginia and North Carolina assured his election to the presidency.

See S. G. Kurtz, *Presidency of John Adams* (1957), excellent; R. Beeman, *Old Dominion in New Nation* (1972); N. E. Cunningham, Jr., *Jeffersonian Republicans* (1957); W. Chambers, *Political Parties in New Nation* (1963); and D. Gilpatrick, *Jeffersonian Democracy in North Carolina* (1931).

RAYMOND W. CHAMPAGNE, JR.
University of Scranton

ELECTION, PRESIDENTIAL, OF 1800. Of the 16 states in the Union, four southern states plus Rhode Island had electors chosen by the people either in districts or by general ticket, methods that increased the importance of state party organization and advanced the process of political development. Although overshadowed by other issues, particularly the Alien and Sedition Acts and the quasi war with France, North-South sectional differences figured in the preelection campaign and seem to have had an effect on the outcome. Of the 73 electoral votes cast for THOMAS JEFFERSON and Aaron Burr, 53 were from the South, whereas John Adams and CHARLES COTESWORTH PINCKNEY achieved a total of only 12 votes from that region. The tied vote in the electoral college between Jefferson and Burr showed the effectiveness of Republican party organization. The election was thrown into the House of Representatives, where neither Jefferson nor Burr was able to win a majority of the states after five days of balloting. On the thirty-sixth ballot, Federalists in four state delegations (three of which were southern) abstained, thereby giving Jefferson the victory. In the congressional contests, well over half the new Republican majority came from the South. The election, therefore, represented not only a triumph for Jeffersonian republicanism but the achievement of southern political dominance in the nation.

See H. Adams, *U.S. in 1800* (1955), general background; M. Borden, *Federalism of Bayard* (1955); S. G. Kurtz, *Presidency of John Adams* (1957); N. E. Cunningham, Jr., *Jeffersonian Republicans* (1957); J. C. Miller, *Federalist Era* (1960), political background; and D. Sisson, *American Revolution of 1800* (1974).

GEORGE DARGO
City College, City University of New York

ELECTION, PRESIDENTIAL, OF 1804. The power of the southern-dominated Republican coalition reached new heights as THOMAS JEFFERSON and George Clinton of New York won 162 of a possible 176 electoral votes. This election victory represented a national referendum on Jefferson's first term. Budgetary retrenchment, debt reduction, and repeal of the Judiciary Act of 1801

were popular measures especially in the South. In particular, the LOUISIANA PURCHASE opened vast new territories, which, it was thought, would be colonized by southerners sympathetic to Republican party policies and principles. Opposition to Louisiana and to Jefferson's reelection was centered in the Northeast. The Federalist party defeat signified the political isolation of New England, where sentiment was drifting toward constitutional revision and even outright secession in some quarters.

See N. E. Cunningham, *Jeffersonian Republicans in Power* (1963); D. H. Fischer, *Revolution of American Conservatism* (1965), on Federalists; J. S. Young, *Washington Community* (1966), resists importance of party; M. Smelser, *Democratic Republic* (1968), political background; and D. Malone, *Jefferson* (1970).

GEORGE DARGO
City College, City University of New York

ELECTION, PRESIDENTIAL, OF 1808. The southern Republicans split in 1808. The "old Republicans" supported JAMES MONROE for the presidency against JAMES MADISON on the grounds that the party threatened to outdo the Federalists in centralizing authority in Washington, favoring northern commercial interests, and enhancing executive power. Since 79 congressional Republicans boycotted the "caucus," Monroe and the old Republicans argued that no candidate had the required sanction to run as the party's choice. Monroe waged a sedate campaign, stressing foreign policy issues, and the old Republicans followed his lead, saying little about the apostasy of the party under Madison from the "principles of '98." Despite the split and the efforts of the Federalists to exploit it, most southerners voted for Madison. Monroe received no electoral votes and polled only 3,408 popular votes in his home state of Virginia as compared with Madison's 14,665. Subsequently, most old Republicans returned to the fold in the face of a resurgent Federalist party.

See N. K. Risjord, *Old Republicans* (1965), fullest account; N. E. Cunningham, *Jeffersonian Republicans in Power* (1963); H. Ammon, *Monroe* (1971); R. Hofstadter, *Idea of Party System* (1969); T. P. Abernethy, *South in New Nation* (1961); W. N. Chambers, *Political Parties in New Nation* (1963); N. K. Risjord, *Journal of Southern History* (Nov., 1967); and H. Ammon, *William and Mary Quarterly* (Jan., 1963).

GEORGE M. DENNISON
Colorado State University

ELECTION, PRESIDENTIAL, OF 1812 was sectionally oriented. JAMES MADISON, the Republican candidate, got only Vermont's six electoral votes in the northeastern states, whereas De Witt Clinton, the antiwar Republican and Federalist candidate, got only nine in the South, part of Maryland's and all of Delaware's. In Delaware, Clinton won easily, though Madison carried commercial New Castle County. In politically divided Maryland, Madison won six of the 11 districts, aided by dissension among the Federalists. Madison carried Virginia and North Carolina easily. The Federalist strongholds in this, as in previous presidential elections, were the peninsula between the Delaware and Chesapeake bays, the Potomac-Shenandoah watershed, and the Cape Fear River valley. In South Carolina the Republican electors routed their Federalist opponents, even in previously Federalist Charleston. And, in Georgia, Kentucky, Tennessee, and Louisiana, Clinton received only a few scattered votes.

See N. K. Risjord, in A. M. Schlesinger, Jr. (ed.), *History of American Presidential Elections* (1971), I.

DAVID J. RUSSO
McMaster University

ELECTION, PRESIDENTIAL, OF 1816 followed a close contest in the last meaningful national nominating caucus of the dominant Republican party between supporters of two southerners, JAMES MONROE of Virginia and WILLIAM H. CRAWFORD of Georgia. Despite Crawford's last-minute withdrawal, he still received 54 votes to Monroe's 65. The hardworking Monroe, who was James Madison's private choice, had won endorsements from various state party organizations; but the Virginia caucus refrained from officially nominating Monroe to prevent him from being labeled Virginia's candidate. Many New York Republicans, objecting to Virginia's long hegemony, rallied around Daniel D. Tompkins. As he was virtually unknown to southerners—a majority of the caucus—they switched to Crawford and secured Tompkins' nomination as vice-president. The Federalists, hurt by wartime actions of northern leaders and by the Republican takeover of their major programs, informally nominated RUFUS KING, who received only 34 electoral votes, all from north of the Potomac, to Monroe's 183.

See H. Ammon, *Monroe* (1971); J. Parton, *Jackson* (1860); and S. Livermore, *Twilight of Federalism* (1962), ignores South.

CHARLES ELLIS DICKSON
King College

ELECTION, PRESIDENTIAL, OF 1820. The almost unanimous electoral vote for JAMES MONROE

was indicative of superficial harmony; for the turbulent Era of Good Feelings witnessed the development of new issues and alignments that would reduce southern dominance over national politics. Many argued that the Missouri controversy (MISSOURI COMPROMISE) was permitting RUFUS KING and De Witt Clinton to form a new alliance against the South. Monroe, fearful for the Union's future and for his own reelection, worked discreetly for a quick compromise in Congress and put pressure on state party leaders, particularly in Virginia, to accept compromise and support his candidacy. Nomination rested entirely with the states because the national caucus, opened to all congressmen, was too poorly attended to make a national nomination practical. With no effective opposition, less than 2 percent of the white population bothered to vote; but, at the congressional vote-counting ceremony, Missouri's disputed ballots created more than an hour-long uproar.

See H. Ammon, *Monroe* (1971); S. Livermore, *Twilight of Federalism* (1962); G. Moore, *Missouri Controversy* (1953); and C. S. Sydnor, *American Historical Review* (April, 1946), contains voting statistics.

CHARLES ELLIS DICKSON
King College

ELECTION, PRESIDENTIAL, OF 1824. After 1816 only the Republican party existed nationwide. Because presidential aspirants were in general agreement on a common economic program (tariff, bank, and internal improvements), presidential preferences evolved around personalities. Of the five major contenders, four were from the South: JOHN C. CALHOUN and WILLIAM H. CRAWFORD represented the Southeast; ANDREW JACKSON and HENRY CLAY represented the Southwest. The fifth principal was Massachusetts' John Q. Adams. Calhoun ultimately withdrew to become a vice-presidential candidate. The congressional caucus endorsed Crawford, but this action proved detrimental to his cause when all other aspirants argued that his endorsement was an infringement on the people's rights. The election sustained their contention. Nationwide, as in the South, no candidate received an electoral majority. Jackson captured 55 of his 99 electoral votes from among the South's 111 total; Adams garnered 6 of his 84 electors there; Crawford, 36 of 41; and Clay, 14 of 37. Absence of a national majority placed responsibility for the final choice of president in the House of Representatives, which ultimately selected Adams; in that balloting the 12 southern states were evenly split among Jackson, Adams, and Crawford.

See J. F. Hopkins, in A. M. Schlesinger, Jr. (ed.), *History of American Presidential Elections* (1971), I; and C. G. Sellers, *American Historical Review* (April, 1957).

JAMES A. KEHL
University of Pittsburgh

ELECTION, PRESIDENTIAL, OF 1828. President John Q. Adams sought reelection although he had done little to solidify the Republican party behind him. His only significant opponent, AN-DREW JACKSON, believed that he had been victimized in 1825, when the House selected Adams as president over him. Only months later the Tennessee legislature nominated Jackson for the presidency. He promptly resigned his Senate seat and began a letter-writing campaign to win the endorsement of politicians across the nation. Almost ignoring substantive issues, Jackson's managers worked diligently to build a machine. Organization was particularly important at this time because the electorate had been democratized by the removal of most restrictions on male suffrage. Adams' ambitious vice-president, JOHN C. CAL-HOUN, concluded that his future was brighter in the Jackson camp and switched. Rewarded with the vice-presidential nomination, Calhoun strengthened the Jackson ticket immeasurably in the Southeast. Additional Jackson support was provided by Martin Van Buren of New York, foremost Jackson spokesman in the North. He was also instrumental in converting hesitant southerners, especially the RICHMOND JUNTO headed by Thomas Ritchie. This Jackson–Van Buren–Calhoun coalition swept to victory. In the 12 northern states, Jackson almost equaled Adams in the quest for presidential electors (73 to 74). In the 12 southern states, Adams was overwhelmed by Jackson, 105 to 9.

See R. V. Remini, *Election of Jackson* (1963); and R. P. McCormick, *Second American Party System* (1966).

JAMES A. KEHL
University of Pittsburgh

ELECTION, PRESIDENTIAL, OF 1832. President ANDREW JACKSON defeated HENRY CLAY in 1832 by a larger popular and electoral vote than he had received in 1828. National statistics, however, obscure the weakened position of the Democratic party in the South. Each time Jackson won eight southern states (Missouri, Louisiana, Mississippi, Alabama, Georgia, North Carolina, Tennessee, and Virginia). In both elections Delaware voted against Jackson and the Maryland electors split, with the majority against Jackson. But, in 1832 Kentucky and South Carolina broke

with Jackson. The Kentucky loss can be attributed to two major occurrences. The first and probably more important was that this was Clay's home state and power base. The second was Jackson's MAYSVILLE ROAD VETO, which not only was a slap at Clay but also alienated some Kentucky voters. The South Carolina loss resulted from JOHN C. CALHOUN being removed from the national ticket in 1832. The major breach occurred between Jackson and Calhoun over the NULLIFICATION issue. This was further compounded by the PEGGY EATON affair, with the final break coming when Vice-President Calhoun broke the Senate tie depriving Martin Van Buren of confirmation as minister to England. The sum of these fragmentations was that, though in 1828 Jackson received 109 out of 118 southern electoral votes, in 1832 he received only 87 out of 121.

See E. A. Miles, in A. S. Link and R. W. Patrick (eds.), *Writing Southern History* (1965), excellent bibliography; J. A. Munroe, *Louis McLane* (1973); R. P. Formisano, *American Political Science Review* (June, 1974); L. L. Marshall, *American Historical Review* (Jan., 1967); C. G. Sellers, Jr., *American Historical Review* (April, 1957); and R. P. McCormick, *Second American Party System* (1966).

STANLEY B. KLEIN
Long Island University

ELECTION, PRESIDENTIAL, OF 1836. Martin Van Buren was chosen by Andrew Jackson to be his successor. In 1836 Van Buren won but lost a majority of southern electors. The John Q. Adams–Henry Clay–John C. Calhoun groups were joined by HUGH L. WHITE, an early Jackson supporter from Tennessee. In the absence of a unified national party, the Whigs chose to run a slate of men against Van Buren in different states with the hope of forcing the election into the House of Representatives, where Jackson's personal influence could be more easily counteracted. The plan almost worked. Van Buren won six southern states (Missouri, Louisiana, Mississippi, Alabama, North Carolina, and Virginia). The Clay forces delivered Delaware, Maryland, and Kentucky to William Henry Harrison (HARRISON FAMILY). The Calhoun electors in South Carolina voted for WILLIE P. MANGUM of North Carolina, and White carried Tennessee and Georgia. Thus, Van Buren had six southern states with 58 electors, and the Whigs had six states and 63 electoral votes. Virginia stayed loyal to Jackson's Van Buren, although the Virginia electors voted against RICHARD M. JOHNSON for vice-president and forced that election into the U.S. Senate, where Johnson won.

See J. H. Harrison, Jr., *Journal of Southern History* (Nov., 1956); P. Moore, *Journal of Southern History* (Aug., 1936); L. L. Marshall, *American Historical Review* (Jan., 1967) and *Mid-America* (Oct., 1965); T. P. Abernethy, *East Tennessee Historical Society Publications* (Jan., 1931); J. N. Averitt, "Democratic Party" (Ph.D. dissertation, University of North Carolina, 1956); W. W. Smith, *Maryland Historical Magazine* (Dec., 1967); W. S. Hoffman, *Jackson and North Carolina* (1958); C. G. Sellers, Jr., *Public Opinion Quarterly* (Spring, 1965) and *American Historical Review* (June, 1954; April, 1957); P. Murray, *Whig Party in Georgia* (1948); and R. P. McCormick, *American Historical Review* (Jan., 1960) and *Second American Party System* (1966).

STANLEY B. KLEIN
Long Island University

ELECTION, PRESIDENTIAL, OF 1840 consolidated and extended Whig strength from 1836, thus establishing a competitive two-party system in the South that lasted until 1852. William H. Harrison (HARRISON FAMILY) carried eight slave states with 78 electoral votes to five (Virginia, South Carolina, Alabama, Arkansas, Missouri) with 48 electors for the incumbent Democrat Martin Van Buren. The Whigs' popular margin in the South was a decisive 54 percent, slightly above their national average. Van Buren's independent treasury had alienated conservative Democrats favoring continuation of federal deposits in state banks, a defection partially offset by John C. Calhoun's return to the Democrats on the same issue. Undoubtedly, the greatest factor in the further southern shift to the Whigs (as elsewhere) was the depression following the PANIC OF 1837. The Whigs successfully blamed the collapse of credit, along with cotton and land prices, on their opponents, masking their own lack of agreement over remedies behind enthusiasm for "Tippecanoe and Tyler Too." Both parties ardently wooed the South, each claiming devotion to states' rights and accusing the other's candidate of abolitionism. Outside of Virginia, South Carolina, and Louisiana the voter turnout averaged an astonishing 82.3 percent.

See R. P. McCormick, *Second Party System* (1966), excellent on state-national relationships; R. G. Gunderson, *Log-Cabin Campaign* (1977), fullest general study; W. N. Chambers, *History of American Presidential Elections, 1789–1968* (1971), best analysis; J. R. Sharp, *Jacksonians Versus Banks* (1970); and J. C. Curtis, *Fox at Bay* (1970).

JAMES S. CHASE
University of Arkansas

ELECTION, PRESIDENTIAL, OF 1844 pitted candidates from the Upper South against one another: JAMES K. POLK, a Tennessee Democrat, and HENRY CLAY, a Kentucky Whig. At the Baltimore convention southerners denied Martin Van Buren the nomination because of his hostility to the annexation of Texas, supporting instead the thoroughgoing expansionist Polk. The Democrats joined in writing a platform that coupled the annexation of Texas with the acquisition of Oregon. Clay initially sidestepped the Texas issue, but subsequently found it necessary to assuage his southern supporters by making a limited commitment to southwestern expansion. Both parties succeeded in generating voter turnouts above 1840 levels: the Whigs rallied only 6,518 more voters, and the Democrats garnered 82,387 additional supporters. The surge of Democratic strength carried Georgia, Louisiana, and Mississippi from the Whig column; however, the total popular vote in the South was close. Polk held a 12,925-vote majority out of 728,893 votes cast, but he carried no state except Arkansas by as much as 60 percent of the vote. Of 114 electoral votes, Polk won 67, including nine registered by the South Carolina legislature. The returns suggest the maturation of a well-developed two-party system in equilibrium. The injection of the Texas issue into the election was a portent of future sectional crisis, but party identification rather than annexation motivated southern voters.

See C. G. Sellers, *James K. Polk* (1966); C. S. Sydnor, *Development of Southern Sectionalism, 1819–1848* (1948); C. G. Sellers, *Public Opinion Quarterly* (Spring, 1965); E. A. Miles, *Mississippi Valley Historical Review* (Sept., 1957); and W. D. Burnham, *Presidential Ballots* (1955).

KERMIT L. HALL
Wayne State University

ELECTION, PRESIDENTIAL, OF 1848. Despite sectional tensions, southern Democrats brushed aside JOHN C. CALHOUN's candidacy and Alabamian WILLIAM L. YANCEY's call for a guarantee of slavery in the territories. Instead they helped nominate Lewis Cass of Michigan for the presidency and urged the application of POPULAR SOVEREIGNTY to the territorial question. The Whigs convinced themselves and Mexican War hero ZACHARY TAYLOR, a Louisiana slaveholder, that he shared enough of their principles to become their presidential nominee. Taylor, who received 106 of his 171 convention votes from the slave states, avoided discussion of the slavery issue but managed because of his background to appeal to many southerners. In the election, Taylor captured eight of 15 southern states and 66 of their 121 electoral college votes. The Whigs won two states that had voted Democratic in 1844, increased their margins in four others, maintained their strength in one, and cut substantially into the Democratic majorities in five states. Taylor's victory in the South did not prove to be the determining factor in his election. Yet, his appeal in the South and the expressions of distrust for Cass foreshadowed "the decline of rational moderation" about the slavery issue and the increasing importance of the sectional perspective in the southern mind.

See H. Hamilton, *Zachary Taylor* (1951), most definitive; B. Dyer, *Zachary Taylor* (1946); W. D. Burnham, *Presidential Ballots* (1955); W. F. Dunbar, *Lewis Cass* (1970); and J. G. Rayback, *Journal of Southern History* (Aug., 1948).

JAMES C. DURAM
Wichita State University

ELECTION, PRESIDENTIAL, OF 1852. The struggle over the acceptance of the COMPROMISE OF 1850 had a disruptive effect on political parties in the South. By the 1852 presidential election, however, the Democratic party had regained its earlier cohesion and also enjoyed the support of numerous states' rights Whigs, who were repelled by the abolitionist tendencies of the northern Whig party. On the other hand, the comparative freedom of northern Democrats from abolition heresies made southern cooperation with the national party easy. Southern Democrats enthusiastically approved the platform's endorsement of the compromise, including the Fugitive Slave Act (FUGITIVE SLAVE LAWS) and the nominees Franklin Pierce and Alabama's WILLIAM R. D. KING. Southern Whigs generally showed little enthusiasm for their candidate WINFIELD SCOTT, and some leading Whigs openly opposed him. In November, Pierce carried the South by more than 80,000 votes; only Tennessee and Kentucky went for Scott. Overall, Whig votes in the South had declined from the 1848 level by 16 percent, and Democratic votes increased by 9 percent.

See A. C. Cole, *Whig Party* (1913); A. O. Craven, *Southern Nationalism* (1953); W. B. Hesseltine, *South in American History* (1960); and H. H. Simms, *Decade of Sectional Controversy* (1942).

FRANK M. LOWREY
Georgia Southwestern College

ELECTION, PRESIDENTIAL, OF 1856 found the South divided politically much along traditional lines. The Whig party was practically nonexistent, but most southern Whigs entered the KNOW-NOTHING or American party. Making its chief appeal to the South, the American convention nominated Millard Fillmore and ANDREW

JACKSON DONELSON, popular choices among most former southern Whigs. The Democratic party also took a prosouthern turn, and its candidates, James Buchanan and JOHN C. BRECKINRIDGE, as well as its stand on congressional noninterference with slavery in the territories, were highly pleasing to southerners. As the campaign progressed, it became increasingly apparent that Fillmore had virtually no chance for election and that a division of the southern vote might make possible the election of the Republican, John C. Frémont. Thus, southern Democrats stressed the need for a united southern vote in order to defeat the Republicans. As the election neared, a steady stream of Know-Nothings abandoned their party and came to Buchanan's support. On election day, Buchanan won 56 percent of the southern popular vote and carried every southern state except Maryland.

See A. C. Cole, *Whig Party* (1913); A. O. Craven, *Southern Nationalism* (1953); W. B. Hesseltine, *South in American History* (1960); W. D. Overdyke, *Know-Nothing Party* (1950); and H. H. Simms, *Decade of Sectional Controversy* (1942).

FRANK M. LOWREY
Georgia Southwestern College

ELECTION, PRESIDENTIAL, OF 1860. In April the Democratic CHARLESTON CONVENTION failed to satisfy southern demands for a platform committed to federal protection of slave property in the territories, and party unity collapsed. The northern-dominated BALTIMORE CONVENTION, which reassembled in June, nominated Stephen A. Douglas of Illinois and HERSCHEL V. JOHNSON of Georgia. Southern dissidents countered by nominating JOHN C. BRECKINRIDGE of Kentucky and Joseph Lane of Oregon at meetings in Baltimore and Richmond. Fearing disunion, other southerners, especially in the border states, had already joined the new CONSTITUTIONAL UNION PARTY, which in May nominated JOHN BELL of Tennessee and Edward Everett of Massachusetts. The new party counted on Unionist sentiment north and south and on support from former Whigs and Know-Nothings. The campaign in the South was bitter, with Abraham Lincoln and the Republicans portrayed as abolitionist threats to southern survival and extremists committed to secession if Lincoln were elected. Douglas campaigned in the South with little success. Breckinridge disavowed secession, but disunion sentiment grew, especially when Republicans won the October elections in the North. Bell offered himself as the best hope for peace and Union. The voting revealed little southern unity except in opposition to Lincoln. He received no popular votes in ten states and finished last even in the border states. Breckinridge won 72 electoral votes (the Lower South plus Delaware, Maryland, and North Carolina), but failed to take a majority of the popular vote of the South. Bell totaled 39 votes (Tennessee, Kentucky, and Virginia). Douglas took only 12 votes (Missouri and three in New Jersey). Lincoln won 180 electoral votes in the North and the election. Almost immediately South Carolina began the process of secession, and most southern states followed before Lincoln's inauguration.

See W. D. Burnham, *Presidential Ballots* (1955); A. Craven, *Growth of Southern Nationalism* (1953); and O. Crenshaw, *Slave States in Election of 1860* (1945).

MARIO R. DINUNZIO
Providence College

ELECTION, PRESIDENTIAL, OF 1864. Abraham Lincoln's political skill and public appeal deflected challenges to his nomination from within the Republican party. Nevertheless, fears of defeat persisted among Republicans and worried Lincoln himself. The party, apparently with behind-the-scenes encouragement from Lincoln, moved to strengthen the ticket with the nomination of ANDREW JOHNSON, war governor of Tennessee and former Democrat. The Democrats adopted a platform calling for peace and reunion, but nominated General George B. McClellan, who insisted that preservation of the Union must be part of the price of peace. Despite McClellan's stand many southerners hoped his election would end the war and preserve the Confederacy. A dissenting southern view argued that Lincoln's reelection would stiffen Confederate determination to fight for survival and feared that McClellan's election would lead to reconciliation with the North. None openly favored Lincoln. W. T. Sherman's capture of Atlanta in September was a great boost to Lincoln's campaign. Efforts by southern agents and COPPERHEADS to disrupt the election failed, and Lincoln swept to victory in November. McClellan won only the electoral vote of two border states (Kentucky and Delaware) and New Jersey. Tennessee and Louisiana, in Union hands, voted for Lincoln, but those votes were not counted in official results.

See M. Davis, *Image of Lincoln in South* (1971); and W. F. Zornow, *Lincoln and Party Divided* (1954).

MARIO R. DINUNZIO
Providence College

ELECTION, PRESIDENTIAL, OF 1868 climaxed a campaign marked by sectional hostility

and bitterness. Republican presidential nominee Ulysses S. Grant had been commanding general of Union Civil War forces; his running mate, Schuyler Colfax of Indiana, was the Radical Speaker of the House. Opposing them were Democrats Horatio Seymour, former governor of New York, and former congressman Francis P. Blair, Jr., of Missouri (BLAIR FAMILY). Both were strong Unionists, but both were also vocal critics of Radical Reconstruction policies. Grant received 214 (of 294) electoral votes, but only 52.7 percent of the popular vote. Florida's three Grant electoral votes were cast by its legislature, and three other southern states (Mississippi, Texas, and Virginia) were still unreconstructed. Seymour carried five of the remaining 12 southern states (Delaware, Georgia, Kentucky, Louisiana, and Maryland) and received 57 (of 94) southern electoral votes and 54 percent of the region's popular vote. These figures, combined with Seymour's northern strength, indicate that the Democratic ticket was supported by a majority of white Americans, who viewed Grant's candidacy as an endorsement of Radical Reconstruction. Thus, Grant owed his victory largely to the continued disfranchisement of potential Seymour voters in the South.

See J. H. Franklin, in A. M. Schlesinger, Jr. (ed.), *History of American Presidential Elections* (1971), II; and C. H. Coleman, *Election of 1868* (1933). Few studies of this election exist.

MARGARET S. THOMPSON
Knox College

ELECTION, PRESIDENTIAL, OF 1872 resulted in the victory of incumbent President Ulysses S. Grant (Republican) over New York *Tribune* editor Horace Greeley. Greeley, nominated first by the Liberal Republicans and subsequently endorsed by the Democrats, was the standard-bearer for an uneasy coalition of civil service reformers, "independent" editors (including HENRY WATTERSON of the Louisville *Courier-Journal*), GREENBACKERS, silverites, resumptionists, former abolitionists, and ex-Confederates. Indeed, it was an alliance founded almost exclusively upon antipathy toward Grant and toward Radical Reconstruction. Grant received all but 66 of 352 electoral votes, although the popular vote margin was much smaller (56 to 44 percent nationwide, and 51 to 49 percent in the South). All six states that Greeley carried were southern: Georgia, Kentucky, Maryland, Missouri, Tennessee, and Texas. The electoral votes of two other southern states (Arkansas and Louisiana), which would have gone to Grant, were disallowed by Congress.

See biographies of prominent participants, such as J. F. Wall, *Henry Watterson* (1956). See also W. Gillette, in A. M. Schlesinger, Jr. (ed.), *History of American Presidential Elections* (1971), II. Few studies specifically on this election exist.

MARGARET S. THOMPSON
Knox College

ELECTION, PRESIDENTIAL, OF 1876. At the Republican convention, meeting in Cincinnati June 14–16, Rutherford B. Hayes won on the seventh ballot, and William A. Wheeler of New York was selected as his running mate. The platform called for vigorous enforcement of the Civil War amendments, the end of federal land grants to railroads, a sound fiscal policy, and national harmony. Democrats meeting in St. Louis on June 27–29 nominated Samuel J. Tilden of New York and Thomas A. Hendricks of Indiana and ran on the slogan Retrenchment and Reform. The dreadful result, as far as Republicans were concerned, was captured in the headline of the Chicago *Tribune*: "Lost. The Country Given Over to Democratic Greed and Plunder." The Democratic National Committee, however, betrayed its doubts by asking the New York *Times* to verify returns from Louisiana, Florida, and South Carolina. This simple question touched off a bizarre chain of events that left the election in doubt until March 2, 1877.

Nineteen electoral votes from Louisiana, Florida, and South Carolina, plus one from Oregon (on a different issue), were questioned. Each party claimed the disputed votes and sent "visiting statesmen" southward to ensure victory. Tilden needed only one of the 20 votes to win; Hayes required every contested vote. The disputed states submitted dual returns, each purporting to be valid. Election chaos was compounded by Congress' failure to agree on a counting procedure. Earlier in the year the Senate had failed to renew the twenty-second joint rule, and the Senate's Republican majority was not prepared to permit the Democratic House to reject electoral returns without Senate concurrence. The question Who was empowered to count the electoral votes? became the focal issue. Whoever counted the votes possessed the power to choose one certificate over the other—and thus select the winner.

Partisans wisely agreed to a compromise, placing the decision in the hands of an electoral commission, composed of five representatives, five senators, and five associate justices of the Supreme Court. The commissioners were to weigh the evidence and make a decision, which could be reversed only by concurrent vote of both houses. To strengthen their cause the Democrats wanted the commission to go behind state returns, that is, to investigate the actual vote cast rather than to accept without investigation the results of the state returning or canvassing boards. But the Republicans maintained that the Constitution gave the several states control over elections and that the federal government had no authority to question the decision of the state returning boards. Thus both parties reversed their traditional roles regarding states' rights and became completely opportunistic about gaining the presidency.

During February, 1877, the commissioners refused to go behind the returns, thereby giving Hayes the presidency. In each case partisanship determined the eight-to-seven vote in favor of the Republican certificates. With the House and Senate divided between the two parties, it was impossible to gain a concurrent vote to override the commission.

Confusion over the election gave southern moderates an opportunity to secure political and economic benefits. In accepting the Republican nomination, Hayes had promised to "wipe out forever the distinction between North and South." L. Q. C. LAMAR, BENJAMIN H. HILL, and others saw the promise as an opening wedge for troop removal, home rule, and economic betterment; specifically, federal recognition of Democratic administrations in Louisiana and South Carolina. Likewise railroad men, such as Tom Scott, saw the disputed election as an opportunity to gain at least one more federal land grant, this one for the Texas & Pacific. The proposed railroad held out the promise of a happy marriage between southern principle and interest. After all, if Hayes were true to his letter of acceptance, he would be more favorably disposed to the railroad than Tilden. Almost in soap opera fashion the various forces came together. The list of prizes expanded to include a southerner in Hayes's cabinet (DAVID M. KEY, postmaster general), various internal improvements, organization of the House in favor of the Republicans, the railroad, home rule, and troop removal.

Southerners supported the electoral commission bill and then helped to curb a filibuster in the House that threatened to delay the count past inauguration day, March 4. By the astute use of dilatory tactics, they extracted a high price from the nervous Republicans. The Wormly House conference was the last in a series of meetings designed to cement the various promises and agreements. The Compromise of 1877, beginning with the electoral commission bill and culminating with the inauguration, ranks with the other great political compromises in American history. Although historians still debate the priority of motivation, political or economic, there can be no doubt that the measures taken removed serious obstacles to governmental stability. Southerners "redeemed" their land, and northerners surrendered for a time the concept of federal intervention. In the final analysis leaders of both parties saw themselves as winners but failed to realize the ultimate cost of expediency.

See C. V. Woodward, *Reunion and Reaction* (1966); K. I. Polakoff, *Politics of Inertia* (1973); *Congressional Record*, 44th Cong., 2nd Sess., V, Pt. 4; *House Miscellaneous Documents*, No. 31, 45th Cong., 3rd Sess., partisan but useful; H. Barnard, *Rutherford B. Hayes* (1954); and A. C. Flick, *Samuel J. Tilden* (1939).

NORBERT A. KUNTZ
St. Michael's College

ELECTION, PRESIDENTIAL, OF 1880 was the first since the Civil War in which there was no federal interference. The result was the emergence of a solidly Democratic South, casting its electoral votes exclusively for Winfield Scott Hancock. Nationally James A. Garfield, the Republican nominee, barely won with just 10,000 more popular votes than his opponent. From the so-called Compromise of 1877 until after the off-year elections of 1878, President R. B. Hayes had followed a lenient policy toward the South. When the returns revealed the emergence of a SOLID SOUTH and, conversely, the total failure of Hayes's moderate policy, which was aimed at bringing the South into the Republican camp, a resurgence of BLOODY SHIRT rhetoric set in. More than half the Republican campaign textbook of 1880 was devoted to bloody shirt material. Neither U. S. Grant, who prior to the Republican convention had pleaded moderation and toured the South, nor the GREENBACKER MOVEMENT was of significance in the outcome.

See J. Kousser, *Shaping of Southern Politics* (1974), new material and interpretations; S. P. Hirshson, *Farewell to Bloody Shirt* (1962); V. P. De Santis, *Republicans Face Southern Question* (1959); and H. J. Clancy, *Presidential Election of 1880* (1958).

RICHARD A. BARTLETT
Florida State University

ELECTION, PRESIDENTIAL, OF 1884, with the victory of a Democratic candidate for president, was of great significance to the South. It was another step in the decline of sectionalism as an issue, a decline that had been apparent as early as President Chester A. Arthur's annual message to Congress in December, 1881. His attempts to split the section through aiding malcontents from the Democratic party—GREENBACKERS, INDEPENDENTS, and others—were failures, and the selections of James G. Blaine and Grover Cleveland as candidates in 1884 were made with virtually no concern for southern interests. The BLOODY SHIRT was just barely waved. Republican infighting and Blaine's tarnished public record, plus a solidly Democratic South, gave the election narrowly to Cleveland. In the South guns were fired, fireworks were set off, speeches were made, and the whites rejoiced while some blacks feared that slavery would be restored. Finally, Cleveland's conservatism assured the nation that it was safe under Democratic leadership even with L. Q. C. LAMAR of Mississippi and A. H. GARLAND of Arkansas in his cabinet.

See S. P. Hirshson, *Farewell to Bloody Shirt* (1962); V. P. De Santis, *Republicans Face Southern Question* (1959); A. Nevins, *Grover Cleveland* (1933); and H. C. Thomas, *Return of Democratic Party to Power in 1884* (1919).

RICHARD A. BARTLETT
Florida State University

ELECTION, PRESIDENTIAL, OF 1888 witnessed a change in Republican strategy to split the SOLID SOUTH. The party's defeat in 1884 had caused a reassessment of its policies, and Grover Cleveland's decision to make the tariff the main issue of the campaign of 1888 provided the key for change. Although a minority of Republicans continued to raise the subject of the DISFRANCHISEMENT of the Negro and waved the BLOODY SHIRT, insisting that their hearts lay with the voteless blacks, leadership of the party abandoned that old argument and instead emphasized in its southern strategy the protection of industry. The aim was to appeal to the rising business interests of the South on the grounds that, in fighting for a high tariff, the Republican party was the true defender of southern interests. The strategy almost worked: Benjamin Harrison received more southern votes than any Republican presidential candidate since Reconstruction, and West Virginia did go Republican. Southern fears about the new administration were groundless. A modest federal election bill (derogatorily called the FORCE BILL) died in the Senate in 1891.

See S. P. Hirshson, *Farewell to Bloody Shirt* (1968); P. H. Buck, *Road to Reunion* (1937); A. Nevins, *Grover Cleveland* (1933); and V. P. De Santis, *Republicans Face Southern Question* (1959).

RICHARD A. BARTLETT
Florida State University

ELECTION, PRESIDENTIAL, OF 1892. The major party candidates for president were Democrat Grover Cleveland of New York and Republican Benjamin Harrison of Indiana. Although the main national issue was the protective tariff, the most significant aspect of the campaign in the South was the appearance of a new political party, the POPULIST PARTY. Populists advocated an expanded role for government in areas such as currency and banking, transportation, and land ownership. Most southern Populist leaders were substantial, informed citizens, but the party's greatest appeal was to farmers in serious economic distress. With organizations and tickets in nearly every southern state, populism presented the first serious challenge to entrenched Democratic power since Reconstruction. The southern strategy of the Populists was to form expedient alliances of discontented white Democrats and Republicans with blacks. Considering this an assault on white supremacy, many conservative Democrats used intimidation, social and economic pressure, corruption of the ballot box, manipulation of black voters, and incidents of violence (particularly in the Lower South). The Populists did best in Alabama and Virginia but officially polled no more than 37 percent of the vote in any southern state. Cleveland won the election, carrying every southern state, and the Democrats remained in control of the South.

See C. V. Woodward, *Origins of New South* (1951); G. H. Knowles, *Presidential Campaign and Election of 1892* (1942); H. U. Faulkner, *Politics, Reform, and Expansion* (1959); J. M. Kousser, *Shaping of Southern Politics* (1974); and H. W. Morgan, in A. M. Schlesinger, Jr. (ed.), *History of American Presidential Elections* (1971), II.

MARY JANE MCDANIEL
University of North Alabama

ELECTION, PRESIDENTIAL, OF 1896 climaxed a dozen years of bitter conflict in the South. Beginning in the mid-1880s, farmers and small planters rebelled against the BOURBONS who dominated the economic and political systems. Farm organizations such as the FARMERS' ALLIANCE demanded expanded educational facilities and regulation of railroads and banks. Some Alliance leaders turned to third-party politics and joined the POPULIST PARTY in 1891–1892. TOM WATSON of Georgia and LEONIDAS L. POLK of North Carolina became national Populist leaders. Yet, though the Populists made some inroads in the South, most farm leaders, such as JAMES S. HOGG in Texas and BENJAMIN TILLMAN in South Carolina, remained in the Democratic party. The white farmers and small planters stood divided on the third-party movement and on cooperation with Republicans and with blacks.

The Democratic National Convention of 1896 nominated William Jennings Bryan on a free-silver platform. The Republicans nominated William McKinley on a gold-standard and high-tariff platform. The Populists, finding their platform usurped by the Democrats, nominated Bryan with Watson as the vice-presidential candidate. Bryan disavowed the Populists, however, leaving Watson to carry on a futile campaign.

The election in the South reflected not only the debate on national issues, but also deep-seated divisions along racial and class lines. The Bourbons fought the "farmers' revolt" with intimidation and violence. They previously had enacted DISFRANCHISEMENT legislation in several states. Appealing to the latent racism of the farmers, they deprived "illiterates" access to the ballot box, thereby drastically reducing the number of eligible voters, both black and white.

Bryan waged an effective campaign, appealing to the Democratic loyalty of the region, while McKinley's supporters devoted considerable energy to the border states. The results show the success of both strategies. Bryan carried the Deep South, but McKinley, in winning the presidency, won four of the border states. Watson received 27 electoral votes for the vice-presidency on the Populist ticket. The election was the last hurrah for the Populist party.

See G. C. Fite, in A. M. Schlesinger, Jr. (ed.), in *History of American Presidential Elections* (1971), II; C. V. Woodward, *Origins of New South* (1951); and J. M. Kousser, *Shaping of Southern Politics* (1974).

KEITH L. BRYANT, JR.
Texas A. & M. University

ELECTION, PRESIDENTIAL, OF 1900 was a tepid replay of the heated contest of 1896. President William McKinley was endorsed by his party, and Theodore Roosevelt, war hero and governor of New York, was drafted as his running mate. The Democratic party again chose William Jennings Bryan. Although urged by his advisers to shelve the free-silver issue in view of rising prices and the consequent decline in pressure for inflation, Bryan insisted on a reendorsement of the party platform of 1896. American control of offshore territories acquired in the recent war with Spain was opposed, and Bryan termed imperialism "the paramount issue." Public response to the issue of imperialism was apathetic, so Bryan switched to attacks on the new gold standard law and on corrupt business practices. Lack of focus on a dominant issue confused the voters. In the South, rising prices and the memory of five-cent cotton, coupled with the Republican cry of "let well enough alone," reduced Democratic pluralities. Moreover, free trade with the newly acquired offshore possessions was as attractive to the cotton-growing South as it was to the industrial North. McKinley received 292 electoral votes, Bryan 155. McKinley's plurality was 861,657.

See P. E. Coletta, *William Jennings Bryan* (1964), I; and T. A. Bailey, *Mississippi Valley Historical Review* (June, 1937).

JOSEPH GOULD
St. Andrew's School, Boca Raton, Fla.

ELECTION, PRESIDENTIAL, OF 1904 pitted incumbent Republican Theodore Roosevelt against conservative Democrat Alton B. Parker, who carried the SOLID SOUTH while Roosevelt led a nationwide landslide. Southern issues remained in the background. Roosevelt's southern family ties, shrewd federal appointments, and Rough Rider charisma had buoyed Republican hopes, but only a few Republican pockets broke the electoral pattern: North Carolina "business Republicans" and mountaineers; Louisiana "sugar Republicans" (who approved Republican high tariff policy and a Panama Canal treaty that promised to increase southern sea trade); and the border states of Maryland, West Virginia, and Missouri. Roosevelt's consultations with black Alabama educator BOOKER T. WASHINGTON, cultivation of black delegates in the national convention, and appointments of blacks to southern federal offices proved intolerable to southern white voters. Thus the election, even though Roosevelt won, helped turn his party and his administration toward a southern policy of racial conservatism and demonstrated the persistence of southern fealty to the Democratic party.

See T. Cripps, "Lily White Republicans" (Ph.D. dissertation, University of Maryland, 1967), good bibliography; E. Morison (ed.), *Letters of TR* (1954–58); S. McCall, *Atlantic* (Oct., 1904); E. Mims, *South Atlantic Quarterly* (Jan., 1905); D. W. Grantham, *Tennessee Historical Quarterly* (June, 1958); H. F. Pringle, *Virginia Quarterly Review* (Jan., 1933); S. M. Scheiner, *Journal of Negro History* (July, 1962); G. B. McKinney, "Mountain Republicanism, 1876–1900" (Ph.D. dissertation, Northwestern, 1971); and J. B. Wiseman, "Dilemmas of Party Out of Power, 1904–1912" (Ph.D. dissertation, University of Maryland, 1967).

THOMAS CRIPPS
Morgan State University

ELECTION, PRESIDENTIAL, OF 1908. After a lifeless campaign, the election returns seemed to indicate a comfortable victory for William Howard Taft over William Jennings Bryan. The electoral vote was 321 to 162. However, considering Bryan's numerous handicaps and lack of a vital issue, the Republicans had cause for concern. Taft's popular majority was less than half that of Theodore Roosevelt's in 1904, and Republican factionalism was spreading. The returns from the South were, therefore, a reason for cautious optimism. Taft had broken precedent by becoming the first GOP presidential candidate to campaign in the South. His efforts were rewarded by increased support everywhere, ranging from a few thousand in the Deep South states to near victory in Tennessee, Kentucky, and North Carolina. The election also increased the number of southern Republican congressmen. This success would encourage Taft to renew the "southern strategy" of his predecessors (TAFT ADMINISTRATION).

See C. V. Woodward, *Origins of New South* (1951); P. E. Coletta, in A. M. Schlesinger, Jr. (ed.), *History of American Presidential Elections* (1971), III; H. F. Pringle, *Taft* (1939); and P. Coletta, *Bryan* (1964).

DAVID C. NEEDHAM
Presbyterian College

ELECTION, PRESIDENTIAL, OF 1912. All three leading contenders for the Democratic nomination in 1912 claimed southern origins. Speaker of the House CHAMP CLARK (Missouri), a provincial man who provided little leadership or legislation, swept the time-serving state organizations of the border South and seemed to have more national delegate strength than any other contestant. The sudden triumph of Governor WOODROW WILSON (native Virginian) over machine politics in New Jersey, along with his enactment of such Progressive reforms as regulation of railroads and utilities, had a powerful appeal for the growing liberal Democratic movement in the South. Although these reformers were unable to achieve control of their own states, they were successful enough in the primaries to provide Wilson with a plurality of southern delegates at the convention. OSCAR UNDERWOOD (Alabama), chairman of the House Ways and Means Committee, appealed to southerners on the basis of sectional pride and tariff reform and won control of four southeastern delegations. His candidacy faltered, probably because of a widespread feeling among southern party leaders that the nation would not support a Deep South candidate who was too conservative for the times anyway. Underwood's delegates played a crucial role in the convention, however, by refusing to join the Clark bandwagon and by opting for Wilson on the decisive ballot. Theodore Roosevelt and President William H. Taft vied for southern delegates at the Republican convention. Taft's "theft" of them was one reason Roosevelt bolted the party. Roosevelt's new Progressive party hoped to appeal to southerners by inviting only whites to join the ranks. However, Roosevelt's ties to northern blacks, the high tariff, and centralized government were too much for southerners to swallow. Wilson won the election, easily carrying all the southern states.

See A. S. Link, "South in 1912" (Ph.D. dissertation, University of North Carolina, 1945), and *Wilson: Road to White House* (1947); G. Mowry, *Journal of Southern History* (May, 1940); and Wilson, Roosevelt, and Taft Papers, Library of Congress.

GEORGE NORRIS GREEN
University of Texas, Arlington

ELECTION, PRESIDENTIAL, OF 1916. WOODROW WILSON's administration maintained its high popularity in the South in 1916, though there were occasional rumblings of discontent. Southern conservatives were alarmed over the CHILD LABOR bill, and they provided over four-fifths of the opposition to it in Congress. Also, rural progressive Democrats from the South were dismayed at Wilson's preparedness measures, but the issue faded when relations with Germany stabilized. Southern prominence in the administration was even a minor election issue. It was used by Republicans to defeat a Maine Democrat in September, 1915. At their national convention (1916) the Democrats prudently decided that "Dixie" might be sung in moderation, but not as often as the "Star-Spangled Banner." Wilson united the West and the South (except West Virginia and Delaware) to squeeze back into office on a mandate for peace, prosperity, and progressivism.

See A. S. Link, *Wilson: Campaigns for Progressivism* (1965); and Wilson Papers, Library of Congress.

GEORGE NORRIS GREEN
University of Texas, Arlington

ELECTION, PRESIDENTIAL, OF 1920. Warren G. Harding, the Republican candidate, predicted that the GOP would make inroads in the SOLID SOUTH, especially in Virginia, North Carolina, South Carolina, Georgia, and Louisiana. During his campaign he pledged support for the industrial development of the region, and he actively

sought southern votes at the national convention and in the general election. Shortly before his inauguration, Harding characterized himself as "highly sympathetic with Southern aspirations." The Democratic candidate, James M. Cox, attempted to counter Harding's strategy and his front porch campaign technique by appearing at rallies in every state in the nation—speaking even in Marion, Ohio, Harding's hometown. Cox's exertions and his defense of the League of Nations and other programs of the Wilson administration were unsuccessful as Harding carried every state outside the South and received more than 40 percent of the major party vote in Arkansas, Georgia, Kentucky, and North Carolina; he carried Tennessee.

See R. M. Scammon (ed.), *America at Polls* (1965), I; A. Sinclair, *Available Man* (1965); and R. K. Murray, *Harding Administration* (1969).

ROGER M. OLIEN
University of Texas, Permian Basin

ELECTION, PRESIDENTIAL, OF 1924. The incumbent president, Calvin Coolidge, won his only full term in office with about 54 percent of the major party vote (COOLIDGE ADMINISTRATION). Running as the "economy and common sense" candidate, Coolidge received professional advice from such southern party leaders as C. Bascomb Slemp (the president's secretary and a former congressman) and Rentfro Banton Creager (head of the Texas GOP). The most significant advantages of the Republican were the weaknesses of his opponents: Democrat JOHN W. DAVIS of West Virginia and Progressive Senator Robert Marion La Follette. Davis was not nominated until the 103rd ballot at the national convention. As a conservative compromise candidate, he carried all the southern states, but he lost the backing of labor and midwestern farmers' organizations, which tended to support La Follette. Senator La Follette won only in Wisconsin, his home state. Coolidge carried all other eastern and western states. In the South, La Follette attracted significant numbers of Democratic voters in Texas, Florida, and Kentucky, and he took Republican votes in Virginia, Tennessee, and North Carolina.

See D. R. McCoy, *Coolidge* (1967); J. L. Bates, *American Historical Review* (Jan., 1955); and K. MacKay, *Progressive Movement of 1924* (1947).

ROGER M. OLIEN
University of Texas, Permian Basin

ELECTION, PRESIDENTIAL, OF 1928 saw Republican Herbert C. Hoover decisively defeat Democrat Alfred E. Smith. Although Smith's popular vote exceeded that of previous Democratic contenders, he carried only eight states: Massachusetts, Rhode Island, Alabama, Arkansas, Georgia, Louisiana, Mississippi, and South Carolina. Yet Smith broke the Republican hold on the nation's northern urban centers. Hoover, reversing the northern trend, ran better in the urban than in the rural areas of the South and shattered the once SOLID SOUTH. Intrigued by Smith's urban gains, Samuel Lubell posited a "Smith Revolution" as a prelude to the "Roosevelt Revolution" of the 1930s. Jerome M. Clubb and Howard W. Allen, however, convincingly demonstrated that Smith's urban votes constituted a personal victory. The 1928 contest was simply a deviating election.

Al Smith—a Catholic of immigrant extraction, an avowed foe of PROHIBITION, and a product of New York City's Tammany Hall—was anathema to the Protestant, dry, native, rural South. His determined opposition to Prohibition and his appointment of John J. Raskob, a fellow Catholic formerly associated with both the Republican party and the Association Against the Prohibition Amendment, as chairman of the Democratic National Committee made it easier for many southerners openly to oppose him. Although the southern defection was initiated by the clergy, most notably Methodist Bishop JAMES CANNON, JR., it was not confined to them. A minority of the prominent southern politicians, among them Senators FURNIFOLD M. SIMMONS of North Carolina and THOMAS HEFLIN of Alabama, also deserted the party.

In the absence of real economic differences between the parties, the contest centered upon social issues. The bolters assailed Smith for the whole complex of urban values he represented. The loyalists countered with pleas for party loyalty and employed the race issue effectively. Faced with a choice between Hoover, representative of an older America, and Smith, candidate of the party of white supremacy, the South fragmented. As V. O. Key has shown, in general the whites of the black belt maintained their party regularity, whereas those rural areas with few blacks swung to Hoover.

See V. O. Key, Jr., *Southern Politics* (1949); D. Burner, *Politics of Provincialism* (1968); E. A. Moore, *Catholic Runs for President* (1956); J. M. Clubb and H. W. Allen, *American Historical Review* (April, 1969); D. B. Kelley, *Journal of Mississippi History* (April, 1963); H. D. Rea-

gan, *Alabama Review* (Jan., 1966); and R. L. Watson, Jr., *North Carolina Historical Review* (Oct., 1960).

MARCILE TAYLOR
Wesleyan College

ELECTION, PRESIDENTIAL, OF 1932 saw Franklin Roosevelt crush Republican Herbert Hoover. The real struggle in 1932 was not between the depression-burdened Hoover and Roosevelt. Rather, the important contest was for the Democratic nomination, and the South determined the nominee. Despite his advocacy of Al Smith's cause throughout the 1920s, Roosevelt maintained a cordial relationship with southern political leaders. In 1932 he hoped to heal the rift between his party's rural and urban wings by grafting Smith's urban support to his own southern following. Smith, however, was reluctant to surrender his leadership, and he and Democratic Chairman John J. Raskob sought to commit the party to the repeal of Prohibition prior to the 1932 convention. Led by CORDELL HULL, southerners rallied behind Roosevelt in an effort to end the wets' domination of the party and to prevent another Smith campaign. With virtually solid southern and western support, Roosevelt captured the nomination over the opposition of the urban delegations. Ironically, Roosevelt, who eventually forged a political coalition with the city as its nucleus, had first to defeat the personification of urban America—Al Smith.

See C. Hull, *Memoirs* (1948), I; F. B. Freidel, *FDR: Triumph* (1956); Hull Papers, Library of Congress; and Roosevelt Papers, Hyde Park.

MARCILE TAYLOR
Wesleyan College

ELECTION, PRESIDENTIAL, OF 1936. Few campaigns have presented a clearer contrast of political position and philosophy than that crucial 1936 test of the New Deal and its apparent political realignment. Stressing government responsibility for public welfare and criticizing economic privilege, Franklin Roosevelt's NEW DEAL had attracted the support of Negroes, Jews, Catholics, labor unions, relief recipients, and a SOLID SOUTH. By contrast, the GOP criticized federalism and charged FDR with mismanaging the economy. Hoping to attract middle America and the farm vote, Republicans nominated Kansas Governor Alf Landon. A recovering South gave FDR 75 percent of its vote, a record 98.5 percent in South Carolina. Nationally, he polled 27.7 million to Landon's 16.6 million and an electoral count of 523 to eight. The new Democratic majority had a broad base. Class, not sectionalism, was the measuring rod.

See G. B. Tindall, *Emergence of New South* (1967), excellent; S. F. Lubell, *Future of American Politics* (1952), classic analysis; V. O. Key, *Responsible Electorate* (1968), superb analysis; W. E. Leuchtenburg, in A. M. Schlesinger, Jr. (ed.), *History of American Presidential Elections* (1971), III; and D. W. Grantham, *Democratic South* (1963).

H. E. EVERMAN
Eastern Kentucky University

ELECTION, PRESIDENTIAL, OF 1940.

By 1940, Franklin Roosevelt's NEW DEAL expenditures, court-packing plan, attempted "purge" of southern leadership, enigmatic third-term position, and a farm recession had combined to revive Republican hopes. International problems induced the GOP to nominate liberal internationalist Wendell Willkie. Nationally, Roosevelt easily defended his popular labor and relief programs, and Willkie evoked enthusiasm—especially among ethnic voters—with his antiwar speeches. The South, although bitter over Roosevelt's political tactics, rallied to his foreign policy and interventionist stand, thus augmenting his 1936 totals and providing much of his 27.2 million to 23.3 million popular margin over Willkie. The electoral count, 449 to 82, was more decisive.

See S. F. Lubell, *Future of American Politics* (1952); V. O. Key, *Southern Politics* (1949) and *Responsible Electorate* (1968), excellent critical analyses; and D. W. Grantham, *Democratic South* (1963), superb bibliography.

H. E. EVERMAN
Eastern Kentucky University

ELECTION, PRESIDENTIAL, OF 1944.

Despite some talk of a southern revolt in 1944, Franklin D. Roosevelt's bid for a fourth term in the White House received strong support from voters throughout the South. The president and his new running mate, Senator HARRY S. TRUMAN of Missouri—a compromise candidate more acceptable to most southerners than Vice-President Henry A. Wallace—captured over 64 percent of the South's popular vote. The Republican challengers, Governors Thomas E. Dewey of New York and John W. Bricker of Ohio, gained an increased percentage of the popular vote in every southern state except Texas, but did not win a majority in any. Once again, as in 1936 and 1940, President Roosevelt won all the South's electoral votes. Thus, despite small Republican gains, the South remained solidly Democratic in 1944.

See R. A. Garson, *Democratic Party* (1974); and L. Friedman, in A. M. Schlesinger, Jr. (ed.), *History of American Presidential Elections* (1971), IV.

LAWRENCE H. CURRY
University of Houston

ELECTION, PRESIDENTIAL, OF 1948.

Growing southern dissatisfaction with the economic and civil rights policies of the national Democratic party culminated at that party's nominating convention. When northern liberals overrode party moderates to win adoption of a militant and uncompromising civil rights plank, the entire Mississippi delegation and half the Alabama delegation walked out. Although President HARRY S. TRUMAN chose Kentucky's Senator ALBEN BARKLEY to be his vice-presidential running mate, Deep South conservatives went ahead with the organization of the DIXIECRAT PARTY. They nominated Governor STROM THURMOND of South Carolina and, in a four-party race, hoped to throw the election to the U.S. House of Representatives. The Dixiecrat slate did win in Alabama (where Truman's electors did not even appear on the ballot) and in Louisiana, Mississippi, and South Carolina. Truman, however, won every other southern state except Delaware and won a surprise victory over Republican Thomas Dewey nationally.

See C. Phillips, *Truman Presidency* (1966); E. B. Ader, *Dixiecrat Movement* (1955); and W. C. Berman, *Politics of Civil Rights* (1970).

ELECTION, PRESIDENTIAL, OF 1952

was marked by Democratic efforts to heal the divisions caused by the DIXIECRAT movement of 1948. Two southerners, ESTES KEFAUVER of Tennessee and Richard Russell of Georgia, seriously sought the Democratic nomination, which went eventually to Adlai Stevenson. To mollify former Dixiecrats and party conservatives, the language of the party's civil rights platform was moderated and Senator JOHN J. SPARKMAN of Alabama was made Stevenson's running mate. More significant to the outcome of the election, however, were the actions of the Republican National Convention. The GOP also adopted a weaker civil rights plank than the one it had run on in 1948, and the convention nominated Dwight D. Eisenhower, a popular war hero, for president. When campaigning through the South, Eisenhower emphasized that he was "somewhat" opposed to further fair employment practices legislation. Three southern governors—JAMES F. BYRNES of South Carolina, Robert Kennon of Louisiana, and Allen Shrivers of Texas—endorsed the Republican's candidacy, and Virginia's Senator HARRY F. BYRD "went fishing." Continuing southern dissatisfaction with Democratic civil rights and economic policies and the popularity of Ike permitted the Republicans to break the SOLID SOUTH. Eisenhower won 25 electoral votes in the border states of Delaware, Maryland, and Missouri and 56 electoral votes in Florida, Tennessee, Texas, and Virginia. He ran exceptionally well in the middle- and upper-income suburbs of southern cities; the Democratic margin of victory in Louisiana and South Carolina was the support of the relatively small number of registered and voting blacks.

See D. S. Strong, *Journal of Politics* (Aug., 1955) and *Urban Republicanism in South* (1960); P. T. David *et al.*, *Presidential Nominating Politics in 1952* (1954), III; A. F. Westin (ed.), *Uses of Power* (1962); and A. P. Sindler (ed.), *Change in Contemporary South* (1959).

ELECTION, PRESIDENTIAL, OF 1956. The two Eisenhower-Stevenson elections shattered the Democratic SOLID SOUTH. Dwight D. Eisenhower had carried seven southern states in 1952, but he ran even better in 1956, winning nine states, 97 electoral votes, and 51.8 percent of the total southern vote. Democrat Adlai Stevenson carried only Alabama, Arkansas, Georgia, Mississippi, Missouri, North Carolina, and South Carolina (73 electoral votes). As in 1952, Eisenhower ran best in urban and suburban areas, primarily on economic issues. Black support for Eisenhower increased to an estimated 50 percent in the South (lower nationally), reflecting discontent with Stevenson's equivocations on civil rights and the success of such Republican appeals as "a vote for Stevenson is a vote for Eastland." Again in 1956, Eisenhower's coattails proved short; despite an increase in the number of Republican candidates throughout the region, southern congressional delegations and state and local governments remained overwhelmingly Democratic.

See D. Strong, *Urban Republicanism in South* (1960); A. Campbell, *Public Opinion Quarterly* (Fall, 1960); and O. D. Weeks, *Journal of Politics* (Feb., 1964).

GARY W. REICHARD
Ohio State University

ELECTION, PRESIDENTIAL, OF 1960, although usually viewed as reinstating the NEW DEAL coalition, did not totally restore traditional voting patterns in the South. The Democratic ticket of John F. Kennedy of Massachusetts and LYNDON JOHNSON of Texas carried 11 states (114 electoral votes) and 51.7 percent of the two-party vote in the region. Yet four states (Florida, Kentucky,

Tennessee, Virginia) went Republican, and six independent electors from Alabama and eight from Mississippi ultimately cast their votes for Senator HARRY F. BYRD. Southern turnout increased by 25 percent over 1956, probably because large numbers of southern Protestants went to the polls specifically to vote against the Catholic candidate, Kennedy. Republican candidate Richard Nixon ran better in many rural areas than Dwight Eisenhower had in 1956, even though Johnson's presence on the Democratic ticket undoubtedly helped to reduce Democratic defections. Nixon also retained considerable Republican support in southern cities and suburbs. On the other hand, Kennedy's symbolic support for arrested civil rights leader MARTIN LUTHER KING, JR., and his liberal civil rights position helped regain for the Democrats the strong support of black voters, which may have been decisive in three southern states. Republicans held five congressional seats (all metropolitan districts) but otherwise made few inroads on Democratic dominance in the region. The closeness of the presidential election in most states in the region, however, completed the nationalization of southern politics that began in the 1950s.

See P. E. Converse *et al.*, *American Political Science Review* (June, 1961); B. Cosman, *Journal of Politics* (May, 1962); and O. D. Weeks, *Journal of Politics* (Feb., 1964).

GARY W. REICHARD
Ohio State University

ELECTION, PRESIDENTIAL, OF 1964. Senator Barry Goldwater, the Republican presidential candidate, sought to exploit southern white "backlash" reaction to increased black voter registration and pressure for school desegregation. He campaigned in part by ruminating aloud about what to do with social security and denouncing the federal government as too big and powerful. John Kennedy's assassination gave Goldwater LYNDON JOHNSON as an opponent, a man from the South and West who had been enormously popular in the region. But many white southerners disapproved of his handling of civil rights issues, and voter turnout increased not only among blacks but also among conservative and poorly educated whites.

Goldwater's vote correlated highly with STROM THURMOND's of 1948. He did much better than had Richard Nixon in 1960 in the BLACK BELT, where racial issues were crucial. His vote was below Nixon's in Mexican Texas, west Texas, the mountains, south Florida, and metropolitan areas, where voters were offended by perceived racism or questions about social security or federal aid. He won five Deep South states (Louisiana, Mississippi, Alabama, Georgia, and South Carolina), 55 percent of the two-man vote in the Deep South, and 38 percent in the border South. He carried with him seven new Deep South Republican congressmen, five in Alabama and one each in Georgia and Mississippi, but Republicans lost a seat in Kentucky and two in Texas. Small Republican gains in the Georgia and Tennessee legislatures were offset by losses in the border states. But the Goldwater campaign left the old southern New Deal coalition a shambles.

See B. Cosman, *Five States for Goldwater* (1966); N. V. Bartley and H. D. Graham, *Southern Politics* (1975); R. F. Hamilton, *Class and Politics in U.S.* (1972); W. C. Havard, *Changing Politics of South* (1972); and J. Bass and W. de Vries, *Transformation of Southern Politics* (1976).

ROBERT W. SELLEN
Georgia State University

ELECTION, PRESIDENTIAL, OF 1968. Third-party candidate GEORGE WALLACE of Alabama symbolized the South's weakening Democratic party loyalties and dislike of LYNDON JOHNSON's push for desegregation and failure to win the Vietnam War. Denouncing liberals and appealing to "plain people," Wallace sought to win all the southern electoral votes to create a stalemate and a bargaining position for himself. Richard Nixon, the Republican candidate, differed from Barry Goldwater in emphasizing border areas rather than the DEEP SOUTH. He gained regional support by promising to ease federal pressure for school desegregation. Nixon chose as a running mate the little-known Governor SPIRO T. AGNEW of Maryland, who would not offend the South. Democratic candidate Hubert Humphrey echoed the New Deal and Great Society, but southern support dropped sharply after a party convention marred by riots. Southern voter turnout rose nearly 10 percent, with Wallace winning traditional rural Democrats and urban working-class voters, Nixon the white bourgeoisie and traditional Republicans, and Humphrey the blacks and liberals. In the Deep South Wallace carried five states and 41 percent of the vote; Nixon, three states and 31 percent; Humphrey, no states and 28 percent. In the border South Wallace won no states and 18 percent; Nixon, five states and 42 percent; Humphrey, three states, the District of Columbia, and nearly 40 percent. The regional result was Nixon 36.6 percent, Humphrey 34.7 percent, and Wallace 28.7 percent. Republicans won new U.S. Sen-

ate seats in Florida and Maryland, gained a net of three U.S. House seats and a net of 61 state legislature seats, making a two-party South a real possibility.

See K. P. Phillips, *Emerging Republican Majority* (1969); L. M. Seagull, *Southern Republicanism* (1975); R. J. Whalen, *Catch Falling Flag* (1972); R. M. Scammon and B. J. Wattenberg, *Real Majority* (1971); T. H. White, *Making of President, 1968* (1969); and T. F. Pettigrew *et al., Psychology Today* (Feb., 1972).

ROBERT W. SELLEN
Georgia State University

ELECTION, PRESIDENTIAL, OF 1972. President Richard M. Nixon slowed school desegregation, sought conservative southerners for the U.S. Supreme Court, and used "code words" appealing to the South. GEORGE WALLACE looked strong at first, winning 45.6 percent of the region's primary vote to Hubert Humphrey's 26 percent, but the Alabamian was crippled by an assassination attempt in May. Senator George McGovern of South Dakota became the Democratic nominee, alien to southerners because of his opposition to the Vietnam War and his favoring of minority groups. Nixon won 61 percent of the national vote, 72.5 percent in the Deep South, 63.7 percent in the border South, and 67.6 percent regionally. He carried the whole South except for the District of Columbia. Republicans won U.S. Senate seats in North Carolina, Delaware, and Kentucky, a net gain of eight U.S. House seats, and 85 state legislature seats, making the South a two-party region.

See E. R. May and J. Fraser (eds.), *Campaign '72* (1973); M. L. Billington, *Political South in 20th Century* (1975); N. V. Bartley and H. D. Graham, *Southern Politics* (1975); and W. C. Havard, *Changing Politics of South* (1972).

ROBERT W. SELLEN
Georgia State University

ELECTION, PRESIDENTIAL, OF 1976. In an extremely close national election, JAMES E. CARTER defeated Gerald Ford to become the first president from the DEEP SOUTH. Carter's quest for the presidency began with his entry into the caucuses and primaries of all 50 states. A crucial primary victory was achieved, however, when he defeated GEORGE WALLACE in Florida, a contest that many observers regarded as signaling Carter's ability both to carry the South and to win in urban areas. Although the past several elections had witnessed the growth of the REPUBLICAN PARTY in the South and the use of a so-called southern strategy for Republican presidential victories, nomination of Carter gave Democrats their own southern strategy. Carter carried every state of the South except Virginia and came closer than any Democrat since 1944 to carrying the SOLID SOUTH. Moreover, the Republicans lost the governorship of North Carolina, a U.S. Senate seat in Tennessee, and two U.S. House seats in Texas, and their representation in the legislative bodies of southern states fell from 15 to only 10 percent. Yet Carter generally trailed the rest of the Democratic ticket in most southern states; and, in Maryland, Missouri, Florida, Louisiana, Mississippi, Texas, and Kentucky, the heavy black vote for Carter probably represented his margin of victory.

See B. A. Campbell, *American Journal of Political Science* (Feb., 1977); P. Williams and G. K. Wilson, *Political Studies* (June, 1977); and E. C. Ladd, Jr., in S. M. Lipset (ed.), *Emerging Coalitions* (1978).

ELECTRICITY. Development of the electrical industry in the South began in 1904, when James B. Duke (DUKE FAMILY) founded the Southern Power Company. In 1906 the Alabama Power Company was organized and continued to grow through consolidations and plant expansions until by 1926 it was the single largest utility company in the South. Others followed quickly—the Georgia Power Company (1928), the Mississippi Power & Light Company (1927), Arkansas Power & Light (1926), and many more—so that by 1930 the use of electricity in the home and factory was commonplace. But the region had a serious shortage of electricity; less than 10 percent of the farms had service, and the power companies were hard pressed to keep pace with urban population and industrial growth. The shortage was ironic since the South was blessed with an abundance of waterways conducive to the generation of power.

The creation of the TENNESSEE VALLEY AUTHORITY in 1933 was the turning point in the development of power for a huge portion of the South, for it brought electricity to the farms, to the cities, and to the factories at remarkably low rates. Beginning in 1936 with the creation of the RURAL ELECTRIFICATION ADMINISTRATION, rural areas received service on a larger scale, and by 1955 rural electrification was complete. The same effect was seen in a smaller way with the creation of the Southwestern Power and Southeastern Power administrations, established respectively in 1943 and 1950. Private electrical interests became aware of the mass consumer market and began an extensive expansion program still under way today. Competition from the public institutions, moreover, forced the utility companies to lower their

rates, and consumption increased even more. Inhabitants throughout the South, rural and urban, enjoyed real improvements in their standard of living.

Despite the expansion of public power, privately owned steam-powered plants accounted for the lion's share of electricity in the South, except in the TVA area, where hydropower was abundant. Nuclear power has already begun to make real headway with eight plants in service as of 1974. That same year the TVA and the electric companies operating in the South had announced plans for another 30 nuclear plants scheduled for operation no later than 1979. As the encouragement and incentive for energy development become more important every day, private enterprise will gain an even larger share of the southern electrical market.

See J. W. Jenkins, *James B. Duke* (1927); T. W. Martin, *Story of Electricity in Alabama* (1952); and A. N. Sanders, "Regulation of Public Utilities in South Carolina" (Ph.D. dissertation, University of North Carolina, 1956).

D. CLAYTON BROWN
Texas Christian University

ELIZABETHTOWN, KY. (pop. 11,748), 40 miles south of Louisville, was first settled in 1780, when three separate stockades were constructed by groups of Virginians. Thirteen years later, Colonel Andrew Hynes laid out a town near one of the stockades and named it after his wife. When Thomas Lincoln, father of ABRAHAM LINCOLN, lived here, the town had 22 lawyers and a reputation as a center for litigation of property disputes. During the Civil War, several skirmishes occurred in the area and, in December, 1862, General JOHN H. MORGAN's cavalry captured the town and its federal garrison. Modern Elizabethtown is the market and shipping point for area limestone quarries and growers of corn, wheat, and burley tobacco. Local industry produces textiles and metal products.

See files of Elizabethtown *News-Enterprise* (1869–), available on microfilm; S. Haycraft, *History of Elizabethtown* (1921, 1960), personal recollections; G. McMurtry, *Elizabethtown, 1779–1879* (1938); T. D. Winstead, *Chronicles of Hardin County* (1974); Hardin County Historical Society, *Who Was Who in Hardin County* (1946); and Historical Library of Brown-Pusey House, which has files on families, homes, and churches of area, plus microfilm copies of area deeds (1795–1876), marriages (1793–1896), wills (1793–1915), census records (1810–80), and court orders (1793–1869).

ELKINS, STEPHEN BENTON (1841–1911). Twenty years before his birth near New Lexington, Ohio, Elkins' family had moved from Virginia partially because of his parents' opposition to slavery. While he was still a young boy, the family moved from Ohio to Westport, Mo. He was graduated from the University of Missouri in 1860 and, although his father and his brother joined the Confederate army, Elkins enlisted in the Missouri infantry as a Union captain. After being admitted to the Missouri bar in 1864, he moved to New Mexico, where he served in the territorial legislature (1864–1866), as territorial district attorney (1866–1867), U.S. district attorney (1867–1870), and territorial delegate to the U.S. Congress (1872–1877). Despite accumulating numerous mining, railroad, and banking interests in New Mexico, Elkins moved his home to West Virginia after marrying in 1875 the daughter of that state's U.S. senator, H. G. DAVIS. In the late 1880s, Elkins, W.Va., was founded to be the headquarters of his growing railroad and financial properties. After serving as secretary of war (1891–1893) in the HARRISON ADMINISTRATION, Elkins won election to the U.S. Senate (1895–1911), where he was an ardent defender of protective tariffs and a spokesman for railroad interests.

See O. D. Lambert, *S. B. Elkins* (1955); and Washington, D.C., *Evening Star* (Jan. 5, 1911).

ELLENDER, ALLEN JOSEPH (1891–1972), was for many years one of the most colorful and influential men in the U.S. Senate. Chairman of the Senate Agriculture Committee and a member of the powerful Senate Inner Club, he often used his influence to help defeat civil rights bills and other liberal legislation. A native of Terrebonne Parish in southwestern Louisiana, Ellender was well known in Washington for his famous CAJUN dishes such as jambalaya and crawfish bisque. He frequently went on world tours and was known as the most traveled man in the Senate. On his trips abroad, Ellender often made such insightful observations as, in Holland, "the canals are filled with water" and "the South of France has a Mediterranean climate." He was also known for his segregationist remarks: *e.g.*, "Africans are incapable of leadership without white assistance." In 1924 Ellender was elected to the Louisiana house of representatives. During his 12 years as a state legislator, he became one of HUEY LONG's closest political associates. In 1937 Ellender was elected to the U.S. Senate, where he served for 35 years. He died in the midst of a difficult campaign for reelection.

See Ellender Manuscripts, Nicholls State University; T. H. Williams, *Huey Long* (1969); and A. P. Sindler, *Huey Long's Louisiana* (1956).

MICHAEL L. KURTZ
Southeastern Louisiana University

ELLICOTT, ANDREW (1754–1820), mathematician, astronomer, and surveyor, was born in Pennsylvania. Although he had resided in Maryland since 1775, Virginia appointed him a commissioner in 1784 to extend the MASON-DIXON LINE to ascertain the Virginia-Pennsylvania boundary. While living in Baltimore, he taught mathematics, became a member of the American Philosophical Society, and was elected (1786) to the Maryland legislature. In 1791 George Washington selected Ellicott to survey the area that was to comprise the District of Columbia. Following the Treaty of San Lorenzo (1795), Washington chose him chief commissioner to determine the thirty-first parallel boundary with the Spanish possessions from the Mississippi River eastward. During this time (1796–1800), Ellicott maintained a chronological account describing virtually everything he encountered: inhabitants, flora, fauna, climate, topography, etc. His *Journal* (1803) is a primary source of incalculable value. From 1811 to 1812, Ellicott surveyed Georgia's boundary with South Carolina. He spent his remaining years at West Point as professor of mathematics.

See C. V. C. Mathews, *Ellicott* (1908).

MARTIN HARDWICK HALL
University of Texas, Arlington

ELLIOTT, HARRIET WISEMAN (1884–1947). Born in Carbondale, Ill., she earned an A.B. degree in history from Hanover College in Indiana and an M.A. degree in political science from Columbia University and in 1913 began teaching at the Woman's College of the University of North Carolina (WOMEN'S COLLEGES). In 1935 she became dean of women, a position that she held until her death. She worked for woman suffrage in North Carolina (WOMEN'S RIGHTS MOVEMENT) and was active in the state Federation of Women's Clubs, the League of Women Voters, and the American Association of University Women. On the administrative board of the state legislative council, she promoted reform in education, better race relations, and social legislation. An active Democrat, she served with the state Emergency Relief Administration, and in 1935 she helped implement an organizational and educational program for the women's division of the national

Democratic party. In the 1940s she served on several national defense boards and, as organizer and chairperson of the women's division in the Treasury Department, promoted the sale of war stamps and bonds.

See V. T. Lathrop, *Educate a Woman* (1942); and E. F. Barnard, *New York Times Magazine* (July 21, 1940).

SUSAN M. HARTMANN
University of Missouri, St. Louis

ELLIOTT, ROBERT BROWN (1842?–1884). There are several conflicting descriptions of the background of this black congressman from South Carolina. His biographer has suggested on the basis of his fine Spencerian script, the historical and literary references in his prose, and his formal oratorical style that he probably was reared and educated in England. Indeed, he may not even have been a citizen of the United States. What is known is that he moved from Boston to Charleston in March, 1867, to work as an associate editor of the *South Carolina Leader*. Entering the turbulent politics of Reconstruction, he was a delegate in 1868 to the state's constitutional convention. He then served in the lower house of the state legislature (1868–1870), two terms in the U.S. House of Representatives (1871–1874), and concluded his elected political career as Speaker of the South Carolina house of representatives (1874–1876). He also served the administration of Governor R. K. SCOTT as assistant adjutant general (1869–1870) and was credited with playing a key role in recruiting and organizing the new (and largely black) state militia. A polished writer and speaker, Elliott labored in behalf of compulsory public education and the KU KLUX KLAN ACTS. He consistently opposed AMNESTY for former Confederates and the use of a poll tax or a literacy test as a qualification for the franchise. Although elected as state attorney general in the contested ELECTION OF 1876, he was forced to leave office after WADE HAMPTON became governor. Thereafter, he worked for the U.S. Treasury Department as a special customs inspector (1879–1882) and practiced law until his death in New Orleans from malaria.

See P. Lamson, *Glorious Failure* (1973), good bibliography; R. Bardolph, *Journal of Negro History* (July, 1955); and J. Williamson, *After Slavery* (1965).

ELLIS, JOHN WILLIS (1820–1861), was born in Rowan County, N.C. He attended Randolph-Macon College and graduated from the University of North Carolina in 1841. He studied law under Judge Richard M. Pearson and was admitted to the bar. A states' rights Democrat, he served as a member of the North Carolina legislature (1844–1848) and as judge of the state superior court (1848–1858). In 1859 Ellis was elected governor of North Carolina. Fearing the Lincoln administration might use coercion against states that attempted secession, he favored a conference of southern states to prepare for possible war. On January 10, 1861, against the advice of Ellis, federal installations were seized in North Carolina. When Secretary of War Simon Cameron requested North Carolina troops to suppress the southern "insurrection," Governor Ellis declared such action to be "in violation of the Constitution and a gross usurpation of power."

See B. G. Crabtree, *North Carolina Governors* (1958); J. C. Sitterson, *Secession in North Carolina* (1939); H. T. Lefler and A. R. Newsome, *North Carolina* (1973); and J. H. Boykin, *North Carolina* (1961).

DONALD M. RAWSON
Northwestern State University of Louisiana

ELLISON, RALPH WALDO (1914–), was born in Oklahoma City and attended Tuskegee Institute from 1933 to 1936. While there, he majored in music composition, and this background, especially jazz and the blues, helped shape the structure of his subsequent writing. After college, he drifted northward to New York City, where he became friends with RICHARD WRIGHT. There he joined the FEDERAL WRITERS' PROJECT and the COMMUNIST PARTY. His disillusionment with the latter group eventually found expression in his works.

During the thirties and forties, Ellison wrote first for the "little magazines" like the *Masses*, but he soon moved to such journals as the *Atlantic* and *Harper's*. These early writings mark him as a member of the Richard Wright school, with a strong emphasis on naturalism and protest. In 1952, Ellison suddenly became a nationally known author with the publication of *Invisible Man*, winner of the National Book Award. In terms of a literary tradition, Ellison borrows from all schools, but with this novel he developed both a personal vision and a personal idiom. Even his choice of style is an attempt to show the chaos of the modern world.

Throughout the first half of *Invisible Man*, the grotesqueries, the outrages, and the humor of the experience suggest the southern school of Gothic writing. But they also suggest such writers as Franz Kafka and James Joyce. In the second half of the novel, the scene moves progressively northward, ultimately leaving the South for good. The main character goes from innocent boy to enlightened man of the world. In short, the novel quickly transcends its regional beginnings. Ellison has not proved a prolific writer. A collection of his essays makes up *Shadow and Act* (1964), his only other book-length work.

See L. D. Rubin, *Bibliographical Guide to Southern Literature* (1969); J. Baumbach, in *Landscape of Nightmare* (1965); J. M. Reilly, *Twentieth Century Interpretation of Invisible Man* (1971); and J. R. Hersey, *Ralph Ellison* (1974).

WILLIAM H. YOUNG
Lynchburg College

EL PASO, TEX. (pop. 322,261), near the westernmost corner of the state, sits on the northern bank of the Rio Grande opposite the Mexican city of Juarez. Prior to the MEXICAN WAR, both cities were a single entity known as El Paso or El Paso del Norte for the nearby pass through the Franklin Mountains. The first permanent settlements in the area were Spanish missions begun in the late seventeenth century (the first as early as 1659). Gradually a Spanish community developed on the south bank of the river, and not until 1827 did this city spread across the river to the present site of the American city. After being seized by the U.S. Army in 1846 and cleaved in two by the peace treaty, the city became the site of a U.S. Army post established in 1849 (now known as Ft. Bliss). The fort attracted American settlers to the area, and by 1852 two American communities, Hart's and Franklin, had grown up around the older Mexican community. Not until 1859, when the city on the Mexican side of the river was known as Juarez, did the three communities on the American side of the river accept the shared name El Paso.

During the 1850s, thousands of California-bound miners passed through the city, and El Paso thrived as a stagecoach station and supply point. It was the coming of several railroads in the 1880s, however, that effectively ended the city's relative isolation and made it a major transportation center. Modern El Paso continues to be a shipping center both for east-west traffic and for commerce with Mexico. Through it is imported Mexican lumber, and metal ores are exchanged for foodstuffs. Moreover, the city is a manufacturer of refined oil and metals and a market for the fruit, vegetables, and cotton produced on the irrigated lands of the surrounding countryside.

See C. L. Sonnichsen, *Pass of the North* (1968), 1528–1968 period; F. Mangan, *El Paso in Pictures* (1971) and *Bordertown* (1964); C. Bryson, *Land Where We Live*

(1973); C. Calleros, *El Paso* (1954), collection of news columns; W. W. Mills, *40 Years at El Paso, 1858–1898* (1901, 1962); O. White, *Out of Desert* (1923); and files of El Paso *Times* (1879–) and *Herald-Post* (1880–). El Paso Public Library maintains Southwest Archives, a collection of original manuscripts and papers of individuals and businesses.

EMANCIPATION, COMPENSATED, embraced proposals that either private philanthropists or governments pay masters for lost investment when their slaves were freed. Public plans were debated in southern states (Virginia, 1831–1832; Tennessee, 1834; Kentucky, 1849) but were never adopted. Private plans (*e.g.*, Frances Wright's NASHOBA) freed few slaves. The most extensive plans were those of the Union government during the Civil War to retain border state support and simultaneously satisfy antislavery sentiment.

In December, 1861, and March, 1862, Abraham Lincoln proposed that states adopting compensated emancipation be reimbursed with federal bonds. In December, 1862, he proposed full emancipation by 1900 and in January, 1865, suggested that compensation be paid in all states provided the war ended by April 1, 1865. Lincoln's proposals, like those that Congress debated in 1862 and 1863, failed to win border state support.

In 1862 Delaware rejected two specific executive plans to end slavery either by 1867 or 1893. In 1864 Maryland's constitutional convention rejected compensated emancipation. Missouri rejected federally aided emancipation in June, 1862. No other border state seriously considered the issue. The Civil War brought compensated emancipation only to the District of Columbia when Congress acted in April, 1862.

Moralists differed on compensated emancipation, with some advocating any means to end slavery and others, especially abolitionists, damning recompense for slaveholding. Loyal southerners divided similarly, with some arguing that funds could better be used to prosecute the war militarily, others seeking to salvage what they could when emancipation became inevitable. These divisions defeated compensated emancipation as an effective part of federal war policy.

See *Congressional Globe* (1862–63); R. P. Basler (ed.), *Works of Lincoln* (1953–55); L. P. Curry, *Blueprint for Modern America* (1968); H. L. Trefousse, *Lincoln's Decision for Emancipation* (1975); W. E. Parrish, *Turbulent Partnership* (1963); E. C. McReynolds, *Missouri* (1962); E. M. Violette, *Missouri* (1918, 1951); C. L. Wagandt, *Mighty Revolution* (1964); H. C. Reed, *Delaware Notes* (1931); C. C. Mooney, *Journal of Southern History* (Nov., 1946); A. Zilversmit, *First Emancipation* (1967); C. D. Goldin, *Journal of Economic History* (March, 1973);

J. V. Lombardi, *Hispanic American Historical Review* (Nov., 1969); and B. L. Fladeland, *Journal of Southern History* (May, 1976).

JANE H. PEASE and
WILLIAM H. PEASE
University of Maine, Orono

EMANCIPATION PROCLAMATION of January

1, 1863, by Abraham Lincoln, liberating the slaves in Confederate-controlled territory, served an unenforceable purpose and drew an inconsequential response. The preliminary report of September 22, 1862, however, hit the South like a thunderbolt. Lincoln's comment that the government "would not act to repress those newly emancipated in any efforts they may make for their actual freedom" was taken to mean that he called for a slave insurrection. It drew instant nationwide criticism. Southern editorialists saw Lincoln's action as pernicious and himself as a weak, wicked, and desperate despot. All sensed from the proclamation new objectives for the war: the complete annihilation of slavery, the destruction of $400 million in personal property, and a "blow at the foundation of Society in the South."

The slaves heard about the proclamation and their supposed freedom from varied sources: newspapers, discussion by their masters, and word of mouth. Those in the hinterlands did not take the matter seriously and continued in their servile state. Many in the border states and near federally controlled territory, however, quit their labors, acted as if free, and in some instances left their plantations for the nearest city.

Lincoln's proclamation drew such heavy criticism that he altered it drastically before it became official. He deleted the section that seemed to call for insurrection, thereby removing much of its sting. Jefferson Davis in late January, 1863, stated before the Confederate Congress that the document spelled the extermination of the Negro race and encouraged them to assassinate their former masters. He sought recourse by pledging to turn over all captured Union officers to respective southern states for them to deal with according to their laws. Some states were prepared to treat them as invaders inciting insurrection and encouraging murder.

Because the document received only passing notice from editorialists and politicians, the furor soon abated and became history. It is known, however, to have caused a crushing diplomatic blow to the South in thwarting its efforts to obtain European intervention.

See F. Donovan, *Lincoln's Proclamation* (1964); J. H. Franklin, *Emancipation Proclamation* (1963), slightly biased but thorough; H. Wish, *Journal of Negro History* (Oct., 1938); and J. E. Randall and D. Donald, *Civil War and Reconstruction* (1961).

E. RUSS WILLIAMS
Northeast Louisiana University

EMBREE, ELIHU (1782–1820), Tennessee abolitionist and manufacturer, was founder and editor of a general reform newspaper, the *Manumission Intelligencer* (1819), and of the *Emancipator* (1820), probably the first American periodical to be devoted exclusively to abolitionism. As a birthright Quaker and early member of the Tennessee Manumission Society, Embree condemned slavery as a moral wrong and advocated political action against it. His outspoken journalism met welcome response in many parts of the nation, but aroused intense opposition from certain southerners. With his brother Elijah he also operated extensive ironworks and nail factories in east Tennessee. His plan to coordinate these enterprises into a complex commercial venture involving Alabama cotton, Tennessee wheat, and eastern goods and credit was disrupted by the PANIC OF 1819.

See *Emancipator* (1932); P. M. Fink, *East Tennessee Historical Society's Publication* (1938); and Embree Papers, Historical Society of Pennsylvania.

MERTON L. DILLON
Ohio State University

EMERGENCY BANKING ACT (1933) was the first of the recovery measures passed by the New Deal Congress. As with much of the NEW DEAL, the essential provisions of the act originated in the HOOVER ADMINISTRATION or Congress. Title 1 ratified the bank holiday proclaimed by President Franklin D. Roosevelt under authority of the Trading with the Enemy Act of 1917. The holiday had been considered and rejected by the Hoover administration. Title 2 provided a modified form of receivership that permitted some assets to be released from banks with impaired capital. Title 3 allowed national banks to raise new capital and permitted the RECONSTRUCTION FINANCE CORPORATION to purchase the stock. The most creative measure, Title 4, was intended to head off "wild" schemes for sudden inflation. Proposed by George Leslie Harrison, a treasury official, it permitted the Federal Reserve banks to make new loans to banks against a wide range of securities formerly deemed ineligible. The new loans would provide cash in Federal Reserve notes rather than scrip or a new paper currency.

The Emergency Banking Act of 1933 was not written specifically to meet the banking problems of the South, although the region did have numerous small banks and the second-highest suspension rate in the period 1921–1932. Indeed, it was but a tardy national response in a sector where many states had already acted, notably Louisiana. But, in combination with the Glass-Steagall Act, it provided dramatic relief, and southern banks opened again at the same rate as banks in other areas of the country. When the nation's suspension rate dropped from 13.5 banks per hundred in 1933 to practically zero in 1934, it was the former Populist strongholds of the middle border states and the South that benefited most because they had suffered the most.

See S. F. Kennedy, *Banking Crisis, 1933* (1973), best account. See also J. O'Connor, *Banking Crisis* (1938); C. Bremer, *American Bank Failures* (1935); and *Federal Reserve Bulletin* (Dec., 1937). A good model for further research is L. Muchmore, *Journal of Economic History* (Sept., 1970).

WILLIAM D. REEVES
New Orleans Bicentennial Commission

EMORY, WILLIAM HEMSLEY (1811–1887), was a respected topographer and U.S. Army officer. A product of Maryland's tidewater gentry and a graduate of West Point (1831), Emory served under Stephen Kearny during the Mexican War. His published survey of a route to California via the Gila River indicated the unsuitability of slavery in the Southwest, a fact much discussed in the congressional debates of 1850. During the Civil War Emory commanded Union forces in the West and helped save N. P. Banks's army from defeat at the battle of SABINE CROSSROADS. Emory later defended Washington against Jubal Early's attack (July, 1864) and served as the city's military commander after the war. An important witness at the trial of Andrew Johnson, Emory refuted claims that Johnson sought to destroy Congress and establish a military dictatorship.

See W. Goetzmann, *Army Exploration of American West* (1959); *Official Records, Armies*, Ser. 1, 2, Vol. XXXVII; E. Ross, *Impeachment of Johnson* (1896); and Emory Manuscripts, Yale University.

JOHN R. WENNERSTEN
University of Maryland, Princess Anne

EMORY UNIVERSITY (Atlanta, Ga. 30322) traces its origins to the founding of the Georgia Conference Manual School in 1834. When Emory College received its charter two years later, it absorbed the manual school and established a campus in Oxford, Ga. Sponsored by the Methodist church and named for Bishop John Emory of Maryland, the college offered a standard classical curriculum. Although beset by doctrinal disputes and financial difficulties during the prewar years, it managed to survive until the Civil War. Reopening in 1866, Emory relied heavily on state funds paid the school to educate Confederate veterans. Under the leadership of Atticus G. Haygood (1875–1884) enrollment, endowment, and physical facilities increased primarily as a result of gifts from a New York banker. With the election of Warren A. Candler to the presidency in 1888, the college turned away from an experiment with technical and normal education and reemphasized the liberal arts curriculum.

In 1914 Methodist officials severed church connections with Vanderbilt University and decided to found a new church-related college. After the Emory trustees had offered the Oxford institution as the "academic department" of the new college and Coca-Cola magnate ASA G. CANDLER had promised $1 million for an endowment, the Methodists voted to establish Emory University in Atlanta. That same year, the Candler School of Theology became the first division of the school to open. The next year Emory absorbed the Atlanta Medical College and in 1916 opened a law school. By 1919 undergraduate, graduate, and business schools had opened. During the 1920s and 1930s, Emory received substantial gifts from the GENERAL EDUCATION BOARD, the ROSENWALD FUND, and the Candler family.

After World War II Emory grew and changed dramatically. Large grants from another Atlanta family with Coca-Cola ties, the Woodruffs, aided the school's continued growth. The school's first Ph.D. graduated in 1948, coeducation came to the campus in 1953, and Emory admitted its first black student in 1962. By the early 1970s, Emory had distinguished schools of liberal arts, medicine, dentistry, law, theology, nursing, librarianship, and business administration as well as a junior college division at nearby Oxford. The present enrollment is 5,500 students.

See H. M. Bullock, *Emory University* (1936); and T. H. English, *Emory University, 1915–1965* (1965).

THOMAS G. DYER
University of Georgia

ENCHANTRESS AFFAIR. The northern brig *Enchantress* was taken on July 6, 1861, by the Confederate ship *Jeff Davis* and then retaken by the Union warship *Albatross* 16 days later. The Confederate prize crew was taken to Philadelphia, imprisoned, tried for piracy (October 22–28, 1861), and convicted. However, they were exchanged as prisoners of war along with the crew of another captured Confederate privateer, *Savannah*, when Confederate authorities threatened retaliation by executing high-ranking Union prisoners.

See F. T. Miller, *Photographic History of Civil War* (1911), VII, brief description; W. M. Robinson, Jr., *Confederate Privateers* (1928); *Southern Historical Society Papers* (Jan.–Dec., 1903); D. F. Murphy, *Jeff Davis Piracy Case* (1861); *Official Records, Navies*, Ser. 1, Vols. I, V, VI; Records of U.S. District Court for Eastern District of Pennsylvania, Box Nos. 11, 12, 16, 140, in Record Group 21, National Archives; and T. McFadden, *Cadwalader's Cases* (2 vols.; 1907). There is no adequate study of the *Enchantress* affair.

WILLIAM N. STILL, JR.
East Carolina University

ENGLAND, JOHN (1786–1842), Roman Catholic bishop of Charleston, S.C., was born and ordained in Ireland. He has been described as the "founder of the Catholic church in Australia" because it was through his arousal of public opinion that non-Anglican clergy were permitted in the penal colonies. His list of firsts is impressive: founded the first Catholic newspaper in the United States, the *United States Catholic Miscellany*; was the first member of the Catholic clergy to address the U.S. Congress; founded the first Catholic workingmen's society in the United States, the Brotherhood of San Marino; was the first United States bishop appointed an apostolic delegate. This mission to Haiti was the great failure of his life.

See P. Guilday, *John England* (2 vols.; 1927), detailed study; J. England, *Writings* (1908); E. M. O'Brien, *Australian Catholic Record* (April, 1928); J. G. Shea, *Catholic Church in U.S.* (1892); R. H. Clarke, *Deceased Catholic Bishops* (1888); and manuscripts in Archives of Diocese of Charleston.

WILLARD E. WIGHT
Georgia Institute of Technology

ENGLISH TURN. After establishing a French fort at Biloxi Bay in 1699, IBERVILLE returned to France after leaving his brother BIENVILLE second-in-command to Sauvolle de La Villantry. Bienville explored the lower reaches of the Mississippi River in search of a more permanent site for a settlement. About 18 miles below present-day New Orleans, he met the English ship *Carolina Galley* coming up the river. He informed the new arrivals that the French were already in control of the Mississippi and named that point at which the English were persuaded to turn back and not challenge French claims the Detour des Anglais, the English Turn.

See R. A. McLemore (ed.), *History of Mississippi* (1973), I.

EPISCOPAL CHURCH (Protestant Episcopal church) was organized from the remnants of the Church of England following the War for Independence. In general, during the colonial era the Anglican church in the South functioned as an integral component of politics and society. From Maryland to Georgia, eighteenth-century Anglicanism gained a reputation for orthodoxy in religious style and quiet accommodation to prevailing politics. Although some controversies, such as those that punctuated the tenure of Commissary JAMES BLAIR of Virginia (1689–1743), the Anglican church in the South usually cooperated with and supported civil authority. By the time of the Revolution, native Americans occupied the vast majority of southern Episcopal pulpits. Attached to the colonial political establishments by both law and tradition and sympathetic to American interests by virtue of both upbringing and social connections, most Anglican ministers in the South joined in an easy alliance with the Americans in the War for Independence. The Tory sentiments that characterized the Episcopal leadership in the North have too often, and incorrectly, been used to describe the southern churchmen.

With the onset of the Revolutionary War, the Episcopal church entered a period of decline. In the North, deterioration of the church stemmed from war-induced hostility toward an institution closely identified with Britain. The process that led to the disestablishment of the Episcopal church in the southern states began with the proliferation of dissenting religious denominations during the GREAT AWAKENING, received additional strength in the 1750s during the controversies that surrounded proposals for an American episcopate, and was finally accelerated by the Enlightenment ideals that surrounded the Revolution. The church lost both communicants and clergy and emerged from the war in such a depressed condition that the Reverend James Madison, first bishop of Virginia, proclaimed it "too far gone ever to be revived."

The new Protestant Episcopal church was ill-equipped to face the challenge of denominational competition for voluntary memberships. In an era of popular religion, BAPTISTS and New Light PRESBYTERIANS rapidly expanded; even the American METHODISTS, who possessed a high level of enthusiasm and mass appeal, abandoned their Episcopal parent church in 1784 in favor of independent denominational status.

In contrast to the enthusiasm of the competing denominations, Episcopal sermons lacked emotion, their rituals discouraged spontaneous involvement, and the ecclesiastical hierarchy appeared undemocratic. Additionally, the parish system of church organization worked best in conditions characterized by a stable and sizable population. The rapid westward migration of southerners in the nineteenth century created settlement patterns inhospitable to the Episcopal church structure. Consequently, the church drew its support from the upper classes of the well-established communities, a condition that remained both its strength and its weakness.

Attempts to expand Episcopal influence into the West met with limited success. Not until the 1835 appointment of the Reverend LEONIDAS POLK to the diocese of Louisiana did the Southwest have a bishop. Historians generally agree that the very real decline and disorganization that accompanied the Revolution left the Episcopalians with neither the personnel nor the resources to organize a strenuous missionary campaign. Furthermore, the Oxford movement, which began in 1833, promoted a High Church sentiment that produced divisions between the northern Episcopalians and their more evangelical southern counterparts.

As sectional controversies became more acute and the Civil War approached, the Episcopal church in the United States remained remarkably free of the bitter sectional disputes that produced schism within other denominations. Episcopalians emphasized political realities rather than debating theological questions. In 1861, Bishop Leonidas Polk stated that political boundaries determined ecclesiastical jurisdictions and supported the call for a separate southern church. Polk's declaration, "Separated, not Divided," reflected the view of most southern churchmen. As organized in 1861, the Episcopal church in the Confederate states retained, with few modifications, the form and content of the United States church. When the war ended, so did the independent status of the southern church.

With the exception of denominational historians, few scholars have exhibited an interest in the history of the church following the Civil War. Indeed, the Episcopal church exerted little influence upon southern Protestantism in the nineteenth and the twentieth centuries. It remained numerically small and essentially removed from the evangelical Protestantism that typified the larger denominations. And yet, its importance in the South looms larger than mere numbers indicate, for it drew prestige from the social position of its membership, and it derived strength from its ability to accommodate change (RELIGION).

See R. W. Albright, *History of Episcopal Church* (1964); W. B. Posey, *Journal of Southern History* (Feb., 1959), good analysis of colonial and antebellum years; W. S.

Perry, *Historical Collections* (4 vols.; 1870); J. B. Cheshire, *Church in Confederate States* (1912); S. S. Hill, *Southern Churches in Crisis* (1966); N. R. Burr, *Critical Bibliography of Religion* (2 vols.; 1971); and General Theological Seminary Library, New York City.

THOMAS GAGE
Lincoln University

ERLANGER LOAN was a Confederate States of America loan originally negotiated on October 28, 1862, between JOHN SLIDELL, commissioner of the Confederacy to France, and Emile Erlanger & Company, a Parisian banking house. In the contract as finally signed on January 8, 1863, the Erlanger firm agreed to market a £3,000,000 ($14,550,000) bond issue abroad, and the Confederacy consented to make the 20-year 7 percent bonds convertible at face value into cotton at a rate of sixpence sterling per pound of cotton. This meant that the bonds were redeemable for cotton at a price well below the world market price of almost two shillings. If the investor wished to make the exchange while the war was still being waged, the Confederacy agreed to deliver the cotton to "within ten miles of a railroad or stream navigable to the ocean." Erlanger & Company was permitted to purchase the bonds at a rate of only £77 for each £100 bond. The banking house was further guaranteed a 5 percent commission for handling the sale of the bonds. Since Erlanger planned to offer the bonds to the public at 90, the opportunities for huge profits were obvious.

The Erlanger loan was authorized by the Confederate Congress on January 29, 1863. The bonds were put on sale at Paris, London, Amsterdam, and Frankfurt on March 19, 1863, and they were an immediate success. Suddenly, however, on March 23, bond values began to fall. Confederate officials suspected Union agents of working to undermine the market. In a few days the bonds dropped from 92 to 85. The value of the bonds then fell to 60 after the news of the Confederate losses at Vicksburg and Gettysburg in July, 1863. During the remainder of 1863 and in 1864 a few more of the bonds were purchased by speculators, and by February, 1865, about five-sixths of the issue had been disposed of. This famous loan has in the past usually been referred to as a "failure" by most historians; but more recent writers have noted that the Confederate government cleared from the sale in cash or its equivalent a total variously estimated at from $6,000,000 to $8,535,000, which it used to buy desperately needed war goods and to pay old debts owed to European suppliers. With the defeat of the Confederacy, the securities, of course, became valueless.

See P. P. DuBellet, *Diplomacy of Confederate Cabinet of Richmond* (1963), contains copy of contract and other primary materials; R. C. Todd, *Confederate Finance* (1954); J. F. Gentry, *Journal of Southern History* (May, 1970), most accurate; and E. M. Lerner, *Journal of Political Economy* (Dec., 1954).

(1971); Greene Papers, New York Public Library, microfilm at W. L. Clements Library; and Cornwallis Papers, microfilm at Colonial Williamsburg.

FRANKLIN B. WICKWIRE
University of Massachusetts, Amherst

ETHERIDGE, EMERSON (1819–1902), was born in Currituck, N.C. In 1831 the family moved to Dresden in west Tennessee. Etheridge practiced law after admission to the bar in 1840 and entered Whig politics. He served one term in the state house (1845–1847) and three terms (1853–1857, 1859–1861) in Congress, being defeated in 1857. In his last term he rejected affiliation with the Know-Nothing party and was the last Whig to serve in Congress. In that same term, he was chairman of the Committee on Indian Affairs. In 1861 the slaveholder Etheridge became a Conservative Unionist, being clerk of the House of Representatives until December, 1863. He supported the Democratic ticket in 1864 and in late 1865 suffered imprisonment in Kentucky for his opposition to WILLIAM G. BROWNLOW, Tennessee's Reconstruction governor. In 1867, as the Conservative candidate against Brownlow, he won only 23 percent of the vote. After one term (1869–1871) in the state senate, he abandoned politics. From 1891 to 1894 he was surveyor of customs at Memphis.

See S. J. Folmsbee, *Tennessee* (1969); M. R. Campbell, *Tennessee Historical Quarterly* (Dec., 1960); *Congressional Globe*, 36th Cong., 1st Sess., Pt. 1; E. Etheridge, *Speeches in Congress* (1857); C. M. Cummings, *Tennessee Historical Quarterly* (June, 1964); J. W. Patton, *Unionism and Reconstruction in Tennessee* (1934); and T. B. Alexander, *Political Reconstruction in Tennessee* (1950).

B. G. J. WALTON
Western Carolina University

EUTAW SPRINGS, BATTLE OF (September 8, 1781), was the last major battle in South Carolina during the American Revolution. Nathanael Greene with 2,300 men attacked a British force of perhaps 1,200 under Alexander Stewart. Greene drove the British back, but his troops scattered to loot, which allowed the British to regroup and counterattack, driving Greene from the field. The British were so weakened that they retreated to Charleston, where they remained cooped up until the end of the war. Eutaw Springs was a tactical defeat and strategic victory for Greene, whose constant pressure forced the British during 1781 to abandon the interior of South Carolina.

See C. Ward, *War of Revolution* (2 vols.; 1952); T. Thayer, *Nathanael Greene* (1960); E. Thane, *Fighting Quaker*

EVANGELISTS are a type of Protestant Christian leadership whose goal is to convert individuals to Christianity, delivering them from a state of sin entailing punishment and alienation to a new standing of forgiveness and salvation. The term itself appears in the New Testament, meaning literally one who proclaims the good news (the gospel of Christ). Moreover, it had currency during the centuries of ecclesiastical domination in Europe, usually being considered as one among several ministries and not the primary one. Both the term and the function acquired new prominence, however, with the breakup of Christendom and the emergence of secularism. Especially in the American colonies and the newly founded Republic did the churches carry on evangelism.

Although Christianity had no formal rival in the New World, Christendom had ceased to exist inasmuch as many were unchurched and even religiously illiterate. This was particularly the case in the interior areas of New England, the middle colonies, and the South. Throughout these extensive reaches, the church was often not even in existence, much less effective. Evangelistic activity abounded in these places under such conditions. The Protestant churches, especially METHODIST and BAPTIST, moved with the people, providing pastoral service to the faithful and evangelistic ministry to the unconverted. The southern GREAT AWAKENING erupted first in the 1740s among PRESBYTERIANS, near Richmond, Va., with the Reverend Samuel Davies and the Reverend William Robinson as principal leaders. The Baptist phase began in central North Carolina, sparked by the Reverend Shubal Stearns, but quickly spread throughout the Carolinas and Virginia and even into Georgia. The Methodist branch of Anglicanism caught fire from the Reverend Devereaux Jarratt in southside Virginia.

The southern phase of the Second Awakening (GREAT AWAKENING, SECOND) in 1800–1810 occurred west of the mountains in Kentucky and Tennessee. From this development resulted vast Baptist and Methodist strength in the area, a lessening of Presbyterian and Congregational force, and, a little later, the DISCIPLES OF CHRIST denomination, which came to life in Kentucky and spread quickly into neighboring states.

Evangelists came to be a major class of Protestant leadership in a frontier society. Their task was largely limited to making Christians, forsaking traditional ministries like religious nurture, theological activity, and contribution to the quality of civilization. They have been referred to as "consecrated functionaries."

Although this approach to Christianity emanated from a society where most people were unbaptized, unconverted, and unchurched, it has become widespread, perhaps even normative, in the many-churched South. By the 1920s, the Southern Baptist Convention, now the nation's largest Protestant body, had virtually identified ministry with evangelism. Before and after that decade, a number of sects emerged for the express purpose of evangelizing the unconverted, many of whom held membership in churches deemed lifeless and heretical. The Nazarenes and the several Churches of God and Assemblies of God are among the denominations that exist to carry on that enterprise (PENTECOSTAL CHURCHES). In the South, "revival meetings" and evangelistic crusades remain popular in main line and sectarian churches alike.

Some individual evangelists, those for whom such activity is a full-time professional occupation, have achieved regional and even national fame. Sam P. Jones of Alabama was acclaimed the "Moody of the South" for his successes in the region and nation between 1880 and 1900. In 1927 Bob Jones, Sr., founded the college bearing his name in Tennessee (later a university in South Carolina), which trains evangelists for service in the region and nation and as overseas missionaries. MORDECAI F. HAM itinerated throughout the South and Southwest between 1905 and 1950 and reached thousands by radio. BILLY GRAHAM is the South's principal evangelist gift to the entire world. It should be emphasized though that most southern evangelists are settled pastors who carry on that work weekly in their own congregations and occasionally through invited visitations to other churches.

See W. G. McLoughlin, Jr., *Modern Revivalism* (1959); B. A. Weisberger, *They Gathered at River* (1958); P. Cartwright, *Autobiography* (1857); and W. W. Sweet, *Religion on American Frontier* (1931, 1936, 1946), I, II, IV.

SAMUEL S. HILL, JR.
University of Florida

EVANS, CLEMENT ANSELM (1833–1911), began his career as a lawyer in Stewart County, Ga., a state senator (1859–1861), and a presidential elector (for John C. Breckinridge, 1860). Commissioned a major in the 31st Georgia Infantry (1861), he fought in Virginia, rising to brigadier general and commanding a division at Appomattox. He served as a Methodist minister from 1866 until war wounds forced his retirement (1892); he remained active as a businessman, college trustee, and prison commissioner. He led the UNITED CONFEDERATE VETERANS and promoted the Confederate Memorial Institute at Richmond. Evans edited and contributed to *Confederate Military History* (12 vols.; 1899). Biased and uneven, this state-by-state account by prominent southerners is still useful for its brief biographies of almost all the Confederate generals. He wrote *Military History of Georgia* (1895) and with A. D. Candler edited *Georgia* (3 vols.; 1906).

See C. A. Evans, *Confederate Military History* (1899), VI; W. J. Northen, *Men of Mark in Georgia* (1911), III; and *Official Records, Armies*, XXI, XLII, XLIII, LI.

ALDEN B. PEARSON, JR.
University of Alabama, Huntsville

EVERGLADES, THE, a broad depression of saw grass and tree hammocks, 30 to 40 miles wide, stretch some 100 miles in an arc from Lake OKEECHOBEE southwestward to the Gulf of Mexico. In predrainage days, the Everglades could be described as a vast saw grass marsh growing on a bed of peat and muck soils.

Evidence indicates that the marsh was inhabited only for short periods of time by the Indians, perhaps as early as 1100 B.C. The Everglades remained relatively unsettled and uncharted until the Seminoles, who had been pushed deep into Florida from the Carolinas and Georgia, and the federal government made them a place of fighting (SEMINOLE WARS) and eventually a reservation for the few surviving Indians (mainly Mikasuki). With the establishment of the Everglades National Park (1947), the Mikasuki (about 430) have been forced onto a narrow strip of land along U.S. Route 41 (Tamiami Trail).

The U.S. Army Corps of Engineers, to protect the urban east coast from the Everglades' flood waters, has developed a system of water storage and drainage within the Everglades. Basically it has made Lake Okeechobee a reservoir area, established a large agricultural region south of the lake, and created three water conservation districts. This system has interrupted the natural surface water discharge and has placed the Everglades National Park in serious danger from lack of fresh water. Indeed, even the agricultural lands are eventually doomed, for the peat soils oxidize when drained. The River of Grass is no more. Only the park and water conservation areas remain, and their future is not secure. The problem of "alligators or people" will continue as long as urban growth in south Florida remains unchecked.

See C. Tebeau, *History of Florida* (1971); P. Gleason (ed.), *Environments of South Florida* (1974); P. Caufield, *Everglades* (1970); and M. Douglas, *Florida* (1967) and *Everglades* (1947).

PAUL SANFORD SALTER
University of Miami

EVOLUTION CONTROVERSY. Until the publication of Charles R. Darwin's *Origin of Species* in 1859, the balance of scientific opinion was against the theory of evolution. Consequently the volume caused a sharp debate among scientists and theologians in Europe. The evolution controversy soon bridged the Atlantic, but the low literacy rate, abolitionism, primitive communications, a critical presidential election, and the approaching Civil War combined to restrict it primarily to academic and theological circles in the Northeast. Virtually all religious groups rejected Darwin's theory, however, and relegated it to a "puerile fancy" status. As Darwin gained credibility, evolution surfaced periodically and caused isolated unrest. In 1878 a geologist at Vanderbilt University was asked to resign after he expressed belief in a pre-Adam origin of man. A professor at the Southern Baptist Seminary at Louisville was asked to resign in 1879 for interpreting the Old Testament in the light of modern science. In 1888 JAMES WOODROW, uncle of Woodrow Wilson, was forced from his position at Southern Presbyterian Seminary after stating that a sympathetic understanding of evolution did not lead to doubt.

The strength of the antievolutionists was greatly increased in 1909, when conservative Protestants, fundamentalists, united to resist "modernism" in theology. Most fundamentalists were antievolutionists, and in 1918 they founded the World's Christian Fundamentals Association. The purpose of the WCFA was to defend the primacy of the biblical gospel and to check all "anti-Christian" tendencies. The organization opposed the teaching of evolutionary theories in the public schools and colleges and sought local, state, and federal legislation to prohibit such instruction. The antievolutionists rapidly became one of the most vocal and adamant pressure groups in the nation and experienced their greatest success in the South.

The strength of southern antievolutionists surfaced in South Carolina in 1921, when an unsuccessful rider was attached to a general appropriations bill. The measure would have prohibited "the cult known as Darwinism" from being taught in the public schools of that state. William Jennings Bryan, a nationally acknowledged antievolutionist leader, addressed a joint session of the Kentucky legislature in 1922 and advocated passage of an antievolution law. Three days later such a measure was introduced but failed of passage by a single vote. Then the Southern Baptist Convention of 1922 declared that the textbook was the anvil upon which evolution was to be crushed. Subsequently, on March 26, 1923, Oklahoma adopted a free textbook measure, which stipulated that no text be used that taught "the Darwin Theory of Creation vs. the Bible Account of Creation." Oklahoma was the first state to adopt an "anti-Darwin" law. In May of 1923, the Florida legislature adopted a resolution, drafted by William Jennings Bryan, which declared that "it is against the interests of the State to teach any theory that relates man in blood relationship with any lower animal." The most widely known of all antievolution laws, however, was enacted in March of 1925 by Tennessee. John Thomas Scopes was indicted and convicted for violating this statute in a trial (SCOPES TRIAL) that attracted national attention. Mississippi became the next state to enact prohibitory legislation. It adopted a law in 1926 that prohibited "the theory that man descended from a lower order of animals" from being taught in state-supported schools. Arkansas was the last state to enact a statewide antievolution law, and it was accomplished by referendum. The statute read in part "that it shall be unlawful for any teacher . . . to teach . . . that mankind ascended or descended from a lower order of animals." The electorate approved the measure by a margin of 108,000 to 63,000 votes.

Oklahoma, Florida, Tennessee, Mississippi, and Arkansas were the only states to legislate against evolution, but during the period 1921–1929 no less than 37 antievolution bills, resolutions, or riders were introduced in states stretching from coast to coast. Moreover, many local school boards passed antievolution rulings, and the Texas state textbook commission officially banned texts relating the theory of evolution, and several other states did so unofficially. The legislatures of Alabama, California, Delaware, Georgia, Kentucky, Louisiana, Maine, Minnesota, Missouri, North Carolina, North Dakota, New Hampshire, South Carolina, West Virginia, and Texas rejected the prohibitive measures.

See K. K. Bailey, *Southern White Protestantism* (1964); S. G. Cole, *History of Fundamentalism* (1931); N. F. Furniss, *Fundamentalist Controversy* (1954); W. B. Gatewood, Jr., *Preachers, Pedagogues, and Politicians*

(1966); R. Halliburton, Jr., *Proceedings of Oklahoma Academy of Science* (1962, 1963, 1965); *Southwest Social Science Quarterly* (Sept., 1960); *Arkansas Historical Quarterly* (Autumn, 1964); *Register of Kentucky Historical Society* (April, 1968); *Journal of Mississippi History* (May, 1973); and *Malaysian Journal of Education* (Dec., 1975).

R. HALLIBURTON, JR.
Northeastern Oklahoma State University

EWELL, RICHARD STODDERT (1817–1872), was born in Georgetown and grew up in Prince William County, Va. He graduated from West Point in 1840, was commissioned in the dragoons, and saw action in the Mexican and Indian wars. He resigned from the U.S. Army April 24, 1861, accepting a lieutenant colonel's commission in the Confederate cavalry. On June 17, he was promoted brigadier general and in October major general commanding a division with which he joined STONEWALL JACKSON in the valley, fighting with distinction there and later on the peninsula. In August, he lost a leg from a wound received at Groveton. Although slow in recovering, he was promoted to the command of the II Corps following Jackson's death. "Old Bald Head" then led the II Corps to GETTYSBURG, where on July 1, 1863, he elected not to commit his badly disorganized troops against the equally disorganized federals on Cemetery Hill, a decision strongly debated since. He performed reasonably well in the WILDERNESS CAMPAIGN and at SPOTSYLVANIA, but was relieved on May 29, 1864, for ill health. Robert E. Lee then gave him the Richmond garrison. Trapped at SAYLER'S CREEK, Ewell surrendered what remained of that force. He was released from prison largely through the efforts of U. S. Grant, whom he admired and of whom he had predicted great things. The Ewells then moved to Spring Hill, Tenn., where he became a successful farmer. D. S. Freeman describes Ewell as a "strange unlovely bird," bald, popeyed, long beaked, with a sharp tongue and an odd sense of humor, yet gallantly generous, chivalrous, and a spirited fighter.

See P. G. Hamlin, *Letters of Ewell* (1935), best insight into personality with good life summary; D. S. Freeman, *Lee's Lieutenants* (3 vols.; 1943); L. Chambers, *Stonewall Jackson* (1959); E. B. Coddington, *Gettysburg Campaign* (1968); B. Davis, *They Called Him Stonewall* (1954); J. Selby, *Stonewall Jackson* (1968); E. Steere, *Wilderness Campaign* (1960); and K. P. Williams, *Lincoln Finds a General* (1956).

DOUGLAS V. JOHNSON II
U.S. Military Academy

EXODUS OF 1879. In the spring of 1879, some 20,000 Afro-Americans from Tennessee, Mississippi, and Louisiana migrated (NEGRO MIGRATION) to the state they knew as "Free Kansas," the land of John Brown. A few months later, several thousand blacks from Texas followed. In this unplanned, leaderless, and popular movement, entire families fled in the fear that Democrat-controlled state legislatures would soon impose conditions reminiscent of slavery. In Louisiana, blacks regarded the convening of a constitutional convention with apprehension; elsewhere they foresaw a resurgence of night-riding in the likely event of a Democratic victory in the presidential ELECTION OF 1880. Flocking to the Mississippi River's banks, "exodusters," as the migrants were called, believed the Kansas fever idea, which promised free transportation, free land, and free subsistence for the first year, to be furnished them by the federal government. Exodusters neither laid plans nor carried provisions; they traveled on the strength of their faith. The sheer intensity of their conviction, their startling numbers, and their neediness attracted nationwide attention. Immigrant aid societies formed in St. Louis and Kansas in response. Although not all reached Kansas, in mid-1880 approximately 8,000 exodusters remained in Kansas, where poverty denied the majority their aim of owning land.

The sensational, panic-ridden exodus belonged to a broader tide of blacks leaving the old slave states. Between 1876 and 1881 Afro-Americans migrated west and southwestward. Like other Americans, they shaped their course well ahead, designating guides and sometimes employing professional conductors. Whether they migrated in this deliberate fashion or fled precipitously as exodusters, only the tenor of their migration differed. The deterioration of their political and economic status pushed them out of the South, as the promise of citizenship rights, public schools, and family farms attracted them to the West.

During the winter of 1879–1880 two black men gave testimony before the Senate Select Committee on the Exodus and came to be known as the leaders of the movement: Benjamin ("Pap") Singleton (1809–1892) of Nashville, Tenn., and Henry Adams (1843–late 1880s) of Shreveport, La. Claiming the title "Father of the Exodus," Singleton showed that he had conducted migrants from Tennessee to Kansas since the mid-1870s and had organized two settlements ("colonies"): one just south of Topeka in Morris County; the other in Cherokee County, in the southeast corner of the state. (Two groups of black Kentuckians had independently organized the Graham County colony of Nicodemus in 1877.) Although Adams never visited Kansas, he revealed the existence of the

Colonization Council claiming almost 100,000 adherents in northern Louisiana and the adjacent portions of Texas and Mississippi. Since the late 1860s the council had grown from an underground organization of black veterans concerned for the welfare of their race into a Liberian immigration group. Adams supported the Kansas exodus as a short-term expedient, but he continued to advocate immigration to Africa as the ultimate solution to Negro oppression. During the 1880s Singleton came to support immigration to Africa as well. Neither Singleton nor Adams led the exodus of 1879. The movement's lack of organization and its reliance on charity embarrassed respectable black observers such as FREDERICK DOUGLASS, though Richard T. Greener of Howard University staunchly defended the exodus.

See U.S. Senate, *Report 693*, 46th Cong., 2nd Sess.; A. Bontemps and J. Conroy, *They Seek a City* (1945); N. I. Painter, *Exodusters* (1976); and G. Schwendemann, *Kansas Historical Journal* (Autumn, 1960; Spring, 1963; Spring, 1968).

NELL IRVIN PAINTER
University of Pennsylvania

EXPANSIONISM, TERRITORIAL, initially was a movement eliciting national enthusiasm, unrelated to the divisive sectional issue of slavery. Although segments of the Federalist party opposed Thomas Jefferson's LOUISIANA PURCHASE because it would add materially to southern political power based on slavery, there is little evidence that southerners supported the purchase for the same reason. Both North and South in 1820 accepted the MISSOURI COMPROMISE. Florida was added, with little reference to slavery, through the Adams-Onís Treaty (1819).

Mounting tension over the slavery issue in the 1830s, resulting from Nat TURNER'S REBELLION and the abolitionist activities of William Lloyd Garrison, crystallized southern attitudes. Southerners became increasingly concerned with maintaining their distinctive economic and social systems and their national political power, all based on the institution of slavery; and slavery and expansionism became inextricably linked.

In 1844 JAMES K. POLK, Tennessee Democrat, was elected president on an expansionist platform national in appeal: Texas for the slaveholding South, Oregon for the free North, California ports for the northeastern commercial interests. Expansionism was the temper of the times. Included in the ranks of expansionists were southerners. Some were expansionists per se, favoring the acquisition of Oregon as well as Texas. Others were motivated primarily by the desire to expand the area of slavery and saw no contradiction between that goal and extending the blessings of freedom, the creed of manifest destiny.

The issue of slavery figured in the battle over the annexation of Texas. Northern abolitionists accused southerners of a slavery plot—to colonize Texas, free it from Mexico, then add it to the United States, carving it perhaps into five slave states to augment southern political power. There was no such plot. When Polk permitted to stand John Tyler's joint resolution, passed by Congress in February, 1845, northerners as well as southerners seemed to welcome Texas as the fifteenth slave state.

Slavery figured in a more subtle way in the negotiations with England over Oregon. The compromise resolution setting 49° as the boundary was sponsored by a southerner, JOHN C. CALHOUN, and was supported in Congress by a combination of Whigs and southern Democrats. Van Buren Democrats later accused Polk of catering to southern interests in failing to press for 54° 40', and southern Democrats were consistent in voting against the 1848 congressional bill barring slavery from the Oregon Territory.

Major territorial additions resulted from the MEXICAN WAR (1846–1848). The controversy over slavery extension into these territories began in 1846. Whether motivated by political considerations or true humanitarian concerns, David Wilmot, Pennsylvania Van Buren Democrat, repeatedly introduced into Congress but never secured approval for his famed WILMOT PROVISO, barring slavery from any territories acquired from Mexico. Neither did John C. Calhoun secure approval for his resolutions offered in rebuttal, asserting that the territories belonged to all the states and that Congress had no right to close them to southern slaves.

The issue of slavery in the Mexican Cession was settled by the COMPROMISE OF 1850, invoking the principle of popular sovereignty, a symbolic rather than a real concession to the South. It recognized the right of southern slaveholding settlers to participate in deciding the slave or free status of a territory; but climate, soil, and terrain frequently kept slaveholding settlers out. Although POPULAR SOVEREIGNTY originated as a simple, straightforward doctrine, attempts to implement it aroused widely divergent interpretations, especially after the Missouri Compromise was repealed by the KANSAS-NEBRASKA ACT of 1854. The acrimony of the debate led to party realignments. The Whig party split over the slavery issue and disintegrated. By 1860 the Democratic party was in disarray, in spite of the valiant efforts of Stephen A. Douglas to preserve it as a national party, appealing to southern Democrats by supporting the dictum of the Supreme Court in the 1857 DRED SCOTT decision, trying to placate northern Democrats with his FREEPORT DOCTRINE. The Republican party took up the banner of the short-lived Free-Soil party; and with the election of ABRAHAM LINCOLN, southern states seceded.

Controversy over the extension of slavery into the territories exacerbated real sectional differences between the North and the South and raised the emotions of the contending parties to a fever pitch. More explicitly, the determination of the South to extend slavery was based on sheer survival. Were slavery contained in the states where it already existed, the economic and social systems of the South would be destroyed. Expansion was necessary to provide fresh land for slave cultivation and to disperse the slave population so that white southerners could maintain adequate social control over an enslaved race.

The issue of slavery settled by the Civil War, expansionism could become again a national rather than a sectional question, with divisions many times drawn solely according to party affiliation. Between 1865 and 1903, however, the character of American expansion changed, becoming commercial more than landed; and territorial acquisitions were noncontiguous. The South, in the throes of Reconstruction, concerned with the attempt to attain prewar levels of production and trade, paid scant attention to the 1867 Alaska Purchase. Many southerners, however, supported American imperialism in Latin America, hoping to find markets for agricultural surpluses there. Southern planters and new textile manufacturers favored the construction of an isthmian canal, secured by Caribbean bases on the east and an American-owned island chain across the Pacific, to provide quick access to the profitable China cotton market. Some southern leaders defended the 1898 annexation of Hawaii, Puerto Rico, and the Philippines and the virtual protectorate over Cuba (so desired by southerners in pre–Civil War days) on the grounds that it was the destiny of Anglo-Saxons to rule inferior peoples; others pointed to the difficulties of reconciling races of different color and cultural heritage.

See standard works by N. A. Graebner, F. Merk, J. H. Smith, A. K. Weinberg, W. LaFeber, and R. Van Alstyne. W. Barney, *Road to Secession* (1972); H. Hamilton, *Prologue to Conflict* (1964); R. F. Nichols, *Disruption of American Democracy* (1948); and G. G. Van Deusen, *Jacksonian Era* (1959), offer valuable insights into slavery extension controversy.

JOSEPHINE MOORE
Guilford College

EXPATRIATES, CONFEDERATE, settled in many foreign lands. Encouraged by Maximilian's imperial government, several thousand southerners established colonies in Mexico. Among these were former governors HENRY W. ALLEN and Thomas O. Moore of Louisiana, ISHAM G. HARRIS of Tennessee, Pendleton Murrah of Texas, and Thomas C. Reynolds of Missouri. They were joined by at least 17 Confederate generals: Hamilton P. Bee, William P. Hardeman, THOMAS C. HINDMAN, Clay King, EDMUND KIRBY-SMITH, Danville Leadbetter, B. H. Lyon, John McCausland, JOHN B. MAGRUDER, STERLING PRICE, Joseph O. Shelby, James E. Slaughter, Walter H. Stevens, Alexander W. Terrell, John G. Walker, Oscar M. Watkins, and CADMUS M. WILCOX. Other well-known southerners who sojourned in Mexico included Judge John Perkins of Louisiana, Beverley Tucker of Virginia, and scientist-oceanographer MATTHEW F. MAURY, who became an honorary counselor of state to Maximilian and also the director of the Mexican astronomical observatory and imperial commissioner of immigration.

Probably between 8,000 and 10,000 Confederates immigrated to Latin America, with between 3,000 and 4,000 of those settling in agricultural colonies in Brazil. Others sought refuge in Venezuela, in Honduras, and in West Indian island colonies like Cuba and Jamaica. Many went to Canada, among them former vice-president JOHN C. BRECKINRIDGE of Kentucky, former senator JAMES M. MASON of Virginia, and JUBAL EARLY.

JUDAH BENJAMIN went to England, where he became a highly respected barrister. Other prominent former Confederates, including JOHN SLIDELL, took up residence in Paris. Some, including three former Confederate generals, C. W. FIELD, WILLIAM W. LORING, and HENRY H. SIBLEY, took service in the army of the caliph of Egypt. A handful of refugees even migrated to Japan.

Characteristic experiences of Confederate expatriates included economic deprivation, prolonged separation from their families, and involvement in numerous quarrels among themselves. Many became destitute. Some took up their pens in defense of the LOST CAUSE. Most of the survivors eventually returned to the United States, with the vanguard filtering back from Mexico during the summer of 1867 as Maximilian's empire collapsed. A few were able to resume careers in American politics, but federal appointments were scarce until Grover Cleveland became president in 1885.

See L. F. Hill, *Diplomatic Relations Between U.S. and Brazil* (1932); A. F. Rolle, *Lost Cause: Confederate Exodus to Mexico* (1965); A. J. and K. A. Hanna, *Confeder-*

ate Exiles in Venezuela (1960); and L. F. Hill, *Southwestern Historical Quarterly* (Oct., 1935).

NORMAN B. FERRIS
Middle Tennessee State University

EXPLORATION. Spain was the first European power to undertake exploration and settlement of the South. In 1513, JUAN PONCE DE LEÓN, conqueror of Puerto Rico, discovered and coasted the Florida peninsula. In the following year he secured permission to colonize Florida, but not until 1521 was he able to renew exploration, which ended in personal disaster on the west coast of Florida.

Meanwhile, Governor Francisco de Garay of Jamaica commissioned Alonzo Alvarez de Piñeda to explore the entire Gulf coast from the Rio Grande to the Florida Keys. Coasting back and forth, Piñeda discovered the mouth of the Mississippi River in 1519. Also in 1519 another agent of Garay's, Diego Camargo, attempted a settlement, probably on the banks of the Rio Grande, and made the first interior exploration along that river. The settlement failed.

As successor to Ponce de León and Garay, Judge Lucas Vázquez de Ayllón in 1521 sent Francisco Gordillo from Hispaniola to explore the Florida coast. Gordillo fell in with a slave hunter, Quejos, and they extended geographical knowledge as far as Cape Fear. In 1525 Ayllón sent Pedro de Quexos along the same coast to perhaps 40° north latitude. Simultaneously Esteban Gómez, seeking a fabled strait through North America, traced the coast from Nova Scotia to Florida. In the following year Ayllón established a colony at Chicora in Carolina with about 500 colonists, but within two years it failed.

Not discouraged by repeated failure, the Spaniards next commissioned the experienced Pánfilo de Narváez. In 1528 he landed near Tampa Bay and with half his command penetrated the Florida interior seeking fabled Apalachen, while others went north by ship. Apalachen turned out to be a poor Indian village near what is today Tallahassee, but the party continued to explore inland until men and supplies were exhausted. Returning to the coast at the Bay of Horses, Narváez and party built makeshift vessels of horsehide intending thereby to follow the coast to Pánuco. Construction miscalculations and nautical inexperience resulted in disaster, with a few castaways finally finding shelter on the Texas coast. Leadership of the survivors devolved upon expedition treasurer ALVAR NÚÑEZ CABEZA DE VACA. First as slaves to the local Indians, next as traders, and finally as medicine men, the four survivors spent six years, mostly in the Texas area, then wandered westward and south, finally arriving at the Pacific coast in Sinaloa.

The Narváez grant was next given to veteran conquistador HERNANDO DE SOTO, who carried out the first major penetration into the southern interior. Between 1539 and 1542, lured from place to place in hope of conquest of rich civilizations, de Soto scoured the interior. Starting also at Tampa, the explorers marched north along the Gulf coast, heading for Apalache in northern Florida, then due north through Georgia to South Carolina, crossing the Great Smoky Mountains into North Carolina. Swinging southward they entered Alabama, cut across a corner of Mississippi, and hit the Father of Waters at Chickasaw Bluffs, where a difficult crossing was made. West of the Mississippi the explorers penetrated Missouri, Arkansas, possibly Oklahoma, Texas, and Louisiana. In mid-1542 the leader died, and command was assumed by Luis Moscoso. He tried first to lead the remnants across Texas on foot, an effort that brought the explorers as far southwest as the BRAZOS RIVER and back again. Next Moscoso went downstream on the Mississippi and along the Gulf of Mexico to Pánuco, where he arrived in 1543.

Spain renewed its exploratory interest in 1559 by sending Tristán de Luna to occupy Coosa and Santa Elena. After disembarking at Pensacola, the party penetrated upriver on the Alabama and established Santa Cruz de Nanipacana, but later returned to Pensacola. An effort to occupy Santa Elena on the Carolina coast miscarried. By 1561 the colony disintegrated, and Spain decided to abandon any further efforts.

French intrusion along the South Atlantic coast resulted in a revised opinion and brought about permanent occupation of St. Augustine by PEDRO MENÉNDEZ DE AVILÉS. Under his leadership the French were summarily expelled, the colony was extended from Tampa Bay to Virginia, and exploration was carried out. Particularly noteworthy were the several attempts to link the Spanish Southeast with Mexico. The Spanish penetrated inland under such leaders as Juan Pardo and Hernando Boyano in the 1560s, and later in explorations of 400 miles inland in 1624 and 600 miles in 1628 under Pedro de Torres, who spent four months exploring the Georgia and Carolina backcountry.

Spain's near monopoly of southern exploration was broken by unofficial explorers, the trappers, traders, and slave raiders of Virginia and later of the Carolinas and Georgia. A German immigrant, John Lederer, made three visits to the "impenetrable" Blue Ridge in 1669–1670. Associated with frontier explorer and military leader Abraham Wood, Thomas Batts and Robert Fallam made a similar but documented exploration to the Blue Ridge in 1671, and in 1673 James Needham and Gabriel Archer headed far to the west and reached the Cherokee land on the upper Tennessee. By 1698 trader Thomas Welch had reached the mouth of the Arkansas by a backcountry route. Officially, in 1713, Virginia Governor Alexander Spotswood with his KNIGHTS OF THE GOLDEN HORSESHOE explored and took symbolic possession of the Blue Ridge and the Shenandoah Valley.

Following discovery of the upper Mississippi by Jacques Marquette and Louis Jolliet, the French began southward exploration. Leaders were LA SALLE and his cousin Henri de Tonty. After descending the Mississippi in 1682, La Salle planned occupation of its mouth, but the effort miscarried and resulted in a short-lived settlement at Matagorda Bay, Tex., and the murder of La Salle by his own men. The Spanish response was 11 separate expeditions in a wilderness manhunt by both land and sea along the Texas coast, the leading explorers being Alonso de León and Andrés de Pez.

Subsequent French occupation of the Gulf at Biloxi (1699) and Spanish settlement of Pensacola (1698) led to exploitation and trade penetration into an interior that was largely known in its general geography. Exploration ceased to be a principal factor of regional history, being replaced by three-cornered rivalry, forest diplomacy, and even outright warfare.

See C. W. Alvord and L. Bidgood, *First Exploration of Trans-Allegheny Region by Virginians, 1650–1674* (1912); J. F. Bannon, *Spanish Borderlands Frontier, 1513–1821* (1970); H. E. Bolton, *Spanish Borderlands* (1921); C. Hallenbeck, *Alvar Núñez Cabeza de Vaca: Journey* (1940); F. W. Hodge and T. H. Lewis (eds.), *Spanish Explorers in Southern U.S., 1528–1543* (1907); R. S. Weddle, *Spanish Search for La Salle* (1973); and manuscripts in Archivo General de Indias, Seville, and in Museo Naval of Spanish Naval Ministry, Madrid.

DONALD C. CUTTER
University of New Mexico

EXPOSITION OF 1828, SOUTH CAROLINA,

was a classic account of state sovereignty, penned anonymously by Vice-President JOHN C. CALHOUN in answer to the Tariff of Abominations. In 1831 Calhoun revealed his authorship, after his native South Carolina legislature had accepted his protest, but rejected his exposition. Other southern states also repudiated Calhoun's argument. This argument was based on Calhoun's novel doctrine of concurrent majorities, added to a contract theory. It contended that the states, voting to form the Union, contracted with each other to surrender only part of their individual sovereignties. All other portions of sovereignty were reserved; states could interpose their own power between their own citizens and the national authority whenever the national government appeared to exceed its delegated responsibility. INTERPOSITION would effectively nullify the law, especially should several states agree that their individual interests were attacked. Concurrent majorities of the smaller states could force Congress to reconsider legislation. The exposition helped to bring about the tariff of 1832, made Calhoun spokesman for nullifiers and secessionists, and called forth opposition from Daniel Webster and others in the North.

See G. M. Capers, *John C. Calhoun* (1960, 1969); and A. O. Spain, *Political Theory of John C. Calhoun* (1968), for incisive analyses of the exposition.

SISTER MARIE CAROLYN KLINKHAMER, O.P.
Norfolk State College

EXPUNGING CONTROVERSY.

During the dissension created by President ANDREW JACKSON's veto of a bill to recharter Nicholas Biddle's second Bank of the United States, HENRY CLAY, with the strong backing of such leaders as Daniel Webster and JOHN C. CALHOUN, introduced a resolution in the Senate censuring the president basically for ordering his secretary of the treasury to remove federal deposits from the bank. The resolution of censure passed on March 28, 1834, but the battle did not end there. Determined to wipe out this insult to the president, THOMAS HART BENTON, at the next session of Congress with the support of an administrative majority in the Senate, began a long struggle to push through a resolution to remove Clay's resolution from the official journal. When on January 16, 1837, the clerk of the Senate marked the earlier censure "expunged," Jackson considered it one of his greatest personal triumphs.

See M. James, *Andrew Jackson* (1937); P. Moore, *Journal of Southern History* (Aug., 1936); and W. G. Sumner, *Andrew Jackson* (1899).

F

FACTOR was the financial agent who handled primarily cotton but also such staples as rice, tobacco, and sugar for planters. He performed numerous functions: furnishing funds, discounting notes, procuring bills of exchange, and acting as commission merchant in purchasing supplies. The factorage system began in the West Indies. With modifications it was transferred to the southern colonies, where it became the cornerstone of staple agriculture.

The factor's most important service was marketing COTTON (COMMERCE). In reality, he was a jack-of-all-trades. He served as supplier for the plantation, extended credit through a system of advances, and acted as personal agent, investment counsel, and stockbroker. Because planters and farmers needed money to meet current expenses until crops were harvested, the factor provided loans at interest rates of from 8 to 12 percent. He was repaid in cotton at the prevailing price, and he sold any surplus beyond the debt for the planter. For this service the factor deducted a brokerage fee of .5 to 2.5 percent and a commission of 2.5 to 4 percent. Other charges were made for hauling, storage, freight, and insurance. To protect himself against loss, the factor insisted upon a minimum number of bales that must be delivered, and a penalty of up to $4 a bale was charged for any shortage. The factor required that he be consigned every cotton bale grown by the planter. New York speculators who bought cotton offered no better terms than those of the southern factors.

Harmony between planter and factor was the rule, and disagreement was the exception. Disputes, however, did arise over issues connected with marketing, purchasing, banking, commissions, and interest charges. Quarrels occurred over the quality of cotton, and discrepancies between plantation and market weights caused disputes. "Customary" fees also were controversial; these were interest charges and commissions for advancing and carrying over unpaid accounts. Factors often had problems collecting debts, and planters sometimes owed several creditors. Contracts, written or verbal, were not customary.

Capital was concentrated in the few southern cities that were important factorage centers. These cities also served as large supply depots for distribution of staples to the interior South. Most factors lived in the commercial towns along the coast and up the rivers as far as Louisville and St. Louis. The factorage system outlived the antebellum era by at least four decades. However, the decline of the seaboard system began after the Civil War, owing to the spread of railroads and the growth of land mortgage companies.

Many contemporaries regarded the factors as conservative businessmen and trusted friends of the planter. Neither side, planter or factor, had a definite advantage. The antebellum factorage system, based on tradition, was not receptive to innovations. Even with its defects, the practice was more satisfactory than alternatives such as direct trade with Europe. In summation, the system was characterized by mutual benefits between planter and factor.

See A. H. Stone, *American Historical Review* (April, 1915); R. W. Haskins, *Agricultural History* (Jan., 1955); L. C. Gray, *History of Agriculture* (1933); Singleton and Heard Papers, University of North Carolina Library; and Liddell Papers, Department of Archives, Louisiana State University.

ARLAN K. GILBERT
Hillsdale College

FAIRHOPE, ALA. (pop. 5,720), was founded in the early 1890s by a group of Iowans who wished to put into practice the single-tax theory of Henry George. It was incorporated in 1908, and it retained the single tax until 1937. Located on the eastern shore of Mobile Bay, the town produces grandfather clocks and is both a summer and a winter resort.

See P. and B. Alyea, *Fairhope, 1894–1954* (1956); D. and H. Franke, *Safe Places* (1972); G. H. Beggs, "Fairhope" (M.A. thesis, University of Arizona, 1967); and *Southern Living* (March, 1969). Fairhope Public Library maintains a collection of pamphlets, articles, books, and biographies on the town, its settlers, and similar single-tax communities.

FAIR OAKS, BATTLE OF. See SEVEN PINES, BATTLE OF

FALL LINE is a line drawn on small-scale maps connecting the points where "falls" or, more precisely, rapids appear in the major rivers as they leave the Piedmont and enter the coastal plain. The line is supposed to approximate the lithological boundary between the old crystalline rocks of the Piedmont and the sedimentary materials of the coastal plain. Away from the rivers, this "line" is indistinct, and little significance would be attached to it, but the attention of historians and geographers has been focused on those sites where urban places have developed in apparent association with the river falls. "Fall-line towns" have been designated from New England to Alabama or even Texas, but consensus would limit the range somewhat more narrowly, perhaps from Trenton, N.J., to Columbus, Ga. The ubiquity of streams and, eventually, of towns has caused some writers—*i.e.*, those working at the scale of textbooks and of associated small-scale maps—to magnify the importance of location on or near the fall line. However, close examination of the site and situation of each town indicates that any generalization that would link Trenton with Columbus, or even Richmond with Petersburg, is likely to be misleading and unproductive. Towns such as Raleigh, N.C., and Camden, S.C., have been erroneously identified as fall-line towns, and the largest southeastern city, Atlanta, has developed away from the fall line and its alleged benefits. Even in the prerailroad era, when water power and river transport were more important, the fall line did not play a causal role in directing settlement and economic activities. The functional significance of the fall line continues to be debated by historians and geographers; somewhat ironically, it is a geographer, Professor H. Roy Merrens of York University, Toronto, who has most effectively challenged the traditional view that the fall line had a definite role to play in the founding of towns in the Southeast. He has called this matter a "pseudoissue" and has attempted to steer the discussion of the urbanization (or nonurbanization) of the South along more profitable avenues.

See H. R. Merrens, *Colonial North Carolina* (1964) and *William and Mary Quarterly* (Oct., 1965); J. A. Ernst and H. R. Merrens, *William and Mary Quarterly* (Oct., 1973); H. Wellenreuther, *William and Mary Quarterly* (Oct., 1974); R. E. Grim, "Virginia Fall-Line Towns" (M.A. thesis, University of Maryland, 1971); and G. L. Holder, "Fall Zone Towns of Georgia" (Ph.D. dissertation, University of Georgia, 1973).

G. S. DUNBAR
University of California, Los Angeles

FAMILY. In spite of the failure of historians to deal explicitly with this topic, several persistent images have spawned some powerful myths about the family in southern history. The slave household has been portrayed as disorganized and unstable and matrifocal in nature, allegedly the case during and after slavery. Recent research, though not denying the presence of significant numbers of broken families, reveals the nuclear family of father, mother, and children, sometimes supplemented by the addition of outsiders or relatives, to be the dominant, indeed vital, form of both slave and postwar domestic groups.

An equally insidious, if more obscure, set of myths on the white family has seeped into the writings of historians of the South, who often make a sharp distinction between the "best class"—comprising the genteel, mannerly, patriarchal families of prideful ancestry, strong family ties, and close bonds of kinship (ARISTOCRACY)—and the lower class, comprising primitive and crude laboring families whose fathers loved drink more than home and who often lacked pride or any strong sense of family solidarity (POOR WHITES). Little historical work exists on the white family, YEOMEN FARMERS and the MIDDLE CLASS, but those interested will find great value in the ignored renditions of novelists and a wealth of detail in the untapped records of southern courts.

See E. Genovese, *Roll, Jordan, Roll* (1974), in which the slave family and the planter concept of family is treated admirably; this should be read with R. M. Myers (ed.), *Children of Pride* (1972). Also useful are E. Fogel and S. Engerman, *Time on Cross* (1974); J. Blassingame, *Slave Community* (1972); and E. S. Morgan, *Virginians at Home* (1952). H. G. Gutman, *The Black Family, 1750–1925* (1976), is a welcomed revision to E. F. Frazier's *The Negro Family in the United States* (1939), standard. See also Gutman, *Journal of Negro History* (Jan., 1975) and *Annales* (July, 1972). For other new findings on the postwar black family, see C. A. Shifflett, *Journal of Interdisciplinary History* (Autumn, 1975). Works of social scientists include: N. E. Whitten, Jr., and J. F. Szwed (eds.), *Afro-American Anthropology* (1964); C. S. Johnson, *Shadow of Plantation* (1966); W. E. B. Du Bois, *Negroes of Farmville, Virginia* (1898); R. T. Smith, *Journal of Comparative Family Studies* (Autumn, 1970); J. Dollard, *Caste and Class in Southern Town* (1949); and D. P. Moynihan, *Negro Family* (1965). On black women, see J. Carson, *Silent Voices* (1969); and the novel of A. Walker, *Third Life of G. Copeland* (1970). The novels of R. Ellison, *Invisible Man* (1952), and R. Wright, *Native Son* (1940), give deep insight. White family images are found in A. O. Craven, *Journal of Negro History* (Jan., 1930), poor whites and Negroes; P. A. Bruce, *Contemporary Review* (1900); and Twelve Southerners, *I'll Take My Stand* (1930). Devastating challenges are in J. Agee, *Let Us Now Praise Famous Men* (1941), and R. Coles, *Migrants, Sharecroppers, Mountaineers* (1971). Novelists like E. Welty, F. O'Connor, and W. Faulkner, as well as J. Agee's *Death in the Family* (1938), destroy old myths. For writings of social scientists, see A. Davis *et al.*, *Deep South* (1948); and E. M. Matthews, *Neighbor and Kin* (1965). On white women, compare A. F. Scott's *Southern*

Lady (1970) to M. Hagood's *Mothers of South* (1939). Childhood, black and white, is beautifully treated in R. Coles, *Children of Crises* (3 vols.; 1967).

CRANDALL A. SHIFFLETT
University of Texas, San Antonio

FANNING, DAVID (1755?–1825), was born in Amelia County, Va. Prior to the Revolution, he was engaged in trade with the CATAWBA INDIANS in the North Carolina backcountry. Initially a Whig, Fanning turned against the patriots and joined Tory raiding parties in 1775, after a Whig band robbed him. Until the summer of 1781, Fanning variously campaigned, was imprisoned, or sat out the fighting. On July 5, 1781, he was commissioned colonel in the Tory militia in North Carolina. Fanning then undertook a series of bold and bloody raids highlighted by his capture of Governor Thomas Burke at Hillsboro, N.C., in September, 1781. The following year, he withdrew southward and was in Florida at the close of hostilities. Fanning was one of three men exempted from the general amnesty issued in North Carolina after the war. He died in Nova Scotia.

See W. Clark (ed.), *State Records of North Carolina* (1894–1914), XXII; L. Sabine, *Biographical Sketches of Loyalists* (1864); and J. J. Crow, *Chronicles of North Carolina* (1975).

MARVIN L. MICHAEL KAY
University of Toledo
WILLIAM S. PRICE, JR.
North Carolina Division of Archives and History

FARMER, JAMES (1920–), a leader in numerous civil rights organizations, was born in Marshall, Tex. After training for the Methodist ministry and graduating from Howard University's School of Religion in 1941, he refused ordination because of the church's practice of segregation. During the next few years he held several positions simultaneously: race relations secretary for a pacifist group (1941–1945), labor organizer for two unions, and founder and national director of the CONGRESS OF RACIAL EQUALITY. He organized nonviolent sitins to desegregate several Chicago businesses in 1943 and sought to challenge bus segregation in the Upper South during 1947. While working for the NATIONAL ASSOCIATION FOR THE ADVANCEMENT OF COLORED PEOPLE (1959–1961), he tried unsuccessfully to get that organization to test desegregation of interstate transportation. He therefore resigned his position with the NAACP and organized the much publicized Freedom Rides through the Deep South in 1961 under the aegis of CORE. He was in the forefront of the CIVIL RIGHTS MOVEMENT of the 1960s and served as assistant secretary of the Department of Health, Education, and Welfare (1969–1970) during the NIXON ADMINISTRATION.

See E. A. Toppin, *Biographical History of Blacks* (1969).

FARMERS' ALLIANCE, a part of the agrarian crusade, arose in the 1880s after the GRANGE lost strength and disintegrated in the 1890s with the appearance of the POPULIST PARTY. The Alliances reflected rural hostility to high freight rates, excessive middlemen's charges, and the practices of big business (AGRICULTURAL ORGANIZATIONS). Southern farmers carried the additional burdens of one-crop farming, SHARECROPPING, and the CROP LIEN SYSTEM. All of these grievances were made more acute by ruinous declines in farm prices and by a steady decay in the place of agriculture in American life.

The Farmers' Alliance consisted of two main branches, plus a number of independent groups. The Northern Farmers' Alliance, established in Chicago in 1880 by Milton George, gained significant strength in the prairie states. Among its more prominent leaders were Ignatius Donnelly of Minnesota and Jay Burrows of Nebraska. The much larger and better-organized southern Farmers' Alliance stemmed from obscure clubs in Texas in the mid-1870s. These local groups formed the Texas Farmers' Alliance, an organization that grew rapidly in the 1880s under the leadership of CHARLES W. MACUNE. His goal of uniting all cotton farmers was made easier by the existence of other groups, with which he was able to arrange mergers. The Louisiana Farmers' Union had appeared in 1885, and two years later it and Macune's group combined to form the National Farmers' Alliance and Cooperative Union. Other mergers followed. The Agricultural Wheel had been launched in Arkansas in 1882, and after absorbing the Brothers of Freedom it united with the Texas organization in 1888 under the title Farmers' and Laborers' Union of America. Meanwhile, LEONIDAS L. POLK created the North Carolina Farmers' Association in 1887 and the next year led it into the rapidly growing southern Alliance. Finally, in 1889 at St. Louis, the northern and southern Alliances made an unsuccessful attempt to merge into a national farm organization. As a step toward that goal, the southern group changed its name to National Farmers' Alliance and Industrial Union, a title that it retained throughout the remainder of its existence.

Among the more important independent groups was the Colored National Farmers' Alliance and

Cooperative Union, which originated in Texas in 1886. During most of its existence, that organization was headed by Richard M. Humphrey, a white Baptist minister. By 1891 the black order claimed a huge membership, but it was weakened by the existence of rival groups, by controversies with its white counterpart, and by racism.

The organizational structures of the different groups followed a common pattern. The basic unit was the local Alliance, Wheel, or Union, consisting of neighbors meeting in local schoolhouses or in private homes. Other organizations existed on the county, state, and national levels. Some groups had complex rituals, the southern Alliance was secret, and most welcomed women. All of the organizations claimed to be exclusively farm orders, but most admitted people whose connection with agriculture was vague.

The objectives of the Alliance movement were much like those of the Grange. It sought to provide a social outlet for farm families, help farmers improve their operations, and strengthen their economic position. Local meetings were both entertaining and educational, with speakers lecturing on crop diversification, better breeds of cattle, and the need for maintaining soil fertility. Unlike the Grange, however, the Farmers' Alliances were political from the outset. Until 1890, however, they acted in a nonpartisan manner, educating farmers to vote wisely and using petitions to voice their political demands. Among the more important were those for better regulation or government ownership of railroads, abolition of national banks, the inflation of the currency, more equitable taxation, and a prohibition of alien landownership and of trading in futures. Southern Alliance men contributed a demand for the subtreasury plan, a scheme that they contended would provide low-interest loans, inflate the currency, and permit more orderly marketing of farm produce.

The continued deterioration in economic conditions and disgust with traditional politicians led western Alliance leaders to establish independent parties in 1890, but southerners were more inclined to work within the Democratic party. By such means BENJAMIN R. TILLMAN of South Carolina, JAMES S. HOGG of Texas, and THOMAS E. WATSON of Georgia rose to power. These successes, however, only encouraged those who favored third-party action, and the establishment of the Populist party destroyed the Alliances. From an estimated family membership of 1.1 million in 1890, their strength fell to 60,526 in 1892 and to 26,315 a year later.

See *National Economist* (1889–94), available on microfilm; N. A. Dunning, *Farmers' Alliance* (1891); W. S.

Morgan, *Wheel and Alliance* (1889); T. Saloutos, *Farmer Movements* (1960); J. D. Hicks, *Populist Revolt* (1931); W. F. Holmes, *Journal of Southern History* (May, 1975); H. C. Dethloff, *References* (1973); and R. C. McMath, *Populist Vanguard* (1975).

ROY V. SCOTT
Mississippi State University

FARMERS' UNION, officially the Farmers' Educational and Cooperative Union, was organized in Rains County, Tex., in 1902 by Newton Gresham and nine associates. They sought to systematize production and distribution by farmers, maintain stable prices, discourage the mortgage and credit systems, assist farmers in buying and selling, further scientific farming, and raise farming to the standards enjoyed by other industries. Gresham, an organizer of the FARMERS' ALLIANCE, was anxious to avoid the mistakes of the GRANGE and especially of the Alliance. Formation of state organizations in Texas, Arkansas, Louisiana, and Georgia and many unaffiliated locals in other states hastened the establishment of the National Farmers' Union in 1905. State organizations appeared in every state of the region by 1910, and the idea of organizing the Union in the states of the Middle West and Far West spread.

Membership was open to "a white person or Indian of industrious habits" who was of sound mind and believed in a Supreme Being. Farmers, farm laborers, rural mechanics, rural schoolteachers, physicians, and ministers of the gospel were eligible for membership, but bankers, merchants, lawyers, and those identified with trusts and combinations who speculated in farm products were not. Efforts were made in 1904, 1906, and 1907, and in other years as well, to set a minimum price on cotton by curtailing the planted acreage and withholding portions of the crop from market. The program seems to have backfired. Many after receiving the instructions planted more instead of fewer acres in the belief that a cotton shortage would develop, and they wanted a good supply on hand to reap a profit. Opportunism, the failure to establish a good working relationship between the poorer and more substantial farmers, and the general dissatisfaction with the business programs were the causes for the decline of the Farmers' Union in the South beginning about 1909–1910. Nevertheless, the Union, by stressing the need for more rational methods of production and distribution, better credit and warehousing facilities, and more effective ways of organizing the farmers, exerted a positive influence.

See C. S. Barrett, *Mission, History, and Times of Farmers' Union* (1909), memoirs; C. B. Fisher, *Farmers' Union*

(1920), sketchy and statistical; E. Wiest, *Agricultural Organization in U.S.* (1923); R. L. Hunt, *Farmer Movements in Southwest* (1935); T. Saloutos, *Farmer Movements* (1960); and W. P. Tucker, *Agricultural History* (Oct., 1947).

THEODORE SALOUTOS
University of California, Los Angeles

FARM SECURITY ADMINISTRATION

FARM SECURITY ADMINISTRATION was created by the Bankhead-Jones Act (1937) to succeed the RESETTLEMENT ADMINISTRATION. Allocated nearly $200 million annually, the FSA was instructed to provide "loans, relief, and rural rehabilitation for needy persons." The intent of the legislation was to encourage rehabilitation of poor farmers, principally TENANT FARMERS, by refinancing and reeducating them. Each FSA loan contract was long-term and binding on the specific individual to whom it was made.

Under the loan agreement, the government acted as the tenant's landlord and overseer for a five-year period. During this probationary period, the tenant had to follow the recommendations of agricultural experts provided him by the FSA. If in the view of the FSA the tenant was a success at the end of five years, it converted the contract to a fee-simple 40-year loan with interest set at 3 percent annually.

Candidates for the tenant contracts far outreached the ability of the FSA to fund them. At the close of the fiscal year 1940, a total of 71,736 southern farmers had applied for tenant contracts, but the FSA had funded only 5,470 contracts, or one for every 13 applicants. The candidates for the FSA tenant contracts were screened carefully. Therefore it is no surprise the default rate was small: in eight southern states there was a default rate of only 3 percent, and in three other southern states it was 9 percent.

One of the chief reasons the FSA made as few loans as it did was that the U.S. Department of Agriculture did not sympathize with the intent of the Bankhead-Jones Act. Agreeing with southern economist Rupert Vance that there were already too many small farms in the South, the USDA worked quietly through the FSA to direct congressional appropriations into projects it considered more important. New rural communities comprised of resettled poor farmers were organized where it was hoped industries would move. Because the latter expectation never materialized, the FSA funded works projects in these communities. A second community program led to the creation of suburbs adjacent to major southern cities. Poor farmers were resettled here, and the FSA helped them find jobs in the city. A final program developed in the South large-scale community farms, which were leased to large bodies of farmers who operated them as groups.

Even these programs touched only a small percentage of the South's rural poor. At the close of the fiscal year 1940, 9,657 southern families had been relocated on FSA resettlement projects. At that time, there was a total of 581,870 acres of land scattered over 58 major FSA community projects in the South.

Because the Bankhead-Jones Act was considered by the USDA to be "half-a-loaf" legislation, the FSA's executives never believed the act would fund a comprehensive and aggressive attack on chronic farm poverty. But they had hoped it would provide a beginning. By 1941, even this hope began to fade. From 1941 to 1944, Congress progressively sliced larger and larger chunks from the budget of the FSA and forced the agency to curtail all but its loan programs.

See S. Baldwin, *Poverty and Politics* (1968); P. Conkin, *Tomorrow a New World* (1959); R. Lord and P. Jonstone, *A Place on Earth* (1942); J. Madox, "Farm Security Administration" (Ph.D. dissertation, Harvard, 1950); and U.S. Farm Security Administration, *History of FSA* (1941).

HARRY C. MCDEAN
San Diego State University

FARMVILLE AND HIGH BRIDGE, BATTLE OF

FARMVILLE AND HIGH BRIDGE, BATTLE OF (April 7, 1865). April 7 was a day of fatal delay for the Army of Northern Virginia. After the virtually complete loss of two corps on the sixth at SAYLER'S CREEK, the remnants of Robert E. Lee's army continued retreating toward Farmville, Va. There, with the Appomattox River between himself and U. S. Grant, Lee hoped to obtain rations and to gain a day's march on Grant, perhaps enough to escape and join with JOSEPH E. JOHNSTON. A. A. Humphreys' II Corps of federals was able to capture the bridges across the Appomattox at nearby High Bridge before William ("Little Billy") Mahone's Confederates could burn them down. Once across the river, Humphreys caught Lee's army at Farmville receiving rations. With the bridges at Farmville destroyed, only George Crook's cavalry was able to ford the river there. FITZHUGH LEE's cavalry supported by HENRY HETH's infantry immediately attacked and defeated Crook's lead brigade. The noise of this skirmish led Humphreys to attack in the belief that there was a general Union advance south of Farmville. Humphreys and Crook were repulsed, but Lee had lost the time he needed to break clear of the encircling Union force. This delay enabled Philip H. Sheridan to capture Lee's next supply point at Appomattox Station and block further retreat.

See D. S. Freeman, *Lee's Lieutenants* (1944), III; A. A. Humphreys, *Virginia Campaign* (1883); and B. Davis, *To Appomattox* (1959), useful anecdotes for teachers.

JAMES WILLIAM STRYKER
U.S. Military Academy

FARRAGUT, DAVID GLASGOW (1801–1870),

the first admiral in the U.S. Navy, was born at Campbell's Station near Knoxville, Tenn. Young Farragut was commissioned a midshipman in the navy on December 17, 1810. During the War of 1812 he served on the *Essex*. He was made prize master of the *Alexander Barclay* when only twelve and distinguished himself in battle. He was promoted lieutenant in 1822 after spending five years on Mediterranean duty. Except for some uneventful sea duty, Farragut spent most of the time from 1822 until 1854 at Norfolk. He was promoted commander on September 9, 1841, and captain on September 14, 1855. He saw no combat duty in the Mexican War, but in August, 1854, was sent to California to establish the Mare Island navy yard. Back in Norfolk in 1861 he immediately moved north with his family when Virginia seceded.

On January 9, 1862, Farragut was appointed to command the West Gulf Blockading Squadron. He commenced an assault against NEW ORLEANS on April 18, 1862. Acting against all advice, he decided to run his fleet past the well-defended forts. The next day he destroyed the Confederate fleet, forcing the city's surrender. Undoubtedly because of this splendid victory he was commissioned rear admiral on July 30, 1862.

In early 1864 Farragut received orders to make an attack on MOBILE BAY. In this assault made on August 5, 1864, he pushed his ships through the channel that ran under the heavy guns of Ft. Morgan. When the monitor *Tecumseh* struck a mine and sank, Farragut, with the same daring he had shown at New Orleans, said, "Damn the torpedoes, full speed ahead," and he successfully drove his force right through the Confederate minefield. Once inside the bay he fought and eventually defeated the Confederate squadron led by the ironclad *Tennessee*. On December 23, 1864, Farragut was appointed to the newly created office of vice admiral, and on July 26, 1866, he was commissioned admiral.

See C. L. Lewis, *D. G. Farragut* (2 vols.; 1941), best; A. T. Mahan, *Admiral Farragut* (1892); and L. Farragut, *D. G. Farragut* (1879), journal and letters edited by his son.

FRANK LAWRENCE OWSLEY, JR.
Auburn University

FAUBUS, ORVAL EUGENE (1910–), six times

governor of Arkansas (1955–1967), was born in Combs, Ark. He was elected circuit clerk in Madison County in 1938 and rose to the rank of major in World War II. Returning to Arkansas in 1947, he bought the *Madison County Record.* He was appointed to the state highway commission and then named director of highways. In 1954 he won the Democratic nomination for governor over incumbent Francis Cherry. As governor, Faubus was considered moderately progressive until, in 1957, he used National Guard troops to prevent court-ordered integration of Central High School in Little Rock. President Dwight D. Eisenhower reacted by sending federal troops to ensure that the court's decree was carried out, but Central was closed in 1958. Faubus' defiance of federal authority won him great popularity in Arkansas and election to four additional terms. In the 1960s his racist image was diminished while he worked to industrialize Arkansas. He did not seek reelection in 1966; however, when Faubus attempted political comebacks in 1970 and in 1974, he was defeated in the gubernatorial primaries. Undoubtedly, his personal life hurt him politically in those years. In 1969 he divorced his wife of 38 years and married a younger woman. Although unsuccessful in the two primaries, Orval Faubus dominated Arkansas politics for more than a decade.

See *Newsweek* (Sept. 15, 1958); *Time* (Aug. 10, 1962; Sept. 21, 1970); New York *Times* (May 30, July 28, 1974); and *Arkansas Gazette* and *Arkansas Democrat* (1954–64). Faubus' papers are in private possession.

DAVID E. RISON
Baptist College at Charleston

FAULKNER, WILLIAM CUTHBERT (1897–

1962), was born at New Albany, Miss., into an illustrious and well-to-do north Mississippi family. His great-grandfather Colonel W. C. Falkner was a lawyer, planter, author, soldier, and railroad builder whose exploits in the Mexican War, the Civil War, and locally (including two killings and his own eventual murder on the streets of Ripley, Miss.) helped fire the imagination and literary hopes of the child born into the family's waning days as a power in the state. Faulkner, who deliberately added the *u* to the family name when he was a young man, grew up in Oxford, Miss., where the family moved in 1902. The University of Mississippi, contiguous to Oxford, played a small role in Faulkner's life, but local influences on the youth were numerous and important.

He enlisted in the Royal Air Force in Canada

and trained, without soloing officially or earning wings, in Toronto in 1918. He lived and worked for a short time in New York City in 1921. He interrupted a sojourn in the literary bohemia of New Orleans with the young artist's obligatory pilgrimage to Europe. In New Orleans he published sketches in the *Times-Picayune* newspaper and in the *Double Dealer*, a well-conducted "little magazine." He had come to New Orleans with a slim volume of poetry to his credit; *The Marble Faun* (1924) had been published with the financial aid of Phil Stone, the young Oxford lawyer who had been Faulkner's friend, literary adviser, and mentor. By the time the volume appeared, however, Faulkner apparently already was turning his attention to prose.

With encouragement and perhaps some tangible assistance from Sherwood Anderson in New Orleans, Faulkner wrote his first novel, *Soldiers' Pay* (1926). *Soldiers' Pay* was accepted by Anderson's publisher while Faulkner was abroad, and so he returned to America as a full-fledged, if not soaring, novelist. He lived on the Mississippi Gulf Coast for a while, near New Orleans, and wrote his second novel *Mosquitoes* (1927), a *roman à clef* satirizing aspects of the New Orleans literary bohemia. Although he had lost Anderson's personal friendship, he continued to benefit from the older writer's advice; as Anderson had suggested, Faulkner set out to explore the material with which he was most familiar, returning to Oxford to write a long family chronicle novel entitled "Flags in the Dust." It obviously drew upon his great-grandfather and other family lore, but it also generally exploited the material of north Mississippi with which Faulkner was broadly and deeply familiar. After Faulkner's first publisher rejected "Flags," the book was shopped around and eventually published in a shortened version, entitled *Sartoris* (1929). It was still the book that contained, as Faulkner later said, "the germ of my apocrypha"; it brought him to Yoknapatawpha County and the characters and history he would explore, with a few side trips, until his death.

With his fourth novel, *The Sound and the Fury* (1929), written while "Flags" was seeking a publisher, Faulkner made a quantum jump in the mastery of material and form. He had by now fully absorbed the tenets and approaches of modernism revealed in the work of such writers as James Joyce and T. S. Eliot, and he had found both his subject matter and his true voice. In the next 12 years his demonic creativity drove him hard, and he produced novel after novel, each different in subject, themes, characters, and artistic form: *As I Lay Dying* (1930), *Sanctuary* (1931), *Light in Au-*

gust (1932), *Pylon* (1935), *Absalom, Absalom!* (1936), *The Unvanquished* (1938), *The Wild Palms* (1939), *The Hamlet* (1940), and *Go Down, Moses* (1942). During this extraordinary period he also published two volumes of stories, *These 13* (1931) and *Doctor Martino* (1934), and a volume of poems, *A Green Bough* (1933). Meanwhile, he spent increasing amounts of time and frustrated energy (from 1932 onward) in Hollywood, where he worked as a very reluctant screenwriter to earn the money his serious fiction did not yield.

World War II deeply affected Faulkner; it conspired, along with his screen-writing occupation, to produce an uncharacteristic silence in his distinguished career, but it was during this period, mostly spent in Hollywood, that he conceived and worked on the novel he, though not his critics, would call his magnum opus, *A Fable* (1954). He reemerged in the public eye after the war first, however, with *Intruder in the Dust* (1948), which won a Pulitzer Prize and was made into a successful film; *Knight's Gambit* (1949), a collection of related mystery stories with the garrulous Gavin Stevens as detective; *Collected Stories* (1950); and *Requiem for a Nun* (1951). He was awarded the Nobel Prize for literature in 1950, an event that changed his economic status favorably and also brought him more into public view, because he accepted the honor as an obligation to speak on public issues and to serve his country as unofficial ambassador. He completed the Snopes trilogy— which he had begun in *The Hamlet* in 1940—with *The Town* (1957) and *The Mansion* (1959). In the interim he collected versions of his hunting stories in *Big Woods* (1955). His last novel was *The Reivers* (1962).

See J. Blotner, *Faulkner* (1974). Useful critical studies are C. Brooks, *Faulkner: Yoknapatawpha Country* (1963) and *Toward Yoknapatawpha County* (1978); and M. Millgate, *Achievement of Faulkner* (1966). Annotated guides are J. Bassett, *Faulkner: Annotated Checklist of Criticism* (1972); and T. L. McHaney, *Reference Guide to Faulkner* (1976). Faulkner criticism and research are evaluated and summarized by J. B. Meriwether in *Sixteen Modern American Authors* (1973). Ongoing surveys of work on Faulkner are in annual volumes of *American Literary Scholarship*. Besides extensive collection of Faulkner's papers and typescripts at the University of Virginia, the University of Texas, New York Public Library, and Princeton Library have holdings.

THOMAS L. MCHANEY
Georgia State University

FAYETTEVILLE, ARK. (pop. 30,729), founded in 1828, is 50 miles northeast of FT. SMITH and situated in the OZARK PLATEAU region. The town was burned during the Civil War, and several battles, including one at PEA RIDGE, occurred in its vicinity. Several small colleges had located there prior to the war, and it was selected in 1871 as the site of the new University of Arkansas. Today, in addition to being a college town, Fayetteville is a resort area, a trade center for poultry raisers and fruit growers, and a producer of light manufactures.

See W. S. Campbell, *Fayetteville* (1928). Washington County Historical Society publishes *Flashback* (1963–) regularly and occasionally a bulletin series on families and places in the area. *Northwest Arkansas Times* (1892–) is available on microfilm.

FAYETTEVILLE, N.C. (pop. 53,510), is approximately 50 miles south of Raleigh on the Cape Fear River. When first settled in 1739 by Scottish colonists, it was called Campbelltown. In 1783 it and the neighboring village of Cross Creek merged to form a single political entity named to honor the marquis de Lafayette. Although it served briefly (1789–1793) as the new state's capital, its development during the nineteenth century was as an agricultural market and as a producer of lumber and turpentine. The town was almost totally destroyed in 1831 by the greatest urban fire in American history to that date. Parts of it were destroyed again when occupied in 1865 by the forces of General W. T. Sherman (CAROLINAS CAMPAIGN). Much of the character of modern Fayetteville, however, dates from the location here in 1918 of Ft. Bragg, a U.S. Army reservation. During World War II, it and Pope Air Force Base transformed the town into a center of supplies and services. Continued use and expansion of these military facilities during the Korean and Indo-Chinese conflicts directly contributed to roughly tripling the city's population during the 1950s and 1960s.

See J. A. Oates, *Story of Fayetteville* (1972); and files of Fayetteville *Observer* (1816–).

FEDERAL ART PROJECT, established in 1935 by the WORKS PROGRESS ADMINISTRATION, was designed to provide jobs for unemployed artists who eventually supplied taxpayers with over 2,500 murals, 17,000 pieces of sculpture, and 108,000 easel paintings. They also produced 22,000 plates for the Index of American Design—superbly accurate copies of such objects as ship figureheads, cigar-store Indians, weather vanes, and other bits of vanishing Americana. Although 75 percent of project personnel were employed in eight metropolitan areas, the project operated in 38 states by virtue of its creation of over 100 community art centers. These centers, designed in part for the South, were essentially gallery-workshops manned by a small staff—sometimes only a single artist-teacher—whose purpose was to provide instruction in painting, drawing, ceramics, and photography, not in order to train professional artists but to create an art-conscious, visually sensitive public. Beginning in North Carolina, where ten such centers were located, the southern art centers stretched from Key West, Fla., northward and westward to Texas. Housed in quarters provided by local communities, these centers offered free work space and instructions as well as traveling exhibits from major urban museums. Separate, unequally equipped centers were established for blacks in Greensboro and Raleigh, N.C., and Jacksonville, Fla. Although public institutions in the South were recipients of project murals and easels, it was the community art centers that FAP Director Holger Cahill hoped would become as indispensable as the public library. Despite their considerable popularity, few survived World War II, when WPA funds were withdrawn and the FAP was phased out.

See J. D. Mathews, *Journal of American History* (Sept., 1975); and R. D. McKenzie, *New Deal for Artists* (1973).

JANE DE HART MATHEWS
University of North Carolina, Greensboro

FEDERAL EMERGENCY RELIEF ADMINISTRATION (1933–1935). Prior to the creation of the Federal Emergency Relief Administration on May 12, 1933, responsibility for the administration of aid to the victims of the GREAT DEPRESSION rested entirely with the state and local governments, assisted by private agencies and individuals. Overwhelmed by the burden, the states welcomed the new $500 million agency. Harry Hopkins took charge of the duties of passing on state applications, establishing grant guidelines, and supervising disbursements.

During the winter of 1933–1934, the Civil Works Administration, a temporary public works effort, augmented the FERA. After the CWA was terminated in March, 1934, the FERA set up a works division that took over a portion of the CWA clients. Other divisions of the FERA included Rural Rehabilitation, concerned with reducing the number of dependent farm families by relocating them on new fertile land and lending them necessary equipment and supplies in order to make them self-sufficient.

The FERA also set up a series of transients' camps at major railroad towns to assist displaced families and individuals. The FERA paid schoolteachers' salaries in bankrupt Arkansas, started adult education classes, and furnished seeds for small vegetable gardens and canning centers for preserving. During the drought of 1934, the FERA extended special help to the stricken counties and purchased cattle that had insufficient grazing.

Hopkins tried to prevent the use of relief as a political reward by urging the professionalization of state agencies, a proposal that met with considerable opposition. In April, 1935, conflicts with Senator HUEY LONG of Louisiana and Governor EUGENE TALMADGE of Georgia led to the federalizing of the programs to bypass the governor's office. As the Works Progress Administration took over relief work, the FERA passed out of existence in December, 1935.

See T. Whiting, *Final Statistical Report of FERA* (1942); E. A. Williams, *Federal Aid for Relief* (1939); J. Brown, *Public Relief, 1929–1939* (1940); D. Carothers, *Chronology of FERA* (1937); and Record Group 69, National Archives, for in-depth research.

STEPHEN F. STRAUSBERG
University of Arkansas, Fayetteville

FERA APPROPRIATIONS BY STATE

	Payments	People on Relief	Monthly Avg./Person
Ala.	$50,546,780	396,766	$17.33
Ark.	46,980,969	350,490	12.33
Del.	2,399,777	17,011	21.19
D.C.	16,999,716	63,346	30.43
Fla.	49,890,781	300,900	13.48
Ga.	53,072,004	383,014	14.62
Ky.	36,410,956	483,014	11.04
La.	49,813,381	274,397	25.98
Md.	35,667,069	174,840	30.59
Miss.	34,793,392	279,495	12.83
Mo.	70,997,300	586,433	18.93
N. C.	39,898,184	355,929	11.88
S. C.	37,251,842	295,941	8.35
Tenn.	37,251,842	337,055	16.45
Tex.	98,456,763	1,020,554	16.35
Va.	26,302,851	208,385	12.53
W. Va.	45,871,141	378,868	16.41

FEDERAL HOUSING ADMINISTRATION. On June 28, 1934, Congress, seeking to revive the foundering building industry, created the Federal Housing Administration to insure loans that private financial institutions granted for new construction, repairs, alterations, and improvements. From its inception the agency identified with real estate brokers, the building industry, and financial institutions and relied upon these groups for both personnel and policy. FHA bureaucrats operated on a profit-making basis and adopted lending practices that favored low-risk loans, new single-family dwellings, and the preservation of

residential segregation. The FHA's *Underwriting Manual* explicitly objected to loan insurance for neighborhoods with "adverse influences" and "inharmonious racial and nationality groups" and advocated the use of racial zoning, particularly restrictive housing covenants, to keep out undesirables.

During the depression the FHA was largely ineffective, but after World War II the agency was vital to the national suburban boom. Postwar prosperity, rising birth rates, the search for cheap land, and the federal highway program joined with FHA lending practices to foster new construction and a flight to the suburbs. Simultaneously, the absence of urban planning and the lending policies of the FHA contributed to the decay of the inner cities and affixed federal approval to residential segregation. After 1945 suburban growth in the South and the rest of the country greatly outstripped the development of the central cities. Yet between 1946 and 1959, less than 2 percent of all housing that received federal mortgage assistance was open to Negroes.

Civil rights organizations protested the FHA's discriminatory racial stance, but their efforts were generally unsuccessful until the 1960s. In 1961, however, federal legislation forced the FHA to extend mortgage assistance to housing for lower-income families and the rehabilitation of buildings. FHA Commissioner Neil Hardy, reflecting the agency's newfound concern for urban renewal, created the post of assistant commissioner for multifamily housing programs. Although these changes did not immediately reverse the conservative trends of the past, they did begin to add a social consciousness to the agency's traditional operations.

See M. I. Gelfand, *Nation of Cities* (1975), best; J. Jacobs, *Death and Life of Great American Cities* (1961); G. B. Tindall, *Emergence of New South, 1913–1945* (1967); and K. T. Jackson, in R. A. Mohl and J. F. Richardson (eds.), *Urban Experience* (1973).

EDWARD F. HAAS
Louisiana State Museum, New Orleans

FEDERALIST PARTY was a loosely organized political formation that successfully contested Jeffersonian Republican dominance of the South only during the years 1797–1801. The origins of the Federalist party in the South may be traced to those politicians, planters, merchants, speculators, lawyers, newspaper editors, and their clients and followers who assumed the identity of "friends of government" and attached themselves specifically to the persons and policies of GEORGE WASH-

INGTON and Alexander Hamilton. Southern Federalists often benefited directly from Hamilton's domestic economic policies even as they found philosophical comfort and support for their elitist view of social order in the foreign policies of Washington and John Adams.

Instinctively opposed to the course of the French Revolution, yet sincerely desirous of ensuring the neutrality of the Republic in the ongoing European struggle between reaction and radicalism, southern Federalists found little opportunity to rouse the generally apathetic late eighteenth-century electorate throughout most of Washington's administration. However, with the publication of Jay's Treaty and the resultant quasinaval war with France in 1797–1798, southern Federalists found a ready public audience for a philosophy and program of nationalism divorced from a reliance upon either British power or French ideology. As late as the ELECTION OF 1796, friends of government below the Potomac had found it difficult to differentiate between sectional and party difference; many had supported a split Jeffersonian-Federalist ticket emphasizing southern candidates. But the decisive swing of the Jeffersonians to the support of France after 1797 crystallized a firm sense of party and ideological identity within Federalist ranks. For the next three years, southern Federalists moved haltingly but unmistakably in the direction of crude party organization while increasingly seeking out public support by means of propaganda, mass appeal, public meetings, and other forms of modern party activity. Dominant in South Carolina, the Federalist party also made strong strides in Virginia and North Carolina. Available statistics seem to indicate that in the last years of the century, the party secured the support of roughly 40 percent of the electorate in these latter two states. In Maryland, the electorate seemed roughly divided between Federalists and Jeffersonians. Only Georgia was firmly in the Republican camp as a result of the identification of many prominent friends of government with the earlier YAZOO LAND FRAUDS.

With the loss of national power after 1800, the Federalist party in the South waned rapidly. Party activity was but fitfully maintained by a small group of younger politicians, and throughout the Jeffersonian era Federalists never seriously contested their opponents' control of either section or nation. But in their reluctant acceptance of primitive party organization and technique, southern Federalists made a lasting contribution to the development of the American party system.

See L. A. Rose, *Prologue to Democracy* (1968), southern Federalists to 1800; D. H. Fischer, *Revolution of Ameri-* can *Conservatism* (1965), Federalist activities in South after 1800; G. C. Rogers, *W. L. Smith* (1962); M. Zahniser, *C. C. Pinckney* (1967); J. W. Cox, *Champion of Southern Federalism* (1972), two previous books excellent biographies of leading South Carolina Federalists; U. B. Phillips, *American Historical Review* (Oct., 1898; July, 1909); W. C. Ford, *South Carolina Historical Magazine* (July, 1901); H. Wagstaff, *Sprunt Historical Publications* (1910); and N. K. Risjord, *Journal of Southern History* (Nov., 1967).

LISLE A. ROSE
U.S. Department of State

FEDERAL THEATRE PROJECT, established in 1935 by the WORKS PROGRESS ADMINISTRATION, had a dual purpose: to conserve the talents of unemployed theatrical people and to provide first-rate productions at nominal cost. Under the energetic leadership of Hallie Flanagan, as many as 13,000 professionals were engaged in productions ranging from classical and modern drama to children's plays, puppet shows, and circuses. Other projects included a Negro theater, dance drama, radio broadcasts of dramatic works, and those theatrically innovative but politically controversial documentaries, the Living Newspapers. Although the South contained few jobless actors, units were established in New Orleans, Atlanta, Miami, Jacksonville, and Tampa. In Texas, Arkansas, and northern Louisiana, the only regular productions were those supplied by minstrel and vaudeville companies. Similar groups played the Civilian Conservation Corps circuit in Virginia, Delaware, and Maryland. In the Southeast, activities took a somewhat different form. In South Carolina the WPA restored Charleston's Dock Street Theatre; in Georgia, directors from New York City worked with the recreational division of the WPA to establish community theaters in the impoverished area of the state's major cities. And in North Carolina, where FTP directors also worked with community groups, the major effort centered around *The Lost Colony,* Paul Green's historical drama of the first English settlement in North America, which opened in 1937 with a company consisting largely of Federal Theatre personnel. Plans to establish a southern regional theater in Chapel Hill were under consideration in 1939, when the entire Federal Theatre Project was abolished by Congress following a series of controversial investigations by the House Un-American Activities Committee and the Subcommittee on Appropriations.

See H. Flanagan, *Arena* (1940); and J. D. Mathews, *Federal Theatre* (1967) and *Journal of American History* (Sept., 1975).

JANE DE HART MATHEWS
University of North Carolina, Greensboro

FEDERAL WRITERS' PROJECT, part of the WORKS PROGRESS ADMINISTRATION, began in 1935 supplying work for jobless writers, editors, and research workers. Directed by Henry G. Alsberg, it employed as many as 6,600 people in the production of over 1,000 books and pamphlets. Most important were the American Guide series. Prepared for all 48 states as well as major cities and scores of towns and villages, these guides provided not only travel information, but detailed explorations of the area's history, economy, geology, ethnic and racial makeup, social life, and culture. Other projects of particular importance to the South were folklore studies, which resulted in such publications as *Bundle of Troubles and Other Tarheel Tales* (1943); over 900 life histories, some of which appeared in *These Are Our Lives* (1939); and the former slave narratives, portions of which were subsequently published in *Lay My Burden Down: A Folk History of Slavery* (1945). Pioneering efforts in ORAL HISTORY, the life histories and slave narratives, gained further uniqueness as the stories of ordinary southerners, black and white, whose memories spanned the entire period from the Civil War to the Great Depression. Other projects that contributed to the history of blacks—and of the South—were local studies such as *The Negro in Virginia* (1940) and the anthropologically oriented *Drums and Shadows: Survival Studies Among the Georgia Coastal Negroes* (1940). Additional studies in Afro-American history envisioned by the Howard professor and poet, Sterling Brown, were curtailed when federal sponsorship ended in 1939, even though the project continued under state sponsorship until 1943.

See J. Mangione, *Dream and Deal* (1972); and J. D. Mathews, *Journal of American History* (Sept., 1975).

JANE DE HART MATHEWS
University of North Carolina, Greensboro

FELTON, WILLIAM HARRELL (1823–1909) and **REBECCA LATIMER** (1835–1930). William Felton was born in Oglethorpe County, Ga. He graduated from the University of Georgia in 1842 and the Medical College at Augusta in 1844, but poor health forced him to abandon the practice of medicine at the close of the Civil War. Primarily a farmer, he was also a licensed Methodist minister. Rebecca Latimer was born in DeKalb County, Ga. Her father, a great influence in her life, operated a tavern, general store, and plantation. Rebecca was educated in a private community school, boarding schools at Oxford and Decatur, and Mad-

ison Female College. Rebecca and William met when he delivered the commencement address at her college, and they were married in 1853.

Before the Civil War, William served one term in the Georgia legislature in 1851. In the 1870s he emerged as a leader of Independent Democrats and, aided by his campaign-manager wife, tongue-lashed the Bourbons from the hustings and through the press. He served three terms in Congress (1875–1881), but by 1880 the INDEPENDENT MOVEMENT had declined and Felton was defeated in his bid for reelection. Felton was elected to the Georgia house of representatives in 1884 and served for six years. In the state legislature he criticized the CONVICT LEASE SYSTEM and supported the railroad commission, prison reform, prohibition, and greater expenditures for higher education.

Although an agrarian and ardent supporter of the GRANGE, Felton did not affiliate with the powerful FARMERS' ALLIANCE, regarding some of their demands as too radical and the leadership as demagogic. He joined the POPULIST PARTY and became its nominee for Congress (Seventh District) in 1894. Felton lost the election and then retired from active political life.

As her husband's career declined, Rebecca Felton's participation in public life increased. She was appointed in 1890 as one of two lady managers from Georgia for the World's Columbian Exposition in Chicago. She served in that capacity for four years and later participated in other fairs. Her most enduring and significant influence came from her writings. She was an inveterate writer of letters to editors of numerous newspapers, and she wrote a column, "The Country Home," for the Atlanta *Journal* from 1899 until the early twenties. She gave opinions and advice on practical, personal, and political matters. She wrote three books: *My Memoirs of Georgia Politics* (1911); *Country Life in Georgia* (1919); and *The Romantic Story of Georgia Women* (1930). Rebecca Felton was an ardent lecturer and feminist, and her most zealous crusade was for WOMEN'S RIGHTS. In 1922 she was given a token appointment to the U.S. Senate, the first woman named to that body. She took the oath of office, spoke briefly, and then retired.

The Feltons achieved prominence for their independent spirit and crusades for a few liberal reforms. However, their racism, respect for property rights, and religious fundamentalism revealed their parochialism and basically conservative philosophy.

See J. B. Bone, "R. L. Felton" (M.A. thesis, University of North Carolina, 1944); W. P. Roberts, "W. H. Felton"

(Ph.D. dissertation, University of North Carolina, 1952); and J. E. Talmadge, *R. L. Felton* (1960).

LALA C. STEELMAN
East Carolina University

FENCE LAWS. The earliest Virginia fence law appeared in 1632. It required farmers to erect a 4¼-foot fence around their fields or else "to plant uppon theire own Perill." In South Carolina and Georgia these laws were more meticulous as to the trial and punishment of owners of offending animals, and they often included regulations of brands and marks. Most of these laws had their earlier counterpart in Jamaica. The most common type of fence was the rail or "worm" fence, constructed in a zigzag fashion and then "staked and ridered." As timber became scarce in the early decades of the nineteenth century, experiments were made with cedar, hawthorn, wild brambles, and ditches. On some older plantations appeared the mortised post and rail fence, which conserved both timber and space. Rock fences appeared in parts of Kentucky, Tennessee, and Missouri. Paling and plank fences were common around dwellings, cemeteries, and town commons. Wire fences were undergoing experimentation by the beginning of the Civil War.

Laws requiring the fencing of arable land were never universally popular with large landowners, who preferred the enclosure of animals instead. Stock penning originated in Virginia in the late seventeenth century as a result of systematic fertilization of soil with manure. Interest in artificial pastures and improved breeding later reinforced the practice. Because of the scarcity of rail timber, Georgia in 1809 required that all enclosures on Harris' Neck on the seacoast be made around pasture lands instead of cultivated fields. This principle of local option was soon adopted in other states, and livestock was confined by running palings across narrow necks of land.

During the Civil War many areas suffered the destruction of fences, and people were forced to plant in open fields. A general movement was begun to amend the open-range law by requiring the universal enclosure of animals. This became a local political issue, and it bore many similarities to the contest between ranchers and farmers on the western plains. Arrayed against the old fence law permitting open range were the larger landowners, urban interests, and railroads, which sought relief from damage suits where livestock had been destroyed on railroad tracks. Tenants and small farmers resisted any change in the law.

During the 1870s legislatures began to permit counties to hold local option referenda on the question. Later local option voting by militia districts was permitted. Thus a piecemeal adoption of the "no fence law" followed. By the end of the nineteenth century the old fence laws had disappeared in a majority of the counties of the South, although the open range persisted in forest areas and in districts dominated by small farmers. Significantly, these districts showed a heavy Populist vote in the 1890s. The open range did not completely end until after the mid-twentieth century.

See L. C. Gray, *History of Agriculture in Southern U.S. to 1860* (1941); J. C. Bonner, *Georgia's Last Frontier* (1971); and C. O. Cathey, *Agricultural Developments in North Carolina, 1783–1860* (1956).

JAMES C. BONNER
Georgia College

FERGUSON, JAMES EDWARD "PA" (1871–1944) and **MIRIAM "MA"** (1875–1961), were a major political team in the personality-ridden, one-party politics of Texas from 1914 to 1940. As a boy, James was one of the rural poor. He had ambition, however, and grew to be a man of considerable ability, if little education. He took a degree in law (1897) and married Miriam Wallace (1899), the daughter of a local wealthy landholder. By 1913 he was president of Temple State Bank, had two daughters, a home, and a farm, and presented the picture of prosperous middle-class America. But Ferguson's ambitions went beyond financial security. He decided to enter politics. His first campaign for governor (1914) called for reforms benefiting tenant farmers and rural Texans, and some reforms were actually passed during his first term of office (1915–1917). In these early years Ferguson established a base of power for himself by skillfully winning the support of discontented rural elements and anti-Prohibition groups. This latter group included the political bosses of south Texas, who could deliver a considerable vote to their candidate. Ferguson was reelected in 1917 but was then impeached, tried, convicted, and barred from ever holding office in Texas again.

The impeachment stemmed from a controversy over control of the University of Texas, his anti-Prohibition stand, his radical views on rural reform, and his financial indiscretions. Despite his impeachment Ferguson kept his name before the public by seeking various offices and, in 1924, he returned to power by running his wife for governor in his stead. The Fergusons opposed the Ku Klux Klan candidate. The combination of his loyal rural supporters, anti-Prohibitionists, and anti-Klan voters proved successful.

But Miriam was governor in name only, for Jim Ferguson did not even favor women's suffrage. The Fergusons were reelected again in 1932, largely with the help of the depression. Their last administrations (1925–1927, 1933–1935) were devoid of important social legislation and plagued by scandals associated with financial dealings of the state and their liberal pardoning policy. The Fergusons played an important role in Texas politics, but the promise of rural reform their presence suggested never came to fruition.

See L. L. Gould, *Progressives and Prohibitionists* (1973), best bibliography; S. S. McKay, *Texas Politics, 1906–1944* (1952), useful; S. A. MacCorkle, *Southwestern Social Science Quarterly* (Dec., 1934); R. W. Steen, *Southwestern Social Science Quarterly* (March, 1955); F. M. Stewart, *American Political Science Review* (Aug., 1930); J. L. Calbert, "J. E. and M. A. Ferguson" (Ph.D. dissertation, Indiana, 1968); J. E. Ferguson Diary, University of Houston; and Ferguson Manuscripts, University of Texas Archives and Barker Texas History Center.

BARBARA THOMPSON DAY
University of Houston, Downtown

FERTILIZER INDUSTRY. The South has long been the heart of the fertilizer industry because of its consumption and of the availability of PHOSPHATES, labor, and transportation. When early settlers abandoned fertile fields depleted of nutrients and there was no other land to exploit, they began to enrich the soil with ashes, shells, fish, garbage, lime, manures, and bone. Then a method, developed in Europe, of dissolving bones and rock in sulfuric acid established a scientific process of producing fertilizer that was the basis for experimentation and tests in the South from the 1840s to the 1860s. Guano was imported from Peru and Mexico, bones and bone black were imported from the West Indies, and sulfur for the preparation of sulfuric acid was imported from Sicily. About 1854 Baltimore became the first city to establish a large trade in fertilizers.

During the Civil War the industry lagged. The Patapsco Guano Company, Baltimore, erected the first model factory in the country about 1864, however, and after the war new plants were erected in Baltimore, Richmond, and Charleston. Factories sprang up throughout the South as the working of the phosphate fields in South Carolina in 1870 (discovered in 1837) brought in northern capital. At that time, standard fertilizer contained 8 percent nitrogen, 2 percent phosphate, and 1 percent potash and was sold to the farmer for cash or cotton (330–400 pounds of cotton for a ton of fertilizer). Imports of potash from Germany and nitrate of soda from Chile were available in the late 1870s, and working of the Florida and Tennessee phosphate fields was begun about 1888.

The depression of 1893 closed small fertilizer plants, and many were sold to the Virginia-Carolina Chemical Company, which stabilized the business in the South. Beginning about 1900 more organization and control prevailed, resulting in increased production and consumption and the formation of the Southern Fertilizer Association. In 1926 the country's first plant to produce fertilizer from atmospheric nitrogen was built in Belle, W.Va., reducing the need for imported Chilean nitrate. In 1927 the South had 602 plants manufacturing or mixing fertilizers, with North Carolina leading in sales with 1,171,499 tons (more than all states outside the South combined).

The GREAT DEPRESSION slowed the industry, and recovery was incomplete until after World War II. By 1950, however, the effects of the TENNESSEE VALLEY AUTHORITY's fertilizer research program were evident. Commercial companies provided new granular fertilizers, custom application, and financing. By the 1960s food shortages reported in parts of the world fostered increased production, and heavy investments in fertilizer plants were made by oil companies. The industry responded to world markets, with heavy exports of products and technology to the developing countries, while the home market continued to expand.

Today, the fertilizer industry continues to thrive in the South. In 1974 Texas and Louisiana produced 83 percent of the U.S. sulfur. These two states had plant capacity for 39 percent of U.S. ammonia production and supplied natural gas to numerous ammonia plants in other states. Florida and North Carolina produced 82 percent of the U.S. phosphate rock. The South Atlantic states applied fertilizers at a rate one and one-half times higher per acre than any other region in the U.S. The forecast is bright for the industry through the 1970s. Since raw material reserves are adequate for many years, research teams can provide technology for products with prices that will offer the farmer fair returns on investments.

See R. W. L. Rasin, *American Fertilizer* (Jan., 1894); B. B. Ross, *American Fertilizer* (Feb., 1901); H. R. Smalley, *American Fertilizer* (July, 1929); A. L. Mehring, *Commercial Fertilizer Yearbook* (1934); and V. Sauchelli, *Fertilizer Review* (March, 1951).

JAMES W. ALDRIDGE
Tennessee Valley Authority,
National Fertilizer Development Center

FEUDS exist when several families, usually over a span of more than one generation, seek revenge on each other even when the precipitating episode has been forgotten. In most instances a simple argument, fight, or murder does not result in a feud, as most families resort to the courts for final adjudication. Therefore, where feuds occurred, a special set of social conditions existed. Probably the most outstanding prerequisite was strong patriarchal families (clannishness). Along with this tradition went a distrust of the law and political and civil unrest.

This combination of conditions existed in the mountain regions of eastern Kentucky, West Virginia, eastern Tennessee, northeast Alabama, northwest Georgia, western North Carolina, and southwest Virginia during the middle of the nineteenth century. The families were of homogeneous, Anglo-Saxon stock, which preserved the traditions of Scottish clans. Because they were largely isolated from the rapid development of the rest of the nation, their life-style was dependent upon farming, distilling, logging, mining, and some stock raising. Most families lived the life-style of the frontiersman. Education, respect for the law, and religious morality were not permitted to interfere with the moonshining or with these people's essentially clannish family life. The Civil War divided the loyalty of families. The area was neither "solid North" nor "solid South," and the stage was set for some outstanding bloody feuds.

The most famous was the Hatfields-McCoys feud (1865–1895). It resulted in 26 or 27 known deaths. During this post–Civil War period Morehead, Ky., had a feud of such nature that troops were necessary to quell it. With similar social conditions, Texas also had many bitter feuds, such as the El Paso Salt War and the Early-Halsey feud in Bell County. As the times changed, so did feuding, but memories of them are perpetuated each summer in such outdoor dramas as the *Hatfields and McCoys* near Beckley, W.Va.; *The Wilderness Road* at Berea, Ky.; and the *Trail of the Lonesome Pine* at Big Stony Gap, Va.

See H. W. Coates, *Stories of Kentucky Feuds* (1942); V. C. Jones, *Hatfields and McCoys Feud* (1948); H. C. McCoy, "Rise of Education in Tug River Valley of West Virginia and Kentucky" (M.A. thesis, Marshall College, 1950); C. L. Sonnichsen, *Ten Texas Feuds* (1957); S. C. MacClintock, *American Journal of Sociology* (July, 1901); and R. C. Woods, *West Virginia History* (1960).

JAMES S. WITTMAN, JR.
Western Kentucky University

FEW, WILLIAM (1748–1828). Few's career illustrates the rise of new leaders during crisis times. Born in backcountry Maryland, brought to Orange County, N.C., by his Quaker father and Catholic mother in 1758, he procured a sketchy education and legal training. After defeat of the REGULATORS at ALAMANCE in 1771, the Fews fled to Georgia. William joined them in 1776 to practice law in Augusta. The Revolution thrust him into leadership with political service on the executive council and in the legislatures of 1777, 1779, and 1783. He also saw military service against East Florida and as a partisan leader after the British captured Savannah. Appointment in 1784 as a trustee of the University of Georgia brought recognition. He also began eight years in Congress. Few served faithfully, but silently, at the Philadelphia CONSTITUTIONAL CONVENTION. After working for ratification in Georgia, he became U.S. senator (1789–1793). He served in the Georgia house (1793–1795) but failed reelection as a U.S. senator in 1796. The following year George Washington appointed him a circuit judge. In 1799 Few began anew in New York, entering state politics and banking.

See W. Few, *Magazine of American History* (Nov., 1881); *Revolutionary Records of Georgia* (1908); M. Farrand, *Records of Federal Convention* (1911–37); and W. Powell, *Regulators in North Carolina* (1971).

JOAN R. GUNDERSEN
St. Olaf College

FEW, WILLIAM PRESTON (1867–1940), was born in Sandy Flat, S.C. He received the Ph.D. degree in modern languages from Harvard University (1896). He then became professor of English in Trinity College, a Methodist institution in Durham, N.C., and in 1910 its fifth president. Few was anxious for Trinity to become a university; J. B. Duke, a trustee, was anxious to establish his philanthropies during his lifetime, and in 1924 he created the Duke Endowment, of which Trinity (to be named Duke University at the suggestion of Few) was the principal beneficiary. Thus Few became the first president of Duke and remained its guiding force until his death.

See R. H. Woody (ed.), *Papers of W. P. Few* (1951); E. W. Porter, *Trinity and Duke* (1964); R. F. Durden, *Dukes of Durham* (1975); and Few, Duke, and Trinity College papers, Duke University Library.

ROBERT H. WOODY
Duke University

F.F.V. Descendants of the earliest settlers of the Old Dominion are sometimes satirically and sometimes proudly identified as First Families of (or in) Virginia. During the Civil War, some Unionists and northerners parodied the initials as

"Fast-Footed Virginians" to denigrate the courage of the state's Confederate soldiers.

FIELD, CHARLES WILLIAM (1828–1892). Born near Lexington, Ky., he graduated from the U.S. Military Academy (1849) and saw frontier service with the 2nd Cavalry. He returned to West Point as a cavalry instructor in 1856. Field resigned to become a Confederate cavalry captain (May, 1861). He rose to major general and command of John B. Hood's division (February, 1864). Field participated in the battles of the SEVEN DAYS, COLD HARBOR, DEEP BOTTOM RUN, and the RICHMOND-PETERSBURG CAMPAIGN. His unit was the only organized division at Appomattox. At second BULL RUN he suffered a hip wound. During his convalescence he was superintendent of the Bureau of Conscription. After the war Field went into business. In 1875 he became colonel of engineers in the Egyptian army and later inspector general. In 1877 he returned and was appointed doorkeeper of the U.S. House during the Forty-fifth and Forty-sixth Congresses (1877–1881). In 1885 Field was appointed superintendent of the Hot Springs, Ark., Reservation. When he died in Washington, Field was a compiler for the *Official Records*.

See New York *Times* (April 11, 1892); E. J. Warner, *Generals in Gray* (1959); and H. B. Simpson, *Hood's Texas Brigade* (1970).

EDWARD K. ECKERT
St. Bonaventure University

FIFTEENTH AMENDMENT (1870) forbids federal and state governments to deny or abridge the right to vote "on account of race, color, or previous condition of servitude" and empowers Congress "to enforce this article by appropriate legislation." The amendment was for many years thwarted, principally in the southern states, both by intimidation, violence, and fraud and by legally enacted measures. Among the latter were laws that required, or authorized political parties or local election officials to require, qualifications that, usually without mentioning race, were intended to bar blacks from voting but were selectively enforced so that they rarely disqualified whites (DISFRANCHISEMENT). Examples are the literacy test, POLL TAX, GRANDFATHER CLAUSE, and WHITE PRIMARY. By the late 1960s all of these were virtually eliminated as barriers to black voting, thanks to federal laws and federal court decisions grounded either upon the Fifteenth Amendment or the FOURTEENTH AMENDMENT's equal protection clause.

At first federal legislation (notably the CIVIL RIGHTS ACT OF 1964 and the CIVIL RIGHTS ACT OF 1965) against literacy tests was designed chiefly to weaken such measures, but in time they were categorically struck down by the courts, even when impartially applied, because past discriminations (especially in educational opportunity) were held by judges to have produced disproportionately high illiteracy rates among blacks. The white primary, which excluded blacks from voting in Democratic primaries, was declared unconstitutional chiefly on equal protection clause grounds, and the grandfather clauses, by virtue of the Fifteenth Amendment. The use of the poll tax to keep blacks from voting in federal elections was ended in 1964 by the Twenty-fourth Amendment; and in 1966 the principle was applied, on the strength of the Fifteenth Amendment, to state and local elections as well.

By 1972 the objects of the Fifteenth Amendment had been largely achieved, and by that time nearly two-thirds of the South's blacks were registered voters. That year there were approximately 1,500 elected black public officials in the South alone, and in 1976 some 130 American cities, including Atlanta, Los Angeles, Gary, Newark, Detroit, and Washington, had black mayors. There were also at that time more than a dozen black members in the U.S. House of Representatives (including members from Georgia and Texas) and a U.S. senator from Massachusetts.

See R. Bardolph, *Civil Rights Record* (1970); J. Greenberg, *Race Relations and American Law* (1959); D. R. Mathews and J. W. Prothro, *Negroes and New South Politics* (1966); and L. Miller, *Petitioners* (1966).

RICHARD BARDOLPH
University of North Carolina, Greensboro

FILLMORE, MILLARD, ADMINISTRATION (1850–1853) was inaugurated at a moment when congressional struggles over the disposition of Mexican War acquisitions had precipitated a national crisis. Abandoning his predecessor Zachary Taylor's opposition, Fillmore first supported Henry Clay's "omnibus" proposal to resolve sectional grievances and later worked with Democratic congressional leaders to speed action on separate bills embodying the COMPROMISE OF 1850. Administration efforts were directed to enforcing the FUGITIVE SLAVE LAW. Notorious escapes and well-publicized failures to convict fugitive-slave rescuers in the Shadrack rescue (Boston, February, 1851), the Jerry rescue (Syracuse, October, 1851), and the Christiana, Pa., riot (September, 1851) marred the administration's enforcement record. But the equally prominent renditions of Henry

Long (New York City, January, 1851) and Thomas Sims (Boston, April, 1851) balanced these failures. During Fillmore's entire administration, 81 percent of fugitives taken before federal tribunals were successfully remanded to their owners, and only 7 percent escaped. Moreover, Fillmore and his entire cabinet stumped New York in support of the Compromise of 1850 (May, 1851), and the president and two southern cabinet members performed the same service in New England (September, 1851). The Fillmore administration generally succeeded in muffling sectional discord over slavery under a cloak of political nationalism.

In foreign affairs, peaceful economic expansion was supported through treaties with Mexico giving protection to employees of a New Orleans firm surveying a railroad across the Isthmus of Tehuantepec. Simultaneously the administration opposed filibusters using U.S. soil as bases to forcibly wrest Cuba from Spain. This enraged southern Democrats but conformed to the antiannexationism of southern Whigs, who cast a solid sectional vote for Fillmore at the 1852 Whig National Convention.

See R. J. Rayback, *Fillmore* (1959), standard, useful bibliography; H. Hamilton, *Prologue to Conflict* (1964); S. W. Campbell, *Slave Catchers* (1970); J. Meador, *Florida Historical Quarterly* (July, 1960); D. Long, *Alabama Historical Quarterly* (Spring–Summer, 1963); R. F. Broussard, *Journal of Mississippi History* (May, 1966); and M. R. Williams, *North Carolina Historical Review* (Winter, 1970).

DAVID E. MEERSE
State University of New York, Fredonia

FILSON, JOHN (1753?–1788), whose book *Kentucke* (1784) included the first map of the territory and the famous Boone "autobiography," was born in Chester County, Pa. This story of DANIEL BOONE became the archetypal myth of the American frontier and had enormous influence on the course of American literature. Published and plagiarized abroad, Filson's work was responsible for a stereotyped image of Daniel Boone in Paris. While engaged in founding Cincinnati, which he called Losantiville, Filson mysteriously disappeared.

See W. R. Jillson (ed.), *Filson's Kentucke* (1929); J. Walton, *John Filson of Kentucke* (1956) and *Filson Club History Quarterly* (Oct., 1973); and R. Slotkin, *Regeneration Through Violence* (1973), scholarly treatment of frontier mythology with Filson as central figure.

JOHN WALTON
Johns Hopkins University

FILSON CLUB (118 W. Breckinridge St., Louisville, Ky. 40203), founded in 1884 in Louisville, has over 2,400 members (1976). The club supports a manuscript collection and a library of 40,000 books and pamphlets on the history of Kentucky and nearby areas. It includes genealogical data, historical files, photographs, maps, newspapers, and manuscripts with major holdings on numerous important Kentuckians as well as academic, business, government, and ecclesiastical records. The society maintains a fine Victorian residence, with valuable period furnishings, which it operates as a museum. The *Filson Club History Quarterly*, circulation 2,500, publishes scholarly articles on topics related to Kentucky history.

See J. Bull, *Kentucky Historical Society Register* (Jan., 1949).

FINLEY, ROBERT (1772–1817), a Presbyterian clergyman and educator, was one of the early leaders of the AMERICAN COLONIZATION SOCIETY, an organization that allowed thousands of antebellum slaves and freedmen to immigrate to Liberia. He graduated from Princeton in 1787 and taught for five years, first in New Jersey and then later in South Carolina. In 1792 he returned to Princeton for theological study and was licensed to preach two years later. The following spring, he was ordained in the church at Basking Ridge, N.J., where he served as a minister and educator for the next 22 years. In 1816 Finley published a pamphlet, *Thoughts on the Colonization of Free Blacks*, which stimulated the formation of the ACS. At the first organizational meeting, he was elected one of the vice-presidents. In April, 1817, he resigned his pastorate and accepted the presidency of the University of Georgia. The trustees hoped Finley could revitalize the struggling school, but shortly after moving to Athens he contracted a fever and died while traveling the state seeking funds and support for the university.

See I. V. Brown, *Memoirs of Finley* (1819), biased but best available; H. N. Sherwood, *Journal of Negro History* (July, 1917); and P. J. Staudenraus, *African Colonization* (1961).

JAMES M. GIFFORD
Western Carolina University

FIRE-EATERS were radical southern political leaders who spoke vehemently and acted decisively for proslavery interests in the antebellum period. In the face of the abolitionists' attack upon slavery, the fire-eaters championed states' rights as a means of protecting southern interests and worked for secession rather than have these interests threatened. Sometimes led by JOHN C. CALHOUN (South Carolina), the fire-eaters included

WILLIAM L. YANCEY (Alabama), ROBERT BARN-WELL RHETT (South Carolina), ROBERT TOOMBS (Georgia), LOUIS T. WIGFALL (Texas), ALBERT GALLATIN BROWN (Mississippi), and EDMUND RUFFIN (South Carolina). Until about 1860, fire-eating radicalism was impotent, but incidents, including John Brown's HARPERS FERRY RAID and the election of ABRAHAM LINCOLN as an anti-slavery president, gave the fire-eaters more credibility. Although a minority, they helped disrupt the Democratic CHARLESTON CONVENTION of 1860 and prevent southern acceptance of Stephen A. Douglas. After Lincoln's election, the fire-eaters, especially those in the U.S. Senate, thwarted compromise and led the way to secession. Within the Confederacy, several fire-eaters, including Toombs, Rhett, and Wigfall, were leaders in the opposition to Jefferson Davis.

See W. J. Cash, *Mind of South* (1956); C. Eaton, *Freedom of Thought in Old South* (1951) and *Mind of Old South* (1964); R. Hofstadter, *Paranoid Style in American Politics* (1965); D. W. Hollis, *South Carolina College* (1951); A. L. King, *Louis T. Wigfall* (1970) and *Louisiana Studies* (Spring, 1968); G. M. Capers, *John C. Calhoun* (1960); and C. M. Wiltse, *John C. Calhoun* (1944).

ALVY L. KING
University of Missouri, St. Louis

FISH AND FISHING, FRESHWATER, have played important roles in the activity and dietary patterns of the South from the period of earliest occupance. The Indians utilized a variety of methods in catching fish, although weirs, traps, and spears were most common on the Atlantic coast and small nets and spears were more common in the Mississippi Basin. Scattered accounts of the use of fishhooks, especially in the Chesapeake Bay area, poisons, torchlight, and bows and arrows are also found. The most important species for the Indians were the buffalo fish and catfish in the Mississippi Basin, sturgeon and various members of the herring family on the Atlantic coast, and various members of the sunfish family, such as the crappie and bass, throughout the region as a whole. In spite of the wide variety and quantities available, however, fish constituted the dominant aboriginal food source only in southern Florida and portions of the Gulf coast.

European settlers and farmers also found freshwater fish an important addition to their diets. Although little statistical data about freshwater fish consumption exists from the period of early settlement, numerous diary, travel, and other accounts indicate that fish were important additions to the diet in many areas. Catfish was an especially important food source in the Mississippi Basin, as

well as buffalo fish and sunfish, and Atlantic coast residents consumed various freshwater and anadromous herrings, bass, and sturgeon.

Commercial fisheries grew up quite early, but were relatively restricted until the development of better preservation techniques. The most important commercial freshwater species in a 1908 survey included catfish, buffalo fish, shad, and sturgeon. Carp, which had been introduced from Germany in 1877, was just becoming important. By the 1970s the freshwater fish industry had grown into a multimillion-dollar enterprise. In the Chesapeake and South Atlantic districts it was dominated by shad and catfish, in the Gulf district by catfish, crawfish, and buffalo fish, and in the Mississippi Basin by catfish and bullheads, buffalo fish and mussels. Arkansas leads in the production of buffalo fish and catfish, primarily through aquaculture, and commercial freshwater mussels are produced only in Tennessee and Alabama, and commercial crawfish solely in Louisiana.

Some species have tended to decline in recent years, especially shad and sturgeon, because of problems with pollution and water impoundment projects. The Mississippi Basin has had tremendous problems with agricultural and industrial chemicals, as well as poorly treated urban sewage, which has been an important factor leading to the growth of aquaculture in the region.

Aquaculture, or fish farming, is both one of the newest and oldest changes in the fish industry. The earliest recorded mention of aquaculture was in 472 B.C. in China, but it was rarely used in the United States before the twentieth century, other than for noncommercial holding ponds to keep live fish for later consumption. True aquaculture had little real impact on the South until the 1930s. The primary centers today are in Arkansas, Louisiana, and Mississippi, which account for about 80 percent of the region's total. Although 19 species of food fish are presently being raised by farmers, the industry is dominated by only a few species. Earliest large-scale efforts at fish farming concentrated on buffalo fish, raised in conjunction with rice, and paddlefish. Both were favored because they were relatively low on the food chain, but unfortunately paddlefish could not spawn in standing water and the mortality rate of the buffalo fish during handling was quite high. In 1970 the predominant species was catfish with 37,000 acres of ponds in the region. Other important species include minnows (28,866 acres), mixed (8,652 acres), buffalo fish (1,366 acres), and goldfish (750 acres). Commercial aquaculture of crawfish began in the late 1940s in Louisiana, usually in rotation with rice production. In 1970 total commercial production from all sources had risen to 2.5 million pounds.

Sportfishing has been an important activity since earliest times, and the literature and culture of the region are steeped in its tradition. On the basis of freshwater licenses issued, the popularity of freshwater sportfishing in the South, especially in those states without coastlines, is greater than the national average. Although freshwater sport fishermen have tended to concentrate on the same species as commercial fishermen, some game fish such as bass have received special interest. An entire industry of specialized boats and fishing tackle has developed to pursue the wily bass. In recent years fishing clubs sponsoring contests with large cash prizes have become increasingly popular.

See E. Rostlund, *Freshwater Fish and Fishing in Native North America* (1952); S. Shapiro (ed.), *Our Changing Fisheries* (1971); J. E. Bardach *et al.*, *Aquaculture* (1972); and U.S. National Oceanic and Atmospheric Administration, *Fishery Statistics of U.S.* (annual).

RICHARD PILLSBURY
Georgia State University

FISHER'S HILL, BATTLE OF (September 22

1864). During the SHENANDOAH VALLEY CAMPAIGN, Philip H. Sheridan, with over 40,000 troops, decisively defeated JUBAL EARLY's 12,000 Confederate veterans at WINCHESTER on September 19, 1864. Although Early was able to retreat southward to Fisher's Hill overlooking Strasburg, Va., his corps was reduced by at least one-third. Early indicated later that he was merely making "a show of a stand here, with the hopes that the enemy would be deterred from attacking me in this position." When it became apparent that Sheridan was going to attack, "orders were given for my troops to retire, after dark," but the attack took place that same afternoon of September 22. Sheridan turned Early's left flank and then successfully carried through with a massive frontal assault. The Confederate troops gave up the field and continued their retreat. Over 1,200 of Early's troops and 12 artillery pieces were lost. Sheridan suffered over 500 casualties.

See D. S. Freeman, *Lee's Lieutenants* (1944); M. K. Bushong, *Old Jube* (1955); and F. E. Vandiver (ed.), *Early's War Memoirs* (1960), provide southern emphases. Also see G. E. Pond, *Shenandoah Valley in 1864* (1883); R. O'Connor, *Sheridan the Inevitable* (1953); and E. J. Stackpole, *Sheridan in Shenandoah* (1961), northern perspectives.

JOHN Q. IMHOLTE
University of Minnesota, Morris

FISK UNIVERSITY (Nashville, Tenn. 37203) was founded in 1866 as a black institution and named for General Clinton B. Fisk of the FREEDMEN'S BUREAU. It is Nashville's oldest college, and its library maintains an extensive collection of Negro history materials. Notable are the papers of CHARLES W. CHESNUTT, JOHN MERCER LANGSTON, Julius Rosenwald, and Charles S. Johnson as well as the archives of the American Missionary Association (1839–1879).

See T. E. Jones, *Progress at Fisk* (1930); and J. M. Richardson, *Tennessee Historical Quarterly* (Spring, 1970).

FITZHUGH, GEORGE (1806–1881), lived most of his life in Port Royal, Va., practicing law. He is best known as the militant proslavery author of *Sociology for the South* (1854) and *Cannibals All!* (1859) and of numerous articles for DE BOW'S REVIEW. Fitzhugh justified slavery and southern civilization by attacking free society as it existed in the North. He argued that the principles of freedom and equality operating in the North encouraged cutthroat competition and class warfare and rendered the inhabitants "cannibals all." Free laborers were in fact "slaves without masters," since they were deprived of the protections that he believed the South offered its slaves. Instead of a free society, Fitzhugh advocated a patriarchal society that recognized "slavery as right in principle, and necessary in practice, with more or less of modification, to the very existence of government, of property, of religion, and of social existence." It was, he contended, just such a social structure that made the South not only distinctive but superior to the North. In 1861 Fitzhugh was a reluctant secessionist. After the Civil War he served as an associate judge of the Virginia freedmen's court and opposed the Radical Republicans, especially their capitalistic spirit and doctrines of racial equality. Ironically, in his last writings for *Lippincott's* magazine, he advanced ideas similar to those of the later New South prophets.

See H. Wish, *George Fitzhugh* (1943); E. D. Genovese, *World Slaveholders Made* (1969); and G. Fitzhugh, *Cannibals All!*, ed. C. V. Woodward (1960).

ANNE C. LOVELAND
Louisiana State University

FITZPATRICK, BENJAMIN (1802–1869), was born in Greene County, Ga., and died at Wetumpka, Ala. He practiced law and engaged in local politics at Montgomery, Ala., until the late 1820s, when ill health forced him to retire to his plantation. Entering the governor's race in 1841 as a Democrat, he was elected. Fitzpatrick was reelected in 1843 without opposition. Twice, in 1848 and 1853, he was appointed to the U.S. Senate to fill out unexpired terms. He was elected to a full Senate term in 1856 and served as president pro tem. At the 1860 Democratic BALTIMORE CONVENTION, he was nominated vice-president on the ticket with Stephen A. Douglas. Previously a Douglas supporter, he cited irreconcilable differences regarding slavery in the territories and refused the nomination. Although not a secessionist, Fitzpatrick resigned from the Senate in 1861 and returned to Alabama. He was briefly arrested in 1865. In that same year he was a delegate to the state constitutional convention and was elected president of that body.

See W. W. Duncan, "B. Fitzpatrick" (M.A. thesis, University of Alabama, 1930); S. H. Roberts, *Publications of Alabama Historical Society* (June, 1901); and T. M. Owen, *Dictionary of Alabama Biography* (1920).

WILLIAM WARREN ROGERS
Florida State University

FIVE FORKS, BATTLE OF (April 1, 1865).

Located 12 miles southwest of Petersburg, Va., Five Forks was the junction of the north-south road leading to the Southside Railroad, the last supply link of the Army of Northern Virginia, and the White Oak Road, leading to the flank and rear of Petersburg's fortifications. U. S. Grant wanted to force Robert E. Lee's besieged army to fight outside its fortifications or stretch Lee's line until his forces were too thin to resist an assault. Grant pushed his left flank westward under the command of Philip H. Sheridan with three divisions of cavalry and the V Corps commanded by Gouverneur K. Warren. In response, Lee sent about 10,000 men commanded by GEORGE E. PICKETT to "hold Five Forks at all hazards." The assault started at 4 P.M. (while Pickett was attending a shad bake), and the 27,000 Union soldiers smashed Pickett's lines, capturing more than 5,000 prisoners. On hearing the news, Grant ordered "an immediate assault along the lines" and captured Petersburg the following day. Eight days after Five Forks, Lee surrendered.

See D. S. Freeman, *Lee's Lieutenants* (1944); B. Catton, *Grant Takes Command* (1968); P. H. Sheridan, *Memoirs* (1891); B. Davis, *To Appomattox* (1959); P. V. D. Stern, *End To Valor* (1958); and *Official Records, Armies*, Ser. 1, Vol. XLVI.

DAVID L. WILSON
Southern Illinois University

FLAGLER, HENRY MORRISON (1830–1913).

A native of Hopewell, N.Y., he joined his half-brother Daniel M. Harkness in Ohio at age fourteen and, within a few years, accumulated a fortune from speculating in grain. He lost his money in a salt-manufacturing venture in Michigan and returned to Ohio and the grain business. Flagler joined with John D. Rockefeller and Samuel Andrews to form an oil-refining company in 1866. This became the Standard Oil Company in 1870. Flagler began to invest in east coast Florida RAILROADS and hotels in the 1880s. He built the Florida East Coast Railway to Miami in 1896 and then effectively promoted that area as a resort. In addition, his companies actively encouraged the development of Florida agricultural products. Flagler next undertook the construction of a railroad from Miami to Key West. This was a tremendous task because much of the construction was over water; however, the line was completed in 1912. He also established a steamship line to Key West and Nassau and built two hotels in the latter city. It is estimated that Flagler spent approximately $50 million in Florida and that his profits were small in comparison.

See S. W. Martin, *Florida's Flagler* (1949); A. Nevins, *Study in Power: John D. Rockefeller* (1953); P. K. Yonge Library of Florida History, University of Florida, Gainesville; and St. Augustine Historical Society Library.

DUDLEY S. JOHNSON
Southeastern Louisiana University

FLATBOATMEN

worked their flat-hulled, shallow-draft vessels in the South from before the Revolution through the Civil War. Their ships were used exclusively in floating with the current (50,000 miles were floatable in the Mississippi Valley) since they possessed no means of counter-current navigation. Flatboatmen preferred spring travel to benefit from the more rapid current at flood stage and the reduced incidence of snag damage. Their craft were disassembled at the voyage's end and sold for scrap lumber or firewood. By 1820 flatboatmen furnished the cities of the South with the preponderance of their foodstuffs, whiskey, and tobacco. Flatboating served as seasonal employment for farmers and tradesmen, who averaged $50 per month in wages through the first half of the nineteenth century. Constant danger appeared from snags, eddies, disease, storms, pirates, Indians, and the ominous return trip north along the NATCHEZ TRACE. Medical care for boatmen was practically nonexistent before the 1837 congressional establishment of marine hospitals along the Ohio and the Mississippi. Flatboatmen utilized their craft in riverine commerce, as store boats, as rental craft for the government to transport military equipment and supplies, as wood boats, and to salvage steamboat hulks. Semipermanently or temporarily moored flats served as hospitals, saloons, gristmills, sawmills, theaters, retail shops, and bordellos. The reputation of flatboatmen for thievery, intemperance, debauchery, and quarrelsomeness has been rhapsodically balanced by George Caleb Bingham's murals of antebellum flatboating on the Missouri featuring dancing, music, song, and laughter. Most emigrant families prior to the Civil War traveled downstream from Pittsburgh, Brownsville, or Wheeling sharing their flats with their livestock and home furnishings.

See L. Baldwin, *Keelboat Age* (1941); C. Ambler, *History of Transportation in Ohio Valley* (1932); W. Carson, *Mississippi Valley Historical Review* (June, 1920); and H. Hoagland, *Journal of Political Economy* (May, 1911).

JAMES T. BANNON
St. Louis University

FLEMING, WALTER LYNWOOD (1874–1932), was a pioneer in the writing of modern southern history. Trained in the new ways of "scientific" methodology, Fleming, the son of a Confederate veteran, studied under George Petrie at the Alabama Polytechnic Institute (1893–1897) and with WILLIAM A. DUNNING at Columbia University (1900–1904). He became the perfect expression of Dunning's view that southern history must be written by those with "an inherent sympathy with Southern society." Fleming taught at West Virginia (1904–1907), Louisiana State (1907–1917), and Vanderbilt (1917–1929) universities, and he served as dean of the College of Arts and Sciences and director of graduate study at the latter institution. As author and editor Fleming produced three major works: *Civil War and Reconstruction in Alabama* (1905); *Documentary History of Reconstruction* (2 vols.; 1906–1907); and *The Sequel of Appomattox* (1921). Fleming showed the new directions of his age with his strong emphasis on economic and social factors, and he made excellent use of oral and written evidence. If he transcended the more partisan prejudices of his day, his work still reflected a conservative support of the southern white and a denial of the role of the southern black. Fleming's views have been superseded, but his solid data still constitute a starting point for the student of southern history.

See W. L. Fleming Collection, New York Public Library, largest source of primary materials; F. M. Green, *Journal of Southern History* (Nov., 1936), complete bibliography; W. C. Binkley, *Journal of Southern History* (May, 1939); and W. H. Stephenson, *South Lives in History* (1955).

ROBERT DAVID WARD
Georgia Southern College

FLETCHER, DUNCAN UPSHAW (1859–1936), was the son of a modest plantation owner in Monroe County, Ga. He attended Vanderbilt, where he completed both undergraduate and law studies. In his new home of Jacksonville, Fla., he was elected councilman and mayor by a reform movement that included blacks and the Knights of Labor. In 1908 he defeated a former ally, NAPOLEON B. BROWARD, for the senatorship and served in the U.S. Senate continuously until his death. His financial support came primarily from banking and corporate interests in Florida, but he also won backing among small farmers. He supported OSCAR W. UNDERWOOD for the Democratic nomination in 1912, but subsequently became an enthusiastic Wilsonian. He authored a plan to provide farmers long-term agricultural credit; and, despite modifications, the Federal Farm Loan Act of 1916 was primarily the result of Fletcher's theory and effort. He also sponsored legislation to provide federal control of the merchant marine and unsuccessfully resisted return of shipping to private firms during the 1920s. His basic conservatism underwent considerable stress during the 1930s, when he served as chairman of the Senate Banking and Currency Committee. He presided over a lengthy investigation of financial and banking irregularities and expedited passage of NEW DEAL banking reforms. Although he retained some philosophical reservations concerning the New Deal, he believed that the national crisis demanded substantive reform.

See J. W. Flynt, *D. U. Fletcher* (1971); and W. J. Wells, "D. U. Fletcher" (M.A. thesis, Stetson, 1942).

WAYNE FLYNT
Samford University

FLETCHER, THOMAS CLEMENT (1827–1899), was born in Jefferson County, Mo. At the age of nineteen he was elected deputy circuit clerk of Jefferson County and later circuit clerk. While in this office he studied law and was admitted to the bar in 1857. At the same time, he became land agent for the southwest branch of the Pacific Railroad. Forming an early alliance with the antislavery Republicans, he was a strong supporter of Abraham Lincoln in the ELECTION OF 1860 and became one of Lincoln's chief Missouri advisers. During the war, he took an active part in raising the 31st Regiment, of which he was colonel. In November, 1864, he was elected the first Republican governor of Missouri. When the state's constitutional convention passed an ordinance freeing Missouri slaves, Governor Fletcher issued his emancipation proclamation early in 1865.

See *Messages and Proclamations of Missouri Governors* (1924), IV; Fletcher Papers, Missouri Historical Society, Columbia; T. C. Fletcher, *Inland Monthly* (Aug., 1872); and G. Anderson, *Story of Border City During Civil War* (1908).

GOSSIE H. HUDSON
Lincoln University

FLETCHER V. PECK (6 Cranch 87 [1810]) was a collusive suit among land speculators who succeeded in raiding the U.S. Treasury for over $4 million. The Georgia legislature in 1795 sold 35 million acres of land for one and a half cents an acre after all but one legislator had been bribed (YAZOO LAND FRAUDS). The next session of the legislature rescinded the sale. In the meantime, the original purchasers sold most of the land to New England speculators, who undertook to defend their land titles in the federal courts. The main issue centered on the scope of the clause in the U.S. Constitution forbidding states to impair "the obligation of contracts" (Art. 1, Sec. 10). This clause had been put in the Constitution to prevent states from interfering with contracts made between private persons, but Chief Justice John Marshall expanded it to include state governments. The 1795 statute that sold the land was defined as a contract protected by the U.S. Constitution, and the 1796 statute that rescinded the sale was declared unconstitutional. It was the first time a state statute had been voided by the U.S. Supreme Court. The effect of the decision was to weaken the powers of state governments by expanding the scope of review by federal courts over state laws, and it extended the protection of the federal courts over land speculators, who at that time were important interstate businessmen.

See C. P. Magrath, *Yazoo: Case of Fletcher v. Peck* (1966); and C. G. Haines, *Role of Supreme Court* (1944).

RONALD E. SEAVOY
Bowling Green State University

FLOOD, HENRY DE LA WARR (1865–1921), lawyer and congressman, was born in Appomattox County, Va., the son of a Confederate army major. After receiving his law degree from the University of Virginia in 1886, he served two terms in the Virginia house of delegates (1887–1891) and three

in the state senate (1891–1900). From 1902 until his death he was a member of the U.S. Congress. He sponsored considerable new legislation and was particularly active in foreign policy, where he vigorously supported President WOODROW WILSON. As congressman, Flood was chairman of the Committee on Territories (1910–1913) and the Committee on Foreign Affairs (1913–1918). He was author of the resolution that admitted New Mexico and Arizona to statehood, and he introduced the resolution declaring war on Germany and Austria in World War I. Flood was a close friend of THOMAS STAPLES MARTIN, U.S. senator from Virginia. With the aid of railroads and other business interests in the state, the two men created a political machine (BYRD MACHINE), which controlled the state beginning in 1893 and not ending until Flood's death, when control passed to his nephew HARRY FLOOD BYRD. Flood was also a member of Virginia's constitutional convention of 1901–1902.

See H. D. Flood Papers, Library of Congress; B. I. Kaufman, "Henry De La Warr Flood" (Ph.D. dissertation, Rice, 1966); V. Dabney, *New Dominion* (1971); A. W. Moger, *Bourbonism to Byrd* (1968); and W. E. Larsen, *Montague* (1965).

CATHERINE SILVERMAN
Institute for Research in History

FLOOD CONTROL. The necessity of flood control was recognized immediately by the early settlers in the lower Mississippi River valley. The French engineer Vitrac de La Tour opposed locating the city of New Orleans at its present site, because he knew that the settlement would be periodically flooded by the river. BIENVILLE, the city's founder, overruled this objection, and La Tour undertook one of this country's earliest flood control systems: a 5,400-foot-long LEVEE along the Mississippi, completed in 1727. As settlements developed along the river valley and as destructive floods continued to inundate property and croplands, JOHN C. CALHOUN declared flood protection a national problem. Flood control began to gain official public recognition in 1847, when THOMAS H. BENTON, ABRAHAM LINCOLN, Calhoun, and Horace Greeley attended conventions advocating federal flood control.

Despite congressional attempts to secure flood protection (Swamp Acts of 1849 and 1850), lack of coordination among several states and levee districts resulted in an unsuccessful control program. Great floods in 1849, 1858, and 1859 plus the Civil War left the already inadequate Mississippi River levee system badly damaged or destroyed. In

1879, as the federal government recognized the need for a more substantial and coordinated flood control effort, Congress established the Mississippi River Commission, which had among its assigned duties "to prevent destructive floods." Although levee work under the MRC began in 1882, inadequate financial support limited its effectiveness primarily to levee repair and navigational channel maintenance. Finally, the flood of 1916 resulted in the passage of the Flood Control Act of 1917, which authorized the construction of flood control levees and affirmed the policy of local cooperation along the lower Mississippi and its tributaries.

The flood of 1927, which caused about $236 million in damages (equivalent to over $1 billion today), took 214 lives, and displaced 637,000 persons, precipitated the Flood Control Act of 1928, which committed the federal government to a definite program of flood control in the alluvial valley of the lower Mississippi River. From 1928 to 1970, 22 additional flood control acts authorized corrective works on the Mississippi River and its tributaries: levees for containing flood flows; floodways for the passage of excess flows past critical reaches; channel improvement for increasing the river channel capacities; and tributary basin improvements, providing for DAMS, reservoirs, pumping plants, auxiliary channels, etc.

With the creation of the TENNESSEE VALLEY AUTHORITY in 1933, flood control was extended into the heart of the South, along the Tennessee River and its tributaries. A new concept of storing unwanted floodwaters behind dams for power, navigation, and other purposes allowed potential flood damage to be converted to regional development. Emphasis on engineering works reached its peak after passage of the Flood Control Act of 1936. For almost 30 years after 1936, the traditional solution to flood control involved keeping water away from people by the use of engineering structures. However, in the 22 years after 1936, flood losses amounted to about $6.6 billion. Even though the federal government, through the Corps of Engineers, TVA, and the Soil Conservation Service, has spent well over $7 billion for flood control works since 1936, present flood losses are currently amounting to $1 billion annually. This does not mean that engineers have not built well; money invested in flood control works has been money well spent, recaptured many times over from damages averted. However, as the population in the South expands into unprotected areas and as "protected" floodplains become inundated from time to time with unusual floods, flood damages continue to accumulate.

Recognition of continued flood damage despite expensive traditional flood control measures of keeping the water away from the people led the federal government to change its approach to reducing flood damages. In 1966 President Lyndon Johnson recommended a "unified program for managing flood losses." Basically, the new approach is toward a more comprehensive floodplain management program, which integrates traditional flood control measures with other available methods such as floodplain regulations designed to keep the people away from the water (zoning, subdivision ordinances, and building codes); flood insurance; evacuation and warning schemes; tax adjustment; education; and many other devices. As a result, many communities in the South, aided by technical assistance from federal agencies such as TVA and the Corps of Engineers, are leading man's quest to adapt to nature's way.

See Water Resources Council, *Nation's Water Resources* (1968); *Unified National Program for Managing Flood Losses*, House Document 465, 89th Cong., 2nd Sess.; G. R. Wall, *Establishing Engineering Basis for Floodplain Regulations* (1969); and Water Resources Council, *Regulation of Flood Hazard Areas to Reduce Flood Losses* (1971, 1972).

BRUCE A. TSCHANTZ
University of Tennessee, Knoxville

FLORENCE, ALA. (pop. 34,031), approximately 100 miles north of BIRMINGHAM, was settled about 1779 as a trading post by rivermen at a rapids on the Tennessee River. They named the rapids Muscle, or Muscle Shoals, possibly because of the strong arms needed to paddle through the rapids. At the junction of the Tennessee River and NATCHEZ TRACE, the land was purchased from the federal government in 1818 by the Cypress Land Company. After a young Italian surveyor had laid out the city, the firm sold lots notably to Andrew Jackson, James Madison, and James Monroe. Although a canal constructed to bypass the shoals was completed in 1836, the irregular water levels of the river made use of it impractical, and the canal was closed in 1837. Yet the town flourished as a shipping and transportation center, and in 1883 a sister city, Sheffield, was founded on the opposite bank of the river. During World War I, the federal government undertook construction of a hydroelectric dam and two nitrate plants at Muscle Shoals. The facilities were not completed in time to produce nitrates needed for the war effort, but they later became the foundation for the TENNESSEE VALLEY AUTHORITY.

See files of Florence *Herald* (1884–); and Florence *Times Tri-City Daily* (1869–), on microfilm (1917–).

FLORENCE, S.C. (pop. 25,997). The area surrounding present-day Florence in northeastern South Carolina was settled in the 1730s by Scottish and Welsh colonists. The principal market town was the community of Mars Bluff. In the 1850s the residents of Mars Bluff, led by Colonel Eli Gregg, opposed construction of a rail line to their town and forced the Wilmington & Manchester Railroad to construct its depot several miles out of town on a place known as "the Wilds." The depot soon became a rail junction, and the site grew into the city of Florence. A shipping point, troop center, and site of a Confederate prison during the Civil War, the city fell to W. T. Sherman's troops on March 5, 1865. The war and the occupation by federal troops did nothing, however, to thwart the continued development of Florence as a rail center and shipping point. Moreover, excellent transportation facilities have served to attract industry to the city, which manufactures a variety of textiles and lumber products.

See files of Florence *News* (1923–), on microfilm.

FLORENCE PRISON. Florence, a junction for three railroads in northeastern South Carolina, was one of the sites selected to receive prisoners from ANDERSONVILLE in the fall of 1864. The chaotic experience of the camp reflected the rapid disintegration of the Confederacy. After the stockade was completed, conditions did not improve significantly. The compound was typical: the walls were of upright timbers sunk into the ground covering a rectangular area of about 23.5 acres, of which six were swamp. A deadline ran around the inside about ten or 12 feet from the palisade. A small stream that traversed the interior served as both water supply and waste disposal. Confederate authorities, local citizens, and prisoners all testified to the odious conditions. None was as eloquent as the death statistics. The peak prison population reached over 12,000. During its five-month existence, some 2,802 prisoners died. Yet these conditions did not indicate a conscious policy of the Confederate government. Rather they mirrored the increasingly brutal nature of a war in its fourth year and the turmoil in the South.

See W. D. Woods, *Notes on Confederate Stockade of Florence* (1947), by guard.

G. WAYNE KING
Francis Marion College

FLORIDA is sometimes described as a southern state with a difference. Although geographically a part of the South, Florida was settled by Europeans earlier than any of the English colonies to the north and by the time of the FRENCH AND INDIAN WAR had almost two centuries of history as part of the Spanish Empire. Both its Indian and European populations have experienced great turnover due to wars, changes of sovereignty, and remarkably rapid tides of emigration and immigration. When Florida became attached to the United States in 1821, virtually none of its earlier Spanish or English inhabitants remained, and its Indian population was composed largely of recently arrived SEMINOLES unrelated to the aboriginal inhabitants present when Europeans first arrived. From the slaveholding states came most of the antebellum populace, with South Carolinians and Georgians predominating. After the Civil War, and after each of the great wars since, immigrants from the northern states flowed into Florida in considerable numbers. Markedly after World War II this tide of "yankees" virtually changed the face of the state, whole areas in the south-central part of the state appearing to be transplanted midwestern communities and the lower east coast taking on the appearance of urban northeastern regions. Refugees from Fidel Castro in Cuba most recently gave the Miami area a Spanish presence unmatched in the state in almost two centuries. One result has been evident in voting patterns. Today conservative Republicans are at home in the Orlando–Tampa Bay area, liberal Democrats do well on the lower east coast, and Old South voting patterns—similar to those in Alabama and south Georgia—prevail in the panhandle. Modern Florida is a complex cosmopolitan state having more in common with states such as California or Texas than with its Old South neighbors.

Origins and geography. "Florida" was the name given by JUAN PONCE DE LEON to the land that he sighted on March 27, 1513, and on which he landed during the first week of April. The name referred to the "feast of the flowers," or the Easter season, during which the landing was made. Although the peninsula appeared on previously published maps and probably was visited by earlier explorers, Ponce de León usually is credited as the discoverer, because he named it and officially laid claim to it for the Spanish crown. The early Spaniards regarded all of the North American continent as Florida, but in the seventeenth and eighteenth centuries English intrusions to the north and French expansion in the Mississippi Valley defined Florida more narrowly. At the close

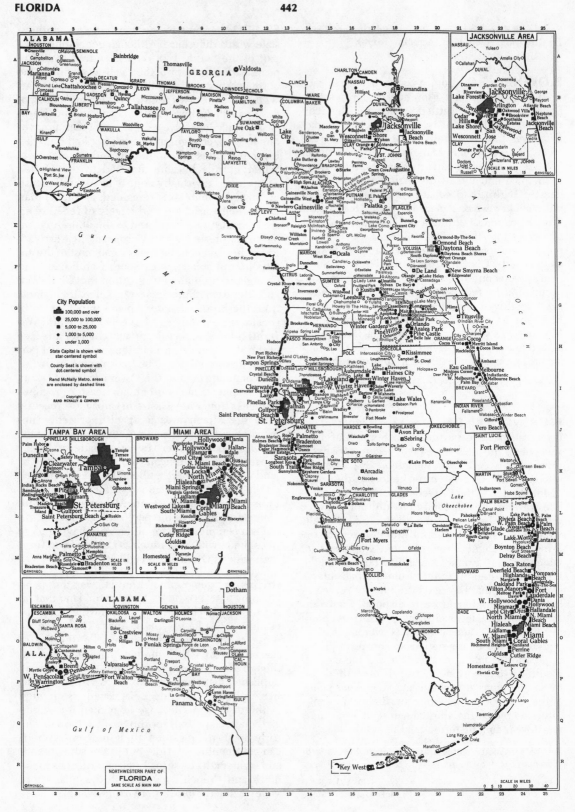

City Population
■ 100,000 and over
● 25,000 to 100,000
● 5,000 to 25,000
• 1,000 to 5,000
• under 1,000

State Capital is shown with
star-centered symbol

County Seat is shown with
dot-centered symbol

Rand McNally Metro. areas
are enclosed by dashed lines

Copyright by
RAND McNALLY & COMPANY

TAMPA BAY AREA

MIAMI AREA

JACKSONVILLE AREA

NORTHWESTERN PART OF
FLORIDA
SAME SCALE AS MAIN MAP

of the French and Indian War in 1763, Florida was transferred to England, which made two provinces of it and delineated its borders. West Florida was bounded by the Mississippi River on the west, the Chattahoochee and the APALACHI-COLA rivers on the east, and the Gulf of Mexico on the south. On the north a line was drawn at about 32° 28' from the mouth of the Yazoo River due east to the Chattahoochee. East Florida was bounded on the west by the Apalachicola River, flowing to the Gulf from the confluence of the Flint and Chattahoochee rivers, and on the north by a line drawn from the junction point of those streams due east to the headwaters of the ST. MARY'S RIVER and down that stream to the Atlantic Ocean.

In 1783 the Treaty of Paris returned Florida to Spain and provided for the independence of the British colonies to the north. A dispute between the United States and Spain over the northern boundary of West Florida was settled in favor of the United States by Pinckney's Treaty of 1795, which established the line at the 31° latitude. After the LOUISIANA PURCHASE in 1803, however, the United States claimed that part of West Florida between the Mississippi and the Perdido rivers as a part of that purchase. Not until 1810, however, was United States authority ordered extended over the region, and not until 1813 was it actually exercised over the entire area. Thus by the latter year was Florida delineated in its present-day boundaries.

Today Florida encompasses about 58,560 square miles, of which 4,298 square miles are inland water areas. Its shape is such that no point is more than 60 miles from either the Gulf of Mexico or the Atlantic Ocean. Six physical regions may be identified within the state. The coastal lowlands include the entire coastline and the Florida Keys. The western highlands include most of the panhandle west of the Apalachicola River and between the Alabama line and the coastal lowlands. In it is located the highest point in the state, an elevation of 345 feet in Walton County. The Marianna lowlands compose a triangular area, encompassed within the latter region, northwest of the Apalachicola. A rolling sinkhole region with numbers of small lakes, it boasts rich soil and is a well-populated rural region.

The Tallahassee Hills region, east of the Apalachicola between the Georgia line and the coastal lowlands, extends eastward to the Withlacoochee River. A gently sloping hilly region, it was once the heart of the cotton plantation belt. The central highlands are a high ridge and lake region on the interior of the peninsula reaching about 250 miles from the Georgia border to Lake OKEE-CHOBEE. It contains thousands of lakes large and small. The EVERGLADES Swamp area is a broad depression about 1,200 square miles in size south of Lake Okeechobee. This "river of grass" is drained by a number of short rivers flowing into the Gulf.

Mean annual Fahrenheit temperatures in Florida range from the upper 60s in the northern regions to the middle 70s in the southern peninsula and 78 degrees at Key West. Summers are long, hot, and humid with mean temperatures about 82 degrees; winters are mild with temperatures running about 13 degrees lower in the north than in the south in the coolest months, January and February. Rainfall varies widely, from year to year and region to region, but 53 inches is a frequently cited average. Tropical storms, to which Florida is particularly exposed, occasionally produce copious rainfall over large regions and dangerously high winds. Snowfall is an almost unknown phenomenon in Florida, the only significant recorded snowfalls having occurred in 1899, 1958, and 1977.

Spanish colonial development, 1513–1763. No permanent Spanish settlement was made in Florida until 1565. In 1513, Ponce de León after his initial sighting of the peninsula went ashore a few miles south of the mouth of the St. John's River and then proceeded to explore the east and west coasts, landing at several points. Before he could attempt to colonize the lands he had discovered, the king ordered him on an expedition to subdue Carib Indians in the lower Antilles. For over half a century numerous other Spanish explorers and/or colonizers, such as Francisco de Garay, Lucas Vázquez de Ayllón, Pánfilo de Narváez, HERNANDO DE SOTO, Tristán de Luna y Arellano, and Angel de Villafañe, probed the Atlantic and Gulf coasts of Florida, but were unsuccessful in establishing a settlement (EXPLORATION).

The growth of nationalism in France in the late sixteenth century led the French to challenge Spanish supremacy in America, and it was this, in turn, that led to the first permanent Spanish settlement in Florida. In 1562 Jan Ribault landed at the mouth of the St. John's River with a band of 150 French HUGUENOTS and eventually erected Ft. Caroline. To break up this French intrusion, colonize the land for Spain, and promote Christianity among the natives, Spain sent an expedition to Florida under PEDRO MENÉNDEZ DE AVILÉS. He reached Florida August 28, 1565, with five ships carrying 700 soldiers and sailors and 100 civilians. Sailing north from the Cape Canaveral area, where he had sighted Florida, Menéndez found the

French settlement on the St. John's River. Turning back some 30 miles, he landed his expedition and on September 8, 1565, ceremoniously founded ST. AUGUSTINE on a safe anchorage called by the French the River of Dolphins (Matanzas River). After sending to Havana for reinforcements, Menéndez prepared his defenses for an expected attack. On September 10, Ribault sailed against St. Augustine, but a hurricane drove his expedition ashore south of the Spanish settlement. Menéndez meanwhile moved overland against Ft. Caroline, seized it, and later slaughtered or made prisoner all other remaining Frenchmen in Florida. Although a French expedition in 1567 destroyed the Spanish garrison at Ft. Caroline, Menéndez had secured Florida for Spain, and no further foreign colonies were attempted. Though he attempted to establish friendly Indian relations and extend Spanish settlement, the city of St. Augustine was the only permanent impress that Menéndez left upon Florida.

Twenty years after its founding, St. Augustine had a government house, a church, some stores and commercial buildings, and houses for its 300 inhabitants. The British buccaneer Sir Francis Drake sacked and destroyed the city in 1586, but it was soon rebuilt and strengthened. Around 1600, however, the abandonment of Florida was seriously considered. Accepting the thesis that a white population could not be attracted to Florida in significant numbers, Spain gave new direction to its policy in Florida. It was decided to "Christianize" and "hispanicize" the Indians through the instrument of the Catholic church and its missionaries. The king and the Council of the Indies were to direct and finance the missions through the bishop of Cuba, supported militarily by the governor at St. Augustine. Governor Menéndez, in the sixteenth century, had attempted to establish Jesuit missions, but that order abandoned the field in 1572, and Florida was put in the charge of the Franciscans. Thirteen members of the order arrived in 1587 and established missions in the main Indian towns north of St. Augustine as far as the upper Sea Islands of Georgia. Following a visit of the bishop of Cuba in 1606, renewed support for the missions was forthcoming, and the most successful extension of the system, into West Florida, was undertaken. By the 1670s the missions were at the peak of their influence. In 1674, Bishop Gabriel Díaz Vara Calderón spent more than ten months visiting the 32 missions in Florida and reported that he counted 13,152 Christian Indians in them. By 1680 there were 52 missionaries.

English settlement of Charleston in 1670 meant trouble for Florida and its Franciscan mission chain. Increasingly the Indians came under English influence, and by 1685 those from the Georgia missions were going over to the British in great numbers. Won by goods, guns, and money, they turned hostile toward the Indians of northeast Florida and clashed with them. In 1702 and 1704, Governor James Moore of South Carolina, invading Florida with Indian allies, first laid waste the coastal missions as far as St. Augustine and later eradicated the Apalachee missions. In these forays perhaps 10,000 Indians were carried away as slaves by the English. During the hostilities only the great stone Castillo de San Marcos (begun in 1672) in St. Augustine had defied destruction. The missions never recovered, and Spain's authority over Florida was never completely restored.

About the same time that the English challenge appeared north of Florida, French pressure spread eastward from the Mississippi Valley. To check that influence, Spain decided to fortify Pensacola Bay on the Gulf coast, and construction was begun in November, 1698. Early in 1699 a French expedition was turned away but withdrew only to settle at Biloxi and later Mobile. Never able to sustain itself, the Spanish garrison at PENSACOLA lived even more precariously than that at St. Augustine. It was frequently undermanned, was subjected to raids by pro-English Indians, and occasionally had to turn to the French in Mobile for food because of irregular and uncertain supply shipments. In 1719, in consequence of the European War of the Quadruple Alliance (1719–1721), a French fleet seized Pensacola and held it until 1723.

The settlement of Georgia in 1733 in the no-man's-land between the Carolinas and Florida renewed the urgency of the threat from the English. The alarmed Spaniards built two small forts on the St. John's to protect communication lines to western Florida and strengthened the defenses of St. Augustine. In 1740 Governor JAMES OGLETHORPE of Georgia invaded Florida in consequence of the War of Jenkins' Ear, which had begun the previous year. He took the small posts on the St. John's and in May assaulted St. Augustine. In June the fortress there was besieged in an action that ended in July, when Spanish warships arrived. In September, 1742, Oglethorpe reappeared but, being no more successful in taking the Castillo than in his earlier attack, he abandoned his campaign.

From 1743 until the end of Spanish rule in 1763, St. Augustine was peaceful and almost prosperous. Stores, warehouses, and homes of the durable coquina rock were becoming numerous. Although agriculture and fishing never flourished, the development of naval stores, ranching, and commercial pursuits was promising. Attempts were made to cultivate good Indian relations, but English influence among the tribes was too strong for Spain to combat. Beyond the vicinity of the forts in Pensacola and St. Augustine, and the tiny garrison in St. Mark's in Apalachee country, Spanish authority was feeble indeed.

Florida played no part in the French and Indian War, but it did become a pawn in the peace settlement. The 1763 Treaty of Paris gave to England French Canada to the north of its American holdings and Spanish Florida to the south of them. Spain received Louisiana from France and had actually traded off Florida for Cuba, which Britain had seized in the war. Thus, as a result of what had been primarily an Anglo-French military struggle, Florida emerged as a British province.

Estimates of the numbers of aboriginal Indians in Florida when Europeans first arrived vary from 25,000 to 100,000. They had by 1500 developed fairly complex cultures with political, military, and religious classes, and most lived in settled communities. They carried on trade over great distances. At the time of discovery there were five principal groups of Indians in Florida. The most numerous were the Timucua, who lived in the area from southeastern Georgia, stretching southwestwardly across the peninsula down to the Tampa Bay area. The APALACHEE INDIANS were numerically second and lived in the panhandle region between the Aucilla and Ochlockonee rivers. It was among these two groups that the Franciscan missions made their greatest headway in the seventeenth century, and it was these groups who suffered most severely from the English attacks beginning in 1702. Third in numbers were the Calusa Indians, who lived on the west coast south of Tampa Bay. They were fishermen who lived in rather large villages with well-developed social structures. They developed a reputation for fierceness and hostility to the white man. The two smallest groups were the Ais, who occupied the east coastal region south of Cape Canaveral, and the Tequesta, who occupied the southernmost coastal region in southeast Florida. The Tequesta were fishermen, probably politically subordinate to the Calusa, and engaged in no agriculture.

Of these aboriginal Indians, almost none remained at the end of the eighteenth century. Their numbers were decimated by warfare, disease, and slave catchers. Some of the survivors placed themselves under Spanish protection and departed with them in 1763, when Britain assumed control. The lands they left soon attracted Indians from Geor-

gia and Alabama. Tribes of CREEK INDIANS soon known as Seminoles began arriving in the early 1700s and continued to come for a century.

Florida in transition, 1763–1821. British rule, which began in 1763, was to be brief, ending in 1783 by terms of the same treaty that recognized the independence of the United States. Although Spain again assumed sovereignty over the region, its authority was never complete. British trading interests continued to operate, and Britain's influence over the Indians continued. Under terms of the 1763 peace settlement, England received all the French holdings east of the Mississippi except New Orleans. Hence Florida's panhandle was extended to the Mississippi River, and Britain created two Floridas from the enlarged colony. East Florida, extending west to the Apalachicola River, had its capital at St. Augustine. West Florida, west of the Apalachicola, was governed from Pensacola. In 1764 the northern boundary of West Florida was pushed north to 32° 28' so that the province included what is now west Florida plus Louisiana east of the Mississippi and the southern third of both Alabama and Mississippi.

Before the transfer, St. Augustine counted 3,046 inhabitants, including 89 Christian Indians, 95 free blacks, and 315 black slaves. Pensacola counted fewer than 800 people, which included about 100 civilians and like numbers of convicts and Indians. Three hundred fifty French subjects lived in Mobile. After the transfer the Spanish and their dependents left almost to a man. Only the French remained for the period of English rule.

West Florida's first civil governor, George Johnstone, arrived in 1764 with instructions to govern the province with an appointive council and to make provision for a representative assembly. Yet both East and West Florida were royal colonies with generous financial support by London. In the circumstances little dependence on the assemblies was necessary, and they played a small role in either colony. The difficulties in West Florida grew in some measure from its size, small population, and lack of good internal transportation. Some of the most attractive but most inaccessible lands were those along the Mississippi, where agricultural patterns were suggestive of the plantation system that developed later. By 1774, some 2,500 whites and 600 slaves lived in that area, and some estimate that the population doubled after the American Revolution started. Like East Florida, West Florida received a large share of LOYALIST refugees. In 1774 the population of all West Florida was about 5,000; approximately 2,000 were in the Biloxi-Mobile-Pensacola area. The major export of the colony was pelts (FUR TRADE), with NAVAL STORES taking second place. No significant cash agricultural crop was developed. When Spain entered the war against England as a de facto ally of the United States in 1779, West Florida became a legitimate target for the Spaniards in Louisiana. Governor Bernardo de Gálvez moved, seizing Natchez in 1779, Mobile in 1780, and Pensacola in 1781.

In East Florida James Grant, a Scot from South Carolina, assumed the governorship in 1764 with instructions similar to those Johnstone had in Pensacola. Although Grant created a distinguished council, no assembly was called until 1781, apparently because he and his successors needed no funds from such a body and feared that it might reflect the radical spirit of the colonies to the north. More than 100 estates were established in northeast Florida and in the St. John's Valley, but the most ambitious effort at settlement was that by Dr. Andrew Turnbull at New Smyrna. After visiting East Florida in 1767, he procured a grant of land and recruited over 1,200 Greeks, Italians, and Minorcans from the Mediterranean. By 1769 the colony was producing CORN, COTTON, sugarcane (SUGAR INDUSTRY), RICE, and INDIGO. Inadequate preparation for the large colony, however, led to hardships and consequent recriminations and dissension. By 1778 most of the New Smyrna settlers were in St. Augustine, where many of their descendants have remained.

Grant was succeeded in the governorship by Patrick Tonyn, a haughty autocrat, who nonetheless called the first assembly in 1781. A majority of those elected were Loyalist refugees. Already the problem of refugees in East Florida had become acute; the year 1783 saw 5,000 more whites and 8,300 more blacks arrive to swell the resident population of 2,000 whites and 3,000 blacks. East Florida, however, saw no serious military action during the Revolution. The great stone fort in St. Augustine served only as a prison for military prisoners and three signers of the Declaration of Independence: Arthur Middleton, EDWARD RUTLEDGE, and Thomas Heyward, Jr.

To the horror and dismay of the thousands of American Loyalists who had sought refuge there, the Treaty of Paris of 1783 returned the Floridas to Spain. Of the British inhabitants, only the Turnbull colonists, called Minorcans, remained in any number after the change of flags. The possession of both Louisiana and the Floridas after 1783 gave Spain again a vast North American empire, but essentially the Spanish were unable to govern it. In the Floridas, to forestall American influence among the Indians, Spain allowed a British firm—PAN-TON, LESLIE & COMPANY—to monopolize the Indian trade to maintain good Indian relations. This firm alone had the goods, capital, and experience that the Indian trade required. A key to control of their trade was ALEXANDER MCGILLIVRAY, Creek chief and British army colonel, who in the last quarter of the eighteenth century was perhaps the most influential man among the Indians of the Southeast. Until 1795 this organized Indian trade kept the United States' southern border area in a state of tension and kept the loyalties of many Indians there turned toward Britain and Spain.

The activities of both English and American adventurers, as well as Indian problems, were main concerns during the second Spanish period. Despite Spanish mercantile policy, more and more trade went to the United States, whose markets were more accessible than any of imperial Spain. In East Florida several important English landholders remained after 1783, and some Americans filtered down into the region. The development of a LUMBER and naval stores industry in East Florida was more often than not associated with names that were not Spanish. Retrocession of Louisiana to France in 1800 and its subsequent acquisition by the United States in 1803 seem to have indicated a growing American expansionist spirit that should have ended Spanish hopes of retaining Florida.

Responding to popular clamor, and after a "revolution" in West Florida, President James Madison in 1810 declared Florida from the Mississippi to the Perdido River to be part of Louisiana and occupied all save the Mobile district. In 1813 Mobile was taken. Meanwhile, Governor Juan Vicente Folch of West Florida had indicated a willingness to deliver up the rest of his province should he not get orders or reinforcements, and Congress secretly authorized the president to take the Floridas if local authorities should offer them or a foreign power should threaten them. Thereafter, however, Governor Folch receded from his earlier offer. In East Florida, Amelia Island on the Georgia border was growing in importance as a center of piracy and international intrigue beyond the control of Governor Juan de Estrada. It had been a smuggling center since Thomas Jefferson's presidency and a hotbed of illegal slave trade.

In 1812 George Mathews, a former Georgia governor, conspired with influential Florida residents for a revolution to be assisted by U.S. military forces. Mathews brought off his revolution, but only a token U.S. force was committed and was soon withdrawn. Seizing Fernandina (on Amelia Island) instead of St. Augustine, the rebels established a "republic of Florida," which expired in 1813. American involvement in war with England in June, 1812, helps explain the withdrawal of support for the rebels.

In May, 1814, an English expedition landed on Amelia Island and from there attacked St. Mary's and Cumberland Island in Georgia. In an advance up the St. Mary's River, however, they were repulsed. Meanwhile, in West Florida, English forces occupied Spanish installations at Pensacola in August, 1814. In November, Andrew Jackson led U.S. forces into the city and drove them away. That done, Jackson moved his army westward, where in 1815 he won his decisive victory over the British in the battle of NEW ORLEANS. A British fort established in 1814 on the Apalachicola River at Prospect Bluff, which was well stocked with munitions, was occupied after their departure by Indians and blacks and became a refuge for runaway slaves. Since these were viewed as a hazard to river travel and a threat to the Georgia frontier, an American gunboat destroyed the fort and most of its inhabitants in 1816.

Meanwhile South American revolutionaries considered Florida as a site for bases for their movements against Spain. In 1817 Gregor Mac-Gregor seized Fernandina in the name of Simón Bolívar and Francisco Miranda (AMELIA ISLAND AFFAIR). When the men and supplies he expected did not materialize, he deserted the region, which was soon after seized by Luis Aury in the name of the Republic of Mexico. Aury was little more than a pirate and, to end his operations, a U.S. naval squadron seized Amelia Island in December, 1817. Thereafter it remained under the American flag.

Andrew Jackson concurrently was moving to establish "law and order" in northern Florida. On April 6, 1818, he seized the Spanish outpost at St. Mark's and executed some British subjects in the area. He inspected the region as far east as the Suwannee River before turning west toward Pensacola, arriving there May 22. Surrendering after five days, the Spanish were shipped off to Havana, and U.S. officers were put in charge. Refusing to sustain Jackson's actions, President James Monroe returned the posts to Spain, but Secretary of State John Quincy Adams' negotiations with Spain were probably furthered by this demonstration of its weakness in Florida. On February 22, 1819, the Adams-Onís Treaty was signed, in which Florida was ceded to the United States, the northern boundary of Mexico was delineated, and the United States was committed to assume Spain's debts to U.S. citizens up to a total of $5 million. A delay in the exchange of treaty ratifications held up the actual transfer of Florida until July, 1821.

Antebellum Florida, 1821–1865. President Monroe named Andrew Jackson to receive Florida and to serve as its provisional governor responsible for organizing the civil administration. Details of the transfer did not go smoothly in Florida, and Jackson's patience was sorely tried. Making his capital at Pensacola, he created counties and their administrative and judicial offices and appointed persons to them. President Monroe himself named the territorial officials, including the members of the legislature. Jackson was not content in Florida, however, and by early October, 1821, he returned to Nashville. In 1822 WILLIAM P. DUVAL of Kentucky was named governor, a post he held for 12 years.

Following Jackson to Florida was a horde of speculators, adventurers, office seekers, and cronies. The Florida into which they came probably had fewer inhabitants than at any time since 1513. The aboriginal Indians had been replaced by some 5,000 Seminoles, a few restless Americans and runaway slaves had filtered in before 1821, but virtually no remnants of earlier European settlement were left. Only 713 inhabitants were in Pensacola in 1820 (including but seven from the first Spanish period), and most of these left in 1821 with their governors. In East Florida some Minorcans remained from the British period, but there too most of the Spanish left in 1821. There was virtually no continuity of cultural institutions, and the expansionist Americans came unfettered by any need to adjust to the ways of a respected, established native civilization.

After 1821, however, the population grew rapidly; a territorial census in 1825 counted about 13,500 persons. About 5,800 were west of the Apalachicola; some 2,400 were in "middle Florida" (between the Apalachicola and Suwannee rivers); and around 5,000 were in northeast Florida. South Florida (a vague region roughly including everything south of New Smyrna) held only a few more than 300 persons. A striking feature of Florida's first American decade was the rapid development of middle Florida. In the federal census of 1830, west Florida had 9,748 inhabitants; middle Florida, 15,779; and east and south Florida, 9,473. By 1840 middle Florida had more population than all the rest of Florida east and west of it. Eighty percent of the cotton was grown there, the largest concentration of slaves was there, and political and social life flourished. It was Florida's black belt, and every elected antebellum governor save one was from this populous plantation area.

Although the Florida legislature was made elective by Congress in 1826 and became bicameral in 1838, sectionalism, rooted in the vast distances and divergent interests of the people of the territory, early manifested itself. West Florida recurrently felt the attraction of annexation to Alabama; statehood sentiment first appeared in middle Florida; opposition to both lingered longest in east Florida. Almost immediately territorial officials addressed themselves to overcoming sectionalism. The second legislative council asked Congress for roads and directed Governor Duval to place a new capital halfway between the east-west extremities of the territory. Commissioners John Lee Williams and William H. Simmons explored the old Apalachee area and recommended Tallahassee as the seat of government. In 1824 the government was established there, and in the same year Congress authorized a Pensacola to St. Augustine road. Although a few other roads were built and canals planned, the greatest impetus to road building came in the Second Seminole War (1835–1842), when the army crisscrossed Florida with military and post roads reaching down to the Everglades.

Indian problems had preoccupied both the Spanish and English rulers of Florida, and Andrew Jackson early had urged the removal of the Seminole from those portions of the territory where they might stand in the way of white settlement. The 1823 Treaty of Moultrie Creek confined them to a reservation in the interior south of present-day Ocala and north of Charlotte Harbor. In less than a decade white expansion brought more Indian clashes and demands that they be sent west of the Mississippi. The signing of an unpopular removal treaty led a fiery young brave, Osceola, to repudiate the old chiefs and rally his people to full-scale war against the whites in 1835. Jackson, now president, pitted the army's best men and leaders against the Indians in a long, difficult war (SEMINOLE WARS). During the war as groups of Indians surrendered or were captured they were sent west, and after the surrender of the militant chief Coacoochee in 1842, Colonel William J. Worth declared the war at an end. In all, 3,800 Indians had been removed, $20 million had been spent, and some 1,500 American lives had been lost.

When Jackson had received Florida in 1821, national political parties were in disarray and no formal parties immediately emerged in Florida; factionalism and personalism prevailed. In 1838, however, at a state constitutional convention in St. Joseph, two political parties appeared, the Democrats and the Whigs. The Whigs were strong in middle Florida and among the older, entrenched political and economic leaders, many of whom had come to Florida as Jackson's cronies. The

leadership included RICHARD KEITH CALL, Thomas Brown, Edward Carrington Cabell, William P. Duval, George T. Ward, and David S. Walker. The Democrats emerged from the 1838 meeting, calling for economic reform, led by DAVID LEVY YULEE, James D. Westcott, and Robert Raymond Reid. Most of the appointive governors of the territorial period—Duval, Call, John H. Eaton, and John Branch—were "Whiggish" in their philosophies. Only Martin Van Buren's appointee, Reid, was a doctrinaire Democrat.

Although a constitutional convention was held in 1838, the financial PANIC OF 1837 and the ravages of the Seminole War delayed Florida's entry into the Union until 1845. Democrats made a clean sweep of the elections, and the first state legislature elected Yulee to the U.S. Senate, forcing him to vacate the congressional seat he had won in the general election. The vigorous young Virginia Whig, Edward Cabell, was elected to replace him and proved the most popular Whig politician in the state. Cabell held his seat until 1852. The most important local issues dividing Whigs and Democrats at statehood had been the fate of local banking corporations, Democrats opposing and Whigs supporting them. The return of prosperity after 1845 and the rapid growth of the state led to an emphasis on national issues, centered around slavery.

The 1852 election was the death blow to the Florida Whigs. After 1852, with the election of James E. Broome, radical Democrats dominated Florida politics. Broome was seen as champion of the "South Carolina separationists," and his popularity probably owed something to patterns of immigration. Between 1850 and 1860 the South Carolina–born population of Florida almost doubled, and the Georgians increased by 50 percent. Together, they constituted one-third of the 1860 population.

During the antebellum era slaves usually made up about 40 percent of the population, and free blacks were a tiny fraction of the people. From 560 in 1845, they increased to 932 in 1860. Most free blacks lived in Key West, Pensacola, or Jacksonville and were laborers, craftsmen, seamen, or farmers. Although they were few in number, their free status caused much concern among whites, and they were subject to increasingly stringent regulation.

By 1860 secessionist Democrats, in unshakable control of state government, were calling for disunion. A convention, which convened January 3, 1861, passed a secession ordinance 62 to seven on January 10, and Florida became the third state to leave the Union. Its role in the Civil War was relatively unimportant due to its small population, scarce resources, and relative isolation from the rest of the Confederacy. Its economy was primarily agricultural and extractive, though a cattle industry of promise was growing north of Lake Okeechobee. Industry was negligible. Throughout the war, Key West and the main forts guarding Pensacola Bay remained in federal hands. Other port cities were held by the federals during much of the war. Some salt, beef, and pork were produced and sent to the Confederates overland by wagon. Perhaps the most important battle in Florida resulted from an attempt to disrupt these supplies. On February 7, 1864, federal forces moved west from Jacksonville along the railroad to Tallahassee. Near the village of OLUSTEE on February 20, they met a force of 5,000 Confederates. Although equal in numbers the federals were unable to proceed and withdrew with heavy losses.

The war brought economic ruin to Florida. Major ports had been destroyed, and the railroads, notable beginnings of which had taken place in the 1850s, were in shambles. Banking and credit facilities had been destroyed, slaves were free, and property values had drastically declined.

New directions, 1865–1930. A. K. Allison, president of the state senate, succeeded to the governorship after the suicide of Governor John Milton at war's end. Allison's attempt to continue government as usual was unacceptable, and President ANDREW JOHNSON jailed him, naming as his replacement WILLIAM MARVIN, a Key West Unionist. Marvin shared authority with the federal military commander, and the two supervised the calling of a constitutional convention in the fall of 1865. The old leaders, appearing prominently among the delegates, agreed to annul secession, abolish slavery, ratify the Thirteenth Amendment, and repudiate the war debt, but they refused to take steps to protect the rights of blacks. The 1866 legislature curbed those rights, enacting restrictive BLACK CODES and appearing to want to preserve all that was "good" about slavery. At Johnson's urging, the Fourteenth Amendment was rejected. David S. Walker, a former Whig, was elected governor in November, 1866, taking office in January, 1867. Walker opposed black suffrage and countenanced more restrictive black legislation.

Southern attitudes in 1865–1866 appeared defiant and unrepentant; in March, 1867, all southern states save Tennessee were restored to military rule, and army officers were to direct the construction of new state governments. Colonel John T. Sprague took over Florida on April 1, 1867. Republican opportunists used military rule and Freedmen's Bureau influence to achieve control of the state, though intraparty bitterness and factionalism were rampant. Local Republicans, northern newcomers, and federal officeholders vied for dominance. Another convention to write a constitution was elected in 1867. Only 11,000 apathetic whites registered to vote, compared with 15,000 blacks. Only 14,500 votes were cast to choose 43 Republican and three Democratic convention delegates; 18 of the Republicans were blacks.

Meeting in January, 1868, the convention split into radical and moderate groups. In a coup the moderates seized the hall on February 10 and ousted the radicals, with no interference from Governor Walker, whom the military government still nominally recognized. After attempting conciliation, the military ruled in favor of the moderate element. The 1868 constitution was written by this group and was conservative enough to be used by the Democrats for a decade after Reconstruction. Enfranchisement of the blacks was its most radical feature. The Republicans elected HARRISON REED, a Wisconsin treasury agent, and William H. Gleason, also from Wisconsin, as governor and lieutenant governor. The party also had clear control of the legislature. Reed won the enmity of his party by his proplanter leanings and reluctant concessions to the radicals. He survived four impeachment attempts at Republican hands, but failed to win Democratic support despite appointment of Democrats to cabinet and judicial posts.

Radical Republicans never won the governorship; both Ossian B. Hart (an old-line Florida Unionist Whig) and Marcellus L. Stearns were moderate governors who worked with a Democratic-Republican coalition in the legislature. Moreover, Florida, with blacks composing about 47 percent of its population, never experienced "Negro rule." The FREEDMEN'S BUREAU was administered relatively evenhandedly and appears to have encouraged continuation of plantation agriculture under a contract labor system. It operated to relieve the distress of needy whites as well as blacks. Provision of medical services met with enthusiasm. The 1868 constitution authorized a state public school system, but not until 1870 were measurable results seen. Freedmen's savings banks were fostered by the bureau, but most failed in the PANIC OF 1873. The bureau also assisted some blacks in the acquisition of land under HOMESTEAD ACTS. Despite bureau efforts, the labor policy that evolved was the SHARECROPPING or TENANT FARMING system, open to many abuses and ultimately impoverishing to all.

During 1870–1871, native whites waged a terrorist campaign (KU KLUX KLAN) in northern Florida to discourage Republican voters, but violence declined after federal prosecution of the troublemakers. By 1873, however, Republican strength was ebbing. Party representation in the legislature was evenly divided in 1875, and Democratic prospects were greatly enhanced by renewed Republican factionalism. Both parties requested the presence of federal troops to supervise the ELECTION OF 1876, and units (company size or smaller) were stationed in eight Florida cities. The contest was heated and the election both corrupt and confused, but the troops did not interfere with the voting. The state supreme court ultimately gave state offices to the Democrats, and the federal electoral commission gave Florida's electoral votes to the Republican Rutherford B. Hayes. The new governor, GEORGE F. DREW, was an old Unionist Whig who had lived in the South since before the war. His administration was hailed as the end of Reconstruction and the return of "home rule." After Drew's peaceful inauguration, the federal troops were withdrawn on January 18, 1877, and no Republican governor again sat in the capitol until 1967.

As a largely rural state on the periphery of the war zone, Florida had suffered comparatively less disruption than had other states. Population grew during the war decade almost 34 percent. In the same period, however, cotton production dropped by half; the value of farms fell by almost 45 percent; and the decline in livestock dangerously depleted breeding stock. BANKING in Florida remained disorganized throughout Reconstruction. Private banking prevailed until 1874, when the first nationally chartered bank in the state opened in Jacksonville. After 1880, banks rapidly proliferated. Railroads, usually closely associated with banking institutions, stagnated through the era, only 16 additional miles being built. Manipulation of railroad securities by politicians and adventurers undermined recovery. By the latter part of the 1870s, however, the age of the developers was dawning. Already wealthy northerners were becoming interested in Florida and investing in it.

During the governorship of Drew, austerity was pursued with a vengeance. Services were slashed, taxes and expenditures were minimized, and generous inducements were offered to outside capitalists to develop the state's resources (REDEEMER GOVERNMENTS). The white leaders felt secure in their prospects of dominating and developing the state and of even controlling the blacks to those ends.

Drew's successor, WILLIAM D. BLOXHAM, took office in 1881 dedicated to positive prosperity policies, emphasizing immigration, education, and transportation. Bloxham found the Internal Improvement Fund, a state agency created to aid railroad construction, in receivership resulting from federal court action upon petition of the creditors of the railroads. The fund had used state lands to back railroad bond issues. Selling Philadelphia millionaire Hamilton Disston 4 million acres for $1 million, Bloxham raised the money to pay the claims of the bondholders against the fund, clearing the title to the lands that it controlled and initiating a new era of railroad development. Bloxham also involved Disston in canal and riveropening projects that furthered water transport and opened more areas to settlement.

Since Reed's administration, the state had officially encouraged immigrants to Florida, and state agencies had published quantities of promotional literature. Under Bloxham, the state employed traveling immigration agents to recruit in the North. They were close collaborators with the railroads in promoting sales of their land grants, but beyond settlers the agents cast their nets for tourists, sportsmen, invalids, and investment-seeking capitalists. Until the early twentieth century, the immigrants were courted, and virtually every political leader was dedicated to "development." By 1900, the population stood at almost 529,000, an increase of 389,000 over the year 1860.

RAILROAD construction was Florida's most pervasive single industry in the last two decades of the nineteenth century. Although short lines had been operated as early as 1836, the earliest significant railways were opened on the eve of the Civil War. By 1861 a line connecting Jacksonville with Tallahassee was operating, and the Florida Railroad, an impressive venture of Senator David L. Yulee, ran from Fernandina on the Atlantic to Cedar Key on the Gulf. By the end of the century rails led into almost every corner of the state and were instrumental in the development of coastal cities and interior agricultural regions. Cities such as West Palm Beach, Miami, and Tampa owe much to the iron horse.

Four railroad developers at the century's end overshadowed all others. In the panhandle, William D. Chipley and the Louisville & Nashville Railroad developed a network centering on Pensacola but serving Alabama, Georgia, and east Florida. HENRY B. PLANT welded a number of short lines in South Carolina, Georgia, and Florida into the Plant System, which reached down to the Tampa Bay area and operated over 600 miles of track in Florida alone when incorporated into the Atlantic Coast Line in 1902. A competing system headed by John Shelton Williams tied lines from Richmond and Columbia into the old Yulee system, as well as a few other short lines in Florida, to build a system that became the Seaboard Air Line in 1903. Unique to Florida, however, were HENRY M. FLAGLER and his Florida East Coast Railway. They made the eastern coast of Florida an urban resort and bridged the watery distances of the Keys. First interested in resort hotels in St. Augustine, Standard Oil millionaire Flagler saw railroads as serving his hostelries and inexorably moved southward until there were no longer even any islands for his rails to reach.

A new constitution (1886) produced in the age of the developers reflected some of the discontents that would surface in the later Populist era. The new document vastly increased the number of elective officers—to include not only county officials but the governor's cabinet as well. The governor was limited to one term; limited railroad regulation was authorized; and the POLL TAX sparked the start of the legal DISFRANCHISEMENT of blacks.

The 1890s witnessed a surfacing of the anticorporation spirit festering among agrarian groups. The FARMERS' ALLIANCE held a national convention in Ocala in 1890 (OCALA PLATFORM), and Alliance influence was strong in the 1891 legislature. Elimination of blacks from politics and the disappearance of real Republican opposition are often cited as factors enabling this dissent from conservative Democratic dominance. Senator Wilkinson Call, sharing many of the agrarian principles of the Alliance, was reelected in 1891, but this Alliance movement did not survive the nineties. The strength of conservatism reasserted itself in the return to the governorship in 1897 of William D. Bloxham, who lent his influence to the defeat of Senator Call in the same year.

At the dawn of the twentieth century Florida was well recovered from the ravages of war and the handicaps of frontier isolation. Although steamboats had operated on the navigable streams since the late 1830s, the real solution to transport problems was the railroads. By 1900 there were more than 3,000 miles of track, which had greatly facilitated the lumber, naval stores, and PHOSPHATE industries and had eased the expansion of agriculture. By that year, Jacksonville was becoming the world's chief port for the export of naval stores and Pensacola was becoming a major export center of lumber. The total annual product of the forests of Florida in 1900 was $19 million, about half the value of the state's annual manufactures. In that year fishing loomed large with an annual production of over $1.2 million and an employment of about 7,000 persons. TOBACCO MANUFACTURES grew rapidly after the Civil War, centering first in Key West but largely shifting to Tampa by the twentieth century. Just before 1890 phosphate was discovered in quantity in interior regions ranging from 150 miles north of Tampa Bay to 150 miles south of it. By 1900 a total of over 5.5 million tons had been removed, and production had exceeded that of all other states. Value of farm products in that year exceeded $18.5 million. Cotton and tobacco were major export crops, but livestock and citrus fruit production had made spectacular gains. There were 765,000 beef cattle in 1900 and 30,000 dairy cows producing 3 million gallons of milk annually. In the 1890s citrus fruits had peaked, with over 5 million boxes being produced in 1894, but severe freezes in 1895 dealt disastrous blows to citrus trees and permanently destroyed groves in the northernmost regions. Recovery was slow, and less than 1 million boxes were produced in 1901.

The Spanish-American War of 1898 was a brief, relatively cheap war for Americans, but Florida was nearest a main battle area, Cuba, and was excited by the "splendid little war." The state was a center for training camps; Tampa was the embarkation point for the Cuba-bound troops; and Key West was the center for naval operations. The war began in late spring of 1898 and was over in late summer, but in its brief course Florida had become better known, millions of dollars had been spent there, and Tampa, Key West, and Pensacola had emerged with improved harbors and defenses.

Political PROGRESSIVISM struck Florida early in the twentieth century, and the new century brought the post–Civil War generation to power. Turn-of-the-century liberal Democrats dealt a blow to boss control by introduction of the primary election method of nominating party candidates. This "white" primary also effectively excluded the black voters from politics, because they were barred from the Democratic party and the general elections were perfunctory. William Sherman Jennings, elected governor in 1901, was an Illinois native resident in Florida only 15 years, a cousin of William Jennings Bryan, and an anticorporation Democrat—of the breed who were to direct Florida politics until World War I. Although akin to national progressivism, the Florida movement was in large measure a reaction against the "developers" who had directed the state since 1877. Railroads were the center of their target. Jennings' major accomplishment was to block railroad corporation claims on the public lands and to lay the foundations of a Progressive organization beneficial to his successor NAPOLEON BONAPARTE BROWARD.

Broward was the preeminent Progressive on the Florida political scene. Elected in 1904, pledged to regulate the trusts and save the public lands for the people, he projected an impression of honesty . and fearlessness and was enormously popular. During his term support for education was increased, and higher education was reorganized with the collection of state colleges being merged in 1905 into three universities: all-male University of Florida; Florida State College for Women; and black Florida Agricultural and Mechanical College. CHILD LABOR laws were enacted, programs of land reclamation in the Everglades were begun, and pure food laws and automobile regulatory laws were initiated. Broward's philosophy and program also dominated the administrations of his two successors, Albert W. Gilchrist and Park Trammell. Under the latter a major reform of primary election laws took place and a state road department was created.

The election of 1916 featured religious and class prejudices never before tapped in Florida. SIDNEY J. CATTS, a former Baptist minister from DeFuniak Springs, showed that a skilled manipulator of bigotry could win the governorship even outside the Democratic fold. Though less than 3 percent of the state's population was Catholic and though Florida had elected both Jews and Catholics to public office, Catts stumped the rural areas peddling a populistic program and anti-Catholicism. Although counted out in the Democratic primary, he went to the general election as an independent and defeated the Democratic and Republican candidates. Catts's governorship reflected more populism than bigotry, however. Despite his sensationalism, his program was a logical extension of the principles of the Broward era. Catts's accomplishments included compulsory school attendance, abolition of the state convict lease system, aid to dependent children, creation of an asylum for mentally handicapped whites, increased road-building activity, and adoption of the Eighteenth Amendment to the federal Constitution.

World War I served to stimulate economic activity in the state. Training bases for all the services were established, agriculture flourished under increased demands, lumber and naval stores industries expanded, shipbuilding at Tampa and Jacksonville temporarily prospered, revived interest was shown in sugar production, and despite inflation the wages of laboring men increased. An unexpected follow-up of the war was the Florida land boom. With the automobile and growing miles of highways, Florida was more accessible than ever, and the prosperity of the early 1920s fostered promoters and developers on a scale heretofore unknown.

Between 1920 and 1930 the population grew from about 970,000 to over 1,460,000, the most rapid increases appearing in the lower peninsula. Jacksonville remained the largest city, but Miami in the decade rose from fourth place to second place with 110,637. Tampa and St. Petersburg had achieved third and fourth place respectively. Nine of 13 new counties created in the 1920s were in south Florida. Railroad construction had a brief new spurt of growth with the Seaboard Air Line expanding into Miami and the Florida East Coast double-tracking its Jacksonville to Miami line. The big transportation news, however, was the great growth in state highways: From about 700 miles of paved road at the start of the decade, the number of paved miles grew to 3,254 by 1930.

In the fall of 1925 the purchase and sale of real estate on the lower east coast reached frenzied proportions. Transportation to the region broke down as the railroads became unable to handle the volume of freight to Miami. Building costs skyrocketed, construction was delayed, and much capital was withdrawn. Revelation of fraudulent promotions resulted in widespread disillusionment. A severe hurricane in 1926 followed by a devastating one in 1928 further disrupted development and left Florida an already prostrate victim for the national financial collapse of 1929. Despite financial setbacks, the state made more population gains during the decade than in any comparable earlier period.

From rural to modern Florida, 1930–1970. Most local and state governments were as slow as the Herbert Hoover administration to respond to the enormity of the economic crisis. To provide badly needed revenue Florida legislators would support only a tax on legalized horse and dog racing. When Congress created the RECONSTRUCTION FINANCE CORPORATION in 1932, Governor Doyle Carlton asked for $500,000 from it, a gross underestimate, for almost $2 million was spent for welfare by the end of the year. Carlton preferred private measures and boasted of the confidence Alfred I. Du Pont (DU PONT FAMILY) was showing in Florida. Buying valuable properties at low prices, Du Pont was building a sound banking chain that marked the entry of the powerful Du Pont presence into Florida political and economic life.

By 1933 per capita income in the state had dropped to $289, and more than a quarter of the people were receiving public assistance. During the administration of Brooklyn-born David Sholtz, great headway was made in the area of social legislation, and impressive increases were made in the support of public education. Substantial amounts of New Deal funds were expended in the state, and some state agencies such as the board of public welfare were greatly enlarged to administer federal relief. State welfare appropriations on a significant scale, however, did not come until 1935.

By 1935, though the nation's economic outlook was better, Floridians were saddened to receive the Labor Day news that a hurricane had irreparably damaged the Overseas Railroad, with the loss of hundreds of lives of World War I veterans building a highway to Key West. Coincidentally President Franklin Roosevelt on the same day announced the start of the Florida Ship Canal project, which temporarily gave employment to hundreds and sparked a minor land boom. Surveyed as early as 1822, the canal had been a long-dreamed-of project, though one of rapidly declining utility in the twentieth century. For lack of funds, work ceased in 1936, but the scheme would not die; it appeared again during the administration of Lyndon B. Johnson, this time as a barge canal. Funding problems and objections from environmental groups caused a last cessation of work in 1971.

The legacy of Sholtz, Florida's most "New Dealish" executive, was a vast increase in governmental agencies to administer expanded state functions. In addition to the welfare board, there was created an industrial commission, a state employment service, a planning board, a tuberculosis board, a conservation commission, a forest service, a state park service, a state beverage department (following repeal of Prohibition), and a citrus commission.

With World War II under way in Europe, Floridians sent SPESSARD L. HOLLAND to the governorship in 1940. Formidable financial problems stemming from boom-time local government debts and expanded state expenditures were tackled with dispatch. Excise taxes were raised, property taxes were reserved for local governments, and a portion of the gasoline tax was reserved to counties for road construction debts. Wartime prosperity and near full employment made surpluses grow in the Holland treasury. Military installations were built on a great scale in Florida, and hundreds of miles of roads and many bridges were built at federal expense. All of Florida's normal growth rates were greatly accelerated. Untold thousands who might never have seen Florida came to know it, and during the 1940s the population increased by 46 percent. The citrus industry moved into a dominant place, with the development of a frozen concentrate process that solved major problems of shipment and storage. Migrant laborers from the Bahamas, Jamaica, and Barbados solved wartime labor shortages for sugar, vegetable, and fruit producers. Importation of these migrants continued after the war, occasionally giving rise to political and social problems.

In 1944 Millard Fillmore Caldwell, a Tennessee-born former congressman from the panhandle, became governor and inherited a treasury general fund surplus of $8 million along with an accumulation of problems in education, institutional care, health, welfare, and natural resources. At war's end Caldwell instituted a $40 million state building program and vastly expanded social services. The report of a citizens' committee on education led to state assumption of a larger share of the costs of schools and an apportionment of funds to counties on the basis of need. The two white universities, undergoing rapid expansion, were made coeducational in 1947, and Florida State College for Women became Florida State University. Although the committee recommended junior colleges in all population centers, little progress was made toward this goal until after 1960. In 1947 the Everglades National Park was officially dedicated.

Fuller Warren, a perennial Democratic candidate for governor, was elected in 1948 amid growing national concern with civil rights. A dissatisfied element of conservative Democrats, called DIXIECRATS, split off to support STROM THURMOND of South Carolina for the presidency. HARRY S. TRUMAN won Florida's electoral votes, but the opposition, split among Thomas E. Dewey, Thurmond, and Henry A. Wallace, accumulated 296,150 votes to Truman's 281,988. Increasingly in the future, Floridians discontent with the Democrats were to become Republicans rather than join splinter groups.

The Warren years were turbulent. Unlike his immediate predecessors, Warren represented a populist philosophy akin to that of the Broward era but was faced suddenly with wide-ranging problems of a rapidly urbanizing state with which his agrarian philosophy left him ill equipped to cope. Wartime surpluses were gone, and urgent needs for funds had to be met. Much against his will, the governor approved a 3 percent sales tax. The growth of organized crime in Florida and its revelation by the Kefauver committee proved a real nemesis to Warren. Refusing to appear before the committee, Warren became a victim of efforts to link him with the underworld, but attempts to impeach him failed. Although politically more flamboyant than effective, Warren's governorship was a bridge to modern Florida. A step was made toward new tax policies, funds were found to implement education programs of the Caldwell regime, citrus-grading regulations were enacted, reforestation programs were begun, the Ku Klux Klan was barred from public places, cattle were removed from the highways, considerable progress in road building was accomplished, and a bill to close integrated colleges and universities was vetoed.

At mid-century Florida stood on the verge of explosive growth. The next 20 years would exceed the most optimistic forecasts. In 1900, with about half a million people, Florida had ranked thirty-second among the states. By 1950 it ranked twentieth with 2,771,305 persons, and in the following decade a 78.7 percent absolute growth raised that total to a figure of 4,951,560. The 1970 census listed a total of 6,789,443 persons, ranking Florida ninth among the states. Growth was accompanied by rapid shifts southward of the center of population. Small north Florida counties continued to lose people while central and south Florida counties mushroomed. URBANIZATION also proceeded more rapidly in Florida than elsewhere. In 1970 one-third of the population was centered in the contiguous southeastern counties of Palm Beach, Broward, and Dade. A notable addition to the population in the 1960s was the more than 300,000 Cubans, refugees from Fidel Castro's regime. Dade County received the bulk of them.

By the 1950s liberalism seemed to have run its course in Florida as well as in the nation, and the increased population of the state included many Republican voters from northeastern and midwestern states; a swing to conservatism seemed inevitable. Liberal Democrat CLAUDE PEPPER lost his U.S. Senate seat in 1950 to George A. Smathers, a Democrat who had the support of business, the major newspapers, the medical profession, and reputedly the Du Pont interests. And in 1952 Daniel T. McCarty, a businessman involved in citrus and livestock, won the governorship on a platform calling for law and order and economical, businesslike government. Two years later, Floridians chose as their governor LeRoy Collins of Tallahassee, a man of great personal magnetism. Although Collins had a distinguished and progressive legislative record, he was not identified with any radical political groups, and his image in 1954 was more conservative than in later campaigns. In the same election William C. Cramer of St. Petersburg was the first Republican named to Congress since Reconstruction; six Republicans won seats in the legislature. Cramer held office

until 1970. Edward J. Gurney, later elected as a Republican congressman from the Orlando area, defeated Collins in 1968 in a U.S. Senate race.

In his two-year term, however, Collins was enormously successful in creating an aura of progressive leadership. In the first primary of 1956, he defeated five opponents, amassing 51.7 percent of the vote. In the general election, even though the state gave its electoral votes to Dwight Eisenhower, Collins defeated his Republican opponent three to one. His greatest strength lay in those liberal bastions, the counties of the lower east coast and Hillsborough County, and his home county of Leon. During his six years Collins made an extremely favorable education record, including establishment of a network of junior colleges, better funding for public schools, expansion of the university system, and establishment of a committee of jurists and lawyers to study the consequences of the 1954 school desegregation decision. His moderation prevailed over legislative intransigence, and desegregation was largely peaceful. In one major effort the governor failed. Acutely aware that shifting population patterns called for legislative reapportionment, Collins waged a continual struggle for it. Under a 1923 constitutional amendment a decennial reapportionment was mandatory, but the dominant "pork chop gang" of rural and north Florida legislators tenaciously refused to make any significant redistribution of power. Not until 1967 was reapportionment accomplished, by a U.S. district court decree.

In 1960 conservative lawyer-businessman Farris Bryant won the governorship despite Collins' support of an opponent. He strongly supported tourism and business expansion, road building, and a cross-Florida canal, but showed little interest in urban problems. Racial problems centered on desegregation of public facilities, and Bryant on several occasions used the highway patrol and National Guard to support his firm stand against violence. Jacksonville Mayor Haydon Burns succeeded Bryant in 1965 and followed a policy of fiscal conservatism. Burns's term was a two-year stint due to a constitutional amendment moving gubernatorial elections from presidential years to the midterm years. The short term was largely a campaign for reelection, which the conservative incumbent lost to the liberal Miami mayor, Robert King High. High, in turn, was defeated in 1966 by Republican Claude R. Kirk. Kirk's four-year term was a running battle with his elected Democratic cabinet and the predominantly Democratic legislature. The most flamboyant governor since Fuller Warren, Kirk brought much publicity to Florida but could point to little achievement except the revitalization of two-party politics.

During Kirk's term, the Democratic legislature did adopt, and the people did ratify, a revised constitution, but the 1968 rewrite of the 1886 document was not widely hailed. Major changes included allowing the governor to succeed himself (once); provision for a lieutenant governor; provision for limited state bonded indebtedness; annual sessions of the legislature (with reforms in its procedures); and mandatory constitutional revision in ten years and every 20 years thereafter. Governor Kirk ran for reelection in 1970 facing state senator Reubin Askew, a moderate liberal. Askew won decisively. In the U.S. Senate race former legislator Lawton Chiles (also moderately liberal) defeated Republican Congressman William Cramer. As the seventies began, Florida voters seemed to show signs of turning to new political faces speaking with voices of moderation, but the rapidly changing growth patterns command caution in any generalizations.

The economy of Florida since World War II has had two dominant characteristics: growth and increased diversification. Between 1929 and 1969 personal income grew from $573 million to almost $22.4 billion. It was largely based upon tourism, manufacturing, agriculture, and government disbursements. Although expanding, agriculture represented a rapidly declining proportion of the state's economic activity. Within agriculture, citrus fruit was the most valuable cash crop, with Florida dominating world markets. In 1973–1974 Florida's crop accounted for 75.3 percent of the nation's production, amounting to 230,250,000 boxes. Citrus fruits were grown commercially in 35 of 67 counties. TRUCK FARMING and cattle production were next in importance. Sugarcane in 1973 was the most valuable of the field crops produced. Commercial production is limited to four counties around Lake Okeechobee, but more than 14,000 people were employed and the 1973 crop was valued at almost $191 million. Cotton continued to decline, 89 percent of the state's total in 1973 being produced in one panhandle county. At the end of that year beef and dairy livestock totaled 2.49 million head. A total of 282,000 dairy cattle produced 1,843,000 pounds of milk.

The value of manufactured products in Florida grew apace, over 10,000 industrial establishments employing 327,500 people in 1972 with an annual payroll of more than $2.5 billion. The areas of production most important were processing of food and kindred products, making of electric and electronic equipment, manufacture of apparel and textiles, printing and publishing, manufacture of transportation equipment, and the making of fabricated metal products. The seafood industry was prominent, employing more than 12,000 persons and producing annual catches valued at over $50 million. Production of minerals, mostly nonmetallic minerals such as phosphate, limestone, dolomite clays, and sand and gravel, was valued in 1971 at $343,731,000. Oil, first important in 1943, had been produced to a cumulative total of over 75 million barrels by 1973, more than 50 million of which had been pumped since 1971.

TOURISM left its impact in terms of large increases in income from wholesale and retail trade, building construction, transportation, and services. It helps explain a state tax structure heavily dependent on the sales tax. It both supports and benefits from such developments as Florida's Disney World and lesser imitators. Desirable features of the state, which persuade many tourists to return or to stay, help explain a growth in population density from 91.5 per square mile in 1960 to 125.5 in 1970 and a total estimated population in mid-1974 of 8,090,000.

Government expenditures from all levels in Florida accounted for more than one-seventh of all personal income by 1970. Defense and space facilities, social security, and veterans' benefits accounted for the major share of federal monies. The growth of state and local services, education, and broadening social welfare explain state and local expenditures.

All the phenomenal growth since World War II has produced serious problems. The pressures for improved roads, police and fire protection, schools, and environmental protection have sorely tried the leadership of the state. By the mid-1970s a faltering economy had resulted in faltering support for many expanded government programs and, despite bright prospects at the start of the decade, political leadership with answers to the problems had not yet appeared.

Manuscripts and printed primary sources. There are two principal collections for Florida history: P. K. Yonge Library of Florida History, University of Florida, Gainesville; and Florida Historical Society Library, University of South Florida, Tampa. The former, having extensive holdings of film and photocopies of documents from European archives, is more valuable; both have important newspaper, manuscript, and rare book holdings. The Federal Regional Archives in East Point, Ga., has important federal documents relating to Florida courts and customhouses. Until very recent years, no state archives have been maintained. Significant printed sources include C. E. Bennett, *Laudonnière and Fort Caroline* (1964); J. T. Connor (trans. and ed.), *Colonial Records of Spanish Florida* (1925, 1930); and A. P. Whitaker (trans. and ed.), *Documents Relating to Commercial Policy of Spain in the Floridas* (1931). Volumes XXII–XXVI of C.

FLORIDA POPULATION, 1830–1970

Year	Total	White	Nonwhite Slave	Nonwhite Free	% Growth	Rank U.S.	Rank South
1830	34,730	18,385	15,501	844		25	13
1840	54,477	27,943	25,717	817	56.9	27	14
1850	87,445	47,203	39,310	932	60.5	31	15
1860	140,424	77,746	61,746	932	60.6	31	14
1870	187,748	96,057		91,691	33.7	33	15
1880	269,493	142,965		126,528	43.5	34	15
1890	391,422	224,949		166,473	45.2	32	15
1900	528,542	297,333		231,209	35.0	32	15
1910	752,619	443,634		308,985	42.4	34	15
1920	968,470	638,153		330,317	28.7	33	15
1930	1,468,211	1,035,205		433,006	51.6	31	15
1940	1,897,414	1,381,986		515,428	29.2	27	14
1950	2,771,305	2,166,051		605,254	46.1	20	9
1960	4,951,560	4,063,881		887,679	78.7	10	2
1970	6,789,443	5,719,343		1,070,100	37.1	9	2

E. Carter (ed.), *Territorial Papers of U.S.* (1956–65), reprint documents and papers for 1821–1845.

Contemporary accounts. Early accounts include A. N. Cabeza de Vaca, *Journey of Cabeza de Vaca* (1905); J. Ribault, *Whole and True Discouerye of Terra Florida* (1964); and *Jonathan Dickinson's Journal* (1945), account of shipwrecked Quaker. Accounts of British era include J. Bartram, *Diary*, ed. F. Harper (1942); W. Bartram, *Travels*, ed. F. Harper (1958); B. A. Romans, *Concise and Natural History*, ed. R. W. Patrick (1962); and W. Stork, *Account of East Florida* (1766). For Seminole War, see M. M. Cohen, *Notice of Florida and Campaigns*, ed. O. Z. Tyler, Jr. (1964); and J. T. Sprague, *Origin, Progress, and Conclusion of Florida War*, ed. J. K. Mahon (1964). J. L. Williams, *View of West Florida* (1976) and *Territory of Florida* (1962), was a perceptive reporter of geography and human events. See E. C. Long, *Florida Breezes*, ed. M. Chapman (1962), for antebellum social life. Civil War and postwar years are chronicled by M. E. Dickison, *Dickison and His Men*, ed. S. Proctor (1962); L. Bill, *Winter in Florida* (1870); H. B. Stowe, *Palmetto Leaves* (1968); J. Wallace, *Carpetbag Rule in Florida*, ed. A. Nevins (1964); J. C. Ley, *Fifty-two Years in Florida* (1899), life of a frontier preacher; F. Warren, *How to Win in Politics* (1949), unconventional; and M. K. Rawlings, *Cross Creek* (1939), rural Florida in 1930s.

Histories. Best survey of state history is C. W. Tebeau, *History of Florida* (1971). Older histories are C. M. Brevard, *History of Florida* (2 vols.; 1925–26); and J. E. Dovell, *Florida* (4 vols.; 1952). For the Spanish periods, see C. W. Arnade, *Florida on Trial* (1959); V. E. Chatelain, *Defenses of Spanish Florida* (1941); M. J. Curley, *Church and State in Spanish Floridas* (1940); M. V. Gannon, *Cross in Sand* (1965); J. J. TePaske, *Governorship of Spanish Florida* (1964); and P. C. Brooks, *Diplomacy and Borderlands* (1939). Studies of British period are R. L. Gold, *Borderlands in Transition* (1969); C. Johnson, *British West Florida* (1943); C. L. Mowatt, *East Florida as British Province* (1943); E. P. Panagopoulos, *New Smyrna* (1966); and J. L. Wright, Jr., *Florida in American Revolution* (1975). Valuable studies of antebellum Florida are R. W. Patrick, *Florida Fiasco* (1954); H. J. Doherty, Jr., *Whigs of Florida* (1959); A. W. Thompson, *Jacksonian Democracy on Florida Frontier* (1961); J. K. Mahon, *Second Seminole War* (1967); S. W. Martin,

Florida During Territorial Days (1944); E. C. McReynolds, *Seminoles* (1957); and C. T. Thrift, *Florida Circuit Rider* (1944). Post–Civil War Florida is well delineated in G. R. Bentley, *Freedmen's Bureau* (1955); J. H. Shofner, *Nor Is It Over Yet* (1974), Florida Reconstruction; E. E. Johns, *Florida During Civil War* (1963); J. M. Richardson, *Negro in Reconstruction of Florida* (1965); G. W. Pettengill, *Story of Florida Railroads* (1952); and A. F. Blakey, *Florida Phosphate Industry* (1973). Solid works on twentieth century are rare. Notable, however, are B. Kendrick, *Florida Trails to Turnpikes* (1964); H. D. Price, *Negro and Southern Politics* (1957); and W. C. Havard and L. P. Beth, *Politics of Misrepresentation* (1962). V. O. Key, *Southern Politics* (1949), should be read in conjunction with H. J. Doherty, Jr., *Journal of Politics* (Aug., 1952), for Florida voting patterns. Important biographies include T. Maynard, *De Soto and Conquistadores* (1930); A. Manucy, *Florida's Menéndez* (1965); H. J. Doherty, Jr., *Richard Keith Call* (1961); J. T. Durkin, *Stephen R. Mallory* (1954); M. V. Gannon, *Augustin Verot* (1964); S. Proctor, *N. B. Broward* (1950); S. W. Martin, *Florida's Flagler* (1941); G. E. Bigelow, *Marjorie Kinnan Rawlings* (1966); R. Holt, *Mary McLeod Bethune* (1964); M. James, *Alfred I. Du Pont* (1941); and G. Plowden, *Amazing Ringlings* (1967).

Articles. Indispensable articles, book reviews, and references are found in *Florida Historical Quarterly* (1908–09, 1924–). General indices are available through Vol. XXXV. Also useful is *Tequesta* (1941–), published annually by Historical Association of Southern Florida. Worthy of note are special numbers of *Florida Historical Quarterly* devoted to Osceola (1955), to Pensacola quadricentennial (1959), and to Florida quadricentennial (1965).

Dissertations and theses. Unpublished work of graduate students holds much good Florida history, especially for modern period. Some notable studies include: W. G. Fouraker, "Administration of Robert Raymond Reid" (Florida State, 1949); A. W. Thompson, "David Yulee" (Columbia, 1954); S. J. Weinberg, "Slavery and Secession in Florida" (University of Florida, 1948); J. M. Richardson, "Freedmen's Bureau" (Florida State, 1959); E. H. Atkins, "History of Jacksonville" (Duke, 1941); N. G. Carper, "Convict Lease System in Florida" (Florida State, 1964); R. L. Carson, "William Dunnington Bloxham"

FLORIDA GOVERNORS

Governor	Party	Term
FIRST SPANISH PERIOD, 1565–1763		
Pedro Menéndez de Avilés		1565–1574
Hernando de Miranda		1575–1577
Pedro Menéndez Marqués (interim)		1577–1578
Pedro Menéndez Marqués		1578–1589
Gutierre de Miranda		1589–1592
Rodrigo de Junco		1592
Domingo Martínez de Avendaño		1594–1595
Gonzalo Méndez de Canzo		1596–1603
Pedro de Ybarra		1603–1609
Juan Fernández de Olivera		1609–1612
Juan de Tribiño Guillamas		1613–1618
Juan de Salinas		1618–1623
Luis de Rojas y Borja		1624–1629
Andrés Rodríguez de Villegas		1630–1631
Luis Horruytiner		1633–1638
Damián de Vega Castro y Pardo		1639–1645
Benito Ruiz de Salazar Ballecilla		1645–1646, 1647
Nicolás Ponce de León (interim)		
Pedro Benedit Horruytiner (interim)		
Diego de Rebolledo		1655–1659
Alfonso de Aranguiz y Cortés		1659–1663
Francisco de la Guerra y de la Vega		1664–1670
Manuel de Cendoya		1670–1673
Pablo de Hita Salazar		1675–1680
Juan Marqués Cabrera		1680–1687
Diego de Quiroga y Lozada		1687–1693
Laureano de Torres y Ayala		1693–1699
Joseph de Zúñiga y Cerda		1699–1706
Francisco de Córcoles y Martínez		1706–1716
Pedro de Olivera y Fullana		1716
Juan de Ayala Escobar (interim)		1716–1718
Antonio de Benavides		1718–1734
Ignacio Rodríguez Rozo (interim)		1726
Francisco del Moral y Sánchez		1734–1737
Manuel Joseph de Justis (interim)		1737
Manuel de Montiano		1737–1749
Melchor de Navarrete		1749–1752
Fulgencio García de Solis (interim)		1752–1755
Alonso Fernández de Heredia		1755–1758
Lucas Fernando de Palacio y Valenzuela		1758–1761
Alonso de Cárdenas (interim)		1761–1762
Melchor Feliú		1762–1764
ENGLISH PERIOD		
East Florida		
James Grant		1763–1770
John Moultrie (lieutenant governor)		1771–1774
Patrick Tonyn		1774–1783
West Florida		
George Johnstone		1763–1767
Montforte Browne (lieutenant governor)		1767–1769
John Eliot		1769
Elias Durnford (lieutenant governor)		1769–1770
Peter Chester		1770–1781
SECOND SPANISH PERIOD		
East Florida		
Manuel de Zéspedes		1783–1790
Juan Quesada		1790–1796
Bartolome Morales (acting governor)		1795

Governor	Party	Term
Enrique White		1796–1811
Juan de Estrada		1811–1812
Sebastián Kindelan		1812–1815
Juan de Estrada		1815–1816
José Coppinger (acting governor)		1816–1821
West Florida		
Arturo O'Neill		1781–1793
Enrique White		1793–1795
Paula Gelabert		1795–1796
Juan Vicente Folch		1796–1811
Francisco St. Maxent		1811–1812
Mauricio de Zúñiga		1812–1813
Mateo González Manrique		1813–1815
José Masot		1816–1819
José Callava		1819–1821
TERRITORIAL PERIOD		
Andrew Jackson		1821
William P. Duval		1822–1834
John H. Eaton		1834–1836
Richard K. Call		1836–1839
Robert R. Reid		1839–1841
Richard K. Call		1841–1844
John Branch		1844–1845
GOVERNORS SINCE STATEHOOD		
William D. Moseley	Dem.	1845–1849
Thomas Brown	Whig	1849–1853
James E. Broome	Dem.	1853–1857
Madison Perry	Dem.	1857–1861
John Milton	Dem.	1861–1865
William Marvin (provisional)	Dem.	1865–1867
David S. Walker	Dem.	1867–1868
Harrison Reed	Rep.	1868–1873
Ossian B. Hart	Rep.	1873–1874
Marcellus L. Stearns	Rep.	1874–1877
George F. Drew	Dem.	1877–1881
William D. Bloxham	Dem.	1881–1885
Edward A. Perry	Dem.	1885–1889
Francis P. Fleming	Dem.	1889–1893
Henry L. Mitchell	Dem.	1893–1897
William D. Bloxham	Dem.	1897–1901
William S. Jennings	Dem.	1901–1905
Napoleon B. Broward	Dem.	1905–1909
Albert W. Gilchrist	Dem.	1909–1913
Park Trammell	Dem.	1913–1917
Sidney J. Catts	Dem.	1917–1921
Cary A. Hardee	Dem.	1921–1925
John W. Martin	Dem.	1925–1929
Doyle F. Carlton	Dem.	1929–1933
David Sholtz	Dem.	1933–1937
Fred P. Cone	Dem.	1937–1941
Spessard L. Holland	Dem.	1941–1945
Millard Caldwell	Dem.	1945–1949
Fuller Warren	Dem.	1949–1953
Daniel T. McCarty	Dem.	1953
Charley E. Johns	Dem.	1953–1955
LeRoy Collins	Dem.	1955–1961
C. Farris Bryant	Dem.	1961–1965
W. Haydon Burns	Dem.	1965–1967
Claude R. Kirk, Jr.	Rep.	1967–1971
Reubin O. Askew	Dem.	1971–1979

(University of Florida, 1945); L. W. Cory, "Florida's Farmers' Alliance" (Florida State, 1963); J. R. Deal, "Sidney J. Catts" (University of Florida, 1949); J. E. Dovell, "History of Everglades" (University of North Carolina, 1947); J. W. Flynt, "Duncan U. Fletcher" (Florida State, 1965); A. F. Malafronte, "Claude Pepper: 1950 Senatorial Primary" (University of Miami, 1963); S. Proctor, "University of Florida, 1853–1906" (University of Florida, 1958); and F. B. Sessa, "Real Estate Expansion in Miami Beach During 1920's" (Pittsburgh, 1950).

HERBERT J. DOHERTY, JR.
University of Florida

FLORIDA, UNIVERSITY OF (Gainesville, 32601), was chartered in 1845 but did not open until 1853 in Ocala, when it was known as East Florida Seminary. It has expanded markedly during the twentieth century (approximately 25,000 students currently enrolled), but it remained essentially a men's school until 1947. Its library of 1.25 million volumes is the repository of two major collections of interest to historians: the Austin Cary Memorial Collection on Forestry and the P. K. Yonge Library of Florida History. The latter includes copies of Spanish, British, and Mexican archival records (1518–1821) relating to Florida, and the papers of numerous governors (R. K. CALL, N. B. BROWARD, SPESSARD L. HOLLAND) and business leaders (DAVID L. YULEE, Samuel A. Swann, Thomas E. Will).

See S. Proctor, "University of Florida, 1853–1906" (Ph.D. dissertation, University of Florida, 1958); A. H. Adams, "Public Higher Education in Florida, 1821–1961" (Ph.D. dissertation, Florida State, 1962); and C. L. Crow, *Florida Historical Quarterly* (Oct., 1936).

FLORIDA HISTORICAL SOCIETY (University of South Florida, Tampa, 33620), organized initially at St. Augustine in 1856, was revived in 1902. With a current membership of 1,750, the society houses its library of books, manuscripts, and maps pertaining to Florida history at the University of South Florida Library at Tampa. Among the manuscripts are the Horsey Papers, Blankenship Papers, documents of the Indian trading firm PANTON, LESLIE & COMPANY, records of two Florida plantations, and the letterbooks and papers of several governors. The society (since 1908) at the University of Florida at Gainesville publishes the *Florida Historical Quarterly*, which is limited to scholarly articles on Florida history. In addition, the society is the coordinating center for the Florida Historical Confederation, an organization of over 160 local and regional historical bodies of the state. It offers yearly to authors publishing in the area of Floridiana the Book Award, the Junior Book Award, and an award for the most distinguished article published in the *Quarterly*.

FLORIDA STATE UNIVERSITY (Tallahassee, 32306) was established in 1857 as the Seminary West of the Suwannee. Now a state-supported coeducational institution, it was a women's college until 1947, known variously as Florida Female College or Florida State College for Women. It has an enrollment of approximately 20,000 students, and its library houses such notable manuscript collections as the Pine Hill Plantation Papers (1840–1909) and the Dr. Edward Bradford Papers (1830–1871).

See A. H. Adams, "Public Higher Education in Florida, 1821–1961" (Ph.D. dissertation, Florida State, 1962); D. S. Sheridan, *Florida State College, 1941–1957* (1964); and W. G. Dodd, *West Florida Seminary* (1952).

FLORIDA TIMES-UNION in Jacksonville was created in 1883 by the merger of the weekly *Florida Union* (1875–1883) and the *Florida Daily Times* (1881–1883). In 1897 this paper was merged with the *Daily Florida Citizen* (1893–1897) and was known for the next six years as the *Florida Times-Union and Citizen*. Called simply the *Florida Times-Union* since 1903, the daily currently has a circulation of approximately 150,000 copies.

See bound copies at Library of Congress (1876–77, 1881–), Jacksonville Public Library (1879–96, 1901–), University of Florida Library (1887–1902, 1907–), and Ohio Historical Society (1923–); microfilm available from Bell & Howell (1882–) and Library of Congress (1876–77, 1888–).

FLOWERS AND SHRUBS. The South is blessed with a bountiful quantity of beautiful plants for use in the landscape. A large proportion of plants used in the landscape plantings throughout the southern states are broad-leaved evergreens. These are far more predominant than the deciduous plants or the narrow-leaved evergreens such as pines, junipers, and others.

The colorful *Camellia japonica* was first introduced from China to England in the early 1700s and later to northeastern America for greenhouse plants. It later was introduced to the gardens of Charleston, S.C., and from there its fame spread throughout the South. The large, waxy flowers bloom from October to April, depending upon cultivar, and vary from white to pink, red, or variegated in singles and doubles. Also depending upon cultivar, it is grown widely in partially shaded gardens from North Carolina southward to eastern Texas. The glossy evergreen-foliaged camellias are large shrubs or small trees in the garden. The southern camellia enthusiasts are fortunate to have the American Camellia Society offices, surrounded by the society's large camellia garden, near Marshallville, Ga. The fall-flowering *Camellia sasanqua* is also important to the landscape. Contrary to popular belief, it is not cold hardy, perhaps less so than *C. japonica*, yet the colorful single to double flowers often receive little or no frost damage compared with some cultivars of *C. japonica*.

The South is also noted for its spectacular azalea gardens. The large-flowered, evergreen Southern Indian hybrid azaleas were the first introduced to the United States. The hybrids were developed in Belgium as greenhouse plants from several species native to Japan. They were introduced to Magnolia Gardens, near Charleston, in 1840 and soon found to be hardy to the Deep South; thus they spread throughout the coastal regions. Many southern cities (*e.g.*, Mobile, Savannah, Charleston) are noted for their azalea trails, street plantings, and gardens lined with the large, colorful masses of the violet-red azalea Formosa, the Fielder's White, the pink Pride of Mobile, and many other cultivars.

The hardier small flowers of Kurume azaleas were first introduced from Japan in 1915. The plants were found to be hardy as far north as Kentucky and Maryland and are very popular. There are 15 or more cultivars commonly grown in the South, many of which have been given English names. Some favorites are Christmas Cheer (Imashojo), Hino (Hino de-giri), Pink Pearl (Asuma-ka-gami), Snow, and Salmon Beauty. Several other hybrid groups of evergreen or persistent-leaved evergreen azaleas are noted in the South for their mid-season to late flowering, often into May or June. Notably, these are the Glenn Dale hybrids, the Back Acres hybrids, and the Satsuki hybrids.

In the Appalachian areas, the flame azalea *Rhododendron calendulaceum* is typical, but throughout most of the South, the Piedmont azalea *Rhod. canescens* is abundant. The plants are commonly referred to as "wild honeysuckle," but they belong to the same group as the introduced azaleas. The native azaleas include the pink to white forms of *Rhod. nudiflorum*, the Pinxterbloom azalea; the white, fragrant flowers of the Alabama azalea *Rhod. alabamense*; and the sweet swamp and hammock-sweet azaleas. The nonfragrant, orange-to-red-flowered Oconee azalea, *Rhod. speciosum*, is found in a narrow band, extending east and west through Georgia. The rare, late, red-flowering plumleaf azalea, *Rhod. prunifolium*, is used extensively in the native plantings at Callaway Gardens.

The South is equally noted for its beautiful evergreen boxwood hedges and the large, compact specimen plants. There are two species commonly found in gardens. *Buxus microphylla*, a native of Japan, is considered hardier and lower in growth; it is notably adaptive to the warm areas of the Gulf states. *B. sempervirens* was introduced from Europe and is more common in the cool areas of the South; the cultivar Suffruticosa is the popular dwarf plant known as the "true dwarf Box," notably in the gardens of Williamsburg and of Mount Vernon.

Each region of the South has its own important plants. The summer fragrance of gardenias is noted in the middle and Deep South. *Elaeagnus* and tea olive are adaptable (ubiquitous throughout the South), though the colorful oleander is only for the Deep South. Equally, broad-leaved evergreens are noted for their attractive fruit, such as the Chinese holly and its cultivar Burfordii, the aucubas, and the nandinas. Frequently seen are the many excellent ground covers of English ivy, liriope, *Vinca minor*, and pachysandra. In every region, among the wealth of plant material are jasmine, euonymus, viburnum, yucca, Japanese hollies, and other introduced plants.

In the broad-leaf evergreen group are various species of holly (American yaupon, cassine, and others), rhododendrons, mountain laurel, cherry laurel, leucothoe, and devilwood osmanthus. The South equally has a wealth of attractive deciduous shrubs. Two outstanding native shrubs are the oakleaf hydrangea and the native azaleas. The oakleaf hydrangea with its large leaves has an upright panicle of white flowers, typical of the introduced hydrangeas, such as the P. G. hydrangea, used in the cooler areas of the South. The large, blue French hydrangeas are more typical in the South than the pink forms, since the soils are usually acid. With the native azaleas, there are several species that can be found growing in the cooler regions all the way to the lower Gulf areas.

Of the many cultivated deciduous ornamental plants, the crape myrtle is one of the best. The crape myrtle (*Lagerstroemia indica*) is often referred to as the "lilac of the South" and can be seen as a large shrub or small tree from the middle cotton belt through all the tropical regions. The plants are noted for their handsome, strong trunk formation. The huge terminal panicles of white, pink, red, or purple flowers are borne in early to late summer. Of equal importance in recent years is the so-called dwarf crape myrtle. It is not a true dwarf, but is slower growing than the typical forms.

The flowering quince or "japonica," *Chaenomeles speciosa* (lagenaria), is noted for its very colorful white to pink or red flowers in the very early spring, before the yellow, bell-like flowers of forsythia and the mass of clustered white blooms of the spireas. The above plants are common both to the temperate region as well as to the South.

There are a number of herbaceous plants used extensively. The one typical of the whole region is the *Hemerocallis* or day lily, an outstanding perennial with a wide range of color forms from the yellows to the near reds. Irises are found, depending on the species, throughout the South; in the cooler areas the bearded iris is abundant, and, as one approaches the Deep South, the Louisiana iris and Japanese iris are more commonly seen. Numerous species of bulbous plants are also found. The colorful narcissus are heralds of spring throughout the South. Roses are important, too, and the South is again fortunate in having the American Rose Society headquarters in Shreveport, La.

There are many colorful annuals such as pansies, which planted in the late fall flower spasmodically during the winter and then turn into a mass of color in the spring. Various other bedding annuals, such as marigolds, petunias, zinnias, salvias, and coleus, with its colorful foliage, are all important. Yet one is continually aware that the summer temperatures (and the fluctuating winter temperatures) are limiting factors for some plants.

See F. C. Galle, *Azaleas* (1974); R. G. Halfacre and A. R. Shawcraft, *Carolina Landscape Plants* (1975); H. H. Hume, *Camellias in America* (1946); J. V. Watkins and H. S. Wolfe, *Your Flower Garden* (1958); C. E. Whitcomb, *Know It and Grow It* (1975); B. E. Wigginton, *Trees and Shrubs for Southeast* (1963); and D. Wyman, *Wyman's Gardening Encyclopedia* (1971).

FRED C. GALLE
Callaway Gardens, Pine Mountain, Ga.

FLOYD, JOHN BUCHANAN (1806–1863), was born in Smithfield, Va. He was graduated from South Carolina College in 1825 and admitted to the bar in 1835. After briefly practicing in Wytheville, Va., he went to Arkansas only to return financially and physically ruined. Resuming his practice in Abingdon, he was elected to the general assembly (1847, 1848, 1855). A states' rights Democrat, he served three terms as governor (1849–1852). Appointed secretary of war by James Buchanan (1857–1861), he left office in a cloud of rumor and accusations regarding his alleged transfer of federal arms to the South (supposedly for its use in case of civil war) and the mismanagement of Indian trust bonds. When Virginia seceded he became a brigadier general but was removed from command by Jefferson Davis after his abrupt withdrawal from Ft. Donelson. Appointed a major general by the Virginia general assembly, he died near Abingdon. His papers were destroyed in a Union raid.

See W. A. Swanberg, *American Heritage* (Feb., 1963); E. A. Pollard, *Lee and His Lieutenants* (1867), contains remaining fragment of Floyd's diary; and R. M. Hughes, *Virginia Magazine of History and Biography* (Oct., 1935) and *William and Mary Quarterly* (Oct., 1925).

CARLTON B. SMITH
Madison College

FOLK, JOSEPH WINGATE (1869–1923), son of a Tennessee lawyer, graduated from Vanderbilt Law School and subsequently moved to St. Louis. There he joined other young Democrats to form the Jefferson Club and from this power base won election as circuit attorney in 1900. His investigations of bribery and corruption in the municipal assembly brought him into conflict with city boss Edward Butler and to the attention of Lincoln Steffens, writing for *McClure's*.

Although Folk exposed bipartisan corruption, the Democrats, then in power, were most affected. Supported by reform-minded Democrats, independents, and Joseph Pulitzer's *Post-Dispatch*, Folk won the gubernatorial nomination and defeated Cyrus Walbridge in 1904. He inaugurated his "Missouri idea": honesty in government, prosecution of corruption, an informed citizenry. During four years as governor, Folk secured an antilobby law, a general primary law, maximum freight and passenger railroad rates, a public utilities corporation law, and approval of state constitutional amendments for the initiative and referendum.

Folk unsuccessfully sought his party's senatorial nomination from incumbent William J. Stone. To prevent his running in 1910 for the second senatorial seat, party regulars promised him support for the presidency in 1912, but later reneged to support CHAMP CLARK. Folk served under Woodrow Wilson in Washington, briefly as solicitor for the State Department and then as chief counsel for the Interstate Commerce Commission.

See L. G. Geiger, *Joseph W. Folk* (1953); Folk Papers, Western Historical Manuscript Collection, Columbia, Mo.; and N. C. Burckel, "Progressive Governors" (Ph.D. dissertation, University of Wisconsin, 1971).

NICHOLAS C. BURCKEL
University of Wisconsin, Parkside

FOLKLORE in the South is a continually evolving blend of transplanted Old World and assimilated New World traditional conceptions and expressions, its distillate of accumulated wisdom inseparable from its residue of anachronisms. As it perpetuates oral traditions, customs, and patterns of material culture, it provides a fuller context for studying the southern experience: the life of the antebellum plantations, the Civil War and its aftermath, and the frontier-type life of the southern uplands. Folk memory, truer to spirit than to fact, exaggerates, romanticizes, and stereotypes historical personalities and events, but even so brings into sharper focus the shaping forces that made them significant.

A mélange of minority influences accounts for much that is picturesque and memorable, including such perennial favorites as MARDI GRAS festivities. The dominant character of southern folklore nonetheless derives from intermingled British and African influences in the Deep South and from predominantly Scotch-Irish and Palatine German influences in the mountain regions (APPALACHIA). The geographical and social features of a new environment naturally affected both survivals and mutations.

Serious collecting and scholarship, beginning in the twentieth century, have produced a rich harvest of oral traditions, customs, and material culture. The lore abounds in tragic and comic violence, in themes of deliverance and tales of daring. The diversity of southern folk narrative includes European-derived cycles of "Jack tales" and African-derived animal tales of clever underdog tricksters, native tall tales, innumerable anecdotes, and local legends. Riddles, charms, proverbs, and beliefs, whatever their ultimate origin may be, frequently acquire a regional flavor. The harvest of traditional songs abounds in both religious and secular reflections of southern experience: white and black spirituals, transplanted British ballads, game songs, work songs, blues, and native songs about cowboys and outlaws, Civil War battles, train wrecks, betrayals, murders, love, and death.

Much southern folklore attaches to seasonal work and rites of passage. The ritualized hunt, charivaris (shivarees), graveyard meetings (Deco-

ration Day), all-day singings with dinner-on-the-ground, trading and court days, sorghum making, and hog killing are typical folk gatherings. FOLK MEDICINE (boneset tea), food preparation (country ham), structures (dogtrot houses), arts and crafts (patchwork quilts), and MUSIC (mountain dulcimers) exemplify the adaptation to local environment that distinguishes traditional practices and products of the South.

See, for collection and interpretation of southern folklore, such periodicals as *Journal of American Folklore*, *Publications of American Dialect Society*, and *PMLA*. *Frank C. Brown Collection of North Carolina Folklore* (7 vols.; 1952–64) serves as an index to mainstream of southern oral traditions. Best repository of folk narratives and songs is Folklore section of Library of Congress. Prestigious publications by Texas Folklore Society (PTFS) deal with Texas oral traditions, folk history, folk life, and scholarly views of field. Leading regional journal is *Southern Folklore Quarterly*, which devotes an issue annually to bibliography; established state journals are *Tennessee Folklore Society Bulletin*; *Kentucky Folklore Record*; *North Carolina Folklore*; *Mississippi Folklore Register*; and *Mid-South Folklore* (Arkansas). C. Haywood's *Bibliography of North American Folklore and Folksong* (1961) is dated but useful. Excellent reference materials on southern balladry and folk song are included in B. Bronson, *Traditional Tunes of Child Ballads* (4 vols.; 1959–70); and J. Hickerson, in D. Emrich (ed.), *American Folk Poetry* (1974). Representative of best early song collections are C. Sharp, *English Folk Songs from Southern Appalachians* (1932); J. and A. Lomax, *Cowboy Songs* (1938); V. Randolph, *Ozark Folk Songs* (4 vols.; 1946–50); J. Combs, *Folksongs du Midi des Etats-Unis* (1925); H. M. Belden, *Ballads and Songs* (1940); and G. P. Jackson, *White Spirituals from Southern Uplands* (1933). For short entries on all folklore genres, see M. Leach (ed.), *Standard Dictionary of Folklore, Mythology, and Legend* (2 vols.; 1949–50). Notable regional folktale collections include V. Randolph, *We Always Lie to Strangers* (1951); R. Chase, *Jack Tales* (1943); M. Campbell, *Tales from Cloud-Walking Country* (1958); and L. Roberts, *South from Hell-fer-Sartin* (1955). A. H. Eaton, *Handicrafts* (1937); H. Glassie, *Pattern in Material Folk Culture* (1968); and E. Wigginton, *Foxfire* (1972), have spurred others to study folk life. Unpublished collections on university campuses throughout South (Western Kentucky, Georgia State, Texas, Duke, North Carolina) and relevant holdings of Smithsonian Institution provide further resources for study.

MARY WASHINGTON CLARKE
Western Kentucky University

FOLK MEDICINE in the South has always been one of the most widespread and tenacious of folk beliefs and practices. The reasons are obvious. The southern states, because of climate and economic conditions, throughout their history have had more than the national average of illnesses.

Combating these, the folk have been pragmatic; if an ill person tried a medicine and felt better, the medicine was given the credit. Although the philosophy behind folk remedies is universal, diseases and cures for a region as large as the South differed rather widely because of local conditions, though all people in a given area—rich and poor, black and white—because of a shortage of medical doctors received virtually the same treatment. But there were some differences. Home remedies were influenced by national origins of the people, by availability of flora and fauna, and by accident. Scotch-Irish practices differed somewhat from English. Cures, and sicknesses, among Negroes and Indians—two other dominant cultural strains in the South—contrasted sharply with those of white people and with each other. Ethnic origins as well as religious and educational backgrounds also shaded beliefs and remedies, though less in the South than in other parts of the United States.

Studying folk beliefs and practices in the South, as elsewhere, is an inexact science, and it is unlikely that geographical typologies will ever be completed. Southern beliefs and practices, however, have been more widely studied than those from any other section of this country. These studies reveal some interesting flows in and from the region. For example, the practice of applying a freshly killed chicken to a snakebite was commonly accepted throughout the South, as well as virtually everywhere else in the United States; but that of applying the gall of an eagle to rattlesnake bites is unreported except from North Carolina. Wearing a string of beads about the neck as a cure for goiter has been widely practiced in the South and Midwest, whereas wearing chinaberry seeds for the same illness seems to have been limited to the South, where chinaberry trees abound.

One cornerstone of folk medicine in the South, as elsewhere, is the age-old belief in homeopathic (or mimetic or imitative) magic stated in the dictum *similia similibus curantur,* "similar things are cured by similar means." By loose logic or association, it seems that an object in nature that resembled the disease in one way or another would be the one God intended as a cure. Thus in the South jaundice was cured by eating yellow plants; "puniness"(looking pale) was set right by eating red plants; weak blood was strengthened by drinking berry wine; bad complexion was cleared up by eating onions. Some diseases that covered areas of the body were cured by poultices, which resembled the affected areas. So a poultice made of feverweed was good for "risings" (skin eruptions). In North Carolina and Mississippi, kerosene oil was applied to burns. Mud as a cure for burns has been reported so far only from North Carolina.

Tied in somewhat with this belief was another general feeling that, if a disease resulted from the introduction of something "bad" into the human body, it could be cured by introducing something else "bad." For example, in North Carolina a tea of cherry and apple bark was taken for fever.

Another important folk medicine cure, in the South as elsewhere, resulted from transferal or contagious magic. In this practice some object is brought into contact with the diseased area and then disposed of. In the South a string was bloodied on warts or tied into knots and buried; as the string rotted the warts went away. Another cure for the same trouble was touching a kernel of corn to warts and feeding it to a chicken. Goiter was cured by wearing Job's tears seed around the neck.

Another strong southern belief in folk medicine, especially a Negro contribution, included verbal incantations and charms used to "conjure" away diseases. To "take the fire out" of a burned spot, for example, one spat on the spot and blew it while saying, "In the name of the Father, the Son and the Holy Ghost, come out of there fire and turn to frost." Somewhat more loosely associated with the charms and incantations was simply the power of associative language.

Although southerners may of necessity have depended more on home remedies than did people in other parts of the country, many in the South viewed the home medical practices with humorous incredulity and derision. How much this disbelief was genuine and how much social pressure is difficult to ascertain. Even though such people swore they would have nothing to do with home remedies, they in fact remembered them, passed them on to other persons, and even—with varying degrees of faith and hope—resorted to them in extreme cases. Generally, however, mention of the cures brought on laughter. In North Carolina, for example, a cure for "sore eyes" was kissing a "red-headed girl." Throughout the South to cure a toothache one "walked around a 'simmon tree three times and didn't think about a 'possum."

Regardless of the general feeling now about the efficacy of home remedies, they in fact had a much sounder basis in reality than other superstitions. For example, a pharmacological analysis of 100 frontier cures, which would have been valid for those from the South whence many undoubtedly had come, demonstrated that more than half would have had some medicinal value and all others except one were folk placebos and would have no effect either adverse or beneficial.

In evaluating the effect of folk medicines one should remember that most scientific medical practitioners are still investigating, and relying on, the same herbs our ancestors used. And, as has been stated many times by medical doctors and historians of medicine, perhaps the single greatest good done by home remedies was that they kept people away from medical doctors.

See R. B. Browne, *Popular Beliefs and Practices from Alabama* (1958) and *Indian Doctor* (1964); W. D. Hand, in *Frank C. Brown Collection of North Carolina Folklore* (1961), Vols. VI–VII; and T. P. Coffin (ed.), *Our Living Traditions* (1968).

RAY B. BROWNE
Bowling Green State University

FOLSOM, JAMES ELISHA "BIG JIM" (1908–), governor of Alabama (1947–1951, 1955–1959), represented a persistent strain of populism in Alabama politics. In the 1946 gubernatorial contest, he forged a coalition of small farmers and urban laborers to defeat conservative forces centered in the BLACK BELT and the industrial centers. Folsom's legislative program of expanded social services, of increased expenditures for education, roads, and old-age pensions, of abolition of the POLL TAX, and of constitutional revision met intransigent opposition from dominant conservative forces in the legislature. He further angered conservatives by opposing the DIXIECRAT revolt of 1948 and by his liberal views in racial matters. The personal scandal of a paternity suit further weakened Folsom politically.

Nonetheless, in 1954 he easily won a second term. He succeeded in pushing through much of his legislative program in the first half of his second term; but, when he refused to cater to the rising tide of segregationist sentiment, his political stock once again plummeted. He appointed voting registrars who would register qualified blacks and dismissed the legislature's "nullification" of the U.S. Supreme Court's 1954 school desegregation decision as futile—"like a hound dog baying at the moon." When he ran for an unprecedented third term as governor in 1962, he was initially considered the strongest contender. Racial sentiment was at a peak in the state, however, and Folsom ran third, losing to a former supporter, GEORGE C. WALLACE.

See V. O. Key, *Southern Politics* (1949); W. D. Barnard, *Dixiecrats and Democrats* (1974); and Folsom Papers, Alabama Department of Archives and History, Montgomery, of limited value.

WILLIAM D. BARNARD
Alabama Commission on Higher Education

FOODS AND BEVERAGES. The general character of the southern diet emerged during the colonial period. The English settlers discovered that HOGS, of all livestock, fared best and that pork, of all meats, was most satisfactorily preserved. Since it also appeared that CORN grew much better than the English grains, pork and corn became the two great southern staple foods. Pork was supplemented by chickens, turkeys, game, and near the coast by fish and shellfish. Relatively little beef, lamb, and mutton were eaten. In addition to venison, bear, and smaller mammals, the colonists ate such diverse birds as wild turkeys, ducks, swans, herons, pigeons, and robins.

Dairying was limited by the poor pastures and the use of cleared land for profitable crops. Most of what milk there was went to make butter, buttermilk, and sour milk. Apples grew poorly, but peaches did well in the Piedmont, and there were native figs, persimmons, and wild berries. Vegetables were neglected, in part because of the inherited English fear of them as unwholesome, though sweet potatoes became important as did beans, cowpeas, rice, and later turnips. Corn played an immense role in breads, hominy, and mush.

Although the poorer settlers of necessity drank water, or water mixed with molasses, others tried to reproduce the beverages they knew and liked. Beer was made from such ingredients as persimmons, corn, and pumpkins. Apples were converted into cider, pears were converted into perry, and honey was converted into mead and metheglin. Since endemic diseases destroyed imported grapevines, the well-to-do bought Spanish, Portuguese, or French wines. Madeira in winter and claret in summer became the most popular. For strong beverages, rum was imported from the West Indies, French or Spanish brandies were imported from Europe, and peach brandy was distilled in the home. By the mid-eighteenth century the Scotch-Irish in the Piedmont were making whiskey (BOURBON).

Imported foods gave variety to middle- and upper-class tables. From northern colonies came corned beef, wheat, apples, cider, cheese, flour, biscuits, onions, hops, and dried fish. The West Indies provided tropical fruits, pimiento, chocolate, coffee, molasses, sugar, and ginger. And from France, Spain, and Portugal came olive oil, lemons, spices, sugar, currants, and raisins.

The slaves ate the food of the poor. Their usual rations consisted of corn, field peas, beans, and sometimes sweet potatoes, but rarely any meat until the nineteenth century, when pork was usually included. Most families were allowed gardens and the right to raise chickens or even a pig. Although forbidden guns, the slaves could fish, snare, and hunt with dogs to obtain catfish, rabbits, opossums, raccoons, and squirrels.

By the mid-nineteenth century there were several distinct and mature culinary regions in the South where the wealthier inhabitants enjoyed fine cooking. Of all the sections of the United States, the South had the greatest number of professional cooks: black slaves, normally women, of whom many were sensitive and skillful culinary artists.

Much of the finest southern cooking was based on seafood. In eastern Maryland and Virginia the oysters, crabs, shrimp, fish, and terrapin were all featured as delicacies together with canvasback and other ducks and ham. Recipes bearing the names Maryland or Baltimore as adjectives spread throughout the country for fried chicken, beaten biscuits, and many other dishes.

Coastal South Carolina and Georgia formed another special section of good cooking, with Charleston and Savannah as centers. Here rice was served with shellfish and in pilaus, soups, puddings, and as flour in breads, biscuits, and cakes. The cookery had absorbed French, West Indian, and African influences and used such ingredients as turtles, oysters, shrimp, crabs, eggplants, sweet potatoes, tomatoes, okra, palmetto cabbage, and benne seeds.

Along the Gulf coast from Florida into Texas both rice and seafood were important. The culinary center of this coast was New Orleans, a cosmopolitan city where Creole cooking, basically French, had been shaped by contributions of the native Indians, Spaniards, African slaves, West Indians, and inhabitants from every part of the United States. The city obtained seafood, fruits, and vegetables from local sources and additional foods from Europe, the East Coast, and the Mississippi Valley. Although meats, other than pork, were inferior, fine fish and shellfish were made into bouillabaisse, chowders, GUMBOS, jambalayas, and other Creole dishes with distinctive flavorings of garlic, sassafras, onions, celery, bay leaves, peppers, and other herbs and spices.

The majority of antebellum white southerners, farmers and laborers, remained dependent on pork and corn, supplemented by such additions as chickens, game, cowpeas, collards, turnips, cabbages, sweet potatoes, pokeweed, and beans. The peas, beans, and various greens were boiled with bacon, and the "potlikker" was consumed as a broth. Some vegetables, such as okra, potatoes, or eggplant, might be fried. Molasses from the West Indies or Louisiana served for sweetening or flavoring. Water was the beverage of the poor, claret was commonly drunk by the more affluent, and whiskey was cheap and widely used by all classes.

The Civil War brought hunger to many southerners. Northern sources of grains, meat, salt, and other foods were cut off, and scarcities were increased by the blockade, hoarding, speculation, deteriorating transportation, military actions, and the unwillingness of farmers to sell for depreciated Confederate currency. Meats, fat, and even fruits and vegetables disappeared from city markets. The soldiers rarely ate better than the civilians, and some, especially during active campaigning, endured extreme hunger.

Following the Civil War and into the twentieth century the use of pork may have increased. The eating of fruits and vegetables probably declined as plantation orchards deteriorated and the sharecroppers planted cotton to the exclusion of garden space. There was also a growing scarcity of game. Southerners with money, of course, benefited by improved transportation of foods from distant places, better refrigeration, and the variety available through canned foods. During the early 1870s iced tea appeared in the South and soon became a year-round beverage. The cola drinks began their tremendous growth in the 1880s. Alcoholic beverages, however, were increasingly discouraged, in part to keep them from the black population.

The southern diet in the twentieth century came more and more under the influence of the national food industry. Canned, refrigerated, fast-frozen, processed, and ready-to-eat foods all gained. These changes lessened the labor of food preparation and increased the variety of foods available. At the same time they reduced the overall quality of foods, limited cooking as a creative activity, and submerged regional differences under the universal pall of uniformity.

See L. C. Gray, *History of Agriculture* (1941); S. B. Hilliard, *Hog Meat and Hoecake* (1972); R. O. Cummings, *American and His Food* (1941); R. B. Vance, *Human Geography of South* (1932); M. E. Massey, *North Carolina Historical Review* (July, 1949); and B. I. Wiley, *Plain People of Confederacy* (1943).

RICHARD J. HOOKER
Roosevelt University

FOOTE, HENRY STUART (1804–1880), lived in Virginia until he moved to Alabama in 1825. Then he moved to Mississippi and remained in the state until 1854. Foote became well known as a journalist, criminal lawyer, orator, and one of the most colorful politicians in Mississippi history. In 1847 Foote and Jefferson Davis went to Washington, D.C., as senators. The two men became and remained personal and political enemies. Foote, one of the principal architects of the COMPROMISE OF 1850, was the only Mississippian in Congress who supported these measures. In 1851 he campaigned successfully for governor against Davis on a platform promising that Mississippi would accept the Compromise of 1850 and remain in the Union. Foote's gubernatorial administration (1852–1854) was a failure, and in 1854 he moved to California. In 1857 Foote moved to Tennessee. During the Civil War he represented the Nashville district in the Confederate Congress and won notoriety as a leading critic of the Davis administration. Foote thought of himself as a peacemaker and was expelled from the Confederacy early in 1865. After the war he became a Republican and was appointed superintendent of the mint in New Orleans in 1878, a post he held until his death.

See J. E. Gonzales, "Foote" (Ph.D. dissertation, University of North Carolina, 1957), only complete study. See also Foote's four books: *Texas and Texans* (1841), *War of Rebellion* (1866); *Casket of Reminiscences* (1874); and *Bench and Bar* (1876).

JOHN EDMOND GONZALES
University of Southern Mississippi

FORCE BILL (1833). In January, 1833, President ANDREW JACKSON startled Washington by asking Congress to grant him powers to subdue NULLIFICATION in South Carolina. In this "Force Bill" message Jackson asked Congress to empower him to collect federal customs duties off the Carolina coast and to circumvent South Carolina's state courts in case of legal protest by the nullifiers. The president also requested approval for previous military preparations that included contingency plans for invasion of South Carolina should fighting erupt. The warlike tone of the message and the president's refusal to support tariff reform alarmed even some of his closest political allies. When Jackson's archenemy HENRY CLAY seized leadership of Congress and successfully engineered a compromise tariff, Jackson insisted even more vehemently on passage of the Force Bill. Congress let the president have his way, approving the bill in early March, 1833. At the same time the legislature passed Clay's compromise tariff, which provided for eventual settlement of the nullification crisis.

See W. Freehling, *Prelude to Civil War* (1966); J. C. Curtis, *Andrew Jackson* (1976); and Andrew Jackson Papers, Library of Congress.

JAMES C. CURTIS
University of Delaware

FORCE BILL (1890). The Republican platform of 1888 had described the widespread DISFRANCHISEMENT of southern blacks as "a criminal nullification of the Constitution and laws of the United States." As the HARRISON ADMINISTRATION had pledged itself to protecting the freedom of the ballot and as the Republicans enjoyed majorities in both houses of Congress, the Republican party was under considerable pressure to enact some form of election reform. Of several election reform bills presented to the House, that introduced by Henry Cabot Lodge of Massachusetts received the most attention. Dubbed by opponents the "Force Bill," Lodge's measure provided for federal supervision of congressional elections. In response to petition by citizens of a congressional district, federal circuit courts were to appoint a board of canvassers to examine the election returns. Where the canvassers disagreed with the returns reported by state election officials, the findings of the former group were to be regarded as prima facie evidence of election.

Northern and southern Democrats alike opposed the bill. Although most Republicans paid at least lip service to the measure, some opposition to it was voiced by a number of southern LILY-WHITE Republicans, who argued that such a statute would only harden racial lines and rekindle political strife. Despite vigorous opposition to the bill and numerous efforts to delay consideration and to emasculate its provisions, it was passed by the House of Representatives by a vote of 155 to 149. In the Senate, however, the bill was lost in the competition for consideration with the McKinley tariff and with silver legislation. Despite continued pledges in Republican campaign platforms to enforce the FIFTEENTH AMENDMENT, Lodge's bill was the last effort by his generation to protect black voting rights in the South. Lodge himself soon became an imperial advocate of the need for Americans to assume "the white man's burden," and the principal effect of his bill was to hasten southern consideration of additional legal devices by which to disfranchise blacks. Indeed, not until consideration of the CIVIL RIGHTS ACT OF 1957 would Congress again seriously consider legislation to protect the franchise in federal elections.

See V. P. De Santis, *Republicans Face Southern Question* (1959); and R. W. Logan, *Betrayal of Negro* (1954).

FOREIGN AFFAIRS. In the early national period, southern interests focused on a favorable overseas commercial market and on attaining frontier security. When John Jay proposed a treaty with Spain in 1785, which gave up American claims to navigate the Mississippi River for 25 years in return for commercial concessions, southern congressmen helped secure its defeat. This experience prompted southern representatives at the CONSTITUTIONAL CONVENTION to insist upon adoption of the two-thirds rule for treaty passage in the Senate. The George Washington administration mollified southern fears in 1795 by concluding Pinckney's Treaty, by which Spain relinquished extensive claims in the old Southwest and permitted Americans the use of New Orleans as a port for three years, tax free.

Sympathetic to the ideals of the French Revolution and tied closely to agrarianism, southerners increasingly supported the Jeffersonian Republicans. With this party's dominance after 1800, the South benefited from an expansionist program. Most significant was the LOUISIANA PURCHASE in 1803. Thomas Jefferson's pressure on France came partly from southern anxiety that New Orleans would become a hostile base, cutting off both commerce and territorial expansion. Southerners enthusiastically backed Jefferson's diplomacy in the purchase, as well as his abortive efforts to acquire WEST FLORIDA. With the Napoleonic Wars threatening commercial interests and freedom of the seas, southerners loyally supported Jefferson's embargo decision of 1807, although it hurt the region's exports. By 1811 a younger breed of southern war hawks had rebelled against economic coercion and were calling on President James Madison for decisive action to halt insults to the national honor. The South solidly backed the WAR OF 1812, and General ANDREW JACKSON's victories helped make the old Southwest a secure area for a major postwar agrarian boom.

By the 1820s southern nationalism ebbed, as the region's growing identification with the cotton culture and slavery shaped its posture on foreign policy in ways that aroused more suspicion than loyalty to the Union. In reality the South still predominated in America's international actions. The acquisition of Florida in 1819 ended Indian threats to Georgia, and in the Southwest settlers, in quest of high cotton profits, moved into Coahuila-Texas. Belated opposition from Mexican officials sparked Texas' war for independence in 1836, though President Jackson sagely avoided the issue of annexation, fearing it could spark controversy over slavery in an election year. Southern congress-

men, with some exceptions in declining cotton areas, were in the forefront of the manifest destiny movement of the 1840s. The consequent MEXICAN WAR of 1846, ostensibly fought over the Texas border dispute, vastly enlarged the national domain—a conflict many northerners opposed as a plot to enlarge the empire of the "slavocracy."

Their further expansionist goals thwarted in the 1850s, and under great stress from northern attacks on slavery, southerners left the Union in 1861. Faith that KING COTTON would bring British assistance proved a tragic delusion. Alternate sources for their mills plus British investments in the North proved to be the boll weevils in the South's cotton diplomacy.

Over the hundred years after 1865, the South exerted less direct influence in America's foreign policy. The major paradox is that, although stigmatized as the region of disloyalty, the South developed a strong sense of nationalism on foreign policy issues. Reliance on agriculture inclined southerners to support the quest for overseas markets as the nineteenth century ended, though a number of leaders warned against territorial acquisitions in the wake of the SPANISH-AMERICAN WAR. This caution stemmed largely from the region's internal problems in handling racial tensions.

Southern support for both world wars was strong, arising partly from close ties with the Anglo-Saxon heritage. Although chauvinistic once the nation was at war, southerners exhibited both internationalist and isolationist streaks in the twentieth century. They moderately favored Woodrow Wilson's League of Nations and strongly responded to America's lead in establishing the United Nations. However, Franklin Roosevelt found that in the depression years most southern congressmen put domestic programs well ahead of proposals to face Fascist dangers.

The two world wars helped bring the South more into the American mainstream. With significant industrial growth after 1940, the South gained a new impetus for nationalism, which evidenced itself mainly in the cold war years. Much of the South's new prosperity was linked to postwar military spending, which was abetted by southern Democrats' power in key congressional committee posts. Over the next 20 years, the South could be found in the forefront of cold war patriotism, as its politicians usually took a determined stand in opposing communism around the globe. However, in the aftermath of the Vietnam War, southerners joined their countrymen in wondering what the future held.

See S. F. Bemis, *Pinckney's Treaty* (1926); A. P. Whitaker, *Mississippi Question* (1934); M. D. Peterson, *Jefferson* (1970); R. A. Young, *Hispanic American Historical Review* (Nov., 1963); M. P. Adams, *Journal of Southern History* (May, 1955); N. K. Risjord, *William and Mary Quarterly* (April, 1961); J. W. Pratt, *Expansionists of 1812* (1925); M. L. Latimer, *American Historical Review* (July, 1956); P. C. Brooks, *Diplomacy and Borderlands* (1939); W. D. Jones, *Journal of Southern History* (Feb., 1956); C. Seller, *Polk* (1966); H. E. Landry, *Journal of Southern History* (May, 1961); N. A. Graebner, *Journal of Southern History* (May, 1953); F. Merk, *Monroe Doctrine and Expansionism* (1966); H. Blumenthal, *Journal of Southern History* (May, 1966); C. P. Cullop, *Confederate Propaganda* (1969); F. A. Logan, *Journal of Southern History* (Nov., 1958); F. L. Owsley, *King Cotton Diplomacy* (1959); W. A. Williams, *Roots of American Empire* (1969); C. Lash, *Journal of Southern History* (Aug., 1958); R. Gregory, *W. H. Page* (1970); A. S. Link, *Wilson* (1947–); W. F. Kuehl, *Seeking World Order* (1969); T. A. Bailey, *Wilson and Peacemakers* (1947); J. W. Pratt, *Hull* (1964); A. DeConde, *Journal of Southern History* (Aug., 1958); R. A. Divine, *Second Chance* (1971); and A. O. Hero, *Southerner in World Affairs* (1965).

T. M. CAMPBELL
Florida State University

FORESTRY in the South has a unique 375-year history. Exploitation of the virgin forest began with the NAVAL STORES industry about 1600 and the first sawmill at Jamestown in 1608. The LUMBER INDUSTRY developed slowly until the 1880s, when it moved from the lake states into the South. By 1900 the nation depended greatly on southern timber, and in 1909 almost half the lumber was produced in the South. Over the next two decades, production declined as the vast southern pinery was cut and lumber companies moved west.

Even in this era of exploitation, a few pioneers realized the potentials for a second forest. The first American forester, Gifford Pinchot, began scientific forest management on the Biltmore estate near Asheville, N.C., in 1892. Pinchot was soon succeeded by the German Carl A. Schenck, who also established the Biltmore Forest School, the first in the South, in 1898. About 350 early foresters received technical forestry training before Biltmore closed in 1913.

Henry E. Hardtner, president of Urania Lumber Company of Louisiana and the father of southern industrial forestry, visualized the second forest when he authored the Louisiana Reforestation Act of 1910 and entered his lands under it in 1913. Other lumbermen soon followed Hardtner's lead with the counsel of early foresters such as W. W.

Ashe, Austin Cary, and H. H. Chapman. In 1920 the Great Southern Lumber Company of Bogalusa, La., began reforestation of cutover lands, and by 1929 some 23,000 acres had been reforested. Great Southern and its successor companies created the largest man-made forest in the United States.

In the early 1900s southern states began to enact legislation to promote forest fire protection and forest regeneration. The first state forestry agency for forest fire protection was created by Louisiana in 1904. Alabama adopted a general forest administration law in 1907. National forests were established, and state and regional forestry associations organized. Formed in 1914, the Southern Pine Association held the first Southern Forestry Congress (1916) to promote state legislation for forestry and sponsored the Cutover Land Conference of the South (1917) to encourage better utilization of the millions of acres of cutover land.

By 1925 forestry practices to make lands more productive had been started on 82 properties totaling 4.7 million acres. But wildfires were still rampant in southern forests. In 1927 the American Forestry Association launched the three-year Southern Forestry Education Project, in which teams of "Dixie Crusaders" traveled in trucks to carry forest fire prevention messages throughout the hinterlands of Florida, Georgia, Mississippi, and South Carolina. Better control of wildfires by state forestry agencies and tree planting by the CIVILIAN CONSERVATION CORPS and farsighted forest owners were largely responsible for regrowth of the South's second forest. But forestry did not become economical until the expansion of the PULP AND PAPER INDUSTRY to utilize small trees from the second forest. The first pulp and paper mill was built in 1891 at Hartsville, S.C.; the use of southern pines for manufacture of kraft paper began in 1909 and for manufacture of newsprint in 1931. The Southern Forest Survey of 1932 documented the comeback of pine and provided the impetus for rapid expansion of the pulp and paper industry. Pulpwood production increased fourfold between 1946 and 1967.

The manufacture of plywood from southern pines started in 1963 and is today another booming forest industry. As a result, the South is now entering the era of the third forest—an intensively managed and intensively utilized forest needed to supply an ever-increasing share of the nation's wood needs by the year 2000.

See H. E. Clepper, *Professional Forestry* (1971); S. T. Dana, *Forest and Range Policy* (1956); H. E. Clepper and A. B. Meyer, *American Forestry* (1960); and publications of Forest History Society, Santa Cruz, Calif.

NORWIN E. LINNARTZ
Louisiana State University

FORREST, NATHAN BEDFORD (1821–1877), commanded the Confederate cavalry corps in the western theater of the Civil War. He was born in Bedford County, Tenn. The death of his father, a blacksmith, in 1837 left Forrest the responsibility of supporting his family. He worked as a farm laborer and as a horse and cattle dealer; then, as a trader in slaves and real estate, he earned enough to buy cotton plantations in Mississippi and Arkansas.

Forrest entered Confederate service as a private in June, 1861, but was appointed lieutenant colonel in October after he recruited a cavalry battalion and equipped it at his own expense. At Ft. Donelson (FTS. HENRY AND DONELSON CAMPAIGN) he opposed the decision to surrender and successfully led his men through the encircling Union troops. Wounded during the retreat from SHILOH, he was subsequently appointed brigadier general in July, 1862, and began a series of cavalry raids (FORREST'S RAIDS) that became his trademark. Whether or not Forrest actually made the statement attributed to him, that his success lay in "getting thar fustest with the mostest," he clearly practiced the formula. Soon after the CHICKAMAUGA campaign, Forrest had a strong disagreement with his superior, BRAXTON BRAGG. JEFFERSON DAVIS resolved the dispute by promoting Forrest to major general and transferring him from Bragg's command. The only blemish on Forrest's reputation for military genius was the alleged massacre of black soldiers by his troops at FT. PILLOW on April 12, 1864. As was his custom, he sought the surrender of the fort by threatening the garrison with "no quarter." Forced to attack, his men slaughtered many of the fort's defenders while supposedly shouting, "Forrest's orders!"

In February, 1865, he was promoted to lieutenant general and, in a losing struggle, opposed federal cavalry operations until his final defeat in April. After surrendering, he returned to his plantations. Forrest reputedly was made grand wizard of the Ku Klux Klan. Although there is evidence that he was aware of certain Klan activities, in June, 1871, Forrest testified before a congressional committee that he had never been a member of the Ku Klux Klan. For several years he was president of the Selma, Marion & Memphis Railroad. He died in Memphis. Although he had little formal education, Forrest's innate abilities made him one of America's greatest military leaders.

See J. A. Wyeth, *Life of Forrest* (1899), eyewitness, but uncritical; *Official Records, Armies*, Ser. 1, Vols. XXXII, XXXIX, XLIX; R. S. Henry, *"First with the Most" Forrest* (1944); A. N. Lytle, *Bedford Forrest* (1931); and J. H. Mathes, *General Forrest* (1902).

JAMES C. SHEPARD
U.S. Army, Carlisle Barracks

FORREST'S RAIDS. Great distances, primitive communications, a generally prosouthern population, absence of continuous military lines, and inept federal cavalry permitted raids into Union-held territory to become a major form of Confederate cavalry activity in the West. Such raids disrupted federal campaigns, destroyed supply bases, broke up lines of communication (mainly railroads), damaged Union morale, and yielded recruits and supplies for the Confederacy.

The first of Forrest's raids occurred in July, 1862. Skill, guile, bluff, and threats enabled NATHAN B. FORREST to capture Murfreesboro and damage the railroad that nourished General Don Carlos Buell's east Tennessee campaign. This, plus exaggerated rumors of Forrest's strength and uncertainty about his movements, halted Buell's campaign. In December, 1862, U. S. Grant drew supplies over two railroads for his overland advance on Vicksburg. Forrest halted the advance by destroying 70 miles of railroad to Grant's rear; he was defeated at Parker's Crossroads on his return, but the damage to the railroad and the destruction by EARL VAN DORN of the federal supply base at Holly Springs wrecked Grant's campaign and postponed the federal capture of Vicksburg by several months (VICKSBURG CAMPAIGN).

In early 1863, Forrest led several raids in the direction of Nashville. Their cumulative effect was to immobilize 20,000 federal troops, deployed to guard a line from Memphis to Corinth. In November, 1863, Forrest raided the Jackson, Tenn., area to collect recruits and supplies. Hemmed in by Union troops, Forrest nevertheless escaped. In the following March he captured Paducah, Ky. On the defensive during the summer, he raided Memphis in August and thereby caused General A. J. Smith to give up his invasion of northern Mississippi. In September, Forrest severely damaged the Nashville & Decatur Railroad; later, at Johnsonville, Tenn., he destroyed federal gunboats, steamers, and huge warehouses filled with army supplies.

Forrest's raids succeeded because of careful planning and his intensely personal, aggressive leadership. Doing the unexpected, confusing the enemy, taking advantage of every opening, Forrest always kept military realities in view; all his raids had a practical military objective.

See A. N. Lytle, *Bedford Forrest* (1931); R. S. Henry, *"First with the Most" Forrest* (1944); J. A. Wyeth, *That Devil Forrest* (1959); T. Jordan and J. P. Pryor, *Campaigns of Forrest* (1868); J. W. Morton, *Artillery of Forrest's Cavalry* (1909); *Official Records, Armies*; and *Memoirs of W. T. Sherman* (1875).

STEPHEN Z. STARR
Cincinnati Historical Society

FORSYTH, JOHN (1780–1841), was born at Fredericksburg, Va., and moved with his family to Augusta, Ga., in 1785. He practiced law in Augusta after 1802, became attorney general of Georgia in 1808, entered Congress in 1813, and then moved to the Senate in 1818. The next year he went as U.S. minister to Spain to negotiate the ratification of the Adams-Onís Treaty, a post in which he was largely ineffectual. After another period in Congress (1823–1827) he became governor of Georgia in 1827 and in that office attempted to extend Georgia's authority over the CHEROKEE. In the Senate again (1829–1834), he emerged as a southern Unionist in the crisis over NULLIFICATION and voted for the compromise tariff of 1833 and the FORCE BILL. He was a master of oratory, a skilled Jacksonian tactician, and a leader in the war against the national bank. Andrew Jackson made him secretary of state in 1834, where he served until 1841. Forsyth moderated Jackson's policies in settling the French spoliation claims, negotiated with Spain in the *Amistad* controversy, and delayed the annexation of Texas.

See A. L. Duckett, *John Forsyth* (1962), scholarly biography; E. I. McCormac, *American Secretaries of State* ed. S. F. Bemis (1928), IV; and J. F. Jeffries, *Forsyth Family* (1920).

RONALD E. SHAW
Miami University

FT. BISLAND AND IRISH BEND, BATTLES OF (April 13–14, 1863). Nathaniel P. Banks, en route to capture the Confederate fortification at Port Hudson, La., led his Union forces from lower Louisiana via Bayou Teche toward the Red and Mississippi rivers. RICHARD TAYLOR, with a small Confederate force, halted Banks's cautious advance at Ft. Bisland on April 13, 1863. Banks then tried an encircling movement and temporarily trapped Taylor at Irish Bend. Here, on April 14, in the muddy cane fields along the Teche, the timorous federal commander C. C. Grover was defeated. Both battles consisted of intense artillery fire and short, faltering Union infantry advances.

Federal casualties numbered 577, and Confederate losses were negligible. Taylor slipped safely through the Union lines.

See J. D. Winters, *Civil War in Louisiana* (1963), extensive bibliography; R. B. Irwin, *Nineteenth Army Corps* (1892), excellent; J. W. De Forest, *Volunteer's Adventures* (1946); and *Official Records, Armies*, Ser. 1, Vol. XV, indispensable.

JOHN D. WINTERS
Louisiana Tech University

FT. FISHER, BATTLES OF (December 24–27, 1864; January 13–15, 1865), were two major engagements for control of Ft. Fisher, located near the tip of the peninsula between the Cape Fear River and the Atlantic Ocean below Wilmington, N.C. The fort protected Wilmington, the most important port in the Confederacy for BLOCKADE-RUNNERS. By 1864 the fort consisted of two series of earthworks, 44 guns, and a garrison of 1,600 men.

In the fall of 1864 General U. S. Grant and Admiral David D. Porter prepared a joint expedition against Ft. Fisher. General Benjamin F. Butler was selected to lead 6,500 troops while Porter would command 48 warships. An old ship, the *Louisiana*, was filled with gunpowder. It would be grounded near the fort and exploded. The shock of the explosion might paralyze the garrison and enable federal troops to capture the fort. Butler's troops arrived at New Inlet on December 16; the fleet joined them on the eighteenth. The *Louisiana* was exploded early on the twenty-fourth without any effect. The experiment failed because the ship was floating free of the bottom, and the shock of the explosion was lost in the water. On December 24 the fleet began to bombard the fort. The fort replied effectively, damaging a number of ships. At noon on the twenty-fifth troops landed three miles above the fort. However, they reembarked on December 25–26 and soon left after their leaders concluded that an assault would fail.

Grant sent a second expedition, 8,000 men under General Alfred H. Terry, which arrived off Ft. Fisher on January 12, 1865. On the thirteenth troops were landed north of the fort. Two lines of earthworks were quickly built across the peninsula. One line faced south to serve as a base for the assault, and the other faced north to prevent reinforcements for the beleaguered garrison. General BRAXTON BRAGG, department commander, withdrew his support troops as the federals invested the fort. He did not believe it was in much danger, if boldly defended. The fort's garrison, reinforced by 350 South Carolinians on January

15, now contained 1,950 men. The fleet bombarded the fort on January 13–15. On the fifteenth General Adelbert Ames's 3,000-man division attacked the land face, while a naval force of 2,000 assaulted the sea face. The naval column, although repulsed, drew the attention of the garrison, while the federal infantry captured the land face near the Cape Fear River. The infantry held its position despite a severe enfilading fire and a counterattack by troops under General William H. C. Whiting, who was severely wounded in the fighting. The Confederate defenders withdrew to Battery Buchanan at the tip of the peninsula, where they surrendered at 10:30 P.M. The capture of Ft. Fisher closed the Cape Fear River to blockade-runners, although Wilmington did not surrender until February 22.

See Wilmington (N.C.) *Daily Journal* (1864–65); Zebulon B. Vance Papers (1864) and Confederate Military Telegrams, North Carolina Division of Archives and History; Miscellaneous Collection of Telegrams and Letters, Catherine McGeachy Papers, John B. Foote Papers, James Otis Moore Papers, and William Read, Sr., Papers, Duke University; James W. Albright Diary, Southern Historical Collection, University of North Carolina; *Official Records, Navies*, Ser. 1, Vol. X; J. M. Merrill, *North Carolina Historical Review* (Oct., 1958); C. B. Denson, *Memoir of Major-General W. H. C. Whiting* (1895); C. B. Boynton, *History of Navy During Rebellion* (1869); I. Price, *History of Ninety-seventh Regiment, Pennsylvania Volunteer Infantry* (1875); J. B. Jones, *Rebel War Clerk's Diary* (1935); W. Lamb, in R. U. Johnson and C. C. Buel (eds.), *Battles and Leaders* (1956); H. M. Rogers, *Memories of Ninety Years* (1928); and G. Dewey, *Autobiography* (1916).

RICHARD W. IOBST
Western Carolina University

FORTIER, ALCÉE (1856–1914), born in St. James Parish, La., was a professor of Romance languages at Tulane University (1894–1914), where he gained a reputation as one of the South's leading educators. His desire to maintain and cultivate the French tongue in Louisiana moved him to write a number of ·vorks in that language, most notably *Histoire de littérature française* (1893) and *Précis de l'histoire de France* (1899). Of more local historical value were his *Bits of Louisiana Folklore* (1888), *Louisiana Studies* (1894), and *Louisiana Folk-tales* (1895), which explicitly examined the Creole linguistic and literary tradition and implicitly extolled French culture. Fortier's major achievement, however, was his four-volumed *A History of Louisiana* (1904), a largely uncritical, pro-Creole, episodic work, which placed him with FRANÇOIS XAVIER MARTIN and CHARLES GAYARRÉ as the foremost historians of the state. A leader in

the American Folklore Society and the Modern Language Association, Fortier was also instrumental in the 1894 reorganization of the LOUISIANA HISTORICAL SOCIETY, of which he was president until his death.

See P. Butler, in W. L. Fleming (ed.), *South in Building of Nation* (1909), XI; G. King, *Creole Families* (1921); and E. M. F. Cochran, *Fortier Family* (1963).

ROBERT L. PAQUETTE
University of Rochester

FT. LAUDERDALE, FLA. (pop. 139,590), 25 miles north of Miami, is an Atlantic port joined by navigable canals to Lake OKEECHOBEE. It grew up around the location of a SEMINOLE WAR fort commanded by Major William Lauderdale. Incorporated in 1911, the town has grown rapidly since the 1920s as a popular resort, an active shipping center for foodstuffs, and a manufacturer of furniture, boats, construction materials, fertilizer, and electrical equipment.

See P. Weidling and A. Burghard, *Checkered Sunshine* (1966), history of city's area (1793–1955); and files of Ft. Lauderdale *News* (1910–), on microfilm.

FT. MOULTRIE, BATTLES OF. Built in 1811 and situated at the northern entrance to Charleston harbor, Ft. Moultrie was seized by South Carolina troops on December 27, 1860. Additional heavy guns, interior improvements, a thick sand cover, and new connecting batteries enabled Moultrie, combined with FT. SUMTER, Battery Gregg, and Ft. Wagner, to turn Charleston harbor into a bristling cul-de-sac. Nonetheless, S. F. Du Pont (DU PONT FAMILY) on April 7, 1863, attacked with eight ironclad monitors. He sailed into a hurricane of projectiles that scored some 500 times, battering five of the monitors so badly that further Union operations were called off the same night. Admiral J. A. Dahlgren fared no better in his assault late that summer, complaining on September 1 that Moultrie had inflicted upon his ships "70 hits, very hard." On the seventh, despite losing 26 killed and wounded when a shell detonated a magazine, Moultrie's garrison under Colonel William Butler continued to "fire like the devil," helping to blunt Dahlgren's offensive. The fort saw relatively little action for the rest of the war. The last Union shots in Charleston were lobbed at a flag over empty Moultrie on February 18, 1865, all the city's defenses having been evacuated the night before.

See *Official Records, Navies*, Ser. 1, Vol. XIV; E. M. Burton, *Siege of Charleston* (1970), best account; J. Johnson,

Defense of Charleston (1890); S. Jones, Siege of Charleston (1911); S. Foote, *American Heritage* (June, 1963); S. F. Du Pont, *Civil War Letters* (1969); H. A. Du Pont, *S. F. Du Pont* (1926); M. Dahlgren, *Memoirs of Dahlgren* (1882), his widow; C. S. Peterson, *Dahlgren* (1945); and G. Welles, *Diary* (1909), strongly anti–Du Pont.

DAVID F. LONG
University of New Hampshire

FT. PILLOW MASSACRE (April 12, 1864).

More than a century after the event, it is still not exactly clear what happened when Ft. Pillow, Tenn., fell to Confederate soldiers under NATHAN B. FORREST. When the garrison refused to surrender to the Confederate advance guard, Forrest ordered an assault. The attacking troops lost 14 killed and 86 wounded. Among the defenders, 231 died, 100 were wounded, and 226 surrendered. Beyond these few facts, much controversy remains.

On one side are those who maintain that the federal troops were slaughtered after they surrendered. In support of this position, the relative casualties of the two sides are cited as well as the disproportion of dead to wounded. Moreover, it is pointed out that 127 of 295 white soldiers were casualties and 204 of 262 blacks fell. Congress concluded that there was a massacre and collected testimony of wanton killing and other atrocities inflicted on men who had laid down their arms. Others note that Confederate authorities, including Forrest, had previously decreed that black soldiers would be treated not as prisoners of war, but as criminals engaging in servile insurrection. Finally, mention is made of Forrest's purported later creation of the KU KLUX KLAN.

The opposite point of view holds that the casualties (with minor exceptions, perhaps) were the result of acceptable military activity. Badly outnumbered and beyond the aid of their gunboats, the Union troops refused to lay down their arms. The inability of black soldiers to fight effectively increased their casualties. Some have charged that the disaster was compounded because many of the northerners were drunk. They add that President Abraham Lincoln was cautious in his pronouncements and ultimately conceded that the affair was within the bounds of legitimate warfare.

See *Official Records, Armies*, Vol. XXXII; A. Castel, *Civil War History* (March, 1958); and J. L. Jordan, *Tennessee Historical Quarterly* (June, 1947).

ARTHUR E. BARBEAU
West Liberty State College

FT. PULASKI, CAPTURE OF (April 11, 1862).

Nearly 20 years had been spent in the construction of this massive masonry fortification, which, sited on Cockspur Island, was believed to provide an invulnerable defense bastion for Savannah, Ga. When a Union naval reconnaissance in December, 1861, revealed that nearby Tybee Island had been abandoned by Confederate forces after the capture of PORT ROYAL SOUND, Union troops under Quincy A. Gillmore established batteries of mortars and rifled artillery on the marshy island. Thirty hours of bombardment by the rifled guns sufficed to breach Pulaski's walls on April 10–11, 1862, whereupon Colonel Charles H. Olmstead surrendered the fort. Held by the Union for the remainder of the war, Pulaski closed Savannah to shipping more effectively than naval blockade. The Confederacy, having learned that masonry forts could not withstand rifled projectiles, began to rely on cheaper and less vulnerable earthworks, and the Union ultimately ceased to use heavy mortars because of their inaccuracy at Pulaski and elsewhere.

See *Official Records, Armies*, Ser. 1, Vol. VI; Q. A. Gillmore, *Official Report* (1862); R. U. Johnson and C. C. Buel (eds.), *Battles and Leaders* (1887), II; A. Williams, *Investment of Fort Pulaski* (1887); and J. D. Hayes (ed.), *Du Pont Civil War Letters* (1969), I.

ROBERT ERWIN JOHNSON
University of Alabama

FORTS.

From earliest times man has sought defensive positions to protect himself from foes. Evidence of early ones by Indians in America exists in mounds, prehistoric forts, and cliff dwellings. When Europeans came to the New World they erected forts as a defense against both Indians and European rivals. These forts and their successors in what is now the South have played a significant role in America's history.

Ft. Raleigh on ROANOKE ISLAND was erected in 1585 to protect SIR WALTER RALEIGH's first settlers. A generation later, the day colonists disembarked at Jamestown in May, 1607, they began "in the name of God to raise a Fortresse." This stockade would sustain the first permanent English foothold on the continent through dreadful times.

Through colonial days quickly erected citadels like the foregoing, sometimes of earth but usually of wooden palisades, protected pioneers as they pushed toward the setting sun. However, France and Spain, struggling with England for empire early erected some more enduring forts at strategic locations like a harbor entrance or river crossing. Castillo de San Marcos at St. Augustine, built 1672–1756 of native coquina rock, is our nation's oldest masonry fort.

During the world wars of the eighteenth century, the great powers built an increasing number of masonry forts at strategic coastal sites. These could hold off an attack by ships or an amphibious expedition until relief arrived from overseas—if navies were strong enough. The prize of America could only be won or retained by strength at sea. In essence a fleet is a group of mobile forts that can bring to bear an enormous concentration of guns. Only the strongest fort, or one situated in a particularly difficult position, could be sure of standing up to a fleet and a well-led expeditionary force.

FT. MOULTRIE, guarding Charleston, was not masonry but had a favorable position. Quickly thrown up of over a 16-foot thickness of sand sandwiched between palmetto logs, it turned back a British naval attack in 1776. In the War of 1812, after burning Washington's public buildings, the British moved against Baltimore. Ft. McHenry, of masonry, withstood a 24-hour bombardment and "in the dawn's early light the flag was still there." Later Ft. Jackson, on the swift-flowing Mississippi, helped save New Orleans. It presented such an obstacle to sailing warships that the attackers undertook a slow, marshy land route to approach the city. Without ship gunfire support, this ended in bloody disaster in January, 1815 (NEW ORLEANS, BATTLE OF). During Texas' struggle with Mexico in the 1830s, the defenders of the ALAMO wrote a chapter of heroism in battling to the death against overwhelming odds.

A quarter of a century later, an attack upon FT. SUMTER, a strong masonry fort opposite Ft. Moultrie, ignited the Civil War. Afterward, supported by Moultrie and several other forts, the Confederate defenders of Ft. Sumter held at bay powerful Union ironclads, an expeditionary force, and artillery emplaced ashore. Only when W. T. Sherman invested Charleston from the land did the defenders retire.

During the war the federals ringed Washington, D.C., with the largest concentration of forts any city in America has had: over 60 forts, most of earth and timber, plus batteries, blockhouses, and entrenchments. The strongest was Ft. Washington on the Potomac, a heavy masonry reconstruction of an earlier fort built after the War of 1812.

FT. FISHER, massive and unconquered for years, protected the port of Wilmington, N.C., vital to General Robert E. Lee because of supplies brought by blockade-runners. It finally fell in January, 1865, to the heavy bombardment of a great fleet and amphibious assault.

Yet in other cases ships quickly overwhelmed or ran by forts to make them untenable. This was so because in 1861 the world steered into the early stages of a portentous revolution at sea. Centuries earlier sails had freed warships from the limitations of oar propulsion. They had made possible long endurance afloat and the development of large, sturdy craft to navigate distant oceans. In combating forts, sailing ships normally enjoyed the advantage of mobility, a moving target hard to hit, and concentration of great guns in a fleet that no fort could equal. However, if wind and tide failed, the wooden hull ships could then become easy targets. Now a revolution of far-reaching import was eliminating this weakness. In the 20 years before 1861, the age of steam, iron, and rifled guns at sea began to gain headway. The effect on the future would be as potent as that from oar to sail. Nowhere would it prove more significant than in ships' increased capabilities to fight against fortifications. The independence from wind and tide that steam brought to attack from the sea gave increased speed of concentration, flexibility, and precision. Iron began to provide ships something of the stout resistance of the walls of forts. Rifled guns enabled warships to fire from longer ranges with more accuracy while themselves becoming even more difficult targets to hit. Thus the historic superiority that powerful forts had enjoyed over warships was changing. Had the Civil War broken out two decades earlier, how different the conflict would have been. Some of the great federal victories spearheaded by warships against fortifications could not have occurred.

Consider two all-important campaigns on the western rivers involving forts, where power afloat made possible giant drives that fatally severed the South. That from the north struck in February, 1862, behind hastily built semi-ironclads under Flag Officer Andrew H. Foote. Serving with General U. S. Grant in combined operations that used the rivers as swift highways, the gunboats captured poorly situated Ft. Henry on the Tennessee River in short order. This and the subsequent capture of Ft. Donelson (FTS. HENRY AND DONELSON CAMPAIGN) on the Cumberland by Grant, with Foote's support, brought catastrophe to the South. Before the forts fell, the Confederate lines extended from east Tennessee far up into Kentucky and were anchored on the Mississippi at Columbus, Gibraltar of the West. The fall of the forts was like the breaching of a dike by a wild sea. The whole Confederate line collapsed. The gunboats swiftly sped upriver spreading fire and destruction. Thousands of soldiers, vast stocks of military stores, and many cannon fell to the Union. Supported by the warships, Grant's troops plunged deep into the Confederacy. Within a few weeks a large seg-

SOME PRINCIPAL FORTS OF THE SOUTH

Name	Date Begun	Built By	Principal Material	Location
ALABAMA				
Ft. Blakely	1865	CSA	earth	Blakely (near Mobile)
Ft. Bowyer	1813	USA	earth	Mobile Point
Ft. Charlotte	1763	Br	masonry	Mobile, site of Ft. Condé
Ft. Condé de la Mobile	1711	Fr	stockade	Mobile (rebuilt of brick in 1717)
Ft. Confederacíon	1780	Sp	stockade	Jones Bluff
Ft. Confederation	1802	USA	stockade	Jones Bluff
Ft. Deposit	1814	USA	stockade	on Tennessee River
Ft. Gaines	1822	USA	masonry	Dauphin Island, Mobile Bay
Ft. Jackson	1814	USA	stockade	junction, Coosa & Tallapoosa rivers
Ft. Louis	1702	Fr	stockade	mouth of Mobile River
Ft. Mims	1812	Pi	stockade	near Montgomery
Ft. Morgan	1819	USA	masonry	east side of Mobile Point
Ft. St. Stephen's	1714	Fr	stockade	Tombigbee River–St. Stephen's
Ft. Seraf	1803	Sp	earth	Mobile Point
Old Spanish Fort	1780	Sp	earth	Spanish Fort
Ft. Stoddert	1799	USA	stockade	on Alabama River near Tombigbee River
Ft. Strother	1814	USA	stockade	on the Coosa River
Ft. Tombeckbee	1714	Fr	stockade	White Rock Bluff
Ft. Tombigbee	1735	Fr	stockade	on Coosa River
Ft. Toulouse	1714	Fr	stockade	on Coosa River near Tallapoosa River
Ft. York	1763	Br	stockade	on Coosa River near Tallapoosa River
ARKANSAS				
Fort at Arkansas Post	1686	Fr	stockade	Arkansas Post
Ft. Charles III	1763	Sp	stockade	Arkansas Post
Ft. Esperanza	1797	Sp	stockade	Arkansas Post
Ft. Hindman	1862	CSA	earth	on site of Ft. Charles III
Ft. Smith	1817	USA	stockade	Ft. Smith
DELAWARE				
Ft. Altena	1655	Du	stockade	Dutch renamed Ft. Christina
Ft. Casimir	1651	Du	stockade	New Castle
Ft. Christina	1638	Sw	stockade	Wilmington
Ft. Delaware	1814	USA	masonry	on Pea Patch Island
Ft. Du Pont	1899	USA	masonry	Delaware City
Ft. Miles	1936	USA	masonry	Cape Henlopen
Ft. Saulsbury	1896	USA	masonry	Slaughter Beach
Ft. Trefaldighet (Trinity)	1654	Sw	stockade	Swedes renamed Ft. Casimir
Ft. Union	1812	USA	earth	Wilmington
Ft. Zwaanendael	1631	Du	stockade	Lewes
FLORIDA				
Ft. Barrancas	1839	USA	masonry	Pensacola, site of Ft. San Carlos
Battery Point	1861	CSA	earth	Torreya State Park
Ft. Blount	1814	exs	stockade	Bartow (built under British direction)
Ft. Brooke	1823	USA	stockade	Tampa
Ft. Caroline	1564	Fr	stockade	St. John Bluff
Castillo de San Marcos	1672	Sp	masonry	St. Augustine
Ft. Clinch	1847	USA	masonry	on Amelia Island, Fernandina
Ft. Dade	1835	USA	stockade	near Bushnell
Ft. Fannin	1838	USA	stockade	Fannin Springs
Ft. Gadsden	1818	USA	stockade	on Apalachicola River
Ft. Gatlin	1837	USA	stockade	Orlando
Fort on George Island	1567	Sp	stockade	Ft. George Island
Ft. Harrison	1841	USA	stockade	Clearwater
Ft. Hartstuff	1838	USA	stockade	Wanchula
Ft. Jefferson	1846	USA	masonry	Dry Tortugas
Ft. Jupiter	1838	Pi	stockade	Jupiter
Ft. King	1825	USA	stockade	Ocala
Ft. Lauderdale	1838	USA	stockade	Ft. Lauderdale
Ft. McRae	1834	USA	masonry	Pensacola, Foster Bank
Ft. Maitland	1838	USA	stockade	Maitland
Ft. Marion	1825	USA	masonry	on site of Castillo de San Marcos
Martello Tower East	1861	USA	masonry	Key West
Martello Tower West	1861	USA	masonry	Key West
Ft. Mason	1837	USA	stockade	Ft. Mason
Ft. Matanzas	1736	Sp	masonry	Matanzas Inlet

Name	Date Begun	Built By	Principal Material	Location
Ft. Meade	1837	USA	stockade	Ft. Meade
Ft. Myers	1839	USA	stockade	Ft. Myers
Ft. Ogden	1841	USA	stockade	Ft. Ogden
Redoubt at Pensacola	1771	Br	earth	Pensacola
Ft. Peyton	1836	USA	stockade	Moultrie
Ft. Pierce	1838	USA	stockade	Ft. Pierce
Ft. Pickens	1834	USA	masonry	Santa Rosa Island, Pensacola
Ft. St. Francis de Pupa	1737	Sp	stockade	Green Cove Springs
Ft. St. Luis	1740	Sp	stockade	Tallahassee
Ft. St. Mark's	1763	Br	masonry	Castillo de San Marcos (Ft. San Mateo)
Ft. San Carlos	1698	Sp	masonry	Pensacola
Ft. San Carlos	1781	Sp	masonry	site of earlier Ft. San Carlos
Ft. San Carlos	1784	Sp	masonry	Fernandina
Ft. San Nicholas	1740	Sp	stockade	Jacksonville
Ft. Santa Lucia	1568	Sp	stockade	Jensen
Ft. Taylor	1844	USA	masonry	Key West
Ft. Walton	1838	USA	stockade	Ft. Walton
Ft. White	1838	USA	stockade	Ft. White

GEORGIA

Name	Date Begun	Built By	Principal Material	Location
Ft. Augusta	1736	Br	masonry	Augusta
Ft. Cornwallis	1778	Br	masonry	British name for Ft. Augusta
Ft. Defense	1790	USA	stockade	Doctortown
Ft. Delegal	1736	Br	masonry	St. Simon's Island
Ft. Edwards	1789	Pi	stockade	Watsonville
Ft. Fidius	1783	USA	stockade	Milledgeville
Ft. Frederica	1736	Br	masonry	St. Simon's Island
Ft. Gaines	1800s	Pi	stockade	Ft. Gaines
Ft. George	1761	Br	stockade	Cockspur Island, Savannah harbor
Ft. Greene	1794	USA	masonry	Cockspur Island, Savannah harbor
Ft. Grierson	1780	Br	stockade	Augusta
Ft. Hawkins	1806	USA	stockade	Ocmulgee River, Macon
Ft. Hughes	1816	USA	earth	Bainbridge
Ft. Jackson	1808	USA	masonry	Savannah
Ft. James	1797	USA	stockade	Altamaha
Ft. King George	1721	Br	stockade	Darien
Ft. McAllister	1861	CSA	earth	near Savannah
Ft. Morris	1776	USA	stockade	Sunbury
Ft. Mountain	1540	Sp	earth	Cohutta Mountain
Ft. Pulaski	1829	USA	masonry	Cockspur Island, Savannah harbor
Ft. St. Andrew	1736	Br	masonry	Cumberland Island
Ft. St. Simon	1736	Br	masonry	St. Simon's Island
Ft. Scott	1816	USA	stockade	mouth of Flint River
Ft. Screven	1898	USA	masonry	Tybee Island
Ft. Tyler	1861	CSA	earth	West Point
Ft. Walker	1864	CSA	earth	Atlanta
Ft. Wayne	1762	Br	masonry	Savannah
Ft. Wilkinson	1796	USA	stockade	Milledgeville
Ft. William	1736	Br	masonry	near Cumberland Island
Ft. Wimberly	1741	Br	masonry	Isle of Good Hope

KENTUCKY

Name	Date Begun	Built By	Principal Material	Location
Ft. Anderson	1861	USA	earth	Paducah
Boone's Fort	1775	Pi	stockade	Boonesboro
Harrod's Fort	1775	Pi	stockade	Harrodsburg
Ft. Jefferson	1779	Va	stockade	5 miles below Cairo, Ill.
Ft. Knox	1917	USA	masonry	Ft. Knox
Logan's Fort	1775	Pi	stockade	Stanford
Ft. Mitchell	1862	USA	earth	Ft. Mitchell
Ft. Nelson	1781	Va	stockade	Louisville
Ft. Thomas	1887	USA	masonry	Ft. Thomas

LOUISIANA

Name	Date Begun	Built By	Principal Material	Location
Fort at Baton Rouge	1719	Fr	stockade	Baton Rouge
Bienvenue Battery	1826	USA	masonry	Bayou Bienvenue, near New Orleans
Ft. Bourbon	1730?	Fr	masonry	Plaquemine Bend, Mississippi River
Ft. Bourgogne	1730?	Fr	masonry	New Orleans
Ft. Claiborne	1806	USA	stockade	Natchitoches
Ft. Dupres Tower	1830	USA	masonry	Bayou Dupres, near New Orleans

Name	Date Begun	Built By	Principal Material	Location
Ft. Iberville	1700	Fr	stockade	Phoenix
Ft. Jackson	1815	USA	masonry	Plaquemine Bend, Mississippi River
Ft. Jesup	1822	USA	stockade	Ft. Jesup
Ft. Livingston	1835	USA	masonry	Grand Terre Island, Barataria Bay
Ft. McComb (Wood)	1819	USA	masonry	Chef Menteur Pass, near New Orleans
Ft. Pike	1818	USA	masonry	Petites Coquilles Island
Fort at Petites Coquilles	1793	Fr	masonry	Petites Coquilles Island
Presidio de Nuestra Señora del Pillar de Los Adais	1721	Sp	masonry	Robeline
Proctor's Tower	1856	USA	masonry	Shell Beach, near New Orleans
Ft. St. Charles	1730?	Fr	masonry	New Orleans
Ft. St. Ferdinand	1730?	Fr	masonry	New Orleans
Ft. St. Jean	1730	Fr	masonry	New Orleans
Ft. St. Jean-Baptiste	1721	Fr	stockade	Natchitoches
Ft. St. John	1730?	Fr	masonry	Lake Pontchartrain
Ft. St. Leon	1730?	Fr	masonry	15 miles below English Bend
Ft. St. Louis	1730?	Fr	masonry	New Orleans
Ft. St. Philip	1795	Fr	masonry	Plaquemine Bend, Mississippi River
Ft. San Carlos	1779	Sp	masonry	Baton Rouge
MARYLAND				
Ft. Carroll	1848	USA	masonry	Sollers Point Flats, Baltimore
Cresap's Fort	1740	Pi	stockade	North Branch, Potomac River
Fort at Cumberland	1754	Br	stockade	Ft. Mount Pleasant
Ft. Federal Hill	1861	USA	earth	Baltimore
Ft. Frederick	1756	Br	masonry	Frederick
Ft. Foote	1861	USA	earth	Rosier's Bluff, opposite Alexandria, Va.
Ft. Howard	1900	USA	masonry	North Point, below Baltimore
Ft. McHenry	1794	USA	masonry	Baltimore
Ft. Madison	1808	USA	masonry	Annapolis
Ft. Severn	1808	USA	masonry	Annapolis
Ft. Warburton	1794	USA	masonry	Potomac River, near Washington
Ft. Washington	1815	USA	masonry	site of Ft. Warburton
Ft. Whetstone	1776	USA	earth	Potomac River, near Washington
MISSISSIPPI				
Ft. Adams	1798	USA	stockade	Loftus Heights, Wilkinson County
Ft. Dearborn	1802	USA	stockade	Washington
Ft. McHenry	1798	USA	stockade	Vicksburg
Ft. Massachusetts	1859	USA	masonry	Ship Island
Ft. Maurepas	1699	Fr	stockade	Biloxi
Ft. Mount Virgie (Hill)	1791	Sp	stockade	Vicksburg
Ft. Nogales	1791	Sp	stockade	Walnut Hills
Patton's Fort	1813	USA	stockade	Winchester
Ft. Pemberton	1861	CSA	earth	Greenwood
Ft. Rosalie	1716	Fr	stockade	Natchez
Ft. St. Peter	1718	Fr	stockade	on Yazoo River
MISSOURI				
Fts. A, B, C, & D	1861	USA	earth	Cape Girardeau
Ft. Bellefontaine	1805	USA	stockade	Missouri River, near St. Louis
Ft. Buffalo	1811	USA	stockade	Louisiana
Ft. Carondelet	1784	Sp	stockade	Vernon County
Ft. Clemson	1812	USA	stockade	Mineola
Cooper's Fort	1812	Pi	stockade	Boonville
Ft. Davidson	1861	USA	earth	Pilot Knob
Ft. d'Orleans	1723	Fr	stockade	Carroll County
Ft. Howard	1812	USA	stockade	mouth of Cuivre River
Ft. Juan del Misuri	1790	Sp	stockade	near Dutzow
Ft. Osage	1806	USA	stockade	Sibley
Fort at Portage des Sioux	1799	Sp	stockade	St. Charles
Ft. San Carlos	1778	Sp	stockade	St. Louis
Ft. Wyman	1861	USA	stockade	Rolla
Ft. Zumwalt	1812	USA	stockade	Ft. Zumwalt State Park
NORTH CAROLINA				
Ft. Amory	1862	USA	earth	James City
Ft. Anderson	1862	CSA	earth	Brunswick Town

Name	Date Begun	Built By	Principal Material	Location
Ft. Bragg	1922	USA	masonry	Fayetteville
Ft. Butler	1838	USA	stockade	Cherokee County
Ft. Caswell	1825	USA	masonry	on Oak Island, Cape Fear River
Ft. Clark	1861	CSA	earth	Hatteras Inlet
Ft. Dobbs	1755	Pi	stockade	near Statesville
Ft. Embree	1838	USA	stockade	Hayesville
Ft. Fisher	1861	CSA	earth	on Federal Point, mouth Cape Fear River
Ft. Granville	1753	Br	stockade	Portsmouth
Ft. Hampton	1808	USA	masonry	Bogue Island, Beaufort
Ft. Hatteras	1861	CSA	earth	Hatteras Inlet
Ft. Johnston	1764	Br	stockade	Southport
Ft. Johnston	1794	USA	masonry	site of British Ft. Johnston
Ft. Macon	1826	USA	masonry	site of Ft. Hampton
Ft. Nohoroco	1713	In	stockade	Snow Hill
Ft. Raleigh	1585	Br	stockade	Roanoke Island
Ft. Totton	1863	USA	earth	New Bern

SOUTH CAROLINA

Name	Date Begun	Built By	Principal Material	Location
Beaufort Battery	1794	USA	masonry	Beaufort
Ft. Beauregard	1861	CSA	earth	Phillips Island, near Port Royal
Ft. Charlesfort	1562	Fr	stockade	Parris Island
Ft. Charlotte	1765	Br	masonry	on Savannah River
Ft. Dearborn (Lawn)	1802	USA	masonry	Ft. Lawn
Old Ft. Dorchester	1696	Pi	masonry	near Summerville
Fort at Folly Island	1861	CSA	earth	Folly Island
Ft. Frederick	1731	Br	masonry	Cat Island
Ft. Fremont	1898	USA	masonry	St. Helena
Ft. Galpin	1760	Br	masonry	Silver Bluff
Ft. Johnson	1704	Br	masonry	James Island, Charleston
Ft. Lyttelton	1758	Br	masonry	near Beaufort
Ft. Martello Tower	1808	USA	masonry	on Sullivan's Island, Charleston
Ft. Mechanic	1794	USA	masonry	Charleston
Ft. Moultrie	1776	USA	masonry	on Sullivan's Island, Charleston
Ft. Ninety-six	1759	Br	stockade	Ninety-six
Ft. Pemberton	1861	CSA	earth	on Stone River, Charleston
Ft. Castle Pinckney	1797	USA	masonry	Charleston harbor
Ft. Prince George	1753	Br	stockade	Pickens
Ft. Randall	1861	CSA	earth	Tilghman's Point
Ft. Rutledge	1776	USA	masonry	Clemson
Ft. San Marcos	1577	Sp	stockade	Parris Island
Ft. Santa Elena	1566	Sp	stockade	Hilton Head
Ft. Starr	1780	Br	earth	Ninety-six
Ft. Sumter	1828	USA	masonry	Charleston harbor
Ft. Wagner (Battery)	1862	CSA	earth	Morris Island, near Charleston
Ft. Walker (Wells)	1861	CSA	earth	Hilton Head
Battery White	1861	CSA	earth	Georgetown
Fort at Windmill Harbor	1706	Br	stockade	Charleston

TENNESSEE

Name	Date Begun	Built By	Principal Material	Location
Ft. Adams (Pike)	1803	USA	stockade	Memphis
Ft. Assumption	1739	Fr	stockade	Memphis
Ft. Blount	1788	Pi	stockade	near Flynn's Lick
Redoubt Brannon	1863	USA	earth	Murfreesboro
Ft. Craig	1785	Pi	stockade	Maryville
Ft. Donelson	1861	CSA	earth	Dover, on Cumberland River
Gillespie's Fort	1802	Pi	masonry	Mentor
Ft. Granger	1864	USA	earth	Franklin
Ft. Henry	1861	CSA	earth	Ft. Henry, on Tennessee River
Ish's Fort	1793	Pi	stockade	near Maryville
Ft. Johnson	1862	CSA	stockade	Nashville
Ft. Loudon	1756	Br	stockade	Loudon
Ft. Nashborough	1780	Pi	stockade	Nashville
Ft. Negley	1862	USA	earth	Nashville
Old Stone Blockhouse	1788	Pi	masonry	New Providence
Old Stone Fort	1450s	In	masonry	Manchester
Ft. Patrick Henry	1775	Pi	stockade	site of Ft. Robinson
Ft. Pickering	1801	USA	stockade	Memphis

Name	Date Begun	Built By	Principal Material	Location
Ft. Pillow	1861	CSA	earth	on Mississippi River, 40 miles below Memphis
Ft. Prudhomme	1682	Fr	stockade	Henning
Ft. Robinson	1761	Pi	stockade	Kingsport
Ft. San Fernando de Las Barrancas	1795	Sp	stockade	Memphis
Ft. South Westport	1792	USA	stockade	Kingston
Ft. Union	1780	USA	stockade	Madison
Virginia Fort	1756	Pi	stockade	on Little Tennessee River
Ft. Watauga	1772	Pi	stockade	Elizabethton
White's Fort	1786	Pi	stockade	Knoxville

TEXAS

Name	Date Begun	Built By	Principal Material	Location
Ft. Alamo	1835	Tex	masonry	San Antonio
Ft. Belknap	1851	USA	stockade	on Brazos River
Ft. Bliss	1854	USA	stockade	El Paso
Old Ft. Bliss	1849	USA	stockade	Franklin
Ft. Boggy	1840	Pi	stockade	on Brazos River
Ft. Brown	1846	USA	earth	Brownsville
Ft. Chadbourne	1852	USA	stockade	on Oak Creek
Ft. Clark	1852	USA	stockade	Brackettville
Ft. Concho	1867	USA	stockade	San Angelo
Ft. Crockett	1899	USA	masonry	Galveston
Ft. Croghan	1849	USA	stockade	Burnet
Ft. Davis	1854	USA	stockade	Ft. Davis
Ft. Duncan	1849	USA	stockade	on Rio Grande at Eagle Pass
Ft. Ewell	1852	USA	stockade	on Nueces River
Ft. Gates	1849	USA	stockade	Gatesville
Ft. Graham	1849	USA	stockade	south of Blum, Hill County
Ft. Griffin	1867	USA	stockade	Ft. Griffin
Ft. Houston	1837	Tex	stockade	near Palestine
Ft. Inge	1849	USA	stockade	on Leona River, Uvalde County
Ft. Jackson	1861	CSA	earth	Galveston
Kenney's Fort	1839	Tex	stockade	near Round Rock
Ft. Lancaster	1855	USA	stockade	on Pecos River, Crockett County
Ft. Leaton	1846	Pi	stockade	on Rio Grande
Ft. Lincoln	1849	USA	stockade	north of D'Hanis, Medina County
Ft. McIntosh	1848	USA	stockade	Laredo
Ft. McKavett	1852	USA	stockade	McKavett
Ft. Martin Scott	1849	USA	stockade	south of Fredericksburg, Gillespie County
Ft. Mason	1851	USA	stockade	Mason
Ft. Merrill	1850	USA	stockade	on Nueces River
Ft. Milan	1840	Tex	stockade	on falls of Brazos River
Parker's Fort	1830	Tex	stockade	Taylor, Limestone County
Ft. Phantom Hill	1857	USA	stockade	north of Abilene, Taylor County
Ft. Point (San Jacinto)	1898	USA	masonry	Galveston
Ft. Preston	1840	Tex	stockade	near Denison
Ft. Quitman	1858	USA	stockade	on Rio Grande
Ft. Richardson	1867	USA	stockade	Jacksboro
Ft. Riley	1852	USA	stockade	Ft. Clark
Ft. Ringgold	1848	USA	stockade	Rio Grande City
Ft. St. Louis	1685	Fr	stockade	Matagorda Bay
Ft. Sam Houston	1879	USA	masonry	San Antonio
Ft. San Jacinto	1898	USA	masonry	Galveston
Ft. Stockton	1850	USA	stockade	at Comanche Springs
Ft. Terrett	1852	USA	masonry	12 miles from Roosevelt
Ft. Travis	1898	USA	masonry	at Bolivar Point, Galveston
Ft. Worth	1849	USA	stockade	Ft. Worth

VIRGINIA

Name	Date Begun	Built By	Principal Material	Location
Algernourne Fort	1609	Br	stockade	Jamestown
Boone Cabin Fort	1767	Pi	stockade	near Tazewell
Ft. Boykin	1812	USA	earth	on James River, near Richmond
Burke's Fort	1774	Pi	stockade	near Tazewell
Ft. Calhoun (Wool)	1830	USA	masonry	Hampton Roads
Ft. Charles	1644	Pi	stockade	Richmond
Ft. Chiswell	1760	Pi	stockade	Pulaski
Ft. Christanna	1714	Br	stockade	Lawrenceville
Ft. Christian	1774	Pi	stockade	near Tazewell

Name	Date Begun	Built By	Principal Material	Location
Ft. Collier	1861	CSA	earth	near Winchester
Ft. Converse	1864	USA	earth	Hopewell
Ft. Darling	1861	CSA	earth	on Drewry's Bluff, near Richmond
Ft. Davis	1864	USA	earth	before Petersburg
Ft. Defiance	1753	Pi	stockade	Milboro Springs
Ft. Dickenson	1756	Br	stockade	Milboro Springs
Ft. Dinwiddie	1755	Br	stockade	near Warm Springs
Ft. Early	1864	CSA	earth	Lynchburg
Ft. Edward Johnson	1862	CSA	earth	near Churchville
Ft. George	1727	Br	masonry	Old Point Comfort
Ft. Harrison	1861	CSA	earth	Richmond
Ft. Henry	1646	Pi	masonry	Petersburg
Ft. Hoke	1861	CSA	earth	Richmond
Hood's Fort (Powhatan)	1776	USA	masonry	Little Brandon
Ft. Hunt	1898	USA	masonry	on Potomac River, opposite Ft. Washington
Hupp's Fort	1755	Pi	masonry	Strasburg
Ft. Lewis	1758	Br	stockade	Ft. Lewis Mountain
Ft. Lewis	1759	Pi	stockade	Bath Alum Springs
Ft. Loundoun	1756	Br	earth	Winchester
Ft. Mahone	1861	CSA	earth	Petersburg
Martin's Fort	1768	Pi	stockade	Rose Hill
Ft. Monroe	1819	USA	masonry	Hampton Roads
Ft. Nelson	1794	USA	masonry	Norfolk
Ft. Norfolk	1794	USA	masonry	Norfolk harbor
Ft. Patrick Kelly	1864	USA	earth	Petersburg
Ft. Powhatan	1776	USA	masonry	Little Brandon
Russell's Fort	1774	Pi	stockade	Dickensonville
Ft. Sedgewick	1864	USA	earth	Petersburg
Smith's Fort	1609	Br	stockade	Surry
Ft. Star	1862	USA	earth	Petersburg
Ft. Stedman	1864	USA	earth	Petersburg
Ft. Story	1840	USA	masonry	Hampton Roads
Ft. Wadsworth	1864	USA	earth	Petersburg
Ft. West	1609	Br	stockade	Richmond
Ft. Witten	1767	Pi	masonry	near Tazewell
Wynne's Fort	1772	Pi	masonry	near Tazewell

WEST VIRGINIA

Name	Date Begun	Built By	Principal Material	Location
Ft. Ashby	1755	Pi	stockade	Ft. Ashby
Ft. Beech Bottom	1775	Pi	stockade	Beech Bottom
Beeler Station	1779	Pi	stockade	near Cameron
Ft. Boreman	1863	USA	earth	Parkersburg
Bush's Fort	1773	Pi	stockade	Buckhannon
Ft. Buttermilk	1756	Pi	stockade	near Old Fields
Ft. Chapman	1784	Pi	stockade	New Cumberland
Cook's Fort	1770	Pi	stockade	near Greenville
Ft. Currence	1774	Pi	stockade	Mill Creek
Ft. Donnally	1771	Pi	stockade	near Richland
Ft. Edwards	1750	Br	stockade	Capon Bridge
Ft. Evans	1755	Pi	stockade	Big Spring
Ft. Green Bryer	1755	Br	stockade	Marlinton
Ft. Hadden	1774	Pi	stockade	Elkwater
Ft. Henry	1774	Br	stockade	Wheeling
Ft. Hinkle	1761	Pi	stockade	Riverton
Kelly's Fort	1774	Pi	stockade	Cedar Grove
Ft. Lee	1788	Br	stockade	Charleston
McIntire's Blockhouse	1773	Pi	stockade	Enterprise
Ft. Martin	1773	Pi	stockade	near Maidsville
Ft. Milroy	1862	USA	earth	White Top Mountain
Ft. Neal	1785	Pi	stockade	Parkersburg
Nutter's Fort	1772	Pi	stockade	Nutter's Fort
Ft. Ogden	1755	Br	stockade	Allegheny Front
Ft. Ohio	1749	Pi	stockade	Ridgeley
Ft. Pearsall	1753	Pi	stockade	Romney
Ft. Pierpont	1769	Pi	stockade	Morgantown
Ft. Pleasant	1756	Pi	stockade	Old Fields
Ft. Randolf	1774	Pi	stockade	mouth of Great Kanawha River

Name	Date Begun	Built By	Principal Material	Location
Ft. Richards (Lowthar's)	1774	Pi	stockade	Clarksburg
Ft. Seybert	1758	Pi	stockade	Oak Flat
Ft. Shepherd	1777	Pi	stockade	Middle Wheeling Creek
Ft. Statlers	1770	Pi	stockade	Core
Ft. Tackett	1787	Pi	stockade	St. Albans
Ft. Van Meter	1774	Pi	stockade	Short Creek
Ft. Warder	1758	Pi	stockade	Wardensville
West's Fort	1770	Pi	stockade	Jane Lew
Wilson's Fort	1774	Pi	stockade	Elkins

KEY British=Br, French=Fr, Spanish=Sp, Dutch=Du, Swedish=Sw, Indian=In, Pioneer=Pi, ex-slave=exs, Virginia=Va, United States=USA, Confederacy=CSA, Texas=Tex

NOTE: Every effort has been made to assure the accuracy of the information in this table, but sources often do not agree. This confusion occurs for a variety of reasons, most frequently because many forts were planned for a particular time but were not built immediately; or they were built and at a later date rebuilt, often by another nation. An attempt has been made here to indicate the correct information at the time construction was actually started on each fort. (Table compiled by the editors.)

ment of the South's territory, population, and resources was lost.

Two months later a Union fleet struck up the Mississippi. Flag Officer DAVID FARRAGUT achieved the seemingly impossible. With seagoing wooden warships he ran past Fts. Jackson and St. Philip, mounting a hundred guns. Surging on upriver, he captured the South's largest and richest city, New Orleans, with a handful of ships manned by under 3,000 men. This was the South's principal port and principal hope for overseas commerce to feed the ravenous hunger of war. The disasters on the Mississippi marked the beginning of the end for the Confederacy.

The great era of building forts in the United States ended with the Civil War. The Spanish-American War caused a brief flurry that led to the construction of a few in the South, such as Ft. Hunt in Virginia.

Developments in range and power of weapons have caused forts as separate strongholds to become obsolete. The United States has properly come to depend upon the navy as a distant first line of defense against attack on its coasts. Backing up the first line are air force aircraft and army guided missiles. In the twentieth century older forts have tended to become historic relics, such as revered Ft. McHenry. Numerous other "forts" by name still exist. Most forts, however, are army posts used as education, training, experimental work, or administration centers. Ft. McNair in Washington, D.C., houses several educational activities, including the prestigious National War College.

Now that the United States has allowed the Soviets to forge ahead in most elements of seapower, the situation is different and most dangerous. Should our country ever sink to the disastrous weakness of having to defend itself against assaults on its coast, it is possible, but unlikely, that

forts would play a key role in the last desperate struggle.

See V. Dabney, *Virginia* (1971); *Official Records, Armies*; *Official Records, Navies*; Navy Department, *Civil War Naval Chronology* (1971); D. H. Mahan, *Treatise on Field Fortifications* (1861); V. E. R. K. von Schelike, *Treatise on Coast Defense* (1868); and individual fort brochures.

E. M. ELLER
U.S. Navy

FTS. HENRY AND DONELSON CAMPAIGN

(1862). Fts. Henry and Donelson, located in northern Tennessee, guarded two important natural arteries into the western Confederacy: the Tennessee and Cumberland rivers. Commanded by Lloyd Tilghman, the two works were manned by about 5,000 soldiers.

On February 6, 1862, Andrew H. Foote's Union naval flotilla attacked Ft. Henry, and after a three-hour artillery duel Tilghman surrendered the position. The Confederate departmental commander, ALBERT SIDNEY JOHNSTON, now abandoned his fortifications at Bowling Green, Ky., and withdrew south to form a new line below the Tennessee River. He ordered an additional 13,000 or more men into Ft. Donelson. The senior officer here became Brigadier General JOHN B. FLOYD; his chief subordinates were Brigadier Generals GIDEON PILLOW and SIMON BOLIVAR BUCKNER, in that order of rank.

On February 12, the Union movement against Ft. Donelson began. Two days later the defenders repulsed Foote's gunboats in a spirited artillery contest. Meanwhile, U. S. Grant laid siege to the position with about 15,000 men. A Confederate counterattack before daybreak on the fifteenth momentarily defeated a portion of the investing force and opened the road to Nashville. But instead of attempting to escape as originally ordered and as now urged by Buckner, Floyd yielded to Pillow's importunities to continue the defense.

This decision doomed the garrison. At first elated over their success, the Confederate generals soon became demoralized by the knowledge that Grant was being steadily reinforced. That night they decided to surrender without further resistance. After staging a travesty of military protocol by passing the command successively to Buckner, the two senior generals abandoned the fort and its defenders. Floyd took out his Virginia troops, about 1,000, by steamer to Nashville, and Pillow and his staff escaped by crossing the river in a small boat. A then obscure cavalry colonel, NATHAN BEDFORD FORREST, led his command and a few other soldiers to freedom through the icy backwaters. At dawn the hapless Buckner acceded to Grant's demand for unconditional surrender.

The loss of Fts. Henry and Donelson exposed the western Confederacy to invasion. The loss of troops in Ft. Donelson critically weakened the Confederate army in the showdown at SHILOH almost two months later.

See *Official Records, Armies*, Ser. 1, Vols. IV, VII; W. P. Johnston, *Albert Sidney Johnston* (1880); C. P. Roland, *Albert Sidney Johnston* (1964) and *Journal of Southern History* (Feb., 1957); T. H. Williams, *P. G. T. Beauregard* (1954); T. L. Connelly, *Army of Heartland* (1967); and S. Horn, *Army of Tennessee* (1941).

CHARLES P. ROLAND
University of Kentucky

FT. SMITH, ARK. (pop. 62,802), located on the Arkansas River along the Oklahoma state line, was established in 1817 as a military outpost intended to separate the warring OSAGE and CHEROKEE Indians from one another. Construction of a permanent fort here was never completed, but the town that developed around the old outpost became an important transportation center. Gold-hungry forty-niners came upriver, equipped themselves at Ft. Smith, and then set out for California. The city was a major terminal for the overland stage and, in the 1870s and 1880s, it became a regional rail center. Although it changed hands several times during the Civil War, no major battles occurred here. What violence Ft. Smith knew resulted instead from the assorted bandits, gamblers, rowdies, and toughs who came to or through this city. Federal Judge Isaac C. Parker, the "Hanging Judge," was sent to Ft. Smith in 1875 to establish order. Assisted by as many as 200 U.S. deputy marshals, Judge Parker sentenced 151 men to the gallows during his 21-year tenure on the bench. Today Ft. Smith is Arkansas' second-largest city and its leading manufacturing center. More than 250

plants produce a diversity of goods including furniture, textiles, glass, bricks, smelted zinc, electric stoves, wood pulp and paper, tin cans, bedding, petroleum products, and natural gas.

See W. J. Butler, *Fort Smith* (1972); R. Mapes, *Old Fort Smith* (1965); E. C. Bearss, *Little Gibraltar* (1969); and C. Dollar, *First Fort Smith Report* (1966). The Arkansas Collection of the Ft. Smith Public Library maintains special collection of books on city and state history. *Southwest Times Record* (1882–), an independent Democratic daily, is on microfilm.

FT. STEDMAN, BATTLE OF (March 25, 1865). By mid-March Robert E. Lee had 55,000 tired, ill-fed, and poorly supplied troops in Richmond and Petersburg facing a force of about 150,000 well-fed and equipped northerners. In council with Jefferson Davis, he decided to attack U. S. Grant before withdrawing to join JOSEPH E. JOHNSTON in North Carolina. Lee picked Union Ft. Stedman, a strong point on the Union right, east of Petersburg and 150 yards from a Confederate position named Colquitt's Salient. If the Union line could be broken, Grant would be forced to move troops from his left, opening the way for Lee's withdrawal. JOHN B. GORDON was to direct the attack. The obstructions before the salient were removed, and 50 axmen opened paths in front of Stedman. At 4:00 A.M. three 100-man Confederate columns captured Stedman and breached the Union line. Additional Confederates poured through and advanced as far as Harrison's Creek, 650 yards behind Stedman. When federal forces counterattacked, the Confederates ran a murderous cross fire returning to their line. Lee lost over 4,000 killed, wounded, and missing; Grant, less than 1,500. Lee had no alternative but retreat.

See D. Freeman, *Lee's Lieutenants* (1942–44); J. B. Gordon, *Reminiscences* (1903); and U. S. Grant, *Personal Memoirs* (1885–86).

RICHARD W. LYKES
University of Virginia, Northern Regional Center, and
George Mason University

FT. SUMTER, built on the shoal opposite Ft. Moultrie to protect Charleston, S.C., by subjecting its ship channel to cross fire, was begun in the winter of 1828–1829. It was an imposing pentagon with five-foot-thick brick walls resting on a granite foundation and rising 50 feet above low water. Only 15 of Sumter's 135 projected guns were mounted, however, on December 26, 1860, when Major ROBERT ANDERSON abandoned Ft. Moultrie and secured his 85 men with four months' provisions in Sumter. Over the next few months he mounted 45 additional guns. After South Carolina on January 9, 1861, prevented James Buchanan's attempt to reinforce Sumter, the federal government did little until Abraham Lincoln resolved on April 4 to provision but not reinforce the fort. Lincoln made certain that if war came the Confederates would start it by firing on "bread." The Confederate government authorized General P. G. T. BEAUREGARD on April 10 to attack Sumter if it were not abandoned. When Anderson refused to evacuate the fort, Beauregard commenced the Civil War by bombarding Sumter at 4:30 A.M. on April 12. The firing continued for 33 hours until Anderson agreed on April 13 to evacuate. The Union failed repeatedly in 1863 and 1864 to capture the fort but succeeded in smashing it to rubble. The Confederates abandoned Sumter on February 17 and 18, 1865, and on April 14, 1865, only hours before Lincoln's assassination, Anderson raised above Ft. Sumter the identical flag he had lowered four years earlier.

See W. A. Swanberg, *First Blood* (1957); R. N. Current, *Lincoln and First Shot* (1963); K. M. Stampp, *And War Came* (1950); D. M. Potter, *Lincoln and Party in Secession Crisis* (1942); J. G. Randall, *Lincoln, Liberal Statesman* (1947); C. W. Ramsdell, *Journal of Southern History* (Aug., 1937); L. H. Johnson, *Journal of Southern History* (Nov., 1960); and A. Hoogenboom, *Civil War History* (Dec., 1963).

ARI HOOGENBOOM
Brooklyn College, City University of New York

FORTUNE, TIMOTHY THOMAS (1856–1928), a noted black newspaper editor and publicist, was born a slave in Marianna, Fla. Between 1872 and 1880 Fortune worked for several newspapers including the Jacksonville *Union* (later the *Courier*), the *People's Advocate* of Washington (1877). and the *Weekly Witness* in New York City. He spent two years (1875–1877) at Howard University before returning to Florida in 1879 to teach school. In 1880 he edited the weekly *Rumor* in New York with George Parker and William W. Simpson. The name was changed to the *Globe* (1881), which the three men edited together until 1884, when disagreements dissolved the partnership and Fortune established the New York *Freeman*. He later gave up sole ownership to work for the New York *Evening Sun*, a leading white newspaper. The name of the *Freeman* was changed to the New York *Age*, and ownership was shared with Jerome Peterson. Fortune continued to edit the *Age* until 1907. After 1907 he was associated with a number of newspapers, either as editor or contributor, including editing Marcus Garvey's *Negro World* from 1923 to his death. He was a brilliant, pointed, and often aggressive writer, and

his outspoken criticism occasioned frequent conflicts with both Republican and Democratic administrations. Fortune also published books and pamphlets on black constitutional rights and assisted in establishing the NATIONAL AFRO-AMERICAN LEAGUE (1887) as an equal rights association that antedated the Niagara movement (1905) and the NATIONAL ASSOCIATION FOR THE ADVANCEMENT OF COLORED PEOPLE (1909).

See E. L. Thornbrough, *T. Thomas Fortune* (1972); I. G. Penn, *Afro-American Press* (1891); and A. Meier, *Negro Thought* (1963).

JAMES E. HANEY
Tennessee State University

FT. WORTH, TEX. (pop. 393,476), is approximately 30 miles west of Dallas at the confluence of the forks of the Trinity River. Four years after the site's settlement in 1843, a military camp was established here to keep watch on area Indians. The town became an important supply point for cattle drivers immediately after the Civil War and, after completion of a rail line in the 1870s, a major meat-packing center. Although the city remains a livestock market of national significance to this day, its economic base has grown increasingly diversified throughout the current century. Development of the fertile prairie land east of the city has made it one of the nation's principal grain markets; the discovery of petroleum in 1912 has led to construction of a massive complex of pipelines and oil refineries; and the dredging of the Trinity River begun in 1965 promises to make it an inland seaport. TEXAS CHRISTIAN UNIVERSITY, Southwestern Baptist Theological Seminary (1905), and Wesleyan College (1891) are all located here.

See O. Knight, *Fort Worth* (1953); B. B. Paddock (ed.), *Fort Worth* (4 vols.; 1922); S. L. Myres, *Southwestern Historical Quarterly* (Oct., 1968); and files of Ft. Worth *Herald* (1855–81), *News* (1861–66), *Express* (1865–1920), *Correro Mexicano* (1891–1915), *Evening News* (1918–), and *Star Telegram* (1909–), all on microfilm.

FORTY ACRES AND A MULE was a phrase popularly used in the post–Civil War era to describe the idea that the national government was going to give land to the freedmen, presumably by expropriating it from their former masters. During the war the government acquired about 800,000 acres that had been "abandoned" by Confederates. It was turned over to the FREEDMEN'S BUREAU with the charge that blacks be settled on it, but most of it was later returned to its original owners by President ANDREW JOHNSON. As the debate over Reconstruction accelerated, a few congressmen, notably Thaddeus Stevens, argued that land should be taken from the planters and given to the freedmen in 40-acre plots. Because of the charge to the bureau, the speeches of congressmen, and reports circulated by black soldiers who had seen a few freedmen farming abandoned lands in the Sea Islands during the war, the rumors of "forty acres and a mule" spread across the South. Believing that the division was to be made on Christmas, 1865, some blacks were reluctant to make labor contracts. Anxious whites feared that an uprising was about to occur. When Christmas passed without notable incident, the blacks went back to the fields as laborers in 1866. Few blacks ever received any land but the phrase endured.

See G. R. Bentley, *Freedmen's Bureau* (1955); W. S. McFeely, *Yankee Stepfather* (1968); J. H. Franklin, *From Slavery to Freedom* (1947); and bibliography in J. G. Randall and D. Donald, *Civil War and Reconstruction* (1961).

JERRELL H. SHOFNER
Florida Technological University

FOSTER, STEPHEN COLLINS (1826–1864), was born in Lawrenceville, Pa. His formal musical training was slight. He was acquainted with the touring minstrel shows and at seventeen wrote his first published song, "Open Thy Lattice Love," typical of his parlor ballads. He achieved his greatest fame writing tunes for the minstrel stage (MINSTRELSY). For a time Foster even allowed the noted E. P. Christy to claim authorship of the numbers his troupe performed, since the writer himself was reluctant to associate his name with "the Ethiopian business."

His songs for the stage include "Old Folks at Home," "O Susannah," "De Camptown Races," "My Old Kentucky Home," and "Old Black Joe"; "I Dream of Jeanie with the Light Brown Hair" and "Beautiful Dreamer" are among his best love songs. Although many of Foster's tunes deal with southern plantation life, he visited the South only once briefly. Earlier he had spent two years in Cincinnati as a bookkeeper and doubtlessly heard much of the lore that wafted across the river from Kentucky. The name "Swanee River" was used for "Old Folks at Home" because it sounded more lyrical than the "Pedee" he originally intended. Curiously enough, Foster's plantation songs are his most honest, for he transferred his own sadness and his nostalgia for the paternal home he never emotionally left to a southern setting. Certainly the negroid element in his work is scant, essentially shaped by stereotyped notions of the Negro character. A poor businessman, Foster ended his life in poverty. At the time of his death he was living in New York City, separated from his wife and daughter, suffering from alcoholism and prolonged despair.

See J. T. Howard *Stephen Foster* (1953); E. F. Morneweck, *Chronicles of S. Foster's Family* (1944); F. Hodges, *Swanee River and a Biographical Sketch of Foster* (1958); and R. C. Toll, *Blacking Up* (1974).

RONALD L. DAVIS
Southern Methodist University

FOUNDATIONS FOR SOUTHERN HISTORY. Foundations are private, nonprofit organizations devoted to channeling their wealth into socially useful projects. Although they have roots in the past and have been set up in other countries, it was in the late nineteenth and early twentieth century America that they achieved their greatest number, size, and importance. The Carnegie Corporation of New York, Twentieth Century Fund, Rockefeller Foundation, John Simon Guggenheim Memorial Foundation, and Ford Foundation are a sampling of the large, national foundations created in this period. These foundations have sponsored a wide range of educational activities in the South including financial support for research and writing in southern history. The Guggenheim Foundation, for example, has consistently supplied fellowships for research and writing in this area, resulting in the publication of such outstanding works as FRANK L. OWSLEY's *King Cotton Diplomacy*. In addition, a number of these foundations have, over the years, provided grants to various councils, such as the American Council of Learned Societies and the Social Science Research Council, which have and are conducting similar aid programs and projects. More recently, the U.S. government's National Endowment for the Humanities, although a public agency, has embarked on a wide-ranging foundation type of support for the humanities, which includes aid in the area of southern history.

Regionally and locally, there are a considerable number of foundations, indigenous to the South, that have sponsored important work in the field of southern history. Various projects conducted by the (Virginia) Colonial Williamsburg Foundation and the (Alabama) David Warner Foundation Trust's subvention for Hudson Strode's biography of Jefferson Davis are significant examples. Also, many of the major southern colleges and universities have ancillary foundations that have been aid sources for southern historical scholarship. The Littlefield Fund of the University of Texas, for example, aided in the publication of the ten-volumed *History of the South* by the Louisiana State University Press. Although the national foundations and councils are more highly publicized sources of aid, those seeking financial support for research and writing in southern history should give increased attention to this growing number of regional and local foundations.

See *Foundation Directory* (5th ed.; 1975); *Foundation Grants Index* (bimonthly); and *Foundation News* (bimonthly), published by Council on Foundations and Foundation Center, 888 Seventh Ave., New York, N.Y. The center is leading depository of information on foundations, and it has established regional branches and reference collections throughout the U.S., which are listed in *Foundation Directory*. See also F. E. Andrews, *Philanthropic Foundations* (1956), excellent general account; and J. C. Kiger, *Operating Principles of Larger Foundations* (1953) and *Journal of Higher Education* (March, 1956).

JOSEPH C. KIGER
University of Mississippi

FOURTEENTH AMENDMENT (1868). Originating in the abolitionist doctrine that the federal government had the power and responsibility to protect civil rights from abridgement by the states, this constitutional amendment declared: "All persons born or naturalized in the United States . . . are citizens of the United States and of the State wherein they reside. No State shall abridge the privileges or immunities of citizens of the United States; nor . . . deprive any person of life, liberty, or property, without due process of law; nor deny to any person within its jurisdiction the equal protection of the laws." In addition, it presented a plan for the restoration of the South to the Union requiring: (1) representation in Congress based on population, though states disfranchising blacks would have membership proportionately reduced; (2) disfranchisement of former Confederates who had sworn an official oath to uphold the United States Constitution, but then had rebelled or aided in rebellion; (3) repudiation of the Confederate debt; and (4) enforcement through appropriate legislation by Congress.

Although the amendment was not fully acceptable to any member of the Joint Committee on Reconstruction and although it was offered as a compromise measure requiring neither universal Negro suffrage nor unconditional amnesty, southern whites soon mounted a campaign to thwart ratification. Encouraged by President Andrew Johnson, they argued that the article provided no guarantees for readmission, conferred unlimited power on Congress, disfranchised the best leaders in the South, and was "a nefarious conspiracy to transfer . . . the government of these states from the white race to negroes." Terming the proposal "unwise," "unjust," "un-constitutional," and "unacceptable," the southern provisional governments established by President Johnson rejected it almost without debate. Such intransigence prompted an increasingly radical Congress to demand military supervision of new elections and the universal enfranchisement of blacks. Under this pressure, all but four southern states officially ratified the amendment. It was adopted July 28, 1868; afterward the remaining states added their consent.

Despite the ringing phrases concerning equal rights and despite the efforts by Congress to protect freedmen, the amendment quickly became dormant in the South. Whites soon mounted a campaign of violence, intimidation, and economic coercion to strip blacks of their newly acquired citizenship rights (DISFRANCHISEMENT). And in 1882 Roscoe Conkling, who had helped draft the article, argued convincingly though erroneously before the U.S. Supreme Court that the framers had intended the word *persons* also to mean *corporations*. The Court then struck down civil rights laws, desegregation statutes, and the equal protection clause, thereby paving the way for southern JIM CROW laws and for systematic, legalized discrimination against Negroes. In recent years, however, the Court has overturned these discriminatory statutes and has reasserted the original principles of the amendment, declaring that individual states have the responsibility to protect the life, liberty, and property of all citizens, whether white or black.

See R. Bardolph, *Civil Rights Record* (1970); H. E. Flack, *Adoption of Fourteenth Amendment* (1908); J. B. James, *Journal of Southern History* (Nov., 1956); A. Kelly, *American Historical Review* (April, 1959); L. Levy (ed.), *Fourteenth Amendment* (1970); B. Nelson, *Fourteenth Amendment and Negro* (1946); J. Ten Broek, *Antislavery Origins* (1951); T. Emerson, D. Haber, and N. Dorsen (eds.), *Political and Civil Rights* (2 vols.; 1967), best documents source; and H. Graham, *Everyman's Constitution* (1968), excellent essay collection.

LOREN SCHWENINGER
University of North Carolina, Greensboro

FOX HUNTING. Native foxes and wolves were hunted as predators and for sport by colonial Americans afoot or astride a horse and accompanied by mongrel dogs in seventeenth-century Maryland and Virginia. As colonial planters grew wealthy, they sought to imitate the formalized hunts of the English gentry. They imported English foxes, thoroughbred horses, and dogs.

Fox hunting flourished where there was enough open ground for hard, cross-country riding. It became the favorite sport of the pleasure-pursuing southerner, combining his love of horses and hounds and the out-of-doors with his desire for good fellowship. The hunt might begin with an "eye-opener" and end with "a night's debauch." After a chase near Charleston in 1761, a Carolinian wrote, "We spent the afternoon very merry, after killing two foxes." Typical of the southern revolutionary elite who rode to hounds were Thomas Jefferson and George Washington. Between 1760 and 1774 Washington hunted foxes on more than 200 occasions. Although most colonial fox hunters wore no prescribed costume, Washington hunted in an imported blue coat and scarlet waistcoat.

By the early nineteenth century, enthusiasts of the chase were the new-rich of the southwestward-spreading cotton kingdom. New hunt clubs were formed, sporting magazines promoted the sport, and fox hunting became one of the trappings of the southern chivalric cult. In 1859 a South Carolinian predicted that if war came an excellent cavalry corps could be formed from the South's fox hunters. Four years later a sporting editor of Upson County, Ga., averred: "Hunting is what makes the true Southern gentleman . . . and soldier."

Due to the economic impact of the Civil War on the South, the scattering of packs of hounds, and the killing or carrying off of the best horses, formalized fox hunting declined sharply. However, in the late nineteenth century, northeastern sportsmen and sportswomen who came South to hunt and a returning prosperity rekindled interest in the more ceremonious fox hunt. And into the twentieth century, whether afoot fox hunting by moonlight with "a dawg or two" or astride a blooded horse and dressed in the habit of an elite hunt club, southerners continued to hunt for many of the same reasons as in earlier times.

See J. B. van Urk, *American Foxhunting* (1940–41); K. Slater, *Hunt Country* (1967); R. G. Osterweis, *Romanticism and Nationalism* (1949); C. Bridenbaugh, *Myths and Realities* (1952); W. H. Gaines, Jr., *Virginia Cavalcade* (Autumn, 1953); and W. Pafford, *Emory University Publications* (Feb., 1955).

WALTER J. FRASER, JR.
The Citadel

FRANCIS, DAVID ROWLAND

FRANCIS, DAVID ROWLAND (1850–1927), a businessman in politics, is representative of the post–Civil War generation of urban politicians who came to power in the 1880s and 1890s. Born in Kentucky, Francis moved to St. Louis in 1866 to complete his education. He entered his uncle's grain commission business, established the D. R. Francis Company in 1877, and attracted Democratic party leaders' attention by his unprecedented election, at age thirty-four, to the presidency of the Merchants' Exchange. He entered politics, becoming mayor of St. Louis (1885–1889) and gov-

ernor of Missouri (1889–1893). His administrations were noted for the introduction of efficient management techniques. He succeeded in reducing the cost of natural gas while mayor, and twice reduced taxes while governor. Francis was rewarded for his unflagging support of Grover Cleveland by an appointment as secretary of the interior (1896–1897). But his political conservatism deprived him of election to the Senate by agrarian Missouri. Francis organized and promoted the St. Louis world's fair (1904). After two unhappy years as ambassador to Russia (1916–1918), he retired from public life.

See W. B. Stevens, *Missouri Historical Review* (April, 1919); D. R. Francis, *Universal Exposition of 1904 (1913) and Russia from American Embassy* (1921); and D. R. Francis Papers, Missouri Historical Society, St. Louis.

GEOFFREY F. MORRISON
Clayton High School, Clayton, Mo.

FRANK, LEO, CASE. Leo Max Frank (1884–1915) was born in Paris, Tex., but moved at an early age to Brooklyn, N.Y. At the invitation of an uncle, Frank moved to Atlanta and became superintendent of the newly formed National Pencil Factory. He was prominent in the Jewish community in that city. In 1913 Mary Phagan, a thirteen-year-old employee of the factory, was brutally murdered in the building, and Frank was accused of the crime. The evidence against him was weak, but a strong public clamor for punishment and the rabid and sensational stories in the press led to his conviction. Frank was sentenced to death by hanging. Concerned citizens in Georgia and throughout the nation condemned the proceedings against him as a travesty of justice. Nevertheless, appeals to the Georgia supreme court and the U.S. Supreme Court brought no relief. Convinced that Frank was not fairly tried and that strong doubt existed as to his guilt, Governor John Slaton commuted Frank's sentence to life imprisonment. Much of the population was enraged by the governor's decision. State troops were necessary to protect Slaton until he could leave the state for an extended tour. In August, 1915, a well-organized mob broke into the penitentiary at Milledgeville, transported Frank across the state to a site near the home of Mary Phagan at Marietta, and hanged him from a tree. The case against Frank and his subsequent LYNCHING smacked heavily of anti-Semitism. Politically, several men rode to high office on the issue. THOMAS E. WATSON, a violent anti-Semite, was elected to the U.S. Senate, and Hugh Dorsey, the prosecutor, became governor of Georgia. John Slaton's political career was wrecked as a result of his commutation.

See L. Dinnerstein, *Leo Frank Case* (1968); C. Moseley, *Georgia Historical Quarterly* (March, 1967); W. C. Rogers, "Coverage of Frank Case" (M.A. thesis, University of Georgia, 1950); C. V. Woodward, *Tom Watson* (1938); N. E. Harris, *Autobiography* (1925); W. E. Thompson, *Short Review of Frank Case* (1914); H. Alexander, *Murder Notes in Frank Case* (1914); C. P. Connolly, *Truth About Frank Case* (1915); and H. Golden, *Little Girl Is Dead* (1965).

C. CHARLTON MOSELEY
Georgia Southern College

FRANKFORT, KY. (pop. 21,356), has been the state's capital since admission in 1792 to the Union. Located astride the Kentucky River approximately 50 miles east of Louisville, the site was surveyed in 1773 by order of Virginia's governor, Lord Dunmore. Thirteen years later, General JAMES WILKINSON formally organized the town and named it after a pioneer who had been slain by Indians. Early Frankfort prospered both as a seat of government and as a river port (with rail connections after 1835). It was a major shipping point for BOURBON whiskey. In the fall of 1862, General Braxton Bragg occupied the city and installed in office a provisional Confederate government. After the battle of PERRYVILLE, however, Confederate military and political forces withdrew from the city. Modern Frankfort is the site of Kentucky State University (1886), numerous antebellum homes, and the Old State Capitol (1827–1830). It is a major commercial market for tobacco, dairy, and livestock producers in the BLUEGRASS area and a center for distilleries and limestone quarries.

See L. F. Johnson, *Franklin County* (1912), most complete; W. R. Jillson, *Early Frankfort* (1936); A. E. Trabue, *Corner in Celebrities* (1958); M. W. Woodson, *Register of Kentucky Historical Society* (July, 1963); and A. Beckley, *Register of Kentucky Historical Society* (Oct., 1962).

FRANKFORT ARGUS OF WESTERN AMERICA (1806–1838). Joseph M. Street served as the early publisher of this weekly newspaper, located at the site of the capitol. His successors included William Gerrard, Moses G. Bledsoe, and Elijah C. Berry. The staunch supporters of Andrew Jackson were Amos Kendall, from 1816 to 1830, and Francis P. Blair, Sr., beginning in 1829. R. A. Ferguson served as editor in 1835.

See microfilm in Kentucky Historical Society, Frankfort; University of Kentucky Library; and University of California Library, Berkeley.

DWIGHT MIKKELSON
Taylor University

FRANKFORT COMMONWEALTH (1833–1872). A. G. Hodges owned this publication through its extended career, and Orlando Brown served as editor from its inception until 1842. Brown was a devoted Whig who focused primary attention upon national issues and more limited attention upon state politics and foreign affairs. With the rise of the Republican party, subsequent editors (Thomas M. Green, J. H. Johnson, Henri Middleton, and Samuel R. Smith) waved the party banner. The *Commonwealth* at different times was a weekly, semiweekly, tri-weekly, and daily.

See C. E. Duesner, "Brown: Whig Editor of Kentucky" (Ph.D. dissertation, University of Kentucky, 1962); and bound volumes, University of Kentucky Library and Kentucky Historical Society, Frankfort.

DWIGHT MIKKELSON
Taylor University

FRANKLIN, JOHN HOPE (1915–), is perhaps the most universally honored black historian now alive. The Oklahoma native received his A.B. degree from Fisk University and the M.A. and Ph.D. degrees from Harvard. His regular teaching posts include Fisk, Howard, Brooklyn College, and his present position at the University of Chicago. He has been honored with numerous foundation research grants, the presidencies of the Southern Historical Association and the Organization of American Historians, three dozen honorary degrees, and visiting professorships at numerous universities.

Most of Franklin's books and articles deal with black history or southern themes. *From Slavery to Freedom* (1947; 4th ed., 1974) is the most highly respected one-volumed general history of Afro-Americans. *The Militant South, 1800–1861* (1956) presents a major interpretation. Franklin asserts that the South was dominated by militant white men with a predilection for violence nourished by their defense of slavery. This violent militance helped make secession possible and has dramatic manifestations in more recent eras of southern history.

Franklin makes a significant contribution to historiography in *Reconstruction After the Civil War* (1963). Although reinforcing the older Beard-Beale economic interpretation, he places strong emphasis on black participation, though not domination, in Reconstruction politics. The main flaw in the Reconstruction process was the failure of the nation to enable freedmen to develop economic independence. This is in strong contrast to the traditional Dunning interpretation (W. A. DUNNING). Other major works by Franklin are *Free*

Negro in North Carolina, 1790–1860 (1943) and *Emancipation Proclamation* (1963).

ROBERT J. MOORE
Columbia College, Columbia, S.C.

FRANKLIN, BATTLE OF (November 30, 1864), one of the bloodiest of the Civil War, was part of the panorama of retreat from Atlanta to Nashville by the Confederate Army of Tennessee under JOHN B. HOOD. Hood had served gallantly, yet this battle must represent a failure of command. He allowed the federal forces under John M. Schofield to slip away in the night from Spring Hill and thus establish itself at Franklin, Tenn., interposing its force between Hood and Nashville. This mistake evidently distorted Hood's judgment for, ignoring the advice of his staff members, including N. B. FORREST, he threw his total force of some 20,000 men in a frontal assault against well-entrenched federal lines at Franklin. Moreover, this was done without substantial artillery aid and on a level approach of some two miles. The Army of Tennessee suffered some 6,000 casualties in this conflict with 12 of its general officers killed, wounded, or captured. It never recovered its morale or strength.

See S. F. Horn, *Army of Tennessee* (1941), best; J. D. Cox, *Battle of Franklin* (1894), most complete, Cox was participant; S. Crownover, *Tennessee Historical Quarterly* (Dec., 1955); D. M. Robison, *Tennessee Historical Quarterly* (March, 1963); J. I. Robertson, Jr., *Tennessee Historical Quarterly* (Spring, 1965); and Tennessee State Library and Archives, leading repository.

SAM B. SMITH
University of Tennessee, Nashville

FRANKLIN, STATE OF (1784–1789). Before and during the Revolution, frontiersmen who had pushed beyond the Appalachians into the western lands of North Carolina (now eastern Tennessee) had chafed under alternate periods of eastern neglect and interference with their land titles, Indian relations, taxation, and local government. When North Carolina ceded its western lands to the Continental Congress in 1784, Tennessee Valley leaders, who feared the collapse of their land schemes, organized a meeting that declared the independence of the "state of Franklin" and called a constitutional convention. Although North Carolina withdrew its cession and sought to restore its sovereignty over the area, Franklinites drew up a constitution and requested admission to the Union.

By late 1785, Franklinites had begun to divide in the face of congressional disinterest and North Carolina pressure. Leadership struggles and dissension over the wisdom of persisting in independence, democratic reform, and the source and extent of land titles prepared the way for restoration of North Carolina sovereignty, the cession of the area to the new federal government in 1789, and the organization of the area as a federal territory in 1790. Historians have interpreted Franklin as demonstrating both the presence and absence of frontier democracy, the challenge of squatter rights to state sovereignty, the threat of western separatism to the new nation in the late eighteenth century, and dominance of land speculation in the trans-Appalachian West.

See S. C. Williams, *Lost State of Franklin* (1933); T. P. Abernethy, *From Frontier to Plantation in Tennessee* (1932); C. S. Driver, *John Sevier* (1932); W. F. Cannon, *East Tennessee Historical Society Publications* (Spring, 1950); and J. D. Barnhart, *Valley of Democracy* (1953).

RICHARD M. CLOKEY
Indiana State University

FRANKLIN & ARMFIELD COMPANY of Alexandria, Va., purchasers of border state slaves in the 1830s, was the largest trading firm in the Old South. It shipped usually by water over 1,000 slaves annually to the New Orleans and Natchez markets.

See W. Stephenson, *Isaac Franklin, Slave Trader* (1938), accurate and informative; F. Bancroft, *Slave Trading* (1931), questionable statistics; E. A. Andrews, *Slavery and Domestic Slave Trade* (1836); F. Bancroft, *Journal of Negro History* (Oct., 1920); and W. Calderhead, *Civil War History* (March, 1972).

WILLIAM L. CALDERHEAD
U.S. Naval Academy

FRAYSER'S FARM, BATTLE OF (June 30, 1862). After SAVAGE STATION, George B. McClellan concentrated behind White Oak Swamp on a line running to Malvern Hill, Va. He intended to block ROBERT E. LEE's pursuit while his supply wagons continued to HARRISON'S LANDING on the James River. Lee, meanwhile, dispatched converging columns to destroy the exposed Union column. None of Lee's separate columns attained their objectives. Poor staff work prevented proper coordination of Lee's seven divisions against McClellan's widely dispersed column. Lee concentrated only the divisions of JAMES LONGSTREET and A. P. HILL, and they, unable to get underway before late in the day, were stymied by strong federal resistance. Federal casualties numbered 2,853; the Confederates lost 3,615. The stalemate at Frayser's Farm cost Lee an opportunity to destroy McClellan's army. The stage was now set for the federal withdrawal to MALVERN HILL and the final, bloody battle of the SEVEN DAYS' operation.

See C. Dowdey, *Seven Days* (1964), best emphasis on emergence of Lee; J. P. Cullen, *Peninsula Campaign, 1862* (1973), good on contrasting commanders; *Official Records, Armies,* Ser. 1, Vols. XI, LI, original sources; R. U. Johnson and C. C. Buel (eds.), *Battles and Leaders* (1887), II, analysis by veterans; J. W. T. Leech, *Southern Historical Society Papers* (1876–1910), XXII, personal account, La. troops; and General Service Schools, Army, *Source Book: Peninsula* (1921), anthology.

B. FRANKLIN COOLING
U.S. Army Military History Research Collection

FRAZIER, EDWARD FRANKLIN (1894–1962),

was born in Baltimore. After being graduated *cum laude* from Howard University (B.A., 1916), he earned degrees in sociology from Clark University (M.A., 1920) and the University of Chicago (Ph.D., 1931). Meanwhile he had taught at Tuskegee Institute and at Morehouse College in Atlanta and had served as director of Atlanta's School of Social Work. While completing his dissertation on the Negro family in Chicago, he held an appointment in the sociology department at Fisk University. His first two books, his dissertation and a study *The Free Negro Family,* were both published in 1932 and earned for him the position as department head at Howard University. Except for occasional research leaves and visiting professorships, he remained at Howard until his retirement in 1960. He was a dedicated and prolific scholar who used a historical approach in his sociological studies. *The Negro Family in the United States* (1939) and *Black Bourgeoisie* (1957) are probably his best-known and most frequently cited works. Other major studies published by Frazier include *Negro Youth at the Crossroads* (1940); *The Negro in the United States* (1949); and *The Negro Church in America* (1964).

FREDERICK, MD. (pop. 23,641), the hometown

of ROGER B. TANEY and of BARBARA FRITCHIE, was first settled by Palatine Germans and laid out in 1744 by Daniel Dulany. It is located in western Maryland, approximately 20 miles southeast of Hagerstown. The town changed hands several times during the Civil War, with Confederate and Union forces clashing July 9, 1864, just southeast of town during EARLY'S WASHINGTON RAID. After a day of fighting near the Monocacy River, Jubal Early's 14,000 men easily routed 6,000 federal soldiers commanded by General Lew Wallace. Union casualties totaled 1,880 (including 1,188 missing), and Confederate casualties totaled fewer than 700 men. Modern Frederick is a trade center for area agriculture and an industrial city producing glass, electrical supplies, castings, and clothing.

See T. J. Williams, *History of Frederick County* (2 vols.; 1910); J. R. Holt, *Historic Frederick* (1949); E. S. Delaplaine, *Maryland in Law and History* (1964); and files of Frederick *Examiner* (1849–1913), *News* (1883–), and *Post* (1910–), all on microfilm.

FREDERICKSBURG, BATTLE OF (December 13,

1862). One of the most thoroughly one-sided battles of the American Civil War was fought in and around the Virginia city of Fredericksburg. The federal Army of the Potomac was led to the vicinity by General Ambrose Burnside in mid-November of 1862. General R. E. Lee placed a part of his 75,000-man Army of Northern Virginia on the hills behind Fredericksburg, between the federals and the roads to Richmond. Burnside's initial opportunity to cross the Rappahannock River near the town and attack Lee or to slip past him was soon lost as Confederate strength reached the area from the lower Shenandoah Valley.

Burnside finally crossed the river with the majority of his 110,000 men on December 11 and 12, after overcoming a stalwart delaying action by Mississippians under General William Barksdale. The town of Fredericksburg was heavily damaged by bombardment and then looted by the occupying army on the eleventh and twelfth.

The battle of the thirteenth was remarkable for the incredible fortitude displayed by the federal infantry and the equally amazing ineptitude of its generals. Lee was able to fight the battle without employing a large proportion of the strength at his command. From late morning until dark, federal columns streamed west from the town and formed up to assault the Confederate-held ridges behind the town. They had to cross a long, sloping plain into a storm of fire from southern artillery on the hills and from infantry in the protection of a sunken road fringed with a stone wall. None of the attackers reached the wall, though some 8,000 of them were shot in the attempt. One of the Confederate commanders bluntly summarized the advantages of his position: "If you put every man on the other side of the Potomac on that field to approach me . . . and give me plenty of ammunition, I will kill them all before they reach my line."

Another federal attack was directed against less formidable Confederate ground five miles south of the bloody sunken road. After two assaults were thrown into disorder by artillery, a third found an undefended stretch of front and several thousand northern soldiers poured through. Their temporary success was illusory, however, for General T. J. Jackson's corps was four divisions deep, and the extent of the federal penetration resulted only in increased losses during their subsequent retreat.

After a Confederate counterattack was halted, the rest of the day on this southern end of the field remained quiet.

The Army of the Potomac paid a high price in blood without any tangible returns. Federal casualties of 12,500 compared with Confederate losses of less than 5,000. On no occasion during the war was Lee able to win a victory with greater ease.

See G. F. R. Henderson, *Campaign of Fredericksburg* (1886); V. Whan, *Fiasco at Fredericksburg* (1961); and C. E. Dornbusch, *Military Bibliography of the Civil War* (1973), III, pp. 115–17 contain a list of sources on the battle. No definitive scholarly history of the Fredericksburg campaign has ever been written.

ROBERT K. KRICK
Fredericksburg National Military Park

FREDERICKSBURG, VA. (pop. 14,450), is located at the FALL LINE of the Rappahannock River, 50 miles south of Washington, D.C. Established in 1727, Fredericksburg prospered as a major inland port for seagoing vessels during the eighteenth century. The town was probably named in honor of Frederick, Prince of Wales. Among the major exports of the colonial town were iron, dried fish, flax seed, TOBACCO, wood products, foodstuffs, military stores, and NAVAL STORES. The town's convenient location on the major overland route from the northern colonies to Williamsburg and other southern capitals brought commercial business and made it attractive to businessmen and political leaders. The Washington family had extensive landholdings in and near the town.

Westward migration during the first quarter of the nineteenth century and the construction of a north-south railroad through Virginia in the 1840s brought a decline in prosperity by the beginning of the Civil War. The town's location at the midpoint between Washington, D.C., and the Confederate capital at Richmond made it a battleground for most of the war. Four major battles were fought in or near the city: FREDERICKSBURG (1862), CHANCELLORSVILLE (1863), WILDERNESS (1864), and SPOTSYLVANIA (1864). The war left the city severely damaged, but by the end of the century Fredericksburg had recovered and restored its position as a commercial-trading and light-manufacturing center in the Rappahannock River watershed.

The city's large inventory of eighteenth- and nineteenth-century buildings qualified the portion of the town within the 1740s boundary for designation as a National Historic District in 1971.

See O. H. Darter, *Colonial Fredericksburg* (1957), exaggerates importance of town but provides useful data; and S. J. Quinn, *History of Fredericksburg* (1908).

RONALD E. SHIBLEY
Historic Fredericksburg Foundation

FREEDMEN'S AID SOCIETIES. At least 80 separate private societies dedicated to freedmen's aid grew up in the North during the Civil War. By mid-1864, however, the larger societies began to consolidate, and funds for the benefit of the freedmen came to be channeled predominantly into about ten different societies. The American Missionary Association was the first organized—a strictly antislavery missionary society founded in 1846—and the first to respond to the plight of the "contraband" at Fortress Monroe in early September, 1861. The Port Royal work of the New England Freedmen's Aid Society began in March of 1862. The New England society was newly formed in Boston, presaging similar freedmen's aid societies in New York, Philadelphia, Baltimore, Washington, Cincinnati, Cleveland, Chicago, Detroit, and other cities. The work of these societies came to be predominantly educational, though a great deal of it was distribution of relief, supervision of labor, and evangelical preaching.

By the time of Appomattox, the New England society supported 180 teachers among the freedmen; the New York society, over 200; Cincinnati, 80; Chicago, 50; Baltimore, 50; and the American Missionary Association, 327. Most of these teachers were young ladies, and financing was obtained through private donations as well as from the government's FREEDMEN'S BUREAU. Early in the war these teachers taught in many hastily built elementary day schools. With time, these societies tended to concentrate their educational work at strategic spots where academies and colleges for the freedmen emerged. Most of the great private black colleges in the South trace their origins to the activities of the freedmen's aid societies of this period: ATLANTA, FISK, Talladega, HAMPTON, DILLARD.

Immediately following the war, with the encouragement of the Freedmen's Bureau, two great overall alliances of societies attempted to organize all the freedmen's aid work. The American Missionary Association attempted to coordinate the work of the church-related societies: the Freewill Baptists, Wesleyan Methodists, Congregationalists in both the U.S. and England, Dutch Reformed, Presbyterians, and Methodists. The union of the various regional aid societies came to be known as the American Freedmen's Union Commission; it combined the work of the New England, New York, Philadelphia, Chicago, Cincinnati, and other secular aid societies. To a remarkable degree this division, which persisted from 1866 to 1869, paralleled the old abolitionist division between the evangelical or church-oriented abolitionists and the humanitarians or Garrisonians.

As the excitement of the Reconstruction revolution began to wear thin, the various societies associated with the American Freedmen's Union Commission began to fall by the wayside. The American Missionary Association gradually became a missionary agency of the Congregational church, and other denominations with northern clienteles formed separate aid societies. Northern Baptists established the American Baptist Home Missionary Society in 1862, and other denominations—the Episcopalians, Friends, Presbyterians, Methodists, Freewill Baptists, and Dutch Reformed—followed their lead. With time, the work of these denominational groups became as much evangelical as educational. By 1869 perhaps 10,000 teachers, most of them from the North, had made themselves available to what BOOKER T. WASHINGTON called a race that began to go to school overnight. Between 1861 and 1889, northern benevolent groups contributed perhaps as much as $21 million in support of freedmen's aid in the South.

See W. L. Rose, *Rehearsal for Reconstruction* (1964); H. L. Swint, *Northern Teacher in South* (1941); J. H. Parmalee, in T. J. Jones, *Negro Education* (1917); O. S. Heckman, "Northern Church Penetration of South" (Ph.D. dissertation, Duke, 1939); and R. B. Drake, "American Missionary Association" (Ph.D. dissertation, Emory, 1957) and *Journal of Southern History* (May, 1963). See also Freedmen's Bureau Papers, National Archives; AMA Archives, Dillard University; and journals, *American Missionary* and *Freedmen's Record.*

RICHARD B. DRAKE
Berea College

FREEDMEN'S BANK or Freedmen's Savings Bank (officially the Freedmen's Savings & Trust Company) was founded in March, 1865, specifically to serve black soldiers and former slaves. Its creators, mostly white Christian humanitarians of whom John W. Alvord was the most influential, intended the bank to instill the bourgeois values of thrift, patience, and honest work in the freedmen. With the help of the American Missionary Association and the FREEDMEN'S BUREAU, with which it was often confused, the bank established branches throughout the South, eventually total-

ing 37 branches in 17 states and the District of Columbia. Under Alvord's presidency, the bank struggled against heavy operating costs and limited deposits from 1865 to 1869. Black soldiers' pay and bounty money were the primary elements in the deposits. After 1870, the advertising campaigns, the employment of black cashiers, clerks, and publicity agents, and the increasing willingness and ability of blacks to deposit small sums considerably extended the bank's business. By June, 1873, total deposits and withdrawals approximated $49 million and $45 million, respectively.

Unfortunately, the success of the bank made it a desirable prey for capitalist speculators. In 1870 the trustees, now dominated by Henry Cooke (of Jay Cooke & Company), amended the charter to permit loans on real estate security, a privilege that was grossly abused by some of the bank's officers. The PANIC OF 1873 unmasked drastic weaknesses, caused by incompetent branch personnel and corruption at the central office. Belatedly, a reform movement succeeded in replacing the fleeing speculators with honest black trustees and replaced the well-meaning but weak Alvord with FREDERICK DOUGLASS. Nothing could have saved the bank, however, and it failed in July, 1874. After several years, many of the bank's 61,000 depositors received up to 62 percent of their money back, but the losses made it one of the worst savings bank failures in the late nineteenth century. The fruitless hope of persuading the U.S. Congress to reimburse the depositors kept the memory of the Freedmen's Bank tragedy alive all over the South up to 1910.

See C. R. Osthaus, *Freedmen, Philanthropy, and Fraud* (1976); W. L. Fleming, *Freedmen's Savings Bank* (1927); *Freedman's Bank*, H.R. 502, Ser. 1710, 1st Sess., 44th Cong.; *Report of the Select Committee to Investigate Freedman's Savings and Trust Company*, S.R. 440, Ser. 1895, 2nd Sess., 46th Cong.; and Records of Freedman's Savings & Trust Company, National Archives.

CARL R. OSTHAUS
Oakland University

FREEDMEN'S BUREAU was created by an act of Congress on March 3, 1865, to supervise southern blacks' transition from slavery to freedom. Because congressional policy makers considered the bureau only a temporary agency, they placed it in the War Department and made it largely dependent on the army for personnel. Consequently, General O. O. Howard, the bureau's commissioner, and his assistant commissioners never obtained an adequate number of men to serve in the field as agents. At the apex of its strength, the bureau employed only 900 persons (350 of whom were clerks) to deal with such matters as justice, labor relations, relief, medical care, and education in 15 southern states.

The results of the bureau's efforts were mixed. The agency's attempt to provide freedmen legal protection enjoyed little success because it possessed limited judicial authority. President Andrew Johnson permitted the bureau to assume jurisdiction of legal cases involving freedmen only when state judges denied freedmen the right to testify against whites. During much of 1865 state judges enforced discriminatory antebellum testimony statutes, and agents responded by adjudicating minor cases involving freedmen and referring serious cases to army officials for trial by military commission. During late 1865 and 1866, however, bureau judicial activity diminished as states permitted freedmen to testify against whites and agents were forced to return jurisdiction to state courts. Even in 1867–1868, when the Reconstruction Act authorized military officials to try civilians in military courts, army commanders were reluctant to permit bureau agents to resume jurisdiction of cases involving freedmen or to order such cases tried by military commission.

In the area of labor relations, the Freedmen's Bureau was also largely unsuccessful. Congress gave the bureau control of some 850,000 acres of land seized by federal officials under the Confiscation Act of 1862 and the Abandoned Property Act of 1863 and authorized it to divide this land into 40-acre tracts, which it could lease and eventually sell to freedmen. But during the summer of 1865 Johnson ordered the bureau to return abandoned and confiscated property to its original owners. Frustrated in their attempt to provide even a few freedmen with land, bureau officials redoubled efforts begun early in the summer of 1865 to establish a system of contract labor. Agents perennially encouraged and supervised the drafting of contracts and sought to guarantee that both parties fulfilled their contractual obligations. In 1866 and after, however, agents generally lacked sufficient authority to prevent planters from dealing unfairly with freedmen. As a result, the contract system left most freedmen impoverished and dependent on white landowners.

Although bureau officials feared that government-sponsored relief would undermine freedmen's self-reliance, the widespread destitution that prevailed in the postwar period compelled them to sponsor an extensive social welfare program. The bureau established a number of "home farms" throughout the South, which provided food and shelter for elderly freedmen, women with small children who were separated from their husbands, and able-bodied men and women who were unable to find employment. After 1865, the number of home farms declined, but the bureau actually expanded its relief activity. Between 1866 and 1868, bureau officials distributed over a million dollars' worth of food to blacks and whites left destitute by crop failures. In addition to feeding the hungry, the Freedmen's Bureau obtained the services of a sufficient number of army surgeons and civilian doctors to operate almost 100 hospitals and dispensaries. Moreover, bureau officials played an important role in helping black veterans collect bounties and pensions that the government owed them.

The bureau was also active in freedmen's education, providing extensive aid to northern benevolent associations (FREEDMEN'S AID SOCIETIES) that sent hundreds of teachers to the South to organize FREEDMEN'S SCHOOLS. Between 1866 and 1870, bureau officials, supported by several congressional appropriations for freedmen's education, spent nearly $5 million to pay teachers, construct and rent school buildings, and establish Negro colleges and normal schools.

A temporary agency with a wide range of responsibilities but limited authority, the Freedmen's Bureau terminated all but its educational and bounty-collecting activity in January, 1869, and concluded those branches of its work in June, 1870, and June, 1872, respectively.

See G. R. Bentley, *Freedmen's Bureau* (1955); C. F. Oubre, *Forty Acres and a Mule* (1978); J. A. Carpenter, *O. O. Howard* (1964); W. S. McFeely, *Yankee Stepfather* (1968); J. L. and L. W. Cox, *Journal of Southern History* (Nov., 1953); H. L. Belz, *Civil War History* (Sept., 1975); D. G. Nieman, "Freedmen's Bureau" (Ph.D. dissertation, Rice, 1975); M. L. Abbott, *Freedmen's Bureau in South Carolina* (1967); H. A. White, *Freedmen's Bureau in Louisiana* (1970); D. G. Nieman, *Journal of Southern History* (August, 1978); O. O. Howard, *Autobiography* (1907); O. O. Howard Papers, Bowdoin College Library; and Bureau Records, Record Group 105, National Archives.

DONALD G. NIEMAN
Kansas State University

FREEDMEN'S SCHOOLS (1861–1877). Black schools, generally illegal and always circumscribed before 1860, became viable institutions during Reconstruction. In the first flush of freedom grandparents and grandchildren thronged the crude schoolhouses to secure the magic of reading and writing. Some of the earliest education work was done by Union Army soldiers and chaplains, who taught slaves who had congregated at their camps. Soon their work was supplemented by benevolent societies such as the American Missionary Association and the National Freedmen's Relief Association. By 1865 there were approximately 75,000 black pupils in Union-occupied territory.

In 1865 the FREEDMEN'S BUREAU began to play a significant role in freedmen's education. During its five years of operation the bureau was instrumental in supervising more than 9,000 schools with 247,000 students. In 1870 alone there were approximately 150,000 black students in 2,677 bureau–benevolent association schools. Although the schools were still reaching little more than one-tenth of school-aged black children, tenth of school-aged black children, the black literacy rate leaped from less than 10 percent to more than 25 percent in a single decade.

Most of the instructors in the first black schools were northern whites, who were frequently ostracized, mistreated, and even assaulted. A few actually lost their lives. By 1870, however, blacks trained in the early schools were becoming the teachers, and a few others were receiving college educations at black colleges such as Fisk, Hampton, Howard, and Atlanta founded during Reconstruction. These colleges trained much of the black leadership during the following century.

When the Freedmen's Bureau and benevolent associations severely restricted their work in 1870, black education did not abruptly cease. Several societies continued their work, and other schools were absorbed into the public school systems. The development of public education was the most outstanding achievement of the Republican state governments in the South. Although public education discriminated against black children (in 1900, Adams County, Miss., spent 11 times more for the education of each white child than for each black child), the public school system had been too widely accepted during Reconstruction to permit its total destruction.

See W. P. Vaughan, *Schools for All* (1974); W. L. Rose, *Rehearsal for Reconstruction* (1964); H. L. Swint, *Northern Teacher in South* (1941); J. W. Alvord, *Reports on School for Freedmen* (1866–70); and U.S. Commission of Education, *Reports* (1870–80).

JOE M. RICHARDSON
Florida State University

FREEMAN, DOUGLAS SOUTHALL (1886–1953),

was born in Lynchburg, Va. He graduated from Richmond College in 1904 and received his Ph.D. degree from Johns Hopkins. From 1915 to 1949 he was editor of the Richmond *News Leader*.

He simultaneously followed an academic career, teaching journalism at several universities. After 1949 he devoted himself primarily to historical writing. Freeman's published works are among the finest produced by an American and rank him as one of the leading historians of his day. His four-volumed biography of ROBERT E. LEE (1934) won the Pulitzer Prize. He considered *Lee's Lieutenants* (1942–1944), however, to be his best work. This superb trilogy on the Army of Northern Virginia is subtitled *A Study in Command*. It reveals Freeman's great knowledge of Civil War military history. His *George Washington* began to appear in 1948, and five of the projected seven volumes were published before his death. The biography was completed by John A. Carroll and Mary W. Ashworth. It won the Pulitzer Prize in 1958.

See obituary, *American Historical Review* (Oct., 1953); *Time* (June 22, 1953); A. S. Link and R. W. Patrick (eds.), *Writing Southern History* (1968); and P. W. Edmunds, *Virginians* (1972).

JOHN G. BARRETT
Virginia Military Institute

FREEMASONRY is a worldwide fraternity tracing its roots to the guilds of stonemasons of the Middle Ages. It teaches the fatherhood of God, the brotherhood of man, and basic moral truths, using builders' tools as symbols and the building of King Solomon's Temple as the vehicle for the lessons taught. In all English-speaking nations Freemasonry is nonpolitical and nonsectarian. In its present form the organization dates from 1717, when four London lodges organized the Grand Lodge of England. Following the American Revolution, the lodges in the United States began organizing Grand Lodges in each state. In 1975 the 17 southern states and the District of Columbia had about 1,221,000 members.

In 1826 William Morgan, an itinerant worker then living in Batavia, N.Y., attempted to publish an alleged "exposure" of Masonic ritual. His subsequent unexplained disappearance caused the Masons to be accused of his abduction and murder. He was never heard of again. The matter propelled the Anti-Masonic party onto the national political scene. In the ELECTION OF 1832 that party ran WILLIAM WIRT against Democratic incumbent Andrew Jackson, a Past Grand Master of Tennessee, and Whig Henry Clay, a Past Grand Master of Kentucky, with Jackson winning. This party never had much prestige in the South, and elsewhere many of its members were absorbed into the WHIG PARTY and eventually into the REPUBLICAN PARTY. Among these were William H.

Seward and Thaddeus Stevens, a leader in the movement to impeach President ANDREW JOHNSON, a Mason. The anti-Masonic furor caused many southern lodges to succumb, but a revival soon occurred.

Among prominent southerners who have been Masons are GEORGE WASHINGTON, JAMES OGLETHORPE, Joseph Hewes and William Hooper of North Carolina and George Walton of Georgia (signers of the Declaration of Independence), JOHN BLAIR of Virginia, JOHN MARSHALL; JOHN C. BRECKINRIDGE; ALBERT SIDNEY JOHNSTON; ROBERT TOOMBS; HUGO L. BLACK; and HARRY S. TRUMAN (Past Grand Master of Missouri).

Southerners especially prominent in Masonic affairs have been Albert G. Mackey of South Carolina, Masonic historian and encyclopedist; Rob Morris of Mississippi and Kentucky, founder of the Order of the Eastern Star for the female relatives of Masons; and ALBERT PIKE of Arkansas and Washington, D.C., Sovereign Grand Commander of the Supreme Council, thirty-third degree, from 1859 to 1891.

See H. W. Coil, *Freemasonry Through Six Centuries* (1967), best general history; W. R. Denslow, *Famous Freemasons* (1957–61); R. I. Clegg and H. L. Haywood (eds.), *Mackey's Encyclopedia of Freemasonry* (1946); C. McCarthy, *American Historical Association Annual Report* (1902), best on political anti-Masonry; J. F. Newton, *Builders* (1951), history and philosophy of Freemasonry; A. Roberts, *House Undivided* (1961), best on Freemasonry and Civil War; Library Supreme Council 33°, 1733-16th St. NW, Washington, D.C. 20009; and Iowa Masonic Library, Box 276, Cedar Rapids, Iowa 52406.

CHARLES SNOW GUTHRIE
Western Kentucky University

FREEPORT DOCTRINE (1858), enunciated by Stephen A. Douglas during his famous debates with Abraham Lincoln, was an effort to accommodate the principle of POPULAR SOVEREIGNTY to the DRED SCOTT decision of 1857. The U.S. Supreme Court, in holding that Congress lacked constitutional authority to forbid slavery in federal territories, had more or less implied that territorial legislatures were likewise without such power. Douglas could scarcely accept the implication without deserting the principle that had become the trademark of his political career. Yet any semblance of disagreement with the Court's decision would further antagonize southern Democrats and President James Buchanan, who were already angry at the Illinois senator because of his opposition to the proslavery LECOMPTON CONSTITUTION for Kansas. Facing this dilemma, Douglas fell back on a distinction between right

and power that had originated with certain southern politicians. At Freeport, Ill., on August 27, 1858, when Lincoln asked him whether the people of a territory could exclude slavery from its limits, Douglas replied that, whatever the Supreme Court might decide, slavery could not exist anywhere without the protection of local police regulations. By "unfriendly legislation," a territory could always prevent the introduction of slavery if it so wished. The consequences of this response have probably been exaggerated, but it did aggravate southern hostility to Douglas and widen the sectional breach in the Democratic party.

See P. M. Angle (ed.), *Created Equal?* (1958); D. E. Fehrenbacher, *Prelude to Greatness* (1962); R. W. Johannsen, *Stephen A. Douglas* (1973); and Douglas Papers, University of Chicago.

DON E. FEHRENBACHER
Stanford University

FREIGHT RATES caused disputes between shippers and carriers for many years in the South. During the nineteenth century, the railroad companies divided the nation into rate territories. A basing system for the southern territory was established from crossings on the Ohio and Potomac rivers to certain distribution points in the South. Low population density and seasonal fluctuation of cargo were factors that helped determine the rate structure; however, the most important factor was competition with water rates from the eastern seaports to southern coastal cities and river rates on southern rivers. Also, some railroads adopted a policy of developing certain cities to the detriment of others. The complicated rate structure, understood by only a few experts and railroad men, worked to the disadvantage of those industries that manufactured finished products, whereas certain producers of raw and semifinished goods were favored. This led to the exportation of resources from the region and discouraged the establishment of new industries. During the twentieth century, politicians blamed poverty, low wages, bad houses, and other ills on the high freight rates. An investigation revealed that southern rates generally were from 39 to 71 percent higher than those in other territories. During the 1930s southern governors and the Roosevelt administration became interested in the problem. A publicity campaign plus legal and legislative action led to a revision of rail rates in the 1940s and early 1950s.

See W. H. Joubert, *Southern Freight Rates in Transition* (1949); S. Daggert, *Railroad Reorganization* (1908); L. G. McPherson *Railroad Freight Rates* (1909); W. Z.

Ripley, *Railroads: Rates and Regulations* (1912); J. H. Alldredge, *Interterritorial Freight Rate Problem* (1937); and *Supplemental Phases of Interterritorial Freight Rate Problems of U.S.* (1939); H. H. Odum, *Southern Regions* (1936); M. Ferguson, *State Regulation of Railroads in South* (1916); and Interstate Commerce Commission reports and documents (1887–1950).

DUDLEY S. JOHNSON
Southeastern Louisiana University

FRENCH AND INDIAN WAR. (1754–1763).

From the founding, in 1607 and 1608, of Jamestown and Quebec it was perhaps inevitable that in time Great Britain and France would do battle for the trans-Appalachian West they both claimed. By 1754 New France was a riverine empire of villages and trading posts strategically located to control the fur trade and to block English access to the interior. North of the Ohio, whenever the mercantilistic policy that declared the West closed to English traders succeeded, its success was due largely to French-Indian alliances. French colonial officials were adept at Indian diplomacy. French traders accepted Indians as men like themselves.

South of the Ohio, the French had fewer advantages. The governor of Louisiana was hampered conducting Indian affairs and regulating trade by the lack of authority and shortage of funds and troops. France did not control the Gulf coast, and save for the Mississippi River posts, had only Ft. Toulouse at the headwaters of the Alabama. Southern Indians had never been won to the French as had most of the tribes north of the Ohio. Their country did not produce much fur, and what little French trade goods they acquired, southern Indians rated generally inferior to English goods.

Yet as the French in Louisiana and Illinois must have known, if they were to hold the West and prevent the English from severing Louisiana from Canada, they had to win the CHEROKEE to their side: the Tennessee River, second only to the Ohio as a water route west, rose and flowed through Cherokee country to its juncture with the Ohio. A moment before the French capture of Virginia's uncompleted fort at the forks of the Ohio in 1754, the Cherokee were of two minds; they were fearful of Englishmen who came among them one year as traders and returned the following year as settlers with families and friends, fencing the Indians off their tribal lands. They were impressed with evidence of French strength. But French alliances with northern tribes they counted traditional enemies inclined them to support the British. Tongue-in-cheek, they had bargained their assistance in return for protection of their

towns against probable French retaliation. To their surprise, in 1753, Ft. Prince George was built near their Lower Towns, and in 1756 South Carolinians built Ft. Loudon on the Tennessee near their Overhills Towns (FORTS).

Cherokee war parties joined George Washington in the Ohio campaign of 1756, fought with the colonial militia on the Pennsylvania and Virginia frontiers the next year, and joined John Forbes's campaign against Ft. Duquesne in 1758. Each time colonial authorities reneged on promises of payment of bounties and trade goods. Each year, coming and going between their towns and the battlegrounds, the Cherokee were set upon and murdered by settlers who did not care to distinguish between Indian allies and enemies. The pro-French CREEK brought promises of ammunition in return for English scalps from the French at Ft. Toulouse and Ft. Massac in Illinois. When South Carolina cut off its supply of ammunition to them in the summer of 1759, the Cherokee were ready at last to join the French against the English. But by then the war in Canada was lost; the French could not send aid. In 1760 under Colonel Archibald Montgomery and in 1761 under Colonel James Grant, 1,200 or so British soldiers with colonial militia and some CATAWBA campaigned in Cherokee country, destroying all but the Overhills settlement. Cherokee leaders signed a peace treaty made in the name of all the English colonies December 17, 1761.

See W. R. Jacobs, *Indians of Southern Colonial Frontier* (1954); E. L. Lee, *Indian Wars* (1963); J. R. Alden, *John Stuart* (1944); W. J. Eccles, *France in America* (1972); and A. D. Candler, *Colonial Records of Georgia* (1904–16), for relations of southern Indians to French and English. Otherwise, this subject has received little attention from scholars, and information is widely scattered.

NATALIA M. BELTING
University of Illinois, Urbana

FRENCH BROAD RIVER

FRENCH BROAD RIVER rises on the eastern edge of the Great Smoky Mountains, near the southern boundary of Henderson County, N.C. (approximately 35.3° N, 82.7° W). The drainage divide forms the boundary line between part of North Carolina and South Carolina. It flows in a northerly direction across a broad basin in the mountains that centers on the city of Asheville, N.C. After some 70 miles the river drops rapidly down to the Great Valley of Tennessee, gradually swinging to the west. A major tributary, the Nolichucky, follows a similar route through the mountains to the north. A smaller tributary, the Big Pigeon, drains an area south of the French Broad. The total area of the main river and its tributaries is around 5,750 square miles. The French Broad joins the Holston at Knoxville, Tenn., to form the TENNESSEE RIVER, flowing some 210 miles in probably the wettest region in the eastern United States with an average rainfall of around 55 inches and no dry season. Its passage through the Great Smoky Mountains from east to west makes it an important routeway. A major TENNESSEE VALLEY AUTHORITY power dam was built on its lower course.

See W. Dykeman, *French Broad* (1955).

RICHARD F. LITTLE
University of West Virginia

FRENCH INFLUENCE on the South was limited because relatively few Frenchmen came and more of them returned home than any immigrant people. Moreover clannish Frenchmen did not readily mix with Anglo-Americans. The most significant migrants, the HUGUENOTS and refugees of the Revolutionary period, came involuntarily. Most of the refugees went home; without that option Huguenots, on the whole, assimilated fairly quickly. Colonial rivalry, and aversion to Catholicism, generated among Anglo-Americans a nearly universal hatred of France, which lasted until the 1770s, when dramatic changes in Franco-American relations followed France's intervention in the American Revolution. The French Revolution was greeted with immense enthusiasm in the South, as indeed throughout America. While Enlightenment thought streamed in, French influence reached unprecedented proportions. But the radicalization of the French Revolution and the Bonapartist dictatorship revived intense Francophobia.

In the 1790s thousands of refugees from revolutionary France and Santo Domingo settled in the French enclaves of southern cities. Representing an extremely heterogeneous lot politically and socially, they contributed importantly to the spread of French "culture." *Petits-maîtres* opened schools, and the aristocratic refugees had entrée to the highest strata of southern society. Their sophistication and elegance generated a rage for French manners and dress.

French influence on the South was often elusive. British influence greatly overshadowed it, and southern life inhibited penetration of French thought. For the southern upper classes, the English country gentleman served as their model. French influence filtered into the southern "aristocracy" indirectly through the English gentry's absorption of French manners and dress. The southern elite's reading up to 1914 was over-whelmingly English literature, regarded as respectable and in tune with southern ways in contrast to the alleged immorality of French literature. Some French was taught in southern colleges, but essentially Greek and Latin held sway until the twentieth century. Contemporary doctrines of racial inequality came essentially from the Germanic world, not from Joseph Arthur de Gobineau's France. New or radical ideas encountered fierce resistance, and so the rich French thought of the nineteenth and early twentieth centuries made little headway in the South.

Long before the Civil War, American views of the French had crystallized into unfavorable stereotypes held by most Americans to this day. The French were regarded simultaneously as atheists and sinister Catholics, politically unstable and unfit for democracy. They were dismissed as immoral, decadent, and inferior. Elegant French fashions, superb wines and cheeses might not be denied. But for all their snob appeal, they were thought frivolous and unmanly. Nor was it to France that the post–Civil War South looked for technological, scientific, and educational guidance, but to the North and Germany.

Louisiana long constituted the most celebrated French redoubt in America. Purchased in 1803, it already had a solidly established "Creole civilization." Creoles resisted the tidal wave of Anglo-American immigrants by speaking French and by sending their sons for education to France or Canada; above all, the church run by French priests exerted a profound influence on them. Many of the ACADIANS expelled by the English from Canada settled in Louisiana. Their descendants, the CAJUNS, today form part of the Gallic influence in Louisiana. French rule left lasting marks. Louisiana's civil law is partly French in derivation. Despite cultural dilution and varying degrees of assimilation, nearly half a million people in Louisiana speak French today. Smaller Creole communities in Mobile and Mississippi River towns inundated by Americans were assimilated by the mid-nineteenth century.

New Orleans around the mid-nineteenth century became the Paris of the New World, the most European of American cities. The French Quarter even today is regarded as French, but the architecture is a mixture of Spanish, French, and American and the "culture" is more generally Latin than French. Still many traits of the French way of life—*douceur de vivre*, lightheartedness, love of pleasure, and fashionable vice—have long been attractions of the city. Ironically the city's intellectual life was essentially the expression of its Anglo-American elements.

In America the French clergy played a crucial role in the establishment of a Catholic church. The first seminary in America, St. Mary's, was founded in 1791 at Baltimore by French monks. But French Catholicism did not influence southern thought, and its missionaries made few converts. French socialism also had virtually no impact on the South. Victor Considérant established an ephemeral Fourierist colony in Texas, and several abortive Icarian communes, tenaciously French, left no mark.

In ARCHITECTURE, city planning, and painting, however, French influence was striking and often profound. French architectural influence appeared early in the lower Mississippi Valley, through French settlers who raised ground floors and encircled their homes with porches to counteract heat and humidity. Classical buildings and continental-style churches owed much to French influence. During the nineteenth century many talented American architecture students, including southerners like Richard Hunt, studied in Paris' École des Beaux-Arts, whose standards and training were considered the finest in the world. Some of them, influenced by Eugène Viollet-le-Duc, turned their interest to French and European Gothic and Romanesque. Thomas Jefferson's neoclassical style was followed by a number of romantic revivals whose creations were prominent in the South: these include Gothic castles and the Greek-style temple used in churches, state capitols, and planters' mansions. Second Empire Paris fascinated Americans observing the urban planning that transformed it. Wide tree-lined boulevards, recreational parks, the mansard roof, and French-style apartment houses were imitated by American cities like St. Louis.

It is difficult to exaggerate the influence of France on American painting from 1875 to 1939. French preeminence in painting brought thousands of American art students to Paris, which also became the mecca of many American writers, intellectuals, and bohemians, among them southerners like Mary Cassatt. Nor were southerners lacking in the "lost generation" of the twenties.

See H. Blumenthal, *France and U.S.* (1970); F. Childs, *French Refugee Life* (1940); M. Giraud, *Histoire de la Louisiane Française* (1953–); H. M. Jones, *America and French Culture* (1927); and E. White, *American Opinion of France* (1927).

BORIS BLICK
University of Akron

FRENCH LICK, a major saline located on the southeast side of the Cumberland River and known initially as the Great Buffalo Lick, was the inter-section of all traces among the numerous salt licks in middle Tennessee. The French arrived in 1714 to hunt and trade for furs. This spring later drew Anglo-American hunters and a French-Canadian trading post (1760). Land speculators followed: RICHARD HENDERSON and associates purchased the area from the CHEROKEE in the Treaty of SYCAMORE SHOALS, and GEORGE ROGERS CLARK claimed the lick tract in 1779 under Virginia authority. In 1779–1780, James Robertson, of Watauga, John Donelson, and their followers erected a settlement, later named Nashborough, on the bluff above French Lick. Nashborough eventually became NASHVILLE, TENN.

See J. A. Jakle, 'Salt and Initial Settlement" (Ph.D. dissertation, University of Indiana 1967); A. Henderson, *Tennessee Historical Magazine* (Sept., 1916) and *Founding of Nashville* (1932); H. S. Arnow, *Seedtime on Cumberland* (1960); S. C. Williams, *Tennessee Historical Magazine* (April, 1919); J. G. M. Ramsey, *Annals of Tennessee* (1853); A. W. Putnam, *History of Middle Tennessee* (1859); and J. Haywood, *History of Tennessee* (1891).

JOHN E. STEALEY III
Shepherd College

FRITCHIE, BARBARA (1766–1862), was born in Lancaster, Pa. Moving to Frederick, Md., she married a glove maker, John Fritchie. Widowed in 1849, she lived on in Frederick. In September, 1862, a part of Robert E. Lee's army under STONEWALL JACKSON passed through her city in an invasion of the North. Doughty Barbara Fritchie was known as a staunch Unionist. Therefore, when one or two younger women neighbors may have defiantly waved Union flags at the invaders, their deeds were garbled and represented as Barbara's own. Union sympathizers needing to bolster morale spread the rumor that Barbara Fritchie had defied the mighty Jackson himself. Barbara Fritchie died only three months after her supposed heroics, but she gained immortality when in 1863 John Greenleaf Whittier made her the heroine of a poem.

See R. B. Harwell (ed.), *Union Reader* (1955); B. Catton, *Mr. Lincoln's Army* (1956); and B. Fritchie Scrapbook, Maryland Historical Society.

RALPH J. ROSKE
University of Nevada, Las Vegas

FRONTIER. From the founding of St. Augustine (1565) to the great Texas trail drives of the 1870s, four separate cultural strains came together on the southern frontier, each surviving to a degree today. The native Americans had occupied the South for thousands of years before the arrival of the Europeans. The presence of the Indians did much to direct patterns of European (and later American) settlement and expansion. Especially noteworthy were the Indian agricultural crops taken over by the Anglo-Americans: corn (maize), tobacco, beans, and squash. SPANISH INFLUENCE in Texas and Florida was strong, for the South lay on the northern fringes of the great Spanish Empire in the New World. The French expanded into the South from a base on the St. Lawrence waterway by way of the Mississippi. LA SALLE reached the mouth of the Mississippi in 1682, where he took possession of the region for France (FRENCH INFLUENCE). Anglo-American settlements in what would become the South began in the early seventeenth century, expanded slowly, remained generally compact, and were predominantly agricultural.

After unsuccessful attempts by SIR WALTER RALEIGH and Sir Humphrey Gilbert, the London Company established a settlement at JAMESTOWN in 1607. TOBACCO became the basis of commercial agriculture; private ownership of the land spread almost as rapidly as tobacco. Other southern colonies were established by the turn of the century, and the frontier advanced slowly toward the interior, subject to imperial policy, political unrest, and increasingly hostile Indian tribes. In the generation from 1730 to 1760 a large-scale immigration down the Great Valley of the Appalachians swelled the population of the "backcountry."

By the time of the American Revolution, pioneers had pressed through the Appalachians into Kentucky and Tennessee. Their settlements initially centered in "stations" around the bluegrass and Nashville basins, survived the intense Indian wars of the Revolution, and expanded after 1781. The 1780s saw two institutional features of the greatest importance for the southern frontier: the Land Ordinance of 1785 laid down the basic rules for the distribution of the public domain and the administrative system associated with it (LAND SURVEY SYSTEM); and the Ordinance of 1787 became the basis of government for new territories in the South (SOUTHWEST ORDINANCE). Thomas Jefferson's LOUISIANA PURCHASE in 1803 dramatically changed the shape, direction, and institutional development of the southern frontier. For the southern frontier, the WAR OF 1812 was largely a struggle between militia units and the Indians. It was highlighted by a substantial loss at Ft. Mims in Alabama and a dramatic victory at Horseshoe Bend. The frontier militia units, especially from Kentucky and Tennessee, made a significant contribution to Andrew Jackson's victory at NEW ORLEANS in 1815.

The Great Migration to the South and West after 1815—one of the largest mass migrations in the history of the world—resulted from several forces that came into focus with the close of the war: the depletion of tobacco lands in the Upper South and the desire of planters to find new and more profitable outlets for their capital and labor; the opening of large tracts of new lands in Alabama and Mississippi as a direct result of military victories and treaties in the war; a generation of prosperity (slowed by the PANIC OF 1819), in which the demands of the English mills made the cultivation of cotton extremely profitable; and the appearance of steam on the waterways of the South, easing the transportation of cotton to market. The frontier societies that emerged were remarkably homogeneous, with interests centered on agriculture, the current price of land, staple crops (COTTON, RICE, and SUGAR), and slaves. The acquisition of Florida by treaty (1819) ended a period of border intrigue and contrived revolution.

The frontier generation before the Civil War (1830–1860) continued the themes of land, staple crops, slavery, and expansion (interrupted by the PANIC OF 1837). Central to this experience was the expulsion of the several Indian tribes from northern Mississippi and portions of Alabama and Georgia in the 1830s and their systematic removal west of the Mississippi. The frontiers of these newly settled areas, called "new counties," were more southern than western. The SEMINOLE WARS (1835–1842) slowed Florida's growth. Amid rising sectional tensions, many southerners remained firmly convinced of their right to settle the new frontiers of Kansas and Nebraska with their slave property.

Texas was long a part of the Spanish Empire and later (after 1821) the newly independent Mexico. Fifteen years of Anglo-American immigration followed Mexican independence. Tensions appeared, grounded in the divergence of the American frontier experience from that of the Mexican (Spanish influenced), as well as in rising racial antagonism and the changing and sometimes contradictory policy of the Mexican government on immigration, slavery, and local governments. This increasing friction led to revolt in the name of constitutional government (1835) and later (1836) for independence. Sam Houston's victory at SAN JACINTO secured Texas' independence, and after annexation in 1845, Texas became a part of the South. The Texas frontier stretched from agriculture and cotton in the humid East across the line of semiaridity, necessitating changes there in traditional agriculture. The grazing industry that was already in process of development before the Civil War boomed after 1865.

The frontier of the South was almost exclusively agricultural, and the impact of the frontier experience in the South was enhanced by an agrarian tradition that remained a feature of southern life long after the transformation of other sections The southern frontier was also characterized by its several cultural strains—Indian, Spanish, French, and Mexican—giving the region a diversity and surviving influences that are unlike those of other sections.

See, for manuscripts, Alabama Department of Archives and History, Montgomery; P. K. Yonge Library, Gainesville; Margaret I. King Library, Lexington; Filson Club, Louisville; Department of Archives, Louisiana State University Library, Baton Rouge; Mississippi Department of Archives and History, Jackson; State Historical Society of Missouri, Columbia; University of North Carolina Library, Chapel Hill; Tennessee Historical Society, Tennessee State Library and Archives, Nashville; University of Texas Library, Austin; and State Historical Society of Wisconsin, Madison.

MALCOLM J. ROHRBOUGH
University of Iowa

FRONT ROYAL, VA. (pop. 8,211), is at the northern terminus of the Skyline Drive near the confluence of the south and north forks of the Shenandoah River. Settled in the eighteenth century as a frontier village known as Hill Town, it was incorporated under its present name in 1788. During the SHENANDOAH VALLEY CAMPAIGN of 1863, Belle Boyd, a Confederate spy, provided STONEWALL JACKSON with such accurate information on the number of Union defenders and the location of federal supplies that the town was easily overwhelmed by Jackson's forces (May 23, 1863). Although 16,000 Confederates suffered approximately 50 casualties, almost the entire federal force of 1,000 men was either killed or captured. Seven days later, captured federal supplies, valued at approximately $300,000, were destroyed when Confederate defenders panicked at the approach of a federal counterattack and set fire to the materials before retreating toward Winchester. The modern town manufactures rayon and furniture and processes limestones and foodstuffs.

See files of *Warren Sentinel* (1869–).

FRUIT AND BERRY INDUSTRY. During the colonial era commercial growing of fruit and berries in the South existed to only a limited extent with most of the output being for home consumption. This pattern of development was not signifi-

cantly different from that of the North, but in the early nineteenth century northern growers commercialized more rapidly. The only significant exceptions were Maryland and Virginia with their close proximity to the growing urban market of the East Coast. After the Civil War, with expansion of the railroad system, commercial growing spread in the South, and by the early twentieth century a specialization by area had been brought about, though the farm orchard remained the basic unit of production.

This concentration developed earliest in the citrus industry, with Florida developing the nation's first extensive commercial citrus groves in the latter part of the nineteenth century. However, disastrous freezes in the mid-1890s retarded the industry for several years, and leadership passed to California. Finding a growing market in processed oranges, Florida reemerged in the 1940s as the leading producer and presently grows about three-fourths of the nation's oranges. It also enjoys a similar dominance of grapefruit growing. In fact, Florida's total citrus production is so great that it accounts for about 30 percent of all fruit grown in the United States. Minor citrus-growing areas also developed in the South, the most successful being the lower Rio Grande Valley of Texas. Concentrating on grapefruit, this region by the mid-1940s, was producing nearly 40 percent of the nation's output, but severe freezes killed much of the acreage. Since then, production has not regained its former level, but is now more balanced between oranges and grapefruit.

In the production of deciduous fruits, the South has never been as important as the West Coast or North, but still has grown substantial quantities of apples and peaches. Apples are an important crop throughout the Appalachia belt of the Upper South, but the heaviest production is concentrated in the Shenandoah Valley of Virginia and parts of West Virginia. Overall the South now produces about 15 percent of the nation's apples. Favored with a mild climate, the South has been relatively more important in peach growing, with an output totaling about 20 percent of the nation's production. Georgia was long the leading peach state of the South, but since World War II has yielded first place to the Spartanburg region of South Carolina.

In berry production, the South has been most successful with strawberries. Although the growing of this crop has always been highly diversified, the Upper South produced about half the nation's output prior to World War II. Faced with a tightening labor supply, this region went into a precipitous decline as production shifted to the West Coast; but Florida and Louisiana still are important producers for the early spring market, and the South continues to produce about 10 percent of the nation's supply.

Since the 1930s fruit and berry production in the South, as elsewhere, has shifted increasingly to the big, highly specialized producers in the prime growing areas. This increasing specialization has generally worked against the South and in favor of the West Coast except that it has also favored those choice areas of the South, particularly Florida, the Rio Grande Valley, and the Appalachia belt, which possess special advantages of their own.

See J. W. Herbert and L. Dexter, *Citrus Industry* (1967); C. W. Olmstead, *Economic Geography* (July, 1956), perceptive; S. W. Fletcher, *Strawberry in North America* (1917); V. P. Hedrick, *Horticulture in America to 1860* (1950); and U.S. Department of Agriculture, *Agricultural Statistics* (annual).

G. K. RENNER
Missouri Southern State College

FUGITIVES, NASHVILLE, constituted a small community of poets centered among the faculty and students at Vanderbilt University. They had no formal connection with the university and in fact owed their existence as a group to the sympathetic interest of a few Nashville citizens, including Sidney Mttron Hirsh. It was Hirsh who suggested to the circle of poets, after they had been meeting informally for six years, that they organize themselves into a group and jointly edit and publish a small poetry magazine. The suggestion was realized in the *Fugitive*, issued four times a year from 1922 through 1927. The *Fugitive* (which took its name from a poem by Hirsh depicting the poet as a wanderer or outcast) published a variety of poems, but the most significant ones were by the chief Fugitives: JOHN CROWE RANSOM, DONALD DAVIDSON, ALLEN TATE, and ROBERT PENN WARREN. Save for those by Ransom, these poems do not mark high achievements in the art of poetry. Nor do they constitute a body of poetry devoted in any specific way to the South. But, together with the editorials and reviews in the *Fugitive*, they indicate a serious and informed alienation from the major premises of modern scientific and industrial civilization (REGIONALISM). Theirs was a reaction to modernity in which Ransom, Tate, and Davidson in particular associated their defense of poetry with a defense of a South they conceived as embodying the true civilizational order, that of the traditional agrarian society. The result was the formation of the Agrarian group, which wrote the manifesto I'LL TAKE MY STAND (1930). Although the Agrarians must be carefully distinguished from the Fugitives, the four most-prominent Fugitives (Ransom, Davidson, Tate, and Warren) were among the 12 authors of this work.

See L. Cowan, *Fugitive Group* (1959); *Fugitive*, repr. with intro. by D. Davidson (1967); D. Davidson, *Southern Writers in Modern World* (1958); A. Tate, *Princeton Library Chronicle* (April, 1942); *Fugitives' Reunion*, ed. L. D. Rubin, Jr., and R. R. Purdy (1959); D. Davidson and A. Tate, *Literary Correspondence*, ed. J. T. Fain and T. D. Young (1974); V. Rock, "Making and Meaning of *I'll Take My Stand*" (Ph.D. dissertation, University of Minnesota, 1961); J. L. Stewart, *Burden of Time* (1965); W. Pratt, *Fugitive Poets* (1965); and L. D. Rubin (ed.), *Guide to Southern Literature* (1969).

LEWIS SIMPSON
Louisiana State University

FUGITIVE SLAVE LAWS. Before the Civil War southerners felt wronged by northern interference in the recovery of fugitive slaves. The Constitution stated that a slave did not become free by escaping to another state. Southerners believed, moreover, that abolitionist agitation was a principal cause for the problem. Congress enacted two laws to aid in the recovery of fugitive slaves. The Fugitive Slave Act of 1793 was enacted to facilitate the extradition of fugitives from justice and the rendition of fugitive slaves. Antislavery sentiment in the North, however, made the law regarding fugitive slaves difficult to enforce. Personal liberty statutes in several northern states rendered the law a virtual dead letter. Although the U.S. Supreme Court ruled a Pennsylvania statute unconstitutional in 1842, the result was negative for the South. New personal liberty laws prohibited state officers from cooperating in the process of returning fugitive slaves.

As part of the COMPROMISE OF 1850 Congress passed a new and more stringent fugitive slave law. It made federal marshals liable for slaves in their custody and theoretically improved the process for recovering fugitive slaves. Believing that compromise did not serve southern interests, southern nationalists like Jefferson Davis had little faith in the law. The hostile reaction to the law in the North did little to assuage their fears. The GEORGIA PLATFORM, adopted in December, 1850, and widely supported in the South, made preservation of the Union dependent upon "faithful execution" of the Fugitive Slave Act of 1850. Soberminded conservatives in the North realized the danger to the Union and pleaded for acquiescence in the compromise. By midsummer, 1851, northern passions cooled regarding enforcement of the hated law. Perhaps a majority now supported the compromise settlement.

After passage of the KANSAS-NEBRASKA ACT in 1854, northern public opinion became increasingly hostile to the return of fugitive slaves. Several northern states enacted new and more sweeping personal liberty laws. Enforcement of the Fugitive Slave Act became increasingly difficult.

It is estimated that between 1,200 and 1,500 slaves ran away each year, but the number that fled to the free states is unknown. Of 332 fugitive slave cases reported in the 1850s, federal tribunals remanded 47.3 percent; 42.5 percent were captured and returned without due process of law. Only 6.6 percent (22 slaves) were rescued from federal custody in the same period. Newspaper reports of those rescues, however, helped convince southerners that the Fugitive Slave Act was not being enforced. Because of their belief that the North had not lived up to its pledge in the Compromise of 1850, southern extremists, feeling the institution of slavery was jeopardized, found additional justification for SECESSION from the Union.

See S. W. Campbell, *Slave Catchers* (1970); H. Hamilton, *Prologue to Conflict* (1964); L. Lara, *Liberty Line* (1969); A. O. Craven, *Growth of Southern Nationalism* (1953); and N. L. Rosenberg, *Civil War History* (March, 1971).

STANLEY W. CAMPBELL
Baylor University

FULBRIGHT, JAMES WILLIAM (1905–), served in the U.S. House of Representatives (1943–1945) and in the Senate (1945–1975), becoming best known for his combativeness (for which he was fired as president of the University of Arkansas in 1941) and for his commitment to internationalism. Over the years he sponsored such important measures as the 1943 Fulbright Resolution, calling for international cooperation after World War II, and the 1946 Fulbright Act, establishing international study fellowships, as well as writing five books on American foreign and security policy. A member of the Foreign Relations Committee from 1949 (chairman, from 1959), Fulbright articulately supported the foreign policies of Presidents Dwight Eisenhower, John Kennedy, and Lyndon Johnson. After breaking with Johnson over the Vietnam War in 1966, Fulbright emerged as a champion of antiwar liberals. In the 1970s he abandoned his long cooperation with the southern anti–civil rights bloc and became one of its leading liberal opponents. At the time of his defeat in the 1974 Arkansas primary, Fulbright was widely regarded as the most statesmanlike member in the Senate.

See H. Johnson and B. M. Gwertzman, *Fulbright* (1968), best source; T. Coffin, *Senator Fulbright* (1966); N. B. Lynn and A. F. McClure, *Fulbright Premise* (1973); and Fulbright Papers, University of Arkansas Library.

GARY W. REICHARD
Ohio State University

FULLER, MINNIE URSULA OLIVER SCOTT RUTHERFORD (1869–1946). An Arkansas social reformer, Minnie Oliver was born in Ozark and reared in Magazine, Ark., before marrying Omer H. Scott at the age of fourteen. When Scott died in 1887, she married William B. Rutherford, an attorney. They were divorced in 1909, and six years later Minnie married Dr. Seaborn Jennings Fuller, a Magazine physician. She studied widely in the United States and in Europe and she was entitled to practice law, but instead she threw her energies into social reform. She was active in the work of the Arkansas WOMAN'S CHRISTIAN TEMPERANCE UNION, as well as being a crusader for legislation regulating CHILD LABOR. She lobbied for women's suffrage and supported governor Charles H. Brough, under whose administration Arkansas ratified the Nineteenth Amendment. Minnie Rutherford Fuller also led in urging legislation to create a girls' industrial school and a state prison farm for women. She died in Brookline, Mass., at the age of seventy-eight.

See H. Brough Papers, University of Arkansas; F. Lisemby, *Arkansas Historical Quarterly* (Spring, 1970); and R. L. Niswonger, "Arkansas Politics, 1896–1920" (Ph.D. dissertation, University of Tennessee, 1974).

DAVID E. RISON
Baptist College at Charleston

FURMAN, FARISH CARTER (1846–1883), was born in Milledgeville, Ga., and studied science under Joseph Le Conte (LE CONTE FAMILY) at the University of South Carolina. He returned to his home to practice law and subsequently became active in local and state politics; but he turned to farming in 1878. At that time southern agriculture was faced with serious problems of labor shortage and depleted soil. To overcome these, Furman utilized his scientific training to formulate a compost designed to produce large cotton crops on reduced acreage. Within five years his intensive-farming system resulted in an eightfold crop increase. Highly publicized by the NEW SOUTH journalist HENRY W. GRADY, "Furman's Formula" was widely adopted in Georgia and other southern states and played a significant role in reforming agricultural methods in the 1880s.

See L. D. Stephens, *Agricultural History* (April, 1976); and Furman Papers, University of North Carolina Library and Georgia Historical Society.

LESTER D. STEPHENS
University of Georgia

FURMAN, RICHARD (1755–1825), supporter of the Revolution and a member of the South Carolina constitutional convention (1790), became a staunch Federalist. From his position as pastor of the First Baptist Church in Charleston, he emerged as the most prominent BAPTIST leader of his generation in the South. His educational concerns led to the establishment, after his death, of FURMAN UNIVERSITY (1826). As president of the South Carolina Baptist State Convention, he wrote a response to the VESEY PLOT, which had wracked Charleston in 1822. The declaration reassured nervous planters that Christianity, far from encouraging slaves to rise against their masters, taught submission to authority, and urged the acceptance of slavery as a biblically sanctioned positive good.

See Furman Papers, University of South Carolina; R. Furman, *Views of Baptists* (1823); H. S. Smith, R. T. Handy, and L. A. Loetscher, *American Christianity* (1963), II, reprint of essentials of *Views* and useful introduction; R. S. Starobin, *Denmark Vesey* (1970), reprint of Furman letter to Governor T. Bennett; and H. T. Cook, *Richard Furman* (1923), thin.

KLAUS J. HANSEN
Queen's University, Kingston, Ont.

FURMAN UNIVERSITY (Greenville, S.C. 29613) is the oldest Baptist college in the South. Founded in 1826 as Furman Academy and Theological Institute, it first was located in Edgefield. After numerous moves, it located permanently in Greenville in 1851. A graduate school was added in 1879, but the school remains primarily a coeducational, liberal arts college with an enrollment of approximately 2,000 students. Its library keeps a small collection of papers relating chiefly to South Carolina Baptists.

See R. N. Daniel, *Furman University* (1951); and A. S. Reid, *Furman University, 1925–1975* (1976).

FURNITURE INDUSTRY. American furniture making began, and has remained, largely craft oriented and family owned. Although most fine furniture used in the South was imported from England or from large northeastern cities prior to the late nineteenth century, the growing wealth of southern planters and traders and their demands for fashionable furniture attracted numerous cabinetmakers from Europe and the Northeast into areas such as Charleston, S.C., even before the Revolution. Some craftsmen became itinerants, some established shops, and others were employed on large plantations. Several of these craftsmen, such as Joseph Sayre of Kentucky and THOMAS AFFLECK of Charleston, gained particular prominence for their work. THOMAS JEFFERSON, a master designer of furniture, employed cabinetmakers at Monticello. The less affluent made their own roughhewn furniture, or they purchased it from local carpenters.

The austere, straight-line styles of furniture made in the South during the seventeenth century gave way to curved lines, comfort, and elegance during the eighteenth century. Chippendale styles dominated fine furniture construction from about 1750 until 1780, but following the Revolution southern cabinetmakers turned toward the functional designs of Hepplewhite and Duncan Phyfe. Richmond and Baltimore joined Charleston as important centers of cabinetmaking, but the South remained deficient in skilled craftsmen, since the market for fine furniture was limited to wealthy planters and traders who preferred the prestige of European makes.

The modern furniture industry of the South began in 1888, when several local businessmen built a furniture factory in High Point, N.C. Although small factories had been established a few years earlier at Nashville, Tenn., and Danville, Va., High Point became the growth center for the industry. Abundance of low-cost wood and labor gave High Point furniture a decided cost advantage over northern competition in supplying the southern Piedmont, where a rapidly growing textile industry was accentuating regional purchasing power. Furniture manufacturing spread from High Point into nearby Thomasville and Statesville and into southwestern Virginia. In 1913 the first Southern Furniture Exposition convened at High Point, signaling efforts to improve the quality of furniture made in the area. By that time the cheapest grades were being manufactured in Little Rock, Pine Bluff, and Ft. Smith, Ark. The major centers of furniture manufacturing, however, remained in the North.

Following World War I southern manufacturers expanded their market beyond the South by using to advantage styles copied from northern factories and lower production and selling costs. Thereafter, the Piedmont industries of North Carolina and Virginia began a period of spectacular growth and steady improvement in product quality. Following World War II North Carolina challenged and surpassed New York as the leading maker of household furniture, currently accounting for about 20 percent of the nation's output. Virginia, Tennessee, Texas, Arkansas, Georgia, and Mississippi also have large and growing industries.

The fragmented and craft-oriented nature of the furniture industry may be short-lived, since large companies have been purchasing smaller competitors and a few corporations have recently entered furniture manufacturing in response to the industry's high returns on capital investments. These financial giants plan to capture a major share of the market through national brand-name advertising. Whether it operates as in the past or as part of a corporate structure, however, the climate for growth in southern furniture manufacturing remains favorable.

See V. S. Clark, *History of Manufactures* (1929); P. H. Burroughs, *Southern Antiques* (1931); B. F. Lemert, *Economic Geography* (April, 1934); T. O'Hanlon, *Fortune* (Feb., 1967); Federal Trade Commission, *Report on Home Furnishings* (1923–25); North Carolina Department of Conservation, *Economic Report No. 57* (1926); and *U. S. Census of Manufactures*.

SIDNEY R. JUMPER
University of Tennessee, Knoxville

FUR TRADE was an extremely important part of the founding of each of the southern colonies. After initial trade with the Indians for food, each colony acquired furs as one kind of export welcomed by sponsors at home. Virginia drew on the Appalachian backcountry and eventually the Ohio Valley for beaver, otter, ermine, and fox as well as lynx, wolf, and bear. English customs records show as much as £2,433 value of furs from Virginia in 1700, although Pennsylvania, New York, and later Canada supplied by far the greater amount. For South Carolina, the principal "fur" was really deerskins, imported by England for the leather. This was South Carolina's first "cash crop." Later supplanted by rice and indigo, deerskins remained third in value of exports. Drawing on the southern Appalachians and the tramontane South, an average of more than 50,000 deerskins were exported from Charleston each year from 1690 to 1770. A high point was reached in the early 1740s, when over 200,000 skins went out in one year.

The fur trade was one of the most important points of contact between colonists and Indians, for the Indians quickly became dependent on European trade goods. Complaints about conduct of the trade ranked with encroachment upon Indian land as an irritant between the races. Colonial authorities attempted to license traders and appointed commissions to enforce laws on the trade, but with little success.

Rivalries between colonies over the trade and access to particular tribes provoked frequently tense relations among the colonies. Virginia's efforts to enter the CHEROKEE trade and South Carolina's law of 1711 requiring all outside traders to come to Charleston for a license and to post bond for bringing skins to the Charleston market are but one example. The British government did not take up the idea of imperial supervision of Indian affairs until the 1750s. Then a northern and a southern district were created with a superintendent in each. John Stuart was the first to be given the full and independent commission in the South in 1761.

International rivalries were involved, too, particularly with the French. Trade provided cement for an alliance of a given tribe to the English or French. Apparently the Indians preferred French personnel and tactics in general. French emissaries from New Orleans, Natchez, Mobile, or some up-country post were frequent visitors among the Cherokee, CREEK, and CHICKASAW and rather dominated the CHOCTAW. However, the French simply could not deliver the quantity and quality of goods provided by the English and could not hold the tribes to a solid alliance.

In the nineteenth century, a change of styles reduced European demand at the same time that removal of the Indians reduced the supply of skins from the South. In the twentieth century, the fur trade still has some importance, particularly in Louisiana, which produced about 6 million muskrat pelts in 1965. This does not place furs very high on the economic ladder, and even this number is said to be declining.

See J. R. Alden, *John Stuart* (1944); C. W. Alvord, *Mississippi Valley in British Politics* (2 vols.; 1917); *Colonial Records of South Carolina, Documents Relating to Indian Affairs* (2 vols.; 1958, 1962); R. L. Morton, *Colonial Virginia* (2 vols.; 1960); *Statistical History of U.S.* (1965); and V. W. Crane, *Southern Frontier* (1929).

CLARENCE J. ATTIG
Westmar College

G

GABRIEL'S INSURRECTION (August–October, 1800), the first of the three great slave insurrections of the nineteenth century, occurred in Henrico County, Va. It was led by Gabriel Prosser (1775?–1800) and had an elaborate plan and a large though uncertain number of conspirators. It attempted to end slavery in the region by capturing Richmond and slaying area slave owners. The insurrection was secretly organized in the spring to take place on August 30. A heavy rainstorm, the warning of two informing slaves, and Governor JAMES MONROE's quick military action prevented success. Gabriel Prosser escaped but was captured on board a ship in Norfolk harbor, refused to give any information, and was executed October 7. Approximately 35 conspirators were hanged. The insurrection resulted in the tightening of laws governing slaves and free blacks, gave an impetus to colonization thoughts, and helped kill antislavery activity in the South.

See G. Mullin, *Slave Resistance* (1972); J. Marszalek, *Negro History Bulletin* (March, 1976); *Calendar of Virginia State Papers* (1934–36); IX; *Writings of Monroe* (1900), III; W. Jordan, *White over Black* (1968); and J. C. Carroll, *Slave Insurrections* (1938).

JOHN F. MARSZALEK
Mississippi State University

GADSDEN, CHRISTOPHER (1724–1805), of Charleston, S.C., a merchant and a radical member of the provincial commons house, was one of the foremost leaders of the Revolution. His ideas for independence originated in 1762 in a contest with Governor Thomas Boone, who had interfered with the freedom of the assembly. In attending the Stamp Act Congress, Gadsden advocated unity of all the American colonies, and at the CONTINENTAL CONGRESS with John Adams he was a leading mover for separation from Great Britain, the construction of a colonial navy, and general armament. At home in South Carolina he earned the enmity of the more moderate planters, but he possessed the backing of the volatile mechanics of Charleston until 1778 and was enabled to effectuate the largely democratic state constitution (1778) containing popular election of senators and disestablishment of the Anglican church. Afterward he advocated nationalism and order with liberty based on representative government. In 1788

he voted for the Constitution in the ratifying convention and took part in the local convention of 1790. He ended his years a staunch Federalist.

See R. Walsh (ed.), *Writings of Gadsden* (1966), for additional references.

RICHARD WALSH
Georgetown University

GADSDEN, JAMES (1788–1858), was born in Charleston, S.C., and was briefly engaged in business there. An army engineer during the War of 1812, he was later appointed aide-de-camp to Andrew Jackson and served with him in the Florida campaign of 1817–1818. During the campaign Gadsden captured the papers that resulted in the trial and execution of Robert C. Ambrister and Alexander Arbuthnot (ARBUTHNOT AND AMBRISTER, CASE OF). His association with Jackson brought him rapid military advancement by 1820.

When Gadsden's nomination as adjutant general of the army in 1821 was rejected by the U.S. Senate, he resigned from service and settled in Florida. His later defense of NULLIFICATION cost him the friendship of Jackson, and he returned to Charleston in 1839. As president of the Louisville, Cincinnati & Charleston Railroad, he reorganized it in 1842 as the South Carolina Railroad Company.

Active in the southern commercial CONVENTIONS, he championed a southern railroad to the Pacific. With the aid of Jefferson Davis, he was appointed minister to Mexico in 1853. Beyond his acquisition of the territory known as the Gadsden Purchase, he accomplished little else in that position.

See P. N. Garber, *Gadsden Treaty* (1923), best; and F. Rippy, *U.S. and Mexico* (1925).

DONALD M. RAWSON
Northwestern State University of Louisiana

GADSDEN, ALA. (pop. 53,928), is on the upper reaches of the Coosa River approximately 60 miles northeast of Birmingham. The site was first settled in the 1830s as a farm village known as Double Springs. The area was rich in coal and iron ore, but residents lacked both the capital and the inclination to develop these resources. The town was renamed in 1845 to honor JAMES GADSDEN, who had spoken favorably of the town and of its economic prospects. By the time of the Civil War it was a shipping center served by steamboats and by six coach lines. Real growth did not come to the town, however, until after its incorporation in 1871 and development of the area's mineral resources. Today the city's foundries produce heavy steel, iron, and manganese (IRON AND STEEL INDUSTRY), and its factories manufacture tires, textiles, tractors, lumber, construction materials, and processed foods.

See files of Gadsden *Times* (1867–); Community Centennial Commission, *History of Etowah County* (1968); and C. A. Donehoo, *Public Schools, Gadsden, 1895–1951* (1951).

GAG RULES sought to suppress any discussion of slavery in the U.S. House of Representatives. A swelling flood of abolitionist petitions in the mid-1830s prompted Congressman H. L. Pinckney, a South Carolina Democrat, to initiate the first gag rule, which was adopted May 18, 1836. It provided that all such petitions "be laid upon the table." A coalition of Democrats and southern Whigs, arguing that slavery was a local issue, combined to reenact a similar rule in subsequent sessions of Congress. On January 28, 1840, the House adopted Standing Rule 21, which stood until its appeal on December 3, 1844. The gag rules failed to accomplish their end. A small group of northern Whigs, led by "Old Man Eloquent," John Quincy Adams, fought the gag and kept the slavery issue alive. By joining the issues of slavery and civil liberties, the gag rules actually strengthened the antislavery movement. The vote that repealed the gag rule divided along sectional lines. The depth of feeling and the sectional alignment that the issue produced were ominous portents for the next decade.

See R. B. Nye, *Fettered Freedom* (1963); S. F. Bemis, *John Q. Adams and Union* (1956); J. M. McPherson, *Journal of Negro History* (July, 1963); and G. H. Barnes, *Antislavery Impulse* (1933).

WILBERT H. AHERN
University of Minnesota, Morris

GAINES, EDMUND PENDLETON (1777–1849), a Virginian, spent his 50-year military career in command positions mainly in the South, where he was occupied with implementing federal policies on defense, Indian affairs, and the slave trade. As a result, Gaines became embroiled in numerous feuds. His fierce nationalism led him to dispute War Department orders, which he grudgingly followed to the letter. His record was marred by highly publicized military court proceedings, and though he was exonerated from serious wrongdoing, he was chastised for improper accounting procedures during the SEMINOLE WARS and for exceeding authority at the outbreak of war with Mexico. Much of his fame rests on his having surveyed GAINES' TRACE, but his greatest contribution lay in expressing humanitarian views toward the Five Civilized Tribes, who he felt could have been admirable citizens in the South. He was at his outraged best in castigating ANDREW JACKSON for implementing the Indian removal policy. Few of his peers, especially General WINFIELD SCOTT, escaped his cutting tongue, yet he was respected for devotion to country.

See Record Groups 94, 98, and 159, National Archives; and J. W. Silver, *Edmund P. Gaines* (1949).

RICHARD D. GAMBLE
Green Mountain College

GAINES, GEORGE STROTHER (1784–1873), a pioneer of Alabama, was the brother of EDMUND PENDLETON GAINES. He was a factor (1806–1819) of the government trading house at St. Stephen's on the Tombigbee River, and his honest and faithful service to the CHOCTAW INDIANS earned him their respect and loyalty. Gaines assisted Chief Pushmataha in having Choctaws accepted into the army after the Creek massacre of 500 Americans at Ft. Mims (August 30, 1813). Resigning as factor, he became a merchant at Demopolis, but resumed the Choctaw trade when the government factory closed. To quiet discontent aroused by the Treaty of DANCING RABBIT CREEK (1830), Gaines led Choctaw elders in an exploration of their new trans-Mississippi territory. After superintending the migration of the Choctaw from Mississippi, Gaines became a respected merchant, president of the Mobile branch of the Alabama State Bank, and promoter of the Mobile & Ohio Railroad.

See G. S. Gaines, *Alabama Historical Quarterly* (Fall, 1964); A. Plaisance, *Alabama Historical Quarterly* (Fall, 1954); and G. Foreman, *Indian Removal* (1932).

ALAN V. BRICELAND
Virginia Commonwealth University

GAINES' MILL, BATTLE OF (June 27, 1862), was the third of the SEVEN DAYS' BATTLES of the PENINSULAR CAMPAIGN. After Robert E. Lee failed to destroy Fitz-John Porter's isolated V Corps at MECHANICSVILLE and Beaver Dam Creek on June 26, George B. McClellan withdrew his right wing to high ground east of Gaines' Mill, Va., and south of Cold Harbor. Lee had dispatched Stonewall Jackson's corps on a northward flanking movement to cut off Porter from the main federal army beyond the Chickahominy. Porter's strong defensive position behind Boatswain's Swamp offered good fields of fire. Lee attacked with the major portion of his army under A. P. HILL, but was repulsed with heavy loss. After Stonewall Jackson's dilatory forces arrived, the Confederates finally breached the federal lines with JOHN B. HOOD's Texas brigade in the van. Twenty-two federal guns fell into Confederate hands, and arrival of federal reinforcements failed to stem the defeat. Losses at Gaines' Mill included 893 killed, 3,107 wounded, and 2,836 missing of 34,214 federals engaged. Confederate losses numbered 8,751 killed and wounded in a force of 57,018. Lee's victory permitted continuation of harassment of McClellan's transfer of base from the Pamunkey to the James River. It also permitted the reoccupation of all ground north of the Chickahominy and substantially diminished the threat to Richmond, the Confederate capital.

See C. Dowdey, *Seven Days* (1964), best emphasis on emergence of Lee; J. P. Cullen, *Peninsula Campaign* (1973), contrasts in command; *Official Records, Armies*, Ser. 1, Vols. XI, LI; R. U. Johnson and C. C. Buel (eds.), *Battles and Leaders* (1887), II; J. P. Cullen, *Civil War Times, Illustrated* (April, 1964), short, popular; T. H. Evans, *Civil War Times, Illustrated* (Aug., 1967), personal account; and General Service Schools, U.S. Army, *Source Book: Peninsula* (1921), anthology.

B. FRANKLIN COOLING
U.S. Army Military History Research Collection

GAINES' TRACE, connecting the Tennessee River near Muscle Shoals, Ala., with the Tombigbee River at Cotton Gin Port, provided an important link in the military-trade route from the Ohio River to Mobile. The original route, following a well-known Indian trail, was laid out in 1801 by ED-MUND P. GAINES. It was used by early settlers along the Tombigbee who were angered by Spanish restrictions on immigration and wanted to avoid taxes imposed on trade goods brought in through Mobile. Later, Gaines and his brother GEORGE S. GAINES, factor at St. Stephen's, convinced the War Department that the route should be surveyed and extended toward the Gulf to Plymouth. The survey was completed in 1808, but delays in concluding a treaty with the CHICKASAW INDIANS prevented opening the road even as a horse path until 1810.

Gaines' Trace played an important role in the development of the entire Southeast, particularly during the period 1810–1830. It became the major route by which settlers entered the Tombigbee River valley, and after it was expanded into a wagon road, it provided a practical and economic route to and from the northeastern states. By encouraging trade and settlement, the road helped secure northeastern Mississippi and southwestern Alabama for the United States. Reinforcements from Tennessee followed this route to join Andrew Jackson just before the battle of NEW ORLEANS (1815).

See C. E. Carter (comp.), *Territorial Papers of U.S., Territory of Mississippi, 1809–1817* (1938), VI; J. H. Stone, *Cotton Gin Port, Miss.* (1969); and W. A. Evans, *Journal of Mississippi History* (April, 1939).

RICHARD FARRELL
University of Maryland

GAINESVILLE, FLA. (pop. 64,510), approximately 65 miles southwest of St. Augustine, was first settled in 1830 as a trading post. Known as Hog Town until 1853, when it was formally laid out, it was named to honor EDMUND P. GAINES, a general in the SEMINOLE WARS. Completion of the Yulee Railroad in the 1860s opened the area to widescale cultivation of cotton and greatly stimulated the town's growth. The location here of the University of Florida, the development of lumber and naval stores industries, and in the twentieth century the growth of tourism have given the town a varied economic base.

See C. H. Hildreth, "History of Gainesville" (Ph.D. dissertation, University of Florida, 1954); F. Hussain, "Gainesville, Florida" (Ph.D. dissertation, University of Florida, 1959); M. Gresham, *Cemetery Records* (1972); J. G. Davis, *History of Gainesville* (1966) and *History of Alachua County* (1969); F. Buckholz, *History of Alachua County* (1929); and files of Gainesville *Sun* (1876–).

GAINESVILLE, GA. (pop. 15,459), 53 miles northeast of Atlanta, was first settled in 1804 as a trading post deep within CHEROKEE INDIAN territory. As the Indians gradually were pushed westward, white settlers built homes around the old trading post until, in 1818, the Georgia legislature made it the seat of a newly created county. On the fringe of the Georgia goldfields, the town grew moderately during the 1830s but was virtually destroyed by fire in 1851. Brenau College (first known as Georgia Baptist Female Seminary) was founded here in 1878, and several cotton mills had been opened, but real prosperity awaited development in the 1890s of the area's POULTRY INDUSTRY. Now known as the Broiler Capital of the

World, Gainesville also is the headquarters for the Chattahoochie National Forest.

See M. Powell, *Hall County Through Years* (1968), illustrated; and S. W. McRay, *This 'n That of Hall County* (1973).

GALLUSES.

A humorous play on the English word *gallows*, the word *gallus* or its plural *galluses* has at least two different meanings in the South. A farmer's suspenders are referred to as his galluses, a one-gallused farmer being indeed a poor fellow. Whether singular or plural, the term recalls the erect posts from which English criminals were hanged. Galluses are also the frameworks used to stack cornstalks, sorgum, or some similar crop that was kept and stored as fodder. By tying the old vine of a squash or pumpkin plant around several stalks of corn, for example, a frame or gallus was created, against which additional stalks could be stacked. When the pile or hock was large enough, it was tied into a bundle, the foundation stalks of the gallus were cut from their roots, and the stack was ready to be stored.

GALPHIN CLAIM

(1765–1790) was at the center of a long boundary dispute between Georgia and the CREEK INDIANS. Part of a promotion by Indian trader George Galphin (?–1780), it placed settlers illegally on the valuable Creek hunting grounds between the Ogeechee and Oconee rivers west of Savannah and provoked continuous tension. It was claimed by Georgia in treaties in 1773, 1783, and 1785, which a majority of Creek leaders repudiated, and was finally ceded to Georgia in the Treaty of New York (1790).

See S. Proctor (ed.), *Eighteenth Century Florida* (1975); E. R. R. Green, *William and Mary Quarterly* (April, 1960); J. R. Alden, *John Stuart* (1944); J. Caughey, *Mc-Gillivray of Creeks* (1938); and D. H. Corkran, *Creek Frontier* (1967).

RICHARD M. CLOKEY
Indiana State University

GALVANIZED YANKEES

was a sobriquet applied to about 6,000 Confederate prisoners of war who obtained their freedom by enlisting in Union regiments used mainly on the western frontier against Indians. Their official name was U.S. Volunteers. Captured Union soldiers who enlisted in the Confederate army were known as Galvanized Confederates but were sometimes confusingly called Galvanized Yankees. An estimated 1,300 to 2,000 captured Union soldiers took the oath of allegiance to the Confederate army. Most were foreign-born recruits. Several escaped from James Island to rejoin the Union command on Hilton Head, S.C., and 254 others surrendered to Union forces after a fight at Egypt Station, Miss.

See D. A. Brown, *Galvanized Yankees* (1963).

DEE ALEXANDER BROWN
University of Illinois

GALVESTON, CAPTURE OF

(1862–1863). Confederate Texas, virtually untouched by Union forces 18 months after FT. SUMTER, was the target of an important Union naval assault in October, 1862. DAVID G. FARRAGUT sent two gunboats and two converted ferries into Galveston harbor, the Confederacy's most valuable port between the Mississippi River and the Rio Grande, captured the island city on October 5 almost without resistance, and occupied it with 260 men. Nathaniel P. Banks, Union commander of the Department of the Gulf, was determined to occupy larger areas of Texas in order to funnel cotton to idle New England textile mills, and he accordingly strengthened the garrison at Galveston Island with three companies on Christmas Eve. But JOHN B. MAGRUDER, Confederate commander of the District of Texas, Arizona, and New Mexico, assembled a force of about 800 men and two cotton-clad steamboats, attacked shortly after midnight on January 1, 1863, and captured the city after a sharp fight. The Confederates destroyed one federal gunboat, captured another, inflicted 600 casualties while suffering 143, and reoccupied Galveston for the remainder of the war.

See S. Foote, *Civil War* (1958–74); R. L. Kerby, *Kirby-Smith's Confederacy* (1972); and H. Henderson, *Texas in Confederacy* (1955).

RICHARD LOWE
North Texas State University

GALVESTON, TEX.

(pop. 61,809), is a major port city off the Texas coast approximately 45 miles southeast of Houston. In 1785, Spanish surveyors named both the island and the bay in honor of BERNARDO DE GÁLVEZ, viceroy of Mexico. A Mexican settlement and garrison established here in 1816 were seized the following year by JEAN LAFFITE, who used the site's fine natural harbor as a pirate base until he was driven away in 1821 by an American naval force. Used by the Republic of Texas as an immigration point, as a naval base, and briefly as its capital, Galveston grew steadily in importance as a major coastal port. In the Civil War, after twice repulsing federal naval attacks, the city fell to federal authorities without resistance on October 5, 1862. Galveston was retaken by Confederate forces on January 1, 1863, however, and did not surrender to federal authorities until June 2, 1865. Shipments of the growing volume of cotton cultivated in the area became the principal economic activity of postwar Galveston. To accommodate this expanded commerce, the city's harbor facilities were renovated, and its channel to the Gulf was deepened between 1889 and 1896. The benefits derived from these facilities were short-lived, however, since the city was hit on September 8, 1900, by the most devastating hurricane in its storm-ridden history. Over 6,000 people lost their lives during the hurricane, and much of the city was completely destroyed. While dealing with this crisis, the city adopted the GALVESTON COMMISSION PLAN of government, the first instance of what became an increasingly popular form of municipal governance. The sea level of the city was raised several feet prior to being rebuilt, and a massive seawall was constructed to protect the city and its harbor from future storms. Dredging of the Houston Ship Channel (1912–1914) augmented Houston's function as a port while diminishing Galveston's relative significance as a shipping point and port of entry. Nevertheless, the city remains an important port for shipments of cotton and grain and a manufacturer of wire and nails.

See files of Galveston *Civilian* and *Gazette* (1838–72), Galveston *News* (1842–), *Flake's Daily Bulletin* (1865–72), and the German *Die Union* (1857–70), all on microfilm; B. Axelrod, *Southwestern Historical Quarterly* (Oct., 1966); and M. Huff and H. B. Carroll, *Southwestern Historical Quarterly* (Jan., 1962).

GALVESTON CIVILIAN

GALVESTON CIVILIAN began publication in Houston in 1838, but it moved that same year to the coastal seaport. The paper was edited by Hamilton Stuart, a native of Kentucky, who chose the name to protest the prevailing practice of adopting such honorific military titles of address as "Major," "Colonel" and "General." A weekly and semiweekly newspaper closely associated with SAM HOUSTON, it became a daily in 1857. Although it suspended publication in 1862, it resumed printing in 1865 and continued until 1886.

See S. Acheson, *35,000 Days in Texas* (1938); and Galveston *Civilian* (1838–45), bound copies in Library of Congress.

GALVESTON COMMISSION PLAN

GALVESTON COMMISSION PLAN. At the turn of the century Galveston, Tex., had the reputation of being one of the most poorly governed cities in America. Mounting debts and declining city services had prompted business leaders in the 1890s to change the city charter to provide for the election of aldermen at large rather than by wards, the expectation being that this would result in the selection of officials responsive to community-wide issues and pledged to governmental efficiency. Meeting with only limited success, reformers seized upon the crisis caused by the tropical storm of September, 1900, that left the city virtually bankrupt to gain both local consensus and state legislative approval of a bill establishing a five-man commission to administer municipal affairs in the manner of the "modern business corporation." The government of the District of Columbia and similar commissions of more temporary nature in Memphis and Baltimore served as models for the Galveston plan, which when adopted provided for the election of two commissioners and the appointment by the governor of the other three. Each commissioner was charged with sharply defined responsibility for one or more functions of city government, and acting together they formed a city council that established general policy.

No doubt the commission plan was partly responsible for the remarkable recovery of Galveston. It also attracted the interest of municipal reformers elsewhere and received wide publicity through the muckraking press. An early court case (1903) led to the repeal of the appointive provision in the Galveston charter, and all commissioners were henceforth elected at large. No panacea for municipal government problems, the commission plan had weaknesses, which led municipal reformers to move to the city manager form of government around World War I.

See J. A. Tinsley, "Progressive Movement in Texas" (Ph.D. dissertation, University of Wisconsin, 1954); B. R. Rice, *Southwestern Historical Quarterly* (April, 1975); J. Weinstein, *Journal of Southern History* (May, 1962); and S. P. Hays, *Pacific Northwest Quarterly* (Oct., 1964).

JAMES A. TINSLEY
University of Houston

GALVEZ, BERNARDO DE

GALVEZ, BERNARDO DE (1748–1786), a nephew of the celebrated minister of the Indies José Gálvez, was Spanish governor of Louisiana during the trying period of the American Revolution. Youthful, courageous, and imaginative, he enjoyed greater popularity with the French Creoles than any previous Spanish administrator. Although unsympathetic to the aspirations to liberty and independence in the English colonies to the north, he realized their profound need for unofficial support. GEORGE ROGERS CLARK's expedition to the Northwest was clandestinely supplied from New Orleans. The outbreak of the war between

Spain and Great Britain furnished the opportunity for the display of Gálvez's exceptional talents as a strategist and a tactician, resulting in the capture of Baton Rouge, Mobile, and Pensacola. His action was decisive in the elimination of the British control of the Floridas, which might have blocked the extension of the frontiers of the southern states to the Gulf.

See J. W. Caughey, *Bernardo de Gálvez* (1934; 1972); and G. Múñoz Porras, *Gálvez* (1952). See also microfilm of Audiencia de St. Domingo Records, Sp. Archives, Loyola University, New Orleans.

J. PRESTON MOORE
Louisiana State University

GAMBLE, HAMILTON ROWAN (1798–1864), was the youngest son of Irish immigrants. He was born in Winchester, Va., educated at Hampden-Sydney College, and admitted to the bar at eighteen years of age. After serving briefly as secretary of state (1824–1825), he located at St. Louis, where he gained a well-deserved reputation as a lawyer. In 1846, he served one term in the U.S. House of Representatives; and from 1851 until 1854 he was a member of the state supreme court. Although sixty-three years old and in failing health, he accepted the responsibility as provisional governor between 1861 and 1864. He kept Missouri in the Union by conservative and moderate measures. At all times, he opposed the demands of the radical Unionist element in the state.

See *Messages and Proclamations of Missouri Governors* (1922), III; W. R. Jackson, *Missouri Democracy* (1935); M. Potter, *Missouri Historical Review* (Oct., 1948); J. F. Phillips, *Missouri Historical Review* (Oct., 1910), most definitive; and G. Anderson, *Story of Border City During Civil War* (1908).

GOSSIE H. HUDSON
Lincoln University

GARDEN, ALEXANDER (1685?–1756), was born in Scotland and received an M.A. degree from the University of Aberdeen. He became rector of St. Philip's Church, Charleston, in 1719 and served in that capacity until 1753. In 1729 he was appointed commissary to Edmund Gibson, bishop of London. Noted for his devotion and piety, Garden carried out his duties with a strong hand. With the aid of Governor FRANCIS NICHOLSON, he was able to revitalize the Church of England in the colony. Through the establishment of an ecclesiastical court, Garden was able to discipline the Anglican clergy under his jurisdiction. His most famous prosecution was that of George Whitefield, which resulted in the suspension of the celebrated

preacher. Although the sentence did not silence Whitefield, it does illustrate the vigor of Garden as commissary. Resigning his commissarial duties in 1749, Garden returned briefly to England before spending the few remaining years of his life in South Carolina.

See A. L. Cross, *Anglican Episcopate* (1902); M. E. Sirmans, *Colonial South Carolina* (1966); E. L. Pennington, *Historical Magazine of Protestant Episcopal Church* (1934); and Q. B. Keen, *Historical Magazine of Protestant Episcopal Church* (1951).

GERALD E. HARTDAGEN
Concordia College, Moorhead, Minn.

GARDEN, ALEXANDER (1730–1791), was the Charleston physician and naturalist for whom the flowering shrub *Gardenia* was named. Born near Aberdeen, Scotland, he became a surgeon's mate in the Royal Navy and studied botany and medicine at Edinburgh. In 1752 he immigrated to South Carolina, where he lived until the Revolution. As a Loyalist, Garden withdrew to England in 1783, serving there on the council of the Royal Society. During three decades in America, despite imperfect health and an extensive medical practice, Garden traveled widely and pursued diverse scientific interests. Like Benjamin Franklin, he was fascinated with ocean currents and meteorology. Garden corresponded with American naturalists— C. Colden, J. and W. Bartram, J. Clayton—and sent specimens of plants, fish, reptiles, and minerals to members of the international scientific community, accompanied by elaborate notes and drawings. Although he published little, Garden's correspondence with Carolus Linnaeus assisted a scientific classic.

See E. and D. S. Berkeley, *Dr. Alexander Garden* (1969), definitive; U. P. Hedrick, *History of Horticulture in America* (1950), for background; and M. Denny, *Isis* (1948).

PETER H. WOOD
Duke University

GARDENS in the South trace their origin to the earliest permanent settlers of the coastal regions. The very first efforts were utilitarian, to provide sources of food and fiber, to expand seed and stock supplies for settlers to the hinterlands, to test the adaptability of species to the new land, and to determine requirements for cultivation. No sooner were the necessities of life provided than were gardens of pleasure established. The colonists followed the traditional methods for design from their homeland and introduced favorite plants, such as boxwood, camellias, and azaleas from gardens in Europe (FLOWERS AND SHRUBS). These together with fine indigenous plants including live oak and magnolia (TREES) formed a horticultural wealth of plant material for them to establish gardens to surround their homes. The geographical area encompassing the South, from Florida to the high elevations of the southern Appalachians, includes climatic zones conducive to the development of diversified gardens with a great range of plant material.

Many of the early gardens perished in turbulent times and with the changing fortunes of their owners. New gardens, however, have been created, and some old ones have been restored. Today's gardens in the South reflect a variety of styles, with a tendency away from the European heritage. New and original designs perhaps better suited to the present culture are being used throughout the area. The English informal plan, utilizing wide lawns, clumps of trees, and vistas, has persisted and is evident in many gardens, large and small.

The South is renowned for many splendid public and private gardens. Public gardens presently maintained to preserve the historic qualities of the colonial planters include Colonial Williamsburg, Monticello, Brandon, Mount Vernon, Middleton, Hermitage, and other plantation sites. Estate gardens, reminiscent of Europe's finest, include Dumbarton Oaks, Biltmore, and the Elizabethan Garden. Others designed to delight the visitor with a harmony and profusion of bloom through the seasons are represented by Callaway, Hodges, Bellingrath, Longue Vue, Cypress, Rip Van Winkle, and Magnolia gardens. Brookgreen is unique, being designed around an old plantation garden as an outdoor museum for an extensive collection of American sculpture. Fairchild, near Miami, and the Plant Introduction Station at Savannah are truly botanical gardens, where, in addition to their beauty in the landscape, introduced plants are studied to determine their adaptability and value for use by others. Private gardens are a traditional source of pride in the South, and many offer exquisite examples of fine landscaping. The cities of Charleston, Savannah, New Orleans, Nashville, Memphis, and Atlanta are especially well known in this regard.

See J. Wedda, *Gardens of American South* (1971); L. W. Briggs, *Charleston Gardens* (1951); E. Lawrence, *Southern Garden* (1942); N. S. Grayson, *South Carolina Gardens* (1973); E. T. H. Shaffer, *Carolina Gardens* (1939); and James River Garden Club, *Historic Gardens of Virginia* (1930).

GURDON L. TARBOX, JR.
Brookgreen Gardens

GARDNER, FRANKLIN (1823–1873), son of Charles Kitchel Gardner, was born in New York City. As an 1843 West Point graduate and lieutenant colonel in the Confederate army, Gardner served at SHILOH and in Braxton Bragg's 1862 Kentucky campaign. As major general, he commanded PORT HUDSON, La., until that post capitulated after a stubborn defense following Vicksburg's surrender. Exchanged, the general served until 1865 in Mississippi. Following Appomattox, he became a planter near Vermillionville (now Lafayette), La., where he died. In a family split by the war, Gardner's father supported the Union cause and his brother actively fought for the North.

See E. J. Warner, *Generals in Gray* (1959), best; W. F. Amann (ed.), *Personnel of Civil War* (1961), listed as Frank Gardner; and A. Johnson and D. Malone (eds.), *Dictionary of American Biography* (1931), for father's biography and ancestry.

JOHN S. PAINTER
Northern State College, Aberdeen, S.D.

GARDNER, OLIVER MAX (1882–1947). Gardner's term as governor of North Carolina (1928–1932) was characterized by the reorganization and centralization of state government and the concentration of power in the chief executive's office. The legislature completed the state's control of the public school system, assumed full responsibility for the maintenance of the county road network, and began exercising close supervision of local finances. Gardner persuaded the legislature to reorganize numerous state agencies, particularly the highway and revenue departments, and create new ones, with the supervisory positions made appointive rather than elective in almost every instance. Through his newly acquired appointive powers, his voice in the distribution of federal patronage as Democratic national committeeman, and his friendship with the state's moneyed establishment, Gardner built a political machine that dominated Tar Heel politics for several years. After he left office and moved to Washington, D.C., to become a lawyer-lobbyist with considerable influence in the Roosevelt administration, his power remained sufficient for his personally selected candidates, J. C. B. Ehringhaus and CLYDE HOEY, to win the governorship in 1932 and 1936 respectively. All three were from Shelby, N.C., thus making the "Shelby dynasty" a byword in the state's politics.

See J. L. Morrison, *Governor O. Max Gardner* (1971); and E. L. Puryear, *Democratic Party Dissension in North Carolina, 1928–1936* (1962).

RONALD E. MARCELLO
North Texas State University

GARFIELD, JAMES A., ADMINISTRATION

(1881). Garfield hoped, as had his predecessor, Rutherford B. Hayes, to break up the one-party system in the South and to increase Republican strength and success in this section. The assassination of Garfield within a few months after he became president abruptly ended his plans, but not before he had time to discuss them and to implement them somewhat. Garfield intended to abandon Hayes's pacificatory policy toward southern Democrats and to give up the possibility of conciliating the South through such an approach. In his opinion the "final cure" for the SOLID SOUTH lay in the education of its youth and development of its business interests. But since both of these things required time, the country was likely to have a "southern question" for many years to come.

Garfield's major problem in the South was whether he should recognize and aid the independent Democrats in the South who had increased since 1878. In particular he had to deal with WILLIAM MAHONE in Virginia, who with his READJUSTER party victory in the state in 1879, provided a test case for Republican policy in the South. Hayes had not cooperated with Mahone, whom he regarded as a repudiator of the state debt. At first, Garfield followed the policy of his predecessor. But, with an offer from Mahone to cooperate with the Republican party and under pressure from a number of Republicans within and outside Virginia, Garfield consented to an alliance between Republicans and Readjusters, but he would not acquiesce in the abandonment of the Republican organization in Virginia, nor would he turn over to Mahone the patronage in the state. There is no way to measure the results of Garfield's southern policy, because he was not in office long enough.

See V. P. De Santis, *Republicans Face Southern Question* (1959), and *North Carolina Historical Review* (Oct., 1959), fullest account; and S. P. Hirshson, *Farewell to Bloody Shirt* (1962).

VINCENT P. DE SANTIS
University of Notre Dame

GARLAND, AUGUSTUS HILL (1832–1899), was

born in Tipton County, Tenn., but moved while still an infant with his family to Arkansas. After being admitted to the Arkansas bar in 1853 and practicing law in Little Rock, he entered politics as a supporter of the Bell-Everett ticket in the ELECTION OF 1860. Although he originally was opposed to secession, he supported the Confederacy after the shelling of Ft. Sumter and served in the Confederate Congress as a representative (1861–1864) and a senator (1864–1865). He was elected to the U.S. Senate in 1866, but was denied his seat by the Republican majority of that body. Moreover, upon seeking reinstatement to practice law before the U.S. Supreme Court, he was disqualified by the test oath required by Congress. In *ex parte Garland*, he challenged the constitutionality of congressional RECONSTRUCTION. As a leader of the Arkansas Redeemers, he held the posts of governor (1874–1876) and U.S. senator (1877–1885). As U.S. attorney general (1885–1899) in the first CLEVELAND ADMINISTRATION, he held the most prominent federal administrative post of any southern Democrat since the Civil War.

See F. Newberry, *Life of Mr. Garland* (1908).

GARNER, JAMES WILFORD (1871–1938), was

born near Summit, Miss., and was educated in local schools and the Mississippi Agricultural and Mechanical College. The University of Chicago awarded him a master's degree (1900) in history and political science. In 1902 he received the Ph.D. Degree from Columbia, where he worked under the direction of WILLIAM A. DUNNING. A career teacher and scholar, Garner held positions at the University of Pennsylvania, Columbia, and several European institutions, but his home base was the University of Illinois. In 1906, Garner and Henry Cabot Lodge produced the four-volumed "popular" *History of the United States*. He soon abandoned history, however, becoming an indefatigable scholar and producing hundreds of works on foreign affairs. Although Garner won international fame as a political scientist, his major contribution to southern historiography rests on his *Reconstruction in Mississippi* (1901). This work is considered "one of the best and most important studies of southern reconstruction." Unlike many of the Dunning group, he has a good word for Mississippi CARPETBAGGERS. "As a class," he judged them "superior in character to the 'carpet-baggers' in South Carolina and Louisiana." Yet he criticized them for fiscal irresponsibility and opportunism in government and racial policies.

See V. L. Wharton, *Negro in Mississippi, 1865–1900* (1947); W. G. Brown, *American Historical Review* (April, 1902); E. R. Mechelke, *Journal of Mississippi History* (Feb., 1971); W. G. Hartley, *Journal of Mississippi History* (Feb., 1973); S. M. Higgenbotham, *Journal of Mississippi History* (July, 1958); and A. A. Taylor, *Journal of Negro History* (Jan., 1938).

H. E. STERKX
Auburn University, Montgomery

GARNER, JOHN NANCE (1868–1967), the thir-
ty-second vice-president of the United States, was
born in a log cabin on the northeast Texas prairie
and reared on the individualistic-minded frontier.
After briefly attending Vanderbilt University, he
was admitted to the Texas bar at the age of twenty-
one. In 1893 he moved to the southwest Texas
town of Uvalde to begin his practice of law and
became editor of the local newspaper, the *Leader*.
Following two terms as a Texas legislator, Garner
was elected in 1902 to Congress.

Throughout his 30-year congressional career,
Cactus Jack remained essentially consistent on
most basic issues. He constantly strove for economy in government, held an evident distrust for
eastern banking interests, and worked as a strong
spokesman for agriculture. Always persistent in
his concern for a strong national defense, he also
became a steadfast advocate of law and order,
shown by his clash in 1927 with the KU KLUX
KLAN. Perhaps above all else, however, he never
wavered in his staunch loyalty to the Democratic
party, an allegiance that permitted him to ascend
through the party's hierarchy and to wield tremendous influence on Capitol Hill. After serving
as chairman of the powerful Ways and Means
Committee, he was elected House minority leader in 1929 and Speaker of the House in 1931. At
the 1932 Democratic convention, he received the
vice-presidential nomination in return for releas-
ing his Texas and California delegates to Franklin
D. Roosevelt.

During his first term under Roosevelt, Garner
took an active role in policy discussions and generally supported the NEW DEAL. He became the
first vice-president to attend cabinet meetings
regularly, and while elevating the importance of
his office he served as a valuable liaison between
the president and congress. Yet Garner was angered by the continuation of deficit spending and
alienated by administrative silence concerning
union sit-down strikes. He refused to support the
Supreme Court packing bill of 1937. Subsequently enraged by Roosevelt's attempted "purge" of
Democratic congressional opponents in 1937 and
by FDR's ensuing decision to seek a third term,
Garner gradually broke with the president. First
he became the leader of the conservative coalition
that blocked New Deal legislation after 1936;
then he openly campaigned against Roosevelt for
the Democratic presidential nomination. After
losing the nomination, the old patriarch retired to
his home in Uvalde, where he died.

See G. R. Brown, *Speaker of the House* (1932); B. N.
Timmons, *Garner of Texas* (1948); M. James, *Mr. Garner*
(1939); I. Williams, *Rise of the Vice-Presidency* (1956);
J. T. Patterson, *Congressional Conservatism* (1967); and
M. J. Romano, "J. N. Garner" (Ph.D. dissertation, St.
John's, 1974).

NEVIN E. NEAL
Texas Christian University

GARY, MARTIN WITHERSPOON (1831–1881),
was born in Abbeville County, S.C. After being
graduated from Harvard (1854) and admitted to
the South Carolina bar (1855), he practiced law
and became a leading figure in the state's secession movement. While seeking service at first and
second BULL RUN, ANTIETAM, FREDERICKSBURG,
CHICKAMAUGA, Bean's Station, Campbell's Station, and the KNOXVILLE CAMPAIGN, he was promoted from the rank of captain through to brigadier general. He was the last general officer to
withdraw from Richmond and, after joining Jefferson Davis at Greensboro, he accompanied what
remained of the Confederate government to his
mother's home near Cokesbury, S.C. He adamantly opposed Republican Reconstruction and blamed
the failure of whites to regain control of the state
upon the temporizing strategies of the Democratic party's Tidewater leadership. In 1876 he led the
state's "straight-out" movement, refusing to permit Democratic cooperation with any group of Republicans or any part of the GOP slate. Against
the wishes of WADE HAMPTON, the Democrats'
candidate for governor, Gary emphasized race in
a blatant campaign for white supremacy and organized armed and mounted groups of Redshirts to
disrupt Republican campaign meetings. Although
he was widely credited with leading the Democrats to victory in the election of 1876, he never
received what he believed was proper recognition. He served four years in the state senate, but,
when he tried for the U.S. Senate in 1876 and for
the Democratic party's nomination for governor in
1880, he was defeated by men more agreeable to
Wade Hampton and the South Carolina Bourbons.
Besides their gentlemanly disapproval of his campaign tactics, they found him suspect for his desire to repeal the state's Reconstruction debt and
his support of a usury law lowering the legal rate
of interest. He finally broke openly with Hampton
in 1879, but party loyalty prevented him from supporting the independents. His legacy to South
Carolina was his political lieutenant and Redshirt
associate BENJAMIN TILLMAN.

See W. A. Sheppard, *Red Shirts Remembered* (1940), po-
lemical defense of Gary; F. B. Simkins and R. W. Woody,
South Carolina During Reconstruction (1932); W. J.
Cooper, *Conservative Regime* (1968); D. D. Wallace,
Journal of Southern History (Aug., 1942); and M. W.
Gary Papers, University of South Carolina Library.

GASTON, WILLIAM JOSEPH (1778–1844), was born in New Bern, N.C. Educated as a Catholic at Georgetown (1791), he graduated from Princeton in 1796 and was admitted to the bar in 1798. Gaston served four terms in the North Carolina Senate (1800, 1812, 1818–1819) and seven in the state's House of Commons (1807–1809, 1824, 1827–1829, 1831). Chosen as a Federalist presidential elector in 1808, he later served as a Federalist U.S. congressman (1813–1817), when he opposed the War of 1812. Gaston was elected a justice of the state supreme court in 1833 and served until his death.

See Gaston Papers, University of North Carolina Library, Chapel Hill; J. H. Schauinger, *William Gaston* (1949); P. K. Guilday, *John England* (1927); W. H. Battle, *North Carolina University Magazine* (April, 1844); S. A. Ashe, *Biographical History of North Carolina* (1905), II; R. Strange, *William Gaston* (1844); W. D. Lewis (ed.), *Great American Lawyers* (1907), III; W. B. Hannon. *Journal of American Irish Historical Society* (1911); J. F. McLaughlin, *Proceedings of American Catholic Historical Society of Philadelphia* (1895); and L. Baker, *John Marshall* (1974).

W. ALLAN WILBUR
State University of New York, Albany

GASTONIA, N.C. (pop. 47,142), is in the Piedmont, approximately 20 miles west of Charlotte. The city was first incorporated in 1877, and its growth and prosperity always had been tied directly to the TEXTILE INDUSTRY. In 1929, national news coverage given the GASTONIA STRIKE revealed many of the problems and working arrangements of a one-industry town. In addition to milling textiles and cotton yarn and thread, the city manufactures textile machinery and tire fabric.

See R. F. Cope, *County of Gaston* (1961); M. S. Puett, *History of Gaston County* (1939); J. Separk, *Gastonia and Gaston* (1936); R. L. Stowe, *Early History of Belmont and Gaston* (1951); and files of Gastonia *Gazette* (1880–), on microfilm. Gaston County Public Library maintains collection of published and unpublished works on area history, including oral history tapes, census records, Ph.D. dissertations, and cemetery records.

GASTONIA STRIKE. On April 1, 1929, a strike occurred at the Loray Mill of the Manville-Jencks Corporation in Gastonia, N.C. Although the strike grew out of conditions at the mill, the principal issue soon became the Communist leadership of the National Textile Workers Union. The strike was effectively broken within two weeks, but the continued presence of some of the union's strikers aroused bitter anger.

On June 7, a clash between police officers and strikers occurred at a tent colony set up by the union for strikers evicted from company housing. Shots were exchanged, and the police chief was killed. The area was gripped with hysteria as a mob turned against the strikers and their Communist leaders. Eventually 16 union members, including Fred E. Beal, the Communist leader of the strike, were put on trial for murder. A mistrial occurred when one of the jurors went insane. Again a local mob terrorized Gaston County, beating strikers and suspected sympathizers. A few days later a truck carrying a group of strikers to a mass rally was stopped, and shots were fired by vigilantes, killing Ella May Wiggins, a twenty-nine-year-old mother of five, whose songs had been a rallying force for the strikers. No one was convicted of the crime.

A second trial ended in the conviction of seven of the strike leaders, but the convicted men jumped bail during their appeal and fled to the Soviet Union. Beal became disillusioned with communism and returned to the United States. He was arrested in 1938 and imprisoned until pardoned in 1942.

See F. E. Beal, *Proletarian Journey* (1937); T. Tippett, *When Southern Labor Stirs* (1931); and L. Pope, *Millhands and Preachers* (1942).

JOHN SCOTT WILSON
University of South Carolina

GATES, HORATIO (1728–1806), was born in England, but saw service in North America in the French and Indian War. In 1772 he moved to Virginia and bought a 700-acre plantation. The CONTINENTAL CONGRESS in June, 1775, appointed him adjutant general with the rank of brigadier. Later he was given command of the Northern Department and gained full credit for the victory at Saratoga. George Washington, sensitive from defeats, believed there was a conspiracy, the Conway Cabal, to replace him with Gates. The intrigue was disavowed, and Congress in June, 1780, appointed Gates to head the Southern Department. Two months later he suffered a disastrous defeat at CAMDEN, and his hurried flight from the field further denigrated his military reputation. In 1782 he was given a command on the Hudson River. At the war's end he returned to Virginia and his dying wife. In 1790 he sold his farm, manumitted his slaves, and, with the support of his wealthy second wife, moved to the outskirts of New York City, where until his death he lived as country gentleman.

See S. W. Patterson, *Horatio Gates* (1941), biased; P. D. Nelson, *General Horatio Gates* (1976), based on archival research; C. Ward, *War of Revolution* (1952); G. A. Billias (ed.), *Washington's Generals* (1964); and compare B. Knollenberg, *Washington and Revolution* (1940), and J. T. Flexner, *George Washington* (1968).

CHARLES L. ANGER
The Citadel

GATLING, RICHARD JORDAN (1818–1903),
inventor, was born in Hertford County, N.C. His early inventions included several useful agricultural machines, which he began to manufacture and sell in 1844 in St. Louis and, subsequently, elsewhere with considerable success. He also studied medicine, but never practiced. In 1862 he developed the revolving rapid-fire machine gun that bears his name. This was adopted by the U.S. Army in 1866, but Gatling continued to improve it for another 30 years until it could fire 1,200 rounds per minute. During this period, he also developed a new gunmetal, additional farm machines, and other devices and in 1891 became the first president of the American Association of Inventors and Manufacturers.

See P. Wahl and D. R. Toppel, *Gatling Gun* (1965); and A. C. McCarty, *Annals of Medical History* (Sept., 1940).

STANLEY L. FALK
Department of the Air Force

GAYARRÉ, CHARLES ÉTIENNE ARTHUR
(1805–1895), historian and public official, was born near New Orleans of Spanish and French descent. He graduated from college in New Orleans and studied law in Philadelphia. He served in the state legislature and held appointive offices as assistant attorney general, presiding judge of the city of New Orleans, and secretary of state for Louisiana. While in Europe (1835–1843), he searched the archives for materials on the history of Louisiana. As secretary of state he enriched the holdings of the state library with such materials, and he continued the historical writing he had begun with the *Essai historique sur la Louisiane* (1830). His *Histoire de la Louisiane* (1846, 1847) is mainly a printing of documents. In 1848 appeared *The Romance of the History of Louisiana*, the first volume of his *History of Louisiana*. His best work is in the remaining three volumes, which deal with the periods of French (1852), Spanish (1854), and American domination (1866). Gayarré wrote also a political satire, *The School for Politics* (1854), a biography of Philip II of Spain (1866), and the novels *Fernando de Lemos* (1872) and *Aubert Dubayet* (1882). He was president of the LOUISIANA HISTORICAL SOCIETY (1860–1888).

See E. N. Saucier, "Charles Gayarré" (Ph.D. dissertation, Peabody, 1935). Letters and other manuscripts are in the Tulane and Louisiana State University libraries.

ARLIN TURNER
Duke University

GAYOSO DE LEMOS, MANUEL (1747–1799),
Portuguese born, was the Spanish colonial governor in the Mississippi Valley (1789–1799). He came to Natchez, amid the rash of filibuster and separatist attempts by southwesterners, to create a buffer district of primarily Anglo-Americans to check U.S. expansion. Aided by liberal economic policies, a "hot line" to Madrid, toleration of Protestants, absence of taxation, homesteads for settlers, and low tariffs, he increased the population of the Natchez district and maintained Indian alliances to check southwestern frontiersmen. A bon vivant who practiced banquet diplomacy, he won the respect of red and white man alike. He encouraged a type of town meeting for Natchez, in which the leading settlers proposed laws that would best meet their needs under the general framework of Spanish policy. He succeeded in encouraging diversification of agriculture, the advent of the cotton gin in Mississippi, the care and regulation of Negro slaves, and town planning complete with early zoning laws. Following the Natchez revolt of 1797 and the transfer of Natchez to the U.S., Gayoso became governor general of Louisiana and West Florida at New Orleans. He guarded the Mississippi Valley against the plans of people like GEORGE ROGERS CLARK and WILLIAM BLOUNT. He so ruled Natchez that the people spoke of the days of the dons with much nostalgia and appreciation. In the final analysis, however, he was unable to make loyal Spaniards out of American frontiersmen.

See J. D. L. Holmes, *Gayoso* (1965); A. P. Whitaker, *Spanish-American Frontier* (1927) and *Mississippi Question* (1934); and L. Kinnaird, *Spain in Mississippi Valley* (3 vols.; 1946–49), documents to 1794. Most archival information on Gayoso is in the Archivo General de Indias, Seville, Archivo General de Simancas, and Archivo Histórico Nacional, Madrid.

JACK D. L. HOLMES
University of Alabama, Birmingham

GENERAL EDUCATION BOARD. John D.
Rockefeller, Jr., as administrator of his father's fortune, toured black schools in the South in 1901 on a train chartered by Robert C. Ogden (OGDEN MOVEMENT). Plans were prepared the following year by the Rockefellers for a program of aid to

education in the South. The result was the General Education Board, a philanthropic corporation endowed by the Rockefellers and chartered by Congress for "the promotion of education in the United States of America, without distinction of race, sex, or creed." The gifts of John D. Rockefeller to the GEB totaled $129.2 million. The emphasis of the GEB varied with the interests of the directors and the exigencies of the period. Frederick T. Gates, chairman, and Wallace Buttrick, secretary, set the early patterns of programs for the GEB until 1923. Raymond B. Fosdick left his imprint on the later years. General and black education and science and medical education benefited the most from this Rockefeller philanthropic corporation. The earliest programs supported the improvement of rural education in the South. Traveling teachers and JEANES FUND supervisors were sponsored so that each southern state could elevate the quality of public education. In the years before World War II, the GEB worked within the framework of segregated schools, its directors believing that there was no alternative. Most grants were conditional and required matching public funds.

In 62 years of activity (1902–1964), the directors expanded their programs to include increasing teachers' salaries, enlarging endowments for over 290 colleges and universities, creating full-time staffs in medical schools, building and equipping libraries and laboratories, and providing fellowships to support promising scholars in their research. Of the $325 million appropriated, 20 percent financed a variety of GEB programs for black education at all levels. This included large appropriations to the United Negro College Fund, the consolidated colleges of Atlanta University, Meharry Medical School, and Fisk and Dillard universities. Soon after the nonprofit corporation was organized it was decided to expend principal as well as interest, which put the focus on solving current problems rather than conserving funds for indefinite problems of the future. Programs spanned the range from farm demonstration projects in the rural South to the expansion of graduate education at Atlanta, Duke, Emory, Tulane, and Vanderbilt universities.

See R. B. Fosdick and H. F. and K. D. Pringle, *Adventures in Giving* (1962); H. S. Enck, "The Burden Borne" (Ph.D. dissertation, Cincinnati, 1970); GEB, *Review and Final Report, 1902–1964* (1964); and Rockefeller Archives, Hillcrest Center, North Tarrytown, N.Y.

A. GILBERT BELLES
Western Illinois University

GEOGRAPHY. As an academic discipline, geography in America and the South first appeared in the curricula of the colleges in the colonial era, where it was an advanced, well-developed subject emphasizing the nature and properties of the earth in which astronomy and the use and study of globes were prominent elements. This position gave way after the Revolution, however, when a growing emphasis on locational geography and on descriptive detail led colleges to dismiss the subject on the ground that it failed to offer adequate intellectual rigor. For most of the nineteenth century, geography was almost exclusively a public school subject; only in the last two decades of that century did it regain a measure of significance in college curricula. The numerous public school geography texts emphasized rote memory, especially those published in the first half of the century, and most displayed unabashed pro-American, pro-Protestant, and pro-Caucasian biases. Regional prejudices were frequently encountered in geography books published prior to 1840. Most of these texts were written by northerners who were critical of the South.

Scholarly geographical works on the South first appeared in the colonial period. The earliest comprehensive study of the region was William Gerard DeBrahm's *Report of the General Survey in the Southern District of North America*, written in 1771–1773 but never published until 1971. The initial state geography was Thomas Jefferson's *Notes on the State of Virginia* (1785). This work, plus his pioneer speculations in climatology and support of geographical exploration of the vast territory between the Appalachians and the Pacific, give Jefferson valid claim to the title "father of American geography."

Works of geographical scholarship in the nineteenth century were few and far between. However, some of the early works of the twentieth century were regional studies on the South. The earliest example is ELLEN CHURCHILL SEMPLE's "Anglo-Saxons of the Kentucky Mountains" (*Geographical Journal*, 1901). Studies on this and other Kentucky regions followed in the 1920s, all published by the Kentucky Geological Survey: D. H. Davis, *The Geography of the Jackson Purchase* (1923), *The Geography of the Mountains of Eastern Kentucky* (1924), and *The Geography of the Blue Grass Region of Kentucky* (1927); W. G. Burroughs, *The Geography of the Western Coal Field* (1924) and *The Geography of the Kentucky Knobs* (1926); and Carl O. Sauer, *The Geography of the Pennyroyal Region, Kentucky* (1927). Also dating from this decade is Sauer's *Geography of*

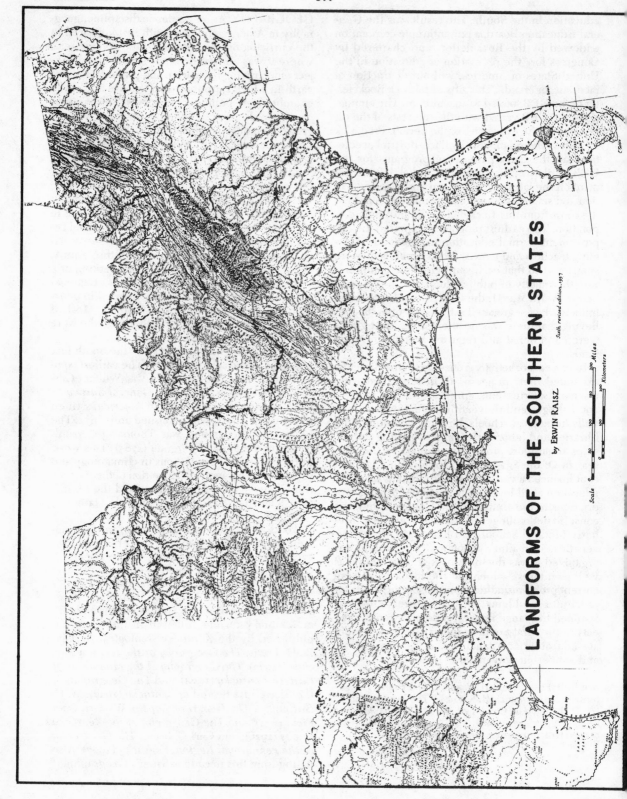

LANDFORMS OF THE SOUTHERN STATES

by ERWIN RAISZ

Sixth revised edition, 1957

Scale

Miles

Kilometers

the Ozark Highland of Missouri (1920), a work that served as an important model for American regional geography for many years. A trilogy of regional monographs on Florida by Roland M. Harper was published by the Florida Geological Survey: *Geography and Vegetation of Northern Florida* (1914), *Geography of Central Florida* (1921), and *Natural Resources of Southern Florida* (1928). Thus, by the end of the 1920s, Kentucky and Florida had geographical monographs on all their regions. Such studies, cast in the framework of physical (natural) regions and sometimes with environmentalist overtones, reflect the character of American geography at that time.

Following World War I the subfield of economic geography came to occupy a place of increasing importance in geographic research. The research of most economic geographers appeared in the form of commodity or land-use studies, some of which focused on the rural South. These genres prevailed in the 1930s and into the 1940s and 1950s. This is reflected in the leading geographical periodicals (*Annals of the Association of American Geographers, Geographical Review, Journal of Geography* and especially *Economic Geography*), where studies appeared on a variety of topics related to the agricultural geography of the South, including row crops (particularly cotton and tobacco), tree crops (mainly citrus), county land-use analysis, and the plantation. The New Deal era gave particular emphasis to federal land-use planning projects; and professional geographers, both in and out of government, were heavily involved in research on and administration of these projects. Major programs for the Tennessee and Mississippi valleys in particular enlisted the expertise of numerous geographers.

Research on the rural South continues, but in the 1960s and 1970s this interest has been shared increasingly with topics on the urban-industrial South. This trend is best seen in the *Southeastern Geographer*, published twice each year by the southeastern division of the Association of American Geographers. This journal has provided a medium for research on the geography of the South since its charter issue in 1961.

Also in the 1960s and 1970s, scholars in the subfields of historical and cultural geography have generated a number of book-length studies on southern regions and topics. For the colonial period these include Louis DeVorsey, Jr.'s *Indian Boundary in the Southern Colonies* (1966) and H. Roy Merrens' *Colonial North Carolina in the Eighteenth Century* (1964). The antebellum period has attracted few geographers. Almon E. Parkins' presidential address to the Association of

American Geographers, "The Antebellum South: A Geographer's Interpretation" (*Annals of the Association of American Geographers*, 1931), stood almost alone until the appearance of Sam B. Hilliard's *Hog Meat and Hoe Cake: Food Supply in the Old South, 1840–1860* (1972). Given its economic and demographic importance in the nation, Texas has until recently been largely neglected by geography scholars. This oversight is being rectified with studies such as Terry G. Jordan's *German Seed in Texas Soil: Immigrant Farmers in Nineteenth-Century Texas* (1966) and Donald W. Meinig's *Imperial Texas* (1968).

There are few substantive, comprehensive geographic works covering the entire South or a single state. The most extensive work by a geographer embracing all of the South is now outdated: Almon E. Parkins' *The South: Its Economic-Geographic Development* (1938). A recent work, less comprehensive and written in a semipopular vein, is John Fraser Hart's *The South* (1976). Recent state geographies include Fred B. Kniffen's *Louisiana: Its Land and People* (1968), Jean Gottmann's *Virginia in Our Century* (1969) and *Kentucky: A Regional Geography* (1973).

Departments of geography in the 1970s have made many excellent contributions to the modern mapping of southern states in thematic atlas format. These include the *Atlas of Louisiana* (1972), *Atlas of Alabama* (1973), *Atlas of Arkansas* (1973), *Atlas of Texas* (1973), *Economic and Social Atlas of Maryland* (1974), *New Florida Atlas* (1974), *Atlas of Mississippi* (1974), *Historical Atlas of Alabama* (1975), and *North Carolina Atlas* (1975). In addition, two urban-oriented atlases have been produced, the *Metrolina Atlas* (1972), focusing on Charlotte, N.C., and *Atlas of Atlanta* (1974).

In the twentieth century, graduate geography programs in southern colleges and universities have developed and grown to meet the need for trained geographers in research and teaching. This can be seen in the increase in the number of Ph.D. programs in geography in the region. The first geography Ph.D.'s were conferred in the 1930s at George Peabody College, Washington University, and Louisiana State University. Of these institutions, only LSU continues to offer doctoral work in geography. In each subsequent decade, other schools have conferred, and continue to confer, Ph.D. degrees in geography: the universities of North Carolina and Maryland and Johns Hopkins University in the 1940s; the universities of Florida and Tennessee in the 1950s; the universities of Texas and Georgia in the 1960s; and Texas A. & M. University and the University of Kentucky in the 1970s. George Washington University and the University of Southern Mississippi each conferred a token number of geography doctorates after World War II but no longer do so. Today, the number of professional geographers in the United States teaching in colleges and universities exceeds 3,000; one-fourth of these teach in the South.

See A. D. Bushong, *Southeastern Geographer* (April, 1969), for detailed analysis of geographical literature for major part of South. See American Geographical Society's *Research Catalog* (1962, supplement 1972) and *Current Geographical Publications* (monthly except July and Aug.) for best bibliographies.

ALLEN D. BUSHONG
University of South Carolina

GEOLOGY has to do with the natural materials and processes of a planet, generally excluding most of biology and meteorology, and therefore constitutes a study of the platform on which history is enacted and of some of the constraints that modify that history. The South, extending from Delaware to Texas, has CLIMATE and bedrock characteristics that control SOILS formation, physiography, water supply, erosion potential, and even economic potential. Precipitation varies from roughly 200 centimeters per year in the higher AP-PALACHIANS to less than 20 centimeters per year in extreme west Texas; the sea level maximum, exceeding 140 centimeters a year, extends from the Florida panhandle to southwestern Louisiana. This variability coupled with moderate-to-warm temperatures produces in the weathering process a spectrum of clay types, from montmorillonite and illite in the West (dry) to kaolinite in the East (humid). Likewise, there is much organic matter in the East and little organic matter in the West. Organic matter combines most effectively with montmorillonite, which decreases in quantity both eastward and westward from about the MISSISSIPPI RIVER.

Clay plus organic matter is a powerful binder, or "glue," in soils and sediments, hence material in stream transport in the East tends to be cohesive, whereas stream sediments in the West tend to be loose. This fact translates into well-defined, reasonably deep, more or less meandering channels in the East and into poorly defined, shallow-braided channels in the West. There is also a runoff contrast: high runoff and more even annual flow (East), and low runoff, with irregular annual flow (West). Therefore western streams tend to have wide shallow channels full of sand, with little or no visible water in them much of the time.

Along the coasts the interplay between binder (clay plus organic matter) and runoff provides in the West few inlets, long, sandy barrier islands (Padre Island, Tex.), and saline lagoons. In the East, on the other hand, there are many inlets, estuaries, and small islands (SEA ISLAND coast of Georgia), as well as coastal marshes, except where wave energy levels are unusually high (SWAMPS).

The combination of clay content and organic matter means thin soils in the West (which may be quite productive, if irrigated) and deep soils in the East. Erosion is lowest where a good tree cover and its root system provide almost perfect protection against rainfall and runoff. Agricultural practices introduced from Europe modified this relationship, and therefore the region's soil reserve has been diminished, especially in the East, where rainfall is heavier and where the history of plowing has been longer.

The important physiographic units in the South are the following. (1) The coastal plain extends landward to altitudes of 100–300 miles. By one estimate, this area contains close to 940,000 square kilometers of surface. There is the humid type (Delaware to Louisiana) and the dry type (Texas). The FALL LINE, the boundary between coastal plain and mountains, was the upstream limit to steamboat traffic. (2) The mountains are broken down into the linear (Appalachians), the not markedly linear (Ozarks, OUACHITAS), and the foothills. (3) The plateaus include parts of Kentucky, Tennessee, Missouri, and Texas. (4) The interior plains are mostly in Texas (including prairies). (5) The river valleys include the Mississippi River valley, primarily; there are other smaller examples.

The humid coastal plain has been historically important agriculturally because of high soil fertility coupled with ample water. In the dry coastal plain, as in the prairie belt, agriculture is much more precarious, requiring larger farm (or ranch) units for survival. The humid coastal plain also provided perennial streams as avenues for early transportation; the Mississippi River system is the outstanding example, but other rivers east of the Mississippi were important (*e.g.*, for cotton shipping).

Mountains have several significant effects. They modify the precipitation patterns (the downwind side is drier; the magnitude of the effect is proportional to the height and linear continuity of the mountains); they provide steeper slopes (which makes agriculture, among other things, more difficult); they provide hydroelectric power; they impede surface transportation and therefore help to determine the local sense of regionality; and they provide for a remoteness proportional to the ruggedness of terrain and lack of good transportation routes. Although inhabitants of the original southern colonies pushed westward across the southern Appalachians, they established convenient east-west routes at only a few places, and even today (despite the network of modern highways) people in mountain states look outward to the plains, thinking of the mountains as "behind" them.

Plateaus, where highly dissected, have many of the attributes of mountains. Where not highly dissected, they are more like plains. The interior plains, both tree-covered plains and prairie, have been handicapped primarily by low rainfall. Irrigation from groundwater has been particularly important in areas such as the high plains (Llano Estacado) of west Texas, and large-scale wheat farming, without irrigation, has also been effective. These activities do not support large metropolitan centers, which were traditionally located near river mouths (New Orleans, Mobile, Savannah, Norfolk), the fall line (Little Rock, Columbus, Columbia), the ends of linear mountains (Atlanta), or great mineral wealth (Houston).

See N. M. Fenneman, *Physiography of Eastern U.S.* (1938); R. E. Grim, *Clay Mineralogy* (1953); and L. B. Leopold, M. G. Wolman, and J. P. Miller, *Fluvial Processes in Geomorphology* (1964).

WILLIAM F. TANNER
Florida State University

GEORGE, JAMES ZACHARIAH (1826–1897),

one of Mississippi's most powerful politicians after Reconstruction, came from a humble background. Self-educated, he read law and was admitted to the bar in 1846. He fought in the Mexican War as a private. A member of the 1861 secession convention, he later served in the Confederate army. He was wounded, captured, and imprisoned. After the war he practiced law in Jackson. As chairman of the Democratic state executive committee in 1875, George engineered the overthrow of Republican rule (MISSISSIPPI PLAN). Named chief justice of the state supreme court in 1879, he was elected to the U.S. Senate in 1880. There he worked (1881–1897) for lower tariffs, regulation of railroads and corporations, civil service reform, and federal aid to schools. He helped frame the Sherman Antitrust Act and was known in Mississippi as the "father of the Department of Agriculture." He played a leading role in the 1890 Mississippi constitutional convention, which disfranchised blacks, and then he defended that work on the floor of the U.S. Senate. Although a wealthy railroad lawyer, he never lost touch with the small farmers of Mississippi. They affectionately called him the Commoner and Old Trace Chains.

See A. D. Kirwan, *Rednecks* (1951); W. D. Halsell, *Journal of Southern History* (Nov., 1945); and M. S. Ringold, *Journal of Mississippi History* (July, 1954).

CHARLES SALLIS
Millsaps College

GEORGE, WALTER FRANKLIN (1878–1957),

was born near Preston, Ga., of tenant-farming parents. After being graduated from Mercer University (B.S., 1900; B.L., 1901) and admitted to the Georgia bar, he practiced law in Dooly County and became active in the Democratic party. He served as circuit court solicitor (1907–1912), circuit court judge (1912–1916), and court of appeals judge (1917) before taking a seat on the state supreme court (1917–1922). In 1922 he left the bench to spend the remaining 35 years of his life as a U.S. senator. In the Senate, George defended segregation and supported tariff protection for southern industries. Although he backed most of Franklin D. Roosevelt's early relief measures, he grew increasingly estranged from the NEW DEAL and adamantly opposed the president's plan to "pack" the federal judiciary in 1937. Roosevelt, in turn, sought to purge George and other southern conservatives from the Senate. While traveling through Georgia in 1938, the president endorsed the senator's primary opponent by pointing out his many differences with George. The attempted purge failed, however, and George returned to his seat confirmed in his opposition to the increasingly liberal direction of the national Democratic party.

See J. Shannon, *Journal of Politics* (Aug., 1939); and G. Tindall, *Emergence of New South* (1967).

GEORGE PEABODY COLLEGE FOR TEACHERS (Nashville, Tenn. 37203) was founded in 1875 with a gift from the PEABODY EDUCATION FUND, but the school has some claim to much older antecedents, dating to the establishment in 1785 of Davidson Academy. In 1806 this latter institution was reorganized as Cumberland College and renamed the University of Nashville in 1826. Today Peabody is a private, coeducational teachers' college with an enrollment of approximately 1,800 students. Notable holdings of the library include the records of Cumberland College and the University of Nashville and also the manuscripts of James Robertson, frontiersman and Indian agent.

GEORGETOWN, KY. (pop. 8,629), is 12 miles north of Lexington on a branch of Elkhorn Creek. Settled in 1776 as McClelland's Station, it was incorporated and renamed by the Virginia assembly in 1790 in honor of George Washington. George-

town College, founded as a Baptist seminary, opened here in 1829. Its proximity to Lexington has prevented the town from becoming a major commercial or manufacturing center. Nevertheless, light industries here mill flour, manufacture precision tools, and distill whiskey.

See R. Peter, *History of Bourbon, Scott, Harrison and Nicholas Counties* (1882, 1957); B. O. Gaines, *History of Scott County* (2 vols.; 1904, 1957); and files of Georgetown *News* (1887–) and *Times* (1867–), Democratic weeklies.

GEORGETOWN, MD., now part of the city of Washington, D.C., was settled as early as 1665. The town, however, was not laid out until 1751, when as George Town it quickly grew into a major shipping point for area wheat and tobacco. The town reached its peak in the value of its commercial exports in 1792–1793, and even completion of the Chesapeake & Ohio Canal (1828) failed to revive Georgetown as a port of entry. By 1850, with a population of over 8,000, its flour mills and tobacco warehouses were less vital to the town's prosperity than were the whiskey, grain, lumber, and coal shipped down the Potomac and the fish, slate, dry goods, and groceries sent up the canal. Since its annexation in 1878 by the capital city, Old Georgetown has been thoroughly integrated into the rest of the metropolitan area. Recently, restoration of the old warehouses, homes, and townhouses has made the Georgetown area a popular (and expensive) residential area for Washington residents.

See G. D. Ecker, *Portrait of Old Georgetown* (1951); H. R. Evans, *Old Georgetown* (1933); Federal Writers' Project, *Washington, City and Capital* (1937); M. S. Waggoner, *Long Haul West, 1817–1850* (1958); and G. W. Ward, *Early Development of C & O Canal* (1899).

GEORGETOWN, S.C. (pop. 10,449), was settled in 1735 and named for the Prince of Wales, later King George II of England. Located on Winyah Bay, 15 miles from the Atlantic Ocean, the city developed as a port and prospered as an exporter of naval stores, rice, and indigo. The American Revolution cut off trade with Georgetown's established customers, Great Britain and the West Indies, and changing patterns of commerce during the nineteenth century gradually diminished its role as an exporter of cotton and lumber. Although still a port of entry and a shipper of lumber, pulp, and paper, since World War II it has grown in popularity as a year-round resort and yachting basin. Several old buildings, including a church constructed in the 1740s and a unique rice museum, survive as points of architectural and historic interest.

See G. C. Rogers, Jr., *History of Georgetown County* (1970); J. S. Bolick, *Georgetown Houselore* (1944); and files of Georgetown *Times* (1797–). Georgetown County Historical Society and Georgetown County Memorial Library maintain collections of various local history materials.

GEORGETOWN UNIVERSITY (Washington, D.C. 20007) was founded by Bishop John Carroll (CARROLL FAMILY) and chartered as a Roman Catholic college in 1789 by act of the U.S. Congress. Rechartered in 1815 as a university, the antebellum school functioned largely as a primary and preparatory academy for a student body enrolled largely from the sons of Maryland's planter gentry. The formation in 1851 of the Georgetown Medical School was part of a gradual shift on the eve of the Civil War toward greater emphasis on higher learning. In April, 1861, however, the school's enrollment plummeted (100 students withdrawing in a single day) as the southern sympathies of its students caused many to don the Confederate gray or at least to leave Washington, D.C.

Despite considerable financial duress and laboring under a reputation for having been pro-Confederate, the postwar school grew gradually with increasing emphasis on college levels of instruction. Courses on literature, botany, physics, and constitutional history were added to the college's classical Jesuit curriculum. Beginning in 1879, the university gave special emphasis to modern science, requiring two years of chemistry and at least one year of physics of all prospective graduates. Moreover, the creation of a school of law in 1870, of a university hospital in 1898, and of a school of foreign affairs in 1919 marked the emergence of a mature university. The university retains its close ties to the Catholic church and presently has a coeducational enrollment of over 11,000 students. Its library houses the archives of the institution, including papers of John Carroll.

See J. T. Durkin, *Georgetown University* (1964) and *Georgetown: Middle Years, 1840–1900* (1963); J. M. Daley, *Georgetown: Origins* (1957); J. S. Easby-Smith, *Georgetown* (1907); P. K. Guilday, *Life and Times of J. Carroll* (1922); and J. F. McLaughlin, *Colonial Days at Georgetown* (1899).

GEORGIA, the largest state east of the Mississippi River with 58,876 square miles and a 1970 population of 4,589,575 (estimated to be over 5 million in 1976), was first explored by the Spaniards, when Francisco Gordillo and Esteban Gómez traveled the island-fringed coast. Later the interior was penetrated by HERNANDO DE SOTO.

The absence of gold and the failure of the earliest colonies nearby discouraged serious effort to settle the area until 1566. In that year PEDRO MENÉNDEZ DE AVILÉS, founder of St. Augustine only one year before, arrived on Santa Catalina (St. Catherine's) Island and conferred with the local Indian chief Guale, by whose name the entire section ultimately came to be known. First the Jesuits and then later the Franciscans acted as missionaries to the natives. After the nearly disastrous Juanillo revolt of 1597, the Spanish reconstituted Guale so effectively that in 1606 Bishop Altamirano of Cuba made an official episcopal visitation and confirmed more than 1,000 natives in their Roman Catholic faith.

The half-century following Altamirano's visit is usually looked upon as the golden age of the Spanish in Georgia. During this period the priests at the missions, protected by Spanish troops, catechized the Indians and instructed them in settled agricultural ways. Periodic attempts were made to expand the mission system into the interior (Tama), but Guale remained throughout the Spanish period an exposed, lightly defended mission province that never, so far as is known, attracted "permanent" European settlers.

With the coming of the English to Charles Town (Charleston) in 1670, Guale was immediately threatened. The Carolina traders in the interior and the raids against the missions by English and French pirates signaled the end for the Spanish in Georgia. They had little choice but to fall back on St. Augustine, and by 1686 had retreated beyond the St. Mary's River (later part of Georgia's southern boundary). Old Guale became land disputed by Spain, England, and France.

English period. At first the English in Carolina had much their own way with the Indians, but the Yamassee War, which broke out in 1715, nearly destroyed Carolina and caused its influence to suffer. The Spanish reasserted their position on the Chattahoochee, and the French built Ft. Toulouse in the heart of the Alabama country in 1717.

There had been many English schemes to settle old Guale, including Sir Robert Montgomery's AZILIA, but they had all come to naught. So the Carolinians cooperated with a group of philanthropists, members of Parliament, and merchants, who in the late 1720s and early 1730s seemed to have an excellent chance of bringing a new British colony to reality. The leaders of this movement were Sir John Perceval (earl of Egmont) and JAMES EDWARD OGLETHORPE. Initially Oglethorpe, who made a national name for himself as chairman of a parliamentary jails committee, thought of a new

American colony as a refuge for released debtors, but as the movement gained momentum the debt-or-province idea was pushed aside by other philanthropic, mercantile, and imperial motives. As finally constituted, Georgia was peopled not by debtors but by small merchants and shopkeepers, unemployed laborers, and a few gentlemen.

A royal charter for Georgia, named in honor of George II, was granted to 21 trustees on June 9, 1732. Georgia's chartered limits were defined as lying between the Savannah and Altamaha rivers and extending from their origins to the western sea. The power of the trust was restricted to 21 years, after which time governmental power reverted to the crown.

Oglethorpe volunteered to escort the first settlers to the colony. He moved to a high bluff on the south bank of the Savannah River, arriving there February 1, 1733 (February 12, New Style). Here Oglethorpe formally received Tomochichi of the YAMASSEE and proceeded, through the good offices of trader John Musgrove and his half-breed wife Mary, to make an alliance of friendship. His initial success with the natives was followed by a treaty with the CREEK in May. Later understandings were reached with the CHEROKEE, CHICKASAW, and even the remote CHOCTAW. Oglethorpe's Indian diplomacy, based upon an acute awareness of the importance of friendly relations along the southern frontier, was climaxed by his trip to Coweta in the heart of Creek country just prior to the outbreak of the War of Jenkins' Ear in 1739.

One of Oglethorpe's most noted successes was his town plan for Savannah, with its wards and tithings focused upon squares placed at regular intervals. The basic design was used at various other settlements including Ebenezer, Darien, and later Brunswick, but nowhere has the original layout survived so well as in Savannah.

Georgia proved to be a haven for both British and continental political and religious refugees. The Salzburg Lutherans, who arrived in 1734, fled persecution at the hands of their Roman Catholic archbishop. They were industrious and frugal, and their settlement at Ebenezer was the most prosperous Georgia town during the trusteeship period. The Highland Scots first came in a group in 1735, and founded New Inverness (Darien). In the same year the first MORAVIANS to come to America arrived in Savannah. They soon opened a school for Indians at Irene, which, however, did not survive the Moravians' departure from the colony by 1740. According to the charter, "liberty of conscience" was permitted to all "in the worship of God," but Roman Catholics were specifically excluded from entering Georgia. In

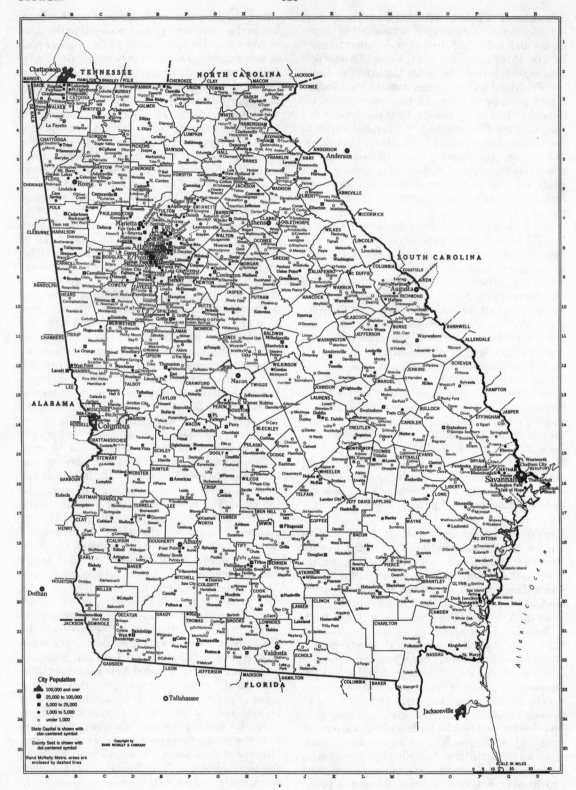

City Population
▲ 100,000 and over
● 25,000 to 100,000
■ 5,000 to 25,000
• 1,000 to 5,000
○ under 1,000

State Capital is shown with
star-centered symbol

County Seat is shown with
dot-centered symbol

Rand McNally Metro. areas are
enclosed by dashed lines

Copyright by
RAND McNALLY & COMPANY

SCALE IN MILES
0 5 10   20   30   40

July, 1733, a group of Jewish immigrants was welcomed by Oglethorpe in spite of what he knew would be trustee disapproval. JEWS were not singled out for exclusion, however, so he used this oversight as the basis upon which to permit them.

After escorting the first transport of Salzburgers (under John Martin Bolzius) to Ebenezer in 1734, Oglethorpe returned to England. From the trustees he secured passage of three acts that would give Georgia the distinctive character he wanted it to assume. The presence of Negroes or Negro slavery was forbidden, rum was outlawed, and a third act regulated the Indian trade in Georgia's chartered limits. It was clear from the start that the trustees' regulations would not be docilely accepted. The restriction on rum was impossible to enforce, and the act became a dead letter by 1742; the interdicts against the size and nature of landholding were gradually withdrawn, and even the Indian Act was emasculated when the apprehensive South Carolinians resorted to legal action in Britain. The Negro Act was abandoned too in spite of support from the Salzburgers and the Highland Scots.

Oglethorpe originally was instructed by Robert Walpole to make no belligerent moves on the frontier, but the English and Spanish drifted into war by the fall of 1739. Oglethorpe had returned to America in 1738 with his own regiment and was anxious to seize Florida, but his 1740 expedition against St. Augustine failed and he fell back to his Ft. Frederica base. The Spaniards invaded Georgia in 1742 and captured part of St. Simon's Island but, after several sharp skirmishes on July 7, they beat a hasty retreat to Florida. Thus Spain's last serious effort to regain its old mission territory was repelled. In 1743 Oglethorpe made another unsuccessful effort to take St. Augustine, and shortly afterward he sailed to England for the last time.

By 1741 Georgia had grown so that it was divided administratively into two counties, one centered at Frederica and the other at Savannah. Oglethorpe was entrusted with the southern district, and William Stephens the northern, but as long as Oglethorpe remained in the province he assumed overall control. After Oglethorpe's departure, Stephens was made president of a united colony and presided over a group of assistants until 1751. In that same year the trust called together Georgia's first elected assembly; although it had no power to legislate, it made sensible recommendations to London.

Religion and men of the cloth played a large role in the founding and forwarding of Georgia. The Church of England was expected to be prominent in the colony and an Anglican priest accompanied the first settlers, but this faith never prospered. Usually the ministers died, left the colony, or were found unsuited to their posts. Charles and John Wesley crossed with Oglethorpe in 1735–1736, but both became disillusioned and left Georgia; George Whitefield was more often out of the colony than in it, and he was more interested in his orphanage at Bethesda than in traditional pastoral cares. From the beginning the dissenters outnumbered the Anglicans. The Scottish Presbyterians and the Lutheran Salzburgers were the most homogeneous religious groups in trustee Georgia.

Efforts to secure competent schoolmasters for the colony proved unsatisfactory. Whitefield's school at the Bethesda orphanage was the most reliable during the period prior to the American Revolution, but his plans to see it develop into a colonial college never materialized. Georgians were too busy hacking a place in the wilderness to engage in *belles lettres*. However, there was much polemical literature written about Georgia, some of it by people who actually lived in the colony. One of the finest satires in eighteenth-century America was done by a group of Georgia "refugees" in Carolina. *A True and Historical Narrative of the Colony of Georgia*, first published in Charleston in 1741, was a general attack on trustee policy preceded by a witty mock dedication to Oglethorpe. William Stephens produced a lively and topical journal, and Francis Moore published one of the century's best travel accounts. The Wesleys' journals and diaries, similar to Whitefield's, reveal more about their authors than about Georgia.

These and other records of the period show that one of the striking failures of the trustees was their inability to establish a firm economic foundation for their colony. They did little to create a practical alternative to a staple crop economy. It was impossible to initiate a rum-sugar-molasses for staves-shingles-lumber trade with the West Indies, and Oglethorpe's idea of a province of subsistence farmers was not feasible on a warlike frontier. The economic situation seemed desperate during the Spanish war, but an upturn was apparent before the trust relinquished its charter.

The experiment with SILK, upon which the trustees pinned so many hopes, seemed to be approaching success in the 1750s, but sericulture, which prospered only with subsidies, declined when those subsidies were withdrawn. The same held true for indigo. Some RICE and COTTON were grown for home use during the trusteeship, but the periods of significant production of both crops lay in the future. Various timber products were the most valuable Georgia exports during trustee years, and, although Savannah was hardly more than a crude village, by the 1740s it had begun to develop a distinctive life of its own. In response to its growth, merchants such as the Moravian John Brownfield, Francis Harris, and James Habersham engaged in a bustling trade that belied the comments of the province's critics that it was a wasteland. Although Georgia was largely undeveloped both politically and economically, the trustees surrendered a colony of about 3,500 people—perhaps as many as 1,000 of them black—to the king in 1752. After the surrender of the charter, Georgia, with the Negro and land restrictions removed, was free to develop as a colony reliant upon a staple crop economy supported by the institution of slavery.

With the coming of royal rule Georgia had for the first time a governor and a bicameral legislature comprised of an elected lower and an appointed upper house. The crown provided Georgia with effective courts, and a battery of royal officials saw to the running of government. The governor was a stronger official than in most of England's royal colonies. The salaries of Georgia's crown officials were provided by the British treasury, so they were less dependent upon the legislature than in other provinces.

Governor John Reynolds, who arrived in Savannah in 1754, had a highly unsatisfactory two-year term, during which he alienated virtually all political factions. He was succeeded by the clever and politic Henry Ellis, whose three years in office saw Georgia experience growth and prosperity as its internal affairs steadied. Ellis was followed by James Wright, who served from 1760 to 1776. His personal popularity, his obvious fondness for Georgia, and the respect in which he was held help explain why the colony was slow to join the Revolutionary movement.

Georgia was spared the hostilities associated with the FRENCH AND INDIAN WAR (1754–1763), but profited enormously by its outcome. The southern boundary was extended to the St. Mary's River, and the Spanish and French were removed from Georgia's borders. Governor Wright, whose key words for the colony were expansion and defense, was able to secure an Indian cession in 1763 of all lands between the Ogeechee and Savannah to a point even north of Augusta. At the same time the natives gave up their claims to coastal lands south of the Altamaha River. Ten years later other significant cessions were made by the Creek and Cherokee, and settlers poured into these newly opened regions. Upper Georgia, in fact, was developing quite differently from the low country, where more organized settlement patterns still prevailed. In the latter area a large and well-equipped group of Puritans moved into the Midway district and prospered so that their town of Sunbury was in 1761 designated an official port of entry; the Scotch-Irish located on the Ogeechee at Queensborough; more Germans came into Georgia and settled north of Savannah; a Quaker colony was created at Wrightsborough.

Revolution and early national period. By 1775 Georgia contained about 50,000 people, probably not quite half of them slaves. These blacks were concentrated in the low-country parishes, where rice and indigo were grown. Although there were some large slaveholders and landholders in Georgia, among them Wright, most people lived on small- to medium-sized farms. Augusta, with its strategic location on the Savannah, was the "metropolis" of the backcountry. Larger and more sedate Savannah prospered as the center of Georgia's administrative machinery. Its wharves hummed with activity, and its architecture reflected the prosperity of Oglethorpe's onetime modest creation. Georgia's first printer, James Johnston, arrived in Savannah in 1762 and began publication the following year of the GEORGIA GAZETTE. Dancing masters, booksellers, cobblers, peruke makers, and teachers of all descriptions advertised in its pages, reflecting the vivid life of the town.

Politically all went smoothly for Wright until the STAMP ACT CRISIS. Although he weathered that storm, it had sharply divided the colony and made a complete return to the harmonious days before 1765 impossible. The lower house began to assert powers it had not claimed before. In 1771–1772 it engaged in a struggle over Wright's rejection of a Speaker for that body, and in 1773 a committee of correspondence was created. Georgia's reaction to the Intolerable Acts put the province more into the stream of the Revolutionary movement. Still Georgia failed to name delegates to the First CONTINENTAL CONGRESS (1774).

Wright used every legal means to keep Georgia out of the Revolution. He prorogued the assembly in January, 1775, to prevent it from appointing delegates to the Second Continental Congress, but this was his last effective step. Wright lingered on until January, 1776, but royal government was replaced during 1775 by a council of safety, a provincial congress, and organizations at the local level. Meeting in the summer of 1775, Georgia's second provincial congress named delegates to the Continental Congress. LYMAN HALL, George

Walton, and Button Gwinnett ultimately signed the DECLARATION OF INDEPENDENCE.

By no means all Georgians thought that this action was a good thing. Royal officials, those recently arrived in America, numerous Anglicans, and many others counseled patience. Dissenters (in a large majority by 1775), small merchants and businessmen, much of the youth, and farmers in the backcountry seemed to favor the more radical party. It is likely that Georgia radicals outnumbered the Loyalists; however, the large undecided group might weight the scales in favor of either at a given time.

The radical camp drew up a constitution in 1776 and another in 1777, the latter vesting a unicameral legislature with most authority. A judiciary and a weak executive were provided, the state was carved into eight counties, and the franchise was broadened. Religious freedom was granted to all, but non-Protestants could not sit in the assembly. Trial by jury as well as other customary privileges were assured in a bill of rights.

The hostilities threatened to destroy Georgia. In the backcountry there was civil warfare where quarter was neither asked nor given. On the coast unsuccessful forays were made against Florida, but Savannah itself was seized by British forces late in 1778. Augusta was captured also, but the English were disappointed when the up-country did not embrace George III. A Loyalist band was defeated by ELIJAH CLARKE and others at KETTLE CREEK in 1779, but this was largely offset by an English victory at Brier Creek in March of the same year. The crowning blow for American hopes in Georgia came in the autumn at the bungled siege of Savannah. Liaison between the French commander Count d'Estaing and the Americans was sadly lacking; a final assault against the British on October 9, 1779, was a disaster. Among the numerous allied casualties were Sergeant William Jasper and Count Casimir Pulaski. Only a few up-country partisan bands continued harrying tactics.

As the war raged, Georgia's Revolutionary government was riddled by factionalism, which weakened Georgia's war effort. At times the Revolutionary government was forced to roam through the backcountry, having been expelled even from its de facto capital of Augusta. So strong was the factional division that in 1779, in spite of the desperate situation, Georgia had two Revolutionary regimes that contended with one another almost as violently as they did the redcoats. The British on their part brought Governor Wright back and charged him with reconstituting Georgia. He worked astutely, but by late 1781, as the British position in the South crumbled, Wright was confined to governing a shrinking perimeter around Savannah. He evacuated in July, 1782.

The war had not been won without great personal suffering and privation. Commerce, agriculture, and the economy had suffered badly. Loyalist estates were confiscated, but often such property was returned if the person recanted or paid a fine. Although some large estates were broken up, there was no massive land redistribution. All told, Georgia lost in the neighborhood of 1,000 whites and perhaps as many as 4,000 slaves at the time of Savannah's evacuation, and probably a good many before that. The state ran up a large debt in financing the war. Ultimately these debts were either repudiated or only partially paid.

The Revolution had a dramatic effect on Georgia. In religion, the Church of England lost both membership and prestige. On the lusty frontier, where thousands moved even during the war, the new and more emotional faiths of the Baptists and Methodists came to predominate. These same new up-country settlers brought with them to northeast Georgia the culture of tobacco, a crop supplanted by cotton in the early 1800s. Politically, Augusta had been the seat of government and the center of resistance to the British in the war's last phases. It was made capital of the state of Georgia in 1785, and the backcountry became politically dominant over Savannah and the low country.

After the war the state was in a strongly nationalistic mood. Georgia promptly ratified the U.S. Constitution, which it was hoped would create a government to help with the Indians on the frontier. The Indians occupied lands Georgians wanted badly. In addition, the natives were being manipulated by the Spanish in Florida. Another indication of nationalistic fervor was the state constitution of 1789, which provided for a more centralized government and a stronger executive. The constitution of 1798 went even farther and was to last over 60 years.

Georgia earlier showed an awareness of the need for higher education by chartering the first state-supported university in 1785 and by encouraging an academy movement in each county. The academies did not prosper, but the University of Georgia, which opened its doors in 1801, achieved distinction even though it received only a handful of public funds during the first century of its life.

In the late eighteenth and early nineteenth centuries there were two dominant interrelated issues facing Georgians: physical expansion and the problem of Indian removal. White Georgians generally felt the Indians hampered progress. The state presumed that the federal government felt the same way, but often there were differences of policy. Such conflicts colored state-federal relations and local politics until after the final Cherokee removal in 1838. A large land cession was wrung from the Creeks at the Treaty of New York in 1790, but pressure on the frontier continued as Georgia's population virtually doubled between 1790 and 1800. Treaties in 1801 and 1804 pushed the western boundary to the Ocmulgee River, and a baker's dozen new counties were set up.

Land grants were often shot through with fraud and corruption during the 1790s, first on the local and finally on the state level. The YAZOO LAND FRAUDS of 1796 stemmed from Georgia's continuing claim to the huge stretch of land from the Chattahoochee west to the Mississippi. Speculators convinced the legislature to grant more than 30 million of these acres to various land companies for about $500,000. The stench of corruption hung over the assembly, and the people of the state became enraged. The assembly of 1797, following the lead of the dynamic JAMES JACKSON, rescinded the grants. Before this action, however, some of the Yazoo property was sold to people who wanted to occupy their grants. The whole issue was ultimately decided by the U.S. Supreme Court in the case of FLETCHER V. PECK (1810). By 1802 Georgia was chastened by the Yazoo experience and ceded its western claims to the central government with the understanding that Indian land titles east of the line of the Chattahoochee be extinguished as quickly as possible.

Early in the nineteenth century the state adopted a unique arrangement to replace the old HEADRIGHT SYSTEM. Lands were surveyed in advance in plots of varying size and were granted free (save for a slight fee) to citizens of Georgia on a lottery basis. Each person was to have an equal opportunity to receive land, but such elements in the population as war veterans, heads of families with one or more children, and widowed heads of families received additional chances. The system worked well, and, although it has been criticized for not bringing money to Georgia's treasury, it was at least as democratic and efficient as the systems used elsewhere. Under the lottery the state's lands were parceled out until there were no more to distribute.

In the political arena, the state became outspokenly Jeffersonian once party lines emerged, backing the VIRGINIA DYNASTY until 1828. James Jackson became Georgia's first popular political leader, and his party developed close ties with the Jeffersonians. After Jackson's death in 1806 WILLIAM H. CRAWFORD and George M. Troup assumed leadership of the faction. Crawford spent most of his time in various cabinet positions in

Washington and was also ambassador to France; Troup, in addition to serving in Congress, became one of the strongest governors in the state's history.

Opposition to the Jackson-Troup faction was headed by JOHN CLARK. At first the Troupites triumphed, and then there was a period of general understanding that everyone should work to drive the Spanish from Florida. All raids into Florida during the WAR OF 1812 aborted, but Georgians reveled in Andrew Jackson's sweeping victory over the Creeks at Horseshoe Bend. At the peace table the Indians surrendered claims to southern Georgia, thus isolating themselves from their former supply base in Pensacola. The Spanish realized their position was hopeless and ceded their colony to the United States in 1819. Georgia's southern boundary was set at the St. Mary's River.

Now that Georgia had reached the Chattahoochee in the southwest, pressure mounted to clear all remaining Creek Indian claims in the state. A voluntary cession to the Flint River in 1821 temporarily staved off the inevitable. In 1825 Governor Troup, who had berated federal officials for their delay, secured the surrender of the Lower Creeks' remaining land in Georgia. When the Upper Creeks (and the national government) questioned the legality of this Treaty of Indian Springs, Troup denounced Washington and threatened war. Feeble efforts by the national government to block implementation of the treaty were useless, and by the end of 1827 the Creeks had been forced from Georgia. The lands that had been ceded were fertile and ideal for cotton culture. Macon and Columbus were settled in 1823 and 1828 respectively, and both towns quickly became marketing and transportation centers first for river navigation and then for railways. In addition, the power of the Ocmulgee and the Chattahoochee rivers was harnessed to operate the mills built at these sites.

By the time the crisis with the Cherokee had developed, Georgia's factions had been replaced by Union and States' Rights parties brought on by the tariff and NULLIFICATION fight. In general Clarkites were pro-Jackson Union party men, and Troupites were more attracted to the pro-Calhoun States' Rightists. JOHN FORSYTH followed Troup as governor, serving 1827 to 1829. He was no exception in his attitude toward the Indians, urging prompt Cherokee removal once the Creeks were gone.

The Cherokee would not give in to the whites without a fierce struggle. By 1830 they had their own written language, a constitution, and a capital at New Echota. As a sedentary people living under a government modeled upon that of the whites, the Cherokee claimed to be a nation. When it was apparent that Georgia would neither observe their border nor respect their lives and after the discovery of gold in the mountains seemed to seal their fate, the Indians appealed to the U.S. Supreme Court. In CHEROKEE NATION V. GEORGIA (1831) the Court refused to forbid Georgia from extending its laws over the Indians because the Cherokee were not a sovereign power. However, in 1832 in WORCESTER V. GEORGIA, the state's laws were declared inoperative on Cherokee land. So violent was Jackson's and Georgia's anger over this decision that the executive order enforcing it was not issued. In effect the Indians were left to fend for themselves. As a result of intimidation and a series of treaties of questionable validity, the Cherokee had been forcibly removed by the end of 1838.

Andrew Jackson's policy on Indian removal increased his popularity among Georgians, who had long been his admirers. They supported him particularly strongly after 1824, when it was clear that Crawford's chances for the White House were gone. Jackson's familiarity with frontier life and his apparent distaste for the second Bank of the United States also appealed to most Georgians. With JOHN C. CALHOUN's articulated philosophy of STATES' RIGHTS many Georgians could also agree, but his dour personality, political ambitions, and rivalry with Crawford turned some against him. So when the nullification conflict arose, Georgia was divided. Following a short, severe struggle, the Jacksonians emerged winners.

Inferences should not be drawn that Georgia was protariff. The state resented the imposts of 1828 and 1832, but leaders such as Forsyth felt a federal constitutional convention should be called before taking radical action. Nor did Georgians deplore all banking institutions. By 1837 Georgia had more than 20 commercial banks, some with branches, and the state's system of regulation had worked so well that the effects of the PANIC OF 1819 had been minimized. The state could not have experienced the enormous growth in people, size, and wealth that it had through the 1830s without properly extended commercial credit, agricultural loans, bank notes issued by state-chartered institutions, and activities of the state's own Central Bank of Georgia.

In a brawling, frontier state such as Georgia before 1838, it is unreasonable to expect a flowering of culture. Colleges were few, and enrollments were small; there were probably less than 40 academies in the state in 1820 (and not many more assorted private schools). Academies were weighted to Latin and Greek, and girls' schools empha-

sized the more "gentle" sciences. However, Georgia Female College (1836), later Wesleyan College, was a leader in higher education for women in the South. In the 1830s the state's main religious groups—the Baptists, Methodists, and Presbyterians—founded Mercer, Emory, and Oglethorpe colleges respectively, and in 1859 a law school was established at the University of Georgia. Georgia Medical College was set up in Augusta in 1828. For basic educational needs, tutoring at home was still important.

NEWSPAPERS had begun to flourish in Georgia by the 1820s, and most of the reading done by literate Georgians was from their pages. THEATER was confined largely to the older settled areas, but traveling puppet shows, carnivals, and "circuses" made their way into the backcountry. One play, *The Mysterious Father* by William Bulloch Maxwell of Savannah, dates from 1807, and Hugh McCall's two-volumed *History of Georgia* antedates 1820. A. B. LONGSTREET (*Georgia Scenes*) was probably the best of the Georgia humorists who used local color in their writings, but William T. Thompson was a capable writer. Richard Henry Wilde and Thomas Holley Chivers were Georgia's first poets of note. Some of the most competent writing was done by William B. Stevens in his *History of Georgia*, produced a generation after McCall's work. The GEORGIA HISTORICAL SOCIETY was formed in Savannah in 1839 and encouraged the interest of Georgians in their history, and library societies, debating groups, and literary organizations advanced knowledge throughout the state.

Georgia's homes began to take on more pretensions in the eastern segment of the state with the coming of William Jay to Savannah in 1817. In the Piedmont, Daniel Pratt built fine houses in the countryside and in Milledgeville, which became the capital of the state in 1806. Athens boasted its distinguished Old College, and handsome townhouses appeared in Savannah and Augusta. Still, the typical Georgia house throughout the antebellum period was rural and simple. By 1860 some of these early houses had additional rooms added and Greek Revival façades imposed.

During frontier days—and most of Georgia was hardly more than two generations from frontier by 1860—families often slept in a one- or two-room cabin, sharing common sleeping quarters and meals with their slaves. Although these rugged folk appeared to enjoy their religion immensely, it was for many an exercise in emotional release. The Baptist itinerant preacher and the Methodist circuit rider did what they could to bring God to the frontier, but the rest of organized religion in

Georgia made little effort to conquer the back-country. By the time of the Civil War there was an increase in church membership, some of which may have been organization of southern branches of the Methodist and Baptist churches. All things considered, however, Georgians were not a religious people.

Antebellum Georgia. In 1793 Eli Whitney's cotton gin, invented at Mulberry Grove plantation on the Savannah River, made profitable the cultivation of the green seed, short-staple cotton throughout most of Georgia and the South. This coincided with the incorporation by Georgia of large chunks of Indian lands, and when Columbus was established in 1828 there was already an incipient "plantation belt" stretching across the state. Significant numbers of Negro slaves were introduced into the backcountry to cultivate and harvest the crop. The size of the average plantation, held down initially by the limited grants under the lottery system, soon tended to grow larger, especially in the lower Piedmont. In some instances small farmers were forced out, but even in the 1850s many white yeomen were found in the areas of large landholdings. In fact, throughout antebellum days the small farmer, usually working with little or no black labor, remained the typical Georgian. By 1860 about 60 percent of Georgia's farm families owned no slaves although plantation life remained the white ideal.

As cotton boomed, other crops were often neglected, and tobacco, once a staple in northeast Georgia, all but disappeared from that section. It did well in south Georgia, however, and by 1860 the state was producing approximately 1 million pounds annually. But it was cotton culture that took on an almost mystic quality, and by the mid-1820s Georgia was the world's largest cotton producer; in 1839 it grew 326,000 bales. Although trailing Alabama's total in 1850, the state's production stood at almost 500,000 bales; the 1860 crop was greater than 700,000. Corn and other grains were widely grown, largely for local consumption. Although crop diversification was more common than is usually thought, upland cotton along with rice in the low country and long-staple cotton on the SEA ISLANDS provided Georgia's primary cash crops.

There is little question that planters dominated Georgia's politics in the antebellum period. Although frequently falling out among themselves, these men all agreed on the question of the right of an individual to own slaves. The state's economic and social system, in spite of flirtations with liberal eighteenth-century thought, became more closely entwined with the South's "peculiar institution" as the nineteenth century advanced. By the time of the Civil War, even the areas where slaveholding was not predominant were willing to follow the planters in secession.

Socially the state was overwhelmingly MIDDLE CLASS; most of the prosperous planters were self-made men. They had little time for leisure or refinements, and hence Georgia's antebellum cultural life appeared to be fairly restricted to Savannah, Augusta, and Athens. If Georgia had anything that might be called an ARISTOCRACY, it was made up of a few planters and merchants along the coast and up the river to Augusta.

Where adequate books were kept and sensible business practices followed, slavery was a profitable institution in Georgia. It is true that Georgia, in 1860, had more plantations of over 1,000 improved acres than any other state, but only one planter owned more than 500 slaves. Twenty-three men owned in excess of 200 Negroes, and 212 planters had 100 or more. Therefore only 236 men owned more than 100 slaves each. Most farms were below 100 improved acres in size, many of them employing no Negroes. All told there were about 50,000 farms in Georgia under 500 improved acres, and only 3,500 that were larger. It was on the smaller plots that the YEOMEN FARMERS lived. In the towns and cities the artisan and mechanic groups grew as did the numbers of lawyers, doctors, and ministers, all adding to Georgia's middle-class orientation.

Below the middle class were the POOR WHITES, some of whom owned small farms, usually in marginal or abandoned areas. They hunted and fished and often hired themselves out as seasonal laborers to planters or yeomen farmers and performed menial tasks in the towns. Not to be confused with the poor whites were the "poor white trash," scorned by blacks as well as whites. These were the drifters, the diseased, the illiterate, living on the periphery of society. The state was saddled with a 20 percent illiteracy rate among the whites. The poor were particularly penalized by the fact that Georgia had no real system of public education prior to the Civil War.

There was also a number of free Negroes in Georgia, but they were feared and were discriminated against. They concentrated in the towns and cities, especially Savannah and Augusta. Although they were usually employed as unskilled labor, there are examples of intelligent and skilled free blacks in Georgia holding positions of respect and prominence within their communities. With slavery the obvious exception and with the odds heavily against free Negroes, Georgia society was mobile and fluid.

By 1860 there were roughly 465,000 slaves in Georgia. This institution was given its rules by state and local codes, which prescribed the limits and fashion of Negro behavior. Although in theory the slaves were carefully regulated, in practice many of the strictures in the statute books were not enforced. The individual slave owner exercised wide latitude, for good or ill, among his chattels. There are examples in Georgia of extreme cruelty by the owner to his slave as well as acts of generosity. Most of Georgia's slaves lived in houses that were barely adequate, ate food of about the same degree, and were shabbily clothed and often unshod. The plantation system did provide the slave with a certain amount of "free time," and it was during these periods that the blacks refined their rich subsociety that contributed so much of value and spontaneity to the mainstream of American life. In the final analysis, slavery by 1860 appeared to be alive and well in Georgia. Although most of the planters had been wasteful with the soil, causing erosion and/or depletion, slavery seemed to thrive wherever the land was fertile and wisely used.

Even before Georgia reached its ultimate boundaries it was obvious that an effective system of transportation and communication was needed. Road building was slow and expensive, and upkeep was always a problem, so Georgia naturally turned to its rivers. Because of increasing traffic and cargo flow and the need for service to and from the backcountry, steamboats began to ply Georgia's major streams after 1820 (RIVERCRAFT). These boats gave Columbus, Macon, and Milledgeville relatively quick and reliable contacts with the coast. (Augusta had enjoyed river traffic with Savannah since the 1730s.) The CANAL frenzy hardly touched Georgia, primarily because a state board of public works recommended other types of public expenditures, particularly for the construction of RAILROADS. It was the railroad boom that knitted the state together by 1860.

The two largest private antebellum railways, the Georgia Railroad and the Central of Georgia, were both chartered in 1833 and immediately prospered. At about the same time a strong movement to build a line to connect the Chattahoochee and the Tennessee valleys caused the creation of the state-owned Western & Atlantic Railroad. Although construction on all roads was delayed by depression in the early 1840s, the W & A reached Chattanooga in 1851, completing its main line.

The southern terminus of the W & A, at Zero Milepost, became Atlanta. When it was clear that the W & A would succeed, the rival Georgia and Central systems vied with one another to see which could reach Atlanta first, thereby linking up with the Mississippi-Ohio system. Augusta's Georgia Railroad won the race in 1845, but Savannah's Central of Georgia was only a year behind. The Atlanta & West Point reached out to tap the flow of northern Alabama railroads, and in south Georgia the Atlantic & Gulf system, connecting the Eastern Seaboard directly with south Georgia and Alabama, was virtually complete by 1861. From these main routes were built feeder lines and connectors, which gave Georgia in 1860 over 1,200 miles of track and a system that had no rival in the Deep South.

Georgia was slow in developing its industrial potential, due largely to the emphasis on agriculture. Although there were numerous earlier mills in the state, TEXTILE mill construction prospered in the 1830s, especially in the fall-line cities, and by 1860 Georgia was a leader in the southern textile field. Other industries included numerous tanneries, a few brickworks and iron foundries, nail factories, machine shops, and the like. Savannah was the state's main industrial city, with lumber interests being particularly important, but upstart Atlanta was in 1860 already producing about half the value of the older center. Atlanta's rolling mill and machine shops were to be crucial during the Civil War, as were Augusta's powder works and Columbus' foundries. Georgia produced industrial goods in 1860 valued at almost $17 million. Dahlonega had been a center of gold mining and the location of a branch U.S. mint since 1838. Iron and clays, coal and marble were all being taken from Georgia's hills. On the eve of the Civil War, however, the state's image was largely agricultural, but the economy was more diversified than is generally thought.

Georgia's political structure became even more complex during the years leading to secession. In the 1840s there were two well-organized and evenly balanced parties. Many of the old Troupite–States' Rights faction became Whigs and carried the state for William Henry Harrison in 1840. Most of the Clark-Unionist element gravitated to the Democratic pole. Each group evolved able leaders: the Whigs had John Mcpherson Berrien, ALEXANDER H. STEPHENS, George W. Crawford, and ROBERT TOOMBS; the Democrats relied on HOWELL COBB, HERSCHEL V. JOHNSON, and JOSEPH E. BROWN. The Whigs tended to be more cautious with state financing, but the parties agreed on many points. The Whig Crawford saw to the creation of a state supreme court during one of his terms as governor and also pushed construction of the W & A. Howell Cobb, in the 1850s, was an important railroad booster, but he also broadened the state's tax base, increased expenditures for schools, and expanded state services. Brown, a Democratic dark horse nominee in 1857, instituted needed reforms in the state railroad and advocated larger allocations of funds for public education. This popular man from the north Georgia hill country was reelected in 1859 and twice during the Civil War.

Many Georgia Whigs were thrown on the defensive by the issue of the annexation of Texas. Stephens, Berrien, and Toombs all opposed the Mexican War that followed, but found it difficult to stay in the same party with the now-strident antislavery northern Whigs who backed the WILMOT PROVISO. Georgia Whigs opposed the proviso and were able to concentrate party strength to carry the state for popular war hero Zachary Taylor in 1848.

The Democrats were having troubles too. A schism developed between the Calhounites and the moderates. Cobb, elected Speaker of the U.S. House, took the lead in rallying the moderate Democrats to the cause of the COMPROMISE OF 1850. Stephens and Toombs, also in Congress, backed the compromise as well, and all three men worked hard to convince the Georgia electorate they had acted properly. Old political labels disappeared as these men and their allies appeared under the name CONSTITUTIONAL UNION PARTY OF GEORGIA; the radicals chose the Southern Rights party as their standard. The Unionists stumped the state counseling acceptance of the GEORGIA PLATFORM, adopted by a state convention in December, 1850. This document called for Georgia voters' approval of the compromise but also issued a stern warning that if the North failed to live up to its guarantees then the South would no longer feel bound. Georgia gave the platform and the Union a ringing endorsement at the polls; the state's position became a model for Union supporters in the rest of the South.

The furor over the compromise effectively destroyed the Whigs, and although Stephens and Toombs were deeply suspicious of Democrats, they had little choice but to cooperate with them, particularly after the formation of the Republican party. The close call James Buchanan had at the hands of the politically inexperienced Republican, John C. Frémont, a Savannah native, in the presidential election of 1856 demonstrated the danger ahead for the Democrats. John Brown's HARPERS FERRY RAID convinced many Georgians that, should a Republican be elected in 1860, the state would be better off out of the Union than in it.

Georgia, 1860–1900. At the Democrats' CHARLESTON CONVENTION in 1860, most of Georgia's delegation walked out when southern demands that slavery be protected in the territories were not met, a tactic repeated at the BALTIMORE CONVENTION. Stephen A. Douglas was nominated for president by this second convention with loyalist Herschel V. Johnson of Georgia as his running mate. Most Georgia Democrats backed the candidacy of JOHN C. BRECKINRIDGE of Kentucky, and many old Whigs and Know-Nothings supported JOHN BELL of Tennessee, the CONSTITUTIONAL UNION PARTY candidate. Abraham Lincoln had no open supporters in Georgia. If Bell's and Douglas' votes in Georgia had been combined, Breckinridge would have lost the state, but the moderate votes were split. Lincoln's election caused Governor Brown to call for a state convention to evaluate Georgia's ties with the Union. The vote for delegates to this convention was no clear-cut mandate for secession, but Brown, Cobb, Toombs, and others chose to interpret it as such. Stephens, Johnson, BENJAMIN H. HILL, and others fought the inflamed rhetoric of the secessionists. A key issue was rejected, 164 to 133, after which a secession ordinance was passed on January 20, 1861.

Because Georgia was the most populous and wealthy state of the Deep South, it seemed only appropriate for its role in the early days of the Confederacy to be a significant one. Howell Cobb's brother, the jurist T. R. R. COBB, was one of the framers of the Confederate constitution; Howell was presiding officer of the Montgomery convention; Stephens was picked as Confederate vice-president; Toombs was chosen secretary of state.

Governor Brown clashed with the Confederate government on its use of Georgia troops, seizure of state goods and munitions, the right to use of the writ of habeas corpus, the appointment of militia officers, and especially conscription. His public postures may have encouraged desertions and a general lowering of morale in Georgia as well as in Confederate military and administrative circles. Still, well over 100,000 Georgians ultimately served in the army, and the state's rich farmlands helped supply Confederate commissaries. Many plantations became self-sufficient and grew more grains and foodstuffs (and less cotton) than previously. Wartime demand stimulated manufacturing and trade, but there was a shortage of skilled labor, and replacement parts for machinery were almost nonexistent. Georgia's railroads were used extensively, the rolling stock wore out, and no new track was laid during the war.

As the war progressed the state found it increasingly difficult to provision its troops. There were acute shortages of medical supplies, salt, and other necessities. The legislature levied new taxes, but as the Confederate cause waned coins disappeared from circulation and paper money became highly inflated. SHERMAN'S MARCH virtually wrecked Georgia's economy and left the state prostrated.

Life in Georgia, until the coming of William T. Sherman, did not alter radically from prewar days. Newspapers operated without censorship, but many were forced to close because of paper shortages. The black work force remained on the plantations and was even pressed into semimilitary service if the occasion demanded. When Union forces drew near, many slaves did leave the plantations, and black colonies were set up on the Union-occupied coastal islands early in the war. All men's colleges except Mercer closed, but the WOMEN'S COLLEGES stayed open. Schooling on the lower level continued as it had until near the end of the war.

With the exception of early action on the coast (resulting in the surrender of FT. PULASKI and the isolation of Savannah's port in April, 1862), there were no military encounters in Georgia between large numbers of troops until 1864. Efforts in 1862 and 1863 to cut the W & A Railroad were frustrated, but Sherman led an army of 100,000 men into Georgia in late spring, 1864, with intent to divide the Confederacy and cripple Georgia's war effort. He marched down the main line of the W & A toward Atlanta, consistently outflanking JOSEPH E. JOHNSTON's smaller army. After a sharp encounter at KENNESAW MOUNTAIN Johnston fell back upon Atlanta's defenses. He was replaced by JOHN B. HOOD, whose efforts to break through federal lines were bloodily repulsed. All but surrounded, Hood withdrew from Atlanta on September 1. Sherman took the city, regrouped his forces, burned most of the town, and set off on his virtually unopposed and highly destructive march to the sea. Savannah fell by mid-December, 1864. The war, as far as Georgia was concerned, had ended.

In defeat Georgia suffered severe economic, political, and social dislocation. But the sheer necessities of survival dictated that by 1870 man and land had gotten together again to the point that cotton production approached the 500,000-bale mark. Various systems of landowner-tenant relationships were attempted, but the one that came to be used most frequently was SHARECROPPING.

Although the tenant was clearly the more oppressed by the system, few landowners actually profited from the arrangement. Both landlord and cropper were hit by periodic agricultural depressions, high interest charges, deflation, and other economic circumstances they could neither understand nor alter. Much of the unrest in Georgia during the last decades of the nineteenth century is incomprehensible unless viewed in the light of these conditions.

The people of the state seemed willing to accept military defeat with some equanimity. Georgia did what was necessary to reenter the Union under President Andrew Johnson's plan, but the rise of the Radical Republicans in Congress doomed presidential efforts at Reconstruction. A military government was instituted in 1867, and a purged convention drew up a new state constitution. The document granted the franchise to the blacks, and although it provided for general public education, it was left to subsequent governments to develop the system. Atlanta was made Georgia's capital, signifying its growing importance and the state's continued population swing north and west. Republican Rufus Bullock was inaugurated governor in 1868, but that autumn the state voted for Democrat Horatio Seymour and the house turned out its black members, thus bringing about a return of military rule. After additional Radical requirements were met, Georgia was again allowed to reenter the Union (1870) for the third time in four years.

By 1872 Georgia had returned to Democratic control and Bullock had left the state in temporary disgrace. His legacy was an administration that was careless with the W & A and with state bonds, but his sins were not so vile as the Democrats claimed. In fact his Reconstruction government broadened the scope of state activity and did worthwhile groundwork in education and allied fields. The FREEDMEN'S BUREAU was effective in helping the former slave adjust to his new status, and it took an active part in establishing Atlanta University in 1867. Perhaps the bureau's finest achievement was to bring into the state a number of dedicated teachers, who worked without hope of material reward to offer education to the blacks.

With the exception of the Union-repaired and state-owned W & A, the main Georgia railroads were bankrupt in 1865. And yet so swift was the state's economic recovery in this area that the biggest systems were soon making profits again. By 1873 almost 1,000 miles of new track had been put down, and a second railroad boom was in the making. Savannah once again exported vast amounts of cotton, although its leadership was threatened for a time by competition from the deepwater port of Brunswick.

By the end of the century Georgia was first in the country in naval stores, and its timber remained important. New industries had grown up to transform cottonseed into stock food and FERTILIZER. The textile mills along the fall line were rebuilt or retooled, and by 1890 this industry was turning out goods worth more than $12.5 million. The growth of Atlanta, however, eclipsed other economic developments. The city was the focal point of Georgia's surge, and HENRY W. GRADY, editor of the Atlanta *Constitution*, with his NEW SOUTH philosophy became the man of the hour. Atlanta's spirit of bustle and optimism was well illustrated by the successful expositions held there in 1887 and 1895 (COMMERCIAL EXPOSITIONS). Still, in spite of the trumpetings of the heralds of the New South, Georgia industry in 1900 was not the sort that attracted or required skilled labor. In fact, important considerations for northern capital to move South were low taxes and even lower wage scales. At the turn of the century Georgia remained overwhelmingly agrarian and lagged behind most states in all economic indicators.

Culturally the Gilded Age in Georgia offered more dross than gold. Indicative of the times, the best prose authors were also journalists. JOEL CHANDLER HARRIS got his early training on the *Countryman*, a magazine printed on Joseph Addison Turner's Putnam County plantation, but Harris' stories of Uncle Remus did not appear until 1879. At the same time another writer on the *Constitution*, Bill Arp (Charles H. Smith), spun tall tales in the rural Georgia tradition. SIDNEY LANIER was Georgia's most talented poet. Several of his best poems deal intimately with the state, notably "The Song of the Chattahoochee" and "The Marshes of Glynn." Charles C. Jones, Jr., was a prominent historian, although he wrote with a strong southern bias.

Church membership up to 1900 increased regularly. After the war the blacks formed their own churches, overwhelmingly Baptist or Methodist. Sectarian efforts at higher education were continued, but Oglethorpe College was a victim of the war. Emory at Oxford and Mercer increased in size; the University of Georgia reopened in 1866 and soon broadened its horizons and curriculum. An offshoot of the university was founded in Dahlonega in 1871, and an agricultural school was created in Athens. Along New South lines, the state chartered the Georgia Institute of Technology in 1885 to teach effective industrial practices in the state. Four years later a women's college was founded at Milledgeville to train young women in similar practical skills such as the teaching of "telegraphy, stenography, typewriting, photography, bookkeeping," and so on.

After Bullock left Georgia, many of the old Confederate leaders regained control, although it took Joe Brown some time to convince the state that he was cleansed of his Reconstruction Republicanism. The postwar politicians were more interested in keeping themselves in power than in helping the Georgia farmer, so it was not long before INDEPENDENT Democrats were challenging "regular" Democratic candidates for Congress and seats in the legislature. WILLIAM H. FELTON was the advance guard of independency, being first elected to Congress in 1874; and Emory Speer won election in 1878. The independents denounced the Atlanta-based politicians and pledged the farmer—Georgia's forgotten man—a fair hearing. In 1882 the independents nearly convinced Stephens to be their candidate for governor, but the regulars, sensing disaster, prevailed upon him to be their candidate instead. With the wind taken from their sails the independents declined. But they had set in motion an opposition movement that was to bear fruit in the 1890s.

In the meantime, the state drew up its "home rule constitution" in 1877. The document tried to ensure fiscal economy and by so doing wound itself in knots that had to be untied by generations of subsequent lawmakers. It was at last replaced in 1945. The work of 1877, however, is also important for what it did not do: it made no serious attempts to reverse the movement for public education, nor did it attack the right of the blacks at the polls.

With independency scotched the old line was once again in control. Brown, old war hero JOHN B. GORDON, and ALFRED H. COLQUITT composed a threesome that dominated the governorship and the senatorial posts for almost 15 years. Government was best that governed least, but what "least" there was should be in the interests of the group in power. The CONVICT LEASE, begun under Reconstruction, was abused during this period; Georgia's archaic tax laws were retained; the newly formed school system was inadequately funded; rural roads were a disgrace; and freight rates seemed pegged to discriminate against the little man.

Against such a background, heightened by agricultural depression, an organization called the FARMERS' ALLIANCE carried all before it. By 1890 the Georgia Alliance was so strong that it dominated the general assembly of that year. A torrent of legislation was pushed through, mainly aimed at state government taking a positive role in the lives of Georgia's citizens. Some leaders, such as THOMAS E. WATSON, elected to Congress in 1890, had misgivings about working within the Democratic party. Watson became a Populist, but most of the Alliance men were afraid to leave the Democrats lest the Republicans and blacks take advantage of the split in white ranks to assume control. Gradually the concept grew that if whites were to have open political disagreement, then the power of the blacks at the ballot box must be eliminated.

The POPULIST PARTY never assumed control of Georgia; its high point came in 1896, and Watson, the party's candidate for the vice-presidency that year, became increasingly disillusioned. Embittered and frustrated, he retired to his home at Hickory Hill and from there issued a steady stream of magazines, books, and political propaganda. No single man, with the possible exception of Eugene Talmadge (who modeled himself on Watson), has ever so dominated Georgia politics.

Georgia, 1900–1945. The new century started calmly, but 1906 saw one of Georgia's most bitter gubernatorial primary battles. The main contestants were newspapermen: HOKE SMITH, onetime owner of the Atlanta *Journal*, with Watson's support, and Clark Howell of the *Constitution*. The mood was such that a violent race riot claiming 17 lives broke out in Atlanta during the same year (ATLANTA RACE RIOT). Fear of the black man was never far below the surface of Georgia life, and Smith's promise to disfranchise the Negro appealed to Watson as well as to Georgia's white voters. Smith was overwhelmingly elected, but in addition to DISFRANCHISEMENT he pushed through the assembly a program of progressive legislation. The convict lease system was outlawed (although experiments with substitute solutions proved almost as offensive), and statewide PROHIBITION was enacted. In addition, state controls over railroad and corporate activities were broadened.

With the help of disfranchisement the Democrats reinforced their hold on Georgia politics. The Democratic WHITE PRIMARY became the de facto election in Georgia, and the county unit arrangement, which heavily favored the agricultural areas, was embraced as a rule of the party. In 1917 the COUNTY UNIT SYSTEM was given legal status as a law of the state. In such an atmosphere it is no surprise that the dominance of personal factions within the party from 1900 to 1950 reinforced an early characteristic of Georgia's political life. This kind of elitist politics caused a decline of interest by the electorate, invitations to DEMAGOGUERY, do-nothingism, and the occasional use of questionable administrative practices. At about the same time as the phenomena occurred elsewhere, nativism, anti-Semitism, and anti-Catholicism appeared in Georgia. The KU KLUX KLAN was resurrected to capitalize on these feelings. Such sentiments were also indicated by the sensational LEO FRANK murder trial in Atlanta.

In the 1920s Georgia slipped farther behind the rest of the nation in most categories, and even behind other states in the South. By 1920 the BOLL WEEVIL raged uncontrolled in Georgia's fields; cotton production, which had reached almost 2 million bales in 1909, fell by more than 300,000 bales ten years later. In 1924 barely 1 million bales were raised in the state. Although tobacco enjoyed an enormous increase, the drop in the cotton dollar was a major one. In fact, a general agricultural depression caused thousands to go to the cities seeking employment, but many Georgians simply left the state. As one example of this migration, there were more blacks in Georgia in 1920 than there were in 1970. Political leadership from the governor's mansion was at its nadir; the state seemed powerless. During the 1920s Georgia, always a southern leader in population and manufacturing, saw its top position in the former usurped by North Carolina, and it fell even more dramatically in the latter category. The state lagged in highway construction, health care, and other state services; the state university, which opened the century with bright promise under Walter Hill, stagnated. Illiteracy was still high in Georgia's rural districts, and the state stood last in support of its public schools. By 1930 over 60 percent of all Georgia's farms were of the tenant variety, but some of the countryside was virtually abandoned. For the state's paralysis during the decade a lackluster assembly must bear much of the blame.

Georgia began to come out of its lethargy under the leadership of the young Richard B. Russell, who became governor in 1931 and presided over an effective program of reorganization. The number of state boards was reduced to 18, and businesslike practices were introduced. Probably Russell's finest act as governor was to take the various boards of trustees that ran the numerous state-supported colleges and combine them under a single board of regents with final authority over the policies of the entire system. To show his disdain for the Klan, Russell appointed Hughes Spalding, Atlanta attorney and Roman Catholic, as the board's first chairman. Reorganization followed; weaker schools were eliminated or absorbed by stronger ones. The result was to create a university the state could understand and afford to support.

Russell was succeeded in the governor's office by EUGENE TALMADGE, a flamboyant figure whose postures and words conjured up images of days gone by. He detested Franklin Roosevelt and fought the various agencies and relief measures of the NEW DEAL. The electorate loved the show he put on, but twice denied him the U.S. senatorship. In 1936 Russell defeated Talmadge handily, and in the same year Eurith D. Rivers, a strong New Dealer, was elected governor over Talmadge's handpicked choice. Rivers supported health services, old-age pensions, teacher pay raises, free texts, an extended school year, and other measures opposed by Talmadge, and his program was enacted. After reelection in 1938, Rivers had trouble financing his policies and ran afoul of the powerful highway department. Talmadge returned in 1940, but again he made a serious blunder. He tried to manipulate the board of regents and the university system in the same way he had intimidated other state officials. The university's accreditation was removed and Talmadge found himself confronted by an electorate incensed by his attacks. The result was a stunning victory for Ellis G. Arnall in the gubernatorial campaign of 1942. Prosperity, brought along by WORLD WAR II, helped Arnall get a program that took the university system largely out of politics and that revamped state government. Arnall's fight to secure equal freight rates, his educational efforts, his prison reforms, and the new constitution in 1945 all gained national attention. But no single act of his administration claimed the public imagination as much as granting the vote to qualified eighteen-year-olds. In this particular, Georgia was first in the nation.

Recent Georgia. The year 1946 saw Arnall, Georgia's first four-year-term governor, unable to succeed himself. Although for a second time Talmadge failed to secure a majority of the popular votes, he won the county unit votes in the Democratic primary. A constitutional crisis occurred when Talmadge died after the election but before his inauguration. (The Republicans had no candidate on the ballot in the general election.) Was the lieutenant governor elect Melvin Thompson to be the new governor, should Arnall remain as caretaker chief executive, or should the person with the next highest number of votes for governor in the general election be designated? The general assembly, reflecting the county unit system that had made Talmadge the Democratic candidate, decided on the last. It was no coincidence that the man who trailed Talmadge in the voting was his own son Herman Talmadge. The state supreme

court decided that the assembly had gone too far, and Thompson, who had been sworn in as lieutenant governor, took possession of the governorship. Talmadge then narrowly defeated Thompson in a special election called in 1948 and again in 1950 for a full four-year term.

The basic issue, even more in 1948 and 1950 than in 1906, was one of race, with Talmadge vowing as strongly as Hoke Smith that Georgia would remain a white citadel. Also like that of Smith, Talmadge's record as governor was one of a relatively progressive nature. More money than ever before was put into public education—including a futile effort to build up the state's black schools to something resembling a "separate but equal" status with the whites'. In some ways Herman surprised his father's followers by expanding state services and by securing passage of a sales tax to help pay for new programs.

Progressive or conservative though the individuals concerned might be, the first half of the twentieth century demonstrated that Georgia politics, based upon personal followings within the Democratic party, had changed hardly at all. Gradually, however, even the Democratic party and the general assembly had to recognize that the practices of the past were gone. Industry and commerce boomed during the 1940s and 1950s, and tens of thousands of new people moved to the state. A better-educated electorate began to ask more questions and expect rational answers. Georgians were chagrined by the state's position in education and undertook to remedy it. A seven-month obligatory school term, authorized in 1935, was increased to nine months in 1952. Herman Talmadge's sales tax helped boost quality education in the state through the Minimum Foundation Association, and school consolidation made the system of public education more efficient. By the 1950s free textbooks were provided for public school children.

The boll weevil and the New Deal brought lasting change to rural Georgia. The RURAL ELECTRIFICATION ADMINISTRATION ran electric lines to many areas not served before, bringing not only lighting and labor-saving machinery, but radio (and later television). The various agricultural and financial programs of the Roosevelt years helped tide the farmers over difficult times, and extension services and county agents spread the word of sensible use of Georgia's soil. Tractors and farm machinery, along with automobiles and trucks, made their appearances; roads were paved to connect market towns with outlying areas. POULTRY, livestock, corn, tobacco, pecans, and peanuts (NUTS) all surpassed cotton in importance. Forest products, spurred by Charles Herty's experiments developing newsprint from pine (PULP AND PAPER), poured new money into the state. SOYBEANS, to become a dominant crop by the 1970s, began to be widely grown some two decades earlier, and in the 1950s Georgia led the nation in the production of broilers. Naval stores continued to be prominent, but old King Cotton declined to fewer than 500,000 bales annually in the 1950s, until by the 1970s each succeeding year showed a marked decrease in acreage planted. In 1975 only 210,000 of Georgia's acres were devoted to cotton, roughly half the size of the 1974 planting.

Industry expanded significantly after the 1930s. Textiles remained important, with the state holding fourth place nationally, but new plants and manufacturing interests challenged the old. Attracted to the urban center of Atlanta—with its key location, transportation facilities, favorable tax structure, and source of relatively inexpensive labor—automobile assembly plants, chemical firms, trucking lines, and other businesses made Georgia's capital their regional headquarters. The state's permissive attitude toward industry meant that pollution of the rivers and air for the first time came to be a problem.

Aiding and abetting the industrial-commercial emphases of the post–World War II years was the state's unquestioned position as a regional leader in transportation and communication. The railroads, which made Atlanta, helped move the city past other national urban centers in the 1940s and 1950s. When airline passenger and airfreight services developed fully, Atlanta led in these aspects of transportation (AIR TRANSPORT). Construction of the interstate highway system triggered land speculation and real estate booms in Atlanta's metropolitan area. By the 1970s the four main interstate roads into the city, as well as the perimeter highway around it, were paralleled by light and heavy industry interspersed by apartment developments. The city remained a railway freight hub although track mileage in the state, due to various mergers, is less than it was 50 years ago. As for shipping, the state port and docks in Savannah have been successful and have helped boost the commercial life of Georgia's oldest city. State wharves have revived Brunswick somewhat as a port, but similar terminals elsewhere have fared less well. Augusta, Macon, and Columbus have grown enormously, as have the smaller cities of Albany, Rome, Athens, Valdosta, and others.

In the field of religion, Baptists and Methodists still dominate Georgia's religious spectrum, there being approximately twice as many of the former as of the latter. Presbyterians lagged far behind, but were well organized and influential. By mid-century Roman Catholics ranked fourth in number, being concentrated mainly in the urban centers of Atlanta, Savannah, and Augusta. Lutherans, many of them descendants of the early Salzburgers, are present in some strength, and there are significant Jewish elements in the state's cities.

Georgia writers have lent distinction to the state in the twentieth century. Byron Herbert Reece used local mountain themes in his poetry and prose, and LILLIAN SMITH shocked the state with *Strange Fruit*. In south Georgia, Caroline Miller's *Lamb in His Bosom* won the 1934 Pulitzer Prize. ERSKINE CALDWELL in the 1930s wrote *Tobacco Road* and *God's Little Acre*. Combining social purpose, humor, and realism, Caldwell chronicled rural and textile mill Georgia and America. Conrad Aiken, from Savannah, was one of the best poets America produced in the twentieth century. With an Atlanta newspaper background similar to Harris' and Caldwell's, Margaret Mitchell wrote her best-seller GONE WITH THE WIND. RALPH MCGILL of the *Constitution*, Pulitzer Prize winner, was an effective spokesman for southern liberals. In the study of history, ULRICH B. PHILLIPS, whose field was the South and slavery, was a Georgia native, and Gainesville's FLETCHER M. GREEN, of the University of North Carolina, trained more southern historians than any other man. Conversely the University of Georgia's distinguished and prolific historian, E. MERTON COULTER, was born in North Carolina. CARSON MCCULLERS, from Columbus, wrote *The Heart Is a Lonely Hunter* and *Member of the Wedding*, and Calder Willingham was the author of *End as a Man*. Atlantan James Dickey's poetry has been well received as has his novel *Deliverance*, but no author in Georgia, and perhaps none in the nation, has recently equaled the talent of Milledgeville's FLANNERY O'CONNOR.

Atlanta became the cultural as well as the economic and sports center of the state. The Atlanta Symphony Orchestra rose to national eminence under Robert Shaw. The High Museum of Art is the largest in the state, but the University of Georgia Museum of Art is also distinguished. MUSEUMS in Savannah, Augusta, and Columbus possess important holdings. The University System of Georgia, which has roughly sextupled in size since the 1950s, has seen its budgetary allocations rise in proportion.

By and large the higher standards of living enjoyed by most Georgians are owing to the commitment by the state to education at all levels. Even so, Georgia still ranks forty-third in the nation in expenditures per pupil in its public schools.

When it's realized that funds for education make up about one-half the total budget, this rating seems to indicate that Georgia needs to overhaul its tax structure to uncover newer sources of revenue.

World War II changed Georgia drastically. Society was more fluid, and certain industries, such as aircraft construction, became important in the state's economy for the first time. Thousands of people, many of them young blacks, left the state, a migration pattern that began in the 1920s and continued into the 1970s (NEGRO MIGRATION). The number of blacks in relation to the state's total population was about 33 percent in 1940 and dipped to approximately 25 percent in 1970. In some of Georgia's cities, however, the black population has found itself in the majority. Even in the midst of Mayor Ivan Allen's Forward Atlanta campaign in the 1960s, whites left the city for the suburbs while blacks poured in from the countryside. Faced by a lack of job opportunities, by discrimination, by exposure to drugs, and by deplorable living conditions, many blacks experienced disillusionment and anger and turned to violence in the late 1960s. The decline of Atlanta's inner city has continued since that time. Reflecting black voting power in Atlanta in the 1970s, Andrew Young represented the Fifth Congressional District in Washington and Maynard Jackson was elected the first black mayor of the city in 1974.

In one fashion or another, though, race was injected into almost every political contest from 1940 to the 1970s. Harry Truman's executive order to desegregate the armed forces had a minimum effect on most Georgians, but the passing of the white primary seemed serious indeed. There were clear warnings before 1954 that PLESSY V. FERGUSON would be overturned, so the actual shock of the BROWN V. BOARD OF EDUCATION decision was not overwhelming. Many Georgians construed "all deliberate speed" to mean "never," and Marvin Griffin, elected governor in 1954, pledged eternal loyalty to the county unit system and segregation, promises repeated by his successor Ernest Vandiver. Vandiver wrestled with the problems of keeping Georgia's colleges and schools open even though integrated and did not buckle under extremist pressure. Integration was accomplished, and the school systems survived. Desegregation of Atlanta's public schools began in 1961 and was carried out in an orderly fashion, a pattern followed by Athens, Brunswick, and other cities.

To lead the fight against local segregation, MARTIN LUTHER KING, JR., returned to Georgia and blanketed the state with demonstrations. Although Vandiver and the assembly assumed hardline stances, municipal officials usually reached reasonable accords with integration leaders (CIVIL RIGHTS MOVEMENT). By 1976 legal de jure segregation had disappeared in Georgia, but busing to achieve racial balance in the state's schools appeared to have had the opposite effect from that desired. Combined with the rising crime and violence rates in the public schools, busing accelerated the white flight to the suburbs and to private schools. In the rural counties, where school systems had been consolidated, many white students were placed in private academies. The effect has been to resegregate the public schools. In Atlanta the situation developed in roughly the same way, with blacks composing about 90 percent of the registered students in the 1975–1976 academic year.

That single-party politics helped hold Georgia in the grip of the past can scarcely be doubted by those who study the state's history since the Civil War. There was no chance the general assembly, which each year became less responsive to the majority will, would willingly alter the county unit rule, which gave the least populous counties control of the legislature and the primary. But in the spring of 1962 the county unit system was invalidated by the courts (BAKER V. CARR), and the legislature was ordered to reapportion itself on a mere representative basis. The effect of the decision was felt immediately, when Carl Sanders swept Georgia's urban areas and defeated Marvin Griffin in a popular vote primary. In Atlanta, Charles Longstreet Weltner, a liberal young lawyer who later voted in favor of the Civil Rights Act of 1964, turned out the incumbent congressman, who would have won if the county unit system had still been operative. Encouraged by the drift of opinion, by the disorganized opposition, and by the prosperous suburbs, the Georgia Republican party roused itself. Instead of presenting themselves as the party of Georgia moderation, the Republicans decided to "out right-wing" the Democrats. At first the strategy seemed successful, and in 1964 Georgia, which had never gone Republican in a presidential year, cast its electoral votes for Barry Goldwater. The Democrats were in their usual disarray, and in the gubernatorial primary the favorite, Ellis Arnall, was forced into a runoff by Lester Maddox; Maddox defeated Arnall handily. The contested general election that followed was exceedingly close. Maddox, with his folksy style, captured the imagination of the nonurban voter, but Republican Howard ("Bo") Callaway did well in the cities. Thousands of Georgians rejected both men and wrote in Arnall's name on election day.

The error of the Republicans in ignoring the disillusioned moderate voters proved fatal: neither Callaway nor Maddox received a majority of the votes cast, so the legislature was left to decide. And there Maddox was chosen.

While in office Maddox provided a minimum of executive leadership. He lacked political *savoir* and did not relish the details of office. He did, however, appoint blacks to state positions and by so doing helped soften some of his own strident race-baiting.

His successor was JAMES E. CARTER, who ran a strong third in 1966 and put together an unbeatable coalition of urban and rural voters to beat Carl Sanders in the 1970 primary. To some he seemed the heir to Maddox and a follower of GEORGE WALLACE, who had carried Georgia in the presidential election of 1968, but Carter soon gave notice that he was his own man. As governor he presided over a tough state reorganization plan, developed cordial relations with Georgia's black leaders, attacked racial discrimination with energy and effectiveness, created the Heritage Trust program to purchase properties and sites essential for an understanding of Georgia's past, rammed through a campaign financial disclosure act, and encouraged state environmentalists by making difficult decisions on issues weaker men might have avoided. In addition, Carter commissioned the writing of a new history of the state. Carter's meteoric rise to national prominence was capped by his unexpected seizure of the Democratic nomination and his subsequent election to the presidency of the United States. It was a victory in which the entire state took pride. His triumph on the national level seemed to symbolize the final success of the principles of the New South.

George Busbee, who followed Carter, had the misfortune to be governor during a time of recession and declining state revenues. But in his primary runoff victory over Maddox in 1974, he showed agility and restraint. His landslide majorities in the cities were no surprise, but his breaking even with Maddox in rural Georgia may have indicated the ultimate decline of the brand of provincial politics once so dominant in the state.

In some ways the physical face of Georgia has changed little since the days of the Indian and the Spanish mission. Lumber and pulpwood companies own about one-half of the state, and approximately 70 percent of Georgia is covered by trees in the 1970s; the deer, the bear, the alligator, and other wild creatures have returned. However, resemblance to the past ends with the physical appearance. A population of 5 million in 1976 is concentrated in about ten metropolitan areas. The number of farms decreases yearly just as the average farm size increases; agriculture represents only 20 percent of the gross value produced by Georgia industry in a society that becomes more and more urban. Yet in some ways Georgia is still basically a rural state—almost pastoral, in fact. In this respect it is extraordinarily fortunate; because of its space, ample rains, and generous rivers the state has escaped having its environment ruined. For the future, however, the guidance of an enlightened electorate and a responsive government would have to guard against the philosophy of growth for its own sake. As Georgia's open spaces and unspoiled rivers, beaches, islands, and mountains attract thousands of new visitors, the question thoughtful citizens are inclined to ask themselves is whether the state can stand so much unplanned prosperity and at the same time retain its appeal and its individuality.

Manuscript sources. Major depositories for Georgia history are University of Georgia and Emory University libraries; Georgia Department of Archives and History; Southern Labor Archives at Georgia State University; Georgia Historical Society; Russell Library at University of Georgia; and Atlanta Historical Society. Out-of-state depositories include South Carolina Department of Archives and History; South Carolina Historical Society; University of North Carolina; Duke; Library of Congress; and National Archives. Various depositories in London and Seville also contain much pertinent material. Additions to major MS depositories in Georgia can be found in "Accessions Registry" printed each spring since 1974 in *Georgia Historical Quarterly*.

General works. Best early studies are W. B. Stevens' *History of Georgia* (2 vols.; 1847–59) and C. C. Jones, Jr.'s *History of Georgia* (2 vols.; 1883). More recently, E. M. Coulter's *Short History of Georgia* (1960) and J. C. Bonner's *Georgia Story* (1958) have held the field. See K. Coleman (ed.), *History of Georgia* (1977), written by six faculty members from University of Georgia. See also A. Johnson, *Georgia as Colony and State* (1938); W. Cooper, *Story of Georgia* (4 vols.; 1938); and A. Hewatt, *Rise and Progress of South Carolina and Georgia* (1779). Much valuable primary source material is found in *Colonial Records of Georgia* (1904–); *Revolutionary Records of Georgia* (1908); and *Confederate Records of Georgia* (1909–10). Valuable interpretive works are A. B. Saye, *New Viewpoints in Georgia History* (1943); and M. Heath, *Constructive Liberalism* (1954). Bibliographical aids include J. Simpson, *Georgia History: Bibliography* (1976); and R. Rowland, *Bibliography of Writings on Georgia History* (1966). K. Coleman's *Georgia History in Outline* (1960) is a useful short guide, as is J. Cook's *Governors of Georgia* (1977).

Pre-Columbian and Spanish periods. Among many studies of Indians, a few only can be cited. J. Adair's *History of American Indians* (1755) is valuable, as are C. Jones's *Antiquities of Southern Indians* (1873) and J. Swanton's *Early History of Creek Indians* (1922). More recently, see J. Corry, *Indian Affairs in Georgia* (1936); and C. Hudson, *Southeastern Indians* (1976). For Spanish period, J. T. Lanning, *Spanish Missions of Georgia* (1935); and H. Bolton and M. Ross, *Arredondo's Historical Proof of Spain's Title to Georgia* (1925), are indispensable. See also Coulter (ed.), *Georgia's Disputed Ruins* (1937); and J. TePaske, *Governorship of Spanish Florida* (1964).

English period. Developing tensions in Georgia are best outlined in V. Crane, *Southern Frontier* (1928). Much has been written about the Georgia movement, among the best being articles by Coulter, Saye, and Crane in *Georgia Historical Quarterly*. T. Reese, *Colonial Georgia* (1963), is effective; and J. McCain's *Georgia as Proprietary Province* (1917) is a good administrative account of trustee years. Best full biography of Oglethorpe is A. Ettinger (1936); P. Spalding, *Oglethorpe in America* (1977), deals most closely with his Georgia career. Crisis with Spain is seen in J. Lanning, *Diplomatic History of Georgia* (1936); and L. Ivers, *British Drums on Southern Frontier* (1974). H. Davis, *Fledgling Province* (1976), covers social and cultural history in colonial period. A good brief overview of royal period is W. Abbot, *Royal Governors of Georgia* (1959). K. Coleman's *Colonial Georgia* (1976) is standard general work dealing with entire period through Revolution. Same author's *American Revolution in Georgia* (1958) is essential and more detailed. C. F. Jenkins' *Button Gwinnett* (1926) is best biography of any of Georgia's signers, but it is none too good. Religion is handled by R. Strickland, *Religion and State of Georgia* (1939). P. Strobel's *Salzburgers of Georgia* (1855) and A. Fries's *Moravians in Georgia* (1905) are old but useful. Also refer to H. Malone, *Episcopal Church in Georgia* (1960); and A. Pierce, *History of Georgia Methodism* (1956). S. Henry, *George Whitefield* (1957); J. Wade, *John Wesley* (1930); and M. Brailsford, *Tale of Two Brothers* (1954), are also helpful.

Early national period. Far less work has been done on this period than on British and Revolutionary periods. Many of the political and economic issues relate to the land. Refer to S. McLendon, *History of the Public Domain of Georgia* (1924); and P. Magrath, *Yazoo* (1966). Saye's *Constitutional History of Georgia* (1948) is well done; and on individuals W. Foster's *James Jackson* (1960) is helpful. See also H. White, *Abraham Baldwin* (1926). L. Hays's biography of Elijah Clarke (1946) needs to be supplemented. E. M. Coulter's *Old Petersburg and Broad River Valley of Georgia* (1965) is a fine study in local history. On frontier problems in period, see R. Murdock, *Georgia-Florida Frontier* (1951), as well as L. Wright, *William A. Bowles* (1967); and J. Caughey, *McGillivray of the Creeks* (1938). D. Corkran, *Creek Frontier, 1540–1783* (1967), is good for background. M. Pound's *Benjamin Hawkins* (1951) is a superior study.

Antebellum period. Georgia's agricultural history is ably treated in J. C. Bonner, *History of Georgia Agriculture* (1964); and W. Range, *Century of Georgia Agriculture* (1954). For antebellum emphases, see particularly U. B. Phillips, *History of Transportation in Eastern Cotton Belt to 1860* (1908); and R. Flanders, *Plantation Slavery in Georgia* (1933). Phillips' *Life and Labor in Old South* (1929) and *American Negro Slavery* (1918) have much material immediately relevant to Georgia, the author's home state.

For settlement of up-country, G. Gilmer, *Sketches of Some of First Settlers of Upper Georgia* (1855), is indispensable. Coulter's *Auraria* (1956) chronicles gold rush

in Cherokee country. Indians are handled in W. Lumpkin, *Removal of Cherokee Indians from Georgia* (1907). For recent assessments, see H. Malone, *Cherokees of Old South* (1956); G. Foreman, *Indian Removal* (1953); and G. Woodward, *Cherokees* (1963). G. Foreman (1959) and R. Radford (1969) have done biographies of Sequoya.

In Georgia politics, H. Montgomery, *Cracker Parties* (1950), is excellent, as is U. B. Phillips, *Georgia and State Rights* (1902); and R. Shryock, *Georgia and Union in 1850* (1926). Biographies are of uneven quality. Some of better ones include C. Mooney, *William H. Crawford* (1974); P. Stovall, *Robert Toombs* (1892); W. Thompson, *Toombs* (1966); J. Simpson, *Howell Cobb* (1973); P. Flippin, *H. V. Johnson* (1931); A. Duckett, *John Forsyth* (1962); R. von Abele, *Stephens* (1946); and J. Parks, *Joseph E. Brown* (1977). In agriculture, see Coulter, *Thomas Spalding* (1940); and in education see same author's *William Montague Browne* (1967) and *College Life in Old South* (1951). D. Orr, *History of Education in Georgia* (1950), is handy. J. Wade's *A. B. Longstreet* (1924) and F. Taylor's *Crawford Long* (1928) chronicle lives of two of Georgia's best-known nonpolitical men. Georgia's extraordinary Jones family has been adequately memorialized by Coulter in *Wormsloe* (1955). More recently, collections of Jones letters have appeared in print as M. Myers (ed.), *Children of Pride* (1972) and *Georgian at Princeton* (1976). J. Simpson (ed.), *Jones Family Papers* (1976), deals primarily with an earlier period. There are several successful local studies of antebellum communities, notably E. Hynds, *Antebellum Athens and Clarke County* (1974), but there is no study devoted solely to secession movement in Georgia. J. Linley, *Architecture of Middle Georgia, Oconee Area* (1972), and F. Nichols, *Early Architecture of Georgia* (1976), contribute much to understanding state. L. Griffith and J. Talmadge, *Georgia Journalism* (1951), is an adequate general history, as is R. Wilson, *Drugs and Pharmacy in Life of Georgia* (1959).

Georgia, 1860–1900. Military affairs in and around Georgia are covered in a number of works, including S. Carter, *Siege of Atlanta* (1973); A. Hoehling, *Last Train from Atlanta* (1958); M. Lane (ed.), *War Is Hell* (1974); G. Tucker, *Chickamauga* (1961); B. Mathews, *McCook-Stoneman Raid* (1976); J. Jones, *Yankee Blitzkrieg* (1976); and A. Murray, *South Georgia Rebels* (1976). There are several good studies of cities and counties during the period. See W. Rogers, *Thomas County During Civil War* (1964); D. Standard, *Columbus, Ga., in Confederacy* (1954); K. Coleman, *Confederate Athens* (1967); A. Lawrence, *Present from Mr. Lincoln: Savannah from Secession to Sherman* (1961); and B. Fleming, *Autobiography of a City in Arms: Augusta, 1861–1865* (1976). *Savannah Revisited: Pictorial History* (1969) covers 1733–1900. F. Garrett, *Atlanta and Environs* (2 vols.; 1969), is also useful. On state level, see C. Bryan, *Confederate Georgia* (1953); L. Hill, *Joseph E. Brown and Confederacy* (1939); and H. Montgomery, *Howell Cobb's Confederate Career* (1959). O. Futch's *History of Andersonville Prison* (1968) is probably best work on subject.

As for Reconstruction, M. Thompson's *Reconstruction in Georgia* (1915) still has merits, but should be supplemented by A. Conway's *Reconstruction of Georgia* (1966). D. Roberts, *Joseph E. Brown and Politics of Reconstruction* (1973), is valuable. Much of the best work dealing with this period remains either unpublished or unworked, but see O. Shadgett, *Republican Party in Georgia from Reconstruction Through 1900* (1964); E. Nathans, *Losing Peace: Georgia Republicans and Reconstruction, 1865–1871* (1968); and E. Coulter, *Negro Legislators in Georgia During Reconstruction* (1968). Helpful biographies, in addition to those previously mentioned, include A. Tankersley, *John B. Gordon* (1955); and H. Pearce, *Benjamin H. Hill* (1928). In education, see R. Mathis, *College Life in Reconstruction South* (1974); and W. Range, *Rise and Progress of Negro Colleges in Georgia, 1865–1949* (1959). D. Orr, *History of Education in Georgia* (1950), is also useful. E. Coulter's *James M. Smith* (1961) contains a useful account of convict lease system. R. Nixon, *Henry Woodfin Grady* (1943), helps render New South period understandable, as does J. Talmadge, *Rebecca Felton* (1960). See also P. Cousins, *Joel Chandler Harris* (1968). For politics, economics, and rise of agricultural discontent, refer to P. Brooks, *Agrarian Revolution in Georgia* (1914); and E. Banks, *Economics of Land Tenure in Georgia* (1905). C. V. Woodward's *Tom Watson* (1938) is full of valuable insights. A. Arnett's *Populist Movement in Georgia* (1922) is old but sound.

Georgia, 1900–1945. In addition to Woodward's *Watson*, refer to D. Grantham, *Hoke Smith* (1958). For a sound work dealing with a more recent figure, see W. Anderson, *Wild Man from Sugar Creek: Eugene Talmadge* (1975). For noted Georgia miniaturist, refer to S. Forbes, *Lucy M. Stanton* (1975). Corra Harris' biography has been done by J. Talmadge (1968), and Juliette Low's was written by G. Shultz (1958). For a distinguished woman educator's life, refer to H. Kane's work on Martha Berry, *Miracle in Mountains* (1956). See too P. Brooks, *University of Georgia* (1956); C. Bacote, *Story of Atlanta University* (1969); T. English, *Emory University* (1966); and M. Brittain, *Story of Georgia Tech* (1948). L. Dinnerstein's *Leo Frank Case* (1968) is revealing. For Georgia's county unit system, refer to L. Holland, *Direct Primary in Georgia* (1949); and J. Bernd, *Grass Roots Politics in Georgia* (1960). New Deal in Georgia has received recent attention in M. Holmes, *New Deal in Georgia: Administrative History* (1975), but see also A. Raper's *Preface to Peasantry* (1936) and *Tenants of the Almighty* (1943). For a vivid account of sharecropping, see J. Maguire, *On Shares* (1976). An entertaining and informative history of Coca-Cola has been done by E. J. Kahn, Jr., *Big Drink* (1960). L. Ball's *Georgia in World War II* (1946) is not adequate, but is the only book done on that topic. *Yesterday's Atlanta* (1974), by F. Garrett, is particularly interesting for the photographic record it chronicles. So too is R. Rowland and H. Callahan, *Yesterday's Augusta* (1976).

Recent Georgia. *Georgia Statistical Abstract*, published biennially, offers a wealth of information on a number of topics. J. Belcher, *Dynamics of Georgia's Population* (1964); C. Floyd, *Georgia Regional Economies* (1974); and J. R. McGregor, *Delimiting Industrial Specialization in Georgia* (1967), give a fairly clear idea of trends at work in present-day Georgia. J. Walker, *Sit-ins in Atlanta* (1964); and D. Lewis, *King* (1970), present a good picture of desegregation struggle. C. Trillin reports his impressions in *Educator in Georgia* (1964), dealing with integration of University of Georgia in Athens. Recent works in women's history include B. Reitt, *Georgia Women: A Celebration* (1976); and M. Barber, *Historic Georgia Mothers, 1776–1976* (1976). Of Georgia's fine recent literary figures, Carson McCullers enjoys by far the best biography, *Lonely Hunter* (1975), by V. Carr.

Georgia politics in recent years has had several good studies, including N. Bartley, *From Thurmond to Wallace: Georgia, 1948–1968* (1970). One governor has been treated fully and with insight: *Riddle of Lester Maddox* (1968), by B. Galphin. There are many works dealing with Jimmy Carter phenomenon, but it is too early to make any kind of objective assessment. *Why Not the Best?* (1975) is a good beginning. With current interest in Georgia mounting, attention is being focused on fields largely ignored in the past. For example, see K. Krakow, *Georgia Place Names* (1975); H. Brinkley, *How Georgia Got Her Names* (1973); and such items as R. Killion and C. Waller, *Treasury of Georgia Folklore* (1972), as well as the various *Foxfire* books.

Georgia Historical Quarterly regularly devotes its pages to articles on Georgia history. *Georgia Review* in

GEORGIA POPULATION, 1790–1970

| Year | Total | White | Nonwhite | | % Growth | Rank | |
			Slave	Free		U.S.	South
1790	82,548	52,886	29,264	398		13	5
1800	162,686	102,261	59,406	1,019	97.1	12	6
1810	252,433	145,414	105,218	1,801	55.2	11	7
1820	340,989	189,570	149,656	1,763	35.1	11	7
1830	516,823	296,806	217,531	2,486	51.6	10	6
1840	691,392	407,695	280,944	2,753	33.8	10	5
1850	906,185	521,572	381,682	2,931	31.1	9	4
1860	1,057,286	591,550	462,198	3,538	16.7	11	5
1870	1,184,109	638,926	545,183		12.0	12	5
1880	1,542,180	816,906	725,274		30.2	13	5
1890	1,837,353	978,357	858,996		19.1	12	4
1900	2,216,331	1,181,294	1,035,037		20.6	11	3
1910	2,609,121	1,431,802	1,177,319		17.7	10	3
1920	2,895,832	1,689,114	1,206,718		11.0	12	3
1930	2,908,506	1,837,021	1,071,485		0.4	14	4
1940	3,123,723	2,038,278	1,085,445		7.4	14	4
1950	3,444,578	2,380,577	1,064,001		10.3	13	4
1960	3,943,116	2,817,223	1,125,893		14.5	16	6
1970	4,589,575	3,391,242	1,198,333		16.4	15	6

GEORGIA GOVERNORS

Governor	Party	Term
COLONIAL PERIOD		
James E. Oglethorpe (resident trustee)		1733–1743
William Stephens (president)		1743–1751
Henry Parker (president)		1751–1752
Patrick Graham (president)		1752–1754
John Reynolds		1754–1757
Henry Ellis		1757–1760
James Wright		1760–1776
REVOLUTIONARY PERIOD		
William Ewen (president of council of safety)		1775
George Walton (president of council of safety)		1775–1776
William Ewen (president of council of safety)		1776
Archibald Bulloch (president)		1776–1777
Button Gwinnett (president)		1777
John A. Treutlen		1777–1778
John Houstoun		1778–1779
William Glascock (president of executive council)		1779
Seth J. Cuthbert (president of supreme executive council)		1779
John Wereat (president of supreme executive council)		1779–1780
George Walton (elected by irregular assembly)		1779–1780
James M. Prevost (British military governor)		1779
James Wright (British occupation governor)		1779–1782
Stephen Heard (president of executive council)		1780
Myrick Davies (president of executive council)		1780–1781
Nathan Brownson		1781–1782
John Martin		1782–1783
AMERICAN PERIOD		
Lyman Hall		1783–1784
John Houstoun		1784–1785
Samuel Elbert		1785–1786
Edward Telfair		1786–1787
George Mathews		1787–1788
George Handley		1788–1789
George Walton		1789–1790
Edward Telfair		1790–1793
George Mathews		1793–1796
Jared Irwin		1796–1798
James Jackson		1798–1801
David Emanuel (president of senate)		1801
Josiah Tattnall, Jr.		1801–1802
John Milledge		1802–1806
Jared Irwin		1806–1809
David B. Mitchell		1809–1813
Peter Early		1813–1815
David B. Mitchell	Dem.-Rep.	1815–1817
William Rabun	Dem.-Rep.	1817–1819
Mathew Talbot (president of senate)	Dem.-Rep.	1819
John Clark	Dem.-Rep.	1819–1823
George M. Troup	Dem.-Rep.	1823–1827
John Forsyth	Dem.-Rep.	1827–1829
George R. Gilmer	Dem.-Rep.	1829–1831
Wilson Lumpkin	Union Dem.	1831–1835
William Schley	Union Dem.	1835–1837
George R. Gilmer		1837–1839

Governor	Party	Term
Charles J. McDonald	Dem.	1839–1843
George W. Crawford	Whig	1843–1847
George W. Towns	Dem.	1847–1851
Howell Cobb	Union Dem.	1851–1853
Herschel V. Johnson	Union Dem.	1853–1857
Joseph E. Brown	Dem.	1857–1865
James Johnson (provisional)		1865
Charles J. Jenkins		1865–1868
General Thomas H. Ruger (provisional military)		1868
Rufus B. Bullock (provisional)	Rep.	1868
Rufus B. Bullock	Rep.	1868–1871
Benjamin Conley (president of senate)	Rep.	1871–1872
James M. Smith	Dem.	1872–1877
Alfred H. Colquitt	Dem.	1877–1882
Alexander H. Stephens	Dem.	1882–1883
James S. Boynton (president of senate)	Dem.	1883
Henry D. McDaniel	Dem.	1883–1886
John B. Gordon	Dem.	1886–1890
William J. Northen	Dem.	1890–1894
William Y. Atkinson	Dem.	1894–1898
Allen D. Candler	Dem.	1898–1902
Joseph M. Terrell	Dem.	1902–1907
Hoke Smith	Dem.	1907–1909
Joseph M. Brown	Dem.	1909–1911
Hoke Smith	Dem.	1911
John M. Slaton (president of senate)	Dem.	1911–1912
Joseph M. Brown	Dem.	1912–1913
John M. Slaton	Dem.	1913–1915
Nathaniel E. Harris	Dem.	1915–1917
Hugh M. Dorsey	Dem.	1917–1921
Thomas W. Hardwick	Dem.	1921–1923
Clifford Walker	Dem.	1923–1927
Lamartine G. Hardman	Dem.	1927–1931
Richard B. Russell, Jr.	Dem.	1931–1933
Eugene Talmadge	Dem.	1933–1937
Eurith D. Rivers	Dem.	1937–1941
Eugene Talmadge	Dem.	1941–1943
Ellis G. Arnall	Dem.	1943–1947
Melvin E. Thompson	Dem.	1947–1948
Herman E. Talmadge	Dem.	1948–1955
Marvin Griffin	Dem.	1955–1959
Ernest Vandiver, Jr.	Dem.	1959–1963
Carl E. Sanders	Dem.	1963–1967
Lester G. Maddox	Dem.	1967–1971
James E. Carter	Dem.	1971–1975
George Busbee	Dem.	1975–1979

the past contained some useful contributions as well. There are perceptive articles about the colonial period in *William and Mary Quarterly, American Historical Review, South Carolina Magazine of History, Florida Historical Quarterly, Agricultural History,* and other journals. Other appropriate items have been published in *Journal of Southern History, Phylon, Journal of Negro History, South Atlantic Quarterly, History of Education Quarterly, North Carolina Historical Review, New South, Southern Voices,* and *Southern School News.*

For information on recent dissertations and theses, see Boney (ed.), *Georgia Historical Quarterly* (Winter, 1975; Summer, 1977). Some excellent Ph.D.'s include M. Ready, "An Economic History of Georgia" (University of Georgia, 1970); R. Martin, "John J. Zubly" (University of

Georgia, 1976); R. McCrary, "John M. Berrien" (University of Georgia, 1971); L. Cleveland, "George Crawford" (University of Georgia, 1974); G. Cates, "Medical History of Georgia" (University of Georgia, 1976); F. Huffman, "Old South, New South: Continuity and Change in a Georgia County" (Yale, 1974); C. Mohr, "Georgia Blacks During Secession and Civil War" (University of Georgia, 1975); F. Mathews, "Politics of Education in Deep South: Georgia and Alabama, 1830–60" (Columbia, 1965); E. Sweat, "Free Negro in Ante-Bellum Georgia" (Indiana, 1957); J. Brumgardt, "A. H. Stephens and Peace Issue" (University of California, Riverside, 1974); J. Ward, "Georgia Under Bourbon Democrats" (University of North Carolina, 1947); C. Wingo, "Race Relations in Georgia, 1872–1908" (University of Georgia, 1969); M. Evans, "History of Organized Labor Movement in Georgia" (Chicago, 1929); O. Adams, "Negro and Agrarian Movement in Georgia, 1874–1908" (Florida State, 1973); A. Jones, "Progressivism in Georgia, 1898–1918" (Emory, 1963); R. Fossett, "Impact of New Deal on Georgia Politics, 1933–41" (University of Florida, 1960); C. Bacote, "Negro in Georgia Politics, 1880–1908" (Chicago, 1955); C. Moseley, "Invisible Empire: History of KKK in 20th Century Georgia, 1915–65" (University of Georgia, 1968); and P. Bolster, "Civil Rights Movement in 20th Century Georgia" (University of Georgia, 1972).

B. PHINIZY SPALDING
University of Georgia

GEORGIA, UNIVERSITY OF (Athens, 30602), was chartered in 1785 and opened in 1801 largely because Yale graduates like Governor Lyman Hall and Abraham Baldwin hoped the molding influence of higher education would preserve the new state from barbaric human nature. Georgia's was the first state university chartered in the nation, and its charter called for a unified scheme of education from the elementary through the university level with supervision from the top. But Georgia's public institutions of higher education were not effectively unified until after 1932, when the one board of regents, as governing body of the entire University System of Georgia, replaced the separate boards of trustees at each state college and university.

After protracted debate from 1799 to 1801, the university was seated in northeast Georgia on the wilderness site that became Athens. Aside from income from the original land grant of 40,000 acres, the state assumed no responsibility for regular appropriations until early in the twentieth century. The antebellum university was little more than a small, classical, liberal arts college named Franklin. Although the law school was founded in 1859, other colleges in the university had to await the twentieth century: pharmacy (1903), agriculture (1906), forestry (1906), education (1908), graduate (1910), business (1912), journalism (1915), home economics (1933), veterinary medicine

(1946), social work (1964), and environmental design (1969).

After 1900 the institution gradually achieved modern university status. From 1960 to 1974, enrollment in professional schools increased more than 300 percent and in graduate programs about 500 percent. In 1973–1974, the budget of the university in Athens ran some $121 million, and enrollment was about 21,000 students. In 1971 the university library contained almost 1.8 million volumes, and its recent expenditures for acquisitions are among the top 25 in the nation. The library's manuscript collections include the Keith Read, Egmont, Telamon Cuyler, Howell Cobb, Charles Colcock Jones, and Margaret Mitchell papers, as well as an unsurpassed collection of Confederate imprints. On national politics in the twentieth century, the Senator Richard B. Russell Library contains over 45 tons of material.

See E. M. Coulter, *College Life in Old South* (1951), excellent to 1870; R. P. Brooks, *University of Georgia, 1785–1955* (1956), flawed but best overview; T. W. Reed, "University of Georgia" (University of Georgia Library), typescript over 4,000 pages; *University of Georgia Fact Book* (1974); G. R. Mathis, "W. B. Hill" (Ph.D. dissertation, University of Georgia, 1967); G. R. Mathis (ed.), *College Life in Reconstruction South* (1974); and *Reed's University of Georgia* (1974).

RAY MATHIS
Troy State University

GEORGIA ARCHIVE, a semiannual scholarly journal established by the Society of Georgia Archivists in 1972, is only the second periodical in the United States devoted largely to the needs of archivists. Its purposes are to promote knowledge and understanding of archival enterprise and to make available information on archival resources for Georgia studies. Every issue carries at least one article describing the holdings of a repository in Georgia, the Georgia holdings of an out-of-state institution, or materials appropriate for the study of a given Georgia topic.

DAVID B. GRACY II
Georgia State University

GEORGIA COLLEGE AT MILLEDGEVILLE (31061) was known until 1967 as the Women's College of Georgia. Founded in 1889 as a state-supported women's college, today it is a coeducational, liberal arts college with an enrollment of about 2,000 students. In addition to the papers of FLANNERY O'CONNOR and the early minutes of the Baptist church, its library houses numerous plantation records, account books, and ledgers.

GEORGIA GAZETTE, the first newspaper published in the state, was founded in Savannah in 1763 by James Johnston (1738–1808), a Scot printer. It was a crude and unpolished publication issued in conjunction with Johnston's work as official printer for the colonial government. After passage of the STAMP ACT in 1764, Johnston suspended publication rather than become embroiled in political controversy. He resumed publication after repeal of the tax was assured, but he closed his shop and his publication again in 1776 after being visited by the local committee on public safety and being asked to submit his publication to censorship. Later that year Johnston followed the royal governor into exile. He returned to Savannah after British forces gained control of the city, reclaimed his position as the public printer, and resumed publication of his weekly, rechristened the *Royal Georgia Gazette* (1779–1782). He again suspended publication one month prior to the return to authority of the American patriots. Despite his ties with the Loyalists and the royal government, he served briefly as the public printer for the state government and, in 1783, resumed publication of the *Gazette of the State of Georgia*. The death of Johnston's son and partner in 1802 and his own ill health forced the publication out of business in 1802.

See L. T. Griffith and J. E. Talmadge, *Georgia Journalism, 1763–1950* (1951); and *Georgia Gazette*, available on microcards (1763–70) from Readex Microprint, N.Y., and Massachusetts Historical Society, Boston.

GEORGIA HISTORICAL SOCIETY (501 Whitaker St., Savannah, 31401). Founded in 1839, with 2,200 members in 1975, it is a branch depository of the Georgia State Department of Archives and History with a library of 30,000 volumes, microfilms, maps, and papers, including letters of Pleasant A. Stovall (publisher) and John M. Berrien (attorney general under President Andrew Jackson), as well as plantation, land lottery, and business records. The society publishes books, pamphlets, a quarterly newsletter, and *Collections*, a series of source material books. The *Georgia Historical Quarterly*, published since 1917, prints book reviews and articles on Georgia, the South, Civil War, and Reconstruction. The society offers an annual award for the best article in the *Quarterly* and an award for the best paper on Georgia history by a Georgia college student.

See A. S. Britt, Jr., *Overture to Future* (1974); and P. Spalding, *Atlanta Journal and Constitution Magazine* (May 6, 1973).

GEORGIA INSTITUTE OF TECHNOLOGY (Atlanta, 30332), one of the premier engineering institutions in the nation, was founded in 1885 and first opened in 1888. The school has grown from its original enrollment of 85 students studying mechanical engineering to university status with over 8,000 students in 46 different programs of study, 1,000 of whom are in graduate school.

See R. B. Wallace, Jr., *Dress Her in White and Gold* (1969); and M. L. Brittain, *Story of Georgia Tech* (1948).

GEORGIANA COLONY (1772–1773), to honor King George and proposed for a location west of Vandalia, was to be 150 to 200 miles wide and to lie along the east bank of the Mississippi south from the Ohio to approximately 33° north latitude. It was believed tobacco, silk, hemp, indigo, flax, cotton, and tea could be profitably produced here. Origin of the Georgiana idea is uncertain, although specific proposals were made about the same time by Phineas Lyman of Connecticut, Indian trader JAMES ADAIR, and British officer CHARLES LEE.

See C. W. Alvord and C. E. Carter, *New Régime* (1916); J. Adair, *American Indians* (1775); New York Historical Society, *Collections: Lee Papers* (1875), IV; and C. W. Alvord, *Mississippi Valley* (1917), II.

ETHEL E. RASMUSSON
Central Connecticut State College

GEORGIA PLATFORM (1850) supported the COMPROMISE OF 1850. Its passage 239 to 19 by a specially elected convention in a cotton state ended effective opposition to the compromise. The text affirmed the value of the Union and of the compromise as a "permanent adjustment" of the sectional problem. It threatened disunion, however, if slavery should ever be abolished in any federal jurisdiction, if slaves could not be taken into Utah or New Mexico, if the slave trade between states were suppressed, or if the Fugitive Slave Act were repealed, modified, or not enforced. Opponents of the platform called it a party move to support the CONSTITUTIONAL UNION PARTY OF GEORGIA (formed by Whigs and Unionist Democrats at night meetings during the convention). Twentieth-century accounts are based on Unionist newspapers and exaggerate the platform's appeal to southern rights Democrats. The platform was reaffirmed as state policy by the general assembly in 1856.

See *Federal Union* (Dec. 10, 17, 24, 1850; Jan. 7, 1851), for election returns, stenographic reports, and minority delegates' analysis; *Journal of Georgia Convention* (1850), in Georgia Archives, State Library of Georgia, and University of Pennsylvania Library; P. Murray, *Whig Party in Georgia* (1948); and H. Montgomery, *Cracker Parties* (1950).

FRANK M. ALBRECHT
Atlanta, Ga.

GEORGIA REVIEW (University of Georgia, Athens, 30602), a quarterly journal with a circulation of about 1,800 and founded in 1947, publishes fiction and poetry as well as book reviews in the area of the arts, history, and literature. Payment of $.50 per line for poetry and $4.00 per printed page for prose are made upon publication. It receives about 5,000 or 6,000 manuscripts annually with only about 10 percent of them from Georgia. Its circulation is also less than one-third Georgian; its subscribers are drawn from all over the United States and from 29 foreign countries.

GEORGIA TRIUMVIRATE. JOSEPH E. BROWN, General ALFRED H. COLQUITT, and General JOHN B. GORDON dominated Georgia's political life in the two decades after the Democrats "redeemed" the state in 1872. Gordon and Brown alternated in one of Georgia's U.S. Senate seats between 1873 and 1897; Colquitt held the other from 1883 to 1894; and either Colquitt or Gordon was governor for all but four years between 1876 and 1890. Not politicians only, but also officers of several railroads and mining and other corporations, they were first termed a "triumvirate" in 1880 after an alleged corrupt exchange of business and political favors. The phrase, not necessarily invidious, had earlier been applied to BENJAMIN H. HILL, ALEXANDER H. STEPHENS, and ROBERT TOOMBS.

See C. V. Woodward, *Tom Watson* (1939); I. W. Avery, *History of Georgia* (1881); L. B. Hill, *Joseph E. Brown* (1939); R. B. Nixon, *Henry W. Grady* (1943); and W. Anderson, *Georgia Historical Quarterly* (Dec., 1968).

PETER WALLENSTEIN
University of Toronto

GEORGIA V. STANTON (6 Wallace 58 [1868]) was the second attempt by a southern state to halt the execution of the RECONSTRUCTION ACTS by enjoining a federal official from implementing them. In April, 1867, while the analogous case MISSISSIPPI V. JOHNSON was pending, representatives of the state of Georgia filed a bill in equity to enjoin Secretary of War Edwin M. Stanton and Generals U. S. Grant and John Pope from carrying out the Reconstruction Acts. In order to make a stronger case, the petitioners also sought protection for the state's real and personal property amounting to more than $5 million. Counsel for Georgia maintained that the purpose of the bill was to safeguard the existence of the state, which, he emphasized, was about to be "Africanized."

Although the U.S. Supreme Court dismissed the case on May 13, it did not publish its reasons until February, 1868. Justice Samuel Nelson, speaking for the majority, agreed with the attorney general that "these matters call for the judgment of the court upon political questions." Pointing out that the references to property had only been added "by way of showing one of the grievances resulting from the threatened destruction of the State," he held that the Court lacked jurisdiction. The chief justice concurred. This case and its companion suit *Mississippi* v. *Johnson* have often been cited as examples of the Supreme Court's alleged retreat during Reconstruction. This opinion, however, is no longer generally held. The decision was legally sound and not rendered to appease the Radicals. Moreover, the justices seem to have been divided on the property question in an amended version of the *Mississippi* case and may have been unwilling to become involved.

See C. Warren, *History of Supreme Court* (1922); S. Kutler, *Judicial Power and Reconstruction Politics* (1968); and C. Fairman, *Reconstruction and Reunion* (1971).

HANS L. TREFOUSSE
Brooklyn College, City University of New York

GERRYMANDERING represents the manipulation of electoral district boundaries in order to juggle populations for partisan advantage. This art of political cartography has not been confined to one group or region, despite its New England origin. Both political parties in most parts of the country have practiced it. Until the 1950s this was usually the Republicans in the North and the Democrats in the South. The South, however, has been a particularly fertile setting for the gerrymander. For example, throughout the South the COUNTY UNIT became practically sacrosanct as a basic building block for the construction of electoral districts. Since the county was first introduced in the southern colonies, it proliferated in number and maintained a special importance. County spokesmen vigorously insisted on maintaining individual county representation in at least one house of the state legislature, and small rural counties subsequently wielded a disproportionate share of political power. District shapes, particularly on the congressional level, were severely contorted to correspond to partisan needs and to county boundaries that were sometimes of odd configuration. An especially favored tactic was the use of the silent gerrymander, whereby state legislatures neglected to redistrict through one decennial census after another. The result was severe district population inequality, which promulgated "barnyard government": rural legislative domination by representatives from constituencies with "more pigs than people." The gerrymander therefore became an effective device in political maneuvering and was used to help reinforce a number of political traits prevalent throughout the region's historical evolvement: the protracted rural political domination over more rapidly growing urban centers; frequent frustration of the growth of the Republican party by incumbent Democrats; and the accumulation of unparalleled seniority by elected officials—as so vividly demonstrated in Congress.

When the judiciary ushered in the reapportionment revolution through its one-man, one-vote decisions of the 1960s (BAKER V. CARR), it was perhaps indicative of the South's gerrymandered status that the landmark decisions emanated from two southern states, Tennessee and Georgia. The wave of subsequent decisions, reapportionments, and new district alignments that followed ended finally the era of the silent gerrymander. On the other hand, alternative forms of gerrymandering still very much persist. The court mandate for population equality simply constrains its unlimited freedom of application. Despite frequent congressional committee efforts, there is still no requirement that districts be compact, contiguous, or represent community of interest. And the Supreme Court has refused to rule on the partisan gerrymander, that drawn strictly for political advantage. The gerrymander thus remains an elusive opponent to representative government.

See A. Hacker, *Congressional Districting* (1966); D. M. Orr, Jr., *Congressional Redistricting: North Carolina Experience* (1970); G. E. Baker, *Rural Versus Urban Political Power* (1955); R. W. Dietsch, *Saturday Review* (June 3, 1972); C. Sauer, *American Political Science Review* (1918), landmark article; and G. Schubert, *Reapportionment* (1965).

DOUGLAS M. ORR, JR.
University of North Carolina, Charlotte

GETTYSBURG, BATTLE OF (July 1–3, 1863).

After his victory at CHANCELLORSVILLE on May 1–4, ROBERT E. LEE invaded Pennsylvania. To carry the war to the North would provide new sources of supplies and enable Lee to maintain the initiative. It might also relieve the pressures against Confederate armies in the West, and a decisive victory could even lead to a compromise peace. R. S. EWELL's advance units had reached the Susquehanna when he was ordered on June 30 to rejoin the rest of Lee's army, then concentrating in the vicinity of Cashtown or Gettysburg. G. G. Meade's Union Army of the Potomac had recently crossed the Potomac and was closing in rapidly from the south. Lee's army numbered 76,000; Meade's army totaled 115,000.

The battle began when Confederate General HENRY HETH's division of A. P. HILL's III Corps, advancing eastward along the Chambersburg Pike, encountered JOHN BUFORD's dismounted Union cavalry on McPherson's Ridge. Union General J. F. Reynolds' I Corps next arrived to join the battle, and at 2:30 P.M. Hill's second division entered the fight in support of Heth. North of the town two of Ewell's divisions tangled with the Union XI Corps. The Confederates were successful on both fronts and drove the two Union corps through the town onto the high ground known as Cemetery Hill.

Lee's plans for July 2 were compromised by the absence of General JEB STUART's cavalry, not yet returned from his raid beyond the Union line of advance. Not knowing exactly where the Union left flank was located or how many troops he faced, Lee ordered JAMES LONGSTREET's I Corps to attack and envelop the Union left. After a controversial delay of several hours, Longstreet struck, driving Daniel Sickles' III Corps from its exposed position in the Peach Orchard but failing to capture the key to the Union position, Little Round Top. That evening Ewell attacked the northern end of the Union line but could not hold Culp's Hill.

Ewell renewed his assault the next morning, again without success. At 3:00 P.M., July 3, after an unprecedented artillery bombardment, 10,500 Confederates from the divisions of GEORGE E. PICKETT and J. J. PETTIGREW assaulted Meade's center. Braving a withering blast of canister and rifle fire as they marched across the fields, the Confederates actually penetrated the Union center but, lacking artillery support and reinforcements, they could not maintain their position. At a cost of perhaps 7,500 casualties, Pickett's charge failed. Meanwhile Jeb Stuart's cavalry, which had arrived at noon on the previous day, likewise failed to drive off the Union cavalry that protected Meade's rear. Both armies remained on the ground for another day, and then Lee fell back to Virginia. Tactically the battle was a draw; strategically it ended Lee's offensive operations in the North. Psychologically, especially in retrospect and when coupled with the fall of VICKSBURG, it marked a turning point in the war. Casualties for the Union were 23,049; Confederate casualties numbered roughly 28,000.

See E. Coddington, *Gettysburg Campaign* (1968); W. Hassler, *Crisis at Crossroads* (1970); J. S. Montgomery, *Shaping of Battle* (1959); G. R. Stewart, *Pickett's Charge* (1959); and G. Tucker, *Lee and Longstreet at Gettysburg* (1968).

JAY LUVAAS
Allegheny College

GIBBONS, JAMES CARDINAL (1834–1921), ninth archbishop of Baltimore (1877–1921), was the most influential churchman in the history of U.S. Roman Catholicism. Born in Baltimore of Irish immigrant parents, he was ordained a priest in 1861 and a bishop in 1868. In the latter capacity he served the few Catholics in North Carolina and Virginia until 1866, when he succeeded to the premier archbishopric of Baltimore, where he would remain until his death. On June 30, 1886, he was elevated to a cardinalate by Pope Leo XIII. Gibbons is remembered especially for the role he played in accommodating public church policy to the exigencies of the American situation. He defended the formation of the Knights of Labor, conciliated differences between Irish and German elements in the U.S. church, and persuaded large numbers of Protestants of the U.S. Roman Catholic commitment to democratic institutions.

See J. T. Ellis, *Cardinal Gibbons* (1952); J. Gibbons, *Faith of Our Fathers* (1876) and *Retrospect* (1916); and H. J. Browne, *Knights of Labor* (1949).

MICHAEL V. GANNON
University of Florida

GIBBS, JONATHAN (1826–1874), was born in Philadelphia, the son of a free Methodist minister who apprenticed him to a carpenter. Gibbs joined the Presbyterian church before reaching the age of majority, and the church assisted him in attending Dartmouth College. After graduation he spent two years at Princeton Theological Seminary. Turned down by the church for an African mission, he was sent to Troy, N.Y., and then to Philadelphia. When the Civil War ended he became a missionary in North Carolina, finally arriving in Florida in 1867. An educated Negro with a compulsion to public service, he saw a need for leadership among the Florida freedmen. He was elected to the 1868 constitutional convention, where he won praise from white newspaper reporters for his decorum, speaking ability, and persuasive powers. Appointed secretary of state by Governor HARRISON REED in 1868, he became a loyal supporter and trusted adviser of the governor and a respected member of the cabinet. In 1873 he became superintendent of public instruction and did yeoman work in establishing the state's infant public school system. Appearing on the program of the National Education Association at Elmira, N.Y., he won national recognition for both the content and delivery of his speech. His sudden death by apoplexy was regarded as a regrettable loss by black and white Floridians alike.

See M. W. Gibbs, *Shadows and Light* (1902); J. M. Richardson, *Negro in Florida Reconstruction* (1965); and J. H. Shofner, *Nor Is It Over Yet* (1974).

JERRELL H. SHOFNER
Florida Technological University

GILES, WILLIAM BRANCH (1762–1830), a well-born Virginian and Princeton graduate, studied law under GEORGE WYTHE and enjoyed success as a planter, lawyer, and politician. Although governor (1827–1830) and a member of Virginia's constitutional convention of 1829–1830, he served most effectively in legislative chambers. An arch-Republican in the U.S. House in the 1790s, he was later one of President Thomas Jefferson's chief lieutenants there and in the Senate. Intermittently he was in the Virginia general assembly. A vigorous debater, pugnacious critic, and partisan "old" Republican, Giles castigated Jay's Treaty, the national bank, and—with other Invisibles—many of President James Madison's diplomatic and war policies. His notable enemies included Alexander Hamilton, Albert Gallatin, James Monroe, and the Adamses. Giles spearheaded Jefferson's attack on the federal judiciary and was an early war hawk and a states' rights essayist. He was a powerful legislator, though often in a negative sense.

See D. R. Anderson, *William Branch Giles* (1914), scholarly, sympathetic, dated; J. S. Pancake, *Journal of Southern History* (Feb., 1955), on Invisibles; and G. M. Betty, *John P. Branch Historical Papers of Randolph-Macon College* (June, 1911).

DANIEL P. JORDAN
Virginia Commonwealth University

GILMER, THOMAS WALKER (1802–1844), legislator and governor, first distinguished himself as a lawyer in his native Albemarle County, Va. Elected to the Virginia legislature (1829, 1833, 1835, 1838, 1839), he was Speaker of the lower house in the latter two years. Elected governor (1840), he displayed an avid interest in internal improvements. Gilmer resigned in 1841, when the legislature refused to support his extreme efforts to extradite from New York three men charged with slave stealing in Virginia. A friend and devotee of JOHN C. CALHOUN, Gilmer applauded the South Carolina nullifiers. Gilmer transferred allegiance from the Democratic to the Whig party in 1834 and was elected in 1841 to Congress, where he staunchly backed President JOHN TYLER. He published in 1843 a controversial letter calling for annexation of Texas. Although THOMAS HART BENTON charged the letter was meant to promote Calhoun's presidential candidacy, there is no proof that this was Gilmer's prime purpose. Appointed secretary of the navy in 1844, he died in the explosion on the steamer *Princeton*.

See T. H. Benton, *Thirty Years' View* (1854–56); and J. Floyd, *Life and Diary*, ed. C. H. Ambler (1918).

PATRICK S. BRADY
Bloomington, Ind.

GINSENG, a perennial herb and mild drug, is a wild plant once commonly found among the craggy ravines and slopes of the Ozark and Allegheny mountains. Its aromatic leaves and roots were valued by the Indians for their curative powers, and frontiersmen often adopted it as part of their FOLK MEDICINE. Although ginseng is a demulcent and a very mild stimulant, modern medicine neither uses it nor credits the fantastic powers often attributed to it. The Chinese, however, have prized the several species of ginseng at least as far back as Confucius. They believe that the root begets pleasant dreams, acts as a potent aphrodisiac, and guarantees longevity. Roots of the North American species (*Panax quinquefolius*) were first exported to China in 1716 and thereafter became an important commodity in the China trade. By the time of the American Revolution, New England had been stripped of most of its wild ginseng, and the Carolinas, Kentucky, Tennessee, and ultimately Arkansas became in turn principal sources of supply. Although frontiersmen raised few crops that could be profitably transported across the mountains, wild ginseng always commanded a cash value. Today choice gatherings of the wild root sell in the U.S. for between $10 and $15 per pound; and a perfect root, shaped in the image of a man and cured to a clear translucency, may bring as much as $400 an ounce in the Orient. In 1968 the U.S. exported over 130,000 pounds of untreated ginseng, valued at almost $4.5 million, principally to Hong Kong, Singapore, and Taiwan.

See C. J. Hylander, *World of Plant Life* (1956); C. M. Skinner, *Myths and Legends of Flowers and Plants* (1925); and E. Gibbons, *Stalking Healthful Herbs* (1966).

GIST, CHRISTOPHER (1706?–1759), was born in Maryland, moved to the Virginia frontier in 1745, and moved to the Yadkin River region in North Carolina in 1749. In 1750–1751 and 1751–1752, he was employed by the OHIO COMPANY OF VIRGINIA to explore and map the Ohio River valley. He accompanied GEORGE WASHINGTON on his famous journey to order the French out of the Ohio lands in 1753. Late in 1752 he established Gist's Plantation in the Monongahela country, the first English settlement west of the Appalachians. After its destruction by the French in 1754, he served as a guide on Edward Braddock's march in 1755 and later became captain of a company of scouts in the Virginia Regiment. In 1757 Gist was appointed deputy superintendent of Indian affairs for the southern colonies. He died of smallpox in Virginia.

See W. M. Darlington (ed.), *Gist's Journals* (1966), important for introductory material; D. B. Trimble, *Virginia Magazine of History and Biography* (Jan., 1965; April, 1966); A. P. James, *Ohio Company* (1959); L. Mulkearn, *George Mercer Papers* (1954); and K. P. Bailey, *Christopher Gist* (1976).

HERBERT R. PASCHAL
East Carolina University

GLASGOW, ELLEN ANDERSON GHOLSON (1873–1945), a novelist of manners and social history, was the first of the twentieth-century southern writers to subject the South to ironic scrutiny and critical evaluation. She was born in Richmond, Va., where she lived most of her life. Always in uncertain health and suffering from growing deafness, she educated herself through extensive, wide reading. She began writing as a child, wrote and destroyed a novel at seventeen, and published a novel, *The Descendant*, in 1897. In 1900 she published *The Voice of the People*, the first of her fictional chronicles of the social history of Virginia. Between 1900 and 1922 she wrote seven novels dealing with Virginia history, the best being *The Deliverance* (1904), *The Miller of Old Church* (1911), and *Virginia* (1913). In 1925 she published *Barren Ground* and between 1925 and 1932 three comedies of manners, *The Romantic Comedians*, *They Stooped to Folly*, and *The Sheltered Life*. Her fame rests upon these four books. Two other novels came—*Vein of Iron* (1935) and *In This Our Life* (1941), which received the Pulitzer Prize—as well as a collection of critical essays, *A Certain Measure* (1943). Her autobiography, *The Woman Within*, was published in 1954. Ellen Glasgow was a fine stylist, a loving but angry critic of southern traditions, and a social historian of impressive scope.

See B. Rouse (ed.), *Letters of E. Glasgow* (1958); M. Parent, *E. Glasgow* (1962); E. S. Godbold, *E. Glasgow* (1972); J. R. Raper, *Without Shelter* (1972); F. P. W. McDowell, *E. Glasgow and Ironic Art of Fiction* (1960); C. H. Holman, *Three Modes of Modern Southern Fic-*

tion (1966); and W. W. Kelly, *E. Glasgow: Bibliography* (1964).

C. HUGH HOLMAN
University of North Carolina, Chapel Hill

GLASS, CARTER (1858–1946), first gained prominence in Virginia as owner-editor of the Lynchburg *News*. His political career dates from the 1890s, when he became an exponent of free silver and white supremacy. In 1902 Glass helped forge the disfranchising clause of the Virginia constitution and began his long involvement in national affairs as a militant defender of the peculiar heritage of the South. From 1902 until 1918, when he was appointed secretary of the treasury by Woodrow Wilson, Glass served in the U.S. House of Representatives and aided in the creation of the Federal Reserve System in 1913. Upon the death of THOMAS S. MARTIN in 1919, Glass won appointment to the Senate, where he served until his death. A product of the bitter Civil War and Reconstruction era, Glass attributed many southern social and political problems to northern meddling and to the addition of blacks and poor whites to the electorate. With the advent of the NEW DEAL in 1933, Glass associated himself with other congressional conservatives in defending states' rights and damning the growth of government bureaucracy. In 1934 Franklin D. Roosevelt accurately described Glass as an "unreconstructed old rebel."

See Carter Glass Papers, University of Virginia Library; R. Smith and N. Beasley, *Carter Glass* (1939); J. T. Patterson, *Congressional Conservatism* (1967); A. W. Moger, *Virginia* (1968); R. H. Pulley, *Old Virginia Restored* (1968); C. Glass, *Constructive Finance* (1927); and H. E. Poindexter, "From Copy Desk to Congress" (Ph.D. dissertation, University of Virginia, 1966).

RAYMOND H. PULLEY
Appalachian State University

GLEBE LANDS were parish farms in the colonial period worked by the Anglican rector or his slaves and intended to supplement the income he derived from taxation. Partly as a result of the fervor of the Revolution as well as the hostility of the newer evangelical sects, these glebe lands were eventually confiscated beginning in 1802 in Virginia, but they continued to exist in other southern states for some time. Many ministers were forced to turn to teaching to increase their incomes once they were deprived of these lands.

See E. C. Chorley, *Men and Movements in American Episcopal Church* (1946); and W. W. Manross, *Episcopal Church in U.S., 1800–1840* (1967).

GOEBEL, WILLIAM (1856–1900), was born in Pennsylvania of German parents, who moved to Covington, Ky., during the Civil War. Graduating from Cincinnati Law School in 1877, he practiced law, first independently and then with John G. Carlisle. Both as a state senator (1887–1899) and as delegate to the constitutional convention of 1890, he argued for governmental regulation of the railroads. In particular, he worked to strengthen the state railroad commission, to prohibit rebates and long- and short-haul rate discrimination, and to enact a "fellow servant" law compensating injured railroad workers. In 1899 Goebel won the Democratic gubernatorial nomination after 26 ballots at a divisive party convention. A group of "honest election" Democrats led by former governor JOHN YOUNG BROWN bolted the regular party, leaving Goebel to face a strong Republican candidate, William S. Taylor. Running as much against the Louisville & Nashville Railroad as against Taylor, Goebel narrowly lost the popular election. With evidence of possible fraud on both sides, Goebel contested the election, and the strongly Democratic legislature declared him governor. But before he could assume office he was shot as he approached the capitol. Although he died within three days, he was administered the oath of office, thus assuring his lieutenant governor J. C. W. Beckham the governorship.

See T. D. Clark, *Journal of Southern History* (Feb., 1939); N. C. Burckel, *Filson Club History Quarterly* (Jan., 1974); U. Woodson, *First New Dealer* (1939), biased account by Goebel's secretary; and R. E. Hughes *et al.*, *Kentucky Campaign* (1900).

NICHOLAS C. BURCKEL
University of Wisconsin, Parkside

GOFF, NATHAN, JR. (1843–1920), a lawyer and banker of Clarksburg, was a leader of the West Virginia Republican party. A Union major during the Civil War, he was captured, imprisoned, and later exchanged. His discussion of southern prison conditions with President Abraham Lincoln contributed to a more lenient exchange policy. His public career included appointments as U.S. attorney (1868–1882), briefly as secretary of the navy (a gesture to southern Republicans by President R. B. Hayes in 1881), and as U.S. circuit judge (1892–1913). Elective offices included three terms in the U.S. House of Representatives (1882–1888) and one in the Senate (1913–1919). Twice a candidate for governor, he claimed victory in the 1888 campaign, but the Democratic-controlled legislature awarded the election to the Democrat, Aretas Brooks Fleming. After this defeat Goff surrendered leadership of the state Republican party to

STEPHEN BENTON ELKINS and accepted appointment to the Fourth Judicial Circuit. In *Mills* v. *Green* (1895) he declared unconstitutional a South Carolina voter registration law that disfranchised blacks, but the decision was reversed by higher courts.

See G. W. Smith, *Nathan Goff, Jr.* (1959), definitive, good bibliography; L. M. Davis and J. H. Henning, *West Virginia History* (July, 1951); J. H. Jacobs, *West Virginia History* (April, July, 1946); F. A. Burr, *Nathan Goff* (1882); and Nathan Goff Papers, West Virginia University.

JERRY BRUCE THOMAS
Shepherd College

GOLD. The founders of the colonies had high hopes of discovering mineral deposits, but it was not until after the Revolution that gold was discovered in significant quantities. The first commercially important deposits were discovered in 1802 in Cabarrus County, N.C., on the farm of John Reed, an unimaginative Hessian mercenary who had been using a 17-pound nugget as a doorstop. Subsequently, gold was discovered in every southern state with territory bordering the Appalachians, although large-scale commercial mining was confined to the Carolinas and Georgia.

In the years following 1802, the search for gold accelerated, and in the 1820s North Carolina became the scene of the nation's first full-scale gold rush. Boomtowns accommodating from 600 to 5,000 miners sprang up overnight. A similar rush took place in northern Georgia after gold was discovered on CHEROKEE lands in 1829. As output rose, southern mines began to attract the attention of northern and English investors, providing the capital for the smelters and the more expensive deep-shaft mining when the initial placer deposits began to play out. In 1835 Congress authorized the establishment of the nation's first branch mints in New Orleans, La., Dahlonega, Ga., and Charlotte, N.C. These mints remained in operation until 1861, when they were seized by the Confederacy and the Civil War brought an end to mining. Accurate statistics on southern output before the Civil War are not available, but reliable sources estimate that mines in North Carolina produced at least $20 million, and Georgia ranked second with an output of about $15 million. Mining was resumed after the war and has continued sporadically to the present, but the output of the southern states has been dwarfed by mines in the West and Alaska.

See E. M. Coulter, *Auraria* (1956); F. Green, *North Carolina Historical Review* (Jan., 1937); and *South in Building of Nation* (1909), V.

ROBERT J. PARKS

GOLDBERGER, JOSEPH (1874–1929), was born in Hungary and brought to New York when he was six. He attended the City College of New York and Bellevue Hospital Medical College (M.D., 1895). In 1899 he became an assistant surgeon in the U.S. Public Health Service, and in 1914 he became director of an extensive investigation of PELLAGRA, a debilitating disease that often resulted in death. The disease was a major public HEALTH problem in the rural South. In 1914, for instance, Mississippi recorded 1,192 deaths from pellagra. Goldberger became convinced that it was a nutritional disease resulting from an unbalanced diet, and he and his colleagues experimented on the diets of inmates of public institutions in Alabama, Georgia, and Mississippi. In 1915 he managed to produce pellagra by restricting the diet. Then he demonstrated that diets with fresh milk and meat would prevent pellagra or clear it up where it already existed. His long campaign to improve the diet eventually helped to eliminate the threat of pellagra, especially as living standards increased in the twentieth century.

See E. W. Etheridge, *Butterfly Caste* (1972); J. Goldberger, *Goldberger on Pellagra* (1964); M. F. Goldberger, *Journal of American Dietary Association* (1956); and R. P. Parsons, *Trail to Light* (1943).

MARTIN KAUFMAN
Westfield State College

GOLDEN, HARRY (1902–), was born in New York City as Harry Goldenhurst. He attended City College of New York without graduating and, after teaching school and working as a reporter for the New York *Post*, he moved to North Carolina in 1939. He worked briefly as a reporter for the Charlotte *Observer* and the Hendersonville *Times-News* before deciding in 1941 to publish his own paper, the *Carolina Israelite*, from his home in Charlotte. Issued irregularly—whenever Golden believes he has something to write—the publication quickly attained a widespread readership among political leaders and intellectuals interested in his comments and observations on the South, JEWS, and national politics. His satirical attacks on segregation during the 1950s were often quoted and reprinted. In addition to the *Israelite*, Golden has written numerous books including *The Jew in the South* (1951), *Jewish Roots in the Carolinas* (1954), *The Pattern of American Philo-Semitism* (1955), and *Only in America* (1958), a prizewinning collection of essays. He is at his best when writing in a jocularly irreverent manner but with serious purpose.

GOLDSBORO, N.C. (pop. 26,810), is on the state's coastal plain, approximately 45 miles southeast of Raleigh. It was founded as a rail station in 1840 and named for one of the railroad's civil engineers. The post–Civil War development of the bright leaf tobacco industry resulted in considerable expansion of the city's role as a market town and shipping center for area agriculture. The factories of the modern city produce lumber products, metals, and textiles.

See E. B. Powell, *Wayne County* (1976); and files of Goldsboro *News-Argus* (1885–), on microfilm.

GOLIAD, TEX. (pop. 1,709). Known originally as La Bahia, this historic community developed around a Spanish mission and a presidio established in 1749. Located approximately 85 miles southeast of San Antonio, the community and its garrison were important links in the defense and communications systems of Spanish Mexico. After being seized and briefly held by American filibusters in 1812 and in 1821, the town was occupied by Texans at the outset of the Texas revolution. The first Texas declaration of independence was issued from here in December, 1835. The following year, however, Mexican forces retook the town, capturing Colonel J. W. Fannin and over 300 Texans. All were executed, and "Remember Goliad!" was used by Texans in conjunction with the more familiar battle cry "Remember the Alamo!" The mission has been restored, and the fort's ruins are now part of a state park.

See I. Friedrichs, *History of Goliad* (1961, 1967); K. O'Conner, *Presidio La Bahia* (n.d.); and files of Goliad *Advance-Guard* (1855–).

GONE WITH THE WIND burst upon the world an instant phenomenon on its publication date, June 30, 1936. Immediately it began breaking sales records. Within a month film rights were bought by David O. Selznick for $50,000, then a record price for a first novel. By Christmas over a million copies were sold. Its author was Margaret Mitchell (Mrs. John R. Marsh), an Atlanta housewife and former newspaperwoman. *GWTW* was written to fill time during a long convalescence, 1926 to 1928. Not intending it for publication, she left it untitled and incomplete until she was persuaded by Harold S. Latham of the Macmillan Company to let him see the manuscript in 1935. It was quickly accepted by Macmillan. Miss Mitchell then spent several months revising it and meticulously checking its historical accuracy.

GWTW was enthusiastically received by reviewers and public, with the intellectual and liberal press contributing dissenting votes. It was awarded the Pulitzer Prize for fiction in 1937. Its 1,037 pages are vividly filled with a Confederate story of Civil War and Reconstruction told from the viewpoint of its protagonist Scarlett O'Hara. It struck a responsive chord in the depression years, but its appeal has outlived the depression and three more American wars. It has been published in virtually every civilized language, and its world sales are estimated in excess of 21 million copies.

The film was famous before a scene was shot. A nationwide talent search for a newcomer to play Scarlett magnified interest already high. Vivien Leigh was selected to act opposite Clark Gable, with Olivia de Havilland and Leslie Howard in the other principal roles. The film had an elaborate premiere in Atlanta December 15, 1939. It rivals the book in length and has achieved comparable success. It probably has been seen by more people than have seen any other motion picture.

GWTW drastically changed its author's life. Her correspondence relating to it was massive. She was overwhelmed with fan mail and with requests for autographs, endorsements, help in getting into the cast of the film, and public appearances. It was several years before she could return, even relatively, to the quiet, unassuming life she preferred. She made few public appearances and wrote no other book.

See F. Farr, *Margaret Mitchell* (1965) and *Atlanta Historical Society Bulletin* (May, 1950); R. Flamini, *Scarlett, Rhett and Cast of Thousands* (1975); G. Lambert, *GWTW* (1973), on the film; R. Harwell (ed.), *Margaret Mitchell's GWTW Letters* (1976); F. Watkins, *Southern Literary Journal* (Spring, 1970); and M. Mitchell Marsh Manuscripts, University of Georgia Library.

RICHARD HARWELL
University of Georgia

GONZALES, NARCISO GENER (1858–1903), was born at Edingsville, on Edisto Island, S.C. He was the second child of Harriet Rutledge Elliott Gonzales, daughter of wealthy planter William Elliott, and Ambrosio José Gonzales, a Cuban revolutionary. Attracted to journalism at an early age, Gonzales served the Charleston *News and Courier* as correspondent from 1880 to 1890. In January, 1891, he helped found and became editor of a daily newspaper, the *State*, to lead the opposition to BENJAMIN R. TILLMAN and his farmers' movement. Although Gonzales was an articulate spokesman for women's suffrage, limitations on child labor, fair treatment for the Negro, and other social and political reforms, his zealous—some said fanatical—anti-Tillman campaign overshadowed all other issues in his newspaper. He died from a gunshot wound inflicted by Tillman's nephew, Lieutenant Governor James Hammond Tillman, who blamed Gonzales for his defeat in the Democratic gubernatorial primary in 1902. Tillman, however, was acquitted of murder in a sensational trial.

See L. P. Jones, *Stormy Petrel* (1973); L. M. Matthews, "N. G. Gonzales" (Ph.D. dissertation, Duke, 1971); and Elliott-Gonzales Papers, University of North Carolina Library.

LINDA M. MATTHEWS
Emory University

GOODLOE, DANIEL REAVES (1814–1902), was born in Louisburg, N.C. The recipient of an indifferent education, he failed in early efforts as journalist and lawyer. As early as 1832, however, influenced by the Virginia Debates, Goodloe concluded that slavery was wrong (ANTISLAVERY SENTIMENT). In 1841 he began publishing anonymous antislavery tracts; in 1844 he settled in Washington, D.C., and began a significant career as an abolitionist spokesman. A prolific writer, he was associated with several prominent newspapers (including editing the *National Era*), but is probably best known as an author of some ten significant pamphlets or books. Most notable was his *Inquiry into the Causes Which Have Retarded the Accumulation of Wealth and Increase of Population in the Southern States* (1846). Unlike northern abolitionists who attacked slavery on moral grounds, Goodloe opposed the "peculiar institution" as impractical and detrimental to all southerners. He concluded that slavery degraded labor, monopolized capital, limited home markets, and discouraged immigration. His methods and arguments anticipated HINTON HELPER's *Impending Crisis*, but unlike Helper he never advocated removal of blacks. Goodloe successively advocated compensated EMANCIPATION, adequate protection for freedmen, and suffrage for qualified blacks. He served both Abraham Lincoln and Andrew Johnson, the latter as federal marshal in North Carolina. He joined Conservative Republicans in opposing W. W. HOLDEN, but his demeanor and character earned the respect of most North Carolinians.

See J. S. Bassett, *Anti-Slavery Leaders in North Carolina* (1898), excellent; C. N. Degler, *Other South* (1974), places Goodloe in context of southern dissent; and Goodloe Papers, University of North Carolina Library.

MAX R. WILLIAMS
Western Carolina University

GORDON, JEAN (1865–1931) and **KATE** (1861–1932), of New Orleans, were two leaders in the New South's social justice movement. Afforded the advantages of education and social position, they helped form the Era Club in 1896 to promote women's suffrage and to initiate projects for the betterment of New Orleans. CHILD LABOR reform, better working conditions, improved municipal physical facilities, better public HEALTH, political democracy, and women's suffrage (WOMEN'S RIGHTS MOVEMENT) comprised the Gordons' main pursuits.

A leader of the National Consumers' League, Jean Gordon focused on child labor, industrial conditions, and mental retardation. She lobbied the Louisiana legislature to secure factory inspector appointments for women and served as the first factory inspector in New Orleans. This position acquainted her with the extent of child labor and stiffened her determination to seek legislative regulation. Convinced that the problems were southwide, she participated in the Southern Textile Conference in Nashville, Tenn., in 1907. She inspired the conference on uniform child labor legislation held in New Orleans in 1909. She deserves major credit for the acceptance of the concept of uniform standards in child labor regulation.

Although both advocated women's suffrage, Kate Gordon worked more actively for this cause. She served as corresponding secretary of the National American Woman Suffrage Association from 1901 until 1909 but opposed the national suffrage amendment out of her fear of the black franchise and her devotion to STATES' RIGHTS. She successfully battled to have women admitted to the Tulane University Medical School.

See Louisiana Scrapbook, XXV, XLVIII, Tulane University Library; N. A. King, *Warrington Messenger* (Oct., 1938); M. McCulloch-Williams, *American Magazine* (April, 1925); and M. E. Sanders, "Sanders" (M.A. thesis, Louisiana State University, 1955).

BETTY J. BRANDON
University of South Alabama

GORDON, JOHN BROWN (1832–1904), was a Confederate general and postwar statesman of the New South. A Georgian and graduated (law) from the state university, he was engaged in mining when the war began. Elected captain of the 6th Alabama, he rose to command of the regiment. Thereafter, his rise was steady, and his combat participation is a catalog of the Army of Northern Virginia's battles. Wounded five times at Sharpsburg, he won permanent command of a brigade. Following the WILDERNESS CAMPAIGN, he led a division and commanded the II Corps at Cedar Creek. By the end of the war, he led one-third of

Robert E. Lee's army and served as one of three officers in carrying out the surrender agreement. D. S. Freeman and others consider Gordon to have been one of the ablest of southern officers. A solid commander with the full respect of his men, he was said to have "anticipated . . . by fifty years . . . the tactics of the breakthrough." After the war, Gordon was twice senator from Georgia, governor for two terms, and a member of the dominant GEORGIA TRIUMVIRATE. From 1890 until his death he was commander-in-chief of the CONFEDERATE VETERANS and worked for national reunification.

See J. B. Gordon, *Reminiscences of Civil War* (1903); and D. S. Freeman, *R. E. Lee* (1934–35) and *Lee's Lieutenants* (1944–45).

ARTHUR E. BARBEAU
West Liberty State College

GORGAS, JOSIAH (1818–1883), army officer and educator, was born in Dauphin County, Pa. Graduated from the U.S. Military Academy in 1841, he was commissioned in the Ordnance Corps and subsequently rose to the rank of captain despite a relatively undistinguished career. In 1853, while stationed in Alabama, he married Amelia Gayle, daughter of the former governor. In 1861, at the start of the Civil War, Gorgas resigned his commission and became chief of Confederate ordnance, with the rank of major. With great energy, imagination, and administrative skill, he did an extraordinary job of developing, practically from nothing, an arms and ammunition industry in the South and of supplementing it with significant ordnance imports run through the Union blockade. It was due primarily to his efforts that the Confederacy had sufficient weapons and ammunition. Although he rose to the rank of brigadier general, the war's end left him unemployed and practically destitute. Gorgas soon turned to teaching, eventually becoming president of the University of Alabama.

See F. E. Vandiver, *Ploughshares into Swords* (1952), best single source; J. Gorgas, *Civil War Diary* (1947); and S. L. Falk, *Journal of Southern History* (Feb., 1962).

STANLEY L. FALK
Department of the Air Force

GORMAN, ARTHUR PUE (1839–1906), was born in Woodstock, Md., and began his lifelong career in politics in 1852 serving first as a page in the U.S. House of Representatives and then in the Senate as Stephen A. Douglas' personal secretary. His support of President Andrew Johnson lost him his position as postmaster of the Senate in 1866, but Johnson made him collector of internal reve-

nue. In 1869 he won election to the Maryland house of delegates, becoming Speaker in 1873. During the same period he consolidated his position in the Democratic party by assuming the presidency of the politically powerful Chesapeake & Ohio Canal Company. After three terms in the state senate (1875–1881), he succeeded William P. Whyte in 1880 as U.S. senator and won two successive terms (1886, 1892). Although defeated for reelection in 1898, he returned to the Senate in 1903, where he developed a reputation as a cautious politician. He helped elect Grover Cleveland to his first term while serving as chairman of the Democratic National Committee. Mentioned as a possible presidential nominee in 1892, he nevertheless supported Cleveland when the convention chose him.

He received national attention for his efforts to win silver Republican opposition to the FORCE BILL of 1890 in return for support of a bill calling for free coinage of silver. In 1894 he amended the Wilson-Gorman Tariff Act to add coal, iron ore, and sugar to the duty list in spite of Cleveland's opposition. Party loyalty was his hallmark, and he served as chairman of the Democratic caucus during his last two terms.

See J. R. Lambert, *Arthur Pue Gorman* (1953) and *Maryland Historical Magazine* (April, 1963); Gorman Papers, Maryland Historical Society and University of North Carolina.

NICHOLAS C. BURCKEL
University of Wisconsin, Parkside

GOVERNMENT, STATE AND LOCAL. THOMAS JEFFERSON and JOHN C. CALHOUN were particularly influential in enunciating the role of governments below the national level. Jefferson of Virginia, in the late eighteenth and first quarter of the nineteenth century, stressed the need for democracy at the grass roots. Calhoun of South Carolina, in the pre–Civil War era, posited a model of federal-state relations aimed at preserving local autonomy. It would probably be fair to say that the views of Calhoun received more support from southern politicians than Jefferson's ideas on participatory democracy. Yet experimentation with new governmental arrangements has been continuous, and the direction today seems to be toward adoption of those institutions that will permit greater access to government by all citizens.

The average southern state has had five constitutions since entering the Union. Most of the current constitutions were adopted near the turn of this century, although four states have adopted new charters recently (Florida, North Carolina, Virginia, and Louisiana, in this order). The older documents are long (averaging about 60,000 words) and contain numerous restrictions on state and local governmental action. Amendments come frequently—the southern constitutions have been amended an average of 137 times. Movements for comprehensive constitutional reform are relatively frequent, but progress has been slow.

The legislature has traditionally been the principal policy-forming agency. The upper house is everywhere the senate, the lower is the house of representatives in all states except Maryland and Virginia (house of delegates). Senates and houses range from 21 and 41 members in Delaware to 56 and 180 in Georgia. Distribution of legislative seats has occasioned much controversy, often culminating in federal court orders requiring reapportionment according to the one-person, one-vote principle.

Several long-recommended legislative reforms are gaining more adoptions in the South. A majority of the legislatures now meet annually. When special problems arise between sessions, extraordinary meetings can be convened (even without gubernatorial approval in a majority of states). More rational legislative consideration of bills is facilitated by prefiling procedures now authorized in most states. There are still a number of limitations on legislative effectiveness, however. Only North and South Carolina put no limit on the length of regular sessions. In the other states the legislatures most normally adjourn after a set period of time, whether they have completed their work or not. Staff support services are generally inadequate, thus increasing disproportionately the role interest groups are able to play in the legislative process. Committees are frequently not used in an effective way. The common pattern is to have numerous committees but to assign bills in such a manner that a few committees handle most important legislation.

The policy-making role of the governor has increased greatly since his figurehead days at the beginning of the Republic. In all states except Arkansas a four-year term is provided, and in nine succession is now permitted. Three states (Delaware, Florida, and Maryland) now follow federal procedures in providing for joint election of the governor and lieutenant governor, an arrangement likely to encourage cooperation and an orderly succession should the office of governor become vacant.

Executive power traditionally has been very fragmented, and this is still a problem. The average southern state elects 11 executive officials, including the governor. Some (members of boards of education, for example) may not be chosen statewide. In addition to the governor, most states elect an attorney general (15 states), a lieutenant governor (14), a treasurer (12), a secretary of state (11), and a commissioner of agriculture (9). The seriousness of executive fragmentation is diminished by the fact that the treasurer, secretary of state, and several other elective officials may have little or no policy-making responsibilities. Still, their popular election does contribute to an excessively long ballot. Abolition of some elective offices or change in their status from constitutional to statutory is widely advocated but extremely difficult to achieve.

An increasing number of administrative officials is appointed by the governor. The most common administrative units are those concerned with budgeting and the functional areas of public health, public assistance, employment security, corrections, highways, economic development, and military affairs. The governor has at least some role in the selection of two-thirds of the heads of these units. In most states the governor has principal budget-making authority and an item veto power over appropriations bills. In two states (Maryland and West Virginia) the legislature is powerless to increase administrative appropriations above the sums requested by the governor.

Southern judiciaries also tend toward fragmentation, although three principal levels of courts can be identified. The court of last resort is the supreme court in all states except Kentucky and Maryland (court of appeals). Most states also have intermediate appellate courts. The major trial courts are most commonly called circuit courts. The principal controversy surrounding the judicial branch concerns judicial selection. Half the southern states elect judges on a partisan ballot. Missouri pioneered a plan providing for appointment by the governor from a list of carefully screened nominees and subsequent popular balloting on the basis of judicial records. The Missouri plan has found little popular support, however.

Principal local governments in the southern states are municipalities and counties. Special district governments are also numerous, however. School districts have been on the decline due to consolidations, but new districts have been created to deal with other functions. The most popular form of municipal government in the South is the mayor-council plan (52.6 percent of cities over 2,500). The council-manager plan is growing in popularity, however, and is currently utilized in 42.4 percent of the municipalities (CITY-MANAGER PLAN). The commission form is on the decline, only 5 percent presently using it (GALVESTON

COMMISSION PLAN). Forms of southern county government largely defy classification. Many offices, boards, and commissions may operate with little if any executive coordination. Generally, in southern counties there is a popularly elected commission, which exercises such general legislative and administrative power as has been delegated by the state legislature.

The District of Columbia Self-Government and Governmental Reorganization Act of 1973 gives its residents greater home rule than they have enjoyed in a century. Voters now elect a mayor and 13-member council to exercise the executive and legislative powers granted to them by a reluctant Congress.

See current editions of *Book of States* and *Municipal Yearbook*, with ongoing updating of information on state and local governments. For overview, consult C. R. Adrian, *State and Local Governments* (1976); H. Jacob and K. Vines, *Politics in American States* (1976); and M. S. Stedman, *State and Local Governments* (1976).

WILLIAM H. STEWART, JR.
University of Alabama

GRADY, HENRY WOODFIN (1850–1889), the son of a Georgia colonel who lost his life at the battle of Petersburg, grew to manhood during the Civil War and Reconstruction. He attended the public schools of Athens, Ga., was graduated from the University of Georgia (1868), and studied law at the University of Virginia. He returned to his native state in 1871 and embarked on a career in journalism, which included a brief stint as a reporter for the New York *Herald*. After a period of apprenticeship, he secured a loan from the northern financier Cyrus W. Field and bought a part ownership of the ATLANTA CONSTITUTION. From then on, the paper would be his home, his joy, his ruling passion as he fashioned it into one of the best newspapers in the country.

In addition, Grady articulated in editorials and acclaimed speeches a deeply felt need of the time. He urged southerners, particularly the men of property, to seek prosperity and the rebuilding of the South by developing local resources, diversifying agriculture, and cooperating with northern capitalists. To the North Grady promised that the South was now ready to work, to look to the future, to put aside the LOST CAUSE. "There was a South of slavery and secession—that South is dead," he announced in 1886. "There is a South of union and freedom—that South, thank God, is living, breathing, growing every hour." That was the NEW SOUTH. From that moment on, Grady's name was linked with the desire for sectional reconciliation and a progressive South. He was, in fact,

conservative on most issues, particularly the race issue, and his words, however uplifting, were mortgaged to an uncritical acceptance of the ethic of white supremacy and to the continued dominance of the social order by planters and businessmen.

See G. Dugat, *Life of Henry Grady* (1927); R. B. Nixon, *Henry W. Grady* (1943); and P. Gaston, *New South Creed* (1970).

BRUCE CLAYTON
Allegheny College

GRAHAM, FRANK PORTER (1886–1972), was born outside Fayetteville, N.C., the son of a school superintendent of Scotch Presbyterian descent. Educated at the University of North Carolina and at Columbia, Chicago, and London universities, he devoted most of his life to the University of North Carolina at Chapel Hill, first as professor of history (1915–1930) and then as president (1930–1949). Appointed to the U.S. Senate in 1949, Graham failed to win renomination in the Democratic primary in 1950. Later he served the United Nations as representative in the Kashmir dispute. Inspired by simple beliefs in the fundamental principles of American democracy and the Christian religion, Graham was a liberal activist, interested especially in education, labor and race relations, civil liberties, and world peace. His associations with numerous agencies for social and economic change, both within the South and beyond, contributed to the liberal reputation of his university. He was elected chairman of the SOUTHERN CONFERENCE FOR HUMAN WELFARE in 1938, and President Harry Truman appointed him to the Committee on Civil Rights in 1946.

See G. W. Johnson, *Survey Graphic* (April, 1942); and F. P. Graham Papers, University of North Carolina Library.

JOSEPH HERZENBERG
University of North Carolina, Chapel Hill

GRAHAM, WILLIAM ALEXANDER (1804–1875), was born in Lincoln County, N.C. He reputedly held more offices of public trust than any other man in North Carolina history. Scion of sturdy Scotch-Irish ancestors, distinguished by their Revolutionary opposition to George III, Graham attended classical academies and graduated from the University of North Carolina in 1824. After reading law with the eminent THOMAS RUFFIN, he settled in Hillsboro and became a successful attorney. He was a founder of the Whig party and an apostle of HENRY CLAY's American System. Graham was successively a state commoner (1833–

1840), Speaker in the 1838 and 1840 sessions; a U.S. senator (1840–1843); a North Carolina governor (1845–1849); a secretary of the navy (1850–1852); an unsuccessful Whig vice-presidential candidate (1852); a state senator (1854); a founder of the CONSTITUTIONAL UNION PARTY; a delegate to the 1861 secession convention; a state senator (1862); a Confederate senator (1864–1865); a state senator (1865), though he declined participation while awaiting pardon; an unseated U.S. senator (December, 1865); an original trustee of the PEA-BODY EDUCATION FUND; a counsel in the w. w. HOLDEN impeachment trial; and an arbitrator of the Virginia-Maryland boundary dispute. He would have been a delegate to the constitutional convention of 1875, except for his unexpected death. Although Graham filled no elective office after 1865, he continued, as elder statesman, to be a dominant force in North Carolina politics and was influential in the conservative faction that eventually "redeemed" the state.

As commoner and governor, Graham promoted public education, humanitarian institutions, and internal improvements. As secretary of the navy he supported the COMPROMISE OF 1850, while proving an able administrator. Long an opponent of JOHN C. CALHOUN's political doctrines, he worked diligently, but futilely, to preserve the Union. After Ft. Sumter he contended that revolution was the proper remedy to northern actions but eventually agreed to secession. Seeing no honorable alternative, he supported the war effort. Nevertheless, while avoiding implication in Holden's peace movement, Graham opposed the infringement of civil rights and worked for reunion by negotiation. Disappointed by the Reconstruction process, which he considered unjust, Graham came to embody the frustration of many southern whites.

See M. McGehee, *Life and Character* (1877), informative but laudatory; M. R. Williams, "William A. Graham" (Ph.D. dissertation, University of North Carolina, 1965); and J. G. de R. Hamilton and M. R. Williams, *Graham Papers* (1957–), I–VI, VII–VIII projected.

MAX R. WILLIAMS
Western Carolina University

GRAHAM, WILLIAM FRANKLIN "BILLY"

(1918–), is the most famous and successful evangelist of the twentieth century. Although he was born and reared in Charlotte and is a permanent resident of Montreat, N.C., his work has been national and international in scope. He holds membership in a Southern BAPTIST CHURCH. Converted in 1934, he was graduated from Wheaton

College (Illinois) and began his career as a recruiter for Youth for Christ in 1945, then served as president of a complex of fundamentalist schools in Minneapolis. Graham's electrifying success as a preacher in the Los Angeles crusade in 1949 made him the best-known name in American Christianity. In addition to his numerous crusades and extensive television and radio ministries, he was spiritual adviser to Presidents Dwight Eisenhower, Lyndon Johnson, and Richard Nixon. His skills as a preacher and organizer are outstanding, the latter best reflected in the Billy Graham Evangelistic Association, which manages the multimillion-dollar evangelistic enterprise. Conservative but not extremist, his theology is based on a literal interpretation of Scripture and in declaring to every person that he is lost in his sins and needs to be saved through conversion.

See J. Pollock, *Billy Graham* (1966); W. G. McLoughlin, Jr., *Billy Graham* (1960); J. E. Barnhart, *Billy Graham Religion* (1972); and Billy Graham Collection, Southern Baptist Theological Seminary, Louisville.

SAMUEL S. HILL, JR.
University of Florida

GRANDFATHER CLAUSE.

Although most framers of the laws and constitutional amendments that restricted suffrage (DISFRANCHISEMENT) in the South in the period from 1880 to 1912 favored excising lower-class whites as well as blacks from the electorate, the disfranchisers realized the difficulty of getting such measures passed in legislatures and referenda without apparent loopholes for whites. They therefore invented the "grandfather clause," adopted in Louisiana, North Carolina, and Oklahoma, which temporarily exempted from literacy or property requirements all men who could vote before 1867 (before Negroes were allowed to vote in the South) and all descendants of such voters; and the "fighting grandfather clause," adopted in Alabama and Georgia, which similarly exempted veterans and descendants of veterans of any American war (including former Confederates). As intended, the escape clauses, which also included the UNDERSTANDING CLAUSE, did not enable many otherwise unqualified whites to register, either because registrars exercised their wide administrative discretion or because illiterate, propertyless men were too ashamed to advertise their ignorance and poverty. The Oklahoma grandfather clause was declared unconstitutional by the U.S. Supreme Court in *Guinn and Beal* v. *U.S.* (238 U.S. 347 [1915]).

See J. M. Kousser, *Shaping of Southern Politics* (1974); W. A. Mabry, "Disfranchisement of Negro" (Ph.D. dissertation, Duke, 1933); E. McCrady, Jr., *Registration of Electors* (1880); *Alabama Constitutional Convention Proceedings* (1901), III; J. H. Stone, *Journal of Southern History* (May, 1972); J. L. W. Woodville, *Political Science Quarterly* (June, 1906); and W. B. Hixson, Jr., *Journal of American History* (Dec., 1968).

J. MORGAN KOUSSER
California Institute of Technology

GRAND OLE OPRY is the premier country music radio show in the United States. It was introduced on WSM in Nashville, Tenn., on November 28, 1925, by announcer George D. Hay, who acted as master of ceremonies for a program of old-time tunes played by eighty-year-old fiddler Uncle Jimmy Thompson. From this humble beginning, the show grew to have a cast of over 100 with a popularity enjoyed throughout the world. The show received its name sometime in 1926, when Hay announced, following the conclusion of NBC's "Musical Appreciation Hour," that WSM would next present, not music from grand opera, but "the Grand Ole Opry." Exposure on the 50,000-watt, clear-channel WSM carried the show into homes throughout the South and Midwest, and a 30-minute segment on NBC after 1939 gave the program national recognition. Through the years the show was held at a variety of sites, the most famous being Ryman Auditorium, where the Opry held sway each Saturday night from 1941 to 1973. The Grand Ole Opry is now performed in an ultramodern auditorium at Opryland, a Disneyland-like complex on the outskirts of Nashville.

Throughout its history the Grand Ole Opry has been a repository of the most important southern white folk music styles, but until World War II the show was principally an arena for old-time string bands. Its current status as a haven for individual stars began in 1938, when Roy Acuff joined the show. Although an affiliation with the show is no longer necessary for stardom, the average fan still envisions the Grand Ole Opry as the mecca of country music.

See G. D. Hay, *Story of Grand Ole Opry* (1953), source material; C. Wolfe, *Grand Ole Opry, 1925–1935* (1976); and B. C. Malone, *Country Music, USA* (1968). John Edwards Memorial Foundation, Los Angeles, and Country Music Foundation, Nashville, contain data on early Opry history.

BILL C. MALONE
Tulane University

GRANGE (Order of the Patrons of Husbandry) identifies the secret, ritualistic farmers' order that first appeared in 1867 and still exists today. The idea originated with Oliver Hudson Kelley, an agent of the federal Department of Agriculture, while on a tour of the South shortly after the Civil War. Moved by the backwardness and isolation of the region, he envisioned an organization that would educate and elevate farmers. Kelley and several able associates perfected the structure, ritual, philosophy, and goals, then set about the task of organizing local granges. For five years progress was exceedingly slow—until a swell of nationwide agrarian discontent found in the Grange a willing medium for protest. The order in 1875 counted at least 850,000 individual members.

First in the Midwest and then in the South, the Grange became associated with antirailroad, antibank, antimonopoly sentiments. "Pecuniary benefits" nonetheless soon emerged as the central economic issue. The hard-pressed farmer felt frustration and anger that prices for his products steadily declined while his debts either remained the same or increased. The Grange's principle of fraternal cooperation logically led to the establishment of buying and selling cooperatives as a means of combating exploiters of the farmer. In the South the most successful cooperative associations were the southwestern (Arkansas, Tennessee, Louisiana, Mississippi) in the 1870s and the Texas between 1880 and 1897. Although nearly all such ventures failed after brief careers, the farmer's realization of "pecuniary benefits" was long remembered and its lesson learned.

Social and educational progress ranked equal to economic gain. Grange meetings stirred interest, encouraged tolerance, and fostered cooperation. Patrons of Husbandry in Georgia and Kentucky called for crop diversification; in Alabama and North Carolina it sponsored private academies for rural youth; in Mississippi it played a vital role in founding the agricultural and mechanical college; in North Carolina and West Virginia it led in the creation of state departments of agriculture; and in the nation's capital it provided strong support for the Hatch Act establishing agricultural experiment stations.

Among southern Grange leaders were D. Wyatt Aiken of South Carolina, who served as a pioneer organizer and as a member of the national body's executive committee; and John T. Jones of Arkansas (1875–1877) and Putnam Darden of Mississippi (1885–1888), who were national masters of the order. At its peak, Grange membership in the South reached about 350,000, 41 percent of the national total. After 1875 the Patrons of Husbandry experienced a sharp loss of members. The numerous reasons included economic depression, power of the vested interests, and competition of the FARMERS' ALLIANCE. Between 1883 (Florida) and 1923 (Kentucky), every state Grange in the South expired save four: Missouri, West Virginia, Maryland, and Delaware.

A carefully planned, energetic campaign between 1928 and 1935 revived the Grange in Virginia, North Carolina, South Carolina, Tennessee, Arkansas, and Texas. In 1961 Florida was added. The new leadership was well exemplified in North Carolina. CLARENCE POE, editor of the *Progressive Farmer*, contributed the initial boost; W. Kerr Scott and Robert W. Scott, father and son, served as state masters before becoming governors of the state; Harry B. and Margaret H. Caldwell, husband and wife, were elected state masters for 23 and 14 years respectively. Patrons in the South have shown special interest in commodity programs, transportation problems, youth work, and community service.

See S. J. Buck, *Granger Movement* (1913); D. S. Nordin, *Rich Harvest* (1974), Grange, 1867–1900; C. M. Gardner, *Grange* (1949); C. C. Taylor, *Farmers' Movement* (1953); T. Saloutos, *Farmer Movements in South* (1960); W. D. Barns, *West Virginia Grange* (1973); and S. Noblin, *Grange in North Carolina* (1954).

STUART NOBLIN
North Carolina State University, Raleigh

GRANT, ULYSSES S., ADMINISTRATION

(1869–1877) covered the period also known as "later Reconstruction." Grant, elected on the strength of his Civil War military record, proved a naïve and inept politician, whose presidency was tainted by scandal. At the same time, however, the continued process of reconstructing the South engaged the attention of both the president and Congress. Despite their general neglect by historians, some of the most radical and controversial pieces of Reconstruction legislation were considered during Grant's tenure in office. Among these were the KU KLUX KLAN ACTS of 1870 and 1871 (under the authority of which Grant sent troops into South Carolina, Arkansas, and Louisiana). The CIVIL RIGHTS ACT OF 1875 granted Negroes equal rights in most public places and forbade their exclusion from jury duty, but a controversial school integration provision was defeated by northern and southern representatives alike. The 1872 AMNESTY Act restored the rights of most former Confederates, but at least 500 individuals remained disfranchised. Grant himself issued executive pardons to many of them. A proposed 1875 amnesty law, which would have covered all who remained, was defeated when it was amended to exclude Jefferson Davis. And the debate that

surrounded this measure was a heated reminder that sectional bitterness was still strong.

Simultaneously, however, Reconstruction was coming to an end. In 1875, the Forty-fourth Congress convened with the first Democratic House majority since 1859, including 87 southern Democrats (82 percent of all southern representatives and 48 percent of all House Democrats). Many of these were former Confederate soldiers and officials, including ALEXANDER STEPHENS. By the summer of 1876, only three southern states (Florida, South Carolina, and Louisiana) remained under Radical rule, and within six months even these had returned to the Democratic fold.

See K. M. Stampp, *Era of Reconstruction* (1965); W. B. Hesseltine, *U. S. Grant* (1935); M. S. Thompson, "Spider Web: Congressional Lobbying in Age of Grant" (Ph.D. dissertation, University of Wisconsin, 1977); and B. Wyatt-Brown, *Western Political Quarterly* (Dec., 1965).

MARGARET S. THOMPSON
Knox College

GRANVILLE TRACT was a strip of land in colonial North Carolina about 60 miles wide, bordering Virginia on the north and running from the coast west to the Appalachians. It contained about half the colony's population. The district went to John Carteret, Earl Granville (1690–1763), after he refused to sell his share of the colonial proprietorship to the crown in 1729. The tract proved an unceasing source of friction. The colony as a whole lost revenue because of it. Granville also profited little because his agents cheated him while squeezing exorbitant fees from settlers. Proposals from North Carolina that the crown purchase the district fell on deaf ears. The dissatisfaction of the Granville people contributed importantly to the REGULATOR movement. After American independence, the state confiscated ungranted land in the tract.

See H. T. Lefler and A. R. Newsome, *North Carolina* (1963); D. Clarke, *Arthur Dobbs* (1957); W. L. Sanders, *North Carolina Colonial Records* (1887), V, (1888), VI; and pamphlets of Herman Husband in W. K. Boyd, *Eighteenth Century Tracts* (1927).

FRANKLIN B. WICKWIRE
University of Massachusetts

GRASSES have become a major part of the southern farmers' diversified agricultural programs for forage, hay, and soil management. Climatic factors have influenced the distribution of approximately 1,200 species of native and introduced grasses in the United States. On colonial southern farms, lack of natural forage and hay kept livestock thin, weak, and susceptible to disease. During the eighteenth and nineteenth centuries an agricultural revolution led southern farmers to adopt foreign grasses to such an extent that most present important grasses are imported.

Kentucky BLUEGRASS, introduced by early settlers, became a valuable grass for winter and summer. Timothy (herd's-grass) is the most widely cultivated hay grass on southern farms. Bermuda grass, a creeping perennial, is widely used for forage and soil improvement. Meadow foxtail grass is extensively cultivated on clayey soils. Italian ryegrass has been praised for long seasonal grazing. Orchard grass is widely used in shaded areas. African guinea grass is used for forage and hay along the Gulf Coast. Johnson grass (Means grass) is a useful sorghum-type perennial, but its creeping stock roots often make it a pest. Syrian millet and Egyptian millet produce tall forage and hay crops. South American Para and Spanish gama grasses are praised for hay and grazing on prairie lands.

Through cultivation of these and other imported grasses, sometimes mixed with clovers, southern farmers have often realized more profit from forage and hay than from cotton, corn, and other major crops. Moreover, they have helped feed the world's growing populations and improved the land for future generations.

See L. Carrier, *Beginnings of Agriculture in America* (1923); L. C. Gray, *History of Southern Agriculture* (1941); H. L. Kerr, *Agricultural History* (April, 1964); K. H. Klages, *Ecological Crop Geography* (1949); C. V. Piper, *Forage Plants* (1914); and T. Shaw, *Grasses* (1903).

HOMER L. KERR
University of Texas, Arlington

GRAYSON, WILLIAM JOHN (1788–1863), is best known for his proslavery poem *The Hireling and the Slave* (1854). A Sea Island South Carolinian, he led his district for NULLIFICATION and served as congressman (1831–1837) and as collector of customs in Charleston (1841–1853). His unionism, expressed in *Letter to Governor Seabrook* (1850) and *Letters of Curtius* (1851), led to forced retirement. He then wrote historical and political essays for *Russell's* magazine, as well as some interesting poems besides *The Hireling and the Slave*, notably *Chicora* (1856) and *Marion* (1860). His memoir of JAMES L. PETIGRU and his autobiography are useful documents in antebellum social history. Grayson saw the Union as a product of God's direct providence. To oppose it was sinful. He believed slavery more efficient and humane than "hireling" labor systems and hoped the slaves would someday return to Africa to redeem their brothers from savagery and paganism.

He agreed with Petigru that slavery must survive within the Union or not at all. A disciplined and vigorous craftsman in the neoclassical style, Grayson was as opposed to romanticism as to secession.

See complete bibliographies in J. B. Hubbell, *South in American Literature* (1954); and L. Rubin, *Bibliographic Guide* (1969). F. Albrecht has annotated *The Hireling and the Slave* and written an unpublished analysis of Grayson's life and works; these are available from author.

FRANK M. ALBRECHT
Atlanta, Ga.

GREAT AWAKENING, although best known in association with Jonathan Edwards and New England Congregationalism, also caused dramatic changes in religious institutions and practices in the South (RELIGION). The movement was characterized by an emphasis on individual salvation, a reassertion of the concept of salvation by grace, and an expression of man's inherently sinful nature. Often utilizing an extemporaneous method of conveying a highly personalized message, the exhorters and preachers of the revivalist faiths abandoned the traditional structure of a settled ministry in favor of itinerancy, thereby expanding their audiences and potential influence. Their methods appealed to southerners who had wearied of the highly formalized theological expositions generally presented by the clergy of the established Church of England (EPISCOPAL CHURCH).

The Great Awakening in the South began in Virginia in the 1740s and quickly spread to neighboring colonies. Three separate religious groups contributed to, and benefited from, the movement's widespread appeal: New Light PRESBYTERIANS, BAPTISTS, and METHODISTS. Probably because of the legitimacy derived from their connection with the Church of England, the Wesleyan societies experienced the greatest growth.

The causes of revivalism are elusive. Traditional interpretations, such as W. Gewehr, *The Great Awakening in Virginia* (1930), view the Awakening as a western, lower-class rebellion against the planter-dominated established church of the Tidewater region. More recent studies, exemplified by G. M. Brydon, *Virginia's Mother Church* (1947–1952), attribute the popularity of religious dissent to the structural deficiencies of the Church of England. Actually, the Great Awakening extended into all geographic regions and attracted some adherents from all social classes. Population growth and rapidly changing internal conditions provided the essential opportunities for the revivalists. With an inadequate supply of clergymen, particularly in North Carolina and Georgia, the Anglican church lacked the ability to serve the religious needs of many sparsely populated areas. In the South, the Awakening survived the Revolutionary era, joining with the forces of rationalism to achieve separation of church and state and establishing an enduring tradition of popular religion.

See W. Gewehr, *Great Awakening in Virginia* (1930), questionable interpretations but still valuable; W. W. Sweet, *Revivalism in America* (1944) and *Men of Zeal* (1935); W. T. Thom, *Struggle for Religious Freedom* (1900); G. W. Pilcher, *Samuel Davies* (1971), recent analysis of important figure; Southern Historical Collection, University of North Carolina Library; Garrett Theological Institute, Evanston, Ill.; and Methodist Publishing House Library, Nashville, Tenn.

THOMAS GAGE
Lincoln University

GREAT AWAKENING, SECOND, was an early nineteenth-century expression of renewed interest in experiential religion. The movement exerted its greatest influence in the South, creating a distinctively southern religious style characterized by a Low Church orthodoxy within a denominational setting dominated by the METHODIST and BAPTIST churches.

The CAMP MEETING, a device particularly suited to the sparsely settled West, was one of the most interesting innovations of the Second Awakening. The first extended revival of that type occurred in August, 1801, at Cane Ridge, Bourbon County, Ky., with an estimated attendance of 10,000 to 25,000 persons. Because of the extreme emotionalism and physical gesticulations that accompanied the revivals, the Awakening was condemned by the staid, sophisticated denominations. Indeed, the PRESBYTERIANS, who had organized the Cane Ridge revival, abandoned the practice and thereby lost the initiative to the Methodist circuit riders and the Baptist farmer-preachers.

Although the Second Awakening served to spread popular religion into the West, it was not strictly a western phenomenon. All of the major participating denominations launched their attacks upon irreverence in the West from firmly established bases in the East, and the exhorters of the great revival drew heavily from the precedents established during the GREAT AWAKENING of the eighteenth century.

See W. W. Sweet, *Religion on American Frontier* (4 vols.; 1931–46), good collection of documents; S. S. Hill, *Southern Churches in Crisis* (1967); B. A. Weisberger, *They Gathered at River* (1958); and E. R. Sandeen, *Roots of Fundamentalism* (1970).

THOMAS GAGE
Lincoln University

GREAT DEPRESSION (1929–1941). The collapse of the stock market in 1929 ushered in a decade that would reshape southern life. The financial empire of Rogers Caldwell of Nashville, "the Morgan of the South," failed in 1930, wrecking banks in Tennessee, Kentucky, North Carolina, and Arkansas. Municipal real estate values collapsed. Prices for cotton and sugarcane fell to levels unprecedented in the twentieth century. And in the summer of 1930, the first of a series of devastating droughts hit Arkansas and Texas, destroying the hopes of those who had hoped to "live at home."

President Herbert Hoover's attempt to stabilize agricultural values with the support of cooperatives by the Farm Board and by halting foreign imports with the Hawley-Smoot tariff (1930) were fruitless. Similarly, efforts of southern governors to limit cotton production by restricting planting were ineffectual. By 1932, per capita yearly INCOME had slipped 45 percent from $372 in 1929 to $203. Only the tobacco industry retained its clientele.

The shrinkage of the tax base resulted in cutbacks in municipal, county, and state expenditures. Schools closed, road construction ceased, and government workers were fired as a result of falling revenues. Arkansas faced technical default on its highway bonds. Southern Governors John Garland Pollard in Virginia, Richard Russell in Georgia, O. MAX GARDNER in North Carolina, and J. Marion Futrell in Arkansas pared state expenditures to bolster sagging revenues. Sales taxes were enacted. By the mid-thirties southern governors such as Hugh White of Mississippi and Carl Bailey of Arkansas sought new industry to strengthen the tax base by advertising special tax advantages.

The massive numbers of unemployed had exhausted the limited financial resources of voluntary agencies. The back-to-the-land philosophy proved inadequate to sustain displaced families. In the fall of 1932, the RECONSTRUCTION FINANCE CORPORATION offered limited federal aid for relief. Increasing desperation brought about strikes of coal miners in Harlan County, Ky., textile workers in Virginia, and sharecroppers in Alabama.

The election of Franklin D. Roosevelt and JOHN NANCE GARNER of Texas in 1932 brought increased federal assistance to the South (NEW DEAL). The FEDERAL EMERGENCY RELIEF ADMINISTRATION provided minimal aid to states to finance welfare programs, including money for transient camps, small gardens, support of teachers' salaries, and distribution of commodities. The Rural Rehabilitation Division of the FERA assisted drought-stricken farmers with loans. In 1935 the WORKS PROGRESS ADMINISTRATION offered work relief that built roads, libraries, schools, and airports as well as a multitude of cultural projects. Overall, the relief expenditures in the South totaled $193,061,860. The TENNESSEE VALLEY AUTHORITY revitalized an economically depressed region by building a series of multipurpose dams generating electricity, producing superphosphate fertilizer, and providing FLOOD CONTROL. By the late thirties an Arkansas Valley authority was being proposed for the Southwest.

The massive injection of federal money frightened conservatives such as Governors EUGENE TALMADGE of Georgia and Futrell of Arkansas. Influential congressional leaders, such as Senators JOSEPH T. ROBINSON of Arkansas, ALBEN W. BARKLEY of Kentucky, and B. P. HARRISON of Mississippi, ensured that southern workers on relief projects were paid on a lower scale in order not to undermine prevailing wages. In contrast, firebrand Louisiana Senator HUEY LONG offered his SHARE OUR WEALTH program for a redistribution of income. Administration critics, such as the SOUTHERN GOVERNORS' CONFERENCE, blamed discriminatory railroad freight rates for sectional economic retardation.

The New Deal's AGRICULTURAL ADJUSTMENT ADMINISTRATION sought higher prices for cotton, rice, and tobacco by an acreage retirement program. Moreover, Secretary of State CORDELL HULL of Tennessee tried to expand foreign markets by reciprocal trade agreements. Storable surpluses were purchased by the Commodity Credit Corporation. Despite these efforts, agricultural receipts did not rise substantially until World War II. Nevertheless, governmental efforts at soil restoration and crop diversification lessened dependence on a single cash crop.

An unfortunate by-product of the AAA was the displacement of SHARECROPPERS as a result of the land retirement program. Barely surviving on $180 to $417 a year in cash and commodities, they attracted national attention through the novelistic efforts of ERSKINE CALDWELL and John Steinbeck, the studies of Arthur Raper and WILL ALEXANDER, and the photographers of the FARM SECURITY ADMINISTRATION. The Socialist-oriented SOUTHERN TENANT FARMERS' UNION, organized in 1934 in Arkansas, agitated for special governmental assistance for these "forgotten farmers." In 1937 Congress enacted the Bankhead-Jones Farm Tenancy Act, granting sharecroppers loans on easy terms and establishing a series of experimental farm colonies.

The New Deal's National Industrial Recovery Act humanized factory conditions by ending child labor and instituting a $12 a week minimum wage and a 40-hour week. In 1935 the U.S. Supreme Court decision declaring the act unconstitutional resulted in a loss of some of these gains. Organizational drives of the American Federation of Labor and the Congress of Industrial Organizations met fierce resistance throughout the South. The La Follette committee's investigation revealed a pattern of intimidation of LABOR UNION organizers. Despite these obstacles, union membership in 11 southern states (excluding Texas) rose to almost half a million by 1938. Yet wages in the South remained substantially below the national average.

See G. Tindall, *Emergence of New South, 1913–1945* (1967), best synthesis; Federal Writers' Program of Works Progress Administration, American Folkways series and *These Are Our Lives* (1939), unique studies; H. Odum, *Southern Regions of U.S.* (1936); W. J. Cash, *Mind of South* (1941), brilliant insights; National Emergency Council, *Report on Economic Conditions of South* (1938); and K. D. P. Lumpkin, *South in Progress* (1940), a liberal critique. See also Record Group 16 (Agriculture), 44 (National Emergency Council), 69 (FERA-WPA), and 83 (Bureau of Agricultural Economics), National Archives. FDR Library, Hyde Park, N.Y.; and Southern Historical Collection, University of North Carolina Library, are rich sources.

STEPHEN F. STRAUSBERG
University of Arkansas, Fayetteville

GREAT SMOKY MOUNTAINS occupy a region on the Tennessee–North Carolina border between the Big Pigeon River to the east and the Little Tennessee River to the west. They are the highest block of mountains in the southern Appalachian highlands, occupying an area of some 70 miles in a nearly east-west direction and about 25 miles in a north-south axis. Most of the major crestline is above 5,000 feet with several peaks above 6,000 feet. These mountains are composed of very old metamorphic rocks. Their present elevations have been lowered from much higher mountains by erosion and weathering over millions of years. The region is located in an area of the highest rainfall in the eastern United States. Some locations have over 90 inches of rain a year. This heavy rainfall, in a moderate temperature regime, supports one of the most diverse mid-latitude forests in the world. The rich flora and fauna amid the striking terrain were the major reasons for the establishment of the National Park dedicated in 1940, but thought of as early as 1885. The land was the home of the CHEROKEE INDIANS. White settlers pushed into the mountains in the 1790s and eventually removed most of the Cherokee. It is still a major center for Indian culture east of the Mississippi. The violence of the frontier wars was followed by the bloodshed of the Civil War, when loyalties were divided between North and South, splitting both families and communities. In the late 1800s lumber companies began cutting the rich forests. Railroads and highways encouraged the growth of tourism, recreation, and light industries, which have largely displaced the traditional subsistence farming, hunting, and gathering occupations.

See M. Frome, *Strangers in High Places* (1966); R. Peattie, *Great Smokies and Blue Ridge* (1943); and L. Thornborough, *Great Smoky Mountains* (1956).

RICHARD S. LITTLE
West Virginia University

GREAT WAGON ROAD began as a "warrior's path," an Indian trail used for hunting and trading and attacking tribal enemies. By the mid-eighteenth century it became important to the American settlers because it linked Philadelphia and the Lancaster area with Frederick, Md., and Winchester, Va., and (via the Shenandoah Valley of Virginia) with the Yadkin River area of North Carolina. It afforded a principal route for Pennsylvania emigrants of English, German, and Scotch-Irish extraction to the North Carolina Piedmont. The road stretched over 430 miles long to this area. After 1760 it covered 800 miles in all, counting a somewhat less famous portion extending on through Pine Tree (Camden), S.C., to Augusta, Ga. Also after 1775, the famous WILDERNESS ROAD branched off from the main route in southeastern Virginia to carry settlers through the CUMBERLAND GAP toward Kentucky and Tennessee. According to some authorities the Great Wagon Road was at one time used by more travelers than any road in the colonies. It also played a significant role in the American Revolution. With the coming of the railroads, however, its importance declined.

See G. Shumway, E. Durell, and H. C. Frey, *Conestoga Wagon, 1750–1850* (1964); P. Rouse, *Great Wagon Road* (1973); and C. Bridenbaugh, *Myths and Realities* (1952).

GREEN, DUFF (1791–1875), born in Kentucky, moved to Missouri in 1816, where he became a government land surveyor, a lawyer, and an influential member of the constitutional convention of 1820. In 1823 he purchased the St. Louis *Enquirer* and supported ANDREW JACKSON in the ELEC-

TION OF 1824. In 1825 he obtained control of the (Washington, D.C.) *United States Telegraph*, which served as the semiofficial national spokesman of the Jacksonian Democrats until December, 1830, when it was replaced by the Washington *Globe* because Green vigorously advocated JOHN C. CALHOUN's cause.

During the 1830s Green was highly critical of Jackson and became a strong advocate of STATES' RIGHTS and free trade. In 1840 he founded the Baltimore *Pilot* and played an important role in getting JOHN TYLER placed on the Whig ticket. When Tyler became president the following year, he sent Green to England and France as an unofficial representative of the United States to help work out a commercial treaty; in 1844 Tyler appointed him consul to Galveston, Tex. Following the war with Mexico, Green served as an agent of the United States to that country under the terms of the Treaty of Guadalupe-Hidalgo.

An important proslavery spokesman and advocate of southern expansion, Green was not an agrarian idealist. Throughout his career he engaged in all kinds of business ventures: land speculation, banks, the development of railroads and iron and coal mines. He constantly advocated the industrialization of the South and advised the Confederate government in its financial and foreign policies.

See F. M. Green, *Journal of Southern History* (Feb., 1936) and *American Historical Review* (Jan., 1947); and Duff Green Papers, Library of Congress and University of North Carolina Library.

RICHARD E. ELLIS
University of Virginia

GREEN, FLETCHER MELVIN (1895–), a native Georgian, was educated at Emory University, the University of Chicago, and the University of North Carolina. He spent the major part of his career at the University of North Carolina, where he became Kenan Professor. Green is recognized as an authority on the South and as a superior teacher, but his productive scholarship is sometimes overlooked. It covered such diverse subjects as the American Revolution, the antebellum South, the Civil War, the post–Civil War South, general American history, social and cultural history, and business history. Green's reputation, however, rests upon his success with graduate students, who soon made places for themselves in leading southern institutions and in ranking institutions across the nation. One hundred one doctoral students and more than 150 master's students earned degrees under his direction. Within this group there developed no school of interpretation or theory of history; perhaps Green's insistence upon a search for facts and the student's freedom to interpret offer partial explanation. Consistent with his high standards, Green never used his students or their research for his own writing or to promote his own interests.

See F. M. Green, *Democracy in Old South*, ed. J. I. Copeland (1969); A. C. Howell, *Kenan Professorships* (1956); A. Link and R. Patrick (eds.), *Writing Southern History* (1965); and W. L. Stephenson, *Southern History in Making* (1964).

J. ISAAC COPELAND
University of North Carolina, Chapel Hill

GREENBACKER MOVEMENT, a political effort in the 1870s and 1880s by farmers and laborers to improve their economic condition through an inflation of the currency, took its name from the fiat paper currency issued by the Union during the Civil War. After that struggle, hard and soft money men fought over monetary policy, the hard money advocates seeking to withdraw the greenbacks, the soft money men favoring their retention. The Resumption Act of 1875 represented a compromise of sorts, but by that time debtor groups and others, suffering from the PANIC OF 1873 and devoted to the quantity theory of money, were arguing that the federal government should abolish the national banks and assume responsibility for providing the nation with an adequate volume of currency through an expanded use of paper money.

The Greenbacker movement can be traced to the National Labor Reform party of 1872, which had an inflationist plank in its platform, but the movement soon came to be dominated by agrarians. Disturbed by the Resumption Act, leaders called a convention at Cleveland in March, 1875, where the Independent (Greenback) party was organized. A nominating convention at Indianapolis in May, 1876, named philanthropist Peter Cooper of New York as the new party's presidential candidate and drafted a platform calling for the repeal of the Resumption Act and the issuance by the federal government of U.S. notes redeemable in bonds paying 3.65 percent interest. Cooper garnered only 81,737 votes, practically all of them in the Middle West. Many southerners, including such prominent figures as Georgia's John B. Gordon, were inflationists, but they chose to work within the Democratic party. Cooper, in fact, appeared on the ballot in only four southern states, where he won a mere 5,764 votes.

A Greenback-Labor party was more successful in 1878. Economic conditions remained severe and, freed from the motions of a presidential campaign, voters were more willing to support independents. Congressional candidates won over a million votes, and 15 Greenbackers, including three from the South, were elected. But this represented the high-water mark. In 1880, with indications of returning prosperity apparent, presidential candidate James B. Weaver of Iowa got 307,700 votes, a third of them in the South, while running on a platform that called for currency inflation as well as for protection of workingmen's rights, forfeiture of unearned railroad land grants, federal regulation of interstate carriers, and a graduated income tax.

The party's last appearance in national politics came in 1884, when it joined with the Anti-Monopoly party to nominate Benjamin F. Butler of Massachusetts for president. Absalom M. West of Mississippi was his running mate. Appealing more to laborers than to farmers, Butler attracted 133,825 votes, 10,228 of them in the South. Some of his labor followers went to the Union Labor party in 1888, but many of those who had supported the Greenbacker movement ultimately became POPULISTS, hoping to accomplish with silver what they had failed to do with paper money.

See T. Saloutos, *Farmer Movements* (1960); I. Unger, *Greenback Era* (1964); and C. C. Taylor, *Farmers' Movement* (1953).

ROY V. SCOTT
Mississippi State University

GREENE'S SOUTHERN CAMPAIGNS (1781–1782) were the culmination of the military career of General Nathanael Greene (1742–1786). Greene had distinguished himself at the battles of Trenton, Brandywine, and Monmouth. After Monmouth he served for two years as quartermaster general of the Continental army and for a few weeks as commandant of Fortress West Point. In the fall of 1780 he was appointed to command the American army in the Carolinas. He accepted with reluctance because the army had suffered a shattering defeat at the battle of CAMDEN. Unable to obtain adequate reinforcements, he was obliged to retreat from North Carolina into Virginia when Lord Cornwallis launched an offensive in January, 1781. Yet Greene's retreat was disastrous for Cornwallis; it drew the British far from their bases, cost them hundreds of men who succumbed to severe winter weather, and cost them 800 men killed or captured at COWPENS by a detachment of Greene's troops commanded by DANIEL MORGAN.

Upon reaching Virginia, Greene's army was

reinforced until its numbers had doubled. Greene promptly advanced into North Carolina and pursued the weakened British army. At GUILFORD COURTHOUSE he formed for battle, and Cornwallis accepted his challenge and stormed his hillside defenses. British valor carried the day, but the victors suffered such losses that they were forced to retreat to the seaport of Wilmington.

After giving his army a rest, Cornwallis led it into Virginia. Meanwhile, Greene invaded South Carolina. He fought and lost a battle at HOBKIRK'S HILL near Camden but maneuvered the British into evacuating the town. Operating in cooperation with FRANCIS MARION's militia, he captured the British posts on the Santee and Congaree rivers. But his attempt to take Ninety-six by storm was repelled. Nevertheless, the garrison evacuated their post.

Greene's next objective was to drive the British into Charleston. To that end he attacked them at EUTAW SPRINGS in September and fought a battle that resulted in heavy losses on both sides. Shortly thereafter the British withdrew into the vicinity of Charleston, and Greene was able to contain them there until they evacuated the town in December, 1782.

See G. W. Greene, *Life of N. Greene* (1871), laudatory but useful; G. W. Kyte, *North Carolina Historical Review* (July, 1960); E. Thane, *Fighting Quaker* (1972); T. Thayer, *N. Greene* (1960), excellent, scholarly; and F. and M. Wickwire, *Cornwallis* (1970).

GEORGE W. KYTE
Northern Arizona University

GREENEVILLE, TENN. (pop. 13,722), in the state's eastern mountains, was first settled in 1775 and is Tennessee's second oldest community. Named for General Nathanael Greene, the city has a history of association with separatism. It served from 1785 to 1787 as the capital of the secessionist state of FRANKLIN. Almost 75 years later, in 1861, Greeneville hosted a convention of UNIONISTS opposed to secession and in favor of separate statehood for east Tennessee. Like the town's most famous citizen ANDREW JOHNSON, most residents remained fiercely loyal to the Union throughout the Civil War. Modern Greeneville differs little from its past economic character: it is a trade center for area agriculture, a tobacco market, and the home of Tusculum College (1794). Andrew Johnson's home, his tailor shop, and his grave are maintained as national monuments.

See R. H. Doughty, *Greeneville, 1775–1875* (1975); R. S. Rankin, *East Tennessee Historical Society Publications* (1929), Tusculum; S. C. Williams, *Dawn of Tennessee* (1937); A. C. Holt, *Economic and Social Beginnings of Tennessee* (1923); and files of Greeneville *Sun* (1879–).

GREENSBORO, N.C. (pop. 144,076), in the Piedmont region of the state, was first settled in 1749. A town was not laid out, however, until 1808, when the state legislature picked the site as the new county seat for Guilford County and named the town in honor of General Nathanael Greene. Although most residents of the town and county opposed secession, Greensboro was used as a supply depot for Confederate forces throughout the Civil War. The postwar town actively promoted industrialization. Factories of the modern city produce hosiery, work clothes, textile machinery, chemicals, fertilizer, and lumber. The city also serves as headquarters for several insurance and trucking companies and as the home of the University of North Carolina at Greensboro (1891), North Carolina Agricultural and Technical College (1891), Bennett College (1873), and nearby Guilford College (1834).

See E. S. Arnett, *Greensboro* (1955); P. O. O'Keefe, *Greensboro* (1977); and files of Greensboro *Daily News* (1905–) and *Record* (1890–), both on microfilm.

GREENSBORO DAILY NEWS, when first published in 1905, was known as the *Daily Industrial News* and was the official organ of the state Republican party. Despite being one of the most modern and most cosmopolitan journals then printed in North Carolina, the paper floundered for insufficient advertising revenue. Reorganized in 1909 as the *Daily News*, it became politically independent in 1911. Since then it has maintained a moderately liberal viewpoint in politics and has developed a circulation of approximately 80,000 copies daily throughout the state's north-central Piedmont.

See D. C. Roller, "Greensboro *Daily Industrial News*" (M.A. thesis, Duke, 1962); complete run of bound volumes, University of North Carolina and Duke libraries; and microfilm (1909–), from Bell & Howell.

GREEN SPRING, BATTLE OF (July 6, 1781), occurred near Jamestown, Va. The day before, the marquis de Lafayette sent Anthony Wayne to scout ahead with 500 troops. The British commander, Lord Cornwallis, fed Wayne false information that the main British force had already crossed the James River, leaving only a small detachment behind. Meanwhile, Cornwallis chose an extremely advantageous position with ponds on his right, a morass on his left, and swampy woodland in his front, connected to Green Spring Farm only by a narrow causeway. After two hours of skirmishing, Wayne sustained a charge by overwhelming numbers, suffering 145 casualties to the British 75. Darkness prevented Cornwallis from sending cavalry in pursuit.

See F. and M. Wickwire, *Cornwallis* (1970); H. E. Wildes, *Anthony Wayne* (1941); L. Gottschalk, *Lafayette* (1942); H. P. Johnston, *Yorktown Campaign* (1881); and C. Ward, *War of Revolution* (1952).

MARY B. WICKWIRE
University of Massachusetts, Amherst

GREENVILLE, MISS. (pop. 39,648), is approximately 50 miles west of Greenwood on the Mississippi River. It remained relatively undeveloped until after the Civil War, when LEVEES first permitted extensive farming. It was incorporated in 1870 and grew as a river port and a market for cotton growers of the Yazoo delta region. After the great flood of 1927, Lake Ferguson was created by a cutoff of the river. It remains primarily a cotton processing and shipping center, noted as the hometown of both WILLIAM ALEXANDER PERCY and HODDING CARTER.

See files of Greenville *Delta Democrat-Times* (1888–), on microfilm; W. A. Percy, *Lanterns on Levee* (1941); H. Carter, *Where Main Street Meets River* (1953); W. McCain and C. Capers (eds.), *Memoirs of Henry T. Ireys* (1954); and B. Keating, *History of Washington County* (forthcoming).

GREENVILLE, N.C. (pop. 29,063), founded in 1786 and named to honor General Nathanael Greene, is in the eastern portion of the state on the Tar River. It always has served as a market for area agriculture and, since the Civil War, primarily as a market for bright leaf TOBACCO. The state normal school established here in 1907 has grown into East Carolina University.

See H. T. King, *Sketches of Pitt County, 1704–1910* (1911); and files of Greenville *Reflector* (1882–), on microfilm.

GREENVILLE, S.C. (pop. 61,208), near the Blue Ridge Mountains, originally was part of the CHEROKEE INDIAN lands ceded to South Carolina in 1777. Twenty years later Lemuel J. Alston laid out the town of Pleasantburg on this site, and in 1831 it was renamed Greenville. Besides being a market town for area agriculture and, after 1835, a railroad depot, the antebellum community was popular among lowland planters' families as a summer resort. Residents opposed secession in 1860 and made Greenville an island of Unionist sentiment in the state. After the Civil War the city grew rapidly into a major manufacturer of textiles and a processor of foodstuffs and lumber, activities that it continues to this day. The city is the home of FURMAN UNIVERSITY (1825) and Bob Jones University (1927).

See files of Greenville *Piedmont* (1829–) and *News* (1874–), both on microfilm.

GREGG, WILLIAM (1800–1867), was a prosperous jewelry merchant in Columbia, S.C., who retired from his business when he saw the advantages manufacturing could bring to the South. After touring New England textile plants in 1844, he used the columns of the CHARLESTON NEWS AND COURIER to encourage southerners to give up their cotton culture and adopt manufacturing to modernize their region and help the poor whites. In 1845 Gregg was granted a charter to incorporate the Graniteville Manufacturing Company in the Horse Creek Valley, and he served (without pay) as president, chief engineer, and general manager. Following the Lowell model, he established a total factory community over which he exercised a constant and benevolent paternalism. When the Civil War broke out, Gregg hoped the South would diversify its economy and support local industry. To his great disappointment, the Confederacy failed to encourage the construction of new factories and imported foreign goods instead. Graniteville survived the war intact, and in spite of hard times Gregg made plans for increased postwar production. After 20 years' service he retired from the presidency of Graniteville in April, 1867.

See W. Gregg, *Essays on Domestic Industry* (1845); B. Mitchell, *William Gregg* (1928); and T. P. Martin, *Advent of William Gregg* (1945).

THOMAS H. O'CONNOR
Boston College

GRIERSON'S RAID (April 17–May 2, 1863) was the most successful of the three diversions General U. S. Grant undertook in April, 1863. These were calculated to divert General JOHN C. PEMBERTON's attention from the march of Grant's columns south from Milliken's Bend, La., to the Mississippi 30 miles south of Vicksburg. The raid's initial success was assured by thrusts that pinned down Confederate forces in northwest Mississippi and northwest Alabama.

Colonel Benjamin H. Grierson headed south from La Grange, Tenn., into Mississippi on April 17 with three cavalry regiments and a six-gun battery, 1,700 raiders in all. His orders were to cut the east-west railroad linking Vicksburg with Meridian. On April 21 one regiment was detached and sent east to raid the north-south Mobile & Ohio Railroad. It failed to break up the railroad, but, in returning to La Grange, it was pursued by the Confederate cavalry posted in northeast Mississippi. His way cleared, Grierson thundered deeper into Mississippi.

On April 24 the raiders entered Newton Station, on the east-west railroad. Rolling stock, bridges, trestles, and track were destroyed. Grierson pushed on, turning his column southwest. The New Orleans, Jackson & Great Northern Railroad was cut at Hazlehurst on the twenty-seventh. Intercepted by Confederate cavalry at Union Church, Grierson headed southeast and then south. Pursued by converging Confederate forces, he overwhelmed a southern roadblock at Wall's Bridge and reached Baton Rouge, La., on May 2.

Grierson's success should not be measured in the 500 miles traveled or the physical damage to communication lines, which was quickly repaired. Its importance was disruption of the dispositions Pemberton was making to oppose Grant's crossing of the Mississippi. Pemberton's strategic reserve, assembling at Big Black Bridge, was scattered in ill-conceived efforts to destroy the raiders. Cavalry, watching the Mississippi, was sent in pursuit. For five critical days, April 24–28, General Pemberton all but ignored Grant's army, massing to cross the Mississippi, and focused his energy on Grierson.

See D. Brown, *Grierson's Raid* (1954); *Official Records, Armies*, Ser. 1, Vol. XXIV; S. A. Forbes, *Illinois State Historical Society Transactions* (1907); R. W. Surby, *Grierson's Raids* (1865); and L. B. Pierce, *History of Second Iowa Cavalry* (1865).

EDWIN C. BEARSS
National Park Service

GRIMKÉ, SARAH (1792–1873) and ANGELINA

(1805–1879), as daughters of the prominent Charleston judge John Faucheraud Grimké, grew up in the most advantaged circumstances in a mature slave society. Conversion to Quakerism and an unorthodox aversion to slavery caused them to move to Philadelphia as young adults, Sarah in 1821 and Angelina in 1829. Dismayed by the violence that greeted the oratory of William Lloyd Garrison, Theodore D. Weld, and other abolitionists, Angelina Grimké wrote a letter of encouragement to Garrison on August 30, 1835, which he reprinted in the *Liberator*. That letter and her *Appeal to the Christian Women of the Southern States* (1836) catapulted Angelina to the front ranks of the abolitionist movement. Sarah Grimké fol-

lowed with *An Epistle to the Clergy of the Southern States* (1836). The sisters began lecturing against slavery in December, 1836. For the next 18 months, Angelina's oratorical power and the sisters' unique background made them the most interesting antislavery speakers in New England. In the Garrisonian spirit, they attacked prejudice even among their coworkers. Although they fervently criticized race prejudice, their resistance to restraints on women had a more immediate impact. In her *Letters on the Equality of the Sexes* (1837), Sarah Grimké identified the attempts to constrain women's public activities with the slaveholding mentality.

With Angelina Grimké's marriage to Theodore Weld on May 14, 1838, however, the sisters ceased lecturing. In their last public attack on slavery until the Civil War, they joined Weld in the preparation of *Slavery As It Is* (1839). The Grimké sisters' withdrawal from public activity left to a new generation the organization of the women's rights movement, but the sisters continued to support this crusade through correspondence and Angelina's membership on the central committee. The public careers of the Grimké sisters thus revealed the intertwining of the antislavery and early feminist movements.

See G. Lerner, *Grimké Sisters* (1967); K. D. P. Lumpkin, *Angelina Grimké* (1974), does not supersede Lerner; G. H. Barnes and D. L. Dumond (eds.), *Weld-Grimké Letters, 1822–1844* (2 vols.; 1934, 1970); Weld-Grimké Collection, Clements Library, University of Michigan; A. S. Kraditor, *American Abolitionism* (1967); C. Birney, *Grimké Sisters* (1885); and B. P. Thomas, *Theodore D. Weld* (1950).

WILBERT H. AHERN
University of Minnesota, Morris

GROVEY V. TOWNSEND (295 U.S. 45 [1935]).

The 1927 and 1932 NIXON decisions invalidated exclusion of black voters from Texas Democratic primaries by state law or by party action under legislative authorization. However, the CIVIL RIGHTS CASES (1883) had held the Fourteenth Amendment inapplicable to private discrimination. Therefore the Texas Democratic state convention declared the party a private group limited to whites. Richard Randolph Grovey, a black, sued the Harris County clerk for refusal of an absentee ballot. The U.S. Supreme Court dismissed the action, thereby temporarily legalizing the WHITE PRIMARY. Justice Owen J. Roberts cited *Bell* v. *Hill*, 74 S.W. 113 (1934), in which the supreme court of Texas held Texas' Democratic party "a voluntary political association" that could define its membership. The plaintiff argued that exclusion from primaries that were tantamount to election rendered his vote in the formal election "insignificant and useless"; but Justice Roberts distinguished "private" primaries from general elections, which were state functions. In SMITH V. ALLWRIGHT (1944), however, the Court reversed this decision, holding Texas primaries integral parts of the electoral process and subject to the Fifteenth Amendment's nondiscriminatory requirements.

See *U.S. v. Classic*, 313 U.S. 299 (1941); and, overturning efforts to revive the white primary, *Rice v. Elmore*, 165 F.2d (5th Cir. 1947); *Brown v. Baskin*, 78 F. Supp. 933 (1948); and *Terry v. Adams*, 345 U.S. 631 (1953). See also *Shepard's U.S. Citations*; *Shepard's Southern Reporter Citations*; *Index to Legal Periodicals*; H. J. Abraham, *Freedom and Court* (1972); R. Bardolph (ed.), *Civil Rights Record* (1970); R. J. Harris, *Quest for Equality* (1960); V. O. Key, Jr., *Southern Politics* (1949); and J. W. Peltason, *Federal Courts in Political Process* (1955).

KEMP P. YARBOROUGH
Texas Woman's University

GRUNDY, FELIX (1777–1840), Democratic statesman of the Upper South, was born in western Virginia. His family moved to Kentucky in 1780. After admission to the Kentucky bar in 1795, Grundy served as commonwealth's attorney (1796–1806) and state legislator (1800–1802). In 1807 he became chief justice of the Kentucky supreme court. Shortly thereafter he moved to Nashville, Tenn., where he began the practice of criminal law. Elected to Congress (1811–1814), Grundy sat on the House Foreign Relations Committee. He advocated land preparations for war with Great Britain and the conquest of Canada, but his views in private were more moderate than his public reputation as a war hawk indicated. Resigning from Congress in 1814, he returned to Tennessee advocating debtor relief after the PANIC OF 1819. Beginning in 1822 he supported Andrew Jackson's candidacy for the presidency. Although related to John C. Calhoun by marriage, by 1833 he opposed Calhoun in the NULLIFICATION crisis, thus repudiating his support of Calhoun's ideas in 1830. Appointed to a vacancy in the U.S. Senate in 1829, he was reelected in 1833, where he defended Jackson's policies concerning patronage and the Bank of the United States. Martin Van Buren appointed him U.S. attorney general in 1838, but Grundy resigned in 1839 to become U.S. senator from Tennessee. Exhausting himself while campaigning for Van Buren in the ELECTION OF 1840, he died shortly after Benjamin Harrison's victory. A man of shifting views, he was typical of many Jacksonian leaders.

See H. Parks, *Felix Grundy* (1940), authoritative; Grundy Papers, University of North Carolina Library, Chapel Hill; and C. G. Sellers, Jr., *Eastern Tennessee Historical Society Publications* (1953).

KENNETH W. KELLER
Ohio State University, Marion

GUILFORD COURTHOUSE, BATTLE OF (March 15, 1781). Nathanael Greene positioned his mostly untested troops (1,670 Continentals; 2,750 militiamen) around Guilford Courthouse, N.C., in three lines with militia in the first and second and Continentals in the third. Lord Cornwallis confidently moved his 1,900 veteran soldiers to the battlefield, and two British brigades attacked across an open field routing the North Carolina militia. Effective fire from William Washington's and Henry Lee's legions on the flanks temporarily halted the attack. Cornwallis committed his reserves against the second line, manned by Virginia militia who offered resistance but were driven back. The British attack against the third line was stopped by the capable 1st Maryland Regiment and Robert Kirkwood's Delaware Company, followed by a bayonet attack that momentarily confused the British advance. Two subsequent attacks on the third line and counterattacks by the Continentals brought heavy British casualties. Had Greene known how badly Cornwallis was crippled, he might have continued the battle and won a victory. Not wishing to risk his army, Greene ordered a withdrawal, leaving Cornwallis in control. Without provisions and after the loss of one-fourth of his army (143 killed, 389 wounded), Cornwallis left for Wilmington. Although Greene lost the battle and suffered 261 killed and wounded, he won the campaign (GREENE'S SOUTHERN CAMPAIGN).

See M. F. Treacy, *Prelude to Yorktown* (1963), provocative; C. Ward, *Revolution* (1952), II, and *Delaware Continentals* (1941), good descriptive chapters; G. W. Greene, *Life of N. Greene* (1871), III; D. Higginbotham, *American Independence* (1971), interpretative; W. M. Wallace, *Appeal to Arms* (1951), brief; B. Davis, *Cowpens-Guilford Campaign* (1962), popular; H. Lee, *Memoirs* (1812), first-hand account; and B. Tarleton, *Campaigns of 1780 and 1781* (1787), British side.

JAMES H. EDMONSON
Union University, Jackson, Tenn.

GULF COAST HISTORY AND HUMANITIES CONFERENCE (c/o John C. Pace, Librarian, University of West Florida, Pensacola, Fla. 32504) was founded in 1969, meets every 18 months with about 250 in attendance, and publishes its proceedings after each meeting. No articles are solicited except for those papers presented at the meetings. Support for the conference rests with the University of West Florida, Pensacola Junior College, Escambia County School Board, and the Historical Pensacola Preservation Board. The society is interested in the history and "humanities" of the Gulf Coast "from Florida to Texas" and in 1974 received an award from the American Association for State and Local History for achievement in the area of local history. Typical conference topics have been "In Search of Gulf Coast Colonial History," "Indians of the Lower South," and "The Cultural Legacy of the Gulf Coast, 1870–1940."

GULFPORT, MISS. (pop. 40,791), 12 miles west of Biloxi, is a deepwater port and year-round resort on the Gulf of Mexico. The site was picked in 1887 to be the Gulf terminus of the Gulf & Ship Island Railway. First settled four years later, it was incorporated as a town in 1898 and as a city in 1904. By 1911, it was shipping more yellow pine than any other port in the world. Although the lumber supplies have long since been exhausted, the state-owned port now ships cotton and seafood while importing minerals and bananas, in 1974 handling more than 800,000 tons of goods. Portions of the city were hard hit by the devastating hurricane Camille in 1969, but the area has come back strongly.

See W. H. Hardy, *No Compromise with Principle* (1946), by a railroad builder and city founder; M. B. Rowe, *Captain Jones* (1942), biography of a founder; J. Lang, *History of Harrison County* (1936); and files of Biloxi-Gulfport *Daily Herald* (1898–), on microfilm.

GULLAH NEGROES are those blacks of the Georgia and South Carolina SEA ISLANDS and TIDEWATER area who hold to and preserve relatively distinctive cultural traditions. The Sea Islands in particular have long been populated by a black majority: in 1840 there were roughly nine black slaves in the Georgetown district for every white resident. Moreover, lacking any bridges to the mainland until after World War I, the islands have been especially remote and isolated from the cultural influences of modernism. Consequently the Gullahs' language, culture, and way of life retain numerous Africanisms and many survivals from slavery. The origin of the name itself appears to be a survival derived either from the word Angola or from a Liberian tribe known as the Gola or the Gora. Although the dialect spoken by these people also is often referred to as Gullah, it sometimes is described as Geechee, a name probably taken from the nearby Ogeechee River.

See L. D. Turner, *Africanisms in Gullah Dialect* (1949, 1969); M. Crum, *Gullah* (1940, 1968); G. Carawan and C. Carawan, *Ain't You Got a Right* (1966); P. Conroy, *Water Is Wide* (1972); and J. Jackson *et al.*, *Black Scholar* (March, 1974).

GUMBO (or gombo) is the Bantu African name for okra. The term is used particularly in and around Louisiana with a variety of meanings. A gumbo may be a thick soup made with a variety of ingredients (often crawfish and crabmeat) but always including quantities of the vegetable giving the stew its name. Gumbo also was used to refer to a runaway slave, any black, or a person of French and Indian ancestry. A dialect that is a patois of French, Spanish, and African languages may also be called gumbo.

GUTHRIE, JAMES (1792–1869), born in Bardstown, Ky., was elected to the lower house of the Kentucky legislature in 1827, then to the state senate in 1831. In 1841 he retired from political office to devote himself to his already growing business interests. Chosen secretary of the treasury in 1853, Guthrie was demanding and mildly reformist, though abrasive and unpopular. He concentrated on his department and had little impact on the national policies of the PIERCE ADMINISTRATION. After 1857, Guthrie built up the moribund Louisville & Nashville Railroad, which under his management during the Civil War was crucial to Union success in the western theater. He favored sectional compromise in 1860–1861 and supported Kentucky's effort at neutrality. His conversion to unionism came less from political conviction than from economic necessity. As a U.S. senator (1865–1868), he was an active supporter of ANDREW JOHNSON.

See R. S. Cotterill, *American Historical Review* (July, 1924); K. Herr, *Louisville and Nashville* (1943); A. Nevins, *Ordeal of Union* (1947–71); R. F. Nichols, *Franklin Pierce* (1958); and Guthrie Manuscripts, Filson Club, Louisville. A full-scale biography is needed.

RICHARD S. CRAMER
San Jose State University

GWIN, WILLIAM McKENDREE (1805–1885), born in Sumner County, Tenn., was trained in law and then earned a medical degree at Transylvania College. Moving to Mississippi, he practiced medicine at Clinton and Vicksburg. In 1833 Andrew Jackson appointed him U.S. marshal for the southern district of Mississippi. Elected to the U.S. House of Representatives in 1840, he served one term and was appointed commissioner of public works at New Orleans in 1846. He also advised James K. Polk on political matters in the Mexican Cession and speculated in Texas lands. In 1848 Gwin sought political opportunity in California, expecting the gold discovery to make it a state. He was chief architect of the California constitution of 1849, and in 1850 the legislature elected him to the U.S. Senate. Serving until 1861, Gwin directed the "chivalry" wing of California's divided Democratic party in opposition to David C. Broderick, who led its "northern" faction. Senator Gwin aided his adopted state in acquiring a branch mint and Mare Island navy yard. An expansionist, he pristinely exhorted the purchase of Alaska. During the Civil War he intrigued to establish a French protectorate in Sonora, Mexico, to be settled by southerners. When his plans failed, he returned to the United States and was imprisoned. After his release and an exile in France, he returned to California in 1868. He died in obscurity in New York.

See L. Thomas, *Between Two Empires* (1969), useful but partially inaccurate; J. O'Meara, *Broderick and Gwin* (1881); H. M. McPherson, "William M. Gwin" (Ph.D. dissertation, University of California, 1931); W. H. Ellison, *California Historical Society Quarterly* (March–Dec., 1940); and E. J. Coleman, *Overland Monthly* (May, 1891).

BENJAMIN F. GILBERT
San Jose State University

H

HABERSHAM FAMILY was significant in the commercial and political development of Savannah, Ga. Its progenitor, James Habersham (1715–1775), accompanied George Whitefield from England to Savannah in 1738 as a missionary-schoolteacher. Subsequently he entered a Savannah-Charleston shipping partnership to obtain adequate supplies for Bethesda Orphanage in the commercially insecure trustee colony. Prosperity of this business venture led him into planting and politics. In the 1750s he became senior councilor; from 1771 to 1773 he served as acting governor.

In 1742 Habersham married Mary Bolton of Philadelphia. Three sons of this union had reached maturity when the Revolution began. Habersham remained a Loyalist, but his son Joseph (1751–1815) led the Liberty Boys. By 1775 all three sons promoted the patriot cause after their father's death. Joseph and John (1754–1799) became officers in the Georgia Battalion and James, Jr. (1745–1799), became an assemblyman. During the Confederation era, the Habershams supported, in state assembly and Congress, a stronger union. In 1788 Joseph helped draft Georgia's approval of the Constitution; later he accepted an appointment from George Washington as postmaster general, a position he held until Thomas Jefferson's removal of Federalists.

Joseph survived his brothers into the nineteenth century and revived the Habersham name in Savannah commerce. His offspring and those of his brothers were prominent in business and planting throughout the new century. Robert Habersham & Company became synonymous with Savannah's import-export trade, and the firm of Alexander Wylly Habersham developed tea and coffee importation into Baltimore. No family members bearing the Habersham name remain as merchants in Savannah in the twentieth century, but descendants from intermarriage with other prominent families exist throughout the Southeast.

See J. G. B. Bulloch, *History and Genealogy* (1901); W. C. Smith, "Georgia Gentlemen" (Ph.D. dissertation, University of North Carolina, 1971); W. B. Stevens, *Georgia Historical Quarterly* (Dec., 1919); Georgia Historical Society, *Collections* (1840ff.); C. C. Jones, *Bio-graphical Sketches* (1891); W. B. Stevens, *Georgia* (1859); and U. B. Phillips, *Georgia Historical Quarterly* (June, 1926).

W. CALVIN SMITH
University of South Carolina, Aiken

HADLEY, HERBERT SPENCER (1872–1927), was reared in a prosperous Unionist Kansas family. He graduated from Kansas University (1892) and Northwestern Law School (1894) before settling in Kansas City (1894). Combining oratory, legal imagination, and political expertise with Republican devotion, he was appointed assistant city counselor (1898) and elected prosecuting attorney (1900). Elected attorney general (1904), he won national prominence for his successful prosecutions of Standard Oil, International Harvester, and Missouri's lumber, fire insurance, and railroad companies. He was elected governor (1909–1913). Democratic legislators defeated his Progressive proposals, but Hadley publicized them for future elections. He also promoted Ozark development and reformed prisons and police. Retiring from active politics, he returned to private practice in Kansas City (1913–1917) and served as professor of law at Colorado University (1917–1923) and chancellor of Washington University, St. Louis (1923–1927). Hadley's PROGRESSIVISM was essentially legalistic. He prosecuted the rich (like corporation managers) and powerful (like policemen), emphasized rehabilitation instead of punishment, and promoted criminal law reform in the 1920s.

See L. E. Worner, "Hadley" (Ph.D. dissertation, University of Missouri, 1946); H. T. Long, "Hadley" (M.A. thesis, University of Missouri, 1939) and *Missouri Historical Review* (Jan., 1941); H. Hahn, *Missouri Historical Review* (July, 1965); and Hadley Papers, University of Missouri, Columbia.

DAVID P. THELEN
University of Missouri, Columbia

HAGERSTOWN, MD. (pop. 35,862), in the Cumberland Valley, is approximately 55 miles east of Cumberland. It is located in the midst of a rich agricultural area, which also produces slate and limestone, and its factories manufacture aircraft parts, truck engines, shoes, clothing, sheet metal, and fertilizers. The town was first settled in 1740 on the property of Jonathan Hager and was laid out in 1762 as Elizabeth Town, named for Hager's wife. It was renamed in 1814. Although the town was not directly engaged in any battles of the Civil War, after ANTIETAM over 5,000 Confederate dead were buried here.

See T. J. C. Williams, *History of Washington County* (2 vols.; 1906); J. T. Scharf, *History of Western Maryland* (2 vols.; 1882); H. C. Bell, *History of Leitersburg District* (1898); and files of Hagerstown *Mail* (1828–), *Maryland Herald* (1802–25), *Torch Light* (1821–1906), *Herald of Freedom* (1839–51), and *Herald* (1873–), all on microfilm.

HAGOOD, JOHNSON (1829–1898), the son of South Carolina planter aristocrats, was an alumnus of The Citadel (1847) who studied law under Judge Edmund Bellinger of Charleston. During the Civil War, he served as a colonel at FT. SUMTER and at the first battle of BULL RUN. Promoted brigadier general in July, 1862, he fought in the WILDERNESS CAMPAIGN and in the battles of WELDON RAILROAD and Petersburg, losing almost two-thirds of his men in 63 days of the latter engagement. After the war he was a scientific farmer and the president of the state agriculture society (1869–1872). Elected state comptroller general in 1876 and 1878, he owed his nomination and election as governor in 1880 largely to his association with WADE HAMPTON. While governor, Hagood continued Hampton's assurances of political and civil rights for blacks. He supported government regulation of railroads, but he did nothing to anger conservative leaders. His was a governorship of unobtrusive conduct. He declined reelection and retired to Barnwell, his plantation. Although he assisted Hampton against BEN TILLMAN in 1890, Hagood remained aloof from politics except to serve for 14 years as a trustee of The Citadel and twice as chairman of the state board of agriculture. Considered haughty and cold, a calculating incisive thinker, he had "few positive ideas on anything."

See W. J. Cooper, Jr., *Conservative Regime* (1968), best; Elliott-Gonzales Papers, University of North Carolina Library, for personality; C. A. Evans (ed.), *Conference of Military History* (1899), V; A. B. Williams, *Hampton* (1935); D. D. Wallace, *History of South Carolina* (1934); and M. W. Gary Papers, Duke Library.

DAVID W. BISHOP
North Carolina Central University

HAHN, MICHAEL (1830–1886), lawyer, editor, Unionist war governor of Louisiana, and congressman, was born in Bavaria, Germany; his family settled in New Orleans about 1840. After graduating from the University of Louisiana in law, he began practice in 1851. He was a Democrat but opposed JOHN SLIDELL's faction. An adherent of Stephen A. Douglas in 1860, after the election he canvassed the state against secession. When federal troops occupied New Orleans, he immediately took the oath of allegiance and in December, 1862, was elected as a Unionist to the U.S. House of Representatives. The Free-State party elected him governor in February, 1864; he resigned in March, 1865, to enter the U.S. Senate but was not seated. A newspaper editor and sugar planter, he was a state legislator (1872–1876), state registrar of voters (1876), superintendent of the United States Mint in New Orleans (1878), and a district judge (1879–1885). In 1884 he was elected as a Republican to the U.S. House of Representatives but died during his term.

See J. G. Taylor, *Louisiana Reconstructed* (1974); and W. M. Caskey, *Secession and Restoration of Louisiana* (1938).

NORMAN D. BROWN
University of Texas, Austin

HALL, LYMAN (1724–1790), was the only Georgian elected to the First Continental Congress and one of three Georgia congressmen to vote for the DECLARATION OF INDEPENDENCE. Born in Connecticut, Hall studied theology at Yale. He later moved to South Carolina and eventually to Georgia, where he settled among Puritans at Sunbury and instituted a medical practice. Although elected to Congress in 1774, he refused to attend since he represented only one parish. Nevertheless, he was elected to five additional terms. The Georgia assembly elected Hall governor in 1783. His administration was notable chiefly for the attention he devoted—without immediate success—to the establishment of an educational system. By the end of his term a college had been chartered, trustees selected, and land for the school acquired. But the UNIVERSITY OF GEORGIA did not commence classes until 1801, more than a decade following Hall's death.

See C. C. Jones, *Biographical Sketches of Delegates from Georgia to Continental Congress* (1891); and K. Coleman, *American Revolution in Georgia* (1958).

JOHN FERLING
West Georgia College

HAM, MORDECAI FOWLER (1877–1961), was an itinerant Protestant EVANGELIST of BAPTIST membership who is best known for being the preacher in the service at which BILLY GRAHAM was converted in 1934. Born in Allen County, Ky., he made the Louisville area his headquarters. He conducted hundreds of revival campaigns between 1903 and 1941, almost all in the South. His most notable successes came in Texas and Oklahoma (1911–1919), in Kentucky and Tennessee (1907, 1920–1921), and in the Carolinas, Virginia, and Georgia (1908, 1922–1925). Following in the tradition of "modern revivalism" with Charles G. Finney, Dwight L. Moody, and Billy Sunday, his crusades featured advance planning, modern advertising and organization, and the use of an evangelistic song leader. Theologically, Ham was premillenial, biblically literalist, and doctrinally scholastic. Among the objects of his vigorous attacks were dancing, drinking, modernistic biblical interpretation (EVOLUTION CONTROVERSY), and the Antidefamation League. In his late years he carried on an extensive radio broadcast ministry.

See E. E. Ham, *M. F. Ham* (1950); and E. E. Ham (ed.), *Sermons That Brought Revival by M. F. Ham* (1950).

SAMUEL S. HILL, JR.
University of Florida

HAMBURG RACE RIOT (July 8, 1876). This event might more appropriately be termed a massacre. It grew out of the campaign of white Democrats, the so-called Conservatives, to wrest control of South Carolina from the Reconstruction government of Governor DANIEL H. CHAMBERLAIN. As part of the campaign, "rifle" and "saber" clubs were employed to nullify the black vote by terrorizing blacks. In response, the dormant militia unit of Hamburg, a nearly all-black town close to the Georgia border, was reactivated, and 80 men began drilling with firearms. Whites, led by former Confederate general MATTHEW C. BUTLER, demanded that blacks give up their arms and apologize for their behavior. The blacks refused and retreated to their armory. Military club units from the surrounding area streamed into town and that night attacked the armory, using cannon fire to overcome and capture the defenders. The town itself was sacked, and more prisoners were taken. Some captured black leaders were killed in cold blood, and others were saved by Georgians present who took them over the border to jail. On the way to the local county jail, the remaining prisoners were ordered to run, whereupon the whites fired into them. The number of casualties is not known. Outrage in the North was so strong that the GRANT ADMINISTRATION felt compelled to send troops into South Carolina, and white terrorism

was curbed temporarily. It was not eliminated. Among other reasons, the army had too few troops to enforce the laws.

See J. Williamson, *After Slavery* (1965); and G. B. Tindall, *South Carolina Negroes* (1952).

ROBERT CRUDEN
Lewis and Clark College

HAMILTON, ANDREW JACKSON (1815–1875), Civil War southern UNIONIST and first Reconstruction governor of Texas, was born and reared in Alabama. During the 1840s, he moved to Texas, eventually settling in Austin where he became a widely renowned lawyer, orator, and Democratic politician. Hamilton went to Congress in 1859 as an opponent of extreme proslavery Democrats and in time sided with SAM HOUSTON in opposition to Texas' secession. In 1862 Abraham Lincoln appointed him military governor of Texas with orders to reestablish federal authority in the state. However, Union campaigns, in which he had a role, failed to win control of the Rio Grande Valley or east Texas. After the war, President Andrew Johnson appointed Hamilton provisional governor of Texas, and, though he later broke with Johnson to become a Republican, he was regarded as a conservative on racial questions. He sought the Republican nomination for governor in 1869 but lost to E. J. Davis. During these years, he promoted railroad building, served on the Texas supreme court, and was a delegate to the Republican National Convention in 1868.

See J. L. Waller, *A. J. Hamilton* (1968), full but uncritical; W. P. Webb and H. B. Carroll, *Handbook of Texas* (2 vols.; 1952); B. H. Procter, *John H. Reagan* (1962); and J. H. Reagan, *Memoirs* (1968).

KENNETH B. SHOVER
University of Texas, El Paso

HAMILTON, JAMES (1786–1857), planter, businessman, and politician, served as governor of South Carolina (1830–1832) and president of the state's nullification convention. A nationalist congressman (1822–1829), Hamilton later became an ardent defender of an extreme states' rights position and was an influential force in organizing popular backing for NULLIFICATION within the state. Frequently a supporter of JOHN C. CALHOUN, Hamilton nonetheless maintained an independent course, breaking with his more distinguished associate over the banking issue after the PANIC OF 1837. In the 1840s, however, Hamilton strongly pushed Calhoun's bid for the presidency. An early proponent of Texas independence,

Hamilton became politically and economically involved and even represented the short-lived Texas republic in Europe. Witty, captivating, impetuous, and an accomplished political intriguer, Hamilton fell deeply into debt in the 1830s as a result of his speculations, and he spent his last years attempting to recoup his fortune.

See W. Freehling, *Prologue to War* (1966); L. White, *Robert Barnwell Rhett* (1965); J. F. Jameson (ed.), *American Historical Association Annual Report* (1899), II; and C. S. Boucher and R. P. Brooks, *American Historical Association Annual Report* (1929).

JAMES ROGER SHARP
Syracuse University

HAMILTON, JOSEPH GRÉGOIRE DE ROULHAC (1878–1961), was born in Hillsboro, N.C., and educated at the University of the South (M.A., 1900) and Columbia University (Ph.D., 1906). He joined the history department of the University of North Carolina at Chapel Hill in 1906, serving as chairman (1908–1930) and Kenan Professor from 1920 until retirement in 1948. *Reconstruction in North Carolina* (1914), best known of 30 books he wrote or edited, secured Hamilton's reputation as a leading member of the Dunning school of RECONSTRUCTION HISTORIOGRAPHY. His most enduring achievement, however, was building the Southern Historical Collection, which he founded in 1930 and directed until retirement, into a great research repository of more than 3 million private manuscripts covering every aspect of southern history. He personally collected many of them, driving a half-million miles and, clad in overalls, searching dusty attics and musty cellars. Edward Weeks, editor of *Atlantic Monthly,* described Hamilton as "the most famous explorer of manuscripts in North America," and Allan Nevins correctly said, "All historians have reason to be grateful to Dr. Hamilton."

See A. C. Howell, *Kenan Professorships* (1956); and Hamilton Papers, University of North Carolina Library.

ORVILLE W. TAYLOR
Georgia College

HAMMOND, JAMES HENRY (1807–1864), was born in Newberry District, S.C. Soon after graduating from South Carolina College in 1825, he entered politics as a nullificationist. Upon marrying an heiress in June, 1831, he moved to her plantation on the Savannah River and became a successful planter. Elected to the U.S. House of Representatives in 1834, Hammond served for two months. Following a tour of Europe to restore his

health, he became a candidate for governor, was elected in 1842, and served a two-year term. A personal scandal caused him to retire to the plantation, where he occupied his time practicing scientific agriculture, carrying on an extensive correspondence, attacking the state bank, and writing a widely reprinted defense of slavery, in which he called it a positive good and the very cornerstone of republican government. He was a delegate to the NASHVILLE CONVENTION in 1850 and was elected to the U.S. Senate in 1857, where he proved to be a moderate, believing that no other state would support South Carolina if it were to secede alone. On November 11, 1860, he resigned. Poor health did not permit him to serve the Confederacy actively. An intelligent man who was both egotistical and insecure, Hammond was a political and social leader and patriotic South Carolinian who is best remembered for his strong defense of slavery.

See R. C. Tucker, "James Henry Hammond" (Ph.D. dissertation, University of North Carolina, 1958); E. Merritt, *James Henry Hammond, 1807–1864* (1923); and J. H. Hammond Papers (1823–75), Library of Congress, and (1795–1935), University of South Carolina Library.

ROBERT C. TUCKER
Furman University

HAMMOND, SAMUEL (1757–1842), was born in Richmond County, Va. After volunteering for DUNMORE'S WAR and a Cherokee expedition, he became a Revolutionary hero at the sieges of Savannah and Augusta, the fall of Charleston, and the battles of Cedar Springs, Musgrove's Mills, KINGS MOUNTAIN, COWPENS, and EUTAW SPRINGS. After the Revolution he pursued a long public career, interspersed with private ventures. In Georgia (1781–1804) he commanded militia against the CREEKS and served as state legislator, surveyor general, commissioner, and congressman. In 1805 he moved to St. Louis and assumed the post of colonel commandant of the district of Louisiana. During his Missouri residency he accumulated considerable property and served as a bank president, judge, president of the territorial legislative council, land office receiver, and temporary president, Missouri constitutional convention. After moving to South Carolina in 1824, he was arrested (1825) for defaulting (offering repudiated bank notes to the treasury while receiver). Released on bond he disposed of his Missouri property to satisfy his obligations. Exonerated, he served South Carolina as surveyor general and secretary of state before retiring in 1835 to his beloved Varello Farm near Hamburg, S.C.

See "Memoir," in J. Johnson, *Traditions and Reminiscences* (1851); C. E. Carter (ed.), *Territorial Papers* (1939, 1948–51), VII, XIII–XV, indispensable; S. M. Drumm, *Missouri Historical Society Collection* (1923), IV, best article; Charleston *Courier* (Sept. 27, 1842; June 21, 1859); F. C. Shoemaker, *Missouri Struggle for Statehood* (1916); and L. C. Draper, *King's Mountain* (1881).

JOHN L. HARR
Northwest Missouri State University

HAMMOND, WILLIAM ALEXANDER (1828–

1900), was born at Annapolis, Md. Shortly after graduating in medicine from New York City University in 1848, he entered the U.S. Army Medical Department. He resigned in 1860 to become a professor in the University of Maryland Medical School, but in 1861 reentered the army. His reformist attitudes won the attention of the U.S. Sanitary Commission, whose officers were dissatisfied with the management of the Medical Department. Early in 1862, through the commission's influence, he was appointed surgeon general, going at one jump from lieutenant to brigadier general. Many who were passed over were affronted. Hammond reorganized the department considerably. His brusque banning of calomel from the army enraged many doctors. His most powerful enemy, War Secretary Edwin Stanton, brought him to a court-martial and dismissal (1864). Hammond then practiced and taught psychiatry and neurology in New York and Baltimore. In 1878 the government reversed his court-martial and cleared his name. Having become rich and professionally esteemed, he then retired to Washington, where he died.

See G. W. Adams, "Health and Medicine" (Ph.D. dissertation, Harvard, 1946) and *Doctors in Blue* (1952); W. Q. Maxwell, *Lincoln's Fifth Wheel* (1956); A. Stillé, *History of U.S. Sanitary Commission* (1867); and L. C. Duncan, *Military Surgeon* (Jan., Feb., 1929).

GEORGE W. ADAMS
Southern Illinois University, Carbondale

HAMPDEN-SYDNEY COLLEGE (Hampden-

Sydney, Va. 23943), the tenth oldest college in the nation, was founded in 1776 with Patrick Henry and James Madison among others on its first board of trustees. This Presbyterian college was named after John Hampden and Algernon Sydney, English patriots and supporters of religious and constitutional liberties. Hampden-Sydney has been traditionally a small, male, liberal arts college, and its library's manuscript holdings concern chiefly the history of the school and area churches.

See L. W. Topping, "History of Hampden-Sydney, 1771–1883" (M.A. thesis, Union Theological Seminary, 1950);

and A. L. Carlson, "John Holt Rice" (Ph.D. dissertation, University of Virginia, 1954).

HAMPTON, WADE (1752–1835), born into an

old Virginia family, had no formal education and came to South Carolina before the Revolution. Although a LOYALIST until 1781, he quickly thereafter became a rebel military and political leader and profited from confiscated Loyalist estates. He speculated heavily in YAZOO LANDS and public securities, experimented with upland cotton, and before 1800 was extremely wealthy. Later he bought an enormous Louisiana sugar plantation and died one of the richest men in America. Hampton held local offices after 1781, opposed the Constitution, and helped organize the local Republican party. Twice elected congressman (1794, 1803), he voted loyally with his party but was defeated for reelection. A presidential elector in 1800, he declined appointment as Thomas Jefferson's postmaster general. Reentering the army in 1808, Hampton became major general and fought on the Canadian front in 1813, but quarreled with JAMES WILKINSON and resigned, remaining thereafter in private life.

See C. E. Cauthen, *Family Letters of Three Wade Hamptons* (1953).

JAMES H. BROUSSARD
Southwest Texas State University

HAMPTON, WADE (1818–1902), a planter, Con-

federate officer, governor, and U.S. senator, was born at Charleston, S.C., and reared at Millwood plantation near Columbia. He graduated at South Carolina College in 1836. As a cotton planter, he ran Millwood and several Mississippi plantations, acquired by his father, so successfully that his 1861 crop reached 5,000 bales. A member of South Carolina's legislature (1852–1856) and state senate (1856–1861), he questioned slavery's economic efficiency and opposed the 1857 drive to reopen the African slave trade. In 1860 he thought Abraham Lincoln's election insufficient cause for secession. But, when South Carolina seceded, he vigorously supported the Confederate cause, raising troops at his own expense and offering his cotton for exchange in Europe for arms.

Large in size with broad shoulders and a barrel chest, Hampton commanded an infantry unit at first BULL RUN, where he was wounded. Promoted brigadier general in May, 1862, he helped defend Richmond, suffering another wound at SEVEN PINES. Shifting to the cavalry of the Army of Northern Virginia, he became second in command and fought in virtually all the eastern campaigns of 1862–1865. He rose to major general on J. E. B. STUART's death in 1864 and later to the rank of lieutenant general. In the Civil War's closing campaign he cooperated with JOSEPH E. JOHNSTON in the Carolinas and even urged continuing resistance west of the Mississippi.

In the postwar era he supported President Andrew Johnson's Reconstruction plan and came close to being elected South Carolina's governor in 1865. He spent much time on his private affairs, especially his Mississippi properties. Along with other southern whites, however, Hampton fumed in anger over Radical Reconstruction. Finally, in 1876, conservative Democrats nominated Hampton for governor. He mounted a vigorous campaign and appealed for Negro votes, while assuring blacks their rights were safe. At the same time private rifle clubs and Red Shirts intimidated blacks, carpetbaggers, and scalawags in a drive to prevent their voting. In the election's confusing outcome, the Democrats appeared to have won, but Republican canvassing boards canceled many local returns and seemingly secured a Republican victory. During the tense months that followed, Hampton restrained his more excited followers until Rutherford Hayes's accession as president brought removal of federal troops followed by Hampton's installation as governor in a white supremacist regime. Reelected governor in 1878, he was shortly elevated to the U.S. Senate, where he served until beaten by the rising forces of BEN TILLMAN in 1890. He died at Columbia in a house presented by admirers to replace one destroyed earlier by fire.

See H. W. Jarrell, *Wade Hampton and Negro* (1949); A. B. Williams, *Hampton and Red Shirts* (1935); E. L. Wells, *Hampton and Reconstruction* (1907); and M. W. Wellman, *Giant in Gray: Hampton* (1949).

DAVID LINDSEY
California State University, Los Angeles

HAMPTON, VA. (pop. 120,779), opposite Norfolk and seven miles northeast of Newport News, was first settled in 1610, making it one of the oldest continuously inhabited English communities in America. Laid out as a town and formally named in 1680, it was greatly enlarged in 1755, when over 1,000 ACADIANS moved here. Because of its strategic location on Hampton Roads, the town was attacked and occupied by the British in 1813 and burned by its own residents in August, 1861, to deny it to the Union. Rebuilt after the war, it became the site of Hampton Institute in 1868, Langley Air Force Base in 1917, and a major shipyard during World War II. Hampton is economi-

cally interlocked with Newport News, and its industries process seafood, construct maritime vessels, and manufacture brick and paint.

See files of Hampton *Home-Bulletin* (1884–1900), *Monitor* (1876–1919), and Newport News *Times-Herald* (1900–), all on microfilm.

HAMPTON INSTITUTE (Hampton, Va., 23668) was founded in 1868 by SAMUEL CHAPMAN ARMSTRONG of the FREEDMEN'S BUREAU, with help from the American Missionary Association, as a normal school with heavy emphasis on industrial training and quasi-military discipline. Armstrong led the school until his death in 1893 and set the tradition of white control. Under its second principal Hollis Burke Frissell (1851–1917), Hampton increased its emphasis on job training and inculcating moral values and increasingly accommodated itself to southern mores. On Frissell's death, W. E. B. DU BOIS wrote scathingly that blacks felt Hampton "belongs to the white South and to the reactionary North . . . a center of that underground and silent intrigue which is determined to perpetuate the American Negro as a docile peasant and peon."

During the 1920s the school changed directions, becoming more of a college. It experienced severe growing pains and unrest, caused partly by the faculty's inability to deal with older, more self-assured students and partly by the rise of a virulent racial purity campaign led by pianist-composer John Powell in Virginia. By 1929 the institute no longer accepted precollege students and in 1932–1933 won accreditation as a Class A college. Alonzo Graseano Morón became Hampton's first black president in 1947 and served until 1959. Graduate programs were begun in 1956. Current enrollment is almost 3,000 students. Its most distinguished early alumni were BOOKER T. WASHINGTON and Robert Russa Moton (1868–1939), both principals of Tuskegee Institute. Moton, along with Thomas Jesse Jones (1873–1940), a Welshman who had served on the Hampton staff from 1902 to 1909, planned and founded the COMMISSION ON INTERRACIAL COOPERATION (1919–1943).

See W. H. Robinson, "History of Hampton Institute, 1868–1949" (Ph.D. dissertation, New York University, 1953); L. R. Harlan, *Booker T. Washington* (1972); R. R. Moton, *Finding Way Out* (1919); W. H. Hughes and F. D. Patterson, *Robert R. Moton* (1956); and R. Wolters, *New Negro on Campus* (1975).

CARL S. MATTHEWS
Georgia State University

HAMPTON ROADS is the channel by which the JAMES, the Nansemond, and the Elizabeth rivers enter the Chesapeake Bay. Approximately four miles (six kilometers) in length, its course forms one of the finest natural harbors in the world. A major shipping and shipbuilding center since the late seventeenth century, it is the headquarters of the U.S. Navy's Atlantic Fleet. Three cities— NEWPORT NEWS, NORFOLK, and PORTSMOUTH— compose the Port of Hampton Roads, a facility serviced and governed by Virginia's Hampton Roads Port Authority.

HAMPTON ROADS CONFERENCE (February 3, 1865), which occurred on the steamer *River Queen* anchored at Hampton Roads, Va., was the only meeting during the Civil War between official representatives of the United States and those of the Confederacy, in the hope of effecting peace. For four hours ABRAHAM LINCOLN and William H. Seward talked with ALEXANDER H. STEPHENS, ROBERT M. T. HUNTER, and JOHN ARCHIBALD CAMPBELL. Lincoln insisted, as fundamental conditions, that the Confederates must return to the Union, accept emancipation, and disband their armies. The Confederate trio could not accept these demands, for the instructions given to them by JEFFERSON DAVIS had authorized them to negotiate "with a view to secure peace to the two countries." The meeting therefore ended in failure.

See A. H. Stephens, *Constitutional View of Late War* (1870), II; Roy P. Basler (ed.), *Collected Works of Lincoln* (1953), VIII; and J. G. Randall and R. N. Current, *Last Full Measure* (1955).

JAMES RABUN
Emory University

HAMPTON'S CATTLE RAID (September 14– 17, 1864). By late summer of 1864, the Confederates were virtually besieged in both Richmond and Petersburg. The food shortage was critical. WADE HAMPTON learned that the Union beef cattle were lightly guarded near the large supply base at City Point and received permission from Robert E. Lee to attempt their capture. This would mean traveling about 50 miles behind nearly 60,000 Union soldiers encircling Petersburg and returning the same distance with the cattle. It was felt that the morale value of the food was worth the risk.

Early on September 14, Hampton with between 3,500 and 4,000 cavalrymen, engineers, and horse artillery marched from their encampments west of Petersburg. On the fifteenth, they crossed Blackwater Swamp and approached their goal. At 5:00

A.M. the next day, they struck the Union troops and within two hours had started their return with the herd. Union attempts to stop Hampton on September 16–17 were weak and disorganized and were all beaten back. At 9:00 A.M., September 17, Hampton was back behind the Confederate lines. Losses were ten killed, 47 wounded, and four missing. They had captured 304 prisoners. Hampton put the number of cattle seized at 2,468. It was certainly over 2,400.

See *Official Records, Armies*, Vol. XLII, Pts. 1, 2; J. M. Hansen, Richmond *Times-Dispatch* (Aug. 1, 8, 1943); and R. W. Lykes, *Civil War Times, Illustrated* (Feb., 1967) and *Military Affairs* (Spring, 1957).

RICHARD W. LYKES
University of Virginia, Northern Regional
Center, and George Mason University

HANNIBAL, MO. (pop. 18,609), famous as the boyhood home of SAMUEL CLEMENS, is on the Mississippi River approximately 100 miles northwest of St. Louis. It was founded in 1819 and named in the classical fashion popular at the time. River trade, a post road, and subsequent rail connections permitted the city to thrive as a commercial center. The first locomotive built west of the Mississippi River was assembled here. Modern Hannibal is the home of Hannibal–La Grange College (1858). It is a rail and trade center, and its factories produce shoes, steel, cement, and lumber.

See Hannibal *Courier-Post* (1838–).

HANOVER COURTHOUSE, BATTLE OF (May 27, 1862), also known as Slash Church or Kinney's Farm, took place 16 miles north of Richmond during George B. McClellan's PENINSULAR CAMPAIGN. This area was protected by two Confederate brigades (about 2,000 men) under Lawrence O'Bryan Branch and J. R. ANDERSON. It was crucial for communications to northern Virginia and the Shenandoah Valley. A Union division (about 11,000 men) under General Fitz-John Porter was ordered to disrupt this line, remove the force on McClellan's right, and open the way for a possible juncture with Irvin McDowell's army. The Union force was completely successful. McClellan was pleased with the results, and especially with Porter. Branch admitted to Robert E. Lee that he had decided before the battle not to engage his entire force so retreat would be easier. Confederate losses were estimated at 200 killed, 200 wounded, and 730 prisoners plus a large quantity of arms, commissary stores, and one howitzer. Union losses were reported as 62 killed, 223 wounded, and 70 missing.

See *Official Records, Armies*, Ser. 1, Vol. II; A. S. Webb, *Peninsula* (1881); W. W. Hassler, *McClellan* (1957); and D. S. Freeman, *R. E. Lee* (1934).

EDWARD K. ECKERT
St. Bonaventure University

HANSEN'S DISEASE, or leprosy, was introduced into the South by the region's explorers and settlers. It was brought to Texas by sixteenth-century Spanish settlers and nineteenth-century German and Czechoslovakian immigrants, to Louisiana by eighteenth-century French refugees from Acadia, and to Florida by its Spanish founders. Not until the end of the nineteenth century, however, can its incidence be gauged with any degree of certainty. In 1894, pressure from the public and the medical profession prompted the Louisiana legislature to establish the nation's first leper home at Carville. This facility was purchased in 1921 by the United States and designated the national leprosarium. From its establishment, it has won international acclaim for its service in the fight against Hansen's disease. Here in the 1940s, for example, Dr. Guy H. Faget demonstrated the efficacy of sulfone therapy, which revolutionized the treatment of leprosy. The Leprosy Registry maintained at Carville shows that in the period 1894–1968 the infection was diagnosed in every southern state and that three of the five states reporting the greatest incidence were in the South. Of the 3,461 cases recorded in the continental United States, 715 were in Louisiana, 673 in Texas, and 226 in Florida. This pattern has also held true for recent occurrences: of 95 new continental cases reported in 1968, 29 were in Texas, 16 in Florida, and four in Louisiana. Today, despite a national infection rate of less than 0.1 for every 1,000 people, Hansen's disease remains a significant health problem in the South, particularly in Texas, Louisiana, and Florida, where it is still endemic.

See E. H. Ackerknecht, *History and Geography of Most Important Diseases* (1965); and HEW, Public Health Service, *National Communicable Disease Center, Leprosy Surveillance* (1970).

JAMES O. BREEDEN
Southern Methodist University

HANSON, JOHN (1715–1783), of Maryland was a prominent figure during the American Revolution, yet only the outline of his career is known because of a paucity of personal papers. An Angli-

can member of the antiproprietary political faction, he was elected repeatedly from 1757 to 1779 to the assembly first from Charles and then from Frederick County; he also held elected offices in both counties. He participated in numerous county and provincial revolutionary activities and organizations from 1765 to 1776. Although primarily a local politician, he was appointed a delegate to the CONTINENTAL CONGRESS by the legislature for three consecutive years beginning in 1779 and served as president of Congress for one year (1781–1782).

See G. H. Ryden and A. B. Benson, *American-Scandinavian Review* (July, 1920); *Congressional Record* (1903), XXXVI; *Maryland Gazette* (Nov. 27, 1783); G. S. Hanson, *Old Kent* (1876); J. T. Scharf, *Western Maryland* (1882); T. J. C. Williams, *Frederick County* (1910); H. D. Richardson, *Side-Lights on Maryland* (1913); H. F. Powell, *Tercentenary History of Maryland* (1925); Maryland Archives; E. C. Burnett (ed.), *Letters of Members of Congress* (1921–36), V, VI; and W. C. Ford (ed.), *Continental Congress Journals* (1904–37), XVI–XXIII.

LARRY R. GERLACH
University of Utah

HARBEN, WILLIAM NATHANIEL (1858–1919), was one of the most popular novelists in America during his 30-year career. Born and raised in Dalton, Ga., he pursued a business profession until the age of thirty. Encouraged by JOEL CHANDLER HARRIS and HENRY GRADY, he experimented during the 1890s with different types of novels: romances, religious works, science fiction, and detective stories. He was simultaneously publishing short stories about his native region, stories that culminated with *Northern Georgia Sketches* (1900), a collection of ten of the best and most representative of his stories. On the advice of William Dean Howells, he began to write novels primarily about mountaineers, averaging one a year; he soon became a best-selling writer. Will Harben excelled in authentic, realistic portrayals of the north Georgia mountain people he knew well. The sentimentality of some of his stories may not appeal to modern readers, but the accuracy of his depictions of mountaineers transcends the usual LOCAL COLOR treatment of regional peculiarities.

See R. Bush in L. Rubin (ed.), *Bibliographical Guide to Southern Literature* (1969); K. M. Roemer, *Mississippi Quarterly* (Winter, 1972–73); R. Bush, *Mississippi Quarterly* (Spring, 1967); and J. K. Murphy, *Mississippi Quarterly* (Winter, 1975–76) and *Southern Folklore Quarterly* (Sept., 1975).

JAMES K. MURPHY
West Georgia College

HARBORS. The Atlantic and Gulf coasts in the South are characterized by low plains of geologically recent sedimentary origin. The land is low and often flat; the rivers are shallow and, except for the Mississippi, relatively short. The river and tidal currents along these coasts have combined to form natural harbors and bays at the mouths of nearly all southern tidal rivers. The partially protected bays can be regarded as enlargements of the lagoons lying along most of the Atlantic and Gulf coasts between the shore and the offshore bars.

The low-lying shoreline with its offshore bars, intermittently broken by tidal inlets, concealed river mouths, and delta creeks, has historically provided shelter for pirates during colonial times and smugglers, especially during the Civil War. The difficulty encountered in finding the mouth of the Mississippi (MISSISSIPPI DELTA) from the Gulf approach is thought to have impeded early French colonization of Louisiana. Initial settlement of the American South, like that of many colonial territories, proceeded inland from port settlements situated on natural harbors. These ports (except for those on the Mississippi and Savannah) are located on rivers immediately above tidal estuaries or bays (*e.g.*, Mobile), on the bay itself (*e.g.*, Tampa), or in a few cases on the outer sandbar (*e.g.*, Galveston). Savannah is situated a dozen miles from the open sea on the first high ground along the Savannah River. The same can be said of New Orleans, if the natural levee may be regarded as high ground. Both are situated on the outside of curves in the river, where natural undercutting of the stream reduces the need for artificial dredging. The only other major exceptions to these generalizations among major ports are Baton Rouge, located at the head of deepwater navigation on the Mississippi, and Houston, some miles up the Buffalo Bayou, a small tidal creek now canalized to form the Houston Ship Channel.

Port development in the South reflects in part the presence of natural harbors. Most of the larger harbors are the sites of ocean ports, although all major ports are not on natural harbors. The position, as well as the composition of trade through the major ports, reflects the presence of important raw materials, the locational relation of the port to regional manufacturing activity, the direction of overseas markets and raw materials sources, or a combination of these. Thus the ports of the Texas-Louisiana Gulf coast are all important shippers of petroleum products, most of which move in coastwise shipping to the Northeast and by barge to the Midwest. Such raw materials as sulfur, phosphates, and coal move into deepwater trade from

ports near their sources, such as the Louisiana ports, the ports of central Florida (especially Tampa), and those of Hampton Roads, respectively. Likewise large quantities of grain move south from the Midwest for export through Gulf ports: New Orleans and Baton Rouge for corn and soybeans, and Houston for wheat, especially. The inbound movement of raw materials for regional industries, some of which were predicated originally on the local presence of raw materials, includes the import of iron ore through Mobile and crude oil to the Texas ports. Imported iron ore is also received at Baltimore, as is aluminum ore and concentrates at Mobile, Baton Rouge, New Orleans, and Corpus Christi. A wide variety of related manufactured products moves through these ports in waterborne domestic as well as foreign trade.

See U.S. Army Corps of Engineers, *Waterborne Commerce of U.S.* (annual), Pts. 1, 2; G. Alexandersson and G. Norstrom, *World Shipping* (1963); and J. Bird, *Seaports and Seaport Terminals* (1971).

JAMES KENYON
University of Georgia

WATERBORNE TONNAGE AT MAJOR SOUTHERN PORTS, 1974
(thousands of short tons)

Port (Harbor)	Total[a]	Foreign	Coastwise
Baltimore	59,891	38,106	8,504
Hampton Roads	73,102	53,802	3,337
Wilmington	7,466	3,837	3,497
Charleston	8,993	4,415	3,077
Savannah	9,699	6,233	1,963
Brunswick	1,966	1,155	–
Jacksonville	14,795	7,036	4,855
Palm Beach	1,097	976	–
Port Everglades	11,556	4,097	7,396
Miami	4,141	–	–
Tampa	40,919	18,686	21,550
Pensacola	2,239	374	179
Mobile	33,154	13,379	4,219
Pascagoula	13,073	3,577	3,535
New Orleans (and below)	112,755	30,477	12,428
Baton Rouge (to but not incl. N.O.)	69,519	53,728	15,462
Sabine-Neches (Beaumont–Port Arthur)	86,589	21,320	24,603
Houston Ship Channel	89,106	34,671	24,940
Texas City	20,156	2,262	5,740
Galveston Channel	7,171	5,204	1,076
Freeport	8,898	3,206	1,995
Matagorda Ship Channel (Port Lavaca–Point Comfort)	4,931	4,162	485
Corpus Christi (incl. Harbor Island)	37,781	17,791	11,513
Brazos Island (Brownsville)	3,016	897	191

SOURCE: U.S. Army Corps of Engineers, *Waterborne Commerce of U.S.* (1974).
[a]Barge traffic included in totals

HARDEE, WILLIAM JOSEPH (1815–1873), born of an established, landed family in Camden County, Ga., graduated from the U.S. Military Academy in 1836. After a short tour of duty in the Seminole War, he attended the Royal Cavalry School at Saumur, France (1840–1841). Following distinguished service in the Mexican War and against the Indians on the frontier, Hardee was assigned to prepare a tactics manual for the army in 1853. This work, *Rifle and Light Infantry Tactics* (1855), "Hardee's *Tactics*," was used by both Union and Confederate officers in the Civil War.

In 1861 Hardee resigned his commission and joined the forces of Georgia. He rose rapidly in rank from colonel to lieutenant general. He led the attack at SHILOH, and at PERRYVILLE and STONES RIVER proved himself a superior corps commander. In November, 1863, he saved the Confederates from annihilation at Missionary Ridge (CHATTANOOGA CAMPAIGN).

When he subsequently was offered the command of the Army of Tennessee, Hardee declined in favor of JOSEPH E. JOHNSTON. He served Johnston well in the retreat before Sherman's advance into Georgia in the spring of 1864, but when John B. Hood succeeded Johnston, Hardee saw his corps destroyed in ill-advised attacks. Late in the autumn he defended Savannah skillfully but vainly against Sherman and also served as a corps commander in resisting Sherman in the final CAROLINAS CAMPAIGN.

See N. C. Hughes, *W. J. Hardee* (1965); S. F. Horn, *Army of Tennessee* (1953); W. D. Pickett, *Military Career of Hardee* (1910); and I. A. Buck, *Cleburne and His Command* (1908).

N. C. HUGHES, JR.
Girls' Preparatory School, Chattanooga, Tenn.

HARDING, WARREN, ADMINISTRATION (1921–1923), which lasted less than 900 days, was characterized by the strong leadership of Charles Evans Hughes (State Department), Andrew Mellon (secretary of the treasury), Henry Wallace (Department of Agriculture), and Herbert Hoover (Commerce Department). Harding busied himself to a great extent with routine political business, giving close attention to patronage disputes and Republican party business, though his policies were not clearly defined. Thus, even though he showed occasional consideration for black Republican aspirants to office, he also gave LILY-WHITE factions encouragement in their disputes with BLACK AND TAN Republicans in the South. Along with most Republicans, Harding supported the Dyer bill and antilynching legislation and advo-

cated the protection and expansion of the constitutional, economic, and educational rights of Negroes, at the same time that he expressed public disapproval of general social integration.

See A. Sinclair, *Available Man* (1965); and R. K. Murray, *Harding Administration* (1969).

ROGER M. OLIEN
University of Texas, Permian Basin

HARLAN, JOHN MARSHALL (1833–1911), was born in Boyle County, Ky., and was educated at Centre College and at Transylvania University. He practiced law in Frankfort and Louisville and supported the Whig party. Opposed to secession, he was a colonel in the Union army. After the war Harlan became an active Republican. In 1877 President Rutherford B. Hayes appointed him to the U.S. Supreme Court. During his long service on that tribunal, Harlan often differed with his conservative brethren, and he deplored the Court's tendency to override the legislative branch on social and economic matters. In vigorous dissents, he upheld the federal income tax (*Pollock* v. *Farmers' Loan*, 1895) and maximum-hour legislation (*Lochner* v. *New York*, 1905). Although a former slave owner, he became a firm champion of civil rights for all, as he showed in his rejection of the separate but equal doctrine laid down in PLESSY V. FERGUSON (1896). Sometimes described as a "premature New Dealer," Harlan stood forth as a liberal nationalist in an age of judicial conservatism.

See L. Filler, in L. Friedman and F. L. Israel (eds.), *Justices of U.S. Supreme Court* (1969), most thorough study, good bibliography; and Harlan Papers, Library of Congress and University of Louisville Law School.

WILLIAM H. GAINES, JR.
Virginia State Library

HARLAN COUNTY (Bloody Harlan), in mountainous southeastern Kentucky, existed on primitive agriculture and lumbering until 1911, when it emerged as a nationally important coalfield. During the 1920s, a decade of labor peace, the county attained the highest homicide rate in the nation. Not until the 1930s, however, when a decade-long struggle erupted between the United Mine Workers and the local coal operators' association with its privately employed deputy sheriffs (many of whom were convicted felons) did the county achieve national notoriety. Although the homicide rate declined and labor strife caused only 13 deaths, investigations by notable literary figures such as Theodore Dreiser and John Dos

Passos and by the La Follette Civil Liberties Committee made the county a national symbol of murderous resistance to labor's right to organize. Robert La Follette's exposé resulted in abolition of the private deputy system and opened the county to successful unionization.

See P. F. Taylor, "Coal and Conflict" (Ph.D. dissertation, University of Kentucky, 1969); J. W. Hevener, "New Deal for Harlan" (Ph.D. dissertation, Ohio State, 1971), both balanced with bibliographies; G. J. Titler, *Hell in Harlan* (n.d.); T. Bubka, *Labor History* (Winter, 1970); T. Draper, *Dissent* (Spring, 1972); and *Harlan Miners Speak* (1932).

JOHN W. HEVENER
Ohio State University, Lima

HARPE BROTHERS, Micajah "Big Harpe" (?–1799) and Wiley "Little Harpe" (?–1804), were pathological, purposeless killers on the early American frontier. They migrated from North Carolina to east Tennessee about 1795, bringing two women with them. It appears that they proposed to settle near Knoxville; however, they soon devoted their energies not to agriculture, as initially intended, but to cattle rustling and horse stealing and eventually to the wanton murder of migrants along the frontier trails of Tennessee and Kentucky. Their later criminal activities centered along the Ohio River between what is now Owensboro and Henderson, Ky. Ultimately Big Harpe was shot and beheaded by a posse and Little Harpe was hanged.

See J. W. M. Breazeale, *History of Harpes* (1842); and O. A. Rothert, *Outlaws of Cave-in-Rock* (1924).

BURTON J. WILLIAMS
Central Washington State College

HARPER, ROBERT GOODLOE (1765–1825), was born in Fredericksburg, Va. His life spanned the early national period and is a case study in the dynamics of early southern society. After Revolutionary War service and a modest South Carolina law practice, he attached himself to a reapportionment movement, and by 1794 he was in Congress, where he identified with the Federalists. Foregoing his earlier moderate views, he became majority leader and shepherded the Alien and Sedition Acts of 1798 through the House and warned of a French-inspired domestic conspiracy. Quitting Congress in 1801, he married the daughter of CHARLES CARROLL OF CARROLLTON and joined the Baltimore bar, then dominated by Federalist attorneys. Harper practiced before the U.S. Supreme Court and federal and state courts and appeared in the trials of Justices SAMUEL CHASE and

John Pickering, the Aaron Burr trial, and *Martin v. Hunter's Lessee*. Harper played a major role in the renaissance of Maryland federalism after 1800. A charter member of the Maryland Colonization Society, he also opposed efforts to resume the importation of slaves. He remains a classic southern Federalist representative of the region and the times.

See Harper Papers, Maryland Historical Society, Library of Congress, and South Carolina Archives; J. Cox, *Champion of Southern Federalism* (1973); and L. Rose, *Prologue to Democracy* (1968).

JOSEPH W. COX
Towson State College

HARPER, WILLIAM (1790–1847), was born on Antigua. After graduating from South Carolina College in 1808, he taught school and studied medicine for a short time; turning later to the study of law, he was admitted to the bar in 1811. Soon after he moved to Missouri Territory, where he served as equity court chancellor (1818–1823) and as a member of the state constitutional convention (1821). In 1823 he returned to South Carolina to practice law and in 1826 was appointed as a states' rights Democrat to the U.S Senate to complete an unexpired term (March 28–December 7) created by the death of John Gaillard. In 1828 he was elected to the South Carolina house of representatives and soon became Speaker of the house. Elected chancellor of the house in 1828, he served in that position until 1830 and again from 1835 to 1847. He was judge of the court of appeals (1830–1835) and a member of the state convention of 1832 that passed the NULLIFICATION ordinance. Harper was an extensive writer, orator, advocate of the doctrine of nullification, and zealous slavery proponent.

See W. S. Jenkins, *Pro-Slavery Thought* (1935), includes Harper's memoir on slavery; W. Harper and T. R. Dew, *Memorial Remonstrating Against Tariff* (1831); and J. B. O'Neal, *Biographical Sketches of Bench and Bar of South Carolina* (1859).

HENRY MARSHALL BOOKER
Christopher Newport College

HARPERS FERRY, W.Va., is situated at the easternmost edge of the state's eastern panhandle and at the lowest point of elevation in the state. Joined here by the Shenandoah River, the Potomac River has cut a channel through the Blue Ridge Mountains as it flows eastward. Thomas Jefferson, in his *Notes on the State of Virginia*, declared that "this scene is worth a voyage across the Atlantic."

Before the Civil War the town served as a trading and manufacturing center for adjacent portions of the Shenandoah Valley. Its transportation needs were met by the arrival of the Chesapeake & Ohio Canal in 1833 and the Baltimore & Ohio Railroad in 1834. The community's major prewar industry, however, was a federal armory and arsenal established in 1796, which provided the lure for John Brown's raid of 1859 (HARPERS FERRY RAID). In 1850, with a population of 1,747, Harpers Ferry was the third largest town in present West Virginia.

The first institution of higher learning for black students in West Virginia, Storer College, was established at Harpers Ferry in 1867 and provided instruction until 1955.

The ravages of the Civil War and of recurring floods caused a serious decline in the economy and population of Harpers Ferry in the postbellum period. Tourist trade became the major business of the town. The most important recent development in the community has been the establishment, in the 1950s, of Harpers Ferry National Historical Park.

See M. K. Bushong, *Historic Jefferson County* (1972); F. B. Sarles, Jr., *Harpers Ferry National Historical Park: Virginius Island* (1969); West Virginia Writers' Program, WPA, *West Virginia: A Guide* (1941); and W. D. Barns, *West Virginia History* (April, 1973).

WILLIAM D. BARNS
West Virginia University

HARPERS FERRY RAID (October 16–18, 1859). Believing himself to be "an instrument of God," John Brown sought to establish a militant black government in the mountains of Virginia and Maryland, which might force the emancipation of almost 4 million slaves. In 1858 a convention in Chatham, Canada, adopted a provisional constitution and elected Brown commander-in-chief. Financed by prominent northeastern abolitionists, Brown selected as his target the U.S. armory and arsenal at Harpers Ferry, Va. (now in West Virginia), located at the junction of the Shenandoah and the Potomac rivers. Brown assembled supplies and 21 men, including three of his own sons and five blacks, at the Kennedy farm across the Potomac and, on the evening of October 16, began his ill-fated expedition.

About a dozen slaves were "liberated," but no slave joined Brown voluntarily. Ironically the first casualty was a free black baggagemaster at the Harpers Ferry railroad station who refused to join Brown's scheme. A number of citizens were taken hostage, including "Colonel" Lewis W. Washington, grandnephew of the general. By midday of October 17 the local militia from the county seat of Charlestown arrived and closed off Brown's only way of escape. Meantime Brevet Colonel ROBERT E. LEE was summoned from his Arlington home to the White House and given command of a detachment of marines, who were promptly dispatched from the Washington naval yard. When Lee arrived at Harpers Ferry he canceled orders for additional troops from Fortress Monroe and did not issue a now-lost presidential proclamation that authorized temporary martial law.

On the morning of October 18 and with several thousand spectators on the scene, Lieutenant JEB STUART demanded Brown's surrender. Then Lieutenant Israel Green led 11 men in a successful three-minute attack on the engine house. In all, the insurgents had killed five persons including one marine and had lost ten men (either dead or mortally wounded, including Brown's sons Oliver and Watson). Brown and the other prisoners were sent to the Charlestown jail, where one week later Brown was indicted for "treason to the Commonwealth, conspiring to commit treason and murder." As expected, the jury after three-quarters of an hour's deliberation found Brown guilty, and Judge Richard Parker sentenced him to be hanged on December 2. Seventeen affidavits from neighbors and relatives claiming Brown to be insane left Virginia Governor HENRY A. WISE unmoved, and the execution took place as scheduled with Brown handing a guard the prophecy of civil war: "I John Brown am now quite *certain* that the crimes of this *guilty land will* never be purged *away* but with Blood. I had as I now *think vainly* flattered myself that without *very* much bloodshed it might be done." Four other conspirators were hanged December 16 and two others on March 16, 1860. Five conspirators, including Brown's son Owen, had escaped capture and punishment.

Lee's official report concluded, "The result proves that the plan was the attempt of a fanatic or madman," though Ralph Waldo Emerson claimed that Brown would make "the gallows glorious like the cross." Abraham Lincoln may well have given the definitive judgment in his Cooper Union speech of February 27, 1860: "That affair, in its philosophy, corresponds with the many attempts, related in history, at the assassination of kings and emperors. An enthusiast broods over the oppression of a people till he fancies himself commissioned by Heaven to liberate them. He ventures the attempt, which ends in little else than his own execution."

See J. Abels, *Man on Fire* (1971); A. Keller, *Thunder at Harper's Ferry* (1958); F. Landon, *Journal of Negro His-*

tory (April, 1921); S. B. Oates, *To Purge This Land with Blood* (1970); B. Stavis, *John Brown* (1970); and O. G. Villard, *John Brown* (1910).

JOHN D. DUNCAN
Armstrong State College

HARRIS, GEORGE WASHINGTON (1814–1869),

popular newspaper humorist and satirist, has been enjoyed by Mark Twain, admired by William Faulkner and Flannery O'Connor, denounced by Edmund Wilson, and evaluated by Brom Weber as pivotal in the analysis of American and southern culture. Harris' one book, *Sut Lovingood: Yarns Spun by a "Nat'ral Born Durn'd Fool"* (1867), sketches of east Tennessee hill country life, is told by a hard-drinking, grotesquely prankish protagonist whose perspective is one of low comic defiance of civilization and celebration of the human animal's capacity for chaos, squalor, and physical joy. The richly metaphoric style, in formidably difficult dialect, broadly exploits the forms and techniques of the culture of folk humor. Early sketches appeared in the 1840s in the New York *Spirit of the Times* and, in the 1850s and 1860s, in the Nashville *Union and American*. Harris himself was formal in manner, a strict Presbyterian. Reared in Knoxville by his half-brother Samuel Bell, Harris was a metalworker, steamboat captain, small businessman, and local politician. Although his foster father was a Union Whig, Harris was a Democrat and early secessionist. During and after the Civil War he wrote anti-Lincoln and antinorthern satires for various newspapers. Sketches not included in his own book have been collected and edited by M. Thomas Inge as *High Times and Hard Times* (1967).

See W. Blair, *Native American Humor* (1960); H. Cohen and W. B. Dillingham, *Humor of the Old Southwest* (1964); B. H. McClary (ed.), *The Lovingood Papers* (1962–65); O. Plater, *Appalachian Journal* (Spring, 1973); M. Rickels, *George Washington Harris* (1965) and "Harris," in L. D. Rubin (ed.), *Bibliographical Guide to Southern Literature* (1969).

MILTON RICKELS
University of Southwestern Louisiana

HARRIS, ISHAM GREEN (1818–1897),

was born near Tullahoma, Tenn. At the age of fourteen he went to Paris, Henry County, where his older brother was already an attorney. He was admitted to the bar by 1841 and was elected to the Tennessee senate in 1847 and to Congress in 1849 and 1851. He moved to Memphis in 1853 to continue his law practice. He was elected governor as a Democrat in 1857, 1859, and 1861. Refusing Abraham Lincoln's call for troops in 1861, Harris was firmly in favor of the state joining the Confederacy. After the occupation of Nashville by federal troops following the Union victories at FTS. HENRY AND DONELSON, he served on the staff of ALBERT SIDNEY JOHNSTON and was with Johnston at the time of his death at SHILOH. After the war, he went first to Mexico and then to England. He returned in 1867 to Memphis where he practiced law and was elected as a Democrat to the U.S. Senate in 1877. He remained in the Senate until his death.

See *Memorial Addresses on Isham G. Harris* (1898); and J. W. Caldwell, *Sketches of Bench and Bar in Tennessee* (1898). Also see Isham G. Harris Papers, Tennessee State Library and Archives, Nashville.

J. MILTON HENRY
Austin Peay State University

HARRIS, JAMES HENRY (1830?–1891),

prominent black North Carolina politician, was born in Granville County, N.C. After serving as an upholsterer's apprentice and foreman, he started his own business in Raleigh. Later he attended school for two years in Oberlin, Ohio, and then traveled to Canada, Liberia, and Sierra Leone. Upon returning to the United States in 1863, he was commissioned to help raise the 28th Regiment of U.S. Colored Troops. In June, 1865, Harris returned to Raleigh as a teacher for the New England Freedmen's Aid Society. But Harris quickly realized that blacks needed legal and political equality to ensure their freedom. Therefore he entered politics, playing a major role in the 1865 and 1866 North Carolina freedmen's conventions, the state's Equal Rights League, and the national equal rights conventions of 1865 and 1867. During congressional Reconstruction, he became a charter member of the state's UNION LEAGUE, one of the founders of the state's Republican party, a delegate to the state's 1868 constitutional convention, a state legislator for several terms, a Raleigh city alderman for many years, and a deputy tax collector. In the 1880s, Harris edited and published the *North Carolina Republican*. Throughout his career, Harris believed blacks and whites had to work together, but, though often urging moderation, he always insisted that blacks fight to keep their political rights and to gain equality before the law.

See W. H. Quick, *Negro Stars* (1898); Jerome Dowd, *Sketches* (1888); Harris Papers, North Carolina State Archives, brief but helpful; and E. Balanoff, *North Carolina Historical Review* (Jan., 1972.)

ROBERTA SUE ALEXANDER
University of Dayton

HARRIS, JOEL CHANDLER (1848–1908), son of a seamstress, was apprenticed at thirteen as printer to the publisher of an Eatonton, Ga., newspaper. There his humble position and lifelong shyness attracted whites and blacks of all classes, who instructed and shielded him, providing the characters and materials for his best work. In Macon and Savannah, Harris developed into a writer determined to make some contribution to southern literature. In 1876, he took his family to Atlanta, and the reputation and popularity of his LOCAL COLOR writing grew steadily. Folklorists, dialect specialists, historians of children's classics, and the corrupt Disney versions have kept alive the folktales "told by Uncle Remus," but most of his other work is long out of print. That critics in the second half of the twentieth century erroneously label him romanticist is as much due to revisionist history as to changing social attitudes. When a collected edition becomes available, it will be obvious that he used real literary skills to effect a portrait gallery of middle Georgia men and women, white and black, antebellum and Reconstruction, with respect, compassion, and insight that explain the affection accorded them internationally in his own day.

See Harris autobiography, *On Plantation* (1892); his daughter-in-law Julia C. Harris, *Life and Letters of Joel Chandler Harris* (1918) and *Harris, Editor and Essayist* (1931); P. M. Cousins, *J. C. Harris* (1968), significant new basic material; and S. B. Brookes, *Harris: Folklorist* (1950). See also C. A. Ray's annotated bibliography, in L. D. Rubin (ed.), *Bibliographical Guide to Southern Literature* (1969); and Harris Manuscripts, Emory University Library.

HARRIET R. HOLMAN
Clemson University

HARRISON, BENJAMIN, ADMINISTRATION (1889–1893). As a Republican leader, Harrison had watched the unsuccessful efforts of his predecessors in the presidency to build up the Republican party in the South. He thought that there was a large potential Republican vote in the South but that it was dormant owing to the illegal methods of Democrats in suppressing it (DISFRANCHISEMENT). In his view the Republican party could regain its majority position in the South by extending federal protection to southern Republicans when voting. His major effort to recapture the South for the Republican party centered around the federal elections bill of 1890. This was a proposal to regulate federal elections by supervising every registration office and polling place where the law was in effect. Because the president was empowered to use the army and navy to enforce the measure, its opponents labeled it the FORCE BILL.

By supporting the bill, Harrison rejected the HAYES ADMINISTRATION's plan to conciliate southern whites and the ARTHUR ADMINISTRATION's program of cooperation with southern independents. His advocacy of the Force Bill was a reversion to Reconstruction tactics. Republican leadership under Speaker Thomas B. Reed pushed the Force Bill through the House by a slender margin. But in the Senate the measure met a different fate. Here certain groups within the Republican party preferred to see the bill die rather than block the passage of the McKinley tariff and the Silver Act or injure northern investments in the South. By the end of Harrison's administration, the Republicans still had failed to find a way to rebuild their party in the South.

See V. P. De Santis, *Republicans Face Southern Question* (1959) and *Indiana Magazine of History* (Dec., 1955), fullest account; S. P. Hirshson, *Farewell to Bloody Shirt* (1962); and H. J. Sievers, *Benjamin Harrison* (1968).

VINCENT P. DE SANTIS
University of Notre Dame

HARRISON, BYRON PATTON "PAT" (1881–1941), born in Crystal Springs, Miss., served his native state in Congress for 30 years. He brought to his post as chairman of the Senate Finance Committee during the NEW DEAL enormous influence based not only upon congressional longevity, dating from his entry into the House of Representatives in 1911 and the Senate in 1919, but also upon a happy combination of personal qualities that made him perhaps the most popular man in the Senate during his time. Never the author of any major legislation, Harrison was a master tactician, and under his tutelage the Finance Committee handled for Franklin D. Roosevelt many of the major measures of the decade. Defeated by one vote in 1937 for the position of majority leader, Harrison was named president pro tem in January, 1941, six months before his death. As a Democratic partisan and a clever debater, Harrison was a floor leader of the Senate during the Republican administrations of the 1920s. Rising rapidly in party circles he played a prominent role in national conventions, serving as the keynoter at the 1924 Democratic convention. By 1940 his influence in convention politics diminished somewhat because of his conservative opposition to the taxation and spending policies of the New Deal. He remained, however, a power in the Senate and was at the zenith of his influence in 1938 and 1939. By 1940 he had reconciled his differences with Roosevelt because of their mutual agreement on preparedness legislation.

See M. H. Swain, *Pat Harrison* (1978); W. S. Coker, *Journal of Mississippi History* (Oct., 1963); J. T. Patterson, *Congressional Conservatism and New Deal* (1967); and Harrison Papers, University of Mississippi.

MARTHA H. SWAIN
Texas Woman's University

HARRISON FAMILY. The first Harrison on these shores, Benjamin (1600?–1648/49), settled south of the James River at Wakefield in Surry County, Va. This hardworking farmer became clerk of the Virginia council and in the early 1640s was elected to the HOUSE OF BURGESSES. Benjamin and his wife Mary managed to acquire several tracts of land, laying the foundations for their son's rise to the well-to-do planter class.

Benjamin Harrison II (1645–1712/13), a successful planter and merchant, held several important offices including sheriff, local justice, militia colonel, charter trustee of William and Mary College, and member of the House of Burgesses. Finally, in 1698, he was appointed to the prestigious Virginia council. Benjamin and Hannah Harrison were well established in the ruling class, and their children matured as aristocrats. One daughter, Sarah, married the Reverend JAMES BLAIR, founder and first president of the College of William and Mary. Another married Philip Ludwell and, through the marriage of her daughter, became the grandmother of RICHARD HENRY LEE and ARTHUR LEE of Revolutionary fame. Nathaniel (1677–1727), the second son, inherited a plantation in Prince George County and was the ancestor of a branch of the family known as the Harrisons of Brandon. His younger brother Henry (?–1732) took charge of the old plantation at Wakefield and was active in Virginia politics.

The oldest son, Benjamin Harrison III (1673–1710), studied law in England. Upon his return to Virginia, he established his line of the family at Berkeley, a tobacco-rich area extending for miles on the north side of the James River. His involvement in Virginia affairs included the following high posts: His Majesty's council at law, Speaker of the House of Burgesses, and treasurer of the colony. He died at the age of thirty-seven. His widow, Elizabeth Burwell Harrison, managed the plantation until her son Benjamin IV (1700?–1744) was able to assume control.

The young Harrison further extended the family's influence by marrying Anne, daughter of Robert ("King") Carter (CARTER FAMILY), one of the richest men in America. Harrison served as militia colonel, county sheriff, and member of the House of Burgesses. His distinguished career came to an untimely end when a bolt of lightning struck his house, instantly killing him and his two youngest daughters, Lucy and Hannah.

Benjamin Harrison V (1726?–1791) took over the vast estate, married Elizabeth Bassett, and in the late 1740s made his first appearance in the House of Burgesses. As an active member of the first and second Continental Congresses (1774–1777), he sat on several committees dealing with foreign and military affairs. Serving as chairman of the Committee of the Whole, he presided over the debates that culminated in the DECLARATION OF INDEPENDENCE and, in due course, appended his signature to this momentous document. Upon his retirement from Congress Harrison returned to Virginia and served as a member of the house of delegates, Speaker, and governor (1781–1784). His son William Henry Harrison (1773–1841) of Ohio and his great-grandson Benjamin (1833–1901) of Indiana both became presidents of the United States.

See C. Dowdey, *Great Plantation* (1957), popular but informative, and *American Heritage* (April, 1957), summary of book; E. C. Burnett, *Continental Congress* (1964); H. J. Henderson, *Party Politics in Continental Congress* (1974), definitive; D. B. Goebel, *William Henry Harrison* (1926), covers early Harrisons; F. Cleaves, *Old Tippecanoe* (1939), genealogical chart; and H. J. Sievers, *Benjamin Harrison* (1952–68).

NEIL T. STORCH
University of Minnesota, Duluth

HARRISON'S LANDING (also known as Berkeley Hundred), the ancestral home of the Harrison family on the James River in Virginia, was the base for the Army of the Potomac from July 2 to August 16, 1862. After the final engagement of the SEVEN DAYS' BATTLES at MALVERN HILL, George B. McClellan moved his 90,000 men to this easily defended peninsula 18 miles southeast of Richmond. McClellan planned to remain there and renew the advance on Richmond as soon as he received reinforcements. When Abraham Lincoln visited the camp on July 7, McClellan handed him the "Harrison's Landing letter," which offered political and military advice on the future conduct of the war. The conservative thrust of the letter probably hastened McClellan's downfall. On August 3, he was ordered to remove his army to Aquia Creek.

See W. W. Hassler, *McClellan* (1957), pro-McClellan; G. B. McClellan, *McClellan's Own Story* (1887); R. U. Johnson and C. C. Buel (eds.), *Battles and Leaders*

(1888), II; and U.S. War Department, *Atlas to Accompany Official Records* (1891–95).

CAM WALKER
College of William and Mary

HARRODSBURG, KY. (pop. 6,471), the state's oldest town and the seat of Mercer County, lies near the state's geographical center. It was settled by James Harrod and 40 Virginians in June, 1774, and permanently occupied after May, 1775; its population reached 198 by 1777. In December, 1776, when Virginia created Kentucky County, Harrodsburg became its seat. Under GEORGE ROGERS CLARK the town withstood an Indian siege through much of the summer of 1777. Harrodsburg and the bluegrass region flourished after 1790 by growing HEMP and burley TOBACCO. A Greek Revival hotel and mineral spa made the town an antebellum resort. It avoided Civil War destruction, but an 1883 arsonist's fire did great damage. Harrodsburg's 1970 population was almost half the county's total. Although agriculture remained important, over 4,000 workers were on area payrolls by 1973. Half were employed in manufacturing, notably clothing, pottery, and automotive parts. Local 1972 retail sales were $25 million. An outdoor drama, *The Legend of Daniel Boone*, and a replica of the original fort are tourist attractions.

See T. D. Clark, in T. C. Wheeler (ed.), *Vanishing America* (1964); K. H. Mason, *James Harrod* (1951); and *U.S. Census for 1970*, with supplements.

RICHARD G. STONE, JR.
Western Kentucky University

HARROWER, JOHN (1733–1777), was a Scottish merchant who became an indentured servant in Virginia. Ruined by the panic of 1772, he left the Shetland Islands to seek work. Unsuccessful in Great Britain, he signed a four-year indenture and sailed for Virginia. Colonel William Daingerfield of Belvidera bought the indenture and installed Harrower as tutor for his children and those of neighboring planters. He was a successful tutor. Harrower's journal is unique. He alone of the thousands of indentured servants who came to Virginia has left us a record of his daily life. He also recorded information about agricultural practices, plantation schooling, and social life among the gentry and their servants.

See E. M. Riley (ed.), *Journal of John Harrower* (1963); J. F. Jameson, *American Historical Rview* (Oct., 1900); and A. E. Smith, *Colonists in Bondage* (1947).

EDWARD M. RILEY
Colonial Williamsburg Foundation

HART, NANCY (1735?–1830), was born Ann Morgan and lived in frontier Pennsylvania and North Carolina, where she married Benjamin Hart. The Harts settled in Wilkes County, Ga., about 1771. Mrs. Hart's most celebrated feat, first publicized in 1825, was the capture of a group of five or six Tories, who, after killing a patriot, appeared at the Hart home demanding food. "Aunt Nancy" plied them with liquor and then killed one, wounded another, and held the rest until help arrived.

See E. M. Coulter, in *Notable American Women* (1971) and *Georgia Historical Quarterly* (June, 1955), definitive; E. F. Ellet, *Women of American Revolution* (1848), first widely circulated account; and G. White, *Historical Collection of Georgia* (1854).

JULIA ANNE SZABO MEARS
University of Iowa

HARVEY, WILLIAM HOPE "COIN" (1851–1936), gained national prominence in 1894, when he published *Coin's Financial School*, which won thousands of voters to the cause of free and unlimited silver coinage. In a witty style, *Coin's Financial School* presented the argument for currency inflation, and although it was a fictional account, the publication appealed to the distressed. The book depicts a young financier, Coin, who lectures on the money question at the Chicago Art Institute. Representations of bankers, politicians, and leading businessmen debate Coin, who exposes the evils of the gold standard. The book sold as many as 1.5 million copies, and Harvey became the "Tom Paine of the Free Silver Movement." Born in Buffalo, Va., he sought his fortune in the West. Failing in the practice of law and silver mining, Harvey moved to Chicago in 1893. After supporting William Jennings Bryan for the presidency in 1896, he settled in northern Arkansas and founded a resort, Monte Ne, near Rogers. The enterprise collapsed, and during the 1920s he promoted the Ozark Trails Association, a "good roads" organization.

See R. Hofstadter's introduction to W. H. Harvey, *Coin's Financial School* (1963); J. P. Nichols, *Ohio History* (Oct., 1958); and C. B. Kenman, *Arkansas Historical Quarterly* (Winter, 1948).

KEITH L. BRYANT, JR.
Texas A. & M. University

HASTIE, WILLIAM HENRY (1904–), born in Knoxville, Tenn., at an early age moved with his family to Washington, D.C., where his father became a federal clerk. He enrolled at Amherst College (B.A., 1925) and Harvard (LL.B., 1930; J.D.,

1933). In 1930 he joined the faculty of the Law School at Howard University. During the NEW DEAL, President Franklin Roosevelt solicited the assistance of black specialists to advise the various departments of the government. These well-educated blacks, often referred to as the "black cabinet" or "black brain trust," included, in addition to Hastie, ROBERT WEAVER and MARY MCLEOD BETHUNE. In 1937 President Roosevelt appointed Hastie judge of the federal district court for the Virgin Islands. In 1939 he returned to Howard as professor of law and dean of the Law School. From November, 1940, to January, 1943, he was on leave from Howard serving as civilian aide to Secretary of War Henry L. Stimson. Hastie took his responsibilities seriously and urged the elimination of racial discrimination in the armed forces. Confronted with the excuses and inaction of Stimson, Hastie in protest resigned his position. Returning to his post at Howard, he remained for three years until President Harry Truman appointed him governor of the Virgin Islands (1946–1949) and judge of the Third Circuit U.S. Court of Appeals (1949–1971).

AL-TONY GILMORE
University of Maryland

HATCHER, ORIE LATHAM (1868–1946), was a pioneer in vocational guidance in the South. She grew up in an atmosphere of learning and social service. Her father William Eldridge Hatcher was a Baptist minister in Richmond, a founder of a boys' school, and a college trustee. Her mother, Oranie Virginia Snead Hatcher, wrote on religious topics and was a trustee of Hartshorn College for Negro girls. After graduating from Vassar College in 1888, Miss Hatcher returned to teaching. In 1903 she received a Ph.D. degree in English literature from the University of Chicago. The next year she joined the faculty of Bryn Mawr College, where from 1910 to 1915 she was head of the department of comparative literature. Dr. Hatcher resigned from Bryn Mawr in 1915 to head the Virginia Bureau of Vocations for Women, which she had helped to found. In 1920 the bureau became the Southern Woman's Educational Alliance and in 1937 the Alliance for Guidance of Rural Youth, with Dr. Hatcher as its president. Its headquarters remained in Richmond, but branches developed in Chicago, New York, and Washington. The alliance first concentrated on securing vocational and educational opportunities for southern women and girls, but it later turned largely to training vocational guidance teachers and counselors for underprivileged rural girls and boys. Research and publication were two of the fundamental activities of the alliance, and Dr. Hatcher wrote extensively on occupational guidance and related subjects.

See Alliance for Guidance Files and Papers, Duke University Library; Richmond *News-Leader* (April 2, 1946); Richmond *Times-Dispatch* (April 2, 3, 1946); New York *Times* (April 3, 1946); and *Leaders in Education* (1941).

MATTIE UNDERWOOD RUSSELL
Duke University

HATCHER'S RUN, BATTLE OF (October 27–28, 1864). On October 27, U. S. Grant and G. G. Meade advanced 24 brigades against the Boydton Road and Southside Railroad, important Confederate supply routes below Petersburg, Va. Rain, woods, underestimated distances, unexpected entrenchments, and Confederate vigilance prevented J. G. Parke's and G. K. Warren's Union corps from defeating HENRY HETH's Division north of Hatcher's Run. W. S. Hancock's three federal divisions did reach Boydton Road just south of the run, but there they halted to await reinforcements, which never arrived. When A. P. HILL's nine southern brigades counterattacked in late afternoon, Hancock, in this his final battle, again displayed tactical mastery in parrying attacks from four directions; but nearly surrounded, low on ammunition, Hancock finally had to withdraw southeastward overnight, eluding the Confederate trap. All northern forces retired to their former positions near Petersburg on October 28. The secessionists hardly pursued. Hatcher's Run cost Meade 1,800 casualties, Hill approximately 1,500. Results were more lopsided. Bluecoats gained neither territory nor advantage there or during simultaneous fighting on the Peninsula. However, this ultimate evolution of Grant's two-pronged strategy of striking on both sides of the James approximately simultaneously, by failing totally, helped shift him toward massive single strikes, which brought victory in 1865.

See A. A. Humphreys, *Virginia Campaign* (1883); *Official Records, Armies*, Ser. 1, Vol. XLII; F. A. Walker, *Second Corps* (1886); U. R. Brooks, *Butler's Cavalry* (1909); and A. Badeau, *Grant* (1885).

RICHARD J. SOMMERS
U.S. Army Military History Research Collection

HATTIESBURG, MISS. (pop. 38,277), is on the Leaf River approximately 85 miles southeast of Jackson. Settled in the early 1880s by Captain W. H. Hardy, a Mississippi lumberman, the town was named for his wife and developed essentially as a lumber town. The University of Southern Mississippi (1910) is located here. The modern city is a producer of lumber products, explosives, and naval stores and is a processing center for area cotton, corn, and truck farmers.

See G. Watson, *Historical Hattiesburg* (1974); G. C. Neff, *Historical Geography of Hattiesburg* (1968); H. Price, *Illustrated Magazine of Hattiesburg* (1908); and files of Hattiesburg *American* (1907–), on microfilm.

HAYES, RUTHERFORD B., ADMINISTRATION (1877–1881).

When Hayes was president, he dreamed of building in the South a strong RE-PUBLICAN PARTY no longer dependent upon the Negro for its main strength, as had been the case during Reconstruction, and capable of commanding the esteem and support of southern whites. He planned to achieve his goal by diminishing Negro and carpetbagger leadership in the Republican party in the South while conciliating southern conservative whites in the hope of converting them to the party. Military Reconstruction, however, blocked any efforts to ingratiate the Republican party with the white South. Thus Hayes launched a new policy in the South, and it was a sharp departure from the one the Radicals had put into effect in 1867.

He appointed DAVID M. KEY, a southern Democrat and a former Confederate officer, to his cabinet. Then he removed the last of the federal troops from the South, ending military Reconstruction there and restoring home rule to southern whites. Although he recalled the troops primarily for political reasons—as a move to rejuvenate the Republican party in the South—he was influenced by other reasons. He acted to restore harmony between North and South and between whites and blacks. He responded to a general demand in the country for a change in policy in the South from that of military Reconstruction. And he also had reached the conclusion that the remaining Radical Republican state governments in the South had lost so much support they were no longer able to sustain themselves even with the use of force.

With these two spectacular moves, Hayes inaugurated his new policy in the South. Just as audacious and vital to the success of the new policy was his experiment of appointing Democrats and former Whigs to positions in the South in the hope of conciliating the white South. But he discovered it was not always feasible to abandon the Negro and the carpetbagger, and he was reluctant to repudiate entirely the old leadership of the Republican party in the South. Neither did Hayes attempt to create a new party in the South nor to revive the Whig party in that section despite the support for this policy in some quarters.

Hayes was seldom credited with any honest motives for his new southern policy, because the public in 1877—and for many years to come—believed what he had done was part of the bargain making him president in the Compromise of 1877. What Hayes tried to do in the South was almost a total departure from the strategy of the Radicals during Reconstruction; had it worked, the Democratic SOLID SOUTH might not have come into being.

See V. P. De Santis, *Republicans Face Southern Question* (1959) and *Journal of Southern History* (Nov., 1955), fullest account; S. P. Hirshson, *Farewell to Bloody Shirt* (1962); and K. E. Davison, *Presidency of R. B. Hayes* (1972).

VINCENT P. DE SANTIS
University of Notre Dame

HAYNE, ISAAC JOHN

(1745–1781), South Carolina soldier and patriot, was taken captive by the British at Charleston on May 12, 1780. The British paroled Hayne and other militiamen and permitted them to return to their homes. Hayne abided by his parole for approximately a year, but in June, 1781, he was ordered to sign an oath of allegiance to the crown. He refused, since it could require him to bear arms against his countrymen; upon receiving verbal assurances that he would not be called to His Majesty's service, Hayne signed the oath. Shortly thereafter, he was summoned to military service for Great Britain. He viewed the verbal contract breached, rejoined the patriot forces, and was again taken captive by the British. On August 4, 1781, the British hanged Hayne for violating his oath.

See T. D. Jervey, *South Carolina Historical and Genealogical Magazine* (July, 1904); H. Lee, *Memoirs of War* (1869); R. G. Rhett, *Charleston* (1940); D. Ramsay, *Ramsay's History of South Carolina* (1858); J. B. O. Landrum, *History of Upper South Carolina* (1897); F. B. Heitman, *Historical Register of Officers* (1967); R. W. Gibbes, *Documentary History* (1853); Y. Snowden, *History of South Carolina* (1920); E. Boudinot, *Journal of Historical Recollections* (1894); and A. S. Salley, Jr., *South Carolina Historical and Genealogical Magazine* (Oct., 1902).

LARRY G. BOWMAN
North Texas State University

HAYNE, PAUL HAMILTON

(1830–1886), was a romantic poet, magazine editor and critic, and promoter of post–Civil War literary understanding and reconciliation. He was born into a prominent Charleston family and graduated from the College of Charleston in 1850. With HENRY TIMROD he studied law briefly before undertaking a literary career. Although he edited several antebellum southern magazines, he received little remuneration from this or his first three books of poems published in the late 1850s. After 1865 Hayne experienced moderate recognition from northern literary magazines, but he still found it necessary to live in rural Georgia during his last 20 years, maintaining his family with occasional book reviews, monetary gifts from northern friends, and the produce raised on his farm. Two more books of poems, *Legends and Lyrics* (1872) and *The Moutain of the Lovers* (1875), and a final collected edition of poems in 1882 capped Hayne's publishing career. At his death Hayne held the respect of a few who appreciated his romantic southern landscape verse, his ornate diction, and his graceful sonnets, but New South LOCAL COLOR and realism had already left him behind, a representative of bygone southern literary ideals.

See R. S. Moore, *Paul Hamilton Hayne* (1972); J. B. Hubbell, *South in American Literature, 1607–1900* (1954), best short treatment and bibliography; and Hayne Manuscripts, Duke University Library

WILLIAM L. ANDREWS
University of Wisconsin, Madison

HAYNE, ROBERT YOUNG (1791–1839), was born in the Colleton District into the South Carolina lowland aristocracy. Marriage and association with LANGDON CHEVES's law office enhanced his career. Hayne served in the legislature (1814–1818) and held the post of attorney general of his state (1818–1822). Alliance with the JOHN C. CALHOUN faction in state politics enabled him to receive appointment to the U.S. Senate in 1822, where he remained until 1832. Hayne was initially an economic nationalist, but changed to opposition to the tariff by 1824. He is best remembered for his 1830 Senate debate with Daniel Webster in which Hayne defended states' rights and NULLIFICATION. He was governor of his state (1832–1834) when it adopted the ordinance of nullification and was an important member of the nullification convention. Although he was prepared to have his state defend its position by force, he eventually supported the compromise tariff of 1833. Prior to his death, he was working for an alliance of the South and West by promoting a railroad between South Carolina and the Ohio Valley.

See W. W. Freehling, *Prelude to Civil War* (1968), good discussion of Hayne and nullification; T. D. Jervey, *Robert Y. Hayne* (1909), poor but only full-length study; and manuscripts at University of South Carolina, Clemson College, and Duke University

LOUIS B. GIMELLI
Eastern Michigan University

HEADRIGHT SYSTEM of awarding land grew out of the concept of "adventure," by which a person coming to the colonial area qualified for a free share of stock in the colonizing company. Headrights originated in 1618 with the Virginia Company's offer of 50 acres of land to those who transported themselves to the colony; later the concept was extended to include grants to those who transported servants and slaves. There were many abuses, such as persons claiming grants for each trip they made to the colony, persons taking up headrights in several counties, and the secretary of the colony selling headrights for small sums. Around 1715 the headright in Virginia was largely superseded by the treasury right, by which 50 acres could be secured for the payment of five shillings to the government, in effect the legitimating of an earlier abuse. Servants at times got land grants upon release from their indentures. Sometimes they received the grants originally made to their masters, sometimes an additional grant from other lands. All the southern British colonies, including Florida after 1764, used the Virginia system, and Louisiana had a somewhat similar system. Several colonies at times offered more than 50 acres. Carolina had a graduated system, offering 150 acres to the earliest arrivals and progressively less to later arrivals, according to a state schedule.

See L. C. Gray, *Agriculture in Southern U.S.* (1932); M. Harris, *Origin of Land Tenure System in U.S.* (1953); W. F. Craven, *Southern Colonies in Seventeenth Century* (1949); and F. Harrison, *Virginia Land Grants* (1925).

MAURICE A. CROUSE
Memphis State University

HEALTH, PUBLIC. From the settlement of Virginia through the eighteenth century, white immigrants and Negro slaves of differing genetic and immunologic backgrounds brought various diseases to the southern colonies. The fluxes, fevers, and pleurisies of "seasoning"—a continuous process of biosocial adaptation—were early names for dysentery, MALARIA, and respiratory diseases. These became endemic and were the principal causes of sickness and mortality. Other infections in descending order of importance included diphtheria, scarlet fever, measles, whooping cough, and mumps. Epidemics were mitigated by dispersion of population in a region having but one principal city. Like other colonial cities, however, Charleston was stricken periodically by fatal epidemics of disease including smallpox and YELLOW FEVER. There, as in the country, provision for general sanitation was barely rudimentary (MEDICINE).

Following the Revolution, and especially after 1815, migrants from former southern colonies established new frontiers of endemic disease, notably malaria, in the interior valleys of the West. Regional economic development promoted rapid growth of cities, river towns, and hinterland communities, where the historical patterns of endemism were repeated on a different scale. Again malaria, dysentery, and respiratory diseases became major causes of sickness and mortality followed by the train of lesser infections mentioned above. After 1830, parallel with domestic migration and a rising emigration from Ireland and Europe, yellow fever's principal foci shifted from the Middle Atlantic cities to the growing South Atlantic and Gulf Coast ports. During the next four decades New Orleans was scourged repeatedly by yellow fever; nearly 10,000 persons died during the great epidemic in 1853. Frequently the virus spread to nearby coast and river towns in Alabama, Mississippi, and Texas. Moreover, in 1832, 1849, 1866, and 1873, cholera ravaged southern cities, towns, and plantations. The widening spread of both diseases throughout the region accompanied the development of railroads.

Prior to the 1840s, traditional concepts of health, sickness, and death remained intact. Historians agree that the regional death rate was high by present standards, yet the related question of significant racial differentiation is disputed. What limited health administration existed was confined to cities, and this consisted of minimal public works, a few ordinances prohibiting nuisances, and, during epidemics, hastily contrived boards of health and quarantine measures that were abandoned afterward. However, increasingly severe cholera and yellow fever epidemics brought infusions of ideas from England by way of Massachusetts, and traditional concepts began to erode. The New Orleans Howard Association, following an earlier Boston model, organized in 1837 to relieve the poor during epidemics. Various societies formed in other towns for similar purposes. By the 1850s some physicians and laymen influenced by Edwin Chadwick and Lemuel Shattuck began advocating sanitary reform based on a numerical calculus of human life as capital to be conserved. Although the District of Columbia created a board of health in 1822, Louisiana established the nation's first permanent state board of health in 1855. Between 1857 and 1860, reform-minded southerners were active in national quarantine and sanitary conventions.

After the Civil War the modern concept of public health became an integral part of the NEW SOUTH creed. Permanent health organization at the state level was effected in Virginia (1872); Maryland (1874); Alabama (1875); Mississippi, North Carolina, and Tennessee (1877); and Kentucky and South Carolina (1878). Following the great Mississippi Valley yellow fever epidemic in 1878, the region's cities and towns rapidly established permanent boards of health, and philanthropic relief societies reorganized as auxiliary sanitary associations. During 1879 urban businessmen and health officers founded the Sanitary Council of the Mississippi Valley, and southern congressmen, notably Senator ISHAM G. HARRIS of Tennessee, provided leadership in creating the short-lived National Board of Health and in establishing modern federal quarantine policy. Permanent state boards of health were organized in Delaware (1879); Arkansas and West Virginia (1881); Missouri (1883); Florida (1889); Georgia (1903); and Texas (1909).

Rapid growth of the urban South after 1880 brought water supply, sewerage, waste disposal, and street-paving improvements, which have undergone continuous extensions and technical refinements. By 1900 city mortality rates showed significant reductions in consequence of biosocial adaptation, more effective control of infectious diseases, bacteriological analysis of milk and food, public and private hospital development, industrial sanitation, and more efficient registration of vital statistics. At the same time, however, there was conclusive evidence to show excessive morbidity and mortality among Negroes, a disparity that continues in the present.

Tuberculosis, pneumonia, typhoid, and malaria were major causes of sickness and death in the rural South at the turn of the century. Then, between 1900 and 1910, extensive prevalence of HOOKWORM and PELLAGRA was discovered. During the Progressive era and subsequent to World War I, the Rockefeller philanthropies and the U.S. Public Health Service cooperated with state health authorities to bring these two debilitating diseases under control. After 1920 county health organization proceeded more rapidly in the South than in any other part of the nation. This development, accompanied by federal and state FLOOD CONTROL and lowland drainage programs, resulted in substantial control of malaria and respiratory diseases on the eve of World War II.

In the cities, as in rural areas, antituberculosis measures, immunization programs, and health education have been major tools of health administration since 1945. In the last quarter-century the region's morbidity and mortality statistics are comparable with those of the nation as a whole. Similarly, attitudes concerning public health in the South have a national character. The idea of health is inextricably bound up with the concept of state responsibility for social welfare. In this connection cancer, heart disease, stroke, mental health, industrial and occupational diseases, and provision of adequate health care services are widely considered to be urgent problems. This conceptual transformation parallels the region's industrial development, urbanization, extension of public and higher education, and rising per capita income. If the South's regional distinctiveness has all but disappeared, this is due in no small measure to the idea of public health.

See, for general introduction, G. Rosen, *History of Public Health* (1958); R. Dubos, *Mirage of Health* (1959); and W. G. Smillie, *Development of Public Health in U.S.* (1955). See also J. Duffy, *Epidemics in Colonial America* (1953); R. C. Wade, *Urban Frontier* (1959); D. Drake *Treatise on Principal Diseases of Interior Valley of North America* (1850–54); J. Duffy (ed.), *Rudolph Matas History of Medicine in Louisiana* (1958–62); W. D. Postell, *Health of Slaves on Plantations* (1951); R. C. Wade, *Slavery in Cities* (1964); R. W. Fogel and S. L. Engerman, *Time on Cross* (1974); J. S. Chambers, *Conquest of Cholera* (1938); L. J. Warshaw, *Malaria* (1949); G. Williams, *Plague Killers* (1969); E. W. Etheridge, *Butterfly Caste* (1972); *Atlanta University Publications* (1968); M. J. Bent and E. F. Greene, *Rural Negro Health* (1937); G. Rosen, *Journal of History of Medicine* (Oct., 1953); D. East, *Louisiana History* (Summer, 1968); R. J. Hopkins, *Georgia Historical Quarterly* (Sept., 1969); J. H. Ellis, *Bulletin of History of Medicine* (May–June, July–Aug., 1970); J. H. Cassedy, *Bulletin of History of Medicine* (March–April, 1971); and L. P. Curry, *Journal of Southern History* (Feb., 1974). For unpublished materials, see F. R. Allen, "Public Health Work in Southeast" (Ph.D. dissertation, University of North Carolina, 1946); C. V. Stabler, "Alabama Public Health System" (Ph.D. dissertation, Duke, 1945); G. E. Gillson, "Louisiana State Board of Health" (Ph.D. dissertation, Louisiana State University, 1960); J. A. Carrigan, "Yellow Fever in Louisiana" (Ph.D. dissertation, Louisiana State University, 1961); J. H. Ellis, "Public Health in Memphis" (Ph.D. dissertation, Tulane, 1962); B. B. Jackson, "Public Health Administration in Kentucky" (Ph.D. dissertation, Indiana University, 1963); B. M. Jones, "Search for Health in Development of Southwest" (Ph.D. dissertation, Texas Tech, 1963); M. S. Legan, "Public Health Services in Mississippi" (Ph.D. dissertation, Mississippi University, 1968); H. F. Farmer, Jr., "Hookworm Eradication Program" (Ph.D. dissertation, University of Georgia, 1970); and F. B. Hildreth, "Howard Association of New Orleans" (Ph.D. dissertation, UCLA, 1975). For bibliography, see R. B. Austin, *Early American Medical Imprints* (1961); G. Miller (ed.), *Bibliography of History of Medicine of United States and Canada* (1964); *Bibliography of History of Medicine* (1965–74); and *Index Medicus*. Original source materials are in state and local

health departments, in university archives, and in medical and public libraries. Leading depository is National Library of Medicine, Bethesda, Md.

JOHN H. ELLIS
Lehigh University

HEFLIN, JAMES THOMAS (1869–1951), gained notoriety as one of the South's most flamboyant demagogues. Heflin, a well-educated member of a substantial hill-county family in Alabama, defeated the Populist candidate for the state legislature in 1896. At the state constitutional convention of 1901, he joined with representatives of the black belt in framing a constitution that both disfranchised blacks and threatened the franchise of many poor whites of north Alabama.

Heflin's record in the U.S. House of Representatives (1904–1920) and Senate (1920–1931) was barren of legislative accomplishment. He was distinguished only by his theatrical dress and his vitriolic oratory directed against Negroes, wets, Wall Street, Tammany, and the Roman Catholic church. His active opposition to Al Smith's 1928 presidential bid constituted a direct challenge to Democratic solidarity and conservative rule in Alabama. After barely carrying the state for Smith, Alabama's black belt conservatives punished Heflin for his apostasy by barring him from the 1930 Democratic primary. Drawing support from the Klan and the Anti-Saloon League, both strong in the old Populist areas of north Alabama, Heflin ran for the Senate as an independent in the general election. He was decisively defeated, however, and served only in several appointed offices until he retired from public life in 1942.

See J. M. Thornton, *Alabama Review* (April, 1968); G. T. Harper, *Historian* (May, 1968); A. B. Moore, *History of Alabama* (1934); and M. C. McMillan, *Constitutional Development in Alabama* (1955).

MARCILE TAYLOR
Wesleyan College

HELENA, ARK. (pop. 10,445), called "Arkansas' only seaport," is a river and railroad shipping center. Originally the site of an Indian village, which may have been visited in 1541 by HERNANDO DE SOTO, it is on the Mississippi River approximately 50 miles southwest of Memphis, Tenn. Settled around 1820, it was named for the daughter of Sylvanus Phillips (1766–1830), one of the town's founders. The home of seven Confederate generals, including THOMAS C. HINDMAN and PATRICK R. CLEBURNE, Helena occupied a strategic position during the Civil War and was captured by federal troops July 12, 1862. The following summer, Confederate General T. H. Holmes attacked the federals at Helena, hoping to divert Union pressure from the VICKSBURG CAMPAIGN. On July 4, 1863—the day Vicksburg surrendered—Holmes launched a mismanaged assault in which he lost about 400 dead and 1,200 captured, compared with federal losses of only 239 men (HELENA, BATTLE OF).

See *Phillips County Historical Quarterly* (1962–); Phillips County Historical Society, *Historic Helena* (1973), pictorial history; T. Worley, *Arkansas Historical Quarterly* (June, 1967); H. and E. Purdue, *Pat Cleburne* (1973); C. E. Nash, *Reminiscence of Cleburne and Hindman* (ca. 1890); and J. H. Shinn, *Pioneers and Makers of Arkansas* (1908).

HELENA, BATTLE OF (July 4, 1863), was an attempt by the Confederacy to relieve federal pressure on besieged Vicksburg during the VICKSBURG CAMPAIGN. On June 22, 1863, Theophilus H. Holmes began moving toward Helena with a force of about 4,400 infantrymen, 3,200 calvalrymen, and seven batteries of artillery with 28 guns. Helena, on the west bank of the Mississippi River, was occupied by Union troops. Moving into position around Helena on July 3, the Confederate forces began their attack early the next morning. The Union force under Benjamin Prentiss, including about 4,100 men and 24 pieces of artillery, occupied strong defensive positions around the town. Moreover, the federal positions were within range to receive support from the gunboat *Tyler*, which was patrolling the river at Helena. The assault began at daybreak and ended with a general Confederate retreat before noon. The Confederate converging attack was weakened by inadequate intelligence of the enemy's defenses, misunderstanding by one division of the time to advance, and failure of the cavalry to give sufficient support to the infantry assaults. Confederate losses were approximately 1,636, and the federal losses were about 239. Since there was no federal pursuit, the Confederate survivors were able to withdraw into central Arkansas.

See *Official Records, Armies*, Ser. 1, Vol. XXII, Pts. 1, 2, XXIV, Pt. 1, XXVI, Pt. 2, most complete account; J. Parks, *E. Kirby-Smith* (1954); J. Harrell, *Confederate Military History of Arkansas* (1899); and E. C. Bearss, *Arkansas Historical Quarterly* (Fall, 1961).

CHARLES W. CRAWFORD
Memphis State University

HELLMAN, LILLIAN (1905–), a popular and significant American playwright in the mid–twentieth century, was born in New Orleans and educated there and in New York. Her father's New Orleans family and her mother's Alabama family provided her with rich dramatic material. Her plays are in general noted for incisive and explicit social comment, well-drawn characters, firm and accurate dialogue, and a blend of realism with the traditions of melodrama and the well-made play. Except for the first, all her important plays are laid in the South—in Washington and its environs, Alabama, the Gulf Coast, New Orleans. Her major plays are *The Children's Hour* (1934), *The Little Foxes* (1939, likely to be best remembered), *Watch on the Rhine* (1941), *Another Part of the Forest* (1947), *The Autumn Garden* (1951), and *Toys in the Attic* (1960). She has also published two enlightening autobiographical studies: *An Unfinished Woman* (1969) and *Pentimento* (1973).

See J. H. Adler, in L. D. Rubin and R. D. Jacobs (eds.), *South: Modern Southern Literature* (1961), and *Lillian Hellman* (1969); R. Moody, *Lillian Hellman, Playwright* (1972); J. Gould, *Modern American Playwrights* (1966); M. C. Harriman, *Take Them Up Tenderly* (1945); and J. Phillips and A. Hollander, *Paris Review* (Winter–Spring, 1965). Manuscripts of her plays are in University of Texas Library.

JACOB H. ADLER
Purdue University

HELPER, HINTON ROWAN (1829–1909), was born in Rowan County, N.C., the son of yeomen parents. After indenture to a Salisbury merchant, he unsuccessfully sought gold in California (1851–1854), a state he excoriated in *The Land of Gold* (1855). Returning to North Carolina, Helper wrote *The Impending Crisis* (1857), which by statistical comparisons sought to demonstrate that in myriad ways the slave states were inferior to the free, a condition he ascribed to slavery. He hoped to induce rebellion among the nonslaveholders, which would lead to abolition and, left to themselves, the blacks' destruction. Although banned in the South, in 1859–1860 Helper's work was widely distributed by the Republican party.

Helper was rewarded with the consulship at Buenos Aires (1862–1868), after which he returned to North Carolina to write three little-noticed, militantly antiblack books: *Nojoque* (1867), *The Negroes in Negroland* (1868), and *Noonday Exigencies in America* (1872). Helper spent much of the 1870s collecting two claims against Latin American governments, an account of which is in *Oddments of Andean Diplomacy* (1879). He concluded that the hemisphere's greatest need was for an Arctic to Argentina railroad, and he devoted the remainder of his life to its promotion. The concept was fully developed in *The Three Americas*

SOUTHERN HEMP PRODUCTION, 1850–1950
(in tons)

State	1850	1860[a]	1870	1880	1890	1900	1910	1920	1930	1940	1950[b]
Ark.	15	447				*					
Ga.		31									
Ky.	17,787	39,409[c]	7,777	4,583	10,794	4,600	2,866	260	97	85	10
La.		1					*				
Md.	63	272					*				
Miss.	7		3					2			
Mo.	16,028	19,267	2,816	209	31	1	2				
N.C.	39	3,016		2							
Tenn.	595	2,243	1,033				*				
Tex.		179	5								
Va.	139	15	31				1				
W.Va.			37								

[a] Florida and South Carolina each produced one ton of hemp in 1860.   *Less than 1 ton
[b] Census discontinued statistic after 1950.   SOURCE: U.S. Census
[c] Some authorities question the accuracy of this figure.

Railway (1881). The Pan-American Conference endorsed the concept and the U.S. government underwrote surveys proving its feasibility, but highway construction precluded its development.

See Helper's books; H. C. Bailey, *Helper* (1965); C. Eaton, *Freedom of Thought Struggle* (1964); and J. A. Caruso, *Hispanic America Historical Review* (Nov., 1951).

HUGH C. BAILEY
Francis Marion College

HEMP (*Cannabis sativa*), a plant of Asiatic origin, was introduced into the South at the beginning of the colonial period when England, seeking a dependable source of fiber for sails and cordage, encouraged the first colonists to grow it. Virginians found tobacco a more profitable crop, however. Several colonial governments in the South, as well as Britain, offered bounties to encourage the growth of hemp and flax, but the objective was never achieved.

Hemp production increased during the Revolutionary period, and afterward, in 1789, Congress granted protection to the crop by levying a duty on imported fiber. Settlers in trans-Appalachia planted hemp, which grew well in the fertile soils of Kentucky and Tennessee. It became the chief money crop of bluegrass Kentucky, and factories sprang up there to process the fiber. After the War of 1812 the industry spread into Missouri, where it came to rival that of Kentucky. The greatest stimulus to production was the expansion of cotton culture, which generated a demand for vast quantities of bale rope and bagging. Most of these products were obtained from Kentucky and Missouri, although cotton planters complained of their quality and of the tariff that raised the price of imported baling materials.

Southern hemp was usually not well prepared.

The process of water rotting (or retting) was occasionally used by some farmers attempting to turn out a product acceptable to the navy, but the common practice was to dewret the crop, which yielded an inferior grade of fiber. In either case, slave labor was considered essential to every stage of the industry. After the Civil War the production of cotton resumed, but metal ties and cheap jute bagging ended the demand for baling materials from domestic fiber. A brief revival of interest in hemp occurred during World War II, when imported fibers became scarce. The United States instituted a crash program; a few crops, primarily for seed, were grown in Kentucky and Missouri; but the center of the industry in this period was in the Midwest.

Hemp survives in a wild state in almost every area where it was once cultivated. The plant is now an outlaw, grown as a source of marijuana and hashish. The latter by-product was known in the earlier period, but, judging from meager evidence, it created few problems in the antebellum South.

See M. W. Eaton, *Missouri Historical Review* (July, 1949); L. C. Gray, *History of Agriculture* (2 vols.; 1933); J. F. Hopkins, *Hemp Industry in Kentucky* (1951); and B. Moore, *Hemp Industry in Kentucky* (1905).

JAMES F. HOPKINS
University of Kentucky

HENDERSON, JAMES PINCKNEY (1808–1858), was born in Lincolnton, N.C., educated at the state university, and admitted to the bar in 1829. After briefly locating in Mississippi, he recruited a company of volunteers for service in Texas, though they arrived after the conclusion of the revolution. Appointed attorney general in President SAM HOUSTON's first cabinet, he later served as secretary of state. In 1837 he went abroad and negotiated treaties of recognition and commerce with England and France. Resuming his law practice, in 1844 he was back in Washington and is credited with devising the joint resolution strategy that effected the annexation of Texas. In 1846 Henderson was elected governor but resigned almost immediately to command Texas volunteers against Mexico. Decorated for bravery, he completed his term in 1848 but refused to run again. In 1857 he was the unanimous choice of the state legislature to succeed THOMAS RUSK in the Senate. In frail health from the inception of his term, he died in Washington.

See F. Merk, *Slavery and Annexation of Texas* (1972); R. G. Winchester, *James P. Henderson* (1971); and F. R. Lubbock, *Six Decades in Texas* (1900).

STANLEY E. SIEGEL
University of Houston

HENDERSON, JOHN BROOKS (1824–1913),

was born in Virginia and moved to Pike County, Mo., in 1832, where he was elected to the legislature in 1848 and 1856. In 1861 he was elected a Union delegate to the state convention on secession and was chosen by the convention to represent Missouri at the border state convention at Frankfort, Ky. Appointed to the U.S. Senate in 1862, he supported Abraham Lincoln's compensated emancipation and later authored the THIRTEENTH AMENDMENT to the Constitution. His acquittal vote at the trial of ANDREW JOHNSON was partially responsible for his being defeated in campaigns for the Senate in 1869, 1871, and 1873 and for governor in 1872. Although never elected to another office, Henderson was appointed special U.S. prosecuting attorney for the Whiskey Ring cases in St. Louis by President Ulysses Grant. He was president of the Republican National Convention in 1884 and appointed chairman of the American delegation to the Pan-American Conference in Washington in 1889. Henderson served as regent of the Smithsonian Institution until just before his death.

See A. H. Mattingly, "John B. Henderson" (Ph.D. dissertation, Kansas State University, 1971); and J. B. Henderson, *Century* (Dec., 1912).

A. H. MATTINGLY
Southeast Missouri State University

HENDERSON, RICHARD (1735–1785),

migrated as a youth with his family from Hanover County, Va., to Bute (later Granville) County, N.C. He read law in the office of John Williams, a relative,

and later formed a legal partnership and a land company with Williams. Henderson's practice, his temporary attorney generalship, and his position as associate justice of the superior court informed him about western lands and endowed him with an uncanny ability to enlist competent frontiersmen in his ventures.

In the late 1760s, the treaties of Ft. Stanwix and Hard Labour and the Watauga lease encouraged Henderson and his associates, who operated successively as the Louisa Company and the TRANSYLVANIA COMPANY, to seek Indian lands. In the treaty of SYCAMORE SHOALS his group purported to acquire all Cherokee land between the Kentucky and Cumberland rivers and an access way through Cumberland Gap. Thwarted, however, by Virginia in Kentucky, he encouraged colonization of the Cumberland Basin in Tennessee in 1779–1780 when he reasserted proprietary control. He was one of the boundary commissioners between North Carolina and Virginia. Also, he served in 1781 in the North Carolina legislature and in 1782 on the council of state. He died in Vance County, N.C.

See A. Henderson Papers, University of North Carolina Library; Draper Papers, State Historical Society of Wisconsin, Madison; A. Henderson, *American Historical Review* (Oct., 1914), *Mississippi Valley Historical Review* (Dec., 1914), *Tennessee Historical Magazine* (Sept., 1916), and *Conquest of Old Southwest* (1920), all filiopietistic but useful; G. W. Ranck, *Boonesborough* (1901); S. C. Williams, *Tennessee Historical Magazine* (April, 1919); and W. S. Lester, *Transylvania Colony* (1935).

JOHN E. STEALEY III
Shepherd College

HENDRICK, BURTON JESSE (1871–1949),

took the B.A. and M.A. degrees from Yale. Working as a journalist in New York, he became one of the most influential muckrakers for *McClure's*. Having established himself as a man of letters, he received commissions to write books on a wide variety of topics. These included *The Age of Big Business* (1919) in the Chronicles of America series; *Victory at Sea* (1920), written in collaboration with Admiral W. S. Sims; *William Crawford Gorgas* (1924), Marie D. Gorgas coauthor; *The Life and Letters of Walter H. Page* (3 vols.; 1926); *The Training of an American: The Earlier Life and Letters of Walter H. Page, 1855–1913* (1928); *The Life of Andrew Carnegie* (2 vols.; 1932); and *Lincoln's War Cabinet* (1946). In southern history, Hendrick published *The Lees of Virginia* (1935) and *Statesmen of the Lost Cause: Jefferson Davis and His Cabinet* (1939). The former emphasizes the importance of kinship patterns in American society, and the latter provides a hostile interpretation of Davis. Despite the title, the book treats the diplomatic history of the Confederacy as well as its government. The author thought the Confederacy fell because of factionalism and internal strife, not because of military weakness. The books on Page likewise deal with southern history, since Page grew up and was educated in the South. Hendrick won three Pulitzer prizes, one for each of the titles on Page and the other for *Victory at Sea*.

See A. S. Link and R. W. Patrick (eds.), *Writing Southern History* (1965).

WALTER RUNDELL, JR.
University of Maryland

HENRY, PATRICK (1736–1799), unsuccessful at business and farming, turned to the law; in 1760 after a short period of study, he began practice. He came to public notice in 1764, when he argued the popular side in the PARSONS' CAUSE, a case concerning the salaries of Anglican clergy. Elected to the House of Burgesses in 1765, he secured the passage of several resolutions against the Stamp Act after his famous threat against George III. He represented Virginia at the First CONTINENTAL CONGRESS and, briefly, at the Second. While a member of the Richmond convention (March, 1775), he supported, with his famous liberty or death speech, resolutions urging the arming of the colony. He was elected first governor of the state by the constitutional convention in June, 1776. Serving three terms, he strongly supported George Washington and sent GEORGE ROGERS CLARK to the Northwest, securing it for the United States.

While serving again as governor in 1784, he protested strongly the projected Jay-Gardoqui treaty, temporarily denying the Mississippi River to American commerce. Formerly a nationalist, he vigorously opposed the Constitution in the Virginia ratifying convention, decrying the excessive power of the central government and the lack of a bill of rights. Reassured by the BILL OF RIGHTS and Washington's prudent administration, Henry became a Federalist. Henry's achievements have been clouded by hero worship, but he deserves to be remembered as more than an orator; he was a competent governor, a consistent exponent of human rights, and a successful practitioner and profound student of the law; and, for a quarter-century, he dominated Virginia politics.

See W. W. Henry, *Patrick Henry* (1891), for letters and speeches; M. C. Tyler, *Patrick Henry* (1898); R. D. Meade, *Patrick Henry* (1957), best biography yet but covers only

to 1775; B. Mayo, *Myths and Men* (1959); H. Grigsby, *Virginia Convention of 1776* (1855); J. Elliot, *State Conventions on Federal Constitution* (1861); J. R. Alden, *South in Revolution* (1957); T. P. Abernethy, *South in New Nation* (1961); and *American Historical Review* (Oct., 1921). For evidence of Henry's ability as a lawyer, see his plea in *Ware* v. *Hylton* (3 Dallas 199).

ROBERT F. JONES
Fordham University

HENSON, JOSIAH (1789–1883), often assumed to be the model for Uncle Tom in Harriet Beecher Stowe's UNCLE TOM'S CABIN, was born into slavery in Charles County, Md. According to his narrative, he was a bright, ambitious, and hardworking young man, anxious to please his masters and worthy of their confidence. He became a plantation overseer in Maryland and, after transporting 18 of his master's slaves to Davis County, Ky., in 1825, he achieved the same position there. On this trip he refused to consider escaping; and later, when being taken to New Orleans to be sold, he drew back from killing his captors. Finally, in 1830, he took his family and fled to Canada, making Dawn, Ontario, his home, founding a manual labor school, and returning twice to Kentucky to lead slaves to freedom. He had a complex and dissembling personality, but his abilities as a Methodist preacher, his trustworthiness, and his rejection of violent abolitionism led many to conclude that he was the original Uncle Tom. Mrs. Stowe was evasive on this point, and not until 1878 did Henson himself make the claim. A series of widely read autobiographies appeared over his name after 1849, all of them ghostwritten, and the later versions were greatly modified to fit the characters and the circumstances of the famous novel.

See R. W. Winks (ed.), *Autobiography of Josiah Henson* (1969).

JOHN M. MATTHEWS
Georgia State University

HEROES OF AMERICA, ORDER OF, also called the Red Strings because of a red badge worn in members' coat lapels, was a UNIONIST secret society in North Carolina for whites only. The society had a small membership, but it ably exploited loyalist feeling and the disaffection that the April, 1862, Conscription Act provoked. During the summer of 1863, the Heroes held over a hundred peace meetings throughout the state. Initially the society's object was to protect Union sympathizers, to supply the Union forces with information, and generally to organize anti-Confederates. However, in 1864 it supported WILLIAM W. HOL-

DEN's candidacy for the governor's race against ZEBULON VANCE. Holden's "treasonous" link to the order helped produce a disastrous defeat for him and tarnished the order for the remainder of 1864, but in 1865 it increased its membership and in the postwar era merged with the UNION LEAGUE.

See J. G. R. Hamilton, *Publications of Southern History Association* (Jan., 1907) and *Reconstruction in North Carolina* (1914); H. R. Raper, *North Carolina Historical Review* (Oct., 1954); G. L. Tatum, *Disloyalty in Confederacy* (1934); and R. E. Yates, *North Carolina Historical Review* (Jan.–April, 1940).

LESTER G. LINDLEY
Kendall College

HESSELTINE, WILLIAM BEST (1902–1963), a graduate of Washington and Lee, Virginia, and Ohio State, spent most of his adult life on the faculty of the University of Wisconsin. Renowned as a stimulating lecturer and seminar leader and a skilled writer, he was an authority in the field of the American Civil War and Reconstruction. Among his best-known works were *Civil War Prisons* (1930), still definitive in its field; *Ulysses S. Grant* (1935); *History of the South* (1936); *Lincoln and the War Governors* (1948), in which he developed the theme that all the states, in the North and South alike, lost the Civil War to a newly predominant national authority; *Rise and Fall of Third Parties* (1948); *Confederate Leaders in the New South* (1950); *Lyman C. Draper* (1954); *Abraham Lincoln* (1959); *Lincoln's Plan of Reconstruction* (1960); (ed.), *Three Against Lincoln: Murat Halstead Reports the Caucuses of 1860* (1960); with Hazel Wolf, *The Blue and the Gray on the Nile* (1961); (ed.), *The Tragic Conflict* (1962); and *Third Party Movements in the United States* (1962).

See W. B. Hesseltine, *Sections and Politics*, ed. with intro. R. N. Current (1968).

PHILLIP R. SHRIVER
Miami University

HETH, HENRY (1825–1899), a Virginian, graduated from West Point in 1847. He saw extensive service as an infantry officer on the Kansas frontier prior to the Civil War. Resigning his captaincy in 1861, Heth joined the Confederate forces. After serving under JOHN B. FLOYD and EDMUND KIRBY-SMITH, he transferred to the Army of Northern Virginia just before the battle of CHANCELLORS-VILLE and remained with that organization for the rest of the war. A division commander in A. P. HILL's corps, Heth played a major role in initiating the battle of GETTYSBURG. Although brave and tenacious, he was too impetuous and careless to rise above mediocrity as a field general. Despite his spotty performance, however, he enjoyed the unwavering support of Robert E. Lee and Jefferson Davis. After Appomattox Heth joined Ambrose Burnside, his West Point roommate, in a Virginia coal-mining venture. Failing in this and other commercial pursuits, he obtained several appointments with the federal government. At his death Heth was engaged in collecting Confederate material for the *Official Records* of the war.

See Heth Manuscripts, University of Virginia; J. L. Morrison, Jr. (ed.), *Memoirs of H. Heth* (1974); and J. L. Morrison, Jr., *Civil War History* (March, Sept., 1962).

JAMES L. MORRISON, JR.
York College of Pennsylvania

HEYWARD, DUBOSE (1885–1940), novelist, poet, and playwright, was born in Charleston of a distinguished, recently impoverished family. Although handicapped by frail health and an interrupted education, he prospered as an insurance broker. After cursory experiments with short stories he turned to verse about 1920, was a founder of the Poetry Society of South Carolina, and published three volumes of verse: *Carolina Chansons* (with Hervey Allen), *Skylines and Horizons*, and *Jasbo Brown and Selected Poems*. His first and best-known novel *Porgy* (1925), a story of violent Negro life on the Charleston waterfront, was well received. Heyward adapted it for the stage and then into the libretto for the folk opera *Porgy and Bess*, with music by George Gershwin. Although the novel can stand on its merits, it is the connection with the opera that ensures its and Heyward's place in literary hitory. Five other novels followed: *Angel, Mamba's Daughters, Peter Ashley, Lost Morning, Star-Spangled Virgin*; as well as a long short story "The Half Pint Flask," and a stage adaptation of *Mamba's Daughters*. Only *Mamba's Daughters* (probably his best novel) and "The Half Pint Flask" are of a quality to compare with *Porgy*.

See F. Durham, *DuBose Heyward* (1954), *Mississippi Quarterly* (Spring, 1966), and "Heyward" (Ph.D. dissertation, Columbia, 1953); and H. M. Cox, "Poetic Renascence, 1920–1930" (Ph.D. dissertation, Pennsylvania, 1959).

HEADLEY MORRIS COX
Clemson University

HEYWARD, NATHANIEL (1766–1851), was born near Port Royal, S.C. He married the Charleston heiress Harriet Manigault, who brought a dowry of $50,000 to the union and enabled Heyward to buy land and slaves while prices were low and eventually to amass a fortune in rice plantations and slaves. When he died he was the owner of at least 14 rice plantations with almost 4,400 acres in crops and well over 1,600 slaves to cultivate them. As a result of his success with rice, he was also able to acquire a cotton plantation, some forest land, nine houses in Charleston, and a fortune in fine furniture, silver, and securities. He was undoubtedly the richest planter in the Carolinas, leaving an estate of almost $3 million, greater even than the Virginia tobacco dynasties of the BYRD FAMILY and CARTER FAMILY.

See U. B. Phillips, *American Negro Slavery* (1918); M. Crum, *Gullah* (1940); D. D. Wallace, *South Carolina* (1961); and C. D. Rice, *Rise and Fall of Black Slavery* (1975).

HEYWARD, THOMAS, JR. (1746–1809), was born near Charleston, S.C. For 18 years he sat in the assembly (1772–1775), provincial congress (1775–1776), council of safety (1775, 1776), Continental Congress (1776–1778), and state legislature (1776–1789). He coauthored the South Carolina association, constitution of 1776, and ARTICLES OF CONFEDERATION. He shared extraordinary powers during adjournments of the provincial congress. In the CONTINENTAL CONGRESS, he signed the DECLARATION OF INDEPENDENCE. In 1779 he fought General George Prevost's invasion and was wounded. Elected lieutenant governor in 1779, he refused to serve. Besieged at Charleston, he was captured, paroled, and exiled. As a circuit judge (1779–1790), he upheld "Sumter's law" (THOMAS SUMTER) and the confiscation and amercement of Loyalist property. His Charleston home (still standing) was George Washington's official residence in 1791. In 1790 Heyward left government, concentrating on law and family property.

See J. B. Heyward, *Heyward Family* (1907); *Journal of Continental Congress*; and South Carolina Archives, stub entries, legislative journals.

W. ROBERT HIGGINS
Johns Hopkins University

HIGHER EDUCATION. See COLLEGES AND UNIVERSITIES

HIGHLANDER FOLK SCHOOL, located in Grundy County, Tenn., at the southern tip of the Cumberland Mountains, was the leading training center for southern labor and civil rights leaders from 1932 to 1961. Established as an adult education school to train rural and industrial workers, Highlander became during the 1930s and 1940s an outpost on the frontier of southern LABOR UNIONISM. Combining teaching and active organizing, Highlander emerged as the major training center for southern labor organizers. In 1953 Highlander began holding resident and extension classes in race relations and by the end of the decade had become the foremost meeting place for the major civil rights organizations in the South. In 1961 the school's charter was revoked by the state of Tennessee for irregularities in its operation as a nonprofit organization. Within a few weeks, the school reopened in Knoxville, Tenn., under another charter granted to the Highlander Research and Education Center. In 1972 the institution moved to its present location near New Market, Tenn.

See F. T. Adams and M. F. Horton, *Unearthing Seeds of Fire* (1975); A. I. Horton, "Highlander Folk School" (Ed.D. dissertation, Chicago, 1963); H. G. Thomas, *Tennessee Historical Quarterly* (Dec., 1964), *New South* (Summer, 1968), and "Highlander Folk School" (M.A. thesis, Vanderbilt, 1963). See also manuscripts at Tennessee State Library and Archives and State Historical Society of Wisconsin.

H. GLYN THOMAS
West Georgia College

HIGH POINT, N.C. (pop. 63,204), approximately 14 miles southwest of Greensboro, is a major manufacturer of hosiery, textiles, and lumber products and a wholesale market for furniture. The town was first laid out in 1853 as a station for the North Carolina & Midland Railway. Because the site represented the highest elevation on the company's rail lines between Charlotte and Goldsboro, it was christened High Point.

See files of High Point *Enterpise* (1885–), on microfilm.

HILL, AMBROSE POWELL (1825–1865), born at Culpeper, Va., graduated from the U.S. Military Academy (1847) and saw action in Mexico and later in the SEMINOLE WARS. On the eve of the Civil War, he resigned his regular army commission, accepting the colonelcy of the 13th Virginia Infantry Regiment. His promotion to brigadier on February 26, 1862, was followed by a distinguished performance against Joseph Hooker in the PENINSULAR CAMPAIGN. He was promoted major general and divisional commander on May 26, 1862, fought tenaciously through the SEVEN DAYS' BATTLES, and was from that time onward associated with Stonewall Jackson's command. He was of great value to Jackson at Cedar Mountain (second BULL

RUN), and it was Hill's "light division," reinforcing Robert E. Lee at the critical moment at ANTIETAM, that blunted Ambrose Burnside's thrust. Wounded at CHANCELLORSVILLE, Hill was promoted lieutenant general after Jackson's death and given command of the newly organized III Corps of the Army of Northern Virginia. He led that corps through GETTYSBURG and the WILDERNESS CAMPAIGN and on to the PETERSBURG CAMPAIGN, where he was killed in action. Lee considered Hill the finest divisional commander in the Army of Northern Virginia.

See D. S. Freeman, *Lee's Lieutenants* (1942); W. W. Hassler, *A. P. Hill* (1957); M. Schenk, *Up Came Hill* (1958); and E. J. Warner, *Generals in Gray* (1959).

PHILIP J. GIOIA
U.S. Army

HILL, BENJAMIN HARVEY (1823–1882), was born in Jasper County, Ga. He was a lawyer, state representative (1851–1852), and state senator (1859–1860), and his politics were Whig, then Know-Nothing, and finally Unionist. In January, 1861, at Georgia's secession convention, Hill initially opposed but then supported SECESSION. In February, 1861, he was a delegate to the Provisional Congress of the Confederacy at Montgomery, Ala. A Confederate senator during the Civil War (1861–1865), he defended President Jefferson Davis against critics. After postwar imprisonment by Union troops (May–July, 1865), Hill practiced law and shunned controversy until mid-1867, when he began to attack Radical Reconstruction in newspaper articles and speeches. However, in December, 1870, he urged acceptance of Reconstruction and, in 1871, forecast a new, industrial South. In 1872 he led the New Departure movement, which endorsed the Liberal Republican presidential ticket (ELECTION OF 1872). A congressman (1875–1877), Hill championed both the South and the compromise settlement of the Hayes-Tilden electoral dispute (ELECTION OF 1876). A U.S. senator (1877–1882), he died in office.

See B. H. Hill, Jr., *Senator Ben H. Hill* (1893), many documents; H. J. Pearce, Jr., *Benjamin H. Hill* (1928), outdated but useful; and E. M. Coulter, *Georgia Historical Quarterly* (Summer, 1973).

ROBERT D. PARMET
York College, City University of New York

HILL, DANIEL HARVEY (1821–1889), was born in South Carolina. Early in life his interest in mathematics and science reflected a considerable intelligence and prepared him for West Point, where he graduated in 1842. After serving in the Mexican War with gallantry, he resigned his commission and became a professor of mathematics at Washington College. He also taught at Davidson before he assumed the superintendency of the North Carolina Military Institute. Approximately two years later he entered Confederate service July 10, 1861. After participating in the first "battle" of the war at BIG BETHEL, Va., he went on to distinguish himself as a composed and resourceful leader in such battles as WILLIAMSBURG, SEVEN PINES, second BULL RUN, ANTIETAM, and CHICKAMAUGA. In the latter, he sharply criticized his commander Braxton Bragg and was relieved by Jefferson Davis. Thereafter he was relegated to secondary posts, surrendering in 1865. His postwar career included publishing and higher education. He edited *The Land We Love*, a monthly magazine of literature, military history, and agricultural interests. He also served as president of the University of Alabama (1877–1884) and the Middle Georgia Military and Agricultural College (1886–1889).

See L. H. Bridges, *Lee's Maverick General* (1961), best, extensive bibliography.

DAVID A. WILLIAMS
California State University, Long Beach

HILL, LISTER (1894–), as a U.S. representative (1923–1939) from a conservative BLACK BELT district in Alabama, nonetheless championed such measures as the TENNESSEE VALLEY AUTHORITY, federal aid to education, and the NEW DEAL. In 1938, with the support of liberal elements in the Democratic party in Alabama, he was elected to the U.S. Senate (1939–1969) to fill the vacancy created by the appointment of HUGO BLACK to the U.S. Supreme Court. He broke with powerful southern colleagues to propose federal control of offshore oil (TIDELANDS OIL CONTROVERSY) with revenue devoted to education. As his party's position on civil rights and on other issues became increasingly incompatible with preponderant sentiment in Alabama, Hill relinquished his position of Senate majority whip (1941–1947). Similarly, as education became the focal point of the civil rights struggle in the 1950s, he turned his primary domestic interest from education to health. As chairman of the Senate Committee on Labor and Public Welfare, he was the chief architect of expanded federal aid to medical education and research. His economic liberalism and racial moderation contributed to the narrowness of his reelection in 1962, when southern reaction to the civil rights movement was at a peak. In 1969 Hill retired to his home in Montgomery.

See V. O. Key, *Southern Politics* (1949); W. D. Barnard, *Dixiecrats and Democrats* (1974); W. D. Burnham, *Journal of Politics* (Nov., 1964); and Lister Hill Papers, University of Alabama at Tuscaloosa and at Birmingham.

WILLIAM D. BARNARD
Alabama Commission on Higher Education

HILLABEE TOWNS. The Hillabee Indians, perhaps the "Ilapi" encountered in Georgia by Hernando de Soto in 1540, developed in Alabama as an important Upper CREEK community within the Muskogee Confederacy. Buffeted by various white nations and seeking an alternative to intratribal and intertribal rivalries, many Hillabee were attracted to Shawnee proposals of Indian unity as early as the 1740s. Inspired by the Shawnee Tecumseh, some fought the United States in the 1813–1814 CREEK WAR. When the Hillabee tried to surrender to ANDREW JACKSON's army, another army destroyed their homes and massacred at least 60. The Hillabee later defeated Jackson (January 24, 1814), but then were among those he overwhelmed at Horseshoe Bend. After the war, Hillabee efforts failed to prevent Creek removal to Oklahoma.

See J. R. Swanton, *Early History of Creek Indians* (1922); D. H. Corkran, *Creek Frontier, 1540–1783* (1967); Angie Debo, *Road to Disappearance* (1941); and manuscripts in National Archives and University of Michigan Library.

ROBERT W. VENABLES
State University of New York, Oswego

HILLIARD, HENRY WASHINGTON (1808–1892), was born in Fayetteville, N.C. He left the legal profession in 1830 to edit the Columbus (Ga.) *Enquirer* and became a professor of English at the University of Alabama (1831–1834). As a Whig he was elected to the state legislature (1838–1839). After his defeat for Congress in 1841, Hilliard was appointed chargé d'affaires in Belgium (1841–1844). In 1845–1851 he was the only Whig elected to Congress from Alabama. While in Congress, he opposed the STATES' RIGHTS policy of the South and supported the COMPROMISE OF 1850. He was the outspoken political opponent of WILLIAM L. YANCEY. Although a leader in the fight against secession in 1861, he raised Hilliard's Legion of 3,000 men and entered the Confederate army as a colonel. After resigning in 1862, he resumed his duties as pastor of the Methodist Protestant Church of Montgomery and practiced law in Alabama and Georgia. His Republican party loyalty earned him

the appointment of minister to Brazil in 1877. Hilliard was the author of several books.

See E. C. Johnson, "Political Life of Hilliard" (M.A. thesis, University of Alabama, 1947); T. Cozart, *Alabama Historical Society Publications* (1904); and T. M. Owen, *History of Alabama* (1921).

ALLEN W. JONES
Auburn University

HILLSBORO, N.C. (pop. 1,444), the summer capital of the colony during the late eighteenth century and the meeting place of four of the state's first general assemblies, is approximately 12 miles northwest of Durham. Although the area was settled as early as 1700, the town was not laid out until 1754. First known as Orange, its name almost immediately was changed to Carbinton, then to Childsboro (1759), and finally to Hillsborough (1766) after Britain's secretary of state for colonial affairs. On September 24, 1768, the town was seized and plundered by the REGULATORS. Thirteen years later it was occupied by General Charles Cornwallis and then raided by area Tories. After the state's capital was permanently moved to Raleigh, the town's development was brought to a halt. The village remains the political seat of Orange County, and an inn and several old homes from the colonial period survive.

HINDMAN, THOMAS CARMICHAEL (1828–1868), was born in Knoxville, Tenn., but moved to Mississippi in 1841. He served as an officer in the Mexican War, then returned to Ripley, Miss., to practice law. Although politically active in Mississippi, Hindman moved to Arkansas in 1854. Elected to Congress in 1858 and 1860, he served as a guiding force behind Arkansas' secession. After being commissioned a colonel in Confederate service, Hindman was appointed brigadier general in September, 1861, and major general in April, 1862. He commanded a division at SHILOH, then headed the Trans-Mississippi Department until July, 1862. He fought the stalemated battle of PRAIRIE GROVE, Ark., in December, 1862, then was transferred to the Army of Tennessee. He commanded a division from CHICKAMAUGA until June, 1864, but saw no further field duty after a disagreement with General John B. Hood. Active in postwar politics, Hindman was assassinated by an unidentified assailant in Helena, Ark.

See B. L. Roberts, "Hindman" (M.A. thesis, University of Arkansas, 1972), definitive; C. W. Nash, *Cleburne and*

Hindman (1898); and B. Hindman, *Confederate Veteran* (March, 1930)

CHARLES F. BRYAN, JR.
University of Tennessee, Knoxville

HISTORICAL SOCIETIES. Since the founding of the VIRGINIA HISTORICAL SOCIETY in 1831, historical societies in every part of the South have been active in the effort to care for the records of the past. It may indeed be, as James Franklin Jameson once suggested, that in the twentieth century such societies have come to fulfill a role not unlike that once played by monastic houses and later by members of a wealthy leisure class, royal societies, and religious orders especially devoted to the tasks of history, such as the Maurists and Bollandists.

More certain, perhaps, are Jameson's further suggestions: that such societies exist because we "believe History to be a useful and important pursuit" and "that certain parts of [the] work are best carried on by organization." For the South, organized professional scholarly study of the region's past traditionally has been spearheaded by the SOUTHERN HISTORICAL ASSOCIATION (New Orleans). Other organizations, though differently oriented, such as the AMERICAN ASSOCIATION FOR STATE AND LOCAL HISTORY (Nashville), share that concern to encourage historical awareness. Rather impressively documenting the value of such widely varied efforts is the recent rapid growth both in the number of historical societies and of the membership involved in them. Presently, there are more than 850 historical societies in the South. Significantly, only 43 of these existed prior to 1900; but even more astonishing is the fact that nearly one-half the total now operating have come into existence since 1960!

Beyond these simple statements, however, serious generalization seems virtually impossible, so great is the variation among societies in matters of stated purpose, structure, and special interests. For instance, though the overwhelming number of the societies in the South are privately sponsored and directed, some (*e.g.*, Kentucky Historical Society, STATE HISTORICAL SOCIETY OF MISSOURI) are supported by public funds and have official functions to perform. There are specifically genealogical societies (examples range from the Virginia Genealogical Society, Richmond, to the Huxford Genealogical Society, Homerville, Ga.). Some specialize in erection of monuments and markers (*e.g.*, Preservation Society of Charleston) or in preservation and restoration of historic buildings or districts (as in Savannah) or entire towns (as in Williamsburg), and others emphasize MU-

SEUM and archeological collections (as do the Museum of the Confederacy, Richmond, and the Archeological Society of Virginia). More familiar to the researcher are those that concentrate on library and archival collections and possibly research-publication activities (typical here are the FILSON CLUB, Louisville, or most of the state-named societies, such as GEORGIA HISTORICAL SOCIETY). The work of these last in particular has been greatly affected by the growth of state departments of archives and history, most commonly introduced around the turn of the century.

What is especially important for the researcher to be aware of is that, although nearly all the historically oriented societies do specialize, few remain exclusively devoted to a single function for long. Organizations that were founded to pursue one specialty have frequently grown to include others little reflected in their official names (*e.g.*, South Carolina Genealogical Society, Charleston, and the Mississippi Coast Historical and Genealogical Society, Biloxi, carry on museum, historical sites and markers, and oral history programs). Further to this point, many choice collections in local history or highly specialized topics are to be found in the societies scattered throughout the region (*e.g.*, Winston S. Churchill Memorial Library in the U.S., Fulton, Mo.; American Canal Society, Glen Echo, Md.; Moravian Music Foundation, Winston-Salem, N.C.). Overall, more than half the South's historical organizations (about 450 of them) have library, archival, or oral history collections. A good many, though only citywide or countywide in scope, have all three. What can be equally helpful is that nearly a quarter of the societies (about 200) publish their own journals, magazines, or proceedings in addition to newsletter-type circulations.

Variations in size, staffing, and services available among historical organizations are equally great. They range from the national "sons" and "daughters" societies (the National Society of the Daughters of the American Revolution claims nearly 200,000 members), through the state-level societies, which commonly number 2,000–6,000 members (though some are larger, *e.g.*, the State Historical Society of Missouri counts 14,000 members), down to the hundreds of county and local societies, which typically have but a few dozen members. Indeed, some two-thirds of the 850 societies cited number *less* than 250 members. Whereas the larger organizations sometimes employ numerous full-time staff (*e.g.*, H. F. Du Pont Winterthur Museum, Delaware, has between 300 and 400 professionals, and the unique Colonial Williamsburg, Inc., has about 3,400), the great majority of societies, being smaller, can afford little or no professional staff. There is a special point here: approximately one-half the societies holding library-archival-oral history resources are actually in this latter class, operating with minimal staff at widely scattered locations.

Obviously, this can be a problem; but it is also a trend that will presumably continue. The understandable urge to retain local history collections in their "home" locale rather than allow them to be buried in remote depositories appears strong and growing, judging from the rapid expansion in the number of societies. That judgment is continually reinforced by the appearance of new societies every month.

Yet this same trend may also be a blessing for history and for historians in that it makes good research opportunities more widely available and that there is an increasing history consciousness on the part of the general populace. Even further, it increases the likelihood that documents of historical value will be preserved, since the means for doing so are growing at the grass-roots level. Whatever else, it appears virtually certain that the role of the smaller societies will continue its present expansion for some time and that the problem of location and retrieval of sources will expand with it.

Worth special mention for the function they perform, even though they are technically not historical societies, are the numerous government-sponsored agencies that are significantly historical in character. For instance, 62 of the country's approximately 170 national historical parks or monuments are in the South (HISTORIC SITES AND PARKS). There are also several notable military museums in the region (e.g., Army Aviation Museum, Ft. Rucker, Ala., and Naval Aviation Museum, Pensacola, Fla., are but two of more than a dozen) and three expanding National Archives and Records centers (East Point, Ga.; Kansas City, Mo.; Ft. Worth, Tex.), each of which provides unique research opportunities not easily duplicated elsewhere.

See D. McDonald (ed.), *Directory of Historical Societies and Agencies in U.S. and Canada* (1975), indispensable in gaining access to sources; and F. L. Roth and M. R. O'Connell, *Historic Preservation: A Bibliography* (1975), Vol. I of a projected six.

ROGER K. WARLICK
Armstrong State College

HISTORIC SITES AND PARKS. Historic preservation in the South is little more than a century old but is accelerating at a rapid pace today. The first significant efforts occurred in the same year,

1856, in Virginia and Tennessee. That year Virginia chartered the Mount Vernon Ladies Association, which raised the money to purchase and preserve George Washington's home, and the Tennessee legislature passed an act to authorize the purchase of the Hermitage, Andrew Jackson's home.

After the Civil War the South turned primarily to local, state, and the federal government in its historic preservation efforts. The one exception was the ASSOCIATION FOR THE PRESERVATION OF VIRGINIA ANTIQUITIES, founded in 1888 (similar organizations were formed later in other states), which among other projects purchased and preserved Jamestown Island. An interest then developed for the preservation of Civil War battlefields, and, since most southerners believed the South lacked the necessary financial resources for a project of this magnitude, they relied on the federal government. The first such parks were Chickamauga and Chattanooga National Military Park in Tennessee (1890), Shiloh National Military Park in Tennessee (1894), and Vicksburg National Military Park in Mississippi (1899).

In 1926 a new era in the private historic preservation movement dawned when John D. Rockefeller, Jr., decided to finance a project for the complete restoration of colonial Williamsburg, Va. This had immense influence and led to similar efforts in such places as Charleston, S.C.; St. Augustine, Fla.; and Savannah, Ga.

Despite these private efforts, general leadership and coordination for the historic preservation movement were lacking, even though Congress had passed the Antiquities Act in 1906 to authorize the president to set aside "historic landmarks, historic and prehistoric structures" and in 1916 the act to establish the National Park Service to administer most of these new areas. However, leadership was assumed by the federal government in 1935 with the passage of the Historic Sites Act, which established it as a national policy to preserve for public use historic sites, buildings, and objects of national significance for the inspiration and benefit of the people and placed with the secretary of the interior the responsibility for national leadership in the field of historic preservation. This policy was broadened in 1966 with the passage of the Historic Preservation Act, which also authorized matching financial grants to state and local governments and the National Trust for Historic Preservation, a private foundation chartered by Congress in 1949.

Some other significant sites are: Abraham Lincoln Birthplace National Historic Site, Ky.; Appomattox Courthouse National Historical Park, Va.;

Castillo de San Marcos National Monument, Fla.; Cumberland Gap National Historical Park, Ky.-Tenn.-Va.; Ft. Raleigh National Historic Site, N.C.; Ft. Sumter National Monument, S.C.; George Washington Birthplace National Monument, Va.; Monticello, Va.; Ash Lawn, Va.; Woodrow Wilson Birthplace, Va.; Custis-Lee Mansion, Va.; Stratford Hall, Va.; Gunston Hall, Va.; Moore's Creek National Military Park, N.C.; Russell Cave National Monument, Ala.; Wright Brothers National Memorial, N.C.; and Yorktown Battlefield, Va.

See C.B. Hosmer, Jr., *Presence of Past* (1965); F. Tilden, *National Parks* (1968); American Heritage Book of *Great Historic Places* (1957); C. Vanderbilt, Jr., *Living Past of America* (1955); J. T. Schneider, *Report to Secretary of Interior on Preservation of Historic Sites and Buildings* (1935); M. Curti, *Roots of American Loyalty* (1946); R. Goodwin, *Brief and True Report Concerning Williamsburg in Virginia* (1940); and J. Morrison, *Historic Preservation Law* (1957).

JOSEPH P. CULLEN
National Park Service

HIWASSEE RIVER rises in the Blue Ridge Mountains of north Georgia, moves north to North Carolina and northwest into Tennessee, and then flows southeast until joining the Tennessee River approximately 30 miles above Chattanooga. In all it is 132 miles long. In addition to Chickamauga Dam at its mouth, three additional dams have been built upstream and are operated by the TENNESSEE VALLEY AUTHORITY.

HOBKIRK'S HILL, BATTLE OF (April 25, 1781). After GUILFORD COURTHOUSE, Lord Cornwallis abandoned the Carolinas, and Nathanael Greene opened his campaign to reduce the British garrisons in the South (GREENE'S SOUTHERN CAMPAIGNS). With the main body of his troops (about 1,200 men) he moved on the British post at Camden, where the young Lord Rawdon commanded a 900-man garrison. Francis Marion and Henry Lee were detached to reduce Ft. Watson and prevent reinforcements reaching Rawdon. After Greene took position on Hobkirk's Hill near Camden, Rawdon learned of his dispositions from a deserter and launched a surprise attack on April 25, 1781. The Americans were encamped in battle formation and reacted quickly, Greene attempting to envelop the flanks of the British force in a counterattack. The plan failed when first a Maryland regiment and then a Virginia regiment of the Continental line broke in confusion. Greene was forced to withdraw from the field, though in good order. Casualties were about even, the British reporting 258, the Americans 266. The British victory proved to be meaningless, since the fall of Ft. Watson to Lee and Marion made Rawdon's position untenable and he abandoned Camden to Greene on May 10.

See C. Ward, *War of Revolution* (1952); and T. Thayer, *Nathanael Greene* (1960).

ROBERT W. COAKLEY
U.S. Army

HOBSON, RICHMOND PEARSON (1870–1937), congressman and reformer, was born in Greensboro, Ala. He graduated first in his class in the U.S. Naval Academy in 1889 and won popular acclaim during the Spanish-American War by leading and miraculously surviving a suicide mission in Santiago Bay, Cuba. In 1903 he left the navy and quickly became one of the great orators of his generation, prophesying war and pleading for a great battle fleet. Turning to politics he fought the Alabama Democratic machine to wrest the congressional nomination from John Bankhead (BANKHEAD FAMILY) in one of the earliest Alabama primaries.

In Congress from 1907 to 1915 he continued his fight for a larger navy, citing probable war with Japan and the "yellow peril." Although a supporter of most Progressive reforms and a leader in the national Prohibition movement, Hobson incurred wide criticism with his alarmist warnings. These, along with his occasionally liberal racial views and his active support of woman suffrage, weighed heavily against him when he ran for the Senate in 1914. Defeated by OSCAR UNDERWOOD, he turned to the Anti-Saloon League and other pressure groups to promote his favorite reforms. During the 1920s and 1930s Hobson formed several organizations to crusade for criminal drug laws and fight such threats as communism. He died suddenly while directing a publicity campaign against President Franklin Roosevelt's court-packing bill.

See R. N. Sheldon, *Alabama Review* (Oct., 1972) and "Richmond Hobson" (Ph.D. dissertation, Arizona, 1970); W. E. Pittman, *Alabama Historical Quarterly* (Fall, 1972); and Hobson Papers, Library of Congress.

RICHARD N. SHELDON
National Historical Publications and
Records Commission

HODGES, LUTHER HARTWELL (1898–1974), was born in Pittsylvania County, Va., and moved with his parents to Leakesville-Spray, N.C., at an early age. After working his way through the University of North Carolina, he joined the North Carolina textile operations of Marshall Field &

Company, where he rose to important executive positions before his retirement to enter public service in 1950. Appointive positions in the Office of Price Administration and the State Department during and after World War II preceded his entry into politics in 1952, when he was elected lieutenant governor. Succeeding to the governorship upon the death of William B. Umstead (1954), he was reelected in 1956. His administration was characterized by increased industrial development, enlarged public school appropriations, and reorganization of the executive branch. He weathered the school integration controversy by transferring public school authority to local areas. Appointed secretary of commerce (1961–1965) by President John Kennedy, he was noted for development of international trade and investment and foreign tourism. Upon retirement from government, he served as president of Rotary International and devoted attention to the Research Triangle Park, which he had promoted in North Carolina.

See L. H. Hodges, *Businessman in Statehouse* (1962), *Messages, Public Papers* (1960–63), and *Business Conscience* (1963); A. G. Ivey, *Luther H. Hodges* (1968) for young people; C. Rieser, *Fortune* (Aug., 1961); H. Rowen and J. J. Barry, *Newsweek* (July 24, 1961); and *Business Week* (Nov. 2, 1957).

THOMAS S. MORGAN
Winthrop College

HOEY, CLYDE (1877–1954), the brother-in-law of former North Carolina governor O. MAX GARDNER, was a product of the Gardner political machine. He was the third in a succession of Tar Heel governors known collectively as the "Shelby dynasty" because they all hailed from the town by that name. Hoey was an advocate of sound, conservative government, depicting the kind of politics desired by the state's moneyed establishment. As an attorney he at one time represented the Duke Power Company, was a private prosecutor in the GASTONIA STRIKE cases, and defended the Marion County sheriff and deputies in the Marion strikes of 1929. Hoey defeated the antimachine candidate Dr. Ralph McDonald in the Democratic gubernatorial primaries of 1936 in the most malicious campaign in the modern history of the state, one typified by vilification and character assassination on both sides. Hoey's administration (1936–1940) continued the "progressive plutocracy" in state government initiated by his predecessors from Shelby, Gardner and J. C. B. Ehringhaus, an administration based upon respectability, economy, and sympathy for corporate capital. With Gardner's support, Hoey was overwhelmingly

elected to the U.S. Senate in 1944, where he served until his death.

See J. L. Morrison, *Governor O. Max Gardner* (1971); and E. L. Puryear, *Democratic Party Dissension in North Carolina, 1928–1936* (1962).

RONALD E. MARCELLO
North Texas State University

HOGG, JAMES STEPHEN (1851–1906), was born near Rusk, Tex. His father, a lawyer-planter who had supported SAM HOUSTON and the annexation of Texas, was author of some sections of the constitution of 1845 and a brigadier general, C.S.A. With the help of a widowed sister Hogg began publishing a newspaper in Longview. When the Texas & Pacific Railroad started toward Dallas, he moved his paper to Quitman and opposed a railroad subsidy, corruption in the Grant administration, and lawlessness. After serving as justice of the peace (1873–1875), Hogg became a licensed attorney. His only defeat was by General John Griffith for a legislative seat in 1876. After serving as county and district attorney, he began private practice in Tyler. As attorney general (1887–1891), he regained thousands of acres for the state, increased school funds, forced railroads to fulfill contracts, closed several "wildcat" insurance companies, obtained an antitrust law, and used it against the Texas Traffic Association, a rate-fixing pool. He then made a strong railroad commission the main issue in his successful campaign for governor, though Jay Gould and some oil interests opposed him.

Hogg was one of the forerunners of PROGRESSIVISM. The "Hogg laws" included an appointive railroad commission; the railroad stock and bond law; a law to force land corporations to sell holdings in 15 years; an alien land law; and a law restricting county and municipal indebtedness. A prolonged depression blocked efforts to obtain a nine-month school year, but he did create a state archive. After SPINDLETOP, he became a founder of the Texas Company.

See R. C. Cotner, *J. S. Hogg* (1959) and (ed.), *Addresses and State Papers of J. S. Hogg* (1951); and H. P. Gambrell, *Southwest Review* (Spring, 1928).

ROBERT CRAWFORD COTNER
University of Texas

HOGS (*Sus scrofa*) apparently were not introduced to this hemisphere until the second Christopher Columbus expedition. Later explorers, particularly HERNANDO DE SOTO, brought pigs in larger numbers to the mainland, some of which escaped. Wild American hogs developed from these stocks.

The climate and the availability of mast, or feed nuts, allowed hogs to thrive in colonial America particularly in the southern regions. Included in the first Virginia colonists' possessions were three pregnant sows. In 18 months the hog population at Jamestown had increased to 60. Two years later the number had increased to 600. To provide protection from wolves, bears, and Indians, early colonists confined their livestock in pens and sties close by their settlements. Hogs multiplied so prodigiously, however, that it became necessary to turn them loose to forage for themselves. In this semiwild state, pigs created numerous problems. Not only were they the object of ownership disputes and sometimes warfare between Indians and colonists, but they also frequently created a general nuisance by uprooting corn and tobacco fields. This latter characteristic caused the proprietors of North and South Carolina to restrict swine raising in their colonies to protect valuable RICE and INDIGO crops.

As the colonial population increased and particularly after the American Revolution, large numbers of settlers began moving west into Kentucky and Tennessee. Hogs, because of their hardiness and ability to forage for themselves, were an important part of the western movement. As the nineteenth century progressed these "wood hogs" or razorbacks became an indispensable part of the western economy. A thriving business developed in driving the hogs, nourished on roots, acorns, and beech mast, back to eastern markets.

Over the years, new dietary habits and scientific breeding combined to bring a significant change. Prior to the Civil War "fat" hogs were desired for their production of lard, which was used in various ways including fuel oil for lighting and cooking. However, the development of refrigeration and petroleum products in the post–Civil War era, as well as new consumer demands, led to an emphasis upon the "bacon" hog characterized by a longer, leaner body. Abundant corn production in the Midwest proved to be an important ingredient in developing the bacon-type hog, and southern states were quickly overshadowed in the new market. Bacon-type breeds came to dominate the industry by the 1940s.

The years since World War II brought still further demands on hogs. Vegetable shortening increasingly replaced lard in cooking, and consumers became interested in a variety of meat cuts. The result was a new breed of hog, the meat type, which blended the features of the lard and bacon types. Breeds of this type currently dominate the pork market. The United States ranks among the top five nations in world hog population, and about 70 percent of the domestic production comes from eight midwestern states. Southern states, led by North Carolina, Texas, and Georgia, raise approximately 25 percent.

See C. W. Towne and E. N. Wentworth, *Pigs from Cave to Corn Belt* (1950), best general account; L. C. Gray, *History of Agriculture in Southern U. S.* (1930), standard; V. A. Rice, *Breeding and Improvement of Farm Animals* (1957); W. E. Carrol *et al.*, *Swine Production* (1962); E. M. Ensminger, *Stockman's Handbook* (1970):

SOUTHERN HOG PRODUCTION, 1850–1969
(thousands of heads)

	1850	1860	1870	1880	1890	1900	1910	1920	1930	1940	1950	1959	1969	% U.S. total
										on farms only				
Ala.	1,905	1,748	718	1,252	1,422	1,474	1,320	1,615	831	752	1,061	1,224	861	1.60
Ark.	837	1,172	841	1,565	1,505	1,766	1,575	1,457	776	847	753	499	247	.45
Del.	56	48	40	48	45	51	53	41	30	23	39	38	48	.08
Fla.	209	272	159	287	374	480	832	802	567	481	459	423	283	.50
Ga.	2,169	2,036	989	1,471	1,396	1,464	1,836	2,179	1,357	1,125	1,537	1,835	1,581	2.85
Ky.	2,891	2,331	1,838	2,225	2,037	2,009	1,532	1,585	1,035	1,053	1,530	1,653	1,251	2.26
La.	597	635	338	633	570	812	1,368	912	759	681	628	353	122	.22
Md.	353	388	258	335	312	360	326	340	205	159	245	217	167	.30
Miss.	1,583	1,533	814	1,152	1,163	1,313	1,336	1,444	733	826	875	812	384	.70
Mo.	1,703	2,354	2,306	4,553	4,987	4,635	4,517	4,036	3,861	2,347	3,912	4,777	4,250	7.66
N.C.	1,813	1,883	1,075	1,454	1,251	1,340	1,278	1,362	839	709	1,231	1,660	1,393	2.50
S.C.	1,066	966	396	628	495	631	678	892	471	439	598	673	414	.74
Tenn.	3,105	2,347	1,829	2,160	1,923	2,060	1,444	1,978	1,002	1,062	1,366	1,610	1,099	2.00
Tex.	692	1,372	1,202	1,950	2,252	2,779	2,430	2,367	1,561	1,514	1,292	1,159	1,007	1.80
Va.	1,830	1,600	675	956	797	999	836	1,026	700	486	797	786	536	.97
W.Va.	incl. in Va.	incl. in Va.	268	511	411	465	354	383	222	172	197	148	60	.11

S. M. Shepard, *Hog in America* (1896); and F. McDonald and G. McWhiney, *Journal of Southern History* (May, 1975), excellent on drovers.

C. FRED WILLIAMS
University of Arkansas, Little Rock

HOLDEN, WILLIAM WOODS (1818–1892), the most controversial state leader during North Carolina's Reconstruction era, was born in Hillsboro under the most humble conditions. At the age of ten, Holden was apprenticed as a printer's devil and worked his way up in the newspaper world until he purchased control in 1842 of the *North Carolina Standard*, an official organ of the Democratic party. As editor, he had a brilliant record, his influence being unsurpassed as he championed reforms of equal suffrage, internal improvements, universal education, and improved labor conditions for an industrial economy. By the 1850s he was the tactical leader of the Democratic party, having made it into the dominant party in the state. In 1858, denied both the gubernatorial and senatorial nominations because of his humble origin and his vigorous support for the "common folk," Holden broke with the Democratic party.

Throughout the 1850s he strongly advocated southern rights on slavery expansion and the right of secession, but by 1860 he shifted to a position of loyalty to the Union. During the Civil War he waged a continuous battle for individual liberty and was the state leader of the peace movement. Sensing the futility of the war, he worked for an honorable peace rather than unconditional surrender. For such views he was denounced as traitor, and the *Standard* office was destroyed by Georgia troops. He was defeated in 1864 in the gubernatorial race on the peace issue. In 1865 Holden was appointed provisional governor by President Andrew Johnson and exerted capable leadership in restoring federal authority and economic prosperity, but once again he was denied his political aspiration of being elected governor for a regular term. Later, as the Radical Republicans gained control over Reconstruction policies, Holden believed that it would be disastrous to resist congressional control. He then organized the Republican party in the state and led it to victory in 1868.

As governor, Holden faced many problems in reorganizing local governments, establishing an integrated public educational system, enacting penal reform, rebuilding and expanding the railroads, and obtaining equal justice for all persons. Although his administration was tainted with corruption, he remained above reproach, and it is generally agreed that his rule was one of the best in the South. Nevertheless, when civil rights and suffrage were extended to the Negro, resistance developed and a vigorous Ku Klux Klan committed many infamous depredations throughout the state. His attempt to maintain civil authority in Caswell and Alamance counties failed, and in the KIRK-HOLDEN WAR he declared the counties to be in a state of insurrection. Holden lost in his effort to bring the Klansmen to trial and, in fact, was impeached for his actions, found guilty, and removed from office. In 1872 he was appointed postmaster in Raleigh, a position he retained until 1883. Many attempts were made to remove his political disabilities, but Holden refused to initiate such action or to work on his own behalf, insisting that any such movement must come from the people and without political friction.

See E. E. Folk, *North Carolina Historical Review* (Jan., 1942) and "W. W. Holden" (Ph.D. dissertation, Peabody, 1934); J. G. deR. Hamilton, *Reconstruction in North Carolina* (1914); W. W. Holden, *Memoirs* (1911); W. K. Boyd, *William W. Holden* (1899); H. W. Raper, "William W. Holden" (Ph.D. dissertation, University of North Carolina, 1951) and *North Carolina Historical Review* (Oct., 1954); A. A. Wilkerson, Durham *Sun* (July 14, 1946); and J. H. Wheeler, *Reminiscences* (1884).

HORACE W. RAPER
Tennessee Technological University

HOLLAND, SPESSARD LINDSEY (1892–1971), was born in Bartow, Fla. He was a Polk County judge (1920–1928); a state senator (1932–1940); governor of Florida (1941–1945); and a U.S. senator for nearly 25 years (1946–1971). Although usually considered a social and fiscal conservative, as a state senator during the 1930s he was instrumental in gaining passage of a state workmen's compensation act, an old-age assistance program, and an act abolishing Florida's POLL TAX. In the U.S. Senate, however, he was a staunch supporter of states' rights and economic conservatism. He was most active in Congress as a spokesman of the cattle and citrus industries. Holland sponsored the Tidelands Act, which returned rights to submerged coastal lands (and their oil deposits) to the states. He cosponsored legislation creating the Everglades National Park and Alaskan and Hawaiian statehood. Holland is perhaps best known nationally for his sponsorship of the Twenty-fourth Amendment to the Constitution.

See *Florida Highways* (Dec., 1944), officially authorized; and L. Holland Papers, University of Florida Library.

JAMES W. DUNN
Hillsborough Community College

HOLLY SPRINGS, MISS. (pop. 5,728), approximately 40 miles southeast of Memphis, Tenn., was originally a spring surrounded by holly trees used by the CHICKASAW INDIANS. After the Indians ceded the territory in 1832, William Randolph, a settler from Virginia, founded the town in the midst of a rapidly developing cotton area. During the Civil War the town was raided 61 times by Confederate and Union forces, the most devastating being the Confederate raid of December 20, 1862. General U. S. Grant was using the town as a federal supply depot for his VICKSBURG CAMPAIGN. While N. B. FORREST was raiding Union rail lines between Bolivar, Tenn., and Columbus, Ky., EARL VAN DORN raided Holly Springs with 3,500 Confederate cavalrymen. They totally surprised the town's federal defenders but withdrew after destroying $1.5 million worth of supplies. The raid undoubtedly delayed the success of Grant's operations against Vicksburg. Sixteen years later the town was badly shaken by a YELLOW FEVER epidemic that cut its population in half. Never totally rebounding from this latter blow, the modern town remains primarily a market for area farmers and the home of Rust College (1866) and Mississippi Industrial College (1905). Several fine antebellum homes survive.

See O. R. Pruitt, *It Happened Here* (1950); and files of *South Reporter* (1865–), weekly on microfilm. The Marshall County Historical Society and public library both maintain collections of local historical materials.

HOLSTON RIVER is formed in northeastern Tennessee by the confluence of two forks, both rising in southwestern Virginia. From its farthest headwaters, it flows 235 miles to a point just above Knoxville, where it and the FRENCH BROAD RIVER merge to form the TENNESSEE RIVER. First settled on its upper waters by Stephen Holston in 1746, it was explored and surveyed by DR. THOMAS WALKER in 1748 as far as the present site of Kingsport. After the formation in 1749 of the LOYAL COMPANY, settlement gradually pushed downstream and, despite halted development during the French and Indian War, the valley served as a major avenue for pioneers entering present-day Tennessee. The TENNESSEE VALLEY AUTHORITY operates two major dams on the Holston.

HOLT, JOSEPH (1807–1894), was born in Breckinridge County, Ky. After attending St. Joseph's and Centre colleges, he studied law with Robert Wickcliffe in Lexington, was admitted to the bar in 1831, and began practice in Elizabethtown. He moved to Louisville to become the assistant editor of the Louisville *Advertiser* (1832–1833) and commonwealth attorney (1833–1835). After a sojourn in Port Gibson, Miss. (1832–1842), he returned to Louisville, toured Europe and the East (1848–1849, 1850–1851), and in 1857 was appointed commissioner of patents, then postmaster general (1859); in January, 1861, he succeeded JOHN B. FLOYD as secretary of war. A staunch UNIONIST he helped keep Kentucky in the Union and in 1862 was appointed the first judge advocate general. He was instrumental in the arrest and trial of civilians during the war and was the chief prosecutor of the Abraham Lincoln assassins. He has been accused of suppressing evidence. Brevetted a major general in 1865, he retired in 1875 and died in Washington.

See Holt Papers, Library of Congress; M. B. Allen, "Joseph Holt" (Ph.D. dissertation, Chicago, 1927); and A. Nevins, *War for Union* (1959–71).

CARLTON B. SMITH
Madison College

HOMESTEAD ACTS were blocked in Congress by the antebellum South when the issue became linked to antislavery. A homestead bill (25 cents per acre) was finally passed in 1860, only to be vetoed by President James Buchanan, a southern sympathizer. Thus, enactment of the first Homestead Act of 1862 had to await the withdrawal of many southerners from Congress and the administration of Abraham Lincoln.

Alabama, Arkansas, Florida, Louisiana, and Mississippi contained 47,726,851 acres of public land scattered among the pine forests where soil was poor. Cash sales of these lands ceased during the Civil War; afterward, Radical Republican George W. Julian, seeking farms for freedmen, pushed through the Southern Homestead Act of 1866. Similar to the act of 1862 (except for a two-year period during which entries were limited to 80 acres), it retained the IRONCLAD OATH for one year so that freedmen could have first choice of lands. Difficulties in reopening land offices and consolidating them into one per state after the war negated the effectiveness of this provision. Only four entries were made in 1866. By October 20, 1869, only 4,000 freedmen had registered claims. Over 3,000 were in Florida, where the FREEDMEN'S BUREAU provided rations until harvest; elsewhere assistance was limited to transportation to the claim and one month's subsistence. Distance from settlements, lack of both rations and implements, and white resistance doomed this aspect of the legislation to failure.

After ten years a nearly unanimous South, arguing that the act was punitive in nature and unfavorable to the growth of their LUMBER INDUSTRY, joined northern timber interests in its repeal. Dummy entries had been used earlier to cut wide swaths through the forests; but after repeal hordes of lumbermen and speculators, including major timber dealers in Wisconsin, Michigan, and Minnesota, bought huge tracts of land. Instead of economic expansion, northern control of most of the section's resources was the result. By 1888–1889 opposition to speculators and interest in conservation forced the adoption throughout most of the nation of a policy restricting entry under the Homestead Act, a policy first tried out in the South in 1866. Although homesteading continued for another generation, the most valuable stands of timber were already in the hands of nonresident lumbermen and speculators.

See P. W. Gates, *Journal of Southern History* (Aug., 1940); C. F. Pope, *Agricultural History* (April, 1970); T. D. Donaldson, *Public Domain* (1884), source materials and statistics; G. R. Bentley, *Freedmen's Bureau* (1955); P. W. Riddleberger, *Agricultural History* (July, 1955); and P. W. Gates, *American Historical Review* (July, 1936).

CHRISTIE FARNHAM POPE
Bloomington, Ind.

HONEY WAR was a boundary dispute beginning in 1836 between Missouri and the territory of Iowa involving an area lying between an Indian boundary line recognized since 1816 by the federal government as Missouri's northernmost limits and a line, which was farther north, resulting from a survey undertaken in 1836 by Missouri. Both Governors Robert Lucas of Iowa and L. W. Boggs of Missouri instructed county officers to enforce the laws of their respective territories in the area. In carrying out their duties they met with much hostility, until an episode involving the felling of three bee trees in the disputed region by a Missourian and the subsequent levying by the Iowa court of a fine against him sparked a strong show of force on both sides. Negotiations continued, but it was not until after Iowa had become a state and the dispute could be heard before the U.S. Supreme Court as a case between two states that a compromise was reached in 1851.

See P. McCandless, *History of Missouri* (1972), II; and S. Larzelere, *Mississippi Valley Historical Review* (June, 1916).

HOOD, JAMES WALKER (1831–1918), born in Chester County, Pa., became an active black abolitionist at the age of fifteen. He became a preacher for the New England conference of the AFRICAN METHODIST EPISCOPAL CHURCH, which in 1863 sent him to North Carolina "as the first of his race appointed as a regular Missionary to the Freedmen in the South." In addition to working with his congregation in New Bern and as an assistant superintendent with the FREEDMEN'S BUREAU, Hood served as a delegate to North Carolina's constitutional convention of 1868. A prominent and influential advocate of strong HOMESTEAD ACTS and of public education, he was commissioned by Governor W. W. HOLDEN as assistant state superintendent of public instruction (1868–1871). By 1870 he had 49,000 black children enrolled in schools and had established schools for the black deaf, mute, and blind. Hood's primary interest, however, remained his church. While holding state office he founded AME Zion churches in Raleigh and Charlotte, and in 1872 he was consecrated bishop (1872–1918).

See W. J. Walls, *AME Zion Church* (1974); D. H. Bradley, *History of AME Zion Church* (1956); and J. W. Hood, *100 Years of AME Zion Church* (1895).

J. REUBEN SHEELER
Texas Southern University

HOOD, JOHN BELL (1831–1879), was born at Owingsville, Ky. He graduated from West Point in 1853. After brief assignments in New York and California, he joined the famous 2nd Cavalry in Texas. After further frontier duty Hood resigned on April 17, 1861, in order to accept a commission as lieutenant in the Confederate regular army. His subsequent rise was spectacular, and he obtained the rank of army commander by July, 1864. Along the way he valiantly led the Texas Brigade at GAINES' MILL. He was outstanding in divisional leadership at second BULL RUN and ANTIETAM. Wounds at GETTYSBURG and CHICKAMAUGA, respectively, cost him the use of his left arm and the amputation of his right leg. Hood returned to action in 1864 as a corps commander under JOSEPH E. JOHNSTON. When President Jefferson Davis relieved Johnston on July 18, 1864, he directed Hood to command the Army of Tennessee in efforts to halt W. T. Sherman. Courageous and daring, but inexperienced in corps and army command, the ill-fated Hood unsuccessfully attacked the federal left at PEACH TREE CREEK. Furious battles around Atlanta eventually resulted in Confederate evacuation of that important rail junction. Hood's campaign into Tennessee to strike Sherman's communications failed completely. After disheartening defeats at the battles of FRANKLIN and NASHVILLE, Hood asked to be relieved of his command. After the war, he engaged in unsuccessful business ventures in New Orleans. He died in New Orleans of yellow fever.

See J. B. Hood, *Advance and Retreat* (1880); J. P. Dyer, *Gallant Hood* (1950); R. O'Connor, *Hood* (1949); F. E. Vandiver, *Military Affairs* (Spring, 1952); T. L. Connelly, *Autumn of Glory* (1971); E. Warner, *Generals in Gray* (1959); T. R. Hay, *Hood's Tennessee Campaign* (1929); and H. B. Simpson, *Hood's Texas Brigade* (1970).

JAMES L. NICHOLS
Stephen F. Austin State University

HOOKWORM (*Necator americanus*, or "American killer") is an intestinal parasite spread by the careless disposal of human excrement. As many as 2,000 eggs a day may be produced by the mature female. If the eggs fall upon porous, moist, and shaded ground, they develop into larvae and, if the larvae come into contact with a human foot, they burrow into the skin and enter the host's circulatory system. They are carried benignly through the circulatory system to the lungs, where they are passed upward by ciliary action into the throat. When swallowed, they enter the digestive system, molt, and adhere to the inner wall of the host's intestine. Adult worms grow to about a third of an inch and may live as long as five years, although most are eliminated in a short period of time. Within a few weeks the female produces eggs, which pass through the lower intestine, and the cycle repeats itself.

In only a few especially severe cases has hookworm been a direct cause of death from heart failure or chronic diarrhea. Infected persons usually develop a protruded abdomen and become generally listless. They suffer from irregular pulse, heart palpitations, and often acute anemia. Youths may even find their growth stunted. Thus, unwitting hosts, in their debilitated condition, are made lethargic workers and highly vulnerable to other far more deadly diseases.

At the Pan-American Sanitary Congress of 1902, Dr. Charles W. Stiles made known the widespread existence of hookworm in the South and attributed to it many of the region's health problems. Few southerners liked being told that they had worms. Some, mocking Stiles's belief that perhaps as many as 2 million southerners carried the disease, credited him with the discovery of the "laziness germ." After opening a clinic in Columbia, S.C., however, Stiles quickly demonstrated both the prevalence and the cure for hookworm. Inadequate financing of public health programs handicapped efforts to treat the disease until, in 1908, John D. Rockefeller was persuaded to fund with $1 million the Rockefeller Sanitary Commission for the Eradication of Hookworm Disease. Between 1909 and 1914, clinics supported by the commission examined 1,087,666 persons in 578 counties of 11 southern states and treated 440,376 patients.

Control of hookworm emphasized breaking the parasite's life cycle through the use of footwear and sanitation. But, like many of the South's ills, the problems posed by hookworm overlapped with the more fundamental problem of regional poverty. Shoes, boots, and even crude privies, all essential to control of the parasite, were relative luxuries to many sharecroppers, tenant farmers, and mill workers in the early years of this century. After the Rockefeller commission disbanded in 1914, improved local public health programs continued that agency's excellent work and, although various species of hookworm continue to infect parts of Central and South America, the parasite is, though not extinct, at least under control in the southeastern United States.

See C. W. Stiles's report, in *Child Conference for Research and Welfare* (1910); *McClure's* (Oct., 1909); W. H. Page, *World's Work* (Sept., 1912); *Annual Report of Rockefeller Sanitary Commission for Eradication of Hookworm* (1910–15); U.S. Bureau of Labor Statistics *Bulletin* (1915); *American Journal of Public Health* (Aug., 1925); *Science Newsletter* (Sept., 1965); G. N. Sisk, *Alabama Historical Quarterly* (Spring, 1962); and H. F. Farmer, "Hookworm, 1909–1925" (Ph.D. dissertation, University of Georgia, 1970).

HOOPER, BEN WADE (1870–1957), Tennessee's only Republican governor between 1883 and 1921, was born in Newport, Tenn., the illegitimate child of Sarah Wade and Dr. L. W. Hooper. His first years were spent in poverty with his mother, who placed him in a Knoxville orphanage; he was then adopted by his father, who reared him in Newport. Graduating from Carson-Newman College (1890), he studied law, ran successfully for state representative in 1892 and 1894, became a captain in the Spanish-American War, and served as assistant U.S. attorney for east Tennessee (1906–1910). When Tennessee's Democrats divided over the liquor issue, Hooper, backed by a coalition of Republicans and temperance Democrats, won the governorship in 1910 and 1912. Contentious but able, he frustrated moves to modify the state PRO-HIBITION and fair election laws and maneuvered a hostile legislature into passing stronger antisaloon measures. Essentially conservative, he supported many goals of PROGRESSIVISM while governor. Denied a third term in 1914 and a Senate seat in 1916, he was appointed by President Warren G. Harding to the U.S. Railway Labor Board, where he served with distinction. Returning to

Newport in 1926, Hooper worked for the creation of the Great Smoky Mountains National Park and practiced law until his death.

See E. R. Boyce, *Unwanted Boy* (1963); P. E. Isaac, *Prohibition and Politics* (1965) and *Tennessee Historical Quarterly* (Fall, 1968); R. L. Stockard, *East Tennessee Historical Society's Publications* (1954, 1960); and Hooper Papers, University of Tennessee, Knoxville.

PAUL E. ISAAC
Lamar University

HOOPER, JOHNSON JONES (1815–1862), was a lawyer, newspaper editor, and author. *Some Adventures of Captain Simon Suggs* (1845) comically recreates the east Alabama frontier of 1835. Of a distinguished family, a migrant from North Carolina, a Whig, sympathetic to the Creek Indians, Hooper in his mock campaign biography denounced the speculators and satirized democracy and the morals and culture of the settlers. His book's rogue protagonist Suggs, whose motto is "it is good to be shifty in a new country," burlesques the career of Andrew Jackson. Hooper's use of dialect, the comic oral tale, and reductive imagery skillfully utilizes the culture of folk humor. He also wrote *A Ride with Old Kit Kuncker* (1849), *The Widow Rugby's Husband* (1851), and other works. As Hooper's ambition grew, he was embarrassed to be known as a comic writer. His Montgomery *Mail* (1854–1861) supported first the Know-Nothing party, then the Rights of the South movement, then became opposition party to the Democrats and strongly secessionist. He was elected secretary to the Provisional Congress of the Confederacy. After moving with the government to Richmond, he became a Catholic convert shortly before his death.

See W. Blair, *Native American Humor* (1960); W. S. Hoole, *Alias Simon Suggs: Life and Times of Johnson Jones Hooper* (1952); F. T. Meriwether, "Rogue in Life and Humor of Old Southwest" (Ph.D. dissertation, Louisiana State University, 1952); N. W. Yates, in L. D. Rubin (ed.), *Bibliographical Guide to Southern Literature* (1969); and N. W. Yates, *William T. Porter and Spirit of Times* (1957).

MILTON RICKELS
University of Southwestern Louisiana

HOOVER, HERBERT, ADMINISTRATION (1929–1933). Even during the GREAT DEPRESSION, Hoover maintained his disdain for federal intervention, and his program reflected his reliance on voluntarism and local initiative. The Agricultural Marketing Act (1929) created the federal Farm Board with power to supervise the marketing of agricultural products, to aid cooperatives, and to set up stabilization corporations to purchase market surpluses. Hoover urged farmers to reduce production voluntarily. Unfortunately, while the government stored burgeoning surpluses and southern wheat, cotton, and tobacco cooperatives obtained millions of dollars, farmers increased production and prices plummeted. The Louisiana and Texas legislatures limited cotton production, but other states procrastinated and the courts invalidated the restrictive legislation. The Farm Board ceased its purchases in 1932, and cotton markets collapsed.

During the severe drought of 1930, the president urged Red Cross intervention and an extension of all agricultural loans by banks and businesses. Congress, exceeding the administration's initial request, appropriated $45 million for seed, feed, and fertilizer loans. Hoover next concluded a protective tariff would aid southern agriculture. In 1931, one-fourth of the southern congressmen violated their traditional low tariff stand and voted for the Hawley-Smoot Act. Although it included numerous amendments protecting local items, the record schedules on ten times as many nonagricultural items easily negated the South's advantage. As economists warned, the tariff accelerated decline. Hoover moved leftward on agricultural relief, financial loans, and public works, as southern leaders deserted his antifederal position and urged greater intervention. However, even Hoover's RECONSTRUCTION FINANCE CORPORATION and Federal Home Loan Bank acts, saving corporations and homes, failed to generate broad recovery. The Emergency Relief and Construction Act (1932) went further and supplied states with relief loans and public works projects, but these limited policies failed the South as well as the nation. Finally, Hoover's patronage policies alienated even the traditional Negro support of the GOP. As the 1932 election neared, it was evident that Hoover had failed.

See G. B. Tindall, *Emergence of New South* (1967), excellent; J. A. Schwarz, *Interregnum of Despair* (1970), superb on Congress; H. G. Warren, *Hoover and Depression* (1959), general; H. E. Everman, "Hoover and New Deal" (Ph.D. dissertation, Louisiana State University, 1970), philosophy; and A. U. Romasco, *Poverty of Abundance* (1965).

H. E. EVERMAN
Eastern Kentucky University

HOPE, JOHN (1868–1936), of mixed white and black blood, might easily have lived as a white in his native Augusta, Ga. After his father's death in 1876 and the HAMBURG RACE RIOT in South Carolina, however, he gravitated increasingly toward the black world. He worked his way through Worcester Academy in Massachusetts (1886–1890) and Brown University, where he graduated in 1894 as class orator. From 1894 until his death, he dedicated himself to the education of black youth. He was professor of classics at Atlanta Baptist College (later Morehouse College) from 1898 to 1906; in the latter year, he became the school's president (1906–1929). From 1929 to 1936 he served as the first president of Atlanta University, the nation's first black graduate school. Shortly after BOOKER T. WASHINGTON delivered his ATLANTA COMPROMISE address in 1895, Hope began to demand publicly complete equality for blacks. He was the only college president to attend the Harpers Ferry Conference (1906), a forerunner of the NATIONAL ASSOCIATION FOR THE ADVANCEMENT OF COLORED PEOPLE. He helped organize the COMMISSION ON INTERRACIAL COOPERATION and was its first black president (1932). Hope also served as a member of the advisory board of the NAACP and as a member of the executive committee of the National URBAN LEAGUE. In his work in behalf of blacks, he sought to challenge the intellect rather than appeal to the emotions.

See R. Torrence, *Story of John Hope* (1948); and W. W. Alexander, *Phylon* (1st Quarter, 1947).

L. MOODY SIMS, JR.
Illinois State University

HOPKINS, JULIET OPIE (1816–1890), was born in Virginia but moved to Mobile, Ala., upon her marriage to Judge A. F. Hopkins, Whig leader and railroad president. Early in the Civil War the Hopkinses became interested in the care of sick soldiers, financing their efforts with donations and their own resources. In November, 1861, the Alabama legislature created the offices of agent for hospitals and superintendent, naming the Hopkinses to the offices and eventually appropriating more than $73,000. Mrs. Hopkins administered the Alabama hospitals in Virginia, employing surgeons, nurses, and stewards, distributing supplies, answering a voluminous mail, and soliciting donations in Alabama. She received high praise from private citizens and high officials. She died in modest circumstances in Washington, D.C., and was buried with military honors at Arlington.

See W. Garrett, *Public Men in Alabama* (1872); T. C. Leon, *Belles, Beaux, and Brains* (1907); T. M. Owen, *Alabama* (1921); L. B. Griffith, *Alabama Review* (April, 1953); H. E. Sterkx, *Partners in Rebellion* (1970); and Hopkins Papers, Alabama State Archives.

LUCILLE GRIFFITH
Montevallo, Ala.

HORSE RACING, as a sport, originated in England in the twelfth century during the reign of Henry II (1154–1189). It was introduced in America in 1610, when the London Company sent seven horses to its colony in Jamestown. America's first racecourse was established in 1665 on Long Island by Colonel Richard Nicolls, governor of New York, near the site of present-day Aqueduct racecourse. Horse racing, "the sport of kings," is the nation's leading spectator sport. Yearly attendance at America's 97 racetracks exceeds 50 million, and annual wagering totals over $4 billion. Thoroughbred horse racing is conducted in 29 states, of which seven (Maryland, Kentucky, West Virginia, Delaware, Arkansas, Florida, and Louisiana) are southern.

Virginia, the pioneer state for horse racing in the South, initially limited racing to quarter horses. This changed in 1730, when a stallion, Bulle Rocke, was imported, providing the colony with its first "bred" horse. The common distance raced was four miles; the age, five years old and upward. The Tayloes of Mount Airy, Va. (close friends of President James Madison), and the Bowies of Maryland were two prominent racing families in colonial times. South and North Carolina also were centers for horse racing, Charleston claiming to have established America's first jockey club in 1734, a date that precedes the first jockey club in England.

By the 1790s horse racing was also popular in Tennessee and Kentucky. ANDREW JACKSON was the dominant figure in early Tennessee racing, and in Kentucky, where breeding figured more prominently, it was Elisha Warfield, Jr. (1781–1859). A fierce interstate rivalry soon developed. It was this rivalry and a trip to the racecourses of Europe that in 1875 caused Colonel W. Lewis Clark of Louisville, Ky., to propose a test between Kentucky's and Tennessee's best three-year-old horses: the Kentucky Derby. The Derby, run at Churchill Downs in Louisville, has since become the world's most famous three-year-olds race classic. Thoroughbred racing also has deep historical antecedents in Florida, Louisiana, Arkansas, and Maryland. All four have historic racecourses: Hialeah (Fla.); the Fairgrounds (La.); Oaklawn (Ark.); and Pimlico (Md.).

The breeding of thoroughbreds has long been one of the South's leading industries. Kentucky, Maryland, Florida, and Louisiana, in that order, lead the way. In 1973 the Keeneland Horse Sales in Kentucky grossed a record $59,423,300, and in July, 1976, an unheard-of $1.5 million was paid for a two-year-old colt. It is estimated that in Kentucky alone the horse-breeding industry is a $625 million a year business, and in the South the total exceeds $3 billion. Horse racing, which is conducted year-round in America, has become the nation's leading sports industry.

See *American Turf Register* (annual) and *American Stud Book* (every 4 yrs.), individual horses; *American Racing Manual* and *Daily Racing Form* (annual and daily), official statistics and records; Keeneland Association Library, Lexington, Ky., and National Museum of Racing, Saratoga Springs, N.Y., outstanding source collections; and *Thoroughbred Record* and *Blood-Horse*, top periodicals.

JAMES C. CLAYPOOL
Northern Kentucky University

HORSES. As early as 1528, CABEZA DE VACA landed horses at Tampa, Fla. In 1565, with the founding of St. Augustine, more horses were brought to Florida; and, beginning in 1610, they were brought into New Mexico. Horses were adopted by the western Indians and quickly spread over the southern plains. According to some accounts, the Spanish horses in Florida spread northward to the borders of the English settlements. The English brought horses to Jamestown in 1607, but were forced to eat them during the starving times. Another supply arrived in 1610, but they were few in number for several decades. Whether they came north from Florida or moved west from the coast, by 1670 droves of horses were running wild along the western frontiers of Virginia and the Carolinas. Most of these animals had deteriorated in size and were of little value. After the turn of the century, however, Scotch-Irish and Germans from Pennsylvania moved south along the Piedmont, bringing good horses with them.

About the mid–eighteenth century, southern horses were further improved by importations from England. During the Revolutionary War, the exploits of the southern cavalry units demonstrated the value of the improved breeds of saddle horses. After the war, emphasis was given to further improvement, and prices of good saddle, carriage, and race horses went up. Agricultural societies imported outstanding stock, and John Stuart Skinner of Baltimore started the first journal devoted to the improvement of American horses in 1829 with his *American Turf Register and Sporting Magazine*. The excellent BLUEGRASS pastures of Kentucky and Tennessee permitted those states gradually to dominate the breeding of both saddle and draft animals.

The Civil War was the great romantic period of the southern horse. Traveller, ROBERT E. LEE's gray mount, was almost as well known as his master. The exploits of General JOHN S. MOSBY and other southern cavalry leaders were possible, at least in part, because of the quality of their mounts. However, the war took a fearsome toll of southern horses. In 1860, the South had 2.2 million; in 1867, 1.6 million.

After the Civil War, farmers generally adopted horse-drawn machinery. This first American agricultural revolution was reflected by an increase in the number of horses. The South had 1.9 million in 1870 compared with 4.6 million in 1910, the peak year for horses on American farms. Several American breeds of horses developed over the years. For example, the Tennessee Walking Horse was recognized as a breed in 1935.

The horse, however, even as new breeds and improved strains were developed, was, except for those animals destined for racing, recreation, and a limited amount of range work, giving way to the automobile, truck, and farm tractor. From its high point in 1910, the number of horses on farms in the South declined to 2.8 million in 1930 and 1.2 million in 1955, the last year in which a count was made.

See R. M. Denhardt, *Horse of Americas* (1947); F. Haines, *Horses in America* (1971); R. W. Howard, *Horse in America* (1965); and P. C. Welsh, *Track and Road* (1967).

WAYNE D. RASMUSSEN
U.S. Department of Agriculture

HORTICULTURE is often referred to as a branch of agriculture, but in reality the latter is surely the offspring of horticulture. Taken literally from the Latin, *horticulture* means cultivation of a garden. As popularly applied, it refers to the art of growing fruits, vegetables, flowers, or ornamental landscaping.

Horticulture has a long and exceedingly important history in the South. Pre-Columbian horticulture, as practiced by virtually every tribe of southern Indians, was predicated on the highly developed horticulture and agriculture of several Central and South American Indian cultures. Certain extremely important plants that had been domesticated, selected, and improved by the Indians were unknown to Europeans before Columbus. These include corn, cotton, tobacco, potato, sweet potato, tomato, peanut, squash, sunflower, pepper, and various beans of the genus *Phaseolus*. Corn had been so long cultivated and so modified that its wild progenitors had become an enigma.

The cultivation of plants by southern Indians was chronicled and illustrated by early explorers, colonists, and travelers such as John White at Roanoke Island, Captain John Smith in Virginia, and William Bartram in Georgia and surrounding states. The CHEROKEE were especially noted for their gardening ability. Indian-grown foodstuffs saved the English colony at Jamestown.

The first Europeans to practice horticulture in the South may have been Spanish settlers in the El Paso, Tex., area as early as 1540. French HUGUENOTS established a colony in Florida in 1562 and began gardening. Two years later they were wiped out and succeeded by the Spanish, who founded St. Augustine in 1565. From this base, which they held for two centuries, the Spaniards established missions, complete with gardens, as far west as Alabama and northward along the coast of "Guale" to North Carolina. As early as 1577, reports to the king of Spain described the very successful horticultural endeavors at Santa Elena (in South Carolina), where both European and American crops in variety were being grown.

Almost at the outset the Indians acquired the peach, the cucumber, the watermelon, and probably the orange from the Europeans. The propagation and dissemination of these plants among the tribes was much more rapid than direct contact between the two cultures. Meanwhile, plants native to the New World became very important to the Europeans. Tobacco, corn, cotton, and an enormous variety of other plants were planted for food, fiber, medicinal purposes, and as curiosities or ornamentals. This latter aspect of horticulture was rather neglected by early colonists and pioneers concerned with survival, but there was a great desire by European gardeners to grow the new plants from America.

The South has a very rich native flora. Botanists, plant collectors, and horticulturists early turned their attentions to discovering, describing, collecting, and growing these plants. Throughout the southern region men such as J. Tradescant, J. Bannister, J. Clayton, M. Catesby, J. Custis, J. Mitchell, A. Garden, J. Bartram, A. Michaux, J. Lyons, and J. Fraser explored, collected, endured hardships, and overcame enormous logistical problems to introduce southern native plants to European gardens.

The growth of the colonial South resulted in, or indeed from, the expansion and improvement in horticultural and agricultural capability. Numerous early attempts to grow European grapes, olives, dates, and silkworms were unsuccessful, but tobacco, rice, sugarcane, cotton, and indigo were each, in their own time and place, very successful, and great plantations devoted to these crops were established. Wealthy owners built and furnished fine homes and laid out gardens combining the current horticultural fashions in Europe with native plants suitable to local climatic conditions and individual tastes. During the nineteenth century a flood of new exotic plants, ornamentals from eastern Asia, reached the South. Many of these have become mainstays of ornamental landscape plantings in the region.

Today in the South each branch of horticulture is both a source of pleasure for millions of people and annually contributes to a multimillion-dollar economic resource. Horticulture's long and interesting history is glimpsed in fine old gardens throughout the South; and state and federal agencies, universities, and land-grant colleges pursue active research and teaching programs in this vital field.

See U. P. Hedrick, *History of Horticulture* (1950); R. Wright, *Story of Gardening* (1934); E. G. Swem, *Brothers of the Spade* (1957); W. Bartram, *Travels* (1791); T. Jefferson, *Garden Book* (1944); E. and D. S. Berkeley, *Dr. John Mitchell* (1974); *Southern Agriculturist* (Charleston, 1828–46); and *Southern Farmer* (Montgomery, 1840–).

ROBERT B. MCCARTNEY
Colonial Williamsburg Foundation

HOSPITALITY, SOUTHERN, refers to the marked willingness of southerners to assist total strangers and to provide them with such material assistance as food and accommodations. Two important points should be remembered regarding southern hospitality. The first is that Americans in general are noted for their outgoing natures and generosity. Southern hospitality has become the ultimate symbol of these characteristics. Second, because of the relatively rigid social structure of the South, the graciousness with which hospitality was extended depended in large measure upon the position of the recipient within that structure. Thus, aristocratic planters would extend unlimited hospitality to persons of a rank equal to themselves from all parts of the United States and abroad. Persons lower in the social structure would be welcomed, but they would receive only limited attention directly from the host. Those of the lowest rank would, quite likely, be provided material assistance outside the main house. Persons below the planter class would be equally liberal with their peers or those of higher rank, but they carefully maintained a similar reserve toward their "lessers." The result was a delicate web of social relationship but also a system that succeeded in providing friendship and assistance to anyone wishing or needing it.

Southern hospitality has its roots in the geography and economy of the South. Agriculture was the main source of wealth, and most successful farms and plantations were large and widely separated. Poor roads and slow transportation emphasized this distance. Visits of kinfolk, friends, or total strangers brought companionship and news from "outside." In antebellum days planters, and frequently others as well, would hold parties lasting several days, at which time the host family shared room and board with the guests. Such sharing was also common during "the season" in cities such as New Orleans and Charleston. Hospitality was so prodigal that EDMUND RUFFIN complained it was causing difficulty through the formation of a "despicable race of loungers and spongers."

The tradition of hospitality remained strong in the South after the Civil War despite the travails of Reconstruction and a depressed agricultural economy. The romanticism indulged in by southerners regarding their past helped reinforce their proud tradition. In the minds of most southerners one was never too poor to extend hospitality to a stranger or to aid an unfortunate. Anyone could afford to invite a stranger to "come in and sit a spell." Not to do so would mark a person as "poor white trash" or, at the very least, one who was not a true southern gentleperson. Even in the face of growing industrialization, population movement, and urbanization, the tradition remains strong today.

See W. J. Cash, *Mind of South* (1941); C. Eaton, *Mind of Old South* (1964); F. L. Olmsted, *Cotton Kingdom* (1861); U. B. Phillips, *Life and Labor* (1929); and W. S. Tryon, *Mirror for Americans* (1952).

RICHARD W. LYKES
University of Virginia, Northern Regional Center

HOTCHKISS, JEDEDIAH (1828–1899), was born near Windsor, N.Y., and graduated in 1846 from the Windsor Academy. He moved to Virginia because of a growing interest in the geology and geography of its diversified topography. Here he taught himself the principles of topographical engineering and acquired an interest in mineral development, the two endeavors that occupied him during and after the Civil War. He taught in several schools, including Mossy Creek Academy and Loch Willow. When the war began Hotchkiss served the Confederacy under Colonel Jonathan Heck and General ROBERT E. LEE, but illness forced him into temporary retirement following the summer's activities. When he returned to the field in March, 1862, Hotchkiss served as a staff member and aide to the great STONEWALL JACKSON. Daily he recorded valuable information about the weather, troop movements, gossip, and anecdotes about the general, as well as serving him as perhaps the best topographical engineer in the

Confederate army. Following Jackson's death in May, 1863, Hotchkiss was assigned to the successive commanders of the II Corps, including A. P. HILL, RICHARD S. EWELL, and JUBAL A. EARLY.

Following the war, Hotchkiss engaged in business and in promoting the development of western Virginia. He made two trips abroad to lure investment capital and immigrants to the state. He was also active in collecting and publishing books and articles on the Civil War; most notably he wrote Volume III, *Virginia*, in Clement Evans' *Confederate Military History*.

See manuscripts, Library of Congress; and A. P. McDonald (ed.), *Make Me a Map of Valley* (1973) and *Virginia Magazine of History and Biography* (April, 1967).

ARCHIE P. MCDONALD
Stephen F. Austin State University

HOT SPRINGS, ARK. (pop. 35,631). Several Indian tribes are reputed to have believed that the Great Spirit was present in the naturally heated water of area springs and to have regarded the valley as neutral ground where braves of all tribes might lie undisturbed in the soothing, hot mud. President Thomas Jefferson commissioned Dr. George Hunter and William Dunbar to investigate the legendary springs, and they found that a number of temporary huts already had been erected by white visitors drawn by reports of the healing powers of the springs. The first hotel was in operation by 1820. In 1832 Andrew Jackson set aside four sections of land as a federal reservation, which in 1921 became the basis for the more than 1000-acre Hot Springs National Park. The Civil War cut the springs off from northern visitors; although the town served for three months in 1862 as the unofficial capital of Arkansas' Confederate government, most of its 200 permanent residents resettled in Texas for the duration of the war. Postwar construction of a railroad and of new hotels and bathhouses revived the spa and marked the beginnings of a modern health resort. Approximately a million gallons of radioactively hot water (143° F.) flow daily from the 47 mineral springs situated within the park.

See files of Hot Springs *New Era* (1890–) and *Sentinel Record* (1877–).

HOUSE, EDWARD MANDELL (1858–1938), interrupted his studies at Cornell University in 1879 and returned to his native Texas to manage his deceased father's estate. Rancher, farmer, and businessman, he handled a substantial inheritance wisely. A decade later he retired from active business, financially independent for life. He then managed the campaigns of Governors JAMES HOGG, Charles Culberson, Joseph Sayers, and Samuel Ianham. As each governor's unofficial adviser, House accepted no position save an honorary colonelcy. He met WOODROW WILSON in 1911 and worked for his election. Serving as the president's confidant, unofficial adviser, and emissary abroad, the Texan was catapulted onto the national and international stage. At the Versailles peace conference the famous friendship deteriorated; thereafter they never saw each other again. His public career over, House resided in New York his remaining years.

See R. N. Richardson, *Colonel House: Texas Years* (1964), best on Texas years, helpful bibliography; A. L. and J. L. George, *Wilson and House* (1956); A. Barr, *Texas Politics* (1971); C. Seymour, *Intimate Papers* (1926), sympathetic but most extensive; A. D. H. Smith, *House* (1918) and *House of Texas* (1940), both uncritical; A. S. Link, *Southwestern Historical Quarterly* (Oct., 1944); [E. M. House], *Philip Dru* (1912), political novel; R. S. Rifkind, *American Heritage* (Feb., 1959); and House Papers and "Reminiscences," Yale University Library.

PARKER BISHOP ALBEE, JR.
University of Maine, Portland-Gorham

HOUSE OF BURGESSES,

meeting in Virginia in 1619, was the first representative legislative body in the New World. The assembly served as an arena in which the Virginia aristocracy exercised increasing power. When the British challenged their power in the eighteenth century, the burgesses became leaders in the movement for independence.

See L. Griffith, *Virginia House of Burgesses* (1968); J. P. Greene, *William and Mary Quarterly* (Oct., 1959) and *Quest for Power* (1963); T. W. Tate, *William and Mary Quarterly* (July, 1962); R. Detweiler, *Virginia Magazine of History and Biography* (July, 1972); S. M. Pargellis, *William and Mary Quarterly* (April–July, 1927); C. S. Sydnor, *Gentlemen Freeholders* (1952); T. J. Wertenbaker, *Give Me Liberty* (1958); R. E. and B. K. Brown, *Virginia* (1964); and *Journals of House of Burgesses* (1915).

ROBERT DETWEILER
San Diego State University

HOUSTON, DAVID FRANKLIN (1866–1940),

born in Monroe, N.C., studied at Harvard and taught political science before serving successively as president of Texas A. & M., the University of Texas, and Washington University. Although Houston spent most of his life as an educator and a businessman, he is remembered more for his role in the WOODROW WILSON administration. His friendship with EDWARD HOUSE of Texas led to an appointment as secretary of agriculture, and in 1920 he became secretary of the treasury. He was not an influential adviser in the cabinet, but within the Agriculture and Treasury departments he was a strong and effective executive. He reorganized the Department of Agriculture and expanded its marketing services. Economically he was quite conservative, but he contributed significantly to the establishment of several federal grant-in-aid programs for agriculture. His most controversial stand came during his tenure as secretary of the treasury, when he served as an ex officio member and chairman of the Federal Reserve Board. The board adopted some restrictive fiscal policies, and when an agricultural depression occurred Houston was severely criticized.

See J. W. Payne, "David F. Houston" (Ph.D. dissertation, University of Texas, 1953); D. F. Houston, *Eight Years with Wilson's Cabinet, 1913 to 1920* (1926); R. N. Richardson, *Colonel House: Texas Years* (1964); and A. S. Link, *Wilson* (1947, 1956, 1960, 1964, 1965).

ADRIAN N. ANDERSON
Lamar University

HOUSTON, GEORGE SMITH (1808–1879),

was a Tennessean by birth, a lawyer by training, and a politician by profession. He served as an Alabama legislator and district solicitor, U.S. congressman (1841–1849, 1851–1861), state governor (1874–1878), and U.S. senator (1878–1879). Houston was a national Democrat. A personal and political friend of President JAMES K. POLK, he was an expansionist who speculated in Texan land and enthusiastically supported the Mexican War. He rejected the sectionalism of John C. Calhoun and his south Alabama followers. In 1860 he supported Stephen Douglas and opposed secession. His Unionist and north Alabama identifications and years of private engagement during the Civil War and Reconstruction caused the Democrats to seek him out to "redeem" Alabama in 1874 (REDEEMERS). The party won by making issue of white solidarity and resorting to unscrupulous practices. Houston's gubernatorial administrations were marked by retrenchment, disastrous to education since a disproportionate share of the state's limited revenue went to service the debt. Supposedly the Democrats' permanent act of "redemption" was the constitution of 1875, but it was little changed from the Reconstruction document of 1868.

See R. B. Draughon, Jr., *Alabama Review* (July, 1966); V. P. Koart, "Houston" (M.A. thesis, Auburn, 1963); G. S. Houston Papers, Duke; and T. M. Owen, *History of Alabama* (1921), III.

JIMMIE FRANK GROSS
Armstrong State College

HOUSTON, SAMUEL (1793–1863), was born in Rockbridge County, Va. Following his father's death, the family moved to Tennessee, where as a youth Houston lived with the CHEROKEE and bore the Indian name meaning "raven." Wounded at the battle of Horseshoe Bend in 1813, he pursued the study of law and became politically active as a disciple of ANDREW JACKSON. Successive terms in the U.S. House of Representatives (1823–1827) were followed by his election as governor of Tennessee (1827–1829). In 1829 he abruptly resigned because of an unhappy marriage and fled to Arkansas, where he again lived with the Cherokee.

In 1832 Houston crossed the Red River into Texas. Active in land speculation, he soon became prominent in the political struggle against Mexico. A signer of the Texas declaration of independence, he was later named to head the republic's armies. Although the twin disasters at the ALAMO and Goliad presaged defeat, Houston's decisive victory at SAN JACINTO earned independence on the battlefield. Elected the first president of Texas (1836–1838), he was successful again (1841–1844) while endorsing annexation to the United States. Upon the completion of annexation, he was elected to the U.S. Senate (1845–1859).

Houston's senatorial career was marked by a strong devotion to the Union. He was the only southern senator to vote for every feature of the COMPROMISE OF 1850 and against the KANSAS-NEBRASKA ACT. Censured by the state legislature for that vote, he sustained his only political defeat in the 1857 gubernatorial race, though he did prevail in 1859. Attempting to pursue an evenhanded policy, Houston rejected Abraham Lincoln's offer of federal troops to keep Texas in the Union while also refusing to take the oath of allegiance to the Confederacy after Texas seceded. Deposed as governor in 1861, he remained a critic of SECESSION until his death.

See A. W. Williams and E. C. Barker (eds.), *Writings of Sam Houston, 1813–1836* (8 vols.; 1938–43); L. Friend, *Sam Houston* (1969); M. James, *Raven* (1929); M. K. Wisehart, *Sam Houston* (1962); and D. Day and H. H. Ullom, *Autobiography* (1954).

STANLEY E. SIEGEL
University of Houston

HOUSTON, TEX. (pop. 1,300,000), entered the century with 44,663 people and now ranks as the nation's sixth largest city. When the Allen brothers established Houston on Buffalo Bayou in 1836, the city had access to the sea as well as to inland trade routes. The temporary capital of the new Republic of Texas grew in boomtown proportions during its initial years.

Although subjected to intense summer heat and frequent epidemics, Houston challenged GALVESTON for economic supremacy over Texas. During the 1850s Houston upstaged its island rival when it became the hub of the Texas railroad network. Within three decades, Houston had major rail connections throughout the nation. But its commercial supremacy was not guaranteed until the Houston Ship Channel was dredged to a 25-foot depth in 1914. The Magnolia City's economy depended on cotton and lumber processing throughout the nineteenth century. After 1901, when SPINDLETOP came in, Houston became a major industrial center. Oil and gas fields surrounded the city, and by the Great Depression Houston had eight refineries, valued at over $200 million, all near the ship channel. During the first 30 years of the twentieth century, Houston sustained a sixfold increase in population.

A combination of federal money and freewheeling though politically conservative businessmen made Houston the largest city in the South. Most notably, political connections, capital, technology, and educational resources brought NASA's Manned Spacecraft Center to Houston in 1961. The 8,000 new jobs and brilliant publicity brought Houston national prominence, as did the construction of the Astrodome, the first major domed sports stadium.

See D. McComb, *Houston* (1969); M. M. Sibley, *Houston Port* (1968); K. W. Wheeler, *City's Crown* (1968); R. Cotner, *Texas Cities* (1973); and A. F. Muir, *Southwestern Historical Quarterly* (Oct., 1943; April, 1944; July, 1960).

HARRY JEBSEN, JR.
Texas Tech University

HOUSTON, UNIVERSITY OF (Houston, Tex. 77004), was founded in 1927 as a community junior college. It became a four-year college and university only seven years later, and the current enrollment of this rapidly growing, coeducational state university is over 25,000 students. The library's holdings include the W. B. Bates Collection of nineteenth-century Texana and western Americana and the Texas Gulf Coast Historical Association Collection of area business history.

HOUSTON POST, an independent Democratic daily with a circulation of 300,000 copies, has been in publication under varying titles since 1880. Known first as the *Post* (1880–1884), then as the *Chronicle* (1884–1885), the *Post* (1885–1923), and the *Post-Dispatch* (1924–1932), it has been known again by its original name since 1932.

See bound copies at Library of Congress (1898–1908, 1930–) and microfilm from Bell & Howell (1880–).

HOUSTON TELEGRAPH.

In 1835 Gail and Thomas Borden began publishing the *Telegraph and Texas Register* in San Felipe de Austin. As the semiofficial organ of the Texas revolutionaries, the paper fled San Felipe before the arrival of Antonio de Santa Anna's army and followed SAM HOUSTON's forces throughout the Texans' war for independence. It settled finally at Houston in 1837. Along with the GALVESTON CIVILIAN and that same city's *Daily News*, the *Weekly Telegraph* was one of the three most influential journals in antebellum Texas. During the days of the republic, the paper generally was critical of MIRABEAU LAMAR and supportive of the Sam Houston faction in Texas politics. The paper remained a loyal defender of the general until 1857, when he sought another term as governor. The *Telegraph* endorsed secession after the election of 1860 and continued as a weekly publication until 1877.

See S. Acheson, *35,000 Days in Texas* (1938); complete bound files, Library of Congress (1836–60); and microfilm from Microfilm Center, Inc. (1835–52).

HOWARD, JOHN EAGER

(1752–1827), born of a prominent Maryland family, served in the Revolution from White Plains to EUTAW SPRINGS, distinguishing himself at COWPENS. After the war he rose quickly in Maryland politics, holding several Baltimore offices and finally the governorship (1788–1790). Howard was a hard-money man in state politics, a supporter of the Constitution, and later a loyal FEDERALIST. In the U.S. Senate (1796–1803), his only major deviation from Federalist party policy was to vote against the Sedition Act. During the War of 1812 he helped defend Baltimore and was the Federalist vice-presidential nominee in the ELECTION OF 1816. Howard was a long-time president of the state Society of the Cincinnati, a proponent of internal improvements, and president of the Maryland Colonization Society.

See C. Howard, *Maryland Historical Magazine* (Sept., 1967); and Howard Manuscripts, Maryland Historical Society, Baltimore.

JAMES H. BROUSSARD
Southwest Texas State University

HOWARD UNIVERSITY

(Washington, D.C. 20059) was founded in 1867 and named for General Oliver Otis Howard of the FREEDMEN'S BUREAU. Although initially supported by the Freedmen's Bureau and, since 1879, partially funded by the federal government, Howard always has been and remains a private institution. Traditionally one of the most prestigious black institutions in the nation, it and FISK UNIVERSITY have trained well over half the country's black professionals. The library, a major collection of Negro history materials, houses the papers of BLANCHE K. BRUCE, Francis Grimké, Oliver O. Howard, P. B. S. PINCHBACK, Arthur and Joel Spingarn, and the records of black Civil War soldiers.

See R. W. Logan, *Howard University, 1867–1967* (1968); W. Dyson, *Howard University* (1973); W. S. McFeely, *O. O. Howard* (1968); and A. Meier, *Journal of Negro Education* (Spring, 1960).

HOWELL, CLARK

(1863–1936), was born in Barnwell County, S.C., and grew up in post–Civil War Atlanta. After graduating from the University of Georgia in 1883, he embarked upon a career in journalism. His father Evan P. Howell had purchased the Atlanta *Constitution* and in 1889 named Clark managing editor after the death of HENRY GRADY. Under Clark Howell the *Constitution* continued to preach Grady's NEW SOUTH doctrine.

In a parallel political career, Howell won election to the general assembly at twenty-three and became Speaker of the house before moving on to the senate in 1900, where he served as president until 1906. That year Howell ran unsuccessfully for governor against HOKE SMITH. Smith, backed by the fiery Populist TOM WATSON, demanded a state law disfranchising black voters. Howell believed that, because blacks were already "white-primaried," such a law was unnecessary, if not unconstitutional.

Howell and the *Constitution* enjoyed a reputation for racial moderation. In fact, Howell was a segregationist, a paternalist who frowned upon any black movement to the left of BOOKER T. WASHINGTON. The *Constitution*, however, rarely indulged in the racist harangues that were the staple of many a southern newspaper. Indeed, Howell editorialized against lynch law and took on the KU KLUX KLAN in the 1920s. In his later years he wrote and edited a four-volumed history of Georgia (1926) and in 1931 accepted a Pulitzer Prize for the *Constitution*'s exposé of an Atlanta city hall graft ring. He organized one of the first Roosevelt for President clubs in 1930, remaining a strong supporter of FDR until his death.

See F. M. Garrett, *Atlanta and Environs* (1954); H. A. Steed, *Georgia: Unfinished State* (1942); D. Grantham,

Hoke Smith (1958), and C. V. Woodward, *Tom Watson* (1938), for 1906 campaign; and Clark Howell Papers, University of Georgia and Emory University libraries.

JOHN DITTMER
Tougaloo College

HUGER FAMILY (pronounced Hu-gee) of South Carolina was a prominent HUGUENOT family of the eighteenth- and nineteenth-century Tidewater districts of Georgetown and Charleston. The first of the Carolina Hugers, Daniel Huger (?–1711), moved there from France in the 1680s. His son, also Daniel Huger, had four sons: Daniel (1742–1799), Isaac (1743–1797), John (1744–1804), and Benjamin (?–1779). All but John saw military action during the American Revolution; in fact, Benjamin died while defending Charleston. John held positions of administrative importance, first as a member of the council of safety and subsequently as secretary of state for South Carolina. Daniel Huger enjoyed more political success than his brothers, for he served in the Confederation Congress (1786–1788) and thereafter in the U.S. House of Representatives (1789–1793).

Of the fourth generation of Hugers, Daniel Elliott Huger (1779–1854) was among the most prominent. Son of the third-generation Daniel, he began the practice of law in Charleston. He soon became involved in politics, serving several terms in the legislature and subsequently as judge of the circuit court. Huger achieved notoriety as a leader, along with JOEL POINSETT, of the Unionist element during the days of the NULLIFICATION controversy in South Carolina. Elected to the state nullification convention in 1832, Huger pleaded for nonparticipation: "If we take seats in the convention, we shall be the means of keeping the Nullification party together." Nevertheless, Huger and other Unionists did attend the conclave. He later served a two-year stint in the U.S. Senate (1843–1845).

The above-mentioned Benjamin had two sons of note: Benjamin (1768–1823), a Federalist who served in the U.S. Congress (1799–1805, 1815–1817); and Francis K. (1773–1855), who earned a medical degree but occupied himself as a rice planter and local politician. Benjamin Huger (1805–1877), son of Francis, graduated from the U.S. Military Academy in 1821 and served in the Mexican War as Winfield Scott's chief of ordnance and in the Civil War as a Confederate major general.

See G. C. Rogers, Jr. *History of Georgetown County, S.C.* (1970); W. W. Freehling, *Prelude to Civil War* (1966); J. B. O'Neall, *Biographical Sketches of Bench and Bar of South Carolina* (1859); and T. T. Wells, *Hugers of South Carolina* (1931).

PAUL H. BERGERON
University of Tennessee, Knoxville.

HUGHES, HENRY (?–1862), was a Gibson, Miss., lawyer and proslavery extremist who published his *Treatise on Sociology* in 1854 to expound his position that slavery had advanced in southern society to a kind of "warranteeism," wherein the master exercised control only over the labor of the slave rather than over his body and that such a view could lead eventually to the perfect society. His enthusiasm even caused him to favor the revival of the African slave trade. He was the first to employ the word *sociology* in a book title and is regarded by some as the father of American sociologists.

See R. McLemore *History of Mississippi* (1973); and A. Craven, *Growth of Southern Nationalism, 1848–1861* (1953).

HUGHES, PRICE (?–1715), came to South Carolina from Montgomeryshire, Wales, probably in 1712. He survived for only three years, but in that brief time became one of the South's most significant leaders on the frontier. Disappointed with the lands set aside for him for a Welsh settlement near Port Royal, he eagerly set out westward in 1713 to acquire for the British crown and the Carolina traders most of the land and Indian trade then loosely controlled by the French on the Mississippi. His plan was to establish a new province to be settled by Welshmen near present-day Natchez or Vicksburg and to be named Annarea in honor of Queen Anne. To this end he intrigued with the CHOCTAW and CHICKASAW Indians and most of the other tribes living between the Illinois River and the Gulf of Mexico. He made new trade alliances with them and successfully persuaded most of them to give up their ties with the French. Alarmed at this attempt by the British to displace the French, BIENVILLE fought back and even held Hughes captive at Mobile for a time. Unfortunately for the British, Hughes, on his return trip from Mobile to the east, decided to travel alone through Alabama country. Near the mouth of the Alabama River he was killed by Indians, and the hopes of the British and the Carolina traders temporarily died with him.

See V. W. Crane, *Southern Frontier* (1928); and D. D. Wallace, *South Carolina* (1951).

HUGUENOTS, the French Protestants of the Calvinist faith, emerged as a powerful religious minority in France during the first half of the sixteenth century. Their interest in what is now the southern United States dates from the attempts of Gaspard de Coligny, a leading Huguenot nobleman, to found a Huguenot refuge in America that would also be a base for attacks on Spanish America. After a failure in Brazil (1555–1558), Coligny sent an expedition under the Huguenot corsair Jan Ribault, who established an outpost on the present Parris Island, S.C., in 1562. This settlement was abandoned after a year. Another expedition of 1564 built Ft. Caroline on the St. John's River in Florida, but Spain, alarmed by these French intrusions, responded in 1565 by founding St. Augustine and massacring the French settlement. In the seventeenth and eighteenth centuries, of the thousands of Huguenots who fled France because of religious persecution, probably no more than 10,000 found their way to British North America, but by the mid–eighteenth century pockets of them could be found in every British colony. The most significant settlements in the southern colonies were in South Carolina, where, though never more than a fifth of the population, the Huguenots exercised a permanent influence on the life of the colony as evidenced by the prominence of French names among the elite of revolutionary South Carolina and by the French flavor of the state's early architecture.

See D. D. Wallace, *South Carolina* (1951), most valuable modern work. Older but still useful are C. W. Baird, *Huguenot Emigration to America* (1885); and A. H. Hirsch, *Huguenots of Colonial South Carolina* (1928).

MARTIN E. LODGE
State University of New York, New Paltz

HULL, CORDELL (1871–1955), was born in Overton County, Tenn. At nineteen he had completed the prescribed law program at Cumberland University and returned to Celina to practice law. He was elected as a Democrat in 1892 to the lower house of the legislature, where he served for two terms. After service in the Spanish-American War, he moved to Gainesville, where he served as circuit court judge from 1903 until 1907, when he was elected to the U.S. House of Representatives. There he served continuously (except for 1921–1923) until his election to the U.S. Senate in 1930. He remained in the Senate until his appointment as secretary of state in 1933, an office he held until his resignation in 1944.

Hull's accomplishments were numerous. He always considered his authorship of a graduated income tax measure in 1913 to be among his most significant legislative achievements. As a con-

gressman he also championed free trade and, after becoming secretary of state, was responsible for the Reciprocal Trade Agreements Act, sometimes referred to as the Hull Trade Agreements Act. He took keen interest in improving Latin American relations and was partly responsible for the Good Neighbor policy. He supported Franklin D. Roosevelt's rearmament program, played a major role in America's preparedness program, and proposed the establishment of a united nations organization early in the war. President Harry Truman termed him "Father of the United Nations." For his efforts, he was awarded the Nobel Peace Prize in 1945.

See Cordell Hull Manuscripts, Library of Congress; and C. Hull, *Memoirs* (2 vols.; 1948). See also H. B. Hinton, *Cordell Hull* (1942); J. L. Johnson, "Congressional Career of Hull" (M.A. thesis, University of Tennessee, 1965); C. Milner, "Public Life of Hull, 1907–1924" (Ph.D. dissertation, Vanderbilt, 1960); and J. W. Pratt, *Cordell Hull*, Vols. XII and XIII of *American Secretaries of State* (1964).

ROBERT E. CORLEW
Middle Tennessee State University

HUMOR can be smothered in definitions or modish theorizing. Two specific problems nevertheless deserve analysis. First, is there a southern (or even American) species of humor or, to narrow the scale, any indigenous variety in a state or subregion? More incisively, do the differences between the regional schools of humor outweigh the similarities? Second, what is the mainstream of southern humor: the printed tale or oral tradition; the belletristic or the journalistic? The antebellum humor most admired today was once held beneath the dignity of cultivated readers, and the comic stories among slaves and freedmen never directly reached the status of print. Ranking somewhere between these lower rungs of materials, the almanacs, joke books, stage companies, and minstrel shows (MINSTRELSY) brought humor to city and hamlet, to merchant and farmer.

In the written record humor was first (and from the first) incidental to the accounts of travelers like Captain John Smith; it also inevitably crept into political jousting. By William Byrd's time southern humor had become both earthier in tone and yet more urbane in perspective than that of New England. This tension grew vibrant in the humorists of the old Southwest. Unsurprisingly their origins are complex, including a gusto for the oddities and crudenesses of a disappearing frontier, an anxiety over instabilities in the Greek-like-Whig dream of a hierarchy, and a partly self-satiric intention to apply eighteenth-century ideals of style to the raw present. Centered in Georgia if anywhere, they saw themselves as urbane historians of the unkempt ways and speech set loose by mobility, as gentlemen tolerant enough to appreciate hunters and bully boys and sharpers. They did not wonder if their measured comedy about brawls or cruel horseplay verged on the sadistic. At their finest they developed toward a realism of incident and language that learned from itself to burst its envelope of gentility and soar into audacity of subject and a rhetoric dazzling for its extravagance and vernacular pungency. A. B. LONGSTREET, J. G. BALDWIN, J. J. HOOPER, W. T. Thompson, and G. W. HARRIS—to name the most gifted—would be still better known if Mark Twain (SAMUEL CLEMENS) had not learned so richly from them.

The Civil War, paradoxically, lessened the sectional differences in humor, with Bill Arp (Charles Henry Smith) matching his northern counterparts in tone and device. On principle the postbellum schools of LOCAL COLOR each played up the flavor of their regions. However, the South had to sacrifice most in order to meet the standards of the mass-circulation magazines (PERIODICALS) of the Northeast. Their genteelist editors would not accept joviality toward rogues or sots, much less sexual adventurers. Likewise, though comedy became a staple of local color fiction, it had to harmonize with the melodrama and pathos that mass audiences usually demand. Finally, the vernacular bristling within the box of the southwestern yarn was muted to merely quaint and then tedious dialect. Such enervation allowed lasting substance only to GEORGE WASHINGTON CABLE and JOEL CHANDLER HARRIS, who maybe is best seen against the submerged black lore that he exploited.

After 1875 or so, a type of anecdotist and mock pundit who had already charmed his way into northern newspapers began to appear in the reviving South. As the market firmed up, the professional humorist was born. By the 1890s he was being syndicated, which brought the further muting of sectional tonalities or what merely seemed its opposite, a posturing in provincial costume. All too soon a gallery of stereotypes froze into a tableau ready for Hollywood: the orotund colonel and his toothy butler, the belle in hoopskirts, the drawling redneck, the bosomy and outspoken mammy. Furthermore, the cheapness of books and the voracious demand for material to fill the magazines kept creating outlets for humorists along with other hack writers. Opie Read and Irvin S. Cobb will perhaps last longest out of this horde,

who started receding only as their public turned its eyes toward television.

If the South has had a true second coming of humor it runs through the serious novelists of the twentieth century. As ELLEN GLASGOW pointed out, romanticizing over the Lost Cause drives the tough-minded into a vein of irony. The irony is diverse, now and then almost self-pitying but often acidic or raucous, as in some moods of THOMAS WOLFE or in ERSKINE CALDWELL's *Tobacco Road* or in WILLIAM FAULKNER, FLANNERY O'CONNOR, and EUDORA WELTY. Although irony is hardly a regional product, humor in modern southern fiction distinctively blends earthiness, morality, wryness, and daring. Faulkner's tragic effects intertwine with his debts to the yarn spinners of the old Southwest as in using a heightened vernacular to sustain narratives that verge on the tall tale.

For readers as well as for writers and their characters, southern humor has been mostly a man's world. Although comedy can be elitist or denigratory (as in racist jokes), it has democratic thrust against pretensions and pomposity. Of its many strains in the South, truth telling couched in a vigorous idiom has lasted best, whereas the taste for stretching toward the fabulous has found an easy kinship with the humor of the absurd.

See W. Blair, *Native American Humor* (Rev. ed.; 1960), standard, and *American Quarterly* (Summer, 1953); H. Cohen and W. Dillingham (eds.), *Humor of Old Southwest* (Rev. ed.; 1974), full bibliographies; L. Rubin (ed.), *Bibliographical Guide to Southern Literature* (1969) and *Comic Imagination in American Literature* (1974); J. Hubbell, *South in American Literature* (1954); A. Turner, *Georgia Review* (Winter, 1958); and J. Q. Anderson, *Mississippi Quarterly* (Spring, 1964).

LOUIS J. BUDD
Duke University

HUMPHREYS, BENJAMIN GRUBB (1808–1882),

was born in Claiborne County, Mississippi Territory, son of a prominent planter. He took time to study law and enter politics as a Whig member of the legislature from 1838 to 1844. Humphreys opposed secession but raised a company of volunteers for the Confederate service. Serving in the Army of Northern Virginia, he participated in most of the major battles in that theater, and at the battle of GETTYSBURG he assumed command of the celebrated Barksdale Brigade when its commander was killed.

His military popularity and his background as a Union Whig resulted in his election as governor in October, 1865. He approved the oppressive BLACK CODE of late 1865, although he later asked the legislature to "relax the rigidity" of these laws.

He especially promoted policies designed to restore the credit standing of the state and to encourage the extension of needed capital to business and planting enterprises. When Congress gained control of Reconstruction in 1867, Humphreys' authority was superseded by a military commander, but he was permitted to continue as a caretaker governor, exercising most of the administrative functions of the office. However, his candidacy as governor on the Democratic ticket in 1868 resulted in his removal from office by the district commander.

See P. L. Rainwater, *Mississippi Valley Historical Review* (Sept., 1934); W. C. Harris, *Presidential Reconstruction in Mississippi* (1967); and Governors' Records, Vols. LXV–LXIX, Mississippi Department of Archives and History.

WILLIAM C. HARRIS
North Carolina State University

HUNT, GALLIARD (1862–1924), archivist, historian, and editor, served several federal government departments in Washington. Born in New Orleans, he was educated in Connecticut and finished Emerson Institute in Washington. Financially unable to enter Yale College, he secured employment at age twenty in the Federal Pension Office as a clerk. In 1887 Hunt transferred to the State Department, where he remained until his death except for the years 1909–1917, when he served as chief of the Manuscripts Division of the Library of Congress. Filling these capacities led to his involvement in historical and biographical writing. He wrote *Life of James Madison* (1902), *John C. Calhoun* (1908), *History of the Seal of the United States* (1909), and *Life in America One Hundred Years Ago* (1914). His edited works include *The Writings of James Madison* (9 vols.; 1900–1910); *The Journals of the Continental Congress* (1910–1922), Vols. XVI–XXV; *Debates in the Federal Convention of 1787 Reported by James Madison* (1920); and the letters of Mrs. Samuel Harrison Fish, entitled *The First Forty Years of Washington Society* (1906).

ROBERT R. SIMPSON
Coker College

HUNTER, ROBERT MERCER TALIAFERRO (1809–1887), was born in Essex County, Va. He attended the University of Virginia and studied law with HENRY ST. GEORGE TUCKER. Hunter turned to politics, being elected to the Virginia house of delegates (1834–1837) and to Congress (1837–1843, 1845–1847). He was elected Speaker (1839–1841), making him the youngest man ever

elected to that position. Later, in the Senate (1847–1861) he was bracketed with JEFFERSON DAVIS and ROBERT TOOMBS as the "southern triumvirate." As the Civil War approached, Hunter resigned as senator (1861) to attend the CONFEDERATE CONGRESS. Soon he accepted the position as secretary of state of the Confederacy. He resigned this position to become a Confederate senator (1862–1865) and president pro tem of the Senate. Hunter suffered greatly from the war. For his remaining years he worked to restore his former position. He succeeded in being elected treasurer of Virginia (1874–1880), but when he died the only position he held was that of collector of the port of Tappahannock, Va.

See H. H. Sims, *M. T. Hunter* (1935), limited study; J. E. Fisher, "R. M. T. Hunter and Sectional Controversy" (Ph.D. dissertation, University of Virginia, 1968); J. L. Anderson and J. Schroeder, *Virginia Cavalcade* (Fall, 1968); J. L. Anderson and M. Crouch (eds.), *Correspondence of R. M. T. Hunter* (1967), microfilm; J. L. Anderson and W. E. Hemphill, *Journal of Southern History* (Aug., 1972); J. E. Fisher, *Virginia Magazine of History and Biography* (Oct., 1973); C. H. Ambler (ed.), *Correspondence of R. M. T. Hunter*, American Historical Association Annual Report (1918); D. W. Bartlett, *Presidential Candidate* (1859); M. T. Hunter, *Memoir* (1903); and D. R. Anderson, *J. P. Branch Historical Papers of Randolph-Macon College* (1906).

JAMES LAVERNE ANDERSON
University of Georgia

HUNTINGTON, W.VA. (pop. 73,315), located on the Ohio River 190 miles southwest of Pittsburgh, Pa., was included in a tract of land used to reward veterans of the FRENCH AND INDIAN WAR. First settled in 1796 by Thomas Buffington, who operated a ferry across the Ohio, it grew as a river town named Guyandotte. Marshall College was founded here in 1837. During the Civil War, Guyandotte was sympathetic to secession, and it was burned in 1861 by federal troops. Anxious to become the railhead of the Chesapeake & Ohio Railroad after the war, the town was renamed in 1871 after Collis P. Huntington, president of the railroad. After prospering as a railroad terminus and a shipping point for coal and lumber, the city later grew as a processor of natural gas and as a manufacturing center. Modern Huntington manufactures a variety of metals, glass, dyes, stoves, furniture, and freight and mining cars.

See D. S. Lavender, *Great Persuaders* (1970); D. C. Miller, *Centennial History of Huntington* (1971); G. S. Wallace, *Huntington Through 75 Years* (1947); and files of Huntington *Advertizer* (1889–, Democratic daily) and *Herald Dispatch* (1903–, Republican daily), both on microfilm.

HUNTSVILLE, ALA. (pop. 137,802), the largest city in northern Alabama, is situated between the Tennessee River and the Tennessee state line. First settled by John Hunt, a Virginia Revolutionary War veteran, it was named Twickenham after the home of English poet Alexander Pope. In 1811, however, animosity against the English caused residents to rename the town in honor of its first settler. In 1819 it was the site of Alabama's first constitutional convention and for three months served as the state's first capital. An important shipping and trading center, the town has grown steadily since the opening of a stage line (1820), completion of its first railroad (1851), and formation of the TENNESSEE VALLEY AUTHORITY (1933). It is a varied city with numerous antebellum homes, the U.S. Army's Redstone Arsenal, a campus of the University of Alabama, and numerous industries.

See F. Roberts, *Alabama Review* (Jan., 1965); E. H. Chapman, *Changing Huntsville* (1972); T. Taylor *History of Madison County* (1880); and files of Huntsville *Times* (1910–).

I

IBERVILLE, PIERRE LE MOYNE, SIEUR D'
(1661–1706), was the founder of the French colony of Louisiana. Iberville had earlier settled colonies in Acadia and Cape Breton Island. During
King William's War he captured several English
forts in the Hudson Bay area. Instructed to establish a colony near the mouth of the Mississippi
River, he made his base at SHIP ISLAND, off Biloxi
Bay. Iberville explored the coastline and, in March,
1699, made the first known entry into the Mississippi from the Gulf of Mexico. He built a temporary fort at Biloxi Bay and returned to France. He
made two other voyages to the colony in 1700–
1701 with colonists and supplies. War with England was imminent in 1701, so the colony was
moved to Mobile Bay to coordinate defenses with
the Spanish at Pensacola, and in 1702 Iberville secured an alliance with the CHOCTAW and CHICK-
ASAW Indians against the English. Illness and
military duty prevented his return to the struggling colony. The colony of Louisiana had not produced material gain for France, but his efforts
gave confirmation to French claims to the Mississippi Valley.

See N. M. Crouse, *LeMoyne d'Iberville* (1954); "Iberville's Journal," in B. F. French (ed.), *Historical Collections of Louisiana and Florida* (1976), VII; and Mississippi Provincial Archives, French period, I; Mississippi
Department of Archives and History, Jackson.

WALTER G. HOWELL
Mississippi College, Clinton

ILLITERACY. Data on illiteracy were first collected when the U.S. decennial census of 1840 asked
the head of the household the number of illiterates in the family. The censuses of 1850 through
1920 employed individual enumeration, asking
ability to read and to write, but defining illiteracy
as inability to write. The 1930 decennial census
was the last to determine illiteracy, but the Current Population Survey asked the question in 1947,
1952, 1959, and 1969. The latter provides a basis
for estimating crude illiteracy rates by state by applying the age, sex, school attendance, and specific illiteracy rates for the nation to the state population, so classified, and assuming those with more
than five years of schooling to be literate.

For periods prior to 1840, illiteracy rates may be

estimated by using the percent of signatories to
legal documents (deeds, marriage licenses) who
used marks. Other useful measures of levels of literacy in households include working with the average number of magazine subscriptions and with
the percentage of people subscribing to newspapers.

The availability of schooling to youth is the
most significant influence upon the illiteracy of an
age cohort, more important than adult education
programs. Indeed the poor educational system in
southern states available to youth five to fourteen
years of age during the Civil War produced higher
illiteracy rates for those aged forty-five to fifty-four
in 1900. Illiteracy of various waves of migrants,
particularly from southern and eastern Europe, affected rates where they settled.

Nationally, nonwhite illiteracy has shown the
greatest improvement, from 79.9 percent in 1870
to 3.6 percent in 1969. Customarily, the older
population has had higher rates than the younger,
and rural residents in agricultural pursuits have
had higher rates than the urban population and
those following industrial and commercial occupations.

In pre–Civil War censuses, literacy of slaves
was not enumerated; they were assumed to be illiterate. When schooling was generally unavailable to females, their illiteracy rates exceeded
those of males, but, with improved attendance of
females, female illiteracy decreased to the point
that, in 1969, it was below the male. Illiteracy
among females has been associated with higher
birth rates and higher infant mortality rates, un-
derscoring the social significance of the skill.

Functional illiteracy far exceeds illiteracy. In
1960 there were 3 million illiterates in the United
States but an estimated 8 million functional illiterates. Currently, educators are attempting to define functional illiteracy by tests using problems
in everyday life requiring reading comprehension.

Because literacy provides the means for improving cognitive skills and acquiring utilitarian
knowledge, it stimulates improvement in socioeconomic status and facilitates the transmission of
ideas. The decrease in illiteracy accompanies UR-
BANIZATION, INDUSTRIALIZATION, and the increased differentiation of occupations. Since many

PERCENTAGE OF ILLITERACY IN THE SOUTHERN STATES, 1840–1960

	1840	1850	1860	1870	1880	1890	1900	1910	1920	1930	1950	1960	1970
U.S.	22.0	22.0	19.0	20.0	17.0	13.3	11.3	8.3	6.5	4.8	3.3	2.4	1.2
Ala.	53.0	55.7	54.6	54.2	50.9	41.0	35.1	24.2	17.8	14.0	6.2	4.2	2.1
Ark.	37.0	43.3	39.5	30.2	38.0	26.6	21.3	13.4	10.2	7.6	5.0	3.6	1.9
Del.	27.3	26.3	25.6	24.9	17.5	14.3	13.2	9.0	6.6	4.4	2.7	1.9	0.9
D. of C.	29.5	23.9	21.1	28.6		13.2	9.4	5.4	3.0	1.7	1.8	1.9	1.1
Fla.	49.6	55.5	47.9	54.8	43.4	27.8	23.4	14.4	10.2	7.7	3.9	2.6	1.3
Ga.	52.4	53.2	52.7	56.6	49.9	39.8	32.1	22.1	16.7	10.4	6.9	4.5	2.0
Ky.	34.5	37.6	31.0	35.7	29.9	21.6	18.1	13.1	9.4	7.3	4.3	3.3	1.6
La.	53.5	56.7	53.3	52.5	49.1	45.8	39.6	29.9	23.4	15.1	9.8	6.3	2.8
Md.	28.7	28.0	22.3	23.5	19.3	15.7	12.1	7.6	6.1	4.2	2.7	1.9	0.9
Miss.	57.4	57.5	60.9	53.9	49.5	40.0	34.1	24.4	18.8	14.8	7.1	4.9	2.4
Mo.	26.5	24.2	19.8	18.4	13.4	9.1	n7.0	4.7	3.4	2.5	2.1	1.7	0.8
N.C.	49.5	51.9	47.2	51.7	48.3	35.7	30.1	20.2	15.0	11.5	5.5	4.0	1.8
S.C.	63.8	62.7	60.6	57.6	55.4	45.0	37.4	27.6	20.9	16.7	7.9	5.5	2.3
Tenn.	39.5	42.0	38.1	40.9	38.7	26.6	21.9	14.7	11.3	8.0	4.7	3.5	1.7
Tex.		37.6	35.7	37.1	29.7	19.7	15.6	10.6	8.9	7.3	5.4	4.1	2.2
Va.	47.4	46.0	44.0	50.1	40.6	30.2	24.3	16.2	12.2	9.7	4.9	3.4	1.4
W.Va.				26.4	19.9	14.4	12.6	9.2	7.2	5.5	3.5	2.7	1.4

NOTES: 1840–1860 rates are for population twenty years of age and over. 1840 rates are for whites only; 1850 and 1860 are for free population.
1870–1890 rates are for ten years of age and over.
1900 rates are for fifteen years of age and over.
1910 and later rates are for fourteen years of age and over.

1940 rates are unavailable. Beginning 1950, rates are estimated.
SOURCES: 1840–1860, S. G. Brinkley, *Journal of Experimental Education* (Sept., 1957).
1870–1890, S. Winston, *Illiteracy in U.S.* (1930).
1900–1970, U.S. Census Bureau

southern states have recently experienced this transformation, they provide laboratories for relating literacy to other institutional changes.

See S. G. Brinkley, *Journal of Experimental Education* (Sept., 1957); S. Winston, *Illiteracy in U.S.* (1930); J. K. Folger and C. B. Nam, *Education of American Population* (1967); U.S. Census Bureau, *Current Population Reports*. Ser. P. 13, No. 6 (Nov., 1959), No. 8 (Feb. 12, 1903), Ser. P-20, No. 99 (March, 1959), No. 217 (March 10, 1971); *Historical Statistics of U.S. to 1970* (1975); and H. S. Shryock, J. S. Siegel *et al.*, *Methods and Materials of Demography* (1971).

ABBOTT L. FERRISS
Emory University

I'LL TAKE MY STAND

I'LL TAKE MY STAND was published in late 1930 by "Twelve Southerners." The leading figures in its inception were JOHN CROWE RANSOM, ALLEN TATE, DONALD DAVIDSON, and ROBERT PENN WARREN, all of them poets and former members of the FUGITIVE poetry group centered at Vanderbilt University, and the future novelist Andrew Nelson Lytle. Other contributors to the volume were FRANK LAWRENCE OWSLEY, John Donald Wade, STARK YOUNG, John Gould Fletcher, Henry Blue Kline, Lyle Lanier, and Herman Clarence Nixon. The symposium sought to caution southerners against the uncritical worship of materialistic modernism in the name of Science and Progress. In a statement of principles and 12 essays, the Agrarians declared that the industrial dispensation, with its exploitation of natural re-

sources and its mechanization of the labor force, could only result in dehumanization and spiritual famine. As a corrective to the business civilization of the 1920s they offered the example of the agrarian community of the preindustrial South, in which men were close to nature and with ample time for leisure.

The near-collapse of the national economy just as *I'll Take My Stand* appeared had the effect of making it seem to be more literal in its economic recommendations than some of its leading contributors intended. Exposed to considerable ridicule for their apparent impracticality and ignorance of the actual low estate of southern agriculture (REGIONALISM), some of the Agrarians retorted by attempting to justify the book's recommendations through debates, articles, and essays. Ultimately they published another symposium, *Who Owns America?* (1936), edited by Herbert Agar and Allen Tate, in which most of the Agrarians joined forces with the English Distributists. In retrospect the importance of *I'll Take My Stand* lay in its vigorous reaffirmation of religious humanism and its farseeing critique of the abuses of unchecked industrial exploitation. In certain crucial respects it is far closer in spirit and intent to works such as Henry David Thoreau's *Walden*, Edward Bellamy's *Looking Backward*, and T. S. Eliot's "The Waste Land" in its rebuke to an acquisitive business society. This, and not its topical prescriptions for the southern economy of the day, largely accounts for its continuing importance.

See *I'll Take My Stand* (1962), reprint edition, contains biographical sketches of 12 essayists; V. Rock, "Making and Meaning of *I'll Take My Stand*" (Ph.D. dissertation, University of Minnesota, 1961), best overall study; and V. Rock, in L. D. Rubin (ed.), *Bibliographical Guide to Southern Literature* (1969).

LOUIS D. RUBIN, JR.
University of North Carolina, Chapel Hill

IMBODEN, JOHN DANIEL (1823–1895), Whig politician (Virginia house of delegates, 1851–1852, 1855–1856), was born near Staunton, Va. In April, 1861, he led the Staunton Artillery in seizing the Harpers Ferry arsenal and commanded the battery at first BULL RUN. Appointed a Confederate brigadier in January, 1863, Imboden in April and May co-led a successful raid along the Baltimore & Ohio Railroad; in July he safeguarded Robert E. Lee's wagons and ambulances on the retreat from GETTYSBURG; and in October he captured the garrison at Charlestown, W.Va. In 1864 Imboden served conspicuously at NEW MARKET and during JUBAL EARLY's campaign in the Shenandoah Valley. After the war he practiced law in Richmond, fostered the Virginia mining industry, and founded Damascus, Va., where he spent his final years.

See H. H. Abbot, *West Virginia History* (Jan., 1960); E. J. Warner, *Generals in Gray* (1959); *Confederate Veteran* (Sept., 1895; Nov.–Dec., 1921); J. D. Imboden, in R. U. Johnson and C. C. Buel (eds.), *Battles and Leaders* (4 vols.; 1887–88), contributed five articles; and Imboden Papers, University of Virginia, University of North Carolina, and Virginia Historical Society.

EDWARD G. LONGACRE
Temple University

IMMEDIATISM, or immediate emancipation, was the doctrine of American abolitionists of the late 1820s and 1830s and was incorporated into the declaration of sentiments issued at the founding of the American Anti-Slavery Society. The term carried a wide range of meanings. For some abolitionists it signified a repudiation of gradualist antislavery methods such as colonization and gradual emancipation. For others it meant taking a moralistic, evangelical approach to the abolition of slavery. Relying on "moral suasion," these reformers urged immediate repentance of the sin of slavery. They appealed not only to southern slaveholders but to all Americans implicated in the "national sin" of slavery. However, most Americans were hostile to immediate emancipation, believing that it meant freeing the slaves without delay or preparation and without regard to consequences. In addition, evangelical southerners par-

ticularly resented being condemned as sinners, and they accused abolitionists of perverting the Scriptures in branding slavery a sin. Thus the emergence of immediatism contributed to the conflict of moralities that ultimately resulted in civil war.

See A. C. Loveland, *Journal of Southern History* (May, 1966); D. B. Davis, *Mississippi Valley Historical Review* (Sept., 1962); G. H. Barnes, *Antislavery Impulse* (1953); B. Wyatt-Brown, *Lewis Tappan* (1969); and D. L. Dumond, *Antislavery Origins* (1939).

ANNE C. LOVELAND
Louisiana State University

INCOME. The most comprehensive measure of economic activity and economic welfare available on a subnational basis is personal income. In terms of usefulness, it is the regional counterpart of gross national product. Personal income is the income received by residents of an area from all sources during a specified period. It consists of wages and salaries, the net profits of unincorporated businesses, supplementary labor income, investment income, and transfer payments. Per capita, or average, income is calculated by dividing total income by total population. (All income figures used herein are expressed in 1972 dollars. That is, changes in the value of the dollar have been eliminated so that one dollar of income in 1929 has the same value as a dollar of income in 1975.)

Personal income in the South in 1975 totaled just over a quarter of a trillion dollars—$288,583 million—or 29 percent of the nation's total. Among individual states income ranged from about $3 billion in Delaware to $52 billion in Texas. With a population of 70,166,000—approximately one-third of the national total—per capita income in the South in 1975 amounted to $4,113. This was 11 percent less than the national average of $4,641 and 16 percent below the average of all states outside the South. Among component areas, per capita income ranges from $3,215 in Mississippi to $5,410 in Delaware and $6,166 in the District of Columbia. These figures reflect the region's current position on a continuing long-term uptrend that has seen the South consistently outpacing the remainder of the nation in the rate of income growth.

Personal income in the South rose from $45.3 billion in 1929 to $288.6 billion in 1975, an increase of 537 percent in real income over four and a half decades. In the remainder of the country, personal income rose 287 percent over the same span. By far the largest relative increase was scored by Florida, where personal income ex-

Total Personal Income
in South and Non-South, 1929–1975
(millions of 1972 dollars)

Area	1929	1940	1950	1959	1975	% increase 1929–75
U.S.	226,393	250,391	398,264	545,119	989,111	337
Non-South	181,097	194,623	297,922	405,432	700,528	287
South	45,296	55,768	100,342	139,687	288,583	537
Ala.	2,248	2,538	4,738	6,766	13,102	483
Ark.	1,496	1,590	2,773	3,477	7,378	393
Del.	646	881	1,204	1,709	3,132	385
D.C.	1,646	2,651	3,151	3,108	4,414	168
Fla.	2,000	3,112	6,336	13,206	36,679	1,734
Ga.	2,675	3,356	6,292	8,871	19,473	628
Ky.	2,707	2,910	5,072	6,656	12,611	366
La.	2,277	2,731	5,319	7,611	14,263	526
Md.	3,338	4,179	6,641	9,910	20,985	529
Miss.	1,512	1,506	2,893	3,710	7,543	399
Mo.	6,034	6,327	9,986	12,611	20,413	238
N.C.	2,755	3,702	7,428	9,733	20,820	656
S.C.	1,232	1,833	3,320	4,528	10,134	723
Tenn.	2,575	3,147	5,801	7,817	15,878	517
Tex.	7,293	8,857	18,462	25,626	52,442	619
Va.	2,778	3,990	7,165	10,142	22,410	707
W.Va.	2,084	2,458	3,761	4,206	6,906	231

SOURCE: Based on current dollar data from Bureau of Economic
Analysis, U.S. Department of Commerce

Per Capita Personal Income
in South and Non-South, 1929–1975
(1972 dollars)

Area	1929	1940	1950	1975	% increase 1929–75	% of Non-South 1929	% of Non-South 1975
U.S.	1,859	1,890	2,634	4,641	150	85	95
Non-South	2,185	2,183	2,898	4,901	124	100	100
South	1,165	1,288	2,044	4,113	253	53	84
Ala.	850	892	1,549	3,625	326	39	74
Ark.	808	813	1,452	3,487	332	37	71
Del.	2,737	3,275	3,754	5,410	98	125	110
D.C.	3,408	3,842	3,910	6,166	81	156	126
Fla.	1,384	1,625	2,255	4,389	217	63	90
Ga.	921	1,076	1,820	3,953	329	42	81
Ky.	1,039	1,018	1,727	3,714	257	48	76
La.	1,092	1,152	1,972	3,762	245	50	77
Md.	2,059	2,272	2,820	5,121	149	94	104
Miss.	757	692	1,329	3,215	325	35	66
Mo.	1,666	1,671	2,519	4,286	157	76	87
N.C.	879	1,036	1,826	3,819	334	40	78
S.C.	708	964	1,572	3,596	408	32	73
Tenn.	989	1,072	1,750	3,792	283	45	77
Tex.	1,266	1,379	2,375	4,286	239	58	87
Va.	1,146	1,467	2,162	4,512	294	52	92
W.Va.	1,214	1,289	1,875	3,831	216	56	78

SOURCE: Based on current dollar data from Bureau of Economic
Analysis, U.S. Department of Commerce

panded more than 17 times: from $2 billion to more than $36.5 billion. Next largest increases were in South Carolina (723 percent) and Virginia (707 percent). Smallest gains occurred in the District of Columbia (168 percent), West Virginia (231 percent), and Missouri (238 percent).

The exceptionally large relative income increases combined with only slightly above-average population growth to push per capita income in the South ahead much more rapidly than in the rest of the country. In the South per capita income increased two and a half times between 1929 and 1975, double the rate of growth in the non-South. The largest per capita income increase occurred in South Carolina, where average incomes expanded 408 percent. North Carolina, Georgia, Alabama, Mississippi, and Arkansas each scored a per capita gain of 300 percent or more.

Perhaps most indicative of the economic progress of the South are the figures of per capita income in the South as a percent of per capita income in the non-South. As noted, in 1929 average income in the South was only slightly more than half that in the rest of the country; in South Carolina, per capita income was only one-third as large; in Mississippi, it was 35 percent. Except in Delaware, Maryland, Missouri, and the District of Columbia, per capita incomes ranged from one-third to two-thirds the non-South average. By 1975, however, unusually rapid growth brought per capita income in the South to within 16 percent of that in the non-South, a reduction of two-thirds in the region's income gap.

Four major factors account for the South's impressive income progress. First, AGRICULTURE, a slow-growth industry characterized by below-average money returns, accounted for 16 percent of personal income in the South in 1929, but only 3 percent in 1975. This diminution of a large, slowly growing industry limited total income growth significantly. At the same time, it lessened its depressive effect on per capita income. Second, over the 46-year span the South became much more industrialized, nearly doubling its share of the nation's manufacturing activity. Third, beginning with the establishment of numerous military installations in the South during WORLD WAR II, a new "industry"—the federal government—developed. With almost half of all federal payrolls disbursed in the South, this new industry contributed significantly to the region's rapid income growth. More important, the expansion of the federal government with its above-average pay scales boosted the region's per capita income relative to the rest of the nation. Fourth, the last two developments—increased INDUSTRIALIZATION and the expansion in federal employment—provided full-time employment for many who otherwise would have been unemployed or underemployed. These factors have moved the income structure of the South to one much closer in composition to that of the nation generally and to a per capita income level closer to parity.

See U.S. Department of Commerce, *Survey of Current Business* (monthly) and *Area Economic Projections, 1990* (1975). There are no official state personal income statistics prior to 1929; for estimates, see *Population Redistribution and Economic Growth, 1870–1950* (1957).

ROBERT E. GRAHAM
University of South Carolina

INDENTURED LABOR was that institution in which the labor of those persons unable or unwilling to pay for their passage to America was sold to meet the cost of transportation. The name derived from the contract between laborers and masters, which was written in duplicate on a large sheet of paper and divided along a jagged or indented line. Bound labor probably accounted for one-half to two-thirds of all persons who immigrated to the southern colonies before the Revolution.

Indentured labor included indentured servants, redemptioners, and convicts. Indentured servants, usually poor and single, often sold their services by contract to a merchant or ship captain before embarking and were resold upon arrival in America. Redemptioners, who began to appear in the eighteenth century, originated principally on the European continent, emigrated in families, brought tools and provisions, paid part of their fare, and thus secured more favorable contracts. Royal pardon of criminal offenders and, after 1717, transportation of criminals for punishment occasioned the conveyance of convicts from England to America, most of whom reached Maryland and Virginia.

Although laborers were considered chattel property of their masters, the terminability of their contracts and the possession of civil rights distinguished them from slaves. According to the contracts, servants promised faithful service for a specified period of time, generally one to seven years, in return for lodging, food, and clothing. At the end of the indenture, masters owed servants "freedom dues." If contracts were broken, servants and masters had recourse to the courts. Attempts to terminate indentured labor in the aftermath of the Revolution failed, and servants, usually skilled individuals, continued to come to America well into the nineteenth century.

See M. W. Jernegan, *Laboring and Dependent Classes* (1931); R. B. Morris, *Government and Labor* (1946), detailed; A. E. Smith, *Colonists in Bondage* (1947), good bibliography; E. S. Morgan, *William and Mary Quarterly* (April, 1971); and E. M. Riley (ed.), *Journal of John Harrower* (1963), excellent original account.

ALAN D. WATSON
University of North Carolina, Wilmington

INDEPENDENCE, MO. (pop. 111,662), adjacent to Kansas City, was settled in 1825 and plotted two years later. It was the eastern terminus of the Sante Fe Trail and the starting point for many wagon trains of west-bound pioneers. In 1831 the MORMONS announced that this section of Missouri was the Promised Land and established a colony here. Non-Mormans resented the influence of the Mormons and objected to their faith. In 1834, after numerous fights and the burning of nearly 300 Mormon homes, the colony moved away. The city remains a holy place to Mormons, however, and is the headquarters of the Reorganized Church of Jesus Christ of Latter-Day Saints. The California gold rush of 1849 brought new life to the community, but during the 1850s Kansas City gradually overshadowed Independence as a center of commerce and industry. Modern Independence is partly a suburb of Kansas City. Its factories produce farm machinery, stoves, furnaces, and textiles.

See Independence *Examiner* (1898–), a daily Democratic paper, on microfilm.

INDEPENDENT MOVEMENTS (1874–1884) were a series of anti-BOURBON political revolts in the South occurring between Reconstruction and the Populist revolt. The monopolizing of state government by the ultraconservative brigadiers and their business and planter allies was extremely galling to idealistic political reformers. Independents renamed the old black-Unionist coalition of Reconstruction and also utilized the political arm of the GRANGE, the GREENBACK party. The result was a new second party in a number of southern states.

Independent candidates were usually bolting Democrats. Their first success was in north Georgia in 1874, when, despite the opposition of the powerful GEORGIA TRIUMVIRATE, WILLIAM H. FELTON was elected to Congress. In Alabama in 1876, reform-minded Mayor Noadiah Woodruff made a strong race as an independent for governor. Independentism won in north Alabama in 1878, when William Lowe was elected to Congress as a Greenback Democrat.

Virginia was the only state in which the independents, called READJUSTERS, gained control. After a Bourbon governor vetoed the debt adjustment bill in 1878, the next year the Readjusters, led by General WILLIAM MAHONE, gained control of the state. They supported a number of reform measures; however, the Bourbons accused Mahone of uniting Negroes and ignorant whites to rule Virginia.

Mahone's success in 1879 was a catalyst causing independent movements to appear in Mississippi, North Carolina, South Carolina, Texas, and Florida. In the early 1880s the ARTHUR ADMINISTRATION supported these movements, with the exception of the one in Florida, with patronage and funds. In 1880 Wash Jones, a Texas Greenbacker, made a strong race for governor. In 1882 General JAMES R. CHALMERS, called the Mahone of Mississippi, was elected as an independent to Congress. In Florida in 1884, political unknown Frank Pope, supported by a coalition of independent Democrats, anti–Ring Republicans, and blacks, ran a vigorous race for governor. President Chester Arthur refused to abandon the Ring Republicans. Without his support, Pope lost in a disputed election.

After 1884, the independent movements disintegrated. Their Achilles' heel was white supremacy. Then the election of Democrat Grover Cleveland in 1884 meant that they would be deprived of federal patronage. Furthermore, without the support of the South's business and planter interests, they were doomed to die on the vine. In retrospect, the independent movement was a forerunner of the PROGRESSIVE and POPULIST revolts. It was usually moderate on race and strong on reform, including public education, fair elections, insane asylums, and more democratic government. Its success would have meant a more enlightened South.

See W. D. Halsell, *Journal of Southern History* (Feb., 1944); E. C. Williamson, *Florida Historical Quarterly* (Oct., 1948); R. C. Martin, *Southwestern Historical Quarterly* (Jan., 1927); W. P. Roberts, "Dr. William H. Felton" (Ph.D. dissertation, University of North Carolina, 1952); N. M. Blake, *William Mahone* (1935); F. Roberts, *Alabama Review* (April, 1952); C. N. Degler, *Other South* (1974); S. P. Hirshson, *Farewell to Bloody Shirt* (1962); A. S. Link and R. W. Patrick (eds.), *Writing Southern History* (1965); and C. V. Woodward, *Origins of New South* (1951).

EDWARD C. WILLIAMSON
Auburn University

INDIANS of the South were composed of diverse linguistic and cultural stocks. When the Europeans arrived late in the sixteenth century, the southern native Americans operated from an agri-

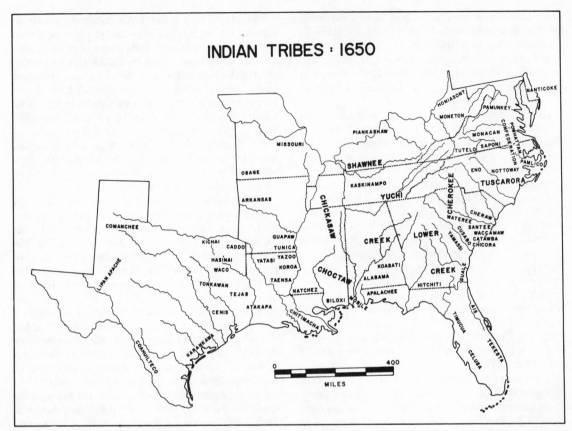

INDIAN TRIBES · 1650

cultural economic base, which they supplemented by hunting, fishing, gathering, and trading. Fundamental to all the tribes was the cultivation of corn in their river bottom plots. Trade, too, was a part of their lives, an exchange between native American groups that transcended geographical boundaries, with lead from the West, pipestone from the North, wampum from the Northeast, and finely dressed deerskins or turkey feathers from the South being common items of exchange.

The arrival of the Europeans brought destructive forces among the native Americans of the South. Trade with the Europeans, rum, and the quest for land became an unholy trinity of dispossession with which the white man harassed the Indian. Desire for such manufactured commodities as guns, knives, axes, kettles, cloth, and blankets drove the native hunters into the forests at such a rate that the deer population was declining as early as 1730. Rum was a useful lubricant to smooth the way when whites wanted to secure more acres or more pelts from the tribes. By the time of the American Revolution, alcoholism was already a problem in certain villages and tribes.

From the earliest contacts, political relations between the whites of the South and the Indians centered on the land problem. In the European perception, the Indians "did live like deer in herds and waste the land." That viewpoint brought over by the settlers has never changed appreciably. From Captain John Smith to Andrew Jackson and into the present day, the assumption that white use of the land was more efficient and hence better has driven the southern Indians away from the Atlantic shore, the Gulf plains, and the Appalachians, across the Mississippi, and into the waste places of the land. The establishment of the Indian Claims Commission after World War II brought some monetary settlement for tribal lands lost, but deceit and degradation cannot be changed by the mere payment of money.

The most publicized and romanticized episodes in southern Indian history came during the removal period. Based on the Jeffersonian adage that separation was best for both cultures, the United States Indian policy was aimed at removing the Indians from the South and across the Mississippi into Indian Territory (present-day Oklahoma). Although Andrew Jackson has been blamed for the implementation of removal policy (a blame not entirely undeserved), it had been conceived by Thomas Jefferson and delivered by John C. Calhoun. Thanks to these three leaders and their anti-Indian constituents, thousands of native Americans were wrested from their southern homelands and driven along the Trail of Tears to the Indian Territory.

In the nineteenth and twentieth centuries it became common practice for the whites to speak of the Five Civilized Tribes in the South. This white nomenclature referred to those groups who aped white ways in order to survive: the CHEROKEE; the CHICKASAW; the CHOCTAW; the CREEK; and the SEMINOLE. Perhaps most successful at copying the white man were the Cherokee, who not only adopted slaveholding monoculture, but also drew up a tribal constitution modeled after that of the United States; in addition, they published a newspaper in their own language using an alphabet perfected by Sequoya. However much they copied the white, they could not change his ethnocentrism, nor therefore could they escape removal. Only the Seminole did so, but only after a long war (SEMINOLE WARS), which forced them to abandon their lands and hide in the recesses of the EVERGLADES.

The other four tribes either emigrated as tribes or were left behind on small plots of wasteland to compete with their aggressive white neighbors. Some Choctaw have eked out an existence in the shadows of Mississippi, though the rest of their tribe, the Creek, and the Chickasaw became a part of the native American potpourri in Oklahoma. The most active of the southern tribes after removal were the Cherokee, who have become two rather distinct groups, the Eastern Cherokee and the Western Cherokee in Oklahoma.

Thanks to twentieth-century tribal renewal movements, there is new emphasis on native American culture, language, and religion. Young Indians can grow up in pride to take their places alongside their white and black neighbors in the South.

See C. M. Hudson, *Southeastern Indians* (1976); J. H. O'Donnell, *Southern Indians in American Revolution* (1973); D. H. Corkran, *Cherokee Frontier* (1962) and *Creek Frontier* (1967); A. M. Gibson, *Chickasaws* (1971); A. H. DeRosier, *Choctaw Removal* (1970); V. W. Crane, *Southern Frontier* (1929); J. Adair, *American Indians* (1775); W. Bartram, *Travels* (1791); and L. DeVorsey, *Southern Indian Boundary* (1966).

JAMES H. O'DONNELL III
Marietta College

INDIGO CULTURE was firmly established in three southern English colonies in North America in the eighteenth century. An important source of dye for the textile industry, the staple was grown in South Carolina with little success prior to successful experimentation by ELIZA LUCAS PINCKNEY in the late 1730s. Bounties by that colony and the British government provided additional encouragement by 1748 since exports of indigo from Charleston amounted to 138,344 pounds annually. It was grown mainly in the middle country of South Carolina and on parts of the SEA ISLANDS. Production reached its peak by 1775, with shipments of over 1 million pounds or 35 percent of South Carolina's total exports.

Indigo was introduced jointly with RICE in Georgia after 1747 but never really became an important export commodity. Georgia exported a little less than 30,000 pounds annually by the late 1760s. Indigo from Savannah amounted to only about 12,000 pounds in 1774, though undoubtedly some Georgia indigo was exported out of Charleston. Although indigo was the principle commercial staple in Florida during the British occupation following the Peace of Paris in 1763, the crop was never large. In the last five years of the colonial period, production varied from 20,000 to 60,000 pounds annually. It was also cultivated to some degree for home use in Virginia and other colonies, especially when conditions stimulated domestic manufactures. During the Revolution it furnished the dye for the blue of the Continental uniform. Production declined sharply in the 1780s and 1790s due to several factors: destruction resulting from military action, end of the British bounty and protection, British encouragement of indigo production in the East Indies, and the expansion of short-staple COTTON, which grew well on former indigo land.

Some indigo was being exported from Louisiana as early as 1725, and by 1738 plantations in the neighborhood of New Orleans were producing some 70,000 pounds annually. By 1785 production had exceeded 200,000 pounds. The next few years, however, also saw the rapid decline of the industry in Louisiana. At the time of the Louisiana Purchase a few planters were still clinging to indigo, but it was rapidly being abandoned.

See K. Coleman, *American Revolution in Georgia* (1958); L. C. Gray, *History of Agriculture in Southern U.S.* (1958); H. H. Ravenel, *Eliza Lucas* (1896); B. Romans, *Concise Natural History of East and West Florida* (1775); A. H. Hirst, *Agricultural History* (Jan., 1930); G. T. Sharrer, *South Carolina Magazine of History* (Oct., 1971); M. L. Ready, "Economic History of Colonial Georgia" (Ph.D. dissertation, University of Georgia, 1970); and British Public Records Office, Colonial Office.

G. MELVIN HERNDON
University of Georgia

INDIGO NEGROES were slaves in the eighteenth century whose health had been so injured by engaging in the culture and manufacture of indigo that they had been rendered valueless. Blacks so employed were said to live an average of only five years.

See A. Moody, *Louisiana Historical Quarterly* (April, 1924).

INDUSTRIALIZATION. The historiography of the industrialization of southeastern United States is not easily described. Although industrialization is often perceived historically as a series of episodes or "stages" linked in a causal pattern, it is often difficult to put the diffuse nature of historical change into simplified models without doing violence to historical realities. In any consideration of regional development, ideas such as "industrial revolution" should be avoided. Not all technological, social, and economic changes are easily identified as to origin and rate of development. The tendency is to overlook or minimize essential stimuli—interregional as well as intraregional—which may have occurred outside the immediate area of concern. James Watt's successful steam engine, for example, was the culmination of a series of developments in mining, metallurgy, and armaments manufacture. And when the textile spindle came to public notice in southern cotton fields in 1880, it was not evidence of an industrial revolution but only of economic maturation of the industry on a national level.

In considering the theoretical aspects of industrialization, one must clearly understand that the resulting industrial society will be shaped by and within the confines of the prevailing value system. Particularly in the initial stages of development, community response will be heavily influenced by the values of the dominant group—often a group threatened with displacement from power, both economic and political. The willingness of the community to accept or tolerate change will often place limits on the conditions under which capital can be utilized in the organization of the industrial process.

Many variations are possible in structuring a methodological approach to the study of the history of regional industrialization. The format suggested here is only one of many approaches

Foremost in effects accompanying industrialization are changes in productive relationships and institutions. Constant shifts in market structure occur, inducing far-reaching changes in area economic activity, displacing some, creating new,

minimizing others. It is important to avoid the assumption that the appearance of new economic activities and new technologies results in the disappearance of the old. New industries often do displace older activities; however, not all change results in an increase in aggregate industrial employment. Sometimes only shifts in employment occur. Shifts in the economic activity of a region will bring about movement between agriculture, manufacturing, and service sectors. The extent and variety of these shifts tend to be specialized according to regional characteristics. The South has been historically oriented toward resource-processing manufacturing such as LUMBER, COAL, and PULP AND PAPER. These tend to be low wage, low skill activities. Movement from agriculture into and out of these activities was relatively easy. In some areas, the rural population could engage in both activities on a seasonal basis.

Work patterns are dramatically affected by changes in the industrial process. Old skills, however minimal, cease to be the norm. New technology requires new work habits. Moving from the individualistic pattern of low income TENANT FARMING to the group-oriented and supervisory situation of the factory or mill had, and still has, far-reaching consequences. The use of family labor in the textile mill was a significant alteration of life-style for poor white farmers (MILL TOWNS). The cash wage of the mill was purchased with the surrender of the family to the discipline of the mill. The change from the rhythms and style of the farmer, however poor, to the mill hand working in place from ten to 12 hours was dramatic. Although such drastic changes usually accompany industrialization, they do not necessarily imply a deterioration of the quality of life.

Employment distribution and worker characteristics (age, race, sex) are important indicators of economic change. Demographic data have the advantage of being the most stable of census definitions and therefore more comparable over time. The composition and distribution of the work force provides a means of relating changes in the regional economic structure to the national economy. The migration of people in response to economic opportunity—or lack of opportunity—is a notable feature of economic change. The southern resource-processing industries such as ore refining, lumbering, and textile production have a lower urban requirement than fabricating industries and may not so quickly build up urban concentrations as was typical of the northeastern United States. Although the typical response to industrialization has been URBANIZATION, in recent years fabricating industries, particularly high skill,

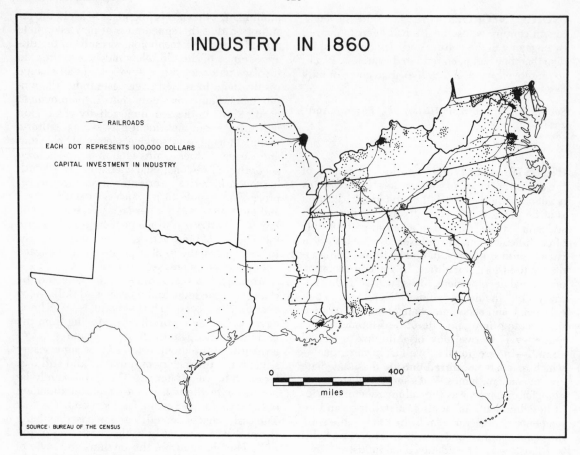

INDUSTRY IN 1860

RAILROADS

EACH DOT REPRESENTS 100,000 DOLLARS

CAPITAL INVESTMENT IN INDUSTRY

0   400

miles

SOURCE: BUREAU OF THE CENSUS

high value industries, have been moving to less urbanized regions of the South.

To complete an analysis of industrialization, consideration should be given to FAMILY organization, educational patterns, mobility of residence, community relations, and social or special interest groups. The appearance of LABOR UNIONS and employer organizations alters traditional agrarian patterns. The long dominance of agrarian traditions in the South has often been cited as a serious obstacle to economic development. The shift of families to urban concentrations produced new political conditions.

Southern disciples of "Progress" had an effect on politics, if not on the development of industry. Legislation to accomplish industrial goals, effective or not, often has an impact beyond the immediate area of concern. Laws designed to inhibit labor organization run counter to national trends. Racial inequality and denial of opportunity conflict with national equal opportunity statutes.

These conflicts are all part of the process of industrialization. One observer recently summed up the situation in this manner: "the modern South cannot accept the advantages offered by industrialism without adapting many of its social and political ideas and forms."

The southern states are frequently compared to underdeveloped nations, needing similar remedies to secure development. "Underdevelopment" is only a comparative term assuming an alternative course of economic change or alternative choices, when, in fact, such may not be the case. Little insight is gained by using this model for the South, since it suggests the possibility of duplicating the pattern of other regions or of displacing those regions in productive capacity. The regional economic patterns that have developed in the United States have tended to persist over time and, given the nationalizing quality of the American economy, are likely to continue.

Another favorite model used in describing

southern industrial development is based on the theme of the "colonial economy." The idea that the South was a colony of the North was specifically formulated by Rupert Vance in his pioneer work and has been developed in more elaborate fashion by other historians. The facts that the southern industrial growth has been of a lesser magnitude than that of other regions, is resource-processing oriented, and has been developed heavily by outside capital (BANKING) are taken as evidence of the colonial nature of the South.

This concept overlooks the fundamental nature of American capitalism and the processes of capital formation and investment. The amounts of capital required to initiate industrial technology are quite large—usually beyond local savings ability. This is particularly true when the economy is dominated by low income farmers with minimal capital invested in their agricultural activities. Accordingly, the long-run tendency of American business enterprise in all sections of the country has been toward centralization of productive facilities and centralization of ownership. The rapid development of the American economy after 1865 was a product of regional specialization, efficiently linked together in a continent-wide market, characterized by rising albeit varying rates of regional development. The unevenness of development, political sectionalism, and the separatist tendencies of southern historical development have tended to obscure the organic relationship of the South to the industrial and financial North. The southeastern United States must be considered as a region within a national context.

Promotional campaigns to secure new industries have been popular throughout the South (COMMERCIAL EXPOSITIONS; CONVENTIONS, COMMERCIAL AND POLITICAL). It is doubtful whether such campaigns have resulted in more than the attraction of marginal firms to whom tax subsidies and low wages were significant. The textile industry did remove South, but less wage-sensitive industries have not duplicated this move. Industrial expansion has tended to be an extension of multiplant firms. Since 1870 five states in the North have accounted for almost half the nation's industrial production. As other regions have developed, the share of the total production of these five states has declined moderately. The many factors involved in industrial location are likely to continue to exert a bias in the direction of historical tendencies.

Observable changes can be noted in the dramatic shift away from agricultural employment. In 1870 some 19.6 percent of the northeastern labor force was employed in agriculture. By 1920 it had declined to 9.1 percent. By contrast, the southern agricultural work force steadily expanded and by 1910 had reached 54.8 percent of the work force, declining slowly to 47 percent in 1950, still higher than the 1870 figure of 43.7 percent. Since 1950 the agricultural work force of the South has declined swiftly in response to mechanization and now more closely approaches the national norm.

Another evidence of development is found in the recent rapid growth of the industrial work force. Although still below national norms in 1970, the region was converging on the national average. In 1970, 23.1 percent of the southern work force was in the manufacturing sector, compared with a national average of 25.9 percent. Another difference between southern development and other regions is reflected, however, in the INCOME data. The South is still a low income region, significantly below other regions. The median family income for the South in 1970 was approximately $8,000 compared with approximately $10,000 for other regions. Some 16.2 percent of all southern families were below the poverty level of income in 1970, reflecting the continuing significance of relatively low wage industries and agriculture.

The present status of the southern industrial economy indicates a more favorable pattern of industrial development, more closely approaching national norms. The region has substantially increased its utilization of the regional work force. The labor force participation rate has increased to 33.7 percent in 1970, compared with 36.7 percent for the nation. The region may have reached a point where new industrial activity will be offset by declines in older activities. Industrial growth is not simply an additive process, but a constantly changing mixture of activities. The absolute and relative gains of the region indicate, nonetheless, a firm base of industrial activity.

See E. Beechert, "Southern Industrialization" (Ph.D. dissertation, Berkeley, 1957); T. Till, "Rural Industrialization and Rural Southern Poverty" (Ph.D. dissertation, University of Texas, 1972); American Academy of Political and Social Science, Coming of Industrialization to South (1931), summary of early period; V. S. Clark, Manufacturing in South, 1880–1905 (1929), VI, pioneer study; L. E. Carbert, State and Local Taxes in South East (1957), impact of taxation in industrialization; V. Fuchs, Location of Manufacturing Since 1929 (1962), comparative regional analysis; M. Greenhut and W. Whitman, Southern Economic Development (1964); H. Herring, Southern Industrialization (1940); C. B. Hoover and B. U. Ratchford, Economic Resources of South (1951); B. F. Hoselitz and W. Moore, Industrialization and Sociology (1963), one of best theoretical studies; M. Jensen (ed.), Regionalism in America (1952); S. Kuznets et al., Population Redistribution and Economic Growth, 1870–1950 (1960), summary of regional data; F. R. Marshall, Labor

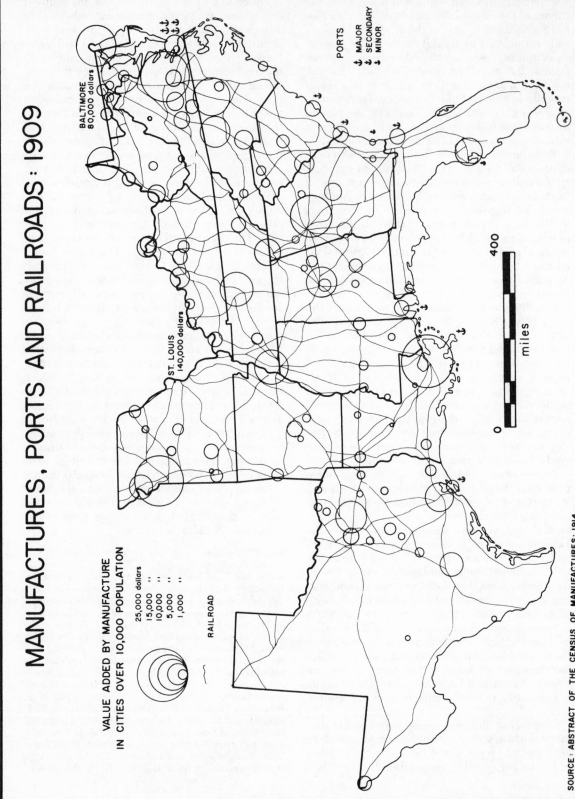

MANUFACTURES, PORTS AND RAILROADS: 1909

BALTIMORE
80,000 dollars

ST. LOUIS
140,000 dollars

PORTS

MAJOR

SECONDARY

MINOR

VALUE ADDED BY MANUFACTURE
IN CITIES OVER 10,000 POPULATION

25,000 dollars
15,000 "
10,000 "
5,000 "
1,000 "

RAILROAD

400

miles

0

SOURCE: ABSTRACT OF THE CENSUS OF MANUFACTURES: 1914

MANUFACTURES AND PORTS : 1970

VALUE ADDED BY MANUFACTURE
IN CITIES OVER 25,000 POPULATION

1,500,000 dollars
750,000   "
250,000   "
75,000   "
< 50,000 "

PORTS

⚓ MAJOR
⚓ SECONDARY
⚓ MINOR

0   400

miles

SOURCE : BUREAU OF THE CENSUS, COUNTY AND CITY DATA BOOK : 1972 *in South* (1967); W. H. Nichols, *Southern Tradition* (1960); H. Odum, *Southern Regions* (1936); and H. Perloff, *Regions and Economic Growth* (1960), outstanding.

EDWARD D. BEECHERT
University of Hawaii

INMAN, JOHN HAMILTON (1844–1896) and **SAMUEL MARTIN** (1843–1915), were from Jefferson County, Tenn. John went to New York City in 1865, took a job with a cotton house, and in 1870 founded his own cotton firm: Inman, Swann & Company. Samuel worked in an Augusta bank and in 1870 started S. M. Inman & Company in Atlanta, which became one of the world's largest cotton dealerships. Despite geographical separation, both advocated southern INDUSTRIALIZATION and invested heavily in the region. John was an organizer of the TENNESSEE COAL, IRON & RAILROAD COMPANY, and he bought heavily in southern COAL and iron lands, in the Louisville & Nashville and Central of Georgia RAILROADS, and with his brother in lines that they later merged into the Southern Railway. Both were active in INSURANCE and BANKING. John helped establish the New York Cotton Exchange and was a member of the New York Rapid Transit Commission. Samuel, friend of HENRY W. GRADY, was a director of the Atlanta *Constitution* and an important educational benefactor. The brothers are credited with attracting $100 million of northern capital into the South.

See New York *Times* (Nov. 6, 1896); Atlanta *Constitution* (Nov. 28, 1880; Jan. 13, 1915); M. Klein, *History of Louisville & Nashville Railroad* (1972); and F. M. Garrett, *Atlanta and Environs* (1954).

JAMES A WARD
University of Tennessee, Chattanooga

INNES, HARRY (1752–1816), was judge of the U.S. Court for the District of Kentucky (1789–1816). Born in Virginia, he studied under GEORGE WYTHE and was admitted to the bar in 1773. He moved to Kentucky in 1783 upon appointment as a judge of the Virginia court for the Kentucky district. For the rest of his life, Innes viewed all issues from the perspective of Kentucky. He advocated immediate and unconditional separation from Virginia, opposed adoption of the Constitution, and- supported Thomas Jefferson in the emerging party structure. As federal judge, he delayed effective enforcement of the internal revenue acts until the government secured peace with the Indians and free navigation of the Mississippi. His willingness to condone communication with Spain in the 1790s and his refusal to prosecute

Aaron Burr in 1806 aroused the deepest suspicions of his lifelong enemy Humphrey Marshall, who threatened him with impeachment. Marshall's popular but biased *History of Kentucky* (1812, 1824) has obscured Innes' reputation as a respected leader and conscientious interpreter of the law.

See M. K. B. Tachau, "Federal Courts in Kentucky, 1789–1816" (Ph.D. dissertation, University of Kentucky, 1972); J. P. Boyd *et al.* (eds.), *Papers of Jefferson* (1974), XIX; A. P. Whitaker, *Mississippi Valley Historical Review* (Sept., 1928); Innes Papers, Library of Congress; Innes Papers, Filson Club, Louisville; and Thomas J. Coolidge Collection, Massachusetts Historical Society, Boston. H. Marshall's viewpoint was repeated by T. M. Green, *Spanish Conspiracy* (1891); it was countered by J. M. Brown, *Political Beginnings of Kentucky* (1889); W. Littell, *Reprints of Littell's Political Transactions in and Concerning Kentucky* (1926); T. Bodley, *History of Kentucky* (1926); and P. Watlington, *Partisan Spirit* (1972), historiographic analysis.

MARY K. BONSTEEL TACHAU
University of Louisville

INNES, JAMES (1754–1798), was born in Caroline County, Va. He organized Williamsburg's first volunteer militia company and in 1775 faced Lord Dunmore's armies at Hampton. He spent the next two years serving as a lieutenant colonel in George Washington's army, fighting at Trenton, Princeton, Brandywine, Germantown, and Monmouth. Most of Innes' activities after the Revolution—his law practice, his service on the board of visitors of William and Mary, his years in the Virginia house of delegates (1780–1782, 1785–1787), and as attorney general of Virginia (1786–1796)—were centered in Williamsburg. His greatest fame came from his speech defending the federal Constitution at the Virginia ratifying convention of 1788. Innes usually shunned government service outside of Virginia. He did, however, accept an assignment to meet with British agents in Philadelphia to implement aspects of Jay's Treaty, and there he died.

See J. Carson, in D. Rutman, *Old Dominion* (1964), best; and H. B. Grigsby, *History of Virginia Federal Convention of 1788* (1890).

RICHARD R. BEEMAN
University of Pennsylvania

INSECTS. The ancestry of insects is not definitely known but is believed to have originated from some aquatic ancestor. They belong to the phylum Arthropoda, which includes their near relatives such as spiders, mites, scorpions, shrimp, millipedes, and centipedes. They are further divided into a class by themselves called Hexapoda or Insecta. The phylum itself consists of about 80 percent of all the species in the animal kingdom with insects sharing the largest portion. In all the world, there are about a million known kinds of insects, and more are discovered each year.

Insect species arise in particular habitat niches all over the world, and from these isolated spots they spread as far as the environment allows. Species with wide temperature and humidity tolerances and with a wide range of food preferences can occupy a wider territory, and their range of territory is only limited by oceans or mountains or other large barriers. The southern United States has a range of climate and plant life that is suitable for a wide selection of insect life. There are few land barriers to inhibit migration of insects from neighboring areas, and modern transportation has weakened the effects of the oceans as barriers for many foreign insects. So the South does indeed have a rich insect fauna.

Some insects have a great capacity to reproduce when conditions are favorable. Theoretically a pair of houseflies could increase their numbers during a single breeding season to cover the entire earth to a depth of 47 feet, if all their offspring lived and reproduced normally. Other insects take a long time to complete their life cycles. Some of the periodical cicadas take 17 years to develop from the egg stage to adults. In the South, the 13-year periodical cicadas are most common, but when they do appear they seem to be everywhere in great numbers.

Most insect species remain limited in number or do not compete with man for the things he values, but some insects feed on us, our crops, our livestock, our stored materials, and even our homes, and they can cause millions of dollars of damage annually and untold suffering. To some extent, southern agriculture is shaped by crop pests. PEANUTS replaced COTTON as a main crop in some areas because of BOLL WEEVIL problems. CORN is not grown as extensively because of corn insect problems. But in many instances man has won out over insects in the South. The screwworm, which is so costly to livestock, was eradicated in most states using the novel technique of sterile male fly releases; the winter tick, although not an insect but a close relative, was also eradicated. The Mediterranean fruit fly has been accidentally imported several times and has threatened the FRUIT INDUSTRY, particularly the citrus fruit industry, but each time the pest was eradicated. Mosquito-borne MALARIA and YELLOW FEVER plagued the South from time to time, but when the mosquitoes' role as vector of the disease be-

came known, their control significantly reduced the frequency of these diseases.

For all the devastation that some insects can incur, there are others, such as the honey bee, on which our agriculture and our varied life depend. Some of the finest honey flavors, such as sourwood, tupelo, and orange blossom, are produced in the South, but honey is really only a by-product of the more important pollinating done by bees. The breeding and rearing of queen and nuclei bees is primarily a southern industry. Other insects are also considered beneficial to man because they are predators or parasites of pest insects. Ladybird beetles and praying mantids are well-known examples, but there are many others that also help keep pest insects in check. These types of insects are often reared or collected in the South for sale in areas where these beneficial insects are not so common.

In general, insects of the South differ little from insects of the North except in their life cycles. In the warmer climates of the South, insects continue to reproduce the year around and are continuous pests, thus causing more of an economic drain on resources than in the North. Although northern and southern insects of the same species are about the same size, certain species of beetles and cockroaches of the South are the largest found in the United States. Some beetles and cockroaches will measure greater than three inches in length, and one species of walking stick measures greater than six inches in length.

See, for good lay discussions of insects, D. J. Borrow and R. E. White, *Field Guide to Insects* (1970); P. Farb *et al.*, *Insects* (1962); G. S. Fichter, *Insect Pests* (1966); USDA Yearbook, *Insects* (1952); R. T. Mitchell and H. S. Zim, *Butterflies and Moths* (1962); and V. J. Stanek, *Pictorial Encyclopedia of Insects* (1969). More specialized entomological studies are C. S. Brimley, *Insects of North Carolina* (1963); A. Darlington and M. J. D. Hirons, *Plant Galls* (1968); E. I. Fanning, *Insects Close Up* (1965); S. W. Frost, *Insect Life* (1969); W. J. Holland, *Moth Book* (1968); M. T. James and R. F. Harwood, *Herm's Medical Entomology* (1969); C. L. Metcalf *et al.*, *Distinctive and Useful Insects* (1962); and J. J. Quayle, *Insects of Citrus and Subtropical Fruits* (1938). Major professional journals include *Annals of Entomological Society of America*; *Applied Entomology and Zoology*; *Entomologist's Gazette*; *Entomology News*; *Journal of Economic Entomology*; *Journal of Environmental Entomology*; *Journal of Medical Entomology*; *Mosquito News*; and *Entomologist's Monthly Magazine*.

F. W. KNAPP and
R. A. SCHEIBNER
University of Kentucky

INSTITUTE FOR SOUTHERN STUDIES (P.O. Box 230, Chapel Hill, N.C. 27514) was founded in

1970. Beginning in 1973 the institute has sponsored the quarterly journal *Southern Exposure*, which now has a circulation of 5,000 and pays up to $100 for book reviews and articles, both scholarly and popular, focusing on regional problems of southern people. It examines such contemporary topics as black politics, southern women, labor history, industrialization, and religion but usually treats them in an historical perspective. The institute maintains files of information on the operations of social change organizations and corporations in the South. It also puts out a syndicated column, "Facing South," appearing in dozens of southern newspapers.

INSTITUTE OF EARLY AMERICAN HISTORY AND CULTURE (P.O. Box 220, Williamsburg, Va. 23185), sponsored by the College of William and Mary and the Colonial Williamsburg Foundation, was founded in 1943. It publishes an occasional newsletter, books, and the *William and Mary Quarterly*, which has a circulation of 4,100. The *Quarterly* places its major emphasis on the publication of documents, articles, and book reviews on the colonial and early national periods of American history and culture to 1815 and related topics in English, European, and Caribbean history. It is generally recognized by scholars as the leading journal in its field. The institute has an active book-publishing program and offers postdoctoral fellowships and the Jamestown Award, a $1,500 annual prize for an unpublished book-length manuscript in early American studies. The archival holdings of the institute are largely in the Swem Library of the College of William and Mary.

INSURANCE INDUSTRY. Rural agrarianism in the South with consequent low income limited the market for both life and property insurance in the past and has discouraged the creation of locally owned insurers. In 1970 not one of the top 20 insurers was based in the South. Since the close of World War II, however, the South has outpaced the national growth rate in most categories, including insurance purchases. Between 1940 and 1974 life insurance in force in the South has grown from 21 percent to 31 percent of the nation's total, and southern insurers by the 1960s collectively transacted a sizable share of the region's life and property insurance.

In the antebellum period, the extremely high mortality rate for white males discouraged the sale of life insurance. Northern-based companies restricted the magnitude of their southern business.

The Baltimore Life Insurance Company, organized in 1830, was the first successful effort to establish a southern life insurance enterprise, but after it added a trust department in 1838 the company wrote little life insurance. Other southern life insurance companies operated to a limited extent during the pre–Civil War years, particularly in Mobile, New Orleans, and the border state of Kentucky.

Insurance on slaves was made widely available and was purchased principally by those transporting slaves or hiring them out for railroad construction or industrial use. A few companies were launched to specialize in this segment of the business, notably the Phoenix Insurance Company of St. Louis and the Southern Mutual Insurance Company.

In maritime cities along the coast as well as rising river towns such as St. Louis and Memphis, the pressing need to insure high-risk vessels and cargo led to the formation of a number of marine insurance companies. One was chartered in Charleston as early as 1797; another was organized in Norfolk in 1802, capitalized at $400,000. Fire insurance companies were launched in Baltimore, Richmond, Charleston, and New Orleans. Although a few survived, most were unable to withstand their first heavy loss, such as the great Charleston fire in 1840.

Despite aggressive competition of northern-based companies, between 1830 and 1860 a large number of property insurers were established in the South, at least 56 in Virginia alone. Some survived into the twentieth century, and a few expanded operations to the North. In 1854 at least two Charleston-based fire and marine insurers maintained agencies in Boston. For the great majority, however, existence was ephemeral. Reckless management, the miscalculation of risks and premiums, and the fraudulent practices of some promoters and agents led to the beginnings of insurance regulation during the 1840s. In 1856 statutory regulation was launched in Virginia and Tennessee and in 1858 in Maryland.

No more than 65 southern property insurers continued to operate through the Civil War. About three-fifths of the surviving companies were based in Washington, D.C., Maryland, and Missouri. In the Reconstruction period an era of "wildcat" insurance flourished, during which domestic stock companies chartered with negligible amounts of capital waged a bitter struggle for business with foreign companies, lowering rates below sound levels. The Underwriters' Association of the South was established in 1871 to advance insurance principles, and a number of southern states adopted legislation requiring insurers to accumulate a reserve fund and to issue annual reports of their business and financial conditions. This helped eliminate unsound practices, but even well-managed companies failed to survive the severe financial depression of the 1870s. During the 1880s the mortality rate of southern property companies was 27 percent. By the turn of the century the reputation of southern insurers had declined and the industry had become dominated by the larger, more responsible northern-based companies.

The flow of southern policyholders' premiums outside the region led to the charge that the South was being kept in thralldom to northern financial centers. The charge had little validity since nationwide insurers were, in fact, making large investments within the South. Nonetheless, the agitation led to various attempts to restrict northern-based firms in their southern operations. In 1907, Texas' Robertson Act required out-of-state life insurance companies to invest in Texas securities and real estate at least 75 percent of their reserves against policies written in the state.

The most significant development of the postbellum era was the launching of a large number of mutual assessment, sick, and accident companies designed to extend burial and health insurance to low-income southerners. Impetus for this development derived from the spread of industrial life insurance throughout urban America after 1875. Southern companies stressed the marketing of small policies to women and children with the contracts being sold and serviced on the debit or home service plan. Enticed to the industry by negligible capital requirements and an absence of regulatory restrictions, the pioneer promoters of these enterprises primarily adopted the mutual assessment form of organization. Many began by concentrating on the Negro market at a time when the first generation after slavery lacked the paternalism of the plantation and feared pauper burials. A number of black-owned and -operated enterprises emerged at about the same time, evolving out of mutual aid societies, often affiliated with churches or fraternal orders. Black-controlled companies confined their operations to the black clientele. After World War I both white- and black-controlled sick and accident insurers were converted into stock companies, offering straight life as well as health insurance.

In 1910 a group of white-owned debit companies organized the Southern Casualty & Surety Conference as a trade association. The total income of the 18 member companies was $3.5 million. By 1947, the year before the organization's name was changed to Life Insurers Conference, the income of its 79 member companies was $384 million. In 1971, indicative of the growth of the southern insurance industry in the post–World War II era, premium income of 88 member companies totaled $4.5 billion. By the 1970s the black-controlled National Insurance Association had more than 40 members. The dozen largest companies in the trade association produced almost 90 percent of the total volume of business; eight of the 12 were based in the South.

Since the mid-1960s the white-owned companies have extensively integrated their agency and clerical staffs and have moved aggressively to capture a larger share of the Negro market. Following conservative sales and investment policies, black-owned companies have lagged in investing in higher-yield mortgage loans, continue to stress the sale of small premium industrial life insurance, and have only recently exploited the potential of group insurance. Concern has been expressed regarding the future of black-owned companies in the southern market unless prevailing trends are sharply reversed.

See J. Blicksilver, *Industrial Life Insurance in U.S.* (1968); T. R. A. Atkinson and W. M. Davis, *Savings and Investment Function of Life Insurance Companies in Sixth Federal Reserve District* (1956); W. R. Vance, in *South in Building of Nation* (1909); C. B. Hoover and B. U. Ratchford, *Economic Resources and Policies* (1951); C. G. Woodson, *Journal of Negro History* (April, 1929); J. M. Duker and C. E. Hughes, *Journal of Risk and Insurance* (June, 1973); and R. C. Puth, *Challenge* (May–June, 1974).

JACK BLICKSILVER
Georgia State University

INTERPOSITION, a constitutional doctrine denying that the federal government is the sole judge of its powers and asserting the right of the states to point out usurpations of power, was first proclaimed in the VIRGINIA AND KENTUCKY RESOLUTIONS of 1798. Although the doctrine has been appealed to in numerous political crises, its exact meaning is debatable.

Paragraph 3 of the Virginia Resolutions of December 24, 1798, written by JAMES MADISON, read as follows: "That this Assembly doth explicitly and peremptorily declare that it views the powers of the federal government as resulting from the compact to which the States are parties . . . and that, in case of a deliberate, palpable, and dangerous exercise of other powers not granted by the said compact, the States . . . have the right and are in duty bound to interpose for arresting the progress of the evil, and for maintaining within their respective limits the authorities, rights, and liberties appertaining to them." A similar resolution, written by THOMAS JEFFERSON, had passed the Kentucky legislature on November 16, 1798. Both resolutions were prompted by congressional enactment of the Alien and Sedition Acts.

The Alien and Sedition Acts were extreme measures; if freedom was to survive in America, these acts would have to be opposed. The nature of the federal union at the time was highly debatable, and it is not surprising that Jefferson and Madison looked to the state legislatures as proper bodies to resist federal encroachments. Yet the Virginia and Kentucky Resolutions of 1798 did not specify any means of resisting federal usurpation other than denunciation and appeal to the people to elect members of Congress who would repeal the unconstitutional laws. There is no evidence that Madison or Jefferson advocated extreme action such as session from the Union. In a second set of resolutions passed on November 22, 1799, the Kentucky legislature went further and proclaimed that "a nullification by those sovereignties, of all unauthorized acts done under color of that instrument, is the rightful remedy" (NULLIFICATION). In this some see the planting of the seed from which extreme doctrines of state sovereignty would develop.

The Embargo Act of 1807 brought forth interposition resolutions from the legislatures of Massachusetts and Connecticut. The Massachusetts resolution held the embargo to be "unjust, oppressive, and unconstitutional, and not legally binding upon the citizens of this State." The Connecticut legislature proclaimed the right of state legislatures "to interpose their protecting shield between the rights and liberties of the people and the assumed power of the general government."

In the development of American constitutional law, the U.S. Supreme Court has come to exercise final authority in interpreting the "supreme law of the land," albeit resort to military force has occasionally been used. Some would conclude that decisions like COOPER V. AARON, enforced by federal troops, marked the end of any doctrine of state power. But no successful attempt has been made to blot out freedom of expression, and interposition in the form of resolutions by state legislatures remains an influential force in American politics.

See F. M. Anderson, *American Historical Review* (July, 1900); A. C. McLaughlin, *Consititutional History* (1935); S. E. Morrison, *Harris G. Otis* (1913); and C. B. Swisher, *American Constitutional Development* (1954).

ALBERT B. SAYE
University of Georgia

INTRACOASTAL WATERWAY consists of two canal systems along the Gulf and Atlantic coasts, interrupted only on the Florida Gulf coast. The Atlantic Intracoastal Waterway extends from Hampton Roads, Va., south to the St. John's River, Fla., a distance of 739 miles. An extension of the system reaches another 349 miles to Miami. The Gulf Coast Intracoastal Waterway stretches 1,109 miles from Apalachee Bay, Fla., to the Mexican border. For many years there have been efforts to connect the two canal systems across Florida, although to date this has not been done. The canals lie a few miles inland of the coasts, in or near the system of lagoons behind offshore sandbars. The Gulf Intracoastal Waterway connects directly with the Inland Waterway System, on the Mississippi River and its major tributaries. This sytem also provides commercially viable (nine-foot) channels to such widely separated inland points as Catoosa, Okla. (near Tulsa), Minneapolis, Chicago, Pittsburgh, and Knoxville. In addition, the intracoastal waterways connect with canals extending up most of the larger rivers on the two coasts.

Canal traffic is generally limited to bulky, low-value per ton materials, for which speed of transit is not essential. Along the Gulf Coast volumes are far higher than along the Atlantic, since the Texas-Louisiana coastal region not only produces large volumes of crude oil, sulfur, and SALT but is also an area of cheap fuel in the form of natural gas, which together have led to considerable growth in PETROLEUM-refining, various CHEMICAL, and petrochemical industries. Traffic on the Gulf Intracoastal Waterway is closely tied to the needs of these industries and is especially important in the movement of their output eastward and northward to market. Thus residual fuel oil, gasoline, and distillate fuel oil move in largest volume. These are followed by a variety of chemical products, most of which are higher in value per ton.

Traffic on the Atlantic Intracoastal Waterway is lighter. It consists of such low-grade materials as pulpwood and logs, of which the Southeast is a major producer (PULP AND PAPER INDUSTRY). Large quantities of IRON ORE and concentrates move up the Chesapeake Bay to Baltimore; the largest flow consists of the various petroleum products, though sand, gravel, and crushed rock also move by barge in substantial quantity.

Where cheap water transportation is combined with cheap fuel and power costs and where important raw materials are produced, there may be a basis for anticipating the growth of heavy industry. The presence of these elements in the South, particularly along the Gulf Coast, suggests contin-

INTRACOASTAL WATERWAY TONNAGE, 1974
(thousands of short tons)

ATLANTIC INTRACOASTAL WATERWAY	Total	Northbound	Southbound
Consolidated Total	3,511	1,565	1,928
Norfolk, Va.–N.C. line	1,118	417	679
North Carolina section	2,045	645	1,389
Little River, S.C.–Port Royal, S.C.	1,574	521	1,043
Port Royal, S.C.–Cumberland Sound	1,232	922	294
Fernandina Hbr.–St. John's River	871	685	172
INTRACOASTAL WATERWAY	**Total**	**Inbound**	**Outbound**
Jacksonville–Miami, Fla.	1,442	1,220	14
GULF INTRACOASTAL WATERWAY	**Total**	**Eastbound**	**Westbound**
Consolidated Total	102,582	62,043	38,910
Apalachee Bay, Fla.–Panama City, Fla.	1,864	1,369	83
Panama City–Pensacola, Fla.	4,186	3,410	403
Pensacola–Mobile, Ala.	7,783	6,595	816
Mobile–New Orleans, La.	21,307	13,832	7,082
New Orleans–Sabine River, La.	60,742	35,405	24,830
Sabine River–Galveston, Tex.	40,034	23,750	16,245
Galveston–Corpus Christi, Tex.	23,310	15,743	7,280
Corpus Christi–Mexico border	2,711	1,107	1,604

NOTE: Intrasection (local) movements are included in totals but not in directional figures.

SOURCE: U.S. Army Corps of Engineers, *Waterborne Commerce of U.S.* (1975).

uation of the process of INDUSTRIALIZATION, especially along the midsection of the Gulf Intracoastal Waterway.

See U.S. Army Corps of Engineers, *Waterborne Commerce of U.S.* (annual), Pts. 1, 2; A. H. Wright, *Atlantic-Gulf or Florida Ship Canal* (1941); J. Hartog, *Waters of New World: Houston to Nantucket* (1961); and C. Goodrich, *Canals and American Economic Development* (1961).

JAMES KENYON
University of Georgia

INVENTION. The history of technology in the South remains one of the least developed sectors of southern historiography. The neglect has left unexamined a stereotypic picture of the South as a region where cultural factors inhibited invention and where engineering and highly technical enterprises languished at least until recently. New and important insights should emerge from an intensive study of the relationships of technology to southern culture, especially if such studies are linked to larger themes and similar studies of other regions with differing resource endowments or cultural patterns.

The cotton gin constitutes probably the most familiar example of an invention made in the South that is alleged to have altered drastically the subsequent history of the region. Aside from the complex issue of technological determinism, the internal history of the cotton gin seems ripe for reconsideration by historians of southern technology. The traditional interpretation of Eli Whitney's role in the introduction of interchangeable-parts manufacture in the North has already been revised substantially. Even a cursory examination of patent records suggests that the cotton gin, like interchangeable-parts manufacture, did not spring fully developed from the mind of one man but went through an evolutionary development over a period of decades.

The reports of the Confederate patent commissioner are among the more interesting documents relating to southern inventors. The Confederate Patent Office was established in Richmond in May, 1861, with a former examiner of the U.S. Patent Office, Rufus R. Rhodes, as commissioner. A total of 266 patents were issued through December, 1864. Residents of Virginia received the most with 81, followed by Georgia with 29, Alabama with 27, and North Carolina with 24. In comparison, the U.S. Patent Office issued 16,051 patents during 1861–1864. The South had had a poor patent record even before the war, although the disparity then was less. In 1857 a citizen of Massachusetts had been ten times as likely to receive a patent as a Virginian and 26 times as likely as a North Carolinian. The ratio of total southern patents to total United States patents in 1860 had been 10.3 percent. The Confederate patent reports shed some light on whether the war caused inventive activity to be directed exclusiviely toward weaponry. Of the 266 patents, 84 were classified under the category of firearms and implements of war, followed by agriculture with 27, chemical processes with 24, and leather with 16.

Commissioner Rhodes's interpretive remarks in the reports are quite revealing. He wrote in the report for 1862 that there was now "conclusive proof . . . that in all that relates to the practice of the Mechanic Arts, the Southern people are the equals of any other race in the world." He predicted that southerners would "quickly transcend Yankee craft and ingenuity in the boasted department of invention and discovery." A contrasting assessment was given by D. P. Hollaway, the U.S. patent commissioner, in his report for 1863. He reported that his office had received a near record number of applications despite the South's having "contributed nothing to invention or human improvement." He attributed the lack of interest in labor-saving devices in the South to labor having been "degraded in these States." However, Hollaway forecast a "happy future" once the South adopted a "just system of labor . . . and when a whole race shall be taught to think, contrive and create."

Despite Hollaway's optimism, the South's patent record continued to lag after the war. The ratio of total southern patents to total United States patents was under 10 percent for each census year from 1870 through 1930. The South's share of textile equipment patents was even lower despite the highly publicized migration of the textile manufacturing industry into the Southeast.

Although such patent data document a regional disparity, much remains to be done before many generalizations can be supported adequately. A microanalysis of patent records should reveal whether there is a correlation between inventiveness and level of URBANIZATION in the South. A more thorough analysis of classes of invention may reveal whether the southern inventor did better in areas related to the region's "peculiar climate and products." More data are needed on the black southern inventor. It may prove illuminating to compare the southern inventor with the inventor in regions other than New England, especially undeveloped regions.

See L. F. Schnore, *New Urban History* (1975); R. S. Woodbury, *Technology and Culture* (Summer, 1960); I. Feller, *Technology and Culture* (Oct., 1974); and J. E. Brittain, "History of Technology in South," paper, History of Science Society Convention (Dec., 1975).

JAMES E. BRITTAIN
Georgia Institute of Technology

IREDELL, JAMES (1751–1799), was the son of a Bristol merchant. His father's financial misfortunes led young Iredell to accept an appointment as comptroller of customs at Edenton, N.C. Arriving in 1768 he began the study of law and soon achieved local prominence. Before 1776 he wrote in support of the American cause and later served his new state as superior court judge (1777), attorney general (1779–1781), and member of the state council (1787) and in revising the laws. Despite North Carolina's lack of enthusiasm for the federal constitution, Iredell strongly defended the new government and helped lead the Federalists in the state ratifying convention of 1788. His activities caused President George Washington to appoint him (1790) an associate justice of the U.S. Supreme Court, a position he held until his death. Iredell advocated policies sometimes described as "states' rights Federalism." Long before *Marbury* v. *Madison* he insisted that an act of Congress not in agreement with the Constitution should be rendered void by the courts. In his famous dissent to CHISHOLM V. GEORGIA (1793) he contended that the states existed before the national government and could not be sued by citizens of another state because such proceedings were not authorized by the Constitution.

See G. J. McRee, *Life and Correspondence* (2 vols.; 1857); and Iredell-Johnson Families Papers, North Carolina State Department of Archives and History, Raleigh.

DAVID AMMERMAN
Florida State University

IRON AND STEEL INDUSTRY is located in all of the southern states with the greatest concentration of works in the areas of Birmingham, Ala.; Sparrows Point, Md.; and Wheeling, W.Va. Established at Falling Creek near Jamestown, Va., in 1619, the first southern ironworks were destroyed by an Indian attack in 1622 after producing only a small amount of iron. The next effort did not come until 1716, when Governor Alexander Spotswood erected a blast furnace near Germanna in Orange County, Va. Within a few years other works were established in both Virginia and Maryland, the foremost being those of the PRINCIPIO COMPANY in Maryland. From these early facilities the southern iron industry spread westward and southward with the expanding frontier. By 1800 ironworks in the form of furnaces, forges, or rolling mills were located from Delaware southward to Georgia and across the Appalachians into Tennessee and Kentucky. During the next 60 years the industry continued to spread westward, locating in Alabama, Arkansas, Missouri, and Texas.

Until approximately 1860, the iron industry in the South remained relatively primitive. Iron was smelted from a variety of ores found in small quantities throughout the region. The greatest quantity of metal was produced in small blast furnaces, which used locally produced charcoal as fuel. Because of its high carbon content and brittleness, the pig iron coming from these furnaces was limited in use to cast iron products. Much of the pig iron was refined in bloomery forges, where it was heated and then beaten with large triphammers to eliminate the carbon and other impurities. The resulting product was a small slab, or bloom, of wrought iron, a malleable metal that might be rolled into plates, cut into strips, or fashioned by blacksmiths into a variety of products.

Although less productive than the furnaces and bloomeries, numerous small Catalan forges were used in many parts of the South during the eighteenth and nineteenth centuries. Conforming in their basic characteristics to the bloomeries, the Catalan forges were used by farmers and blacksmiths to smelt small quantities of ore directly into wrought iron. The product was limited in quantity and quality, but it served the needs of a frontier society that was isolated from more abundant sources of iron. Other types of ironworks of the eighteenth and early nineteenth centuries included rolling mills and rail mills, which converted the heated blooms of wrought iron into plate, bars, and rails. Often naileries were operated in conjunction with rolling mills, cutting nails from the finished plate. By 1860 southern iron production had reached 125,000 tons, or 15 percent of the national total.

During the Civil War the iron industry experienced substantial growth as it expanded to meet the military demands of the Confederacy. The largest establishment in the South was the Tredegar company in Richmond where cannon, shells, shrapnel, plate and other matériel of war were fashioned. The most important developments took place in central Alabama, where small frontier works were transformed into relatively large and complex industries, the most notable examples being at Shelby, Brierfield, Selma, and Oxmoor. The wartime success of the iron industry was short-lived as invading armies overran the South, destroying most of its industrial capacity. By the spring of 1865 the southern iron industry lay in ruins.

Gradually recovering from the devastation of war, the industry began to abandon the scattered, small blast furnaces and forges and to construct larger and more productive furnaces and mills, concentrating in those areas possessing the most abundant supplies of iron ore and coal. The most notable developments were in northern Alabama, eastern Tennessee, and western Virginia.

The principal technological changes coming during the last of the nineteenth century were the development of larger and more efficient blast furnaces; the utilization of heated air at higher pressures in the blast; the consumption of the more abundant red hematite ores, replacing the brown limonite and magnetite ores used earlier; and the replacement of friable charcoal with coke, a sturdier and more efficient fuel. Southern pig iron production began to increase rapidly during the decade of the 1880s with the construction of a large number of new furnaces especially in the Birmingham area. Pig iron production rose from 397,000 tons in 1880 to 1,953,000 tons in 1890, or about 20 percent of the nation's total.

The rapid expansion of iron production was not accompanied by a comparable increase in the southern market. Consequently, much of the iron had to be shipped to consumers in the North. Bearing heavy freight charges, this iron could not have competed with the northern product if southern production costs had not been exceedingly low. In the Birmingham area, low costs were obtained because of the proximity of coking coal and iron ore and the availability of abundant and inexpensive labor, including convicts who were employed in mining coal for iron companies in both Tennessee and Alabama. In 1897 production costs for iron reached a low of $5 a ton in Birmingham.

During the 1880s as the national demand for steel began to increase, there was a commensurate decline in the market for southern iron, much of which was unsuitable for conversion into steel by the then dominant Bessemer process. In 1890, after numerous experiments, southern iron was successfully converted through the use of the basic open-hearth process. But because of the financial stringency of the 1890s, large-scale production did not begin until 1899 with the development of ten open-hearth furnaces at Ensley, Ala.

During the 1890s many of the southern iron enterprises experienced shifts from southern to northern control. At the same time several of the leading companies merged their interests, creating fewer but larger businesses. The most notable development was the expansion of the TENNESSEE COAL & IRON COMPANY. Originating as a coal-mining company in eastern Tennessee in 1852, it absorbed several smaller Tennessee firms before shifting its main operations into Alabama in 1886 with the purchase of the Pratt Coal & Iron Company. After expanding through the acquisition of other properties to become the largest of the southern iron enterprises, it was absorbed in 1907 by the United States Steel Corporation. Although its capacity was surpassed during World War II by the Sparrows Point facilities of the Bethlehem Steel Corporation, the T.C. & I. Division (now the

Fairfield works of U.S. Steel) has remained the dominant factor in the southern iron and steel industry.

Between 1900 and 1940 the southern iron and steel industry continued to expand. Even so its rate of growth did not match that of the North. In 1914 southern pig iron had dropped to only 11 percent (2.7 million tons) of the national production; southern steel amounted to only 6 percent (1.2 million tons) of the national total. The basic difficulty in the southern iron and steel industry was the lack of a large industrial market in the still predominantly agrarian South. But another factor that slowed southern production was the pricing system known as PITTSBURGH PLUS, whereby southern iron (even that sold near its production point) was priced according to the Pittsburgh rate, plus the freight charges from Pittsburgh to the point of consumption. The effect was to protect the northern industry in the southern market and to eliminate the advantages that the southern product might have in its own territory because of less expensive labor and raw materials. Even though the Pittsburgh Plus system was terminated by order of the Federal Trade Commission in 1924, the subsequent "basing point" system of pricing continued to discriminate against southern iron and its consumers until it was halted by court action in 1948.

During World War I and World War II, southern iron and steel facilities were expanded to fill the enormous demand created by the military. Not only were works such as T.C. & I. and Sparrows Point expanded, but through federal funding new plants were developed, notably in Texas by Armco and Lone Star Steel. By the end of World War II the southern pig iron production had risen to 15 percent (6.7 million tons) and its steel to 14 percent (12.7 million tons) of national production.

Since 1945 the iron and steel industry has undergone several significant changes in the South. Because of the decreasing iron content of southern ores (30 to 40 percent iron), companies have shifted to the use of foreign ores (60 to 70 percent iron), primarily from Venezuela, Chile, and Liberia. At the same time there has been a significant increase in the use of scrap in the steel furnaces. Automation and computer control in all phases of production have led to the need for highly skilled and better-trained workers. The most notable development, however, has been the adoption in the mid-1960s of the basic oxygen furnace (BOF) process for steelmaking. In the 1970s a more advanced oxygen process known as the Q-BOP has been adopted at U.S. Steel's Fairfield works in Alabama. Many smaller plants have turned to the electric furnace for steelmaking, with the Georgetown Steel Company of South Carolina being the first in the nation to convert processed ore directly into steel with this type of furnace.

After World War II the South began a significant shift away from an agrarian economy toward an industrial one. At the same time the region's rate of economic growth was greater than the average for the nation. One result was a major increase in demand for iron and steel products, especially in the most rapidly growing areas of Texas and the South Atlantic states. To fill this demand the iron and steel industry has expanded the number of small, independent steel plants, which tend to serve a localized market. Decentralization of the industry has been made possible by changes in technology, particularly the refinement of the electric furnace, and by decreasing dependence on local ore and coal supplies. For the South the result has been a gradual rise in its share of the nation's iron and steel, with 18 percent (16 million tons) of the pig iron produced in 1970 and 19.5 percent (25 million tons) of the steel. Also, the industry has become widely based and highly diversified, with production ranging from relatively simple castings reminiscent of the frontier days to specialized alloys for a space-age technology.

See W. T. Hogan, *History of Iron and Steel Industry* (1971), most recent and comprehensive work; H. H. Chapman, *Iron and Steel Industries of South* (1953); J. M. Swank, *Manufacture of Iron in All Ages* (1892); J. P. Lesley, *Iron Manufacturer's Guide* (1866); G. W. Stocking, *Basing Point Pricing* (1954); E. C. May, *Principio to Wheeling* (1945); K. Bruce, *Virginia Iron Manufacture* (1931); V. S. Clark, *Manufactures in U.S.* (1929); E. M. Armes, *Coal and Iron in Alabama* (1910); J. Fuller, *Alabama Review* (April, 1964); C. E. Hatch, *Virginia Magazine of History and Biography* (July, 1962); F. E. Vandiver, *Alabama Review* (Jan., April, July, 1948); E. C. Eckel, *Annals of American Academy of Political and Social Science* (Jan., 1931); L. J. Cappon, *Journal of Economic and Business History* (Feb., 1930); J. Fuller, "Tennessee Coal, Iron and Railroad Co." (Ph.D. dissertation, University of North Carolina, 1966); R. H. McKenzie, "Shelby Iron Co." (Ph.D. dissertation, University of Alabama, 1971); and American Iron and Steel Institute, *Annual Statistical Report* (1867–).

JUSTIN FULLER
University of Montevallo

IRONCLAD OATH, adopted first by Congress in 1862, required all federal officeholders to affirm loyalty to the Union. This oath differed radically from that used by President Abraham Lincoln and from the oath Congress imposed on federal officeholders in 1861, in that it looked to past as well as

IRON ORE PRODUCTION IN SOUTH, 1880–1974 (excluding by-product ore)
(thousands of long tons)

State	First reported iron-making furnace	1880	1890	1900	1910	1920	1930	1940	1950	1960	1970	1974	Latest year of reported production
Ala.	1818	171	1,898	2,759	4,801	5,894	5,738	7,316	7,300	4,235 }	} 1,484	} 287	1975
Ga.	1790	81	244 }	} 132	314	105	52	101	202	128 }			1975
N.C.	1725	3	23 }		65	72	a			2			1974
Tenn.	1790	93	466	594	732	376	28 }	} 23					1957
Va.	1716	163	543 }	} 922	903	321	20 }		5				1954
W.Va.	1798	55	25 }		} 64								1917
Ky.	1792	58	78	53 }									1914
Md.	1724	125	35	26	14	1							1920
Del.	1725	2											before 1890
S.C.	1773												1901
Mo.	1815	345	181	41	78	55	133	54	194	404	b	1,862	1975
Tex.	1850	3	22	17	30			5	1,182	b	b	b	1975
Ark.	1850?								1			b	1975
Miss.	1913				(1913–14) 22			50 (tons)					1967
Fla.	1862?												1862?
La.													
Total, southern states (listed figures only)		1,099	3,515	4,544	7,001	6,824	5,971	7,499	8,884	4,769	1,484	2,149	
Total U.S.		7,120	16,036	27,553	56,890	67,604	55,201	73,696	98,045	88,784	89,760	84,355	

[a] less than ½ unit
[b] not available or withheld to avoid disclosing company confidential information
SOURCES: *Mineral Resources of U.S.* (1889–1930)
Minerals Yearbook (1940–74)

future conduct. The state legislatures quickly followed the lead of the congressional Republicans, and the ironclad oath became a basic weapon used by Republicans against their political adversaries.

In 1863 President Lincoln announced that erstwhile rebels in occupied areas had merely to swear future loyalty to secure a presidential pardon and participate in politics. When Andrew Johnson succeeded to the presidency, he followed Lincoln's plan, with minor modifications. Despite the fact that 1862 and 1864 statutes required the ironclad oath of all federal officeholders and congressmen, Johnson's reconstructed governments of 1865 included men who obviously could not comply. Confrontation between the president and Congress over this issue began in December, 1865, and culminated in the impeachment effort of 1868.

Congress itself departed from the ironclad oath requirement in the exclusion clause of the Fourteenth Amendment, and the U.S. Supreme Court in CUMMINGS V. MISSOURI and *ex parte Garland* ultimately ruled both the national and state forms of the oath unconstitutional. Nonetheless the ironclad oath remained a vital element in Republican policy until finally repealed in 1884.

See H. Hyman, *Era of the Oath* (1954), fullest account, and *To Try Men's Souls* (1959), broadest perspective; J. G. Randall, *Constitutional Problems Under Lincoln* (1951); C. Fairman, *Reconstruction* (1971); and A. W. Bishop, *Loyalty on Frontier* (1863).

GEORGE M. DENNISON
Colorado State University

IRON ORE is a mineral substance that, when heated in the presence of a reductant such as carbon, will yield metallic iron. Because iron is the metal most widely used by man, iron ore is one of the world's most important mineral commodities. World production in 1974 was estimated at 880 million long tons. Production of iron ore in the United States in 1974 totaled 84.4 million tons, valued (f.o.b. mine) at about $1.3 billion. Approximately 4 percent of U.S. output in 1974 was produced in the southern states.

Iron ore was first reported in America by an English expedition that landed on Roanoke Island in 1585. Ore was found 80 to 120 miles from the island, but no samples were reportedly taken. In 1608 a sample of ore from Virginia or Maryland was smelted in England; the iron was found to be of good quality, and this led to the first attempt to establish an ironworks in the colonies. A works was built at Falling Creek, near Richmond, but was destroyed in 1622 in an Indian raid before production could begin. It was not until 1716 that iron making began in Virginia (IRON AND STEEL INDUSTRY).

Iron ore has been mined in almost all southern states, but most production has come from Alabama, Georgia, Tennessee, Virginia, Missouri, and Texas. Total production from southern states since colonial times is estimated at 525 million long tons (excluding by-product ore). Of this total, Alabama produced about 72 percent; Missouri, 8 percent, Tennessee, Virginia, and Texas, about 5 percent each; Georgia, 3 percent; and the remaining states, 2 percent. Maryland, West Virginia, and Kentucky were significant producers prior to 1921. North Carolina produced over 2 million tons, but mining virtually ceased in 1930. Texas became an important producer in 1947, and Missouri has been the leading southern producer since 1965. In late 1975 only Missouri, Texas, Georgia, and Arkansas were producing iron ore.

Although magnetite ore, mined in Missouri, now constitutes the bulk of southern production, hematite and limonite ores have been more important historically. Red fossiliferous hematite ore, found as sedimentary beds in Silurian formations of the Appalachian Mountains, was the principal iron ore mined in Alabama. It was mined in the Birmingham district from 1860 to 1971 and, together with the coal deposits of the Warrior River basin, led to the establishment of Birmingham as the leading southern iron-making and steelmaking center. This ore usually contains 35 to 40 percent iron and is the South's principal iron ore resource, but it is no longer mined because it cannot be concentrated cheaply enough to compete with higher-grade ores produced elsewhere in the United States and abroad.

Brown ore, consisting of goethite or limonite and usually derived from alteration of siderite, has been mined in most southern states and was the ore used in most of the earliest iron-making furnaces. Brown ores are found over broad areas west of the Appalachians and in the coastal plain region from Maryland to Texas. Important iron-making industries were based on brown ores, especially in Maryland, Virginia, and Tennessee. These ores are still mined in Georgia and Texas.

Other iron ores mined in the South included "black band" or "clay ironstone" ores, which consisted mainly of siderite and were mined from coal-bearing strata principally in Kentucky, West Virginia, and Maryland prior to 1900. Also, large quantities of iron oxide have been recovered as a by-product from processing sulfides of iron and copper at Ducktown, Tenn., since 1925.

See *Mineral Resources of U.S.* (1882–1931), esp. J. M. Swank, *American Iron Industry, 1619–1886* (1886); U.S. Bureau of Mines, *Minerals Yearbook* (1931–73); H. H. Chapman, *Iron and Steel Industries of South* (1953); and E. N. Hartley, *Ironworks on Saugus* (1957).

F. L. KLINGER
U.S. Bureau of Mines

IVERSON, ALFRED (1798–1873), born in eastern Georgia, attended Princeton, practiced law in central and western Georgia, and served as a legislator and jurist. He entered the U.S. Senate in 1855 as a Democrat. Iverson attracted attention in 1859 with a Senate speech in which he predicted secession unless Congress protected slavery in the territories. Defeated for reelection, he told the Senate in December, 1860, that the sections were irreconcilable. Ironically, he was still in the Senate when Georgia seceded in January, 1861, and ROBERT TOOMBS promptly joined him in resigning. Iverson took no active part in the Confederacy, though his son and namesake (1829–1911) became a brigadier general and was responsible for the capture of General George Stoneman and some 600 of his raiders near Macon.

See R. F. Nichols, *Disruption of Democracy* (1948); K. M. Stampp (ed.), *Causes of Civil War* (1959); and Milledgeville *Federal Union* (July 26, 1859).

HORACE MONTGOMERY
University of Georgia

J

JACKSON, ANDREW (1767–1845), born in the Waxhaws, S.C., settled in the "southwest" territory in 1788. He allied himself with the WILLIAM BLOUNT faction and served as a delegate to the Tennessee constitutional convention in 1796, as U.S. congressman from Tennessee (1796–1797), and briefly as U.S. senator (1797). His congressional career was notable only for his extreme opposition to concessions to either England or the Indian tribes of the West. After his return to Tennessee, Jackson served for six years as a superior court judge, but devoted most of his attention to his plantation and business ventures.

The War of 1812 dramatically changed Jackson's political fortunes. Obtaining a commission, Jackson led Tennessee troops to victory against the CREEK INDIANS at Horseshoe Bend in 1814 and the British at New Orleans in 1815. The battle of NEW ORLEANS transformed "Old Hickory" from a minor and retired Tennessee politician to a national hero. A subsequent military expedition against the SEMINOLE INDIANS in 1818 occasioned a storm of controversy when Jackson invaded Spanish Florida and executed two British subjects (ARBUTHNOT AND AMBRISTER, CASE OF).

Jackson served briefly as the first American governor of Florida in 1821. In 1822 the Tennessee legislature nominated him for the presidency of the United States and in 1823 elected Old Hickory to the U.S. Senate. Although Jackson received a plurality of both the popular and electoral votes in the presidential ELECTION OF 1824, the U.S. House of Representatives chose John Quincy Adams. Determined to win the presidency in 1828, Jackson and his supporters forged a political coalition in alliance with Martin Van Buren and JOHN C. CALHOUN that led to the rebirth of the national two-party system. Jackson's successful presidential campaign in the ELECTION OF 1828 was vague on specific issues, but won broad popular support through an effective propaganda campaign that portrayed Jackson's defeat in 1824 as the result of an "aristocratic conspiracy" to thwart the people's will.

Jackson served two terms in the White House (1829–1837). In keeping with his campaign to vindicate the principle of popular rule, he openly defended the principle of "rotation in office" (termed the "spoils system" by his opponents) as essential to prevent the subversion of democracy by a permanent office-holding class. Jackson set an important precedent by extensive use of the veto power to disallow legislation he deemed unconstitutional. However, despite his veto of the MAYSVILLE ROAD bill (1830), Jackson's administration did not actually reduce federal expenditures for internal improvements. His administration's TARIFF policy was equally equivocal. Although his southern supporters had represented Jackson as an opponent of protective duties, no action was taken to provide any substantial reduction of duties until after the passage of South Carolina's ordinance of NULLIFICATION in 1832. Following Jackson's proclamation on nullification, which asserted both the legitimacy of the tariff and the sanctity of the Union, Congress passed a compromise tariff bill in 1833, which left the issue of protectionism unresolved. Jackson's statements, in response to the nullification controversy, illuminated both his conception of states' rights and of the office of the president. Rejecting Calhoun's theory that states possessed the power to prevent the enforcement of federal statutes they deemed unconstitutional, Jackson argued that it is incumbent on the federal government to respect the constitutional limits on national power and asserted that the president, as the elected representative of all the people, is charged with special responsibility to defend the Constitution. That premise was also advanced by Jackson as a justification for his veto of the recharter of the second Bank of the United States in 1832. Jackson's opposition to the bank apparently grew out of long-standing suspicion of banks of issue, compounded by resentment of antiadministration political activities of some of the bank's officers. Although he attempted to foster a hard money policy by issuance of the Specie Circular, which forbade payment by bank note of obligations to the federal government, his administration failed to establish a consistent banking policy.

Although Jackson's administration did not formulate a consistent federal policy on the tariff, the currency, or internal improvements, Jackson's bold assertions of presidential power and responsibility established precedents for subsequent chief executives and profoundly influenced the evolution of the presidency.

See J. Parton, *Andrew Jackson* (1860); J. S. Bassett, *Andrew Jackson* (1911); M. James, *Andrew Jackson, Border Captain* (1933) and *Andrew Jackson, President* (1937); R.

Remini, *Andrew Jackson* (1966); J. C. Curtis, *Andrew Jackson* (1976); J. W. Ward, *Andrew Jackson* (1953); M. Meyers, *Jacksonian Persuasion* (1957); A. M. Schlesinger, *Age of Jackson* (1945); E. Pessen, *Jacksonian America* (1969); G. van Deusen, *Jacksonian Era* (1969); and Jackson Papers, Library of Congress.

ALFRED A. CAVE
University of Toledo

JACKSON, CLAIBORNE FOX (1806–1862),

leader of Missouri's secessionist government at the outset of the Civil War, was a native Kentuckian. He moved to Saline County, Mo., in 1830 and thereafter pursued various business enterprises while marrying in succession three sisters, the daughters of Dr. John Sappington. His main love was politics, however, and he was regularly in and out of the Missouri legislature over the next 20 years. He played a leading role in the overthrow of THOMAS HART BENTON as the leader of Missouri's Democratic party in 1850 through his "Jackson resolutions" in the assembly, which instructed the state's senators to vote in favor of slavery extension.

Elected governor in 1860, his prosouthern leanings quickly became evident. Although failing to secure secession by the convention route, he helped provoke a confrontation with the Union military command at St. Louis in May and June, 1861, which resulted in his government being driven from Jefferson City. After several skirmishes and two major battles, he and his Missouri State Guard under STERLING PRICE were forced to leave the state at the end of 1861. In the meantime, he had secured recognition from the Confederacy and formally withdrew Missouri from the Union by action of a rump legislative session at Neosho in November. He maintained a government in exile until his death at Little Rock.

See W. E. Parrish, *History of Missouri, 1860 to 1875* (1973); W. H. Lyon, *Missouri Historical Review* (July, 1964); and A. R. Kirkpatrick, *Missouri Historical Review* (Jan., April, July, 1961).

WILLIAM E. PARRISH
Westminster College, Fulton, Mo.

JACKSON, JAMES (1757–1806), was born in

Devonshire, England. At age fifteen he came to Savannah, Ga., studied law, and became a Whig when revolutionary troubles erupted. As a member of the state military forces he fought at Savannah (1778), COWPENS (1781), and the recovery of Augusta from the British (1781) and received the final British surrender of Savannah (July, 1782). After the war he rose from colonel to major general (1792) in the state militia, practiced law, and

was a planter. In 1788 he refused his election as governor on the grounds that he was too young and inexperienced. He served in the U.S. House (1789–1791) and in the Senate (1793–1795), from which he resigned to fight the YAZOO LAND FRAUD in the Georgia legislature. He was an important member of the state constitutional convention (1798), became governor (1798–1801), and returned to the U.S. Senate (1801–1806). His successful opposition to the Yazoo land fraud made him a great power in Georgia politics and furnished the excuse for several duels. With WILLIAM H. CRAWFORD and George M. Troup, he founded and headed the Georgia Republican party, the dominant party in the state.

See W. O. Foster, *James Jackson* (1960).

KENNETH COLEMAN
University of Georgia

JACKSON, THOMAS JONATHAN "STONEWALL" (1824–1863), was born at Clarksburg, Va.,

now W.Va. Since his parents died in poverty during his early childhood, he was reared by an uncle. After graduating from West Point in 1846, he entered the Mexican War, where he served with distinction at Veracruz, Cerro Gordo, and Chapultepec. Within 18 months after leaving West Point, he was brevetted major. In 1851 Jackson was appointed professor of artillery tactics and natural philosophy at the Virginia Military Institute in Lexington. He commanded the VMI Cadet Corps at the hanging of John Brown in 1859. Although not active in public affairs, he was a Democrat in politics and owned a few slaves.

When hostilities broke out in 1861, Jackson took the cadets to Richmond, where they served as drillmasters for the mobilizing Virginia troops. After he was appointed colonel of infantry in the Confederate army, Jackson was sent to Harpers Ferry, where he organized the famous Stonewall Brigade. He was promoted brigadier general on June 17, 1861, and participated with distinction in the first battle of BULL RUN. The sobriquet "Stonewall" was received by his brigade and himself as a result of a remark made by General Barnard E. Bee in this engagement. His promotion to major general followed on October 7, 1861, and on November 5 he assumed command in the Shenandoah Valley with headquarters at Winchester. After an unsuccessful winter campaign against Bath (Berkeley Springs) and Romney, he conducted his famous SHENANDOAH VALLEY CAMPAIGN of 1862, one of the most brilliant exploits in history.

Jackson's military star continued to shine as a

result of the victory at second BULL RUN. Promoted lieutenant general on October 10, 1862, he assumed command of the II Corps, Army of Northern Virginia. He distinguished himself at the battles of FREDERICKSBURG and CHANCELLORSVILLE. Unfortunately he was wounded by his own men while riding in front of his lines and, weak from the loss of blood, he died of pneumonia at Guiney's Station.

Jackson's greatness as a military commander is due to several characteristics. He was unusually aggressive and seized the initiative. He covered ground so quickly that his infantrymen were known as the "foot cavalry." He was a firm believer in two principles of war that he thought every military commander should observe. One is to mystify, mislead, and surprise the enemy so as to cause him to flee and then to continue to pursue him as long as possible. The other rule is to avoid fighting against superior numbers if it is possible to maneuver and fight part of the enemy's force. He was a strict disciplinarian and would condone no remissness in the performance of one's duty. On the other hand, he was an unreasonable taskmaster, did not confide in his subordinate officers, and even found it difficult to get along with such able generals as A. P. HILL and C. S. Winder.

See *Official Records, Armies*; R. L. Dabney, *Jackson* (1864–66); H. K. Douglas, *I Rode with Stonewall* (1940); D. S. Freeman, *Lee's Lieutenants* (1946); G. F. R. Henderson, *Stonewall Jackson* (1949); and F. Vandiver, *Mighty Stonewall* (1957).

MILLARD K. BUSHONG
Shepherd College

JACKSON, MISS. (pop. 153,968), began as a trading post on the Pearl River operated by Louis LeFleur. Chosen in 1821 as the site of the new state's capital, LeFleur's Bluff was rechristened to honor Andrew Jackson. Before the Civil War the town had become an important rail center. During the VICKSBURG CAMPAIGN, the city was twice the site of conflict (May 14, July 9–16, 1863) with bloodletting again the following year (July 3–9, 1864) during the MERIDIAN CAMPAIGN. Although the capital had been moved temporarily to Columbus during the war, postwar Jackson resumed its role as the seat of state government and an important rail center. Encouraged in part by the discovery of natural gas fields in the 1930s, Jackson's population tripled during the period between 1920 and 1950. Jackson is the home of MILLSAPS COLLEGE, Belhaven College (1894), and Jackson College (1877). It produces petroleum, natural gas, valves and fittings for drilling rigs, plumbing, and lumber products.

See files of *Clarion-Ledger* (1837–), *News* (1892–), *Advocate* (1941–68), *Mississippian* (1834–63), and *Vardaman's Weekly* (1908–23), all on microfilm.

JACKSON (MISS.) CLARION-LEDGER began publication in 1837 as the *Eastern Clarion*, a weekly sheet published in Paulding, Miss. Locating in Jackson after the Civil War, the paper became a daily and grew into one of the most widely distributed newspapers in Mississippi. Editor ETHELBERT BARKSDALE made it a key weapon in the overthrow in 1875 of the state's Reconstruction Republican government. In 1877 the *Clarion* openly condoned the LYNCHING of Judge W. W. Chisholm (a while Republican judge in Kemper County) and of his fifteen-year-old daughter, his fourteen-year-old son, and his friend (an English citizen). By 1889, however, the paper urged curtailing political violence and an end to lynchings.

Like most Mississippi dailies, the *Clarion* was closely associated with the state's conservative Bourbon leadership, yet it never became an organ of the machine. It opposed "free silver" in the 1890s, but it supported railroad regulation and it campaigned against the CONVICT LEASE SYSTEM. It also opposed the calling of the state's consititutional convention of 1890 and was extremely critical of such provisions in the new constitution as its UNDERSTANDING CLAUSE and its formula for apportionment, which shifted representation from the planter counties of the Delta to the largely white counties of the hills and the piney woods. As the *Clarion* feared, the new constitution resulted in the gradual loss of leadership by such men as Anselm McLaurin and in the eventual rise of such populistic spokesmen as JAMES K. VARDAMAN and T. G. BILBO. Although the political influence of the *Clarion* waned as the fortunes of Vardaman and Bilbo rose, the paper remains today the Mississippi newspaper with the largest circulation in the state, over 60,000 copies daily.

See A. D. Kirwan, *Revolt of Rednecks* (1951); complete bound files at Mississippi State Department of Archives; and microfilm from Bell & Howell (1865–78, 1890–1902, 1922–).

JACKSON (MISS.) DAILY NEWS was founded in 1892. In continuous publication since that date, it currently is a Democratic journal with an average daily circulation of approximately 50,000 copies.

See J. R. Skates, *Journal of Mississippi History* (May, July, Oct., 1967); bound copies at University of Mississippi (1908–); and microfilm from Bell & Howell (1902–).

JACKSON (MISS.) MISSISSIPPIAN began publication as a weekly newspaper in 1832. An early advocate of the NASHVILLE CONVENTION and states' rights, the *Mississippian* endorsed J. C. BRECKINRIDGE in the election of 1860. Soon after Abraham Lincoln's election, it called for secession. The *Mississippian* inaugurated a daily edition in 1861, but beginning in August, 1863, it was published in Selma, Ala., as a refugee newspaper. It returned to Jackson prior to the end of the war, and in 1865 it endorsed the suggestion to permit blacks to testify in Mississippi courts. It was merged with the Vicksburg *Herald* in 1867 and passed from the Jackson scene.

See assorted bound copies at Library of Congress and Mississippi State Department of Archives (1862–65); and microfilm from Bell & Howell (1834–56, 1859–63).

JACKSON, TENN. (pop. 39,996), on the Forked Deer River approximately 75 miles northeast of Memphis, was first settled in 1819. Since many of its residents were veterans who had served under ANDREW JACKSON, the town was named in his honor. The early town developed primarily as a market for area cotton growers. After completion to this point of the Illinois Central Railroad in 1858 and of the Mobile & Ohio in 1861, Jackson became equally important as a rail junction. The city exchanged hands several times during the Civil War after the fall of FTS. HENRY AND DONELSON in early 1862. On December 19, 1862, Union defenders successfully drove off an attack by NATHAN B. FORREST's cavalry, and on April 10, 1864, Confederate forces under J. R. CHALMERS left from here en route to their attack on FT. PILLOW. Continuing in its tradition as a railroad town, modern Jackson is a major transportation and shipping center for western Tennessee. Casey Jones, the legendary railroad engineer, is buried here. The city also is the home of Lambuth College (1843), Lane College (1882), and Union University (1834). Its factories manufacture aluminum foil, textiles, airconditioners, furniture, clothing, and wood veneers.

See E. I. Williams, *Historic Madison* (1946, 1972); J. G. Cisco, *History of Madison County* (1902); B. W. Overall, *Story of Casey Jones* (1956); S. C. Williams, *Beginnings of West Tennessee* (1930); S. V. Clement, *College Grows* (1972), Lambuth; and files of Jackson *Sun* (1888–).

JACKSONVILLE, FLA. (pop. 528,865), is a deepwater port near the mouth of the ST. JOHN'S RIVER on the Atlantic Ocean. Originally settled in 1740 when the Spanish built Ft. St. Nicholas, the surrounding community was called Cowford by the British after 1763. The town was severely burned in 1812 by American patriots. In 1821, after the purchase of Florida by the United States, a new city was planned and named for ANDREW JACKSON, the territorial governor. Although its growth was interrupted by the SEMINOLE WARS, antebellum Jacksonville developed rapidly as a market and shipping point for area cotton, naval stores, and lumber. A federal raiding party briefly occupied the city (March 23–31, 1863) during operations up the St. John's River. Prior to the battle of OLUSTEE, the city was again occupied by Union troops (February 7, 1864). During Reconstruction, the city began to gain popularity as a winter resort: Harriet Beecher Stowe and Stephen Crane both resided here. And by the end of the nineteenth century, rail connections and construction of improved harbor facilities assured the city of its position as one of the South's major coastal commerical centers. Modern Jacksonville exports lumber, naval stores, fruits, and machinery. It is a popular tourist resort, and its varied industries produce furniture, fertilizer, boats, cigars, glassware, construction materials, and processed meats.

See T. F. Davis, *History of Jacksonville, 1513–1924* (1925); P. D. Gold, *History of Duval County* (1928); Jacksonville Historical Society, *Papers* (1947–69); R. A. Martin, *City Makers* (1972); Jacksonville Sesquicentennial Commission, *Out of Cowford, 1822–1972* (1972), largely pictorial; *Florida Times-Union* (Dec. 27, 1964), centennial edition; W. Merritt, *Century of Medicine in Jacksonville* (1949); and files of *Florida Times-Union* (1864–) and *Journal* (1887–), both on microfilm. Jacksonville Public Library and Jacksonville Historical Society both maintain collections of local historical materials.

JACKSONVILLE FLORIDIAN began publication in 1828 as a weekly newspaper printed in Tallahassee. Also known as the *Floridian and Advocate* (1831–1848) and as the *Floridian and Journal* (1849–1864), it briefly attempted a daily edition in the spring of 1891. Since 1898 the *Floridian* has been published in Jacksonville, Fla.

See bound volumes at Library of Congress, J. C. Yonge Library in Pensacola, and Walker Memorial Library in Tallahassee; and microfilm from Bell & Howell (1831–60) and University of Florida Library (1865–88).

JACK TURNERISM was a term used in Alabama during the elections of 1882. Turner, a former slave, had become the political leader of the blacks in Choctaw County, and his successes were a standing affront and challenge to the white hierarchy. With the defeat of the Democrats in the county in the gubernatorial election of 1882, Turner was arrested, charged with conspiracy to kill all the whites in the county, and hanged in front of the courthouse at Butler on August 19. The case aroused national attention, and Alabama Democrats preyed on white fears by discovering other "Jack Turners" throughout the state planning revolt and murder. This intimidated blacks and assured a large turnout of white voters in the November elections.

See W. W. Rogers and R. D. Ward, *Journal of Negro History* (Oct., 1972) and *August Reckoning* (1973).

ROBERT DAVID WARD
Georgia Southern College

JACOBS, PATTIE RUFFNER (1875–1935), was born in West Virginia. She attended Ward Seminary in Nashville and Birmingham Training School for Teachers; she studied voice in Paris and commercial art in New York. In 1898 she married Solon Harold Jacobs, a Birmingham railroad executive. Mrs. Jacobs served as president of the Alabama Equal Suffrage Association (1912–1916, 1918–1920) and was an official in the National American Woman Suffrage Association. After ratification of the Nineteenth Amendment, the latter was transformed into the League of Women Voters. Always interested in politics but never a candidate for public office, she was chosen the first national Democratic committeewoman from Alabama. She strongly supported state PROHIBITION, CHILD LABOR legislation, abolition of the CONVICT LEASE SYSTEM, and better working conditions for women. But she opposed the adoption of a progressive income tax for Alabama and was generally silent on racial injustices. While doing public relations work for the Tennessee Valley Authority, she died.

See L. N. Allen, *Alabama Review* (April, 1958); Pattie R. Jacobs Scrapbook, Birmingham Public Library; and Alabama Equal Suffrage Association File, Alabama Department of Archives and History, Montgomery.

KENNETH R. JOHNSON
University of North Alabama

JAMES RIVER was named for King James I of England. Probably the best-known section is the 100-mile stretch that runs from the FALL LINE at Richmond to its mouth at HAMPTON ROADS. In 1607, approximately 30 miles upstream, English colonists began the colonization of Virginia at JAMESTOWN. In the eighteenth century this tidewater section of the river was a major artery of colonial COMMERCE, and in the nineteenth century during the Civil War it was used by Union forces as an avenue of attack on Richmond. An additional 250 miles of the James go from western Virginia to Richmond, however. Formed in the mountains by the confluence of Jackson River and Cowpasture Creek, the James flows through the Blue Ridge Mountains, past Lynchburg, and then generally southeast toward the fall line at Richmond. Its chief tributaries are the Chickahominy and the Appomattox rivers. Early nineteenth-century Virginians envisioned development of the upper reaches of the James River as a transportation link with the state's westernmost counties. Beginning in 1816, the general assembly authorized construction of an ambitious system of canals and turnpikes connecting the James with the KANAWHA RIVER in present-day West Virginia. Although the canals were completed to Lynchburg by 1840 and to Buchanan in 1851, the link with the Kanawha was never finished, and the James River canals were abandoned in the 1880s.

See B. Niles, *James River* (1939).

JAMESTOWN, VA., the site of the first permanent English settlement in the United States, served as the capital of colonial Virginia from 1607 to 1699. The founding expedition of the Virginia Company of London selected the peninsula in the James River, which proved to be good for defense but unhealthy with its marshy and malarial conditions.

The first few years after the landing on May 14, 1607, were extremely difficult. Fire destroyed the fort and storehouse in 1608, and the substantial number of nonworking "gentlemen" in the colony contributed to the difficulty of building adequate shelters and providing needed supplies. John Smith was able to impose discipline and also negotiated with the nearby POWHATAN Indians, who were at times hostile, at other times friendly. So severe was the "starving winter" of 1609 that the settlers almost abandoned Jamestown in June, 1610, but the arrival of new supplies turned them back.

There were many events of historic significance. The first representative assembly in the area of the United States was convened at Jamestown in 1619 by Governor George Yeardley in the frame church of that time. The brick church tower that is Jamestown's most significant ruin today was constructed later in the seventeenth century. In the same year of the first assembly, Virginia received the first blacks imported from Africa. Threatened by the devastating Indian attacks of 1622, Jamestown was spared the main fury of the assault because of the warning of a friendly Indian. It did not, however, escape the torch in BACON'S REBELLION in 1676.

Following the removal of the capital to Williamsburg in 1699, Jamestown declined in population and reverted to wilderness. In 1893 the ASSOCIATION FOR THE PRESERVATION OF VIRGINIA ANTIQUITIES began to reclaim the area and continues today to contribute to its preservation along with the National Park Service, which has included it in the Colonial National Historical Park. The Virginia 350th Anniversary Commission joined with a federal commission in arranging an elaborate celebration in 1957 with a visit by Queen Elizabeth II. The anniversary commission's successor, the Jamestown Foundation, continues as an agency of the commonwealth of Virginia. Its purpose is to extend knowledge of the Jamestown settlement, and it now includes among its activities the exhibition of Jamestown Festival Park adjacent to the original historic site.

See W. F. Craven, *Southern Colonies in Seventeenth Century* (1949); R. L. Morton, *Colonial Virginia* (1960); J. L. Cotter and J. P. Hudson, *New Discoveries at Jamestown* (1957), an archeological report; and E. G. Swem (ed.), *Jamestown 350th Anniversary Historical Booklets* (23 vols.; 1957).

W. STITT ROBINSON
University of Kansas

JANNEY, SAMUEL McPHERSON (1801–1880), was born in Loudon County, Va. He tried two or three business ventures before opening a boarding school for girls called Springdale in Loudon County in 1839. At the same time he began to find time to travel in the ministry among the QUAKERS. The author of more than a dozen volumes, he made a major contribution to the intellectual and spiritual development of his denomination. He is best remembered for his biography of William Penn (1851), which went through six editions, but his *History of the Religious Society of Friends* in four volumes (1859–1867) was also influential. Janney participated in various programs to bring an end to slavery. He supported the Union cause during the Civil War, but gave help to the wounded on both sides. He served as superintendent of the northern region of Indian reservations from 1869 to 1871 and then returned to Loudon County, where he remained until his death.

See *Memoirs of Samuel M. Janney* (1881); "Dictionary of Quaker Biography," Quaker Collection, Haverford College; and Janney Papers, Friends Historical Library, Swarthmore College.

EDWIN B. BRONNER
Haverford College

JAZZ is a very large word. It can be a noun or a verb, even an adjective. It can be improvised MUSIC, or it can be composed. There is a definite repertoire of jazz tunes, but any song can be played as jazz. Moreover jazz keeps changing and developing until at one end of the spectrum we have modern, complicated, progressive jazz and at the other end the original Dixieland of the early 1900s, very much alive and accepted by purists as the only authentic jazz. The origins of the word are vague. It was probably in use as early as 1900 meaning coitus, and it definitely appeared during 1913 in San Francisco denoting a kind of music. Most experts agree that the first use of the word to describe a band occurred at Lamb's Cafe in Chicago in June, 1915, when Tom Brown's Band from New Orleans was accused of playing jass or bawdy house music. But the band that was to make the word famous was another group of New Orleans musicians who opened in January, 1917, at Reisenweber's Restaurant in New York. They were at first advertised as the "Jasz Band" [*sic*] but by February they were calling themselves the "Original Dixieland Jazz Band." However, when they made their first big recording, they titled one side the "Dixieland Jass Band One-Step." But in their advertising the Victor Company said, "Spell it Jass, Jas, Jaz or Jazz—nothing can spoil a Jass band." Unless of course one deleted the first letter. And that is why the band finally chose "jazz."

See D. Holbrook, in *Storyville* (Dec., 1973–Jan., 1974), best and most recent study.

HENRY A. KMEN
Tulane University

JEANES FUND, or legally the Negro Rural School Fund (Anna T. Jeanes Foundation), was endowed in 1907 with $1 million. In carrying out the purpose of its Quaker benefactress to aid southern rural schools for Negroes, the fund's basic work became the sponsorship of a Jeanes teacher in all southern counties requesting assistance. Originally, within her county, this Jeanes representative instructed teachers in techniques of teaching simple industrial arts and domestic skills. Gradually the Jeanes teacher evolved into an academic supervisor and ultimately an unofficial assistant to the school superintendent, responsible for directing Negro schools. In 1937, after giving additional varied halp to Negro education, the fund was merged with the Slater and other foundations into the Southern Education Foundation (SOUTHERN EDUCATION BOARD), which continued Negro aid. During its existence the Jeanes Fund, with financial assistance from counties and other foundations, placed Jeanes teachers in almost one-half the counties in the South, saw its teacher model copied in several African countries, and became the prime force in program development for Negro rural schools.

See A. D. Wright, *Negro Rural School Fund* (1933), most complete; L. G. E. Jones, *Jeanes Teacher* (1937); J. W. Dillard, *South Atlantic Quarterly* (July, 1923), for early years; and C. W. Dabney, *Universal Education in South* (1936), acceptable overview.

GEORGE A. DILLINGHAM
Western Kentucky University

JEFFERSON, THOMAS (1748–1826), was a native Virginia planter. While living in Williamsburg as an undergraduate at William and Mary and later as a law student, he encountered a relatively sophisticated and cosmopolitan intellectual environment. In this capital he also observed Virginia's colonial politics. He entered the House of Burgesses in 1769 and actively participated in protests against British policies. Local leadership and publication of his pamphlet, *A Summary View*, made him a prominent politician.

In 1775 the provincial convention made him a delegate to the CONTINENTAL CONGRESS, where he distinguished himself as author of the DECLARATION OF INDEPENDENCE. In 1776 he returned home and actively participated in reforming the laws of his state, most notably with his proposal, the statute for religious freedom, which received final approval under James Madison's leadership in 1786. Jefferson served as governor from 1779 to 1781, but a disastrous British invasion tainted his gubernatorial record. After a brief retirement during the fatal illness of his wife Martha Wayles Skelton, he reentered national politics as delegate to the Continental Congress from 1783 to 1784. His proposals on the decimal system of coinage and on government for the western territories laid foundations for future policies.

In 1784 he went to Europe to negotiate commercial treaties and later became minister to France. His *Notes on Virginia*, published in 1785, enhanced his international reputation and provided guidelines for later Virginia reformers. In 1790 he became George Washington's secretary of state. Because of clashes with Alexander Hamilton on foreign and fiscal policies, Jefferson resigned in 1793. John Adams narrowly defeated him for the presidency in the ELECTION OF 1796, though Jefferson became vice-president and assumed leadership in the developing DEMOCRATIC-REPUBLICAN PARTY.

He finally won the presidency in 1801 in a bitter campaign (ELECTION OF 1800), and his first administration won general approval. Western expansion received renewed impetus not only from the LOUISIANA PURCHASE, but also from Georgia's land cession and a series of Indian treaties. His second term brought disappointments: failure to buy Florida or enforce American neutral rights during the Napoleonic Wars. Jefferson continued to receive wide southern support, although prices on two major southern staples, rice and cotton, dropped sharply because of the Embargo Acts. In 1809 Jefferson retired to Monticello and to the role of a political consultant to later Virginia presidents.

Jefferson's broad interests were shown by his leadership in successfully establishing the University of Virginia, his enthusiasm for Palladian architectural designs, which left its mark on American architecture, and his promotion of scientific agriculture. He bequeathed a rich legacy of belief in human freedom, faith in democracy, and patronage of "enlightened" goals. There were ambivalences in his attitude toward Negroes as a race and a lack of public support for antislavery programs, but his philosophical opposition to slavery as an institution was strong. His overall support of civil liberties, despite some inconsistencies, inspired later democrats.

See D. Malone, *Jefferson and His Time* (1948–), detailed, still incomplete, full bibliographies, somewhat uncritical; F. Brodie, *Thomas Jefferson* (1974), effort at psychohistory; M. D. Peterson, *Thomas Jefferson* (1970), best short biography and bibliography; L. Levy, *Jefferson and Civil Liberties* (1963), highly critical; J. P. Boyd (ed.), *Papers of Thomas Jefferson* (1950–), excellent but unfinished; A. A. Lipscomb *et al.* (eds.), *Writings of Thomas Jefferson* (20 vols.; 1903); and Jefferson Papers, Library of Congress (microfilm), Massachusetts Historical Society (microfilm), and University of Virginia (calendar available).

FRANCES L. HARROLD
Georgia State University

JEFFERSON BIRTHDAY TOAST (April 13, 1830). "Our Union! It must be preserved!" declared Andrew Jackson, looking straight at John C. Calhoun. Later he allowed the word *federal* to be placed before *Union*. "The Union! Next to Liberty most dear," replied Calhoun. These toasts occurred at a subscription banquet in Washington, gotten up in part by friends of Calhoun who wished to associate Thomas Jefferson's principles, and Jackson himself, with their theories of NULLIFICATION. Two and one-half years later, Jackson's toast became a slogan of those who supported the Union in the nullification controversy.

See M. James, *Andrew Jackson, Portrait of a President* (1937); J. C. Fitzpatrick (ed.), *Autobiography of Martin*

Van Buren (1920); and T. H. Benton, *Thirty Years View* (1854).

WILLIAM S. HOFFMANN
Saginaw Valley College

JEFFERSON CITY, MO. (pop. 32,407), approximately 110 miles west of St. Louis on the right bank of the Missouri River, was chosen in 1821 to be the state's capital because of its central location. The town developed very slowly, however, and after the capitol burned in 1837 other cities clamored for the capital to be moved. Although Jefferson City was tied by rail to St. Louis in 1855, real growth did not begin until after the turn of the century. The modern city is the home of Lincoln University and is a processor of poultry, grain, and fruit, but the state government remains its principal business.

See files of *Post-Tribune* (1865–), *Capital News* (1910–), and *Jeffersonian Republican* (1831–40), all on microfilm.

JENKINS, CHARLES JONES (1805–1883), born in Beaufort, S.C., and educated in Schenectady, N.Y., played a significant role in Georgia politics. He served two decades in the state legislature (1830–1850) and one year as attorney general and led the Georgia Whig party throughout. He is recognized as the major contributor to the GEORGIA PLATFORM of the state convention that endorsed the COMPROMISE OF 1850 and as a leader of southern unionism. In 1856 Jenkins switched to the Democratic party and sat on the Georgia supreme court during the Civil War. Elected governor under presidential Reconstruction in 1865 and in office until removed in 1868, he virulently opposed military Reconstruction. When Jenkins left office, he took the Georgia state seal, his own administration's records, and $600,000 in state revenue and deposited them in a New York bank to avoid handing them over to his Republican successor. He received a gold replica of the seal and a vote of thanks from the legislature in 1872, and he died peaceably after serving as president of the Georgia constitutional convention in 1877.

See C. C. Jones, *Life of Ex-Governor Jenkins* (1884); W. J. Northern, *Men of Mark in Georgia* (1910); H. M. Montgomery, *Georgians in Profile* (1958); and R. M. McCray, *Georgia Historical Quarterly* (Spring, 1970).

PETER D. KLINGMAN
Daytona Beach Community College

JEWS in the South have been a significant but small minority for more than 240 years. Never composing more than 1 percent of the total south-ern population, they have contributed substantially to the development of this region. Many prospered as financiers, merchants, artisans, and professionals. Particularly since the Civil War, southern Jewish families participated in creating an expanding economy. The Riches of Atlanta, the Thalheimers of Richmond, and the creators of Neiman-Marcus in Dallas serve as outstanding examples of Jewish merchant activity.

Antebellum Jewish history began in 1733 with the arrival of 40 Spanish-Portuguese and German Jewish refugees in Savannah. Although Jewish names appear in southern annals long before this date, the Savannah immigrants constituted the first Jewish community in the South. By 1740 most of these residents departed, and many resettled in Charleston. In 1820 the 500 Jews in Charleston composed one of the largest Jewish communities in America. Here they prospered and assimilated many of the characteristics of their Gentile neighbors.

The agrarian economy of the South accounts for the small number of Jews who settled there. Despite the influx of German Jews to America after 1836, the southern Jewish population amounted to less than 15,000 by 1860. As they became more prosperous, they gained greater acceptance in the pre–Civil War South. With the exception of North Carolina, where full political rights were denied them until 1868, Jews had been granted complete civil freedom by the end of the antebellum period. Notwithstanding initial political barriers, southern Jews participated in government. In 1845 DAVID L. YULEE from Florida became the first Jew elected to the U.S. Senate. The most prominent southern Jewish politician was JUDAH P. BENJAMIN, a U.S. senator and member of Jefferson Davis' Confederate cabinet.

Although few Jews owned plantations, they supported the institution of slavery. Rabbi David Einhorn of Baltimore was the only notable southern Jew to advocate emancipation. Most accounts indicate that Jews in the South wholeheartedly supported the southern cause by serving in the Confederacy and by making generous financial contributions. During the Civil War though, Jews in both the North and South became the target of anti-Semitic attacks. Fear of these "outsiders" intensified in the provincial South as economic conditions steadily worsened and fundamentalist Protestants looked for a scapegoat.

After the war, overt antagonism toward the Jews subsided as they contributed to the formation of the New South. Immigrant peddlers traversed the rural areas, and many eventually became prosperous merchants. Urban Jews congregated in such places as Miami, Atlanta, Houston, Dallas, and the suburbs of Washington, D.C.

By 1900, however, conditions for the laboring poor equaled those of the sharecroppers, and frustrations caused by poverty led to increased unrest. Jewish residents of Atlanta witnessed one of the worst outbreaks of anti-Semitism in American history when a prejudiced jury convicted LEO FRANK of killing a young white female laborer in 1912. In contrast to their coreligionists in the North, the Jews in the South kept silent about the unjust treatment of Frank and huddled in their homes fearing outbursts by the alienated white supremacists. As the twentieth century progressed, complete social acceptance of Jews proved elusive, and it is nowhere more apparent than in New Orleans. Mardi Gras marks the height of the social season there; and, although the first king of Rex, Lewis Solomon, was a Jew, they are now excluded from the elite clubs and social functions.

The civil rights era of the 1950s and 1960s marked another period of anxiety for southern Jews. While their northern brethren vociferously advocated equal rights, most southern Jews remained timidly neutral. Even so, they once again became a target for terrorism; and, during a ten-year period from 1960 to 1970, 12 dynamite explosions and nine fire bombings destroyed or damaged Jewish temples located for the most part in the South.

Nowhere in America has the "tyranny of the majority" been more evident than in the South. Yet the small minority of Jews who dwell there have resisted total assimilation. Their future as a thriving community in the South is far from certain, but their tenacity over the past 200 years augurs well for the days ahead. The attitude of Jews toward their adopted region is best expressed by E. N. Evans: "I am not certain what it means to be both a Jew and a Southerner—to have inherited the Jewish longing for a homeland while being raised with the Southerner's sense of home.... But I respond to the Southerner's commitment to place, his loyalty to the land, to his own tortured history, to the strange bond beyond color that Southern blacks and whites discover when they come to know one another."

See L. Dinnerstein and M. D. Palsson (eds.), *Jews in South* (1973), most comprehensive, includes bibliographical essay; E. N. Evans, *Provincials* (1973); American Jewish Archives, Cincinnati; and American Jewish Historical Society, New York City.

MARY DALE PALSSON
University of Arizona

JIM CROW for over a century has referred to laws, policies, and practices providing for racially segregated public facilities in the United States. Specifically, it refers to those educational, recreational, transportation, lodging, and dining institutions and services reserved for the use of black persons. The name Jim Crow derives originally from a northern white minstrel show performer, Thomas Dartmouth Rice (MINSTRELSY). "Daddy" Rice attributed one of his most popular acts to Jim, an old crippled slave of a Mr. Crow, who owned a stable in Louisville next door to the theater where Rice was performing. Rice's "Jump Jim Crow" song and dance act, first performed in 1828, became so popular that the actor billed himself, and rose to fame, as Jim Crow Rice. Ultimately he toured Europe, and according to one author "Jim Crow" became the song hit of the century in England.

See C. V. Woodward, *Strange Career of Jim Crow* (1966).

ALAN W. C. GREEN
Charlotte, Vt.

JOE BROWN'S PIKES. Thinking that these spearlike weapons would be valuable in combat, Georgia Governor JOSEPH E. BROWN commissioned the manufacture of thousands in 1862. Often made of ash, they consisted of poles from six to seven feet long with either a foot-long, double-edged blade or a hooked knife attached. The latter "bridle cutters" supposedly could be used to pull a man from his horse or, when detached from the pole, used like a Bowie knife. Because of the shortage of muskets and rifles, the Confederate Congress called for the formation of several companies to be equipped with these pikes. The weapon was apparently never used in battle.

See E. M. Coulter, *Confederate States of America* (1950).

JOHNS HOPKINS UNIVERSITY (Baltimore, Md. 21218) was founded in 1867 by Johns Hopkins (1795–1873), a childless Maryland merchant and Quaker who willed his $7 million estate to establish the school and a hospital. When opened in 1876, this private, nonsectarian university was primarily an undergraduate college for males. Daniel C. Gilman, the school's first president, modeled the institution after European universities, however, and Johns Hopkins quickly came to emphasize graduate training and research rather than collegiate instruction. Johns Hopkins University Press, inaugurated in 1878, was the first university press in the nation. The school currently has an enrollment of about 10,000 students, and its outstanding library houses, among other things, the papers of poet SIDNEY LANIER.

See H. Hawkins, *History of Johns Hopkins, 1874–1889* (1960); R. P. Sharkey, *Johns Hopkins* (1961); J. C. French, *History of University Founded by Johns Hopkins* (1946); W. C. Ryan, *Studies in Early Graduate Education* (1939); L. F. Barker, *Maryland Historical Magazine* (March, 1943); G. Connor, "Basil L. Gildersleeve" (Ph.D. dissertation, University of Wisconsin, 1960); G. Dykhuizen, *Journal of History of Ideas* (March, 1961), John Dewey; A. Flexner, *Daniel Coit Gilman* (1946); W. Conrad Gass, "Herbert Baxter Adams" (Ph.D. dissertation, Duke, 1962); and W. S. Holt, *New England Quarterly* (Sept., 1938), Henry Adams and Johns Hopkins University.

JOHNSON, ANDREW (1808–1875), born in Raleigh, N.C., settled in Greenville in 1826, where he opened a tailor shop, learned to write, and eventually became a small slaveholder. He entered politics as a Jacksonian Democrat, a champion of the common white men against the "stuck-up aristocrats." He advanced from alderman (1828–1830) and mayor of Greenville (1830–1834) to the state legislature (1835–1837, 1839–1843), to the U.S. House of Representatives for five terms (1843–1853), to the Tennessee governorship for two terms (1853–1857), to the U.S. Senate (1857–1862). An accomplished stump speaker, Johnson gained a reputation as a radical advocate of political reform, of state-supported public education, and of a federal homestead act—all intended, he said, to build up and sustain "the middle portion of society."

Although Johnson defended slavery and, in 1860, supported JOHN C. BRECKINRIDGE for president, he bitterly opposed Tennessee's secession and refused to resign his Senate seat. In 1862 he accepted an appointment as military governor of Tennessee. In 1864 Abraham Lincoln chose him to be vice-presidential candidate on the Union party ticket. On April 15, 1865, after Lincoln's assassination, he became president and thus inherited the enormous task of restoring the Union and determining the fate of 4 million emancipated slaves.

Johnson was poorly equipped for these responsibilities. He was still a traditional states' rights Democrat, and his Reconstruction policies showed him to be indifferent to the welfare of the freedmen and vulnerable to the blandishments of former Confederates whom he pardoned with unseemly haste. His refusal to compromise with Congress, his tactless affronts to Republican leaders, his public opposition to the FREEDMEN'S BUREAU and the FOURTEENTH AMENDMENT, and his ignorance of northern public opinion all contributed to his crushing defeat in the congressional elections of 1866. After the election, with more

than a two-thirds majority in both houses, the Republicans repudiated Johnson's conservative southern governments and launched their own Reconstruction program based on civil and political rights for the freedmen (RECONSTRUCTION, CONGRESSIONAL). In 1868 the House impeached Johnson for an alleged violation of the TENURE OF OFFICE ACT, for conduct unbecoming to a president, and for attempting to bring the Congress into disgrace. The validity of the case against Johnson depended upon whether one accepted a narrow or broad interpretation of the impeachment power. In any case, thanks to the opposition of seven Republicans, the Senate vote fell one short of the two-thirds majority required for conviction. After completing the last months of his term, Johnson returned to Tennessee. In 1874 the Tennessee legislature sent him back to the U.S. Senate. In his last speech (March 22, 1875) a few months before his death, he bitterly attacked Republican Reconstruction policies, finishing with a cry: "God save the Constitution."

See although there is no satisfactory biography of Johnson, G. F. Milton, *Age of Hate* (1930); H. K. Beale, *Critical Year* (1930); M. Lomask, *Andrew Johnson* (1960), all warmly sympathetic; E. L. McKitrick, *Johnson and Reconstruction* (1960); L. and J. H. Cox, *Politics, Principle, and Prejudice* (1963); K. M. Stampp, *Era of Reconstruction* (1965); and M. L. Benedict, *Impeachment and Trial of Johnson* (1973), all more critical.

KENNETH M. STAMPP
University of California, Berkeley

JOHNSON, BUSHROD RUST (1817–1880), was born of Quaker parents near Morristown, Ohio. Graduating from West Point in 1840, he served as an infantry officer in the SEMINOLE and MEXICAN wars. In 1847 he resigned his commission to teach at the Western Military Institute, Georgetown, Ky. He was appointed superintendent when WMI merged with the University of Nashville in 1855. In 1861 Johnson entered Confederate service as a colonel of engineers and was appointed brigadier general in January, 1862. Although captured at Ft. Donelson (FTS. HENRY AND DONELSON CAMPAIGN), Johnson managed to escape. Severely wounded at SHILOH, he nevertheless was able to lead his brigade at PERRYVILLE and STONES RIVER; he succeeded to division command at CHICKAMAUGA and KNOXVILLE. Transferred to the East and promoted major general in May, 1864, Johnson led a division throughout the RICHMOND-PETERSBURG CAMPAIGN and surrendered at APPOMATTOX. After the war, Johnson was chancellor of the University of Nashville from 1870 until his retirement to a farm in Illinois shortly before his death.

See C. M. Cummings, *Yankee Quaker* (1971), most definitive; T. M. Kegley, *Tennessee Historical Quarterly* (Sept., 1948); and J. D. Porter, *Confederate Veteran* (Jan., 1906).

CHARLES F. BRYAN, JR.
University of Tennessee, Knoxville

JOHNSON, CAVE (1793–1866), was an astute politician, born in Robertson County, Tenn. He was instrumental in engineering JAMES K. POLK's nomination for president at the Democratic convention in 1844. Johnson became postmaster general (1845–1849) in the Polk administration, starting a trend of postmasters general being selected for their political and patronage skills. He had previously been a Tennessee congressman (1829–1837, 1839–1845). Johnson remained active in national politics and served as a circuit judge from 1853 until his service was terminated when he chose to support the Confederacy.

See D. G. Fowler, *Cabinet Politician* (1943); N. A. Graebner, *Mississippi Valley Historical Review* (June, 1951); L. H. Barrett, *American Historical Review* (Oct., 1924); G. L. Sioussat, *Tennessee History Magazine* (Sept., 1915; March, 1917); L. D. White, *Jacksonians* (1954); C. A. McCoy, *Polk and Presidency* (1960); C. G. Sellers, Jr., *Polk, Jacksonian, 1795–1845* (1957) and *Polk, Continentalist, 1843–1846* (1966); and Polk Papers, Library of Congress.

CHARLES A. MCCOY
University of North Florida

JOHNSON, EDWARD (1816–1873), of Chesterfield County, Va., and the West Point class of 1838, achieved the rank of major general, C.S.A. (February, 1863). He served in the SEMINOLE WAR, in the Mexican War, and in Kansas and the West in the 1850s. He entered Confederate service June 10, 1861. Under STONEWALL JACKSON, his defense of the mountain crest won him the appellation "Allegheny." Wounded in defense of MCDOWELL, May 8, 1862, he returned to duty in June, 1863, as commander of Jackson's old division, which he led through GETTYSBURG and the WILDERNESS. Captured on May 2, 1864, he was exchanged in August and assigned command of a division of the Army of Tennessee. In JOHN B. HOOD's vain thrust toward Nashville, Johnson was captured again. After the war he farmed in Chesterfield County until his death.

See D. S. Freeman, *Lee's Lieutenants* (3 vols.; 1942–44), stresses Johnson's soldierly professionalism; J. I. Robertson, *Stonewall Brigade* (1963); S. F. Horn, *Army of Tennessee* (1941); M. B. Chesnut, *Diary from Dixie*, ed. B. A. Williams (1949), character sketch; and B. W. Duke,

History of Morgan's Cavalry, ed. C. F. Holland (1960), prison ship and exchange.

R. E. FORDERHASE
Eastern Kentucky University

JOHNSON, GEORGE W. (1811–1862), a wealthy planter from Scott County, Ky., was a conspicuous advocate of the Confederate cause in Kentucky. He participated as a delegate in the Russellville convention, which declared itself the "Provisional Government of Kentucky" and passed resolutions seceding from the Union and petitioning for admittance to the Confederacy. Johnson was appointed first provisional governor. Operating with funds borrowed from the Confederacy, Johnson headquartered temporarily in Bowling Green and attempted to collect taxes and recruit troops. His authority was never recognized beyond Confederate lines. He volunteered for service in the Confederate army after his "government" was driven from Kentucky by advancing Union troops. He was fatally wounded in the battle of SHILOH.

See L. Collins and R. Collins, *History of Kentucky* (1966), Russellville convention and activities in Bowling Green; E. M. Coulter, *Civil War and Readjustment in Kentucky* (1926); and L. Harrison, *Civil War in Kentucky* (1975).

MICHAEL T. DUES
California State University, Sacramento

JOHNSON, GERALD WHITE (1890–), was born in the rural community of Riverton, N.C. The son of a newspaperman, he was educated at Wake Forest College and worked briefly for two small newspapers before joining the Greensboro *Daily News* in 1913. His writing caught the eye of Baltimore newspaperman H. L. Mencken, who proclaimed him "the best editorial writer in the South." After two years as professor of journalism at the University of North Carolina (1924–1926), he joined Mencken on the Baltimore Sunpapers as an editorial writer. Although he became widely respected as a national political analyst after 1930, his greatest contribution to southern life was his work as an iconoclastic essayist in the 1920s. He was second only to Mencken in his indictment of southern literary poverty and his call for a new southern spirit. His subjects were religious frenzy, racial prejudice, the POOR WHITE, and the subculture of the southern mill town. His freewheeling prose style equaled and sometimes surpassed Mencken's own. Since 1943 he has been a news commentator and free-lance journalist. He has also written novels and works of history.

See E. Clark, *Innocence Abroad* (1931); and F. Hobson, *Serpent in Eden* (1974).

FRED HOBSON
University of Alabama

JOHNSON, HERSCHEL VESPASIAN (1812–1880), caught up in the sectional conflict that grew out of the Mexican War, remained something of a moderate yet completely devoted to southern rights. He interpreted the division in the democratic party at the CHARLESTON CONVENTION (1860) as a distinct threat to the Union. In June he accepted the nomination for vice-president on the Stephen Douglas ticket. Johnson commented on the bitterness that greeted his decision, but he insisted the interests of Georgia and the South would best be served by rallying to Douglas, the "idol of the Great Northwest," the leading man of the section destined to dominate the country, and representative of the natural comity between South and West.

Johnson opposed immediate secession, preferring instead a convention of southern states. When Georgia seceded, he followed his state. Never optimistic about the Confederacy's probable success, he served in the Confederate Senate from the fall of 1862 until the end of the war. He maintained his states' rights views but was considered a supporter of Jefferson Davis. In 1866 he was elected to the U.S. Senate but, as a former Confederate official, was denied his seat. In 1873 he became judge of the middle circuit and served in that office until his death. He was remembered by friends as a man of generous tendencies and high principles.

See P. S. Flippen, *Herschel V. Johnson* (1931); R. H. Shryock, *Georgia and Union* (1926); and R. F. Nichols, *Disruption of American Democracy* (1948).

JOHN T. HUBBELL
Kent State University

JOHNSON, JAMES WELDON, (1871–1938), was born in Jacksonville, Fla., of parents whose devotion to American middle-class standards, joined to a sense of mission, lifted them above the common lot of Negroes. He pursued several careers. Graduated from Atlanta University, he returned to Jacksonville as principal of the grammar school that he had attended; read law and was admitted to the Florida bar; and founded and edited a weekly newspaper, which failed after a year. Meantime, he wrote poetry and in 1900 composed "Lift Every Voice and Sing," which, set to music by his brother Rosamond, became widely known as the Negro national anthem. In 1901 he joined Rosamond in New York City, and their collaboration on Negro musical plays and "coon songs" brought them immediate success.

But Jim Johnson had his parents' sense of mission, of doing something "meaningful for the benefit of his [Negro] people." In 1905 he campaigned for Theodore Roosevelt, "the best friend Negroes had in public life." Johnson's reward was an appointment as U.S. consul in Venezuela and subsequently in Nicaragua. During the seven years (1906–1913) he lived abroad, he contributed poems to magazines, and he wrote his only novel, *The Autobiography of an Ex-Coloured Man* (1912). In 1914 Johnson became field secretary for the NAACP, and in 1930 he accepted a professorship—more congenial to writing—at Fisk University. He was killed in an automobile accident.

Besides the novel, Johnson published three volumes of poetry: *Fifty Years and Other Poems* (1917); *God's Trombones* (1927), the volume for which he is most esteemed; *Saint Peter Relates an Incident of the Resurrection Day* (1930); and three of prose: *Black Manhattan* (1930); an autobiography, *Along This Way* (1933); and *Negro American, What Now?* (1934). Also, he edited *The Book of American Negro Poetry* (1921) and, with his brother, *The Book of American Negro Spirituals* (1925) and *The Second Book of American Negro Spirituals* (1926). In all of his works, excepting only the "coon songs," which he regretted having written, Johnson wanted to identify and evaluate the Negroes' contributions to American life and to depict their place in it. He succeeded to a marked degree.

See S. Brown, in J. W. Johnson (ed.), *Book of American Negro Poetry* (Rev. ed; 1969); J. W. Johnson, *Along This Way* (1933); and Johnson Papers, Yale University.

SAUNDERS REDDING
Cornell University

JOHNSON, LYNDON BAINES (1908–1973), was born in Gillespie County, near Stonewall, Tex., of a backcountry, middle-class, and politically known family. He graduated from Southwest Texas State Teachers College in 1930. By 1931 he was in Washington as a legislative assistant and soon married to Claudia ("Lady Bird") Taylor, who would rank among the most politically active of first ladies. From 1935 to 1937 he served as director of the Texas NATIONAL YOUTH ADMINISTRATION until his election to Congress as a Democrat and ardent New Dealer. He became a protégé of Franklin Roosevelt and such powerful congressmen as Carl Vinson and SAM RAYBURN. Although defeated in his first bid for the U.S. Senate in 1941, he was elected in 1948 after a restless career in the House (1937–1948). In January, 1951, he became Democratic majority whip in the Senate and in January, 1953, was elevated to minority leader. He stepped to national power in January, 1955, as majority leader of the Senate. The "Johnson system" of coercion and persuasion dominated Senate legislation. As vice-presidential candidate he campaigned in 1960 energetically, particularly in the South, where his support probably won the election for John Kennedy (ELECTION OF 1960).

Johnson's national image was that of "just a politician and a Southern politician at that." He had shifted on domestic issues in the 1940s and 1950s from the left to the center and then more to the right, mirroring the defection of his Texas constituency from the national party. As president, following the assassination of Kennedy in 1963, Johnson moved to shed his tag as a southern conservative. His presidency furthered the greatest period of reform since the New Deal, a program he called early in 1964 the Great Society. From 1964 through 1966 Congress passed measure after measure, such as Medicare and federal aid to health agencies, federal aid to education, urban assistance programs, an antipoverty war, a broad housing program, and the beginning of significant environmental legislation. In the ELECTION OF 1964 he defeated Barry Goldwater by the largest plurality in American history, 62.1 percent.

His other great achievement, ironically for a southern president, lay in civil rights. Johnson helped engineer passage of the weak 1957 voting law. In 1964 and 1965 he strongly supported passage of the effective public accommodation and voting rights laws. In 1968 at administrative urging, Congress passed an open-housing law (CIVIL RIGHTS ACT OF 1957; CIVIL RIGHTS ACT OF 1964; CIVIL RIGHTS ACT OF 1965; CIVIL RIGHTS ACT OF 1968). Johnson, the southern country-boy president, became a national spokesman for black progress and racial justice. By the end of his administration, an aggressive legal and administrative policy had also given new strength to school desegregation in the South and equal opportunity in the marketplace and had helped to further black political power. Yet his support of liberal change had eroded badly his popularity in the South.

Johnson's cold war heritage dogged his presidency. Although making promising steps toward disarmament and using international negotiation rather than confrontation, Johnson continued to support an independent, non-Communist South Vietnam. On August 7, 1964, he obtained from Congress the Tonkin Gulf Resolution, which granted him the authority to use military force in Vietnam. In February, 1965, Johnson ordered the bombing of North Vietnam and in April, 1965, American combat troops entered the conflict. By 1968 the U.S. had well over 500,000 people in Vietnam. The war destroyed his domestic coalition, and he himself suffered a hard-hitting attack from the antiwar movement and estranged intellectuals. On March 31, 1968, he announced his intention not to run for another term.

Johnson's years left many sharply differing views of his career. Among many was that of an arrogant, personally crude man who blindly clung to old visions of power and destroyed a generation of liberalism. Another is that of an activist and courageous leader tragically falling into the Vietnam quagmire at the expense of his inspiring and skilled leadership of a national breakthrough in social, economic, and racial justice. Johnson himself thought that future events would vindicate his programs. His last major state paper closed with the line: "But I believe that at least it will be said that we tried."

See, for clear chronological record, A. Steinberg, *Sam Johnson's Boy* (1968); and J. Heath, *Decade of Disillusionment* (1975), comprehensive bibliography. For interpretative accounts, see B. Mooney, *Lyndon Johnson Story* (1960); W. White, *Professional: LBJ* (1964); R. Evans and R. Novak, *Lyndon B. Johnson* (1966); P. Geyelin, *Lyndon B. Johnson* (1966); R. Sherrill, *Accidental President* (1967); L. Heren, *No Hail, No Farewell* (1970); and H. McPherson, *Political Education* (1972). See also Johnson's memoirs, *Vantage Point* (1971); and Johnson Papers, Lyndon B. Johnson Library, Austin, Tex.

JAMES A. HODGES
College of Wooster

JOHNSON, REVERDY (1796–1876), was one of Maryland's most distinguished lawyers of the nineteenth century. Admitted to the bar in 1816, he rose rapidly in his profession. His legal career embraced many of the important federal cases of the period, including DRED SCOTT V. SANDFORD and a role in the defense of Mary Surratt. Intermittently he was active in both state and national politics. Originally a DEMOCRATIC-REPUBLICAN, he later became a Whig. With its collapse, Johnson, opposing Know-Nothingism, joined the Democratic party. Early in his career he was elected to the state senate (1821–1828) and later to the U.S. Senate (1845–1849), only to resign to serve as attorney general (1849–1850) under Zachary Taylor. During the Civil War he supported the Union and was elected to Maryland's house of delegates (1861–1862) and once again to the U.S. Senate (1863–1868). Johnson, a conservative Unionist, was often critical of Abraham Lincoln. Following the war, with notable exceptions, he supported Johnsonian Reconstruction and defended the president in the impeachment proceedings. In 1868, resigning his Senate seat, he was appointed ambassador to Great Britain. There he negotiated the ill-fated Johnson-Clarendon Convention.

See B. C. Steiner, *Reverdy Johnson* (1914), dated but useful; and A. Cook, *Maryland Historical Magazine* (June, 1966).

RICHARD R. DUNCAN
Georgetown University

JOHNSON, RICHARD MENTOR (1780–1850),

Kentucky's first native son elected to its general assembly (1804), was catapulted into the national political arena, where he served in the House of Representatives (1807–1819) and the Senate (1820–1837). A war hawk, he led a regiment of Kentucky mounted volunteers in the battle of the Thames (October 5, 1813) and was severely wounded while killing the Indian chief Tecumseh. Educated in the law, Johnson, a Democrat, introduced the bill that abolished imprisonment for debt in the nation (1832). Nominated for the vice-presidency on the ticket with Martin Van Buren (1836), he failed to receive a majority of the electoral votes, but was elected by the Senate (February 8, 1837). Never married, Johnson acknowledged two daughters born to his slave mistress Julia Chinn. Founder of the Choctaw Academy for Indian youth, he was also a founder and trustee of Georgetown College, Ky.

See L. W. Meyer, *Richard M. Johnson* (1932); and W. Emmons, *Biography of R. M. Johnson* (1833).

BETTY CAROLYN CONGLETON
East Carolina University

JOHNSON, RICHARD W. (1827–1897), Union

general, was born in Livingston County, Ky. After graduating from West Point in 1849, he performed duty on the western frontier, including field service with the celebrated 2nd Cavalry in Texas until that department was surrendered to rebel insurgents on the eve of the Civil War. He was appointed brigadier general of volunteers in October, 1861, and afterward commanded a brigade at CORINTH. Taken prisoner by JOHN HUNT MORGAN in August, 1862, he was exchanged and advanced to divisional command in the Army of the Cumberland, fighting gallantly at CHICKAMAUGA, CHATTANOOGA and NASHVILLE. For meritorious conduct, he was subsequently promoted brigadier general in the regular military establishment. After retirement, he taught military science at the uni-

versities of Missouri and Minnesota and wrote articles and books, including his memoirs.

See R. W. Johnson, *Soldier's Reminiscences* (1886); Johnson's Military Service Record, National Archives; and R. U. Johnson and C. C. Buel (eds.), *Battles and Leaders* (1888), III, IV.

JAMES W. MCKEE, JR.
East Tennessee State University

JOHNSON, THOMAS (1732–1819), was an able

lawyer who spent his life in the service of his native Maryland. The Revolution occasioned his greatest contributions. After serving on revolutionary committees, he was prominent in the CONTINENTAL CONGRESS and, as Maryland's first governor (1777–1779), demonstrated consummate skill in furnishing the Continental army with arms, men, and supplies. Subsequently, he served in the state assembly (1780–1781, 1786–1787); in the state convention to ratify the new federal Constitution (1788); as chief justice of the Maryland general court (1790–1791); and as associate justice of the U.S. Supreme Court for a brief and undistinguished term (1791–1793). An early southern entrepreneur, he collaborated with his old friend GEORGE WASHINGTON in establishing the Potomac Company in 1785, a joint Maryland-Virginia effort to open the Potomac to east-west trade. In 1791 Washington appointed him to the commission to establish the District of Columbia on that river. When poor health forced his retirement in 1794, he declined public office and devoted his remaining years to his lands and ironworks at Frederick, Md.

See E. S. Delaplaine, *Thomas Johnson* (1927), thorough; and L. Friedman and F. L. Israel, *Justices of U.S. Supreme Court* (1969), on judicial career.

FRANCIS N. STITES
San Diego State University

JOHNSON, WILLIAM (1771–1834), born in

Charleston, graduated from Princeton and studied law with CHARLES COTESWORTH PINCKNEY. A state legislator and judge, he was President Thomas Jefferson's first appointee to the Supreme Court, a position he held for 30 years. A judicial pragmatist and an advocate of positive, legislative law, he was the most frequent dissenter on the Marshall Court. As a nationalist, he upheld the war powers of Congress, wrote a strong concurring opinion in *Gibbons* v. *Ogden* (1824), and later opposed NULLIFICATION. He read the obligation of contracts clause narrowly, wrote the lead opinion in *Ogden* v. *Saunders* (1827), and advocated reform of bankruptcy law. He rejected common law federal crimes in *United States* v. *Hudson* (1812). In *Gilchrist* v. *Collector* (1808) he restrained by mandamus presidential enforcement of the Embargo Act. In admiralty cases, he restricted the jurisdiction. Overshadowed by Joseph Story and JOHN MARSHALL, Johnson was an independent judge whose central principle was legislative supremacy controlled by the electoral process.

See D. G. Morgan, *Harvard Law Review* (Jan., 1944) and "William Johnson" (Ph.D. dissertation, Harvard, 1942); and C. Warren, *Supreme Court* (1922).

BRADLEY CHAPIN
Ohio State University

JOHNSON CITY, TENN. (pop. 33,770), founded in 1777, was first known as Blue Plum. Soon renamed Haynesville, it and nearby JONESBORO were two of the important settlements in early Tennessee history. As the political, commercial, and population centers of the state moved westward, however, the community declined in importance along with many other mountain towns in east Tennessee. Railroads brought new life to the community when Haynesville became a railroad junction in the middle of the nineteenth century. Located approximately 100 miles north of Knoxville, it developed first as a major market town and shipping point for area lumber industries and then as a focal point for east Tennessee's IRON AND STEEL INDUSTRY. Soon after being incorporated in 1869, the town changed its name to Johnson City to honor its first mayor. East Tennessee State College (1911) is located here.

See S. C. Williams, *Dawn of Tennessee* (1937); J. A. Caruso, *Appalachian Frontier* (1959); and files of Johnson City *Press Chronicle* (1910–), on microfilm.

JOHNSON FAMILY of Arkansas was part of a Democratic political combination that dominated the government of the territory and state until the close of the Civil War. Patriarch of the family was Benjamin Johnson (1784–1849), who came to Arkansas from Kentucky in 1821 to accept an appointment to the superior court. Benjamin was a younger brother of RICHARD MENTOR JOHNSON, vice-president under Martin Van Buren. Two other brothers, James Johnson and John T. Johnson, served in Congress from Kentucky.

Benjamin Johnson spent 15 years on the superior court. After Arkansas became a state in 1836, President Andrew Jackson appointed him federal district judge, a position that Johnson retained until his death. Robert Ward Johnson (1814–1879), the most prominent of Benjamin's sons, was attor-

ney general of Arkansas prior to his election to Congress (1846–1853). He then moved up to the U.S. Senate (1853–1861), where he was a strong proponent of southern rights. After Arkansas seceded he became a delegate to the Confederate Provisional Congress. He was Confederate senator from 1862 until the end of the war. Another son, Richard H. Johnson (1826–1889), edited the influential Little Rock *True Democrat* and was narrowly defeated for governor in 1860. Juliette, daughter of Benjamin Johnson, married Ambrose H. Sevier, territorial delegate to Congress and one of the state's first U.S. senators. Their daughter Anna Maria married THOMAS J. CHURCHILL.

The ascendancy of the Johnsons and their allies the Conways began while Arkansas was a territory. Henry W. Conway was delegate to Congress from 1823 until his death in 1827. Henry's brother James S. Conway became first governor of the state in 1836 and served four years. Elias N. Conway, another brother, served two terms as governor (1852–1860). Ambrose H. Sevier, son-in-law of Benjamin Johnson, was a cousin of the Conways. The Rector family was also a part of the Conway-Johnson dynasty. Ironically, it was Henry M. Rector who bolted the combination in 1860 and was elected governor as an independent Democrat. Two years later the family returned to power with a hand-picked governor, but the defeat of the Confederacy destroyed its fortunes. James B. Johnson, a younger son of Benjamin, was killed in service with the Confederate army.

See J. Hallum, *History of Arkansas* (1887); and J. H. Shinn, *Pioneers and Makers of Arkansas* (1908).

JOHN L. FERGUSON
Arkansas History Commission

JOHNSTON, ALBERT SIDNEY (1803–1862), was born at Washington, Ky. He graduated from the U.S. Military Academy (1826) and served in the Black Hawk War. General THOMAS J. RUSK of the Republic of Texas appointed him adjutant general (1836), and he was raised to brigadier general (1837) to replace Felix Huston, who challenged Johnston to a duel, wounding him. Texan President MIRABEAU LAMAR named Johnston secretary of war. He resigned (1840), moved to Kentucky, and later returned to Texas, where he entered the Mexican War, serving as colonel in the U.S. Army. Johnston became paymaster of the army (1849) and assumed command of the Department of Texas (1856) as colonel of the 2nd Cavalry. Johnston commanded in Utah (1858–1860) as brevet brigadier general, subduing peacefully a threatened Mormon uprising. He accepted com-

mand of the Department of the Pacific at San Francisco (1860), but resigned (April 10, 1861) on learning of Texas' secession and returned to the South. President JEFFERSON DAVIS appointed him general over the Western Department. Johnston took Bowling Green, Ky., and formed and drilled an army. At MILL SPRINGS (January 19, 1862), he was defeated by G. H. Thomas. Johnston withdrew to near Nashville and then to Corinth, Miss. He planned to defeat U. S. Grant before Grant could be joined by D. C. Buell. Johnston moved from Corinth (April 3, 1862) and on April 6 struck Grant at SHILOH Church near Pittsburg Landing, Tenn., where the federals outnumbered him. Strenuous Confederate attacks forced the federals back against the Tennessee River, but Johnston was killed in the engagement.

See C. P. Roland, *Albert S. Johnston* (1964); W. P. Johnston, *Life of Albert S. Johnston* (1878); and *Official Records, Armies*, Ser. 1, Vols. III, IV, VII, VIII, X, XII.

WILLIAM CURTIS NUNN
Texas Christian University

JOHNSTON, JOSEPH EGGLESTON (1807–1891),

was born in Prince Edward County, Va., and graduated from West Point (1829). In April, 1861, he resigned as quartermaster general of the U.S. Army to join the Confederacy. He was an individualist with a retentive mind and reserved personality; some contemporaries considered him moody and deeply sensitive about personal honor and dignity. Johnston first assumed command of the Army of the Shenandoah. He joined P. G. T. BEAUREGARD at the first battle of BULL RUN and, as ranking officer, received credit for this Confederate victory. But his promotion to full general on July 4 ranked Johnston only fourth in seniority, a fact he felt violated Confederate law and constituted a personal affront.

In 1862 Johnston commanded the Army of Northern Virginia in the PENINSULAR CAMPAIGN until seriously wounded at SEVEN PINES. After recovery, he received an ill-defined command in the western theater, including the armies of BRAXTON BRAGG and JOHN C. PEMBERTON. He warned Pemberton to evacuate Vicksburg to avoid the capture of his troops, but President Jefferson Davis insisted Pemberton hold at all costs. Lacking manpower, Johnston could not relieve Vicksburg; on the surrender of the city Davis reprimanded Johnston and greatly reduced his command. Following Bragg's resignation after the CHATTANOOGA CAMPAIGN, Davis appointed Johnston to lead the Army of Tennessee. Badly outnumbered, Old Joe conducted a masterful retirement through

north Georgia before the forces of William T. Sherman. Confederate political leaders, critical of Johnston for being too cautious and unaggressive, replaced him on July 17, 1864, with JOHN B. HOOD before Atlanta.

Johnston remained inactive until restored to command the remnant of the Army of Tennessee (then in North Carolina) by R. E. Lee in the closing months of the war. After delaying Sherman's northward march at BENTONVILLE, Johnston surrendered on April 26 at Durham Station. The caliber of Johnston's generalship has been a subject of dispute, with modern scholars assigning him new stature for his defensive skill and strategic understanding. He was held in high respect by Union commanders and enjoyed the admiration of the soldiers serving under him. He suffered, however, from an inability to convince others of the wisdom of his recommendations and from the protracted feud with the president of the Confederacy. After the conflict Johnston entered the business field. He won election to the U.S. House of Representatives for one term (1879–1881) and in 1885 received an appointment from President Grover Cleveland as commissioner of railroads. To justify his military record, Johnston in 1874 published his *Narrative of Military Operations*.

See G. E. Govan and J. W. Livingood, *A Different Valor* (1956); R. M. Hughes, *General Johnston* (1893); B. Johnson, *Joseph E. Johnston* (1891); A. Jones, *Confederate Strategy* (1961); and T. L. Connelly, *Autumn of Glory* (1971).

JAMES W. LIVINGOOD
University of Tennessee, Chattanooga

JOHNSTON, JOSIAH STODDARD (1833–1913),

farmer, soldier, journalist, and historian, was born in New Orleans. He received his formal education at Western Military Institute, Georgetown, Ky., and Yale College (1853). He was, for a time, a planter in Arkansas (1855–1859) and a farmer in Scott County, Ky. (1859–1862). Prosouthern in sympathy, he served with distinction as a major on the staffs of Generals Braxton Bragg, S. B. Buckner, John C. Breckinridge, and John Echols of the Confederate army, attaining the rank of lieutenant colonel early in 1865. In 1867 he became editor of the Frankfort *Yeoman* (1867–1886), where his facile pen, courtly demeanor, political acumen, and social skills greatly strengthened the Democratic party in Kentucky. After losing the nomination for governor (1875) he was secretary of state under Governor James B. McCreary (1875–1879), whose victory he had made possible. In 1889 Johnston moved to Louisville, where he wrote editorials for the *Courier-Journal* and gave himself increasingly to historical writing. His publications include the memorial *History of Louisville* in two volumes (1896), *Confederate History of Kentucky* (1898), and many articles on the early settlement of the commonwealth. In writing and speaking on economic subjects he urged a fuller development of Kentucky's industrial potential.

See J. S. Johnston Manuscripts, Filson Club Library, Louisville; *Courier-Journal* (Oct. 5, 1913); and J. C. Morton, *Register of Kentucky Historical Society* (Jan., 1914).

JUDGE WATSON
Florida Southern College

JOHNSTON, MARY (1870–1936), was the author of 23 novels; a history, *Pioneers of the Old South* (1918); and a verse drama, *The Goddess of Reason* (1907). Best known for her vastly popular and successful historical romances, such as *To Have and To Hold* (1900), this tiny, frail, patrician Virginian spinster, daughter of a Confederate major, was an ardent feminist, outspoken pacifist, and practicing mystic. Her historical novels were carefully researched, the most ambitious project in that genre being the two-volumed opus of the Civil War, *The Long Roll* (1911) and *Cease Firing* (1912). Less well known are her feminist novels, *Hagar* (1913) and *Foes* (1918), and works of her later, mystical phase, such as *Michael Forth* (1919) and *Sweet Rocket* (1920). Five of her novels are still in print.

See E. Wagenknecht, *Sewanee Review* (April–June, 1936); L. G. Nelson, *Southern Writers* (1964); L. D. Rubin (ed.), *Bibliographical Guide to Southern Literature* (1969); and Mary Johnston Papers, University of Virginia, Charlottesville.

DOROTHY SCURA
Virginia Commonwealth University

JOHNSTON, OLIN DEWITT (1896–1965), was born of tenant-farming parents near Honea Path, S.C. He received an A.B. degree from Wofford College and LL.B. and master's degrees from the University of South Carolina by 1924. He began a law practice the same year, combining it with a political career that took him from South Carolina's house of representatives (1923, 1924, 1927–1930) to the governor's office (1935–1939, 1943–1945) and thence to the U.S. Senate (1945–1965).

As governor, he "temporarily" foiled a precedent-setting U.S. Supreme Court decision allowing blacks to vote in state primary elections (WHITE PRIMARY) by having his state's primary laws repealed and subjugating the primaries to the state's Democratic party, a "private organization." Capitalizing on his resulting popularity, Johnston won a seat in the U.S. Senate. Here he usually voted with his party except on civil rights legislation. Disapproving HARRY TRUMAN's proposed civil rights program in 1948, he opposed his nomination for the presidency. After Truman's selection, however, Johnston campaigned for his election, as he did for subsequent Democratic presidential nominees.

Senators who knew him well explained that he was not as conservative as he appeared to be. Johnston sensed that, with inevitable increases in Negro voting, the South would change. To help his state during an era of flux, he mastered the art of double-talk, which allowed him to mouth phrases of white supremacy while covertly appealing to blacks.

See O. D. Johnston Papers, University of South Carolina; and E. M. Lander, *South Carolina* (1960).

RICHARD C. ETHRIDGE
East Central Junior College, Decatur, Miss.

JOHNSTON, SAMUEL (1733–1816), born in Scotland, immigrated to North Carolina during his infancy, eventually (1754) settling in Edenton, N.C. Wealthy lawyer, merchant, and planter, he was appointed to important provincial offices and in 1759 was elected to the assembly, serving until 1775. During the Revolution, he served on the first four provincial congresses in North Carolina, presiding over the third and fourth, and from 1779 to 1786 he alternately sat in the state senate and the CONTINENTAL CONGRESS. Strongly favoring ratification, Johnston presided over the 1788 and 1789 federal constitutional conventions in North Carolina and from 1787 through 1803 he consecutively served as governor, U.S. senator, and superior court judge. Although he drafted the Riot Act of 1770 to suppress the REGULATORS, he may have written the "Atticus" letter attacking Governor William Tryon's mishandling of the Regulator problem. Although elected to the U.S. Senate as a Federalist, he opposed Alexander Hamilton's plan of funding the debt.

See W. Saunders (ed.), *Colonial Records of North Carolina* (1886–90), V–X; W. Clark, *State Records of North Carolina* (1894–1914), XI–XXV; S. Ashe (ed.), *Biographical History of North Carolina* (1905–17); and G. McRee, *Life and Correspondence of James Iredell* (1857–58).

WILLIAM S. PRICE, JR.
North Carolina Division of Archives and History

MARVIN L. MICHAEL KAY
University of Toledo

JONES, ANSON (1798–1858), was born at See-konkville, Great Barrington, Mass. He received his M.D. degree in 1827 and moved to Brazoria, Tex., in 1833, where he signed the petition for consultation at San Felipe in 1835 and presented the resolution calling for a convention to declare independence from Mexico. He enlisted as a private and participated in the battle of SAN JACINTO. Jones returned to Brazoria after the war and was elected to the second congress, from which he was appointed Texas minister to the United States. One of his first acts was to withdraw the unaccepted offer of Texas annexation. He returned to Texas to fill a vacancy in the senate, then was elected president pro tem of the senate in the fifth congress. SAM HOUSTON appointed him secretary of state in 1841. Houston respected Jones's judgment and education and strongly supported him for president in 1844. Jones oversaw the admission of Texas to the Union, then retired to his plantation near Washington-on-the-Brazos. When he received no votes for the U.S. Senate in 1857 he committed suicide.

See H. Gambrell, *Anson Jones* (1948), generally favorable account; A. Jones, *Memoranda and Official Correspondence* (1859); G. P. Garrison (ed.), *Diplomatic Correspondence* (1905–11); and J. H. Smith, *Annexation of Texas* (1911).

RON TYLER
Amon Carter Museum of Western Art

JONES, HUGH (1691–1760), was born in Hereford County, England. After graduating from Oxford in 1716, he was appointed professor of mathematics of the College of William and Mary and additionally chaplain of the House of Burgesses and minister of Jamestown. His outspoken support of Governor Alexander Spotswood led to a confrontation with Commissary JAMES BLAIR. Under pressure, he returned to England in 1721; however, by 1725 he was back in Virginia at St. Stephen's, King and Queen County. A dispute with the vestry in 1726 forced him to leave for William and Mary Parish, Charles County, Md. He again built his political connections and with the help of the CALVERT FAMILY moved to North Sassafras Parish, Cecil County, in 1731. He repaid their aid by serving as their chief mathematician during the Pennsylvania boundary dispute. Jones is best known for his perceptive *The Present State of Virginia* (1724). He also published a practical English grammar and an essay on calendar and numerical reform.

See H. Jones, *History*, ed. R. Morton (1956); and R. L. Morton, *William and Mary Quarterly* (Jan., 1950).

KEVIN P. KELLY
Bowdoin College

JONES, JESSE HOLMAN (1874–1956), born in Tennessee and raised in Kentucky, came to Texas in his late teens. During the next 30 years he became a millionaire several times over in real estate and as owner of the Houston *Chronicle*. One of the major real estate developers in Houston, he was largely responsible for the making of the city's skyline with his construction of 33 multistory buildings. He was best known for his service on the RECONSTRUCTION FINANCE CORPORATION from 1932 to 1945; he served as its head after 1933. In 1940 he entered Franklin Roosevelt's cabinet as secretary of commerce, but he also retained control over the RFC. In 1945 he resigned from the cabinet at Roosevelt's request to make room for Henry Wallace, who had been rejected by the Democratic party for vice-president. He also resigned from the RFC at the same time. Jones once estimated that he distributed $50 billion in loans to American business to save it from collapse during the GREAT DEPRESSION. The greatest criticism of him as RFC director was that he was too cautious and businesslike in the distribution of government loans.

See J. H. Jones with E. Angly, *Fifty Billion Dollars* (1951); and R. F. Fenno, *American Political Science Review* (June, 1958).

DONALD W. WHISENHUNT
Eastern New Mexico University

JONES, MARVIN (1882–1976), was born near Valley View, Tex. After practicing law in Amarillo, the boyish-faced Jones won election to the U.S. House of Representatives in 1916, where he became a skilled parliamentarian and an expert practitioner of the art of politics (1917–1940). As chairman of the Agriculture Committee (1931–1940), Jones controlled House agricultural legislation during the NEW DEAL and also sponsored the Emergency Farm Mortgage Refinancing Act (1933), Farm Credit Administration Act (1933), Jones-Connally Cattle Purchase Act (1934), Soil Conservation and Domestic Allotment Act (1936), Bankhead-Jones Farm Tenancy Act (1937), Jones-Costigan Sugar Act (1934), and the Agricultural Adjustment Act of 1938. Yet, his major legislative interests concerned farm finance and soil conservation. In 1940 Franklin Roosevelt appointed

Jones to the U.S. Court of Claims, but Jones served in the Office of Economic Stabilization with JAMES BYRNES and as director of the War Food Administration (1943–1945). Returning to the court (1945), Jones became chief judge in 1947 and continued until his appointment as senior judge in 1964. A devout Methodist and agrarian, Jones combined knowledge of agricultural legislation, administration, and law with an agricultural philosophy.

See M. Jones, *Memoirs* (1973); and I. May, *Agricultural History* (April, 1977) and "The Panhandle Kid and His Constituents," paper, TSHA convention (March, 1974).

IRVIN MAY, JR.
Texas Agricultural Experiment Station

JONES, THOMAS GOODE (1844–1924), personified the southern BOURBON leader. Before his gubernatorial election in 1890, Jones had served in the Confederate army, practiced law, farmed, and served two terms in the Alabama legislature (1884–1888). Although he won the election handily, he secured the nomination because leading business interests sought to head off the nomination of Populist REUBEN F. KOLB. Two years later Jones ran against Kolb and won by what historians agree were fraudulent returns. Jones hired Pinkerton detectives and called out the state militia in 1894 to protect the property of mine and railroad interests from strikers. In the 1901 constitutional convention, Jones opposed the GRANDFATHER CLAUSE but nevertheless went along with DISFRANCHISEMENT explaining that high standards for voting would give blacks incentive to qualify. In the same year President Theodore Roosevelt appointed Jones to an Alabama federal district judgeship. He took an active if lenient role in the 1903 PEONAGE cases and later helped sponsor BAILEY V. ALABAMA. As federal judge, he consistently defended business interests, especially in the railroad rate dispute.

See T. G. Jones Papers, Alabama Department of Archives and History; C. R. Huggins, "Bourbonism and Radicalism in Alabama" (Ph.D. dissertation, Auburn, 1968); P. Daniel, *Shadow of Slavery* (1972); S. Hackney, *Populism to Progressivism in Alabama* (1969); W. W. Rogers, *One-Gallused Rebellion* (1970); and R. D. Ward and W. W. Rogers, *Labor Revolt in Alabama* (1965).

PETE DANIEL
University of Tennessee, Knoxville

JONES, WILLIAM ATKINSON (1849–1918), a Confederate veteran, was graduated from the University of Virginia Law School with honors in 1870 and returned to Warsaw, Va., in the Northern

Neck of the commonwealth to practice law. Between 1870 and 1890 with the aid of his newspaper, the *Northern Neck News*, Jones eased into Virginia politics by being elected commonwealth's attorney and by becoming actively involved in the READJUSTER MOVEMENT and the reorganization of the Conservative Democratic party in 1883. As a result, Jones emerged as a prominent Democratic politician by 1890. In that year he was elected to Congress, an office he held until his death. During the height of his political career, Jones was committed to the restoration of political democracy in the Old Dominion. With the election of THOMAS S. MARTIN to the U.S. Senate by the legislature in 1893 and the subequent rise of the Martin machine in Virginia politics, Jones began his long struggle for reform by means of a statewide senatorial primary. After enduring several defeats, the primary was finally adopted in time for the senatorial election of 1905. However, Martin continued to defeat his opponents, including Jones in 1911.

See H. G. Wheatley, "Jones" (M.A. thesis, University of Virginia, 1953); W. A. Jones Papers, University of Virginia Library; R. H. Pulley, *Old Virginia Restored, 1870–1930* (1968); V. Dabney, *Virginia, New Dominion* (1972); and A. W. Moger, *Bourbonism to Byrd, 1870–1925* (1968).

THOMAS E. GAY, JR.
Edinboro State College

JONES, REPUBLIC OF, was, in southern folklore at least, the most famous Unionist stronghold in the Confederacy. According to the legend, Jones County, located in the southeastern part of Mississippi, seceded from the South in late 1862, established an independent republic with a bicameral legislature, and elected one "Nathan" Knight as president. Knight allegedly raised an army of some 10,000 men and made Jones a haven for disaffected Unionists and deserters. The myth of the "Jones County Confederacy" was exploded around 1900. The truth is that Jones County, although a center of strong anti-Confederate sentiment where Newton Knight led a gang of deserters, at no time attempted to establish an independent republic. Indeed, the regular county government seems to have operated smoothly throughout the war.

See G. N. Galloway, *Magazine of American History* (1886), exaggerated version; G. Montgomery, *Mississippi Historical Society Publications* (1904), early corrective; and J. K. Bettersworth, *Confederate Mississippi* (1943), authoritative.

EVERETTE SWINNEY
Southwest Texas State University

JONESBORO, TENN. (pop. 1,510), is the oldest town in the state. After being laid out in 1779, it served until 1785 as the first capital of the state of FRANKLIN. ANDREW JACKSON practiced law here for two years (1788–1790), but by then the town clearly had lost its early commercial and political importance.

See S. C. Williams, *Dawn of Tennessee* (1937) and *Tennessee Historical Magazine* (April, 1932); M. Fink, *American Historical Magazine* (Jan., 1896); J. A. Caruso, *Appalachian Frontier* (1959); and files of Johnson City *Press Chronicle* (1910–).

JOUETT'S RIDE (1781). Unknown to the governor of Virginia, THOMAS JEFFERSON, Colonel Banastre Tarleton, on orders from Lord Cornwallis had succeeded in penetrating to within 45 miles of Monticello to Louisa, Va., in a plot to seize the governor and the legislature then sitting at Charlottesville. Rebel Captain John ("Jack") Jouett, who happened to be staying at the Cuckoo Tavern in Louisa on the night of June 3, discovered the British troops and, guessing their purpose, raced all night by back roads to warn the governor. Jefferson received him in the early dawn, offered him a glass of madeira, and sent him on to nearby Charlottesville to alert the legislators. Jefferson and most of the members of the legislature thus escaped capture.

See S. K. Padover, *Jefferson* (1942); and F. M. Brodie, *Thomas Jefferson* (1974).

JOURNAL OF BLACK STUDIES, founded in 1970 as a quarterly organ of the Center for Afro-American Studies at the University of California at Los Angeles, is now sponsored by the Black Studies Department at the University of New York at Buffalo and is published by Sage Publications (275 S. Beverly Dr., Beverly Hills, Calif. 90212). It concerns itself with questions of economics, politics, sociology, literature, philosophy, and history involving persons of African descent. With a circulation of 2,500, the *Journal* has included book reviews and a bibliographic guide to periodicals and books on topics of interest involving black people.

JOURNALS, HISTORICAL, of the South date from the Virginia Historical Society's *Virginia Historical Register and Literary Companion* (1848–1853). It was an eclectic publication, stressing the state's colonial history. It and the brief (12 issues only) *South-Western Monthly* (1852) represent the only southern contributions before the Civil War. As elsewhere in the nation, extensive historical materials were appearing in general magazines, such as the SOUTHERN LITERARY MESSENGER and DE BOW'S REVIEW.

The aftermath of the Civil War produced approximately ten "Lost Cause" journals, beginning with the *Land We Love* (1866–8169). Although seeking to justify the South's attempted secession, their basic purpose was to preserve the exploits of the Confederate army and its leaders. Most of the articles were brief and reminiscent in nature. The most significant was the *Southern Historical Society Papers* (1876–1959), although its monthly publication pattern soon gave way (1885) to an annual publication. Too exclusively devoted to Confederate history, the *Papers* only partially met the need for a regional journal. To fulfill more completely this desire, the *Publications of the Southern History Association* appeared in 1897, patterned after the new *American Historical Review*, but inadequate financial support limited its existence to a decade.

It was not sectional but state historical journals that would provide the major channel for historical articles in the period following the decline of the Lost Cause journals. Between 1820 and the Civil War, state societies were organized in 11 of the slaveholding states, but only Virginia's (see above) had sponsored a periodical. Following the Civil War, limited financial resources remained an obstacle, and not until 1893 did the first state journal still published today appear: the *Virginia Magazine of History and Biography*. Within a decade state society journals had appeared in nine additional southern states. In these journals, brief articles were contributed by members of the society or by the editors, and research was minimal. Much documentary material was reproduced, but it was fragmentary in scope. Most of these state journals, however, remain currently published and are becoming steadily more professional. This trend has been stimulated by the extensive growth of research-oriented teachers of history as a major group of contributors. Numerous local HISTORICAL SOCIETIES also emerged, with approximately 125 county, city, or intrastate regional groups currently reporting some periodical-type publication.

In 1915 a new dimension was added to southern historical magazines with the appearance of the *Journal of Negro History*. A successful return to the regional journal was made in 1935, when the revived Southern Historical Association began publishing the *Journal of Southern History*, a thoroughly professional periodical. If the South was relatively slow in comparison with the Northeast and Middle West in entering the field, by the mid–twentieth century its contributions to American state and regional historical journals had become a significant one.

See *Writings on American History* (1902–75), journal titles and/or descriptive commentary; A. H. Shearer, *American Historical Association Annual Report* (1916), I; C. C. Crittenden and D. Godard (eds.), *Historical Societies in U.S.* (1944); M. O. White, "History of American Historical Periodicals, 1741–1895" (Ph.D. dissertation, University of Iowa, 1946); D. McDonald (ed.), *Historical Societies and Agencies* (1972); and *Ulrich's International Periodicals Directory* (16th ed.; 1975).

MAXWELL O. WHITE
Northeastern Oklahoma State University

JUDICIARIES, SOUTHERN, developed during the colonial era in a fashion at once similar to, yet different from, those in the northern colonies. Both reflected the difference between frontier and mother country by not evolving quite Stuart England's extraordinary hodgepodge of diverse courts, each possessing jurisdiction over narrow areas of the law. And both avoided the mother country's greatest procedural excesses—though, it should be noted, more successfully during the seventeenth than the eighteenth century, when until the Revolution formalism was on the rise. But equally apparent were the differences within the colonies. Prerevolutionary southern courts dealt with a law somewhat more codified than England's, yet less so than the northern colonies'. The southern judiciaries inclined to greater procedural formalism and tended more swiftly to develop some of the task differentiations of the English juridical system—*e.g.*, separate equity courts.

The effects of the Revolution were twofold. The first, stemming from identification of judiciary with imperial authority, was a short-lived debilitation of juridical power in favor of "popularly based" legislative power. The second was to make possible the development of an idiosyncratic juridical system devoted to sustaining the "peculiar institution." Yet perhaps the most noteworthy feature of the evolution of the southern judiciary between the 1780s and the Civil War is that it did not become, relative to the rest of the nation, more idiosyncratic than it did. The persistence of slavery in the South could well have brought about a well-orchestrated defense of the peculiar institution, one that took precedence over judicial maintenance of other legal-political values—*e.g.*, measured and orderly administration of the rule of law. Equally, it could have caused enormous divergence from the basic drive of nineteenth-century American law toward increasing its penetration into society, toward bringing more and more types of social, economic, and personal conflict within the ambit of the judiciary.

Some historicans have emphasized these aspects of defense and divergence, pointing to the circumstance that most slaves remained in practice outside the formal legal system and even urging that there was a breakdown in due process, an increasing resort to violence, after about 1830. Such a view ignores the countervailing growth of a tendency to litigate slavery issues within the formal judicial structure, one that far outstripped population increase. It also ignores the tendency of many southern judges to find "openings" in existing statutory law in order to free slaves, let off free Negroes from repressive charges, and so on.

Space does not permit detailed analysis of the jurisprudence created by southern supreme courts in wrestling with the peculiar institution. However, some quotations and rulings of the most influential judges illustrate the diversity of opinion persistent to the outbreak of the Civil War:

"The prisoner has been severely whipped ... do the humane principles of the common law demand anything further? Sure am I they do not. If the prisoner was a white man ... could such a course receive the countenance of anyone?" (Justice John Belton O'Neall of South Carolina, in *Nathan*, 5 Richardson 219 at 232–33 [SC, 1851]).

"An officer ... having a notice to serve on the defendant without any authority whatsoever, arrests him and attempts to tie him! ... Was he to submit tamely?—Or was he not excusable in resorting to the natural right of self-defense." (North Carolina Chief Justice Richmond Pearson, reversing the conviction of a tax-delinquent free black who had resorted to "self-help" against police brutality. The black had beaten up the town constable. *Davis*, 52 NC 52 at 54–55 [1859]).

"Suppose that Ohio ... should be determined to descend another grade in the scale of her peculiar humanity, and ... confer citizenship on the ourang-outang, are we to be told that 'comity' will require of the States not thus demented." (Judge William Harris of Mississippi, refusing to uphold a will bequeathing property to a former Mississippi slave living in Ohio, in *Mitchell*, 37 Miss. 235 at 263 [1859].) The decision resurrects "the barbarian rules which prevailed in the dark ages." (Judge Alex Handy, dissenting.)

"Birds of prey ... upon the wing." (North Carolina Chief Justice Frederick Nash, overruling litigants attempting to defeat a manumission, in *Mayo*, 2 Jones 239 [1855].)

A slave "is made after the image of the Creator. He has mental capacities ... equal to his owner ... but the law under which he is held as a slave

. . . cannot extinguish his high-born nature." (Judge Nathan Green, in *Ford* 26 Tenn. 92 at 95 [1846], rejecting the contention that a slave could not sue for freedom.) There is no good reason to regard Green's point of view as less a classic exposition of the law of southern slavery than *Cresswell's Executors*, wherein the Alabama court of 1861 asserted the slave "has no legal mind, no will." (37 Ala. 229 at 236.)

The antebellum southern judiciary never was really able to resolve its most difficult task: agreement on whether the black should be treated as human or as propery (SLAVE CODES).

See D. Flanigan, *Journal of Southern History* (Nov., 1974); L. Friedman, *History of American Law* (1971); and K. Nash, *Virginia Law Review* (Feb., 1970), *North Carolina Law Review* (Feb., 1970), and *Journal of American History* (Dec., 1971).

A. E. KEIR NASH
University of California, Santa Barbara

K

KANAWHA RIVER begins as the New River in North Carolina. From there it flows northward through Virginia to Radford, where it turns northwestward across West Virginia to join the Ohio River at Point Pleasant. Its total length is 430 miles, and it drains a third of West Virginia. Charleston is the most important city on its shores. The river probably derives its name from the Conoy Indians, who lived along the Potomac and New rivers. As early as 1750 there were a few scattered settlers in the area, but by 1769 and 1770 there were enough people in the valley of Virginia to establish the settlements of Lewisburg and Peterstown.

George Washington secured land claims totaling 33,000 acres in the region and in 1770 personally toured the Kanawha. Daniel Boone settled at Point Pleasant and in 1791 moved to Charleston; from there he was sent to the Virginia assembly to represent Kanawha County. He moved on to Kentucky in 1795. By 1800 Charleston was a settlement of a dozen houses and nearby began the Kanawha Salines (now Malden), which eventually produced annually millions of bushels of the finest quality salt. Other economic pursuits by the beginning of the nineteenth century included tobacco, pork, cattle, and lumber. The coal industry, now dominant, began in this era, and since World War II over 14 million tons per year have been shipped. Other industries that have been added include glass, paint, paper, flour and feed, sand, cement, concrete, iron, steel, and chemicals.

One of the perennial concerns of the people has been to improve the navigation of the river and to develop the basin. From that day in 1819 when the steamer *Robert Thompson* failed to conquer the swift current at Ted House, improvement of the Kanawha has continued unabated. Today, there is a significant, coordinated, regional water resources planning effort, which involves federal departments as well as officials of three states. The program is to be implemented from 1985 to 2000 and when completed, with its plans for economic development, irrigation, flood control, and hydroelectric power, it will help the Kanawha Valley fulfill the promise it has held for its people.

See O. K. Rice, *Allegheny Frontier* (1970), thorough and well documented; H. Reynolds, *West Virginia Review* (May, 1936); R. W. Dayton, *Pioneers on Upper Kanawha* (1948); T. Walker, *Journal of Expedition in 1750* (1888); O. K. Rice, *Journal of Southern History* (Nov., 1965); E. Comette and F. Summers (eds.), *Thirty-Fifth State* (1966), good collection of sources; J. A. de Gruyter, *Kanawha Spectator* (1953); G. Summers, *Pages from Past* (1935); C. W. Butterfield (ed.), *Washington-Crawford Letters* (1877); T. Abernethy, *Western Lands and American Revolution* (1959); and J. P. Hale, *History of Kanawha Valley* (1891).

ROBERT D. ARBUCKLE
Pennsylvania State University

KANNAPOLIS, N.C. (pop. 36,293), was founded as a company town in 1906 by J. W. Cannon of Cannon Mills. It is in the central portion of the state, approximately 20 miles north of Charlotte, and is one of the largest producers of towels, sheets, and blankets in the world.

See files of Kannapolis *Independent* (1927–), on microfilm.

KANSAS CITY, MO. (pop. 487,799), sprang from business on the border: fur, Indian, and far western trade and land speculation. François Chouteau established a fur post in 1821 near the juncture of the Kaw and Missouri rivers. Westport, now part of Kansas City, supplanted Independence by 1845 as the start of the Santa Fe Trail. (SANTA FE TRADE). By the Civil War, population in Kansas City was 5,000. Proslavery advocates failed to annex Kansas City to Kansas in the 1850s. Residents supported Stephen Douglas and JOHN BELL in the ELECTION OF 1860. The battle of WESTPORT (1864) ended threats to Union control of the city during the war. A railroad bridge in 1869 over the Missouri tied Kansas City to Chicago. Transportation, jobbing, and the cattle and grain trade were economic pillars. The city planned its elaborate park and boulevard system in the 1890s. Thomas J. Pendergast succeeded his brother Jim at the head of a growing political machine (PENDERGAST MACHINE). Gambling by Boss Tom and inflated contracts and fraudulent votes preceded the machine's downfall. L. P. Cookingham, city manager, for 19 years orchestrated a reform period that ended in 1959. Reform government returned to city hall in 1963.

See A. T. Brown and R. R. Wohl, *Huntington Library Quarterly* (May, 1960), evaluates usable past; H. C. Haskell and R. B. Fowler, *City of Future* (1950), best survey; W. L. McCorkle, "Nelson's *Star*" (Ph. D. dissertation, University of Texas, 1968); A. T. Brown, *Frontier Community* (1963), scholarly; L. W. Dorsett, *Pendergast Machine* (1968); W. M. Reddig, *Tom's Town* (1947); H. N. Monnett, *Action After Westport* (1964); C. P. Blackmore, "Joseph B. Sahnnon" (Ph.D. dissertation, Columbia, 1954); and Kansas City Public Library.

WILLIAM L. MCCORKLE
Kansas City Star

KANSAS-NEBRASKA ACT, approved by Congress in the spring of 1854 and signed into law by President Franklin Pierce on May 30, 1854, created two new territories out of the old Louisiana Purchase and opened to settlement the vast area between the Missouri River and the Rocky Mountains that had earlier been designated a "permanent" Indian reservation. Passage of the legislation was one of the most significant issues in the sectional conflict over the extension of slavery and has been viewed by some historians as a key element in the coming of the Civil War. Written by Democratic Senator Stephen A. Douglas of Illinois, chairman of the Senate Committee on Territories, the act was thought by many Americans to be long overdue. Douglas himself had sought the organization of this area since early 1844. The acquisition by the United States of Oregon and California and the subsequent rush of population to the Pacific coast had focused attention on the status of the intervening area; its unorganized character had thwarted plans for a Pacific railroad along a central route and had hampered development of the country along the heavily traveled emigrant trails.

In its treatment of the slavery question, however, the act proved to be highly controversial. The area of the Louisiana Purchase in which the two territories lay was subject to the terms of the MISSOURI COMPROMISE of 1820, by which slavery was forever excluded from territory north of the parallel 36° 30'. Douglas, who played a leading role in the passage of the COMPROMISE OF 1850, had become persuaded that the Missouri Compromise was no longer a viable solution to the slavery extension issue. He belived that slavery was a local domestic institution and that the people of the territories, like those of the states, must be allowed to decide for themselves whether they wanted slavery (a doctrine that came to be known as popular sovereignty). In addition, Douglas as a spokesman for western interests, was sensitive to the desires of frontiersmen for an increased measure of self-government within the territorial system.Thus he used the Kansas-Nebraska Act to introduce a number of changes that would allow the people of the territories to exercise a greater control over their own institutions.

In his original version of the bill, Douglas specified that the principle of the Compromise of 1850, which left the residents of Utah and New Mexico free to decide the slavery question for themselves, would apply to Kansas and Nebraska, an indirect negation of the Missouri Compromise. Southerners in Congress, however, seized the opportunity to get rid of an odious restriction on the expansion of slavery and insisted that the Missouri Compromise be explicitly and directly replaced. Douglas acquiesced, and in its final terms the Kansas-Nebraska Act formally repealed the slavery provisions of the Missouri Compromise.

The repeal of the Missouri Compromise raised a storm of protest in the North; coming in the midst of the reaction to the Fugitive Slave Act and the publication of *Uncle Tom's Cabin*, it aroused the antislavery movement to new heights of agitation. Douglas was bitterly denounced for his "betrayal" of freedom in the West, even though he repeatedly pointed out that slavery could not flourish in the new territories and that popular sovereignty would probably result in its exclusion. Debate over the bill in both houses of Congress was prolonged, acrimonious, and exciting. On March 3 it passed the Senate by a vote of 37 to 14, and on May 22 it was approved by the House of Representatives by the close margin of 113 to 100. In the final tally, southern senators and congressmen, regardless of party, voted almost solidly in favor of the bill. Only two southern senators (Sam Houston of Texas and John Bell of Tennessee) voted against it, and only nine southern representatives (all but one from the Upper South) sided with the opposition, believing for the most part that the repeal of the Missouri Compromise would ultimately prove of little benefit to the South.

The passage of the Kansas-Nebraska Act had immediate consequences for the sectional conflict: it ushered in a period of turmoil and violence in Kansas Territory as proslavery and antislavery settlers vied for control, and it brought a new and ominous realignment of political parties in the nation. The Whig party, already weakened and now hopelessly divided by reactions to the act, suffered its demise; in its place emerged the new Republican party, pledged to the restriction of slavery and reflecting the growing antislavery mood of the North. The Kansas-Nebraska Act has been the subject of a great deal of study and interpretation by historians of the Civil War; widely divergent views have been expressed, especially on the subject of Douglas' motives. It seems clear, however, that the Illinois senator viewed popular sovereignty as a fair and just solution to the disturbing question of slavery and that he hoped its acceptance would not only strengthen the Democratic party but would also heal the breach between the sections. He also regarded the act as an important part of his broader program for the promotion of western, hence of national, development.

See R. W. Johannsen, *Stephen A. Douglas* (1973); A. Nevins, *Ordeal of Union* (1947); R. F. Nicholas, *Mississippi Valley Historical Review* (Sept., 1956); J. C. Malin, *Nebraska Question* (1953); F. H. Hodder, *Mississippi Valley Historical Review* (June, 1925); and R. R. Russel, *Journal of Southern History* (May, 1963).

ROBERT W. JOHANNSEN
University of Illinois, Urbana-Champaign

KEFAUVER, CAREY ESTES (1903–1963), was born in Madisonville, Tenn., of a locally prominent family. A graduate of the University of Tennessee and Yale Law School, he practiced law in Chattanooga. In 1939 he served briefly as state commissioner of finance and taxation and later was elected first to the U.S. House of Representatives (1949) and then to the U.S. Senate (1949–1963). In 1948, after E. H. CRUMP derided him as a "pet coon," he campaigned for the Senate in a coonskin cap, which later earned national renown, and he won the primary and general elections. In Congress, Kefauver was a liberal internationalist and a stout advocate of the TENNESSEE VALLEY AUTHORITY. His support for modest civil rights measures embittered die-hard segregationists. Disturbed by the growth of economic concentration, he cosponsored the 1950 Celler-Kefauver Act (to amend the Clayton Act); while head of the Subcommittee on Antitrust and Monopoly after 1956, he investigated numerous monopoly practices. His probe of the drug industry yielded dramatic findings regarding drug safety, led to the 1962 Kefauver-Harris Drug Act, and fueled the rising consumer movement. Kefauver's greatest fame came with his 1950–1951 investigation of organized crime. Televised hearing conveyed images of the underworld to a fascinated public and launched Kefauver's 1952 presidential bid. His tireless campaigning won 11 primaries and the largest single bloc of delegates, but party leaders, unhappy with his independence and the crime probe, chose Adlai E. Stevenson instead. Kefauver's 1956 presidential quest, his last, stalled in the primaries, but he was nominated for vice-president.

See J. B. Gorman, *Kefauver* (1971), most thorough; W. H. Moore, *Kefauver Committee* (1974), insightful; R. Har-

ris, *Real Voice* (1964), drug probe; and J. Anderson and F. Blumenthal, *Kefauver Story* (1956). Kefauver helped write, with J. Levin, *Twentieth-Century Congress* (1947); with S. Shalett, *Crime in America* (1951); and with I. Till, *In a Few Hands* (1965). See also Kefauver Papers, University of Tennessee.

RICHARD M. FRIED
University of Illinois, Chicago Circle

KELLER, HELEN ADAMS (1880–1968), internationally famous deaf and blind lecturer, was the daughter of Arthur Keller, a newspaperman and Confederate veteran, and Kate Adams, a relative of Robert E. Lee's. Helen was a normal child until the age of eighteen months, when an illness, described as "acute congestion of the stomach and brain," deprived her of both sight and hearing. Her arduous and eventually successful efforts to learn to read, write, and speak remain one of the best-known stories of personal triumph over physical handicaps. Although she became most widely known for her work in behalf of the American Foundation for the Blind, in her early years she was an ardent feminist, a spokesman for women's suffrage, and in politics a confirmed Socialist and a critic of World War I. Her birthplace, Ivy Green, is exhibited and maintained by the city of Tuscumbia, Ala.

See V. W. Brooks, *Helen Keller* (1956), insufficient; P. S. Foner (ed.), *Keller: Her Socialist Years* (1967); W. S. Vance, *Alabama Review* (Jan., 1971); and Keller Papers, Randolph-Macon College, Library of Congress, and American Foundation for the Blind, New York.

KELLEY, WILLIAM DARRAH (1814–1890), a native of Philadelphia, became the foremost congressional advocate of the protective tariff. In 1845 Pig-Iron Kelley was elected to local public office as a Democrat. Shifting to the Republican party, he was elected in 1860 to the first of 14 consecutive terms as a U.S. congressman. His legislative actions were guided by his advocacy of industrialization, support for the laboring classes, and sympathy for the black people. Favoring the tariff as protection for American workers, he also supported greenback currency as an aid to the working class. An outspoken Radical, he played a major role in the passage of Reconstruction legislation and was the foremost proponent of federally guaranteed Negro suffrage. He toured the South in 1867 speaking in support of the Radical Republican program. In 1887 on a return trip through the NEW SOUTH, Kelley was welcomed by southerners as he praised in both speeches and articles the region's economic renaissance.

See I. V. Brown, *Pennsylvania Magazine of History and Biography* (July, 1961); S. W. Wiggins, *Alabama Review* (Jan., 1970); New York *Times* (Jan. 10, 1890); W. D. Kelley, *Old South and New* (1888) and *Speeches* (1872); and H. T. Lefler, "Preacher of Protectionism" (Ph.D. dissertation, University of Pennsylvania, 1931), only the abstract survives.

JUSTIN FULLER
University of Montevallo

KELLOGG, WILLIAM PITT (1830–1918), was born in Orwell, Vt., attended Norwich Military Institute, practiced law in Illinois, became chief justice of Nebraska Territory, served as a brigadier general in the Union army, and then came to Louisiana as collector of the port of New Orleans in 1865. He was elected U.S. senator in 1868 and then, after a disputed election finally settled by presidential fiat, Republican governor of Louisiana in 1873. As governor, Kellogg tried to reorganize the state debt, reform the New Orleans city charter, improve social welfare services and institutions, and implement an ambitious internal improvements program. His initiatives were doomed, however, by rampant factionalism within the Republican party and by the implacable opposition of the Democrats, who viewed him as a fraudulent usurper. Kellogg's heavy-handed patronage policies and alleged peculations contributed to his failure. His greatest achievement was sheer survival; despite two assassination attempts, a White League insurrection, and an impeachment attempt, Kellog managed to serve out his term. He returned to the Senate from 1877 to 1883, served one term in the House, then retired in 1885 to a behind-the-scenes role in state and national Republican politics.

See J. E. Gonzales, *Louisiana Historical Quarterly* (April, 1946); and E. Lonn, *Reconstruction in Louisiana* (1918).

ROGER A. FISCHER
University of Minnesota, Duluth

KEMBLE, FRANCES ANNE (1809–1893), was a famous British actress who in 1834 married Pierce Butler, Jr., of Philadelphia at the conclusion of an American theatrical tour. The Butlers inherited a cotton and rice plantation on two islands in the estuary of the Altamaha River; and in 1838–1839 Mrs. Butler visited this property with her husband and spent four months there. While in Georgia she recorded her experiences for Elizabeth Sedgwick, a New England friend, in a series of 31 letters. These provided a harrowing and intimate account of the life of black people, especially women,

under slavery. Mrs. Butler refused to publish her letters for nearly 25 years on the grounds that the information they contained was privileged. Appearing finally as *Journal of a Residence on a Georgian Plantation in 1838–1839* (1863), they constitute a private record written by a keen observer, not, as critics have often charged, an antislavery polemic. The *Journal* remains a fundamental source for the study of the antebellum South.

See R. A. Kemble, *Journal of Residence on a Georgian Plantation* (1961), for full text, history, and guide to sources; and J. A. Scott, *Journal of Negro History* (Oct., 1961) and *Fanny Kemble's America* (1973).

JOHN ANTHONY SCOTT
Rutgers University

KEMPER, JAMES LAWSON (1823–1895), graduated from Washington College, read law, and saw duty in the Mexican War. He served ten years in the Virginia house of delegates (1853–1863), championing BANKING and CURRENCY reform and southern unity. Largely through his leadership in reforming the militia, Virginia was in a relatively advanced state of readiness in 1861. Kemper participated in major battles from first BULL RUN to GETTYSBURG, where he was seriously wounded. The war over, Kemper urged Virginians to "let the past severely alone." In 1873 he was elected governor on the Conservative party ticket. His failure to obtain federal financial assistance or recapitalization of the state debt prevented further development of public services, especially education, and necessitated a policy of frugality and retrenchment (READJUSTER MOVEMENT). Kemper believed in white superiority, but sought (*e.g.*, through the Petersburg Charter veto) to protect the equality of blacks before the law. He also worked to ensure honesty, promoted sectional reconciliation, and strove to bring Virginia into conformity with a modern industrial nation.

See R. R. Jones, "Kemper, 1823–1865" (M.A. thesis, University of Virginia, 1961), "Post-war Career of Kemper" (Ph.D. dissertation, University of Virginia, 1964), *Virginia Magazine of History and Biography* (Oct., 1966), and *Journal of Southern History* (Aug., 1972); J. P. Maddex, Jr., *Virginia Conservatives, 1867–1879* (1970), well informed and insightful; and C. C. Pearson, *Readjuster Movement in Virginia* (1917), solid.

ROBERT R. JONES
University of Southwestern Louisiana

KEMPER, REUBEN (1800–1826), exemplified American resistance to Spanish-British colonialism in the lower Mississippi Valley from 1803 to 1817. He was a militia officer at New Orleans. When Spanish officials remained 18 months beyond the date for the American occupation of Louisiana, he urged their departure. With his brothers Nathan and Samuel, he resisted eviction by the Spanish at Bayou Sara. An attack made upon Baton Rouge in 1804 by his followers was unsuccessful, but the Kemper brothers nevertheless issued a declaration of independence for West Florida. In 1805 Spaniards kidnaped the Kempers across the border, creating an international incident. Reuben Kemper participated in the successful capture of Baton Rouge in 1810 and in a convention that created the "West Florida Republic." That same year he led an unsuccessful revolt at Mobile and was arrested by U.S. authorities. He served at the battle of New Orleans and later collected claims of West Florida inhabitants against the U.S. government.

See S. C. Arthur, St. Francisville (La.) *Democrat* (July 8, 15, 22, 29, 1933) and *Story of West Florida Rebellion* (1935); J. W. Monette, *History of Valley of Mississippi* (1846); C. E. Carter, *Territorial Papers* (1934–62), V–VI; D. Rowland, *History of Mississippi* (1925); I. J. Cox, *West Florida Controversy* (1918); and A. Latour, *Historical Memoir of War in West Florida* (1916).

M. JAMES STEVENS
Mississippi Coast Historical and Genealogical Society

KENDALL, AMOS (1789–1869), was born in Dunstable, Mass., and graduated from Dartmouth. After studying law two years, he migrated to Kentucky in 1814. In 1816 he became editor of the influential *Argus of Western America* in Frankfort. After the PANIC OF 1819, he identified himself with the debtor relief party. At first a supporter of Henry Clay, he shifted his support to Andrew Jackson prior to the ELECTION OF 1828. Appointed fourth auditor of the treasury in 1829, he also became a member of the Kitchen Cabinet. As Jackson's adviser and frequent amanuensis, he helped produce numerous state papers. While postmaster general (1835–1840), he condoned the exclusion of abolitionist propaganda from the mails and received bitter criticism from antislavery groups. In 1845 he became business manager for Samuel F. B. Morse, inventor of the telegraph, and helped make both wealthy. He argued against the right of secession and supported the Union during the war.

See W. Stickney (ed.), *Autobiography* (1872); J. D. Daniels, "Amos Kendall" (Ph.D. dissertation, University of North Carolina, 1968); L. L. Marshall, "Early Career"

(Ph.D. dissertation, California, 1962); A. M. Schlesinger, Jr., *Age of Jackson* (1949); and C. G. Bowers, *Party Battles* (1922).

JOHN M. MARTIN
West Georgia College

KENNEDY, JOHN F., ADMINISTRATION (1961–1963) devoted much of its energy to cold war matters, and its domestic accomplishments were few. Unlike Dwight D. Eisenhower, however, Kennedy endorsed the principle of the BROWN V. BOARD OF EDUCATION decision, and his eloquent rhetoric in support of racial equality helped to set the tone of the civil rights demonstrations that continued throughout his presidency.

In his successful 1960 presidential campaign, Kennedy ran considerably better in the South than in the rest of the nation (ELECTION OF 1960). As president, he dealt cautiously with the problem of black civil rights in the South, in part because he was reluctant to antagonize the powerful southern Democrats in Congress. The administration did offer encouragement to the CIVIL RIGHTS MOVEMENT in public comments and White House conferences and, more tangibly, by providing federal protection for freedom riders and for the students who desegregated the universities of Mississippi and Alabama. The Kennedy administration gave priority to voting rights. The Justice Department, under the president's brother, Attorney General Robert F. Kennedy, attempted to expand political opportunities for southern blacks by prosecuting dozens of voting suits under the CIVIL RIGHTS ACT OF 1957 and CIVIL RIGHTS ACT OF 1960. The administration also supported the measure banning the payment of a POLL TAX in federal elections, which became the Twenty-fourth Amendment to the Constitution.

Protest demonstrations forced the administration to make a stronger commitment to civil rights. In the backwash of the highly publicized demonstrations in Birmingham, Kennedy said in a television speech in June, 1963, that he would ask Congress for comprehensive civil rights legislation, stating: "We are confronted primarily with a moral issue. It is as old as the scriptures and is as clear as the American Constitution." In August, 1963, a quarter of a million people marched in Washington in support of the civil rights bill, which ultimately became the CIVIL RIGHTS ACT OF 1964 but which was still in congressional committee when Kennedy was assassinated in Dallas on November 22, 1963.

See A. M. Schlesinger, Jr., *Thousand Days* (1965); and T. C. Sorenson, *Kennedy* (1965), which should be balanced by D. Halberstam, *Best and Brightest* (1973). See also T. H. White, *Making of President* (1961); J. L. Sunquist, *Politics and Policy* (1968); H. Golden, *Mr. Kennedy and Negroes* (1964); J. C. Harvey, *Civil Rights During Kennedy Administration* (1971); A. Wolk, *Presidency and Black Civil Rights* (1971); and C. M. Braur, *JFK and Second Reconstruction* (1977).

NUMAN V. BARTLEY
University of Georgia

KENNEDY, JOHN PENDLETON (1795–1870), born in Baltimore to an Irish immigrant father and a Virginian mother, was always conscious of the pulls between his plantation heritage and the mercantilism of his city. In 1812 he began the practice of law but soon turned to what would remain his chief interests: politics and literature. His political career included terms in the U.S. House of Representatives (1838–1839, 1841–1845) and brief service as secretary of the navy (1852–1853). As an active Whig he satirized Jacksonianism in *Quodlibet* (1840) and *Defense of the Whigs* (1844); a major political biography was the *Life of William Wirt* (1849). During the Civil War Kennedy supported the North in *Mr. Ambrose's Letters on the Rebellion* (1865).

It is on his literary productions, however, that Kennedy's reputation now rests. His first major work, *Swallow Barn* (1832), drew on memories of a Virginia plantation to reveal both his amused observation of a provincial society and his appreciation of the legend of an aristocratic past. In 1835 he published *Horse-Shoe Robinson*, which examines the divided loyalties of Americans in the 1780s. A second historical romance, *Rob of the Bowl* (1838), is of lesser interest. Perhaps because of the southern notion that creative writing was only an avocation for a gentleman, he failed to keep pace with the nation's developing literature; yet his accomplishment was not trifling. In *Swallow Barn* and *Horse-Shoe Robinson* he left revelatory accounts of the myriad problems that the American experiment—especially in the South—had created by the 1830s.

See C. H. Bohner, *J. P. Kennedy* (1961); J. V. Ridgely, *J. P. Kennedy* (1966); L. W. Griffin, *Maryland Historical Magazine* (Dec., 1953); and Kennedy Papers, Peabody Institute, Baltimore, Md.

J. V. RIDGELY
Columbia University

KENNEDY ASSASSINATION (November 22, 1963). After embracing the nation's CIVIL RIGHTS MOVEMENT, President John F. Kennedy faced dismal prospects of carrying the South again in 1964. Even Texas, where the Democrats were bitterly disunited, was in some doubt—despite the certain presence of its native son LYNDON JOHNSON on the ticket. Democratic fortunes in the South, especially Texas, were also plagued by a growing right-wing movement that cursed the administration as part of the Communist conspiracy. The extremist heartland, as well as the murder capital of the nation, was the burgeoning city of Dallas. During his political sojourn in Texas, Kennedy was cordially received in Dallas on the fateful day; but the city's strident aura possibly affected the thinking of the assassin, Lee Harvey Oswald, a dejected psychotic who was greatly desirous of attention and well aware of the popularity of the anti-Kennedy right-wing leaders.

The personal impact of the assassination on most southern citizens was much the same as the national reaction—genuine shock and grief. Yet the South had a higher proportion of people who cheered the slaying of the "nigger lover." Even in urbane Atlanta a group of insurance men "laughed and applauded" the event. Ironically for the hate-mongers, the only permanent effect of the tragedy on the South's domestic affairs was that it made passage of the administration's rights bill inevitable (CIVIL RIGHTS ACT OF 1964). Regarding short-term effects, of the 11 southern states carried by the Democrats under Johnson in the ELECTION OF 1964, only one or two would have voted for Kennedy; much of the Johnson vote hinged on regional pride. But the South soon resumed its drift away from the Democratic party.

See G. Green, in R. D. Marcus, *How Many Roads?* (1972); Atlanta *Constitution* (Nov. 23–25, 1963); W. Manchester, *Death of President* (1967); and T. C. Sorenson, *Kennedy* (1965).

GEORGE NORRIS GREEN
University of Texas, Arlington

KENNESAW MOUNTAIN, BATTLE OF (June 27, 1864), was the most costly defeat suffered by W. T. Sherman in the ATLANTA CAMPAIGN. After successfully maneuvering J. E. JOHNSTON's Confederates southward from Chattanooga to just north of Atlanta, Sherman decided to launch a frontal assault against the Confederate center on Kennesaw. He believed the position was weak and its collapse would bring the quick capture of Atlanta. One of his generals later reported that Sherman struck because of his desire to share newspaper headlines with U.S. Grant.

Early on the twenty-seventh, federal troops took Johnston's rifle pits at the mountain's base, but failed in their assault on his second line. Stout Confederate defense, scorching heat, and rugged terrain halted further Union advance. Federal troops dug in a few yards from Johnston's position. On the twenty-ninth, Confederates failed in an attempt to dislodge XIV Corps troops. On July 1 Sherman resumed his campaign of maneuver, and Johnston withdrew from Kennesaw to prevent his lines from being outflanked. At Kennesaw the federals suffered 2,051 casualties; the Confederates, 442.

See L. Lewis, *Sherman* (1932), for Sherman's motivation; G. E. Govan and J. W. Livingood, *Different Valor* (1956); R. M. McMurry, "Kennesaw Mountain" (M.A. thesis, Emory, 1964); J. E. Johnston, *Narrative* (1959); W. T. Sherman, *Memoirs* (1957); and *Official Records, Armies*, Ser. 1, Vol. XXXVIII, Pt. 3.

JAMES P. JONES
Florida State University

KENTON, SIMON (1755–1836), a frontiersman and Indian fighter, was born in Fauquier County, Va., but escaped to the frontier and assumed the name Simon Butler because he believed he had killed a rival in love. In 1775 Kenton joined DANIEL BOONE's settlement (Boonesboro) and helped in defending it against Indian attacks. He participated in the GEORGE ROGERS CLARK expedition to Kaskaskia, Cahokia, and Vincennes in 1778. Although he was captured by the Indians and taken to the British at Detroit, he soon managed to escape. Until the end of the Revolutionary War, Kenton remained a fierce Indian fighter. He resumed his original name on learning that the man he thought he had killed was still alive. He established his family at Limestone (Maysville); eventually settled in Ohio, where he was appointed a militia brigadier general in 1804; and served in the War of 1812. Kenton died in poverty, after losing most of his lands "through ignorance of the law."

See E. Kenton, *Simon Kenton* (1930); P. Jahns, *Violent Years* (1962); T. Clark, *Frontier America* (1959); and S. W. Price, *Old Masters of Bluegrass* (1902).

YASUHIDE KAWASHIMA
University of Texas, El Paso

KENTUCKY, a border state in historical, geographical, and political perspective, has yet developed and still retains its own unique personality. Its tramontane location let it play a key national role from the American Revolution through the Civil War, but for the next century a hesitancy toward involvement vitiated its early leadership and deterred internal growth. Geographically closer to Canada than to the Gulf of Mexico, Kentucky is more southern than northern, in both sentiment and politics. The people, split into distinct political and geographical blocs, listen as rural and urban legislators clash bitterly over limited funds and reapportionment. From intense pride in early achievements to complaints of stagnation, awakening from a long preoccupation with localism to a current germination of progress, Kentucky is a fascinating study for the historian or the general reader.

Origins and geography. The word *Kentucky* has been given different origins. Some suggest a derivation from an Indian description of a "DARK AND BLOODY GROUND"; some imply a contraction of *cane* and *turkeys*, each found in abundance by early settlers; others argue that it is Cherokee for "prairie" or Iroquois for "great meadows"; officially, it is from the Wyandot *Kah-ten-tah-teh*, "the land of tomorrow."

Kentucky, approximately 40,000 square miles in area, is smaller than the average southern state and ranks thirty-seventh nationally. Its shape is most irregular: the Ohio River for 664 crooked miles is the northern border; the Big Sandy and Tug Fork rivers mark a boundary with West Virginia; Allegheny peaks help delineate a boundary with Virginia; and the Mississippi River changes the western line constantly. The straightest border is with Tennessee, but even it has variations. The Ohio has caused long contention with Ohio, Indiana, and Illinois, since in 1784 Virginia ceded to the Confederation Congress its claims north of the low-water mark on the northern shore, and in 1792 the national government confirmed this mark as Kentucky's line. The original western boundary was the Tennessee River, but in 1818 Andrew Jackson and ISAAC SHELBY concluded a treaty with the Chickasaw for the lands west to the Mississippi.

Physiographically, the state has six natural divisions. A triangle covering the eastern one-fourth is the CUMBERLAND PLATEAU, also called the eastern coalfields or the mountains. Special features include Big Black Mountain, at 4,150 feet the state's highest, and Cumberland Falls. West of the plateau and south from the Ohio, then bowing back northward, is the Knobs, an area of conical hills. Inside the Knobs is the BLUEGRASS, the inner portion of which contains the world-renowned horse farms. West of the Knobs is a large two-pronged area, the Pennyroyal. The northern prong angles toward the Ohio, the southern projects toward the Tennessee. The best-known feature of the "Pennyrile" is Mammoth

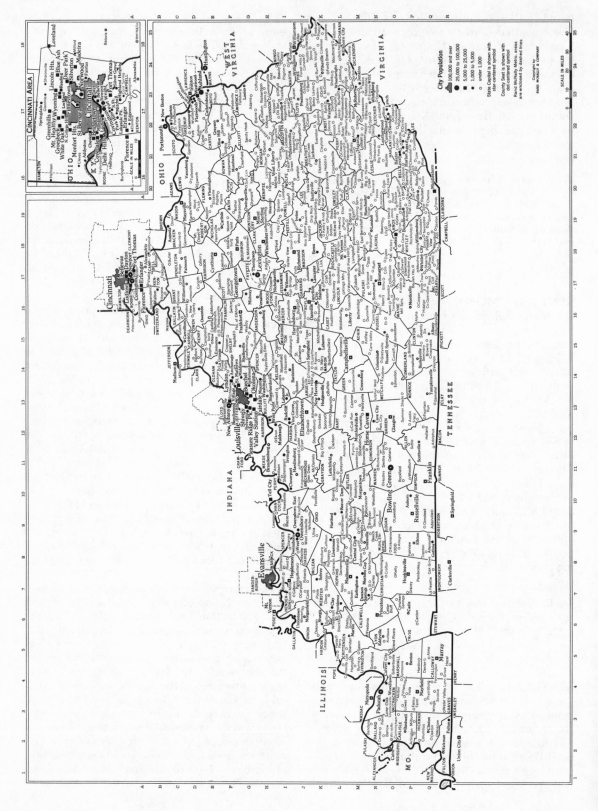

Cave. Between the prongs is the western coalfields, and the final division is the Jackson Purchase.

Exploration and settlement. France and England were the first to vie for the region. The French built forts and traded in a great southwestward-sweeping arc from the St. Lawrence to the Mississippi delta. Englishmen, however, moved only as overpopulation and worn-out lands forced them, so a century and a half of settlement left them still east of the Appalachians.

The first Englishmen in Kentucky came unwillingly as Indian captives, so English interest technically began in 1750, when the LOYAL COMPANY engaged THOMAS WALKER and five others to explore the Cumberland Plateau. Coming through Cave Gap (CUMBERLAND GAP), they confirmed bountiful game, fine timber, good lands, and few Indians—four reasons to conquer a wilderness. Delayed momentarily by the French and Indian War, the colonists ignored the crown's PROCLAMATION OF 1763, which would contain them east of the mountains to pacify the Indians.

DANIEL BOONE made his first visit in 1767. Two years later he returned for a two-year stay, and in 1773 he attempted to lead families to the "Great Meadows," but was repulsed by Indians before reaching Cumberland Gap. Here he lost the first of his sons to the red man, but the "Kentucky fever" was already enveloping too many people to frustrate settlement much longer. From North Carolina came the LONG HUNTERS for furs and pelts. From Virginia came the adventurers SIMON KENTON, Thomas Bullitt, Hancock Taylor, and the McAfee brothers, usually surveying for speculators such as George Washington, Patrick Henry, and the Virginia governor, Lord Dunmore. From Pennsylvania in 1774 came James Harrod, who began what is called, or questioned as, Kentucky's first settlement (HARRODSBURG, KY.)

The first big name in settlement was RICHARD HENDERSON, a North Carolina judge who turned to speculation. In 1774, aflame from Boone's reports, Henderson organized the TRANSYLVANIA COMPANY and, eschewing the usual pattern of seeking a royal grant, the following year purchased from the Cherokee the eastern half of the future Kentucky. This area was chosen because it was reserved by both northern and southern tribes for hunting, not settling, a circumstance that permitted the whites to establish themselves before retaliation. Henderson's friend Boone employed 30 axmen to help him cut a pathway later known as the WILDERNESS ROAD, and on April 1 they reached the Kentucky River. On April 20 Hender-

son brought more men and began a fort he named BOONESBOROUGH. To establish his control, he called into session on May 24 a convention with representatives from Boonesborough, Harrodstown (Harrodsburg), Boiling Springs (Danville), and St. Asaph's (Stanford). In September Boone and others brought their families to Boonesborough, an action long accepted as the symbol of progress and permanency.

Henderson's dreams were short lived, since his scheme of government was too medieval in scope and too monarchical in practice for free-spirited settlers. Many had come to escape government; others wanted land free of such encumbrances as QUITRENTS; and some questioned Henderson's ownership. All were individualists too involved with frontier dangers to accept his concepts and restraints. Additionally, the Virginia and North Carolina governors were upset that he had purchased lands they claimed. On December 31, 1776, Virginia carved Kentucky County from Fincastle County, itself formed only in 1772. His plan shattered, Henderson accepted lands farther west and slowly disappeared from Kentucky history.

Revolution and statehood, 1775–1815. Virginia's creation of Kentucky County officially brought the American Revolution to the West, and the Indians, spurred by the British administrator Lieutenant Governor Henry Hamilton, increased their attacks on forts and isolated cabins. Only four forts withstood these onslaughts through 1777, so drastic measures were designed by GEORGE ROGERS CLARK, the West's first military hero. Determining that relief was possible only by carrying the battle to the enemy, he and his recruits moved northwestward and in 1778 and 1779 captured the British outposts of Kaskaskia, Cahokia, and Vincennes, also taking Hamilton prisoner.

In the meantime, Indian depredations within Kentucky had continued. Just before Hamilton's capitulation, Boone and several other men were captured on a salt expedition, but Boone later escaped to warn Boonesborough of impending attack, and the fort survived a 13-day siege. Possibly the decisive battle in Kentucky during the war, it was neither the last nor the bloodiest. In August, 1782, British-led Indians, failing to destroy Bryan's Station, were pursued and caught at BLUE LICKS, where heavy Indian losses ended large organized raids on Kentucky.

An estimated 30,000 people moved into Kentucky County during the Revolution. Forts and cabins sprang up as timbers fell, and farms replaced meadows and the canebrakes. By 1783 the central area was filling up. Newcomers, bypassing the poor lands and the isolation of the mountains, jammed the Wilderness Road; others crowded the Ohio with boats and rafts. Grasping for the better life, with landownership as the big attraction, these nomads were not dispelled by the unknown or the Indian; after all, most had faced these enemies along earlier frontiers. Tales of lands for the taking brought such numbers that the 1790 census listed over 70,000 people in Kentucky, and two years later 75,000 inhabited a district void of whites 17 years earlier. Virginians predominated, but North Carolinians, Pennsylvanians, and Marylanders were prominent.

Land, the magnet drawing settlers, became also Kentucky's big problem, for no orderly system of surveys existed. A plat might be claimed by a squatter, a French and Indian War veteran, a purchaser from the Transylvania Company, a later arrival finding no one "at home," or a Revolutionary War pensioner. A 1779 Virginia law required claimants to register their surveys by purchasing land warrants, but ignorance of the law and dangers in travel deterred filing. Daniel Boone surveyed, claimed, then lost 100,000 acres by not processing his warrants. Schemers living off the misery of others grabbed unregistered parcels for themselves or their employers. Some areas remained unregistered, and several counties even today contain lands one may claim through searches of state title records. A traveling four-man land court faced an impossible task in adjudicating ownership, thereby creating demands for lawyers. Such opportunities brought the young legal minds, HENRY CLAY and JOHN C. BRECKINRIDGE, but not all lawyers and their clients had the acumen or ethics of these two men. Certain land cases clogged court dockets for decades. Moreover, all major cases and appeals had to be heard in Richmond.

The citizens of Kentucky County sent two delegates to the Virginia assembly and elected local officials, but the various problems of distance, time, expense, and population growth required some form of constitutional reform. In 1780 the Virginia assembly subdivided Kentucky into the counties of Jefferson, Fayette, and Lincoln, then three years later gave a four-man superior court limited appellate jurisdiction. But what the Kentuckians gained in local government they lost in self-rule, for the legislation of 1780 made all local officials, except the county clerk, appointees of the governor. And the new political structure did nothing to abate the continuing land squabbles among individuals, Virginia, and the Confederation Congress. Kentuckians argued that the laws of the Old Dominion were written for the settled

East, not for the frontier. Non-Virginians voiced their dissatisfaction with laws and interpretations that differed from those of their home states. The grant of appellate powers to the superior court helped the situation somewhat, but only the well-to-do could afford the expenses and time for major appellate action. Kentuckians were looking down the path toward statehood without necessarily knowing it. All that was needed to put this step into focus was an additional problem—the Indian—which the Virginia assembly would be unable to resolve.

England had signed a treaty in 1783 and had recognized the United States of America, but its ally of the forest had done neither. He still claimed and fought for his ancestral lands. Murder of immigrants, scalpings, and kidnapings, burning of homes and crops, stealing and slaughter of livestock continued. A county militia lieutenant could organize citizens for protective purposes and pursuit of marauders, but he could cross county boundaries only with permission from Richmond. This was a stultifying arrangement, since the Indian did not recognize the white man's boundaries. By 1784 conditions had so worsened that Colonel BENJAMIN LOGAN called for a convention at Danville to study alternatives. In December appointed delegates planned for a common defense and petitioned for permission to attack the enemy on his own grounds. Before adjourning, they called for a second convention.

From the next session emerged the four factions fighting for the political future of Kentucky. One, believing that the mother state could meet all exigencies, saw fewer risks in remaining a part of Virginia. A second wanted statehood within the Confederation, even though its fate was uncertain. Another suggested separating and chancing nationhood. The fourth preferred annexation by some strong European empire. Delegates swayed by the last two proposals dominated and petitioned for no affiliation with the Confederation, but Virginia, wisely and adamantly, would agree only to either of the first two proposals.

Surely one of Virginia's fears centered on General JAMES WILKINSON. Brilliant, dangerously ambitious, vain, and utterly unscrupulous, this Marylander "made intrigue a trade and treason a profession." A personal magnetism, however, kept friends about him. Now a powerful influence at the conventions, he began readying his most nefarious act. Soon after Spanish authorities withdrew from tradesmen free use of the Mississippi and right of deposit at New Orleans, he showed up in Lexington with claims that he had quadrupled the usual price for his tobacco by playing the game under Spanish rules. The lesson was clear: cut all ties with the United States. This had strong appeal for farmers and commercial interests, since the Mississippi was already considered their life-blood. Wilkinson was so assured of his position that at the seventh convention he forcefully argued for separation, then turned to John Brown for presentation of a proposed annexation by Spain.

Delegates were spellbound, however, when Brown immediately exposed Wilkinson and other conspirators, including himself, then begged that the Kentuckians turn to Congress for relief. His plans permanently shattered, Wilkinson would not recognize defeat for another two years. A letter to Louisiana's Governor General Esteban Miró callously suggested that for a mere $16,500 he could still buy Kentucky's leaders and reverse the move toward statehood. Included were his coconspirators Benjamin Sebastian, Harry Innes, and Brown ($1,000 each), Isaac Shelby and James Garrard (destined to be the first two governors) for $800, and Benjamin Logan for a like amount. The general had lost this war, however.

The Virginia assembly apprehensively passed a series of four enabling acts detailing standards for separation, the constant being union with the United States. Both Thomas Jefferson and James Madison cautioned against hasty release, and the last Confederation Congress refused statehood. When a ninth convention (1790) accepted Virginia's terms, however, President George Washington recommended admission. Congress approved in 1791, a tenth convention produced an acceptable state constitution, and on June 1, 1792, Kentucky became the fifteenth state, the first west of the Appalachians.

Kentucky's first constitution gave the franchise to free white males with no reference to property or religion. Using the federal Constitution as a guideline, the framers organized the state government around executive, legislative, and judicial branches. With no lieutenant governor, the Speaker of the senate would preside during the governor's absence. The governor and senators were chosen for four-year terms by an electoral college, elected, as were the representatives, by the people. Members of the highest court, elected for life or during good behavior, had both original and appellate jurisdiction. The most original thought in the document was Article 11, which permitted the people after five years to vote their opinion on its effectiveness.

Slavery was an important issue before the constitution makers, since the Declaration of Independence and an ensuing fervor concerning the natural rights of man had aroused strong abolition-

ist sentiments. The several clergymen helping write the constitution argued for a no-slavery clause, but owners of the 13,000 slaves and their friends were too influential; only one other member supported their losing appeal. The majority then decreed the unconstitutionality of any later legislative action against slavery. Members of the first legislature so heeded the threats that they did not even provide for a chaplain! They wanted no prayers with contaminated abolitionist overtones.

Kentucky's first officials neither campaigned nor were appointed on national persuasions. Dedicated to local, state, and regional issues, most worked to organize a strong political framework and develop the precedents for a new state. The first two legislative sessions were in Lexington, the state's largest town, while appointed commissioners mulled over a permanent homesite. Three towns had the most to offer: Lexington, already being used and centrally located; Louisville, at the fall of the Ohio a promising commercial and industrial base; and Danville, site of the constitutional conventions, also centrally located. Within the Lexington-Louisville-Danville triangle and on the Kentucky River, however, was the community of Frankfort, much of it owned or controlled by General James Wilkinson. Persuasions, including transfer of lots and cash, aided the commissioners' decision to locate the seat of government there. The die for Judge James H. Mulligan's oft-cited "And politics the damnedest/In Kentucky" was being cast!

Governor Isaac Shelby (1792–1796), confronted with more problems than any chief executive before the Civil War, merited plaudits for his tenure. Substituting dedication and "horse sense" for formal legal training, the old Revolutionary War hero charted tax programs, supervised the organization of a court system, helped local government expand from nine to 25 counties, and again fought Indians.

Large-scale Indian attacks had ended in 1782, but small raids against outlying areas and on shipping seemingly multiplied thereafter. Harry Innes recorded that in the years 1783–1790 a minimum of 1,500 people within or en route to the region had been killed or captured. Ineffective efforts under George Rogers Clark in 1786, General Josiah Harmar in 1790, and General Arthur St. Clair in 1791 had caused more bitterness between regular army personnel and volunteers than curtailments of Indian abuses. The individualistic frontiersmen charged regulars with a lack of aggressiveness and questioned the military skills of the generals; however, impetuous volunteers both in command and in the ranks often blundered into fatal traps. Fortunately, when President Washington decided on overwhelming strength to secure the frontier and dispatched General Anthony Wayne and 2,600 regulars westward, Governor Shelby in 1794 sent 1,600 Kentucky volunteers to join Wayne. On August 30 at Fallen Timbers the whites won such a decisive victory that Indian threats to Kentucky ended for good.

Governor Shelby's last major problem came from the complexities of the French Revolution. The republicans, recognizing the value of international goodwill, began courting the nation of Ben Franklin and Jefferson and sent Edmond Charles Genêt as their representative. They also posted five agents under the guise of "scientists" to Kentucky, rapidly becoming a stronghold of Republicanism and anti-Federalist sympathies. With letters of introduction from Jefferson and Senator John Brown, Genêt moved westward. George Rogers Clark, deeply embittered by recent military reverses, loss of public adulation, and severe personal tragedies, easily succumbed to the Frenchman's guile and a fancy military title. When he began subscribing for funds and advertising for recruits, ironically the newspapers simultaneously carried his appeals and General Wayne's admonitions against such actions. Governor Shelby became by circumstances a participant in the mess. Encouraged by Jefferson and swayed by his own antipathies toward Alexander Hamilton's economic policies, he refused to impede Clark even when President Washington cautioned that negotiations with Spain over the Mississippi were progressing. The whole disagreeable matter collapsed with Genêt's removal, but another venture in intrigue brought no glory to any Kentuckian.

Jefferson resigned his cabinet post during the Genêt affair to lead an antiadministration movement, but returned to office in 1797 as vice-president, just in time to bring Kentucky into the spotlight again. His Republicans advocated those issues that appealed to frontiersmen: agriculture over industry and commerce, extension of the franchise, increased state power at the expense of national power, and foreign relations more geared to French sympathies than to the British monarchy. The Alien and Sedition Acts, passed to slow criticism of the Adams administration, backfired; and Jefferson, from his contempt for these repressive laws, penned his "secret" objections. John Breckinridge edited Jefferson's notes; Governor James Garrard incorporated each objection into his message to the general assembly; and Breckinridge pushed the objections through as resolutions (VIRGINIA

AND KENTUCKY RESOLUTIONS). The assembly's action introduced the concept of NULLIFICATION, a declaration that a federal law was null and void if state legislatures voted such to be an infraction of the Constitution.

Kentucky ended the eighteenth century by adopting a second constitution. The one of 1792 had guaranteed revocation should the people approve, and discontent surfaced early against the lack of local court jurisdiction, the selection of too many officials by an electoral college, squabbles over legislative-judicial powers, and an insufficient extension of democracy. The abolitionists were also crying for change. The constitution of 1799 provided for popular election of governors and senators, eliminated the electoral college, created the office of lieutenant governor, and decreed only appellate jurisdiction for the court of appeals. The legislature was directed to organize additional lower courts as needed. These advances, however, were negated by other provisions, deletions, or omissions. Slavery clauses were retained; amending procedures were so tightened that change would be virtually impossible; and public education was ignored. Conservatism was far from dead in Kentucky.

Kentucky's population passed 200,000 in 1800, with 42 counties in operation. Agriculture and industry boomed, especially after Spain had guaranteed in 1795 free use of the Mississippi and right of deposit at New Orleans. With the LOUISIANA PURCHASE in 1803, the last apparent obstacle to Kentucky's growth had been removed. Or, at least, it so appeared until the arrival of Aaron Burr.

Was there a BURR CONSPIRACY? If so, what was it? Unfortunately, no definitive answers to these questions are possible. A man of consummate abilities fed by avaricious ambition, Burr had joined Jefferson in 1800 to defeat the Federalists, but he had little in common with Jefferson and soon perceived that he could neither rise to the presidency nor be Jefferson's running mate in 1804. After his famous duel with Alexander Hamilton, he came west. His western contacts and associates were a formidable group: Anthony Merry, an English agent; Harman Blennerhassett, a well-to-do but muddle-headed English-Irishman; Senator John Brown; Andrew Jackson and John Eaton of Tennessee; and the ubiquitous General Wilkinson, now governor of the Louisiana Territory and commander of all western military forces. Unfortunately, Burr seldom committed his plans to paper, and the degree of complicity—if any—by each of his associates is unclear.

In Kentucky, the editors of the KENTUCKY GAZETTE and the Frankfort *Western World* began asking questions about Burr's intentions. Joseph H. Daveiss, a federal attorney, sought to bring Burr to court, but Henry Clay successfully defended his client. Burr soon floated southward with a contingent of followers, but Wilkinson had by now switched sides and ordered his arrest. Acquittals by a Mississippi Territory grand jury and by a U.S. circuit court in Richmond in 1807 brought honor neither to Burr's schemes, to his trials, nor to the participants. Yet the last serious attempt to separate Kentucky from the Union until the Civil War was crushed.

If the Burr conspiracy had divided and embarrassed Kentuckians, the War of 1812 at least unified them. England's impressment of American seamen, its refusal to abandon posts in the Northwest Territory, and its continued support of the Indians combined to aid the growth of a martial Kentucky spirit, typified by Henry Clay, who, as leader of the war hawks and Speaker of the House, eventually forced President James Madison's belated call for a declaration of war. Westerners had not waited for such a declaration, however, and at Tippecanoe in 1811 already had won a resounding victory over Indians armed with new British guns. Once war was declared, 7,000 Kentuckians volunteered, but once again inept leadership, conflicts between regulars and volunteers, and impetuous movements led to defeats and ignominies. In the first months of the war, General William Hull disgracefully surrendered near Detroit. In January, 1813, a group of Kentuckians was massacred at Raisin River, and in May another contingent was ambushed near Ft. Meigs. After Commodore Oliver Perry's victory over the British on Lake Erie, Isaac Shelby personally led 4,000 Kentuckians as part of General William Henry Harrison's forces into Canada. In October, 1813, at the River Thames, Kentuckians exacted partial revenge for the Raisin River massacre. Other Kentucky volunteers also participated in the last action of the war, the battle of NEW ORLEANS; and Henry Clay, "Mr. War Hawk," appropriately served as one of this nation's commissioners negotiating the treaty of peace at Ghent.

Northern versus southern state, 1815–1890. In 1811 the *City of New Orleans* began the steamboat era southward between Louisville and New Orleans; four years later the *Enterprise* made the run from New Orleans to Louisville. By 1830, when the Portland Canal around the falls at Louisville linked Pittsburgh with the Gulf, Kentuckians transported their surpluses east and south, and also imported needs and luxuries. State funds developed the internal rivers, but roads were or-

dinarily left to local speculators with their tolls. Louisville gradually replaced Lexington as the commercial, industrial, and financial capital.

The panic of 1819 brought such critical times that most banks folded and left the citizens in perilous circumstances. Of the 59 banks operating in 1818, only the two national branches survived. The Bank of Kentucky was absorbed into the new state-owned Bank of the Commonwealth, and private banks disappeared, to be remembered as "wildcats" or the "forty thieves." National party affiliations dissolved largely into local relief and antirelief groups. The legislature effected various relief measures, the main one a replevin act to postpone foreclosures, but the courts ruled this unconstitutional since it violated the contract clause in the federal Constitution. Anticourt sentiment in 1824 led the legislature to vote out the court of appeals and replace it with a relief-minded "new" court. A constitutional impasse lasted until 1827, when a new legislature returned the "old" court to power.

Recovery from the panic and resulting governmental crisis launched developments that would be interrupted only by the Civil War. In 1830 a railway company was organized in Lexington; by 1834 tracks ran to Frankfort; and in 1852 service opened between Lexington and Louisville. Two years later Cincinnati began challenging Louisville for the bluegrass trade with a line into Lexington, and in 1859 trains began service between Louisville and Nashville. By 1861 approximately 600 miles of track interlaced the state. State funds were still developing the vast internal waterway systems with locks and the removal of navigation hazards.

Manufacturing and industry burgeoned. In 1819 New Orleans received over 200,000 gallons of the famous Kentucky BOURBON whiskey, and deliveries increased annually. Coal production increased, the iron industry flourished, and Kentucky ranked fifth in salt production. Over 30,000 men were employed in factory and home manufactures by 1850. Agriculture was showing equal gains. Henry Clay helped develop better animal husbandry, and in 1838 a state agricultural society was organized. Kentucky was first in flax and hemp, second in corn. Tobacco was a huge cash crop, and the state ranked next to Virginia in 1850. Beef and pork sales soared, mules were transported to the cotton fields, and sheep provided needed wool. In 1860 farmers reported huge gains in total production.

A common school system was being financed by 1850. Political and hypocritical use by governors and legislators of early education funds had become a Kentucky scandal. As an example, Governor Joseph Desha helped switch appropriated education monies in 1826 into turnpike construction. Immediate construction should convince travelers that formal education was no substitute for physical comfort on fast roads! An investigation of education, however, by President Alva Wood and Professor Benjamin Peers of Transylvania in 1829 galvanized the people and their legislators into action.

The Wood-Peers report showed that five of the 83 counties had no schools and that three-fourths of the 140,000 children between five and fifteen were denied educational opportunities. It recommended a poll tax of 50 cents, a small assessment on real property, and local control of education to remove funds from the "Frankfort gang." From these figures and guidelines, an education convention in 1833 drafted a common school plan. Five years later the legislature appropriated $850,000 for education and created the office of superintendent of education. The most influential early superintendent was Robert J. Breckinridge, who convinced the delegates of Kentucky's third constitutional convention in 1849 that education was a child's right and that state funds must provide that right. Unfortunately, education would become an early victim of the "impending conflict."

Higher education, mainly supported by churches and philanthropy, had handicaps. TRANSYLVANIA UNIVERSITY was victimized by Governor Desha's contention that it was a stronghold of aristocracy and by rural fears that Lexington was a Sodom and Gomorrah ensnaring youth of the hinterlands. Another problem arose over administrative and curricular matters; supporting churches had since its inception fought each other and the state for control. The Presbyterians had withdrawn support in 1818, but the great furor came later. Under Horace Holley (1818–1827) Transylvania was one of the nation's most prestigious, but he was hounded out because he was a Unitarian. With his departure went much of the dream for continued greatness.

The Presbyterians, with state financial support, organized CENTRE COLLEGE in 1819, but turmoil over a divided governance ended with complete Presbyterian control in 1824. Two other colleges organized during this period were St. Joseph's in 1819 by the Roman Catholics and Georgetown by the Baptists ten years later. From a medical institute dating from 1837 came the University of Louisville in 1846. BEREA COLLEGE, organized by abolitionists in 1855, had operations later temporarily suspended because of racial issues.

Kentuckians had access to several newspapers, but only two had wide circulation. Shadrack Penn's *Public Advertiser* became the state's first daily in 1826, but in 1830 the pro-Jacksonian Penn got a formidable rival in George D. Prentice, a Clay supporter and editor of the Louisville *Journal*. The *Journal* after the Civil War would be combined with two other papers to become the *Courier-Journal*. Literary magazines were numerous, but only the *Transylvanian* continues. Two state histories were written by Humphrey Marshall (1812, revised in 1824) and by Lewis Collins (1847). Theodore O'Hara, the poet, composed "The Bivouac of the Dead," a tribute especially dedicated to Kentucky's fallen in the Mexican War. Novelists were few and of minor talent. This period was possibly Kentucky's greatest for the arts, however; portrait painter Matthew Harris Jouett, sculptor Joel T. Hart, and architect Gideon Shryock received international prominence.

Kentucky history, 1815–1867, is essentially built around one issue—slavery. Many migrating southerners brought slaves with them, and as conditions developed favorably, more and more Kentuckians accepted human bondage as a fundamental in an agrarian economy. The free man of ambition found too many available acres to remain a hired hand for long, and success often meant becoming a slaveholder. By 1840 over 182,000 slaves signaled a ratio of one bondsman to three whites. Only Virginia and Georgia had more owners. The black population reached a quarter of a million in 1860. However, not all whites were receptive. Futile endeavors at the constitutional conventions had not altered efforts to eradicate this "mournful evil."

Presbyterians, Methodists, and Baptists (not all of them, to be sure) carried the antislavery banner, organized abolitionist societies, opened their churches to blacks, even ran rudimentary slave schools, since Kentucky did not deny such. Until Garrisonianism began fragmenting North-South friendships, most Kentuckians favored emancipation if owner compensation and acceptable accommodations for the freedmen could be arranged. Many owners, though holding that abolition could harm blacks more than bondage, could accept emancipation of slaves with self-supporting skills. Henry Clay, a president of the American Colonization Society, held this position, but JAMES G. BIRNEY decried Clay's gradualism. Joining William Lloyd Garrison's American Anti-Slavery Society and hoping to operate a Kentucky corollary to the *Liberator*, he hurriedly departed to ensure his own safety. By the late 1830s the abolitionists had so alarmed the voters that earlier demands for a new constitution to change slavery provisions were in 1838 resoundingly rejected.

CASSIUS MARCELLUS CLAY, possibly Kentucky's most colorful personality, fronted the state's abolitionist forces and survived gun, knife, and fist assaults. He differed from abolitionists who would end slavery by any means. His short-lived newspaper, the *True American*, was open to both proslavery and antislavery writers to help Kentuckians understand controversial issues. He donated to abolitionists the land on which Berea College was built but was angered that they supported the UNDERGROUND RAILROAD, an illegal circumvention of the law of the land.

Kentucky, settled and won by immigrants, stipulated in its constitutions free immigration, so many immigrants and their offspring moved on. The state also served as a way station for restless, nomadic easterners. The troubles in Missouri involved former Kentuckians, so Henry Clay faced more than just resolving the matter of bondage in some western territory. So many Kentucky bachelors followed the Austins into Texas that many females seeking husbands followed! Kentuckians died at the Alamo in 1836, but others helped assure Texas independence, and 2,400 volunteers later fought the Mexicans. California gold then lured hundreds westward.

A third constitution was adopted in 1849. Earlier slavery provisions were retained, but the legislature was empowered to strengthen or add laws inhibiting agitators. Free Negroes were denied entry, and emancipated slaves were to move north. Ministers were denied the governorship or legislative membership, and amending procedures became more restrictive. Some liberalizing features were incorporated, however. More legislators were apportioned to growing areas, with federal censuses as guidelines. All court members and county officials were to be elected. An oath of office had officials swear that during their tenure they would neither fight nor second a duel! At long last, a constitution sanctioned education by organizing an inviolable educational fund, authorizing taxation for additional monies, determining allocation policies, and calling for quadrennial election of a state superintendent of public instruction.

Kentuckians in 1849, sensing imminent national dangers, returned a reluctant Henry Clay, the "Great Pacificator," to the Senate. From his groundwork and Stephen A. Douglas' follow-up came the COMPROMISE OF 1850, granting the North an extra free state and the South a stronger fugitive slave law, but neither area was jubilant. Sectionalism soon doomed nationalism with the passing of the "American triumvirate" (John C. Calhoun in 1850, Daniel Webster and Clay in 1852). In 1852 *Uncle Tom's Cabin* helped irrationalism override reason. Kentuckians were incensed that some harrowing action in the novel was centered in their state and certain characters were developed from Harriet Beecher Stowe's observations during visits. Kentucky emigrants later helped create the BLEEDING KANSAS issue.

Kentucky soon faced its decision of a lifetime: union or disunion. Senator JOHN J. CRITTENDEN, Clay's successor, saw his compromise resolutions rebuffed on December 18, 1860, South Carolina's secession two days later, then formation of the Confederate States of America. Kentuckians debated what mood to adopt—pride over accomplishments of two native-born sons, Abraham Lincoln and Jefferson Davis, or agony that one had migrated northward to the presidency of the Union, the other southward to the presidency of the Confederacy. Compounding the situation were the forced surrender of Ft. Sumter by a native son, Major Robert Anderson, on April 14, 1861, and war.

BERIAH MAGOFFIN typified the concerned border state governor. He called for a convention to analyze public sentiments, sought a strong neutralist stand by all border states, backed Virginia's WASHINGTON PEACE CONFERENCE, but failed. On May 20 he issued his own neutrality proclamation, but on September 3, General LEONIDAS POLK led Confederate troops into the state, and U. S. Grant countered with Union detachments. Lincoln's enemies taunted him, saying he would prefer Kentucky to God on his side; but Lincoln's assertion that "to lose Kentucky is nearly the same as to lose the whole game" was echoed by southerners. Kentucky had too many assets to expect neutrality: the nation's best river transportation system; railroads; food; horses; a divided people; a possible arena for battle; and over 100,000 men of military age. These men chose sides, approximately two-thirds donning the blue. A star in the Confederate flag represented the state, but government policy was dictated by military power, and the North triumphed.

The Kentucky tragedy was that this conflict became a brothers' war, a father-son war, a relatives' war, a neighbors' war. Every county suffered divisions of loyalty, and guerrillas often took advantage of deteriorating situations. Confederate efforts to gain the state consistently failed. Skirmishes were commonplace, but few bloody encounters by large forces materialized. The southerners' greatest successes came from the lightning-fast strikes by the Kentuckian JOHN HUNT MORGAN, who revolutionized cavalry tactics into

far-ranging independent raids by mounted infantrymen; however, his victories were more psychological than military.

Governor Magoffin, after failing at neutrality,
supported the Confederacy, so the Union-con-
trolled legislature demanded his resignation. In
August, 1862, he left office and, the lieutenant
governor having died, was succeeded by James F.
Robinson, Speaker of the house, a man more Union
oriented. He was governor in name only, since the
federals virtually assumed a military occupation.
Suspected Confederate sympathizers were imprisoned, fined, or kept under house arrest; and
invidious rumors by their enemies often brought
serious problems to dedicated Unionists. Confiscation of property and goods reached major proportions. In fact, abuses were primary causes for
Kentucky's subsequent southern orientation.

Most Kentuckians could chance Lincoln as their
chief executive because they wanted to preserve
the Union, but they would not vote Republican.
In 1860 Lincoln polled only two votes in Lexington, his wife's hometown, and in 1864 George B.
McClellan convincingly carried the state. One-
quarter million slaves, however, posed a problem.
What was their status in a nonseceding state?
Federal authorities made the determination by
forming work battalions to build fortifications and
roads, to repair railway lines, or to work in army
encampments. Objecting owners were subject to
arrest or imprisonment. An 1862 law freed such
workers and their families, then later the president authorized free Negro enlistments. Many
Kentuckians, fearing that slaves could soon enlist,
withdrew from the Union cause; some slipped
south to join the Confederates; others turned to
guerrilla warfare. The THIRTEENTH AMENDMENT
was heatedly rejected by both houses, again signifying opposition to enforced abolition and to
federal intervention in state matters. Military rule
continued longer here than in other border states,
and voters vented their ill feelings by keeping the
state solidly Democratic until 1895. Confederate
monuments and memorials far outnumbered those
for Unionists, another attestation of changing sympathies.

Peace found the state in deep distress. More
than 10,000 men had died in action, other thousands returned maimed or ill. Destruction of or
damage to industry and real estate, a serious drop
in food production with the end of free labor, and
huge losses of livestock retarded economic growth.
Education was in financial shambles. A critical
factor was the continued alienation within families and among neighbors, which fostered murders, torturous legal battles, and some notorious
feuds. Battles ahead over railroad legislation,
agricultural depressions, the Negro ballot, temperance, third parties, and monetary standards
aggravated matters. A Democratic split into conservatives and liberals added to the confusion, all
of which kept Kentucky from retaining its earlier
national status.

A search for selfhood, 1891–1941. The third constitution prevented easy change by prohibiting a
new constitutional convention except under the
most stringent circumstances. A legislature had to
issue a call, the eligible voters in two successive
regular elections had to approve, and the next legislature had to agree. From 1867 to 1884 all proposals failed simply because most eligible voters
shunned the polls! In 1886 the legislature, tired
of such shenanigans, defined "eligibility" in terms
of those balloting in the forthcoming 1887 elections. This permitted constitutional delegates to
convene in September, 1890. Many forces, led by
HENRY WATTERSON of the *Courier-Journal*, fought
the proposed constitution, but the electorate overwhelmingly accepted it. Slave-related clauses were
obviously omitted. The state was officially termed
a commonwealth. Controls over railroads and industries were broadened to check their political
and economic clout. The legislature gained new
taxing authority, but the executive and judicial
branches received few alterations. Oaths of office
retained the antiduel declaration, and amending
processes, even though liberalized somewhat,
permitted simultaneous submission of only two
unrelated proposals. City charters were revoked,
and a classification of cities based on population
was adopted. Another liberalizing feature was
adoption of the secret ballot.

Section 183 declared, "The General Assembly
shall, by appropriate legislation, provide for an efficient system of common schools throughout the
state." Unfortunately, the legislature long defined
"common" as "elementary," so secondary and
higher education was still primarily maintained
by churches and philanthropy. The University of
Kentucky, an outgrowth of the Morrill Act of 1862,
received little encouragement until after 1900.

Kentucky's most crucial episode since the Civil
War centers on the "Goebel affair." In 1895 William O. Bradley, the state's first Republican chief
executive, was elected by bolting Democrats (still
the one sure way for a Republican to become governor), and William McKinley carried the state
over William Jennings Bryan in 1896. Democrat
WILLIAM GOEBEL vowed vengeance on the Republicans, who had in his mind stolen both elections. A man of invective and "a deceitful trick-

ster," he was a state senator from 1886 until 1900. In 1898 he rammed through the Democratic-controlled legislature a bill "to further regulate elections," which would set up a three-man board to canvass returns, then carried it into law over Bradley's veto. Politicians realized too late its import— through it Goebel was going to make himself the next governor. At least he kept Kentucky from much involvement in the Spanish-American War!

The 1899 gubernatorial election was spotlighted across the nation. Anti-Goebel Democrats unwilling to support the Republican William S. Taylor splintered and ran two more Democrats. After a campaign considered the state's most corrupt and venal, Taylor won and was inaugurated, but the drama was not over. Goebel's allies, alleging that the Louisville & Nashville Railroad and other interests had bought the election, demanded implementation of the Goebel election law. On January 30, 1900, its author was shot from ambush. Governor Taylor proclaimed a state of insurrection, but the Democrats, now united by an unknown sniper, backed their controlled election canvass committee and had the oaths of office administered to a dying Goebel and his colleague J. C. W. Beckham. After local, state, and federal courts successively ruled in the Democrats' favor, Taylor resigned, and Beckham became governor. The episode was over, but its ghost long haunted Kentucky politics.

The politicians were just crawling from cover after the Goebel affair when another crisis sent people scurrying to avoid the more generalized violence of the BLACK PATCH WAR. Tobacco prices had plummeted because of overproduction and independent marketing, so the new Tobacco Growers' Association decreed that companies had to meet its prices and that all growers had to join. Nonjoining growers were visited by night riders, who destroyed crops, burned barns and homes, beat and tortured victims (NIGHT-RIDING). When such actions failed to stop the independents, the night riders severely damaged several cities with tobacco warehouses. From 1901 to 1907 the tobacco war raged unchecked and subsided only when Republican Governor Augustus E. Willson declared martial law and got some legislative action to regulate the power of the tobacco companies. Such Kentucky authors as ROBERT PENN WARREN had a new source of plots for their novels.

Except for involvement in World War I, Kentucky very much isolated itself, created its own problems, and did little for half a century to resolve many of them. A 1904 school law did decree a minimum term of six months, and in 1906 normal schools for teacher training were organized at

Bowling Green and Richmond, with each slowly moving toward college status. Similar colleges were organized at Morehead and Murray in 1922. Kentucky State at Frankfort, the "colored" school begun in 1886, received just enough support to operate. The general assembly in 1908 replaced the old local trustee system with an elected county board of education empowered to select a county superintendent, place teachers, determine school tax policies, and organize or close schools. Each county now had to maintain at least one high school. The state college in Lexington was elevated to university status, more in name than in financial aid.

The legislature in 1912, realizing the evils of internal isolation and fragmentation, organized Kentucky's first highway department with the responsibility of connecting all county seats with all-season roads. Despite excessive hiring of party members as employees prior to elections and issuance of contracts with political overtones, the department began providing a road network especially beneficial where rail and river transport was unavailable. Financing was later augmented by the creation of a state tax commission and the use of gasoline taxes as automobiles multiplied.

Progress between the Goebel fiasco and World War II was often deterred by political personalities and factional politics. Old-timers still laugh about the 1914 gubernatorial race between Democrat Augustus O. Stanley and Republican Edwin P. Morrow, personal friends touring together and exciting the crowds with their "dog" speeches. Morrow injected the "Old Ring" issue by attacking a Democratic-passed dog tax, but Stanley won "by a dog hair." Morrow won in 1918 on the same issue and ended the tax! In 1923 the Democrats split over legalizing pari-mutuel betting at racetracks. The Jockey Club, organized in 1874 and beginning the prestigious Kentucky Derby the following year, had become an adjunct of the Democratic party. Congressman ALBEN BARKLEY challenged the horsemen, lost the governor's race, but became a national figure. The thirties featured the Democrats Ruby Laffoon and Albert B. ("Happy") Chandler. When Governor Laffoon procured a sales tax to help finance a depression government, his lieutenant governor, Chandler, campaigned for and won the governorship by promising repeal.

World War I helped break the self-centeredness of Kentuckians. Over 80,000 men were in uniform, with fatalities and casualties exceeding 5,000. The best-known serviceman was Sergeant Willie Sandlin, whose exploits against the Germans rivaled those of Tennessee's Alvin York. Civilians joined groups aiding the military, oversubscribed their shares in war loans, worked in factories and shipyards, or entered the mines. War and the succeeding boom spurred the coal industry, especially in the mountains. Descendants of original settlers, joined by incoming non-Anglo-Saxons, opened the rich veins; and "coal drags" meandering the narrow valleys carried the tonnage northward. Unionizing efforts brought murderous disturbances. Companies and laborers turned from negotiations to guns and dynamite, but the National Guard and federal investigations prevented much violence and maintained an uneasy truce into World War II.

The Roaring Twenties did not affect Kentuckians as did the depression thirties. Relief programs alleviated some distress, but unemployment and a general malaise, compounded by several devastating floods, were not eased until support for American allies again sent workers into the fields. the mines, and the factories.

Kentucky on the move, 1941–1976. Kentucky lost approximately 10,000 men in World War II, but helping assuage the sorrow was the return of 300,000 veterans. Jobs elsewhere led to much emigration, but an internal migration also began changing the state's complexion from rural to urban. The biggest shift was from nonindustrial mountain counties, but recent demands for coal and the national recession have reversed this migration.

Urbanization and the concept of one man, one vote have brought heated legislative clashes over both state and national redistricting. Other problems have centered on determining taxes and budgets for ever-expanding programs modernizing the different levels of government. A proposed new constitution was soundly defeated by conservatives in 1966, but occasional amendments and court interpretations have brought some changes to the document of 1891. State employees still worry about the power each governor wields over the state's merit system. By terminating or altering programs staffed by antiadministration personnel, a governor can develop his own staff positions, choose party friends, and then declare them under the system. Nonmerit employees face possible turnovers every four years.

The big political problem is that there are three factions: the Republicans and two Democratic branches. Seldom are the governor and the lieutenant governor of the same faction, so the lieutenant governor can spend four years politicking for the governorship. Today's Kentucky politician rarely develops the statesmanship that carries him to national prominence. Since Alben Barkley, only JOHN SHERMAN COOPER has achieved real stature at national and international levels. Neither was ever governor.

In public education the key words have been consolidation, integration, busing, and financing. Adequate roads are eliminating one-room elementary and isolated secondary schools. Since 1954 a reluctant integration has worked fairly well, but court-ordered busing for "balance" is now causing great disquiet in Louisville and Jefferson County. Financing received impetus in 1956 with the adoption of the minimum foundation law, which dispenses funds on average daily attendance rather than on annual school-age census figures. New instructional and administrative concepts and improved salaries have increased budgets, and the state no longer loses teachers to other states as it did for years.

Higher education has seen the five state colleges reconstructed into regional universities, and another has been organized in northern Kentucky. Also, the University of Louisville is now state supported. The University of Kentucky has developed several two-year community colleges, and vocational schools are now located across the state. Private colleges have retained their academic traditions in spite of financial woes.

Social and medical programs have mushroomed. The state now cares for most orphans and juvenile delinquents through special centers and foster family projects. County health services now relieve private organizations, such as the Frontier Nursing Service, of many responsibilities. This mountain philanthropy organized by Mary Breckinridge in 1925 has a remarkable record in midwifery, home treatment, and hospital services.

Even with the interruptions of the Korean and Vietnam wars, the state has made industrial and agricultural headway. Industries are locating in smaller towns with ready labor supplies. Tobacco remains the big crop, but an increase in other farm products from grains to beef is evident. Kentucky is a leader in interstate and intrastate highway construction, and new and enlarged airfields have increased commercial aviation (AIR TRANSPORT). Two new elements have kept coal in the spotlight. The first has been a struggle between union and nonunion groups; the other has been strip mining. Poor reclamation has polluted streams and destroyed homes, farms, and roads, but regulations for rebuilding stripped areas have been loosely enforced, strictly because of politics. A related tragedy permits a company with a so-called broad form deed to get to the coal regardless of other damages, and court battles to overturn these

KENTUCKY POPULATION, 1790–1970

Year	Total	White	Nonwhite		% Growth	Rank	
			Slave	Free		U.S.	South
1790	73,677[a]	61,133	12,430	114		14	6
1800	220,955	179,873	40,343	739	199.9	9	5
1810	406,511	324,237	80,561	1,713	84.0	7	4
1820	564,317	434,826	126,732	2,759	38.8	6	3
1830	687,917	517,787	165,213	4,917	21.9	6	2
1840	779,828	590,253	182,258	7,317	13.4	6	3
1850	982,405	761,413	210,981	10,011	26.0	6	3
1860	1,155,684	919,484	225,483	10,684	17.6	9	2
1870	1,321,011	1,098,692	222,319		14.3	8	1
1880	1,648,690	1,377,179	271,511		24.8	8	1
1890	1,858,635	1,590,462	268,173		12.7	11	2
1900	2,147,174	1,862,309	284,865		15.5	12	3
1910	2,289,905	2,027,951	261,954		6.6	14	3
1920	2,416,630	2,180,560	236,070		5.5	15	4
1930	2,614,589	2,388,452	226,137		8.2	17	6
1940	2,845,627	2,631,425	214,202		8.8	16	5
1950	2,944,806	2,742,090	202,716		3.5	19	7
1960	3,038,156	2,820,083	218,073		3.2	22	10
1970	3,218,706	2,981,766	236,940		5.9	23	10

[a]Population of that part of Virginia taken to form Kentucky in 1792

deeds have so far been futile to landowners. The state now returns to coal-producing counties a percentage of taxes levied against the companies, and county-levied taxes on companies are now before the courts.

Leisure has become an expected daily routine. Television spans the state for the stay-at-home. Vacationers overcrowd an exceptional state park system, and sportsmen swarm to well-stocked lakes and hunting preserves. Outdoor dramas, fairs, and festivals are offered throughout the state. A current strength is TOURISM; annually millions of outsiders join the citizens to enjoy the natural and man-made wonders of the Bluegrass State. Tourism is a big factor in helping Kentuckians see a new, brighter, more progressive image of themselves.

Manuscripts and printed primary sources. Indispensable sources for primary as well as secondary materials is J. W. Coleman, Jr., *Bibliography of Kentucky History* (1949), a replacement for W. R. Jillson, *Early Kentucky Literature* (1931). Principal manuscript depository for Kentucky history is still Wisconsin Historical Society (Draper Papers), but invaluable primary materials are also at Filson Club, Louisville; Kentucky State Historical Society, Frankfort; State Archives, Frankfort; and University of Kentucky Library. Transylvania, Centre, and Berea colleges and state's regional universities have smaller but important collections. At the Kentucky State Historical Society are papers of all governors; these are now being codified and published. The first issue is R. Sexton and L. Bellardo (eds.), *Public Papers of Louie B. Nunn* (1976). Extant order books of county courts until 1851 have been collected by the Church of Jesus Christ of Latter-Day Saints and are on microfilm at University of Kentucky Library.

Contemporary accounts. J. S. Johnston, *First Explorations of Kentucky* (1898), contains journeys of Thomas Walker and Christopher Gist; but best study of period is C. W. Alvord and L. Bidgood, *First Explorations of Trans-Allegheny Region by Virginians, 1650–1674* (1912), since it both interprets the history and reproduces parts of these and other journals, diaries, and pamphlets. J. Filson, *Discovery, Settlement, and Present State of Kentucke* (1784), contains Daniel Boone's "own memoir," account of major Indian tribes, geography, table of distances, and good early map. Another reliable contemporary source is articles from the *Kentucky Gazette*, later published as J. Bradford's *Historical Notes on Kentucky* (1932). Two books by W. Littell, *Political Transactions in Kentucky* (1806) and *Statute Laws of Kentucky* (5 vols.; 1809–19), embody excellent political and legal source materials for years 1783–1819. Chief source for Virginia's acts concerning Kentucky is W. W. Hening, *Statutes at Large of Virginia, 1619–1792* (13 vols.; 1819–23).

Histories. First general account is H. Marshall, *History of Kentucky* (2 vols.; 1824), but the Federalist Marshall was strongly prejudiced. Better volume is M. Butler, *History of Commonwealth* (1834). Excellent insight on general history, counties, and personalities is L. Collins, *History of Kentucky* (1847), later revised by his son R. H. Collins in 1884. Best recent study is T. D. Clark, *History of Kentucky* (1960). Fine history to 1783 is D. K. Rice, *Frontier Kentucky* (1975). For photographic history, see J. W. Coleman, Jr. (ed.), *Historic Kentucky* (1968) and *Kentucky, Pictorial History* (1972).

Invaluable study of local government under first three constitutions is R. M. Ireland, *County Courts in Antebellum Kentucky* (1972); and a fascinating, at times controversial, volume on early settlers' attitude toward government and society in general is A. K. Moore, *Frontier Mind* (1957). Two later governmental presentations touching on politics are V. O. Key, Jr., *Southern Politics* (1949); and J. H. Fenton, *Politics in Border States* (1957).

KENTUCKY GOVERNORS

Governor	Party	Term
Isaac Shelby	Dem.-Rep.	1792–1796
James Garrard	Dem.-Rep.	1796–1804
Christopher Greenup	Dem.-Rep.	1804–1808
Charles Scott	Dem.-Rep.	1808–1812
Isaac Shelby	Dem.-Rep.	1812–1816
George Madison	Dem.-Rep.	1816
Gabriel Slaughter	Dem.-Rep.	1816–1820
John Adair	Dem.-Rep.	1820–1824
Joseph Desha	Dem.-Rep.	1824–1828
Thomas Metcalfe	Dem.-Rep.	1828–1832
John Breathitt	Dem.	1832–1834
James T. Morehead	Dem.	1834–1836
James Clark	Whig	1836
Charles A. Wickliffe	Whig	1836–1840
Robert P. Letcher	Whig	1840–1844
William Owsley	Whig	1844–1848
John J. Crittenden	Whig	1848–1850
John L. Helm	Dem.	1850–1851
Lazarus Powell	Dem.	1851–1855
Charles S. Morehead	Know-Nothing	1855–1859
Beriah Magoffin	Dem.	1859–1862
James F. Robinson	Union-Dem.	1862–1863
Thomas Bramlette	Dem.	1863–1867
John L. Helm	Dem.	1867
John W. Stevenson	Dem.	1867–1871
Preston H. Leslie	Dem.	1871–1875
James B. McCreary	Dem.	1875–1879
Luke P. Blackburn	Dem.	1879–1883
J. Proctor Knott	Dem.	1883–1887
Simon B. Buckner	Dem.	1887–1891
John Young Brown	Dem.	1891–1895
William O. Bradley	Rep.	1895–1899
William S. Taylor	Rep.	1899–1900
William Goebel	Dem.	1900
J. C. W. Beckham	Dem.	1900–1907
Augustus E. Willson	Rep.	1907–1911
James B. McCreary	Dem.	1911–1915
Augustus O. Stanley	Dem.	1915–1919
James D. Black	Dem.	1919
Edwin P. Morrow	Rep.	1919–1923
William J. Fields	Dem.	1923–1927
Flem D. Sampson	Rep.	1927–1931
Ruby Laffoon	Dem.	1931–1935
Albert B. Chandler	Dem.	1935–1939
Keen Johnson	Dem.	1939–1943
Simeon S. Willis	Rep.	1943–1947
Earle C. Clements	Dem.	1947–1950
Lawrence Wetherby	Dem.	1950–1955
Albert B. Chandler	Dem.	1955–1959
Bert T. Combs	Dem.	1959–1963
Edward T. Breathitt	Dem.	1963–1967
Louis B. Nunn	Rep.	1967–1971
Wendell H. Ford	Dem.	1971–1975
Julian M. Carroll	Dem.	1975–

Best publication on agriculture is J. H. Hopkins, *Hemp Industry in Kentucky* (1957). For tobacco, see W. F. Axton, *Tobacco and Kentucky* (1975); and J. C. Robert, *Story of Tobacco* (1949). The tobacco war is well told by J. O. Nall, *Tobacco Night Riders* (1939); and J. G. Miller, *Black Patch War* (1936).

Industry, commerce, and travel are treated well in F. A. Ogg, *Opening of the Mississippi* (1904); A. B. Hurlburt, *Ohio River* (1906); C. H. Ambler, *Transportation*

in Ohio Valley (1932); W. A. Pusey, *Wilderness Road* (1921); J. W. Coleman, Jr., *Stage-Coach Days* (1934); T. D. Clark, *The Kentucky* (1942); and M. Verhoeff, *Kentucky River Navigation* (1917). Two interesting related works are W. Blair and F. Meine, *Mike Fink* (1933); and O. A. Rothert, *Outlaws of Cave-in Rock* (1924). A multiplicity of county and city histories gives valuable insight to local industries as well as outside contacts. The best daily sources since Civil War are Louisville *Courier-Journal* (since 1868) and Lexington *Herald* (since 1895).

Biographies of Kentucky personalities and relevant adjuncts must include J. Bakeless, *Daniel Boone* (1930); L. Elliott, *Long Hunter: Daniel Boone* (1976); G. W. Ranck, *Boonesborough* (1901); L. Harrison, *John Breckinridge* (1969); T. P. Abernethy, *Burr Conspiracy* (1954); V. B. Reed and J. D. Williams, *Case of Aaron Burr* (1960); J. A. James, *George Rogers Clark* (1928); C. M. Clay, *Life and Memoirs* (1886); D. L. Smiley, *Lion of White Hall* (1962); H. E. Richardson, *Cassius Marcellus Clay* (1976); C. Eaton, *Henry Clay* (1956); B. Mayo, *Henry Clay* (1937); G. Van Deusen, *Henry Clay* (1937); J. F. Hopkins and W. M. W. Hargreaves, *Papers of Henry Clay* (5 vols. to date; 1972–75); A. D. Kirwan, *John J. Crittenden* (1962); L. W. Meyer, *Richard M. Johnson* (1932); and E. Kenton, *Simon Kenton* (1930).

F. L. McVey, *Gates Open Slowly* (1950), is best educational history, but A. F. Lewis, *Higher Education* (1899), is worthwhile. Another survey is B. Hamlett, *Education in Kentucky* (1914). For long-standing problems of Transylvania, see R. Peter and J. Peter, *Transylvania University* (1896); and, for early religious matters, see N. H. Sonne, *Liberal Kentucky, 1780–1828* (1968). C. G. Talbert, *University of Kentucky* (1965); and E. S. Peck, *Berea's First Century* (1955), are good. An excellent account of integration is O. Carmichael and J. Weldon, *Louisville Story* (1957).

Cultural and social life is treated in D. Drake, *Pioneer Life* (1870); E. Ellet, *Pioneer Women* (1873); and earlier cited J. Bradford, *Notes* (1932). Notorious feuds are related in C. Mutzenberg, *Kentucky's Famous Feuds* (1917); L. F. Johnson, *Famous Kentucky Tragedies* (1922); and J. F. Day, *Bloody Ground* (1941). Mining difficulties of 1920s and 1930s are covered by T. Dreiser *et al.*, *Harlan Miners Speak* (1932), colorful but biased. For Appalachians, see E. Poole, *Nurses on Horseback* (1933); and M. Breckinridge, *Wide Neighborhoods* (1952), both good studies of Frontier Nursing Service. Controversial studies of present-day Appalachia are H. M. Caudill, *Night Comes to Cumberlands* (1963) and *Darkness at Dawn* (1976); J. E. Weller, *Yesterday's People* (1965), adds insight into mountaineers' problems.

Religious histories, written primarily by members of denominations or of local churches, generally praise saints and forget sinners. Best is F. Asbury, *Journal* (3 vols.; 1829). Sister R. Mattingly, *Catholic Church on Kentucky Frontier* (1936); J. H. Spencer, *Kentucky Baptists* (2 vols.; 1886); A. H. Redford, *Methodism in Kentucky* (3 vols.; 1868); and R. Davidson, *Presbyterian Church* (1847), are worthwhile.

J. E. Reeves, *Kentucky Government* (7th ed.; 1973), is far the best and is used in secondary and college courses. G. L. Willis, *Kentucky Democracy* (3 vols.; 1935), is valuable. For infamous Goebel episode, see R. E. Hughes *et al.*, *Kentucky Campaign* (1900); Caleb Powers, *My Own Story* (1905); and I. S. Cobb, *Exit Laughing* (1941).

Daily newspapers now provide best sources on government and politics.

Best general treatment of the Negro is *Kentucky's Black Heritage* (1971), compiled by Commission on Human Rights, exceptionally good bibliography. A most interesting and excellent study is J. W. Coleman, Jr., *Slavery Times in Kentucky* (1940). See also A. E. Martin, *Anti-Slavery Movement Prior to 1850* (1918); and I. E. McDougle, *Slavery in Kentucky, 1792–1865* (1918). Negro's problem since Reconstruction is well depicted by publications of Commission on Human Rights.

For War of 1812, see J. W. Hammack, Jr., *Kentucky and Second American Revolution* (1976). Indispensable work on Kentucky is E. M. Coulter, *Civil War and Readjustment* (1926). L. H. Harrison, *Civil War in Kentucky* (1976), is helpful. Lincoln and Kentucky are given good coverage in J. G. Nicolay and J. Hay (eds.), *Complete Works of Lincoln* (12 vols.; 1905). Best biographies of John Hunt Morgan are C. Holland, *Morgan and His Raiders* (1942); and E. H. Thomas, *Morgan and His Raiders* (1976). A. M. Stickles, *Simon Bolivar Buckner* (1940), is good military biography.

Journals and special publications. Best coverage of historical facets aside from newspapers is *Filson Club History Quarterly* (1926–) and *Register of Kentucky Historical Society* (1903–). The Legislative Research Commission has provided scores of detailed studies on a wide variety of subjects such as education, child welfare, finance and taxation, health, roads, public utilities, flood insurance, social security and retirement for governmental and public use. University Press of Kentucky, controlled by both state and private higher educational systems, has published several studies and is now concentrating on a library of bicentennial materials.

QUENTIN BEGLEY KEEN
Eastern Kentucky University

KENTUCKY, UNIVERSITY OF (Lexington, 40506).

The institution now known as the University of Kentucky was founded in 1865, when the state of Kentucky decided to take advantage of the opportunity offered by the Morrill Act of 1862. An "agricultural and mechanical college of Kentucky" was created by the legislature and attached to a denominational school at Lexington, which was known as Kentucky University. This arrangement was never satisfactory, and in 1878 the state school was detached from the denominational university, but it remained in Lexington under its original title.

The college's first president was James K. Patterson, a classical scholar who placed great emphasis upon Latin, Greek, and philosophy. By 1908 this school had developed to a point where it wished to be known as a university. The legislature complied but gave it an extremely awkward name: State University, Lexington, Kentucky. It had colleges of arts and sciences, agriculture, law, civil engineering, mechanical engineering, and mining engineering. After ten years the last three were combined into a single college of engineering. In 1911 Henry S. Barker succeeded Patterson as president. A former judge of the Kentucky court of appeals, he was totally devoid of experience in educational administration. His main achievement was the initiation and encouragement of agricultural extension.

In 1916 the school was given its present name, the University of Kentucky. In the following year Frank L. McVey became its president. McVey took an institution that was a university in name and made it a university in fact by strengthening the faculty and the library and by encouraging research. During his administration a college of commerce and a college of education were added. Although a graduate school had been added in 1912, it was not until 1929 that the first doctorate was granted.

McVey's successor Herman L. Donovan came to the institution in 1941 and remained until 1956. He was largely responsible for the creation of colleges of pharmacy, medicine, nursing, and dentistry. Frank G. Dickey, who was president of the University of Kentucky from 1956 until 1963, had been dean of the college of education. He presided over a period of great physical growth.

John W. Oswald became president in 1963 and continued in that office until 1968. In the second year of his administration the university created a community college system, which soon had two-year schools in operation in 13 campuses across the state. Albert D. Kirwan, long associated with the institution, served as president for 13 months and was succeeded in 1969 by Otis A. Singletary. The University of Kentucky in 1975 had on its Lexington campus 15 colleges and a graduate school. Current enrollment is 22,000 students. Its library contains 1 million volumes. Major collections are the Wilson Collection of Kentuckiana, the Cartot Collection of Musicology, the John Milton Collection, the Horine Collection on Daniel Drake, and the papers of Chief Justice Fred M. Vinson, Vice-President Alben Barkley, and Senators Albert B. Chandler, John Sherman Cooper, Thruston B. Morton, and Augustus O. Stanley.

See J. F. Hopkins, *University of Kentucky: Origins and Early Years* (1951); and C. G. Talbert, *University of Kentucky: Maturing Years* (1965).

CHARLES G. TALBERT
University of Kentucky

KENTUCKY GAZETTE (1787–1848),

in Lexington, was the second newspaper established west of the Allegheny Mountains, appearing weekly and semiweekly. John Bradford and four members of his family were among the 21 editors. It provided a sheet for the liberal political forces of the Jeffersonian Republicans and the Democrats. As a supporter of Andrew Jackson in the hometown of Henry Clay, the paper experienced violence when Charles Wickliffe killed editor Thomas R. Benning. His successor George James Trotter took Wickliffe's life in a duel. Bradford's "Notes on Kentucky" appeared in 66 numbers through intermittent issues during 1826–1829. These portray the historic development of Kentucky during the last half of the eighteenth century, treating such issues as Kentucky statehood, the Mississippi question, and the rise of Transylvania University. At least three men demonstrated editorial ability superior to the Bradfords: Thomas Smith, John Norvell, and Joshua Cunningham. The former also edited the opposition *Kentucky Reporter*, Norvell became a U.S. senator from Michigan, and the latter served as the final *Gazette* editor.

See D. L. Mikkelson, *"Kentucky Gazette"* (Ph.D. dissertation, University of Kentucky, 1963); and files and microfilm, University of Kentucky and West Virginia University libraries.

DWIGHT MIKKELSON
Taylor University

KENTUCKY RIVER flows generally westward from its source near Beattyville in southeastern Kentucky. It skirts the south edge of the BLUE-GRASS, where its meanders become deeply entrenched in uplifted Ordovician limestones, and then turns north to join the Ohio at Carrollton, some 259 miles downstream. The river was more an obstacle than a route for early transport. The channel, where not clogged with trees and sand, was narrowed by rocky shoals during extended months of low water. Near the bluegrass the river flowed through a deep gorge with near-vertical 400-foot walls, which disrupted overland trails and effectively isolated the small river settlements. BOONESBORO, the first town established in the state, was sited along the river. Frankfort, alone of the early river towns, survived, primarily because it was designated the state capital in 1792. The state began open-channel work in 1818 to attract steamboat traffic, but large boats could not manage the narrow and twisting route. In turn, occasional cargoes of salt from various licks, tobacco from bluegrass farms, iron and timber from the eastern mountains, and whiskeys from bluegrass distilleries were shipped during the nineteenth century, but volume was never significant or prolonged. During the twentieth century only stone and gravel barges and recreational craft utilize the federally constructed system of locks and dams.

See M. Verhoeff, *Kentucky River Navigation* (1917).

KARL B. RAITZ
University of Kentucky

KERNSTOWN, FIRST BATTLE OF (March 23, 1862). When Confederate troops evacuated Manassas in early March, 1862, STONEWALL JACKSON was forced to abandon Winchester and retire up the Shenandoah Valley. N. P. Banks, Union commander in the region, thinking Jackson had left the valley, began moving his troops across the Blue Ridge to reinforce Irvin McDowell for the PENINSULAR CAMPAIGN. To prevent such a move, Jackson decided to take the offensive. However, at Kernstown, Va., near Winchester, he was soundly repulsed by James Shields's division of Banks's command. Jackson had attacked under a misapprehension of his opponent's strength. Jackson, however, gained a strategic victory. Federal authorities, alarmed over his bold moves, retained in northern and western Virginia troops that otherwise would have fought on the peninsula.

See *Official Records, Armies*, Ser. 1, Vol. XII; L. Chambers, *Stonewall Jackson* (1959); M. F. Steele, *American Campaigns* (1922); and D. S. Freeman, *Lee's Lieutenants* (1942–44).

JOHN G. BARRETT
Virginia Military Institute

KERNSTOWN, SECOND BATTLE OF (July 23–24, 1864). George Crook had approximately 11,000 Union soldiers encamped around Winchester, Va. On July 23 he moved south to Kernstown, Va., and went into position on the site of the 1862 battle. When JUBAL EARLY, after his Washington raid, learned of Crook's advance, he put his army in motion for Kernstown. The main Confederate attack on the twenty-fourth, under the personal leadership of General JOHN C. BRECKINRIDGE, drove the Union troops from the field in confusion. Crook was not able to rally his men until the Potomac was crossed on July 25.

See *Official Records, Armies*, Ser. 1, Vol. XXXVII; J. A. Early, *Autobiographical Sketch* (1912); and W. C. Davis, *Breckinridge* (1974).

JOHN G. BARRETT
Virginia Military Institute

KERSHAW, JOSEPH BREVARD (1822–1894), came from a prominent Camden, S.C., family. His early life was spent as a lawyer, legislator, and soldier in the Mexican War. In 1854 he was a staunch defender of STATES' RIGHTS and by 1860 attended the Charleston secession convention. Rising to major general, C.S.A., by May, 1864, he served at Morris Island (SUMTER), first BULL RUN, the PENINSULAR CAMPAIGN, SEVEN DAYS', second BULL RUN, ANTIETAM, FREDERICKSBURG, CHANCELLORSVILLE, GETTYSBURG, CHICKAMAUGA, the WILDERNESS, SPOTSYLVANIA, COLD HARBOR, PETERSBURG, the Shenandoah, the retreat toward APPOMATTOX and was captured near SAYLER'S CREEK. He was temporarily imprisoned in Ft. Warren. Returning home, he was elected to the state senate, serving as its president one year. As a member of the Union Reform party, he advocated the Reconstruction acts. In 1877 he was elected to the bench of the fifth circuit, resigning in 1893. He was then postmaster of his native Camden until his death.

See J. B. Kershaw Papers, University of South Carolina, small collection; E. J. Warner, *Generals in Gray* (1959); J. E. McDowell and W. C. Davis, *Civil War Times Illustrated* (Feb., 1970); R. U. Johnson and C. C. Buel (eds.), *Battles and Leaders* (1884), III; T. J. Kirkland and R. M. Kennedy, *Historic Camden* (1926), II; and D. D. Wallace, *History of South Carolina* (1935), II.

JAMES W. POHL
Southwest Texas State University

KETTLE CREEK, BATTLE OF (February 14, 1779), was according to ANDREW PICKENS, commander of the patriot militia, "the severest check & chastisement the tories ever received in South Carolina and Georgia" and the hardest fought battle of his career. Waged in the canebrakes of Big Kettle Creek, southwest of present Washington, Ga., the battle turned when ELIJAH CLARKE outflanked the Loyalist right. The destruction of Colonel John (or James) Boyd's force of 700 to 800 prevented implementation in 1779 of the British "southern strategy," a plan to hold Georgia with Loyalist militia and free the British regulars to campaign northward.

See R. S. Davis and K. H. Thomas, "Kettle Creek" (1975), report, Georgia Department of Natural Resources, Atlanta, sources; C. R. Ferguson, "Andrew Pickens" (Ph.D. dissertation, Duke, 1960), good narrative; and O. Ashmore and C. H. Olmstead, *Georgia Historical Quarterly* (June, 1926), good.

CLYDE R. FERGUSON
Kansas State University

KEY, DAVID McKENDREE (1824–1900), born in Greene County, Tenn., graduated from Hiawassee College in 1850 and was admitted to the bar. An active Democrat, he was a presidential elector in 1856 and 1860. In the Civil War he served as colonel of the Confederate 43rd Tennessee Infantry, and afterward, in 1870, he was elected chancellor of the third judicial district. In 1875 Key was appointed to fill a U.S. Senate seat vacated by the death of ANDREW JOHNSON. A sincere advocate of sectional reconciliation, Key urged this course in the Senate, even backing Republican measures he believed would further this end. Following Key's defeat for election to his Senate seat in 1877, President Rutherford B. Hayes, who was anxious to name a southerner to his cabinet as a gesture of national unity, selected the independent-minded Key to be postmaster general. In 1880 Key resigned and became federal district judge for eastern and middle Tennessee, a post he held for the rest of his life.

See D. M. Key Papers, Chattanooga Public Library; D. M. Abshire, *South Rejects a Prophet* (1967); C. V. Woodward, *Reunion and Reaction* (1951); and R. I. Polakoff, *Politics of Inertia* (1973).

ROBERT B. JONES
Middle Tennessee State University

KEY, FRANCIS SCOTT (1779–1843), born in Maryland (Carroll County), attended St. John's College (1789–1796) in Annapolis, studied law, and then went with fellow student ROGER B. TANEY, later chief justice, to practice in Frederick. In 1802 Key moved to Georgetown, D.C., to practice law with an uncle. During the War of 1812, in the aftermath of the British capture of Washington (1814), Key went on a mission to secure release of a well-known Maryland physician held prisoner in Chesapeake Bay aboard a ship of the British fleet then preparing to attack Baltimore. The British freed the prisoner, but detained the exchange party until completion of their attack. Key thus became a spectator to the intensive bombardment (September 13–14) of Ft. McHenry guarding Baltimore harbor. His sighting the following morning of the American flag still flying over the fort became the inspiration for composition of "The Star-Spangled Banner," shortly thereafter set to the well-known English tune, "To Anacreon in Heaven," attributed to John Stafford Smith. Although Key continued his literary efforts as well as practice of law, he left no other writings of importance. From 1833 to 1841, he served as U.S. attorney for the District of Columbia.

See F. S. K. Smith, *Francis Scott Key* (1911); O. G. T. Sonneck, *Report on Star Spangled Banner* (1909); and V. Weybright, *Spangled Banner, Story of F. S. Key* (1935).

VINCENT C. JONES
Center of Military History, Department of Army

KEY, V. O., JR. (1908–1963), was the leading student of American politics in his generation. His most significant work was *Southern Politics in State and Nation* (1949), which won the Woodrow Wilson Foundation Award for the best publication of the year about government and democracy. Key analyzed the political evolution of each former Confederate state along with regionwide political phenomena. His conclusions centered on the significance of blacks in the population and on the consequences of the resulting one-party politics.

Key was born in Austin and spent early years in Lamesa in west Texas. His capacious mind and formidable mastery of analytical tools were fortified by canny intuition. His experiences in Lamesa, where his father was active in local politics, gave him sensitivity to political processes that proved valuable when he later studied them systematically in more complex settings. He attended McMurry College in Abilene (1925–1927), the University of Texas (A.B., 1929), and the University of Chicago (Ph.D., 1934), where he worked under Charles E. Merriam. His doctoral dissertation, "The Techniques of Political Graft in the United States," examined that subject as a form of social influence. He was prolific, writing swiftly and accurately. By the time he began *Southern Politics*, he had published *The Administration of Federal Grants to States* (1937), *The Initiative and Referendum in California* (1939, with W. W. Crouch), *The Problem of Local Legislation in Maryland* (1940), and the first of five editions of his widely used textbook, *Politics, Parties, and Pressure Groups* (1942). His subsequent work built on professional interests developed in his southern studies: *A Primer of Statistics for Political Scientists* (1954), *American State Politics: An Introduction* (1956), *Public Opinion and American Democracy* (1961), and *The Responsible Electorate: Rationality in Presidential Voting, 1936–1960* (1966, posthumously). He wrote influential articles, served federal agencies, taught at UCLA, Johns Hopkins, and Yale before becoming in 1951 Jonathan Trumbull Professor at Harvard, and was elected president of the American Political Science Association in 1958.

ALEXANDER HEARD
Vanderbilt University

KILBY, THOMAS ERBY (1865–1943), was born into a planter family in Wilson County, Tenn. He received limited education in Atlanta public schools, then came to Anniston, Ala., in 1887 as agent of the Georgia & Pacific Railroad. Two years later he entered the steel business, becoming president of his own company and of the City National Bank. As mayor from 1900 until 1908 he gained a reputation as a skilled administrator who saved the town from bankruptcy. He served a term in the state senate before his election as lieutenant governor in 1914 and governor in 1918. His major support came from prohibitionists in northern and eastern Alabama and from small-town newspapers. He was known as a "businessman" governor who instituted a state budget system, proposed a depletion tax on coal and forest products, and favored a graduated income tax and equalization of tax assessments. He supported the better roads campaign and harbor improvements at the port of Mobile. Despite improvement in state financial conditions, conservative interests bitterly contested this program. As a social reformer, Kilby opposed the CONVICT LEASE SYSTEM and favored construction of modern penal facilities. He increased expenditures for mental hospitals and education, secured enactment of a workmen's compensation law, and created a child welfare department. Despite these reforms, his administration ended negatively for workers when he used his office to break a strike in the Birmingham district in which the United Mine Workers sought company recognition.

See E. Owen, "Thomas E. Kilby," (M.A. thesis, University of Alabama, 1942); and T. E. Kilby Papers, Department of Archives and History, Montgomery.

WAYNE FLYNT
Samford University

KILPATRICK-DAHLGREN RAID TO RICHMOND (February 28–March 2, 1864). Judson Kilpatrick persuaded Abraham Lincoln to order a cavalry raid to free federal prisoners within Richmond while also distributing Lincoln's amnesty proclamation. Kilpatrick planned to attack with 3,000 men from north of Richmond while Ulric Dahlgren, with 500 men, attacked from the south. Kilpatrick attacked on March 1, met stiff resistance, and retreated toward federal lines east of Richmond. Arriving too late, Dahlgren retreated, with his column inadvertently separating into two parts in the darkness. Three hundred men were able to rejoin Kilpatrick; the remainder were ambushed and Dahlgren was killed. The raid cost 340 federal casualties with few southern losses. Mutilation of Dahlgren's corpse and bloodhounds hunting down his men caused a sensation in the North. Papers allegedly taken from Dahlgren's body, ordering the burning of Richmond and the killing of Jefferson Davis and his cabinet, caused a sensation in the South. Federal officials, disclaiming the purported orders, charged forgery. The original documents vanished, and the charges are unresolved.

See B. Catton, *Stillness at Appomattox* (1953); J. Moore, *Kilpatrick* (1865); V. C. Jones, *Eight Hours Before Richmond* (1957); and *Official Records, Armies*, Ser. 1, Vol. XXXIII.

DAVID L. WILSON
Southern Illinois University

KIMBALL, HANNIBAL INGALLS (1832–1895), entrepreneur, developer, and financial power behind the Republican administration in Georgia during Reconstruction, was born in Maine, entered the carriage-making trade, and in 1867 came to Atlanta as manager of the southern branch of the Pullman Palace Car Company. He soon allied himself with Republican Governor RUFUS B. BULLOCK, lobbied to have the state capital moved from Milledgeville to Atlanta, and began a series of daring financial dealings. He bought an uncompleted opera house, furnished it, and leased and later sold it to the state as a capitol. He gained control of several railroad lines in Georgia and secured from the Republican legislature the state's endorsement of $4.5 million in construction bonds for them. Kimball's railroads were badly managed, however, and after Democrats repudiated the endorsements in 1872 his shaky financial empire collapsed. He left the state under the cloud of scandal that ended the Bullock administration. Kimball returned to Atlanta in 1874, withstood the charges that the sale of the capitol and the state assistance to his railroads were fraudulently obtained, and became a popular businessman, a New South promoter, and a friend of HENRY GRADY's. He founded the Atlanta Cotton Mills in 1874, organized the International Cotton Exposition in 1881, and in 1884 helped develop Peters Park, a residential subdivision. He narrowly lost an election for mayor of Atlanta in 1880. His career illuminates the role of business interests in Reconstruction politics in the South and the financial connections between Reconstruction and Redemption.

See W. Range, *Georgia Historical Quarterly* (June, 1945); E. M. Mitchell, *Atlanta Historical Bulletin* (Oct., 1938); and C. M. Thompson, *Reconstruction in Georgia* (1915).

JOHN M. MATTHEWS
Georgia State University

KING, MARTIN LUTHER, JR. (1929–1968). Growing up in Atlanta's black middle class did little to protect Martin Luther King, Jr., from racism and discrimination. During his attendance at Morehouse College, he decided on the ministry, continuing his education at Crozier Seminary and Boston University, where he earned a Ph.D. degree in 1955 in systematic theology. While at Boston he married Coretta Scott and in 1954 accepted a call from the Dexter Avenue Baptist Church in Montgomery, Ala. The MONTGOMERY BUS BOYCOTT, which catapulted him into national prominence, began in December, 1955. In 1957 King, sensing the need for similar action throughout the South, helped establish the SOUTHERN CHRISTIAN LEADERSHIP CONFERENCE to supplement the work of CORE and the NAACP. Two years later he resigned his Dexter Street pastorate and moved to Atlanta, serving with his father as copastor of Ebenezer Baptist Church and devoting full time to SCLC.

Despite threats, bombings, and assassination attempts, King clung to the philosophy of nonviolence. His ideology grew from the idealism of Walter Rausenbusch's Social Gospel, the pacifism of Henry David Thoreau, the realism of Reinhold Niebuhr's neoorthodoxy, and Mahatma Ghandi's nonviolence and civil disobedience. Fully realizing that nonviolence meant acceptance of physical abuse and suffering, King established institutes to teach the techniques of passive protest and self-protection. Finally, King emphasized the individual's right to a meaningful occupation. In addition to his philosophy of nonviolent civil disobedience, King's oratorical talents played a key role in his successes. His homiletical training and his keen intellect produced speeches such as the "I have a dream" address during the 1963 march on Washington.

Throughout his public career as a leader in the CIVIL RIGHTS MOVEMENT, King stressed the importance of biracial cooperation, the ballot, and desegregation, hoping that southern white moderates would be willing to accept federal laws. To change southern society he staged marches, boycotts, and peaceful protests, leading blacks and whites to resist the evils of segregation. One of King's techniques was imprisonment to protest unfair treatment, and this resulted in 17 jailings. His most famous imprisonment occurred during the 1963 Birmingham campaign, when King wrote his *Letter from Birmingham Jail* renouncing the white moderates who failed to take a stand and who loved law and order more than justice.

By the mid 1960s when the younger, more militant leaders rejected nonviolence, King shifted from integrating lunch counters in the South to open housing in the North. He also vehemently opposed the American military intervention in Vietnam, despite the objections of advisers who feared the loss of White House support, because he felt the need for a fundamental reordering of American priorities. By the spring of 1968 SCLC was planning the Poor People's Campaign, which along with Operation Breadbasket would aid the poverty-stricken and perhaps reverse American economic policy. In April, 1968, while discussing civil rights, pacifism, and the class struggle, King intervened in the Memphis garbage strike and was assassinated.

The results of King's efforts are mixed. On the local level marches and boycotts were only partially successful in reordering southern society, but nationally they dramatized the plight of southern blacks and helped force passage of several significant pieces of legislation, including the CIVIL RIGHTS ACT OF 1964 and the CIVIL RIGHTS ACT OF 1965. Furthermore, they won for King international acclaim and the 1965 Nobel Peace Prize. Despite limited concrete achievements King remains America's most dynamic and charismatic black leader. He provided leadership for blacks and whites alike, offered hope and dignity to the black masses, and translated legal changes into social and economic realities.

See D. L. Lewis, *King* (1970), best, excellent bibliography; C. S. King, *My Life with M. L. King* (1969); and C. E. Lincoln, *M. L. King* (1970). Manuscript collections are at Mugar Library, Boston University, and M. L. King Center for Social Change, Atlanta. King's writings include *Stride Toward Freedom* (1958), *Why We Can't Wait* (1964), and *Where Do We Go from Here?* (1967).

DUNCAN R. JAMIESON
University of Alabama

KING, WILLIAM RUFUS DE VANE (1786–1853),

was born in Sampson County, N.C. Educated at the University of North Carolina, he later studied law and entered the state house of commons in 1808. After serving two terms in that body and briefly as circuit solicitor, he entered the U.S. House of Representatives in 1811, where he became one of the lesser war hawks. After serving in a minor diplomatic post (1816–1818), he moved to Alabama and became a member of the state constitutional convention of 1819 to which he made major contributions. Elected to the U.S. Senate (1819–1844), he supported land legislation beneficial to western settlers, a low tariff, and Indian removal. After 1828 he was a supporter of Andrew Jackson. Although he was an advocate of states' rights, he opposed NULLIFICATION. He became minister to France at the time the Texas question was a central concern (1844–1846). Reentering the Senate in 1848, he became presiding officer (1850) and exercised a significant moderating influence on debates. Following adoption of the COMPROMISE OF 1850, he was instrumental in helping to secure its acceptance. Elected to the vice-presidency in 1852, he died shortly after assuming office.

See J. M. Martin, "William R. King" (Ph.D. dissertation, University of North Carolina, 1955), *Alabama Review* (Jan., 1963; Oct., 1965), and *North Carolina Historical Review* (Autumn, 1962); W. M. Jackson, *Alabama's First Vice President* (1952); and A. J. Pickett, *History of Alabama* (1851).

JOHN M. MARTIN
West Georgia College

KING COTTON.

With the invention of the cotton gin in 1793, the cultivation of short-staple cotton began to spread, covering most of the South by the late 1850s. Cotton became the chief export of the United States and the chief fiber for the manufacture of cloth. Southern leaders were led to contend and the people to believe that industrialized countries were so dependent upon a continuing supply of it that, in the words of Senator JAMES H. HAMMOND, "no power on earth dares to make war upon it. Cotton *is* king." During the Civil War, much suffering resulted from the cotton famine, which was one factor causing agitation in England and France to recognize the Confederacy (KING COTTON DIPLOMACY); but Union victory proved the belief in King Cotton to be a delusion.

See F. L. Owsley, *King Cotton Diplomacy* (1931); C. Eaton, *Growth of Southern Civilization, 1790–1860* (1961); and M. Ellison, *Support for Secession* (1972).

ROBERT C. TUCKER
Furman University

KING COTTON DIPLOMACY

considered cotton a powerful instrument of policy. In 1858 Senator JAMES H. HAMMOND of South Carolina echoed David Christy's *Cotton Is King* (1855). This notion assumed that "no power on earth dares to make war upon it." Countries dependent on southern cotton, especially England and France, were expected to extend prompt recognition to the seceded Confederate states and in case of a northern blockade to react vigorously. Actually, Europe remained neutral, withheld recognition, used inferior Indian and Algerian cotton, and ameliorated local economic hardships caused by the war in America. Miscalculations hurt KING COTTON. When secession was proclaimed, European cotton mills were amply stocked. Moreover, Confederate policy of withholding cotton to compel recognition merely accelerated Europe's search for substitute supplies.

See F. L. Owsley, *King Cotton Diplomacy* (1931); J. L. Watkins, *King Cotton* (1908); and H. Blumenthal, *Journal of Southern History* (May, 1966).

HENRY BLUMENTHAL
Rutgers University

KINGS MOUNTAIN, BATTLE OF (October 7, 1780). British attempts to reintegrate the southern provinces into the empire required successful utilization of local LOYALISTS. No incident demonstrates the failure of this reliance on the king's friends more than this engagement. With approximately 100 Loyalist regulars and 1,000 militiamen and operating as the left flank of Lord Cornwallis' main force, which had moved to Charlotte, N.C., overconfident Lieutenant Colonel Patrick Ferguson threatened to lay waste to the Carolina backcountry that did not support the king. This aroused the OVERMOUNTAIN MEN of the Watauga, Holston, and Nolichucky River headwaters, who marched against Ferguson. These frontiersmen, reinforced by Carolina militiamen to total 1,790, surrounded Ferguson's camp on a hogback ridge known as Kings Mountain in South Carolina. The Loyalists' muskets and bayonets were no match for the patriots' rifles in the densely wooded terrain. Loyalist losses were 157 dead, including Ferguson, 163 seriously wounded, and 700 prisoners, to the Americans' 28 killed and 62 wounded. The defeat forced Cornwallis to withdraw from Charlotte and constituted the beginning of the end of the British southern campaign. Since 1931 the site has been a National Military Park.

See L. C. Draper, *King's Mountain and Its Heroes* (1881; repr., 1929, 1967); G. C. Mackenzie, *Kings Mountain National Military Park* (1955); and R. F. Weigley, *Partisan War* (1970).

DAVID CURTIS SKAGGS
Bowling Green State University

KIRBY, JOHN HENRY (1860–1940), a native of east Texas, was one of the first to recognize the potential commercial value of the area's thousands of acres of virgin pinelands. Through connections with a group of Boston investors in east Texas lands, Kirby by 1900 had become a wealthy landowner in addition to promoting the Gulf, Beaumont & Kansas City Railway. In 1901 he organized the Kirby Lumber Company, which owned over 300,000 acres of east Texas pinelands and operated 13 sawmills. Kirby served two terms as president of the National Lumber Manufacturers' Association, was a founder and five-time president of the Southern Pine Association, and served briefly during World War I as southern lumber director of the U.S. Shipping Board Emergency Fleet Corporation. Active in local and state politics, Kirby served two terms in the Texas legislature and was delegate to the 1916 Democratic National Convention.

An adherent of the Gospel of Wealth and a paternalistic employer, Kirby steadfastly fought against unionism. A self-proclaimed patriot, he was an ultraconservative Democrat who equated liberalism with socialism. Franklin D. Roosevelt's NEW DEAL particularly repelled Kirby, who was a principal founder of the Southern Committee to Uphold the Constitution as well as a contributor to the American Liberty League. Forced into bankruptcy in 1933, Kirby lost managerial control of his lumber company and of the Kirby Petroleum Company, which he had organized in 1920; but he continued to serve as chairman of the boards of both companies.

See J. O. King, *Houston Oil Company* (1959), best discussion of beginnings of Kirby Lumber Company; G. T. Morgan, *Labor History* (Spring, 1969) and *Southwestern Historical Quarterly* (Oct., 1971); and J. H. Kirby Papers, University of Houston Library.

GEORGE T. MORGAN, JR.
University of Houston

KIRBY-SMITH, EDMUND (1824–1893), soldier and educator, son of Joseph Lee and Frances Kirby Smith, was born in St. Augustine, Fla. Both the Smith and Kirby families were of New England stock. In 1821 Joseph Lee Smith had been appointed federal judge in the eastern district of the territory of Florida. In 1836 young Edmund enrolled in Benjamin Hollowell's school in Alexandria, Va., preparatory to admission to the U.S. Military Academy, from which he graduated in 1845, ranking twenty-fifth in his class. Commissioned brevet second lieutenant, he was assigned to the 5th Infantry, which was already en route to join General Zachary Taylor's army moving into Texas. He saw action with Taylor through the battle of Monterrey, after which, now a member of the 7th Infantry, he was transferred to General Winfield Scott's command. He participated in the battles of Cerro Gordo, of Contreras, and in the vicinity of Mexico City and emerged as brevet captain. Throughout the 1850s Kirby-Smith saw service at several western posts.

When Florida seceded he resigned, accepted the Confederate rank of colonel, and was assigned to recruiting service at Lynchburg, Va. In May, 1861, he joined Joseph E. Johnston's command in northern Virginia and was soon promoted to brigadier. He was wounded in the battle of MA-

NASSAS. While recuperating at Lynchburg he married Cassie Selden, to which union would be born 11 children. Promoted major general in October, 1861, he was assigned to command a division in the army on the Potomac. In the spring of 1862 he assumed command of the Department of East Tennessee, where the vital Virginia railroad was threatened by both federal troops and local Unionists. In the fall of 1862 his army joined Braxton Bragg in a two-pronged invasion of Kentucky and won several minor victories but was not at PERRYVILLE. Upon return to Tennessee, Kirby-Smith was promoted lieutenant general, but, discouraged and disgusted with Bragg's failure, he no longer wished to have any connection with Bragg's leadership. He assumed command of the Trans-Mississippi Department in the spring of 1863. For two years he exercised both civil and military command in that vast area, where lack of transportation facilities and much civilian disloyalty made success almost impossible. He was unable to import adequate supplies or to export sufficient cotton to pay for imports and was plagued by the activities of speculators and dissension among civil and military leaders, and his problems continued to multiply. He was promoted general in February, 1864. His most important military victory was the defeat of N. P. Banks in the RED RIVER CAMPAIGN. He officially surrendered the department on June 2, 1865, and fled to Mexico, thence to Cuba. In November, 1865, he returned to Lynchburg and took the amnesty oath. After unsuccessful terms as president of an insurance company and then a telegraph company, he joined BUSHROD JOHNSON in an attempt to revive the University of Nashville. When that institution became the Peabody Normal School in 1875, he moved to the University of the South, where he taught mathematics until his death.

See A. H. Noll, *General Kirby Smith* (1907); J. H. Parks, *General Kirby Smith, C.S.A.* (1954); and R. L. Kerby, *Kirby Smith's Confederacy* (1972). The only collection of Kirby-Smith Papers is at the University of North Carolina.

JOSEPH H. PARKS
University of Georgia

KIRK-HOLDEN WAR (1870). After North Carolina Republicans had won convincing victories in the elections of 1868, the activity and membership of the state's KU KLUX KLAN expanded markedly. Throughout 1869, threats against white and black officeholders became commonplace and whippings and beatings increasingly frequent. Yet Governor W. W. HOLDEN felt powerless to deal with the problem. When witnesses were willing

to testify against indicted Klansmen, local juries were unwilling to convict. The state's new constitution empowered the governor to declare martial law, but prohibited him from suspending writs of habeas corpus and from substituting military tribunals for trials in local civil courts. Moreover, the state's organized militia was notoriously inept.

Accordingly, Holden attempted to bring the Klan under control by both threatening to declare martial law (meaningless except in a psychological sense) and by seeking to conciliate conservative Democratic leaders. For example, when Holden sent a company of 25 militiamen into Lenoir County, the militia's only act was to disarm local blacks; and, in the same county, 35 Klansmen indicted for the murder of the local sheriff were freed on bail and never brought to trial. This mixture of threats and conciliatory efforts failed to bring Klan violence under control, however. In Alamance County, a black member of the Graham town council and his father and brother were each slain by the Klan. And in May, 1870, a white state senator from neighboring Caswell County was murdered in the county courthouse while in the company of the county sheriff (a Klansman) and while county Democrats were holding their convention upstairs.

With no federal assistance forthcoming and under mounting Republican criticism for his perceived timidity, Holden decided to act. On June 8, 1870, he proclaimed martial law in Alamance and Caswell counties; he organized a special unit of 600 volunteer militiamen; and he placed the volunteers under the command of Colonel George W. Kirk of Jonesboro, Tenn. In addition to having commanded a regiment of Unionists in east Tennessee and western North Carolina during the Civil War, Kirk had assisted Tennessee's Governor W. G. BROWNLOW in suppressing Klan activity in that state.

Even prior to the arrival of Kirk's volunteers in mid-July, Klan violence in the two counties was greatly abated. Kirk and his lieutenants quickly arrested approximately 100 individuals, including the sheriffs of two counties. Also arrested was Josiah Turner, editor of the Raleigh *Sentinel*. Although Turner had given editorial encouragement to the Klan, he had not participated in Klan violence, nor was he even within the district governed by Kirk at the time of his detention. Local judges almost immediately issued writs ordering the release of the prisoners pending their trials, but Kirk—acting on orders from Holden—refused to comply. The Republican chief justice of the state's supreme court was sympathetic to Holden, but the suspension of the writs of habeas corpus clearly violated the state's constitution, and he too ordered the prisoners released. Still Holden refused to comply. Finally a federal district judge, mindful of the due process clause of the recently ratified FOURTEENTH AMENDMENT, ordered the Klansmen's release. Denied support from President U. S. Grant, Holden had no choice but to comply with the federal court order.

The Democrats, led by editor Turner, berated Holden's "villainous," "high-handed," and "tyrannical" interference with the civil liberties of the state. Turner even advanced the argument that the murder of Republican officeholders was a Republican campaign tactic intended to discredit the Democrats. In statewide elections that August, the Democrats gained substantial majorities in both houses of the legislature. The lower house proceeded to impeach the governor. In the upper house a number of Republicans joined with the Democrats to convict Holden of a clear violation of the state constitution's prohibition against any suspension of writs of habeas corpus. Meanwhile, of the 49 Klansmen indicted in Alamance and Caswell counties, not one was ever convicted.

See A. W. Trelease, *White Terror* (1971); *Trial of W. W. Holden* (3 vols.; 1871); and O. H. Olsen, *North Carolina Historical Review* (Summer, 1962).

KIRWAN, ALBERT DENNIS (1904–1971), football coach, university administrator, teacher, and American historian, was born in Louisville. After graduating from the University of Kentucky, he returned to Louisville to coach high school football, teach English, and attend law school in the evenings. He was a football coach at the University of Kentucky for six years before entering Duke University where he earned his Ph.D. degree in history with a dissertation later published as *The Revolt of the Rednecks* (1951). Returning to the University of Kentucky, he served as dean of men and later dean of students (1947–1954), professor of history (1954–1960), dean of the graduate school (1960–1966), president (1968–1969), and again professor of history until his death.

In addition to his book *The Revolt of the Rednecks*, which C. Vann Woodward called "an outstanding contribution to . . . recent American political history," Kirwan ably edited the diary of a Confederate soldier, published as *Johnny Green of the Orphan Brigade* (1956), and a series of nonmilitary documents entitled *The Confederacy* (1959). His major work was the biography *John J. Crittenden: The Struggle for the Union* (1962), a thorough and well-balanced account of the distinguished senator from Kentucky. This volume stands as the definitive work on CRITTENDEN. Kirwan also collaborated with THOMAS CLARK in writing *The South Since Appomattox* (1967), a useful textbook for the period, and edited *The Civilization of the Old South: Writings of Clement Eaton* (1968), published as a tribute to EATON on the occasion of his retirement.

See F. F. Mathias, *Albert D. Kirwan* (1975); and A. S. Link and R. W. Patrick (eds.), *Writing Southern History* (1965).

JOHN D. WRIGHT, JR.
Transylvania University

KITCHIN, CLAUDE (1869–1923), member of a prominent North Carolina family, first attracted public attention in the 1890s when he joined with other Tarheel politicians to shatter the fusion of Republicans and Populists by uniting whites in a bloc under the Democratic banner. After DISFRANCHISEMENT of the Second District's black majority, he easily won election to GEORGE H. WHITE's former seat in Congress in 1900 and then in 1911 received a post on Ways and Means, from which position he helped perfect the Underwood-Simmons Tariff Act of 1913. Almost immediately upon becoming majority leader (1915–1919), Kitchin announced his opposition to President Woodrow Wilson's reversal on preparedness; despite his influential position, his only success was inclusion of munitions taxes to finance the armament program. As the nation moved closer to war, Kitchin assumed the role of chief House critic of administration foreign policy. On April 6, 1917, his opposition culminated in his speech and vote against American involvement and swelled to 50 the number of nay votes in the House. With the exception of conscription, Kitchin proved a loyal supporter of the war effort; he favored a pay-as-you-go fiscal policy, which resulted in a corporate excess profits tax, the first in American history and one he intended to be permanent.

See A. M. Arnett, *Kitchin* (1937); H. L. Ingle, "Kitchin" (Ph.D. dissertation, University of Wisconsin, 1967) and *North Carolina Historical Review* (Jan., 1967); and manuscripts, University of North Carolina and National Historical Publications Commission microfilm.

H. L. INGLE
University of Tennessee, Chattanooga

KNIGHTS OF THE GOLDEN CIRCLE was a secret society devised by George Bickley in Cincinnati during the 1850s and envisioned as an agency to "colonize and finally annex northern Mexico." Hounded by creditors, Bickley left Cincinnati in 1860, first for a tour of the East and then of the

South, ineptly promoting his vague filibustering fancy. He failed in an effort to transfer his paper-based organization into one that would "repel invasion and guarantee Southern rights." After a short stint as a surgeon in the Confederate army, the garrulous pretender deserted and lived with a backwoods belle in the Shelbyville, Tenn., area. Northerners, with a phobia of subversive secret societies, fabricated several exposés, which circulated as booklets, made the Golden Circle a household term, and gave it a reputation as a supposedly leading prosouthern COPPERHEAD organization in the North. Republicans used the KGC as a bogeyman, providing justification for organizing the Union League and concocting election-eve exposés that linked antiwar Democrats to treasonable plots. Although not a single "castle" was established north of the Ohio River, Golden Circle myths survived the war and gained respectability, becoming the base for historical novels (exemplified by C. Robertson's *The Golden Circle* and W. Blake's *The Copperheads*) and being repeated as fact by historians.

See O. Crenshaw, *American Historical Review* (Oct., 1941); F. L. Klement, *Cincinnati Historical Society Bulletin* (Spring–Summer, 1974); and C. A. Bridges, *Southwestern Historical Quarterly* (Jan., 1941).

FRANK L. KLEMENT
Marquette University

KNIGHTS OF THE GOLDEN HORSESHOE. This romantic label of recent concoction refers to events during Colonel Alexander Spotswood's administration (1710– 1722). In 1710 Spotswood ordered rangers to explore beyond the Blue Ridge for a route to the Great Lakes from which British trade, fortification, and settlement could counter French expansion. In 1714 he encouraged settlement to move out of the TIDEWATER and into the PIEDMONT by touring Virginia's frontier and organizing the fortified mining and farming hamlet of Germanna. In August, 1716, Spotswood led 64 men—Virginia rangers and Indian scouts, political notables and land speculators, soldiers and servants—out of Germanna, up the Rapidan and along its South Branch, through the Swift Run Gap in the Blue Ridge, and down the Iroquois trail to the Shenandoah. There, on September 5, he took possession of the whole country from the mountains to the lakes for George I. Back in Williamsburg, Spotswood "presented each of his companions with a golden horse-shoe ... with this inscription on the one side: *Sic juvat transcendere montes* And on the other is written the Transmontane Order." Following this expedition,

he persuaded the Virginia legislature to form Spotsylvania County and to request British troops and forts for the Western passes. Peace and politics meant that the plan was not implemented for a generation, but the "knights of the golden horseshoe" helped open the path to territorial empire and colonial revolution.

See *Journal of the Lieutenant Governors Travells & Expeditions,* Colonial Office Group 5, Pt. 1358, No. 209, D, and Board of Trade Reports to the King, Pt. 1365, No. 229–36, British Public Records Office; R. A. Brock (ed.), *Spotswood Letters* (1882); L. J. Cappon (ed.), *Virginia Magazine of History and Biography* (April, 1952); R. L. Morton, *Colonial Virginia* (1960); A. Maury (ed. and trans.), *Huguenot Family* (1852, 1907); W. W. Scott, *William and Mary Quarterly* (July, 1923); and H. Jones, *Present State* (1724, 1956).

STEPHEN SAUNDERS WEBB
Syracuse University

KNOTT, JAMES PROCTOR (1830–1911), was born in Marion County, Ky., but moved when he was twenty years old to Memphis, Mo. There he practiced law, served in the Missouri legislature (1857–1859), and accepted appointment as state attorney general (1859–1860). With the beginning of the Civil War, Knott returned to Kentucky and to the private practice of law. He returned to active politics after the war and was elected to six terms in the U.S. House of Representatives (1867–1871, 1875–1883). After serving as governor (1883–1887) and as a delegate to Kentucky's constitutional convention of 1891, he retired permanently from politics to teach civics, economics, and law at Centre College (1893–1901).

See *J. P. Knott Letterbook* (1885–86), University of Kentucky Library.

KNOW-NOTHING PARTY, officially the American party, served in the evolution of the U.S. two-party system as a bridge whereby southern Whigs crossed over into the Democratic party and northern Whigs into the Republican in the mid-1850s. When the WHIG PARTY disintegrated, American nativism reappeared. By exploiting this emotional force, nativists thought to sidetrack the slavery issue and so save the Union. This antiimmigrant impulse had been injected into American politics several times in the preceding decades, but by 1854 it was organized as the Order of the Star-Spangled Banner and set for itself the goal of becoming a national party whose mission was to enlighten the electorate to the "real" danger facing the country—the corruption of American institutions by the foreign-born. As a substitute for confrontation over slavery in the territories, nativism appealed to southerners because the vast majority of immigrants were thought to be abolitionists. These same foreigners were held to be corrupters of the electoral system, since many of them were organized to vote before naturalization. The fact that this could occur only through the organizing efforts of those who controlled the electoral machinery (usually Democrats) was never the important part of the rhetoric. It was the foreigner who was the abuser, and therefore it was he who endangered the institutions of the Republic.

The American party started as a secret organization and was soon dubbed Know-Nothing, for the standard response of members when queried by the uninitiated was, "I know nothing." The secrecy was dropped by 1855. The party was organized enough to intervene in a Maryland election in 1853, but generally 1854 was the year in which it was organized in most southern states. Its biggest effort was to try to get Millard Fillmore elected president in 1856. In this it failed handsomely; Fillmore received eight electoral votes. As a result of the 1856 election there were about 30 congressmen and two senators who could be called Know-Nothings. By 1857 the party was moribund in all but five southern states: Louisiana, Missouri, North Carolina, Kentucky, and Maryland.

As is usually the case in American politics, local issues often reveal more about electoral returns than campaign rhetoric. In New Orleans, for instance, the party was a front behind which the American sector of the city united to wrest control from the section of the city dominated by Creoles and Democrats. The Americans succeeded, and the party continued to win all elections in the city until it was invaded by federal troops. Although New Orleans is the only city that has been studied from the perspective of local issues, there is some evidence that similar dynamics might account for the Know-Nothings' continued existence in cities such as Baltimore and Louisville long after the death of the national party.

See W. D. Overdyke, *Know Nothing Party in South* (1950); L. C. Soulé, *Know Nothing Party in New Orleans* (1962); A. W. Thompson, *Journal of Southern History* (Fall, 1949); H. J. Carman and R. H. Luthin, *South Atlantic Quarterly* (April, 1940); and A. C. Cole, *Mississippi Valley Historical Association* (1913).

LEON C. SOULÉ
Cleveland State University

KNOXVILLE, TENN. (pop. 174,587), in the northeastern portion of the state, sits on the banks of the Tennessee River, approximately 100 miles northeast of Chattanooga. The University of Tennessee, Knoxville College (1863), and the administrative headquarters of the TENNESSEE VALLEY AUTHORITY are all located here. In addition to being a major manufacturer of textiles, aluminum, chemicals, metals, furniture, and wood products, it is a shipping point for area tobacco and livestock growers, lumber companies, marble quarries, and coal, iron, copper, and zinc mines. First settled in 1786 by Captain James White, the community was known for five years as White's Fort until renamed to honor Secretary of War Henry Knox. While serving as capital of the old Southwest Territory (1792–1796) and of the new state (1796–1812, 1817–1819), the city became the principal commercial center in eastern Tennessee. Not until 1855, however, did the first RAILROAD penetrate the surrounding mountains to Knoxville. Although a majority of the city's residents were staunch UNIONISTS, it was occupied by Confederate forces until September 2, 1863, and almost immediately (November 17) thereafter placed under a seven-week siege by JAMES LONGSTREET (KNOXVILLE CAMPAIGN). Despite considerable damage to the city, to its railroads, and to the surrounding area, Knoxville quickly was rebuilt and rapidly began its postwar industrialization.

See S. J. Folmsbee and L. Deaderick, *Founding of Knoxville* (1941); B. B. Creekmore, *Knoxville* (1958); M. U. Rothrock (ed.), *History of Knox County* (1946); and files of Knoxville *Journal* (1839–, independent Republican) and *News Sentinel* (1886–).

KNOXVILLE CAMPAIGN (November, 1863). On September 2, 1863, Ambrose E. Burnside's Army of the Ohio occupied Knoxville. Confederate troops had been withdrawn to reinforce BRAXTON BRAGG's Army of Tennessee at Chattanooga. By October 1 Burnside had more than 20,000 men, including 4,500 cavalrymen, scattered through east Tennessee with about half assigned to the defense of Knoxville. Meanwhile, Bragg had won the battle of CHICKAMAUGA and had penned the Union Army of the Cumberland in Chattanooga. On November 4 he detached JAMES LONGSTREET's corps of 12,000 men and JOSEPH WHEELER's cavalry corps of 5,000 to drive Burnside out of Knoxville. He believed that Longstreet could accomplish this and return to Chattanooga before the Union army could be reinforced and resupplied in Chattanooga. When Longstreet approached Louden, 25 miles southwest of Knoxville, on November 13, he learned that some 5,000 federal soldiers were posted there. He made plans to cut them off from Knoxville, but the yankees, aided by a strong rearguard action at Campbell's Station, succeeded in retiring behind the strong Knoxville fortifications. Meanwhile, Wheeler's cavalry defeated and drove the Union cavalry into Knoxville.

Longstreet then besieged the city, but actions elsewhere forced him to change this strategy. Bragg's army was defeated at Chattanooga and driven into Georgia and, on November 27, William T. Sherman with 20,000 federal troops left Chattanooga to relieve Knoxville. Thus, Longstreet did not have time for a protracted siege. At dawn on November 29 the Confederates made a desperate assault on Ft. Sanders, an earthwork salient in the defenses, but were repulsed with severe losses. Realizing the defenses were too strong and aware of Sherman's approach, Longstreet abandoned the siege and withdrew to the northeast along the railroad from Virginia, establishing headquarters 40 miles from Knoxville. A bitter winter cavalry campaign with battles at Dandridge, Mossy Creek, and Sevierville followed this withdrawal, ending with the Union in firm control of east Tennessee by April, when Longstreet's corps left to rejoin Robert E. Lee's army in Virginia.

See *Official Records, Armies*, Ser. 1, Vol. XXXI, Pt. 1; H. S. Fink, *East Tennessee Campaign and Battle of Knoxville* (1957); J. Longstreet, *Manassas to Appomattox* (1896); J. P. Dyer, *"Fighting Joe" Wheeler* (1941); and B. P. Poore, *Ambrose E. Burnside* (1882).

JOHN W. ROWELL
Columbus, Ind.

KNOXVILLE WHIG, the personal paper of W. G. BROWNLOW, began publication in 1839 in Elizabethton, Tenn. Although Brownlow moved the paper in 1840 to Jonesboro and in 1849 to Knoxville, its character and flavor remained unaltered. It was a partisan and often unpolished advocate of Whigs in both state and national politics, a crude and bitter critic of Democrats, and a Unionist paper both before and after secession. Yet, for all its journalistic shortcomings, the *Whig* probably was the most influential newspaper in eastern Tennessee at the beginning of the Civil War. Brownlow's arrest and imprisonment by Confederate authorities in 1861 forced a suspension in the *Whig's* publication, but, after General Ambrose Burnside's federal troops occupied Knoxville in 1863, the *Whig* resumed publication as *Brownlow's Whig and Rebel Ventilator*. Although Brownlow continued publishing the paper throughout his term as governor and, for a time, during his term in the U.S. Senate, ill health and the press of his duties in Washington forced him to discontinue the paper in 1872. Three years later, the paper's name and goodwill were sold to the *Weekly Chronicle*

(1870–1875), a Republican newspaper that then was published until 1883 as the *Whig and Chronicle*.

See bound copies at Library of Congress, Waltham Public Library, Boston Athenaeum, and Lawson-McGhee Library, Knoxville.

KOLB, REUBEN FRANCIS (1839–1918), the central figure in the populist struggle in Alabama, was born in Eufaula, Barbour County. He was graduated from the University of North Carolina and served in the Confederate army, a credential that was useful when he ran for public office. In 1887 Governor Thomas Seay appointed Kolb the state's second commissioner of agriculture (1887–1891). He proved innovative and zealous to a degree unexpected in a bureaucracy. Alabama on Wheels was a Kolb production, a special railway car painted yellow, containing Alabama products and pamphlets, pulled through more than half a dozen states, promoting tourism, migration to Alabama, and investment in the state. In 1890 Kolb sought the Democratic gubernatorial nomination, but the state convention instead nominated the conservative THOMAS G. JONES. Later Kolb formed the Jeffersonian party, which represented the Alabama populists (with a small *p*). Alabama also had a group calling itself the Populists (with a capital *P*), but it was never larger than the Jeffersonians, and both groups generally supported Kolb in his gubernatorial campaigns of 1892 and 1894.

Racial questions as well as economic and political reforms were important elements in Kolb's three attempts at the governorship in the 1890s. It is apparent that the vote of the blacks was manipulated in favor of Bourbon forces. Thus the Kolb campaigns of the nineties were directly related to the systematic DISFRANCHISEMENT of blacks in the constitution of 1901. Kolb's career far outlasted Alabama populism. From 1911 to 1915 Kolb was once more Alabama commissioner of agriculture, and in 1914 he ran for governor in the Democratic primary. In 1914 Kolb clearly lost, but in 1892 and 1894 it is quite possible that he was counted out, as claimed by so many.

See S. Hackney, *Populism to Progressivism in Alabama* (1969); W. W. Rogers, *Agrarianism in Alabama* (1970); and C. G. Summersell, *Alabama Review* (Jan., 1955).

CHARLES G. SUMMERSELL
University of Alabama

KUDZU (*Pueraria thunbergiana*), a climbing, perennial legume indigenous to the Far East, was introduced into the South at the Japanese pavilion of the New Orleans exposition (1884–1886). It rapidly gained popularity as a decorative outdoor vine used to shade family porches until, at the turn of the century, attention shifted to its possibilities as a source of fodder and hay. The vine allegedly grew as much as a foot a day. As hay it could be harvested, cured, and stored within a 24-hour period, and kudzu leaves were equal in protein content to alfalfa, imported largely from the Middle West. In 1935 the U.S. Soil Conservation Service began promoting kudzu for the additional purpose of erosion control. Highway departments and farmers made extensive use of the vine to stabilize the soil of gullies and slopes and also to build up the nitrogen content of the soil. Kudzu was hailed as a "miracle plant" throughout the countryside of the depression-era South, but the plant's many drawbacks gradually made it seem more an annoyance than a miracle. Its rapidly growing vines choked trees, burdened power lines, and hindered efforts at reforestation. Greater specialization of agriculture led southern farmers to seek more suitable feed crops, and the development of less troublesome, deep-rooted grasses reduced kudzu's use in erosion control. Since the mid-1950s, new plantings of kudzu have been less frequent than efforts to eradicate it.

See J. J. Winberry and D. M. Jones, *Southeastern Geography* (Nov., 1973); P. R. Cargould, *Crops and Soils* (Dec., 1952); and R. McKee and J. L. Stephens, *Farmers Bulletin*, No. 1923 (1948).

KU KLUX KLAN ACTS.

There were three such laws enacted by Congress in 1870 and 1871 in response to widespread terrorism employed by such secret white organizations as the KU KLUX KLAN against black and white Republicans in the South and those who worked with them, such as school-teachers. The laws outlawed terrorist "conspiracies," made interference with voting a federal offense punishable in federal courts, and put elections of congressmen under federal control. The president was authorized to suspend the writ of habeas corpus and to use the army to enforce the laws. Strict enforcement of the laws in South Carolina resulted in 82 convictions and a sharp drop in terrorist activities. In Mississippi, where terrorists had been on a rampage of burning black schools and churches, torturing and killing teachers, and otherwise enforcing a "reign of terror" in some counties, the prospect of federal prosecution sufficed to bring about a sharp decline in terrorism. Enforcement of the laws had the support of leading southern planters and businessmen, who saw in the terrorists a menace to their rapprochement with northern business and political leaders.

With terrorism subdued, the rapprochement went on, symbolized by the prowhite South platform adopted by the Liberal Republicans in the ELECTION OF 1872. In that year also, an alliance between Democrats and Liberal Republicans in the House of Representatives weakened enforcement of the Ku Klux Klan Acts. In succeeding years the second GRANT ADMINISTRATION showed little interest in enforcing such of the laws as remained in force, and antiblack terrorism revived, especially in Mississippi and South Carolina. It played a significant role in the overthrow of Republican governments in those states in 1875–1876.

See R. Cruden, *Negro in Reconstruction* (1969); V. L. Wharton, *Negro in Mississippi* (1947); J. Williamson, *After Slavery* (1965); and W. E. B. Du Bois, *Black Reconstruction* (1935).

ROBERT CRUDEN
Lewis and Clark College

KU KLUX KLAN OF RECONSTRUCTION

existed at least briefly in every former Confederate state and in Kentucky as well. It was not, however, a single organization or even a loose confederation of local, state, and regional groups. Inspired by the notoriety of the Klan in Tennessee, several different Ku Klux Klans—with different relationships to one another—developed throughout the South. Indeed, North Carolina at one point had three independent orders of the KKK (the White Brotherhood, the Constitutional Guard, and the Invisible Empire), often with overlapping memberships. Moreover, several totally independent organizations grew up in various parts of the South, some of which used their own names interchangeably with that of the Klan: the Moderators in Kentucky, the Black Cavalry in Alabama, the Order of the Pale Faces in Tennessee, the Young Men's Democratic Clubs of Florida, the Knights of the Rising Sun in Texas, and the Knights of the White Camellia in Louisiana, Alabama, Texas, and Arkansas. All of these organizations inherited a tradition of vigilantism and flourished in an environment of VIOLENCE that they did not create. All drew their memberships from a broad range of white social and economic backgrounds. All practiced intimidation, coercion, whippings, beatings, and even murder in defense of white supremacy. But unlike previous vigilante groups in southern history, all functioned to a greater or lesser degree as paramilitary arms of the DEMOCRATIC PARTY.

The first organization formed and known as the Ku Klux Klan was founded by six Confederate veterans in Pulaski, Tenn., during May and June, 1866. After young men from the surrounding countryside sought initiation into the Klan, additional dens were organized in nearby localities. The original character and intent of this Klan was as undeniably innocent as were the oaths and rituals it borrowed from Kappa Alpha, a college social fraternity. Within weeks, however, members tired of playing pranks on one another and began finding greater sport in bullying local blacks and in intimidating those believed guilty of violating the region's traditional racial code. Then in April, 1867, the Klan was adopted and reorganized by the state's Democratic party leadership. Congress had passed the military Reconstruction Acts the previous month, and Generals JOHN C. BROWN and George W. Gordon, both natives of Pulaski, viewed an expanded version of the Klan as a possible instrument for mobilizing Democratic strength in the coming elections. The codes and rituals of the Klan took on a considerable resemblance to those of the Masons, and NATHAN BEDFORD FORREST was named its first (and only) Grand Wizard.

Whatever were the Klan's contributions and achievements in Democratic campaigns of the summer of 1867, it was neither credited with nor blamed for any of the state's acts of political violence. Following the reelection of Republican Governor W. G. BROWNLOW, however, political positions hardened, white vigilantism mounted, and the membership and activity of the Klan became more general during the winter of 1867–1868. Fearful that Brownlow might proclaim martial law, the leadership of the Conservative Democratic party sought to bring the rising level of violence under control. The state Grand Dragon of the KKK (General George Gordon?) ordered Klan members to cease all acts of violence, and there is some evidence that three members of the Klan were executed by their own organization for violations of that order. Yet Klan activity grew more frequent and more outrageous throughout 1868. Sporadic acts of violence continued past the presidential election and into the following winter. Finally, on February 20, 1869, Brownlow proclaimed martial law in nine counties of middle and western Tennessee. The proclamation was rescinded within a week, after Brownlow resigned to take a seat in the U.S. Senate; and, after the election (with Democratic support) of a moderate Republican governor that August, the Klan formally disbanded. Not until after the election of J. C. Brown as governor in November, 1870, however, was criticism by Democratic leaders effective enough to gradually end Klan violence in Tennessee.

Local units of the Klan and Klan-like organizations often engaged in terrorism to coerce social control over and economic advantage from their victims (sometimes as part of horse-stealing rings). Yet most victims were Republicans, and the general pattern of all Klan activity waxed and waned in accord with the political events in an area. In Virginia, for example, the Klan was organized in March, 1868, but, after the state's elections and constitutional convention were put off for at least one year, the Klan disappeared totally. Arkansas held its constitutional convention and its elections in 1868. Although that state's Klan focused most of its activity on disrupting voter registration, over 300 political killings were reported in the three months prior to the fall elections, including the murder of Little Rock's U.S. congressman J. M. Hinds.

In Louisiana the KKK was most extensively organized in the parishes above New Orleans. Within that city and in parishes to the south of it, the stronger organization was the Knights of the White Camellia. Organized by Colonel Alcibiade De Blanc in May, 1867, the Knights retained a greater degree of discipline than did any of the Ku Klux Klans. But greater discipline did not mean less violence. In New Orleans, where the Knights enlisted half the adult white male population, at least 63 persons were killed on the eve of the election of 1868. Statewide, over 1,000 killings marked electioneering between the time of the local elections in April and the presidential election in November. The results were dramatically tallied at the polls: 21 parishes that had cast 26,814 votes for Governor H. C. WARMOUTH delivered only 501 votes for U. S. Grant. Once the election was over, both the Louisiana Klan and the Knights of the White Camellia were formally disbanded.

Although the political outrages of vigilante groups tailed off markedly by the spring of 1869 in Louisiana, Texas, Arkansas, and Florida, in other states a mounting surge of terrorism rose to new peaks. North Carolina's Klans had been relatively orderly throughout the elections of 1868, but after inauguration of Republican Governor W. W. HOLDEN the gradually escalating acts of political terrorism reached a climax in the KIRK-HOLDEN WAR of 1870. Alabama's Knights of the White Camellia disbanded after the 1868 elections, and the state's Klan leadership ordered that organization dissolved in 1869. Thereafter, Klan activity in the state grew relatively less political in character but no less frequent. In April, 1869, Klansmen disrupted the reopening of the university at Tuscaloosa, and repeated violations of the peace throughout 1870 led several Democratic spokesmen to argue for election of their candidate as governor in order to put an end to Klan terror. Although ROBERT LINDSAY, the Democrat, won in 1870, the principal change noted by both Democratic and Republican observers was that its membership became more restricted to the "lower" and "meaner" elements of the state. Even though the Republicans recaptured the governorship and the statehouse in 1872, the Alabama Klan gradually wilted under mounting Democratic criticism and an increasingly hostile public opinion. Mississippi had little notable Klan activity prior to 1869, in part because not until that year did the state elections ratify a new constitution. Most volatile in seven counties along the Alabama state line, Mississippi's campaign of terror was directed against the new Republican public school system (and its agents) rather than against officeholders.

By the spring of 1871, a reluctant GRANT ADMINISTRATION and a hesitant Congress agreed on additional enforcement legislation. In May, 1870, Congress had enacted an enforcement act to support the Fifteenth Amendment. Although Section 6 of that act had made it a felony for two or more persons to enter into a conspiracy or to disguise themselves in order to deny anyone the franchise, Grant had been reluctant to invoke the military powers given him by that act. Moreover, Klan violence had become increasingly less political in the sense of Fifteenth Amendment rights. Accordingly, on March 23, 1871, Grant asked Congress for legislation to enforce the more general rights promised in the FOURTEENTH AMENDMENT. The KU KLUX KLAN ACT, as it was called, was enacted April 20, yet the president continued to hope that the act's presence on the statute books would suffice by itself and obviate the necessity of military action. In a few instances troops were dispatched to suppress Klan violence. Federal district attorneys utilizing this legislation found that federal juries, with members drawn from a larger geographical area than local juries, were less easily intimidated and more inclined to indict and convict. Yet more effective than this belated federal effort to suppress the Klan was the growing refusal of southern whites, particularly leaders of the Democratic party, to countenance the continued and indiscriminate terrorism of the Klan. By the end of 1872 only sporadic Klan activity remained scattered across the South.

Apologists for the Ku Klux Klan have argued that the organization was necessary during Reconstruction to control the lawless behavior of the freedmen. If so, black crime was punished at the cost of a massive rise in white crime. And, unless one is willing to maintain a spurious distinction between the criminal activity of defenders of different races, opposing political parties, and conflicting social philosophies, such a defense of the Klan and related organizations is insupportable. NIGHT-RIDING, BULLDOZING, and WHITECAPPING continued to be parts of the southern social and economic environment into the twentieth century. The organized intimidation of voters and an occasional political riot continued to be used by Democratic party leaders until the wholesale DISFRANCHISEMENT of blacks one and a half generations later. Yet never again would leaders of the Democratic party employ secret organizations that might take on a life independent of party needs to accomplish victory at the polls.

See A. W. Trelease, *White Terror* (1971), standard and comprehensive; S. F. Horn, *Invisible Empire* (1939), undocumented and pro-Klan; W. P. Randel, *KKK* (1965), undocumented and anti-Klan; J. C. Lester and D. L. Wilson, *KKK: Origin, Growth, and Disbandment* (1884, 1905), by two of original founders; and *Senate Reports*, 42nd Cong., 2nd Sess., No. 41 or *House Reports*, 42nd Cong., 2nd Sess., No. 22.

KU KLUX KLAN OF TWENTIETH CENTURY.

Taking its name from the terrorist organization that opposed black voting in the South during Reconstruction, the Klan was revived by an Alabama-born fraternalist "Colonel" William J. Simmons. Stimulated by tales of the Reconstruction Klans and by the success of D. W. Griffith's epic movie *The Birth of a Nation* (based on THOMAS DIXON's 1905 novel *The Clansman*), Simmons rededicated the Klan on Thanksgiving eve, 1915, at STONE MOUNTAIN, Ga. He hoped for a mildly successful fraternal order to which he could sell memberships, robes, and insurance.

After World War I, two hard-driving salesmen, Edward Y. Clarke and Elizabeth Tyler, turned the Klan into a national success. Newspapers headlined the Klan, and it spread through the South and Southwest, out to the West Coast, into the Great Lakes states, and up the Atlantic seaboard. Everybody talked about it. The New York press, led by the *World*, attacked it, and inland America rushed to join it.

The main appeal of the Klan was as a fraternal lodge, a protector, and a refuge for old-stock America. The Klan promised to clean up politics, enforce PROHIBITION, and defend small-town morality and traditional American values. Although the Klan was also anti-Negro, anti-Jew, and anti-Oriental, it focused on immigrant Roman Catholicism as the principal threat. It was most popular in the small towns, but the Klan spread also into the growing cities.

Directed from its Imperial Palace on Peachtree

Street in Atlanta, the Klan at its peak in 1924 had more than 2 million members. It was strongest in Georgia, Alabama, Louisiana, Texas, Oklahoma, California, Oregon, Colorado, Kansas, Missouri, Illinois, Indiana, Ohio, Pennsylvania, New Jersey, and New York. Many policemen and politicians belonged or deferred to the Klan, and it helped elect 11 governors and 16 U.S. senators, some of them Klan members. Senators whom the Klan helped elect included Earle Mayfield (Texas), HUGO BLACK and TOM HEFLIN (Alabama), William J. Harris (Georgia), L. D. Tyson (Tennessee), and Frederick Sackett (Kentucky). Among the governors were Clifford Walker (Georgia), Bibb Graves (Alabama), and Austin Peay (Tennessee). The Klan tended to be Democratic in the South and Republican in the North. In 1924 a bitter fight over the Klan split the Democratic National Convention.

The Klan brought excitement and violence, mainly against fellow white Protestant southerners, rather than against blacks and outsiders. Although there were some Klan floggings and terrorism elsewhere and battles with anti-Klansmen in the Northeast, the chief violence was in Texas, Oklahoma, Alabama, Georgia, North Carolina, Florida, and Louisiana. Klan leadership turned out to be inept and exploitive. Corruption, immorality, violence, internal Klan conflict, and community disruption destroyed Klan power. The Memphis *Commercial Appeal*, Columbus (Ga.) *Enquirer-Sun*, and Montgomery *Advertiser* each received a Pulitzer Prize for their Klan coverage.

During the GREAT DEPRESSION Klan strength narrowed to the Southeast, where it had friends such as Georgia Governors E. D. Rivers and EUGENE TALMADGE. It focused its attack on the Negroes, Jews, communism, NEW DEAL, and LABOR UNION organizers in the industrializing Piedmont. There was occasional national publicity over the Joseph Shoemaker murder in Tampa, Fla. (1935), and the appointment of Hugo Black to the U.S. Supreme Court (1937).

Hiram Wesley Evans, the Dallas dentist who had captured the Klan from Simmons in 1922, reportedly sold it to Terre Haute, Ind., veterinarian James A. Colescott in 1939. Back taxes, protest over association with the German-American Bund, and World War II led Colescott to dissolve the Klan. An Atlanta obstetrician, Dr. Samuel Green, revived the Klan in the Southeast after the war, but when he died in 1949 the Klan splintered out of control. States and cities passed antimask laws, and Klan floggers went to jail. Dynamite became a Klan weapon and anti-Semitism its credo, but the Klans remained more a group striving for social recognition than an anti–civil rights movement.

In the 1960s Tuscaloosa rubber worker Robert M. Shelton, Jr., established leadership over most of the southern Klans. Although Klan highway patrollers were responsible for murdering Colonel Lemuel Penn (1964) and Viola Liuzzo (1965), Shelton generally kept his United Klans under control, aided by new Klan-stimulated civil rights laws and FBI pressure, lack of community support, and a greater likelihood of jury conviction. The most violent Klansmen were Mississippi's independent White Knights, who killed three civil rights workers in Philadelphia, Miss. (1964), and others, before being broken up by the FBI. In the 1970s new young Klansmen sought a slightly improved image and recruits in racially troubled northern cities, but Klan forces remained small, cautious, divided, and politically impotent. Since the 1920s Klans have continued to exist, but no one has been able to put together a Klan movement.

See C. C. Alexander, *KKK in Southwest* (1965), best state/regional study; K. T. Jackson, *KKK in City* (1967), valuable information but overstates urban uniqueness; and D. M. Chalmers, *Hooded Americanism* (1965, 1968) and *Mississippi Quarterly* (1965).

DAVID M. CHALMERS
University of Florida

L

LABADISTS followers of the French mystic theosophist Jean de Labadie (1610–1674), established the second Protestant commune in America (PLOCKHOY) in 1684 at the head of the Chesapeake in Bohemia Manor, Md. They were led by two Dutchmen, Jasper Dankärts and Petrus Sluyter, who thought they were settling in Pennsylvania. Recruits arrived from Germantown near Philadelphia, mostly disaffected MENNONITES. All material things were held in common, and the regimen was extremely ascetic. But the common property was divided in 1698, and, when Conrad Beissel of the Ephrata commune in Pennsylvania visited the Labadists in 1721, the community was in a state of disintegration. Bishop Sluyter died 1722.

See B. B. James, *Labadist Colony in Maryland* (1973); H. C. Murphy's Long Island Historical Society, *Memoirs* (1867), I; and J. F. Sachse, *German Sectarians of Pennsylvania* (1899), I.

E. GORDON ALDERFER
Washington, D.C.

LABOR UNIONS. In the antebellum South the widespread use of slave labor and the development of an agricultural economy slowed the urban and industrial growth critical to the development of a strong, mature labor movement. The Civil War and Reconstruction exacerbated already existing imbalances in the southern economy, but the war was a necessary catharsis, and during the 1880s the South experienced a mini-industrial revolution (INDUSTRIALIZATION). Although the southern economy grew slowly thereafter, the origins of the modern southern labor movement can be found in those post-Reconstruction years.

Although labor organization began on a local basis in the South during the early years of the nineteenth century, it remained shallow and localized. Following the Civil War the Knights of Labor was the first national organization to launch a sustained campaign to unionize the South. Because of its horizontal method of organization, the Knights had considerable success, especially among blacks and farmers. But its strength was also its weakness. The inclusive and reformist nature of the Knights tilted it toward political and cooperative ventures, inhibiting the development of collective bargaining and stable trade union-

ism. Nevertheless, the Knights had a significant impact on the South; at its peak, as many as 50,000 southern workers held Knights of Labor membership cards. Its highly publicized activities, including such dramatic conflicts as the 1886 Augusta, Ga., textile strike and the Southwest railroad strike instigated by Jay Gould, introduced the idea of trade unionism and collective action to large numbers of southern laborers.

The greatest benefactor of this groundwork was the American Federation of Labor and its constituent national trade unions. A number of influential AFL national unions first organized in the South. Atlanta, for example, give birth to the dominant section of the International Brotherhood of Boilermakers, Iron Shipbuilders, and Helpers in 1888 as well as the International Association of Machinists and the International Brotherhood of Blacksmiths, Drop Forgers, and Helpers in 1889. Other national unions originating in the South include the Brotherhood of Maintenance of Way Employees (Demopolis, Ala., 1887); the Brotherhood of Painters, Decorators, and Paperhangers of America (Baltimore, 1887); the Paving Cutters' Union of the United States of America and Canada (Lithonia, Ga., 1901); the National Association of Postal Supervisors (Louisville, 1908); and the Glass Bottle Blowers Association of the United States and Canada (Baltimore, 1890).

The entry of the AFL into the southern labor scene introduced a new note of stability and longevity. Skilled craftsmen, especially in the building trades and among printers, railroaders, and dock workers, built effective local unions. Moreover, most cities organized central labor unions, and by 1919 state federations existed in all southern states. Organization, however, remained shallow and failed to encompass many of those workers most in need of the cloak of trade unionism, especially in the growing TEXTILE INDUSTRY.

Closely following the pattern of the national trade union movement, organized labor in the South grew rapidly during World War I but fell into an extended period of decline and disintegration during the 1920s. Only unions composed of the most skilled workers survived the decade, and even those were severely tested by the GREAT DEPRESSION of the thirties. During the depression decade, the South was not only, in the words of

Franklin D. Roosevelt, "the Nation's No. 1 economic problem," but became also the American labor movement's most glaring failure. After the depression, however, favorable federal government policies, continuing industrialization, and the emergence of the Congress of Industrial Organizations all contributed to the resurgence of organized labor in the South. Moreover, both the national labor movement and the various international unions extended their efforts to organize the South. Southern organizing drives, such as the much publicized Operation Dixie after WORLD WAR II, were usually disappointing, but they reflected a growing commitment to unionize the South. Although membership in the area grew steadily after the mid-thirties, 40 years later the South remained the least organized section of the United States.

The retarded growth of the southern labor movement resulted primarily from the South's comparatively slow economic development. Employers not only made effective use of such traditional antiunion weapons as blacklisting, espionage, yellow-dog contracts, injunctions, welfare capitalism, and governmental strikebreaking, but also took advantage of circumstances peculiar to the South. Whether or not race was or remains the CENTRAL THEME of southern history, it was a major barrier to union organization. Until the 1930s employers remained proficient in the art of dividing the working class by playing off one race against the other.

The nature of southern industry also inhibited labor organization. Until recently, the single-plant firm, often dispersed throughout rural areas, was the predominant industrial unit, and it proved highly resistant to trade unionism. Typically, a close, almost paternalistic relationship developed between management and labor. The millowner often assumed an influential role in the operation of schools, churches, chambers of commerce, local elections, and other community affairs. When necessary, the owner unleashed these reserves against trade union organizers, threatening the existing pattern of labor relations. Extensive employment of women and children in the industrial labor force, antiunion attitudes and activities of numerous religious leaders, and the antagonistic attitude of many local and state officials further retarded the growth of trade unionism in the South. Conversely, trade union organizers had their greatest success in organizing the southern units of large multiplant firms headquarters outside the south.

Trade unionism has had a significant, long-term impact on the following southern industries: coal, construction, lumber, printing, railroads, textiles, and water transportation.

The Knights of Labor first entered the coalfields of Tennessee, Alabama, West Virginia, and Kentucky, and the United Mine Workers of America, after its organization in 1890, continued the effort. Recognizing that nonunion mines in the South constantly threatened the stability of their organizations in the North, UMW officials made special efforts to organize the South. Until the late 1930s, these efforts proved largely futile. Unlike in most other southern industries, race was a relatively minor handicap to the organization of coal miners. Nevertheless, the highly competitive nature of the coal industry, the use of convicts as strikebreakers, the existence of company towns, and the utilization of traditional antiunion weapons retarded organization for many years. By the end of World War II, however, North-South differentials ended as coal miners became one of the best-organized groups of workers in the South.

Construction unions contributed the largest membership to the southern labor movement. Carpenters, painters, bricklayers and various stoneworkers first organized during the mid-nineteenth century, and they were followed much later by electricians, plumbers, and other craftsmen in the building trades. The growth of building-trades unions in the South closely paralleled national patterns, normally growing during prosperous times and declining during periods of recession and depression. The building-trades unions actively discriminated against black workers and made a strong effort to restrict them to nonunion trades.

The Industrial Workers of the World had its greatest impact in the South among workers in the Texas and Louisiana lumber industry. In 1910 IWW supporters organized the Brotherhood of Timber Workers, which had a brief but dramatic history. Due in part to an open membership policy, the union grew rapidly. This so alarmed employers that the Southern Lumber Operators' Association was revived to spearhead the fight against the union. Unsuccessful strikes in 1912 against mills owned by the Santa Fe Railroad in Louisiana revealed not only increasingly effective employer resistance but growing community opposition to the IWW; the union disappeared shortly thereafter. Effective organization awaited the 1930–1940 period and the emergence of the International Woodworkers of America as a strong and stable national union.

New Orleans typographers organized the first known printing trade union in the South in 1810. During the following years, similar unions organized in cities throughout the South, and many of them affiliated with the National Typographical Union (later the International Typographical Union) after its organization in 1852. The Civil War temporarily disrupted the relationship between the ITU and its southern locals, but shortly thereafter the southern locals reaffiliated and became strong local units of the national union. As technological change gradually introduced new crafts and skills, national unions of printing pressmen, stereotypers, electrotypers, photoengravers, compositors, and bookbinders emerged. These unions were subject to varying economic vicissitudes but grew steadily stronger in part due to their enlightened resolution of the divisive race issue.

In the railroad industry, southern locals of the four major operating trades—engineers, firemen, conductors, and trainmen—were organized shortly after the creation of the national unions. Moreover, a number of national unions of workers closely associated with the railroad industry originated in the South, including machinists, blacksmiths, boilermakers, telegraphers, and maintenance of way employees. By 1900 relatively strong and stable unions represented most skilled workers on southern railroads, and, as a result of sympathetic federal policies during World War I, union organizations encompassed virtually all southern railroad workers. After the war, however, the failure of the national shopmen's strike of 1922 signaled a precipitant decline, especially among nonoperating unions. The failure of the railroad unions to organize the large number of black workers made a large, potential strikebreaking force available to antiunion employers.

Organized labor's greatest failure in the South lay in its efforts to organize textiles, the South's leading manufacturing industry. During the late nineteenth century, the highly competitive textile industry began moving South in search of lower taxes, reduced transportation costs, and cheap labor. The history of textile organizing efforts contains a lengthy recital of lost strikes characterized by such dramatic failures as the conflicts at Augusta in 1898 and 1902; Danville, Va., 1901; Atlanta, 1913; Kannapolis and Concord City, N.C., 1921; Elizabethtown, Tenn., 1929; Gastonia and Marion, N.C., 1929 (GASTONIA STRIKE); and the historic general strike of 1934. Although the Communist-inspired National Textile Workers Union conducted the bitter strike in Gastonia, the predominant union during these years was the United Textile Workers of America. Textile employers effectively resisted union organization in spite of the National Labor Relations Act of 1935; the CIO, which launched a major organizing offensive in 1937 through the Textile Workers Organizing Committee; and the organizing competition between the UTW-AFL and the Textile Workers Union of America-CIO. Bringing the textile workers of the South under the trade union umbrella has been a long, difficult, expensive, and so far uncompleted undertaking.

Because of the large, bulky exports of cotton and tobacco, waterfront unions of screwmen, who compressed cotton bales, and longshoremen appeared very early in the ports of the Gulf Coast, but the race issue was a source of constant disruption. Large numbers of black laborers worked the docks after the Civil War, and employers often succeeded in dividing the labor force through appeals to racial fears and antagonism. In an effort to resolve this problem, the waterfront unions organized black workers (usually in segregated locals), introduced work sharing, and promoted coordinated bargaining. Like so many other unions, the waterfront unions prospered during World War I, but unsuccessful strikes during the early 1920s virtually eliminated trade unionism in several important Gulf Coast ports. Trade unionism was not revived until the 1930s, when the maritime unions also began vigorous organizing activities.

See, for best survey of southern labor, F. R. Marshall, *Labor in South* (1967). See also G. B. Tindall, *Origins of New South* (1967); A. Berglund, G. T. Starnes, and F. T. deVyver, *Labor in Industrial South* (1930); D. McCracken, *Strike Injunction in New South* (1931); L. R. Mason, *To Win These Rights* (1952); F. Meyers, *Southern Economic Journal* (April, 1940), Knights of Labor; R. B. Morris, *Labor and Nation* (May–June, 1948), Old South: and U.S. Department of Labor, *Bulletin No. 898* (1946). Accounts of state and local movements include H. Head, "Alabama" (Ph.D. dissertation, University of Alabama, 1954); G. G. Kundahl, Jr., "Alabama" (Ph.D. dissertation, University of Alabama, 1967): R. D. Ward and W. H. Rogers, *Labor Revolt in Alabama* (1965); W. E. Cullison, "Union Membership in Arkansas, Louisiana, and Oklahoma" (Ph.D. dissertation, University of Oklahoma, 1967); M. G. Evans, "Georgia" (Ph.D. dissertation, University of Chicago, 1929); W. Flint, *Labor History* (Winter, 1968), Florida, 1919–20; K. M. Thompson, *Louisiana* (1959); R. W. Shugg, *Louisiana Historical Quarterly* (April, 1938), New Orleans, and *Louisiana* (1931); A. R. Pearce, "New Orleans" (Ph.D. dissertation, Tulane, 1938); D. C. Mosely, *South Atlantic Quarterly* (July, 1935), Mississippi, and *Social Forces* (May, 1933); H. E. Jolley, *North Carolina Historical Review* (July, 1953), North Carolina; B. R. Skelton, "North Carolina and South Carolina" (Ph.D. dissertation, Duke, 1965); Y. Snowden, *South Carolina* (1914); L. R. Tripp et al., *Labor-Management Relations in Western Kentucky* (1954); K. A. Harvey, *Maryland Coal Region* (1969) and *Labor History* (Fall, 1969), Knights of Labor in Maryland; G. M. Fink, *Missouri* (1974) and *Missouri Historical Review* (July, 1970); L. Meriwether, *Missouri Historical Review* (Oct., 1920);

E. J. Forsythe, "St. Louis" (Ph.D. dissertation, University of Missouri, 1956); K. Born, *West Tennessee Historical Society Publications* (1967), Memphis; G. L. Mullenix, "Texas" (Ph.D. dissertation, University of Texas, 1954); J. V. Reese, *Labor History* (Winter, 1970), Texas; R. A. Allen, *Organized Labor in Texas* (1941); H. Shapiro, *Southwestern Social Science Quarterly* (Sept., 1955), San Antonio; G. H. Haines, "Virginia" (Ph.D. dissertation, Clark, 1946); E. L. K. Harris and F. J. Krebs, *West Virginia* (1960); C. P. Anson, "West Virginia" (Ph.D. dissertation, University of North Carolina, 1940); and T. E. Posey, "West Viginia" (Ph.D. dissertation, University of Wisconsin, 1949). Labor in textile industry can be found in O. Carlson, *Current History* (Nov., 1934); B. M. Cannon, "Social Deterrents to Unionization" (Ph.D. dissertation, Harvard, 1952); W. F. Dunne, *Gastonia* (1929); C. A. Gulick, Jr., *Quarterly Journal of Economics* (Aug., 1932); H. J. Lahne, *Cotton Mill Worker* (1944); M. A. McLaurin, *Paternalism and Protest* (1971); K. Meiklejohn and P. Nehemkis, *Southern Labor in Revolt* (1930); B. Mitchell, *Rise of Cotton Mills in South* (1921) and *Harvard Business Review* (April, 1930); G. S. Mitchell, *Textile Unionism* (1931); M. E. Reed, *Labor History* (Spring, 1973), Augusta strike, 1886; G. T. Schwenning, *Journal of Political Economy* (Dec., 1931); and T. Tippett, *When Southern Labor Stirs* (1931). Waterfront unions have been analyzed by R. C. Francis, *Opportunity* (March, 1936); C. G. Miller, "New Orleans Longshoremen's Union" (Ph.D. dissertation, Louisiana State University, 1962); and H. R. Northrop, *Political Science Quarterly* (Dec., 1942). For lumber and paper unions, see C. Hall, *International Socialist Review* (July, Dec., 1912); H. Lathan, Jr., "Union Organization in Two Southern Paper Mills" (Ph.D. dissertation, Louisiana State University, 1961); and M. E. Reed, *Labor History* (Winter, 1972), lumberjacks and longshoremen. For accounts of black workers in South, see H. Cayton and G. S. Mitchell, *Black Workers and New Unions* (1939); F. R. Marshall, *Negro and Organized Labor* (1965); G. S. Mitchell, *Southern Economic Journal* (Oct., 1931); E. W. Rogers, *Labor History* (Summer, 1969). There are two major collections of documentary materials: Southern Labor Archives, Georgia State University, Atlanta; and Labor Archives, University of Texas, Arlington. Of the major national collections, see Archives of Labor History and Urban Affairs, Wayne State University, Detroit.

GARY M. FINK
Georgia State University

LADIES' GUNBOAT SOCIETIES

were the outgrowth of popular support in the South, especially in early 1862, for building ironclads, the Confederate navy's new weapon. Patriotic women's associations, the first in New Orleans in 1861, were organized to solicit contributions and to raise money in a variety of ways—bazaars, auctions, and gunboat "fairs"—to build these boats. Amid much publicity, strong competition developed among all the southern states, and several vessels were constructed either entirely or at least partially with such funds.

See W. Still, *Iron Afloat* (1971); and M. B. Chesnut, *Diary from Dixie*, ed. B. A. Williams (1949).

LAFAYETTE, LA. (pop. 68,908), was settled by French ACADIANS about the time of the American Revolution. Approximately 50 miles southwest of Baton Rouge on the Vermilion River, the community—originally known as Vermilionville—remained little more than a village until connected to Houston, Tex., in 1878 by rail. The city has since thrived first as a shipping point and market for area agriculture and later as a manufacturing town and a producer of petroleum, sulfur, and salt. Renamed Lafayette in 1884, the city is the home of the University of Southwestern Louisiana (1898). It is a major center for the petroleum industry and a thriving rail and river port, yet the city retains much of its CAJUN character and French is commonly spoken.

See H. L. Griffin, *Attakapas Country* (1959) and *History of Lafayette* (1936), both standard; W. H. Perrin, *Southwest Louisiana Biography* (1891, 1971); and Q. M. Anders, *Some Early Families* (1970) and "History of Institutions and Organizations of Lafayette," mimeo manuscript, Lafayette Public Library.

LAFFITE, JEAN (1780?–1825?), also spelled Lafitte, was a leader of Louisiana privateer-pirates who preyed on Spanish and probably neutral shipping in the Gulf of Mexico (1810–1814), selling the plunder in New Orleans. During the WAR OF 1812 (September, 1814), the British, trying to establish a presence in the lower Mississippi Valley by taking New Orleans, sought Laffite's help. Essentially out of self-interest rather than principle, Lafitte chose to aid the United States instead, since he wanted pardon for commercial irregularities and restoration of confiscated goods. The Americans needed his military supplies, men, and topographical knowledge. His artillery was particularly significant in repulsing the British before the city, January 8, 1815 (NEW ORLEANS, BATTLE OF). Laffite resumed his former activities, eventually moving near Galveston, and disappeared in the early 1820s. Literature on him is voluminous and myth laden.

See L. Saxon, *Lafitte the Pirate* (1930), most satisfactory biography; S. C. Arthur, *Jean Laffite* (1952), details a later Laffite career, including association with Karl Marx, though historians hedge on authenticity of family papers used by author; and *Journal of Jean Lafitte* (1958), a rambling reminiscence, also in these papers. Robert C. Vogel of Minneapolis has compiled a Laffite bibliography.

PAUL WOEHRMANN
Milwaukee Public Library

LA GRANGE, GA. (pop. 23,301), 39 miles north of Columbus, is a textile and lumber center and the home of La Grange College. When the marquis de Lafayette visited this log settlement in 1825, he favorably compared the surrounding countryside with that of his estate, La Grange in France. The village adopted the name to honor the marquis, and it flourished during the antebellum period as a cotton market. The town escaped destruction during the Civil War, permitting the survival of many Greek Revival homes.

See files of La Grange *News* (1842–).

LAIRD RAMS were two warships built at the Laird shipyard in Birkenhead, England, for Captain James D. Bulloch, a resourceful Confederate agent. To raise the BLOCKADE of southern ports and to maximize its offensive capabilities, the Confederate government authorized Bulloch in the summer of 1862 to order the Laird rams. Acting as a private citizen, Bulloch contracted this "commercial transaction" for delivery the following spring. To avoid violation of British laws, the design of the rams facilitated installment of appliances of war after departure from Britain, and their ultimate destination was kept secret. In cooperation with Laird engineers, Bulloch planned these rams, capable of a speed of ten knots, to pierce ships below their protective armor and thus "Sweep away the entire blockading fleet of the enemy." Together with corvettes and ironclads secretly being built in France, the Laird rams were to form the nucleus of the Confederacy's offensive naval power.

Once alert northern agents kept their watchful eyes on these projects, Bulloch took precautionary measures. Concerned about possible British government intervention and aware of northern determination to block the development of a Confederate navy, he arranged the legal transfer of the Laird rams to a French firm. But this ruse failed when, unexpectedly, Napoleon III decided against any entanglement in these Confederate schemes. To the North's relief, moreover, the British government's detention and subsequent seizure of the rams in October, 1863, led to the complete collapse of Bulloch's undertaking.

See F. J. Merli, *Great Britain and Confederate Navy* (1970), excellent; W. D. Jones, *Confederate Rams* (1961); J. D. Bulloch, *Secret Service* (1883); B. Adams, *Massachusetts Historical Society Proceedings* (Dec., 1911); and D. H. Maynard, *Mississippi Valley Historical Review* (June, 1958). Also useful are C. F. Adams, *Charles Francis Adams* (1900); G. Welles, *Diary* (1911); and J. Bigelow, *Confederate Navy* (1888).

HENRY BLUMENTHAL
Rutgers University

LAKE CHARLES, LA. (pop. 77,998), and the lake on which it fronts are both said to have been named for one Carlos Salia (or Charles Sallier), who settled here about 1781. By the time of the Civil War, a small town had grown up on the lakefront approximately 55 miles east of Beaumont, Tex. Active development of the town, however, awaited the postwar completion of the Southern Pacific's rail link to Houston and New Orleans. Although prospering as a shipping point for area lumber and rice, the city became something of a boomtown after the discovery of nearby petroleum and sulfur early in the twentieth century. A deepwater port since 1926, modern Lake Charles manufactures fertilizers, turpentine, chemicals, synthetic rubber, and construction materials while continuing to serve as a processing and shipping point for rice, lumber, cattle, and a variety of petroleum products.

See Lake Charles *American Press* (1895–).

LAKELAND, FLA. (pop. 41,550), is approximately 30 miles east of Tampa. Although first settled in the 1870s, the town did not begin to develop until 1884, when the South Florida Railway completed a line to this site. Its central location in the state, its relatively high altitude, and the availability of pure water combined to make Lakeland a national railroad center. The closing of the large railroad shops in 1926 and 1927 dealt the city a serious economic blow, but Lakeland had developed by that time a far more diversified economy. Nearby phosphate deposits and the area citrus industry had been developed, and the many small lakes that surround the town had made it a popular inland resort. Besides Florida Southern College (1885), the Florida Citrus Commission is located here. The modern city also continues to serve as a shipping center for citrus fruits, and its industries produce fertilizer, leather goods, boats, trailers, and canning machinery.

See files of Lakeland *Ledger* (1924–).

LAMAR, CHARLES AUGUSTUS LAFAYETTE (1823–1865), was a member of a pominent Georgia family that included MIRABEAU B. and LUCIUS

Q. C. LAMAR. Charles was active in attempts to annex Mexico and Cuba and to remove federal restrictions on the importation of slaves. Between 1857 and 1860 he organized a company that sent the ships *Rawlins, Richard Cobden,* and *Wanderer* to the coast of Africa. In 1858, after landing 750 slaves at Savannah, the *Wanderer* was seized and Lamar arrested. Within a few months both were released. It is thought that Lamar landed a final cargo in 1860, which would make him one of the last of the American slavers. He raised a Georgia regiment and saw action through the Civil War. On April 16, 1865, he was shot by Union troops and is called the last man killed in combat in the Civil War.

See *North American Review* (Nov., 1886), Lamar papers.

ROBERT T. BROWN
Westfield State College

LAMAR, JOSEPH RUCKER (1857–1916), was born in Elbert County, Ga. He attended Richmond Academy and the University of Georgia and graduated from Bethany College, in West Virginia, in 1877. After briefly studying law at Washington and Lee, he was admitted to the Georgia bar in 1878. Lamar practiced law in Augusta and was twice elected to the state legislature (1886–1887, 1888–1889). In 1893 he was appointed one of three commissioners to rewrite the law codes of Georgia and soon after was named an associate justice of the state supreme court. After an illustrious career on the state bench (1902–1905), Lamar was appointed an associate justice of the U.S. Supreme Court (1911–1916) by President William Howard Taft. In 1914 President Woodrow Wilson appointed Lamar a commissioner to represent the United States at the Niagara Falls Conference at which Argentina, Brazil, and Chile were mediating a serious dispute between the United States and Mexico.

See C. P. Lamar, *Life of J. R. Lamar* (1926); L. Dinnerstein, in L. Friedman and F. Israel (eds.), *Justices of U.S. Supreme Court* (1969); W. J. Northen, *Men of Mark in Georgia* (1908); and G. S. Price, *American Bar Association Journal* (Dec., 1948).

C. CHARLTON MOSELEY
Georgia Southern College

LAMAR, LUCIUS QUINTUS CINCINNATUS (1825–1893), although popularly known as a southern advocate, was a nationalist as well as a sectionalist and is perhaps best remembered as a conciliator. His plea in his eulogy of Charles Sumner for reconciliation between the North and South and between black and white and his support of Rutherford B. Hayes for president cast him in the latter role. Before the Civil War he was a staunch defender of states' rights, and he was the principal author of Mississippi's ordinance of secession. He served the Confederate States of America as an army officer and diplomat, but he was a pragmatist in politics.

A native of Putnam County, Ga., Lamar came to be identified with Mississippi. He represented that state as a congressman in the late 1850s and again from 1873 to 1877 and as a senator from 1877 to 1885. He resigned from the U.S. Senate to be secretary of the interior, and in 1888 he became an associate justice of the U.S. Supreme Court. As secretary he was a competent administrator and was reform minded on Indian policy and conservation. While associate justice he wrote few dissenting opinions, which suggests that his judicial philosophy was very similar to that of the other members of the Court.

In private life Lamar was at various times a lawyer, university professor, and planter. His health was never robust, and illness cut short his service with the 19th Mississippi Regiment during the Civil War. He never reached Russia as the Confederate commissioner to that country, but he spent several months in England and France studying European attitudes toward the Confederacy before he was recalled. Between the end of the war and his return to Congress in 1873, he worked to restore home rule in Mississippi.

In Congress, Lamar was considered a moderate on sectional issues, but in supporting fusion politics in Mississippi he did not abandon white supremacy. An outstanding orator, he was a leading spokesman for the NEW SOUTH. He came to be widely regarded as an eminent statesman, and as a conciliator he is still honored. In 1969 a group of progressive southerners organized as the L. Q. C. Lamar Society to influence the development of the economic and social potential of the South.

See W. A. Cate, *L. Q. C. Lamar* (1935); E. Mayes, *L. Q. C. Lamar* (1896), life and speeches; J. B. Murphy, *L. Q. C. Lamar* (1973); New York *Times* (April 20, 1970); and Lamar-Mayes Papers, Mississippi Department of Archives and History.

MATTIE UNDERWOOD RUSSELL
Duke University

LAMAR, MIRABEAU BUONAPARTE (1789–1859), born in Georgia, became a poet and journalist and entered politics as secretary to Governor George Troup. After the death of his wife, he traveled to Texas, arriving in time to fight at SAN JACINTO and then to be named secretary of war.

He was elected vice-president of the Republic of Texas in 1836 and then president in 1838. Lamar began his administration (1838–1841) with a vision of a strong, independent Texas extending all the way to the Pacific. His aggressive foreign policy resulted in recognition by major European powers, but it failed to secure either foreign loans or Mexican acceptance of independence. He was more successful at pacifying the Indians and organizing frontier defenses. He also encouraged legislation providing for public education and earned the title Father of Education in Texas. Lamar's fiscal policies, which left Texas near bankruptcy, and the disastrous Santa Fe expedition both contributed greatly to a decline in his popularity. He also served in the Mexican War and was U.S. minister to Nicaragua in 1858 and 1859.

See C. Gulick (ed.), *Lamar Papers* (1921), originals in University of Texas Archives; K. Sexton, *Texana* (Summer, 1973); P. Graham, *Lamar* (1938), a literary biography; and H. P. Gambrell, *Lamar* (1934).

RAY F. BROUSSARD
University of Georgia

LAND GRANTS. The British, like other Europeans, acknowledged only the Indian's right of occupation, when any claim was recognized, and asserted the "exclusive right" to extinguish that title. The British crown usually made grants in America to organized companies or to proprietors for colonization, and they in turn passed on titles to individuals. The southern colonies included primarily grants to individuals rather than the community-oriented town and township in New England. Vestiges of the feudal system were evident in the proprietary grants of some 60 manors in seventeenth-century Maryland.

Most land was granted by HEADRIGHT, by direct purchase or "treasury right," by reward for public service such as military bounties after the American Revolution, and by encouragement to frontier colonization such as the OHIO COMPANY in 1749. The headright provided most often for only 50 acres for each person, but the abuse of the system and the transition to direct purchase both contributed to the growth of large plantations in the South.

French grants (including seignorial estates) along the Mississippi River in Louisiana and Spanish grants from Florida to Texas were usually recognized by the British and the Americans after transitions in jurisdiction. The vagueness of boundaries, however, and the questions of full validation of titles led to many years of litigation, such as the Clamorgan grant in Arkansas and the claims by the baron de Bastrop along the Ouachita River, which were later acquired by Aaron Burr during his controversial activities in the West. Following the introduction of the orderly system of LAND SURVEYS of the Land Ordinance of 1785, the SOUTHWEST ORDINANCE of 1790 extended these provisions for surveys to areas in the South and Southwest that had not already been granted by states or been included in earlier French or Spanish grants.

See L. C. Gray, *History of Agriculture in Southern U.S.* (1933); A. M. Sakolski, *Land Tenure and Land Taxation* (1957); M. Harris, *Origin of Land Tenure System* (1953); P. A. Bruce, *Economic History of Virginia* (1896); and W. S. Robinson, *Land Grants in Virginia* (1957).

W. STITT ROBINSON
University of Kansas

LAND SPECULATION constitutes a major theme throughout southern history. Royal and proprietary grants and the HEADRIGHT and QUITRENT systems initiated great holdings: the Calverts' and Carrolls', GRANVILLE TRACT, MISSISSIPPI BUBBLE, CAROLANA, CROZAT GRANT, and CÔTE DES ALLEMANDS. Prominent families successively engrossed the choice lands from the tidelands to the Great Valley: the Washingtons, Lees, Randolphs, Byrds, Carters, and Wade Hamptons. Rival groups formed companies to obtain trans-Allegheny grants—OHIO COMPANY, MISSISSIPPI COMPANY, LOYAL COMPANY, GEORGIANA COLONY, WATAUGA ASSOCIATION, and TRANSYLVANIA COMPANY—involving leading colonials and British officials. Restrictive royal policies (PROCLAMATION OF 1763; TRYON'S LINE) thwarted their success. Speculators fanned the revolutionary flames and influenced state cessions of western land claims, public domain, and Indian policies of the new republic.

Postrevolutionary ventures featured the state of FRANKLIN, the Spanish intrigues, Muscle Shoals (1783), and Yazoo (1789) fiascoes; Kentucky grant duplications, title controversies, and "bluegrass barons," involving machinations of prominent southwestern speculators JOHN SEVIER, ELIJAH CLARKE, WILLIAM BLOUNT, JAMES WILKINSON *et al.*; Georgia's pine barren episode and the colossal YAZOO LAND FRAUDS.

KING COTTON ignited rushes for lands in Alabama, Florida, and Mississippi across to Missouri, Arkansas, and empresario grants in Texas. Land sales boomed to new peaks in 1816–1819, 1834–1837, and 1854–1857. Indian land cessions and removal treaties generated episodes unsurpassed for chicanery and violence. New companies appeared (Chickasaw, American Land, New York & Mississippi, Galveston Bay & Texas Land, Wimico & St. Joseph), benefiting from all aspects of the land policies. Influential speculators, such as ROBERT WALKER, JOHN SLIDELL, and WADE HAMPTON, lent respectability.

By 1900 public lands were virtually extinguished by extravagant grants, vast sales of timber and mineral tracts in the Gulf states and Arkansas, and imperial cattle domains. New facets of speculation emanated from oil strikes in Texas and from all aspects of the many real estate ventures of "bulldozer revolution". Building upon the prototype of Florida's fabulous promoters like HENRY M. FLAGLER brought boom and bust by the mid-twenties, recovery after 1940, and spectacular advance since 1960. Capitalizing on climate, transportation improvement, tourism, retiree attraction, federal projects, and new industries, southern growth has been phenomenal (*e.g.*, Miami, Atlanta, Houston, Dallas). Soaring land values inevitably produced charlatanism and deception, but speculators and developers have been catalyzers, as well as beneficiaries, of economic growth throughout southern history.

See P. W. Gates, *Public Land Law* (1968); T. P. Abernethy, *Western Lands and Revolution* (1937) and *Frontier to Plantation in Tennessee* (1932); M. E. Young, *Redskins, Ruffleshirts, Rednecks* (1964), for comprehensive bibliographies; A. M. Sakolski, *Great American Land Bubble* (1932); T. L. Miller, *Public Lands of Texas* (1975); R. A. Billington, *Western Expansion* (1949); C. E. Harner, *Florida's Promoters* (1973); C. E. Carter (ed.), *Territorial Papers of U.S.* (1937–62), IV–VI, IX, XIII–XV, XVIII–XXVI, invaluable.

JOHN L. HARR
Northwest Missouri State University

LAND SURVEY SYSTEM. Although in no two American colonies was the system for disposing of lands exactly alike, a distinctly southern land survey system, as opposed to the New England system, developed during British rule in all of the colonies south of Pennsylvania and became known as the "indiscriminate survey" (or "indiscriminate location and subsequent survey") method. This system began with the Virginia Company, which had the contractual right to issue patents of land as it saw fit. Since the company had little to offer as an inducement to settlers other than land, it dispensed it with a lavish hand and without great concern for legal impedimenta. In contrast to the discriminate survey system in New England, which required that the land be surveyed prior to settlement, laid off boundaries precisely with due reference to adjoining allotments, and kept very careful records, the Virginia method left much to private initiative. The colonial or state government rarely made any preliminary surveys before the land was sold. An individual, having purchased or otherwise obtained a warrant, could select a tract of unappropriated land without concerning himself too carefully about its relationship to other people's property or the possibility of creating overlapping claims. Only then must the land be surveyed and described (usually by "metes and bounds"). The survey was recorded in the land office, and the claimant was issued a patent or grant covering the land. His claim was then valid on condition that it had not already been claimed by someone else. This haphazard system, combined with the faulty recording of titles, inaccurate surveying, and use of natural features like trees, rivers, and heights of ridges to mark boundaries, afforded little security of title and led to continual arguments and lawsuits. Since only the choicest lands were claimed first, another effect of this system was the scattering of farms and plantations up and down the coast and along the banks of the major streams, rather than in concentrated settlements. This coincided with the emergence of strong county governments rather than towns. With some variations this Virginia practice also prevailed in most of the other original southern states, as well as Tennessee and Kentucky east of the Tennessee River.

The remainder of the South, except for Texas, fell under the federal rectangular grid, which originated with the famous Land Ordinance of 1785 (SOUTHWEST ORDINANCE). This rectangular method, which formerly received lavish praise from historians, has been shown by more recent writers to have worked somewhat less than perfectly in its actual application to this part of the South. Because of the numerous conflicting and ill-defined grants made during the periods of French, British, and Spanish rule and because of fraud and careless surveying done in the first years of American ownership, the supposedly more efficient rectangular land survey system as applied to this area did not spare it the problems of overlapping private land claims and the legal snarls so familiar in the older South. Vague titles to hundreds of thousands of acres of land distributed by earlier colonial governments had to be clarified before the United States could, in 1807, even begin to sell some of its public domain in the Mississippi-Alabama area, and thereafter the litigation over conflicting claims was enormous. The first public land sales in Missouri could not be undertaken until 1818; in Louisiana, not until 1820;

and in Florida none were made until 1825, all for the same reasons.

In Texas, early methods of surveying varied considerably. Distances were sometimes stated as a "day's walk" or even in "cigarette lengths." At the time of American colonization STEPHEN F. AUSTIN refused to issue land titles until surveys had been completed using the Mexican unit of land measure, the vara, but the surveys then as well as later were done crudely and the land was not laid out with any precision. The Texas legislature has over the years enacted reforms, however, and a workable grid reference system with some rough similarity to that of most of the rest of the United States has been gradually adopted.

The story of the untangling of land titles throughout the southern states became almost a part of the region's folklore. Many lawyers received a large portion of their income from representing claimants before federal departments and boards or in the courts. The open hearings held in thousands of such cases in the South were a major source of entertainment for a rural people.

See P. J. Treat, *National Land System* (1910), standard authoritative work; M. Rohrbough, *Land Office Business* (1969); E. Dick, *Dixie Frontier* (1948); B. H. Hibbard, *History of Public Land Policies* (1924); V. Carstensen, *Public Lands* (1963); R. M. Robbins, *Landed Heritage* (1942); H. L. Coles, *Mississippi Valley Historical Review* (June, 1956); P. W. Gates, *Journal of Southern History* (May, 1956); H. D. Mendenhall, *Surveying and Mapping* (Oct.–Dec., 1950); F. Daniell, *Surveying and Mapping* (April–June, 1948); E. V. Coonan, *Surveying and Mapping* (Jan.–June, 1947); and R. S. Cotterill, *Mississippi Valley Historical Review* (March, 1930).

LANGSTON, JOHN MERCER (1829–1897), black Republican politician, was born in Louisa County, Va., on the plantation of his white father Ralph Quarles. His mother Lucy Langston, the mother of Quarles's four children, had been freed by Quarles in 1806. Therefore, John Mercer was born free. When both Quarles and Lucy died in 1833, the father left the children his entire estate. John, the youngest, moved with his brothers to Ohio, although during most of his youth he lived with a white family, under whose guardianship he was placed. He was graduated from Oberlin College with high honors in 1849 and received an M.A. degree in theological studies in 1852. It was from this training that Langston developed the great oratorical skills for which he was known throughout the rest of his life. In 1854, after studying law with a judge in Elyria, Ohio, Langston became the first black west of the Alleghenies to be admitted to the bar. His Lorain County law prac-

tice grew rapidly; he began to speak for the abolition of slavery and equal rights for northern blacks; and he entered politics. Despite the fact that his was the only black family in the area, he won his race for township clerk, becoming the first black ever to be elected to public office in the United States. In 1856 he moved to Oberlin, where he was elected township clerk, a member of the city council, and a member of the board of education.

During the Civil War, Langston was a recruiting agent. In 1867 O. O. Howard appointed him a general inspector for the FREEDMEN'S BUREAU. In 1868 he helped organize the Howard University Law School and became its first dean and, from 1873 to 1876, vice-president and acting president. In 1877 he became the U.S. minister and consul general to Haiti; and from 1885 to 1887 he served as president of Virginia Normal and Collegiate Institute in Petersburg. In 1888 he was elected to Congress. However, because of fraud and intimidation by local Democrats, the tally showed that his opponent had won. Langston was not seated until September, 1890, when the House voted in his favor and made him the first black representative from Virginia.

See J. M. Langston, *From Virginia Plantation to National Capitol* (1894), autobiography, and *Freedom and Citizenship* (1883), selected speeches; W. J. Simmons, *Men of Mark* (1887); J. M. Langston Papers, Fisk University; and F. J. Grimké Papers, Howard University.

ROBERTA SUE ALEXANDER
University of Dayton

LANIER, SIDNEY (1842–1881), often ranked next to EDGAR ALLAN POE as the leading poet of the South, is now remembered chiefly for a few anthology pieces such as "The Marches of Glynn" and "The Song of the Chattahoochee." Of his prose works the most popular survival is *The Boys' King Arthur* (1880), one of his several efforts to retell medieval stories for children. He was also a gifted musician and served for a time as first flutist of the Peabody Orchestra in Baltimore. His life was a struggle against the overpowering odds of tuberculosis and the untoward circumstances besetting the would-be artists who emerged in the South immediately after the Civil War.

Born in Macon, Ga., and educated at Oglethorpe University, Lanier early enlisted in the Confederate army and capped his adventures as a signal corps officer by being captured and subjected to the horrors of a prison camp. Returning to a Georgia ravaged by W. T. Sherman's troops, he ventured farther south as a tutor and hotel clerk, failed to adjust to the family profession of the law, and eventually gravitated to Baltimore, where he added to his income as musician by producing hack work for the periodicals and lecturing on literary topics. An amateurish novel, *Tiger-Lilies* (1867), was his first book. The only volume of his verse to appear during his lifetime, *Poems* (1877), contained merely a few pieces reprinted from *Lippincott's* magazine. Of his lectures and other prose the more eminent examples are *The Science of English Verse* (1880), undertaken to establish a tonal basis for metrical effects, and *The English Novel* (1883), brilliantly conceived in terms of Spencerian evolution but dwindling to a superficial critique of George Eliot as its author's powers were sapped by increasing hemorrhages of the lungs. The principal collection of his poems was edited by his wife in 1884. Subsequently several additions have been made, most recently by C. R. Anderson. His verse is well within the range of subject and manner of the eminent Victorians, particularly Alfred, Lord Tennyson and the Pre-Raphaelites, but certain later manuscripts published as *Poem Outlines* (1908) reveal a more independent talent that was never fulfilled.

See C. R. Anderson *et al.* (eds.), *Centennial Edition of Writings of Sidney Lanier* (1946); A. H. Starke, *Life of Sidney Lanier* (1933); and Lanier Manuscripts, Johns Hopkins University.

CLARENCE GOHDES
Duke University

LANIER UNIVERSITY in Atlanta was founded in 1917 by C. Lewis Fowler (1877–1974), a Baptist minister and Klansman who had been president of two other colleges: Cox College in Atlanta, and Lexington College in Missouri. He organized the new institution for the ostensible purpose of providing Atlanta with its first Baptist-oriented, co-educational college and the South with its first "all-southern" center of higher learning. The unaccredited college offered a broad array of courses designed to promote the values of southern culture as perceived by the founder. Among the faculty members was William J. Simmons, Imperial Wizard of the KU KLUX KLAN and "special lecturer in southern history." The college received the enthusiastic support of many of Atlanta's prominent commercial and professional leaders as well as the encouragement of local Baptist churches and the chamber of commerce. A 53-acre campus in the fashionable suburb of Druid Hills featured a replica of Robert E. Lee's home. Lanier claimed enrollments of several hundred students and graduated four classes before it succumbed to eco-

nomic difficulties in late 1921. The Klan, operating in the background until then, assumed the debts of the institution, named Simmons president, and made Fowler a national organizer for the masked order. With Klan ownership openly acknowledged, local support evaporated, and Lanier permanently closed its doors in 1922.

See B. J. W. Graham, *Baptist Biography* (1914); *Lanier University Bulletin* (1920); A. S. Rice, *Ku Klux Klan* (1962); and K. T. Jackson, *Ku Klux Klan in City* (1967).

THOMAS G. DYER
University of Georgia

LAREDO, TEX. (pop. 69,024), opposite Nuevo Laredo, Mexico, is on the Rio Grande approximately 140 miles south of San Antonio. One of the first Spanish settlements in Texas not founded as a mission or a presidio, Villa de Laredo was established in the 1750s by a Spanish rancher. It developed primarily as a market town on the road to Mexico's settlements in Texas. In 1848 it was ceded to the United States, and Camp Crawford (later U.S. Army Ft. McIntosh) was founded here. The completion in the 1880s of two railroads through Laredo greatly expanded the city's commercial importance, and the irrigation of area farmland in the 1890s made it a significant market for truck farming. Further expansion of the city's economic base occurred with the discovery of natural gas in 1908 and of petroleum in 1921. Modern Laredo remains a trade center, shipping cattle, vegetables, coal, and petroleum to Mexico. Moreover, since the completion in 1936 of the Inter-American Highway between here and Mexico City, Laredo has become a major tourist gateway to Mexico.

See Laredo *Times* (1881–).

LA SALLE, RENÉ ROBERT CAVELIER, SIEUR DE (1643–1687), was born in Rouen, France, and came to America in 1666. He became a trader, trapper, farmer, and explorer. La Salle explored the Great Lakes and discovered the Ohio River in 1671. He was the first European to descend the Mississippi to its mouth (1682) and the first to recognize the size and importance of the river for a French empire in America. He took possession of the Mississippi for Louis XIV in 1682. He named Louisiana and gave the region its first geographic concept. First to realize the importance of a settlement at the mouth of the Mississippi, La Salle envisioned a chain of French forts extending from Quebec thence along the Great Lakes and the Mississippi to the river's mouth. Such a system,

LAURENS, JOHN

La Salle believed, would assure French sovereignty over the heartland of North America. La Salle was a dreamer and a nationalist. Despite his efforts, France failed to realize control of North America. His chief weakness was his inability to effectively communicate his ideas to his subordinates.

See T. Falconer, *Discovery of Mississippi* (1844), translation from original manuscripts; and A. Fortier, *History of Louisiana* (1901), I, objective account using secondary sources.

NOEL GRAY
Southern University

LATROBE, BENJAMIN HENRY (1764–1820), British architect and engineer, immigrated to Virginia in 1796 and became a contributor to America's architectural and industrial development. His admiration for Greek and Roman Revival ARCHITECTURE stimulated his use of the neoclassical style in his first commissions, particularly the Richmond Penitentiary (begun 1797), which incorporated the advanced idea of humane penology. In Philadelphia he completed the earliest neoclassical structure, the Bank of Pennsylvania (1798–1800), and the steam-powered waterworks. The Baltimore Cathedral (begun 1804), influenced by Roman models, is his finest surviving project. Befriended by Thomas Jefferson, he began the completion of the Capitol in Washington, and after the British burned it he restored the interior, but was forced to resign from the project in 1815. His last commissions were the New Orleans waterworks and the construction of steamboats to travel rapidly on the Ohio and Mississippi rivers. His legacy to later architects was a high standard of craftsmanship and engineering and an appreciation of the neoclassical style.

See T. Hamlin, *Latrobe* (1955); and American Association of Architectural Bibliographers, *Benjamin Henry Latrobe* (1972).

AARON SHEON
University of Pittsburgh

LAUREL, MISS. (pop. 24,245), 27 miles north of Hattiesburg, began in 1881 as a sawmill and railroad station in the middle of a pine forest. The lumber community that had grown up around the mill by the 1890s was named for the many laurel shrubs that grew among the pines. Today the economy of the town continues to revolve in large part around lumber. It also is a market for the agriculture, which has grown up on the cleared forest land, and a manufacturer of farm machinery.

See files of Laurel *Leader-Call* (1911–).

LAURENS, HENRY (1724–1792), born in Charleston, ranked by 1770 among the wealthiest men in America with extensive landholdings (20,000 acres) in South Carolina and Georgia and a large import-export business. Vain, argumentative, and aggressive, the nouveau riche aristocrat was also an urbane man of integrity. A patron of the American Philosophical Society, he served as an officer in the provincial militia during the French and Indian War and as a ranking member of the commons house of assembly almost continuously from 1757 to the Revolution. A moderate Whig, he was a leader of the independence movement in Carolina as president of the provincial congress and council of safety (1775–1776) and first vice-president (1776–1777) of the new state. Laurens was a delegate to the CONTINENTAL CONGRESS (1777–1779), and his term as president (1777–1778) was marked by contentions over personalities and policies. Appointed envoy to the Netherlands in 1780, he was captured at sea and imprisoned. Released in early 1782, he first assisted in negotiating the peace treaty with Britain and then acted as unofficial ambassador to England.

See P. M. Hamer and G. C. Rogers, *Papers of Henry Laurens* (1968–), definitive edition; D. D. Wallace, *Henry Laurens* (1915), detailed biography, extensive bibliography; P. M. Hamer, *Transactions of Huguenot Society of South Carolina* (1965) and *Proceedings of Massachusetts Historical Society* (1965); R. B. Morris, *Peacemakers* (1965); J. P. Greene, *Quest for Power* (1963); G. E. Frakes, Laboratory for Liberty (1970); M. E. Sirmans, *South Carolina* (1766); E. C. Burnett, *Continental Congress* (1941) and *Letters of Members of Congress* (1921–36); W. C. Ford, *Continental Congress Journals* (1904–37); and F. Wharton, *Revolutionary Diplomatic Correspondence* (1889).

LARRY R. GERLACH
University of Utah

LAURENS, JOHN (1754–1782), solider, diplomat, and member of the South Carolina legislature during the Revolutioanry War, was born in Charleston (son of HENRY LAURENS) and educated in London and Geneva. He accompanied George Washington as aide-de-camp in the campaigns of 1777 and 1778; served in South Carolina and Georgia in 1779; was captured at Charleston in 1780; and, on being exchanged, was sent to France to secure money and supplies for Congress. He rejoined Washington for the YORKTOWN CAMPAIGN and was killed ten months later fighting the British in South Carolina. In his brief career Laurens proved himself a zealous patriot and republican; a man, rash in battle and importunate in negotiations, who repeatedly risked his life and reputation for American independence.

See D. D. Wallce, *Henry Laurens* (1915); W. G. Simms (ed.), *Correspondence of John Laurens* (1969); and P. M. Hamer (ed.), *Papers of Henry Laurens* (1968), includes essay on manuscripts.

IRA D. GRUBER
Rice University

LEA, LUKE (1879–1945), was a member of a prominent Tennessee family. Although his only public office was U.S. senator (1911–1917), Lea became a power in the state Democratic party. Prior to World War I he was a leader of the independent-Democratic wing (fusionist-prohibitionist) and generally opposed Boss E. H. CRUMP of Memphis. After defeat in the 1916 primary by KENNETH MCKELLAR, he raised and led the 114th Field Artillery, 30th Division, AEF. Lea became best known as leader of a group of officers who unsuccessfully attempted to capture the kaiser in Holland and return him for trial as a war criminal. Owner of the Nashville *Tennessean*, Memphis *Commercial Appeal*, and Knoxville *Journal*, he gave statewide press support to his candidates for office. He was associated with Rogers Caldwell in various financial institutions, and his ties with Governor H. H. Horton led to the deposit of large amounts of state revenues in Caldwell's banks. The 1930s depression witnessed the banks' failures, the loss of $7 million of state monies, and the end of Lea's empire. After serving two years in a North Carolina prison for conspiracy to defraud, he was pardoned in 1937 and lived quietly until his death.

See C. Tidwell, *Tennessee Historical Quarterly* (Spring, 1969); P. E. Isaac, "Prohibition and Politics in Tennessee" (Ph.D. dissertation, University of Texas, 1961); and J. T. MacPherson, "Democratic Progressivism in Tennessee" (Ph.D. dissertation, Vanderbilt, 1969).

CHARLES W. JOHNSON
University of Tennessee, Knoxville

LEAGUE OF UNITED SOUTHERNERS was a southern nationalist movement proposed in 1858 by EDMUND RUFFIN. It was hoped that it would be a rallying point for southerners and, through "discussion, publication and public speeches" by prominent leaders in the organization, would help prepare public opinion in the South for secession. Ruffin prepared a written "Declaration and League" for supporters to sign and drafted a proposed constitution. He quickly won the support of WILLIAM L. YANCEY and a few other FIRE-EATERS.

Some local clubs were organized, and the movement won some attention in the newspapers; but most of the South's political leaders balked at the idea for fear it would frighten off the northern Democrats, wreck the Democratic party, and destroy any chance the South had for electing a southern president in 1860. Ruffin soon gave up, and his hoped-for league was largely forgotten in the succession of fast-moving events after 1858 that led into the Civil War.

See W. K. Scarborough (ed.), *Diary of Edmund Ruffin* (1972), I; and A. Craven, *Edmund Ruffin* (1932).

LECOMPTON CONSTITUTION of Kansas was a response to a territorial popular referendum (October, 1856) and a territorial legislative law (February, 1857). But by the time of their working sessions (November, 1857) the 60 convention delegates—of whom 34 were Democrats, 48 slave-state natives, and seven presently or formerly slave owners—no longer reflected popular feelings. Their constitution contained controversial sections on banking, officeholding, public lands, constitutional amendments, and the future status of Kansas' approximately 200 slaves. An equally controversial ratification section prohibited voter rejection of the constitution and allowed voters to decide how many more slaves would be subsequently admitted to the state. In a fraud-marked election (December, 1857), 6,226 slavery supporters ratified the constitution with unlimited future admission of slaves, but in a nonbinding special referendum (January, 1858), 10,226 free-state voters rejected the document.

Illinois Senator Stephen A. Douglas denounced Lecompton as not complying with his POPULAR SOVEREIGNTY doctrine and led a minority of northern Democratic congressmen in demanding resubmission of the constitution to a popular vote. Citing the legality of the convention action, President James Buchanan joined southerners in urging congressional acceptance of Lecompton with modifications. After a three-month deadlock, a compromise required Kansans, if they wished immediate statehood under Lecompton, to vote to accept a sharp reduction in requested federal land grants; rejecting reduction temporarily barred further statehood proceedings. Immediate statehood was decisively rejected (August, 1858), and Kansas statehood disappeared as a national political issue. But the Buchanan-Douglas feud, persisting in the Democratic party, strengthened southern disunionist elements and resulted in the irreconcilable division of the party at the CHARLESTON CONVENTION (April, 1860).

See R. F. Nichols, *Disruption of Democracy* (1948), standard; A. O. Craven, *Southern Nationalism* (1953); J. A. Rawley, *Race and Politics* (1969); R. W. Johannsen, *Kansas Historical Quarterly* (Autumn, 1957) and *Douglas* (1973); and P. S. Klein, *Buchanan* (1962).

DAVID E. MEERSE
State University of New York, Fredonia

LE CONTE FAMILY. Descended from French Huguenots who settled in New York, Louis Le Conte (1782–1838) was educated at Columbia College and studied medicine at the College of Physicians and Surgeons in New York. In 1810 he took possession of 3,000 acres of land acquired by his father in Liberty County, Ga., and established a large rice and cotton plantation worked by over 200 slaves. An accomplished naturalist, he developed an internationally recognized botanical garden on his Woodmanston plantation. Two of his sons, John (1818–1891) and Joseph (1823–1901), became prominent scientists. Each was graduated from the University of Georgia, and both subsequently earned M.D. degrees at the College of Physicians and Surgeons. From 1846 to 1855 John served as professor of physics at the University of Georgia and from 1856 to 1869 at the College of South Carolina. Joseph, who studied geology and zoology under Louis Agassiz at Harvard University from 1850 to 1851, served as professor of natural history at the University of Georgia from 1852 to 1856 and then joined his brother in South Carolina as professor of chemistry and geology.

During the Civil War both John and Joseph were employed by the Confederate government. Although they resumed their academic duties at the college after the war, they were dissatisfied with the Reconstruction regime and sought to leave the South. Thus, in 1869 they moved to the newly founded University of California, where they achieved considerable fame. Their departure from the South contributed to the decline of science in postwar southern institutions. Author of scores of books and articles on physiological optics, geology, evolutionary theory and philosophy, Joseph acquired the greater scientific reputation, but John also published numerous articles, particularly in medicine and physics.

See J. Le Conte, *Autobiography* (1903), *'Ware Sherman* (1937), and *National Academy of Sciences Biographical Memoirs* (1894), III, memoir of John Le Conte, contains selected bibliography; E. W. Hilgard, *National Academy of Sciences Biographical Memoirs* (1906), VI, memoir of Joseph Le Conte, includes evaluation and list of writings; T. D. Bozeman, *Journal of Southern History* (Nov., 1973); L. D. Stephens, *Historian* (Feb., 1976), lists private source collections; E. M. Coulter, *Georgia Historical Quarterly* (March, 1969); J. S. Lupold, "From Physi-

cian to Physicist" (Ph.D. dissertation, University of South Carolina, 1970), valuable bibliography; and manuscripts, in University of California Library, University of North Carolina Library, University of South Carolina Library, Lewis R. Gibbes Papers in Library of Congress, Smithsonian Insitution Archives, and Georgia Historical Society, Savannah.

LESTER D. STEPHENS
University of Georgia

LEE, ARTHUR (1740–1792), born at Stratford, Va., the youngest son of Thomas Lee (LEE FAMILY), studied at Lincoln's Inn and the Middle Temple and was admitted to the London Bar in 1775. He wrote the Monitor Letters and later the Junius Americanus, defending the American cause. From 1777 to 1780 Lee was a diplomat on the Continent, working to get aid for America. Most of the time he served as a commissioner to the court at Versailles (with Benjamin Franklin and Silas Deane). His diplomatic career was marred by his suspicions of and quarrels with the other commissioners. Congress recalled Lee in 1780. Afterward he served in the Virginia legislature and in Congress and on commissions to negotiate the Indian treaties of Fts. Stanwix and McIntosh. Fiercely patriotic, but suspicious and quarrelsome, he often defeated his own admirable purposes.

See C. H. Lee, *Arthur Lee* (1894); C. Isham, *Deane Papers* (1897–99); F. Wharton, *Diplomatic Correspondence* (1889); W. C. Ford, *Letters of W. Lee* (1891); J. C. Ballagh, *Letters of R. H. Lee* (1914); L. W. Potts, "Arthur Lee" (M.A. thesis, Duke, 1968); A. R. Riggs, *Virginia Magazine* (July, 1970); and manuscripts, University of Virginia (microfilm) and Virginia Historical Society.

LUCILLE GRIFFITH
Montevallo, Alabama

LEE, CHARLES (1731–1782), was born in Chester, England, and was no relation to the distinguished Virginia Lees. He was commissioned an ensign in the 55th (later 44th) Foot Infantry of England (1746). Lee's regiment, commanded by Thomas Gage, was ordered to America (1754) and was defeated (1755) under Major General Edward Braddock at Ft. Duquesne. While quartered in Albany, he married the daughter of a Seneca chief (1756) and was given the name Ounewaterika (boiling water). He was wounded in the attack on Ft. Ticonderoga (1758) and returned to England (1760). Lee was granted 20,000 acres in East Florida (1766) and returned to America (1773). Sympathetic to the colonists, he wrote *Strictures upon a "Friendly Address to All Reasonable Americans"* (1774) striking down Tory arguments advocated by Dr. Myles Cooper. Lee resigned from the British army (1775) and was appointed by the Continental Congress one of two major generals who were immediately subordinate to General GEORGE WASHINGTON. That year, Lee purchased land in Berkeley County in Virginia (now West Virginia). He was given command of the Southern Department (1776), and Congress congratulated Lee for the defeat of the British during their CHARLESTON EXPEDITION (1776). Lee was captured by the British (1776) and exchanged just before the battle of Monmouth (1778), at which Lee's order to retreat and his map reportedly given to Lord Howe may have led to the American defeat. A court-martial, Major General William Alexander presiding, found Lee guilty of disobedience, disrespect, and misbehavior and suspended him one year. Lee returned to Virginia and was dismissed from the army (1780).

See J. R. Alden, *General Charles Lee* (1951), excellent, most recent; J. Sparks, *Lives of Charles Lee and Joseph Reed* (1846), dated but highly useful; and *Lee Papers* New York Historical Society (1872–75).

DONALD G. BROWNLOW
Haverford School

LEE, CHARLES (1758–1815), brother of LIGHT-HORSE HARRY LEE, served as a naval officer from 1777 to 1789 and was admitted to the bar in 1794. A friend and lawyer of George Washington's after the Revolution, he was appointed by Washington collector of the port of Alexandria (1789–1793) and U.S. attorney general (1795–1801). Mild and unforceful, Lee was a poor administrator, but his anti-French and anti-Jefferson attitudes made him a bulwark of John Adams' administration. As one of the "midnight judges," he was returned to private life by the repeal of the 1801 Judiciary Act (1802). Lee later participated in several celebrated legal battles: for the plaintiff in *Marbury* v. *Madison* (1803); and for the defense in the trials of Justice Samuel Chase (1805) and Aaron Burr (1807).

See A. J. Beveridge, *John Marshall* (1919); J. C. Fitzpatrick, *Diaries of Washington* (1925) and *Writings of Washington* (1931–44); and C. F. Adams, *Works of John Adams* (1854).

JOHN L. MOLYNEAUX
Rockford College

LEE, FITZHUGH (1835–1905), was born at Clermont, Fairfax County, Va. After graduating from West Point in 1856 he served with the 2nd Cavalry in Texas, where he was wounded in action against the Indians. He later served at the U.S.

Military Academy until his resignation from the army on May 3, 1861. He served with credit in the Confederate army during the first BULL RUN CAMPAIGN. In August, 1861, he became a lieutenant colonel and served in the PENINSULAR CAMPAIGN with J. E. B. STUART. He earned a brigadier's star on July 25, 1862, and was promoted major general on September 3, 1863. On November 19, 1864, he was seriously wounded in action but returned to take J. B. Hood's cavalry in January, 1865. At the close of the war, he commanded the remnants of the Cavalry Corps of the Army of Northern Virginia. He was considered one of the most gifted cavalry officers of the War. After the war he became a farmer in Stafford County, Va. His election as governor (1886–1890) strengthened Democratic control of his state. He was named consul general to Havana in 1896 and was commissioned major general of volunteers on May 5, 1898, during the Spanish-American War.

See E. J. Lee, *Lee of Virginia* (1895), genealogy and western duty; and Papers of Fitzhugh Lee and related Lees (restricted), Alderman Library, University of Virginia, on microfilm (5,000 items).

AGNES DOWNEY MULLINS
National Park Service

LEE, FRANCIS LIGHTFOOT (1734–1797), was born at Stratford, Westmoreland County, Va., son of Thomas (1690–1750) and Hannah Ludwell Lee, brother of Philip, Thomas, RICHARD HENRY, WILLIAM, and ARTHUR. Francis married Rebecca Tayloe (1796) and purchased the plantation Menokin. He served in the Virginia HOUSE OF BURGESSES, representing Loudoun County (1758–1768) and Richmond County (1769–1776). He signed the Westmoreland Association (1766) protesting the Stamp Act, participated in the Virginia committee of correspondence, and became a member of the Virginia convention of 1774. Lee was a delegate to the CONTINENTAL CONGRESS (1775–1779), signed the DECLARATION OF INDEPENDENCE, and helped draw up the ARTICLES OF CONFEDERATION. After Lee retired from the Congress, he served briefly in the Virginia senate, supporting the ratification of the federal CONSTITUTION.

See B. J. Hendrick, *Lees of Virginia* (1935); E. G. Swem and J. W. Williams, *Register of General Assembly of Virginia* (1918); E. C. Burnett, *Letters of Members of Continental Congress* (1921–28), I–IV; and Lee Family Papers and Tayloe Family Papers, Virginia Historical Society.

DONALD G. BROWNLOW
Haverford School

LEE, GEORGE WASHINGTON CUSTIS (1832–
1913), the eldest son of ROBERT E. LEE, was born at Fortress Monroe, Va. He graduated first in his class at West Point. Torn like his father between dismay at the destruction of the Union and loyalty to Virginia, Custis resigned his commission in the Corps of Engineers on May 2, 1861.

Although he served from August 31, 1861, as Jefferson Davis' chief adviser on engineering and defense and rose to the rank of major general, Custis longed for a field command. After the fall of Richmond, he joined General R. S. Ewell's corps in the retreat from Petersburg. He was captured at SAYLER'S CREEK.

In October, 1865, he became professor of military and civil engineering at Virginia Military Institute. A shy, retiring man who never married, Custis succeeded his father in 1871 as president of Washington and Lee University. Plagued by poor health and self-doubt, he provided little leadership for the struggling school. Although he tendered his resignation several times, not until 1897 did the trustees consent to sever the Lee connection. Custis gratefully retired to Ravensworth in Fairfax County, Va.

See J. L. Howe, *Virginia Magazine of History and Biography* (Oct., 1940), sympathetic; O. Crenshaw, *General Lee's College* (1969); and R. E. Lee Papers, Virginia Historical Society, Richmond.

CAM WALKER
College of William and Mary

LEE, HENRY "LIGHT-HORSE HARRY" (1756–
1818), was prepared for his cavalry command by his education as a Virginia gentleman and in classics at the College of New Jersey (1770–1773). His troop of Virginia light dragoons joined George Washington's army in October, 1776. Lee rose in rank to lieutenant colonel as his cavalry raided British supply wagons and posts, performed reconnaissance duty, and shared the hardships of Valley Forge. "Lee's legion" served importantly under Nathanael Greene in the South in 1781. Crediting Lee with originating Greene's brilliant startegic move into South Carolina is erroneous. He felt ignored by Greene and left the army in 1782. Neither a strategist nor an accomplished tactician, Lee was a daring and inspiring commander, cruel to Tories and deserters, and overly sensitive about his honor.

Because of his wartime experiences and his friendship with Washington, Lee was one of the most prominent Virginia Federalists. He argued for the ratification of the Constitution and defended Washington's foreign policy. While governor of Virginia (1791–1794) he commanded the expedition to suppress the Whiskey Rebellion. In Congress (1799–1801) he advocated nationalistic programs. Financial blunderings, injury in a Baltimore riot, and separation from his family after 1813 made tragic Lee's last years. He was neither as skillful nor as stable as ROBERT E. LEE, who hardly knew but greatly admired his father, yet he was more devoted to his nation.

See N. B. Gerson, *Light-Horse Harry* (1966), uncritical; M. F. Treacy, *Prelude to Yorktown* (1963); R. M. Beeman, *Old Dominion and New Nation* (1972); and H. Lee, *Memoirs*, ed. R. E. Lee (1870).

BENJAMIN H. NEWCOMB
Texas Tech University

LEE, HENRY (1787–1837), son of Light-Horse
Harry Lee, served in the Virginia house of delegates (1810–1813) and in the War of 1812. His career prospects were ruined by a widely publicized affair with his sister-in-law. After an association with JOHN C. CALHOUN, he became a political publicist for ANDREW JACKSON in 1826, beginning a campaign biography of the general and helping ghostwrite Jackson's 1828 inaugural address. Appointed consul general to Algiers in 1829, but rejected by the Senate in 1830, Lee spent the balance of his life in Paris. Among his writings, all strongly polemical, are *Campaign of 1781 in the Carolinas* (1824) and *Observations on the Writings of Thomas Jefferson* (1832).

See B. J. Hendrick, *Lees of Virginia* (1935); J. Parton, *Life of Jackson* (1861); R. B. Davis, *Jefferson's Virginia* (1964); and J. Daniels, *Randolphs of Virginia* (1972).

JOHN L. MOLYNEAUX
Rockford College

LEE, JESSE (1758–1816), Virginia's "Apostle of
Methodism," preached from Georgia to Canada and wrote the first history of the American METHODIST CHURCH. Appoined to the first New England circuit in 1789, he led the Methodist assault on New England Congregationalism. While spearheading the transformation of Methodism from a predominantly southern denomination into a national organization, Lee also took an active role in shaping the government of the Methodist Episcopal church in America. Lee was less successful in his lifelong campaign for primitive simplicity in Methodist churches. He was elected chaplain by the Republican U.S. House of Representatives four times (1810–1813) and U.S. Senate chaplain in 1813.

See J. Lee, *History of Methodists* (1810); M. Thrift, *Lee* (1823); L. M. Lee, *Lee* (1848); J. M. Buckley, *Constitutional History* (1912); G. C. Baker, Jr., *Early New England Methodism* (1969), especially bibliography; and *Tyler's Quarterly* (July, 1921), partisan but suggestive.

JUDITH H. WILSON
Washington University

LEE, MARY ANNE RANDOLPH CUSTIS (1808–1873),

daughter of George Washington Parke Custis (grandson of Martha Washington) and Mary Lee Fitzhugh, was born at Annfield in present-day Clarke County, Va. She married ROBERT E. LEE, later commander of the Army of Northern Virginia, on June 30, 1831, and they had seven children. She was a gentle woman educated in the values of family traditions, which she jealously guarded. Although afflicted with rheumatism and confined to a wheelchair in later years, she asserted a gentle but positive rule at home. She died at Lexington, Va.

See R. M. E. MacDonald, *Mrs. R. E. Lee* (1939); D. S. Freeman, *R. E. Lee* (1934): J. W. Wayland, *R. E. Lee and Family* (1951); and manuscripts, Virginia State Library and Virginia Historical Society, Richmond.

LOUIS H. MANARIN
Virginia State Library

LEE, RICHARD HENRY (1732–1794),

brother of ARTHUR, WILLIAM, and FRANCIS LIGHTFOOT LEE, was elected to the House of Burgesses in 1758 as a representative of Westmoreland County. He served until the burgesses disbanded in 1775 and earned the reputation of a hardworking and eloquent legislator. By 1774, due to his opposition to the Stamp Act, the Townshend duties, and other royal policies, he emerged as one of the prominent leaders in Virginia political affairs. He was among the men elected to the Continental Congress in 1774. As a member of Congress, Lee introduced the resolution calling for American independence in 1776. He retired from Congress in 1779 and involved himself in local Virginia affairs. Reelected to Congress in 1784, Lee helped to enact the famous Northwest Ordinance of 1787. He also served as president of Congress in 1784–1785. He again left Congress in 1787 and opposed ratification of the new Constitution. Lee's *Letters of the Federal Farmer* became one of the noted statements against ratification. He did, however, serve as a U.S. senator from 1789 to 1792.

See J. C. Ballagh, *Letters of Lee* (2 vols.; 1911–14); E. J. Lee, *Lee of Virginia* (1895); H. J. Eckenrode, *Revolution in Virginia* (1916); R. H. Lee, *Memoirs of Lee* (1825); C. R. Lingley, *Transition in Virginia* (1910); R. H. Lee, *Observations* (1787); J. C. Matthews, "Lee and American Revolution" (Ph.D. dissertation, University of Virginia, 1939); B. J. Hendrick, *Lees of Virginia* (1935); P. C. Bowers, "Lee and Continental Congress" (Ph.D. dissertation, Duke, 1965); M. P. Cubbison, "Virginia Antifederalists" (M.A. thesis, Duke, 1961); L. B. Griffith, "House of Burgesses" (Ph.D. dissertation, Brown, 1957); and O. P. Chitwood, *Richard Henry Lee* (1967).

LARRY G. BOWMAN
North Texas State University

LEE, ROBERT EDWARD (1807–1870),

born at Stratford, Westmoreland County, Va., was the fifth child born to LIGHT-HORSE HARRY LEE and his second wife Anne Hill Carter (CARTER FAMILY). He entered West Point in 1825 and graduated second in his class in 1829. On June 30, 1831, he married Mary Anne Randolph Custis.

As an officer in the engineers Lee saw active duty on fortification, navigation, and boundary assignments. He was promoted second lieutenant in 1832, first lieutenant in 1836, and captain in 1838. Appointed chief engineer on General John E. Wool's staff in 1846, he served with distinction in Mexico and was brevetted colonel in 1848. After a tour at Baltimore he was assigned as superintendent at West Point in 1852. In 1855 he was promoted lieutenant colonel and ordered to Texas. He commanded the detachment of marines sent to Harpers Ferry to capture John Brown in 1859 (HARPERS FERRY RAID). In 1861 he was promoted colonel and resigned his commission on April 20, 1861. Three days later he was appointed major general and commander-in-chief of Virginia military forces. On May 14, 1861, he was appointed lieutenant general in the Confederate army.

Lee's duties in the first year of the war included administrative duties of organization and supply. When he assumed command of the Virginia forces in April, 1861, he created administrative departments and mobilized the manpower and resources of the state. In August, 1861, he went to western Virginia with the nominal title of coordinator. There he encountered the problems involved in coordinating two separate armies against an enemy committed to definite routes of advance. While he remained with one army, he allowed the other, torn by dissension between its ranking generals, to undertake independent action. Failure to coordinate the armies was a mistake.

His next command was in the Department of South Carolina, Georgia, and Eastern Florida from November, 1861, to March, 1862. There he had to establish a defensive system to protect the coast against an uncommitted enemy. He established military districts as he had in Virginia and coordinated his defenses. He defended the rail line at the points of possible advance and retained a mobile reserve to be moved by rail to any threatened point.

In March, 1862, Lee became adviser to President JEFFERSON DAVIS and concluded that the pressure on Richmond could be reduced by applying pressure in another area, the Shenandoah Valley. He encouraged, suggested, advised, and directed General STONEWALL JACKSON to assume the offensive aggressively. Successfully executed, the offensive reduced the pressure and the enemy's superiority.

In June, 1862, in the middle of G. B. McClellan's PENINSULAR CAMPAIGN, Lee assumed command of the Army of Northern Virginia, when JOSEPH E. JOHNSTON was wounded, and succeeded in preventing the capture of Richmond by striking McClellan's right flank and by driving his army back in a series of engagements known as the SEVEN DAYS' BATTLES. This successful campaign and victories at Cedar Mountain, second BULL RUN, FREDERICKSBURG, and CHANCELLORSVILLE won him worldwide fame. As commander he never was able to employ the massive hard-hitting tactics associated with total war. His only alternative to counter the superiority of his opponent was to maneuver, and in the fall of 1862 and the summer of 1863 he felt driven to invade and (unsuccesfully) to seek victory on enemy soil (ANTIETAM, GETTYSBURG). Throughout the war Lee sought to battle his opponent by maneuvering to advantage, to force him to disperse, to strike when opportunity presented, and to destory him or disrupt his campaign. He had the remarkable ability to anticipate his opponent and to maneuver his forces so as to harass or defeat him. Scarcity of supplies, transportation, equipment, artillery, and men in arms, in the presence of a powerful enemy, restricted Lee's ability to maneuver. In 1864 he was forced on the defensive to protect the Confederate capital and was unable to maneuver except to assume a new defensive position (RICHMOND-PETERSBURG CAMPAIGN). He was finally forced to surrender at APPOMATTOX on April 9, 1865. Following the war he assumed the presidency of Washington College in Lexington, Va.

See C. Dowdey and L. H. Manarin, *Wartime Papers of R. E. Lee* (1961); D. S. Freeman, *R. E. Lee* (1934) and *Lee's Lieutenants* (1944); R. E. Lee, Jr., *Recollections and Letters of General Robert E. Lee* (1904); L. H. Manarin, *Virginia Cavalcade* (Spring, 1976); and manuscripts, Virginia State Library, Virginia Historical Society, Richmond, and National Archives.

LOUIS H. MANARIN
Virginia State Library

LEE, SAMUEL PHILLIPS (1812–1897), was born in Virginia, a grandson of RICHARD HENRY LEE. Phillips entered the navy in 1825, gaining recognition during the 1850s through his able direction of Atlantic oceanographic surveys. He opted for the Union, commanding with what was called "great coolness and judgment" the *Oneida* in David Farragut's April, 1862, assault on New Orleans. He was rewarded with promotion to acting rear admiral and given the North Atlantic Blockading Squadron from 1862 to 1864 and later the Mississippi Squadron. During December, 1864, Lee was unable to bar the escape of J. B. Hood's Confederates, shattered at Nashville, across the Tennessee River near Florence, Ala. General G. H. Thomas officially thanked him for his "efficient cooperation," but another Union officer ascribed his failure to "the natural timidity of a deep-water sailor in a shoal-water river." Lee was promoted to rear admiral in 1870 and retired in 1873.

See S. P. Lee, *Cruise of Dolphin* (1854), Senate Executive Document No. 59, 32nd Cong., 1st. Sess.; *Official Records, Navies*, Ser. 1, Vols. VIII–X, XVIII, XXVI–XXVII; G. Welles, *Diary* (3 vols.; 1911), highly uncomplimentary to Lee; R. M. Thompson and R. Wainwright, *Correspondence of G. V. Fox* (2 vols.; 1918–19); J. H. Wilson, *Recollections* (2 vols.; 1902); W. E. Smith, *Blair Family* (2 vols.; 1933); F. Cleaves, *George Thomas* (1948); and New York *Times* (June 6, 1897).

DAVID F. LONG
University of New Hampshire

LEE, STEPHEN DILL (1833–1908), was born at Charleston, S.C., a distant relative of the Lees of Virginia. He attended West Point, graduating in 1854. Service, until 1861 with the 4th U.S. Artillery, included the third Seminole War (1856–1857). In the Confederate army, he rose through every rank to lieutenant general, attained at the age of thirty. Jefferson Davis said that Lee was "one of the best all-round soldiers which the war produced." An organizer, a master of logistics and training, and a disciplinarian, methodical and quiet, Lee could win confidence and cooperation; any organization he led turned into a better outfit. He carried only baggage he could tie behind his saddle, and on campaigns he shared meals and shelter with the troops. As a corps commander he outperformed his peers but showed some weakness in independent operations and a need for more experience and seasoning. His principal achievements in battles occurred at second BULL RUN, CHICKASAW BAYOU, and in the battle of NASHVILLE. After the Civil War he established a home in Mississippi, tried farming, joined other Confederate veterans in various projects, and became an active and productive historian, a politician, a champion of women's rights, a preserver of the Vicksburg battle area, chairing the federal Military Park Commission, and a founder and commander-in-chief (1904–1908) of the UNITED CONFEDERATE VETERANS. As the first president of the A. & M. College of Mississippi from 1878 to 1897 (now Mississippi State University), he worked for revitalization of his region through mechanization, industrialization, and rejuvenation of soil fertility. Admirers bestowed upon him the title Father of Industrial Education in the South.

See H. Hattaway, *Lee* (1976), extensive bibliography.

HERMAN HATTAWAY
University of Missouri, Kansas City

LEE, WILLIAM (1739–1795), son of Thomas Lee and brother of RICHARD HENRY LEE, was born at Stratford, Va. Moving to London in 1768, he became a prosperous tobacco merchant in the Virginia trade and a London officeholder. With the final break with the colonies, Lee welcomed a congressional appointment as commercial agent to Nantes and later as commissioner to Vienna and Berlin. Because of contradictory instructions, ill-defined delineation between the commercial and diplomatic, quarrels within the commission to Versailles, and his own outspoken personality, he was unsuccessful on the Continent. Recalled by Congress, he chose to settle in Brussels, hoping to rebuild his mercantile business. In 1783 he returned to Virginia, living out his life at Green Spring plantation.

See W. C. Ford, *Letters of W. Lee* (1891); J. C. Ballagh, *Letters of R. H. Lee* (1914); R. H. Lee, *Arthur Lee* (1829); E. J. Lee, *Lee* (1895); F. Wharton, *Diplomatic Correspondence* (1898); London newspapers; and manuscripts, University of Virginia (microfilm), Virginia Historical Society, and Stratford Hall. See also correspondence of B. Franklin and J. Adams, scattered locations.

LUCILLE GRIFFITH
Montevallo, Ala.

LEE, WILLIAM HENRY FITZHUGH (1837–1891), second son of ROBERT E. LEE, was called Rooney to distinguish him from his cousin Fitzhugh. He left Harvard in 1857 to join the army, serving in the Mormon campaign. He returned to farming in 1859. At the outbreak of the Civil War, Rooney organized a cavalry company, rising to the rank of major general. Wounded at BRANDY STATION, he was later captured and imprisoned at Fortress Monroe until exchanged in March, 1864.

He served with his command until the surrender at Appomattox. Calm under fire, he distinguished himself in several engagements, including Turner's Gap, CHANCELLORSVILLE, and the APPOMATTOX CAMPAIGN. After the war, he returned to farming and politics, serving in the Virginia state senate, as president of the Virginia State Agricultural Society, and in the U.S. Congress (1887–1891). He died at Ravensworth, his plantation near Alexandria. Tall and powerfully built, with a long, flowing beard, Rooney was a quiet, courteous southern gentleman whose wartime reputation probably suffered from being the son of Robert E. Lee.

See D. S. Freeman, *Robert E. Lee* (1934–35) and *Lee's Lieutenants* (1943–44); *Official Records, Armies*, Ser. 1, Vols. XXI, XXV, XXVII, XLII, XLVI; R. U. Johnson and C. C. Buel (eds.), *Battles and Leaders* (1884–87), III, IV; and New York *Times* (Oct. 16, 1891).

CAREY W. BRUSH
State University College, Oneonta, N.Y.

LEE FAMILY. John Adams wrote, "The family of Lee . . . has more merit in it than any other family." That merit was an amalgam of ambition, political and intellectual ability, landed wealth, sound marriages, and the ability to survive defeat with dignity and grace.

Richard Lee (1613–1664), founder of the family, came to Virginia in 1638. An English gentry background combined with support for royal and gubernatorial policies aided his rise to social and political prominence. A successful tobacco planter and factor, Richard served as clerk of the quarter court, colonial secretary of state, and member of the council. At his death he left eight children, extensive landholdings in Virginia and Maryland, and a residence in England. His grandsons Thomas (1690–1750) and Henry I (1691–1747) established the most famous branches of the family.

Thomas headed the Stratford line. Occupying high political positions, he was colonial rather than English in outlook. His ambitions were shaped by the western frontier; they culminated in his establishment of the OHIO COMPANY in 1748. Four of his sons—RICHARD HENRY (1732–1794), FRANCIS LIGHTFOOT (1734–1797), WILLIAM (1739–1795), and ARTHUR (1740–1792)—were especially prominent in the American Revolution.

The son of Henry I of Westmoreland County, Henry II (1729–1787), firmly established the Leesylvania branch. He was a member of the assembly and held other political offices, but it was the military and political activities of his son HENRY

"LIGHT-HORSE HARRY" (1756–1818) that brought particular recognition to this line. Other sons were CHARLES (1758–1815), Richard Bland (1760–1827), and Edmund Jennings (1772–1843).

Numerous ironies color Light-Horse Harry's life. He joined the two branches of the family by marrying the heiress to Stratford, Matilda Lee (1764–1790). The peculations of their son HENRY IV, known as "Black-Horse Harry" (1787–1837), resulted in the sale of the estate. Land speculation brought wealth and prominence to Henry III's forebears; it brought him imprisonment for debt and a life of genteel poverty for his second wife Ann Hill Carter (1773–1829). He was an optimist and a nationalist. His most famous son, ROBERT EDWARD (1807–1870), was a pessimist and a state particularist.

The political and military influence of the Lee family diminished following the Civil War; the implicit merit of the family increased and became legend.

See P. P. Hoffman (ed.), *Lee Family Papers* (1966); D. S. Freeman, *R. E. Lee* (4 vols.; 1934–35); B. J. Hendricks, *Lees of Virginia* (1935); and C. G. Lee, Jr., and D. M. Parker, *Lee Chronicle* (1957).

MILES M. MERWIN
University of Santa Clara

LEGARÉ, HUGH SWINTON (1797–1843), born in Charleston to an aristocratic planter family, graduated from South Carolina College in 1814, read law for three years, and then went to Edinburgh to continue his study. Returning to South Carolina in 1820, he served eight terms in the state legislature. Although a defender of states' rights and an opponent of the protective system, he became a leader of the Union party in opposition to the nullificationists. Typical of the aristocratic Tidewater Unionists, Legaré was suspicious of democracy, unenthusiastic about political organization to meet the threat of NULLIFICATION, and offered no concrete solutions to deal with the tariff question. As a result, he and the other Unionists were easily outmaneuvered and defeated. In 1832, eager to escape the frustrations engendered by the nullification controversy, he accepted an appointment as chargé d'affaires in Belgium. Upon returning to the United States in 1836, he was elected to Congress as a Democrat, but his opposition to Martin Van Buren's independent treasury led him to join the Whig party. In 1841 President John Tyler appointed him attorney general and, after Daniel Webster's resignation, secretary of state.

See W. W. Freehling, *Prelude to Civil War* (1965); M. S. Legaré, *Writings of Legaré* (1846); and L. G. Tyler, *Letters and Times of Tylers* (1896).

WALTER HUGINS
State University of New York, Binghamton

LETCHER, JOHN (1813–1884), was the Civil War governor of Virginia and a staunch Confederate. Born in Lexington, Va., he studied law and became an ardent Jacksonian Democrat. In 1851 he helped write a liberal constitution for Virginia. The same year he was elected to the U.S. House of Representatives, where for four consecutive terms (1851–1859) he championed moderation and compromise as sectional hostilities increased. After a bitterly contested election in 1859, Letcher began his four-year term as governor of Virginia on January 1, 1860. He opposed secession, but when war erupted he followed his state out of the Union. Letcher cooperated with the Confederate government and tried to channel Virginia's vital resources into the centralized war effort. He was one of the most effective state governors within the fatally disunified Confederacy. Union troops burned his home in 1864, and he was briefly jailed when the war ended, but Letcher championed sectional reconciliation. He practiced law again, served briefly in the Virginia house of delegates (1875–1877), and died in Lexington.

See F. N. Boney, *John Letcher* (1966), definitive biography, and *Civil War History* (June, 1964); Executive Papers (1860–63), Virginia State Library, Richmond.

F. N. BONEY
University of Georgia

LEVEES, embankments built to control flooding in the lower Mississippi River valley from Cape Girardeau, Mo., to the Gulf of Mexico, were started by early French settlers and were the responsibility of the landowners whose property fronted on the river. In the 1830s and 1840s, as American settlers cleared the rich Delta lands of Mississippi and Arkansas, they built scattered, unconnected levees, but their efforts emphasized local responsibility in keeping with Jacksonian Democracy and the realities of frontier life. The increasing importance of the Delta region and the destructive floods led to the first federal involvement, albeit indirectly, when Congress passed the Swamp Acts of 1849 and 1850 giving Louisiana, Mississippi, and Arkansas all unsold swamp and overflowed federal lands within their boundaries to be used to raise funds for FLOOD CONTROL. This encouraged some standardization of levee construction and state control, and between 1850 and 1858 considerable progress was made. Gaps remained, however, and most levees were earthen embankments only slightly over four feet high and four feet wide at the top.

Floods in 1858 and 1859, as well as the neglect and destruction caused by the Civil War, wiped out most of what had been accomplished. During Reconstruction, Louisiana tried to rebuild its levees by chartering a private company, Arkansas issued state bonds, and Mississippi returned to local and district initiative; little lasting protection resulted. In 1879 Congress established the Mississippi River Commission involving the U.S. Army Engineer Corps, and in 1881 the River and Harbor Act provided direct federal assistance to levee construction, although only as an aid to navigation on the premise that levees would help "flush" out the channel during flooding. In 1917 the Randsdell-Humphreys Flood Control Act provided the first direct federal aid for local, district, and state levee boards, which had been mainly responsible for trying to protect some of the South's most valuable agricultural regions from flooding. After the mammoth flood of 1927, the Jones-Reid Act established a comprehensive flood control program for the whole Mississippi River valley and its tributaries. Levees are now augmented by a complex flood control system and a broad research program, which includes the U.S. Waterways Experiment Station at Vicksburg, Miss.

See *Mississippi River* (June, 1940); D. O. Elliott, *Improvement of Lower Mississippi River* (1932); R. W. Harrison, *Levee Districts and Levee Building in Mississippi* (1951); and R. W. Harrison and W. W. Kollmorgen, *Arkansas Historical Quarterly* (Spring, Winter, 1948).

LILLIAN A. PEREYRA
University of Portland

LEVER, ASBURY FRANCIS (1875–1940), was born near Springhill, S.C., and was graduated from Georgetown University's School of Law (1899). After serving in the South Carolina legislature (1900–1901), he was elected to an unexpired term in the U.S. House of Representatives. During the next 18 years in Congress, Lever was one of the more effective spokesmen for the Farm Bloc and for agricultural relief. He was the principal House sponsor of the Federal Farm Loan Act (1916), extending long-term, low-interest loans to farmers through a system of 12 federal land banks. Lever also was the chief sponsor of the Lever Act (1917), emergency wartime legislation governing agriculture and foodstuffs. He resigned from Congress in 1919 to become a member of the Farm Loan Board (1919–1922) and later served as

a field representative for the same organization. During the 1930s he was the public relations director of the Farm Credit Administration.

See A. F. Lever Papers, Clemson College Library.

LEWIS, DAVID PETER (1820–1884), was Republican governor of Alabama between 1872 and 1874. Shortly after his birth in Charlotte County, Va., his parents migrated to Madison County, Ala., where he was educated. He studied law at Huntsville and practiced successfully in Lawrence County. As a delegate to the state convention in 1861, he voted against secession. He declined to serve in the Confederate Provisional Congress, but in 1863 accepted the judgeship of the circuit court of Alabama. Early in 1864, he fled through Union lines to Nashville. After the war, he affiliated with the Republican party and, following his election as governor, sought military support for the contested Republican "courthouse legislature" and for the election of George Spencer to the U.S. Senate. Despite his administration's generally tarnished reputation, it achieved some reform, notably in education. He resumed his law practice following Reconstruction.

See T. M. Owen, *History of Alabama* (1921); W. L. Fleming, *Civil War and Reconstruction in Alabama* (1905); and S. V. Woolfolk, *Alabama Review* (Jan., 1964) and "Role of Scalawag" (Ph.D. dissertation, Louisiana State University, 1965).

ROBERT GILMOUR
Princeton University

LEWIS, MERIWETHER (1774–1809), was born at Locust Hill, Albemarle County, Va. After his father's death in 1779, Lewis lived for several years in a colony of former Virginians on the Broad River in Georgia and then returned to Albemarle County. He was commissioned ensign in the regular army in 1795 and served briefly in a rifle company commanded by WILLIAM CLARK. Early in 1801 Captain Lewis was at Pittsburgh when he received Thomas Jefferson's letter with its offer of the post of private secretary at a salary of "500D." For two years he lived in the White House and performed duties like those of an aide-de-camp.

Sometime in 1802 Jefferson and Lewis began planning the expedition they had envisioned for a decade. Lewis, the leader, chose his army friend Clark as his companion. The Corps of Discovery started up the Missouri in May, 1804, and reached the Mandan villages in North Dakota in time to spend the winter there. In the autumn of 1805 Lewis and Clark reached the Pacific. They recrossed the continent and arrived in St. Louis in

September, 1806. Jefferson appointed Lewis governor of Upper Louisiana Territory in November, 1806. After a year's delay, during which he represented the president at the Aaron Burr trial in Richmond (BURR CONSPIRACY), Lewis reached St. Louis to begin his duties. He was soon plagued by Indian problems, contested vouchers, and quarrels with the territorial secretary. Despondent and ill, he left for Washington in 1809 to try to untangle his affairs. Traveling through Tennessee, he stopped on October 10 at Grinder's Stand, a wilderness inn on the NATCHEZ TRACE. Next morning Lewis was found dead by the roadside, a victim of suicide or possibly robbery and murder.

See J. Bakeless, *Lewis and Clark* (1947); and R. Dillon, *Meriwether Lewis* (1965).

JOHN PAYNE
Sam Houston State University

LEWIS, WILLIAM BERKELEY (1784–1866), born in Virginia, settled in Nashville about 1809. Through his marriage and service as quartermaster (1812–1813), he became closely connected with ANDREW JACKSON. Major Lewis helped launch Jackson's first bid for the presidency in the ELECTION OF 1824, and in the ELECTION OF 1828 he worked effectively as organizer and propagandist. Living in the White House, he was more influential in political management than in public policy. He backed PEGGY O'NEALE EATON in her battle for social recognition and initiated the movement for Jackson's second term. He created the occasion for Jackson's final break with John C. Calhoun. At his suggestion, the first Democratic National Convention met in 1832. Although opposed to Jackson's war against the national bank, he remained loyal. President Martin Van Buren ignored Lewis but continued his appointment as second auditor of the treasury, as did John Tyler, who used him to enlist Jackson's support for Texas annexation. Lewis returned to Tennessee in 1845 after being dismissed by James K. Polk as untrustworthy. Lewis reemerged long afterward as a moderate Unionist, serving briefly in the first Reconstruction legislature (1865–1866) of Tennessee.

See L. R. Harlan, *Tennessee Historical Quarterly* (March, June, 1950), definitive; and J. S. Bassett, *Life of Jackson* (1931) and *Correspondence of Jackson* (1926–35).

JAMES S. CHASE
University of Arkansas

LEXINGTON, KY. (pop. 108,137), in the center of the state's BLUEGRASS region, is approximately 75 miles east of Louisville. The site was named in 1775 by a group of hunters who first heard news of the battles of Lexington and Concord while camped here. The town was founded four years later and chartered in 1782. Early Lexington was the principal industrial city in the state until about 1820, when the paddle-wheeler transferred that honor to Louisville. TRANSYLVANIA UNIVERSITY moved here in 1787, and the city's public library, opened in 1795, is the oldest such institution west of the Alleghenies. Hemp, tobacco, and horse breeding were among the city's principal economic activities in the nineteenth century. Although breeding thoroughbred horses and processing loose-leaf burley tobacco remain central to the economy of modern Lexington, important also is the presence of the University of Kentucky (1861), the production of asphalt and insecticides, the distilling of alcohol, and the manufacture of sheet metals, tools, furniture, toys, and automobile parts.

See C. R. Staples, *History of Pioneer Lexington* (1939); J. W. Coleman, *Squire's Sketches of Lexington* (1972); R. Peter, *History of Fayette County* (1882); G. W. Ranck, *History of Lexington* (1872); and files of Lexington *Leader* (1888–), *Herald* (1870–), *Stewarts Kentucky Herald* (1795–1801), *Kentucky Gazette* (1793–1819, 1822–30, 1833–44), *American Statesman* (1811–13), *Western Monitor* (1814–16), and *Morning Journal* (1896–1903), all on microfilm.

LEXINGTON (KY.) OBSERVER AND REPORTER, published between 1832 and 1872, also was sometimes called the Lexington *Observer and Kentucky Reporter.* The paper was created by the merger of the *Observer* (1831–1832) and the much older *Kentucky Reporter* (1808–1832).

See microfilm files (1850–72), University of Kentucky.

LEXINGTON, VA. (pop. 7,597), the home of WASHINGTON AND LEE UNIVERSITY and of VIRGINIA MILITARY INSTITUTE, is an agricultural market and college town in the Shenandoah Valley of western Virginia. After being founded in 1777, it was totally destroyed by fire in 1796 and rebuilt with the proceeds of a public lottery.

See H. Boley, *Lexington in Old Virginia* (1936, 1974); R. Lyle, Jr., and P. M. Simpson, *Architecture of Historic Lexington* (1977); and files of Lexington *Intelligencer* (1823–30) and *News-Gazette* (1801–), both on microfilm.

LIBBY PRISON in Richmond, Va., was used by the Confederates from 1862 to 1865 mainly to house Union officers. It was also familiar to captured enlisted men who were registered there. The three-story brick warehouse on the banks of the James River received its name from Libby & Son, its former business occupant. Libby was most crowded and controversial between May, 1863, when the regular exchange of officers ceased, and May, 1864, after which the Confederates used Libby only for transients. In those months the more than 1,000 inmates complained of short rations and uncomfortable conditions. Yet hardships never approached those at camps for enlisted men, and the officer prisoners frequently could use money to improve their situation. Nevertheless, because the prisoners often combined social prominence with literary ability, their complaints reached a large audience.

The prisoners' attempts to escape and the jailers' countermeasures stimulated mutual hostility. The most successful break occurred on February 9, 1864, when 109 prisoners tunneled out. Thereafter the guards tightened security. In March, when the KILPATRICK-DAHLGREN RAID threatened Richmond, the Confederates buried several hundred pounds of gunpowder in the cellar and informed the prisoners of their action. A Confederate congressional committee characterized this as a bloodless intimidation of the inmates from any uprising. The federal authorities on the other hand made much of the Libby powder mine in propaganda and postwar investigations. After the fall of Richmond, Libby served as a Union prison for Confederates and then reverted to commercial uses. In 1889 it was demolished and rebuilt in Chicago as a museum. Remnants are in the Chicago Historical Society.

See F. L. Byrne, *Journal of Southern History* (Nov., 1958) and *Civil War History* (June, 1962); F. F. Cavada, *Libby Life* (1865); W. B. Hesseltine, *Civil War Prisons* (1930); *Official Records, Armies*, Ser. 2; and National Archives.

FRANK L. BYRNE
Kent State University

LIBRARIES. The earliest libraries established in the South followed the European pattern of private and university collections. The Virginia planter William Byrd II (BYRD FAMILY) assembled one of the finest collections in colonial America, as did Thomas Jefferson, whose library became the basis of the LIBRARY OF CONGRESS. The College of William and Mary which began its library in the seventeenth century, the University of Virginia, and South Carolina College each developed collections comparable with most institutions beyond the region.

Reverend Thomas Bray, one of the founders of the Society for the Propagation of the Gospel in Foreign Parts, initiated the first attempt to provide free library service in the southern colonies. Appointed commissary to Maryland in 1696, Bray initially intended to develop only parish libraries for the use of missionaries and ministers; however, he later extended his plans to include laymen's libraries. Bray sent libraries to Maryland, Virginia, the Carolinas, and Georgia, and some of them were administered as free circulating libraries. The Bray Library at Annapolis may have been the first free circulating library in the colonies.

Subsequent circulating libraries in the eighteenth and nineteenth centuries took the form of social or subscription libraries. Although not free, social libraries were public in that they were open to anyone who paid dues or purchased stock in the library. The CHARLESTON LIBRARY SOCIETY founded the earliest social library in the region in 1748, and other groups followed suit. In Annapolis in 1762, William Rind established perhaps the earliest circulating library that appealed to popular tastes. Although social libraries grew in importance, the South did not develop a tradition of free public library service. An exhaustive Office of Education report issued in 1876 listed only seven free public libraries in the region.

As the South industrialized and became increasingly urban, demands for public services, including libraries, intensified. By 1895, conditions were favorable for a widespread free public library movement. In that year, the Cotton States and International Exposition in Atlanta focused attention on libraries by including among its exhibits a model library. This exhibit introduced thousands to the idea of library service, an idea that they carried back to communities throughout the South. In conjunction with the exposition, the Congress of Women Librarians met to foster interest in library development. With women's clubs, librarians, and progressive businessmen providing the initial leadership, the free library movement gained momentum. Cities throughout the region established free public libraries, many in buildings provided by Andrew Carnegie, and traveling libraries increasingly served rural areas. Librarians formed state associations, which successfully lobbied for state library commissions, extension services, state aid, and legislation allowing municipalities to levy library taxes.

One obstacle to library development was the scarcity of trained librarians. To remedy this situation, several libraries began apprentice-training programs. Aided by a Carnegie gift, the Carnegie Library of Atlanta established the first such program, the Southern Library School, in 1905. After 1920, academic institutions offered library training. Programs accredited by the American Library Association were established at Women's College in North Carolina (1924), Hampton Institue (1925), Peabody and Tennessee (1928), Emory (1930), North Carolina and William and Mary (1931), and Atlanta University (1941). Prior to the Hampton Institute program, the Louisville Free Public Library offered the only library training for Negroes in the South.

Segregation barriers kept Negroes out of most southern libraries until after 1954. However, many urban libraries provided Negro branches, and rural Negroes benefited somewhat from extension programs and from Rosenwald demonstration libraries. Financed by the ROSENWALD FUND, these libraries provided county-wide service without regard to race. The Southeastern Library and American Library associations focused attention on the problem and provided leadership in eliminating the barriers.

Regional associations—the Southeastern founded in 1920 and the Southwestern in 1922—took the lead in formulating plans and goals for library growth on a regional basis. Two depression-era programs, the WORKS PROGRESS ADMINISTRATION and the TENNESSEE VALLEY AUTHORITY, further expanded library service and consciousness in the South, paving the way for additional state aid when federal aid was terminated. By 1950, 75 percent of the southern people had access to library service. With the demise of segregation and the influx of federal and state funds in the subsequent two decades, library service was extended and improved until few southerners were beyond its scope.

See U.S. Office of Education, *Public Libraries* (1876), indispensable; M. E. Anders, "Public Library Service" (D.L.S. dissertation, Columbia, 1958, excellent survey; E. A. Gleason, *Southern Negro and Public Library* (1941); L. R. Wilson and M. A. Milczewski, *Libraries* (1949); L. R. Wilson and E. A. Wight, *County Library Service* (1935); *Library Journal* (1876–); and *Library Literature* (1921–), nearly definitive bibliography.

WILLIAM THOMAS MILLER
Birmingham Public Library

LIBRARY OF CONGRESS. The founding fathers were book oriented. Most of them were lawyers used to consulting codes and statutes. When the CONTINENTAL CONGRESS first convened in Philadelphia (1774), one of its first acts was to ask for library privileges from the Library Company of Philadelphia, which were courteously granted. The same procedure was followed in New York, but at other meetings there were no library facilities available. The delegates, therefore, thought of having their own library.

A start was made in Washington in a rented room. Subsequently it was housed in various rooms in the Capitol. A librarian was employed at $1,000 per annum, and he disposed of a $500 book budget. The library was in the Capitol when that building was burned by the British in 1814. The purchase of THOMAS JEFFERSON's library for $24,000 (1815) made up for much of the loss. But after the fire of 1851 in which the Jefferson Library was destroyed with almost all of the other books, the library room had to be rebuilt.

The library was housed in its own building under the librarianship of Herbert Putnam in 1897. It has since expanded into an annex (1939), and in 1976 a second annex was completed, the Madison Memorial Library. A card catalog is now available. Duplicate cards are printed for subscribers; there is also a union catalog of printed books in the leading research libraries in this country. It also offers photoduplication services. None of these services are perfect. Classification and organization are far in arrears, search room service is slow, photoduplication is expensive, and errors are found in the printed cards. The library has a budget of $87 million, it has 73 million items, and it has a staff of over 4,000 persons (1974).

See C. A. Goodrum, *Library of Congress* (1974); L. H. Evans, *Report of Library of Congress* (1946); and W. D. Johnson, *History of Library of Congress* (1904), I, 1800–1861.

MORRIS L. RADOFF
Library of Congress

LICKING RIVER flows 320 miles through eastern and central Kentucky to its mouth on the Ohio River just east of COVINGTON. Although it was used as an artery of trade by area Indians and traveled in the very early nineteenth century by westward-bound pioneers, steamboat traffic was limited and no major towns developed along its banks. Its most common use during the nineteenth century was as a carrier of timber floated downstream to Covington and Cincinnati.

LIEBER, FRANCIS (1800–1872), after receiving a Ph.D. degree at Jena, Prussia, in 1820, was imprisoned because of his liberal activities. In 1826 he fled to England and then to the United States, where he edited the *Encyclopedia Americana*. In 1835 he was appointed professor of history and political economy at South Carolina College. Interested in penal reform, he translated Alexis de Tocqueville and Gustave de Beaumont's *On the*

Penitentiary System in the United States. His most famous works on political science, especially *On Civil Liberty and Self-Government* (1853), were written during his stay in South Carolina. He was unfairly suspected of abolitionist views, so he was neither happy nor popular in the South. Resigning his post in 1856, he was appointed to a chair at Columbia College in New York; he became an active Republican and held several federal appointments during the last decade of his life.

See F. Friedel, *Francis Lieber* (1947); J. Dorfman and R. G. Tugwell, *Columbia University Quarterly* (1938); and T. S. Perry (ed.), *Life and Letters of Lieber* (1882).

WALTER HUGINS
State University of New York, Binghamton

LILY-WHITE MOVEMENT, from post–Civil War Reconstruction to the 1928 Republican National Convention, pursued a policy of excluding Afro-Americans from the Republican party in the South. The movement included antebellum Whigs, reformers, businessmen, and racists who opposed black suffrage. The term was coined in 1888 by black politician NORRIS WRIGHT CUNEY during a Texas Republican convention. Most Republican presidents owed a patronage debt to black delegates for their votes in national conventions; thus lily-whites were often at odds with national administrations and sent contesting delegations to conventions. In Louisiana they were called "national" or "sugar" Republicans and in North Carolina "business" Republicans to distinguish them from black Republicans. Gradually in the twentieth century Republicans began to hope for future electoral victories in the South without the votes of blacks, who had been disfranchised. Despite a brief anti-lily-white movement led by BOOKER T. WASHINGTON between 1901 and 1904, Presidents Roosevelt, Taft, Harding, Coolidge, and Hoover cultivated the lily-white Republicans and precipitated an eventual drift of Negro voters to the Democratic party.

See T. R. Cripps, "Lily White Republicans" (Ph.D. dissertation, University of Maryland, 1967), good bibliography.

THOMAS CRIPPS
Morgan State University

LINCOLN, ABRAHAM (1809–1865), sixteenth president of the United States (1861–1865), was born near Hodgenville, Ky. His parents, Thomas Lincoln and Nancy Hanks, were natives of Virginia. Following the death of Lincoln's mother in southern Indiana, Thomas Lincoln married Kentuckian Sarah Bush Johnston. In 1830 the family moved to east-central Illinois, where the majority of the population was southern in origin. In 1832 Lincoln moved to New Salem and in 1837 to Springfield, where he found southern-dominated societies. In 1842 he married Mary Todd of Kentucky.

He was surrounded by southerners, and his views were shaped in some measure by them, but these views were not those of southern slaveholders. Lincoln noted that among the reasons his father left Kentucky was abhorrence of slavery. Lincoln's political views were influenced by HENRY CLAY, a southern Whig slaveholder who advocated colonization of the nation's blacks.

In the Illinois house of representatives (1834–1840), Lincoln was a leading proponent of state internal improvements. In 1846 he was the only Illinois Whig elected to the U.S. House of Representatives. There he incurred the enmity of many southern members of Congress by introducing in opposition to the Mexican War the "spot resolutions," asking where American blood was shed on American soil. That enmity was deepened when he supported the WILMOT PROVISO. Lincoln served one term before returning to his successful law practice, having been admitted to the bar in 1836.

The KANSAS-NEBRASKA ACT caused Lincoln to resume active political participation. Careful not to blame southerners for their insistence on the right to carry slaves to the territories—"If we were situated as they are, we should feel and act as they do"—he denounced it as an act calculated to expand the area of slavery at the expense of freedom. Unsuccessful in his effort to secure election to the U.S. Senate in 1855, he supported Lyman Trumbull, who was elected.

Lincoln joined the Republican party, and in 1858, as the "first and only choice of the Republicans of Illinois for the U.S. Senate," he delivered his ringing "house divided" speech. In debates with Stephen A. Douglas, he continued to oppose the expansion of slavery into the territories. Although the general assembly chose Douglas, Lincoln gained considerable national notice. When William Seward failed to secure the Republican presidential nomination, the convention turned to Lincoln. His subsequent election precipitated the long-threatened southern SECESSION (ELECTION OF 1860).

Before and after his inauguration, secession demanded Lincoln's attention. Privately he assured ALEXANDER STEPHENS that slavery in the southern states would not be attacked and that laws respecting the return of fugitive slaves would be enforced. Lincoln gave similar views to Trumbull for insertion in an address known to have the president-elect's approval. While assuring the South that its institutions would remain free from federal interference, Lincoln counseled his supporters against an alleged Union-saving compromise extending the MISSOURI COMPROMISE line. When he assumed office, however, he did not object to the organization of several western territories with no mention of slavery in the acts (*i.e.*, in effect accepted a qualified POPULAR SOVEREIGNTY) in an effort to keep the border states from joining the Confederacy. During the early months of the Civil War, Lincoln formulated his other policies and actions to the same purpose.

Restoration of the Union remained Lincoln's chief goal for the next four years. Although he never presented a comprehensive reconstruction plan, he believed there should be few conditions placed on the southern states before they could resume their rightful relationship within the Union. Perhaps the most important change he desired was southern acceptance of the EMANCIPATION PROCLAMATION and the THIRTEENTH AMENDMENT to the Constitution. Before he could develop a comprehensive program he was assassinated by the southern sympathizer, actor JOHN WILKES BOOTH.

See B. Thomas, *Abraham Lincoln* (1952), best one-volumed biography; J. G. Randall, *Lincoln the President* (4 vols.; 1945–55), scholarly, well written, and *Lincoln and South* (1946); M. Davis, *Image of Lincoln in South* (1971), first two chapters good on Lincoln's southern influence; A. Cole, in *Lincoln Centennial Association Papers* (1928); J. Monaghan, *Lincoln Bibliography, 1839–1939* (2 vols.; 1943–45), comprehensive for dates included; and *Lincoln Lore* (1929–), annually lists Lincoln bibliography additions. Major Lincoln manuscripts are in Library of Congress, National Archives, Illinois State Historical Library, especially Illinois years and source for virtually everything printed about Lincoln, Lincoln National Life Foundation, and Lincoln Memorial University.

ROGER D. BRIDGES
Illinois State Historical Library

LINCOLN, MARY TODD (1818–1882), born in Lexington, Ky., of a prominent family, went in 1839 to live with her married sister in Springfield, Ill. Intelligent and vivacious, she became a local belle, with wit enough to see beyond the rusticity of young ABRAHAM LINCOLN. After their marriage in 1842 their devotion endured through life. It had much to endure. Politics and law absorbed her husband's attention and physically separated them for months at a time. High-strung by nature, she grew increasingly temperamental, especially after their second son's death in 1850 and the dif-

ficult birth of their fourth son in 1853, the physical effect of which troubled her thereafter. The strain of her position as first lady (1861–1865) coincided with that of menopause to bring out a latent neuroticism, worsened by the deaths of her third son in 1862 and her husband in 1865. During the war she was accused unjustly of disloyalty and justly of extravagance. In bereavement she swung irrationally between parsimony and wild spending and was briefly confined as insane. With all its tragedy, her life was exalted by a great man's well-attested and by no means irrational love.

See R. P. Randall, *Mary Lincoln* (1953); J. G. and L. L. Turner, *Mary T. Lincoln* (1972); W. A. Evans, *Mrs. Abraham Lincoln* (1932); E. Keckley, *Behind the Scenes* (1868); D. Donald, *Lincoln's Herndon* (1948); and W. H. Townsend, *Lincoln and Bluegrass* (1955).

ROBERT V. BRUCE
Boston University

LINCOLN ASSASSINATION. JOHN WILKES BOOTH shot ABRAHAM LINCOLN on April 14, 1865, at Ford's Theatre in Washington, D.C., during a performance of *Our American Cousin*, a play by Tom Taylor. Booth then jumped onto the stage and escaped. He had fatally wounded Lincoln using a single-shot derringer pistol. The unconscious president was moved across the street to the house of William Petersen and died the next morning, April 15, at 7:22.

Booth originally planned to kidnap the president and take him to the Confederacy. For this purpose he recruited a group of conspirators: Samuel Arnold, George Atzerodt, David Herold, Michael O'Laughlin, John Surratt, and Lewis Paine (born Powell). In the spring of 1865 Booth substituted murder for kidnaping. Paine was assigned to assassinate William H. Seward, secretary of state. On the night of April 14, he wounded Seward but not fatally. Atzerodt was supposed to kill Vice-President ANDREW JOHNSON but lacked the courage to attempt it. Booth was killed in Virginia on April 26, 1865, but Arnold, Atzerodt, Herold, Paine, and O'Laughlin were all captured. Surratt was not in Washington during the assassination. In a military trial held in Washington, Paine, Atzerodt, and Herold were found guilty and hanged on July 7, 1865. Executed with them was Mary E. Surratt, mother of John, at whose house Paine turned up after attacking Secretary Seward. Arnold and O'Laughlin, along with Edward Spangler (a friend of Booth's from Ford's Theatre) and DR. SAMUEL A. MUDD (who had set Booth's broken leg after the assassination), were all imprisoned in the Dry Tortugas.

See Investigation and Trial Papers Relating to Assassination of Lincoln, National Archives, microfilm; B. Pitman, *Assassination of Lincoln and Trial of Conspirators* (1865), summary of trial transcript; D. M. DeWitt, *Assassination of Lincoln* (1909); G. S. Bryan, *Great American Myth* (1940); L. Lewis, *Myths After Lincoln* (1929); O. Eisenschiml, *Why Was Lincoln Murdered?* (1937), suggests unfairly that E. M. Stanton was involved in plot; and L. J. Weichmann, *True History of Assassination* (1975), his testimony mainly responsible for Mrs. Surratt's execution.

JOSEPH GEORGE, JR.
Villanova University

LINCOLN HERALD, a quarterly journal founded in 1937 as successor to the *Mountain Herald* (1900), publishes historical research in the field of the Civil War, especially Lincolniana. With a circulation of 740, it is funded through subscriptions and allocations from the Lincoln Memorial University in Harrogate, Tenn.

LINDSAY, ROBERT BURNS (1824–1902), was Democratic governor of Alabama between 1870 and 1872. A native of Scotland, he received his education there and distinguished himself at the University of St. Andrews. He traveled to America in 1844 and assumed the mastership of a North Carolina academy. At the same time he began to read law and in 1849 moved to Tuscumbia, Ala., and established a legal practice. During the 1850s he served in the Alabama general assembly and in the state senate. An opponent of secession, he nevertheless rode with P. D. Roddey's cavalry. He returned to the state senate after the war and was elected governor in 1870 over the protest of the Republican incumbent WILLIAM H. SMITH. Lindsay fought government extravagance with limited success. He lowered the tax rate and cut expenditures, but the state debt grew; nor was his administration able to check corruption among Republicans or Democrats. He refused to run for a second term. Shortly after he left office, he was stricken with paralysis, which left him an invalid.

See T. M. Owen, *History of Alabama* (1921); and W. L. Fleming, *Civil War and Reconstruction in Alabama* (1905).

ROBERT GILMOUR
Princeton University

LITERATURE. The notion of a distinctively southern literature, like so much else that involves southern regional self-consciousness, is a product of the rise of the sectional tensions of the nineteenth century. Yet, from the time of the Jamestown colony onward, there had been imaginative writing going on in the South.

The extent of the intellectual activity in the southern colonies and the presence of talented men and women who committed their thoughts to paper have generally been underestimated. Only in recent years have literary historians begun to apprehend the merits of the formidable body of writing produced by southerners in the seventeenth and eighteenth centuries. The Hudibrastic satire by Ebenezer Cook of Maryland, "The Sotweed Factor," has now been recognized as a highly sophisticated, deftly wrought verse satire. The writings, public and secret, of William Byrd II of Westover (BYRD FAMILY) are the observations, meditations, and imaginative effusions of a distinguished man of letters. Indeed Byrd had infinitely more to say about early American life, and could say it with far more skill and less pretension, than someone such as Cotton Mather. The writings of other colonial southerners—the sermons and occasional verse of Samuel Davies, the prose and verse of RICHARD BLAND, the elegant diaries of Landon Carter, the histories and commentaries of ROBERT BEVERLEY—go far toward demonstrating that, despite the scarcity of printing presses and the virtual absence of urban communities, the early southerners were by no means deficient in either literary training or artistic inclination.

In the early decades of the nineteenth century, the rural character of the Old South made it difficult for a professionalism in literature to develop such as began to characterize the literary scene in places such as New York City and Boston. There were few literary coteries, no major LIBRARIES, and little encouragement of literary PERIODICALS. Southerners were uninterested in reading and fostering southern authors; the English periodicals, and a little later those of the Northeast, were what gentlemen subscribed to and read. Moreover, as the slavery controversy grew in magnitude, so did a corresponding disinclination to develop any kind of searching artistic inquiry into the underlying assumptions of southern society. Thus the writings of the single major literary imagination that the Old South produced, EDGAR ALLAN POE, are characteristically set "out of time, out of space," and involve an intense portrayal of the tortured inner soul, while Poe's slashing literary criticism, unique on the American literary scene in its time, emphasizes formal craft with little or no concern expressed for content.

The leading man of letters of the Old South, WILLIAM GILMORE SIMMS of Charleston, spent the better part of a lifetime energetically attempting to encourage southern taste and develop regional literary consciousness. There began developing around Simms, in Charleston during the 1850s, the ingredients for an authentic professional literary situation, centered on John Russell's bookstore. Here, for the only time in the history of the antebellum South, was a group of poets whose interests and standards gave promise of transcending the amateurism of the day. The magazine they published, RUSSELL'S, provided a forum for the earlier work of HENRY TIMROD as well as for that of its editor PAUL HAMILTON HAYNE. Other participants in the group were marginal but interesting literary talents such as William John Grayson, William Elliott, and the classicist Basil Lanneau Gildersleeve. There seemed to be the makings of genuine literary ferment in antebellum Charleston. But *Russell's* fell victim to the preoccupation of the secession crisis in South Carolina, and soon thereafter the advent of the war wrecked whatever chance there was for a solidly professional literary group to develop in the nineteenth-century South.

The Charlestonians, of course, were by no means the only poets on the southern scene. There was a host of them, of whom perhaps the best was Philip Pendleton Cooke, by profession a lawyer, as indeed were most of the others, including FRANCIS SCOTT KEY, Richard Henry Wilde, Edward Coote Pinkney, Alexander B. Meek, and James Mathewes Legaré, the last a distant cousin of HUGH SWINTON LEGARÉ, editor of the erudite if rather ponderous Charleston SOUTHERN REVIEW (1828–1832). Other poets included the physicians Thomas Holley Chivers and Samuel Henry Dickson. Save for a few well-turned lyrics, however, the work of none of these survives.

The chief literary accomplishment of the Old South lay in its novelists, who drew upon the material of the southern scene as the poets largely did not. Other than Simms, the most talented was JOHN PENDLETON KENNEDY of Baltimore, whose first novel *Swallow Barn* (1832) was one of the earliest and best examples of the popular plantation novel subgenre, which has recurrently offered a pastoral rebuke to the materialism of American commercial and industrial democracy. *Swallow Barn* is set in Virginia, which was also the scene of two colonial romances by William Alexander Caruthers, of the earlier novels of JOHN ESTEN COOKE, and of GEORGE TUCKER's early *The Valley of Shenandoah* (1824), an attempt to deal with the social and economic problems of the contemporary Virginia scene with less than memorable artistic success. The model for the southern historical romancers was the fiction of Walter Scott, James Fenimore Cooper, and Washington Irving,

but their subject matter came from the history and manners of their own region. Far more propagandistic than these were the several novels of Nathaniel Beverley Tucker, whose *The Partisan Leader* (1836) predicted a civil war between North and South well in advance of the event. Equally propagandistic in intent was the work of the first American Negro novelist, William Wells Brown, an escaped slave, who produced two versions of a protest novel, *Clotel; or, The President's Daughter* (1853), published in England, and *Clotelle: A Tale of Southern States* (1864), brought out in the United States during the Civil War.

From the Old South also came a prose genre that, far more than the formal literary writings of the period, drew closely upon the vernacular speech and everyday experience of rural southerners: HUMOR. For the most part the writing of the so-called southwestern humorists was considered journalism rather than literature and was customarily published first in NEWSPAPERS rather than in literary magazines. The authors were usually Whigs, men of education and standing, who offered humorous reports on the odd doings, droll habits of speech, and highly pragmatic ethics of low-life characters in a crude and vigorous frontier society. The *Georgia Scenes* (1835) of A. B. LONGSTREET is perhaps the best product of a lively prose narrative form based upon the tall tale, the racy and sometimes even bawdy anecdote, and the comically exaggerated character sketch. Other practitioners included JOSEPH G. BALDWIN, JOHNSON JONES HOOPER, Charles F. M. Noland, GEORGE WASHINGTON HARRIS, Thomas Bangs Thorpe, DAVY CROCKETT (or his ghostwriters), George W. Bagby, William Tappan Thompson, and many another connoisseur of rural high jinks. Violence, cruelty, frailty, and vice were presented with unabashed relish and chronicled in language ranging from Baldwin's tongue-in-cheek formality and self-deflating circumlocutions to the comically atrocious vulgarity of Harris' dialect renditions of the backwoods exploits of Sut Lovingood. Although not unique to the South, such writing has enjoyed a prominent place in the southern imagination since William Byrd II's accounts of the dividing line expeditions.

The Civil War itself produced little memorable literature in the South. The single author whose wartime writings are of genuine importance was the poet Henry Timrod, who found in the Confederate cause the public theme that enabled him to do most of his best work. Some few of his poems got beneath the patriotic excitement of the occasion to suggest the undercurrents not only of pride and hope but also of apprehension and despair, which imaged the South's secession and subsequent defeat and ruin. By contrast, most Confederate war poetry was rhetorical and declamatory patriotic verse.

There was little continuity between the prewar and postwar literary generations in the South. During the years immediately after 1865, as might be expected, there was almost no place for the southern author to publish his work. Such southern magazines as had existed were all defunct, even including the SOUTHERN LITERARY MESSENGER (1834–1865). The better-paying northern periodicals desired no contributions from former Confederates. Only toward the close of the Reconstruction years did southern authors begin to find that editors in New York City, Boston, Philadelphia, and other such places were becoming receptive.

Once this began happening, however, the growing American vogue for LOCAL COLOR literature offered them unparalleled opportunity. The readers of the leading magazines of the day, such as *Scribner's Monthly, Century, Harper's, Atlantic, Lippincott's,* and *Putnam's,* had developed an apparently insatiable appetite for fiction that took for its setting the odd ways, quaint customs, and variant character types of the various American regions and subregions. The newly affluent upper-middle-class readership of the Northeast found great delight in dialect-laden tales of languorous New Orleans Creoles, picturesque CAJUNS, rugged Applachian mountaineers, courtly Virginia planters, and the like. GEORGE W. CABLE's stories of Louisiana; MARY NOAILLES MURFREE's accounts of the mountaineers of Tennessee; THOMAS NELSON PAGE's tales of antebellum Virginia plantation chivalry as recounted by faithful black retainers; JOEL CHANDLER HARRIS' fables of rabbit, terrapin, fox, wolf, and bear contending for subsistence and reputation; as well as lesser fiction by a host of other southern local colorists— such was the vogue for their work in the leading magazines that, by 1888, ALBION W. TOURGÉE complained that "our literature has become not only Southern in type but distinctly Confederate in sympathy."

By no means all local color literature was sweetness and light, however. Cable undertook an increasingly overt critique of southern racial attitudes. A black writer, CHARLES W. CHESNUTT, cleverly turned the plantation stereotype inside out in a series of dialect tales of antebellum life that revealed the cruelty and inhumanity of slavery. Another remarkable writer, KATE CHOPIN, began writing in the local color medium, but in her novel *The Awakening* (1899) she moved through it into a psychological exploration of the desire for sexual fulfillment, which scandalized turn-of-the-century reviewers. The single important southern poet of the post-Reconstruction years, SIDNEY LANIER, tended in his best work to infuse south Georgia landscape portraiture with a passionate mysticism almost pantheistic in its throbbing intensity.

The one southern-born writer of the period whose work achieved major literary stature, however, was SAMUEL LANGHORNE CLEMENS, whose greatest art grew not out of his adult experience in the Far West but out of his earlier years. Almost all of his best work is set either in the little slave-holding Missouri town that he called St. Petersburg or else upon the great river that linked St. Louis and Cairo with the Deep South, and which he had traversed as a riverboat pilot. His greatest novel, *Huckleberry Finn,* not only explored southern racial views but drew masterfully upon the vernacular speech modes of the lower Mississippi, in a way that showed American writers how to use the language they actually spoke to deal with and document their own experience. In his love-hate relationship with the values, attitudes, and sensuous surfaces of the society he knew and remembered so well, Clemens became in effect the first modern southern writer. Not for several more decades would a generation of southern authors arise who were sufficiently distanced from the powerful loyalties and attitudes of the southern community to be able to write literature that could image the life they knew in universal terms.

The literary generation that made up what came to be known as the southern literary renascence of the 1920s and afterward arrived on the literary scene following several decades of the regional literary barrenness that occasioned H. L. Mencken's famous essay "THE SAHARA OF THE BOZART," in which he branded the early twentieth-century South as "almost as sterile, artistically, intellectually, culturally, as the Sahara Desert." With the dwindling of the vogue of local color in the 1890s, southern literature did indeed enter upon a fallow time. Although writers of historical costume romance such as MARY JOHNSTON and facile ironists of plot such as WILLIAM SYDNEY PORTER (O. Henry) achieved widespread popular success, the authors of the New South participated only marginally in the dominant currents of American letters. The modes of critical realism and naturalism seemed basically uncongenial to the southern imagination; only ELLEN GLASGOW of Richmond sought successfully to use "blood and irony," as she later put it, in examining the political, social, economic, and psychological actualities of everyday southern life. Her somewhat younger fellow Richmonder JAMES BRANCH CABELL chose instead to develop elaborate and wickedly humorous tales, ironically romantic, of gallant gentlemen and lovely ladies in faraway medieval lands. Upon closer inspection, though, it was noted that Cabell's characters tended to behave remarkably like bored and bemused moderns as they went about weaving a tapestry of legend and myth that bore a startling resemblance to the attitudes of contemporary Virginians to their much-honored pantheons of civic heroes.

It was a band of young poets at Vanderbilt University who first augured the achievement of modern southern literature after the First World War. JOHN CROWE RANSOM, ALLEN TATE, DONALD DAVIDSON, and ROBERT PENN WARREN were the important figures in a remarkable little group (FUGITIVES) that in 1922 began publishing a poetry magazine, *The Fugitive*, in which for the first time southern poetry appeared fully to enter the mainstream of world literature. Here at last was a group of professionals. *The Fugitive* lasted only four years, but its leading participants went on to become important figures in twentieth-century American letters. Ransom, Tate, and Warren, together with Cleanth Brooks, became central figures in the development of what Ransom later named the New Criticism, an approach to the reading of poetry that focused on a close reading of the actual imagery, language, and tropes of the poem itself, rather than on its thematic, ideological, or biographical aspects. By the 1950s the New Criticism had all but revolutionized the teaching of poetry in American colleges and universities. Toward the end of the 1920s Ransom, Tate, Davidson, and Warren began to concern themselves with their identity as southerners in a modern world and together with Andrew Nelson Lytle were the moving spirits in the formulation of a symposium, I'LL TAKE MY STAND (1930).

It was with fiction, however, that the writers of the modern South were to have their greatest ascendency. In 1926 appeared *Soldier's Pay*, the first novel of the man who is today considered the premier American novelist of the twentieth century and one of the great masters of fiction in English. When in 1929 WILLIAM FAULKNER of Oxford, Miss., published *Sartoris*, he commenced creating the saga of Yoknapatawpha County, the mythical "postage-stamp's worth" of native earth that he made into the scene of more than a dozen novels and many more short stories. Faulkner was but one, the greatest, of a score or more of talented contemporaries who from the late 1920s onward produced a body of fiction that for several decades made the states of the onetime Confederacy the creative center of American literary achievement. So numerous and distinguished were the literary southerners of the post–World War I generation that only a bare listing of names is possible here: THOMAS WOLFE, ERSKINE CALDWELL, RICHARD WRIGHT, Robert Penn Warren, Allen Tate, KATHERINE ANNE PORTER, John Peale Bishop, ELIZABETH MADOX ROBERTS, Margaret Mitchell, Hamilton Basso, STARK YOUNG, DUBOSE HEYWARD, Jesse Stuart, Andrew Lytle, Julia Peterkin, Zora Neale Hurston, Caroline Gordon, JEAN TOOMER, Evelyn Scott, Arna Bontemps. These and others wrote fiction at once unmistakably original and individual, yet at the same time exhibiting certain common characteristics that seemed to set the southern writer apart from much of the other American fiction of the day.

Critics noted their pervasive historical sense, the joy they took in the lavish surface textures of life, their fascination with the ordered patterns of community identity and also with the explosive shattering of such order through violence, their sure grasp of social complexity, their willingness to call upon the full resources of the southern rhetorical tradition and their reliance upon the old ethical absolutes that gave the rhetoric credence and authority, their disposition to confront evil on individual as well as social terms, and their skill at tale telling with its roots in the family legendry and tribal chronicling of a folk tradition. It was as if, from the confusion and the turmoil attendant upon the South's tardy entrance into the modern world, its writers were able to extract human definition that gave their stories universal dimensions previously lacking in much southern writing.

The literary generation that followed these writers, and whose work began appearing in the 1940s and 1950s, showed little diminution in intensity. Among its leading figures were CARSON MCCULLERS, JAMES AGEE, FLANNERY O'CONNOR, Shelby Foote, Madison Jones, Shirley Ann Grau, George Garrett, Peter Taylor, RALPH ELLISON, WILLIAM STYRON, Truman Capote, WALKER PERCY, Elizabeth Spencer, Reynolds Price, Guy Owen, John Barth, Ernest J. Gaines, and the poets Randall Jarrell, William Jay Smith, and James Dickey. Robert Penn Warren, who was the youngest of the Fugitives, continued to develop as a writer long after the others had ceased; the poetry he wrote in the 1960s and 1970s is perhaps his best. Most impressive of all the writings of the second generation of the renascence, perhaps, is the fiction of EUDORA WELTY of Jackson; the delight and wisdom with which she portrayed the daily doings of Mississippians in loneliness and community, in terms of the ultimate dimensions of human time and place, gave to her work a depth of meaning that few other American writers have ever attained.

The achievement of the twentieth-century South in fiction, poetry, and criticism was not accompanied by a comparable flowering in drama. Although yet another Mississippian, TENNESSEE WILLIAMS, produced some of the most impressive plays of the post–World War II American stage, and LILLIAN HELLMAN, Laurence Stallings, Paul Green, and DuBose Heyward all attained considerable success with their dramatic writings, it cannot be said that the southern imagination has ever been as proficient in creating for the stage as it has for the printed page.

In recent years, as the South's economic, political, and social life has appeared to be drawing ever closer to the national patterns and as the region has become more urban and less self-consciously sectional, critics have wondered what the effect will be upon the literary imagination of southerners. If social and historical transition helped to produce the renascence in southern writing, has it therefore run its course? Has there been a falling off in quality, and is the work produced by southern-born authors of the 1960s and 1970s still importantly different in crucial respects from the general run of American writing? Opinions differ; but if one thing is certain, it is that such questions are not the concerns of the poets and novelists upon whom the answers will depend. Literature in the South is still very much an ongoing activity. The extent to which it is importantly "southern" literature, as we have grown accustomed to think of it, or whether that is either desirable or possible, will be for future critics to decide.

See J. B. Hubbell, *South in American Literature* (1974), best survey through nineteenth century. There is no overall history of twentieth-century renascence, but see F. J. Hoffman, *Art of Southern Fiction* (1967); L. D. Rubin, Jr., *Faraway Country* (1963); and two collections of essays edited by Rubin and R. D. Jacobs, *Southern Renascence* (1953) and *Modern Southern Literature* (1961). L. P. Simpson, *Dispossessed Garden* (1975), is a provocative and imaginative interpretation of southern literary mind. Other works of importance include C. H. Holman, *Roots of Southern Writing* (1972); W. Sullivan, *Requiem for Renascence* (1976); and G. Core (ed.), *Southern Fiction Today* (1969). L. D. Rubin, Jr. (ed.), *Bibliographical Guide to Southern Literature* (1969), contains checklists by period, topic, and author. See also annual checklists published since 1968 in spring issues of *Mississippi Quarterly*.

LOUIS D. RUBIN, JR.
University of North Carolina, Chapel Hill

LITTLEFIELD, GEORGE WASHINGTON (1842–1920), born in Mississippi, moved to Texas with his family in 1850, attended Baylor University, and fought with the 8th Texas Cavalry. He was later active in Confederate veteran affairs and helped erect the Jefferson Davis monument in Kentucky. After the war he realized a fortune in the cattle trade, established the LIT and LFD ranches in Texas and New Mexico, and was active (1882–1887) in the Texas Cattle Raisers Association. He moved to Austin in 1882 and founded the American National Bank in 1890, from which he directed his other business affairs, including the Littlefield Lands Company (1912–1920), which sold his ranchland to farmers and created Littlefield, Tex. An active Democrat, he was appointed to the first Texas library and historical commission (1909–1911) and to the University of Texas board of regents (1911–1920). To the university he presented the Littlefield Fund for Southern History (1914)—which continues to build an already preeminent collection, the incomparable Wrenn Library of English literature (1918)—and a considerable portion of his large estate.

See D. B. Gracy II, "Littlefield" (Ph.D. dissertation, Texas Tech, 1971); and J. E. Haley, *Littlefield* (1943).

DAVID B. GRACY II
Georgia State University

LITTLEFIELD, MILTON SMITH (1830–1899), Union general and "Prince of Carpetbaggers," was born in Orondaga County, N.Y., but moved to Grand Rapids, Mich., in 1851 and later to Jerseyville, Ill. During the Civil War, he rose from captain to brevet brigadier general, winning citations for the battles of Pittsburg Landing and Shiloh. In private life Littlefield was a business promoter with close alliances with leading Rupublican and northern financiers. He was also active in the UNION LEAGUE, serving as state chairman in North Carolina in 1868 and presiding over the 1870 national convention.

In 1867 he moved to North Carolina to work with state leaders in securing northern aid in rebuilding the state's railroads and in other internal improvement projects. During the Republican administration of WILLIAM W. HOLDEN (1868–1870), he was recognized as the chief lobbyist-agent for all party projects. Within two years, Littlefield allegedly paid out $240,000 to state legislators and received a 5 percent fee for securing a multimillion-dollar issue of state bonds to finance several North Carolina railroads. In 1869 he joined George W. Swepson, the state's leading conservative Democratic banker and railroad promoter, in a scheme using bonds of the Western North Carolina Railroad to secure control of three Florida railroads. Both men escaped prosecution for their parts in the fraudulent deals. Littlefield was indicted for bribery of members of the Florida legislature, but the case was dismissed because of lack of witnesses, and North Carolina's efforts to bring him to trial were thwarted by Florida's Republican chief executives. In the 1880s Littlefield lived in Morristown, N.J., but maintained an office in New York City as a "promoter of business enterprises." When he died he was virtually forgotten, and his grave remained unmarked for more than half a century.

See J. Daniels, *Prince of Carpetbaggers* (1958); C. K. Brown, *State Movement in Railroad Development* (1928); J. G. D. Hamilton, *Reconstruction in North Carolina* (1914); P. E. Fenlon, *Florida Historical Quarterly* (April, 1954); and C. L. Price, *East Carolina Publications in History* (1964).

HORACE W. RAPER
Tennessee Technological University

LITTLE ROCK, ARK. (pop. 132,483), capital and major center of the state, is centrally located, situated near the OUACHITA uplands and commanding a view of the Arkansas River and delta. Its 1970 metropolitan area population was 323,296. The original site had the first small rock formation visible along the river, hence its name. The Frenchman Bernard de La Harpe reputedly named the place in 1722, but this has no basis in fact. Native inhabitants for some time commonly called it "point of rocks." Settled in 1819, it became the territorial capital in 1821. Incorporated in 1831, with its head count rising from 13 to 430, the city thrived on politics and the steamboat. It claimed attention in 1840 as the largest urban complex west of the Mississippi, but hopes of its becoming the distribution point for the western hinterland never materialized.

Residents of Little Rock expressed less interest in SECESSION in 1860 than Arkansans generally. They consistently courted Whig favor and feared disruption of the marketplace. Abraham Lincoln's actions changed this position. Isolated, the city suffered little from war, prospered with federal occupation (1863), and observed a mild postwar boom with the railroad (1869) and cotton speculation. Its population increased from 12,000 in 1870 to over 38,000 by 1900. Cultural life kept pace. The ARKANSAS GAZETTE is the oldest newspaper in the western two-thirds of the United States. Modern Little Rock has experienced new life with completion of the Arkansas River Navigation Project, but the city's social image appears in disarray

after the severe 1957 federal-state confrontation over court-ordered school integration.

See I. Richards, *Rivertown* (1969); *Arkansas Gazette* (1819–); and D. Herndon, *Little Rock* (1933).

IRA DON RICHARDS
Henderson State University

LITTLE TENNESSEE RIVER, one of several tributaries forming the headwaters of the TENNESSEE RIVER, rises in the Blue Ridge Mountains of Georgia, flows north to North Carolina, and then winds around the Great Smoky Mountains into Tennessee. Early French explorers and trappers, after visiting the Cherokee Indian village of Tenase, named the river simply the Tennessee. Later, under the mistaken impression that this was the mainstream of the larger river, they extended use of this name to the Ohio River. After it was realized that other tributaries of the Tennessee were larger and after considerable confusion in nomenclature, the Tennessee state legislature in 1819 began using the designation Little Tennessee for the branch of the stream above its confluence with the HOLSTON RIVER. Researchers using eighteenth-century maps, treaties, or land grants may be confused by this change in nomenclature.

LOCAL COLOR is a term often applied to fiction or verse that examines the mores, speech, landscape, or habits of thought found in a locale or region. In this country it is specifically applied to writings of that kind which appeared, usually as short stories, from the 1870s through the early years of the twentieth century, in efforts to familiarize a national audience with the homely, usually lovable characteristics of people who lived in newly settled or relatively unknown sections of the country. Although it followed trends in realism set abroad by such writers as Gustave Flaubert and Guy de Maupassant, it also responded to an apparent desire by post–Civil War American readers to learn more of the habits and circumstances of countrymen in out-of-the-way enclaves of the newly united Union, thus helping to mend wounds that war had made.

Influences on the movement were varied: local color writers built on the emphases of locale and local idiosyncracies made popular by earlier writers of Down East yarns or tall tales of the frontier; they followed examples of characters sometimes almost caricatured in the writings of Washington Irving in this country and of Charles Dickens in England; and they responded to the critical admonitions of Hippolyte Taine in France, who argued for a closer attention by writers to materials found close at home. Although part of what is called the realistic movement of the late nineteenth century, most local color writing of this period lacked the high seriousness of realism and was content to be entertainingly instructive about surface, often quaint mannerisms of language, dress, superstitions, and local traditions of characters who were somehow eccentric and usually sentimentalized, in a romantic narrative set against an unusual but realistically presented background.

Although a national movement, many of the most effective local colorists were from the South. Following Bret Harte, whose stories of California mining camps in the 1860s set a pattern, came GEORGE WASHINGTON CABLE, with tales of Creole Louisiana a decade later, and then JOEL CHANDLER HARRIS of Georgia, MARY NOAILLES MURFREE of Tennessee, John Fox of Kentucky, and THOMAS NELSON PAGE of Virginia. The movement then spread through writings of James Whitcomb Riley and Edward Eggleston of Indiana, Hamlin Garland of Iowa and South Dakota, O. Henry (WILLIAM SYDNEY PORTER) of New York, Lafcadio Hearn of Ohio, New Orleans, and the West Indies (and after that, Japan), and, perhaps the most talented of all, Sarah Orne Jewett of New England, whose tales, like those of SAMUEL L. CLEMENS and later of Willa Cather and WILLIAM FAULKNER, are important for reasons other than portrayal of locale. The term local color is often confused with the older and more inclusive term REGIONALISM, which is usually more seriously concerned with observed fact, is less often a sentimentalized attempt to depict the characteristics of a region, and may take nonfictional forms, as in James Kirk Paulding's *Letters from the South* (1817), Horace Greeley's *An Overland Journey from New York to San Francisco* (1860), or Wilbur J. Cash's *The Mind of the South* (1941).

See M. Jensen, *Regionalism in America* (1951); and H. Bernard, *Le Roman Régionalist aux États-Unis* (1949), though there is no adequate full-length study of the local color movement.

LEWIS LEARY
University of North Carolina, Chapel Hill

LOGAN, BENJAMIN (1742–1802), was born in the Shenandoah Valley to David and Jane Logan, immigrants from Ulster. He took part in Henry Bouquet's Indian campaign of 1764 and in DUNMORE'S WAR in 1774. After living for a time in Virginia's Holston River settlements he took his family to Kentucky. He established a home at St. Asaph's in what soon became Virginia's Kentucky County. Because he led the way in building a fort

there, St. Asaph's was often referred to as Logan's Fort. Logan advanced through the militia ranks of Kentucky County from captain to colonel. After that county was subdivided, his home was in Lincoln County. He soon became county lieutenant of the Lincoln militia and continued in that command until 1788. Logan served on campaigns against the SHAWNEE INDIANS under John Bowman in 1779 and GEORGE ROGERS CLARK in 1780 and 1782 and led his own Shawnee campaign in 1786. He was a member of eight of the ten conventions that led to statehood for Kentucky. In 1796 and again in 1800 he was an unsuccessful candidate for governor of the new state.

See C. G. Talbert, *Benjamin Logan* (1962); and T. D. Clark, *History of Kentucky* (1960).

CHARLES G. TALBERT
University of Kentucky

LONG, EARL KEMP (1895–1960), was one of the most colorful and interesting politicians in Louisiana history. He was eccentric, ribald, sarcastic, and funny. He was as likely to be found purchasing 300 pairs of cowboy boots and 900 alarm clocks as he was conducting state business. Once Long characterized his political opponent DELESSEPS MORRISON as "smoother than a peeled onion." He described Governor Robert Kennon as "a man with perfectly good ears. He can hear an election coming two years away."

Often depicted by the press as a clown and a buffoon, especially after his 1959 confinement to a mental institution, Earl Long was actually a progressive reformer. During his administration, teachers' salaries were increased, new roads, schools, and charity hospitals were constructed, and welfare payments to the old, poor, and disabled were raised. Earl Long was also one of the earliest champions of Negro voting rights and led a successful fight in the state legislature to prevent the DISFRANCHISEMENT of Negro voters in Louisiana. Long served as lieutenant governor (1936–1939) and as governor (1939–1940, 1948–1952, 1956–1960). He lost three elections for lieutenant governor (1932, 1944, 1959), and he lost a try for the governor's chair in 1940. In August, 1960, Long won election to the U.S. House of Representatives, but died a few days after the election.

See A. J. Liebling, *Earl of Louisiana* (1961); R. McCaughan, *Socks on a Rooster* (1967); B. Hebert and B. Read, *Last of Red Hot Poppas* (1961), a record; and M. Kurtz, "Demagogue and Liberal" (Ph.D. dissertation, Tulane, 1971) and *Louisiana History* (Summer, 1969).

MICHAEL L. KURTZ
Southeastern Louisiana University

LONG, HUEY PIERCE (1893–1935), was born in northern Louisiana. Although he built a political machine (LONG MACHINE) upon the votes of poor whites of that rural region, his family was middle class. After only one year of law school, he was admitted to the state bar and became an outstanding lawyer. His political career began in 1918 with his election to the Louisiana railroad commission. There he made a name for himself by attacking large Louisiana-based corporations, especially the Standard Oil Company. In 1924 Long ran for governor and lost, but he had begun to build an extremely effective political machine that would carry him to the governor's chair in 1928.

As governor of Louisiana Huey Long brought about the most sweeping "revolutionary" reforms that had ever taken place in the state. He began a massive road construction program, and by 1932 more people were employed building roads in Louisiana than in any other state in the Union. He supplied free textbooks to all school-aged children, established free public night schools, and began a statewide program to improve dramatically the health standards of the people. The money for these programs came from heavy taxation of large corporations.

In 1930 Long was elected senator from Louisiana. While in Congress he allied himself with progressive Republicans. He worked hard to help Franklin Roosevelt win the presidency in 1932, but broke with him in 1933 because he believed Roosevelt was moving too slowly with his programs to end the depression. In 1933 Long proposed his SHARE OUR WEALTH program, a massive overhaul of the tax structure in order to bring about a redistribution of wealth. The Kingfish, as Long liked to refer to himself, hoped his Share Our Wealth program and attacks upon large corporations would carry him to the presidency in 1936 or 1940. On September 8, 1935, however, he was fatally wounded while entering the capitol in Baton Rouge. His assassin, Dr. Carl Austin Weiss, was killed on the spot by Long's bodyguards, and thus his reasons for killing Long remain a mystery.

Huey Long has been referred to as a dictator, a Fascist, and a Communist; a pragmatic politician would no doubt be a better label. He built a massive political machine in Louisiana along class lines, gaining the support of poor whites. He deducted money from public employees' paychecks to support this machine. He had the power and used it to appoint the legal staffs of all district attorneys and many parish sheriffs. Nor was Long above calling out the National Guard to make sure votes were counted his way in hostile New Orleans. Although the Long machine was filled with

some corruption and dishonesty, Long himself never gained wealth illegally. He was a man who appeared to have no racial or religious prejudices and who never indulged in "nigger baiting" in order to win votes. Long was a man who sought power in order to do good and eventually came to equate power with good.

See H. Carter, *Aspirin Age* (1949), scathing attack on Long; H. P. Long, *Every Man a King* (1964); A. P. Sindler, *Huey Long's Louisiana* (1956), highly critical; G. L. K. Smith, *As We Saw Thirties* (1967); R. P. Warren, *All King's Men* (1953), a novel; and T. H. Williams, *Huey Long* (1969), good in-depth biography.

HARRY H. EDWARDS
Port Clinton, Ohio

LONG HUNTERS. Learning of the vast game preserve that was Kentucky, Tennessee, and the Lower South, eastern adventurers as early as the 1760s, sometimes traveling alone but more often in groups of ten to 40, ventured into the area to hunt, trap, and trade for periods ranging from several months to as long as two or three years. Among the more famous of these long hunters were Abraham Bledsoe, DANIEL BOONE, Elisha Walden, and James Knox. These men explored many new regions of the South and opened the way to future migration and settlement.

See E. Dick, *Dixie Frontier* (1948); M. W. Lafferty, *Lure of Kentucky* (1971); and R. L. Kincaid, *Wilderness Road* (1947).

LONG MACHINE refers to the Democratic political faction forged in Louisiana by HUEY P. LONG. The system's three chief attributes—Democratic bifactionalism, the "ticket" system of statewide slates in Democratic primaries, and gubernatorial dominance over the legislature—all had historic antecedents that were vastly accelerated by Long. Gubernatorial dominance of the state bureaucracy and the legislature was rooted in Louisiana history and was reinforced by the constitutional revisions of 1897, 1898, 1906, and 1921. The ticket system of statewide slates in the Democratic primaries was begun by the Choctaw machine in New Orleans and became common practice under Long and his successors. Bifactionalism had origins in the abortive dirt-farmer revolt of the 1890s. Long tapped this smoldering class resentment with a program of rural liberalism, which included massive highway and toll-free bridge construction; lower utility and public transportation rates; free school books, school lunches, and hospital care; and opposition to reapportionment, civil service, and the BOURBON tradition of minimal public service and low taxation. Support of Longism's rural liberalism was strongest in the cutover uplands of north and west-central Louisiana, and anti-Long sentiment was centered in the urban, Delta, and Sugar Bowl parishes.

Longite regimes dominated Louisiana from 1928 to 1940, when the corruption scandals unearthed by federal prosecutors in 1939 enabled the anti-Long reformer Sam H. Jones to defeat Huey's younger brother EARL K. LONG for the governorship. Jones was succeeded in 1944 by anti-Long JIMMIE H. DAVIS, but in 1948 Earl Long defeated Jones, and Russell B. Long, Huey's son, was elected to the U.S. Senate. The anti-Longs returned in 1952 under Robert F. Kennon, but Earl triumphed again in 1956. By 1960 the politics of race and religion had supplanted the old politics of class, and for the first time since 1928 a Longite failed to make the gubernatorial runoff and the old Long bifactionalism succumbed to the turmoil over racial desegregation.

See A. P. Sindler, *Huey Long's Louisiana* (1956); T. H. Williams, *Huey Long* (1969); and P. H. Howard, *Political Tendencies in Louisiana* (1971).

HUGH DAVIS GRAHAM
University of Maryland, Baltimore County

LONGSTREET, AUGUSTUS BALDWIN (1790–1870), was born in Augusta and educated at Moses Waddel's Willington Academy, Yale, and Tapping Reeve and James Gould's law school. He began the practice of law in Georgia in 1815 and served in the state legislature and as a judge. Remembered chiefly for his *Georgia Scenes*, Longstreet was successful as lawyer, planter, editor, minister, educator, and author. He served as president of four southern colleges: Emory, Centenary, the University of Mississippi, and the University of South Carolina. *Georgia Scenes* is an insightful view in a series of sketches of one of the United States' earliest frontiers. It was first published in 1835 and since then has been almost constantly in print. After the death of his eldest child in 1824 he turned increasingly religious and was ordained a Methodist minister in 1838. His career as an educator began with his appointment as president of Emory College in 1839. He retired from college administration in 1861 and spent his last years in Mississippi, though he was a refugee during much of the Civil War in Georgia. Longstreet's later publications were largely religious or political. His one novel, *Master William Mitten*, was a failure. His place in literary history, however, is as-

sured by *Georgia Scenes*, the premier book of southwestern HUMOR in both time and influence.

See J. S. Wade, *Augustus Baldwin Longstreet* (1924); and J. Blanck, *Bibliography of American Literature* (1973).

RICHARD B. HARWELL
University of Georgia

LONGSTREET, JAMES, "OLD PETE" (1821–1904), was born in Edgefield District, S.C., of Dutch ancestry. He graduated from West Point in 1842, fought gallantly in the Mexican War, and subsequently rose to the rank of major. Resigning in June, 1861, Longstreet was appointed the same month a brigadier general in the Confederate army and rose rapidly to the rank of lieutenant general. He participated in most of the significant encounters of the Army of Northern Virginia from first BULL RUN to APPOMATTOX. Temporarily detached from Robert E. Lee's forces, he was not at CHANCELLORSVILLE in May, 1863. After GETTYSBURG, where his performance became the focus of postwar criticism, Longstreet was sent to reinforce Braxton Bragg's army in Tennessee. His troops fought capably at CHICKAMAUGA but subsequently found only disappointment, defeat, and frustration in operations before KNOXVILLE and elsewhere in eastern Tennessee. Returning to the Virginia front in April, 1864, Longstreet resumed his position as Lee's senior and most trusted lieutenant.

After the war Longstreet remained in the South, joined the Republican party, and was rewarded by appointments to several different offices over the next 30 years including postmaster, federal marshal, and American minister to Turkey. Understandably, Longstreet's meritorious wartime record came under close scrutiny from biased southerners, who commonly characterized him as overcautious, disobedient, sulky, and inordinately slow in moving his troops. The embattled general's intemperate rebuttals to his critics additionally damaged his postwar reputation. But Longstreet's military contribution has been largely restored by recent scholarship. No longer a villainous SCALAWAG, he is regarded as a fearless, skillful, and inspiring combat officer who may have had no peer in either army as a superb defensive tactician. Once again Lee's unswerving confidence in his senior lieutenant has been vindicated.

See D. S. Freeman, *R. E. Lee* (1935), biased, and *Lee's Lieutenants* (1944), more balanced; H. J. Eckenrode and B. Conrad, *Longstreet* (1936), critical; J. I. Robertson, Jr., intro. to Longstreet's memoirs, *From Manassas to Appomattox* (1960), best brief account; D. R. Sanger and T. R. Hay, *Longstreet* (1952); and G. Tucker, *Lee and Longstreet* (1968), both favorable.

CHARLES P. CULLOP
East Carolina University

LORING, WILLIAM WING (1818–1886), born in North Carolina, practiced law and served as a legislator before entering the Mexican War. He afterward pursued a military career, but later resigned from the regular army in sympathy with states' rights. Commissioned a brigadier general, C.S.A., he participated in West Virginia operations. Involved in an incident with STONEWALL JACKSON resulting in Jackson's recommendation that Loring be cashiered, he was transferred to the West. In the VICKSBURG CAMPAIGN, Loring gained the nickname "Old Blizzards" by his spirited repulse of Union gunboats on the Tallahatchie. His slowness in responding to repeated calls from General JOHN PEMBERTON, ordering him to the rebel left at CHAMPION HILL, brought accusations of blame for the defeat. He served creditably as a corps leader in Georgia and was second-in-command at the battles of FRANKLIN and NASHVILLE. After the war Loring was a banker, a brigadier general in the service of the khedive of Egypt, and the author of many articles and a book on his war experiences.

See W. P. Deese, "General William Loring" (M.A. thesis, Abilene Christian College, 1973); W. L. Wessells, *Military Career of Loring* (1971), undocumented but useful; S. Foote, *Civil War* (1958–74), II; and *Official Records, Armies*.

J. L. MCDONOUGH
David Lipscomb College

LOST CAUSE is a phrase that refers to the southern states' unsuccessful attempt to secede from the United States. An early use of the phrase was made in the title of a history of the Civil War published in 1866 by a southern newspaper editor, EDWARD A. POLLARD. According to him the "cause" was the principle that the federal Union was an association of sovereign states. The war's conclusion not only destroyed this principle, he declared, but it also abolished slavery and would threaten the whole southern way of life. Later interpretations of the phrase have varied, including references to cultural and material "losses" such as southern traditions generally, slavery, and the Confederate military (as seen for example in the periodical *The Lost Cause: A Confederate War Record*, which was published at the turn of

the century by the UNITED DAUGHTERS OF THE CONFEDERACY). All these "causes" are secondary to the primary Lost Cause of the states' vain assertion of sovereignty and of independence from the Union.

See E. A. Pollard, *Lost Cause* (1866), contemporary view; and J. G. Randall and D. Donald, *Civil War and Reconstruction* (1969), standard text, extensive bibliography.

WESTLEY F. BUSBEE, JR.
Belhaven College

LOUISIANA contains three separate identifiable areas. Cosmopolitan New Orleans, the state's largest and best-known city, forms one political and social entity. Another unit is formed by a triangular-shaped area from Lake Charles in southwest Louisiana to New Orleans in the east and Alexandria in the north. This triangle is inhabited by French descendants, mostly Roman Catholic. The area of the state above Alexandria plus the area once known as West Florida is populated mostly by Protestant Anglo-Saxons. This geographic and ethnic mixture has produced a volatile political and social environment.

Even today, as the twenty-first century nears, all areas outside New Orleans look upon the city with suspicion. The northern part of the state is not comfortable with the French Catholics in the south, and the citizens of the south do not really understand their Protestant brethren in the north. For the good of all, the state legislature must compromise extensively. The tensions caused by the mixture of ethnic background, religion, and geographical identity make Louisiana's politics colorful and interesting. Perhaps Louisiana is, as A. J. Liebling called it, closer to Lebanon than to other southern states. At times it has appeared to be another banana republic accidentally located in North America.

Origins and geography. In the early sixteenth century, Spanish explorers, while searching for precious metals, discovered the Mississippi River; because they did not find what they sought, Spain lost interest in the northern Gulf Coast. For over a century after the Spaniards abandoned the area, the Mississippi waited for someone to claim its vast valley. When the area was claimed, it was by France, not Spain; and Louisiana would be claimed by way of Canada, not the Gulf of Mexico.

The present state of Louisiana has an area of 48,523 square miles, of which over 3,000 square miles are inland water areas. The highest elevation is 535 feet above sea level, and the lowest

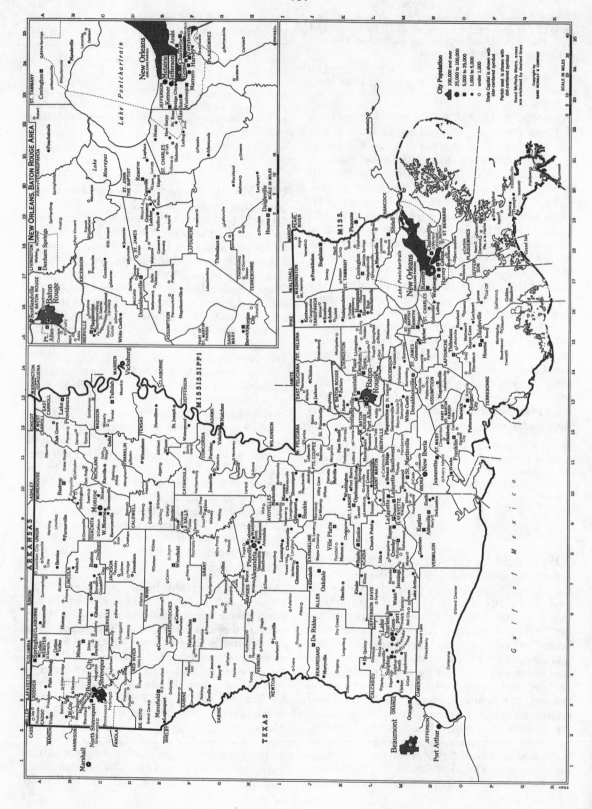

point is five feet below sea level. The physiography of the state includes tidal marshes along the Gulf of Mexico; the ridges along the Mississippi River; the prairies of the southwestern part of the state; sandy-clay hills in the north-central, west-central, and southeastern part of the state; reddish brown alluvial soil along the Red River; and the black, rich alluvial soil bordering the Mississippi River and its smaller tributaries.

Colonial development. The first of the French explorers were Louis Jolliet, the fur trader, and the Jesuit priest Father Jacques Marquette. They discovered that the "Great River" flowed south instead of west. The river was not the Northwest Passage. ROBERT CAVELIER DE LA SALLE, a settler in Canada, envisioned a French empire from Canada to the Gulf. He descended the river to its mouth in 1682 and claimed all the land draining into the Mississippi River for France, naming the vast area Louisiana in honor of King Louis XIV. It was not La Salle's fate to be the one to establish a permanent French colony in the area he had claimed. That task fell to the Le Moyne brothers. La Salle's expedition had been in part an attempt to establish a base from which the French could launch expeditions against the Spanish; the expedition in 1699 of PIERRE LE MOYNE D'IBERVILLE was for the same reason. Iberville, following the northern coast of the Gulf of Mexico, found the Mississippi and sailed upriver. He explored the area but found no mines of precious metal, a prime concern of his venture. Because of the strategic location of the colony, France could not afford to abandon it; however, France never gave the colony adequate support.

Iberville decided to establish the permanent settlement at modern-day Ocean Springs, Miss. JEAN BAPTISTE LE MOYNE DE BIENVILLE explored the Mississippi River further upstream. While returning from one of his explorations, he met a British ship sailing upriver. The British were investigating the possibility of establishing a colony on the river. Bienville informed them that France possessed the area and that the river they searched for was farther west. Shortly thereafter the French erected a fort about 50 miles from the river's mouth. France now had tangible evidence of its possession of the Mississippi River and the area drained by the river. The headquarters of the colony were moved to Mobile Bay, a safer and more accessible site than Biloxi.

Meanwhile France and England engaged in the conflict known in England as the War of the Spanish Succession and in America as Queen Anne's War. During this conflict, as in all other wars, the Louisiana colony suffered. Internal problems added to the misery of the small settlement. Bienville, in command of the colony after Iberville's death in 1706, quarreled with officials and the colonists. The colonists blamed him for all their problems. They brought formal charges against him, and he was recalled to France. An investigation cleared him before he left the colony, and he remained there until Antoine de la Mothe Cadillac replaced him. The French government had spent limited amounts of money and supplies on the colony and had received no return. It did not want to leave the colony to England or Spain, but neither did it wish to have the colony as a constant drain on the French treasury.

Luckily the French government found a rich merchant willing to accept Louisiana as a propriy etary colony. Antoine Crozat, hoping to profit from mineral resources and commercial agreements with Mexico, accepted Louisiana from the French crown (CROZAT GRANT). The land between the Gulf of Mexico to Illinois in the north and from Carolina to Texas in the west was given to Crozat. Under the terms of the charter Crozat received all mines, all cultivated and reclaimed land, and all manufacturing plants he would build. In addition, he received all furs, except beaver, plus a monopoly on all trade with the area. As frosting on the cake, the French government would pay all expenses of the colony for a period of nine years. In return for these privileges, Crozat had to send two shiploads of colonists to Louisiana per year. The king would receive a percentage of all gold and silver discovered. The laws of France were also to be the laws of Louisiana.

Up to this time Louisiana had been a military outpost with a military governor in control. From 1702 onward the governor had to share his power with a civilian commissary (later, under Crozat, the commissaire-ordonnateur). The result was rivalry between the governor and the ordonnateur, whose powers included control of finance, commerce, internal improvement, the royal warehouses, justice, the police, and first judge of the superior council. Added to the conflict between the governor and the ordonnateur, a conflict developed between the Capuchin and Jesuit religious orders for supremacy of Louisiana's spiritual life. It was almost inevitable that factionalism develop. The governor and the ordonnateur each had his supporters, and the religious orders also chose sides. The factionalism that developed during those early years proved to be a preview, for factionalism of some kind continued into the twentieth century. At times the factionalism had been detrimental. For example, during the Seven

Years' War, Governor Louis Billouart, the baron de Kerlerec, attempted to regulate prices. The ordonnateur, Vincent Gaspare Pierre de Rochemore, frustrated the attempt because he controlled commerce.

Crozat added to the governmental structure by establishing the superior council. This addition reflected the change of Louisiana from a military outpost to one that was supposed to return a profit to the proprietor. The superior council arbitrated commercial disputes and successions involving property and served as the court of last resort in minor cases.

The governmental reorganization did not help Crozat make a profit. Trade with Mexico did not materialize, although efforts to establish such a trade led to the founding of the first permanent settlement in present-day Louisiana, Natchitoches in 1714. To protect Louisiana from the English, the French built Ft. Rosalie at Natchez. The entrance of Negro slaves led to enactment of a BLACK CODE, modeled after the one of Santo Domingo. Slaves would continue to enter the colony, but by the summer of 1717 Crozat had not made any profit in Louisiana; in fact, he had squandered a fortune. He decided to return the colony to the French government. It in turn granted a charter to John Law, a Scottish gambler, who formed the Company of the West, later reorganized into the Company of the Indies (MISSISSIPPI BUBBLE). Because one of the more important needs for the colony was additional settlers, the new company launched a propaganda campaign depicting Louisiana as a garden of Eden. When those who believed the propaganda arrived in Louisiana, they found a sparsely settled frontier environment. Their reports to France overemphasized the negative aspects. The result of the bad publicity was a lack of volunteer colonists. The company, therefore, searched the jails and streets for settlers. These dregs of society were sent to Louisiana; they made poor colonists. Only the famous CASKET GIRLS (girls provided with little trunks of clothes) and some German immigrants proved to be valuable colonists, for the girls became wives and the Germans engaged in much needed agricultural endeavors.

The company failed to attract desirable settlers, but it did manage to build a city near the mouth of the Mississippi River. Bienville had been lobbying for such a city, and in 1718 New Orleans became a reality. Streets were laid out, surveyed, and given the names of saints, royalty, prominent people, or institutions. The original city is what is now known as the French Quarter or Vieux Carré. In spite of the new city, problems multiplied.

French suppression of the Natchez Indians cost the colony dearly because the company could not afford the added expense of an Indian war. Additional troubles, such as crop failures, convinced the company that no profit could be made in Louisiana. In 1731 the colony of Louisiana was returned to the French crown.

Both proprietors, Crozat and the Company of the Indies, had failed for many reasons. Perhaps the most important was the lack of the right kind of colonists: farmers. Those who would have been good settlers did not wish to leave France. France's policy of religious and political orthodoxy prevented some, such as the HUGUENOTS, from settling in Louisiana. The desire for quick profit by both the company and the individuals did not provide the atmosphere for success. The French government must also accept part of the blame, for it did not provide the needed aid.

The French crown again owned Louisiana in 1731 after the Company of the Indies gave up the colony. France had to keep the colony to prevent its enemies from acquiring the area. Expenses kept increasing, and profits continued to prove elusive. An Indian war against the CHICKASAW INDIANS, usually a pro-British tribe, proved costly and inconclusive. After the failure of France to defeat the Chickasaw decisively, Bienville at his own request was relieved of his duties. He retired to France. Pierre François de Rigaud, the marquis de Vaudreuil-Cavagnal, replaced him as governor.

Vaudreuil presided over the colony during the War of the Austrian Succession or King George's War. He tried to turn New Orleans into a frontier Versailles, but "culture" did not provide a profit, and Louisiana continued to be a drain on the French treasury. During the Seven Years' War or the French and Indian War, as in all the others, Louisiana proved to be outside the theater of operations. The only activity was neglect. The French government had its hands full and could not adequately provide for the colony. France in the Treaty of Paris of 1763 gave Louisiana west of the Mississippi River plus the Isle of Orleans to Spain. England received the remainder of Louisiana and Canada. With the end of the conflict, France was eliminated as a colonial power in North America and Louisiana belonged to Spain. It is ironic that one group of immigrants who came to Louisiana because it was a French possession arrived after Spain had title to the area. The ACADIANS, exiled from Nova Scotia by the British in 1755, made their way to Louisiana beginning in the mid-1760s. Henry W. Longfellow romanticized their plight in *Evangeline*. Their descendants today include almost one-third of Louisiana's population.

The economy of Louisiana when Spain received it left much to be desired. As in other colonies, subsistence agriculture had occupied settlers during the early period. The colony exported indigo, tobacco, naval stores, fur, rice, and sassafras. Unfortunately, the settlers produced only small quantities of these export crops mainly because the people refused to do this type of work. The labor problem was relieved somewhat with the importation of African slaves. However, Louisiana was never self-sufficient and always depended upon France, Spain, or the West Indies for supplies.

When Spain received Louisiana, it was in no hurry to assume actual control of the colony. France continued to rule the area, but with a greatly reduced force. The French-descended people in the Louisiana colony did not want to become citizens of a Spanish colony. Therefore, they called a public meeting in New Orleans and adopted a petition asking the French king to retain Louisiana. Jean Milhet, a rich merchant, carried the petition to France. The French government refused to retain the colony, but the Louisianians hoped to change the government's mind, especially since Spain seemed reluctant to take over the colony. Finally, in 1765, the superior council in Louisiana received a letter from Don Antonio de Ulloa informing the Louisianians that upon his arrival he would assume control of the colony for Spain. He did not arrive until the spring of 1766. Because he had been led to believe that the French troops in Louisiana would join his command, Ulloa brought only two infantry companies, an inadequate military force to take over the rebellious colony. His reception in New Orleans was correct, but cool. The superior council demanded inspection of Ulloa's credentials, and his defiant refusal set the tone of his administration. He governed through French Captain Charles Philippe Aubry, who was then the senior French officer in Louisiana.

The problems of the Spanish governor were numerous. For years the lack of specie in Louisiana had been alleviated with paper money. Now the colonists feared that the Spanish would abolish their wealth. This the new government did not do, but the Spanish redemption of paper money fell below the value placed on it by the colonists. The settlers also feared abolishment of the normal commercial links of Louisiana. Ulloa, in general, wanted regulations that would bring Louisiana into the Spanish orbit of trade instead of trading with France and French possessions. Although the regulations did not go into effect immediately, the political damage was done. Secret meetings were held to discuss means of driving out the Spanish. Merchants, local French officials, planters, and some officers of the French armed forces led the movement against the Spanish. Armed men from various parts of the colony poured into New Orleans. There were not enough Spaniards or loyal French troops to defend the Spanish administration, and Ulloa, on the advice of Aubry, boarded a ship in the Mississippi River for safety. Meanwhile, the superior council ordered the governor out of the colony. Ulloa left Louisiana and, for the time being, the leaders of the rebellion were in control. Commercial regulations, rather than a quest for political liberty, had affected the desire of the Louisianians to remain French.

With Ulloa gone the superior council ran the colony. The council again to no avail sent a petition to Louis XV asking that France reclaim Louisiana. Some individuals active in the rebellion even talked of establishing a republic or gaining the aid of England. These matters were not part of any overall plan but rather an attempt to find some way out of the dilemma.

Ulloa, now in the West Indies, informed his superiors of the situation in Louisiana, and Spain decided to crush the rebellion. Don Alexander O'Reilly, an Irish soldier of fortune, then a general in the army of Spain, would reestablish Spanish authority in Louisiana. While O'Reilly prepared his expedition, the Louisianians were having second thoughts about their rebellion. A Spanish fleet arrived at the mouth of the Mississippi River in the summer of 1769. From that base O'Reilly arrived at New Orleans with his 24 ships and the next day took formal possession of the colony. His 2,000 troops ensured a peaceful transfer, and after taking control O'Reilly arrested the rebel leaders. They were tried, convicted, and sentenced. A few received the death penalty; the remainder were sent to jail for varying terms but later released by the Spanish king. O'Reilly left behind a tarnished reputation for his alleged harshness toward the rebel leaders. Early Louisiana historians also condemned the action; however, if the time in which he lived is taken into account, O'Reilly was indeed lenient.

After suppressing the rebellion, O'Reilly abolished the superior council and established the cabildo in its place. When possible, he appointed Frenchmen to positions of authority, thereby allaying the fear of complete Spanish tyranny. Louisianians accepted the fact that Spain indeed controlled the area and would not tolerate resistance. They might refuse to learn the Spanish language and to accept Spanish customs, but their political rulers would, without a doubt, be Spanish.

The years that followed were generally prosperous ones for the colony. Population increased, Spanish officials closed their eyes to illegal trade when they saw the necessity for it, and the economy improved during the period of Spanish control. O'Reilly was succeeded by mild-mannered Don Luis de Unzaga, who did his utmost to reconcile the Louisianians to Spanish rule. Like all goernors, he had his share of problems, but he dealt with his subjects in a conciliatory manner. Not until the American Revolution did the preservation of Spanish authority require a stronger hand at the helm. This stronger hand, perhaps the best of Louisiana's colonial governors, appeared in the successor to Unzaga, Don BERNARDO DE GÁLVEZ.

Gálvez, twenty-nine years old and able, with the right political connections in Spain, proved to be an asset to Spain and Louisiana. About 15,000 people occupied the territory over which he governed. Obviously Louisiana needed more people to make it an asset to the Spanish crown. Liberal concessions were made to those who wished to settle in Louisiana, and emigrants came from France and the Canary Islands. Spain allowed ships of other countries to enter Louisiana and sell Negro slaves. Less rigid commercial restrictions also bolstered the prosperity of the colony. However, the desire and need for a prosperous Louisiana had to take a back seat to the pressing need for defense when the American Revolution began and threatened to involve Spain.

Although Spain refused to become officially involved at the beginning of the Revolution, it provided secret aid to the Americans fighting Spain's old enemy England. Gálvez allowed American ships to purchase provisions in New Orleans and permitted Oliver Pollock to act as an agent for the Americans. Through Pollock, supplies were provided for some of the American expeditions in the West. Meanwhile Gálvez improved defenses for Louisiana should England and Spain engage in open warfare.

In May, 1779, Spain declared war on England. Gálvez planned an offensive action against British posts on the Mississippi River and along the Gulf coast. He led about 1,400 men (whites, Indians, and Negroes) in the capture of Ft. Bute, a little over 100 miles above New Orleans. After this force also captured Baton Rouge and Natchez, Spain controlled both sides of the Mississippi River north to Natchez. Gálvez moved next against the British possessions along the Gulf coast. He captured Mobile and planned to occupy Pensacola, a well-fortified position. Upon entering Pensacola harbor, however, one of the Spanish ships ran aground.

The naval officers refused to cross the sandbar at the entrance of the harbor. Not until the expedition from Mobile and New Orleans arrived could Gálvez attack the fort. He assumed command of the two forces, sailed the ships into the harbor, and laid siege to the town. The siege of Pensacola lasted until a powder storehouse inside the fort exploded when hit by a Spanish shell. Confronted with the impossibility of further resistance, the fort surrendered. The whole Gulf coast now belonged to Spain. Gálvez's actions laid the basis for the claim of Spain to the area when the American Revolution ended, and in the peace treaty Spain did get Florida. In 1785 Gálvez received the viceroyalty of Mexico for his efforts.

Events occurring during the remaining years of Spanish control of Louisiana were important ones, but not as dramatic as those of the American Revolution. Louisiana's rulers were relatively able; however, because they governed in peaceful times and in the shadow of O'Reilly and Gálvez, their visibility was not as great as their predecessors'. Much time was spent trying to blunt the obvious expansion tendencies of the new United States. Spanish officials in Louisiana tried to obtain the friendship of the Indians in the Southeast, hoping that the Indians would act as a buffer between themselves and the American. The Indians could also be used if war should break out between the United States and Spain. Spain even hoped that some of the western Americans would secede from the United States and unite with Spain. None of the plans succeeded because diplomacy finally settled the question.

Trade improved, a limited commerce with the Indians developed, and immigration was encouraged. Perhaps the most important economic development of the post-Revolution period in Spanish Louisiana was the development of a granulated sugar industry. Étienne Boré purchased the necessary equipment and proved successful in giving birth to a whole new industry. Louisiana at last had a valuable export crop in quantity.

Economic development was not the only problem facing the Spaniards. The French Revolution created apprehension for the Spanish administrators in Louisiana, most of the citizens of which were of French origin. With a rather steady hand, however, the Spaniards managed to keep passions in the colony at low tide. Some French royalist refugees were allowed to settle in Louisiana, offsetting the balance of French republican sentiment. Once France and Spain began to fight, the problems of defense made the situation even more complex. Defenses were prepared in case the area should become a combat zone, and Spanish officials walked a tightrope. A decade of Spanish rule had not altered the French character of the colony. The first newspaper in Louisiana was published during this period, *Moniteur de la Louisiane*, and the culture remained French. Spanish administrators managed the situation very well, for an overly conciliatory policy would likely have allowed the citizens to get out of hand and a policy of extreme repression would probably have produced a rebellion.

This fact of Spanish jurisdiction and French cultural dominance in Louisiana did not matter at all to the Americans. Western Americans were more interested in the right of deposit at New Orleans and the right to navigate the Mississippi River than they were in the question of which culture predominated. America received the right of deposit in Pinckney's Treaty. The same treaty also settled the southern boundary of the United States at the thirty-first parallel. Under intense American pressure, Spain relinquished its forts north of the boundary line.

By the time Thomas Jefferson became president of the United States in 1801, France had pressured Spain to cede Louisiana to France in a secret treaty, but a slave uprising in Santo Domingo delayed French plans to assume physical possession of Louisiana. When the French proved unable or unwilling to suppress the rebellion in the West Indies, the Spanish continued to administer Louisiana. Eventually France sent the colonial prefect Pierre Clement Laussat to begin the administrative control of Louisiana. In June of 1803 Prefect Laussat received instructions to accept formal possession of Louisiana from Spain, and in November the ceremony took place.

Jefferson believed French control of the area to be a greater threat to the United States than Spanish control had been. He therefore instructed the American ambassador to France, Robert Livingston, to buy New Orleans and West Florida, if at all possible. Negotiations moved slowly, but France (Napoleon) finally decided to sell the whole of Louisiana to the United States for the sum of $15 million (LOUISIANA PURCHASE). On December 20, 1803, Laussat turned Louisiana over to President Jefferson's appointed representatives, and the size of the United States just about doubled.

During the third of a century of Spanish rule, Louisiana's population had almost doubled. The overwhelming majority was located in the southern portion of this vast colonial territory, and slaves and free blacks now outnumbered white Louisianians. The Spanish regime had enacted a more stringent black code, but fear of a black insurrec-

tion remained constant. Nevertheless, Louisiana's free blacks probably had more legal rights than did those in most other slaveholding areas of the United States. For example, free blacks in Louisiana had the right to sue in the courts, to testify against whites, to own property, and even to own slaves.

The period of Spain's colonial rule had also been a prosperous one for Louisianians. In an effort to encourage the colony's economic self-sufficiency, Spain had agreed to purchase all the tobacco Louisiana produced at a set price. Despite a similar government policy concerning indigo, production of that crop actually decreased during the final years of Spanish Louisiana, and other goods replaced indigo in the export market: cotton, sugar, hides, lead, tobacco, flour, salt beef and pork, and molasses. Despite its rather extensive exports, Spanish Louisiana had yet to establish a favorable balance of trade. Spain provided subsidies and the colony was more self-sufficient than it had been under the French regime; but Louisiana continued to import more than the value of its exports.

Spanish rule had done relatively little, moreover, to alter the essentially French character of Louisiana's culture. The people had refused to learn the Spanish language, to attend Spanish schools, or to change any facet of their way of life. Even the Spanish architecture in New Orleans today is in the French Quarter. French culture had absorbed the Spanish influences instead of the other way around. With the cession of Louisiana to the United States, however, a different political, economic, and social order would operate.

An American territory and state. President Jefferson appointed W. C. C. CLAIBORNE temporary governor of the Louisiana Territory. On leave from his position as governor of the Mississippi Territory, Claiborne governed alone until Congress passed an act dividing Louisiana into two territories: the district of Louisiana and the territory of Orleans. The district of Louisiana encompassed the area north of the thirty-third parallel, and the territory of Orleans included the area south of the same parallel to the Gulf of Mexico. It also included the Isle of Orleans and the area west of the Mississippi River to the Sabine River. Louisiana's western boundary was actually somewhat more ambiguous than this, however. The United States and Spain, being unable to agree on a boundary, had created a neutral zone between the Calcasieu and the Sabine rivers. This no-man's-land became a haven for pirates and outlaws until 1819, when Spain ceded the territory to the United States.

In addition to delineating physical boundaries, the act creating the territory of Orleans provided for the appointment of a governor by the president of the United States. Some Louisianians objected to the act because they had expected immediate statehood, and they vented their disappointment on the appointed governor. Jefferson had tried to recruit General Lafayette and James Monroe for the job. These two men had refused, and many Louisianians refused to serve in the government of Claiborne, a Virginian who knew no French. If they could not have statehood or a governor of their liking, they wanted at least a more liberal form of government with some representation. Congress reacted with a new territorial act, which provided for an elected house of representatives in addition to the officials appointed under the previous act. One provision promised statehood whenever the territory had at least 60,000 free inhabitants. As expected, when the territorial house of representatives met, those representatives of French ancestry were in the majority.

Although Louisiana now had an elected and American government, some people contemplated a future that did not include statehood. During 1805–1806 Aaron Burr, former vice-president of the United States, traveled extensively in the West and down the Mississippi River. He conferred with General JAMES WILKINSON, military commander of the Mississippi River region, and he was very well received in New Orleans. Later Wilkinson informed President Jefferson that Burr planned treasonous activities. Burr was arrested, tried for treason, and found not guilty. Meanwhile, in Louisiana, Wilkinson exaggerated the conspirary, thereby providing a pretext for him to declare a state of martial law and to supersede Claiborne. Wilkinson was later reprimanded for his actions, but Claiborne had to bear the stigma of having had his authority taken from him.

Shortly after Burr's trial, a real revolt rather than some murky conspiracy attracted the attention of many Louisianians. The United States and Spain disagreed over Louisiana's eastern boundary with Spanish Florida (WEST FLORIDA CONTROVERSY). Congress in 1804 authorized the president to assume control of lands west of the Perdido River. Although a growing number of Americans had settled in the area, nothing definite was done. Spain meanwhile sought to organize and to incorporate the area into Florida. The predominantly American settlers in and around Baton Rouge resisted Spanish designs by declaring their independence. In 1810, under the command of Colonel Philemon Thomas, the settlers captured Baton Rouge, raised a blue banner with a white star in the middle, and proclaimed the West Florida Republic. A constitution was written, a chief executive, FULWAR SKIPWITH, was elected, and annexation by the United States was requested. The United States did seize that part of the disputed territory west of the Pearl River, and in December, 1810, Governor Claiborne divided the area into four parishes to be governed as part of the territory of Orleans.

The Louisiana residents, claiming that they had the required population for admission into the Union, still labored for statehood. The census of 1810 showed that the territory had over 70,000 people, though roughly half were slaves and free blacks. Congress nevertheless did pass an enabling act authorizing the territory of Orleans to prepare for statehood. West Florida was not included in the area preparing for statehood because, some claimed, it was still in dispute with Spain. Some congressmen, led by Josiah Quincy of Massachusetts, argued against statehood for Louisiana because it was not part of the original United States. In spite of the protests, President James Madison signed the enabling act for the area from the Sabine to the Mississippi River and from the thirty-third parallel to the Gulf of Mexico. The only area east of the Mississippi included in the original state was the Isle of Orleans. The necessary requirements were fulfilled by the Louisianians, and on April 8, 1812, President Madison signed the statehood bill. A few days later he signed a bill adding West Florida to the original state of Louisiana with the Pearl River as the eastern boundary.

Louisiana's constitution, which had been written without the predominantly American residents of West Florida, created the normal state government with legislative, executive, and judicial branches. Payment of a tax, which meant property ownership, was required to vote for state officials. Representatives, senators, and governors had to possess at least $500, $1,000, and $5,000 worth of property, respectively. In addition, the legislature chose the governor from the two men who received the most popular votes. So cumbersome was the process of amendment that the constitution of 1812 was never amended.

Except for the American settlers, the people of Louisiana had had no experience in self-government. The governors had run the colony when it belonged to France and Spain. Claiborne had governed until a territorial house of representatives was provided for in 1805. Now, in 1812, Louisiana was a state. The tradition of a strong governor had been engraved upon the state through at least a century. From statehood until Reconstruction,

Louisiana followed the national standards for gubernatorial powers, but a strong governor reemerged during Reconstruction and the Huey Long era. This tradition continues in the last quarter of the twentieth century. Any Louisiana governor willing to use the power at his disposal can be a strong governor.

W. C. C. Claiborne, elected governor over Jacques Villère in the state's first election, immediately had problems. In June the United States declared war on England. New Orleans would be vulnerable, for the city was almost without defenses. The U.S. government made no strong effort to fortify the city, and Governor Claiborne had domestic problems of his own in the persons of JEAN LAFFITE and company. These pirates sold their booty in New Orleans openly, and the governor posted a reward for the arrest of Laffite. Laffite offered a reward for Claiborne. The people of New Orleans thought it a good joke, and the state legislature would not provide the necessary aid to stop the pirates. The British, however, were actively trying to obtain the aid of Laffite in a projected British attack on New Orleans. Although tendered money and other compensations to help the British, Laffite refused and offered his services to the United States. General ANDREW JACKSON, who had come to New Orleans to prepare the city for a spirited defense, accepted Laffite's offer. Jackson needed all the help he could get, for New Orleans was totally unprepared, physically and psychologically, for a British attack. The main battle of NEW ORLEANS took place on January 8, 1815. Jackson defeated the British and saved the city. The Treaty of Ghent ending the war had been signed two weeks earlier, but this took nothing away from the adulation showered upon him.

Until he received official notification of peace, however, Jackson refused to lift the martial law that he had imposed upon his arrival. In fact, several militiamen and a Louisiana judge were arrested during the latter period of martial law. Upon the lifting of martial law, Jackson was arrested and fined for his high-handed actions. Nevertheless, Louisiana had acted in concert with the rest of the nation in fighting the British. Its introduction into the nation had been dramatic, but the functioning of the state during peacetime had not yet been tried.

Claiborne ended his term in office in 1816. He had earned his retirement, for he had crossed swords with Generals Wilkinson and Jackson as well as with French citizens of Louisiana who refused Americanization by maintaining their language and culture. The election to choose Claiborne's successor developed into a contest between the "Americans" and the "French." Jacques Villère successfully carried the banner for the French faction, and Joshua Lewis represented the American group. A breakdown of the voting showed Lewis carrying the sections where the Americans dominated (such as the Florida parishes). Villère carried the predominantly French areas. This voting by nationality continued until national political parties expanded into Louisiana, and even then nationality remained a consideration. The question of ancestry surfaced from time to time, even in the gubernatorial elections of 1972, when Edwin Edwards ran a campaign that stressed his residence in the southern part of the state and his French blood. Edwards won because the southern part of the state solidified behind his candidacy. Thus, nationality is not out of the picture after more than a century and a half of statehood. It is therefore understandable that it played an important part in the early state elections. Although Louisiana has a sizable number of non-French and non-Anglo-Saxon citizens, the French designation still dominates as though French and Anglo-Saxons were the only two groups in the state. Whatever other cultures have provided has been absorbed under the general designation of French.

During the years after the War of 1812, Louisiana adjusted to being an American state. Legislation enacted during the early years represented attempts to move Louisiana, except for New Orleans, away from frontier living and toward becoming a lawful, civilized society. Inundated by an influx of Americans in search of economic opportunity, Louisianians came to grips with the increasing number of Protestants entering the state. Roman Catholicism was losing its dominant position in the spiritual life of the state. Methodists, Baptists, and Presbyterians organized churches. The state legislature could grant divorces although the Catholic church prohibited divorce. Slowly the state fell into step with the remainder of the nation. Too many Americans were moving in, and inevitably the old ways were modified, but slowly. For example, the Catholic church, while losing influence, still controlled most of the educational efforts in the state.

Economically the state prospered. The Bank of the United States established a branch in New Orleans. The state granted charters to insurance companies, other banks, and additional business endeavors. The creation of a board of internal improvements launched Louisiana, like the rest of the nation, into the economic boom of the 1820s and 1830s. New companies formed for every conceivable purpose from canals to towboats to railroads. In many cases the state government either bought stock in some of these internal improvement companies or else guaranteed the bonds of such companies. Therefore, when the PANIC OF 1837 arrived, the state, as well as private individuals, lost money. With the advent of the depression, the state government made some attempt to restore prosperity. The state created boards to oversee banks, forcing the weak ones to liquidate. Governor A. B. Roman vetoed state-funding bills for internal improvement. Slowly the state lifted itself out of the depression. The memory would remain, but by 1852 the state Democratic party was again pushing internal improvements. Tax exemptions and stock purchases were again offered to those companies that would improve transportation and communication.

Unfortunately, education did not progress as fast as railroad building. There were no public colleges or universities in Louisiana. Private colleges existed, but public schools were few and underfunded, for the state provided only matching funds for the local public school systems. By the time of the Mexican War, Louisiana had approximately 30,000 youngsters of school age. Of that number less than 5,000 attended public schools. In 1848 a special session of the legislature provided additional funds for public education, and by 1850 school enrollments had quadrupled. But not until 1853 did the legislature provide for a "seminary of learning," which later became Louisiana State University. Educational advancement in Louisiana was measured in inches instead of miles during the pre–Civil War period.

While the state indulged in economic expansion and neglected education, immigrants poured into the state from foreign countries and from other states of the Union. Many of the immigrants settled in the cities, and many "Americans" settled in New Orleans and in the northern part of the state. These Americans usually had had experience in active democracy, and they added their voices to the growing cry for a new constitution. This demand bore fruit in 1845, when a more democratic document replaced the old 1812 constitution. Property qualifications for voting were removed; more officials were now elected by the populace; and provision was made for free public schools together with a state superintendent of education. Soon people demanded still another constitution. The new document, the constitution of 1852, provided for the election of even more state and local officials. Representation in the legislature, however, would now be based upon total population, including slaves, rather than upon the number of free whites. District judges were to be popularly elected, but legislative power was now weighted in favor of the big planters.

Louisiana had owned slaves under France, Spain, and the United States. State public officials denounced abolitionists almost from the beginning of statehood. Several governors had condemned abolitionist literature. They argued that to free the slaves would disrupt the society of the state. Accordingly, they held that each state had the power to control its internal affairs, including slavery. The WILMOT PROVISO, according to officials in Louisiana, was unconstitutional, for Congress had no authority to control slavery in any area. By 1850 politicians predicted that, if the antislavery agitation continued, Louisiana should prepare itself to join the other slave states in possible secession from the Union. Six years later a Louisiana governor, Robert C. Wickliffe, suggested the acquisition of Cuba, Mexico, and Central American as areas for future potential slave states. By this time Louisiana was indeed a southern state desiring the expansion of slave territory.

Secession, rebellion, and Reconstruction. Louisiana's Democrats did not win a gubernatorial election until 1842, and the Whigs, once dominant in statewide elections, never elected a governor after that date. State politics prior to the Civil War were, therefore, largely the politics of the Democratic party. The Whig party had ceased to exist by 1856, and the KNOW-NOTHING PARTY had only a very brief career in heavily French-Catholic Louisiana. In 1856 the Know-Nothings, stressing their opposition to foreign immigrants, attempted to challenge the Democratic hegemony. After their defeat, Louisiana had only one party both in fact and in name. In the absence of formal political opposition, Democratic intraparty factionalism came to the foreground. JOHN SLIDELL and PIERRE SOULÉ, leaders of opposing factions of the state's Democratic party, vied for power and political control. In Louisiana, both the presidential ELECTION OF 1860 and the secession crisis that followed were intertwined with the factional politics of the Democratic party.

Slidell's gubernatorial candidate, Thomas O. Moore, won the governor's race in 1860, but the presidential election was deemed more important both for the nation and for the two contending party factions. In an election with four candidates for president, Slidell was backing J. C. BRECKINRIDGE, for, if Breckinridge lost the election and Abraham Lincoln won, Louisiana probably would secede. Soulé and his faction backed S. A. Douglas. If Douglas won, Soulé would then gain control of federal patronage in Louisiana, thus undermining Slidell's power and influence. Breckinridge carried Louisiana with a plurality of the vote, besting JOHN BELL, a Unionist, by only 2,000 ballots. the combined totals of Douglas and Bell were much greater than the vote for Breckinridge. Most Louisianians appear to have opted for the more moderate candidates, but Douglas faltered nationally and Lincoln was elected president. The principal question for Louisianians at that point was no longer whether the state should secede but when it would secede.

Governor Moore called the legislature into a special session to meet in December, 1860. The legislature in turn issued a call for a special convention to meet the crisis of Lincoln's election. Meanwhile the governor seized federal installations and property in Louisiana, including the forts and the arsenal. A majority of the delegates elected to the special convention favored immediate secession from the Union. When those delegates met, Governor Moore informed them of his actions against Union property in Louisiana. Alexander Mouton, the state's first Democratic governor elected in 1842, won the presidency of the secession convention. Since the vote on secession was a foregone conclusion, Mouton appointed a committee to draft the ordinance of secession. Those against immediate secession put up a spirited though losing defense. The ordinance passed. Louisiana declared itself to be a free, sovereign, independent republic on January 26, 1861. The state left the Union it had wanted so much to enter in 1812.

The secession convention elected John Perkins, Jr., Alexander Declouet, Charles M. Conrad, Duncan Kenner, Edward Sparrow, and Henry Marshall to attend a convention of seceded states in Montgomery, Ala. There the Louisianians participated in the formation of the Confederate States of America. The Louisiana secession convention, refusing to submit the Confederate constitution to the people of the state for ratification, instead ratified the constitution itself. Louisiana then turned over to the Confederacy all the federal property it had confiscated in the state.

With the fall of FT. SUMTER in April, 1861, Louisiana's officials prepared for war. Spirit was high and there was no dearth of volunteers in those early days of the war. Louisiana strengthened its forts along the Mississippi River. Before long, however, the federal BLOCKADE of New Orleans began to choke the state's economy. The governor ordered banks on the verge of bankruptcy to suspend specie payments and to accept Confederate money at face value. Louisianians thus felt the consequences of secession early, though the war did not come into the area until 1862.

Admiral DAVID G. FARRAGUT led his fleet up the Mississippi River toward New Orleans (NEW ORLEANS, BATTLE OF). Defense preparations of the forts south of New Orleans proved inadequate, and on April 25, 1862, the federal fleet appeared at New Orleans. The Union army and navy gathering against the Confederate forces were much too superior to risk an engagement, so the city was evacuated, but the civilian mayor of New Orleans refused to surrender his city to military officers of the Union. The dispute ended on May 1, 1862, when General Benjamin F. Butler and his troops landed in the city. The Union controlled New Orleans and thereby controlled the mouth of the Mississippi.

Union troops moved into other parts of south Louisiana. Expeditions took place in the Bayou Lafourche area, the Atchafalaya River area, and the Bayou Teche area. By May of 1863 federal troops marched into the Alexandria area and the next year attempted, though unsuccessfully, to capture Shreveport.

While military operations were taking place, General Butler governed New Orleans. His Order No. 28 (WOMAN ORDER) proclaiming that intentional disrespect toward Union soldiers by the women of New Orleans allowed those women to be treated as prostitutes, infuriated the population. It ensured that Butler would leave behind a tarnished reputation in spite of the fact that he did aid the city in many ways, including cleaning streets and restoring commerce. Meanwhile, attempts to restore civilian government began almost immediately, and in December, 1862, elections were held in federally occupied Louisiana for Congress.

At the same time Confederate Louisiana remained under the control of Governor Moore. He served until 1864, when HENRY WATKINS ALLEN succeeded to the governorship. Elections for governor of federally occupied Louisiana were also held in 1864. The voters elected Michael Hahn, an opponent of slavery and secession before the war. Louisiana now had two governors. A constitutional convention, called in 1864 in federally occupied Louisiana, abolished slavery but did not enfranchise the newly freed blacks. This new government ratified the Thirteenth Amendment to the U.S. Constitution. When Andrew Johnson became president after the assassination of Lincoln, he accepted the elections in federal Louisiana as valid. In the meantime Hahn was elected to the U.S. Senate, and Lieutenant Governor J. Madison Wells succeeded to the governorship. Wells, like Hahn, had opposed secession and followed the Union army throughout both its successes and its failures in Louisiana.

Although Wells was elected governor in his own right in 1865, a large number of former Confederates also won state elections in that year. State officials were more Confederate than at any time since before the fall of New Orleans, and the legislature proceeded to restrict the rights of the freedmen. A vagrant law forced unemployed freedmen to work. BLACK CODES prohibited blacks from carrying weapons and serving on juries and restricted other rights. Governor Wells, sensing the will of the Radicals in Congress, suggested another constitutional convention to produce a document more in line with the prevailing attitude in Congress. The former Confederates blocked the convention call, so Wells decided instead to reconvene the constitutional convention of 1864. Large crowds, mostly black, gathered in New Orleans in favor of the convention. Mayor John Monroe of New Orleans called upon the people to take up arms and prevent the convention from meeting. A bloody riot resulted (NEW ORLEANS RIOT) in which over 30 people were killed and over 100 were wounded. The riot had an adverse effect upon northern public opinion. It appeared that the South was still in a state of rebellion, so more Radicals were elected to Congress in 1866. Radical Reconstruction of Louisiana was about to begin.

The Radical-sponsored Reconstruction Act of March, 1867, divided the South into five military districts. Philip H. Sheridan, military commander of Louisiana, removed Wells from office and appointed Benjamin F. Flanders to the governorship. Under the privision that disfranchised former Confederates and enfranchised Negroes, Louisiana's voter registration figures totaled 82,907 Negroes and 44,732 whites. Negroes would continue to outnumber whites in registration until 1890. HENRY CLAY WARMOTH was elected governor in 1868, and at the same time voters ratified a new constitution. The constitution of 1868 provided access to public facilities to all races. It also extended the suffrage to all adult males who agreed that secession was a moral wrong. This new liberal document also included the first bill of rights for Louisiana.

During Governor Warmoth's administration, political corruption became almost a way of life. Warmoth wanted whites to control the Republican party in the state. WILLIAM P. KELLOGG led the anti-Warmoth faction, which Warmoth claimed wanted to turn the state over to Negro control. By 1870 the conflict between the Republican factions moved into the open. When the lieutenant governor died, there was a fight over his successor; P. B. S. PINCHBACK, a black backed by the Kellogg faction, won the battle. The conflict culminated in 1872, when the anti-Warmoth faction in the legislature impeached Warmoth. He was not convicted, but he was removed from office during the trial. During that time, Pinchback served as governor—the only black to achieve that office.

Kellogg ran for the governorship in 1872. Warmoth joined with the Democrats in supporting John McEnery for the position. Both gubernatorial candidates claimed victory; both proceeded to organize state governments; but the official returning board declared Kellogg the winner. The Kellogg faction took over the statehouse and called upon the president for federal troops; the McEnery government disbanded and accepted defeat.

Continued corruption and increased hostility to the Radicals marked Kellogg's administration. Warmoth and Confederate General P. G. T. BEAUREGARD found themselves united against the incumbent administration. The White League, a Louisiana relative of the Ku Klux Klan, proposed and used violence to rid the state of Radical domination. On September 14, 1874, the streets of New Orleans witnessed a battle between Kellogg's metropolitan police and the White Leaguers. The police dispersed, leaving the field to the White League. Kellogg then asked for and received the support of federal forces, and with their aid he was able to resume control. The battle of September, 1874, signaled the high point of Radical rule in Louisiana. In local areas the Radicals were forced out of power, sometimes peacefully, but violently at other times. Violence and the threat of violence had weakened the Republican regime to the point where it could no longer govern effectively unless enough soldiers were stationed in Louisiana to enforce its laws and policies.

By 1876 Democrats controlled enough parishes to mount a genuine political threat to Republican control of the state government. FRANCIS T. NICHOLLS, a Confederate general, carried the banner for the Democrats as their gubernatorial candidate. STEPHEN B. PACKARD, the Republican candidate, promised to protect the rights of the blacks, whom both parties courted. Fraud and violence marked the election, with both parties claiming victory. The returning board, composed of a four-to-one Republican majority, declared Packard's slate elected. The Democrats, however, refused to accept the returning board's conclusion and organized their own government. Again two separate groups claimed to be the legal government of Louisiana. Moreover, the Democrats claimed that Samuel Tilden had carried the state's presidential election while the Republicans maintained that Rutherford B. Hayes had won (ELECTION OF 1876). Under the Compromise of 1877, Hayes received the electoral votes of Louisiana and, two weeks after taking office, removed the remaining federal troops from duty at the statehouse and assigned them to their barracks. Packard's government could not function without federal troops, so it disbanded. Reconstruction in Louisiana was over, and the Democrats were in control.

Conservative and Progressive Democratic eras. The conservative Democrats remained in power until after the turn of the century. They did not spend as much and probably were less guilty of corruption than had been the Republicans. Economy became a watchword, especially when the needs of blacks and poor whites were under consideration. Those who governed the state after Reconstruction ran it for their own self-interests.

The economy measures supported by the conservatives were reflected in the constitution of 1879, which reduced salaries, placed limits on property taxes, and limited the public debt. BOUR-BONS did not provide better roads, schools, or river levees. Public monies spent for services were dispensed with the generosity of a Scrooge. The conservatives kept much of the Reconstruction legislation, however. Negroes continued to vote, only now they voted or were voted Democratic. A returning board still declared the winners in political contests, and the constitution still had a bill of rights. But the goal of those in office had changed. Those who redeemed the state from the Radical Republicans in the long run proved through inaction to be as great a disaster as had been the war (REDEEMERS).

Life changed little for the average Louisianian during the years of conservative rule. Instead of slaves, sharecroppers now worked the plantation. The plantation store received the money the sharecropper earned. Freed blacks often lived in the same home they had occupied as slaves, and the economic status of both the white and black lower classes changed little. The planter owed money to those who furnished the goods he needed, and he lived in the shadow of a crop lien. He owned more and lived better than most farmers, but debt haunted him from year to year. The small farmer in most cases had little education, lived on a subsistence level, worked hard, and had little money. Those living in Louisiana's cities saw more changes than did the rural dwellers. Indoor plumbing, electric lights, and paved roads were available to the city dweller. Some of these do not yet exist for some rural Louisianians. New Orleans, as before the war, dominated the commerce of the state.

By 1890 discontent began to be widespread as people demanded a better life. The levee system did not prevent floods, prices for crops were low, over one-third of the state's population was illiterate, roads were in deplorable condition, crime ran high, and state government did nothing but practice economy. The seeds for an outburst of reform were ready to sprout.

The black, once a slave, was about to become a victim of the reformer. After the Civil War the rural black for the most part became a tenant farmer; his income generally averaged less than white incomes. A few blacks owned farms with some even owning plantations, but they were the exception rather than the rule. The Negro continued to participate in the political life of the state, for he still had the franchise. Many served in the legislature and in local offices until the 1890s. There were black newspapers, a black labor movement, no major public segregation by law, worship in either black or white churches, and schools on both the primary and higher education levels. However, in many instances, the politicians counted the black votes without the Negro casting a ballot. In 1890 the JIM CROW laws entered the scene, and the constitution of 1898 completed the job of disfranchising the blacks. The reform movement of the 1890s reformed the blacks right into second-class citizenship. The Populists believed that the elimination of blacks from voting would help reform because the conservatives would thereby lose the black vote. The conservatives believed that the disfranchisement of the blacks would help prevent the Populists from gaining power. Both groups believed that DISFRANCHISEMENT would be a reform move.

Among the items needing reformation was the LOUISIANA STATE LOTTERY COMPANY. Chartered in 1868 during Reconstruction, it was given a monopoly in the constitution of 1879. In addition the lottery paid no state taxes, although it did pay the state $40,000 yearly to support charity hospitals and public schools. Lottery money distributed as campaign funds ensured its perpetuation, and many Louisianians blamed their troubles on the lottery, which they claimed controlled the state. When the lottery company applied for a charter renewal in 1890, it promised to pay over $1 million to the state annually. The vast amount of money involved helped to bring the antilottery people together, many of whom made the lottery a scapegoat for the many ills of Louisiana. City reformers claimed that the lottery controlled government and that no services or public improvements would occur until the lottery was destroyed. Many farmers believed the same thing. They held the lottery responsible for the lack of suitable debt relief, roads, schools, and levees. The people organized to fight the lottery.

Farmers joined farm organizations such as the GRANGE and the Louisiana Farmers' Union. Eventually they combined with others into the southern FARMERS' ALLIANCE. The Alliance voted to join the Anti-Lottery League, but the dissidents organized the People's party (POPULIST PARTY) of Louisiana. In the gubernatorial election of 1892 the Populists ran a candidate as did the antilottery Democrats, the prolottery Democrats, the antilottery Republicans, and the prolottery Republicans. The issue in 1892 was indeed the lottery. The antilottery Democrats won the election. When the legislature met, it prohibited the renewal of the lottery charter. In the meantime Congress had enacted a law prohibiting the use of the United States mail by lotteries. The death knell of the company had sounded. On January 1, 1895, it died.

The death of the lottery did not, as many people had hoped, lead to improvements in schools, roads, or levees. A national depression intensified the discontent. In Louisiana the Populists gained seats in the legislature; some protariff sugar planters joined the Republican party; and some reform-minded New Orleanians left the Democratic party. The discontented were blaming the party in power for their ills, and they were searching for solutions in other alliances. By 1896 Populists and Republicans presented a fusion candidate against the regular Democratic candidate for governor. Fraud, mostly by the Democrats, helped give the governorship to the Democrats. Populists gathered arms and threatened to take over some towns by force. State troops prevented large-scale violence, but the point was made—something had to change. Among the gains of the reformers was adoption of secret ballots and a new city charter for New Orleans. With emotions spent, those who had left the Democratic party began to drift back to their former allegiance hoping that the party would become more Progressive.

In New Orleans the Progressive reformers won some battles for more and better municipal services; more citizens had electricity and sewage systems improved. The Progressives were ascendant in the state's largest city, but the rise of reformers in New Orleans was not paralleled in state government. Louisiana's farmers would have to wait a while yet for needed social and economic assistance. The gubernatorial platforms began to show signs of PROGRESSIVISM in 1900. Antitrust regulation, federal aid for levee improvements, and a law allowing municipalities to own utilities were all part of gubernatorial platforms. During the Progressive years the state built schools, teacher training and certification began, the state enacted CHILD LABOR laws, which protected working women as well as children, and it abolished the convention system of nominating candidates for state office in favor of a party primary.

JOHN M. PARKER, a leader in the New Orleans reform movement, even became a vice-presidential candidate on the Progressive party ticket in 1916. In 1920 the people elected Parker governor of Louisiana and continued the Progressive trend. Although the Progressives were an improvement on the conservatives, they moved too slowly for many citizens of the state. They were gentlemen who believed in good business practices. Many people needed and wanted more, and they cared nothing about gentlemanly business practices. Among those who claimed that the Progressives did too little too slowly was Huey P. Long.

Huey Long's Louisiana. Forty years after HUEY LONG's death he is still viewed as either a saint or an abominable sinner. Other governors have sat in the capitol Long built, but they operated in his shadow. Whenever they look out over the capitol grounds, they see Long's statue over his grave. A light illuminates the statue, and his birthday remains an official state holiday. The shadow of Huey Long probably will remain a permanent fixture over the state of Louisiana.

Born in 1893 on a 340-acre north Louisiana farm, Long attended the Baptist College of Oklahoma, then the University of Oklahoma. He became a salesman, studied law for a year at Tulane, and passed a special bar examination that allowed him to practice law in Louisiana. He ran for the railroad commission (known later as the public service commission) and won. His record on the commission was controversial, for he became involved in a bitter dispute with Standard Oil Company of New Jersey. While on the public service commission Long classified pipelines as public carriers subject to the regulations of the commission. The governor and the legislature overturned his victory. The major issue, however, was a severance tax on petroleum. The governor did not agree on as high a severance tax as Long desired. In 1924 Long ran for governor and lost, but he ran again in 1928 and won. He wanted results rather than the gentlemanly business practices of the Progressives. Under his administration boards that had been created for good government became political tools, and Long used all the potential powers of Louisiana governors to gain his ends. New Orleans got natural gas; the state's schoolchildren received free textbooks; he added over 12,000 miles of paved, asphalt, or gravel roads; he constructed numerous bridges over the state's main waterways; and he also built a new governor's mansion and a new state capitol. The costs were borne by a higher seveance tax on petroleum.

Long's methods led to an attempt to impeach him. When he convinced 15 of the 39 state senators to pledge their support to him, the impeachment move disintegrated. In 1930 he won election to the U.S. Senate but continued to govern the state. "Huey Long for President of the United States" was no longer a pipe dream of a backwoods clown. In 1932 Long had one of his supporters elected governor; however, he continued to run the state from Washington. His SHARE OUR WEALTH clubs sprouted across the nation, and Huey Long became a threat to the Roosevelt administration. On September 8, 1935, Dr. Carl Weiss allegedly shot Huey Long in the state capitol. Long died of the wounds and became a martyr.

The power that he had acquired passed into the hands of his subordinates. In 1936 Richard W. Leche became governor. During his term of office Louisiana lost about $100 million to corrupt public officials. Scandals broke all over the state. Leche resigned, eventually taking up residence in a federal penitentiary. The president of Louisiana State University, a Long appointee, later joined Leche in the penitentiary. The house that Long built had tumbled to the ground. Reformers won the gubernatorial elections of 1940 and 1944, but the basic Long programs of schools, roads, and bridges continued. The programs were too popular to dismantle, even in the wake of the scandals. By 1948 Huey's brother EARL LONG had rebuilt the Long faction sufficiently to win election to the governor's office. Earl added to the services offered by Huey, and like him delivered on his promises. In the same election, Huey's son Russell won a seat in the U.S. Senate. The anti-Long segment of the Democratic party gained the governorship in 1952, but Earl returned in 1956. When Earl died in 1960, so also did much of the strength of what had been Longism. The federal government has assumed control and responsibility for too many of the Long programs, such as schools, roads, and

welfare. There was no heir apparent for Longism after Earl died. Russell Long remains in the Senate today. Other kinfolk held various political offices, but Longism is no longer strong enough to gain the governorship.

Was Longism good or bad? It depends upon the person asked, but more Louisianians lived better lives because of Huey Long and Longism. If those who came before him had done a competent job of caring for the needs of the population, a Huey Long would not have been necessary. He helped lift people out of the mud and out of illiteracy. For that, many sins can be forgiven.

But Longism was finished in 1960. By that time the federal government had not only taken over the welfare programs, but it demanded that there be integration of the races. In the early sixties Louisiana fought integration. The politicians failed to stop it as they knew they would, but they fought anyway. By the seventies the integration fight was over. Political power, which had been concentrated in the northern portion of the state (with few exceptions) since Huey Long, moved south. Population, industry, and ethnic identity indicated that the southern part of the state, if it desired, could maintain political power.

The problems facing the leaders during the last quarter of the twentieth century will be major, for Louisiana has depended on petroleum and its ancillary industries for much of its revenue. A small severance tax placed on oil during the 1920s was raised by Long to build the welfare state in Louisiana. Those who have continued to provide state services have also used severance taxes to help defray a large part of the cost. Because of oil, the Mississippi River between New Orleans and Baton Rouge is an industrial complex filled with petrochemical plants. When the oil is depleted, the state may well lose much of its industry, and it will have to find some new source of revenue or drastically curtail services. If indeed modern Louisiana's services are based in large part on the severance tax, the state may be headed into an era of neoconservatism personified by a lack of state services such as education, nonfederal highways, and charity hospitals before the end of this century.

General sources. Two excellent indexes list most important books and articles: B. Cruise, *Index to Louisiana Historical Quarterly* (1956), pre-1956 publications; and G. Conrad and J. Roque, *Name 'and Subject Guide to Louisiana History* (1975), 1960–75 publications. Journals besides *Louisiana Historical Quarterly* and *Louisiana History* include *Louisiana Studies* and *McNeese Review*. Principal manuscript depositories are University of Southwestern Louisiana, for French colonial period; Loyola, for Spanish period; Louisiana State Museum in New Orleans, for French and Spanish eras; Louisiana

State University; Louisiana State Archives in Baton Rouge; New Orleans Public Library; Tulane; and Historic New Orleans Collection, New Orleans. Outdated but still useful histories include A. Fortier, *History of Louisiana* (4 vols.; 1904); C. Gayarré, *History of Louisiana* (4 vols.; 1903); H. E. Chambers, *History of Louisiana* (3 vols.; 1925); and F.-X. Martin, *History of Louisiana* (1882). More recent surveys are G. W. McGinty, *History of Louisiana* (1949); and E. A. Davis, *Louisiana* (1960). Popular surveys of New Orleans are H. Asbury, *French Quarter* (1936); and S. Longstreet, *Sportin' House* (1965).

Colonial period. French era is capably covered by M. Giraud, *History of French Louisiana*, trans. J. C. Lambert (4 vols. to date; 1953–). Other surveys include W. J. Eccles, *France in America* (1972), emphasizing Canada; N. W. Caldwell, *French in Mississippi Valley, 1740–1750* (1941); W. E. Dunn, *Spanish-French Rivalry in Gulf Region, 1678–1702* (1917); E. W. Lyon, *Louisiana in French Diplomacy, 1759–1814* (1934); H. Gravier, *Colonisation de la Louisiane, 1717–1721* (1904); H. Carter, *John Law Wasn't So Wrong* (1952); J. Delanglez, *French Jesuits in Lower Louisiana, 1700–1763* (1935); C. O'Neill, *Church and State in French Colonial Louisiana to 1732* (1966), excellent; R. Baudier, *Catholic Church in Louisiana* (1931); N. M. M. Surrey, *Commerce of French Regime, 1699–1763* (1916); and O. Winzerling, *Acadian Odyssey* (1955), less romanticized than other studies. Biographies during French era include A. C. Laut, *Cadillac* (1931); N. M. Crouse, *Lemoyne d'Iberville* (1954); R. Phares, *Louis Juchereau de St. Denis* (1952); G. Fregault, *Rigaud de Vaudreuil* (1952); E. R. Murphy, *Henry De Tonty: Fur Trader* (1951); E. H. McNeil, *Tonty of Iron Hand* (1926); E. G. King, *Bienville* (1892), unsatisfactory; and C. E. O'Neill, *Louisiana History* (Fall, 1967), Bienville. For Spanish era, no such survey such as Giraud's exists. Good specialized studies are J. A. James, *Oliver Pollock* (1937), an American in New Orleans; D. K. Texada, *Alejandro O'Reilly* (1970), New Orleans rebellion of 1768; J. W. Caughey, *Bernardo de Galvez in Louisiana, 1776–1783* (1934); C. M. Burson, *Don Esteban Miro, 1782–1792* (1940); and J. D. L. Holmes, *Gayoso, 1789–1799* (1965).

Also see J. P. Moore, *Louisiana History* (Summer, 1967), Ulloa; D. E. Everett, *Louisiana History* (Winter, 1966), free blacks; J. D. Hardy, *Louisiana History* (Winter, 1967), church and state; R. I. Matthews, *Louisiana Studies* (Summer, 1965), New Orleans revolution, 1768; J. D. Holmes, *Hispanic American Historical Review* (Nov., 1962), economic problems; and J. D. L. Holmes, *Louisiana History* (Fall, 1967), indigo.

Territorial era. This is a neglected period in need of study, but important studies include C. E. Carter (ed.), *Territorial Papers of U.S.*, Vol. IX, *Territory of Orleans, 1803–1812* (1940); J. L. de Grummond, *Baratarians and Battle of New Orleans* (1964); I. J. Cox, *West Florida Controversy, 1793–1813* (1918); S. C. Arthur, *West Florida Rebellion* (1938); T. P. Abernethy, *Burr Conspiracy* (1954), remains standard; and J. G. Clark, *New Orleans, 1718–1812* (1970), an economic history.

Antebellum and Civil War eras. Together, W. Adams, *Whig Party of Louisiana* (1973); and J. G. Tregle, "Louisiana in Age of Jackson" (Ph.D. dissertation, University of Pennsylvania, 1954), capably study politics of 1830s. See also V. L. S. Jeanfreau, *Louisiana Studies* (Fall, 1965), Know-Nothings, 1855–56; and L. C. Soulé, *Know-Nothing Party* (1961), nativism in the Crescent City. Biographies include H. Hamilton, *Zachary Taylor* (1941); R. Meade, *Judah P. Benjamin* (1943); L. Sears, *John Slidell* (1925); and F. L. Dorsey, *Henry Shreve* (1941). R. W. Shugg, *Origins of Class Struggle in Louisiana, 1840–1875* (1939, 1966), is influential but needs revision. J. Duffy, *Sword of Pestilence* (1966), is excellent study of yellow fever epidemic of 1853. Recent studies of slavery and the Negro include J. G. Taylor, *Negro Slavery in Louisiana* (1963), standard work, and *Louisiana History* (Winter, 1967), Civil War slavery; H. E. Sterkx, *Free Negro in Louisiana* (1972); M. Christian, *Negro Ironworkers in Louisiana* (1972); R. C. McConnell, *Negro Troops of Ante-Bellum Louisiana* (1968); S. Northup, *Twelve Years a Slave*, ed. S. Eakin and J. Legsdon (1968); and F. J. Woods, *Colored Family Through Ten Generations* (1972). Civil War studies include J. D. Winters, *Civil War in Louisiana* (1963), standard study; C. L. Dufour, *Night the War Was Lost* (1960), capture of New Orleans; J. D.

LOUISIANA POPULATION, 1810–1970

Year	Total	White	Nonwhite		%	Rank	
			Slave	Free	Growth	U.S.	South
1810	76,556	34,311	36,660	5,585		19	8
1820	153,407	73,867	69,064	10,476	100.4	17	8
1830	215,739	89,441	109,588	16,710	40.6	19	9
1840	352,411	158,457	168,452	25,502	63.4	19	11
1850	517,762	255,491	244,809	17,462	46.9	18	11
1860	708,002	357,456	331,726	18,647	36.7	17	9
1870	726,915	362,065	364,210		2.7	21	11
1880	939,946	454,954	483,655		29.3	22	11
1890	1,118,588	558,395	559,193		19.0	25	12
1900	1,381,625	729,612	650,804		23.5	23	10
1910	1,656,388	941,086	713,874		19.9	24	10
1920	1,798,509	1,096,611	700,257		8.6	22	9
1930	2,101,593	1,322,712	77,326		16.9	22	9
1940	2,363,880	1,511,739	849,303		12.5	21	9
1950	2,683,516	1,796,683	882,428		13.5	21	10
1960	3,257,022	2,211,715	1,039,207		21.4	20	9
1970	3,641,306	2,541,498	1,086,832		11.8	20	9

LOUISIANA GOVERNORS

Governor	Party	Term
FRENCH PERIOD		
Pierre Le Moyne, Sieur d'Iberville		1699
LeSieur de Sauvole		1699–1701
Jean Baptiste Le Moyne, Sieur de Bienville		1701–1713
Antoine de la Mothe Cadillac		1713–1716
Jean Baptiste Le Moyne, Sieur de Bienville (acting)		1716–1717
Jean Michiele, Seigneur de l'Epinay (Lepinay)		1717–1718
Jean Baptiste Le Moyne, Sieur de Bienville		1718–1724
Pierre du Bugue (Gue), Sieur de Boisbriant (acting)		1724–1725
Etienne de Perier		1725–1733
Jean Baptiste Le Moyne, Sieur de Bienville		1733–1743
Pierre Rigaud		1743–1753
Louis Billouart, Chevalier de Kerlerec		1753–1763
Jean Jacques Blaise D'Abadie (director)		1763–1765
Charles Philippe Aubry (acting)		1765–1766
SPANISH PERIOD		
Antonio de Ulloa		1766–1768
Charles Philippe Aubry (acting)		1768–1769
Alexander O'Reilly (captain general and governor)		1769
Luis de Unzaga		1769–1777
Bernardo de Gálvez		1777–1785
Estevan Miro		1785–1791
Francisco Luis Héctor de Carondelet		1791–1797
Manuel Gayoso de Lemos		1797–1799
Francisco Bouligny (acting)		1799
Sebastian Calvo de la Puerta y O'Faril (acting)		1799–1801
Juan Manuel de Salcedo		1801–1803
PERIOD OF TRANSFER		
Pierre Clement de Laussat		1803
TERRITORIAL PERIOD		
William Charles Cole Claiborne		1803–1812
STATE PERIOD		
William C. C. Claiborne	Rep.	1812–1816
Jacques Philippe Villère	Rep.	1816–1820
Thomas B. Robertson (resigned)	Dem.-Rep.	1820–1824
Henry S. Thibodaux (president of senate)		1824
Henry S. Johnson	Know-Nothing	1824–1828
Pierre Derbigny (died in office)		1828–1829
Armand Beauvais (president of senate)		1829–1830
Jacques Dupre		1830–1831
André B. Roman	Whig	1831–1835
Edward D. White	Whig	1835–1839
André B. Roman	Whig	1839–1843
Alexander Mouton	Dem.	1843–1846
Isaac Johnson	Dem.	1846–1850
Joseph Marshall Walker	Dem.	1850–1853
Paul O. Hebert	Dem.	1853–1856
Robert C. Wickliffe	Dem.	1856–1860
Thomas O. Moore	Dem.	1860–1864
George F. Shepley (Union military governor)		1862–1864
Henry W. Allen (elected governor within Confederate lines)		1864–1865
Michael Hahn (elected Union governor resigned)	Free-State	1864–1865
James M. Wells (lieutenant governor)	Free-State	1865–1867
Benjamin F. Flanders (appointed by military authority)	Unionist-Rep.	1867–1868
Joshua Baker (appointed by military authority)	Dem.	1868
Henry C. Warmoth	Rep.	1868–1872
P. B. S. Pinchback (acting)	Rep.	1872–1873
John McEnery (elected, but ruled out)	Dem.	1873
William P. Kellogg	Rep.	1873–1877
Francis T. Nicholls	Dem.	1877–1880
Louis A. Wiltz (died in office)	Dem.	1880–1881
Samuel D. McEnery (lieutenant governor)	Dem.	1881–1884
Samuel D. McEnery	Dem.	1884–1888
Francis T. Nicholls	Dem.	1888–1892
Murphy J. Foster	Dem.	1892–1900
William W. Heard	Dem.	1900–1904
Newton C. Blanchard	Dem.	1904–1908
Jared Y. Sanders	Dem.	1908–1912
Luther E. Hall	Dem.	1912–1916
Ruffin G. Pleasant	Dem.	1916–1920
John M. Parker	Dem.	1920–1924
Henry L. Fuqua (died in office)	Dem.	1924–1926
Oramel H. Simpson (lieutenant governor)	Dem. (Ind.)	1926–1928
Huey P. Long	Dem.	1928–1932
Alvin O. King (president of senate)	Dem.	1932
Oscar K. Allen (died in office)	Dem.	1932–1936
James A. Noe (lieutenant governor)	Dem.	1936
Richard W. Leche (resigned)	Dem.	1936–1939
Earl K. Long (lieutenant governor)	Dem.	1939–1940
Sam H. Jones	Dem.	1940–1944
James H. Davis	Dem.	1944–1948
Earl K. Long	Dem.	1948–1952
Robert F. Kennon	Dem.	1952–1956
Earl K. Long	Dem.	1956–1960
James H. Davis	Dem.	1960–1964
John J. McKeithen	Dem.	1964–1972
Edwin W. Edwards	Dem.	1972–1980

Bragg, *Louisiana in Confederacy* (1941); V. H. Cassidy and A. E. Simpson, *Henry Watkins Allen* (1964); E. Cunningham, *Port Hudson Campaign* (1963); T. H. Williams, *P. G. T. Beauregard* (1955); W. Arceneaux, *Alfred Mouton* (1972); J. H. Parks, *General Leonidas Polk* (1962); and C. P. Roland, *Louisiana Sugar Plantations During Civil War* (1957).

From Reconstruction to progressivism. See J. G. Taylor, *Louisiana Reconstructed, 1863–1876* (1975), standard modern work. Older works include J. R. Ficklen, *Reconstruction in Louisiana Through 1868* (1910); E. Lonn, *Reconstruction in Louisiana After 1868* (1918); H. C.

Warmoth, *War, Politics, and Reconstruction* (1930), a memoir; H. L. Trefousse, *Ben Butler* (1957); S. O. Landry, *Battle of Liberty Place* (1955); D. W. Davis, *Louisiana History* (Summer, 1965), constitution of 1868; A. D. Pitre, *Louisiana History* (Spring, 1965), Warmoth regime; and G. A. Reed, *Louisiana History* (Fall, 1965), race legislation, 1864–1920. W. I. Hair, *Bourbonism and Agrarian Protest, 1877–1900* (1969), is standard for late nineteenth century. See also H. C. Dethloff, "Populism and Reform in Louisiana" (Ph.D. dissertation, University of Missouri, 1964), differs with Hair; J. Jackson, *New Orleans, 1880–1896* (1969); D. A. Somers, *Sports in New Orleans, 1850–1900* (1972); H. C. Dethloff, *Louisiana History* (Spring, 1965), Alliance and lottery; J. A. Carrigan, *Louisiana Studies* (Spring, 1967), yellow fever panic, 1897; and C. W. Lord, *Louisiana Studies* (Summer, 1971), farmers' institutes and fairs. For Progressive period, see M. J. Schott, "John M. Parker" (Ph.D. dissertation, Vanderbilt, 1969); and G. M. Reynolds, *Machine Politics in New Orleans, 1897–1926* (1936).

Era of Huey Long. A. S. Sindler, *Huey Long's Louisiana, 1920–1952* (1956), is best overall survey. Also see H. T. Kane, *Louisiana Hayride* (1941); T. H. Williams, *Huey Long* (1969); and H. Long, *Every Man a King* (1933, 1964). Earl Long's biographies are R. B. McCaughan, *Socks on a Rooster* (1967); and A. J. Liebling, *Earl of Louisiana* (1970), successful at conveying flavor of Louisiana politics. Also see E. Haas, *DeLesseps S. Morrison, 1946–1961* (1974), New Orleans politics; G. Jeansonne, *Louisiana History* (Summer, 1970), racism and Longism, 1960; and P. F. Dur and D. M. Kurtz, *Louisiana Studies* (Spring, 1971), voting patterns, 1948–68.

ALLEN E. BEGNAND
University of Southwestern Louisiana

LOUISIANA HISTORICAL ASSOCIATION

(929 Camp St., New Orleans, La. 70130) was originally founded largely by Confederate veterans and was incorporated in April, 1889. Present membership is almost 2,000. The library at TU-LANE UNIVERSITY in New Orleans is the repository for its collection of some 150,000 items devoted mainly to the Civil War period, with the papers of Jefferson Davis composing a major part. There are also records of various executive departments of the Confederate government, battle plans and maps, and the papers of several CONFEDERATE VETERANS organizations. There was a long period of inactivity after the turn of the century, but in 1958 the association was reorganized. Since 1960 the association has published the quarterly journal *Louisiana History* (P.O. Box 2949, University of Southwestern Louisiana, Lafayette, 70501), which limits itself to articles on the history of Louisiana. It offers an annual prize of $100 for the best article of the year. The association also cooperates with the Historic New Orleans Collection (533 Royal St., New Orleans, 70130) to sponsor two other prizes: for the best published work in

Louisiana history; and for the best manuscript on Louisiana by an unpublished author. The association also publishes books and a newsletter.

See Historical Records Survey, *Guide for Louisiana* (1938); K. T. Urquhart, *Louisiana Historical Association Papers* (March 21, 1959), Howard-Tilton Library, Tulane; and W. M. Whitehill, *Independent Historical Societies* (1962).

LOUISIANA HISTORICAL SOCIETY

(509 Cotton Exchange Bldg., 231 Carondelet St., New Orleans, La. 70130) was organized in 1836, although there were many years thereafter when it was inactive. Although its membership has always maintained an interest in Louisiana history generally, it has devoted itself particularly to the colonial period. The society's archives of historical documents includes records relating to Louisiana from 1678 to 1769 and in 1803. From 1895 to 1917 the society published ten volumes of the *Publications of the Louisiana Historical Society*. Between 1917 and 1965 it published the *Louisiana Historical Quarterly*, with the aid of a modest state subsidy; but it eventually lost its state appropriation, and after 1965 issues of the *Quarterly* became irregular until 1973, when they were suspended altogether. Since 1974 the society has once again begun to issue its annual volumes of the *Publications of the Louisiana Historical Society*, now known as Series 2. These volumes contain both popular and scholarly monographs with emphasis still on the colonial era. The society at present has a membership of approximately 800.

See Historical Records Survey, *Guide for Louisiana* (1938); J. S. Kendall, *North Carolina Historical Review* (Oct., 1930); and W. M. Whitehill, *Independent Historical Societies* (1962).

LOUISIANA LEGAL CODE

was composed in reaction to Thomas Jefferson's attempt in 1805, through Governor WILLIAM C. CLAIBORNE, to introduce common law into civilian ORLEANS TERRITORY (present Louisiana). Established residents demanded retention of familiar Spanish customary law, in use since 1769. The legislature ordered compiled a "digest of the civil laws of Orleans Territory" in 1808, revised in 1825 as the "Civil Code of Louisiana," which remains Louisiana's basic law. Based on Roman law and the Spanish colonial Siete Partidas and Recopilacion de Indias, it borrowed the Napoleonic Code's format. Edward Livingston's simplified Code of Practice was also adopted, but proposed commercial and penal codes were not. Notable features include its mortgage enforcement organization, mineral leases, ultimate equity decisions by judges in all civil matters not covered by the code, lenient black code (purged in 1870 revision), community property provisions, facile legitimation of bastards, allodial landholding, continuing judicial review of testamentary guardians, and absence of juries in civil cases. The "code" was a digest, not a true code, being a compilation of existent law rather than a substitution by newly devised statutes. It served as a model for the Code Quebec in 1857.

See G. Dargo, *Jefferson's Louisiana* (1975), excellent overview of code's inception; E. G. Brown, *American Journal of Legal History* (Jan., 1957); and J. H. Tucker *Code Napoleon and Common Law in Louisiana* (1956).

JAMES T. BANNON
St. Louis University

LOUISIANA PURCHASE was both a symbol of the potential "empire for liberty," which Thomas Jefferson envisaged for America, and a diplomatic coup that transformed the nation. The early stages of the purchase, however, seemed to promise no such happy results. The idea of a purchase began in the information relayed to Washington by British Intelligence that Napoleon had signed a secret treaty with Spain in 1800 whereby the Spanish crown would return to France the Louisiana lands lost by the Bourbons in 1763 in exchange for territory in Italy. For the United States this news was ominous. Although Spain had been an obnoxious neighbor, it was also a weak one, fearful of American strength and open to American intimidation.

Jefferson's forebodings increased when the Spanish government in New Orleans, presumably under French instructions, closed the port to American shippers in 1802, forcing the administration to take a stand on the danger in the West. Jefferson's choices were limited. To wage war risked raising both new taxes and the threat of militarism once again. It could also play into the hands of Britain, the country Jefferson still considered to be America's primary enemy. His solution was to purchase New Orleans and the Floridas for $2 million.

To help Robert R. Livingston, minister to France, in his mission, Jefferson sent JAMES MONROE, an experienced diplomat with strong ties to France. Earlier, Pierre Samuel Du Pont (DU PONT FAMILY), a French philosopher residing in the United States, went to Napoleon bearing information from the president that the future of Franco-American relations hung on the solution to the problem. Should France balk, the United States would be forced to resort to an Anglo-American alliance, a distasteful but necessary consequence of the French presence on the Mississippi. Jefferson appealed to the memory of a common bond against Britain to induce Bonaparte's compliance.

The diplomatic techniques seemed to work magnificently. Bonaparte, who up to this point had never admitted possession of Louisiana, surprised Livingston and Monroe with an offer to sell all of the territory for $15 million. The American ministers accepted, and Jefferson responded by his approval of a treaty of cession despite his scruples over the constitutionality of the act. Although a constitutional amendment would have been preferable, the time required by the process might be too long and the results too unpredictable. Bonaparte might change his mind; the Federalists in the East might defeat the amendment.

Jefferson was never to learn the reasons for France's generous action. To him it was simply a triumph of his diplomacy. He was correct, but only in part. Bonaparte sold Louisiana because war was about to break out again with Britain in 1803, and he knew that the British could capture Louisiana in the absence of a French occupation army. As it was, the French needed funds for the new war and could afford to wait until they had defeated Britain to think again about recovering their American empire. Jefferson knew nothing of these considerations.

In the short run, Jefferson's exaggeration of his own diplomatic skills invited the difficulties he was to suffer with the superpower in his next administration. In the long run the Louisiana Purchase represented America's good fortune in being able to extract benefits from Europe's difficulties.

See E. W. Lyon, *Louisiana in French Diplomacy, 1759–1804* (1934); A. P. Whitaker, *Mississippi Question, 1795–1803* (1934), western point of view; and L. S. Kaplan, *Jefferson and France* (1967).

LAWRENCE S. KAPLAN
Kent State University

LOUISIANA SPECIE RESERVE SYSTEM (1842–1862), established by a Louisiana banking act of 1842, was one of several bank reform measures (BANKING) enacted by states after the PANIC OF 1837. It represented a shift away from expansive credit toward a more restrictive policy (CURRENCY). A board of currency gained supervisory powers over all state banks, and a series of "fundamental rules" required banks to divide their loans into two classes: those made from capital ("dead weight") and those made from deposits ("movement of the bank"). Capital loans could be made in long-term investments, but loans from deposits were limited to 90-day, nonrenewable terms. Each bank had to maintain a specie reserve of one-third its total cash liabilities. The reform measures originated in the 1837 report of a legislative committee written by Edmond Jean Forstall (1794–1873), New Orleans merchant and banker. He developed the proposals in 1836 from wide reading, especially Albert Gallatin's *Considerations on the Currency* (1831) and histories of the banks of England, France, and Amsterdam, and from practical experience. The Louisiana system flourished until the Civil War and was widely praised and imitated, especially in the national banking system and the federal reserve act (1913).

See F. Redlich, *Molding of American Banking* (1951); I. D. Neu and G. D. Green, *Explorations in Economic History* (1970), revisionist; B. Hammond, *Banks and Politics* (1957); and L. C. Heldernman, *National and State Banks* (1931).

A. V. HUFF, JR.
Furman University

LOUISIANA STATE LOTTERY COMPANY

(1868–1895) was chartered by the Republican legislature of Louisiana in 1868. In return for a 25-year charter, a monopoly of the lottery business in Louisiana, and tax-exempt status, the company paid $40,000 annually to the state. Under the leadership of Charles T. Howard, the company developed a large clientele throughout the United States, became involved in political corruption in Louisiana, and enjoyed large profits. To create a good public image, it engaged former Confederate Generals PIERRE G. T. BEAUREGARD and JUBAL EARLY to represent the company. After Reconstruction the company developed support among New Orleans machine Democrats and Bourbon Democrats in the Delta and sugar parishes. Farm protest groups, for whom the lottery became a symbol for all the ills they suffered, and patrician urban reformers became the strongest opponents. In 1878 the Louisiana legislature repealed the company's charter, but the federal courts ruled this action a violation of contract. To prevent further legislative meddling, the company arranged to have its charter included in the 1879 Louisiana constitution.

In 1890 the company succeeded in getting a constitutional amendment through the legislature extending its charter but increasing its annual payment to $1,250,000. The lottery issue dominated state politics for the next two years, and the constitutional amendment was defeated. National opposition also increased, and Congress in 1890 strengthened a long-standing prohibition on using the mails to conduct lotteries and in 1895 prohibited lotteries in interstate commerce. After 1890 the company's profits declined, and it moved in 1895 to Honduras, where it functioned as the Honduras National Lottery Company until 1907.

See B. C. Alwes, *Louisiana Historical Quarterly* (Oct., 1944); R. H. Wiggins, *Louisiana Historical Quarterly* (July, 1948); H. C. Dethloff, *Louisiana History* (Spring, 1965); W. I. Hair, *Bourbonism and Agrarian Protest* (1969); and T. H. Williams, *Beauregard* (1954).

JUDITH FENNER GENTRY
University of Southwestern Louisiana

LOUISIANA STATE UNIVERSITY (Baton Rouge,

70803), first located at Pineville, was founded in 1860 as the Louisiana State Seminary of Learning and Military Academy. In 1869, after fire destroyed its original building, it was moved to Baton Rouge and given its present name. With a current enrollment of 25,000, it is the largest of six institutions in the Louisiana State University system, including the University of New Orleans (1958). The library at the Baton Rouge campus maintains one of the richest collections of materials on the history of Louisiana and the lower Mississippi Valley. Among the more notable of its holdings are the Charles F. Heartman Collection on Negro culture, the Burguieres Sugar Collection, the Warren L. Jones Collection of Lincolniana, and the personal and family papers of Thomas Butler (state district court judge), Edward J. Gay (planter, manufacturer, and U.S. senator), WILLIAM P. KELLOGG, PIERRE G. T. BEAUREGARD, Joseph Jones (Confederate army surgeon), JOSEPH E. RANSDELL (U.S. representative and senator), James H. Dillard (president of the Jeanes Foundation), and historians WALTER L. FLEMING and CHARLES E. A. GAYARRÉ. As a custodian for the state's archives, the library also houses the records of the executive department (1832–1928), secretary of state (1873–1930), state auditor (1823–1933), department of education (1825–1931), railroad commission (1898–1919), penitentiary board (1879–1930), and board of control of state leper home (1892–1921), as well as the records of several parishes (1786–1933).

See V. L. Bedsole and O. Richard (eds.), *LSU* (1959), pictorial; J. L. Barnidge, *Louisiana History* (Summer, 1969); W. L. Fleming, *LSU, 1860–1896* (1936); and M. M. Wilkerson, *Thomas Duckett Boyd* (1935), president, 1896–1927.

LOUISIANA-TEHUANTEPEC COMPANY

(1857–1861) was established in New Orleans under the presidency of Emile La Sère at 45 Carondelet St. Leading backers were Peter A. Hargous of New York and JUDAH P. BENJAMIN, JOHN SLIDELL, and La Sère of New Orleans, commercial expansionists dreaming of tapping Asiatic trade via San Francisco and Tehuantepec. The company emerged from four rival groups claiming ownership of Mexico's 1842 isthmian land grant to Don José de Garay. Despite the opposition of PIERRE SOULÉ, the company succeeded in gaining a new charter from the Mexican government in August, 1857, partly by bribery and by pressure from the Buchanan administration. From September passenger steamship services operated from New Orleans to Suchil, Coatzacoalcos River. A one-year mail contract was awarded in November, 1858. Gold fever struck the isthmus the next year. But the season of prosperity ended. The company split into sectional cliques and also lost the mail contract. Hargous withdrew his vessels, and the company collapsed financially. Powerful southern commercial expansionists using northern capital had attempted and failed to dominate Mexico's isthmian route before the outbreak of the Civil War.

See J. F. Rippy, *Mississippi Valley Historical Review* (March, 1920); J. P. Moore, *Hispanic American Historical Review* (Feb., 1952); J. Phillips, "American Interest Tehuantepec" (M.A. thesis, University of Alabama, 1951); Shufeldt Papers, Box 20, Library of Congress; P. A. Hargous, New York *Herald* (Aug. 12, 1856); and P. Butler, *Judah P. Benjamin* (1906).

FREDERICK C. DRAKE
Brock University, Ontario

LOUISVILLE, GA.

LOUISVILLE, GA. (pop. 2,691), was founded in 1786 as the new state capital, succeeding Augusta and Savannah. The state buildings were completed in 1796, but the capital was moved in 1805 to Milledgeville. Today the town is a small market for area lumber and cotton growers and also the manufacturer of some textiles.

See files of Louisville *News and Farmer and Wadley Herald* (1867–).

LOUISVILLE, KY.

LOUISVILLE, KY. (pop. 361,472). GEORGE ROGERS CLARK and his soldiers built a blockhouse here in 1778. Its strategic location near a falls on the Ohio River caused Clark to use it for his headquarters and, in 1782, as a supply base for his operations against the British north of the Ohio. After the British and later the Indians were cleared from the Ohio Valley area, Louisville grew along with the expanded volume of river traffic. In 1830 the completion of a canal ended in the portage

around the falls and made possible uninterrupted voyages up the river as far as Pittsburgh. The arrival of two rail lines in the 1850s stimulated additional commerce and solidified the city's position as Kentucky's principal center of trade and manufacturing. Despite the acute division of the residents' loyalties during the Civil War, Louisville was an important supply base for Union forces in the West.

Today the city named for King Louis XVI of France is one of the principal educational, financial, commercial, and industrial centers in the South. In addition to the University of Louisville (1798), the oldest municipal university in the country, Louisville is the home of Southern Baptist Theological Seminary (1859), the College of Pharmacy of the University of Kentucky (1870), Louisville Presbyterian Seminary (1901), and the Jefferson School of Law (1905). River traffic remains a significant element in the city's commerce, and the only inland station of the U.S. Coast Guard is here. Louisville is one of the nation's principal producers of tobacco products and distilled whiskey (BOURBON). Its varied industries manufacture electrical appliances, foodstuffs, textiles, construction materials, leather goods, petrochemicals, furniture, plastics, synthetic rubber, and farm equipment.

See R. C. Riebel, *Louisville Panorama* (1960), illustrated chronology; H. McMurtrie, *Sketches of Louisville* (1819), includes botanical catalog; B. Casseday, *History of Louisville* (1852); J. S. Johnston (ed.), *Memorial History of Louisville to 1896* (2 vols.; 1896); S. W. Thomas (ed.), *Views of Louisville* (1971), 436 illustrations; J. P. Sullivan, "Louisville, Her Southern Alliance, 1865–1890" (Ph.D. dissertation, University of Kentucky, 1965); and files of numerous city newspapers, notably *Courier-Journal* (1868–), on microfilm. University of Louisville Library has archive of photographs; Filson Club Library keeps local manuscripts; and public library has newspapers on microfilm since 1818, city directories from 1832, census reports from 1810, and annual city reports from 1866.

LOUISVILLE (KY.) COURIER-JOURNAL

LOUISVILLE (KY.) COURIER-JOURNAL was formed in 1868 by the merger of two newspapers that previously had engaged in one of the classic competitions of American journalism. The *Courier* (1844–1868), edited by W. N. Haldeman, had been a staunchly Democratic newspaper that supported JOHN C. BRECKINRIDGE in the ELECTION OF 1860 and had looked favorably upon the Confederate cause. G. D. Prentice, editor of the *Journal* (1830–1868) was equally as vigorous an advocate of the Whig party, of JOHN BELL's candidacy in 1860, and of the need to preserve the Union. The financial problems caused by competition for advertising revenues and the demise of old issues and personalities suggested the logic of merging these two journalistic foes. It was HENRY WATTERSON's masterful editing (1868–1918) of the *Courier-Journal*, however, that made the paper both an influential oracle and a widely recognized symbol of the NEW SOUTH movement during the late nineteenth and early twentieth centuries.

See M. F. Schmidt, *Filson Club History Quarterly* (Oct., 1966), Louisville printers, 1800–60; microfilm of *Courier* (1844–68), *Journal* (1830–68), and *Courier-Journal* (1868 to date) available from Bell & Howell; assorted bound copies of *Courier*, Louisville Free Public Library and University of Chicago Library; bound copies of *Journal*, Filson Club, Louisville Free Public Library, and Library of Congress; and bound copies of *Courier-Journal* (1868–), Kentucky State Library and Louisville Free Public Library.

LOUISVILLE, UNIVERSITY OF (Louisville, Ky.

40208), is the oldest municipal university in the nation. Started in 1798 as Jefferson Seminary, it became a university in 1846 with an academic department, a medical school, and a school of law. Since World War II the school has expanded both its offerings and enrollments and presently serves over 16,000 students, most of whom are commuters. Housed in the university law school library are the papers of LOUIS D. BRANDEIS and JOHN MARSHALL HARLAN.

See Federal Writers' Project, *Centennial History of University of Louisville* (1939).

LOWNDES, RAWLINS (1721–1800), was born

on the island of St. Christopher, British West Indies. The family migrated to South Carolina, where his father failed in business and died in 1736. Trained in the law, Lowndes was named provost marshal in 1745 and subsequently engaged in planting and land speculation, through which he rebuilt the family fortune. Elected to the provincial legislature in 1749, he rose rapidly in politics, becoming house Speaker in 1763 and chief judge of the provincial courts by 1767. Consistently defending colonial rights, he participated in the Gadsden election, STAMP ACT, Wilkes fund, and REGULATOR controversies. Although Lowndes resisted the trend toward revolution, he firmly supported the patriot cause after independence was declared and was elected president of South Carolina in 1778. Ineffectual in the office owing largely to factional opposition, he shunned reelection and remained politically inactive during the war. In 1788 Lowndes closed his political career as the

Cassandra of South Carolina, warning in vain of northern aggrandizement under the proposed Constitution and eventual subordination of the South.

See G. B. Chase, *Lowndes of South Carolina* (1876), genealogical; Mrs. S. J. Ravenel, *William Lowndes* (1901); Lowndes Papers, Library of Congress, thin; William Lowndes Papers, University of North Carolina Library, esp. 1754–55 journal of Rawlins Lowndes, though attributed to his brother; C. J. Vipperman, *South Carolina Historical Magazine* (Oct., 1969) and "William Lowndes" (Ph.D. dissertation, University of Virginia, 1966); South Carolina Commons House and Council Journals (1749–76), South Carolina Archives; *South Carolina Gazette and Country Journal* (Feb. 28, 1769); and J. Elliott, *Debates* (1941), IV.

CARL VIPPERMAN
University of Georgia

LOWNDES, WILLIAM (1782–1822), settled at

his birthplace, Colleton County, S.C., after an early education in Britain and study of law in Charleston. He soon turned to Jeffersonian Republican politics (although he married Elizabeth, daughter of Federalist THOMAS PINCKNEY) and served in the South Carolina legislature (1806–1810), where he wrote a significant reapportionment bill. He was elected U.S. representative in 1810. His endeavors reflected his constituents' interests: naval and military preparedness for the WAR OF 1812. He favored the second Bank of the United States as relevant to national defense and a moderate tariff to prevent foreign dependence. He, like JOHN C. CALHOUN, was an economic nationalist. He refused administrative and diplomatic posts offered him by Presidents James Madison and James Monroe, but did serve as chairman of the House Ways and Means Committee and did help to negotiate the admission of Missouri to the Union. In 1821 the South Carolina legislature nominated him for president of the United States; low-country legislators had battled up-country supporters of Lowndes's friend Calhoun. This nomination, however, had little viability because Lowndes's health was failing; he suffered increasingly from "rheumatic fever," contracted as a boy in England. He resigned from Congress in the spring of 1822 and died in October en route to Europe. The Charleston *Courier* reported the death of a "statesman who cherished the Union of these States . . . and promoted all the salutary and stable defences of the Republic."

See Mrs. S. J. Ravenel, *Life and Times of William Lowndes* (1901). A major portion of Lowndes's papers were destroyed by fire in 1861. The remainder, mostly letters written from Washington, D.C., to his wife, are available on microfilm, University of North Carolina Library. Library of Congress also holds small collection.

MARGARET K. LATIMER
Auburn University

LOYAL COMPANY

LOYAL COMPANY was a major force in late eighteenth-century land politics. On July 12, 1749, near the end of Governor William Gooch's administration, the Virginia council granted "eight thousand acres in one or more surveys, beginning on the Bounds between this Colony and North Carolina, and running to the Westward and to the North" to the Loyal Land Company of Virginia, whose members, mainly from Albemarle County, included DR. THOMAS WALKER, John Lewis, Peter Jefferson, and later EDMUND PENDLETON. The grant required payment of fees and completion of surveys within four years. The Loyal company's more famous rival, the OHIO COMPANY, and four others received grants the same day.

Dr. Walker, the company's leading agent until his death (1794), explored southwest Virginia and Kentucky for it in 1750, and then the company began selling land at £3 per 100 acres, but all land sold—200,000 acres by 1773—was east of the Appalachians. Its members' great political power in Virginia enabled the company to survive the FRENCH AND INDIAN WAR, the PROCLAMATION OF 1763, and failure to fulfill the 1749 terms. Squatters and rival speculators challenged the company's titles, but in 1783 the Virginia court of appeals validated company surveys made before 1776. The company became the "successors of the Loyal Company" in 1818; it was in a lawsuit as late as 1871.

See A. Henderson, *Dr. Thomas Walker and Loyal Company* (1931); T. P. Abernethy, *Western Lands and American Revolution* (1937); and C. W. Alvord, *Mississippi Valley in British Politics* (1917).

JOSEPH A. DEVINE, JR.
Stephen F. Austin State University

LOYALISTS

LOYALISTS (Tories) in the South, less noticed at first than their northern counterparts, became the key element in British strategy after 1779. They were strongest in Georgia and South Carolina, likely to be recent immigrants, planters, or professional men in the low country and disgruntled frontiersmen to the westward. North Carolina Loyalists were weaker and lived mostly in the backcountry, where many had been involved in the REGULATOR movement. Nowhere was loyalism weaker than Virginia, where the few Tories were found around Norfolk and on the Eastern Shore. Eastern Maryland was home to numerous Loyalists, but they were never an effective force.

When war began, Sir Henry Clinton hoped to rally the many backcountry Tories, but a strong base on the coast was needed. He arrived at Cape Fear in March, 1776, to learn that the North Carolina Tories had just suffered a crushing defeat at MOORE'S CREEK BRIDGE. Clinton moved on to Charleston, where his ill-planned attack was repulsed. The patriots were able to organize state governments and suppress the southern Loyalists at leisure.

Only after the war reached a stalemate in the North did the British turn again to the South, encouraged by exiles in London and hoping once again to rally the many Loyalists supposedly waiting to serve their king. Lieutenant Colonel Archibald Campbell captured Savannah in December, 1778, and soon occupied all Georgia. Governor James Wright returned in July, 1779, and restored the civilian royal government. Clinton captured Charleston in 1780, and the British, now under Lord Cornwallis, soon occupied most of South Carolina and advanced in North Carolina, offering generous terms. Loyalists came forward by the thousands, but never as many as expected and never strong enough to protect their homes when embodied as militia. Resurgent patriots hit hard at isolated posts, and a vicious civil war developed, in which the Loyalists suffered the greater losses. When Cornwallis marched to Yorktown, the patriots regained full control except for a few garrisoned towns crowded with Loyalist refugees. Cornwallis had never been able to protect those who admitted their Tory beliefs, and they suffered greatly, many fleeing into exile when Charleston and Savannah were evacuated from July to December, 1782.

See W. Brown, *Good Americans* (1969); P. H. Smith, *Loyalists and Redcoats* (1964) and *William and Mary Quarterly* (April, 1968); and G. McCowen, Jr., *British Occupation of Charleston* (1972).

PATRICK J. FURLONG
Indiana University, South Bend

LUBBOCK, TEX.

LUBBOCK, TEX. (pop. 179,295), is an industrial and commercial center in the northwest section of the state, approximately 250 miles west of Ft. Worth. Besides shipping and processing poultry, grain, cattle, oil, and diary products, Lubbock is the third largest inland cotton market in the world. The town was founded in 1891 as the result of a merger and relocation of two older communities: Lubbock and Monterey. It is the seat of Texas Technological College (1923).

See L. L. Graves (ed.), *History of Lubbock* (1963); and files of Lubbock *Avalanche-Journal* (1900–), on microfilm.

LUMBER INDUSTRY. Lumber manufacturing is the South's oldest industry, having originated in every state soon after settlement by Europeans. Commercial lumbering began at Jamestown in 1608, when the colonists sawed clapboards for Captain Christopher Newport to carry back to England. Subsequently, until TOBACCO became the colony's main export, supply ships returned home from Virginia laden primarily with timber. Sawmilling machinery was introduced into Virginia around 1620 by the London Company, which offered land grants as inducements for the construction of water-powered sawmills. During the seventeenth and early eighteenth centuries, however, southern yellow pine lumber was manufactured largely for home consumption because English craftsmen preferred easily worked northern white pine. Nevertheless, the southern colonies gradually developed an important trade with the West Indies in timber, lumber, shingles, and barrel staves.

During the final century of the colonial period, lumbering was carried on in the southern colonies as an adjunct to agriculture with farm workers employed in the woods and mills when not needed in the fields. Sawmills of that era utilized water-powered sash saws, which cut about 1,000 linear feet of lumber daily. North Carolina was the South's leading manufacturer of lumber, exporting about 3 million linear feet annually. The other southern colonies shipped from 1 million to 2 million feet each, except for Maryland, which imported lumber for shipbuilding.

During the eighteenth century the forests of Florida generally were neglected, but the French and Spanish exploited the cypress forests along the lower Mississippi River for the benefit of their possessions in the West Indies. In fact, cypress lumber was the economic mainstay of colonial Louisiana.

The American Revolution cost the southern states most of their lucrative lumber trade with the West Indies. Similarly, Louisiana cypress lumber manufacturers had to turn to the domestic American market after 1803. Fortunately, development of the cotton kingdom and the settlement of the old Southwest created a rapidly expanding domestic market. During the westward movement small sawmills, often powered by steam engines, followed closely behind immigrants pouring into western Georgia, Alabama, Mississippi, and Tennessee, permitting the settlers to replace their original log cabins with frame buildings. On many of the new cotton plantations, sawmills driven by the same source of power as the cotton gins were used to manufacture lumber from logs obtained when clearing the fields for cultivation. These planters rafted surplus lumber and timber to the ports for sale in the coastal or foreign trades. By 1840 every town of consequence boasted at least one sawmill, and many others scattered along the rivers served local markets.

Between 1800 and 1860 improvements in technology and growth in the domestic market for lumber made great changes in the southern lumber industry. In 1803, for example, the nation's first steam-powered sawmill was erected at Donaldsonville, La., using one of Oliver Evans' recently invented high-pressure engines. Subsequently, steam power was applied to a great many mills throughout the South where adequate sources of water power were lacking. Mills using circular saws became common during the 1840s, with the new device being utilized in portable sawmills that could be moved to sources of timber as well as in stationary mills of various sizes. By the 1850s earlier types of sash saw mills producing around 1,000 linear feet of lumber daily had been superseded by mills manufacturing from 15,000 to 25,000 feet of semifinished lumber. Sawmills like one operated at Natchez by Andrew Brown and the Vale Royal sawmill at Savannah, Ga., were typical of the larger southern sawmills of that period. Both of these establishments were equipped with three gang saw mills, a circular saw mill, and a planing machine with capacities of 25,000 feet of edged and planed boards daily. The Savannah mill was powered by three 30-horsepower steam engines; and the Natchez mill, by a single 100-horsepower steam engine. Both mills were capitalized at $60,000 and employed about 40 slaves. In the late 1850s both mills cleared about $25,000 annually.

Between 1820 and 1860 the southern export trade in lumber expanded gradually as markets opened in Europe, the Middle East, South America, Central America, and the West Indies. Professional lumbermen, many of whom had learned their trade in Maine, moved their operations southward along the Atlantic coast exhausting the stands of timber near rafting streams as they went. By the last decade of the slavery era, Norfolk, Wilmington, and Charleston were declining as lumber ports, while Savannah, Jacksonville, Pensacola, and Mobile were gaining in importance. In the late 1850s both Savannah and Pensacola were shipping more than 30 million linear feet of yellow pine lumber annually.

The Civil War interrupted the growth of the southern lumber industry. Invasion by northern armies threw the formerly booming internal lumber market of the southern states into disarray, and the federal BLOCKADE of southern ports choked the foreign trade in timber and lumber. During the first postwar decade the industry recovered very slowly because depression reigned in the former Confederate states and foreign customers had found other sources of supply. Nevertheless, southern mills manufactured approximately 1.5 billion board feet of yellow pine lumber in 1869 and 2.7 billion board feet in 1879.

With the exhaustion of the white pine forests in the Great Lakes states, northern lumbermen turned their attention in the late 1870s to the South's yellow pine forests. Acquiring vast tracts of timberlands during the 1880s, northern lumber manufacturers erected enormous sawmills near the railroads and constructed spur railways to transport logs from the forest to the mills. Equipped with twin-opposed circular saw mills, multibladed gang saw mills, and in the late 1880s with fast-cutting band saw mills, the lumber manufacturing establishments of this period dwarfed the largest mills of the 1850s. In Virginia, for example, the Camp sawmill produced 12 million feet of lumber in 1887. The Camp mill paled into insignificance, however, when the Gulf Lumber Company mill went into operation in Louisiana during 1906. Utilizing five band saw mills, this establishment produced about 120 million feet annually. The Great Southern plant at Bogalusa, La., equipped with four band saw mills and a gang saw mill had a capacity of 1 million feet a day after 1908. The production of yellow pine lumber crested in 1909, with southern mills turning out more than 16 billion board feet that year.

Very extensive logging operations were carried on by the lumber companies with the aid of vastly improved steam-powered machinery. Steam skidders, for example, dragged huge logs from where the trees were felled to the logging railroads, and other machinery loaded them onto the cars. Such operations as these converted stands of timber into cutover lands with astonishing speed and efficiency. When the timber supply was exhausted, the whole operation was moved to a new location.

By 1920 most of the extensive tracts of virgin yellow pine had gone the way of northern white pine, and many of the great mills had been transferred to the West Coast. Nevertheless, lumber production continued in the southern states on a reduced scale. Large numbers of small sawmills were able to obtain logs from timberlands too small to sustain the large mills of the preceding era by using trucks and crawler tractors. In 1929 these small establishments produced 7 billion board feet of lumber, while large mills manufactured 4 billion feet. During the 1930s, however, lumber manufacturing declined drastically, reaching a low point in 1932 of only 3 billion feet.

In the depressed 1930s southern lumbermen became aware that second growths of timber were springing up on the cutover pinelands. The surviving large lumber companies accordingly adopted improved methods of managing their forest lands so that they could supply their mills indefinitely. In this fashion, the southern lumber industry transformed itself from an exploitive industry into one based on conservation of natural resources.

In the period since World War II, pine trees have been raised in the South like crops of cotton or corn. Lumber and paper manufacturers acquired millions of acres on which to grow trees scientifically. In cooperation with federal and state agencies, these corporations developed effective methods of forestry and shared their technology with small owners of timberlands. To date, however, owners of large landholdings, especially lumber and paper corporations and state and federal governments, have been far more successful than small owners in growing trees for pulp and saw timber.

The South's hardwood lumber industry, smaller and more diversified than the yellow pine industry, reached its heyday somewhat later than the latter. The specialized cypress industry of the Mississippi Valley was prostrated by the Civil War, but finally revived during the late nineteenth and early twentieth centuries. On the eve of World War II the annual production of cypress lumber was more than 200 million board feet. The story of other varieties of hardwoods was quite different from cypress. In the 1880s northern hardwood manufacturers invaded the Upper South seeking walnut timber, which they culled from the forests and manufactured with small sawmills. When the supply of walnut was used up, the hardwood lumbermen turned next to poplar and oak. More recently, cottonwood, redgum, pecan, hackberry, and even magnolia have become marketable for manufacture of furniture and building supplies.

In the twentieth century, North Carolina developed an important FURNITURE INDUSTRY utilizing oak, cherry, yellow poplar, and walnut from the mountains of that state. In 1955, 300 factories produced furniture valued at nearly $300 million. In the Mississippi Valley, Memphis emerged as the South's principal center for manufacturing of hardwood flooring and building materials. During the 1920s at least 50 sawmills were operating in the city. For most of the present century, the southern states have supplied the nation's furniture manufacturers with much of their hardwood lumber. In 1947, for example, the South produced 68 percent of the country's hardwood.

Before World War II hardwood manufacturers generally bought their logs from small landowners rather than maintaining extensive tracts of timberlands like the yellow pine manufacturers. After the war, however, it became apparent that some hardwoods, including the valuable walnut trees, were reaching maturity much faster than had previously been believed. On fertile bottom lands, walnut trees were attaining diameters of 25 inches in as many years. Inspired by this discovery, the larger hardwood manufacturers acquired forest lands and planned to operate their mills on a sustained-yield basis like the yellow pine producers.

Because both hardwoods and pines can be harvested in a shorter time in the South than in other regions, the southern states are rapidly recapturing the leading role in the lumber industry that they lost to the Northwest earlier in the century. In 1970 southern mills produced about 15 billion board feet of lumber, while converting 75 percent of the waste materials into commercially valuable pulp. At the same time, hardwood and pine lumber manufacturers have had to adjust to much smaller logs of lower quality than they utilized during the first half of the century. Improved forestry methods can produce enough timber to meet the nation's needs indefinitely. Since raising trees to maturity is prohibitively expensive, however, high-quality hardwoods and yellow pines are gone forever.

See S. F. Horn, *This Fascinating Lumber Business* (1951); J. M. Collier, *Southern Pine Association* (1965); C. W. Goodyear, *Bogalusa Story* (1950); N. W. Hickman, *Mississippi Harvest* (1962); W. W. Kellogg, *Kellogg Story* (1969); J. H. Moore, *Cypress Lumbering* (1967); J. Pikl, *Georgia Forestry* (1966); M. Curtis, *Louisiana History* (Fall, 1973); R. Douglas, *Tennessee Historical Quarterly* (Spring, 1966); J. A. Eisterhold, *Louisiana History* (Winter, 1972), *Georgia Historical Quarterly* (Winter, 1973), *Alabama Review* (April, 1973), *Florida Historical Quarterly* (Jan., 1973), *South Carolina Magazine of History* (April, 1973), and *Southern Lumberman* (Dec., 1971); J. E. Fickle, *Journal of Southern History* (Feb., 1974); P. Gates, *Journal of Southern History* (Aug., 1940); M. Herndon, *Georgia Historical Quarterly* (Spring, 1973); N. W. Hickman, *Journal of Mississippi History* (July, 1957; Oct., 1958); J. D. Hodge, *Journal of Mississippi History* (Nov., 1973); E. F. Keuchel, *Florida Historical Quarterly* (Spring, 1974); R. S. Maxwell, *Forest History* (April, 1973); D. J. Millet, *Louisiana History* (Winter, 1966); J. H. Moore, *Journal of Southern History* (May, 1961); R. E. Norgress, *Louisiana Historical Quarterly* (Winter, 1947); J. W. Silver, *Journal of Southern History*

(Nov., 1957) and *Journal of Mississippi History* (April, 1957); S. A. Schulman, *Tennessee Historical Quarterly* (Fall, 1973); and *Pioneer America* (Jan., 1974); C. W. Crawford, "R. F. Learned Lumber Company" (Ph.D. dissertation, University of Mississippi, 1968); H. P. Easton, "Texas Lumbering Industry" (Ph.D. dissertation, University of Texas, 1947); N. W. Hickman, "Forest Industries in East Louisiana and Mississippi" (Ph.D. dissertation, University of Texas, 1958); H. King, "Long-Bell Lumber Company" (M.A. thesis, Louisiana State University, 1936); O. T. Mouzon, "Wood and Paper Industry of South" (Ph.D. dissertation, University of North Carolina, 1940); J. P. Oden, "Southern Pulp and Paper Industry" (Ph.D. dissertation, Mississippi State University, 1974); and G. A. Stokes, "Lumbering in Southwest Louisiana" (Ph.D. dissertation, Louisiana State University, 1954). *Forest History* is scholarly journal of lumber industry, and *Southern Lumberman* is foremost trade journal of southern lumber industry. Southern university libraries designated as depositories by Forest History Society are collecting records of the industry.

JOHN HEBRON MOORE
Florida State University

LUMPKIN, JOSEPH HENRY (1799–1867), was born in Oglethorpe County, Ga. Son of a prosperous superior court clerk, he attended the University of Georgia and Princeton, was admitted to the Georgia bar in 1820, and moved to Athens. An effective, eloquent attorney, he served two terms in the state legislature (1824 and 1825) and assisted in promulgating the Georgia Penal Code in 1833. A frequent lecturer at the University of Georgia Law School (named for him), Lumpkin urged elevation of POOR WHITES through manufacturing, temperance reform, and, in the crisis of 1850, southern separation from the Union. Elected chief justice of the first Georgia supreme court in 1845 (serving in that office until his death), he established the court's appellate jurisdiction and the doctrine of binding precedents against the local prerogatives of superior court justices. His decisions, often delivered orally, reveal a preference for substantive justice rather than technical legal procedures.

See W. J. Northen, *Men of Mark in Georgia* (1910), II; J. R. Lamar, *24th Georgia Bar Association Reports*; L. L. Cody, *Lumpkin Family* (1928); and *Georgia Reports*, I–XXXV, for Lumpkin's opinions.

RICHARD ALLAN GERBER
Lehman College, City University of New York

LUMPKIN, WILSON (1783–1870), was born in Pittsylvania County, Va., and raised in northeast Georgia. He read law and was admitted to the bar in 1804. That same year he was elected to the Georgia legislature, where he served a decade. After a term in Congress (1815–1817), he was appointed commissioner to run the line of the Creek cession in Georgia. After two additional terms in Congress (1827–1831), he resigned to run for governor of Georgia, a position he held for two terms (1831–1835) at the height of the Indian removal controversy. He exhibited a strong states' rights attitude toward federal interference. After a part term in the U.S. Senate (1837–1841) he returned to Georgia and devoted his time to the Western & Atlantic Railroad, then being built from today's Atlanta. During the rest of his life spent in Athens, Ga., he was attentive to the developing sectional struggle. His advanced age prevented him from taking an active part in the Civil War.

See W. Lumpkin, *Removal of Cherokee Indians* (1907); and C. J. Vipperman, "Wilson Lumpkin and Cherokee Removal" (M.A. thesis, University of Athens, 1961).

RICHARD K. MURDOCH
University of Georgia

LUNDY, BENJAMIN (1789–1839), New Jersey-born Quaker abolitionist, spent most of his life in the South and West promoting emancipation, chiefly by means of the *Genius of Universal Emancipation*, a newspaper that he founded in 1821 in Ohio but soon transferred to east Tennessee as a successor to ELIHU EMBREE's *Emancipator*. An advocate of gradual emancipation, Lundy developed a comprehensive critique of slavery, emphasizing its immorality but also condemning its political, economic, and social consequences. For many years he principally addressed southerners in the belief that southern nonslaveholders could be persuaded to end slavery through state legislative action. He moved his newspaper to Baltimore in 1824 and to Washington in 1830, but with each passing year he found fewer southerners receptive to antislavery argument. Lundy advocated immigration of free blacks to Haiti, Canada, and Mexico. Besides providing blacks a better life, such settlements, he believed, would encourage emancipation by demonstrating the efficiency of free labor. His plan to develop such a colony in Texas was frustrated by the outbreak of the Texas revolution. His pamphlet, *The War in Texas*, interpreting that event as the result of a slaveholders' conspiracy, proved convincing to abolitionists as well as to other northerners, thereby helping to delay the annexation of Texas and to strengthen the concept of "the slave power."

See T. Earle, *Life of Benjamin Lundy* (1847); and M. L. Dillon, *Benjamin Lundy* (1966), full account and bibliography. Most important collections of Lundy Papers are at Ohio Historical Society, Library of Congress, and Historical Society of Pennsylvania. Most complete file of

Genius of Universal Emancipation is at Boston Public Library, also on microfilm.

MERTON L. DILLON
Ohio State University

LUTHERANISM in the South began with the Palatine immigration into Virginia in 1717. Earlier appearances of Lutherans were either legendary (St. Augustine) or temporary (New Bern, N.C.). Settlement by Pennsylvania Germans and by additional immigrants brought Lutherans into the Shenandoah Valley in 1727. The tide continued southward into North Carolina (1747), central South Carolina (1749), and east Tennessee (1780). A group of Protestant refugees from Salzburg settled at Ebenezer, just north of Savannah, in 1734, and other immigrants arrived through Charleston, where a congregation was worshiping by 1742. The earliest pastors were called from Europe, and the congregations tried to maintain the heritage of their homeland.

Following the Revolution, Lutherans in the South moved toward independent organization and indentification with American culture. After preliminary efforts for a common organization in the Carolinas in 1788, the North Carolina Synod held its first meeting in 1803. Other synods gathered Lutherans in Maryland-Virginia (1820), South Carolina (1824), southwest Virginia (1842), Kentucky (1854), Mississippi (1855), and Georgia (1860). By 1825 English had replaced German in most congregations, and the pattern of church life resembled that of most other groups in American evangelical Protestantism. A seminary opened in South Carolina in 1830, and colleges were founded in Virginia (Roanoke College, 1842) and South Carolina (Newberry College, 1855). A vocal minority, led by members of the Henkel family, resisted the loss of German and the modification of traditional Lutheran doctrines, and by the Civil War their Tennessee Synod (1820) had congregations in several southern states.

Conservative forces grew as the result of the massive immigration of Germans to America after 1840. Settlers flocked into the Mississippi Valley, bringing with them German hymnals, catechisms, pastors, and attitudes. In contrast to the Americanized Lutherans along the Eastern Seaboard, these recent immigrants spoke a foreign language, tolerated the use of beer and wine, and shunned cooperation with other denominations. The largest group settled in Perry County and St. Louis, Mo., where they founded a seminary (1839) and published a newspaper. Under the leadership of C. F. W. Walther, they organized the German Evangelical Lutheran Synod of Missouri, Ohio, and Other States (now the Lutheran Church–Missouri Synod) in 1847. A smaller concentration of Lutherans around San Antonio established the Texas Synod in 1851.

The Civil War forced most of the older Lutheran synods along the Atlantic coast to unite in an organization called the General Synod in the Confederate States of America (1863). After the war they continued as a separate body, adding the conservative Tennessee Synod in 1886 and changing their name to the United Synod, South. This body merged with its sister bodies in the North to form the United Lutheran Church in America in 1918. Southern Lutherans were becoming more conscious of their denominational identity during this period. Worship services became more liturgical, doctrine more important, and catechetical instruction more prominent. Preaching robes were introduced; central pulpits gave place to altars. Auxiliaries for women, children and finally men appeared as fund-raising agencies for missionary work at home and overseas (Japan, Liberia). Another college was chartered in 1880 in North Carolina (now Lenoir Rhyne College). Attempts to provide religious services for the small percentage of black Lutherans after the Civil War proved inadequate; Missouri Synod missionary efforts resulted in the founding of two educational institutions for blacks in 1903 (Emanuel Lutheran College, Greensboro, N.C., and Luther College, New Orleans).

Industrialization, particularly after World War II, brought Lutherans from Pennsylvania and the upper Midwest into most southern cities. The result was a burst of home mission activity. Florida also received many retired couples, and by 1975 the state had approximately equal representation of the three major Lutheran bodies—the American Lutheran Church, the Lutheran Church in America, and the Lutheran Church–Missouri Synod.

See C. Nelson, *Lutherans in North America* (1975), general bibliography; H. G. Anderson, *Lutheranism in Southeastern States* (1969); W. Eisenberg, *Lutheran Church in Virginia* (1967), also covers Maryland and east Tennessee; P. McCullough, *History of Lutheran Church in South Carolina* (1971); and C. S. Meyer, *Moving Frontiers* (1964), Missouri Synod.

HUGH GEORGE ANDERSON
Lutheran Theological Southern Seminary

LYCEUMS were public gatherings or meetings for the purpose of promoting popular education by means of lectures, concerts, and demonstrations. Lyceums in the South received their impe-

tus from an article by Josiah Holbrook containing a plan for a "society for mutual education" in the October, 1826, *American Journal of Education*. As outlined by Holbrook, then living in Massachusetts, two principal objectives of the lyceum were "to procure for youths an economical and practical education and to diffuse rational and useful information through the community generally" and "to apply the sciences and the various branches of education to the domestic and useful arts, and to all the common purposes of life." Unlike the Mechanics Society and the athenaeum, the lyceum was directed to the mutual improvement of the whole community, rather than of selected groups.

The lyceum movement found its full fruition during the 1830s and 1840s. Virginia, Delaware, and the District of Columbia were early southern leaders: Delaware's center for lyceums was Wilmington; Virginia had lyceums in Norfolk, Alexandria, Charlottesville, and Richmond; and in the District of Columbia, the Smithsonian Institution became a focus for lyceum activities by the 1840s. Georgia had 13 lyceums in 1834 and by 1843 had lyceums in at least four towns. Centers of population—Baltimore, New Orleans, Little Rock, and St. Louis—were the homes of the principal lyceums in Maryland, Louisiana, Arkansas, and Missouri. North Carolina and Florida apparently did not engage in the movement, and South Carolina showed little interest. Alabama and Tennessee had some activity in Mobile and Nashville. Kentucky, however, had lyceums in three towns by the early 1830s. Mississippi showed great interest in the lyceum movement, having formed a total of 54 lyceums in 36 towns by 1848, including the Ladies Institute and Lyceum. The early lyceums depended principally upon resident scientists and other scholars for their lectures; later lyceums, upon traveling lecturers. Interest in lyceums dwindled during and after the Civil War, but a similar desire for popular education led to the CHAUTAUQUA MOVEMENT in a later era.

See C. Bode, *American Lyceum* (1956, 1968); New York *Christian Advocate* (May 13, 1831); L. D. S. Harrell, *Journal of Mississippi History* (Aug., 1969); and *Southwestern Journal* (1837–38), I.

LAURA D. S. HARRELL STURDIVANT
Mississippi Department of Archives and History

LYNCH, JAMES (1838–1872), was born in Baltimore to a free mulatto merchant and a slave mother. He was educated at Kimball Union Academy, Hanover, N.H., after which he entered the ministry of the Methodist church in the North. During the Civil War he followed W. T. Sherman's army into Georgia, serving as a missionary to blacks. In 1867 he moved to Mississippi to serve, as he expressed it, "my mission as a religious and moral educator of my race." He soon became involved in the politics of Reconstruction, however. A brilliant orator, Lynch by 1868 had become the leading Negro politician in the state and a threat in the black community to the influence of the carpetbaggers who resisted his rise to political prominence. He joined white moderate Republicans in capturing control of the state Republican party, and in 1869 he was elected secretary of state on the Republican ticket headed by JAMES LUSK ALCORN. As the first black man to hold a state office in Mississippi, Lynch served ably; after his death even his conservative opponents accorded a measure of praise to him for his honesty and competency.

See W. C. Harris, *Historian* (Nov., 1971); V. L. Wharton, *Negro in Mississippi* (1965); and J. R. Lynch, *Facts of Reconstruction* (1970).

WILLIAM C. HARRIS
North Carolina State University

LYNCH, JOHN ROY (1847–1939), was born in Concordia Parish, La., the son of a wealthy white planter and a Negro slave. Taken to Natchez during the Civil War, he was freed by the Union army in 1864. Enrolling in a night school for blacks, he quickly became functionally literate. In 1867 he assisted in the organization of the local Republican party and in 1869 won election to the Mississippi house of representatives, where he performed with such ability that his colleagues elected him to the speakership in 1872. Even state conservatives admitted that he served well. In the fall of 1872 Lynch was elected to represent the Natchez district in the U.S. House of Representatives (1873–1879). He worked mainly for the enactment of Charles Sumner's civil rights bill, which in emasculated form became law in 1875. He continued into the 1890s as an influential leader in the declining Republican party of the state. He also served briefly in a minor federal position in Washington, and from 1898 to 1911 he served as a junior officer in the army. In 1912 he settled in Chicago, where he practiced law, dabbled in the real estate business, and wrote of his Reconstruction experiences.

See J. R. Lynch, *Facts of Reconstruction* (1970), *Autobiography of John Roy Lynch* (1970), *Some Historical Errors of James Ford Rhodes* (1922); and S. D. Smith, *Negro in Congress, 1870–1901* (1940).

WILLIAM C. HARRIS
North Carolina State University

LYNCH, THOMAS, JR. (1749–1779), was born in Berkeley County, S.C., the son of a wealthy planter and statesman, Thomas Lynch. He was educated in England. Returning to South Carolina he took up farming on a plantation his father gave him and joined the growing protest against British policies. Lynch was elected to the first and second provincial congresses (1774–1776) and the first state legislature (1776). He was briefly a captain in the army but caught a fever that forced him to leave the service. Elected to the Second CONTINENTAL CONGRESS in 1776, he signed the DECLARATION OF INDEPENDENCE but his health rapidly failed thereafter. He sailed for France in 1779, hoping to find relief, but his ship was lost at sea.

JAMES H. BROUSSARD
Southwest Texas State University

LYNCHBURG, BATTLE OF (June 17–18, 1864). On June 6, 1864, U. S. Grant ordered David Hunter, commander of the Department of West Virginia, to destroy the vital rail center of Lynchburg, Va., noting "it would be of great value to us to get possession of Lynchburg for a single day." The convalescing Confederate commander of the Department of Southwest Virginia, JOHN C. BRECKINRIDGE, requested Brigadier General John C. Vaughn to assume temporary command. Hunter's troops attacked the outworks of Lynchburg on June 17 and again the following day, only to receive a counterattack in their center, which Hunter described as "so unexpected and rapid as almost to amount to a surprise." Fearing more Confederate reinforcements and short on ammunition, Hunter quietly withdrew that night, reporting his losses as "comparatively light" though a Confederate report noted "the flight was so rapid that all but the slightly wounded were left behind, together with many small arms and some cannon."

See C. M. Blackford, *Campaign and Battle of Lynchburg* (1901); H. A. Du Pont, *Campaign of 1864 to Lynchburg* (1925); M. W. Humphreys, *History of Lynchburg Campaign* (1924); and *Official Records, Armies*, Ser. 1, Vol. XXXVII, Pt. 1.

JOHN D. DUNCAN
Armstrong State College

LYNCHBURG, VA. (pop. 54,083), in the foothills of the Blue Ridge Mountains, is approximately 40 miles east of Roanoke on the James River. First settled as a ferry crossing in 1757 by John Lynch, the town was laid out in 1786 and incorporated as a city in 1852. Antebellum Lynchburg was an important center for dark leaf tobacco, and its transportation facilities made it a useful Confederate supply base during the Civil War. In June, 1864, Union forces under General David Hunter began to move against Lynchburg. General R. E. Lee, however, sent General JUBAL EARLY's cavalry overland from Richmond to Charlottesville and then by train to Lynchburg to reinforce General J. C. BRECKINRIDGE's brigades. Early's cavalry began to arrive in Lynchburg at noon, June 18, the same day that Hunter launched his main attack. Failing to capture the city and concerned about Early's presence in the west, Hunter disengaged that night and withdrew to Salem. The Confederates then launched EARLY'S WASHINGTON RAID. Postwar Lynchburg resumed its activity as a major tobacco market and also became an educational center as the home of Randolph-Macon Woman's College (1891), Lynchburg College (1903), and Sweet Briar College (1901). Today the city also produces nuclear reactors, batteries, machine parts, cosmetics, drugs, and clothing.

See D. P. Halsey, *Historic and Heroic Lynchburg* (1935); P. L. Scruggs, *History of Lynchburg, 1786–1946* (1971); R. F. Yancey, *Lynchburg and Its Neighbors* (1935); and files of Lynchburg *Virginian* (1822–92), *Advance* (1880–), and *News* (1866–), all on microfilm.

LYNCHING

LYNCHING is a particularly brutal and cruel manifestation of the tradition of VIOLENCE in American society. It has been most frequently inflicted upon blacks, and, though lynchings have occurred in all sections of the country, they have been most numerous in the South. The origin of the word is probably found in the activities of Judge Charles Lynch (1736–1796) of Bedford County, Va., during the Revolutionary War. The invasion of Virginia by Lord Cornwallis' army encouraged a conspiracy to overthrow patriot rule in Bedford County. The plot was uncovered, and those involved were brought before Lynch and sentenced to jail terms ranging from one to five years. Following the war, Tories charged that Lynch had exceeded his powers, but the Virginia legislature in 1782 found that the measures taken to suppress conspiracy "may not be strictly warranted by law, although justifiable from the imminence of the danger."

The first written reference to "Lynch's law" is believed found in a book by WILLIAM WIRT published in 1818. Wirt defined the term as "thirty-nine lashes, inflicted without trial or law, on mere suspicion of guilt, which could not be regularly proven." By the 1840s the term "lynch-law" was found in dictionaries such as Brande's *Dictionary of Science, Literature and Art* (1842) and in the 1845 University Edition of *Webster's*. In these early definitions no reference was made to death as the usual result of lynching.

Prior to 1830 lynching most often involved whipping the victim and perhaps banishment from the community. Following 1830, however, lynching took on a new severity as it was employed to suppress abolitionism among both blacks and whites. In 1835 whites in Madison County, Miss., lynched five whites and at least ten blacks believed to be planning a slave insurrection. Also in 1835 a white mob in St. Louis seized a black prisoner, tied him to a tree, set a fire, and roasted the victim. At least 26 blacks were summarily executed between 1850 and 1860, nine of the victims being burned at the stake.

Lynching was first commonly associated with inflicting death in connection with widespread vigilantism occurring during the 1850s in the territories of the Far West and Southwest. The definition of lynching as murder by mob action was confirmed during the Reconstruction era when hundreds of blacks and white Radicals were murdered by white supremacists determined to overthrow Radical Reconstruction. Such groups as the KU KLUX KLAN and the Knights of the White Camellia mounted a campaign of terror aimed at intimidating Radical voters and officeholders, destroying such political organizations as the UNION LEAGUES and forcing black militia companies to disband. During Reconstruction, the pretext given to justify lynching was that whites were threatened by black insurrection and that the black freedmen sought domination of southern society. "Negro domination" was the catchword used to infuriate the white mob.

Lynching played a part in crushing Reconstruction, but it did not pass from the scene with the end of Radical rule. From the 1880s on, it clearly emerged as a regularized, routine feature of the New South, which could be used to punish "uppity" blacks and to consolidate the rule of white property. In the 21-year interval 1882–1903, lynchings numbered 3,337; the number of persons lynched in the South was 2,585. Of these, 1,985 were blacks (including 40 black women) and 23 were white women.

The major pretext for lynchings from the post-Reconstruction era onward was that mob action was necessary to control black sexual assaults upon white women. The facts show the falseness of the claim. Statistics assembled by James Elbert Cutler in his careful study *Lynch-Law* (1905) indicate that, from 1882 to 1903, no more than 34 percent of blacks lynched in the South either actually had committed rape or were allegedly guilty of the crime. In fact, blacks have been lynched for real

NUMBER OF PERSONS LYNCHED, 1882–1951

Year	Whites	Negroes	Total
1882			114
1883			134
1884			211
1885			184
1886			138
1887			122
1888			142
1889			176
1890			128
1891			195
1892			235
1893			200
1894			197
1895			180
1896			131
1897			165
1898			127
1899			107
1900			115
1901			135
1902			97
1903			104
1904			87
1905			66
1906			73
1907			63
1908			100
1909			87
1910			74
1911			71
1912			65
1913			51
1914			52
1915			67
1916			54
1917			38
1918			64
1919			83
1920			61
1921	5	59	64
1922	6	51	57
1923	4	29	33
1924	0	16	16
1925	0	17	17
1926	7	23	30
1927	0	16	16
1928	1	10	11
1929	3	7	10
1930	1	20	21
1931	1	12	13
1932	2	6	8
1933	4	24	28
1934	0	15	15
1935	2	18	20
1936	0	8	8
1937	0	8	8
1938	0	6	6
1939	1	2	3
1940	1	4	5
1941	0	4	4
1942	0	6	6
1943	0	3	3
1944	0	2	2
1945	0	1	1
1946	0	6	6
1947	0	1	1
1948	1	1	2
1949	0	3	3
1950	1	1	2
1951	0	1	1

SOURCES: J. E. Cutler, *Lynch-Law* (1905); A. F. Raper, *Tragedy of Lynching* (1933); and *Negro Yearbook* (1952).

or alleged offenses ranging from cases of rape, murder, theft, and arson to instances of mistaken identity, grave robbery, incendiary language, testifying on behalf of another black person or refusing to give testimony, and bad reputation. In many instances lynching has occurred simply because the mob sought a victim and any black person would serve its purpose.

During its history, lynching operated to buttress the JIM CROW system of SEGREGATION and black political DISFRANCHISEMENT. WALTER WHITE noted that lynching was "more an expression of Southern fear of Negro progress than of Negro crime" and that "lynching has always been the means for protection, not of white women, but of profits." This analysis is supported by evidence that poor whites were sometimes impelled into the lynch mob by fear of black economic competition, but that lynching was most often at least tolerated by the South's propertied classes, which seldom used their considerable power to restrain or punish the mob. Records kept for the years between 1900 and 1930 show only 12 instances of conviction for lynching with 67 individuals involved. Only eight-tenths of 1 percent of lynchings during those 30 years were followed by conviction. Punishment ranged from suspended sentences to life terms.

The frequency of lynchings substantially decreased after 1900. Agitation and educational efforts against lynching succeeded in making mob violence a public national issue. A pioneering role was played by the journalist and platform lecturer IDA WELLS-BARNETT who, beginning in the early 1890s, began a crusade to expose the facts concerning lynching. Her work was continued and extended by the NATIONAL ASSOCIATION FOR THE ADVANCEMENT OF COLORED PEOPLE. The antilynching campaign mounted by the NAACP led to the introduction in Congress in 1919 of the Dyer bill, which would make lynching a federal offense. The bill, after passing the House, was defeated by filibuster in the Senate, but the antilynching campaign made progress in creating a public climate of opinion hostile to lynching. In the 1920s, also, groups of southern liberals (ASSOCIATION OF SOUTHERN WOMEN) organized to generate an antilynching movement. Yet, during the period 1900–1921, 36 was the smallest number of blacks lynched in any one year. The frequency of lynchings did drop during the 1920s, but the depression years saw some resurgence of lynching; in 1930, 21 persons were lynched and 20 of the victims were blacks. Lynching, as known earlier in American history, has not been completely eradicated from modern American society. Such episodes as the 1955 lynching in Mississippi of the black youth Emmett Till and the 1964 murders of civil rights activists in Neshoba County, Miss., are evidence of lynching's persistence as a threat to democracy and human decency.

See I. Wells-Barnett, *On Lynchings* (1969); J. H. Chadbourn, *Lynching and the Law* (1933); J. E. Cutler, *Lynch-Law* (1905); A. F. Raper, *Tragedy of Lynching* (1933); D. L. Grant, *Anti-Lynching Movement, 1883–1932* (1975); J. S. Reed, *Social Forces* (Fall, 1968); W. White, *Rope and Faggot* (1929); R. S. Baker, *Following Color Line* (1964); T. W. Page, *Atlantic Monthly* (Dec., 1901); and for best account of KKK, A. Trelease, *White Terror* (1971).

HERBERT SHAPIRO
University of Cincinnati

M

McADOO, WILLIAM GIBBS (1863–1941), was born in Georgia and educated in Tennessee. In 1892 he moved to New York City, where he achieved fame as the developer of the Hudson River tunnels. A man consumed by energy and ambition, McAdoo emerged as one of the most prominent members of the Wilson administration. His activities as secretary of the treasury (1913–1918) and as director general of the railroads (1917–1919) won him a large following among his party's Progressive wing. In 1920 McAdoo's presidential ambitions were thwarted when Wilson refused to renounce any desire for a third term. Seeking the nomination again in 1924, McAdoo, although innocent of any involvement, became publicly identified with the Teapot Dome scandal. He entered the southern primaries against OSCAR UNDERWOOD, an outspoken critic of the Klan. Although McAdoo was no Klansman, he refused to denounce the order and was again denied the presidential nomination. Seeking support for the 1928 nomination, he found that he appealed only to his party's fanatical drys. McAdoo withdrew from the contest in the fall of 1927. He ended his public career as U.S. senator from California (1933–1938).

See McAdoo Papers, Library of Congress; W. M. Bagby, *Road to Normalcy* (1962); B. Noggle, *Teapot Dome* (1962); L. N. Allen, *Journal of Southern History* (May, 1963); and R. M. Posner, *California Historical Society Quarterly* (Winter, 1960).

MARCILE TAYLOR
Wesleyan College

McCARDLE, EX PARTE (7 Wallace 506 [1869]), was the U.S. Supreme Court case to which opponents of congressional Reconstruction looked for relief after the RECONSTRUCTION ACTS of 1867 had substituted military control for presidential Reconstruction. The court took jurisdiction under authority of the habeas corpus act of 1867 and heard arguments in February, 1868. The case originated in the trial of a civilian by military tribunal in Mississippi. The leading judicial precedent was *ex parte* MILLIGAN, a case involving the military trial of a civilian in Indiana at a time when civil courts were operating. Application of principles enunciated in the *Milligan* case might cause the entire military Reconstruction of the

South to be declared unconstitutional. To avoid this possiblity, Congress quietly inserted in a general bill a rider repealing the jurisdiction of the Supreme Court specified by the 1867 habeas corpus act. The presidential veto was immediately overriden, and the Court—which had earlier avoided confrontation with Congress—dismissed the *McCardle* appeal because of no jurisdiction. How the Court would have ruled had it decided *McCardle* will never be known, but Congress obviously was fearful of a judicial challenge.

See C. Fairman, *Reconstruction and Reunion* (1971); R. E. and R. F. Cushman, *Cases in Constitutional Law* (1968); and J. G. Randall and D. Donald, *Civil War and Reconstruction* (1969).

JOSEPH B. JAMES
Wesleyan College

McCULLERS, CARSON (1917–1967), born Lula Carson Smith and reared in Columbus, Ga., is popularly known as a leading southern Gothic novelist. She treats experiences of troubled adolescents, dwarves, deaf mutes, grotesques, psychotics, and sexual inverts, but seldom for purely sensational purposes. Her abiding theme is intense loneliness, resulting from the paradoxes of unreciprocated Platonic love. Her best works are *The Member of the Wedding* (1946) and *The Ballad of the Sad Café* (published with collected short stories, 1955), both quasi-allegorical treatments of this theme. *The Heart Is a Lonely Hunter* (1940) and *Clock Without Hands* (1961) blend that approach with social realism and controversial current issues like poverty and racial injustice. *Reflections in a Golden Eye* (1941) comes closest to unrelieved Gothic horror.

See O. Evans, *Ballad of Carson McCullers* (1966); and C. McCullers, *Mortgaged Heart*, ed. M. G. Smith (1971), contains previously uncollected writings.

FRANK BALDANZA
Bowling Green State University

McDONOGH, JOHN (1779–1850). One of the South's earliest and greatest educational philanthropists, this native of Baltimore came to New Orleans in 1800 and by the time of his death had accumulated a fortune in excess of $3 million.

Nearly all of his estate was bequeathed for the education of white youths in New Orleans and Baltimore. McDonogh owned brickyards and plantations, but made most of his money as a real estate speculator, merchant, and factor for other planters. Foreseeing possible tragedy over the slavery issue, he became a member of the AMERICAN COLONIZATION SOCIETY and sent many freed Negroes to Liberia. Despite legal restrictions, he taught his slaves to read and to write. Among southern planters he was a pioneer in the use of farm machinery, flood control and "scientific" farming.

See McDonogh Papers, Tulane University; John Minor Wisdom Collection of McDonogh Documents, New Orleans; McDonogh Papers, Duke University; William Taylor Papers, Library of Congress; and A. G. Nuhrah, "John McDonogh" (Ph.D. dissertation, Tulane, 1950).

ARTHUR G. NUHRAH
Gardner-Webb College

McDOWELL, BATTLE OF (May 8, 1862), was crucial in the SHENANDOAH VALLEY CAMPAIGN of STONEWALL JACKSON. The merging of Jackson's 6,000 men with the 2,800 of EDWARD JOHNSON west of Staunton, Va., halted the advance of John Charles Frémont's 3,700-man vanguard under Robert Milroy. Withdrawing to McDowell, Va., and reinforced by Robert Schenck's brigade of 2,300, Milroy was protected by the Bull Pasture River. Sitlington's Hill, on the left of the turnpike descending from Bull Pasture Mountain, dominated the area. Jackson placed Johnson's infantry there. A federal attack of over four hours' duration blocked development of a flanking movement. Ultimately 4,000 Confederates (498 casualties) repulsed 2,500 federals (256 casualties). Milroy and Schenck withdrew northward toward Frémont's army. Jackson failed to destroy his enemy, but accomplished his mission. Freed of the western threat, he could return to the Shenandoah Valley and defeat N. P. Banks.

See *Official Records, Armies*, Ser. 1, Vols. I, XII, Pt. 1; W. Allan, *Valley Campaign* (1878); and G. F. R. Henderson, *Jackson* (2 vols.; 1898).

RAYMOND C. DINGLEDINE, JR.
Madison College

McDUFFIE, GEORGE (1790–1851), was a U.S. representative from South Carolina from 1821 to 1834. His congressional career epitomized the shift that a number of southern politicians made from nationalism to states' rights during the years after the War of 1812. McDuffie defended the nationalist position against the economy-minded and states'-rightist WILLIAM CRAWFORD faction (1821) and gave the most impressive speech among nationalist-minded southerners in suport of the survey bill (1824). But he reassessed his nationalistic stance in the late 1820s in response to what he considered to be the abuse of federal power revealed in the high protective tariff proposals of those years and, in 1828, publicly embraced the doctrine of NULLIFICATION. But, he also supported the Bank of the United States and presented the bank's memorial for recharter in 1832. McDuffie followed John C. Calhoun into opposition to the Jackson administration and its policies in 1831. McDuffie's inconsistent positions reflected pressures that were not always in harmony: the interests of his constituents and the political ambitions and philosophizing of Calhoun. McDuffie resigned from Congress in 1834 to become governor of South Carolina (1834–1836) and was later a U.S. senator (1842–1846).

See E. L. Green, *George McDuffie* (1936); and A. R. Newsome (ed.), *North Carolina Historical Review* (Oct., 1930), letters on campaign of 1824.

DAVID J. RUSSO
McMaster University

McENERY, SAMUEL DOUGLAS (1837–1910), personified the coalition of plantation owners and urban politicians that dominated Louisiana after Reconstruction. Born at Monroe, La., to a planter family, McEnery graduated from a New York law school in 1859. He joined the Confederate army, but he spent most of the war at a training camp near Monroe. Beginning in 1866 McEnery became politically active as a Democrat. His elder brother John was the Democratic nominee for governor in 1872 and claimed to be the state's chief executive during the term of WILLIAM PITT KELLOGG (1873–1877). Elected lieutenant governor in 1879, Samuel McEnery became governor when the incumbent died in 1881, was elected to a full term in 1884, and was then defeated for renomination by his party's state convention in 1888. During his administration (1881–1888) he allied himself with the LOUISIANA STATE LOTTERY COMPANY and the New Orleans machine known as the Ring; foes referred to him as "McLottery." Upon leaving the governorship, McEnery was appointed associate justice of the state supreme court. In 1892 he again became the gubernatorial candidate of the lottery faction of the Louisiana Democratic party, but was defeated. Four years later, as state Democrats coalesced against Populist and Republican opposition, he was elected to the U.S. Senate (1897–1910). Not a prominent senator, he defended Louisiana's economic interests and denounced Negro suffrage.

See A. Fortier, *Louisiana* (1909), II; and W. I. Hair, *Bourbonism and Agrarian Protest* (1969).

WILLIAM I. HAIR
Georgia College

McGILL, RALPH EMERSON (1898–1969), was a native of Tennessee and charter member of the SOUTHERN REGIONAL COUNCIL. As editor of the ATLANTA CONSTITUTION, he endorsed a series of socioeconomic programs consistent with the New South tradition. He supported moderate, law-abiding leadership in the changing South while emphasizing education as the key to regional progress. Initially an adherent to the separate but equal doctrine, he described segregation in 1950 as "undemocratic" and "un-American." "Those who array themselves on the wrong side of a moral issue not merely end up in defeat but in bitterness and ruin of spirit," he wrote of Little Rock's desegregation problems. In 1959 McGill won a Pulitzer Prize for his editorials on racial terrorists, whom he condemned as "rabid, mad dogs." His attitudes regarding the South's racial problems represented significant adaptation and placed McGill in the vanguard of southern liberals.

See Atlanta *Constitution* (1929–69); Nashville *Banner* (1922–29); R. E. McGill, *South and Southerner* (1959), autobiography; R. E. McGill and T. C. David, *Two Georgians Explore Scandinavia* (1938); and D. C. Kinsella, "Southern Apologists" (Ph.D. dissertation, University of St. Louis, 1971), excellent bibliography.

DOROTHY C. KINSELLA
NETWORK, Washington, D.C.

McGILLIVRAY, ALEXANDER (1745?–1793), was the son of a Georgia Indian trader and his French-Creek wife. Accordingly, he grew to manhood between two worlds: from his mother's clan he drew tribal status, while his father's connections were useful in white society. Rejected by the Americans in 1775 because of his father's loyalism, Alexander McGillivray soon put his talents to work among the CREEKS. By 1777 he had assumed tribal leadership positions and had obtained a clerkship at a British trading post. Then, in 1783, he assumed a major role that made him a powerful influence on the southern frontier. McGillivray's opposition to American expansion prevented any major Creek treaty until the Treaty of Washington (1790).

See J. W. Caughey, *McGillivray* (1938), documents; J. H. O'Donnell III, *Georgia Historical Quarterly* (June, 1965); J. L. Wright, *Georgia Historical Quarterly*

(Dec., 1967); C. R. Ferguson, *Kansas Quarterly* (Fall, 1971); and L. Milfort, *My Sojourn* (repr., 1972), contemporary, but biased.

JAMES H. O'DONNELL III
Marietta College

McGREADY, JAMES (1758–1817), the "Father of the Western Revival," is a significant transitional figure in the evolution of the Calvinistic revivalism of the eighteenth century into its antiintellectual offspring of the nineteenth century. Raised in North Carolina, he was educated in Pennsylvania under two evangelical Presbyterian graduates of the College of New Jersey, the Reverend John McMillan and the Reverend Joseph Smith. His career as a revivalist began in North Carolina after 1788 but culminated in Kentucky, whence he had moved in 1796, with the first CAMP MEETING revival in 1800. His later life was marred by controversies with both the antirevival Presbyterian clergy and the more Arminian of his evangelical colleagues. He died while serving as a missionary in Indiana.

See J. Opie, Jr., *Church History* (Dec., 1965), best interpretation; E. T. Thompson, *Presbyterians in South* (1963), I, especially useful; J. McGready, *Posthumous Works* (1837); J. Smith, *Old Redstone* (1854); and E. H. Gillett, *History of Presbyterian Church* (1864), I.

MARTIN E. LODGE
State University of New York, New Paltz

McINTOSH, WILLIAM (1775–1825), was a Lower Creek Indian chief and a brigadier general, U.S.A., in the War of 1812. He was a son of a Scottish captain in the British army and a full-blood CREEK Indian woman. In the War of 1812, he fought under ANDREW JACKSON against the hostile Creeks at Horseshoe Bend, Ala. Despite a tribal resolution decreeing the death penalty to anyone who ceded Creek land without authority, he signed five treaties of cession. In the Treaty of Indian Springs (February 12, 1825), at which only one-seventh of the Creek towns were represented, all remaining Creek lands in Georgia were ceded, and McIntosh was awarded $25,000 for his property. On April 30, 1825, he was shot by a Creek band, which surrounded and burned his home in Carroll County, Ga.

See H. T. Corbin, "History and Genealogy of Chief William McIntosh, Jr." (1967), uncritical account, at Newberry Library; E. J. Harden, *Life of George M. Troup* (1859), contains relevant documents; and A. Debo, *Road to Disappearance* (1941), best general account.

VIRGIL J. VOGEL
Truman College, City Colleges of Chicago

McIVER, CHARLES DUNCAN (1860–1906), was born in rural Moore County, N. C. Educated at the University of North Carolina, he made education his chosen profession. After gaining experience as a teacher, principal, and superintendent, McIver was employed by the state board of education in 1889, with EDWIN A. ALDERMAN, to conduct county teachers' institutes throughout the state. For two years these young men visited every county, imparting an enthusiasm and respect for teaching as a profession and literally preaching a gospel of public education. McIver's speeches increasingly emphasized the necessity of educating women equally with men. He popularized the quotation— "If you educate a man you educate a citizen. If you educate a woman you educate a family."— which North Carolinians credit to him. His most outstanding single accomplishment was in persuading the state legislature to establish a normal school for women in 1891, and his exemplary success as the first president (1891–1906) of the North Carolina State Normal and Industrial School (now the University of North Carolina at Greensboro) attests to his administrative ability. He was a loyal Democrat, active in politics, and he never ceased to campaign for a strong system of public schools (OGDEN MOVEMENT), serving as secretary and field agent of the SOUTHERN EDUCATION BOARD. Next to Calvin H. Wiley (1819–1897), the state's first superintendent of common schools, McIver remains the most influential educational leader in North Carolina's history.

See F. G. Satterfield, *Charles D. McIver* (1942); R. H. Holder, *McIver of North Carolina* (1957); *C. D. McIver Memorial Volume* (1907); and McIver Papers, University of North Carolina, Greensboro, almost complete.

WILLIAM E. KING
Duke University

McKELLAR, KENNETH DOUGLAS (1869–1957), moved to Memphis from Alabama as a young man and practiced law until his election to Congress in 1911. Defeating the incumbent LUKE LEA in the Democratic senatorial primary in 1916 and former governor Ben Hooper in the general election, he began the first of six continuous terms (1917–1953). As an ally of E. H. CRUMP of Memphis, chairman of the Senate Post Office Committee, and acting chairman of the Appropriations Committee, he wielded extensive power in the U.S. Senate. He probably reached his greatest influence, however, as a staunch supporter of the NEW DEAL, especially in matters of relief, agricultural policy, and Court reform. He differed with Franklin Roosevelt on Prohibition and civil rights.

With Senator George Norris, he led the fight for the TENNESSEE VALLEY AUTHORITY. The split between McKellar and FDR in the late 1930s resulted from differences over control of TVA, patronage, Douglas Dam, and TVA Director David Lilienthal. He was tenacious and imaginative in using political power to crush enemies and reward friends, and his feuds with Herbert Hoover, Andrew Mellon, AUBREY WILLIAMS, and Lilienthal are legendary. Weakened by political losses of the Crump machine in 1948, McKellar was defeated in the primary in 1952 by Albert Gore.

See G. Felsenthal, *West Tennessee Historical Society Publications* (1966); and R. Mark, Jr., "McKellar" (M.A., thesis, University of Maryland, 1964).

CHARLES W. JOHNSON
University of Tennessee, Knoxville

McKELWAY, ALEXANDER JEFFREY (1866–1918), although born in Pennsylvania, moved to Virginia in 1867 and considered himself a southerner. Educated as a Presbyterian minister, he served in North Carolina until his appointment in 1898 as editor of the *Presbyterian Standard* terminated his active ministry but initiated his career as a reformer. McKelway and EDGAR GARDNER MURPHY originated a correspondence, which led to Murphy's recommending McKelway to the National Child Labor Committee in 1904 as its assistant secretary for the southern states. Following his resignation as editor, McKelway moved to Atlanta to direct the southern CHILD LABOR campaign. In 1909 the NCLC transferred McKelway to Washington as its principal congressional lobbyist. Two pioneering legislative acts, the 1912 children's bureau law and the 1916 Keating-Owen Child Labor Act, rewarded his persistent efforts and represented the supreme achievement of his life. McKelway typified PROGRESSIVISM by his essential pragmatism and his promotion of the meliorative society. A white supremacist, he shared progressivism's strain of racism. Affiliated with the National Conference of Charities and Correction and the SOUTHERN SOCIOLOGICAL CONGRESS, he tirelessly crusaded for human betterment through legislative action.

See A. J. McKelway, "Legislative Hints for Social Reformers," McKelway Papers, Library of Congress, interpretive; B. J. Brandon, "McKelway" (Ph.D. dissertation, University of North Carolina, 1969); and H. J. Doherty, *Journal of Southern History* (May, 1958).

BETTY J. BRANDON
University of South Carolina

McKINLEY, JOHN (1780–1852), born in Virginia and reared in Kentucky, moved in 1819 to Huntsville, Ala., where he rose to political prominence. He was elected to the first state legislature in 1820 and was elected in 1826 to fill a vacancy in the U.S. Senate as a Jacksonian Democrat. Reelected to the legislature in 1831, he was in 1832 elected to the Twenty-third Congress, where he vigorously supported ANDREW JACKSON's programs and the Martin Van Buren ascendancy. McKinley was then reelected to the Senate in 1837; however, prior to taking his seat, Van Buren appointed him associate justice of the U.S. Supreme Court. For over a decade he seldom dissented from the majority on the ROGER TANEY Court. He is best remembered for his dissent in *Bank of Augusta* v. *Earle* (1839). By the late 1840s, he was unable to participate fully in the Court's work because of poor health.

See J. M. Martin, *Alabama Historical Quarterly* (Spring, 1966); T. W. Campbell, *Forgotten Men* (1950); and J. Hicks, *Alabama Review* (July, 1965).

J. KENT FOLMAR
California State College, California, Pa.

McKINLEY, WILLIAM, ADMINISTRATION (1897–1901). McKinley's victory over William Jennings Bryan in the ELECTION OF 1896 elevated to the White House a Republican advocate of the gold standard, protective tariffs, and laissez faire capitalism and crushed the hopes of reform southern and western Democrats. The economic policies of McKinley's administration adhered to the Republican platform. The Currency Act of 1900 sealed the doom of free silver, making gold the single standard for all U.S. currency. The Dingley tariff enacted in 1897 reinstated protectionism, raising tariff schedules to record levels. Although McKinley voiced concern over corporate power, he called for no restraining legislation and Congress failed to initiate any. Such policies dismayed progressive southern Democrats (PROGRESSIVISM) but reassured southern industrialists and BOURBONS, many of whom had favored McKinley's election.

The South supported the administration's expansionist foreign policy. The SPANISH-AMERICAN WAR provided southerners an opportunity to prove their loyalty to the Union, acquire Cuba—desired since the antebellum era—and open the markets of the Far East to the region's expanding textile industry. McKinley used the conflict to promote sectional harmony, obtaining major generalships for former Confederates JOSEPH WHEELER of Alabama and FITZHUGH LEE of Virginia. The South also backed administration efforts, which resulted in the Hay-Pauncefote Treaty of 1900, to secure British approval of a canal through Central America built and operated by the United States.

McKinley courted the South in his distribution of patronage both to further reconcile sectional animosities and to enhance his party's standing. He appointed James Gray of Maryland postmaster general, placed southerners on the U.S. Industrial Commission, and consulted conservative Democrats such as Senator JOHN L. MCLAURIN of South Carolina about federal appointments in the region. The administration also acquiesced in JIM CROW legislation and the DISFRANCHISEMENT of blacks. The attempts to placate the South proved politically unproductive, for Bryan swept the former Confederate states in the ELECTION OF 1900. McKinley's death by assassination on September 14, 1901, shocked both the region and the nation and removed from office the nineteenth-century Republican president the South most respected.

See H. W. Morgan, *William McKinley* (1963); M. Leach, *In Days of McKinley* (1959); O. H. Shadgett, *Republican Party in Georgia* (1964); and P. D. Uzee, "Republican Politics in Louisiana" (Ph.D. dissertation, Louisiana State University, 1950).

MELTON A. MCLAURIN
University of South Alabama

McLANE, LOUIS (1786–1857), was born in Smyrna, Del. As ANDREW JACKSON's minister to Britain (1829–1831), he successfully negotiated for an opening of the American trade with the West Indies and, as JAMES K. POLK's minister to Britain (1845–1846), contributed to the peaceful resolution of the Oregon dispute. His career included a decade (1837–1847) as president of the Baltimore & Ohio Railroad. McLane was at first a Federalist but before the ELECTION OF 1824 had allied himself to Martin Van Buren and to the ill-starred presidential campaign of WILLIAM H. CRAWFORD. A member of the U.S. House of Representatives from 1817 to 1827, McLane maneuvered to prevent the House's election of John Quincy Adams as president early in 1825. Looking ahead to 1828, McLane, like Van Buren, hitched his wagon to Andrew Jackson's rising star. As secretary of the treasury (1831–1833) in Jackson's second cabinet, McLane emerged as one of the principals in the bank war. Indeed, his opposition to the presidential plan to chastise the Bank of the United States resulted first in his being transferred to the secretaryship of state (1833–1934) and then, a year later, to his complete withdrawal from the Jackson administration.

See J. A. Munroe, *Louis McLane* (1973), definitive; and J. C. Fitzpatrick (ed.), *Autobiography of Martin Van Buren* (1920).

ROBERT P. HAY
Marquette University

McLAURIN, JOHN LOWNDES (1860–1934), was born in Marlboro County, S. C. He began a law practice at Bennettsville in 1883. Almost by chance he heard BENJAMIN TILLMAN speak in 1885 to the joint session of the state Agricultural Society and the state Grange. He recalled jumping up and yelling, "Go Ahead, Captain," and then he organized a pro-Tillman group. In 1890 McLaurin won election to the state legislature, in 1891 he became attorney general, and in 1892 he was elected, with Tillman's support, to the U.S. House of Representatives. During three terms in the House (1893–1897), he was regarded as well informed on financial questions. Moreover, he increasingly voted independently of Tillman.

Appointed in 1897 to the U.S. Senate, he won election for a full term in 1898. His votes for repeal of the Sherman Silver Act, protectionism, ship subsidies, a larger army, and Philippine annexation widened his breach with Senator Tillman. He cast a crucial vote to annex the Philippines, a vote likely influenced by pressure from the cotton textile industry. Tillman's subsequent reference to vote secured by "improper" means led to an exchange of blows with McLaurin on the Senate floor. His break with Tillman sealed McLaurin's chance for reelection in 1902. After an unsuccessful business venture in New York, he returned to South Carolina and was elected to the state senate, where in 1914 he wrote the cotton warehouse bill. Subsequently, from 1915 to 1917, he was warehouse commissioner. From 1917 until his death, he farmed and practiced law.

See R. H. Davis, "South Carolina Cotton Manufacturers in U.S. Far Eastern Policy" (M.A. thesis, University of South Carolina, 1966); R. D. Stroud, "Congressional Career of John L. McLaurin" (M.A. thesis, University of South Carolina, 1972); F. B. Simkins, *Pitchfork Ben Tillman* (1944) and *Tillman Movement* (1926); J. L. McLaurin Scrapbook, South Caroliniana Library; E. M. Lander, *History of South Carolina* (1960); and D. D. Wallace, *South Carolina* (1951).

ROGER M. BURTS
Carson-Newman College

McLAWS, LAFAYETTE (1821–1897), born in Augusta, Ga., graduated from West Point in 1842. He served on the frontier and in the Mexican War. With Georgia's secession, McLaws entered Confederate service, rising to the rank of brigadier general in September, 1861. His performance during the PENINSULAR CAMPAIGN led to promotion to major general in May, 1862. He participated in the major campaigns of R. E. Lee in 1862–1863. After GETTYSBURG McLaws was sent west, where during the KNOXVILLE CAMPAIGN he was charged by JAMES LONGSTREET with insufficient preparations for the assault on Ft. Sanders and court-martialed. The decision was reversed by Jefferson Davis, and McLaws was assigned to the District of Georgia in 1864. As a division commander, McLaws was at his best in fighting from defensive positions, particularly when supervised by a capable corps commander. Lee thought McLaws hesitant, unaggressive, and unable to extemporize. After the war McLaws entered the insurance business in Augusta. Later he served as collector of internal revenue and then postmaster in Savannah.

See D. S. Freeman, *Lee's Lieutenants* (1942–44); *Official Records, Armies*, Ser. 1, Vols. XXIX–XXXIII, LI–LIII; and C. A. Evans (ed.), *Confederate Military History* (1899).

MARION B. LUCAS
Western Kentucky University

MACON, NATHANIEL (1758–1837), Republican congressman and senator, was born in Edgecombe (now Warren) County, N. C., attended the College of New Jersey (1774–1776), fought with the militia in 1777 and 1780, and served in the North Carolina senate (1781–1786). He refused, though elected, to serve in the Continental Congress and opposed ratification of the federal Constitution. Macon represented the Hillsboro District of North Carolina in Congress (1791–1815) and served as Speaker of the House (1801–1807). In 1815 he moved to the Senate and was president pro tem from 1826 until retiring in 1828. He supported William H. Crawford for president in the ELECTION OF 1824. A states' rights man, Macon opposed Jay's Treaty, the Alien and Sedition Acts, Alexander Hamilton's fiscal policies, preparations for war with France, protective tariffs, and internal improvements, but, an advocate of Thomas Jefferson, he supported the LOUISIANA PURCHASE. Macon and Jefferson were briefly estranged after JOHN RANDOLPH's attempt to split the Republicans. Macon's Bill No. 1 and No. 2 were not written by Macon; the latter he actively opposed. Although often labeled a negative radical, Macon was a man of integrity, genuinely concerned for his countrymen.

See W. E. Dodd, *Life of Nathaniel Macon* (1903); J. M. Helms, Jr., "Early Career of Nathaniel Macon" (Ph.D.

dissertation, University of Virginia, 1962); A. B. Lacy, "Jefferson and Congress" (Ph.D. dissertation, University of Virginia, 1963); and D. Malone, *Jefferson* (1974), V.

EDWIN M. GAINES
University of Arizona

MACON, GA. (pop. 122,423), is a commercial and industrial center 78 miles southeast of Atlanta at the FALL LINE on the Ocmulgee River. It produces textiles, paper, and lumber products as well as processes peaches, pecans, peanuts, and cotton. The first settlement here was Ft. Hawkins, constructed in 1806 to protect Georgians from possible Indian uprisings. The village of Newtown grew up on the east bank of the river, but in 1822 the state legislature ordered that another town, named for NATHANIEL MACON, be established on the west bank. Macon prospered as a cotton market and inland water port, and in 1828 it annexed the older, original settlement. In May, 1864, when CONFEDERATE PRISONS were threatened by federal attack, a new prison was constructed here (MACON PRISON). The city is the home of MERCER UNIVERSITY and Georgia Wesleyan College for Women (1836).

See I. Young *et al.*, *History of Macon* (1950); J. C. Butler, *Historical Record of Macon* (1879, 1958); W. H. Parish Publishing Co., *Art Work of Macon* (1894); S. Dowell, *History of Mercer University, 1833–1953* (1958); *Georgia Journal and Messenger* (1823–69), on microfilm; Macon *News* (1844–), on microfilm since 1901; and Macon *Telegraph* (1826–), on microfilm.

MACON PRISON (also called Camp Oglethorpe) was a short-lived but important Confederate prison for Union officers at Macon, Ga. Opened in May, 1864, the prison was a large, roofless, wooden stockade enclosing three acres. In the center of the enclosure was a hospital and quarters for the imprisoned generals. Prisoners of lower rank built sheds or shanties for their shelter. The diet, made up primarily of bacon and cornmeal, lacked variety but was adequate; and officers were allowed to spend their own money to buy additional items from the sutler. Health conditions were generally good for a prison camp although numerous cases of diarrhea and scurvey were reported. In mid-June the camp had 1,000 prisoners; by late June that figure had risen to 1,400 prisoners and may have reached as high as 1,900 before evacuation of the prison began in July as a result of W. T. Sherman's advance toward Atlanta.

See *Official Records, Armies*, Ser. 2, Vols. VII, VIII; A. C. Roach, *Prisoner of War* (1865); W. W. Glazier, *Capture, Prison Pen and Escape* (1868); and W. B. Hesseltine, *Civil War Prisons* (1930).

WILLIAM G. EIDSON
Ball State University

MACON TELEGRAPH, with a number of variations on its original and present name, has been published continuously since 1826. The daily edition was begun in 1860 and currently has a circulation of over 50,000 copies. In 1850 the *Telegraph* was one of the first southern newspapers to discuss openly the desirability of secession. Although partisanly Democratic during most of its career, the paper was highly critical during the 1890s of William Jennings Bryan in the elections of 1896 and of 1900.

See nearly complete bound copies (1826–), Library of Congress and University of Georgia Library; and microfilm from Bell & Howell.

McREYNOLDS, JAMES CLARK (1862–1946), Kentucky-born jurist, was educated at Vanderbilt and the University at Virginia Law School. Although he was a Democrat, his prominence as a Nashville lawyer brought an assistant attorney generalship (1903–1907) from the Republican Theodore Roosevelt. Next, he practiced law in New York (1907–1913) and was special counsel in the government's tobacco trust prosecution. Seemingly a Progressive foe of monopolies, he became one of numerous southerners selected for Woodrow Wilson's administration, serving as attorney general (1913–1914). In spite of certain antitrust prosecutions, McReynolds favored big business. Elevated to the U.S. Supreme Court by Wilson, McReynolds rendered an occasional majority opinion safeguarding Fourteenth Amendment liberties, but his long tenure (1914–1941) is remembered for a stubborn opposition to the NEW DEAL. In vigorous dissents he declared TVA, Social Security, and the Wagner Act unconstitutional. Part of the conservative bloc, the industrious justice espoused a constitutional fundamentalism that opposed most social legislation that threatened property rights or rugged individualism. Critics have called him cynical and irascible, "a lonely and crusty Southern bachelor." Yet, Chief Justice C. E. Hughes praised his forthright and independent defense of constitutional principle.

See A. S. Link, *Woodrow Wilson* (1963); and A. M. Schlesinger, Jr., *Politics of Upheaval* (1960).

JAMES R. CHUMNEY
Memphis State University

MACUNE, CHARLES W.

MACUNE, CHARLES W. (1851–1931), a leader in the FARMERS' ALLIANCE, was born in Wisconsin and reared in Illinois. After residing in California and Kansas, he settled in Texas. He taught himself pharmacy, medicine, and law and practiced all of them before becoming involved in the Alliance movement. In 1886, when the Texas Alliance divided on political issues, Macune became its acting president. He reunited the Texas Alliance and merged it with the Louisiana Farmers' Union and the Arkansas Wheel. He then enlarged the organization to include farmers throughout the South. After serving as president of the southern Alliance, Macune became editor of its official organ, the *National Economist*, with offices in Washington, D.C. He originated the innovative but controversial SUBTREASURY PLAN. Believing that the Alliance should be nonpartisan, Macune opposed its support of the POPULIST PARTY. In the election of 1892 he was accused of accepting bribes to aid the Democrats. As a result, he gave up the editorship of the *National Economist* and withdrew from the Alliance. He retired to Waco, Tex.

See R. Smith, *Southwestern Historical Quarterly* (Jan., 1945); J. D. Hicks, *Populist Revolt* (1961); and *Handbook of Texas* (1952).

MARILYN M. SIBLEY
Houston Baptist University

MADISON, DOLLY

MADISON, DOLLY (1768–1849), was born in North Carolina, but spent her childhood in Hanover County, Va. Her father John Payne, a conscientious Quaker, after manumitting his slaves in 1783 followed an unprosperous business career in Philadelphia. She was a twenty-six-year-old widow with a two-year-old son when she married Congressman JAMES MADISON on September 15, 1794. Her first husband John Todd, Jr., and an infant son had died in 1793. When Madison was secretary of state and president, she arranged and presided over the social life of the capital. She was universally acknowledged to be a delightful and impartial hostess. During her husband's declining years, she cared for him tenderly, protectively, and devotedly. After his death, she lived in Washington, D.C.

See K. Anthony, *Dolly Madison* (1950); A. C. Clark, *Life and Letters of Dolly Madison* (1914); M. G. Smith, in *National Portrait Gallery*, ed. J. B. Longacre and J. Herring (4 vols.; 1834–39, 1970), III; and *Memoirs and Letters of Dolly Madison*, ed. L. B. Cutts (1887).

HAROLD S. SCHULTZ
University of Vermont

MADISON, JAMES

MADISON, JAMES (1751–1836), was born in King George County, Va. His public life began in 1774, when he became a member of the committee on public safety for Orange County, Va. During and after the Revolutionary War he served in the Virginia legislature (1784–1786), and the CONTINENTAL CONGRESS (1780–1783, 1787–1788). Although convinced that Virginia alone could not provide for its future economic growth and overcome its immediate financial difficulties, he did not, before 1787, advocate drastic changes in the Confederation. He expected the ANNAPOLIS CONVENTION, which he promoted and attended in 1786, to accomplish little. After November, 1786, as delegate-elect to the CONSTITUTIONAL CONVENTION of 1787, he became an active champion of fundamental and far-reaching changes in the Articles, including proportional representation in Congress and a national veto of state laws. The Virginia Plan of Union incorporated his proposals.

Often called the "Father of the Constitution," Madison himself rejected the idea that the Constitution was "the offspring of a single brain." After the "great compromise" deprived Virginia of proportionate representation in the Senate, Madison followed a strategy of transferring powers from that body to the House and to the president. Between November, 1787, and March, 1788, in cooperation with Alexander Hamilton and John Jay, Madison published in New York newspapers 29 letters on the Constitution, which were subsequently known as *The Federalist*. In June, 1788, he was in Richmond, where he was a persuasive speaker in the convention that ratified the Constitution by a vote of 89 to 70.

As a member of the U.S. House of Representatives (1789–1797) he played a major role in adding a BILL OF RIGHTS to the Constitution and in passing legislation that provided the first taxes, executive departments, and federal courts. Although a trusted adviser to George Washington during 1789, he became thereafter a leading organizer of the congressional opposition to the financial and foreign policies of his administration. He was preeminent among the men who founded the first Republican party. In 1798 he prepared a set of resolutions which, in a slightly amended form, were adopted by the legislature of Virginia protesting the constitutionality of the Alien and Sedition Acts. In a report adopted by the legislature in January, 1800, he argued that the VIRGINIA AND KENTUCKY RESOLUTIONS had meant that state governments could merely propagandize against unconstitutional acts of Congress.

In 1801 Madison became secretary of state in Thomas Jefferson's administration, and in 1809 he succeeded Jefferson as president. His presidency was dominated by a prolonged diplomatic struggle and war with Great Britain. Since 1794 Madison had repeatedly advocated economic retaliation in order to obtain diplomatic concessions from belligerents in the European war. In supporting war in 1812 he did not abandon economic retaliation as a weapon of diplomacy, and his objectives were much the same as they had been since 1807. The purpose of invading Canada was to occupy territory that could be used as a hostage in bargaining for British acceptance of American terms for settling the maritime disputes. Despite numerous military failures and continuing condemnation of "Mr. Madison's war" by a sizable minority, Madison was reelected president in 1812, and his party kept control of Congress throughout the war. With the restoration of peace and prosperity during the last two years of his presidency, Madison readily turned to long-term policies affecting the future economic growth and unity of the nation. His opinions on the national debt, taxes, the army, the navy, protective tariffs, a U.S. bank, and internal improvements contrasted sharply with those he had expressed in the 1790s. Policies enacted into legislation in 1816 with his approval were to prevail until the presidency of Andrew Jackson.

See I. Brant, *James Madison* (6 vols.; 1941–61) and *Fourth President* (1970); R. L. Ketcham, *James Madison* (1971); W. C. Rives, *History of James Madison* (3 vols.; 1859–68); H. S. Schultz, *James Madison* (1970); *James Madison Papers*, ed. W. T. Hutchinson and W. Rachel (9 vols.; 1962–75); and *Writings of James Madison*, ed. G. Hunt (9 vols.; 1900–10).

HAROLD S. SCHULTZ
University of Vermont

MAFFITT, JOHN NEWLAND (1819–1886), reared near Fayetteville, N.C., was appointed a navy midshipman in 1832. He spent the majority of his naval service as a hydrographer. With the coming of the Civil War, he accepted a lieutenancy in the Confederate navy, where he eventually rose to fame in command of the commerce raider *Florida* (August, 1862). Maffitt was a spectacular commander surpassed only by RAPHAEL SEMMES of the *Alabama*. The *Florida* steamed through a Union blockade into Mobile Bay to outfit then out again to capture 25 ships. Temporary illness led eventually to a new command for Maffitt, a blockade-runner the *Owl* (September, 1864). Maffitt's seamanship saved the *Owl* from capture at both fallen Wilmington and Charleston. He ran the *Owl* into blockaded Galveston. From here he passed for the last time through the blockade to carry his command to England and internment. Maffitt died near Wilmington.

See H. C. Cochran *Blockade Runners* (1958); E. M. Maffitt, *Life and Services of John Maffitt* (1906); J. D. Bulloch *Secret Service of Confederate States in Europe* (1883), standard reference for naval affairs; *Official Records, Navies*, Ser. 1, Vols. I–IV, VII, IX–XIII, XVII–XX, XXII, XXVII, Ser. 2, Vols. I–III; and P. V. D. Stern, *Confederate Navy* (1962), good pictorial source.

BERTRAM HAWTHORNE GROENE
Southeastern Louisiana University

MAGNOLIA was a monthly magazine, published first in Macon as the *Southern Ladies' Book* (January, 1840–January, 1841), by George Foster Pierce, editor. Editor Philip C. Pendleton moved it, as the *Magnolia*, to Savannah in January of 1841. WILLIAM GILMORE SIMMS edited it at Charleston from July, 1842, until the *Magnolia* ceased publication in June, 1843. In its pages Simms published his "Settlements of Coligny" (part of his GEORGIA HISTORICAL SOCIETY lectures), "Cooper: His Genius and Writings," "First English Voyage to Virginia," Henry Laurens' letters, "Hays' Station massacre (1781)," "Journals of the Charleston Siege (1780)," and Georgia Historical Society news. Benjamin Franklin Perry's "Revolutionary Incidents," Alexander Beaufort Meek's historical poems, and Augustus Baldwin Longstreet's "Georgia Sketches," second series, also appeared in various issues. In the longer-lived *Southern and Western Monthly Magazine and Review*, popularly known as *Simms's Magazine*, Simms continued to express his views on the southern economy, as he had for one golden year in the *Magnolia*.

See *Magnolia* (July, 1842–June, 1843), Pratt Library, Baltimore; F. L. Mott, *History of American Magazines* (1938); W. G. Simms, *Letters* (1952); W. S. Hoole, *Georgia Historical Quarterly* (March, 1935); J. B. Hubbell, *South in American Literature* (1954); E. W. Parks, *Simms as Literary Critic* (1961); and J. L. Wakelyn, *Politic of Literary Man* (1973).

JOHN CHARLES BODGER
Whitneyville, Maine

MAGOFFIN, BERIAH (1815–1883), a native of Harrodsburg, Ky., began a law practice there in 1839 and was appointed police judge in 1840. A Democrat, he ran unsuccessfully for lieutenant governor in 1855 and was elected governor in 1859. Magoffin hoped that Kentucky, by proclaiming neutrality, might prevent war by standing between the hostile parties or, failing that, serve as mediator to restore peace and union under the

Constitution. Republican charges that he secretly sought secession created enough suspicion about his motives that it became impossible for him to govern effectively. Hence, he resigned in August, 1862. He later served two terms in the state legislature.

See E. M. Coulter, *Civil War and Readjustment in Kentucky* (1926); A. D. Kirwan, *John J. Crittenden* (1962); L. Harrison, *Civil War in Kentucky* (1975); and M. Dues, *Filson Club History Quarterly* (Jan., 1966), detailed discussion of Magoffin's neutrality stance.

MICHAEL T. DUES
California State University, Sacramento

MAGRUDER, JOHN BANKHEAD (1810–1871), was born in Winchester, Va. He graduated from West Point in 1830 and was promoted lieutenant colonel for "meritorious conduct" during the Mexican War. While in command of Ft. Adams in Rhode Island after the war, he acquired the nickname Prince John for his courtly bearing, military parades, and fashionable entertainments. When Virginia seceded in 1861, Magruder entered the Confederate army as colonel of a corps of infantry. In May he fought and won the first battle of the Civil War at BIG BETHEL, which earned him a promotion to brigadier general and the command of all forces on the Virginia peninsula between the York and James rivers. He was promoted major general in October, 1861, for his defense of the peninsula, but his failure to command efficiently in the SEVEN DAYS' BATTLES around Richmond brought censure from General R. E. Lee. In October, 1862, Magruder was sent to command the District of Texas, where he fortified the Texas coast, seized the revenue cutter *Harriet Lane*, and on January 1, 1863, captured Galveston. When the war ended, he was in command of the District of New Mexico and Arizona. Refusing to seek parole, Magruder went to Mexico and served as a major general in the army of Maximilian. After the downfall of the emperor, he returned to Houston, where he died.

See A. L. Long, *Southern Historical Society Papers* (1884); B. P. Lee, *Southern Historical Society Papers* (1891); C. A. Evans (ed.), *Confederate Military History* (1899); and manuscripts, University of Texas Library.

ALLEN W. JONES
Auburn University

MAHONE, WILLIAM (1826–1895), was one of the most dynamic and controversial figures in Virginia history. Born in Southampton County, this tavern keeper's son graduated from Virginia Military Institute in 1847 and rose to prominence as a surveyor and railroad executive in the 1850s. During the Civil War he became a major general in the Confederate army, leading his troops with particular distinction during the 1864–1865 Petersburg campaign. After the conflict he returned to the railroad business, and he devoted his energies to reorganizing three war-ravaged companies whose lines stretched across Virginia from Norfolk to Bristol. In 1870 he consolidated these units under his management, thus laying the foundations for the modern-day Norfolk & Western Railroad. He lost control of the line during the 1873 depression, however, and began a new career in politics. He became involved in the burgeoning READJUSTER MOVEMENT, and he managed the new party's successful 1879 campaign for control of the legislature. Elected to the U.S. Senate, he took his seat in 1881 and announced his decision to align himself with the national Republicans. This move enabled him to control Virginia's Negro vote, but it also alienated thousands of his white supporters. Completing his senatorial term in 1887, he suffered a crushing defeat in his 1889 Republican bid for the governorship. His influence collapsed thereafter. He died from a paralytic stroke.

See N. M. Blake, *William Mahone* (1935), dry but informative; J. T. Moore, *Virginia Debt Controversy* (1974); C. C. Pearson, *Readjuster Movement* (1917); and Mahone Papers, Duke University, a massive collection.

JAMES T. MOORE
Virginia Commonwealth University

MALARIA is a parasitic disorder, caused by the protozoa *Plasmodium*, transmitted by infected mosquitoes of the genus *Anopheles*, and characterized by recurrent attacks of fever, chills, and sweating. In the colonial period three common strains were identified on the basis of the intervals between fever bouts: quotidian, in which the fever occurred daily; tertian, every second day; and quartan, every third day—hence the names intermittent or remittent fever or the more descriptive term, "fever and ague." The disease has a long history, dating back at least to ancient Greece. It was transmitted to the American colonies relatively early and was widespread by the eighteenth century. It began receding from New England by the Revolution but remained a major problem in the middle and southern colonies. In the nineteenth century it followed settlers westward, ravaging the inhabitants of the entire Ohio and Mississippi valleys and reaching California in the 1850s. By this date virtually all of America save the New England states and the Appalachian areas was infested.

The Civil War, through the enormous movement of troops and civilians, intensified the malaria problem, bringing renewed outbreaks even into areas of New England that had been free of it for a hundred years. The disease peaked around 1870 and began receding from the northern states. By 1900 malaria was essentially a southern problem, with only a few scattered foci of the disease in the northern states.

Throughout its history, fever and ague was so common along the riverbanks and lowland areas of the South that it was scarcely considered a sickness. In endemic areas the chief mortality occurs among infants, and those who survive are seldom free of the disease; hence most southerners accepted the recurrent fever and chills as a fact of life. Travelers' descriptions of the sallow-skinned, debilitated inhabitants in the southern states leave little doubt as to the extent of malaria.

By 1898 the work of Charles Laveran, Ronald Ross, and Giovanni Grassi had demonstrated both the causative agent and the vector of malaria, and it was now possible to attack the disease rationally. The U.S. Public Health Service initiated the first major antimalarial campaign in the South in 1912–1913 in North Carolina, Virginia, Mississippi, and Arkansas, and shortly thereafter it enlisted the aid of the Rockefeller Foundation. The need to protect army camps in World War I gave a further stimulus to these efforts, and by 1930 a drastic reduction had been made in the morbidity from malaria. Creditable as were the antimalarial campaigns, the decrease in malaria in the southern states, as was true in the North, was attributable as much to the general improvement in social and economic conditions. Illustrating this point, the Great Depression brought a renewed wave of the disease.

The onset of World War II brought radical changes to the southern economy, and this factor, combined with an energetic antimalarial campaign utilizing the insecticide DDT, eliminated malaria from the United States by the 1960s. The rural shacks, lacking windows or screens, that housed both blacks and poor whites in the 1930s and early 1940s have largely disappeared, and along with them have gone the omnipresent highway signs advertising antimalarial tonics. The work of the U.S. Public Health Service and the Rockefeller Foundation with the emerging state and county public HEALTH units during the twentieth century contributed to the decline of malaria, but the rising standard of living, which meant better food, housing, plumbing, and sewerage and drainage facilities, played at least as great a role.

See E. H. Ackerknecht, *Ciba Symposium* (June–July, 1945); St. J. R. Childs, *Malaria and Colonization in Carolina Low Country* (1940); D. Drake, *Malaria in Interior Valley of North America* (1964); and J. Duffy, *Epidemics in Colonial America* (1953).

JOHN DUFFY
University of Maryland

MALLORY, STEPHEN RUSSELL (1813?–1873),

born in Trinidad, grew up in Florida, where he helped his widowed mother run a Key West boardinghouse. Entering the law and politics, he won election to the U.S. Senate in 1851, serving until 1861. Although lukewarm toward secession, he was nonetheless named secretary of the navy in the newly organized Confederacy by Jefferson Davis, who was impressed by Mallory's experience as chairman of the Senate Committee on Naval Affairs. Since the Confederacy had no navy to speak of and scant prospects of building one, Mallory's problems were formidable. He did not solve them all, but he did display considerable energy and skill, especially in his appreciation of such technological innovations as ironclads, mines, and SUBMARINES. Mallory was the only cabinet officer to remain at the same post throughout the entire life of the Confederacy, an indirect testimonial to his effectiveness. He resumed his legal practice in Florida after the war.

See J. T. Durkin, *Stephen R. Mallory* (1954); J. T. Scharf, *History of Confederate Navy* (1887); O. Clubbs, *Florida Historical Quarterly* (Oct., 1946; April, 1947); and P. Melvin, *Journal of Southern History* (May, 1944).

ALLAN PESKIN
Cleveland State University

MALVERN HILL, BATTLE OF (July 1, 1862).

After the battle of FRAYSER'S FARM, Va. (June 30, 1862), the federal Army of the Potomac, under George B. McClellan, withdrew south to the James River. By July 1 it was in position on Malvern Hill. McClellan, having made his dispositions and leaving Fitz-John Porter in charge, boarded a gunboat to select a base of supplies. Determined to destroy the enemy, ROBERT E. LEE ordered up his artillery to soften the opposing line; but too few roads, swampy and wooded terrain, defective staff work, and federal gunfire prevented the artillery from taking position. The insufficient artillery preparation notwithstanding, in mid-afternoon Lee's gray-clad troops began advancing piecemeal across a broad, open rise and into the mouths of Porter's concentrated cannon supported by massed infantry. "It was not war," wrote D. H. HILL, "it was murder." Before the Confederates were repulsed, they had suffered 5,000 casualties. The federals lost about half that. Although Porter wanted to hold Malvern, McClellan, who had returned to the hill during the battle, ordered him to withdraw to HARRISON'S LANDING, the new federal base of supplies.

See D. S. Freeman, *Lee* (1934), II; W. W. Hassler, Jr., *McClellan* (1957); C. Dowdey, *Seven Days* (1964); B. Catton, *Lincoln's Army* (1951); R. U. Johnson and C. C. Buel (eds.), *Battles and Leaders* (1887), II; and *Official Records, Armies*, Ser. 1, Vol. XI, Pts. 1, 2.

JOHN D. MILLIGAN
State University of New York, Buffalo

MAMMALS AND BIRDS. The first attempt to list natural resources of the South was made by Thomas Hariot, sent to North Carolina by SIR WALTER RALEIGH. Hariot's *Brief and True Report* (1588) mentioned mammals such as deer, conies (rabbits), "Saquenucket and Maquowoc" (opossum and raccoon), squirrels, bear, "lyon," wolves, and "wolfish dogges." Porpoises he listed under "Fishe." He also saw the furs of otter, marten, and skunk. Among the birds, he mentioned "Turkie[s], Stockdoves [wild pigeons], partridges, cranes, Hernes [herons], & in winter great store of swannes and geese . . . also Parats [parrots], Faulcons, & marlin hawkes."

Captain John Smith first described raccoons, muskrats, and flying squirrels as being native to Virginia. His description of the female opossum was the first from North America. It had, he said, "a head like a swine . . . a tail like a rat and [was] of the bigness of a cat. Under her belly she hath a bagge, wherein she lodgeth, carryeth, and suckleth her young." Some information in Smith's *General Historie of Virginia* (1624) was borrowed from others, notably Raphe Hamor, whose *True Discourse of the Present State of Virginia* (1615) listed 15 mammals, including "squirrels flying." John Lawson's *A New Voyage to Carolina* (1709) included a detailed account of its mammals and birds. MARK CATESBY produced the two-volumed *Natural History of Carolina, Florida, and the Bahama Islands* (1729, 1742), describing 100 species of birds and 24 mammals, together with fish, amphibians, reptiles, insects, and plants of these regions. His work marks the high point of development in American descriptive zoology prior to the Revolution.

THOMAS JEFFERSON's *Notes on the State of Virginia* (1781) was drafted originally in response to the interest of France in its new ally after 1778. Part of Jefferson's book refuted assertions by the comte de Buffon that American animals were inferior in number and quality to those of Europe. In his celebrated *Travels* (1791), William Bartram described 215 birds and over 30 mammals. His accounts of the wildlife of Virginia, the Carolinas, Georgia, and Florida are classic. Early in the nineteenth century, Alexander Wilson produced seven volumes of his *American Ornithology* (1808–1814) dealing with the birds of the Eastern Seaboard. His work was thorough and accurate, and the paintings of this self-taught Scot were often charming. The last two volumes of his work were completed by George Ord. JOHN JAMES AUDUBON included many accounts of southern birds in his *Birds of America* (1839–1844). His *Viviparous Quadrupeds of North America* (1849–1854), completed in collaboration with the Reverend John Bachman, a South Carolinian, was sounder from a scientific standpoint. There were a number of excellent early twentieth-century studies, such as A. H. Howell's *A Biological Survey of Alabama* (1921).

About 460 of the 700 full species of breeding birds in North America are found in the southern states at some point during the year. Many subspecies are also present. Because of the varied geography of the South, the avian fauna of the region is diversified. Some species, such as the Common Crow, are found throughout the South all year; others winter in the South but migrate elsewhere during the breeding season. Brown Pelicans are found on or near saltwater, whereas Green-winged Teal locate on freshwater ponds and lakes. Red-tailed Hawks nest in wooded areas, but feed in open fields. Among the rarer birds in the South are the Whooping Crane, whose population has hovered at between 20 and 50 individuals for half a century; and the Everglade Kite, a member of the hawk family, of which there are perhaps less than a dozen living in the interior of Florida. Commoner birds range in size from the huge White Pelican to the tiny hummingbird.

The mammals of the South include about 170 of the nearly 400 full species in the United States. There are also a number of geographic variants. As with birds, biogeographic factors limit the ranges of certain forms. Southern mammals range in size from the tiny Winnemanna Pigmy Shrew to the American Black Bear. Largely extirpated in much of its former range, the latter now occupies swampy areas and dense brush country where man seldom ventures. Some species have disappeared altogether from the South, such as the elk and the buffalo, which once ranged into most southern states except Florida. The Eastern Cougar is also probably extinct, and the Florida Cougar has been reduced to perhaps 100 individuals in Everglades National Park. The tiny Key Deer is also quite scarce, with perhaps 300 living on the islands off the southern tip of Florida. Some species have become extinct through excessive hunting, others because of the great quantities of land that have been cleared in the past 350 years, a process that has altered or eliminated the ground cover needed by many forms. Other forms have managed to hold their own, and a few, such as the coyote and armadillo, have even extended their range into areas where they were not found 50 years ago.

See, for general works on birds, T. G. Pearson, *Birds of America* (1936); E. H. Forbush and J. B. May, *Natural History of American Birds of Eastern and Central North America* (1939); and F. M. Chapman, *Handbook of Birds of Eastern North America* (1940). For studies of individual species, see A. C. Bent, *Life Histories* (1919–58). For excellent field guides, see R. T. Petersen, *Field Guide to the Birds* (1947) and *Field Guide to the Western Birds* (1961); and C. S. Robbins, B. Bruun, and H. S. Zim, *Birds of North America* (1966). For state studies, see T. Imhof, *Alabama Birds* (1962); R. J. Longstreet (ed.), *Birds in Florida* (1969); T. D. Burleigh, *Georgia Birds* (1958); G. H. Lowery, Jr., *Louisiana Birds* (1974); A. Stupka, *Birds of Great Smoky Mountains National Park* (1963), North Carolina; A. Sprunt, Jr., and E. B. Chamberlain, *South Carolina Bird Life* (1970); and H. C. Oberholzer, *Bird Life of Texas* (1974). For southern mammals, see W. J. Hamilton, Jr., *Mammals of Eastern U.S.* (1943), excellent, covers all but Louisiana and Texas; G. H. Lowery, Jr., *Mammals of Louisiana* (1974); and W. B. Davis, *Mammals of Texas* (1960). For life histories, see E. T. Seton, *Lives of Game Animals* (1925–28), classic. For detailed taxonomic treatment, see E. R. Hall and K. Kelson, *Mammals of North America* (1959). Excellent field guide is W. H. Burt and R. P. Grossenheider, *Field Guide to Mammals* (1976). State studies include F. B. Golley, *Mammals of Georgia* (1962); A. V. and R. W. Linzey, *Mammals of Great Smoky Mountains National Park* (1971); and R. H. Manville, *Mammals of Shenandoah National Park* (1956), Virginia.

KEIR B. STERLING
Pace University

MANASSAS, FIRST AND SECOND BATTLES OF. See BULL RUN CAMPAIGN, FIRST; BULL RUN CAMPAIGN, SECOND

MANCHAC POST (Ft. Bute, 1764–1779) was a military and trading post on the Mississippi at the southwest extremity of British West Florida. It was garrisoned until 1768 but subsequently allowed to decay. Traders here dealt with the Span-

ish and French along the river and Indians in the hinterland. A town was plotted (1772) but never materialized. Manchac was seized by raiding Americans (1778), retaken by local loyalists, then regarrisoned. In 1779 it was surrendered to Spain and finally was annexed to the United States in 1810.

See H. M. Lydenberg, *Archibald Robertson* (1930); C. Johnson, *British West Florida* (1943); *Mississippi Historical Society Publications* (1925), V; and W. Bartram, *Travels* (1791).

ETHEL E. RASMUSSON
Central Connecticut State College

MANGUM, WILLIE PERSON (1792–1861), was an important North Carolina politician. He was a legislator, judge, congressman, and senator. He belonged to the old Republican faction that supported William H. Crawford in 1824 and Andrew Jackson in 1828. Although twice voting against rechartering the Bank of the United States, he openly broke with Jackson and became the leading Whig in North Carolina during the battle over removal of the deposits. He was instructed to support the resolution expunging the censure of Jackson, but refused to obey. In 1836 he received South Carolina's electoral votes for president. From the time he openly became a Whig he was an ardent ally of Henry Clay. He resigned from the Senate in 1836, but returned in 1840, serving until 1853. He supported recharter of the national bank, distribution, the Mexican War, and the Compromise of 1850. He twice supported Winfield Scott for the presidential nomination.

See H. T. Shanks, *Papers of Mangum* (5 vols.; 1950–56), valuable; P. McDuffie, *Trinity College Historical Papers* (1925); and W. S. Hoffmann, *Journal of Southern History* (Aug., 1956) and *Andrew Jackson and North Carolina Politics* (1971).

WILLIAM S. HOFFMANN
Saginaw Valley College

MANN, AMBROSE DUDLEY (1801–1889), was one of three commissioners dispatched in 1861 to Europe to obtain recognition of the Confederacy (CONFEDERATE DIPLOMACY). His appointment was due to his long experience in the U.S. diplomatic service and his friendship with the Confederate president. Upon the failure of the mission, he was assigned in 1862 as agent to Belgium. King Leopold's open advocacy of the southern cause and the suspension of northern enlistments in that country were the chief fruits of his efforts. His mission to the papacy in 1863 was a fiasco. Vigorous and resourceful but grandiose in his ideas, he

proved unduly credulous in the conduct of diplomacy. An "irreconcilable," he spent the remainder of his life in Paris, writing his memoirs, which were unfortunately never published.

See J. P. Moore, *Letters of Mann to Davis* (1960), esp. introduction; F. L Owsley, *King Cotton Diplomacy* (1931); and F. Balace, *La Guerre de Sécession et la Belgique* (1969), latest treatment.

J. PRESTON MOORE
Louisiana State University

MANNERS. See CUSTOMS AND MANNERS

MANNING, RICHARD IRVINE (1859–1931),

was born at Holmesley plantation in Sumter County, S. C. After two years at the University of Virginia, he returned in 1881 to Holmesley and began farming. As a prominent member of a local GRANGE he won election to the state house of representatives (1892–1896) and subsequently served eight years in the state senate (1898–1906), supporting such Progressive legislation as the Australian ballot, education, fiscal reform, county health facilities, and road improvement. After an unsuccessful bid for the governorship in 1906 and the turbulent, sometimes reactionary administration of COLE BLEASE, Manning won the governorship in 1914 on a platform that promised to help the state "catch step" with the currents of progress. As governor (1915–1919) he reformed and secured increased appropriations for the state hospital for the insane; he increased support for all education; and he signed legislation implementing the tax commission, compulsory school attendance, the Australian ballot, a state highway commission, stricter law enforcement, regulation of insurance companies, a girl's reformatory, a state board of charities and corrections, a land registration law, and a school for the mentally retarded. He thought that the Negro's improvement would have to come as a concomitant of the upgrading of the social, economic, and educational status of the whites. Under Manning, South Carolina received its strongest single, concentrated impetus in social and economic progress since the Civil War.

See R. M. Burts, *Richard I. Manning* (1974); D. W. Grantham, *Hoke Smith* (1958) and *Democratic South* (1963); G. B. Tindall, *Emergence of New South* (1967); F. B. Simkins, *Pitchfork Ben Tillman* (1944); E. M. Lander, *History of South Carolina* (1960); Y. Snowden, *History of South Carolina* (1920); J. C. Hemphill, *Men of Mark* (1909); and D. D. Wallace, *South Carolina* (1951).

ROBERT M. BURTS
Carson-Newman College

MANUMISSION is the formal release of an individual or group from slavery. Although similar in meaning to emancipation, manumission is granted by a person, whereas emancipation is usually indicative of mass liberation by governmental act or of legal abolition of particular kinds of servitude. Manumission was achieved through wills, written deeds of manumission, special legislative acts, and self-purchase (which included "benevolent slaveholding" by free Negroes). Wills typically offered freedom for "good and faithful service." Many carefully designed wills, however, such as that of John Randolph, were wrecked on the shoals of legal technicalities, greed, or racial prejudice. Written deeds of manumission might reflect a master's affection for a slave or free his children by a slave woman or represent an attempt to abandon aged or other "profitless" slaves. Occasionally a state legislature would manumit a slave for some meritorious act saving life or property. Finally, extra jobs, especially in the cities, provided some ambitious slaves with savings enough to purchase their freedom.

The legal right to manumit a slave issued from the right of a citizen to sell his property; therefore, only direct legislative action could restrict that right. The colonies initiated restrictive action and the states expanded it until slavery ended. Manumission, for example, was barred if the slave would become a public charge; nor could an insolvent owner manumit his slaves to the damage of his creditors. Pressures on slavery after 1830 brought increasingly stringent restrictions against manumission. Although chances of achieving manumission were never high, by 1850 the rate had fallen to 0.45 per thousand slaves.

See T. R. R. Cobb, *Law of Negro Slavery* (1858), valuable southern legal views; H. T. Catterall (ed.), *Cases Concerning Slavery* (4 vols.; 1926–36), manumission examples unlimited; L. P. Jackson, *Journal of Negro History* (July, 1930); J. M. England, *Journal of Southern History* (Feb., 1943); S. E. Matison, *Journal of Negro History* (April, 1948); and F. F. Mathias, *Journal of Southern History* (May, 1973).

FRANK F. MATHIAS
University of Dayton

MAPS. Although Juan de la Cosa, pilot to Christopher Columbus, made a map of the New World (1500), the first known printed map of America was the world map by Matteo Giovanni Contarini (1506). One of the earliest printed maps exclusively dealing with the New World was produced by Martin Waldseemüller in 1513.

Regional maps soon began to appear and show more detail than the earlier world maps. Florida was named by PONCE DE LEÓN in 1513, and the name soon applied to the whole southeastern region. Ortelius' Florida map (1584) was based on information from the Spanish royal cartographer Alonso de Chaves and included the area south of Virginia and west to New Mexico. Gerhardus Mercator's work of 1569 was the first to show the Appalachians as a continuous mountain range running parallel to the coast southwest to northeast.

By the end of the sixteenth century, important English contributions were made by Humphrey Gilbert, Martin Frobisher, Michael Lok, Robert Thorne, Francis Drake, WALTER RALEIGH, Emery Molyneux, and William White. The manuscript of White's map of Virginia (1590) is in the British Museum. Jacques Le Moyne de Morgues' map of Florida (1591) showed the area from North Carolina south to the Cape of Florida, including the French settlement area on St. John's River (1564).

The seventeenth century produced such items as John Smith's map of Virginia and the Chesapeake region (1608) and map of Virginia (1612). In the following century the wars between France and England encouraged work by military and naval engineers. In his Carte de la Louisiane (1718), Guillaume Delisle showed the Gulf region from Mexico to Florida and first mentioned Texas on a map. Englishman Herman Moll published a number of maps of Carolina. Manuscript materials for some of Moll's maps are in the British Public Records Office.

It was John Mitchell's Map of the British and French Dominions in North America (1755) that used some of the data collected by Colonel Tuscarora Jack Barnwell some 30 years before and Joshua Fry and Peter Jefferson's map from the Virginia–North Carolina boundary commission (1749) published by Captain John Dalrymple in London in 1755. Politically and historically, the Mitchell map is the most important in American history. Editions were used by the negotiators of the Treaty of Paris (1783) and in later English and American boundary dispute settlements.

In 1757 William Gerard DeBrahm published his Map of South Carolina and a Part of Georgia. His appointment by the king marks the transition to professional surveyors in map making. Bernard Romans worked with DeBrahm and produced the Chart of the Coast of East and West Florida (1774). Joseph Frederick Wallet des Barres used the work of these men, John Stuart, and his own admiralty surveys to produce the Atlantic Neptune (1774–1781). With the American Revolution, native map makers became more active. George Washington and Thomas Jefferson had had mapping experi-

ence. British maps were used by the American forces as well as maps by native map makers. Des Barres' work was not surpassed until the Coast and Geodetic Survey maps (1878) and the development of new techniques like aerial photography and satellite surveys since World War II.

See most large libraries, state universities, and state archives for map collections. Among the best in U.S. are Huntington Library and Bancroft Library, California; Newberry Library, Chicago; Library of Congress, Geography and Map Division; U.S. Coast and Geodetic Survey, Map Service Branch, Maryland; J. F. Bell Library, Minneapolis; W. L. Clements Library, Ann Arbor; J. C. Brown Library, Providence; and New York Public Library. The Casa de Contratación in Seville has important materials for Spanish America. Also see E. J. Burrus, *Kino and Cartography of Northwestern New Spain* (1965); D. K. Carrington, *Map Collections in U.S. and Canada* (1970); W. P. Cumming, *Southeast in Early Maps* (1962); W. P. Cumming, R. A. Skelton, and D. B. Quinn, *Discovery of North America* (1972); L. DeVorsey, Jr., *North America at Time of Revolution* (1974); P. J. Guthorn, *British Maps of American Revolution* (1972) and *American Maps and Map Makers of Revolution* (1966); K. Nebenzahl and D. Higginbotham, *Atlas of American Revolution* (1974); R. V. Tooley, *Maps and Map-Makers* (1970); and C. I. Wheat, *Mapping the American West, 1540–1857* (1957–63).

MARY EMILY MILLER
Salem State College, Salem, Mass.

MARDI GRAS celebrations officially begin on the "twelfth night" after Christmas, January 6, and culminate on Fat Tuesday, the last day before Lent. The tradition began with the Roman celebration of Lupercalia, which later became the Catholic Carnevalamen. In New Orleans, however, Mardi Gras is a year-long preoccupation. It is a major element of the city's aesthetic and cultural life and, according to critics, the reason for New Orleans' lack of museums and other cultural institutions. The city boasts over 200 Carnival clubs, called krewes, structured in an elaborate social hierarchy with considerable distinctions existing in the social standing of the different krewes.

New Orleans' sporadic celebration of Mardi Gras first became regularized in 1857 with the parade of the Mistick Krewe of Comus. More than a century later, Comus remains socially the most prestigious of the krewes and enjoys the honor of being the last krewe to parade on Mardi Gras night. Rex, the largest and most influential of the city's krewes, was founded in 1872, and the king of Rex is the city's official "king of Carnival." Mardi Gras officially ends when the courts of Rex and Comus meet at midnight and sing the anthem of Mardi Gras, "If Ever I Cease to Love." In the final two weeks of Carnival, there are over 50 parades in which masked krewe members throw beads, doubloons, and even coconuts into the crowd (a modern version of masked, medieval nobility who threw wheat to bystanders at parades in the Middle Ages). At the end of each parade, there is a by-invitation-only ball given by the host krewe; even onlookers are required to dress formally, and a ball invitation is a prized social commodity.

Despite its concerns for rank and status, New Orleans' Carnival has tended to be democratic. Truck krewes of ordinary citizens traditionally follow the elaborate Rex parade on Mardi Gras day. Neighborhood krewes, women's krewes, and suburban krewes continue this tradition. Such businessmen's krewes as Bacchus and Endymion are further widening the scope of Mardi Gras; they have imported show business celebrities as "kings," have held more elaborate parades, and have even hosted public balls. Carnival is constantly changing in New Orleans, but it retains its popularity and its hold upon the city's imagination.

See P. Young, *Mistick Krewe* (1969); C. I. Du Four and L. Huber, *If Ever I Cease to Love* (1970); A. La Cour and S. Landry, *New Orleans Masquerade* (1952); R. Tallant, *Mardi Gras* (1948); and O. Evans, *New Orleans* (1959).

RICHARD H. COLLIN
University of New Orleans

MARIETTA, GA. (pop. 27,216), is today a small industrial town and a residential suburb of Atlanta. Founded in 1832, antebellum Marietta prospered as a summer resort in the foothills of the Blue Ridge Mountains. General W. T. Sherman was defeated here (KENNESAW MOUNTAIN, BATTLE OF) in his advance on Atlanta.

See files of Marietta *Journal* (1866–).

MARION, FRANCIS (1732–1795), of Huguenot ancestry, was born in Berkeley County, S.C. His first military experience was fighting the CHEROKEE in the FRENCH AND INDIAN WAR. In 1775 he was selected one of the captains of the 2nd South Carolina Regiment and rose to the rank of lieutenant colonel in the Continental service, participating in the defense of Charleston in 1775 and the siege of Savannah in 1779. Because of a broken ankle he was not with his regiment when Charleston surrendered in 1780, and he escaped the debacle at CAMDEN when HORATIO GATES sent him back to his home country to rally the militia. From bases in swampy areas he knew well, he soon began a relentless guerrilla campaign, beginning with an action at Great Savannah (August 20,

1780) when he freed some of the prisoners taken at Camden. He subdued the local Tories at Blue Savannah, Black Mingo Creek, and Tearcourt Swamp in the weeks following and engaged in numerous skirmishes with British troops. After GUILFORD COURTHOUSE he worked closely with HENRY LEE in the progressive reduction of British posts in South Carolina, successfully capturing Ft. Watson, Ft. Motte, and Georgetown. He participated in the siege of Ninety-six and commanded Nathanael Greene's militia force at EUTAW SPRINGS. Commissioned by Governor EDWARD RUTLEDGE as brigadier general of South Carolina militia, he acted virtually as military governor of his region until civil government was restored late in 1781. In 1781, 1782, and 1784 he was elected to the state senate. Even before his death he had become a living legend as the Swamp Fox.

See romantic biographies by W. D. James (1821), W. G. Simms (1844), and Parson M. L. Weems (1845), who adapted material of Peter Horry, which contributed to the legend. Recent biographies by R. D. Bass, *Swamp Fox* (1959); and H. F. Rankin, *Francis Marion* (1973), place Marion in proper perspective.

ROBERT W. COAKLEY
U.S. Army

MARION STRIKE. One of the most violent of the strikes (LABOR UNIONS) that swept through the southern TEXTILE INDUSTRY in 1929 occurred at the Baldwin Manufacturing Company in Marion, N.C. In June of that year some Baldwin workers joined the United Textile Workers union and organized a mass public meeting to discuss working conditions at the mill. Twenty-two unionists were shortly discharged. The union's demands for reinstatement of dismissed workers, a reduction of the workday from 12 to ten hours, and the creation of a grievance committee were rejected, and a strike began July 11. The UTW, however, was unable to give either relief or effective leadership to the strikers. The Conference for Progressive Political Action of A. J. Muste contributed most to the effort. By September the strike was effectively ended when a compromise favorable to the company was reached through the efforts of mediators. State troops, which had been sent to the area, were withdrawn; but R. W. Baldwin, president of the company, refused to honor the commitment to rehire most of the union members, and over 100 strikers were blacklisted. On October 2 the night shift at the Baldwin mill walked out and attempted to convince the day shift to refuse to work. The county sheriff fired tear gas into the crowd assembled at the mill, and his deputies opened fire into the backs of the fleeing workers. Six workers were killed, and 25 were seriously wounded. R. W. Baldwin applauded the sheriff's actions. The sheriff and his deputies were quickly acquitted of the murder charges against them.

See T. Tippett, *When Southern Labor Stirs* (1931); and I. Bernstein, *Lean Years: History of American Worker, 1920–1933* (1960).

JOHN SCOTT WILSON
University of South Carolina

MARK TWAIN, SAMUEL CLEMENS' pen name, is derived from riverboat parlance signifying a measured depth of two fathoms or 12 feet. A steamboat's landsman regularly measured a river's depth and called his findings to the captain. On a course into gradually deepening water, he might have called out thus: "Half twain [six feet], quarter less twain [one and three-quarters fathoms], mark twain, no bottom."

MARMADUKE, JOHN SAPPINGTON (1833–1887), the son of M. M. Marmaduke (Missouri governor, 1844), was born near Arrow Rock, Mo. He attended Yale, Harvard and West Point and joined the 7th U.S. Regiment. On April 17, 1861, he resigned and joined the pro-Confederate Missouri Home Guard. After a defeat at BOONVILLE, he traveled to Richmond and was commissioned in the Confederate cavalry. He distinguished himself at SHILOH and was promoted brigadier general. At HELENA (July, 1863), he blamed General L. M. Walker for the defeat. Walker demanded satisfaction and was mortally wounded. Marmaduke was arrested but soon returned to command. In the fall of 1864, he led his cavalry division in PRICE'S RAID ON MISSOURI. At WESTPORT (October 23) he helped save STERLING PRICE's army but was captured at Mine Creek, Kan. (October 25), while protecting Price's retreat. While imprisoned he was confirmed as a major general. Released in July, 1865, he returned to St. Louis, where he became a successful businessman and newspaper editor. He was elected governor in 1884. Noted for his handling of serious railroad strikes, the bachelor governor died before completing his term.

See J. Lee, *Missouri Historical Society Collection* (July, 1906); *Kansas City Times* (Nov. 24, 1962); M. Plummer, *Missouri Historical Review* (Oct., 1964); and S. Oates, *Confederate Cavalry* (1961).

MARK A. PLUMMER
Illinois State University

MAROONS, Indian Negroes and, after *ca.* 1750, Seminole Negroes, were members of military-agrarian communities comprising fugitive black slaves and their descendants, Indianized Negroes, and Africanized Indians. They resided beyond the limits of the plantation heartland in areas occupied by Indian confederacies. Benjamin Brawley first called attention to their significance for southern history; Herbert Aptheker employed the term loosely to embrace temporary camps of fugitive slaves within the plantation heartland; Kenneth W. Porter investigated the Seminole Negroes and their role in the Seminole Wars (1835–1842) in studies that have set a high standard; J. Leitch Wright points to their military participation in border warfare along the Gulf coast. After 1815, maroons were confined largely to the Floridas.

See J. R. Giddings, *Exiles of Florida* (1858); B. Brawley, *Social History of American Negro* (1921); H. Aptheker, in R. Price (ed.), *Maroon Societies* (1973); K. W. Porter, *Negro on American Frontier* (1971); and J. L. Wright, *Journal of Southern History* (Nov., 1968).

RODERICK BRUMBAUGH
Troy, N.Y.

MARSHALL, JOHN (1755–1835), was born and reared in Fauquier County, Va., and always bore the influence of the frontier on his life and thought. In 1783 he married Mary Willis Ambler (Polly) and lived the remainder of his life in Richmond, where—until 1797 when he accepted President John Adams' request to help represent the nation in France—he was deeply involved in state political and legal affairs. He served intermittently on the council of state, in the house of delegates, on the Richmond city council, as a delegate to the Virginia ratifying convention in 1788, and after 1793 as a brigadier general of the state militia. Marshall and a handful of his contemporaries dominated the state court bar; Marshall practiced before the state courts, the U.S. circuit court for Virginia, and the U.S. Supreme Court, where he argued the famous case *Ware* v. *Hylton* in 1796. After his involvement in the XYZ affair and his return from France in 1798, he was persuaded by George Washington to run for Congress. He was elected in 1799 but resigned in 1800 to become first secretary of war and then secretary of state, a position he held when President Adams nominated him chief justice of the United States on January 20, 1801.

Marshall sat as chief justice until 1835, longer than any other person, and during his tenure he persuaded the justices to abandon their practice of writing *seriatim* opinions and to begin speaking as one voice. The Court emerged as a strong, effective part of national government interpreting the Constitution as a grant of broad power to Congress, especially in the area of commerce. The most significant opinions Marshall delivered as chief justice were those in *Marbury* v. *Madison* (1803), FLETCHER V. PECK (1810), *McCulloch* v. *Maryland* (1819), *Dartmouth College* v. Woodward (1819), COHENS V. VIRGINIA (1821), and *Gibbons* v. *Ogden* (1824).

See A. J. Beveridge, *Life of Marshall* (4 vols.; 1916–19); H. A. Johnson and C. T. Cullen (eds.), *Papers of John Marshall* (1974–); E. S. Corwin, *John Marshall and Constitution* (1919); and W. M. Jones (ed.), *Marshall: A Reappraisal* (1956).

CHARLES T. CULLEN
Institute of Early American History and Culture

MARSHALL, THURGOOD (1908–), civil rights lawyer and associate justice of the U.S. Supreme Court, was born in Baltimore. He received a B.A. degree *cum laude* from Lincoln University in Pennsylvania in 1930 and graduated at the head of his class from Howard University Law School in 1933. After engaging in private practice in Baltimore, he was appointed in 1936 to the legal staff of the NATIONAL ASSOCIATION FOR THE ADVANCEMENT OF COLORED PEOPLE, becoming in 1938 the organization's chief legal officer. From 1940 until 1961 he served as director-counsel of the NAACP legal defense and educational fund. During his affiliation with the NAACP, he argued 32 cases before the Supreme Court, winning all but three of them. Some of the cases that were turning points in the elimination of segregation were: SMITH V. ALLWRIGHT (1944); *Morgan* v. *Virginia* (1946), declaring unconstitutional segregated seating on buses engaged in interstate travel; SHELLY V. KRAEMER (1948); SWEATT V. PAINTER (1950); and BROWN V. BOARD OF EDUCATION (1954), in which Marshall's arguments played a commanding role.

In 1961 Marshall was nominated by John F. Kennedy for appointment to the Second Circuit Court of Appeals, being confirmed by the Senate a year later over the strenuous objections of several conservative white southern senators. In 1965 Lyndon B. Johnson named him solicitor general. The peak of Marshall's career occurred in 1967, when Johnson appointed him an associate justice of the Supreme Court, thus making him the first black to sit on the highest court of the nation. From the outset he became a member of the liberal activist wing of the Court.

See *Official Congressional Directory*, 94th Cong., 1st Sess., p. 747; U.S. Senate, Committee on Judiciary, *Nom-*

ination of Thurgood Marshall (1967); and L. Friedman and F. L. Israel (eds.), *Justices of Supreme Court* (1969), IV.

ARNOLD S. RICE
Kean College of New Jersey

MARSHALL UNIVERSITY (Huntington, W.Va. 25701). After residents of Wyandotte County became dissatisfied with the three-month term of area schools, they incorporated Marshall Academy in 1837. The academy became a private college in 1858 but insufficient finances and the Civil War threw the school's future into doubt until it became a state normal college in 1867. A university since 1961, Marshall has a coeducational enrollment of approximately 8,000 students.

See V. A. Smith, *West Virginia History* (Oct., 1963).

MARTIN, FRANÇOIS XAVIER (1762–1846), was born in Marseilles, France. As a youth he settled in New Bern, N.C., where he founded a newspaper, served in the legislature and studied law. In 1809, James Madison named him first to the superior court of Mississippi Territory and then to the same post in the territory of Orleans. In 1813 he was Louisiana's first attorney general and in 1815 became a justice of the state supreme court, where he served until 1846. Martin was an indefatigable compiler and antiquarian who published histories of both North Carolina and Louisiana. While on the Louisiana bench he published fine collections of the reports of that court. His knowledge of the French language and law aided the court in untangling the confusing influences of Spanish, French, and common law that made Louisiana law a no-man's-land.

See F. X. Martin, *History of Louisiana* (1827) and *History of North Carolina* (1829); W. B. Yearns, *North Carolina Historical Review* (Jan, 1959); E. L. Tinker, *Bulletin of New York Public Library* (1935); and H. A. Bullard, in B. F. French (ed.), *Historical Collections of Louisiana* (1850), II.

HUGH F. BELL
University of Massachusetts

MARTIN, LUTHER (1744–1826). A Maryland lawyer and jurist born in New Jersey, he graduated from Princeton College in 1766. In 1771 he began practicing law in Maryland and Virginia. An ardent patriot, he wrote several pamphlets and served as state attorney general (1778–1805, 1818–1822) and delegate to the CONSTITUTIONAL CONVENTION in 1787. There he was a strong supporter of state sovereignty, strongly influencing, however, the wording of Article 6, Section 2, the "supreme law" clause. His objections are given in "The Genuine Information." He was also judge of a Baltimore county court (1814–1818). Martin was always a busy, prosperous attorney, and he helped defend SAMUEL CHASE during his 1805 impeachment trial and Aaron Burr during his 1807 treason trial. He also participated in FLETCHER V. PECK (1810) and *McCullough* v. *Maryland* (1819). His pleadings exhausted all possible precedents and were notable more for their matter than the manner in which they were delivered. In 1796 Maria Cresap, his wife, died leaving him with two daughters, each of whom made unsuccessful marriages (see *Modern Gratitude* [1802]). His faculties ruined by drink and a stroke, he died while living with Burr in New York.

See C. Evans, *American Bibliography* (14 vols.; n.d.), Nos. 15112, 15389, 16329, 21220; P. S. Clarkson and R. S. Jett, *Luther Martin* (1970), pedestrian but complete; P. A. Crowel, *Johns Hopkins Studies in Historical and Political Science*, LXI, No. 1 (1943); E. A. Obrecht, *Maryland Historical Magazine* (Sept., 1932); J. F. Essary, *Records of Columbia Historical Society* (1916); and H. P. Goddard, *Maryland Historical Society Fund Publications* (1887).

ROBERT F. JONES
Fordham University

MARTIN, THOMAS STAPLES (1847–1919), railroad lawyer, U.S. senator, and cofounder of the modern Virginia Democratic party, was the son of a merchant-manufacturer in western Virginia. While at the Virginia Military Institute he fought in the battle of NEW MARKET. When defeat and Reconstruction forced the transformation and rebuilding of the state's economy, Martin with lawyers for the railroads and corporations led a process of consolidation and systematization, first in the railroad industry and then in politics. In 1893 Martin won a U.S. Senate seat through manipulation of the Virginia senate. During his five terms (1893–1919) he compiled a conservative, pro-business, hard-money record; yet he also supported the Hepburn Act, Pure Food and Drug Act, Federal Reserve System, and the Child Labor Act. From 1917 to 1919 he served as majority leader of the U.S. Senate. In Virginia the Democratic organization, Martin's organization, continued for 40 years after his death along the lines that he established: centralized, probusiness, antilabor, anti-Negro, and committed to a philosophy of states' rights and limited governmental services (BYRD MACHINE).

See R. H. Pulley, *Old Virginia Restored* (1968), excellent; A. Moger, *Virginia, 1870–1925* (1968), excellent; A. F. Scott, *Journal of Southern History* (Feb., 1963); G. B. Tindall, *Emergence of New South* (1967); and J. A. Bear, "T. S. Martin" (M.A. thesis, University of Virginia, 1952).

JOSEPH P. HARAHAN
U.S. Government Historian

MARTINSBURG, W.VA. (pop. 14,625), is approximately 17 miles south of Hagerstown, Md. The surrounding area was settled during the eighteenth century by German and English pioneers. Prior to the American Revolution, General Adam Stephen founded the town on land of the Fairfax estate and named it for J. B. Martin, nephew of Lord Fairfax. When the Baltimore & Ohio Railroad ran its track through town in 1837, the city began to flourish as a rail and shipping point. Belle Boyd, a Confederate spy, lived here and was imprisoned here during the Civil War. Because of the town's strategic importance as a rail center it was subjected to several raids and was the site of a skirmish during the SHENANDOAH VALLEY CAMPAIGN. The end of the war did not bring peace. In 1877, during the great railway strike, President R. B. Hayes sent federal troops into the town to break the strike. The modern city remains a shipping center for area limestone, apples, livestock, grain, and dairy products. It also manufactures hosiery and automobile parts.

See W. T. Doherty, *Berkeley County, U.S.A.* (1972); W. F. Evans, *History of Berkeley County* (1928); H. H. Hardesty, *Hardesty's West Virginia Counties* (1973), III; F. V. Aler, *History of Martinsburg* (ca. 1888); and files of Martinsburg *Journal* (1907–, Republican daily), *News* (1929–, Democratic daily), *Statesman* (1874–1913), and *Gazette* (1810–54), all on microfilm.

MARVIN, WILLIAM (1808–1902), a native New Yorker, first served Floridians in 1835 as a territorial district attorney and from 1845 to 1863 as a U.S. district judge. Then on July 13, 1865, President Andrew Johnson appointed Marvin provisional governor of Florida. While preparing Floridians for presidential Reconstruction, Marvin told blacks to thank God for their freedom and reminded them they were not equal to whites. At the same time he assured white Floridians, particularly the constitutional convention delegates, that government was a task for whites only. He urged the delegates to meet President Johnson's minimal demands for Reconstruction, to guarantee freedmen their civil rights, and to enact a vagrancy law as a necessary stimulant to Negro initiative. Following Marvin's advice the delegates drafted a prowhite constitution. The new general assembly adopted a series of harsh BLACK CODES

designed to preserve the "beneficial aspects" of slavery. It then completed the remaining steps for presidential Reconstruction. Although Marvin faithfully carried out President Johnson's charge, Floridians lost an opportunity for a smooth transition from military to civilian authority when the Radical Republican Congress refused to accept presidential Reconstruction. Perhaps Marvin could not have prevented the Radical Reconstruction of Florida, but his actions and sentiments gave impetus to the black codes and to the ruling elite's attitude of defiance toward Congress (RECONSTRUCTION, CONGRESSIONAL). On January 18, 1866, Marvin resigned as governor, later returning to New York, where he died.

See J. M. Richardson, *Negro in Reconstruction* (1965), excellent content and bibliography; J. H. Shofner, *Florida Reconstruction* (1974); P. D. Ackerman, "Florida Reconstruction" (M.A. thesis, University of Florida, 1948); and Governor's Letter Books, Florida State Library, Tallahassee and P. K. Yonge Library, Gainesville.

N. GORDON CARPER
Berry College

MARY BALDWIN COLLEGE (Staunton, Va. 24401), founded in 1842 by the Reverend Rufus W. Baily, a Presbyterian minister, was first known as Augusta Female Seminary. Joseph Wilson, father of WOODROW WILSON, briefly headed the school during his pastorate in Staunton, and William McGuffey, author of *McGuffey's Readers*, served here as a counselor. The individual with the greatest impact on the school's development, however, was Mary Julia Baldwin. After becoming principal in 1863, she guided the school through the difficult Civil War and postwar years, which witnessed the closing of many schools with a seemingly more secure financial base. In 1895 the academy was renamed to honor its former principal, and in 1923 the school became a full college. Still affiliated with the Presbyterian church, it has a present enrollment of approximately 550 students.

See M. Walters, *History of Mary Baldwin College* (1942); and J. A. Waddell, *History of Mary Baldwin Seminary* (1905).

MARYLAND, like Missouri and New Jersey, is a state with a split regional identity. A small but densely populated state with a moderate-sized immigrant population, Maryland always has differed demographically from the South; but its constant preoccupation with slavery and the Negro has made it different from the North as well. To many of its citizens, especially those living on the Eastern Shore or in the lower Potomac Valley, it is a southern state. Among Baltimoreans and those living in the western mountains, however, there is a definite attachment to the North. Its economic and cultural life has been dominated since the Revolution by Baltimore, while its politics have been controlled by men whose philosophy differs greatly from the commercial, industrial, and intellectual life of that city. At one with neither the North nor the South, Maryland is a state with an intriguing and distinctive historical, ethnic, and occupational pluralism.

Origins and geography. "Terra Mariae" was the name given by King Charles I to the tract of wilderness he bestowed upon George Calvert, first baron of Baltimore. Named in honor of his queen, Henrietta Maria, the original grant awarded all land between the southern shore of the Potomac River and 40° north latitude and from the Atlantic Ocean westward to the river's "first fountain." The Roman Catholic nobleman's princely domain originally included all of what is now the DELMARVA PENINSULA, southern Pennsylvania (including Philadelphia), the District of Columbia, and a sizable piece of West Virginia. The first of a series of territorial cessions occurred even before the charter was put into final form when part of the Eastern Shore, already settled by Virginians, was returned to the Old Dominion. A later award of proprietary rights to the Penn family further reduced Maryland's size and subsequently set the northern and eastern limits at the MASON-DIXON LINE. A mistaken notion that the northern branch of the Potomac constituted the river's "first fountain" resulted in another loss to its southern neighbor, and the cession of land to the federal government for its new capital concluded the partition of the original grant.

The modern state encompasses nearly 10,000 square miles of land and 2,400 square miles of inland water, including the Chesapeake Bay and its inlets and tidewater rivers. It ranks forty-second in size in the Union, and only Delaware is smaller geographically in the South. Maryland is divided into three physiographic provinces. The coastal plain province or TIDEWATER includes all of the Eastern Shore (that part of the state lying on the Delmarva Peninsula) and the part of the Western Shore between the bay and the FALL LINE. The PIEDMONT region encompasses the hill country above the fall line (which runs roughly between Baltimore City and Georgetown, D.C.) and Parrs Ridge. West of the Piedmont Plateau lies the Appalachian province, which includes the Blue Ridge

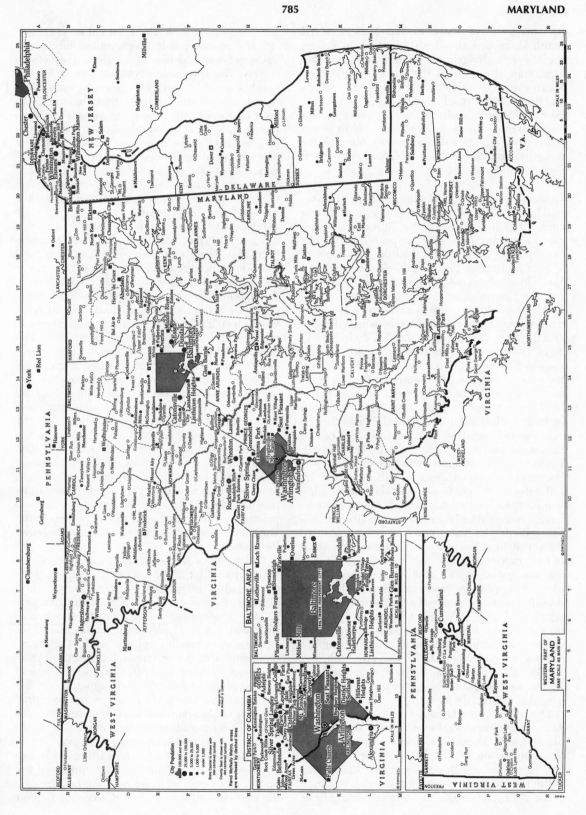

(the extension of which in Maryland is called South Mountain), the Great Appalachian Valley, the Allegheny Ridges, and the Allegheny Plateau. Maximum elevation in the state is 3,360 feet. Mean annual temperature for the state is 52° F., and the average annual rainfall is 43 inches. Maryland's climate is similar to that of other border states. Winters by New England or midwestern standards are quite mild, but metropolitan Baltimore has an average of 24 inches of snow each year. Summers are hot and humid.

Colonial development. Cecilius Calvert, the second Lord Baltimore, received the original charter from King Charles because his father died before the document had passed the privy seal. Under his direction from London and the local leadership of his brother Leonard, the first governor of the colony, Maryland prospered in the years before the Cromwellian revolution. Governor Calvert led the first 200 settlers who, after a long, difficult voyage on two small vessels named the *Ark* and the *Dove*, landed at St. Mary's City in March, 1634. The expedition was well equipped and well managed to meet the exigencies involved in initial contact with the wilderness and the few Indian tribes of the region. The result was that Maryland never underwent the "starving time" faced by early settlers of Jamestown and Plymouth.

Religious toleration became a precept of the Baltimore proprietorship. From the beginning, Roman CATHOLICS were a minority in the colony, and recent scholarship finds no indication that the Calverts ever sought to use the palatinate as a haven for their coreligionists. Such a policy would have been politically and economically inexpedient. Roman Catholics were not being persecuted in Britain at the time (witness the open grant of the proprietorship to the Calverts and the fact that the queen was a Catholic); and the church hierarchy opposed migration to Maryland because it could hurt the chances of a Catholic restoration when the Prince of Wales, whom they expected his mother to bring up in their faith, assumed the crown. Although the leadership of the original settlers was predominantly of Calvert's faith, the family's chief desire was to see their colony settled as soon as possible so that they might gain from it economically.

The intent of the famous Maryland Toleration Act of 1649 was to continue a policy already traditional with the proprietor and to procure additional protection for a badly outnumbered Catholic minority faced with a growing Protestant threat to their political, economic, and social dominance of the colony. Although the "Act concerning Religion" required toleration, it did not accept diversity as a positive good; it represented only an initial step toward the idea of pluralism in American society. The very necessity of passing such a law pointed out the intellectual diversity that existed from the foundation of this colony in contrast to most of seventeenth-century America. Thus, from its origin, Maryland would be more tolerant, more diverse, and thereby unique in the South. But the narrowness of seventeenth-century "toleration" endured into the twentieth century, when jurors were required to believe in a supreme being and the state's officers (Jews excepted) took their oaths "on the faith of a Christian."

Whatever the progressivism embodied in this act, however, the colony's charter and the intentions of its proprietor in economic, political, and social matters were medieval. Under their charter the Lords Baltimore were entitled to all the medieval powers accorded the north English palatinate of the bishop of Durham including the territorial, legislative, judicial, regal, ecclesiastical, military, and financial rights of that officer. The only restriction upon the arbitrary use of this power was that the settlers were entitled to give their advice and consent to all laws. In theory the proprietor had more power than the king of England possessed in 1632. The literal implementation of these powers, however, was hardly within the realities of seventeenth-century life. Thus the Calverts had to combine their desire to maintain firm control over their colony with common-sense concessions to the political situations in both Maryland and England. Their success was illustrated by the fact that Maryland was the only proprietary government based on the powers of the Durham palatinate to endure until the American Revolution.

The governor served as lieutenant general, admiral, chancellor, chief justice, land officer, grantor of public offices, dispenser of honors, and director of commercial life. The centralized proprietary government held as many powers as possible, and only slowly did responsibility and power devolve upon smaller political units. Local government during the seventeenth century fell upon the county officers (sheriff, clerk, surveyor, and justices of the peace) who were appointed by the governor. The legacy of this policy has been that the state of Maryland still has one of the most centralized administrations in the Union.

To assist in the administration, the governor had a council of close advisers who, during the first 50 years of Maryland history, were members of the proprietor's family or its intimate friends. In 1669 the council consisted of three Calverts, a Calvert brother-in-law, and two close family friends. The only challenge to the Calvert oligarchy came from the lower house of the Maryland assembly, which after 1650 consisted of four delegates from each county elected by the freeholders. The council constituted the upper house. This bicameralism gave the proprietor effectively three vetoes over the lower house: one in the council, which was always under the governor's control; one in the person of the governor; and one in his own right.

The original intent of George and Cecilius Calvert was to create certain aspects of medieval life in the New World. Thus they tried to build manors and govern them with courts baron and leet. Ordinarily, freeholds farmed by the planter, his indentured servants, and a few slaves constituted the basic form of ownership. The proprietors did not grant title in fee simple and thus were able to collect QUITRENTS, which became a valuable income for the family in the eighteenth century.

The bountiful Chesapeake provided the basic source of sustenance for the region. From its fecund waters came fish, oysters, and crabs for the table, and its many inlets allowed TOBACCO culture to dominate agricultural life. It was neither climate nor soil, but rather topography that allowed Maryland and Virginia to become the tobacco centers of the colonial world. The shallow-draft vessels of the period could sail easily up most of the 150 rivers, creeks, and branches that fed the bay. Every planter had his private dock to which he conveniently rolled the half-ton hogsheads of tobacco prior to their being transported across the Atlantic. The planter's home faced the water, not the muddy road behind the house that led inland, because it was from the bay that came news and cargoes from Europe, the West Indies, Africa, and the other colonies. So much was this society dependent upon water transport that one observer referred to the colonial Chesapeake region as a "sylvan Venice." To this day tobacco is the most valuable crop cultivated in the state.

In the initial 40 years of settlement the population rose at a rate of over 100 percent per decade until it reached 16,000 by 1670. In the next 60 years the rate of growth continued rapidly and steadily but at a lower rate (between 30 and 50 percent per decade), reaching 82,000 by 1730. Principal causes of this decline lay in the opening of settlement of new English colonies and trading posts throughout the world and the immigration limitations imposed by the various wars for empire. In the first years Maryland, like Virginia, was peopled mostly by persons of British origin. Although slavery existed from the opening of the colony, indentured servitude was the com-monest source of labor used by the freeholders.

The exclusion of an emerging Protestant elite and a decline in tobacco prices after the passage of the Navigation Acts combined to support a challenge to the Calvert-Catholic control of Maryland not unlike BACON'S REBELLION in Virginia. Internal dissent began 15 years earlier, but by 1689 a legitimate excuse for rebellion emerged when a series of misfortunes ended with a prolonged delay by the proprietary governor in acknowledging the accession of William and Mary. John Coode of Charles County organized the young Protestants who had migrated to the colony ten to 30 years earlier and who, as the younger sons of English gentry, expected the reigns of political power to come into their hands as readily as financial prosperity had. Seizing control of the government in July, 1689, Coode's Protestant association petitioned the crown for and received a royal charter (COODE'S REBELLION).

A quarter-century of royal rule brought considerable change. The capital was moved from St. Mary's in the center of Catholic settlement and sentiment to Anne Arundel Town, later renamed Annapolis, closer to the population center. The locus of power gradually shifted from the governor and council to the lower house. Roman Catholics were denied the right to hold office, vote, serve as lawyers, proselyte, or hold religious services outside their own homes. Despite opposition from Catholics and Quakers, the Anglican church was established in 1702, and with this action came a strengthening of local institutions and government. The elected vestrymen carried out not only ecclesiastical functions but also certain civil duties. Economically, this period saw a shift from small farming enterprises toward the development of large plantation units with much labor being done by slaves. By the time of the proprietary restoration in 1715, nearly a quarter of the population was in slavery. Coode's Rebellion resulted in leadership by a new colonial elite but did little to aid the development of either a democratic economic or social system. The descendants of the 1689 rebels constituted the ruling gentry of the colony through the revolutionary era.

While political power rested in the drawing rooms of Tidewater plantations and Annapolis townhouses, eighteenth-century Maryland saw a significant shift from dependence upon tobacco as the sole staple crop. The traditional customer of the Eastern Shore's dark, rank Orinoco tobacco was France. By the end of King George's War, this trade was virtually extinguished and no new buying public emerged. For its principal export that shore then turned to wheat and flour, lumber and wood products, and barreled pork and beef. But more significant growth and development occurred on the Western Shore. Here the cultivation of the finest Orinoco along the Tidewater was combined with the development of a large granary in the Piedmont. An entirely new form of commerce arose out of the iron furnaces and forges emerging from the Susquehanna River to Antietam Creek. British investments in the PRINCIPIO COMPANY and Maryland and Virginia investors behind the Baltimore Iron Works Company backed the first of a number of such enterprises that resulted in this colony becoming one of the three leading iron-producing centers in North America. Shipbuilding also became important. In the last quarter-century before the Revolution, Maryland built 126 vessels of over 100 tons. Any survey of the planter-merchants shows that a significant portion of the family fortunes of the Chews, Galloways, Carrolls, Dulanys, Taskers, Ridgelys, and Ringgolds came from manufacturing and shipping ventures. Marylanders' investment in shipping, mercantile, and manufacturing enterprises was little different from that engaged in by a Virginian like Robert Carter of Nomini Hall or a South Carolinian like Henry Laurens; but for Maryland this would be a harbinger of future development rather than an economic bypath taken outside the mainstream of southern life. At mid-century, the Calverts' colony had the most heterogeneous and second largest population in the South, and it was fourth largest among the 13 colonies. The population reached 153,000 in 1752 and 223,000 on the even of the Revolution. The growth rate was about 25 percent per decade after 1730. Approximately 25 percent of the population were slaves, 5 percent were white indentured or convict servants, 5 percent were free persons of color, and 65 percent were white freemen. The number of Negro freemen was unexceeded elsewhere in the South, and it portended even greater voluntary emancipation in the future.

Few colonies, except Pennsylvania, exhibited the religious diversity that found Anglican, Roman Catholic, Presbyterian, Quaker, German Reformed, Lutheran, and Baptist congregations scattered throughout the colony. Undoubtedly, the established Church of England enjoyed the nominal support of the largest number of colonists. Vestry membership was allowed all Protestants, and the vestry's civil functions—such as appointing the tobacco inspectors—were important to everyone regardless of religious affiliation. The lord proprietor, however, had the charter right to name all rectors, and the abuse of this power was to damage seriously the church's reputation. Despite the enactment of several penal laws to restrict the Catholics, that denomination was able to maintain itself with about 8 percent of the population throughout the eighteenth century. Occasional outbursts of anti-Catholicism emerged during the wars for empire, but no "papist" was ever persecuted under these statutes, and after the French and Indian War the Jesuits built churches separate from their residences in open violation of these laws.

Ethnic pluralism was also characteristic of eighteenth-century Maryland. Although settlers from England, Scotland, Wales, and northern Ireland predominated in the white population, the colony also had the largest concentration of Celtic Irish in North America and the largest percentage of Germans in the South. One of the important events of the century was the movement of population out of the Tidewater into the Piedmont. Men like Daniel Dulany, the elder, and Jonathan Hagar brought thousands of German, Scotch-Irish, Scottish, and English farmers into the rich Monocacy, Antietam, and Conococheague valleys. Many of the great planters of the Western Shore owned huge tracts in this region, but they had them cultivated by tenants rather than slaves. In western Maryland, the ethnic diversity, the dominance of grain and forage crops, and the need for highly developed transportation networks resulted in a change from a tobacco- and plantation-oriented society of the Tidewater to one more closely resembling Pennsylvania, whence many of the backcountry settlers came.

The settlement of this region required a seaport, and Baltimore Town filled the need because of its easy ability to tap commerce along the Philadelphia road running up the Monocacy Valley to the Pennsylvania city. Starting from 200 dwellers in 1750, Baltimore rose in size to 3,600 in 1770 and 5,700 a decade later. Its closest rivals were the Piedmont towns of Frederick and Hagerstown, whose population reached about 1,500 each in 1776.

Recent research indicates that a trend toward more rigid social-economic stratification and a decline in social mobility occurred in the third quarter of the eighteenth century, despite all the western movement and urbanization. Only 40 percent of white adult males were landowners, and it was increasing tenancy not freeholding that characterized the late colonial years. Many of the colony's young men migrated to the Carolina frontier, where greater economic opportunities beckoned.

Revolutionary ferment, 1763–1815. Within Maryland politics there arose a threefold division. Those persons and families profiting from the multitude of lucrative patronage posts at proprietary disposal were members of a loosely knit faction called the "court party." Their opponents, who usually controlled the lower house of the general assembly, were known as the "country party." The latter group (which got its name from its supposedly pro-Maryland bias at a time when one referred to his home colony as "my country") contained a dominant Whig faction and a vocal but less politically powerful democratic wing. The Whig faction desired the preservation of traditional gentry leadership without the odious restrictions of proprietary interference, and the latter demanded greater economic, social, and political opportunity in the colony.

United in a common cause against supposed British tyranny, Marylanders joined in riots, petitions, extralegal associations, and congresses typical of the revolutionary ferment in all of British America. Daniel Dulany's *Considerations* (1765) and the return of Roman Catholics to the political arena under the leadership of CHARLES CARROLL OF CARROLLTON added certain peculiarities to the colony's participation.

The internal struggle for political control that followed the decision for independence saw an unequal battle between the Democrats (allied with many militia battalions and recent emigrants from Pennsylvania), representing the northwestern Chesapeake counties, and the Whigs, who depended upon the traditional deference of the electorate to gentry leadership to control Baltimore Town, Annapolis, the Eastern Shore, and southern Maryland. The struggle saw a few outbursts against gentry-dominated political life such as the burning of the PEGGY STEWART in October, 1774 (where "Annapolis out-Bostoned Boston" at its tea party), the arson of the *Totness* in July, 1775 (a "second burnt-offering to liberty"), and militia demands for a more egalitarian society in the summer of 1776. But the Whigs lost neither their nerve nor their control of the situation, and they so dominated the 1776 constitutional convention that the new state emerged with the nation's most conservative fundamental law.

Like most of the early constitutions this document placed most political power in the bicameral general assembly, which had a popularly elected house of delegates (four from each county) and a 15-member senate chosen by an electoral college. Strict property qualifications for voting and officeholding denied the franchise to nearly half the adult white males and the governorship (elected by the assembly for one-year terms) to all but the very wealthiest landowners. Gentry dominance was further ensured by abolishing the religious establishment (which terminated the only locally elected officers, the parish vestrymen) and making all local officers except the sheriff appointed by the governor. But the Whig triumph did not go uncontested. The spirit of egalitarianism fostered by the Revolution and demonstrated to Marylanders in neighboring Pennsylvania resulted in continued assaults upon the constitution and a series of constitutional amendments in the early years of the nineteenth century.

Although its national political directions were somewhat blurry and sometimes contradictory, the Whig leadership pursued a centralistic course. Symbolizing this tendency was its resistance to ratification of the Articles of Confederation until after Virginia's cession of what became the old Northwest Territory. Similar support for the 1785 Mount Vernon Conference (ALEXANDRIA CONFERENCE) and the ANNAPOLIS CONVENTION (1786) prior to the Philadelphia Convention indicated a continued concern with nationalism. However, internal political quarrels between Carroll and SAMUEL CHASE, both Whigs, resulted in an undistinguished and ambiguous delegation to the 1787 convention in which LUTHER MARTIN constituted a vocal but rather unrepresentative Maryland voice for state sovereignty. Knowing that the economic well-being of the state demanded a strong national government, most of Maryland's conservative leaders supported ratification of the new federal constitution. To the Federalist government the self-proclaimed Old Line State gave several men of moderate importance and ability—Chase, James McHenry, WILLIAM WIRT, and William Vans Murray for example.

Internal migration within the state toward Baltimore City and the western counties and an outward immigration to southern and western states resulted in a significant shift in economic power in Maryland. By 1798 Baltimore had become the nation's third most populous city. During the 1780s Baltimore was the fastest-growing city on the continent. Certainly no other southern state and probably no state in the Union was so dominated demographically and economically by one urban center. Baltimore merchants engaged in trade with West Indian planters and British and French traders for the state's grain, flour, tobacco, and wood products. By 1805 over 50 flour mills were located in or near the city, many using the latest techniques for quick processing. The great mercantile families like the Smiths, Pattersons, and Olivers directed fleets of clipper ships that circled the globe. By 1815 the value of Baltimore's exports exceeded that of Philadelphia.

Partisan political conflict arising out of the impact of this urban development saw both Federalists and Republicans appeal for popular support and urge a more egalitarian political system. Suffrage was given to all white adult males, thus making Maryland the first of the original states to do so. Property and religious qualifications for office-holding were eliminated, and popular election of the justices of lower courts was initiated in the decade before the War of 1812.

To Marylanders the second British conflict presented opportunities for profit and patriotism. From the Chesapeake Bay came hundreds of privateers that wreaked havoc upon the British merchant marine. As part of major British offensives during 1814 (the Royal Army assaulted New York along Lake Champlain and a combined army-navy operation maneuvered against New Orleans), Vice Admiral Sir Alexander Cochrane attacked the center of the Atlantic seaboard. British regulars under Major General Robert Ross stormed ashore on the Patuxent River, marched through Upper Marlboro, and on August 24 defeated a superior American force in a series of engagements at BLADENS-BURG. That night they burned the public buildings in Washington in revenge for an earlier American burning of Lower Canada's capital of York (Toronto).

Ross's remarkable feat allowed Major General, U.S. Senator, and Baltimore merchant Samuel Smith enough time to coordinate and reinforce the defenses of the Patapsco River port. The British assault of September 12–14 resulted in the frustration of an army attempt to outflank Baltimore's harbor defenses by an attack east of the city and in the failure of a naval bombardment to open a path into the harbor by silencing the guns of Ft. McHenry. With the loss of General Ross and several hundred other personnel, Cochrane withdrew. He left behind FRANCIS SCOTT KEY, a prominent Georgetown attorney who had been temporarily aboard one of his vessels, and Key's first draft of a poem entitled "The Star-Spangled Banner." By defending Baltimore and popularizing Key's poem, Maryland made its final contribution to early American nationalism.

Revolutionary ferment also affected the social structure of the state. Dislocation of fortunes wrought by wars, new investment opportunities, and the introduction of new men into political and economic leadership contributed to a lessening of the social stratification that existed before 1776. The rapid expansion of Methodism easily made it rather than Episcopalianism the dominant church in the state. Adroit leadership by the Right Reverend John Carroll, first archbishop of Baltimore, did much to make Roman Catholicism acceptable to Protestant America. During these years the Germans took advantage of the existing state of flux to become part of the mainstream of life in the state rather than the isolated, inward-looking group they had been before. Pangs of conscience, plus the economic liability of slavery in a period of declining dependence on tobacco as a staple crop, brought a rapid increase in the number of free Negroes, until by 1810 Maryland had the largest number and the second highest percentage (next to Delaware) of freedmen in the whole South.

Southern versus Middle Atlantic state, 1815–1867. As a result of the changes wrought in the previous decades, the state found itself torn with a schizophrenic desire to be both southern and Middle Atlantic in its orientation. With its southern and Eastern Shore counties oriented toward agrarianism, slaveholding, and a static, stratified, stable society held together by deference to gentry leadership, the Tidewater was decidedly southern. On the other hand, Baltimore City and the counties bordering Pennsylvania were urban, commercial, industrialized, peopled by free blacks and immigrants, mobile, changing, and directed by an emerging ambitious, enterprising set of economic and political speculators.

New factories sprang up along the Patapsco River. Boots and shoes, refined sugar, packed oysters, clothing, and the products of foundries and furnaces poured forth from these enterprises in such quantities that by 1850 the value of Maryland's manufactured goods ranked first in the South and was worth twice the value of its agricultural production. But the emigration of native sons and daughters left a significant void in the state's development. The southern tobacco-growing counties had fewer whites in 1860 than in 1790. Charles and St. Mary's counties lost an estimated $1.5 million in property and cash due to migration in one 18-month period (1836–1837). The net loss was so great that one-third of native-born Marylanders lived outside their home state. What population gain there was came as a result of foreign immigration and interstate migration to Baltimore and to the northwestern counties. The agricultural revival after 1840 stemmed the tide of emigration as demands for grains, tobacco, seafood, coal, and industrial products kept many of the young and industrious in the state. Yet, for the first century and a half of statehood, Maryland's relative population position in both the Union and the South declined.

Saving the state from an absolute decline in population was the rapid growth of Baltimore. By

1860 its population was 212,000, and combined with the surrounding Baltimore County it comprised 40 percent of the state's population. Besides its extensive manufacturing interests, the metropolis was the center of wholesaling, shipping, and culture for a region including the Susquehanna Valley, Shenandoah Valley, and Chesapeake Bay. With a fourth of its population foreign born (Germans, Irishmen, Englishmen, and Scots in that order of size) and a sixth colored, it was the only southern city of such a heterogeneous composition.

This was the golden age of industrial and commercial magnates whose names are still bywords in the state: Robert Gilmor, Jr. (1774–1848), merchant; Johns Hopkins (1795–1873), merchant, industrialist, financier, and philanthropist; George Peabody (1764–1834) and Robert Garrett (1783–1857), both merchant-financiers; and the latter's son John Work Garrett (1820–1884), railroad developer.

To continue expansion, Baltimoreans backed a multitude of projects designed to promote interior communications and trade. In particular the Susquehanna & Tidewater Canal (completed 1840), Baltimore & Susquehanna Railroad (constructed 1832–1854), Chesapeake & Delaware Canal (completed 1829), Chesapeake & Ohio Canal (constructed to Cumberland in 1850), and Baltimore & Ohio Railroad (completed to Wheeling in 1853) brought about a transportation revolution that bound Maryland as much to the Middle Atlantic states as it did to the South.

Avant-garde cultural developments usually occur in places of economic prosperity. Baltimore was no exception to this rule. It was the center of an extensive publishing industry headed by such newspapers as the BALTIMORE AMERICAN (founded 1799), *Patriot* (1812), BALTIMORE SUN (1837), and *Clipper* (1939). German-language publications were extensive in number and importance in Baltimore, Frederick, and Hagerstown. Leading literary periodicals included the *Baltimore Monument* (1836–1840) and the *Saturday Visitor* (1832–1847). The latter journal's most famous article, "MS. Found in a Bottle," came from the pen of the most notable literary figure of the metropolis, EDGAR ALLAN POE. Although the latter's eccentric life provided a considerable number of romantic legends for the city, probably more important for the time was JOHN PENDLETON KENNEDY (1797–1870), Poe's mentor. From the beginning, Kennedy cast his lot with the restless, acquisitive, cosmopolitan life of Baltimore while his novels romanticized the Old South. Maryland's literary sons also included two of the country's most noted glorifiers of the revolutionary patriots, Reverend MASON LOCKE WEEMS and WILLIAM WIRT. On the stage of the Holliday Street Theater, packed houses saw everything from *Hamlet* to the latest trivial comedy.

Despite Baltimore's cosmopolitanism and the fact that nearly half its Negroes were free in 1860, Maryland's geographic location below the Mason-Dixon Line forced most Americans to look upon it as a southern state. Reinforcing this southernness was a political structure allowing the eastern and southern counties to dominate the scene despite their declining population.

By the 1830s the quest for a realignment of the constitutional structure from one that guaranteed the gentry's control of the government to one more closely resembling the ideals of egalitarian democracy was the major political issue. A complicated political impasse was reached between the Democrats and Whigs, which ended with a series of semireform compromises. After 1837 the governor was elected by popular vote, a third of the senate was chosen biennially by the electorate, the house of delegates was reapportioned to reflect population shifts more closely, and the governor's council was abolished. These changes plus a few additional concessions to Baltimore City were confirmed in the 1851 constitution. Still the political structure continued to give the counties a dominant role. County politics were often run by great families like the Howards of Anne Arundel, the Bowies of Prince George's and Montgomery, and the Goldsboroughs of Talbot and Dorchester. But recent studies show that it was neither kinship nor class that determined political developments. As always, personal inclination, ambition, and geographic location were significant factors in political orientation.

The internal political conflict of the northern and western counties against the southern and eastern ones reached its acme during the sectional crisis. Political party disintegration and reorganization in Maryland were typical of the rest of the country. One of the indications of the political troubles may be seen in the careers of HENRY WINTER DAVIS and Montgomery Blair (BLAIR FAMILY). The former rode the coattails of Know-Nothingism into Congress. Hating Democrats and slaveholders, he became the personification of Baltimore's abolitionism. Blair, a close confidant of President Abraham Lincoln, favored gradual, compensated emancipation. Despite their mutual dislike for one another, the two united with men like REVERDY JOHNSON and John W. Garrett to form a loose confederation of Republicans, war Democrats, and loyalists into a Unionist party. The principal adhesive for the organization was the hope of federal patronage and political influence. In the midst of the necessities of war, the Unionists forced through the constitution of 1864, which abolished slavery, denied the vote to Confederate sympathizers, and initiated a strong program of public education. Supported by Union troops and Lincoln's executive orders, the Republicans reconstructed the state during the war.

Redemption came with peace. Democrats regained their traditional control of Maryland politics and quickly pushed through the constitution of 1867, which accepted abolition but abolished the loyalty oath and canceled the progressive education provisions. With amendments, this document remains the fundamental law of the Old Line State. Although more concessions were made reflecting Baltimore City's increasing dominance, it never received the political power deserved by its percentage of population. When the federal courts forced a wholesale legislative reapportionment in the 1960s, it would be the suburban counties, not the city, that would benefit from a one-man, one-vote rule.

With the constitutional issue settled, the state continued its split personality. Economically it was a member of the Middle Atlantic states; politically and socially it was still southern. To those from south of the Potomac it was a "yankee" state; to those from north of the Mason-Dixon Line it was southern.

The Free State, 1867–1930. The nationalism of the state during the early years of the Republic greatly declined by the time of Republican ascendancy following the Civil War. For Marylanders these were years of internal decline and change, years when many citizens wanted to withdraw and turn their attention to local affairs. With the deaths of Johns Hopkins and John W. Garrett no new men of vision and risk-taking enterprise seemed to emerge. The banker's 6 percent became more important than the risk taking of the entrepreneur. Undoubtedly much of this attitude was caused by the fact that Maryland in general and Baltimore in particular suffered grievously during the Civil War years. The constant disruption of the port's ties with the Ohio Valley and the South resulted in a serious decline in trade with Britain, the Caribbean, and South America.

Immediately after the conflict, business leaders attempted to reestablish the old trade and to secure new commercial connections. In 1868 regular steamship commerce with Bremen launched Baltimore in the transatlantic freight and passenger trade. The Baltimore & Ohio Railroad erected its huge Locust Point and Canton wharves to accommodate this new business. These facilities, coupled with rail connections to Chicago in 1874 and its shorter route to the Midwest, gave the B & O a shipping advantage over the New York and Philadelphia railroads. By 1880 Baltimore established itself as the world's sixth largest port specializing in heavy, bulk cargo for transshipment to and from the South and the Middle West. This dependence on bulk goods contributed to the reestablishment of the state's IRON AND STEEL INDUSTRY at Sparrows Point, where today Bethlehem Steel operates the world's largest Tidewater steel plant.

All was not sweetness, however. New York gradually dominated the Brazilian coffee trade that had long been a mainstay of Baltimore commerce. The West Indian sugar trade declined rapidly after the four largest refineries went bankrupt in 1879. The tariff of 1869 cut off the copper trade with South America. Shipbuilding declined to the point that the port, which once built the magnificent Baltimore clippers, was forced to purchase 80 percent of its barkentines from Belfast, Maine.

The expanded European commerce also brought a wave of new immigration to the city and state. In 1860 roughly 6,000 foreigners landed. In 1868 this figure was above 10,000; in 1882 it rose to over 42,000; and in 1907, to 67,000. That year saw the largest single immigration wave into the state, and Baltimore stood third only to New York and Boston in the number of annual arrivals. Although most immigrants passed through the state for the West, in 1900 8 percent of the state's population was foreign born. Some 94,000 Marylanders were former aliens, over half of them from Germany and Austria. Other large segments of the state's foreign born came from Ireland, Russia, Britain, and Poland. Maryland had both the largest percentage and largest total number of immigrants in the South. This influx made Baltimore a city of heterogeneity not found elsewhere in the South. Ethnic groups speaking their native tongue crowded into self-made ghettos. In 1890 the entire German-American community was estimated at 100,000, a good portion of which normally spoke German and read the *Deutsche Correspondent*. Other foreign-language journals catered to diverse ethnic tastes.

In the rest of the state the economic picture was much the same. Changing patterns of agriculture, fishing, and mining brought some prosperity and redistribution of the wealth, but the outlying counties were in a general state of decline. On the whole, major population increases were in the

Baltimore area; other areas either remained relatively static or actually declined. Despite the immigration rate, the relative population position of Maryland in relation to the rest of the South and the nation continued to decline. This trend continued until the 1930s.

The Eastern Shore was traversed by railroads, which brought truck gardens into importance as suppliers to Philadelphia and New York. The "immense protein factory" that was the Chesapeake Bay provided perch, oysters, and crabs for the whole East Coast. From May to October the bay area had one great crab feast, and from November to April oysters were in season. Men like Albanns Phillips (?–1949) of Cambridge, owner of the Phillips Packing Company, dominated the local economic and political scene. The use of the bay as a seaway, sewer, and playground—combined with destructive fishing techniques and a failure of cooperation among the oystermen, fishermen, and conservationists—resulted in a decline in the oyster catch of from 14 million bushels in 1875 to 1 million bushels in 1963. The fish catch dropped from 64 million pounds in 1890 to 17 million pounds in 1929. Conservation efforts since then have brought the total up to over 300 million pounds in 1966. Throughout this century there has been a steady decline in the number of persons engaged in the bay fishing, and there was a net decline in the industry's economic impact on the shore. The crab catch, on the other hand has grown well during the twentieth century. Although there are wide fluctuations due to dramatic shifts in crab population, the industry is on a solid foundation.

Southern Maryland also continued to lose population as its continued dependence upon tobacco brought little prosperity. The western portion of the state grew rapidly and prospered greatly due to the transportation revolution and the rise of extractive industries, especially COAL MINING. The peak year of production was reached in 1907 with 5,532,000 tons mined. It declined to a low of 648,000 tons in 1951 and rose to 1,789,000 tons in 1973. In the latter year virtually all the coal was stripmined, since only two underground mines remained. Significant long-term economic revival of the region from coal production is doubtful because of limited reserves and fewer employment opportunities in surface mines.

Strikes by both railroaders and miners of the western counties became increasingly common and bitter. The Baltimore & Ohio strike of 1877 and the soft-coal miners' strikes of 1894 and 1922 were especially momentous in the state's history. Their occurrence marks the real beginning of or-

ganized labor. Economically, Maryland now faced problems in this regard well before its fellow southern states.

The traditional grain cultivation in the central counties declined as competition from the Great Plains made such farming less profitable. Instead the region turned to hay and fodder for the horses of Washington and Baltimore as well as to dairying for the same cities. By the 1960s light industry moved into the Frederick-Hagerstown area.

Political dominance remained with the Democratic party, which demonstrated an adaptability allowing it to move with the political winds. Its leadership slowly changed from Bourbon REDEEMERS to machine spoilsmen to mild Progressives as the political climate shifted. Despite the taint of Reconstruction *à la* the 1864 constitution, the Republican party remained a strong minority force combining the Negroes, western Marylanders, and Baltimore Whigs. The Democrats, however, were able to maintain almost continuous control of the governor's mansion and the statehouse.

After less than a decade of direction, the elitist Democrats who wrote the constitution of 1867 were pushed aside by a new force within the party. Under the leadership of I. Freeman Rasin (1833–1907) of Baltimore and ARTHUR PUE GORMAN of Howard County, the Democratic party ruled and misruled the state except for rare instances when the Republicans were briefly given the reins of power. Rasin controlled both the slum and elite wards of the metropolis while serving as clerk of the court of common pleas. Gorman, from his position as president of the Chesapeake & Ohio Canal Company (by then a state-controlled corporation), dispensed patronage that eventually gave him control of the various county organizations. The combination of Rasin and Gorman, plus the recipients of the vast array of appointive plums they controlled, resulted in a group variously termed "the Organization" or "the Ring."

The major countervailing power against this combination was the two major railroads, the Baltimore & Ohio and the Pennsylvania. Usually the Ring was able to play one off against the other. For the most part it kept taxes low, services few, and profiteering rampant. Only a combination of dissident Democrats, Baltimore *Sun*, Baltimore & Ohio Railroad money, and effective Republican candidates routed the Democrats in the elections of 1895 and 1897. The governorship, both houses of the assembly, and the Baltimore mayoralty all fell to the opposition. Gorman lost his U.S. Senate seat from 1897 to 1902.

By 1900 the Ring returned to power but confronted a new generation of Democrats who challenged the traditional leadership. New men like Isidor Rayner of Baltimore and Francis Preston Blair Lee of Montgomery County moved to the fore, and the whole Progressive urge demanded public services that had hardly existed earlier. Here, as in the rest of the South, PROGRESSIVISM meant a public service commission, better educational facilities, and legalized segregation. To many Marylanders it also meant an end to the favoritism and alleged corruption of the Ring.

While Gorman returned to the Senate and Rasin controlled the Baltimore Courthouse, the appearance of the Ring's restoration belied the reality of new leadership. Men of the new and old Democratic party combined for the final implementation of SEGREGATION. Although separate education began in 1872, rigid segregation did not begin until after the restoration of 1900, when the Ring seized the Negro issue in an attempt to curb a principal source of Republican votes and the Progressives employed it to keep the black in his place while they used white power to secure reform. For the first time Jim Crow legislation appeared in the statute books. The culmination of this onslaught came with the Poe amendment of 1905. Designed to restrict Negro voting by a literacy test and a GRANDFATHER CLAUSE, the amendment threatened not only Negroes but also the immigrants of Baltimore. Charles J. Bonaparte led the Republicans, in an alliance with the *Sun* and others who feared "bossism," in a reform league that ended in the amendment's resounding defeat. Rasin was noncommittal about the amendment, a fact that undoubtedly aided the amendment's opponents.

The Progressive age in Maryland was hardly a time of radicalism but rather one of mild reform. Leaders like Rayner, Lee, and ALBERT C. RITCHIE were more in the ideological tradition of the past than of the future. They continued a growing characterization of Maryland as "the Free State." This apellation described an attitude reflecting the drift away from the nationalism that had characterized the state before the Civil War. Perhaps it was Republican control in Washington that no longer granted the bounties of public works that the prewar Democrats and Whigs variously supported; perhaps it was the growing dependence upon private enterprise rather than the publicly supported economic development of the earlier period; perhaps it was the desire to keep federal hands off the touchy Negro issue; or perhaps it was just a general political apathy. Whatever the causes, Maryland no longer supported the nationalism of pre–Civil War years but instead took pride in its belief in states' rights, separation of powers, and economy in government.

But economy in government and demands for educational, highway, consumer protection, and conservation services did not necessarily go hand in hand. They constituted a dilemma for those desiring to reform state government. The quest for a public education system of merit was long delayed by the rural counties' fear of excessive taxation. From 1840 to 1850 the number of white illiterates doubled, but not until 1868 was a general school law passed providing county districts for white-only education. In 1872 colored schools came into being. With the overthrow of the Ring in 1895, change came more rapidly: free textbooks, minimum salary schedules, a teachers' pension system, standardized certification procedures, and improved Negro education all occurred before the First World War. Under Governor Ritchie's long tenure, 1920 to 1935, the much heralded "Maryland plan" brought reforms at the primary, secondary, and collegiate levels. The beginning of school busing resulted in a dramatic increase in high school enrollments. By 1928 expenditures for public education reached $3.9 million, and they constituted 11 percent of the state budget.

For years Maryland depended upon private education or individual initiative to provide the state with trained intellectual leadership. For some time there had been a private University of Maryland but it consisted mostly of a loose confederation of professional colleges. In 1920 the legislature merged the professional schools in Baltimore and the state agricultural college (which had already acquired schools of engineering, arts and sciences, education, home economics, and graduate education) into the University of Maryland. Thus the state set out to build an institution similar to those of the Middle West and a few southern states. While JOHNS HOPKINS UNIVERSITY and St. John's College provided the nation with education for an elite, the university began its route toward educational democracy.

Ritchie's shadow dominated Maryland conservatism. A Baltimore-bred aristocrat of ability and integrity, Ritchie rose through the public service commission to become a figure representative of the Bourbon ideal. Thrice the subject of a boomlet for the presidency, Ritchie turned the Democratic party away from the Ring's corruption into the Organization's honesty, operating a system similar to the BYRD MACHINE of Virginia. The Ritchie administrations reformed the state government, cleaned up a corrupt Baltimore police department, helped private investors build a power system, maintained labor peace by a judicious application of power on both sides, and reduced taxes 30 percent. He made both himself and his Free State ideology more popular by refusing to cooperate with the enforcement of the Eighteenth Amendment because it represented an unwarranted interference in Maryland's internal affairs.

But the GREAT DEPRESSION brought an end to the age of the Free State. No longer could a single state cope with the demands placed upon it. In 1930 the electorate voted to convene a new constitutional convention. The assemblymen failed to provide for such a body both then and in 1950 because they knew that their own seats would be endangered. This disregard by the Organization of popular demands and an animosity between the governor and the NEW DEAL contributed to the defeat of Ritchie in 1935. The voters approved of Franklin Roosevelt although the Organization and the Sunpapers did not.

The triumph of suburbia, 1930–1975. For the first time since the emergence of Baltimore City in the late eighteenth century, a major demographic shift in population occurred in the middle third of this century. Baltimore, Anne Arundel, Prince George's, and Montgomery counties began to expand in population at significantly high rates while the metropolitan city remained either relatively stable or declined. In 1910 half the state's population was urbanized; by 1960 it reached 73 percent. Maryland became one of the fastest growing states in the Union, exceeded in the South only by Florida.

The population rise in the suburban counties was unprecedented in the state's history. Between 1930 and 1940, Baltimore and Anne Arundel counties rose 24 percent; between 1940 and 1950, some 72 percent; and between 1950 and 1960, another 80 percent. Growing even more rapidly were the two Washington, D.C., suburban counties, Montgomery and Prince George's. They rose some 60 percent in the depression decade, another 108 percent during WORLD WAR II, and over 94 percent in the 1950s. All four counties plus Howard, Harford, Carroll, and Frederick continued rapid expansion in the 1960s. In 1970 the estimated state population was 3,922,000, ranking it eighteenth in the Union, of which 77 percent could be classified suburban. During the 1970s the growth rate declined rapidly, so that the state's increase was less than half the 23.5 percent annual growth rate of the 1960s.

Not only was the population expanding in numbers, it also rose in quality. In the 1960s Maryland had the largest number of physicians per capita in the South and the fifth highest nationally. Its primary and secondary educational system contained districts that were the envy of the nation. Prince George's County had the country's largest suburban school system. Montgomery County boasted the highest per capita income in the nation. With 81 percent of their houses containing plumbing in 1960, Marylanders were the best housed of all southerners.

The fact that the state had never undergone the local political subdivision of power that characterized the Jacksonian era made its county governments and school boards more effective (but no less susceptible to corruption and favoritism) in dealing with the problems of suburbanization than many localities throughout the nation. Home rule or charter government has been accepted by Baltimore City (1915) and Montgomery (1948), Baltimore (1956), Anne Arundel (1964), and Wicomico (1964) and Harford (1972) counties. Multigovernment cooperation emerged with such agencies as the Baltimore Metropolitan Council, the Washington Suburban Sanitary Commission, and the Maryland–National Capital Park and Planning Commission.

Suburbanization fed upon itself, demanding ever more changes. The automobile revolution forced the first major transportation change since the building of the railroads. The construction of interstate highways, the Washington Beltway, and the Baltimore-Washington Parkway have been graphic examples of the transformation of the Western Shore. For the future, planners talk of an outer beltway around both Washington and Baltimore. Equally significant has been the building of two connections to the Eastern Shore—the Chesapeake Bay Bridge (completed 1952) and the Chesapeake Bay Bridge-Tunnel (completed 1964)—providing ease of access, which has modified the region's traditional isolation. Not only has Baltimore been affected by the automotive transportation network, but it also has been linked to the world with the finishing of Friendship International Airport south of the city.

Suburbanization has created problems. It has been accompanied by the usual sprawl associated with the megalopolis stretching from Boston to Richmond: rising crime rates, high taxes, spoilage of natural beauty, irresponsible profiteering, lack of foresight, and racial and economic segregation. It is heartening to note, however, that one Marylander, James W. Rouse, has taken it upon himself to develop one of the nation's first new cities. From the crossroads community of Columbia in Howard County is rising a city of 125,000 planned to meet the needs of the twenty-first century. Many hope this new departure in urban planning will be the harbinger of future America.

Meanwhile, Maryland's relative position as the industrial leader of the South has declined greatly. Despite its long tradition of investment in such heavy industries as shipbuilding and steel manufacture, the state is being outstripped by the South in heavy industrial development. Newer investment opportunities, however, are opening up in chemical, electronic, and space industries, which have higher wages and require greater education for employees than do the traditional manufacturers. For instance, space technology places the state in competition with California, Texas, Florida, and Massachusetts for income from this new field.

While suburbia grew, new problems emerged regarding the central city of Baltimore. Two major areas were involved: revitalization of economic life in the downtown area and the place of the Negro in the community. To solve the first problem, extensive construction was made in an automobile transportation network through and around the city. The Baltimore Harbor Tunnel, the Baltimore Beltway, and the Jones Falls Expressway caused a major transformation of traffic patterns. During the 1960s the development through private and public funds of the Charles Center project constituted the first major construction downtown since the aftermath of the fire of 1904. It gave the city architectural gems that are the envy of the world.

But bricks and cement were not about to solve the problems emerging from the increasing concentration of Negroes in the core city. Not only were these people repressed by typical Jim Crow laws, but they also faced the rigid ethnic ghettos of Baltimore, which were more typical of northern than southern cities. Final emancipation came slowly as the result of World War II, Korean and Vietnamese military experiences, Supreme Court decisions, and a grudging admission by the state government of Negro equality. In 1967 school integration was virtually complete, except that the white flight to the suburbs threatened to resegregate the Baltimore City schools. The legislature repealed the antimiscegenation law of 1661 and passed the first statewide open-housing law in the South. But for many Negro activists this was too little, too late. They demanded more than tokenism and equality by requesting redress for the effects of three centuries of discrimination. Negro frustrations burst forth in rioting and looting in Baltimore and Cambridge in 1968. Still, Maryland, Delaware, and Florida were the only southern states to increase in Negro population in the postwar decades, and blacks played ever-larger roles in the state's legislature and congressional delegation.

The net effect of the suburban and Negro revolutions was a profound change in the nature of Maryland government. The Free State ideal declined in importance as thousands of citizens looked to the federal government for employment and millions hoped Washington would solve problems of transportation, housing, welfare, education, pollution, and defense. No longer was the federal government a menace in Washington; it was an inhabitant and employer in Maryland. A growing federal bureaucracy meant a growing Maryland. Among the major federal offices affecting this attitude were not only those in the District of Columbia but also such Maryland installations as the National Institutes of Health, the Bureau of Standards, the Atomic Energy Commission, Ft. George G. Meade, the Agriculture Research Center, the Goddard Space Flight Center, Andrews Air Force Base, Aberdeen Proving Grounds, Patuxent Naval Air Station, and the U.S. Naval Academy.

Post–World War II politics involved a three-way conflict among conservative and liberal Democrats and the opportunistic Republicans. Although Marylanders demanded better education, highways, and other public services, they continued to resent their cost. When a Democratic governor backed a sales tax to provide needed services, outraged voters turned to the Republican candidate (who did not repeal the sales tax). Because the suburban counties have never voted in similar patterns, they have never held corporately the same power that the rather consistent voter behavior in Baltimore City secured. Instead there has been a rather pronounced conflict between Baltimore's suburbia and Washington's suburbia. The best examples of this conflict occur in such elections as the 1966 Democratic gubernatorial primary (Baltimore County supported George P. Mahoney's Your Home Is Your Castle campaign in contrast to the Washington suburbs) and the 1968 constitutional ratification vote (Montgomery and Prince George's counties were the only ones to back the new document). Led by maverick Democrat Mahoney, the conservative wing of the party brought together Baltimore City and County ethnic voters and others frightened by Negro advances, federal expansion, and rapid change to frustrate the trend toward New Frontier liberalism. On the other hand, the liberals possessed enough votes to deny most general elections to an unacceptable conservative. When the Democratic candidate was too objectionable, the Republican party usually won an election. Thus the major Re-

MARYLAND POPULATION, 1790–1970

| Year | Total | White | Nonwhite | | % Growth | Rank | |
			Slave	Free		U.S.	South
1790	319,728	208,649	103,036	8,043		6	3
1800	341,548	216,326	105,635	19,587	6.8	7	4
1810	380,546	235,117	111,502	53,927	11.4	8	5
1820	407,350	260,223	107,327	39,730	7.0	10	6
1830	447,040	291,108	102,994	52,938	9.7	11	7
1840	470,019	318,204	89,737	62,078	5.1	15	8
1850	583,034	417,943	90,368	74,723	24.0	17	10
1860	687,049	515,918	87,189	83,942	17.8	19	11
1870	780,894	605,497	175,397		13.7	20	10
1880	934,943	724,693	210,250		19.7	23	12
1890	1,042,390	826,493	215,897		11.5	27	13
1900	1,188,044	952,424	235,620		14.0	26	13
1910	1,295,346	1,062,639	232,707		9.0	27	13
1920	1,449,661	1,204,737	244,924		11.9	28	14
1930	1,631,526	1,354,170	277,356		12.5	28	14
1940	1,821,244	1,518,481	302,763		11.6	28	15
1950	2,343,001	1,954,975	388,026		28.6	24	11
1960	3,100,689	2,573,919	526,770		32.3	21	10
1970	3,922,399	3,194,888	727,511		26.5	18	8

MARYLAND GOVERNORS

Governor	Party	Term
PROPRIETARY		
Leonard Calvert		1634–1644
Richard Ingle		1644–1646
Edward Hill		1646
Leonard Calvert		1646–1647
Thomas Greene		1647–1649
William Stone		1649–1652
parliamentary commissioners		1652
parliamentary commissioners		1654–1657
Josias Fendall		1657–1660
Philip Calvert		1660–1661
Charles Calvert		1661–1676
Jesse Wharton		1676
Cecil Calvert		1676
Thomas Notley		1676–1679
Charles Calvert, 3rd Lord Baltimore		1679–1684
Benedict Leonard Calvert		1684–1688
William Joseph		1688–1689
John Coode		1689–1690
Nehemiah Blackiston		1690–1692
ROYAL		
Sir Lionel Copley		1692–1693
Sir Thomas Lawrence		1693
Sir Edmund Andros		1693
Nicholas Greenberry		1693–1694
Sir Edmund Andros		1694
Sir Thomas Lawrence		1694
Sir Francis Nicholson		1694–1699
Nathaniel Blackiston		1699–1702
Thomas Tench		1702–1704
John Seymour		1704–1709
Edward Lloyd		1709–1714
John Hart		1714–1715
PROPRIETARY		
John Hart		1715–1720
Thomas Brooke		1720
Charles Calvert		1720–1727
Benedict Leonard Calvert		1727–1731
Samuel Ogle		1731–1732
Charles Calvert, 5th Lord Baltimore		1732–1733
Samuel Ogle		1733–1742
Thomas Bladen		1742–1747

Governor	Party	Term
Samuel Ogle		1747–1752
Benjamin Tasker		1752–1753
Horatio Sharpe		1753–1769
Robert Eden		1769–1776
Convention and Council of Safety		1776–1777
STATE		
Thomas Johnson		1777–1779
Thomas Sim Lee		1779–1782
William Paca		1782–1785
William Smallwood		1785–1788
John Eager Howard	Fed.	1788–1791
George Plater	Fed.	1791–1792
Thomas Sim Lee	Fed.	1792–1794
John H. Stone	Fed.	1794–1797
John Henry	Fed.	1797–1798
Benjamin Ogle	Fed.	1798–1801
John Francis Mercer	Fed.	1801–1803
Robert Bowie	Dem.-Rep.	1803–1806
Robert Wright	Dem.-Rep.	1806–1809
Edward Lloyd	Dem.-Rep.	1809–1811
Robert Bowie	Dem.-Rep.	1811–1812
Levin Winder	Fed.	1812–1816
Charles Ridgely	Fed.	1816–1819
Charles Goldsborough	Fed.	1819
Samuel Sprigg	Dem.-Rep.	1819–1822
Samuel Stevens, Jr.	Dem.-Rep.	1822–1826
Joseph Kent	Dem.-Rep.	1826–1829
Daniel Martin	Anti-Jackson	1829–1830
Thomas King Carroll	Jacksonian Dem.	1830–1831
Daniel Martin	Anti-Jackson	1831
George Howard	Anti-Jackson	1831–1833
James Thomas	Anti-Jackson	1833–1836
Thomas W. Veazey	Whig	1836–1839
William Grason	Dem.	1839–1842
Francis Thomas	Dem.	1842–1845
Thomas G. Pratt	Whig	1845–1848
Philip Francis Thomas	Dem.	1848–1851
Enoch Louis Lowe	Dem.	1851–1854
Thomas Watkins Ligon	Dem.	1854–1858
Thomas Holliday Hicks	Am.	1858–1862
Augustus W. Bradford	Unionist	1862–1866
Thomas Swann	Unionist, later Dem.	1866–1869
Oden Bowie	Dem.	1869–1872

Governor	Party	Term
William Pinkney Whyte	Dem.	1872–1874
James Black Groome	Dem.	1874–1876
John Lee Carroll	Dem.	1876–1880
William T. Hamilton	Dem.	1880–1884
Robert M. McLane	Dem.	1884–1885
Henry Lloyd	Dem.	1885–1888
Elihu E. Jackson	Dem.	1888–1892
Frank Brown	Dem.	1892–1896
Lloyd Lowndes	Rep.	1896–1900
John Walter Smith	Dem.	1900–1904
Edwin Warfield	Dem.	1904–1908
Austin L. Crothers	Dem.	1908–1912
Phillips L. Goldsborough	Rep.	1912–1916
Emerson C. Harrington	Dem.	1916–1920
Albert C. Ritchie	Dem.	1920–1935
Harry W. Nice	Rep.	1935–1939
Herbert R. O'Conor	Dem.	1939–1947
William P. Lane, Jr.	Dem.	1947–1951
Theodore R. McKeldin	Rep.	1951–1959
J. Millard Tawes	Dem.	1959–1967
Spiro T. Agnew	Rep.	1967–1969
Marvin Mandel	Dem.	1969–1979
Harry R. Hughes	Dem.	1979–

publican winners of recent years—Harry W. Nice, Theodore R. McKeldin, SPIRO T. AGNEW, and Charles Mathias—owed their positions largely to Democratic liberals. Republican success has been tied to the nomination of moderates rather than reactionaries.

The Democrats never succumbed to Republican dominance largely because they refused to stand on principle; there was no serious cry of "massive resistance" or "never" during the 1950s. Instead, the Democrats adapted to a pragmatic state of gradual change. Both the Negro and the suburbanite capitalized upon Supreme Court decisions to force desegregation and reapportionment on a grudging old guard. The modification of the state's ruling party was carried on mainly by men like William Preston Lane, Jr., whose governorship saw the enactment of a sales tax; elderly J. Millard Tawes, whose governship marked the gradual dominance of suburban control; and young Senator Joseph D. Tydings, probably the personification of the new generation in Maryland politics. At the end of the 1960s, the Democrats controlled the governor's mansion, the statehouse, and most courthouses. The congressional delegation was evenly split between the parties, but it was decidedly liberal in voting trends.

Prodded by the Supreme Court and the liberals, Tawes brought about the beginnings of constitutional reform. The constitutional convention of 1967–1968 rewrote the century-old fundamental law. It gave home rule to all counties, a decentralization necessary since 46 percent of the legislature's work had been devoted to county problems.

It inaugurated a strong, independent executive branch, thereby eliminating legislative dominance of the government. It wrote a bill of rights incorporating the latest in civil liberty guarantees, made most local officials appointive rather than elective, and lowered the voting age to nineteen. Liberalism had its limits, however. It was just too progressive a step for the state to take. Riots in Baltimore just before the election, student demonstrations that made young people look unsuited for political participation, fear of rising taxes, and an unwillingness to try the unknown left Marylanders with enough opposition to reject the document 366,000 to 283,000.

Thus, as it enters the last quarter of this century, Maryland remains in a position of representing both the hopes and fears of a new South. It prides itself on being "America in miniature." Part big city, part suburb, part rural; stretching from seacoast to mountain; industrial, commercial, governmental, and agricultural: Maryland remains as it has since the rise of Baltimore—an enigma to those who want to label it northern or southern, liberal or conservative.

Manuscripts and printed primary sources. Two principal depositories are Maryland Historical Society, Baltimore, and Hall of Records, St. John's College. See A. J. Pedley, *Manuscripts Collections of Maryland Historical Society* (1968); and, for archival, land, and church records, see *Publications of Hall of Records Commission* (17 vols. to date; 1943–). Other institutions with notable holdings are Baltimore Cathedral Archives (see J. T. Ellis, *Catholic Historical Review*, 1946); Peabody Institute Library and Enoch Pratt Public Library, Baltimore; Johns Hopkins; University of Virginia; New York Public Library; and University of North Carolina. Maryland State Library, Annapolis, has best collection of state governmental publications. *Archives of Maryland* (71 vols. to date 1883–) contain considerable material on legislative, executive, and court proceedings of colonial period. This series is being expanded to include materials from early statehood years. Maryland Historical Society's *Fund Publications* (1867–1901) contain a number of significant items, especially colonial literary reprints. Microfilmed collections include the papers of Charles Carroll of Carrollton, Robert Goodloe Harper, and Benjamin Henry Latrobe.

Contemporary accounts. Observations of Maryland life begin with Father A. White, *Lord Baltimore's Plantation* (1634); C. C. Hall (ed.), *Narratives of Early Maryland* (1910); E. Cook, *Sot-weed Factor* (1704); and Dr. A. Hamilton, *Intinerarium* (1906, 1948). Excellent Loyalist commentaries are J. Boucher, *American Revolution* (1797, 1967) and *Reminiscences* (1925, 1967); and W. Eddis, *Letters* (1792, 1969). J. V. L. McMahon, *Government of Maryland* (1831, 1968), provides insight into evolution of Maryland politics. For later political developments, see E. S. Riley, *General Assembly of Maryland, 1635–1904* (1905, 1970); F. R. Kent, *Maryland Politics* (1911); P. M. Winchester, *Men of Maryland* (1923); and C. J. Bonaparte, *Defects in Public Education* (1885). Interesting observations appear in H. L. Mencken's trilogy *Happy Days* (1940), *Newspaper Days* (1941), and *Heathen Days* (1943).

Histories. No well-rounded general survey of Maryland history exists. M. L. Radoff (ed.), *Old Line State* (1956, 1971); and R. Walsh and W. L. Fox (eds.), *Maryland* (1974), contain articles of varying quality describing the state's growth.

Excellent monographs covering early developments include N. D. Mereness, *Proprietary Province* (1901); M. P. Andrews, *Founding of Maryland* (1933); L. G. Carr and D. W. Jordan, *Maryland's Revolution, 1689–1692* (1974); D. M. Owings, *Patronage in Colonial Maryland* (1953); C. A. Barker, *Revolution in Maryland* (1940, 1967); H. B. Adams, *Maryland's Influence upon Land Cessions* (1885, 1968); D. C. Skaggs, *Roots of Maryland Democracy* (1973); R. Hoffman, *Revolution in Maryland* (1973); and P. A. Crowl, *Maryland and Revolution* (1943). Latter is part of Johns Hopkins University Studies in Historical and Political Science (1883–); consult for relevant material. Little major work has been written on political developments since the Revolution, but W. J. Evitts, *Maryland from 1850 to 1861* (1974); J. H. Baker, *Maryland Political Parties, 1858 to 1870* (1973); and C. L. Wagant, *Mighty Revolution* (1964), are excellent for Civil War era. J. B. Crooks, *Urban Progressivism in Baltimore* (1968), provides introduction to this century's politics.

Nationally oriented studies making important comments on the state's early development include D. S. Lovejoy, *Glorious Revolution in America* (1972); J. T. Main, *Upper House* (1967) and *Political Parties* (1973); D. H. Fischer, *Revolution of American Conservatism* (1965); T. B. Alexander, *Sectional Stress* (1967); and R. P. McCormick, *Second American Party System* (1966). Only early volumes of *History of the South* series include more than passing references to Maryland.

J. H. Fenton, *Politics in Border States* (1957), provides observations on recent politics, but best analyses are in Studies in Government series published (1946–65) by University of Maryland's Bureau of Governmental Research. These thoroughly researched pamphlets combined with *Report of Constitution Convention Commission* (1967) and A. Rosenthal, *Strengthening Maryland Legislature* (1968), are indispensable source books and scholarly introductions to state and local government. F. F. White, Jr., *Governors of Maryland* (1970), is survey without much analysis. The biennially published *Maryland Manual* is useful for recent governmental developments and organization.

Among the better works on economic affairs are A. P. Middleton, *Tobacco Coast* (1953); B. W. Bond, *Quit-Rent Systems* (1919, 1965); E. I. McCormac, *White Servitude in Maryland* (1904); V. W. Brown, *Annapolis, 1748–1775* (1964); A. O. Craven, *Soil Exhaustion* (1926, 1965); E. C. Papenfuse, *Annapolis Merchants, 1763–1805* (1975); P. L. Payne and L. E. David, *Savings Bank of Baltimore* (1956); J. W. Livingood, *Philadelphia-Baltimore Trade Rivalry* (1947); W. S. Sanderlin, *Chesapeake and Ohio Canal* (1946); R. D. Gray, *Chesapeake and Delaware Canal* (1967); J. Rubin, *Canal or Railroad?* (1961); E. Hungerford, *Baltimore and Ohio Railroad* (2 vols.; 1928); and T. C. J. Whedbee, *Port of Baltimore, 1828 to 1878* (1953). Considerable information is in R. B. Morris, *Government and Labor in Early America* (1946); D. T. Gilchrist (ed.), *Seaport Cities, 1790–1825* (1967); and B.

Hammond, *Banks and Politics* (1957). Good recent labor history is K. A. Harvey, *Best-Dressed Miners* (1969).

Important biographical studies are J. W. Foster and B. K. Manakee, *Lords Baltimore* (1961); A. C. Land, *Dulanys* (1955, 1968); E. H. Smith, *Charles Carroll* (1942); T. O. Hanley, *Charles Carroll* (1970); J. S. Pancake, *Samuel Smith* (1972); F. A. Cassell, *Samuel Smith* (1971); S. W. Bruchey, *Robert Oliver* (1956); P. S. Clarkson and R. S. Jett, *Luther Martin* (1970); P. P. Hill, *William Vans Murray* (1971); F. Parker, *George Peabody* (1971); W. Lewis, *Roger Brooke Taney* (1965); J. R. Lambert, *Arthur Pue Gorman* (1953); and E. F. Goldman, *Charles J. Bonaparte* (1943). F. F. Bierne, *Amiable Baltimoreans* (1951), covers many modern figures.

The cultural and intellectual history of Maryland is best seen in biographical analyses like R. R. Beirne and J. H. Scarff, *William Buckland, Architect* (1958); C. C. Sellers, *Charles Willson Peale* (2 vols.; 1939–47); T. F. Hamlin, *Benjamin Henry Latrobe* (1955); C. H. Bohner, *John Pendleton Kennedy* (1961); A. H. Quinn, *Edgar Allan Poe* (1941); D. C. Stenerson, *H. L. Mencken* (1971); and J. Tharpe, *John Barth* (1974). H. A. Williams, *A. Aubrey Bodine* (1971), is good analysis of outstanding photographer. J. A. L. Lemay, *Men of Letters* (1972), merits special attention by students of colonial literature, as does J. W. Reps, *Tidewater Towns* (1971), for colonial urban planning.

Three studies of journalism merit considerable attention, although they decline in quality from L. C. Wroth, *Printing in Colonial Maryland* (1922); to J. T. Wheeler, *Maryland Press, 1776–1790* (1938); and finally A. R. Minick, *Printing in Maryland, 1791–1800* (1949). All contain superb bibliographies of early Maryland imprints. Also see G. W. Johnson et al., *Sunpapers* (1937), for century of journalistic development and political comment.

Among better ethnic studies are D. Cunz, *Maryland Germans* (1948); and M. L. Callcott, *Negro in Maryland Politics, 1870–1912* (1969). Racial attitudes can be seen in P. Campbell, *Maryland in Africa* (1971); and in biographies of prominent blacks: S. A. Bedini, *Benjamin Banneker* (1972); and B. Quarles, *Frederick Douglass* (1948).

G. H. Callcott, *University of Maryland* (1966); and Hugh Hopkins, *Johns Hopkins University* (1960), cover higher education with insights into Maryland history. Religious history may be seen in such monographs as N. W. Rightmyer, *Maryland's Established Church* (1956); and J. T. Ellis, *Catholics in Colonial America* (1965). Excellent biography is Ellis, *James Cardinal Gibbons, 1834–1921* (2 vols.; 1952). Most other religious histories lack critical analysis. Two county histories are valuable: O. Tilghman, *Talbot County* (2 vols.; 1915, 1967); and G. Johnston, *Cecil County* (1881, 1967). L. J. Hienton, *Prince George's Heritage* (1972), does a fine analysis of that county's first century. V. R. Filby, *Savage* (1965), is unusually good treatment of rise and fall of a mill town.

Articles. No student can omit a detailed study of *Maryland Historical Magazine* (1906–) for the most complete scholarly analyses of the state's history. Unfortunately, no general index exists other than a card file in Maryland Historical Society. For other articles, see D. M. Brown and R. H. Duncan, *Maryland Historical Magazine* (Fall, 1974). For lists of theses and dissertations, see R. Duncan and D. M. Brown, *Master's Theses* *and Doctoral Dissertations on Maryland History* (1970); and R. J. Cox, *Maryland Historical Magazine* (June, 1978).

DAVID C. SKAGGS
Bowling Green State University

MARYLAND, UNIVERSITY OF (College Park, 20742), is a state-supported, coeducational institution with a total enrollment of almost 40,000 students. The present institution traces its origins to the formation in 1807 at Baltimore of the College of Medicine of Maryland. A proprietary school run by its faculty and supported by funds from a public lottery, the college became a university in 1812 with the addition of schools of divinity and law and, at least on paper, a college of arts and sciences. Although the three professional schools easily recruited both faculty and students, the university's uncertain finances and its inability to inaugurate an undergraduate college led the state legislature in 1826 to purchase the university from its faculty and to lodge control in a state-appointed board of trustees. To offer finally undergraduate levels of instruction, the board in 1830 purchased the already established Baltimore College (1798). Conflict between the board and the faculty of the medical college in particular was resolved in 1839, when the state relinquished its ties to the institution and returned ownership to the faculty. Throughout the rest of the nineteenth century the University of Maryland remained essentially a proprietary institution of several loosely linked colleges located in Baltimore.

Meanwhile, the state government grew increasingly interested in launching a public institution that would emphasize an agricultural curriculum. In 1856 the legislature chartered Maryland Agricultural College (later called Maryland State College) to be located outside Baltimore at College Park. This institution officially became tied to the federal system of land-grant colleges in 1864 and gained an AGRICULTURAL EXPERIMENT STATION under the Hatch Act in 1887. After fire destroyed much of the campus in 1912, rebuilding plans included a considerable expansion of the school's offerings, and interest in a merger with the university (still located in Baltimore) was renewed. In 1920, after complex negotiations and several false starts, arrangements were made for acquiring the University of Maryland with its main campus being located at College Park and with the schools of medicine, dentistry, law, pharmacy, and nursing in Baltimore.

See G. H. Callcott, *History of University of Maryland* (1966); and E. F. Cordell, *University of Maryland, 1807–1907* (2 vols.; 1907).

MARYLAND GAZETTE has been the name of four separate newspapers published in the state's capital, Annapolis. The first *Maryland Gazette* and the first newspaper published in the South was founded in 1727 by William Parks. After Parks moved to Williamsburg, Va., to begin the *Virginia Gazette*, the paper floundered and ceased publication in 1734. A second *Maryland Gazette* was established in 1745 by Jonas Green and, except for a suspension after enactment of the STAMP ACT (1764), continued publication until 1839. The tradition established by these first two *Gazettes* undoubtedly led a third paper, published between 1842 and 1862, to adopt the same name. In 1922 a fourth newspaper, one that had been in print since 1809. adopted the venerated name of its former competitors. Known as the *Maryland Republican* from 1809 to 1908 and then as the *Advertizer* from 1908 to 1922, the present version of the *Maryland Gazette* is normally published as a weekly newspaper but is issued semiweekly during sessions of the state legislature.

See W. White, *Journalism Quarterly* (Fall, 1958); Jonas Green's *Gazette* (1745–1839), on microfilm from Datamics, Inc., New York; and *Maryland Republican*, bound files (1821–40) at Library of Congress and microfilm (1809–) at Library of Congress.

MARYLAND HISTORICAL SOCIETY (201 W. Monument St., Baltimore, Md. 21201) was founded in 1844 and has a present membership of 4,500. It supports a museum in the 1847 Greek Revival Pratt House, which contains an impressive collection of Maryland furniture, principally of the Federal period. It also maintains an art gallery and a library of more than 70,000 volumes strong in local and genealogical history and large manuscript collections on the colonial, revolutionary, War of 1812, and Civil War periods. Numbering among them are the Calvert Papers and those of important military and political leaders, major holdings of business records, ship departures and arrivals, early Maryland newspapers, sheet music, and graphics. The society has published the quarterly *Maryland Historical Magazine* since 1906 and is especially interested in articles derived from its own manuscript collections. The magazine has a circulation of 4,700.

See *Manuscripts Collections of Maryland Historical Society* (1968); R. Manakee, *Maryland Historical Magazine* (March, 1965); R. J. Cox, (Dec., 1974); and R. S. Somerville, *Antiques* (March, 1975; May, 1976); and P. W. Filby, *Notes* (March, 1976).

MARYLAND TOLERATION ACT (1649) was originally hailed as a landmark in religious freedom, but recent historians have considered it to be a more limited step toward toleration. Although Maryland had offered shelter to Catholics from its founding, the colony had a Protestant majority. Concurrent with the English civil war, which threatened the CALVERT FAMILY's hold on the Maryland charter, the colony's Catholics and Protestants engaged in religious civil war. Governor Leonard Calvert had to flee and returned only with military aid from Virginia. Lord Baltimore, as proprietor, steered a neutral course by pressuring the Catholic clergy to give up land, appointing a Protestant governor, and offering refuge to Puritans forced from Virginia. In 1649 he sent the assembly a toleration act protecting all Christians, which the assembly apparently altered to include a number of penalties for Sabbath breaking, blasphemy, and religious name-calling. The act had a short life in factional Maryland, for Puritans overthrew the Calvert government in 1652 and repealed the Toleration Act in 1654, replacing it with one protecting Protestants. In 1658 Lord Baltimore regained control of Maryland, reinstated the act of 1649, and tried to restore harmony. Religious mistrust remained central in Maryland politics, however, and during the Glorious Revolution anti-Catholic forces repealed the act for a final time.

See W. F. Craven, *Southern Colonies in Seventeenth Century* (1949); G. Johnson, *Maryland Act of Religious Toleration* (1649); T. Hanley, *Their Rights and Liberties* (1939); old but unreplaced is B. Steiner, *Maryland During English Civil Wars* (1906–07) and *Maryland Under Commonwealth* (1911); and *Archives of Maryland* (1883–), contain many pertinent documents.

JOAN R. GUNDERSEN
St. Olaf College

MASON, GEORGE (1725–1792),

of Gunston Hall was a man, Thomas Jefferson wrote, "of the first order of greatness." He was also a "reluctant statesman," and this characteristic, the product of poor health and personal inclination, along with his opposition to the federal Constitution, has tended to place Mason's historical reputation below that of other revolutionary statesmen. But to his contemporaries Mason was known and respected for insights and skills displayed both before and after the momentous days of May and June, 1776, when he wrote the VIRGINIA DECLARATION OF RIGHTS and was the principal author of the Virginia constitution of 1776.

Mason was born into a family known for "wealth and leadership, talent and taste" (MASON FAMILY). Largely self-educated, he became so well versed in the law that he was frequently sought for legal advice even though he was not licensed as a lawyer. Despite his inclination to avoid public office, Mason did take time from management of extensive properties (75,000 acres in Virginia and the Ohio country) to serve as justice of the peace, vestryman, trustee for Alexandria (1754–1779), delegate to the Virginia house (1858–1761), and during the Revolution as a member of the council of safety. On several occasions, including the Philadelphia CONSTITUTIONAL CONVENTION, Mason spoke out against slavery, which he felt a malign influence "upon the Manners & Morals of our People." He never ceased his advocacy of the rights of man, but after the Revolution his concern that state governmental powers be protected against possible losses to central authority led him to oppose ratification of the federal Constitution.

See H. H. Miller, *George Mason* (1938, 1975); R. A. Rutland, *George Mason* (1961); R. A. Rutland (ed.), *Papers of Mason* (1970); and K. M. Rowland, *George Mason* (1892).

ALAN S. BROWN
Western Michigan University

MASON, JAMES MURRAY (1798–1871),

grandson of Revolutionary War patriot GEORGE MASON, graduated from the University of Pennsylvania (1818), then studied law at William and Mary. He established a law practice at Winchester in 1820 and served five years in Virginia's legislature (1826–1831). A member of Virginia's constitutional convention (1829), he took the part of the valley against his native Tidewater. An Andrew Jackson elector (1832), he later served a term in the U.S. House of Representatives (1837–1839). In the U.S. Senate (1847–1861) Mason chaired the Foreign Relations Committee for ten years and emerged as one of the most powerful senators. A strict constructionist Democrat and a follower of JOHN C. CALHOUN, he believed inevitable the clash between northern industrialism and southern agrarianism. He drafted the COMPROMISE OF 1850's fugitive slave law; then read enfeebled Calhoun's speech in the Senate debate that ensued. Mason was known as a hard worker, not as an author of clever speeches or pivotal legislation.

He resigned his Senate seat when Virginia seceded and shortly accepted appointments as Confederate diplomatic commissioner to England. He sailed with JOHN SLIDELL, who was on his way to France aboard the British mail steamer *Trent*. Seized by U.S. authorities, Mason and Slidell were released as part of the TRENT AFFAIR settlement. Mason served the Confederacy well in Britain until the war's end. He remained there until 1866, then lived in Canada until Andrew Johnson's amnesty proclamation (1868) provided him an opportunity to return to Virginia.

See V. Mason, *Public Life and Diplomatic Correspondence of James M. Mason* (1903). Virtually nothing else has been published on Mason. See F. L. Owsley, *King Cotton Diplomacy* (1931); bibliographic references to *Trent* affair; Calhoun's works; and Jefferson Davis' works. Diplomatic correspondence is in Pickett Papers and Mason Papers, Library of Congress.

ROBERT H. JONES
University of Akron

MASON, JOHN YOUNG (1799–1859), was born in Greensville County, Va. He was admitted to the Virginia bar in 1819. Finally settling in Southampton County in 1822, he practiced law profitably, was elected to the Virginia assembly in 1823, and was chosen a representative to the state constitutional convention in 1830. Running as a Democrat, he won election to Congress in 1831 and served three consecutive terms in the House. Mason resigned his seat in 1837 to become U.S. district judge for eastern Virginia. Then, on March 14, 1844, President JOHN TYLER appointed him secretary of the navy. And with the accession of JAMES K. POLK to the presidency, Mason was made attorney general in 1845 and secretary of the navy in 1846, conducting naval affairs during the Mexican War. Although regarded as an ardent expansionist, Mason opposed the annexation of Mexico. Retiring from the cabinet in 1849, he resumed the practice of law in Richmond, was elected to the constitutional convention of 1850, and became its presiding officer. Mason served as U.S. minister to France until his death. He signed, along with James Buchanan and Pierre Soulé, the famous OSTEND MANIFESTO of 1854.

See S. J. Bemis, *American Secretaries of State* (1928), V, VI; E. I. McCormac, *James K. Polk* (1922); K. J. Bauer, *Mexican War* (1974); R. F. Nicholas, *Franklin Pierce* (1931); A. A. Ettinger, *Pierre Soulé* (1932); and P. S. Klein, *James Buchanan* (1962).

J. MICHAEL QUILL
Viterbo College

MASON, LUCY RANDOLPH (1882–1959), was for 17 years (1937–1954) in charge of public relations for the Congress of Industrial Organizations in the Southeast. Her effectiveness as a labor negotiator in Operation Dixie, the CIO's organizing effort in the South, won for her in 1952 the annual Social Justice Award of the National Religion and Labor Foundation. In that year also appeared her *To Win These Rights: A Personal History of the CIO in the South*. Born in an Episcopal rectory in Fairfax County, Va., the daughter of the Reverend Landon Randolph and Lucy Ambler Mason, she was related to a number of Virginia's most distinguished families. Early in her career she began working to improve the lot of women, underprivileged children, and factory workers. Starting out as a secretary in a Richmond law office, she became active in the Richmond Equal Suffrage League and the League of Women Voters. She served as the first industrial secretary of the Richmond Young Women's Christian Association (1914–1918) and as its general secretary (1923–1932). For the next five years she was general secretary of the National Consumers' League. Upon joining the CIO in 1937 she moved to Atlanta, which remained her home until her death.

See L. R. Mason Papers, Duke University; New York *Times* (May 8, 1959); and Atlanta *Constitution* (May 9, 1959).

MATTIE UNDERWOOD RUSSELL
Duke University

MASON-DIXON LINE, traditionally recognized as the division between the South and the North, originated from a boundary controversy caused by ambiguities of the respective 1632 and 1681 charters of the proprietary colonies of Maryland and Pennsylvania. When William Penn acquired present-day Delaware in 1682, the precise demarcations of this region were equally unclear. The boundary issue was submitted to the English court of chancery in 1735, but it was not until 1760 that the Calvert and Penn families compromised and agreed to engage Charles Mason (1730–1787) and Jeremiah Dixon (?–1767), prominent English surveyors and astronomers, to determine the exact jurisdictions. Arriving in America in 1763, Mason and Dixon first calculated the eastern boundary of Maryland with Delaware. On the bases of complex computations, they subsequently fixed the border between Maryland and Pennsylvania at parallel $39°43'17.4''$ north, commencing at the Maryland-Delaware frontier. By 1767 they had surveyed westward approximately 230 miles, which (though they did not know it) extended approximately 32 miles beyond Maryland's limit. They proceeded no farther because of the threat of hostile Indians. Mason and Dixon marked each mile of their survey with English-quarried limestones (34 inches high, 12 inches wide, and 11 inches thick), every fifth one of which bore the crests of the Calvert and Penn families. In 1784 a subsequent commission continued the line westward to complete the survey between Pennsylvania and Virginia (now West Virginia). By the time of the MISSOURI COMPROMISE, all states north of this division had abolished slavery. As a result, the Mason-Dixon Line was soon popularly accepted as the boundary between the South and the North, a designation that still prevails. DIXIE, a term synonymous with the South, may have originated from a corruption of the Mason-Dixon Line.

See *Journal of Charles Mason and Jeremiah Dixon* (1969); and J. H. B. Latrobe, *History of Mason and Dixon's Line* (1855).

MARTIN HARDWICK HALL
University of Texas, Arlington

MASON FAMILY was an energetic family prominent among the early architects of the tobacco society that developed along the shores of the Potomac in the seventeenth and eighteenth centuries. The first Mason, George Mason I (1629–1686), immigrated to Virginia from Pershore, England, in 1652 and acquired lands in Westmoreland and Stafford counties, which, together with early political offices, laid the foundation for the family's estates and its political power in northern Virginia. His oldest son George Mason II (1660–1716) strengthened the family's political and social leadership in Stafford. With a dozen allied families, he contributed to the transition of northern Virginia from a frontier to a plantation economy. Through marriage to Mary Fowke he aligned the Mason family with Maryland Protestants in their struggle (1686–1688) against proprietary rule and subsequently fell heir to the vast Fowke estates in Maryland. His success in Indian affairs, tight control over the militia and county offices in Stafford, and later marriages into the Waugh and Taliaferro families established the Masons in a position of prominence in the northern Tidewater.

His oldest son George Mason III (1690–1735) solidified this position through careful husbandry and shrewd land investments. The third Mason also established some of the earliest trade connections with London tobacco merchants only to witness the attending consequence of planter debt that lasted until after the Revolution. Upon his death his wife Anne Thompson Mason, a strong and resourceful woman, administered the family's business until her oldest son, GEORGE MASON IV (1725–1792), attained his majority in 1746.

George Mason IV continued his family's inclination for business expansion especially in the West. He was one of the early members of the OHIO COMPANY and an advocate of internal improvements. In the 1750s and 1760s he sold lands in Stafford and acquired properties in Fairfax County, where he built stately Gunston Hall. Elected to the Virginia HOUSE OF BURGESSES in 1759, he took an influential stand against the British position. A leading figure in the CONSTITUTIONAL CONVENTION (1787), he campaigned against ratification of the Constitution. Prominent among his descendants were John Mason (1766–1849) and JAMES MURRAY MASON (1798–1871), lawyers and businessmen.

See P. C. Copeland and R. K. MacMaster, *Five George Masons* (1975); F. Harrison, *Landmarks of Old Prince William* (1924); K. M. Rowland, *Life of George Mason* (1964); R. A. Rutland (ed.), *Papers of George Mason* (1970); and C. Sydnor, *Gentlemen Freeholders* (1952).

JOHN A. TREON
Merrill Lynch, Pierce, Fenner & Smith, Minneapolis

MASSEY, JOHN EDWARD "PARSON" (1819–1901), a Baptist clergyman and politician, was born in Spotsylvania County, Va. After two years at the Baptist Seminary (now University of Richmond), he read for the law and in 1843 was admitted to the bar. Simultaneously he served as a preacher in the Shenandoah Valley region. Originally a Whig, Massey became a Democrat in 1854 and in 1860 an ardent secessionist. Although he did not participate militarily in the Civil War, he supported the Confederacy by raising foodstuffs and buying bonds. After serving two terms in the Virginia house of delegates (1873–1877), he was elected to the state senate in 1877. His opposition to the funding act passed by the REDEEMERS earned him the title "Father of the READJUSTER MOVEMENT." Working with the Readjusters until WILLIAM MAHONE attempted to move them into the Republican party, Massey led a revolt and was an important element in ultimately defeating the movement in 1883. In 1885 he was elected lieutenant governor and in 1889 superintendent of public instruction. In the latter spot he espoused the view that education for blacks should be limited in proportion to taxes paid by them.

See E. H. Hancock, *Autobiography of John E. Massey* (1909); I. B. Patterson, "Massey" (M.A. thesis, University of Virginia, 1929); N. M. Blake, *Mahone* (1937); C. C. Pearson, *Readjuster Movement* (1917); J. P. Maddex, Jr., *Virginia Conservatives* (1972); V. Dabney, *New Dominion* (1971); and W. Holt, *Virginia Magazine of History and Biography* (Jan., 1968).

CATHERINE SILVERMAN
Institute for Research in History, New York

MATAGORDA ISLAND is a 36-mile-long barrier beach off the coast of Texas between San Antonio and Espiritu Santo bays. Varying in width a distance of between one and four miles, it was visited by LA SALLE in 1685 during his last voyage to the New World. Little effort has been made to use or develop the sandy strip, and of late it has been a bombing and gunnery range for the U.S. Air Force.

MAURY, DABNEY HERNDON (1822–1900), a typical gentleman-soldier of antebellum Virginia, was raised by an uncle, William Lewis Maury (not as is sometimes stated MATTHEW FONTAINE MAURY, a better-known uncle). After graduation from the University of Virginia, he attended West Point, establishing friendships with many future generals on both sides in the Civil War. In the Mexican War he was recognized for gallantry at Veracruz and Cerro Gordo. Between wars he taught at West Point, served in Texas, and was superintendent of the cavalry school at Carlisle, Pa. After FT. SUMTER, he joined the Confederate army, soon becoming a major general. His most responsible position was commander of the District of the Gulf, headquarters at Mobile, which city he held even after David Farragut's capture of the bay. He finally evacuated it on April 12, 1865, and on May 4 surrendered the remnants of his command. Financially ruined, he taught school, engaged in business, and in 1868 helped organize the SOUTHERN HISTORICAL SOCIETY to preserve southern war records, becoming chairman of its executive committee in 1873. Under Grover Cleveland he served as minister to Colombia.

See *Southern Historical Society Papers*, esp. XXVII; and D. H. Maury, *Recollections of Virginian* (1894).

WILLIAM HANCHETT
San Diego State University

MAURY, MATTHEW FONTAINE (1806–1873), was born near Fredericksburg, Va. After his seagoing career was cut short by an accident in 1839 that left him lame, he wrote vigorously in the causes of naval reform and southern expansion. The former brought Maury a naval shore command in 1842: the Depot of Charts and Instruments in Washington. Here he turned his organizational talents to empirical science, annexing the Naval Observatory on its completion in 1844 and acquiring in 1849 a fleet to carry out deep-sea soundings. From observations made at sea he constructed charts that presented a climatic picture of surface winds and currents for all the oceans. To these he added sailing directions, which he brought together in *The Physical Geography of the Sea* (1855), one of the most popular books of science ever published. At the Brussels conference of 1853 Maury organized worldwide weath-

er reporting at sea; it was extended to the land after his death. He drew the route for the first Atlantic cable of 1858. Maury served the Confederacy as naval agent in England from 1862 until the war ended, when he went to Mexico to establish a "new Virginia" of southern EXPATRIATES. In 1868 Virginia summoned him home from England to teach physics at its military institute and to superintend its physical survey.

See J. Leighly, in M. F. Maury, *Physical Geography of Sea* (1963), and *Bulletin de l'Institut Océanographique* Special Issue 2 (1968); and F. L. Williams, *Matthew Fontaine Maury* (1963).

HAROLD L. BURSTYN
U.S. Geological Survey, Reston, Va.

MAUVILLA, BATTLE OF (October 18, 1540), is sometimes called the battle of Alabamo. HERNANDO DE SOTO led his expedition into the territory of the Mauvilla Indians, seized their leader, the legendary Tuscaloosa, and demanded burden carriers and 100 Indian women. Under pretense of giving in to the requests, Tuscaloosa invited de Soto to Mauvilla, a small fortified town possibly located in present-day Clarke County, Ala. Mauvilla was an armed camp, and Tuscaloosa had obviously laid plans to dispense the Spaniards. A frenzied skirmish broke out within the confines of the town and soon developed into a full-blown battle. The Spanish suffered 170 casualties, and the Indian force of some 3,000 was virtually wiped out. De Soto's force left Mauvilla on November 14, 1540, and moved northwestward.

See P. J. Higginbotham, *Mobile Indians* (1966); J. A. Robertson (ed.), *True Relation of Fidalgo of Elvas* (1933); and E. G. Bourne, *Narratives of De Soto* (1904).

JAMES P. PATE
Livingston University

MAVERICK, MAURY (1895–1954), born into an old, prominent Texas family, was educated in Virginia and Texas. An ancestor who took unbranded cattle had added the family name to American slang. Maury proved to be a true maverick by his independent style throughout life. Although he was educated in the law, his first love was politics. In 1930 he was elected tax collector of Bexar County and then in 1934 was elected to Congress, where he became known as a leading New Dealer and a crusading liberal. He actively supported the TENNESSEE VALLEY AUTHORITY, conservation, slum clearance, and the antilynching bill. After serving two terms, he was defeated for reelection. In 1939 he was elected mayor of San Antonio. During World War II he was director of the government division of the War Production Board and chairman of the Smaller War Plants Corporation. He apparently added the word *gobbledygook* to the language—a word he used to describe unintelligible government language. His greatest contribution was as a champion of freedom and civil liberties, a lifelong obsession for him.

See R. B. Henderson, *Maury Maverick* (1970); S. L. Weiss, *Journal of American History* (March, 1971); D. W. Whisenhunt, *Texana* (1971); and M. Maverick, *Maverick American* (1937).

DONALD W. WHISENHUNT
Eastern New Mexico University

MAXEY, SAMUEL BELL (1825–1895), was born and reared in Kentucky. He graduated from West Point in 1846. He served in the Mexican War, but resigned his commission afterward to enter law practice with his father. In 1847 he moved to Lamar County, Tex. When the Civil War began, Maxey joined the Confederate army and rose from colonel to brigadier general. He fought in battles in east Tennessee, at VICKSBURG, and in the RED RIVER CAMPAIGN. For a time, he commanded the Confederacy's Indian Territory Military District. He returned to Texas after the war to practice law, and in 1875 was elected as a Democrat to the U.S. Senate for the first of two terms.

See W. P. Webb and H. B. Carroll, *Handbook of Texas* (2 vols.; 1952); B. H. Procter, *John H. Reagan* (1962); F. R. Lubbock, *Six Decades in Texas* (1900); and E. Eliot, Jr., *West Point in Confederacy* (1941).

KENNETH B. SHOVER
University of Texas, El Paso

MAYS, BENJAMIN ELIJAH (1894–), born in Epworth, S.C., received degrees at Bates College (B.A., 1920) and the University of Chicago (M.A., 1925; Ph.D., 1935). Ordained a Baptist minister in 1921, he taught at Morehouse College (1921–1924) and at South Carolina State College (1925–1926). He worked as executive secretary of the Tampa Urban League (1926–1928) and as national student secretary of the YMCA (1928–1930), and as dean of the School of Religion at Howard University (1934–1940). As president of Morehouse College (1940–1967) May worked to develop a "tradition of excellence" for the predominantly black student body. He was able to increase the proportion of Ph.D. faculty members from 8.7 percent to 54 percent, to quadruple the endowment, to add students to college administrative committees in the early 1940s, to develop study–travel abroad programs for both students and faculty, and to qualify Morehouse for a Phi Beta Kappa

chapter (installed January, 1968). An active opponent of racial segregation, Mays was mentor to MARTIN LUTHER KING, JR., and delivered the eulogy at King's nationally televised funeral in 1968.

See B. E. Mays, *Born to Rebel* (1971), autobiography; E. A. Jones, *Candle in Dark: Morehouse College* (1967); B. E. Mays and J. W. Nicholson, *Negro's Church* (1933); B. E. Mays, *Negro's God* (1938); and T. G. Rush, *Black American Writers* (1975).

DE WITT S. DYKES, JR.
Oakland University, Rochester, Mich.

MAYSVILLE, KY. (pop. 7,411), located on the Ohio River approximately 50 miles southeast of Cincinnati, was first settled in 1782. DANIEL BOONE and his wife operated a tavern here between 1786 and 1789. Although initially known as Limestone, the town was renamed to honor a local landholder when it was chartered in 1787 by the Virginia assembly. It was an important shipping and shipbuilding point for river traffic during the early nineteenth century. Today its industries manufacture electrical equipment, textiles, bicycles, motorcylces, cigars, and tin cans.

See files of Maysville *Ledger-Independent* (1892–).

MAYSVILLE ROAD VETO was delivered by Andrew Jackson on May 27, 1830. Shortly after he became president, Jackson indicated that he had strong reservations about a policy of federal aid for internal improvements, in part because it endangered his plan to pay off the national debt. He favored instead a policy whereby the surplus revenue of the federal government should be distributed to the states to be used at their own discretion. Despite this, under Henry Clay's leadership, Congress passed a bill authorizing the federal government to buy stock in a company building a road from Maysville to Lexington, Ky. The president immediately vetoed it, indicating that—since the road was entirely within Kentucky—it was not a "national" project. In one of his most important ideological statements, Jackson stressed his strict constructionist view of the Constitution, his hostility to measures that would lead to logrolling, and his desire to curtail government spending.

In addition to considerations of principle, personalities and politics also were involved. Jackson loathed HENRY CLAY, and since the Maysville Road went through Clay's hometown of Lexington it was added incentive for the president to veto it. The veto also had an important impact on the struggle between Martin Van Buren and JOHN C. CALHOUN, whom Jackson was growing to dislike, over who was to become the president's successor. Calhoun hoped to develop an alliance between the southern and western wings of the party, but the two sections disagreed over internal improvements. It was in Calhoun's interest therefore to see the internal improvement question avoided at all costs. When Jackson refused to do this and actually allowed Van Buren to draft the Maysville Road veto, it clearly indicated the New Yorker's ascendancy and the failure of Calhoun's strategy.

See J. D. Richardson, *Messages of Presidents* (1896–99), II; C. G. Sellers, *James K. Polk* (1957), I; and G. R. Taylor, *Transportation Revolution* (1951).

RICHARD E. ELLIS
State University of New York, Buffalo

MECHANICSVILLE, BATTLE OF (June 26, 1862),

the first major battle of the SEVEN DAYS' BATTLES, erupted during G. B. McClellan's PENINSULAR CAMPAIGN. ROBERT E. LEE planned a massive turn to the southeast *en échelon* from the left, aided by a detached flanking maneuver, which would disrupt the Union army threatening Richmond. A. P. HILL would cross the Chickahominy River and attack Union General Fitz-John Porter's 35,000 men on Beaver Dam Creek. D. H. HILL and JAMES LONGSTREET would then follow, while STONEWALL JACKSON's army moved up from behind to menace Porter's right flank, thus necessitating a federal retreat. Properly executed, the maneuver would have cut McClellan's railway communications and involved minimal casualties. But too much depended on Jackson's weary men making a forced march through seas of mud. Twelve hours after the scheduled hour of attack, with Jackson still not in position, Hill impetuously launched a frontal assault, losing about 1,400 men to the federals' 361 within six hours. Although Lee blamed Jackson for being late and historians have castigated Hill, responsibility for the disaster belongs to Lee, who failed to keep his commanders informed of the changed situation and set an impossible schedule for Jackson.

See D. S. Freeman, *R. E. Lee* (1934–35), II, sympathetic to Lee, but good; B. Catton, *Terrible Swift Sword* (1963); F. Vandiver, *Mighty Stonewall* (1957); R. U. Johnson and C. C. Buel (eds.), *Battles and Leaders* (1956), II, Porter's account; and J. Longstreet, *Manassas to Appomattox* (1896).

GORDON H. WARREN
Central Washington State College

MECKLENBURG RESOLUTIONS. On May 31,

1775, citizens in Mecklenburg County, N.C., met and drew up 20 resolutions declaring that all laws and commissions deriving their authority from king or Parliament were annulled and vacated; all civil and military commissions issued under them were void; and the constitution of each colony was wholly suspended. Henceforth, all legislative and executive power within each colony was to be vested in its provincial congress under the direction of the CONTINENTAL CONGRESS. Any person who thereafter received a commission from the crown or who exercised any previous commission or who refused to obey these resolutions was declared an enemy of the county and was to be apprehended and punished. These resolutions were to be in effect until otherwise provided by the provincial congress or until Parliament should give up its "unjust and arbitrary Pretensions with respect to America." The resolutions were apparently sent to the North Carolina delegates in the Continental Congress but were never presented to that body.

In 1819 an account of these resolutions was published. Inasmuch as they contained phrases that had later appeared in the Declaration of Independence of July 4, 1776, a myth grew up of a previous Mecklenburg "declaration of independence," supposedly proclaimed on May 20, 1775 (and not to be confused with the Mecklenburg Resolutions). Most historians today agree that the Mecklenburg "declaration" is a spurious document.

See W. L. Saunders and W. Clark (eds.), *North Carolina Colonial Records* (26 vols.; 1886–1906), IX; *Documents Illustrative of Formation of Union of U.S.*, 69th Cong., 1st Sess., House Doc. 398; H. S. Commager, *Documents of American History* (1949); W. H. Hoyt, *Mecklenburg Declaration of Independence* (1907); and *Writings on Amerian History* (1904–), for numerous sources dealing with controversy over this document.

PHYLLIS R. ABBOTT
Mankato State University

MEDICINE. Medical care was not provided the

seventeenth-century South by colonial agencies; and, since English physicians were reluctant to emigrate voluntarily and colonists generally did not travel to Europe to seek medical education, the practice of medicine for nearly a century after the founding of Jamestown fell largely to self-trained "doctors" or former apprentices of such doctors unrestricted by any serious licensing requirements. Although aware of and influenced by medical theories, the chief interest of these men and women was the practical treatment of illness. For much of the eighteenth and nineteenth centuries physicians frequently combined their medical studies with a general interest in natural science, but the *materia medica* of seventeenth-century doctors (learned in part from the Indians, whose medicine was alternately viewed as wise and barbaric) was developed in the main without any such broader theoretical concerns. During the colonial period, such simples as sassafras, tobacco, GINSENG, and snakeroot were held to be especially efficacious (FOLK MEDICINE).

The apprentice system of training was significant for what there was of a democratic and utilitarian orientation of medicine in the South, but the eighteenth-century vogue of attending medical lectures in European schools wrought a separate and more important tradition. The number of southern students in European medical schools is not known, but in the period 1749–1800 at least 78 of the 122 Americans graduating from Edinburgh were southerners, mainly from Virginia and South Carolina. This training had two related effects: it introduced southern physicians to European systems, which were considered purer science and hence closer to an integrated world view than was the craft of medicine as practiced by unschooled doctors; and, in consequence, it elevated the status of degree holders over that of preceptor-trained doctors. As early as 1736 a Virginia law required higher fees for the former group, and by the end of the century it was medical school trained physicians who sought to organize medical societies in an effort to exclude unschooled doctors and enhance their own prestige.

Between 1800 and 1860, professionals organized and staffed nearly two dozen medical departments and colleges in the South, excepting Missouri and all sectarian medical schools. Aimed at producing general practitioners rather than specialists, curricula usually included institutes of medicine, *materia medica*, anatomy, physiology, surgery, obstetrics, and chemistry. But, relatively isolated and often poorly administered, only a few southern medical schools survived the century. Although they attracted capable teachers, their meager resources told against them and southern students preferred to go north. Thus, over two-thirds of the graduates of Philadelphia's two major medical schools before 1860 were southerners. Increasing sectional feeling, however, encouraged the founding of no less than eight medical schools in the South between 1850 and 1859 and underlay the famous "secession" of southern medical students from Philadelphia to Richmond in 1859.

A specifically southern medicine was often cited as a real need to be satisfied by southern schools, but no such medicine evolved beyond the racist physiology of Samuel Cartwright, and it generated as much incredulous denunciation as praise within the South. Similarly divisive were the theories of polygenesis and diversity, actively supported by Josiah Nott, William Stump Forwood, and others but by no means a majority of the profession. The relation of slavery to medicine was exceedingly complex. Slaves were never used as "guinea pigs" for experiments, but in the absence of hospital facilities their availability for instructional purposes was occasionally cited as an advantage in medical school advertisements. Southern physicians benefited from slavery in its affording them a ready practice with which to accumulate experience and maintain a steady income. Yet slavery tended to retard southern physicians in their ability to assess innovative researches in human biology objectively; it enforced commitments to nonscientific values in the name of professionalism.

Professionalism in the antebellum years did not bring more efficacious treatment than formerly, although Ephraim McDowell's successful ovariotomy in 1809, James Marion Sims's cure of vesico-vaginal fistula, and Crawford Long's celebrated discovery of ether as a surgical anesthesia are exceptions. However, southern diseases, and particularly epidemic diseases, resisted successful treatment until early in the twentieth century. Based on rational etiologies, such therapeutics as purgings, irritants, bleedings, and narcotics were generally ineffective, which accounts both for the nadir in the prestige of the medical profession and the popularity of heterodox schools of medicine in the middle period of the nineteenth century.

Southern physicians made some interesting observations in epidemiology, but they were generally fruitless and, except for smallpox, epidemics persisted with appalling consequences down to the beginning of the twentieth century. These were largely responsible for the growth of the public HEALTH movement in the South, which in the 1870s and continuing into the twentieth century generated the establishment of state health boards in all the southern states. At first poorly financed and directed mainly to seeking improvements in sanitation, their work was stimulated by outside agencies: the U.S. Army's virtual conquest of YELLOW FEVER and MALARIA; the Rockefeller-financed Sanitary Commission for the Eradication of HOOKWORM Disease; and the U.S. Public Health Service, which in 1914 established PELLAGRA as a dietary deficiency disease and initiated programs to allevaite the problem. Before, during, and after World War I state appropriations to health boards increased dramatically; and, during and after the war, disease prevention services, handled increasingly by county health boards, extended beyond sanitation reform to mosquito control, distribution of vaccines, and dissemination of information. Although educational and clinical services were limited, the Johns Hopkins School of Medicine, established in 1893, provided a model for national medical education reform. Yet, by 1930, there were still only 95.1 physicians per 100,000 people in the southeastern states, compared with 125.2 nationally, and mortality statistics in the 1920s indicated that the death rate in the South was generally above the national average. This was largely due to economic conditions that did not alter significantly until the World War II period and after.

See H. B. Shafer, *American Medical Profession* (1936); R. Shryock, *Medicine and Society* (1960); W. F. Norwood, *Medical Education* (1944); F. R. Packard, *History of Medicine in U.S.* (1931); J. Duffy (ed.), *Rudolph Matas History of Medicine in Louisiana* (1958, 1962); D. Long (ed.), *Medicine in North Carolina* (1972); J. I. Waring, *History of Medicine in South Carolina* (1964–71); W. B. Blanton, *Medicine in Virginia in Seventeenth Century* (1930) and *Medicine in Virginia in Eighteenth Century* (1931); E. F. Cordell, *Medical Annals of Maryland* (1903); H. H. Cunningham, *Doctors in Gray* (1958); E. W. Etheridge, *Butterfly Caste* (1972); P. Allen, *Journal of History of Medicine and Allied Sciences* (Autumn, 1947); J. H. Cassedy, *Journal of History of Medicine and Allied Sciences* (April, 1973); J. Duffy, *Journal of Southern History* (Feb., 1959; May 1968); R. Shryock, *South Atlantic Quarterly* (April, 1930); W. Fisher, *Journal of History of Medicine and Allied Sciences* (Jan., 1968); M. C. Mitchell, *Journal of Southern History* (Nov., 1944); W. D. Postell, *South Atlantic Quarterly* (July, 1952); R. Shryock, *Journal of Medical Education* (1956); and F. R. Allen, "Public Health" (Ph.D. dissertation, University of North Carolina, 1946). Important manuscript collections include Tait Family and J. Y. Bassett papers, Alabama Archives; Ashby Papers, Virginia Historical Society; J. L. Cabell Papers, University of Virginia; C. A. Hentz and W. S. Forwood papers, University of North Carolina; and J. C. Trent Collection of History of Medicine, Duke University Hospital.

WILLIAM H. LONGTON
University of Toledo

MEDICINES, PATENT, imported from England during the eighteenth century, were advertised in Charleston and Williamsburg newspapers just as they were advertised in Boston and Philadelphia. When the Revolution sharply curtailed sales of Turlington's Balsam and Hooper's Female Pills, native American brands largely took their place. Northern manufacturers dominated the southern market from the start of the new nation. One of the first brands, Lee's Bilious Pills, made in Connecticut, soon was advertised in Georgia, and so it went through the antebellum years: yankee nostrum vendors urging residents of Dixie, especially

planters, to buy their certain cures. When P. T. Barnum toured the South he bought New York–made Brandreth's Pills in Mississippi and Louisiana. Patent medicines formed part of the health care system (HEALTH, PUBLIC) on many plantations. The few patent medicines made in the South received virtually no promotion in the North.

Well into the Civil War, southern newspapers continued to run advertising for northern nostrums, although Confederate patriotism stimulated the creation of some southern brands. A Charleston druggist promoted the Memphis-made Cherokee Remedy and other "SOUTHERN PREPARATIONS" at the sign of the Negro and the Golden Mortar. After Appomattox, northern patent medicine makers quickly sought to regain their southern markets. An Ohio proprietor promoted a panacea called Hasheesh Candy with purported testimonials from Ulysses S. Grant and Robert E. Lee. A Columbia, S.C., editor rebuked his fellow publishers for selling advertising space at cut rates to yankee "patent blood-suckers."

Relatively easy to make, patent medicines played a key role in New South industrialization. Virtually every city sent forth its brands: Black Draught and Wine of Cardui from Chattanooga; Dr. Tichenor's Antiseptic Refrigerant (flying on its label the Stars and Bars) from New Orleans; Botanic Blood Balm and Swift's Sure Specific from Atlanta. Atlanta's Coca-Cola began as a headache remedy but soon gave up therapy for sheer refreshment. Patent medicine money, it has been said, provided the initial capital fueling Atlanta's surge forward in economic development.

Wartime and postwar poverty, an inadequate diet that worsened for those moving to the new MILL TOWNS, and the warm climate combined to give the South a high incidence of disease. The educational level was low, and superstitions about health were abundant. Circumstances were propitious for the strident appeals made in nostrum advertising. Even today many southerners without money for adequate food buy proprietary tonics. Many nostrums have aimed at black buyers, including purported skin whiteners and hair straighteners.

Huey Long once peddled Wine of Cardui, and another Louisiana politician, Dudley J. LeBlanc, in the late 1940s conducted one of the twentieth century's most colorful patent medicine campaigns in behalf of his iron and vitamin tonic, Hadacol. Aided by show business stars and steam calliopes, LeBlanc sought wealth and the Louisiana governorship with his gaudy revival of the old-time medicine show that toured the South. The governorship eluded LeBlanc, although he once forced the LONG MACHINE to market Vita-Long, a competing patent medicine.

See J. H. Young, *Toadstool Millionaires* (1961) and *Medical Messiahs* (1967); F. M. Clay, *Coozan Dudley LeBlanc* (1973); and B. McNamara, *Step Right Up* (1976).

JAMES HARVEY YOUNG
Emory University

MEHARRY MEDICAL COLLEGE (Nashville, Tenn. 37208)

was originally established as the medical department of Central Tennessee College. It became a separate institution, Walden University, in 1900, and it was reorganized and renamed in 1915 after a family who greatly contributed to its financial support. Although it has an enrollment of fewer than 500 students, this coeducational and largely black institution has long been one of the most prestigious of black medical schools in the nation.

See J. J. Mullowney, *America Gives a Chance* (1940).

MELUNGEONS

or Malungeons are a people, probably descended from a frontier mixture of whites, Indians, and free blacks, whose uncertain origins have long been a subject for speculation. Favorite theories have hypothesized their descent from Phoenician sailors, from a twelfth-century Welsh prince, and from survivors of Sir Walter Raleigh's lost settlement at Roanoke. Many Melungeons themselves prefer to claim descent from the Croatan or from the Cherokee Indians. During the 1870s, however, a Chattanooga attorney successfully defended them against the charge of a Negro heritage by convincing a jury that his clients were descended from shipwrecked Portuguese sailors. Their name, he argued, was a corruption of the Portuguese word *melungo*, meaning shipmate. Melungeons have lived in various parts of the Appalachian Mountains since the 1790s. Their dark hair and olive complexions set them apart from other settlers, and they lived in clanlike clusters, the most central and often studied being the several hundred Melungeons of Newman's Ridge in Hancock County, Tenn. The census of 1830 counted them as "free colored," but in 1840 most of these same families were listed as "white." Since World War II, intermarriage, urbanization, and migration from Appalachia have seriously weakened family ties and greatly reduced the size and numbers of remaining Melungeon communities.

See W. A. Dromgoole, *Arena* (May, 1891); E. T. Price, *Geographical Review* (April, 1951); and "Melungeons," Federal Writers' Project manuscript in Knoxville Public Library.

MEMMINGER, CHRISTOPHER GUSTAVUS

(1803–1888), lawyer, statesman, and entrepreneur, was born at Nayhingen, Germany. Migrating to America, he was orphaned at age four and placed in the Charleston Orphanage until eleven, when adopted by Thomas Bennett (later governor of South Carolina), who provided him advantages of a wealthy home. Memminger graduated from South Carolina College (1819) and was admitted to the Charleston bar (1824). Vitally concerned with education, he was founder of the public school system in Charleston; instrumental in having the state legislature provide education for the deaf, mute, and blind; a South Carolina College trustee; and a Charleston Orphanage benefactor.

Memminger was elected to the South Carolina house of representatives (1836–1860, except 1853–1854). As chairman of the ways and means committee, he began a long struggle to disassociate the state from banking corporations and to force the banks to maintain specie payments on pain of forfeiture of their charters. In these contests he won considerable reputation as a "sound money man." From 1861 to 1864 he was secretary of the treasury, Confederate States of America. Although ably filling this office, he was subjected to much criticism. He resigned June 15, 1864, and went to Rock Hill, his country home at Flat Rock, N.C., where he lived until granted amnesty January 7, 1867. Memminger then returned to Charleston, resuming the practice of law, but devoted much of his remaining life to business enterprises, becoming president of Etiwan Phosphate Company and president of the Spartanburg & Asheville Railroad.

See H. D. Capers, *Memminger* (1893); R. C. Todd, *Georgia Review* (Winter, 1958); J. C. Schwab, *Yale Review* (Nov., 1893); B. J. Hendrick, *Jefferson Davis and Cabinet* (1939); and R. C. Todd, *Confederate Finance* (1954).

RICHARD C. TODD
East Carolina University

MEMPHIS, TENN.

(pop. 623,587), approximately 235 miles south of St. Louis, Mo., is situated on a bluff overlooking the Mississippi River. A trading post (1794) and U.S. Army Ft. Adams (1797) preceded the formal laying out of a town in 1819, but—after the removal of area Indians—the town developed rapidly into a major river port and cotton market. The city fell to a Union naval force commanded by Charles H. Davis on June 6, 1862. Although the assault itself occasioned little physical damage to the city, the prolonged disruption of Mississippi River trade and the region's cotton commerce was disastrous. Even before recovering from these blows, the city was hit in 1878 with one of the nation's most serious YELLOW FEVER epidemics. Not until after the turn of the next century, during the era of E. H. CRUMP, did Memphis truly rebound and resume its development.

Today Memphis is one of the most modern cities in the South. Served by systems of rail, truck, and AIR TRANSPORT and assisted by renewed use of the Mississippi as an inland waterway, Memphis is the world's largest inland market for both cotton and lumber. It is the home of Southwestern at Memphis (1848), Memphis State University (1909), LeMoyne College (1870), Siena College (1923), and Christian Brothers College (1871). Moreover, the research and therapeutic activities of the city's several hospitals and of the medical college of the University of Tennessee make Memphis the premier medical center of the mid-South.

See G. Capers, *Biography of River Town* (1939, 1966); W. Miller, *Mr. Crump of Memphis* (1964), and *Memphis During Progressive Era* (1957); S. McIlwaine, *Memphis Down in Dixie* (1948); J. M. Keating, *History of Memphis* (3 vols.; 1888); J. M. Davis, *History of Memphis* (1873); and files of Memphis *Commercial Appeal* (1840–) and *Press-Scimitar* (1880–), both on microfilm.

MEMPHIS AVALANCHE

MEMPHIS AVALANCHE was founded in 1858 by local Democrats who were dissatisfied with the Memphis *Commercial Appeal*'s support of Stephen A. Douglas. The *Avalanche*'s editor, M. C. Gallaway, embraced extreme southern positions, backed J. C. BRECKINRIDGE in the election of 1860, and called for secession almost immediately after Abraham Lincoln's victory. Despite the paper's Confederate loyalties, it was published throughout the period of federal occupation, though under the name *Bulletin*. At the end of the Civil War, the *Avalanche* led the fight of Memphis Democrats against the Reconstruction government of W. G. BROWNLOW. It continued as the journalistic competitor of the *Commercial Appeal* until that paper purchased the *Avalanche* in 1890 to form the *Appeal-Avalanche*.

See T. H. Baker, *Memphis Commercial Appeal* (1971); and *Avalanche* (1861–95), on microfilm from Bell & Howell.

MEMPHIS COMMERCIAL APPEAL

MEMPHIS COMMERCIAL APPEAL was founded in 1841 by Henry Van Pelt as the *Weekly Appeal*. As a Democratic paper published in a predominantly Whig town, the *Appeal* was partisan in character but moderate in tone. It was equally critical of southern FIRE-EATERS and of KNOW-NOTHINGS, and it championed Stephen A. Douglas throughout the 1850s as the best hope for de-

fending the South within the national Democratic party. Benjamin Franklin Dill, editor from 1855 to 1866, approached secession with considerable reluctance. After 1861, however, he was a staunch defender of the Confederacy. Prior to the occupation of Memphis by federal troops in 1862, Dill loaded the *Appeal*'s boiler, presses, and print onto a railroad boxcar and fled the city. For the next three years he published his daily as a refugee newspaper in ten different towns and four states. Returning to Memphis at the end of the Civil War, Dill and his *Appeal* preached patience and endurance to the defeated Memphians.

After Dill's death in 1866, the new proprietors and editors of the *Appeal* published it as an organ of the NEW SOUTH movement. Exuding optimistic boosterism, the *Appeal* pushed for diversification of agriculture, sanitation reform, and industrialization. In politics the paper was identified with the so-called BOURBON element of Tennessee's Democratic party, favoring interests of the state's western planters over the Whiggish supporters of ARTHUR COLYAR. In the aftermath of the PANIC OF 1893, the *Appeal* purchased the *Daily Commercial* (1889–1894) and adopted its present name. It preserved its traditionally moderate political stance throughout the 1890s by endorsing the popular issue of free silver but at the same time backing the candidacies of conservative goldbug Democrats. Under the editorship of C. P. J. Mooney, however, the *Commercial Appeal* became one of Tennessee's more progressive dailies. As editor between 1908 and 1926, Mooney was an early supporter of both E. H. CRUMP and WOODROW WILSON, a vigorous defender of the League of Nations, and a Pulitzer Prize winner in 1923 for his campaign against the KU KLUX KLAN.

See T. H. Baker, *Memphis Commercial Appeal* (1971); and *Commercial Appeal* on microfilm (1843–) from Bell & Howell.

MEMPHIS RIOT

MEMPHIS RIOT (1866). A minor accident involving a Negro and a white erupted into a riot on May 1. A huge influx of immigrants and black freedmen had almost doubled Memphis in size between 1863 and 1865. Immigrants controlled the city's government while 4,000 black troops at Ft. Pickering represented the U.S. government. Job competition inflamed relations between Negro and Irish residents, and black troops feuded continuously with Irish policemen. Former Confederates were without political power, and they despised all symbols of northern economic and political intervention. These antagonisms were exacerbated by an uncontrolled crime rate and because police authority was divided between the black troops and Irish police. When four black regiments were mustered out of the army without pay, the situation worsened. The former soldiers and police clashed on April 30, and then the May 1 accident touched off fighting, burning, and looting by an assorted rabble, which cost the lives of 46 Negroes and two whites.

See J. D. L. Holmes, *Tennessee Historical Quarterly* (June, 1958), best study; *Congressional Report on Memphis Riots*, 39th Cong., 1st Sess.; A. A. Taylor, *Negro in Tennessee* (1941); and T. A. Alexander, *Political Reconstruction* (1950).

JAMES MURPHY
Southern Illinois University

MENÉNDEZ DE AVILÉS, PEDRO (1519–1574), was born in Avilés, Asturias, Spain. After distinguished service in Europe, he was named frontier captain or adelantado of Florida, where he was granted 300,000 acres of land on condition that he recruit and transport 500 settlers, build two fortified towns, and expel foreigners who had colonized there. Arriving in September of 1565, he founded St. Augustine, the first European settlement in the United States. Promptly, Menéndez in a surprise attack destroyed the intrusive French HUGUENOT colony of Ft. Caroline on the St. John's River, slaying many of its defenders and renaming the site San Mateo, which he occupied. Subsequently, though not always personally present, Menéndez expanded Spanish holdings northward into Georgia, the Carolinas, and Virginia; introduced Jesuit priests, who set up Catholic missions among the southeastern Indians; sponsored interior explorations by Juan Pardo and Hernando Boyano; and initiated coastal reconnaissance from the Florida Keys to Chesapeake Bay. Native resistance and a French counterattack in 1567 inhibited more complete exploration and occupation of the Southeast. Pedro Menéndez de Avilés was succeeded by his nephew Pedro Menéndez Marqués as leader of Spanish Florida, while the uncle returned to Spain. Named commander-in-chief of the Invincible Armada destined to attack England, he died while in Santander preparing the ill-fated invasion.

See W. W. Dewhurst, *History of St. Augustine* (1885, 1968); J. T. Conner (ed.), *Pedro Menéndez de Avilés* (1923); and B. Barrientos, *Pedro Menéndez de Avilés* (1965).

DONALD C. CUTTER
University of New Mexico

MENNONITES are a religious group that had its beginnings in Switzerland in the 1520s during the Protestant Reformation. Some of Huldreich Zwingli's followers emphasized the baptism of adult believers; since they were rebaptizers they became known as Anabaptists. Many different types of Anabaptists developed; the Mennonites owed their organization and their name to Menno Simons, a former Catholic priest. They proposed to live in accordance with the Bible and to reject military service. Because they rejected the state church, they were persecuted in most of Europe. They fled to places where they were tolerated, including the Netherlands.

Beginning in the 1680s groups of Mennonites immigrated to Pennsylvania. Some of them established Germantown, outside of Philadelphia, and some of them moved into the interior. By the early 1700s they were immigrating into Virginia, where they established permanent settlements in the western river valleys, such as the Shenandoah. Also, some Mennonites were settling in Maryland and in the Carolinas during the colonial period, but evidently no permanent settlements were established that early.

Many different groups of Mennonites live in the South. The Amish, who developed from a European division in the seventeenth century, are one of the best known, but there are several groups of Amish. The Beachy Amish, for example, have settlements in ten of the southern states. The largest group in the South is the Old Mennonite sect, especially strong in Virginia and Maryland. They have developed a center of activities, including Eastern Mennonite College, at Harrisonburg, Va.

The Mennonites have been characterized by their mobility, and by the 1970s Mennonite congregations had been organized in all the southern states. In about two-thirds of these states this activity has taken place in the twentieth century. Florida provides a good example, for the Mennonites began to arrive in the 1920s but no organizations were established before the 1940s; by the 1970s there were more than 20.

The Mennonites have also been characterized by their pacifism, sectarianism, and conservatism. During the twentieth century some of these characteristics have been modified in some of the Mennonite groups, but apparently the most liberal groups have not yet become very numerous in the South. Thus the Mennonites in the South continue to be "different" in some ways from southern society.

See H. A. Brunk, *Mennonites in Virginia* (1959, 1972); R. E. Sappington, *Mennonite Quarterly Review* (April, 1968); and *Mennonite Encyclopedia* (1955–59).

ROGER E. SAPPINGTON
Bridgewater College

MENTAL HEALTH. Until the period immediately following the Second World War, mental health treatment and concern focused primarily on the mental hospital systems of the states. Although the establishment of the Worcester, Mass., hospital for the insane in 1833 is generally credited as the beginning of the state mental hospital movement, the first public attempt to treat mentally disordered patients in the United States came in Virginia before the American Revolution, and four southern states opened hospitals for the insane before 1830 (Maryland, 1797; Kentucky 1824; Virginia, 1825; South Carolina, 1828). The Louisiana state system (1840) was an outgrowth of the New Orleans Charity Hospital program begun in 1820. By 1860 Georgia, Alabama, Tennessee, Missouri, North Carolina, Mississippi, and Texas had opened mental hospitals.

Although southern states led the nation in the institutionalization of the mentally ill, public concern for care and treatment of the insane was shaped less by medical and social concerns than by political and administrative problems inherent in the mental hospital programs themselves. The first 125 years (1820–1945) of institutionalized care of the insane in the South is best characterized as a period of meager state appropriations, which resulted in inadequate facilities, overworked and poorly trained staff, low salaries, and the political structuring of the hospital systems that fostered patronage and produced institutions oriented to custodial care. Appropriations for the maintenance of patients during this period clearly indicate that, despite substantial increases in the total allotments, hospitals still afforded only bare subsistence. When prorated with the hospitals' population, apparent increases were in many instances marked decreases. Low per capita costs were regarded as a measure of efficiency.

Overcrowding was an accepted practice because of efforts to hospitalize emergency cases who could no longer be cared for at home or in county jails. Furthermore, during the employment of moral therapy routines, administrators were convinced that early hospitalization and treatment would afford a rapid recovery for a majority of patients, and admission was provided for more than the systems could bear.

Overcrowding reached such proportions in most southern hospitals by 1900 that the progressive program of moral therapy had to be abandoned for the practice of custodial care of inmates. Even though the unit cost per patient was continually being reduced to the satisfaction of public officials, the low discharge rate and rising patient load forced most hospital officials to request more and more funds for buildings to house patients. In a system dependent directly on the legislature for capital and operational funds, superintendents found it expedient to acquiesce to the wishes of individual legislators, governors, and other state politicians who sought special admission of patients for friends. This practice led to unchecked and unavoidable political patronage, which characterized the southern hospital systems between 1900 and 1945.

Since World War II, however, the South has experienced unprecedented growth in its population and economy. New leadership in the medical and social services has joined forces with progressive and enlightened political leaders to meet the demands for expanded and improved therapeutic programs. Without exception, the result has been well-organized administrative structures that are providing direction as well as continuity to the complex hospital and community mental health service programs. With the support of the Department of Health, Education, and Welfare, the National Institute of Mental Health, the Southern Education Board, and increased federal and state appropriations, the southern states have assumed a leadership role in the development of administrative techniques and treatment programs. Discharge rates from hospitals now exceed admission rates. Expenditures for daily patient care in southern hospitals rose from an average of 1.4 to 4.6 percent of the total daily maintenance cost between 1955 and 1960. The mental health movement begun by Clifford Beers has taken on a new life in the South under the leadership of citizens who recognize the need to combine the forces of medical treatment, training, and research with political leadership in order to breed a continuity of support and service.

See state and federal documents, archives; American Psychiatric Association journals; Southern Education Board publications; G. N. Grob, *Mental Institutions in America* (1973), best early-period bibliography of hospital, state, and local government documents; N. Dain, *Concepts of Insanity* (1964); H. E. Marshall, *Dorothea Dix* (1937); J. K. Hall, *Southern Medicine and Surgery* (Nov., 1938); A. Deutch, *Mentally Ill in America* (1938); L. Bellak, *Handbook of Community Psychiatry* (1963); I. Belknap, *Human Problems of State Mental Hospital* (1956); S. K. Weinberg, *Society and Personality Disorders* (1952); D. L. Dix Papers, Harvard; W. S. Jenkins, *Guide to Microfilm Collection of Early State Records, Library of Congress* (1950); J. S. Tarwater, *Alabama State Hospitals* (1964); E. Wisner, *Social Welfare in South* (1970); H. S. Cochrane, *Georgia Historical Quarterly* (June, 1948); E. B. Thompson, *Tennessee Histori-*

cal Quarterly (Dec., 1944); and C. Beers, *Mind That Found Itself* (1937).

CLARK R. CAHOW
Duke University

MERCER UNIVERSITY (Macon, Ga. 30217) was opened in 1833 as a Baptist theological seminary and named for Jesse Mercer (1769–1841), a Georgia clergyman and one of the school's founders. In 1871 the school was moved from Penfield to its present home in Macon. Under the leadership of Spright Dowell, president from 1928 to 1953, Mercer underwent considerable growth and today has a enrollment of almost 4,000 students. As the repository of the Georgia Baptist Convention, its library houses a rich collection of original and microfilm materials on Baptist church history.

See S. Dowell, *History of Mercer University, 1833–1953* (1958).

MERIDIAN, MISS. (pop. 45,083), is approximately 80 miles east of Jackson and 16 miles west of the Alabama state line. The site was first settled by Richard McLemore in 1831 as a plantation. Gradually a small agricultural community clustered around McLemore's home, and in 1861 the town became the junction of the Mobile & Ohio and the Vicksburg & Montgomery railroads. Although the presence of the railroads promised prosperity, it also brought bitter conflict that divided the town into farm folk versus railroaders. The division was symbolized in a fight over the town's name: farmers preferring Sawashee, and the railroad mechanics wanting Meridian. After federal occupation of Jackson, Meridian briefly served as the Confederate state capital in 1863. The following year, the town was occupied and largely destroyed by W. T. Sherman (February 14–19, 1864) as part of his MERIDIAN CAMPAIGN. The town was rebuilt after the war as a rail center and an agricultural market, but since the turn of the century it has become an industrial city as well.

See files of Meridian *Star* (1896–), on microfilm.

MERIDIAN CAMPAIGN (February 3–March 5, 1864). In the spring of 1864, Meridian, Miss., represented the seat of Confederate military power in the state. Headquarters of LEONIDAS POLK, Meridian served as the hub of southern resupply efforts to its forces in western Mississippi. Unable to support N. P. Banks's RED RIVER CAMPAIGN until March (the Yazoo and Red rivers were too low for navigation), William T. Sherman decided to strike eastward through Jackson to Meridian. He sought to isolate Mississippi, prevent resupply efforts westward, and break the only railroad connection between Mississippi and the east. In conjunction with this move, Sherman directed William Sooy Smith to strike south from Memphis with his 7,000 cavalrymen along the Mobile & Ohio Railroad, linking up with Sherman at Meridian. Confederate forces under Polk numbered 20,000, including NATHAN B. FORREST's cavalry in northern Mississippi. After several skirmishes but little determined resistance en route, Sherman's 25,000-man force entered Meridian on February 14–15, 1864. They remained five days, destroying roads, bridges, and railroad tracks and trestles in all directions. Without hearing from Smith, Sherman withdrew his force on February 20 to Canton, Miss., and thence to Vicksburg (March 5, 1864). Federal casualties totaled 170. Confederate losses were 600 (400 killed, 200 prisoners). Late starting south, Smith's cavalry was routed by Forrest at West Point, Miss., on February 21, 1864.

See S. Foote, *Civil War* (1963); A. Nevins, *War for Union* (1971); and J. B. Walters, *Merchant of Terror* (1973), biased but useful.

JOHN G. FOWLER, JR.
U.S. Army

MERIWETHER, ELIZABETH AVERY (1824–1916), was born on a farm in Bolivar, Tenn., and moved to Memphis in 1835. Following her parents' deaths in 1846 and 1847, she and her two sisters conducted a school in their home. In 1850 she married Minor Meriwether, a civil engineer. As the wife of a Confederate army officer, she was banished from Memphis when W. T. Sherman occupied the city in 1862. Pregnant, she traveled with her two small sons, managing to stay near the Confederate army in Mississippi, where she gave birth to her third son. After the war the Meriwethers returned to Memphis, remaining there until 1883, when they moved to St. Louis. In the 1870s she began her public advocacy of PROHIBITION and woman suffrage (WOMEN'S RIGHTS MOVEMENT), addressing audiences throughout the South and New England and participating in state and national suffrage organizations. A meeting with Henry George in 1881 converted her to the single-tax theory, which she supported in speeches and writing. She published several novels dealing with the South and southern culture.

See E. A. Meriwether, *Recollections of 92 Years* (1916); and E. C. Stanton and S. B. Anthony, *History of Woman Suffrage* (1886, 1902), III, IV.

SUSAN M. HARTMANN
University of Missouri, St. Louis

MERRIMACK. See MONITOR AND MERRIMACK, BATTLE OF

MERRYMAN, EX PARTE (17 Fed. Cas. 144 [1861]), a decision rendered by ROGER B. TANEY in his individual capacity as chief justice of the United States, held unconstitutional President Abraham Lincoln's suspension of the privilege of the writ of habeas corpus. Declaring invalid the military arrest and detention of John Merryman, a Maryland militia lieutenant suspected of Confederate sympathies, Taney held that only Congress, not the president, can suspend the writ and condemned military arrests of civilians. Pro-Union legal authorities, including Horace Binney, U.S. Attorney General EDWARD BATES, REVERDY JOHNSON, and Joel Parker, defended presidential suspension. Congress in 1863 ambiguously declared that the president "is authorized" to suspend the writ. The question has never been definitively resolved. Despite Taney's prosecession sympathies and the short-run futility of his act, his *Merryman* opinion stands as a monument of judicial hostility to presidential and military encroachment on individual liberties in wartime

See *Official Records, Armies*, Ser. 2, Vol. I; J. G. Randall, *Constitutional Problems Under Lincoln* (1951); H. M. Hyman, *More Perfect Union* (1973), critical of Taney; and C. B. Swisher, *History of Supreme Court* (1974), sympathetic to Taney.

WILLIAM M. WIECEK
University of Missouri, Columbia

METHODIST CHURCH. Shortly after a discouraging two-year stay in Georgia as an unflinching High Churchman, the Reverend John Wesley had an intensely personal religious experience in London on May 28, 1738. Two years later he formed the United Methodist Society for the purpose of infusing into the Church of England a personal inner dimension of faith. This aspect of the evangelical revival appeared in the American colonies 25 years later, becoming a major factor in the GREAT AWAKENING in the South. By 1775 the society numbered 4,000 colonial members, but when Wesley's Toryism forced him to recall his English preachers, all left except Francis Asbury. Nonetheless, under the direction of American preachers the movement nearly quadrupled during the

American Revolution, with 80 percent living south of the Mason-Dixon Line. Pressure to form an independent organization was contained until 1779, when the Annual Conference began to ordain its own clergy.

At the close of the Revolution, Wesley recognized the status of the former Anglican church in America and also decided that it must have considerable independence. Accordingly in 1784, acting contrary to English canon law, he ordained two men for American service and assigned Thomas Coke as superintendent. In Baltimore that Christmas, 60 Methodist preachers met and formed the Methodist Episcopal church, electing Coke and Asbury superintendents, though the title was soon changed to bishop. Still claiming loyalty to Wesley and his guidelines, a denomination was born that, utilizing circuit riders as well as lay preachers, was soon to become the largest in the South and was to hold that position until exceeded by the total of the various BAPTIST denominations in the early twentieth century.

There were years of discouragement following the Revolution, however, including the defection of the Republican Methodists in 1792 in a challenge to the hierarchical structure (a similar movement led to the Methodist Protestant church in 1830); yet the denomination could still claim 65,000 members at the turn of the century with seven circuits in the old Southwest. Then, with the impetus of the Second GREAT AWAKENING together with the introduction of the CAMP MEETING, it was possible to spread the denomination so that by 1830 it became the most numerous religious body in America.

In 1844 the church divided over the issues of slavery and discipline, centering on the slaveholding of Bishop James Andrews of Georgia. Originally of a strong antislavery stance, the Methodists had accommodated to the prevailing southern scene until the issue could no longer be avoided. The General Conference attempted an amicable division, and in 1845 the Methodist Episcopal Church, South, came into existence affirming the slave society to be a positive good as well as biblically supported. Following the Civil War, separate Negro churches were formed from among the 200,000 Negro Methodists in the South. These new congregations affiliated primarily with the Methodist Episcopal church that had moved into the South, the AFRICAN METHODIST EPISCOPAL and African Methodist Episcopal Zion churches, or the Colored (after 1954, Christian) Methodist Episcopal church formed in 1870.

The war did not bring about a collapse of southern religious tradition, though the southern Methodists experienced a one-third loss of membership. Admittedly the Wesleyan influence declined, the distrust of northern ideas and industrialism continued, and the emphasis increased on the virtues of "old-time religion," including revivals and a heavy accent on a moral code denouncing dancing, tobacco, alcoholic beverages, gambling, card playing, and theater going.

Although priding itself on a clergy primarily without formal education, the Methodist church founded or reorganized academies and colleges in nearly every southern state. A central university, Vanderbilt, was established at Nashville in 1875, but it severed ties in 1914 after a long struggle. Also by the mid-1870s the southern church was becoming a church of the rising middle class, reflecting the mores of this segment of the population. In the 15 years following the war, the church doubled its membership. It was then challenged by the Holiness movement, which sought to reassert Wesleyan perfectionism, claiming that the church had veered from its traditional path. This resulted in considerable defections to new denominations, a story to be continued until World War I and becoming in the later years a movement to various new PENTECOSTAL CHURCHES.

A static conservatism in theology based on rigid biblicism, however, remained basically unchallenged particularly in the rural and small-town areas. Then revivalists like Samuel P. Jones led mass evangelism into the new urban areas developing from rural migrations and secured a hold for the denomination by stressing the validity of rural values for city life. Noticeably, the Social Gospel, so prominent in sections of the northern church, never achieved such status in the southern church, though a more liberal theological trend was developed at Emory, Duke, and Southern Methodist universities. Also in the pre–World War I era, the denomination gave unstinting support to the PROHIBITION movement and supplied considerable leadership in Bishop JAMES CANNON.

Then in 1939 the northern and southern churches, along with the Methodist Protestant church, merged to form the Methodist church with 8 million members, again becoming the largest Protestant denomination in America until the early sixties. Included in the new church were the jurisdictional conferences, which were actively used in the South to retain southern traditions. In the late forties and fifties the reunited Methodists enjoyed a general church resurgence, building to a membership of nearly 10 million by 1960 but experiencing a much slower rate of growth in the South. Segments within the denomination agonized through the social turmoil accented by the

Supreme Court's school desegregation decision of 1954 (BROWN V. BOARD OF EDUCATION), continuing through the sixties. In 1968 a further merger took place with the inclusion of the Evangelical United Brethren church to form the United Methodist church. In the seventies, this denomination, like so many of the large church bodies, suffered membership losses, bringing a halt to the marked growth that had been experienced over the past quarter-century.

See F. A. Norwood, *Story of American Methodism* (1974); E. S. Bucke (ed.), *History of American Methodists* (3 vols.; 1964); W. B. Posey, *Religious Strife on Southern Frontier* (1965); H. D. Farish, *Circuit Rider Dismounts* (1938); and K. K. Bailey, *Southern White Protestantism in 20th Century* (1964).

MYRON J. FOGDE
Augustana College, Rock Island, Ill.

MEXICAN-AMERICANS. The Spanish-speaking people of the United States, who are usually called Mexican-Americans, have their historical and cultural origins in Spain, Mexico, and the Spanish-Mexican borderlands (Texas, Arizona, California, New Mexico, and parts of Colorado). This phrase, like any chosen to characterize the Spanish speaking, is misleading and also condescending, but it is frequently used to include all those people who are sometimes called Spanish Americans, Latin Americans, Spanish colonials, Mexicans, Hispanos, CHICANOS, or other names.

The history of Mexican-Americans in the United States is usually considered to begin in the 1840s with the annexation of Texas in 1845, the war with Mexico in 1846, and the Mexican cession of 1848. But the story or chronicle of Mexican-Americans properly begins with the expansion of Europe and the meeting in the early sixteenth century of ethnically heterogeneous individuals known as Spaniards and various tribal members of Indian societies in what would become the central and northern fringe of the viceroyalty of New Spain. Mexican-American history thus includes not only the history of the Southwest—where two frontiers collided and a fusion began—but also the Iberian and Indian past of the area that became Mexico in 1821 and a regional area of the United States in 1848.

By this definition the Mexican-American experience stretches over four and a half centuries. It encompasses the Spanish conquest of the Indian civilization of Mexico and the creation of Mexican colonial society resulting from mestization, acculturation, and the eventual formation of regional Mexican cultures predominantly Spanish in language, religion, technology, political institutions, and artistic expression. In addition, because of intermarriage and cultural contact with the Anglo-American population of the Southwest since the nineteenth century, Mexican-Americans today "defy categorical classification as a group and no term or phrase adequately describes them."

Between 6 million and 9 million people of Spanish-Mexican ancestry live in the United States. Mexican-Americans are thus the largest minority group in the Southwest and the second largest minority population in the country. Ninety percent of the Mexican-Americans live in the Southwest, and in 1970 more than 1.5 million Mexican-Americans resided in Texas. No more than 10 percent of this population lives outside the Southwest. Very little research has been done on the Mexican-American population of the South, but Frederick Law Olmsted observed as early as 1857 that the "mingled Puritanism and brigandism, which distinguishes the vulgar mind of the South, peculiarly unfits it to harmoniously associate with the bigoted, childish, and passionate Mexicans."

The minority status of the Spanish-speaking people of the Southwest was an apparent fact by 1900 and is largely explained by the influx of new peoples into the region and by the economic order that replaced the older agrarian and pastoral economy. Mexican-Americans remain a heterogeneous ethnic group, but their relationship of subordination to the dominant majority population does give cohesion to the group, along with the use of the Spanish language and a certain community of psychological makeup. On many issues Mexican-Americans are more divided than united; and on others the social distance between generations of Mexican-Americans is greater than the social distance between Mexicans and Anglos. These generational differences, accompanied by local regionalism, have made for a low degree of solidarity within the larger ethnic group. Division remains in spite of the Chicano movement of recent years and will continue until the problems of discrimination and poverty and their attendant ills are overcome and equal opportunity ends the limitations of lower status in a generally affluent middle-class Anglo society.

See R. Acuña, *Occupied America* (1972); J. F. Bannon, *Spanish Borderlands Frontier, 1513–1821* (1970); C. E. Castañeda, *Our Catholic Heritage in Texas, 1519–1936* (7 vols.; 1936–58); D. Fernández-Florez, *Spanish Heritage in U.S.* (1965); C. Gibson, *Spain in America* (1967); C. McWilliams, *North from Mexico* (1949); M. Mörner, *Race Mixture in History of Latin America* (1967); S. Ramos, *Profile of Man and Culture in Mexico* (1963); and R. Rosaldo *et al., Chicano* (1973).

RALPH H. VIGIL
University of Nebraska, Lincoln

MEXICAN WAR (1846–1848) occurred so near the Civil War that it often seems neglected. Yet the war revealed many things, including America's desire to rule the continent. Because of this war the United States became almost half again as large, acquired a significant share of its mineral wealth, and complicated its own internal struggle over the expansion of human slavery.

The causes of the Mexican War are complex and are rooted in the feeling of most Americans in the inevitable realization of manifest destiny. Many applauded the acquisition of additional territory because it provided room for the expansion of slavery and the "southern way of life," and many feared it for the same reason. The immediate issue was the annexation of Texas. As early as the 1790s filibusters from the United States penetrated Spanish territory and in the 1820s other Americans (MOSES AUSTIN) received empresarial grants to locate immigrants in Texas. Because of established migratory trends, most of those who came were southerners, and they brought slavery with them. The early and genuine efforts by the Americans to Mexicanize themselves were stymied by two forces: too many Americans and a Mexican reaction to loss of population superiority in Texas. Resultant Mexican restrictions, plus the nationalistic reaction of the Americans, produced the Texas revolution and the natural desire to reunite with the United States. The Mexicans refused to recognize Texas and threatened war against the United States should Texas be admitted to the Union. Antislavery northeasterners blocked Texas' admission more than the Mexican threat, however, and the question dragged on for a decade.

The issue became embroiled in the presidential ELECTION OF 1844, when the Whig candidate HENRY CLAY and Martin Van Buren, a leading contender for the Democratic nomination, agreed to omit the expansion question from the contest. This cut against the grain of the public's feeling and enabled JAMES K. POLK to obtain the presidency following a campaign that called for the "reannexation" of Texas and the "reoccupation" of Oregon. The Oregon question had been pending since 1818, when Great Britain and the United States agreed that joint occupation of the territory would be acceptable until one power had a clear advantage. Thus Polk entered office facing a potential war against two foreign powers. By the time he assumed office the process of Texas' admission under congressional joint resolution was already underway, and Texas became the twenty-eighth state on December 29, 1845. Polk's own desires went even farther. Already Americans were casting covetous eyes toward California. With the country determined on expansion, the stage was set for bold plays. Polk had a three-pronged policy: give England notice that joint occupation would terminate at the end of 1846; have Commodore R. F. Stockton poised to seize California should war erupt with Mexico, while John C. Frémont's topographical party stood ready to help on land; and send JOHN SLIDELL to Mexico to resolve the differences between the two countries with American dollars. Adding pressure to Slidell's mission was the presence of General ZACHARY TAYLOR's command along the Nueces River, the traditional boundary between Texas and the Mexican state of Coahuila. An area of disagreement was the territory between the Nueces and the Rio Grande. President Antonio de Santa Anna had agreed by the Treaty of Velasco (May 14, 1836) to transfer the lands between the two rivers to Texas, and now the United States pressed that claim. Slidell was to offer for the U.S. to assume damage claims against Mexico, as much as $5 million for the cession of New Mexico and up to $25 million for California. The Mexicans would not receive Slidell. Oregon ceased to be a problem when the British suggested and Polk accepted an extension of the forty-ninth parallel, and now Polk could turn his entire attention to the Mexican problem.

On January 13, 1846, Taylor was ordered into the disputed territory, and in May word came from him that a clash had occurred between Mexican and U.S. troops. Polk asked Congress for a declaration of war, and on May 13 it was granted, 40 to two in the Senate and 174 to 14 in the House.

Polk took the lead in planning offensive strategy. First, Taylor led his troops into action in northern Mexico. Despite his success in taking Monterrey, he felt that badly needed supplies were denied in favor of General WINFIELD SCOTT, who was organizing a force to land at Veracruz. Polk may have judged Taylor less able than Scott, or he may have been attempting to block the popular Taylor from a presidential bid. After landing at Veracruz, Scott took the city on March 27, 1847. With 14,000 men he moved via the pass at Cerro Gordo where he defeated the Mexican resistance, to Chapultepec, where he captured another fortress before moving into Mexico City. Meanwhile, Stephen W. Kearny organized a march from Leavenworth, Kan., to Santa Fe and then on to California to take command of the American operations there. Colonel A. W. DONIPHAN branched southward from Kearny and rendezvoused with Taylor.

With American forces victorious on all fronts, NICHOLAS TRIST was sent to Mexico to negotiate the Treaty of Guadalupe-Hidalgo, which was completed on February 2, 1848. Mexico agreed to cede California and New Mexico to the United States and to accept the Rio Grande boundary, and the United States agreed to settle claims against Mexico and to pay $15 million. At home the war had further pointed out a growing sectional division. Congressman David Wilmot's rider banning slavery from territory gained by the war, although it did not pass, alarmed many southerners, who bore the greatest burden of the war in manpower and finance.

See A. F. Bill, *Rehearsal for Conflict* (1947); R. S. Henry, *Story of Mexican War* (1950); R. S. Ripley, *War with Mexico* (2 vols; 1949); G. L. Rives, *U.S. and Mexico, 1821–1848* (1913); J. H. Smith, *War with Mexico* (2 vols; 1919); and S. V. Conner and O. B. Raulk, *North America Divided, 1846–1848* (1971), fine bibliography.

ARCHIE P. MCDONALD
Stephen F. Austin State University

MIAMI, FLA. (pop. 334,859). Located on Biscayne Bay approximately 70 miles south of West Palm Beach, the site has been favored since earliest times by visitors. Several groups of Indians built small villages here; the Spanish coveted the location but could not hold it; and the U.S. government built Ft. Dallas here in 1836 during the SEMINOLE WAR. Hurricanes, the shortage of fresh water, and difficulties in farming the land combined to thwart permanent development of the area until 1870, when William Brickell and Julia A. Tuttle bought land on both sides of the small Miami River. A drainage system was begun, and the rich soil of the hammocks was prepared for cultivation. Miami's future was not to be as an agricultural town, however. In 1895 HENRY M. FLAGLER became interested in developing the town of 260 people. He made it the southern terminus of his railroad (1896), dredged the harbor, and began promoting Miami as a winter resort. The village grew quickly into a city, and during the 1920s, after completion of U.S. Route 1, Miami's real estate boom spilled over into three new suburbs: Miami Beach, Coral Gables, and Hialeah. Metropolitan Miami continues to be one of the nation's most popular resorts and recreation areas. It also is a major aviation center, port of entry, and shipping point with connections to the West Indies and South America. The University of Miami (1925) is in Coral Gables.

See N. Smiley, *Yesterday's Miami* (1973); H. Muir, *Miami, U.S.A.* (1953); C. E. Nash, *Magic of Miami Beach* (1938); J. G. Du Puis, *History of Early Medicine, Public Schools, and Agriculture* (1954); F. W. DeCroix, *Historical, Industrial, and Commercial Data* (1911?); I. Cohen, *Historical Sketches* (1925); E. V. Blackman, *Miami and Dade County* (1921); K. Ballinger, *Miami Millions* (1936);

annual numbers of *Tequesta* (1941–), published by Historical Association of South Florida; and files of Miami *News* (1896–), *Herald* (1910–), and *Diario Las Americas* (1953–).

MIAMI HERALD has been in continuous publication since 1910. Regarded by many newspapermen as the most progressive journal printed in the South, it has a circulation of over 400,000 copies daily, which ranks it the twelfth largest paper in the nation.

See bound copies at University of Florida Library (incomplete 1910–27, complete 1928–) and microfilm from Microfilm Corporation of America (1911–).

MIAMI NEWS began publication in 1896 as the Miami *Metropolis* and was known as the *News Metropolis* between 1923 and 1925. It is a Democratic daily with a circulation of approximately 70,000 copies.

See bound copies at publishers and microfilm from Bell & Howell (1896–).

MIDDLE CLASS has constituted one factor in southern society since colonial times, but until the mid–twentieth century the middle class did not dominate either the region's economy or its culture. In this respect, the South remained distinct from the North and West. The southern middle class consisted of persons engaged in commerce; members of professions, such as doctors, ministers, and lawyers; and manufacturers. Small farmers might be included in the middle class to the extent that they were dependent upon the market, but for the majority of antebellum small farmers market involvement was minimal. For the most part, the middle class remained dependent upon and auxiliary to the planters, who set the tone of southern life and dominated all major institutions. Despite the Herculean efforts of such men as WILLIAM GREGG and J. D. B. De Bow (DE BOW'S REVIEW) to encourage industrial development, manufactures remained a poor stepsister to southern agriculture through the end of the nineteenth century.

In the 1880s and 1890s, the southern middle class began to emerge as an independent class with its own ethos and aspirations, perhaps most forcefully articulated by HENRY GRADY's NEW SOUTH movement. Although they honored the LOST CAUSE and never repudiated their past, these members of the middle class perceived their interests and needs as distinct from those of the planters. The development of railroads, tobacco and textile factories, coal mines, and iron and steel mills provided sources of economic power to rival the planters' traditional hegemony.

Spokesmen for the middle class stressed economic and social integration of the South with the rest of the nation. They pushed for improved transportation facilities, better education, more modern prisons and asylums, and amelioration of racial friction. Led by the middle class, thousands of southerners subscribed to community funds in the late nineteenth century to build cotton mills, tobacco factories, and railroads, but the South remained dependent on cotton in an era when international developments deflated cotton prices and made it impossible to rely on southern financing alone. The early twentieth century witnessed the influx of considerable northern investment attracted by low taxes, favorable laws, and cheap labor. The southern middle class had created and maintained this hospitable environment for business development, but, because they had to share with outside investors both control of new industries and the profits of expansion, the southern middle class remained dependent and unfulfilled.

See H. Woodman, *Journal of Southern History* (Aug., 1963); C. V. Woodward, *Origins of New South* (1951); S. Hackney, *Populism to Progressivism* (1971); D. Grantham, *Hoke Smith* (1958); J. Daniels, *Tar Heel Editor* (1941); and P. Gaston, *New South Creed* (1970).

JANICE HARDING-MCGOWAN
University of Rochester

MIDDLETON FAMILY stemmed from the merchant class of London. Edward Middleton (?–1685) settled in Charleston, S.C., in 1678 and was joined later by his brother Arthur (?–1685), who had been an interloping slave trader in Barbados. Before their deaths, both had acquired large grants of land and taken part in colonial politics as members of the Barbadian, antiproprietary faction known as the "Goose Creek men." Edward left a four-year-old son Arthur (1681–1737), whose political patrimony was nurtured by his stepfather Jacob Howes, another Goose Creek man. This Arthur became the leader of the revolution of 1719 that resulted in the overthrow of the lords proprietors. As president of the council, he was acting governor from 1725 to 1730, during which the colony was beset with economic troubles and Indian wars.

In the third generation, Henry Middleton (1717–1784) built a fortune in rice and indigo production through slave labor. He was no placeman in politics, however, resigning from the council, on which he had served from 1755 to 1770, to protest an encroachment on colonial rights and handling the exchange of money when the Commons voted £1,500 sterling to the Wilkes fund. Henry was a noted philanthropist, contributing heavily to religious and educational bodies. Through his children's marriages, the Middletons became connected with other powerful families, including the Izards, Rutledges, Manigaults, DRAYTONS, and PINCKNEYS. During the Revolution, Henry and his son Arthur (1742–1787) were leaders in the provincial movement. Henry also served as president of the CONTINENTAL CONGRESS (1774–1775) but resigned from the South Carolina delegation in 1776. He was replaced by Arthur (1776–1778, 1781–1783), who signed the DECLARATION OF INDEPENDENCE.

Later prominent Middletons include Henry (1770–1846), who served as state representative, senator, and governor (1810–1812), member of Congress, (1815–1819), minister to Russia (1820–1830), and Unionist leader in the NULLIFICATION controversy; and Williams (1809–1883), who signed the ordinance of secession. Other members of his generation served the Confederate cause in the military. Thus, through this representative family of South Carolina, one can see the birth, growth, and death of southern civilization built on slave labor and states' rights.

See M. E. Sirmans, *Colonial South Carolina* (1966); D. D. Wallace, *History of South Carolina* (1935); and L. Cheves, *South Carolina Magazine of History* (July, 1900).

DIXON K. DURHAM
University of South Carolina

MIGRANT WORKERS became an important element in the agricultural economy after 1900. Prior to this time the demand for seasonal labor on American farms was small. Very little outside labor was required, and then it was usually provided by persons hired from the local area. In the twentieth century, however, the mechanization of the preharvest operations in many crops altered the traditional labor requirements. The resident labor force using machines could plant and cultivate more acres than it could harvest. As a result, there was a great need for seasonal labor during the harvest period.

The South became the main source of migrant farm workers. In this region, there was a large reservoir of laborers who could not find full-time employment in the areas in which they lived. In the South the decline of the TENANT FARMING system contributed to the building up of this pool of underemployed labor. In addition, the presence of thousands of Mexican immigrants and MEXICAN-AMERICANS in south Texas created a labor force

that could not find sufficient employment close to home. These workers became increasingly mobile with the introduction of the automobile and the development of a better highway system. Using automobiles, workers could follow the crops as they matured throughout the nation, working only a few days or weeks on each farm.

During the winter months, many migrants find employment in the fruit and vegetable industries of Florida and south Texas. Each spring, as the demand for seasonal labor develops farther north, large numbers of farm workers from the South begin migrating in search of jobs. The movement of workers grows in size and flows over the boundaries of the southern states and spreads to the rest of the nation. When the season is over, the migrants generally come back to their homes in various parts of the South. In recent years, the demand for migrant labor has been reduced by the mechanization of cotton harvesting and the continual invention of machines for harvesting fruits and vegetables.

See G. B. Tindall, *Emergence of New South* (1967); C. McWilliams, *Ill Fares the Land* (1942, 1967); T. E. Moore, *Slaves We Rent* (1965); R. Coles, *Uprooted Children* (1970); and G. Coalson, *Migrant Farm Labor System in Texas* (1977).

GEORGE O. COALSON
Texas A. & I. University, Kingsville

MIGRATION, NEGRO. See NEGRO MIGRATION

MIKASUKI INDIANS. See SEMINOLE INDIANS

MILITARY TRADITION. The prominent, possibly unique role of the South in the nation's military history has long been accepted. According to the familiar story, most of the great generals— GEORGE WASHINGTON, ANDREW JACKSON, ROBERT E. LEE, STONEWALL JACKSON, John J. Pershing, and Omar N. Bradley—have been southerners. Others who happened not to be born in the South, including George C. Marshall and George S. Patton, Jr., were often educated at the VIRGINIA MILITARY INSTITUTE, or perhaps at the CITADEL in Charleston, S.C. The South, it is commonly said, had an aristocratic planter style, which produced an abundance of dashing, imperious West Pointers who on the eve of the Civil War occupied the bulk of the regular army's senior posts. At the lower social level, no less accustomed to shoot and to ride, came the farmers who formed the composite portrait of ragged, reckless Johnny Reb. Even hostile northerners at the time of the Civil War bowed to the legend of a distinctive and formidable southern military tradition. The battle of New Orleans (1815) was conceded as a largely southern victory, together with the achievement of Texas independence (1836) and the élan that led to the defeat of Mexico (1846–1848). In abolitionist eyes the whole antebellum South was an armed camp, constantly engaged in suppressing slave discontent.

There is obviously a measure of truth in this view of southern military prowess. The Confederacy displayed battlefield talents of a remarkable order. After Appomattox, the events of the war were remembered and cherished in the South much more conspicuously than in the North. New military schools were opened in the South, particularly in Virginia. When West Point was again opened to southerners, they began to attend in increasing numbers. The same was true of the U.S. Naval Academy at Annapolis, Md., which had likewise had a southern tinge in antebellum days. In the twentieth century the South has contributed manpower to the army, navy, and air corps, among both officers and enlisted men, somewhat in excess of its proportion of the U.S. population.

However, the story is more complicated than might appear. Before the outbreak of the Civil War, southern regular officers were undoubtedly prominent in the cavalry, among West Point staff, and in senior administrative posts. Thus WINFIELD SCOTT, general-in-chief from 1841 to 1861, was a Virginian. JEFFERSON DAVIS of Mississippi, a West Pointer, was secretary of war (1853–1857), and was succeeded (1857–1861) by JOHN B. FLOYD of Virginia. In Floyd's era the commandant of cadets at West Point was WILLIAM J. HARDEE of Georgia. Even so, of the 950 staff and line officers serving in 1860, only 41.6 percent were from slave states (including the District of Columbia and nonseceding states), a figure rather below the ratio of northern to southern white population in 1860. Between 1802 and 1861 New York contributed 317 West Point graduates; Pennsylvania, 187; and Massachusetts, 124, against the 142 of Virginia, the South's leading state.

It has often been said that volunteer companies and military schools were a marked feature of the pre–Civil War South. But there was in fact little difference between the sections. DUELING, tournaments, and filibustering were commoner in the South; yet other forms of VIOLENCE were at least equally evident in the free states.

In military matters, then (to use the word *military* in a broad sense), the South's antebellum tradition was in part a myth, stimulated by sectional rivalry. The element of myth, powerfully reinforced by the military record of the Confederacy, was heightened and embellished by the Civil War. Historians have tended to repeat it, somewhat uncritically. The point is not that the Old South was lacking in military ardor, but that the differences between North and South, seen detachedly, may seem less striking than the similarities. The South's postbellum military prowess is of course a separate and undeniable phenomenon, though it may have built upon the lineage so lovingly fashioned by chroniclers of the LOST CAUSE— and at times so sourly invoked by northerners who, seeking to explain why the outnumbered Confederacy held out for four long years, depicted the Old South as one vast quasi-military conspiracy. If the Civil War is the key episode in the nation's history, it is also the central determinant in shaping the concept of a unique southern military tradition. And the extraordinarily appealing figure of Robert E. Lee, the gallant son of a gallant Revolutionary War cavalryman, is probably the main factor in fixing the notion of a romantic warrior South upon our historical imaginations.

See R. D. Meade, *Current History* (April, 1929); J. C. Bonner, *Georgia Review* (Spring, 1955); J. H. Franklin, *Militant South* (1956); S. P. Huntington, *Soldier and State* (1957); E. J. Warner, *Generals in Gray* (1959); and M. F. Cunliffe, *Soldiers and Civilians* (1968). For background, see E. J. and R. W. Crooks, *Ring Tournament* (1936); and R. G. Osterweis, *Romanticism and Nationalism* (1949).

MARCUS CUNLIFFE
University of Sussex, England

MILLEDGE, JOHN (1757–1818), first entered politics as a Liberty Boy participating in a 1775 raid on Savannah's powder magazine. He remained active in the revolutionary cause, both as a soldier and, despite his youth, as state attorney general. After serving in Georgia's general assembly (1789–1790), the young lawyer became a representative in the U.S. Congress in 1792. When the YAZOO LAND FRAUDS scandal shocked state politics, he joined his friend, the fiery JAMES JACKSON, in seeking repeal of the Yazoo grant. In 1802 these two helped negotiate with United States commissioners the cession of Georgia's trans-Chattahoochee lands, thus ridding the state of responsibility for Yazoo claims. Later that year Milledge was elected governor. During his term the state capital moved to a new town named Milledgeville in his honor. From 1806 until the illness of his wife forced his retirement in 1809, Milledge, a strong Jeffersonian, served as U.S. senator. He used some of his considerable wealth for agricultural experimentation and donating a site for Georgia's new state university.

See *Correspondence of John Milledge* (1949), contains biographical sketch and bibliographical information, most useful; G. White, *Historical Collections of Georgia* (1854); and *Investigation of Claims of John Milledge* (1807), anonymous pamphlet.

FRANCES L. HARROLD
Georgia State University

MILLEDGEVILLE, GA. (pop. 11,601), was laid out in 1803 to replace Louisville as the state's capital. Thirty miles northeast of Macon on the fall line at the Oconee River, it remained the seat of Georgia's government until 1868. Except for the burning of the penitentiary, the city escaped destruction during SHERMAN'S MARCH TO THE SEA, and many fine antebellum homes survive to this day. Modern Milledgeville is the home of Georgia State College, and its industries produce woolen goods, mobile homes, and brick, tile, and clay products.

See L. S. Beeson, *History of Milledgeville* (1943) and *100 Years of Old Governor's Mansion* (1938); A. M. G. Cook, *History of Baldwin County* (1925); and files of weekly *Union-Recorder* (1819–). Mary Vinson Memorial Library maintains Beeson Collection (Indian lore, churches, and local biographies), Bonner Collection (published works of J. C. Bonner, historian), and DAR collection of colonial records of Georgia.

MILLIGAN, EX PARTE (4 Wallace 2 [1866]). In October, 1864, L. P. Milligan of Indiana and others were arrested by federal military authorities for conspiring to release Confederate prisoners of war. Tried in Indiana by a federal military tribunal established by President Abraham Lincoln, Milligan was convicted and sentenced to be hanged. He appealed his conviction, and his case was reviewed by President Andrew Johnson, who commuted Milligan's sentence to life imprisonment.

Milligan's attorneys argued that his arrest, trial, and conviction by military authorities were unconstitutional violations of his rights as a civilian far removed from a theater of war. Government attorneys based their case on the Habeas Corpus Act of 1863 (authorizing a suspension of writs) and on the government's inherent power to defend itself against a planned insurrection. All justices upheld the constitutionality of the statute authorizing a suspension of writs of habeas corpus during periods of grave emergency. Moreover, all justices agreed that Lincoln's military tribunals were unconstitutional, but they divided in their reasons for upholding this portion of Milligan's appeal. In a split five-to-four decision, a majority of the U.S. Supreme Court, speaking through Justice David

Davis, denied both presidential and congressional authority to establish military tribunals except at a place and during a time of an actual invasion. "Martial law," opined Davis, "can never exist where the courts are open and in the proper and unobstructed exercise of their jurisdiction."

The decision was delivered in December, 1866, and it seemed to place the Court on a collision course with the Radical Republican members of Congress. Radical Republicans believed (and most Democrats and southerners hoped) that the Court intended to challenge congressional Reconstruction. A few weeks later, the Court's decision in *ex parte Garland* seemed to confirm that suspicion and belief. In MISSISSIPPI V. JOHNSON, in GEORGIA V. STANTON, and in *Texas* v. *White*, however, the Supreme Court avoided any such direct confrontation and upheld the Reconstruction powers of both the executive and the legislative branches.

See S. Klaus (ed.), *Milligan Case* (1929, 1970); H. H. Burton, *American Bar Association Journal* (Feb., 1955); and H. H. Hyman, *More Perfect Union* (1973).

MILLSAPS COLLEGE (Jackson, Miss. 39210) was founded in 1890 and named for Reuben Webster Millsaps, the school's benefactor and a Jackson merchant. Today this small, Methodist, liberal arts college has an enrollment of fewer than 1,000 students. Its library maintains specialized collections on Methodist church history and on theater, music, and the other arts.

MILL SPRINGS, BATTLE OF (January 19, 1862). Felix Zollicoffer, commanding Confederate forces in eastern Kentucky, advanced in late November, 1861, from Cumberland Ford to Mill Springs in order to improve his supply situation while observing the federals and covering the routes into eastern Tennessee. However, he crossed the Cumberland, placing this large river at his back while superior forces lay in his front. GEORGE CRITTENDEN, his superior, arrived with reinforcements and prepared to withdraw across the river. Before he could accomplish this, GEORGE THOMAS was ordered to concentrate his Union forces and drive back the Confederates. Crittenden determined to attack Thomas before the concentration was effected. Advancing some nine miles to Logan's Crossroads, he attacked about dawn on January 19. A three-hour battle ensued in which Zollicoffer was mortally wounded. Driven in disorder from the field, Crittenden retreated across the Cumberland. His force largely broke up in retreat. The Confederate losses were 533; the federal, 246. This first significant federal victory cleared eastern Kentucky of Confederate forces.

See *Official Records, Armies*; K. P. Williams, *Lincoln Finds a General* (1952); S. F. Horn, *Army of Tennessee* (1953); H. M. Cist, *Army of Cumberland* (1882); C. P. Roland, *A. S. Johnston* (1964); F. F. McKinney, *Education in Violence* (1961), good biography of Thomas; W. Thomas, *George H. Thomas* (1964); and R. U. Johnson and C. C. Buel (eds.), *Battles and Leaders* (1884–88).

ROBERT S. QUIMBY
Michigan State University

MILL TOWNS emerged in the late nineteenth century when cotton TEXTILES developed as the major nonagricultural industry of the South. Concentrated in the Piedmont region of the Carolinas and Georgia, the industry grew rapidly from fewer than 7,000 workers producing $2 million worth of goods in 1890 to 261,000 workers turning out $830 million worth of textiles in 1927. Most mills operated almost entirely with white labor.

Early mill sites, chosen for their accessibility to water power, were often in country towns or rual areas that lacked housing adequate for the influx of mill operatives. Even when mills were built near towns, factory owners usually constructed a separate mill village for their workers, in part because company housing facilitated supervision and control of workers and partly because this practice was less expensive than paying workers enough to provide their own housing. Rent was often free and always cheap compared with whatever private housing was available. Standards of sanitation and comfort ranged from good to miserable, but mills generally provided accommodations similar to the small farms in the area. It was the drabness and uniformity of mill villages that depressed most contemporary observers.

Life in mill villages revolved around the factory, which usually ran 12 to 14 hours daily. As in New England, the family was employed by the mill as a unit with the father and all children over ten years of age working in the factory. Mills often required families to provide one worker per room, which encouraged small families to take in lodgers or relatives. Many factory owners built churches and grade schools and paid ministers and teachers for their services; naturally they selected ministers who preached hard work and teachers who did not object when their pupils were called from the classroom to work in the mills. Workers fought periodically to unionize the mill towns (LABOR UNIONS). Bitter struggles surrounded these attempts because most southern mill owners were and still are adamantly opposed to organization of their labor force. The owners'

complete control of the mill towns was a powerful weapon in resisting unionization, and the isolation of mill workers from both farmers and town residents impeded their attempts to gain support for shorter hours, better wages, and restriction of CHILD LABOR. After World War I, many operatives bought their own houses; private merchants replaced company stores; movie houses and YMCAs added variety to town life; and the automobile gave access to life beyond the mill village.

See A. McLaurin, *Paternalism and Protest* (1971); H. Thompson, *Cotton Field to Cotton Mill* (1906); M. E. Reed, *Labor History* (Spring, 1973); H. L. Herring, *Welfare Work* (1929); and M. Potwin, *Cotton Mill People* (1927).

JANICE HARDING-MCGOWAN
University of Rochester

MIMS, EDWIN (1872–1959), born in Richmond, Ark., attended Vanderbilt University. In 1894 he became professor of English literature at Trinity College in North Carolina. During the late 1890s he completed his doctoral work at Cornell, and in 1912 became chairman of the English department at Vanderbilt. Mims's lifelong religious enthusiasm fed his desire to be of service to his beloved but backward South. Believing that cultural uplift was essential to progress, he sought to promote through lecturing and writing a "cosmopolitanism and openmindedness" based on the cultural heritage of Victorian Britain. Perennially the scholar-activist and NEW SOUTH progressive, he became coeditor of the *South Atlantic Quarterly* and published *Sidney Lanier* (1905); he campaigned for better public schools, academic freedom, and anti-lynching laws. Amid the upsurge of racial and religious bigotry in the 1920s, Mims rushed into print *The Advancing South*, asserting that despite setbacks progress was being made.

See M. O'Brien, "To Seek a Newer World" (M.A. thesis, Vanderbilt, 1973); M. L. Park, "Edwin Mims" (M.A. thesis, Vanderbilt, 1964); and Mims Papers, Joint University Libraries, Nashville.

WALTER J. FRASER, JR.
The Citadel

MINOR, VIRGINIA LOUISA (1824–1894), was born in Caroline County, Va. She grew up in Charlottesville and in 1843 married a lawyer who established a practice in St. Louis. During the Civil War, she worked in the war relief effort of the St. Louis Union Aid Society, an affiliate of the Western Sanitary Commission. After the war, she joined the WOMEN'S RIGHTS MOVEMENT and helped to organize the Missouri Woman Suffrage Association. She served as president for many years and was Missouri's best-known suffragist until her death. She gained national attention when she and her husband filed a lawsuit claiming that the Fourteenth Amendment granted suffrage to women. The U.S. Supreme Court ruled unanimously in 1875 (*Minor v. Happersett*) that the right of suffrage was not a privilege of citizenship under the Constitution. This notable case practically ended the suffragists' hopes of gaining the franchise quickly through the courts.

See E. C. Stanton *et al.*, *History of Woman Suffrage* (1881); and H. R. Pinkney, in *Notable American Women* (1971).

PAUL E. FULLER
Wesleyan College, Macon, Ga.

MINSTRELSY. Commonly thought to have originated among the black slave populations of the pre–Civil War South, blackface or "Negro" minstrelsy was probably the product of northern white entertainers. As early as 1796 blackface was donned by white singers to sing "Negro" songs on stage and in circuses. By the 1820s most of the basic ingredients that were to compose the minstrel show had been developed in theaters from New York to Louisville, Ky. Thomas Dartmouth Rice, a New Yorker, is generally credited with being the father of American minstrelsy. Known as JIM CROW or Daddy Rice, it was he who first constructed an entire act around the black-faced performer.

The first full-fledged "Ethiopian" minstrel show first appeared in 1843. Almost from the beginning it followed a set pattern. It was divided into two parts—eventually three as olio acts became more important—the first of which featured the dandy "darky" or big-city Negro with his big talk, flashy clothes, and womanizing ways. The plantation or "Jim Crow" Negro was relegated to the second part. He spoke the same dialect as his urban counterpart, but was as ragged as the dandy was gorgeous. Once an evening a pompous speech was delivered, displaying abysmal ignorance of language, grammar, and subject matter. Dances and musical accompaniments were interspersed throughout the performance, as were conundrums and question-answer jokes. The "interlocutor" or master of ceremonies was generally the only white-faced performer on stage, and his position was at the center of the front line of performers.

Minstrel shows continued popular well into the twentieth century, finally giving way before the objections of people who saw them as perjorative caricatures, offensive to human dignity.

See E. L. Rice, *Monarchs of Minstrelsy* (1911); R. C. Toll, *Backing Up* (1974); D. Paskman, *Gentlemen, Be Seated!* (1976); and G. D. Engle (ed.), *This Grotesque Essence* (1978).

ALAN W. C. GREEN
Charlotte, Vt.

MINT JULEP. Although juleps—sweetened drinks prepared for medicinal or pleasurable purposes—are many centuries old, the mint julep prepared with whiskey is of a distinctively southern evolution. Like many southern traditions, consensus on its ingredients, preparation, and service is impossible to attain. Essentially it is a highly individualized mixture of whiskey, ice, mint leaves, and sugar, prepared in a silver or pewter goblet and served after being thoroughly chilled and frosted. One classic version of the mint julep is prepared by first rolling the moistened lip of the goblet in powdered sugar and then filling the glass with alternating thin layers of freshly cut young mint leaves, powdered sugar, and finely cracked ice. When the container is nearly full, the finest available BOURBON whiskey is poured over the layers, and the entire concoction is stirred vigorously until the sides of the goblet are thoroughly frosted (the entire process may take the better part of an hour). Then, while slowly rotating the drink, the person sips the prepared nectar over the goblet's sugared lips.

Marylanders traditionally preferred rye to bourbon whiskey, and some lovers of the mint julep float a dollop of rum on the drink after all stirring is finished. Some people insist that virginal mint leaves with the stems cut short bleed sufficiently to flavor the drink. HENRY CLAY, however, argued that the leaves should be slightly bruised against the side of the goblet with the backside of a spoon. Many people actually prefer to crush or pummel the leaves to ensure the mintyness of the finished beverage. One vigorous dissenter, who believed that this practice released the more bitter juices of the mint, held that a man who would "crush the leaves would put scorpions in a baby's bed." Clay and many others also have argued that the sugar must be mixed with a small amount of spring water to prevent lumps of undissolved sugar from intruding on the pleasurable sipping of a properly mixed drink.

At Churchill Downs, where volume production and high standards must be merged to mix the traditional drink of the Kentucky Derby, the following recipe is used: one or more tablespoons of sugar and a tablespoon of water are muddled with a sprig of mint leaves to form a thick green paste; after a chilled julep cup is half filled with shaved ice, the mint syrup and two ounces of bourbon are stirred in; the goblet is then filled with ice, and a sprig of fresh mint and straws are set into the ice; then the entire drink is frosted in a refrigerator for at least half an hour. However it is made, the mint julep is one of the finest symbols of southern tradition and hospitality.

MISCEGENATION was first effectively introduced into the American language by David Goodman Croly and George Wakeman of the New York *World* in a pamphlet entitled *Miscegenation: The Theory of the Blending of the Races, Applied to the American White Man and Negro*. Published anonymously in 1863, it was a cynical attempt to win northern white voters over to the Democrats by making a Radical Republican appear to be the author of this tract, which championed the hated concept of intermarriage between blacks and whites. The word has retained its original black-white emphasis, but broadly it designates the universal tendency of diverse peoples to interbreed when thrown together by the forces of history.

In the American South the process began when Europeans first probed the southeastern fringes of North America. In nascent Virginia it was symbolized by the marriage of POCAHONTAS and John Rolfe. Their son Thomas became the ancestor of a host of southerners who remained in the white world. Many ordinary whites and Indians also commingled over the generations, especially in rugged frontier areas. Some of the offspring of these unions like Thomas Rolfe blended into the white population; others remained Indian. A few "breeds" like ALEXANDER MCGILLIVRAY and William Weatherford of the CREEKS and John Ross of the CHEROKEES led red resistance to white encroachment, but by the 1830s the Indian tribes were removed from most of the South.

Blacks suffered a harsh fate too, but they remained a much more prominent part of the overall southern population. Some interbreeding with whites and to a lesser extent with Indians occurred as a few blacks were brought into the early colonial South, but only when whites began importing masses of West African slave laborers late in the seventeenth century did miscegenation become extensive.

Throughout the antebellum period, white social and legal restrictions against "amalgamation" were ineffective. Interbreeding between black men and white women was not unknown, despite terrible risks, but the overwhelming majority of interracial unions was between white men of every class and black women who, as "inferior beings" and "property," were very vulnerable. Some of these affairs were simply rape, most were probably casual liaisons, but a few were lasting unions of mutual affection. For example, prominent Georgia planter David Dickson lived openly with his Amanda and their children and left her part of his estate after the Civil War, and Kentuckian RICHARD M. JOHNSON, vice-president of the United States from 1837 to 1841, made no secret of his only family, his slave Julia Chinn and their two daughters (who married whites).

But as with Indians and whites, antebellum black-white interbreeding was poorly documented. Miscegenation in the American South was probably less extensive than in Latin America, but it was certainly less condoned and recognized. Even late antebellum federal censuses made only vague "black" and "mulatto" designations, and the 1860 estimate that approximately 12 percent of the nation's over 4 million "colored" people were "mulattoes" is probably too low. Southern courthouses contain clues, such as divorce proceedings based on infidelity with a black and wills with emancipation provisions intimating or stating that the freed blacks were the children of the deceased. But the overall uncertainty remains and is well illustrated by the scholarly debate over whether widower THOMAS JEFFERSON really did father several children by his slave Sally Hemings, the half-sister of his dead wife.

Antebellum slavery disintegrated during the Civil War, and miscegenation may have increased in this tumultuous period, but in the long run it probably decreased somewhat. Free blacks gained more control over their own private lives even as legal SEGREGATION evolved to separate the races further. Although traditional interbreeding between white males and black females probably lessened, more blacks were able to try the old strategy of "passing over" into the privileged white world.

Miscegenation remains an imprecise and uncertain process in contemporary times. The crumbling of legal segregation and a resurgence of ethnic pride among blacks are only two of many recent developments, but long-standing trends will probably not change drastically. Over the centuries the red and especially the black and white folk of the South have lived simultaneously together and apart, gradually blending enough to create a "southern way of life." And this is only one dramatic aspect of a general American trend, which has drawn peoples together from all over the earth and shaped a culture that is both uniform and diverse.

See G. Myrdal, *American Dilemma* (1962), good overview; G. M. Fredrickson, *Black Image* (1971), origin of word; J. H. Johnston, *Miscegenation* (1970), best antebellum documentation; A. Haley, *Roots* (1976), black genealogy; H. G. Gutman, *Black Family* (1976); C. N. Degler, *Neither Black Nor White* (1971); G. B. Nash, *Red, White, and Black* (1974); and W. D. Jordan, *White over Black* (1968).

F. N. BONEY
University of Georgia

MISSISSIPPI, more even than other southern states, is the victim of a stereotype. To the unreconstructed romantic, it is a land of magnolias and mansions, plantations and cotton fields, a state museum straight from Al Jolson and Tin Pan Alley or *Gone with the Wind*. To the unknowledgeable modern liberal puritan, it is a state populated by violent rednecks and oppressed blacks, a sinister and grotesque Faulknerian place that is both mystifying and morally troublesome. It is, of course, neither, and it never has been.

Yet like most stereotypes, there is enough truth to make them persist. There are in Mississippi's past and present some plantations, some magnolias, some violence and oppression. Certainly one of the major themes of the state's history is the tension and intertwined fortunes of blacks and whites. With the exception of early Spanish and French influences, which still persist along the Gulf Coast, the white population has always been of British descent, Protestant, and ethnically homogeneous. Balanced against and thrown with them has been a large black population. Both groups have been until recently tied to the land and to cotton. Both have been rural; and, with the exception of a few large planters of the Delta and the bottoms, both, in contrast to the rest of the United States, have been remarkably poor. In all these ways Mississippi may be seen, then, as the most southern of southern states—a prototype where is mixed all of the peculiar forces and tensions that have made the American South unique in the nation.

Geography. The geography of Mississippi has been a major determinant in the economic and cultural development of the state. Although Mississippi has been within its black-white framework ethnically unified, the state has never been politically and economically monolithic. SOIL quality has imposed upon the state a rough division of interests between planters and small farmers, between political and economic conservatism and a sort of Jacksonian populism. Since the territorial period, planters, blacks, and cotton have dominated the fertile areas in the west, while small hill farmers

have prevailed in the red clay hills and piney woods of the east. It is no coincidence that today the bulk of the state's blacks still live in the western counties and that the last stronghold of KING COTTON is in the Delta region of northwest Mississippi.

Mississippi today spreads over 47,338 square miles. The climate is moderate with hot summers and mild winters. The average temperature in January is 48.7 degrees F. In July it is 81.3 degrees F. The growing season ranges from 200 days in the north to 270 days on the Gulf Coast. Rainfall in the four seasons is almost evenly distributed: almost 15 inches each in the winter, spring, and summer in the planting and growing seasons and slightly below ten inches in the fall, when crops are harvested. Obviously this is an ideal climate for agriculture, the economic base that has dominated most of the state's history.

Geographically Mississippi may be divided into six soil regions. For a depth of 30 miles inland from the coast is a relatively flat plain of sandy infertile soil thickly grown over with pine trees. Although the Gulf Coast was the first area settled by the French in the eighteenth century, until this century the population was sparse and the chief resources were timber and seafood. Only in the last five decades has the Gulf Coast blossomed as a result of the growth of TOURISM and INDUSTRIALIZATION. To the north of the coastal plain between the Pearl River and the Alabama line, the terrain becomes rolling and the pine trees grow taller. Piney woods soil is thin and sterile. Only after 1880, when lumbermen drove railroads through this immense forest of virgin pines, did the area attract a dense population and begin to develop economically. Neither the soil of the coast nor that in piney woods was fertile enough to attract planters, their slaves, and COTTON. Hence, the inhabitants of southeast Mississippi never shared many of the economic and political characteristics of their fellow Mississippians to the north.

The heartland of Mississippi is in the red clay and bluff hills, which fan out from central Mississippi northward through the center of the state to the Tennessee line. The soil is fertile only in the bottomlands of the river and creek beds. Planters and slaves carved plantations from the bottoms, and the more numerous hill farmers were relegated to the inhospitable (and later gullied) red clay hills. This is the land of WILLIAM FAULKNER's fictional world, Yoknapatawpha County, where the Compsons, Snopeses, blacks, and Indians were thrown together for better or worse.

In the northeast corner of Mississippi the land

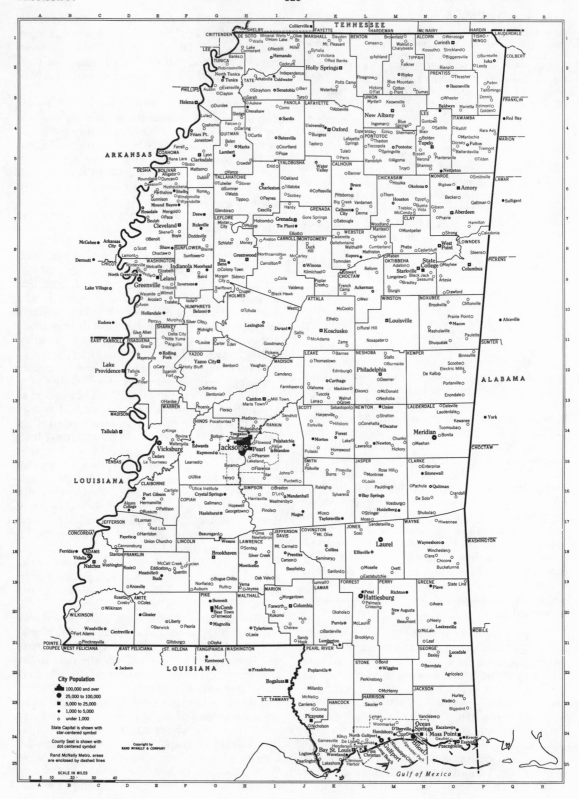

City Population

■ 100,000 and over
● 25,000 to 100,000
■ 5,000 to 25,000
□ 1,000 to 5,000
○ under 1,000

State Capital is shown with
star-centered symbol

County Seat is shown with
dot-centered symbol

Rand McNally Metro. areas
are enclosed by dashed lines

Copyright by
RAND McNALLY & COMPANY

SCALE IN MILES
0 5 10   20   30   40

rises to its highest point; Mount Woodall in Tishomingo County is 806 feet above sea level. Culturally akin to their highland cousins in northern Alabama and eastern Tennessee, these hill people historically had little in common with their fellow Mississippians to the south. Independent, poor, small subsistence farmers, these high-country Mississippians never held many slaves or planted much cotton. Even today blacks in the population of Alcorn, Itawamba, and Tishomingo counties number respectively only 11.7, 5.6, and 4.4 percent of the population. Only the TENNESSEE VALLEY AUTHORITY after the 1930s unbound this area from its Appalachian-like poverty.

In the east, between the high country and the red clay hills, jutting northward in a 30-mile-wide arc along the western side of the Tombigbee River, is the prairie. Relatively open, rolling, fertile country, the prairie is in reality a finger of the Alabama BLACK BELT, that fertile cotton kingdom of the Old South. Devoted mostly to grazing CATTLE today, the prairie was a land of cotton until the Second World War. Conservative in their politics, the planters and farmers there tried to emulate the Natchez barons but never reached the heights of their wealth or arrogance.

Perhaps the most important soil region in the state, at least in the minds of Mississippians, stretches flatly over the northwestern quarter of Mississippi. A part of the lower Mississippi River floodplain, the Yazoo-Mississippi Delta (YAZOO RIVER BASIN) should not be confused with the delta at the mouth of the Mississippi River. Although it is geographically little different from adjacent alluvial soil regions in Arkansas and Louisiana, the Delta has occupied an uncommon role in Mississippi history. Because of flood problems it was settled extensively only after the Civil War. Hence the Delta developed as the archetypical plantation-sharecropping-cotton kingdom not of the Old South but of the New. Delta planters who cleared and drained and diked the land achieved the same sort of grandiose style as their antebellum counterparts. Even to the present, the plantation system (now with machines and chemicals rather than sharecroppers) dominates. Cotton is still important here, though since World War II it has been challenged by SOYBEANS and cattle.

The indigenous Mississippians. When the first Europeans came, perhaps 30,000 Indians lived in what is now Mississippi. They were grouped into three large tribes and a number of smaller tribes. The CHOCTAW numbered 20,000 and controlled lands in the central and southeastern portions of Mississippi. Some 4,500 CHICKASAW, culturally kin

to the Choctaw, controlled the extreme north; and an equal number of Natchez lived in the southwest, with their principal settlement near the town that now bears their name. Numerous smaller groups—the Acolapissa, Bayogoula, BILOXI, Pascagoula, Chakchiuma, and Tunica—lived as satellites around the larger tribes.

At peace with their environment, the Mississippi Indians subsisted from the wilderness. Their contacts with European civilization affected their culture in two ways. As the Spanish, the French, and finally the English penetrated the area, they introduced European axes, weapons, textiles, and other accouterments of civilization. Inevitably, the Indians became more dependent on the superior European goods, and their native culture was overwhelmed. As contact between the two cultures increased and widened and as the Indians became more important to the Europeans, the tribal structure was destroyed. Ultimately, the Indian faced three alternatives: extinction; adoption of European ways; or, by 1830, removal from his ancestral lands by the federal government.

The process began in 1729–1731, when the Natchez were virtually exterminated in a war with the French. Under increasing pressure to give up their rich lands to French settlement, the Natchez in 1729 rose and massacred the garrison at Ft. Rosalie. In retaliation the French sent an army from their capital at New Orleans. By 1731 only a few Natchez survived to live with the Choctaw or to be sold into slavery in the French West Indies. Bienville, the French governor of Louisiana, launched three campaigns against the Chickasaw in the north in 1720, 1736, and 1739. The Chickasaw persisted in trade with the British, and Bienville wished to teach them a lesson. In each campaign the French were roundly defeated.

Ironically, the more the Indians adapted to European ways, the more they were pressured to give up their lands. This pressure grew irresistible after statehood. The Choctaw had already vacated the southern one-third of Mississippi by the treaties of Ft. Adams in 1801 and Mount Dexter in 1805. In 1816 the Chickasaw ceded from their northern lands a small area west of the Tombigbee River. The Choctaw chiefs met in 1820 with United States representatives at Doak's Stand, north of what is now Canton, and ceded a vast area in west-central Mississippi in return for lands in Indian Territory. At DANCING RABBIT CREEK, the Choctaw gave up the remainder of their lands in 1830; and in 1832 the Chickasaw, always the most independent tribe, gave up their lands in the north in the Treaty of Pontotoc. After 1850 only a few

Choctaw remained on lands they were allowed to retain by the terms of the Treaty of Dancing Rabbit Creek. Within 150 years, the Indians had lost the domain that they alone occupied when the first French settlers stepped ashore at Biloxi Bay in 1699. Only their musical names for counties and rivers remind us that they lived here before the white man.

A pawn of Europe, 1699–1798. Of the Europeans, the Spanish came to Mississippi first. Sailing from their New World bases in Havana and Santo Domingo, first Alonzo Alvarez de Piñeda (1519), then Pánfilo de Narváez (1529), and last HERNANDO DE SOTO explored the Gulf Coast. From 1539 to 1543 this tenacious conquistador wandered aimlessly through Florida, Georgia, North Carolina, Tennessee, Alabama, Mississippi, and Arkansas. He found little of interest and paid for his efforts with his life. Not until late in the seventeenth century did another European power, this time France, become interested. Led by the expeditions of Father Jacques Marquette and Louis Jolliet (1673) and of RENÉ ROBERT CAVELIER, SIEUR DE LA SALLE (1681), the French hoped by controlling the Mississippi Valley to expand their fur trade and cut off the expansion of Britain's seaboard colonies into the interior. In the fall of 1699 a French expedition, under the command of PIERRE LE MOYNE, SIEUR D'IBERVILLE, arrived at Biloxi Bay and built Ft. Maurepas. After a tenuous beginning, in which the colonists died in great numbers from starvation and disease, the French, now under Iberville's young brother BIENVILLE, gradually expanded their holdings. In 1702 they built a settlement at Mobile Bay, in 1716 they erected Ft. Rosalie on the Natchez bluffs, and in 1718 they laid out New Orleans, the city that would soon become the keystone to their Louisiana empire. Only after they moved away from the sterile soil of the coastal plain and began to carve out plantations along the fertile banks of the Mississippi north of New Orleans did the colony begin to prosper. Yet, when France lost the FRENCH AND INDIAN WAR to Great Britain and thus its New World empire, Louisiana still contained fewer than 5,000 Frenchmen.

Ceding New Orleans and that portion of Louisiana west of the Mississippi to its ally Spain, in 1763 France formally handed Canada and the coastal strip of Louisiana east of the river over to the victorious British. Thus, the southern one-third of what is now Mississippi, or the Natchez District as it was then called, became part of the new British colony of West Florida.

The British, operating from their capital at Pensacola, immediately recognized the importance of the Natchez area, which had been largely vacated by the French after the Natchez War of 1729–1731. There the British authorities granted lands liberally and otherwise promoted settlement. By the opening of the American Revolution, the Natchez District had become so distinctly British that it became a haven for Tories who were forced to flee their homes in the Atlantic colonies. The British held the Natchez District and West Florida for fewer than 20 years, yet in that short time they placed such an Anglo-Saxon, Protestant stamp on it that, though the Spanish would hold it afterward from 1781 until 1798, the new area would inevitably and eventually drift toward the new nation to the north, the United States.

In 1779 Spain, following France's lead, declared war on Great Britain. Striking from its territories on the west bank of the river, from 1779 to 1781 Spain almost effortlessly wrested West Florida from Great Britain. In rapid succession the British garrisons were driven from the forts at Baton Rouge, Natchez, Mobile, and Pensacola. Quickly the Natchez settlers found themselves governed by still a third European power. The Spanish were feared as Catholic tyrants by the pro-British settlers, but the inhabitants soon learned that they had little to fear from the rather light-handed benevolent Spanish authorities. British land titles were confirmed, and Spain, despite its prohibitions against Protestantism, winked at continued Protestant practice. Even better, the settlers found Spanish rule economically rewarding. The planters prospered from a Spanish subsidy on TOBACCO, then from INDIGO culture, and finally from cotton, for it was late in the Spanish period when that future blessing and curse was introduced to Mississippi.

Since 1783, however, the United States had pressed a claim to that portion of West Florida that lay within the confines of 31° latitude on the south, 32°28' on the north, the Mississippi River on the west, and the Chattahoochee River on the east. From 1783 to 1795 Spain denied it. Then suddenly in 1795, as part of a general settlement with the new American nation, it acceded. Not only did Spain allow American traders to navigate the Mississippi and to deposit their goods duty free at its New Orleans port, but it validated the United States claim to the Natchez District in the Treaty of San Lorenzo de Real. Yet not until March, 1798, did the Spanish garrison at Natchez board vessels and sail away downriver to New Orleans. Simultaneously, the U.S. Congress created the Mississippi Territory and gave it the boundaries of the Natchez District.

A part of the American frontier, 1798–1840. In the years of the territory (1798–1817) and for the first two decades of statehood, Mississippi was not "southern"; it was western. The institutions, the settlers, the violence, and the freewheeling opportunism all were characteristics shared by the entire American frontier. Mississippi as a frontier was little different.

Territorial government began to be organized in August, 1798, with the arrival of the first territorial governor, Winthrop Sargent. A New England Federalist appointed by President John Adams, Sargent had problems from the very beginning. LAND GRANTS had been made by the French, the British, and the Spanish, and the litigation of these awaited the arrival of three territorial judges (LAND SURVEY SYSTEM). Three men were appointed: Daniel Tilton of New Hampshire; William McGuire of Virginia; and PETER BRYAN BRUIN, a planter who lived at Bruinsburg, north of Natchez. Only Bruin was on hand immediately to serve. Tilton did not arrive until January, 1799, and McGuire finally came in the summer of 1799. Hence, the problem of land titles went largely unsolved. Then too, these judges were supposed to sit with Sargent in a territorial council to issue laws and attend to other legislative matters. Sargent was a Federalist, and most of the Natchez planters were Jeffersonians. Finally he was perceived by the natives as arrogant and arbitrary. Although political intriguing and infighting continued, administration of the territory was placed on a sounder footing in 1801, when President Thomas Jefferson replaced Sargent with the young and energetic WILLIAM CHARLES COLE CLAIBORNE. Claiborne moved the capital from Natchez to the little village of Washington, six miles to the north. Territorial courts operated to settle conflicting land claims. Already in 1800 Congress had approved the second stage of territorial government for Mississippi. This meant that the settlers were allowed to elect a territorial legislature.

The territory grew rapidly both in population and in land area. As originally formed, the territory included all lands between 31° on the south and 32°28′ on the north. The western limit was the Mississippi River, and the eastern boundary was the Chattahoochee. In 1804 all lands north to the Tennessee line were placed in the territory. In 1813 by annexation the Mississippi Territory acquired the former Spanish lands south of 31° between the Pearl and Perdido rivers. With these additions, the Mississippi Territory included all lands presently within the states of Mississippi and Alabama. Within 15 years, the territory had almost tripled in size. Population growth was equally dramatic. The last Spanish census had shown a population of less than 5,000. In 1800 there were about 7,500 in the territory. By 1810 the population was 31,000. The 1820 census showed 75,000 inhabitants in the newly formed state.

This rapid territorial expansion produced the first sectionalism in the state, an east-west split that would persist in varying forms well into the twentieth century. The planters of the river counties already had become prosperous and politically conservative. Newcomers who filtered into the area east of the Pearl generally farmed subsistence crops and, as frontiersmen, were characteristically more radical.

By 1815, with the end of the WAR OF 1812 and the crushing of a Creek Indian uprising (CREEK WAR) in the eastern counties (now Alabama), the territory was ready for statehood. The east-west sectionalism, however, posed an obstacle, as did the size of the territory. Settlers east of the Pearl were reluctant to enter a state that would be dominated by the more conservative river counties. Congress was reluctant to admit so large a territory as one state. By 1816 both problems had been compromised by a division of the territory along the present Mississippi-Alabama boundary. Early in 1816 Congress passed legislation authorizing the western counties of the territory to write a constitution and form a state government. The eastern counties were organized into the Alabama Territory.

The electors in the territory chose delegates to a constitutional convention in the summer of 1817. The delegates gathered at the Methodist Church in the little village of Washington and began their labors in the midsummer heat. By August they had completed a document favoring the interests of the older, richer river counties. Characterized by such provisions as property qualifications for voting and holding office, election of judges by the legislature, and life tenure for judges, this conservative instrument was not destined to survive the Jacksonian revolution of the next decade. Following the acceptance of the constitution of 1817 by Congress, David Holmes, the last territorial governor, was elected first governor of the state, and Mississippi entered the Union as the twentieth state.

Hectic expansion and change marked the first two decades of Mississippi's statehood. The Indian cessions of 1820, 1830, and 1832 opened a vast domain to purchase and settlement. As the Choctaw and Chickasaw vacated the northern two-thirds of Mississippi, their lands were rapidly filled with speculators and farmers. These newly arrived, land-hungry backwoodsmen almost to a man were followers of Andrew Jackson, and as their numbers increased they politically submerged the older river counties. They demanded that the capital be removed from Natchez, and it was. A new capital was planned in central Mississippi, and the backwoodsmen named it Jackson in honor of their hero.

Their ascendancy was confirmed in the 1830s. First, they demanded a new constitution, one that would embody universal white manhood suffrage, the election of all officials, limited tenure, legislative supremacy, and other Jacksonian goals. They won a sweeping victory with the creation of the constitution of 1832. Furthermore, they turned state government to their own interests by electing Jacksonians to the legislature from all the new counties carved out of the newly settled Indian lands. By promoting easy money and easy credit, the state government sponsored a backwoods boom in land sales and speculation, which culminated in the PANIC OF 1837 and finally in the virtual bankruptcy of the state. In the short term, the fiscal bungling of the Jacksonians made them slightly ridiculous. Yet, in the long run, the 1830s were one of the most important eras in Mississippi history.

The flush times of that decade marked Mississippi for the future. In the 1830s emerged the social, political, and economic patterns that would dominate under different names for the next 100 years. King Cotton expanded into the new areas in the north. With it went the institution of slavery. While the general population grew 175 percent, the slave population of Mississippi increased nearly 200 percent between 1830 and 1840. Jacksonian politics became dominant. Mississippi developed as an agrarian state with a large black population kept in economic and social bondage by the spread of slavery, hitherto largely limited to the southwest corner of the state. Neither the Civil War nor the agrarian revolt nor the New Deal changed these institutions. Only the names changed. Slavery became SHARECROPPING and JIM CROW; cotton remained king; and almost the same percentage of Mississippians still lived in rural areas on farms in 1940 as had in 1840. The ratio of blacks to whites remained significantly unchanged from 1840 to 1940. Mississippi was hardly any more industrialized in 1940 than in 1840. It was in the 1830s that Mississippi ceased to be "western" and became "southern," that, indeed, it developed the institutions that have since marked the South as peculiar in the nation. Mississippi developed them to a greater degree than its sister states of the South, kept them longer, and gave them up more reluctantly.

Peculiar institutions, 1840–1940. Mississippians faced their first crisis in defense of their new institutions in the aftermath of the Mexican War. After defeating Mexico, ostensibly to confirm the annexation of Texas, the nation acquired a vast new empire in California and the Southwest. Immediately the question arose, Should the new territories be open to slaves, or not? The WILMOT PROVISO, introduced in Congress in 1848, would have closed to slavery the territories acquired from Mexico. The gauntlet was down, and Mississippians began to talk of secession. Efforts were made by the FIRE-EATER Governor JOHN A. QUITMAN, elected in 1849, to carry Mississippi out of the Union. Meanwhile, Congress wrestled with the issues in the COMPROMISE OF 1850. For the moment the issue waned after 1851, when Mississippi voters returned a Unionist majority to Quitman's secession convention and elected the Unionist HENRY S. FOOTE to the governorship over the secessionist JEFFERSON DAVIS.

Only briefly were the secessionists in retreat. The great national controversies of the 1850s—BLEEDING KANSAS, DRED SCOTT, and the HARPERS FERRY RAID—all worked to build fire-eater strength and to make the ground of the Unionists untenable. Foote, in disgust, left the state for California in 1854, Davis was returned to the U.S. Senate in 1857, and Quitman already was serving in the U.S. House, having returned there in the elections of 1855. John Jones Pettus was elected governor in 1859 on a secessionist platform. No longer, apparently, as in 1850, were Mississippians willing to compromise.

The final crisis came in 1860. ABRAHAM LINCOLN was elected, and on January 9, 1861, Mississippi left the Union. Even then, however, the decision was not unanimous. JOHN BELL of Tennessee and Stephen Douglas of Illinois, both Unionist presidential candidates in 1860, together received nearly 30,000 votes while JOHN C. BRECKINRIDGE polled 40,000. Moreover, at the secession convention, Unionists captured nearly one-third of the seats. Against this strong minority, the secessionists prevailed. In March, 1861, when Mississippi joined the Confederacy, Jefferson Davis had already taken his oath as president and war was only days away.

Mississippi occupied a strategic place in Union war plans and, as the war progressed, in Confederate defensive dispositions. By early 1862, as a result of SHILOH and Memphis, the war had already entered northern Mississippi. Vicksburg, the Confederate defensive bastion on the Mississippi, assumed a crucial importance. Ulysses S. Grant, located in western Tennessee, moved on Vicksburg in the early fall of 1862 (VICKSBURG CAMPAIGN).

The city sits atop high bluffs on the eastern bank of the Mississippi. A few miles north, the Yazoo River enters the Mississippi. As it winds down from the northeast, the Yazoo too is lined by high hills. To the west and north of both rivers, the land is low, swampy, and flooded in the winter and spring. Grant's engineering skills were put to a severe test throughout the winter of 1862–1863 as he tried every conceivable method to get his Union army on high ground behind the city. Only in mid-April, when he ran his gunboats past the batteries to get below town, did Grant begin to seal the doom of Vicksburg. It then, however, took him only two weeks to take Jackson, to defeat the forces of John C. Pemberton when he came out to meet the federals at CHAMPION HILL, and finally to envelop Vicksburg. By May 19, 1863, the fortress was besieged. The siege lasted until July 4, 1863, when, short of rations and ammunition, Pemberton surrendered his command.

The war would go on for nearly two more years, and there would be other campaigns in Mississippi. Yet with the fall of Vicksburg the western half of the state, the more populous and richer, was in Union hands. Despite the depredations of W. T. Sherman later in 1863 and the wizardry of N. B. FORREST in keeping the federals at bay in northeast Mississippi in 1864, Vicksburg was the high point of the war in Mississippi. From then on strategic action shifted to other theaters.

Mississippi paid a high price defending its peculiar institutions. More than 75,000 Mississippians served in the war, and perhaps 25,000 of them died. If that was a dear price to pay in manhood, the toll seemed to be even higher in institutional destruction. Slavery, the system on which Mississippians depended for social control and economic benefit, was gone. The political system was in disorder, and nobody knew what would replace it. But the land was still there and cotton brought good prices, if one only had the capital, labor, and equipment to grow it.

RECONSTRUCTION was a bitter period for Mississippians. Yet whites had one early opportunity to control their own destinies and to avoid Radical Republicanism. When the war ended, Lincoln's 10 percent plan was still in effect, and it was with that blueprint that Mississippi first complied. Told by President ANDREW JOHNSON to get a civil government reestablished before the end of 1865 so that he could present the returning Congress with a *fait accompli*, Mississippians wrote a constitution and elected state officers by October. Things then started to go awry. Johnson had also suggested that the freedmen should be granted some token civil rights and that the THIRTEENTH AMENDMENT be ratified. These the first meeting of the legislature refused to do.

Instead the unreconstructed legislature passed a series of acts that became known as the BLACK CODE. It was certain that the freedmen were no longer slaves, but the federal government had not specified what rights they did have. The legislature took it as its duty now to do so. In an effort to force the freedmen back onto the land, the law decreed that any freedman not having a contract to work could be arrested for vagrancy and his services sold to the highest bidder. In another act the legislators reenacted the prohibitions against liquor, weapons, and assembly that had previously applied to slaves. It was a grave miscalculation. The black code infuriated the Radicals, who returned to Washington in 1866 more than ever dedicated to the destruction of presidential Reconstruction.

In 1867 Congress threw out the 10 percent government and placed a military governor in charge of the state. The first duty of General E. O. C. Ord was to register voters. He had accomplished this by September, placing on the rolls 79,000 blacks and 58,000 whites. The new electorate chose delegates to a constitutional convention, which met for the first six months of 1868. They wrote a constitution that survived until 1890. Conservative by the standards of the prewar Democrats, it provided for a strong executive branch, many appointive officers, and no limitation on tenure. The constitution of 1868 represented well the views of the Republican CARPETBAGGERS and their SCALAWAG allies, most of whom were prewar Whigs.

Republicans dominated state government in Mississippi for only six years. The first Republican administration, headed by Governor JAMES L. ALCORN, took office in January, 1870. Republican rule ended when Governor ADELBERT AMES was driven from office by a newly elected Democratic legislature in the spring of 1876. The interim dramatically illustrated all the divisions, personal and partisan, that came to afflict Mississippi politics during Reconstruction. The native scalawag faction under Alcorn pursued moderate policies and prevailed until the elections of 1873. Then power passed to Ames's more radical Republican faction. It mattered little to the Democrats which faction ruled. Their aim from the beginning was to regain power. They got their chance in the elections of

1875. Led by L. Q. C. LAMAR and JAMES Z. GEORGE and aided by the reluctance of President Grant to intervene in support of Ames, the Democrats intended to win the legislature. Win they did, but with tactics of fraud, violence, and intimidation that would haunt Mississippi politics for years (MISSISSIPPI PLAN).

Although it had changed few basic institutions, Reconstruction left a bitter legacy. The freedman had been first a pawn of the Republicans. Now he was at the mercy of his former masters. The myths of black incompetence and of carpetbag and scalawag venality still persist, and for a hundred years served the Democrats well by creating among the whites an artificial solidarity, which defied economic interests. More important, however, Mississippi emerged from the war and Reconstruction little changed. The state was still rural, wedded to cotton, and unindustrialized. There were still six blacks to every four whites and, though no longer slaves, they would soon be just as oppressed by sharecropping and Jim Crow as if they were. During the last quarter of the nineteenth century, the old institutions rehardened; and this time not only blacks, but also many small white farmers, filled the roles of the peasants.

The Democrats who pitched the Republicans from power in 1875 came as near as any politicians in Mississippi history to creating a political machine. Conservative, linked to the planters, railroad barons, and lien merchants, they pursued policies of favoritism to business and large-scale agriculture and dreamed of industrializing the state. They kept themselves in power by manipulating the convention system for choosing Democratic nominees. When the small hill farmer grew restless, the leaders reminded him that they had saved him from the Republicans and from the freedmen and that white men must stick together. At the same time they controlled the black vote much as the Republicans had during Reconstruction.

It worked until 1890, when events combined against the conservatives. First the cry arose to revise the Republican constitution of 1868. The small farmers understood that, until the blacks were removed from politics, they could not hope to factionalize the Democratic party and drive the conservatives from power. Then too, many were tired of the fraud of Mississippi elections. They reasoned that, as long as blacks voted, they would have to be controlled. In other words, the white man could only afford to conduct honest elections if the black man was made politically impotent.

Hence, in 1890 a new constitutional convention met to write the black man out of the political sys-

tem. The constitution provided for a literacy test that allowed white illiterates to slip through, a poll tax, and long registration and residency requirements; in the years after 1890 blacks were almost to a man eliminated from the political system (DISFRANCHISEMENT). Nor did they lose only their political rights. Segregation laws reestablished the social controls of the old slave system; and, as the CROP LIEN SYSTEM and declining cotton prices degraded formerly independent white farmers into sharecropping, the Negro's material existence became ever more precarious. Now he was forced to compete even for the most menial stations.

But the impotence of the blacks allowed the Democrats to divide. The "revolt of the rednecks," as A. D. KIRWAN called it, began in the 1890s and culminated in the first 15 years of the twentieth century. Their aims and frustrations personified by the agrarian leaders JAMES K. VARDAMAN and THEODORE G. BILBO, the hill farmers forced new issues in Mississippi politics. They owed their new control of state politics to the enactment of a direct primary election law passed in 1902, which eliminated the convention system for choosing Democratic nominees.

Vardaman, governor from 1904 to 1908, and Bilbo, governor from 1916 to 1920, led the revolt. Openly racist, they were Progressive on all other issues. If it was a "progressivism for whites only," that was all the better to their constituency. Drawing their strength mainly from the hill farmers in the east, Vardaman and Bilbo advocated greater support for public education, penitentiary reform, tax equalization, child labor legislation, public health, and social reform. They accomplished some of these, but the old conservative faction was not yet completely dead, and the first two decades of the twentieth century were marked by the hottest factionalism in the history of the state. Some changes came. Public education was strengthened; state institutions for the care of the handicapped were created; the scourge of tuberculosis began to come under control; and the brutal treatment of convicts under the lease system was ended. Yet by 1920, after World War I killed PROGRESSIVISM in Mississippi as it had in the nation, the social, economic, and political institutions remained largely unaltered.

The 1920s were largely a period of stagnation in Mississippi history. The tenant-sharecropping system of agriculture grew, and Jim Crow laws were strengthened. Total population for the first time in history actually declined slightly. At the mercy, as always, of the vagaries of the cotton market, Mississippians did not share in the prosperous

Roaring Twenties. Mississippi was not yet in the mainstream of American life.

If the 1920s were a decade of stagnation, Mississippians in the period from 1930 to 1940 suffered an economic disaster. Cotton prices dipped toward 5¢ per pound, and by 1932 one Mississippi farm in every ten was going under the auctioneer's hammer. By the middle of that decade more than one-half of all Mississippi farmers were tenants or sharecroppers.

The frantic activity of the NEW DEAL is supposed to have worked a revolution in the nation. It did not in Mississippi. In 1940 Mississippi's institutions were the same ones that had developed a hundred years earlier. Eight of every ten Mississippians still lived in the country. Dependence on cotton had, if anything, increased. Although the black man's legal status had changed, in reality he had exchanged slavery for the serfdom of sharecropping.

Yet the disaster of the Great Depression reawakened a long-dormant theme in Mississippi history and gave it a new immediacy—the need for industrialization and agricultural diversification. In 1936, with Governor HUGH WHITE's Balance Agriculture with Industry plan, the state government not only recognized the need for industrial development but also promised to subsidize the process. Resembling more the conservatives of the late nineteenth century than his agrarian predecessors, White sought to entice new industry to Mississippi through tax exemptions and a unique device allowing municipalities and counties to finance plant construction for industrial tenants through public bond issues. Industrial tenants then leased the facilities from the local government, which in turn used these proceeds to retire the bonds. The community got a new payroll, and industry got public subsidy. Despite the BAWI's depression origins, its impact was not generally felt until after the Second World War.

Mississippi rejoins the mainstream, 1940–present. The Second World War was the watershed of modern Mississippi history. Before it there was institutional continuity stretching back 100 years. After it nothing remained the same. This is not to say that World War II was the cause of all change, but it is a convenient dividing line.

In fact, World War II did work in some ways to erode the old institutions. Although Mississippi profited less than other southern states, the war did bring a prosperity unknown since before the Civil War. Former sharecroppers working in the Pascagoula shipyards made more money in a week than they had seen in a year before the war, and

they would not go back in 1946 to walk behind a mule. The war broke down Mississippi's long insularity. Army camps and air force bases dotted the landscape. During World War II many Mississippians encountered their first yankees, and soldiers from the North and West were introduced to Mississippi. Traditional provincialism declined. An exodus of blacks began for the first time since 1841 to alter significantly the racial ratio (NEGRO MIGRATION).

Since World War II, every one of Mississippi's long-cherished major institutions has been destroyed. King Cotton has lost his throne. Only in the Delta is cotton still important, and even there its place is challenged by soybeans, rice, and livestock. Everywhere mechanization and diversification have triumphed. Tenancy and sharecropping have disappeared altogether, and in their places have come commercialized agricultural businesses not unlike those in the rest of the nation. Perhaps even more important, agriculture has lost its primacy in Mississippi's economy. No longer is it the chief employer and income producer. Manufacturing now employs more workers and produces more income than does agriculture.

No governor has campaigned in Mississippi since 1940 without pledging more industry and better-paying jobs. By any criteria Mississippi must now be called an industrial state, albeit with some qualification. Largely lacking heavy industry, the industrial economy is still dominated by the apparel and wood products industries, the lowest-paying industries in the country.

Perhaps most important of all, it is in the realm of race relations that change has been most obvious. Reluctantly and under duress, the old racial system, which prevailed from slavery, has been swept away. In the last 25 years Mississippi blacks gained entry into the political system, and segregation has crumbled. The single most distinguishing and noticeable of the old institutions is disappearing.

In demographics, too, Mississippi is becoming more like the rest of the nation. Rural residents, who stood at 80 percent of the population in 1940, now number only 55 percent. The historically high ratio of blacks to whites in the population has reversed since 1940. Mainly because of the migration from the state by young blacks, the ratio in the 1970 census stood at 63 percent white to 37 percent black.

Lest the point be overstated, there persist in Mississippi many characteristics of the old institutions. Mississippians have historically been poor. By national standards they still are. Judged by the state's own past, per capita income in the last 35 years has risen dramatically, while falling farther behind the national average. Race has not been eliminated from politics or from the minds of Mississippians. Mississippi lacks heavy, high-wage industries. The tax base is narrow, public revenues are consequently low, and government services are not elaborate. Politics is still personal and Jacksonian in quality.

Nonsoutherners tend to regard Mississippi as the last bastion of the South. Perhaps there is some truth in that. It is true that Mississippi's institutions were peculiar, insular, and provincial for 100 years. Because of the state's peculiarity, many have felt compelled to remold it in the national image—to produce a new Mississippi. They need not bother. That process began during World War II, and it is still proceeding.

Papers, collections, and manuscripts. The best collection of Mississippiana is at Mississippi Department of Archives and History at Jackson (papers of governors; WPA county histories; provincial, territorial, and state archives). Important collections are papers of Bank of Mississippi, J. F. H. Claiborne, Jefferson College, L. Q. C. Lamar, John A. Quitman, and Eudora Welty. Important manuscript collections are at Mississippi college and university libraries: Delta State University has Walter Sillers Papers; Millsaps College houses Methodist Historical Collection; Baptist Collection is at Mississippi College. Mississippi State University has important collections: Cully Cobb Papers on Agricultural Adjustment Administration; George L. Sheldon Papers on lily-white Republicanism; and John C. Stennis Papers. University of Mississippi Library contains papers of David L. Cohn, William Faulkner, Pat Harrison, John E. Rankin, and William M. Whittington. University of Southern Mississippi houses Theodore G. Bilbo Collection, William M. Colmer Papers, and Railroad Collection with manuscripts from Mississippi Central, Illinois Central, and Gulf, Mobile & Ohio railroads.

Books. Best general survey is R. A. McLemore (ed.), *History of Mississippi* (2 vols.; 1973); Vol. II contains outstanding bibliography. Older and less valuable are J. F. H. Claiborne, *Mississippi as Province, Territory, and State* (1880); and D. Rowland, *Mississippi* (1925). Two best-known modern texts are J. K. Bettersworth, *Mississippi* (1959); and C. Sallis and J. Loewen, *Mississippi: Conflict and Change* (1974).

Monographs on Indians include H. B. Cushman, *History of Choctaw, Chickasaw, and Natchez Indians* (1899); A. H. DeRosier, *Removal of Choctaw Indians* (1970); and J. R. Swanton, *Indians of Southeastern U.S.* (1946).

Best studies of European dominion are D. Rowland (ed.), *Mississippi Provincial Archives, 1701–1743: French Dominion* (1927–32) and *Mississippi Provincial Archives, 1763–1766: English Dominion* (1911), in ten volumes (1763–83) in Mississippi Department of Archives and History. C. E. Gayarré, *History of Louisiana* (1854–64), is old but complete. C. Johnson, *British West Florida, 1763–1783* (1971), is best monograph on that subject. See also J. D. L. Holmes, *Gayoso: Spanish Governor in Mississippi Valley, 1789–1799* (1965); and A. P.

Whitaker, *Spanish American Frontier, 1783–1795* (1927) and *Mississippi Question, 1795–1803* (1934).

On territorial period, see D. C. James, *Antebellum Natchez* (1968); M. Swearingen, *Early Life of George Poindexter* (1934); and C. E. Carter, *Territorial Papers of U.S.* (1934–), V, VI.

For period from 1817 to 1860, see E. A. Miles, *Jacksonian Democracy in Mississippi* (1960); J. H. Moore, *Agriculture in Ante-Bellum Mississippi* (1958); H. Weaver, *Mississippi Farmers, 1850–1860* (1945); and classic C. S. Sydnor, *Slavery in Mississippi* (1933). Biographies include D. C. Dickey, *Sargent S. Prentiss* (1945); W. R. Hogan and E. A. Davis, *Barber of Natchez* (1954), fascinating account of free Negro; J. B. Ranck, *Albert Gallatin Brown* (1937); J. O. Shenton, *Robert John Walker* (1961); and C. S. Sydnor, *Benjamin L. C. Wailes* (1938). J. G. Baldwin's *Flush Times of Alabama and Mississippi* (1853) is humorous account of 1830s and 1840s. Personal recollections include R. Davis, *Recollections of Mississippi* (1889); and H. S. Foote, *Casket of Reminiscences* (1874) and *Bench and Bar of South and Southwest* (1876), interesting anecdotes and candid biographical sketches. See also H. S. Fulkerson, *Random Recollections of Early Days in Mississippi* (1835).

For secession, best work is P. L. Rainwater, *Mississippi: Storm Center of Secession, 1856–1861* (1938). Military accounts of war are E. C. Bearss, *Decision in Mississippi* (1962); D. A. Brown, *Grierson's Raid* (1954); and S. Foote, *Civil War* (1963), II, Vicksburg campaign. Nonmilitary accounts of war in Mississippi are J. K. Bettersworth, *Confederate Mississippi* (1943); and P. F. Walker, *Vicksburg: People at War, 1860–1865* (1960). See also J. K. Bettersworth, *Mississippi in Confederacy: As They Saw It* (1961); and J. W. Silver, *Mississippi in Confederacy: As Seen in Retrospect* (1961).

Traditional study of Reconstruction is J. W. Garner, *Reconstruction in Mississippi* (1901). A revisionist study is W. C. Harris, *Presidential Reconstruction in Mississippi* (1967). His companion study on congressional Reconstruction will soon be published. L. A. Pereyra, *James Lusk Alcorn, Persistent Whig* (1966), is biography of state's most famous scalawag.

Outstanding books for late nineteenth century are A. D. Kirwan, *Revolt of Rednecks* (1951); and V. L. Wharton, *Negro in Mississippi, 1865–1890* (1947). See also W. A. Cate, *Lucius Q. C. Lamar* (1935); and R. L. Brandfon, *Cotton Kingdom of New South* (1967), Yazoo-Mississippi Delta region.

Best for twentieth century are W. F. Holmes, *White Chief: J. K. Vardaman* (1970); and W. A. Percy, *Lanterns on Levee* (1941, 1975), one of best autobiographies ever written by southerner. Dull but complete is G. C. Osborn, *John Sharp Williams* (1943). A. W. Green, *The Man Bilbo* (1963), is short and inadequate. Best accounts of modern civil rights movement are subjective and personal: J. W. Silver, *Mississippi: Closed Society* (1964); W. Lord, *Past That Would Not Die* (1965); R. H. Barrett, *Integration at Ole Miss* (1965); and F. Smith, *Congressman from Mississippi* (1964).

Articles. *Journal of Mississippi History* is best for articles on Mississippi history. Each volume is indexed separately; in preparation is a cumulative index to first 30 volumes. See also unindexed *Publications of Mississippi Historical Society*. On Indians, see J. O. McKee, *Southern Quarterly* (Jan., 1971); D. A. Phelps, *Tennessee*

MISSISSIPPI POPULATION, 1790–1970

Year	Total	White	Nonwhite Slave	Free	% Growth	Rank U.S.	South
1790	4,500						
1800	7,600	4,146	2,995	459	68.9	21	9
1810	31,306	16,602	14,523	181	311.9	21	10
1820	75,448	42,176	32,814	458	141.0	22	10
1830	136,621	70,443	65,659	519	81.1	23	11
1840	375,651	179,074	195,211	1,366	175.0	17	10
1850	606,526	295,718	309,878	930	61.5	15	9
1860	791,305	353,899	436,631	775	30.5	14	8
1870	827,922	382,896		445,026	4.6	18	8
1880	1,131,597	479,398		652,199	36.5	19	9
1890	1,289,600	544,851		744,749	14.0	21	9
1900	1,551,270	641,200		910,070	20.3	20	9
1910	1,797,114	786,111		1,011,033	15.8	21	9
1920	1,790,618	853,962		936,656	0.4	23	10
1930	2,009,821	998,077		1,001,744	12.2	23	10
1940	2,183,796	1,106,327		1,077,469	8.7	23	10
1950	2,178,914	1,188,632		990,282	−0.2	26	12
1960	2,178,141	1,257,546		920,595	−0.04	29	13
1970	2,216,912	1,393,283		823,629	1.8	29	13

Historical Quarterly (June, 1957); and G. I. Quimby, *American Antiquity* (Jan., 1942). On colonial period, are J. W. Caughey, *Louisiana Historical Quarterly* (Jan., 1932; Jan., 1933); and W. S. Coker, *West Virginia History* (1969). Information on territorial period is in J. A. Padgett, *Louisiana Historical Quarterly* (Jan., 1938); and C. S. Sydnor, *Journal of Southern History* (Feb., 1935). For the period 1817–1860, see W. M. Drake, *Journal of Southern History* (Aug., 1957); W. H. Stephenson, *Mississippi Valley Historical Review* (Dec., 1936); and M. Swearingen, *Journal of Southern History* (May, 1935). For secession and Civil War, see E. C. Bearss, *Civil War History* (March, 1959; Dec., 1962) and *Military Affairs* (1960). For Reconstruction, see D. Donald, *Journal of Southern History* (Nov., 1944); and S. I. Kutler, *American Historical Review* (April, 1967). For last quarter of nineteenth century, examine J. S. Ferguson, *Journal of Southern History* (Nov., 1942); W. D. Halsell, *Journal of Southern History* (Feb., 1941; Feb., 1944; Nov., 1945); and W. A. Mabry, *Journal of Southern History* (Aug., 1938). Although there are many magazine articles on Mississippi in twentieth century, especially on race relations, there are few in scholarly journals other than *Journal of Mississippi History*.

Dissertations and theses. Published annually in *Journal of Mississippi History* since 1953 is a bibliography of theses and dissertations relating to Mississippi. See F. A. Dennis, *Journal of Mississippi History* (Feb., 1976), for bibliography of theses and dissertations. Those dealing with periods or subjects on which little has been published are L. T. Balsamo, "T. G. Bilbo" (Ph.D., University of Missouri, 1967); J. M. Bentley, "Financial Institutions and Economic Development in Mississippi, 1809–1860" (Ph.D., Tulane, 1969); W. M. Drake, "Constitutional Development in Mississippi, 1817–1865" (Ph.D., University of North Carolina, 1954); D. East, "Land Speculation in Chickasaw Cession" (M.A., University of Wisconsin, 1964); J. S. Ferguson, "Agrarianism in Mississippi, 1871–1900" (Ph.D., University of North Carolina, 1952); J. E. Gonzales, "Henry S. Foote" (Ph.D., University of North Carolina, 1957); C. G. Hamilton, "Missis-

MISSISSIPPI GOVERNORS

Governor	Party	Term
TERRITORIAL		
Winthrop Sargent	Fed.	1798–1801
William C. C. Claiborne	Jeff. Rep.	1801–1805
Robert Williams	Jeff. Rep.	1805–1809
David Holmes	Dem.-Rep.	1809–1817
STATE		
David Holmes	Dem.-Rep.	1817–1820
George Poindexter	Dem.-Rep.	1820–1822
Walter Leake	Dem.-Rep.	1822–1825
Gerard C. Brandon	Dem.-Rep.	1825–1826
David Holmes	Dem.-Rep.	1826
Gerard C. Brandon	Dem.-Rep.	1826–1832
Abram M. Scott	Dem.	1832–1833
Charles Lynch	Dem.	1833
Hiram G. Runnels	Dem.	1833–1835
John A. Quitman	Whig	1835–1836
Charles Lynch	Dem.	1836–1838
Alexander G. McNutt	Dem.	1838–1842
Tilgham M. Tucker	Dem.	1842–1844
Albert G. Brown	Dem.	1844–1848
Joseph M. Matthews	Dem.	1848–1850
John A. Quitman	Dem.	1850–1851
John I. Guion	Dem.	1851
James Whitfield	Dem.	1851–1852
Henry S. Foote	Union-Dem.	1852–1854
John J. Pettus	Dem.	1854
John J. McRae	Dem.	1854–1857
William McWillie	Dem.	1857–1859
John J. Pettus	Dem.	1859–1863
Charles Clark	Dem.	1863–1865
William L. Sharkey (provisional)		1865
Benjamin G. Humphreys	Dem.	1865–1868
Adelbert Ames (military)	Rep.	1868–1870
James L. Alcorn	Rep.	1870–1871
Ridgley C. Powers	Rep.	1871–1874
Adelbert Ames	Rep.	1874–1876
John M. Stone	Dem.	1876–1882
Robert Lowry	Dem.	1882–1890
John M. Stone	Dem.	1890–1896

Governor	Party	Term
Anselm J. McLaurin	Dem.	1896–1900
Andrew H. Longino	Dem.	1900–1904
James K. Vardaman	Dem.	1904–1908
Edmond F. Noel	Dem.	1908–1912
Earl L. Brewer	Dem.	1912–1916
Theodore G. Bilbo	Dem.	1916–1920
Lee M. Russell	Dem.	1920–1924
Henry L. Whitfield	Dem.	1924–1927
Dennis Murphree	Dem.	1927–1928
Theodore G. Bilbo	Dem.	1928–1932
Martin S. Conner	Dem.	1932–1936
Hugh White	Dem.	1936–1940
Paul B. Johnson	Dem.	1940–1943
Dennis Murphree	Dem.	1943–1944
Thomas L. Bailey	Dem.	1944–1946
Fielding L. Wright	Dem.	1946–1952
Hugh L. White	Dem.	1952–1956
J. P. Coleman	Dem.	1956–1960
Ross R. Barnett	Dem.	1960–1964
Paul B. Johnson	Dem.	1964–1968
John B. Williams	Dem.	1968–1972
William L. Waller	Dem.	1972–1976
Cliff Finch	Dem.	1976–1980

sippi Politics in Progressive Era, 1904–1960" (Ph.D., Vanderbilt, 1958); W. B. Hamilton, "American Beginnings in Old Southwest: Mississippi Phase" (Ph.D., Duke, 1938); P. Hardin, "Edward C. Wallthal" (M.A., Duke, 1940); J. T. Hatfield, "W. C. C. Claiborne" (Ph.D., Emory, 1962); R. V. Haynes, "Political History of Mississippi Territory" (Ph.D., Rice, 1959); J. Honeycutt, "Mississippi in Mexican War" (M.A., University of Southern Mississippi, 1970); W. D. McCain, "Populist Party in Mississippi" (M.A., University of Mississippi, 1931); J. N. McLendon, "John A. Quitman" (Ph.D., University of Texas, 1949); F. E. Melton, "David Holmes" (M.A., Emory, 1966); D. C. Mosley, "Labor Unions in Mississippi" (Ph.D., University of Alabama, 1965); J. E. Prince, "Mississippi Balance Agriculture with Industry Program, 1936–1958" (Ph.D., Ohio State, 1961); D. M. Rawson, "Party Politics in Mississippi, 1850–1860" (Ph.D., Vanderbilt, 1964); and D. Young, "Mississippi Whigs, 1834–1860" (Ph.D., University of Alabama, 1968).

JOHN R. SKATES
University of Southern Mississippi

MISSISSIPPI, UNIVERSITY OF (University, 38677), one mile west of Oxford, was chartered by the state legislature February 24, 1844, and inaugurated its first session November 6, 1848, with 80 students and four faculty members. Notable early presidents include southern author AUGUSTUS BALDWIN LONGSTREET (1849–1856), under whose administration a law school was established, and nationally known educator F. A. P. Barnard (1856–1862). The Civil War closed the university, and its buildings served as a hospital for wounded soldiers from the South and North. In 1882 the university became coeducational. Intercollegiate football, an important aspect of life at Ole Miss, was first introduced in 1893. Subsequent years witnessed attempts to make the university more than a liberal arts college with the establishment of schools of engineering, education, medicine, pharmacy, business administration, and the graduate school. In 1955 the medical school was moved to Jackson, where it became the nucleus of the University of Mississippi Medical Center, later including schools of nursing, health-related professions, and dentistry.

Political interference posed serious problems on two occasions. In 1931–1932 the university temporarily lost accreditation when Governor THEODORE G. BILBO had the board of trustees dismiss the chancellor and several professors and appoint candidates of his own choosing. In 1962 Governor Ross Barnett's resistance to federally ordered racial integration caused a confrontation that helped induce a serious riot. National guardsmen maintained order for some months thereafter. The university library houses the Senator Pat Harrison Collection, and its Mississippiana Collection includes the papers of Judge Stone Deavours. Present enrollment is approximately 11,000 students.

See A. Cabaniss, *History of University of Mississippi* (1971); and R. Barrett, *Integration at Ole Miss* (1965).

ROBERT R. SIMPSON
Coker College

MISSISSIPPI BUBBLE, an economic nightmare of gargantuan proportions, overwhelmed the French in 1720, when the public desperately tried to sell stock that it had eagerly been buying from the Company of the Indies. This frenzied action, coupled with a truly wild run on the royal bank, had been caused by one of the most remarkable and colorful financiers in history, John Law (1671–1729). Law was notorious throughout Europe as a gambler. Obliged to leave England because of one serious escapade, he found refuge in Paris around 1715. Ready to inject new life into a bankrupt royal treasury with his proposal to the regent, the duc d'Orléans, Law was welcomed with open arms. Simply stated, Law's scheme consisted of establishing a bank, with royal backing, to serve as the receiver for all of the nation's tax revenues. Especially noteworthy was the feature providing for the issuance of paper money to replace specie, which was "payable on demand." Having obtained permission for his royal bank in 1718, Law next created the Company of the Indies, the new owner of the monopoly of trade in French Louisiana, formerly held by Antoine Crozat (CROZAT GRANT). Frenchmen bought stocks with ever greater expectations from Louisiana's expected but unrealized resources. The bubble burst in 1720, following a bank run. Law fled with moments to spare and died an unknown in Venice.

See F. L. Paxson, *History of American Frontier* (1924); and F. C. Green, *Eighteenth-Century France* (1929).

C. RICHARD ARENA
Mary Star of the Sea High School, San Pedro, Calif.

MISSISSIPPI COLLEGE (Clinton, 39058) was

chartered in 1826 as Hampstead Academy and became a municipal college in 1830. The school was taken over in 1842 by the Presbyterian church, which then turned it over to the Baptist church in 1850. With a coeducational enrollment of almost 2,000 students, it is one of the oldest and largest Baptist liberal arts colleges in the country. Its Mississippi Baptist Historical Collection houses church records, histories, and documents dating from the early nineteenth century to the present.

MISSISSIPPI COMPANY OF VIRGINIA was

formed in 1763 by certain members of the OHIO COMPANY. Its purpose was to expand land speculation in the area recently won by England in the Treaty of Paris and to capitalize on the land bounties granted soldiers in the colony's militia. The company was composed of 50 subscribers (including the LEE FAMILY, the Fitzhughs, and GEORGE WASHINGTON), each of whom contributed funds to send Thomas Cumming as their bargaining agent to London to solicit a grant. In September, 1763, the company requested a 2.5 million-acre grant near the confluence of the Ohio and Mississippi rivers. It promised to settle the region within 12 years in return for protection from the Indians by British troops. For five years Cumming and later ARTHUR LEE lobbied in England but were unable to secure the grant due to the cessation of settlement required by the PROCLAMATION OF 1763.

See S. Livermore, *Early American Land Companies* (1939); C. E. Carter, *American Historical Review* (Jan., 1911); and A. Hulbert, *Ohio Archeological Society Publications* (Oct., 1908).

D. DUANE CUMMINS
Oklahoma City University

MISSISSIPPI DELTA. The generic "delta" has

been adopted to describe various regions within the Mississippi alluvial valley. Herodotus (fifth century B.C.) was the first to apply the term to a topographic feature—the mouth of the Nile enclosed by its distributary channels—shaped like the Greek symbol Δ. Geologists state the "delta" begins near Cape Girardeau, Mo., and is synonymous with the Lower Mississippi Alluvial Valley. Within Louisiana, however, the toponym defines a fan-shaped area apexed at the head of the Atchafalaya River—called both "delta" and "deltaic plain." It encompasses an active delta (Balize) and six relic deltaic lobes.

Social scientists most often encounter the words "Mississippi Delta" when investigating the riverine bottomlands of northeast Louisiana, southeast Arkansas, and northwest Mississippi. One of the richest agricultural regions in the world, it is an area of slight relief where conspicuous features are natural levees, cutoff lakes, and backswamps. Initially settled from the Southeast, the Delta was ideal for plantation agriculture. Later immigrants came from the Midwest. During the Great Depression, thousands of hill farmers moved into the bottomlands. Throughout the antebellum, Reconstruction, and sharecropper eras, cotton was king. Today, farming is large-scale, highly mechanized, and diversified. Important are COTTON, CORN, oats, RICE, SOYBEANS, CATTLE, and the LUMBER INDUSTRY. Small farms are uneconomical, as machinery is expensive. Of great concern today is the environmental impact of chemicals that destroy pests, pollute streams, control grass, and fertilize crops. Light, labor-intensive industry is being attracted by an abundant labor supply.

See E. A. Davis, *Rivers and Bayous of Louisiana* (1968); R. W. Harrison, *Alluvial Empire* (1961); Mississippi River Commission, *Lower Mississippi Region Comprehensive Study* (1974); Y. Phillips, "Settlement Succession" (Ph.D. dissertation, Louisiana State University, 1952); R. J. Russell, *Louisiana Geological Survey Bulletin* (Nov., 1936); F. P. Shepard, *Our Changing Coastlines* (1971); and F. E. Smith, *Yazoo River* (1954).

RANDALL A. DETRO
Nicholls State University

MISSISSIPPI HISTORICAL SOCIETY (Archives

and History Bldg., P. O. Box 571, Jackson, 39205), founded in 1858 and with an intermittent existence, has since 1902 been under the aegis of the Mississippi State Department of Archives and History and presently has a membership of 1,900. The department is the official repository for holdings that include almost 1,300 collections of private manuscripts and extensive county records, plus Mississippi newspapers from 1805, military records of the Civil War, and records of Mississippi as a French, English, and Spanish province. Included are papers of WILLIAM C. C. CLAIBORNE and John F. H. Claiborne, JOHN A. QUITMAN, JEFFERSON DAVIS, LUCIUS Q. C. LAMAR, EUDORA WELTY, and other citizens, records of commission merchants and other businesses, and plantation journals. In addition to the department newsletter, the society and the department jointly sponsor, since 1939, the quarterly *Journal of Mississippi History*, circulation 2,500, which publishes articles relating to the state and to the area of which it was formerly a part.

See *Guide to Official Records in Mississippi Department of Archives and History* (1974); and Mississippi Department of Archives and History, *Annual Reports*.

MISSISSIPPI PLAN

MISSISSIPPI PLAN (1875) was the strategy of white Democrats to regain political control of their state after about five years of Republican rule during Reconstruction. The Democrats employed whatever devices they deemed necessary for victory in that year's elections. They appealed for white unity and created fear of a race war by spreading exaggerated or mythical accounts of the blacks' political powers and of black officials' corrupt and violent actions. Local party clubs and committees persuaded or intimidated blacks and resorted to fraudulent acts to obtain an overwhelming triumph. Subsequently the Democratic legislature used impeachment and other methods to secure the "restoration" of white rule in Mississippi.

See W. C. Wells, *Mississippi Historical Society Publications* (1906), biased but primary evidence; J. W. Garner, *Reconstruction in Mississippi* (1901); and R. A. McLemore (ed.), *History of Mississippi* (1973), I, chapters by W. C. Harris and D. G. Sansing.

WESTLEY F. BUSBEE, JR.
Belhaven College

MISSISSIPPI QUARTERLY: THE JOURNAL OF SOUTHERN CULTURE

MISSISSIPPI QUARTERLY: THE JOURNAL OF SOUTHERN CULTURE (Mississippi State, 39762), begun in 1948 as the bulletin of the Social Science Research Center of Mississippi State University, has a circulation of 600 and since 1963 has focused on the life and culture of the entire American South. The *Quarterly* continues to be supported by Mississippi State University. It accepts scholarly material in the areas of history, literature, politics, sociology, folklore, art, and music and publishes book reviews on southern subjects, review essays, and edited documents. Since 1964 it has devoted each summer issue to WILLIAM FAULKNER; and from 1969 the spring issue has included an annual annotated checklist of articles and books of literary scholarship prepared by the Society for the Study of Southern Literature. In the past few years the *Quarterly* has sponsored (via the University Press of Mississippi) a series of books entitled the Mississippi Quarterly Series in Southern Literature. Among the first were ones on Andrew Nelson Lytle and on William Faulkner.

MISSISSIPPI RIVER

MISSISSIPPI RIVER. This greatest of North American rivers and its hundreds of tributaries drain 1,244,000 square miles. It originates in Lake Itasca, Minn., and flows southward for 2,348 miles to enter the Gulf of Mexico through five passes at its mouth in Louisiana. After its conjunction with its two major tributaries, first the Missouri and then the Ohio, it becomes broad and muddy, sometimes stretching over a mile wide, frequently curving, building up sandbars, and rising menacingly in spring. This is the portion of the river that flows through the southern states. It is the Old Man River of song and legend whose turbulent waters carried settlers into the heart of the continent. The word *Mississippi*, of ALGONQUIN Indian derivation, means "big waters" or "father of waters." Indian tribes lived along the Mississippi in prehistoric times. Its southern banks were occupied by the CHOCTAW, CHICKASAW, Tunica, Yazoo, Natchez, Koroa, Taensa, Pascagoula, BILOXI, and Alabama.

The first known white man to reach the Mississippi upriver (near Memphis) was HERNANDO DE SOTO in 1541. French explorers Father Jacques Marquette and Louis Jolliet traveled in 1673 down the Mississippi as far as the St. Francis River in Arkansas. Between 1679 and 1682, RENÉ ROBERT CAVELIER, SIEUR DE LA SALLE journeyed to the Gulf of Mexico. He grasped the importance of this vast waterway and claimed the entire Mississippi Valley for France, naming it Louisiana. French settlements were established at New Orleans (1718) and Ft. Rosalie (1716), later the site of Natchez, Miss.

In 1763 Spain acquired New Orleans and the Louisiana Territory west of the Mississippi from France in the Treaty of Paris. The British received the territory east of the Mississippi. St. Louis, which became a base for FUR TRADE up the Missouri River for almost a century, was founded in 1764 on the Spanish side of the river. Settlers from the English seaboard migrated over mountains and down the eastern tributaries of the Mississippi to Ohio, Kentucky, and Tennessee. By 1783, when the United States became independent, American backwoodsmen were using the Mississippi to float their farm produce on flatboats to New Orleans, where it could be shipped to market. But the Spanish at New Orleans, alarmed by the growth of American settlements, periodically withdrew the right of DEPOSIT of American goods. The Mississippi and most of its tributaries were finally united politically as well as geographically in 1803, when, after acquiring Louisiana from Spain, France sold Louisiana to the United States (LOUISIANA PURCHASE). Population growth in territories along the Mississippi swiftly brought statehood to Louisiana (1812), Mississippi (1817), Missouri (1821), and Arkansas (1836). By the 1830s there were large-scale removals of Indian tribes along the Mississippi and its eastern tributaries to new homes west of its banks.

The lower Mississippi Valley was profoundly influenced by the spread of COTTON cultivation westward after 1803 to the MISSISSIPPI DELTA, which proved a fertile area for cotton growing and slavery. Along with the founding of new river towns and the building of spacious plantation houses behind the river levees, the lower Mississippi Valley saw a tremendous change in river transportation between 1803 and 1860. Indians and early explorers had used canoes and pirogues. White settlers built flatboats and keelboats. But the greatest advance came in 1811–1812 with the introduction of the steamboat, the workhorse of the river in carrying cargoes to and from New Orleans (RIVERCRAFT). In the last year before the Civil War, 1859–1860, the total cotton bales received at New Orleans via the Mississippi River reached a record-breaking 2,139,425.

As the plantation system developed in the lower Mississippi Valley, many southerners migrated northward into Indiana, Illinois, and Ohio. The farm animals and many foodstuffs sold to southern plantations along the Mississippi River came from their northern farms. During the Civil War many of these settlers or their descendants wished to end hostilities that interfered with their commerce. Union victory in the struggle to control the Mississippi River was assured by the capture of NEW ORLEANS, VICKSBURG, and PORT HUDSON in 1863, isolating Louisiana, Arkansas, and Texas from the rest of the Confederacy.

In the post–Civil War period, commerce slowly recovered along the Mississippi from the war's devastation. It was 30 years after 1859–1860 that cotton receipts at New Orleans finally topped that antebellum year with 2,149,370 bales received from upriver in 1889–1890. The late 1800s were the golden age of steamboats. Many remained small, uncomfortable, and unsafe. But lines of sleek, large floating palaces also made their appearance. Showboats offering dramatic performances and calliope music became respectable family entertainment by the 1880s. Aiding ocean vessels to enter the Mississippi was James B. Eads, who designed the jetties at the Mississippi's mouth deepening the passes in 1879. Responsibility for keeping the Mississippi navigable along its entire

course and providing FLOOD CONTROL was given to the Mississippi River Commission in 1879. It supervises river work done by the U.S. Army Corps of Engineers.

By the 1890s river traffic greatly declined as railroads switched the pattern of commerce from north-south river-borne cargo to west-east rail-borne cargo. By the First World War the steamboat had almost disappeared. But, since World War II, towboats and barges have recaptured much of the lost cargo from the railroads, and in the decade of the 1960s river commerce reached record highs. The main bulk cargo carried on the Mississippi today includes grain, petroleum and its by-products, coal, coke, iron, steel, and chemicals.

See H. Carter, *Lower Mississippi* (1942); N. L. Wayman, *Life on River* (1971); T. Severin, *Explorers of Mississippi* (1968); and W. Havighurst, *Voices on River* (1967).

JOY J. JACKSON
Southeastern Louisiana University

MISSISSIPPI STATE UNIVERSITY (Mississippi State, 39762), near Starkville, was first organized in 1878 under the Morrill Land-Grant College Act as the Mississippi Agricultural and Mechanical College. It first opened in 1880 and two years later began granting an engineering degree. When a program of graduate studies was inaugurated in 1930, the school was renamed Mississippi State College. It has been a university since 1951. Its library maintains a varied collection of manuscripts, diaries, and newspapers related primarily to the agricultural, family, and business history of Mississippi.

See J. K. Bettersworth, *People's College* (1953).

MISSISSIPPI V. JOHNSON (4 Wallace 475 [1867]). After all southern states but one had refused to ratify the Fourteenth Amendment, Congress, over the president's veto, passed the Reconstruction Acts remanding these states to military rule and requiring them to introduce black suffrage (RECONSTRUCTION, CONGRESSIONAL). Because the laws declared existing southern governments merely provisional, on April 5, 1867, WILLIAM L. SHARKEY and ROBERT J. WALKER, counsel for Mississippi, sought relief from the U.S. Supreme Court by asking leave to file a bill for an injunction. Attorney General Henry Stanbery protested the propriety of receiving the bill. On the grounds that the president could not be enjoined in an ordinary court, he held that the only remedy against the chief executive was the power of impeachment. It followed that the mere reception of the bill would be legally "scandalous." In view of the administration's bitter opposition to the Reconstruction Acts, this argument was especially forceful.

The Court substantially agreed with Stanbery. Declaring that in carrying out laws of Congress the president had duties that were not merely ministerial, as asserted by Sharkey, but executive and political, the chief justice denied permission to file the bill. "An attempt on the part of the judicial department . . . to enforce such duties of the President might be justly characterized . . . as 'an absurd and excessive extravagance,'" he said (April 15, 1867). This case and its companion actions were formerly cited as examples of the Supreme Court's increasing timidity during Reconstruction. In recent years, however, this view has been substantially corrected to show that the decisions were legally sound and not a response to Radical pressure.

See C. Warren, *History of Supreme Court* (1922); S. Kutler, *Judicial Power and Reconstruction Politics* (1968); and C. Fairman, *Reconstruction and Reunion* (1971).

HANS L. TREFOUSSE
Brooklyn College, City University of New York

MISSOURI. In the late 1920s, U. B. Phillips wrote that Missourians, like Kentuckians and Marylanders, were "Southerners in main sentiment." Missouri had been a slave state with an initial power elite that voiced a strong southern orthodoxy. On the eve of the Civil War, two-thirds of its populace had originated from southern ancestry. And, though not a land of large plantations, the state was long preoccupied with slavery and with its free black population. Other commentators, struck by the dualism of northern and southern influences in its makeup, have preferred to describe Missouri as a "border state." But even this characterization fails to indicate the true complexity of Missouri with its French and Spanish colonial heritage, its pluralistic immigrant populations, and its east-west sectional diversity.

Situated in the heart of the nation at the confluence of two great rivers, Missouri early became a "gateway to the West." ST. LOUIS, near the convergence of the Missouri and Mississippi rivers, was equally important in the East-West and in the North-South commerce of these natural transportation routes. KANSAS CITY, at the confluence of the Kansas and Missouri rivers, was a western boomtown proud of its very qualities most disdained by conservative, French-founded St. Louis. Separately, St. Louis and Kansas City respectively

illustrate the staid and the vigorous within Missouri's urban development. Together they represent not only the early urbanization of the state, but their drive for political and economic dominance created an urban-rural rift in Missouri politics that is significant to this day. If one eschews facile characterizations, Missouri, the Show Me State, probably is best viewed as a localized case study of America's antebellum predicaments, its trans-Mississippi expansion, and its post–Civil War urban-industrial growth.

Origins and geography. The name of the state was taken from the MISSOURI RIVER and probably came from the Indian word meaning the "town of the large canoes." First a part of the French and then the Spanish mid-continental empires, Missouri was acquired by the United States in 1803. Americans began to filter into the area in the late eighteenth century, but French influences predominated in the region's early history. Missouri experienced a traumatic entry into the Union as the twenty-fourth state in 1821 (MISSOURI COMPROMISE), its present boundaries being established with the addition of the state's northwest corner by the Platte Purchase of 1836. Nineteenth in size among the states, Missouri encompasses 69,686 square miles including 691 square miles of inland water.

North of the Missouri River, which bisects the state from east to west, are the dissected till plains. Once covered by glaciers, this area is largely prairie land, especially suited to corn and livestock production. To the south and west, between the Missouri and Osage rivers, are found the Osage Plains. The soil is less rich here, and the chief crops are corn and other grains.

The state's largest land region, an important mineral area south of the Missouri and Osage rivers, is the OZARK PLATEAU. A major tourist attraction, the area is dotted with fruit orchards, springs, caves, and streams. The St. François Mountains in the southeast cover about 70 square miles and are the most rugged terrain in Missouri. The peak of Taum Sauk Mountain (1,772 feet) is the state's highest point.

The Mississippi alluvial plain covers the southeastern corner of the state. The floodplain soil is extremely rich, and the area is Missouri's land of cotton. The southernmost and least populated section of the floodplain, jutting into Arkansas, is known as the bootheel because of its shape. Except for the bootheel, Missouri lies north of latitude 36°30′ N. Average July temperatures range from 81 degrees F. in the bootheel to 79 degrees F. in the north and at higher elevations; January

MISSOURI

temperatures vary from an average of 38 degrees F. in the bootheel to 29 degrees F. in the north. Average yearly precipitation ranges from about 50 inches in the southeast to about 30 inches in the northwest, and the growing season is about 55 days longer in the southeast than in the north. Because of its geographic position and its diverse climatic conditions, Missouri played host to the competitive cultures of both North and South.

French and Spanish colonization, 1673–1804. The French period of Missouri history began in 1673, when Jacques Marquette and Louis Jolliet reached the area during their expedition down the Mississippi to the mouth of the Arkansas River. Their greatest achievement was the discovery of the junction of the Mississippi and Missouri rivers.

French activity in Missouri increased under Louis XIV, whose policies to develop an interior American empire were directed at containing the British east of the Appalachians while searching for a northwest passage to the Pacific. Important also in French colonization were the combined motivations behind the missionary zeal of the Jesuits, the lure of the profitable FUR TRADE, and the desire to exploit the dreamed-of wealth of unknown civilizations as Spain had done in Central and South America. In 1682 LA SALLE descended the Mississippi to its mouth, claimed its drainage territory for Louis XIV, and named it Louisiana in honor of his monarch. La Salle envisioned a series of settlements on the great river linking the St. Lawrence with the Gulf of Mexico. Other French explorers followed in rapid succession. By the end of the 1600s trade with Indians in the Missouri region was well established, and several *coureurs des bois* delivered reports of lead ore to French officials in Illinois.

In the early 1700s during the War of the Spanish Succession, financial strain forced a withdrawal of French governmental assistance to Louisiana, and independent financiers filled the gap. Louis XIV granted Antoine Crozat (CROZAT GRANT) exclusive commercial privileges in France's North American empire in 1712, and Crozat appointed Antoine de la Mothe Cadillac governor of Louisiana. When a French explorer sojourning from Canada reached Mobile with ore samples containing high percentages of silver, an expedition under the governor set out for southeastern Missouri. His miners discovered no silver, but they uncovered rich lead veins. Cadillac remained there for nine months making observations and taking astronomical bearings. By 1716 Crozat realized that his economic enterprise had

failed, and his commercial grant was restored to the crown.

Speculation in Louisiana continued with the formation in 1719 of the Company of the Indies, a plan devised by John Law. Law manipulated the company's stocks with unsubstantiated reports of mineral discoveries in Louisiana, but the MISSISSIPPI BUBBLE eventually burst, and many investors went broke. Nevertheless, indirect benefit was derived from increased migration of skilled workers to interior Louisiana from France and French Canada.

Penetration of Missouri was finally achieved on a greater scale in 1719–1720, when Philippe François Renault (Renaud) with 200 workers and slaves launched the Company of St. Philippe. Before returning to France in 1742, Renault extracted large amounts of lead from southeastern Missouri. Moreover, Étienne Venyard, Sieur de Bourgmont, who had explored the Missouri River from 1712 to 1718, constructed Ft. Orleans in 1724 on the north bank of that river in today's Carroll County. The site was abandoned after six years, and Bourgmont's hope to establish trade with the Spanish in Santa Fe was not realized until 1739, when the Mallet brothers reached that outpost on the Spanish northern frontier.

The first permanent settlement in Missouri was Ste. Genevieve. Established about 1735, the town developed because of the lead mines and the salt springs in its vicinity. Unlike later American settlers, who wrenched the land from the Indians at their earliest opportunity, the French clustered in small towns nestled along the Mississippi and cultivated trade with the Indians. The growth pattern of Ste. Genevieve followed that of a feudal French village. Most French settlers were engaged in mining and the fur trade, but agricultural pursuits occupied a part of almost every colonist's time. The early development of the town moved at a slow pace, for a 1752 census showed only 20 permanent residents and three slaves there. But by the early 1770s the town's population had grown to approximately 600.

The most significant early settlement in Missouri and interior Louisiana came about from an economic partnership between Pierre Laclède Liguest and Antoine Maxent. Maxent and Laclède had obtained an eight-year franchise to trade with the Indians on the Missouri River. While Maxent remained in New Orleans, Laclède, a southern Louisiana soldier-planter and civil engineer, voyaged up the Mississippi with thirteen-year-old René Auguste Chouteau and a company of *voyageurs*. In February, 1764, Chouteau and 30 workers began to clear the chosen trading post site. Shortly after his arrival in April, Laclède named the future city St. Louis in honor of reigning Louis XV, for his name saint Louis IX. It was founded upon trade with the Indians, and between 1,200 and 1,500 packs of furs were exported from St. Louis annually by 1769. St. Louis rapidly eclipsed Ste. Genevieve as the economic and political center of colonial Missouri, and the foundations for urbanization were laid in the state by the late eighteenth century.

With the conclusion of the French and Indian War in 1762, the secret Treaty of Fontainebleau transferred Louisiana to Spain. Frenchmen living east of the Mississippi quickly removed themselves to Missouri's French settlements to avoid British dominion in the Illinois country. St. Louis, then, was founded at an opportune time to receive this influx of settlers. Settlement in Missouri continued during Spanish dominion, but the new villages were largely French. Florissant was established in 1786 by French Canadians, and Cape Girardeau was founded in 1793 by a Montreal-born Frenchman.

The proximity of Spanish Missouri to the American colonial scene was demonstrated during the American Revolution by the battle of St. Louis on May 26, 1780. Missouri's French settlers naturally favored the Americans in the conflict, for France was an official ally of the colonies. The British military in Canada engineered a campaign to recapture the forts in the Illinois country that had been taken by the American GEORGE ROGERS CLARK. The action included a plan for taking St. Louis as well. An attack was mounted on St. Louis, but the Spanish garrison and French settlers held the city and reversed the British assault on interior America.

In addition to repelling the British, Spain allowed Americans to settle in Missouri if they swore allegiance to the Spanish crown and the Catholic church. MOSES AUSTIN, for example, whose son later established a colony in Texas, obtained a land grant from the Spanish in 1797 after migrating from Virginia. Within two years he had constructed a shot factory at Mine à Breton and was manufacturing lead and shot until 1804. Agricultural and mining productivity as well as population increased more dramatically in Missouri under Spain's rule than during the French period.

By the Treaty of San Ildefonso in 1800, Charles IV of Spain traded Louisiana to France for the province of Tuscany in Italy. Almost as abruptly, France sold the Louisiana territory to the United States in 1803, never even having occupied it (LOUISIANA PURCHASE). Thus, on March 9, 1804, Captain Amos Stoddard, acting as representative for both France and the United States, took possession of upper Louisiana from the Spanish governor in St. Louis.

Territorial growth and early statehood, 1803–1865. In 1804 the Louisiana Purchase was divided into two sections. The northern territory, which encompassed Missouri, was part of the territory of Indiana with its capital at Vincennes. A meeting was held in St. Louis that year to complain that Missouri's citizens had no voice in their government because territorial officials were too far away. The meeting also disappointingly noted that slavery, an important labor force in Missouri, was not adequately protected by law. The following year the U.S. Congress reacted by creating the first-class territory of Louisiana, with its capital at St. Louis. Missourians were closer to their officials, but they still had no more political rights than they had known under Spain. Not until 1812, when Missouri became a second-class territory, did its citizens gain the right to vote. The War of 1812 brought no major repercussions to Missouri. Pointing to the increased importance of the fur trade that had begun with the French, the Missouri Fur Company was organized in St. Louis in 1808. It merged with the American Fur Company in 1813, a branch of which was established in St. Louis in 1819. WILLIAM CLARK became the final territorial governor in 1813 and served until statehood was realized eight years later.

The population of Missouri increased from about 10,000 in 1804 to over 65,000 in 1820. The early settler had several alternatives in acquiring land, including squatting, filing a claim on government land and purchasing it at auction at a minimum of $1.25 an acre for at least 80 acres, buying already claimed and improved land, or securing New Madrid land certificates. This final procedure demonstrates the federal government's involvement in frontier aid. The New Madrid certificates were issued by the U.S. government after the 1811 earthquake to help those settlers whose land had been devastated. Speculation and fraud abounded, however, and ultimately five times more certificates were honored in federal land offices than were originally issued.

Missouri's first American settlers came primarily from Indiana Territory, Kentucky, Tennessee, Virginia, and North Carolina, and the state was quickly engulfed in a process of Americanization. The dramatic extension of southern culture into Missouri was predicted by Virginia's state treasurer, who commented in 1816 that "with every intelligent person I have met, and many others Missouri has been the subject of conversation." Early settlement came from the Upper South and followed the Missouri River, making the river counties the oldest, most prosperous, most populous, and most powerful politically in the state. Missouri's greatest contributor to American literature, Mark Twain (SAMUEL CLEMENS) had good reason to write that "in Missouri a recognized superiority attached to any person who hailed from Old Virginia; and this superiority was exalted to supremacy when a person of such nativity could also prove descent from the First Families of that great commonwealth."

As the Americanization of Missouri was in full swing, other social forces were also at work. In the early 1820s Paul Wilhelm, the duke of Württemberg, noted that, though the French in St. Louis were growing closer to the Americans in bonds of friendship and ties of marriage, when one traveled from an urban setting it was a "rare occurrence to find French people living near the farms of Anglo-Americans." French farmers scoffed at American innovation and technology. On the other hand, Wilhelm was much impressed by the culture of St. Louis, where the French Creoles and the "immigrated Anglo-Saxons" vied with each other to excel in courtesy at social gatherings.

Even more significant were the German nobleman's observations regarding slavery in Missouri. Slavery had been introduced into the state by Renault and De Lochon with the earliest mining operations. In 1819 Henry R. Schoolcraft noted that many Missouri "plantations" and mines were worked by slaves. Slavery flourished in Missouri during the French and Spanish periods, and by the time of statehood Wilhelm could note that, "as in Louisiana and other states in which black slavery still exists . . . so also in Missouri there is a sharp separation between the white and the colored races. However, this relation applies more to the higher than the lower classes. It does not reach that ridiculous situation as in the far south where even the most wretched person of unmixed European blood would regard it a great degradation to eat at the same table with the richest quadroon." Wilhelm found more free blacks in St. Louis than slaves. In the early 1820s, too, the price of black slaves in Missouri was much higher than in Florida, Louisiana, or Georgia, and day labor in Missouri was less expensive than in the South.

Slavery may have been on the decline in St. Louis, but it was a growing institution in other areas of antebellum Missouri. In the Missouri River counties, a political clique known as the Boonslick Democracy gradually gained control of the Democratic party and state politics from the 1830s through the 1850s. These leaders revered southern culture and the position of the planter class within it. In the minds of Boonslick leaders like STERLING PRICE and William Napton, slavery was the foundation of a more lofty civilization.

In addition to the standard defense of slavery voiced by many Missourians, the peculiar institution also provided an easy road to economic aggrandizement in the state. In Jackson County, located in the northwest on the Kansas border, slaveholders composed by 1860 the most prosperous segment of the population, slave prices were at their highest level, and the slave population was greater than it had ever been. Unlike eastern Missouri, the western part of the state experienced little population growth until the 1830s. As in the Missouri River basin, Jackson County was settled largely by pioneers from the Upper South. And as in St. Louis in the early 1820s, slaves in Jackson County were selling well above the Virginia average by the mid-1830s, but they were apparently in much greater demand in agricultural areas than in the urban center.

Missouri was basically a state of small slaveholdings. Family servants composed the bulk of slaves; social habits were those of the farm rather than the plantation; and white owners often labored in the fields alongside their slaves. With only about 260 overseers in the entire state in 1860, the system was more patriarchal than in the Deep South. Even so, the state had a long tradition of antiblack legislation. The 1820 constitution directed the legislature to keep free Negroes and mulattoes out of the state. An 1835 free Negro code required the licensing of free blacks. Restrictions on free blacks entering the state were reimposed in 1843, and an 1847 law forbade the teaching of free blacks. The DRED SCOTT case originated in the state courts of Missouri in 1846, 11 years before reaching the U.S. Supreme Court.

But Missouri was not a slaveholder's paradise, and the national repercussions that institution created often found expression in state politics. Although the antislavery movement in Missouri was for the most part a failure, it did exist. Mormon settlers in Jackson County during the 1830s were adamant in their abolitionist sentiment and were forced to leave the area by supporters of slavery. In 1835 the Presbyterian Synod of Missouri condemned slavery and advocated emancipation. Reaction to Missouri abolitionism led to the 1837 state law prohibiting "the publication, circulation, and promulgation of abolition doctrines." During the 1840s Iowa brought antislavery pressure to bear on Missouri's northern counties, and passage of the KANSAS-NEBRASKA ACT in 1854 opened the door to free-soil settlers with abolitionist designs who became Missouri's neighbors. This led to an increased loss of slave property in Jackson County, firing the hostility of proslavery alarmists over free Negroes in the region.

Although slavery occupied a significant place in Missouri's pre–Civil War politics, it was not the only important issue. Standard historical interpretations maintain that Senator THOMAS HART BENTON dominated the Missouri Democratic party and state politics from 1820 to 1850. A Jacksonian Democrat from Tennessee, Benton in 1818 became the editor of the St. Louis *Enquirer*, a sounding board for his advocacy of the nation's manifest destiny. Benton attempted to place himself at the head of a movement that gave Andrew Jackson 70 percent of Missouri's vote in the presidential election of 1828. But there was no cohesive Jacksonian party in the state, for a coalition of diverse interests supported Old Hickory. Benton doubtlessly epitomized Jacksonianism to many Missourians, but the lack of organized party machinery often left him ineffective in internal state affairs. After 1830 he avoided intervention in state political contests when numbers of his supporters were divided among all of the diverse contending factions.

In 1835 the Boonslick politicians began to establish a tightly knit Democratic party organization. By 1840 they had taken control of the newly created, oligarchic party structure from their political capital in Fayette. The same year also saw hostility begin to grow in the Democratic party between the out-state agrarian forces and the St. Louis business interests over the acceptance of depreciated currency by the state bank, an economic tactic favored by the urban, business Democrats. St. Louis newspapers attacked the Boonslick group as a "central clique" that controlled the state to the detriment of the Missouri metropolis. In yet another realm of state politics, Boonslick leaders began to suspect Senator Benton of free-soil sympathies. In 1849 the Missouri assembly passed a set of proslavery resolutions, introduced by the future state governor and Confederate leader, CLAIBORNE F. JACKSON. Benton appealed to the Missouri electorate to allow him to ignore the Jackson resolutions, but this cost him the support of the Boonslick leaders, who transferred their allegiance to the victorious Whig candidate, who favored slavery's entrance into the territories. When the issue of slavery replaced orthodox Jacksonianism, Benton alienated the pro-

southern, Democratic oligarchy and thus lost his seat in the Senate.

Despite the political difficulties revolving around the slavery question, urban development continued in Missouri. The town of Westport was founded in 1833 four miles south of the Missouri River near its junction with the Kansas. After two decades of precarious growth it became the town of Kansas, enduring two more decades of severe tests before it emerged as Kansas City. As early as 1821 an American Fur Company depot was located near the site. Kansas City's location meant control of the Santa Fe trade as well as Indian trade to the south and southwest. In 1850 alone, 600 wagons started from Kansas City bound for Santa Fe, and by 1860, with a population of about 4,400, over 16 million pounds of freight passed through the city. The Kansas City levee was a busy place, the steamboats lying at its wharves being the principal mode of transport in early Missouri.

Kansas City obtained a charter from the state legislature in 1853, and the town got a permanent newspaper in 1854, the Kansas City *Enterprise,* later named the *Western Journal of Commerce.* In standard city-building fashion, a board of trade was created in 1856; a chamber of commerce was organized in 1857; and branches of the Mechanics' Bank and the Miners' Bank of St. Louis brought needed credit and capital to the expanding town in 1859.

Portending coming difficulties, however, the effects of slave flight from Jackson County forced Kansas City lawmakers to strengthen local ordinances concerning slaves, free blacks, and runaways in 1855. After a decade of growing prosperity, the Civil War hit Kansas City with disastrous economic dislocation. Half the population left, and financial problems abounded. But adroit postwar entrepreneurial leadership made the city a railroad center. When Kansas City's rival towns, St. Joseph and Leavenworth, were unable to unite internally, the Cow Town's promoters successfully secured the first bridge across the Missouri River and in 1869 negotiated a transcontinental railroad connection linking their city to Chicago. From an emigrant supply base, Kansas City emerged a regional city in 1870.

St. Louis, however, remained the predominant manufacturing and population center of the state. Incorporated as a town in 1808, it retained much of its French character as late as the early 1850s, when its population was around the 90,000 mark, or almost one-seventh of Missouri's total. A writer in *Harper's* in late 1888 observed that "the growth of the city has always been solid, unspeculative, conservative in its business methods, with some persistence of the old French influence."

In 1819 the merchant Henry Shaw noted an integrated St. Louis environment with all the wealthy families and primary business establishments located on Main Street. This pattern changed rapidly, however, as the old "French town" near the river became the city's first blighted district. The city's wealthy elite quickly moved to more desirable neighborhoods as the business center of St. Louis expanded. Already in 1850 the upper class was taking steps to create stable, fashionable neighborhoods segregated from the business core, for the city could be a dangerous as well as unsightly place to live. In 1849 alone, a cholera epidemic took over 4,000 lives and a fire on the levee destroyed most of the buildings and boats. In the wake of these disasters, private neighborhoods like Lafayette Park and Lucas Place were instigated, and the first suburban development was begun in Kirkwood, well out from the city on the route of the Pacific Railroad. Thus, the seeds for suburbanization and urban sprawl were planted in St. Louis a decade before the Civil War.

One force prompting the outward movement of the wealthy from St. Louis was increased foreign immigration. During the decade and a half preceding the Civil War, there was a large influx of Germans and Americans from northern states, which created a solid bloc of antislavery votes. By 1860 the German population amounted to 10 percent of Missouri's total (total foreign born amounted to 14 percent), and northerners contributed another 15 percent. Although not large enough to wrest political control of the state from the Boonslick leadership, this group elected St. Louis area leaders, who supported northern interests. When the state's proslavery government was ousted during the Civil War, this faction provided strong ties to the Union.

In the 1860 election, Douglas Democrats and the Constitutional Union party polled a combined total of over 85 percent of the votes cast in the presidential election. Although this vote indicates a more moderate stance in Missouri than that espoused by either the antislavery Republicans or the proslavery Breckinridge Democrats, a majority of Missouri citizens still favored slavery and also elected the secessionist Jackson to the governorship in 1860. Slaves composed only 10 percent of the state's population on the eve of the Civil War, and Missouri chose to remain in the Union because of its economic ties with the North. It was in the hotbed of Unionist support, St. Louis, that the first blood of the war was spilled on May 10, 1861, as Captain Nathaniel Lyon marched captured prosouthern state guardsmen to the federal arsenal for incarceration. Without authority, Lyon and Unionist troops had surprised the Missouri State Guard at Camp Jackson in a move to hold Missouri in the Union. Unionist Congressman Francis P. Blair, Jr. (BLAIR FAMILY), had correctly determined that St. Louis would be the key to keep Missouri in the sphere of the North.

Nevertheless, Governor Jackson and secessionist state officials gained admission into the Confederacy for Missouri in November, 1861. Jackson's government was quickly exiled, finally establishing headquarters in Marshall, Tex. Following the battle of PEA RIDGE, Ark., in March, 1862, the federal forces gained titular control of Missouri, but Confederate troops didn't cease operations in the state until the conclusion of the war. Missouri bushwackers, including WILLIAM C. QUANTRILL and others, kept Union sympathizers busy. Over 109,000 Missourians, many of them enlistees who came to Missouri when their own state's quotas were filled, fought for the Union, while the state supplied about 30,000 men to the Confederate forces. Two Missourians, Attorney General EDWARD BATES and Postmaster General Montgomery Blair, served in Lincoln's cabinet. On the whole, the war virtually brought a halt to railroad construction in the state. St. Louis relied more heavily upon river transportation than the iron horse, perhaps a contributing factor to its later loss of predominating regional metropolis status to railroad-building Chicago. The state's educational system almost totally collapsed, and agriculture was devastated in many counties during the war.

Political dissension continued under Radical Republican rule from 1864 to 1870. The new 1865 constitution freed the slaves even before ratification of the Thirteenth Amendment. But at the same time it circumscribed the liberties and voting rights of former Confederate supporters. State radicalism was neither as traumatic nor as long-lived as in the Deep South. A Negro suffrage amendment was passed in 1867. In addition to reflecting a concern for public education and for black civil rights, the new constitution also encouraged corporate expansion and the development of Missouri's natural resources. Radical political strategy effectively employed the vote of Union veterans, enjoying its greatest support in the northern and southwestern counties. The Missouri River counties, St. Louis, and southeastern Missouri early turned against Radical policies by narrow margins, thus revealing an opposition that soon brought a demise to Radical voting restrictions and vindictiveness.

Urban-industrial maturation, 1866–1930. Missouri recovered from the Civil War rapidly. In 1870, with the election of a Liberal Republican state administration, a popular vote removed the restrictions placed upon former Confederates. In the same year, however, coincidental with the organization of the farmers' Grange, the KU KLUX KLAN emerged in Missouri and spread across the state from the bootheel to Boonville. From 1874 to the turn of the century, the Democratic party dominated during a period when Missouri politics primarily revolved around railroad regulation, lowering the state debt, cheap money and inflation, and establishing law and order in the wake of the disruptive Civil War.

In the midst of dramatic growth, the 1880 federal census dealt a serious blow to the status of St. Louis as the first city of the West, when it placed Chicago ahead of its Missouri rival by 125,000 people. In several respects the hinterland of the river city added to its staid image. Its most important area of economic hegemony, the New South of Mississippi, Louisiana, Texas, Arkansas, Kentucky, and Tennessee, gave the city an obvious southern image. Established family business firms contributed to this conservative hue. Nevertheless, the business elite of St. Louis was becoming younger, more yankee, and more foreign born. In the early 1870s, 36 percent of the city's residents were foreign born, the Germans composing 55 percent of this group. Irish, British, Swiss, French, Canadian, and later Slavic nationalities also made up significant foreign minorities.

Even though the river city was discriminated against in railway rates, its woodenware, hardware, sugar-refining, lager-beer-brewing, clothing, and cotton trade industries were among the leaders of the nation by the late 1880s. Within yet another spectrum of development, St. Louis became a center for Hegelian philosophy, a reporter once commenting that such speculation "was a leaven that had a marked effect in the social, and especially in the educational, life of the town." The city was famous for advanced educational methods: the kindergarten and a manual-training school were both early, innovative institutions in its public school system.

Along with a slightly greater voice in state government for urban areas, the new state constitution of 1875 gave St. Louis independent status. Almost doubling in population between 1860 and 1870, St. Louis in the closing decades of the nineteenth century was transformed from a commercial entrepôt to a diversified manufacturing center. By 1900, as the nation's fourth largest city, Missouri's industrial metropolis contained 6,750 different manufacturing businesses, with a capital of $150 million and employing over 110,000 persons. But a new business elite had emerged in St. Louis decades before 1900. And the private neighborhoods of the wealthy rose and fell in rapid succession as the industrial and immigrant city engulfed them. The phenomenon of uncontrolled urban growth, which led ultimately to the present-day massive suburban ring surrounding the deteriorating core of St. Louis, was evident already in the late nineteenth century.

Indeed, as early as 1822 St. Louis, the first city west of the Mississippi to be Americanized, was regarded as "the dirtiest place in the Mississippi Valley." By the 1880s and 1890s, the St. Louis Engineers' Club, which had been organized in 1868, saw a definite need for constructively dealing with the city's air pollution from a technical point of view. But the smoke lingered over the river metropolis for another four decades, even through the three-year antipollution efforts of the Citizens' Smoke Abatement League of St. Louis, which was formed in 1926. It took the influence of the press—especially the ST. LOUIS POST-DISPATCH, which won the Pulitzer Prize for its campaign—combined with Black Tuesday (November 28, 1939) and the 20 days of darkness surrounding it, before St. Louis lawmakers made it illegal to burn soft coal, thus eliminating heavy smoke by finally determining that social problems could be handled more effectively by city government than by hoped-for technological panaceas.

That the problems of black-white relations had not been totally solved by the Civil War and Reconstruction in Missouri also surfaced in St. Louis during this time when its citizens were demanding that their city government be more democratic. Innovative in many areas of education, St. Louis demonstrated its southern mentality with a statute requiring separate schools for whites and blacks during Reconstruction. In 1914 the initiative was incorporated in the city charter, and two years later St. Louis became the first city to initiate and vote for mandatory residential segregation. The idea, which had originated in Baltimore in 1910, was heavily supported by St. Louis Polish-Americans and the white wards closest to Negro residential areas. Although the law was opposed by 23 of the 28 aldermen, the St. Louis press, and the Jewish community, it passed by a vote of 52,220 to 17,877. Almost immediately a temporary injunction was issued, enjoining the city from following the conditions of the ordinance. By the end of 1917, the U.S. Supreme Court had decided such segregation ordinances were unconstitutional, and the St. Louis law was abolished. Private restrictive covenants, however, adopted by property owners, achieved the desired result almost as effectively.

As the urban problems of St. Louis began to multiply, a new city sprang into existence in the southwest corner of the state to serve as a supply center for the miners flooding the area to extract the bountiful lead deposits discovered there. In 1873 Joplin was incorporated with a population of 4,000. In another two years, the "Klondike of Missouri" boasted dozens of prosperous business establishments and 75 saloons. The population of the state climbed steadily during the late nineteenth century but, as evidenced by Joplin's amazing growth, urban centers were increasing at a faster rate than rural areas.

The percentage increase in total state population from 1870 on, however, remained less than that for the country as a whole. Although by 1920 its population exceeded 3 million, making it second only to Texas west of the Mississippi, Missouri in its growth rate was extremely retarded. The fourteenth federal census revealed that 89 of the state's 114 counties and one independent city, St. Louis, had decreased in population between 1910 and 1920. It is highly significant to note that 66 of the state's counties contained no urban population whatsoever in 1920, even though the state was 46.6 percent urban. Three-fourths of the state's urban population resided in St. Louis, Kansas City, and St. Joseph alone. With so many small counties limiting the area a city might dominate, the proportional representation of rural areas was much greater than that of cities, a problem that exists to a degree in Missouri today.

When it became apparent that the state was not attracting a great tide of immigration and was not destined to be the hub of the nation, promoters in the 1920s and 1930s sought to veil their unrealized predictions in a belief that "the real Missourian is the man on the farm." One writer took comfort in his observation that "95% of Missourians are native born Americans and 75% are native born Missourians. Here in Missouri there has developed a remarkably pure American type." Although agriculture had long been mechanized and geared to market production, the Missouri farmer faced hard times in the 1920s. Between 1930 and 1934, approximately 18,000 farms, over 2.5 million acres, were lost by foreclosure in the state. As Missouri's "pure American type" was catapulted into the quagmire of the Great Depression, the state's urban population exceeded its rural numbers for the first time.

From depression to affluence, 1930–1975. Machine politics and the economic miseries of depression cast a long shadow over Missouri during the 1930s. Boss politics was not a new phenomenon in the state, but it achieved an unparalleled dimension in Kansas City under Thomas J. Pendergast, the chief personage in Kansas City's Democratic party (PENDERGAST MACHINE). Boss Tom's political philosophy was that "people work for a party because they can get a job or get a favor, special privilege gets the votes." That this formula was effective was demonstrated throughout the late 1920s and the 1930s with Democratic victories in Kansas City and the extension of the machine into rural Jackson County. By relying upon the leadership of HARRY S. TRUMAN, destined to be the first president from Missouri, Pendergast pulled together a well-disciplined machine that could deliver the largest bloc of votes in the state. Truman was a Jackson County native with WASP appeal. As an administrative judge from the early twenties until his election to the U.S. Senate in 1934, he controlled almost all of the county patronage and used it to aid those willing to work for Boss Pendergast in the county districts. And in 1933, when Guy B. Park, a machine nominee, gained the state governorship, Pendergast began to build a statewide organization.

Missouri, like other areas in the nation, felt the imprint of the NEW DEAL during the 1930s. Since Pendergast had supported Franklin D. Roosevelt "from the start," federal relief programs became an added boon to the boss's patronage in the state. But months before the New Deal could have been of any benefit to Kansas City, the western Missouri city had a definite impact upon the New Deal in that its relief programs served as a model for the Civil Works Administration. In 1931 Kansas Citians had approved a $50 million bond issue, initiating a "10-year plan" advocating massive public works to fight the Great Depression. Added to this, New Deal relief modernized and beautified Kansas City. Since Pendergast and his director of federal work relief, Matthew S. Murray, oversaw the federal relief programs in Missouri, Kansas City and its surrounding areas saw a larger share of federal funds than other areas in the state.

Corruption in machine politics, however, eventually brought the downfall of Pendergast. In 1939 he was found guilty of income tax evasion. Once the broker-politician was removed from the political scene, the Democratic party in Missouri began to fall apart. The Republican party was returned to predominance by the electorate in the 1940s. A Republican governor was elected in 1940, and the GOP held a majority in the general assembly from 1942 to 1948. For the first time since the 1870s, the state had two Republican U.S. senators from 1947 to 1951.

A fourth constitution was adopted in 1945 to replace the much amended 1875 version. Although the major divisions of Missouri government—the bicameral legislative, the judicial, and the executive—remained constant, the new constitution instituted a "nonpartisan plan" for the election of judges, replaced justice of the peace courts with magistrate courts staffed by licensed lawyers, and gave the cities slightly more voice in the state senate in Jefferson City, Missouri's capital. Nevertheless, the rural areas of the state retained their disproportionate, larger representation in the house. Rural counties held onto as much power as possible, realizing that, from the post-1920 period on, the number of farms in the state had declined right along with farm tenancy. In 1930 almost 35 percent of the state's farmers were tenants; this had dropped to about 18 percent in 1955. During the 1950s also, the number of farms in Missouri declined by almost 90,000 as the size of the average farm increased from 119 acres to 170 acres in response to mechanization and large-volume production. The surplus rural population flowed into urban areas, adding to the process of suburbanization now fully under way in the state's two metropolitan areas.

The 1960 federal census was a repeat performance of the 1920 census. The trend toward urbanization continued with 61.3 percent of Missouri's population being urban, but the state's total population again increased during the 1950s at less than half the national rate. Eighty-four counties declined in population, though the greatest gains were realized in the suburban areas of St. Louis, Kansas City, and Springfield. Another significant factor regarding suburbanization in Missouri was the decline of white population in central cities in relation to an increase in black urban population. Between 1960 and 1970 white population in central cities declined 12.1 percent while Negro population in the same areas increased by 22.9 percent. In addition, the increase in black population inside Missouri's standard metropolitan statistical areas was almost three times greater than the white increase during the sixties, when the total Negro population of the state grew by 25.7 percent compared with a 6.5 percent increase in the number of whites. By 1970 Missouri's population was more than 70 percent urban.

Apparently still combating the negative implications inherent in a conservative image, the state's booster mentality reemerged unencumbered in the mid-1970s under the banner that "today's Missouri is young and energetic." While neglecting to mention that Missouri has one of the largest lists of old-age pensioners in the nation, a 12-page promotional advertisement in *Fortune* magazine during 1975 stressed the youthfulness of Missouri's corporate leaders, epitomized in state government by thirty-seven-year-old Republican Governor Christopher Bond. Repeating the centralized promotional thesis of the early 1900s, with a new slant on low corporate taxes and urban renewal, Missouri once again had "all the right ingredients, and in the right place." Perhaps most significant was an unquestioned recognition by state promoters of the St. Louis–Kansas City urban axis as an overriding force in terms of the future development of the state.

Missouri's central location makes it an important linkage point or common ground between the North and the South as well as the East and the West. In this sense, the state has never demonstrated an all-pervasive sectional image. Like the diverse terrain encompassed within its borders, the variety of Missouri's population, politics, and culture does not lend itself to a particular regional categorization. Missouri's major concentrations of population and its governmental, educational, economic, and cultural institutions have been and remain today in the mid-region of the state firmly tied to the St. Louis–Kansas City latitudinal artery. Since these cities provided the directive force in Missouri's history, they will become increasingly important in its future.

Manuscripts and primary sources. Two major manuscript depositories are the State Historical Society of Missouri, in Columbia, and the Missouri Historical Society, in Jefferson Memorial Building, St. Louis. Latter has largest manuscript collection on colonial and territorial periods including Valle Papers, Ste. Genevieve Papers, New Madrid Archives, Chouteau Collections, Amos Stoddard Papers, and Louisiana Territorial Papers. Important collections on poststatehood era include Hamilton R. Gamble Papers, Charles Gibson Papers, Edward Bates Papers, and William B. Napton Papers. The State Historical Society has files of most Missouri newspapers and manuscript census materials. It also has valuable Charles D. Drake manuscript autobiography and Robert T. Van Horn Papers; its Western Historical Manuscripts Collection houses papers of important Missouri politicians.

Universities with holdings on Missouri history include the libraries of St. Louis University and Washington University (St. Louis). The University of Missouri-St. Louis is developing an archives and manuscripts collection pertaining especially to St. Louis. Significant are Harry S. Truman Library in Independence and Kansas

City and St. Louis public libraries; all contain materials on state history.

Published manuscripts and documents for colonial period are L. Houck, *Spanish Regime in Missouri* (2 vols.; 1909); A. P. Nasatir (ed.), *Before Lewis and Clark: Documents, 1785–1804* (2 vols.; 1952); and J. F. McDermott (ed.), *Early Histories of St. Louis* (1952) and *Old Cahokia* (1949). Also see *Missouri Historical Society Documents* (1906–12); and C. C. Carter (ed.), *Territorial Papers of U.S.* (1948–54), XIII–XV.

For further information, see *Laws of State of Missouri*; B. Leopard and F. C. Shoemaker (eds.), *Messages and Proclamations of Governors of Missouri* (20 vols.; 1922); *Reports of Cases Argued and Determined in Supreme Court of State of Missouri*; and W. H. Taft, *Missouri Newspapers, 1808–1963* (1964), guide to all known holdings.

Contemporary accounts. First-hand observations of Missouri life are extensive. See edited accounts in Missouri Historical Society's *Glimpses of the Past* (1933–44); *Mississippi Valley Historical Review*; *Journal of Southern History*; *Missouri Historical Review*; and *Bulletin*. See especially John Shaw, *Missouri Historical Review* (Jan., 1912), New Madrid earthquake; and D. O. Jensen (ed.), *Bulletin* (Oct., 1956; April, Oct., 1957; April, Oct., 1958), diary of a yankee farmer.

Valuable though sometimes biased early accounts are A. Stoddard, *Sketches, Historical and Descriptive of Louisiana* (1812); H. M. Brackenridge, *Views of Louisiana* (1814) and *Recollections* (1834); J. Bradbury, *Travels in Interior of America* (1817); and H. R. Schoolcraft, *View of Lead Mines of Missouri* (1819) and *Journal of Tour into Missouri and Arkansaw* (1821). Of particular interest is Paul Wilhelm, duke of Württemberg, *First Journey to North America* (1835), trans. W. G. Bek, University of North Dakota, 2 vols., typescript.

Contemporary accounts of attitudes toward blacks are J. A. Lyon, *Address on African Colonization* (1850); and N. L. Rice, *Ten Letters on Slavery* (1855). Commentary on free blacks by a black is C. Clamorgan, *Colored Aristocracy of St. Louis* (1858), ed. L. O. Christensen in *Bulletin* (Oct., 1974).

Important urban promotional piece is L. U. Reavis, *St. Louis: Future Great City* (1875). Outstanding reminiscence of St. Louis is G. Anderson, *Border City During Civil War* (1908). Participants' narratives on war are in R. U. Johnson and C. C. Buel (eds.), *Battles and Leaders of Civil War* (4 vols.; 1887–88).

Magazine articles reflecting booster mentality include C. D. Warner, *Harper's* (Oct., 1888); E. L. Eames, *Magazine of Western History* (April, May, June, 1889); J. W. Paramore, *Magazine of Western History* (July, 1889); and W. Clendenin, *Great Southwest* (April, 1908).

T. H. Benton's *Thirty Years View* (2 vols.; 1859) is informative on early Missouri politics, as is W. V. N. Bay's *Reminiscences of Bench and Bar of Missouri* (1878). Useful for Radical Republican politics is *Reminiscences of Carl Schurz* (3 vols.; 1908). More recent and of broader scope is H. S. Truman, *Memoirs* (1955).

Histories. Comprehensive and each with helpful essay on sources are W. E. Foley, *History of Missouri, 1673 to 1820* (1971); P. McCandless, *History of Missouri, 1820 to 1860* (1972); and W. E. Parrish, *History of Missouri, 1860 to 1875* (1973). Good account of state's development is D. D. March, *History of Missouri* (4 vols.;

1967). D. Meyer, *Heritage of Missouri* (rev. ed.; 1970), is best single-volumed study. Other recent works are E. C. McReynolds, *Missouri: Crossroads State* (1962); and L. Larkin, *Vanguard of Empire: Missouri's Century of Expansion* (1961), for western settlement. L. Houck's *History of Missouri from Earliest Explorations* (3 vols.; 1908) is helpful on territorial period. An early history of value is F. C. Shoemaker, *Missouri and Missourians: Land of Contrasts* (5 vols.; 1943).

Important monographs include J. F. Ellis, *Influence of Environment on Settlement of Missouri* (1929); and J. E. Collier, *Geography of Northern Ozark Border Region* (1953). Pertinent Indian nations are covered in W. T. Hagen, *Sac and Fox Indians* (1958); and J. J. Mathews, *Osages* (1961). On French influences, see J. F. McDermott (ed.), *French in Mississippi Valley* (1965). F. J. Yealy explores first permanent settlement in *Ste. Genevieve* (1935).

Useful studies of St. Louis are J. T. Scharf, *St. Louis City and County* (2 vols.; 1883); W. B. Stevens, *St. Louis, 1764–1909* (1911); and E. Krischten, *Catfish and Crystal* (1960), popularly written. Western urban rivalry is discussed in W. W. Belcher, *St. Louis and Chicago, 1850–1880* (1947). St. Louis is compared with other cities in R. C. Wade, *Urban Frontier* (1959).

An older study is D. Garwood, *Crossroads of America: Kansas City* (1948). Two excellent works are A. T. Brown, *Frontier Community: Kansas City to 1870* (1963); and C. N. Glaab, *Kansas City and Railroads* (1962), post–Civil War economic development.

On early history, see F. C. Shoemaker, *Missouri's Struggle for Statehood, 1804–1821* (1916); J. Monaghan, *Civil War on Western Border, 1854–1865* (1955); J. V. Mering, *Whig Party in Missouri* (1967); P. McCandless, *Constitutional Government in Missouri* (1971); F. L. Klement, *Copperheads in Middle West* (1960); W. H. Ryle, *Missouri: Union or Secession?* (1931); W. E. Parrish, *Missouri Under Radical Rule, 1865–1870* (1965); and L. W. Dorsett, *Pendergast Machine* (1968), excellent.

Studies related to blacks in Missouri are extensive. Early and useful works are H. A. Trexler, *Slavery in Missouri, 1804–1865* (1914); and W. W. Elwang, *Negroes of Columbia, Mo.* (1904). See also B. G. Merkel, *Anti-Slavery Controversy in Missouri, 1819–1865* (1942); and V. C. Hopkins, *Dred Scott's Case* (1967). History of black university is W. S. Savage, *Lincoln University* (1939). R. C. Wade's *Slavery in Cities: The South, 1820–1860* (1964) contains references to St. Louis.

Important economic studies include P. C. Phillips, *Fur Trade* (2 vols.; 1961); I. Lippincott, *Fur Trade at St. Louis* (1916); J. N. Primm, *Economic Policy in Development of Western State: Missouri, 1820–1860* (1954); H. M. Chittenden, *Steamboat Navigation on Missouri River* (2 vols.; 1903, 1962); E. L. Lopata, *Local Aid to Railroads in Missouri* (1937); J. D. Norris, *Frontier Iron: Meramec Iron Works* (1964); L. E. Atherton, *Frontier Merchant in Mid-America* (1971); and T. Hubbard and L. E. Davids, *Banking in Mid-America: Missouri's Banks* (1969).

Some significant biographies are W. N. Chambers, *Old Bullion Benton* (1956); M. R. Cain, *Edward Bates* (1965); M. L. Dillon, *Elijah P. Lovejoy* (1961); J. F. McDermott, *George Caleb Bingham* (1959); N. L. Peterson, *B. Gratz Brown* (1965); C. M. Fuess, *Carl Schurz* (1932); R. E.

Shalhope, *Sterling Price* (1971); and W. A. Swanberg, *Pulitzer* (1967).

Excellent contemporary literary accounts of life in the nineteenth century are found in much of the fiction of Mark Twain. See also E. L. Jacobs and F. E. Wolverton, *Missouri Writers: Literary History of Missouri, 1780–1955* (1955); W. H. Lyon, *Pioneer Editor in Missouri, 1808–1860* (1965); E. R. Bowen, *Theatrical Entertainment in Rural Missouri* (1958); C. A. Phillips, *Education in Missouri* (1911); and F. Stephens, *History of University of Missouri* (1962). On religion, consult J. Rothensteiner, *History of Archdiocese of St. Louis* (2 vols.; 1928); R. S. Douglass, *Missouri Baptists* (1934); F. C. Tucker, *Methodist Church in Missouri, 1798–1939* (1966); and G. C. Peters, *Disciples of Christ in Missouri* (1937). On Anglo-Saxon migration, see W. O. Foster, *Zion of the Mississippi* (1953). On role of the attorney, consult W. F. English, *Pioneer Lawyer and Jurist in Missouri* (1947). One aspect of social reform is in F. O. Boan, *History of Poor Relief in Missouri* (1941).

Articles. Check indexes to *Missouri Historical Review* and *Bulletin*. Useful studies of early developments include J. M. Espinosa, *Missouri Historical Review* (April, 1938), Ste. Genevieve District during Spanish period; M. J. Kedro, *Bulletin* (April, 1973), Three-Notch Road; D. Rickey, Jr., *Missouri Historical Review* (Oct., 1960), British attack on St. Louis, 1780; G. C. Din, *Southwest-ern Historical Quarterly* (Oct., 1969), immigration policy of Governor Esteban Miró; A. P. Nasatir, *Iowa Journal of History and Politics* (April, 1931), Anglo-Spanish frontier, 1786–1796; H. Wish, *Mid-America* (July, 1941), French assimilation, 1804–1821; J. F. McDermott, *Bulletin* (Jan., 1967), St. Louis as military headquarters; K. L. Gregg, *Missouri Historical Review* (Oct., 1938; Jan., April, 1939), War of 1812; and R. J. Swartzlow, *Missouri Historical Review* (April, July, Oct., 1934; Jan., April, 1935), most complete account of early lead mining.

Early Missouri politics are examined in D. D. March, *Missouri Historical Review* (July, 1971), statehood; A. Lightfoot, *Missouri Historical Review* (Jan., 1967), Henry Clay and Missouri question; R. E. Shalhope, *Bulletin* (April, 1969), T. H. Benton, and *Civil War History* (Sept., 1969), Jacksonian politics and McCormick thesis; H. Ershkowitz and W. G. Shade, *Journal of American History* (Dec., 1971), excellent study of six state legislatures during Jacksonian era; S. Carroll, *Bulletin* (Oct., 1972), secession question; W. Ehrlich, *Journal of American History* (Sept., 1968), Dred Scott; M. J. Kedro, *Bulletin* (April, 1971), St. Louis Presbytery under martial law during Civil War.

Studies of post–Civil War political developments include J. N. Primm, *Journal of Southern History* (Aug., 1954), G.A.R., 1866–1870; M. C. Morris, *Missouri Historical Review* (Oct., 1930), women's suffrage, 1867–1901;

MISSOURI GOVERNORS

Governor	Party	Term	Governor	Party	Term
LIEUTENANT GOVERNORS OF MISSOURI REGION UNDER FRANCE AND SPAIN			Hancock L. Jackson	Dem.	1856–1857
			Robert M. Stewart	Dem.	1857–1860
Francisco Rios de Rive (or Rivers)	Fr.	1767–1769	Claiborne F. Jackson	Dem.	1860–1861
			Hamilton R. Gamble	Unionist	1861–1864
Pierre Joseph (Pedro) Piernas	Sp.	1770–1775	Willard P. Hall	Unionist	1864
			Thomas C. Fletcher	Radical Rep.	1864–1868
Don Francisco Cruzat	Sp.	1775–1778	Joseph W. McClurg	Radical Rep.	1868–1870
Ferdinand De Leyba	Sp.	1778–1780	B. Gratz Brown	Liberal Rep.	1870–1872
Don Silvio Francisco de Cartebona	Sp.	1780	Silas Woodson	Dem.	1872–1874
			Charles H. Hardin	Dem.	1874–1876
Don Francisco Cruzat	Sp.	1780–1787	John S. Phelps	Dem.	1876–1880
Emenuel Perez	Sp.	1787–1792	Thomas T. Crittenden	Dem.	1880–1884
Zenon Trudeau	Sp.	1792–1799	John S. Marmaduke	Dem.	1884–1887
Charles Dehault Delassus	Sp.	1799–1804	Albert P. Morehouse	Dem.	1887–1888
			David R. Francis	Dem.	1888–1892
TERRITORIAL			William J. Stone	Dem.	1892–1896
Amos Stoddard		1804	Lon V. Stephens	Dem.	1896–1900
James Wilkinson		1805–1806	Alexander M. Dockery	Dem.	1900–1904
Meriwether Lewis		1807–1809	Joseph W. Folk	Dem.	1904–1908
Benjamin Howard		1810–1812	Herbert S. Hadley	Rep.	1908–1912
William Clark		1813–1820	Elliott W. Major	Dem.	1912–1916
			Frederick D. Gardner	Dem.	1916–1920
STATE			Arthur M. Hyde	Rep.	1920–1924
Alexander McNair	Dem.-Rep.	1820–1824	Sam A. Baker	Rep.	1924–1928
Frederick Bates	Dem.-Rep.	1824–1825	Henry S. Caulfield	Rep.	1928–1932
Abraham J. Williams	Dem.-Rep.	1825	Guy B. Park	Dem.	1932–1936
John Miller	Dem.-Rep.	1825–1832	Lloyd C. Stark	Dem.	1936–1940
Daniel Dunklin	Dem.	1832–1836	Forrest C. Donnell	Rep.	1940–1944
Lillburn W. Boggs	Dem.	1836–1840	Phil M. Donnelly	Dem.	1944–1948
Thomas Reynolds	Dem.	1840–1844	Forrest Smith	Dem.	1948–1952
Meredith M. Marmaduke	Dem.	1844	Phil M. Donnelly	Dem.	1952–1956
			James T. Blair, Jr.	Dem.	1956–1960
John C. Edwards	Dem.	1844–1848	John M. Dalton	Dem.	1960–1964
Austin A. King	Dem.	1848–1852	Warren E. Hearnes	Dem.	1964–1972
Sterling Price	Dem.	1852–1856	Christopher S. Bond	Rep.	1972–1976
Trusten Polk	Dem.	1856	Joseph P. Teasdale	Dem.	1976–

MISSOURI POPULATION, 1810–1970

| Year | Total | White | Nonwhite | | % | Rank | |
			Slave	Free	Growth	U.S.	South
1810	19,783	16,696	2,480	607		23	11
1820	66,586	56,017	10,222	347	236.6	24	12
1830	140,455	114,795	25,091	569	110.9	22	11
1840	383,702	323,888	58,240	1,574	173.2	16	9
1850	682,044	592,004	87,422	2,618	77.8	13	8
1860	1,182,012	1,062,555	113,977	5,480	73.3	8	2
1870	1,721,295	1,603,068		118,227	45.6	5	1
1880	2,168,380	2,022,928		145,452	26.0	5	1
1890	2,679,185	2,528,730		150,455	23.6	5	1
1900	3,106,665	2,944,843		161,822	16.0	5	1
1910	3,293,335	3,134,932		158,403	6.0	7	2
1920	3,404,055	3,225,044		179,011	3.4	9	2
1930	3,629,367	3,403,876		225,491	6.6	10	2
1940	3,784,664	3,539,187		245,477	4.3	10	2
1950	3,954,653	3,655,593		299,060	4.5	11	3
1960	4,319,813	3,922,967		396,846	9.2	13	4
1970	4,676,501	4,177,495		499,006	8.3	13	4

F. DeArmond, *Missouri Historical Review* (April, 1967), Reconstruction; J. Muraskin, *Bulletin* (April, 1969), municipal reform; T. K. Evans, *Bulletin* (July, 1972), M. S. Murray; and L. W. Dorsett, *Bulletin* (Oct., 1964), *Arizona and West* (Summer, 1966), and in J. Braeman *et al.*, *New Deal* (2 vols.; 1975), three studies of Kansas City and Pendergast machine.

Social and cultural history are found in J. F. McDermott, *Missouri Historical Review* (July, 1956), frontier culture; L. E. Atherton, *Missouri Historical Review* (July, 1971), Missouri in 1821; W. Keil and H. R. Grant, *Missouri Historical Review* (Oct., 1971), utopian communities; H. R. Grant, *Bulletin* (July, 1971), freethinkers and spiritualists; on boosterism and state promotion, L. W. and M. Dorsett, *Bulletin* (Jan., 1972); and W. E. Unrau, *Bulletin* (Oct., 1970). See also B. Murphy, *Journal of the West* (Jan., 1975), on wide range of problems brought on by Civil War; J. C. Burnham, *Bulletin* (April, 1971), on St. Louis prostitution laws of 1870s; R. E. Oglesby, *Bulletin* (April, 1970), on St. Louis air pollution; and S. J. Raiche, *Missouri Historical Review* (Oct., 1972), on St. Louis and world's fair.

Several studies ably cover urban development: S. F. Voss, *Missouri Historical Review* (Oct., 1969; Jan., April, 1970), on towns of central Missouri, 1815–1860; C. Van Ravenswaay, *Bulletin* (July, 1967), St. Louis, 1850s; H. D. Holmes and R. L. Davis, *Journal of the West* (July, 1974), St. Louis, 1870–1910; C. N. Glaab, *Business History Review* (Summer, 1959), Kansas City real estate; and P. E. McLear, *Bulletin* (Jan., 1972), Kansas City and panic of 1857.

Articles on black Missouri history include E. Oberholzer, *Bulletin* (Jan., April, July, 1950), legal aspects of slavery; A. E. Strickland, *Missouri Historical Review* (July, 1971), slavery in 1821; G. E. Lee, *Missouri Historical Review* (April, 1971), slavery in Lewis County; L. W. Dorsett, *Bulletin* (Oct., 1963), slaveholding in Jackson County; J. W. Blassingame, *Missouri Historical Review* (April, 1964), recruitment of Negro troops; G. H. Wamble, *Missouri Historical Review* (April, 1967), Negroes and Missouri Protestants; J. Day and M. J. Kedro, *Bulletin* (Jan., 1974), St. Louis free blacks; D. D. Bellamy, *Missouri Historical Review* (Jan., 1973), free blacks, 1820–1860; W. S. Savage, *Journal of Negro History* (July, 1931), Negro schools, 1865–1890; R. and M. Fletcher,

Journal of Negro History (July, 1935), Negro occupations in St. Louis, 1866–1897; and D. T. Kelleher, *Bulletin* (April, 1970), St. Louis segregation ordinance of 1916.

Selected ethnic histories include M. Sullivan, *Bulletin* (July, 1972), Irish-American nationalism, 1902–1914; G. R. Mormino, *Bulletin* (Oct., 1973), Italo-Americans and WWI; and V. C. Blum, *Missouri Historical Review* (Jan., 1948), German-Americans in St. Louis, 1859–1861.

Dissertations, theses, and unpublished papers. See W. E. Foley, "Territorial Politics, 1804–1820" (Ph.D., University of Missouri, 1967); N. J. Tice, "Territorial Delegate, 1794–1820" (Ph.D., University of Wisconsin, 1967); R. E. Forderhase, "Jacksonianism, 1820–1836" (Ph.D., University of Missouri, 1968); R. E. Glauret, "Education and Society in Ante-Bellum Missouri" (Ph.D., University of Missouri, 1973); G. H. Kellner, "German St. Louis, 1830–1860" (Ph.D., University of Missouri, 1973); R. I. Brigham, "Education of Negro" (Ph.D., University of Missouri, 1946); W. R. Houf, "Protestant Church, 1820–1870" (Ph.D., University of Missouri, 1967); D. L. Craig, "Decision Not to Secede" (M.A., University of Missouri, 1970); A. R. Kirkpatrick, "Twelfth Confederate State" (Ph.D., University of Missouri, 1954); L. O. Christensen, "Black St. Louis, 1865–1916" (Ph.D., University of Missouri, 1972); R. J. Plavchan, "Anheuser-Busch, 1852–1933" (Ph.D., St. Louis University, 1970); S. McConachie, "Community Planning for the Wealthy" (paper at Twelfth Missouri Conference on History, St. Louis, 1970); M. J. Kedro, "University of Missouri at St. Louis" (typescript, Missouri at St. Louis Archives, 1970); R. L. Gerlach, "Cultural Islands in Ozarks" (Ph.D., University of Nebraska, 1974); and D. B. Oster, "St. Louis and Kansas City" (Ph.D., University of Missouri, 1969).

M. JAMES KEDRO
State Historical Society of Colorado
LYLE W. DORSETT
University of Denver

MISSOURI, STATE HISTORICAL SOCIETY OF

(Hitt and Lowry Sts., Columbia, 65201), was founded in 1898 under the aegis of the Missouri Press Association and has since 1899 received state aid. The society supports an excellent art collection, a museum, a library of almost 400,000 volumes of books and other publications, and an archival collection comprising 150,000 pieces of state records, 300,000 original manuscripts, and over 600 reels of microfilmed manuscripts relating to Missouri and the Middle West. Among these are the papers of artist George C. Bingham and his family and journals and ledgers on business and social history, including a collection of Ozark folk songs and the largest state newspaper collection in the nation. Since 1906 the society has published the quarterly *Missouri Historical Review* (circulation of over 14,300 in 1976), which offers a yearly prize of $100 for the most interesting and scholarly article.

See *Missouri Historical Review* (Oct., 1973), seventy-fifth anniversary issue.

MISSOURI, UNIVERSITY OF, is composed

of four semiautonomous campuses: Columbia (65201), Kansas City (64110), Rolla (65401), and St. Louis (63121). The oldest of the affiliated institutions is the school at Columbia. Established in 1839 at a site near the geographical center of the state, it was the first state-supported school of higher education to be founded west of the Mississippi River. Its school of journalism, created in 1908, was the first of its kind in the world. Although the school had only two students who were graduated at its first commencement in 1843, it presently has an enrollment of approximately 20,000 full-time students in a wide range of graduate and undergraduate programs.

The University of Missouri at Rolla, founded in 1870, was first known as the Missouri School of Mines and Metallurgy. The two youngest institutions are those in the state's two principal cities: the University of Missouri at Kansas City (1933) and the University of Missouri at St. Louis (1965). Approximately 4,000 students are enrolled in programs of mining and metallurgy at Rolla, and each of the newer schools serves approximately 6,000 students in a variety of educational programs.

The Western Historical Collection at the Columbia campus specializes in the history of Missouri and the trans-Mississippi West. Besides the papers of numerous political figures in Missouri history, the collection includes the papers and records of banks, general stores, and mining, lumber, and railway companies, as well as extensive materials on breeding and animal husbandry.

See F. Stephens, *History of University of Missouri* (1962); R. M. Sawyer, "Gaines Case, 1936–1950" (Ph.D. dissertation, University of Missouri, 1966); H. O. Severance, *Richard H. Jesse* (1937), president, 1891–1908; and J. Viles, *University of Missouri* (1935), all deal with Co-

lumbia campus. Also see C. R. Decker and M. Bell, *Place of Light* (1954), Kansas City campus; and C. V. Mann and B. H. Mann, *Brief History of Missouri School of Mines* (1939), Rolla campus.

MISSOURI COMPROMISE (1820) put an end

temporarily to the first major airing of the slavery controversy in antebellum America. It settled a crisis, portentous for the future, that had been occasioned by the movement of settlers into the newly acquired territory of the LOUISIANA PURCHASE. Those who settled at the confluence of the Ohio and Mississippi rivers found themselves directly astride an imaginary extension westward of the MASON-DIXON and Ohio River line, which by tacit consent had separated free states from slave within the original boundaries of the United States. When these settlers petitioned Congress to be allowed to draw up a constitution and enter the Union as the state of Missouri, the balance of free and slave states stood at 11 each. When the Missouri bill reached the U.S. House of Representatives in 1819, Congressman James Tallmadge of New York moved an amendment to prohibit slavery in the new state. Southerners objected violently to the idea that Congress could impose such a ban on an incoming state. Nonetheless, the House passed the amendment; the Senate refused to concur; and amid scenes of increasing acrimony the issue was put off until the following year.

Two new factors made the compromise possible in 1820. In the Senate the Missouri bill, without the Tallmadge amendment, was attached to a bill to separate Maine from Massachusetts, thus maintaining the balance of free and slave states; and the combined bill was further sweetened for northern consumption by the Thomas Proviso, which outlawed slavery forever in the remaining territory of the Louisiana Purchase north of 36°30'. Even this bill would not have passed the House without an adroit maneuver by Speaker HENRY CLAY, who separated the three bills so that southern congressmen could provide a slim three-vote margin of victory for the unrestricted Missouri bill, while opposing to the end the Thomas Proviso, which many insisted was both unconstitutional and intolerable, threatening in the long run to dam them up in a land of slaves.

In 1821 a majority in the House of Representatives was unwilling to accept a provision in the new Missouri constitution that prohibited free Negroes and mulattoes from entering the state, necessitating a "second Missouri Compromise." Again the handiwork of Henry Clay, the reprise made final admission to the Union contingent on an act by the Missouri legislature agreeing never to impair the rights of the citizens of any state.

.Neither settlement was so much a compromise as a feat of legislative legerdemain that put to rest the immediate crisis but left open for future altercation questions fraught with peril: whether Congress had the right to impose on new states conditions that could not be imposed on existing ones and, even more difficult, whether Congress either could or should ban slavery in the territories. The public polemics and prophecies that accompanied the crisis startlingly illustrated the divisive power of the slavery issue and prefigured many of the arguments that would subsequently be made on both sides—including the famous natural law argument, soon to be picked up by the abolitionists, which held for the first time that slavery was morally wrong and should be banned everywhere. Equally significant, the crisis prefigured the major developments in American politics for the next 40 years. It gave rise to a resuscitation in the South of "Old Republicanism," committed to strict construction of the Constitution. Convinced that the Missouri crisis had been precipitated by Federalists capitalizing on the one-party government of the Era of Good Feelings, the Old Republicans eventually marched back to power under the banner of ANDREW JACKSON, recreating an old Jeffersonian party system that kept the slavery issue quiet for another generation and protected southern interests in national government. Forged in the fires of the Missouri crisis, the Jacksonian party was committed both to the annexation of Texas to rectify the imbalance of the Thomas Proviso and ultimately to the repeal of the proviso itself, which was accomplished in 1854 with the KANSAS-NEBRASKA ACT. In 1857 the U.S. Supreme Court ruled in DRED SCOTT V. SANDFORD that the proviso had been unconstitutional all along, as the Old Republicans had argued in 1820, and the stage was set for civil war.

See G. Moore, *Missouri Controversy* (1953), definitive but limited in implications; G. Dangerfield, *Era of Good Feelings* (1952); and R. H. Brown, *South Atlantic Quarterly* (Winter, 1966).

RICHARD H. BROWN
Newberry Library

MISSOURI DEMOCRAT, in St. Louis, began in 1852 as a free-soil Democratic newspaper. Amid the turmoil in this border community, the paper, under the management of William McKee, moved gradually into the Republican party. A small businessman, McKee viewed slavery mainly as a blight on the commercial growth of St. Louis. Following the war, after briefly supporting the harsh policies of Radical Republicans, the *Democrat* turned to

the Liberal Republican movement. In 1875 it merged with the recently established *Globe* to form the modern *Globe-Democrat*, still in publication.

See J. A. Hart, *Globe-Democrat* (1961); W. B. Stevens, *Missouri Historical Review* (Oct., 1930; April, 1934); L. E. Guese, *Missouri Historical Review* (Jan., 1942); G. Grover, *Missouri Historical Review* (Oct., 1913); and S. B. Laughlin, *Missouri Historical Review* (April, 1929; Jan., 1930).

JULIAN S. RAMMELKAMP
Albion College

MISSOURI EX REL. GAINES (305 U.S. 337 [1938]) required the admission of a Negro to the University of Missouri Law School. Lloyd Gaines, a Negro, had been refused admission to the law school and instructed to apply for an out-of-state scholarship to enable him to attend a law school in any adjacent state. Missouri, like Maryland, had denied Negroes admission to the state's white law school but had provided them with an opportunity to obtain legal education via this out-of-state arrangement. Gaines petitioned the U.S. Supreme Court to compel his admission to Missouri's white law school. Justice Charles Evans Hughes, in delivering the opinion of the Court, stressed the "equal" provision of the separate but equal doctrine set down in PLESSY V. FERGUSON. He noted that the basic issue was not "what sort of opportunities other states provide" but what opportunities Missouri "provides to white students and denies to Negroes wholly upon the ground of color." He asserted that the admissibility of laws separating the races "in the enjoyment of privileges afforded by the state" was based "wholly upon the equality of the privileges" that state laws gave to the separated groups within the state. The Court, holding that admission to the state's white law school was the only "appropriate remedy consistent with the constitutional standard of equality," ordered Gaines's admission "in the absence of other and proper provision for his legal training within the state."

See R. M. Sawyer, "Gaines Case, 1936–1950" (Ph.D. dissertation, University of Missouri, 1966).

H. REN KENT
Southwestern University, Georgetown, Tex.

MISSOURI HISTORICAL SOCIETY (Jefferson Memorial Bldg., St. Louis, Mo. 63112), founded in 1866, has 3,000 members. It maintains a museum, a library of over 100,000 volumes, a substantial graphics collection, and an archive containing 1.5 million manuscripts dating from 1664 related to the history of Missouri and the West. These include the papers of major explorers, fur traders, military leaders, and pioneers in the theater, medicine, journalism, art, and literature. Also among them are business records, Civil War papers, tax and court records, and the Missouri Governors Collection. Since 1944 the society has published the quarterly *Bulletin of the Missouri Historical Society* (circulation 3,300), which accepts articles related to Missouri and westward expansion.

MISSOURI REPUBLICAN of St. Louis, begun as the weekly *Missouri Gazette* in 1808 by Irish immigrant Joseph Charless, was renamed the *Republican* in 1822. In 1828, as the voice of the merchant classes, it joined the Whigs. In 1836 it became a daily and soon was sold to George Knapp, owner until his death in 1885. In the late 1850s the *Republican* supported the pro-Union wing of the Democratic party. After 1865, as a Democratic party organ, it became the most influential paper west of the Mississippi. In 1888 it was taken over by Charles H. Jones, renamed the St. Louis *Republic*, and dedicated to free silver. Jones was ousted in 1893 and replaced by Charles W. Knapp. However, its close alliance with powerful financial interests aggravated its continued loss of circulation, and in 1919 it was sold to its old rival, the *Globe-Democrat*.

See J. T. Scharf, *History of St. Louis* (1883); J. Cox, *Old and New St. Louis* (1894); W. B. Stevens, *St. Louis* (1909) and *Missouri Historical Review* (April, 1923; July, 1925; Jan., 1928); T. S. Graham, "Charles H. Jones" (Ph.D. dissertation, University of Florida, 1973); and *Missouri Gazette, Missouri Republican, Missouri Republic*, in Missouri Historical Society, St. Louis.

JULIAN S. RAMMELKAMP
Albion College

MISSOURI RIVER, flowing 2,714 miles from its farthest headstream to its mouth, is the longest river in the United States and the major tributary of the MISSISSIPPI RIVER. Rising at an altitude of 4,000 feet above sea level in Montana's Rocky Mountains, it moves through the Dakotas, Iowa, Nebraska, and Kansas before reaching Kansas City and bisecting the state of Missouri. From Kansas City and Independence it winds in an easterly direction past Jefferson City and enters the Mississippi approximately 17 miles above St. Louis. Because of its steep descent and because of the irregular rainfall of the northern plains, the Missouri remains essentially untamed. Each spring it rushes with torrents of water and refuse; each summer it becomes a quiet stream marked by numerous sandbars. Throughout the year, however, it carries away many millions of tons of topsoil, giving it its nickname, Big Muddy.

Despite the hazards of navigating so changeable a stream, the Missouri was much traveled by area Indians. Jacques Marquette and Louis Jolliet in 1673 were probably the first Europeans to discover the river and, after Lewis and Clark's expedition (1804–1806), the river became an important artery for westward-bound pioneers in the early nineteenth century. Steamboat traffic on the Missouri began in 1819, and in 1832 one paddlewheeler successfully traveled the length of the river upstream to Yellowstone. It was the lower portion of the Missouri, however, that was most heavily used prior to the Civil War. Settlers bound for Oregon or for California frequently traveled by river through Missouri to Independence and moved overland from there to their destinations.

Railroads relegated river commerce to a subordinate role during the latter half of the nineteenth century, and, although some barge traffic still uses the lower part of the river, the Missouri's principal value today is as a source of water for irrigation and as a producer of hydroelectric power. In 1944 the U.S. Congress authorized the Missouri River Basin Project, an enterprise modeled after the TENNESSEE VALLEY AUTHORITY. Its objective has been to improve FLOOD CONTROL, irrigation, navigation, water supplies, pollution, and CONSERVATION. Yet engineers estimate that at least 100 major dams will be necessary to tame the Missouri, and work on the project has been seriously curtailed by the costs of so gigantic an undertaking.

See W. S. Campbell, *Missouri River* (1945); J. M. Hanson, *Conquest of Missouri* (1946); and P. E. Chappell, *History of Missouri River* (1905).

MITCHELL, BROADUS (1892–), economic historian, educator, and proponent of southern industrialization, was born in Georgetown, Ky., the son of historian Samuel Mitchell. He received his doctorate from Johns Hopkins University in 1918 and joined the economics faculty there the following year. Leaving Hopkins in 1939, he taught at Rutgers, Occidental College, and Hofstra before retiring in 1967. Among his publications are a two-volumed biography of Alexander Hamilton (1957–1962) and *Depression Decade* (1947), a study of the depression and New Deal. Mitchell's first work, *Rise of Cotton Mills in the South* (1921), portrays an epic folk movement. Led by mill owners, who sought prosperity for their region and a means to remove poor whites from competition with blacks, a devastated South began to enter the nation's economic mainstream. *The Industrial Revolution in the South* (1930), written with his brother George, reiterates these themes. Mitchell also notes that persisting values of the old agrarian order, including racism and religious fundamentalism, deterred acceptance of an industrial society. These works, with *William Gregg* (1928), a biography of an antebellum textile manufacturer, established Mitchell as a prominent NEW SOUTH historian.

See P. M. Gaston, in A. S. Link and R. W. Patrick (eds.), *Writing Southern History* (1965).

MELTON MCLAURIN
University of South Alabama

MOBILE, ALA. (pop. 190,126), the state's only seaport and second largest city, lies at the entrance of Mobile River to Mobile Bay in the southwestern part of Alabama. Although the site was visited during the sixteenth century by several Spanish expeditions, it was not successfully settled until 1702, when the French Le Moyne brothers, IBERVILLE and BIENVILLE, founded Ft. Louis de la Mobile (the latter name a local Indian derivative) upriver at Twenty-seven-Mile Bluff. The colony moved to its present site in 1711. Although the capital of Louisiana until the 1717 hurricane shoaled the Gulf pass, Mobile remained a small Indian supply depot until the British obtained it in 1763 as part of Florida. Recaptured by the Spanish in 1780, the area was seized by the United States in 1813. Alabama incorporated Mobile in 1819.

Mobile grew into a major cotton-exporting port and cultural center of colleges, theaters, and Greek Revival buildings. With a federally maintained ten-foot ship channel offsetting the shallow bay and river, its population (county) increased from 2,672 in 1820 to 41,131 in 1860 (30.6 percent black). Steamboats, supplemented by the Mobile & Ohio Railroad, freighted to the interior. Although antisecessionist in 1860, the city supported the Confederacy and continued shipping until 1864 (MOBILE CAMPAIGN). Following the war, the port declined and the city experienced scandals, bankruptcy (1879), and rechartering. Despite the resumption of federal dredging and the construction of additional railroads, the population actually declined in the 1880s. After the turn of the century, however, the city rebounded. Increased trade (because of banana shipments), river improvements, shipbuilding (1917), and completion of the INTRACOASTAL WATERWAY and state docks revived the city's economy. Although its social

structure remained comparatively the same until 1939, the PULP AND PAPER and ALUMINUM industries, TOURISM, and New Deal programs predisposed changes. During World War II, the city's social and economic life was transformed when the population increased two-thirds and overtaxed housing, services, and education. Brookley Field remained the largest single employer until 1964, when termination began, but chemical plants, educational facilities, and tourism have largely counterbalanced the economic loss of Brookley.

See B. K. Loftin, "Social History" (Ph.D. dissertation, University of Southern Mississippi, 1971); C. G. Summersell, *Mobile* (1949); Mobile Public Library; H. Amos, "Social Life" (Ph.D. dissertation, Emory, 1976); A. Thompson, "Social and Economic Characteristics of Mobile, 1850–1861" (Ph.D. dissertation, University of Alabama, 1977); and J. Higginbotham, *Old Mobile, 1702–1711* (1977).

BERNADETTE KUEHL LOFTIN
Middle Georgia College

MOBILE BAY, BATTLE OF (August 5, 1864), commenced when Admiral DAVID G. FARRAGUT's fleet—composed of four monitors, 14 wooden ships, and numerous small gunboats—forced its way into the bay through a narrow channel that was protected by the guns of Ft. Morgan and a minefield. The wooden ships were lashed together in pairs to reduce casualties. During the passage into the bay, the monitor *Tecumseh* struck a mine and sank with most of its crew. At this the fleet hesitated, but saying, "Damn the torpedoes; full speed ahead," Farragut ordered his flagship *Hartford* to take the lead. He correctly believed that most of the Confederate mines (torpedoes) were waterlogged and inoperative. Once in the bay, Farragut fought a Confederate squadron of three small wooden gunboats and the heavy ironclad *Tennessee*, commanded by Admiral FRANKLIN BUCHANAN. The small gunboats were soon chased off, and eventually the *Tennessee*, its steering chains and smokestack shot away, surrendered. Ft. Morgan surrendered August 23, and Mobile was finally closed.

See E. B. Potter and C. Nimitz, *Seapower* (1960), excellent battle account; M. C. McMillan, *Alabama Confederate Reader* (1963), good documentary account from both sides; and C. L. Lewis, *David G. Farragut* (1941).

FRANK LAWRENCE OWSLEY, JR.
Auburn University

MOBILE CAMPAIGN (March–April, 1865). When Ft. Morgan was captured on August 23, 1864, by Admiral DAVID FARRAGUT and federal land forces (MOBILE BAY, BATTLE OF), the North had finally closed Mobile Bay to blockade-runners. The Confederacy, however, still controlled Mobile, located 30 miles from the Gulf of Mexico. Not until March, 1865, did the North begin military operations against Mobile, which was commanded by DABNEY MAURY. His army consisted of 9,000 soldiers, most of them young and inexperienced. According to JOSEPH E. JOHNSTON, Mobile was one of the best-fortified cities in the Confederacy.

The task of capturing Mobile for the Union was given to EDWARD CANBY. On March 17, 1865, he left Ft. Morgan with approximately 30,000 Union soldiers to begin the campaign. Dispatched from Pensacola, Frederick Steele moved west with 15,000 men toward BLAKELY, ten miles north of Mobile. Another Confederate stronghold on the outer defenses of Mobile was Spanish Fort, located seven miles east. Here nearly 3,000 men, most of them from JOHN HOOD's late army, engaged the federals in a fierce artillery duel, which began March 27. The Confederates were outnumbered eight to one at Blakely and Spanish Fort, but it took 12 days for the federals to break through the defenses and force a surrender. Finally, on April 9, 1865, the Confederate troops at Blakely and Spanish Fort surrendered, the same day that Robert E. Lee surrendered at APPOMATTOX.

Meanwhile, Canby and his men proceeded toward Mobile, and on March 28 he placed the city under siege. On April 8, assisted by the navy, Canby launched a heavy assault against the inner defenses of Mobile. Two days later he was joined by the victorious federals from Blakely and Spanish Fort. Realizing that capture by the federals was imminent, Maury evacuated the city, moving his men by gunboats up the Alabama River. On April 12, civil authorities surrendered Mobile. When the Confederates departed from Mobile, they destroyed valuable resources, including cotton and steamboats. However, the North captured nearly 20,000 bales of cotton, 400 cannon, and considerable ammunition and commissary stores. Thus, once again, the North controlled one of the most strategic ports in the Lower South.

See *Official Records, Armies*, Ser. 1, Vol. XLIX; *Official Records, Navies*, Ser. 1, Vol. XXII; A. Mahan, *Gulf Waters* (1883), biased but informative; W. Fleming, *Civil War in Alabama* (1905), indispensable; A. Nevins, *War for Union* (1971), IV; T. Holt, Jr. (ed.), *Waring's Journal* (n.d.); and J. Newton, *Alabama Historical Quarterly* (Winter, 1958).

ROBERT C. HARRIS
University of West Florida

MOBILE REGISTER began publication in 1821 as a daily newspaper except during the summer, when it was issued triweekly. Although the paper endorsed W. H. CRAWFORD in the ELECTION OF 1824, it was more vitally interested in trade and in business news than in politics. In 1860, while being edited by John Forsyth, it was perhaps the most polished and best-edited newspaper in the South. Much more political in nature than the *Register* was the *Daily Advertizer* (1833–1861). It argued against extreme states' rights positions by equating them with NULLIFICATION and by arguing that southern nationalism might ultimately destroy the Union. Both the *Advertizer* and the *Register* opposed Alabama's drift toward secession after the ELECTION OF 1860. The merger of the two papers in 1861 to form the *Advertizer and Register* resulted in a reorganization of the daily and in a definite change in its journalistic viewpoint. The new paper's spirited defense of the Confederacy caused it to be suppressed briefly by federal occupation authorities during the Civil War. Unbowed by defeat, it vowed after the war to accept no compromise with white supremacy despite ratification of the Fourteenth and Fifteenth amendments. Known simply as the *Daily Register* since 1868, the paper presently is edited as an independent journal with a circulation of 45,000 copies daily.

See bound copies of the *Register* (1833–48, 1857–59, 1862–64, 1869–) at Library of Congress; and microfilm from Bell & Howell (1822–1969) and from Microfilm Corporation of America (1970–).

MOBILE RIVER links the Alabama River system to the shallow Mobile Bay and Gulf of Mexico. Formed by the heavily forested junction of the Alabama and Tombigbee rivers, the river flows 45 miles to its mouth at Mobile, where it is crossed by Cochran Bridge (1917), Bankhead Tunnel (1941), and twin tunnels (1973). HERNANDO DE SOTO (1540) defeated the Mauvilla (Mobile) Indians, who lived along the banks. Despite sandbars at the mouth, the river served as a major route inland for the French (1702) and the British (1763). Spanish occupation led to difficulties over free navigation, particularly after the establishment of Ft. Stoddert (1799) at the river's intersection of the American boundary. United States seizure (1813) inaugurated a flourishing steamboat river traffic, and the Army Corps of Engineers maintained a ten-foot channel until the Civil War. Confederate fortifications and shoaling hindered traffic until the dredging of a 13-foot channel (1876), but railroads continued to divert waterborne freight. River transportation improved with the Warrior-Tombigbee lock and dam system (1915) and state docks (1923). Completion of the Tennessee-Tombigbee Waterway will tie the Mobile to the Midwest. The presently maintained channel (1977) is 40 feet deep, 500 feet wide, and 33 miles long (including bay) to the Gulf outlet.

See Mobile Public Library; Mobile U.S. Engineers; and E. L. Ullman, *Mobile: Industrial Seaport* (1943).

BERNADETTE KUEHN LOFTIN
Middle Georgia College

MONITOR AND MERRIMACK, BATTLE OF

(March 9, 1862). The *Merrimack*, or *Virginia* as it was commissioned in the Confederate navy, was converted from a burnt hulk into an armored warship. The vessel left the yards at Portsmouth, Va., on March 8, 1862, for its trial run. However, FRANKLIN BUCHANAN, its commanding officer, had determined to take advantage of the element of surprise and attack federal vessels off Newport News in Hampton Roads. The *Virginia*, supported by wooden gunboats, destroyed the *Cumberland* and *Congress* before retiring into Elizabeth River. The following day, under the command of Catesby ap R. Jones (Buchanan was wounded March 8), the *Virginia* returned to complete the destruction of enemy vessels. The ironclad *Monitor*, however, had fortuitously arrived in Hampton Roads during the night.

The *Monitor*, designed by John Ericsson, was commissioned on February 25, 1862, and left New York early in March in tow of a tug. Commanded by John Worden, it originally was to join David Farragut's squadron in the Gulf, but the alarming news of the *Virginia's* progress persuaded the Navy Department to send it to Hampton Roads. It was a fortunate coincidence that the *Monitor* arrived before the Confederate vessel could finish its destructive work.

For four hours the two armored vessels fought each other, usually at close range, before breaking off the engagement. Neither ship was seriously damaged, although the *Virginia* lost two killed and 19 wounded and the *Monitor's* captain was seriously wounded. Tactically the battle was a victory for the *Monitor*; the Confederate ironclad retired without destroying additional Union vessels. The strategic consequences, however, favored the *Virginia*. For two months it controlled the river approaches to Richmond, delaying George McClellan's campaign to take the Confederate capital. The battle did not revolutionize naval warfare, but it was the first time that ironclad ships had

fought each other. The *Virginia* was destroyed by its own crew on May 9, and the *Monitor* foundered off Hatteras on New Year's Eve, 1862.

See the most useful W. C. Davis, *Duel Between First Ironclads* (1975); R. W. Daly, *How Merrimac Won* (1957); and W. N. Still, Jr., *Iron Afloat* (1971). See also H. P. Nash, Jr., *American Neptune* (July, 1963); W. Tindall, *Virginia Magazine of History and Biography* (Jan., April, 1923); J. P. Baxter III, *Introduction of Ironclad Warship* (1933); W. C. Church, *Life of John Ericsson* (1890); R. S. McCordock, *Yankee Cheese Box* (1938); H. A. Trexler, *Confederate Ironclad Virginia* (1938); and C. White, *Tin Can on Shingle* (1957). Accounts by participants include J. R. Eggleston, *Southern Historical Society Papers* (Sept. 1916); C. ap R. Jones, *Southern Historical Society Papers* (Jan., 1883); H. B. Littlepage, *Civil War Times Illustrated* (April–March, 1974); V. Newton, *Southern Historical Society Papers* (Jan., 1892); W. H. Parker, *Recollections of Navy Officer* (1883); H. A. Ramsay, *Confederate Veteran* (July, 1907); A. Sinclair, *Hearst* (Dec., 1913); J. T. Wood and D. B. Phillips, in R. U. Johnson and C. C. Buel (eds.), *Battles and Leaders* (1888), I; H. A. Ramsay, J. L. Worden, and S. D. Greene, *Monitor and Merrimac* (1912); W. F. Keeler, *Aboard USS Monitor* (1964); F. B. Butts, *Monitor and Merrimac* (1890); and T. O. Selfridge, Jr., *Memoirs* (1924). See also *Official Records, Navies*, Ser. 1, Vols. VI, VII; *Report of Secretary of Navy in Relation to Armored Vessels* (1864); J. L. Worden Papers, Lincoln Memorial University and Library of Congress; L. M. Goldsborough Papers, Duke University; Area 7 Files (NA microfilm M-625), Log of *Monitor*, and letters of North Atlantic Blockading Squad (NA microfilm M-89), in Record Group 45, National Archives. See also G. P. Watts, "Monitor of New Age" (M.A. thesis, East Carolina University, 1975).

WILLIAM N. STILL, JR.
East Carolina University

MONROE, JAMES

(1758–1831), was born in Westmoreland County, Va. He entered the College of William and Mary in June, 1774, but left to enlist as a lieutenant in the Virginia line. He was wounded at Trenton and became a major on Lord Stirling's staff (1777–1778). Unable to secure further appointment, he studied law (1780–1783) with Thomas Jefferson, forming a lasting friendship.

Monroe was elected to the Virginia legislature (1782) and represented Virginia in Congress (1783–1786), where he became a friend of JAMES MADISON. In 1787 he reentered the legislature and became an ANTI-FEDERALIST delegate to the convention to ratify the Constitution. In 1788 he purchased an estate near Monticello and ran unsuccessfully against Madison for Congress. In the U.S. Senate (1790–1794) he became increasingly critical of FEDERALIST policy and organized DEMOCRATIC-REPUBLICAN opposition. He was minister to France (1794–1796) and governor

(1799–1802). During GABRIEL'S INSURRECTION (1800), Monroe proposed leniency toward slaves less involved, but was overridden. He believed that slavery was an evil, but the dangers of abolition greater. He later became an advocate of colonization. In 1803 he was envoy to France, assisting in negotiating the LOUISIANA PURCHASE, and to Spain and minister to England (1803–1807). An unsuccessful candidate for president in 1807, Monroe broke with Madison, who did not appoint him to the cabinet because of Senate opposition. In 1811 the two reconciled their differences, and Monroe became secretary of state.

In 1816 Monroe's only serious opponent for the presidency was W. H. CRAWFORD. As president he adopted the politics of consensus, repudiating the party system. In his cabinet appointments he attempted to balance the sections and presidential aspirants. Negotiations for Florida were interrupted in 1818 by ANDREW JACKSON's invasion. Monroe admitted Jackson had exceeded his instructions but refused to repudiate him. A treaty was signed in February, 1819. That month, the Tallmadge amendment to the Missouri statehood bill precipitated a national debate on slavery. Publicly, Monroe took no position but privately determined to veto any bill restricting Missouri and worked with Congress for compromise legislation (MISSOURI COMPROMISE). Reelected without opposition in 1820, Monroe supported the Bank of the United States. In the debates over Indian policy (1823–1824) he defended the right of Indians to control their lands, recommending in 1825 voluntary resettlement west of the Mississippi.

In 1825 Monroe left office on the verge of bankruptcy. Seeking federal reimbursement for expenses dating back to 1794, he received $30,000 in 1831. He served on the University of Virginia board of visitors until his health failed in 1830 and presided over the Virginia constitutional convention in 1829.

See the definitive H. Ammon, *James Monroe* (1971); the older W. P. Cresson, *James Monroe* (1964); and the presidential period studies by G. Dangerfield, *Era of Good Feelings* (1963) and *Awakening of American Nationalism, 1815–1828* (1965). Chief manuscript collections are in Library of Congress and New York Public Library. Published works include S. M. Hamilton (ed.), *Writings* (7 vols.; 1898–1903); and S. G. Brown (ed.), *Autobiography* (1959).

A. V. HUFF, JR.
Furman University

MONROE, LA. (pop. 56,374), is situated on the Ouachita River approximately 95 miles east of Shreveport. Although white settlers had located along the banks of the river during the early eighteenth century, this site was not occupied until 1785, when Jean Baptiste Filhial settled here. Five years later, Filhial erected a fort, which he named Fuerte Miro in honor of the Spanish governor, Don Esteban Miró. The settlement grew slowly as a cotton and trade center and was renamed (*ca.* 1818) in honor of the first steamboat, the *James Monroe*, to arrive at this point. After completion of rail links to the city in the 1860s, the town enjoyed a steady commercial growth. In 1916, however, the discovery of one of the largest known natural gas fields nearby made the town an industrial center as well. Its factories produce textiles, chemicals, paper, lumber, metals, and construction materials.

See files of Monroe *News-Star* (1909–) and *World* (1929–).

MONTAGUE, ANDREW JACKSON (1862–1937), was born near Lynchburg, Va. Soon after his graduation from the University of Virginia Law School in 1885, he became active in state Democratic politics. In 1892 he was given a federal patronage appointment as district attorney of the Western Judicial District of Virginia. It was during the POPULIST period that Montague's attitude toward laissez faire began to change. By 1897 he was a silverite and was privately supporting a senatorial primary and moving toward the more progressive element in his party. During his term as state attorney general (1898–1902), he openly fought for the primary and thereby openly challenged the machine of THOMAS S. MARTIN. In the 1901 gubernatorial campaign, Montague ran on a platform calling for a primary, better schools, better roads, and the enactment of an employer's liability law. As a result of his election, Montague became the undisputed leader of the "independent" faction of the Democratic party. He interpreted his victory as an outcry against the Martin machine and proceeded to lay plans to challenge Martin in the senatorial election of 1905. After Montague lost this political battle, his political career went into eclipse. He continued, however, to be extremely active in public service for the next 30 years as an educator, foreign diplomat, congressman (1913–1937), and constitutional lawyer.

See W. Larsen, *Montague of Virginia* (1965); R. H. Pulley, *Old Virginia Restored, 1870–1930* (1968); and A. J. Montague Papers, Virginia State Library, Richmond.

THOMAS E. GAY, JR.
Edinboro State College

MONTGOMERY, ALA. (pop. 133,386), the state's capital since 1846, is located on the Alabama River 85 miles southeast of Birmingham. Originally it was the site of two Indian villages. The first white settler arrived in 1716, but not until a century later was a town established. Then two towns developed almost simultaneously: Philadelphia, established by a group of New England speculators, and East Alabama, founded by a similar group of Georgians. The rivalry of the two settlements was resolved by merger and incorporation in 1819 under the name Montgomery. After the state's secession convention, representatives of six southern states met here in February, 1861, to form the CONFEDERATE STATES OF AMERICA and named Montgomery the provisional capital of the Confederacy. Since its founding it has been a market for area cotton growers; however, modern Montgomery also produces fertilizers, foodstuffs, textiles, lumber products, and air conditioners.

See C. W. Williams, "History of Montgomery, 1817–1846" (Ph.D. dissertation, Vanderbilt, 1938); R. H. Hines and J. E. Pierce, *Phylon* (Summer, 1965); files of Montgomery *Advertiser* (1828–) and *Alabama Journal* (1888–); Society of Pioneers, *History of Montgomery in Pictures* (1963) and *100 Years, 100 Families* (1958); and W. J. MacWilliams, *A Growing City* (1953).

MONTGOMERY ADVERTIZER began publication in 1828 as a newspaper more interested in commercial news than in politics. In 1854 the *Daily Mail* went into competition with the *Advertizer* as decidedly the more political of the two dailies. Avowedly Democratic and secessionist in sentiment, the *Mail* also made a special contribution to southern humorous literature by publishing the writings of JOHNSON JONES HOOPER under the pseudonym Simon Suggs. Despite the *Mail*'s secessionist fervor, in 1864 the paper began to warn of impending defeat and to hint about the desirability of a quick peace.

In 1872 the *Advertizer* and the *Mail* were merged into a single daily called the *Advertizer and Mail* until 1882 and then known simply as the *Advertizer*. Drawing on the commercial tradition of the old *Advertizer* and the political past of the *Mail*, the postwar paper was a partisan defender of Alabama's Conservative Democratic party and a promoter of the state's industrial development. It urged Alabamians to accept the results of the Civil War—including the enfranchisement of southern blacks—and to concentrate instead on the building of a NEW SOUTH. With close ties to state and community business leaders, the *Advertizer* decried independent movements and farm-

ers' reform groups during the late nineteenth century. It also was perhaps the state's leading journalistic foe of the populistic REUBEN KOLB. Presently published as an independent paper, it has a circulation in excess of 50,000 daily copies.

See bound copies at Alabama Department of Archives, Montgomery, and at Library of Congress; and microfilm from University of Alabama (1854–82) and from Library of Congress (1882–).

MONTGOMERY BUS BOYCOTT (1955–1956). By refusing to relinquish her seat, a spontaneous decision that stemmed from past abuses, Rosa Parks touched off the Montgomery bus boycott. Immediately after her arrest, Montgomery's black ministers and lay leaders, including E. D. Nixon, pullman porter and former president of the Alabama NAACP, convened to form the Montgomery Improvement Association, electing MARTIN LUTHER KING, JR., to direct the boycott's efforts. Originally scheduled as a one-day affair (Monday, December 5, 1955), the boycott continued, with the black leaders and their white sympathizers using car pools, mass meetings, publicity campaigns, and fund raisings. Threats, intimidation, bombings, KU KLUX KLAN marches, white CITIZENS' COUNCIL meetings, police harassment, and legal delays were the white opposition's techniques. With King at the helm this massive nonviolent movement brought national attention to the civil rights struggle. It cut across socioeconomic lines, tying nearly all blacks together. The initial goals were limited to courteous treatment on buses, a first-come, first-served seating arrangement with whites from the front and blacks from the back, and black drivers on the black routes. The leaders did not call for an end to segregation; they planned to operate within the system. By May, 1956, however, an NAACP suit filed in federal court called for a complete end to bus segregation. The U.S. Supreme Court upheld a lower court ruling, which approved the NAACP action on the same day (December 19, 1956) a local court enjoined the car pool, a ruling that otherwise might have killed the boycott. The boycott catapulted King into national prominence and brought public attention to the plight of the southern black.

See M. L. King, *Stride Toward Freedom* (1958); G. Barrett, *New York Times Magazine* (Dec. 16, 1956); W. Dykeman, *Nation* (Jan. 5, 1957); and W. A. Emerson, Jr., *Newsweek* (May 5, 1956).

DUNCAN R. JAMIESON
University of Alabama

MONTGOMERY CONVENTION assembled at Montgomery, Ala., February 4, 1861, to organize the Confederate States of America. Six states of the Lower South (in the order of secession)—South Carolina, Mississippi, Florida, Alabama, Georgia, and Louisiana—answered the first roll call. Texas delegates arrived March 2. Four other states (Arkansas, Virginia, North Carolina, and Tennessee), admitted after FT. SUMTER, had little to do with the formation of the Confederacy. The convention, which elected HOWELL COBB of Georgia as its presiding officer, worked speedily and mostly in secret session, as it wished to present the Lincoln administration with a *fait accompli* on March 4. It drafted a provisional constitution and shortly thereafter a permanent constitution, both very much like the Constitution of the United States. As WILLIAM L. YANCEY said, the Confederacy wanted to take with it the U.S. Constitution as "the ark of the Covenant of her liberties."

JEFFERSON DAVIS was elected president over the Georgia triumvirate (ROBERT TOOMBS, Cobb, and ALEXANDER STEPHENS) but the latter, who had been a Unionist, was elected vice-president in order to try to bring about unity and as a consolation prize to the Georgians. Davis was inaugurated on February 18, 1861, amid a throng of about 10,000 people. The convention declared itself the Provisional Congress of the Confederate States and held its sessions in Montgomery until May 21, 1861, when it adjourned to meet in Richmond. It acted interchangeably as a powerful constitutional convention and a legislative body. Beginning July 20, 1861, it continued to meet in Richmond as the CONFEDERATE CONGRESS until the permanent government elected by the people in November, 1861, was inaugurated February 22, 1862. The Provisional Congress was a unicameral body; the latter, a bicameral Congress.

See M. C. McMillan, *Alabama Confederate Reader* (1963); R. F. Nichols, *Disruption of American Democracy* (1948); C. Eaton, *History of Southern Confederacy* (1954); and *Journal of Congress of Confederate States of America, 1861–65* (7 vols.; 1904).

MALCOLM C. MCMILLAN
Auburn University

MOORE FAMILY of North Carolina was descended from James Moore (1640?–1729) of South Carolina, who emigrated from Ireland in 1665 and was governor of the colony. Two of Moore's sons, James (1667–1740) and Maurice (1670–after 1740), settled in North Carolina. Maurice's son Maurice (1735–1777), jurist and revolutionary patriot, was active in provincial government, serving a number of terms in the house of commons, on the governor's council, and as an associate judge of the province. Another son of Maurice, James (1737–1777), Revolutionary War soldier, was a member of the provincial house of commons (1764–1771, 1773). He was selected colonel of the 1st North Carolina Continental Regiment and in 1776 was made brigadier general in command of forces in North Carolina. He won fame in the battle of MOORE'S CREEK BRIDGE. Son of the second Maurice, Alfred (1755–1810), Revolutionary War soldier and jurist, participated in the battles of Moore's Creek Bridge, Charleston, and FT. MOULTRIE. He served in the state senate (1783), as attorney general (1782–1791), and in the house of commons (1792–1795). John Adams appointed him an associate justice of the U.S. Supreme Court in 1799. He resigned in 1804 because of poor health.

See S. A. Ashe (ed.), *Biographical History of North Carolina* (1905), II; J. Sprunt, *Chronicles of Cape Fear River* (2nd ed.; 1916); L. Friedman and F. L. Israel, *Justices of U.S. Supreme Court* (4 vols.; 1969), I; and manuscripts, North Carolina Historical Commission.

DWIGHT F. HENDERSON
Indiana University–Purdue University, Ft. Wayne

MOORE'S CREEK BRIDGE, BATTLE OF (February 27, 1776), was fought between some 1,100 North Carolina Whig militiamen under Colonel RICHARD CASWELL and about 1,600 Loyalists, including Highland Scots, under command of Brigadier General Donald MacDonald. Directed by royalist governor Josiah Martin, the mission of these Loyalists was to march to the sea at Wilmington, there to join British regular troops to subdue the rebellion. This intention was frustrated by the maneuvers of Whig Colonel James Moore (MOORE FAMILY), who ordered a junction of militia to block the Loyalist march at a bridge on Moore's Creek, a tributary of the Black River. The Loyalists launched an attack across the bridge, which had been greased to make footing precarious. Whig fire routed them with a loss of perhaps 50 dead and wounded. The British Loyalist threat to North Carolina had been broken at a cost of one Whig killed. All thoughts of reconciliation with Britain vanished, and within two months the provincial congress empowered its delegates in the CONTINENTAL CONGRESS to vote for independence.

See H. Rankin, *North Carolina Historical Review* (Summer, 1953), definitive, and *North Carolina Continentals* (1971); and D. Meyer, *Highland Scots* (1957).

KENNETH B. WEST
University of Michigan, Flint

MORAVIANS. Although not formally organized until 1457, the Unitas Fratrum (Unity of the Brethren) had existed since the fourteenth century as a group of the followers of John Hus. Eager to evangelize among the American Indians, a group from Saxony settled in Georgia in 1735, but their refusal to bear arms for the British against Spain and a high mortality rate in the southern colony soon led their leader, Augustus Gottlieb Spangenberg, to move the settlement to Pennsylvania. The Brethren purchased their own land and in 1741 occupied their first building in Bethlehem.

In 1749 an act of Parliament declared the Brethren church to be an "Ancient Protestant Episcopal Church," thereby securing its right to function as an organized church in Britain and its colonies. Referring to the members of this church as "Moravians," the act conferred upon the Brethren the name eventually adopted by the denomination as its official title. Legal recognition brought a number of invitations to establish settlements in other areas. Lord Granville offered to sell 100,000 acres in North Carolina, and after touring this colony in 1752 Spangenberg selected a site in what is now Forsyth County. Named Wachau by the Moravians because of its resemblance to the Austrian valley owned by the Zinzendorf family, the area was inhabited in 1753 by 15 settlers from Bethlehem and is now known by its anglicized name Wachovia. Settlements were established at Bethabara (1753), Bethania (1759), and Salem (1766). Old Salem has in modern times been largely restored as a historic site.

Restrictions placed upon the American Moravians in 1779 by their European leaders prevented them from organizing new congregations. The denomination had been divided into geographical regions or provinces, however, and in 1857 the two American provinces succeeded in gaining for all provinces the autonomy that American Moravians had repeatedly sought. The Moravians soon joined in the westward migration to the American frontier and established new churches across the continent. The administrative offices, archives, and principal educational institutions of the American provinces are at Bethlehem, Pa., and Salem (now Winston-Salem), N.C. Moravians are popularly known for their interest in church music. They published the first Protestant hymnal in 1501 and have written much of the best music used in corporate worship.

See A. L. Fries and J. K. Pfohl, *Moravian Church* (1926); J. T. Hamilton, *History of Church Known as Moravian* (1900, 1967); S. K. Hutton, *By Patience and Word* (1935); E. Langton, *Moravian Church* (1956); W. G. Malin, *Catalogue of Books* (1881); *Moravian Historical Society Transactions* (1858–); *Moravian Music Foundation Publications* (Nos. 1–6); and A. W. Schattschneider, *Through 500 Years* (1956, 1974).

PAUL I. CHESTNUT
Duke University

MOREHEAD CITY, N.C. (pop. 5,233), an ocean port on the Newport River, is approximately 30 miles south of New Bern. The city was founded in 1857 by Governor John Motley Morehead and was the eastern terminus of the Atlantic & North Carolina Railway. Although never developed as extensively as its founder expected, it is an increasingly popular summer resort and a center for commercial fishing and canning.

See B. A. Konkle, *John Motley Morehead* (1922); P. W. Fisher, *One Dozen Eastern North Carolina Families* (1958); and files of *Carteret County News-Times* (1912–).

MORGAN, DANIEL (1736–1802), was perhaps the best tactician and leader of light infantry in the Revolution. A hot-tempered frontiersman, he lived most of his life near Winchester, Va., serving before the Revolution in the FRENCH AND INDIAN WAR and DUNMORE'S WAR. He possessed many faults, but he was steadfastly loyal to friends and country. When the Revolutionary War broke out, Morgan joined Benedict Arnold in America's invasion of Canada, was captured at Quebec, and was exchanged in 1776. Placed in command of a rifle regiment, he marched the following year to the assistance of HORATIO GATES at Saratoga. After an absence from the army, in 1780 he reentered the service by joining Gates's Southern Army at Charlotte and was promoted to a brigadier generalship. Put in charge of a "flying army" by Nathanael Greene, who replaced Gates, Morgan marched into western South Carolina, where at COWPENS in January, 1781, he routed a British force led by Banastre Tarleton in a tactically superb battle. He then retired from the service because of health problems. During his last years, Morgan lived on a farm near Winchester. In 1794 he helped suppress the Whiskey Rebellion and later served one term in Congress, where he supported Federalist programs and referred to the Jeffersonians as a "parsell of Egg sucking Dogs."

See D. Higginbotham, *Morgan* (1961), best; J. Graham, *Morgan* (1856); N. Callahan, *Morgan* (1961); and Myers Collection, New York Public Library.

PAUL DAVID NELSON
Berea College

MORGAN, JOHN HUNT (1825–1864), a Confederate cavalry officer, gained fame for daring raids during the Civil War. He was born at Huntsville, Ala., but his family moved to Kentucky in 1829. He attended Transylvania College in Lexington and served in the Mexican War, participating in the battle of Buena Vista. Returning to Lexington, Morgan entered business, owned a hemp factory and a woolen mill, and became active in local civic and political affairs. In 1857 he organized the Lexington Rifles, a militia troop. In late 1861 he joined the Confederate army. By April, 1862, he was a colonel of cavalry. He raided with success through Mississippi, Tennessee, and Kentucky, taking 1,700 federal prisoners at Hartsville, Tenn., on December 7, 1862. Promoted brigadier general in December, 1862, he began his famous raid into Ohio in June, 1863. His force of over 2,000 traveled 1,100 miles and fought one major engagement, the battle of Buffington Island (July 19, 1863), where his tired men were badly defeated. Morgan and 364 of his remaining troopers were captured in Columbiana County, Ohio, on July 26 and he was sent to the Ohio penitentiary. He escaped on November 27 and returned to the Confederacy. In April, 1864, he commanded the Department of Southwest Virginia. He continued to raid against federal forces into Kentucky and Tennessee. Morgan was killed on September 4 at Greenville, Tenn.

See B. W. Duke, *Story of Morgan's Cavalry* (1867); C. F. Holland, *Morgan and His Raiders* (1943); and E. H. Thomas, *Morgan and His Raiders* (1975).

THOMAS H. SMITH
Ohio Historical Society

MORGAN, JOHN TYLER (1824–1907), an Alabama BLACK BELT lawyer, was active in secession and served in the 5th Alabama Infantry and 51st Cavalry during the Civil War. He participated in the "redemption" election of 1874 and two years later was elected to his first of five terms in the U.S. Senate (1877–1907). His ardent adherence to states' rights left an extraordinarily negative record: opposition to the Pendleton Act, the Interstate Commerce Act (and its revision in the Hepburn Act), the BLAIR BILL, and the FORCE BILL. He believed in the innate inferiority of blacks and supported the colonization of Negro Americans in the Belgian Congo and the Philippines. He supported free and unlimited coinage of silver, but not as a Populist agrarian, and he opposed a high tariff. His greater achievements were in foreign policy. As an expansionist and a member of the Foreign Relations Committee, he supported naval construction, the isthmian canal through Nicaragua, and overseas expansion (Cuba, Hawaii, Puerto Rico, and the Philippines), though he disagreed with Republican policies governing these territories.

See A. C. Radke, Jr., "John Tyler Morgan" (Ph.D. dissertation, University of Washington, 1953); John Tyler Morgan Papers, Library of Congress; J. O. Baylen, *Alabama Review* (April, 1962); and A. L. Venable, *Southwestern Social Science Quarterly* (March, 1939).

JIMMIE FRANK GROSS
Armstrong State College

MORMONS. The Church of Jesus Christ of Latter-day Saints, organized in New York (1830) by Joseph Smith, Jr., looked to the South first as a missionary field. Missionaries commenced work in rural areas of Kentucky, Tennessee, and Virginia in the 1830s. Most early converts migrated to the Mormon gathering places in northern Ohio, western Missouri (1831–1839), and Nauvoo, Ill. (1839–1846). Despite a general lack of hostility toward itinerant Mormon preachers, antagonism did develop when Smith attempted to establish a communitarian city in Missouri. Prior settlers saw the influx as a threat to their political and economic influence, and the Mormon settlers were forcibly expelled from Jackson County in 1833 and from northern Missouri in 1839. Very few remained elsewhere in the South after 1846. After Brigham Young led the major body to Utah, others formed the Reorganized Church of Jesus Christ of Latter-day Saints in 1852, with headquarters at Independence, Mo. Lyman Wight led another small group to Texas in 1844.

From their new base in Utah, the Mormons reentered the South after Reconstruction with redoubled effort. This higher profile during a time of general social unrest probably contributed to increased violence and threats. Perhaps 15 Latter-day Saints, five of them missionaries, were killed between 1879 and 1900. This included the much-publicized murder of Joseph Standing (1879) in Georgia and five deaths in the Cane Creek Massacre (1884) in Tennessee. Membership grew rapidly after 1895, paralleling a multiplication of the missionary force, until by 1900 the church counted 10,000 southern members. Until that time most converts migrated to Utah or to Mormon enclaves for southerners in Colorado and Arizona. After 1900, however, authorities began to encourage the strengthening of local wards (congregations). Membership in the South was 54,372 in 1950 and

225,000 in 1975 (when world membership totaled 3.4 million). Largest concentrations were in Texas (47,774), Florida (28,915), Virginia (22,002), North Carolina (17,839), and Georgia (14,360).

See R. J. Robertson, *Missouri Historical Review* (April, July, 1974); L. C. Berrett, "Southern States Mission" (M.S. thesis, Brigham Young, 1960); W. W. Hatch, "Mormon Civil Relations" (M.S. thesis, Utah State, 1965); G. A. Sessiona, *South Atlantic Quarterly* (Spring, 1976); W. A. Jennings, "Expulsion from Missouri" (Ph.D. dissertation, University of Florida, 1962) and *Missouri Historical Review* (Oct., 1969); D. Bitton, *Reminiscences and Civil War Letters* (1970) and *Arizona and West* (Spring, 1969); L. H. Gentry, "LDS in Northern Missouri" (Ph.D. dissertation, Brigham Young, 1965); B. M. Durning, "Mormon Church in Texas" (M.A. thesis, East Texas State, 1964); and Max Parkin, "LDS in Clay County, Mo." (Ph.D. dissertation, Brigham Young, 1976).

LEONARD J. ARRINGTON
Historical Department, Church
of Jesus Christ of Latter-day Saints

MORRISON, DELESSEPS STORY (1912–1964). To his friends Chep Morrison was a "white knight" who would purge Louisiana politics of its corruption and evil. To his enemies he was "little boy blue," a city slicker, and as EARL LONG noted, "about the cutest little ol' thing I've ever seen." Morrison evoked such responses, for he was a complex and controversial man. Mayor of New Orleans (1946–1961), ambassador to the Organization of American States (1961–1963), three times unsuccessful candidate for governor of Louisiana, Morrison was generally acknowledged as a liberal reformer and a racial moderate. As mayor, he effected many projects that greatly changed the physical image of New Orleans and that won for himself favorable publicity in the national press. As a leader of the anti-Long faction, Morrison created a city political machine more potent than its Long-dominated predecessors. At times he was a political ally of such diverse individuals as Leander Perez, Hale Boggs, and Jimmie Davis. Morrison was a 1950s and 1960s predecessor of many southern progressives of today.

See Morrison Papers, Tulane and New Orleans Public libraries; E. Haas, *DeLesseps S. Morrison* (1974); M. Kurtz, "Demagogue and Liberal" (Ph.D. dissertation, Tulane, 1971) and *Louisiana History* (1975); J. Parker, *Morrison Era* (1974); and A. J. Liebling, *Earl of Louisiana* (1961).

MICHAEL L. KURTZ
Southeastern Louisiana University

MORRISTOWN, TENN. (pop. 20,318), is situated approximately 40 miles northeast of Knoxville, between the Holston and Nolichucky rivers. First

settled in 1783 by brothers for whom the town is named, it is one of the oldest communities in the state. It long has been an important tobacco center and, since the Civil War, a market and shipping point for lumber producers. The city manufactures textiles and furniture and is the home of Morristown College (1881).

See C. D. Brooks, *Records of Hamblen County* (1940); Works Progress Administration, *Diary of Kate Livingston, 1859–1868* (1938); M. Fisk, *American Heritage* (Jan., 1897); S. C. Williams, *Dawn of Tennessee* (1937); and files of *Gazette-Mail* (1866–).

MOSBY, JOHN SINGLETON (1833–1916), was a soldier and Confederate partisan leader. Born in Powhatan County, Va., he practiced law at Bristol until the Civil War. Enlisting in the Virginia cavalry (1861), he participated in first BULL RUN, was commissioned a lieutenant (1862), and undertook scouting missions for J. E. B. STUART. After serving with Stuart in the PENINSULAR, second BULL RUN, and ANTIETAM campaigns, Mosby obtained his permission to organize a band of irregulars for guerrilla operations. Designated Partisan Rangers, Mosby's irregulars, beginning in 1863, employed hit-and-run tactics to harass Union forces, seizing supplies, disrupting communications, and taking prisoners. Operating in an area that came to be known as "Mosby's Confederacy," comprising Virginia and Maryland counties adjacent to Washington, his Partisan Rangers for more than two years carried out a series of daring raids that kept the Union army in a constant state of anxiety concerning their whereabouts. After Robert E. Lee's surrender (1865), Mosby, who had risen to the rank of colonel, disbanded his Rangers and was paroled. Resuming the practice of law, he joined the Republican party, campaigned for U. S. Grant, and served as U.S. consul at Hong Kong (1878–1885) and in the Department of Justice (1904–1910).

See J. S. Mosby, *War Reminiscences* (1887), based on lectures; J. J. Williamson, *Mosby's Rangers* (2nd ed.; 1909); V. C. Jones, *Ranger Mosby* (1944); and J. S. Mosby, *Memoirs*, ed. C. W. Russell (1917, 1959).

VINCENT C. JONES
Center of Military History, Department of the Army

MOSES, FRANKLIN J., JR. (1838–1906), was born to a prominent family in Sumter District, S.C., and attended South Carolina College. During the Civil War he was an army enrolling officer, and in the immediate postwar years he practiced law and edited the Sumter *News*. Initially a supporter of President ANDREW JOHNSON, Moses changed his political stand after the RECONSTRUCTION ACTS were passed. He became a Republican, and, after serving as Speaker of the state house of representatives, he won the governorship in 1872. Moses was actively identified with the cause of racial equality, and many blacks regarded him as a special friend. He was an opportunist, however, and one of the worst corruptionists in the South. He used his power to enhance his personal wealth and appointed to local judicial offices many incompetent persons, including those whom he called "good political niggers." He liberally granted pardons to criminals whose support he expected. So flagrant was the corruption under Moses that his party denied him renomination in 1874. After leaving the governorship, Moses practiced law for a short time. His friends in the legislature secured his election to a judgeship, but Governor DANIEL H. CHAMBERLAIN prevented him from taking the office. When Reconstruction ended, Moses left South Carolina, and he resided in a number of northern states. A drug addict and petty swindler, he served a number of jail sentences, and he died impoverished.

See R. H. Woody, *North Carolina Historical Review* (April, 1933); F. B. Simkins and R. H. Woody, *South Carolina During Reconstruction* (1932); and J. Williamson, *After Slavery* (1965).

ROGER P. LEEMHUIS
Clemson University

MOSSBACK. A hopelessly outdated person or set of beliefs was often described simply as a "mossback Baptist," a "mossback Democrat," or a "mossback Republican." The term implies an indifference to changing realities, ignorance of newer conditions or developments, and a remoteness from the hub of current activity. Its origin is usually credited to people of the swampy, coastal region of North Carolina, who allegedly disparaged poorer whites of the cypress swamps by comparing them to old turtles and crayfish, which moved so seldom and so slowly that moss was said to grow on their backs.

MOULTRIE, WILLIAM (1730–1805), resided in St. John's Berkeley in South Carolina. His early military service included a captaincy during the Cherokee War. As a colonel he defended Charleston in June, 1776 (the fort on Sullivan's Island being named in his honor), and Beaufort in February, 1779. Held prisoner by the British between May, 1780, and February, 1782, he later served until peace was signed, having achieved the rank of major general in October, 1782. His public service included seats in the South Carolina house of commons for a decade before the Revolution, the provincial congresses (1775–1780), the house of deputies (1783), the state senate (1787–1791), and the convention that ratified the federal Constitution in 1788. He served as lieutenant governor in 1784 and as governor twice (1785–1787, 1793–1795).

See W. Moultrie, *Memoirs of American Revolution* (2 vols.; 1802); E. McCrady, *History of South Carolina in Revolution* (2 vols.; 1901–02); and W. M. Wallace, *Appeal to Arms* (1951).

FRANK C. MEVERS
New Hampshire Historical Society

MOUNTAINEERS, like southern highlanders or Appalachians, identifies residence and/or nativity as the critical element in a definition of the people of APPALACHIA as a people. Like the appellations New Englander and Italian-American, it also implies that they compose one of the "ethnic groups" (standard usage before the 1930s referred to "racial types") in the American population, possessing cultural, social, ethnic, and anthropometrical characteristics, which may be used to define such a group more precisely. Yet neither the substantial literature on who are the mountaineers nor personal observation reveals what such superresidential characteristics are. Some mountaineers are tall, and others are not. Some may well have one leg shorter than the other, but it is doubtful whether this group forms a greater proportion than persons with the same defect in the American population at large. Even those archetypical activities of the comic-strip mountaineer (FEUDING and moonshining), like those archetypical activities of the "real" mountaineers (banjo picking and ballad makin', weaving and basket making, snake handling and GINSENG gathering), give evidence of a high degree of social and economic specialization that contradicts the assumption of social and economic homogeneity.

In the same way, the ethnic origins of the mountaineers are uncertain, and even appear unascertainable. Indeed, the issue of ethnic origins has been a matter of antiquarian interest only, except at such times—as at the end of the nineteenth century—when "degenerate origins" have been offered as an explanation for the alleged "peculiarities" of the mountaineers. At such times, attempts have been made to prove that the mountain people were of English, Scottish, Scotch-Irish, or sometimes French Huguenot (*i.e.*, nondegenerate) ancestry. Such "research" has almost inevitably been inconclusive. In addition, contemporary accounts from the nineteenth century, as well as more recent studies and common sense, suggest that patterns of in-migration and out-migration—including the in-migration of "new stock" immigrants following the economic development of Appalachia's mineral wealth during the 1800s—have seriously muddled the picture, which could in any case have been no more clear than elsewhere in the nation.

The mountaineers of Appalachia were not regarded as a separate people until the 1880s, when home missionaries of northern Protestant denominations found it desirable to legitimate their work in the mountains by distinguishing their clientele of "mountain whites" from the so-called POOR WHITES, then of such concern as a result of the revelation of massive illiteracy in the South by the federal census returns for 1880. As the name of a people, mountain whites persisted well into the twentieth century, despite the efforts of William Goodell Frost of Berea College to introduce the term Appalachian Americans and of John C. Campbell of the Russell Sage Foundation to introduce the term southern highlanders in attempts at naming as explaining. Appalachians is of more recent usage, largely a product of the ethnic revival of the 1960s, and is frequently employed to designate mountain people who have become part of the labor force in the industrial cities of the Midwest, especially Cincinnati, Cleveland, and Detroit. Appalachians is also the term preferred by the promoters of Appalachian festivals, by the authors of social service agency reports, and by the enumerators of minority participation in employment pools. In Appalachia itself, "hillbilly" is used generally among rural and quasi-rural peoples in referring to themselves with ironic deprecation; and the assertion, "I am as mountain as they come," is often heard, most recently from the lips of a well-known writer and college administrator.

See J. C. Campbell, *Southern Highlander* (1921); and H. D. Shapiro, *Appalachia on Our Mind* (1977). Identification of manuscript materials for study of Appalachia is only in beginning stages; among places with materials are libraries of Berea College, University of North Carolina, West Virginia University, University of Kentucky, Appalachian State (Boone, N.C.), Alice Lloyd College, and Harvard. There also are papers at New York Public Library, Russell Sage Foundation, Presbyterian Archives (Montreat, N.C.), and John C. Campbell Folk School.

HENRY D. SHAPIRO
University of Cincinnati

MUDD, SAMUEL ALEXANDER (1833–1883),

practiced medicine and raised tobacco with slave labor on part of his father's land near Bryantown, Md. During the Civil War, Mudd's neighborhood lay on a major underground route to the Confederacy, with which he sympathized. JOHN WILKES BOOTH, professedly seeking land but actually planning to kidnap Abraham Lincoln (LINCOLN ASSASSINATION), was introduced to Mudd on November 20, 1864, and spent the night at his home. On December 23, Mudd encountered Booth in Washington and talked with him privately. Early on April 15, 1865, Booth, fleeing in disguise after murdering Lincoln, was treated for a broken leg by Mudd at his home. Noticeably evasive on later questioning, Mudd swore he had not recognized Booth. Nevertheless he was convicted of complicity and sentenced to life imprisonment. Probably privy to the kidnap plot, but not the assassination, Mudd very likely had indeed recognized the fugitive and panicked. After more than three years at Ft. Jefferson, where he did heroic service during a yellow fever epidemic, Mudd was pardoned by President Andrew Johnson in 1869 and returned home.

See S. Carter, *Riddle of Dr. Mudd* (1974); N. Mudd, *Life of Mudd* (1906); B. Pitman, *Assassination of Lincoln and Trial* (1865), record of testimony; and T. Roscoe, *Web of Conspiracy* (1959).

ROBERT V. BRUCE
Boston University

MUD MARCH. Following the Union repulse by Robert E. Lee at FREDERICKSBURG, Va. (December, 1862), Major General Ambrose E. Burnside underwent strong pressure to resume operations. Northern morale, the White House and War Department insisted, demanded action. Accordingly, Burnside advanced on Falmouth, above Fredericksburg, intending to cross the Rappahannock and threaten Confederate communications. Launched January 20, 1863, the move degenerated into a "mud march." His troops bogging down in heavy rains, Burnside recalled them January 22. He forthwith issued orders cashiering several dissentient subordinates. President Abraham Lincoln demurred, superseding Burnside with Joseph Hooker and a strategy culminating in federal disaster at CHANCELLORSVILLE.

See *Official Records, Armies*, Ser. 1, Vol. XXI; F. Moore (ed.), *Rebellion Record* (1864), VI; and J. H. Stine, *Army of Potomac* (1892).

LESLIE ANDERS
Central Missouri State University

MUDSILL. Although the term has several uses and various meanings, all denote favorably or opprobriously membership in a low-income or working class. The plank or sill of a frame building closest to the ground is the one most often splashed with mud by rain falling off the roof. Accordingly, the term was used derisively to identify southern poor whites and also to denigrate northerners who, regardless of their wealth, were deemed outsiders without the status bestowed by local "breeding." During the 1850s the term was used to identify supporters of Stephen Douglas' popular sovereignty, derogatorily in the South, though favorably in the western free states.

MULES. Although mules were the principal draft animal used in the post–Civil War South, they played only a secondary role in antebellum agriculture. Oxen and horses had been used to clear the frontier, and not until after the American Revolution was the mule, long an object of jest and derision, seriously regarded by Americans as a potential work animal. George Washington, starting with a jackass given to him by the king of Spain, was one of the earliest Americans to engage in the systematic husbandry of these animals.

During the 1820s and 1830s, farmers in Kentucky and then in Tennessee followed Washington's example. After importing jacks and jennets from Europe, they turned the Nashville and bluegrass basins into preeminent centers for breeding quality mules. Kentucky mules, often foaled by thoroughbred mares, were reputedly showy and sprightly animals with fine hair and upright heads. The Tennessee mules, usually taller and bigger boned, were considered to have greater stamina. Missouri, a third center of American mule breeding, did not attain its leadership of the industry until after the Civil War. Its initial prominence resulted not from breeding mules for the westward overland wagon trains but from being the eastern depot for mules and asses imported from Santa Fe and the Mexican Southwest. As Mexican jackasses were much smaller than the fine breeding stock that had been developed in Tennessee and Kentucky, Missouri's mules were deemed scrawny by comparison. After the Civil War, Missourians developed special breeding mares with quantities of Percheron and Clydesdale draft horse blood. Larger jacks and bigger mares permitted Missouri breeders to produce a mule that eventually became an American standard synonymous with their state.

By 1860 Tennessee (the principal breeding area), Kentucky, and Missouri annually sold tens of thousands of mules to cotton belt farmers through a complex pattern of trade marked by considerable specialization. Mules, which had represented only 21 percent of the draft animals in the Lower South in 1850, accounted for 33 percent of that region's work animals in 1860. A good mule generally cost 10 to 20 percent more than a horse, but a farmer regained that extra investment in an animal that lived almost twice as long as a horse, enjoyed greater immunity from disease, and (it was believed) required less and cheaper fodder.

The popularity and the significance of mules soared throughout the final three decades of the nineteenth century. A mule for every 40 acres of farmland had been a numerical impossibility during Reconstruction (FORTY ACRES). The nation's mule population almost tripled between 1870 and 1900, however, and the South, which at the turn of the century had almost 70 percent of the nation's total, had almost three mules for every 100 acres of harvested cropland. Between 1900 and 1925, cotton prices climbed from 6 cents to over 30 cents per pound and the South's mule population rose from approximately 2 million to over 3 million. But 1925 was the peak of the South's and the nation's mule population. The BOLL WEEVIL and declining cotton prices were followed by reduced cotton acreage during the New Deal and then by manpower shortages occasioned by World War II. By 1950, mules were reduced to half their former numbers in the Upper South. Where draft animals continue to be used today, it is still likely as not a mule that is in harness. But the recent trends toward larger farming units and ever-increasing mechanization have displaced the mule permanently from its former primacy in southern agriculture.

See R. B. Lamb, *Mule in Southern Agriculture* (1963), good but not definitive; G. C. Fite, *Agricultural History* (Jan., 1950); L. C. Gray, *Agriculture to 1860* (1933); R. L. Jones, *Mississippi Valley Historical Review* (June, 1946); L. W. Knight, *Jacks, Jennets and Mules* (1902); and H. Riley, *Mule* (1867).

MULES IN THE SOUTH

	Lower South		Upper South		U.S.
	# in 1,000s	% of Draft Animals	# in 1,000s	% of Draft Animals	% of Draft Animals
1850	266	21	229	12	9
1860	529	33	427	17	12
1870	380	35	386	20	12
1880	614	40	594	25	14
1890	738	49	735	27	11
1900	1,049	51	912	32	15
1910	1,310	57	1,042	31	13
1920	1,733	65	1,388	40	21
1925	1,687	73	1,400	48	26
1930	1,807	80	1,255	52	27
1940	1,531	75	1,074	50	28
1950	1,103	69	772	47	29

SOURCE: Based upon figures in R. B. Lamb, *Mule in Southern Agriculture* (1963).

MUMFORD, WILLIAM B. (1820?–1862), a professional gambler and patriotic Confederate citizen, on April 27, 1862, pulled down the federal flag that had been raised on the Mint Building in New Orleans. The flag had been removed apparently after the Union navy had appeared before the city and while Admiral DAVID G. FARRAGUT was negotiating its surrender, but before any actual occupation had taken place. Following the entry of the U.S. Army into New Orleans, General Benjamin F. Butler had Mumford arrested and tried for treason. Upon his conviction, Butler had Mumford hanged on June 7. Southerners were outraged, and President JEFFERSON DAVIS issued a proclamation on December 24, 1862, declaring Butler to be a common outlaw and subject to be executed immediately if captured by Confederate troops.

See *Official Records, Armies*, Ser. 2, Vols. IV, V; and E. M. Coulter, *Confederate States of America* (1950).

MUNFORDVILLE, BATTLE OF (September 14–17, 1862). Advance forces of the Confederate invasion of Kentucky under JAMES R. CHALMERS were repulsed by a 4,000-man Union garrison protecting the Louisville & Nashville Railroad bridge on Green River at Munfordville, Ky. General BRAXTON BRAGG, "unwilling to allow the impression of a disaster," surrounded the fort with his army of 27,000 and convinced the inexperienced Union Colonel John T. Wilder to surrender. Bragg was criticized for not blocking Don Carlos Buell's retreat to Louisville and for wasting valuable time, but recent interpretations emphasize factors other than Bragg's Munfordville decisions for the failure of the campaign.

See L. H. Harrison, *Civil War in Kentucky* (1975); T. L. Connelly, *Army of Heartland* (1967); S. C. Williams, *John T. Wilder* (1936); G. McWhiney, *Braxton Bragg* (1969); and *Official Records, Armies*, Ser. 1, Vol. XVI, Ser. 3, Vol. II.

JAMES A. RAMAGE
Northern Kentucky State University

MURFREE, MARY NOAILLES (1850–1922), better known under her pseudonym Charles Egbert Craddock, was born at Grantland, a family estate near Murfreesboro, Tenn. In 1854 an attack of fever left her partially crippled. For many years the family spent from May to October at Beersheba, where Mary Murfree developed a love for the scenic beauty of the Cumberland Mountains.

Between 1884 and 1900 she published 15 books, including eight novels and five volumes of short stories that deal exclusively with Tennessee mountain life. Her best work belongs to this period. *In the Tennessee Mountains* (1884), a volume of some of her best short stories, brought her immediate fame both in America and in England and went through 14 printings. Also published during this period were *The Prophet of the Great Smoky Mountains* (1885), her most powerful as well as most popular novel, and *In the 'Stranger People's' Country* (1891), artistically her best novel. Her use of mountain dialect is natural and lively; her descriptions of mountain scenery and the mountaineer are for the most part detailed and powerful, but she never learned to restrain description to the best purposes of fiction. In an age that expected it, she tended to moralize heavily.

See E. W. Parks, *C. E. Craddock* (1941), judicious; M. T. Adkins, *Magazine of American History* (1890); M. S. Mooney, "Mary N. Murfree" (M.A. thesis, Peabody, 1928); A. Cowie, *Rise of American Novel* (1951); and R. Cary, *Mary N. Murfree* (1967).

MARION MICHAEL
Texas Tech University

MURFREESBORO, BATTLE OF (December 7, 1864), a part of the FRANKLIN and NASHVILLE campaign, began when Union commander Lovell H. Rousseau ordered R. H. Milroy to move out the Salem pike and contact the Confederate forces under NATHAN B. FORREST. After a spirited artillery duel, Milroy withdrew in order to have Fortress Rosecrans to his rear and then organized his forces into two attacking lines. The federals came within short range of the rebel infantry, which, with the exception of T. B. Smith's brigade, fled in panic. Seizing the colors of one of the broken regiments, Forrest sought unsuccessfully to rally his forces. W. H. Jackson then led a Confederate cavalry counterattack, and, although he was repulsed, Rousseau ordered Milroy to withdraw. The federals lost 22 killed and 186 wounded; the Confederates lost 19 killed, 73 wounded, and 207 prisoners.

See *Official Records, Armies*, Ser. 1, Vol. XL, Pt. 2; E. L. Drake, *Western Armies* (1879); and J. A. Wyeth, *Forrest* (1959).

THELMA JENNINGS
Middle Tennessee State University

MURFREESBORO, TENN. (pop. 26,360), one of the oldest communities in central Tennessee, is approximately 30 miles southeast of Nashville on a fork of Stones River. After being incorporated in 1817, the town served briefly (1819–1825) as the state's capital. A railroad connecting Murfreesboro to the Tennessee River, Chattanooga, and north-

eastern Alabama made the city a prosperous antebellum cotton and tobacco center. Yet that same
railroad connection made the city a strategic point
in BRAXTON BRAGG's defense of east Tennessee
and in Union efforts to break the Confederacy.
From December 30, 1862, to January 3, 1863, over
75,000 Union and Confederate soldiers contested
control of Murfreesboro in one of the bloodiest
battles of the Civil War (STONES RIVER, BATTLE
OF). The postwar community lacked the transportation facilities of Nashville and failed to keep
pace with the growth of its sister city. Today Murfreesboro is the site of Middle Tennessee State
University (1911) and is a producer of baked foods,
hosiery, and lumber.

See C. C. Henderson, *Murfreesboro* (1929); C. C. Sims,
Rutherford County (1947); J. G. M. Ramsey, *Annals of
Tennessee* (1853); H. Pittard, *First 50 Years* (1961), Middle
Tennessee State University; J. Burt, Jr., *East Tennessee
Historical Society Publications* (1951), Nashville &
Chattanooga Railroad; and files of Murfreesboro *News-
Journal* (1849–).

MURPHY, EDGAR GARDNER (1869–1913).
Born in Arkansas, he graduated from the University of the South (1889) and studied at New York's
General Theological Seminary (1889–1890). As an
Episcopal priest, he held pastorates in Texas, Ohio,
and New York before accepting a call to St. John's
Parish in Montgomery, Ala., in 1898. In 1901,
however, he resigned from St. John's to become
executive secretary of the SOUTHERN EDUCATION
BOARD and to spend full time on reform activities.
A founder of the Alabama Child Labor Committee, he wrote pamphlets attacking CHILD LABOR
and published his comprehensive *Problems of the
Present South* (1904). At the initial meeting of the
National Child Labor Committee in 1904, the organizers named Murphy temporary secretary. In
1906 he broke with the NCLC, however, on the
issue of federal legislation and resigned from the
committee's board of trustees to crusade for state
regulation. Racism was indigenous to Murphy's
South, and he conformed to that standard in *The
Basis of Ascendancy* (1910), a defense of white supremacy. Although he subscribed to BOOKER T.
WASHINGTON's program of industrial education,
he adamantly opposed the Fourteenth and Fifteenth amendments. In spite of this blemish, he
was a thoughtful reformer and a positive influence
in southern society.

See H. C. Bailey, *E. G. Murphy* (1968), disappointingly
saccharine; and A. J. Going, *Historical Magazine of
Protestant Episcopal Church* (Dec., 1956).

BETTY J. BRANDON
University of South Alabama

MURPHY, ISAAC (1802–1882), was born near
Pittsburgh, Pa., and moved to Tennessee in 1830,
before settling in Fayetteville, Ark., in 1834. Prior
to leaving for California in 1849, he taught school,
practiced law, and served in the legislature. He
returned to Arkansas in 1854, settled in Huntsville, resumed his legislative activities, and was
later elected to the state secession convention.
One of five delegates who voted initially in opposition to secession, Murphy alone refused to alter
his vote so the secession ordinance could gain
unanimous support. A representative of UNIONIST
sentiment in northwest Arkansas, he then joined
the Union army, in which he served until the occupation of Little Rock. Involved in the formation
of the loyal Arkansas government, Murphy was
elected governor in 1864. He served in that office
through the implementation of congressional Reconstruction and the inauguration of Governor
POWELL CLAYTON in 1868. He then retired from
politics, although he supported Clayton's efforts to
repress the state's KU KLUX KLAN.

See T. S. Staples, *Reconstruction in Arkansas* (1923);
D. Y. Thomas, *Arkansas in War and Reconstruction*
(1926); and R. A. Wooster, *Secession Conventions* (1962).

RICHARD L. HUME
Washington State University

MUSEUMS. The Charleston Museum in South
Carolina, established in 1773, is the oldest in the
United States. The Peale Museum, Baltimore, occupies the oldest American building erected as a
museum (1814). Today the South, with 32 percent
of the nation's population, has 27 percent of its
museums. In 1966, the latest year for which a
state-by-state survey is available, this region had
767 bona fide museums—115 art, 396 history, 105
science, and 151 general. They employed 2,956
professional staff members and spent $111,996,000
on operations. The number of museums has increased since 1966. So have collections, facilities,
and programs. Although the rate of growth has
been fastest among art museums, history museums remain the most numerous. Annual attendance at southern museums surely exceeds 80
million visitors.

These museums compose a rich resource for
teaching, cultural enlightenment, and scholarly
research. At least 90 percent of them supplement
their exhibits with educational or cultural activities. Museum programs, of which the statewide
services of the Virginia Museum of Fine Arts are
one example, often extend into schools and community centers throughout the areas being served.
Museum collections provide much of the essen-

tial data on the material culture of southern Indians and of the Spanish, French, and English colonists. For other aspects of regional and local history, they verify or amplify verbal evidence and offer relatively untapped sources of new knowledge. Specimens preserved in museums document the South's flora and fauna, undergirding both systematic and ecological studies. Art collections also generate research.

Southern museums represent a variety of recognizable types. The National Gallery of Art and the principal art museums of such large cities as Atlanta, Baltimore, Dallas, Houston, Kansas City, Richmond, and St. Louis have collections of wide scope. Other art museums specialize, for example, in African art, the decorative arts, folk art, modern art, or textiles. Major history museums limit their interests to particular areas and periods. For the National Museum of History and Technology these cover the whole country from colonization to the present. Others concern a state or smaller unit. Many history museums deal effectively with single sites such as an Indian or colonial settlement or a battlefield. The South has many furnished historic-structure museums providing unique insights of persons, ways of life, or events. Mount Vernon, saved through the efforts of a southern woman, set an early pattern for these. Colonial Williamsburg became the prototype of American open-air museums, of which the South has a growing number. The Corpus Christi Museum, the Cumberland Museum and Science Center, and the Ft. Worth Museum of Science and History, which began as children's museums, represent another category of especially active ones.

See American Association of Museums, *Official Museum Directory* (1975), descriptive list by states; L. V. Coleman, *Museum in America* (1939); C. E. Guthe, *Management of Small History Museums* (1964); National Endowment for Arts, *Museums USA* (1974); F. L. Rath, Jr., and M. R. O'Connell, *Guide to Historic Preservation, Historical Agencies, and Museum Practices* (1970), bibliography; and L. E. Rogers, *Museums and Related Institutions* (1969).

RALPH H. LEWIS
National Park Service

MUSIC, FOLK AND COUNTRY. Southern folk music drew its sustenance from the musical traditions of the British Isles and Africa, traditions that have interrelated while preserving much of their own identity. Other important pockets of ethnic music, such as those of the CAJUN French in southwest Louisiana and the Mexican-, German-, and Polish-Americans of south-central Texas, survive in the late twentieth century, but there has

been a strong tendency for them to be absorbed or modified by the dominant Anglo culture. British settlers took their music to all parts of the American mainland, but it has endured most persistently in the rural and socially conservative South. Much has been made of the MOUNTAINEER's passion for song, but his musical commitment was shared by his flatland rural cousins. British folk songs have been collected everywhere in the South. Southerners may have leaned toward the sad and tragic songs of their inheritance—the "lonesome tunes" as they were called in the mountains—but they also drew upon an immense legacy of nonsense and bawdy songs, as well as dances and instrumental traditions. A jovial children's song, such as "Froggy Went a-Courtin'," or a raucous tune like "Our Goodman" was as much a part of the imported British song bag as was the beautiful and melancholy ballad "Barbara Allen."

Research is still lacking on the musical interaction among southern blacks and whites, but it can be reasonably assumed that such sharing began very early in the colonial period and that there was in fact a common folk culture and a common reservoir of songs shared by poor people of both races. Black slaves did learn from whites, but whites also heard, and often absorbed, the work songs and field hollers, the dance tunes and instrumental styles, as well as the spirituals and gospel tunes, of the blacks. Such cultural interchange continued when the two peoples moved to the cities. It is particularly difficult to determine the racial origin of a piece of music coming from the nineteenth century, because songs and styles then moved freely from one group to another. Songs like "John Henry" and "John Hardy," which were about black characters and probably created by black musicians, have been just as common among white musicians.

Drawing from Old World resources and from indigenous reserves, southern folk musicians developed songs and styles that increasingly reflected life in the American environment. Often the songs were merely "Americanized" versions of British songs, as in the case of the 1744 ballad "The Berkshire Tragedy" (best known today as "The Knoxville Girl"). But more typically, American songs described native conditions, as in "Arkansas Traveler," or chronicled heroic or notorious characters, as in "Jesse James." Everywhere on the southern frontier the country dance or house party prevailed as a major form of social diversion, and the fiddle, common among both blacks and whites, reigned as the king of folk instruments. Generally of anonymous origin, the fiddle tunes were often transmitted from father to son, and as such they have constituted the "truest" folk tunes in the southern repertory. Many of the oldest tunes are still cherished and played by fiddlers today, and at least one of them, "The Eighth of January," served in 1960 as the melody of the hit pop tune "The Battle of New Orleans."

As popular as the fiddle might be, it could never overcome a suspicion by many rural southerners that it was "the devil's instrument," a device that diverted Christians from their faith. Calvinist Protestantism did not prevent southerners from singing and dancing; it did, however, color the kind of music that they made. Religion probably had a stronger impact on southern folk music than any other phenomenon, shaping singing styles, choices of songs, and the nature of lyrics. Songs emerging from the great CAMP MEETINGS of the early nineteenth century are still loved by southerners. These songs often drew upon earlier folk melodies and were marked by choruses and repetitive phrases and were therefore easily learned. Developing parallel to the camp-meeting songs was a type of musical instruction, known as the shape-note method, which was ultimately to prevail throughout the rural South (SHAPE-NOTE SONGBOOKS). Using diamond, circle, triangle, and rectangular symbols to denote musical pitch, rural singing teachers after 1800 fanned out from Pennsylvania and eventually ranged as far west as Texas, teaching the shape-note method and encouraging people to sing in four-part harmony. Rural southerners listened to and loved both the secular and religious forms of music around them. These musical genres constantly interacted and, as in the case of the black- and white-derived folk songs of the nineteenth century, it is often difficult to distinguish a religious tune from a secular one.

Southern rural life was never totally isolated from the city, and urban musical forms occasionally made their way among country people and were frequently accepted and preserved. Such professionally composed songs as "Wildwood Flower" and "The Little Rosewood Casket" moved into the southern folk repertory alongside the venerable British ballads. The southern folk were never as intolerant toward these "sentimental parlor tunes" as have been the scholars and collectors of folk songs. Neither have the southern folk been averse to the commercialization of their music. Talented folk entertainers, such as the itinerant balladeer or street singer, had always tried to obtain monetary rewards for their art, and their communities in turn had often recognized their abilities and had rewarded them. Occasionally, such a performer became part of a medicine show, a minstrel (MINSTRELSY) or vaudeville group, or per-

haps a traveling tent show. The real commercial discovery of folk performers, however, did not come until the 1920s, when the radio and recording industries began their exploitation of the southern folk market. Between 1920 and 1923 folk entertainers began playing on such radio stations as WSB in Atlanta, WBAP in Ft. Worth, and WSM in Nashville and likewise began making phonograph records for such labels as Okeh, Columbia, Victor, and Brunswick. The music was then described as "hillbilly," a designation that it carried at least until the late forties, when it was superseded by "country" or "country and western."

The year 1927 was a milestone for hillbilly music, because two of its most influential acts, the Carter Family and Jimmie Rodgers, made their first recordings for Victor in Bristol, Tenn. The Carter Family, comprising A. P. Carter, his wife Sara, and their sister-in-law Maybelle, came out of the Virginia hills to represent the domestic, down-home image of country music, a tradition now best reflected by bluegrass music. Jimmie Rodgers, a former railroad worker from Mississippi, represented the drifter tradition of country music, singing of hoboes and trains, convicts and rounders, and footloose lovers. This tradition is today preserved by such singers as Waylon Jennings, Johnny Cash, and Merle Haggard. Before his untimely death from tuberculosis in 1933, Rodgers became the first superstar of country music, inspiring such an uncountable number of apostles that he is now acknowledged as the "Father of Country Music."

It was perhaps inevitable that country music would be affected by the romantic cowboy image; even Jimmie Rodgers occasionally posed for publicity pictures in cowboy hat and chaps. But the most powerful "western" influence came from Texas singers after the mid-thirties. After 1934 Gene Autry, a hillbilly singer from Texas, made the nation conscious of the "singing cowboy" through his many motion pictures. He spawned both a breed of similar singers, such as Roy Rogers and Tex Ritter, and a vogue for dude cowboy costumes, which remained common among country entertainers until the early sixties. A more genuine western influence came from such important Texas musicians as Bob Wills and Ernest Tubb. These men were all inheritors of southern rural music traditions, but they also embodied the diverse and shifting influences of the Southwest, a land of contrasting cultures and varied economic patterns. Wills was a fiddler who drew his music from his southern white rural ancestors and from his black neighbors. The resulting fusion was a brand of music known as "western swing," a danceable music that demonstrated both rural and

JAZZ roots. Tubb, an ardent disciple of Jimmie Rodgers, created his own individualistic vocal style in the taverns and dance halls of Texas, a milieu that promoted important changes in both the lyrics and instrumentation of country music. The product of these forces was "honky-tonk" or "beer-drinking music," oriented toward transplanted rural southerners who wanted a tradition-based music that at the same time mirrored their contemporary concerns. Western swing and honky-tonk country bands pioneered in the electrification of instruments and in the adoption of pianos and drums, innovations that did much to make the music commercially acceptable. These western-derived styles, distinguished by the ubiquitous electric steel guitar, dominated the entire country music scene until at least the mid-fifties.

World War II was the catalyst that accelerated country music's transition from a regional genre to a nationally popular phenomenon. Southern servicemen and civilian defense workers carried their musical preferences to the North and all over the world. Roy Acuff became the best-known country singer of the war years, and the show where he was based, Nashville's GRAND OLE OPRY, came to symbolize country music as a whole. Country music's first real boom period came in the ten years immediately following the war, when such singers as Eddy Arnold, Hank Williams, Webb Pierce, and Kitty Wells became superstars and carried the music to every sector of North America. Capitalizing on the popularity of country music, Nashville became one of the major recording centers of the United States and gained the designation Music City, U.S.A.

Country music survived the rock-and-roll inundation of the late fifties, but was permanently affected by the newfound national emphasis on youth. The resulting fusion of pop and country styles became known as "the Nashville sound," a style deliberately aimed at the broadest possible audience, which often had little or no direct experience with southern rural life. The music has survived and prospered, but its success has encouraged a dilution of the original rural sounds and a consequent blurring of identity. The country music industry has lured individuals who have no commitment to the music's survival and little devotion to rural sounds. Country music now encompasses numerous substylings, which reflect varying degrees of commitment to tradition. They range from country-pop music (a bland, sophisticated style aimed at urban middle-class listeners) to progressive country (which caters to youth weaned on rock music) to the more mainstream country styles, such as honky-tonk and bluegrass (which adhere to the older and more rustic-derived sounds). But whatever the style, country music still demonstrates to a remarkable degree the marks of its southern origin and orientation.

See B. C. Malone, *Country Music USA* (1968), best scholarly survey available; B. C. Malone and J. McCulloh (eds.), *Stars of Country Music* (1975), good collection of original essays; A. Lomax, *Folk Songs of North America* (1960); and G. P. Jackson, *White Spirituals* (1933), two best studies of folk background. See also *Journal of American Folklore* (July–Sept., 1965); *Western Folklore* (July, 1971); and C. Townsend, *San Antonio Rose: Life and Music of Bob Wills* (1976). John Edwards Memorial Foundation, Los Angeles, and Country Music Foundation, Nashville, are two best depositories for country music.

BILL C. MALONE
Tulane University

MUSIC, JAZZ AND POPULAR. Probably the most important contribution of the South to American music has been JAZZ. Although it would be inaccurate to say that jazz, in any or all of its myriad forms, is exclusive to the South, it remains true that the most important early developments in the form occurred in the South.

Traditionally, it has been more or less standard to say that jazz began in New Orleans and simply moved up the Mississippi River to points north. As with all such generalizations, the statement contains some truth. Since a great number of slaves were funneled through New Orleans, it is safe to say that blacks significantly influenced musical forms there from the early eighteenth century onward. These slaves, mainly from West Africa and various Caribbean islands, especially Haiti, brought with them their tribal customs, including complex, non-European, rhythmic patterns. Added to this was the fact that New Orleans was a center of French culture until the LOUISIANA PURCHASE of 1803. In addition, some Spanish influences were active in the city also. Thus, much of the city's early music probably resembled that found in Martinique or Haiti, a unique blending of European and African musical styles.

Not all the slaves brought to New Orleans, however, remained there. Most were quickly sold to plantations away from urban centers. Because these slaves had little contact with the changing music of the cities, much original African music survived well into the nineteenth century.

Those slaves who did remain in New Orleans were gradually made part of the lively, growing city. Its tolerant racial attitudes were coupled with a cosmopolitan society. Creoles—those who combined French, Spanish, and African parentages—

actually achieved a certain social status until the end of the Civil War. In an attempt to assure this elite ranking, the Creole community imported leading musical talent and maintained a city opera, complete with a European conductor. Thus, fashionable urban musical styles, at least in early nineteenth-century New Orleans, were basically European, performed for a sophisticated audience.

The continued influx of slaves, however, brought about a subtle change in the music of the city. Slowly, West African rhythms and tonalities began to insinuate their way into New Orleans culture. Via religious rites (especially the African-Caribbean voodoo, or *vodun*) and public performances by blacks (especially in Congo Square, and encouraged by city officials), the slave heritage became a musical force to be reckoned with. Added to these influences was a predilection on the part of the black community to organize into various open and secret societies and fraternities. Many of these organizations boasted marching bands, and the resultant music further blended European and African elements (even today, such bands survive in New Orleans; a funeral, particularly for someone active musically, will still occasionally involve several of these distinctive groups).

The outgrowth of this blending was ultimately called "jazz," the linguistic roots of which are still argued. Jazz was essentially European melodies and harmonies with greatly modified African rhythmic bases. In addition, most of the early performers lacked extensive musical training, and the sound achieved on individual instruments, particularly horns, therefore resembled the human voice more than it did the tone espoused by traditional academic techniques. The result was the unique "jazz sound."

Jazz grew rapidly in New Orleans. Legendary performers like Buddy Bolden, Ma Rainey, Bunk Johnson, King Oliver, and Bessie Smith helped establish the form. But any roster of great jazz musicians, both past and present, would have to include a disproportionate number from the South (not just New Orleans, by any means) who have carried on the music's influence. For instance, such disparate figures as Louis Armstrong, Cannonball Adderley, Sidney Bechet, Thelonious Monk, Dizzy Gillespie, and Lester Young all originally came from the South.

In a discussion of jazz, however, several other areas of southern music must be touched on, because each influenced the form jazz would take. First would be the work song, or "field holler," performed by black field hands from the 1700s onward. A simple call and response, the work song

served both as a respite from exhausting labor and as a form of covert communication. A simpler form of the work song would be the cry, or holler, in which an individual vocalizes various emotions. A holler can be anything from a moan to a complex series of sliding, slurring sounds, not unlike the results later achieved by brass and reed players in many early jazz bands.

Rural black churches, located primarily in the South but not exclusive to the region, also used variations on both the holler and the call-and-response pattern. The church leader would exhort the congregation, and they in turn would punctuate his speech by individual and unison responses ranging from simple grunts to entire phrases. Again, this church tradition could be heard in most black bands playing jazz.

Spirituals and gospel songs constituted a more complex southern religious music. The roots of these forms are hazy, but they probably grew out of traditional European hymns and were blended, in varying degrees, with African rhythmic concepts. Whereas jazz and its related forms were not easily assimilated by white performers, spirituals, with their emphasis on European form, found quick acceptance. In fact, white composers were soon writing "spirituals" that were completely European in rhythm and harmony. The same process of assimilation occurred with gospel songs, a shorter, more rhythmic variant on the spiritual. Originally, gospel music was improvised (as were most early spirituals) by the singer(s) who, in a sense, delivered a musical sermon (the "gospel"). Today, of course, gospel music flourishes in many evangelical and fundamentalist churches throughout the country, and it has become a broad-based, established musical form.

Ragtime, a strong influence on jazz, was also popular in the South. Simply stated, ragtime is traditional, notated piano music with the addition of a strong rhythm. Although ragtime initially achieved popularity in the 1890s along the Mississippi River, it was around St. Louis and not in the Deep South that it was born. Performers like Jelly Roll Morton, however, quickly adopted the style and took it to New Orleans, where it was incorporated into the developing musical form that would ultimately be known as jazz.

One final aspect of the southern jazz tradition deserves mention: the blues. The blues are actually only one part of the larger jazz idiom. For musicians the term suggests, among other things, a tonality, a tendency to play certain notes or chords in such a way as to give them a sad or "blue" sound. However, since there are infinite variations on the blues (including a great number of "happy" blues songs), any definition of the blues must simply suggest an approach to the music rather than being final. The blues, nonetheless, were initially strongest in the South, and many of the earliest southern jazz musicians demonstrated great skill and feeling within this particular idiom. W. C. Handy, himself a southerner, probably did more to popularize the form than any other individual. The blues have long since transcended their southern roots and appear today, in one form or another, in most jazz and in much popular music.

In the years following World War I, the "jazz age" can be said to have arrived. From its birth in New Orleans, it spread quickly to Memphis and St. Louis and then on to points north and west. And, although the music might be associated with the South, its popularity was nationwide. The term Dixieland was early used to denote a usually fast, usually raucous music, and groups like the Original Dixieland Jass (original spelling) Band attained a large following—but in places like New York and Chicago. In the South, jazz continued its evolution and development but it could no longer be thought of as a regional musical form.

Jazz, however, was not the only popular music to emerge from the South. During the second half of the nineteenth century, another southern-based form achieved tremendous international popularity. This was the minstrel show. MINSTRELSY's roots go back to the late 1700s, when occasional white performers appeared in blackface, much to the amusement of their audiences. By the early 1800s, blackface acts were becoming commonplace in the South and along the border states. Gradually, the dancing and singing that characterized these shows caught the nation's fancy. Vaudeville eventually sprang from the minstrel show and, along with other new entertainment forms, finally eclipsed the parent form in the early twentieth century. But minstrelsy lived on in the South. It was not until recently, however, that the last traveling show disappeared. On the one hand, these shows introduced white American audiences to at least certain elements of Negro music of the period. Yet these same shows, with their coarse humor and demeaning blackface routines, involved racial stereotyping of the worst kind.

In the area of popular music, the South has enjoyed something of a boom since the early 1950s. At this time, a small but steady stream of recordings by largely unknown performers began issuing from various studios located throughout the South. At first, these records were contemptuously referred to as "race records" (a term used in the 1920s and thereafter to designate recordings that presumably sold only to black audiences), then as "rhythm 'n' blues." As more and more people began to listen, the music quickly became national, becoming "rock 'n' roll" and, finally, just "rock." In a short period, a regional music mushroomed to become a national fad. But the southern heritage can be found clearly in the rhythm 'n' blues (or "R & B" as it came to be called) of the era and in much of the later rock.

One reason for the national awareness of this music involved the continued migration of rural southerners, white and black, northward to urban centers. As they moved, they took their regional preferences with them and created vast new audiences for the music. Another reason is purely technological: radio, television, and recordings are a ubiquitous fact of American life. What is regional one moment is national the next. Nonetheless, popular entertainers like Elvis Presley, Johnny Cash, Ray Charles, and Muddy Waters, southerners all, continue to remind their audiences of the lasting impact the South has had on American popular music.

See J. Eisen (ed.), *Age of Rock* (1969); L. Jones, *Blues People* (1963); G. Schuller, *Early Jazz* (1968); N. Shapiro and N. Hentoff, *Hear Me Talkin' to Ya* (1955); M. Stearns, *Story of Jazz* (1958); and H. Kmen, *Music of New Orleans, 1791–1841* (1966).

WILLIAM H. YOUNG
Lynchburg College

MUSKOGEE INDIANS. See CREEK INDIANS

MYERS, ABRAHAM CHARLES (1811–1889),

born in Georgetown, S.C., was graduated from West Point in 1833 and was chief quartermaster of the U.S. Army of Mexico from April to June, 1848. As quartermaster in New Orleans in 1861, he surrendered his stores to Louisiana state officials and was appointed quartermaster general of the Confederate army. Contending with many problems—particularly currency depreciation and poor transportation—Myers ran a reasonably effective department but failed to see the need for military regulation of the railroads. He enjoyed strong support in the Confederate Congress, and his removal by Jefferson Davis in August, 1863, was resented by many. He left the army in 1863 and died in Washington, D.C.

See R. D. Goff, *Confederate Supply* (1969); J. L. Nichols, *Confederate Quartermaster in Trans-Mississippi* (1964); War Department Collection of Confederate Records,

Record Group 109, National Archives; and Quartermaster General's Office Records, Virginia Historical Society, Richmond.

JEREMY P. FELT
University of Vermont

MYERS, ISAAC (?–?). Although he was a major figure in the early history of black labor organization, little is known about his personal history. It is known that, as a ship caulker in Baltimore in the 1860s, he was outraged by existing labor unions, which excluded blacks and sought to prevent skilled black workers from pursuing their occupations. Myers responded in two ways. First, in 1865 he was a leading spirit in the formation of a drydock company in Baltimore, which employed 300 blacks and thrived for 12 years. Second, Myers participated actively in the developing union movement among black workers and in 1869 was elected president of the National Colored Labor Union. Under his leadership, the NCLU sought an end to job discrimination not only in the North, but also in the South. The organization was also concerned with the plight of southern black SHARECROPPERS. It urged Congress to distribute public lands to such people so that they might become economically independent. In 1870 Myers was replaced by FREDERICK DOUGLASS as president, and the NCLU gradually lost interest in bread-and-butter issues while promoting Republican causes. Myers faded into obscurity.

See P. Foner, *History of Labor Movement* (1947), I; S. D. Spero and A. L. Harris, *Black Worker* (1969); and C. H. Wesley, *Negro Labor in U.S.* (1927).

ROBERT CRUDEN
Lewis and Clark College

N

NASHOBA COMMUNITY was a 640-acre plantation established in 1825 by Frances Wright, feminist and utopian reformer. Begun with the aid of George Flower, Nashoba was located on the Wolf River, 13 miles east of Chickasaw Bluffs (Memphis, Tenn.).

The plantation had the dual objectives of providing both a model training center where blacks might purchase their freedom and a white cooperative community based on the ideas of Robert Dale Owen. Wright's utopian community, named after the Chickasaw word for wolf, commenced operation in December, 1825. On her plantation she established nine adult slaves and several children. Managed by ten trustees, the settlement never grew beyond 15 slaves, had no school established, and suffered from neglect and mismanagement. Nashoba's agricultural production centered on the planting of corn and cotton and the production of butter and eggs.

The community's death knell came with Wright's espousal of miscegenation and advocacy of the abolition of marriage. In April, 1828, she left Nashoba for New Harmony, Ind., an Owenite community, in the wake of increasing hostilities from residents in the Memphis area. She turned the affairs of the community over to Richesson Whitbey, husband of her sister Camilla, but the settlement failed to operate after the winter of 1829. Upon phasing out Nashoba, Wright had her slaves transported to Haiti, where she made arrangements for their housing and future employment.

See A. J. G. Perkins and T. Wolfson, *Frances Wright* (1939); W. R. Waterman, *Frances Wright* (1924); and scattered Frances Wright letters at University of Illinois, University of Chicago, and Duke University, plus the Working Men's Institute at New Harmony, Ind.

FRANK R. LEVSTIK
Ohio Historical Society

NASHVILLE, BATTLE OF (December 15, 16, 1864). The Union army, 50,000 strong under GEORGE H. THOMAS, formed a semicircle south of Nashville, Tenn., with both flanks resting on the Cumberland River. JOHN B. HOOD's Confederate forces, suffering 6,200 casualties at FRANKLIN, did not have sufficient strength to justify accepting battle at Nashville. Because of losses from fighting, disease, stragglers, and detachments sent to Murfreesboro, it is doubtful that Hood had 20,000 effectives when the battle began. Nevertheless, in desperation the Confederates entrenched on the southern outskirts of the city, defending a line stretched longer than their strength warranted, made worse because it was concave to the enemy, thus depriving the rebels of interior lines. There they waited in the vain hope of reinforcements or some favorable development.

General Thomas, after several delays that had federal authorities in Washington perturbed, attacked the southerners early on the morning of December 15. The Union left feinted an attack on the rebel right, while their main assault was made at the other end of the line. There the Union hurled more troops against the Confederate left (some 35,000) than Hood had in his whole army. The rebels were beaten back to a new line about a mile farther south. With a shorter line and good defensive terrain, Hood prepared to fight again the next day.

Uncertain whether the Confederates would retreat, Thomas apparently issued no orders during the night for the continuation of the struggle. On the sixteenth the northern corps commanders aligned their units for battle and probed the new enemy position. Decisive action did not come until afternoon, when federal cavalry gained the left rear of the southern line, thus threatening the whole flank. Following an artillery barrage, the main Union infantry assault overwhelmed the Confederate left at Shy's Hill. The rebel center then gave way, and the southerners fled in confusion with federals pursuing until after dark. The Union army suffered slightly over 3,000 casualties. Confederate losses are not known, but the federals captured 4,500 prisoners.

See S. F. Horn, *Decisive Battle of Nashville* (1956), most extensive account; S. Foote, *Civil War* (1974), III; J. L. McDonough, *Schofield* (1972); *Official Records, Armies*, Ser. 1, Vol. LXV.

JAMES L. MCDONOUGH
David Lipscomb College

NASHVILLE, TENN. (pop. 447,877), was founded in 1780 as Ft. Nashborough by James Robertson. As a port city on the Cumberland River and the northern terminus of the NATCHEZ TRACE, the city rapidly developed into one of the most impor-

tant commercial centers in the new West. RAIL-
ROADS later augmented its commercial significance. In part because of its central location and
its superior transportation facilities, it was made
the state's capital in 1843. Abandoned in February, 1862, by Confederate authorities after the fall
of Ft. Donelson 70 miles to the northwest (FTS.
HENRY AND DONELSON CAMPAIGN), the city became an important Union communications and
supply base for the remainder of the war. A Confederate effort by J. B. HOOD to retake the city in
December, 1864, was successfully repulsed by
Union General G. H. THOMAS (NASHVILLE, BAT-
TLE OF). Combining the twin advantages of excellent transportation and being the state's capital,
postwar Nashville continued its development as a
commercial center. Today it is the headquarters of
numerous area firms and the manufacturer of air-
plane parts, fertilizer, boats, barges, and bridges.
A major educational center, it is the home of FISK
UNIVERSITY, VANDERBILT UNIVERSITY, MEHARRY
MEDICAL COLLEGE, GEORGE PEABODY COLLEGE,
David Lipscomb College (1891), and Tennessee
Agricultural and Industrial State University (1912),
among other institutions.

See J. C. Burt, Jr., *Nashville* (1959) and *East Tennessee
Historical Society Publications* (1951); H. McRaven,
Nashville (1949); F. G. Davenport, *Journal of Southern
History* (Aug., 1937); A. Henderson, *Tennessee Histori-
cal Magazine* (Sept., 1916); W. W. Clayton, *History of
Davidson County* (1880); and files of Nashville *Tennes-
sean* (1812–) and *Banner* (1876–), both on microfilm.

NASHVILLE BANNER began publication in 1876,
assuming the name abandoned by its competitor,
the Nashville *American*. A conservative Democratic daily, it opposed convict lease labor in the
1880s, free silver in the 1890s, prohibition at the
turn of the century, and the policies of governors
Austin Peay and LUKE LEA in the 1920s. It was
once said of the *Banner*'s competition with the
Tennessean that the two papers could agree on
nothing except the time of day; when the state
and the *Tennessean* adopted daylight savings time,
however, even the time became an issue between
the two papers.

See bound copies at Library of Congress, Tennessee
State Library, Nashville, and Carnegie Library, Nashville; and microfilm from Bell & Howell (1949–).

NASHVILLE CONVENTION (June 3–12, November 11–18, 1850). Influenced by JOHN C. CAL-
HOUN, a Mississippi convention in October, 1849,
issued the call for a convention of slaveholding

states to be held in Nashville the following June.
The stated purposes were to promote southern
unity and "adopt some mode of resistance" to
northern "aggressions," especially the attempt to
exclude slavery from territory acquired in the
Mexican War. With the subsequent introduction
in Congress of Henry Clay's compromise resolutions (January, 1850) and Daniel Webster's conciliatory speech of March 7, the initial enthusiasm
for the convention waned, particularly among
Whigs. Only nine of 15 slave states were represented at Nashville in June; of the 175 delegates
attending, 102 were from Tennessee. The great
majority were Democrats, slaveholding planters
and/or lawyers of substantial wealth, and men of
prominence in state or local, if not national, affairs.

Moderates dominated the proceedings. Twenty-eight resolutions were approved, the most important of which demanded the opening of all territories to slavery but, "as an extreme concession,"
also consented to accept extension of the Missouri
Compromise line of 36°30′ to the Pacific. Resolving to await the final action of Congress, the convention then adjourned until November. The
second session, attended by 59 delegates and
generally unrepresentative of public sentiment,
denounced the recently enacted COMPROMISE OF
1850, affirmed the right of secession, and recommended yet another convention. The Nashville
Convention failed to attain its objectives but, in
the view of recent scholars, it did serve as a warning to the North, thus strengthening the position
of moderates in Congress and helping to assure
passage of Clay's proposals.

See T. Jennings, "Reappraisal of Nashville Convention"
(Ph.D. dissertation, University of Tennessee, 1968), most
informative, good bibliography; *Resolutions, Address,
and Journal of Proceedings of Southern Convention*
(1850), official journal of first session, at Harvard University Library; and *Resolutions and Address Adopted by
Southern Convention, June 3d to 12th, with a Preamble
and Resolutions, Adopted November 18th, 1850* (1850),
at University of North Carolina Library.

RICHARD H. HAUNTON
Appalachian State University

NASHVILLE JUNTO was the name given to the
personal friends of ANDREW JACKSON who inspired the Tennessee legislature to nominate him
for the presidency in 1822. The wealthy and influential Judge JOHN OVERTON, Major WILLIAM B.
LEWIS, and Senator JOHN H. EATON persuaded a
reluctant Jackson to enter presidential politics,
probably to boost the sagging political fortunes of
the Overton faction in the state. Surprised by

Jackson's national popularity, the three men became his closest advisers in the election campaigns of 1824 and 1828. During the 1830s, however, Jackson's banking policies cooled their enthusiasm for the president.

See S. G. Heiskell, *Andrew Jackson* (1918); T. P. Abernethy, *Tennessee* (1932); C. G. Sellers, Jr., *Mississippi Valley Historical Review* (June, 1954) and *American Historical Review* (April, 1957); and R. V. Remini, *Election of Jackson* (1963).

EDWARD K. SPANN
Indiana State University

NASHVILLE REPUBLICAN-BANNER and **UNION-AMERICAN** are two nineteenth-century newspapers that merged in 1875 to form the Nashville *American*. The *Republican-Banner* dates back through several mergers and name changes to the founding of the *Tennessee Gazette* in 1800. In 1809 the *Gazette* merged with the Nashville *Clarion* (1806–1809) to create a weekly known variously as the *Clarion and Tennessee Gazette* (1809–1821), the *Clarion* (1821–1823), and the *Republican* (1824–1837). In 1837 the *Republican* merged with the *Banner and Nashville Whig* (1812–1837) to form the *Republican-Banner* (1837–1875). Moving gradually away from the JAMES K. POLK wing of the state's Democratic party and toward affiliation with the Whig party, the *Republican-Banner* defended the institution of slavery, opposed the KANSAS-NEBRASKA ACT (1854) and "squatter sovereignty," and regularly denounced southern FIRE-EATERS and all talk of secession. The paper supported JOHN BELL in the ELECTION OF 1860. After Abraham Lincoln's election and inauguration, it urged patience with the new administration, but, after the firing upon Ft. Sumter, it became an ardent advocate of secession. Its vigorous defense of the Confederacy led Unionist Governor ANDREW JOHNSON to suspend its publication after federal authorities assumed control of Nashville in 1862.

One of the *Republican-Banner*'s principal competitors in Nashville was the *Union-American* (1835–1875), a Democratic party paper that supported J. C. BRECKINRIDGE in 1860. Yet as former Whigs and antebellum Democrats joined together in politics to form the postwar Conservative Democratic party, so also did the *Republican-Banner* and the *Union-American* merge in 1875 to form a single newspaper, the *American* (1875–1910). Closely associated with A. S. COLYAR and the industrialists' wing of the Conservative Democrats, the *American* was for 35 years one of the state's leading NEW SOUTH presses. In 1910, how-

ever, the *American* was itself merged with the NASHVILLE TENNESSEAN.

See bound copies of these newspapers at Library of Congress, Carnegie Library, Nashville, and Tennessee State Library, Nashville.

NASHVILLE TENNESSEAN began publication in 1812. In 1910 its merger with the *American* created the paper that for ten years was known as the *Tennessean and Nashville American*. Since 1920, however, the paper has been called simply the *Tennessean*. It was closely associated during the 1920s with LUKE LEA in state politics, and throughout most of the twentieth century it has been considered one of Tennessee's more liberal and progressive newspapers. Within Nashville, its competition with the conservative *Banner* is a classic in the annals of southern journalism. The *Tennessean* presently enjoys a daily circulation in excess of 130,000 copies.

See bound copies at Library of Congress, Tennessee State Library, Nashville, and State Historical Society of Wisconsin, Madison; and microfilm from Bell & Howell (1949–).

NATCHEZ, MISS. (pop. 19,704), is on a bluff overlooking the Mississippi River approximately 60 miles south of Vicksburg. The site was first settled in 1716, when BIENVILLE built Ft. Rosalie. Thirteen years later the Natchez Indians massacred the French settlers and garrison, an action that caused the French to launch a series of campaigns to exterminate the Natchez. An English town from 1763 to 1779 and then under Spanish rule, Natchez was part of the territory recognized by Spain in 1795 as belonging to the United States. In 1797 Andrew Endicott, a surveyor, raised the U.S. flag, and the following year Congress named Natchez the capital of the Mississippi Territory. Because it was a seat of government and a bustling river port, thousands of settlers poured into and through the city. Although the capital was moved in 1817, when Mississippi achieved statehood, steamboats and the expanding demand for cotton brought the city even greater prosperity. Bombarded and then occupied by federal forces during the Civil War, Natchez never regained its prewar position as a premier cotton market and river port. The modern city, with many eighteenth-century and antebellum homes, is a popular tourist attraction, especially during its annual spring festival. It is a market for area cattle, oil, and cotton.

See D. C. James, *Antebellum Natchez* (1968); H. T. Kane, *Natchez on Mississippi* (1947); J. W. Cooper, *An-*

tebellum Houses of Natchez (1970); E. A. Davis, *Barber of Natchez* (1973); T. Marshall, *They Found It in Natchez* (1939); M. S. Power, *Memento Old and New, 1700 to 1897* (1897); J. D. Shields, *Natchez: Early History* (1930); C. S. Sydnor, *A Gentleman of Old Natchez* (1938); R. Smith and J. Owens, *Majesty of Natchez* (1930); and files of Natchez *Courier* (1830–71), *Democrat* (1865–), *Mississippi Free Trader* (1835–61), and *Mississippi Gazette* (1813–33).

NATCHEZ DEMOCRAT began publication as a weekly in 1865 and as a daily newspaper in 1874. A conservative Democratic organ, it generally supported L. Q. C. LAMAR, A. J. McLaurin, and the state's Bourbon machine against independent farmers' movements and reform groups. The prevailing violence in Mississippi politics and the mounting use of LYNCHINGS to intimidate blacks became subjects of criticism in *Democrat* editorials as early as 1886. Like most Delta dailies, the paper opposed calling the constitutional convention of 1890 and objected to DISFRANCHISEMENT by the UNDERSTANDING CLAUSE as an unnecessary and absurd subterfuge. The paper currently has a circulation of 12,000 daily copies.

See A. D. Kirwan, *Revolt of Rednecks* (1951); and microfilm from Bell & Howell (1865–) and Library of Congress (1874–1930).

NATCHEZ FREE TRADER began publication in 1838 as a semiweekly newspaper called the *Mississippi Free Trader and Natchez Gazette*. It began to issue a daily edition in 1851. A Democratic party paper throughout its career, the *Free Trader* was a strong advocate of secession.

See bound files at University of Mississippi, Oxford; and microfilm from Bell & Howell (1843–60).

NATCHEZ TRACE is a famous frontier road or trail extending from Natchez on the Mississippi River in a northeasterly direction through about 300 miles of the present state of Mississippi, 40 miles of the northwest corner of Alabama, and approximately 100 miles of Tennessee to Nashville. The importance of the Natchez Trace derived from the fact that almost all the navigable rivers in the lower Mississippi Valley flowed in a southerly direction. Travelers could negotiate the turbulent waters when floating with the current, but until the invention of steam navigation the return trip to the North had to be overland. It was a dark, fearsome, and laborious route through the wilderness, and many men, Indian and white, died from illness, accident, or foul play before they reached their destinations; but for more than three decades it was to thousands of settlers an important link among the Gulf, the Great Lakes, and the Atlantic seaboard.

The city of NATCHEZ was under Spanish occupation between 1779 and 1798; and, although the Natchez Trace was used occasionally prior to this time, it was during this Spanish period that its history really started. Flatboats loaded with farm products from Pennsylvania, Virginia, and Kentucky began floating down the river to stop at Natchez as well as New Orleans. After 1803, when NEW ORLEANS and the outlets of the Mississippi passed permanently into American hands, the flow of traffic became enormous. Meanwhile, the application of steam power in England to the spinning and weaving of goods—with its consequent growth in demand for raw cotton—and the arrival in 1795 of the first COTTON GIN at Natchez provided further stimuli to the economic growth of the region. Each year hundreds of boatmen and helpers after depositing their cargo at New Orleans worked their way back along the banks of the Mississippi to Natchez and then headed on foot or horseback over the Trace toward their homes. In early 1800 Congress declared the trail a post road and inaugurated a regular monthly POSTAL SERVICE over the route even though at the time it was still little more than a path. Hostelries for post riders and travelers remained crude and inadequate, and later government "improvements" to the road did not always include even removing the stumps from between the wagon ruts.

Other than its use by returning boatmen and an occasional merchant, the Natchez Trace had surprisingly little economic importance in history. It was not often used by farmers or planters for moving produce to market or even by immigrants entering the region to settle. As a result, with the arrival of the first steamboats on the Mississippi after the War of 1812, the trail declined in importance rather quickly and in time almost disappeared from the memory of man. In 1935, partly as a work relief project, President Franklin Roosevelt allotted over $1 million to begin construction of a new national road following the general route of the old path. This came to be known as the Natchez Trace Parkway.

Among other names, the Natchez Trace has been called at various times the Natchez Road, the Columbian Highway, the Massac Trace, the "road cut by the federal troops," the Big South Road, and even the Path of Peace. The name Natchez Trace seems to have been its official designation rather late in its history.

See L. M. Jamison, *Journal of Mississippi History* (April, 1939); D. A. Phelps, *Journal of Mississippi History* (Jan., 1949; July, 1953), *Tennessee Historical Quarterly* (Sept., 1954), and *Alabama Review* (Jan., 1954); J. Daniels, *Devil's Backbone* (1962); and R. G. Hall, "Natchez Trace" (M.A. thesis, University of Wisconsin, 1914).

NATCHITOCHES, LA. (pop. 15,974), was settled by Louis Juchereau de St. Denis in 1714 as Ft. St. Jean Baptiste. The oldest settlement within the Louisiana Purchase territory, Natchitoches (pronounced nak'-uh-tish) gradually developed from an Indian trading post into a shipping center on the Red River. It is approximately 68 miles southeast of Shreveport. The modern city serves primarily as a market for area farmers. It also is the site of Northwestern State University of Louisiana (1884), a state fish hatchery, and factories producing mobile homes, brick, cottonseed oil, and lumber products.

See K. Bridges and W. DeVille, *Louisiana History* (Spring, 1963); and files of *Courrier* (1824–27), Natchitoches *Times* (1859–73, 1903–), *Louisiana Populist* (1894–99), and *Enterprise* (1888–).

NATIONAL AFRO-AMERICAN COUNCIL was a revival of the earlier NATIONAL AFRO-AMERICAN LEAGUE. Because of the deteriorating status of blacks in the South, plans for the council were laid at a meeting in Rochester, N.Y., in September, 1898. The council was to incorporate existing black religious, political, and benevolent organizations. The statement of objectives was basically the same as the platform of the earlier league. The first national convention was held in Washington, D.C., in December, 1898, and thereafter conventions were held annually in different cities for approximately a decade. The two men most prominently identified with the council were Bishop Alexander Walters of the AME Zion church of New York and T. THOMAS FORTUNE, editor of the New York *Age*. Between them they held the presidency and chairmanship of the executive council during almost the entire history of the council.

The council unsuccessfully sought to initiate a suffrage test case in New Orleans (1900–1901). It took partial credit for bringing the Alabama suffrage cases (*Giles* v. *Harris*, 189 U.S. 475) before the U.S. Supreme Court in 1903. Although the council attracted more Negro leaders than the league, it failed to win mass support and was able to accomplish little because of insufficient funds. Internal dissension was also a source of weakness. The history of the council was inextricably linked with the divisions among blacks over the role of

BOOKER T. WASHINGTON as race leader. Behind the scenes, Washington sought to dominate the council, and by 1902 all of the officers were persons who were subservient to his wishes in varying degrees. W. E. B. DU BOIS and IDA WELLS-BARNETT, who earlier had been prominent in the council, ceased to support it, and the anti-Washington press denounced the council as a tool used by him to advance his own reputation and to further his accommodationist philosophy and methods. Washington sought to use the council to counteract the Niagara movement, which his critics founded in 1905, but the council languished and some of its leaders, including Bishop Walters, affiliated with the Niagara movement and later with the NATIONAL ASSOCIATION FOR THE ADVANCEMENT OF COLORED PEOPLE, which Washington also opposed. The last convention of the council appears to have been held in 1908 in Baltimore.

See E. L. Thornbrough, *T. Thomas Fortune* (1972) and *Journal of Southern History* (Nov., 1961).

EMMA LOU THORNBROUGH
Butler University

NATIONAL AFRO-AMERICAN LEAGUE was an early attempt at a national civil rights organization with emphasis upon the grievances of southern blacks. It was proposed by T. THOMAS FORTUNE in 1887. He listed as the grievances that it would combat: the suppression of voting rights in the South; lynch and mob law; inequities in the funding of schools for blacks and whites; the chain gang and convict lease system; discrimination by railroads; the denial of accommodations in hotels, restaurants, etc. The organization would center its activities in the South, where most Negroes lived and where grievances were most acute. It was to be a federation of state leagues to which local leagues would belong.

In January, 1890, delegates from 23 states, mostly in the North but including South Carolina, North Carolina, Georgia, Texas, Tennessee, and Virginia, met in Chicago. They adopted a constitution along lines suggested by Fortune, which said that the organization was to be nonpartisan and that it would seek its objectives by educating public opinion and through test cases in the courts. Joseph C. Price, president of Livingstone College in North Carolina, was chosen president, with William A. Pledger of Georgia as vice-president and Fortune as secretary.

In spite of the high hopes on which it was founded, the league lacked vitality and accomplished little. A second national convention in

Knoxville, Tenn., in 1891, at which Fortune was elected president, was sparsely attended. In August, 1893, Fortune announced that the league was defunct. It had failed to attract mass support, and, because Fortune had insisted that it be nonpartisan, few black political leaders supported it. Most important, the league lacked funds to support test cases in the courts. The attempt to organize the league was premature, although it was revived in 1898 as the NATIONAL AFRO-AMERICAN COUNCIL. But the idea of the league foreshadowed the direction that the civil rights movement was to take in the twentieth century.

See E. L. Thornbrough, *T. Thomas Fortune* (1972) and *Journal of Southern History* (Nov., 1961); and Booker T. Washington Papers, Library of Congress.

EMMA LOU THORNBROUGH
Butler University

NATIONAL ASSOCIATION FOR THE ADVANCEMENT OF COLORED PEOPLE.

Although northern white liberals and black activists created the NAACP in 1908, the local groups have always been predominantly black. Ideologically opposed to BOOKER T. WASHINGTON's moderate philosophy, its early goals included greater police protection for southern blacks, defense against LYNCHING, jury service and fair court proceedings, equal employment opportunities, and open recreational facilities. Although the laws it sought were not passed, its vigorous support of antilynch legislation at least reduced the number of such atrocities.

Seeing themselves as the spiritual descendants of the abolitionists, NAACP leaders perpetuated the philosophy of immediacy; in their legal attacks on Jim Crow SEGREGATION, however, they adopted a gradualist approach. Early legal successes included a 1915 decision striking down the GRANDFATHER CLAUSE in Oklahoma and Maryland and a 1917 victory in which the U.S. Supreme Court declared unconstitutional a Louisville statute requiring residential segregation. Throughout the 1920s and 1930s the association fought, unsuccessfully at first, the Texas WHITE PRIMARY, and it also suffered a setback in the famous SCOTTSBORO CASE, when it lost the field to the Communists.

In 1940 the association emphasized ending sharecrop PEONAGE and DISFRANCHISEMENT while supporting equal employment and educational opportunities. In the last instance legal victories in the 1930s and 1940s opened southern graduate and professional schools, preparing the way for an attack on public school segregation, where its only major gain had been a decision outlawing Virginia's separate pay scales for white and black teachers. In 1950, using inequality in educational opportunity to attack the very nature of segregation, it initiated suits resulting in the BROWN V. BOARD OF EDUCATION decision in 1954. Throughout its history the NAACP had been viewed with disfavor, and following the 1954 pronouncement most southern states instituted legal proceedings to curtail its activity, an action that simply drove the association underground.

Until the 1960s CIVIL RIGHTS MOVEMENT, the NAACP reigned supreme; during that decade, however, organizations that appealed to the masses, helping them protest instead of protesting for them (CONGRESS OF RACIAL EQUALITY, SOUTHERN CHRISTIAN LEADERSHIP CONFERENCE, STUDENT NONVIOLENT COORDINATING COMMITTEE), eclipsed the more traditionalist NAACP. Preoccupied with rooting out discrimination, the association saw civil rights as exclusively a white affair, contending that the problem would be solved when the whites granted blacks their rights. Further, the association lacked popular appeal and charisma—until the 1940s it made no concerted effort to reach the blue-collar masses, remaining dedicated to the social elite. Even after opening its membership to anyone willing to pay the dollar annual dues, the association did little to involve its company in the civil rights struggles. During the 1960s the NAACP continued to labor behind the scenes in the courts while the newer groups enjoyed publicity and popular appeal. In several major civil rights confrontations it was NAACP financial and legal talent that raised bail money and provided demonstrators with legal protection.

The NAACP's strength remains legal; it prefers to win court battles and leave street demonstrations and picket lines to others. In many ways the association's quiet, prosaic, and sometimes dreary court cases laid the proper foundation for the more flamboyant and charismatic campaigns of the 1960s. Its underlying goal remains integration. In the late 1960s it blasted the separatists who opposed integration, going so far as to suspend the officers of its Atlanta chapter when they took action to end a 15-year court battle and gain control of local school boards by conceding that some public schools would always be black.

See C. F. Kellogg, *NAACP* (1967), excellent for early years; A. M. Duster (ed.), *Crusade for Justice* (1970), autobiography of Ida Wells-Barnett; R. L. Zangrando, *Journal of Negro History* (April, 1965); C. V. Woodward, *Strange Career of Jim Crow* (1974); R. Brisbane, *Black Vanguard* (1970); and C. Silberman, *Crisis in Black and White* (1964).

DUNCAN R. JAMIESON
University of Alabama

NATIONAL FARMERS' ALLIANCE. See FARM-ERS' ALLIANCE

NATIONAL LABOR RELATIONS BOARD.

Using the National Industrial Recovery Act, the Roosevelt administration established two successive administrative boards to create a national collective-bargaining policy, the National Labor Board (1933–1934) and the first National Labor Relations Board (1934–1935). The National Labor Relations Act (Wagner Act, 1935) created the permanent NLRB and made explicitly legal the right of labor to bargain collectively. The NLRB, comprising three members appointed by the president, investigated disputes. Its cease-and-desist orders, after possible federal judiciary review, became national labor law. On April 27, 1937, five of the board's decisions were upheld by the U.S. Supreme Court (the leading case was *NLRB* v. *Jones & Laughlin Steel Corporation*, 301 U.S. 1) and since then the board's decisions, and the court decisions surrounding them, have defined in detail unfair labor practices and proper bargaining units. In 1947 the Labor-Management Relations Act (Taft-Hartley) increased the NLRB to five members, defined unfair labor practices by unions, and created a quasi-independent general counsel of the board to prosecute cases.

In the South after 1937, there was no organized attack, other than ideological disagreement, on the board; the region's employers used other means to defeat LABOR UNIONS and keep the South underunionized by national standards. The NLRB decisions have not reflected or created any southern labor practices distinctive from the rest of the country, though many southern cases have been important in the ever-increasing web of labor law created by the thousands of cases the board handles annually. Since the 1930s, controversy has swirled around the board's broad policy power and the alleged prounion bias despite changing composition by presidential appointment.

See I. Bernstein, *Turbulent Years* (1969); J. Rosenfarb, *National Labor Policy* (1940); B. Taylor and F. Witney, *Labor Relations Law* (1971); G. Bloom and H. Northrup, *Economics of Labor Relations* (1973); NLRB, *Annual Report*; *Decisions and Orders of NLRB* (annually); and *Court Decisions Relating to National Labor Relations Act* (annually). From 1950 *Labor Law Journal* has published many interpretative articles on NLRB decisions.

JAMES A. HODGES
College of Wooster

NATIONAL RECOVERY ADMINISTRATION.

With the country in deep depression, the National Industrial Recovery Act became law on June 16, 1933. Congress intended to increase purchasing power through public works and minimum wages and to reduce unemployment by spreading work through lowering the hours worked per day. To achieve these goals without damaging corporate profits, NIRA, Title 1, suspended the antitrust acts. The trade association of each industry was permitted to govern that industry, theoretically in partnership with labor and government. Section 7a reaffirmed labor's right to organize and the employer's obligation to bargain collectively.

The National Recovery Administration was established to administer Title 1. NRA evolved from an agency reflecting the NIRA's balanced approach to representing the views of corporate interests, and finally it attempted to cast off the hold of business. General Hugh Johnson, administrator of NRA, considered the NIRA unconstitutional. To avoid court conflicts with industry, he relinquished government's licensing enforcement measures retained by the act and depended upon voluntary compliance and social pressure. To put NRA into operation quickly, he made additional compromises.

The result was an embryonic and short-lived cartelization of the economy. Trade associations dominated NRA code authorities, the administering agent for each industry, and a few large corporations controlled each trade association. Federal representatives on code authorities did not vote and divided their energies by simultaneously working with numerous code authorities. Small business, the consumer, and labor were virtually eliminated from code authorities. Of the more than 700 codes, only 23 had voting union representatives and only three permitted consumers a vote. Business self-government, unhampered by countervailing forces, resulted in coordinated price increases unrelated to demand and various devices to limit production. By the beginning of 1935, 568 codes had minimum price provisions of some kind, and a large number of the remaining maintained prices in other ways.

Although some labor leaders remained satisfied with NRA, others did not. In addition, the agency was under fire from small business and from numerous progressives in Congress. Most significant, the NRA simply did not draw the country out of the depression. The result was a gradual shifting of NRA's role beginning in mid-1934.

Johnson resigned October 1, 1934, and a board that gradually ended enforcement of production limits and other monopolistic practices replaced him. The position of small business was also strengthened. In addition, price increases became subject to investigation, the power of the National Labor Board was strengthened, and influential leaders were added to the NRA board.

There was insufficient time to reform the NRA; for on May 27, 1935, in a unanimous decision, the Supreme Court ruled the National Industrial Recovery Act unconstitutional and with it destroyed the NRA.

See A. M. Schlesinger, Jr., *Coming of New Deal* (1959); W. E. Leuchtenburg, *Franklin D. Roosevelt and New Deal* (1963); B. Mitchell, *Depression Decade* (1947); B. Bellush, *Failure of NRA* (1975); and J. P. Johnson, *Journal of American History* (Dec., 1966), bituminous coal.

NEIL BETTEN
Florida State University

NATIONAL ROAD. See CUMBERLAND ROAD

NATIONAL UNION CONVENTION (1866).
Supporters of ANDREW JOHNSON sought a new organization to promote the conservative program of conciliatory reunification. Mainly the movement appealed to moderate Republicans, war Democrats, and old Unionists prominent in the southern state governments. The coalition's pull across party lines constituted its weakness as well as its strength. Republicans and Democrats found it difficult to weaken their respective parties to support a union with former political opponents. Northerners and southerners found common cause to be embarrassing and suspect. Johnson's supporters therefore favored a "movement" rather than a third party. The wartime Union party coalition purged of "radicals" appeared to offer the best opportunity.

The Philadelphia meeting in August was the first national convention in six years. National representation, as well as a symbolic arm-in-arm entry of the Massachusetts and South Carolina delegations, set the tone, and the convention adopted a platform calling for immediate restoration of the Union. In the critical November election, however, the radicals overwhelmed the moderates. If Johnson had effectively used his patronage power, moderates might have done better. He made matters still worse in his ill-fated "swing around the circle." Continued emotionalism from the Civil War inflamed by southern recalcitrance combined to wreck union chances.

See M. Perman, *Reunion Without Compromise* (1973); T. Wagstaff, "National Union Movement" (Ph.D. dissertation, University of Wisconsin, 1967); H. K. Beale, *Critical Year* (1930); and E. L. McKitrick, *Andrew Johnson* (1960).

JAMES MURPHY
Southern Illinois University

NATIONAL URBAN LEAGUE. See URBAN LEAGUE, NATIONAL

NATIONAL YOUTH ADMINISTRATION was
created in June, 1935, as a division of the WORKS PROGRESS ADMINISTRATION charged with the task of alleviating the problems of unemployed and needy young people. It became fully autonomous in 1939. The agency was headed by the deputy director of the WPA, AUBREY W. WILLIAMS, who ran a small Washington office. NYA offices were also quickly established in each state and in thousands of localities throughout the nation. From its inception, then, it was an essentially decentralized operation.

There were two main divisions in the NYA project. One, student work, was geared specifically at enabling needy college and high school students to complete their education through the provision of stipends in return for useful community work. The program was virtually run by the educational institutions themselves, and by 1942 nearly 2 million young people had been assisted by it. The second NYA division was formed to aid young people who were both out of school and out of work. The agency's aim was to provide both relief and vocational training for these people, through work on tasks of relevance to the communities in which they lived. Advisory councils of local citizens were appointed to assist NYA officials in developing appropriate projects. NYA enrollees worked on a variety of jobs: construction, machine shop work, carpentry, power sewing, and home economics, to name a few.

By 1937 NYA leaders realized that many of the nation's neediest young folk were not being reached by either program. These were rural youth. To meet this need, hundreds of residence centers were set up, places to which young country people could come to receive training in a variety of vocations, which could aid them in securing employment away from the home farm if they so desired. Southern young people, in particular, benefited from this development.

With the onset of war in Europe, Williams moved the NYA systematically into the area of defense training. By 1942 the agency was operating solely as an adjunct of the defense effort, introducing young people to machines, training them in shop practice, and then sending them to areas of labor demand. Again, southern youth participated more than proportionally in this aspect of the program.

The NYA was abolished in 1943 as part of a congressional economy drive. By then it had assisted many millions of young people and had achieved an enviable record of accomplishment. Moreover, it was one of the few New Deal agencies that made a particular attempt to treat both black and white Americans on an entirely equal footing. One measure of its success is that, when President LYNDON B. JOHNSON was establishing his own youth programs in 1965, it was to the NYA he turned as a model.

See NYA Records, National Archives; A. Williams Papers, FDR Library; E. Roosevelt Papers, FDR Library; E. and B. Lindley, *New Deal for Youth* (1968); and S. L. Charles, *Minister of Relief: Hopkins* (1963).

JOHN A. SALMOND
La Trobe University, Melbourne, Australia

NAVAL STORES, an industry based on the exploitation of the pine woods for their resinous juices, developed early in the South. Of prime importance to the British navy during the era of wooden sailing vessels, turpentine, tar, and pitch were supported by bounties from 1705 to the American Revolution (COMMERCE). Production declined after the Revolution until the 1830s, when new uses in painting, printing, as a solvent for rubber, and especially as an illuminant to replace dwindling whale oil caused a revival that lasted until the Civil War. Colonial production was largely by small farmers as an adjunct to agriculture. After the 1840s, however, larger planters entered production using slave labor, and in 1860 annual production was valued at $12 million, third behind cotton and tobacco in the export trade of the South. That it was a staple principally associated with North Carolina down to the Civil War is confirmed in the nickname Tarheel State.

The longleaf pine (*Pinus palustris*) was the principal source. It grew along a coastal belt approximately 100 to 150 miles wide from southern Virginia to Texas. As the forests became exhausted, the industry migrated southward: South Car-olina led in the 1870s; Georgia, 1889–1899; and Florida, 1909–1919. Production currently centers in southeastern Georgia and northern Florida.

Regular chipping of the trees during summer caused resin to flow into a box cut into the base of the tree. Crude resin was distilled in a copper still to produce spirits of turpentine and rosin. Tar was made by smoldering dead pine wood in an earthen kiln. These crude methods often destroyed the trees and were not improved until after 1901. Further improvements occurred after World War II, but petroleum- and coal-based chemicals superseded the use of turpentine. Since 1950 turpentine and rosin have been obtained primarily from old longleaf pine stumps by dry distillation and as a by-product of sulfate wood pulp and are considered products of the CHEMICAL INDUSTRY.

See C. C. Crittenden, *Commerce in North Carolina* (1936); P. Perry, "Naval Stores" (Ph.D. dissertation, Duke, 1947) and *Journal of Southern History* (Nov., 1968); and T. Gamble (ed.), *Naval Stores* (ca. 1920).

PERCIVAL PERRY
Wake Forest University

NEGRO, FREE. Through emancipation, self-purchase, mixed racial unions (if they were the progeny of a free black mother), and running away, bondsmen and bondswomen in the pre–Civil War South secured their freedom, though exactly how many is difficult to determine. A 1755 Maryland census counted 1,800 free blacks (2 percent of the population) in that colony; and later federal censuses officially enumerated for the South: 32,000 (1790), 61,000 (1800), 108,000 (1810), 134,000 (1820), 182,000 (1830), 214,000 (1840), 238,000 (1850), and 262,000 (1860). Yet, some blacks, though slaves by law, achieved a quasi freedom through cunning or economic enterprise, and others, though legally free, committed themselves to long-term contracts, living in virtual slavery. In

VALUE OF TAR GUM, SPIRITS OF TURPENTINE, AND ROSIN, 1840–1940
(thousands of dollars)

State	1840	1850	1860	1870	1880	1890	1900	1910[a]	1920[a]	1930[a]	1940[a]
N.C.	$1,484	$2,476	$5,356	$2,338	$1,758	$1,706	$1,057	$674	$167	$690	
S.C.	2	236	1,097	774	1,896	1,524	788	406	168	691	$379
Ga.		55	236	96	1,456	4,242	110	6,939	10,875	18,076	10,207
Fla.		28	101	26	296	192	6,470	11,938	21,509	11,728	4,922
Ala.		18	642	280	372		2,034	2,472	5,892	2,244	1,239
Miss.	6	2	2	9	97	282	1,772	1,475	5,548	1,558	469
La.	6	21	21	3		115	1,174	5,591	1,295		
Total	$1,498	$2,836	$7,455	$3,526	$5,875	$7,946	$12,346	$25,078	$49,750	$36,282	$17,216

[a] Wood-distilled turpentine and rosin excluded
SOURCE: U.S. Census Bureau

addition, groups of runaways (MAROONS) lived in isolated regions while other fugitives successfully posed as freedmen, especially in urban areas. These quasi-free and fugitive blacks may have actually outnumbered indentured Negroes; and census takers almost certainly underestimated the total free Negro population. Nonetheless, several generalizations about this anomalous group can be made: free blacks constituted only a small fraction (perhaps 1 percent) of the South's colonial population; they usually gained free status during this period as a result of miscegenation; their numbers increased rapidly after 1785, and by the early nineteenth century they constituted about 6 percent of the region's population; three out of five lived in the border states; and they remained disproportionately (two of five) urban compared with southern whites and slaves. The rapid increase in the free black population after the American Revolution was the result of ideals of liberty and equality prompting slave owners to liberate their bondsmen; emigration of free colored people from the Caribbean during the 1791–1801 Haitian revolution; and the ability of industrious blacks to take advantage of an expanding southern economy by hiring out and purchasing their own freedom. By 1810 perhaps one of ten blacks in the South claimed free status.

Southern whites entertained ambivalent feelings toward free Negroes. In the Upper South, especially before 1830, when there was more ANTISLAVERY SENTIMENT (as opposed to abolitionism) than in the North, some whites held genuinely liberal feelings toward free Negroes, praising them as "steady," "industrious," and "intelligent." But most whites, accepting the current theories of black inferiority, agreed with the Tennessee judge John Catron, who castigated free blacks as "indolent," "thieving," "ungovernable," and "depraved." Their attitudes were best reflected by the comprehensive legal codes, which early in the nineteenth century outlawed black emigration from the West Indies, prohibited emancipation (in some states) without a special act of the legislature, and after TURNER'S REBELLION in 1831 denied free blacks the right to visit slaves, travel without a pass (both on penalty of being sold into bondage), secure an education, drink liquor, play cards, or enter certain apprenticeships. On the eve of the Civil War, southerners first proposed legislation to colonize free blacks in Africa, then to remand them to slavery, though both proved impractical. In short, whites created a complex legal system to regulate every aspect of free Negro life.

But the system failed to curtail the activities of many free blacks, who traveled through different regions, moved about without passes, engaged in numerous economic pursuits, and attended slave gatherings. Some Negroes lived in a state of illegal quasi freedom. Perhaps part of the reason for this failure was the seemingly incongruous acquiescence of whites, but more significant was the ability of ambitious free blacks to achieve a degree of economic independence. Working as laborers, factory workers, teamsters, carpenters, domestics, blacksmiths, coopers, cooks, stewards, washerwomen, barbers, and at a host of other jobs, a sizable minority became self-sufficient, and a few, especially in southern cities, accumulated great wealth. The well-known William Johnson, a barber in Natchez, for instance, purchased a sprawling plantation and secured a contingent of slaves. Nor was Johnson the only free black slave owner, as a number of Louisiana free Negroes also managed plantations. This black elite founded African churches, schools, benevolent associations, and paternal organizations; they stood at the center of the free Negro community; and they assumed positions of leadership during Reconstruction.

Whether a member of this elite, the economically independent middle class, or the vast majority who lived subsisting from day to day, free Negroes yearned for full acceptance in American society, valuing, as did most whites, hard work, frugality, religious piety, close family ties, and a strict moral code. Yet, no matter how hard they tried, they could not achieve that goal. The aging free black John H. Rapier, Sr., a wealthy Alabamian who had toiled a lifetime to gain such acceptance, wrote in 1854: "I am Satisfied that [white southerners] would not care if all the free negros in the United States was at the Botom of the Sea," just "So they was out of the United States."

See I. Berlin, *Slaves Without Masters* (1974), outstanding, and *Journal of Social History* (Spring, 1976). Also excellent are L. P. Jackson, *Free Negro Labor in Virginia* (1942); and J. H. Franklin, *Free Negro in North Carolina* (1943). See also E. Davis and W. Hogan (eds.), *William Johnson* (1951); M. Wikramanayake, *Free Black in South Carolina* (1973); and L. Schweninger, *Civil War History* (March, 1974), brief survey of recent periodical literature.

LOREN SCHWENINGER
University of North Carolina, Greensboro

NEGRO EDUCATIONAL REVIEW (West Bay Annex, Jacksonville, Fla. 32203), originally affiliated with the National Teachers Research Association, was begun in 1950 in response to the difficulties Negro scholars felt they were experiencing in getting the results of their work published. The *Review*, currently with a circulation of 3,000, accepts scholarly articles and research in a variety of areas including history, political science, education, business, language, music, the arts, and current problems, with emphasis placed on topics relating to racial discrimination in America. One feature of the *Review* is the annual compilation of masters' theses under way in selected southern institutions of higher learning (1950–1961, 1974–).

NEGROES. The first 20 Negroes in the English mainland colonies arrived at Jamestown, Va., in 1619 aboard a Dutch frigate and were sold to the colonists as INDENTURED LABOR, not as slaves. Others followed, and though many were freed when their period of indenture was up, very early (certainly by 1640) some were being kept in permanent servitude as slaves, a status that received statutory recognition in Virginia in 1661. It was easy for the institution of black slavery to spread to the other southern colonies as they were established, or soon thereafter; and it did, including Georgia in 1750, after almost 20 years of being forbidden there. By that date, black SLAVERY had become an integral part of the South's economic system and would remain so, amid growing controversy, until the Civil War settled the question once and for all.

Free blacks were, of course, not unknown in the South, having been freed by their owners, having purchased their own freedom, or being the descendants of other free blacks (NEGRO, FREE). They were generally to be found in the larger towns and cities, with more than half of them in Virginia and Maryland alone. In a position of increasing precariousness, they were hemmed in by restrictive legislation and lived always with the threat that they might be reenslaved for some minor infraction or by kidnaping. Even so, free blacks occasionally voted in Maryland until 1810, in Tennessee until 1834, and in North Carolina until 1835.

On the eve of the Civil War, the slave population of the southern states (plus the District of Columbia) was approximately 4 million, and there were 262,000 free blacks. Whether slave or free, however, blacks in the South had served perforce largely as the region's hewers of wood and drawers of water. In both slavery and freedom, many had come to fill economic roles far different from those of either field hands or house servants: as carpenters, masons, smiths of various kinds, coopers, wheelwrights, seamen, etc. By 1860 the race

had also produced in Maryland's free BENJAMIN BANNEKER a self-taught clockmaker, mathematician, astronomer, and surveyor; and in James Derham (1762–?), onetime New Orleans slave, a linguist and physician praised by Dr. Benjamin Rush. Doubtless there were other southern blacks whose talents went unrecognized or who never met opportunity face to face. Finally there were southern blacks who, as free men or as slaves given their freedom as a reward, had served the colonies in the American Revolution as both soldiers and sailors. Later wars and Indian engagements down to the Civil War also saw free southern blacks and even a handful of slaves (NEGRO TROOPS), some later to be freed, in the service of their country.

In the Civil War, blacks continued to serve the white South: in the fields and on plantations, in factories and in the army, as cooks, laborers, teamsters, and body servants. Military service was a more thorny problem, with that question anxiously and fearfully debated until just a month before the Confederacy fell, when in March, 1865, a Confederate law first authorized recruitment of both slaves and free blacks as soldiers. It was too late, leading only to increased numbers of blacks fleeing to the Union forces. Reports that blacks participated in combat as Confederate soldiers, however, were not confirmed.

The end of the Civil War, together with ratification of the THIRTEENTH AMENDMENT (December, 1865), meant freedom for all the South's blacks. The end of the war saw thousands leave the plantation or other scenes of their oppression, most often for the towns and cities in search of opportunity, or just to roam and "test" their freedom. Soon, though, the BLACK CODES of the newly constituted state governments were forcing blacks back into a position of semislavery. These laws, though most of them were shortly repealed—plus white southern intransigence and the determination of the so-called Radicals in the North that the white South should be punished and Negroes in the South awarded near if not full civil rights—led to the establishment of congressional RECONSTRUCTION in March, 1867. New state governments were then established, with Negroes voting and holding office—though usually minor ones and almost always as a minority. Then came the FOURTEENTH AMENDMENT (July, 1868), which made the Negro a citizen and in theory guaranteed him equal protection of the law; and the FIFTEENTH AMENDMENT (March, 1870), which proclaimed that no one might be denied the vote on the basis of "race, color, or previous condition of servitude." The millennium for blacks was not nigh, however. The new constitutional amendments and supporting legislation were often flouted by the white South, while increasingly the North ignored such lawbreaking as it grew tired of the "Negro question" and turned to the economic and political healing of the nation even at the expense of the Negro. In the South, meanwhile, annually fewer and fewer Negroes were elected to office, Radical-dominated governments friendly to them were toppled, and by 1877 all the former Confederate states had been "redeemed" by conservative governments (ELECTION OF 1876).

Economically the position of blacks came to be even more agricultural—usually as a SHARECROPPER, not as owner or renter—than had been the case in slavery, as more and more of the crafts and skilled trades once open to blacks were closed to them. Where once black slaves occasionally had been used to operate southern cotton mills, the TEXTILE INDUSTRY now became the most segregated of all, with whites claiming that "Negroes just can't work with machinery." In fact, the cotton mills had become a refuge for poor, often sharecropping whites eager to leave the worn-out land, and there was no room for racial competition for the same jobs (MILL TOWNS). Consequently, blacks not on the land were forced into the roughest, lowest-paying jobs in the mines, tobacco factories, flour mills, and LUMBER INDUSTRY.

Politically, the Negro's "place" was assumed, by both blacks and whites, to be in the REPUBLICAN PARTY, an ever weaker minority in the South after the early 1870s. In fact, more and more Negroes came to see the "wisdom" of voting Democratic, or else ceased political activity altogether. The POPULIST revolt of the early and mid-1890s briefly promised to restore the Negro to a meaningful position in southern politics, as poor whites and poor blacks warily sought political union on grounds of their common economic plight. In the end, the Populist party failed in the South largely because of its alleged threat to white supremacy.

Socially, situations from the end of the Civil War to the late 1890s were not nearly so clear-cut as were those in the economics and politics of race. Although there undoubtedly was a distinct preference by the white South for racial SEGREGATION in public places and whereas such segregation was probably more often the practice than not—except possibly on the railroads—massive, monolithic segregation by statute did not come about until near and just after the turn of the century.

At the same time or a little earlier, and making such segregation possible, there was the move to disfranchise Negroes by statute or by constitution, "so that the white man would not have to continue to steal the Negro vote" and so that the Negro might not ever again even threaten to hold the balance of political power, as he had during the Populist revolt (DISFRANCHISEMENT). Helping to make such a move both possible and safe were a complacent North, which had embraced the philosophy of social Darwinism; the Republican party, which abandoned the Negro; and a narrowly legalistic and conservative U.S. Supreme Court. So, beginning with Mississippi in 1890 and culminating about 1910 in the last remaining southern states, the Negro was disfranchised by such devices as the GRANDFATHER CLAUSE, POLL TAX, and literacy tests.

Thus, by the outbreak of World War I, the southern Negro was both disfranchised and segregated and, in a word, frozen into a castelike status or "place," which was to see little change for the better for a generation, or until after World War II. For rapidly on the heels of disfranchisement and segregation in public, the KU KLUX KLAN was reborn in 1915, and the first city ordinances decreeing residential racial segregation were enacted.

The entry of the United States into World War I saw southern Negroes drafted into the armed forces for the first time. At home, wartime industrial opportunities marked the beginning of the twentieth-century exodus of Negroes from the South (NEGRO MIGRATION), a process that would not be reversed until sometime in the 1960s. In the 1920s the exodus was further encouraged by the spread of the BOLL WEEVIL through the South, wiping out the jobs of thousands in the cotton fields. In the GREAT DEPRESSION of the 1930s, NEW DEAL legislation designed to curb farm production paid the landowner not to produce but in the process sent more thousands of unemployed black farmhands north, as compensatory funds meant for them often did not find their way into black hands. Many of the New Deal programs did, however, aid the southern Negro, but rarely in proportion to the number of blacks in the population.

World War II once more witnessed southern blacks, in segregated service or combat units commanded by white officers, fighting for the democracy that they rarely enjoyed at home. But the war also meant the beginning of the modern CIVIL RIGHTS MOVEMENT, for once the war was over, the white South, try as it might, would never again know the security of the segregated world of earlier years. With increasing success—largely through the efforts of the NATIONAL ASSOCIATION FOR THE ADVANCEMENT OF COLORED PEOPLE—the WHITE PRIMARY and other voting restrictions,

teacher salary differentials, inadequate educational opportunities, and finally segregated education
itself (BROWN V. BOARD OF EDUCATION, 1954) were
all challenged in the federal courts and ultimately
met their doom. Successive legislation, notably
the CIVIL RIGHTS ACT OF 1964 and the CIVIL
RIGHTS ACT OF 1965, spelled the end of the segregated and disfranchised black world that the
white South had forged at the turn of the century,
thus constituting a second Reconstruction with
little or no chance of being undone like the first.
Even so, the decade of the 1970s would mark a
turning from the zealous pursuit of the ideals of
the 1950s and 1960s in the face of an increasing
national mood of conservatism—including that in
the courts—new and growing economic problems, and the waning of enthusiasm for reform,
together with increased divisiveness among reformers, both black and white (NEGROES, HISTO-
RIOGRAPHY OF).

CHARLES E. WYNES
University of Georgia

NEGROES, HISTORIOGRAPHY OF.

The study
of Afro-American history was confined to a relatively small group of specialized scholars prior to
the civil rights revolution of the 1960s, but black
historiography is no recent development. James
W. C. Pennington, a fugitive slave, attempted as
early as 1841 to tell the history of the Afro-American. Other amateur black historians of the nineteenth century made more significant efforts. Although they violated many of the canons of
historical scholarship, they frequently engaged in
prodigious research and sometimes published
valuable records that would have been lost without their efforts. Furthermore, they pointed out
the neglected aspects of American history as written by their nonblack contemporaries and developed the major themes of black history.

These amateurs were followed in the early
twentieth century by scholars such as W. E. B. DU
BOIS, Benjamin Brawley, and CARTER G. WOOD-
SON. These and other men and women published
their articles in the *Journal of Negro History* and
their monographs through the Associated Publishers, both of which Woodson served as editor
while directing the ASSOCIATION FOR THE STUDY
OF AFRO-AMERICAN LIFE AND HISTORY. These
scholars expanded and documented the pioneer
work of the amateurs, studying all facets of the
black experience and culture. Although these
studies were uneven in quality and were too frequently inspirational and purpose history, the
scholarship improved as more of the young au-

thors pursued degrees in graduate schools. Woodson provided a synthesis of these studies in *The
Negro in American History*, which was first published in 1922 and has been republished in 19 revised editions.

Black historiography was thus well established
as an important field of scholarship prior to World
War II, but this was recognized by only a very few
nonblack historians. The one area of black life that
captured the attention of white historians was
slavery, and here voluminous studies were published (SLAVERY, HISTORIOGRAPHY OF). These
were generally marked by notions of racial inequality and a predilection to look at the institution through the eyes of the southern white. Many
historians of the South were attracted to studying
Reconstruction, but the traditional interpretation
of this period was also marked by racist bias, and
the freedmen were given a subordinate and stereotyped role (RECONSTRUCTION, HISTORIOGRA-
PHY OF). In short, Afro-Americans were generally
ignored by white historians in the early decades
of the twentieth century, except in slavery and Reconstruction, where they were portrayed in distorted images.

Evidence of change first appeared in the 1930s.
Black historians had already indicated the richness and variety of subjects to be studied, but before these were recognized, there had to be
changes in attitudes in the historical profession.
Historians trained in the early graduate seminars
of American universities were indoctrinated with
the philosophy of social Darwinism and the imperialist belief in the "white man's burden." But,
in the 1930s, reaction to Nazi racial ideology forced
many Americans to take a new look at American
principles and practices. The sociological studies
by HOWARD ODUM, RUPERT VANCE, Charles S.
Johnson, E. FRANKLIN FRAZIER, and others destroyed racial myths and stereotypes and raised
new questions about the southern past. Influential also was the growing militancy and discontent
among Afro-Americans. Following World War II,
the rise of African nations and America's new position in international affairs emphasized the importance of bringing domestic practices closer in
line with pronouncements.

The first indication of change came in the historiography of Reconstruction. The traditional
interpretation, generally known as the Dunning
school interpretation, had been challenged by Du
Bois in his address to the American Historical Association in 1909, in publications in 1913 and
1917 by JOHN R. LYNCH, and by Alrutheus A. Taylor's studies of the Negro during Reconstruction
in South Carolina and Virginia, published in the

1920s. But these works, which were considered defensive, did not receive the attention that came with the publication, in 1932, of the detailed and expert study of Reconstruction in South Carolina by FRANCIS BUTLER SIMKINS and ROBERT H. WOODY. Simkins, in 1938, and HOWARD K. BEALE, in 1939, strongly and effectively called for reevaluation of Reconstruction. The wave of the future is perhaps best illustrated by Vernon L. Wharton's *The Negro in Mississippi, 1865–1890* (1947). Wharton, through fair-minded use of new and old sources, showed the freedmen as central and often constructive figures in Reconstruction. Since 1947 revisionism has taken over the historiography of Reconstruction and has, in fact, become the orthodox interpretation. This has resulted largely from a change of attitude, but the new research of scores of historians has also been important, especially in the area of state and local studies.

The revisionist studies of slavery that have come since World War II have also been significant, but they have followed a more tortuous and controversial route than the reinterpretation of Reconstruction. Although no new single interpretation has replaced the old orthodoxy, that orthodoxy has been destroyed. Today's writers have gone beyond slavery as an institution and seen the slave as a person who was affected by and responded to the institution in a variety of ways. Equally important have been the recent studies of other aspects of black history that were previously almost totally ignored by white historians. For example, the group of Civil War historians who were called revisionists had by 1945 practically eliminated Afro-Americans as a cause of the Civil War and treated them as negligible factors in the war itself. Black writers had earlier portrayed the black soldier in the Civil War, but BELL I. WILEY's study, published in 1938, of Negroes on the home front and as soldiers was a major breakthrough in black historiography. Although somewhat condescending in attitude, Wiley investigated every aspect of black life and clearly showed how the Afro-American affected the war and was affected by it. This study has been followed by significant and unbiased studies of the slave and freedmen during the period by Dudley T. Cornish, Benjamin Quarles, James M. McPherson, James H. Brewer, and many others. They have shown that, far from being a passive participant, the Afro-American was an important factor in winning his freedom.

The courage and patriotism of the Afro-American have been documented in studies of his participation in other wars, including the American Revolution, the War of 1812, the Seminole War, the Spanish-American War, and both world wars.

Scholars have also produced valuable studies of black troops in the West in the late nineteenth century, and these have been paralleled by pioneer studies of the black cowboy. The period between Reconstruction and the First World War, in fact, has been a particularly fruitful field for studying the black experience, with emphasis on the development of Jim Crow and treating black disfranchisement in some cases and black participation in the politics of the period in others. Of importance also have been studies of black thought and programs during this period, centering on the differences in philosophy that characterized the debate between Du Bois and BOOKER T. WASHINGTON. Many scholars have shown that a viable, though segregated, black society developed during this period.

The recent deluge of publications in black history, accompanied by wide public interest in the black experience, has resulted largely from civil rights activities in the late 1950s and 1960s. There is a clear line of development, however, in black historiography from the nineteenth century, with important landmarks along the way, such as the formation of the Association for the Study of Afro-American Life and History in 1915 and the gradual awakening of white scholars in the 1930s and 1940s to the importance of black history. Contemporary scholars have frequently followed paths of study charted earlier by black scholars. White racism and race relations have replaced slavery in recent years as the field that attracts most attention from white scholars. Studies in this area, which began in the 1930s and 1940s and increased greatly in the 1950s and 1960s, have explored the development of American racism from the earliest colonial period to the present day. They have also shown that racism is not exclusively a southern trait.

A second major area of interest, which has grown steadily since the 1950s, is black biography. At the close of World War II there were few biographies of Afro-Americans based on scholarly research. Most black biographies were designed primarily for young people and were inspirational, often fictional, in nature. The advancement in this area of study is best illustrated by the excellent scholarly and critical biography of Booker T. Washington by Louis Harlan. This growing interest in black biography is illustrative of perhaps the most significant development in recent black historiography, the ability of white scholars to see Afro-Americans as individuals. On the other hand, there remains the tendency among both black and white historians to lean too much toward purpose history when writing about the black experience. The cause of race relations becomes more important than factual history.

There is no doubt that black historiography is firmly established as a field of scholarship and that it will continue to challenge standard interpretations. There are many areas that require further investigation, particularly black institutional life and the development of black leadership in the South. National leaders and institutions have received much more attention than those located primarily in the South. The greatest need, however, in both southern and American history is to make the black experience an integral part of the general history. Throughout most of their history the overwhelming majority of Afro-Americans has lived in the South. However, black history and culture have been described again and again with little attention to their effect on southern history and culture. On the other hand, historians have often examined the response of Afro-Americans to their environment and have continued, even in very recent studies, to portray them as passive participants in the general history. For most historians, *southern* still means *white*, the southern mind is the white mind, southern culture is white culture. Actually, the Afro-American may well be the most southern of all southerners.

See A. S. Link and R. W. Patrick (eds.), *Writing Southern History* (1965); J. M. McPherson *et al.*, *Blacks in America* (1971), bibliographical essays; L. D. Reddick, *Journal of Negro History* (Jan., 1937); and E. E. Thorpe, *Black Historians* (1971).

CLIFTON H. JOHNSON
Amistad Research Center, New Orleans

NEGRO HERITAGE (11372 Links Dr., Reston, Va. 22070) is a bimonthly illustrated magazine begun in 1961. It aims to inform the public about the accomplishments of Negro Americans. It contains biographical sketches, popular articles, and an occasional scholarly one (if it does not include footnotes) on a wide variety of topics national in scope, as well as recipes for African foods and lists of recent books about Negroes. Beginning in 1974 with *Blacks in History*, the magazine has made available a limited number of cassettes and filmstrips on the Negro in history.

NEGRO LAND-GRANT COLLEGES. Four states, Mississippi, Virginia, South Carolina, and Kentucky, established separate Negro colleges partially supported by funds from the first Morrill Act (1862). Only after the second Morrill Act (1890) mandated that funds be equitably divided when segregated schools were maintained did the re-

maining southern states and Oklahoma undertake the support of Negro institutions for the "agriculture and mechanic arts." In some states, existing private Negro schools were assigned the funds; in others, existing state normal schools or new institutions benefited.

Because of the poor primary and secondary education available to Negroes, Negro land-grant colleges had to do extensive college preparatory work. In 1916 only 12 of 4,895 students were taking college-level courses; and, as late as 1928, two-thirds still were enrolled in subcollegiate work. These Negro institutions, with few exceptions, were funded at lower levels than were their white counterparts. Those in the region where the Southern Association gave accreditation were placed in a special Class B category for Negro colleges, a rating phased out only in the 1960s. The National Association of Land-Grant Colleges and Universities even refused to admit Negro representatives, but the Conference of Presidents of Negro Land-Grant Colleges (1924–1954) worked steadfastly to improve educational opportunities for Negroes in segregated states. In 1954 the conference was dissolved when its presidents accepted the invitation to join the larger association. Collegiate programs were extended during these years to include teacher training, liberal arts and sciences, and business curricula.

Since 1954, only token integration in reverse has occurred in most of these institutions, although two, West Virginia State College and Lincoln University (Missouri), now have a white majority. In 1957 West Virginia State surrendered land-grant status, a decision justified by conditions unique to that state. The remaining 16 institutions now serve more than 50,000 students.

See J. W. Davis, *Journal of Negro Education* (July, 1933); R. B. Atwood, *Journal of Negro Education* (Summer, 1958); W. Payne, *Civil Rights Digest* (Spring, 1970); D. O. W. Holmes, *Evolution of Negro College* (1934); C. L. Orr, "Conference of Presidents of Negro Land-Grant Colleges" (D.Ed. dissertation, University of Kentucky, 1959), valuable appendices; H. A. Bullock, *Negro Education in South* (1967), good perspective; and reports by U.S. Office of Education, esp. *Survey of Land-Grant Colleges and Universities* (1916, 1930) and *Statistics of Land-Grant Colleges and Universities* (1955).

JAMES A. DURAN, JR.
Canisius College

NEGRO MIGRATION. Immediately after emancipation, there was only slow and patternless movement by the South's black population. By the late 1860s and early 1870s, however, this movement had taken on a distinctly westward migratory character in conjunction with the expansion of numerous railway systems. The black populations of Texas and Arkansas increased significantly during the 1870s, and the EXODUS OF 1879 drew still additional numbers of blacks out of the lower Mississippi Valley and into the dominant pattern of westward migration.

Although much has been written about the migration of southern blacks to the Oklahoma Territory between 1880 and 1910, the more frequent path followed by black migrants was northward. While migration into Oklahoma increased that territory's black population by 136,400, black migration into the North (Middle Atlantic and east north-central states) resulted in a net increase there of 318,400 blacks. The numbers of people involved in both the westward and the northern routes, however, were relatively small, and the South, the home of 92.7 percent of the nation's black population in 1880, continued to have 89.2 percent in 1910.

The massive migration of blacks out of the South did not occur until World War I, and then it fol-lowed a distinctly northward and urban pattern with little westward migration. Between 1910 and 1930, migration resulted in a net loss of 1,143,000 blacks in the South's population while the North experienced a net gain of 1,035,700 due to black migration. The percentage of blacks in the nation continuing to reside in the South had fallen to 79.2 percent in 1930. During these same two decades, blacks, whether they moved north or remained in the South, increasingly shifted from rural to urban areas. Between 1880 and 1910, the percentage of blacks within the South living in urban areas had climbed from 15.3 percent to 21.2 percent; by 1930, 31.7 percent of the South's black population resided in urban areas.

The GREAT DEPRESSION of the 1930s failed to stop the flow of black migrants out of the South, but it turned migration from a flood to a trickle. Despite this interruption in the migratory pattern of the previous decades, World War II led to its revival on a massive scale. The migration figures for the 1940s resulted in a net loss of black population for the South of 1,180,000; almost 900,000

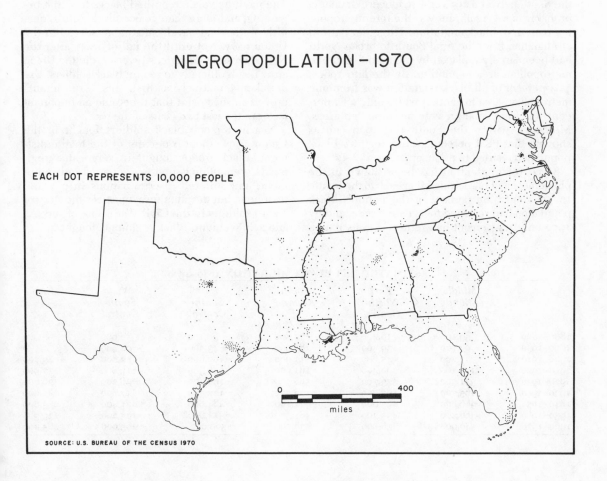

NEGRO POPULATION – 1970

EACH DOT REPRESENTS 10,000 PEOPLE

0   400

miles

SOURCE: U.S. BUREAU OF THE CENSUS 1970

of that figure migrated to the North while the Pacific states of Oregon, Washington, and California became residences for an additional 283,800 blacks due to migration. The emigration of blacks from the South on this scale further reduced the percentage of the nation's black population living in the South to 68.9 percent by 1950. Almost all of the emigrant population moved to urban areas of the northern and Pacific states. And those blacks remaining in the South paralleled at least the urban aspect of this migration: the percentage of southern blacks living in urban areas climbed from 31.7 in 1930 to 46.3 in 1950.

Between 1950 and 1970, the emigration of blacks out of the South reached record proportions. The South's black population had a net decline of 2,527,300 due to migration, and by 1970 only 54.4 percent of the nation's black population resided there. Meanwhile, migration resulted in a net increase of 1,727,700 in the North's black population and of 494,500 in the black population of the Pacific coast states.

Although the numbers of blacks migrating from the South between 1950 and 1970 were dramatic, probably more significant was the intermetropolitan pattern of black migration. The older pattern of migration from the rural South to urban North had been largely replaced by migration from one metropolitan area to another. By the late 1960s, 42.4 percent of all black migration was from one metropolitan area to another while only 28.2 percent was from rural areas to metropolitan areas. Moreover, within the South the 1970 census showed that 68.8 percent of the region's black population resided in urban areas.

Since 1970, attention has been drawn to the phenomenon of blacks migrating back to the South. In 1960 only .85 percent of the nation's black population had returned to its native state, and by 1970 only 1.4 percent had returned to its native state. Even if all returning migrants were going to southern states, which of course is not true, the percentage is so small that it is impossible at this point to talk of a demographic trend or pattern of significant proportions.

See U.S. Census Bureau, *Negro Population, 1790–1915* (1918); W. C. Calef and J. H. Nelson, *Geographical Review* (Jan., 1956); H. C. Hawkins, *Phylon* (June, 1973); E. J. Scott, *Negro Migration During War* (1920, 1969); A. Miller, "Black Migrant" (Paper, W. E. B. Du Bois Institute Conference, Oct., 1974); C. E. Lincoln, *Negro Pilgrimage* (1969); D. O. Price, *Negro Population* (1960); and C. G. Woodson, *Century of Negro Migration* (1917).

HOMER C. HAWKINS
Michigan State University

NEGRO TROOPS IN THE CIVIL WAR.

Although northern free Negroes and liberated southern slaves constituted a potentially large manpower resource for Union armies, race prejudice and political exigencies prevented their enlistment during the first year and a half of the war. The navy, however, recruited blacks from the beginning, and more than 20,000 black sailors, one-fifth of the total naval enlistment, served in the Union navy. Not until the fall of 1862, after the North had suffered serious reverses, did the Union army begin officially to recruit black soldiers. Undertaken tentatively at first, this "experiment" proved so successful that it became an important factor in the last two years of the war.

Nearly 180,000 black soldiers fought in the Union army, about 9 percent of the total enlistment. Black troops fought in segregated regiments, were often issued inferior arms and equipment, and suffered discriminations in pay and treatment, but despite these injustices the story of Negro soldiers in the Civil War is one of success and achievement. Black regiments fought in 449

ESTIMATED NET BLACK MIGRATION, 1880–1970

	Middle Atlantic	East North-Central	South Atlantic	East South-Central	West South-Central	Pacific
1880–1890	39,100	16,400	−72,500	−60,100	56,600	0
1890–1900	90,700	39,400	−181,600	−43,300	−22,400	0
1900–1910	87,200	45,600	−111,900	−109,600	−2,800	13,700
1910–1920	170,100	200,400	−161,900	−246,300	−19,800	17,900
1920–1930	341,500	323,700	−508,700	−180,100	−26,200	36,800
1930–1940	165,700	107,700	−175,200	−122,500	17,600	42,900
1940–1950	386,800	493,800	−424,100	−484,600	−271,400	283,800
1950–1960	396,400	435,300	−464,500	−524,600	−175,200	229,500
1960–1970	540,000	356,000	−538,000	−560,000	−265,000	265,000

engagements, of which 39 were major battles. Twenty-three Negro regiments fought in the Army of the Potomac and 15 in the Army of the James during the Union campaigns in Virginia, 1864–1865. Black soldiers were among the first Union troops to enter Charleston and Richmond when these cities fell in 1865. More than 37,000 Negroes lost their lives fighting for the Union. Seventeen black soldiers and four Negro sailors won congressional Medals of Honor for outstanding bravery. More than any other single factor, the contribution of black soldiers and sailors won the respect of the North for their race, made emancipation secure, and paved the way for the gains in civil and political rights after the war.

Even the Confederacy in the end was sufficiently impressed with the value of black troops—and sufficiently desperate for new recruits—to take the once-inconceivable step of enrolling Negro soldiers. As the South headed toward military collapse in early 1865, Robert E. Lee threw his decisive support behind the idea of black soldiers. On March 13, Jefferson Davis signed a "Negro soldier law" providing for the enlistment of slaves. A few companies were enrolled, but the war ended before the questionable theory that they would fight for the Confederacy could be tested.

See D. T. Cornish, *Sable Arm* (1956), most scholarly study; B. Quarles, *Negro in Civil War* (1953); J. M. McPherson, *Negro's Civil War* (1965); R. F. Durden, *Gray and Black* (1972), Confederate debate over whether to recruit blacks; and B. I. Wiley, *Southern Negroes, 1861–1865* (1938), treats military employment of blacks by both Union and Confederacy.

JAMES M. MCPHERSON
Princeton University

NELSON, THOMAS, JR. (1738–1789), born of a wealthy merchant family in Yorktown, Va. (NELSON FAMILY), became involved in politics as a member of the House of Burgesses, a delegate to the Continental Congress (1775–1777), a signer of the Declaration of Independence, and a member of the Virginia house of delegates (1779, 1780). After resigning from Congress in 1777, he was appointed brigadier general and commander of the Virginia militia; and in 1781 he was named governor to succeed the militarily inept Thomas Jefferson. After taking part in the Yorktown campaign in 1781, Nelson retired from military and political life.

See E. G. Evans, *Thomas Nelson of Yorktown* (1975); *Biographical Directory of American Congress*; G. E.

Ross, *Know Your Declaration of Independence and 56 Signers* (1963); and *Daughters of American Revolution Magazine* (Jan., 1952).

PHYLLIS R. ABBOTT
Mankato State University

NELSON, THOMAS A. R. (1812–1873), grew up in Knoxville, studied law, and by 1832 had become a solicitor in east Tennessee. He became prominent in the Whig party, backing William Henry Harrison in 1840 and HENRY CLAY in 1844. At the age of twenty-eight he was a national figure in the party. Nelson favored seeking the consent of Mexico to annex Texas. He was elected as a Unionist to Congress in 1858 and 1860. He was captured by Confederate troops in 1861 and taken to Richmond as a prisoner of war. After the war Nelson was a delegate to the Union National Convention of 1866 and the Democratic National Convention in New York in 1868. In the same year he defended ANDREW JOHNSON in the impeachment proceedings in Congress. During the last years of his life he had an active, extensive law practice in Tennessee. He was a skilled orator and a man whose caution and conservative stance on issues often earned him great popularity.

See T. B. Alexander, *Thomas A. R. Nelson* (1956); S. Nelson, *Virginia Magazine of History and Biography* (April, 1910); Nelson Papers, Lawson McGhee Library, Knoxville; T. A. R. Nelson, *Secession* (1864); and J. W. Caldwell, *Sketches of Bench and Bar of Tennessee* (1898).

ARNOLD A. SHERMAN
Virginia Polytechnic Institute and State University

NELSON FAMILY. The first member of the family to come to Virginia from England (around 1700) was Thomas ("Scotch Tom") Nelson (1677–1745). He founded Yorktown in 1705 and became a prosperous merchant and planter.

By 1738 one of his sons, "President" William Nelson (1711–1772), had become the sheriff of York County and a burgess between 1742 and 1744. He was on the colony's council from 1744 to 1772 and was president of the council for part of that period. After Governor Botetourt's death, Nelson was acting governor from October, 1770, to August, 1771. He opposed British taxation of the colonies and was on the assembly's committee of correspondence. Like his father he became a prominent merchant in Yorktown and acquired land in many parts of Virginia.

One of William Nelson's sons was THOMAS NEL-

SON, JR. (1738–1789), member of the House of Burgesses and Continental Congress (1775–1777), signer of the Declaration of Independence, and governor of Virginia (1781–1782). He supported the Revolution and spent much of his personal fortune raising troops in Virginia. In 1781 he joined George Washington in the siege of Yorktown.

One of his sons was Hugh Nelson (1768–1836), who became an attorney in Albemarle County, which he represented in the Virginia assembly from 1805 to 1809. He served in Congress from 1811 to 1823, when President James Monroe appointed him minister to Spain. Hugh returned to Virginia in 1825 and served in the house of delegates from 1828 to 1829. Through his father's contacts he came to know most of Virginia's prominent revolutionary leaders, including Thomas Jefferson.

The other side of the Nelson family descended from "Secretary" Thomas Nelson (1716–1782), a brother of William and second son of Scotch Tom. His three sons, Colonel William Nelson (1746–1807), Captain Thomas Nelson (1748?–?), and Major John Nelson (1748?–?), were all present at the battle of Yorktown, and they carried their father into the American lines under a flag of truce. John Nelson's eldest son was Major Thomas M. Nelson (1782–1853), who served with distinction in the War of 1812.

See E. G. Evans, *Thomas Nelson of Yorktown* (1975); R. C. M. Page, *Genealogy of Page Family* (1965); H. J. Eckenrode, *Revolution in Virginia* (1916); and E. G. Swem, *Virginia Historical Index* (1965), II.

ARNOLD A. SHERMAN
Virginia Polytechnic Institute and State University

NEUSE RIVER is a 300-mile stream located entirely within North Carolina. It starts as the Flat River, 500 feet above sea level in the PIEDMONT near Roxboro. Just north of Durham, the Eno and Flat rivers join to form the Neuse, which then flows southeast through the fall zone between Raleigh and Goldsboro. A general eastern flow through the upper coastal plain past Kinston, the head of navigation, brings it to New Bern, where it is joined by the Trent River. From there the Neuse becomes a five-mile-wide estuary extending 35 miles before discharging into the Pamlico Sound. German and Swiss pioneers began to settle near the mouth of the Neuse River by 1703. New Bern was founded in 1710, and as settlers moved upstream other colonial towns developed at Ft. Barnwell near Kinston and at Hillsboro near

Durham. SHERMAN'S MARCH of 1865 crossed the Neuse at Goldsboro, and battles were staged at BENTONVILLE and Kinston. The Caswell Memorial and Confederate gunboat *Neuse* at Kinston are current reminders of the Civil War.

See J. Clay, *North Carolina Atlas* (1975); and U.S. Army Corps of Engineers, *Neuse River Basin* (1965).

H. DANIEL STILLWELL
Appalachian State University

NEW BERN, N.C. (pop. 14,660), is situated at the confluence of the Neuse and Trent rivers, approximately 30 miles west of Pamlico Sound. Laid out in 1710 by Baron Christopher de Graffenried as a colony for persecuted German MORAVIANS, it was named after the capital of de Graffenried's native Switzerland. Many of the original settlers either were killed during an attack by the TUSCARORA INDIANS or fled soon after, but the town survived and English colonists soon became dominant. The town was the site of meetings of the colonial assembly from 1745 to 1761 and the official residence of royal governors from 1770 to 1774. Although it lost a chance of becoming a permanent seat of government during the American Revolution, the town became during the antebellum period an important shipbuilding center. Confederate authorities fortified New Bern and used the port as a center for BLOCKADE-RUNNING until the city fell to General Ambrose BURNSIDE'S NORTH CAROLINA EXPEDITION in 1862. Its importance as a port and as a shipbuilding center declined after the war. In addition to some commercial fishing, the production of wood veneer, fertilizer, and dairy products provides the basis for the modern city's economic support. Among the surviving colonial buildings is Tryon Palace (1767–1770).

See M. Basinger, *Gateway to New Bern* (1960), pamphlet; A. T. Dill, *Governor Tryon and His Palace* (1955); J. Kittinger, *Diary, 1861–1865* (1963); and files of New Bern *Sun-Journal* (1876–).

NEW DEAL. In 1938 Franklin D. Roosevelt announced that the South was the nation's number one economic problem. That remark may have exaggerated conditions, but the South had unquestionably been hard hit by the GREAT DEPRESSION. The depression also had the indirect effect of giving southerners more influence on the national scene than they had had since the First World War. While governor of New York, Roosevelt, with his eyes on the presidency, developed strong political ties in the South. Southerners as diverse as CORDELL HULL, HUEY LONG, and CARTER GLASS turned toward FDR; and, in the Democratic convention in 1932, southerners and westerners combined to give JOHN NANCE GARNER of Texas the vice-presidential nomination and Roosevelt the nomination for president.

Roosevelt and congressional Democrats won overwhelmingly. Except for Speaker of the House Henry T. Rainey (Illinois), congressional leaders were southern. When Rainey died in 1935, Joseph W. Byrns of Tennessee became Speaker, and William B. Bankhead of Alabama (BANKHEAD FAMILY) moved into Byrns's place as majority leader. In the Senate, J. T. ROBINSON of Arkansas served as majority leader until his death in 1937, when ALBEN BARKLEY of Kentucky replaced him. Southerners held nine of 14 important committee chairmanships in the Senate and 12 of 17 in the House. Roosevelt, however, appointed only three southerners to his original cabinet: Hull of Tennessee as secretary of state; CLAUDE SWANSON of Virginia as secretary of the navy; and Daniel C. Roper of South Carolina as secretary of commerce.

The grimmest problem of the 1930s was that of the unemployed. The New Deal's first relief agency, the FEDERAL EMERGENCY RELIEF ADMINISTRATION, provided grants to states, which helped more than 4 million unemployed in the South in 1933. A winter crisis in 1933–1934 led to the creation of the Civil Works Administration and provided work administered by the federal government again through local agencies. The WORKS PROGRESS ADMINISTRATION (1935) tried to institutionalize work relief suitable for individual skills; thus resulted not only construction projects but also state guidebooks, slave narratives, and art, music, and drama programs. The CIVILIAN CONSERVATION CORPS established more than 100 camps in the South for unemployed youth. Although these projects had idealistic goals, they were modified by regional realities. Pressures from southerners, for example, resulted in lower wage scales in that region and in distinctions between blacks and whites.

Although southerners complained that northern cities were favored with relief funds, New Deal defenders claimed that the South and West were compensated by farm programs. The Agricultural Adjustment Act (1933), for example, aimed at increasing prices of crops (including southern-grown cotton, rice, and tobacco and later sugar, peanuts, and cattle) by restricting production. At first restriction was voluntary, but compulsory features

were added with the Bankhead Cotton Control and Kerr-Smith Tobacco Controls acts (1934). In 1936 the U.S. Supreme Court declared the processing tax that financed the first AAA unconstitutional. Within a few months, the Soil Conservation and Domestic Allotment Act was passed, which provided payments from general tax revenues to farmers using soil conservation practices. Although this legislation reduced soil erosion, it did not prevent surpluses. Thus MARVIN JONES of Texas, chairman of the House Committee on Agriculture, and John Bankhead of Alabama designed the second AGRICULTURAL ADJUSTMENT ADMINISTRATION (1938).

Although the agricultural program was the New Deal's most important action to promote recovery in the South, the National Industrial Recovery Act (1933) also was significant. It provided for the PUBLIC WORKS ADMINISTRATION and the NATIONAL RECOVERY ADMINISTRATION. The PWA was designed to revive the construction industry. Between 1933 and 1938, it spent in the South over half a billion dollars of the total of $2.1 billion allocated for nonfederal projects. Twenty-one of 57 slum clearance projects, for example, were in the South. At first, southern industrialists supported the NRA, which established industrial codes to regulate production, prices, and wages and, in Section 7a of the act, required collective bargaining. Opposition to federal regulation, led by such southern senators as Glass (Virginia) and JOSIAH BAILEY (North Carolina), however, soon found support among southern industrialists who advocated growth rather than the stability that was the keynote of NRA. When the Supreme Court declared the NRA unconstitutional in 1935, it appeared to have failed. In the TEXTILE INDUSTRY, however, the work week was shorter, wages were higher, and CHILD LABOR was abolished. In COAL MINING the NRA, reinforced by the Guffey-Snyder Coal Conservation Act (1935) and the Guffey-Vinson Coal Conservation Act (1937), had reduced hours and abolished child labor. Section 7a, furthermore, led to temporary LABOR UNION victories in southern coal mines, steel mills, tobacco plants, and oil fields, but unionization failed in textiles.

Of the agencies of the early New Deal, perhaps the most controversial was the TENNESSEE VALLEY AUTHORITY, designed to rehabilitate the Tennessee River's drainage basin, much of it poverty-stricken areas of seven southern states. Under the TVA the Tennessee became navigable, flood damage was reduced, electricity cost less, and living standards rose. Yet conflict developed within the agency over goals, and the sale of public power irritated private utilities. The internal conflict resulted in a deemphasis of regional planning, but the Supreme Court supported the agency against the private utilities, and private electrical appliance companies profited from sales to users of public power.

Conflicts developed within almost every program of the New Deal, and usually the best-organized interests won. In the farm program, for example, the larger farm owners, usually members of the AMERICAN FARM BUREAU FEDERATION, molded a program that almost ignored tenants, sharecroppers, and migrants, who lacked the power to protect their rights. An attempt to develop that power was the organization of the SOUTHERN TENANT FARMERS' UNION in 1934. The STFU was at first so successful in organizing blacks and whites that it led to violence in Arkansas and Oklahoma. The publicity resulting from this violence, reinforced by economic and sociological studies and the fiction of ERSKINE CALDWELL and John Steinbeck, led to some palliative measures.

Actually rural poverty had not been ignored in the early New Deal. The NIRA and the FERA had financed subsistence homesteads, rural communities, and relief projects. The RESETTLEMENT ADMINISTRATION (1935) established 99 rural communities, 61 in the South, and provided loans and grants to resettle farmers. The most important attempt to help the poorer farmers was the Bankhead-Jones Farm Tenancy Act (1937). Inspired by a presidential committee on farm tenancy, it was a compromise forced by the agricultural establishment and southerners in Congress. Although inadequate, it provided loans, grants, and services to small farmers, tenants, and migratory workers. More than half the loans went to southerners for rehabilitation or purchases of farms. At the same time, the RURAL ELECTRIFICATION ADMINISTRATION provided loans to cooperatives, which helped increase the percentage of rural dwelling units with electricity from 12.6 to 35 between 1935 and 1941.

An element of the agrarian heritage was hostility to unionism, and the New South's effort to escape that heritage generated a belief that cheap and unorganized labor offered the most effective lure for new industry. These beliefs help explain opposition in the South to the New Deal's labor program. This program, after the NIRA, consisted primarily of three enactments: the National Labor Relations Act (1935), which authorized the NATIONAL LABOR RELATIONS BOARD to protect labor against "unfair labor practices"; the Social Secu-rity Act (1935), which among other things encouraged states to set up unemployment insurance programs and provided grants-in-aid for welfare programs; and the Fair Labor Standards Act (1938), which regulated wages and hours and outlawed child labor in interstate commerce.

Almost every facet of the New Deal in the South was touched by the issue of race. The implementation of most of the acts responded to local prejudices, and blacks usually found discrimination in pay, promotion, and hiring practices. CCC camps were segregated, and some local administrators had to be ordered to enroll blacks. The TVA likewise posed restrictions on where blacks could live and work. An unusual number of LYNCHINGS in the 1930s, moreover, led to a renewed demand for a federal antilynching law. The House passed such a measure, but southern senators filibustered it to death. In spite of urging from the NAACP, Eleanor Roosevelt, and others, the president never pressed for passage. He condemned lynching, indicated that the bill should come to a vote, but refused more active support lest southern committee chairmen "block every bill I ask congress to pass to keep America from collapsing." Black people, however, received support from the federal courts. Indeed, decisions in cases brought by the NAACP laid the groundwork for undermining the WHITE PRIMARY and the separate but equal principle (SEGREGATION) and for providing equitable treatment for minorities in courts.

Critics on both right and left have faulted the New Deal. The right decried increasing expenditures and centralization of government. The left called for a new social order or, through Huey Long, for a program to "share the wealth." In more recent years, the New Left criticized the insensitivity to blacks and poor farmers, claimed that regulatory agencies favored the businesses to be regulated, and complained that little redistribution of wealth occurred. Defenders of the New Deal argue that, in spite of discrimination against blacks, the New Deal relieved their economic plight; that the complex farm problem was attacked with unprecedented success; that the regulatory measures were compromises and the alternative of no regulation was unacceptable; and that the New Deal was supported at the polls.

The key to the compromising of the New Deal was the southern leadership in Congress. Roosevelt had long hoped to forge a new party consisting of the "progressive" elements of the old parties. In the elections of 1938, he vainly attempted to purge several congressmen, including Senators

WALTER GEORGE of Georgia, MILLARD TYDINGS of Maryland, and E. D. SMITH of South Carolina, whom he considered hostile to his liberal goals. These attempts, coming after an effort to reconstitute the Supreme Court in 1937, brought reinforcements to conservative southern Democrats such as Smith, Glass, Bailey, and HARRY BYRD. Even JAMES BYRNES, hitherto a reliable New Dealer, began to feel that the New Deal had gone far enough. Although opposition to the New Deal was probably more consistently rural than southern, J. T. Patterson has found that "southern Democrats composed the chief Democratic opposition to the New Deal in the House" and that "most Senate Democratic conservatives came from the South and West." Yet pragmatic southerners such as Byrnes of South Carolina, SAM RAYBURN of Texas, and LISTER HILL and the Bankheads of Alabama were essential ingredients in the earlier coalition that had forged the New Deal.

See G. B. Tindall, *Emergence of New South* (1967), most useful; J. T. Patterson, *Congressional Conservatism and New Deal* (1967); T. Saloutos, *Journal of American History* (Sept., 1974); S. Baldwin, *Poverty and Politics* (1968); D. E. Conrad, *Forgotten Farmers* (1965); D. H. Grubbs, *Cry from Cotton* (1971); R. Wolters, *Negroes and Great Depression* (1970); F. Freidel, *FDR and South* (1965); P. K. Conkin, *New Deal* (1967); J. S. Auerbach, *Journal of Southern History* (Feb., 1969); T. S. Morgan, *North Carolina Historical Review* (July, 1975); and P. E. Mertz, *New Deal Policy and Southern Rural Poverty* (1978).

RICHARD L. WATSON, JR.
Duke University

NEW HOPE CHURCH, BATTLE OF (May 25, 27, 1864), was part of the ATLANTA CAMPAIGN. New Hope Church, near Dallas, Ga., was the center of the Union attack on the twenty-fifth. The clash occurred when W. T. Sherman, realizing J. E. JOHNSTON's Confederate position at Allatoona Pass was unassailable, shifted his attack westward. Johnston discovered the movement and hurried his men into position to block. On May 25, Union troops (J. W. Geary's division of Joseph Hooker's XX Corps) assaulted J. B. HOOD's corps only to be repulsed by concentrated infantry and artillery fire at a spot dubbed Hell Hole by federals. Next day Sherman reinforced Hooker with units from the IV and XIV corps. On the twenty-seventh those reinforcements struck P. R. CLEBURNE's division of W. J. HARDEE's corps. When that attack failed, Cleburne counterattacked, forcing a withdrawal. Failing to flank Johnston at Dallas, Sherman swung eastward again. Johnston followed, still determined to save Atlanta by de-

fensive maneuvers that would force the superior enemy to attack on terms favorable to the Confederates.

See L. Lewis, *Sherman* (1932); G. E. Govan and J. W. Livingood, *Different Valor* (1956); W. T. Sherman, *Memoirs* (1957); J. E. Johnston, *Narrative* (1959); and *Official Records, Armies*, Ser. 1, Vol. XXXVIII, Pt. 3.

JAMES P. JONES
Florida State University

NEW IBERIA, LA. (pop. 30,147), is one of the major producers of petroleum in the state and a major sugar market for the BAYOU TECHE area. Located approximately 50 miles southwest of Baton Rouge, the area was settled by both French and Spanish colonists in the middle of the eighteenth century. After experimenting with flax and cattle raising, they turned to the cultivation of sugarcane. The town was laid out in 1835 by Frederick W. Dupérier, a local planter, and incorporated four years later as Iberia. It was occupied by federal troops during the RED RIVER CAMPAIGN and was renamed New Iberia in 1868. The city continues to be a shipping point for area rice and sugar and also for seafood, salt, petroleum, and lumber.

See H. L. Griffin, *Attakapas Country* (1975); H. T. Kane, *Bayous of Louisiana* (1944), popular; W. H. Perrin, *Southwest Louisiana* (1891, 1971); and D. J. LeBlanc, *Acadian Miracle* (1966). See also *Attakapas Gazette* (1966–), published by Attakapas Historical Association, and files of *Iberian* (1895–).

NEW MADRID AND ISLAND NO. 10, CAPTURE OF (March 3–April 8, 1862). Early March, 1862, found Confederate forces at New Madrid, Mo., and Island No. 10 preparing to defend an inverted S bend in the Mississippi River. Federal General John Pope with 18,000 soldiers invested New Madrid on March 3. During the 11-day siege, Pope repulsed a sortie by General M. Jeff Thompson and brought heavy artillery to bear. After Commodore George Hollins' Confederate gunboats withdrew, steamers evacuated the garrison upriver to Island No. 10. On March 15, the federal flotilla, under Flag Officer Andrew H. Foote, arrived above the island's defenses commanded by General William W. Mackall. Two of Foote's gunboats ran past the island at night and on April 7 silenced the Confederate batteries along the Tennessee shore below New Madrid. Pope's army then crossed the river and severed the land communications to Island No. 10. The resulting surrender cost the South 6,000 prisoners, many mu-

nitions, and control of the Mississippi down to Ft. Pillow, Tenn.

See J. C. Mullen, *Missouri Historical Review* (April, 1965); K. P. Williams, *Lincoln Finds a General* (1952), III; J. D. Milligan, *Gunboats* (1965); R. U. Johnson and C. C. Buel (eds.), *Battles and Leaders* (1887), I; *Official Records, Armies,* Ser. 1, Vol. VIII; and *Official Records, Navies,* Ser. 1, Vol. XXII.

JOHN D. MILLIGAN
State University of New York, Buffalo

NEW MARKET, BATTLE OF (May 15, 1864).

In order to protect his flank and in turn to threaten R. E. Lee's, U. S. Grant ordered a Union attack up the Shenandoah Valley. Franz Sigel commanded the federal forces. Facing him were 4,500 soldiers under JOHN C. BRECKINRIDGE. Procrastination and confusion marked the 6,000-man advance, which was further weakened by Confederate cavalry raids on its communications. Near New Market, Va., the armies met on a cold, wet day. After Breckinridge's assault, Sigel withdrew to Bushong Hill, where he spread his defenses too thinly. At this point, he counterattacked with his cavalry under the sluggish Julius Stahel. The charge was halted by Confederate artillery. Another Confederate assault then carried the day. The battle is often remembered because of the presence of cadets from the Virginia Military Institute.

See W. C. Davis, *Battle of New Market* (1975), standard; E. R. Turner, *New Market Campaign* (1912), good account; J. W. Wayland, *Battle of New Market* (1926), brief; J. S. Wise, *Battle of New Market* (1882), reminiscence; W. Couper, *V.M.I. New Market Cadets* (1933), biographical sketches; and B. Stanard, *Letters of New Market Cadet* (1961), poignant letters from boy killed in battle.

JAMES W. POHL
Southwest Texas State University

NEW MEXICO AND ARIZONA OPERATIONS (1861–1862).

In late 1861 a force of Texas mounted volunteers, consisting of the 4th, 5th, and 7th regiments, led by Brigadier General HENRY HOPKINS SIBLEY, moved westward from San Antonio with the objective of conquering "New Mexico," which territory then included Arizona and part of Nevada. Sibley's orders were to drive out the federals and establish a military government in the territory. In advance of Sibley, Colonel JOHN R. BAYLOR on August 1, 1861, created the Confederate territory of Arizona from the southern part of New Mexico. Confident that Confederates would soon be welcomed as liberators in New Mexico, Sibley occupied El Paso in mid-December. With his Army of New Mexico now proclaimed, he moved up the Rio Grande, defeating a federal force of 3,800 under Colonel E. R. S. Canby at Val Verde on February 21, 1862. Meanwhile, Baylor had directed the occupation of Tucson by Captain Sherod Hunter's Arizona Volunteers. After taking Albuquerque and Santa Fe, Sibley's forces met disaster on March 26 and 28, 1862, at Glorieta Pass, where their supply train was destroyed. With a remnant of his brigade, Sibley returned to San Antonio in the summer of 1862. An early Confederate dream had been shattered.

See, for best accounts, T. Noel, *Campaign from Santa Fe to Mississippi,* ed. M. H. Hall and E. A. Davis (1961); and M. H. Hall, *Sibley's New Mexico Campaign* (1960). For convenient compilations of sources, see C. T. Horn and W. S. Wallace, *Confederate Victories in Southwest* and *Union Operations in Southwest* (1961). Other accounts include R. C. Colton, *Civil War in Western Territories* (1959); R. L. Kerby, *Confederate Invasion of New Mexico and Arizona, 1861–1862* (1958); A. Hunt, *Army of Pacific* (1951); and W. C. Whitford, *Colorado Volunteers* (1906, 1971).

JAMES L. NICHOLS
Stephen F. Austin State University

NEW NATION, HISTORIOGRAPHY OF THE SOUTH AND THE.

There are no general works dealing exclusively and precisely with the history of the South from the end of the REVOLUTION to the MISSOURI COMPROMISE (1781–1820). For an overall view, the best places to begin are the relevant chapters in C. Eaton, *A History of the Old South* (1975); and F. B. Simkins and C. P. Roland, *History of the Old South* (1972). These volumes are well balanced and both had up-to-date bibliographies when they went to press. For more extended general treatment, the following volumes in the series entitled *A History of the South,* edited by W. H. Stephenson and E. M. Coulter, are relevant: J. R. Alden, *The South in the Revolution, 1763–1789* (1957); T. P. Abernethy, *The South in the New Nation, 1789–1819* (1961); and C. S. Sydnor, *The Development of Southern Sectionalism, 1819–1848* (1948). In his book on the South in the Revolution and even more explicitly in *The First South* (1961), JOHN ALDEN argued that a distinctive region with particular interests appeared as early as 1775. THOMAS ABERNETHY, on the other hand, maintained that a well-defined sectional consciousness did not evolve until the debates over the Missouri Compromise. The earlier struggles were not concerned with the defense of institutions peculiarly southern. Abernethy devotes the major part of his volume to such topics as the acquisition of West Florida (WEST FLORIDA

CONTROVERSY) and the western part of the South, the YAZOO LAND FRAUDS, the WILLIAM BLOUNT conspiracy, the BURR CONSPIRACY, the intrigues of JAMES WILKINSON, and the battle of NEW ORLEANS. Neglecting internal developments of the Atlantic states and slighting social and economic developments, Abernethy in the preface to his volume expressed the hope that these deficiencies would be compensated by Sydnor's volume. Part of what Sydnor says on social and economic developments by implication applies to an earlier period, but of course he did not and could not cover the period that the editors assigned to Abernethy.

Since the publication of the volumes in *A History of the South*, there have been major contributions of cultural, social, and political history. In *Intellectual Life in Jefferson's Virginia, 1790–1830* (1964), R. B. Davis deals with science, fine arts, law, and literature of the period. The origins and structure of the party system have been traced by N. Cunningham in *The Jeffersonian Republicans, 1789–1801* (1957) and *The Jeffersonian Republicans in Power, 1801–1809* (1963), and the conservative branch of the party has been examined by N. Risjord in *The Old Republicans* (1965). The southern Federalists have been treated in L. Rose's *Prologue to Democracy* (1968).

Since the 1960s, slavery and civil rights have received increasing attention. In *Slavery and Jeffersonian Virginia* (1964), R. McColley maintained that, contrary to assumptions often made, neither slavery nor the plantation system was dying in the South; as president, Thomas Jefferson did little toward limiting or abolishing slavery; agrarian philosophy, which had deep roots in southern thought of the period, favored the plantation and slavery; and Jefferson, along with most of his colleagues, believed that blacks were in some respects inferior to whites. W. D. Jordan in *White over Black* (1968) discusses not only general attitudes but Jefferson's personal dilemma; and the problem of race relations is placed in a broad historical perspective by D. B. Davis, *Slavery in the Age of Revolution* (1975). In *Jefferson and Civil Liberties: The Darker Side* (1963), L. Levy draws a bill of particulars against Jefferson's reputation as the archliberal in the field of civil rights.

Perhaps the area in which there has been the most satisfying progress in the last decade is biography and the publication of the writings of both prominent and lesser figures. Four of the five presidents during the period were southerners, and there are now good, up-to-date biographies of all of them. There are also projects that promise scholarly editions of the works of George Washington, Jefferson, James Madison, and John Marshall, as well as other important southerners. Specific citations to many of these works can be found in the references listed below.

See M. D. Peterson, *Jefferson Image in American Mind* (1960), best historiographical treatment of central figure of period; H. L. Coles, *Indiana Historical Society Lectures* (1969–70); A. S. Link and R. W. Patrick (eds.), *Writing Southern History* (1965); and W. H. Cartwright and R. L. Watson, Jr. (eds.), *Interpreting and Teaching American History* (1961) and *Reinterpretation of American History and Culture* (1973).

HARRY L. COLES
Ohio State University

NEW ORLEANS, BATTLE OF (January 8, 1815), was the most important military engagement in the South during the WAR OF 1812. British strategists, hoping to capture New Orleans in order to control the trans-Appalachian region, sent an army of 9,000 to the Mississippi delta in December, 1814. While these troops encamped on a small plain a few miles downriver from New Orleans, General ANDREW JACKSON gathered a force of 5,000 to defend the city. After several inconclusive battles between December 23 and January 1, General Edward Pakenham ordered a full attack against the American lines on January 8. Securely placed behind a canal and mud wall reaching from the east bank of the Mississippi to a cypress swamp, Jackson's army easily repulsed the British with artillery and small arms fire. After only half an hour, the British withdrew, leaving more than 2,000 casualties, including their three ranking generals, on the field. Jackson's victory helped to ensure British ratification of the peace treaty concluded at Ghent on December 24. By obscuring earlier American military failures, the victory at New Orleans also contributed to a rising spirit of nationalism. The victorious general became a heroic symbol of that spirit.

See R. Horsman, *War of 1812* (1969), concise, based on original sources; W. S. Brown, *Amphibious Campaign for West Florida and Louisiana* (1969), thorough; H. L. Coles, *War of 1812* (1965), brief and reliable; and C. I. A. Ritchie, *Louisiana Historical Quarterly* (Jan.–April, 1961).

MYRON F. WEHTJE
Atlantic Union College

NEW ORLEANS, BATTLE OF (April 18–29, 1862). New Orleans' Confederate defenders, under Mansfield Lovell, relied on poorly armed Fts. Jackson and St. Philip—located on opposite banks just above the Mississippi River's mouth, plus a heavy chain strung between them and a small Confederate naval force—to ward off any attack by sea. Aided by Commander D. D. Porter and a fleet of 44 vessels, Admiral D. G. FARRAGUT began shelling the forts on April 18. The five-day bombardment caused considerable damage, but the defenders did not surrender. Porter would have withdrawn; but Farragut ordered the fleet to proceed under cover of darkness on April 24. That night high winds enabled him to break the chain defense and pass the forts. Although three Union vessels were lost in the operation, Confederate naval opposition proved unavailing. At 1 P.M. on April 25, Farragut arrived before New Orleans, where high waters before the levee gave his battleships a commanding artillery advantage. Although Mayor John T. Monroe answered Farragut's demand for his surrender with the technical objection that the city was under military command and not his to surrender—and despite the hostility of civilian crowds—a federal party raised the United States flag over the mint on April 26. Three days later Farragut ordered marines to occupy the city. This was accomplished in a sullen atmosphere but without other resistance. The troops of General B. F. Butler completed the capture when they marched ashore on May 1.

See C. L. Dufour, *Night War Was Lost* (1960), most detailed account; J. D. Winters, *Civil War in Louisiana* (1963); and H. A. Trexler, *Southwest Review* (1933).

ELISABETH J. DOYLE
St. John's University, Jamaica, N.Y.

NEW ORLEANS, LA. (pop. 592,700), was founded in 1718 on the east bank of the Mississippi River approximately 110 miles from the Gulf of Mexico. It was named for Philippe, duc d'Orléans and regent of France, by BIENVILLE, governor of Louisiana. The first town plan was shaped like a parallelogram and encompassed 66 squares (the Vieux Carré). Envisioning the settlement as a port of deposit for upriver goods, Bienville persuaded the colonial proprietors to move the capital of Louisiana to New Orleans in 1722. In 1731 Louisiana reverted to the French crown. In the next 30 years New Orleans' main exports were INDIGO and TOBACCO, but these cargoes were more bulky than profitable. In 1763 France ceded New Orleans and Louisiana west of the Mississippi to Spain in the Treaty of Paris, and the change of allegiance did not please many Louisianians. New Orleans was the scene of revolution in 1768. The following year five of the rebel leaders were executed and five others shipped to prison in Havana. Although Spanish rule began with these harsh

measures, it proved benign and economically profitable. Trade between New Orleans and Spanish Caribbean ports existed on a regular basis, and illicit trade with the English colonies flourished. City architecture was deeply influenced by Spanish colonial styles, and the intermingling of French and Spanish cultures in New Orleans gave rise to the word *creole*.

Following secret negotiations in 1800 to regain Louisiana from Spain, Napoleon decided to sell it to the United States in 1803. During the War of 1812, Andrew Jackson's army saved the recently acquired city from capture by the British (NEW ORLEANS, BATTLE OF), and New Orleans then entered a golden age as the port of destiny that Bienville had envisioned. New inhabitants from other areas of the nation and from Europe swelled the city's population from 8,000 in 1803 to 116,375 by 1850. The first steamboat to reach New Orleans in 1812 was named for the city. By the 1840s over 400 steamboats were berthed along the city levees. COTTON was the major export.

In physical growth the city had grown out of its original parallelogram. Across Canal Street from the Vieux Carré lay the "American section." By the end of the nineteenth century, numerous other suburbs (called *faubourgs*) were laid out adjacent to the older neighborhoods and on the west bank of the Mississippi. With rapid physical growth came serious sanitary and health problems—faulty drainage, lack of sewerage, and cistern drinking water that was often contaminated. Sporadic outbreaks of cholera and YELLOW FEVER resulted.

New Orleans was captured by Union forces early in the Civil War (NEW ORLEANS, BATTLE OF). The era of Reconstruction in New Orleans, spanning the late 1860s and lasting until 1877, was a time of racial tension, political maneuvering, tremendous municipal indebtedness, and heightened lawlessness. Economic growth and civil rights for blacks regressed in the late nineteenth century. But the city did see some cultural achievements. Major epidemics were eradicated by the early 1900s as quarantine methods and mosquito control programs were adopted. MARDI GRAS became a major holiday with the creation of the Rex parade, and Dixieland JAZZ was born in the musical milieu of late nineteenth-century New Orleans.

By the early 1900s, railroads had drained away much river cargo, and steamboats disappeared. Their place was taken after World War I by towboats and barges capable of carrying cargo equal to that carried by train, but at a cheaper price (INTRACOASTAL WATERWAY). Following World War II, New Orleans was recognized as the second port (HARBORS) in the nation in exports. Patterns of SEGREGATION, which had been rigid since the 1890s, began to be reversed in the 1950s with the integration of public schools. In physical improvements the city has seen extensive changes including drainage, sewerage, and water purification systems, electricity and natural gas, and two bridges spanning the Mississippi River. The port and its allied industries remain the major sources of wealth. But TOURISM is a vital economic factor in the city's economy.

See H. Rightor (ed.), *Standard History* (1900); J. G. Clark, *New Orleans, 1718–1812* (1970); R. C. Reinders, *End of Era* (1964); G. M. Capers, *Occupied City* (1965); and J. J. Jackson, *New Orleans* (1969).

JOY J. JACKSON
Southeastern Louisiana University

NEW ORLEANS BEE, founded in 1827 as *Abeille de la Nouvelle Orleans,* had as its first editor Baron René de Perdreauville, a former page to Marie Antoinette. Printed both in French and in English (and sometimes in Spanish), the *Bee* was a WHIG PARTY paper reflecting many of the views of the French-speaking business community of the New Orleans area. A moderately nationalist daily, it supported JOHN BELL in the election of 1860 and accepted the fact of secession with considerable reluctance. Plagued by declining revenues and a diminishing readership after the war, the *Bee* was forced to discontinue its English edition in 1873. It continued as a French newspaper until 1923.

See bound volumes at Louisiana State Museum (1827–1917), Library of Congress (1836–1902), and New Orleans City Archives (1830–88); and microfilm from Bell & Howell (1827–1923).

NEW ORLEANS CRESCENT was published under slightly varying titles between 1848 and 1869 except during the period of May, 1862, to October, 1865. Originally a Whig party press, the *Crescent* was critical of secessionist talk during the 1850s and hoped to stem the drift toward disunion by backing Stephen A. Douglas in the election of 1860.

See bound assorted copies at New Orleans City Archives (1849–69) and Library of Congress (1850–67).

NEW ORLEANS RIOT (July 30, 1866) occurred after local Radical leaders, alarmed by the neo-Confederate nature of Louisiana government, attempted to reconvene the 1864 constitutional convention to enact Negro suffrage and to disfranchise former rebels. White New Orleanians, an-

gered by the dubious legality of the maneuver, were incited even more by the harangues of Democratic officials and wild rumors spread by the city press. When Negroes parading to celebrate the reconvening were set upon by whites, a distraught marcher fired a shot that set off a massacre. City police and armed civilians (mainly teenagers and former Confederates) began shooting at every Negro in sight. Many blacks sought refuge in Mechanics' Institute, the convention hall, where they were hunted down by the mob. Thirty-eight were killed (34 Negroes, three white Radicals, and a rioter shot accidentally), and 146 were injured. The massacre outraged national Republican leaders and the northern public. A congressional investigation and campaigning Radicals kept the issue alive until November. Then northern voters elected the overwhelmingly Republican Fortieth Congress, which made Negro suffrage, the very phenomenon the New Orleans mob had sought to prevent, the law of the land.

See D. E. Reynolds, *Louisiana History* (Winter, 1964); and J. G. Taylor, *Louisiana Reconstructed, 1863–1877* (1974).

ROGER A. FISCHER
University of Minnesota, Duluth

NEW ORLEANS STATES-ITEM was formed in 1958 by the purchase of the *Daily Item* and its merger with the *States* by the Times-Picayune Publishing Company. The *Daily City Item* had been founded in 1877 as a Democratic afternoon paper devoted primarily to local news. The *States,* established three years later, was founded by Henry J. Hearsey to attack the LOUISIANA STATE LOTTERY after Major E. A. BURKE had maneuvered him out of his earlier post as editor of the *Democrat.* Hearsey's colorful invective and strong opinions made the *States* one of the most often quoted papers in the state during the late nineteenth century. In addition to his opposition to the lottery, Hearsey reveled in recalling the glories of the Old South and the LOST CAUSE. A thoroughly unreconstructed rebel, he advocated rigid states' rights positions and defended (and on one occasion instigated) LYNCHING as a means of controlling unruly blacks and Italians.

During the first half of the twentieth century, competition between the two dailies was both intense and politically significant. The *Item,* which had urged neutrality during World War I, was accused by the editor of the *States* of being in the pay of German spies. At the advent of the HUEY LONG era during the 1920s, the *States* was one of the Kingfish's few early supporters while the *Item* was one of his bitterest foes. In 1931, however, the *Item* switched positions and allied itself with the LONG MACHINE. The *States*, on the other hand, grew increasingly hostile toward the Longs after it was purchased by the publishers of the *Times-Picayune*. In the years after World War II, the once prosperous *Item* found competition with the *States* for limited advertising revenue more and more difficult. It lodged and carried an antitrust suit against the *Times-Picayune* and the *States* all the way to the U.S. Supreme Court. After losing its suit, the *Item* was itself purchased by the Times-Picayune Publishing Company and merged in 1958 with the *States* to form a single afternoon paper, the *States-Item*, with a daily circulation in excess of 120,000 copies.

See J. Wilds, *Afternoon Story* (1976); bound copies of *Item* at Howard Memorial Library, New Orleans (1879–97, 1900–), Louisiana Library Commission (1932–), and Library of Congress (1897–98, 1900–); and microfilm from Bell & Howell of *Item* (1911–58), *States* (1916–58), and *States-Item* (1959–).

NEW ORLEANS TIMES-PICAYUNE was formed in 1914 by the merger of the *Times-Democrat* (1881–1914) and the *Daily Picayune* (1837–1914). The latter paper had been named for a Spanish coin valued at six and one-half cents and was the first New Orleans publication sold for less than a dime. Critical of the emotional character of secessionist sentiment during the 1850s, the *Picayune* urged moderation and caution. It published population tables and industrial indices of northern and southern states after the election of Abraham Lincoln, warning that in the event of a war the South would be mismatched. Yet, after reporting detailed and reasonably objective accounts of the battle of New Orleans, it applauded the "patriotic" act of a group of citizens who tore the national flag from the pole of City Hall.

Although the *Picayune* had the largest circulation of the city's newspapers, it had growing competition from the *Times* (organized in 1863 by New Orleans Unionists) and the *Democrat* (formed in 1875 by John McEnery). An official organ of the state's Democratic party, the *Democrat* regularly criticized the LOUISIANA STATE LOTTERY until 1879, when Major E. A. BURKE—state treasurer and a backer of the lottery—acquired control of the paper to silence the criticism. The *Times* meanwhile had cast its lot with the Democratic party, and in 1881 it too was acquired by Burke to form the *Times-Democrat*. Thus, although the city's principal newspapers were Democratic in their political viewpoints, they competed for reve-

nues and expressed very different positions. The *Picayune* was extremely critical of the lottery and urged the breakup of large sugar plantations to achieve moderate agrarian reform. The *Times-Democrat*, on the other hand, strongly defended the lottery and represented a more conservative viewpoint on social and economic problems.

Competition between the two papers ended in 1914, when the two dailies were merged to form the *Times-Picayune*. An independent Democratic paper, it was hostile during the 1920s to both the KU KLUX KLAN and HUEY LONG. It currently has a circulation in excess of 200,000 copies daily.

See T. E. Dabney, *100 Great Years* (1944); F. Copeland, *Kendall of Picayune* (1943); and microfilm, from Bell & Howell (1837–) and Library of Congress (1886–).

NEW ORLEANS TRUE DELTA was a Democratic daily newspaper published between 1849 and 1866. Like much of the Crescent City's population, it was reluctant to embrace secession, and in the election of 1860 it supported Stephen A. Douglas in the hope of avoiding disunion.

See bound assorted copies at Library of Congress and Louisiana State University Library (1853–66) and at New Orleans City Archives (1849–66).

NEWPORT NEWS, VA. (pop. 138,177), site of one of the largest drydocks and shipbuilding yards in the world, is adjacent to Hampton and opposite Norfolk on HAMPTON ROADS. Although a small settlement had existed here since 1611, the community underwent little development until 1880, when it was chosen as the terminus of a rail line from Richmond. Wharves and warehouses quickly grew up around the railroad shops, and in 1886 the shipbuilding industry got under way. The city's importance as an ocean port has grown throughout the twentieth century, and its shipyards—after a short-term expansion during World War I—have been increasingly significant to the city's growth and prosperity since World War II. It ships tobacco, motor vehicles, lumber, wood pulp, grain, coal, chrome and manganese ore, petroleum, and general cargoes.

See P. Rouse, Jr., *Endless Harbor* (1969); A. L. Jester, *Newport News, 1607–1960* (1961); R. H. Chambers, *Hilton Village* (1967), planned community built by federal government; and files of *Times-Herald* (1900–), on microfilm.

NEW SOUTH is a term that never has been used with much precision. Since 1862 various spokesmen and visionaries ranging from corporation presidents to Communists have employed it to label their pet programs or to signify developments that they believe mark an abrupt change from the past. Thus the term variously defines one of several programs or movements, delimits different time periods, or denotes a set of proposals popular during a specific era.

Apparently first used in print by Union Captain Adam Badeau early in 1862, *New South* was the name of a military newspaper published for federal servicemen stationed at Port Royal, S.C. Not surprisingly, Badeau's vision of the "new" South and his use of the term did nothing to add it to the vocabularies of white southerners either during or after the Civil War. Yet the defeat of the Confederacy left countless southerners casting for an alternative vision of the postwar South to that of the Old South and the South of Reconstruction. Ironically, it was DE BOW'S REVIEW that took the lead in calling for a postwar South that would neither depend upon slavery nor retain the weaknesses that had proved fatal to the cause of secession. J. D. B. De Bow himself and contributors to his journal called for the INDUSTRIALIZATION of the South and for the diversification of AGRICULTURE to replace the staple crop economy of the Old South and KING COTTON.

Proposals similar to those offered in *De Bow's Review* circulated as common currency in the years after the war, yet not until 1870 did this increasingly popular vision of the postwar South gain an appropriate label. It was Edwin De Leon of South Carolina, in an article in *Putnam's*, who first used the slogan "New South." For De Leon and for FRANCIS W. DAWSON, Atticus Greene Haygood, WILLIAM D. KELLEY, HENRY WATTERSON, and in particular HENRY W. GRADY, the New South became an article of faith, a vision of the future, and a blueprint for the regeneration of the post–Civil War South.

Unquestionably, journalists and propagandists will continue in the future to discover the New South. Historians probably will wish to employ it to label a chronological period, while disagreeing as to whether the period begins in 1865, 1877, or 1900 and whether it ends in 1913 or simply with the present. The term is most commonly used, however, to identify the credo of southern journalists and of those political and business leaders who adhered to and worked for implementation of economic proposals similar or identical to those put forth in *De Bow's Review*.

See P. M. Gaston, *New South Creed* (1970); R. D. Little, "Ideology of New South, 1865–1910" (Ph.D. disserta-tion, University of Chicago, 1950); and E. De Leon, *Putnam's* (April, 1870).

NEWSPAPERS. It is doubtful if anyone can be precise about the number of newspapers published in the South over the span of two and a half centuries. No doubt the cumulative number of papers in the region has run into the thousands, but many a journal scarcely survived its first few issues. Editing a purely local journal has required only limited talents, training, and capital, but it also has required some entrepreneurial capability to keep a newspaper solvent. The shifting sands of political fortunes and economic conditions account for the fairly good number of modern local and daily newspapers that bear hyphenated titles. In fact, most journals once depended upon political patronage for survival, and because of this they looked to Washington, the state capitals, and the county seats for support. Especially prior to 1865, the overwhelming majority of newspapers published in the South were purely political in nature, many of them blossoming and fading with the fortunes of individual politicians and splinter political movements.

Over the centuries a veritable army of able editors, and even lesser men, have left their marks on southern history. The first was William Nuthead, who published a religious journal at St. Mary's, Md., in 1689. This tender flower bloomed and withered scarcely known and unmissed. The actual beginning of southern newspaper publication was the appearance in Annapolis of William Parks's MARYLAND GAZETTE in 1727. This was a semi-news-political journal of a purely colonial nature. In time Maryland became the home of several newspapers, including the Annapolis *Gazette* (1750) and the important Baltimore *Advertiser* (1773). William Hunter began publication of the Williamsburg (Va.) *Gazette* in 1751, and newspaper publication then filtered southward from Maryland and Virginia. In 1755 publication of the *North Carolina Magazine of Universal Intelligence* was begun at New Bern. Already Thomas Whitemarsh had published the *South Carolina Gazette* in Charleston in 1730. It was not until 1785, however, that the printing press crossed the Savannah River and John Erdman Smith brought the famous Augusta *Chronicle* into existence. By the end of the American Revolution, newspapers began to appear in almost all of the South. Organization of new territories and states, 1780 to 1820, attracted fairly good numbers of editors and printers to the new country. Across the Appalachians John and Fielding Bradford began publication of the *Kentucke Gazette* in 1787; the Knoxville *Gazette* made its appearance in eastern Tennessee in 1793; and, in the Mississippi Territory, the *Mississippi Gazette* was first published at Natchez in 1800.

A statistical profile of southern newspaper publication prior to 1860 reveals a fairly clear concept of the development and nature of the regional press. In 1828 there were in existence 148 papers, of which 39 appeared daily. A decade later, in 1840, there were 35 dailies and 270 weeklies and semiweeklies. This number grew to 480 by 1850, of which 413 were weeklies. Reflective of the reach of the southern papers in the South in 1860 is the fact that annually there were printed 9,891,391 copies of all papers. This approximated one copy per capita per year. In the two decades of Civil War and Reconstruction, the number of weekly papers had grown to 1,500, and there were 317 dailies. By 1960 there were 435 southern daily papers with widely varying circulation.

Between the establishment of the AUGUSTA CHRONICLE in 1785 and the appearance of the ATLANTA JOURNAL in 1903, there came into existence two-score southern daily papers of major status. Many of these represented fairly long histories of mergers and absorptions. Among the rising number of dailies were the Augusta *Chronicle*, the RICHMOND TIMES-DISPATCH, the LOUISVILLE COURIER-JOURNAL, the ATLANTA CONSTITUTION, the CHATTANOOGA DAILY TIMES, the CHARLESTON NEWS AND COURIER, the CHARLOTTE OBSERVER, the MEMPHIS COMMERCIAL APPEAL, the New Orleans *Times*, and the DALLAS NEWS. Beginning with the fiery uncompromising Dennis Driscoll of the Augusta *Chronicle* into the present, the southern editors have expressed strong views. Among these was A. S. Willington of the Charleston *News and Courier*, who in time was succeeded by a half-dozen men of fire and vigor. There were Thomas Ritchie of the Richmond *Enquirer*, John Hampden Pleasants of the RICHMOND WHIG, GEORGE D. PRENTICE of the Louisville *Journal*, and G. W. Kendall of the New Orleans *Picayune*. Antebellum editors seem to have adopted the idea that they spoke ex cathedra on most matters, and they were able to make themselves heard.

The antebellum tradition of strong editors was carried through the Civil War to the papers of the New South. Some of these were Captain FRANCIS W. DAWSON of the Charleston *News and Courier*, who conceived the South's destiny to be tied up with industry and the development of its human and natural resources. In Louisville HENRY WATTERSON was a fit successor to Prentice as editor of the newly merged *Courier-Journal*. HENRY GRADY made the term NEW SOUTH famous as editor for the Atlanta *Constitution*. In Memphis the Kentucky Irish Catholic C. P. J. Mooney made the *Commercial Appeal* a powerful voice in the mid-South, and in Raleigh JOSEPHUS DANIELS spoke for a large segment of southern democracy in the *News and Observer*. Major W. W. Screws of the MONTGOMERY ADVERTIZER was somewhat ambivalent in his views, but nevertheless a powerful editor. D. W. Tompkins and D. J. Caldwell continued Captain Dawson's fight to industrialize the modern South with their editorials in the Charlotte *Observer*, and in Richmond the erudite DOUGLAS SOUTHALL FREEMAN combined editorial writing with a distinguished career as a major biographer. Among the younger crusaders were Mark Etheridge of the Macon *Telegraph and News* and later of the Louisville *Courier-Journal*, George Fort Milton of the Chattanooga *News*, RALPH MCGILL of the Atlanta *Constitution*, VIRGINIUS DABNEY of the Richmond *Times-Dispatch*, JONATHAN DANIELS of the Raleigh *News and Observer*, and W. W. BALL of the Charleston *News and Courier*.

Throughout southern history the region's newspapers have been outspoken in all matters pertaining to public interests. Sometimes editors have written with an undue amount of anger and bias, but seldom if ever out of disloyalty to southern causes. In treating the subjects of LYNCHING, the CONVICT LEASE SYSTEM, and crime in general, they expressed genuine concern about regional moral aberrations but generally opposed federal intervention in these matters. Almost universally, the southern editors of weekly and daily papers supported development of natural resources and industrialization. Generally they were concerned about conditions that led to heavy migrations of southerners to more prosperous sections of the country. They lamented the southern farmer's dependence upon staple crops, and they cried out in righteous anger at the discriminatory credit and supply policies. They first opposed and then reluctantly supported woman suffrage, straddled the editorial fence on the KU KLUX KLAN issue, and were agitated about the POLL TAX, the wet and dry question, the HOOKWORM crusade, the anti-evolution controversy, the Spanish-American War, and dozens of other current questions. Aside from the strong vein of regional militancy that crept into much editorial writing and news reporting, there was on the whole an appreciable touch of literary quality about the southern newspapers. Editors like Henry W. Grady, Henry Watterson, GEORGE W. CABLE, JOEL CHANDLER HARRIS, Virginius Dabney, Jonathan Daniels, George Fort Milton, and Douglas Southall Freeman all established creditable literary reputations outside their editorial offices.

In the more commonplace area of newspaper publishing was the sprawling grass-roots empire of the country weekly, which collectively was read by more people at the basic levels of southern population than all the other published material put together. No matter how scarce news was in most localities, after 1870 it was possible to fill up two blank pages with legal notices, social notes, obituaries, weather reports, comments on crops, and correspondence from rural stringers or reporters. Two of the four pages could be purchased already printed from syndicates. This "patent" service was first offered to American country newspaper publishers by Ansel N. Kellogg of the Baraboo (Wis.) *Republic* in 1861. By 1890 the readyprint industry had become a substantial national business. Southerners either bought or were supplied practically free two printed and two blank pages. The readyprint was heavily weighted with advertising of all sorts, but principally that of proprietary or patent MEDICINE companies. The textual matter of these sheets consisted of literary selections, descriptions of natural curiosities, strange human physical and psychological phenomena, sermons, and selected editorials from the major regional dailies.

Not until after 1875, however, did any of these country weeklies become something more than a furious little mouthpiece of politicians and parties. After that date a relatively large number of the journals came to merit the designation newspaper. Among them were Sidney Lewis' Sparta (Ga.) *Ishmaelite*, W. H. Lawrence's Livingston (Ala.) *Our Southern Home*, T. Lary Gant's Oglethorpe (Ga.) *Echo*, W. P. Walton's Stanford (Ky.) *Interior Journal*, S. A. Jonas' Aberdeen (Miss.) *Examiner*, J. S. Hall's Fayetteville (N.C.) *Observer*, and Lewis M. Grist's Yorkville (S.C.) *Enquirer*. Nowhere is the average rural southerner's struggle with the social and economic realities of the times better revealed than in the files of the country journals.

On April 12, 1903, 30 representatives of the southern press met in the Piedmont Hotel in Atlanta and organized the Southern Newspaper Publishers Association. This new body was indirectly successor to the Southern Press Association, organized in 1880, and to the Southern Associated Press, organized in 1891. The new organization was created to deal with news transmission, the mechanics of printing and publishing, and all other matters concerning the production of news-

papers. Headquarters were established in Chattanooga with Walter Johnson as general manager. Among the concerns of the SNPA were the development of regionally based sources of newsprint (PULP AND PAPER INDUSTRY), the training of the technical personnel necessary to the production of a modern newspaper, and the encouragement of schools of journalism.

Reflected in the voluminous files of southern newspapers is the history of the day-to-day life of the South. Buried in the bound volumes are the tragedies, the failures, the victories, and the revolutionary changes that have occurred since William Parks first published the *Maryland Gazette* in 1727. No other historical source pieces together more than two centuries of southern history of human foibles, anxieties, heedlessness, and accomplishments in quite the same manner as do the collective efforts of the southern editors.

See F. W. Alsop, *History of Arkansas Press* (1922); T. H. Baker, *Memphis Commercial Appeal* (1971); E. L. Bell and K. C. Crabbe, *Augusta Chronicle* (1960); T. D. Clark, *Rural Press and New South* (1948) and *Southern Country Editor* (1948); J. Daniels, *Tar Heel Editor* (1939); R. C. Ellison, *History and Bibliography of Alabama Newspapers* (1954), nineteenth century; S. A. Fackler, *Country Editor* (n.d.); L. T. Griffith and J. E. Talmadge, *Georgia Journalism, 1763–1950* (1951); R. H. Henry, *Editors I Have Known* (1922); W. C. Johnson and A. T. Robb, *South and Its Newspapers, 1903–1953* (1954); R. B. Nixon, *Henry W. Grady* (1943); H. R. Sass, *News and Courier* (1953); J. F. Wall, *Henry Watterson* (1956); and E. S. Watson, *History of Newspaper Syndicates in U.S., 1865–1935* (1936).

THOMAS D. CLARK
Indiana University

NICHOLAS FAMILY planted its roots in Virginia in 1722, when George Nicholas (1695–1734) of Dorset County, England, was transported to the colony in lieu of being hanged for forging a bank note. Somehow concealing this ignominy, Nicholas used his gentry family background, his education, and a scanty medical training to establish a medical practice in Williamsburg and to win acceptance by the ruling elite. A justice of the peace and a vestryman for Bruton Parish, he also sat in the House of Burgesses. His success was assured in 1724, when he married Elizabeth Carter Burwell, the widowed daughter of Robert ("King") Carter (CARTER FAMILY).

Nicholas was survived by three sons, all of whom served on local county courts and parish vestries, and the eldest two—John (1725–1795) and George (1726–1771)—held offices as clerks of the county courts of Albemarle and Dinwiddie respectively. The most distinguished of the three, Robert Carter Nicholas (1728–1780), practiced law in Williamsburg and long sat in the House of Burgesses, eventually becoming treasurer of the colony in 1766. A reluctant revolutionary, he opposed Virginia's separation from Great Britain until the actual vote for independence in May, 1776. In 1778 he was elected one of the three judges of the high court of chancery.

Of the third generation of Nicholases, four of the sons of Robert proved to be the most prominent. George Nicholas (1754–1799), Kentucky's first attorney general, had held seats in the Virginia house of delegates and the constitutional ratification convention of 1788. Besides matching his brother's service in these Virginia bodies, Wilson Cary Nicholas (1761–1820) also served in both houses of Congress as a Jeffersonian leader (Senate, 1799–1804; House, 1807–1809) and was elected governor of Virginia in 1814. John Nicholas (1764–1819) held positions in the house of delegates and the U.S. House of Representatives (1793–1801) as an impressive Jeffersonian spokesman. After his removal to western New York in 1803, he served briefly in his adopted state's senate. Philip Norborne Nicholas (1776–1849) made his mark as a lawyer, state attorney general, and banker. With the passing of this generation of Nicholases, the family generally retreated from active political roles on the state and national level.

See Wilson Cary Nicholas Papers, Library of Congress and University of Virginia; Robert Carter Nicholas Diaries and Letterbooks, University of Virginia and Virginia Historical Society; V. D. Golladay, "Nicholas Family" (Ph.D. dissertation, University of Virginia, 1973); R. H. Caldemyer, "Career of George Nicholas" (Ph.D. dissertation, Indiana University, 1951); M. J. Dauer, *American Historical Review* (Jan., 1940); and L. P. DuBellet, *Prominent Virginia Families* (1907).

V. DENNIS GOLLADAY
Pensacola Junior College

NICHOLLS, FRANCIS REDDING TILLOU

(1834–1912), a gentlemanly patrician, became Louisiana's Democratic REDEEMER governor whose inauguration (1877) ended the last Republican Reconstruction regime in the South. Born in Donaldsonville, La., he graduated from West Point in 1855 but returned to Louisiana to study law. In 1861 he entered the Confederate army as a captain and lost his left arm at the battle of Winchester (1862). Later promoted brigadier general, he lost a foot at CHANCELLORSVILLE and was assigned to desk duty in the Trans-Mississippi Department for the remainder of the war.

He was installed as Louisiana's governor in 1877 as part of the national compromise that ended Reconstruction, but his term was cut short three years later by Democratic machine politicians, who drew up a new state constitution and then elected a regime friendly to a powerful gambling syndicate, the LOUISIANA STATE LOTTERY COMPANY. In 1888 Nicholls led a "reform Democratic" movement that returned him to the governorship (1888–1892) and ended the lottery's existence. But his halfhearted efforts to achieve racial and political peace in that turbulent state were thwarted by anti-Negro and corrupt elements within his party. He then served on the Louisiana supreme court (1892–1911), retiring to his plantation near Thibodaux a year before his death.

See C. H. Nichols, "F. T. Nicholls" (M.A. thesis, Louisiana State University, 1959); and A. Fortier, *Louisiana* (1909), II.

WILLIAM I. HAIR
Georgia College

NICHOLSON, FRANCIS (1655–1728), was lieutenant governor (1690–1692) and governor general (1698–1705) of Virginia; lieutenant governor (1690–1694) and governor (1694–1698) of Maryland; first royal governor of South Carolina (1719–1728); founder of Annapolis, Md., Williamsburg, Va., the College of William and Mary, and King William's School (St. John's College); and patron of the Church of England in the colonies. He entered the English army in 1678, and in 1686 he became captain of a dominion of New England garrison company. Serving notably on the frontier and for the church, Nicholson was promoted lieutenant governor of the dominion in 1688, with headquarters at New York. There he was overwhelmed by Leisler's Rebellion in the spring of 1689 and fled to England.

Sent out to command Virginia early in 1690, Nicholson won the support of the House of Burgesses for a college to train orthodox leaders for church and colony, for a progressive land and tax policy, and for militia reform and provincial self-defense. Superseded in the Virginia command, he took up his lieutenancy of Maryland, where he was "furiously Zealous for building of Churches and Coledges." Nicholson marked his second Virginia term by moving the colonial capital from Jamestown to the site of the college, a planned town that he named Williamsburg.

Recalled as a Tory extremist in the massive Anglo-American political shift of 1704–1705, Nicholson returned to America as a commander of an abortive attack on Canada in 1709. He captured Port Royal in 1710, commanded again against

Canada in 1711, was commissioned governor of Nova Scotia (1712–1715) and named "Governour of Governours" or inspector general in 1714. In 1719 the South Carolinians overthrew their proprietary government. In 1720 Nicholson was sent out with a garrison company to install royal government, ensure public order, promote orthodox religion, and defend and expand the frontier of empire. Advancing age put an end to his active administration in 1725. Three years later he died in London, a lieutenant general and still governor of South Carolina.

See B. T. McCully and S. S. Webb, *William and Mary Quarterly* (Oct., 1962; Oct., 1966); C. Dalton (ed.), *George the First's Army* (1912); R. L. Morton, *Colonial Virginia* (1960); and M. E. Sirmans, *Colonial South Carolina* (1966).

STEPHEN SAUNDERS WEBB
Syracuse University

NICKAJACK, STATE OF (1861), was an attempt by Union men in several Alabama counties bordering the Tennessee River to maintain their loyalty to the United States during the secession crisis. UNIONISTS hoped to establish the free state of Nickajack (using an ancient Indian name for their region) or possibly to join the still loyal state of Tennessee. When the Alabama convention voted by a narrow majority to secede without a popular referendum, the disgruntled Unionists found they could not act because of a lack of influential political leaders, the inability of Tennessee Union men to prevent the secession of their own state, and the initial pro-Confederate enthusiasm of Alabamians. Later the Nickajack area would provide sustenance to various pro-Union movements and even contribute troops to the Union army.

See E. L. Watson, *Alabama Review* (Jan., 1967); B. Martin, *Desertion of Alabama Troops* (1932); W. L. Fleming, *Civil War and Reconstruction in Alabama* (1905); and E. C. Betts, *Early History of Huntsville* (1916).

WILLIAM L. RICHTER
Tucson, Ariz.

NICKNAMES. See COLLOQUIALISMS AND NICKNAMES

NIGHT-RIDING was a form of unsophisticated terrorism, characterized by moralistic self-righteousness, wanton brutality, and mystical emotionalism, prevalent at the turn of the century in southern agrarian communities (VIOLENCE). Its outer manifestations, such as hoods, gowns, and oaths, were borrowed from the earlier KU KLUX KLAN, although night-riding tended to spring from local conflicts and seldom possessed the purposefulness and discipline of the Reconstruction Klan. In its classic sense, night-riding was rooted in the advent of modernization (corporate capitalism), which disrupted the traditional economic and social patterns of tightly knit, quasi-kinship, rural communities. Resistance to the new enterprises took the form of arson, whippings, looting, and murder. Individuals also took advantage of the upheaval to settle personal grudges, and occasional forays had racial overtones. Riders tended to be poorly educated, Protestant fundamentalists who held a firm sense of a God-given right to pursue an unfettered life founded in nature. Tennessee's Reelfoot Lake witnessed a typical night rider uprising in 1908. The lake, created in 1812 by an earthquake, evolved into a bountiful natural fish hatchery that attracted westward-bound settlers. More than half a century later, profiteers connived to gain legal control of the lake and environs, which they intended to develop as a private sportsmen's haven. The pioneers were ousted from the land and lake they had long worked, and so the law confronted social justice. Reelfoot's settlers responded by night-riding, and it took the state militia to quell the violence. With public sentiment aroused, the riders eventually legalized their lakeside rights through the state supreme court.

See P. Vanderwood, *Night Riders of Reelfoot Lake* (1969).

PAUL VANDERWOOD
San Diego State University

NIXON, RICHARD, ADMINISTRATION (1969–1974) related to the South primarily through the so-called southern strategy, a political plan to enlist and retain southern white Democratic support for the Republican president. In the ELECTION OF 1968, many southerners voted for Nixon because they approved of his conservative political and economic philosophy, particularly his stand on civil rights for blacks. After becoming president, Nixon continued to appeal to southern whites rather than to the nation's black voters by subtly catering to segregationist impulses. The administration encouraged a slowdown of school desegregation progress in the South, and Nixon publicly disagreed with a 1969 U.S. Supreme Court decision demanding that racial school segregation end "at once." Also, the president aligned himself with those southerners who opposed busing to achieve racially balanced schools. Segregationists were pleased to have a friend in the White House.

Continuing to appeal to the South, Nixon filled

a vacancy on the Supreme Court with a conservative southerner. He first nominated South Carolinian Clement Haynsworth, but the Senate rejected the nomination in view of Haynsworth's record on civil rights and some rather careless financial activity. Determined to appoint a justice with the desired qualifications (white, southerner, a strict constructionist with experience on the federal bench, and under age sixty), Nixon then nominated G. Harrold Carswell of Florida. The Senate also rejected Carswell, a mediocre judge who lived in a legally segregated neighborhood. The Senate finally approved Nixon's nomination of Lewis F. Powell, Jr., a Virginia lawyer who was impeccable in every respect, even though he was a conservative in regard to civil rights. The president's style, rhetoric, and tone were important factors in his sustained popularity in the South. In speeches and press releases, Nixon used code words southerners recognized, and the symbolism of his actions was unmistakable. Throughout his first term in office, he carefully cultivated southern white support, but the costs were high: increased racial division, disillusionment of civil rights leaders, and serious problems between the administration and leading members of Congress.

Nixon occasionally spoke of building state and local Republican parties in the South, but his primary concern was his own reelection. During the ELECTION OF 1972, the president made few statements in support of southern Republican senatorial and congressional candidates, fearful of touching off reactions that could take Democratic votes away from his own candidacy. His desire for an overwhelming personal mandate did little to move the South in the direction of a two-party system. He carefully avoided the southern states that had powerful Democratic chairmen in Congress who were heavily favored for reelection. He refused to support Republican opponents of these Democrats for fear of offending southern politicians who would surely return to Congress. Since he needed legislative support from these conservative Democrats, his actions were good politics but they did not build the Republican party in the South.

Governor GEORGE WALLACE of Alabama was the most serious early threat to Nixon's candidacy in the South in 1972. When Wallace won some Democratic primary elections in the South after speaking out strongly against busing to achieve school desegregation, Nixon took an even stronger stand against forced busing, recommending that Congress place a moratorium on new court-ordered busing and adopt strict limits on how the courts could deal with continued school segrega-

tion. Civil rights leaders decried these suggestions, which appeared to be designed to reverse the tide of school desegregation, but in the drive for white southern votes Nixon ignored the protests. Wallace withdrew from the campaign after being seriously wounded by a would-be assassin, and Nixon won the electoral totals of every southern state—an unprecedented feat for a Republican candidate. Until his resignation in August, 1974, Nixon spent much time throughout his second term with the unfolding Watergate scandal. During its final 18 months, the Nixon administration all but ignored the South and the southern strategy.

See R. Murphy and H. Gulliver, *Southern Strategy* (1971); M. Billington, *Political South* (1975); T. H. White, *Making of President, 1968* (1969) and *Making of President, 1972* (1973); and K. Phillips, *Emerging Republican Majority* (1969).

MONROE BILLINGTON
New Mexico State University

NIXON V. HERNDON (273 U.S. 536 [1927]). In 1923 the Texas legislature enacted the first WHITE PRIMARY law, providing that no black person should be eligible to participate in Democratic primaries. Dr. A. L. Nixon, supported by the NATIONAL ASSOCIATION FOR THE ADVANCEMENT OF COLORED PEOPLE, challenged this statute on grounds that it violated the Fifteenth Amendment. Justice Oliver Wendell Holmes, Jr., author of the U.S. Supreme Court's ruling, held that the Fourteenth Amendment forbade a state to exclude a citizen from party membership on the basis of race. Thereupon the Texas legislature enacted a new statute giving the executive committees of political parties the right to prescribe qualifications of members. The Texas Democratic executive committee then ruled that only white Democrats could vote in primaries. In 1932 the Court ruled in a five-to-four decision (*Nixon v. Condon*) that this statute was invalid because the Fourteenth Amendment protected blacks from political discrimination by a group deriving its authority from the state. Three years later, however, the Court held unanimously in GROVEY V. TOWNSEND that party delegates, voting in a convention, could exclude blacks from membership because a political party was a private organization. But in UNITED STATES V. CLASSIC (1941) and in SMITH V. ALLWRIGHT (1944), the Court ruled finally against both restricted conventions and white primaries.

See L. Miller, *Petitioners* (1967); J. Frank and R. Munro, *Columbia Law Review* (Feb., 1950); and D. B. King and

C. W. Quick, *Legal Aspects of Civil Rights Movement* (1965).

VIRGINIA V. HAMILTON
University of Alabama, Birmingham

NORFOLK, VA. (pop. 307,951), one of the nation's largest port cities, is located on HAMPTON ROADS, opposite the cities of Portsmouth and Newport News. Possessing a superb natural harbor and excellent rail and INTRACOASTAL WATERWAY connections, the city is a major shipping point for coal, tobacco, cotton, lumber, truck crops, grain, textiles, metals, and chemicals. It also is the headquarters of the U.S. Navy's Atlantic Fleet. Although Norfolk has been a seaport since it first was settled in the 1680s, its growth during the colonial period was limited, especially in comparison with such ports as Charleston, Boston, and New York. Its prosperity depended directly on TOBACCO exports, and by 1800—when tobacco cultivation in Virginia's tidewater section had declined—Norfolk's 400 residences and the absence of a single bank were hardly the badges of honor one might expect to find in the state's largest commercial port. Yet its strategic location was not lost on the minds of military men in three different wars. In the American Revolution it was seized by Lord Dunmore in 1775 and burned to the ground in 1776. An attack on the city by the British fleet during the War of 1812 was successfully repulsed. During the early weeks of the Civil War it was evacuated by the U.S. Navy (but only after burning the navy yard) and then retaken by federal forces on May 10, 1862. Not until the postwar construction of rail lines, however, was Norfolk able to take advantage of its natural harbor and become both a regional and national port of considerable significance.

See T. J. Wertenbaker, *Norfolk* (1931, 1962); H. W. Burton, *History of Norfolk, 1736–1877* (1877); L. Chambers and J. E. Shank, *Saltwater and Printer's Ink* (1967), newspapers, 1865–1965; M. Schlegel, *Conscripted City* (1951), World War II; H. Rorer, *History of Norfolk Public Schools, 1681–1968* (1968); G. H. Tucker, *Norfolk Highlights, 1584–1881* (1972); F. Wing, *Through the Years* (1936); and files of *American Gazette* (1792–97), *American Beacon* (1815–61), *Gazette and Public Ledger* (1804–16), *Herald* (1805–61), *Landmark* (1873–1911), *Daily Southern Argus* (1848–60), *Journal and Guide* (1899–, black weekly), *Ledger Star* (1876–), and *Virginian-Pilot* (1865–), all on microfilm.

NORFOLK VIRGINIAN-PILOT has been the leading newspaper in this port city since the daily was formed by a merger in 1898. This merger of the Norfolk *Virginian* (1865–1898) and the *Daily Pilot* (1894–1898) was followed in 1911 by yet another merger, this time with the Norfolk *Landmark* (1873–1911). The paper was known for the next 26 years (1912–1938) as the *Virginian-Pilot and Norfolk Landmark*. Since 1939, however, the paper has been known as the *Virginian-Pilot*. It is an independent Democratic paper with a circulation in excess of 130,000 copies daily.

See L. Chambers and J. E. Shank, *Saltwater and Printer's Ink: Norfolk Newspapers, 1865–1965* (1967); bound copies, at Library of Congress (1899–); and microfilm for *Virginian* (1865–98), *Landmark* (1878–1904), and *Virginian-Pilot* (1899–1912, 1945–) from Microfilm Corporation of America, Glen Park, N.J.

NORTH ANNA RIVER, BATTLE OF (May 22–29, 1864). The North Anna River was of importance because it guarded the northern approach to the east-west Virginia Central Railroad. The river assumed its greatest significance in 1864, when U. S. Grant sought to move between Robert E. Lee's army and Richmond. Following the battle of SPOTSYLVANIA, Lee's army retired south of the North Anna. On May 23, Grant's right wing crossed the river and withstood a poorly executed evening attack by A. P. HILL. The following day Grant's left wing crossed the North Anna to the east. The Union center remained north of the river. This unusual position presented Lee with an opportunity to attack either of the extended wings of Grant's army. Reinforcement of either wing would require two crossings of the river. However, Lee and two of his commanders (R. S. EWELL and Hill) were ailing, and a third (R. H. ANDERSON) was inexperienced. Thus the Confederates missed a chance to exploit Grant's overly rapid advance. Grant recognized his vulnerability on May 26 and withdrew. Desultory fighting occurred from May 27 to May 29, when Grant again started to move south. This skirmishing was the prelude to the battle of COLD HARBOR.

See V. Esposito, *West Point Atlas of American Wars* (1959), good account with excellent map; S. Foote, *Red River to Appomattox* (1974); D. S. Freeman, *Lee's Lieutenants* (1942); U. S. Grant, *Personal Memoirs* (1885); and *Official Records, Armies*, Ser. 1, Vol. XXXVI.

JAMES W. HARPER
Texas Tech University

NORTH CAROLINA comprises an area of 52,250 square miles, including 3,670 of inland waterways. Along its stormy coastline, known as the "graveyard of the Atlantic," treacherous currents, CAPES, sand reefs, and narrow inlets repel com-

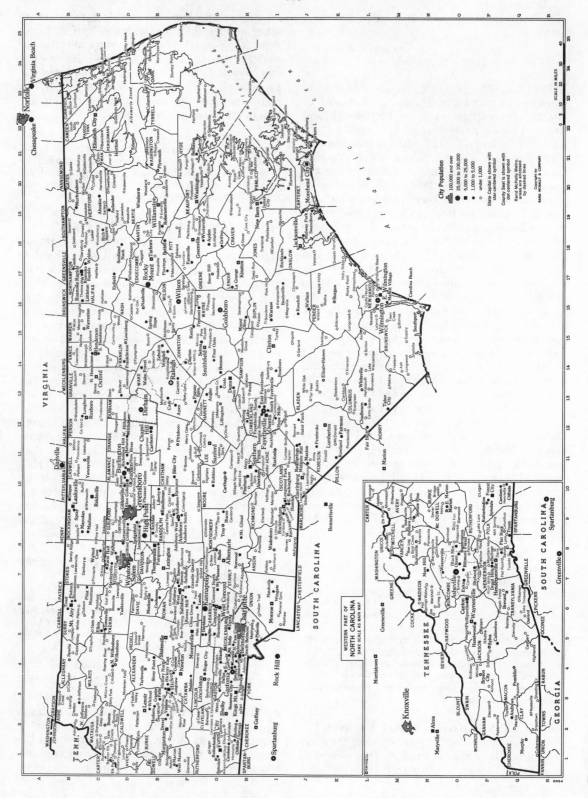

merce. The vast expanses of inland waterways or sounds, by far the largest of the colonies or original states, are shallow and inaccessible to the heavier vessels used in transatlantic shipping. The river systems of North Carolina flow either into the sounds or into South Carolina. Only the CAPE FEAR RIVER empties directly into the Atlantic Ocean, and even its approaches are endangered by the Frying Pan Shoals. Consequently the history of North Carolina has been profoundly influenced by geographic forces. Although it was the site of England's first projected colony in America, it became one of the last to be settled and developed. And, of all the colonists, only the Highland Scots landed directly on the coast in any significant numbers. Others migrated by overland routes from neighboring colonies.

Geography and background. Eastern North Carolina, known as the coastal plain, extends some 100 to 150 miles into the interior to the FALL LINE of the river systems. The abundance of rainfall, level surface of the land, porous soil, ease of clearing fields, and mild climate determined this would become an agricultural section. To the west, from the coastal plain to the foothills of the APPALACHIAN MOUNTAINS, lies the PIEDMONT Plateau. The heavy hardwood forest cover, topography, soils, and extremes of climate determined that this section would be populated by the YEOMAN FARMER class. The abundance of streams that could be dammed and utilized for waterpower influenced the location of early industrial sites in this section. And, since the streams flow in a southerly course into South Carolina, the social and economic life of the Piedmont was more closely integrated with Columbia and Charleston than with the small towns of the coastal plain. The Piedmont was largely settled by colonists from New Jersey, Pennsylvania, Delaware, Maryland, and Virginia, who moved down the SHENANDOAH VALLEY of Virginia, across the Dan River, and through the passes of the BLUE RIDGE into North Carolina. Some few moved up the river valleys from South Carolina. It is also noteworthy that many colonists reversed the usual frontier pattern and moved from west to east. These settlers were principally non-English, either Scotch-Irish or German. They differed from colonists of the coastal plain, mostly of English extraction, in many respects: nationality, language, religion, historical background, customs, size of farms, slaveholding, industrial and agricultural pursuits, and social life generally. All these factors contributed to the existence of sectional rivalries that persist to the present.

The mountain section of North Carolina is relatively small in comparison with other sections; it includes an area of about 6,000 square miles. The highest mountains of eastern America and of the southern Appalachian system are in this region. This chain of mountains diverted population southward during the colonial era. The mountain barrier thwarted westward migration of the settlers and encouraged the development of contiguous communities. The barrier also protected colonists from the nomadic and warlike Indians of the trans-Appalachian frontier. After the immediate menace of the Indians was removed following the FRENCH AND INDIAN WAR, pioneers commenced to settle along the western slopes of the mountains. Far removed from the seat of colonial and early state government, they soon expressed separatist tendencies. Ultimately they achieved their goal with the creation of the territory and state of Tennessee.

A second factor that profoundly influenced the development of colonial North Carolina was the presence of approximately 35,000 Indians at the time the first white colonists arrived. Indians made significant contributions to colonial agriculture; with the exception of wheat and rye, the vegetable and cereal crops successfully cultivated in the colony were principally Indian crops. They schooled the colonists in techniques of clearing fields, girdling trees, planting row crops, and fertilizing plants. Techniques of survival, hunting, trapping, and woodcraft were Indian contributions to whites. They served as gatherers and middlemen in the conduct of an extensive traffic in furs. Concepts of Indian warfare in a wilderness environment were quickly learned by white settlers. In the interminable wars between Indians and colonists, friendly tribes were frequently used by the English to fight hostile Indians. Ultimately the presence of whites destroyed the basis of Indian civilization. Most of the Indians were exterminated, perished from diseases and epidemics, or were forcibly removed to reservations. A few, most notably the CHEROKEE, evaded capture and survived amid the mountain fastnesses.

Various European settlers brought their institutions and ways of living into this comparatively isolated wilderness environment. The frontier experience altered and shaped the distinctive contributions of Englishmen, Scotch-Irish, Scottish Highlanders, French Huguenots, Welshmen, and emigrants from the various German states and Swiss cantons. The history of North Carolina as a colony and state reflected the interplay of these forces. It has been marked by a long and continuing struggle to overcome the adverse effects of geographic forces and the divisive influence of sectionalism.

Exploration and colonial era. Following the voyage of Christopher Columbus, Spain, France, and England conducted explorations of North Carolina. In 1524 Giovanni da Verrazano, who sailed in the interest of France, recorded the first descriptive account of the Carolina coastline. He observed the Cape Fear River, the OUTER BANKS, and the presence of friendly Indians. He assumed mistakenly that the PAMLICO and ALBEMARLE sounds were part of the Pacific Ocean. Verrazano's accounts were subsequently published by Richard Hakluyt in 1584 and influenced the efforts of SIR WALTER RALEIGH and others in planting colonies. In 1525 Lucas Vázquez de Ayllón, of Hispaniola, conducted an exploration of the coastline between the Cape Fear and SANTEE rivers in the interest of Spain. In 1526 he brought a colony of some 500, including women and Negroes, to the lower Cape Fear River. The colony was plagued by loss of supplies and decimated by diseases and in desperation sought to relocate in South Carolina. Within a short time, reduced to 150 survivors, it returned to Santo Domingo.

Subsequent Spanish explorations of the North Carolina mountains were undertaken in 1539–1540 by HERNANDO DE SOTO in a futile search for gold. But Spanish explorations of the coastline and the mountains were inconclusive, and this nation withdrew to its frontier bastions in Florida and the Southwest. Following the unsuccessful explorations of Jan Ribault and René de Laudonnière along the South Atlantic coast in the 1560s, France focused attention upon its colonies in Canada and the Mississippi Valley. The development of North Carolina would be left to English colonizers.

In 1584 Sir Walter Raleigh received a patent from Elizabeth I that authorized the establishment of colonies and gave the settlers the same privileges as natives of England. Raleigh sent Philip Amadas and Arthur Barlow on an exploratory voyage in 1584; landing at ROANOKE ISLAND in July, the party was hospitably treated by Indians. Six weeks later the explorers returned to England and submitted the most favorable accounts to Raleigh and Queen Elizabeth. In 1585 Raleigh dispatched an expedition of seven ships and possibly as many as 600 men to the West Indies, whence it sailed to Roanoke Island. This extraordinarily talented group spent too much time looking for gold and a passage to the South Seas. Factional discord and the prospect of starvation prompted Richard Grenville, the commander, to dispatch vessels to England for supplies. Ralph

Lane was left to command the fort at Roanoke Island and a force of 107 men. In 1586, faced with the prospect of starvation and the threat of an Indian attack, he chose to return to England with the fleet of Sir Francis Drake. Thus ended the first English colony in America.

On July 25, 1587, the John White colony, Raleigh's second attempt to establish an English outpost in America, arrived at Cape Hatteras and proceeded to Roanoke Island. Plagued by hostile Indians and lack of supplies, Governor White returned to England for assistance. Delayed by England's engagement with the Spanish armada in 1588, White did not return to Roanoke Island until August, 1590. He searched in vain for the settlers; and to this day no conclusive evidence has been revealed to account for the fate of the Lost Colony (CROATAN ISLAND).

Following the settlement of Jamestown, Va., in 1607, explorers, trappers, and traders ventured into the Albemarle Sound region. When Virginia became a royal colony in 1624, all ungranted land reverted to the crown. Accordingly Charles I granted to his attorney general, Sir Robert Heath, the land incorporated as the province of CAROLANA between 31° and 36° north latitude, from sea to sea. Heath failed to colonize his 1629 grant and in 1638 transferred it to Lord Maltravers, the duke of Norfolk. The proprietary grant of March 24, 1663, to eight lords proprietors vacated the earlier Heath patent. Charles II thereby rewarded his friends and supporters of the Restoration era. They were men of established reputation and ability, although only one of the original proprietors, Sir William Berkeley, ever came to America. In 1665 the charter was amended to extend northward to 36°30′ north latitude to accommodate settlements already made in the Albemarle Sound; it was also extended southward to 29°.

Extraordinary powers were granted to the proprietors by the charter of 1663. The colony was expected to serve as a buffer against Spanish encroachments on the southern frontier and to provide a reliable source of supply for the NAVAL STORES industry. It was among the most favored and perhaps most heavily subsidized of the English colonies. Emigrants were granted the same rights as the king's subjects at home, were entitled to representation in the lawmaking process, and were granted liberty of conscience. Nevertheless, the indecision of the proprietors, their lack of firsthand knowledge of the colony, and their failure to select competent governors thwarted the colony's growth. They spent far more time and money promoting the development of South Carolina. For more than 30 years the proprietors sought to implement a feudalistic scheme of government, the fundamental constitutions of 1669, based upon an artificially contrived landed aristocracy, before the plan was abandoned altogether. Economic experiments that involved crops unsuited to the colony were launched and abandoned after considerable waste of time and money.

Throughout the proprietary era (1663–1729), politics in North Carolina involved incessant factional squabbles between the popular party (consisting of leaders of the legislative branch) and the party of officialdom (usually led by governors and their hirelings). In a bitter struggle that involved conflicting views over violations of trade and navigation, Albemarle partisans resorted to armed rebellion against the proprietary faction in what was known as CULPEPER'S REBELLION of 1677. Although the uprising led to a change of officialdom, colonists soon found that the administration of Governor Seth Sothel (1683–1689) was the most notoriously corrupt of any in their history. Sothel was tried by the general assembly in 1689, found guilty on 13 charges, and banished forever from politics by an irate citizenry.

From 1689 to 1763, England and France were engaged in a series of intercolonial wars characterized by Lawrence H. Gipson as the "great war for empire." Ultimately North Carolina colonists were involved directly in all of these wars, whether they originated in Europe or America. In a broader sense England's involvement with wars and diplomacy meant that the administration of the colony was neglected. Immediately after the Glorious Revolution, a succession of fairly capable but undistinguished deputy governors was appointed by the proprietors for the county of Albemarle. In this period the settled area gradually extended southward into the Pamlico Sound region, where French HUGUENOTS principally located. In 1706 the legislature incorporated Bath as the first town in North Carolina.

In 1710 New Bern was founded by colonists from Germany, Switzerland, and England under the leadership of Christopher de Graffenried. The settlement of New Bern was launched under the most trying circumstances; almost half the original party died in the Atlantic crossing, and the survivors were plundered by a French privateer upon reaching the Virginia coast. The overland trek to New Bern was arduous, and the settlers arrived too late to plant and harvest crops. Under de Graffenried's dedicated efforts, however, the settlement survived and flourished. New Bern became the largest town in North Carolina during the colonial period.

The CARY REBELLION of 1711 divided the colonists and thwarted growth of the proprietary. It involved a crisis between the Society of Friends (QUAKERS) and the government of the colony over the enforcement of vestry legislation. The issue of separation of church and state was at stake. Ultimately these differences led to armed clashes in which Governor Edward Hyde routed the Quaker forces. This rebellion left the colonists prone to Indian attacks during the Tuscarora War (1711–1713). The fact that the TUSCARORA INDIANS had been eliminated as middlemen in the conduct of fur trade with the Cherokee on the frontier also provoked hostility. Furthermore the Tuscarora resented the encroachment of settlers in the New Bern area upon their hunting grounds. During the war the suppression and banishment of the Tuscarora were accomplished largely by forces of friendly Indians from South Carolina led by John Barnwell and James Moore. A further hindrance to the Carolina proprietary involved the last stand of PIRACY in the Western Hemisphere. Driven from South America and the Caribbean, pirates sought refuge along the sounds and rivers of North Carolina. They used the inland waterways of North Carolina as bases from which to prey upon shipping around Charleston and Norfolk. The heyday of piracy was short-lived. By 1718 practically all of these pirates had been captured and executed.

Conceivably proprietary government might have survived these crises and brought a period of expansion and prosperity to North Carolina. However, the proprietors apparently concluded that the venture was unsuccessful, and in 1729 all the lords except John Carteret, the earl of Granville, sold their shares to James II. At this time North Carolina was the most isolated and sparsely settled English colony in America. In marked contrast, the growth of population and expansion of settled areas were phenomenal from 1729 to 1775. Most of the immigrants after 1729 were of non-English extraction. Highland Scots, given an opportunity to settle in America after they were crushed at the battle of Culloden in 1746, were landed on the lower Cape Fear River and settled upstream in this river valley. Heavily subsidized by the English government, they were instrumental in the development of the naval stores industry.

Scotch-Irish and German immigrants traveled over the GREAT WAGON ROAD from Pennsylvania through the Shenandoah Valley of Virginia to North Carolina. High land prices, exhaustion and erosion of farmlands, overcrowding of the population, and the Indian menace and mountain barriers on the Pennsylvania frontier all influenced the southward migration of these settlers. Practically all the Scotch-Irish had come to America as INDENTURED LABOR and after serving their period of indenture were able to acquire title to free land. The best-known German colonists, the United Brethren or MORAVIANS, settled principally in Forsyth County. Devoutly religious, operating under a system of community ownership and management of property, the Moravians established an impressive record for other colonists to follow.

From 1729 to 1775 the population of North Carolina as a royal colony increased from about 35,000 to 345,000. Of this number there were about 80,000 Negroes in 1775. During this period the Cape Fear Valley was developed, and colonists occupied the fertile farmlands of the Piedmont along the Yadkin and Catawba rivers. This growth was accomplished in spite of the ineptitude of royal governors and the "salutary neglect" of the colony. In 1775 only Virginia, Pennsylvania, and Massachusetts exceeded North Carolina in total population.

The spread of population into the Piedmont did not result in adequate reapportionment of representation in the general assembly. Eastern counties were divided and subdivided to counterbalance the influence of the west. Frontiersmen could therefore rightfully complain of taxation without representation. The frustration of yeomen farmers of the west was also aggravated by corrupt land agents and surveyors, tax collectors, sheriffs, and political opportunists who were allowed to hold multiple offices. The protest movement by REGULATORS of the backcountry in many ways resembled uprisings in other colonies and states, including such well-known events as BACON'S REBELLION in Virginia and Shays's Rebellion in Massachusetts. The vigilante activities of the Regulators of Piedmont North Carolina, which centered in Orange and Alamance counties, were not provoked by more stringent colonial and commercial policies of Parliament after 1763. Nor were the Regulators moved to acts of violence by inadequate representation. Their protests were instead aimed against specific abuses of local and county government, which were particularly severe in the Granville District, lands claimed by the Carteret heirs. The Regulator movement was utterly crushed by Governor WILLIAM TRYON and forces under his command at the battle of ALAMANCE in 1771. Many of the Regulators moved westward; an impressive number joined Whig forces during the Revolution. There is little evidence, contrary to some myths, that Regulators joined the Tory cause after 1775.

Revolution and the new nation. When British colonial and commercial policies became more exacting after the end of the French and Indian War, colonists in North Carolina responded by appealing to their constitutional rights within the empire. They demonstrated little interest in the Albany Plan of union in 1754, but in defying the Stamp Act of 1765 they willingly endorsed the Stamp Act Congress and used force to coerce royal officials. The general assembly acted in concert with other colonies in an economic boycott of Great Britain that forced repeal of the Townshend Acts of 1767. The impetus for colonial unity was further promoted by a committee of correspondence in 1773 and by support of beleaguered Boston and the Massachusetts Bay Colony in 1774. North Carolina patriots, defiantly challenging Governor Josiah Martin, called for a provincial congress that would be independent of royal control. This congress met in New Bern in 1774, endorsed the proposal for the First CONTINENTAL CONGRESS, and elected William Hooper, RICHARD CASWELL, and Joseph Hewes to serve as delegates to Philadelphia. With the outbreak of hostilities at Lexington and Concord in April, 1775, Governor Martin found his position in New Bern to be untenable. Ultimately he took refuge on a British warship stationed off the coast. Thereafter, committees of safety and provincial congresses took over governmental powers.

On April 12, 1776, delegates to the fourth provincial congress at Halifax, N.C., drafted what were known as the Halifax Resolves. The resolves empowered North Carolina's delegates in the Continental Congress to "concur" with representatives of other colonies "in declaring Independency" and in "forming foreign alliances." This may well have been the most significant action for American independence by any revolutionary body at the time. The Continental Congress acted decisively when it adopted the resolution for independence submitted by RICHARD HENRY LEE of Virginia. The DECLARATION OF INDEPENDENCE that followed Lee's resolution was signed by North Carolina's delegates Hooper, Hewes, and John Penn.

A substantial number of North Carolinians were LOYALISTS during the revolutionary era. Highland Scots in particular had many reasons to support the crown. They had taken an oath of allegiance to the house of Hanover before coming to America and were also heavily subsidized producers of naval stores in the Cape Fear Valley. They were promised free land, money, and remission of arrearages in rent, as well as exemption from future rentals, to support the Tory cause. Furthermore, they suspected the motives of Whig political leaders in the Albemarle Sound region. Throughout the Piedmont many colonists were at best neutral in outlook. Whig tactics of violence and intimidation were therefore effective in swaying many of the uncommitted colonists to support the Whig cause even before the outbreak of hostilities. And in many ways Whigs were guilty of excesses fully comparable with alleged British abuses. During the Revolution, Highland Scots recruited military units and in 1776 undertook to rendezvous with British forces along the North Carolina coast. This operation failed utterly when the Scots were crushed at the battle of MOORE'S CREEK BRIDGE on February 27, 1776. The initial British plan to join Tory forces and drive a wedge into the southern colonies was therefore thwarted, and following the battle of FT. MOULTRIE in South Carolina the plan was abandoned. After 1776 Tories within North Carolina posed no major military threat; their efforts were confined largely to harassment of army operations.

After the battle of Moore's Creek Bridge, North Carolina did not become a principal theater of operations until 1780–1781. Its regular army forces, troops of the Continental Line numbering some 6,000, served with distinction under George Washington's command in campaigns across New York, New Jersey, Pennsylvania, and Virginia. An estimated 10,000 North Carolinians served as militiamen who were castigated by their commanders for fleetness of foot in running from the enemy. Both Continentals and militiamen served under General Benjamin Lincoln's command in Georgia and South Carolina in 1779 and 1780, and an inordinately large number was taken prisoner in the ill-advised defense of Charleston. The staggering losses at Charleston and the subsequent battle of CAMDEN left the southern states vulnerable to the British forces led by General Charles Cornwallis. At this juncture the heroic assault by militiamen from the mountain counties upon a British force at the battle of KINGS MOUNTAIN, October 7, 1780, stalled the advance of Cornwallis' army. Under the command of Nathanael Greene, American forces skillfully retreated across North Carolina and maneuvered British troops into position for the battle of GUILFORD COURTHOUSE on March 15, 1781. Although Greene was driven from the field of battle, the British losses were so great that this engagement is regarded as a turning point of the Revolution. Thereafter Cornwallis was engaged in a desperate maneuver to evacuate his army from the South. And, finally thwarted in this effort, he surrendered at YORKTOWN on October 19, 1781.

While the war was under way, the fifth provincial congress at Halifax, which convened on November 12, 1776, launched a new constitution for the independent state of North Carolina. The work of this congress symbolized the transition from colony to commonwealth. Although radical and conservative Whigs were well represented in the congress, neither faction dominated its proceedings. The final draft of the constitution represented a compromise, with moderates holding the balance of power. The constitution of 1776 was based on colonial experience, shaped by English charters and precedents, and drawn in part from the constitutions of other states. The legislative branch dominated the executive and judicial branches and reflected the colonists' dislike and suspicion of governors and judges generally. The framers of the constitution placed considerable emphasis upon a bill of rights. Yet in many ways the document reflected a conservative trend in politics. Property-holding and tax-paying requirements for voting and officeholding were prescribed. Although the separation of church and state was affirmed in principle, the delegates by a curious twist of logic set up religious tests for officeholding, barring ministers from election to the legislature and excluding candidates for any public office who denied the "truth" of the Protestant religion. The constitution cited the obligation of the state to support public schools and higher learning. Ironically, the state failed to take decisive action to support public schools until 1839. The glaring inequities in representation the delegates allowed in 1776, which favored eastern counties and towns, aroused much political disaffection until corrected in the convention of 1835. Furthermore, the constitution contained no provision for amendments and was not submitted to a popular referendum before it was put into effect. The defects of the original state constitution caused incessant controversy between 1776 and 1835.

The rapid recovery of the economy of North Carolina in the aftermath of the Revolution appears to contradict the views of earlier historians that the Confederation era was marked by depression and chaos. The state was occupied with the problems of transition from a wartime to a peacetime economy in attempting to cope with disgruntled veterans and in handling the separatist tendencies of frontiersmen. Disaffection on the frontier was finally resolved when North Carolina ceded its western land claims in 1789. The legislature contented itself with chartering private academies but neglected to support public schools. In 1789 it commenced to erect the apex of an educational pyramid by chartering the state university. When it opened in 1795, the University of North Carolina became the first state institution of higher learning to enroll students. After much haggling, Wake County was finally chosen as the seat of government in 1792, and the first permanent capitol building was completed at Raleigh in 1794.

North Carolina was not prominently represented in the movement that led to the CONSTITUTIONAL CONVENTION of 1787 in Philadelphia. The five delegates who represented the state were drawn from the ranks of the planter aristocracy. They appeared to be principally concerned about restrictions upon the president and sought vainly to provide for his election by Congress. The TARHEEL delegates significantly influenced provisions relating to the power of Congress to override a presidential veto, the method of impeachment of the president, the senatorial term of six years, and the decennial census. Although frequently absent, the delegates voted with the slaveholding states and with the small states for the great compromises of the Philadelphia convention. After the Constitution was submitted to the states, the Hillsboro convention of 1788 refused by a vote of 184 to 84 to ratify the document. After the Federalists promised a BILL OF RIGHTS, conducted a campaign to educate voters on the advantages of a stronger central government, and pointed out that the new government would become operative regardless of the North Carolina vote, a second convention at Fayetteville in 1789 voted to ratify by 195 to 77.

Rural and agrarian interests of North Carolina opposed the economic and diplomatic policies of the FEDERALIST PARTY after 1789. The state electoral vote was cast for THOMAS JEFFERSON for president in the ELECTION OF 1796, and from that time until 1824 the electorate was dominated by the VIRGINIA DYNASTY in presidential politics. Yet in many ways the Jeffersonian Republicans (DEMOCRATIC-REPUBLICAN PARTY) of North Carolina did not share the enlightened views of the founder of the party or his successors. A dissident group of STATES' RIGHTS advocates led by NATHANIEL MACON of Warren County, known as QUIDS, assumed an intransigent role on national issues.

Antebellum era. Archibald D. Murphey, state senator from Orange County (1812–1819), symbolized the spirit of progress and reform that followed the War of 1812. The Murphey program, ably presented in a series of reports to the general assembly, called for the development of a network of CANALS linking the river systems, the opening of inlets to the sounds, and extension of navigable waterways into the Piedmont. Roads were also projected to lead from canals and rivers into the Piedmont and western counties. However, RAILROAD construction soon eclipsed and rendered futile this ambitious program to link together the east and west.

Murphey also undertook to fulfill the constitutional mandate of 1776 for a public school system. He proposed state support for elementary schools for all white children. His plan included ten regional public academies for students of extraordinary ability. Those specially qualified but unable to pay tuition would also receive free education in the state university. Murphey's advocacy of a state school for the deaf and mute, as well as his views on reforming the curriculum of the state university to include more practical and fewer ornamental subjects, indicates a progressive outlook toward learning. An integral part of the state senator's reform program involved revision of the 1776 constitution to allow more equitable representation in government and to remove many defects from the original document.

Although North Carolina was moved by the spirit of patriotism and nationalism after 1815, the legislature hesitated to enact Murphey's proposals. Generally the state did not support the new nationalist measures of Congress or look with favor upon the U.S. Supreme Court decisions of JOHN MARSHALL. In this period North Carolina acquired a reputation for backwardness and inertia and was castigated as the "Rip Van Winkle state." Emigration of population, the high rate of illiteracy, and the low per capita income and standard of living contributed to this image. Tarheels salved their consciences for tardy participation in the War of 1812 by providing for the families of three wartime heroes, and the legislature in a fit of patriotism commissioned a statue of George Washington by Canova. In 1822 the legislature provided modest support to agricultural societies, and between 1824 and 1827 Denison Olmsted and Elisha Mitchell, of the University of North Carolina, prepared and published the first state geological survey in the United States.

Enthusiasm for state spending programs was dampened by the PANIC OF 1819. Nevertheless, North Carolina employed an engineer to survey rivers and sounds and authorized subscription of stock in navigation and canal companies. State funds were also appropriated to construct turnpikes, located principally in the west. Generally the state wasted money on widely scattered local projects, of which only a few were successful. The precedent for state spending on internal improvements was nonetheless established and was later augmented by railroad construction. Indecisive action also characterized the early school program. Long after Murphey left public life, the legislature in 1825 created a literary fund to establish common schools and a literary board to administer it. The fund was derived from dividends, taxes, land sales, and appropriations. However, the receipts were inadequate, some monies were stolen by the state treasurer, and the legislature borrowed heavily from the fund for other than educational purposes. For more than ten years the state languished under a totally inadequate plan for public schools. The legislature, dominated by eastern slaveholding counties, dedicated to parsimony and maintenance of the status quo, and determined to thwart Murphey's program of constitutional and social reform, hampered the impulses for change. Unfortunately, Murphey became insolvent and was imprisoned for debts. It would take North Carolina more than a century to implement and appreciate many of his visionary proposals.

Jeffersonian Republicans dominated state politics after 1815, but sectional animosities and demands for change split the party and led eventually to its demise. Western counties were clamoring for more equitable representation and internal improvements. They resented party caucuses and the general ticket system whereby eastern counties dictated the nomination and election of candidates. The clamor of western counties for constitutional reforms heralded the emergence of a new political era. In 1822 disgruntled legislators called for a convention, and in 1823 an extralegal convention of 47 delegates from 24 western counties met in Raleigh. The general assembly rejected its proposals for a state constitutional convention.

During the presidential ELECTION OF 1824, Charles Fisher of Salisbury mobilized support of western counties for JOHN C. CALHOUN on what was called a "people's ticket." Calhoun supported nationalist measures for internal improvements, including a national road that would run across Piedmont North Carolina, but he found his appeal in northern states eclipsed by the meteoric rise of ANDREW JACKSON. When Calhoun withdrew from the race, Fisher and his followers endorsed Jackson. Consequently those who aligned with the "people's ticket" believed they were supporting a movement to eliminate the Republican machine, congressional caucuses, and the Virginia dynasty in national politics and to institute a broad spectrum of constitutional and social reform in North Carolina. The Jackson ticket won by a commanding majority in the state in 1824.

After 1824 the party of Jackson (DEMOCRATIC PARTY) experienced a metamorphosis in state politics. The base of its support shifted from western to eastern North Carolina, from yeomen farmers of the backcountry to planter aristocrats of the coastal plain. Jackson's views on slavery, state sovereignty, and federal spending programs generally pleased slaveholders. Small farmers became increasingly weary of Jackson during his second term. Therefore advocates of internal improvements, banking interests disturbed by the veto of the recharter bill of 1832, and critics of the president's handling of the NULLIFICATION crisis in South Carolina turned to the anti-Jackson or WHIG PARTY. The North Carolina Whigs were more inclined to support nationalist measures and were less ardent about states' rights issues. They also championed constitutional reform, reapportionment of representation, public school legislation, state aid to eleemosynary institutions, and tax reforms. The state program of the Whig party was one that under ordinary circumstances would most likely be identified with the tenets of Jacksonian Democracy. Yet the party that inherited Federalist political traditions was destined to carry out a program of progress for North Carolina. Whigs championed the interests of undeveloped and underrepresented counties from the western and sound regions. From 1835 to 1850 this party dominated the political life of the state, thereby terminating eastern control.

The constitutional convention of 1835, one of the early accomplishments of the Whig party, represented a turning point in the history of the state. Whigs first secured in 1835 a popular referendum on the call for a constitutional convention. The majority support for this call resulted from strong western support, with opposition generally in eastern counties. Governor David L. Swain, a Whig, was the floor leader, ably assisted by Whigs WILLIAM GASTON and John Motley Morehead and by Charles Fisher from the Democratic ranks. The changes incorporated in the state constitution were subject to popular approval. Borough representation and free Negro suffrage were abolished, thereby satisfying demands of slaveholders, who were apprehensive about abolitionist activities. Poll taxes were equalized; Catholics, but not Jews or atheists, were permitted to hold public office. Provisions were added to allow constitutional amendments by either a convention or legislative action.

Under the new constitution, legislative sessions became biennial instead of annual. Election of the governor was removed from the legislature and placed with the electorate—adult white male taxpayers. Equal county representation in the house of commons was abolished, and the 120 members were apportioned according to federal population, with each county guaranteed one representative. The 50 state senators were to be chosen from districts the size of which was determined by amounts paid in state taxes. In this way the convention allowed western control of the house of commons and eastern control of the senate. Whigs scored a major victory when these changes were ratified by a popular majority in 1835. The activities surrounding the convention, the emergence of two fairly evenly balanced political parties, and the emphasis upon party journalism and campaign activities tended to highlight state problems and issues. Perhaps for the first time the problems confronting North Carolina as a state could be treated in a realistic way.

Whigs promoted railroad construction in their efforts to provide a statewide transportation system. Railroads were believed to be superior and cheaper than canals or turnpikes, and with construction from the coast to the mountains the landlocked counties would finally have access to port facilities. Consequently towns vied for railroads; the legislature chartered many private companies in the 1830s, and the sister state Virginia aroused concern by threatening to encroach upon shipping in the Roanoke River valley. The Wilmington & Weldon Railroad (chartered as Wilmington & Raleigh in 1834) became the first significant line to orient traffic from the Roanoke River to Wilmington, N.C. It was chartered as a private company, and its construction was completed in 1840 by state aid of about $1 million. This 161-mile line was the longest railroad in the world in 1840. Ultimately it became a profitable operation and was described as the "lifeline of the Confederacy" during the Civil War. The Raleigh & Gaston Railroad, an 86-mile line connecting Raleigh and the Roanoke River, was completed in 1840 after receiving substantial state aid. This line was not profitable at first, and the state lost almost $1 million from its investment. The losses from state aid to railroad companies did not dampen enthusiasm for more construction, and in 1849 the most ambitious project of all, the North Carolina Railroad, was chartered to connect Goldsboro and Charlotte. The state subscribed two-thirds of the stock in this venture, which opened for development what is presently known as the Piedmont Crescent. This 223-mile project was completed in 1856 and was the pride of the state. The immediate reduction of freight rates and the expansion of agriculture and industry into the Piedmont would affect the economic prosperity of the 1850s. It is noteworthy that when the Democrats returned to

power in 1850 they expanded the railroad construction program launched under the Whig party.

Whigs next focused attention upon the development of a public school system. Aware of the shortcomings of the literary fund, they capitalized upon the distribution of the federal surplus in 1837 and directed that it be used to support schools. In 1839 the legislature enacted a public school law to permit counties to vote for or against the principle of state support. Those approving schools would receive, for each district, $40 annually from the literary fund, to be supplemented by $20 and a school building provided by the district. Ultimately all counties voted for schools, and by 1850 there were 2,657 public schools with an enrollment of 100,591 students. This notable expansion of educational opportunities was achieved within a decade.

In 1844 the legislature appropriated $5,000 to create a state school for the deaf and the blind. Counties provided $75 a year in supplements for each student enrolled. This institution was launched in Raleigh in 1845 and in 1851 was expanded to include a department for the blind. Whigs also acted to create a state hospital for the insane in 1848, and this institution, located in Raleigh, was opened in 1856. These pioneering efforts to provide eleemosynary institutions fell short of the goals of many reformers, who envisioned state-supported orphanages and a penitentiary. Although Whigs provided for reassessment of property and levied new taxes on inheritances, incomes, licenses, and luxuries, the state income was inadequate to provide for increased services. Consequently in 1848 the party resorted to borrowing by authorizing the sale of state bonds.

Although the record of the Whig party from 1835 to 1850 was one of extraordinary achievement, events during the 1840s led to its decline and eventual disappearance. Some critics maintained that the Whigs failed to carry out an adequate railroad-building program. Others questioned the lack of administration and efficiency in the public school system and pointed to the unequal distribution of state support under a formula based on the federal population. The resurgent Democratic party capitalized upon the issue of free white manhood suffrage, which the Whigs opposed, and under WILLIAM W. HOLDEN's editorship the *North Carolina Standard* depicted the party of Jackson as the party of the common man. This strategy represented a dramatic change from the status quo mentality of the 1830s. The election of JAMES K. POLK to the presidency in 1844, in view of his North Carolina background and upbringing, augured favorably for Democratic party prospects.

But Whig opposition to the Mexican War and expansion of slavery into the territories became perhaps the most telling issues. Increasingly the Democratic party in North Carolina was identified as most favorable to southern and slaveholding interests. And, as the issues involving slavery and territorial expansion became more heated, the nationalist measures identified with the Whig party were less and less appealing to Tarheels.

The election of David S. Reid, a Democrat, as governor in 1850 terminated an era of Whig party domination. The Democrats also won control of the legislature. They pressed immediately for enactment of a free suffrage amendment, but did not secure ratification of their proposal until 1857. On state issues Democrats expanded the railroad construction program significantly and also contributed state aid to plank roads and navigation companies. A plank road craze swept North Carolina in the 1850s. These roads were expected to provide access to railroads and assist farmers in marketing produce; the cost was about $1,500 per mile. Promoters did not reckon with decay of timbers and the mounting cost of maintenance. By 1860 the movement was of little consequence.

In 1852 Democrats created the office of state superintendent of common schools and elected Calvin H. Wiley, a Whig, to fill the position. Under Wiley's brilliant leadership, textbooks were improved, teachers were certified by examination, salaries were augmented, facilities were expanded and vastly improved, and a spirit of professionalism was brought to the public school system. Emphasis upon quality became the singular contribution of Wiley.

Phenomenal economic prosperity during the 1850s brought additional tax revenues for education and for charitable and correctional services. From 1850 to 1860 land values more than doubled; TOBACCO production increased from 12 to 33 million pounds; the COTTON crop increased from 73,845 bales in 1850 to 145,514 bales in 1860; and WHEAT production rose from 2 million bushels in 1850 to 4.7 million bushels in 1860. The bright leaf variety of tobacco was introduced by Abisha and Elisha Slade of Caswell County and with a new curing process became the basis for the bright leaf tobacco industry. New varieties of short-staple cotton facilitated expansion of the cotton economy into Piedmont North Carolina. Much of the agricultural and industrial expansion was made possible by railroad construction. It is noteworthy that between 1850 and 1860 the value of manufactured articles rose from $9.7 million to $16.7 million. There were indications of an industrial transformation before the Civil War. The un-

paralleled prosperity of the 1850s also convinced many slaveholders of the economic advantages of the peculiar institution and strengthened their defensive attitude. Developments in the decade contradicted much of what HINTON ROWAN HELPER described in *The Impending Crisis*.

The great revival movement in religion strengthened the membership and influence of churches in the antebellum period. In its broadest sense the movement included missionary and philanthropic work, Sunday school activities, Bible tract publications and church journals, advocacy of temperance, peace proposals, and defense of the rights of women and children. A major function of churches in the early years of the nineteenth century involved the establishment of academies and colleges for men and women. Through involvement in many social issues and reform movements, the churches came to occupy a more important role in the lives of the people. Only a few denominations, most notably the Society of Friends and the Wesleyan Methodists, supported abolition of slavery. The others either took a neutral role or defended the institution. By 1844 the leading Protestant denominations were establishing southern branches.

Disunion and the Civil War. Although the Democratic party after 1850 expanded the state reform programs initiated by Whigs, its position on the question of slavery placed it in a defensive posture in national politics. The great debates over the COMPROMISE OF 1850 and the KANSAS-NEBRASKA ACT of 1854 made Tarheels aware of their minority interests. And civil crises in Kansas, the emergence of the Republican party in 1854, the spirited debates between Stephen A. Douglas and Abraham Lincoln in 1858, and the wave of hysteria that followed John Brown's HARPERS FERRY RAID in 1859 manifestly contributed to the determination of Democrats to uphold sectional interests.

The division of the Democratic party into northern and southern branches in 1860 assured the election of Lincoln to the presidency. Lincoln had no Republican organization or significant following in North Carolina. Predictably, JOHN C. BRECKINRIDGE, the southern Democratic candidate, received the majority vote and North Carolina's electoral vote. However, JOHN BELL, the CONSTITUTIONAL UNION PARTY candidate who appealed to the nationalist sentiments of old-line Whigs in particular, received 44,990 votes to 48,539 cast for Breckinridge. It is significant that a candidate who espoused nationalism—the Constitution, the Union, and the laws of Congress—almost defeated the prosouthern slaveholding candidate. North Carolinians obviously were not in the vanguard of the SECESSION movement in 1860.

The combined vote for Bell and Douglas, leader of the northern Democrats, exceeded that cast for Breckinridge and indicated that majority sentiment in North Carolina opposed secession. Therefore the Democratic legislature at first refused to call a convention to consider secession. When voters were given an opportunity in February, 1861, to endorse a convention, they rejected the proposal by a vote of 47,323 to 46,672. Conceivably UNIONISTS would have controlled such a gathering, but voters nonetheless feared it might lead to secession. The refusal of Republican leaders to agree to any terms of compromise, as well as Lincoln's determination to reinforce federal garrisons in the South, strengthened the appeal of secessionists in North Carolina. When Confederate troops fired on FT. SUMTER on April 12, 1861, and the president responded by calling upon the states to supply 75,000 soldiers to suppress the insurrection, there remained scant hope that North Carolina could stay in the Union.

Governor JOHN W. ELLIS thereupon ordered that U.S. Fts. Caswell and Johnston, the arsenal at Fayetteville, and the branch mint at Charlotte be seized. The legislature in special session called for election of delegates to a convention that met in Raleigh on May 20. This convention rejected the argument that the state could secede from the Union by right of revolution. Instead it resolved that under the right of secession the Union was dissolved. On May 20 the ordinance of secession was adopted unanimously and Tarheels joined the Confederacy.

Although North Carolina had strong Unionist ties, it was never considered a large slaveholding state with an influential planter aristocracy, and was hardly regarded as wealthy or affluent, it nevertheless supplied a greater number of men to the Confederacy (125,000) than any other southern state. It also sustained a greater number of casualties by far than any other Confederate state. Those killed in battle or who died from diseases numbered 40,275. Yet the position North Carolina occupied in the Confederate government aroused constant political wrangling. Confederates, those who supported without reservation the policies of JEFFERSON DAVIS and the Confederate government in Richmond, were a decided minority. The majority of North Carolinians belonged to a political faction, known as the Conservative party, with strong reservations about the policies of the Confederate government.

Led by ZEBULON B. VANCE, who was elected governor in 1862, the Conservatives criticized the use of North Carolina troops on the Virginia front while much of eastern North Carolina was vulnerable to invasion. Vance demanded that his state have more high-ranking generals in the Confederate ranks, and he particularly resented the presence of Confederate recruiters. He insisted that the supply and provisioning of troops be a state function, and he displayed outstanding administrative talents in directing the war effort. He also maintained that his state should have higher-ranking members of the CONFEDERATE CABINET, its diplomatic service, and strategic committee assignments in the CONFEDERATE CONGRESS.

Vance took exception to the policies of the Richmond government over suspension of the writ of habeas corpus, and his defense of this venerable constitutional guarantee indicated a concern for civil rights in wartime. When the Conscription Act of 1862 exempted from military service all those who owned 20 or more slaves, Vance complained that the conflict had become "a rich man's war, and a poor man's fight." He strongly objected to the insistence of the Confederate government that goods carried through the Union BLOCKADE, principally at Wilmington, be consigned to Confederate account. In 1863 and 1864 Vance determined that peace overtures with the Union were futile, and he sharply criticized William W. Holden, who emerged as a gubernatorial candidate and leader of the PEACE MOVEMENT in 1864.

During the Civil War much of eastern North Carolina, along the rivers, sounds, and Outer Banks, was overrun and occupied by Union forces. Ft. Hatteras was captured in 1861; Roanoke Island, New Bern, Washington, Ft. Macon, and Plymouth fell in 1862 (BURNSIDE'S NORTH CAROLINA EXPEDITION). In 1863 Union forces conducted raids upon the Wilmington & Weldon Railroad, upon Goldsboro, and in the Tar River valley near Tarboro. Governor Vance complained that North Carolina troops, engaged principally on the Virginia front, should be used to drive the invader from the state. After repeated Union naval attacks in 1862 and 1864, FT. FISHER, which commanded approaches to the port of Wilmington and thus protected blockade-runners, fell to naval and amphibious attacks on January 15, 1865. From that point Union forces advanced to Wilmington and over the Wilmington & Weldon Railroad to join William T. Sherman's army advancing from South Carolina (CAROLINAS CAMPAIGN). The "lifeline of the Confederacy" was severed, and the loss of Robert E. Lee's base of supplies and reinforcements made his position in Virginia untenable.

In March, 1865, Sherman's army captured Fayetteville. Advancing toward Goldsboro it defeated Confederate forces at Southwest Creek, at Avarasboro, and in a major battle at BENTONVILLE (March 19–21, 1865). By April 13 Sherman's army passed in review around Capitol Square in Raleigh, and on April 18 General JOSEPH JOHNSTON surrendered what was left of his Confederate army to Sherman. The final terms of surrender were negotiated at Bennett House, near Durham, on April 26. During the final weeks of the war, North Carolina was invaded by General George Stoneman's army, which marched from Tennessee. This campaign involved destruction of small factories, supply bases, and harassment of the civilian population (STONEMAN'S RAIDS). Its principal objective was to capture the Confederate prison at SALISBURY, second only to ANDERSONVILLE in size and by 1865 a veritable deathtrap for most of its occupants. Stoneman seized the prison on April 12. The concept of total war was brought home to North Carolinians by Sherman and Stoneman. Following Lee's surrender at APPOMATTOX and Johnston's surrender at Bennett House, North Carolina was placed under a Union army of occupation commanded by General John M. Schofield on April 29.

Reconstruction and Redemption. ANDREW JOHNSON of Tennessee, a native of Raleigh, undertook to carry on Lincoln's plan for the restoration of the southern states upon succeeding to the presidency on April 15, 1865. He offered amnesty to most Tarheels and in exceptional cases generously extended pardons. William Holden was appointed provisional governor and in this capacity filled offices, processed applications for pardons, and arranged to call a constitutional convention. This convention repealed the ordinance of secession, abolished slavery, and repudiated the state war debt. The heated issue of debt repudiation led to Holden's defeat by JONATHAN WORTH in the gubernatorial election of 1865. The refusal of North Carolina to grant suffrage to freedmen or to provide public schools for their advancement, the enactment by Conservatives of BLACK CODES restricting the rights of freedmen, as well as Holden's defeat and reports of widespread racial violence in the South, convinced Radical Republicans in Congress that harsher measures of RECONSTRUCTION were necessary. President Johnson's intransigence and his failure to win support in the congressional elections of 1866 enabled Radical Republicans to override his vetoes and proceed with their own plans for Reconstruction in 1867.

Under congressional Reconstruction, North Carolina was placed in the second military district. The Republican party state organization coincided with the inauguration of Reconstruction measures. In 1868 Republicans controlled the constitutional convention that drafted a completely new fundamental law for the state. Principally written by ALBION W. TOURGÉE of Ohio, this document was one of the most progressive of the state constitutions. It enfranchised freedmen, provided for popular control of county government through elected commissioners, supported the principles of a public school system, and removed previous religious and property-holding restrictions on voting and officeholding. In April, 1868, the new constitution was ratified. Republicans won control of the legislature and the congressional delegation, and Holden was elected governor over his Conservative party opponent. The principal accomplishment of Reconstruction in North Carolina involved constitutional reform.

Throughout the Reconstruction era, agents of the FREEDMEN'S BUREAU established schools, negotiated labor contracts, provided for clinics, dispensaries, and medical care to freedmen, and distributed food and clothing. The bureau agents failed notably in the distribution of abandoned and confiscated lands to freedmen, and further disappointment came with the failure of the FREEDMEN'S BANK in 1874. Bureau agents were accused of using the agency to promote the Republican party, a charge that has not been substantiated. Instead the UNION LEAGUE was launched for the avowed purpose of encouraging freedmen to register and vote as Republicans. After 1867 the KU KLUX KLAN undertook through violence and intimidation to discourage the political activities of freedmen and white Republican leaders. This organization bequeathed a legacy of hatred and violence to the state.

Although there were several tangible accomplishments by the Reconstruction regime, it was comparatively short-lived and marred by corruption. The most notable failure involved the fraudulent issuance of railroad construction bonds, in which many Conservatives concurred. Subsequent exposure of these railroad schemes by the Bragg and Shipp commissions tarnished the record of Republicans. When Governor Holden sought to suppress Klan violence in the Piedmont and in his zeal denied the writ of habeas corpus, he was overruled by a federal judge and rejected by national leaders of the Republican party. After Conservatives regained control of the legislature in 1870, they impeached Holden and removed him from office. He thus became the only state governor up to that time removed by impeachment.

Conservatives sought to undo much of the Reconstruction program through constitutional amendments, particularly in the convention of 1875. The convention provided a means for Conservative control of county government by replacing popularly elected county commissioners. Instead county commissioners were to be appointed by justices of the peace, who in turn were appointed by the legislature. In this way local self-government and home rule were denied. In the ELECTION OF 1876, Conservatives, in anticipation of Samuel J. Tilden's victory, assented to use the Democratic party label. In this celebrated election Zebulon Vance, the Democratic gubernatorial candidate, defeated his Republican opponent Thomas Settle. Joint debates between the candidates were a memorable feature of the campaign.

The Bourbon Democrats, or REDEEMERS, dominated state politics after the abandonment of Reconstruction. They emphasized economy in government, retrenchment, and scrupulous honesty. No major scandal involving corruption would plague Tarheel Democrats in this period. Bourbons gave special favors to railroads through charters of incorporation and tax exemptions. They either sold or leased valuable state properties to railroads. Generally their tax policies favored business interests, holders of stocks, bonds, and securities, and salaried persons, while bearing down heavily upon farmers and owners of real property. In 1879 Democrats drastically scaled down and repudiated a substantial portion of the state debt, thereby reducing it from about $43,750,000 to some $6,500,000. Shortly thereafter, following the sale of state-owned railroad property, they declared a tax holiday of one year. While these economies were pursued, the party in office neglected public schools, internal improvements, and eleemosynary institutions. If challenged by disaffected interests, Democrats invariably fell back on the campaign slogan of "Radical Reconstruction and Negro misrule," thereby capitalizing on the legacies of Reconstruction, which created an illogical political unity of the white voters. One-party domination was augmented by control of the electoral machinery. Yet IN-DEPENDENT MOVEMENTS represented a constant threat, Republicans regularly cast more than 40 percent of the total vote, and in 1887 a coalition of independents and Republicans actually secured control of the state house of representatives on the issue of repeal of the odious county government system. The coalition failed to enact this reform, and in 1889 Democrats undertook to discourage further independence through enactment of a repressive election law. A substantial decline in the vote attested to the effectiveness of this legislation.

The most effective criticism of Bourbon policies came from farmers, who in 1887 were encouraged by LEONIDAS L. POLK, editor of the *Progressive Farmer*, to organize a state association. The 1887 farmers' lobby was instrumental in securing the charter of the agricultural and mechanical college in Raleigh and, in cooperation with the Knights of Labor, created in 1887 the state bureau of labor statistics. In 1887 the FARMERS' ALLIANCE was organized in Robeson County, and by 1890 it was active in politics throughout the state. Farmers were emboldened to make demands upon legislative and congressional candidates, and the 1891 legislature was accurately called the "farmers' legislature." In creating a railroad commission and in chartering a normal and industrial college for women and an agricultural and mechanical college for Negroes, both in Greensboro, the farmers achieved a noteworthy reform program.

Although most North Carolina Alliance men preferred to work within the Democratic party, the nomination of Grover Cleveland in 1892 alienated farmers generally and hastened the emergence of a POPULIST PARTY ticket at the state level. The Populist state candidates fared badly in 1892, but the combination of Populist and Republican votes exceeded the number cast for Democrats and was an augury of defeat for Bourbon hopefuls in 1894. Instead of making a sincere effort to accommodate Alliance and Populist demands, Bourbon Democrats ignored the advice of their liberal members and assumed a posture of intransigence. They also undertook to repeal the charter of the Farmers' Alliance and to crush its political role. These circumstances made inevitable the coalition of Populists and Republicans in 1894, known to Tarheels as the fusion government. Although the alliance of Populists and Republicans was illogical from the standpoint of national ideology, there were mutual state interests on which the parties could agree. Republicans were preoccupied with reform of the county government system and election machinery. Populists sought restoration of their charter, usury legislation, stronger railroad regulations, and tax reform. Both parties initially made concessions in shaping their state programs and electoral slates.

The record of the fusion government was impressive in securing repeal of the county government system and in restoring local self-government and home rule. Many of the Populist economic reforms were carried out. Negroes were encouraged to take a more active role in politics, although the extent of their vote and officeholding was exaggerated by Democrats. Populists and Republicans were, however, plagued by disagreements over patronage and electoral slates, and by 1897 an open schism over senatorial candidates had developed. Yet, instead of appealing to disaffected Populists, Democrats capitalized upon an emotionally charged "white supremacy" campaign in 1898 to wrest control of the legislature from fusionists. In a campaign marked by violence and intimidation, Democrats regained control of the state. They proceeded in 1899 to draft a suffrage amendment with its infamous GRANDFATHER CLAUSE. In 1900, again pursuing the white supremacy theme, Democrats elected CHARLES B. AYCOCK to replace the fusionist governor Daniel L. Russell.

The twentieth century. In the 1900 election voters ratified the suffrage amendment that disfranchised illiterate blacks and enfranchised illiterate whites (DISFRANCHISEMENT). The hopes of Republicans and Populists were further dashed by the new election law of 1899. Subsequently Populists either returned to the ranks of Democrats or joined the Republicans. And whatever appeal Republicans might have to the electorate was further undermined by bitter factional squabbling after 1900. There is substantial evidence to indicate that patronage brokers in the Republican ranks were content to allow the party to remain small during the early years of the twentieth century.

The Wilmington race riot erupted in November shortly after the 1898 election. Although it had no effect on the outcome of this white supremacy campaign, it intensified the movement to remove blacks from politics and to replace black laborers with whites. FURNIFOLD M. SIMMONS, the Democratic state chairman, devised party strategy in 1898 and 1900. He promised denominational interests that state support for the University of North Carolina and other public institutions would not be augmented. Furthermore he promised railroad interests that the party would not demand rate reductions. These commitments indicated a conservative leaning among Democratic leaders.

When former Populists complained of the number of white illiterates and doubted that all who came of voting age after 1908 would be educated (in order to qualify under the suffrage amendment), Aycock turned this criticism to advantage by highlighting the educational issue. The educational crusade became the most noted aspect of his gubernatorial program—increased school support, construction of schoolhouses, and most important a campaign to persuade counties and school

districts to levy taxes for the support of common schools.

In the absence of effective Republican or Populist opposition, Democrats divided into liberal and conservative factions. U.S. Senator Furnifold Simmons of New Bern, the acknowledged party leader, headed the conservative faction, known usually as the Simmons machine or dynasty, during the time he served as senator (1901–1931). Simmons by no means dictated party candidates or state legislative policies. Governors Aycock, Robert B. Glenn, and William W. Kitchin were not considered machine candidates. The legislative records, particularly the 1907 and 1913 sessions, were far more liberal and Progressive than Simmons' forces generally favored. With the emergence of the Kitchin family, of Scotland Neck, to prominence in state and national politics, mounting pressures were put upon Democrats to remove Simmons, whom many accused of apostasy to his own party. JOSEPHUS DANIELS, editor of the *News and Observer*; Chief Justice WALTER CLARK of the North Carolina supreme court; and Edward J. Justice, most prominent of the Progressive legislators, demanded a reorientation of the party along more liberal lines. In 1912 Aycock, Clark, and Kitchin challenged Simmons in the senatorial primary. Aycock died during the campaign, and Simmons easily defeated his two lesser opponents. Ironically, he soon became a cosponsor of one of the major pieces of legislation in Woodrow Wilson's first administration, the Underwood-Simmons Tariff Act of 1913.

Disfranchisement of Negroes, the overall decline of the electorate, and the reluctance of Democrats to enact a statewide primary law until 1915 qualified in many ways the proud boast that North Carolina was in the mainstream of the Progressive movement and a leader among southern states. The inability of labor to organize, the pervasively low wage scale, the reluctance of the legislature to enact CHILD LABOR laws or compulsory attendance regulations, and the blighting effects of mill town paternalism retarded Progressive forces during the early years of the twentieth century. Although Simmons was identified with tariff reforms of the Wilson era and CLAUDE KITCHIN was instrumental in shaping Progressive tax reforms at the national level, North Carolina Democrats were unable to translate the idealism of Woodrow Wilson into an impressive state reform program. This was perhaps most evident in the failure of the Progressive Democratic convention of 1914 to impress its demands upon the party leaders. The failure of voters to ratify ten proposed constitutional amendments in 1914 revealed basic conservative philosophies of Tarheel Democrats.

During WORLD WAR I the focus upon defense efforts and expansive training and supply operations in North Carolina shifted emphasis from domestic state programs. A total of 86,457 North Carolinians served in the armed forces, of whom 629 were killed in action. A far greater number, 1,542, died from disease, particularly from the influenza epidemic of 1918.

The accomplishments of state government in the 1920s eclipsed earlier records. From 1913 to 1930 North Carolina taxes increased 554 percent; state expenditures from 1915 to 1925 rose by 847 percent; and from 1920 to 1930 the state bonded debt increased from $13,300,000 to $178,265,000. In this decade business-oriented governors focused on new budgeting and accounting methods, higher tax assessments, highway and school bond issues, and significant increases of support for public schools, higher education, and charitable institutions. Much of the debt burden for schools and roads was assumed by counties and municipalities. In this decade North Carolina deservedly earned its reputation as the "good roads" state of the South.

The administration of Governor O. MAX GARDNER (1929–1933) coincided with the GREAT DEPRESSION, and his significant accomplishments in time of crisis attest to an extraordinary political ability. In 1931 the legislature provided for overall state control of the highway system; it also assumed responsibility for the constitutional six-month public school term and directed that taxes other than ad valorem levies be used to support public schools. The legislature also provided for consolidation of the three major branches of the University of North Carolina. The 1931 session enacted controls over local and county debts in an effort to curtail the advancing tax burden. Due largely to the impetus of Gardner and his successor J. C. B. Ehringhaus, the legislature in 1933 provided that revenues from a 3 percent sales tax be placed in a general fund largely to support schools and charitable institutions. Although North Carolina was in the depths of a depression, the public school term was extended from six to eight months in 1933.

Enormous economic and social losses that followed the panic of 1929 required drastic federal programs to carry out relief, recovery, and reform. Public works projects, conservation activities, and direct relief grants were launched by the administration of Franklin D. Roosevelt to provide employment and a stimulus to the economy. From 1933 to 1938 North Carolina received $428,053,000

in various federal relief projects. At the height of the NEW DEAL era, more than 10 percent of the state population was employed in various federal relief activities. The per capita expenditure of $123.82 was, however, the lowest in the nation. Farmers received benefit payments for crop control and soil conservation projects; with curtailment of production and revival of prosperity, the income of farmers more than doubled from 1932 to 1935. Benefit payments to farmers amounted to $99,351,000 from 1933 to 1940.

The New Deal program, particularly after the passage of the Wagner Act of 1935, sought to protect the rights of workers to organize and bargain collectively (LABOR UNIONS). This legislation and subsequent court decisions upholding the powers of the NATIONAL LABOR RELATIONS BOARD became a powerful stimulus to the growth of organized labor in North Carolina. Further gains for labor were secured in the wages and hours legislation of 1938, which provided to workers in the major industries a minimum 25-cent hourly wage and a 44-hour work week. Under the Social Security Act of 1935, retirement benefits were provided to workers, and payments were made to dependent children and to the needy, blind, and aged. By 1939 the New Deal program had contributed manifestly to the recovery of North Carolina. Tarheels indicated their overwhelming support for the Roosevelt program in the ELECTION OF 1936 and the ELECTION OF 1940.

With the outbreak of WORLD WAR II in Europe in 1939, the concerns of North Carolinians became inextricably linked with foreign policies. The peacetime draft of 1940 and strategies to assist Great Britain affected the lives of many Tarheels before the Japanese attack upon Pearl Harbor in 1941 brought the nation into a two-front war in the Far East and Europe. North Carolina became one of the major training areas for army and marine recruits. Altogether 362,000 Tarheels, including more than 7,000 women, served in the armed forces. Of this number more than 7,000 died in service. On the home front industry and agriculture were converted to wartime production. The state became a major supplier to the armed forces, a construction site for naval vessels at Wilmington, and a quartermaster center of major significance.

During the height of the war, Governor J. Melville Broughton worked with the legislature to secure a nine-month school term (1943) and record-breaking appropriations for education. In 1944 the governor launched a medical care program, whose importance was highlighted by the state's having had the highest rate of rejections of draftees for medical reasons of any American state. The increased revenues available to the state allowed the implementation of a five-year hospital plan (1947–1952) to secure modern hospitals and public HEALTH centers for practically every county. Federal matching funds were provided for these projects under the Hill-Burton Act.

The Shelby dynasty in state politics, launched under the aegis of O. Max Gardner in 1928, for 20 years provided the state with a succession of business-oriented governors, half of whom came from the Shelby area. This leadership was known to historians and political scientists as the progressive plutocracy. In 1948 this political machine was challenged successfully by the former state commissioner of agriculture, W. Kerr Scott of Haw River. Scott achieved one of the most notable records in the twentieth century. Under his leadership landmark victories were secured in bond proposals for schools and roads. The state set a world record for road construction between 1948 and 1952. Scott's program included completion of four-year medical and dental schools at the University of North Carolina and a determined campaign to construct hospitals and health centers in all counties of the state. As a farmer he pushed aggressively for rural electrification, improved telephone services, and the concept that all state financial deposits should yield interest payments. Under Scott's administration blacks were first admitted to the University of North Carolina following a federal court order of 1951.

In 1949 Scott appointed the well-known liberal FRANK P. GRAHAM, president of the University of North Carolina, to the U.S. Senate. When Graham was challenged and defeated by Willis Smith of Raleigh in the primary campaign of 1950, the race issue was used extensively in North Carolina politics for the first time since 1900. Smith's race-baiting marked a significant political departure in the history of the state. This tactic was also used by Alton Lennon against Scott's bid for a Senate seat in 1954 and by I. Beverley Lake against gubernatorial candidate Terry Sanford in 1960. In both instances the agitation of the race issue failed. Since 1960 the issue was exploited in 1968 and 1972 variously by Richard Nixon and by the followers of GEORGE WALLACE. Recent political trends, particularly since the victory of JAMES EARL CARTER over Wallace in North Carolina's 1976 presidential primary and Carter's subsequent election, appear to indicate that the race issue has lost much of its emotional impact.

When LUTHER H. HODGES became governor on November 9, 1954, following the death of William B. Umstead, he brought to the office a background of business experience at national and international levels. Perhaps his greatest achievement was the campaign to attract industry to North Carolina. A major focal point of interest was the creation of the 5,000-acre "research triangle" between Raleigh, Durham, and Chapel Hill. The center presently contains a significant number of research laboratories, both public and private, in the industrial, chemical, and medical fields. In spite of significant progress in construction of industries and laboratories, the relocation of business in North Carolina did not improve significantly the state's average per capita wage for industrial workers. There were even indications that new textile and apparel industries depressed wage levels. Yet the legislature in 1959 became the first in the South to enact a minimum hourly wage law of 75 cents for workers in companies that employed more than five people.

In recent years North Carolina's reputation as a progressive state has been greatly enhanced by the leadership of Governors Terry Sanford (1961–1965) and Robert W. Scott (1969–1973). Stressing quality education for all people, Sanford introduced bold and innovative programs involving a school for the performing arts, a governor's school for high school students of extraordinary ability, and an advancement school for underachievers. The movement to create community colleges and technical schools brought opportunities for higher education into every corner of North Carolina. And a major area of educational activity has involved public television. Significantly larger appropriations for school construction and teachers' salaries were provided during the Sanford and Scott administrations. To finance this ambitious program Sanford defended the extension of sales taxes to food and other consumer items. The governor was not as successful as W. Kerr Scott in securing popular approval for school and road bonds. Indeed, the voters in 1961 rejected all ten items that involved a bond issue referendum. Sanford was more successful in securing constitutional amendments to provide court reform, legislative reapportionment, and tax revision. During his administration a number of cities across the state integrated their schools and, following the much publicized sit-ins at Greensboro, lunch counters commenced to serve customers on an integrated basis. To conservative-minded critics who assailed federal programs and raised the issue of states' rights, the governor responded that the state should assume greater responsibilities and function in a more dynamic and creative way.

Archival and manuscript depositories for study of North Carolina history are located in a number of state and private institutions. At Division of Archives and History in Raleigh, state records are classified by various departments and include executive, legislative, and judicial materials. Extensive county and municipal records, either in original files or microfilm copies, are located in state archives. Private manuscript collections deposited in archives division are described in B. Crabtree (ed.), *Guide to Private Manuscript Collections in North Carolina State Archives* (1964). C. C. Crittenden and D. Lacy (eds.), *Historical Records of North Carolina* (3 vols.; 1938–39), is useful reference. Southern Historical Collection at University of North Carolina, Chapel Hill, has extensive manuscript collections relating to North Carolina history. Detailed descriptive analyses of holdings include S. Blosser and C. N. Wilson, Jr., *Southern Historical Collection: Guide to Manuscripts* (1970); and E. H. Smith, *Supplementary Guide to Manuscripts, 1970–1975* (1976). Manuscript department of Duke University has a large collection of North Carolina materials; its catalog is detailed and classified and includes an autograph file. Both Duke and UNC have launched oral history projects involving North Carolina history.

The East Carolina University manuscript collection, Greenville, has materials relating to coastal plain, notably agriculture, Civil War, and military history, with descriptive catalogs and autograph files available. Western Carolina University, Cullowhee, has recently launched a manuscript collection; Appalachian State University and Mars Hill College are engaged in collecting materials relating to southern Appalachian region. These collections have all launched oral history projects. The records of Presbyterian Church in North Carolina are located at Montreat, and Baptist Historical Collection is located at Wake Forest University.

Greatest single depository of printed material relating to North Carolina history is North Carolina Collection at UNC, Chapel Hill. Its resources are listed in M. Thornton (comp.), *Bibliography of North Carolina, 1589–1956* (1958) and *Official Publications of Colony and State of North Carolina, 1749–1939: Bibliography* (1954). H. T. Lefler and A. R. Newsome's *North Carolina: History of Southern State* (1973) is outstanding general history. This may be supplemented by R. D. W. Connor, *North Carolina: Rebuilding an Ancient Commonwealth* (2 vols.; 1929); and H. T. Lefler, *History of North Carolina* (2 vols.; 1956).

W. L. Saunders (ed.), *Colonial Records of North Carolina* (10 vols.; 1886–90), is being reissued with new documentary material under editorship of M. E. Parker and W. S. Price; four volumes have appeared to date (1963–74). W. Clark (ed.), *State Records of North Carolina* (16 vols.; 1895–1901), is major source of documentary material. Earliest explorations of North Carolina are documented in D. B. Quinn (ed.), *Roanoke Voyages, 1584–1590* (2 vols.; 1955). Significant contemporary accounts of early settlement include J. Lawson, *New Voyage to Carolina* (1709); J. Brickell, *Natural History of North Carolina* (1737); J. Schaw, *Journal of Lady of Quality*, ed. C. M. and E. W. Andrews (1921); and W. P. Cumming, *Southeast in Early Maps* (1958). For geographical factors, see C. Camp, *Influence of Geography upon Early North Carolina* (1963); and D. Stick, *Graveyard of Atlantic: Shipwrecks of Carolina Coast* (1952) and *Outer Banks of North Carolina, 1584–1958* (1958). For place-names, consult W. S. Powell, *North Carolina*

Gazetteer (1968). H. R. Merrens, *Colonial North Carolina in Eighteenth Century: Study in Historical Geography* (1964), is first-rate. For contributions of Indians, see D. L. Rights, *American Indian in North Carolina* (1957); C. J. Milling, *Red Carolinians* (1940); and S. A. South, *Indians in North Carolina* (1959).

E. L. Lee, Jr., *Indian Wars in North Carolina, 1663–1763* (1963), highlights major problem of early settlers. W. S. Powell (ed.), in *Ye Countie of Albemarle in Carolina* (1958) and *Carolina Charter of 1663* (1954), focuses on settlement of northeastern North Carolina. H. F. Rankin, *Upheaval in Albemarle, 1675–1689: Culpeper's Rebellion* (1962), treats factional political struggles. W. S. Powell, *Proprietors of Carolina* (1963), presents useful biographical data. Expansion of settlements into southeastern North Carolina is treated in E. L. Lee, Jr., *Lower Cape Fear in Colonial Days* (1965); and J. Sprunt, *Chronicles of Cape Fear River, 1660–1916* (1916). D. Meyer, *Highland Scots of North Carolina, 1732–1776* (1961), focuses on settlement of Cape Fear River valley and development of naval stores industry.

A. L. Fries, K. G. Hamilton, and M. Smith (eds.), *Records of Moravians of North Carolina* (11 vols.; 1922–69), is monumental collection. R. W. Ramsey, *Carolina Cradle* (1964); and C. Hammer, Jr., *Rhinelanders on Yadkin* (1965), deal with settlement of frontier counties.

J. P. Greene, *Quest for Power* (1963), deals with factional political crises, 1689–1776. C. L. Raper, *North Carolina: Study in English Colonial Government* (1904), represents an early study. See also P. M. McCain, *County Court in North Carolina Before 1750* (1954); and C. Parker, *History of Taxation in North Carolina, 1663–1776* (1926). B. P. Robinson, *Five Royal Governors of North Carolina* (1963), provides useful biographical data. C. C. Crittenden, *Commerce of North Carolina, 1763–1789* (1937), develops historical significance of trade records. H. F. Rankin, *Pirates of Colonial North Carolina* (1960), places topic in perspective. S. B. Weeks's *Religious Development in Province of North Carolina* (1892) and *Church and State in North Carolina* (1893) develop beginnings of religious activity. J. C. Spruill, *Women's Life and Work in Southern Colonies* (1938), is major work. F. B. Johnston and T. T. Waterman, *Early Architecture of North Carolina* (1941); J. V. Allcott, *Colonial Homes in North Carolina* (1963); and J. H. Craig, *Arts and Crafts in North Carolina, 1699–1840* (1965), are useful for social history. Perhaps greatest work on North Carolina social history is G. G. Johnson, *Ante-Bellum North Carolina* (1937). D. Long, *Medicine in North Carolina, 1524–1960* (2 vols.; 1972), is of interest.

For indentured servants, see A. E. Smith, *Colonists in Bondage* (1947). D. R. Lennon and J. B. Kellam (eds.), *Wilmington Town Book, 1743–1778* (1973), develops significant phase of social history. E. W. Knight (ed.), *Documentary History of Education in South Before 1860* (5 vols.; 1949–53) and *Public School Education in North Carolina* (1916), are noteworthy. For Regulator movement, see W. S. Powell et al. (eds.), *Regulators in North Carolina: Documentary History, 1759–1776* (1971); see also A. T. Dill, *Governor Tryon and His Palace* (1955). Revolutionary era in North Carolina is treated in R. D. W. Connor, *Revolutionary Leaders of North Carolina* (1916) and *Cornelius Harnett* (1909). H. F. Rankin's *North Carolina Continentals* (1971) and *American Revolution in North Carolina* (1959) give insights into military operations. See also C. G. Davidson, *Piedmont Partisan: William Lee Davidson* (1951); C. W. Troxler, *Loyalist Experience in North Carolina* (1976); J. J. Crow, *Chronicle of North Carolina During American Revolution, 1763–1789* (1975); and L. S. Butler, *North Carolina and Coming of American Revolution, 1763–1776* (1976). E. P. Douglass, *Rebels and Democrats* (1955), is significant political analysis. W. H. Hoyt, *Mecklenburg Declaration of Independence* (1907), treats a venerable myth. F. M. Green, *Constitutional Development of South Atlantic States, 1776–1860* (1930); and E. W. Sikes, *Transition of North Carolina from Colony to Commonwealth* (1898), deal with constitutional developments.

Confederation era problems are related in J. R. Morrill, *Practice and Politics of Fiat Finance: North Carolina, 1783–1789* (1969); A. B. Keith and W. H. Masterson (eds.), *John Gray Blount Papers* (3 vols.; 1952–65); W. H. Masterson, *William Blount* (1954); B. P. Robinson, *W. R. Davie* (1954); and L. I. Trenholme, *Ratification of Federal Constitution in North Carolina* (1932). For early education, see R. D. W. Connor (ed.), *Documentary History of University of North Carolina, 1776–1799* (2 vols.; 1953); C. L. Coon, *Beginnings of Public Education in North Carolina, 1790–1840* (2 vols.; 1908) and *North Carolina Schools and Academies, 1790–1840: Documentary History* (2 vols.; 1915), esp. significant.

G. J. McRee (ed.), *Life and Correspondence of James Iredell* (2 vols.; 1857–58); and D. Higginbotham (ed.), *Papers of James Iredell* (2 vols.; 1976), give insight into life of prominent Federalist and jurist. H. M. Wagstaff, *State Rights and Political Parties in North Carolina, 1776–1861* (1906), traces early political developments. Beginnings of party journalism are treated in R. N. Elliott, Jr., *Raleigh Register, 1799–1863* (1955). D. H. Gilpatrick, *Jeffersonian Democracy in North Carolina, 1789–1816* (1931); H. M. Wagstaff (ed.), *Papers of John Steele* (2 vols.; 1924); and W. E. Dodd, *Life of Nathaniel Macon* (1903), treat aspects of Jeffersonian Democracy. S. M. Lemmon, *Frustrated Patriots: North Carolina and War of 1812* (1973), is carefully researched.

Transportation problems are described in C. C. Weaver, *History of Internal Improvements in North Carolina Previous to 1860* (1903); and C. K. Brown, *State Movement in Railroad Development* (1928). Early agricultural history is described in C. O. Cathey, *Agricultural Development in North Carolina, 1783–1860* (1956). Ideas of major social and economic reformer are treated in W. H. Hoyt (ed.), *Papers of Archibald D. Murphey* (2 vols.; 1914). B. A. Konkle, *John Motley Morehead and Development of North Carolina, 1796–1866* (1922), is study of much significance.

Factional divisions that led to breakup of Jeffersonian Republican party are masterfully told in A. R. Newsome, *Presidential Election of 1824 in North Carolina* (1939). J. G. de R. Hamilton, *Party Politics in North Carolina, 1835–1860* (1916); W. S. Hoffman, *Andrew Jackson and North Carolina Politics* (1958); C. C. Norton, *Democratic Party in Ante-Bellum North Carolina, 1835–1861* (1930); J. G. de R. Hamilton and M. R. Williams (eds.), *Papers of William A. Graham* (6 vols.; 1957–76); J. G. de R. Hamilton (ed.), *Papers of Thomas Ruffin* (2 vols.; 1918–20); H. T. Shanks (ed.), *Papers of Willie P. Mangum* (5 vols.; 1950–56), present data of interest on Democrats and Whigs. See also S. M. Lemmon (ed.), *Pet-*

tigrew Papers, 1685–1818 (1971), first vol. of significant family series.

N. M. Tilley, *Bright Tobacco Industry* (1948); R. H. Taylor, *Slaveholding in North Carolina: Economic View* (1926); N. C. Chaffin, *Trinity College, 1839–1892* (1950); G. W. Paschal, *History of Wake Forest College* (3 vols.; 1935–43); and C. Shaw, *Davidson College* (1923), present significant nineteenth-century economic and social data.

Aspects of abolitionist crusade are developed in J. S. Bassett, *Anti-Slavery Leaders of North Carolina* (1898). A major work is J. H. Franklin, *Free Negro in North Carolina* (1943). North Carolina's role in secession crisis is presented in J. C. Sitterson, *Secession Movement in North Carolina* (1939). F. Johnston (ed.), *Papers of Zebulon B. Vance, 1843–1862* (1963), is first vol. to be published in noteworthy project. N. J. Tolbert (ed.), *Papers of John W. Ellis* (2 vols.; 1964), deals with secession crisis. W. Clark (ed.), *Histories of Several Regiments and Battalions from North Carolina in Great War, 1861–1865* (1901), is monumental contribution. J. G. Barrett's *Civil War in North Carolina* (1963) and *General Sherman's March Through Carolinas* (1956) are authoritative works.

Political and legal problems of Civil War are treated in C. Dowd, *Life of Zebulon B. Vance* (1899); G. Tucker, *Zeb Vance* (1965); and M. F. Mitchell, *Legal Aspects of Conscription and Exemption in North Carolina, 1861–1865* (1965). See also C. P. Spencer, *Last 90 Days of War in North Carolina* (1866); and L. R. Wilson (ed.), *Selected Papers of Cornelia Phillips Spencer, 1865–1900* (1953).

For period since Civil War, useful introductive studies are J. G. de R. Hamilton, *North Carolina Since 1860* (1919) and *Reconstruction in North Carolina* (1914). W. K. Boyd (ed.), *Memoirs of W. W. Holden* (1911); J. G. de R. Hamilton (ed.), *Correspondence of Jonathan Worth* (2 vols.; 1929) and *Papers of Randolph Shotwell* (3 vols.; 1929–36), are widely consulted studies. For a significant recent study, see W. M. Evans, *Ballots and Fence Rails: Reconstruction on Lower Cape Fear* (1967) and *To Die Game: Story of Lowry Band* (1971). O. H. Olsen, *Carpetbagger's Crusade: Albion Winegar Tourgée* (1965), is first-rate. J. Daniels, *Prince of Carpetbaggers* (1958), exposes seamy antics of Milton S. Littlefield. For gubernatorial politics under Conservative party leadership, see R. L. Zuber, *Jonathan Worth* (1965).

Political changes in post-Reconstruction era are recounted in D. J. Whitener, *Prohibition in North Carolina* (1946). J. Daniels, *Tar Heel Editor* (1939), is enormously interesting personal reminiscence. B. J. Hendrick, *Training of an American: Earlier Life and Letters of Walter Hines Page, 1855–1913* (1928), develops theme of journalism and reform. F. A. Logan, *Negro in North Carolina, 1876–1894* (1964), provides fresh insights. S. Noblin, *Leonidas Lafayette Polk* (1949); G. T. Winston, *Builder of New South: Daniel Augustus Tompkins* (1920); W. K. Boyd, *Story of Durham* (1925); H. Thompson, *From Cotton Field to Cotton Mill: Industrial Transition in North Carolina* (1906); and B. Mitchell, *Rise of Cotton Mills in South* (1921), deal with agriculture and industry.

Bourbon era politics are treated in W. B. Yearns (ed.), *Papers of Thomas Jordan Jarvis, 1869–1882* (1969), first vol. in a series. I. W. and J. J. Van Noppen, *Western North Carolina Since Civil War* (1973), is work of considerable interest. R. J. Lanier, *Blanford B. Dougherty* (1974), develops role of founder of Appalachian State University. R. F. Durden, *Dukes of Durham, 1865–1929* (1975), treats role of family of tobacco manufacturers and philanthropists. Negro contributions to Durham's history are developed in W. B. Weare, *Black Business in New South: Social History of North Carolina Mutual Life Insurance Co.* (1973). Aspects of fusion era are treated in H. G. Edmonds, *Negro and Fusion Politics in North Carolina, 1894–1901* (1951). D. L. Russell's political and private activities are treated in R. F. Durden, *Reconstruction Bonds and Twentieth-Century Politics: South Dakota v. North Carolina, 1904* (1962). Campaign for Negro disfranchisement is developed by W. A. Mabry, *Negro in North Carolina Politics Since Reconstruction* (1940); and J. M. Kousser, *Shaping of Southern Politics: Suffrage Restrictions, 1880–1910* (1974). Aspects of race issue are also discussed in B. Clayton, *Savage Ideal, 1890–1914* (1972); and H. S. Smith, *In His Image but . . . : Racism in Southern Religion, 1780–1910* (1972). See also F. A. Bode, *Protestantism and New South: North Carolina Baptists and Methodists in Political Crisis, 1894–1903* (1975).

For specialized studies dealing with twentieth-century education, see L. R. Harlan, *Separate and Unequal: Public School Campaigns and Racism, 1901–1915* (1958); J. F. Gifford, Jr., *Evolution of Medical Center: Medicine at Duke University to 1941* (1972); C. C. Carpenter, *Story of Medicine at Wake Forest University* (1970); L. R. Wilson, *University of North Carolina, 1900–1930* (1957); E. W. Porter, *Trinity and Duke, 1892–1924* (1964); R. H. Holder, *McIver of North Carolina* (1957); and E. A. Bowles, *Good Beginning: First Four Decades of UNC at Greensboro* (1967).

Early twentieth-century political data are developed in J. Daniels, *Editor in Politics* (1941); J. L. Morrison, *Josephus Daniels Says* (1962); O. H. Orr, Jr., *Charles Brantley Aycock* (1949); R. D. W. Connor and C. Poe, *Life and Speeches of Charles Brantley Aycock* (1912); J. F. Rippy (ed.), *Furnifold Simmons: Memoirs and Addresses* (1936); A. L. Brooks, *Walter Clark* (1944); and A. L. Brooks and H. T. Lefler (eds.), *Papers of Walter Clark, 1857–1924* (2 vols.; 1948–50). Opposition to Woodrow Wilson is indicated in A. M. Arnett, *Claude Kitchin and Wilson War Policies* (1937). A more favorable attitude toward Wilson is revealed in J. Daniels, *Wilson Era* (2 vols.; 1944). Works of a political nature spanning years between two world wars include J. R. Moore, *Josiah William Bailey* (1968); and J. L. Morrison, *Governor O. Max Gardner* (1971).

Intellectual climate of 1920s is recalled in S. C. Linder, *William Louis Poteat* (1966); and W. B. Gatewood, Jr., *Preachers, Pedagogues, and Politicians: Evolution Controversy in North Carolina, 1920–1927* (1966). G. B. Tindall, *Emergence of New South, 1913–1945* (1967), highlights business progressivism in North Carolina. Political campaigns are described in E. L. Puryear, *Democratic Party Dissension in North Carolina, 1928–1936* (1962); and J. L. Morrison, *Josephus Daniels* (1966). H. L. Herring's *Welfare Work in Mill Villages* (1929) and *Passing of Mill Village* (1949) are major contributions to understanding mill town life. Significant profiles of North Carolina are developed in S. H. Hobbs, Jr., *North Carolina, Economic and Social* (1930) and *North Carolina: Economic and Social Profile* (1958).

For 30 years D. L. Corbitt edited for North Carolina Historical Commission the messages, papers, letters, and public addresses of state governors. These include Cameron Morrison, 1921–1925 (1927); Angus W. McLean, 1925–1929 (1931); Oliver Max Gardner, 1929–1933 (1937); John Christoph Blucher Ehringhaus, 1933–1937 (1950); Clyde Roark Hoey, 1937–1941 (1944); Joseph Melville Broughton, 1941–1945 (1950); Robert Gregg Cherry, 1945–1949 (1951); William Kerr Scott, 1949–1953 (1957); and William Bradley Umstead, 1953–1954 (1957).

One of major New Deal projects in North Carolina in 1930s is described in H. E. Jolley, *Blue Ridge Parkway* (1969). S. B. King, Jr., *Selective Service in North Carolina in World War II* (1949), highlights high rate of rejections for medical and psychological reasons. For aspects of 1950s, see J. W. Patton (ed.), *Messages, Addresses, and Public Papers of Luther Hartwell Hodges* (3 vols.; 1960–63); and L. H. Hodges, *Businessman in Statehouse* (1962). A significant contemporary analysis of Tarheel politics is J. D. Fleer, *North Carolina Politics: Introduction* (1968). The 1960s are reflected in M. F. Mitchell (ed.), *Messages, Addresses, and Public Papers of Terry Sanford, Governor of North Carolina, 1961–1965* (1966). The dynamic political philosophy of Sanford is revealed in T. Sanford, *But What About People?* (1966) and *Storm over States* (1967). Miles Wolff, *Lunch at Five and Ten: Greensboro Sit-ins* (1970), is significant chapter in race relations. M. F. Mitchell (ed.), *Messages and Public Papers of Dan Killian Moore, 1965–1969* (1971) and *Messages and Public Papers of Robert Walter Scott, 1969–1973* (1974), are of interest for contemporary politics. P. L. Clancy, *Just a Country Lawyer: Senator Sam Ervin* (1974), is noteworthy political study.

Useful political data are available in J. L. Cheney (ed.), *North Carolina Government, 1585–1974: Narrative and Statistical History* (1975). J. W. Clay, D. M. Orr, Jr., and A. W. Stuart's *North Carolina Atlas* (1975) offers wide variety of information on history, politics, population, physical resources and environment, economic trends, transportation, and services and amenities.

Aspects of literary and cultural life of state are treated in T. Stem, Jr., *Tar Heel Press* (1973); R. Walser, *Literary North Carolina* (1970), *Poets of North Carolina* (1963), and *North Carolina Poetry* (1941); and H. G. Jones, *For History's Sake: Preservation and Publication of North Carolina History, 1663–1903* (1966). A major publication relating to social history is *Frank C. Brown Collection of North Carolina Folklore* (5 vols.; 1952–62).

Since 1924 the *North Carolina Historical Review* has published countless articles of significant historical and literary quality. Almost all of the works deal with North Carolina history. A 50-year index is being compiled for publication. The *South Atlantic Quarterly* has been a major source of articles on North Carolina history, as have publications of Trinity College Historical Society. Significant essays on legal problems appear in *North Carolina Law Review*. North Carolina materials are also featured in *East Carolina College Publications in History* (3 vols.; 1964–66).

Doctoral dissertations in North Carolina history, written principally at UNC and Duke, are conveniently listed in W. F. Kuehl's *Dissertations in History* (1972). One of most convenient bibliographies is H. T. Lefler's *Guide to Study and Reading of North Carolina History* (1969).

JOSEPH F. STEELMAN
East Carolina University

NORTH CAROLINA POPULATION, 1790–1970

Year	Total	White	Nonwhite Slave	Nonwhite Free	% Growth	Rank U.S.	Rank South
1790	393,751	288,204	100,783	4,764		3	2
1800	478,103	337,764	133,296	7,043	21.4	4	2
1810	555,500	376,410	168,824	10,266	16.2	4	2
1820	638,829	419,200	204,917	14,712	15.0	4	2
1830	737,987	472,843	245,601	19,543	15.5	5	2
1840	753,419	484,870	245,817	22,732	2.1	7	4
1850	869,039	553,028	288,548	27,463	15.3	10	5
1860	992,622	629,942	331,059	31,621	14.2	12	6
1870	1,071,361	678,470	392,891		7.9	14	6
1880	1,399,750	867,242	532,508		30.7	15	7
1890	1,617,949	1,055,382	562,567		15.6	16	7
1900	1,893,810	1,263,603	630,207		17.1	15	6
1910	2,206,287	1,500,511	705,776		16.5	16	5
1920	2,559,123	1,783,779	775,344		16.0	14	4
1930	3,170,276	2,234,958	935,318		23.9	12	3
1940	3,571,623	2,567,635	1,003,988		12.7	11	3
1950	4,061,929	2,983,121	1,078,808		13.7	10	2
1960	4,556,155	3,399,285	1,156,870		12.2	12	3
1970	5,082,059	3,901,767	1,180,292		11.5	12	3

NORTH CAROLINA GOVERNORS

Governor	Party	Term	Governor	Party	Term
Richard Caswell		1776–1780	Curtis H. Brogden	Rep.	1874–1877
Abner Nash		1780–1781	Zebulon B. Vance	Dem.	1877–1879
Thomas Burke		1781–1782	Thomas J. Jarvis	Dem.	1879–1885
Alexander Martin		1782–1785	Alfred M. Scales	Dem.	1885–1889
Richard Caswell		1785–1787	Daniel G. Fowle	Dem.	1889–1891
Samuel Johnston	Fed.	1787–1789	Thomas M. Holt	Dem.	1891–1893
Alexander Martin	Fed.	1789–1792	Elias Carr	Dem.	1893–1897
Richard D. Spaight	anti-Fed.	1792–1795	Daniel L. Russell	Rep.	1897–1901
Samuel Ashe	anti-Fed.	1795–1798	Charles B. Aycock	Dem.	1901–1905
William R. Davie	Fed.	1798–1799	Robert B. Glenn	Dem.	1905–1909
Benjamin Williams	Dem.-Rep.	1799–1802	William W. Kitchin	Dem.	1909–1913
John B. Ashe	Dem.-Rep.	1802	Locke Craig	Dem.	1913–1917
James Turner	Dem.-Rep.	1802–1805	Thomas W. Bickett	Dem.	1917–1921
Nathaniel Alexander	Dem.-Rep.	1805–1807	Cameron Morrison	Dem.	1921–1925
Benjamin Williams	Dem.-Rep.	1807–1808	Angus W. McLean	Dem.	1925–1929
David Stone	Dem.-Rep.	1808–1810	O. Max Gardner	Dem.	1929–1933
Benjamin Smith	Dem.-Rep.	1810–1811	J. C. B. Ehringhaus	Dem.	1933–1937
William Hawkins	Dem.-Rep.	1811–1814	Clyde R. Hoey	Dem.	1937–1941
William Miller	Dem.-Rep.	1814–1817	J. Melville Broughton	Dem.	1941–1945
John Branch	Dem.-Rep.	1817–1820	R. Gregg Cherry	Dem.	1945–1949
Jesse Franklin	Dem.-Rep.	1820–1821	W. Kerr Scott	Dem.	1949–1953
Gabriel Holmes		1821–1824	William B. Umstead	Dem.	1953–1954
Hutchings G. Burton	Fed.	1824–1827	Luther H. Hodges	Dem.	1954–1961
James Iredell, Jr.	Dem.-Rep.	1827–1828	Terry Sanford	Dem.	1961–1965
John Owen	Dem.-Rep.	1828–1830	Dan K. Moore	Dem.	1965–1969
Montfort Stokes	Dem.	1830–1832	Robert W. Scott	Dem.	1969–1973
David L. Swain	Whig	1832–1835	James E. Holshouser, Jr.	Rep.	1973–1977
Richard D. Spaight, Jr.	Dem.	1835–1836	James B. Hunt, Jr.	Dem.	1977–
Edward B. Dudley	Whig	1836–1841			
John M. Morehead	Whig	1841–1845			
William A. Graham	Whig	1845–1849			
Charles Manly	Whig	1849–1851			
David S. Reid	Dem.	1851–1854			
Warren Winslow	Dem.	1854–1855			
Thomas Bragg	Dem.	1855–1859			
John W. Ellis	Dem.	1859–1861			
Henry T. Clark	Dem.	1861–1862			
Zebulon B. Vance	Dem.	1862–1865			
William W. Holden	Rep.	1865			
Jonathan Worth	Dem.	1865–1868			
William W. Holden	Rep.	1868–1870			
Tod R. Caldwell	Rep.	1870–1874			

NORTH CAROLINA, HISTORICAL SOCIETY OF (Box 2248, Elon College, N.C. 27244), organized in 1945, is sometimes considered to be the descendant of the first state historical society, which was chartered in 1833 but which was only intermittently in existence thereafter. This society is limited to 75 scholars invited to membership because of their publications or sustained interest in history, who meet semiannually to present scholarly papers on North Carolina history. The society sponsors an annual prize for the best article published in the *North Carolina Historical Review* and also the Undergraduate History Award for the outstanding paper written by a student in one of the colleges or universities of the state.

NORTH CAROLINA, UNIVERSITY OF (Chapel Hill, 27511), chartered in 1789, was the first state university in the nation to open its doors. Being first in operation, however, has meant little to the school's success. During the first century of its existence, the university was constantly hindered by uncertain finances and regularly embroiled in state politics. The university's original Federalist sponsors sought to finance its operation through grants of state lands to the institution, but Democratic-Republicans repealed the land-grant legislation in 1805 and refused to authorize alternative forms of financial assistance. They viewed the institution as a Federalist stronghold and regarded its classical curriculum as fit only for sons of the very rich.

During the period of Whig domination of the state's government (1835–1850), increased appropriations for the university were almost as popular with the majority party as were internal improvements. New buildings and additional faculty permitted the student enrollment to grow from 104 in 1835 to over 400 in the 1850s. Yet, as the school grew in public acceptance, so also did it become more reflective of popular opinion. In 1856, for example, after a chemistry professor B. J. Hedrick voiced his opposition to any further expansion of slavery, he was dismissed from the faculty and forced to flee the state. The Unionist inclinations of the university's president David Swain did little to endear the institution to the state's pro-Confederate legislature; and the lending of the university's meager endowment to support the state's war effort resulted only in bankrupting the institution when the state repudiated its Confederate debt. Republican Governor W. W. HOLDEN reopened the university in 1868 as an arm of an expanded statewide system of public education. A new (and Republican) board of trustees was appointed, but political conflict at the Chapel Hill campus forced the school's closing again in 1870. Although the state's REDEEMERS reopened and reorganized the university in 1875, insufficient funds and continuing political and denominational controversy prevented its developing beyond its status as a small liberal arts college.

The rise of the university to its present position as one of the nation's premier institutions of higher learning is a phenomenon of the twentieth century. During the 1920s, a period of spectacular growth, state appropriations were increased by five times the amount given at the beginning of the decade. The size of the school's faculty tripled during this period. Schools of graduate studies, public welfare, and library science and departments of drama, sociology, music, journalism, and psychology were founded. The University of North Carolina Press (the first such press in the South), the Carolina Playmakers (THEATER), and HOWARD ODUM's Institute for Research in Social Science gave the institution a national reputation for the first time in its history. Current enrollment is approximately 20,000 students.

Not the least of the university's recent achievements has been creation of the library's Southern Historical Collection, a massive collection of manuscripts based upon materials originally collected by the Historical Society of North Carolina. Among the approximately 4 million items housed in this collection are the records of plantations and the personal correspondence of countless educators, scientists, physicians, authors, religious leaders, politicians, and military figures. Among the military figures whose papers are in the collection are E. P. Alexander, T. L. Clingman, J. H. Morgan, and J. J. Pettigrew. Other collections of personal papers include those of William Gaston, Thomas Bragg, R. D. W. Connor, W. A. Graham, and Z. Vance, of North Carolina; William Wirt, Edmund Pendleton, William Byrd II, and the Tucker family, all of Virginia; Wade Hampton III, William Lowndes, R. I. Manning, C. G. Memminger, and R. B. Rhett, of South Carolina; A. O. Bacon and Tom Watson, of Georgia; J. A. Campbell, B. B. Comer, and E. A. O'Neal, of Alabama; John Bell, Felix Grundy, and D. M. Key, of Tennessee; R. K. Call, of Florida; A. P. Gorman, of Maryland; J. Guthrie, of Kentucky; J. F. H. Claiborne, J. M. Parker, and H. C. Warmouth, of Louisiana; and J. L. Alcorn, of Mississippi.

See L. R. Wilson, *University of North Carolina* (1957) and *UNC Under Consolidation, 1931–1963* (1964); R. B. House, *Light That Shines* (1964); K. P. Battle, *History of UNC* (1907–12); W. S. Powell, *First State University* (1972), illustrated; and R. D. W. Connor (ed.), *Documentary History of UNC, 1776–1799* (2 vols.; 1953).

NORTH CAROLINA HISTORICAL REVIEW (Historical Publications Section, Division of Archives and History, 109 E. Jones St., Raleigh, N.C. 27611) is a quarterly founded in 1924 and published by the Division of Archives and History of the North Carolina Department of Cultural Resources. In addition to subscribers, the *Review* goes to all members of the North Carolina Liter-

ary and Historical Association. The *Review* followed a long line of North Carolina publications, such as *Our Living and Our Dead* (1873–1876), *North Carolina Historical and Genealogical Register* (1900–1903), *North Carolina University Magazine* (1844–1920), and *North Carolina Booklet* (1901–1926), all of which failed. The illustrated and indexed *Review*, with a present circulation of 2,300, publishes scholarly articles on the history of North Carolina and occasionally other parts of the South if a relationship with North Carolina is apparent, plus documentary materials, book reviews, and an annual North Carolina bibliography. It pays $10 per article upon acceptance for publication. The *Review* relies heavily though not exclusively on writers from institutions of higher learning but welcomes material from a variety of writers in addition to professional historians. A cumulative 50-year index is currently under way. The Historical Society of North Carolina offers an annual prize of $100 for the best article appearing in the *Review*.

The Division of Archives and History publishes not only the *Review* but a wide variety of documentary volumes, pamphlets, maps, and *Carolina Comments*, a bimonthly established in 1952 that includes brief articles on activities of the division's several sections and on local and statewide historical organizations. The division administers programs devoted to archives and records management, historic preservation, historic sites, museums, and archeology as well as historical publications.

NORTH CAROLINA STATE COLLEGE (Raleigh, 27607)

is a coeducational, state-supported institution with an enrollment of approximately 13,000 students. In 1868 the state accepted the terms of the Morrill Act of 1862 and transferred federal scrip for 270,000 acres of western land to the University of North Carolina at Chapel Hill. Yet that institution never created an agricultural college and often failed to offer the few courses in husbandry and agricultural arts listed on its books. Accordingly, in 1887 the legislature created a new institution tied to the federal system of land-grant colleges and universities: North Carolina College of Agricultural and Mechanical Arts. Besides having an excellent School of Agriculture, North Carolina State has developed programs that both reflect and lead toward greater diversification of the state's economy. Its School of Engineering is one of the largest in the nation. And its School of Textiles, School of Forestry, and Center for Pulp and Paper Technology have been invaluable assets to the state's economy. Housed at the college library

are the papers of C. A. Schenck, an important figure in North Carolina FORESTRY.

See D. A. Lockmiller, *History of North Carolina State College, 1889–1939* (1939).

NORTHROP, LUCIUS BELLINGER (1811–1894),

was commissary general of subsistence for the Confederate army. Born in Charleston, S.C., he was graduated from West Point in 1831, served in the Indian Territory, and was wounded in the Seminole War. For a time he engaged in a limited medical practice in Charleston until 1861. In March, 1861, Northrop was appointed commissary general by Jefferson Davis; in this office he had to contend with increasingly serious problems: internal corruption, food speculation, hoarding, the government policy against trade with the enemy, military reverses, the necessity for impressment and price-fixing, currency depreciation, and a poor transportation system. He was an adequate if overly bureaucratic and unimaginative administrator, but his eccentric and cranky personality made him a natural target for those who were either frustrated by defeat or anxious to discredit Davis. He was perhaps the most criticized of Davis' appointments and was replaced by Isaac St. John in February, 1865. In later years Northrop farmed near Charlottesville, Va.

See R. D. Goff, *Confederate Supply* (1969); T. R. Hay, *Civil War History* (March, 1963); J. P. Felt, *Virginia Magazine of History and Biography* (April, 1961); W. E. Wight (ed.), *Virginia Magazine of History and Biography* (Oct., 1960); Northrop Papers, New York Public Library; and Papers Relating to Subsistence Department, Virginia Historical Society, Richmond.

JEREMY P. FELT
University of Vermont

NUECES RIVER

rises in south-central Texas and flows in a southerly and southeasterly course to Nueces Bay, an arm of Corpus Christi Bay, on the Gulf of Mexico. Its name is derived from the Spanish word *nuez* (nut) for the many nut-bearing trees that grew along the river's lower banks. After formation of the Republic of Texas, the river was the subject of a considerable dispute concerning that nation's boundary with Mexico. Texans argued that the Rio Grande should be its southern boundary, and Mexicans held that the Nueces was and should be the line of division. At issue was not only the territory between the two rivers along the coast but also the territory between their headwaters, including much of present-day Colorado, Kansas, New Mexico, Oklahoma, and Texas. The question was resolved at the conclusion of the MEXICAN WAR, when the Rio Grande was made the international boundary.

NUGENT, THOMAS L. (1841–1895), was born in Louisiana of prominent, slaveholding parents. A graduate of Centenary College in 1861, he migrated to Texas in 1862 and volunteered as a private in the Confederate army. Afterward he taught school in Austin and studied for a short time to become a Methodist minister, before deciding to become a lawyer. In 1873 he settled in Stephenville and was a delegate to the Texas constitutional convention of 1875. In 1879 he was appointed district judge. Reelected twice, he resigned in 1888 because of ill health and moved to El Paso. In 1891 he moved to Ft. Worth, established a law office, and took the lead in organizing the POPULIST PARTY. These efforts won him the nomination for governor at the first Texas Populist convention in 1892. The election of 1892 was bitter and hotly contested. The dominating Democrats split, with Governor JAMES S. HOGG heading the regular reform Democrats and Waco attorney George W. Clark leading the splinter conservative group. Although Nugent made a strong showing, he still finished third as Hogg won reelection. Renominated by the Populists in 1894, Nugent had hopes of defeating Hogg's successor, but the Democrats embraced enough reform proposals, primarily free silver, to defeat him soundly. Nugent's untimely death deprived the Texas Populists of their most dignified and respected leader.

See W. Alvord, *Southwestern Historical Quarterly* (July, 1953); C. Nugent (ed.), *Nugent* (1896); A. Barr, *Texas Politics* (1971); R. C. Cotner, *Hogg* (1959); and M. A. Martin, *People's Party in Texas* (1933).

BOB C. HOLCOMB
Angelo State University

NULLIFICATION is the process by which a state seeks to make a federal law inoperable within its borders. Nullification rests upon the theory that the United States originated in an agreement among the states, which retained sovereignty. By ratifying the Constitution, the people of each state acted in their sovereign capacity and conferred certain specified powers and placed certain limits upon the federal government. Should the United States exercise a power not granted or exceed or abuse a granted power, the theory holds, the people of each state as sovereign may rightfully block such federal action. Since the Constitution is silent on who determines whether the federal government is usurping powers beyond those in the Constitution, nullificationists contend that a state

acting in its sovereign capacity can properly do so in voiding such federal acts.

Prior to 1860, many states used nullification as a remedy for excessive or abusive federal acts. First to nullify were Virginia and Kentucky, whose resolutions (1798–1799) sought to void the federal Alien and Sedition Acts (VIRGINIA AND KENTUCKY RESOLUTIONS). Then followed Pennsylvania's use of troops to resist federal court orders (1809); New England states' acting to nullify federal commercial restrictions and military enlistments (1809–1815); Georgia's blocking execution of federal treaties and court orders concerning the state's Indians (1825–1829); northern states' using "personal liberty laws" to thwart federal fugitive slave legislation (1850s).

Most notable, however, was South Carolina's nullification (1832). In the 1820s, as Congress boosted tariff duties, southern opposition to protectionist policy grew. Loudest opposition came in South Carolina, where leaders JAMES HAMILTON and THOMAS COOPER denounced national "consolidation" and called for resistance by nullification, strongly urged by Robert J. Turnbull's *Crisis* (1827). Coming late on the scene, JOHN C. CALHOUN, at the request of South Carolina's legislature, secretly prepared his "South Carolina Exposition and Protest" (1828), which elaborated the nullification theory, resting it on the doctrines of 1798, as the "rightful remedy" against the recently enacted federal "tariff of abominations." In Calhoun's view, the sovereign people of a state, as a party to the constitutional compact, had not granted Congress power to levy a protective tariff and could therefore nullify such an act. When in 1832 still another protective tariff passed, the legislature authorized election of a state convention. The convention (November 19–24) quickly adopted an ordinance of nullification, declaring the tariffs of 1828 and 1832 "null, void . . . nor binding upon this State, its officers or citizens." Further it authorized measures requiring all state officials to obey the ordinance, prohibiting appeals to the U.S. Supreme Court, and barring after February 1, 1833, collection of tariffs within the state (all shortly passed by the state legislature).

President Andrew Jackson's proclamation (December 10) denounced nullification as unconstitutional and invalid. South Carolinians armed in preparation for the expected showdown, as Congress prepared a FORCE BILL to send troops to enforce tariff collections in South Carolina. Meanwhile a matching compromise tariff bill of 1833, reducing duties substantially over the coming years, rolled through Congress. Both bills were signed into law on March 2, 1833. Disaster had been narrowly averted. Nine days later the South Carolina convention reassembled and rescinded its ordinance nullifying the tariff but in a gesture of defiance went on to adopt another nullifying the Force Bill. Washington wisely chose to ignore the latter action, and the crisis passed.

See W. W. Freehling, *Prelude to Civil War* (1966); D. F. Houston, *Nullification in South Carolina* (1967); and D. Lindsey, *Andrew Jackson and John C. Calhoun* (1973).

DAVID LINDSEY
California State University, Los Angeles

NUTS have been an important food for animals and human beings since early times. Native Indian cultures used nuts extensively in their diets. European settlers found black walnuts, hickory nuts, chestnuts, pecans, and chinquapins growing wild in the South. All (except the chestnut, killed by a blight around 1920) still grow, but only the pecan is commercially important. Because of the quality of the nut meat, the quantity produced, relative ease in processing, wide climatic range, and the propagation of improved varieties, the pecan has become unquestionably the "queen of nuts" in the United States and the fifth most important tree nut in the world. The southern states are the only substantial producers other than Mexico.

Over one-half the total pecan crop comes from wild and seedling trees, principally in Texas, Oklahoma, and Louisiana. The area from the Carolinas to Louisiana, on the other hand, is important for improved varieties developed primarily since 1890, with Georgia the chief producer. In flavor, seedlings are as good as improved varieties but yield of the latter is twice as great. Six to ten years are required to establish an orchard. Production is shifting toward the Southwest, with concentration in larger orchards, increasing mechanization, and cold storage.

The largest crop on record, 1963, totaled 341 million pounds in nine leading southern states and was worth $52 million. Great fluctuations in yield and price occur because of the biennial production habit of the tree, but since 1949 the government and cooperative associations have sought to stabilize prices. Traditionally pecans have been marketed in the shell; less than 10 percent are today. Principal users are bakeries (38 percent), confectioners (20 percent), and households (20 percent); less than 3 percent is exported. Fewer than 40 firms dominate marketing.

See J. G. Woodroof, *Tree Nuts* (1967), comprehensive; S. A. and V. C. Childs, *USDA Technical Bulletin 324*; and USDA, *Agricultural Statistics* (annual).

PERCIVAL PERRY
Wake Forest University

PECAN PRODUCTION IN THE SOUTH, 1899–1969
(thousands of pounds)

	1899	1909	1919	1929	1939	1949	1959	1969
N.C.	11	75	146	408	1,379	2,924	1,400	3,000
S.C.	13	160	526	516	2,203	3,200	4,000	3,500
Ga.	27	354	2,544	3,809	20,751	18,000	42,000	83,000
Fla.	47	308	1,026	823	3,225	3,650	4,500	4,600
Ala.	61	228	1,180	1,544	9,264	15,500	15,200	36,000
Miss.	242	637	1,559	1,428	5,611	10,000	5,400	14,000
La.	637	724	2,243	1,303	4,390	17,000	20,000	28,000
Tex.	1,811	5,832	16,755	9,588	10,106	29,000	32,000	30,000
Ark.	86	250	348	248	1,547	4,900	4,600	9,000
TOTAL	2,935	8,568	26,327	19,667	58,476	104,174	129,100	211,100

SOURCES: U.S. Census Bureau; U.S. Department of Agriculture

O

OAK GROVE, BATTLE OF (June 25, 1862). Known also as the battle of King's Schoolhouse, Henrico, French's Field, and the Orchards, this minor engagement nevertheless marked the beginning of the PENINSULAR CAMPAIGN's climactic SEVEN DAYS' BATTLES. Federal General George B. McClellan ordered two divisions to bend the Confederate right, under General Benjamin Huger, in order to secure the western edge of White Oak Swamp and as a preparation for a general Union attack. The assaults began at 8 A.M. and continued with limited success until near nightfall. Federal losses were 516 men; Confederate casualties, 316 men. An irritated Robert E. Lee stated that the Confederate defense "was not well managed"—an obvious criticism of Huger. Yet the following day Lee seized the initiative by delivering heavy assaults on McClellan's exposed right flank at Mechanicsville.

See J. Cook, *Siege of Richmond* (1862); J. P. Cullen, *Peninsular Campaign* (1973); and A. S. Webb, *The Peninsula* (1881).

JAMES I. ROBERTSON, JR.
Virginia Polytechnic Institute and State University

OAK RIDGE, TENN. (pop. 28,319), was created by the U.S. Army Corps of Engineers, Manhattan Engineer District, during World War II. Located some 20 miles northwest of Knoxville, the 59,000 acres of sparsely settled land were claimed in 1942. It was to provide a guarded, fenced, highly secret community and production facilities to separate the rare isotope uranium 235 from the more plentiful U-238. This was accomplished at two plants: K-25, where a process of gaseous diffusion was used by Carbide & Carbon Chemicals Corporation; and Y-12, where Tennessee Eastman Corporation used an electromagnetic process. The concentrated U-235 was sent to Los Alamos, N.Mex., where it was shaped into the atomic bomb dropped on Hiroshima August 6, 1945.

The architectural, engineering, and management firm of Skidmore, Owings & Merrill was chosen to design a town, which by June, 1945, had grown to 75,000 people. The army yielded direct control in January, 1947, to the newly created Atomic Energy Commission. Gates to the town were opened in 1949, and the town took on the appearance of a more "normal" civilian community with a population stabilized at approximately 30,000. It remains a center for the production of enriched uranium, radioactive isotopes, and research in nuclear physics and energy development by Oak Ridge National Laboratories.

See R. Hewlett and O. Anderson, *New World* (1962); L. Fine and J. Remington, *Military Construction* (1972); and C. Jackson and C. Johnson, *Tennessee Historical Quarterly* (Fall, 1973).

CHARLES W. JOHNSON
University of Tennessee, Knoxville

OATES, WILLIAM CALVIN (1835–1910), was born in Pike (now Bullock) County, Ala. Admitted to the bar in 1858, he practiced law and edited a newspaper at Abbeville. During the Civil War he rose from captain to the rank of colonel in Alabama regiments that fought at ANTIETAM, GETTYSBURG, CHICKAMAUGA, and CHATTANOOGA. In 1865 Oates returned to Alabama, resumed his law practice, and entered politics. He was an unsuccessful candidate for governor in 1872, chairman of the judicial committee of the Alabama constitutional convention (1875), and congressman from the Third District (1881–1894). A REDEEMER and gold Democrat, he became governor in 1894, but failed to win a U.S. Senate seat in 1897. After serving as a brigadier general in the Spanish-American War, Oates returned to his law practice in Montgomery. In the 1901 Alabama constitutional convention, he supported limited suffrage but demanded equal treatment for Negroes (DISFRANCHISEMENT). Oates also published articles and a book on the Civil War, plus a collection of his congressional speeches.

See W. C. Oates File, Alabama Department of Archives and History; M. C. McMillan, *Constitutional Development* (1955); W. W. Rogers, *One-Gallused Rebellion* (1970); S. Hackney, *Populism to Progressivism* (1969); Montgomery *Advertizer* (Sept. 10, 1910); and W. C. Oates, *War and Lost Opportunities* (1905, 1974).

D. ALAN HARRIS
Old Dominion University

OCALA PLATFORM was a statement of demands voiced by the supreme council of the National FARMERS' ALLIANCE and Industrial Union at its annual convention at Ocala, Fla., in December, 1890. Similar in most particulars to the platform adopted a year earlier at St. Louis, the Ocala Platform represented a condensation of agrarian demands that had been articulated by local, county, state, and national groups for a decade or more. With only minor modifications, it became the platform of the POPULIST PARTY in 1892.

The Ocala Platform focused attention on the three great interests of discontented agrarians of the late nineteenth century—land, transportation, and money—as well as a number of other issues. It demanded the prohibition of alien landownership and the reclaiming for the use by actual settlers of all land held by aliens as well as the unearned portions of railway land grants. It called for strict government control of railroad and communications systems or, if that proved unsuccessful, government ownership of those systems. The platform denounced the Sherman Silver Purchase Act, demanded instead free and unlimited coinage of silver, called for the abolition of national banks and for an increase in the circulating currency to $50 per capita, and advocated the adoption of the SUBTREASURY PLAN, C. W. MACUNE's scheme by which nonperishable farm commodities stored in government warehouses would serve as collateral for low-interest loans. The platform also called for a graduated income tax, economy in government, prohibition of trading in agricultural futures, and a constitutional amendment providing for direct election of U.S. senators. Finally, it objected to a protective tariff on necessities and denounced all legislation that discriminated against agricultural interests.

See *National Economist* (1889–90); N. A. Dunning, *Farmers' Alliance* (1891); J. D. Hicks, *Populist Revolt* (1931); and T. Saloutos, *Farmer Movements* (1960).

ROY V. SCOTT
Mississippi State University

OCCANEECHI PATH was the Indian path used by seventeenth- and eighteenth-century Virginians as the major route of exploration, trade, and migration into the Carolinas. The path, named for the Occaneechi Indians who controlled the point where it crossed the Roanoke River, was also called the Trading Path, Catawba Path, and Virginia Path. The explorations of John Lederer (1671), James Needham (1673), and John Lawson (1700), together with Nathaniel Bacon's attack upon the Occaneechi Indians (1676), opened the path as the trade route from Virginia to the CATAWBA, CHEROKEE, and interior tribes of the Carolinas. Along the narrow path, Abraham Wood,

William Byrd, and Governor Alexander Spotswood pioneered Virginia's lucrative FUR TRADE with the southern Indians. The path extended from Ft. Henry at Petersburg, Va., to Augusta, Ga. Near Salisbury, N.C., a branch turned westward into Cherokee country.

See D. S. Brown, *Catawba Indians* (1966); W. E. Myer, *Forty-second Annual Report, Bureau of American Ethnology* (1928); and D. L. Rights, *North Carolina Historical Review* (Oct., 1931).

ALAN V. BRICELAND
Virginia Commonwealth University

OCEAN POND, BATTLE OF. See OLUSTEE, BATTLE OF

O'CONNOR, MARY FLANNERY (1925–1964), lived in or near Milledgeville, Ga., except for several years' work at the University of Iowa Writers' Workshop and in the East, until her untimely death from disseminated lupus, a congenital degenerative disease. In the words of Caroline Gordon, "she was the first fiction writer of outstanding talent to look at the rural South through the eyes of Roman Catholic orthodoxy," and, one might add, typically using fictional characters who were Protestant fundamentalist fanatics. In her two short novels, *Wise Blood* (1952) and *The Violent Bear It Away* (1960), God-obsessed BIBLE BELT prophets suffer hideous anguish in struggling with their vocations in the context of an urban secular society permeated with religious apathy, humanism, science, and materialism. In the short stories *A Good Man Is Hard to Find* (1955) and the posthumous *Everything That Rises Must Converge* (1965), one finds a pattern in which supernatural grace (though seldom identified by this name) erupts violently within the experience of ordinary rural people. O'Connor was acutely aware of the dilemma of presenting essentially medieval Catholic assumptions to a body of secularized readers; she consciously employed her somewhat specialized genius for macabre caricature, vicious satire, and violently ludicrous comedy to shock complacent readers into a recognition of her own sense of urgency to accept certain traditional views of Christ, the devil, death, and salvation. Her own convictions are cogently presented in the posthumous collection of occasional writings *Mystery and Manners* (1969). *The Complete Short Stories* (1971) contains all her short fiction including previously uncollected pieces.

See C. W. Martin, *True Country* (1969); M. Orvell, *Invisible Parade* (1973); M. Stephens, *Question of Flannery O'Connor* (1973); K. Feeley, *Flannery O'Connor*

(1972), a valuable survey of O'Connor's reading in theology; and O'Connor Papers, Woman's College of Georgia.

FRANK BALDANZA
Bowling Green State University

O'DANIEL, WILBERT LEE (1890–1969), Ohio born and Kansas raised, became a major Texas political figure between 1938 and 1948. He came to Texas in 1925 after a modest career in the flour business in Kansas and New Orleans. As the manager of a flour mill in Ft. Worth, he became a statewide personality through his radio program, which featured the musical group, the Light Crust Doughboys. Known as Pappy because of his advertising phrase, "Pass the biscuits, Pappy," he effectively used radio and his hillbilly band to win the governorship of Texas in 1938 against 12 opponents and again in 1940. An undistinguished governor, he is best remembered for his unsuccessful proposal for a "transactions tax" to finance pensions of $30 per month for everyone over sixty-five. In 1941 O'Daniel won a special election to the U.S. Senate against 28 opponents. In 1942 he was elected to a full term. In the Senate he was identified with the isolationist, conservative, Republican bloc, often referring to World War II as the "president's war." In 1948 he retired, but in 1956 and 1958 he made two unsuccessful comeback attempts as a candidate for governor.

See G. N. Green, "Far Right Wing" (Ph.D. dissertation, Florida State University, 1967); S. S. McKay, *W. Lee O'Daniel* (1944); and J. T. Yauger, "Rhetorical Study" (Ph.D. dissertation, Louisiana State University, 1969).

DONALD W. WHISENHUNT
Eastern New Mexico University

ODUM, HOWARD WASHINGTON (1884–1954), born on a modest farm near Bethlehem, Ga., graduated from Emory College in 1904. He then taught school in rural Mississippi and collected Negro folk songs and folklore. Odum received an M.A. degree in the classics from the University of Mississippi, a Ph.D. degree in psychology from Clark University, and another in sociology at Columbia University with the dissertation "Social and Mental Traits of the Negro" (1910). Throughout Odum's career, the Negro occupied a prominent place in his writings. From 1910 to 1912, Odum did municipal research in Philadelphia; next he taught at the University of Georgia and then served as dean of liberal arts at Emory. In 1920 he moved to the University of North Carolina, where he established a school of public welfare and a department of sociology. He found-

ed the journal *Social Forces* in 1922 and two years later the Institute for Research in Social Science. The culmination of Odum's research into southern folkways was the development of his theory and methodology of REGIONALISM. His magnum opus *Southern Regions* (1936) criticized the South's shortcomings, but saw hope in a future based on planned development. He was a skillful administrator, an enthusiastic teacher, and a social activist. Odum's first love, creative scholarship, was attested to by his 20-odd books and nearly 200 articles.

See G. B. Tindall, *Journal of Southern History* (Aug., 1958) and *Emergence of New South* (1967); R. B. Vance and K. Jocher, *Social Forces* (March, 1955), good bibliography; W. D. Brazil, "Odum" (Ph.D. dissertation, Harvard, 1975); and Odum Papers, University of North Carolina.

WALTER J. FRASER, JR.
The Citadel

O'FALLON, JAMES (1749–1794), immigrated to North Carolina from Ireland in 1774. After serving in the Revolution as a medical officer, he moved to Charleston. Here he sought, without success, a Spanish grant of 5 million acres to found a colony in Florida. Then, as general agent for the South Carolina Yazoo Company, he planned to recruit settlers for a colony in the Mississippi Valley. Evidence suggests that the company and O'Fallon hoped the colony would eventually proclaim its independence from the United States. In 1791, however, President George Washington publicly unmasked the conspiracy. A year later O'Fallon clandestinely attempted to secure French assistance in order to seize company-claimed lands in the Spanish Southwest. Although Washington's resolute policies again foiled the plot, the United States declined to prosecute O'Fallon.

See J. C. Parish, *Mississippi Valley Historical Review* (Sept., 1930); A. P. Whitaker, *Mississippi Valley Historical Review* (Dec., 1929); G. White, *Accurate Account of Yazoo Fraud* (1852); and T. P. Abernethy, *South in New Nation* (1961).

JOHN FERLING
West Georgia College

O'FERRALL, CHARLES TRIPLETT (1840–1905), was born in Frederick County, Va. He held a series of minor offices from the age of fifteen to the outbreak of the Civil War, when he joined the 12th Virginia Cavalry, rising to the rank of captain. He entered law school in 1868 at Washington College, graduating a year later. In the house of delegates for two terms (1871–1874), he was an opponent of the controversial "funding" bill, but never joined the READJUSTERS (who opposed funding) in their battles with the Democrats. After serving as Rockingham County court judge from 1874 to 1880, he ran for Congress on the Democratic ticket against a Readjuster and won, serving from 1884 until 1893, when he resigned. In Congress, though a strict constructionist, he favored federal aid for public education (BLAIR BILL) based on his view that the federal government had an obligation to the former slaves. As governor of Virginia from 1894 to 1898, he was most noted for his efforts to stamp out LYNCHING, an enterprise in which he was largely successful during the first half of his term, less so in the second half. In a message to the legislature he proposed that the locality where mob violence occurred should be forced to pay into the school fund and that local officials should be removed from office and liable for damages. Less charitable toward labor, in 1895 he was instrumental in breaking a strike of his native Virginians at the Pocahontas coalfield.

See C. T. O'Ferrall, *40 Years of Active Service* (1904); O'Ferrall Papers, William and Mary Library; N. M. Blake, *Mahone* (1937); C. C. Pearson, *Readjusters* (1917); A. W. Moger, *Bourbonism to Byrd* (1968); V. Dabney, *New Dominion* (1971); and W. E. Larsen, *Montague* (1965).

CATHERINE SILVERMAN
Institute for Research in History

OGDEN MOVEMENT, an educational crusade focusing on the development of public schools in the South from 1900 to 1913, acquired its name from Robert Curtis Ogden (1836–1913), its most influential leader. The movement included the Conference for Education in the South, which met annually in various southern states; the SOUTHERN EDUCATION BOARD, an administrative body that met privately; the Bureau of Information and Advice on Legislation and School Organization; and the Summer School of the South, which met in Knoxville, Tenn.

In 1900 the three-year-old Conference for Christian Education in the South changed its name and focus and elected Ogden its president, a position he held until his death. Ogden, general manager of the Wanamaker Department Stores, developed his interest in education as trustee of Hampton Institute and as president of the board of directors of Union Theological Seminary. He brought a private train full of northerners interested in education to the annual southern conferences. This permitted businessmen, churchmen, journalists, professional educators, and politicians from the North and South to meet in a common cause. Through the years such notables as William H. Baldwin, George Foster Peabody, Lyman Abbott, Albert Shaw, John D. Rockefeller, Jr., Oswald Garrison Villard, Felix Adler, WALTER HINES PAGE, Wallace Buttrick, EDGAR GARDNER MURPHY, J. L. M. CURRY, CHARLES D. MCIVER, EDWIN A. ALDERMAN, Seaman A. Knapp, and almost every southern governor traveled the "Ogden Special."

The annual conference was unique. Ogden acknowledged that critics doubted its serious purpose, labeling it a faddish affair "primarily social, incidentally educational." Nothing could have been farther from the truth. These zealous new redeemers possessed a seriousness of purpose and a passionate belief that, in Ogden's phraseology, "the things that make for good character, family peace, clean living, human brotherhood, civic righteousness, and national justice are impossible without general educational progress."

The movement's major vehicle of reform was the statewide campaign, most often focusing on legislative action. Indigenous leadership, a vital ingredient for success, conducted the independent campaigns of varied origin. The educational crusade in North Carolina was first, beginning in 1902. Campaigns followed in Tennessee and Virginia in 1903, Georgia in 1904, Alabama, South Carolina, and Mississippi in 1905, Louisiana in 1906, Kentucky and Arkansas in 1908, and Florida in 1909. In many instances they continued after 1913, but the impetus provided by the Ogden movement waned after 1907. The net results were impressive. Attendance laws were strengthened, consolidation of school districts and local taxation for public education increased dramatically, per capita expenditure for education more than doubled, and corresponding increases in teachers' salaries and length of school terms occurred. The estimated value of public school property in the South more than tripled, with North Carolina building an average of one schoolhouse a day from 1902 to 1910. Illiteracy among white children of school age was reduced to less than half what it had been in 1900. The southern educational system, however, remained far below the national average in 1913; and, in its greatest failing, education for Negroes continued to lag behind that provided for whites. As historian Louis R. Harlan has emphasized, this constructive educational crusade, conducted largely by white leadership, ran parallel to the destructive white supremacy movement, and it resigned itself by default to the growth of separate but unequal schools.

See *Proceedings of Annual Conferences for Education in South* (1898–1913); C. W. Dabney, *Universal Education in South* (1936); L. R. Harlan, *Separate and Un-*

equal (1958); P. W. Wilson, *Robert C. Ogden* (1924); Robert C. Ogden Papers, Library of Congress; and Southern Education Board Papers, University of North Carolina Library, Chapel Hill.

WILLIAM E. KING
Duke University

OGLETHORPE, JAMES EDWARD (1696–1785),

London-born member of a prominent Jacobite family, became interested in America while chairing a parliamentary committee on the condition of English jails. He and others secured a charter for the colony of Georgia (1732). The project captured the public fancy, and the result was that the early debtor-province idea was superseded by imperial, mercantilistic, and religious motivations.

Oglethorpe led the colonists to America, where Savannah was founded (1733). He laid out the town, looked upon as a fine example of urban planning. Oglethorpe defended Georgia against the Spanish during the War of Jenkins' Ear and defeated them on St. Simon's Island (July 7, 1742). In 1743 he returned to England, but maintained his interest in America.

Oglethorpe showed himself an able colonizer, but he was not always a good judge of men. He was compassionate to his settlers and fair toward the Indians, but he could be short-tempered and arbitrary. As a military leader, he reflected indecisiveness in his Florida expedition in 1740, but his defense of Georgia was effective. Although his dream of Georgia as a white, yeoman farmer colony evaporated, his overall leadership was superior and at times inspired.

See Egmont Papers, Phillipps Collection, University of Georgia Library; A. D. Candler (ed.), *Colonial Records of Georgia* (1904–16); *Georgia Historical Society Collections* (1840–48), III; A. E. Ettinger, *Oglethorpe* (1936), best biography; B. P. Spalding, *Oglethorpe in America* (1977); and L. Ivers, *British Drums on Southern Frontier* (1974), military details. See also B. P. Spalding, *Georgia Historical Quarterly* (Fall, 1972) and *South Carolina Historical Magazine* (April, 1968); and *Johnson Society Transactions* (1974).

B. PHINIZY SPALDING
University of Georgia

OGLETHORPE UNIVERSITY (Atlanta, Ga. 33019).

The first institution of this name was a Presbyterian school founded in 1835 and located at Midway, Ga., near the state capital Milledgeville. It had a steady growth until the Civil War destroyed its financial base and forced its closure. Although the school was reopened after the war and even moved to Atlanta, it failed and closed in 1872. Dr. Thornwell Jacobs led a movement to revive the school, and it was reorganized in 1913. Today it is a nonsectarian, private institution with an enrollment of 1,000 students. It also is the site of a time capsule, the Crypt of Civilization, which was sealed in 1940. Containing documents and artifacts of 6,000 years of human history, the crypt is not to be opened until May 28, 8113.

O'HARA, JAMES EDWARD (1844–1905), born

and educated in New York City, came to North Carolina in 1862 on a pleasure trip with some missionaries. After briefly teaching school, he read law in North Carolina and at Howard University and was admitted to the bar in 1873. O'Hara began his political career in 1867, when he became a delegate to the Republican state convention. Twice elected to Congress (1882, 1884), O'Hara was a partisan spokesman for blacks. He was perceptive and articulate and one of the first to recognize that white Republicans in North Carolina were reluctant to support a black Republican against a white Democrat. He sponsored numerous antidiscrimination bills; he also sponsored bills to protect the butter industry from oleomargarine and to protect women's rights. O'Hara was defeated in the 1886 election primarily because of the divided black vote and rumors that he directed dark-skinned blacks to his back door and the lighter-hued ones to the front. He returned to his home in New Bern, where he had a lucrative law practice with his son Raphael.

See M. Christopher, *America's Black Congressmen* (1871), best; F. Logan, *Negro in North Carolina* (1964); G. W. Reid, "George White" (Ph.D. dissertation, Howard University, 1973); J. C. Jones, "James E. O'Hara" (M.A. thesis, North Carolina College, 1957); S. D. Smith, *Negro in Congress* (1966); and W. A. Mabry, *Negro in North Carolina* (1940).

DAVID W. BISHOP
North Carolina Central University

OHIO COMPANY OF VIRGINIA was orga-

nized in 1747 under the leadership of Thomas Lee. The company petitioned the British Board of Trade for a grant of western land and on March 16, 1749, received 200,000 acres bounded by the Ohio and Great Kanawha rivers and the Allegheny Mountains. Provisions of the grant required that 300,000 additional acres would be granted if 100 families were settled within seven years and that a garrison be constructed and maintained at the forks of the Ohio. Efforts to bring immigrants faded, but the Ohio Company engaged in successful trading activities directed by CHRISTOPHER GIST. In 1752 the company requested a charter revision allowing seven more years to secure a total of 300 settlers. Subsequent years were difficult for the company due to an expected German migration that failed to materialize and the threat of war, which deterred settlement on the frontier. Following Pontiac's Rebellion and the PROCLAMATION OF 1763, the Ohio Company was confronted with a British policy that prohibited settlement west of the Alleghenies. The company appointed George Mercer as an agent to help persuade England to reach agreement with western tribes. The treaties of Ft. Stanwix, Lochaber, and Hard Labour in 1768 finally reopened the Ohio region to settlement, and land companies, old and new, were embroiled in feverish activity to renew and secure grants. Samuel Wharton, agent of the Indiana Company, saw consolidation into a "Grand Ohio Company" as an answer to the dilemma. Among the companies that joined the new consolidation in 1769 was the Ohio Company of Virginia. It was proposed that a proprietary colony named Vandalia be developed, but the Revolutionary War ended all hope of the promoters.

See K. Baily, *Ohio Company of Virginia* (1939) and *Ohio Company Papers, 1753–1817* (1947); A. James, *Ohio Company* (1959) and *George Mercer of Ohio Company* (1963); and S. Livermore, *Early American Land Companies* (1939).

D. DUANE CUMMINS
Oklahoma City University

OHIO RIVER is geologically the youngest major river in North America. The Kansan glacial advance is thought to have dammed the Ancient Teays River, which had drained the country west of the Alleghenies and had flowed northward across Ohio, Indiana, and Illinois. The modern-day Ohio runs west and southwest, approximating the glacial ice front, 981 miles from the confluence of the Allegheny and Monongahela rivers at Pittsburgh to a junction with the Mississippi at Cairo, Ill. During the eighteenth century, the French and British contended for control of the strategic point of land where the Allegheny and Monongahela join. The French built Ft. Duquesne there to service their FUR TRADE along the Ohio, but in the FRENCH AND INDIAN WAR of 1756–1763 the site was lost to the British, who erected Ft. Pitt and established the village of Pittsburgh. The Ohio provided access to the West, and a string of forts, supplied by the river and its tributaries, stabilized the Indian frontier. Immigrants, using RIVERCRAFT of all types—barges, keelboats, flatboats, or rafts—made their way from Pittsburgh. Immigrants destined for Indiana or Illinois left the river at Cincinnati, and those en route to Kentucky would disembark at Limestone (Maysville) or Louisville.

Pittsburgh, Wheeling, and Marietta, Ohio—at the mouth of the Muskingum—became major shipbuilding centers, first for emigrant boats but during the 1820s and 1830s for steamboats and later deep-draft, oceangoing craft. Beginning in the 1820s, industrial goods produced along the river, salt from springs along the Kanawha and Wabash, and pig iron, whiskey, soap, and other processed agricultural products were shipped downriver to New Orleans for sale in the cotton South, Atlantic coast cities, or Europe. In 1830 a canal around the falls of the Ohio at Louisville was completed to speed the trip south. But reliable, year-round navigation could not begin until 1879, when Congress provided funds for construction of the first locks and dams on the river. Abundant coal found along much of the river's length has been the basis for heavy industrialization. Forty-six dams and locks and a nine-foot navigation channel are maintained for modern barge traffic, which moves primarily bulk cargoes of coal, grain, steel and iron, gasoline, and sand.

See C. H. Ambler, *History of Transportation in Ohio Valley* (1931).

KARL B. RAITZ
University of Kentucky

OIL INDUSTRY. See PETROLEUM

OKEECHOBEE, LAKE, in Florida is the South's largest lake (730 square miles) and the third largest freshwater lake wholly within the United States. The name, a Hitchiti Indian word, means "big water." Okeechobee is a remnant of the Pamlico Sea, a Pleistocene feature whose shallow waters once covered the present Okeechobee-Everglades Basin. The lake occupies the deeper portion of the ancient sea; the remainder of the sea is known today as the EVERGLADES. Before drainage began in the late 1800s, water flowed from the lake to the south and southwest, forming a "river of grass" (called *Pa-hay-okee*, "grassy water," by the Indians) 100 miles long and 65 miles wide. Although water still flows along much of the former channel, it is controlled by the Central and Southern Florida Flood Control District. A complex series of dikes, floodgates, canals, and pumping stations maintains Okeechobee's level at 15.5 feet above mean sea level at a mean depth of seven feet. Much of the water that used to move southward now irrigates the vegetable and sugarcane fields created by drainage.

See *Water Management Bulletin* (bimonthly), C&SFFCD, West Palm Beach; A. Carr, *Everglades* (1973); and A. J. Hanna and K. Abbey, *Lake Okeechobee* (1948).

ROBERT H. FUSON
University of South Florida

OKEFENOKEE SWAMP is the third largest swamp in the South. It lies for the most part in Georgia, on the Georgia-Florida border, and covers an area of close to 700 square miles. About four-fifths of the swamp is included within the 331,000-acre Okefenokee National Wildlife Refuge established in 1937. One can find in it numerous animals, including alligators, bears, pumas, deer, several species of waterbird, otters, foxes, squirrels, and a variety of snakes and turtles. Georgia also maintains portions of the swamp as a state park.

Geologists technically do not regard the area as a swamp at all, but rather as a great natural bog or "dome of water," for the water in the Okefenokee lies above the surrounding water table and even higher than the water-surface level of the nearby land. The bog acts like a sponge, collecting water by "suction pressure" even when there is a drought or the water level is low in nearby regions. Because of this sponge action, a surplus of water develops, which accounts for the existence of two rivers flowing from the area, the ST. MARY'S and the SUWANNEE. Because the Okefenokee is a bog, the floor of the swamp displays some peculiar characteristics. Much of it is covered with a deposit of water-saturated peat, sometimes 20 feet thick, which is very unstable; therefore, big trees growing in this peat can often be made to sway violently by a person's jumping up and down on the spongy surface. This ground trembling or quaking is what has given the swamp its name; for Okefenokee is a corruption of the Seminole world *Quaquaphenogau*, which means "trembling earth."

Much of the natural attraction of the swamp is derived from the vegetation. The cypress forests are the most important because of their beauty and commercial value. Loggers during the first quarter of the twentieth century brought out almost a half-billion board feet of cypress and other lumber over roads built on pilings. "Prairies," which are large expanses of plant-choked water, appear in the eastern portion of the swamp, where muck prevents the growth of trees. Scattered throughout the prairies, however, are small island clumps of cypress trees or other dense vegetation called "bays," "heads," "houses," or "hammocks" depending on their particular size or other characteristics. Other aquatic plants such as "bon-

nets," pitcher plants, and "never-wets" also grow in abundance in the prairies.

As early as 1539, Spanish explorers led by Hernando de Soto had discovered the swamp and described it as a "great morass" fringed with forests and impassable undergrowth. Years later, in the 1700s, the swamp became the hunting and fishing grounds of many CREEK and SEMINOLE Indians. The latter even built a few of their villages on the islands, one of which, Billy's Island, was named after the famous Seminole chief Billy Bowlegs, who commanded some of the Indians in the SEMINOLE WARS. The Creeks officially ceded the area to the state of Georgia by treaty in 1785, but the Seminole remained after that date for some time. Because of its relative inaccessibility, the Okefenokee has been a sanctuary, a place of escape, for many. In addition to serving the Seminole Indians, who lived there until driven out in 1838 during the Seminole Wars, it later reputedly became a refuge for deserters from the Confederate army. It was also used at this time by area farmers, who wished to hide their cattle from Union soldiers foraging for provisions.

See A. H. Wright, *Our Georgia-Florida Frontier* (1945); and C. H. Matschat, *Suwanee River* (1938). Popular in nature, but apparently accurate, are L. Dietz, *Field and Stream* (April, 1967); F. Harper, *National Geographic* (May, 1934); and J. J. Stophlet, *National Parks* (Oct., 1963).

OLMSTED, FREDERICK LAW (1822–1903), was the son of a Connecticut merchant. Family excursions in New England, private tutoring in topographical engineering, scientific courses at Yale, and extensive study of agriculture (he published *Walks and Talks of an American Farmer in England* in 1852) superbly trained him for critical social analysis. On December 11, 1852, Olmsted set out as a correspondent of the New York *Times* "to report with candor and fidelity the ordinary condition of the laborers of the South." The accounts of his two trips (1852–1853, 1853–1854) were published in the *Times*, in the *Tribune*, and in book form: *A Journey in the Seaboard Slave States* (1856), *A Journey Through Texas* (1857), *A Journey in the Backcountry* (1860), and *The Cotton Kingdom* (1861), a condensation of the three volumes. His descriptive portraits of personalities and customs are unsurpassed in the travel literature of the antebellum South. The discussion of slavery (which he found far less profitable than free labor) possessed a thoroughness and objective detachment that elicited praise from contemporary critics and later historians.

Olmsted firmly supported the Union cause, serving as secretary of the sanitary commission (1861–1863). After the Civil War he emerged as the nation's first professional landscape architect. Among his numerous commissions were plans for parks and residential grounds in Baltimore, Kansas City, Louisville, Natural Bridge, Washington, Wilmington, Del., Montgomery, Atlanta, Richmond, and Hot Springs, at the New Orleans Cotton Exposition, and at G. W. Vanderbilt's Biltmore in Asheville.

See C. E. Beveridge, "Olmsted" (Ph.D. dissertation, University of Wisconsin, 1966); P. W. Bidwell, *American Historical Review* (Oct., 1917); T. H. Clark, *South Atlantic Quarterly* (Jan., 1904); B. Mitchell, *Olmsted* (1924); F. Olmsted and F. Kimball, *Olmsted* (1922–28); L. W. Roper, *FLO* (1973); A. M. Schlesinger, *Journal of Negro History* (April, 1952); and Olmsted Papers, Library of Congress.

JOHN C. DANN
University of Michigan

OLUSTEE, BATTLE OF (February 20, 1864), is also called the battle of Ocean Pond. On February 7, 1864, Union troops under Truman Seymour landed in Jacksonville to encourage Floridians to rally to the Union, to seize and interdict supplies, and to enlist blacks. Overcoming scattered opposition, Seymour seized the rail junction at Baldwin and reconnoitered inland. Although he encountered neither recruits nor support and was then ordered to occupy only Jacksonville and Palatka, he determined to move deep inland to cut the rails at the Suwannee. Seymour's division of 5,500 men met 5,200 Confederates under Joseph Finegan on February 20 at Olustee, three kilometers southeast of Ocean Pond. Maneuvering under fire, the 7th New Hampshire Volunteers became confused and broke ranks. The black 8th U.S. Infantry withdrew only after sustaining 54 percent casualties. Although reinforced, the Union line gave way by dusk, and Seymour quickly retreated to Jacksonville. Seymour had attained none of his objectives and lost 1,861 killed, wounded, and missing. Southern casualties numbered 946.

See W. W. Davis, *Civil War in Florida* (1913); R. U. Johnson and C. C. Buel (eds.), *Battles and Leaders* (1888); *Official Records, Armies*, Ser. 1, Vol. XXXV; M. F. Boyd, *Federal Campaign in East Florida* (1956); and regimental histories.

DONALD M. BISHOP
U.S. Air Force Academy

O'NEAL, EDWARD ASBURY (1818–1890), was born in Madison County, Ala. In 1840 he moved to Florence, where he established a successful practice of law. In the late 1850s, he became a leader in the secessionist movement in Alabama. On June 4, 1861, he left Florence as a captain in charge of three companies of infantry and proceeded to Virginia. After four years of service, where he saw action at SEVEN PINES, CHANCELLORSVILLE, GETTYSBURG, and PEACH TREE CREEK, he returned to Florence as a respected "brigadier general" to resume practicing law. During Reconstruction O'Neal took an active part in restoring the power of the Democratic party and in establishing white supremacy. As a member of the constitutional convention of 1875, he worked to develop public education and a sound financial system to support responsible state government.

Elected governor (1882–1886), he promptly called for the prosecution of the three-term incumbent state treasurer for embezzlement of $250,000. Normal schools for training white teachers were opened at Livingston and Jacksonville, and teacher training for Negroes was expanded at the normal school at Huntsville. Some improvement was also made in public education and public health, and a department of agriculture was created to aid in developing better farm practices. Attempts were also made to improve the treatment of convicts and to regulate railroads operating within the state. Even though he received high praise from the press at the end of his term, O'Neal actually accomplished little in upgrading the basic government services that would have improved education, health, and transportation for all the people. Neither O'Neal nor his immediate successor Thomas Seay saw the need to go beyond the maintenance of the status quo, which called for honesty, economy, and efficiency in government and a policy of white supremacy in race relations.

See J. F. Doster, *Railroads in Alabama Politics* (1957); A. J. Going, *Bourbon Democrats in Alabama* (1951); S. Hackney, *Populism and Progressivism in Alabama* (1969); and C. V. Woodward, *Origins of New South* (1971).

FRANCES C. ROBERTS
University of Alabama, Huntsville

OPECHANCANOUGH (1545?–1646) was the chief of the POWHATAN Confederacy in tidewater Virginia. An implacable enemy of the English, he secretly plotted to annihilate them. On March 22, 1622, the Indians attacked the settlers; 347 whites were killed. The attack almost succeeded in completely destroying the settlement, but Jamestown was warned in time. On April 18, 1644, Opechancanough, aged and infirm, led his warriors in another attack; more than 500 settlers died. The war continued until Opechancanough was captured and killed and the various tribes were completely subdued.

See R. Beverley, *History of Virginia* (1705); J. Smith, *Works*, ed. E. Arber and A. G. Bradley (2 vols.; 1910); and T. J. Wertenbaker, *Virginia Under Stuarts* (1914).

EDWARD M. RILEY
Colonial Williamsburg Foundation

OPELOUSAS, LA. (pop. 20,121), originally was settled by French traders as a post for their commerce with the area's Opelousas Indians. After Spain assumed control of Louisiana, the trading post was made the governing center of the southwestern section of the colony (1769) and known officially as El Poste de Opelousas. The antebellum town drew its economic vitality as a market for area cattle, sugar, and cotton growers. In 1863, after the Confederate state government was forced to flee Baton Rouge, the city served briefly as the state's capital. Completion of the first railroad into the community in 1882 and later the discovery of petroleum have extended the city's economic base. Yet Opelousas remains essentially a market town for area agriculture and a place where French is spoken as commonly as English.

See Opelousas *World* (June 12, 1970), town history since 1720; and W. DeVille, *Opelousas* (1973).

ORAL HISTORY. Although the technology of sound recordings has introduced a new element into the historian's craft, the interview itself has long been a tool of social investigation. Sociologists and anthropologists, for example, have developed an extensive literature on interviewing methods. As early as the 1930s, the WORKS PROGRESS ADMINISTRATION gathered two major interview archives: the Slave Narrative Collection, housed in the Library of Congress; and a series of southern life histories, a selection of which was published in *These Are Our Lives* (1939). Only since the founding of the Columbia Oral History Office in 1948, however, has the term "oral history" gained currency. The formation of the Oral History Association in 1967 provided recognition of a growing oral history movement, and by 1974 almost 400 oral history projects were scattered throughout the country.

The reasons for this evolution can be found in a complex of technological, cultural, and intellectual trends. As changing forms of communication have eroded the substance of written documentation, historians have turned to interviews for the personal revelations once supplied by diaries and confidential letters. Also, the rise of social history has engendered a search for evidence about the lives of people who do not ordinarily leave behind written records. Black historians have pioneered in the use of interviews to counteract the biases of white sources. As scholars of women's history have shifted attention from the contributions of notable women and prescriptive definitions of womanhood to the realities of women's lives, oral life histories have assumed increasing importance.

Oral history projects in the South devoted to the careers of political and military leaders include the LYNDON B. JOHNSON project at the University of Texas and the George C. Marshall Research Library in Lexington, Va. T. Harry Williams' *Huey Long* (1969) is an outstanding example of the application of interview methods to political history. Among the numerous multipurpose projects based on the Columbia model are those of Memphis State and North Texas State universities. The University of North Carolina at Chapel Hill has established an oral history program that sponsors research in the neglected areas of women's and labor history and contributes a range of other source material to the archives of the Southern Historical Collection.

The emergence of Appalachian studies has added impetus to oral history within that region. The interviews collected by the colleges of the Appalachian Consortium provide information on the social history of the mountains. Similarly, under Eliot Wigginton's direction at Rabun Gap–Nacoochee School in north Georgia, high school students have published a four-volumed collection of articles on the folk culture of the mountains (*The Foxfire Book*, 1972, 1973, 1975, 1977). Robert Coles's *Migrants, Sharecroppers, Mountaineers* (1967), William Lynwood Montell's *The Saga of Coe Ridge* (1970), and Kathy Kahn's edited volume *Hillbilly Women* (1973) are important contributions to the field.

Black history projects have generated both primary sources and distinguished published works. Fisk University, which was instrumental in initiating the WPA efforts in the thirties, is now the site of an oral history project on black artists and leaders. Students at Mary Holmes College in West Point, Miss., have gathered data on the lives of over 600 rural Mississippians. The Archive of New Orleans Jazz at Tulane preserves the sound and social context of a unique musical heritage. The Civil Rights Documentation Project in Washington, D.C., and the Martin Luther King Library in Atlanta have amassed oral sources on the southern civil rights movement. Duke University's innovative project is devoted to teaching and research rather than to archival collections.

The publication of the Slave Narrative Collection in its entirety in 1972 served as an index of professional interest in black oral sources (George P. Rawick, ed., *The American Slave*). Lawrence C. Goodwyn's study of the Populist movement revealed black and working-class white perspectives on political conflict (*American Historical Review*, Dec., 1971). Robert Hamburger's *Our Portion of Hell* (1973) and Alex Haley's *Roots* (1976) offer divergent insights into the black experience. Finally, in his life history of an Alabama sharecropper, Ned Cobb (*All God's Danger's*, 1974), Theodore Rosengarten provides an instructive example of the rich human material from which historical analysis must ultimately be shaped—and of the potential of the interview as an avenue into the lives of those who have been hidden from history.

See G. L. Shumway (ed.), *Oral History in U.S.* (1971); A. Meckler and R. McMullin (eds.), *Oral History Collections* (1974); M. Wasserman (comp.), *Bibliography* (1974); *Oral History Review*; and R. L. Gorden, *Interviewing* (1975), most helpful guide to interviewing problems and techniques.

JACQUELYN DOWD HALL
University of North Carolina, Chapel Hill

ORANGEBURG, S.C. (pop. 13,252), is approximately 40 miles south of Columbia on a fork of the Edisto River. Settled in 1735 by Swiss and German colonists, the town was named for William, prince of Orange. Primarily a trade and processing center for area agriculture since its formation, modern Orangeburg ships grain, gins cotton, mills lumber, and prepares meat products. It also is the home of two predominantly black colleges: Claflin College (1869) and South Carolina State Agricultural and Mechanical College (1896).

See A. S. Salley, Jr., *History of Orangeburg County* (1898, 1969), eighteenth century; and files of Orangeburg *Times and Democrat* (1881–), on microfilm.

ORATORY has long had an important place in the values of southerners. W. J. CASH wrote in *Mind of the South* that rhetoric "early became a passion . . . a primary standard of judgment, the *sine qua non* of leadership. The greatest man would be the man who could best wield it." In current usage the stereotypes "southern oratory" and "southern orator" sometimes have derogatory implications, suggesting a flamboyant, spread-eagle speaker who indulges in grandiloquent language, a thundering voice, and an impassioned delivery.

Among the early southerners to win acclaim for their eloquence were PATRICK HENRY and JOHN RANDOLPH of Roanoke. During the golden age of southern oratory (1820–1860), southerners argued great propositions of policy concerning preservation of states' rights and the protection of slavocracy. Foremost among the antebellum speakers was JOHN C. CALHOUN, whose most important speeches were those delivered in his debate (1833) with Daniel Webster and his valedictory delivered March 4, 1850, shortly before he died. Of equal importance was the Daniel Webster–ROBERT HAYNE debate (1830). Other prominent pre–Civil War speakers included WILLIAM C. PRESTON, ROBERT BARNWELL RHETT, HUGH S. LEGARÉ, and JAMES PETIGRU of South Carolina, ALEXANDER STEPHENS and ROBERT TOOMBS of Georgia, HENRY HILLIARD and WILLIAM LOWNDES YANCEY of Alabama, Seargent S. Prentiss of Mississippi, and HENRY CLAY of Kentucky. WILLIAM GARROTT BROWN doubted whether "there has ever been a society in which the orator counted for more than he did in the Cotton Kingdom."

The period from 1865 to about 1900 saw a marked shift in southern public address from deliberative speaking to that of accommodation and reconciliation. Because of domination by outside forces, the speakers often had to limit their proposals to what was acceptable or inoffensive to those who held power. As a result speakers turned to the promotion of heroes and shibboleths and to amplification of popular myths: the Old South, the LOST CAUSE, the SOLID SOUTH, white supremacy, and the NEW SOUTH. In their appearances at dedications of battlefields and monuments, reunions, funerals, and commencements they approached the stereotyped southern orator through excessive emotion and figurative and ornate language. L. Q. C. LAMAR of Mississippi early regained acceptance in national circles and won acclaim in the U.S. House of Representatives for his eulogy of Charles Sumner (April 28, 1874). The two most widely heralded orators of the period were HENRY W. GRADY ("The New South," delivered December 22, 1886) and BOOKER T. WASHINGTON (Atlanta Exposition speech, delivered September 18, 1895). Well known for their pleas for reconciliation were BENJAMIN H. HILL, JOHN B. GORDON ("The Last Days of the Confederacy"), and HENRY WATTERSON.

The agrarian discontent in the late nineteenth century provided a platform for many popular speakers, sometimes called southern demagogues. Astute showmen and manipulators of mass appeals, these rustics exploited racial hatred to consolidate the rural whites and to hold power. Included in this group were TOM WATSON and EUGENE TALMADGE of Georgia, PITCHFORK BEN TILLMAN of South Carolina, JAMES K. VARDAMAN and THEODORE BILBO of Mississippi, JEFF DAVIS of Arkansas, and HUEY LONG and EARL LONG of Louisiana (the Longs made little use of racial rhetoric). ORVAL FAUBUS, Lester Maddox, and GEORGE C. WALLACE are recent additions.

Since 1954 rhetorical patterns seem to be moving toward the national norm. The stereotyped southern orator has given way to such optimistic leadership as JIMMY CARTER, Reuben Askew, John C. West, Dale Bumpers, Julian Bond, and Barbara Jordan.

See W. Braden, *Oratory in Old South* (1970) and *Southern Speech Journal* (Spring, 1961; Summer, 1964); J. D. Saxon, *Southern Speech Journal* (Spring, 1975); and F. P. Gaines, *Southern Oratory* (1946).

WALDO W. BRADEN
Louisiana State University

ORD, EDWARD OTHO CRESAP (1818–1883), was born in Cumberland, Md., and graduated from West Point in 1839. He fought Indians and served in the Mexican War in California. He was commissioned brigadier general of U.S. Volunteers (1861) and major general (1862). Ord fought at Iuka, CORINTH, and VICKSBURG, becoming a U. S. Grant favorite. He captured Ft. Harrison on the Richmond front (1864) and commanded the Army of the James and Department of Virginia (1865). Ord's overnight march of nearly 40 miles forced the surrender at APPOMATTOX. He was commissioned brigadier general of regulars in 1866, holding various commands. In Arkansas he was assistant commissioner of the FREEDMEN'S BUREAU. In the Fourth Military District Ord executed the RECONSTRUCTION ACTS vigorously and precipitated the *ex parte* MCCARDLE case. In Texas he ordered pursuit of marauders into Mexico and pacified the Rio Grande frontier in the 1870s. Retired as a major general by act of Congress in 1880, Ord went to Mexico for the Grant-Gould railroad interests.

See E. O. C. Ord Papers (1850–83), University of California, Berkeley; W. T. Sherman Papers, Library of Congress; Record Groups 59, 94, 98, 105, 108, National Archives; *Official Records, Armies*, Ser. 1; and B. Cresap, *Pacific Historical Review* (Nov., 1952).

BERNARR CRESAP
University of North Alabama

ORDER OF AMERICAN KNIGHTS. See AMERICAN KNIGHTS, ORDER OF

ORLANDO, FLA. (pop. 99,006), like much of the central peninsula, was settled by army volunteers in the aftermath of the SEMINOLE WARS. Growing up around Ft. Gatlin, approximately 75 miles east of Tampa, the early community was a cattle-raising center. It remained unnamed until 1850, when it was christened Jernigan after a family that had moved there from Georgia. The first commercial citrus groves were planted immediately after the Civil War. In 1880 General U. S. Grant presided over ceremonies inaugurating construction of a line of the South Florida Railway, a transportation link that permitted Orlando to develop as a shipping point and packing center for citrus fruits. In the twentieth century, the many small lakes within the city's limits have proved attractive to tourists and have made it a popular inland resort. The city's varied industries manufacture citrus spraying and packaging equipment, fertilizer, missiles, pleasure boats, furniture, mirrors, and sheet metals.

See E. H. Gore, *Florida Sand* (1957), best; W. F. Blackman, *History of Orange County* (1927, 1974); K. Fries, *Orlando* (1938), anecdotal; C. E. Howard, *Early Settlers* (1915); A. G. Breakfast, *Romantic History of Orlando* (1946); files of *Sentinel Star* (1876–), on microfilm; and numbers of *Orange County Historical Quarterly*, published by county historical society.

ORLEANS TERRITORY was organized by Congress on March 26, 1804, following the LOUISIANA PURCHASE. Louisiana was divided into upper and lower territories, the latter becoming Orleans. Orleans included present-day Louisiana except land east of the Mississippi and north of Lake Pontchartrain. Government consisted of a governor (W. C. C. CLAIBORNE), secretary, three judges, and 13 councilors (all presidential appointees), plus a popularly elected legislature. Civil code agitation, congressional petitioning, and JOHN RANDOLPH's remonstrance for liberalized institutions reflected widespread citizen discontent with administration policies. Orleans became the state of Louisiana on April 30, 1812.

See C. Gayarré, *History of Louisiana* (1920); and T. P. Coffey, "Territory of Orleans" (Ph.D. dissertation, St. Louis University, 1956).

JAMES T. BANNON
St. Louis University

ORR, JAMES LAWRENCE (1822–1873), of Anderson, S.C., was a STATES' RIGHTS Democrat in Congress before the Civil War. He was a moderate on sectional issues, but he advocated SECESSION after Abraham Lincoln's election. As a spokesman for the mountainous western part of his state, he criticized as wasteful the economic practices of the planters, favored industrial growth, and led a movement to democratize the state's political structure. A slaveholder, he opposed a legalized foreign slave trade and urged the immigration of white laborers into the South.

A Confederate senator during the war, Orr was a harsh critic of Jefferson Davis. By 1864 he advocated peace negotiations with the Union. Governor of his state from 1865 to 1868, Orr supported the Reconstruction policies of ANDREW JOHNSON. Initially he opposed Negro suffrage, but he came to recognize that the South had to conciliate the North and make concessions to the blacks. After the RECONSTRUCTION ACTS resulted in black electoral majorities and Republican dominance, Orr urged whites to enter and control the ruling party. In 1872 he was a leader of an unsuccessful reform movement against a corrupt element in the Republican party. Also, from 1868 to 1873 he was a state judge and U.S. minister to Russia.

See R. P. Leemhuis, "James L. Orr" (Ph.D. dissertation, University of Wisconsin, 1970); S. A. Channing, *Crisis of Fear* (1970); L. A. Kibler, *Benjamin F. Perry* (1946); H. V. Schultz, *Nationalism and Sectionalism in South Carolina* (1950); F. B. Simkins and R. H. Woody, *South Carolina During Reconstruction* (1932); J. Williamson, *After Slavery* (1965); and W. B. Yearns, *Confederate Congress* (1960).

ROGER P. LEEMHUIS
Clemson University

OSAGE INDIANS, according to tribal legend, first formed in the Piedmont region of Virginia and later settled in the Ohio Valley. Recorded history, however, does not locate the tribe until about 1673, by which time they were comfortably situated on the Osage River in what is now western Missouri. Here they remained, bartering with Frenchmen and Spaniards, until 1802, when they were enticed to the Three Forks region of present-day Oklahoma by the master trader Auguste Chouteau.

All of their claims to the Osage River area were relinquished in treaties of 1808 and 1822 with the U.S. government. The following decades in what was then termed Indian Territory were torturous for the Osage. In addition to bloody confrontations with the Kiowa and Comanche Indians, who were indignant over new pressures on their hunting ranges, there were further cessions of land to the government in 1825. In 1839 the Osage were removed to Kansas, suffered two more land cessions in 1865 and 1870, and returned to Indian Territory in 1872 numbering only 4,000 souls.

In 1904 the tribe followed the national policy of the times and allotted their reservation into separate plots for 2,229 tribesmen. Fortunately the Osage legislation differed from similar acts in that it reserved all mineral rights to the tribe, inasmuch as there were binding oil leases from as early as 1896, which remained in force. These contracts began to pay substantial dividends by 1912, and throughout the 1920s the Osage were the wealthiest people in the world. By the end of that decade every allotted Osage had received $102,534 in royalties and the combined tribal revenues through 1971 amounted to more than $510 million.

See W. D. Baird, *Osage People* (1972), best; and J. J. Mathews, *Osage* (1962), sympathetic treatment by Oxford-educated Osage.

ROBERT C. CARRIKER
Gonzaga University

OSAGE RIVER, approximately 500 miles in length, is formed in western Missouri by the junction of the Marais des Cygnes and the Little Osage rivers. It flows in an easterly direction for 130 miles into the Lake of the Ozarks, an artificial body of water created by the construction (1929–1931) of Bagnell Dam. From there it flows generally northeast for 360 miles to its mouth near Jefferson City on the MISSOURI RIVER. When Jacques Marquette explored the river in 1673, he named it and the Osage Indians in a French corruption of the name of the Washazhe Indian tribe.

OSCEOLA (1804?–1838), of CREEK INDIAN–Scotch lineage, was born in Alabama. In 1814 (CREEK WAR) the anti–United States band, with him in it, migrated to Spanish Florida. Even there it was crushed by U.S. forces in 1818 under ANDREW JACKSON. Although not a hereditary chief, Osceola gradually assumed leadership of the Florida Indians. He entered history when he took a defiant stand against American demands at a council meeting in October, 1834. Thereafter he led the Indian opposition to removal from Florida. He began the Second SEMINOLE WAR on December 28, 1835, with a two-pronged attack on U.S. personnel. His continuing campaign was so successful that the white population was confined in three coastal towns. By late summer, 1836, Osceola, due to illness, was no longer able to unify Indian attacks, but in three months he had shown himself one of the finest war leaders ever to appear among the North American Indians. Finally, however, he was captured on October 21, 1837, under a flag of truce. This treachery, plus the gallant fight the Florida Indians had waged under his command, made Osceola a national figure. But, ill when captured, he soon died at Ft. Moultrie, S.C. In a short 40 months, out of a life of only 34 years, Osceola had come to personify Indian patriotism. As a result, 20 towns, three counties, two lakes, two mountains, a state park, and a national forest have since been named for him.

See W. and E. Hartley, *Osceola* (1973); J. K. Mahon, *History of Second Seminole War* (1967); and entire issue of *Florida Historical Quarterly* (Jan.–April, 1955).

JOHN K. MAHON
University of Florida

OSTEND MANIFESTO. The PIERCE ADMINISTRATION, which came into office in March, 1853, was decidedly prosouthern in attitude, and the new president in his inaugural address proclaimed his sympathy for a vigorous expansionist policy. The acquisition of Cuba in particular, as one more slave state, he considered to be inevitable because of its proximity to the United States and because its ownership was necessary for the continued safety of the institution of slavery in the South. He appointed as minister to England James Buchanan, a DOUGHFACE and an ardent advocate of acquiring Cuba by purchase; for France he chose the like-minded JOHN Y. MASON of Virginia; and, most important, for minister to Spain he appointed the flamboyant PIERRE SOULÉ of Louisiana, leader of the Cuban annexationist movement in the Senate.

In many ways the international situation was ideal for Pierce to achieve his goal. The Spanish government was verging on bankruptcy; France and England were involved in the Crimean War; and a group of wealthy Cuban planters had already invited the United States to overthrow Spanish rule and annex the island. Seemingly at the opportune moment the Spanish authorities in Cuba also virtually invited an American show of force by their harassment of an American steamer in Havana harbor in the famous *Black Warrior* affair. Soulé delivered to the Spanish monarchy, on his own authority, a 48-hour ultimatum in order to bring maximum pressure to bear. Spain, however, failed to be pushed.

To get negotiations for the purchase of Cuba moving, Franklin Pierce and Secretary of State William L. Marcy suggested to Soulé that he arrange a meeting with Buchanan and Mason and that together they draft a confidential memorandum to the president offering their recommendations for future action.

The three ministers conferred in Ostend, Belgium, from the ninth to the eleventh of October, when they adjourned to meet in Aix-la-Chapelle, Prussia, from October 12 to October 18. The result of the conference, drafted on October 18, 1854, was the Ostend Manifesto. It was not issued from Ostend, and it was by no means a public "manifesto"; rather, it was a confidential message to Marcy. The key sentences stated "that an . . . effort ought to be made . . . to purchase Cuba from Spain. . . . If this shall have been refused, it will then be time to consider the question; does Cuba, in the possession of Spain, seriously endanger our internal peace and the existence of our cherished Union? Should this question be answered in the affirmative, then . . . we shall be justified in wresting it from Spain." Accompanying this proposal was a letter from Soulé enthusiastically urging the conquest of Cuba.

The timing of the arrival of the dispatch in America, however, could not have been less opportune. The antislavery forces were greatly incensed over the recent passage, under administrative sponsorship, of the KANSAS-NEBRASKA ACT. To make matters worse, the New York *Herald* was able to publish a reasonably accurate summary of the Ostend Manifesto for all the world to see. The antislavery forces, expressing shock at this ruthless proposal to expand slavery, were in full cry against the administration. The Pierce administration was forced, in the face of the public anger in the North, to retreat quickly from its aggressive Cuba posture. Marcy sent new instructions to Soulé, which in effect repudiated much of the Ostend Manifesto. Soulé was so distressed that he resigned in disgust and left Spain. Southern expansionists continued to dream of adding the island as a new slave state, but the northern reaction to the "Manifesto of the Brigands" killed all hopes in the 1850s of ever obtaining congressional consent to its acquisition.

See F. E. Chadwick, *Relations of U.S. and Spain* (1909), full text of manifesto; S. Webster, *Political Science Quarterly* (March, 1893), old but informative; A. A. Ettinger, *Mission to Spain of Soulé* (1932), definitive; G. B. Henderson (ed.), *Journal of Southern History* (Aug., 1939); B. Rauch, *American Interest in Cuba* (1948); R. F. Nichols, *Franklin Pierce* (1958); P. S. Toner, *History of Cuba and Relations with U.S.* (1963), II; and I. D. Spencer, *Victor and Spoils* (1959).

OUACHITA MOUNTAINS compose a region in southeastern Oklahoma and west-central Arkansas. The Athens Piedmont Plateau, the Novaculite Uplift, and the Fourche Mountains constitute the major subdivisions of the Ouachitas. In Arkansas, Hot Springs National Park and its environs are a well-known vacation and hydrotherapy center. HERNANDO DE SOTO may have visited the Hot Springs area in 1541. Crater of Diamonds State Park, near Murfreesboro, is the only place in North America where diamonds are found in their natural matrix. The gems were mined there in the early twentieth century in commercial quantities. Present-day visitors are allowed to keep the ones they find. Many artificial lakes characterize the region, the largest of which is Lake Ouachita. The Ouachita National Forest covers a significant portion of the region. Minerals include bauxite, the ore from which aluminum is processed. It has been mined there since 1899 and constitutes most of the bauxite production of the United States.

JAMES E. GRINER
Arkansas State University

OUTER BANKS compose a chain of barrier islands that run the length of the North Carolina coast and separate both ALBEMARLE and PAMLICO sounds from the Atlantic Ocean. Counted as parts of the Outer Banks are CAPES Fear, Lookout, and Hatteras. It is at Hatteras that the warm northerly waters of the Gulf Stream meet the colder and southerly waters of the Labrador Current. Although the area's shifting sands and changing currents long have been extremely hazardous to navigation, it is the dense fogs produced by the juncture of the currents that have earned for Cape Hatteras its name as the "Graveyard of the Atlantic."

Sir WALTER RALEIGH in 1585 located the first English settlement in the New World on ROANOKE ISLAND, just inside the Outer Banks, where it would be protected from the ocean and screened from the view of Spanish ships. Except for a few fishing villages and some limited farming, the Outer Banks underwent little development prior to the twentieth century. Because of the area's steady winds and its relative isolation, Orville and Wilbur Wright chose Kill Devil Hill (a 100-foot elevation near the village of Kitty Hawk) as the site for their experiments in heavier-than-air flight. Today the Wright Brothers National Memorial (established in 1927) commemorates their first successful flight in 1905. Farther to the south, the Cape Hatteras National Seashore Recreation Area was created in 1937 as a public beach and campsite, which protects the natural beauty of over 70 miles of the Outer Banks. Both the Wright memorial and the recreation area are important components in a rapidly developing tourist industry.

OUTLIERS, also spelled Outlyers, were either rebels or Loyalists in the Carolina backcountry during the Revolutionary War who fled their homes and families and went into hiding to avoid taking an oath of allegiance to the king or to escape retaliation from rebel militia and their sympathizers. The term is applied specifically to loyal Highland Scots in the Cross Creek country of North Carolina who sought refuge in nearby forests from their rebel tormentors in the winter of 1775–1776.

See H. Rankin, *North Carolina Continentals* (1971).

PETER M. MITCHELL
Seton Hall University

OVERMOUNTAIN MEN were colonists who first settled the area immediately beyond the crest of the Appalachians. They produced exceptional leadership as in the development of the Watauga settlement on the Holston by James Robertson, JOHN SEVIER, and ISAAC SHELBY. RICHARD HENDERSON lent considerable organizing talent to the Transylvania and Cumberland settlements. Strong leadership and the different environment of trans-Appalachia exacerbated friction with the eastern establishment over taxation, protection from Indians, and the extension of state courts. These frontiersmen effected changes in both institutions and values including those concerned with religion and politics. They also provided impetus to the further exploitation of the West.

See J. A. Caruso, *Appalachian Frontier* (1959); Draper Papers, State Historical Society of Wisconsin; C. S. Driver, *Sevier* (1932); and W. H. Masterson, *Blount* (1954).

EDWARD L. HENSON, JR.
Clinch Valley College

OVERSEERS played a vital role in the management of southern plantations. Usually employed on units with more than 20 working field hands, the overseer occupied a position between the proprietor and Negro DRIVERS in the managerial hierarchy of the plantation and was responsible for executing the policies formulated by his employer. Primarily accountable for slave discipline and crop production, he assigned gangs to work, supervised field labor, administered punishment, treated minor ailments, distributed food and clothing, and maintained various record and account books. In many areas, overseers afforded the sparse white population its only security against possible SLAVE INSURRECTIONS.

The typical overseer was white, less than thirty-five years of age, the son of a YEOMAN FARMER, deficient in formal schooling, and devoid of significant property. He had entered the overseeing business to earn a competency—to save enough money to purchase a tract of land and perhaps a few slaves and to establish himself as a small independent farmer. Such a goal was attainable, for, in addition to an annual salary that ranged from $100 on small Virginia tobacco farms to as much as $2,000 on the great rice and sugar estates, he received free housing, a provisions allowance, and the use of one or more black servants. Thus, if he lived frugally and soberly, he could look forward to escaping from the socially distasteful occupation of slave manager before he reached the age of forty. In the meantime, he was doomed to a Spartan existence. Virtually ostracized by his employer, forbidden to fraternize with the slaves, discouraged from entertaining company, and compelled to remain constantly at his post, the overseer was a lonely figure.

Berated by their superiors for a variety of transgressions, real and imagined, and hated intensely by the slaves, overseers were a much-maligned group. Some of the criticism was justified, but planters exacerbated the deficiencies in the system by castigating their overseers at every opportunity, constantly and capriciously changing managers, and refusing to pay fair wages. Because their self-interests did not coincide, a certain degree of friction was inherent in the owner-manager relationship even under ideal conditions. Cognizant of this conflict, the slaves exploited it to their own advantage, thus rendering the overseer's position even more untenable.

See W. K. Scarborough, *Overseer* (1966); J. S. Bassett, *Southern Plantation Overseer* (1925); J. C. Bonner, *Agricultural History* (Jan., 1945); W. K. Scarborough, *Agricultural History* (Jan., 1964); E. D. Genovese, *Roll, Jordan, Roll* (1974); and manuscripts, University of North Carolina Library, Chapel Hill, and Louisiana State University, Department of Archives, Baton Rouge.

WILLIAM K. SCARBOROUGH
University of Southern Mississippi

OVERTON, JOHN H. (1766–1833), was born in Louisa County, Va., went to Kentucky about 1786 and there studied law, and finally migrated to Nashville, Tenn., where he established a lifelong friendship with ANDREW JACKSON. Overton be-

came a leading land-title lawyer, speculated in land (including present-day Memphis), and bought and sold slaves. Between 1795 and 1816 he was federal supervisor of the revenue for the district of Tennessee, a judge of the superior court of law and equity of Tennessee, and a judge of the supreme court of Tennessee. He managed Jackson's bid for the presidency in 1824 and was the chairman of the "whitewashing committee" that was so instrumental in Jackson's successful effort in 1828.

See, in order of importance, *Overton Reports* (1811–16); J. S. Bassett, *Correspondence of Jackson* (1926–31); S. F. Horn, *Tennessee Historical Quarterly* (June, 1947); F. Clifton, *Tennessee Historical Quarterly* (March, 1952); M. T. Orr, *Tennessee Historical Quarterly* (Sept., 1956); H. L. Swint, *Tennessee Historical Quarterly* (Summer, 1967); W. W. Clayton, *Davidson County* (1880); J. Parton, *Jackson* (1859–60); M. James, *Jackson* (1938); J. E. Roper, *Tennessee Historical Quarterly* (Dec., 1962); T. B. Jones, *Tennessee Historical Quarterly* (Spring, 1968); G. L. Lowe, Jr., *Tennessee Historical Quarterly* (June, 1952); and Overton Papers, Tennessee Historical Society.

R. BEELER SATTERFIELD
Lamar University

OWENSBORO, KY. (pop. 50,329), is on the Ohio River in the northwest section of the state. When first settled in 1800, the community was known as Yellow Banks because of the unusual color of the clay. Renamed Rossborough in 1815, the town prospered as an antebellum river port. Not until 1866 did the town adopt its present name, chosen to honor a soldier slain at the battle of Tippecanoe (1811). Long a major tobacco market and producer of BOURBON whiskey, modern Owensboro also manufactures electrical supplies, refined petroleum, furniture, construction materials, foodstuffs, and cellulose. Kentucky Wesleyan College (1860) is located here.

See Owensboro *Messenger and Inquirer* (1874–), on microfilm.

OWSLEY, FRANK LAWRENCE (1890–1956), southern historian, was born near Montgomery, Ala. He was educated at Auburn (B.A., 1911; M.A., 1912) and at the University of Chicago (M.A., 1917; Ph.D., 1924), studying under WILLIAM E. DODD. He served in World War I, taught at Auburn and Birmingham-Southern, then at Vanderbilt (1920–1949). He held the Hugo Friedman Chair in Southern History, University of Alabama (1949–1956).

Owsley published *State Rights in the Confederacy* (1925), the first to stress internal weakness in a new interpretation of the Confederacy. A member of the Agrarians, he published an interpretive essay, "The Irrepressible Conflict," in I'LL TAKE MY STAND (1930). In *King Cotton Diplomacy* (1931, 1959) he advanced a controversial new interpretation stressing economic factors to explain the failure of the British to intervene in the Civil War. In *Plain Folk of the Old South* (1949), a controversial examination of social and economic structure, Owsley tapped new sources and applied statistical methods to break the stereotype of the Old South and reveal the large and substantial middle class of YEOMEN FARMERS. Owsley served as president of the Southern Historical Association in 1940. He died in London.

See Frank Owsley Papers, other material on Agrarians, Joint University Libraries, Nashville, Tenn.; F. L. Owsley, *South: Old and New Frontiers* (1969); B. Cresap, *Alabama Review* (Oct., 1973); and F. Linden, *Journal of Negro History* (April, 1946), critical of Owsley's statistical methods.

BERNARR CRESAP
University of North Alabama

OXFORD, MISS. (pop. 13,846), was first settled in 1835 by John Chisolm, John Craig, and John Martin. They built a log store here, approximately 60 miles southeast of Memphis, Tenn., on land recently ceded by the CHICKASAW INDIANS. The community that grew up around the store was named Oxford, apparently with the hope that the town would be made the site of a new state university. In 1848 the University of Mississippi opened its doors, and Oxford became an educational center. The town was occupied by U. S. Grant's forces in December, 1862. It is the Jefferson of WILLIAM FAULKNER's tales of Yoknapatawpha County and the setting of some of STARK YOUNG's stories. The modern city remains essentially a university town and a market for area agriculture.

See files of Oxford *Eagle* (1867–), on microfilm.

OZARK PLATEAU, or Ozark Mountains, is a land region of about 40,000 square miles encompassing the larger portions of southern Missouri, northern and northwestern Arkansas, and smaller areas in northeastern Oklahoma and southern Illinois. The southernmost section of the Ozarks is the Boston Mountain area, which merges into the hills and ridges along the north side of the Arkansas River. North of this section lie the Springfield Plateau and the Salem Plateau, each of which extends well into Missouri. The François Mountains rise in southeast Missouri and include Taum Sauk (1,772 feet), the highest point in Missouri. Most of the level land of the Ozark Plateau consists of river valleys and tablelands, much of which is suitable for crops and livestock. Mineral wealth is abundant in the Missouri portion.

The Ozarks, as the region is commonly known, are a major tourist and vacation area (TOURISM). Numerous CAVES and other commercialized entertainment, as well as extensive lakes, supplement the moderate climate and beautiful scenery as elements of attraction. Large artificial lakes include Lake of the Ozarks and Table Rock Reservoir. In Arkansas the largest lakes are Bull Shoals, Beaver, and Norfork, all created by dams on the WHITE RIVER. PEA RIDGE National Battlefield Park memorializes the most important Civil War battle west of the Mississippi River. Eureka Springs is a unique historic resort town. Folk festivals, folklore, and local crafts characterize modern forms of "hillbilly" culture. Industrial plants have multiplied in recent decades.

JAMES E. GRINER
Arkansas State University

P

PACA, WILLIAM (1740–1799), born near Abingdon, Md., earned an M.A. degree at the College of Philadelphia (1759) and completed his legal education at the Inner Temple in London. He joined SAMUEL CHASE in opposing the proprietor and in supporting the patriots. He served in the Maryland assembly, committee of correspondence, provincial convention, state constitutional convention, senate, and general court and as governor for three terms (1782–1785). A member of both the First and Second CONTINENTAL CONGRESS (1774–1779), Paca signed the DECLARATION OF INDEPENDENCE and participated actively in committee work and as chief justice of the court of appeals in admiralty and prize cases. At the state ratification convention in 1788, Paca proposed 15 amendments to the Constitution reflecting his ANTI-FEDERALIST sympathies. Although they were rejected by the majority, who doubted their authority to qualify endorsement of the Constitution, most were incorporated later in the Judiciary Act of 1789 and in the BILL OF RIGHTS. Despite his doubts about the Constitution, Paca accepted appointment as U.S. judge for the District of Maryland and held that office for the final decade of his life.

See P. A. Crowl, *William and Mary Quarterly* (Oct., 1947); A. Silverman, *Maryland Historical Magazine* (March, 1942); J. Elliot, *Debates in State Conventions* (1836), II; K. M. Rowland, *Charles Carroll of Carrollton* (1898); Gwathmey Collection, University of Virginia Library; and Lee Family Papers, Virginia Historical Society.

MARY K. BONSTEEL TACHAU
University of Louisville

PACKARD, STEPHEN B. (?–?), was a native of Maine and attained the rank of captain in the Union army during the Civil War. In 1871 he was named U.S. marshal for the District of Louisiana by President Ulysses S. Grant. In Louisiana he quickly became the leader of the Customhouse Ring, that faction of the Radical Republican party opposed to Governor HENRY CLAY WARMOTH. He directed the campaign of WILLIAM PITT KELLOGG for the governorship in 1872. When the election was disputed, Packard saw to it that Warmoth was impeached (thus removing him from office until his term expired) and secured federal recognition

of P. B. S. PINCHBACK as governor for the remainder of Warmoth's term. Kellogg was then recognized as the legitimate governor by the national administration. In 1876 Packard was himself the Radical Republican candidate for governor. Both he and his opponent FRANCIS T. NICHOLLS were inaugurated; but, as a result of the famous Compromise of 1877 (ELECTION OF 1876), the electoral vote of Louisiana was counted for Rutherford B. Hayes and the Hayes administration offered no opposition to Nicholls' complete assumption of the governorship. As a reward for his services to the Republican party, Packard was named U.S. consul at Liverpool.

See J. G. Taylor, *Louisiana Reconstructed* (1975); E. Lonn, *Reconstruction in Louisiana After 1868* (1918); and A. Grosz, *Louisiana Historical Quarterly* (April, 1944).

JOE GRAY TAYLOR
McNeese State University

PADRE ISLAND is a 115-mile-long barrier beach off the coast of Texas. Varying in width between 1,400 feet and four miles, it runs north from Brazos Santiago Pass to a channel southeast of CORPUS CHRISTI, which separates Padre Island from Mustang Island. The Spanish explorer Alonzo de Piñeda named it Isla Blanca in 1519. It was the home of a group of cannibalistic Indians and a refuge for Gulf pirates. In the eighteenth century, a Spanish priest gained title to the entire island, and it since has been known by its present name.

PADUCAH, KY. (pop. 31,627), is at the confluence of the Ohio and Tennessee rivers. GEORGE ROGERS CLARK used the site as a base for his operations against the British in 1778, and 17 years later a grateful Virginia assembly made Clark a gift of almost 73,000 acres of land in this area of western Kentucky. The land was in CHICKASAW INDIAN territory, however, and Clark was unable to do anything with his claim other than to will it upon his death in 1818 to his brother William. Meanwhile, a small trading community known as Pekin had grown up at the mouth of the Tennessee. In 1827, when WILLIAM CLARK made good upon his inherited claim, he laid out the town and named it after his Indian friend Chief Paduke. The town possessed several natural advantages from which it has drawn a relatively stable if unspectacular growth and prosperity: it is near four navigable rivers (the Ohio, Tennessee, Cumberland, and Mississippi); logs could be floated down both the Tennessee and the Cumberland to feed Paducah's lumber and shipbuilding industries; and the warmer waters of the Tennessee made it an ice-free winter harbor for many Ohio River boats.

In September, 1861, General U. S. Grant took control of this strategic river port and thereafter used it as a major transportation center and supply depot. Although General NATHAN B. FORREST successfully attacked the city in 1864, his Confederate troops retired after burning the riverfront warehouses with their stores of federal supplies. Periodic floods have done more damage to the city, however, than any Civil War engagement. Several FLOOD CONTROL projects have greatly reduced this danger to the city since the great flood of 1937. Moreover, the revival of inland waterway commerce since 1920 and the inauguration of the multifaceted services of the TENNESSEE VALLEY AUTHORITY have brought further advantages to Paducah. It is the primary market and distribution center for western Kentucky's dark burley tobacco. The Atomic Energy Commission produces fissionable uranium here, and the city's varied industries manufacture river barges, hosiery, chemicals, machine tools, and concrete products.

See F. G. Neuman, *Story of Paducah* (1927) and *Paducahans in History* (1922); and files of Paducah *Sun-Democrat* (1871–), on microfilm. Paducah Public Library maintains Irvin S. Cobb Collection, works and memorabilia; Kentuckiana Collection, area history; Labor History Collection; and census reports of McCracken County and Paducah since 1810.

PAGE, THOMAS NELSON

PAGE, THOMAS NELSON (1853–1922), a patrician Virginian, grew up in the hard times of war and Reconstruction and attended Washington College and the University of Virginia Law School. As a Richmond attorney, he won instant acclaim in 1884 with "Marse Chan," a poignant story related in the dialect of Negroes of the Virginia Piedmont. Other stories followed, including the semi-autobiographical *Two Little Confederates*, which has never been out of print since. Deteriorating business conditions led him to read his stories on the LYCEUM platform. Seeing libraries and other riches that the impoverished South lacked, he was determined to help the South rise from poverty, rediscover its proud heritage, and achieve national reconciliation. To that end he gave Richmond its first library, urged collection of regional history, and published essays, sketches, and stories, all the while making impassioned public addresses. His best-seller *Red Rock* remains one of the memorable novels of Reconstruction. In 1893 he moved to Washington, D.C., and began to travel abroad, but part of his heart remained at his family home. In 1913 he became ambassador to Rome, serving with vigor and frustration until 1919. A cosmopolitan, he wrote with affection about the people of his region as he remembered them; editors did not want him to write anything else.

See T. N. Page, *Land of Spirit* (1913), *Italy and World War* (1920), *Dante and His Influence* (1922), *Red Riders* (1924), *Washington and Its Romance* (1923), *Mediterranean Winter, 1906* (1971), *North African Journey, 1912* (1970), and *On Nile in 1901* (1969); H. R. Holman (ed.), *John Fox and Tom Page* (1970); R. Page, *Thomas N. Page* (1923), general but basic; T. L. Gross, *Thomas N. Page* (1967), hastily researched; H. R. Holman, "Literary Career of T. N. Page" (Ph.D. dissertation, Duke, 1948); J. N. Fusco, *Diplomatic Relations Between Italy and U.S., 1913–1917* (1970); and Page Papers, Duke, University of Virginia, and William and Mary libraries.

HARRIET R. HOLMAN
Clemson University

PAGE, WALTER HINES

PAGE, WALTER HINES (1855–1918), was born in Cary, N.C., the son of a small planter. After studying at Randolph-Macon College and Johns Hopkins, he taught high school English in Louisville for a year before becoming a reporter for the St. Joseph (Mo.) *Gazette* in 1880. Journalism was his calling. As the result of a series of syndicated articles on the South, he was hired by the New York *World* as a roving reporter and traveled widely throughout the country. In 1883 he became editor of the Raleigh (N.C.) *State Chronicle*, in which he argued for policies associated with the NEW SOUTH movement. In 1885 he returned to the Northeast and a highly successful publishing career, which led to editorship of the *Atlantic Monthly*, to his partnership in the publishing house of Doubleday, Page, and to the founding of a new magazine, *World's Work*. He was one of the inner circle who organized and financed the presidential campaign of WOODROW WILSON, an old friend. An anglophile like Wilson, he was a natural choice as ambassador to Great Britain. At first Page enjoyed an excellent relationship with the president. The coming of World War I changed this. Wilson advocated neutrality, while Page saw the struggle as one between German militarism and British democracy and urged active support for the Allies. Relations between the two men became strained until American entry into the war resolved the situation.

See B. J. Hendrick, *Walter H. Page* (3 vols.; 1922–25); A. S. Link, *Wilson* (5 vols.; 1947–); and W. H. Page, *Rebuilding of Old Commonwealths* (1902), *Publisher's Confession* (1905), and *Southerner* (1909), novel written under pseudonym Nicholas Worth.

HUGH GREGG CLELAND
State University of New York, Stony Brook

PALMETTO ARMS. The Palmetto Armory was established in 1851 by William Glaze & Company in Columbia, S.C., to fill an order for weapons for the state. In addition to Glaze the company included James S. Boatwright, also of Columbia, and Benjamin Flagg, of Millbury, Mass., who was a gun maker and supplied most if not all of the machinery. In fulfilling its contract the Palmetto Armory produced 6,000 U.S. model 1842 muskets with triangular bayonets, 1,000 model 1841 rifles, and 2,000 model 1842 single-shot pistols. The armory also made a limited number of cavalry and long artillery sabers. All weapons made were of the finest quality and were used in the Civil War. The Palmetto Armory appears to have gone out of business sometime in 1854 or 1855 upon completion of the state contract, but Glaze continued his manufactory under different names until 1865, when Columbia was burned by W. T. Sherman's forces and with it Glaze's buildings. It should be noted that the Palmetto Armory was the only private contract manufacturer of weapons in the South prior to 1861.

See W. A. Albaugh III, H. Benet, Jr., and E. N. Simmons, *Confederate Handguns* (1963), illustrated; and R. M. Reilly, *U.S. Military Small Arms, 1816–1865* (1970), has line schematics of weapons.

HUGH BENET, JR.
Star-Spangled Banner Flag House Association, Inc.

PALO ALTO, BATTLE OF (May 8, 1846), was fought in Texas eight miles northwest of Matamoros, Mexico. ZACHARY TAYLOR with an American army of 2,300 men encountered 6,000 Mexican soldiers under Mariano Arista. Situated on slightly higher elevation at Palo Alto (tall timber), Taylor ordered Major Samuel Ringgold and Captain James Duncan with several batteries of extremely maneuverable horse-drawn six-pounders to rake the Mexicans. During the afternoon Duncan's guns set fire to the dry prairie grass, which limited the effectiveness of both armies. At 4:30, however, both Taylor and Arista ordered frontal assaults; yet neither side gained an advantage. Darkness finally ended the battle. Mexican dead and wounded ranged between 229 and 500; American losses were only 53. Because Mexican soldiers were demoralized, Arista retreated early the next morning to RESACA DE LA PALMA, where Taylor severely defeated him. Palo Alto was thus an auspicious American military victory, which helped promote Taylor to the presidency of the United States.

See J. H. Smith, *Annexation of Texas* (1941); O. A. Singletary, *Mexican War* (1960); and A. H. Bill, *Rehearsal for Conflict* (1947).

BEN H. PROCTER
Texas Christian University

PAMLICO SOUND, the largest sound or lagoon on the East Coast, is an arm of the Atlantic Ocean formed by the barrier beaches of North Carolina's OUTER BANKS. Approximately 80 miles in length, it adjoins ALBEMARLE SOUND to the north and receives the waters of the Neuse and the Tar (Pamlico) rivers. There are no major cities on its shores, but New Bern on the Neuse and Greenville on the Tar utilize the sound as part of the INTRA-COASTAL WATERWAY and for access to the Atlantic.

PANAMA CITY, FLA. (pop. 32,096), faces onto St. Andrew Bay on the Gulf of Mexico, approximately 95 miles east of Pensacola. The surrounding area was settled about the time of the American Revolution by homesteaders, many of whom were British Loyalists. The cultivation of indigo, lumbering, and the production of naval stores provided settlers with their earliest livelihoods. Soon the large catches of fish created yet another source of income. During the Civil War, however, federal raiding parties destroyed the fisheries on the bay. Fish and lumber continued to be the bases for rebuilding the area economy, and in 1909, after a merger with two adjacent towns, Panama City was incorporated. The establishment here in 1931 of a paper mill and the post–World War II development of TOURISM have greatly spurred the city's growth.

See B. K. Loftin, "Panama City, 1930–1950" (Ph.D. dissertation, University of Florida, 1971); and files of *News-Herald* (1931–), on microfilm.

PANIC OF 1819 struck most severely and lasted longest in the old Southwest. The second Bank of the United States encouraged land speculation while contracting loans and demanding specie payments from state banks. Falling farm prices and land values collapsed southern agriculture. Northern Alabama was the most distressed district in the country. Southerners generally lost confidence in government as cotton and other staple prices fell by one-third. Nearly one of every three land purchasers in new districts lost their claims. Congress issued relief loans in 1820 and 1821. An 1820 liberalized land law allowed for purchasing less minimum acreage with a smaller sound money outlay. Some southern states adopted appraisal and stay laws, abolished debt imprisonment, and tightened BANKING regulations. Popular distrust of federal and eastern institutions surfaced in the South during the crisis and contributed to molding support for sectionalism and Jacksonian Democracy. Social dislocation in seaboard cities and older settled portions of the South precipitated the nation's third major postrevolutionary wave of westward migration.

See G. Dangerfield, *Era of Good Feelings* (1952), overview; and M. Rohrbough, *Land Office Business* (1968).

JAMES T. BANNON
St. Louis University

PANIC OF 1837 resulted from Jacksonian BANKING policy, LAND SPECULATION, reversal of a rising cotton market, and an excess of imports from Britain. After ANDREW JACKSON's national bank veto, deposits in "pet banks" stimulated inflationary expansion, especially in internal improvements. Western, particularly southwestern, land speculation using inadequately backed paper brought Jackson's Specie Circular of 1836 requiring specie payment for public lands. Specie moved west, and treasury specie was depleted by the act of 1836 to distribute the federal surplus to the states. When British cotton prices fell, businesses failed in the South and a national panic followed. Recent authors have deemphasized speculative expansion and the Specie Circular as causes of the panic, one interpretation ascribing expansion to changes in the silver market. To aid recovery, Congress authorized $47,002,900 in treasury notes by 1843, while Nicholas Biddle's United States Bank of Pennsylvania attempted an unsuccessful cotton speculation. Specie payments were suspended in 1837, cotton prices fell, internal improvements were stopped, and the South was especially hurt in the depression that lasted until 1844.

See R. C. McGrane, *Panic of 1837* (1924); B. Hammond, *Banks and Politics* (1957); D. North, *Economic Growth* (1961); R. Sobel, *Panic on Wall Street* (1968); and P. Temin, *Jacksonian Economics* (1969), challenges traditional interpretation.

RONALD E. SHAW
Miami University

PANIC OF 1857. Because out-of-state bankers regularly withdrew large sums from New York banks in the harvest season to finance the shipment of produce to market, the American financial system was chronically vulnerable to crises in the fall. In 1857 sustained runs by customers on New York banks led to a panic atmosphere and, on October 14, the suspension of specie payments. The panic spread to other states, and for the next two years the volume of economic activity was somewhat reduced. In the South the consequences of the financial crisis were less severe than elsewhere, and recovery began much sooner. Several banks in New Orleans maintained specie payments throughout the crisis. Contemporary defenders of the South invariably cited the section's relatively strong performance in the panic and its aftermath as firm evidence of the superiority of the slave economy. Later historians rejected that explanation and pointed instead to the continued high price of cotton on world markets in the late fifties.

See G. W. Van Vleck, *Panic of 1857* (1943); W. B. Smith and A. H. Cole, *Fluctuations in Business* (1935); G. Green, *Finance in Old South* (1972), best on South, esp. Louisiana; F. Redlich, *Molding of Banking* (1951); and *De Bow's Review* (1857–59).

EDWIN J. PERKINS
University of Southern California

PANIC OF 1873 may be considered a financial crisis brought on by a general BANKING crisis. The tremendous railroad building in the period from 1873 along with liberal credit had led to reckless speculation. The failure of Jay Cooke & Company, respected for its sound banking, precipitated the panic. It had more effect on the North than on the South, which had fewer institutions susceptible to panic. Nonetheless, the panic was reflected in a harder existence for millions of people seeking to catch up with the falling prices paid for their products. In the first six months of 1875, failures in the South amounted to $11 million. Interest rates soared. In South Carolina the rates ran from 25 to 30 percent; and 18 to 24 percent was normal over the South. The CROP LIEN SYSTEM developing after the Civil War because of scarce money was greatly increased by the panic.

Southern RAILROADS, almost completely destroyed by the war, made a rapid recovery until the panic threw many individual railroads into bankruptcy and curtailed further construction. The panic did serve to create consolidations and new combinations. For instance, it helped the Louisville & Nashville extend its dominions and incidentally led to the organization of the Southern Railway Company some years later. It also paved the way for northern railroad interests to secure control of many southern lines. The panic was instrumental in bringing about a unique development—the freight pool—later to be adopted by the whole country. To guard against ruinous competition, the principal southern railroads formed the Southern Railway & Steamship Association. With headquarters in Atlanta, the pool prorated all through traffic among the competing railroads.

The panic struck at a time when the southern people were struggling to recover from the effects of the war. Their losses took on a measure of desperation. The more desperate of them were said by one of their number to be "willing for almost anything to turn up which gives promise or possibility of change." Economic and political carpetbaggers retreated in the face of the panic, leaving to the REDEEMERS empty treasuries. When the Redeemers applied to the federal government for subsidies for dredging and rebuilding harbors, building an adequate LEVEE system, and repairing and extending the railway system (ELECTION OF 1876), they were rebuffed by their northern colleagues in Congress, who began to preach a doctrine of "retrenchment and reform." It was not until the late 1870s that economic conditions began to take an upswing.

See E. M. Coulter, *South During Reconstruction, 1865–1877* (1947), brief summary of effects on South; and C. V. Woodward, *Origins of New South, 1877–1913* (1951), interesting observations.

DONALD J. MILLET, SR.
McNeese State University

PANIC OF 1893 was brought on mainly by too-rapid RAILROAD construction, by the decline in the purchasing power of the farmer (CURRENCY), and by depression conditions abroad, which resulted in the selling of American securities by foreigners. Writers usually have emphasized the panic in terms of stricken cities of the East and the impoverished plains of the West. Yet the depression in the South probably lasted longer and was more heavily felt than in other parts of the country. Here business failures were considerably higher than the national average (the percentage of failures in Mississippi was several times larger than even in Kansas), and as early as 1891 the proportion of failures was already as large as it would be in 1893. Savings banks refused money to depositors without at least a 60-day notice (BANKING), and other banks suspended the honoring of checks entirely. The failure of the Richmond Terminal left the states of the South Atlantic seaboard without a single large, solvent railway system. Cities like Richmond, New Orleans, and Atlanta were especially hard hit by unemployment.

In 1894, the worst year of the depression, there were unprecedented unemployment and rumors of jobless men roaming in armies through the countryside. When coal miners in northern Alabama walked out, the governor ordered a regiment of state troops to the scene, causing "very bitter feeling" among the miners. This scene was reenacted in Birmingham, where railroad workers walked out on a strike inspired by the Chicago pullman strike. Racial violence broke out when Negro strikebreakers were hired by the Tennessee Coal, Iron & Railroad Company. Violent labor disputes came to New Orleans in October, 1894, when English shippers attempted to substitute Negro for white screwmen at the wharves. Race warfare raged along the levees and was followed by greater violence in the early spring of the next year. It was the farmers and the agricultural masses associated with them, however, who suffered most bitterly in the depression following the panic. The South produced record crops in 1894, and prices plummeted. The region did not begin to recover until the closing years of the century, and not until the First World War did southern farmers again know real prosperity.

See C. V. Woodward, *Origins of New South, 1877–1913* (1951), best summary; R. Fels, *American Business Cycles* (1959); and C. Hoffman, *Journal of Economic History* (June, 1956), provides statistics.

DONALD J. MILLET, SR.
McNeese State University

PANTON, LESLIE & COMPANY. In January, 1783, William Alexander, Thomas Forbes, John Leslie, and William Panton formed Panton, Leslie & Company in St. Augustine. In order to retain the Indians' loyalty after Spain's return to the Floridas, Spanish officials agreed that the company could remain until it could be replaced. That day never arrived. In 1785 Panton moved the company headquarters to Pensacola. Through their network of stores and numerous traders, the company extended its trade monopoly to include virtually all of the Indians of the Southeast. During the height of its operations, the company had an annual capital investment of about $400,000 in ships, property, debts, and trade goods. The company enjoyed a special relationship with the Indians and Spain, which enabled it to exercise a tremendous influence in diplomatic as well as commercial affairs.

See M. H. Harris, *Florida History: Bibliography* (1972); and W. S. Coker, in *Eighteenth-Century Florida* (1976).

WILLIAM S. COKER
University of West Florida

PAPER INDUSTRY. See PULP AND PAPER INDUSTRY

PARKER, JOHN MILLIKEN (1863–1939), was governor of Louisiana (1920–1924), long-time leader of governmental reform, spokesman for the commercial and agricultural interests of the lower Mississippi Valley, and friend and supporter of Theodore Roosevelt. He was born of a well-to-do planter family in Bethel Church, Miss. The family moved to New Orleans in the 1870s, and Parker followed his father as owner of cotton properties, planter, and cotton factor.

Emerging in the 1890s as a leader of New Orleans reformers, Parker believed in government led by the "better elements" rather than the professional politicians. Espousing the creed of the NEW SOUTH and the New Nationalism of Theodore Roosevelt, he supported federal flood control and tariff protection. Parker was the foremost southern backer of Roosevelt's PROGRESSIVE party in 1912 and influenced the party's LILY-WHITE organization in the South. Defeated as a Progressive gubernatorial candidate in 1916, he accepted the vice-presidential nomination of the Bull Moose party as a protest against Roosevelt's refusal to head the ticket. Recognizing the futility of his position, however, he campaigned for Woodrow Wilson in the election, making a significant contribution to Wilson's reelection.

Elected as the Democratic governor of Louisiana in 1920, Parker, in the style of the "business progressivism" characteristic of the South in the 1920s, pushed for improved state services financed by new severance taxes on natural resources and vigorously opposed the Ku Klux Klan. An ambitious HUEY LONG assailed the governor as unduly deferential to corporate interests. Parker's lifelong Progressive orientation and his bitter disillusionment at the triumph of Longism can best be understood in light of his elitist and moralistic ideas, his paternal values, and his concern for upper-class economic interests.

See M. J. Schott, "John M. Parker" (Ph.D. dissertation, Vanderbilt, 1969); and Parker Papers, University of North Carolina and University of Southwestern Louisiana libraries.

MATTHEW J. SCHOTT
University of Southwestern Louisiana

PARKERSBURG, W.VA. (pop. 44,208), is a river port at the confluence of the Ohio and Little Kanawha rivers. Although numerous trappers and travelers visited the area during the eighteenth century, the first permanent settlement awaited establishment in 1785 by Captain James Neal of a fortified trading post called Neal's Station. A second settlement grew up nearby called Stokelyville, before John Stokely laid out a new town between the two older settlements after the War of 1812. He called it Newport, but when it was chartered in 1820 the Virginia assembly named it Parkersburg. The town prospered during the 1830s and 1840s because the construction of turnpikes permitted it to grow as a commercial center. The discovery of oil in 1859, however, made the city a prosperous petroleum center for the rest of the nineteenth century. Although the last oil refinery was closed in 1937, the petroleum boom had brought railroads, docking facilities, and highways, which continue to provide the bases for the town's livelihood. It ships by rail and by river bituminous coal, clay, tobacco, lumber, and heavy machinery; and its factories produce rayon, oil well rigging, plastics, and processed foods.

See Parkersburg *Gazette* (1841–72), *State Journal* (1869–1916), *Sentinel* (1889–, Democratic daily), and *News* (1898–, Republican daily), all on microfilm.

PARKS, JOSEPH HOWARD (1903–), was born in Lincoln County, Tenn., and graduated from Middle Tennessee State College (B.S., 1927) and the University of Alabama (M.A., 1930). He did graduate work at the universities of California and Michigan and received his Ph.D. degree from Ohio State in 1937. Parks taught history at Memphis State College (1938–1943), at Birmingham-Southern College (1943–1958), and at the University of Georgia until 1969. At the university he was Foundation Distinguished Professor (1967). He most recently served as visiting professor at the University of Alabama at Birmingham (1971–1974). Professor Parks was president of the Southern Historical Association in 1965. His research and teaching have focused on biographic studies of leading political and military figures of the Jacksonian and Civil War periods. Among his major publications are *John Bell of Tennessee* (1950), *Felix Grundy, Champion of Democracy* (1940), *General E. Kirby Smith, C.S.A.* (1954), *General Leonidas Polk, the Fighting Bishop* (1962), and *Joseph E. Brown of Georgia* (1977). Professor Parks continues his research and writing in southern history at his home in Winchester, Tenn.

STEVE GURR
Georgia Southwestern College

PARRISH, CELESTIA SUSANNAH (1853–1918), was born on a Virginia plantation. Orphaned in 1863, she educated herself from her aunts' library and taught in public schools. In 1886 she graduated from the state female normal school in Farmville, Va., where she remained to teach. Following a year of study in mathematics and astronomy at the University of Michigan in 1893, she began teaching at Randolph-Macon Woman's College. In 1902, after completing a Ph.D. degree at Cornell University and studying with John Dewey at the University of Chicago, she became professor of pedagogic psychology at the state normal school in Athens, Ga., and later supervisor of rural schools for Georgia. She introduced progressive education to the South, established the first southern laboratory school for teacher training, initiated the parent-teacher movement in Georgia, and established schools for adult illiterates. Recognizing the limited opportunities for women, she worked for their admission to southern colleges and for the improvement of WOMEN'S COLLEGES and organized the Southern Association of College Women.

See C. S. Parrish, *My Experience in Self-Culture* (n.d.), pamphlet at University of Georgia Library, and *Grading of Country Schools* (1888); and G. A. Laress and M. Glass, *Virginia Journal of Education* (May, 1942).

SUSAN M. HARTMANN
University of Missouri, St. Louis

PARSONS' CAUSE (1759–1767). Virginia's two-penny act of 1758 made tobacco debts payable in money, at the rate of twopence per pound, in a year when tobacco prices soared from the normal average of one and one-half pence to as much as sixpence. Since a law of 1748 had fixed clerical salaries at 17,280 pounds of tobacco, the 1758 act reduced the value of the 1758 salary from perhaps £432 to £144, still 33 percent above the usual value. The Reverend John Camm secured royal disallowance of the act in 1759, then he and four other clergymen sued their parish collectors, presenting the dubious and unprecedented argument that the two-penny act had been null and void *ab initio*. Thus serious constitutional issues involving the assembly's authority and the legal force of royal instructions entered a local quarrel. In print, Camm charged into battle against Landon Carter and RICHARD BLAND, who published a theory of colonial autonomy in internal legislation that has been called the "great initial paper of the Revolution." Three of the four cases actually brought to court went against the clergy, but in the case of James Maury (1763) the Hanover County court ruled that the act was "no law." When Maury tried to recover damages, however, PATRICK HENRY launched his career by making a brilliantly vicious speech against the clergy and suggesting that no obedience was owed a king who rejected laws enacted for the public good. In 1767 the Privy Council ruled against Camm's attempt to overturn the Virginia general court's decision against his claim.

See R. L. Morton, *Colonial Virginia* (1960), II; W. S. Perry, *Historical Collections* (1870, 1969), I; J. H. Smith, *Appeals* (1950); H. Kemp, "Virginia Polemical Essay" (Ph.D. dissertation, University of Tennessee, 1972); R. Isaac, *William and Mary Quarterly* (Jan., 1973); and W. W. Manross, *Fulham Papers* (1965), index to Fulham Papers available on microfilm.

JUDITH H. WILSON
Washington University

PASCAGOULA, MISS. (pop. 27,264), is approximately 20 miles east of Biloxi on Pascagoula Bay and at the mouth of the Pascagoula River. Growing up around an old Spanish fort erected here in 1718, the community remained a small fishing village until after the Civil War, when RAILROADS and the LUMBER INDUSTRY turned it into a major coastal seaport. The modern city continues to function as a port of entry, but it is also a winter resort, the site of a U.S. Coast Guard base, and a center of both commercial and recreational deep-sea fishing.

See N. N. Oliver, *Gulf Coast of Mississippi* (1941); D. Greenwell, *12 Flags* (1968); M. M. Douglas, *History of Pascagoula Schools* (1966); and files of Pascagoula *Chronicle* (1897–) and *Democrat-Star* (1878–1920), on microfilm.

PASCAGOULA RIVER. The Pascagoula (Choctaw for "bread people") Basin comprises most of southeastern Mississippi and part of southwestern Alabama. Its major headwater streams are the Okatoma, Tallahala, and Leaf rivers in the west and the Chickasawhay in the east. Settlement of the area began in 1717 with the construction of Krebs Fort at the mouth of the Pascagoula. Lower-basin ethnic groups were French, English, and John Law's Germans. In 1772 cotton was grown and a "roller cotton gin" was in operation, perhaps the first in America. Population growth was slow until annexation in 1810, after which Scotch-Irish and American immigrants occupied and settled the region. Population surges resulted from the LUMBER boom of the 1880s and the industrial growth in World War II. Since 1960, except for the coastal counties, there has been a net decrease in population.

The western basin is characterized by loess SOILS planted in cotton, soybeans, corn, and grain sorghums. In addition, a significant portion is woodland: mixed bottomland hardwoods and longleaf pine. Between the Chickasawhay and Tallahala, the area has been subject to erosion, and since 1930 its soils have been a target for CONSERVATION. When drained, the floodplains and gently sloping uplands are well suited for row crops. Beef cattle, dairying, truck farms, and pine timber are also important. Recent FLOOD CONTROL reservoirs add to an emerging recreation industry.

See R. D. Cross, *Atlas of Mississippi* (1974); R. E. Hutchins, *Island of Adventure* (1968); Federal Writers' Project, *Mississippi Gulf Coast* (1939); L. L. Seale, "Indian Place-Names in Mississippi" (Ph.D. dissertation, Louisiana State University, 1939); and U.S. Army Corps of Engineers, *Pascagoula River* (1968).

RANDALL A. DETRO
Nicholls State University

PATRONS OF HUSBANDRY. See GRANGE

PATTERSON, MALCOLM RICE (1861–1935),
practiced law in Memphis, Tenn., and served as local district attorney (1894–1900) and Democratic U.S. congressman (1900–1906) before becoming governor (1906–1910). A moderately progressive governor, he enacted the 1909 general education law, which established Tennessee's present educational system. Leading the state militia to Reelfoot Lake, the scene of much NIGHT-RIDING in 1908, Patterson won national approval for his vigorous response to this VIOLENCE. Unfortunately for Patterson, PROHIBITION spokesmen persuaded the powerful former senator E. W. CARMACK to seek the Democratic nomination in 1908. A bitter campaign divided the state. Cities, party regulars, and important newspapers supported Patterson; rural folk, church groups, and independent Democrats backed Carmack. The candidates debated the issues publicly: Patterson wanted local option and Carmack advocated total abolition of intoxicants. Patterson won, but shortly afterward a Patterson adviser killed Carmack in Nashville. Carmack's martyrdom brought statewide prohibition, and, by pardoning the killer, Patterson finished his own political career. Returning to Memphis, he was later circuit court judge from 1923 until retirement in 1934.

See P. E. Isaac, *Prohibition* (1965); and S. J. Folmsbee *et al.*, *Tennessee* (1969).

JAMES R. CHUMNEY
Memphis State University

PATTERSON, ROBERT (1753–1827), a Pennsylvania-born pioneer, recorded his exploits in a diary subsequently published in the *Ohio National Journal*. He migrated to Kentucky in 1775 and helped construct McClellan's Station. In October, 1776, he led an expedition to Pittsburgh to obtain ammunition for the station's defense. Hostile Shawnee ambushed them, killing or wounding all and incapacitating him for a year following his escape. He served in GEORGE ROGERS CLARK's 1778 Illinois expedition and in John Bowman's Chillicothe raid of 1779. In April, 1779, Patterson built the first house in Lexington as original proprietor. He served as captain in Clark's 1780 campaign on the Little Ohio and Mad rivers. Patterson was second-in-command to DANIEL BOONE at the battle of BLUE LICKS (August 19, 1782). He acted as colonel in Clark's 1783 Miami campaign and with BENJAMIN LOGAN against the Shawnee in 1786. He later negotiated prisoner exchanges with Indians, served as sheriff, and obtained one-third ownership of the site of Cincinnati at its 1788 platting. He died on his farm near Dayton, Ohio.

See J. Walton, *John Filson of Kentucke* (1956), good discussion of later land jobbing; J. Van Cleve, *American Pioneer* (March, 1843); and Draper Papers, Presbyterian Historical Society.

JAMES T. BANNON
St. Louis University

PATTON, ROBERT MILLER (1809–1885), merchant, planter, and industrialist, was Democratic governor of Alabama between 1866 and 1868. Born in Virginia, he migrated with his family to Huntsville, where his father founded one of the first cotton mills in the state. Patton learned the mercantile business and in 1829 moved to Florence, accumulating 4,000 acres and 300 slaves. Opposed to secession, he nevertheless attended Alabama's secession convention and served as Confederate commissioner during the war, in which he lost two sons. A leader of Alabama's "restoration convention" in 1865, he defeated two Unionist candidates in the gubernatorial race that year. As governor, he assumed a moderate racial stance. He vetoed proscriptive legislation against the freedmen and advocated ratification of the Fourteenth Amendment. Moreover, he provided relief at personal expense and issued some $500,000 in "Patton certificates" to finance civil government. His activities as industrial promoter, however (he would become president of the Chattanooga & Meridian and the South & North Alabama railroads), increased state indebtedness.

See W. L. Fleming, *Civil War and Reconstruction in Alabama* (1905); T. M. Owen, *History of Alabama* (1921); and H. M. Bond, *Negro Education* (1939).

ROBERT GILMOUR
Princeton University

PATTON V. MISSISSIPPI (332 U.S. 463 [1947]) was a U.S. Supreme Court decision striking down the exclusion of Negroes from juries as a violation of the Fourteenth Amendment guarantee of equal protection under the law. The case arose out of the indictment and conviction for murder of Patton, a Negro, by all-white grand and petit juries. THURGOOD MARSHALL, arguing Patton's appeal, pointed out that, although Negroes composed more than one-third of the county's population, the jury venires did not contain the name of a single Negro and no Negro had served on a grand or petit criminal court jury in the county in 30 years. Marshall claimed that such "systematic, purposeful, administrative exclusion" of Negroes from jury duty was contrary to the equal protection clause of the Fourteenth Amendment. Justice HUGO BLACK, in delivering the opinion of the Court, cited a "long and unbroken line" of decisions, dating back to 1880, that held that state exclusion of Negroes from juries solely because of race was a denial of Fourteenth Amendment protection. The absence of any Negroes on the county's juries for 30 years "created a very strong showing" that Negroes were thus "systematically excluded" because of race. The Court reversed Patton's conviction and remanded the case for proceedings "not inconsistent with this ruling." The decision did not mean that a defendant found guilty must go free, but that indictment and conviction must be obtained by juries selected "as the Constitution commands."

H. REN KENT
Southwestern University, Georgetown, Tex.

PEABODY EDUCATION FUND or simply the Peabody Fund was founded in 1867 by the banker-mercantilist George Peabody to promote education in the southern states. For 47 years the fund made substantial contributions through fostering educational leadership and stimulating public support for schools. The endowment, the first of several philanthropic endeavors in the South, had a usable principal of $2 million, which provided $3.6 million in revenue. Most of the money went for teacher training in normal schools, for summer teacher institutes, and for large-town public schools, which could serve as models. By 1880 Peabody Normal College, predecessor to George Peabody College for Teachers at Nashville, became the fund's central normal school. Through 1909 it received more than $1 million. Of this sum, one-half provided over 2,000 scholarships for students from every former Confederate state. In 1914 the fund was liquidated, with $1.5 million given to endow the new Peabody College. The SLATER FUND, benefactor of Negro education, was granted $350,000, and $450,000 was divided among southern universities to further teacher training.

See H. Taylor, *Peabody Fund* (1933), good on early years; J. Brouilette, "Peabody Fund, 1904–1914" (Ph.D. dissertation, Peabody, 1940); *Proceedings of Peabody Fund* (1867–1914); and E. Robert, "Peabody Fund, 1880–1905" (Ph.D. dissertation, Peabody, 1936).

GEORGE A. DILLINGHAM
Western Kentucky University

PEACE AND CONSTITUTIONAL UNION SOCIETY, an Arkansas peace group, was the first well-organized resistance movement to form in the South after the outbreak of the Civil War. Loyalists in the state ably exploited Union sentiment, which was especially strong in the north-central region of the state. The Richmond government could offer little aid to the state, which further aroused disaffection and encouraged disloyalty. By the end of 1861 the brotherhood had a constitution, initiation rites and oaths, passwords, and signs and had established communications with the Union army. During the first two years of the war, state officials were moderately successful in combating the society. Many of its members were forced into the Confederate army on the threat of death, but most of them later deserted, often joining the Union army. With the advance of northern troops into the state in 1862 and with their capture of Little Rock in 1863, disloyalty to the Confederacy became pervasive in the northern part of the state. From mid-1863 on, members of the society worked openly to support the Union cause.

See G. L. Tatum, *Disloyalty in Confederacy* (1934); T. R. Worley, *Arkansas Historical Quarterly* (Spring, 1958) and *Journal of Southern History* (Nov., 1958); and A. B. Bishop, *Loyalty on Frontier* (1863).

LESTER G. LINDLEY
Kendall College

PEACE MOVEMENT, CIVIL WAR, was representative of many diverse elements of the population in the South, including nonslaveholding backwoodsmen who resented fighting a war in behalf of slavery and those who felt that during the course of the war the Confederacy, organized on the premise of states' rights, was undermining the "rights" of the states. The movement comprised three societies, one or another of which existed from the earliest days of the war: the PEACE AND CONSTITUTIONAL UNION SOCIETY, the Peace Society, and the Order of the HEROES OF AMERICA. Each of these societies was regional in character, the first drawing its support from the disaffected in Arkansas; the second, from those in Alabama, east Tennessee, Georgia, Mississippi, and Florida; and the third, from those in North Carolina, southwestern Virginia, and east Tennessee.

Characterized by elaborate rituals and signals, these societies were devoted to demoralizing the Confederate war effort by encouraging desertion, spying, organizing a political opposition to the Confederacy, and supporting enlistments in the Union army.

The Order of the Heroes of America was the most significant of the three movements. Headquartered within Union lines, it drew its membership from among leading citizens in the North as well as the South. President Abraham Lincoln and General U. S. Grant were members. The order was so strong that Jefferson Davis asked the Confederate Congress to suspend the writ of habeas corpus in February, 1864, since the order's influence in some localities was so marked that conviction of its members in courts was often impossible.

Union military victories, especially during the last two years of the war, offered perhaps the greatest inspiration to the members of these societies to agitate for reunion and reconstruction. However, the southern leaders, always slow to admit a lost cause, had to conclude that the military effort could not be sustained any longer before peace was finally achieved.

See G. L. Tatum, *Disloyalty in Confederacy* (1970), leading study; F. Vandiver, *Their Tattered Flags* (1970); and J. G. Randall and D. Donald, *Civil War and Reconstruction* (1969), superb bibliography.

CATHERINE M. TARRANT
Houston, Tex.

PEACH TREE CREEK, BATTLE OF (July 20, 1864).

After W. T. Sherman crossed the Chattahoochee River in his advance on Atlanta, Jefferson Davis relieved JOE E. JOHNSTON, replacing him with an aggressive commander, JOHN HOOD. Hood hoped to strike Sherman hard and to secure a great victory like CHICKAMAUGA. Johnston had emplaced his army south of Peach Tree Creek on a strong defensive position just four miles north of Atlanta. Sherman planned to pivot his army around the northeast side of Atlanta and in this fashion force Johnston out of his strong defensive position. Hood's scouts reported the Union movement to him. It was apparent that a dangerous gap existed between the pivot corps under GEORGE H. THOMAS and the next corps to the left under John M. Schofield. After crushing Thomas, Hood would roll up the remainder of the Union line and win a smashing Napoleonic victory. Thomas was a master of the defense and was especially conscious of the value of artillery. His skilled use of his guns helped repel Hood's desperate assaults. The attack was a failure, Hood had seen an opportunity and seized it, but Thomas' veterans had rallied and driven Hood's men back at heavy cost.

See R. U. Johnson and C. C. Buel (eds.), *Battles and Leaders* (1888), IV; J. B. Hood, *Advance and Retreat* (1880); J. Johnston, *Narrative of Military Operations* (1874); and W. T. Sherman, *Memoirs* (1890).

RICHARD SONDEREGGER
Northern Michigan University

PEANUT (*Arachis hypogaea*) or "goober,"

native to Brazil, is properly a member of the pea family and not a nut. After the flowers of this annual legume are fertilized, they grow downward and into the soil. The peanuts then mature underground. It was first imported to Virginia by way of Mediterranean Europe, and its cultivation spread gradually throughout the nineteenth century. After GEORGE WASHINGTON CARVER discovered numerous commercial uses for the peanut and after the BOLL WEEVIL ruined many areas for cotton cultivation, the peanut developed into a major agricultural crop for many sections of the South. As a crop and as a food staple, the peanut has several advantages. Its fruit has ounce for ounce more protein than a steak, more vitamins and minerals than beef liver, more calories than sugar, and more carbohydrates than a potato. Peanuts are often used as a feed for HOGS, and the dried foliage of the plant makes a rich and valued fodder for all animals. Moreover, for whatever purposes it is grown, its leguminous character helps to fix nitrogen in the soil. Internationally the peanut is most often grown as a source of cooking oil, but in the United States almost half the annual crop is ground into peanut butter; most of the remainder is roasted or used in a variety of confections.

PEA RIDGE, BATTLE OF (March 7–8, 1862),

was called by Confederates the battle of Elkhorn Tavern. Early in March, 1862, Major General Earl Van Dorn, commanding the combined Confederate forces of Sterling Price and Ben McCulloch, 16,000

SOUTHERN PEANUT PRODUCTION, 1900–1969
(thousands of pounds)

	1900	1910	1920	1930	1940	1950	1959	1969	% of U.S. Total
Ala.	22,484	34,628	137,258	9,328	144,318	279,810	149,027	273,238	11.0
Ark.		3,718	6,798	638	5,820	2,574	916	844	.03
Fla.	1,716	50,930	30,030	7,700	35,108	48,600	44,898	81,413	3.3
Ga.		56,540	84,414	17,996	371,674	583,513	495,403	901,533	36.7
Ky.	22				29	2	16	1	
La.	1,012	9,064	6,086	286	2,677	752	343	266	.01
Md.					1				
Miss.	2,112	6,270	5,324	462	9,942	2,510	1,495	2,231	.09
Mo.	154	66			45	9,000		8	
N.C.	76,120	131,582	128,810	5,852	273,735	229,600	245,496	341,499	13.9
S.C.	2,904	3,410	2,486	396	9,025	12,234	8,520	20,928	.85
Tenn	16,456	12,034	5,808	352	3,404	2,234	628	89	
Tex.	4,070	13,650	71,104	4,928	112,747	273,299	167,521	388,809	15.8
Va.	81,686	14,248	129,030	3,564	164,815	182,800	177,637	232,930	9.5

in all, including an Indian brigade, launched a counteroffensive against Brigadier General Samuel R. Curtis' 12,000-man Union army, which had invaded northwest Arkansas. Curtis retreated to the north side of Sugar Creek near Pea Ridge. During the night of March 6 Van Dorn tried to gain Curtis' rear by marching northward around the Union right, but was delayed by unanticipated obstacles. Consequently in the morning only Price attacked from the north, while McCulloch struck from the west. Quickly redeploying, Curtis routed McCulloch, who was killed. Price, however, advanced successfully until darkness ended the fighting. The next day Van Dorn resumed the battle, but exhaustion of men and ammunition forced him to break it off and retreat, having lost about 2,000 men. Curtis, who lost one-tenth of his command, did not pursue. Often it is stated that Pea Ridge secured Union control of Missouri. Van Dorn and Price were preparing a new offensive aimed at Missouri when the Confederate high command summoned their troops to the east side of the Mississippi to help resist U. S. Grant.

See A. Castel, *General Sterling Price and Civil War in West* (1968); and W. Brown, *Arkansas Historical Quarterly* (Spring, 1956), provides orthodox view of Pea Ridge.

ALBERT CASTEL
Western Michigan University

PEARL RIVER, rising in the red hills of east-central Mississippi, is approximately 485 miles in length. It flows generally southwest to JACKSON and then south to coastal lagoons, which join the Gulf of Mexico. Although it was named by French explorers impressed with the river's abundant supply of oysters, the pearls produced by these oysters are commercially worthless. The lower part of the river divides into two parallel forks, the East and the West Pearl rivers, with the eastern and main branch forming the Louisiana-Mississippi state line. Between these two streams is the Honey Island Swamp, used during the early nineteenth century as a haunt and haven for outlaws and runaway slaves. Although flatboats and keelboats originally traveled upstream as far as Jackson, modern commerce on the river now stops at BOGALUSA, LA.

PEASE, ELISHA MARSHALL (1812–1883), governor of Texas (1853–1857, 1867–1869), was born in Connecticut. In 1835 he moved to Texas, began studying law, and during the Texas revolution served as both soldier and civil servant. Under the Republic of Texas he was briefly national comptroller of public accounts, and after annexation he served two terms in the state house and one in the senate. He was elected governor in 1853 and reelected in 1855. As a Union Democrat he opposed secession, and when it came he retired from public life. After the Civil War he was an unsuccessful Union party candidate for governor; nonetheless, he was appointed governor by the military in 1867. Pease, now a moderate Republican, opposed disfranchisement of former Confederates and the division of Texas, both of which Radical Republicans favored. In 1872 he helped organize the Liberal Republican party in Texas. After the failure of that party he devoted his time almost entirely to law and banking. In 1879, however, he accepted appointment as collector of the port of Galveston.

See Graham-Pease Collection, Austin Public Library; B. H. Miller, "E. M. Pease" (M.A. thesis, University of Texas, 1927); and C. W. Ramsdell, *Reconstruction in Texas* (1910).

JAMES ALEX BAGGETT
Union University, Jackson, Tenn.

PEBBLES' FARM, BATTLE OF. See POPLAR
SPRING CHURCH, BATTLE OF

PEE DEE RIVER traverses both North and South
Carolina for 435 miles. It starts as the Yadkin River near the Blue Ridge Parkway east of Blowing
Rock, N.C., at about 3,600 feet above sea level. It
flows for a total of 205 miles before becoming the
Pee Dee River just below Morrow Mountain State
Park. The Pee Dee flows for 230 miles, crossing to
South Carolina in the fall zone, thence meandering southeast through the coastal plains. It is joined
by the Little Pee Dee River 20 miles before entering Winyah Bay at Georgetown. The last 91 miles
are navigable. Annual discharge is about 6.8 million acre-feet.

Spanish settlement in 1526 was attempted at
Winyah Bay but failed due to Indian attack and
disease. In the early 1700s, RICE and INDIGO plantations were established in the fertile river bottoms around Georgetown, and the town was
founded in 1734. Meanwhile the Yadkin Valley
was being settled by Highland Scots from the
south and MORAVIANS from Pennsylvania (YADKIN
RIVER SETTLEMENTS). Major economic activities
along the Yadkin–Pee Dee today include resorts
in Blowing Rock, hydropower production in the
lower Piedmont, and one of the world's largest
PULP AND PAPER mills on Winyah Bay.

See J. W. Clay, *North Carolina Atlas* (1975); C. Camp,
Influence of Geography upon Early North Carolina
(1963); and U.S. Corps of Engineers, *Development of
Water Resources in Appalachia* (1969).

H. DANIEL STILLWELL
Appalachian State University

PEGGY STEWART ARSON (October 19, 1774).
After the CONTINENTAL CONGRESS approved an
American boycott of British goods, the *Peggy
Stewart*, a vessel owned by Maryland merchant
Anthony Stewart, docked in Annapolis. Its cargo
included 2,000 pounds of English tea. Radicals in
Maryland openly demanded the destruction of
ship and cargo, but cooler heads prevailed. The
county committee voted to scuttle only the tea, although Stewart was compelled to apologize for
having "committed a most daring insult." Stewart,
however, put the match to his ship and cargo. Perhaps he concluded that only the destruction of the
brig could save his other properties from the mob
or that the conflagration would ingratiate himself
with imperial authorities. This "tea party" did not
provoke British retaliation, but it did result in
Annapolis' rigid adherence to the congressional
boycott.

See R. Hoffman, *Spirit of Dissension* (1973); A. M.
Schlesinger, *Colonial Merchants* (1918); and *Pennsylvania Magazine of History and Biography* (1901).

JOHN FERLING
West Georgia College

PEGRAM, JOHN (1832–1865), was born in Virginia. At eighteen he entered West Point, graduating in 1854. As a young lieutenant he endured
frontier service. Then, on a leave of absence, he
observed Louis Napoleon's Italian war. In 1861
Pegram became the first federal officer to enter
Virginia state service. He was quickly appointed
lieutenant colonel and captured after fighting at
RICH MOUNTAIN. When released in 1862, he was
made colonel and shortly brigadier general. During this period he served as a western cavalry
commander, but then, after disputes with subordinate officers, returned east as an infantry leader.
In the East he served with notable skill, even
commanding a division, although never promoted
major general. His January, 1865, Richmond wedding to Hetty Cary was perhaps the most brilliant
wartime capital social affair. Three weeks later
Pegram was killed in the defense of Petersburg
and buried from the same church where he had
taken his bride.

See Pegram Papers, Virginia Historical Society; H. K.
Douglas, *I Rode with Stonewall* (1940); E. J. Warner,
Generals in Gray (1943); and C. Evans (ed.), *Confeder-
ate Military History* (1962), III.

GEORGE C. BITTLE
Berlin, N.J.

PELLAGRA is a dietary deficiency disease that
was epidemic in the South in the early years of
this century. The specific deficiency was identified in 1937 by researchers at the University of
Wisconsin led by Dr. Conrad A. Elvehjem as the
B-complex vitamin nicotinic acid or niacin, but for
many years its cause was unknown and the search
for a cure frantic. Known as the disease of the four
D's—diarrhea, dermatitis, dementia, and death—
pellagra took a heavy toll in lives and was the
single largest cause of insanity in the South. The
characteristic mark of a pellagrin was a skin rash
that symmetrically marked the hands and feet and
sketched an ugly red butterfly-shaped pattern
across the victim's face. Pellagrins were often ostracized by their friends and families, and some
were even isolated as lepers.

Although pellagra had been described and
studied by European physicians as early as 1735
and pellagroid symptoms had long been identi-

fied in this country, pellagra was not acknowledged as a discrete disease in the United States until 1907, when an epidemic broke out at the Mount Vernon Insane Hospital in Alabama. Within a few years, pellagra was pandemic in the South. In the late 1920s there were more than 200,000 cases annually with a mortality rate of about 3 percent. Because pellagrins were almost invariably poor, the disease became closely identified with the poverty of the South. Gradually the stigma of the disease was transferred from individuals to the South as a whole, and the northern press dubbed the region the "land of hookworm and pellagra."

The cause of pellagra was the subject of much acrimonious debate in the medical profession. The two most popular theoretical causes were corn, both spoiled and unspoiled, and insect-borne bacteria. Medical literature lists more than 200 suggested treatments and cures including arsenic compounds and electric shock. The puzzle of pellagra was unraveled in large part by JOSEPH GOLDBERGER, of the U.S. Public Health Service, who began pellagra research in 1914. Despite frequent setbacks, Dr. Goldberger persisted in his work and found the unbalanced cornmeal, fatback, and molasses diet of the southern poor to be the root of the problem. He correctly associated pellagra with the social and economic conditions of the South, particularly with the one-crop system of agriculture, which perpetuated TENANT FARMING and SHARECROPPING. His study of the incidence of pellagra in South Carolina mill villages (1916–1921), in which he directly linked the disease to low income, is a milestone in the history of epidemiology. He determined that pellagrins did not eat foods with the pellagra-preventive factor, or vitamin P-P, because these foods either were not available on the market or were too expensive. Dr. Goldberger was on the cutting edge of two new fields in medicine—nutrition and social medicine—and thus many southern physicians had difficulty accepting his findings. Southern laymen sometimes rejected his work because to accept it meant acknowledging that the South was poor. To the outrage of southerners, President Warren G. Harding dubbed the South a region of "famine and plague" in 1921, when pellagra reappeared in force after a hiatus during World War I.

Pellagra virtually disappeared during World War II, when the economic condition of the South improved and when the addition of synthetic vitamins, including niacin, to bread and flour as part of the war effort made possible a widespread pellagra-control program.

See M. Terris, *Goldberger on Pellagra* (1964); D. A. Roe, *Plague of Corn* (1973); E. W. Etheridge, *Butterfly Caste* (1972); and R. Parsons, *Trail to Light* (1943).

ELIZABETH W. ETHERIDGE
Longwood College

PEMBERTON, JOHN CLIFFORD (1814–1881), was born into a prominent Philadelphia family. After graduation from West Point (1837), he campaigned against the SEMINOLE, earned brevets for gallantry in the MEXICAN WAR, and served at western posts. Partially because of his long-standing states' rights sympathies, partially because of his marriage to a Virginian, he in 1861 cast his lot with the South. In 1862 he supervised Confederate defenses on the South Atlantic coast, where he encountered a problem that would plague his wartime career—southern suspicion of his northern birth. Late in 1862 he was promoted lieutenant general and given command of the Department of Mississippi and East Louisiana. His principal task was to hold Vicksburg and Port Hudson as links to the trans-Mississippi Confederacy. In the spring of 1863, Ulysses S. Grant threatened to cut Pemberton off from Confederate forces to the east. Torn between conflicting instructions, Pemberton decided to risk his army on President Jefferson Davis' advice that the defense of Vicksburg was a strategic imperative. Rapidly, Union forces pushed the Confederates into Vicksburg and laid it under siege. With no relief in sight and with supplies dwindling, Pemberton surrendered on July 4, 1863. Paroled by Grant, Pemberton sought another command. However, his defeat combined with continuing suspicion of his northern origin to end effectively his military career. After the war, he retired with his family to a farm near Philadelphia.

See J. C. Pemberton, *Pemberton* (1942); E. S. Miers, *Web of Victory* (1955), Vicksburg campaign; *Official Records, Armies*, Ser. 1, Vol. XXIV; and Pemberton Family Papers, Historical Society of Pennsylvania.

WILLIAM B. SKELTON
University of Wisconsin, Stevens Point

PENAL SYSTEMS. Prior to the Civil War, not all southern states had a recognizable penal system, as most felons were confined in local or county jails rather than in a state-managed facility. The few state penitentiaries constructed before 1860 conformed to the "Auburn plan," a nationally imitated New York model, which stressed solitary confinement and industrial labor for the inmates. The structures were large stone and brick buildings with solitary cells on their upper floors and work areas below where inmates engaged in textile making, harness and saddle manufacturing, and the production of basic agricultural implements. They were inhabited largely by whites, because most black offenders were slaves and were punished by their owners outside the normal judicial process (SLAVE CODES). The relatively few black convicts of antebellum days were either free blacks, apprehended slave runaways, or blacks convicted of capital crimes and awaiting execution. They were usually engaged in tending a prison fruit and vegetable garden. The convicts' labor was intended not only to rehabilitate by teaching useful trades but also to make money from the sale of products and thus to cut expenses. Little money was made by these enterprises, however, and several prisons went into the red.

The end of slavery abruptly revolutionized southern penology. The subjection of all black offenders to the judicial process resulted in the rapid substitution of black majorities for white ones and in an equally sudden and dramatic increase in the overall number of convicts to be guarded and provided for. Caught with inadequate facilities and stymied by a war-ravaged economy, southern legislatures quickly abandoned their responsibilities for prison maintenance to private firms or individuals. Southern governments eagerly leased or hired out their convicts to planters, railroad builders, and industrialists. The CONVICT LEASE SYSTEM, a legal postbellum form of slavery, was (with the exception of LYNCHING) the most disgraceful and barbarous practice ever devised by southern Americans. Opposed from the outset by southern humanitarians and northern penologists, the system managed to endure for decades because it satisfied public officials, who wanted penal expenditures reduced; corrupt politicians in league with the lessees; and racists, who forgot that white inmates were also victimized. The first states actually to abolish or phase out convict leasing were Tennessee (1893–1897), South Carolina (1895), and Louisiana (1898–1901). In no case, however, was humanitarianism the principal motive for reform. In Tennessee abolition resulted from violent opposition to leasing from free labor; in the other two states abolition was the outcome of the reforms of PROGRESSIVISM. North Carolina, however, retained aspects of the system into the 1930s. Although the system met its demise over a generation ago, it continues to afflict southern penology with a number of dismal legacies: a general preference by officials and taxpayers alike for low-cost operations; an aversion to "expensive" professional personnel; an "out-of-sight, out-of-mind" psychology, which serves to keep many southern penal institutions in remote, rural areas; a habitual and excessive emphasis upon agricultural labor; and an indifference to violence and brutality so long as there are no "riots" and the institutions remain otherwise out of the headlines. Other Americans may view their prisons similarly, but perhaps not for the same historical reasons as do southerners.

Various and uneven reforms have created within the South a great diversity of penal systems since the 1920s. Texas has perhaps the best system, with 17 separate and specialized adult offender institutions. Alabama, Arkansas, and Louisiana appear to maintain the worst: all three states in the 1970s were ordered by federal courts to upgrade their central facilities comprehensively and immediately. Mississippi's traditional system is the only one in the South that allows conjugal visits of married inmates with their spouses.

Money making and rehabilitation have again become the joint objectives of southern prisons. Balanced results, however, have been difficult to achieve, because many of the activities that inmates want or ought to do—such as learning to read and write, auto and appliance repair, and artwork—have little or no commercial value in a prison environment, while activities from which prisons can make money—agricultural work and the production of mattresses, clothing, license plates, and janitorial supplies—have limited rehabilitational value.

See H. J. Zimmerman, "Penal Systems in South" (Ph.D. dissertation, University of North Carolina, 1947); D. T. Carter, "Convict Lease" (M.A. thesis, University of Wisconsin, 1964); and M. T. Carleton, *Politics and Punishment* (1971).

MARK T. CARLETON
Public Affairs Research Council of Louisiana, Inc.

PENDERGAST MACHINE (1892–1939) originated in the political chaos of Kansas City, Mo., following the Civil War. Thousands of southerners were joined in the burgeoning factories by larger numbers of immigrants. Confronted by a hostile society and the vagaries of an industrial economy, these people needed representation and protection. The machine met these needs. Alderman Jim Pendergast organized the Democrats in the First Ward. When he died in 1911, control of the organization passed to his ambitious brother Tom, who extended the machine's influence from the city hall to the statehouse and the national government.

As a political boss, Tom controlled some events and capitalized upon the unexpected. For example, after obtaining a new city charter in 1925, the machine elected a majority of the city council, which appointed the city manager. Conversely, the depression created opportunities for a machine able to "deliver" large blocs of votes. Pendergast influenced the elections of eight out of 13 congressmen running at-large in 1932, placed Guy Park and Lloyd Stark in the governor's mansion, sent HARRY TRUMAN to the U.S. Senate, and worked for the presidential nomination of Franklin Roosevelt. Patronage inevitably went to Pendergast, and his associate Matthew Murray became state director of the Works Progress Administration. The end, however, had to come. The elections of 1936 were so openly fraudulent that the federal district attorney Maurice Milligan won 259 convictions of election officials. Governor Stark withdrew his support from the machine, ultimately challenging Pendergast's power and bringing in the U.S. Treasury to examine the machine's financial affairs. When Tom and several of his highly placed cohorts were imprisoned in 1939–1940, the machine collapsed.

See L. W. Dorsett, *Pendergast Machine* (1968), scholarly, excellent; W. M. Reddig, *Tom's Town: Kansas City* (1947); and D. D. March, *History of Missouri* (1967), II.

GEOFFREY F. MORRISON
Clayton High School, Clayton, Mo.

PENDLETON, EDMUND (1721–1803), was born in Caroline County, Va. His youthful apprenticeship to the powerful Robinson family together with his own perseverance lifted him into the top sociopolitical echelon in Virginia. Although he did not venture into national politics, he wielded great influence in Virginia as a respected conservative. Despite his cautious stance in the pre-revolutionary dispute and clashes with PATRICK HENRY, Pendleton presided over a number of important patriot organizations including the state convention that sent the resolves for independence to Congress. After 1777 Pendleton increasingly turned his attention from politics to law. Although he served as president of the Virginia ratification convention in 1788, his presidency of the court of appeals (1779–1789) and his judgeship on the state supreme court of appeals (1789–1803) occupied most of his time.

See D. J. Mays, *Edmund Pendleton* (1952), definitive biography, and *Letters and Papers* (1967), contains extant Pendleton letters; and J. P. Greene, *Virginia Quarterly Review* (Spring, 1968).

JOHN A. NEUENSCHWANDER
Carthage College

PENINSULAR CAMPAIGN (March–June, 1862).The plan formulated by George B. McClellan for the peninsular campaign was accepted by Abraham Lincoln reluctantly and against his judgment. McClellan rejected the overland route to Richmond and proposed instead to transport his army by water to Ft. Monroe and from there to Richmond, about 70 miles away. He made no attempt to soothe the president's fears concerning Washington's security. As a result, Lincoln detained Irvin McDowell's corps of over 30,000 men.

On March 17 McClellan began moving 12 divisions by transport to Ft. Monroe, and on April 4 the federal advance up the peninsula began. Moving on Yorktown, McClellan could probably have broken through its defenses had he attacked immediately. Instead, he exaggerated Confederate strength and settled down to a lengthy siege (April 5–May 3) that gave JOSEPH E. JOHNSTON an opportunity to position his 60,000-man army on McClellan's front. Johnston evacuated Yorktown on May 3 and fell back up the peninsula before McClellan's planned bombardment. After the fall of Yorktown, McClellan moved his forces slowly toward Richmond, using the York River as his line of operation. Johnston, who wanted the decisive battle fought near Richmond, continued to retreat as McClellan advanced. On May 5 fighting broke out at WILLIAMSBURG, after which the Confederates continued retiring slowly toward their capital.

Lincoln had agreed to send McDowell's forces by land to assist McClellan in his attack on Richmond, but, when he was informed of STONEWALL JACKSON's SHENANDOAH VALLEY CAMPAIGN, he detained McDowell's corps, although not for the traditional explanation, which held that Lincoln was overly fearful for the safety of Washington. Lincoln's motive was offensive rather than defensive; he hoped that McDowell could pursue and destroy Jackson's force, ending the Confederate threat in the valley. On May 20 McClellan advanced to the Chickahominy, learning four days later that McDowell's reinforcements were suspended. With the federal forces divided by the flooded Chickahominy, the Confederates delivered a series of attacks at SEVEN PINES and Fair Oaks (May 31–June 1). Although the Confederates failed to severely cripple McClellan's army, they did manage to destroy the federal initiative. Johnston was severely wounded in this battle and was replaced by ROBERT E. LEE on June 1. When Lee took command of the Confederate forces, McClellan's army was less than five miles from Richmond. His first action upon taking command was to launch the SEVEN DAYS' BATTLES (June 26–July 1) as a series of counterattacks. Throughout the seven days, sanguinary actions took place at OAK GROVE, MECHANICSVILLE, GAINES' MILL, SAVAGE STATION, and WHITE OAK SWAMP as McClellan changed his base of operations from White House on the York River to Harrison's Landing on the James River and hesitated to take any further offensive action. After beating back Lee's forces at MALVERN HILL, the Union army was withdrawn to reinforce John Pope for the second BULL RUN CAMPAIGN. The immediate threat to Richmond was removed despite the failure of Lee to destroy the Army of the Potomac.

See *Official Records, Armies*, Ser. 1, Vol. XI; D. S. Freeman, *Lee's Lieutenants* (1945); B. Catton, *Mr. Lincoln's Army* (1951); R. U. Johnson and C. C. Buel (eds.), *Battles and Leaders* (1884–87), II; G. B. McClellan, *McClellan's Own Story* (1887); T. H. Williams, *Lincoln and His Generals* (1952); and J. P. Cullen, *Peninsular Campaign, 1862* (1973).

ALVIN R. SUNSERI
University of Northern Iowa

PENSACOLA, FLA. (pop. 59,507), the second oldest city in the state, lies on the northern shore of Pensacola Bay. The city is separated from the Gulf of Mexico by Santa Rosa Island. San Miguel de Panzacola was founded by Spain for protection from French and English encroachment into the upper Gulf of Mexico. The first attempt at settlement was by Tristán de Luna in 1559, but was abandoned in 1561. Resettled by the Spanish in 1696, it became permanent in 1698, when Ft. San Carlos was constructed.

Pensacola was incorporated as an American city in 1822, with a population of probably less than 3,000. In 1824 a naval station was established, located near the mouth of the bay. In 1829 construction began on Ft. Pickens on Santa Rosa Island and was completed in 1834. During the Civil War Pensacola was occupied by the Confederacy, but Ft. Pickens remained in Union hands. On May 8, 1862, Union troops reoccupied the city. The naval station was not effectively developed, with the exception of 1847–1848, but continued to operate until 1911. Reopened in 1914 as the Pensacola Naval Air Station, it became the largest naval air complex in the world and the mainstay of the city's economy.

See Pensacola quadricentennial issue, *Florida Historical Quarterly* (Jan.–April, 1959); Pensacola Bicentennial Series; M. H. Harris, *Florida History: Bibliography* (1972); and J. R. McGovern, *Emergence of a City, 1900–1945* (1976). Best depository is P. K. Yonge Library, University of Florida, Gainesville.

HENRY S. MARKS
Northeast Alabama State Junior College

PENTECOSTAL CHURCHES. Although some Pentecostals claim to trace their origins to apostolic times, it generally is acknowledged that Pentecostalism stems from the teachings of John Wesley. Until the 1890s sanctification or the Holiness movement in America centered mainly in the METHODIST CHURCH. By 1894, however, tensions within Methodism, involving personalities, theological liberalism, and the critical study of the Scriptures in seminaries, prompted most Holiness followers to form separate organizations. Between 1894 and 1905 more than a score of Holiness churches were formed. Four of these developed a significant following in the South: the Fire-Baptized Holiness church; the Pentecostal Holiness church; the Church of God; and the Church of God in Christ. All of these churches were evangelistic and emphasized the doctrines of sanctification, baptism of the Holy Spirit, divine healing, and the Second Coming of Christ. All also imposed ethical strictures against "worldliness" upon their members.

Following the Los Angeles Holiness Revival in 1906, the four major Holiness churches in the South and numerous independent Holiness congregations in the region became Pentecostal. This revival received its stimulation from the teachings of C. F. Parham and W. J. Seymour that "speaking in tongues" was sufficient evidence that one had received the baptism of the Holy Spirit. Most Holiness had considered speaking in tongues as one of many evidences of spirit baptism.

Two doctrinal controversies contributed to factionalism in the Pentecostal movement between 1910 and 1920. One concerned a theological dispute between "finished work" and "second work" advocates pertaining to sanctification; the other focused on the "Jesus only" schism. Finished work Pentecostals claimed that sanctification occurred at conversion; second work advocates taught that sanctification was a second work of grace that followed conversion and prepared one for reception of the Holy Spirit. Although perhaps one-half of all Pentecostals in the country today subscribe to the finished work interpretation, Pentecostal churches in the South have remained predominantly second work, reflecting their traditional or Holiness origin. The Jesus only Pentecostals maintained that Jesus Christ alone was God and that God the Father and the Holy Spirit were only titles for Jesus. Their converts were baptized in the name of Jesus rather than in the name of the Trinity. Jesus only Pentecostals constitute probably 25 percent of the current Pentecostal membership.

Until 1924 most Pentecostal churches were interracial, although some groups began excluding or segregating blacks in 1914. State laws in the South that prohibited racially integrated conventions in hotels contributed to this division. Some individual Pentecostal congregations defied the racial customs of their region, however, as blacks and whites continued to worship together in the decades following 1920. In the 1960s the Church of God and other Pentecostal denominations abandoned segregation and welcomed blacks into their congregations. Blacks have always been an integral part of the Pentecostal movement, and it was estimated that there were more than 1 million black Pentecostal Christians in the United States in 1975.

The Pentecostal movement is probably the largest religious movement to originate in America. Pentecostal students estimate that there are currently more than 4 million Pentecostal Christians in the United States, and observers acknowledge that the Pentecostal groups are the fastest-growing segment of Christendom. The *Yearbook of American and Canadian Churches, 1973* listed 26 Pentecostal denominations. Six of these—the Assemblies of God; the Church of God (Cleveland, Tenn.); the Church of God (Huntsville, Ala.); the Church of God in Christ International; the United Pentecostal Church, Inc.; and the Pentecostal Holiness Church, Inc.—claim a membership in excess of 2.5 million. By 1965 the Church of God (Cleveland, Tenn.) was the third largest denomination in the state of Georgia. Although Pentecostal churches are found in every state, they are more numerous in the South and Midwest than in other regions. Their strength in the South initially came when the leaders of the four major Holiness groups in the area embraced Pentecostalism. Pentecostal churches have been and continue to be popular with mill and factory workers, the poor, and blacks.

Although the distinguishing feature of all Pentecostal groups is speaking in tongues, there are many variations in doctrinal emphases among them. Some are pacifistic; others stress divine healing, the Second Coming of Christ, premillennialism, and other gifts. Some congregations observe foot-washing ceremonies; some baptize by immersion, and others practice pouring or sprinkling. They all expect a strict code of ethical behavior from their members.

See V. Synan, *Holiness-Pentecostal Movement in U.S.* (1971), best; W. J. Hollenwager, *Pentecostals* (1972); S. Durasoff, *Bright Wind of Spirit* (1972); C. H. Jacquet, Jr. (ed.), *Yearbook of American and Canadian Churches* (1973); C. W. Conn, *Like a Mighty Army* (1955); E. T. Clark, *Small Sects in America* (1949); F. E. Mayer, *Religious Bodies of America* (1961); and D. E. Harrell, Jr., *White Sects and Black Men* (1971) and *All Things Are Possible* (1975).

W. HARRISON DANIEL
University of Richmond

PEONAGE. Following the Civil War, the southern states enacted a series of BLACK CODES and contract labor laws aimed exclusively at the Negro, which created a system of debt slavery called peonage. In the turpentine and cotton belts of Florida, Alabama, Georgia, and Mississippi, blacks were shackled physically and spiritually and compelled to labor for white entrepreneurs.

The climate of opinion that fostered black peonage in the South resulted from a series of historical events. During the Civil War–Reconstruction era, the institution of slavery was abolished and blacks won fundamental political rights, but for the South and the freed Negro that era produced more problems than it solved. Institutions of political, social, and economic control were destroyed. Moreover, the northern liberators brought with them their newly developed concepts of an industrial capitalistic society in which labor, regardless of race, was exploited. This, combined with southern slave standards and intensified by racism, made the South a fertile field for peonage.

During the Progressive era the escalating number of peonage violations attracted the attention of Fred Cubberly, U.S. commissioner for the Northern District of Florida. In the first peonage case tried in American courts, Cubberly successfully prosecuted S. M. Clyatt, a wealthy turpentine operator, under the 1867 peonage statutes, which outlawed debt slavery. The case created a national sensation and stimulated muckraking journalists to expose the graft, corruption, and brutality inherent in the system.

Cubberly's efforts encouraged others, including BOOKER T. WASHINGTON, to curtail debt slavery in Alabama. In 1908 the Alabama supreme court found Alonzo Bailey, a black farm laborer, guilty of fraud and upheld that state's contract labor law. The case was appealed to the U.S. Supreme Court. In the majority opinion Justice Charles Evans Hughes ruled that no state could compel a man to labor for another in payment of a debt (BAILEY V. ALABAMA). Alabama's contract labor law violated the Thirteenth Amendment.

With the judicial rulings in the Clyatt and Bailey cases, the legal structure supporting peonage was destroyed. Yet peonage violations continued. In the early 1920s Mose and Alston Brown, Florida turpentine operators, were prosecuted on peonage charges. Testimony revealed the sordid abuses of debt slavery, particularly as they related to women, and demonstrated the relationship between peonage and the CONVICT LEASE SYSTEM. Brown worked peons and leased convicts at the same tasks and housed them in the same camps. If a peon tried to leave he was placed back into the system as a convict. If a convict served his sentence, he found himself in debt via the commissary system and was forced to labor as a peon. For many, death was the only way out.

The abolitionists continued their efforts, however, and attacked the lease system. By 1925 all southern states had abolished convict leasing and removed another impetus to peonage. Although progress has been made, there have been numerous reports of peonage violations from 1925 to the present. The forces of racism and an expanding capitalism with its concomitant need for labor apparently are stronger than the law of the land.

See P. Daniel, *Shadow of Slavery* (1972); N. G. Carper, "Convict-Lease System" (Ph.D. dissertation, Florida State University, 1964); and W. Cohen, *Journal of Southern History* (Feb., 1976), black servitude, 1865–1940.

N. GORDON CARPER
Berry College

PEOPLE'S PARTY. See POPULIST PARTY

PEPPER, CLAUDE DENSON (1900–), born in rural Alabama and a graduate of the University of Alabama and Harvard Law School, began to practice law in Florida in 1925. An enthusiastic supporter of Franklin D. Roosevelt, Pepper was elected senator in 1936 and became a vociferous critic of congressional conservatism. He was never fully accepted by other southerners in Congress, and his interventionist stance before Pearl Harbor was the apex of his harmony with southern opinion. Pepper was an advocate of the "common man"; his liberalism centered on expansion of federal economic and social welfare programs rather than on abstract theory. In the forties, Pepper moved gradually to the national liberal position of guaranteeing civil rights to Negroes and favored a liberal coalition. These attitudes brought him into conflict with southern tradition and vested interests. By favoring postwar cooperation with the Soviet Union, Pepper defied southern opinion on foreign policy. He was defeated in a bitter, emotion-charged Democratic primary in 1950. He was elected to the U.S. House in 1962, but Pepper's significance lies in his years as a liberal southern senator.

See A. R. Stoesen, "Senatorial Career of Claude D. Pepper" (Ph.D. dissertation, University of North Carolina, 1965) and *Florida Historical Quarterly* (Jan., 1972; Oct., 1973); T. G. Paterson, *Cold War Critics* (1971); and R. Sherrill, *Gothic Politics* (1968).

ALEXANDER R. STOESEN
Guilford College

PERCY, WALKER (1916–), orphaned at thirteen, lived his teenage years in the Greenville, Miss., home of his father's cousin WILLIAM ALEXANDER PERCY. There he was raised in an intellectual milieu he later described as "Southern Stoicism." After his undergraduate work at Chapel Hill, N.C., Percy entered the College of Physicians and Surgeons at Columbia University and completed his medical degree in 1941. Shortly thereafter, he contracted tuberculosis, apparently from a laboratory specimen. During the period of rest that followed, Percy found himself with the time to read and to question the sufficiency of the scientific method, a precept that hitherto had guided his life. The period of his convalescence was accompanied by several significant decisions: his marriage; his settling in Covington, La.; his conversion to Catholicism; and his abandonment of medicine in favor of writing for a career. His first publications were essays, either social or metaphysical in nature; he was interested both in the changing South and in the loneliness of modern man when considered to be only a scientific datum. Out of these two disparate interests came Percy's first published novel (after two failures): *The Moviegoer* (1961, National Book Award), the confessions of Binx Bolling as he regretfully rejects the Stoic tradition as inapplicable to his own dilemma. This novel was followed by *The Last Gentleman* (1966), a fable occurring on two different planes as Will Barrett must cope with a present that is meaningless to him and must struggle to understand the southern past that is constricting his mind's freedom. In *Love in the Ruins* (1971), he lays aside the theme of the southern past, at least for a while, and examines the plight of those who refuse to accept a world in which only empirical values count. Percy's most recent novel is *Lancelot* (1977). *The Message in the Bottle* (1975) is a collection of some of his previously published essays.

See M. Luschei, *Sovereign Wayfarer* (1972); R. Coles, *Walker Percy* (1979); A. Kazin, *Harper's* (June, 1971); L. A. Lawson, *Texas Studies in Language and Literature* (Spring, 1969); and S. Byrd and J. F. Zeugner, *Bulletin of Bibliography* (March, 1973), lists Percy's scattered nonfiction publications.

LEWIS A. LAWSON
University of Maryland, College Park

PERCY, WILLIAM ALEXANDER (1885–1942), a

lawyer, author, and poet from Greenville, Miss., ably upheld the genteel traditions of the Delta aristocracy. His poetry was classic in form and unbounded by sectional themes. In politics he was a consistent critic of such figures as J. K. VARDAMAN and T. G. BILBO. On all questions of race relations, Percy both professed and practiced the paternalism associated with members of his class. He also defended sharecropping as the most equitable profit-sharing arrangement in America. *Lanterns on the Levee* (1941, 1975), his autobiography, is a valuable and gracefully written document of the life and views of a member of the planter class seeking to cope with the twentieth century.

See W. A. Percy, *Collected Poems* (1943); D. L. Cohen, *Virginia Quarterly Review* (Fall, 1955); and B. P. Spalding, *Georgia Review* (Fall, 1958) and *Journal of Mississippi History* (Feb., 1965).

PERIODICALS. A southern periodical is not only

one published in the South; it is one that expresses the South as a self-conscious entity. The many periodicals that can be called southern in this sense may be placed in two broad categories: those devoted to literature as an art and discipline; and those given to the various areas of regional life, such as agriculture, commerce and industry, religion, and family and home life. Notable by its absence is a third category: magazines of general literary, intellectual, and societal character like the *Atlantic Monthly* and *Harper's Monthly*. The failure of the South to produce at least one such magazine suggests that the historical evolution of southern periodicals was truncated.

Several reasons for this situation may be advanced: the South's sparseness of population, its low literacy rate, and its lack of cities and publishing centers. But these circumstances are not as fundamental as the antebellum South's abortion of its relationship with the central literary and journalistic authority in modern Western civiliza-

tion—that is, the republic of letters, the cosmopolitan, secular realm of letters and learning that in the fourteenth century began to become clearly differentiated from church and state. Personified in world historical men of letters—for example, Bacon, Locke, and Voltaire—this independent third realm of civilizational order issued the massive revolutionary criticism of church and state that resulted in the American and French revolutions. More or less coincidentally with these events, the improvement of printing technology brought the periodical press into history. By the fourth decade of the American Republic, magazines had become integral to the functioning of the literary order. By this same time, however, the imperatives of a southern self-interpretation demanded by slavery had begun to develop so strongly that the third realm in the South (powerfully represented earlier by THOMAS JEFFERSON) was being assimilated into the realm of the state. This process divested southern periodicals of their primary context, the independent moral order of the republic of letters. How this was so is aptly illustrated in PAUL HAMILTON HAYNE's editorial plea in RUSSELL'S MAGAZINE in 1858 that southern magazines allow "a true literary spirit," which is "essentially liberal," in the reviewing of "purely literary" books by northerners, these books being defined as those that "in no way" interfere "with the 'peculiar institution,' or our rights under it." Hayne's attitude ironically reveals why *Russell's* could not carry out its avowed mission to rival the *Atlantic*, established one year before in Boston. Having in effect become an agency of the state, it could not represent the South in the humanistic polity of letters as the *Atlantic* represented New England. To varying degrees the identification with the politics of slavery clouded the vision of HUGH SWINTON LEGARÉ, WILLIAM GILMORE SIMMS, T. W. White, EDGAR ALLAN POE, J. D. B. De Bow, and all the other able antebellum southern editors, thwarting their efforts to create genuinely distinguished magazines. Several of their ventures were substantial: the first SOUTHERN REVIEW (Charleston), the SOUTHERN LITERARY JOURNAL, the MAGNOLIA, and the SOUTHERN QUARTERLY REVIEW. But even the SOUTHERN LITERARY MESSENGER and DE BOW'S REVIEW, periodicals of considerable vigor and breadth of appeal, failed in their promise to become general magazines of large cultural significance.

After the Civil War the absorption of the periodical press in southern nationalism continued in the nostalgia of the Lost Cause: in, for instance, *The Land We Love* and, more substantively, in the second SOUTHERN REVIEW (Baltimore), edited by

Albert Taylor Bledsoe. When the postbellum southern writers did move toward an identification with the cause of humane letters, they found expression not in southern magazines but in the *Atlantic, Harper's,* the *Century, Scribner's,* and other fast-growing publications that were instituting the golden age of American periodical publishing. In the 1920s the recurrent impulse to establish an independent southern literary periodical resulted in three short-lived but noteworthy magazines. One was the *Fugitive,* the organ of the Nashville FUGITIVES. A larger effort was represented by the New Orleans *Double Dealer.* Calling itself "A National Magazine for the South," this publication, like the *Fugitive,* deplored the "treacly sentimentalities" of southern literature; it also avowed to make New Orleans a cultural center. A contemporary of the New Orleans magazine, the *Reviewer* expressed a similar aspiration for Richmond, Va. In failing condition, this ambitious periodical was moved to Chapel Hill, N.C., in 1925. Soon thereafter it was merged with the SOUTHWEST REVIEW at Southern Methodist University.

The only periodicals in the South that have substantially joined its writers to the modern literary and intellectual cosmopolitanism have been the quarterlies supported by universities. The leading ones are still in existence: the SEWANEE REVIEW, founded in 1890 at the University of the South; the SOUTH ATLANTIC QUARTERLY, founded in 1902 at Trinity College (later Duke University); the *Texas Review,* founded in 1915 at the University of Texas (moved to Southern Methodist University in 1924 as the *Southwest Review*); the VIRGINIA QUARTERLY REVIEW, founded in 1925 at the University of Virginia; and the third SOUTHERN REVIEW (Baton Rouge), founded in 1935 at Louisiana State University, suspended in 1942 and resumed in 1965. Save for the *South Atlantic Quarterly* and the *Virginia Quarterly,* these periodicals are dominated by literary concerns. Southern history, politics, and economics are the province of specialized journals, also with institutional affiliations. All of the present-day southern periodicals of serious literary and intellectual character are limited in circulation. The sole magazine of large circulation currently being published in the South—and bearing a distinct relation to the theme of southern identity—is *Southern Living,* a commercial monthly dominated by nostalgia and tourism.

See F. L. Mott, *History of American Magazines* (4 vols.; 1939–57); J. B. Hubbell, *South in American Literature, 1607–1900* (1954); W. T. Couch (ed.), *Culture in South* (1934); F. J. Hoffman, *Little Magazine* (1974); L. P. Simpson, *Man of Letters in New England and South* (1973); and L. D. Rubin (ed.), *Guide to Southern Literature* (1969).

LEWIS P. SIMPSON
Louisiana State University

PERRY, BENJAMIN FRANKLIN (1805–1886), was born on Choestow Creek in up-country South Carolina. He opened a law office in Greenville, but quickly found himself embroiled in politics. Perry's first fame came as editor of the Greenville *Mountaineer,* when he helped lead the fight against the NULLIFICATION movement between 1830 and 1833. He was elected to the state house of representatives in 1836 and served there through the Civil War, except for three two-year terms, when he chose not to run. He opposed separate state action during the secession movements of 1850 and 1860, but found himself in an extreme minority on both occasions. When the Civil War came, he went with his state and served the Confederacy as district attorney, commissioner under the Impressment Act, and district judge. Appointed by ANDREW JOHNSON as provisional governor in June, 1865, he demonstrated democratic tendencies by providing for the popular election of the governor, lieutenant governor, and presidential electors, but generally refused to carry out the president's suggestions. Later he opposed Radical Reconstruction and aided in its overthrow. In 1877 he retired to his farm near Greenville.

See H. M. Perry, *Letters* (1889); Mrs. B. F. Perry, *Letters* (1890); L. A. Kibler, *Benjamin F. Perry* (1946); W. A. Schaper, *Sectionalism* (1968); A. G. Smith, Jr., *Economic Readjustment* (1958); L. A. Kibler, *Journal of Southern History* (Aug., 1938); W. W. Freehling, *Prelude to Civil War* (1965); E. M. Lander, Jr., *Journal of Southern History* (Aug., 1960); H. S. Schultz, *Nationalism and Sectionalism* (1950); P. M. Hamer, *Secession Movement* (1918); C. N. Degler, *Other South* (1974); and papers, at Alabama State Department of Archives and History and home of Mrs. S. R. Baker, Montgomery, Ala.

R. BEELER SATTERFIELD
Lamar University

PERRYVILLE, BATTLE OF (October 8, 1862), was a Civil War engagement between Union forces commanded by Major General Don Carlos Buell and a Confederate army under General BRAXTON BRAGG, who with 28,000 men had invaded Kentucky in September. The Confederate and Union lines west of Perryville extended north and south a distance of four miles—the Confederates' a mile west of Perryville, the Union's roughly a mile farther west, between the New Mackville and Lebanon roads. Because of scarcity of water, large portions of the Union troops, after taking assigned positions, were ordered toward Doctor's Creek and Chaplin River to reconnoiter and seek water. The battle opened at 2:00 P.M. with a Confederate cavalry charge from the right. Quickly, Bragg's entire right plunged forward, striking and driving back the unsuspecting federals searching for water near Doctor's Creek. The Confederate center, with heavy artillery support, soon moved forward. It pushed back a Union division beyond its original line. The Union's left center was hard pressed until after four o'clock, when effective support arrived. Portions of the Confederate left were then driven into and beyond Perryville. Buell, unaware of the battle until 4:00 P.M., moved sufficient reinforcements, toward dusk, to stabilize the entire broken Union left, driven back a mile. Darkness ended the sanguinary struggle. At midnight the Confederates began a retreat toward Harrodsburg. From that point, they retired into Tennessee. Bragg, able to get all of his 16,000 soldiers into the battle, used them more effectively than did Buell his 22,000 out of a Union total of 54,000. Buell sustained 4,241 casualties; Bragg, 3,396.

See *Official Records, Armies*, Ser. 1, Vol. XVI, Pt. 1; R. U. Johnson and C. C. Buel (eds.), *Battles and Leaders* (1887), III; T. L. Connelly, *Army of Heartland* (1967), new viewpoint and some fresh sources; S. F. Horn, *Army of Tennessee* (1941); F. B. Fry, *Operations of Army Under Buell* (1884); and H. Tapp, *Filson Club History Quarterly* (July, 1935).

HAMBLETON TAPP
Versailles, Ky.

PETERSBURG, VA. (pop. 36,103), approximately 20 miles south of Richmond at the navigational head of the Appomattox River, was first settled in 1646 with the construction of Ft. Henry. Three separate communities grew up near the military post: Petersburg (1748), Blandford (1748), and Pocahontas (1752). The three towns were united as a single political entity in 1784, and by the War of 1812 Petersburg had begun to rival Richmond as a commercial center along Virginia's FALL LINE. In June, 1864, General U. S. Grant sought to approach Richmond by way of Petersburg. After being repulsed by R. E. Lee and P. G. T. Beauregard, Grant laid siege to the city. The battle of the CRATER (July 30, 1864) failed to dislodge the city's Confederate defenders. After the Union victory at FIVE FORKS (April 1, 1865), however, a general assault resulted in the fall of Petersburg (April 3, 1865) the same day as the fall of Richmond. Badly ravaged by the siege and fighting, the city was re-built after the war as an industrial town using the waterpower of the river's falls. The modern city manufactures textiles, luggage, plastics, chemicals, and optical goods and serves as a processing center for area tobacco and peanuts. Blandford Cemetery contains the graves of some 30,000 Confederate soldiers, and Poplar Grove National Cemetery has approximately 6,000 federal graves.

See J. G. Scott and E. Wyatt, *Petersburg's Story* (1960); E. Pollock, *Historical and Industrial Guide to Petersburg* (1884); and files of Petersburg *Progress-Index* (1865–), on microfilm. Public library maintains excellent collection of early newspapers, considerable genealogical material, and city directories (1860–).

PETIGRU, JAMES LOUIS (1789–1863), was born in Abbeville District, S.C. Son of farmers, he learned classics and Jeffersonian principles of constitutional liberty at the "log school" of Dr. Moses Waddel and graduated from South Carolina College (1809). He became JAMES HAMILTON's law partner and the recognized head of the bar. Elected attorney general (1822–1830), he lost the race for state senate as a Unionist during the NULLIFICATION crisis. A consistent nationalist, Petigru forfeited popularity by approving Andrew Jackson's stance on nullification; he won a case overthrowing the requirement that militia officers swear allegiance to a free South Carolina. Petigru and Hamilton patched together a compromise largely responsible for averting bloody confrontation between nullifiers and Unionists in 1832–1834. An ardent Whig, he was one of the few Charlestonians publicly to favor the COMPROMISE OF 1850 and oppose SECESSION in 1860. His final achievement was his codification of the laws of South Carolina.

See J. P. Carson, *Life* (1920); W. J. Grayson, *Petigru* (1866); W. W. Freehling, *Prelude to Civil War* (1965); and W. F. Guess, *South Carolina Annals* (1957).

RICHARD ALLAN GERBER
Lehman College, City University of New York

PETROLEUM has been known to and used by man since at least 4000 B.C. Surface deposits of asphaltic bitumen and seeping crude oil long had been used in embalming Egyptian mummies, lighting Roman crude oil lamps, burning enemy ships with "Greek fire," and oiling ships' riggings. Not until the development of the kerosene lamp in the 1850s, however, was the demand for petroleum great enough to drill in search of subterranean sources. The successful opening of the Pennsylvania oil fields with the Drake well in 1859 was followed by similar developments in California in 1875 and Texas in 1887. These relatively shallow deposits—the Drake well was only 69 feet deep—fulfilled the needs of late nineteenth-century America, but the growth of industry and the expanding use of the internal combustion engine gradually required petroleum and petroleum by-products far in excess of these fields' supply.

The modern petroleum industry in the United States dates from the opening of the SPINDLETOP well near Beaumont, Tex., in 1901. The Drake well in Pennsylvania had "gushed" an average of ten barrels a day before it was capped; Spindletop gushed between 70,000 and 100,000 barrels a day. The discovery of even richer oil deposits in Oklahoma (1907) and California temporarily caused Texas to lose its position as the leading oil-producing state. The development of deposits in western Texas restored that state to its position as the premier oil producer in the 1920s; and, with the discovery of new fields in eastern Texas in 1930, the Lone Star State retains that rank into the 1970s. The inauguration of offshore drilling in the Gulf of Mexico after World War II further expanded the industry in Texas, but also transformed Louisiana in the 1950s into the second largest producer of petroleum in the U.S. In 1972, the peak year of U.S. oil production, two-thirds of all domestic petroleum was drawn from southern wells.

Title to subterranean mineral rights in the U.S. customarily belongs to the owner of the surface property. As a consequence, numerous derricks have been constructed almost side by side to ensure each property holder's being credited with an approximately fair proportion of oil pumped from thousands of feet below the surface. This pattern of property rights also resulted, at least initially, in a generally fragmented and decentralized business structure in the extractive segment of the petroleum industry. Control and construction of the pipelines and refineries, on the other hand, have been achievements of vertically integrated corporations, beginning with the Standard Oil Company, J. W. Gates's Texas Oil Company, and the Mellon family's Gulf Oil Company.

Although the capacity of U.S. and southern oil production was once sufficient to supply both normal and emergency needs, spiraling demand for petroleum, rising exploration costs, and the diminishing volume of known reserves are forcing the nation to seek alternative sources of fuel. The South still retains almost half the proved crude oil reserves in the U.S. and provides almost two-thirds of all domestic production. Further expansion of the southern oil industry appears limited, however, and Alaska rather than the South appears the most promising source of new petroleum.

See H. F. Williamson, *American Petroleum Industry* (2 vols.; 1957–63), and J. S. Clark, *Oil Century* (1958), both general studies; W. K. Ferguson, *Geology and Politics in Frontier Texas, 1845–1909* (1969); J. O. King, *Joseph S. Cullinan: Texas Petroleum Industry, 1897–1923* (1970); R. R. Moore, "Oil Industry in West Texas" (Ph.D. dissertation, Texas Tech, 1965); and A. M. Johnson, *Development of American Petroleum Pipelines* (1956).

PETROLEUM PRODUCTION AND RESERVES, 1972

| | Production | | Reserves | |
	Million Barrels	% U.S. Total	Million Barrels	% U.S. Total
Ala.	10	.29	57	.16
Ark.	18	.52	113	.31
Fla.	17	.49	208	.57
Ky.	10	.29	48	.13
La.	892	25.82	5,029	13.84
Miss.	61	1.77	313	.86
Tex.	1,302	37.68	12,144	33.42
W.Va.	3	.09	34	.09
South	2,313	66.95	17,946	49.38
U.S. Total	3,455	100.00	36,339	100.00

PETTIGREW, JAMES JOHNSTON (1828–1863), descended from an old and prominent North Carolina family, acquired both a degree from the University of North Carolina and an assistant professorship at the Washington Naval Observatory while still only nineteen. He practiced law in Charleston; in 1856 he joined the South Carolina general assembly, where he opposed resumption of the international slave trade. As a militia officer he witnessed the firing on FT. SUMTER. In May, 1861, he became colonel of the 12th North Carolina. Soon appointed a brigadier general, at SEVEN PINES he believed himself to be mortally wounded, refused to leave the field, was captured, and was later exchanged. As one of HENRY HETH's brigadiers in 1863, he made the famous foray toward Gettysburg in quest of shoes, thus bringing on the first contact with Union cavalry on June 30. He led Heth's division on the immediate left of GEORGE PICKETT in the famous charge. During R. E. Lee's retreat to Virginia, Pettigrew was wounded in the groin in a skirmish with federal cavalry at Falling Waters, Md., and died three days later. D. S. Freeman calls him a "magnificent Carolinian" and "a man of large intellectual capacity but of limited field service."

See D. S. Freeman, *Lee's Lieutenants* (1942–44); *Official Records, Armies*; and W. J. Peele, *Lives of Distinguished North Carolinians* (1898).

JAMES E. SEFTON
California State University, Northridge

PETTIT, KATHERINE (1868–1936), a settlement worker in Kentucky's mountains, was born near

Lexington. She early developed an interest in the mountain people when she realized the narrowness of their lives. In 1899 Pettit and May Stone held homemakers' "camp meetings" near Hazard to help the women with cooking, sewing, and home nursing. A similar event was held in Hindman in 1900, but it was not until 1902 that a permanent settlement school was established. In 1913 Pettit left the Hindman work in the hands of Stone and with the help of Ethel de Long established a school at Pine Mountain. Here Pettit stressed crafts and manual skills as well as providing basic health services. She resigned as codirector in 1930, but continued her work on an individual basis until her death.

See L. Furman, *Register of Kentucky Historical Society* (Jan., 1937) and *One Man's Cravin'* (1945); and Pettit's diaries and letters, Berea College.

MARY MARTHA THOMAS
Jacksonville State University

PHILANTHROPY, defined as private giving for public purposes, embraces gifts both of service and of money. Some of America's most celebrated philanthropists, like Benjamin Rush, Dorothea Dix, and MARTIN LUTHER KING, JR., have been doers of good deeds rather than donors of great fortunes. Increasingly, however, philanthropy has come to be associated with giving and raising money for religion, charity, education, research, cultural and eleemosynary institutions, and a variety of public causes.

The South has been both the scene of philanthropic innovations and the object of benevolent concern of other sections. In 1634 Benjamin Syms of Virginia endowed the first free school in the American Colonies. The first orphan home in the present United States opened in New Orleans in 1729. Philanthropic considerations figured in the founding of Georgia; and the evangelist George Whitefield conducted the first intercolonial fund drive to found an orphanage in that colony. Nineteenth-century southerners like JOHN MCDONOGH and Judah Touro established patterns of giving followed by Peter Cooper, Andrew Carnegie, and other practitioners of the gospel of wealth. The Howard Association of New Orleans provided an outstanding example of service-centered benevolence. The organization, composed of young clerks, tended the sick and orphaned in times of yellow fever epidemics. Sympathizers throughout the nation contributed funds to enable the Howards to assist victims of the epidemic of 1853.

During the Civil War, southern civilians, like their northern counterparts, played an important role in furnishing aid to soldiers and relief to refugees. After the war no apologies were offered for the fact that southern efforts were not as well organized as those in the North. "We had no Sanitary Commission in the South," wrote a Confederate veteran. "We were too poor. . . . With us, each house was a hospital." While the war was in progress, northern freedmen's aid societies sent teachers and relief supplies to former slaves in occupied portions of the South. During Reconstruction voluntary associations in the North continued educational activities for blacks and supplemented the work of the U.S. FREEDMEN'S BUREAU in relieving need among both blacks and whites.

In the late nineteenth and early twentieth centuries, philanthropic foundations including the PEABODY EDUCATION FUND, GENERAL EDUCATION BOARD, and ROSENWALD FUND assisted educational development in the South for both races and at all levels. Improvement of southern agriculture and public health were also foundation objectives. Beginning in 1909 the Rockefeller Sanitary Commission assisted southern state governments in a campaign for eradication of HOOKWORM disease. Southerners like J. L. M. CURRY of the Peabody Education Fund and Dr. Wickliffe Rose of the Rockefeller Sanitary Commission and General Education Board exercised strong influence on American foundation policies. The Duke Endowment, founded by the North Carolina industrialist James B. Duke, ranks as one of the largest general purpose foundations (DUKE FAMILY).

One tendency of American philanthropy has been to encourage, assist, and sometimes goad governmental authorities to better performance of civic duties and closer attention to social needs. In recent years, advocacy organizations like the SOUTHERN REGIONAL COUNCIL and the NATIONAL ASSOCIATION FOR THE ADVANCEMENT OF COLORED PEOPLE Legal Defense Fund have marshaled philanthropic support for efforts to protect and advance civil, legal, and human rights in the South.

See *Report of Princeton Conference on History of Philanthropy in U.S.* (1956); R. H. Bremner, *American Philanthropy* (1960); M. Curti, *Proceedings of American Philosophical Society* (April, 1961); M. Curti and R. Nash, *Philanthropy in Shaping of American Higher Education* (1965); R. H. Bremner, *Civil War History* (Dec., 1966); H. L. Swint, *Northern Teacher in the South, 1867–1870* (1941, 1967); G. Bentley, *History of Freedmen's Bureau* (1955); R. B. Fosdick, *Story of Rockefeller Foundation* (1952); W. Weaver, *U.S. Philanthropic Foundations* (1967); and W. A. Nielsen, *Big Foundations* (1972).

ROBERT H. BREMNER
Ohio State University

PHILIPPI, BATTLE OF (June 3, 1861), a minor action at Philippi, Barbour County, W.Va., is generally reputed to be the first land battle of the Civil War. A Confederate force of 1,500 men, stationed at Philippi under the command of Colonel George A. Porterfield, was attacked by Union troops led by Colonels Benjamin F. Kelley and Ebenezer Dumont on the morning of June 3. Surprising the Confederates, who had failed to take proper precautionary measures prior to the assault, the federals drove them from town, inflicting 15 casualties while suffering two themselves. Large amounts of arms, horses, ammunition, provisions, and camp equipage were captured by the federals. The federals' failure to capture the entire Confederate force was due in large measure to weather conditions and physical exhaustion of the men, who had marched 15 miles in pitch darkness through a drenching rain. On June 20, 1861, a court of inquiry was convened at Beverly, Va., to examine the retreat of the Confederate forces led by Porterfield. The court commended him for his coolness and courage during the attack, yet found him lax in taking proper preventive measures. No formal charges were filed against Porterfield, but the court recommended that the actions at Philippi serve as an object lesson for the war.

See P. Conley, *West Virginia History* (Jan., 1959); B. B. Stutler, *West Virginia in Civil War* (1963); and *Official Records, Armies*, Ser. 1, Vol. II.

FRANK R. LEVSTIK
Ohio Historical Society

PHILLIPS, ULRICH BONNELL (1877–1934), historian of the Old South, was born in La Grange, Ga., and graduated from the University of Georgia in 1897. As a student assistant, he manifested an unusual regard for primary sources in history, all but ruining his eyesight by reading intensively a file of newspapers he had been asked no more than to arrange. Phillips took with him this fascination with the history of his native state and of the South to Columbia University, from which he received his Ph.D. degree. His dissertation, "Georgia and State Rights" (1902), won the Justin Winsor Prize given by the American Historical Association.

Phillips taught history at the University of Wisconsin from 1902 to 1908, went on to Tulane University as professor of history and political science, and in 1911 joined the University of Michigan faculty, where he stayed until 1929. That year he transferred to Yale University, where he taught until his death.

His passion for facts was uncompromising and gave his two-volumed *Plantation and Frontier, 1649–1863* (1910) authority in its field. Yet Phillips' love for the South was deep and reflected itself in his writings. He denied that the South had any reason for apologizing for its labor system based on slavery. His famous essay "The Central Theme of Southern History," published in the *American Historical Review* for 1928, insisted that the issue was not slavery but white domination.

Phillips continued his well-esteemed research and writing in *The History of Transportation in the Eastern Cotton Belt* (1908), *The Life of Robert Toombs* (1913), and *American Negro Slavery* (1918), all characterized by a clear writing style, impressive illustrative examples, and high conscientiousness in detail. In 1934 Gilbert H. Barnes dedicated his influential *The Anti-Slavery Impulse* to Phillips, "whose teaching first moved me to begin this study." Phillips' greatest moment of public fulfillment came in 1929, when his *Life and Labor in the Old South* received a prize award from his Boston publishers. A few recent writers have accused Phillips of racial prejudice and have insisted, among other things, that he presented an overly benign view of the master's relationship to the slave; nevertheless, almost all historians of the South freely admit their great debt to the immense labors of this pioneer scholar.

See introduction in E. M. Coulter (ed.), *Course of South to Secession, by U. B. Phillips* (1939); W. Gray, in W. T. Hutchinson (ed.), *Marcus W. Jernegan Essays in American Historiography* (1937); and W. H. Stephenson, *South Lives in History* (1955).

LOUIS FILLER
Antioch College

PHOSPHATES. Three chemical elements—phosphorus, nitrogen, and potassium—are essential to soil fertility and are the most important ingredients in commercial fertilizers. Of the three, phosphorus is perhaps the most difficult to obtain and utilize. In a free or uncombined state it is one of the most destructive substances known. Yet, without the compounds of phosphorus (for which there is no natural or synthetic substitute), plant, animal, and bacterial life would cease. And our supply of phosphorus will be exhausted long before carbon, nitrogen, or oxygen supplies even become critical unless rigorous conservation policies are enacted in the near future.

Over 3 million tons of phosphorus are washed from the land into the seas by the world's rivers

PRODUCTION AND VALUE OF PHOSPHATE, 1870–1970
(thousand long tons and thousands of dollars)[a]

Year	S.C. Quantity	Value	Fla. Quantity	Value	Tenn. Quantity	Value	N.C. Quantity	Value	Ala. Quantity	Value	Ark. Quantity	Value
1870	65											
1880	191											
1890	464	$2,875	46	$330								
1900	329	$1,042	706	$2,980	454	$1,329			334	$534	75	$225
1910	180	$733	2,067	$8,640	398[b]	$1,503[b]						
1920	43	$341[c]	3,369	$19,460	627	$4,425						
1930			3,248	$10,790	611	$2,938						
1940			3,845	$10,230	994[d]	$3,967[d]						
1950			8,086	$45,380	1,344[d]	$9,067[d]						
1960			12,251	$81,920	1,927	$15,319						
1970			28,520	$152,420	3,184	$15,606	3,000[c]	$15,000[c]				

[a] All values rounded
[b] Includes small quantities from Kentucky, Alabama, and Arkansas
[c] Estimated, exact figures not available
[d] Includes Virginia
NOTE: In addition to the above states, marketable quantities of rock are produced in Georgia, Idaho, Montana, Utah, and Wyoming, and smaller quantities have been mined in New Jersey, New York, and Pennsylvania at various times.

annually. This loss occurs through leaching of the soils and from crop production as well. The phosphorus in the soil is transferred to the ripening plant seed, and this in turn is consumed by man and beast alike. Even with dairy or livestock farming, where manure is returned to the soil, there is an unavoidable loss of phosphorus. The loss through human waste is almost total.

There are large reserves of phosphate rock (the primary source of phosphorus) in several southern and western states, but the production of phosphates in America is largely confined to Florida. Other states are active producers, but Florida accounts for over 70 percent of domestic output and about 30 percent of world production. With few exceptions, Florida's experiences are true for the industry as a whole.

The first step in obtaining the mineral after locating a deposit is to remove the overburden (everything covering the ore) with large draglines. The ore is then excavated, dumped into a hole, and fluidized by high-pressure streams of water. The resulting mixture is then pumped to the recovery plant. There the mixture of ore, soil, and water is washed and then screened to recover the large pebbles of rock, and the remaining mixture is sent through flotation units, which further separate the rock from the waste particles. The rock is then dried and ready to be processed into fertilizer. At this point, dangerous emissions result when the phosphorus is chemically separated from accompanying impurities.

Environmental damage occurs throughout the process. Mined-out areas resemble a "moonscape" unless they are reclaimed; waste products have to be contained behind dams, which sometimes break, resulting in water pollution; and emissions (primarily gaseous fluorine) can be ex-

tremely dangerous to plant, animal, and human life. Fortunately, massive investments by the industry in technological improvements have virtually negated these effects while greatly increasing production. Florida and other southern states will continue to furnish the bulk of national production in the foreseeable future. But demands are increasing and national conservation policies will have to be improved if we are not to exhaust this mineral of life.

See A. F. Blakey, *Florida Phosphate Industry* (1973), extensive bibliography, only nontechnical work available; I. Asimov, *Fact and Fancy* (1972); and U.S. Bureau of Mines, *Mineral Resources* (1870–1932) and *Minerals Yearbook* (1932–75).

ARCH FREDRIC BLAKEY
University of Florida

PHYLON (Atlanta University, Atlanta, Ga. 31314) is a quarterly journal founded in 1940 by W. E. B. DU BOIS and subsidized by Atlanta University. It had a circulation of 3,195 in 1976 and publishes book reviews and scholarly articles of ethnic interest, not limited to the South. It makes no payment for accepted articles and does not grant awards or prizes.

PHYSICAL EDUCATION. See SPORTS AND PHYSICAL EDUCATION

PICKENS, ANDREW (1739–1817), was born in Paxton Township, Pa. Moving along the frontier, he made his final home Tamassee plantation on the South Carolina side of the Cherokee boundary. He was probably the most capable revolutionary officer without Continental experience. Some of his notable military actions included Savage Old Fields (1775), the Cherokee expedition of 1776, KETTLE CREEK (1779), and COWPENS and EUTAW SPRINGS (1781). He and other southern militiamen suppressed Loyalists and Indians and thus prevented counterrevolution, Britain's only real chance for reconquest.

Success in war and just treatment in peace earned Pickens the admiration and trust of the red men. Between 1785 and 1802 he repeatedly negotiated with the CREEK, CHEROKEE, CHICKASAW, and CHOCTAW nations. Teaming with Benjamin Hawkins of North Carolina, he worked to preserve their homelands adjacent to the white frontier. By opposing fraudulent state treaties he earned the enmity of Georgia's JAMES JACKSON and Tennessee's JOHN SEVIER and WILLIAM BLOUNT. A recognized expert on judicial and fiscal matters, he served repeatedly in the legislature and helped draft much of the legislation that dealt with development and settlement of the state's interior.

See C. R. Ferguson, "Andrew Pickens" (Ph.D. dissertation, Duke, 1960), best; A. L. Pickens, *Skyagunsta* (1934), good, brief; A. N. Waring, *Fighting Elder* (1962); and C. R. Ferguson, *Kansas Quarterly* (Fall, 1971).

CLYDE R. FERGUSON
Kansas State University

PICKENS, FRANCIS WILKINSON (1805–1869), born in St. Paul Parish, Pendleton District, S.C., was a long-time resident of Edgefield. A lawyer, state legislator, and U.S. congressman (1834–1843), Pickens was early cited by John C. Calhoun as "the most promising young man in the state." An ardent nullificationist, he presided at the state convention in 1832 and promulgated the secession ordinance. Defeated for the U.S. Senate by JAMES H. HAMMOND in 1857, he served as U.S. minister to Russia (1858–1860), then returned to state politics. He became a leader in the conservative secessionist movement and was elected governor in December, 1860. Pickens demanded federal surrender of the Charleston harbor forts and subsequently directed the firing of the shots on FT. SUMTER, which opened the Civil War. Unable to muster popular confidence as a wartime governor, he was forced from office in 1862 by an executive council and retired to his estate Edgewood, emerging in 1865 to assist in Reconstruction.

See E. Milander, in R. K. Ackerman (ed.), *Perspectives in South Carolina History* (1973); S. A. Channing, *Crisis of Fear* (1970); L. A. White, *R. B. Rhett* (1931); J. A. Chapman, *History of Edgefield County* (1897); and L. A. White, *American Historical Review* (July, 1929).

JAMES B. AGNEW
U.S. Army Military History Research Collection

PICKETT, GEORGE EDWARD (1825–1875), born in Richmond, Va., was appointed to West Point from Illinois and graduated in 1846. After serving in the Mexican War, in Texas, and in the Pacific Northwest he resigned in 1861. Pickett received command of the Game Cock Brigade in Virginia and participated in the defense of Richmond under JAMES LONGSTREET until wounded at GAINES' MILL. As a major general, he served creditably but not notably at FREDERICKSBURG and Suffolk. At GETTYSBURG in 1863, three brigades of Pickett's division, together with remnants of North Carolina units, marched in parade-ground formation to assault a Union defensive position, and almost three-fourths of the combined command was lost. Twenty years later there was bitter argument whether Pickett had led or followed his men. In North Carolina in 1864, he failed to capture New Bern but was able to muster enough militia strength at Petersburg to hold off overly cautious Benjamin F. Butler at Bermuda Hundred until relieved by P. G. T. BEAUREGARD. Pickett's musket-armed infantrymen were routed at FIVE FORKS by Philip H. Sheridan, whose unmounted troopers had repeating carbines and overwhelming numbers. Pickett and the remaining members of his command surrendered at APPOMATTOX. Because he had executed after courts-martial a number of turncoat Confederate soldiers captured at New Bern, he was declared a war criminal in Congress by General Butler. He fled to Canada with his family and returned to Virginia only after President U. S. Grant declared the amnesty proclamation made at Appomattox to be all-inclusive. Although pauperized, he refused a commission from the khedive of Egypt and rejected Grant's offer to appoint him marshal of Virginia. Pickett died while living at his ancestral James River plantation and eking out a living as an insurance agent.

See D. S. Freeman, *Lee's Lieutenants* (3 vols.; 1942–44); G. O. Haller, *San Juan and Secession* (1896); J. C. Mayo, *Southern Historical Society Papers* (1906); Richmond *Inquirer* (Aug. 1, 1875); letters of James Longstreet, Robert A. Bright, W. Stuart Symington, Charles Pickett, and Thomas R. Friend, Virginia Historical Society; G. R. Stewart, *Pickett's Charge* (1959); and L. J. Edson, *Fourth Corner* (1951).

REUBEN ELMORE STIVERS
Bethesda, Md.

PIEDMONT region or province is an inland plain running from the FALL LINE, its eastern escarpment, to the base of the BLUE RIDGE and APPALACHIAN mountains. It is closest to the Atlantic Ocean near New York City, where it is a barely noticeable geographic feature. Farther south, however, it begins farther from the coast and becomes gradually much wider, extending ultimately into central Alabama. Most early settlement of the southern colonies remained below the fall line and in the TIDEWATER area, where rich soils and easy transportation supported commercial agriculture. The generally clayey and only moderately fertile soils of the Piedmont combined with insufficient transportation to delay intensive settlement until the late eighteenth and early nineteenth centuries. Piedmont (or up-country) residents had significantly different interests than the population of the tidewater (low country), and political conflict between these two sections was especially evident in the early history of Virginia and the Carolinas. Indeed, much of the turnpike, canal, and railroad construction of the antebellum period represented the political ascendancy of the Piedmont regions of these states. Moreover, the deep valleys and river gorges, which had inhibited commercial development in the seventeenth and eighteenth centuries, became sites for the generation of power that helped the INDUSTRIALIZATION of the nineteenth- and twentieth-century South.

PIEDMONT, BATTLE OF (June 5, 1864), was an engagement in the Lynchburg, Va., campaign (May 26–June 29). As part of a series of diversions planned by U. S. Grant, David Hunter moved rapidly up the Shenandoah Valley from Cedar Creek with two brigades of infantry (one mostly West Virginians) and supporting cavalry and artillery. At Piedmont, Va., his force of approximately 9,000 encountered William E. ("Grumble") Jones and about 6,000 well-posted but largely inexperienced Confederates. A seesaw battle of several hours left Jones dead, 600 Confederates killed and wounded, 1,000 more prisoners, and the remnant retreating to Waynesboro. The next day Hunter, less 800 casualties, entered Staunton without opposition and captured many supplies. The defeat left the upper Shenandoah Valley open to invasion, taught the Confederates a lesson about weak and confused command structure in the area, and prompted R. E. Lee to detach a large force to the valley.

See M. M. Brice, *Conquest of a Valley* (1965), full-scale study, useful·bibliography.

JAMES E. SEFTON
California State University, Northridge

PIERCE, FRANKLIN, ADMINISTRATION (1853–1857). Nominated by a divided Democratic convention, Pierce easily defeated his Whig opponent to become in March, 1853, the fourteenth president. Despite his New Hampshire background, he received his greatest support from the South. Pierce's appointments cemented these regional bonds, for among his cabinet officers were three southerners including his personal friend JEFFERSON DAVIS, and his diplomatic appointments included states' rights advocates such as Pierre Soulé of Louisiana and Solon Borland of Arkansas. Yet Pierce's intentions were to avoid sectional conflict, uphold the COMPROMISE OF 1850, and concentrate on foreign policy—positions most southerners accepted.

Such sectional neutrality was elusive, and Pierce was shortly embroiled in the divisive issue of Kansas. Although the administration did not write the KANSAS-NEBRASKA BILL, Pierce promptly traded support of the bill for congressional votes favoring his appointments and treaties. Soon confronted with disorder, election frauds, and two contending territorial governments in Kansas (BLEEDING KANSAS), Pierce opposed the free-state movement as illegal. Although the president intended to keep order and did remove overtly proslave officials, his Kansas policy, which held northern interests responsible for the continuing disruption in the territory, encouraged the South to expect that Kansas would enter the Union a slave state.

Southerners found less to applaud in the administration's foreign policy, partly because many anticipated annexation of Cuba and support of the filibustering efforts of southerners like WILLIAM WALKER and JOHN QUITMAN. Although the administration gave no support to the latter, the OSTEND MANIFESTO, written in 1854 by three of Pierce's foreign envoys, justified American intervention in Cuba if Spain refused to sell the island. Yet, when Pierce retired from office in 1857, only the Gadsden Purchase—potentially useful for a southern transcontinental railroad—had advanced slavery interests.

On balance, the South supported Pierce's administration, approving his veto of certain internal improvement bills, his efforts to reduce the debt, and his condemnation of the Republicans. Usually it was the administration's ineffectiveness, not its intentions, that caused southern complaints. Accordingly the Lower South provided Pierce's main support in the 1856 Democratic convention; and, although another northern man with southern principles (James Buchanan) was nominated, the alliance between the Democratic party and the South was cemented during Pierce's tenure.

See R. Nichols, *Franklin Pierce* (1931), dated, but exhaustive; A. Nevins, *Ordeal of Union* (1947), censorious; and E. L. Craik, *Kansas Historical Collection* (1922), on South's interest in Kansas.

JEAN BAKER
Goucher College

PIERPONT, FRANCIS HARRISON (1814–1899), born in northwestern Virginia near Morgantown (now West Virginia), became a prosperous lawyer-businessman and a Henry Clay Whig. Identifying with the interests of the West, he opposed secession in 1861 and became governor of the "restored government" of Virginia. Since his government endorsed the separate statehood movement, he became known as the "father of West Virginia." When Abraham Lincoln signed the statehood bill (1863), his administration moved to Alexandria, where it could operate on Virginia soil but under federal protection. Presiding over a government that one witty congressman characterized as the "Common Council of Alexandria," Pierpont secured a new constitution abolishing slavery and successfully challenged General Benjamin Butler's usurpation of civil authority. After Appomattox Pierpont sought to govern from Richmond, but he became the victim of Reconstruction politics and lost the governorship in April, 1868. Moving to West Virginia, he resumed his local political and business activities.

See R. O. Curry, *House Divided* (1964), authoritative; C. H. Ambler, *Francis H. Pierpont* (1937), standard biography; H. T. Shanks, *Secession Movement in Virginia* (1934, 1971); F. N. Boney, *John Letcher* (1966); J. G. Randall, *Constitutional Problems Under Lincoln* (1926); and H. L. Trefousse, *Ben Butler* (1957).

WILLIAM E. DERBY
State University College, Geneseo, N.Y.

PIGS. See HOGS

PIKE, ALBERT (1809–1891), was born and educated in Massachusetts. After teaching several years he traveled in 1832 to Little Rock, Ark., establishing himself in journalism and law. A Whig among Democrats, he nonetheless won station in the Civil War. He brought western Indian tribes under Confederate influence and commanded them as a brigadier general. However, reported Indian atrocities at PEA RIDGE and conflicting authority led Pike to resign in 1862. An inglorious arrest, then semiretirement, filled out the war years. After moving to Memphis and later to Washington, he returned to his prewar professions, wrote several legal treatises, and renewed his lifelong service to Scottish rite Masonry. His poems received moderate acclaim, principally "Hymns to the Gods."

See Pike Papers, Scottish Rite Library, Washington, D.C.; W. L. Brown, "Albert Pike" (Ph.D. dissertation, University of Texas, 1955); W. L. Boyden, *Bibliography of Pike* (1921); and R. L. Duncan, *Reluctant General* (1961).

GARY E. MOULTON
Southwestern Oklahoma State University

PIKE, ZEBULON MONTGOMERY (1779–1813), explorer, was born in New Jersey. At age twenty he was commissioned a second lieutenant in the army. In 1805, under direct orders from General JAMES WILKINSON, he searched for the source of the Mississippi River. Again on Wilkinson's orders he was sent in 1806 to explore the headwaters of the Arkansas and Red rivers and to look over Spanish settlements in the territory. Historians have questioned whether he was involved in the abortive BURR CONSPIRACY, but there is no evidence to indicate that he was. His group ascended the Arkansas River above the Royal Gorge, turned south, and crossed with great difficulty the Sangre de Cristo range, building a small fort on the Rio Grande. Spanish troops "requested" them to go along to Santa Fe and Chihuahua, where they were interrogated but later released. Although his maps and papers were confiscated, Pike secreted some material, and from this and memory he wrote and published his report in 1810. He received promotions and was a brigadier general by the War of 1812. He led the successful charge on York (Toronto), but was killed there in an explosion of gunpowder.

See W. E. Hollon, *Lost Pathfinder* (1949), only good biography; D. Jackson (ed.), *Journals of Pike* (1966); A. P. Hulbert (ed.), *Pike's Arkansas Journal* (1932); and E. Coves (ed.), *Expedition of Pike* (1895).

JOHN A. CAYLOR
Boise State University

PILLOW, GIDEON JOHNSON (1806–1878), was born in Williamson County, Tenn. He graduated from the University of Nashville in 1827 and became a millionaire lawyer (he was never a law partner of James Polk) and planter. He played major roles in securing the Democratic presidential nominations of JAMES POLK in 1844 and Franklin Pierce in 1852. Polk rewarded him with a general's commission in the Mexican War. Pillow's egotism and penchant for intrigue produced an uneven record. With the outbreak of the Civil War, he assisted in the mobilization of Tennessee's armed forces. In November, 1861, he fought the battle of BELMONT, Mo., against Ulysses Grant, who after initial success was driven away. The defense of Ft. Donelson, Tenn., in February, 1862, was complicated by wrangling between Generals JOHN FLOYD and SIMON BUCKNER, who favored abandoning the fort, and Pillow, who wanted to stay and fight. This indecision led to the surrender of the garrison, with Floyd and Pillow escaping.

See T. Connelly, *Army of Heartland* (1967); J. Garrett, "General Pillow and Pillow Family," Columbia, Tenn.; and R. Stonesifer, Jr., *Tennessee Historical Quarterly* (Winter, 1966).

ROY P. STONESIFER, JR.
Edinboro State College

PINCHBACK, PINCKNEY BENTON STEWART

ART (1837–1921), the only Negro ever to be governor of an American state, was Louisiana's most prominent black politician during Reconstruction. He was born in Macon, Ga., to a free woman of mixed ancestry named Eliza Stewart; his father William Pinchback was a white planter. At age nine he was sent by his father to Cincinnati to be educated. Upon his father's death in 1848, Pinchback became a cabin boy on a canalboat; later he worked as a steward on Mississippi River steamboats. Arriving in New Orleans shortly after the occupation by Union forces in 1862, Pinchback organized a black company and joined the federal army as a captain. Within a year he resigned his commission because his troops were subjected to racial discrimination. His own appearance was "just perceptibly African," and Pinchback might have passed for white had he chosen to do so.

After the war's end, Pinchback became active in Republican politics. A member of the Louisiana constitutional convention of 1868, he was elected to the state senate later that year. As president pro tem of the senate in 1871, he became lieutenant governor when the incumbent, Oscar J. Dunn, died. For one month (December, 1871–January, 1872) Pinchback served as governor of Louisiana, after the legislature removed HENRY CLAY WARMOTH from office. In 1873 the Republican legislature elected Pinchback to the U.S. Senate, but the Senate refused to seat him. After Reconstruction his political career subsided; but, as did many of the leading white Republicans of Louisiana,

Pinchback retired wealthy. In 1890 he moved to Washington and lived comfortably there for the remainder of his long life.

See J. Haskins, *P. B. S. Pinchback* (1973); B. A. Weisberger, *American Heritage* (Dec., 1973); and J. G. Taylor, *Louisiana Reconstructed* (1974).

WILLIAM I. HAIR
Georgia College

PINCKNEY, CHARLES (1757–1824), author of the "Pinckney draught" of the federal Constitution, senator (1798–1801), congressman (1819–1821), minister to Spain (1801–1804), and four-time governor of South Carolina (1789–1792, 1796–1798, 1806–1808), was born in Charleston. The son of Colonel Charles Pinckney, he was a cousin of THOMAS PINCKNEY and CHARLES COTESWORTH PINCKNEY (PINCKNEY FAMILY). An officer in the Revolution, Pinckney was captured at the surrender of Charleston (1780). In postwar politics he served three years in the Confederation Congress, where he championed stronger central government. Sent to the CONSTITUTIONAL CONVENTION in 1787, he offered a plan for the new government, although his claims regarding the extent of his contributions to the Constitution have been disputed by historians. In the 1790s Pinckney, alone among his kinsmen, joined the Republican cause. Following his successful management of Thomas Jefferson's South Carolina campaign in 1800, thoroughly embarrassing cousin Charles Cotesworth's bid for the vice-presidency, he headed the state Republican party and became "Blackguard Charley" to his Federalist contemporaries.

See J. F. Jameson, *American Historical Association Report* (1903); A. C. McLaughlin, *American Historical Review* (July, 1904); M. Ferrand, *Records, Federal Convention* (1911), III; J. Elliott, *Debates* (1941), IV; G. C. Rogers, *William Loughton Smith* (1962), best explanation of S.C. political alliances; I. Brant, *James Madison* (1950), III, refutes "Pinckney draught" claims; M. R. Zahniser, *Charles Cotesworth Pinckney* (1967); Charles Pinckney Papers, South Caroliniana Library, Columbia; and A. J. Bethea, *Contribution of Charles Pinckney* (1937).

CARL VIPPERMAN
University of Georgia

PINCKNEY, CHARLES COTESWORTH (1746–1825), was born in South Carolina (PINCKNEY FAMILY) and in 1773 married Sarah Middleton (MIDDLETON FAMILY). In the Revolutionary War he served faithfully but without particular distinction, rising to the rank of brigadier general. In state politics he supported low-country planter interests and the commercial community of Charleston. He represented the state at the national CONSTITUTIONAL CONVENTION and strongly defended slave interests. A moderate Federalist, he was named minister to France in 1796. Although a Francophile, he was expelled from France, returning later in the XYZ mission. He refused to pay France a bribe, saying, "No, no, not a sixpence." Pinckney was named John Adams' running mate in the ELECTION OF 1800. In 1804 and 1808 he became the Federalist presidential candidate. After 1800 he served as state senator, tended his plantations, served as president general of the Order of the Cincinnati, and helped to found a state-supported college at Columbia (1800–1801).

See M. R. Zahniser, *Charles Cotesworth Pinckney* (1967); G. C. Rogers, Jr., *Charleston in Age of Pinckneys* (1969); H. H. Ravenel, *Eliza Pinckney* (1909); Pinckney Family Papers, Library of Congress; and Pinckney Papers, South Carolina Historical Society.

MARVIN R. ZAHNISER
Ohio State University

PINCKNEY, ELIZABETH LUCAS (1722–1793),
was responsible for the introduction of INDIGO CULTURE in South Carolina. She was the daughter of Lieutenant Colonel George Lucas, who saw long service in the West Indies. Eliza was probably born in Antigua and educated in England. She came with her parents in 1738 to South Carolina, where her father acquired Wapoo plantation and control of two others. Colonel Lucas very shortly returned to duty in Antigua, and Eliza, at age sixteen, was left to manage the three plantations. She turned her very active mind to experimentation with various plants, searching for profitable plantation crops. In 1741 her father sent her some indigo seed. After three seasons of effort Eliza adapted a strain of the plant to South Carolina conditions. From a man from Monserrat she learned the techniques of processing indigo as a dyestuff. Her success set off a boom in indigo production. The English government granted subsidies and tariff preference, and indigo soon became the second money crop in South Carolina.

In May, 1744, Eliza married Charles Pinckney, a widower. They had two sons, CHARLES COTESWORTH and THOMAS. Her husband died in 1758, and Eliza resumed the very active role of planter. She was interested in public affairs, and governors and other South Carolina leaders were frequent guests at her home.

See *South Carolina Historical and Genealogical Magazine* (Oct., 1907; Jan., 1913; July, 1916; Jan., July, 1918);

E. L. Pinckney, *Letterbooks* (1972); and H. H. Ravenel, *Eliza Pinckney* (1896).

CLARENCE J. ATTIG
Westmar College

PINCKNEY, THOMAS (1750–1828), educated in
England with his brother CHARLES COTESWORTH, returned to his native Charleston in 1774 to practice law. He served with distinction in the Revolutionary War and was wounded and captured at CAMDEN. As governor of South Carolina (1787–1789), he encouraged the quick ratification of the Constitution. While U.S. minister to Britain (1792–1796), he was sent to Spain, where at San Lorenzo (1795) he obtained freedom of navigation on the Mississippi and a favorable southern boundary settlement. Pinckney's Treaty opened up the choicest slave territory to settlement and, with his consequent popularity in the South and West, earned him second place on the Federalist ticket in 1796. After two terms in Congress (1797–1801), he resumed his law practice but was mainly a planter, frequently publishing the results of his agricultural experiments. Although unsympathetic with the War of 1812, he reluctantly accepted command of the Sixth Military District (the Southeast) and helped defeat the CREEK INDIANS. After the Denmark VESEY PLOT he published an attack on the abolition movement.

See C. C. Pinckney, *Life of Thomas Pinckney* (1895), only biography; J. L. Cross, *London Mission* (1968); and S. F. Bemis, *Pinckney's Treaty* (1926, 1960).

CHARLES ELLIS DICKSON
King College

PINCKNEY FAMILY. As one historian comment-
ed, "No family more fully illustrates the economic, military, and constitutional history of Charleston during the golden century [1730–1830] than does the Pinckney family." Thomas Pinckney came to South Carolina in 1692. A merchant, he married Mary Cotesworth, by whom he had two sons, Charles (1699–1758) and William (1704–1766). Charles became Speaker of the commons house of assembly, was briefly chief justice of the colony, and was later its agent in London. He married ELIZA LUCAS PINCKNEY, developer of indigo planting in South Carolina, by whom he had CHARLES COTESWORTH and THOMAS. The brothers were patriots in the Revolution and prominent state and national politicians.

William Pinckney, a man of public affairs, married Ruth Brewton. Their best-known child was Colonel Charles Pinckney (1731–1782), who was a patriot in the revolutionary crisis but who later wavered in his loyalties. His son CHARLES was a delegate to the Constitutional Convention and governor of the state. Governor Pinckney's son by Mary Laurens, Henry Laurens Pinckney (1794–1863), served as mayor of Charleston and in Congress (1833–1837).

The Pinckney family achieved enormous influence in South Carolina through advantageous marriages, by providing their children with the best possible education, and by identifying itself so closely with low-country, later southern, interests. Chief Justice Charles Pinckney's championship of commons house rights in the 1730s, Thomas Pinckney's negotiation of the Treaty of San Lorenzo in 1795, and Henry Laurens Pinckney's support of the GAG RULE in Congress in the 1830s illustrate how the family moved with the times.

See M. L. Webber, *South Carolina Magazine of History* (Jan., 1938); G. C. Rogers, Jr., *Charleston in Age of Pinckneys* (1969); C. C. Pinckney, *Life of Thomas Pinckney* (1895); H. H. Ravenel, *Eliza Pinckney* (1909); M. R. Zahniser, *Charles Cotesworth Pinckney* (1967); Pinckney Family Papers, Library of Congress; and Pinckney Papers, South Carolina Historical Society.

MARVIN R. ZAHNISER
Ohio State University

PINE BARRENS, sometimes called "piney woods," was the name given by early settlers to the broad coastal plain extending from southern Virginia into eastern Texas on which wiregrass and pine trees flourished. Tidewater planters seeking fertile soil shunned the sandy, infertile barrens, leaving the area during the antebellum period to indigent herdsmen and subsistence farmers who came to be referred to as POOR WHITES, sandhillers, and CLAY EATERS.

Speedy removal of the Great Lakes pine forests in the years following the Civil War and a concurrent increase in railroad construction throughout the South Atlantic and Gulf states sparked the beginnings of wholesale exploitation of the piney woods. Northern lumbermen joined southerners in the rush to acquire the best pinelands and commenced a production that by 1900 made the South the nation's leading producer of softwood lumber (LUMBER INDUSTRY). Rapid cutting of the pineries without thought of reforestation, plus the destruction wrought by steam skidders and recurrent forest fires, not only reduced the original stand of 650 billion board feet to some 139 million feet by 1920 but also left a barren, virtually deserted wasteland despite attempts to establish pastoral and farming enterprises. Today, the desolation that once marked most of the pine barrens has been significantly altered by the adoption of forest management techniques, effective forest fire protection systems, and the widespread popularity of the tree farm movement.

See F. Heyward, *Industrial Forestry in South* (1958); N. Hickman, *Mississippi Harvest* (1962); T. D. Clark, *Emerging South* (1961); G. P. Ahern, *Forest Bankruptcy* (1933); U. B. Phillips, *Life and Labor* (1929); and P. H. Buck, *American Historical Review* (Oct., 1925).

GEORGE T. MORGAN, JR.
University of Houston

PINE BLUFF, ARK. (pop. 57,389), situated on the Arkansas River 43 miles south-southeast of LITTLE ROCK, was settled as a trading post in 1819 by Joseph Bonne, the son of a Frenchman and an Indian woman. Called Mount Marie until 1832, the town was renamed when its growing population desired a more American name for this regional center of the cotton trade. In October, 1863, Union defenders successfully repulsed a Confederate effort to capture the city. In 1874 Pine Bluff was the site of the BROOKS-BAXTER WAR, an incident in Arkansas' Reconstruction. The city continues to be a significant cotton market, but it is also a livestock market, a center of regional commerce, and a producer of chemicals, lumber, wood, and cottonseed products. Pine Bluff boasts the Southeastern Arkansas Arts and Science Center, with two art galleries, a library, and a theater.

See *Southwest Times Record* (1882–), independent Democratic daily.

PINKNEY, WILLIAM (1764–1822). His distinguished career as a Maryland lawyer, as a member of Congress (1815–1816), as senator (1819–1822), and as attorney general in James Madison's cabinet (1811–1814) has never won the attention that his lesser services as diplomatist have achieved. In 1796 he was appointed an American commissioner in London (until 1804) examining claims of American merchants against Britain under the terms of Jay's Treaty. He served as minister to Britain from 1807 to 1811 and as minister to Russia from 1816 to 1818. His major imprint upon American history was a failure of statecraft. He was a logical choice by Thomas Jefferson to treat with Britain over renewed seizure of American ships and impressment of American seamen during the Napoleonic Wars. In 1806 James Monroe and Pinkney as joint commissioners signed a treaty that failed to address the problem of impressment. The treaty was an embarrassment to the president, who refused to submit it to the Senate. To Pinkney the accommodation with Britain was the best that could be achieved. The alternative ultimately was a war, which he vigorously supported in 1812.

See B. Perkins, *Prologue to War* (1961); W. Pinkney, *Life of William Pinkney* (1853); and A. Steel, *American Historical Review* (Jan., 1952). See also papers at Maryland Historical Society and Harvard Library.

LAWRENCE S. KAPLAN
Kent State University

PIRACY is robbery, or any other act held to be criminal by the laws of nations, committed in international waters. Usually piracy has been perpetrated by organized bands operating from armed vessels. It was a sporadic problem during the colonial era, becoming particularly serious during 1695–1700 and 1713–1718, periods after wars when some former privateers turned to piracy. Two favorite stalking grounds for pirates were the entrance of Chesapeake Bay and outside Charleston harbor. When pirate depredations disrupted commerce, concerted action by governments resulted. Great Britain added and systematized naval patrols. Virginia and South Carolina efforts climaxed about 1718 with the killing of BLACKBEARD and the execution of Major Stede Bonnet. Other pirate leaders and crewmen were killed, executed, imprisoned, or simply retired by accepting amnesty. It became too risky for colonial officials in the West Indies and on the mainland to provide illicit havens for piratical operations. By 1720, piracy was fading.

Misconceptions about the age of piracy still abound in legends, in fiction, in popular and even serious histories. In reality pirates were desperate men, sometimes women, who robbed and committed other vicious crimes. Although they seldom felt it necessary to kill their victims, those killed, contrary to popular belief, did not walk the plank. Pirates were sensualists, taking to gratify immediate desires, spending today since tomorrow might bring the end; no quantity of buried pirate gold has ever been found. These individuals, who had turned their backs on civilized standards and had few redeeming qualities, scarcely deserve favorable interpretation much less romanticizing.

See H. F. Rankin, *Golden Age of Piracy* (1969), short, scholarly; C. H. Karraker, *Piracy Was a Business* (1953); P. Pringle, *Jolly Roger* (1953), both popular, sound; L. H. Williams, *Pirates of Colonial Virginia* (1937); H. F. Rankin, *Pirates of Colonial North Carolina* (1960); and S. C. Hughson, *Carolina Pirates* (1894), three informative monographs.

CONVERSE D. CLOWSE
University of North Carolina, Greensboro

PITTSBURGH PLUS was a system of pricing steel by which the price at any point in the United States was fixed at the Pittsburgh price plus the railroad freight charge, whether paid or not, to the point of quotation. Consumers in Birmingham, Ala., a producing point, thus had no price advantage in being close to the source of supply. Quoting delivered prices was a standard practice in the IRON AND STEEL INDUSTRY by 1880, and over the next 20 years the basing point system was gradually extended to all major producers and products in the field. The Pittsburgh Plus system had the virtue of simplicity in understanding and execution, and, although it occasionally broke down, it provided a fairly stable system of price-fixing that helped to bring prosperity to the industry. Its heyday was from 1901, when the United States Steel Corporation was formed, until 1921. The system was already breaking down when it was condemned by the Federal Trade Commission in 1924, and it was replaced by a more complex system of multiple basing points. From the point of view of the buyer, the system smacked of monopolistic price-fixing, and there were loud complaints about charging "phantom freight" and denying the natural advantages of location to steel fabricators. It was wasteful in encouraging crosshauling of steel by railroads and in keeping inefficient steel plants competitive. But it did give a considerable degree of stability to the steel industry.

See Temporary National Economic Committee, Monograph No. 42, *Basing Point Problem* (1941), and Monograph No. 21, *Competition and Monopoly in American Industry* (1940).

JAMES F. DOSTER
University of Alabama

PLANT, HENRY BRADLEY (1819–1899), best known for his development of Tampa, Fla., was born in Connecticut. He began working with express and transportation companies in the late 1830s, and in 1854 he was placed in charge of the southern operations of the Adams Express Company. When the Confederacy was formed, Plant organized the Southern Express Company from properties of the Adams Express Company located south of the Potomac. This company rendered great service to the South during the war, although Plant, for reasons of health, went to Europe in 1863. The company prospered after the war, and in 1879 Plant began to buy and construct RAILROADS. He completed the first line to Tampa in 1884 and then developed Port Tampa, nine miles away. He opened the lavish Tampa Bay Hotel in 1891 to attract the tourist trade (TOURISM), and he established steamship routes to New England, Cuba, and Central America. It was through Plant's influence that Tampa was declared the port of embarkation during the Spanish-American War and his transportation companies handled much of the movement of troops and supplies. After the war Plant became interested in developing the railroads in Cuba, but he died before he could carry out these plans. The Plant System, extending from Florida to South Carolina, was sold to the Atlantic Coast Line Railroad in 1902.

See G. H. Smyth, *Life of H. B. Plant* (1898); K. H. Grismer, *Tampa* (1950); D. S. Johnson, *Florida Historical Quarterly* (April, 1970; Oct., 1966), *Georgia Historical Quarterly* (1972), and *Alabama Review* (Oct., 1968); *Commercial and Financial Chronicle* (1880–1903); and P. K. Yonge Library of Florida History, University of Florida.

DUDLEY S. JOHNSON
Southeastern Louisiana University

PLANTATIONS. The word derives from the Latin *plantare* (to plant) and *plantatio* (the act of planting). In England the metaphor progressed from a term signifying a transplantation of plants, trees, people, or institutions from one place to another; to a migration implying settlement, first without and later with a designated form of settlement; and, finally, as in the American South, to a landed estate producing an export crop and vesting jurisdiction in an established authority. The historical roots of plantation as a migration and settlement in overseas territory go back to the cosmology of the Crusades with their fervor to conquer and convert heathen populations coupled with the commercial purposes of the Mediterranean and Baltic trading factories. Plantation as migration to the other side of a body of water such as the Atlantic Ocean required assistance, direction, and control by sponsoring Englishmen of capital and resolution. Virginia as a plantation colony lost its aspect as a trading factory when trade with the Indians proved impractical and the colony dissolved into a number of "particular plantations." On these the resident entrepreneur, or planter, appeared with the development of tobacco as a profitable export to the European market.

The plantation as an estate underwent an independent development in Virginia and Maryland, but in South Carolina and Louisiana it was transplanted from the British and French West Indies, each giving rise to territorially limited societal systems. Tobacco centered the economic system in Virginia and Maryland; rice and indigo, in South Carolina and Georgia; and sugar, in Louisiana. An approach to a plantation system based upon the production of hemp developed in Kentucky around 1830. By far the most important staple crop produced on a plantation scale was cotton, which after the invention of the cotton gin in 1793 responded to a surging demand for the fiber in England and advanced westward across state boundaries to eastern Texas by 1860.

Its significance in southern life and history is missed if the plantation is not understood as an institution in as real a sense as any institution. It was a completed social movement and a migration ending in a settlement that progressively mobilized capital, people, purposes, and energies at a time and space juncture that southern situations provided. The institution arose in the tension between change and continuity in order to deal with the turnover of generations and survived under the conditions of an expanding economy to continue the purposes, however modified, of those originally investing in the movement. On the southern frontier the English principle of continuity through PRIMOGENITURE underwent swift decline because land to the west was easily obtained but valuable for the production of export staples mainly to the extent that labor was available to work it. Controlled yet movable, inheritable, and transmissible slave property rather than, or along with, land became a prime factor in the continuity of the institution until emancipation shifted the role of the planter from that of master to that of landlord. Change there was, but the plantation maintained its identity as such over a period of several centuries until well into the twentieth century.

It is helpful to view the plantation institution in four interrelated aspects. Initially it was an institution of settlement. At least from 1616 to 1860 and even after the Civil War, in the Mississippi Delta, for example, it spread and arranged a new population along a moving westward frontier in a process of demographic and economic succession. One of slavery's most important contributions was to furnish the large amount of labor required for the clearing of forest lands. In these clearings small population clusters, little isolated camps in the wilderness, became and remained the plantation's most obvious and visible aspect. Its economic and political order was reflected in its spatial pattern and in its characteristic architecture of big house, quarters, and, later, tenant cabins.

Second, it was and remained an economic institution producing agricultural staples for export. It was in this capacity that the plantation oriented the region to the larger community in which the planters sold their staples, obtained their capital, their supplies, and for a period of time their labor, and competed with producing areas elsewhere. Southern statesmen were well aware of their interests in this larger market and of world conditions affecting it. From the days of original settlement into the twentieth century, there was more land in the South capable of profitable cultivation than there was labor available to cultivate it. In these circumstances use was made of such labor as could be obtained under conditions something less than those of a free labor market. White indentured servants from Europe under contract for varying periods of time were first employed (INDENTURED LABOR). Planters then invested capital in labor itself; that is, in Negro slaves. After emancipation they turned to white and Negro sharecroppers. SHARECROPPING is now rapidly being replaced by wage labor and machinery.

In its third aspect the plantation was a political institution; that is, an institution privileged to exercise physical force and other forms of coercion over a subordinate class in a closed territory. There were plantations with jails, police, rules and regulations, chains of command, and systems of reward and punishment extending beyond the hiring and firing practices of modern industry. By both law and custom the planter enjoyed immunities from the laws of the larger state, immunities that, however, were progressively reduced and then eliminated by state and federal action. The most far-reaching action, of course, was the abolition of slavery. The idea of race evolved to rationalize white superiority and authority and to naturalize the enslavement of those of one color only. After emancipation the idea became more powerful than before, since the system then had to deal with its laboring class of another color now increasingly more mobile and competitive.

Finally, the plantation was a cultural institution that over the years achieved a distinctive and intensely local "way of life" participated in by members of all classes and races. The institution functioned as an isolating mechanism by means of which a body of habits and customs and attitudes was fashioned and passed down through generations. Each plantation, and especially the larger ones, tended to develop its own traditions and even its own distinctive dialect. This is the aspect of the plantation depicted in popular and nostalgic literature, the aspect that left a heritage of norms now affirmed or denied even after the physical plantation has passed away. It was inevitable that the plantation, as a frontier and therefore a transient institution, should give way to other institutional forms.

U. B. Phillips spoke of a "climate of coherence," a relational fabric of churches, schools, families, and other institutions centered on the plantations of the Old South continuing into the New. It was a "plantation system" that, in spite of local variations and inconsistencies, gave the South a certain unity and that was, in fact, "the South" itself.

See E. T. Thompson, *Plantation: A Bibliography* (1957), all principal references to time of publication are listed, and *Plantation Societies, Race Relations, and South* (1975).

EDGAR T. THOMPSON
Duke University

PLANTS, WILD. The southern region of the United States from the highlands of the Appalachians to the coastal lowlands and Florida peninsula includes a variety of physiographic and climatic environments that support a flora of great complexity and magnitude. During the ice ages, climatic changes and sea level fluctuations created and destroyed habitats, but, because of the general north-south position of the Appalachian Mountains, plants were able to migrate and follow climatic conditions that favored their survival. In contrast, some mountain ranges in Europe and Asia, which lie in an east-west position, effectively prevented the movement of plants and during these climate changes prevented the development of a flora as rich as that in the southern United States. Components of the region's flora include representatives from the North as well as many from the nearby West Indies. Over 5,000 different species of plants of more than 1,500 genera have been classified in the region.

Early explorers and botanists collected, studied, and sent back to Europe samples of the flora for classification and introduction. Three of the earliest botanists who studied the region's plants were John Bartram, who established a botanical garden in Philadelphia; Thomas Walter, who planted a garden of native plants by his house on the banks of the Santee River in South Carolina; and André Michaux, who had a botanical garden near Charleston, S.C.

Among plants from the South that have added interest and variety to ornamental horticulture include several species of deciduous azaleas (*Rhododendron calendulaceem, Rhod. canescens, Rhod. prunifolium, Rhod. speciosum* and allies) and the Catawba rhododendron (*Rhod. catawbiense*). Unusual insectivorous plants of the genus *Sarracenia* and *Drosera* are found throughout the region. The unique, rare Venus's-flytrap (*Dionaea muscipula*) is found only in specific habitats of coastal North and South Carolina.

See J. K. Small, *Manual of Southeastern Flora* (1933); A. E. Radford, H. E. Ahles, and C. R. Bell, *Flora of Carolinas* (1968); B. E. Dean, A. Mason, and J. L. Thomas, *Wildflowers of Alabama* (1973); H. W. Rickett, *Wildflowers of Southeastern States* (1967); F. Harper, *Travels of William Bartram* (1967); and B. W. Wells, *Natural Gardens* (1932).

GURDON L. TARBOX, JR.
Brookgreen Gardens

PLEASANT HILL, BATTLE OF (April 9, 1864).
After the Confederate victory at Mansfield, La., on April 8, the Union army retreated south to the village of Pleasant Hill, where N. P. Banks formed his reinforced army of no more than 13,000 men facing north to defend a low plateau. RICHARD TAYLOR hurried forward his Confederate reserves and followed the Union flight with about 12,500 men, but could not launch an attack until 4:00 P.M. Taylor probed the Union right with artillery and cavalry and sent three infantry divisions against Banks's left and center, which was driven back into the village. Union reserves counterattacked against the advancing Confederate right wing and drove it back until nightfall. After some debate Banks retreated to Grand Ecore, where he could reunite his army with the federal fleet on the Red River, thus converting a tactical victory into a strategic defeat that sealed the fate of the Union RED RIVER CAMPAIGN of 1864. Banks suffered at least 1,369 casualties. Taylor placed his losses at 1,626.

See L. H. Johnson, *Red River Campaign* (1958), most definitive; J. D. Winters, *Civil War in Louisiana* (1963); *Official Records, Armies*, Ser. 1, Vol. XXXIV; J. Scott, *32nd Iowa* (1896); and R. Taylor, *Destruction and Reconstruction* (1890).

ALWYN BARR
Texas Tech University

PLESSY V. FERGUSON (163 U.S. 537 [1896])
sustained the authority of states to maintain "separate but equal" facilities for the white and colored races. In the opinion of the U.S. Supreme Court, Justice H. B. Brown wrote:

The object of the [Fourteenth] amendment was undoubtedly to enforce the absolute equality of the two races before the law, but in the nature of things it could not have been intended to abolish distinctions based upon color, or to enforce social, as distinguished from political equality, or a commingling of the two races upon terms unsatisfactory to either. Laws permitting, and even requiring, their separation in places where they are liable to be brought into contact do not necessarily imply the inferiority of either race to the other, and have been generally, if not universally, recognized as within the competency of the state legislatures in the exercise of their police power. The most common instance of this is connected with the establishment of separate schools for white and colored children, which has been held to be a valid exercise of the legislative power even by courts of States where the political rights of the colored race have been longest and most earnestly enforced. . . .

We consider the underlying fallacy of the plaintiff's argument to consist in the assumption that the enforced separation of the two races stamps the colored race with a badge of inferiority. If this be so, it is not by reason of anything found in the act, but solely because the colored race chooses to put that construction upon it. . . . The argument also assumes that social prejudices may be overcome by legislation, and that equal rights cannot be secured to the negro except by an enforced commingling of the two races. We cannot accept this proposition. If the two races are to meet upon terms of social equality, it must be the result of natural affinities, a mutual appreciation of each other's merits and a voluntary consent of individuals.

Justice JOHN HARLAN dissented, holding that "our Constitution is color-blind, and neither knows nor tolerates classes among citizens. . . . The law regards man as man, and takes no account of surroundings or of his color when his civil rights as guaranteed by the supreme law of the land are involved."

The *Plessy* case arose from the following circumstances. A Louisiana statute required railroads carrying passengers in that state to provide separate but equal accommodations for the white and colored races. Plessy, seven-eighths Caucasian and one-eighth Negro, insisted upon going into a railroad coach reserved for white passengers. Upon arrest and prosecution, he filed a petition for writ of prohibition, challenging the constitutionality of the statute under which he was being prosecuted.

Prominent cases in which the Supreme Court reaffirmed the constitutionality of separate but equal facilities based on race were *Cummings* v. *County Board of Education* (1899) and *Gong Lum* v. *Rice* (1927). In the latter case the Court held that the question of the power of a state to classify children by race for school purposes was a question that had been "many times decided to be within the constitutional power of the state legislature to settle without intervention of the federal courts under the Federal Constitution."

A change in the attitude of the justices of the Supreme Court toward racial segregation was shown by the opinions in a number of cases dealing with higher education in the 1940s. In SWEATT V. PAINTER (1950) the Court virtually ruled out segregation in higher education. Four years later in BROWN V. BOARD OF EDUCATION it expressly overruled *Plessy* v. *Ferguson*.

See A. M. Bickel, *Supreme Court and Idea of Progress* (1970); and E. F. Waite, *Minnesota Law Review* (March, 1946).

ALBERT B. SAYE
University of Georgia

PLOCKHOY COMMUNE, first of many idealistic communitarian experiments in America, was established in 1663 on the Hoeren Kill off Delaware Bay near ZWAANENDAEL by Pieter Cornelius Plockhoy (sometimes erroneously Plockboy), a Dutch Mennonite with daring Socinian ideas. His mildly religious, socialistic plan was first put forward in 1659 in England, where he is still regarded as a father of the cooperative movement. His commune of 41 persons, supported by the burgomasters of Amsterdam, was destroyed "to a very naile" when the British seized Dutch territories in America (1664).

See L. Harder, *Delaware History* (March, 1949); J. Downie, *Peter C. Plockboy* [*sic*] (n.d.), contains text of Plockhoy's pamphlet; E. Bernstein, *Cromwell and Communism* (1930); and C. A. Weslager, *Dutch Explorers in Delaware Valley* (1961).

E. GORDON ALDERFER
Washinton, D.C.

PLYMOUTH, CAPTURE OF (April 17–20, 1864). On April 17, 1864, a Confederate army and naval force of an estimated 10,000 men commanded by General Robert Hoke attacked Plymouth, N.C., a strategic town on the south bank of the Roanoke River. This was an important supply depot for Union troops in eastern North Carolina, and the assault was part of a vigorous Confederate effort to wrest the state from Union control. Although Plymouth was heavily fortified, Confederate forces penetrated federal defenses on April 18. The next day the rebel ironclad ram *Albemarle*, under the command of James W. Cook, sank the Union gunboat *Southfield* and maintained control of the river. On April 20 Matt Ransom's brigade attacked Plymouth from the east and shelled Ft. Williams, the last remaining Union bastion. Shortly thereafter W. H. Wessells, the Union commander, surrendered 2,500 men and a vast amount of artillery, small arms, and ordnance. Hoke was promoted major general by Jefferson Davis. The fall of Plymouth led to federal evacuation of Washington, N.C., on April 27.

See W. Smith, *New York Commandery Addresses* (1891), I; *Official Records, Armies*, Ser. 1, Vol. XXXIII; and J. Barrett, *Civil War in North Carolina* (1963).

JOHN R. WENNERSTEN
University of Maryland, Princess Anne

POCAHONTAS (1595?–1617), also known as Matoaka, an Indian princess, was the daughter of POWHATAN, overchief of a confederacy of Indian tribes in Virginia. In 1608, one year after the establishment of Jamestown Colony, Captain John Smith was captured by Powhatan and, according to his account, would have been executed had Pocahontas not intervened to save his life. Historians still disagree over the veracity of Smith's tale. In 1613 Pocahontas was abducted and held hostage at Jamestown. The next year she was converted to Christianity and married John Rolfe. In 1616, with her husband and son, she visited England. In 1617, on the eve of her return to Virginia, Pocahontas died at Gravesend.

See P. L. Barbour, *Pocahontas* (1970); G. S. Woodward, *Pocahontas* (1969); M. Fishwick, *American Heritage* (Oct., 1958); E. Arber and A. G. Bradley (eds.), *Travels and Works of Captain John Smith* (2 vols.; 1910); and S. Purchas, *Purchas His Pilgrimes* (4 vols.; 1625).

ROBERT G. WEBB
Northern State College

POE, CLARENCE (1881–1964), was born to a sturdy yeoman family in Chatham County, N.C. Son of a member of the Farmers' Alliance, at age sixteen he penned an eloquent appeal for public schools to the editor of the Alliance's organ, the *Progressive Farmer*. Poe soon became editorial assistant. At eighteen he became editor; and at twenty-two he owned controlling interest. Poe expanded the weekly farm paper (as the Alliance faded away) into five intraregional editions in 1909, and the *Progressive Farmer* became the preeminent agricultural journal of the South. Poe became a respected opinion molder of farm policy, education, and other public matters. He promoted statewide PROHIBITION, boys' reformatories, public ownership of urban utilities, and efficient government. In 1912 he helped establish the SOUTHERN SOCIOLOGICAL CONGRESS. He also founded the North Carolina Conference for Social Service and served as its president (1913–1915). Both groups pioneered in penal, CHILD LABOR, educational, and public HEALTH reforms. Meanwhile Poe campaigned for a "great rural civilization" in which southern farmers would racially segregate themselves and build cooperative enterprises that would ensure the survival of the family farm and the human virtues he associated with farm life. After World War I Poe moderated his schemes and politics, although his interests remained broad.

See Poe's anecdotal *My First 80 Years* (1963); J. T. Kirby, *South Atlantic Quarterly* (Winter, 1969); and Clarence

Poe Papers, North Carolina Department of Archives and History, Raleigh.

JACK TEMPLE KIRBY
Miami University

POE, EDGAR ALLAN (1809–1849), was born in Boston, but his early life was spent chiefly in Richmond, Va., where he was taken into the family of a prosperous merchant, John Allan, after his mother died in 1811. In 1826 he was sent to the new University of Virginia, but his foster father withdrew him after a single term allegedly because young Poe had incurred heavy gambling debts. Finding homelife intolerable, Poe left for Boston in 1827, where he succeeded in publishing *Tamerlane and Other Poems* privately. Finding no employment, he joined the U.S. Army and spent some two years as a soldier. Poe published a second book of poems in Baltimore, *Al Aaraaf, Tamerlane, and Minor Poems* (1829), but received no money and little recognition for his efforts. After a short time in officers' training at West Point, he published a third volume, *Poems by Edgar A. Poe, Second Edition*, which contained most of the poems he was to write throughout his career.

The years following 1831 were difficult. Living in Baltimore, young Poe served his apprenticeship as a writer of fiction, but rewards evaded him until in 1833 he won a literary contest and the friendship of one of the judges, JOHN PENDLETON KENNEDY, who recommended Poe to the publisher of the SOUTHERN LITERARY MESSENGER in Richmond. Becoming assistant editor of the *Messenger* in 1835, Poe quickly earned a reputation as a formidable literary critic as well as a creative writer. He felt secure enough to marry his thirteen-year-old cousin Virginia Clemm in 1836. This happy state of affairs did not continue. His employer objected to Poe's occasional drinking and thought he was unduly severe in his book reviews. By January, 1837, Poe left Richmond for New York and then Philadelphia. In the latter city he became assistant editor of *Burton's Gentleman's Magazine* (1839–1840) and then assistant editor of *Graham's Magazine* (1841). He published his *Tales of the Arabesque and Grotesque* in 1840. In May, 1842, he resigned from *Graham's* to try to fulfill his lifelong ambition of publishing his own journal. Misfortune was constant, however. His financial backer withdrew support from the magazine, and Virginia Poe broke a blood vessel while singing and was never to regain her health. Although widely acclaimed as a writer, Poe was unable to find employment until 1844, when he was given a subordinate position with the New York *Evening Mirror*, a newspaper. It was in the *Evening Mirror* that his most popular poem, "The Raven," appeared on January 29, 1845. He was also able this year to publish a new edition of his poems, *The Raven and Other Poems*, on which modern texts are based, and a new edition of his fiction, entitled simply *Tales*.

With the rapidly declining health of his wife, Poe's situation became increasingly desperate. He moved his family to a cottage in Fordham, N.Y., where Virginia died in early 1847. For most of the remainder of the year Poe was in a state of collapse, but he managed to begin an essay on the nature of the universe, which he published in 1848 under the title *Eureka*. From this time until the end of his life Poe worked furiously to resurrect his project of publishing his own magazine. He finally located a financial backer but, while on a trip seeking subscribers for the magazine, Poe disappeared for a few days. He was found on the streets of Baltimore in a deplorable physical condition, and died without ever being able to reveal what had happened to him.

Misfortune continued even after Poe's death. His literary executor Rufus Wilmot Griswold published in 1850 a scurrilous biographical account of Poe in which forged passages in Poe's letters were used to make him appear to be not only an alcoholic but also an ingrate incapable of friendship and unworthy of trust. Some of these charges were believed until twentieth-century biographers disclosed Griswold's falsifications. Since his death, however, Poe has achieved an international reputation. Poe's total achievement in poetry, fiction, and literary criticism entitles him to be considered one of the classic literary figures of nineteenth-century America.

See A. H. Quinn, *Edgar Allan Poe* (1941), most reliable biography; E. H. Davidson, *Poe* (1957), first good critical study; P. F. Quinn, *French Face of Edgar Poe* (1957), shaped by French criticism; D. Halliburton, *Edgar Allan Poe* (1973), phenomenological interpretation; G. R. Thompson, *Poe's Fiction* (1973), emphasizes Poe's irony, perhaps too much; R. D. Jacobs, *Poe: Journalist and Critic* (1969); E. W. Carlson (ed.), *Recognition of Poe* (1966), critical essays; J. L. Dameron and I. B. Cauthen, Jr., *Poe Bibliography* (1974), criticism through 1967; J. W. Ostrom (ed.), *Letters of Poe* (2 vols.; 1948), excellent; and C. F. Heartman and J. R. Canny, *Bibliography of First Printings* (1943). Important collections of Poe Papers are at University of Texas, University of Virginia, New York Public, Boston Public, and Huntington libraries.

ROBERT D. JACOBS
Georgia State University

POINDEXTER, GEORGE (1779–1853), was born in Louisa County, Va., moved to Mississippi in

1802, and served that territory as attorney general, judge (1813–1817), legislator, and delegate to Congress (1807–1813). He was one of the most influential members of the Mississippi constitutional convention of 1817 and became the first congressman from the new state (1817–1819). After a term as governor (1819–1821) Poindexter in 1822 failed for reelection to Congress and spent the next eight years dogged by illness and personal tragedy. In 1830 he was appointed to fill an unexpired term in the U.S. Senate. A vain, caustic, and vindictive man, he was the embodiment of the personal, particularistic, and frequently flamboyant political style of the antebellum Southwest. While serving in the Senate (1830–1835), he emerged as one of ANDREW JACKSON's most outspoken and severe critics. A patronage dispute and Poindexter's strong support for and close connection with the Bank of the United States, as well as his championing of South Carolina's cause during the NULLIFICATION crisis, led him into a bitter personal feud with the president. Defeated by ROBERT J. WALKER in his bid as a Whig to stay in the Senate in 1836, Poindexter retired from public life.

See J. F. H. Claiborne, *Mississippi as Province, Territory, and State* (1964); M. Swearinger, *Early Life of G. Poindexter* (1934); E. A. Miles, *Jacksonian Democracy in Mississippi* (1960); and J. F. H. Claiborne Collection, Mississippi Department of Archives and History.

JAMES ROGER SHARP
Syracuse University

POINSETT, JOEL ROBERTS (1779–1851), was born at Charleston, S.C. He studied medicine in Edinburgh, Scotland, and military science at Woolrich Military Academy, after which he returned to Charleston to read law. He was asked by President James Madison to go to South America to observe the revolutions there, assess the rebels' chances of victory, and open friendly relations with them. In Chile he openly participated in battles against Spaniards, returning home in 1815 to serve in the South Carolina legislature and two terms in Congress. In 1825 he was appointed American minister to Mexico; there he negotiated a treaty of commerce, promoted Masonic lodges, and took a hand in local politics. Home once again, he openly sided with President Andrew Jackson during the NULLIFICATION controversy, forming a pro-Union volunteer militia and commanding it in Charleston. As a reward he became secretary of war in the VAN BUREN ADMINISTRATION, during which time he tried to improve the artillery and reorganize the militia. Retiring in

1841, he wrote articles on agriculture, manufacturing, science, and botany (the poinsettia is named for him).

See J. R. Poinsett, *Notes on Mexico* (1824); J. F. Rippy, *Joel R. Poinsett* (1935); and C. S. Boucher, *Nullification Controversy* (1916).

ODIE B. FAULK
Oklahoma State University

POINT LOOKOUT PRISON (1863–1865) was located at the confluence of the Potomac River and the Chesapeake Bay in southern Maryland. Originally a summer resort, it was leased in 1862 to the federal government. Initially a hospital was established there, but following the battle of GETTYSBURG a prison camp was added to the complex. It was designed to accommodate up to 10,000 prisoners, but by June, 1864, the figure stood at 15,500 and reached a high of 20,110 in April, 1865. It was administered initially as a separate military district under General Gilman Marston. But later it was included in the Department of Virginia and North Carolina. Marston was replaced by General E. W. Hinks, who in turn was succeeded by Colonel Alonzo G. Draper. The prison compound consisted basically of tents. Living conditions, food, and clothing, especially after federal retaliation for southern prison conditions, were spartan. Exposure was a serious problem. The most prevalent diseases were diarrhea, dysentery, typhoid, fevers, scurvy, and scabies. Officially, although historically debatable, 2,950 Confederates died there.

See E. W. Beitzell, *Point Lookout Prison Camp* (1972); and *Official Records, Armies*, Ser. 2, Vols. VI–VIII.

RICHARD R. DUNCAN
Georgetown University

POINT PLEASANT, BATTLE OF (October 10, 1774), fought at the junction of the Ohio and Kanawha rivers, was the major contest in Lord DUNMORE'S WAR and one of the most fiercely fought engagements between frontiersmen and Indians during the colonial period. Almost completely surprising a unit of 1,100 frontiersmen under command of Colonel Andrew Lewis, about 1,000 Indians led by such chiefs as Cornstalk, Logan, Red Hawk, and Ellinipsico (son of Cornstalk) attacked Camp Point Pleasant. For most of the battle, which lasted from dawn to sundown, both sides fought with great courage and desperation; neither side would retreat, nor could the other really advance. The colonial casualties are known to have been at least 80 dead and 140 wounded, with Indian losses assumed as high. There was no major change until late afternoon, when the Indians did a masterly job of retreating across the Ohio and the colonials fell back to their Point Pleasant defenses—both sides physically exhausted. The battle, sometimes called Kanawha, was significant not only for breaking the power of the SHAWNEE Nation, but also for being a major factor in the opening of the Kentucky region. Soon after the battle, Ft. Blair (later called Ft. Randolph) was built at the junction and later became the town of Point Pleasant, W.Va.

See R. G. Thwaites and L. P. Kellogg, *Documentary History of Dunmore's War* (1905), best; V. A. Lewis, *Battle of Point Pleasant* (1909); T. Roosevelt, *Winning of West* (1889–96); W. DeHass, *Indian Wars* (1851); and K. R. MacDonald, Jr., *West Virginia History* (Oct., 1974).

WILLIAM H. WROTEN, JR.
Salisbury State College

POLK, JAMES KNOX (1795–1849), was born in Mecklenburg County, N.C. His family moved in 1806 to the Duck River valley in Tennessee. Polk practiced law and served in the state legislature (1823–1825), in the U.S. House of Representatives (1825–1839), and as governor (1839–1841). In 1844 he was nominated by the Democratic party and defeated HENRY CLAY to become the eleventh president of the United States. He was determined to be a one-term president, a view from which he only slightly wavered during his four years in office. He came to office with a clear idea of what he wanted to accomplish, not the least of which was the expansion of the boundary of the United States to the Pacific Ocean (EXPANSIONISM). When he left office four years later the nation was half again larger than it had been when he took his oath of office. Territory was acquired out of which would be formed the states of Oregon, Washington, Idaho, California, New Mexico, Arizona, Nevada, Utah, and parts of Colorado, Montana, and Wyoming.

Polk's assumption of presidential power led him to assert actively his authority over the cabinet and lesser officials of the government. This is nowhere more pronounced than in his personal conduct of FOREIGN AFFAIRS and in his exercise of the rule of commander-in-chief. In the latter role he engineered American involvement in the Mexican War, which provides a startling comparison with recent American involvement in Latin America and Vietnam. The parallel between Polk's dismissal of General WINFIELD SCOTT and President HARRY TRUMAN's dismissal of General Douglas MacArthur is also obvious. Nor was Polk's role as chief legislator less assertive. He combined his role as leader of his party with that of chief legislator to assure success of all of his major legislative programs in four years.

His most important shortcoming was his inability to act decisively and mobilize public opinion with regard to the coming division of the nation over slavery. That he was aware of the danger is obvious, being especially apparent in his disapproval of John C. Calhoun. Unfortunately his style as a politician's politician rather than as a popular figure prevented him from providing the leadership so needed on this issue, which more than any other in the nation's history cried out for a charismatic leader. Perhaps Polk believed that the expansion of the nation would provide the space and time that would allow the slavery issue to be settled; this unfortunately did not prove to be the case. The dominant presidency for which Polk was the architect has now reached such magnitude that the need to reassert other agencies of government as a counterweight appears to diminish his record. It took the failure in Vietnam to underscore the ethical weakness of his actions in the Mexican War and the dangers implicit in manifest destiny. It is now possible to assess his presidency with a more balanced perspective.

See B. Devoto, *Year of Decision!* (1942); S. Jenkins, *James K. Polk* (1850); E. McCormac, *James K. Polk* (1922); C. A. McCoy, *Polk and Presidency* (1960); A. Nevins, *Diary of a President* (1929); M. Quaife, *Polk Diary* (4 vols.; 1910); C. Sellers, Jr., *Polk, a Jacksonian, 1795–1843* (1957) and *Polk, Continentalist, 1843–1846* (1966); Polk Papers, Library of Congress; J. H. Schroeder, *Mr. Polk's War* (1968); J. K. Polk, *Correspondence* (1969, 1972), I, II; and J. J. Farrell (ed.), *James K. Polk, 1795–1849* (1970).

CHARLES A. MCCOY
University of North Florida

POLK, LEONIDAS (1806–1864), planter, clergyman, and soldier, was born in Raleigh, N.C. He was educated at the University of North Carolina and the U.S. Military Academy, from which he graduated in 1827 eighth in his class. Choosing the career of a clergyman in the Episcopal church to that of a soldier, he attended the Virginia Theological Seminary and was ordained deacon in 1830. A month later he became assistant to Bishop Richard Channing Moore in Monumental Church, Richmond. Meanwhile, he had married Frances Ann Devereux of Raleigh. When poor health cut short his ministerial activities, he became a planter on land given him by his father in Maury County, Tenn. In 1838 Polk was appointed missionary bishop of the Southwest. In 1841 he purchased Leighton, a sugar plantation near Thibodaux, La., and a year later was appoined bishop of Louisiana.

When cholera, a tornado, and yellow fever destroyed much of his fortune, he sold his plantation and moved to New Orleans in 1854. During 1856–1860 Polk spent much time promoting the establishment of the University of the SOUTH. When Louisiana seceded in 1861 he immediately severed connection between the Diocese of Louisiana and the Protestant Episcopal Church of the United States. He went to Richmond to confer with President Jefferson Davis and while there accepted a commission of major general and command of Department No. 2. He established headquarters at Columbus, Ky., and on November 7, 1861, met the forces of General U. S. Grant in the battle of BELMONT. Following the surrender of Ft. Donelson and the evacuation of Nashville, Polk was ordered to fall back and join A. S. Johnston at Corinth. He commanded a corps at SHILOH and a wing of Braxton Bragg's army in the invasion of Kentucky. As second in rank to Bragg he was left in command while Bragg inaugurated a Confederate governor of Kentucky. Bragg later blamed him for much of the failure at PERRYVILLE, but he was promoted lieutenant general. He commanded a corps of the Army of Tennessee at STONES RIVER and a wing at CHICKAMAUGA, after which, again under Bragg's displeasure, he was removed from command. Dismissing Bragg's charges, President Davis assigned Polk to command W. J. Hardee's corps in the Army of Mississippi and Hardee to Polk's corps in the Army of Tennessee. When J. E. Johnston succeeded Bragg, Polk succeeded Johnston in Mississippi. When W. T. Sherman moved his troops from Mississippi to north Georgia and assumed command there, Polk was ordered to join Johnston and was killed while scouting atop Pine Mountain.

See W. M. Polk, *Leonidas Polk* (2 vols.; 1893); and J. H. Parks, *General Leonidas Polk* (1962). Most Polk Papers are at University of South; some are at University of North Carolina, Chapel Hill.

JOSEPH H. PARKS
University of Georgia

POLK, LEONIDAS LAFAYETTE (1837–1892), began life in Anson County, N.C. His father and mother died by the time the boy was fifteen, yet he received a good local education and attended Davidson College one year. In 1860 he won election to the state house of commons as a Union Whig. During the Civil War he raised militia in Anson, served in two North Carolina regiments, and was again elected to the legislature. After serving as a delegate to the state constitutional convention of 1865, he spent the Reconstruction

years laboring on his farm, caring for a growing family, building the town of Polkton, and editing his weekly *Ansonian*.

In 1877, as a Democrat and friend of Governor ZEBULON B. VANCE, Polk developed a plan for a state department of agriculture and was made the first commissioner. Although this agency served as a model for several other states, its governing board proved unprogressive, and Polk resigned in 1880. In 1886 he launched the *Progressive Farmer*. As both editor and orator he educated rural people, organized farmers' clubs, and advocated reorganization of the state board of agriculture. Most important, however, was his leadership of the movement to establish in Raleigh a land-grant college separate from the state university at Chapel Hill. He likewise gave impetus to the creation of a Baptist girls' school in the capital city.

When the FARMERS' ALLIANCE entered North Carolina in 1887, Polk embraced it and rose to the presidency of this "southern alliance" less than three years later. From headquarters in Washington, D.C., and on extensive tours, he voiced the discontent of southern and western farmers and crusaded against divisive postwar sectionalism. Convinced by 1891 that neither Republicans nor Democrats would legislate reform measures to help American agriculture, Polk joined the POPULIST PARTY. Three weeks before their nominating convention the next year, he died suddenly. At the time it appeared certain that he would be the third party's choice for president.

See S. Noblin, *L. L. Polk* (1949); L. L. Polk Papers, University of North Carolina, Chapel Hill; W. J. Peele, *North Carolina Baptist Almanac* (1893); J. Daniels, Raleigh *News and Observer* (July 29, 1926); and C. Poe, *Colonel Polk* (1926).

STUART NOBLIN
North Carolina State University, Raleigh

POLLARD, EDWARD ALFRED (1831–1872), journalist and historian, was born in Nelson County, Va., on Oakridge Plantation. He became one of the Confederacy's most able writers and advocates, as coeditor of the Richmond *Daily Examiner* (1861–1867) and as author of a number of books on Negro slavery, southern political and military leaders, and the campaigns and battles of the Civil War. Captured in 1864 while attempting to run the Union blockade in the steamer *Greyhound* to get to England to promote the Confederate cause, he was imprisoned for eight months at Ft. Warren and Fortress Monroe. Subsequently paroled, he founded his own weekly newspaper, *Southern Opinion*, in 1867, followed by *Political Pamphlet* in 1868. Neither was successful. Rather, it was through his historical writings that he made his most enduring impact. The best known was his classic *Lost Cause* (1867), sometimes called "the standard Southern history of the Civil War." Pollard's other major works included *Southern Spy; or, Curiosities of Negro Slavery in the South* (1859); *Letters of the Southern Spy* (1861); *Southern History of the War* (1862–1866); *Two Nations* (1864); *Observations in the North: Eight Months in Prison and Parole* (1865); *Lee and His Lieutenants* (1867); *Lost Cause Regained* (1868); *Key to the Ku Klux Klan* (1869); *Jefferson Davis* (1869); and *Virginia Tourist* (1870).

See J. P. Maddex, *Reconstruction of Edward A. Pollard* (1974).

PHILLIP R. SHRIVER
Miami University

POLL TAX, a capitation tax, was first used in the United States following the Revolutionary War when some states substituted the tax for property qualifications and thereby enlarged the suffrage (TAXATION). Gradually tax requirements were eliminated, and few states had them by the Civil War. Between 1889 and 1908, however, southern leaders adopted the tax as one of several devices to disfranchise the Negro and to discourage voting by poor whites (DISFRANCHISEMENT). At the time of adoption the tax was largely overlooked. Attention centered upon literacy and registration requirements. The rise of the POPULIST PARTY had split the white vote; had threatened white or, more accurately, Democratic supremacy; and had led to an increase in violence and fraud in elections.

Poll tax rates ranged from $1 to $2 annually. Alabama, Georgia, Mississippi, and Virginia had cumulative taxes. An Alabama voter could owe $36 since the $1.50 tax was due for each year from ages twenty-one to forty-five. Alabama reduced the cumulative period in 1953 to two years. Georgia's $1 tax accumulated from ages twenty-one to sixty, and with penalties the maximum liability amounted to $47.47. Mississippi and Virginia had two- and three-year cumulative provisions respectively, but Mississippi disallowed a single payment for the significant primary election. Payment was required by February 1 for each of the two years preceding the primary.

Elderly voters and disabled or handicapped persons generally were exempt. Some states also exempted women and veterans. Another restrictive feature of the poll tax was that payment was due several months before both the primary and general elections. In some instances a tax receipt was required when offering to vote, but most states allowed alternative methods of proving payment. Where the poll tax was tied to the suffrage, its purpose was to restrict the electorate and not to raise revenue. The revenue generated was primarily designated for education, but the amount raised was insignificant. Payment was largely voluntary and rarely enforced.

The poll tax was not the chief cause for low voter participation in the South, but it was an important voting restriction. It discouraged and prevented many citizens from voting, especially where it was cumulative. Its repeal encouraged many persons to qualify as voters. It affected white citizens more directly than Negroes.

North Carolina repealed the tax in 1920, and a poll tax repeal movement began in the 1930s when Louisiana (1934) and Florida (1937) removed it and when attention was directed to it by Congress. Georgia eliminated it in 1945, South Carolina in 1951, and Tennessee in 1953. Yet in 1964, when the Twenty-fourth Amendment prohibited poll tax payment as a voting prerequisite for federal elections, Alabama, Arkansas, Mississippi, Texas, and Virginia still required its payment for state and local elections. Arkansas repealed the tax in late 1964. The CIVIL RIGHTS ACT OF 1965 directed the U.S. Department of Justice to challenge the constitutionality of the tax in the remaining four states. In March, 1966, the U.S. Supreme Court voided Virginia's poll tax requirement on the basis that the payment of a fee to vote violates the equal protection clause of the Fourteenth Amendment. Texas voters amended their constitution in November, 1966, to repeal the tax, an insignificant *coup de grace* due to the Supreme Court decision.

See F. D. Ogden, *Poll Tax in South* (1958); T. M. Scott, in *Book of States* (1966–67), XVI, (1968–69), XVII; and *Harper* v. *Board of Elections*, 383 U.S. 663 (1966).

FREDERIC D. OGDEN
Eastern Kentucky University

PONCE DE LEÓN, JUAN (1460?–1521), the founder of Florida and first governor of Puerto Rico, was born in Santervas de Campos, Valladolid Province, Spain. Following military service against the Moors in Granada, he accompanied Christopher Columbus on the second trip to America (1493). Although Puerto Rico was discovered during that voyage, 15 years elapsed before Ponce de León established a settlement (Caparra) on the island. He served as a governor from 1509 to 1511. When Diego Columbus challenged his claim to Puerto Rico, Ponce de León received a royal commission to colonize Bimini, an island of fabulous wealth and the "fountain of youth." In 1513 he commanded three ships sailing northward through the Bahama Channel and along the mainland coast. The *adelantado* named the new area Florida since his discovery coincided with the Easter season (*Pascua Florida*). Sometime after April 2 the Spaniards landed somewhere between the present site of St. Augustine and the mouth of the St. John's River. They claimed Florida for their sovereign and then sailed southward around the peninsula to the Gulf coast, perhaps as far west as Pensacola. Harried by hostile Indians, Ponce de León returned to Puerto Rico without wealth or youth. In 1521, following years of fighting in the Caribbean, he attempted another conquest of Florida. Indians attacked the Spanish force, fatally wounding Ponce de León. He died in Cuba and was buried in Puerto Rico.

See W. Lowery, *Spanish Settlements* (1905), I; J. Winsor, *History of America* (1886); and A. Herrera, *History of America* (1725), I, II.

ROBERT L. GOLD
Southern Illinois University

PONTCHARTRAIN, LAKE, more properly a lagoon, is located near the Gulf coast in Louisiana and was first explored by IBERVILLE in 1699. It is approximately 25 miles by 41 miles in size, and its average depth runs between ten and 16 feet. It is joined to the Mississippi River by a canal at New Orleans. Its natural drainage, however, is through Rigolets and Chef Menteur channels and into the Gulf of Mexico by way of Lake Borgne. Its shore served as a popular antebellum resort area.

See J. P. Baugham, *Louisiana History* (Winter, 1962).

POOR WHITES is a derogatory term applied in antebellum days to that class of nonslaveholders below YEOMEN FARMERS, artisans, and frontiersmen. It was suggested by the descriptive details, subjective comments, and broad generalizations that abound in the travel literature of this period, notably the writings of FREDERICK LAW OLMSTED. The existence of this unfortunate group was recognized by well-to-do southerners, who compared them to northern slum dwellers and applied to them such derisive expressions as "CLAY EATERS," "poor white trash," "peckerwoods," and "crackers." The term thus carried a stigma beyond poverty.

"Poor whites" originally composed a comparatively small group of poverty-stricken white yeomanry, whose number probably never exceeded 10 percent of the South's white population. They found themselves stranded on the ebbing frontier of PINE BARRENS, sandhills, and mountains. Those who lived on the unproductive lands between plantations were considered nuisances, and planters did their best to get rid of them.

Victims of their isolated environment, poor whites generally lived in squalid huts and stayed alive by hunting and fishing; by growing corn, sweet potatoes, collards, and pumpkins; and by keeping a few pigs and steers and a cow, all roaming the woods at little expense to their owners. Many were illiterate, shiftless, and irresponsible; often they were vicious, and nearly always the men were blissful tipplers of "rotgut" whiskey. Common among the sandhillers were dirt eating, snuff dipping, and tobacco chewing.

Modern scholars recognize that among the important causes of the shiftlessness and irresponsibility of poor whites were several diseases that were caused by poverty, a diet consisting principally of corn and pork, and the primitive state of public HEALTH. Most serious of these diseases were HOOKWORM and MALARIA. PELLAGRA may also have existed, though little is known about it before 1900. Hookworm was not limited to the poor, but they were its principal victims, especially those of the sandy soil regions. Victims spoke of this enervating ailment as the "lazy disease." Also widespread by 1800 was malaria. It too was enervating and produced some of the symptoms of hookworm. None of these diseases were brought under control until the twentieth century.

Antebellum life among the poor was comparatively easy for the man. Surrounded by lean hounds, he often spent hours absentmindedly whittling. The woman, on the other hand, was a beast of burden. She married at an early age, bore children, hoed, cooked, and even cut wood. Actually, the economy of the poor whites contained both nomadic and agricultural features. Its patriarchs were primarily hunters, fishermen, and stock raisers, whose mobility was limited by both the plantation and the need to grow food. They were stubbornly independent and intensely proud. Many of their problems have long since merged with the unsolved ones of twentieth-century poverty.

See A. N. J. Den Hollander, in W. T. Couch, *Culture in South* (1935); C. Eaton, *History of Old South* (1966); F. L. Owsley, *Plain Folk of Confederacy* (1949); G. L. Cates, "Medical History of Georgia, 1733–1833" (Ph.D. dissertation, University of Georgia, 1976).

HORACE MONTGOMERY
University of Georgia

POPLAR SPRING CHURCH, BATTLE OF (September 29–October 1, 1864), also known as the battle of Peebles' Farm, was part of U. S. Grant's strategy to encircle Petersburg and force R. E. Lee to surrender it and Richmond (RICHMOND-PETERSBURG CAMPAIGN). Grant launched a two-part attack: one directed at Ft. Harrison, close to the Confederate capital; the second aimed at the Southside Railroad and the two roads (Boydton Plank and Squirrel Level) that supplied Petersburg from the southwest. While Union troops were successfully capturing Ft. Harrison (September 29), 16,000 soldiers struck the Confederate right flank south of Petersburg, commanded by WADE HAMPTON. On September 30 Poplar Spring Church was taken. On October 1 Hampton, reinforced by Henry Heth, was preparing to attack when a false rumor that Union troops had gotten behind him stopped him. Grant had extended his left flank three miles west forcing the Confederates to also stretch their thin lines. Union losses were approximately 2,500; Confederate losses were probably considerably less.

See R. W. Lykes, *Campaign for Petersburg* (1970), concise; R. U. Johnson and C. C. Buel (eds.), *Battles and Leaders* (1888), IV; U. S. Grant, *Memoirs* (1885); and D. S. Freeman, *R. E. Lee* (1935).

RICHARD W. LYKES
University of Virginia, Northern Regional Center,
and George Mason University

POPULAR SOVEREIGNTY was a major political idea of the period 1847 to 1861. It first arose in response to the WILMOT PROVISO, which specifically called for the exclusion of slavery from any territory annexed as a result of the Mexican War. The appeal of free soil in the North prompted northern Democrats to seek an alternative. Lewis Cass, the Democratic candidate of 1848, first defined popular sovereignty on December 29, 1847, in a letter to A. O. P. Nicholson of Nashville, Tenn. It proposed that territorial residents decide whether they wanted slavery.

It was reintroduced politically by Stephen A. Douglas in the New Mexico and Utah acts of the COMPROMISE OF 1850. These acts left it to the residents of a territory whether to introduce or exclude slavery. In 1854 Douglas extended it to the KANSAS-NEBRASKA ACT. The resulting political upheaval smashed the Whigs, divided the Democrats, and gave rise to the Republicans. In Kansas the introduction of the measure precipitated a violent sectional struggle.

In the Lincoln-Douglas debates (1858), Douglas at Freeport, Ill., restated his position that the people of a territory could exclude slavery before they ratified a state constitution. Doulgas' position solidified southern opposition to his presidential nomination in 1860. Thus the issue of popular sovereignty split the Democrats at the CHARLESTON CONVENTION and climaxed the national political rift that ended in the Civil War.

See E. Foner, *Free Soil, Free Labor, Free Men* (1970); C. W. Morrison, *Democratic Politics and Sectionalism* (1967); and D. M. Potter, *Impending Crisis, 1848–1861* (1976).

JAMES P. SHENTON
Columbia University

POPULIST PARTY or People's party of the United States was officially created at Omaha, Neb., on July 4, 1892. The radical Omaha Platform of the new third party tracked platforms promulgated at St. Louis in 1889, at Ocala, Fla., in 1890, and at Indianapolis in 1891 by a mass citizens' institution known as the National Farmers' Alliance and Industrial Union. Much of the institutional and ideological meaning of populism—as the agrarian movement came to be known—was derived from the earlier experience of the FARMERS' ALLIANCE in organizing some 1.5 million farmers in the South and West.

The Alliance had constituted itself as a "national" institution in 1887 when its scope was confined to Texas, where the organizing had taken root through the preceding decade. Emphasizing methods of cooperative marketing and purchasing that had been developed in the founding years, Alliance lecturers fanned out across the South in 1887–1888 and across the West in 1888–1890, recruiting hard-pressed farmers by the hundreds of thousands. At the heart of the agrarian political and economic creed was an ambitious plan to restructure the national monetary system so as to lessen the influence of eastern commercial bankers on the nation's system of credit. The Alliance plan, derived from earlier "greenback" monetary ideas, was known as the SUBTREASURY PLAN, and its details were exhaustively spelled out by its originator CHARLES W. MACUNE, first national president of the Alliance.

Farmers joined what came to be known as the "agrarian revolt" as a means of escaping a national system of usurious credit that had the effect of reducing millions of agriculturalists to impoverishment and landless tenantry. In addition to the elaborate remedies espoused in the subtreasury system, the agrarian platforms of the late 1880s—popularly known as the "Alliance demands"—also called for regulation or government ownership of the railroads and telegraph industries and a series of proposed land reforms aimed at preventing corporate ownership of farmland by railroad, land, and cattle syndicates. These sundry Alliance demands formed the entirety of the 1892 Omaha Platform of the People's party.

The 1892 presidential candidate of the new party, General James B. Weaver, a veteran Greenbacker from Iowa, polled over 1 million votes in 1892, and the party elected hundreds of local officials in the farming districts of the South and West. Countering the post–Civil War sectional feelings that grouped most northern farmers in the Republican party and most southern farmers in the Democratic party, the third party scored impressive gains in the 1894 state and congressional campaigns across the South. The movement was particularly strong in Georgia, Alabama, and Texas. Through "fusion" with the Republican party, populism appeared to have considerable influence in North Caroina as well.

The third-party cause, however, suffered a setback in the West in 1894, which led to a drive by silver mineowners to champion "free silver" as a means of capturing both the Populist and the national Democratic party, the latter having been severely weakened by voter dissatisfaction following the depression of 1893. Assisted by various cooperating Populist officeholders, the silver lobby was instrumental in the 1895–1896 political developments that led to the presidential nomination of William Jennings Bryan by both the Democratic and People's parties. In a celebrated "battle of the standards" between gold and silver, Bryan was defeated by Republican William McKinley in the ELECTION OF 1896. The greenback monetary issues of the Populists were subsumed in this struggle, and the third party ceased to be relevant politically on a national scale after 1896.

See C. V. Woodward, *Origins of New South* (1951), comprehensive on agrarian revolt; L. Goodwyn, *Democratic Promise: Populist Movement in America* (1976); and J. Hicks, *Populist Revolt* (1931). Excellent state histories are A. M. Arnett, *Populist Movement in Georgia* (1922); W. W. Rogers, *One-Gallused Rebellion* (1970), Alabama; W. I. Hair, *Bourbonism and Agrarian Protest in Louisiana* (1969); and R. Martin, *People's Party in Texas* (1933). See also H. G. Edmonds, *Negro and Fusion Politics in North Carolina* (1951); G. B. Tindall, *South Carolina Negroes, 1877–1900* (1952); C. V. Woodward, *Tom Watson* (1963, 1973); S. Noblin, *Leonidas L. Polk* (1949); T. Saloutos, *Farmer Movements in South, 1865–1933* (1960); R. C. McMath, Jr., *Populist Vanguard* (1975); S. Hackney, *Populism to Progressivism in Alabama* (1969); R. F. Durden, *Climax of Populism* (1966); and H. Woodman, *King Cotton and His Retainers, 1800–1925* (1968).

LAWRENCE GOODWYN
Duke University

PORT ARTHUR, TEX.

PORT ARTHUR, TEX. (pop. 57,371), faces onto Sabine Lake, a body of water formed by the Sabine and Neches rivers, approximately 20 miles southeast of Beaumont and 15 miles north of the Gulf of Mexico. Although the general vicinity of this east Texas city was explored in 1543 by HERNANDO DE SOTO and settled by Spanish and American colonists during the eighteenth century, development of this site has been relatively recent. After John Sparks settled here in 1836, a small market village known as Aurora grew up only to be totally destroyed by a combination of disease and hurricanes. In 1895, however, a group of real estate developers founded a new city on the site and named it for Arthur Stilwell, one of the group's backers. Intended to be a rail terminus and deepwater ocean port for the shipment of cattle, the city began dredging a ship channel from Sabine Lake to the Gulf. After the discovery of PETROLEUM at SPINDLETOP in 1901, oil rather than cattle became the city's primary product.

See W. F. Stewart, *Collision of Giants* (1966); Federal Writers' Project, *Port Arthur* (1940); H. L. Hunt, *History of Port Arthur* (1926); F. Leverett, "Stilwell" (M.A. thesis; University of Texas, 1955); K. L. Bryant, Jr., *Southwestern Historical Quarterly* (July, 1971); and files of Port Arthur *News* (1897–).

PORTER, KATHERINE ANNE

PORTER, KATHERINE ANNE (1890–), is a native of Indian Creek, Tex. At the age of sixteen, after convent and other private schooling, she ran away from home to marry. This was the first of three marriages in a peripatetic life marked by sickness and privation until Porter was in her sixties. She traveled widely in early life, especially in Mexico and Germany. Her first story, "Maria Concepcion," was published in 1922; her first book, *Flowering Judas and Other Stories*, in 1930. By 1939 she had written her most important fiction, the best of which appears in *Pale Horse, Pale Rider*. Since then she has published a novel, *Ship of Fools* (1962), parts of which serially appeared from 1944 through 1959; and until 1967 she continued regularly to write the miscellaneous journalism (criticism, biographical sketches, personal essays) that was collected in 1970. *The Collected Stories* (1965) embodies all 26 of Porter's short fictions. Her reputation is essentially based upon this work, and it will continue to be. She is a brilliant stylist whose characteristic fiction is written out of the memory of her past. Her reach is limited, but her grasp is sure.

See L. Hartley (ed.), *Katherine Anne Porter* (1969).

GEORGE CORE
Sewanee Review

PORTER, WILLIAM SYDNEY (1862–1910), known to millions as O. Henry, was born and reared in Greensboro, N.C. A licensed pharmacist, he moved in 1882 to Texas, where for the next 15 years he pursued a varied career. In 1887 he married the stepdaughter of a prominent Austin merchant and began working as a draftsman in the Texas Land Office. Later he became a teller in the First National Bank and, in 1894, began publishing his own humor weekly, *Rolling Stone*. During the next three years Porter's fortunes suffered disastrously: accused of embezzlement in 1895, he was arrested in Houston while writing for the *Post*; he fled to Honduras but returned after a year to stand trial in Austin after his wife's death. Convicted in 1898, many believe unjustly, he began serving time at the federal penitentiary in Ohio, where his professional career as a short-story artist got under way. A dozen or so of his stories written in prison were published nationally; upon his release in 1901, he became a feature writer for the Pittsburgh *Dispatch* and continued publishing stories in New York magazines. Porter moved to New York in 1902 and quickly attained worldwide popularity as hundreds of his stories, appearing first in magazines under the new pseudonym, were reissued in nine volumes beginning with *Cabbages and Kings* (1904) and *The Four Million* (1906). He is buried in Asheville, N.C.

See E. S. Arnett, *O. Henry from Polecat Creek* (1962); E. Current-Garcia, *Studies in Short Fiction* (Fall, 1964) and *O. Henry* (1965); G. Langford, *Alias O. Henry* (1957); and C. A. Smith, *O. Henry* (1916). R. O'Connor, *O. Henry* (1970), is disappointing. Additional references are in P. S. Clarkson, *Bibliography of W. S. Porter* (1938); and E. Current-Garcia, in L. Rubin (ed.), *Bibliographical Guide to Southern Literature* (1969).

EUGENE CURRENT-GARCIA
Auburn University

PORT HUDSON, SIEGE OF (1863), lasted 45 days. It culminated in a Union victory undertaken to eliminate all major Confederate military strength from the Vicksburg, Miss., area. The siege produced no significant military heroics. Tactical strategies used by both sides have been repeatedly criticized. The Union decision to capture Port Hudson had little importance because after the fall of VICKSBURG the military work of Port Hudson was academic. By May, 1863, a federal army of 13,000 men commanded by General Nathaniel P. Banks lay siege to Port Hudson, La., a Confederate stronghold about 20 miles north of Baton Rouge. Confederate defenders commanded by General Franklin Gardner numbered less than 6,000. Three major assaults against Confederate defenses were repulsed with heavy Union losses, weakening the morale of Union troops. Luckily for General Banks, the Confederates ran out of food and, with no likelihood of relief, surrendered on July 9. The last Confederate military obstruction on the Mississippi had fallen.

See E. A. Davis, *Louisiana* (1961), brief account, importance to Louisiana; R. Johnson, *Campfires and Battlefields* (1958), evaluation of military tactics and strategy; and B. Catton, *Hallowed Ground* (1956), human side of war.

NOEL GRAY
Southern University

PORT REPUBLIC, BATTLE OF (June, 1862), did much to establish STONEWALL JACKSON's reputation as one of the great tacticians. The overture to the engagement found strong Union forces, commanded by John C. Frémont and James Shields, operating on separate sides of the South River in the foothills of the Blue Ridge. Jackson seized control of the most significant crossing at Port Republic, Va., thereby enabling himself to operate against either Union group. A part of Jackson's forces under RICHARD EWELL put a bold front across the line upon which Frémont was advancing to hold him in place. Meanwhile Jackson led an assault on Shields in which the Union forces were driven from the field losing some 450 prisoners. More important, Union apprehensions about Washington were strengthened, plans for reinforcing G. B. McClellan's campaign against Richmond were altered, and Jackson's forces were themselves added to the forces defending the Confederate capital. In one authority's judgment, seldom had fewer troops accomplished more.

See D. S. Freeman, *Lee's Lieutenants* (1950); W. Allan, *Jackson's Campaign in Shenandoah Valley* (1912); G. F. R. Henderson, *Stonewall Jackson* (1898); F. Vandiver, *Mighty Stonewall* (1957); and J. C. Ropes, *Story of Civil War* (4 vols.; 1894–1913).

DAVID A. WILLIAMS
California State University, Long Beach

PORT ROYAL SOUND, CAPTURE OF (November 7, 1861). The Confederate forts guarding this sheltered anchorage in South Carolina—Walker on Hilton Head and Beauregard on Bay Point, together mounting 43 guns and commanded by Thomas F. Drayton—were attacked by Samuel Francis Du Pont's 17 Union warships on November 7, 1861. After several hours of bombardment by the fleet's heavy guns, during which attackers and defenders suffered few casualties, both forts were abandoned. Port Royal Sound served as the South Atlantic Blockading Squadron's principal base for the remainder of the war and supported operations against Charleston and the coasts of Georgia and Florida. Du Pont's victory demonstrated that steamers armed with shell guns could fight forts and led ROBERT E. LEE to withdraw the region's coastal defenses farther inland.

See D. Ammen, *Old Navy and New* (1891); J. D. Hayes, *Du Pont Civil War Letters* (1969), I; J. T. Scharf, *C.S. Navy* (1887); J. M. Merrill, *Rebel Shore* (1957); B. Anderson, *By Sea and River* (1962); and R. E. Johnson, *John Rodgers* (1967). *Official Records, Navies*, Ser. 1, Vol. XII, describes battle as planned, not as fought. Works repeating this error include D. Ammen, *Atlantic Coast* (1883); D. Knox, *U.S. Navy* (1936); H. A. du Pont, *S. F. Du Pont* (1926); and H. P. Nash, *Naval History of Civil War* (1972).

ROBERT ERWIN JOHNSON
University of Alabama

PORTSMOUTH, VA. (pop. 110,963), is on the Elizabeth River and HAMPTON ROADS opposite the city of Norfolk. The site was first plotted in 1750, and, after the location here in 1752 of a Royal Navy yard, the town prospered as a shipbuilding center. The opening in 1812 of the Dismal Swamp Canal made Portsmouth a commercial port in its own right, independent of Norfolk and Newport News. Although the British occupied the city during the American Revolution and attacked it during the War of 1812, more destructive to the city than either of these two events were the great fire of 1821 and the decimating YELLOW FEVER epidemic of 1855. Meanwhile the former British navy yard had become an operation of the U.S. Navy. At the outbreak of the Civil War, federal authorities ordered the evacuation and destruction of the navy yard, including the recently commissioned *Merrimack*, which was undergoing engine repairs (April 20–21, 1861). After the duel of the MONITOR AND MERRIMACK (March 9, 1862), Confederate forces withdrew from Portsmouth (May, 1862), but only after setting fire to and once again destroying the navy yards. Subsequently rebuilt, Portsmouth's Norfolk Navy Yard has built and serviced naval craft for each of this nation's wars. The modern city also is a manufacturer of fertilizers, furniture, chemicals, and textiles and is a shipper of processed seafood, cotton, lumber, soybeans, and tobacco. Historic points of interest besides the old navy yard include several eighteenth-century homes, Trinity Church (1762), and the U.S. Naval Hospital (1827–1830).

See M. W. Butt, *Portsmouth Under Four Flags* (1961, 1971); M. M. Holladay, *History of Portsmouth* (1936); E.

Pollock, *Sketch Book of Portsmouth* (1886); W. H. Stewart, *History of Norfolk County* (1902); L. H. Snyder, "Great Depression in Portsmouth" (M.A. thesis, Radford, 1974); L. A. Deans, *Brief History of Public Education in Portsmouth* (n.d.); and E. P. Lull, *History of U.S. Navy Yard* (1874). See also files of Norfolk and Portsmouth *Herald* (1794–1861) and *Ledger-Star* (1876–).

POSTAL SERVICE. The first permanent postal system in the English colonies in North America began in 1693 under the ownership of Thomas Neale, to whom the British government had given the postal monopoly in America. Neither Maryland nor Virginia joined Neale's system, however, and the mails ran no farther south than Delaware in the 1690s. Not until 1732 was regular mail extended to Virginia. By then Neale's monopoly had been taken over by the government in England and deputy postmasters general appointed to oversee the operation of the British post office in America.

In 1753 Benjamin Franklin became one of the deputy postmasters general and subsequently made the service so efficient that in 1761 the post office produced a profit. Franklin, however, was removed from his post in 1774, and the colonists organized an independent postal service, which was soon controlled by the Second Continental Congress. The system, reorganized in 1782, remained in operation through the adoption of the Constitution.

Under the authority given it by the Constitution, Congress took control of the confederation postal system, and by the laws of 1792 and 1794 promulgated the nation's postal policy. The U.S. Post Office was to be self-supporting, but it was not to produce a revenue for the treasury. All profits were to be used to extend the mail service to westering Americans.

By 1836, 11,091 post offices had been established and the mails were being carried over some 112,000 miles of post roads, nearly half of which ran through the 14 slave states. This rapid spread of the mail service made possible the broad dissemination of abolitionist literature and forced the South to censor the mails after 1836. Moreover, the extension of mail service over sparsely settled southern post roads produced postal deficits and forced Congress to decide whether the extension of mail service should take precedence over a balanced postal budget or vice versa. Largely because of southern insistence, Congress opted for a service-first policy in 1851, when it declared that neither existing mail service nor future extensions of the mail service were to be curtailed because of postal deficits.

Postal deficits thereafter became the rule, but

the South profited from the policy. Between 1850 and 1861, largely because of southern influence in the Post Office Department, more than 2,000 post offices and over 25,000 miles of post roads were established in the states of the future Confederacy. In 1859 and 1860 some of this service had to be curtailed, which so angered southern legislators that the mails, according to one historian, became "one of the less tangible factors leading to the Civil War." How expensive the service in the South had become was indicated by the fact that, when it was suspended there during the war, postal revenues exceeded expenditures even though the postal service itself was being modernized with such expensive innovations as city free delivery (1863), a money order system (1864), and railway post offices (1864).

After 1876, when the Democrats periodically controlled the U.S. House of Representatives, southern congressmen again became influential in postal affairs, and the service was rapidly extended through the old Confederacy. Between 1879 and 1891 the star route network was completed in the region, and the number of post offices increased from 11,209 to more than 19,000. Besides securing mail service for their own region, southerners were also instrumental in the establishment of the rural free delivery of mail (1896), postal savings banks (1910), and parcel post (1913).

As in the antebellum period, the mail service in the South did not pay its way, but the South and the nation profited from the expense. The mail service brought catalogs, advertisements, and uncensored northern opinion into southern homes, which helped tie the area into the national economy and heal the wounds remaining from the war. Moreover, the postal service helped woo southerners from the traditional states' rights position so that, almost to a man, southern members of Congress supported the Federal Highway Act of 1916, which provided that the national government could help states build and repair post roads.

Following the establishment of airmail (1918), few major changes were made in the mail service until 1970. In that year, some southern members of Congress vigorously opposed the proposed establishment of a postal corporation and the change in policy that would make a balanced postal budget more important than service, because they feared such a policy would mean a curtailment of their nonpaying postal services. On this measure, however, southerners who had long been successful in securing the postal legislation they desired were defeated and forced to accept a change in the postal policy that had served the area so well.

See C. Eaton, *American Historical Review* (Jan., 1943); C. Scheele, *History of Mail* (1970); and W. E. Fuller, *R.F.D.* (1964), *American Mail* (1972), and *Journal of Southern History* (Nov., 1959).

WAYNE E. FULLER
University of Texas, El Paso

POST OF ARKANSAS, BATTLE OF. See ARKANSAS POST, BATTLE OF

POTOMAC RIVER, one of the most beautiful and historic streams in North America, is formed near Meadow Mountain, W.Va. Rising at a point near the headwaters of the Ohio River system, its branches merge at a point near CUMBERLAND, MD. From there the river cuts through the Blue Ridge Mountains at Harpers Ferry, forms the boundary between Virginia and Maryland, and flows past Alexandria, Georgetown, and the District of Columbia to the Chesapeake Bay. Its entire course runs approximately 290 miles. Early colonists established plantations along its banks below present-day Washington and navigated upstream in oceangoing vessels to that point. Above Washington and Georgetown, however, the Great Falls of the Potomac made further transit impossible. A drop in the river's level of 35 feet in a 200-foot gorge, this cataract is part of an 80-foot descent over a short two-mile stretch of the river. George Washington dreamed of damming the river at this point, using its rapids as a power source, and making the upper river navigable by a system of canals. Although the Chesapeake & Ohio Canal eventually did permit transit upstream to Cumberland, canal commerce was short lived and the Potomac never realized Washington's dreams for it.

See F. A. Gutheim, *Potomac* (1949); M. S. Waggoner, *Long Haul West* (1958); and G. W. Ward, *Early Development of C & O Canal* (1899).

POTTAWATOMIE MASSACRE (May 24, 1856) was the systematic murder of five proslavery Kansas settlers by a small band of Free-Soilers led by John Brown. Brown, an unstable middle-aged ne'er-do-well and avowed abolitionist, went to the troubled Kansas Territory in the summer of 1855 determined to strike a blow against slavery. The massacre was probably a reprisal for the attack on Lawrence by southerners on May 21 (W. C. QUANTRILL) and may have resulted also from local political grievances. Brown, with four sons and two other men, called the victims from their cabins near Dutch Henry's Crossing of Pottawatomie Creek and shot and hacked them to death. The crime was the worst outrage that had yet occurred in Kansas and was responsible for an immediate widening of bloodshed there (BLEEDING KANSAS). Warrants were issued for the arrest of six members of the Brown family and two other men. One participant, James Townsley, was arrested, but the case never went to trial. John Brown himself remained active in local guerrilla warfare through the summer and fall of the year.

See J. C. Malin, *Kansas Historical Quarterly* (May, 1938) and *John Brown* (1942); O. G. Villard, *John Brown* (1910); and A. Nevins, *Ordeal of Union* (1947), II.

STEPHEN G. CARROLL
Missouri Western State College

POTTER, DAVID MORRIS (1910–1971), was born in Augusta, Ga., and educated at Emory (B.A., 1932) and Yale (M.A., 1933; Ph.D., 1940). After teaching at the University of Mississippi and the Rice Institute, he went to Yale in 1942, remaining there until 1961, when he moved to Stanford University. Potter was the author of *Lincoln and His Party in the Secession Crisis* (1942), a revisionist study of the critical period between the election of 1860 and the firing on Ft. Sumter; *People of Plenty* (1954), a brilliant interpretation that singled out "economic abundance" as the main determinant of the American character; *The South and the Sectional Conflict* (1968), a collection of penetrating essays; and *The Impending Crisis, 1848–1861* (1976), an ambitious treatment of the coming of the Civil War. He found the history of the South "perennially compelling," not only because of his southern background but also because historically the region had been the focus of two of the most profound and most difficult problems in the nation's experience—its "enduring distinctiveness and combative sectionalism" and its long adherence to "racial distinctions." Potter rejected the idea of the South as an agrarian society, explaining the survival of its folk culture in terms of its inhabitants' personalism and persistent local attachments. Potter was a seminal contributor to the modern study of the southern past. His work was distinguished by the originality and penetration of his intellect, by his faculty for finding new meaning in even the most familiar phenomena, and by his sensitivity to the complexity of human motivation.

See D. Brogan, in M. Cunliffe and R. W. Winks (eds.), *Pastmasters* (1969); J. A. Garraty, *Interpreting American History* (1970); D. E. Fehrenbacher *et al.*, *Journal of American History* (Sept., 1971); and C. N. Degler, *American Historical Review* (Oct., 1971).

DEWEY W. GRANTHAM
Vanderbilt University

POULTRY INDUSTRY of the South comprises three different activities that for the most part are unrelated: broiler chicken, egg, and turkey production. Broiler chicken production historically has been of greater significance to the southern economy than the other two activities, although in recent years both egg and turkey production have increased in importance. The modern broiler industry as characterized by mass production techniques dates from the 1930s. Prior to that time most chickens produced for meat sale were by-products of egg production and the "spring hatch." Surplus female and male chickens were sold for meat, and almost every farm produced a small number of chickens for sale each year.

Several high density production regions began to emerge in the South beginning in the late 1930s and continuing through the 1950s. These areas were characterized by large-scale operations and the use of specialized production techniques. The first regions to appear were northern Georgia centered in the area of Gainesville and northwest Arkansas in the vicinity of Fayetteville. These two regions have remained major broiler chicken production areas in the South as well as the entire nation. By the late 1940s two additional regions had emerged: south-central Mississippi and central North Carolina. The most recent specialized production region in the South is northern Alabama, centered in Cullman County, which began to develop during the 1950s.

The emergence of these five major broiler regions was related to existing farm conditions. These areas had been characterized by small farms, low farm and family incomes, and the loss of a previous source of farm income such as cotton or fruit production. The growing of broiler chickens was enthusiastically accepted by farmers in these areas as an attractive alternative source of farm income. The reason for the specific localities where the industry emerged (such as Gainesville, Ga.) was related to the role of entrepreneurs like J. D. Jewell and promotional efforts of agricultural officials. North Carolina, Georgia, Alabama, Mississippi, Arkansas, and Texas account for approximately two-thirds of U.S. broiler production. These areas have become dominant broiler supply regions for many of the nation's markets.

Egg production has expanded more recently in the South. Some of the same regions that were major broiler producers have now become important egg production areas. These two different activities utilize similar services and facilities including feed supply units and similar types of chicken houses. The South's important position nationally as an egg-producing region is indicated by the fact that Georgia, North Carolina, and Arkansas are among the five leading egg-producing states. In recent years production has exceeded that occurring in traditional midwestern egg production states such as Minnesota, Iowa, and Indiana.

Although the South has not been as important nationally in turkey production as in broiler and egg production, it nevertheless accounts for an important share of U.S. output. The turkey industry too has developed more recently in the South than the broiler chicken industry. North Carolina is now the second largest turkey-producing state in the nation, with Arkansas and Virginia also being major producers.

See B. F. Lobin and H. B. Arthur, *Dynamics of Broiler Industry* (1964); J. D. Lord, *Southeastern Geography* (April, 1971) and *Professional Geographer* (Nov., 1972); A. Kushner, *Atlanta Economic Review* (June, 1966); and I. A. Moke, *Journal of Geography* (Oct., 1967).

J. DENNIS LORD
University of North Carolina, Charlotte

POWHATAN (1550?–1618), whose correct name was Wahunsonacock, father of POCAHONTAS, was chief of most of the ALGONQUIN tribes in TIDEWATER Virginia when the English settled Jamestown in 1607. The 30-odd tribes under his control lived between the Potomac and James rivers, as well as the Eastern Shore of Virginia, and were known as the Powhatan Confederacy. Approximately 9,000 Algonquin Indians, living in over 200 villages, were members of this confederacy. The large area under Powhatan's rule comprised more than 8,000 square miles, slightly larger than the state of Massachusetts. Powhatan was a crafty, ambitious, often cruel, and capable ruler. John Smith described him as "a tall, well proportioned man, with a sower look, his head somewhat gray, his beard so thinne, that it seemeth none at all, his age [in 1608] neare sixtie, of a very able and hardy body to endure any labour." Although he did not trust the English settlers, he was able to get along with them fairly well, especially after the marriage of his daughter Pocahontas to John Rolfe in 1614. After this event, Indian-white relations were quite peaceful in tidewater Virginia until the great chieftain's death.

See B. C. McCary, *Indians in Seventeenth-Century Virginia* (1957); J. Smith, *Travels and Works of J. Smith* (2 vols.; 1910); and D. I. Bushnell, *Virginia Before Jamestown* (1940).

J. PAUL HUDSON
Colonial National Historical Park

PRAIRIE GROVE, BATTLE OF (December 7, 1862), marked the failure of a Confederate attempt to expel federal forces from Arkansas. James G. Blunt, invading Arkansas in 1862, divided his Union army into two detachments, commanded by himself and Francis J. Herron. Confederate General THOMAS C. HINDMAN moved his I Corps north to meet Blunt. Hindman hoped to crush Blunt's 5,000 soldiers, then turn and defeat Herron. Blunt overpowered Hindman's cavalry under General JOHN S. MARMADUKE at Cane Hill on November 28. As Herron and 6,000 men rushed to Blunt's support, Hindman interposed his army between the two federal forces. On December 7, Marmaduke's cavalry routed Herron's advance

POULTRY PRODUCTION IN THE SOUTH, 1880–1969
(thousands of heads)

	1880 (chickens only)	1890 (chickens only)	1900	1910	1920	1930	1940	1950	1959	1969	% of U.S. Total
Ala.	2,100	6,252	4,867	4,674	6,011	5,571	5,985	5,814	8,113	16,242	4.3
Ark.	1,830	6,264	5,498	5,266	7,029	6,180	6,339	5,487	7,279	24,683	6.6
Del.	269	900	648	794	947	1,612	916	763	1,045	673	.18
Fla.	439	920	1,141	1,263	1,573	2,019	2,053	2,404	5,214	17,067	4.56
Ga.	2,266	7,358	4,653	4,970	7,300	5,459	5,900	5,587	12,251	34,936	9.3
Ky.	3,577	12,741	7,129	8,189	10,646	9,303	8,240	8,209	5,883	2,866	.76
La.	1,113	2,247	4,006	3,312	3,800	4,180	4,205	3,754	3,648	4,237	1.1
Md.	1,061	3,431	2,215	2,711	3,492	4,056	3,191	2,991	2,347	1,973	.5
Miss.	1,936	5,632	5,275	4,656	6,422	5,466	6,089	5,860	7,486	12,430	3.3
Mo.	6,810	22,786	15,370	20,220	25,132	25,442	19,000	16,904	13,748	7,887	2.0
N.C.	2,072	7,508	3,993	4,637	7,490	6,590	7,359	9,023	13,389	18,486	4.9
S.C.	1,108	3,874	2,785	2,759	4,028	3,137	3,408	3,608	5,260	6,980	1.85
Tenn.	3,482	12,062	6,378	7,460	11,441	9,034	8,051	8,059	6,912	5,137	1.37
Tex.	3,128	11,524	14,211	13,083	18,541	25,309	22,507	17,169	19,100	17,588	4.6
Va.	1,987	6,576	4,798	5,833	8,020	8,171	7,094	6,879	12,100	4,791	1.27
W.Va.	1,322	3,197	2,865	3,180	4,089	3,857	3,409	2,988	3,263	1,273	.34

guard near Prairie Grove. Hindman failed to exploit this advantage and took a defensive position at Prairie Grove. In the early afternoon, Blunt's advance arrived. The contending infantries advanced and retreated until night fell. Casualties were about 1,300 on each side. Hindman held the field, but failed to repulse the federal invasion. In the morning darkness, Hindman's demoralized army retreated southward.

See S. B. Oates, *Arkansas Historical Quarterly* (Summer, 1960); *Official Records, Armies*, Ser. 1, Vols. XIII, XXII; R. U. Johnson and C. C. Buel (eds.), *Battles and Leaders* (1887), III; F. Moore, *Rebellion Record* (1861–68), VI; and H. N. Monnett, *Arkansas Historical Quarterly* (Winter, 1962).

LEROY H. FISCHER
Oklahoma State University

PRENTICE, GEORGE DENISON (1802–1870), from Connecticut, wrote the campaign *Biography of Henry Clay* (1830) in Kentucky, where he accepted the editorship of the Louisville *Journal* established to promote Clay's candidacy. First distributed November 24, 1830, the *Journal* attracted readers throughout America and in Europe because of the editor's sparkling wit, humor, and sarcasm. Meanwhile, an editorial war with his Democratic rival Shadrack Penn made the *Journal* a household word throughout the Mississippi Valley. Prentice gained recognition as a party leader while establishing the *Journal* as a significant Whig newspaper. The demise of the Whigs, however, led him to endorse the KNOW-NOTHINGS, and thus his name is indelibly associated with "bloody Monday," Louisville's election riots of 1855. Predicting that the election of Abraham Lincoln would provoke secession, Prentice endorsed the CONSTITUTIONAL UNION ticket in 1860. Following the election he urged southerners to be moderate. The editor's steadfast loyalty to the Union enabled the *Journal* to play an important role in saving Kentucky for the Union.

See B. C. Congleton, "George D. Prentice" (Ph.D. dissertation, University of Kentucky, 1962), *Filson Club History Quarterly* (Oct., 1963; April, 1967), *Register of Kentucky Historical Society* (April, 1964; July, 1965; April, 1967; April, 1969), and *Indiana Magazine of History* (Sept., 1967); G. D. Prentice, *Poems* (1876) and *Prenticeana* (1860); and W. L. Visscher, *Ten Wise Men* (1909).

BETTY CAROLYN CONGLETON
East Carolina University

PRESBYTERIAN CHURCH developed in America partly as a strain of English Puritanism and partly as the church of dissenting Scotch-Irish immigrants. Unlike their Calvinist cousins, the CONGREGATIONALISTS, Presbyterians perceived individual congregations as temporal units of a universal church (not as autonomous and sovereign Christian bodies). Their ministers were ordained as representatives of Christ (not mere pastors of a local congregation), and their laity voiced its views only indirectly through elected members of local benches of elders, area presbyteries, regional synods, and—after the American Revolution—meetings of the national General Assembly.

The first Presbyterian ministers came to the colonies in the 1680s to serve the growing numbers of Scotch-Irish refugees in Maryland, Virginia, and the Barbados. Most such clergy provided itinerate service to small, coastal congregations in the southern colonies, but Francis Makemie—sometimes called the father of American Presbyterianism—also developed a close relationship with Increase Mather and other New England Puritans. Makemie's New England contacts probably helped direct a large branch of American Puritans toward Presbyterianism, but few Puritans had settled in the southern colonies and, except for Delaware and South Carolina, southern Presbyterianism floundered until the second quarter of the eighteenth century.

The GREAT AWAKENING and the continuing immigration of Scotch-Irish settlers helped extend the sway of southern Presbyterianism, especially in the western areas of the settled sections of Virginia and the Carolinas. Indeed, by 1788 there were almost as many congregations in the South as in the North, though the southern churches were twice as likely to be without a minister and their members tended to be both less affluent and less influential than in the northern states. As American settlers pushed the frontier across the Allegheny and Appalachian mountains and into Kentucky and Tennessee, the insistence of the Presbyterians upon formal academic training for their ministers (notably at Princeton University) aggravated the shortage of ordained clergy and handicapped the church in its competition with METHODISTS and BAPTISTS for converts and adherents. At the same time, however, this very emphasis upon education almost predestined the Presbyterians to be the church of the rising new elite of many western communities.

In part to alleviate the chronic shortage of qualified ministers, Presbyterians were more active than most denominations in founding and supporting colleges; Hampden-Sydney (1776), Transylvania (1784), Union Theological (1812), Columbia Theological (1828), Davidson (1837),

Southwestern (1848), Westminster (1851), King College (1866), and Arkansas (1872) are but a few examples. A second device for dealing with the need for more ministers—one practiced after 1801 by the presbyteries of Cumberland (Tenn.) and Transylvania (Ky.)—was to license as ministers men who lacked traditional standards of academic training and whose doctrinal views on such matters as predestination were less than rigorously orthodox. Conflicts over these matters with the General Assembly were resolved in 1810, when these two presbyteries broke away to form the Cumberland Presbyterian church (an especially strong sect in the border states and the Upper South).

The problems of ministering to and evangelizing western communities caused the Presbyterian Church in the U.S.A. to undertake a cooperative program with the Congregational churches. Beginning in 1801, the two churches agreed to avoid establishing competing congregations in the same community. They further agreed to permit congregations of both sects to call ministers from either body. Assisted by this cooperative evangelism, the number of Presbyterian (U.S.A.) communicants grew from approximately 30,000 in 1810 to almost 175,000 by 1830. Cooperation also resulted in a gradual dilution of the orthodoxy of northern and western churches and presbyteries, in augmenting the power of the New England synods, and—in the opinion of some southern Presbyterians—in "yankeeizing" the church.

At the meetings of the General Assembly of 1837, the more orthodox, traditionalist members voted to excind four synods most seriously infected with Congregational heresies. The excinded New School Presbyterians maintained a national organization, but they remained predominantly a northern church: in 1857, fewer than 12 percent of 139,000 New School Presbyterians lived in the South, while over 33 percent of the Old School's 250,000 communicants were in the South. Thus, seven years before the Baptist and Methodist churches divided along sectional lines over the question of slavery, organizational and theological issues caused the removal of a large northern contingent from the Presbyterian Church in the U.S.A. Perhaps as a consequence, the Old School Presbyterians avoided a rupture of their organization until May, 1861; the Cumberland Presbyterians, reflecting their border state character, survived the Civil War without a formal breech.

Following Ft. Sumter and the General Assembly's condemnation of secession, southern Presbyterians of the U.S.A. church withdrew to organize the Presbyterian Church of the Confederate States of America, known since the Civil War as the Presbyterian Church in the United States. The postwar southern church established Stillman College (1876) to train black clergy for a separate synod of black congregations. Outside such metropolitan areas as Atlanta and New Orleans, however, little headway was made in evangelizing southern blacks, and most of Stillman's graduates worked instead as missionaries in Africa. In 1916 the southern church abandoned efforts to develop a synod of black congregations. Beginning in the 1940s, its general assemblies began to question the viability of segregation, and in 1954 the southern Presbyterians became the first church formally to endorse the U.S. Supreme Court's decision in BROWN V. BOARD OF EDUCATION. Nevertheless, the greater relative orthodoxy of the southern (U.S.) Presbyterians, the greater influence of the more numerous northern (U.S.A.) Presbyterians, and continuing differences of opinion on a variety of social and political issues to date have prevented the reunion of these two bodies despite a century of interest in ecumenicalism.

See E. T. Thompson, *Presbyterians in South* (3 vols; 1963–73), definitive on organization of southern church; A. E. Murray, *Presbyterians and Negro* (1966); L. G. Vander Velde, *Presbyterian Churches and Federal Union* (1932); L. J. Trinterud, *Forming of American Political Tradition* (1949), colonial church; P. S. T. Amant, *Presbyterian Church in Louisiana* (1961); W. D. Blanks, "Presbyterian Churches of South, 19th Century" (Ph.D. dissertation, Union Theological Seminary, 1960); F. D. Jones and W. H. Mills, Presbyterian Church in South Carolina (1925); L. C. LaMotte, *Columbia Theological Seminary, 1828–1936* (1937); M. H. Smith, *Studies in Southern Presbyterian Theology* (1962); and T. W. Street, *Story of Southern Presbyterians* (1960).

PRESTON, JOHN SMITH (1809–1881), was born near Abingdon, Va. Educated at Hampden-Sydney College, the University of Virginia, and Harvard, he practiced law in Abingdon for a time before moving to Columbia, S.C. Preston served as a states' rightist South Carolina senator from 1848 to 1856. An ardent secessionist, in 1860 he was elected to the South Carolina secession convention. During the Civil War Preston served in the Confederate army and headed the Bureau of Conscription. After the war and a brief sojourn in Europe, he returned to South Carolina, where he remained an "unreconstructed rebel" until his death.

See *Journals of South Carolina Executive Councils of 1861 and 1862; Official Records, Armies*, Ser. 4, Vol. III; *Address Before Washington and Jefferson Societies of University of Virginia* (1868); A. Moore, *Conscription and Conflict in Confederacy* (1924); and University of South Carolina Library, Columbia, leading manuscript depository.

ALVIN A. FAHRNER
East Carolina University

PRESTON, WILLIAM BALLARD (1805–1862), son and nephew of Virginian governors, spoke to end slavery in the Virginia house of delegates debate (1831–1832). Elected to Congress as a Whig (1846–1848) after serving in the house of delegates (1830–1832, 1844–1845) and the state senate (1840–1844), he was appointed secretary of the navy by ZACHARY TAYLOR in 1848 for party loyalty. Preston called for the admission of California and New Mexico to the Union and ordered naval vessels south to prevent Narciso López' filibusters operating against Cuba (1849). After Taylor's death, he resumed law practice. In 1858 his negotiations for Virginia to open a Norfolk-Nantes shipping line failed. At the Virginia secession convention of 1861, Preston, a moderate, joined the secessionists (April 16) after officially visiting Abraham Lincoln (April 8) to discover his policy on federal forts. His last political activity was as Confederate States senator. Personally wealthy ($383,330 in 1861) he was buried at Smithfield, Montgomery County, the family home.

See Richmond *Enquirer* (Feb. 9, 1832); papers, Virginia Historical Society; M. P. Burg, "Southern Whig Congressional Leaders" (Ph.D. dissertation, University of Washington, 1971); J. P. B. Lamb, *Virginia Magazine of History and Biography* (April, 1939; Oct., 1940); H. Hamilton, *Zachary Taylor* (1951); C. H. Ambler, *Sectionalism in Virginia* (1964); and R. W. Wooster, *Secession Conventions* (1962).

FREDERICK C. DRAKE
Brock University, Ontario, Canada

PRESTON, WILLIAM CAMPBELL (1794–1860), was born in Philadelphia, practiced law for a time in Virginia, and in 1822 moved to Columbia, S.C. He was elected to the lower house of the South Carolina legislature (1828–1834). In 1833 he was elected to the U.S. Senate as a Democratic nullifier and became a renowned orator. In 1837 he was reelected as a Whig and served until 1842, at which time his opposition to Martin Van Buren's fiscal policies led to a loss of support and resulted in his resignation. He privately expressed his feelings of repugnance for the "peculiar institution," but during his tenure of office he was strongly proslavery, supported the GAG RULE, and advocated closing the mails to abolition materials. He concluded his career as president of South Carolina College (1846–1851). He gave his 3,000-vol-

umed classical library to the Columbia LYCEUM, which he founded.

See D. D. Wallace, *South Carolina* (1961); H. S. Schultz, *Nationalism and Sectionalism in South Carolina* (1969); and W. Thorp, *Southern Reader* (1955).

PRICE, STERLING (1809–1867), was the most prominent Confederate general west of the Mississippi. A native Virginian, he established a tobacco plantation near Keytesville, Mo., in the 1830s and in 1844 was elected to Congress as a Democrat. In 1846 he became colonel of a Missouri regiment in New Mexico, where he suppressed an Indian revolt. He was governor of Missouri (1853–1857) and early in 1861 was president of a state convention that rejected secession. When Missouri's Unionists resorted to military force, however, he took command of the state's secessionist troops. On August 10, 1861, he combined with Ben McCulloch's Confederate army to defeat Nathaniel Lyon at WILSON'S CREEK, then captured a Union garrison at Lexington on September 20. Despite these victories he had to retreat into Arkansas, where he and McCulloch, under Earl Van Dorn, suffered defeat at PEA RIDGE (March 7–8, 1862).

Next Price, now a Confederate major general, was transferred to Mississippi, where he escaped an enemy trap at Iuka (September 19) but was repulsed along with Van Dorn at CORINTH (October 3–4). In 1863 he returned to Arkansas, where he participated in a futile attack on HELENA (July 4) and evacuated Little Rock to the federals (September 10). In the spring of 1864 he successfully resisted a Union advance on Shreveport, then took part in a vain effort to crush the retreating enemy at Jenkins' Ferry (April 30).

In the fall of 1864 Price led a large-scale cavalry raid into Missouri but was checked at Pilot Knob (September 27), defeated at WESTPORT (October 23), and routed at Mine Creek, Kan. (October 25). Following Confederate surrender he went to Mexico, then returned in 1867 to Missouri, where he soon died. Called "Old Pap" by his troops, Price was a good fighter but a mediocre commander.

See R. Shalhope, *Sterling Price* (1971), full biography; and A. Castel, *General Sterling Price and Civil War in West* (1968), concentrates on Price's Civil War military career.

ALBERT CASTEL
Western Michigan University

PRICE'S RAID ON MISSOURI (1864). In September, former Missouri governor STERLING PRICE led an army of 12,000 Confederates in an invasion of Missouri. Major General EDMUND KIRBY-SMITH, commander of the Trans-Mississippi Department, ordered Price to capture St. Louis if possible and to gather recruits and supplies. Missouri's exiled "governor," Thomas C. Reynolds, accompanied the expedition in the hope of establishing a Confederate state government. Price organized three divisions headed by J. S. MARMADUKE, J. O. Shelby, and J. F. Fagan. His army entered Missouri on September 19 and encountered stubborn but brief resistance at Pilot Knob on September 27. He then moved toward St. Louis as far as Franklin, where he learned that St. Louis had been reinforced by a detachment of 4,500 of A. J. Smith's Union regulars. Price then turned westward but found the capital, Jefferson City, strongly fortified, and he moved on toward Kansas City. At WESTPORT his army was almost surrounded by Kansas militia (15,000 men) and Missouri Union forces (10,000 men). A great battle ensued (October 23), and each side suffered approximately 1,000 casualties. Price's army, still in possession of a large booty-laden train, escaped southward along the Ft. Scott road. At Mine Creek, Kan. (October 25), he lost most of his train and Generals Marmaduke and W. L. Cabell were captured. Thereafter, the army disintegrated although Price was able to make another stand at Newtonia, Mo., on October 28. He then fled to southern Arkansas via Indian Territory with a few survivors. Governor Reynolds was highly critical of Price's leadership, and a court of inquiry was called but not completed before the war's end.

See A. Castel, *General Sterling Price* (1968), best account of raid; R. Shalhope, *Sterling Price* (1971); J. Monaghan, *Civil War on Western Border* (1955), glib; W. Britton, *Civil War on Border* (1899), by Union participant; and J. Edwards, *Shelby* (1867), by Confederate participant.

MARK A. PLUMMER
Illinois State University

PRIMOGENITURE AND ENTAIL. In feudal England, if called upon by the king to defend the realm, each fief and barony was required to produce a knight or a contingent of fighting men. So that the military requirement would not be diluted among several heirs, the rule of primogeniture evolved, dictating that all of the father's real property should descend to the eldest son. To foster the accumulation of property and to restrain the free alienation of family territory, the practice of entailing estates was introduced. The statute *De Donis Conditionalibus* (1285) in theory allowed a grantor to preclude a grantee, and his heirs forever, from alienating an estate.

Primogeniture and entail became law in all the southern colonies. Under THOMAS JEFFERSON's leadership, the Virginia legislature in 1776 abolished entails. The remaining states followed Virginia's example. Some went further. Georgia in 1777 and North Carolina in 1784 also abolished primogeniture. Virginia did the same in 1785, Maryland in 1786, and South Carolina in 1791. Some historians charge that primogeniture and entail enabled a few southern families to aggrandize and then perpetuate massive estates, capture provincial offices, and curry favor with the crown. Thus they reason that the abolition of the feudal vestiges prepared the way for the creation of a more democratic social order.

Available evidence does not support entirely these claims. First, primogeniture could be (and frequently was) avoided through resort to wills. Second, a customary form of equalized distribution evolved in parts of the southern backcountry. Third, entails often were "docked" (destroyed) by special legislation and writ. These practices approximated the ancient "common recovery" (a collusive action) in England. Fourth, no strong correlation has been proved to exist among entail, primogeniture, and southern political power. Fifth, the quantity of land entailed in the colonies has been exaggerated. The abolition of the systems did not significantly alter landholding patterns in the new southern states. Finally, primogeniture and entail were abolished because they were anomalous in a democratic society, not because of popular clamor or pressure. In sum, primogeniture and entail at times contributed to, but usually were overshadowed by, the larger forces shaping southern society: the plantation economy, cheap land, staple agriculture, and Negro slavery.

See C. R. Keim, "Primogeniture and Entail" (Ph.D. dissertation, University of Chicago, 1926), excellent; and R. B. Morris, *Studies in American Law* (1930), overstates importance.

JAMIL SHAHEEN ZAINALDIN
Northwestern University

PRINCIPIO COMPANY was a partnership of British ironmasters formed in 1720 that owned one of the largest ironworks in the South in the colonial period (IRON AND STEEL INDUSTRY). Its operations began at Principio Furnace, at the head of Chesapeake Bay. Under the direction of John England from 1723 to 1730, the enterprise became firmly established. By 1751 the company owned four furnaces, two forges, and 30,000 acres of land in Maryland and Virginia. The local manager supplied the American revolutionary army with bar iron and cannonballs. The company expired when the state of Maryland in 1780 confiscated that interest belonging to British investors.

See H. Whiteley, *Pennsylvania Magazine of History and Biography* (1887); and E. C. May, *Principio to Wheeling* (1945), popular.

BENJAMIN H. NEWCOMB
Texas Tech University

PRINGLE FAMILY of West Virginia comprised originally Lowland Scots who enlisted in the British army during the FRENCH AND INDIAN WAR. In 1761 two Pringle brothers, John and Samuel, joined by William Childers and Josephy Linley, deserted the British garrison at Ft. Pitt and headed into the southern wilderness. With Childers and Linley the Pringles traveled along the Monongahela River and settled for a time in southwestern Pennsylvania. In 1764 Childers and Linley were captured as deserters, but the Pringles escaped. After months of hunting and trapping with John Simpson, the founder of Clarksburg, the three quarreled, and the Pringles crossed the mountain westward deeper into the forest wilderness. Following Turkey Run Creek to its confluence with the Buckhannon River in present-day West Virginia, the brothers came upon the large hollow sycamore tree in which they lived for over three years.

When the French and Indian War was over and he found that he was no longer wanted as a deserter, John persuaded several families to return with him to his arcadian paradise. John Jackson (great-grandfather of Stonewall), John Hacker, Jesse Hughes, and Sam Radcliffe, all experienced frontiersmen, followed John Pringle across the mountains, where they located on Buckhannon River, Turkey Run, Hacker's Creek, and Bushy Fork. In 1769 and again in 1770, the Pringles brought in other pioneer families from the north branch of the Potomac and located them in the Beverly region. By 1772 the communities of families brought in by the Pringles were permanently settled in the lush Tygart Valley. Starting in the wilderness as deserters, the Pringle brothers had brought civilization to the Tygart Valley of West Virginia in less than a decade.

See J. P. Hale, *Trans-Allegheny Pioneers* (1971), useful; O. K. Rice, *Allegheny Frontier* (1970); and WPA, *West Virginia* (1941), on famous Pringle tree.

MILTON READY
University of North Carolina, Asheville

PRINTING AND PUBLISHING INDUSTRY.
Although Virginia had the first British settlement in America, there, as throughout the South, printing and publishing lagged behind the northern colonies. Geographic and economic factors were not favorable to the development of a printing industry in the South, and neither was the attitude of royal authority. "I thank God we have not free schools nor printing," said Sir William Berkeley, Virginia's governor, in 1671, "and I hope we shall not have them these hundred years. For learning has brought disobedience and heresy and sects into the world; and printing has divulged them and libels against the government. God keep us from both."

The South's first commercial press, begun in 1682 in Gloucester County, Va., was promptly shut down by royal authorities, who chastised the printers, John Buckner and William Nuthead, for publishing without official permission. Nuthead reappeared three years later in St. Mary's, Md., to establish the first ongoing commercial press in the South. Not until 1731, more than 40 years later, was the next southern colony, South Carolina, to have its own printing presses. Eventually, however, colonial authorities came to lend cautious encouragement to some pioneer printers, who were needed to publish compilations of territorial laws and other official documents.

By 1825 a number of PERIODICALS had begun to give direction to the spirited sectional feeling already evolving in the South. These publications survived on small circulations and low profits; however, several southern cities became important publishing centers—Baltimore, Richmond, Charleston, and New Orleans, among them—and some southern periodicals were able to reach influential audiences. Chief among these were *Niles' Weekly Register*, a Baltimore newsmagazine whose most famous editor, Hezekiah Niles, was known throughout the country as a genuine journalist; the *Commercial Review of the South and West*, carefully edited by James D. B. De Bow in New Orleans (DE BOW'S REVIEW); the SOUTHERN REVIEW, whose star contributor was HUGH SWINTON LEGARÉ of Charleston; and the SOUTHERN LITERARY MESSENGER, begun in Richmond in 1834.

As might be expected, the printing and publishing industry collapsed and very nearly died in the South during the Civil War. Accustomed to buying machinery, paper, and inks from northern manufacturers, southern publishers found themselves compelled to produce their own supplies and equipment on short notice and with the Confederacy on a war footing. The ersatz materials were barely adequate—at one time bootblacking was used for ink and wallpaper for printing stock—and military conscription drained off much of the already limited editorial and production manpower. In spite of these difficulties (and the southern publishing industry had never been strong to begin with), some magazines survived and, along with their NEWSPAPER counterparts, helped sustain morale while the fighting wore on. "You must take care of yourself," wrote Robert E. Lee to Dr. Albert Taylor Bledsoe, editor of the *Southern Review*, during one of the Civil War's dark hours. "You have great work to do; we all look to you for our vindication."

After the war, a number of southern writers attained national prominence in what one editor described as a "craze" for articles and fiction about

EARLY PRINTING IN THE SOUTH
When and Where the First Southern Presses Appeared

State	First Press	Comments
Alabama	an unidentified printer, using type "old and much worn," at Wakefield, 1807	The earliest printer whose name is known was P. J. Forster, who began at St. Stephen's early in 1811.
Arkansas	William E. Woodruff, Arkansas Post, 1819	The following year Woodruff moved to the new territorial capital at Little Rock.
Delaware	James Adams, Wilmington, 1761	Prior to this time, Benjamin Franklin in Philadelphia did most of the printing for Delaware.
District of Columbia	Charles Fierer, Georgetown, 1789	This was in the district as it now exists; first printer in the area was actually George Richards in Alexandria, Va., in 1784.
Florida	John and William Charles Wells, St. Augustine, 1783	
Georgia	James Johnson, Savannah, 1763	Like many early printers, Johnson was offered money and was guaranteed printing contracts by the government as inducement to set up his printing plant.
Kentucky	John Bradford, Lexington, 1787	Bradford, a Virginian, was not related to the famous Bradford printing family of New York and Philadelphia, though his printing press did come from their plant in Philadelphia.
Louisiana	Denis Braud, New Orleans, 1764	
Maryland	William Nuthead, St. Mary's, 1685	Nuthead, whose pioneering printing efforts in Virginia had been suppressed, moved to Maryland and became the first printer in each of the two southern colonies.
Mississippi	Andrew Marschalk, Walnut Hills, near Vicksburg, 1798	
Missouri	Joseph Charless, St. Louis, 1808	Like many pioneer printers, Charless' first work was a compilation of the territorial laws, in this case *Laws of the Territory of Louisiana*, of which Missouri was then a part.
North Carolina	James Davis, New Bern, 1749	
South Carolina	George Webb, Charleston, 1731	Some scholars argue that Eleazar Phillips and Thomas Whitmarsh, both of whom opened printing shops about this time, actually began before Webb.
Tennessee	George Roulstone and Robert Ferguson, Hawkins Courthouse (now Rogersville), 1791	Their first publication was a newspaper, the Knoxville *Gazette*, so named because they intended to move when Knoxville became the first capital of the territory, which it did the following year.
Texas	William Shaler and Jose Alvarez de Toledo, Nacogdoches, 1813	These two men published pamphlets and newspapers under at least two titles as organs of a pioneer expedition. Texas' first permanent printer of record was Samuel Bangs, who set up a press in Galveston in 1817.
Virginia	John Buckner, Gloucester County, 1682	Buckner and his associate William Nuthead got in trouble with authorities for printing without a license, and their press was stopped. The first permanent printing press in Virginia was set up by William Parks in Williamsburg in 1730.
West Virginia	Nathaniel Willis, Shepherd's Town (near Harpers Ferry), 1790	

the South. Most of these magazine pieces, however, were destined to be published in the North and East; the South was not inhospitable to its own writers so much as it was unable to develop enough effective periodicals to support them. Only two southern magazines, *Scott's Monthly* of Atlanta and the Louisville *Home and Farm*, reached circulations of 100,000 prior to 1885.

The book industry, too, has been a northern and eastern story. Except for a period before and during the Civil War, when southern writers and printers were urged to develop textbooks reflecting political views prevailing in the region at that time, the South has depended on the rest of the country for most of its books—this despite the fact that the South has produced an astonishing number of best-selling writers. Many southern publishing houses exist today, but most of them are comparatively small, and the overwhelming majority of the nation's book-publishing successes has been achieved outside the South. The largest concentration of southern publishing today is at Nashville, Tenn., the home of a number of religious, educational, and commercial publishers, as well as some 450 firms engaged in music publishing.

See D. C. McMurtrie, *History of Printing in U.S.* (1936) and *The Book* (1943); and F. L. Mott, *History of American Magazines* (5 vols.; 1938–68).

RONALD TRUMAN FARRAR
University of Mississippi

PRISONS. See PENAL SYSTEMS

PRITCHARD, JETER CONNELLY (1857–1921), during the administrations of William McKinley and Theodore Roosevelt, was the only Republican senator from a former Confederate state, the first elected since Reconstruction, and one of only two elected prior to 1960. Although born in Jonesboro, among the eastern mountains of Tennessee, he resided during most of his adult life in western North Carolina. Both sections were bastions of the Republican party, and Pritchard simply adopted the dominant party of his section. After editing a party newspaper and serving several terms in the North Carolina legislature, he was considered by state Democrats and Republicans alike to be one of the GOP's ablest leaders. In 1894 and again in 1896, he successfully led his party in joint, or fusion, campaigns with the state POPULISTS. This cooperation permitted the two parties to control two sessions of the state legislature, to elect a Republican governor, and to elect two U.S. senators: MARION BUTLER (the Populist leader) and Pritchard (1895–1903). After failing to defeat North Carolina's disfranchisement amendment in 1900, he accepted the loss of his Negro constituents. Thereafter, he not only discouraged Negro participation in state politics, he sought to purge the few remaining black voters from all Republican organizations in the South. A dependable party man and the titular spokesman for southern LILY-WHITE Republicans, Pritchard failed to gain reelection in 1903, but Roosevelt appointed him to the supreme court of the District of Columbia and later to the Fourth U.S. Circuit Court of Appeals, a post he held until his death.

See G. B. McKinney, "Mountain Republicanism" (Ph.D. dissertation, Northwestern, 1971); and D. C. Roller, "Republican Party in North Carolina" (Ph.D. dissertation, Duke, 1965).

PROCLAMATION OF 1763 illustrates the emerging "seacoast theory" of British colonial policy. Specific provisions created four new colonies from the territory recently acquired in the war with France—Quebec, East Florida, West Florida, and Granada; prohibited survey or settlement of lands beyond the mountains; required settlers already located in the prohibited area to move; forbade the purchase of Indian lands by private citizens; and instructed all fur traders to obtain a license from colonial governors.

Adopted in part to conciliate the Indians (Pontiac's Rebellion had broken out in May, 1763), the proclamation line was seen as temporary. During the next decade British policy fluctuated from year to year, but restricting settlement in the interior was never abandoned completely. In 1768 and 1772 the Board of Trade recommended that the proclamation line be made permanent. The Quebec Act of 1774 attached a substantial portion of the interior to Canada, indicating that efforts to discourage settlement there continued until the eve of revolution.

Drawing lines on colored maps in the colonial office did not effectively redirect expansion but it did prevent the acquisition of clear titles to land. In the South the policy stimulated interest in the Floridas but hindered the development of other colonies, particularly Virginia. Efforts to confine colonial expansion gave both settlers and speculators a grievance against the British government and contributed to the friction that split the empire in 1776.

See C. W. Alvord, *Mississippi Valley* (1917); T. P. Abernethy, *Western Lands* (1937); J. R. Alden, *John Stuart*

(1944); L. H. Gipson, *British Empire* (1956), IX; and J. M. Sosin, *Whitehall and Wilderness* (1961).

DAVID AMMERMAN
Florida State University

PROFITEERING can be described as taking advantage of public necessity to exact unfair profits. During the Civil War, this was usually called speculation or extortion. The extent and effect of speculation cannot be determined precisely. Many Confederates believed it to be widespread and damaging. In September, 1863, Jefferson Davis said: "The passion of speculation has become a gigantic evil. It has seemed to take possession of the whole country, and has seduced citizens of all classes . . . to a sordid effort to amass money." On the other hand, the line between legitimate profit taking and profiteering was often blurred. Shortages plus currency inflation meant rising prices and a depreciating currency. People were reluctant to part with property that was appreciating in currency value for money that was declining in buying power. Yet holding goods off the market aggravated shortages, helped drive up prices, and produced accusations of speculation. However, there were those who undoubtedly deserved the epithet profiteer, who bought only to sell again. These included minor public officials as well as private citizens. Their activities were often notorious, were injurious to southern morale, and caused actual suffering.

Seven states acted to discourage speculation, but their laws proved to be unenforceable, and the Confederate Congress passed no laws that attacked it directly. In fact, for the entirely laudable purpose of procuring funds abroad and supporting the currency at home, both state and Confederate governments speculated in cotton and specie. Although there is no doubt that speculation, strictly defined, was fairly common, there can also be no doubt that most of the evils attributed to it were the result of the combination of shortages and a redundant currency.

See J. C. Schwab, *Confederate States* (1901); and E. M. Coulter, *Confederate States* (1950), for overview and guides to sources.

LUDWELL H. JOHNSON
College of William and Mary

PROGRESSIVISM. During the first two decades of the twentieth century the South was an active participant in the variegated reform movement in the United States known as progressivism. The magnitude of the region's problems—as well as its peculiar historical experience, economic development, political party alignment, and racial structure—undoubtedly contributed to the distinctiveness of its progressivism; nevertheless, the program and accomplishments of southern reformers were essentially the same as those of Progressives elsewhere. As in the rest of the nation, progressivism in the South was a diffuse, amorphous movement, embracing a complex of reforms designed to promote corporation regulation, political democracy, public health and welfare, efficiency, and morality. Its proponents included a varied assortment of individuals and groups representing a mélange of motives, styles, and backgrounds whose approach to reform ranged from that of the bold innovator to that of the gentle paternalist.

Regardless of differences in style and approach, however, southern Progressives were virtually unanimous in their adherence to the ideology of white supremacy. At a time when the MISSISSIPPI PLAN was rapidly becoming the "American way," southerners espoused a progressivism for whites only, in which racism and reform were complementary rather than contradictory. Convinced that the maintenance of peace and order necessitated more stringent control of the black population, southern Progressives completed the racial settlement begun in the late nineteenth century by constructing an elaborate legal system of disfranchisement and segregation, which eliminated most Negroes and not a few poor whites from the political process. This was the "seminal reform," the prerequisite for purifying the electorate and for securing all other significant reforms.

Reaching maturity in the wake of the traumatic political and economic upheavals of the 1890s, the Progressive movement in the South tended to be dominated by those committed to stability, orderly social change and material development, and honest, efficient government. Such forces of respectability, for whom reform often served a conservative function, determined in large measure the orientation and scope of the region's progressivism. Between 1900 and 1920 loose political coalitions, including businessmen, professionals, certain agricultural interests, and a medley of social uplift agents, emerged in one southern state after another, where they constituted "progressive" or reform factions within the Democratic party. In most states the cohesion and effectiveness of these coalitions depended upon individual political leaders adept at harmonizing the interests of disparate groups and in marshaling popular support for multiple reforms. Political spokesmen of southern progressivism on occasion invoked rhetoric that obscured the novelty and complexity of their reform programs; and some, such as THEO-DORE G. BILBO of Mississippi, pursued Progressive goals by consciously exploiting the frustrations and racial prejudices of the white masses. Although reform politicians in the predominantly rural South could scarcely ignore their "redneck" constituency, the region's Progressive leadership was drawn, to an extraordinary degree, from the ranks of business and professions. Progressive governors such as B. B. COMER of Alabama, HOKE SMITH of Georgia, and CHARLES BROUGH of Arkansas gave the movement a respectable, middle-class cast and made reform palatable to those who had been frightened by the programs of agrarian radicals of the 1890s.

Under the direction of such astute, middle-class politicians the Progressive coalitions either captured control of the Democratic party in the southern states or applied sufficient pressure upon its entrenched "machines" to bring about acquiescence in their reform goals. In any case their presence stimulated intraparty competition in an essentially one-party region and offered white voters a real choice of candidates. The election of southern-born WOODROW WILSON to the presidency in 1912 "was both a reflection of and a contribution to" progressivism in the South. The southern Democratic party became "Wilsonized", and, even if Wilson provided relatively little aid to local and state Progressives in overthrowing their adversaries, he pulled "Southern politicians into the orbit of national politics" and won their support for the reforms of his administration.

Although reformers in the South usually marched under the Democratic banner, the region's progressivism was by no means of a single piece or uniform in its development. Variations within the southern scene not only affected the rate at which reform movements took shape and matured in different states, but also determined in large part their emphasis, success, and duration. In some southern states progressivism inherited a substantial portion of the "intellectual baggage" as well as the clientele of the Populist party; in others such as Alabama the continuity between populism and progressivism was practically nonexistent. No less diverse was the priority given specific reforms such as prohibition and the conservation of natural resources. For example, Virginia's Progressives, though allied with the drys, never made PROHIBITION one of their principal concerns, while in Texas the crusade against liquor became synonymous with progressivism. In two other states, Tennessee and Alabama, as well as in Texas, prohibition virtually disrupted the Democratic party. In a similar vein discrepancies existed in the response of southern states to the cause of CONSERVATION. A half-dozen states undertook relatively comprehensive conservation programs; in others the approach was piecemeal, usually concentrating on forests and wildlife or on drainage and FLOOD CONTROL. The efficient, rational use of regional resources, rather than nostalgia, seems to have been the dominant concern of the enlightened businessmen, scientists, Audubon Society members, and others who led the conservation movement in the South.

If southern progressivism had a focus it was the crusade to control and regulate corporations. Resentful of the "colonial status" of their industry and commerce, southerners of diverse backgrounds united in the effort to free the region from the domination and discriminatory practices of "foreign" corporations. Less radical in its thrust than a similar effort by the agrarians in the 1890s, the regulatory movement in the South during the Progressive era drew much of its impetus and strength from boards of trade, freight bureaus, and other urban agencies primarily interested in securing competitive advantages for a host of emerging industries in the region. In addition to measures designed to regulate public utilities, insurance and oil companies, and other corporate "malefactors," southern Progressives also invoked the regulatory principle to achieve legislation relating to pure food and drugs, CHILD LABOR, and industrial working conditions. But their most sustained efforts were aimed at railroads, whose political as well as economic power was viewed as an obstacle to regional economic progress and independence. The result was a plethora of laws that not only strengthened or revamped state railroad commissions but also tackled specific problems such as discriminatory rates and railroad property tax evaluation. The crusade for "economic democracy" reached a climax in the dramatic legal confrontations between railroad companies and state officials in Kentucky, Alabama, and North Carolina. In Kentucky the clash led to violence and political turmoil.

In the area of political reforms southerners were on occasion in the vanguard of progressivism. For example, they pioneered in the use of the direct primary. Although employed to reinforce the disfranchisement of Negroes, it was hailed as an instrument of political democracy. In fact, an Alabama Progressive proclaimed that "nothing breeds democracy like a primary." In the one-party South the primary was the means for achieving in effect the direct election of U.S. senators and popular preferences for presidential candidates. To augment the democratization of the political process, southern reformers also experimented with the initiative, recall, and referendum. Despite the activities of women's organizations and the strong endorsements of LUKE LEA of Tennessee, WALTER CLARK of North Carolina, and other men, woman suffrage generated little support among southern Progressives in general. In fact, of the former Confederate states only Tennessee was part of the three-fourths majority required for ratification of the federal suffrage amendment. In contrast, southern Progressives displayed enthusiasm for corrupt practices, antilobbying, and other measures designed "to banish all evils from politics."

Those primarily interested in social reforms often won concessions from the same legislators who enacted laws to bring about clean government and greater freedom from outside economic interests. Perhaps more than any other facet of the reform movement, the quest for social justice revealed both the rich diversity and restricted vision of southern progressivism. Spearheaded by a potpourri of paternalistic patricians, clergymen, professional social workers, and clubwomen, the cause of social uplift included a broad spectrum of reforms ranging from the abolition of child labor, illiteracy, and convict leasing to improvements in public health, charitable institutions, and race relations. The SOUTHERN SOCIOLOGICAL CONGRESS, organized in 1912 to serve as a focus for "social uplift forces in the South," promised to substitute the "pew religion" of the various denominations with "the 'do religion' of twentieth century efficiency." Although the congress included among its goals the implementation of "a new order in race relations," it actually effected little change in the region's basic racial settlement. But the degree to which Progressives operated within the whites-only framework was nowhere more evident than in the campaign for "universal education" in the South undertaken with the financial assistance of northern philanthropy. White, rather than black, children reaped the harvest of the educational renaissance. Southern churches, notwithstanding the inroads of the Social Gospel and increasing social awareness of some clergymen, also lent support to the region's racial system. Even the most socially active ministers, EDGAR GARDNER MURPHY and ALEXANDER MCKELWAY, both leaders in the child labor reform movement, subscribed to the prevailing racial creed. In spite of their neglect of blacks and failure to come to grips with the fundamental problems of rural poor whites, southern Progressives nonetheless were responsible for substantial changes in the areas of education, health, penology, and child labor.

The impact of progressivism upon the South was by no means limited to developments at the state level. In cities and towns throughout the region groups dedicated to civic betterment won victories in the name of environmental improvements, moral purity, clean government, and administrative efficiency. The same individuals active in social settlement work and in securing better housing and recreational facilities often participated in local crusades against prostitution, gambling, and liquor. In addition to their use of the primary and other devices of "direct democracy," cities also waged campaigns for home rule and for "the divorcement of policemen and firemen from politics." Some utilized the short ballot in an effort to ensure that the management of schools, police departments, and fiscal affairs would be entrusted to appointed experts rather than elected politicians. Two municipal reforms of the Progressive era that originated in the South were the commission plan of city government (GALVESTON COMMISSION PLAN), first used in Galveston, Tex., following a tidal wave in 1900, and the CITY-MANAGER concept, introduced in Staunton, Va., in 1908. Although municipalities were the chief beneficiaries of Progressive innovations at the local level, the concern for efficient, businesslike administration stimulated interest in county government reform. A pioneer in this area was E. C. Branson, whose Bureau of Research in Social Sciences at the University of North Carolina exposed the antiquated practices and cumbersome organization existing in county courthouses throughout the state. But not until the 1920s, when "business progressivism" and the public service concept of the state reached maturity in the South, did the cause of county government reform, as well as other movements such as good roads, fiscal responsibility, and conservation, receive full attention.

See J. T. Kirby, *Darkness at Dawning* (1972); A. S. Link, *North Carolina Historical Review* (April, 1946); G. B. Tindall, *Emergence of New South* (1967); and C. V. Woodward, *Origins of New South* (1951), all indispensable. See also R. Abrams, *Journal of Southern History* (Nov., 1956); E. H. Atkins, *Florida Historical Quarterly* (Jan., 1957); H. C. Bailey, *Edgar Gardner Murphy* (1968) and *Liberalism in New South* (1969); M. Bigalow, *Journal of Mississippi History* (Aug., 1967); A. L. Brooks, *Walter Clark* (1944); R. E. Burts, "Public Career of Richard I. Manning" (Ph.D. dissertation, Vanderbilt, 1957); E. C. Chatfield, *Tennessee Historical Quarterly* (Dec., 1960; March, 1961); B. Clayton, *Savage Ideal* (1972); E. H. Davidson, *Child Labor Legislation* (1939); H. J. Doherty, *Mississippi Valley Historical Review* (June, 1955) and *Journal of Southern History* (May, 1958); J. F. Doster, *Railroads in Alabama Politics* (1957); J. J. Duffy, "Charleston Politics in Progressive Era" (Ph.D. dissertation, University of South Carolina, 1963); J. L. Eighmy, *Church History* (Sept., 1969); E. W. Etheridge, *Butterfly Caste* (1972); W. Flynt, *Duncan U. Fletcher* (1971) and *Journal of Southern History* (Nov., 1969); P. Gaston, *New South Creed* (1970); W. B. Gatewood, *Eugene Clyde Brooks* (1960) and *Arkansas Historical Quarterly* (Spring, 1973); L. L. Gould, *Progressives and Prohibitionists* (1973); D. W. Grantham, *Democratic South* (1963) and *Hoke Smith* (1958); S. Hackney, *From Populism to Progressivism in Alabama* (1969); L. R. Harlan, *Separate and Unequal* (1958); R. A. Hohner, *South Atlantic Quarterly* (Autumn, 1968); W. F. Holmes, *White Chief* (1970); P. E. Isaac, *Prohibition and Politics* (1965); C. Jacobeson, *Life Story of Jeff Davis* (1925); A. D. Jones, *Georgia Historical Quarterly* (Sept., 1964); A. W. Jones, *Alabama Review* (July, 1968; Jan., 1973); J. T. Kirby, *Westmoreland Davis* (1968); A. D. Kirwan, *Revolt of Rednecks* (1951); W. Larsen, *Montague of Virginia* (1965); A. S. Link, *American Scholar* (Summer, 1951); N. P. McLemore, *Journal of Mississippi History* (Feb., 1967); W. D. Miller, *Memphis in Progressive Era* (1957) and *Mr. Crump* (1964); J. O. Nall, *Tobacco Night Riders* (1939); O. H. Orr, *Charles B. Aycock* (1961); S. Proctor, *Napoleon Broward* (1950); R. H. Pulley, *Old Virginia Restored* (1968); A. F. Scott, *Journal of Southern History* (Feb., 1963), *South Atlantic Quarterly* (Autumn, 1962), and *Southern Lady* (1970); J. B. Sellers, *Prohibition Movement in Alabama* (1943); R. N. Sheldon, *Alabama Review* (Oct., 1972); J. F. Steelman, *North Carolina Historical Review* (Spring, 1977; Spring, 1972) and "Progressive Era in North Carolina" (Ph.D. dissertation, University of North Carolina, 1954); L. C. Taylor, *Virginia Magazine of History and Biography* (Oct., 1962); G. B. Tindall, *South Atlantic Quarterly* (Winter, 1963); J. A. Tinsley, "Progressive Movement in Texas" (Ph.D. dissertation, University of Wisconsin, 1953); F. B. Vinson, "Conservation and South" (Ph.D. dissertation, University of Georgia, 1971); R. H. Wiebe, *Search for Order* (1967); J. Weinstein, *Journal of Southern History* (May, 1962); and J. Zimmerman, *Journal of Southern History* (Nov., 1951). Manuscript collections pertinent to the study of southern progressivism are Southern Education Board, Edgar G. Murphy, B. B. Comer, and John M. Parker papers, University of North Carolina; Trinity College and William G. Brown papers, Duke University; Alexander McKelway, Josephus Daniels, and B. T. Washington papers, Library of Congress; Charles H. Brough Papers, University of Arkansas; Carter Glass and Edwin Alderman papers, University of Virginia; Walter Hines Page Papers, Harvard; Thomas B. Love Papers, Dallas Historical Society, Tex.; and Hoke Smith Papers, University of Georgia.

WILLARD GATEWOOD
University of Arkansas

PROHIBITION. Although the antebellum South had experienced periodic outbursts of temperance activity, not until the late nineteenth century did prohibition become a significant and persistent issue. Led by the METHODIST and BAPTIST churches, southern temperance forces made gradual but steady gains. Local prohibition through special acts of the state legislature became in-

creasingly common, and in the 1880s drys in Georgia, Mississippi, Virginia, Florida, and Missouri secured general local option laws, which enabled local districts and counties to abolish the saloon by special election. Elsewhere, attempts to impose statewide prohibition were defeated in referenda in North Carolina (1881), Tennessee (1887), Texas (1887), and West Virginia (1888). South Carolina, Virginia, North Carolina, and Alabama experimented with the dispensary, or state monopoly of liquor sales; but, discredited by scandal in South Carolina and opposed by many militant drys, it failed to spread. In time, much of the region became dry piecemeal, either by local option or special legislation, such as Tennessee's four-mile law, which banned liquor sale near schools, or by statutes such as those in North Carolina and Virginia, which in 1903 outlawed the saloon in rural areas. By 1907 two-thirds of the counties in the former Confederate states were dry, and by 1908 one-half were dry in the border states of Maryland, West Virginia, Kentucky, and Missouri.

The prohibition movement gained new momentum after 1904, when the militant Anti-Saloon League expanded its southern operations. The league, founded in Washington, D.C., in 1895, soon scored a series of statewide prohibition victories in the South. Georgia acted first (1907), followed in quick succession by Alabama (1907), Mississippi (1908), North Carolina (1908), and Tennessee (1909). After these impressive victories, which launched a national prohibition wave, a period of stalemate and reversal followed. Voters rejected prohibition in referenda in Florida (1910), Missouri (1910), Texas (1911), and Arkansas (1912); and, although West Virginia became dry in 1912, Alabama in 1911 repealed its prohibition law. In 1914, however, Virginia adopted prohibition, followed by Arkansas, South Carolina, and Alabama in 1915 and by the District of Columbia (1917) and Florida (1918). By January, 1919, when the Eighteenth Amendment was ratified, only Delaware, Louisiana, Kentucky, Maryland, and Missouri remained wet. Although the South was thus overwhelmingly dry, most state prohibition statutes permitted the importation of liquor for personal use. Only when federal law closed such loopholes in 1917 did southern prohibition states become "bone-dry."

An ethnocultural issue that often cut across party and ideological lines, prohibition was a reaffirmation of Protestant values. Of particular interest to the middle class, it had special appeal in the South, the population of which, both rural and urban, was overwhelmingly native and evangelical

Protestant. An expression of the Social Gospel, it was also enthusiastically embraced by Progressive political reformers such as Thomas B. Love of Texas, BRAXTON B. COMER of Alabama, and HOKE SMITH of Georgia. The political struggles over prohibition were bitter and protracted, and for many years it was the most divisive question in southern politics. Southern leaders—such as Congressman RICHMOND P. HOBSON of Alabama, Senator MORRIS SHEPPARD of Texas, and the Reverend JAMES CANNON, JR., of Virginia, chief lobbyist for the national Anti-Saloon League—also played significant roles in the adoption of national Prohibition. In Congress southerners in December, 1917, voted disproportionately in favor of the Eighteenth Amendment, and the following month Mississippi, Virginia, Kentucky, and South Carolina were the first states to ratify it.

After Prohibition became effective in January, 1920, the South remained the country's strongest defender of a dry society. In 1928 the worst fears of southern drys were realized when the Democratic party, heedless of their warnings, nominated for the presidency the wet, Roman Catholic governor of New York, Alfred E. Smith. In the turbulent campaign that resulted (ELECTION OF 1928), Bishop Cannon organized the southern opposition to Smith, and the Methodist and Baptist clergy entered politics as never before. The chief concern of the leaders of this revolt was Prohibition, but Smith's urban background, his parochialism, and his religion, which prompted both responsible inquiry and scurrilous attacks, also alienated southern voters. On election day the "Hovercrats" carried ten southern states for the Republicans, including—for the first time since Reconstruction—Florida, Texas, North Carolina, and Virginia.

The dry triumph was short lived, however. In 1929 Cannon's anti-Smith coalition in Virginia suffered defeat, the bishop himself became embroiled in scandal, and Democratic voters in 1930 defeated the political leaders, such as Senator FURNIFOLD SIMMONS of North Carolina, who had bolted the party in 1928. Thus the GREAT DEPRESSION suddenly dealt Prohibition a mortal blow. In the midst of economic disaster and massive unemployment, Prohibition lost its moral urgency and soon seemed irrelevant. Repeal, in part a measure for economic recovery, came in 1933 with astonishing rapidity. In state referenda the voters of 11 southern states, in a striking reversal of public sentiment, joined the electorate elsewhere in demanding repeal. (North Carolina and South Carolina, however, voted against repeal, the only two states to do so.) Thus the "experi-

ment noble in purpose," perhaps the most characteristic of Progressive reforms, came to an abrupt end.

See J. H. Timberlake, *Prohibition and Progressive Movement* (1963), best; E. H. Cherrington (ed.), *Standard Encyclopedia of Alcohol Problem* (6 vols.; 1924–30); R. M. Miller, in E. S. Bucke (ed.), *History of American Methodism* (3 vols.; 1964), III; L. L. Gould, *Progressives and Prohibitionists* (1973), Texas, best state study; D. Burner, *Politics of Provincialism* (1968); and Cannon Papers, Duke University. See also J. R. Gusfield, *Symbolic Crusade* (1963); R. A. Hohner, *South Atlantic Quarterly* (Autumn, 1969); R. M. Miller, *American Protestantism and Social Issues* (1958); K. K. Bailey, *Southern White Protestantism* (1964); J. B. Sellers, *Prohibition in Alabama* (1943); J. S. Blocker, *Retreat from Reform, 1890–1913* (1976); D. J. Whitener, *Prohibition in North Carolina* (1945); P. E. Isaac, *Prohibition and Politics* (1965), Tennessee; C. C. Pearson and J. E. Hendricks, *Liquor in Virginia* (1967); and R. A. Hohner, "Prohibition and Virginia Politics" (Ph.D. dissertation, Duke, 1965) and *Journal of Southern History* (Feb., 1968).

ROBERT A. HOHNER
University of Western Ontario

PROSSER REVOLT. See GABRIEL'S INSURRECTION

PROSTITUTION in the South differed in degree and character from that in other sections of the country. Smaller cities meant in part that commercialized vice, as traditionally understood, would be less prevalent. The more complicated ingredient, however, that set antebellum prostitution in a mold different from that of the North was the factor of race. In Charleston, Mobile, and New Orleans the keeping of mulatto mistresses and the general prevalence of MISCEGENATION tended both to limit and modify the free enterprise character of the commerce in women. Indeed, a traffic in mulatto women for purposes of prostitution was a recognized aspect of the domestic SLAVE TRADE.

More is known of the vice trade of New Orleans than of any other southern city. Thriving on service to the flatboat crews and rivermen in the early nineteenth century, prostitution increased with the commercial growth of the city and flourished during the years of Civil War and Reconstruction. In 1857 New Orleans legalized prostitution, being the first city in the United States to do so. Although the law was declared unconstitutional in 1859, it was renewed in 1897. In that year prostitution was legally confined to a 38-block area of the French Quarter, known as STORYVILLE. With its luxurious and plush bordellos, Storyville was the most celebrated red-light district in the United States and a center for the distribution of prostitutes, black and white, to Galveston, Memphis, Atlanta, and other southern cities.

Prior to the twentieth century no dramatic outcry against prostitution occurred in the United States. During the Progressive period, however, came a new attitude about sex, a growing consciousness about the plight of women, and a belief that the society was ripe for both moral and social improvement (PROGRESSIVISM). There was a belief in some circles that prostitution could be completely abolished. This new outlook generated an unprecedented crusade against prostitution. Unlike in northern cities, however, there are no available studies of "vice crusades" in the cities of the South. This absence suggests that the crusade against prostitution was weaker in southern than in northern cities.

Despite such citizen uprisings, prostitution continued to flourish in the United States throughout the twentieth century in the North and South. New sexual mores, an increased tolerance of sexual deviance, the movement for sexual liberation, and the discovery of male prostitution have all attenuated the public's concern about commercialized vice. It is not so much the moral issue but the increasing incidences of VENEREAL DISEASE and drug addiction among those who trade love for money that have in recent years commanded the most serious attention.

See, for colonial period, scattered references in C. Bridenbaugh, *Cities in Wilderness* (1966) and *Cities in Revolt* (1971); for early racial sexual attitudes, W. D. Jordan, *White over Black* (1968); and for New Orleans, read with caution the valuable H. Asbury, *French Quarter* (1968), and the prostitute's biography, N. Kimball, *Her Life as an American Madam* (1970). For general surveys, see C. Winick and P. M. Kinsie, *Lively Commerce* (1971); and H. B. Woolston, *Prostitution in U.S.* (1969). On Progressive uprising and vice commissions, see J. Addams, *New Conscience* (1912); L. W. Banner, *Women in Modern America* (1974); E. Feldman, *American Quarterly* (Summer, 1967); R. Lubove, *Historian* (Fall, 1962); J. Mayer, *Regulation of Commercialized Vice* (1922); and H. Woods, *America* (May, 1913). For more recent decades, see T. C. Esselstyn, *Annals of American Academy of Political and Social Science* (March, 1968); L. Graham, *Sexual Revolution* (1971); and R. Riegel, *Journal of History of Ideas* (July–Sept., 1968).

EGAL FELDMAN
University of Wisconsin, Superior

PRYOR, ROGER ATKINSON (1828–1919), was born in Dinwiddie County, Va. He followed parallel careers in politics, law, and journalism, editing among others the Washington *Union* and the Richmond *Enquirer*. He was minister to Greece (1855) and a member of Congress (1859–1861). Briefly a Confederate congressman, he served with great distinction in the army as colonel and brigadier general of the 3rd Virginia Infantry and later as a private in FITZHUGH LEE's cavalry. Captured before Petersburg in November, 1864, he was imprisoned five months in Ft. Lafayette but was released on parole by order of President Abraham Lincoln. After 1865 Pryor began life anew in New York, becoming a leader of the bar and serving as judge of common pleas and justice of the supreme court (1890–1899).

See S. A. Pryor, *Reminiscences* (1908), fullest; New York *Times* (July 19, 1908; March 15, 1919); C. A. Evans, *Confederate Military History* (1912), III; T. T. Epes, *Kaleidoscope* (1903); and R. A. Pryor, *Religious and Secular Culture* (1873) and *Essays and Addresses* (1912).

EDWARD M. STEEL, JR.
West Virginia University

PUBLIC HEALTH. See HEALTH, PUBLIC

PUBLIC HOUSES. Seventeenth-century Englishmen stopped overnight at inns when they traveled; at home they drank wine in taverns or ale and beer in less fashionable alehouses. Their inns typically had no common dining or drinking rooms, and "gentlemen" dined in their own rooms, ordering whatever they pleased. Seventeenth-century southern colonists, however, frequented only one type of public house, an all-purpose institution called an ordinary. The word signified a "place of eating at a set price," usually at a common table. Colonial laws required that anyone licensed to serve "strong drink" must also provide ordinary meals, lodging, and stabling for horses. Prices were set by authorities, who ordered them posted "in the common room."

Early company and colony governments discouraged the sale of wine in ordinaries. Later, as wine licenses were issued, keepers renamed their houses taverns. More prestigious, tavern became the popular name for all public houses before 1776, but ordinary lingered later in law books and some rural areas. A few coffeehouses appeared in the late colonial South. The French word *hôtel* was popularized between 1776 and 1793, when the Union Public Hotel was offered as a grand prize in a lottery designed to promote the new "Federal City." By 1825 tavern was used mainly for rural and old, second-rate urban houses.

Significantly, the new hotel served ordinary meals, and its dining room was called the ordinary. Antebellum British travelers were surprised and puzzled by the ordinary, the large common parlor and barroom, and the huge, many-galleried lobby. Several described Barnum's Baltimore City

Hotel (1826) or the New Orleans St. Charles Hotel (1836) as the biggest and best house in the country. This American-plan hotel remained the typical one in southern cities until almost 1900.

The European-plan hotel, which replaced it, provided lodging; but the new restaurant or café, which served à la carte and table d'hôte meals, was frequently a separate business. The new custom of tipping drove many hotel guests to new tipless cafeterias and lunch counters. Those who searched for the barroom frequently found it down the street, transformed into a saloon. Prohibition killed the saloon, but repeal fathered a new species of southern tavern, one licensed to sell nothing stronger than beer or wine, usually on condition that it also serve food. The best of the breed was a good, wine-licensed restaurant. Southern states were reluctant to permit the sale of liquor by the drink, and the cocktail lounge is still illegal in some of them. Few all-purpose colonial tavern buildings survive, and those open to the public usually serve only as restaurants or museums.

The present-day motel evolved from the tourist or motor court composed of several cabins, each with its own garage. The word *motel*, denoting a roadside motor hotel, was used in California in 1925, but the new name and the long one-story building composed of adjoining bedrooms, each with its own front door and parking space, became common in the South only after 1950. The rapid growth in the number and size of motels since 1950 has driven many Mom-and-Pop establishments out of business, and today's typical motel is a link in a corporately controlled chain. Holiday Inns, Inc., the nation's largest motel company, is a Tennessee corporation founded by homebuilders Kemmons Wilson and Wallace E. Johnson. Wilson opened the first Holiday Inn (Memphis) in 1952. In August, 1975, there were 1,706 Holiday Inns in 44 countries. Few downtown hotels were built 1930–1960, but many tall hotel-motel structures have risen more recently in downtown, suburban, and airport areas. This architectural synthesis is evidenced by new high-rise Holiday Inns containing traditional hotel dining, drinking, and meeting rooms and by the practice of adding parking decks and the words *motor inn* to old hotels. The return of the huge, galleried lobby was heralded by architect John C. Portman's design for the 22-story atrium of the Regency-Hyatt House in Atlanta (1967) and reflected in the 1974 announcement that Holiday Inns planned to build some new multistory units around an atrium or "fun dome." Portman's 70-story Peachtree Center Plaza (Atlanta), which features an artificial lake in the lobby, opened in 1976. It is advertised as the world's tallest hotel and the South's tallest building.

See D. E. King, "Hotels of Old South" (Ph.D. dissertation, Duke, 1952), *Journal of Southern History* (May, 1957), *Explorations* (Feb., 1956), *Hotel-Restaurant* (Oct., 1968), "Transformation of the English Inn" (paper, AHA convention, Dec., 1970), and *Never Let People Be Kept Waiting*, King Reprints 1 (1973); G. L. Eskew, *Willard's* (1954); J. L. Sultzby, *Alabama Hotels* (1960); *Southern Hotel Journal*; *Hotel Monthly*; *Tourist Court Journal*; K. Wilson, *Holiday Inn Story* (1972); and Holiday Inns, Inc., annual and quarterly reports.

DORIS ELIZABETH KING
North Carolina State University

PUBLIC WELFARE. See WELFARE, PUBLIC

PUBLIC WORKS ADMINISTRATION was established in June, 1933, in accordance with Title 2 of the National Industrial Recovery Act. Congress, which intended PWA to stimulate the depression-laden economy, appropriated $3.3 billion to achieve this end. Secretary of Interior Harold Ickes, the careful and honest administrator of the PWA, produced few immediate results, since the PWA undertook projects only after lengthy, intensive scrutiny. It did, however, simultaneously move in several directions: it constructed its own projects, provided funds for projects carried out by other federal agencies, and lent money to private corporations (although this program was discontinued) and to state governments for specific projects. In addition, it directly funded some state projects.

If the PWA shortcoming was lack of speed (it therefore was supplemented by other federal agencies), it nevertheless produced an abundance of public works that boosted the economy by the latter 1930s. In the South, PWA built military airports (as part of a larger military construction program), docks, bridges, FLOOD CONTROL projects, hospitals, power plants, schools, and courthouses as well as minor projects. It helped rural people with jobs on the roads (but at a lower pay rate than PWA paid in the North). In two southern states PWA lent money to farmers for seeds and tools. A typical PWA success in the South was the revival of a dying Key West, Fla. An island city that once boasted the highest per capita income in the United States, it fell into bankruptcy in 1934 with 80 percent of its population receiving public assistance. In addition to providing jobs resulting from the rebuilding of the city into a tourist center, PWA provided the capital for a 170-mile highway connecting the island to the Florida mainland. This permitted the state to build what one contemporary called the "largest overseas thoroughfare in the world." Today's prosperous Key West serves as a typical monument to the PWA in the South.

See A. M. Schlesinger, Jr., *Coming of New Deal* (1959); W. E. Leuchtenburg, *FDR and New Deal* (1963); and B. Mitchel, *Depression Decade* (1947).

NEIL B. BETTEN
Florida State University

PUBLISHING INDUSTRY. See PRINTING AND PUBLISHING INDUSTRY

PULP AND PAPER INDUSTRY has exhibited consistent growth since 1920, when 24 small pulp mills in the South had an average daily capacity of 41 tons, which accounted for only six percent of the national total. By 1964, 82 mills had increased the South's share of national capacity to 57 percent. In 1971 the region contained 117 pulp-paper mills whose combined daily capacity of 81,000 tons accounted for about 63 percent of national capacity. Despite these tremendous increases, the industry operated at greater than 94 percent of plant capacity from the close of World War II through 1974, reflecting the long-term growth in the national demand for paper products and the South's role in meeting it.

Although the expanding national market was an underlying factor, the industry's growth was triggered by technological innovations that shifted the industry's resource base from the hardwoods of the southern Appalachians to the vast yellow pine forests on the plains of the South Atlantic and Gulf coasts. Prior to 1920, the small Appalachian plants used pulp from hardwoods to which they applied either the caustic soda or sulfite process to remove lignins and resinous materials. Neither process was effective when applied to the high-resin pines of the coastal plains. The sulfate process, in which sulfuric acid is the principal chemical solvent and which was developed in Germany in 1884, was adapted to produce bleached pulp and newsprint from yellow pine through technological modifications developed by Dr. Charles H. Herty (1867–1938) between 1920 and 1933. Herty's work was sponsored by the U.S. Forest Service. The industry expanded rapidly in the South after 1936 because of regionally low manufacturing costs, an abundant raw material supply, forest regrowth rates more than twice as great as those in other principal U.S. forest regions, climatic conditions that permitted virtually year-round pulpwood harvesting, and a large number of sites with abundant water supplies.

Pulp-paper manufacture is a raw-materials-oriented and bulk-reducing process in which, at one stage, the pulp is in a solution that is more than 95 percent water. Thus, when locating within pine forests of the coastal plains, the industry developed plants at riverside and river mouth sites. By 1950 four areal concentrations of plants had emerged: the South Carolina, Georgia, and northeast Florida coast; the northwest Florida and Alabama coast, centered particularly on Mobile Bay; tidewater Virginia and Albemarle Sound; and adjacent to the Red and Mississippi rivers in Louisiana and southwestern Mississippi. Plants constructed since 1950 have occupied riverside sites as far inland as the fall zone in Georgia, Alabama, and the Carolinas, the great Appalachian Valley in eastern Tennessee and northwestern Alabama, northwestern Texas, and south-central Arkansas. Since World War II the traditional leader in pulpwood cut and mill output has been the South Carolina, Georgia, and north Florida area; it was surpassed for the first time by the mid-South states (Alabama, Mississippi, Arkansas, Louisiana) in 1969. Since 1960 wood residues from other wood products manufactures have become an increasingly important raw material. Received overwhelmingly in the form of wood chips, by 1970 residues accounted for 20 percent of the regional pulpwood supply. Some 900 sawmills and veneer mills were the main sources.

The variety of paper stocks produced has increased since establishment of the initial sulfate mills, producing kraft papers. Semichemical processes for pulping of hardwoods (mostly culls from the pine forests) have been added to many mills, resulting both in an enlarged raw materials base and in greater product variety. Mixed with pine pulp in different amounts depending upon the end product, the hardwood fibers add stiffness and strength to paperboard, smoothness to printing, magazine, book, and business papers, and strength to newsprint. Since 1970 southern plants have produced about 90 percent of the national paperboard output, more than half its newsprint, about one-fourth of printing, writing, business, and book grades of paper, all the cigarette paper, and varying but large proportions of wrapping and bagging as well.

About 86 percent of the southern woodland is privately owned in small tracts averaging less than 200 acres. Pulp mills rarely control forest land sufficient to supply more than 35 percent of their wood requirements. Mills purchase most of their wood from dealers, widely distributed throughout the pine forest area, who in turn purchase from "producers"—small-scale entrepreneurs (mostly blacks) who contract with landowners to cut and market their woodstuffs. Prior to 1950, most pulpwood was hand loaded into boxcars at the dealer's rail siding. In 1952 the first mechanized railside woodyard was installed at Union Point, Ga., and by 1970 more than 1,100 were in operation. In the contemporary dealer's woodyard, pulpwood is moved from the producer's trucks by mechanical loaders to the modified rail flatcar (called a pulpwood "rack") in uniform lots and lengths and then proceeds in trainloads to the recipient mill.

See N. C. Brown, *Forest Products* (1950); J. H. Allen, *Southern Pulp and Paper Journal* (Dec., 1938), history; P. R. Hagenstein, *Pulpwood Annual* (1965); A. I. Jeffords, *Journal of Forestry* (July, 1956), marketing; M. C. Prunty, *Economic Geography* (Jan., 1956), recent expansion; and T. A. Walbridge and L. H. Camisa, *Forest Farmer* (March, 1966), mechanization.

MERLE C. PRUNTY
University of Georgia

Q

QUAKERS are a religious group that was founded by George Fox in seventeenth-century England. Fox emphasized the presence of the Inner Light, "the heavenly guide given directly to inform or illuminate the individual conscience." He believed in a revival of the primitive Christianity of the first-century church, and on that basis he rejected any distinction between clergy and laity or between men and women in the church. He refused to swear an oath, he rejected military service, he refused to pay tithes to the church, and he rejected the outward forms of baptism and the communion. Fox was zealous and enthusiastic, and he quickly gained followers, who became known as the Society of Friends. They shared his zeal and enthusiasm and became missionary minded. The first Quakers arrived in America in 1656 in Boston. The Puritans were vigorously opposed to these new religious ideas and banished the Quakers. The Quakers were persistent, however, even though by 1660 the Puritans had hanged four Quakers, including one woman. Shortly after their arrival in Massachusetts, the Quakers were also entering Maryland and Virginia. They were no more welcome in Virginia than in Massachusetts, and in 1661 a Quaker died in a Virginia prison "after being cruelly scourged and heavily ironed, for a long period." But the Quakers kept coming, including a visit to Maryland, Virginia, and Carolina by Fox in 1672. In the 1670s and the 1680s the Quakers established settlements in the two Carolina colonies, and in the 1750s they finally arrived in Georgia. These seventeenth-century settlements were established near the seacoast.

In contrast, the Quakers established a number of more permanent settlements, especially in North Carolina, in the interior during the eighteenth century by moving down the mountain valleys from Pennsylvania. Some of these settlements were terminated in the early nineteenth century by the extensive migration of Quakers to the Northwest to escape the slavery of the South.

The Quakers have been very reform minded and socially concerned. Under the leadership of John Woolman (1720–1772), they had eliminated slavery from their own group and had become a vigorous antislavery group by 1800. Also, they supported temperance, democracy, and popular education. In North Carolina their schools helped to shape the public educational system. North Carolina has the only Quaker college in the South today, Guilford College. They have been pacifists and have tried to keep their members out of military service and to support peace in every way possible. In 1917 they organized the American Friends Service Committee to render relief and reconstruction in the war-torn world; it has continued to be active.

The problems of adjusting to a changing world have caused divisions among the Quakers. By the 1970s there were at least four major groups: Conservative, Evangelical Friends Alliance, Friends United Meeting, and General Conference. All these groups are represented in the South, where there are about 200 Quaker meetings located in all the southern states except Mississippi. North Carolina has the most meetings with nearly 90. Other states with more than ten meetings are Virginia, Texas, Florida, Maryland, and Tennessee. Many of these southern meetings have been established in the twentieth century.

See S. B. Weeks, *Southern Quakers and Slavery* (1896); F. C. Anscombe, *I Have Called You Friends* (1959); J. F. Moore, *Sources of Quaker History in North Carolina* (1967); and Friends World Committee, *Friends Directory* (1973).

ROGER E. SAPPINGTON
Bridgewater College

QUANTICO, VA. (pop. 719), on the Potomac River, is approximately 30 miles southwest of Washington, D.C. The name is of Indian origin and means "by the long stream." Used as a base to service American naval vessels during the Revolutionary War, the site became a training camp for the U.S. Marine Corps in 1917.

QUANTRILL, WILLIAM CLARKE (1837–1865), alias Charley Hart, was born in Canal Dover, Ohio. He became a schoolteacher prior to his migration to Kansas Territory in 1857 and after his arrival taught in Lawrence. Regarding the euphemistic free-state versus slave-state struggle, Quantrill initially appeared to align with the free-state elements. With the outbreak of the Civil War, however, he joined the Confederate army. He fought at Lexington, Mo., and as a Confederate captain was credited with the capture of Independence, Mo., in August, 1862. On August 21, 1863, he made his famous or infamous guerrilla raid on Lawrence, Kansas Territory, which had served as headquarters for the notorious free-state guerrillas known as the Redlegs. Also, Lawrence was the home of the hated James H. Lane, who had led the Kansas Jayhawkers in bloody guerrilla activities along the Missouri border, climaxed by Lane's sacking and burning of Osceola, Mo., in 1861. With a band of approximately 300 men Quantrill retaliated by sacking and burning Lawrence, killing approximately 150 men. No women were killed. Among those who accompanied Quantrill were William F. ("Bloody Bill") Anderson, Cole Younger, George Todd, Frank James, and possibly Jesse James. Quantrill fled in 1865 to Kentucky, where he was fatally wounded by Union forces in Spencer County.

See A. Castel, *William Clarke Quantrill* (1962), best; and B. J. Williams, *Kansas Historical Quarterly* (Summer, 1968), latest interpretation and motives for sacking Lawrence.

BURTON J. WILLIAMS
Central Washington State College

QUAPAW INDIANS, also called Arkansas Indians, are members of the Hokan-Siouan Indian family. French explorers encountered them in the area of today's state of Arkansas. Forced from that area by U.S. Indian policy, the Quapaw found refuge with other Indians. By 1852 the Quapaw moved to a reserve in Indian Territory. During the 1860s and 1870s they were forced to migrate again. They did not reunite on their reserve until the 1880s. Today most Quapaw engage in farming and business on the Miami Agency, Okla.

See F. Hodge, *Handbook* (1912); M. Wright, *Guide to Indian Tribes* (1951); G. Foreman, in C. Wilson (ed.), *Indians of Eastern Oklahoma* (1956); J. Swanton, *Indians* (1946); V. Thompson, *History of the Quapaw* (1937); James Owen Dorsey Papers, Bureau of American Ethnology Archives; Records of Office of Secretary of War, Record Group 107, Office of Secretary of Interior, Record Group 48, and Bureau of Indian Affairs, Record Group 75, all in National Archives; and Bureau of Indian Affairs Public Information Office, Washington, D.C., helpful for current information.

EDWARD A. LUKES
Hillsborough College

QUARLES, BENJAMIN (1904–), one of the foremost scholars of Afro-American history, was born in Boston, graduated from Shaw University in Raleigh, N.C. (1931), and received his M.A. and Ph.D. degrees from the University of Wisconsin (1933, 1940). From 1939 to 1953 he taught at Dillard University in New Orleans and since 1953 has taught at Morgan State College in Baltimore. His first book, *Frederick Douglass* (1948), is still the standard biography. His second, *The Negro in the Civil War* (1953), and his fourth, *Lincoln and the Negro* (1962), provide the most readable accounts of the role of blacks in the Civil War. For a treatment of blacks in the American Revolution, the student can read nothing better than Professor Quarles's *The Negro in the American Revolution* (1961). Two of his most recent books, *Black Abolitionists* (1969) and *Allies for Freedom: Blacks and John Brown* (1974), provide definitive accounts of Negroes in the abolitionist movement. Quarles has also written a brief general narrative of Afro-American history, *The Negro in the Making of America* (1964), has edited several collections of documents, and is the author of numerous articles in scholarly journals. While teaching at Dillard University he was secretary of the New Orleans Urban League (1947–1951) and has also served as vice-president of the Baltimore Urban League (1957–1959).

JAMES M. MCPHERSON
Princeton University

QUIDS, or tertium quids, a faction of the Republican party, for the most part were southerners who declared that Thomas Jefferson and James Madison had abandoned fundamental Republican principles of 1798. Although the term appears to have been first employed in Pennsylvanian party disputes during 1804, it was enlarged by JOHN RANDOLPH of Roanoke in Congress in his second speech on Andrew Gregg's resolution (March 6, 1806). By the tertium quids or "Quiddists," Randolph signified a "third thing" or "third force" in national politics, opposed both to the Jefferson administration and to the Federalists. The quids of 1806 vehemently protested schemes for compensating the purchasers of Yazoo lands, negotiations with France for acquiring West Florida, and restraints upon trade with Britain. Randolph, NATHANIEL MACON, and Joseph Nicholson were their leaders in the U.S. House of Representatives, and JOHN TAYLOR of Caroline was their principal writer.

See N. Risjord, *Old Republicans* (1965); N. Cunningham, *Mississippi Valley Historical Review* (Sept., 1963); and R. Kirk, *John Randolph of Roanoke* (1964).

RUSSELL KIRK
University Bookman

QUITMAN, JOHN ANTHONY (1799–1858), was born in Rhinebeck, N.Y., and migrated to Mississippi in 1821 after a brief sojourn in Ohio. His marriage to Eliza Turner of a wealthy Mississippi family converted him into a cotton planter, and he became a leading southern FIRE-EATER. He held numerous offices: state representative (1826–1827), chancellor of the state (1828–1835), member of the constitutional convention of 1832, president of the state senate and acting governor (1835–1836), judge of the high court of errors and appeals (1838), governor (1850–1851), and U.S. congressman (1855–1858). In the 1830s during the NULLIFICATION controversy, Quitman led in the formation of the States' Rights party in Mississippi. In the 1840s he deserted the Whigs, rejoined the Democrats, and led the opposition to the COMPROMISE OF 1850. He was a strong supporter of manifest destiny and served as a major general in the Mexican War. He became the first civil and military governor of Mexico City in 1848 after the American occupation. He was a strong advocate of the annexation of Cuba to the United States and was indicted for violating the Neutrality Act of 1818. His only national political office was in the U.S. House of Representatives.

See J. H. McClendon, "Quitman" (Ph.D. dissertation, University of Texas, 1949), best recent work; and J. F. H. Claiborne, *Life and Correspondence of Quitman* (2 vols; 1860).

JOHN EDMOND GONZALES
University of Southern Mississippi

QUITRENTS originated as a commutation of certain feudal obligations, a payment that absolved or made quit a tenant from personal service or other obligations to the feudal overlord. In the American colonies quitrents were due, theoretically, from all landholders as one condition of their tenure in consequence of the theory that all lands belonged to the monarch and were granted according to forms of feudal tenure, some already obsolete in England itself. In the royal colonies, quitrents were usually collected by a receiver general appointed by the crown. Nominal in amount, typically two shillings per 100 acres, payable in real money or its equivalent in produce, they were rarely burdensome unless cash were demanded. Effective collection was hindered by scattered settlement, a prevalent shortage of specie, and outdated or incomplete rent rolls. In the proprietary colonies, the quitrents were payable to the proprietor and constituted private income, the most valuable of the returns from his American holdings. He in turn made token payment, often symbolic, to the monarch, as the two Indian arrows annually rendered by the Calverts for Maryland.

See B. W. Bond, Jr., *Quit Rent System* (1919); C. M. Andrews, *Colonial Period* (1934–38), for individual colonies; and H. L. Osgood, *American Colonies in Seventeenth Century* (1904–07).

GEORGE M. WALLER
Butler University

R

RAILROADS. The southern states were active in their promotion of railroads in the early nineteenth century. As in the rest of the nation, southern commercial cities were early sponsors of the new form of transport. Baltimore businessmen chartered the Baltimore & Ohio Railroad in 1827. Two years later, on Christmas Day, 1830, the American-built locomotive Best Friend of Charleston carried 141 passengers out of Charleston on the first scheduled run of a steam railroad train in the country. Other construction followed, and railroads appeared in Delaware, Virginia, and Louisiana during 1831, Alabama in 1832, and Kentucky in 1834. By 1840 nearly 900 miles of railroad, located in nine states, gave the South nearly a third of the total mileage in the nation.

During the forties construction continued, and by 1850 the total in the South was over 2,400 miles. The network at mid-century was far from complete, but Richmond had rail service down to Wilmington, and farther south Charleston and Savannah had lines as far west as Atlanta and Chattanooga. Even though much of the region was still sparsely settled, more than 8,000 miles of line were built during the prosperous fifties. In 1860 the 15 slave states could claim more than 10,800 miles of railroad, or more than a third of the national total. Still, on the eve of the Civil War, southern railroads lagged well behind those of the North in the quality of original construction, equipment and rolling stock, number of employees, volume of traffic, and the facilities for proper maintenance.

Even with these shortcomings many Confederate railroads enjoyed an expanding traffic and a certain prosperity early in the Civil War. But much of the prosperity on the 8,700-mile Confederate rail network was soon proved unreal because of inflation and the growing expenses of operation. By mid-war a growing deterioration of rail service was caused by general abuse, equipment shortages, and the difficulty of track maintenance. Even in their weakened condition southern railroads continued to serve the military needs of the Confederacy. Sometimes the troop movements were immense. In late July and early August, 1862, General BRAXTON BRAGG moved his entire army of 30,000 men from Tupelo, Miss., to Chattanooga over an indirect rail route via Mobile, Montgom-

ery, and Atlanta. A year later, in September, 1863, Bragg was reinforced when General JAMES LONGSTREET's I Corps of the Army of Northern Virginia moved by rail some 900 miles from Richmond to northern Georgia. As Union forces carried the war into the South, more and more Confederate lines suffered destruction at the hands of one military force or the other. Much of this destruction was in the states of Mississippi, Alabama, Georgia, South Carolina, and Virginia. By the spring of 1865, Confederate rail lines were in as crippled a condition as the armies they had sought to support during the war.

In the summer and fall of 1865, twisted rails, a disintegrating right-of-way, destroyed depots and bridges, and dilapidated or lost rolling stock were typical of the railroads of the defeated Confederacy. However, the restoration of at least some rail service was quite rapid. In the generation after the war southern railroads experienced in turn the corruption of northern carpetbaggers, widespread receivership, the construction of much new mileage, and finally an extensive period of merger and consolidation, which was accompanied by a growing control by northern financiers.

The late sixties and early seventies were years of profitable railroad activity by carpetbaggers and their southern collaborators. The worst corruption was in the four states of North Carolina, South Carolina, Georgia, and Alabama. The carpetbaggers were far more interested in personal profit than in building new lines. Thus many states paid hundreds of thousands of dollars for railroads that were never completed or placed in operation. Southern roads were in a weakened financial condition in the postwar years, and many were hit hard by the PANIC OF 1873. The sequence of default, receivership, and foreclosure became commonplace. By 1876 more than 40 percent of all southern lines were in default on their bond coupons. In the rest of the nation less than a quarter of the railroads were in default.

In the last decades of the nineteenth century, the southern rail network in the 16 states grew from 10,800 miles in 1860 to 15,400 miles in 1870, 24,800 miles in 1880, 48,900 miles in 1890, and 59,600 miles in 1900. In the sixties and seventies new construction in the South was held in check by the Civil War, Reconstruction, and the depression. After 1880 rail construction picked up quickly, and in the eighties southern trackage nearly doubled. This was especially true west of the Mississippi. In both 1870 and 1880 Missouri led the South in rail mileage, an honor that was lost to Texas by 1890. The decade of the eighties was also marked by the shift of southern track to standard gauge, the change occurring in 1886.

In the early postwar years nearly all southern railroads continued to be largely owned and controlled by southern men and money. The trend toward outside or northern control gained headway with the sequence of receivership and reorganization present during the seventies. The growing mergers and consolidations typical of the prosperous eighties found still more southern railway shifting to northern financial management. In the last decade of the century, another period of extensive receivership failed to slow the inevitable trend toward larger rail systems, most of which were northern controlled. Well before the turn of the century northern men and money, as well as management, firmly dominated the railroads of the South.

As in the rest of the nation, several large railroads dominated rail transport in the South by 1900. Three roads—the Baltimore & Ohio, the Chesapeake & Ohio, and the Norfolk & Western—were of major importance in Virginia and the border states to the north. Both the B & O and the C & O also served the region north of the Ohio River. South of the Potomac three railroads—the Atlantic Coast Line, the Seaboard Air Line, and the Southern—served all the South Atlantic states. Three other major roads—the Illinois Central, the Louisville & Nashville, and the Mobile & Ohio—served the four states of Alabama, Mississippi, Tennessee, and Kentucky. West of the Mississippi two additional lines, the Missouri Pacific and the Southern Pacific, had extensive mileage in the region bounded by St. Louis, New Orleans, and El Paso.

Quite early in the twentieth century, southern railroads faced competition from new modes of transport. The passenger train in turn was challenged by electric interurbans, private automobiles, intercity buses, and finally airliners. Freight traffic was lost to larger and larger trucks, a growing network of pipelines of increasing capacity, and improved river and canal barge service. The competition from the new transport facilities did not become too serious until the 1920s and 1930s. During the twenties the railroads still carried about three-quarters of all commercial intercity freight and passenger traffic. By the early 1970s the rail share of such freight traffic was under 40

percent, and rail passenger business had dropped to well under 10 percent of the total commercial traffic.

Railroad mileage in the South increased in the first decades of the new century at a faster rate than in the nation at large. The southern network of 59,600 miles in 1900 grew to 84,600 miles by 1920, an increase of 42 percent. After 1920 total rail mileage in the South gradually declined with the rest of the nation. Some southern states, however, added new mileage during the twenties. Between 1920 and 1930 only five states east of the Mississippi increased their mileage, and four of these (Florida, Kentucky, Maryland, and West Virginia) were southern states. After 1920 the South continued to have almost exactly one-third of the nation's total rail mileage.

Several times during the twentieth century southern railroads served a nation at war. Both in World War I and World War II the contribution to victory made by southern railroads was unique since so large a portion of military-training installations was located in southern states. During World War II southern railways were especially vital since they carried a major share of the oil to the East after German submarines had pinched off coastal and Gulf tanker service.

All American railroads prospered during World War II, but southern lines during the years 1941 to 1945 earned a rate of return well above that typical of northern and western roads. This greater prosperity for southern lines, which continued to be true in the generation following 1945, was partly based upon the increasing rail freight traffic in southern states. Rail freight tonnage originating in the Southern District (east of the Mississippi River and south of the Ohio River and Virginia) in 1947 amounted to only 15 percent of the national total. By 1973 the Southern District was accounting for above 24 percent of such rail freight. The favorable economic health of several southern lines was also helped by such innovations as early dieselization, the increased use of new types of freight equipment, the investment in computerized terminal yards, and the extensive introduction of mechanized track and roadbed maintenance. In the postwar years southern railroads were contributing to, and sharing in, the economic and industrial growth generally present in the region.

Organized in 1889, the **Atlantic Coast Line** consisted of a number of small lines extending from Richmond and Norfolk down into the Carolinas. The first segment of the system was created shortly after the Civil War when two Baltimore businessmen, William T. Walters and Benjamin F.

Newcomer, gained control of two roads connecting Weldon, N.C., with several cities in South Carolina. As a Baltimore commission merchant, Walters was eager to establish a rapid movement of North Carolina garden truck to northern cities. The railroad continued to grow and by 1900 consisted of a system of over 2,100 miles. In 1902 the Atlantic Coast Line acquired the Plant System, which provided important extensions into Georgia, Florida, and Alabama. In the same year a substantial share of the capital stock of the Louisville & Nashville was also purchased. Throughout most of the twentieth century the system was prosperous, paying regular dividends. In 1967 the Atlantic Coast Line merged with the Seaboard Air Line to form the new 9,000-mile Seaboard Coast Line.

Founded in 1827 by business interests in Baltimore to link the Atlantic seaboard with the Ohio River, the **Baltimore & Ohio** was one of the nation's first railroads. The main line to Harpers Ferry was opened in 1834, and service to Washington, D.C., was inaugurated the following year. The line across the mountains to Wheeling on the Ohio River was opened late in 1852. Western extensions were completed to St. Louis in 1857 and Chicago in 1874. During the Civil War the B & O was an important rail lifeline for the North, although often vulnerable to Confederate attack. The postwar development of the road was greatly influenced by two men: John W. Garrett, president from 1858 to 1884, and Daniel Willard, president from 1910 to 1941. By the time of the road's centennial in 1927, the B & O was a rail system of over 5,000 miles. By this time the majority of the road's mileage lay north of the Mason-Dixon Line or the Ohio River. Between 1960 and 1963 the more prosperous Chesapeake & Ohio took over the larger Baltimore & Ohio, creating a combined system of about 11,000 miles.

Chartered in 1835, the **Central of Georgia** was built to funnel the commerce of the state to the port of Savannah. The charter also allowed the railroad to engage in banking, a function that was continued until after the Civil War. The main line to Macon was completed by 1843, and the line, economically built and efficiently managed, was profitable from the start. Service was extended to Atlanta, Chattanooga, and southwestern Georgia before the Civil War. Considering the wartime destruction in the state, the postwar restoration of the Central of Georgia was quite rapid. The line remained prosperous until the late 1880s. Between 1887 and 1891 the Central of Georgia went completely under northern financial control, specifically that of the Richmond & West Point Ter-

minal Company. These were years of an increasing funded debt and lower net earnings, and the railroad was placed in receivership in 1892. When the road was reorganized in 1895, it consisted of more than 1,600 miles serving Georgia and eastern Alabama. The Illinois Central obtained a controlling interest in the company early in the twentieth century, but a subsequent reorganization eventually rendered the investment worthless. In 1963 the Central of Georgia was acquired by the Southern Railway.

The **Chesapeake & Ohio** was the result of an 1868 merger of two earlier Virginia roads, the Virginia Central and the Covington & Ohio. Efforts to build the line over the mountains to the Ohio River were successful only after Collis P. Huntington became interested in the line late in 1869. The 428-mile line from Richmond to Huntington, W.Va., was completed early in 1873. By 1882 the road was built eastward to Newport News, Va., and by the turn of the century the C & O was operating 1,475 miles of route with service to Washington, Lynchburg, Cincinnati, and Louisville. Before 1920 the C & O had extended its service across the Ohio River through Indiana to ports on Lake Michigan and Lake Erie. Its acquisition in 1947 of the 1,900-mile Pere Marquette gave it still more northern mileage. The C & O had always been a major carrier of coal, and by mid-century it was originating more coal traffic than any other railroad in the nation. Even though its large coal business made it reluctant to give up steam power, the C & O had achieved complete dieselization by the late 1950s. The prosperous Chesapeake & Ohio merged with the Baltimore & Ohio in the early 1960s and later in the decade added another important coal carrier, the 800-mile Western Maryland.

The **East Tennessee, Virginia & Georgia** was formed in 1869 out of two roads built in the 1850s. The 270-mile road ran southwestward from Bristol, Tenn., via Knoxville to Chattanooga and Dalton, Ga. During the Civil War the line was a valuable rail link between the western Confederacy and the Virginia front. Between 1865 and 1880 the line remained under southern control, expanded modestly, and paid dividends even during the depression of the seventies. The expansion of the line during the eighties was much more rapid, growing from 592 miles in 1880 to 2,594 miles in 1890. The quality of the financing by new northern managers did not match the rate of expansion, and the road was in receivership by 1885. Later the railroad came under the control of the Richmond & West Point Terminal. When the latter company was reorganized in the early 1890s, the railroad property was included in the new Southern Railway.

The **Illinois Central** was built from Chicago and East Dubuque to Cairo, Ill., in the early 1850s. Wishing to increase its southern traffic, the Illinois Central after the Civil War became financially interested in the Mississippi Central and the New Orleans, Jackson & Great Northern. When these southern lines went bankrupt during the depression, the Illinois Central purchased them under foreclosure in 1877. Merged as the Chicago, St. Louis & New Orleans, the new road gave the Illinois Central control of a rail route to the Gulf. The Illinois Central shifted its southern trackage to standard gauge several years ahead of other southern lines. By 1900 a major portion of its more than 5,000 miles of line was located south of the Ohio River in the states of Kentucky, Tennessee, Mississippi, and Louisiana. Always a prosperous road, the Illinois Central paid regular dividends from the Civil War until the depression of the 1930s. The Illinois Central was one of the first railways to ship southern fruits to northern markets under refrigeration, and it also was an early sponsor of scientific farming, crop diversification, and reforestation. In 1972 the Illinois Central merged with the Gulf, Mobile & Ohio to form the new 9,400-mile Illinois Central Gulf.

The **Louisville & Nashville** was built in the late 1850s for the purpose of diverting traffic to the river port of Louisville. With a total line of over 250 miles on the eve of the Civil War, the L & N prospered greatly during the four years of war. After the war, while other southern roads were facing problems of rehabilitation, the L & N was declaring dividends. In the early postwar years southern control of the road was firm, but northern financial influence became more dominant by 1880 and after. The L & N expanded in these years and by 1884 was a system of over 3,500 miles, with service to St. Louis, Cincinnati, Memphis, Chattanooga, Montgomery, Mobile, and New Orleans. From 1884 until his death in 1921, Milton H. Smith was the dominant personality in the leadership of the L & N. As president, Smith preferred freight traffic to passenger business and saw his system grow to become the second largest railroad in the South with more than 5,000 miles by 1900. In the twentieth century it continued its unbroken record of solvency and became known as the "Old Reliable." In 1971 the Seaboard Coast Line (old Atlantic Coast Line) greatly increased its ownership of L & N stock to become virtually the exclusive owner of the railroad.

Projected at mid-century to help the trade of Mobile, the **Mobile & Ohio**, along with the Illinois Central, benefited from the federal land-grant legislation of 1850. The 483-mile road was completed from Mobile to Columbus, Ky., in the spring of 1861 in time to be used by both armies during the Civil War. Expansion after the war was not rapid, and the road operated only 876 miles at the turn of the century. In 1940 the Mobile & Ohio merged with the Gulf, Mobile & Northern to form the Gulf, Mobile & Ohio. A later addition in 1946 of the Alton Railroad extended service northward to Kansas City and Chicago. In 1972 the 2,700-mile Gulf, Mobile & Ohio was merged with the larger Illinois Central to form the Illinois Central Gulf.

Chartered in 1881, the **Norfolk & Western** was the successor of three short Virginia roads built during the 1850s, whose combined length of 408 miles ran from Norfolk to Bristol, Tenn. The Norfolk & Western expanded quite slowly and in 1900 consisted of about 1,500 miles of line, including a branch to Columbus, Ohio. The growth of this important coal carrier remained quite modest until after World War II. In 1959 it acquired another coal road, the 600-mile Virginian Railway. Later in 1964 the N & W added the 2,100-mile Nickel Plate and by 1970 also had full control over the 2,400-mile Wabash. These last two additions gave the Norfolk & Western a rail system stretching from Norfolk, Buffalo, and Detroit westward to Chicago, Des Moines, Omaha, and Kansas City. By 1970 the enlarged Norfolk & Western was a 7,600-mile line with total assets of $2 billion. Although it had much mileage in Virginia and West Virginia, more than two-thirds of its line was located north and west of the Ohio River.

The **Plant System** was created by Henry B. Plant, a yankee from Connecticut who moved to the South before the Civil War. During the depression of the 1870s Plant became interested in railroads in Georgia. With help from northern capitalists he established in 1882 the Plant Investment Company to purchase southern railroads. Using the Savannah, Florida & Western as the keystone, Plant acquired railway after railway. By the end of the century the Plant System consisted of more than a dozen roads with a total of 2,100 miles of line in the states of South Carolina, Georgia, Alabama, and Florida. Plant died in 1899, and in the spring of 1902 the Altantic Coast Line acquired the entire Plant System.

The **Richmond & Danville** was opened to Danville, Va., in 1856 and extended to Greensboro, N.C., during the Civil War. By 1870 the 190-mile road was one of the major lines in the Upper South. In the next score of years the road was deeply involved in one of the most complicated financial developments in the railroad history of the South. During the early seventies the Richmond & Danville became the cornerstone of the 2,000-mile rail empire the Pennsylvania Railroad was acquiring in seven southern states through its subsidiary, the Southern Railway Security Company. After the Pennsylvania gave up its southern rail ambitions, the R & D continued to be the parent line of a direct rail route from Richmond to Atlanta. During the eighties the Richmond & Danville grew to a system of over 3,000 miles. Much of this expansion was possible through the use of a holding company, the Richmond & West Point Terminal Company. In the mid-eighties northern capitalists in control of the holding company turned the tables on the R & D, and soon the Richmond Terminal controlled the Richmond & Danville. Later the Richmond Terminal also controlled the East Tennessee, Virginia & Georgia as well as the Central of Georgia. In the early 1890s the Southern Railway was formed out of much of the financial wreckage of the Richmond Terminal holdings.

As a system the **Seaboard Air Line** started with the post–Civil War control of the 80-mile Seaboard & Roanoke by a group of northern capitalists headed by John M. Robinson of Baltimore. By the early 1880s the Robinson group controlled four lines serving the region between Portsmouth, Va., and central South Carolina. A decade later the system then known as the Seaboard Air Line consisted of five roads and over 800 miles of line operating from Virginia to Atlanta. Between 1898 and 1900 an additional 1,500 miles of road were added, with most of the new trackage located in Alabama, Georgia, and Florida. At the turn of the century the Seaboard Air Line consisted of 2,600 miles and included 20 formerly separate railroads. Even though it continued to expand to a network of more than 4,000 miles by mid-century, the railroad generally was not as prosperous as other major competing roads. In 1967 it merged with the Atlantic Coast Line to form the new 9,000-mile Seaboard Coast Line.

The **Southern Railway** was created in 1893–1894 out of much of the mileage controlled by the bankrupt Richmond & West Point Terminal Company. Following a reorganization plan drawn up by Drexel, Morgan & Company, the new Southern Railway was chiefly formed out of the former Richmond & Danville plus the East Tennessee, Virginia & Georgia and in 1894 included about 4,500 miles of road. The railroad grew during the early twentieth century and by 1930 had increased to 6,700 miles. The Southern was the largest single railroad in the South and by 1950 served

13 states with a network reaching from Washington, D.C., Cincinnati, and St. Louis to Memphis, New Orleans, Mobile, Jacksonville, and Charleston. With over 7,500 miles in the system in the 1950s the railroad used the slogan: The Southern Serves the South. By the standards of the rail industry the company was both innovative and prosperous. During the 1960s the Southern Railway expanded still further by obtaining complete financial control over the 2,000-mile Central of Georgia.

See, for general treatment of American railroads, G. R. Taylor, *Transportation Revolution, 1815–1860* (1951), excellent on era of internal improvements; S. H. Holbrook, *Story of American Railroads* (1947); R. W. Fogel, *Railroads and Economic Growth* (1964); and J. F. Stover, *Life and Decline of the American Railroad* (1970). For chronological survey of southern railroad development, see U. B. Phillips, *Transportation in Eastern Cotton Belt to 1860* (1908); M. E. Reed, *New Orleans and Railroads, 1830–1860* (1966); R. S. Cotterill, *Mississippi Valley Historical Review* (March, 1924); R. C. Black, *Railroads of Confederacy* (1952), best; A. J. Johnston, *Virginia Railroads in Civil War* (1961); F. P. Summers, *Baltimore and Ohio in Civil War* (1939); R. E. Riegel, *Mississippi Valley Historical Review* (Sept., 1922); C. R. Fish, *Restoration of Southern Railroads* (1919); G. R. Taylor and I. D. Neu, *American Railroad Network, 1861–1890* (1956), good for review of technical advances; S. Andrews, *South Since the War* (1866); W. Reid, *After the War: A Southern Tour* (1866), gives good view of ruined Confederacy; L. P. Curry, *Rail Routes South, 1865–1872* (1969); J. F. Stover, *Railroads of South, 1865–1900* (1955); J. P. Baughman, *Charles Morgan and Southern Transportation* (1968); M. Klein, *Business History Review* (Autumn, 1968); J. F. Doster, *Railroads in Alabama Politics* (1957); E. G. Campbell, *Reorganization of Railroad System, 1893–1900* (1938), reorganizations and mergers of 1890s; M. Ferguson, *State Regulation of Railroads in South* (1916); W. H. Joubert, *Southern Freight Rates* (1949); and E. Hungerford, *Daniel Willard Rides the Line* (1938). For individual southern railroads, see T. D. Clark, *Pioneer Southern Railroad* (1936); C. J. Corliss, *Main Line of Mid-America* (1950); E. M. Coulter, *Cincinnati Southern* (1922); S. M. Derrick, *South Carolina Railroad* (1930); H. D. Dozier, *Atlantic Coast Line* (1920); E. Hungerford, *Baltimore and Ohio* (1928); M. Klein, *Great Richmond Terminal* (1970) and *Louisville and Nashville* (1972); V. V. Masterson, *Katy Railroad* (1952); J. F. Stover, *Illinois Central* (1975); and C. W. Turner, *Chessie's Road* (1956).

JOHN F. STOVER
Purdue University

RAINEY, JOSEPH HAYNE (1832–1887), the first black to be seated in the U.S. Congress, served longer in that body (1870–1879) than any other Negro of the Reconstruction period. Born in Georgetown, he was trained as a barber by his free Negro father. After Confederate authorities impressed him in 1862 into work upon Charleston's fortifications, he escaped and fled to Bermuda. A delegate to the Colored People's Convention in Charleston (1865), he also served as a member of the executive committee of the state Republican party formed in 1867. As a delegate to the state constitutional convention of 1868, he favored payment of a poll tax for educational purposes as one prerequisite to voting, as well as the removal of political disabilities from white citizens. He resigned his seat in the state senate in 1870 to fill a vacancy in the U.S. House of Representatives. In Congress, he favored passage of the Fourteenth Amendment and full civil rights for black citizens, including unrestricted access to all public places and conveyances. He worked as an internal revenue agent in South Carolina from 1879 to 1881, and from 1881 to 1886 he was engaged in the brokerage business in Washington, D.C.

See A. A. Taylor, *Negro in South Carolina During Reconstruction* (1924), useful pioneer study; *Journal of Negro History* (Jan., 1920); and J. Williamson, *After Slavery* (1965).

EDWARD F. SWEAT
Clark College

RALEIGH, SIR WALTER (1552?–1618), Elizabethan courtier, soldier, and author, initiated the first English colony in North America. Born of Devon gentry, he attended Oxford and Middle Temple. An advocate of English expansion and naval action against Spain, he was involved in privateering ventures and major expeditions against Cadiz, the Azores, and the Spanish main. Having served in Ireland, he became a court favorite by 1582, acquiring lucrative monopolies and Irish lands. In 1585 he was knighted and began sitting frequently in Parliament. Beginning in 1584, Raleigh, hoping for both military and commercial success against Spain, poured some £40,000 into the three futile ROANOKE expeditions. By 1589 he transferred his rights to a merchant syndicate. He is also credited with introducing tobacco among England's elite. He was a proud man, and his relations with the Elizabethan court were turbulent, but the accession of James I proved his undoing. He was tried for treason in 1603 and finally executed in 1618 after his Guiana efforts failed. His ventures were unsuccessful but his vision of America as an English dominion remained.

See A. L. Rowse, *Raleigh* (1962), stimulating; D. B. Quinn, *Raleigh and Empire* (1947), essential; W. Raleigh, *Works* (1829); and D. B. Quinn, *Roanoke Voyages* (1955).

RICHARD P. GILDRIE
Austin Peay State University

RALEIGH, N.C. (pop. 121,577). In 1788 the state's constitutional convention mandated the establishment of a permanent state capital in Wake County, near the geographical center of the state. Four years later, a nine-member commission selected a site near Wake Courthouse and the hamlet of Bloomsbury. The commissioners laid out the town, naming it for the founder of ROANOKE, and two years later the government was moved to Raleigh, where it has remained ever since. Although the principal business of the town was the government, after the completion of rail connections in 1840 the city also became a significant market for area agricultural produce. Removed from most scenes of conflict during the Civil War and having little strategic value, it escaped being a battleground and was surrendered to General W. T. Sherman on April 14, 1865, without a shot being fired. After the war the city gradually became an educational and industrial center. Two black schools, Shaw University (1865) and St. Augustine's College (1867), were founded here during Reconstruction; Meredith College for women was opened in 1891; and the North Carolina State College of Agriculture and Engineering was founded in 1889. Textile factories, lumber mills, and printing plants were located here in the late nineteenth century and continue to provide alternative sources of income. Yet the principal business of Raleigh remains the government.

See E. C. Waugh, *North Carolina's Capital* (1967); E. D. Reid, *From Raleigh's Past* (1965) and *History of Wake County* (2 vols.; 1975); Federal Writers' Project, *Raleigh* (1942); D. L. Swain, *Early Times in Raleigh* (1867); K. P. Battle, *Early History of Raleigh* (1893); and H. S. Chamberlain, *History of Wake County* (1922).

RALEIGH NEWS AND OBSERVER evolved from a series of newspaper mergers in North Carolina's capital. Its antecedents date back to publication of the *Daily Carolinian* (1871–1872). The *Carolinian* became the Raleigh *Daily News* (1872–1880) and then merged in 1880 with the *Observer* (1876–1880) to form the *News and Observer*. Yet another merger in 1893 with the *State Chronicle* (1890–1893) briefly changed the name to the *News and Observer Chronicle*. After JOSEPHUS DANIELS purchased the financially unsteady paper in 1894, he restored the simpler name while removing advertisements from the front page and introducing bold-faced headlines. Editing the paper as a highly partisan Democratic sheet and an advocate of Progressive reform, he developed the *News and Observer* into one of the most widely circulated and often quoted papers in the state. In 1933 Daniels was succeeded as editor by his son JONATHAN

DANIELS, who perpetuated the paper's loyalty to the Democratic party and who staunchly supported the New Deal and numerous local and state reform movements.

See bound copies (1872–), at Duke and University of North Carolina libraries; and microfilm (1877–), from Atlantic Microfilm Corp. and Library of Congress.

RALEIGH REGISTER was founded in 1799 as the official organ of the state's Democratic-Republicans. Joseph Gales, its editor, was an émigré Englishman who had been brought to North Carolina from Philadelphia by congressional supporters of Thomas Jefferson. An extremely influential newspaper during the first half of the nineteenth century, the *Register* became aligned with the state's WHIG PARTY during the 1830s. It became a daily newspaper in 1850, the first such paper in the state, but its fortunes and its influence declined with that of the Whig party. While its Democratic counterpart, the Raleigh *Standard*, opposed secession and regularly criticized the Confederate government, the *Register* was a dyed-in-the-wool rebel paper and ceased printing in 1868.

See R. N. Elliott, Jr., "Raleigh *Register*" (Ph.D. dissertation, University of North Carolina, 1955); incomplete bound copies at Library of Congress (1823–67), Duke University Library (1823–68), and University of North Carolina Library (1822–68).

RALEIGH STANDARD, a weekly newspaper, began publication in 1834 and served until the Civil War as the official organ of the state Democratic party. Purchased in 1842 by W. W. HOLDEN, the paper advocated universal education, suffrage reform, internal improvements, and industrialization. Despite the paper's defense of states' rights and Holden's endorsement of J. C. BRECKINRIDGE in the ELECTION OF 1860, the *Standard* vigorously opposed secession. Increasingly critical of Jefferson Davis and of the state's Civil War governors, the *Standard* carried Holden's call for a separately negotiated peace and followed its owner and editor into the Republican ranks during Reconstruction.

See E. E. Folk, *North Carolina Historical Review* (Jan., 1942); and incomplete bound copies, at Library of Congress (1835–67), Duke University Library (1835–70), and Cornell University Library (1834–70).

RAMSAY, DAVID (1749–1815), perhaps the most influential American physician-historian of the late eighteenth century, was born in Lancaster County, Pa. He graduated from the College of New Jersey in 1765 and studied medicine under Benjamin Rush at the College of Pennsylvania. Receiving his medical degree in 1773, he practiced for a year in Maryland before moving in 1774 to Charleston, S.C. As a Charleston physician and an active member of the Medical Society of South Carolina, he tried to improve the quality of medical practice in the state (MEDICINE) and campaigned for vaccination against smallpox. He also wrote tracts advocating various public HEALTH measures. But his major medical contribution was his *Review of the Improvements, Progress, and State of Medicine in the XVIIIth Century* (1801), the first serious effort at medical historiography by an American writer. Ramsay served in the South Carolina legislature during the Revolutionary War, was a delegate to the CONTINENTAL CONGRESS, and supported efforts to strengthen the powers of the national government. A moderate Federalist, he continued to be active in the state legislature through the 1780s and 1790s. During this period, he opposed the reduction of debtor obligations, the issuance of paper money, and the importation of slaves.

Ramsay's chief significance, however, was as a historian of early American national development. His *History of the American Revolution* (1789) stood as a prototype for scholars of his generation. Along with most of Ramsay's other historical publications, it focused on the origins of the new nation and the uniqueness of American national culture. His commitment to a strong, centralized nation was much more intense that that of most other late eighteenth-century American historians. Unlike most of the others, Ramsay lacked a sense of local geographic roots. He never returned to Lancaster County, and he was bitter about South Carolina's cultural shortcomings despite many decades in the state. His history seemed, therefore, to represent an attempt to find rootedness—a sense of place—in the nation itself.

See R. L. Brunhouse, *Transactions of American Philosophical Society* (1965), collection of most intellectually and biographically significant Ramsay letters; R. Y. Hayne, *Analectic* (Sept., 1815); P. Smith, *William and Mary Quarterly* (Jan., 1960); W. R. Smith, *History as Argument* (1966); and A. H. Shaffer, *Politics of History* (1975).

LAWRENCE J. FRIEDMAN
Bowling Green State University

RAMSDELL, CHARLES WILLIAM (1877–1942), was born in Salado, Tex. He received his B.A. (1903) and M.A. (1904) degrees at the University of Texas and his Ph.D. degree (1910) at Columbia University. He taught history (1905–1942) at Texas, where he supervised numerous graduate students. He did much to make the Littlefield Collection at Texas an important depository of southern history and pioneered in planning for the exchange of the holdings of numerous depositories by means of microfilm. Ramsdell was president of the Mississippi Valley Historical Association (1928–1929) and Southern Historical Association (1936) and served on the editorial boards of the *Mississippi Valley Historical Review* and the *Journal of Southern History*. In addition to numerous articles and other works, he wrote *Reconstruction in Texas* (1910) and *Behind the Lines in the Confederacy* (1944) and edited *Laws and Resolutions of the Last Session of the Confederate Congress* (1941). At the time of his death he was coeditor of the cooperative ten-volumed work, *A History of the South*. Although no slave to Frederick Jackson Turner's hypotheses, he documented the influence of frontier and section in American history, emphasizing especially the role of geography in sectional conflict.

See W. C. Binkley, *Mississippi Valley Historical Review* (Sept., 1942); and W. H. Stephenson, *Journal of Southern History* (Nov., 1960).

W. CONARD GASS
Campbell College

RAMSEUR, STEPHEN DODSON (1837–1864),

was the youngest West Pointer to achieve the rank of major general in the Confederate army. A North Carolinian, Ramseur graduated from the academy in 1860, resigning his commission within a year to join the Confederacy. He commanded an artillery battery before being elected colonel of a North Carolina infantry regiment. Severely wounded at MALVERN HILL, he was promoted brigadier general in November, 1862. A brilliant and aggressive combat officer, he enjoyed the strife of battle, acting as though he could not get enough fighting. Ramseur particularly distinguished himself at CHANCELLORSVILLE and SPOTSYLVANIA, earning him his promotion to major general a day after his twenty-seventh birthday. He was mortally wounded at CEDAR CREEK, valiantly trying to stem the Confederate rout.

See W. R. Cox, *S. D. Ramseur* (1891); E. J. Warner, *Generals in Gray* (1959); and J. D. Wert, *Civil War Times Illustrated* (May, 1973).

JEFFRY D. WERT
Penn Valley High School, Spring Mills, Pa.

RAMSEUR'S MILL, BATTLE OF (June 20, 1780),

also spelled Ramsour's, took place in North Carolina northwest of Charlotte about a month after Charleston had fallen to British troops. Although Loyalists in the Carolina interior had been urged by Lord Cornwallis to await support from his army before assaulting their patriot neighbors, they acted prematurely. In mid-June, 1,100 of them from the vicinity of the Catawba River's south fork assembled under Colonel John Moore at Ramseur's Mill. Colonel Francis Locke collected about 400 men and attacked the king's friends, who had situated themselves upon a hill near the mill. After a desperate struggle, Moore's force was dislodged, and loyalism was suppressed in North Carolina. Each army suffered some 35 fatalities and 100 wounded; 50 Loyalists were captured.

See B. Lossing, *Pictorial Field Book of Revolution* (1850); H. Lefler and A. Newsome, *North Carolina* (1954); and J. Sosin, *Revolutionary Frontier* (1967).

PAUL DAVID NELSON
Berea College

RANDALL, JAMES GARFIELD (1881–1953),

during the 1930s and 1940s, was one of the most prominent Abraham Lincoln scholars and revisionist historians of the Civil War era. Born in Indianapolis, he graduated from Butler University and received his M.A. and Ph.D. degrees from the University of Chicago. His first wife died in 1913, and in 1917 he married Ruth Painter, who shared his devotion to Lincoln studies and wrote biographies of Mary Lincoln and her sons. From 1920 until 1949, Randall taught at the University of Illinois, where his graduate seminars were unusually productive of published dissertations and of outstanding scholars. He is best known for his *The Civil War and Reconstruction* (1937) and the four-volumed *Lincoln the President* (1945–1955). His revisionism, which he defined as the disengagement of historical truth from deposits of myth and misunderstanding, minimized the importance of the slavery controversy as a cause of the Civil War and was bitterly critical of Republican radicalism both during and after the war. At the time of his death, he was apparently modifying these views, and his *Constitutional Problems Under Lincoln* (1926) may prove to be his most enduring work.

See *Journal of Illinois State Historical Society* (Summer, 1953), obituary and list of works.

WILLIAM HANCHETT
San Diego State University

RANDOLPH, ASA PHILIP (1889–1979), was one

of the great freedom fighters of our time. Not only did he help build a strong labor movement, but he was among those chiefly responsible for making LABOR UNIONS a force for social progress and racial integration. Born in Crescent City, Fla., he organized the Brotherhood of Sleeping Car Porters in 1925, and in 1936 the union became affiliated with the American Federation of Labor. He was the organizer and director of the first march on Washington in 1941, which led President Franklin Roosevelt to start the Fair Employment Practice Committee. Again in 1958 Randolph organized a youth march on Washington in support of the U.S. Supreme Court's 1954 school desegregation decision and in 1963 directed the 200,000-person march on Washington to protest the lack of jobs and freedom, the largest such demonstration in the history of the United States (CIVIL RIGHTS MOVEMENT). In his behalf Mayor Abraham Beame of New York proclaimed Friday, October 18, 1974, as A. Philip Randolph Day.

See J. Anderson, *A Philip Randolph* (1974), recent and good; B. R. Brazeal, *Brotherhood of Sleeping Car Porters* (1946); and E. Embree, *13 Against Odds* (1946).

GOSSIE H. HUDSON
Lincoln University

RANDOLPH, EDMUND (1753–1813), born in

Williamsburg to one of Virginia's preeminent lines (RANDOLPH FAMILY), had scarcely begun his legal practice when the Revolution divided his immediate family; his uncle PEYTON RANDOLPH was a distinguished patriot, but his father John, the colony's attorney general, fled as a Loyalist. After brief military duty under George Washington, Edmund became the youngest member of Virginia's constitutional convention of 1776 and shortly afterward the state's first attorney general. He was in the CONTINENTAL CONGRESS intermittently (1779–1782). A prime mover in the ANNAPOLIS CONVENTION, he served as governor (1786–1788) and played a leading, if controversial, role in the formation of the U.S. Constitution. He introduced the nationalistic Virginia Plan and then refused to sign the finished product. Later he sensed the issue had been reduced "to the single question of *Union or no Union*" and supported ratification in the Virginia convention of 1788.

An eloquent orator, Randolph was in the state legislature when Washington appointed him the nation's first attorney general. He became a trusted counselor to the president and succeeded Thomas Jefferson as secretary of state. Randolph labored competently until August, 1795, when he resigned under fire, having been unjustly accused of being under French influence. He returned to Richmond and enjoyed great prestige as a lawyer. Portly yet handsome, he was beset by financial difficulties throughout his life and closed his career by serving for the defense in the Aaron Burr treason trial in 1807 (BURR CONSPIRACY) and by writing an important manuscript history of Virginia.

See J. J. Reardon, *Edmund Randolph* (1974), definitive; C. F. Hobson, "Early Career of Edmund Randolph, 1753–1789" (Ph.D. dissertation, Emory, 1971); I. Brant, *William and Mary Quarterly* (April, 1950); and M. D. Conway, *Edmund Randolph* (1888), good for source material.

DANIEL P. JORDAN
Virginia Commonwealth University

RANDOLPH, GEORGE WYTHE (1818–1867),

grandson of THOMAS JEFFERSON and son of THOMAS MANN RANDOLPH, was born at Monticello. Educated at the University of Virginia, he practiced law in Albemarle County and later in Richmond. As a member of the Virginia state convention of 1861, he ardently advocated secession. Randolph became a Confederate officer and rose rapidly to the rank of brigadier general. In March, 1862, he was appointed secretary of war, a post in which he demonstrated considerable organizational ability. His efforts to influence strategy were circumvented by President Jefferson Davis, and in November, he resigned in frustration. Randolph then returned to active duty, but ill health soon forced his retirement to private life.

See G. G. Shackleford, *Collected Papers of Monticello Association* (1965), fullest account; and A. Jones, *Virginia Magazine of History and Biography* (Jan., 1953) and *Journal of Southern History* (Aug., 1960).

WILLIAM H. GAINES, JR.
Virginia State Library

RANDOLPH, JOHN, OF ROANOKE (1773–

1833), Virginia rhetorician, was long the most consistent champion of states' powers as opposed to those of the national government, and near the end of his life he became a principal architect of southern sectionalism and nationalism. As an extemporaneous speaker, he probably has not been excelled in the history of Congress, and selections from his speeches and letters formerly were conspicuous in anthologies of southern literature.

At the beginning radical in his politics, the brilliant Randolph (who regularly subscribed the name of his plantation to his name) entered Congress as a Jeffersonian, becoming leader of the Republican majority in the U.S. House of Representatives in 1801. By 1805, however, when Randolph was prosecuting Judge SAMUEL CHASE before the

Senate, he began dissenting from the Jefferson administration over the YAZOO LAND FRAUDS, the negotiations to purchase West Florida, and a foreign policy hostile toward Britain and endangering the southern agrarian interest. By March, 1806, he had broken with Thomas Jefferson and was leading a congressional faction called the tertium QUIDS, which appealed to the old Republican principles of 1798.

Reacting against the French Revolution and Napoleon, Randolph went into an opposition that lasted all his life. His mordant wit and erratic personality (the consequence, in part, of a disease that occasionally plunged him into periods of madness) prevented him from leading successfully a coherent party, but he was defeated only once (1813) in an electoral contest, sitting in the House for 11 terms (1799–1813, 1815–1817, 1819–1825, 1827–1829) and briefly in the Senate (1825–1827), where he much impressed Vice-President John C. Calhoun. After being an eloquent delegate to the Virginia convention in 1829, he was minister to Russia in 1830–1831.

See J. Randolph, *Letters to Young Relative* (1834); H. Adams, *John Randolph* (1882); P. Bouldin, *Home Reminiscences of Randolph* (1837); W. Bruce, *Randolph of Roanoke* (1922); H. Garland, *Randolph* (1850); R. Kirk, *John Randolph* (1964), with select letters and speeches; W. Stokes, "Randolph of Roanoke" (Ph.D. dissertation, University of Virginia, 1955); and W. Stokes and F. Berkeley, *Randolph, Preliminary Checklist of Texts* (1950).

RUSSELL KIRK
University Bookman

RANDOLPH, PEYTON (1721?–1775), son of John Randolph (RANDOLPH FAMILY), was born at Tazewell Hall in Williamsburg, Va. He was admitted to the Virginia bar in 1744 and rose to the post of king's attorney for Virginia in 1748. He was elected a member of the House of Burgesses in 1748 and served in that body almost continuously until it was disbanded in 1775. When the Speaker, John Robinson, died in 1766, Randolph held that office also until 1775. A conservative in viewpoint and representative of the Virginia aristocracy, Randolph frequently opposed royal policy. In 1773 he was selected chairman of the Virginia committee of correspondence. Randolph presided over the revolutionary conventions in Virginia in 1774 and 1775. He was elected a delegate to the First CONTINENTAL CONGRESS, where he was chosen its president. Reelected president of the Second Continental Congress, he resigned to return home to direct the last session of the burgesses. Randolph died in Philadelphia.

See H. J. Eckenrode, *Randolphs* (1946); H. B. Grigsby, *History of Virginia Convention* (1855); H. J. Eckenrode, *Revolution in Virginia* (1916); J. M. Leake, *Virginia Committee System* (1917); A. W. Weddell, *Memorial Volume* (1930); P. B. Caley, "Dunmore" (Ph.D. dissertation, University of Pittsburgh, 1939); L. B. Griffith, "House of Burgesses" (Ph.D. dissertation, Brown, 1957); N. Norkus, "Francis Fauquier" (Ph.D. dissertation, University of Pittsburgh, 1954); and J. A. Ernst, *Virginia Magazine of History and Biography* (April, 1969).

LARRY G. BOWMAN
North Texas State University

RANDOLPH, THOMAS MANN (1768–1828), was born at Tuckahoe in Goochland County, Va., and was educated at the University of Edinburgh. In 1790 he married Thomas Jefferson's older daughter Martha and was thereafter closely identified with his father-in-law. As a congressman from Virginia (1803–1807), Randolph generally supported the Jefferson administration and so came into conflict with his caustic cousin JOHN RANDOLPH OF ROANOKE. While governor of Virginia (1819–1822) and as a member of the state legislature (1823–1825), he promoted the interests of the University of Virginia, which Jefferson founded. Although an advocate of states' rights, Randolph was progressive for his day and favored manhood suffrage, gradual emancipation, and penal reform. An active farmer, he was interested in new techniques and helped to develop contour plowing.

See W. H. Gaines, *Thomas M. Randolph* (1966), only full-length study; M. D. Peterson, *Thomas Jefferson* (1970); and Edgehill-Randolph Papers, University of Virginia Library.

WILLIAM H. GAINES, JR.
Virginia State Library

RANDOLPH FAMILY. Spirited aristocrats all, the Randolphs of Virginia were eminent in law, politics, and statecraft, though their political views were often diverse. The family was noted for its lavish life-style (masking chronic indebtedness), penchant for intermarriage, sense of *noblesse oblige*, and surplus of both tragedy and eccentricity. The golden age of the clan was the eighteenth century, but it was prominent afterward, most brilliantly in the person of ROBERT E. LEE.

The founding parents were William (1651?–1711) and Mary Isham Randolph of Turkey Island. William had a respectable pedigree and came to the colony about 1673. As a planter and entrepreneur, he acquired a huge estate and helped to found the College of William and Mary. He held numerous political posts, including those of king's attorney and Speaker of the House of

Burgesses—both positions later filled by his son, the scholarly lawyer Sir John. William and Mary Isham had nine children, most of whom married well. Subsequent generations also prospered, and the "web of kinship" soon encompassed many of Virginia's elite families. From the Randolph women came Thomas Jefferson's mother and John Marshall's grandmother.

The Revolution divided part of the family. One of Sir John's sons was PEYTON RANDOLPH, Speaker of the House of Burgesses, patriot, and first president of the Continental Congress; Peyton's brother John was king's attorney and fled as a Loyalist. John's son was Governor EDMUND RANDOLPH, the nation's first attorney general and second secretary of state. The postrevolutionary generation was headed by JOHN RANDOLPH OF ROANOKE, a tempestuous congressman and orator who was *sui generis*, even among the Randolphs.

See H. J. Eckenrode, *Randolphs* (1946); and J. Daniels, *Randolphs* (1971), both popular histories but latter more comprehensive.

DANIEL P. JORDAN
Virginia Commonwealth University

RANDOLPH-MACON COLLEGE (Ashland, Va. 23005) was an all-male, liberal arts college until 1968. Opened in 1832 at Boydton, Va., it is the oldest Methodist college in the United States and was named for JOHN RANDOLPH OF ROANOKE and NATHANIEL MACON. The school was closed during the Civil War, during which most of the railroad connections to Boydton were destroyed. As a result the college was moved in 1868 to Ashland. It has an enrollment of fewer than 1,000 students, but its 55,000-volumed library houses the records of the Methodist Episcopal Church, South, and the the the papers of historian WILLIAM E. DODD.

RANSDELL, JOSEPH EUGENE (1858–1954), was born at Elmwood plantation in Rapides Parish, La. He was reared a Catholic and in later life (1950) was made knight commander of the Order of Saint Gregory by Pope Pius XII. He settled in Lake Providence in the extreme northeastern part of Louisiana, was admitted to the bar in 1883, and from 1884 through 1896 was district attorney. After serving as a delegate to the state constitutional convention of 1898, he was a U.S. congressman (1899–1913) and senator (1913–1931). Defeated for reelection to the U.S. Senate in 1930 by HUEY LONG, he retired from public life to his home in Lake Providence. Ransdell's major activities in Congress focused on rivers and HARBORS legislation, FLOOD CONTROL projects, and public HEALTH issues. Under his prodding, Congress in 1917 accepted responsibility in principle for recurring Mississippi River floods by appropriating funds for LEVEE construction. The appropriations were increased significantly in the decade of the 1920s. In 1906 he committed the federal government to a program that eradicated cattle ticks bearing Texas fever. Of more lasting significance, he was instrumental in 1917 in gaining support for the national leprosarium at Carville, La. (HANSEN'S DISEASE), and in 1930 he won a long battle to establish the National Institute of Health at Bethesda, Md.

See A. P. Laborde, *Ransdell of Louisiana* (1951); and Ransdell Papers, Louisiana State University.

JAMES A. TINSLEY
University of Houston

RANSOM, JOHN CROWE (1888–1974), was born in Pulaski, Tenn. He studied at Vanderbilt and at Oxford. After a year on the faculty of the Hotchkiss School in Lakeland, Conn., he returned to Vanderbilt, where he taught for 23 years and participated in both the FUGITIVE and Agrarian movements. In 1937 he went to Kenyon College as professor of poetry and two years later established the *Kenyon Review*, which under his editorship developed into one of the most distinguished quarterlies in this country. Almost from its inception the journal published essays, stories, and poems from the most significant writers on both sides of the Atlantic. Ransom's publications have been various. His lifelong concern with the conflict between skepticism and belief and his conviction that man needs an inscrutable God, one that cannot be comprehended by his reason or explained by scientific analysis, are fully developed in *God Without Thunder* (1930). Over a period of ten years or so Ransom wrote more than two dozen essays of social commentary and contributed to both of the Agrarian symposia: I'LL TAKE MY STAND (1930) and *Who Owns America?* (1936). Ransom published three books of literary criticism—*The World's Body* (1938), *The New Criticism* (1941), and *Beating the Bushes* (1972)—but much of his speculation on the nature and function of poetry remains uncollected in the various volumes of the *Kenyon Review* and other periodicals. Ransom's volumes of verse—*Poems About God* (1919), *Chills and Fever* (1924), *Grace After Meat* (1924), *Two Gentlemen in Bonds* (1927), *Selected Poems* (1945), *Selected Poems* (1963), and

Selected Poems (1969)—include some of the most original and impressive poetry written in this country.

THOMAS DANIEL YOUNG
Vanderbilt University

RAPE COMPLEX, SOUTHERN, is a hypothesis invoked by several analysts of the region to explain certain hostilities of whites toward blacks. These analysts have traced the rape complex to antebellum plantations and the pervasive characterization of planters' wives and daughters as impeccable, moral, refined "jewels of the universe." Sexually repulsed by "sacred" white women, planters and their sons supposedly insisted upon frequent intercourse with "more natural" slave women. Concurrent with interracial sexual promiscuity, the white male planter class characterized blacks as child-savages—children when under firm controls of a slave system and wild savages wherever slave controls lapsed. Emancipation and perceptions of black "misconduct" during Reconstruction affirmed, for the planter class, the vision that black savagery had become rampant. Drawing upon this vision and refusing to acknowledge that they craved black women, planters charged that savage black men craved and would rape white women.

Almost all analysts who have propounded the rape complex hypothesis have developed it along the foregoing lines. In addition, certain analysts have stressed other variables. In *Caste and Class in a Southern Town* (1937), for example, John Dollard maintained that white male–black female sexual relationships and concurrent references to the "black savage rapist" extended beyond the planter class during the postbellum decades. This rape complex became a general characteristic of white southern culture. Dollard also stressed that the complex was fortified by fears that black males would seek revenge for the white "rapes" of black females. In *The Mind of the South* (1941), W. J. CASH charged that during Reconstruction white southerners perceived regional degradation "as rape itself." This intensified desires to protect white women against black rapists. LILLIAN SMITH focused upon the effects of the rape complex upon white women in *Killers of the Dream* (1949). Over time, Smith noted, pressures upon white women to live up to their purported role—to repress erotic urges and dwell on "lonely pedestals"—mounted. They became brainwashed proponents of white male protection against "the black rapist." Laurence Baughman's *Southern Rape Complex* (1966) stressed a historic white male jealousy of the black man's sexual potency. Baughman also claimed that between 1865 and 1965 there were hundreds of legal executions and thousands of lynchings for the purported rape of sacred womanhood.

There have been serious problems with the way analysts of the rape complex have presented their case. Their discussions have usually been impressionistic and have sometimes been polemical. They have demonstrated neither the frequency nor the pervasiveness of interracial sexual promiscuity on antebellum plantations. Their use of the Freudian theory of defensive projection is subject to challenge. Finally, even if there has been a pervasive southern rape complex, it is not at all certain that it has been a uniquely regional phenomenon.

Systematic research on many fronts is required. Cautious, sustained scholarship may reveal that the rape complex was not exclusively southern, that it involved no more than certain specific groups of people, and that it is only valid as an explanation for human behavior at certain specific points in time and under certain specific conditions. Until thorough studies are conducted, the rape complex must be considered no more than a provocative hypothesis.

LAWRENCE J. FRIEDMAN
Bowling Green State University

RAPIER, JAMES THOMAS (1837–1883), born of free black parents in Florence, Ala., emerged during Reconstruction as one of the South's outstanding political leaders. Educated in Nashville (1845–1851) and in Buxton and Toronto, Canada (1856–1862), he taught school in Canada (1863–1864) before returning to the South. After Appomattox, he delivered a keynote address at the Tennessee Negro suffrage convention asserting that freedmen understood the responsibilities of citizenship. At Alabama's first Republican state convention, he helped draft a document that called for "equal rights for all men." Later, at the state's constitutional convention, he strove to remove the political disabilities of former Confederates as well as to secure equal rights for Negroes. Although defeated in 1870 as the first black candidate for state office, he was elected in 1872 to Congress, where he pushed through legislation making Montgomery a port of customs and delivered an eloquent speech in support of the CIVIL RIGHTS ACTS OF 1875. "Not a few rebel scribblers in the press might envy him," one newspaper said, "for his talent, education, intelligence, and influence."

In later years he was active in Republican politics as well as the Negro emigration movement, but his career was cut short by his untimely death at the age of forty-five.

See L. Schweninger, "James Rapier" (Ph.D. dissertation, University of Chicago, 1972), *Civil War History* (March, 1974), *Journal of Negro History* (Jan., 1975), *Ontario History* (June, 1975), and *Alabama Review* (July, 1975); and E. Feldman, *Black Power* (1968).

LOREN SCHWENINGER
University of North Carolina, Greensboro

RAPPAHANNOCK RIVER rises at Manassas Gap near Front Royal, Va., and flows past Fredericksburg (at the FALL LINE) on its 212-mile course to the CHESAPEAKE BAY. A Spanish mission was established near the river's mouth in 1570. The following year, however, all members of this Jesuit party except a small boy were killed by Indians. Permanent colonization of the river's banks came only after the English settlement of Jamestown. Navigable as far upstream as the site of Fredericksburg, the river was an important artery for colonial commerce with the numerous tobacco plantations along its shores. During the Civil War the Rappahannock took on strategic importance as a defensive line defending the approaches to Richmond. Both the battles of CHANCELLORSVILLE and FREDERICKSBURG occurred on its banks.

RAYBURN, SAM (1882–1961), was born in Roane County, Tenn., but five years later moved with his family to a small farm in Fannin County, Tex. After a boyhood in northeast Texas, Rayburn graduated from East Texas Normal College (now East Texas State University) in 1903. After teaching in the public schools for three years, in 1906 he plunged into Texas politics and was elected to the Texas house of representatives. There he served for six years, with the last term as Speaker.

The election of 1912 brought Rayburn to the nation's capital as a congressman. A protégé of JOHN NANCE GARNER, Rayburn received an appointment to the Interstate and Foreign Commerce Committee. During his apprenticeship, he sponsored the War Risk Insurance Act (1914). After becoming chairman in 1931 and supported by Democratic majorities, Rayburn sponsored other successful legislation: the Truth-in-Securities Act (1933), Securities Exchange Act (1934), Federal Communications Act (1934), Public Utility Holding Company Act (1935), and Rural Electrification Act (1936). In other matters, Rayburn sponsored farm-to-market road legislation and actively participated in the creation of the Southwestern Power Administration.

As a man, Rayburn exhibited traits of small-town rural heritage with streaks of nationalism, individualism, and devout loyalty to the Democratic party. He coolly calculated the mood of the House and was a persuader rather than a compromiser. Rayburn loved power and became majority leader in the House in 1937.

Three years later, upon the death of William Bankhead, Rayburn assumed the speakership of the House. With brief interruptions, he held his position until his death. No other man served as Speaker so long; nor were many as powerful. In this post, Rayburn gave strong leadership, especially in cloakroom conversations. His closest friends included MARVIN JONES and Rayburn's protégé LYNDON JOHNSON. A master politician, Rayburn reached heights of leadership in the 1941 draft crisis and the Rules Committee disputes.

See C. D. Dorough, *Mr. Sam* (1962); A. Sternberg, *Sam Rayburn* (1975); D. C. Brown, *Southwestern Historical Quarterly* (Oct., 1974); L. V. Patenaude, *Texana* (Winter, 1971); A. G. Shanks, "Sam Rayburn and New Deal, 1933–1936" (Ph.D. dissertation, University of North Carolina, 1965); and D. L. Little, "Congressional Career of Sam Rayburn, 1913–1961" (Ph.D. dissertation, University of Cincinnati, 1970).

IRVIN MAY, JR.
Texas Agricultural Experiment Station

RAYNER, JOHN B. (1850–1918), a black teacher, preacher, and political leader from Robertson County, Tex., acted as a spokesman for the Texas Populists in the 1890s, seconded the nomination of THOMAS L. NUGENT as the Populist candidate for governor in 1894, and served as an at-large member of the Texas POPULIST PARTY committee. Some historians contend that such activity by Rayner and other blacks illustrates a unique strain of racial liberalism and political realism on the part of white southern Populists. The evidence to sustain such an interpretation is far from conclusive. Rayner and other southern blacks lacked a viable power base in the Populist party. The symbolic and subordinate roles blacks played—seconding nominations and serving in at-large capacities—indicate the limited extent of black influence within the Populist party structure. White Populist leaders who shared the racial antipathies of other southern whites attempted to attract black voters, who were the potential balance of power in close elections, without antagonizing white supremacists. The fact that white Democratic leaders made many of the same overtures to blacks attests to the significance of blacks retaining the franchise. The ballot gave blacks some leverage against even more racial proscription. Ultimately the efforts and influence of Rayner and other black leaders were inundated by the waves of disfranchisement and *de jure* segregation.

See J. Abramowitz, *Journal of Negro History* (July, 1953); C. Martin, *People's Party in Texas* (1933); and C. V. Woodward, *Origins of New South* (1951).

ROBERT M. SAUNDERS
Christopher Newport College

READ, GEORGE (1733–1798), born in Cecil County, Md., was a champion of the conservative tradition in eighteenth-century American politics. Even his signature on the DECLARATION OF INDEPENDENCE was only reluctantly affixed after he initially voted against the document. As the son of a prosperous Irish immigrant in New Castle, Del., he received a good education and by the early 1760s was a highly regarded lawyer in both Delaware and Maryland. During the prerevolutionary dispute with Britain he was a very influential albeit conservative patriot like his friend John Dickinson of Pennsylvania. After independence, Read concerned himself with helping to write a new constitution for Delaware and as vice-president and then president of his state (1777–1778). During the confederation period and as a delegate to the CONSTITUTIONAL CONVENTION of 1787, he was a staunch nationalist and avid defender of the rights of the smaller states. Before his death he served briefly as Delaware's first U.S. senator (1789–1793) and established the FEDERALIST PARTY on such a firm footing that it controlled the state for the next half-century.

See W. T. Read, *Life and Correspondence of George Read* (1870), useful only for letters; *Timoleon's Biographical History of Dionysius* (1948), contemporary anti-Read political tract; and J. A. Munroe, *Federalist Delaware* (1954).

JOHN A. NEUENSCHWANDER
Carthage College

READ, OPIE (1852–1939), editor and humorist, was born in Nashville, Tenn. As a young printer, he started a newspaper in Carlisle, Ark., called the *Prairie Flower*, but returned to his home state when the newspaper failed. Moving again to Arkansas in 1877, he became city editor of the ARKANSAS GAZETTE. He wrote humorous columns for the *Gazette*, and in 1882 he and his brother-in-law published the first edition of their *Arkansaw Traveler*. The amusing paper was popular in Little Rock and some of the larger towns, but Read's humor often offended rural Arkansans. In 1887 Read

moved his paper, which claimed a circulation of 60,000, to Chicago. Although Opie Read no longer lived in Arkansas, several of his books, such as *An Arkansas Planter* and *Emmett Bonlare*, were set in the state.

See F. W. Alsopp, *History of Arkansas Press* (1922); O. Read, *I Remember* (1930); and J. R. Masterson, *Tall Tales of Arkansas* (1942).

DAVID E. RISON
Baptist College at Charleston

READJUSTER MOVEMENT was the name of a Virginia political revolt in the 1870s and 1880s that sought to achieve a downward "readjustment" of the state debt. Originally contracted to finance antebellum public improvements, the debt had swollen to more than $40 million during the Civil War and Reconstruction years. The state attempted to repay its creditors during the 1870s by raising taxes and by reducing public school expenditures, but the results were disappointing. Depressed economic conditions cut deeply into government revenues, spawning new deficits and making the financial situation even worse. These developments poisoned Virginia's political atmosphere, naturally enough, and by 1879 the debt issue had splintered the electorate into antagonistic "Funder" and "Readjuster" factions. Representing the wealthier agricultural and commercial interests, the Funders insisted that the state should meet its financial obligations, even if it meant the levying of additional taxes. Their Readjuster opponents, by contrast, rejected this approach and called instead for the repudiation of roughly a third of the debt. This radical proposal found its strongest support among the economically deprived and the politically disaffected—among mountaineers and Negroes, poor whites and small businessmen.

Led by WILLIAM MAHONE, an ambitious railroad magnate, the Readjusters won sweeping victories in the 1879 and 1881 state elections. The revolt's partisans took charge of every branch of the government, and they moved rapidly to implement their program. They slashed the debt, reduced taxes on the poor, liberalized voting requirements, and increased expenditures for schools and asylums. At the peak of their influence, however, the Readjusters began to quarrel among themselves. Racial and personal antagonisms flourished, aggravated by Mahone's controversial course in national politics. Elected to the U.S. Senate, Mahone voted with the Republicans there, thus alienating many of his Democratic followers. The resulting furor demoralized the insurgents, and they lost control of the general assembly in 1883 and the governor's mansion in 1885. Their influence faded rapidly in subsequent years, and the state enacted a new debt settlement—one more favorable to the bondholders—in 1892.

See C. C. Pearson, *Readjuster Movement* (1917), good but dated; J. T. Moore, *Virginia Debt Controversy* (1974); N. M. Blake, *William Mahone* (1935); and C. N. Degler, *Other South* (1974), perceptive analysis.

JAMES T. MOORE
Virginia Commonwealth University

REAGAN, JOHN HENNINGER (1818–1905),

was born near Sevierville, Tenn. In 1839 he migrated to Texas and participated in the Cherokee War. He served as a frontier scout before being elected to the state legislature (1847–1849). In the 1850s he defended settler rights in Peters Colony and strengthened the Democratic party against the Know-Nothings. In 1857 he was elected to Congress for two terms (1857–1861). In January, 1861, he helped Texas secede from the Union, then served as postmaster general of the Confederacy. In May, 1865, he was captured and imprisoned at Ft. Warren in Boston harbor, where he wrote the famous Ft. Warren letter that implored Texans to put aside their rancor and rejoin the Union. In 1866 Reagan returned to Texas, where he worked to oust the Republicans and return the Democratic party to power. He was then elected to Congress, serving in the U.S. House from 1874 to 1887 and the Senate from 1887 to 1891. He was coauthor of the Interstate Commerce Act. From 1891 to 1903 he was the first chairman of the Texas railroad commission.

See B. H. Procter, *Not Without Honor: John H. Reagan* (1962); J. H. Reagan, *Memoirs*, ed. W. F. McCaleb (1906); and J. H. Reagan Papers, Texas State Archives, Austin.

BEN H. PROCTER
Texas Christian University

REAMS STATION, BATTLE OF (August 25,

1864), was fought 12 miles south of Petersburg, Va., on the Weldon Railroad, an important supply line for ROBERT E. LEE's half-surrounded army at Richmond and Petersburg. AMBROSE P. HILL's Confederate infantry, supported by WADE HAMPTON's cavalry, attacked Winfield Hancock's II Corps, which had been discovered isolated and loosely disposed while destroying the railroad near Reams Station. The Confederates routed the outnumbered enemy and halted the destruction of the railroad, but they never recovered control of the track between Reams Station and Petersburg.

See C. M. Stedman, *Southern Historical Society Papers* (1891), best Confederate narrative; R. U. Johnson and C. C. Buel (eds.), *Battles and Leaders* (1887–88), IV; *Official Records, Armies*, use General Index; W. Clark (ed.), *North Carolina Regiments* (1901), II, IV, V; W. W. Hassler, *A. P. Hill* (1957); G. Tucker, *Hancock* (1960); U. R. Brooks, *Butler's Cavalry* (1909); E. L. Wells, *Hampton's Cavalry* (1899); and J. F. J. Caldwell, *McGowan's Brigade* (1866).

FREDERICK D. WILLIAMS
Michigan State University

REBEL YELL, initially used at the first battle of BULL RUN, served the double purpose of unnerving the enemy while relieving tension among the rebel soldiers themselves. It is claimed that the yell, a high-pitched holler, was never confused with a yankee shout and that the yell varied from state to state and was particularly fierce when rebels were in battle against Negro troops.

See B. I. Wiley, *Life of Johnny Reb* (1943); and B. A. Botkin (ed.), *Treasury of Southern Folklore* (1949).

RECONSTRUCTION (1865–1877). Destruction, dilapidation, and poverty met the eye almost everywhere in the South in 1865. The greatest sufferers, perhaps, were persons at opposite ends of the spectrum: the antebellum elite, whose investments in slaves and Confederate securities were now abolished; and the freedmen, who faced destitution. Actual suffering for most people was relatively short lived, as the section rebuilt itself and a new labor system replaced slavery.

The staple crops—COTTON, TOBACCO, SUGAR, and RICE—still depended on Negro labor. Most blacks, despite some moving about in 1865, remained in or returned to the vicinity of their former homes. Planters first tried paying them wages, but they had little more ready cash for this purpose than the freedmen had for buying or renting land. Thus the SHARECROPPING and CROP LIEN systems evolved, whereby blacks farmed segments of the plantations on a family basis in return for a share of the crop and received necessary food and supplies as advances against their shares. Productivity fell below prewar levels, and few people prospered, least of all the laborers, for whom slavery was replaced with a form of PEONAGE. Here lay a major limitation to Radical Reconstruction. Despite wartime legislation looking to the confiscation of rebel estates and some talk of dividing them among the freedmen, little land was ever appropriated and it was soon returned.

Federal policy toward the South by 1865 had been aimed at restoring the Union and freeing the slaves. After the war there was widespread concern to make these gains permanent and more than nominal. Republicans, moreover, were loath to see their party undone by its own achievements. A restored South, denying the vote to blacks yet stronger than ever by virtue of emancipation and the abrogation of the old three-fifths apportionment for slaves, might well combine with northern Democrats to sweep away Republican power, undermine emancipation, and restore the conditions that had led to war. Disregarding such possibilities, Presidents ABRAHAM LINCOLN and ANDREW JOHNSON both sought a quick reunion. Successively they established new governments by executive order in every southern state. Few conditions were demanded beyond promising to support the Constitution and accept the THIRTEENTH AMENDMENT. Former Confederates were elected to offices high and low. That a large proportion had been Whigs and reluctant secessionists hardly mitigated their desire to minimize the fruits of the Union victory.

Further developments heightened northern, and especially Republican, misgivings. In spite of the army and the FREEDMEN'S BUREAU, blacks were repeatedly victimized by employers and others who felt a God-given right to exploit their labor and to keep them subservient. Nearly every state enacted BLACK CODES relegating the freedmen to a second-class citizenship. Blacks could not testify against whites in court; they were excluded from juries, the ballot box, and political office; and in some states they were all but required to labor for whites. Bands of Regulators, reminiscent of the antebellum slave patrols, roamed the countryside in many districts, sometimes with official sanction, in order to keep the freedmen "in their place." Intimidation and VIOLENCE were visited upon white UNIONISTS as well. Memphis and New Orleans saw massive race riots in 1866, in which whites deliberately shot down blacks and ravaged their neighborhoods while local authorities either participated or looked the other way (MEMPHIS RIOT; NEW ORLEANS RIOT).

Congressmen responded to these developments with mounting anger (RECONSTRUCTION, CONGRESSIONAL). Failing in efforts to reach a middle ground with Johnson, Republican leaders increasingly took charge of Reconstruction policy, overriding solid Democratic opposition and a succession of presidential vetoes. The Freedmen's Bureau was renewed, and the CIVIL RIGHTS ACT OF 1866, guaranteeing equal protection of the laws to Negroes, was passed. Lest a future Democratic Congress repeal this measure, it was embedded in the new FOURTEENTH AMENDMENT to the Constitution along with a compromise Reconstruction policy, which supplemented rather than supplanted Johnson's. States could obtain representation and electoral votes based on their black populations only if they let them vote. And prewar officials who had supported the Confederacy were temporarily debarred from holding office. Johnson advised the South not to accept these terms. Only his own state of Tennessee, dominated by mountain Unionists, did so, and Tennessee was accordingly readmitted by Congress in 1866. Encouraged by an overwhelming victory in the congressional elections that fall, Republicans pushed on to assure the ratification of the Fourteenth Amendment by replacing Johnson's governments altogether.

The RECONSTRUCTION ACTS of 1867–1868 represented the most conservative means left to accomplish this goal, falling short of indefinite military rule, territorial status, or full Confederate disfranchisement. The essential ingredient was Negro suffrage, which Republicans had hitherto shrunk from imposing. Constitutions were drafted on this basis in the ten remaining states, and in most of them new governments were elected and functioning by the summer of 1868. Congress admitted them as soon as they ratified the Fourteenth Amendment. At the same time it proposed the FIFTEENTH AMENDMENT, intended to make Negro suffrage permanent and nationwide.

In response to the new policy the REPUBLICAN PARTY organized throughout the South in 1867. It won control of every state but Virginia. Negroes supported the party almost unanimously, supplying about 80 percent of its vote but considerably less of its leadership. They held offices chiefly in the BLACK BELTS and won a legislative majority only in the lower house of South Carolina. But two blacks went to the U.S. Senate (from Mississippi) and 20 to the House at different times. The partial dearth of Negro leadership was supplied in some measure by newcomers from the North, dubbed CARPETBAGGERS by the opposition. They too were elected primarily in the black belts, coming South as soldiers or seekers of economic opportunity (the same motivation that peopled the West). The third Republican component, native whites whom the opposition libeled as SCALAWAGS, held a large proportion of the offices and supplied roughly a fifth of the party's votes. Predominantly wartime Unionists, they lived throughout the South but were most numerous in the Appalachian and Ozark mountains, centers of disloyalty to the Confederacy. In Tennessee and North Carolina, where they cast a third of the Republican vote, they had been largely Whigs before the war; elsewhere many had been Democrats. Among them were a few former Whig planters like Governor JAMES L. ALCORN of Mississippi, who hoped (usually in vain) to dominate the Negro vote; like the northerners, these men were more prominent than plentiful. The remaining four-fifths of the white population, rich and poor, Democrat and Whig, bitterly opposed Reconstruction as an outrage on the South. Reflecting its mixed antecedents, the opposition party called itself Conservative more often than Democratic during the postwar generation.

Party lines were never more tightly drawn in American history. Both parties had internal differences over economic policy, but the overriding issue was white supremacy. The vast majority of Conservatives opposed Negro suffrage and most of the rights that accompanied it. These they determined to subvert or destroy as opportunity offered. White Republicans varied markedly in their enthusiasm for black equality, but the party as a whole subscribed to at least legal and political parity and wrote such guarantees into the new constitutions and laws.

Under the Republicans, government became more democratic. More offices were elective, and property qualifications for voting and officeholding disappeared. Former Confederates voted freely after 1868 in all but two or three states. Republican legislators were readier than Conservatives to tax, borrow, and spend money for RAILROADS, EDUCATION, and such institutions as penitentiaries, asylums, and hospitals. (In the North Carolina house, black members favored these measures most heavily, followed closely by the northerners and then by the native white Republicans; Conservatives disapproved all but the most minimal proposals.) Republican zeal for internal improvements led several states to overextend themselves in granting public aid to railways. The party's most lasting achievement was to create in each state an effective public school system for the first time.

Public DEBTS and TAXATION consequently rose far above antebellum levels (but not as high as in the North). The tax burden rested primarily on the landowning class, which had previously governed in its own interest. As in the North, bribery and fraud sometimes accompanied this flow of money. South Carolina and Louisiana saw the greatest corruption, Mississippi perhaps the least. Both parties and races were implicated, and both helped to clean house afterward.

The Radical governments were hardly radical in a modern sense. Subscribing to the trickle-down theory, they encouraged rather than regulated business activity in the public interest; more public money was appropriated to stimulate business enterprise than to sustain the poor. Their record on racial integration was mixed, with laws and customs varying widely from state to state. SEGREGATION was universal in the schools except in New Orleans. On trains and in places of public accommodation it was common but by no means complete.

Conservatives fought Reconstruction with every means at hand: conventional electioneering, social ostracism, economic boycott, terrorism, and murder. In most of the predominantly white districts, Conservatives were in a majority and controlled local governments from the outset. In Tennessee and Arkansas they captured the state governments as soon as Republicans reenfranchised former Confederates. Intimidation and violence yielded the greatest returns, and were adopted most often, in regions where the races or parties were relatively balanced. The KU KLUX KLAN, originating in Tennessee, spread across the South in 1868 as black suffrage and Republican governments came into being. Where this quasi-political vigilante organization flourished it paralyzed the legal process, since whites refused, through sympathy or fear, to check its atrocities. Federal legislation, arrests, and prosecutions were eventually required to suppress the Klan in 1871.

The most effective device in overthrowing Republican majorities was the riot, patterned after those of Memphis and New Orleans. Georgians first used it successfully on a statewide basis in 1870. The rest of the Lower South followed suit in the election campaigns of 1874–1876. Republican meetings were mobbed, blacks were driven from the polls, and officials were forced to resign. These tactics prevailed only because the federal government, and ultimately northern public opinion, acquiesced in them. Conservatives in effect won a war of attrition against an increasingly shaky northern commitment to Negro equality, which required continuing federal support. Other goals, like intersectional harmony and business expansion, came to seem more important. The Compromise of 1877 sealed the transition (ELECTION OF 1876). Southern Conservatives accepted the disputed election of Republican Rutherford B. Hayes in return for his pledge of a free hand in the South and federal money for southern economic development (HAYES ADMINISTRATION). Thereafter the Republican party went into gradual eclipse in the South, along with civil rights and political democracy for many whites as well as the blacks. Reconstruction, as it turned out, wrought a very reluctant, partial, and temporary revolution in Dixie (RECONSTRUCTION, HISTORIOGRAPHY OF).

See K. M. Stampp, *Era of Reconstruction* (1965), best survey; K. Stampp and L. F. Litwack (eds.), *Reconstruction* (1969), anthology of revisionist writings; J. H. Shofner, *Nor Is It Over Yet* (1974), Florida, 1863–77; J. G. Taylor, *Louisiana Reconstructed, 1863–1877* (1974); W. M. Evans, *Ballots and Fence Rails* (1967), superb local study of lower Cape Fear; M. Perman, *Reunion Without Compromise, 1865–1868* (1973); A. W. Trelease, *White Terror* (1971), fullest account of KKK; R. Cruden, *Negro in Reconstruction* (1969), excellent brief survey; T. Holt, *Black over White* (1977), black leaders in South Carolina; and J. Williamson, *After Freedom: South Carolina 1861–1877* (1965), masterful. Among scattered and highly specialized primary sources, perhaps most comprehensive is *Report of Joint Committee to Inquire into Conditon of Late Insurrectionary States* (13 vols.; 1872).

ALLEN W. TRELEASE
University of North Carolina, Greensboro

RECONSTRUCTION, CONGRESSIONAL. The nineteenth-century attempt to transform the South from a slave to a free society began during the Civil War as an assault upon slavery, expanded during the postwar years into a commitment to equal citizenship plus suffrage for black southerners, and ended in 1894 with repeal of legislation designed to provide them with federal protection. Upon the Republican party, not the North as an apolitical entity, rests responsibility for the Reconstruction laws, constitutional amendments, and enforcement acts intended to impose by national authority a drastic change in the pattern of southern race relationships. Reconstruction historiography, both old and new, has focused much attention upon Congress with widely varying evaluations of Republican goals and Republican performance. Scholarship since the 1950s has illuminated not only the internal dynamics of party and the complexity of the political process but also such central issues as the nature of Republican "radicalism," the motivation for party action, and the reasons for limited success in refashioning the South. The conflict between Congress and President ANDREW JOHNSON has been reexamined in the context of the Republican effort to consolidate far-reaching social change through law, an effort made in the face of opposition from white southerners, northern Democrats, and the postwar president. A similar perspective has marked a renewed interest in the functional role of constitutional theory in the Reconstruction process during and after the Civil War.

Despite disavowal in July, 1861, of any purpose to interfere with southern institutions, there was soon evident a shift in intent that found expression in the Confiscation Acts and in the passage of the Wade-Davis bill on July 2, 1864, following defeat in the House of the Republican effort to kill slavery by constitutional amendment. The bill linked destruction of slavery to Reconstruction through required state action and congressional declaration but provided only a minimal protection for freedmen that included neither suffrage nor citizenship, though Republican support for both was considerable and growing. In addition, it would establish interim civil regimes under appointed state governors, in contrast to Abraham Lincoln's military control, and authorize elected governments at war's end based on white majority consent but with severe proscriptions intended to deny power to Confederate leaders. After Lincoln's pocket veto a substantially similar measure, conceding to the president the admission of Louisiana, was formulated with his approval but was not passed by the Thirty-eighth Congress. In its final weeks, Republicans did obtain the necessay two-thirds vote for the THIRTEENTH AMENDMENT, but only with executive help through a lobby that neutralized Democratic opposition. They also passed and Lincoln signed a FREEDMEN'S BUREAU bill, which suggested readiness not only to protect the freedmen but also to weaken the landed aristocracy by promoting small landholdings. During the Thirty-ninth Congress, which met in December, 1865, the party enacted a moderate conciliatory program in view of President Johnson's opposition to a federal grant of land, suffrage, or citizenship to black southerners and his concessions to the old southern leadership. Embodied in the Freedmen's Bureau, CIVIL RIGHTS ACT OF 1866, and FOURTEENTH AMENDMENT, it established citizenship and federal responsibility for basic civil rights but abandoned a land program, provided incentive but no coercion for Negro suffrage, and limited proscription to officeholding.

When the secession states, except Tennessee, refused to ratify the Fourteenth Amendment, Congress passed a series of RECONSTRUCTION ACTS beginning in March, 1867, which remanded them to military control; mandated Negro suffrage, new constitutions, and ratification of the amendment; and temporarily excluded from voting large numbers of former officials. When the reorganized states, even under Republican control reinforced by the FIFTEENTH AMENDMENT, proved ineffectual in protecting the new rights of blacks, the party passed federal enforcement legislation in 1870 and 1871 but largely failed in its objectives when faced with continuing white resistance, adverse U.S. Supreme Court decisions, and loss of power in Congress. A new tactic, retreat from coercion of the white South in favor of seeking voluntary acquiescence in the new political status of blacks, marked the Liberal Republican movement of 1872 (ELECTION OF 1872) and President Rutherford B. Hayes's southern policy of 1877 (HAYES ADMINISTRATION), a policy that proved unrealistic. When Republicans regained briefly the ascendancy lost in the second GRANT ADMINISTRATION, they made a final effort to strengthen enforcement. The federal elections bill of 1890–1891 (FORCE BILL) passed the House but was sidetracked in the Senate with the defection of a few Republican senators to the Democratic opposition. Three years later, with Democrats in control of both houses and the presidency, they repealed existing enforcement statutes, thereby repudiating intervention in the South as a means of fulfilling that freedom and equal citizenship to which Republicans had committed the nation.

See E. L. McKitrick, *Andrew Johnson* (1960); L. and J. H. Cox, *Politics, Principle, Prejudice* (1963); W. R. Brock, *American Crisis* (1963), three landmark studies; H. Belz, *Reconstructing Union* (1969), outstanding for war years and constitutional theory; M. L. Benedict, *Compromise of Principle* (1974), most comprehensive; D. Donald, *Politics of Reconstruction* (1965); C. V. Woodward, *Burden of Southern History* (1960) and *American Counterpoint* (1971), interpretive essays; H. M. Hyman, *More Perfect Union* (1973), monumental reexamination of constitutionalism; and H. Trefousse, *Impeachment* (1975).

LAWANDA COX
Hunter College, City University of New York

RECONSTRUCTION, HISTORIOGRAPHY OF.

The persistent and often bitter historical controversies that have surrounded the Reconstruction era for over a century are testimony to the fact that the issues raised during that era—race, nationalism versus localism, the limits of federal power, the sometimes conflicting claims of liberty and equality—have not yet been resolved. Initially these controversies were dealt with in journalism (*e.g.*, Whitelaw Reid, *After the War* [1866] and James S. Pike, *The Prostrate State* [1874]) and in fiction (*e.g.*, ALBION TOURGÉE's *A Fool's Errand* [1879] and THOMAS DIXON's *The Clansman* [1905]), in which the attitudes held by participants tended to color their judgment. Not until after the turn of the century was the voice of history heard. Surprisingly, it spoke with a southern accent.

From the famed Columbia University seminar of WILLIAM A. DUNNING came a generation of scholars, including WALTER L. FLEMING, JAMES W. GARNER, and J. G. DE ROULHAC HAMILTON, who subjected the Reconstruction process in each southern state to careful scrutiny. Their findings, along with those of such kindred northern histo-

rians as James Ford Rhodes and JOHN W. BURGESS, were in remarkable agreement.

After Appomattox, Abraham Lincoln, compassionate and wise, had planned to restore the chastened South to the Union swiftly and mercifully. After his death, ANDREW JOHNSON attempted to carry out Lincoln's plan but was thwarted and ultimately impeached by the Radical Republicans. These ruthless "Jacobins" desired only to punish and humiliate the prostrate South. To this end, they disfranchised the natural southern leaders and imposed state governments run by illiterate, half-savage Negroes, greedy northern carpetbaggers, and turncoat native "scalawags." The result was an orgy of corruption and misgovernment unique in the annals of English-speaking people. At length, self-respecting southern whites overturned these carpetbag regimes, restored honest home rule, and ended the ill-advised Reconstruction experiment.

Such an interpretation, based as it was on the assumption of Negro inferiority, was likely to appeal to many Americans during the first third of the twentieth century. These were the years when segregation was sanctioned by law and LYNCHING by custom, when theories of racial supremacy had not only achieved some "scientific" respectability but had even been written into the statute books in the form of restrictive immigration legislation. The viewpoint of the Dunning school was incorporated virtually intact in nearly every textbook. It permeated such widely read fiction as GONE WITH THE WIND and helped propel CLAUDE G. BOWERS' lurid popularized history *The Tragic Era* (1929) into the best-seller lists. Even the usually judicious *Encylopaedia Britannica* could conclude that "all the misfortunes of war itself are insignificant when compared with the sufferings of the people during Reconstruction." These alleged sufferings could be cited to justify the continuing racial discrimination in the South.

Only a few dissenting voices were raised. In 1910 W. E. B. DU BOIS published a largely ignored, iconoclastic article "Reconstruction and Its Benefits" in the *American Historical Review*. Most of those who did speak out against the prevailing Dunning interpretation were either Negroes (such as JOHN R. LYNCH and Alrutheus A. Taylor) or Marxists (such as James S. Allen) or both (as was Du Bois) and could too readily be dismissed as biased. A more serious challenge, or rather supplement, to the Dunning school came from Charles A. Beard and his disciples. Although Beard wrote no specific work on Reconstruction, a few provocative pages in his influential work *The Rise of American Civilization* (1927) provided a text that other historians would embellish with copious commentary. Central to Beard's thesis was the concept of the Civil War as the second American Revolution, a revolution in which northern capitalists deposed the southern planters from national power. When applied to Reconstruction this hypothesis helped explain what had been a weak link in the Dunning thesis—the motivation of Radical Republicans. To Dunning, the Radicals had been inspired by "narrow fanaticism" and the spirit of vengeance. Beard regarded the Radicals as the front men for capitalist expansion. They deliberately kept the South out of the Union so as to pass high tariffs, subsidize industry, promote hard money, and centralize the banking system.

To a depression generation, this interpretation, with its implication that economic conflict lay at the heart of reality, seemed to make good sense. It was amplified in HOWARD K. BEALE's influential monograph *The Critical Year* (1930) and in Matthew Josephson's widely read narrative *The Politicos* (1938), and it permeated James G. Randall's familiar textbook *The Civil War and Reconstruction* (1937). C. Vann Woodward frankly acknowledged his debt to Beard in the preface to *Reunion and Reaction* (1951), a study that explained the abandonment of Reconstruction as part of an economic deal between northern and southern conservatives. Although the Beard thesis was in many respects at odds with the views of the Dunning school, the two could nonetheless be merged into some sort of synthesis. The common feature was hostility to Radical Republicans. Liberals could now condemn the Radicals for ther supposedly conservative economic policies, and conservatives could continue to deplore the Radicals' equalitarian racial views.

This synthesis completely dominated the historical literature on Reconstruction throughout the 1930s and 1940s. As late as 1947, E. MERTON COULTER could conclude his monumental study *The South During Reconstruction* with the flat statement that Reconstruction had been "a dismal failure." He insisted, "No amount of revision can write away the grievous mistakes made in this abnormal period of American history."

Coulter's reference to "revision," however, was an indication that new interpretive winds were beginning to stir the field of Reconstruction historiography. In 1939 FRANCIS B. SIMKINS (*Journal of Southern History*), followed by Howard K. Beale in 1940 (*American Historical Review*), had called for a reexamination of the assumptions of the Dunning school. The primary assumption, of course, was white supremacy. If, however, the Negro was not by nature inferior to the white man,

then it might be possible to look at the Reconstruction experiment in a more sympathetic light. Simkins cited the many positive achievements of Reconstruction: public schools, agricultural reform, and religious, commercial, and constitutional innovations. He also suggested that the Radical program might have been too timid rather than too bold. Beale called for a fresh look at Reconstruction. "Is it not time," he asked, "that we studied the history of Reconstruction without first assuming, at least subconsciously, that carpetbaggers and Southern white Republicans were wicked, that Negroes were illiterate incompetents, and that the whole white South owes a debt of gratitude to the restorers of 'white supremacy'?"

By and large, these suggestions were ignored until after World War II. Since race had always been the great touchstone of Reconstruction historiography, it was hardly surprising that the postwar rejection of racism should reverse historians' perceptions of Reconstruction. The war against nazism had helped to discredit all theories of racial superiority. The civil rights movement of the 1950s, which some likened to a second Reconstruction, helped focus fresh attention on the original Reconstruction.

A new series of state studies supplanted the now outdated Dunning monographs. Vernon Wharton's pathbreaking book *The Negro in Mississippi, 1865-1896* (1947) set the tone for state studies by Joel Williamson, Thomas B. Alexander, Joe Gray Taylor, and others, all of which emphasized the constructive features of Reconstruction and examined the black experience free from racial bias. Sympathetic biographies of carpetbaggers began to appear, and a lively debate on the nature of the so-called scalawags was conducted by David Donald and Allen Trelease, which helped rehabilitate this maligned group. The conclusions of this new school were summarized by Kenneth Stampp in *The Era of Reconstruction, 1865-1877* (1965), who argued that "if it was worth four years of civil war to save the Union, it was worth a few years of radical reconstruction to give the American Negro the ultimate promise of equal civil and political rights."

While these studies were overturning the conclusions of the Dunning school, historians on another front were chipping away at Beard's thesis. Utilizing much more subtle tools of economic and social analysis than either Beard or Beale had employed, Stanley Coben (*Mississippi Valley Historical Review* [June, 1959]), Robert P. Sharkey (*Money, Class, and Party* [1959]), and Irwin Unger (*The Greenback Era* [1964]) demonstrated that the Radicals were not united on any common economic program and that northern capitalists were themselves sharply divided on tariff, currency, and banking policies. Fresh biographies of leading Radicals revealed that most were motivated by genuine concern for the security of the newly freed Negro and that, rather than acting as tools of capitalist expansion, they could be considered (as in the subtitle of Hans Trefousse's 1969 collective portrait) "Lincoln's vanguard for racial justice."

As the reputation of the Radicals rose, that of Andrew Johnson declined. Instead of an intrepid defender of the Constitution and proto-Populist champion of the common man, Johnson was now portrayed as a rigid, inept political "outsider" by Eric L. McKitrick in *Andrew Johnson and Reconstruction* (1960) and as a racist, devious politico by John and LaWanda Cox in *Politics, Principle, and Prejudice, 1865–1866* (1963). Carrying this reversal to its logical conclusion, Michael Les Benedict argued that Johnson's impeachment was both politically and constitutionally justified (*The Impeachment of Andrew Johnson* [1973]). To round matters off, the concluding chapter of the orthodox interpretation was also challenged, as Woodward's neo-Beardian explanation of the abandonment of Reconstruction was questioned by Allen Peskin (*Journal of American History* [June, 1973]) and Keith Ian Polakoff (*The Politics of Inertia* [1973]).

By the mid-1970s, the once-dominant Dunning-Beard synthesis lay shattered with scarcely a defender. Yet the new othodoxy was not really a fresh interpretation of Reconstruction; rather it was the old interpretation stood on its head. The Dunning studies had slighted and denigrated the Negro; the newer studies concentrated on southern blacks. In both, the YEOMAN FARMER, whom W. J. CASH had called "the man at the center," was pushed off to one side. Similarly, the heavy concentration of political studies on the early Reconstruction years of 1865 to 1868 may have been an outgrowth of the desire to refute Beale's study of Johnson and the Radicals, yet in the process the important years of the GRANT ADMINISTRATION have been virtually neglected. Furthermore, the traditional time frame of 1865 to 1877 followed by Dunning is still being imposed upon the Reconstruction story, despite such compelling evidence as presented in Willy Lee Rose's *Rehearsal for Reconstruction* (1964) that the process of Reconstruction began during the Civil War itself. Reconstruction historiography still awaits the chronicler who can realize that the years from 1861 to 1890 are all of a piece and who will do what Dunning,

to his credit, attempted: integrate southern events with those in Washington.

See K. Stampp, *Era of Reconstruction* (1965); and D. Donald and J. G. Randall, *Civil War and Reconstruction* (1969), both critical bibliographies. For further historiographic discussion, see A. A. Taylor, *Journal of Negro History* (Jan., 1938); T. H. Williams, *Journal of Southern History* (Nov., 1946); J. H. Franklin, *Journal of Negro Education* (Fall, 1948); B. A. Weisberger, *Journal of Southern History* (Nov., 1959); L. Kincaid, *Journal of American History* (June, 1970); and R. O. Curry, *Civil War History* (Sept., 1974).

ALLAN PESKIN
Cleveland State University

RECONSTRUCTION ACTS. As soon as Robert E. Lee surrendered on April 9, 1865, the issues that had been in the background during the Civil War suddenly came to the fore. Among them were the status and rights of the former Confederate states after the war, the question of whether the legislative body or the executive branch should have the main authority to reconstruct that part of the Union, the reconstruction of the states, and the status of the Negroes and their rights. Consequently, a myriad of legislation was introduced in an attempt to establish a pattern to solve these issues (RECONSTRUCTION, CONGRESSIONAL). Notable were the so-called Reconstruction Acts.

The most significant of these was the First Reconstruction Act or military bill of March 2, 1867, which divided the South into five military districts, all subject to martial law. To achieve restoration in the Union, the southern states were required to hold new constitutional conventions, whose participants were to be elected by universal manhood suffrage and were to establish state governments that would guarantee Negro suffrage and ratify the FOURTEENTH AMENDMENT. Excluded from voting were former Confederates disqualified under the proposed Fourteenth Amendment. Congress reserved for itself the power to review each proposed constitution, to end military rule, and to seat representatives. Although ANDREW JOHNSON vetoed the bill on March 2, 1867, it was passed over his veto by both houses.

Three weeks later, the Radical Republican majority in Congress passed a supplemental or Second Reconstruction Act (March 23, 1867), again overriding a presidential veto. This statute detailed the procedures by which federal military commanders in the South were to reconstruct civil governments. It directed the military commanders to implement a new registration of voters (excluding prominent Confederates), an election of delegates to state constitutional conventions, and a ratification vote requiring "the approval of a majority of all the qualified electors in the State." The Third Reconstruction Act (July 19, 1867) clarified some of the ambiguities of the earlier acts and empowered the commanders of military districts to remove any state official who tried to obstruct the enforcement of congressional legislation.

Many conservative southern whites preferred to remain under military government rather than constitutions drawn under the aforementioned conditions. Most white voters in Alabama boycotted that state's ratification vote. Although the document received the approval of a majority of the votes cast, it failed to gain adoption because less than 50 percent of the state's registered voters had gone to the polls. Congress, deeply embroiled in the impeachment proceedings against Johnson, responded with the Fourth Reconstruction Act. Henceforth, ratification was to "be decided by a majority of the votes actually cast," even if only a minority of the population voted in the election.

The operational results of the Reconstruction Acts indicate that congressional policies toward the southern states were clearly inappropriate (RECONSTRUCTION, HISTORIOGRAPHY OF). The U.S. Congress tried to enforce in the Reconstruction Acts equal rights in a biracial society at a time when most northern states remained unwilling to enfranchise their own black populations. Because of the many irregularities, the acts challenged the democratic institutions then operating in America, and the manner in which they were enforced and opposed discredited the ideal of a color-blind democracy. Lastly, the acts reinforced the determination of conservative, white southerners to resist national authority.

See Andrew Johnson Papers, Library of Congress; E. L. McKitrick, *Andrew Johnson and Reconstruction* (1961); K. Stampp and L. F. Litwack (eds.), *Reconstruction* (1969), revisionist anthology; W. R. Brock, *American Crisis* (1963); D. Donald, *Politics of Reconstruction* (1965); L. Cox, *Mississippi Valley Historical Review* (Dec., 1961); H. K. Beale, *American Historical Review* (July, 1940); M. Lomask, *American Heritage* (Dec., 1959); J. G. Randall and R. N. Current, *American Historical Review* (June, 1955); J. T. Dorris, *Mississippi Valley Historical Review* (June, 1928); L. and J. H. Cox, *Journal of Southern History* (Aug., 1967); G. H. Thompson, *Leadership in Arkansas Reconstruction* (1976); and S. Scheiner, *Reconstruction: A Tragic Era?* (1975)

ANGEL LUIS ORTIZ-GARCIA
University of Puerto Rico

RECONSTRUCTION FINANCE CORPORATION (1932–1957) was established by Congress on January 22, 1932. It was authorized to extend financial aid to agriculture, commerce, and industry by means of direct loans to banks, credit agencies, and railroads. Later legislation broadened the RFC powers to allow it to purchase capital stock of banks, insurance companies, agricultural credit corporations, national mortgage associations, and other governmental agencies.

Between 1932 and 1941, the RFC spent $10.5 billion. JESSE JONES, the Houston financier who headed the agency during its formative years, was sympathetic to the appeals of southerners and located 13 of the 31 RFC offices in the South. In 1941 the RFC underwrote Arkansas' $137 million highway debt. It also financed the building of three bridges over the Mississippi at New Orleans, Natchez, and Greenville. The RFC extended $4.5 million to Crossett Lumber to establish a kraft paper mill and $8.5 million to Southland Paper at Lufkin, Tex., for making newsprint from pine.

With the advent of World War II, Congress gave the RFC responsibility for financing and stimulating the production of synthetic rubber, refined petroleum, planes, tanks, and guns. The Defense Plant Corporation established plants throughout the South. Two of the most important projects were the laying of two pipelines: the Big Inch, carrying petroleum from Longview, Tex., to Philadelphia and costing $79 million; and the Little Big Inch, transporting gasoline from Beaumont, Tex., to Linden, N.J., at a cost of $69 million.

After the war the RFC was authorized to supply credit at reasonable interest rates to finance the conversion to peacetime construction. After a se-

RECONSTRUCTION FINANCE CORPORATION IN THE SOUTH

	No. of Defense Plants	Money Expended
Ala.	16	$73,733,000
Ark.	12	88,853,000
Del.	7	3,383,000
Fla.	14	16,008,000
Ga.	11	4,279,000
Ky.	56	161,432,000
Md.	42	72,598,000
Miss.	5	1,620,000
Mo.	32	161,808,000
N.C.	9	13,420,000
S.C.	11	8,090,000
Tenn.	23	47,545,000
Tex.	92	647,000,000
Va.	10	16,553,000
Washington, D.C.	3	4,850,000
W.Va.	12	93,003,000

ries of scandals, Congress decided to liquidate the RFC on July 30, 1953. On June 30, 1957, the RFC was abolished.

See J. Jones with E. Angly, *Fifty Billion Dollars: My Thirteen Years with RFC* (1951), biased, but best source; B. Timmons, *Jesse H. Jones* (1956); S. Harris, *Economics of America at War* (1943); and National Archives, Record Group 234, for in-depth research.

STEPHEN F. STRAUSBERG
University of Arkansas, Fayetteville

RECREATION. Early settlers in the South, true to their English heritage, were ardent participants in recreational pursuits, those activities that are voluntary and pursued during one's leisure time. Although both northern and southern colonies were founded by Englishmen, the South was not restricted by the Puritan ethic and aversion to play. The popular recreational sports of hunting and fishing served a multiple purpose for the early pioneers. The abundant game and fish were essential sources of food, and knowing how to hunt was vital for survival in the wilderness. By the age of ten most boys owned rifles and knew how to use them effectively.

In England, where legal hunting was restricted to the landed gentry, FOX HUNTING was the premier sport. This tradition carried over to the colonies, where fox hunting became the exclusive domain of the newly established landowners. The red fox and the hounds were imported from England for this purpose and accentuated the differences in social class that were emerging in the South. Another typical English sport that provided recreation and food for the colonists was bird hunting. The forests and lakes were teeming with partridges, wild geese and turkeys, a variety of ducks, pheasants, cormorants, and other game birds.

Horses played a vital role in the Old South, from plow horses to thoroughbreds. The first horses were imported from England, then bred in the colonies. HORSE RACING soon became a popular spectator sport for all classes of people. The English proclivity for gambling encouraged betting on the horses as well as other "sports" such as cockfighting. There was little public opinion against cruelty to animals, and bearbaiting, bullbaiting, goose riding, and cockthrowing were diversions for the populace. In the backwoods regions these activities were replaced by wrestling, boxing, rail splitting, and other displays of strength and endurance.

By the close of the colonial period, many new recreational activities had been introduced, such as boating, bowling, fencing, horseshoe pitching, quoits, cricket, badminton, swimming, and even ice skating. Although the colonials were fond of outdoor sports, they spent some time in home and church socials that included music, dancing, theatricals, and a variety of card games.

After the American Revolution the Old South settled into a way of life that was essentially rural. At the head of this rustic society was the country gentleman, the plantation owner. The very nature of his work provided him with ample leisure time, and his recreational pursuits were rooted in the land and in his horse. Horsemanship came to him naturally, and hunting was still the supreme sport. In the winter season, when work abated, he toured the resorts where the warm mineral springs flowed and in a relaxed way enjoyed both their social and therapeutic values (SPRINGS OF VIRGINIA).

At the other end of the social continuum were the Negro slaves, accounting for more than half the southern population. During the evening rest periods, Sundays, and holidays, torchlight 'possum and 'coon hunts were favorite sports along with rabbit hunting, fishing, and trapping. MUSIC also occupied a large portion of the Negroes' leisure time. The fiddle and banjo were the instruments that were played for lively dances like jigs, clogs, and cakewalks. These musical frolics provided the basic material for that favorite American entertainment, the minstrel show (MINSTRELSY).

Between these two social extremes were the YEOMEN FARMERS. They often found ways to combine work and recreation, such as the state and county agricultural fairs. The fairs were organized for purposes of showing sheep, hogs, and other animals, as well as demonstrating the domestic arts. In the early years the main attraction was the ploughing match, but later horse races and trotting races supplanted them in popularity.

In the postbellum period, the South expanded its recreational horizons, once it had regained its economic stability. Baseball, football, and SPORTS in general became increasingly popular. However, despite the social upheaval and recreational changes that were taking place, hunting remained the epitome of all recreational pursuits for the true southerner.

Gradually the New South became aware of its most attractive asset, a warm, sunny climate that permitted outdoor sports the year round. In time the South became the winter playground for most of the nation. Myriads of tennis courts and splendid golf courses were built to complement its beautiful sandy beaches. To attract older tourists, it added shuffleboard and bowling on the green, as well as fishing and camping. Admirably, the

New South had found a way to take full advantage of its natural recreational facilities.

See J. Betts, *America's Sporting Heritage* (1974), excellent overview; J. Carson, *Colonial Virginians at Play* (1965); F. Simkins, *South Old and New* (1947); W. Thorp, *Southern Reader* (1955); and E. M. Coulter, *South During Reconstruction* (1947).

ROBERT J. KEEFE
Bowling Green State University

REDEEMER GOVERNMENTS. The conservative Democratic politicians whose accession to power ended the Reconstruction experiment in their respective states were often called the REDEEMERS. Their victories in the 1870–1877 years supposedly liberated the South from Negro and carpetbagger oppression and thus restored decent, responsible white home rule. Yet critics referred to the Redeemers and their successors as BOURBONS, implying that, like the backward-looking European monarchs, they had "learned nothing and forgotten nothing." Actually, both Redeemer and Bourbon can be misleading terms. Their regimes hardly restored honesty and tranquillity any more than they resurrected intact the plantation South of 1860.

The first state to be redeemed was Tennessee, which had a Republican government (1865–1870) but was never under military Reconstruction. In 1870 former Confederate general JOHN C. BROWN was elected the first Democratic governor since the war. That same year Tennessee ratified a new constitution, which provided for a POLL TAX. Governor Brown was a neo-Whiggish conservative determined to uphold the state's credit.

Virginia was also redeemed in 1870. Here, the victorious gubernatorial candidate Gilbert C. Walker ran not as a Democrat but as a "Conservative," since his coalition consisted of neo-Whiggish Republicans as well as former Confederate Democrats and some Negro voters. Railroad and bondholding interests dominated Walker's administration. Of all southern Redeemer governments, Virginia's was probably the most probusiness.

North Carolina underwent a semiredemption in 1870, when the Radical Republican governor was impeached by a Democratic legislature and replaced by a Republican conservative. Not until 1876 did North Carolina have both a Democratic governor (ZEBULON VANCE) and legislature. That year, a new law designed to assure white Democratic control of the entire state provided that the principal offices in all counties were to be appointed by justices of the peace, who in turn were named by the legislature.

Georgia's Redeemers captured the governorship in an 1871 special election, after the Republican chief executive fled the state under threat of impeachment from the Democratic legislature. Governor James M. Smith's administration (1872–1876) witnessed a slashing of expenditures and a repudiation of much of the state's Reconstruction-era debt. Governor Smith, however, soon faded into obscurity; from 1876 through the 1880s the so-called GEORGIA TRIUMVIRATE of ALFRED H. COLQUITT, JOHN B. GORDON, and JOSEPH E. BROWN ruled the state, sharing the governorship and the two U.S. Senate posts. All three were businessmen who advocated "progress" through industrialization and exploitation of natural resources, yet Georgia's triumvirate—like Redeemers elsewhere—still upheld the antebellum code of white supremacy and were properly reverential toward the LOST CAUSE.

Texas installed a Democratic governor (RICHARD COKE) and legislature early in 1874, after President Ulysses S. Grant refused to intervene militarily. "Rigid economy" became the watchword of Coke's administration; all expenditures, except for the Texas Rangers and state militia, were slashed. Coke was reelected in 1876 but soon went to the U.S. Senate.

Along with Texas, Alabama and Arkansas also experienced redemption in 1874. Alabama Democrats narrowly elected GEORGE S. HOUSTON, who stood for "home rule" and "white supremacy." Houston's two-term administration severely reduced expenditures, but a settlement of Reconstruction-era debts was arranged favorable to bondholders and railroads.

Redemption in Arkansas came on the heels of a two-year period of governmental anarchy in which rival Republican factions claimed the statehouse (BROOKS-BAXTER WAR). Conservative Democrat AUGUSTUS H. GARLAND, elected in 1874, stabilized the state's shaky finances by issuing bonds and creating a sinking fund. As a fiscal conservative, he opposed repudiation of the Reconstruction debt, despite its questionable legality.

Mississippi's redemption occurred in a two-step process during 1875–1876. White conservatives regained most legislative and local offices in the autumn elections of 1875 by practicing the MISSISSIPPI PLAN, intimidating the black Republican majority with paramilitary demonstrations of white power. Early in 1876 the carpetbagger governor, facing a hostile legislature that threatened his impeachment, departed the state. The legislature replaced him with Democrat John M. Stone, who was elected to a full term in 1877. Stone approved cuts in taxes and expenditures, while encouraging investments of northern and foreign capital, particularly in railroad construction. He remained a power in Mississippi politics, although his influence in the state Democratic party during the next two decades ranked below that of three other Redeemer politicians: L. Q. C. LAMAR, Edward C. Walthall, and JAMES Z. GEORGE.

Redemption came last to Florida, South Carolina, and Louisiana, following the Hayes-Tilden disputed presidential ELECTION OF 1876. But in Florida the Democratic accession to power in January, 1877, was not directly part of the compromise involving the presidential election. Florida's dispute over the governorship was resolved prior to settlement of the Hayes-Tilden question in Washington; a state supreme court ruling led to the inauguration of Democratic Governor GEORGE F. DREW and the installation of a Democratic legislature. As governor, Drew welcomed northern investors and adopted a fiscal policy summed up in his phrase "spend nothing unless absolutely necessary."

The redemption of South Carolina and Louisiana directly resulted from the Compromise of 1877. President Rutherford B. Hayes withdrew troops from both states in April, 1877, and recognized the legitimacy of the Democratic gubernatorial claimants: WADE HAMPTON of South Carolina and FRANCIS T. NICHOLLS of Louisiana. The administrations of Hampton and Nicholls were remarkably similar; both were patricians who evoked memories of the Old South but whose fiscal and tax policies represented the NEW SOUTH business outlook.

See C. V. Woodward, *Origins of New South* (1951); D. W. Grantham, Jr., *South Atlantic Quarterly* (Summer, 1961); J. C. Ward, Jr., *Georgia Historical Quarterly* (Sept., 1957); and P. M. Gaston, *New South Creed* (1970).

WILLIAM I. HAIR
Georgia College

REDEEMERS were the conservative leaders of the white Democrats who opposed Radical Reconstruction and took power after its defeat, thereby "redeeming" their states from Radical rule (REDEEMER GOVERNMENTS). They claimed to represent the old slaveholding class and to have restored most of the traditional policies and social institutions of the slave era. In particular they have been seen as inveterate foes of Negro participation in politics. More recently C. Vann Woodward has shown that redemption "was not a return to an old system, nor the restoration of an old ruling class." The Redeemers worked to integrate their region into contemporary industrial

capitalism and American nationalism. Far from opposing black voting, the Redeemers controlled a captive Negro vote in their own BLACK BELT counties and made it the basis of their own electoral strength. Finally, though the Redeemers claimed to represent a higher form of political virtue than the supposedly corrupt Radicals, they have been shown to have taken part in political corruption, usually involving railroads.

See C. V. Woodward, *Origins of New South* (1951), definitive; D. W. Grantham, *South Atlantic Quarterly* (Summer, 1961); J. P. Maddex, *Virginia Conservatives* (1970); H. M. Bond, *Journal of Negro History* (July, 1938); A. Going, *Bourbon Democracy in Alabama* (1951); W. I. Hair, *Bourbonism and Agrarian Protest: Louisiana* (1969); J. T. Moore, *Journal of Southern History* (Aug., 1978); and R. L. Hart, *Redeemers, Bourbons, and Populists* (1975).

JONATHAN M. WIENER
University of California, Irvine

RED RIVER. Although frequently seen by early explorers, the 1,300-mile river was not fully mapped until Randolph B. Marcy found its source in 1852. Partway upstream it was blocked for over 150 miles by the Great Raft, a centuries-old logjam. Below the raft, the French founded Natchitoches, La., in 1715; above it, STEPHEN F. AUSTIN laid out Fulton, Ark., in 1819. During 1833–1838, the raft was broken for a time by Henry M. Shreve, for whom Shreveport, La., was named. Jefferson, Tex., although 40 miles west of the main channel, was the major river port of Texas until the final breaking of the raft in 1873 lowered the water level in connecting bayous. The lower valley's worth as a cotton-growing area by 1860 is shown by the Union's attempt in 1864 to retake it in the RED RIVER CAMPAIGN. By 1870 cotton was again the chief crop downriver, and by the early 1900s it had spread into the upper valley. After 1945 COTTON remained a major crop upstream, while CATTLE, grain, and SOYBEANS supplanted it in many areas downstream. Long feared for its floods, the river was gradually controlled, beginning in 1944 with Lake Texhoma on the main channel and later with such dams as the Wright Patman and the Millwood on its tributaries.

See W. P. Webb, *Handbook of Texas* (1952); E. A. Davis, *Rivers of Louisiana* (1968); R. L. Jones, *Arkansas Historical Quarterly* (Winter, 1966); G. Rice, *Red River Valley Historical Review* (Spring, 1974); O. L. Barker, "Historical Account" (M.A. thesis, University of Colorado, 1929); R. B. Marcy, *Adventures on the Red* (1937); and L. H. Johnson, *Red River Campaign* (1958).

ROBERT B. WALZ
Southern Arkansas University

RED RIVER CAMPAIGNS of 1863 and 1864 represented Union efforts to acquire cotton, to stimulate Texas unionism, to disrupt Confederate-Mexican trade, and to protect against French activities in Mexico. On April 12, 1863, N. P. Banks advanced up Bayou Teche in southern Louisiana with 16,000 men and drove back 4,000 Confederates under RICHARD TAYLOR (FT. BISLAND AND IRISH BEND, BATTLES OF). Taylor withdrew to Alexandria, while Banks collected cotton and slaves. Banks, along with federal gunboats on the Red River under Admiral D. D. Porter, occupied Alexandria in May 7, while Taylor retreated to Natchitoches. Banks turned east on the fourteenth and crossed the Mississippi River to attack PORT HUDSON.

Union interest again turned to the Red River valley in 1864, although U. S. Grant opposed another expedition. On March 7 Banks advanced up the Teche with 17,000 men while Porter's squadron and 10,000 infantrymen captured Ft. De Russy and Alexandria on the Red River in mid-May. Union forces then collected cotton and held loyal state elections.

On March 26 Banks pushed northwest, while Taylor gathered reinforcements that brought his army to 13,000 men. At SABINE CROSSROADS on April 8, Taylor defeated the Union column, but Banks retreated to PLEASANT HILL and beat off another attack on the ninth. Confederate cavalry blocked the Red River with a sunken riverboat and harassed Porter's return downstream. By April 27 both Banks and Porter had retreated to Alexandria.

In a coordinated effort, 11,000 federal soldiers advanced toward Shreveport from Little Rock and Ft. Smith, Ark., in late March under Frederick Steele. At Prairie d'Ane in early April they skirmished with 7,000 Confederates under STERLING PRICE. Steele turned east to Camden, but lost two foraging expeditions in Confederate attacks at Poison Spring on the eighteenth and at Marks's Mill a week later. He then retreated to Jenkins' Ferry, where he was attacked on April 30 by EDMUND KIRBY-SMITH, commander of the Trans-Mississippi Department. Steele extracted his army and reached Little Rock on May 3.

Banks and Porter built wing dams to raise the river level at Alexandria and allow the gunboats to continue their retreat on May 13. Taylor unsuccessfully assaulted the Union rear guard at Yellow Bayou on the eighteenth, which ended the campaign.

See R. L. Kerby, *Kirby Smith's Confederacy* (1972), most complete; L. H. Johnson, *Red River Campaign* (1958), only 1864; J. D. Winters, *Civil War in Louisiana* (1963);

Official Records, Armies, Ser. 1, Vol. XXXIV; and *Official Records, Navies*, Vol. XXVI.

ALWYN BARR
Texas Tech University

RED RIVER VALLEY HISTORICAL ASSOCIATION (Southeastern Oklahoma State University, Durant, Okla. 74701), founded in 1973, sponsors a library, museum, and archives and publishes in conjunction with the state the quarterly *Red River Valley Historical Review* (since 1974). This journal (circulation 700) publishes book reviews, notes, and both popular and scholarly articles on anthropology, archeology, or history of the Spanish borderlands, the Southwest, the Great Plains, the South, or any of the region's states. Three annual awards are made for the best article published in the *Review*: one on the Spanish borderlands and the Southwest; one on the Great Plains; and one on the South. The association also published in 1976 the *Red River Valley Historical Journal of World History*. The association's museum fosters a Choctaw and Chickasaw Indian arts and crafts program.

RED STICKS WAR. See CREEK WAR

REED, HARRISON (1813–1899), was born in Massachusetts and educated in Vermont. After brief careers in farming, journalism, and business, he held minor political offices in Wisconsin, Washington, D.C., and Florida. His friendliness with President Andrew Johnson's administration and his political and journalistic activity in Florida made him a power in the Union-Republican party, which labored against Radical Reconstruction. In the battle for political control, the moderate Republicans won and Reed became governor in 1868.

Reed's administration reformed the judicial system and established a uniform public school system, a state university, an immigration commission, a state militia, and a state penitentiary. A hostile legislature of Radical Republicans and Conservative Democrats, however, incessantly negated and discredited his program. Inheriting the preceding Conservative administration's problems, including a $523,000 debt, Reed's administration offered few solutions. By 1870 financial difficulty encouraged Reed's administration to lease prisoners to private contractors, originating the inhumane CONVICT LEASE SYSTEM. Although Reed was a moderate on race relations, his prosouthern white views negated most Negro efforts to influence policy. Personally honest, his political ineptitude and his racial and financial naïveté generated severe criticism of his administration and several unsuccessful impeachment attempts. With a record of minor public improvements and a justifiably increased public debt, Reed left office in 1872. He retired near Jacksonville, where he died.

See J. H. Shofner, *Florida Reconstruction* (1974), excellent content and bibliography; W. W. Davis, *Civil War and Reconstruction* (1913), biased, but useful; P. D. Ackerman, "Florida Reconstruction" (M.A. thesis, University of Florida, 1948); and Reed Papers, P. K. Yonge Library, Florida State University.

N. GORDON CARPER
Berry College

REED, WALTER (1851–1902), was born in Belroi, Va., and educated at the University of Virginia Medical School and the Bellevue Hospital Medical College. He became an army officer in 1875, and in 1890 he was assigned to Baltimore, where he came under the influence of William Henry Welch at the Johns Hopkins Hospital. In 1893 he became curator of the Army Medical Museum in Washington, D.C., and professor of bacteriology at the Army Medical School. Seven years later, in 1900, when YELLOW FEVER struck the American troops in Cuba, Reed was named to head the Army Yellow Fever Commission. When the commission proved that the disease was transmitted by the *Aëdes aegypti* mosquito, that set the stage for the successful campaign to eradicate the disease through extermination of the mosquito. In February, 1901, the drive to eliminate the mosquito began, and by 1902 there were no cases of yellow fever in Cuba. The example set in Cuba was followed by many southern cities, which had traditionally been plagued by yellow fever, and the threat from the disease subsided.

See J. Blake and J. Duffy, *Bulletin of New York Academy of Medicine* (June, 1968), studies of yellow fever in eighteenth and nineteenth centuries. See also H. A. Kelly, *Walter Reed and Yellow Fever* (1923); A. E. Truby, *Memoir of Walter Reed* (1943); and L. N. Wood, *Walter Reed* (1943).

MARTIN KAUFMAN
Westfield State College

REGIONALISM. When Reconstruction had run its course and southerners were again in control of their own governments, the young people especially began looking ahead to a new day and a NEW SOUTH. Most leaders thought that they "should forget politics and go forward with their economic affairs." They believed that a prosperous South was necessary for the nation as a whole

and talked of "the immense natural wealth of the South" in climate, timber, minerals, and waterpower. "If ever a people had been sleeping in and on the edge of a land of opportunity, here it was." The task, however, was clearly one of finding a common end toward which all, or at least a majority, might turn their efforts. At first, confusion dominated. Then gradually, in the late 1920s and early 1930s, two new and disparate views of life began to emerge, each from an academic background. One centered at Vanderbilt University and advocated agrarianism; the other centered at the University of North Carolina and advocated regionalism.

Young men at Vanderbilt University, the Agrarians, took their stand in favor of a revived but largely agricultural South. Their theory was that the culture of the soil was the best and most sensitive vocation and that "it should have the economic preference and enlist the maximum number of workers." Twelve young men each wrote an article in support of some phase of the old order, and all were critical of those who would lead the South down the path of modernity. Under the title I'LL TAKE MY STAND, the essayists issued a clear call for the whole South to stand firmly against the surrender of its distinct historical and sectional identity and to hold to the social, moral, and economic ways of the past.

On the other hand, some professors and students at the University of North Carolina decided that it was time to bring the South into line with the modern world and its demands. They found that, in every statistical report, the southern states ranked at the bottom; therefore, change was imperative. The Old South with its plantations and Negro slaves was gone, they argued, and a new day had dawned. The South must wake up to the physical and social realities of the day. It should utilize modern science and technology drawn from the nation as a whole to build a new, diversified, yet regionally distinct pattern of living.

Professor HOWARD W. ODUM of the University of North Carolina was a pioneer in laying the foundation for a wider study of social science and regional planning. He and his colleagues, especially RUPERT B. VANCE, advanced the doctrine of regionalism as a sound and intelligent way to integrate the South into the nation. "It was a way of recognizing differences and encouraging diversity" in the South while treating its problems as ones related to the general national welfare.

In the first place, they said, there was not in the United States a single entity that could be designated "the South." There was, instead, a Southeast and a Southwest, a Northeast and a Northwest, the Middle States, and the Far West. Odum's "Southeast" included all states east of Oklahoma and south of the Potomac and the Ohio rivers (except West Virginia). He thus placed Texas in the Southwest region, West Virginia, Maryland, and Delaware in the Northeast, and Missouri with the Middle States (SOUTH, BOUNDARIES OF). And within the Southeast, said Odum and Vance, an infinite variety of subregions was worthy of study and separate development. Moreover, "the cumulative product of historical and geographic incidence" would permit perpetuation of culturally and economically distinct regions. Taking exception with Frederick Jackson Turner's idea of southern sectionalism, which implied internal conflict, Odum's regionalism meant cooperation and regional planning within a national framework. Under Odum's leadership, regional planners created the Southern Regional Committee of the Institute for Research in Social Science and the Advisory Work Committee. By 1932, 54 studies dealing with the various phases of the existing physical-social order had been published under its editorship.

Then appeared Vance's excellent volume *Human Geography of the South* (1932). "The purpose of regionalism" he said, "was to use the American South as a test of human adequacy to master the resources of a given region and to develop thereon a distinctive and component culture." As Americans had pushed aside the native plants and animals and planted cotton, corn, wheat, and rye, they had created a new agricultural world. As a result, he noted, we have our corn belts, our wheat belts, and our dairy belts, and man had proceeded by stages from the regions as laid down by geology to the regions as transformed by the hand of man. Now the task, through judicious use of technicians and social planning, was to bring about a new southern cultural and material renaissance. Researchers were to inventory not only the South's physical resources—mineral, climate, soil, etc.—but also its human resources (diet, health, and energy).

The South throughout its history had had a colonial status. It had long plundered its raw resources in order to have some immediate modicum of luxury and had thus remained long a debtor economy (CURRENCY). According to Vance and Odum, southern scholars interested in regionalism would now bring together men of intelligence from the academic and civilian population, from all cultural, scientific, and economic groups. Together they would explore the needs of the region and face the task of regional planning for the future in coordination with that of the nation as a whole. The statesman would play his part, and the engineer would play his. That was the way regionalism could work, and the South was now in a position where "wise planning could assure its orderly economic and cultural development."

For a while it seemed that the new regionalism might realize some of its goals under the NEW DEAL in such projects as the TENNESSEE VALLEY AUTHORITY; but, with the coming of the Second World War, many ambitious regional plans had to be shelved, and for a time afterward it seemed that the old lines of sectionalism with its attendant racism, strong local loyalties, and backward economic stance might reassert itself. In the postwar world, however, even though regionalism was almost lost sight of in economic planning, sectionalism was disappearing too; and, as a result of technological advances, demographic shifts, and changing locations of natural resources, southern economic and cultural problems became almost indistinguishable from those of the rest of the nation.

See G. B. Tindall, *Journal of Southern History* (August, 1958) and *Emergence of New South* (1967); F. C. Hobson, *Serpent in Eden* (1974); H. W. Odum and H. E. Moore, *American Regionalism* (1938); H. W. Odum, *American Epoch* (1930) and *Southern Regions* (1936); and R. B. Vance, *Human Geography of South* (1932, 1935).

AVERY O. CRAVEN
University of Chicago

REGULATORS. East-west antagonism was an enduring feature in the South during the late colonial period. This sectionalism—caused in part by differences in national origin, religion, and physiography between the largely English, aristocratic, Anglican, slave-owning Tidewater on the one hand and the Scotch-Irish, more democratic, Baptist-Presbyterian yeomanry of the Piedmont on the other—erupted into open hostility in both North and South Carolina. The movement to "regulate" local government and provide protection for law-abiding frontiersmen was first noticeable in South Carolina when in November, 1767, inhabitants living north of the Santee River petitioned the governor and legislature for a redress of grievances. With the passage of the circuit court act of 1769, many of the frontier complaints were alleviated and the South Carolina Regulator movement collapsed.

Of greater importance and potentially more volcanic was the movement in North Carolina. Formally organized in April, 1768, in Orange County, the Regulators sought to gain the right to "regulate" their own local government. Exploited by a political system that allowed and even encouraged such unfair and undemocratic practices as multiple officeholding, the sale of local political offices, unfair taxation, and an unjust judicial system, the increasingly disgruntled frontiersmen first tried to obtain justice by peaceful and legal means. The mildly sympathetic Governor WILLIAM TRYON responded favorably to their May, 1768, petition but warned against illegal actions and violence. However, a Regulator-inspired riot led by Herman Husband (1724–1795) in the Hillsboro court of Judge RICHARD HENDERSON led to the enactment in January, 1771, of the Johnston riot act and to the calling out of the militia. Tryon marched from New Bern to Hillsboro at the head of 1,400 well-armed militiamen. On March 16, 1771, he was confronted by 2,000 ill-equipped Regulators; and, after an abortive attempt at negotiation, the governor gave the order to fire. The two-hour battle of ALAMANCE was a decisive victory for the governor. Subsequently 12 Regulators were convicted of treason, and six were hanged. With this defeat the North Carolina Regulator movement came to an end. Fifteen hundred frontier families fled to the WATAUGA settlement in northeastern Tennessee, though 6,000 individuals remained to accept Tryon's offer of clemency. Contrary to the long-accepted interpretation, only 5 percent of the Regulators definitely became Tories during the War for Independence.

See J. S. Bassett, *American Historical Association Annual Report* (1894), North Carolina Regulators, standard work but still useful; E. D. Johnston, "War of Regulation" (M.A. thesis, University of North Carolina, 1942); and R. M. Brown, *South Carolina Regulators* (1963), definitive.

JOSEPH C. MORTON
Northeastern Illinois University

RELIGION. The South's distinctiveness as a region endures partially because of its especially pervasive, conservative Protestantism. METHODISTS and BAPTISTS have dominated southern religious life as the result of two generations of explosive growth at the beginning of the nineteenth century and maintenance of a persistent pattern of activity through the 1950s; the DISCIPLES OF CHRIST and PRESBYTERIAN groups have been counted as a poor third and fourth in the numerical ranking of the denominations. But the Holiness and PENTECOSTAL families of religious expression are also a major force in the region quite out of proportion to their power in other parts of the United States. Among the smaller religious bodies are the EPISCOPAL, LUTHERAN, Roman CATHOLIC, MORAVIAN, and QUAKER churches

and the Jewish congregations. The two largest Protestant groups first began to attract great numbers of converts during the revolutionary and early national periods (1760–1800), when great numbers of people began to pour into the South. With them came Separate Baptists, New Light Presbyterians, and a few Methodist (nominally Anglican) itinerants, who already had embarrassed ecclesiastical authorities with preaching that emphasized the "New Birth," a "conversion experience," and a life of disciplined piety or "holiness." The Evangelicals directly attacked Anglican priests as "unregenerate hirelings." They rejected the social primacy of aristocratic values and emphasized instead plainness, moral rigor, and the unostentatious virtues of respectable folk. At one time, the class conflict inherent in Evangelical preaching was expressed in attacks upon slaveholding. But Evangelicals were ambitious as well as relatively "poor," and their interest shifted from emancipation to the conversion of slaves.

Evangelical influence in the antebellum South developed in several ways. First, the churches provided social bondedness for people otherwise isolated from familial and geographic roots. They also contributed a religious ideology that enhanced the self-esteem of people who did not think that the upper classes really valued them as highly as they deserved. And, in an age when the rising democracy wished to demonstrate its respectability, Evangelicals built academies and colleges and provided faculties for state universities throughout the region. Soon the entire literate population of the South had come into contact with teachers whose religious faith was probably more obvious than their learning. To the slaveholding elites of the South—with whom the Evangelicals had made their peace in the late eighteenth century—churchmen offered a way to educate slaves through oral "religious instruction" in values that would stabilize the slaveholding regime. The result of this offer and its acceptance was to wed southern Evangelicalism to a theory of paternalism that rested on the white man's superiority and power. Through the Civil War, white Evangelicals were so sure of their identification with God's plan of salvation that the defeat of the Confederacy seemed only a sign that southern Christians had not been as responsible in their role of slaveholders as they should have been.

Southern religion was given its unique qualities, however, not merely by the activities of whites. Afro-Americans participated in the early revivals not only as converts but also as preachers. In southeastern Virginia, eastern North Carolina, South Carolina, and parts of Georgia, independent black preachers lay the foundations of Evangelicalism. But unqualified independence of black religious leaders in 1822 (VESEY PLOT) and 1831 (TURNER'S REBELLION) led to armed conflict; as a result, blacks were placed under the surveillance of white religious leaders as well as the police. Afro-American Christianity developed, therefore, under severe restraints in the South; but it was powerful enough to provide black and white missionaries from the North and returning fugitive former slaves with a social base and local leadership with which to build Afro-American churches after R. E. Lee's surrender (AFRICAN METHODIST EPISCOPAL CHURCH). There continued to be many similarities between white and black religion: an intense emotionalism; a view of the minister as a leader of his people rather than a professional; a preference for preaching based upon the Bible; and a sense of personal powerlessness before the forces of history. But there were differences, too: the expressiveness of black people at worship became a way of bonding the black community and freeing it from the psychological destructiveness of its oppression until political events and economic change made it possible to use the church as an instrument of nonviolent "revolution." The biblicism of the two peoples differed, too; that of whites often became a dogmatic "literalism" that supported a restricted, mechanical view of life, whereas blacks tended more to interpret present experience in biblical terms and to ignore the question of plenary inspiration of the Scriptures. In both cases, however, southern Christians could agree that religious expression was the genius of social life.

Throughout the nineteenth century and on into the twentieth, religious institutions and movements continued to shape southern life. In the process, class conflict—diverted from confrontations among whites to racial fears—came to be expressed in religious terms. The Holiness and Pentecostal movements in the late nineteenth century were parallel—some even believe complementary—to the Populist revolt. But such religious movements, because they conceived of their goals essentially in terms of participation, personal expression, and self-esteem, could never be translated into political action to achieve goals defined by class interest. Symbolic issues were another matter, however. For over a century after Appomattox, conservative white Christians would employ the issues surrounding temperance and PROHIBITION, the EVOLUTION CONTROVERSY, sex education, and SEGREGATION to establish the normative power of their own canons of social respectability. Consistent with this mood, the pri-

vate, conservative social ethics crafted under slavery and maintained by the doctrines of white supremacy continued to be the prevailing attitude of southern whites' religion.

It is also its very pervasiveness that makes southern religion different from that of the rest of the country. In all social crises the religious institutions of the region are for all races and political persuasions still a significant social factor. The South is probably the only area of the country in which a major political issue, such as the equal rights amendment to the Constitution, will prompt state legislators to ask the opinion of a prominent evangelist's family. And it is the one region of the country where a Protestant minister can lead his people with a new style of politics speaking in traditional cadences and with biblical phrases to effect a social revolution; for MARTIN LUTHER KING, JR., was able to win the Nobel Peace Prize because he understood so well the power of southern religion.

See K. K. Bailey, *Southern White Protestantism* (1964); S. S. Hill, *Southern Churches in Crisis* (1966); J. Fichter and G. Maddox, in J. C. McKinney and E. T. Thompson (eds.), *South in Continuity and Change* (1965).

DONALD G. MATHEWS
University of North Carolina, Chapel Hill

REPTILES AND AMPHIBIANS often require a highly specific environment, and the South—because of its wide range of climates, land forms, and altitudes—sustains a varied population of both. In North America, however, most species of reptiles and amphibians inhabit areas bordered by geographic features (Appalachian Mountains, Mississippi River, Rocky Mountains) that mark east from west rather than north from south.

The only order of North American reptile found exclusively within the South is the Crocodilia. The American alligator (*Alligator mississipiensis*) was once common all along the coast from North Carolina to the Florida Keys and west to Texas. Irresponsible killings for "sport" and for its valuable hides have greatly reduced both its domain and population. The American crocodile (*Crocodylus acutus*), found in the EVERGLADES and the Keys of southern Florida, was never so widespread as the alligator, a fact partially responsible for the mistaken belief that crocodiles are not native to North America. Indeed, the popular notion that the shape of the snout is the best way to distinguish an alligator (broad and stubby) from a crocodile (narrow and pointed) functions consistently only in North America.

Among the North American salamanders (Caudata) and toads and frogs (Salientia), no family of either order is unique to the South, although some species inhabit particular areas of the region. Several species of spotted salamanders (*Ambystoma maculatum, A. laterale*, and *A. jeffersonianum*) and mud puppies (*Necturus maculosus*), for example, thrive in areas scattered throughout the eastern two-thirds of the nation, depending upon the preference of these amphibians for rivers, grasslands, or woods. Yet the ringed salamander (*A. annulatum*) of the Ozarks and the Ouachita Mountains, Mabee's salamander (*A. mabeei*) of the Carolinas, and the flatwoods salamander (*A. cingulatum*) of the Gulf and Atlantic coasts survive only within portions of the South. Two other members of the salamander family, the hellbender (*Cryptobranchus alleganiensis*) and the siren (*Siren lacertina*) are found predominantly but not exclusively within the South. The hellbender—looking much like a wrinkled, fat, two-and-a-half-foot-long snake with legs—thrives in most of the larger southern rivers, yet may also be found as far north as the Hudson River.

Similarly, toads and frogs are an order of amphibians, the families of which more commonly follow east-west rather than north-south territorial limits. The bullfrog (*Rana catesbeiana*), green frog (*R. clamitans*), and leopard frog (*R. pipiens*) are native to most areas east of the continental divide. The distinctive "jug-o'-rum" call of the male bullfrog can now be heard as far west as Hawaii and Taiwan because the fine taste of this animal's legs has encouraged many usually unsuccessful attempts to establish frog farms. The eastern spadefoot toad (*Scaphiopu holbrooki*) and the American toad (*Bufo americanus*) are found throughout the eastern half of the continent, the former as far north as Canada and the latter north to Massachusetts. The carpenter frog (*R. virgatipes*), whose call sounds like a series of rapid hammer blows, is found in ponds and rivers as far north as New Jersey; however, both the pig frog (*R. grylio*) and the river frog (*R. heckscheri*) are local to the lowland waters of warmer areas in the South. The pig frog, an aggressive animal with more toe webbing than a bullfrog and a piglike grunt, is found in an area between South Carolina and Texas. The placid river frog with two calls—a growling snore and an explosive grunt—is native to the rivers of the area between South Carolina and southern Mississippi. The largest toad found in the South (*B. marinus*) is not as large as *B. alvarius* of southern California and Arizona, nor is it native to the South. It was introduced to the region from South America to control the insect populations of southern sugarcane fields.

Although the American public has an exaggerated notion of both the frequency and seriousness of venomous snakebites, the four venomous snakes living east of the Rockies are all found in the South: rattlesnakes, cottonmouths, copperheads, and coral snakes. The copperhead (*Agkistrodon contortrix*) reaches a length of two to three feet at maturity, feeds on small mammals, and hibernates in groups or with other species of snakes. The bite of a single copperhead is rarely fatal, and it seldom is seen, preferring instead to avoid human contact. The cottonmouth (*Agkistrodon piscivorus*) or water moccasin usually grows to three or four feet in length, but may reach six feet. Unlike the copperhead, which prefers high grass, the cottonmouth moccasin is aquatic, it is highly aggressive, and its bite is quite toxic. Of the 13 species of North American rattlesnakes, only three are found in the South: the timber rattler (*Crotalus horridus horridus*), the canebreak rattler (*C. horridus atricaudatus*), and the eastern diamondback (*C. adamanteus*). The eastern diamondback, the largest venomous snake in North America, may reach as much as eight feet in length. It and the smaller canebreak rattler are found only in the South, the former usually within 100 miles of the coastline. The timber rattlesnake, up to six feet in length at maturity, is found as far north as New Hampshire, Wisconsin, and Nebraska. Cottonmouths are native to rivers as far north as Illinois, and copperheads, native to the entire South except for the Florida peninsula, reach as far north as Massachusetts and Nebraska.

Of the South's four kinds of venomous snakes, only the eastern coral snake (*Micrurus fulvius*), found in the grasslands and open woods of the area from the Carolinas to central Texas, is unique to the South. The colorfully ringed markings of the coral snake often cause it to be confused with similarly banded, nonvenomous milk snakes and scarlet snakes. The coral snake bites and chews its victims (unlike other snakes, which inject their poison through fangs), but the bite of the two-foot-long mature eastern coral is far less toxic than that of its western cousin.

Most southern snakes, like those throughout the nation, are nonvenomous and are extremely helpful in keeping the population of unwanted small mammals under control. The eastern indigo snake (*Drymarchon corais couperi*), at eight feet in length, is the largest snake in North America. Found throughout the Lower South from South Carolina to Alabama, the indigo is often passed off at roadside snake farms as a cobra, but it is essentially harmless to man. The rainbow snake (*Abastor erythrogrammus*), found in swamps throughout the southern seaboard, is perhaps the most beautiful snake to be found on the continent.

Most of the remaining nonvenomous snakes found in the South are not limited by the historical boundaries used to define the region. The red-bellied mud snake (*Farancia abacura*) or hoop snake, though found throughout the South, may also be found in parts of Illinois, Indiana, and Ohio. The scarlet (*Cemophora coccinea*) or false coral snake is native as far north as New Jersey. Unlike the true coral, the nonvenomous scarlet snake has a red rather than a black mouth; however, since several banded milk snakes have black noses, the color of the head is not a safe way to distinguish harmless from harmful snakes. Racers (*Coluber constrictor*), eastern worm snakes (*Carphophis amoenus*), rat snakes (*Elaphe obsoleta*), water snakes (*Natrix*), king snakes (*Lampropeltis getulus*), milk snakes (*L. doliata*), and hognose snakes (*Heterodon platyrhinos*) can be found in the eastern two-thirds of the United States wherever suitable habitat and diet for their particular needs exist. In parts of the South that furnish an abundance of food and a longer growing season, they may reach maturity sooner, may grow somewhat larger, and may even exist in a variant subspecies. In the sandy floodplains of the South Atlantic seaboard, for example, the southern hognose (*H. simus*) shares his domain with the eastern hognose, which ranges from New Hampshire to the Rio Grande valley. Both are sometimes mistaken for copperheads; when threatened, both will hiss and flatten their necks like a cobra; and, when captured, both will roll over and play dead like an opossum.

See A. E. Leviton, *Reptiles and Amphibians of North America* (1970), illustrated, valuable general study; J. A. Oliver, *North American Amphibians and Reptiles* (1955); A. d'A. Bellairs, *Life of Reptiles* (1970); D. M. Cochran, *New Field Book of Reptiles and Amphibians* (1970); R. Conant, *Reptiles and Amphibians of Eastern and Central North America* (1974); W. T. Neill, *Ruling Reptiles: Alligators, Crocodiles, and Kin* (1971); R. W. Barbour, *Amphibians and Reptiles of Kentucky* (1971); A. F. Carr, *Reptiles, Amphibians, and Fishes of Florida* (1955); P. Anderson, *Reptiles of Missouri* (1965); and *Journal of Herpetology* (1968–), published by Society for Study of Amphibians and Reptiles.

REPUBLICAN PARTY was first introduced into the South as an alien institution. Few southerners joined the party in the 1850s, and in the ELECTION OF 1860 Abraham Lincoln won votes in only five southern states. The Civil War made the Republicans, as the spokesmen for the enemy of the Confederate states, seem hostile to southern interest. Even in the border states Republicans often found it necessary to neglect their partisan interests and take part in Unionist governments with Democrats.

Reconstruction produced a dramatic change in the position of southern Republicans. During the 1863–1866 period both ABRAHAM LINCOLN and ANDREW JOHNSON were content to work with UNIONIST coalitions that included Democrats and former Whigs as well as Republicans. By March, 1867, therefore, the Republicans had gained control only in Tennessee, Missouri, and West Virginia. In each of these states large Unionist populations in the mountain regions sustained the party. The advent of congressional Reconstruction in 1867 altered the situation in the ten former Confederate states where the Republicans were not in power. Tens of thousands of former Confederate political and military leaders were disfranchised, and approximately 700,000 blacks were given the right to vote. These changes were accompanied by direct military control of the political process.

The new electorate produced powerful Republican parties throughout the former Confederacy. Using groups like the UNION LEAGUE, Republicans appealed to and organized most of the blacks into the party. As a result the Republicans were able to dominate most of the conventions called to write new constitutions for the southern states. These documents encouraged education and business and removed almost all suffrage restrictions. The officials of the new governments were often Republicans, and some were black. Only in Virginia did the Republican party fail to win at least partial control of the state government.

Conservative white reaction to black suffrage and northern Republican politicians, who provided a disproportionate share of party leaders, was violent. Between 1869 and 1876 Democratic terrorist groups such as the KU KLUX KLAN succeeded in racially polarizing the southern electorate. The result was that by 1876 Republicans had lost power in all the southern states except Florida, Louisiana, and South Carolina. The confused presidential ELECTION OF 1876 led to a compromise that ended Republican domination even in those states.

The party, however, remained a significant factor in southern politics between 1876 and 1896. It consistently won some congressional elections in Virginia, Tennessee, and the border states. In other areas where blacks greatly outnumbered whites, fusion arrangements between the two parties allowed Republicans to win local offices. In addition Democratic factionalism occasionally allowed Republicans to win state elections. For example, President Chester A. Arthur encouraged Virginia

Readjuster leader WILLIAM MAHONE to align himself with the Republicans in the early 1880s and attempted to persuade other dissident Democrats to emulate Mahone. At the same time, mountain Republican bosses like Leonidas C. Houk in eastern Tennessee constructed effective local organizations.

The economic difficulties of the 1890s offered great opportunities to the Republicans. The party elected governors and U.S. senators in most border states and in North Carolina. The victory in West Virginia was achieved under the leadership of businessman STEPHEN B. ELKINS and gave the party control of the state from 1894 to 1930. The most startling Republican success came in North Carolina, where fusion with the Populists resulted in Democratic defeats in 1894 and 1896. In the Deep South fusion between Populists and Republicans was common, and only violence and fraud prevented Populist successes in Georgia, Louisiana, and Alabama.

The rise of southern Negrophobia, combined with the Populist challenge, led to concerted efforts to disfranchise blacks (DISFRANCHISEMENT). Starting with Mississippi in 1890 and ending with Georgia in 1908, all of the former Confederate states used POLL TAXES, literacy tests, and discriminatory registration policies to eliminate black voters. To discourage illiterate blacks, border state Democrats passed legislation requiring secret ballots. The greatly weakened southern Republicans split into LILY-WHITE and BLACK AND TAN factions in most states and spent their time fighting for federal patronage. A few Republicans like Congressman C. Bascom Slemp in southwestern Virginia continued to win elections, but only in the border states did the party contest for state offices.

Changes in the national Democratic party in the 1920s presented an opportunity to rebuild the southern Republican party. The candidacy of New York Governor Al Smith, a Catholic, in 1928 alienated many Protestant southerners. The Republicans carried not only the border states but five Deep South states as well. The depression of the 1930s drove the southern Democrats together however. The racial and economic policies of Franklin D. Roosevelt's NEW DEAL and HARRY S. TRUMAN reopened the split between the national and southern Democrats again. In 1948 many southerners joined the DIXIECRAT revolt against the commitment of the Democratic convention to increasing civil rights for blacks.

The candidacy of Dwight D. Eisenhower in 1952 and 1956 allowed the Republicans to exploit Democratic factionalism. Although continuing to vote for Democrats in local elections, many white southerners supported Republican presidential nominees. In 1964 Republican Barry Goldwater won his major victories in the Gulf coast states. Republicans also began to match their success in the presidential campaigns at the state level. Republicans elected governors in all of the border states and in the Deep South states of Arkansas, Florida, North and South Carolina, Tennessee, and Virginia. Democratic converts like STROM THURMOND of South Carolina played an important role in these Republican triumphs. Although still a minority in the South as a whole, the Republicans did carry all of the region in 1972 and could at that point be considered an accepted part of southern political life.

See R. O. Curry (ed.), *Reconstruction in Border States* (1969); and J. H. Franklin, *Reconstruction* (1961). Two excellent books, V. P. De Santis, *Republicans Face Southern Question* (1959), and S. P. Hirschson, *Farewell Bloody Shirt* (1962), discuss policies of national party. For after 1876, see N. M. Blake, *William Mahone* (1935); and G. B. McKinney, "Mountain Republicanism" (Ph.D. dissertation, Northwestern University, 1971). Black disfranchisement is traced in J. M. Kousser, *Shaping Southern Politics* (1974). Republican efforts to remain competitive after 1900 are documented in D. C. Roller, "Republican Party in North Carolina" (Ph.D. dissertation, Duke, 1965); and V. O. Key, *Southern Politics* (1949), includes classic study of twentieth-century party.

GORDON B. MCKINNEY
Valdosta State College

RESACA, BATTLE OF (May 13–15, 1864). Resaca, on the Western & Atlantic Railroad in northwestern Georgia, assumed strategic importance for Confederate operations during early May, 1864. While Confederate General JOSEPH JOHNSTON awaited a frontal assault against strong defenses at Dalton, William T. Sherman sent James McPherson's Union forces around the Confederate left to threaten rail communications at Resaca. Faulty intelligence led Johnston to assume this activity was a feint to divert attention from Sherman's main objective. Delayed reaction to the federal threat was unfortunate, for Johnston's hastily formed position at Resaca offered Sherman an opportunity to trap him against the Connasauga and Oostanaula rivers. On May 14 Sherman attacked LEONIDAS POLK's sector of the Confederate line, but Johnston countered effectively by sending JOHN B. HOOD against the weakened federal left. As Johnston planned to resume attacking on the fifteenth, he discovered Union forces were crossing the Oostanaula six miles south near the rail town of Calhoun. Johnston therefore retreated southward hoping to ambush the pursuing enemy.

See T. L. Connelly, *Autumn of Glory* (1971); G. E. Govan and J. W. Livingood, *Different Valor* (1956); and N. C. Hughes, *William J. Hardee* (1965), all good accounts. See also L. Lewis, *Sherman, Fighting Prophet* (1932); W. T. Sherman, *Memoirs* (1875); J. D. Cox, *Atlanta* (1882); and R. U. Johnson and C. C. Buel (eds.), *Battles and Leaders* (1888), IV.

WILLIAM E. DERBY
State University College, Geneseo, N.Y.

RESACA DE LA PALMA, BATTLE OF (May 9, 1846).

After PALO ALTO, ZACHARY TAYLOR on May 9, 1846, found that Mexican General Mariano Arista occupied the rim of Resaca de la Palma, a concave ravine. Taylor, while deploying the 1st Brigade under Lieutenant Colonel W. G. Belknap, sent forward along the road Captain George A. McCall's unit to draw the fire of Arista's artillery. When Lieutenant Randolph Ridgely's battery did not knock out the Mexican artillery, Taylor ordered Captain C. A. May of the 2nd Dragoons to charge, which he did with such impetuosity that he scattered the crews and captured General Rómolo Diaz de la Vega. Belknap's 8th Infantry then captured and held the battery of seven pieces. Taylor's 1,700 active soldiers then captured the enemy camp and drove Arista's larger army across the Rio Grande. Taylor failed to capture the enemy army and possibly end the war decisively, but he opened up the interior of northern Mexico to invasion.

See T. F. Rodenbough, *Everglade to Cañon* (1875), best; L. Giddings, *Sketches of Campaign* (1853), map; W. S. Henry, *Campaign Sketches* (1847); H. Hamilton, *Zachary Taylor* (1941); N. W. Stephenson, *Mexican War* (1921); O. A. Singleton, *Mexican War* (1960); and W. P. Webb (ed.), *Handbook of Texas* (1952).

KENNETH FRANKLIN NEIGHBOURS
Midwestern State University

RESETTLEMENT ADMINISTRATION,

created by an executive order of President Franklin D. Roosevelt in April, 1935, was viewed by Rexford Tugwell and other agricultural planners in the U.S. Department of Agriculture as a long-range program designed to cure a crippled agricultural economy. Funds for operation of the RA during its first year ($126.5 million) came from $4.888 billion allotted by Congress in the Emergency Relief Appropriations Act of 1935. Similar congressional relief appropriation acts funded the RA in subsequent years.

The original goals of the RA were ambitious. The USDA estimated that 2 million farmers tilled 200 million acres of land unsuited for agricultural production. The RA would coordinate a land-reform and a land-purchase program to phase out agricultural production on all of this land and resettle the farmers who were on it. Tugwell hoped to relocate them in newly constructed federal communities where they would find work as industrial workers. Because this expectation proved impracticable, Tugwell resettled most of them on productive agricultural land.

The South attracted much of the RA's attention. USDA surveys showed that 55 percent of all southern farmers in 1935 were tenants, and 60 percent of all cotton producers were in a similar status. Sixty percent of America's eroded soil was in the South, and the USDA estimated that 34.5 million acres of southern farmland should be removed from cultivation as rapidly as possible. Three-fourths of all farmers who produced annually less than $1,000 worth of farm products were in the South.

In spite of its ambitious goals, the RA generated only minor reforms in the South. It bought 1,275,000 acres of submarginal land through 74 land-purchase projects. It relocated nearly 15,000 farmers, almost half of whom settled on community projects developed or operated by the RA. The RA purchased and leased good farmland to 1,000 tenant farmers in ten select southern states. It provided direct relief to more than 200,000 southern farm families. And it made farm rehabilitation loans averaging $300 each to a select number of southern farmers.

Disappointed by the small funds provided him by Congress, Tugwell resigned as director of the RA in late 1936. From that point until it was reorganized as the FARM SECURITY ADMINISTRATION in September, 1937, the RA used most of its resources to make rehabilitation loans to needy farmers.

See S. Baldwin, *Poverty and Politics* (1968); P. Conkin, *Tomorrow a New World* (1959); and R. Lord and P. Johnstone, *A Place on Earth* (1942).

HARRY C. MCDEAN
San Diego State University

REVELS, HIRAM RHOADES (1822–1901),

was born in Fayetteville, N.C., of free black parents who were of mixed Indian and Negro blood. After working as a barber for several years, he matriculated for two years (1844–1846) in a Quaker seminary at Liberty, Ind. He completed his formal education at Knox College in Illinois and was ordained a minister in the African Methodist church. Before the Civil War he served as a missionary to blacks in Ohio, Illinois, Indiana, Missouri, Kansas, Kentucky, and Tennessee. When the Civil War began,

Revels moved to Baltimore and then to St. Louis, where he taught in black schools and assisted in organizing three Negro regiments for the Union army. In the capacity of a missionary he followed U. S. Grant's army into the lower Mississippi Valley, and after the war he returned to the Natchez area to organize black churches and schools.

Revels entered Reconstruction politics in 1868, when he was appointed by the military commander to serve on the Natchez city council. Elected to the state senate as a Republican in 1869, he made such a profound impression upon members of the legislature with his prayer opening the session that he was selected to fill the short term in the U. S. Senate (reputedly the unexpired term of Jefferson Davis). As a member of the Senate from February, 1870, to March, 1871, Revels, the first black to serve in this august body, was more of a curiosity than a mover of men or an instigator of legislation. He did speak in behalf of the voluntary integration of the public schools in the District of Columbia and also the immediate removal of the political disabilities of former Confederates. After his term expired, Revels served as the first president of Alcorn University (1871–1883) in Mississippi. During the "revolution of 1875," which overthrew Republican rule in the state, Revels joined in the conservative attacks on the administration of carpetbagger ADELBERT AMES, although he continued his allegiance to the Republican party.

See S. D. Smith, *Negro in Congress, 1870–1901* (1940); *Autobiography of John Roy Lynch* (1970); V. L. Wharton, *Negro in Mississippi* (1965); Jackson *Weekly Pilot* (January 22, May 21, 28, 1870); and Washington *New National Era* (1870).

WILLIAM C. HARRIS
North Carolina State University

REVOLUTION, AMERICAN. It is difficult to write of a South as distinct from the English colonies above the Susquehanna in the era of the American Revolution, especially when, as Carl Bridenbaugh notes, there were several societies in the region from Maryland to Georgia in 1763: a plantation hierarchy on the Chesapeake shores; another aristocratic order in the Carolina low country; a backcountry society in the Piedmont and farther west; and possibly still another, less easily defined social mixture in North Carolina. Whatever colony a man hailed from, he identified himself in all likelihood locally—as a Virginian, for instance, and then secondly as an Englishman. If he had proceeded further, which is doubtful, he might have described himself as an American or a British-American, but not as a southerner.

The imperial crisis with Britain after 1763 saw southerners (the word henceforth used in its present sense) resorting to the same arguments as their northern brethren against parliamentary taxation and other measures of the mother country that seemed to violate the British constitution and run counter to a century and a half of colonial development. If the literary outpourings of southerners were fewer than those of the soon-to-be-designated yankees, the former needed to make no apologies for the quality of the essays that flowed from the pens of Daniel Dulany (DULANY FAMILY) of Maryland, Maurice Moore (MOORE FAMILY) and JAMES IREDELL of North Carolina, William Henry Drayton (DRAYTON FAMILY) of South Carolina, RICHARD BLAND and THOMAS JEFFERSON of Virginia. Nor did southern legislative assemblies, already long engaged in a "quest for power," wait for similar bodies elsewhere to point the way in retaliating against Britain.

Virginia soon emerged as a leader, and not simply of the southern provinces. Populous and prestigious, the Old Dominion issued the strongest condemnation of the Stamp Act, called for intercolonial committees of correspondence, joined Massachusetts in appealing for the gathering known as the First CONTINENTAL CONGRESS, and saw one of its delegates, PEYTON RANDOLPH, chosen president of that body. Virginians, moreover, played other key roles. GEORGE WASHINGTON commanded the Continental army, RICHARD HENRY LEE introduced the congressional resolution for severing political ties with Britain, and Jefferson wrote the DECLARATION OF INDEPENDENCE.

Once again it was Virginia that afforded direction in the transition from colony to statehood. GEORGE MASON's Declaration of Rights preceded those of the other states and influenced their contents, just as it served as a model for the later national BILL OF RIGHTS. If all the southern states swept away certain archaic land laws and practices—QUITRENTS, PRIMOGENITURE AND ENTAIL—it was the state of Jefferson and JAMES MADISON that produced the most explicit and far-reaching liberal document on ending church-state relationships, the Statute of Religious Liberty.

Slavery was another matter, where even in Virginia Jefferson acknowledged the futility of introducing in the legislature his draft of a bill for the gradual elimination of the peculiar institution. Yet in every southern state there were sensitive, educated leaders who felt the contradiction between the principles of the Revolution and human bondage. "Especially in view of the way their grandchildren were to talk after 1830," observes Winthrop Jordan, "it is important to bear in mind that

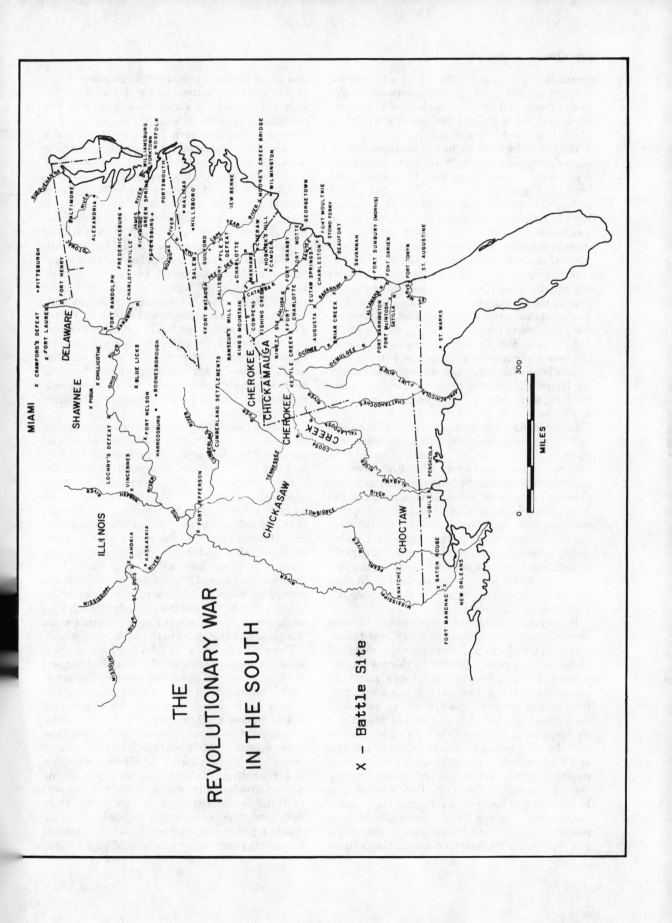

THE
REVOLUTIONARY WAR
IN THE SOUTH

X — Battle Site

during the Revolutionary War, despite the virtual absence of antislavery pronouncements in the Lower South and the cautiousness of Virginians on the subject, no one in the South stood up in public to endorse Negro slavery."

The role of the South in the war itself was largely secondary prior to 1778. Washington, of course, was not the only general from that region, but here too Virginians stand out: HORATIO GATES and CHARLES LEE, former British veterans, had settled in the western section near another future revolutionary general, DANIEL MORGAN, who became perhaps the best combat officer in the Continental army. Most of the prominent field commanders, however, were from the New England and Middle Atlantic states, a reflection of the fact that in the initial years of warfare the bulk of American manpower was drawn from the areas invaded by British troops.

To be sure, Britain had from 1775 onward a kind of southern strategy, which was taken off the back burner briefly in 1776, when an expedition under Sir Henry Clinton put in momentarily at Cape Fear and then moved on to fight an inconclusive naval duel with American shore batteries at Charleston, S.C. The strategy was this: the LOYALISTS, whom the cabinet believed composed a majority of the southern population, would be able to maintain themselves *after* British armies landed and destroyed the Whigs' revolutionary regimes. Clinton, with instructions to return to the North in the summer of 1776, had no real opportunity to test these assumptions. But they remained unchallenged in the minds of London policy makers, and they became the mainspring of British military campaigning following the failure of the king's forces to crush the rebellion in the North and after the entry of France into the conflict on the patriots' side.

If the fundamental assumptions about Loyalist strength were correct, then it made sense to retrench in the North and try to save that segment of the empire most valuable in the mercantile scheme of things, the realm of tobacco, rice, indigo, and naval stores. The real test began on a positive note as the winter of 1778–1779 witnessed the reduction of Georgia, followed in May, 1780, by the capture of Charleston. Even so, the restored royal governments established in Georgia and South Carolina never became viable instruments of control. The patriots proved to be too numerous, scarcely the minority they were said to have been; and the guerrilla war that raged in the backcountry drained Lord Cornwallis of irreplaceable regulars and intimidated countless Tories into concealing their true colors. The destruction of the newly raised American Southern Army at the battle of CAMDEN in South Carolina (August, 1780) was only a temporary setback for the patriots. General Nathanael Greene, assuming direction of the Southern Department, played a masterful cat-and-mouse game with Cornwallis luring His Lordship into North Carolina, where they traded heavy blows at GUILFORD COURTHOUSE (March, 1781) before the British general limped northward into Virginia.

In doing so Cornwallis committed two monumental errors. First, as a result of establishing himself on the Virginia peninsula, he was vulnerable to a French-American land and sea blockade, which Washington and Admiral François de Grasse executed with remarkable skill and precision. While Cornwallis was succumbing to siege operations—he surrendered on October 19, 1781— Greene was capitalizing on His Lordship's second disastrous mistake, leaving his bases isolated and exposed in the Lower South. Greene and the South Carolina partisan fighters picked them off, one by one, until only Charleston and Savannah remained for the British to evacuate at the conclusion of hostilities.

Had the Revolution created a perception among southerners of a common identity and unique concerns? Yes, for some at least, but only to a limited degree. There was disagreement about the northern boundary; Washington, for example, continued to speak of Virginia as one of the "middle states" and of the Carolinas and Georgia as the "Southern states." On the other hand, William Henry Drayton, in the winter of 1777–1778, excluded Maryland but added Virginia to the above-mentioned states, all forming "the body of the southern interest." But it may well be that the prevailing view had become that expressed in 1787 by CHARLES PINCKNEY, another South Carolinian, who stated, "When I say Southern, I mean Maryland and the states to the southward of her."

There was in fact, says John R. Alden, a "First South," set apart not merely by its agriculture and its slavery, but also by certain interests that manifested themselves in the Continental Congress, usually on economic issues. South Carolinians and Georgians fought successfully for the continued exportation of rice, notwithstanding the Continental ASSOCIATION; but they lost their battle to have blacks removed from the Continental army. The most divisive sectional controversy during the war involved the making of the first national constitution, the ARTICLES OF CONFEDERATION. Particularly troublesome was the question—ultimately rejected—of whether to include slaves as property in determining what should be the states' annual financial contribution to the confederation government. Throughout, the greatest fears of the South becoming a subordinate section were voiced by South Carolinians, prophetic of their state's stand in the years 1828–1860.

All the same, for thoughtful, reflective southerners as well as northerners—men with first-hand knowledge of the nation's wartime weaknesses—nationalism was a more potent force than sectionalism. Enlightened southerners believed that the South, with its population increasing, with Tennessee and Kentucky rapidly growing, had little to fear in the long run from a stronger American union. Led in large part by southerners such as Washington and Madison, American nationalists pushed for greater political consolidation, their efforts culminating in the federal Constitution of 1787. In sum, the First South was not the Old South.

See J. R. Alden, *South in the Revolution* (1957) and *First South* (1961); C. Bridenbaugh, *Myths and Realities* (1951); W. W. Abbot, *Royal Governors of Georgia* (1959); J. P. Greene, *Quest for Power* (1963); R. D. Higginbotham, *Daniel Morgan* (1961); D. S. Freeman, *George Washington* (1951–52), III–V; M. F. Treacy, *Prelude to Yorktown* (1963); R. E. and B. K. Brown, *Virginia, 1705–1786* (1964); H. J. Eckenrode, *Revolution in Virginia* (1916); and R. McColley, *Slavery in Jeffersonian Virginia* (1964). Three invaluable multivolumed documentary works are J. P. Boyd (ed.), *Jefferson Papers* (1950–); W. T. Hutchinson and R. Rutland (eds.), *Madison Papers* (1962–75); and J. C. Fitzpatrick (ed.), *Washington Papers* (1931–44).

DON HIGGINBOTHAM
University of North Carolina, Chapel Hill

REVOLUTION, HISTORIOGRAPHY OF THE SOUTH IN THE.

For the most concise bibliography of material to 1957 concerning the South in the Revolution, consult J. R. Alden, *The South in the Revolution* (1957), a book that demonstrates both the local and conservative orientation of the South in this period. Since that time, many fine works have been published. Biographies like T. Thayer's *Nathanael Greene* (1960), H. F. Rankin's *Francis Marion* (1973), R. D. Meade's *Patrick Henry* (1958, 1969), and M. R. Zahniser's *Charles Cotesworth Pinckney* (1967) illuminate the period leadership.

Military topics reveal many war problems. R. Weigley, *The Partisan War* (1970), concerns the local fighting in South Carolina; H. F. Rankin, *The North Carolina Continentals* (1971), discusses military development in one state; P. D. Nelson, *North Carolina Historical Review* (Summer, 1974), reviews the problems in southern military campaigns; and R. L. Ganyard, *North Carolina His-torical Review* (Jan., 1969), deals with the Indian problem.

Political development is another important theme in such books as K. Coleman, *Revolution in Georgia* (1958), which shows the emerging democratic trends in that state; and R. Hoffman, *A Spirit of Dissension* (1973), concerning Maryland. Other valuable studies include such articles as M. D. Pierce, *Virginia Magazine of History and Biography* (Oct., 1972), concerning the patriot movement in Virginia; J. T. Main, *Maryland Historical Magazine* (March, 1968), developing the concept of political parties in Maryland; R. L. Ganyard, *William and Mary Quarterly* (Oct., 1968), discussing political divisions in North Carolina; J. L. Anderson, *Virginia Magazine of History and Biography* (Jan., 1974), interpreting the problems of the older political elite; and E. G. Evans, *William and Mary Quarterly* (July, 1972), discussing the planter debt.

The plight of the southern Loyalist is important too. This theme has been developed for Georgia by R. S. Lambert, *Georgia Review* (Winter, 1963) and *William and Mary Quarterly* (Jan., 1963); and by G. D. Olson, *Georgia Historical Quarterly* (Spring, 1970). Loyalism in Maryland is discussed by A. A. Allan, *Journal of Southern History* (May, 1973); and in South Carolina by G. D. Olson, *South Carolina Historical Magazine* (Oct., 1968), and B. D. Barger, *South Carolina Historical Magazine* (July, 1962). To place the South in perspective about the Revolution, C. G. Sellers, in A. S. Link and R. W. Patrick (eds.), *Writing Southern History* (1965), should be used.

JAMES LAVERNE ANDERSON
University of Georgia

REYNOLDS, ROBERT RICE (1884–1963), U.S. senator from North Carolina, was born in Weaverville, N.C. After graduation from the University of North Carolina in 1907 with a law degree, he began practice in Asheville, specializing in criminal work. Often an aspirant to nomination in the Democratic party, he made unsuccessful bids for lieutenant governor in 1924 and U.S. senator in 1926. Elected to the U.S. Senate in 1932 to fulfill the unexpired term of Lee S. Overman, Reynolds retained that post until he declined to run for reelection in 1944. In 1950 he was unsuccessful in obtaining the Democratic nomination to return to the Senate. As senator he was best known for his strong isolationism prior to World War II, including the founding in 1938 of the American Nationalist party.

See R. R. Reynolds, *Wanderlust* (1914) and *Gypsy Trails* (1925); B. Davis, *Harper's* (March, 1944); T. Schlesinger, *Nation* (April 22, 1950); U. Bell, *American Mercury* (Nov., 1939); R. McCormick, *Collier's* (May 21, 1938); *Newsweek* (May 1, 1939); G. H. Cless, Jr., *Scribner's* (June, 1941); and R. Coughlan *Life* (Sept. 8, 1941).

THOMAS S. MORGAN
Winthrop College

RHETT, ROBERT BARNWELL (1800–1876), was born in Beaufort, S.C., the son of James Smith and Marianna Gough. The family name was changed in 1837 to that of a distinguished colonial forebear, Colonel William Rhett. Rhett's formal schooling ended when he was seventeen. Aristocratic in manner, he was considered well-to-do although he was heavily indebted for many years. Rhett served in the House of Representatives (1837–1849) and in the U.S. Senate (1850–1852). An early disciple of Robert J. Turnbull's gospel of liberty and self-government, Rhett was convinced that revolution was the means of achieving those ends. The support that he aroused caused South Carolina to become known as "Rhettsylvania." Although he temporarily championed John C. Calhoun's view of NULLIFICATION as a constitutional alternative to revolution, he never accepted it with finality. He was a leading FIRE-EATER at the NASHVILLE CONVENTION. His efforts as leader of the secessionist element in South Carolina following the COMPROMISE OF 1850, however, ended in failure. After the southern Confederacy was organized in 1861, Rhett served in the Confederate Congress until 1863 and devoted all efforts to oppose any schemes at reconstruction of the Union. The CHARLESTON MERCURY became the instrument through which he attacked Jefferson Davis for failure to achieve southern independence.

See L. A. White, *Robert Rhett* (1931), only comprehensive biography; N. W. Stephenson, *Day of Confederacy* (1920); and H. S. Schultz, *Nationalism and Sectionalism in South Carolina* (1950).

DONALD M. RAWSON
Northwestern State University of Louisiana

RICE CULTURE in the South dates from the late 1600s at Charleston, spreading gradually along all of South Carolina's coast and by the 1750s into Georgia. The prime habitat during the early years was inland swamps near the coast where earthen dams impounded enough stream water to inundate small fields.

A major shift in site selection came with the development of plantations in the Tidewater area, where planters took advantage of the diurnal variation in tide to flood or drain the fields. When the tide raised the stream above the field level, trunks installed in the rice field dikes were opened to allow water onto their fields; successive high tides were used to flood the fields to the desired height. Draining the fields was accomplished by reversing the process, allowing water to run off the fields during low tide. The area that could be cultivated with this flooding procedure was limited since a location too close to the ocean led to the encroachment of saltwater and streams too far upstream had only diminished tidal effects.

In spring, fields were drained to permit tillage and then row planted. The fields were then flooded to encourage sprouting, but drained within a few weeks for hoeing. The growing season involved alternately flooding and draining in order to provide moisture, inhibit weed growth, prevent pest damage, encourage strong root and stem growth, and facilitate cultivation. Harvest was in late summer. The rice was cut, allowed to dry, and then threshed. Finally, the seed underwent further processing in the rice mill, which removed the husk coating the rice seed.

From the early 1700s to the 1880s rice was the dominant cash crop in the coastal counties of South Carolina and Georgia, and most was plantation grown. It supported a sizable infrastructure of mills, warehouses, and merchants and was an economic mainstay for Savannah, Charleston, and Georgetown, the latter depending exclusively upon rice for its existence. Tidewater rice production peaked around the mid–nineteenth century, but the postbellum period saw a rapid shift to the Gulf Coast and Mississippi Valley.

In Louisiana rice had long occupied an important but minor economic role. Grown on poorly drained sites on backswamps of the lower Mississippi River valley, it remained a poor second to sugarcane until settlement of the prairies, when new irrigation technology and mechanization permitted large-scale production in southwestern Louisiana. In 1870 Louisiana accounted for only about one-fifth of the nation's rice, but by 1890 it was producing over half. By 1910 Louisiana and Texas together accounted for some 90 percent of the nation's total, while that of Carolina and Georgia had dwindled to less than 5 percent. The major new producing areas were and still are southwestern Louisiana, southeastern Arkansas, and southeastern Texas. At the same time the entire process was modernized with the introduction of grain binders, threshers, and irrigation pumps requiring much less labor and permitting larger-scale operations.

RICE PRODUCTION IN THE SOUTH, 1840–1970
(in thousands of pounds)

State	1840	1850	1860	1870	1880	1890	1900	1910	1920	1930	1940	1950	1960	1970
Ala.	149	2,312	493	223	811	399	927	233	643	84	444			
Ark.		63	17	73		7	9	57,727	305,871	313,115	344,305	895,033	1,266,436	2,102,400
Fla.		1,075	234	402	1,295	1,012	2,254	555	1,762	220	115			
Ga.	12,385	38,951	52,508	22,277	25,370	14,556	11,175	6,691	2,687	823	99			
La.	3,605	4,425	6,331	15,854	23,188	75,645	172,732	487,799	720,525	734,286	800,345	1,062,051	1,357,635	2,039,700
Miss.	777	2,720	809	375	1,719	677	739	218	816	42	27		120,571	224,400
N.C.	2,820	5,466	7,594	2,059	5,609	5,846	7,893							
S.C.	60,591	159,931	119,101	32,305	52,078	30,339	47,360	24,371	5,511	1,314	724			
Tenn.	10	259	40	3										
Tex.		88	26	64	62	108	7,187	404,629	238,787	232,134	467,861	1,076,372	1,360,823	2,254,051
Va.	2	17	8			360	4,374							

SOURCE: U.S. Census Bureau. Figure in each instance is actually for year preceding. That is, 1840 data are actually for crop year of 1839, etc.

See L. C. Gray, *History of Southern Agriculture* (1941); D. Doar, *Charleston Museum Contributions* (1936); A. S. Salley, Jr., *Historical Commission of South Carolina Bulletin*, No. 6; S. Hilliard, *Geoscience and Man* (1975); J. H. Easterby, *South Carolina Rice Plantation* (1945); A. R. Childs, *Rice Planter and Sportsman* (1953), both Easterby and Childs based on plantation documents; D. C. Heyward, *Seed from Madagascar* (1937), popularly written by former rice planter; G. C. Rogers, Jr., *Historical Georgetown County* (1970), excellent county history; C. Lee, "Culture History of Rice" (Ph.D. dissertation, Louisiana State University, 1960); and M. K. Ginn, *Louisiana Historical Quarterly* (April, 1940).

SAM B. HILLIARD
Louisiana State University

RICE UNIVERSITY (Houston, Tex. 77001) was founded in 1891 with a gift of $200,000 from William Marsh Rice (1816–1900). Known (until 1960) as William Marsh Rice Institute, the school eventually inherited the bulk of its benefactor's $6 million estate and opened its doors in 1912. After 12 years of operations the trustees decided to limit the school's undergraduate enrollment to 450 students and to emphasize programs of graduate education. After developing especially strong programs in engineering, architecture, science, and mathematics, the institute began a period of rapid growth following World War II. The size of the school's faculty more than tripled in the 20 years after the war. In 1961 the Manned Space Flight Laboratory of the National Aeronautics and Space Administration was located on land made available by Rice, and the following year the school inaugurated a graduate program in space science. The school's growth, however, vastly exceeded its founder's original vision and endowment. The endowment stipulated that the school neither charge tuition nor admit blacks. While running large deficits and fearful of losing federal research funds, the trustees in 1964 successfully began legal action to free the institution of these restrictions. Today the school has an enrollment of approximately 4,000 students. Notable library holdings include the papers of Governor J. S. HOGG and a journal of M. B. LAMAR.

RICHMOND, KY. (pop. 16,861), was first settled in 1784 and named for its sister city in Virginia. Located approximately 25 miles southeast of Lexington, Richmond is the home of Eastern Kentucky University (1906) and a market for area tobacco growers. During the Civil War, the area south of town was the site of the Confederacy's first victory in Kentucky. Approximately 6,500 federal soldiers had been sent to Richmond in August, 1862, in anticipation of an invasion by General EDMUND KIRBY-SMITH's Confederates. After two days of fighting (August 29, 30), the divided federal forces retreated to Louisville having sustained 206 deaths, 844 wounded, and over 4,000 missing. The somewhat smaller force of 6,000 Confederates sustained 78 killed, 372 wounded, and only a single man missing.

See W. Chenault, *Richmond* (1897); J. T. Dorris, *Glimpse at Historic Madison County* (1934); R. A. Hammons, *History of Richmond City Schools* (1949); J. T. Sullivan, *Madison County* (1965); and C. M. Valliant, *Battle of Richmond* (1966). Townsend Room of Eastern Kentucky University Library maintains collection of books, manuscripts, and documents on local government, churches, and personalities.

RICHMOND, UNIVERSITY OF (Richmond, Va. 23173), one of the oldest Baptist colleges in the nation, was founded in 1830 and began instruction in 1832. Although like many church-related schools it frequently suffered from financial uncertainties and like most southern colleges it was forced to close during the Civil War, its growth and development in the twentieth century, especially since World War II, have been reasonably steady. It is a coeducational school supported by the Southern Baptist Convention, and it has an enrollment of approximately 6,000 students in schools of arts and sciences, business, law, and graduate studies. The university library houses the materials of the Virginia Baptist Historical Society, including records, diaries, sermons, letters, and minutes of Baptist associations dating back to 1762.

See R. E. Gaines and G. Taylor, *First 100 Years* (1932).

RICHMOND, VA. (pop. 249,621), the state capital since 1779, is located at the navigational head of the James River approximately 100 miles south of Washington, D.C. Although a small trading post (1637) and Ft. Charles (1645) were built at the falls here in the early seventeenth century, the town was not founded and laid out until the 1730s. It was largely burned by Benedict Arnold in 1781, but it was quickly rebuilt as the seat of government and as a commercial center on the FALL LINE. Made the capital of the Confederacy in July, 1861, it became the constant and principal objective of federal military operations in the eastern theater of the Civil War. Threatened in 1862 by the PENINSULAR CAMPAIGN and in 1864 by the WILDERNESS CAMPAIGN, it finally fell on April 3, 1865, after the RICHMOND-PETERSBURG CAMPAIGN. Despite extensive damage to the city, St. John's Church (1741), John Marshall's home (1793), and the state capitol (1785) designed by Thomas Jefferson are among the old structures that survived. The University of Richmond (1830), Medical College of Virginia (1838), Union Theological Seminary (1812), Virginia Union University (1865), and Richmond Professional Institute (1917) are among the city's several centers of learning. Its significance as a port of entry has declined considerably since the late nineteenth century, but the city remains an important tobacco market and a major manufacturer of cigarettes, cigars, and smoking tobacco. Its factories also produce clothing, paper, steel, and machinery.

See J. C. Pollard, *Richmond's Story* (1954), concise; W. A. Christian, *Richmond* (1912), comprehensive; M. M. P. Stanard, *Richmond* (1923); E. Lutz, *Richmond Album, Pictorial* (1937); A. W. Weddell, *Richmond in Old Prints, 1737–1887* (1932); S. Mordecai, *Richmond in By-gone Days* (1860, 1946); M. W. Scott, *Old Richmond Neighborhoods* (1950); V. Dabney, *Richmond* (1976); and files of *Times-Dispatch* (1850–), *News-Leader* (1896–), *Afro-American Planet* (1888–), *Whig* (1824–88),

Enquirer (1804–77), *Examiner* (1847–67), *Virginia Gazette and Advertizer* (1780–1809), and *Virginia Chronicle* (1786–90), all on microfilm.

RICHMOND (VA.) ENQUIRER AND EXAMINER was created in 1867 by the merger of two much older daily papers. The *Enquirer*, founded by Thomas Ritchie in 1804, had long been one of the principal Democratic presses in the state. Under Ritchie and then under his son, the *Enquirer* developed into one of the few antebellum newspapers to have more than a local readership. During the 1850s, the paper chastised equally northern opponents of slavery and southern advocates of separation. As Virginia moved gradually and reluctantly toward secession, however, so also did the *Enquirer*. The *Examiner*, the younger of the two papers, had been founded in 1847. During the Civil War it was one of the Confederacy's more persistent critics of Jefferson Davis' administration and its war policies. The *Enquirer*, on the other hand, remained until 1863 one of the government's most friendly presses. The merger of the *Examiner* and the *Enquirer* did not resolve all of the problems inherent in publishing in Richmond's crowded field of newspapers. After publishing between 1867 and 1870 as the *Enquirer and Examiner* and from 1870 to 1877 simply as the *Enquirer*, the paper went out of business.

See C. H. Ambler, *Thomas Ritchie* (1913); L. J. Cappon, *Virginia Newspapers, 1821–1935* (1936); bound copies of *Enquirer*, at Library of Congress (1844–77) and Duke University Library (1845–73); microfilm of *Enquirer*, from Bell & Howell (1861–62); and microfilm of *Examiner*, from Bell & Howell (1861–67) and Library of Congress (1860–67).

RICHMOND (VA.) NEWS-LEADER, an independent Democratic paper with a daily circulation of approximately 120,000 copies, was founded in 1868 as the Richmond *Evening News*. In 1903 it merged with its afternoon competitor, the *Evening Leader*, to form the present paper. DOUGLAS SOUTHALL FREEMAN edited the *News-Leader* from 1915 to 1949 and earned for it a national reputation as the conservative counterpart to its morning competitor, the Richmond *Times-Dispatch*.

See L. J. Cappon, *Virginia Newspapers, 1821–1935* (1936); and microfilm, from Microfilm Corp. of America.

RICHMOND (VA.) PLANET was a black weekly published between 1883 and 1945. Although it never achieved the prominence or the influence of many northern black newspapers, the length of its publication period and its location in the Upper South make it a valuable research tool.

See L. J. Cappon, *Virginia Newspapers, 1821–1935* (1936); and microfilm, from Bell & Howell (1890–94, 1896–97, 1899–1938).

RICHMOND (VA.) TIMES-DISPATCH was formed in 1903 by the merger of the *Times* (1886–1903) and the *Dispatch* (1850–1903). The *Times* had been a conservative Democratic paper that during the 1890s opposed the growing influence within the Democratic party of William Jennings Bryan and the silverites. The *Times-Dispatch*, on the other hand, reached the zenith of its national reputation under the editorship (1936–1969) of the moderately liberal VIRGINIUS DABNEY. An independent Democratic daily, the paper currently has a circulation in excess of 140,000 copies.

See L. J. Cappon, *Virginia Newspapers, 1821–1935* (1936); both *Times* (1886–1903) and *Dispatch* (1852–1903) on microfilm, from Library of Congress and Bell & Howell; and *Times-Dispatch* (1903–) on microfilm, from Bell & Howell and Microfilm Corp. of America.

RICHMOND (VA.) WHIG was founded in 1824 by John H. Pleasants. It was a fierce journalistic competitor of the Democratic Richmond *Enquirer*, and Pleasants was killed in a duel with the son of the *Enquirer*'s editor. The *Whig* expressed generally nationalist views and opposed secession until after the firing upon Ft. Sumter and Abraham Lincoln's call for volunteers. During the Civil War, its editorials regularly criticized the leadership of Jefferson Davis and the war policies of the Confederate government. In 1879 the *Whig* was acquired by General WILLIAM MAHONE, and it became the principal organ of Virginia's READJUSTER MOVEMENT until it ceased publication in 1888.

See L. J. Cappon, *Virginia Newspapers, 1821–1935* (1936); bound copies, at Library of Congress (1824–69) and Duke University Library (1824–69); and microfilm, from Bell & Howell (1831–61, 1865–74).

RICHMOND JUNTO is the term applied to a small group (approximately 20) of Virginia's political leaders who through their control first of DEMOCRATIC-REPUBLICAN (and later DEMOCRATIC) party machinery dominated that state's politics through most of the first half of the nineteenth century. Operating secretly through the legislative caucus, the junto—led by Judge Spencer Roane, Wilson Cary Nicholas (NICHOLAS FAMILY), and Thomas Ritchie, editor of the RICHMOND ENQUIRER—dispensed patronage and dictated legislative policies. In national politics it supported Presidents Thomas Jefferson and James Madison, but opposed the nationalistic policies of James Monroe by reviving a strict states' rights doctrine. Although continuing to exert power after 1828, the junto came under attack from both the nationalists prominent in the western part of the state and the supporters of NULLIFICATION in the Tidewater. It lost complete power after 1851, when universal manhood suffrage in Virginia took the election of state officials from the legislature.

See H. Ammon, *Virginia Magazine of History and Biography* (Oct., 1953); and C. H. Ambler, *Thomas Ritchie* (1913).

HERBERT ERSHKOWITZ
Temple University

RICHMOND-PETERSBURG   CAMPAIGN (1864–1865). This 11-month campaign led to the capture of the Confederate capital and the surrender of the Army of Northern Virginia. U. S. Grant's campaign against the Confederate capital consisted of two coordinated movements. One was an attack on Richmond from the South and was led by Benjamin F. Butler. In May his Army of the James, numbering 40,000 men, was cornered at BERMUDA HUNDRED by P. G. T. BEAUREGARD with a much smaller force. Grant later wrote that Butler's army was "as if it had been in a bottle strongly corked." Beauregard commanded the defenses of Richmond-Petersburg with a force of less than 30,000. The other coordinated move was George Meade's Army of the Potomac against ROBERT E. LEE's Army of Northern Virginia. Grant accompanied Meade as overall commander. Union forces at that time numbered 122,000 compared with a Confederate strength of 61,000 to 65,000. Savage but inconclusive battles were fought at the WILDERNESS (May 5–7), 60 miles north of Richmond, at SPOTSYLVANIA Courthouse (May 8–21), and at COLD HARBOR (June 3), eight miles east of Richmond.

Open field maneuver now turned to siege tactics, which were to grind down the outnumbered Confederates. Logical point of Union concentration was Petersburg, 23 miles south, a rail hub of importance. All rail supplies came through Petersburg except those sent via the Richmond & Danville Railroad to the west. Like Richmond, Petersburg was protected by an undermanned defense line. On June 9 General August Kautz, Butler's command, attacked with 4,300 men. His repulse was only a temporary respite. On June 15 a Union corps commanded by William F. Smith opened a mass attack on Petersburg's eastern line. Two days later, 70,000 Union soldiers were attacking 14,000 defenders. The battle ended at nightfall, June 18, with Beauregard forced back to rapidly completed new defenses, where he held. Meanwhile, Lee moved his headquarters to "Violet Bank" near Petersburg and ordered reinforcements from the Richmond area.

The rest of the campaign consisted largely of ponderous Union movements to the west to encircle Petersburg and choke off supplies to both cities. On June 22–24 a Union attempt to capture the Weldon Railroad running south to North Carolina, failed. Siege lines were extended, and CITY POINT (now Hopewell) became a Union supply base. An attempt to break the Confederate line came on July 30, when 8,000 pounds of powder were exploded under a Confederate battery east of the city. Quick action by Lee and General WILLIAM MAHONE repulsed the attack. The Union commander, Ambrose Burnside, resigned shortly after (CRATER, BATTLE OF THE).

Union encirclement continued. Gouverneur Warren captured the WELDON RAILROAD in a four-day battle (August 18–21) leaving only the Richmond & Danville serving Richmond and the Southside serving Petersburg. A short-lived ray of hope appeared on September 17, when WADE HAMPTON and less than 4,000 men returned to Petersburg after circling the Union lines and capturing over 2,400 head of cattle (HAMPTON'S CATTLE RAID). The Union march west continued at POPLAR SPRING CHURCH (September 29–October 1), Boydton Plank Road (October 27), and HATCHER'S RUN (February 5–7, 1865). Coordinated with Poplar Spring Church was the Union capture of Ft. Harrison, a Richmond defense post. This was the only major action taken directly against Richmond after Cold Harbor.

By March, 1865, the fortifications on the Richmond-Petersburg front stretched 37 miles, making this the largest battlefield of the war. Little could be done by Lee with a starving force of 55,000 facing about 150,000 in line or within easy reach. A last desperate gamble was necessary to facilitate an orderly withdrawal from Richmond-Petersburg. On March 25 JOHN GORDON attacked Union FT. STEDMAN, east of Petersburg. The attack met with initial success, capturing the fort and about a mile of line. Then a sharp Union counterattack forced Gordon's troops back with heavy losses.

Spring brought renewed northern action. On April 1 Philip Sheridan defeated GEORGE PICKETT and FITZHUGH LEE at FIVE FORKS, 10 miles southwest of Petersburg. On April 2 heavy Union attacks resulted in cutting the Southside Railroad and rolling up part of the Confederate line. Lee ordered military evacuation of both cities to be made that night. President Jefferson Davis, his cabinet, and his staff left Richmond on April 2. The following day Union troops entered both cities to find that Richmond had suffered severe damage from fire and looting. On April 9 Lee surrendered to Grant 100 miles west at APPOMATTOX Courthouse.

See S. Foote, *Civil War* (1974); D. S. Freeman, *R. E. Lee* (1935), classic; U. S. Grant, *Memoirs* (1885); R. U. Johnson and C. C. Buel (eds.), *Battles and Leaders* (1888), IV; R. W. Lykes, *Campaign for Petersburg* (1970), concise; and F. T. Miller, *Photographic History of Civil War* (1911, 1957).

RICHARD W. LYKES
University of Virginia, Northern
Regional Center, and George
Mason University

RICH MOUNTAIN, BATTLE OF (July 11, 1861).

Topography made this mountain a key to northwestern Virginia (now West Virginia). Confederate Commander JOHN PEGRAM, whose forces were astride a strategic road, knew Union troops appeared to be outflanking his left. He ordered no reconnaissance. Shortly before fighting began, Pegram finally ordered log defenses constructed. Union General W. S. Rosecrans, met by skirmishers whose skillful retreat led northern soldiers directly into a southern artillery position, had not expected a fight. After initial failures, the federal battle line was extended so as to enfilade the Confederate position. Confederate reinforcement attempts failed, and 1,900 Unionists defeated 350 southerners. A possible, but never developed, ensuing federal campaign might well have won the Shenandoah Valley.

See *Official Records, Armies*, Ser. 1, Vol. II; Pegram Papers, Virginia Historical Society; Heuch Papers, University of Virginia Library; D. S. Freeman, *Lee's Lieutenants* (1942); J. W. Thomas, *West Virginia History* (July, 1944); and C. Evans (ed.), *Confederate Military History* (1962), III.

GEORGE C. BITTLE
Berlin, N.J.

RIO GRANDE, known in Mexico as the Rio Bravo del Norte, has been part of the international boundary between the United States and Mexico

since 1848. Occasional changes in the river's course have often been points of disagreement between the two nations. Rising in the Colorado Rockies, the 1,800-mile-long river flows generally south through New Mexico to EL PASO and then toward its mouth on the Gulf of Mexico near BROWNSVILLE. Although the lower portion of the river is navigable, it has been only slightly used as a transportation artery since first being explored by ALVAR NÚÑEZ CABEZA DE VACA in 1536. The upper river was and is totally unsuited for shipments to or from Santa Fe, and the lower river failed to link Spanish Mexico with any of its major settlements in the Texas area. Today the river is closed to navigation by international agreement. The waters of the Rio Grande, however, have long been important to the region's economy as a means of irrigation. Native Indians irrigated their fields with its water, and today, assisted by Falcón Dam (approximately 140 miles from Brownsville), the Rio Grande waters the rich agricultural lands of the lower river valley.

See P. Horgan, *Great River* (2 vols.; 1954); L. P. Graf, "Economic History of Lower Rio Grande Valley, 1820–1875" (Ph.D. dissertation, Harvard, 1942); and J. O. McKee, *Southern Quarterly* (Oct., 1965).

RITCHIE, ALBERT CABELL (1876–1936), best known for his four terms as Democratic governor of Maryland (1920–1935), was descended from a prominent Virginia family and educated at Johns Hopkins and the University of Maryland Law School. While practicing law, he entered public service and subsequently was elected attorney general and governor. As governor he achieved national prominence for his refusal to enforce PROHIBITION. He advocated a states' rights philosophy, opposing expanded federal governmental powers. Ritchie ranked with other Progressive southern governors of the early 1920s, supporting administrative reorganization, road construction, increased aid to public health and education, and civil service reform. Yet, he believed in limited government at all levels, and he was unprepared to cope with the GREAT DEPRESSION. His reluctant response to New Deal programs led to his defeat in 1934.

See D. M. Brown, in R. Walsh and W. L. Fox (eds.), *Maryland, 1632–1974* (1974); F. F. White, Jr., *Governors of Maryland, 1777–1970* (1970); J. B. Levin, "Albert C. Ritchie" (Ph.D. dissertation, City University of New York, 1970); and Ritchie Papers, Maryland Historical Society.

JAMES B. CROOKS
University of North Florida

RIVERCRAFT. The southeastern quadrant of the United States possesses an extensive system of navigable coastal waters, rivers, and tributaries. On these waterways, a colorful variety of rivercraft flourished and then vanished as newer competitors—railroads, highways, pipelines, and airplanes—attracted passengers and freight with greater speed, convenience, and safety (TRANSPORTATION). Today only bulk goods, timber, coal, stone, and the like still use the rivers, often employing a lock and dam system that canalizes the streams.

The first boats on the coastal and tidal waterways were oceangoing sailing ships. As settlement moved inland, the earliest of other types were canoes and mackinaws, apparently brought downstream from the North; bullboats (round coracles of buffalo skins on a wood frame); wide military galleys; and rafts, variously called cotton boxes on the Savannah River, sneak boxes on the Ohio, and segmented rafts on the Cape Fear River. The most popular early boat in the southern waters was the dugout (carrying from two to 15 or 20 men) hollowed from logs up to 60 feet long. Commonly called pirogues, they were known as pettiaugers on South Carolina streams and periaugers on the Cape Fear River, where they were sometimes equipped with sails. Poling barges have been mentioned on the Alabama rivers.

Rowboats and flatboats soon followed, with the usual variety of local names: radeau in Louisiana, bateaux (flatboats with oars) in Louisiana as well as on the Savannah River, where flatboats with sails were known as piraguas and as Petersburg boats. Early flatboats were called arks, broad beams, broadhorns, and Durham boats. Later on the Ohio a distinction was made between partially roofed Kentucky boats, up to 40 feet long and 16 feet wide, and the fully roofed New Orleans boats, up to 50 feet long and 14 feet wide, designed to pass between two large boulders 15 feet apart near Louisville. As few as three to five men, often a farmer and his sons, could safely maneuver a flatboat downstream. In times of high water much larger craft, 18 to 25 feet wide and 50 to 100 feet long, could pass over the falls at Louisville, carrying up to 100 tons of freight.

Keelboats quickly followed (1792), 30 to 70 feet long and seven to nine feet wide, with a draft of 20 to 30 inches on the Ohio-Mississippi, employing three men downstream and six to eight upstream. Keelboats with sails, sometimes called "barges," were noted on the Tennessee River. Although there were no significant changes in the physical characteristics or technical advances in either flatboats or keelboats, they continued in use, as did scows, barges, and rafts on the upper reaches of tributaries and on the smaller streams, especially in periods of low water, into the twentieth century, primarily transporting bulk materials and farm produce.

River steamers appeared on the Ohio-Mississippi as early as 1811–1812, on the Tennessee as early as 1818, on the Savannah River from 1819, on the Red and Arkansas from 1824, on the major Alabama rivers by 1835, on the Chattahoochee by 1836, and on the Cape Fear about the same time. They tended to monopolize the upstream traffic since they offered greater speed and safety, lower labor costs, and half the insurance rates. Keelboats disappeared first, being used only on the upper stretches of tributaries. Ironically, flatboats survived and even flourished as steamboats reduced the return trip and soon gave rise to a more skilled class of flatboatmen: "agent" instead of "dealer" or "peddler" boatmen. Dealer and peddler boatmen were often farmers, millers, or merchants carrying their own produce and others' in crude, self-made craft. Agent boatmen were full-time captains of newer, larger boats, often strongly made by regular shipbuilders and towed upriver by steamers for repeated use. The flatboats reached dimensions up to 24 feet wide by 150 feet long, carrying 120 to 140 tons of freight by the 1850s. Labor costs on flatboats fell by one-half, and improved speed and safety of transit and handling resulted. Federally sponsored river improvements also made night travel feasible on both the Ohio and the Mississippi rivers.

Unlike the flatboats and keelboats, the river steamers underwent major changes in the design and proportions of the hull, an overall reduction of weight of boat and equipment, and a shift from low-pressure condensing engines to high-pressure noncondensing engines of increased size. Boats grew 21 percent longer and 39 percent wider, and new decks were added to increase carrying capacity. More trips per season, less time for loading and unloading, and fewer days for repairs all reduced costs and increased efficiency of the steamers. Steamboat crews ranged from four or five on smaller vessels to over 100 on the largest ones. The development of small steamboats to act as tugs and pushers on shallower streams is less spectacular but equally important as the growth of palatial boats. The flexibility of the smaller steamers enabled them to survive for limited purposes, while the more colorful varieties of rivercraft have vanished.

See Rivers of America series; E. Q. Hawk, *Economic History of South* (1934); C. E. MacGill, *History of Transportation in U.S. Before 1860* (1917); L. Baldwin, *Keelboat Age on Western Waters* (1941); L. C. Hunter, *Steamboats on Western Waters* (1949); H. N. Scheiber, in D. Ellis (ed.), *Frontier in American Development* (1969); J. Mak and G. M. Walton, *Journal of Economic History* (Sept., 1972; June 1973); W. W. Carson, *Mississippi Valley Historical Review* (June, 1920); J. Baughman, *Journal of Southern History* (Aug., 1963); J. A. James, *Mississippi Valley Historical Review* (Dec., 1932); G. Foreman, *Mississippi Valley Historical Review* (June, 1928); and R. L. Jones, *Ohio History Quarterly* (July, 1950).

WALTER S. SANDERLIN
Washington and Jefferson College

RIVERS AND LAKES historically have provided fresh water, transportation routes, fertile agricultural land, waterpower, and natural boundaries. For these reasons, they have had a significant influence on settlement patterns and regional economic activity. The South, because of its CLIMATE and topography, has been endowed with numerous rivers and streams. The occurrence of large natural lakes, however, is notably lacking.

The two largest lakes of the South are OKEECHOBEE and PONTCHARTRAIN, covering 730 and 621 square miles, respectively. Other large lakes of the region are man-made and found in association with water resources development. Several of these are: Toledo Bend Reservoir (284 square miles), between Texas and Louisiana on the Sabine River; Kentucky Lake (250 square miles), between Tennessee and Kentucky on the Tennessee River; Sam Rayburn Reservoir (179 square miles), in Texas on the Angelina River; and Lake Marion (173 square miles), in South Carolina on the Santee River. The Florida peninsula contains the largest concentration of natural lakes in the region. Primarily, their occurrence may be attributed to limestone solution (karst) topography and a relatively high groundwater table.

The rivers of the South drain either to the Atlantic Ocean or to the Gulf of Mexico. With the exception of the ST. JOHN'S RIVER in Florida, the major Atlantic coastal rivers originate in the Appalachian highlands. Headward erosion and stream capture have created many water and wind gaps. These passes, of which CUMBERLAND GAP is most renowned, provided access routes for westward expansion. From the highlands, the rivers flow generally in a southeastward direction across the Piedmont Plateau to the FALL LINE. In this general area they begin their rapid descent to the less resistant Cretaceous sedimentaries of the coastal plain and the sea.

The division between the Piedmont and coastal plain physiographic provinces generally marks the inland limit of river navigation from the ocean. Because of the importance of water transport during colonial times, numerous southern cities were established along rivers in the vicinity of the FALL LINE. Since the colonial period, other important centers have also developed in this general region. Several of the important fall line cities are Washington, D.C. (Potomac River), Richmond (James River), Raleigh (Neuse River), Columbia (Saluda and Broad rivers), Augusta (Savannah River), and Macon (Ocmulgee River).

Inland transportation along many southern rivers of the Atlantic coastal plain is enhanced by the occurrence of numerous estuaries. The area from the NEUSE RIVER in North Carolina northward as far as Cape Cod is known as the embayed section. Coastal submergence in this region was caused by depression of the northeastern portion of the North American continent by the Pleistocene glaciers and the subsequent rise in sea level with glacial retreat. Embayment inland to the fall line exists in the rivers as far south as the James, on which Jamestown, the first permanent English settlement in the New World, was established. In the upper reaches of CHESAPEAKE BAY and Delaware Bay, which are estuaries of the Susquehanna and Delaware rivers, respectively, are found the cities of Baltimore and Wilmington, Del.

Drainage from the inland South to the Gulf of Mexico is overshadowed by the MISSISSIPPI RIVER system, including the major tributaries of the MISSOURI, OHIO, TENNESSEE, KENTUCKY, ARKANSAS, and RED rivers. Other smaller river outlets to the Gulf include the SUWANNEE, Chattahoochee-APALACHICOLA, TOMBIGBEE and MOBILE, PEARL, SABINE, TRINITY, COLORADO, Pecos, and RIO GRANDE. The Mississippi, the principal river in the country, is approximately 2,348 miles in length and maintains an average discharge of about 640,000 cubic feet per second. Since its discovery in 1541 by HERNANDO DE SOTO and further exploration by Jacques Marquette and Louis Jolliet in 1673 and LA SALLE in 1682, the river has served as a major transportation route to the heartland of the continent. Early commerce along its course with the agricultural areas of the Middle West and South, coupled with the concept of manifest destiny, established numerous river cities in the South, such as St. Louis, Memphis, Vicksburg, Natchez, Baton Rouge, and New Orleans. In 1974 over 367 million tons of freight were shipped along the Mississippi system from St. Louis to New Orleans, including large quantities of bauxite, fertilizer, sulfur, feed grain, and oil.

Water resource development within this region of the South has led to numerous FLOOD CONTROL projects, improved navigation, and the low-cost production of ELECTRICITY. The TENNESSEE VALLEY AUTHORITY and the Arkansas River Navigation System are two such projects that have attracted industrial development to the region.

See C. B. Hunt, *Natural Regions* (1974); E. Raisz, *Landforms Map* (1957); W. D. Thornbury, *Regional Geomorphology* (1965); Water Resources Council, *Nation's Water Resources* (1968); and C. L. White, E. J. Foscue, and T. L. McKnight, *Regional Geography* (1974).

PETER S. SEGRETTO
University of South Florida

RIVES, WILLIAM CABELL

RIVES, WILLIAM CABELL (1793–1868), was born in Nelson County, Va. He studied under Thomas Jefferson, served in Virginia's legislature (1817–1820, 1822–1823), and moved to Castle Hill plantation in Albemarle County. Rives entered Congress (1823–1829) and was a leading Virginia Jacksonian by 1828. His reward was the French mission (1829–1832), where he negotiated the Spoliation Claims Treaty. Upon return, he was elected to the Senate (1832–1834) and supported Andrew Jackson on NULLIFICATION and the FORCE BILL. Virginia's 1833–1834 anti-Jackson legislature "instructed" Rives from office. Two years later, Democrats employed "instruction" to return him (1836–1839). He split over Martin Van Buren's independent treasury proposal; and Rives Conservatives, a third party in the state, blocked election of a senator for two years (1839–1841). He endorsed William H. Harrison and proved his most eloquent champion in Virginia. A Whig legislature returned Rives to the Senate (1841–1845). Acting independently, he supported President JOHN TYLER on bank and tariff before fully entering Whig ranks and endorsing HENRY CLAY in 1844. With failure to carry Virginia, Rives's Senate career ended. A second French mission (1849–1853) was unnoteworthy. Involved in agriculture and railroad development, Rives continued a conservative Whig. He wholeheartedly supported the CONSTITUTIONAL UNION PARTY and eloquently pled for the Union at the WASHINGTON PEACE CONFERENCE of 1861. When border state cooperation failed, he remained loyal to Virginia and served in the Provisional and Second Confederate congresses (1861, 1864–1865). In his final years he wrote *The Life and Times of James Madison* (1859–1868), completing three of a projected four volumes.

See R. C. Dingledine, Jr., "Rives" (Ph.D. dissertation, University of Virginia, 1947); R. A. McLemore, *Franco-American Relations* (1941); and W. C. Rives Papers, Library of Congress.

RAYMOND C. DINGLEDINE, JR.
Madison College

ROANOKE, VA. (pop. 92,115), is on the Roanoke River between the Blue Ridge and the Allegheny mountains. Although the surrounding area had been settled since 1740, a town was not laid out on this site until 1834. Known until 1882 as Big Lick, the town's first rail connection was completed in 1852 and its first tobacco factory was constructed in 1858. After gaining additional rail connections in the 1880s, the city developed as an important rail and shipping center. The modern city manufactures electrical equipment, fabricated steel, furniture, and textiles.

See R. P. Barnes, *History of Roanoke* (1968); Federal Writers' Project, *Roanoke* (1942); G. S. Jack, *History of Roanoke County* (1912); W. McCauley, *History of Roanoke County* (1902); F. B. Kegley, *Kegley's Virginia Frontier, 1740–1783* (1938); and files of Roanoke *Times* (1886–), *World News* (1889–), and *Tribune* (black, 1938–).

ROANOKE ISLAND, located between the Outer Banks and the mainland of North Carolina, is the site of the first attempted English colony in America. In 1584 an expedition, the first of three sponsored by Sir WALTER RALEIGH under patent from Elizabeth I, explored the area and returned to England with two Indians and some tobacco and potatoes. The next year 108 settlers arrived, including John White, whose 75 Indian drawings are of immense ethnological significance, but explorations led them to conclude that the Chesapeake would be a superior locale. In 1586, fearing Indian attack, they left for England with Sir Francis Drake. A relief party, finding the colony abandoned, left 15 men to hold England's claim. These men disappeared. In 1587 a colony of some 100 settlers was planted by John White, who then went to England for supplies. Before his return in 1590, the colony had vanished. Recent conjectures suggest Indian reprisals for English provocations.

See D. Quinn, *Roanoke Voyages* (1955), documents; and P. Hulton, *Drawings of White* (1964).

RICHARD P. GILDRIE
Austin Peay State University

ROANOKE RIVER is a 410-mile stream. From its source at about 1,000 feet above sea level in the Shenandoah Valley, it cuts a narrow gap through the BLUE RIDGE Front at Roanoke, Va. It then winds east through the hilly PIEDMONT with impondments first at Smith Mountain Lake and later at Kerr Reservoir, where it straddles the Virginia–North Carolina border. Just south of the border the Roanoke passes through the fall zone at Roanoke Rapids into the coastal plains. It then mean-

ders 112 miles southeast until finally reaching the ALBEMARLE SOUND. English colonists followed the GREAT WAGON ROAD south along the Shenandoah Valley and settled Roanoke in 1834. Near Brookneal, Va., where U.S. Route 501 crosses the river, are an old covered bridge and Patrick Henry's tomb and shrine. In 1829 the 12-mile-long Weldon Canal was opened to extend navigation around Roanoke Rapids but was abandoned in 1850. Today the Roanoke River is managed for comprehensive FLOOD CONTROL and power production as well as for extensive recreational boating and commercial pulpwood movement.

See U.S. Army Corps of Engineers, *Roanoke River* (1969); Virginia Conservation and Development, *Development of Roanoke River* (1949); and J. Clay, *North Carolina Atlas* (1975).

H. DANIEL STILLWELL
Appalachian State University

ROBERTS, ELIZABETH MADOX (1881–1941), was born in Perryville, Ky., and Kentucky remained the focal point of her life as it did of her fiction. She secured her A.B. degree in philosophy from the University of Chicago in 1921 and returned to Springfield, Ky., to write her first and best novel *The Time of Man* (1926). She published seven additional novels, the best of these being *My Heart and My Flesh* (1927), *The Great Meadow* (1930), *He Sent Forth a Raven* (1935), and *Black Is My True Love's Hair* (1938). She was a gifted poet (*Under the Tree* [1922] and *Song in the Meadow* [1940]) and a short story writer who stressed the technique of the epiphany and the exploration of the inner life of her characters. Many articles refer to Roberts as an "Appalachian writer." This is a grave though oft repeated misconception. She was born in the bluegrass region of Kentucky, and all of her work treats of the region (the one exception is "On the Mountain Side"). She had a genuine feeling for the life and speech of the SHARECROPPERS of central Kentucky and a poetic way of presenting them.

See H. M. Campbell and R. E. Foster, *Elizabeth Madox Roberts* (1956); F. P. W. McDowell, *Elizabeth Madox Roberts* (1963); and E. M. Roberts Papers, Library of Congress.

RUEL E. FOSTER
West Virginia University

ROBINSON, JOSEPH TAYLOR (1872–1937), born near the rural Arkansas town of Lonoke, was deeply influenced by rural populism. Beginning at seventeen, he taught school for two years in order to attend the University of Arkansas. In 1892 he took up the study of law and two years later served one term in the Arkansas general assembly. Serving in the U.S. House of Representatives (1903–1913), he strongly advocated antitrust, low-tariff, farm, and CHILD LABOR legislation. In 1912 he campaigned successfully as a reform candidate for the Arkansas governorship, but, after less than two months in that office, he resigned to accept election to the unexpired U.S. Senate term of JEFF DAVIS, who had died in office. As a member of the Senate (1913–1937), Robinson acquired a national reputation by his support of Wilsonian legislation such as the Federal Reserve Act, wartime measures, the Treaty of Versailles, and national FLOOD CONTROL. In 1923 he succeeded OSCAR W. UNDERWOOD as minority leader and in 1933 became majority leader. In the meantime, he had been nominated for vice-president on the 1928 ticket with Alfred E. Smith. In combating anti-Catholic sentiment toward Smith in the South, Robinson made powerful appeals for religious toleration, but was nonetheless defeated. Under Franklin D. Roosevelt, Robinson gained the responsibility for guiding various emergency and NEW DEAL measures through the Senate. Along with JOHN N. GARNER and B. P. HARRISON he differed somewhat with Roosevelt, opposing the Arkansas Valley Authority and other measures, but his loyalty to party and president caused subordination of his personal desires. His last Senate speech was in behalf of the Roosevelt plan to reorganize the U.S. Supreme Court.

See N. E. Neal, "Joseph T. Robinson" (Ph.D. dissertation, University of Oklahoma, 1958); B. E. Pettus, "Joseph T. Robinson" (M.A. thesis, University of Illinois, 1952); B. Ross, "Joseph T. Robinson" (M.A. thesis, University of Maryland, 1950); and E. Watson, "1928 Presidential Campaign" (M.A. thesis, University of Oklahoma, 1954).

NEVIN E. NEAL
Texas Christian University

ROCKY MOUNT, N.C. (pop. 34,284), is near the falls of the Tar River, approximately 50 miles east of Raleigh. Although the immediately surrounding area had been settled during the early nineteenth century, development of the town did not occur until after completion of a rail line in 1840 and the construction here of a rail station. The antebellum village never developed much beyond being a small market town. After the Civil War, however, additional rail lines and the newly found popularity of bright leaf tobacco combined to make Rocky Mount both a major rail junction and a leading tobacco market in the eastern part

of the state. Moreover, several textile mills were located here to take advantage of the power generated by the falls. Modern Rocky Mount continues to be a premier tobacco market and a manufacturer of both natural and synthetic fibers.

See M. O'Quinlivan, *Century of People* (1967), only published history; and files of Rocky Mount *Telegram* (1911–), on microfilm. The Rocky Mount Public Library and Nash County Historical Association maintain collection of news clippings and family genealogies.

RODES, ROBERT EMMETT (1829–1864), was born in Lynchburg, Va. He graduated in 1848 from the Virginia Military Institute and was then appointed an assistant professor. Resigning in 1851 to become a civil engineer, in 1858 he accepted a position as chief engineer of an Alabama railroad. In May, 1861, he was appointed a colonel of Alabama infantry, C.S.A., and won commendation in some early skirmishes. Promoted brigadier general, he commanded at SEVEN PINES, where he was wounded. He later fought at GAINES' MILL, ANTIETAM, FREDERICKSBURG, and CHANCELLORSVILLE, after which he was appointed a major general. He then commanded with great skill at GETTYSBURG, the WILDERNESS, and SPOTSYLVANIA. Sent in June, 1864, with his division to the Shenandoah Valley, he served there with Jubal Early during EARLY'S WASHINGTON RAID and during his defense of the valley against Philip Sheridan. Rodes was killed by a shell fragment at the battle of WINCHESTER in September. Although he had been subject to minor criticism on a few occasions, he had a reputation as one of the Confederacy's finest field commanders.

See D. S. Freeman, *Lee's Lieutenants* (3 vols.; 1945); *Official Records, Armies*, Ser. 1, Vols. II, V, X, XXV; and J. C. Wise, *Military History of V.M.I., 1839–1865* (1915).

RODNEY, CAESAR (1728–1784), born near Dover, Del., is best known for his 80-mile horseback ride on July 2, 1776, to break a tie and give Delaware's vote for independence. His public association with the revolutionary movement began with his activity at the Stamp Act Congress. During the Townshend Acts controversy, the Delaware assembly appointed him to their committee of correspondence. After news of the Intolerable Acts, Rodney, as Speaker of the assembly, called a special session, which elected him to the First CONTINENTAL CONGRESS. Put out of office in the fall of 1776, Rodney turned to military activities, first as chairman of the Kent County council of safety, then as post commander at Trenton in the winter of 1777, and finally as commander of the Delaware militia during the British invasion of the state in September, 1777. He returned to Congress in December, 1777, but was elected president of Delaware (1778–1782).

See Public Archives of Delaware, Dover; Kent County Records, Dover; Historical Society of Delaware, Wilmington; Library of Congress; Genealogical Society of Pennsylvania; and New York Public Library. Also see G. H. Ryden (ed.), *Letters, Caesar Rodney* (1933); *Journal of Continental Congress* (1904); E. C. Burnett (ed.), *Letters of Members of Continental Congress* (1921–36); *Minutes of Council of Delaware State, 1776–1792* (1887); H. Niles, *Principles and Acts of Revolution in America* (1822); *Delaware Archives* (1911, 1912, 1919), I–III; and J. A. Munroe, *Federalist Delaware, 1775–1815* (1954). A biography of Rodney is needed.

WILLIAM RAYMOND SMITH
University of Pittsburgh, Johnstown

ROLL OF HONOR. Although the Confederate Congress desired to reward its men for bravery in action with appropriate medals and a law to this effect was passed October 13, 1862, the Confederate government was never able to provide them. As a substitute, beginning in October of 1863, the adjutant general's office ordered that the names of all officers and men "conspicuous for courage and good conduct on the field of battle ... be inscribed on a Roll of Honor to be preserved in the office of the Adjutant and Inspector General" and that as additions were made to this list the names be read at army dress parades and published in southern newspapers.

See *Journal of Congress of Confederate States* (1904), II; and *Official Records, Armies*, Ser. 1, Vol. XI.

ROOSEVELT, THEODORE, ADMINISTRATION (1901–1909). Its policy toward the South was designed to foster national unity, reinvigorate the Republican party, and soften the harsh treatment of blacks. In an attempt to achieve a responsible, biracial southern Republican organization, Roosevelt courted white southern moderates and made a number of excellent appointments of blacks to federal offices both before and after the election of 1904. He also took action against PEONAGE and denounced LYNCHING. This prompted southern editors and racist politicians to inflame the region over "Roosevelt Republicanism." The president's social courtesies to BOOKER T. WASHINGTON were inflated into a symbolic issue, and by 1904 the enlightened white southerners around whom Roosevelt intended to restructure the GOP had been forced on the defensive.

In these circumstances, Roosevelt reverted to a much more gradualist policy. To promote good-

will, he appointed a few outstanding white southern Democrats to office and tolerated all-white Republican organizations in some states. Partly on Washington's counsel, he refused to support proposals that the South's representation in Congress be reduced in proportion to the DISFRANCHISEMENT of blacks, as provided by the Fourteenth Amendment. He also refused to denounce the ATLANTA RACE RIOT of 1906 and otherwise failed to give moral leadership.

Roosevelt had no clearly defined economic policy toward the South. His party's commitment to high tariffs kept the region hostage to northern industry, and his own acceptance of the merger of the TENNESSEE COAL & IRON and the United States Steel companies in 1907 probably slowed its economic development. Conversely, the Hepburn Act of 1906 resulted in the elimination of some inequities in railroad rates. In the long run, Roosevelt's CONSERVATION program, his support of increased appropriations for AGRICULTURAL EXPERIMENT STATIONS, and certain recommendations of the Country Life Commission of 1908 served the South well.

See Roosevelt Papers, Library of Congress; E. Morison (ed.), *Letters of Theodore Roosevelt* (1951–54); H. Hagedorn (ed.), *Works of Theodore Roosevelt* (1926); W. H. Harbaugh, *Theodore Roosevelt* (1961); W. B. Gatewood, Jr., *Theodore Roosevelt and Art of Controversy* (1960); H. S. and M. Merrill, *Republican Command* (1971); R. B. Sherman, *Republican Party and Black America* (1973); G. Morwy, *Theodore Roosevelt and Progressive Movement* (1946); F. B. Simkins, *Pitchfork Ben Tillman* (1944); and L. R. Harlan, *Booker T. Washington* (1972).

WILLIAM H. HARBAUGH
University of Virginia

ROSENWALD FUND. Julius Rosenwald, president of Sears, Roebuck & Company (1909–1924), met Booker T. Washington in 1911 and thereafter initiated a program of personal beneficence that knew no restrictions of race, creed, or color. The Rosenwald Fund, incorporated in Chicago in 1917, remained for 11 years under the personal control of its founder, but in 1928 Edwin R. Embree became president under a governing board of trustees. Rosenwald launched the philanthropic corporation with a gift of 20,000 shares of Sears stock (worth $35 million before the crash) with the stipulation that the fund expend interest and principle within 25 years of the founder's death. American race relations, black interests, and the South benefited the most from Rosenwald PHILANTHROPY. The earliest program begun by Rosenwald stimulated construction of rural schoolhouses for blacks by providing funds that were matched by money or land from school boards and money or labor from local citizens. Before the fund closed, 4,978 schools had been built. Under Embree's management the fund program expanded to include aid to southern colleges, fellowships for blacks and whites working on problems of the South, Negro health services, book subsidies for libraries, and contributions to agencies working on race relations. By 1948 Embree had exhausted the fund, expending a total of over $22 million.

See E. R. Embree and J. Waxman, *Investment in People* (1949); A. G. Belles, "Julius Rosenwald Fund" (Ph.D. dissertation, Vanderbilt, 1972); Julius Rosenwald Papers, University of Chicago; and Rosenwald Fund Papers, Fisk University.

A. GILBERT BELLES
Western Illinois University

ROSSER, THOMAS LAFAYETTE (1836–1910), was born in Virginia; his family moved to Texas in 1849. Resigning from West Point in 1861, he served the Confederacy with great distinction and bravery in the eastern fighting from BULL RUN to APPOMATTOX and was twice wounded on the battlefield. He became a major general in 1864. He was the epitome of the flamboyant cavalry leader. In 1862 his forces raided J. Pope's headquarters carrying away the Union general's hat. Shortly before Appomattox, Rosser was seen riding the horse and wearing the sword of a fallen Union commander. Following the war he directed railroad construction in the West, eventually becoming the chief engineer of the Canadian Pacific. His investments prospered, and he retired to a farm in Charlottesville, Va.

See D. S. Freeman, *Lee's Lieutenants* (1942), best; E. J. Warner, *Generals in Gray* (1959); *Official Records, Armies, passim*; and T. L. Rosser Papers, University of Virginia Library.

JAMES W. HARPER
Texas Tech University

ROST, PIERRE ADOLPHE (1797–1868), born in France, was a Bonapartist veteran who immigrated to Natchez after 1815. He read law and served a term in the Mississippi legislature before moving to Natchitoches. In 1830 he moved to New Orleans, where marriage into a prominent Creole family helped raise him to the Louisiana supreme court in 1839. In 1861 Jefferson Davis appointed Rost to serve with WILLIAM L. YANCEY and A. DUDLEY MANN as Confederate commissioners in Europe. In May Rost arrived in Paris and began a mission that "earned him more ridicule than respect." Having failed to persuade Napoleon III to

recognize the Confederacy, Rost sought to win the support of the French people for his cause. Unfortunately, his imperfect French and *haute bourgeois* demeanor prejudiced his efforts as a propagandist (CONFEDERATE PROPAGANDA). He was removed from France to Spain in March, 1862, but was no more successful there. Plagued by diabetes and discouraged, Rost retired to Fumel in France in May, 1862. He remained in Fumel until the end of the Civil War permitted his return to New Orleans.

See W. W. White and J. O. Baylen, *Louisiana History* (Summer, 1961); E. Lonn, *Foreigners in Confederacy* (1940); J. M. Callahan, *Diplomatic History of Southern Confederacy* (1901); F. L. Owsley, *King Cotton Diplomacy* (1931); H. P. Dart, *Louisiana Historical Quarterly* (Jan., 1921); and W. L. Fleming (ed.), *South in Building of Nation* (1909), XII.

JOSEPH O. BAYLEN
Georgia State University

ROYALL, ANNE NEWPORT (1769–1854), reared on the Pennsylvania frontier, married William Royall in western Virginia in 1797. To earn a living after his death she traveled widely, writing travel books and editing in Washington, D.C., two successive weeklies (1831–1854): *Paul Pry* and the *Huntress*. She initiated the personal interview in American journalism. Of strong convictions she admired John Q. Adams, idolized Andrew Jackson, loved all Masons, feared a union of church and state, and hated established religion, the Bank of the United States, corruption in government, and hypocrisy. Suspicious and contentious, she was the only woman in our national history to be tried, convicted, and sentenced to be ducked for being a common scold.

See S. H. Porter, *Anne Royall* (1909); G. S. Jackson, *Uncommon Scold* (1937); L. B. Griffith (ed.), *Letters from Alabama* (1969); B. R. James, *Anne Royall* (1972); and L. B. Griffith, *Alabama Review* (Jan., 1968). Files of *Paul Pry* and *Huntress* are in Library of Congress.

LUCILLE GRIFFITH
Montevallo, Ala.

RUBY, GEORGE T. (1841–?), one of only three black Texas state senators during Reconstruction, was born in New York City and in 1851 moved to Portland, Maine, where he attended public school. In 1861 he was employed as a newspaper correspondent in Haiti, but left the island in 1864 for New Orleans, where he became principal of a black grade school. Shortly thereafter, he was appointed a Freedmen's Bureau agent to found schools. In September, 1866, Ruby joined the bureau in Texas, and by early 1867 he was combining his educational work with political activity, especially the founding of local UNION LEAGUES. Ruby in 1868 became deputy collector of customs at Galveston, a delegate to the Reconstruction convention, a delegate to the Republican National Convention, and editor of the *Freedman's Press*, a Negro weekly. Then in 1869 he became president of the Texas Union League and was elected to the state senate. He was appointed to many important committees, and, in addition to supporting civil rights legislation, he favored internal improvements. After his term expired he returned to New Orleans, where he edited a newspaper into the 1880s.

See R. B. Woods, *Red River Valley Historical Review* (Autumn, 1974); Austin *Daily State Journal* (July 27, 1870); and J. P. Newcomb Papers, University of Texas Library.

JAMES ALEX BAGGETT
Union University, Jackson, Tenn.

RUFFIN, EDMUND (1794–1865), a celebrated

agricultural reformer and militant secessionist, was born in Prince George County, Va., the son of a prosperous James River planter. After attending the College of William and Mary and serving briefly in the War of 1812, he embarked upon a career as a gentleman-farmer. During the 1820s and 1830s he spearheaded an agricultural renaissance in the Upper South through his discovery of the beneficent properties of marl, a shell-like deposit that neutralized soil acidity, and his editorship of the *Farmer's Register* (1833–1842). His Virginia farms, Marlbourne and Beechwood, soon became models that others sought to emulate. After retiring from the active management of his properties in 1856, Ruffin devoted the remainder of his life to promoting his dream of southern independence. Through private contacts and voluminous writings in newspapers and periodicals, he expounded the gospel of southern rights. When, in 1861, his labors were crowned with success, he was accorded the honor of firing the first shot at FT. SUMTER. Four years later, broken in spirit and fortune by the demise of the Confederacy, the embittered Ruffin, in a gesture that symbolized not only his personal tragedy but that of his section, took his own life rather than submit to the anticipated indignities of Reconstruction.

See A. O. Craven, *Edmund Ruffin* (1932); W. K. Scarborough (ed.), *Diary of Edmund Ruffin* (3 vols. projected; 1972–); J. C. Sitterson (ed.), *Essay on Calcareous Manures* (1961); manuscript diary, Library of Congress; and Ruffin Papers, Virginia Historical Society, Richmond.

WILLIAM K. SCARBOROUGH
University of Southern Mississippi

RUFFIN, THOMAS (1787–1870), was a Virginia-

born jurist noted for service to courts in North Carolina. A scientific agriculturalist like his kinsman EDMUND RUFFIN, a devout Episcopalian, and a father of 14 children, Ruffin was a practicing lawyer, member of North Carolina's house of commons (Speaker in 1816), judge of the state's superior court (1817–1819, 1825–1828), associate and chief justice of its supreme court (1829–1833, 1833–1852), and writer of influential decisions in equity regarding property rights. Regarded as the peer of John Marshall and Lemuel Shaw, he opposed secession but supported the Confederacy once it was formed. He objected to Reconstruction policies, but spent the last years of his life speaking and writing against violence and the Ku Klux Klan.

See W. A. Graham, *Life of Thomas Ruffin* (1871); and J. G. de R. Hamilton, *Papers of Thomas Ruffin* (1918–20), best source, and *Reconstruction in North Carolina* (1964), incidental, illuminating mentions.

SISTER MARIE CAROLYN KLINKHAMER, O.P.
Norfolk State College

RURAL ELECTRIFICATION ADMINISTRA-

TION, established in 1935, proved to be one of the most successful NEW DEAL agencies, both with regard to realizing the goal of equipping farms and rural homes with electrical service and as a self-supporting lending institution. Until the REA went into operation, only one farm in ten in the United States had electricity, meaning that the single most important ingredient necessary for modern living was not available in rural areas. By 1941 30 percent of America's farms had service, and the completion of rural electrification could be set at 1955, when over 90 percent of the rural market was served. The REA did not act alone, for such public power agencies as the TENNESSEE VALLEY AUTHORITY contributed to the program. Private enterprise, slow to enter the rural market, was spurred into action once the federal government committed itself and supplied electricity for nearly half the electrified rural dwellings of 1955. A lending institution, the REA has an amazing collection record, having less than 1 percent loan defaults since its inception in 1935. Credit for such success lay in the use of the electric cooperative, which made the recipients of service also members of the cooperative. The grass-roots nature of the program, therefore, engendered an enthusiasm and support rare in the case of most federal programs.

The enthusiasm was understandable in view of the impact of electrification on rural life. Running water, indoor plumbing, refrigeration, incandescent lighting, radio, altogether a multitude of comforts and conveniences lifted the farm out of the preindustrial age and thrust it into modernity. Nowhere was the transformation more pronounced than in the South, a region that reflected the general state of rural conditions in the United States, except in more dramatic fashion. A variety of typically rural health problems—PELLAGRA, HOOKWORM, dysentery—vanished with a diet of nutritional foods preserved in refrigerators and the use of modern sanitation facilities. Rural electrification also encouraged diversification of agriculture, even to the point in some areas that modernized POULTRY farming replaced cotton as the mainstay. Not to be overlooked were the promotion of small industries, improved rural schools, and a breakdown of isolationism via electronic media, all important contributions in narrowing the gap between city and country living. Thus, the REA lessened some of the regional distinctions of the South and gave the dirt farmer a larger and improved role in American life.

See Morris L. Cooke Papers, F. D. Roosevelt Library, most thorough collection of sources through 1936; REA Files, Record Group 221, National Archives; Harry Slattery Papers, Duke University Library, excellent look at operations and politics, 1939–45; M. W. Childs, *Farmer Takes a Hand* (1952); C. T. Ellis, *Giant Step* (1966); P. J. Funigiello, *Toward a National Power Policy* (1973); F. W. Muller, *Public Rural Electrification* (1944); and K. E. Trombley, *Morris L. Cooke* (1954).

D. CLAYTON BROWN
Texas Christian University

RUSK, THOMAS JEFFERSON (1803–1857), was born in Pendleton District, S.C. After studying law, he began to practice in Clarksville, Ga., in 1825. He went to Nacogdoches, Tex., in 1834. A signer of the Texas declaration of independence, he was named secretary of war in the new government in 1836 and participated in the battle of SAN JACINTO on April 21. From May 4 to October 31, he was brigadier general of the Texas army. In 1837 and 1838 Rusk was a member of the Texas congress and from December 25, 1838, to June 20, 1840, was chief justice of the Texas supreme court. In 1839 he commanded troops sent to expel CHEROKEE INDIANS from land in east Texas and in 1843 was major general of the militia. President of the convention of 1845, Rusk strongly supported annexation to the United States and the next year was named U.S. senator (1846–1857).

See L. F. Blount, *Southwestern Historical Quarterly* (Jan., April, 1931); M. W. Clarke, *Thomas J. Rusk* (1971),

popular biography; and Rusk Papers, Archives, University of Texas, Austin.

DORMAN H. WINFREY
Texas State Library, Austin

RUSKIN SETTLEMENTS were utopian experiments in communal living conducted in the South at the turn of the last century. Ruskin societies attempting to put into effect some of the ideas of John Ruskin (1819–1900), the English art critic and social theorist, were popular in Great Britain at this time. The originator of the American version was Julius A. Wayland of Greensburg, Ind., who early in 1893 established a successful weekly socialistic newspaper called the *Coming Nation* (1893–1902). He determined to use the income from his printing plant and the newspaper as the financial backbone of a socialistic community. A site chosen three miles from Tennessee City, Tenn., proved to be untillable, however, and after a few months was abandoned in favor of a much better location at Cave Mills, six miles away. Here for a time (1894–1899) the Ruskin Cooperative Association achieved a degree of success raising vegetables, fruits, flower seeds and bulbs, and other crops and engaging in light manufacturing on a basis of complete economic and social equality. The experiment quickly won international attention. Internal dissension, however, eventually led to court action by some of its members, which placed the colony in receivership in 1899. A few faithful then moved to Duke (renamed Ruskin) in Ware County, Ga., but the new colony on an island near OKEFENOKEE SWAMP lasted only a little over a year. In September, 1901, its assets were disposed of at a sheriff's sale.

See F. Butler, *Tennessee Historical Quarterly* (Dec., 1964); W. G. Davis, *Guton's* (Dec., 1901); H. C. McDill, *Guton's* (May, 1902); J. W. Braam, *American Journal of Sociology* (March, 1903); complete file of *Coming Nation*, State Historical Library, Madison, Wis.; and manuscripts, University of Tennessee Library.

RUSSELL'S MAGAZINE was an excellent monthly published in Charleston from April, 1857, through March, 1860. Under the editorship of PAUL HAMILTON HAYNE, it presented southern poetry, serialized fiction, literary criticism, and references to South Carolina society. Reluctantly, *Russell's* also reviewed politics, slavery, and abolition. Although it was never widely circulated, contributors included H. TIMROD, Hayne, W. G. SIMMS, and other literary notables of the South. *Russell's* was forced to cease publication when southern nationalism and SECESSION assumed precedence over the cultural format of the periodical. Historically, *Russell's* provides a literary overview of the late antebellum South.

See F. Kennedy, *South Atlantic Quarterly* (April, 1919); F. Mott, *American Magazines* (1938); M. Oliphant (ed.), *Simms Letters* (1954–56); and W. Trent, *Simms* (1892).

DAVID W. FRANCIS
Chippewa Lake, Ohio

RUTLEDGE, EDWARD

RUTLEDGE, EDWARD (1749–1800), brother of JOHN RUTLEDGE, exemplified the South Carolina low-country elite. Although considered a radical when first elected to the CONTINENTAL CONGRESS (1774–1777), he championed Joseph Galloway's plan of union, opposed (but signed) the DECLARATION OF INDEPENDENCE, and criticized the centralizing tendencies of John Dickinson's ARTICLES OF CONFEDERATION. Military service brought capture and internment at St. Augustine in 1780. Exchanged the following year, he joined his brother-in-law CHARLES COTESWORTH PINCKNEY in dominating local politics for nearly two decades. As a leading member of the state legislature, Rutledge favored confiscation of Loyalists' property and an end to the slave trade. In the state ratifying convention of 1788 and the state constitutional convention of 1790, he respectively supported the U.S. Constitution and the interests of the low country. Distrusting financial manipulators and foreign influence, he condemned Jay's Treaty and served as a Jeffersonian presidential elector in 1796. But the XYZ affair and later Republican attempts to smear Pinckney alienated him, and he was a firm Federalist while serving as governor (1798–1800).

See E. C. Burnett, *Letters of Members of Continental Congress* (1921–36); G. C. Rogers, Jr., *W. L. Smith* (1962); *South Carolina Historical Magazine*; M. R. Zahniser,

C. C. Pinckney (1967); Papers of Continental Congress, National Archives; Governors Papers, South Carolina Archives; E. Rutledge and Pinckney Family Papers, South Caroliniana Library, University of South Carolina; A. Middleton, Pinckney Family, and W. L. Smith Papers, South Carolina Historical Society; and E. and J. Rutledge Papers, Duke University Library and Historical Society of Pennsylvania.

ROBERT M. WEIR
University of South Carolina

RUTLEDGE, JOHN

RUTLEDGE, JOHN (1739–1800), brother of EDWARD RUTLEDGE, was born in Charleston, the son of Dr. John and Sarah Hext Rutledge. He was elected to the provincial assembly in 1762, married Elizabeth Grimké in 1763, and served as attorney general pro tem from 1764 to 1765. He represented South Carolina in both the Stamp Act Congress (1765) and the First Continental Congress (1774–1776). He returned to South Carolina in 1776 to assist in writing a constitution and was elected president. He resigned as president in 1778, but the following year was reelected (1779–1782) and clothed with dictatorial powers to meet a British invasion. He was elected to Congress in 1783 and 1784 and served as a delegate to the CONSTITUTIONAL CONVENTION in 1787. Rutledge was appointed an associate justice of the U.S. Supreme Court but never sat as a justice. He resigned in 1791 to become chief justice of the South Carolina court of common pleas. George Washington nominated Rutledge for chief justice in 1795, but the Senate rejected him by a vote of 14 to ten.

See R. H. Barry, *Rutledge of South Carolina* (1942); and L. Friedman and F. L. Israel (eds.), *Justices of U.S. Supreme Court* (4 vols.; 1969), I.

DWIGHT F. HENDERSON
Indiana University–Purdue University, Ft. Wayne

S

SABINE CROSSROADS, BATTLE OF (April 8, 1864), took place three miles southeast of Mansfield, La., and resulted in the turning back of Nathaniel P. Banks in his RED RIVER CAMPAIGN. After driving RICHARD TAYLOR back for about 200 miles, Banks, with 19,000 strung-out men, was defeated here by Taylor, who commanded a force of only half that number. On that day, Taylor's troops were dispersed to defend the narrow and heavily wooded Mansfield Road. Early that afternoon, after severe skirmishing, the federals massed to turn the Confederate left. At 4 P.M., Taylor ordered a division under Alexander Mouton to charge the Union's right and John G. Walker's Texas division to attack the Union's left. The enemy line crumbled, and its sole retreat route was blocked by a wagon train. Because of this, the wagon train and all Union artillery were captured. The federals were driven back five miles until the XIX Corps made a successful stand at Pleasant Grove. The Union suffered about 3,000 casualties, and the southerners had only about 1,000 losses.

See R. Taylor, *Destruction and Reconstruction* (1879), brilliant account; and J. B. Davis, *Louisiana Historical Quarterly* (Jan., 1941).

ALLAN C. ASHCRAFT
Texas A. & M. University

SABINE PASS, BATTLE OF (September 8, 1863). In order to reestablish U.S. authority in Texas and thus discourage the French-controlled Emperor Maximilian from attempting to reconquer Texas for Mexico and in order to satisfy northern abolitionists' and textile manufacturers' demands to capture Texas, Union General Nathaniel P. Banks planned to occupy Texas by invading the state at the mouth of the Sabine River on the Louisiana border. Four gunboats and 22 transport ships containing 5,000 Union soldiers steamed from the Gulf of Mexico into the river mouth on September 8 but were turned back by only 47 Confederates led by twenty-five-year-old Lieutenant Richard Dowling. Accurately firing their six small cannons from an unimpressive dirt fort, Dowling's men destroyed two gunboats, disabled another, drove the remaining vessels into the Gulf, and captured 350 Union sailors. Hailed then and since as the Confederacy's Thermopylae, this battle ended a serious attempt to occupy Texas, lifted sagging southern spirits, and spread consternation throughout the Union army command.

See A. F. Muir, *Civil War History* (Dec., 1958), best; M. M. Pray, *Dick Dowling's Battle* (1936); F. R. Sackett, *Dick Dowling* (1937); and *Official Records, Armies*, Ser. 1, Vol XXVI, Pt. 1.

RICHARD LOWE
North Texas State University

SABINE RIVER rises in northeastern Texas and flows to the Louisiana line, where it forms the Louisiana-Texas boundary. It continues in a southerly course and enters the Gulf via Sabine Lake and Sabine Pass. The Sabine has played a minor role in the economic progress of the people along its Louisiana bank; however, Texans have built an industrial complex on the lower Sabine. The river provides a valuable resource—fresh water. The completion of the Toledo Bend Dam will eventually make possible better utilization of the fresh water, but the final effects of the dam are yet unknown.

The major interest in the river derives from its geography and history. Spaniards, Frenchmen, and Americans have argued and fought over it. The Sabine, therefore, was important because it was where it was, not because of what it was. From the opening of the eighteenth century until the first quarter of the nineteenth century, the Sabine was involved in important diplomatic negotiations. The Adams-Onís Treaty established the west bank of the Sabine as the boundary between Spanish Texas and Louisiana. It remained there until 1848, when it was moved to midstream. Recently the federal courts decided against Louisiana's plea to move the boundary to the west bank and stated that it should remain as set in 1848. On the military side, the Sabine area has played roles in the Mexican and Civil wars. Americans used military posts on the river as starting points to move to Mexico, and Union forces attempted to gain control of Texas via the Sabine. The future of the area rests upon what is done to develop the recreational and industrial potential that could result from the Toledo Bend Dam.

See E. Davis, *Rivers and Bayous of Louisiana* (1968); F. Van Zandt, *Boundaries of U.S.* (1966); *Sabine River and*

Tributaries, House Document 91–429 (1971); and A. Bertrand and J. Hoover, *Toledo Bend Reservoir* (1973).

RALEIGH A. SUAREZ
McNeese State University

SAHARA OF THE BOZART, THE,

an essay written by social critic H. L. Mencken in 1917 and expanded and included in *Prejudices, Second Series* (1920), was a severe indictment of postbellum southern culture and literature. Mencken claimed that the South was "almost as sterile, artistically, intellectually, culturally, as the Sahara Desert" and that "in all that gargantuan paradise of the fourth-rate there is not a single picture gallery worth going into, or a single orchestra capable of playing the nine symphonies of Beethoven, or a single opera-house, or a single theater devoted to decent plays." Most southern prose and poetry were drivel, Mencken charged, and "when you come to critics, musical composers, painters, sculptors, architects and the like, you will have to give it up, for there is not even a bad one between the Potomac mud-flats and the Gulf." Nor was there, he added, a historian, sociologist, philosopher, theologian, or scientist.

Written in typical Menckenian hyperbole with a disregard for historical accuracy, the essay maintained that the modern southern condition was particularly lamentable because the antebellum South had been the American seat of civilization. Mencken attributed the fall of southern civilization to the POOR WHITES, who he charged had seized control in the South after the Civil War. Particularly to blame were the preachers and the politicians. The hope for the South, he contended, lay in a return to influence of the best of the old aristocracy.

Mencken's "Sahara" received widespread attention in the South in the 1920s. Traditional southerners denounced Mencken as a "modern Attila," a "miserable and uninformed wretch," and a "bitter prejudiced and ignorant critic of a great people." But other southerners—including HOWARD W. ODUM, GERALD W. JOHNSON, Paul Green, and W. J. CASH of North Carolina—pronounced their agreement with the substance of Mencken's indictment. The southern literary renascence followed Mencken's blast, and literary scholars have suggested that the "Sahara" shocked young southern writers into an awareness of southern literary poverty and thus played a seminal role in the revival of southern letters. But as important as Mencken's effect on southern literature was his effect on the general intellectual climate of progressive centers in the South. Menckenism became, as the 1920s progressed, a school of thought for iconoclastic southerners. Mencken himself later wrote numerous other essays on southern thought and culture, but none was to attract the attention of the "Sahara."

See J. L. Morrison, *Southern Literary Journal* (Autumn, 1968); O. Cargill, *Georgia Review* (Winter, 1952); and F. Hobson, *Serpent in Eden* (1974).

FRED HOBSON
University of Alabama

ST. AUGUSTINE, FLA.

(pop. 12,352). PEDRO MENÉNDEZ DE AVILÉS came to Florida in 1565 to expel French intruders and establish a Spanish outpost. He captured Ft. Caroline on the ST. JOHN'S RIVER and established St. Augustine, the oldest European city in the present-day United States. St. Augustine constituted the principal Spanish outpost in Florida for 236 years. Priests and soldiers went forth to exercise influence over southeastern Indians as far north as the Savannah River and as far west as Tallahassee. Foreigners contested Spanish control over the borderland province. Sir Francis Drake sacked the city in 1586, Captain John Davis in 1665, and Captain Robert Searles in 1668, influencing Spain to construct a fortress, the Castillo de San Marcos, which stands today. James Oglethorpe besieged it in 1740. No foreign power ever captured and retained control of the city.

Spain in 1763 ceded Florida to England, which retained it for 20 years; many Loyalists fled there for protection during the American Revolution. Spain got it back in 1783. Inability to keep Indians and escaped slaves from raiding southwest Georgia contributed to Andrew Jackson's decision to capture St. Mark's and Pensacola. Its American empire in revolt, Spain ceded Florida to the United States in 1819.

St. Augustine became a resort in the last quarter of the nineteenth century, when HENRY M. FLAGLER constructed the Ponce de Leon and other luxury hotels where American presidents such as Theodore Roosevelt and Warren Harding vacationed. St. Augustine, county seat of St. John's County, is the home of museums, historic sites, and Flagler College. The commercial life of the city depends on fishing, industry, and tourism.

See M. V. Gannon, *Cross in Sand, 1513–1870* (1965); T. Graham, *Florida Historical Quarterly* (July, 1975); and F. B. Reeves, *Florida Historical Quarterly* (Aug., 1965).

FRED LAMAR PEARSON, JR.
Valdosta State College

ST. CHARLES, MO.

(pop. 31,834). Louis Blanchette, a French Canadian hunter, settled here on the Missouri River in 1769 approximately 15 miles northwest of St. Louis. The settlement that grew up around Blanchette's was called Petites Cotes (little hills) until the 1780s, when the present name was adopted. During the 1790s, many Americans—including DANIEL BOONE and his family—moved in among the French settlers, and after the War of 1812 yet another wave of Americans moved into the area. St. Charles was the temporary capital of Missouri (1821–1826), but it gradually was bypassed by St. Louis as a center of transportation and commerce. Today it is part of metropolitan St. Louis.

See files of St. Charles *Missourian* (1820–22) and *Banner News* (1863–).

ST. DENIS EXPEDITION. In September, 1713, Louis Juchereau de St. Denis and a trading party left Mobile with instructions from Antoine de la Mothe Cadillac, Louisiana governor, to look for Francisco Hidalgo, a Spanish priest who had asked for French aid in establishing missions among the Tejas Indians in east Texas, and to purchase livestock for Louisiana. St. Denis went to the Mississippi and then to the mouth of the Red River. The party traveled in canoes to Grand Ecore, where they built the first log huts of the post of Natchitoches. In early 1714 they crossed the Sabine and reached the Tejas country. For several weeks they traded goods for livestock and hides and then traveled to the Colorado and on to an Indian village near present San Antonio. St. Denis, with nine companions, finally reached San Juan Bautista, the presidio near the Rio Grande, on July 19, 1714. He was sent to Mexico City, where he persuaded the viceroy to appoint him guide for a Spanish expedition of 80 persons, including Hidalgo, that in 1716–1717 founded six missions on the Louisiana-Texas frontier.

See R. Phares, *Cavalier in Wilderness* (1952), readable biography; and S. V. Connor, *Texas* (1971).

JOHN PAYNE
Sam Houston State University

ST. JOHN'S COLLEGE (Annapolis, Md. 21404) was founded in 1696 and known as King William's School. After the American Revolution, however, the name was changed to St. John's College. A private, coeducational school with an enrollment of fewer than 400 students, it is widely known for its classical, liberal arts curriculum.

ST. JOHN'S RIVER, rising near Lake OKEECHOBEE in Florida and flowing north for almost 300 miles, was discovered by Jan Ribault, May 1,

1562. French HUGUENOTS, led by René de Laudonnière, established Ft. Caroline in 1564. PEDRO MENÉNDEZ DE AVILÉS expelled them in 1565. England challenged unsuccessfully Spain's control of the river through expeditions led by James Moore (1702) and JAMES OGLETHORPE (1740). The river attracted the attention of naturalists JOHN AUDUBON and John and William Bartram. Steamboats provided more effective means of getting cotton, fruit, and lumber to market in the 1820s. After the Civil War tourism assumed importance, especially in such towns as Jacksonville and Palatka. Establishment of railroads by HENRY M. FLAGLER and Henry B. Plant and development of resorts brought an end to the steamboat era and hurt tourism. Introduction of the water hyacinth in the 1880s threatened navigation and resulted in expenditure of huge sums to combat it. The river is important today for barge traffic, fishing, and the naval base at Mayport.

See B. Cabell and A. J. Hanna, *St. Johns* (1943) and *River in Distress* (1970).

FRED LAMAR PEARSON, JR.
Valdosta State College

ST. LOUIS, MO. (pop. 622,236), was founded in 1764 by French merchant explorers Pierre Laclede and Auguste Chouteau at the center of 5,000 miles of navigable rivers in the interior of the continent. This advantage in transportation enabled the city to become a focus of the FUR TRADE and military missions in the early years and the gateway city for the settlement of the West. The city began to grow in substantial terms only in the aftermath of the War of 1812. Then large numbers of Americans from the South, especially Virginia and Kentucky, and from the East came due to the movement of the agricultural frontier through the Midwest and to a more efficient exploitation of the rivers through the introduction of the steamboat in 1817. In 1822 the city obtained its first charter and contained about 5,000 inhabitants comprising a cosmopolitan mixture of French, southerners, yankees, and blacks. Beginning with the influx of the Irish in the 1820s and of the Germans in the 1830s, the city's immigrant population increased to the extent that by 1860 St. Louis had the largest percentage of foreign born of any major city with 60 percent. The population mixture accounted for the infection of municipal politics with nativism, Irish-German antagonisms, and anti-Negro sentiments.

The Civil War divided the city between the Unionists and the Confederates. Unionist victory not only secured St. Louis for the North but also, by disfranchising a southern element, initiated the ascendancy of the Germans and the Republican party, which predominated in local affairs until after the turn of the century. During this period, St. Louis was a focus of civic reform, pioneering in public EDUCATION during the superintendency of William T. Harris (1868–1880), in charity through the organization of the Western Sanitary Commission in the 1860s, and in public HEALTH with regulation of food production in the 1880s and smoke abatement in the 1890s. Although growth was temporarily stymied by the war, population continued to increase so that the city was the nation's fourth largest at the turn of the century.

Growth was due to the successful transfer from a commercial to an industrial economy. The process was under way as early as the 1840s and 1850s with the development of food-processing industries such as breweries, sugar refineries, and flour mills as well as foundries and machine shops involved with the building of railroads and steamboats. By 1910 more stoves, chemicals, streetcars, and clay products were manufactured in the St. Louis area than in any other. By the mid-twentieth century, major additions to the economy included aircraft production, electronics, automobiles, and health services. The twentieth century, however, has witnessed the relative decline of St. Louis. A prime factor has been the premature termination of the annexation movement in 1876, which left the city with only 61 square miles. By 1900 there was a significant spillover into the adjacent counties in Missouri and on the Illinois side of the Mississippi. Thus, although the city of St. Louis slipped from fourth place in 1910 to eighteenth in 1970, the St. Louis metropolitan area has retained its regional and national importance, ranking as the eleventh largest metropolis in 1970.

See S. K. Troen, *Guide to Resources on History of St. Louis* (1971); and S. K. Troen and G. E. Holt, *St. Louis* (1977).

SELWYN K. TROEN
University of Missouri, Columbia

ST. LOUIS POST-DISPATCH was established in 1878, a combination of the *Evening Dispatch* and the *Evening Post*. The *Dispatch*, founded in 1862, had been an old-fashioned political journal, the only asset of which was a Western Associated Press franchise. It was bought in 1878 for $2,500 by Joseph Pulitzer, a Hungarian immigrant who fought for the Union and afterward settled in St. Louis as a reporter for the German-language *West-*

liche Post. Pulitzer arranged with John A. Dillon, proprietor of the small *Evening Post*, founded in 1878, to merge the two papers. After a year of publishing the new *Post-Dispatch* in partnership, Dillon sold out to Pulitzer. The *Post-Dispatch* pioneered a new style of independent, crusading journalism dedicated to urban reformism of a middle-class type that prefigured the progressivism of a later generation. In a series of multiple crusades, the paper sought to improve municipal services and facilities, to curb corrupt political bosses and machines, and to bring powerful corporations under public control. These crusades Pulitzer combined with a sensational news style and the development of entertainment features such as sporting news, cartoons, comics, and a Sunday supplement to attract a mass readership. In 1911 Pulitzer died, leaving the *Post-Dispatch* to Joseph Pulitzer, Jr., who with Oliver K. Bovard, managing editor, not only continued the paper's crusading style but brought it to such national prominence during the next half-century that Senator George Norris called it the "Manchester *Guardian* of America." The paper became famous for its exposures of Teapot Dome, the KU KLUX KLAN, the PENDERGAST MACHINE in Kansas City, and corruption in the Truman administration, as well as numerous crusades against corruption in Illinois government, McCarthyism, and defense of civil and minority rights. In 1955 Joseph Pulitzer, Jr., died, and the paper is now published by his son Joseph Pulitzer III. Current daily circulation is more than 286,000 copies.

See W. A. Swanberg, *Pulitzer* (1967); D. C. Seitz, *Joseph Pulitzer* (1924); G. S. Johns, *Joseph Pulitzer* (1932); J. S. Rammelkamp, *Pulitzer's Post-Dispatch* (1967); O. Johns, *Time of Our Lives* (1937); H. W. King, *Pulitzer's Prize Editor* (1965); J. W. Markham, *Bovard of Post-Dispatch* (1954); A. Thomas, *Print of My Remembrance* (1922); C. Wetmore, *Battle Against Bribery* (1904); C. Ross and C. F. Hurd, *Story of St. Louis Post-Dispatch* (n.d.); W. A. Kelsoe, *Missouri Historical Review* (Jan., 1922); W. B. Stevens, *Missouri Historical Review* (April, 1923; July, 1925); T. S. Graham, "Charles H. Jones" (Ph.D. dissertation, University of Florida, 1973); J. Pulitzer Collection, Library of Congress and Columbia University; interview, J. Pulitzer, Jr., Oral History Project, Columbia University; and St. Louis *Post-Dispatch* (1878–).

JULIAN S. RAMMELKAMP
Albion College

ST. LOUIS UNIVERSITY (St. Louis, Mo. 63103), a Roman Catholic institution, was founded in 1818 as the St. Louis Academy. Adopted by the Society of Jesus in 1827, the school received a charter in 1832. It currently has an enrollment of approximately 4,000 students. Its library specializes in manuscripts relating to religious history since the first century B.C. and is an important source of materials for early Catholic settlements in and around St. Louis.

See R. G. Adams *et al.*, *St. Louis University* (1968); T. S. Bowdern, *St. Louis University* (1928); and W. B. Faherty, *History of Education Quarterly* (Winter, 1968).

ST. MARY'S CITY, MD., the oldest settlement in Maryland, was founded in 1634 on the site of a small Piscataway Indian village. It was made the colony's capital in 1676. In 1694, however, the capital was moved to Annapolis, and 16 years later even the county seat was removed. In 1934, memorializing the site's former position of importance, a reproduction of the first capital building was reconstructed on this spot.

See M. P. Andrews, *History of Maryland* (1929, 1965) and *Founding of Maryland* (1933).

ST. MARY'S RIVER rises in OKEFENOKEE SWAMP and follows a 180-mile course to its mouth on the Atlantic Ocean. First flowing generally south, then east, then north, and then east once again, the river forms the small loop in the eastern portion of the Georgia-Florida state line. At the river's mouth are two of the coastal SEA ISLANDS: Amelia to the south (Florida) and Cumberland to the north (Georgia). After an unsuccessful attempt by the French to colonize Amelia Island in 1562, small Spanish missions and forts dotting the St. Mary's area were founded in the late sixteenth and the seventeenth centuries. Although none of these settlements were as important to the Spanish as was ST. AUGUSTINE or the garrisons on the ST. JOHN'S RIVER, the St. Mary's took on a special significance after the American Revolution, when Britain ceded the Floridas back to Spain. Then the river became part of an international boundary, and the cities of St. Mary's, Ga., and Fernandina, Fla., became briefly ports of international trade. Indeed, by 1810, St. Mary's had become the fifth largest city (pop. 585) in all of Georgia. On Amelia Island, Fernandina became a haven for British Tories, smugglers, pirates, and slave runners. Beginning in 1812, the cities also became centers of intrigue by American adventurers seeking to acquire Florida for the United States (AMELIA ISLAND AFFAIR). The area around the river mouth was "captured" in 1817 by Sir Gregor MacGregor, who ruled Amelia Island for several months as his personal possession; later that year the pirate Luis Aury seized the island, claiming it was part of Mexico; and shortly thereafter the United States took the island to hold it in trust for Spain. After

the United States formally gained possession of the Floridas in 1821, the political and commercial importance of the St. Mary's River declined.

See E. C. Nance (ed.), *East Coast of Florida* (1962); C. E. Bennett, *Settlement of Florida* (1968); M. V. Gannon, *Cross in Sand* (1965); W. H. Siebert, *Loyalists in East Florida* (1929); and C. W. Tebeau, *History of Florida* (1971).

ST. PETERSBURG, FLA. (pop. 216,232), is tied to the city of Tampa by two bridges. The first white settler, Antonio Maximo, established a fish "rancho" here in 1843, but the small fishing community that had grown up around Maximo Point was shelled by federal blockaders during the Civil War and its inhabitants fled to Tampa. In 1876 a new community, Pinellas, and some citrus groves were established on the site. After the Orange Belt Line Railway was built to the city in 1888, the name was changed to honor the birthplace of a Russian-born resident. In 1914 a second railroad line was extended to the city, which grew rapidly as a winter resort. Called the Sunshine City for its average annual 360 days of sun, modern St. Petersburg remains a center for tourism. It also is a port of entry, and its factories manufacture electronic equipment, air conditioners, and prepared fruit and seafood.

See K. Grismer, *History of St. Petersburg* (1924, 1948), standard; H. Dunn, *Yesterday's St. Petersburg* (1973), well illustrated; W. Straub, *History of Pinellas County* (1929); J. Bethell, *History of Point Pinellas* (1914); W. Fuller, *St. Petersburg* (1971), illustrated; P. Jackson, *Informal History of St. Petersburg* (1962); unpublished manuscripts, St. Petersburg Public Library; and files of St. Petersburg *Independent* (1907–) and *Times* (1884–), both on microfilm.

SALISBURY PRISON at Salisbury, N.C., was established by the Confederates in 1861. It consisted of a former factory building, several smaller structures, and a few tents surrounded by a board stockade. Conditions were tolerable for the over 1,500 Union soldiers held there until the beginning of regular exchange in 1862. Thereafter the prison housed several hundred southern civilians charged with political offenses, soldiers convicted of desertion or other military crimes, and a few northerners accused of spying or the like. Conditions worsened radically in October, 1864, when Richmond suddenly shipped its accumulated prisoners to Salisbury. Most of the more than 10,000 prisoners who overcrowded Salisbury were enlisted men. Food, wood, and even water were in short supply. Lacking shelter, many prisoners burrowed in the earth. Some desperate captives vainly attempted an uprising on November 25, 1864, and others joined the Confederate army to win release. From October, 1864, until the resumption of exchange in February, 1865, 3,419 prisoners died. Subsequently a few hundred transient prisoners were at Salisbury Prison until its destruction by STONEMAN'S RAID in April, 1865. A U.S. military commission tried the Salisbury commander, Major John H. Gee, and acquitted him of charges of atrocity.

See B. F. Booth, *Dark Days* (1897); O. H. Bixby, *Incidents in Dixie* (1864); A. D. Richardson, *Secret Service* (1865); *Official Records, Armies*, Ser. 2; and National Archives.

FRANK L. BYRNE
Kent State University

SALT was of little economic importance in the South until the Revolutionary War, when imports were disrupted. Several areas quickly became known for salt production: Saltville, Va.; northeastern Kentucky, including the famous Blue Licks; French Lick, now Nashville, Tenn.; the Kanawha Valley near modern Charleston, W.Va.; present-day Clarke, Washington, and Mobile counties, Ala.; and, after the Louisiana Purchase, Ste. Genevieve and Boonslick country, Mo., and modern Bossier, Bienville, and Winn parishes and Avery Island, La.

Salt was often scarce and costly in remote areas, for bulk and weight made it difficult to transport. To make salt available, the government in 1807 began leasing salt springs on public lands; among others, works in Alabama, Missouri, and later Arkansas operated under this land policy. After the War of 1812 and until 1845, the industry was protected by a tariff. Although domestic works supplied local needs, meat-packers preferred the purer, imported salt, which became cheaper as steamboat travel on western waterways quickly reduced transportation costs. The Kanawha producers created a monopoly in the West and made government leases unprofitable, and other works declined. As transportation improved, foreign salt dominated the market, so that by 1861 the only extensive works in the South were at Kanawha, Saltville, and Goose Creek, Ky.

During the Civil War, blockades and the early loss of the Kanawha and Kentucky works resulted in severe shortages of salt in the South. The Confederacy was forced into making solar salt along the Atlantic and Gulf coasts and evaporated salt at springs in Virginia, Alabama, Louisiana, Arkansas, and Texas, especially in Llano and Lampasas counties and at Grand Saline.

Although large-scale production continued at Kanawha and Saltville for a number of years after the war, attention turned almost exclusively in the 1880s to rock salt mining at domes discovered at Avery Island and elsewhere in Louisiana and Texas. Industrial growth brought increased demands for brine in chemical production, so that soon most salt produced in the South was extracted as artificial brine. Louisiana, Texas, West Virginia, Alabama, and Virginia are salt-producing states today, the first two accounting for over half the nation's domestic output.

See J. W. Taylor, "Reservation and Leasing" (Ph.D. dissertation, University of Chicago, 1930); C. A. Fost, "Salt Industry" (Ph.D. dissertation, University of Southern Illinois, 1970); E. Lonn, *Salt as a Factor* (1965); D. W. Kaufmann, *Sodium Chloride* (1960); J. E. Stealey III, "Salt Industry" (Ph.D. dissertation, Louisiana State University, 1952); D. F. Littlefield, Jr., *Arkansas Historical Quarterly* (Winter, 1973); and U.S. Bureau of Mines, *Minerals Yearbook* (1906–72).

DANIEL F. LITTLEFIELD, JR.
University of Arkansas, Little Rock

SAN ANTONIO, TEX. (pop. 654,153), at the head of the Trinity River approximately 190 miles west of Houston, was the most important Spanish and Mexican settlement in early Texas history. It was first settled in 1718 with the establishment of the mission San Antonio de Valero and the presidio San Antonio de Bexar. During the next 13 years, four additional missions and a small settlement, the Villa de San Fernando, were all established in the immediate vicinity of present-day San Antonio. The city was occupied by Texans in December, 1835, but three months later its defenders were massacred within the walls of the old mission, the ALAMO. After the MEXICAN WAR, the city underwent change. Commercially, politically, and intellectually the town began to face north and east rather than south toward Mexico City. Austin, 75 miles to the northeast, became the state's capital; a large influx of German immigrants joined the Mexican and American elements of the city's population, giving it a truly cosmopolitan character; and San Antonio became a major supply point for cattle drivers pushing their herds to American markets.

The modern period of San Antonio's history probably dates from 1877, the year a line of the Southern Pacific Railroad was constructed through the town. The railroad station soon became a rail junction with connections to all points on the compass. Instead of being merely a supply point for cattle drivers, the city became a shipping point for cattle and later for processed meat, cotton, wool, pecans, metals, furniture, and clothing. In the twentieth century the city's existing transportation facilities led to the location here of refineries to process the state's expanding PETROLEUM industry. And, since World War II, the city has become increasingly important as a military and aviation center with U.S. Army Ft. Sam Houston (1865), Brooke Army Medical Center, and four U.S. Air Force bases (Brooks, Kelly, Randolph, and Lackland) all located here.

See A. Curtis, *Fabulous San Antonio* (1955); C. Ramsdell, *San Antonio* (1959), illustrated; and files of San Antonio *Express* (1865–), *News* (1918–), and *Light* (1881–).

SANDBAR DUEL was a famous encounter that took place on an island in the Mississippi River off Natchez on September 19, 1827. Thomas H. Maddox and Samuel Levi Wells went there with the ostensible purpose of just the two fighting a duel with pistols (DUELING), but it soon broadened into a general encounter involving accompanying friends and others in attendance, including JAMES BOWIE. When it was over, two men were dead and three wounded. One of the dead was Major Morris Wright, killed by Bowie with a hunting knife that soon became famous as the "Bowie knife."

See J. F. Dobie, *Southwest Review* (April, 1931).

SANDLAPPERS. See CLAY EATERS

SANFORD, EDWARD TERRY (1865–1930), came from a wealthy merchant family influential in east Tennessee Republican politics. He practiced law in Knoxville and spent his spare time lecturing on law, doing historical writing, and serving on civic and educational boards. Republican friends secured him an assistant district attorneyship (1907–1908). Next, Sanford served as a deliberate and impartial federal judge (1908–1923), who impressed Judge William Howard Taft so favorably that Taft later persuaded President Warren Harding to appoint Sanford to the U.S. Supreme Court (1923–1930). Liberals considered Sanford to be a conservative jurist. Concerned about spreading radical socialism, he consistently sustained the constitutionality of state laws against Communists and others who advocated violent overthrow of capitalist society. Actually, his record on upholding antitrust laws was a moderately liberal one, and he sympathized with working men's compensation laws. On federal versus states' rights questions, he took a nationalist stand. Following his sudden death, both colleagues and press praised Sanford's personal charm, openness of mind, profound learning, and usefulness to the Court.

See A. E. Ragan, *East Tennessee Historical Society Publications* (1943); G. F. Milton, *Outlook* (Feb 14, 1923); *Nation* (March 19, 1930); and New York *Times* (March 9, 1930).

JAMES R. CHUMNEY
Memphis State University

SAN JACINTO, BATTLE OF (April 21, 1836), was the last and decisive engagement of the Texas revolution. When SAM HOUSTON heard on March 13 of the fall of the ALAMO, he led his 380 Texas volunteers from Gonzales in a gradual eastward retreat. His slim hopes for victory depended upon avoiding battle with the Mexican forces, which numbered between 7,000 and 8,000, and upon augmenting his own army with additional volunteers. General Antonio de Santa Anna, mistakenly thinking Houston was attempting to reach the Sabine River, crossed the flood-swollen Brazos River with about 900 effective soldiers and intercepted the Texans on April 20 at a prairie on the San Jacinto River. Houston's forces now numbered just over 800 men, and it was the only chance the Texans would ever have for anything like an equal engagement. Neither army went on the offensive, though Santa Anna kept his troops on the alert through the night and until noon the next day. After the arrival of about 400 Mexican reinforcements, Santa Anna concluded that Houston was not going to attack. He allowed his men to cook a hot meal and to relax from their 24-hour vigil. This was when Houston chose to attack. The Texans charged through the Mexican camp in 17 minutes. While two Texans were killed and 208 were wounded, Houston counted Mexican casualties as 630 killed, 208 wounded, and 730 captured. Among these was Santa Anna himself. Even this decisive victory would not have given Texas independence except for the capture of Santa Anna and for Vicent Filosola's (Santa Anna's second-in-command) decision to withdraw the Mexican army, still about 6,000 strong, below the Rio Grande to save Santa Anna's life.

See S. V. Connor, *Battles of Texas* (1967); E. C. Barker, *Texas Historical Association Quarterly* (April, 1901); and S. V. Connor, *Texas* (1971), extensive bibliography.

SEYMOUR V. CONNOR
Texas Tech University

SANTA FE TRADE. William Becknell, an Indian trader of Franklin, Mo., is acknowledged as the father of the Santa Fe Trail, becoming the first to publicize New Mexico as a trade outlet for Missouri merchants. Following Mexico's independence from Spain in 1822, a regular trade was established, which lasted until the coming of the railroad. Although the trade never involved great numbers of men, the traders unknowingly became the advance agents of manifest destiny. An annual caravan of merchant freighters headed southwestward as soon as the prairie sod was dry enough to support the weight of the heavily laden wagons, which were pulled by eight to 12 MULES or oxen. The 700-mile trip was made through Indian Territory, either by way of the Cimarron Desert or more circuitously via Bent's Fort to the north. Occasionally a U.S. Cavalry escort accompanied the traders as far as the Mexican border, where they were frequently met by an equivalent Mexican military detachment.

Initial gains in the Santa Fe trade were great, but subsequent profits were reduced by competition and by taxation imposed by the government in New Mexico. Westbound trade goods were small-bulk and high-value merchandise including minor hardware, cloth, and wearing apparel, whereas eastbound items included coarse and fine furs, livestock, gold, and silver, with the Mexican coins used to overcome a chronic shortage of fractional currency in the Mississippi Valley.

When in 1843, after over two decades of regular commerce, Mexican President Antonio de Santa Anna ordered closure of trade, the action was resented by both Americans and Mexicans. The significance of the Santa Fe trade lies in its part in breaking down the Indian barrier, in destroying the myth of the Great American Desert, which it crossed, and in softening the Mexican will to resist subsequent U.S. military occupation during the Mexican War. Trade continued after the U.S. conquest of Santa Fe, but without the international complications and benefits. The trade also served to bring a measure of prosperity to Missouri and to train a pool of skilled guides, who would later lead agricultural immigrants to new western homes.

See J. Gregg, *Commerce of Prairies*, ed. M. L. Moorhead (1954); H. Inman, *Old Santa Fe Trail* (1897); and J. D. Rittenhouse, *Santa Fe Trail: Historical Bibliography* (1971).

DONALD C. CUTTER
University of New Mexico

SANTEE RIVER, draining much of central South Carolina, is formed approximately 30 miles southeast of Columbia by the confluence of the Wateree and Congaree rivers. It flows along a 143-mile course, entering the Atlantic Ocean by way of two separate mouths. The lower portion of the river was used on a limited basis for commerce during the colonial period and was joined to the Cooper River and Charleston by a canal constructed between 1792 and 1800. During the nineteenth century the Santee was used increasingly as a power source for area textile mills. Since World War II, however, its principal economic value is as the generator of hydroelectric power.

SARASOTA, FLA. (pop. 40,237), is approximately 45 miles south of Tampa on a shallow lagoon that connects with Tampa Bay. The site was homesteaded by William Whitaker of Tallahassee in 1856. Twenty-five years later, a syndicate of Scottish settlers acquired land here, established the city, and introduced the game of golf as a tourist attraction. After the Seaboard Air Line railway reached Sarasota in 1902, the town grew rapidly as a resort and as a center for growing vegetables and citrus fruits. It is famous as the winter headquarters for the Ringling Brothers, Barnum & Bailey Circus, and the factories of the modern city produce pleasure boats, mobile homes, and electronic parts.

See Sarasota *Herald-Tribune* (1925–), on microfilm.

SAVAGE STATION, BATTLE OF (June 29, 1862), was one of the SEVEN DAYS' BATTLES during the PENINSULAR CAMPAIGN of the Civil War. Following a loss to R. E. Lee at GAINES' MILL, the overcautious G. B. McClellan ordered withdrawal south to the James River. Edwin V. Sumner (II Corps), Samuel P. Heintzelman (III Corps), and William B. Franklin (VI Corps) withdrew toward Savage Station, Va., and formed a rear guard for the federal army crossing White Oak Swamp. After determining McClellan's direction of retreat, Lee ordered a pursuit. STONEWALL JACKSON was to cross the Chickahominy River and, with assistance from J. B. MAGRUDER's division advancing from the west, pressure the Union rear while divisions of Benjamin Huger, JAMES LONGSTREET, and A. P. HILL were to encircle the retreating enemy and attack its flank and rear. Magruder made contact with Sumner's corps early on June 29. Jackson uncharacteristically took the entire day to cross the river and never joined the battle. Magruder attacked cautiously and was repulsed by the federals. Nightfall and a heavy thunderstorm ended the battle. The Union forces retreated across White Oak Swamp during the night, abandoning many supplies and wounded. McClellan was probably spared a serious defeat by Jackson's unexplained inactivity. Casualties were 626 Confederates and 1,590 federals.

See V. J. Esposito, *West Point Atlas* (1959), excellent maps; and *Official Records, Armies*, Ser. 1, Vol. XI.

G. C. BROWN
U.S. Military Academy

SAVANNAH, GA. (pop. 118,349), was founded and laid out in 1733 by JAMES OGLETHORPE and the colony's first settlers. The origin of its name is uncertain, perhaps being derived from the Spanish word *savana* (flat countryside) or from the Sewana (SHAWNEE) Indians, who once inhabited the area. The colonial town thrived as a center of shipping and commerce and—after management of the colony's affairs by a board of trustees in England was replaced with a royal government— served as Georgia's first capital. During the American Revolution, sentiment in Savannah was largely prorevolutionary. The town was captured by the British in 1778, but was retaken in 1782 by the forces of Mad Anthony Wayne. Although Georgia's capital was moved in 1786 to Augusta, Savannah grew as an ocean port with river (and eventually canal and rail) connections with area cotton and tobacco growers. In 1819 the first steamship to cross the Atlantic Ocean sailed from here to Liverpool, England. The city was blockaded early during the Civil War, but not until December, 1864, did it fall into Union hands (SHERMAN'S MARCH TO THE SEA). Postwar Savannah regained some measure of prosperity after the formation in 1882 of the Naval Stores Exchange, which made it the leading shipper of turpentine. The city has become increasingly popular as a winter resort, and its industries produce naval stores, airplanes, fertilizers, chemicals, construction materials, canned foods, pulp and paper, and refined sugar.

See Savannah *Republican* (1802–73); *Advertizer* (1868– 75); *Morning News* (1850–); *Evening Press* (1891–); R. E. Perdue, *Negro in Savannah, 1865–1900* (1973); W. C. Smith, "Georgia Gentlemen" (Ph.D. dissertation, University of North Carolina, 1971); R. H. Haunton, "Savannah in 1850's" (Ph.D. dissertation, Emory, 1968); J. D. Griffin, "Savannah During Civil War" (Ph.D. dissertation, University of Georgia, 1963); J. M. Patrick, *Savannah Theater to 1810* (1952); and M. Granger (ed.), *Savannah River Plantations* (1947, 1972).

SAVANNAH MORNING NEWS began in 1850 as a penny publication modeled after the New York *Sun* and the Baltimore *Sun*. "Old Betsy" or the "South Georgia Bible," as it is sometimes called, has a tradition of independent political conservatism. It supported J. C. BRECKINRIDGE in the election of 1860, Grover Cleveland in the 1890s, and Herbert Hoover in the election of 1928. Published throughout the Civil War, it was known during the federal occupation of Savannah as the *Herald*. It enjoys the largest circulation of any paper in southeastern Georgia with a daily edition in excess of 60,000 copies.

See L. T. Griffith and J. E. Talmadge, *Georgia Journalism, 1763–1950* (1951); bound copies, at Library of Congress, Georgia Historical Society, Savannah, and Savannah Public Library; and microfilm, from Bell & Howell (1944–).

SAVANNAH REPUBLICAN was founded in 1802 as the *Georgia Republican*, a weekly newspaper supporting the programs of Thomas Jefferson and the Democratic-Republican party. Despite several variations on the same name, the *Republican* was published long after its title had become an anomaly. In 1840 it was a supporter of William H. Harrison and the Whig party. It avoided any association with the KNOW-NOTHING movement of the 1850s and was a leading secessionist organ in 1861. In 1873 it merged with the *Advertizer* to form the *Advertizer-Republican*, and in 1875 it was absorbed by the Savannah *Morning News*.

See L. T. Griffith and J. E. Talmadge, *Georgia Journalism, 1763–1950* (1951); and bound copies, at Library of Congress, Georgia Historical Society, Savannah, and Savannah Public Library.

SAVANNAH RIVER, serving as much of the state line between Georgia and South Carolina, is formed by the confluence of the Tugaloo and Seneca rivers. It follows a southeasterly course, moving through approximately 100 miles of the PIEDMONT region to Augusta at the FALL LINE, and from there it flows 212 miles through the coastal plain to its mouth on the Atlantic Ocean. Since James Oglethorpe founded the city of Savannah in 1733 (17 miles upstream from the river's mouth), the Savannah has played an important and a lively role in the area's history. Cockspur Island, at the river's mouth, was first fortified in 1761 by the construction of Ft. George. Although this fort was dismantled during the American Revolution, a second fort, Ft. Greene, stood on the same site (1794–1804) until it was destroyed by a hurricane. Defending the Savannah became the object of a third fortification, Ft. Pulaski, constructed in 1847. The capture of FT. PULASKI in April, 1862, was one of the Union's early successes against the coastal defenses of the Confederacy.

Navigable by shallow-draft vessels as far upstream as the site of Augusta, the Savannah River played a vital role in sustaining colonial Georgia as a carrier of NAVAL STORES, LUMBER, and TO-BACCO. In 1790 the first experimental steamboat floated in southern waters was launched from Augusta. After the steamboat *Enterprise* successfully navigated upstream as far as Augusta in 1816, commercial use of the Savannah expanded markedly. Railroads and shifting population patterns gradually diminished the river's importance as a trade route during the nineteenth century, but above the fall line its role as a power source was vital to the industrialization of Anderson and Augusta. Today dams above Augusta provide the area with FLOOD CONTROL, recreation sites, and hydroelectric power. Approximately 20 miles below Augusta, on the South Carolina bank, the Savannah River plant of the U.S. Atomic Energy Commission produces materials for nuclear research. And at the river's mouth, once busy with shipping, a wildlife refuge preserves some of the Savannah River in a state of nature.

See T. L. Stokes, *Savannah River* (1951).

SAYLER'S CREEK, BATTLE OF (April 6, 1865),

also called Sailor's Creek, was the last major engagement of the APPOMATTOX CAMPAIGN between R. E. Lee's exhausted and starving Army of Northern Virginia and the pursuing Union forces under U. S. Grant. Hard pressed at Amelia Courthouse by George Meade's infantry marching on his rear and Philip Sheridan's cavalry and E. O. C. Ord's Army of the James blocking continued retreat along the Richmond & Danville Railroad, and lacking rations for his troops, Lee sought escape during the night of April 5–6 by twisting west toward Farmville, Va., in hope of receiving rations by rail from Lynchburg. Union harassment caused RICHARD ANDERSON and RICHARD EWELL to halt their corps to cover the wagon trains. In the confusion JAMES LONGSTREET's corps in the van and JOHN GORDON's corps in the rear were separated from Anderson and Ewell. Cut off by Union cavalry and infantry, Anderson's and Ewell's commands were forced to surrender after a gallant but uncoordinated series of fights near Sayler's Creek. Gordon's corps escaped capture but sustained heavy losses. Confederate losses for the day were about one-third of Lee's army, perhaps 8,000 men, plus great quantities of guns, wagons, and equipment.

See D. S. Freeman, *Lee's Lieutenants* (1944) III; A. A. Humphreys, *Campaign of 1864 and 1865* (1883); and P. V. D. Stern, *End to Valor* (1958), map and useful anecdotes for teachers.

JAMES WILLIAM STRYKER
U.S. Military Academy

SCALAWAG, scallawag, or scallywag was the title of derision and contempt given by southern opponents of RECONSTRUCTION to the native white who supported the REPUBLICAN PARTY. The origins of the word are uncertain. Used in the United States before the war as a term for scrawny or undersized cattle, it was also common as a synonym for rascal, scamp, good-for-nothing, or loafer. A century of predominantly racist thought and writing firmly established the scalawag as an intrinsic part of the opprobrious Reconstruction stereotype. Because of its past connotation there are those who now prefer to drop the term altogether, yet it remains in common usage, although increasingly free of negative implications, to designate native white Republicans of the Reconstruction South.

Southern whites often found the scalawag uniquely hateful. The faults of an alien CARPET-BAGGER or member of a supposedly inferior race were considered more understandable than those of a despicable renegade, a traitor to one's own section and people. Since that treachery frequently had extended back into the war years, scalawags also were blamed for the South's defeat. Numbering in the tens of thousands, scalawags blurred a desired racial division, thus providing an indigenous power and respectability to the Republican party that was recognized as crucial. Consequently they were denounced with special vigor and purpose.

The myth that the defeat of the southern Republican party represented the triumph of property, intelligence, and virtue, together with the original meaning of the term scalawag, encouraged a simplistic conception of the class origins of the scalawags. They were primarily thought to have been POOR WHITES who had opposed the slaveholding aristocracy and the Confederacy and who sought class or personal gains through the Republican party. Although this interpretation served the purposes of both the Conservative critics and Radical defenders of Reconstruction, the more diverse origins of the scalawag were recognized by a number of earlier historians and stressed in the Reconstruction novels of ALBION W. TOURGÉE and in W. E. B. DU BOIS' *Black Reconstruction* (1935).

In 1944 David Donald found most scalawags in Mississippi to have been former Whigs from the black belt: "wealthy men—the large planters and the railroad and industrial promoters—who turned naturally to the party which in the state as in the nation was dominated by business interests." Nationalist in orientation and well educated, these former Whigs had opposed SECESSION. They still opposed the egalitarian and STATES' RIGHTS leanings of the Democrats and were anxious to guide the Republican party in safe and sensible directions. Donald believed that most Whigs initially supported the Mississippi Republican party, but they were soon to be alienated by the Radical demands and growing power of blacks and carpetbaggers. They were especially hostile to further racial equality, and their resultant defection was the major cause of Republican defeat.

Donald also suggested the validity of this thesis for much of the rest of the South, but a quantitative study of voting patterns in the South by Allen W. Trelease concluded that most scalawags, including those in Mississippi, were poor farmers and former Democrats from counties that were relatively poor and contained few Negroes. Located mainly in the mountain areas, these counties had remained strongly UNIONIST during the war and, with some exceptions, were identifiable with a radical variant of Jacksonian Democracy. Portions of Trelease's methodology have been challenged, however, and recent studies of Mississippi and Alabama, together with studies of the Whig heritage, have strengthened Donald's thesis.

Although the debate continues, it is apparent that white support for the southern Republican party differed from state to state and varied in origin and goals. Scalawags were a small minority of the total white population. They included former Whigs and Democrats, secessionists and Unionists, members of the upper and lower classes, and both Radical and Conservative elements. Even though much of the scalawag leadership has been clearly identified, estimates of the origins of white Republican votes have been based upon rather speculative correlations. Most commentators consider the race issue primarily responsible for declining white membership in the Republican party, but the class, ideological, and sectional complexities of this entire matter have yet to be properly explored.

See D. Donald, *Journal of Southern History* (Nov., 1944; May, 1964); A. W. Trelease, *Journal of Southern History* (Nov., 1963); O. H. Olsen, *Civil War History* (Dec., 1966); W. Ellem, *Journal of Southern History* (May, 1972); and R. O. Curry, *Civil War Hisory* (Sept., 1974).

OTTO H. OLSEN
Northern Illinois University

SCHURZ, CARL (1829–1906), born near Cologne, Germany, was working on a doctorate in history at the University of Bonn when he was forced to flee following his participation in the abortive democratic uprising of the late 1840s. He arrived at Philadelphia in 1852, became active in the Republican party, and purchased land near Watertown, Wis., in 1856. Appointed ambassador to Spain in 1861, Schurz returned to the United States in 1862, accepted an appointment as an officer, and saw combat at second BULL RUN and CHANCELLORSVILLE during the Civil War. In the summer of 1865, Schurz toured five former Confederate states at President Andrew Johnson's request to observe conditions in the postwar South. His subsequent published report advocated enfranchisement of the freedmen, criticized the course of presidential Reconstruction, and helped to increase northern anxiety over the ineffectiveness of Johnson's southern policies. Although his observations advocated the implementation of congressional Reconstruction, Schurz's later activities as a U.S. senator from Missouri (1869–1875) helped to terminate that experiment. He then split with President U. S. Grant over the issue of corruption and became a leader in the Liberal Republican campaign in the ELECTION OF 1872. After tenure as secretary of interior under President Rutherford B. Hayes, Schurz engaged in journalistic activities and became an outspoken critic of the American acquisition of the Philippines following the Spanish-American War.

See Carl Schurz Papers, Library of Congress; F. Bancroft (ed.), *Speeches, Correspondence, and Papers of Schurz* (6 vols.; 1913); C. Schurz, *Reminiscenses* (3 vols.; 1907–08); J. Schafer (ed.), *Intimate Letters of Schurz* (1928); and C. M. Fuess, *Carl Schurz* (1932).

RICHARD L. HUME
Washington State University

SCOPES TRIAL. Tennessee enacted America's most publicized antievolution law in 1925. Shortly thereafter the AMERICAN CIVIL LIBERTIES UNION offered free legal services to the first person charged with violating the statute. This offer, in turn, encouraged a small group of Dayton business and professional men to conceive a bizarre scheme to "place Dayton on the map." They sought out John Thomas Scopes, a twenty-four-year-old physics teacher and football coach at the Rhea County High School, and asked permission to initiate a test case against him. Scopes reluctantly acquiesced, although he later, in 1960, stated emphatically that he had never taught or even mentioned evolution.

The young teacher was arrested on May 7, received a preliminary hearing on May 10, and was indicted on May 25, and the trial was scheduled to commence on July 10. With the pen of H. L. MENCKEN setting the tone, the press seized upon the "monkey trial" with alacrity. William Jennings Bryan, the acknowledged leader of the anti-evolutionists, offered his services to the prosecution. Clarence Darrow, one of America's most eminent criminal lawyers, then offered his services to the ACLU for Scopes's defense. As the date for adjudication approached, Dayton became encompassed by a half-revival, half-circus atmosphere. The town was inundated with hucksters and vendors, who hawked everything from religious literature to watermelons. The city fathers even appointed a "committee on entertainment for the Scopes trial."

The case for the defense, which rested upon the constitutionality of the antievolution statute, was shattered by the court's refusal to hear expert testimony from a score of America's most eminent scientists. Judge John T. Raulston acquiesced to the prosecution's contention that the law was a valid exercise of Tennessee's police power and that the clarity of the statute precluded any necessity for expert testimony. Since the defense had admitted the charge, the jury declared Scopes guilty, and Judge Raulston imposed a $100 fine. The decision was appealed to the Tennessee supreme court in January of 1927. The tribunal subsequently upheld the antievolution law but reversed the decision against Scopes since Judge Raulston had not been empowered to levy a fine in excess of $50. The principal significance of the trial was that it dramatized the EVOLUTION CONTROVERSY. William Jennings Bryan died in Dayton five days after the trial ended. Although Mississippi and Arkansas passed antievolution laws afterward, antievolutionism became increasingly moribund after the Scopes trial.

See R. Ginger, *Six Days or Forever* (1958); J. T. Scopes and J. Presley, *Center of Storm* (1967); J. R. Tompkins (ed.), *D-Days at Dayton* (1965); H. Allen, *Current History* (Sept., 1926); K. K. Bailey, *Journal of Southern History* (Nov., 1950); and R. Halliburton, Jr., *Proceedings of Oklahoma Academy of Science* (1963).

R. HALLIBURTON, JR.
Northeastern Oklahoma State University

SCOTT, DRED. See DRED SCOTT V. SANDFORD

SCOTT, ROBERT KINGSTON (1826–1900), born in Pennsylvania, migrated to Ohio, where he attended Central College and a medical school before succumbing to the California gold rush in 1850. His indifferent success led him to South America before he returned to Ohio. During the first year of the Civil War, Scott organized the 68th Ohio Infantry, and in 1865 he was brevetted major general. His preeminence in South Carolina was attributed to his excellent administrative performance as assistant commissioner of the FREEDMEN'S BUREAU (1866–1868). Elected the state's first Republican governor in 1868, he supported removal of political disabilities of Confederates, and he attempted to appease the ruling class. He was "notoriously weak and pliant," however, and his incongruent alcoholism and female entanglements caused him to become prey to the scheming "Forty Thieves." During Scott's two administrations (1868–1872), there were numerous legislative and press charges of corruption and fraudulent mismanagement of public funds. He was impeached, but the trial never materialized. Disgraced in office, Scott returned to Ohio in 1877 to escape possible prosecution. He became a Democrat and expressed sentiment for DISFRANCHISEMENT of blacks.

See F. B. Simkins and R. H. Woody, *South Carolina* (1932), best; M. Abbott, *Freedmen's Bureau* (1967); E. P. Mitchell, *Memoirs* (1924); D. D. Wallace, *History of South Carolina* (1934), III; and H. T. Thompson, *Ousting Carpetbaggers* (1969).

DAVID W. BISHOP
North Carolina Central University

SCOTT, WINFIELD (1786–1866), was born near Petersburg, Va. He obtained a captain's commission in 1808 and served in the New Orleans area until 1812. He was assigned to the Niagara frontier in 1812 and was captured at Queenston. He captured Ft. George in 1813. Promoted brigadier general in 1814, Scott played major roles at Chippewa and Lundy's Lane. He was severely wounded in the latter battle and took no further part in the fighting. Scott's talents as a pacifier were especially important during the NULLIFICATION crisis of 1832. By a judicious combination of firmness and conciliation, he did much to calm the heated atmosphere. Scott's campaigns against the SEMINOLE and CREEK Indians in Florida and Georgia during 1836 were only partially successful. Placed in charge of the removal of the CHEROKEE in 1838, he did much to mitigate the unavoidable harshness involved. Scott's military fame rests primarily on the illustrious campaign in Mexico in 1847. His brilliant series of victories led to the fall of Mexico City and peace. He was nominated for president by the Whigs in the ELECTION OF 1852, but party divisions and his own political ineptitude led to a crushing defeat. Scott remained loyal to the Union in 1861. Almost alone, he recognized the immense size of the task facing the federal government. He served usefully until ill health forced his resignation in November, 1861. He was one of the greatest figures in American military history, and no man has exercised greater influence upon the army than he.

See C. W. Elliott, *Winfield Scott* (1937), best biography; W. Scott, *Memoirs* (1864), still valuable; E. D. Mansfield, *Life of Winfield Scott* (1852), best contemporary biography; E. A. Cruikshank, *Campaign upon Niagara* (1896–1908), sources; K. J. Bauer, *Mexican War* (1974); M. M. Quaife (ed.), *Diary of James K. Polk* (1910), presents adverse view; and M. Leech, *Reveille in Washington* (1941), view of last public services.

ROBERT S. QUIMBY
Michigan State University

SCOTTSBORO CASE.

On April 9, 1931, eight black teenagers received the death penalty in a Scottsboro, Ala., courtroom. A mistrial was declared in the case of a ninth youth. The nine were charged with raping two white girls, Victoria Price and Ruby Bates, aboard a freight train as it traveled through the mountains of northern Alabama. The number of defendants, their extreme youth (two were only thirteen), the unfairness of the trial, and the draconian verdicts attracted immediate national attention.

In late 1931 the International Labor Defense, the legal affiliate of the COMMUNIST PARTY, assumed control of the case. With a simultaneous program of legal appeal and national propaganda, the ILD and the Community party sought to depict the "Scottsboro boys" as symbolic victims of a racist, capitalist America. From a narrowly legal point of view, the ILD succeeded. In a landmark decision in 1932 (*Powell* v. *Alabama*), the U.S. Supreme Court granted a new trial on the grounds that the defendants had been denied adequate counsel in the 1931 trial. At the same time, a massive program of rallies, marches, and letter-writing campaigns by the Communist party convinced most Americans outside the South that the Scottsboro defendants were innocent victims of southern racism and repression.

When the state retried one of the defendants in Decatur, Ala., in 1933, Ruby Bates dramatically reversed her earlier account and denied any rape had taken place. Nevertheless, the jury ignored her testimony, found Haywood Patterson guilty, and recommended the death penalty. Presiding Judge James E. Horton, Jr., convinced that the verdict was not supported by the evidence, reversed the jury's decision. Public sentiment led to his defeat at the next election, and the state retried two of the defendants in the fall of 1933. In separate trials, Alabama juries found Patterson and Clarence Norris guilty of rape and sentenced

them to death. Once again the ILD won a reversal, when the Supreme Court reversed the verdicts on the grounds that blacks had been systematically excluded from the state's jury rolls (*Norris* v. *Alabama* [1935]).

Still more retrials followed, but public interest in the case had begun to wane. The ILD relinquished control of the defense to a broad-based coalition of civil rights groups in late 1935, and the state finally agreed to a "compromise" in 1937 whereby four of the defendants were released and the other five received prison sentences. Sponsors of the compromise expected quick paroles for the defendants, but—despite the private intervention of President Roosevelt—Alabama Governor BIBB GRAVES declined to release the defendants. Between 1943 and 1950, the remaining five Scottsboro "boys" were paroled or (in the case of Patterson) escaped.

See D. T. Carter, *Scottsboro* (1969); H. Patterson, with E. Conrad, *Scottsboro Boy* (1950); and A. K. Chalmers, *They Shall Be Free* (1951). For primary materials, see NAACP Papers, Library of Congress; Scottsboro File and Alabama Governors' Papers, Alabama State Archives, Montgomery; Scottsboro Defense Committee Papers, Boston University Library; and International Labor Defense Papers, Schomburg Collection, New York Public Library.

DAN T. CARTER
Emory University

SEAFOOD INDUSTRY.

For centuries man has been fishing, using his hands first, then extending his range with spears, lines, boats, nets, dredges, and automated devices. Fish lured early visitors and settlers to America, and the abundance of fish and shellfish finally helped ease the early settlers' food problems along the Atlantic coast. The Dutch were the first Europeans to appreciate the vast natural oyster beds by the mid-1600s, but there is increasing evidence of the extensive use of mollusks by American Indians prior to European settlement. By the 1800s oysters were very popular. Various states had become known for special oysters: Delaware, Maryland, Virginia, and Louisiana. State agencies were created to handle problems and the inflow of tax funds. Some put out recipe booklets. Cookbooks still contain recipes for the famous New Orleans Oysters Rockefeller.

The inefficiency of early fishing methods did not threaten various species with extinction; but, with the introduction of steam power to vessels in the 1800s, improved efficiency in catches has developed shortages in some popular fish and shellfish. By the end of the 1800s, problems with overfishing, pollution, disease, and competition had developed. Political overtones of the use of steam power can be seen in the long battles in the Chesapeake Bay between Maryland and Virginia for oystering rights. In the 1960s and 1970s, revival of commercial oystering is dependent upon southern oyster seed, and southern beds provide a steady source of oysters for the food-canning and -freezing business.

Suggested fishing fleet improvements were postponed in many instances until after World War II, when an extensive rebuilding program was started. In the late 1940s and early 1950s, new shrimp grounds were discovered in the Gulf of Mexico, and that industry expanded, then declined in the late 1950s. Foreign shrimp production competed with U.S. production, and studies were made in the 1960s to revitalize the industry. Shrimp had overtaken oysters as a popular seafood specialty. The Atlantic coast blue crab was also a popular food, and by the mid-1940s crab fisheries had expanded. The Atlantic coast was yielding some 80 million pounds per year. The Chesapeake Bay produced a little over half of this blue crab catch. South Carolina and Louisiana provided most of the canned crabmeat. Improved transportation and the development of a frozen food market after World War II have increased the demand for oysters, shrimp, and crabs.

The southern United States has been active in a variety of sport and food fish industries. Growing demands for fish protein have led to efforts at aquaculture or mariculture, attempts to produce aquatic plants and fish in a controlled environment or a manipulated ecological system. Some encouraging results have been seen in the raising of pompano, a member of the jack family and a fine eating fish. Improvements in pollution control in rivers and streams have caused various species of fish to reappear in quantity. These signs are hopeful when one views increased world population and growing marginal nutrition. The sea will continue to fulfill its ancient promise to mankind.

See L. M. Alexander (ed.), *Law of Sea Institute Series* (1966–); R. L. Carson, *Sea Around Us* (1954); J. Cousteau, *Ocean World of Cousteau* (1975), excellent and illustrated; V. Lang, *Follow the Water* (1961), Chesapeake; C. Ogburn, Jr., *Winter Beach* (1966), history of beaches from Maine to North Carolina; and H. F. Taylor *et al.*, *Survey of Marine Fisheries of North Carolina* (1951). Also see reports of state seafood or fish and shellfish commissions, of U.S. Fish and Wildlife Service, and of several state universities, notably University of Miami at Coral Gables, Texas A. & M., Clemson, Georgia, Louisiana, North Carolina, and Delaware.

MARY EMILY MILLER
Salem State College

SEA ISLANDS along the coast of Georgia and South Carolina experienced their first white settlement in 1568, when Spain established mission stations among the dozen major islands. Native uprisings and English intrigue ultimately swept away a Spanish presence that ended in the battle of Bloody Marsh. In 1734 JAMES OGLETHORPE brought to this coast Englishmen in "decayed Circumstances," esthetic Salzburger dissidents, and dour Scots, some of whom had left "for the good of their country." They became malcontents, understandably unhappy in their role as insulators between Spanish forces in Florida and rich merchants of Charleston.

Eventually an idyllic plantation life began for a few wealthy families using slave labor to raise cash crops of RICE or COTTON. Some early experiments included production of wine, SILK, and citrus, the latter killed by the great freeze of 1835. When London prices soared to a half-guinea the pound, Sea Island cotton, with its magnificent bolls of long, silky staples, prospered along the Georgia coast. But more devastating than an occasional hurricane was the destruction wrought by the Civil War. Mansions and their fields were left in ruins. This melancholy landscape changed as northern resort owners encouraged tourists and invalids to winter among the Sea Islands.

A growing consciousness of their intrinsic value as wilderness completes a cycle that began when CREEK INDIANS reserved them in treaties for special hunting purposes. Today parks have been established, such as those on Cumberland, Sapelo, and Wassaw Islands, where one can enjoy beauty unequaled elsewhere in the South.

See T. R. Reese, *First Visit in America* (1974); C. C. Lovell, *Golden Isles of Georgia* (1933); and J. Cerruti, *National Geographic* (March, 1971).

ALAN K. CRAIG
Florida Atlantic University

SECESSION was the pivotal political event of southern history. The taproot of secession ran back to the seventeenth century, when slavery became well established both in practice and in law. As a system of labor and of racial accommodation, slavery was central to both the economy and the society of the Old South. Less deeply rooted but more venerated was the South's participation in the American Revolution and the government of the new nation. At first there was little conflict between the South's dual heritage of slavery and the Revolution: in 1790 slavery existed in every state in the Union except Vermont and Massachusetts, and southerners were prominent among the nation's most revered leaders. But from the beginning there was anxiety about how the powers of the federal government might be used against southern interests. From that anxiety arose the idea of secession as the ultimate protection from a hostile central government.

For most of the antebellum period, secession was not an actual strategy to disrupt the Union but was instead a political threat designed to preserve the Union on terms acceptable to the South. The threat of secession was the political specie that legitimated the currency of STATES' RIGHTS principles. ANTI-FEDERALISTS like PATRICK HENRY and GEORGE MASON warned of the dangers of a minority South in a centralized government. Their warnings were echoed by many, including JOHN TAYLOR of Caroline, who flirted with secession as a response to the Alien and Sedition Acts. Although Thomas Jefferson's Kentucky Resolutions did not match James Madison's Virginia Resolutions (VIRGINIA AND KENTUCKY RESOLUTIONS) in coupling an insistence on NULLIFICATION of the partisan acts with professions of fervent unionism, Jefferson opposed talk of secession, admonishing Taylor, "If on a temporary superiority of the one party, the other is to resort to a scission of the Union, no federal government can ever exist."

When southern interests ran parallel to federal policy, states' rights principles were conveniently ignored, as they were for example both in 1817, when JOHN C. CALHOUN supported congressional expenditures for internal improvements, announcing that "he was no advocate for refined arguments on the Constitution," and in the 1850s, when southerners protested the personal liberty laws passed by northern states in response to the federal FUGITIVE SLAVE LAW of 1850. THOMAS COOPER put it precisely when he prophesied in 1827 that "we shall 'ere long be compelled to calculate the value of the union; and to enquire of what use to us is this most unequal alliance." For most southerners, including all but the most extreme southern rights spokesmen, the calculation was sufficiently in favor of the Union that as late as the presidential ELECTION OF 1860 the term "secessionist" was considered an epithet, even by many JOHN C. BRECKINRIDGE Democrats.

As the South became a minority section in population and as federal policy diverged or threatened to diverge from what many southerners perceived to be the "use" of the Union to them, the value of the Union entered political calculations in the red. South Carolina made the first official threat to secede in the ordinance of nullification (November 24, 1832). But congressional mandates for both the FORCE BILL OF 1833 and a reduced TARIFF schedule, coupled with the repudiation of South Carolina's action by the other southern states, killed nullification and outlined the vital considerations in translating secession from a threat into an accomplished fact.

First, federal military coercion was the counterthreat to secession. Second, compromise on policy issues might make secession unnecessary. Calhoun, in his *Disquisition on Government*, advocated the concurrent majority—a southern veto on federal action—as the sole guarantee of compromise acceptable to all sections. Although nullification had proved that state action was at best a cumbersome and inconclusive mechanism, the South did achieve the resemblance of an operational concurrent voice through the Democratic party, by means of the two-thirds rule in presidential nominating conventions (adopted in 1832) and the party's influence on the organization and action or inaction of Congress. Southern response to the COMPROMISE OF 1850 demonstrated both the impotence of secession in the face of compromise and, as the GEORGIA PLATFORM put it, the necessity of the compromise to prevent secession.

The third vital matter in accomplishing rather than merely threatening secession was overcoming the division within the South. In 1860–1861, only the seven Lower South states responded to Abraham Lincoln's election with ordinances of secession (South Carolina, December 20, 1860; Mississippi, January 9, 1861; Florida, January 10; Alabama, January 11; Georgia, January 19; Louisiana, January 26; Texas, February 1). The eight border states stayed in the Union, four of them permanently (Delaware, Kentucky, Maryland, Missouri). The seceding border states were satisfied to hope for compromise, until Lincoln's call for troops in response to the firing on Ft. Sumter made clear that he would not compromise on coercion, and then they took their stand with the Confederacy (Virginia, April 17; Arkansas, May 6; Tennessee, May 7; North Carolina, May 20). Divisions among the states were matched by disunity within the states. In the Lower South, the 113,785 voters for state convention candidates who campaigned against immediate secession represented a 40 percent minority, a larger minority than the one that had elected Lincoln. In the border states, the majority opposed secession, at least until Lincoln's call for troops.

Although the reasons for secession have been debated since 1860, few now deny the importance of slavery. Whereas the Lower South contained 33 percent of the South's white population, the seceding border states 35 percent, and the remaining border states 32 percent, the respective proportions of slaveholders were 47 percent, 31 percent, and 22 percent, of those with ten or more slaves were 58 percent, 31 percent, and 12 percent, and of slaves were 59 percent, 30 percent, and 11 percent. Whereas the South's minority position within the Union helps explain why secession was a remedy for threats to slavery, only the governing power of the slaveholding minority within the South can explain how secession was achieved. The divisions within the South disclosed both the potency of the heritage of the American Revolution and the deep ambiguity about whether one had to be a secessionist to remain a southerner: Was slavery worth disunion? Or was the Union worth threats to slavery? The greater the interest in slavery, the more unsettling was the ambiguity and the more necessary was secession.

See, for interpretive synthesis, D. L. Dumond, *Secession Movement* (1931); U. B. Phillips, *Course of South to Secession* (1939); C. S. Sydnor, *Development of Southern Sectionalism* (1948, 1968), 1968 ed. has updated bibliography; A. O. Craven, *Growth of Southern Nationalism* (1953); C. Eaton, *Growth of Southern Civilization* (1961); W. Barney, *Road to Secession* (1972); and D. M. Potter, *Impending Crisis* (1976). For historiography and bibliography, see T. J. Pressley, *Americans Interpret Their Civil War* (1954); C. E. Cauthen, with L. P. Jones, in A. S. Link and R. W. Patrick (eds.), *Writing Southern History* (1965); and D. M. Potter, *South and Sectional Conflict* (1968). Indispensable information and interpretations are in H. T. Shanks, *Secession Movement in Virginia* (1934); R. W. Shugg, *Origins of Class Struggle in Louisiana* (1939); R. A. Wooster, *Secession Conventions* (1962); G. H. Knoles (ed.), *Crisis of Union* (1965); E. D. Genovese, *Political Economy of Slavery* (1965) and *World Slaveholders Made* (1969); W. W. Freehling, *Prelude to Civil War* (1965), nullification, and *American Historical Review* (Feb., 1972); S. A. Channing, *Crisis of Fear* (1970), South Carolina; C. V. Woodward, *American Counterpoint* (1971); D. M. Potter, *South and Concurrent Majority* (1972); W. L. Barney, *Secessionist Impulse* (1974), Alabama, Mississippi; and C. N. Degler, *Other South* (1974), Unionists. For an unrivaled collection of documents, see G. H. Reese (ed.), *Proceedings of Virginia Convention of 1861* (4 vols.; 1965). See also biographies and papers of southerners of antebellum period.

MICHAEL P. JOHNSON
University of California, Irvine

SECOND GREAT AWAKENING. See GREAT AWAKENING, SECOND

SECTIONALISM. In 1858 Senator JAMES HAMMOND of South Carolina berated his northern colleagues: "The South have sustained you in a great measure. You are our factors. You fetch and carry for us." To Hammond, the South was a separate and self-sustaining community, and southern sec-

tionalism was the product and expression of that situation. In succeeding years, historians have taken Hammond and other antebellum southern leaders at their word. Frederick Jackson Turner called the South "one of the three great interests" of the nation.

There is, nevertheless, great danger in accepting the notion of a monolithic southern sectionalism. It is an example of what Daniel Boorstin has called "the error of homogenization." Recent students of southern history have been more explicit in their warnings. DAVID POTTER criticized the tempting but misleading "dualism" of an "agrarian rural South" pitted against an "urban, industrial North." C. VANN WOODWARD, reviewing WILBUR J. CASH's *The Mind of the South*, called for greater stress upon divergent southern localism. Cash's own up-country pinewoods Carolina freeholders little resembled the aristocratic planters of the Chesapeake or the harried entrepreneurs of the "black bottom" plantations, much less the craftsmen of Richmond and Baltimore or the field hands of the rice land swamps. Diversity of climate, local mores, and terrain nourished a thriving variety of regional cultures. Even during the Civil War, when Confederate administrators in Richmond strained every nerve to unify the South, dissident voices were heard in Alabama, Georgia, North Carolina, and elsewhere.

Yet, for all the real diversity of southern life and heterogeneity of southern opinion, southern sectionalism was a historical fact. In the past, historians and observers have generally attempted to find fundamental differences between the South and other regions and to build explanations of sectionalism upon these. At the beginning of the twentieth century, some scholars attributed the rise of sectionalism to the "cavalier" and "Puritan" origins of the Virginia and Massachusetts colonies. This is an oversimplification, for, as Governor William Berkeley of Virginia constantly complained, the Puritans were always a potent force in the southern settlements.

Other commentators have explained southern sectionalism as the consequence of a restrictive and repressive racism. Although it is true that southern SLAVE CODES were more brutal than northern slave laws and that southern race relations were always tense, the same elements of discrimination and anxiety existed throughout the United States. What is more, until the last three decades before the Civil War, almost as many voices were raised against slavery in the South as in the North.

Another group of historians has viewed sectionalism in the South as a product of the victimization of that region by other parts of the country. This argument parallels Hammond's thesis and may have its origins in the postwar memoirs of leaders like JEFFERSON DAVIS and ALEXANDER STEPHENS. Their coupling of southern sectionalism to northern economic imperialism, political partisanship, and narrow-mindedness reappears in portions of early twentieth-century Reconstruction and Civil War scholarship.

The external forces that would isolate and embitter the southern section were not unique to it. Throughout the new nation, a free, competitive, "atomistic" political and economic system replaced one based, at least in theory, on status and community control. Economic change, whipped onward by unregulated price, land-purchase, and fiscal structures, worried southern planters and exporters while leaving them progressively more dependent upon others to market their goods. The democratization of politics, altering election practices from a recognition of existing power relationships to a real and fierce competition for office, made every political contest the setting for high passions and inflammatory rhetoric. In this atmosphere of unregulated capitalism and unrestricted partisanship, it was not easy for southern leaders to distinguish real from fanciful dangers to southern strength. Psychological factors, including the fear of slave rebellions and anxiety over the future of their "peculiar institution" blended in southern minds with the more universal psychological pressures of rural isolation, premodern medical care, and frequent family separation. Real social and political conflicts acted as resonators of feared social and political unrest.

The way in which contests of real sectional differences could explode into contests of will over imagined insults to sectional pride can be seen in legislative confrontations like the famous Webster-Hayne Senate debates of 1829–1830. ROBERT Y. HAYNE entered the controversy over Augustus Foote's resolution to halt new western land sales as part of a carefully planned reconciliation of southern and western Jacksonian forces. Daniel Webster saw the danger of this political union to New England interests and protested against it. The Massachusetts senator's remarks aroused Hayne's anxiety, and the South Carolinian became defensive. Hayne's "reply" to Webster bristled with hostility and menace and ended with the threat of further southern NULLIFICATION. This oversensitivity and consequent overreaction to the cut and thrust of normal sectional rivalry explain the particular intensity of southern sectionalism. In the MISSOURI COMPROMISE and nullification crises, the GAG RULE debates, the Texas and Cali-

fornia questions, and the specter of BLEEDING KANSAS, manageable contests over sectional interests became almost uncontrollable episodes of sectional paranoia.

Southern congressional leaders' anger and fear genuinely represented the feelings of many of their constituents. The life of the South was slavery. The perpetuation of slavery required new lands, and these must be found in the western territories. Every planter and would-be planter who saw profit and status in the success of southern congressional land policy had the same emotional stake in sectionalism as the leaders of the South.

Defeat in the Civil War added new layers of situational and psychological debris to the ruins of sectional policy. Emotional sectionalism after the Civil War led to excesses in racism, political agitation, and social conservatism, which retarded reunification of the sections. At the same time, real sectional interest drew the South closer to the North. As southern leaders increasingly realized, the future of the South lay in INDUSTRIALIZATION, URBANIZATION, and intranational cooperation. In recent decades, situational and psychological forces have refashioned southern sectionalism into a regional variant of progressive nationalism.

See A. O. Craven, *Growth of Southern Nationalism* (1953); D. M. Potter, *South and Sectional Conflict* (1969); C. Sydnor, *Development of Southern Sectionalism* (1948); and C. V. Woodward, *Burden of Southern History* (1960), on southern sectionalism. C. N. Degler, *Other South* (1974); and E. Wilson, *Patriotic Gore* (1962), prove the South not monolithic in its opinion. Mind of South is discussed in J. Carpenter, *South as Conscious Minority* (1930); and W. Taylor, *Cavalier and Yankee* (1961). On nullification, see W. Freehling, *Prelude to Civil War* (1966). Webster-Hayne debate is traced in P. C. Hoffer, *Missouri Historical Review* (July, 1972). Valuable psychological insights are in S. Elkins, *Slavery* (1959).

PETER C. HOFFER
University of Georgia

SEDDON, JAMES ALEXANDER (1815–1880),

was born in Fredericksburg, Va. In Congress (1845–1847, 1849–1851) he advocated a political coalition of southern rights men, cursing the "bonds of party" that undermined sectional loyalty. He continued to exert political influence in Virginia between 1852 and 1861, when he emerged as a secessionist spokesman at the WASHINGTON PEACE CONFERENCE. A member of the Confederate Provisional Congress (1861), he was defeated in the congressional election of 1862.

In November, 1862, Seddon, a personal friend of President Jefferson Davis, was appointed secretary of war (1862–1865). Despite frail health he exercised considerable influence, often ordering military movements on his own responsibility; and his policy of emphasizing action in the western zone was frustrated only by the overcautious JOSEPH E. JOHNSTON. Seddon in November, 1864, refused to consider enlistment of black troops, contending it would undermine southern society. In 1865, when a congressional delegation from Virginia, hoping to rebuild southern morale, called for reorganization of the cabinet, he resigned. After the war he retired to agricultural pursuits at Sabot Hill.

See R. W. Patrick, *Jefferson Davis* (1964); J. B. Jones, *Rebel War Clerk's Diary* (1866); R. G. H. Kean, *Diary* (1957); *Official Records, Armies*, Ser. 1, Vols. VI, CXIII–CLIII, Ser. 2, Vols. II, III, V–VIII, Ser. 3, Vols. III–V, Ser. 4, Vols. I–III; and Garnett Family Papers, Virginia Historical Society Library.

GERALD SORIN
State University of New York, New Paltz

SEGREGATION, a complex system of laws and mores wherein caste distinctions are expressed in terms of physical distance, evolved in the South for many reasons—white anxieties and squeamishness, political opportunism, above all a white desire to subordinate Negroes through ostracism and public humiliation. Although segregation has been and remains a national phenomenon, only in the South did it develop into a virtually total system of racial control for such a prolonged period of time; only in the South did its defense become a "cardinal test" of regional identity.

Southern segregation was born long before the Civil War. It first appeared not on the plantations and farms, where a color line would have been an unnecessary nuisance, but in the antebellum cities and towns, where large communities of free Negroes and unusually independent slaves combined with white nonslaveholders and transients to create a society totally alien to the plantation tradition of rigid, personal racial control. Many urban whites were annoyed by unwelcomed contact with Negroes in public places and apprehensive about the dangers to slavery and white supremacy posed by interracial fraternization, especially in black bawdy houses and grog shops. Thus patchwork segregation systems made up of municipal ordinances, management policies, and customs began to emerge in such cities as New Orleans, Charleston, Savannah, Mobile, and Richmond. By 1860 most urban blacks were excluded from restaurants, saloons, hotels, and some public grounds and relegated to segregated sections in hospitals, theaters, cemeteries, jails, and public conveyances.

Emancipation created a stronger and more widespread desire to safeguard white supremacy by secondary means now that slavery was dead. The interlude between Confederate rule and the onset of Radical Reconstruction was too brief to permit formulation of a full-scale segregation system, but a beginning was made. Now that freedmen could legally learn to read and write, several legislatures enacted laws excluding Negroes from public schools. Florida, Texas, and Mississippi adopted measures excluding Negroes from first-class railroad coaches. Many municipalities wrote segregationist zoning, vocational, and public accommodations provisions into their local BLACK CODES.

Radical Reconstruction engendered the first serious attacks on segregation. Massive demonstrations by New Orleans Negroes in 1867 put an end to segregated streetcars there, a result soon duplicated in Richmond, Charleston, and Louisville. State laws forbidding segregated places of public accommodation were enacted in Mississippi, South Carolina, and Louisiana in 1868 and Florida in 1873. Racially segregated public schools were outlawed in South Carolina and Louisiana. A stubborn crusade for federal antisegregation legislation by Senator Charles Sumner of Massachusetts culminated in the CIVIL RIGHTS ACT OF 1875, which prohibited racial discrimination in hotels, theaters, conveyances, and other places of public accommodation. In practice, however, the challenge to the color line was much less spectacular. Several public schools in New Orleans were successfully integrated from 1870 to 1877, as was the University of South Carolina from 1873 to 1877, but school desegregation elsewhere was virtually nonexistent. Negroes were allowed to ride with whites on some railroads and steamboats, especially in the seaboard states, and black attempts to test the 1875 Civil Rights Act in theaters, restaurants, and taverns in New Orleans and some North Carolina communities were partially successful. On the whole, however, segregation survived relatively unscathed. Few Negroes asserted their legal rights, and most Radical governments tolerated or even encouraged de facto segregation in institutions under their control.

The threat to segregation eased considerably with the collapse of Reconstruction. The color line was quickly restored in the New Orleans schools and the University of South Carolina, many state desegregation laws were amended or voided, and new public institutions were born segregated. An 1881 Tennessee law required separate first-class seating for black railroad passengers. In general, however, the REDEEMER GOVERNMENTS did not rush to write segregation into their legal codes, for such a course would have been in direct violation of federal law. That barrier fell in 1883, when the U.S. Supreme Court invalidated the 1875 Civil Rights Act in the CIVIL RIGHTS CASES. In 1887 Florida enacted a JIM CROW law requiring "separate but equal" railroad accommodations, an edict duplicated by Mississippi in 1888 and Texas in 1889. After the Supreme Court upheld the Mississippi law in 1890, six other states enacted similar measures within a year. A challenge to the Louisiana law led to the infamous PLESSY V. FERGUSON ruling in 1896, in which the Court sanctified separate but equal as the law of the land.

The *Plessy* decree inspired an epidemic of Jim Crow legislation in the South. All public transportation and depots were segregated by state law, as were most mental hospitals, prisons, homes for the handicapped and the aged, and other state institutions. Municipalities adopted ordinances segregating parks, auditoriums, jails, cemeteries, even neighborhoods. Businesses, with or without legal mandate, improvised their own Jim Crow policies. Little signs reading Whites Only and Colored decorated drinking fountains, toilets, ticket windows, and doors to restaurants and saloons. The code encompassed bawdy houses in New Orleans, telephone booths in Oklahoma, and courtroom Bibles in Atlanta. By the time the nation went to war in 1917 to make the world safe for democracy, Jim Crow had developed into an enormously thorough system that governed Negroes in nearly every public place. After World War I Jim Crow simply kept up with technological and social change, expanding into such facilities as buses and bus depots, taxicabs, ambulances, air terminals, swimming pools, and soda fountains.

This Jim Crow mania developed when it did for several reasons. The tensions created by economic depression and the epic political wars of the 1890s, the helplessness of the newly disfranchised Negroes, the sheer political opportunism of such race-baiting demagogues as PITCHFORK TILLMAN of South Carolina and JAMES K. VARDAMAN of Mississippi, and a rising tide of ethnic intolerance outside the South each played an important part. The paramount factor, however, the *sine qua non* of Jim Crow's dramatic proliferation was simply that a majority of white southerners at long last had official permission to indulge their urge to subordinate and humiliate Negroes through constant reminders of their MUDSILL status. Despite the separate but equal litany of the laws, the slightest trace of equality (or even true separation in some cases) would have negated their basic intent. Thus Negroes rode in the rear of buses, drank from rusted spigots a few inches away from

spotless ones for whites, and buried their dead in weedy, overgrown plots usually separated from neatly trimmed white ones by only a hedge or picket fence. Often Negroes were denied even separate facilities, especially in business establishments, where black restrooms, fitting rooms, and lunch counter sections were uncommon.

Like slavery before it, segregation won the support of most of the South's most eminent intellectual and spiritual leaders. Scientists like Robert Bennett Bean, James Bardin, and Nathan Shaler proclaimed Jim Crow in tune with the laws of nature. Historian PHILIP ALEXANDER BRUCE described it as a manifestation of "the instinct of race preservation." Charles B. Galloway, William Montgomery Brown, and other churchmen practically transformed it into an eleventh commandment. In the process, segregation gradually acquired a symbolic importance to southern whites, which transformed it in their minds from a petty code of caste elitism into a hallowed symbol of the "southern way."

All the while, Jim Crow was developing into a symbol of great significance to black southerners as well. MARTIN LUTHER KING, JR., never forgot a shoe clerk's refusal to wait on him "up front" when he was a child, nor did James Meredith ever forget the humiliation of being moved to a Jim Crow car when the train he was riding home from Detroit reached Memphis. For them and millions more, all racial injustice came to be symbolized by the despised Whites Only signs. When the CIVIL RIGHTS MOVEMENT developed during the 1950s and 1960s, the death of Jim Crow became its first priority. Black children braved mob disorders and "massive resistance" in Little Rock, New Orleans, and elsewhere to put into practice the Supreme Court's epic 1954 ban on separate but equal public schools (BROWN V. BOARD OF EDUCATION). The color line in southern colleges crumbled with a night of terror in Mississippi in 1962 and a faintly absurd "stand in the schoolhouse door" in Alabama ten months later. Jim Crow public accommodations, weakened by a bus boycott in Montgomery, Freedom Rides through the Deep South, and sit-ins nearly everywhere, were finally doomed by the landmark CIVIL RIGHTS ACT OF 1964. Similar changes have taken place, quietly and peacefully for the most part, at hiring windows throughout the South. Dead as a legal precept and dying, however slowly and grudgingly, as a de facto denominator of caste, Jim Crow appears destined to join slavery and the LYNCHING bee as unlamented relics of the southern past.

See C. V. Woodward, *Strange Career of Jim Crow* (1974); I. A. Newby, *Jim Crow's Defense* (1965) and (ed.), *Devel-*

opment of Segregationist Thought (1968); J. Williamson, *After Slavery* (1965) and (ed.), *Origins of Segregation* (1968); G. Myrdal, *American Dilemma* (1944); R. C. Wade, *Slavery in Cities* (1964); L. J. Friedman, *White Savage* (1970); C. H. Nolen, *Negro's Image in South* (1967); L. R. Harlan, *Separate and Unequal* (1958) and *American Historical Review* (April, 1962); O. H. Olsen (ed.), *Thin Disguise* (1967); C. E. Wynes, *Race Relations in Virginia* (1961); F. A. Logan, *Negro in North Carolina* (1964); D. W. Doyle, *Etiquette of Race Relations in South* (1937); B. A. Glasrud, *American Studies* (Spring, 1974); and R. A. Fischer, *Segregation Struggle in Louisiana* (1974), *American Historical Review* (Feb., 1969), and *Journal of Negro History* (July, 1968).

ROGER A. FISCHER
University of Minnesota, Duluth

SELMA, ALA. (pop. 27,379), on the Alabama River, is approximately 40 miles west of Montgomery. Although the site was visited by HERNANDO DE SOTO in 1540 and by SIEUR DE BIENVILLE in 1702, it remained unsettled until after the War of 1812 when it was developed by a land company headed by WILLIAM RUFUS KING. During the town's first two decades, it served primarily as a market for area cotton growers. In 1848 two occurrences significantly altered the course of the town's development: construction of the Alabama & Tennessee Railway; and the arrival of a colony of 300 skilled German ironworkers. Selma quickly became one of the region's principal producers of iron and cast-iron products, including guns. During the Civil War, the city was an important source of munitions and a Confederate supply depot. Captured by Union forces in 1865, the town was largely destroyed, although some antebellum homes survive to this day. Genuine economic recovery had to wait until the introduction of livestock and dairy farming at the turn of the century. In addition to being an agricultural market, modern Selma produces farm machinery, lawn mowers, and paper and textile products. It also benefits from the presence of nearby Craig Air Force Base (1941) with its U.S. Air Force Special Staff School.

See W. M. Jackson, *Story of Selma* (1954); J. Hardy, *Selma* (1879); E. Layton, *Alabama Review* (April, 1966), Confederate arsenal, 1862–65; and files of *Times-Journal* (1827–).

SEMINOLE INDIANS and Mikasuki Indians began to enter Florida from northward about 1730, and in a century there were 5,000 of them there. They lived in scattered bands, some of whom spoke Muskogee and some Mikasuki, but all were of the CREEK culture. When Florida passed from Spain to the United States, the Indians, unconsulted, passed with it. Almost at once, the United

States sought to expel these people. Three SEMINOLE WARS and numberless nameless encounters finally in 1858 reduced the Florida Indian population to about 125. Most of them had been shipped to Indian Territory. The remainder kept out of sight in the EVERGLADES.

About 1878 America began to rediscover the Florida Indians, and various agencies commenced to set land aside for them. Therefore, as of 1975 the United States held 106,500 acres and the state of Florida another 76,000 in trust for them. There are five federal reservations, but the state trust lands are practically unoccupied. The United States assumed it had to use Christianity and education to rescue these people from savagery. Soon many missionaries appeared to convert them, but only Seminole Baptists from Oklahoma were especially successful. A few of the Mikasuki cling to their traditional religion, centering around the annual green corn dance. The earliest efforts to educate the Florida Indians, white style, began in the 1870s. But due to Indian resistance it was 1927 before the first day school was established, and even after a century only a very tiny number of them had been graduated from high school and even fewer from college. As of 1975 the numbers are rising.

Until the 1930s the Indians sustained themselves by hunting and gardening. They got cash from selling alligator hides and egret plumes. White encroachment enforced changes. By 1913 part of the Everglades was drained, and by 1928 the Tamiami Trail had been cut through their hunting grounds. Killing of egrets and alligators was outlawed, and Everglades National Park was established in 1947. One alternative they could turn to was cattle culture beginning in the 1930s, but few families have made their entire living at that. The cattle, although owned by individuals, are managed in tribal herds and pastured on reservation land. Indians not raising cattle work for white employers in agriculture, as cowboys, as truck and tractor drivers, and a few as factory hands. Others make and sell Indian craftwork, and others still are employed by the tribes or by the Bureau of Indian Affairs. Less than 10 percent depend on welfare, but in 1970 60 percent of the families had incomes below $3,000 per year.

Traditionally men led, but hereditary rights to leadership passed through women, and married men lived among their wives' clans. In 1957, prodded by the BIA, part of the Florida Indians adopted a constitution and constituted themselves the Seminole Tribe of Florida. They elected a chairman and a tribal council. Also they incorporated and elected a president and a board of managers for their economic enterprises. The corporation strives to multiply the economic options open to their people. In all their governing bodies, women are involved. In 1962 the BIA approved a second constitution, which brought into being the Mikasuki Tribe of Florida. It occupies a small federal reservation along the Tamiami Trail and has access to 76,000 acres of state trust land. Three-quarters of the Florida Indians speak Mikasuki, but no more than 400 of them are in the Mikasuki tribe. The others either belong to the Seminole tribe or are unaffiliated. Seminole and Mikasuki have increased from 125 in 1858 to about 2,000 in 1975.

See C. H. Fairbanks, *Florida Seminole People* (1973); I. M. Peithman, *Unconquered Seminole Indians* (1957); W. T. Neill, *Florida's Seminole Indians* (1952); E. C. McReynolds, *Seminoles* (1957); and M. S. Garbarino, *Big Cypress* (1972).

JOHN K. MAHON
University of Florida

SEMINOLE WARS.

On November 21, 1817, a U.S. force of 250 men destroyed a Mikasuki village in southwestern Georgia. The Indians withdrew into Spanish Florida, but in January, 1818, the Monroe administration ordered ANDREW JACKSON to punish them. By April, Jackson had conquered the Indians west of the Suwannee River and a couple of Spanish towns besides.

As a result of this, the First Seminole War, Spain ceded Florida to the United States in 1821. The next year the United States sought to press the Indians into a reservation. When this failed, it planned to remove them to Indian Territory. Indian resistance to removal became the Second Seminole War (1835–1842), a confrontation between European and Indian (guerrilla) methods of warfare. Indian resistance lost coordination when the leader OSCEOLA was captured under a flag of truce on October 21, 1837. Gradually U.S. generals changed their tactics in favor of small detachments that relentlessly pursued the foe into remote places. Finally, when less than 300 Indians were left in Florida in August, 1842, the United States called off the fight. There was no formal surrender, no treaty ending the war, and the remnant of Indians slipped back into the EVERGLADES out of sight.

Because Florida still wanted to get rid of its Indians, U.S. Army detachments once more began to penetrate the Indian hideouts. This produced confrontations and finally an attack by 35 warriors on December 20, 1855, led by Billy Bowlegs. The Third Seminole War was under way. In it about 120 warriors were pitted against 800 regular soldiers and 1,300 volunteers. Systematically, small detachments ferreted out the Indians, until most had come into Ft. Myers by March 15, 1858, and agreed to be shipped west. Now no more than 125 of the first Americans remained in Florida.

See C. R. Paine, "Seminole War of 1817–1818" (M.A. thesis, University of Oklahoma, 1938), fullest account; R. W. Patrick, *Duncan L. Clinch* (1963); J. K. Mahon, *History of Second Seminole War* (1965); and J. T. Sprague, *Florida War* (1848, 1964). J. D. Covington, Tampa University, has written unpublished account of Third Seminole War.

JOHN K. MAHON
University of Florida

SEMMES, RAPHAEL

(1809–1877), was born near Piscataway, Charles County, Md. Appointed a midshipman in the U.S. Navy in 1826, he had a relatively uneventful career of almost 35 years. While on extended leave, Semmes read law in his brother's law office and was admitted to the bar in the 1830s. His legal training became extremely useful later in handling the complicated international problems encountered in the cruises of the *Sumter* and *Alabama*. In 1845 he established his home in Alabama, moving in 1849 to Mobile, where he practiced law until recalled by the navy to duty as a lighthouse inspector (1856). In 1858 he was made secretary of the Lighthouse Board in Washington and board member in 1861.

He resigned as a commander, U.S.N., on February 15, 1861, and was commissioned the same rank in the Confederate navy on March 26, 1861. Converting the steam packet *Havana* into the CSS *Sumter*, he sailed on June 30, 1861, to prey upon northern shipping. In six months the *Sumter* captured 18 ships and caused consternation among northern shippers. Blockaded in Gibraltar, it was decommissioned in April, 1862. Semmes then placed in commission a new English-built commerce raider on August 24, 1862, the CSS *Alabama*. In 22 months it cruised 67,000 miles and checked 447 vessels. It captured 66 ships with a combined value of over $5.1 million and fought but two battles, both by choice. The *Alabama* sunk the USS *Hatteras* off Galveston on January 11, 1863, but was in turn sunk by the USS *Kearsarge* off Cherbourg, France, on June 19, 1864. Service on the *Sumter* brought Semmes a meritorious promotion to captain; that on the *Alabama*, rear admiral. Returning to the Confederacy in January, 1865, he commanded the James River Squadron and his naval brigade, organized from his crews, surrendered on April 26, 1865.

Semmes's attempt to lead a peaceful civilian

postwar life was interrupted on December 15, 1865, when he was arrested and taken to Washington. He was held in confinement, without formal charges, until released without explanation or apology on April 7, 1866. After working as a teacher and an editor, he devoted himself to writing, lecturing, and teaching law in Mobile. Semmes left a legacy of a successful career as a commerce raider that stands as a milestone in the history of naval warfare.

See R. Semmes, *Service Afloat* (1851) and *Memoirs of Service Afloat* (1869); R. T. Semmes, *Semmes and Allied Families* (1918); W. A. Roberts, *Semmes* (1938); C. G. Summersell, *Cruise of Sumter* (1865) and *Journal of G. T. Fullam* (1973); G. T. Scharf, *History of C.S.N.* (1887); and E. Bethel, *Journal of Southern History* (Nov., 1956).

RALPH W. DONNELLY
Division of History and Museums, U.S. Marine Corps

SEMPLE, ELLEN CHURCHILL (1863–1932), geographer, was born in Louisville, Ky. After graduating from Vassar (A.B., 1882; M.A., 1891), she studied geography at the University of Leipzig (1891–1892, 1895) with Friedrich Ratzel, a pioneer in anthropogeography (human geography). Semple introduced anthropogeography into the United States through her writing and her teaching as an occasional lecturer at the University of Chicago (1906–1924) and as a professor at Clark University (1921–1932). In both mediums she was highly skilled and effective and, in recognition of her accomplishments, was elected president of the Association of American Geographers in 1921, the only woman to have held that office. Three of Semple's many writings have southern settings. Two focus on cities: Louisville, in the *Journal of School Geography* (1900) and St. Louis, in the *Journal of Geography* (June, 1904). The third study, "The Anglo-Saxons of the Kentucky Mountains," *Geographical Journal* (June, 1901), is an example of explanatory human geography based on field observation and inquiry and of inference from postulated theory; it has become a classic in the geographical literature.

See *Notable American Women, 1607–1950* (1971).

ALLEN D. BUSHONG
University of South Carolina

SETON, ELIZABETH ANN BAYLEY (1774–1821), was a daughter of Dr. Richard Bayley, pioneer surgeon of New York City. In 1794 she married William Magee Seton of the New York mercantile firm Seton-Curson. Cooperating with Isabella Marshall Graham in 1797 to found the So-ciety for the Relief of Poor Widows with Small Children, Mrs. Seton served as its treasurer until 1803. After the death of her husband (1803), she tried to support her children by boarding pupils at St. Mark's School, but her conversion to Catholicism reduced her clientele rapidly. In 1808 she left New York for Baltimore to open a school for young gentlewomen. In 1809 she took religious vows and removed both her school and infant community, the Sisters of Charity of St. Joseph, to Emmitsburg, Md. There in 1810 she opened a free school for local children, which tradition labels the foundation of parochial school education in the United States. In 1975 Pope Paul VI proclaimed her Saint Elizabeth Ann Seton, whose feast day on the liturgical calendar commemorates her death on January 4, 1821.

See J. I. Dirvin, *Mrs. Seton* (1962); A. M. Melville, *Elizabeth Bayley Seton* (1951); and C. I. White, *Mother Seton* (1949).

ANNABELLE M. MELVILLE
Bridgewater State College

SETON, ERNEST THOMPSON (1860–1946), was born in England, moved to Canada as a child, and lived for many years in Connecticut. Trained as an artist, he was most successful with his evocative field sketches. He developed into a naturalist and Indian authority as a result of years of fieldwork in the South, Southwest, and Canada. Although his dramatic animal stories were criticized by some as anthropomorphic, his *Life Histories of Northern Animals* (1909) and *Lives of Game Animals* (1925–1928) are regarded as classics of popular scientific writing. Seton helped found several organizations for boys, including the Boy Scouts of America (1910). He became an American citizen in 1930. He operated the College of Indian Wisdom in New Mexico and lectured widely until his death.

See E. T. Seton, *Trail of Artist Naturalist* (1940), autobiography; F. A. Wiley (ed.), *E. T. Seton's America* (1954); and J. H. Wadland, *Ernest Thompson Seton* (1978).

KEIR B. STERLING
Pace University

SEVEN DAYS' BATTLES (June 25–July 1, 1862) represent the last phase of George B. McClellan's PENINSULAR CAMPAIGN of 1862. Having fought a drawn battle with the Confederates at SEVEN PINES, where southern General JOE JOHNSTON was wounded, McClellan withdrew in the general direction of the federal base on the York River. ROBERT E. LEE, who had replaced Johnston, pursued McClellan, hoping to catch the federals as they lay astride the Chickahominy. On June 25 at OAK GROVE and again on June 26 at MECHANICS-VILLE, Lee was unable to beat McClellan's adroit maneuvering, and the Confederates suffered heavy casualties in their attacks. After STONEWALL JACKSON finally came up in support of Lee, the Confederates moved to assault the new federal position at GAINES' MILL (June 27–28). Unfortunately for Lee, Jackson was unable to get his men off in time, and the full force of the assault was not felt until late afternoon of the first day. By that time McClellan had masterfully strengthened his positions so that the Confederates were thrown back on the second day with 8,751 casualties. Mc-Clellan's army lost 6,837 in killed, wounded, and missing. The battle of Garnett's and Golding's farms (June 27–28) was of relatively minor importance, but at SAVAGE STATION the two armies met again, with McClellan leaving 2,500 sick and wounded federals behind in his retreat. Lee hammered McClellan into retreat again at WHITE OAK SWAMP on June 30, but on July 1 McClellan fought savagely in the hardest contest of the seven days' battles. This last, at MALVERN HILL, brought about mutual withdrawal—Lee to Richmond and Mc-Clellan to the banks of the James River. Lee came out of the fighting with an enhanced reputation even though his handling of troops seemed to lack polish. McClellan, whose retreat was masterful, was given rough treatment by the Committee on the Conduct of the War. Approximate casualties were 20,614 Confederates and 15,849 federals.

See R. U. Johnson and C. C. Buel (eds.), *Battles and Leaders* (1888), II; D. S. Freeman, *R. E. Lee* (1934); and G. F. R. Henderson, *Stonewall Jackson* (1936).

VICTOR HICKEN
Western Illinois University

SEVEN PINES, BATTLE OF (May 31–June 1, 1862), also called the battle of Fair Oaks, took place in the PENINSULAR CAMPAIGN. JOSEPH E. JOHNSTON had withdrawn toward Richmond to protect the city. G. B. McClellan had arrived at a position on the Chickahominy River, about six miles from Richmond. Johnston hastily prepared the defenses of the city. Awaiting arrival of reinforcements, McClellan's III Corps and IV Corps (two-fifths of his army) established bridgeheads south of the river. Richmond was seriously threatened, and, when Johnston realized that Irvin McDowell's army was not joining McClellan but was being sent to the valley, he attacked E. D. Keyes's IV Corps on May 31. The Union forces holding the bridgeheads would have soon been in serious trouble if E. V. Sumner, acting with dis-patch, had not ordered John Sedgwick's division of the II Corps to cross the river to assist Keyes. In the course of the battle, Johnston was seriously wounded and had to relinquish the command. The Union troops that remained north of the river saw no action, partly because heavy rains made crossing the swollen river hazardous. Ths Confederates suffered from delay in making the attack and confusion in executing their plans. JAMES LONGSTREET renewed the attack the next day. On that day ROBERT E. LEE arrived to take command in the field, as did McClellan, who had been ill the first day of the battle. Both sides had failed to make the most of a superb opportunity. The Union army remained a few miles from Richmond. The Confederates had failed to dislodge it. The battle was largely a drawn one. And Lee's career had taken a significant new turn.

See D. S. Freeman, *Lee's Lieutenants* (1943), I, excellent; V. J. Esposito (ed.), *West Point Atlas of Civil War* (1962), excellent, technical; R. U. Johnson and C. C. Buel (eds.), *Battles and Leaders* (1888), II; D. S. Freeman, *R. E. Lee* (1934), II, excellent; G. B. McClellan, *McClellan's Own Story* (1887); and B. Catton, *Terrible Swift Sword* (1963).

DAVID M. SILVER
Butler University

SEVIER, JOHN (1745–1815), one of the founding fathers of Tennessee, was born near Harrisonburg, Va., in the Shenandoah Valley. He emerged as one of the leaders of the Watauga settlements (east Tennessee) in 1773 and represented them in the North Carolina assembly in 1776. Sevier gained fame as a military leader for his participation in the victory at KINGS MOUNTAIN in 1780, and he became a frontier hero for his successful expeditions against the CHEROKEE in the 1780s. In 1788 he launched his colorful political career, when he became governor of the state of FRANKLIN, a statehood movement in the east Tennessee area that failed. He subsequently was elected to the North Carolina senate (1789) and the U.S. House of Representatives (1789–1791) prior to his election as the first governor of Tennessee in 1796. He served as governor through 1801 and again from 1803 to 1809. He returned to Congress in 1811 and served until his death at Ft. Decatur, Ala., while surveying the Creek cession boundary.

See C. S. Driver, *John Sevier* (1932); S. C. Williams, *State of Franklin* (1933); J. Haywood, *History of Tennessee* (1823); and Sevier Papers, Tennessee State Archives, Nashville.

JAMES P. PATE
Livingston University

SEWANEE REVIEW (University of the South, Sewanee, Tenn. 37375) is the oldest literary quarterly in the United States. Founded by William Peterfield Trent in 1892, it now has a circulation of 3,750, including over 700 foreign subscriptions. It is published by the University of the South and is affiliated with the Council of Literary Magazines. In its early period (1892–1943), the *Review* was an academic journal devoted to the humanities in general. Since the editorship of ALLEN TATE (1944–1946) the magazine has been severely literary and critical, publishing short fiction, poetry, essays, essay reviews, and reviews. Tate's editorial procedures, which were formed partly on the examples of the *Southern Review* (First Series) and the *Kenyon Review*, are still largely in force. A few articles are devoted to southern subjects, but the quarterly is by no means regional. Major attention is given to British and American writers from 1500 to the present. The magazine pays its contributors $10 to $12 per printed page for prose and about $.60 per line for poetry.

See G. A. M. Janssens, *American Literary Review* (1968).

SHAKERS (United Society of Believers) were a religious and communal sect founded by a small band of dissident QUAKERS from England who migrated to New York in 1774, settling at Watervliet near Albany. The Shakers believed that Christ had returned a second time in the person of the charismatic leader Mother Ann Lee, who taught that through a life of self-denial, particularly celibacy, man could achieve a life free from sin. In two major missionary thrusts—one into New England (1780–1783), the second into the Ohio Valley (1805)—the Shakers laid the foundations for a communal system that by 1825 comprised about 4,000 inhabitants living in 18 sequestered villages. Two communities, Pleasant Hill near Harrodsburg and South Union near Russellville, were in Kentucky.

To meet the temporal and spiritual needs of a sect practicing community of goods, separation from the world, celibacy, and auricular confession of sins—Shakerism's four cardinal tenets—the Believers developed a thoroughgoing organization of community life known as the "Gospel order." The basic social and economic unit was the "family," a celibate group of approximately 50 to 150 members. Reflecting the Shakers' belief in the dual sexuality of the godhead, each family was governed by elders and eldresses and economic affairs were handled by a parallel deaconate.

The Shakers refused to participate in political life, though their thoroughgoing pacifism many times brought them into conflict with civil authorities. Woman's equality was, of course, total; and the Shakers, ever receptive to reformist currents outside their sequestered villages, adopted prohibition, took up various medical fads, embraced dietary reforms, and practiced Negro emancipation. Both Kentucky communities had black members, whose freedom usually was purchased after they had adopted the Shaker faith. But the Shakers' real impact on contemporary life was their primacy in the development and transmission of a communitarian tradition. By 1900 most Shaker communities were in collapse, though a few continued into the twentieth century.

See E. D. Andrews, *People Called Shakers* (1953), still standard; S. Parsons, in D. D. Egbert and S. Parsons (eds.), *Socialism in American Life* (2 vols.; 1952), I; manuscript collections of Western Reserve Historical Society and Library of Congress; J. Neal, *Kentucky Shakers* (1977); and H. E. Cook, *Shaker Music* (1973).

F. G. HAM
State Historical Society of Wisconsin

SHAPE-NOTE SONGBOOKS. George Pullen Jackson's comprehensive *White Spirituals in the Southern Uplands* (1933), the story of "the fasola folk, their songs, singings, and 'buckwheat notes,'" described a significant movement in southern history and folk life almost overlooked until that time. Subsequent research has revealed a colorful musical tradition of remarkable duration and persistence extending from Virginia to Missouri and Texas and including at one time virtually all the states of the Deep South (MUSIC).

The books of religious folk song, which created a tradition of plain-folk group and community singing, had their origin in the singing-school movement of New England in the late 1800s and of the South and West in the early 1900s. Traveling singing masters, carrying shape-note tune books like *Kentucky Harmony* (1816) and *Missouri Harmony* (1820), taught rural songsters to read music by *fa, sol, la,* and *mi* (and later the *do, re, mi* seven syllables), the syllables linked with the shaped noteheads that indicated pitch. The pupils, who then sang the syllables to get the tune in mind, thus acquired a repertory of standard songs including folk hymns, early American fuguing tunes and anthems, and eventually revival choruses. The songs, almost as many in minor key as in major, were in three- or four-part "dispersed harmony"—each part on a separate staff. Although put to sacred texts, many of the tunes were secular folk airs now "spiritualized," like the famous "Wondrous Love," and thus were often modal.

In their heyday in the mid–nineteenth century, books like the *Sacred Harp* (1844) by Georgians B. F. White and E. J. King and the *Southern Harmony* (1835) by South Carolinian William Walker started nondenominational singings and "conventions" at country churches and county courthouses, where hundreds of participants sat around an open square, divided by harmonic part, and sang without instrumental accompaniment "Amazing Grace," "Northfield," and other favorite tunes. Although these "white spirituals" derived from the predominantly Scotch-Irish, English, and German folk who settled the upland stretches of the Southeast, the *Sacred Harp*, the most durable of the four-shape hymnbooks, was also cherished by groups of black singers in Alabama, Florida, Mississippi, and Texas.

Prior to 1900, instrumental music became generally available, and the shape-note hymnals began to fade. The open harmony of the old songs, with each part given melodic interest, gave way to close harmony. Soon replacing the oblong tune books were thin, manila-backed collections of seven-shape gospel songs, increasingly influenced by jazz, ragtime, and popular secular music. For decades these "little books" were distributed widely throughout the South by such notable names as Ruebush-Kieffer, Showalter, and Stamps-Baxter.

Although the old rural way of life and the era of all-day singing with dinner on the grounds appear threatened, a few old-time tune books, along with some gospel song publications, have survived. The *New Harp of Columbia* is still used in eastern Tennessee, and the *New Harmonia Sacra* is used in Mennonite churches in the Shenandoah Valley of Virginia. The active life of the *Southern Harmony* appears almost over, but singings from the *Christian Harmony*, Walker's 1866 seven-shape compilation, number in the hundreds each year across Mississippi, Alabama, Georgia, and the Carolinas. And, in a vigorous style of singing that has not changed appreciably in over a century, the *Sacred Harp* is used for approximately 700 annual singing assemblies from Georgia to Texas.

See G. P. Jackson, *Story of Sacred Harp* (1944), *White and Negro Spirituals* (1943), and *Spiritual Folk-Songs* (1937); B. E. Cobb, *Sacred Harp* (1977); and D. D. Horn, *Sing to Me of Heaven* (1970), for technical analysis of music.

BUELL E. COBB, JR.
West Georgia College

SHARECROPPING was one of several types of farm tenancy that developed in the South and

helped produce a rigidly stratified social and economic class system. The cash tenant, at the top of the tenancy structure, was not markedly different from any other tenant who rented from a homeowner (TENANT FARMING). Out of his crop each year, he usually paid a specific amount of rent for the use of the land. He owned his own farm equipment and was but a step from actual farm ownership. The share tenant, immediately below him in status, also owned most of his implements and paid a share of the crop for any remaining supplies he got from the landlord. The sharecropper, however, owned nothing. Since the landlord provided everything—including credit and a subsistence "furnish" of food and household needs in advance of the crop—the sharecropper was totally dependent upon him. At the bottom of the tenancy ladder, the cropper therefore was in fact more a hired laborer, receiving payment in kind, than a farm tenant.

Although not exclusively confined to blacks, sharecropping came to be closely identified with Negroes living in the South after the Civil War, when many freed slaves simply exchanged one form of bondage for another. Without land, money, or credit, most newly freed blacks could do little else except become sharecroppers. Whether he was black or white, the lot of the cropper was indeed bleak. At best, the sharecropping system was a paternalistic one, since most poor croppers were illiterate and at the mercy of landlords from the start. More often than not, there was no written contract and rates charged for the furnish by plantation commissaries were usurious. When "settling time" came, the landlord, who always made the calculations (often, the croppers charged, with a "crooked pencil"), frequently informed his cropper that after all payments and deductions were accounted for, he had simply broken even. Unable to maintain himself until the next crop was gathered, the cropper would have to get another credit advancement and—most important—remain in debt while the entire process was repeated the next year. This meant that only rarely was the cropper able to get sufficiently ahead to break out of the system. Thus sharecropping, in a real sense, was little more than debt PEONAGE.

Although this sharecropping arrangement frequently has been described as a semifeudal system, the sharecropper enjoyed little of the reciprocal obligations associated with feudalism. When the price of farm goods was low or the crop risk great, the planter favored the sharecropper method and thus shared with his cropper half the risk of a possible loss. Conversely, when the price of goods was high and its return assured, the planter switched to the cheaper form of day labor. Although vestiges of sharecropping remain even today, the large-scale system was virtually destroyed by farm mechanization and the NEW DEAL's farm program. By indirectly dispossessing many croppers, the AGRICULTURAL ADJUSTMENT ADMINISTRATION accelerated a process already taking place during the 1930s because of farm mechanization.

See J. Agee and W. Evans, *Let Us Now Praise Famous Men* (1960); D. Conrad, *Forgotten Farmers* (1965); H. Kester, *Revolt Among Sharecroppers* (1936); A. F. Raper, *Preface to Peasantry* (1936); and A. F. Raper and I. Reid, *Sharecroppers All* (1941).

LOUIS CANTOR
Indiana University, Ft. Wayne

SHARE OUR WEALTH was a program of income redistribution advocated by Louisiana's Democratic Senator HUEY P. LONG to combat the GREAT DEPRESSION and to further his presidential ambitions. Long formally announced his program in a radio address on February 23, 1934, though his Senate speeches had reflected its assumptions since 1932, as had his political activism in Louisiana since 1918. Long was an increasingly strident critic of Franklin Roosevelt's cautious NEW DEAL, and the Share Our Wealth program promised a radical redistribution rather than mere recovery. Long called for a capital levy on the inheritances and a tax on the income of millionaires to produce the revenue to guarantee a $5,000 homestead for every American family; a $2,000–3,000 guaranteed annual family income; monthly pensions for the elderly; veterans' bonuses; college scholarships; government regulation to limit the hours of labor; and government purchase and storage of agricultural surplus to balance farm supply with demand over time.

Economically, the plan was vulnerable to criticism that it was poorly thought through. It focused on money as the symbol of wealth rather than on the machinery that generates wealth, and its concentration on family wealth and taxation ignored the increasingly corporate evolution of American economic life. Ideologically, Long shunned the Socialist label and defended Share Our Wealth as a reform that would strengthen American capitalism. Politically, the program appealed so broadly across the socioeconomic spectrum of depressed America that by 1935 Long's chief organizer, Gerald L. K. Smith, claimed upward of 27,000 Share Our Wealth clubs containing 4.6 million members and a mailing list of 7.5 million. Club members paid no national dues and received free a pamphlet entitled *Share Our Wealth: Every Man a King*; a copy of Huey Long's autobiography, *Every Man a King*; and a subscription to Long's publicity journal, *American Progress*. Membership distribution was strikingly regional, however, clustering in the Gulf Coast South and the Upper Midwest. Long introduced a Senate bill embodying the principles of Share Our Wealth, but it stood little chance of passing and he made no effort to bring it to a vote, preferring to use it as leverage toward the presidential ELECTION OF 1936. But on September 8, 1935, Long was gunned down by an assassin and died two days later, taking with him his consuming ambition for the presidency, his populist dreams for the American poor, and the personal symbol without which Share Our Wealth disintegrated.

See A. P. Sindler, *Huey Long's Louisiana* (1956); and T. H. Williams, *Huey Long* (1969).

HUGH DAVIS GRAHAM
University of Maryland, Baltimore County

SHARKEY, WILLIAM LEWIS (1798–1873), was born in east Tennessee. At sixteen he fought with Andrew Jackson in the battle of NEW ORLEANS (1814). Soon after the war he settled in Warren County, Miss., where he studued law. In 1825 he moved to Vicksburg and soon was elected to the state house of representatives. In 1832 Sharkey was elected to the state supreme court, and his colleagues immediately chose him chief justice, a position he held until 1851, when he resigned to return to private practice. In 1850 he served as the moderate president of the NASHVILLE CONVENTION, and his influence contributed to the defeat of the southern rights' effort to use the body as a stepping-stone toward secession. As a Union Whig, he resisted secession and refused to aid the Confederate cause. Soon after the war Sharkey was appointed provisional governor of Mississippi with the task of implementing President Andrew Johnson's mild plan of Reconstruction. His success in reducing the authority of the federal army in the state and in restoring the political rights of the old citizens resulted in his selection to the U.S. Senate. Congress, however, in December, 1865, refused to seat Sharkey and other southern representatives. When the military Reconstruction laws were passed in 1867, Sharkey and ROBERT J. WALKER attempted unsuccessfully to obtain a U.S. Supreme Court injunction against their enforcement (MISSISSIPPI V. JOHNSON).

See J. F. H. Claiborne, *Mississippi* (1880); J. W. Garner, *Reconstruction in Mississippi* (1901); W. C. Harris, *Presidential Reconstruction in Mississippi* (1967); D.

Rowland, *Courts, Judges, and Lawyers of Mississippi* (1935); L. M. Hall, *Journal of Mississippi History* (Feb., 1965); R. A. McLemore (ed.), *History of Mississippi* (1973); and Governors' Records, LX–LXIV, Mississippi Department of Archives and History.

WILLIAM C. HARRIS
North Carolina State University

SHAWNEE INDIANS (from *Shawanogi*, southerners) were the most southerly Algonquian-speaking Indian tribe, known for their migratory habits. In the early historic period they were mainly in South Carolina, along the Savannah River opposite the site of Augusta, Ga. Another group was on the Cumberland River about the site of Nashville, Tenn. Because of the Yamassee War, part of the Carolina band, called Hathawekela, moved to Creek territory on the Tallapoosa in present Alabama in 1715 and remained there a century, closely allied to the CREEKS. Simultaneously, the Cumberland group was driven off by the CHEROKEE and CHICKASAW and gradually migrated to the north side of the Ohio River. Other Shawnee, pushed out of South Carolina by the CATAWBA, were living on Delaware lands in eastern Pennsylvania as early as 1678, but by 1756 all the Shawnee except those in Alabama were settled in present Ohio.

The Shawnee fought the English in the FRENCH AND INDIAN WAR and Pontiac's Rebellion (1756–1763) and again in DUNMORE'S WAR (1774). During the American Revolution, they attacked the Kentuckians, and in 1790–1794 they were, with the Miami Indians, the core of the alliance of Northwest tribes resisting white penetration of the Ohio country. After defeating expeditions led by Generals Josiah Harmar and Arthur St. Clair, they lost to Anthony Wayne at Fallen Timbers (near Toledo) August 20, 1794.

In 1793 one band of Shawnee, with Spanish permission, settled near Cape Girardeau, Mo., remaining until 1825, when they exchanged their reserve for another on the Kansas River. Other Shawnee settled in Indiana, where Tecumseh and his brother Tenskawatawa ("the Prophet") joined the Potawatomi at the mouth of Tippecanoe River. During the War of 1812 the Shawnee sided with Great Britain, until Tecumseh was killed in Canada, October 5, 1813.

The remaining Ohio Shawnee were gradually reduced to two reservations totaling 145 square miles at Wapakoneta and Hog Creek. In a treaty branded by the Quaker missionary Henry Harvey as fraudulent, these bands in 1831 ceded their lands in return for a portion of the Kansas reservation and for $13,000 for their improvements.

Meanwhile, part of the Missouri band had settled in Mexican Texas but was expelled by the Anglo-Texans in 1839. In 1845–1846 they were joined in Oklahoma by part of the Kansas group, all becoming known as Absentee Shawnee. The Eastern Shawnee, who had resided with the Seneca at Lewistown, Ohio, removed in 1832 to present Ottawa County, in northeastern Oklahoma. In 1854 part of the Kansas reservation was divided in severalty, and most of the remainder was sold to whites.

Although many Kansas Shawnee joined the Union army in the Civil War, there was mounting pressure for their expulsion. In 1869 they were offered citizenship in the Cherokee Nation, and more than 700 of them settled in eastern Oklahoma. The Absentee Shawnee settled on the Oklahoma Potawatomi reservation until their lands were divided in 1890. The Eastern and Absentee Shawnee are each incorporated under the Oklahoma Indian welfare act of 1936. The number of Oklahoma Shawnee was last reported (1930) as 1,161, of whom 35.5 percent were full bloods. They follow the same economic pursuits as whites, but some traditional activities are preserved.

See T. W. Alford, *Civilization* (1936); J. E. Clark, "Shawnee Migration," American Society of Ethnohistory meeting (Oct., 1974); W. A. Galloway, *Old Chillicothe* (1934); G. W. Harrington, *Shawnees in Kansas* (1937); H. Harvey, *History of Shawnee Indians* (1855); F. W. Hodge, *Handbook American Indians* (1910), II; and G. Tucker, *Tecumseh* (1956).

VIRGIL J. VOGEL
Truman College, City College of Chicago

SHEEP (*Ovis aries*) were first brought to North America in the sixteenth century. Sheep raising appeared to be ideally suited for early Americans bent on self-sufficiency. The most elementary technology allowed woolen fleece to be spun into yarn and woven into material for clothing and household furnishings. Surplus wool was sold or exchanged for needed items, and mutton provided a meat alternative in a rather monotonous diet.

Despite these advantages, the sheep population increased slowly in colonial America. Docile in nature, sheep had a difficult time surviving the harsh conditions faced by the early colonist. Wild dogs and wolves were frequent predators, and their attacks made sheep raising a risky business. As late as 1649 the colony of Virginia could report only 3,000 sheep. British policy also initially hampered the sheep industry. To protect the home market, Parliament passed legislation in 1699 that made it illegal to transport any wool or wool products outside the colonies. Ironically, however, a new policy in the form of a British embargo against the American colonies following the Boston Tea Party generated a boom in sheep raising. Virginia and Maryland in particular produced a surplus in wool for export to their neighbors.

Following the Revolutionary War, sheep were gradually introduced into new regions in the South. Commonly considered something of a luxury, the industry was perpetuated for the most part by "persons of estate," who were primarily interested in sheep for their wool. Mutton and lamb never became significant parts of the southerner's diet. The South's increasing dependence on one crop, cotton farming, during the nineteenth century further reduced the region's interest in sheep.

Even though sheep were never numerically significant in the South, efforts nevertheless were made at scientific breeding. The first sheep brought to America were of the Spanish Merino breed, noted for its dense, fine wool. Numerous crossbreedings with later sheep resulted in varieties of new sheep in America. Most notable of the new types was an American Merino, also known as the Vermont, which found wide acceptance in Maryland, Virginia, Kentucky, Tennessee, and the Carolinas in the first two decades of the nineteenth century. By the 1840s a French breed, the Rambouillet, came to rival the Merino types, particularly in the Southwest. Currently there are more than 200 breeds of sheep throughout the world; however, the industry is dominated by fewer than 30 breeds. Except in Texas, the nation's leading producer, sheep cannot be considered a significant part of southern agriculture. Less than 20 percent of U.S. sheep are produced in the South, and the nation as a whole does not rank in the top ten nations in world sheep production.

See C. W. Towne and E. N. Wentworth, *Shepherd's Empire* (1945), best general account, dated; K. Winifred, *Golden Hoof* (1945), Texas and Southwest; R. Maudslay, *Texas Sheepman* (1951), reminiscences; and J. W. Thompson, *History of Livestock Raising in U.S., 1607–1860* (1942), good.

C. FRED WILLIAMS
University of Arkansas, Little Rock

SHELBY, ISAAC (1750–1826), was born in Washington County, Md. The fall of Charleston to the British (1780) led to his active participation in the war and culminated in the defeat of the Loyalists at KINGS MOUNTAIN (October 7, 1780). Before moving to Kentucky in 1783 he had served briefly in the legislatures of Virginia and North Carolina. Shelby helped frame Kentucky's first constitution and was elected governor (1792–1796). Kentucky's demand for uninterrupted navigation on the Mississippi involved Shelby in the Genêt affair; pressure was applied by George Washington and Thomas Jefferson to prevent Kentucky volunteers from attacking Spain; and Shelby's hesitancy to cooperate was more a matter of political strategy than a lack of respect for the central government. Pinckney's Treaty was a vindication of his policy. The War of 1812 brought the old soldier from retirement to the governorship again (1812–

SOUTHERN SHEEP PRODUCTION, 1850–1969
(in thousands of heads)

Year	1850	1860	1870	1880	1890	1900	1910	1920	1930	1940[a]	1950[a]	1959[a]	1969[a]	% of U.S. Total
Ala.	372	370	242	348	386	323	145	83	69	32	25	36	7	.03
Ark.	91	203	161	247	244	260	145	101	86	90	50	47	9	.04
Del.	28	19	23	22	12	12	8	3	5	2	3	4	2	.01
Fla.	23	30	27	57	98	126	114	66	47	21	4	7	5	.02
Ga.	560	513	419	528	440	342	191	75	50	17	10	28	5	.02
Ky.	1,102	939	937	1,000	937	1,300	1,365	710	1,597	989	982	546	119	.55
La.	110	181	119	136	186	222	181	134	171	190	91	95	26	.12
Md.	178	156	130	171	132	194	238	104	194	56	50	38	27	.125
Miss.	305	353	233	288	452	316	200	166	110	60	67	73	13	.06
Mo.	763	937	1,352	1,411	951	1,096	1,829	1,288	1,750	1,431	1,160	825	281	1.3
N.C.	595	547	463	462	402	303	216	92	146	46	50	53	17	.07
S.C.	286	234	125	119	79	72	38	25	19	7	4	11	2	.01
Tenn.	812	773	827	673	541	499	799	367	626	358	368	261	60	.28
Tex.	101	753	714	2,412	3,455	1,898	1,813	2,591	7,021	8,448	7,750	6,064	4,297	20.0
Va.	1,310	1,043	370	497	495	696	808	345	829	355	454	343	247	1.14
W.Va.	incl. in Va.	incl. in Va.	552	675	785	971	912	514	897	437	422	290	189	.87

[a] on farms only

1816). He personally led 4,000 Kentucky volunteers to Canada and participated in the battle of the Thames (1813).

See Shelby Papers, Library of Congress; L. Collins, *History of Kentucky* (1882), excellent; A. Henderson, *Mississippi Valley Historical Review* (March, 1920), good; S. Wilson, *Register of Kentucky Historical Society* (Jan., 1962); and H. Peters, *Register of Kentucky Historical Society* (Oct., 1925).

WALLACE B. TURNER
Colorado Women's College

SHELLY V. KRAEMER (334 U.S. 1 [1948]). In May, 1941, the U.S. Supreme Court decided by a vote of six to zero that racially restrictive housing covenants were no longer legally enforceable. That decision had a limited impact, for it neither prohibited restrictive housing covenants nor challenged segregated housing patterns. The historic importance of the *Shelly* case rests in the intervention of the Truman administration in the proceedings. The administration, working through the Department of Justice, filed an *amicus curiae* brief in December, 1947, which dovetailed with the positions of the NATIONAL ASSOCIATION FOR THE ADVANCEMENT OF COLORED PEOPLE and other groups seeking judicial relief. Among the points made in the administration's brief, which was endorsed by President Harry Truman, was that housing covenants "cannot be reconciled with the spirit of mutual tolerance and respect for the individual." The administration also stated that the retention of a legal justification for housing covenants would hamper the United States in the execution of its foreign policy. This brief was a political signal to black Americans, demonstrating the administration's willingness to take positive action in their behalf. Clearly, the government's intervention in this case was connected to the president's developing strategy for the ELECTION OF 1948. Thus the politics of civil rights intersected with the pressing claims of minority groups at a time when the Supreme Court was accelerating its own fresh review of American justice in the context of civil rights.

See C. Abrams, *Forbidden Neighbors* (1955); W. C. Berman, *Politics of Civil Rights* (1970); D. McCoy and R. Ruetten, *Quest and Response* (1973); and C. Vose, *Caucasians Only* (1959).

WILLIAM C. BERMAN
University of Toronto

SHENANDOAH VALLEY is the northern and most fertile section of the valley of Virginia. It is 6,500 square miles in area, 180 miles long, ten to 24 miles wide, underlain primarily by limestone, and drained by the Shenandoah River. The valley was first settled during the late 1720s by Europeans, who encountered no resident Indians. By 1776 there were 35,000 settlers of German, Scotch-Irish, and English origins from the middle colonies and western Europe; less than 5 percent of the population was black. By 1800 the population had increased to 84,000; planters from eastern Virginia had moved into the northern (lower) valley; and 18 percent of the population was black. By 1860 the valley's total population of 148,000 remained predominantly white (79 percent) and rural (85 percent), with only one town, Winchester, of more than 4,000 residents.

The colonial economy was based on mixed agriculture with some specialization in CATTLE raising, HEMP, WHEAT, and, in the northern valley, TOBACCO. After the Revolution, agriculture became more specialized and the economy more diversified. The valley was the most important WHEAT-growing region in the Upper South between 1790 and 1850. Late colonial production of pig iron, woolen textiles, and whisky was expanded after 1800 to include leather and wood products. The first Baltimore & Ohio Railroad line reached Harpers Ferry in 1834, although it was another 20 years before railroads penetrated the southern (upper) valley. Growth was severely disrupted by the Civil War. Opinion on the war was divided; the two most northerly counties joined West Virginia in 1863; and STONEWALL JACKSON's successes against Union armies were countered in 1864 by the "scorched-earth" policies of U. S. Grant and Philip Sheridan, who laid waste much of the northern valley. Economic recovery was slow during Reconstruction with emphasis on livestock fattening, dairying, and fodder and orchard crops. Many small manufacturing plants were established between 1870 and 1900, and increasing numbers of summer tourists visited the resort spas that flourished after 1890.

See R. D. Mitchell, *Commercialism and Frontier* (1976); W. Couper, *History of Shenandoah Valley* (1952); J. W. Wayland, *Twenty-five Chapters* (1957); F. H. Hart, *Valley of Virginia* (1942); W. F. Bliss, *Virginia Magazine of History and Biography* (Oct., 1951); C. E. Kemper, *Virginia Magazine of History and Biography* (April, 1922); and J. T. Schlebecker, *Virginia Magazine of History and Biography* (Oct., 1971).

ROBERT D. MITCHELL
University of Maryland

SHENANDOAH VALLEY CAMPAIGN OF JACKSON (1862) was one of the most remarkable accomplishments in the annals of warfare. There is probably no other campaign in history that affords a better example of strategic diversion and the intelligent use of interior lines of communication. With an army never exceeding 17,000 men, STONEWALL JACKSON immobilized 100,000 federals scattered among four armies.

In 1862, with General George B. McClellan in command, the Union was ready for its big push to capture Richmond and bring the war to a successful conclusion. Part of McClellan's strategy was to send General Nathaniel P. Banks to dislodge Jackson at Winchester, Va. Upon the approach of Banks to Winchester, Jackson withdrew southward up the Shenandoah Valley. General James Shields pursued as far as Woodstock, whereupon, believing that Stonewall had fled from the valley, he marched back to Winchester. Banks, supposing he had accomplished his objective by expelling Jackson, left Shields in Winchester and took the remainder of his force east of the Blue Ridge Mountains.

With information supplied by his chief cavalry officer, General Turner Ashby, Jackson marched rapidly northward. Thinking he was facing only the federal rear guard, he launched an attack on March 23, which resulted in the battle of KERNSTOWN. When the remainder of Shields's troops became engaged and Jackson's men were in danger of being overwhelmed, General Richard B. Garnett of the Stonewall Brigade gave the order to retire. Most of the credit for the Union victory belongs to Colonel Nathan Kimball, who led the federals because Shields was hospitalized.

Jackson then retreated southward and took a position near Swift Run Gap. Since the Confederate authorities wanted him to keep Irvin McDowell at Fredericksburg from joining McClellan, they reinforced him with General RICHARD EWELL's division of 8,000 muskets. They also authorized him to call on General EDWARD JOHNSON's force, west of Staunton, giving Jackson a total of 17,000 men. To meet a federal threat and to prevent General Robert Milroy from uniting with Banks, Jackson acted swiftly. He continued westward until he met Milroy's federals, reinforced by General Robert Schenck's brigade, at the village of MCDOWELL on May 8. Since the federals' assault was unsuccessful, they withdrew westward.

Having disposed of this threat, Jackson went to Harrisonburg to engage Banks, who had retreated to Strasburg. Instead of marching northward down the main valley, he marched eastward across the Massanutten Mountains into the Page Valley. Using this range as a screen and aided by Ashby's cavalry, he defeated a small federal force under Colonel John R. Kenly at Front Royal on May 23. When Banks learned of this reverse, he evacuated his position at Strasburg and fell back to Winchester. Jackson intercepted part of the enemy en route and brought on an engagement on May 25 known as the first battle of WINCHESTER.

President Abraham Lincoln and Secretary of War Edwin Stanton planned to trap Jackson by having McDowell from the east and John C. Frémont from the west converge on Strasburg and thus cut off his retreat. The federals were incapable of closing this trap. Having encountered Jackson previously, they were cautious and allowed the entire Confederate army to slip through the noose and retreat up the main valley. General Frémont pursued Jackson southward up the main valley; Shields, on the other side of the Massanuttens, followed up the Page Valley. After the death of Ashby near Harrisonburg, Ewell defeated Frémont at CROSS KEYS on June 8, and Jackson attacked Shields the next day at PORT REPUBLIC and caused him to flee northward. While his opponents in the valley continued to wonder concerning his whereabouts, Stonewall secretly marched to the Virginia Central Railroad and headed for Richmond to help General ROBERT E. LEE launch the offensive against McClellan known as the SEVEN DAYS' BATTLES.

See W. Allan, *Stonewall Jackson* (1880); G. F. R. Henderson, *Stonewall Jackson* (1949); A. P. McDonald (ed.), *Make Me a Map* (1973); J. I. Robertson, Jr., *Stonewall Brigade* (1963) and *Civil War Times Illustrated* (May, 1972); M. F. Steele, *American Campaigns* (1951); and F. Vandiver, *Mighty Stonewall* (1957).

MILLARD K. BUSHONG
Shepherd College

SHENANDOAH VALLEY CAMPAIGN OF SHERIDAN (1864). U. S. Grant had assumed command of the Union armies facing R. E. LEE's Army of Northern Virginia. With this assumption of command, Grant made a number of administrative changes, one being to give Philip Sheridan an independent command of the Army of the Potomac, uniting it in one total unit. Whereas in the past the Union cavalry had hardly been used except for guard, messenger, and scouting duties, now it was to be used as a cavalry force, united for shock action in the spirit of the attack.

While Grant and Lee were fighting the battle of the WILDERNESS, Sheridan was ordered by Grant to move out as a whole cavalry corps in a column to ride south to find and destroy the Confederate army forces in the Shenandoah Valley of Virginia and to bring the war home to the civilian population of the valley, which had been a base of supplies and an avenue of approach used by Confederate armies in their attacks north into Union territory. Sheridan had with him some of the most noted U.S. Army cavalry leaders: Wesley Merritt, James H. Wilson, and George Armstrong Custer. With the Confederate forces in the Shenandoah Valley were such famous leaders as J. E. B. STUART, WADE HAMPTON, and FITZHUGH LEE.

There was a series of raids and battles that led the Union forces within a few miles of Richmond (SHERIDAN'S RICHMOND RAID). These actions were finally climaxed by the cavalry battle at YELLOW TAVERN, where Stuart was killed and the Union forces achieved a notable victory. Sheridan's mission had been carried out: an important part of the Confederate cavalry had been defeated in a major battle; its chief leader had been killed; southern supplies, railroads, and farm crops had been burned and destroyed so that a good part of Shenandoah Valley could not be used again as a base of operations against Washington and the North.

Another Confederate army, however, under the command of JUBAL EARLY had moved into that area and was still not defeated. Confederate forces made a series of sudden surprise attacks that at first were successful. These actions were climaxed at CEDAR CREEK, where Union forces were about to be defeated when Sheridan came into battle after a 20-mile forced ride and turned the tide of battle into a Union success. The Shenandoah Valley campaign was now over—the valley had been destroyed as a source of supplies for the South and the Confederate army in the area had been captured and destroyed or had withdrawn from the area. Sheridan now moved to join Grant in the final attack in 1865 against Lee.

See R. U. Johnson and C. C. Buel (eds.), *Battles and Leaders* (1888), IV; J. Kerr and E. S. Wallace, *Story of U.S. Cavalry* (1953); *West Point Atlas of American Wars* (1959); R. E. Dupuy and T. N. Dupuy, *Military Heritage of America* (1956); and M. Matliff (ed.), *American Military History* (1967).

WILLIAM J. DICKINSON
Lake Superior State College

SHEPPARD, JOHN MORRIS (1875–1941), was

born near Wheatville, Tex. He received the B.A. and LL.B. degrees from the University of Texas and the master of laws degree from Yale. In 1902 he filled the vacancy in the U.S. House of Representatives caused by the death of his father and served until 1912. In January, 1913, he became the last U.S. senator elected by the Texas legislature and held office until his death. A Progressive Democrat, he supported such measures as woman's suffrage, CHILD LABOR laws, infant welfare and maternity benefits, and aid for distressed American farmers. As the author of the Eighteenth Amendment, he is best remembered as the father of national PROHIBITION, a crusade he continued even after repeal in 1933. Sheppard served as a member of the Senate Military Affairs Committee from 1913 and as chairman from 1933 until his death. In 1940 he led the successful Senate fight for the controversial Selective Service Act. Sheppard Air Force Base is named for him.

See Sheppard Papers, University of Texas Library; E. F. Duke, "Morris Sheppard" (Ph.D. dissertation, University of Texas, 1958); and L. S. Keyes, *Morris Sheppard* (1950).

ESCAL F. DUKE
Angelo State University

SHERIDAN'S RICHMOND RAID (May 9–24,

1864) was the first independent operation by Philip H. Sheridan as commander of cavalry, Army of Potomac. With U. S. Grant's approval, he cut loose from the main army near Spotsylvania, leading 10,000 troopers south to threaten the Confederate capital, cut its communications, and lure J. E. B. STUART's cavalry into a finish fight. As anticipated, Stuart pursued, though with fewer than 5,000. Some dogged Sheridan's heels; the majority sought to head him off.

On May 9–11 the raiders skirmished with pursuers along the North and South Anna rivers. They also wrecked 16 miles of track on the Virginia Central and the Richmond, Fredericksburg & Potomac railroads, destroyed millions of dollars in supplies, and freed 378 federals from prison trains. On the eleventh Stuart overtook his quarry, deploying near YELLOW TAVERN, six miles above Richmond. During a six-hour battle the federals captured vital cannon, smashed enemy flanks, and mortally wounded Stuart. Most Confederates fled south, enabling Sheridan to thrash those still at his rear.

Next day Sheridan continued south unmolested, penetrating Richmond's outer works until meeting stiff resistance from defenders along the Mechanicsville Turnpike. Replanking a partially dismantled bridge under fire, his men crossed the Chickahominy River and, marching east and then south, bypassed the capital. On May 14, via Gaines' Mill and Malvern Hill, Sheridan reached Haxall's Landing, a Union supply base on the James River where he was to refit.

After a three-day rest, Sheridan returned north, rejoining Grant at Chesterfield Station. He had suffered over 600 casualties but had devastated

Confederate resources and morale. From this raid may be dated the federal cavalry's permanent superiority over its opponent.

See P. H. Sheridan, *Memoirs* (2 vols.; 1888); L. H. Carpenter, *Journal of U.S. Cavalry Association* (Nov., 1888); R. U. Johnson and C. C. Buel (eds.), *Battles and Leaders* (1888), IV; S. H. Miller, *Civil War History* (March, 1956); E. G. Longacre, *Mounted Raids* (1975); *Official Records, Armies*, Ser. 1, Vols. XXXVI, LI; and Sheridan Papers, Library of Congress.

EDWARD G. LONGACRE
Temple University

SHERMAN'S HAIRPINS. One of the major goals of General William T. Sherman during his famous march through Georgia "from Atlanta to the Sea" in 1864 was to render as much as possible of the state's railroads permanently useless to the Confederacy. His troops discovered that an effective way to accomplish this was to heat the centers of the torn-up rails over a bonfire of rail ties. This made the iron rails sufficiently pliable so that they could be twisted completely around the trunks of nearby trees. The Confederates found that these oversized "Sherman's hairpins" were impossible to straighten out again. Other nicknames for these objects were "Jeff Davis' neckties," "Sherman's neckties," or "iron doughnuts."

See G. E. Shankle, *American Nicknames* (1955); M. M. Mathews, *Dictionary of Americanisms* (1951); and J. D. Cox, *March to Sea* (n.d.).

SHERMAN'S LAND GRANTS. On January 16, 1865, General William T. Sherman, with the approval of Secretary of War Edwin Stanton, issued Special Field Order Number 15. This order set aside for settlement by Negro refugees a large tract of land, which encompassed the Sea Islands from Charleston, S.C., southward to the St. John's River and the land along the coastline for 30 miles into the interior. All abandoned land that had not already been transferred to new owners under the Direct Tax Law was thrown open to settlement by Negro refugees in tracts of 40 acres or less. The blacks were to receive "possessory" titles to the land "until Congress shall regulate their title." Within six months, more than 40,000 freedmen, fired by dreams of their own farms, had moved onto the land under the supervision of General Rufus Saxton. But in August and September, 1865, President Andrew Johnson began restoring to the original owners all lands that had not been sold outright. Former Confederates who obtained a pardon, swore allegiance, and paid their back taxes could reclaim their land. Most black settlers

were turned off the land with nothing but an option to buy 20-acre lots on other federal property in the South, and necessity forced most to return to working for the white plantation owners.

See G. R. Bentley, *History of Freedmen's Bureau* (1955); and W. L. Rose, *Rehearsal for Reconstruction* (1967).

PAUL D. ESCOTT
University of North Carolina, Charlotte

SHERMAN'S MARCH TO THE SEA. Atlanta fell on September 2, 1864. William T. Sherman set to work consolidating his gains while watching JOHN B. HOOD's Army of Tennessee carefully. Although the destruction of Hood's army was his principal objective and had been since early spring, Sherman conceived the plan of a bold thrust to the sea. Actually, Sherman had expressed the concept as early as May, 1864, indicating that, following Atlanta's fall, Savannah or Charleston but surely "salt water" would be his next destination. Therefore, instead of falling prey to the enemy's plan to have him wear out his army protecting long, exposed lines of communication and chasing Hood's elusive army, Sherman confronted the Confederates with a dilemma. They must either chase his coattails across the state of Georgia or "sacrifice the heart of their country."

Sherman destroyed Atlanta and on November 16 set out. His army was divided into two wings under Oliver O. Howard (XV and XVII Corps) and Henry W. Slocum (XIV and XX Corps). Sherman retained direct control of Hugh Kilpatrick's cavalry. The 65,000 men were allotted the minimum in supply wagons, allowing each wing, indeed each corps, to be independent. Mobility was the password. A 15-mile daily advance over separate roads was prescribed, and the troops were expected to feed themselves from the countryside. To accomplish this, every unit quickly organized foraging parties. These foragers, BUMMERS, brought in the provisions, but equally as important they created a wide net of scouts about the army. The enemy was thereby deprived of the element of surprise. "Along with the systematic business of foraging there was a shocking amount of downright plunder and vandalism," creating a belt of destruction 60 miles wide and 200 miles deep.

Unable to ascertain Sherman's strength and baffled as to his objectives, the makeshift Confederate force of 12,000 men offered only token resistance. Sherman's two wings marched from five to 50 miles apart, simultaneously threatening vital centers such as Augusta and Macon. While marching, a corps would leave one of the wings and suddenly change direction, menacing or attacking another objective, as in the capture of Milledgeville, then reverse itself. JOSEPH WHEELER, assigned to Sherman's front, gave up in despair, and WILLIAM J. HARDEE positioned him at Sherman's flank and rear. Other than a sharp encounter with the Georgia militia at Griswoldville (November 22) and rear-guard actions later that week close to Savannah, Sherman's march was a military holiday outing.

Hardee had spent a great deal of effort preparing Savannah's defenses, however, and for three weeks Sherman's efforts were frustrated. Marshaling his forces against Hardee's multiple defense lines, Sherman attacked, feinted, and then discovered that Ft. McAllister was the key to the Savannah positions. When General William Hazen's men reduced the fort on December 13, Savannah's fate was sealed. Hardee evacuated the city on December 21, leaving behind over 200 guns and 35,000 priceless bales of cotton. On December 22 Sherman sent this cheery message to Abraham Lincoln, "I beg to present you as a Christmas gift the city of Savannah." He had shattered Georgia's military potential, threatened the Carolinas and the rear of R. E. Lee's command, and pierced the heart of the Confederacy. In six weeks and at the loss of fewer than 2,200 men, he had won a reputation for innovation in warfare unmatched by any nineteenth-century American military figure save NATHAN B. FORREST.

See R. U. Johnson and C. C. Buel (eds.), *Battles and Leaders* (1888); R. S. Thorndike, *Sherman Letters* (1894); J. D. Cox, *March to Sea* (1882); C. C. Jones Papers, Duke University Library; and N. C. Hughes, *Georgia Historical Quarterly* (March, 1963).

N. C. HUGHES, JR.
Girls' Preparatory School, Chattanooga, Tenn.

SHILOH, BATTLE OF (April 6–7, 1862). U. S. Grant's river invasion of west Tennessee in February drove Confederates back to nearby Corinth, Miss. Twenty-two miles north at Pittsburg Landing, Tenn., Grant assembled 47,000 federals and awaited D. C. Buell's Union army from Nashville before attacking Corinth. Deciding to strike Grant's exposed army, A. S. JOHNSTON ordered 44,000 southerners north on April 3. Although boldly conceived, Johnston's plan required too much of raw soldiers in rough and rain-dampened country. After a difficult three-day march, troops led by W. J. HARDEE, BRAXTON BRAGG, LEONIDAS POLK, and JOHN C. BRECKINRIDGE would charge head on and then sweep the federal left away from its base on the Tennessee River.

At daybreak Sunday, Confederates fell upon federals still in camp and drove them past Shiloh Church, three miles from the landing for which the battle was named. Grant's scattered army retreated, but certain units eventually stood stubbornly at a thickly wooded position dubbed the Peach Orchard and the Hornets' Nest, frustrating Confederate efforts to turn the Union left. Not until twilight did Confederate units, by now hopelessly intermingled, press down to the landing. At this point, P. G. T. BEAUREGARD, in command after Johnston was killed, ordered action stopped until morning. Unknown to Beauregard, however, Buell poured 17,000 soldiers into Union lines during the rainy night; Lew Wallace's fresh division also arrived.

Early Monday, reinforced federals counterattacked, eventually forcing Beauregard to call off the uneven contest at 2 P.M. Exhausted southerners withdrew unpursued toward Corinth. Northern casualties numbered 13,047; southern, 10,699. Did Beauregard's order late Sunday prevent Confederate victory? Actually, his weary army was probably too disorganized for further action that day. Did Buell's timely arrival save Grant? Worried by losses and hints of his incompetence, Grant denied a surprise and near defeat, claiming his army alone could have prevailed. But it seems Grant's unprepared forces were badly mauled Sunday; heavy reinforcements were essential.

See R. U. Johnson and C. C. Buel (eds.), *Battles and Leaders* (1888), I; T. L. Connelly, *Army of Heartland* (1967); and A. Dillahunty, *Shiloh* (1955).

JAMES R. CHUMNEY
Memphis Sate University

SHIP ISLAND is an important sand barrier seven miles long and a half-mile wide, 12 miles across Mississippi Sound from Biloxi and Gulfport. Its deep natural harbor provided a base for the French-Canadian establishment of New Orleans. It served as an American and Spanish fleet rendezvous during the American Revolution. The English used it to attack New Orleans in 1814–1815. On January 13, 1861, Confederate forces seized a Union fort under construction there, but later abandoned it. Union leaders DAVID G. FARRAGUT and Benjamin F. Butler used it as an attack supply base to seize New Orleans in April, 1862. In the last six months of that war it served as a Union prisoner-of-war camp. After 1881 it served as a yellow fever quarantine station intermittently for 40 years. Its harbor was a great lumber-shipping port. Ft. Massachusetts on the island now serves as a tourist attraction as part of the Gulf Islands National Seashore.

See R. P. Weiner, *Journal of Mississippi History* (Nov., 1969); Z. H. Burns, *Ship Island and Confederacy* (1971); and J. E. Steckel "Ship Island and Ft. Massachusetts" (M.A. thesis, University of New Orleans, 1975).

M. JAMES STEVENS
Mississippi Coast Historical and Genealogical Society

SHREVEPORT, LA.

SHREVEPORT, LA. (pop. 182,064), near the Arkansas and Texas state lines, is located on a stretch of the RED RIVER once clogged by a 160-mile jam of driftwood known as the Great Raft. In 1835 Henry Miller Shreve cut a channel through the raft to this point with a steamboat. The town he founded thrived as an antebellum river port, shipping area-grown cotton. It also served as the capital of the state's Confederate government (1863–1865). Accumulations of silt gradually closed the river to steamboats, but the construction of rail lines permitted the city to survive as a center of commercial activity. After the turn of the century, however, the discovery of nearby gas and petroleum transformed Shreveport into a major industrial town. Today its factories produce electrical equipment, chemicals, refined oil, textiles, lumber products, machinery, glass, and construction materials. CENTENARY COLLEGE and a branch of Louisiana State University are located here. Plans to dredge the river and extend the inland waterway to Shreveport, when completed, will result in the city once again becoming a Red River port.

See V. Carruth, *Caddo: 1000* (1970), area history; M. O'Pry, *Chronicles of Shreveport* (1928); L. McLure, *History of Shreveport* (1937, 1951); Federal Writers' Project, *History of Shreveport* (1936); and files of Shreveport *Journal* (1896–) and *Times* (1872–).

SHRUBS. See FLOWERS AND SHRUBS

SIBLEY, HENRY HOPKINS

SIBLEY, HENRY HOPKINS (1816–1886), was born in Natchitoches, La. After graduation from West Point, he served with the 2nd Dragoons in Florida, Mexico, the Texas frontier, Kansas, Utah, and New Mexico. After resigning in 1861, Sibley went to Richmond, where he was commissioned a brigadier general and subsequently commanded the ill-fated Confederate invasion of New Mexico. After a bloody victory at Val Verde, Sibley's Texans were defeated at Glorieta Pass and were forced to evacuate the territory. The controversial Sibley was court-martialed by the U.S. Army and the Confederate army and was dismissed from the Egyptian army for his heavy drinking, a weakness that plagued him throughout his military career. Sibley, inventor of the tent and stove that bear his name, as well as other military apparatus, died at Fredericksburg, Va.

See M. H. Hall, *Sibley's New Mexico Campaign* (1960), definitive; J. D. Thompson, *Military History of Texas and Southwest* (1972), X; J. D. Thompson, *Texana* (1973), No. 4; and C. H. Quenzel, *Virginia Magazine of History and Biography* (April, 1956).

JERRY D. THOMPSON
Laredo Junior College

SILK CULTURE

SILK CULTURE (sericulture) was a sidelight to the development of southern agriculture for more than two centuries. Thomas Hariot noted the existence of indigenous silkworms (nonreeling type) in his *A Briefe and True Report of the New Found Land of Virginia* (1588), and John Gerard mentioned Virginia's red mulberry trees (*Morus rubra*) in his arboricultural study of 1599. The prospects for such an exotic crop titillated both southern planters and merchantilists on the Thames.

Between 1615 and 1650, Virginia planters experimented with silk culture but found little success. In 1654, however, one Edward Digges reported that he had produced eight pounds of silk fiber after importing Armenian workers to tend the crop. By 1668 Virginia's silk production had risen to 300 pounds. The Virginia burgesses tried to encourage silk production in various ways—enacting bounties and requiring mulberry tree plantings. By 1730, however, Virginia's silk production had increased little over the 1668 crop.

Carolina planters attempted to raise silkworms in the same spirit that they tried to produce wine grapes, figs, coffee, sesame, and hops. Colonial and parliamentary bounties promoted silk culture somewhat, but the Carolinians had far greater incentive to produce silk for the protected English market. South Carolina produced its greatest silk crop, only 118 pounds, in 1750.

After 1741 Georgia farmers led in silk production, and from 1755 to 1761 they annually exported an average of 450 pounds. Salzburgers, founding the settlement at New Ebenezer, worked extensively with silk culture from 1736 to 1774. The Revolution, of course, ruined the export market for silk, and Georgia's production declined to almost nothing until about 1840, when a "silkworm craze" caused a brief revival in production. The Civil War brought a final end to silk farming in the South.

Sericulture remained a sidelight of southern agriculture for several reasons. Biologically, reel-type silkworms are delicate creatures, not altogether acclimated to torrid summers. Also frost easily damaged mulberry leaves. Technically, silk culture required not only intensive labor, but also workers with expertise. Perhaps most important, however, silk culture competed with resources that farmers found more profitable to invest in TOBACCO, INDIGO, RICE, and ultimately COTTON.

See L. C. Gray, *Agriculture in Southern U.S.* (1933); J. Ewan and J. C. Bonner, *Agricultural History* (Jan., 1969); P. W. Gates, *Farmer's Age* (1960); and J. D'Homergue, *Report on Growth and Manufacture of Silk*, House Document 126, (1830).

R. G. WALTHER
Smithsonian Institution

SILVER, JAMES WESLEY (1907–), a prominent southern educator specializing in regional, state, and local history, was born in Rochester, N.Y. He received the bachelor's degree from the University of North Carolina, the master's from Peabody, and the doctorate from Vanderbilt in 1934. Between 1936 and 1965 he taught history at the University of Mississippi. His first book *Edmund Pendleton Gaines* (1949) is the study of an influential figure in the early development of the South. During the 1950s, Silver became a frequent contributor to the *Journal of Mississippi History*, the *Journal of Southern History*, and various northern learned journals. Especially active during the Civil War centennial, he produced *Confederate Morale and Church Propaganda* (1957), *Robert A. Moore* (1959), *A Surgeon's Recollections* (1960), and, with John Bettersworth, *Mississippi in the Confederacy* (1961).

Professor Silver attracted national attention when the integration crisis reached Ole Miss in the 1960s. Personally involving himself in the turbulence, he vigorously championed the liberal position. Out of the experience he wrote "Mississippi: The Closed Society" as his 1963 presidential address to the Southern Historical Association and in 1964 published it in book form. A first-hand account of the race riots at Ole Miss, the work examines the origins and force "of the mentality of a closed society." Silver was the recipient of many accolades, as well as condemnation, for this book. In 1965 he left Mississippi to teach at Notre Dame and later at the University of Tampa.

See *America* (Aug., 1965); *Life* (July 17, 1964); *Nation* (July 29, 1964); *New York Times* (July 19, 1964); *New Republic* (Oct. 19, 1968); *Publishers Weekly* (July 29, 1964); *Journal of Mississippi History* (Feb., 1965); and L. Clifford, "Artistic Vision" (M.A. thesis, University of New York, 1968).

H. E. STERKX
Auburn University, Montgomery

SIMKINS, FRANCIS BUTLER (1897–1966), historian of the South, was born in Edgefield, S.C. He received his B.A. degree from the University of South Carolina (1918) and his A.M. (1920) and Ph.D. (1926) degrees from Columbia University. After brief appointments at Randolph-Macon Woman's College, the University of North Carolina, and Emory, he taught at Longwood College in Virginia for 38 years. He was visiting professor at Louisiana State University (1948–1951), Princeton University (1953–1954), and the University of Texas (1957). He was president of the Southern Historical Association (1953–1954). A careful historian whose writings reveal original ideas about the history of the South, he wrote *The Tillman Movement in South Carolina* (1926), *Pitchfork Ben Tillman* (1944), and a college text, *A History of the South* (1947). His pioneering revisionist study *South Carolina During Reconstruction* (1932), which he wrote with ROBERT H. WOODY, was awarded the William A. Dunning Prize by the American Historical Association in 1931. He and James W. Patton published *The Women of the Confederacy* (1936). *The Everlasting South* (1963), a collection of his essays, contains his reflections upon the uniqueness of southern history.

See memorial pamphlet, *Francis Butler Simkins* (n.d.), published by his family.

E. STANLY GODBOLD, JR.
Valdosta State College

SIMMONS, FURNIFOLD McLENDEL (1854–1940), was born in Polloksville, N.C. He was graduated from Trinity College in 1873, practiced law successfully until 1901, and meanwhile had become an active Democratic politician. He was elected to the U.S. House of Representatives in 1886, but was defeated by a black Republican in 1888. He served as chairman of the Democratic state committee from 1892 to 1894. After Republican and Populist victories in North Carolina in 1894 and 1896, he again became party chairman, a position he held until 1907. His two most famous campaigns were the blatant white supremacy campaign of 1898, when the Democrats regained control of the legislature, and that of 1900, which elected CHARLES AYCOCK governor and approved an amendment to the state constitution designed to disfranchise blacks.

Elected to the U.S. Senate (1901–1931), he served on the Committee on Commerce (1906–1931) and paid particular attention to appropriations for the rivers and harbors of his state and for the Atlantic INTRACOASTAL WATERWAY. As chairman of the

Committee on Finance from 1913 to 1919, he guided through the Senate the Underwood-Simmons tariff (1913) and war revenue bills calling for unprecedented bond issues and taxes on incomes, corporations, and profits. During the 1920s, he fought the Republican position on tariffs, dueled with Andrew Mellon over taxes, and stood for "adjusted compensation" for veterans. In the ELECTION OF 1928, Simmons threw his prestige against Al Smith. Simmons was not opposed to Smith's religion, but Catholicism together with Smith's wetness, his support of immigration, his association with Tammany Hall, his choice of J. J. Raskob as campaign manager, and his "northern" attitude toward race convinced Simmons that Smith represented a change that would threaten southern control of the Democratic party. This "bolt" encouraged JOSIAH BAILEY to challenge Simmons in the primary of 1930. By this time, Simmons' organization was shattered by deaths and age; now he could be accused of treachery. Bailey overwhelmingly defeated him. Simmons retired to his farms in New Bern.

See F. M. Simmons and J. Bailey papers, Duke University Library; J. F. Rippy (ed.), *F. M. Simmons* (1936); and R. L. Watson, *North Carolina Historical Review* (Oct., 1960; Winter, 1965; Spring, 1967).

RICHARD L. WATSON, JR.
Duke University

SIMMS, WILLIAM GILMORE (1806–1870), the

most prolific southern antebellum writer, was born in Charleston, S.C., son of an immigrant tradesman. After brief and poor schooling, he was apprenticed to an apothecary and later read law, but began writing in his youth. He was editor of two periodicals before 1830, when he purchased and edited the Charleston *City Gazette*, supporting the Union in the NULLIFICATION controversy. He sold the newspaper in 1832 and went north. His long poem *Atalantis* appeared in 1832, his first novel *Martin Faber* in 1833, and in 1834 the first of his border romances, *Guy Rivers*. In 1835 came *The Yemassee*, his best and most popular novel, and *The Partisan*, the first of seven Revolutionary War romances. In 1836 he married and moved permanently to a plantation 70 miles inland from Charleston. In 1844–1846 he served in the South Carolina house of representatives. He continued writing from 1836 to 1860. producing Revolutionary War and border romances; novels of crime, colonial history, and Spanish history; over 70 short stories; at least 17 volumes of verse and criticism; and biographies of Generals FRANCIS MARION and Nathanael Greene as well as of John Smith and

Chevalier Bayard. He edited ten periodicals and was a vigorous defender of slavery. Left destitute by the Civil War, in his last years he wrote desperately. From his prodigious output little survived its own day, and he remains primarily of historical rather than literary importance.

See M. C. S. Oliphant, A. T. Odell, and T. C. D. Eaves (eds.), *Letters of W. G. Simms* (5 vols.; 1952–56); W. P. Trent, *W. G. Simms* (1892); J. V. Ridgely, *Simms* (1962); C. H. Holman, *Roots of Southern Writing* (1972); and E. W. Parks, *Simms as Literary Critic* (1961).

C. HUGH HOLMAN
University of North Carolina, Chapel Hill

SINGLETON PEACE PLAN (1865). James Wash-

ington Singleton (1811–1892) was a Virginia-born Illinois businessman, politician, and peace Democrat who knew Abraham Lincoln. With Lincoln's permission, he traveled to Richmond in January, 1865, on a self-appointed, unofficial, dual mission to extend peace feelers, probably regarding the terms of reunion and abolition of slavery with federal monetary compensation (EMANCIPATION, COMPENSATED); and to conclude a business arrangement for private profit and national interest by purchasing southern tobacco with northern greenbacks. The mission failed to bring peace or profit, but this and Singleton's earlier and later peace efforts may have slightly influenced Lincoln's attitude toward the HAMPTON ROADS CONFERENCE (February 3, 1865) and his recommendation for a joint resolution on compensation (February 5, 1865).

See T. C. Pease and J. G. Randall (eds.), *Collections of Illinois State Historical Library* (1927–33), XX, XXII; M. G. Baxter, *Orville H. Browning* (1957); R. P. Basler (ed.), *Collected Works of Lincoln* (1953), VIII; M. P. Andrews, *Virginia* (1937), biased, but important; E. C. Kirkland, *Peacemakers* (1927); P. J. Parish, *Civil War* (1975); and R. O. Curry, *Civil War History* (March, 1967).

JEFFREY KIMBALL
Miami University

SIPUEL V. OKLAHOMA BOARD OF RE-

GENTS (332 U.S. 631 [1948]). Ada Sipuel's lawsuit to gain admission to the University of Oklahoma Law School took two years to reach the U.S. Supreme Court. But, only four days after argument, the Court granted the relief she sought in a short four-paragraph opinion. Finding that Sipuel had been rejected "solely because of her color" and that no law school for blacks was available in the state, the Court ruled that the Fourteenth Amendment required her admission. The 1948 opinion did not mention a decision handed down ten years earlier (MISSOURI EX REL. GAINES), which had held that a statute enabling black graduate students to receive tuition to attend out-of-state schools did not meet "separate but equal" standards. The petitioner in that case, Lloyd Gaines, disappeared before he enrolled and was never heard from again. Sipuel was more fortunate. The state court interpreted the Supreme Court's order as requiring her admission only until a law school was provided for blacks. Her lawyers returned to the Supreme Court contending that her admission should be without reservation, but the Court indicated that the issue of whether a law school for blacks would satisfy the separate but equal standard was not before it. Oklahoma did not establish a law school for blacks, and Sipuel entered the university, ultimately was graduated, and was admitted to the Oklahoma bar.

DERRICK BELL
Harvard University

SKAGGS, WILLIAM HENRY (1861–1947), was born in Talladega, Ala. A businessman and banker, he became mayor of Talladega (1884–1890) and obtained municipal improvements: a public school, paved streets, water and sewerage systems, and gas facilities. His view of the NEW SOUTH emphasized public education and honest politics. Widespread fraud in Alabama elections after 1890 precipitated a change in Skaggs's political convictions. In 1894 he became state chairman of the Jeffersonian Democratic (POPULIST) party and campaigned for REUBEN F. KOLB in the gubernatorial election. His party's subsequent defeat embittered Skaggs. Charging that the South was corrupt and would never change without honest politics, he moved to Chicago in 1901. Skaggs's articles and books consistently championed rule by the people. His strong anti-German bias prior to the U.S. involvement in World War I, expressed in *German Conspiracies in America* (1916), emphasized the "conflict . . . between autocracy and democracy." His most important work, *The Southern Oligarchy* (1924), attacked southern leaders for using fraud and perpetuating racism and concluded that it was their rule that had left the South impoverished, illiterate, and despised.

See T. H. Nolan, "William H. Skaggs" (M.A. thesis, Florida State University, 1970) and *Alabama Historical Quarterly* (Summer, 1971); Skaggs File, Alabama Department of Archives and History; and Talladega *News* (Jan. 23, 1947).

D. ALAN HARRIS
Old Dominion University

SKINNER, JOHN STUART (1788–1851), founded and edited Baltimore's *American Farmer*. A weekly begun in 1819 and the first successful agricultural journal in the United States, it published correspondence from distinguished agriculturists including THOMAS JEFFERSON and JOHN TAYLOR of Caroline, advocated a series of innovations, especially in fertilization, and furnished a model for the farm journals that proliferated during the next generation. Skinner also published the *American Turf Register and Sporting Magazine* in Baltimore from 1829 until 1844, conducted journals in New York and Philadelphia from 1845 until his death, and wrote several agricultural books. He held federal appointments through most of his career and was postmaster of Baltimore (1816–1837).

See A. L. Demaree, *American Agricultural Press, 1819–1860* (1941); B. P. Moore, *Plough, Loom, and Anvil* (July, 1854), Skinner's last journal, Moore was acquaintance; and W. E. Ogilvie, *Pioneer Agricultural Journalists* (1927).

DONALD B. MARTI
Indiana University, South Bend

SKIPWITH, FULWAR (1765–1839), a Virginia merchant, was appointed consul in Martinique (1790). As James Monroe's amanuensis when Monroe became minister to France, Skipwith was designated consul general in Paris (1794). He represented claims of American shippers for spoliations occurring before and during the Quasi War (1798–1799); but his efforts were only partly successful owing to rivalries among claims agents. From 1797 to 1799 he was the only legally authorized representative of the U.S. government in Paris. Later serving as commercial agent of the United States in Paris, Skipwith incurred the displeasure of American Minister Robert Livingston, who pressed Napoleon to revoke his exequatur; and Skipwith returned home in 1808. He then purchased a cotton plantation at Feliciana, near Baton Rouge, La., and became a wealthy, much respected planter.

See H. B. Cox, *Parisian American* (1964), full bibliography; Causten-Pickett Papers, Library of Congress; and Skipwith Family Papers, College of William and Mary Library.

HENRY BARTHOLOMEW COX
George Washington University Law School

SLASH CHURCH, BATTLE OF. See HANOVER COURTHOUSE, BATTLE OF

SLATER FUND. John F. Slater, a Rhode Island textile manufacturer, believed that education was necessary for blacks if former slaves were to become responsible citizens. In 1882 he donated $1 million as the endowment for the Slater Fund, the first philanthropic corporation devoted exclusively to black education. An independent board of trustees directed the program of the fund, which included naming the president. After 1903 the president of the fund was also executive director of the JEANES FUND. The Slater Fund worked closely with all other agencies engaged in promoting better education but concentrated on improving opportunities for black Americans. Officials of the fund believed in strong academic education beginning in the secondary schools. This would be possible only if teachers were better trained. Money from the Slater Fund supported improvements in salaries and facilities for public schools and stronger academic preparation for graduates of Fisk, Atlanta, Hampton, and Tuskegee. In 1937 the Slater Fund joined the Jeanes Fund, the PEABODY EDUCATION FUND, and the Virginia Randolph Fund to form the Southern Education Foundation located in Atlanta.

See J. E. McNeal, "James Hardy Dillard" (Ph.D. dissertation, University of Virginia, 1970); H. S. Enck, "Burden Borne" (Ph.D. dissertation, University of Cincinnati, 1970); W. W. Alexander, *Slater and Jeanes Funds* (1934); and Slater Fund Archives, Southern Education Foundation, Atlanta.

A. GILBERT BELLES
Western Illinois University

SLAUGHTERHOUSE CASES (16 Wall. 36 [1873]). Louisiana's Reconstruction legislature limited livestock slaughtering in New Orleans to one corporation's premises, which others could use at prescribed charges. JOHN A. CAMPBELL, former U.S. Supreme Court justice and plaintiffs' counsel, contended that the act violated the Fourteenth Amendment, denying due process and equal protection and abridging privileges and immunities of U.S. citizens, which embraced all civil rights and liberties including occupational pursuit without monopolistic restrictions. Justice Samuel F. Miller, for the Court's majority, held that most civil rights, including fundamental liberties, flowed from state citizenship and lay beyond Fourteenth Amendment protection. Otherwise the Court would become "perpetual censor" upon all state legislation, with radical alteration in the federal structure. He rejected Campbell's arguments, holding that the amendment's "pervading purpose" was protection of freedmen's rights. Thus the southern Democrat had sought the amend-

ment's broadest national application; the northern Republican justice upheld one greatly restricted. The decision affirmed the states' regulatory police power, and its distinction between federal and state citizenship has never been reversed. However, the sweeping federal protection for personal liberties envisioned by Campbell came through reinterpretation of due process and equal protection.

See *Butcher's Union Slaughter-House* v. *Crescent City Co.,* 111 U.S. 746 (1884); *Jurisprudence* (1964), Secs. 445–64; H. G. Connor, *John Archibald Campbell* (1920); J. S. Mann, "Constitutional Thought of Campbell" (Ph.D. dissertation, University of Alabama, 1966); H. J. Graham, *Everyman's Constitution* (1968); and L. P. Beth, *Louisiana Law Review* (April, 1963).

KEMP P. YARBOROUGH
Texas Woman's University

SLAVE CODES constituted the Old South's closest approximations to coherent statutory delineation of the conditions of black subjugation. Detailed of regulation, especially from 1800 to 1865, they sought to fix relations between white and black, both bond and free, over a broad range of activities: from minor provisions proscribing, for example, interracial gambling to major concerns such as manumissions and the trial rights of slaves. Nonetheless, both in construction and administration, southern slave codes were less than completely systematic, less than thoroughly "totalitarian." They lacked the jurisprudential coherence, the deductive interconnectedness from general social principle to particular behavioral provision, of Roman and Continental codificatory traditions. Even southern codes specifically so labeled by their progenitors often resembled compendia of prior legislative enactments. Comparison of early Latin American and Virginian slavery lawmaking illustrates the point. The former appears as a largely unsuccessful series of royal decrees and clerical admonitions seeking to push the realities of South American slave treatment "upward" to the more humane prior prescriptions of the Siete Partidas. Virginia colonial enactments reflected, more than they initiated, emergent societal structures.

Increasing uniformity among southern states and greater restrictiveness over time, though the major statutory trends, were undercut by lesser trends of diversity and relaxation. Defense of the peculiar institution thrust powerfully toward restriction, especially after the rise of northern abolition. Four factors pushed less powerfully in the opposite direction: the very circumstance of a federal political order; the periodicity of insurrectionist scares, which permitted the incremental, adjustive tendency of the Anglo-Saxon legislative tradition to flourish; a curiously filtered diffusion of Enlightenment ideals, tending less toward encouraging freedom than toward developing norms of protection within bondage; and most important, judicial interpretation of legislative rule (JUDICIARIES, SOUTHERN). A few comparisons from two areas of slavery code making and adjudication suggest the resulting "dappled" pattern.

In South Carolina manumission was easy for a master to effect until restrictive statutes were enacted in 1800 and 1820. Yet these acts, though supported by equity chancellors, were undercut by law judges, a practice that was rebuffed by the state legislature in 1841. Nonetheless, some of the law judges continued to seek exceptions up to 1860. (See, for example, *Bynum*, 4 Desaus. Eq. 266 [1812]; *Frazier*, 2 Hill Eq. 304 [1835]; *Carmille*, 2 McMul. 454 [1842]; *Gordon*, 1 Rich. Eq. 61 [1844]; *Willis*, 11 Rich. Eq. 447 [1860].) North Carolina, by contrast, became less restrictive after an 1830 act encouraging out-of-state manumission.

North Carolina provided a relatively high level of protection for the rights of slaves on trial (see acts of 1783, 1794, 1807, 1816, 1825, and 1842). Virginia provided much less legal protection, failing even to give the power of review over such trials to the appeals court until the 1850s.

It is important to note that, despite the general tendencies toward uniformity and restriction, many code provisions were rarely enforced, that many were passed on close legislative votes, and that many bills seeking greater restrictiveness failed to gain passage.

See W. Goodell, *American Slave Code* (1853), northern view; T. Cobb, *Law of Negro Slavery* (1858), southern view; state legislative journals (better); J. B. O'Neall, *Digest of Law of South Carolina* (1848), much neglected critique of South Carolina slave laws by state's dominant judge; and A. E. K. Nash, *South Carolina Law Review* (Spring, 1969).

A. E. KEIR NASH
University of California, Santa Barbara

SLAVE INSURRECTIONS. In the entire history of slavery in North America only three full-scale slave insurrections matured to the point where blacks and whites fought pitched battles. These were Cato's rebellion of 1739 near Stono Creek, S.C. (STONO SLAVE CONSPIRACY); an uprising on several plantations in Louisiana in 1811; and TURNER'S REBELLION of 1831 in Southampton County, Va. In two other elaborate conspiracies, white authorities arrested their alleged leaders before any actual insurrections took place: these were GABRIEL'S INSURRECTION in Richmond (1800) and the VESEY PLOT in Charleston (1822). Until recently, textbooks in American history rarely mentioned conspiracies other than Gabriel Prosser's, Denmark Vesey's, and Nat Turner's, leaving the impression that the large slave population of North America was generally docile. Yet as long ago as 1943 Herbert Aptheker published *American Negro Slave Revolts*, describing "approximately two hundred and fifty revolts and conspiracies in the history of American Negro slavery."

Aptheker reached such a high figure by counting affairs that involved ten or more blacks. As Eugene Genovese has pointed out, Aptheker proved conclusively the continuing will to resist slavery, early and late and in every slaveholding area. American Negroes were not docile as a group, nor were masters free of anxiety about their own safety. But by comparing the scope and violence of North American slave insurrections with those in the Caribbean and Latin America, Genovese shows that North American blacks achieved relatively meager results. This was not for lack of will, but was the result of circumstances. The black population of North America was scattered over a huge area, interspersed with and usually outnumbered by alert, well-armed, and determined whites. In many tropical colonies, on the other hand, black populations lived in extreme concentration, and they heavily outnumbered whites. North American blacks often tried to start insurrections, but they had insuperable difficulties in spreading them. If, like Prosser and Vesey, they tried to coordinate a force large enough to assure success, someone always exposed the plot to white authorities. If, like Turner, they kept their secret among a mere handful, most of the blacks in the surrounding countryside were too frightened or confused to join. The most effective black fighters in the slavery era were runaways who joined the SEMINOLE INDIANS in Florida; but, by fleeing to what was originally foreign territory and later retreating into the swamps, they were not precisely insurrectionaries. The great majority of rebellious slaves chose sabotage, theft, arson, murder, or escape as their modes of resistance, since these could be executed by either an individual or a very small group.

See E. D. Genovese, *Roll, Jordan, Roll* (1974); P. H. Wood, *Black Majority* (1974), Stono Creek rebellion; G. W. Mullin, *Flight and Rebellion* (1974), Gabriel's rebellion; J. Lofton, *Insurrection in South Carolina* (1964), Denmark Vesey; and S. B. Oates, *Fires of Jubilee* (1974), Nat Turner.

ROBERT MCCOLLEY
University of Illinois, Urbana-Champaign

SLAVERY. The word derives from the Latin *sclavus* and the Slavic and Russian *slovene*, indicating the original association with the enslavement of Slavic peoples of central and eastern Europe. It came to mean any person held as the property of another and divested of freedom and personal inalienable rights. In the preemancipation world of the American South, no other socioeconomic relationship affected the lives of all persons, white and black, so profoundly. Southern slavery had a very old heritage, for there are few if any older institutions in recorded human history. Bondage existed in all civilizations of antiquity, both in the biblical Near East and Africa, as well as in India and China. The institution reached its first peak in the West in ancient Greece and Rome. Its origins seem to be connected with war, in which captives, as an act of mercy or expediency, are enslaved rather than slaughtered. Although this early slavery was not associated with race, it had come by the later pre-Christian era to have all the trappings of future Afro-American bondage. In ancient Sicily and southern Italy, white slaves labored in mines and as craftsmen and house servants, as well as on PLANTATIONS that much resembled those to come in the Western Hemisphere. Slave breeding and trading, auctions, and bloody revolts were also commonplace. Although the institution virtually disappeared in the West during the feudal age, it began to reemerge during the great Islamic-Christian wars and by the thirteenth century was vigorously reestablished on Cyprus under the direction of Venetian and Genoese city-state merchants. White Slavs and black Africans labored on Cyprian sugar plantations that became models for sixteenth-century West Indian colonies.

Considering the strong continuity and connection in the history of both slavery and the plantation, it was not surprising that Europeans resorted to these devices to exploit the mineral and agricultural resources of the New World. When ravaging disease and cultural disaffinities undermined the experiment with Indian slavery (SLAVES, INDIAN), the European merchant classes and royal governments quickly overcame religious, cultural, and practical obstacles to inaugurate an accelerating international SLAVE TRADE, which in time transported millions of Africans to Western Hemisphere sugar, coffee, and tobacco plantations. Pejorative racial stereotypes combined with economic greed over the next 400 years to support this, perhaps the greatest forced migration in human history. Early resistance to the importation and enslavement of Africans in Virginia and Maryland eroded by the end of the seventeenth century as these bound laborers came to be regarded as essential instruments for achieving wealth and status. From a coldly economic view, their merits seemed clear. They were evidently in inexhaustible supply, Africa was falsely believed already to be a veritable reservoir of slaves, they could be purchased outright and even more harshly disciplined than white INDENTURED LABORERS, and they were apparently more effective workers and certainly more resistant to European diseases than the aboriginal Indian population.

By the middle of the eighteenth century, slavery existed throughout the American colonies, though it was principally fastened upon those from Maryland southward. The addition of RICE and INDIGO plantations in South Carolina and Georgia added an especially important element. The last quarter of the century, however, proved a decisive period in the history of the institution. Declining soil fertility and profits in the TOBACCO regions and the multiple disruptions wrought by the Revolutionary War combined with rising antislavery ideological pressure to place the institution under severe strain. Proemancipation forces began to triumph in the northern states while voluntary manumissions soared in the Chesapeake district; meanwhile, the Ordinance of 1787 banned future slavery expansion into the northwestern territories. If slavery was to survive, it would now be as a sectional institution. Black bondage was, nevertheless, not truly saved by the introduction of Eli Whitney's fabled cotton gin in the 1790s. Rice and tobacco exports were slowly rebounding, slave-grown WHEAT and other grains were increasing in importance, and a boom in the production of the finer long-staple COTTON plant was already evident in South Carolina during the 1780s. Most important, the rising British and later northern industrial appetite for vast quantities of short-staple cotton virtually assured that slave labor would be in high demand. This is not to mention the subsequent importance of slavery in the production of American sugarcane and HEMP and the role played by skilled slave craftsmen and laborers in both the countryside and the emerging urban and industrial sector of the southern economy. But it was the generally flourishing cotton market that remained the dominant factor in the continuing westward expansion and economic health of slavery. As the principal world source for this most critical raw material, the slave South became an integral link in the economic cycle of the industrial revolution.

Despite the central role played by slavery in the settlement of the southern frontier and the sustained production of key world market crops, the question of profitability has long been a subject of controversy. The argument of unprofitability has been important in the historiography of slavery to sustain the notion of slaveholder paternalism and the implication that planters largely eschewed bourgeois capitalist goals and behavior (SLAVERY, HISTORIOGRAPHY OF). It has also been argued that slavery was only profitable under circumstances of unusual soil fertility and facility of transportation. Westward expansion was therefore essential to its survival, and, since such expansion had allegedly approached its natural limits in eastern Texas by the 1850s, secession and war were needless and avoidable. Contemporary economic analysis suggests, however, that such interpretations have been too sweeping. Taking into account such variables as labor productivity, soil fertility, farm size, market conditions, and the costs of slave owning, it appears that black servitude returned at least a modest rate of profit all across the South. The significant forced migration of slaves toward the southwestern states in the generation before the Civil War reflected the still higher rates

of return and consequent higher value of bound labor on those virgin soils.

At the heart of these phenomena lay the superior productivity of the slave plantation, for the organization and management of capital, land, and labor here created a marked competitive advantage over smaller farming operations. A majority of Afro-Americans resided on farm units near to or greater than 20 slaves per farm, and their owners tended to possess more of the best soils in each state. But as important as any reason for the clear economic superiority of the slave plantation was its more efficient and effective labor management. The successful planter was an agriculturalist, an accountant, a student of the weather and the crop market. Always he depended upon others: FACTORS, stewards, and OVERSEERS among the whites; Negro DRIVERS and the slave folk themselves among the blacks. Above all he had to master the difficult, sometimes literally fatal art of slave management. The two sides, master and servant, alternately tipped and swayed in a delicate balance between the social and economic ambitions and

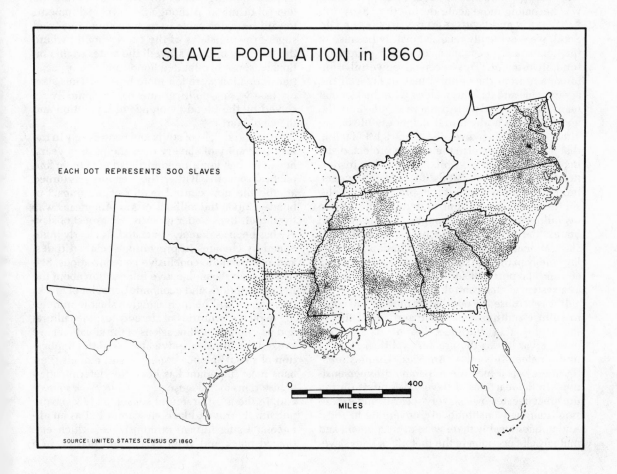

SLAVE POPULATION in 1860

EACH DOT REPRESENTS 500 SLAVES

0   400
MILES

SOURCE: UNITED STATES CENSUS OF 1860

expectations of the former and the individual and group will of the latter. Nothing preoccupied the southern slaveholders more than their endless search for the illusory peaceful and prosperous mean between techniques of terror and humanity. Some employed the task system, making individual work assignments that offered the incentive of an earlier finish to the day's drudgery. Others relied on the greater surveillance of the gang system, in which all labored together. Meanwhile an infinite gradation of similar devices was adopted by slaveholders eager to maximize production, smother discontent, and breed at least the illusion of communalism. Still, the use or threat of violence or more insidious forms of punishment was rarely absent anywhere that black people were compelled to labor for white.

Regardless of means, there is no denying that plantation slavery produced nearly all southern SUGAR and rice and that slavery in general dominated the production of all other crops, including cotton. Investment in land and slaves accordingly did not seem economically irrational. As a result, the relative dominance of larger-scale plantations was becoming more acute during the 1850s. URBANIZATION and INDUSTRIALIZATION in the Old South were evidently retarded mainly because of the comparative economic advantage of agricultural investment. This received powerful reinforcement from the cultural bias in favor of the agrarian life and its values, along with the fact that many planters (and perhaps more significantly the vocal political and cultural defenders of the regime) resisted such diversification, rightly feeling that it would jeopardize the unique protected status of slavery. And so, while the peculiar institution paid good dividends to private owners, brought general agricultural prosperity to the southern region, and contributed significantly to overall economic development in the United States, the benefits to the predominantly nonslaveholding southern white population probably lay chiefly in the ego satisfaction of white supremacy and the personal security afforded by slavery as a system of race control.

It was because the peculiar institution had come to suffuse southern economic and social life so thoroughly that the question of its survival emerged at last as the greatest political issue of mid-nineteenth-century America. Unquestionably there was a measure of paranoid hypersensitivity in the reactions of slavery defenders during the great debates over slavery security and expansion from the Constitutional Convention to 1861. And unquestionably there were overstatement and mutual self-deception in the rhetoric of both slave-

and free-state spokesmen arguing for cultural difference and superiority. Virtually all white Americans profited in some way from slavery, and relatively few were truly concerned about the human aspects of blacks in bondage. Moreover, the political party system had succeeded in retarding outright discussion of the future of the institution in the growing and maturing nation. But, when the issue was finally confronted in the veiled form of territorial EXPANSIONISM, sectional polarization rapidly followed.

Each side came to believe that vital interests and liberties were at stake. It was more than only cultural difference; the Union of their revolutionary fathers appeared threatened with corruption by a conspiracy of either abolitionists or slave power interests. Slavery defenders particularly feared that a ban on expansion would only be the prelude to more direct assaults on the security of the institution to be orchestrated by a Republican-controlled federal government. Anxiety over potential slave unrest and ultimate abolition combined with concern over the continuing loyalty of nonslaveholding whites to push many toward the logic of disunion. Although the principal impetus toward secession came from the cotton-, rice-, and sugar-growing states of the Lower South, where the majority of blacks lived, the states' rights rationale, sense of offended honor, and fear of social transformation were felt more broadly. Thus slavery as a vexing political question was finally resolved by the bloody violence of revolution and the Civil War.

The central field of study and controversy in the historiography of slavery over the past 25 years, however, has gone beyond these economic and political concerns. Rather, the literature has turned around the now central matter of the impact of bondage upon the millions of Afro-Americans who lived their lives under its sway. No aspect of slavery has been as fiercely contested, as clearly influenced by changes in prevailing social attitudes, and as resistant to conclusive generalizations. Statistical analysis of objective information about the living conditions and economic behavior of blacks in bondage will be increasingly valuable in helping to pierce centuries of stereotypes; the cultural and psychological dimensions of the situation have evoked the often sensitive and insightful application of social science concepts and models. Perhaps most important has been the determination of historians to make use of available black sources and, in the most profound sense, to view slavery not simply from a black viewpoint but as an all-encompassing human circumstance, which embraced black and white, slave and master, in a complex and fateful web of interrelationships.

It has been suggested that slavery, particularly in its plantation form, has served together with the twentieth-century urban ghetto as one of the two principal institutional devices employed by the dominant white population to control and shape the lives of blacks. These two exploitative systems imposed significant physical, economic, cultural, and psychological parameters upon the rural black immigrant and growing black child. Slavery certainly subjected the African to relentless pressure to nullify his native culture and adapt him to a life of servitude. Forced to adjust to a new language, new clothing and diet, a new religious cosmology, and even a new Western name, the African was in a distorted sense forcibly Americanized. The experience of the European immigrant only approximates the tribulations of Afro-Americans in bondage. The slave population was subjected to an astonishing range of restrictions and misusages, not the least of which was the attack in law and custom upon black family structure. Not only were North American slave marriages uniquely unsanctified by church or state, but adult and child alike were legally vulnerable to division and separation, and the black woman was in fantasy and reality the victim of sexual abuse.

Recent historiography has shown, however, that the traditional picture of a powerless and infinitely plastic Afro-American culture is invalid. There were, to begin with, important restraints upon white avarice and anxiety: SLAVE CODES, community opinion, and the paternalism emergent in all such power relationships were all factors. More consequential was the fact that slaveholders were dependent upon their bondmen and bondwomen for the labor that promised wealth and status. In addition, American slavery was not monolithic, but an institution that evolved over two and a half centuries and assumed a great variety of forms across the growing and changing South. Within these shifting limits it is clear that the slave population, grown to nearly 4 million by 1860, struggled continuously to create and preserve a distinct Afro-American culture and life-preserving sense of community within slavery. Violent resistance has always dominated this part of the story, with its drama and immediacy. SLAVE INSURRECTIONS, fugitive SLAVES, the private terror of murder, arson, or other acts of passion and day-to-day resistance, there were aplenty. Although patrols and general vigilance might slacken from time to time, the slave regions of the antebellum South were, like all such societies, places where violence was never far from the surface. More important than this, however, was the quieter process by which blacks labored to give meaning and value to their lives. The effort to preserve valued pieces of African culture such as music and dance, folktales, conjuring, and the rituals of life and death; the remarkably successful effort to sustain family life, to create a relevant Christianity, to find satisfaction and even rewards in one's daily labor—these along with accommodation, flight, and rebellion were part of the broad variety of black responses to slavery.

See excellent bibliographies, including A. Link and R. Patrick (eds.), *Writing Southern History* (1965); J. Randall and D. Donald, *Civil War and Reconstruction* (1969); G. Grob, *American Social History* (1970); D. Fehrenbacher, *Manifest Destiny* (1970); and A. Weinstein and F. Gatell, *American Negro Slavery* (1973). Noteworthy recent titles are R. Fogel and S. Engerman, *Time on Cross* (1974); E. Genovese, *Roll, Jordan, Roll* (1974); E. Morgan, *American Slavery, American Freedom* (1975); and J. W. Blassingame (ed.), *Slave Testimony* (1977). W. L. Rose, *Documentary History of Slavery* (1976); and M. Mullin, *American Negro Slavery* (1976), are fine introductions to primary sources preserved in all major southern university libraries and state archives, especially University of North Carolina, Chapel Hill, Duke University, and Louisiana State University.

STEVEN A. CHANNING
University of Kentucky

SLAVERY, DEFENSE OF. The rise of ANTI-SLAVERY SENTIMENT in the 1770s and 1780s made southerners conscious of the unique importance of SLAVERY in their lives and prompted them to articulate a defense for an institution they previously had taken for granted. As this occurred, the creation of the American Union began generating a sense of sectional consciousness (SECTIONALISM). The triumph of abolition in the northern states (1780–1804) and the rise of the cotton kingdom in the Deep South coupled that consciousness with slavery, the most obvious symbol of southern distinctiveness, while the facts of racial demography tied it to a concern over white supremacy.

The defense of slavery was reactive, sporadic, and relatively self-assured until after 1830. Only when their fears or suspicions were aroused, as at the CONSTITUTIONAL CONVENTION (1787) or during the MISSOURI COMPROMISE controversy (1819–1820), did southerners react sharply. The generally sympathetic stance of the federal government during the VIRGINIA DYNASTY and the absence of antislavery militance served to obscure what was really a growing concern. When the national antislavery movement embraced militant abolitionism around 1830, that concern turned to unease and then to fear, and from then until the Civil War the defense of slavery was a major preoccupation of public life in the South.

The defense operated on several levels. Southerners used their influence in national politics and the federal government to guard the institution. JOHN C. CALHOUN formulated an elaborate constitutional defense, while THOMAS R. DEW, WILLIAM GILMORE SIMMS, GEORGE FITZHUGH, and others produced an extensive literature of apology, major items of which E. N. Elliott brought together in *Cotton Is King, and Pro-Slavery Arguments* (1860). One of the important expressions of the antebellum mind, this literature drew upon religious, historical, scientific, and philosophical authorities to argue that slavery was a positive good for blacks and the linchpin of a superior way of life. After the Mexican War, the South's role in national politics was largely dictated by the determination to protect slavery and all that slavery implied in moral, racial, economic, and political terms.

Why were southerners so concerned to defend slavery? The basic reasons were racial, ideological, and economic. By 1830 the economic and political epicenter of the section lay in the DEEP SOUTH and the BLACK BELT, where demographic factors caused whites to consider slavery and abolition as first of all matters of racial security. (In 1860 the population of the six Deep South states was 49 percent black.) Whites feared blacks because they abused them and because they believed them incapable of functioning as responsible citizens or of controlling their baser instincts. The consequence of emancipation, they insisted, would be chaos: the southern way of life—civilization itself in the South—was built around slavery and could not survive abolition. The enormous economic stake in slavery was another important consideration, as was the issue of STATES' RIGHTS, the ability of the southern minority to protect itself in a majoritarian nation.

See, though there is no general history of defense of slavery, D. L. Robinson, *Slavery in Structure of American Politics, 1765–1820* (1971); W. S. Jenkins, *Pro-Slavery Thought in Old South* (1935); D. B. Davis, *Problem of Slavery in Age of Revolution, 1770–1823* (1975); W. D. Jordan, *White over Black* (1968); G. M. Frederickson, *Black Image in White Mind* (1971); W. W. Freehling, *Prelude to Civil War* (1966); S. A. Channing, *Crisis of Fear* (1970); E. D. Genovese, *World Slaveholders Made* (1969); C. G. Sellers, *Southerner as American* (1960); D. Donald, *Journal of Southern History* (Feb., 1971); and R. E. Morrow, *Mississippi Valley Historical Review* (June, 1961).

I. A. NEWBY
University of Hawaii

SLAVERY, HISTORIOGRAPHY OF, began with the writings of the abolitionists, who also encouraged former slaves, most notably FREDERICK DOUGLASS, to write narratives of their experiences. The first historian to encompass the whole story of American slavery was the versatile black Pennsylvanian, George Washington Williams (1849–1891). His *History of the Negro Race in America* (1883) was crowded with political, legal, and constitutional developments. Williams' point of view was in the abolitionist tradition; he also anticipated W. E. B. DU BOIS and CARTER G. WOODSON by claiming for black people a constructive and intelligent role in American history.

The era between 1880 and World War I saw the rise of professionally trained historians. Many, especially at Johns Hopkins, published monographs dealing with slavery in a single colony or state and stressing institutional developments. In keeping with prevailing ideals of scientific history, these were dry and factual in style. Such works became a basis, along with new types of research, for UL-RICH BONNELL PHILLIPS, who dominated the historiography of slavery in the first half of the twentieth century. In *American Negro Slavery* (1918) and *Life and Labor in the Old South* (1929), Phillips reversed the abolitionist tradition by viewing slavery as a useful transition from African primitiveness to modern civilization. His sunny view of the Old South is now in disrepute, but Phillips remains important for his detailed picture, original in its time, of the everyday workings of slave society.

With Kenneth M. Stampp's *The Peculiar Institution* (1956) and Stanley F. Elkins' *Slavery* (1958) the neoabolitionist school took over, dwelling on the deprivations, punishments, and maladjustments that plagued slaves. Stampp also argued the profitability of slavery, which was greatly reinforced by A. H. Conrad and J. R. Meyers in *The Economics of Slavery* (1964). Elkins made suggestive comparisons among North American, Caribbean, and South American slavery, stimulating a series of new comparative studies. The statistical methods of Conrad and Meyers led to an elaborate and highly publicized work, *Time on the Cross* (1974) by R. W. Fogel and Stanley Engerman. Fogel and Engerman held that southern plantations were more efficient than the free farms of the North and that slaves enjoyed better nurture and longevity than free laborers in Europe and North America. After an early wave of enthusiasm, the two-volumed study has met an unprecedented amount of vehement and meticulous criticism. Perhaps of more long-range significance was the trend, beginning in the 1960s, to emphasize the positive contributions of blacks in forming their distinctive American subculture. This approach characterizes John W. Blassingame's *The Slave Community* (1972) and Eugene Genovese's *Roll, Jordan, Roll* (1974), a major synthesis that reflects all the major tendencies of recent writing on slavery and serves as an ideal introduction to scholarship in this field.

ROBERT MCCOLLEY
University of Illinois, Urbana-Champaign

SLAVES, FUGITIVE, although never sufficiently organized to threaten the survival of the peculiar institution, represented a perennial problem for the slave regime. Thousands of slaves ran away each year. They were overwhelmingly young (aged sixteen to thirty-five), and disproportionately skilled. Although groups of two or three and even as many as 50 slaves fled together, at times to establish colonies of runaway slaves in remote areas (MAROONS), most frequently flight was an individual act. Runaways enjoyed considerable support from the slave community in the form of food, shelter, clothing, passes, and refuge from pursuers. Nevertheless, most fugitive slaves remained at large only for a short period of time—a few days or at most a few weeks—before they were captured or returned voluntarily to their owners.

Most slaves ran away because of specific grievances. Most frequently the decision to escape was triggered by the desire to avoid a whipping or as a consequence of having been whipped. Some sought to gain concessions: a lighter work load or cancellation of a threatened whipping. Family ties played a crucial role in the motivations of many fugitive slaves. On the one hand, many slaves fled to rejoin their families or to prevent separation from them by an impending sale. On the other hand, many slaves were reluctant to run away because to do so would separate them from their loved ones.

Fugitive slaves who sought permanent freedom faced almost insurmountable odds. Most were familiar only with local terrain, were confronted by a hostile white population, and possessed few skills and resources with which to effect a successful escape. In addition they were pursued by dreaded bloodhounds and bands of patrollers. Many fugitives headed for cities and towns, which provided greater anonymity and better access to transportation. Although in the Deep South some sought refuge among Indian tribes, those who successfully evaded capture usually headed for the North or Canada and were most likely to have escaped from the border states. Once secure from capture, many fugitives related their experiences under slavery to sympathetic whites, and their published narratives contributed substantially to mounting ANTISLAVERY SENTIMENT.

See B. Drew, *Refugee* (1855); N. R. Yetman, *Life Under "Peculiar Institution"* (1970); G. P. Rawick, *American Slave* (1972); E. D. Genovese, *Roll, Jordan, Roll* (1974); K. M. Stampp, *Peculiar Institution* (1956); J. W. Blassingame, *Slave Community* (1972); G. W. Mullin, *Flight and Rebellion* (1972); and H. Aptheker, *American Negro Slave Revolts* (1943).

NORMAN R. YETMAN
University of Kansas

SLAVES, INDIAN. In the sixteenth century Spaniards from the Caribbean raided the coastal and interior South for slaves, but once they settled Florida (1565) they infrequently enslaved Indians. Henry Woodward of South Carolina initiated in 1674 the slave trade that became a major factor in English-Indian relations. Once the French settled Louisiana in 1699, their intense rivalry with the English caused both sides to dispatch their respective Indian allies to fight and take slaves. The Spanish missions in Georgia and Florida were destroyed by raids from Charleston. Rebellious Indians, such as the TUSCARORA (1711) and the Natchez (1729), were seized as slaves. The French extended Indian slavery into their Mississippi Valley settlements. Great Plains Indians, seized and traded as slaves, reached southern settlements. The Spanish in Texas engaged in the trade especially with Comanche traders. The English legalized Indian slavery though the French and Spanish merely condoned it.

Due to their fierce independent spirit and susceptibility to disease, Indians proved difficult to adapt to plantation labor. As a result they were used as domestic servants or exchanged for black slaves in the West Indies. By 1700 Indian slaves were almost completely replaced by blacks. Yet Indian slavery persisted in the Carolinas and Georgia into the early American period. In Spanish Louisiana, despite Governor Alexander O'Reilly's 1769 decree against it, Indian slavery persisted into the nineteenth century. The Missouri supreme court declared it illegal in 1834.

See D. H. Cockran, *Carolina Indian Frontier* (1970); V. W. Crane, *Southern Frontier* (1929); A. M. Gibson, *Chickasaws* (1971); A. W. Lauber, *Indian Slavery* (1913), classic but dated; R. M. Magnaghi, *Missouri Historical Society Bulletin* (July, 1975) and "Abolition of Indian Slavery in Spanish Louisiana," paper, Missouri Valley History Conference (March, 1974); and S. Winston, *Journal of Negro History* (Oct., 1934).

RUSSELL M. MAGNAGHI
Northern Michigan University

SLAVE TRADE, ATLANTIC, the forced emigration of approximately 10 million to 12 million black persons from Africa to the Western Hemisphere, was one of the largest intercontinental human migrations in history. Preceded by many centuries of trans-Saharan slave trade to the Mediterranean region, the Atlantic trade was initiated by the Portuguese, who began shipping slaves from Africa in the fifteenth century to be used primarily for domestic service in Spain and Portugal. Initially this trade was very small; but, with the spread of sugar plantations from the Mediterranean and Atlantic islands to Brazil and the Caribbean, the "trickle became a flood" during the early seventeenth century. The Atlantic slave trade reached a peak during the 1770s, when as many as 100,000 slaves arrived in the Americas during certain years. A similar high point may have been reached during the period of illicit slaving in the 1840s.

The United States, or British North American mainland colonies, was the recipient of a surprisingly small portion, approximately 6 percent, of these African slaves. By far the largest percentage of the slaves was taken to Brazil, and the various Caribbean island colonies also consumed large numbers. The Spanish mainland colonies had been among the first to exploit African slave labor, but their intake was regulated by the famous Asiento contracts and limited by Spain's failure to achieve a foothold on the African coast until the nineteenth century.

The American need for labor, the African willingness and ability to export fellow Africans, and the European commercial institutions, ships, capital, and manpower all combined into an efficient, cooperative system that brought suffering, humiliation, and premature death to millions of innocent Africans. With a few exceptions, their offspring cannot account for their geographic or ethnic origin. Since the Africans along the coast were frequently involved in the slave trade in a middleman capacity, the majority of the slaves came from a variety of ethnic groups in the interior. Initially the hinterland of the Dahomey coast (formerly called the Slave Coast) and of the Congo River region produced the largest proportion of the slaves, but by the eighteenth century the whole region from Senegal to Angola, and even the east coast of Africa, contributed to the flow of forced emigrants.

Several European nations, along with the United States, participated in the Atlantic slave trade. Because of the length of their involvement, the Portuguese were undoubtedly responsible for the largest share of the slave traffic. England clearly dominated the trade during the eighteenth century. The United States and Spain were involved for relatively short periods only, which accounts for their modest degree of participation.

Although the dreaded "middle passage" has received much attention in slave trade literature, the journey to the coast in coffles and the confinement in coastal slave dungeons and aboard ships may have been equally devastating for the slaves. Many slaves succumbed before they reached their destination. The ocean crossing alone exacted an average toll of in the range of 10 to 20 percent, although there were many exceptions, with death tolls ranging from close to zero to 100 percent. Infectious diseases and length of voyage appear to have been the principle determinants in mortality rates. Studies consistently confirm that white crew members on slave ships died at even higher rates than African slaves.

The economic impact of the slave trade is difficult to assess; it is extremely complex and has ramifications for four continents if not the whole global economy. Profits have often been exaggerated. Although some human cargoes brought returns in excess of 100 percent, others suffered serious losses. Calculations of the British trade, perhaps the most efficient, point to profits of 9.5 percent.

In North America, slaves were imported on a significant scale for only about one century (1690–1808), which explains the low percentage—6 percent, or approximately 600,000 slaves—of the total Atlantic slave trade. The development of RICE culture in the 1690s and INDIGO and TOBACCO afterward stimulated a demand for slave labor in the southern colonies. Virginia and South Carolina attracted the bulk of the slaves initially, with Charleston functioning as the most important American colonial slaving port from which slaves were reexported to other colonies. Initially English ships were the main suppliers, but gradually American captains, especially New Englanders, replaced them. American ships often carried small consignments of slaves fom the West Indies, but the majority of the slaves was brought directly from Africa (COMMERCE).

Eventually the rising tide of humanitarian criticism, bolstered by the liberal opposition to forced labor, brought an end to the Atlantic slave trade. England and the United States abolished the slave trade in 1808. Other countries gradually followed suit, but the traffic was continued illicitly and in some areas legally until the 1860s.

See P. Curtin, *Atlantic Slave Trade* (1969); S. Engerman and E. Genovese (eds.), *Race and Slavery* (1975); P. Emmer *et al.* (eds.), *Atlantic Slave Trade* (1976); J. Hogen-

dorn and H. Gemery (eds.), *Atlantic Slave Trade* (1978);
R. Anstey, *Atlantic Slave Trade* (1975); R. W. Fogel and
S. Engerman, *Time on Cross* (1974); P. Duignan and C.
Clendenen, *U.S. and African Slave Trade* (1963); D.
Wax, *Pacific Quarterly of History and Biography* (April,
1962) and *Georgia Historical Quarterly* (March, 1967);
and R. Higgins, *South Atlantic Quarterly* (Winter, 1971).

JOHANNES POSTMA
Mankato State University

ESTIMATED NUMBER OF SLAVES ARRIVING IN WESTERN HEMISPHERE

Years	Total	Annual Average
1450–1600	275,000	1,800
1601–1700	1,365,000	13,650
1701–1810	6,200,000	56,360
1811–1860	2,300,000	46,000
Grand Total	10,140,000	

ESTIMATED REGIONAL DISTRIBUTION OF DESTINATION OF SLAVES

Destination	%	Total
U.S.A. (North American mainland)	6	600,000
Brazil	39	3,900,000
Spanish colonies	17	1,700,000
British Caribbean	16	1,600,000
French Caribbean	16	1,600,000
Dutch Caribbean	5	500,000
Danish Caribbean	1	100,000

NATIONS PARTICIPATING IN SLAVE TRADE

Nation	%	Total
Portugal	40	4,400,000
England	29	3,100,000
France	18	1,970,000
Holland	6	660,000
U.S.A.	4	440,000
Spain	2	220,000
Denmark and others	1	110,000

SLAVE TRADE, DOMESTIC, was one of the grimmer features of slavery in the antebellum South. Four economic developments enhanced its importance: namely, land expansion into the old Southwest; the increase in southern cotton production; the termination of slave imports in 1808; and the decline in the importance of slave labor in the border states.

Between 1816 and 1860 the states of Virginia, Kentucky, Maryland, Tennessee, and South Carolina provided surplus slaves for the domestic trade.

The major cities of Baltimore, Washington, Richmond, Norfolk, Louisville, and Charleston served as the gathering and shipping sites for those engaged in the trade. The source of slaves in the market came from owners who had surplus chattels, who found slavery no longer competitive, who deliberately sought a large profit in the interstate trade, or who as executors of wills found the southern market a convenient means of disposing of chattel property in settling an estate. Despite the attractions of the trade, there was much reluctance for many owners to sell south. Substantial numbers in Maryland and Virginia manumitted their slaves or found it feasible to hire them out for extensive periods. Still others made firm stipulations that sales were to be made only to local purchasers. Because of these limitations the trade was less than it might have been.

Those who purchased slaves were professional traders and planters seeking chattels for their own use. The latter were active until the late 1820s, moving through the rural areas of the border South, making a series of small purchases, and sending their charges south in coffles by overland trails or riverboats. The professional traders soon overshadowed them. Headquartered in the larger cities, they had agents scouring the countryside for purchases and ads in the local papers promising the biggest cash payments.

Despite their role as economic middlemen, the professional traders quickly aroused the ire of many local citizens as well as northern abolitionists, and they were symbols of fear and oppression to the slave family. It was typical for one large trader to dominate his geographic region for a number of years. Thus the leading figure in Maryland in the 1820s was Austin Woolfolk. He was succeeded by Hope Slatter and Joseph Donovan and then by John Denning and Bernard Campbell in the 1850s. Virginia's major traders were FRANKLIN & ARMFIELD in the 1830s and George Kephart in the 1840s. The chief traders in Kentucky and South Carolina were Tarlton Arterburn and Norman Gadsden, respectively.

Maintenance and shipment were major features of the traders' activities. Slaves awaiting shipment were kept in jail spaces or specially built pens until sufficient numbers were available for the move southward. The period from October to May was the typical shipping season. The major traders usually sent their cargoes by water with New Orleans the chief destination. Smaller traders and planters favored the overland route and the smaller ports like Mobile, Savannah, and Charleston. By land, coffles were sent westward to river ports on the Ohio and then by steamboat to New Orleans, or they might be sent directly south by land to cities like Natchez. The water route was quicker and more convenient. Groups of from 100 to 150 slaves were dispatched, often with the last spaces filled by the slaves of small shippers. The chattels transported were invariably young (ten to twenty-five years old). Although males were mostly in their twenties, the age of females was more evenly ranged. In numbers, males predominated by a 30 percent margin. This ratio was partly rebalanced by the more even distribution of sexes in the shipments of the nontraders. Still, the practice resulted in an imbalance in the sex ratio of slaves in some parts of Maryland and Virginia. Whether this practice was deliberate on the part of the traders or sellers cannot be determined. If deliberate, the retention of the child-bearing element, the female slaves, might lend credence and statistical evidence to the charge of slave breeding.

In contrast to its overall operations, the economics of the slave trade are less clear. The difference in price between slaves in the border South and the Deep South, which monetarily justified the sale of slaves southward, was always substantial. Thus early in the nineteenth century a prime hand who brought $350 in the Virginia market would sell for $500 in New Orleans. By 1860 the comparative prices had moved to $1,000 and $1,500, respectively. If the profit motive alone were involved, border owners would have had a compelling reason to sell.

For the traders, the degree of profits is more difficult to determine. There were many serious hazards in slave trading. Because of the short-term operations of the small traders and their lack of control in the major phases of the business, their endeavors appear to be of limited profits. The major traders undoubtedly fared better. Estimates of profit range from a high of 30 percent to a low of $15 per slave sold, figures well within the range of other successful and more respectable businesses.

As to the actual number of slaves reaching the Deep South, the picture is less certain. The decade of the 1830s witnessed the heaviest movement, followed by the 1820s, the 1850s, and then the 1840s. In those decades a total of perhaps 300,000 reached the Deep South. But, when allowances are made for slaves taken south by emigrating masters and by individual southern planters, the share left to the traders was probably less than 50 percent. Nevertheless, the trade and the trader played a major role in nineteenth-century American history.

See F. Bancroft, *Slave Trading in Old South* (1931), complete, but questionable statistics; E. A. Andrews, *Slavery and Domestic Slave Trade* (1836); W. H. Collins, *Domestic Slave Trade* (1904); W. T. Laprade, *Journal of Negro History* (Jan., 1926); C. Wesley, *Journal of Negro History* (April, 1942); and W. L. Calderhead, *Civil War History* (March, 1972), statistical appraisal of trade in Maryland.

WILLIAM L. CALDERHEAD
U.S. Naval Academy

SLIDELL, JOHN (1793–1871), was born in New York City. He achieved a diploma from Columbia College, traveled in Europe, where he discovered a fondness for the diplomatic arts, and earned a degree in law. Then he went south to New Orleans, where he was by 1823, and became a prominent attorney, a land speculator, and the most powerful politician in Louisiana. In 1843 he was elected to the U.S. House of Representatives, which seat he vacated in 1845 upon assuming the post of President James Polk's special minister to Mexico. In 1853 he became U.S. senator, which he remained until 1861, when he followed his state out of the Union to become before the end of the year the Confederate agent to Napoleon III.

Notable events in his long career included the "Plaquemine frauds" of 1844, in which he helped several voters frustrated in New Orleans to cast perhaps illegal ballots elsewhere for Polk; the diplomatic journey the following year to Mexico, where failure led almost directly to the Mexican War; his guidance of James Buchanan into the White House in 1856; his frustrated endeavors as Confederate emissary to obtain Napoleon's recognition of and assistance to the southern cause; and, above all, the TRENT AFFAIR, which began his mission to France, in which he and JAMES M. MASON were forcibly removed by Captain Charles Wilkes of the USS *San Jacinto* from a British merchant ship, an action that almost brought Great Britain in the Civil War. He was a man of consummate political skill, especially in bringing together warring elements within a party's ranks. He did not return to his native land after the war, and he died in England.

See L. M. Sears, *John Slidell* (1925); B. Wilson, *John Slidell and Confederacy in Paris* (1932); F. L. Owsley, *King Cotton Diplomacy* (1931); and A. L. Diket, "John Slidell in Senate, 1853–1861" (Ph.D. dissertation, Louisiana State University, 1958).

A. L. DIKET
Nicholls State University

SMALLS, ROBERT (1839–1915), best known for his abduction of the Confederate steamer *Planter* during the Civil War, became an active black leader during and after Reconstruction in South Carolina. Born in Beaufort and taken to Charleston as a child, he subsequently acquired a limited education through private tutelage. He was a delegate to the Republican National Convention in 1864, 1872, and 1876. As a delegate to the South Carolina constitutional conventions of 1868 and 1895, he had little to say in the deliberations of 1868, but he bitterly assailed BENJAMIN TILLMAN's movement to disfranchise blacks in 1895. He served one term each in the state house of representatives (1869–1871), the state senate (1871–1873), and the U.S. House of Representatives (1875–1877). Interest in the affairs of his district, civil rights, and South Carolina's election procedures characterized his congressional career. In 1877 he was charged with and convicted of having accepted a bribe while a state senator, but he was pardoned by WADE HAMPTON, the governor, by mutual agreement of state Democrats and federal Republican officials. From 1879 until his death, he was the collector of the port of Beaufort.

See O. E. Uyo, *Smalls* (1971), definitive full-length work; D. Sterling, *Captain of Planter* (1958), written for younger audience; B. Quarles, *Civil War History* (March, 1958); M. Work, *Journal of Negro History* (Jan., 1920); and G. B. Tindall, *South Carolina Negroes, 1877–1900* (1966).

EDWARD F. SWEAT
Clark College

SMITH, ASHBEL (1805–1886), was born at Hartford, Conn., and was educated at Yale. After receiving his medical degree in 1828, he practiced medicine briefly in Salisbury, N.C., studied further in Paris, and moved to the Republic of Texas in 1837. He served the new republic as surgeon general (1837), chargé d'affaires to England and France (1842–1844), and secretary of state (1844, 1845). After Texas gained statehood, Smith served briefly in the Mexican War, was in the legislature three separate terms (1855, 1866, 1878), and became a brigadier general in the Confederate army. He held offices in the Texas medical college board and was president of the board of regents of the University of Texas, which he helped to establish. Dr. Smith at various times delivered the annual address before the Phi Beta Kappa chapter at Yale; was a U.S. commissioner to the London Industrial Exhibition in 1851; was a juror of the Centennial Exhibition in Philadelphia; and was an honorary commissioner from Texas in 1878 at Paris. He was the author of several scientific and historical trea-

tises. He died at Evergreen plantation, his home on Galveston Bay.

See A. Smith, *Reminiscences* (1876); J. H. Smith, *Annexation of Texas* (1919); and papers, Texas State Archives.

ROBERT W. AMSLER
University of Texas, Arlington

SMITH, EDMUND KIRBY. See KIRBY-SMITH, EDMUND

SMITH, ELLISON DURANT "COTTON ED" (1864–1944), U.S. senator from South Carolina (1909–1944), was born at Tanglewood, a family farm near Lynchburg, S.C. After four years in the state house of representatives (1897–1901) and an unsuccessful campaign for Congress in 1901, Smith promoted the organization of cotton farmers throughout the Southeast. His talent for radical rhetoric complemented his "friends and neighbors" approach in South Carolina politics; he was not a Populist. In the Senate, Smith's votes helped sustain Progressive causes and federal assistance to agriculture between 1909 and 1932. Yet he opposed immigration, woman suffrage, and the abolition of child labor, and he accepted the assumptions of racial prejudice that permeated his society. During his last two terms, he was an ineffective senator; his limited support of the New Deal was accompanied by demogogic appeals to white supremacy and states' rights.

See S. K. Smith, "E. D. Smith" (Ph.D. dissertation, University of South Carolina, 1970); D. W. Hollis, "Cotton Ed Smith," paper, SHA Convention (Nov., 1967); M. N. Bouknight, "Senatorial Campaigns" (M.A. thesis, Florida State University, 1961); R. T. Berthhoff, *Journal of Southern History* (Aug., 1951); D. W. Grantham, Jr., *Journal of Southern History* (Nov., 1947); T. Saloutos, *Journal of Southern History* (Nov., 1947); D. W. Grantham, Jr., *North Carolina Historical Review* (April, 1949); and V. O. Key, Jr., *Southern Politics* (1949). No personal papers remain.

SELDEN K. SMITH
Columbia College

SMITH, HOKE (1855–1931), was born in Newton, N.C. He moved to Atlanta and by the 1880s was the most successful railroad damage suit lawyer in Georgia. He purchased the Atlanta *Journal*, and his antitrust, antirailroad policies endeared him to the farmers. As secretary of the interior (1893–1896), he directed the last great land rush in Oklahoma in 1893. Smith was elected governor of Georgia in 1906, and his reform administration abolished the CONVICT LEASE SYSTEM, established statewide PROHIBITION, disfranchised Negroes, sponsored educational advances, reformed penal institutions, established juvenile courts, and gave Georgia a powerful railroad commission to regulate the railroads and eliminate discriminatory practices. Reelected governor in 1910, he continued his program of reform. He resigned in 1912 to fill the unexpired term of U.S. Senator Alexander S. Clay, who had died. Elected U.S. senator in 1914, he sponsored the Smith-Lever bill, which established extension departments within land-grant colleges to give instruction in agricultural and home economic subjects to farmers. The bill provided federal funds the states had to match. The Smith-Hughes bill provided the same type of matching funds for vocational education programs in secondary schools. Smith worked to establish a federal department of education and for federal support for rural schools. His opposition to President Woodrow Wilson's programs helped defeat him in his bid for reelection to the Senate in 1920. Although Smith ultimately adopted HENRY GRADY's New South creed of responsible industry working with the political and economic power of the North, his reforms as governor place him in the line of southern Progressives.

See Hoke Smith Papers, University of Georgia Library; H. W. Grady, *New South* (1890); D. W. Grantham, Jr., *Hoke Smith* (1958); A. S. Link, *North Carolina Historical Review* (April, 1946); T. Carageorge, "Hoke Smith and Tom Watson" (Ph.D. dissertation, University of Georgia, 1963); and J. C. Ward, "Bourbon Democrats" (Ph.D. dissertation, University of North Carolina, 1947).

TED CARAGEORGE
Pensacola Junior College

SMITH, LILLIAN (1897–1966), novelist, teacher, editor, lecturer, columnist, and author of nonfiction books and articles on race relations, was born in Jasper, Fla. She published two novels, *Strange Fruit* (1944) and *One Hour* (1959), and five nonfiction books, *Killers of the Dream* (1949), *The Journey* (1954), *Now Is the Time* (1955), *Memory of a Large Christmas* (1962), and *Our Faces, Our Words* (1964). In 1936 she founded a little magazine, *South Today*, which she edited until 1944. From October, 1948, to September, 1949, she wrote a weekly column, "A Southerner Talking," for the Chicago *Defender*.

See L. Blackwell and F. Clay, *Lillian Smith* (1971); F. H. Marcus, *English Journal* (Dec., 1962); B. DeVoto, *Harper's* (May, 1944); and G. B. Leonard, *Look* (Sept., 1966).

LOUISE BLACKWELL
Florida A. & M. University

SMITH, MARTIN LUTHER (1819–1866), born at Danby, N.Y., graduated from West Point in 1842. As a second lieutenant in the topographical engineers he served in the Mexican War. He also surveyed for government improvement of the Savannah River and for a ship canal across the Florida peninsula. From 1856 to 1861 Smith served as chief engineer for the Fernando & Cedar Keys Railroad in Florida. He resigned from the U.S. Army and was commissioned a major in the Confederate army (March, 1861). He was assigned as engineer-in-chief of the defenses of New Orleans, April 16, 1861, and promoted brigadier general (April, 1862) and major general (November, 1862). After the fall of NEW ORLEANS, he was placed in charge of constructing the defenses of Vicksburg. In December, 1862, as commander at VICKSBURG, he repulsed the attack of General W. T. Sherman. He served as chief engineer of the Army of Northern Virginia (April–July, 1864) and in that same position in the Army of Tennessee (July, 1864–January, 1865), where he constructed the defenses of Mobile.

See W. F. Amann, *Personnel of Civil War* (1961); and C. A. Evans, *Confederate Military History* (1962).

RICHARD W. SADLER
Weber State College

SMITH, MILTON HANNIBAL (1836–1921), was born in New York. After living with his family in Illinois, he moved to the South in 1858 to work as a telegraph operator in northern Mississippi and eastern Tennessee. He worked with federal rail and communications authorities during the Civil War and became thoroughly familiar with the southern RAILROADS between Atlanta and Memphis. Employed by several railroad companies after the war, he rose rapidly from being a division superintendent of the Alabama & Tennessee (1866) to the principal executive officer of the Louisville & Nashville (1882–1921). He was always more interested in the operational details of railroading than in its finances or its executive management. While greatly expanding and improving the properties of the L & N, he regularly was at odds with both state and federal officials interested in public regulation of rail transportation.

See *Railway Age* (March 4, 1921); M. Klein, *Louisville and Nashville* (1972); and J. F. Doster, *Railroads in Alabama Politics* (1957).

SMITH, WILLIAM (1762–1840), a native South Carolinian, served as state senator (1802–1808) and then as judge, gaining the reputation for severity tempered by fairness. In the U.S. Senate (1816–1823) he sided with the WILLIAM CRAW-FORD faction and led the call for a return to STATES' RIGHTS orthodoxy. Both deepened the enmity between himself and the nationalist J. C. CALHOUN and helped to shape state politics for a decade. His greatest triumph over Calhoun came in 1825, when he pushed resolutions through the state legislature condemning high tariffs and internal improvements as unconstitutional. He returned to the U.S. Senate (1826–1830); but resolute opposition to NULLIFICATION, with which Calhoun was now identified, led to Smith's defeat for reelection. Shortly thereafter he moved to Huntsville, Ala., became a wealthy landholder, and served four years in the state legislature. His modest stature and "angelic face" belied an irascible temper, a vindictive spirit, and a grating style of debate.

See C. S. Boucher, *Nullification Controversy* (1916); W. W. Freehling, *Prelude to Civil War* (1965); J. B. O'Neall, *Biographical Sketches* (1859); B. F. Perry, *Reminiscences* (1883); and C. M. Wiltse, *Calhoun* (1944–51).

MAJOR L. WILSON
Memphis State University

SMITH, WILLIAM "EXTRA BILLY" (1797–1887),

was born in King George County, Va. He practiced law in Culpeper, where he was residing when elected to the Virginia senate (1836–1841) and to the U.S. House of Representatives (1841–1843). In 1842 Smith moved his practice to Warrenton. He was elected governor of Virginia by the legislature for the term 1846–1849. Upon stepping down as governor, Smith moved to California but returned to Virginia in 1852. Again Smith was elected to the House of Representatives, where he remained from 1852 to 1861. During the Civil War, he served in the Confederate army, briefly in the Confederate Congress, and as governor from January 1, 1864, to the fall of Richmond. As governor Smith supported the Davis government and was a pillar of the Confederacy. He served in the Virginia house of delegates from 1877 to 1879.

See A. A. Fahrner, "William 'Extra Billy' Smith" (Ph.D. dissertation, University of North Carolina, 1953), comprehensive bibliography, *Virginia Magazine of History and Biography* (Jan., 1966), and *East Carolina University Publications in History* (1965); *Biographical Directory of American Congress* (1974); J. W. Bell, *Memoirs of Governor William Smith of Virginia* (1891); and Virginia State Library, original sources.

ALVIN A. FAHRNER
East Carolina University

SMITH, WILLIAM HUGH (1826–1899), was the

controversial Republican governor of Alabama between 1868 and 1870. Born in Georgia, he was reared and educated in Randolph County, Ala. A successful lawyer, he served before the Civil War in the state legislature. Although he was a Douglas Democrat and an opponent of secession, he stood for election to the Confederate Congress in 1861. His narrow defeat proved a turning point, and after brief Confederate service he fled through Union lines. In 1867 he became supervisor of registration for Alabama. His election as chairman of the Republican convention that June anticipated his victory in 1868. As governor he struggled to maintain a coalition of blacks, native whites, and northern Republicans. Critics charged him with racial duplicity and financial extravagance, but his task was impossibly difficult. He left office in 1870 under protest that his defeat had been secured by fraud.

See, for unsympathetic assessments, W. L. Fleming, *Civil War and Reconstruction in Alabama* (1905); and J. W. DuBose, *Alabama's Tragic Decade* (1940). More balanced are H. M. Bond, *Negro Education* (1939); and S. V. Woolfolk, "Role of Scalawag" (Ph.D. dissertation, Louisiana State University, 1965).

ROBERT GILMOUR
Princeton University

SMITH V. ALLWRIGHT (321 U.S. 649 [1944])

was brought to the U.S. Supreme Court on behalf of Lonnie Smith, a black citizen barred from voting in the 1940 Democratic primary in Texas on the basis of race (WHITE PRIMARY). Lower courts ruled against Smith on the ground that the Supreme Court, in a unanimous decision in 1935 (GROVEY V. TOWNSEND), had held that the Democratic party was a private organization with a right to limit its membership on the basis of race. Speaking for the eight-person majority, Justice Stanley F. Reed held, however, that the right to vote in a primary for nomination of candidates, like the right to vote in a general election, is secured by the Fifteenth Amendment and may not be denied or abridged by a state on the basis of color. Political parties, Reed held, are agents of the state insofar as they determine participants in a primary. In specifically overruling *Grovey*, Reed stated that the Court, when convinced of prior error, "has freely exercised its power to re-examine the basis of its constitutional decisions." Although further efforts to revitalize the white primary system were made in South Carolina and Texas, the *Smith* decision, for all intents and purposes, killed this device for DISFRANCHISEMENT of blacks.

See L. Miller, *Petitioners* (1967); P. E. Jackson, *Dissent in Supreme Court* (1969); and A. T. Mason, *Supreme Court from Taft to Warren* (1968).

VIRGINIA V. HAMILTON
University of Alabama, Birmingham

SOCIAL FORCES (168 Hamilton Hall, University of North Carolina, Chapel Hill, 27514), founded in 1922 largely on the initiative of HOWARD ODUM, is a quarterly journal published under the auspices of the department of sociology at the University of North Carolina at Chapel Hill and the Southern Sociological Society, which sends copies of the journal to all its members. With a circulation of 5,000 (in 1976), the journal publishes empirical research in sociology and related sciences, book reviews, a yearly inventory of propositions culled from the papers published, and a 50-year index to its own articles and reviews. Many of the papers accepted are by southern scholars who are investigating aspects of southern society, but the emphasis is not solely on the South.

SOCIALIST PARTY OF AMERICA. The first active Socialists in the South, notably William Farmer, who organized a Socialist party in Texas in 1898, had been active in the radical, antimonopoly wing of the POPULIST PARTY. When the SPA was founded in 1901, however, it included not only former Populists, but also southern labor leaders like Leon Greenbaum of St. Louis and William Mailly of Tennessee, who served as its first two national secretaries. Party organizers touring the South in 1903 found their warmest response in LABOR UNION strongholds like Sebastian County, Ark., where the United Mine Workers had just won a closed shop after a long struggle. Organizers from midwestern cities played an important role in the early southern development of the SPA, but native southern farmers and workers were primarily responsible for the party's growth. When Eugene Debs toured in the region in 1903, he opposed the organization of racially segregated locals and called for the recruitment of black workers on an equal basis, but his efforts did not lead to the integration of the southern parties.

In 1908 Debs conducted an energetic presidential campaign for the SPA, but he tended to ignore the South, where William Jennings Bryan was expected to bring out the Democratic party faithful. Bryan's neopopulism proved less appealing than before, however, and the Socialists converted some Democratic voters. The SPA's organizational efforts among farmers were also aided by the collapse of the FARMERS' UNION following the panic of 1907. Socialism gained as rural reformism faltered. The SPA also gained recruits from its grassroots organizational efforts, which included the revival of Populist camp meetings and the publication of some 40 weekly newspapers (headed by the *Texas Rebel* with a circulation of 22,000). Southern Socialists called for immediate reforms, like taxes on speculative land holdings, and for an ultimate demand: the abolition of competitive capitalism and the creation of a cooperative commonwealth.

As a result of these efforts, Debs made impressive gains in the presidential ELECTION OF 1912, even though he was running against three reform candidates, including a southern Progressive, WOODROW WILSON. Debs polled his largest totals in the populous midwestern and northeastern states, but he made impressive gains in Florida, West Virginia, and the southern states west of the Mississippi. In most of these southern states Debs outpolled William H. Taft and Theodore Roosevelt. The Socialists were strongest in Oklahoma, where Debs polled 42,000 votes (16 percent) and elected scores of local officials. Debs also ran well in Texas, where he polled 25,743 votes (8.5 percent) mostly from poor white TENANT FARMERS, who had been organized into a renters' union.

The SPA voting constituency in the southern states comprised primarily the following: white tenant farmers, as well as indebted yeomen farmers (including many former Populists); unionized coal miners, railroad workers, and timber workers (who formed a revolutionary union in the Louisiana piney woods), as well as some skilled urban workers, notably German brewers; and a small but articulate group of professionals (renegade preachers, country doctors, lawyers, teachers, and editors) and small-town merchants.

Without Gene Debs leading the SPA ticket in 1916, the party lost votes to Wilson's "peace and prosperity" campaign. In any case, the party's growth was limited by the widespread DISFRANCHISEMENT of its main constituency—poor white tenants and laborers—and by its inability to win the suffrage for women or to help regain it for blacks. Because of SPA opposition to U.S. entry into World War I and the participation of a few party members in antidraft activity, Socialists were stigmatized as traitors; their newspapers were suppressed; their leaders, including Debs, were imprisoned; and their local organizations were destroyed. Like the Socialist party in the Midwest, the SPA in the South never recovered from World War I repression. The last revival of party activity came in the mid-1930s, when two young Arkansas Socialists, H. L. Mitchell and Clay East, organized the SOUTHERN TENANT FARMERS' UNION.

See D. A. Shannon, *Socialist Party* (1967); R. Ginger, *Eugene V. Debs* (1966); O. Ameringer, *If You Don't Weaken* (1940); G. McWhiney, *Journal of Southern History* (Aug., 1954); F. A. Barkey, "Socialist Party in West Virginia" (Ph.D. dissertation, University of Pittsburgh, 1971); J. R. Green, *Grass Roots Socialism* (1978), Oklahoma, Texas, Arkansas, and Louisiana; G. N. Green, "Florida Politics and Socialism" (M.A. thesis, Florida State, 1962); G. Burbank, *Journal of American History* (June, 1971); and J. Weinstein *Decline of Socialism* (1967).

JAMES R. GREEN
Brandeis University

SOCIAL SCIENCE QUARTERLY (University of Texas, Austin, 78712), the oldest publication of an interdisciplinary academic organization, was established in 1920. Formerly the *Southwestern Political Science Quarterly*, then the *Southwestern Political and Social Science Quarterly*, then the *Southwestern Social Science Quarterly*, it published book reviews and articles with a considerable degree of regional emphasis in economics, political science, sociology, geography, and history. In 1968, with the last name change and with its circulation grown to 3,000, the *Quarterly* began to place more emphasis on articles of a national nature. The journal is published by the University of Texas Press in cooperation with the Southwestern Social Science Association.

SOCIETY FOR THE PROPAGATION OF THE GOSPEL IN FOREIGN PARTS. See VENERABLE SOCIETY

SOILS. Few areas on the earth's surface can lay claim to the diversity of soil types that characterize the South. Southern soils have formed upon a wide variety of geologic materials, under vegetation ranging from forest to grassland, and within a milieu of climates encompassing semiarid and humid subtropical regimes. Unlike in areas to the north, where the mantlerock or regolith was refashioned by glacial ice, the South's surface materials have experienced a long history of uninterrupted chemical and physical weathering processes. Heavy leaching, in particular, has produced thoroughly altered mineral soils. Intraregional soils varying in their nutrient status, moisture availability, and agricultural potential are described below.

Coastal plain soils, developed from marine sands and clays, are predominantly sandy or loamy and possess a thick, clay-enriched subsurface. Below the organically darkened topsoil, colors range from yellow to red or brown, depending on the state of oxidation of iron and the presence of organic matter. Olive and gray colors become dominant in areas where the water table is near the surface and organic matter accumulates in the upper few inches.

Piedmont soils are formed from igneous and metamorphic rocks, generally in areas of rolling to steep topography. They are not as deep or as thoroughly weathered as coastal plain soils. In cultivated areas, soil erosion and mixing due to tillage have frequently resulted in the disappearance of the original surface. Uneroded soils tend to have a loamy to clayey surface, with a subsurface of clay enrichment and colors ranging from yellow or brown to dark red.

Mississippi Delta soils, commonly referred to as alluvial soils, form the flood and deltaic plains of the Mississippi River. The soil types are primarily a product of floodwater action. When the streams overflow their banks, large sand particles settle along the channel margins, producing coarse-textured ridges (natural levees) rising five to 15 feet above the floodplain. Adjacent to the ridges the floodplains tend to have silt loam and silty clay soils, which grade into clay soils with distance. This gradation is the result of silt and clay particles being held in suspension by floodwater much longer than sand, until they are deposited by relatively still water over broad, flat areas.

Prairie soils of Texas have an organically rich, dark-colored surface. Occurring in subhumid to semiarid climates, they have accumulations of carbonates, especially calcium, and frequently exhibit signs of alkalinity. Because of their fibrous root systems, grasses are important to prairie soil formation. Many roots decaying in the presence of calcium form products that are resistant to leaching and adhere to soil minerals, especially clays.

Less extensive soils having local significance include desert grassland soils of southwest Texas, which have layers of soft to indurated calcium carbonate or other soluble salt accumulations near the surface; BLUEGRASS areas of Kentucky and Tennessee, where soils are naturally high in phosphate content; the BLACK BELT of Alabama and Mississippi, where parent materials of chalk and marine-deposited clays have fostered the development of heavy clay soils; loessial soils occurring in a narrow belt east of the Mississippi River, which are highly acidic and low in both mineral nutrients and organic matter; hydromorphic (waterlogged) soils in areas of poor surface drainage, most notably occurring in the outer coastal plain; and a variety of upland soils in the Appalachian and Ozark mountains.

Southern soils support diverse land-use functions. Exclusive of western Texas, more than 55 percent of the South is forested. The remainder is primarily in crop and pasture land. A long frost-free period and abundant sunshine permit the production of a wide variety of field, truck, and horticultural crops. Where water is not restrictive, CORN and SOYBEANS are dominant in total cropland acreage, and cash crops such as COTTON, PEANUTS, and TOBACCO are of local significance. In moisture-deficient areas, WHEAT is the most important single crop, and grazing activities occupy the greatest percentage of the land.

Soil exhaustion and erosion by water and/or wind have resulted in land-use changes over large segments of the South. Paradoxically, some soils of the region have been continuously cultivated for more than 200 years and are still productive, while others have experienced severe gullying and complete removal of the topsoil due to improper management. The severest damage has occurred on the undulating surfaces of the PIED-MONT, in the limestone valleys of the Appalachian Plateau, and on parts of the dissected coastal plain. Over the last 50 years, however, enlightened conservationists with the aid of the federal government have halted most soil abuses in the South (CONSERVATION). Damaged and poor cropland is being reverted to permanent pastures and forest cover. Much land that had been abandoned and previously considered useless has been returned to economic productivity and saved from further degradation by farsighted land managers.

See S. W. Buol (ed.), *Soils of Southern States and Puerto Rico* (1973); D. Steila, *Geography of Soils* (1976); and USDA, *Yearbook of Agriculture: Soil* (1957).

DONALD STEILA
East Carolina University

SOLD DOWN THE RIVER. Although its precise origins are uncertain, the phrase reflects the fear, particularly pronounced among slaves in the Upper South, of being "sold south" (especially to the old Southwest—Louisiana, Alabama, Mississippi), where slave conditions were reputed to be most oppressive. Slave sales, especially those involving permanent separation, threatened the fragile but deeply rooted bonds of affection that united the slave family. There was a finality about being "sold down the river," and the separation that it implied made it one of the most extreme and dreaded sanctions with which a recalcitrant slave could be threatened.

See B. Drew, *Refugee* (1855); N. R. Yetman, *Life Under "Peculiar Institution"* (1970); G. P. Rawick, *American Slave* (1972); M. Twain, *Pudd'nhead Wilson* (1894); and H. B. Stowe, *Uncle Tom's Cabin* (1852).

NORMAN R. YETMAN
University of Kansas

SOLID SOUTH is a term popularized during the ELECTION OF 1876 by JOHN S. MOSBY while supporting the candidacy of Rutherford B. Hayes. Since then it has been loosely and variously used to refer to the southern states' support of and loyalty to the DEMOCRATIC PARTY. In precise usage the Solid South is composed of the 11 states of the Confederacy. In every presidential election from 1876 to 1920, the electoral votes of these states went to the Democratic candidate. During this time, the border states of Maryland, Kentucky, and Missouri sometimes supported the national ticket of the REPUBLICAN PARTY, although they have been often considered to be part of the Solid South. In the ELECTION OF 1920, the Solid South was cracked when Warren G. Harding carried Tennessee; and, in the Republican landslide ELECTION OF 1928, Herbert Hoover won the electoral votes of five former Confederate states: Virginia, Tennessee, North Carolina, Florida, and Texas. Although the South remains largely Democratic in local elections, conservative Republican candidates for the presidency have done quite well since 1952. With a stronger advocacy of states' rights and less insistence upon the passage and implementation of civil rights and social welfare legislation, they have taken many traditionally Democratic votes away from their liberal Democratic opponents. In recent elections, the number of former Confederate and border states that have voted Republican in presidential elections has ranged from a low of four in 1960 to a high of all 14 in 1972.

See G. Stimpson, *Book About American Politics* (1952); W. Safire, *New Language of Politics* (1972); F. Elliott and M. Summerskill (eds.), *Dictionary of Politics* (1964); and C. F. Adams, "Solid South," public address, Richmond (Oct., 1908).

ARNOLD S. RICE
Kean College of New Jersey

SOULÉ, PIERRE (1801–1870), arrived in Louisiana from France in 1825. He rose in the New Orleans bar and society on the strength of oratorical brilliance and an astute marriage into Creole society. A consistent spokesman for immigrant concerns, he opposed lengthy residence requirements for officeholding and suffrage at the state constitutional convention of 1844–1845. He served as state senator (1846) and U.S. senator (1847, 1849–1853). From 1848 to the eve of the Civil War, he contested JOHN SLIDELL for control of the Louisiana Democratic machine. Soulé gained notoriety as "young America's" leading exponent in the Deep South, supporting European republicans and Cuban revolutionaries. In 1853 he accepted the Spanish mission, hoping to accomplish Cuban annexation (OSTEND MANIFESTO). In 1856 he helped draft the expansionist national Democratic platform and became connected with WILLIAM WALKER's Nicaragua movement. As attorney for A. G. Sloo, who claimed a Mexican cession to develop a transit across the Isthmus of Tehuantepec, Soulé traveled to Mexico (1857).

A STATES' RIGHTS and proslavery advocate, Soulé attacked the COMPROMISE OF 1850. He became increasingly Unionist, however, and in 1860 headed the Stephen Douglas delegation from Louisiana to the BALTIMORE CONVENTION. During the Civil War, Soulé helped avert a bombardment of New Orleans through negotiations and was active in municipal affairs during the early stages of the occupation. Briefly imprisoned in the North, he escaped to the Confederacy, but it did not bring the active command he sought. Later he associated with William Gwin's Sonoran colonization scheme. His career illustrates that nationalism and sectionalism in the Old South were dynamic and interrelated concepts rather than fixed and mutually exclusive ideologies.

See A. A. Ettinger, *Mission to Spain of Pierre Soulé* (1932); A. Freeman, *Louisiana Historical Quarterly* (Oct., 1942); J. P. Moore, *Journal of Southern History* (May, 1955) and *Hispanic American Historical Review* (Feb., 1952); and F. Gaillardet, *Sketches of Early Texas and Louisiana* (1966).

ROBERT E. MAY
Purdue University

SOUTH, BOUNDARIES OF. Less heated, but no less conclusive, than debates over the South's essential character (CENTRAL THEME) is the unsettled question of the region's boundaries. Some academic definitions include Missouri but not Delaware; others add Oklahoma; and some either include or exclude all three states. A few definitions even challenge the "southernness" of Texas. The Mississippi River and the Allegheny-Appalachian mountains, two of the region's most prominent geographic features, separate East from West,

but no comparable geophysical line serves clearly to divide North from South. Even the MASON-DIXON LINE (39°43'26.3''), often used since the eighteenth century as a symbolic boundary, has no relevance to the region of the Mississippi River valley. The U.S. Census Bureau includes Delaware and Oklahoma in its definition of the South, but it classifies Missouri as a west north-central state. The Department of Health, Education, and Welfare, on the other hand, includes Oklahoma but not Missouri and Delaware. The SOUTHERN GOVERNORS' CONFERENCE not only includes representatives from all of the sometimes questioned states mentioned above, but it counts as well the commonwealth of Puerto Rico and the territory of the Virgin Islands. Businesses are no more authoritative. Bell Telephone Company, for example, encompasses most of the traditional South within three southern districts. These districts include not only Oklahoma and Missouri, but the state of Kansas as well; they also exclude Delaware and parts of Kentucky. Thus, whether for administrative or academic purposes, physical definitions of the South vary widely, proceeding from the needs and perceptions of the user rather than from any working consensus. Accordingly, students of slavery usually include Delaware and Missouri, though twentieth-century scholars, especially those concerned with demography and economics, often exclude these two highly urban former slave states, while including Oklahoma. The editors of this volume, without intending any slight to any other definition, define the South as all the states and the District of Columbia where slavery was legal in 1860.

SOUTH, UNIVERSITY OF THE (Sewanee, Tenn. 37375), was founded in 1857 with the expectation that it would become the southern equivalent to Oxford, Heidelberg, and Göttingen universities. Its founders, notably LEONIDAS POLK, wanted an institution that would strengthen and preserve orthodox southern faiths in religion, politics, and slavery. Plans for the university projected creation of 32 separate schools and departments covering everything from the classics, law, medicine, and religion to mining, agriculture, bookkeeping, and insurance. Although the university was inaugurated with an endowment of almost $500,000 and 10,000 acres of land, the Civil War destroyed both the impetus for and the financial base of the endeavor. The university survived, however, operating as a small Episcopalian college for men. It became coeducational in 1969 and has an enrollment of approximately 1,000 students. The SEWANEE

REVIEW is sponsored and published by this institution.

See R. G. Dudney (ed.), *Centennial Report* (1959); A. B. Chitty, *Reconstruction at Sewanee, 1857–1872* (1954) and *Historical Magazine of Protestant Episcopal Church* (1954); G. R. Fairbanks, *History of University of South* (1905); and M. Guerry, *Sewanee Review* (Summer, 1933).

SOUTH ATLANTIC QUARTERLY (Duke University Press, Box 6697, College Station, Durham, N.C. 27708), founded by JOHN SPENCER BASSETT in 1901 in connection with the "9019" Scholarship Society of Trinity College, is the second oldest review in the United States and is published by the Duke University Press. With a circulation of 1,200 (in 1975), it publishes book reviews and both scholarly and popular articles in the general humanities, social studies, and history. Although a number of its articles and reviews relate to the South, the *Quarterly* by no means limits its interest to that region.

SOUTH CAROLINA. The history of South Carolina has been a recurring search for stability, for a balance in human affairs. It has also been an experiment in black-white relationship: at first brutal, then paternal, after the Civil War black dominance, after Reconstruction white dominance, and now in the post-1954 years the working out of a new way of life that recognizes this unusual past as well as present realities. Each time order has been established some outside force has come along to disrupt that order, but South Carolina's people have never stopped looking for the best arrangements. Over three centuries blacks and whites have developed a distinct loyalty to the land and to the local scene—a pride in history and of place—which will continue to provide the essential stabilizing element. Since the third century of U.S. history will belong to the Sun Belt, this element may become a national characteristic.

Origin and geography. Under English claims stemming from the discoveries of John Cabot in 1497, Charles I gave "Carolana" to Sir Robert Heath in 1629. In 1663 Charles II gave the same lands, now designated "Carolina," to eight lords proprietors, men who had helped restore Charles to the English throne. After rights under the first charter had been voided, a second charter of 1665 confirmed the grant to the lords proprietors and fixed the limits of Carolina as extending from 36° 30' north latitude to 30° south and "to the West as far as the South Seas." In 1710 the first governor for North Carolina was appointed, thus dividing the province into two. With the establishment of Georgia in 1732, the southern boundary became the Savannah River. After South Carolina ceded its western lands in 1787 to the new U.S. government, its boundaries were fixed. The great extent of coastal lowlands with an interior that gradually diminishes toward the mountains explains in part the long ascendancy of the low country over the up-country in the political life of the state.

The FALL LINE, which runs from Aiken to Columbia to Camden to Cheraw, divides the state into low country and up-country. The low country has a coastal strip of barrier islands (called SEA ISLANDS southward of Charleston) backed by interior swamps out of which emerge the black-tinged rivers that flow sluggishly to the sea. Behind the swamps, but still below the sandhills that were the shore of the ancient ocean, there is a belt of fertile soils extending from Allendale on the Savannah to Marlboro in the Pee Dee basin. Above the fall line are the red hills famous at one time for cotton. Out of the PIEDMONT flow the major rivers marked red by the clay soil that they carry as sediment: the SAVANNAH, the Saluda and Broad, which join to form the Congaree, which in turn merges with the Catawba-Wateree to form the SANTEE and the PEE DEE. The small northwestern corner of the state is mountainous, with Mount Sassafras, 3,560 feet, the highest point in the state.

The state is 285 miles long and 215 miles wide. It contains 30,225 square miles of land and 830 square miles of water and ranks fortieth in size among the 50 states of the Union. The annual mean temperature at Charleston on the coast is 65 degrees F. and 61 degrees at Greenville at the foot of the mountains. The average rainfall at Charleston is 49.17 inches; at Greenville, 46.41 inches.

Colonial era. Although South Carolina is more English in its traditions than any other of the 50 states, it was first settled by Spaniards, who came to Winyah Bay in 1526 to establish San Miguel de Gualdape. HERNANDO DE SOTO entered Carolina near present-day Aiken and moved northwestward into the mountains in the 1540s, and from St. Augustine, founded in 1565, Spanish missions were extended along the coast at least as far northward as St. Helena Island. The Spanish presence to the south was always felt and feared until the British acquired East Florida in 1763, but the Spaniards left no descendants within the state.

The attempt of the French HUGUENOTS under Jan Ribault to establish a settlement at Port Royal in 1562 ended in disaster when no one came from home to succor them. Nor did the Huguenots led by René de Laudonnière fare any better, for the

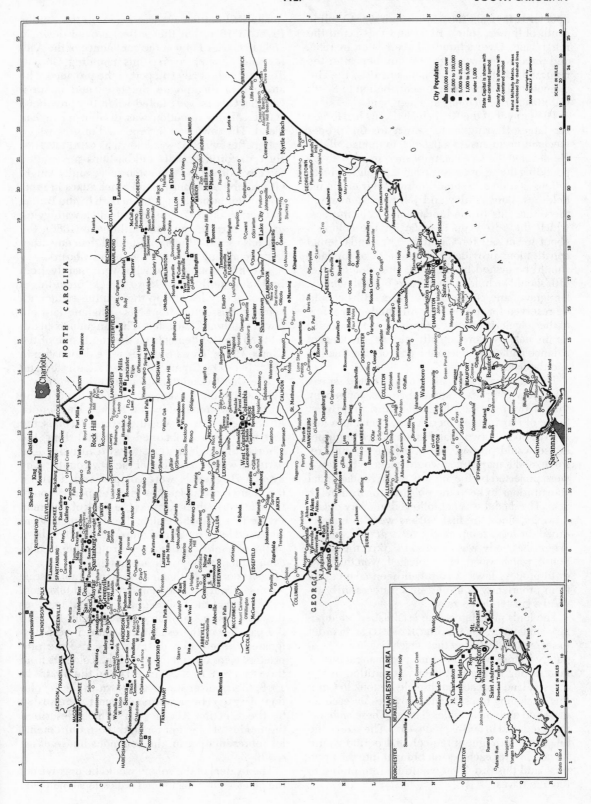

Spaniards in 1565 destroyed their Ft. Caroline south of the St. John's River and massacred the inhabitants. Over a hundred years later, in 1680, and then in somewhat greater numbers after the revocation of the Edict of Nantes in 1685, the Huguenots made a permanent contribution to South Carolina as rice planters and merchants.

The turmoil of the English civil wars had forced Sir James Harrington to search for the proper mechanisms to ensure a balance in human affairs. He devoted the *Oceana*, published in 1656, to expounding the agrarian rule, that the political institutions of a people should mirror their economic holdings. Lord Ashley and John Locke adapted these thoughts in the fundamental constitutions, which they drew up in 1669 for the colonists about to set sail for Carolina. The fundamental constitutions provided that one-fifth of the land should be owned by the lords proprietors; one-fifth should be held by two orders of local nobility, landgraves and caciques; and three-fifths should be reserved for the people. Although only a few of the seigniories for the proprietors and baronies for the nobility were actually laid out, the ideal of balance and order became a part of Carolina life and thought.

The various ranks of society would speak through a complex system of courts, topped by that of the palatine, the senior lord proprietor. Some of Harrington's mechanisms, such as a legislative body of two chambers in which an upper house would propose, a lower house would resolve, and a magistracy would execute the laws, were projected by the authors of the fundamental constitutions to keep the political institutions in gear. The model was not followed in every detail, however, since the first settlers were to be governed, at least temporarily, by a grand council. When that body was divided in 1691, the lower house, which was then established, won the power to propose laws. A step had been taken away from proprietary control, but not necessarily toward a greater democracy.

The lords proprietors also established a temporary land policy, the HEADRIGHT SYSTEM, in order to secure colonists, but that which began as a temporary feature would become a permanent one. A man sailing in the first fleet was entitled to 150 acres of land for each adult male he took to Carolina, including himself, and 100 acres for each female and each male under sixteen. These amounts were reduced in subsequent years. The size of the headright throughout the colonial period would be 50 acres for each person brought into the province, and this provision would be interpreted to include slaves.

The first settlement was made up the Ashley River in 1670, but the settlers moved down in 1680 to Oyster Point at the confluence of the Ashley and Cooper rivers, thus founding Charles Town, the chief city and port of the province. The attempt to incorporate the town and name it Charles City in 1722 failed when the provincial statute of incorporation was disallowed in England. The town was incorporated on August 13, 1783, after which it was known as CHARLESTON. By 1704 fortified walls and bastions surrounded the city. Although Charleston successfully fought off a combined Spanish and French attack in 1706, it was later besieged and taken both by the British and Union forces. Yet, in spite of military struggles, fires, hurricanes, and an earthquake (1886), the city has remained more unspoiled than any other large community along the eastern seaboard.

The first immigrants, who were mainly from Barbados, settled on Goose Creek, providing a core of gentry leadership through the eighteenth century. Dissenters from New England laid out towns south of Charleston. The Huguenots planted their first settlements on the south side of the Santee River. Three counties were designated in 1682. Berkeley County contained Charleston and Goose Creek. Colleton County to the south was the home of the Dissenters. Craven County to the north was dominated by the French Huguenots. After much rivalry among these three factions, the first balance was obtained by establishing the Church of England (EPISCOPAL CHURCH). Ten parishes were carved out of the low country. The French Huguenots were comprehended within the Church of England by granting permission to them to use in their parishes the Book of Common Prayer in a French version. The Dissenters were appeased by permitting their representatives to sit in the assembly without requiring them to take communion in the Anglican church.

Governor Sir Nathaniel Johnson, Chief Justice Nicholas Trott, and Commissary Gideon Johnston, the deputy of the bishop of London, put together this first South Carolina establishment. In 1716 the parishes of the established church were designated the election districts. Because the proprietors were unable to defend the colonists from the YEMASSEE INDIANS in 1715 and the pirates in 1718, their power was overthrown in the revolution of 1719. The new arrangements were sealed by the Election Act of 1721, which described the modes of election for, and the requirements for representation in, the commons house of assembly.

The leaders of the colony would be drawn from the planters, merchants, and professional men who could meet the requirements for holding office. Every free white man over twenty-one professing the Christian religion and possessed of a freehold of 50 acres or paying 20 shillings a year tax might vote. To be a member of the commons house, however, one had to be a white male, twenty-one years of age or over, and possessed of 500 acres and ten slaves or own houses and town lots worth £1,000. Residence in the parish was not required.

The planters and merchants first began to grow rich off the deerskin trade (FUR TRADE), then the trade in NAVAL STORES, in RICE (1730s), and in INDIGO (1740s). The inland waterways tied the low-country plantations to Charleston, where the merchants shipped produce to the world markets (COMMERCE). Deerskins, naval stores, and indigo went almost entirely to Great Britain; rice went to the Rhineland via English Channel ports and, after 1730, directly to ports south of Cape Finisterre.

After the crown bought out the rights of seven of the eight proprietors in 1729 and Governor Robert Johnson established a true royal government for the province, the merchants and planters had a secure base from which to operate. Proprietary land grants were newly enrolled, QUITRENTS were recorded, the local CURRENCY was stabilized at the rate of £7 South Carolina currency to £1 sterling, and a semicircle of interior townships was marked off to defend the coastal region. The ascendancy of the low-country gentry thus established was only challenged after the defeat of the CHEROKEE INDIANS in 1761 opened up the interior to settlement from the north of Scotch-Irish immigrants flowing down the GREAT WAGON ROAD from Pennsylvania, Virginia, and North Carolina. The backcountry men (REGULATORS), having banded together in the Regulator movement, demanded for themselves what the low country had obtained much earlier: representation in the commons house, churches, schools, courts, jails—in fact, law and order. Two of these demands were met by the Circuit Court Act of 1769, which provided for courthouses and jails in seven judicial circuits: Beaufort, Orangeburg, and Ninety-six to the south; Georgetown, Cheraw, and Camden to the north. Charleston remained the home of the central courts of record. The major backcountry leaders such as Andrew Williamson, William Thompson, and Richard Richardson had thus been satisfied before the eve of the Revolution and could be counted upon to support the low country in their coming contest with the mother country.

Yet the province was not unified with ease, for the various ethnic groups that had come to Caro-

lina each had to make a decision for itself. The Swiss who came to Purrysburg, the French to New Bordeaux, the Scotch-Irish to Williamsburg, and the Welsh to the Welsh Tract were generally on the patriot side. The Germans of Orangeburg and of the Dutch Fork wanted to remain neutral. The Scottish Highlanders, at least those who had arrived since the defeat at Culloden in 1746, formed the principal group of LOYALISTS. Both the Regulator troubles of the 1760s and the bitter struggles between the patriots and the Tories of 1780–1782 may have shown the people of this province that they must become one people if they were to hold the fabric of society together, a goal obtained by the 1820s.

Blacks were present in South Carolina from the arrival of the first fleet in 1670. By 1708 there was a black majority in the province, a position blacks would retain until the eve of the Revolution, when the filling up of the backcountry added a mass of white immigrants from the north. These blacks were brought first from the West Indies, then by the Royal African Company and ultimately by independent traders directly from the western coast of Africa, from Gambia to Angola. They brought with them such skills as watermen, agriculturists, and herdsmen possessed, which made a contribution to the planting society of great though indeterminate importance. The link with home was broken somewhere between the purchase of the slaves by the planters in Charleston and the new work routines of the outlying plantations. When the Spaniards at St. Augustine tempted the slaves with promises of freedom, some were willing to take the chance to escape, usually by longboat through the inland waterways to Georgia and Florida. This glimmer of hope sparked the STONO SLAVE CONSPIRACY of 1739. In 1740 the commons house passed a new Negro act that was the basic slave code in South Carolina until the Civil War. The patrol system by which men were ticked off from militia companies for such duty was put on a more permanent basis. No historian has yet explained the acculturation that must have taken place by the eve of the Revolution. Although the blacks were not quiescent during the Revolution, there was no uprising that interfered with the progress of the patriot cause.

Revolutionary and early Federal eras. The merchants and planters who dominated the commons house of assembly were determined to defend their rights as Englishmen, both procedurally in the Gadsden election controversy (1762) and substantively in the STAMP ACT CRISIS (1765). When the new collector of the customs Daniel

Moore and his underlings demanded extortionary fees and detained vessels on specious charges, they were defeated by the strong stance of HENRY LAURENS, and the mercantile community thereupon joined the radical Whigs. The merchants (with the exception of the Scottish element) joined the planters and the mechanics led by CHRISTOPHER GADSDEN to form a committee of 39 to enforce the nonimportation agreement adopted July 22, 1769. When the Carolinians tied their cause to that of John Wilkes in England by sending the Society of the Supporters of the Bill of Rights £1,500 sterling, the English ministry prevented the colonial assembly from doing further business until an apology to the crown was forthcoming for their ill-considered gift to Wilkes. The Carolina patriots were aspiring men who demanded respect; and, drawing upon the works of the English Whig tradition, they made their decision for freedom. The Charlestonians were ahead of Boston in their plans to resist the importation of tea, and the northern tea parties merely strengthened their resolution to stand firm. At a large meeting near the Exchange on July 6, 7, and 8, 1774, two lines of political activity merged: that of private citizens meeting out of doors under the Liberty Tree and that of assemblymen within the legislature. A delegation consisting of JOHN RUTLEDGE, EDWARD RUTLEDGE, Thomas Lynch, Gadsden, and Henry Middleton (MIDDLETON FAMILY) was sent to the first Continental Congress.

The ability of the South Carolina leaders to organize the society for revolution was manifest in the actions taken by the provincial congress, which first met in January of 1775, and of the council of safety, which was formed during the following summer. The provincial congress set up a network of local committees to enforce the Continental ASSOCIATION, demanded that each Carolinian make a commitment to support the patriot cause, and raised two regiments of troops to defend the province. In August and September, 1775, the council of safety sent William Henry Drayton (DRAYTON FAMILY), the Reverend William Tennent, and the Reverend Oliver Hart to win the support of the up-country. On September 15, 1775, the last royal governor Lord William Campbell fled to the protection of His Majesty's ships stationed in Charleston harbor. By November the council of safety had decided to block the navigation of the Cooper River and fortify the port of Charleston to resist invasion. The seizure of powder magazines in Charleston and of powder ships off Savannah and St. Augustine revealed the boldness of the new leaders. They then proved their fighting prowess by defeating the fleet of Sir Peter Parker and the army of Sir Henry Clinton on June 28, 1776, in the battle of FT. MOULTRIE. That victory provided symbols for a new people. Colonel WILLIAM MOULTRIE, who defended the fort, and Sergeant William Jasper, who rescued the flag, were the new heroes. The flag, which Moultrie had designed with a silver crescent (taken from the cap of the uniform of the South Carolina Regiment) on a field of blue, became the flag of the new state after the single addition of the palmetto, the tree whose spongy trunk had made the fort so impregnable. The birth of the new republic, however, was slow, since many were reluctant to cut their ties with the crown. The first constitution of March 26, 1776, was a temporary document looking toward reconciliation. Among those who signed the DECLARATION OF INDEPENDENCE for South Carolina—Arthur Middleton, Thomas Lynch, Jr., THOMAS HEYWARD, JR., and Edward Rutledge—none could be called an ardent revolutionary. Yet with the new oath of allegiance required by a law of February, 1777, and by the new state constitution of 1778, the die was cast.

After Charleston was captured on May 12, 1780, by Admiral Mariot Arbuthnot and Sir Henry Clinton, it looked as though the power and the will of the low-country elite might be broken. The possibility of exploiting the discontent of the back-country folk and the loyalty of the Highland Scots gave the British ministry hope of subduing the state, but the British army pushed forward too rapidly and failed to consolidate the strength behind it. British attempts to smother opposition by the tactics of a Tarleton and a Wemyss only fanned the flames of battle. The British raised up against themselves the fury of the Scotch-Irish, who were led by FRANCIS MARION. Guerrilla bands also rallied around Andrew Pickens and Thomas Sumter. After General Nathanael Greene took over from HORATIO GATES, who had been defeated by Cornwallis at Camden on August 16, 1780, and established a recognizable center of strength in the state, the patriot bands could harry the enemy unmercifully. Greene, turning near-defeats into strategic victories, made his way into the low country, where he remained a menace until the British evacuated Charleston on December 14, 1782 (GREENE'S SOUTHERN CAMPAIGNS).

Although Georgia had succumbed completely to the British forces and had its royal government fully restored, South Carolina had held the southern frontier during the Revolution, parrying many thrusts from the Floridas. This was a signal contribution to the new nation, which was honored in

1787 when concessions in regard to representation and slavery were made to the Deep South in order to create the new union.

But that respect could only rest on new economic strength. After the devastation of the Revolution, the planters borrowed heavily from English merchants in order to resume their planting operations. When these debts came due, the planters passed a loan act, a STAY LAW, and a pine tree law, which were all designed to make it difficult for the agents of the former enemy to collect both old and new debts. In 1785 the Agricultural Society was formed to experiment with new staples (something was needed to take the place of indigo, which had now lost its English bounty), and the Charleston Chamber of Commerce was reorganized to open new avenues of trade, particularly with Holland and France. There was also a conscious effort to assist backcountry development. In 1786 the Santee Canal Company was organized to build a canal between the Santee and the Cooper rivers (CANALS) so that interior farmers might be able to export their surplus more quickly through the port of Charleston. The ultimate solution came more by indirection than by planning. Tories returning to South Carolina from the Bahamas brought cotton seeds, which they planted on the Sea Islands; in 1793 Eli Whitney, while visiting Mrs. Nathanael Greene in Georgia, improved the machines for ginning cotton. Long-staple Sea Island cotton took the place of indigo in the coastal region, and within a decade short-staple cotton would make the backcountry prosperous.

In this period of economic flux, South Carolina leaders decided that a stronger union was needed. The legislature had voted to amend the ARTICLES OF CONFEDERATION to give Congress greater power over commerce; thus South Carolina sent no delegation to the ANNAPOLIS CONVENTION. In 1787 John Rutledge, CHARLES COTESWORTH PINCKNEY, CHARLES PINCKNEY, and Pierce Butler were selected to represent South Carolina at Philadelphia. Once the protection for the interests of the Deep South (slavery) was recognized, these men placed themselves behind those working for a stronger union. Rutledge spoke in favor of basing representation partly upon property, and C. C. Pinckney desired property qualifications for holding office. Clearly, the delegation favored the model of an aristocratic republic like that which they already had established at home. They would eschew titles, but they had a special conception of the role of citizen in the new land. But what probably provided more impetus for a stronger

union than almost anything else was the perennial cry of South Carolinians for fiscal responsibility. Part of the leadership deplored the stay laws of the 1780s, and most wanted the state debt paid off, by the federal government if necessary. South Carolina and Massachusetts had the largest state debts left over from the Revolution. Had not South Carolina made one of the major efforts? Should its debts not be the debts of all? Thus on May 23, 1788, South Carolina ratified the Constitution and became the eighth state to enter the Union. The seven parishes in and around Charleston voted almost unanimously for ratification. The backcountry, suspecting antidemocratic tendencies among the low-country elite, was suspicious of this alien government and cast most of the votes against. Aedanus Burke, Thomas Tudor Tucker, and Thomas Sumter, who represented the more democratic elements in the state in the First Congress, made important contributions to the BILL OF RIGHTS.

At home a new balance was worked out in the Constitution of 1790. The legislature had consented to remove the capital from Charleston to Columbia in 1786; the constitutional convention of 1790 was held in Columbia; the offices of the new state government would open there in January, 1791. Yet there would be two sets of state officials, one sitting in Charleston and one in Columbia. By the new constitution Jews and Catholics were placed on an equality with Protestants; their congregations could now be incorporated under the laws of the state. On February 19, 1791, the congregation of Beth Elohim and that of St. Mary's, both in Charleston, took advantage of the new dispensation. At the same time the legislature abolished the right of PRIMOGENITURE as of May 1, 1791. Although the concessions were made, the representation in the house and the senate still maintained the strength of the low country. It was not until 1808 that representation was divided more evenly between the two sections. In 1810 the state adopted white adult manhood suffrage. Yet the qualifications for membership in the house of representatives were to remain as they had since 1721 in those who were possessed of 500 acres of land and ten Negroes or of real estate of the value of £150 pounds sterling. Thus the concession on representation of 1808 meant little in practice, for by that date the up-country was producing its own elite. The only erosion of legislative power was in the making of some local officers elective in the period 1810–1814 rather than appointive by the legislature. Its continued control over districting, election of U.S. senators, selection of presidential electors, and election of the governor kept power concentrated in the legislature. South Carolina to the present has been dominated by the legislature, and that body by its local elite—whether planter, conservative New South, or county courthouse clique.

During the 1790s the South Carolina Federalists basked in the reflected glory of the national party. Alexander Hamilton and the Federalist administrations passed out patronage through the four aristocratic factions that dominated South Carolina politics in that decade—of whom the Rutledge-Pinckney coalition was the most important. George Washington sent THOMAS PINCKNEY as minister to England, sent C. C. Pinckney as minister to France, and named John Rutledge chief justice of the U.S. Supreme Court (though he was not confirmed). In 1796 Thomas Pinckney ran with John Adams for the vice-presidency; in 1800 C. C. Pinckney ran with Adams. In 1804 and 1808 the Federalists picked C. C. Pinckney to head their ticket. The commercial world of Charleston, which ballooned profits as a result of the strife in Europe, joined the wealthiest rice planters and the old Continental officers to make a strong group that used its power to support Washington and Adams and its wealth to rebuild Charleston in a Federalist style. This decade saw a flowering of culture: two theaters vied with each other for performers and audiences; gentlemen architects like Gabriel Manigault did for Charleston what Charles Bulfinch was doing for Boston; excellent silversmiths and cabinetmakers flourished; and artists such as James Earle, John Trumbull, and the Peales, as well as a host of French emigré miniaturists, painted superb likenesses of prominent South Carolinians. It was a society out of which much of the later artistic talent of the city and state emerged. But this world seemed threatened by the Democratic-Republican societies, the fiery opposition to Jay's Treaty, and the ultimate victory of Thomas Jefferson in 1800.

This unique society, based more upon rice than cotton and thus confined to the littoral, might have been threatened if the backcountry had kept on growing and had not been transformed. The population of the state did grow by 38.8 percent in the 1790s, but the spread of COTTON after 1793 (production increased eightfold by 1803) transformed the farmer into a cotton planter with the consequent squeezing out of many of the lesser folk. Population increased only slightly in the first decade of the nineteenth century. Those who left who hated slavery, like the Quakers, moved northwest across the Ohio; the younger sons or less successful farmers moved southwest to start a new South Carolina in Alabama and Mississippi. The cream of discontent was skimmed off to the westward. WADE HAMPTON, who had been nobody before the Revolution, was reputed to be the richest man in America by 1810, the owner of extensive cotton plantations in Richland County and of sugar plantations along the Mississippi River. These new planters married their sons to the daughters of low-country elite, thus merging the two societies. The South Carolina College, which opened its doors in Columbia in 1805, was consciously designed to homogenize the elite. As Joseph Alston would say in 1808, the low country was ready to make concessions since the up-country men "have assimilated so nearly to the privileged districts below."

It was in this first decade of the nineteenth century that South Carolinians became a churched people. The story of the METHODISTS is the most revealing. Francis Asbury, who first entered the state in 1785, moved back and forth each year over the length and breadth of the state converting people and organizing church congregations. Religion might have become an unsettling factor, because Asbury was opposed to slavery, preached to the slaves, and wanted exhorters appointed among them. In 1795 a group of Methodist ministers meeting in Charleston stated that they would recognize no minister who continued to own slaves. Yet due to GABRIEL'S INSURRECTION in Virginia in 1800 (which coincided with statements issued by the Methodist bishops in favor of emancipation), a crisis was raised and settled only in 1804 by a compromise that permitted Methodist churches in the South to use a discipline that tolerated slavery. The BAPTISTS were to make a similar compromise; and, since their congregations had more autonomy, it was easier to accomplish. The Episcopalians formed the Society for the Advancement of Christianity in South Carolina in order to extend their influence into the interior. Gradually each up-country town was to have an Episcopal church, as well as a PRESBYTERIAN, into which would gravitate over the years many of the leading planters. Thus religion became a tie, not a divider.

The institution of the FAMILY also underwent changes, and as it did it formed another link in the new South Carolina society. Intermarriages between up-country and low-country persons did take place, but more frequently kinship groups flourished within neighborhoods. The society became less mobile and more demographically stagnant from 1810 to 1860; the rate of growth slowed to 2.3 percent in the 1830s. Every county therefore had its group of families. The more frequent use of middle names and the use of surnames as Christian names are proofs that by the 1820s pride in family had grown. Families hearkened back to the revolutionary heroes, perpetuating the patriot names in an unending procession. A sense of place and of family marked the Carolinians down to the end of World War II, if not beyond. In 1960 there were more native-born persons living within South Carolina than within any other state in the Union.

The same processes of religion and family building were manifest among the black population, though there may have been a lag of two decades behind the changes in the white society. The reopening of the slave trade in 1803 for five years brought 40,000 blacks from Africa into the state. Not all remained in South Carolina, but that was the decade in which slavery did spread into the up-country. Thus that decade was more unsettling for the blacks than the whites. The churching of the blacks took place as a result of the mission to the slaves, which was a phenomenon of the 1830s and 1840s, surely completed by the 1850s, when almost all of the largest plantations had their own plantation chapels. By the 1840s the more successful planters had purchased neighboring plantations; thus the slave families living in their separate houses on the slave streets had a greater chance to create a family structure. The fact that the blacks adhered to Anglicized names after emancipation indicates some modeling of the black family along white family lines. That there were many marriages among the slaves can be proved by reference to plantation and parish records. The use of a last name by slaves was not uncommon.

There was an interaction between white and black that grew stronger as one approached the Civil War. This was due partly to living together and to sharing common tasks; it was also partly a forcing together under external pressures. In 1821 Governor Thomas Bennett told the South Carolina legislature: "Associations with the wily aborigine and occasional demonstrations of a spirit of insubordination educed by a sudden transition from the indolence and precarious enjoyments of uncivilized life to labour and servility, coerced our forefathers to the adoption of a system of Law which should deter from crime by a prompt and appalling severity of punishment. This system is still maintained although the necessity which dictated has long since ceased and been supplanted by affections and sympathies whose growth had been cultivated by the active beneficence and humane attentions of their proprietors." The emer-

gence of a distinctive accent shared to a great extent by both black and white Carolinians in the early years of the nineteenth century is evidence of how far the mutuality of life had gone.

Outside pressure upon the state was first apparent in the Missouri controversy of 1820, when the attempt to prevent the expansion of slavery into the Louisiana Territory and at the same time to challenge the right of a state to bar entry to those who might be subversive of the local order (*i.e.,* free Negroes) acted as "a firebell in the night." White uneasiness over the growing slave and free black communities had already begun to build after the Santo Domingo uprisings of the early 1790s. The city of Charleston, as a result, passed ordinances segregating crowds at theaters and controlling public meetings of blacks. In 1800 the state legislature itself made it more difficult for an owner to free a slave and in 1820 decided that only the legislature could grant emancipation. One does not know the extent to which the ideas of the French Revolution made manifest in Santo Domingo or the words spoken in the North at the time of the Missouri controversy affected the local black population, but enough percolated through the alleys and along the wharves of Charleston to create a climate in which the Denmark Vesey insurrection of 1822 (VESEY PLOT) was possible. Vesey was the only free black among 37 persons executed for this abortive insurrection. Historians still disagree on the extent of the conspiracy.

The Vesey scare produced a curious result. First the legislature passed seamen's acts to prevent the introduction of any blacks who might stir up trouble; second, a guardhouse was erected in Charleston in 1825 and on that site later would be placed the Citadel, a military school for young white men, a symbol of power in the heart of the metropolis. But equally demanding was the need to create an image for the young men to model themselves after if they were to take on the role of leaders in a disciplined and restricted society. The tutoring was by indirection. The 1820s saw an enhancement of myths about the American Revolution, most notably in Alexander Garden's *Anecdotes of the American Revolution*, first published in 1822 but added to in 1828. Henry Laurens Pinckney instructed through the editorials of the CHARLESTON MERCURY. The construction of courthouses as replicas of Greek and Roman temples, in every county in the state, was a conscious seeking of republican models. Robert Mills produced the Fireproof Building (1829) to protect the public records, an American structure for a southern purpose. WILLIAM GILMORE SIMMS commenced the most notable career in antebellum letters in South Carolina, devoting his novels, poems, and numerous magazine articles to describing the Revolution as an age in which heroes were formed. John Stevens Cogdell's sculptures and John Blake White's historical canvases were executed with the same feelings and purpose. And DUELING (Governor James Hamilton fought 14 in his lifetime) became the true test of whether one was capable of leading. Private confidence was a public need, but amid the confidence would bloom much arrogance, a trait the North would be quick to note.

There were those who had thought that the national contract, the U.S. Constitution, would always be honored since it had been made by gentlemen. This was the view of the older Pinckneys, but not of the younger Charles, who first cried the alarm in 1819. The second generation of South Carolina leaders, the war hawks JOHN C. CALHOUN, LANGDON CHEVES, and WILLIAM LOWNDES, had been enthusiastic nationalists for they believed that the new republic should be strong. Calhoun as secretary of war under President James Monroe had worked to strengthen the nation by supporting Henry Clay's American System and by advocating the construction of a national network of roads. But in the 1820s, when South Carolina's economic base was eroded by the opening up of new cotton lands in the Southwest, Calhoun lent his incredibly logical mind to formulating constitutional defenses within the framework of the Constitution. Building upon the concept of INTERPOSITION as expressed by Jefferson and James Madison in 1798, he constructed his doctine of NULLIFICATION, a storm shelter for his state. First aimed at the American System, particularly the tariff, it would be used later for other purposes. It was designed to preserve liberty in a world inexorably marching toward equality. Richard Hofstadter called Calhoun the Marx of the master class, an apt identification, for Calhoun, like Alexis de Tocqueville, perceived the mass society coming. The Greek city-state seemed a worthy model to the members of this artistocratic republic. Was there ever a city in America with so many Greek temples as Charleston had on the eve of the Civil War (the College of Charleston, the First Baptist Church, the Hibernian Hall, etc.)?

The nullifiers tried to parry everything that JOHN MARSHALL had done in order to make the Americans one people. In nullifying the tariff acts of 1828 and 1832, South Carolina denied appeals from its state courts into the federal court, denied the use of force against the state, and exacted an oath from its public officials to support the ordinance of nullification. These were designed to undo what had been done to make the peoples of the several states into one nation. Andrew Jackson, a native-born South Carolinian, blocked those moves with a request for a FORCE BILL. This was prelude to civil war. After the crisis, those who had faltered were driven from public life. Calhoun, not willing to apply his doctrines internally, molded the state into a monolith.

Foreseeing the growth of the North, the Carolinians tried to open lines of communication with the West. Robert Mills in 1822 had suggested a rivers and roads connection with the west coast. Between 1829 and 1832 the longest railroad line in the world was built between Charleston and Hamburg on the Savannah River in order to tap the new cotton lands to the southwest. Yet the produce of the Southwest was to find its outlets through the Gulf ports. In the late 1830s the entrepreneurs of Charleston tried to build a railroad to Cincinnati, but it was not completed until after the Civil War. Even so, it was only with the construction of the interstate highway system after World War II that middle America was really tied to the port of Charleston.

Antebellum period. Not succeeding in a transportation or a commercial or an industrial revolution, South Carolina led by Calhoun embarked upon a political game with the North: the politics of the concurrent majority. Beginning with the two-thirds rule adopted for the Democratic National Convention of 1836, the South used its power in national politics for over a hundred years to defend its interest. DAVID POTTER has charted that political course in *The South and the Concurrent Majority* (1972). The nullifiers first worked with the Whigs against Andrew Jackson, but Martin Van Buren's subtreasury scheme sent them back into the Democratic fold. The South then secured for eight years a GAG RULE, which barred full discussion of the question of slavery on the floor of Congress. When JOHN TYLER failed to follow his Whig leads, Calhoun seized the opportunity to join the administration as secretary of state, in which position he negotiated the treaty of annexation with Texas. President JAMES K. POLK, himself the product of the two-thirds rule, campaigned for Texas and Oregon, a low tariff, and internal improvements. By such maneuverings the voice of the South and of South Carolina was maintained in national councils.

Some, however, did not like these compromises on the national level; and, with ROBERT BARNWELL RHETT, "the father of secession," leading the Bluffton movement of 1844, the path to separate state action was taken. By the decade of the 1840s, South Carolina was cocky and confident. Many did leave the state, but that only meant that those who remained were even more of one mind. The mission to the slaves had succeeded; even the Episcopalians had adopted the evangelical stance. It was not U. B. PHILLIPS but Eugene Genovese (SLAVERY, HISTORIOGRAPHY OF) who perceptively captured much of the interactions of discipline and respect that made blacks and whites close to being one people within one state.

The most recent study of the free blacks in South Carolina describes a group caught between the two worlds but taking its origins from the black world and its signals from the white. Free blacks found a modus vivendi that, if not based on principle, was based on survival and that would endure as the core of a new black establishment after the Civil War, providing the bridge that has always made the South Carolina society so different from the other southern states. The Brown Fellowship Society, the black Episcopal churches of Charleston, the respect for genealogy, the love of a locale all provided the free blacks a solid base. Some would leave, like Daniel Payne; some would come back, like Jehu Jones. But it was a group never disloyal during the Civil War and later an essential factor in enabling both blacks and whites to endure Reconstruction and in the mid-twentieth century to adjust with the minimum of friction to the new society.

Although Calhoun tried for a while to base American foreign policy on the recognition of slavery, thus alienating the North, and although John Quincy Adams, Theodore Weld, and the GRIMKÉ sisters sparked a petition movement against the institution of slavery, thereby alienating southerners, there was more self-confidence than ever before. There was little sign that slavery would disappear. Indeed planters were becoming larger operators and more dominant over all phases of the economy. Although they did not need the lands obtained from Mexico, they thought that they should have access to those lands as of right. So argued Calhoun in the Senate and Rhett in the House in 1847 in opposing the WILMOT PROVISO. So convincing and so assertive were these men that even a Henry Clay and a Daniel Webster could see the logic of their course and could lead the nation into the COMPROMISE OF 1850. The desires of Calhoun, Clay, and Webster to see the Republic endure triumphed over the sectionalists, who were just emerging into the limelight.

The FUGITIVE SLAVE LAW of 1850, as it potentially involved all northerners in the maintenance of slavery, could not be enforced in the North as Charles Sumner and Harriet Beecher Stowe proclaimed. On the other hand it was something of a southern victory, followed by the elections of Franklin Pierce and James Buchanan and the DRED SCOTT decision of 1857. While the South wielded that much power in national councils, could South Carolina secede alone? There was a southern rights movement that emerged at the NASHVILLE CONVENTION in June of 1850, waited for the compromises of 1850, hesitated, and then fell apart in 1852. In South Carolina the cooperationists defeated the advocates of immediate and separate secession 25,000 to 17,000, and the meeting of the southern rights forces in Charleston in May, 1852, achieved nothing. Rhett resigned from the U.S. Senate to await events. South Carolina in the 1850s was itself awaiting events. It pushed its railroads, extended the network of agricultural societies (winning prizes for its cotton and rice at the London Exhibition of 1851), supported its own Carolina resorts at Greenville and Flat Rock, published its own magazines (RUSSELL'S), and established the South Carolina Historical Society to preserve its treasured documents.

The Palmetto State watched Kansas and even supported some young men desirous of immigrating there. But the chief event was the famous speech of Senator Sumner on the Kansas question in which he excoriated Senator A. P. Butler to such an extent that South Carolina Congressman PRESTON S. BROOKS took up his cane and hit Sumner over the head 30 times while he still sat at his desk in the Senate. That event, as well as John Brown's actions at Harpers Ferry, crystallized feelings. Henceforth the two sections thought in stereotypes: bleeding Sumner or bully Brooks, John Brown or Simon Legree. In the light of such tensions it is amazing that JAMES L. ORR managed to indicate a different path for his state, a need to work within the Democratic party. He succeeded in leading a South Carolina delegation in 1856 to the Democratic convention in Cincinnati. A promise was obtained there that in 1860 the convention would be held in Charleston. When Orr was elected Speaker of the U.S. House of Representatives in 1857, it seemed as though his path was viable. But in the political climate of the CHARLESTON CONVENTION in April, 1860, the forces of moderation led by Orr in behalf of Stephen A. Douglas could not hope for a fair hearing. When the Alabama delegation determined to seek a congressional slave code for the territories, there was no hope for compromise. The extreme southerners lost the platform fight and walked out of the convention. When Abraham Lincoln won the election in the fall, the South Carolina convention passed unanimously on December 20, 1860, the ordinance of secession.

The role of the political convention has had a special role in South Carolina history. Presumably in Calhoun's philosophy it represented the sovereignty of the state, but in actuality, since South Carolina was a deferential society, the convention was the vehicle of the great men who were willing to accept a call to these special meetings although they were reluctant to attend yearly sessions of the legislature. The largest planters were the most ardent secessionists. It was probably easier in 1860 to secure unity than in 1776, but the leaders of 1860 knew that they were lineal descendants of those earlier patriots and therefore knew how to form pressure groups such as the 1860 Association, vigilance committees, and minute men. They had put together a civilization that held for four long years without noticeably crumbling, but it could not withstand the ultimate strength of the North in its material resources and its allegiance to the new wave of egalitarianism then sweeping over the Western world.

Civil War and postwar periods. The attempt of Buchanan to reinforce and supply FT. SUMTER, the last visible sign of federal power in the state, failed when cadets from the Citadel fired upon the *Star of the West* on January 9, 1861. A second attempt might mean war. Although the Confederate government had been organized in Montgomery without awarding either of the highest offices to a South Carolinian, the key to the future lay in Charleston harbor, where federal forces still held Ft. Sumter. On April 12, 1861, the first shot was fired from Ft. Johnson against Ft. Sumter, and the Civil War began. Two days later Major ROBERT ANDERSON surrendered Ft. Sumter to the Confederate commander.

In the Civil War South Carolina expended onefifth of its fighting manhood. That war drained the state of its talent as World War I drained Britain. Destruction in 1865 at the hands of General W. T. Sherman, who cut a wide swath through South Carolina, coupled with explosions at the railroad depot in Charleston and the burning of Columbia, laid waste much of a state. All money invested in slaves evaporated with their emancipation; the value of lands consequently tumbled. Surplus invested in Confederate bonds was worthless. Although the white citizenry was momentarily stunned, there was enough leadership left to start again under the generous prodding of President ANDREW JOHNSON, and in September, 1865, a new constitution was forged. The governor would

henceforth be popularly elected. But, unmindful of the lessons of the war, the legislature adopted a BLACK CODE, which instituted a new form of servitude rather than a new freedom. The North rightly could not let this happen, and General D. E. Sickles voided the black code as of January 1, 1866. Military rule was to follow.

Under the umbrella provided by the national Reconstruction program, a civilized black community emerged from the class of free blacks, the former slaves, and those returning to their native soil such as Bishop Daniel Payne and FRANCIS L. CARDOZO. The constitutional convention that met in Charleston in January, 1868, consisted of 76 blacks and 48 whites. Cardozo was the most distinguished member; other prominent black delegates were ROBERT B. ELLIOTT, Richard Cain, and JONATHAN WRIGHT. Two able white natives who cooperated with the Radical Republicans were Thomas J. Robertson, a Charleston merchant, and Dr. Albert G. Mackey, who presided over the convention. Among the carpetbaggers the best known were DANIEL H. CHAMBERLAIN, B. F. Whittemore, and J. K. Jillson.

These men drew up the constitution of 1868, which provided for a more democratic structure of government. Universal adult male suffrage was established; representation in the state legislature would be based on population only; more offices were made elective; property qualifications for officeholding were abolished; and a free public school system was set up. The schools and the state militia were immediately opened to members of both races on an unsegregated basis.

These constitutional changes were not matched by an economic revolution. President Johnson had pardoned individually the wealthiest planters, thus securing to them their lands. Many planters, however, did go bankrupt when they could neither meet the payments on money borrowed at high rates of interest nor pay their taxes. Very little of this land could be purchased by the freedmen, nor did the South Carolina land commission, which was established in 1869 to use state funds to buy up large tracts of land and then resell small plots on easy terms to freedmen, succeed in redistributing property. Only in Beaufort County, where the process had begun shortly after the Union invasion of the Sea Islands on November 7, 1861, was there a significant change in landownership from white to black.

During Reconstruction there was much corruption in government. The most corrupt politician was the scalawag Governor FRANKLIN J. MOSES, JR. (1872–1874). Printing scandals, fraudulent bond issues, and bribery went against the tradition of fiscal responsibility. The resulting high cost of government elicited two taxpayers' conventions in 1871 and 1874 at which the opposition to Reconstruction government tried to rally.

A more brutal form of opposition had emerged during the election campaign of 1870 with the appearance of the KU KLUX KLAN. After Governor ROBERT SCOTT had been reelected, the black militia seemed more threatening. On February 12, 1871, a race riot occurred in Union in which several hundred Klansmen took eight Negro militiamen from the jail and shot them after a mock trial. Mob violence occurred in other parts of the state, forcing President U. S. Grant to suspend the writ of habeas corpus in nine upstate counties. The show of federal strength brought the Klan terrors to a quick end.

The prospect for reform seemed more likely under Governor Daniel Chamberlain (1874–1876). He had a good reputation and was able to win support in the Charleston business community and from FRANCIS W. DAWSON, the editor of the Charleston *News and Courier*. But this coalition for reform was undermined by two events. The first was the selection by the legislature of Moses and W. J. Whipper, two of the most corrupt members, as judges. Even though Chamberlain opposed these appointments, the Democrats were not sure if he could control his cohorts. The HAMBURG RACE RIOT of July, 1876, was the second and more crucial event. Governor Chamberlain overreacted and asked for additional federal military support during the coming election campaign in which he ran on the "Fusionist" ticket against General WADE HAMPTON, who was the leader of the "Straightout" ticket. The presence of federal troops heightened racial tensions. Historians do not agree whether the Red Shirts organized by General MARTIN W. GARY intimidated enough blacks to stay away from the polls or whether Hampton's promises of offices and fair play for the blacks won their votes. The election campaign of 1876 was the most violent in South Carolina history. The worst riots occurred at Ellenton on September 16–19 and at Cainhoy on October 16. Both sides were to claim victory. The matter was settled only when President Rutherford Hayes withdrew federal troops as part of the Compromise of 1877 and Chamberlain's carpetbagger government collapsed, permitting Hampton to take office. Hampton had definitely secured some support among the black voters, support that may not have been warranted by events that came later; for he was not able to prevent the emergence of a white farmers' movement led by BENJAMIN R. TILLMAN, which secured control of the state government by 1890, removed Hampton from the U.S. Senate, and disfranchised the blacks.

During the 1880s the shift from agriculture to a modern industrial system was begun. Banks financed new undertakings; the railway system was extended. But more important was the rapid expansion in the 1890s of the TEXTILE INDUSTRY both in the old Piedmont towns such as Greenville, Spartanburg, and Anderson and in the new ones such as Rock Hill, Greenwood, and Gaffney. The whites who could not succeed in growing cotton as sharecroppers became the new mill workers. Most significant for the state was the emergence of a new middle class, the crossroads merchant and the town shopkeeper, along with the mill owners, who became the most prosperous group in the state. The greatest success story was that of James Lide Coker, who was a pioneer industrialist and whose sons successfully experimented with seeds and fertilizers, creating an entirely new industry for the Hartsville area (COKER FAMILY). But this group was to find it difficult to withstand the pressures from the dirt farmers and mill workers, who were organized by Tillman.

The Tillman movement supplied the state with Clemson College for the sons and Winthrop College for the daughters of the Tillmanites, who eschewed the aristocratic state university. In 1893 the dispensary system introduced state control over liquor, which was to be manufactured by the state and sold through state stores. But the most lasting result was the new state constitution of 1895, which by adopting the reading and UNDERSTANDING clauses from the Mississippi constitution of 1890 successfully reduced the number of blacks participating in politics. The constitution banned intermarriage of the races and established the pattern of segregation. Thus was formed the solid South Carolina, which lasted until after World War II.

One of the curious anomalies of the turn-of-the-century years was the arrival of the rich yankees who bought plantations for winter homes. BERNARD BARUCH, South Carolina born and New York bred, put back together the 17,000-acre Hobcaw Barony across Winyah Bay from Georgetown. Aiken and Camden became winter resorts for the yankees and remain centers for training thoroughbred horses. Thus began a new leavening of the South Carolina population with the introduction of conservative, retired northerners.

Twentieth century. The first decade of the twentieth century contained bleak years for blacks. During the presidency of Theodore Roosevelt they held onto the last plums of political patronage; Dr.

W. D. CRUM was the Republican collector of customs at Charleston. No Negro was elected to Congress from South Carolina after 1896; the last black elected to the state house of representatives took his seat in 1900. These were years of LYNCHINGS, the Klan, and complete SEGREGATION—institutions that LILLIAN SMITH so poignantly described as "killers of the dream." The provision for free high school education in 1907 was only a slight break in this monolithic structure.

The attempts of Governor Duncan Clinch Heyward to sow some seeds of reform were nipped in the bud by the administrations of COLEMAN L. BLEASE, who catered to the worst elements of Tillmanism. But when RICHARD I. MANNING won the governorship in 1914 he put through the state legislature a program of reform designed to help the state catch up with the nation. He reorganized the state hospital for the mentally ill; created a board of charities and corrections; secured a workmen's compensation law, a measure requiring textile mills to adopt a weekly payday, a CHILD LABOR law to protect youths under fourteen, a new railway employer's liability act, and equalization of tax assessments; founded the highway department; and promoted public education with a local option law for compulsory school attendance. World War I brought Camp Jackson to Columbia, the marine camp to Beaufort, and an expansion of the Charleston naval yard. Cotton prices remained high until the end of the war, when the price of cotton fell just as the BOLL WEEVIL reached the state. That conjunction of evils marked the end of the agricultural regime that had endured since cotton had first been introduced. The decline in farm values brought many bank failures. The twenties became years of bitter poverty for rural folk, many of whom were black. The first large emigration of blacks (NEGRO MIGRATION), which had begun during the war, increased greatly in the 1920s; 1922 was the year in which the whites became the majority again.

Poverty and segregation had done something to the spirit of the South that the boosterism of civic clubs could not undo. During the twenties the career of William Jennings Bryan reached its nadir in the SCOPES TRIAL. Yet, in the minds of some, these stresses began to release creative insights. In South Carolina in the early 1920s there began a cultural renaissance; Charleston's Poetry Society of South Carolina was its center. The works of Dorothy and DUBOSE HEYWARD, Hervey Allen, Beatrice Ravenel, Josephine Pinckney, and Samuel G. Stoney were the fruits. DuBose Heyward's *Porgy* was the great work that, though written by a white man, seemed to fathom the yearnings of the black man. This novel was turned in the 1930s into *Porgy and Bess*, an American opera, for which George Gershwin wrote the music while visiting the Heywards on Folly Island. The other literary success was that of Julia Peterkin, who after living close to the blacks at Ft. Motte and Murrell's Inlet focused on their lives in *Green Thursday*, *Black April* and *Scarlet Sister Mary*, the last of which won the Pulitzer Prize. Heyward and Peterkin sensed the common humanity that bound the two races together and had done so even in the darkest days. They drew upon two strains that had been present in the three centuries of South Carolina's history and that were not to be united into one society until late in the twentieth century. Both blacks and whites had known high times and low times; neither could claim pasts of unending successes. In 1970 a production of *Porgy and Bess* with a local cast and desegregated audiences seemed a fitting climax to the state's tricentennial celebrations.

South Carolina overwhelmingly supported the NEW DEAL program of Franklin D. Roosevelt, giving him 98 percent of the popular vote in the 1936 election. The state benefited from all of the national programs but most of all from the AGRICULTURAL ADJUSTMENT ADMINISTRATION, the WORKS PROGRESS ADMINISTRATION, the NATIONAL RECOVERY ADMINISTRATION, and the CIVILIAN CONSERVATION CORPS, which provided a minimum price for crops, wages for those out of work, and a minimum wage and maximum hours for textile workers. The Santee-Cooper project was the local TVA.

Yet it was World War II that brought South Carolina out of the depression, for the state became the focal point for many naval, marine, air, and army activities. Ft. Jackson at Columbia, the U.S. Marine Station at Paris Island, the Charleston Naval Base, and the countless air fields attracted by the bright sunny skies of the state brought in federal funds that stimulated the economy. The power of Congressman L. Mendel Rivers in the two decades after the war as chairman of the Armed Forces Committee protected these bases.

Far more than World War I, the Second World War drew the young men and women, black and white, out of their accustomed places in society, providing them with new experiences that broke traditional ties and prejudices. If 1808 had been an important year, certainly 1945 was equally important in the history of the state. The veterans' program and the armed forces educational program lifted up many Carolinians.

Yet the government was still in the hands of the traditional political groups. Change was slow. *Rice*

v. *Elmore* (1948) opened up the primaries to blacks, who began to vote in increasing numbers. Yet in 1948 STROM THURMOND became the Dixiecrat leader. Later JAMES F. BYRNES, after breaking with the Truman administration, came home to govern the state. His great effort was to obtain a state sales tax to raise funds to make black and white schools truly equal. This did not, however, stave off the U.S. Supreme Court decision of 1954, which brought an end to segregation, at least theoretically, in the schools. It was to be a decade, however, before there were concrete results. Then giant steps were made. The lunchroom sit-ins at Rock Hill in 1962 showed that blacks were determined to push their own cause forward. In 1963 the first blacks were enrolled in previously all-white schools, and Harvey Gantt was admitted to Clemson. A technical education program trained the unskilled for new jobs. With the passing of the CIVIL RIGHTS ACT OF 1964 and the CIVIL RIGHTS ACT OF 1965, there were federal observers at elections who could, if necessary, certify blacks to vote. *South Carolina* v. *Katzenbach* (1966) was the final effort of the state to use the doctrines of interposition, which failed. After 1966 the strides were immense, although the affair at Orangeburg, in which three black students were killed, marred the march forward. In 1976 there were 13 blacks in the state legislature.

One of the factors underlying the acceptance of better race relations was demographic change. In 1880 blacks represented 60.7 percent of the state's population. By 1970 the proportion was down to 30.5 percent. The population as a whole has not been increasing significantly. In the 1960s total population increased by 8.7 percent to a total of 2,590,516 by 1970.

The state is now far less rural. In 1945 there were 150,000 farms of an average acreage of 75; in 1970 there were only 52,000 farms with an average acreage of 160. Although the cities themselves have not grown greatly, the metropolitan areas have. In 1970 Columbia had a population of 99,000; Greenville, 64,000; Charleston, 60,000; North Charleston, 49,000; and Spartanburg, 46,300. But the metropolitan area of Columbia contained 330,000 people; Greenville, 298,000; Charleston, 296,000; and Spartanburg, 141,000. These changes in black-white ratios and rural-urban ratios will determine the nature of the new society.

The entire picture of the agricultural sector has changed too. In 1972 farm income was derived from the following divisions: TOBACCO, 20.2 percent; meat animals, 20.1 percent; SOYBEANS, 15.9 percent; vegetables, 10.4 percent; cotton lint and seed, 7.8 percent. South Carolina certainly bears

out Thomas D. Clark's statement about the South: "cotton going west, and cattle coming east." Yet the largest crops in the future may come from the forests, which now cover 64.5 percent of the land.

An economic resurgence has taken place under the direction of four moderate reform governors— Ernest F. Hollings, Donald Russell, Robert E. McNair, and John C. West. Factories of blue-chip American corporations have been spotted in every small town to take up the slack as people moved off the farms. A statewide technical education program has retrained many rural folk for jobs in the new factories. Blacks are now employed in textile mills. A German steel plant, a British-owned paper company, a French-owned rubber tire plant, and dealerships for the sale of Japanese automobiles are evidence of the influx of foreign capital. All of this has been sparked by the state development board, which collects statistics and points out opportunities. The South Carolina ports authority rebuilt the port facilities at Charleston and established modern docks at Port Royal (Beaufort) and at Georgetown. These improvements, with the great system of interstate highways, have brought prosperity to a state that had known little from 1865 to 1939.

Perhaps the newest and largest industry is TOURISM. The Carolina shore from Myrtle Beach to Hilton Head Island, with the exception of a long strip from Dubourdieu Beach to the Isle of Palms, has been developed by a variety of resort concerns, the most unusual being the use of Arab capital from Kuwait to exploit the resources of Kiawah Island. The system of state parks, many of them grouped around the major lakes of the state (Moultrie, Marion, Murray, Hartwell, Clark Hill, and Keowee), under the management of the department of parks, recreation, and tourism has added to the leisure fun of local citizens and visitors from afar.

Equally important in the field of tourism has been the emphasis placed first in Charleston and then throughout the state on preservation and restoration. Charleston in the 1920s led the way in the nation in urban zoning designed to preserve buildings of historic interest. The Manigault House was the first taken over by the Charleston Museum, followed by the Heyward-Washington House. To these have been added the Nathaniel Russell House under the control of the Historic Charleston Foundation and Drayton Hall on the Ashley River under the National Trust. Historic Columbia Foundation has been equally successful in preserving the Ainsley Hall House (a Robert Mills building) and the Hampton-Preston House. At the same time the preservation of cher-

SOUTH CAROLINA POPULATION, 1790–1970

Year	Total	White	Nonwhite Slave	Nonwhite Free	% Growth	Rank U.S.	Rank South
1790	249,073	140,178	107,094	1,801		7	4
1800	345,591	196,255	146,151	3,185	38.8	6	3
1810	415,115	214,196	196,365	4,554	20.1	6	3
1820	502,741	237,440	258,475	6,826	21.1	8	4
1830	581,185	257,863	315,401	7,921	15.6	9	5
1840	594,398	259,084	327,038	8,276	2.3	11	6
1850	668,507	274,563	384,984	8,960	12.5	14	8
1860	703,708	291,300	402,406	10,002	5.3	18	10
1870	705,606	289,667	415,939		0.3	22	12
1880	995,577	391,105	604,472		41.1	21	10
1890	1,151,149	462,008	689,141		15.6	23	10
1900	1,340,316	557,807	782,509		16.4	24	11
1910	1,515,400	679,161	836,239		13.1	26	12
1920	1,683,724	818,538	865,186		11.1	26	12
1930	1,738,765	944,049	794,716		3.3	26	12
1940	1,899,804	1,084,308	815,496		9.3	26	13
1950	2,117,027	1,293,405	823,622		11.4	27	13
1960	2,382,594	1,551,022	831,572		12.5	26	12
1970	2,590,516	1,794,430	796,086		8.7	26	12

SOUTH CAROLINA GOVERNORS

Governor	Party	Term
PROPRIETARY		
William Sayle		1669–1671
Joseph West		1671–1672
Sir John Yeamans		1672–1674
Joseph West		1674–1682
Joseph Morton		1682–1684
Sir Richard Kyrle		1684
Joseph West		1684–1685
Robert Quary		1685
Joseph Morton		1685–1686
James Colleton		1686–1690
Seth Sothell		1690–1692
Phillip Ludwell		1692–1693
Thomas Smith		1693–1694
Joseph Blake		1694–1695
John Archdale		1695–1696
Joseph Blake		1696–1700
James Moore		1700–1703
Sir Nathaniel Johnson		1703–1709
Edward Tynte		1709–1710
Robert Gibbes		1710–1712
Charles Craven		1712–1716
Robert Daniel		1716–1717
Robert Johnson		1717–1719
James Moore		1719–1721
ROYAL		
Francis Nicholson		1721–1725
Arthur Middleton		1725–1730
Robert Johnson		1730–1735
Thomas Broughton (lt. gov.)		1735–1737
William Bull (lt. gov.)		1737–1743
James Glen		1743–1756
William H. Lyttelton		1756–1760
William Bull (lt. gov.)		1760–1761
Thomas Boone		1761–1764
William Bull (lt. gov.)		1764–1766
Lord Charles Montagu		1766–1768
William Bull (lt. gov.)		1768
Lord Charles Montagu		1768–1769
William Bull (lt. gov.)		1769–1771
Lord Charles Montagu		1771–1773

Governor	Party	Term
William Bull (lt. gov.)		1773–1775
Lord William Campbell		1775
STATE		
John Rutledge		1776–1778
Rawlins Lowndes		1778–1779
John Rutledge		1779–1782
John Mathews		1782–1783
Benjamin Guerard		1783–1785
William Moultrie		1785–1787
Thomas Pinckney		1787–1789
Charles Pinckney		1789–1792
William Moultrie	Fed.	1792–1794
Arnoldus Vander Horst	Fed.	1794–1796
Charles Pinckney	Dem.-Rep.	1796–1798
Edward Rutledge	Fed.	1798–1800
John Drayton	Dem.-Rep.	1800–1802
James B. Richardson	Dem.-Rep.	1802–1804
Paul Hamilton	Dem.-Rep.	1804–1806
Charles Pinckney	Dem.-Rep.	1806–1808
John Drayton	Dem.-Rep.	1808–1810
Henry Middleton	Dem.-Rep.	1810–1812
Joseph Alston	Dem.-Rep.	1812–1814
David R. Williams	Dem.-Rep.	1814–1816
Andrew Pickens	Dem.-Rep.	1816–1818
John Geddes	Dem.-Rep.	1818–1820
Thomas Bennett	Dem.-Rep.	1820–1822
John L. Wilson	Dem.-Rep.	1822–1824
Richard I. Manning	Dem.-Rep.	1824–1826
John Taylor	Dem.-Rep.	1826–1828
Stephen D. Miller	Dem.	1828–1830
James Hamilton, Jr.	Dem.	1830–1832
Robert Y. Hayne	Dem.	1832–1834
George McDuffie	Dem.	1834–1836
Pierce M. Butler	Dem.	1836–1838
Patrick Noble	Dem.	1838–1840
B. K. Henagan	Dem.	1840
J. P. Richardson	Dem.	1840–1842
J. H. Hammond	Dem.	1842–1844
William Aiken	Dem.	1844–1846
David Johnson	Dem.	1846–1848
Whitemarsh B. Seabrook	Dem.	1848–1850
John H. Means	Dem.	1850–1852
John L. Manning	Dem.	1852–1854

Governor	Party	Term
James H. Adams	Dem.	1854–1856
R. F. W. Allston	Dem.	1856–1858
William H. Gist	Dem.	1858–1860
Francis W. Pickens	Dem.	1860–1862
Milledge L. Bonham	Dem.	1862–1864
A. G. Magrath	Dem.	1864–1865
Benjamin F. Perry (provisional)		1865
James L. Orr	Conservative	1865–1868
Robert K. Scott	Rep.	1868–1872
Franklin J. Moses, Jr.	Rep.	1872–1874
Daniel H. Chamberlain	Rep.	1874–1876
Wade Hampton	Dem.	1876–1879
W. D. Simpson	Dem.	1879–1880
Thomas B. Jeter	Dem.	1880
Johnson Hagood	Dem.	1880–1882
Hugh S. Thompson	Dem.	1882–1886
John C. Sheppard	Dem.	1886
John P. Richardson	Dem.	1886–1890
Benjamin R. Tillman	Dem.	1890–1894
John G. Evans	Dem.	1894–1897
W. H. Ellerbe	Dem.	1897–1899
Miles B. McSweeney	Dem.	1899–1903
Duncan C. Heyward	Dem.	1903–1907
Martin F. Ansel	Dem.	1907–1911
Coleman L. Blease	Dem.	1911–1915
Charles A. Smith	Dem.	1915
Richard I. Manning	Dem.	1915–1919
Robert A. Cooper	Dem.	1919–1922
Wilson G. Harvey	Dem.	1922–1923
Thomas G. McLeod	Dem.	1923–1927
John G. Richards	Dem.	1927–1931
Ibra C. Blackwood	Dem.	1931–1935
Olin D. Johnston	Dem.	1935–1939
Burnet R. Maybank	Dem.	1939–1941
J. E. Harley	Dem.	1941–1942
R. M. Jefferies	Dem.	1942–1943
Olin D. Johnston	Dem.	1943–1945
Ransome J. Williams	Dem.	1945–1947
J. Strom Thurmond	Dem.	1947–1951
James F. Byrnes	Dem.	1951–1955
George B. Timmerman	Dem.	1955–1959
Ernest F. Hollings	Dem.	1959–1963
Donald Russell	Dem.	1963–1965
Robert E. McNair	Dem.	1965–1971
John C. West	Dem.	1971–1975
James B. Edwards	Rep.	1975–1979
Richard W. Riley	Dem.	1979–

ished documents in the renovated and superbly directed state archives has been a parallel movement of great importance. All of these projects were stimulated or enhanced by the state's celebration of its three-hundredth birthday in 1970. The tricentennial was fittingly marked by the acquisition of Charles Towne Landing, the site of the first settlement on Albemarle Point, miraculously saved by its devoted owners.

But it is in the blending of the old and the new that the state takes its greatest pride. Its past, which has interwoven the lives of blacks and whites, and its bright future in the Sun Belt seem to be marking South Carolina as a place to watch, an example of mutuality in modern living.

Manuscripts and printed primary sources. Principal depositories for South Carolina history are South Carolina Department of Archives and History, 1430 Senate St., Columbia; South Caroliniana Library, University of South Carolina, Columbia; and South Carolina Historical Society, Fireproof Bldg., Charleston. For the first, see M. C. Chandler, *Colonial and State Records in South Carolina* (1973); for the last two, see J. H. Moore, *Research Materials in South Carolina* (1967). *Colonial Records of South Carolina* and *State Records of South Carolina*, divided into subseries, contain material generated by provincial and state governments. For laws of South Carolina, see T. Cooper and D. J. McCord (eds.), *Statutes at Large of South Carolina* (10 vols.; 1836–41). *South Carolina Historical Magazine* (1900–) contains most extensive collection of articles. P. M. Hamer, G. C. Rogers, and D. R. Chesnutt (eds.), *Papers of Henry Laurens* (5 vols. to date; 1968–); and R. L. Meriwether, W. E. Hemphill, and C. N. Wilson (eds.), *Papers of John C. Calhoun* (9 vols. to date; 1959–), are valuable as source materials and for annotation. J. H. Easterby, *Guide to Study and Reading of South Carolina History* (1950, repr. with supplement by N. Polk, 1975), is standard. Briefer and laced with apt comment is L. P. Jones, *Books and Articles on South Carolina History* (1970). Also helpful is R. J. Turnbull, *Bibliography of South Carolina, 1563–1950* (5 vols.; 1956–60). Microfilmed collections include papers of Nathanael Greene, J. H. Hammond, H. Laurens, and B. F. Perry and the Draper Papers relating to American Revolution in South.

Contemporary accounts. Observations of life in provincial South Carolina are found in A. S. Salley (ed.), *Narratives of Early Carolina, 1650–1708* (1911, 1959); L. Cheves (ed.), *South Carolina Historical Society Collections* (1897); J. Lawson, *New Voyage to Carolina* (1709, 1967); J. Glen, *Description of South Carolina* (1761, 1951); R. J. Hooker (ed.), *Carolina Backcountry: Journal of Charles Woodmason* (1953); and B. R. Carroll, *Historical Collections of South Carolina* (2 vols.; 1836, 1973). Observations of life in revolutionary and antebellum South Carolina are found in W. Moultrie, *Memoirs of American Revolution* (2 vols.; 1802, 1968); J. Drayton, *View of South Carolina* (1802, 1972); J. Johnson, *Traditions and Reminiscences* (1851, 1972); and C. Fraser, *Reminiscences of Charleston* (1854, 1969). Post-1860 accounts are M. B. Chesnut, *Diary from Dixie*, ed. B. A. Williams (1949); J. S. Pike, *Prostrate State* (1874, 1935, 1968); E. J. Scott, *Random Recollections* (1884, 1969); B. Robertson, *Red Hills and Cotton* (1942, 1963); and D. E. H. Smith, *Charlestonian's Recollections* (1950).

Histories. Best survey is D. D. Wallace, *South Carolina: Short History* (1951, 1969); this volume is condensation of *History of South Carolina* (4 vols.; 1934). Less successful is Y. Snowden, *History of South Carolina* (5 vols.; 1920). Most readable and perceptive short account is L. P. Jones, *South Carolina: Synoptic History for Laymen* (1970). Two personal views are presented in W. F. Guess, *South Carolina: Annals of Pride and Protest* (1960); and L. B. Wright, *South Carolina: Bicentennial History* (1976).

Excellent monographs on colonial era are W. S. Powell, *Proprietors of Carolina* (1963); E. McCrady, *South Carolina Under Proprietary Government, 1670–1719* (1897, 1969); E. McCrady, *South Carolina Under Royal Government, 1719–1776* (1899, 1969); W. J. Rivers, *Sketch of History of South Carolina to 1719* (1856); M. E. Sirmans, *Colonial South Carolina* (1966); V. Crane, *Southern Frontier* (1928); W. R. Smith, *South Carolina as Royal Province* (1903); R. L. Meriwether, *Expansion of South Carolina, 1729–1765* (1940); C. J. Milling, *Red Carolinians* (1940); R. M. Brown, *South Carolina Regulators* (1963); W. R. Walsh, *Charleston's Sons of Liberty* (1959, 1968); and J. P. Greene (ed.), *Nature of Colony Constitutions* (1970).

Excellent monographs on revolutionary and early federal eras are D. Ramsay, *History of Revolution in South Carolina* (2 vols.; 1785) and *History of South Carolina, 1670 to 1808* (2 vols.; 1809, 1858, 1959–60); E. McCrady, *History of South Carolina in Revolution, 1775–1780* (1901, 1969) and *History of South Carolina in Revolution, 1780–1783* (1902, 1969); R. F. Weigley, *Partisan War* (1970); J. H. Wolfe, *Jeffersonian Democracy in South Carolina* (1940); G. C. Rogers, *Evolution of Federalist* (1962); and W. A. Schaper, *Sectionalism and Representation in South Carolina* (1901, 1968).

Excellent monographs on antebellum period are W. W. Freehling, *Prelude to Civil War* (1966); P. H. Hamer, *Secession Movement* (1918); H. S. Schultz, *Nationalism and Sectionalism in South Carolina* (1950, 1969); and S. A. Channing, *Crisis of Fear* (1970).

Excellent monographs on Civil War and postwar periods are C. E. Cauthen, *South Carolina Goes to War, 1860–1865* (1950); W. L. Rose, *Rehearsal for Reconstruction* (1964); F. B. Simkins and R. H. Woody, *South Carolina During Reconstructon* (1932, 1966); M. Abbott, *Freedmen's Bureau in South Carolina, 1865–1872* (1967); C. K. R. Bleser, *Promised Land: History of South Carolina Land Commission, 1869–1890* (1969); J. Williamson, *After Slavery* (1965); E. M. Lander, *History of South Carolina, 1865–1960* (1960, 1970); and W. J. Cooper, *Conservative Regime: South Carolina, 1877–1890* (1968).

A glimpse of South Carolina thought at mid–twentieth century can be found in W. W. Ball, *State That Forgot* (1932); W. D. Workman, *Case for South* (1960, 1969); and J. M. Dabbs, *Southern Heritage* (1958) and *Who Speaks for South?* (1964). Economic base of South Carolina history has been analyzed in L. C. Gray, *History of Agriculture in Southern U.S. to 1860* (2 vols.; 1933, 1958); C. D. Clowse, *Economic Beginnings in Colonial South Carolina, 1670–1730* (1971); L. Sellers, *Charleston Business on Eve of American Revolution* (1934); D. Kohn (ed.), *Internal Improvements in South Carolina, 1817–1828* (1938); R. Mills, *Statistics of South Carolina* (1826, 1972); A. G. Smith, *Economic Readjustment of Old Cotton State* (1958); U. B. Phillips, *History of Transportation in Eastern Cotton Belt to 1860* (1908, 1968); J. H. Easterby, *South Carolina Rice Plantation* (1945); E. M. Lander, *Textile Industry in Antebellum South Carolina* (1969); D. C. Heyward, *Seed from Madagascar* (1937); and E. W. Pringle, *Woman Rice Planter* (1913, 1961).

Important biographical studies are J. Alden, *John Stuart* (1944, 1966); D. D. Wallace, *Henry Laurens* (1915, 1967); R. D. Bass, *Green Dragoon* (1957), Tarleton, *Swamp Fox* (1959), F. Marion, and *Gamecock* (1961), T. Sumter; M. R. Zahniser, *Charles C. Pinckney* (1967); D. G. Morgan, *Justice William Johnson* (1954, 1971); D. Malone, *Thomas Cooper* (1926, 1961); B. Mitchell, *William Gregg* (1928, 1966); F. Freidel, *Francis Lieber* (1947); C. M. Wiltse, *John C. Calhoun* (3 vols.; 1944–51); L. A. White, *Robert B. Rhett* (1931, 1965); F. B. Simkins,

Pitchfork Ben Tillman (1944, 1964); G. L. Simpson, *Cokers of Carolina* (1956); and W. D. Workman, *Bishop from Barnwell* (1963), Edgar Brown. Valuable twentieth-century autobiographies are J. A. Rice, *I Came Out of Eighteenth Century* (1942); J. F. Byrnes, *All in One Lifetime* (1958); and B. E. Mays, *Born to Rebel* (1971).

For cultural and intellectual history, see F. P. Bowes, *Culture of Early Charleston* (1942); A. Rutledge, *Artists in Charleston* (1949); G. C. Rogers, *Charleston in Age of Pinckneys* (1969); C. S. Watson, *Antebellum Charleston Dramatists* (1976); J. H. Easterby, *History of College of Charleston* (1935); and D. W. Hollis, *University of South Carolina* (2 vols.; 1951, 1956).

Some light is cast on history of journalism in H. Cohen, *South Carolina Gazette, 1732–1775* (1953); W. L. King, *Newspaper Press of Charleston* (1872); L. P. Jones, *Stormy Petrel, N. G. Gonzales* (1973); and S. L. Latimer, *Story of State* (1970). Good ethnic studies are rare; valuable but out of date is A. H. Hirsch, *Huguenots of Colonial South Carolina* (1928, 1962).

For black history, see P. H. Wood, *Black Majority* (1974); H. M. Henry, *Police Control of Slave in South Carolina* (1914, 1968); M. Wikramanayake, *World in Shadow: Free Black in Antebellum South Carolina* (1973); J. Lofton, *Insurrection in South Carolina* (1964); A. A. Taylor, *Negro in South Carolina During Reconstruction* (1924, 1969); G. B. Tindall, *South Carolina Negroes, 1877–1900* (1952, 1963); I. A. Newby, *Black Carolinians, 1895 to 1968* (1973); and J. Nelson and J. Bass, *Orangeburg Massacre* (1970).

For religious history, see F. Dalcho, *Episcopal Church in South Carolina* (1820); A. S. Thomas, *Protestant Episcopal Church in South Carolina, 1820–1957* (1957); G. Howe, *Presbyterian Church in South Carolina* (2 vols.; 1870, 1883); B. A. Elzas, *Jews of South Carolina* (1905); L. Townsend, *South Carolina Baptists, 1670–1805* (1935); A. D. Betts, *History of South Carolina Methodism* (1952); and H. G. Anderson, *Lutheranism in Southeastern States, 1860–1886* (1969).

For county and local histories, see A. Gregg, *History of Old Cheraws* (1867, 1905, 1965); T. Kirkland and R. M. Kennedy, *Historic Camden* (1926); H. K. Hennig, *Columbia, 1786–1936* (1936); A. K. Gregorie, *History of Sumter County* (1954); H. Savage, *Santee* (1956); G. C. Rogers, *History of Georgetown County* (1970); and T. H. Pope, *History of Newberry County* (1973).

Articles. See R. M. Weir, *William and Mary Quarterly* (Oct., 1969), prerevolutionary South Carolina politics; R. M. Calhoon and R. M. Weir, *William and Mary Quarterly* (Jan., 1969), scandalous history of Sir Egerton Leigh; E. M. Sirmans, *Journal of Southern History* (Nov., 1962), legal status of slave, and *William and Mary Quarterly* (July, 1961), royal council; E. Donnan, *American Historical Review* (July, 1928), slave trade; J. P. Greene, *Journal of Southern History* (Feb., 1963), Wilkes fund controversy; P. Maier (ed.), *Perspectives in American History* (1970), Charleston mobs; G. Olson, *South Carolina Historical Magazine* (Oct., 1967; Jan., 1968), Loyalists; G. C. Rogers, *South Carolina Historical Magazine* (Jan., 1970), South Carolina Federalists; M. K. Latimer, *American Historical Review* (July, 1956), South Carolina in War of 1812; E. H. Fitchett, *Journal of Negro History* (Oct., 1947), free blacks; J. Senese, *South Carolina Historical Magazine* (July, 1967), free blacks; T. W. Rogers, *South Carolina Historical Magazine* (Jan., 1967), population movement to Southwest; and D. W. Hollis, *South Carolina Historical Magazine* (Jan., 1969), South Carolina Progressives.

Dissertations. See C. Attig, "W. H. Lyttelton" (University of Nebraska, 1958); R. W. Barnwell, 'Loyalism in South Carolina" (Duke University, 1941); M. L. Cann, "B. R. Maybank and New Deal in South Carolina" (University of North Carolina, 1967); D. R. Chesnutt, "South Carolina's Expansion into Colonial Georgia" (University of Georgia, 1973); J. D. Duncan, "Servitude and Slavery in Colonial South Carolina, 1670–1776" (Emory University, 1971); W. B. Edgar, "Libraries of Colonial South Carolina" (University of South Carolina, 1969); V. L. Glenn, "James Hamilton, Jr." (University of North Carolina, 1964); J. I. Hayes, "South Carolina and New Deal" (University of South Carolina, 1972); R. M. Jellison, "Paper Currency in Colonial South Carolina" (Indiana University, 1953); J. Nadelhaft, "Revolutionary Era in South Carolina" (University of Wisconsin, 1965); D. J. Senese, "Legal Thought in South Carolina, 1800–1860" (University of South Carolina, 1970); W. R. Snell, "Indian Slavery in Colonial South Carolina" (University of Alabama, 1972); R. C. Tucker, "J. H. Hammond" (University of North Carolina, 1958); A. D. Watson, "Quitrent System in Royal South Carolina" (University of South Carolina, 1971); R. M. Weir, "South Carolina and Stamp Act Crisis" (Western Reverse University, 1966); P. F. Wild, "South Carolina Politics, 1816–1833" (University of Pennsylvania, 1949); and C. N. Wilson, "J. J. Petigrew" (University of North Carolina, 1971).

GEORGE C. ROGERS, JR.
University of South Carolina

SOUTH CAROLINA, UNIVERSITY OF (Columbia, 29208), founded in 1801, was intentionally located in Columbia to lessen the political anxieties of up-country Carolinians over the role and influence of Charleston in state affairs. During the presidency of THOMAS COOPER (1820–1834), the school developed a classical liberal arts curriculum considered by many to be one of the finest in antebellum America. In 1862, however, declining enrollments and the pressures of the Civil War forced the school to close. Its buildings were used to house a Confederate hospital until the city's surrender in February, 1865, and were destroyed in the conflagration that swept the city following its occupation by General W. T. Sherman. Although it reopened almost immediately after the war's end, financial and political problems forced six separate reorganizations of the institution between 1865 and 1906. When its agricultural department was moved to Clemson College in 1890, the university was left with an enrollment of fewer than 100 students. In the twentieth century, especially since World War II, the school has fared much better. Today it has over 16,000 students enrolled in a variety of graduate and undergraduate programs of instruc-

tion. Library holdings include copies of church and county records from a wide area of the state and dating back to 1691. Also housed here are the papers of JOHN C. CALHOUN, J. H. HAMMOND, WILLIAM G. SIMMS, HENRY TIMROD, WADE HAMPTON, H. S. LEGARÉ, EDWARD RUTLEDGE, JAMES WOODROW, STROM THURMOND, and the MIDDLETON FAMILY.

See D. W. Hollis, *University of South Carolina* (2 vols; 1951, 1956); E. L. Green, *History of University of South Carolina* (1916); D. Malone, *Public Life of T. Cooper* (1926); and M. Colyer, *History of Higher Education in South Carolina* (1889).

SOUTH CAROLINA GAZETTE began publication in 1732 on a printing press and with an editor, Thomas Whitemarsh, sent to Charleston by Benjamin Franklin. Although the paper failed after only one year of publication, it almost immediately was revived by Lewis Timothée and was continued after his death by his wife and his son Peter Timothy. Under the latter's editorship, the *Gazette* was an early and ardent critic of Parliament. Timothy's vigorous opposition to the STAMP ACT, his support of nonimportation agreements, and his advocacy of independence made the *Gazette* the principal revolutionary press in South Carolina. During the period of British occupation of Charleston, a Loyalist newspaper, the *Royal South Carolina Gazette* (1780–1782), replaced Timothy's publication. Timothy resumed publication of the *South Carolina State Gazette* in 1785, and under several variations on this name the paper continued until 1837, when it was purchased by the *Courier* (CHARLESTON NEWS AND COURIER).

See W. L. King, *Newspaper Press of Charleston* (1872, 1970); and copies on microfilm from Bell & Howell among early miscellaneous newspapers (1732–82).

SOUTH CAROLINA HISTORICAL SOCIETY (Fireproof Bldg., Charleston, S.C. 29401), founded in 1855, maintains a library and an extensive manuscript collection dating from 1668 and centered on the history of South Carolina and its coastal region in the eighteenth and nineteenth centuries. Included are the Laurens Papers; the papers of Robert F. W. Allston, South Carolina rice planter and governor, and of his family (1757–1926); and the papers of such others as Thomas Pinckney, Langdon Cheves, and Arthur Middleton. There are also diaries; plantation, land-grant, business, church, professional, genealogical, and medical records; and military, local government, and private papers of the Confederate and Reconstruction periods. The society has published since 1900 the *South Carolina Historical Magazine* (circulation 2,400 in 1976) and accepts documents and scholarly articles not to exceed 5,000 words on South Carolina and its environs. The society has also sponsored the publication of many of the manuscripts in its library.

See H. G. McCormack, "Provisional Guide to Manuscripts in South Carolina Historical Society," in 10 installments in *South Carolina Historical and Genealogical Magazine*, beginning April, 1944; and consolidated index (1900–39) of *South Carolina Historical Magazine*, subject index (1900–60).

SOUTHEASTERN GEOGRAPHER (Department of Geography, University of Tennessee, Knoxville, 37916), a biannual with a circulation of 850, was founded in 1961. It is published by the Southeastern Division of the Association of American Geographers for its membership and accepts scholarly research papers of general topical or methodological interest; it maintains a particular interest in articles dealing with the South, east of the Mississippi River.

SOUTHEASTERN LIBRARY NETWORK (First National Bank Bldg., Suite 820, 615 Peachtree St. NE, Atlanta, Ga. 30308) is a computerized library network serving over 100 member libraries in ten southeastern states. Patterned on the Ohio College Library Center (OCLC), the network provides on-line bibliographic and cataloging information to member libraries and obligates them to provide such data for titles not in the data base. The network also provides a union catalog showing which libraries own each title. Thus scholars and researchers can have locations of monographs quickly identified. SOLINET was organized by the ASSOCIATION OF SOUTHEASTERN RESEARCH LIBRARIES as the result of a feasibility study conducted in 1972. The organizational meeting, held March 9, 1973, at the University of South Carolina, adopted temporary procedures and elected a board of directors with John H. Gribbin of Tulane as chairman. Ninety-nine charter members pledged $268,891 to begin operations. Grants of $600,000 from the Andrew Mellon Foundation and $10,000 from the Council on Library Resources put SOLINET on a firm financial footing. In 1974 SOLINET signed a tie-in contract with OCLC. The service became operative in 1975 with terminals installed, training given to operators, and practical use beginning. SOLINET will continue to use OCLC services, gradually adding

access to additional capabilities at the regional level as practicable and self-supporting.

See J. P. Kennedy, *Southeastern Librarian* (Spring, 1973); J. H. Gribbin, *Southeastern Librarian* (Fall, 1974); R. W. Frantz, Jr., *Southeastern Librarian* (Fall, 1976); J. H. Gribbin, *College and Research Libraries* (Feb., 1975); and annual reports at Atlanta office.

ELAINE VON OESEN
North Carolina Department of Cultural Resources

SOUTHERN AND WESTERN MONTHLY MAGAZINE AND REVIEW, popularly known at the time as *Simms's Magazine*, was a literary and political journal published in Charleston, S.C., beginning in January, 1845. It was largely written by the talented and ambitious editor, WILLIAM GILMORE SIMMS. The magazine during its short existence became a stout advocate of slavery, scientific farming, war with Mexico, and the industrialization of the South. After the last issue in December of the same year, the journal merged with the SOUTHERN LITERARY MESSENGER.

See J. V. Ridgely, *W. G. Simms* (1962); M. C. S. Oliphant, A. T. Odell, and T. C. D. Eaves (eds.), *Letters of W. G. Simms* (5 vols.; 1952–56), I; F. L. Mott, *History of American Magazines* (1966), I; and J. L. Wakelyn, *Politics of Literary Man, W. G. Simms* (1973).

SOUTHERN BIVOUAC: A MONTHLY LITERARY AND HISTORICAL MAGAZINE was published in Louisville between 1882 and 1887 by the Kentucky branch of the SOUTHERN HISTORICAL SOCIETY. In August, 1883, it was taken over by W. N. and E. H. McDonald and in June, 1885, was acquired by the publishers of *Home and Farm*. It finally in 1887 merged with the *Century*. The publication included historical papers read before the association, short stories about the Civil War, sketches of soldiers distinguished in the war, poetry, and miscellaneous articles related to southern life. The magazine was directed at the Confederate soldier, his family, and friends of the South. It was an attempt to reproduce and preserve in permanent form the life and times of the Confederacy. With so much attention given the Union soldier in the press after the Civil War, it was only natural that the Confederate Johnny Reb be given an opportunity to tell his side of the Civil War.

See F. L. Mott, *History of American Magazines* (1967), III; and complete files of magazine, Louisville Free Public Library, Newberry Library, University of Chicago Library, Iowa State University Library, Kansas State Historical Society, Tulane University Library, University of

Texas Library, and New–York Historical Society. An index is currently under preparation at Youngstown State University.

HUGH G. EARNHART
Youngstown State University

SOUTHERN CHRISTIAN LEADERSHIP CONFERENCE, a Negro rights organization and direct outgrowth of the Montgomery bus boycott (1955–1956), was formed by Dr. MARTIN LUTHER KING, JR., in January–February, 1957. Often considered more militant than the NATIONAL ASSOCIATION FOR THE ADVANCEMENT OF COLORED PEOPLE because it preferred direct-action campaigns and even civil disobedience to legal maneuvers, the SCLC nevertheless avoided the extremism and race chauvinism of the later CONGRESS OF RACIAL EQUALITY and STUDENT NONVIOLENT COORDINATING COMMITTEE. As its organizer, president, and guiding light, King imposed upon the organization his deep philosophic commitments to Gandhian pacifism, Christian reconciliation, and universal brotherhood.

Until the urban race riots of the mid-1960s, SCLC's primary focus was the South, where it conducted voter registration drives, citizenship training classes, and massive protest demonstrations against discriminatory practices. After that date it attempted to address hard-core employment, educational, and housing problems of the black urban masses. But its successes outside the South were rarely tangible, and its principal contribution to the CIVIL RIGHTS MOVEMENT was the dramatization of the southern Negro's plight. In this, as in all aspects of its work, the organization itself was overshadowed by its towering leader. In the Birmingham demonstrations of April, 1963 (which at one point involved several hundred black schoolchildren), King and other SCLC leaders effectively exploited the brutality of local authorities to expose race discrimination in the very citadel of segregation. This action moved President John F. Kennedy to ask Congress for the public accommodations legislation that became the CIVIL RIGHTS ACT OF 1964. Similarly, the SCLC leader's 1965 voter rights demonstrations, climaxed by the Selma-to-Montgomery march, served as the immediate catalyst for the Voting Rights Act (CIVIL RIGHTS ACT OF 1965). The high point of Dr. King's moral leadership and of civil rights unity came with the march on Washington in August, 1963, during which he electrified an audience of 250,000 with his "I have a dream" oration at the Lincoln Memorial. Shortly before a second Washington march, SCLC's Poor People's Campaign of 1968, King was assassinated (April 4, 1968) in Memphis, where he had joined demonstrations in behalf of striking garbage workers. His successor as president of SCLC was Dr. RALPH ABERNATHY.

Unlike CORE or NAACP, SCLC was an organization of affiliates not members. Individuals held membership through such affiliated organizations as churches, fraternal orders, and civic bodies in 16 border and southern states. It was controlled by a 33-member executive board composed almost entirely of black Baptist ministers. It sporadically published a bulletin and in 1970 maintained a full-time staff of 60 workers at headquarters in Atlanta. Annual budgets (ranging from some $200,000 in 1961 to over $1 million in 1970) were supported from benefits, contributions, and collections at the personal appearances of its presidents.

See E. T. Clayton (ed.), *SCLC Story* (1964); M. L. King, Jr., *Where Do We Go from Here?* (1967); H. Walton, Jr., *Political Philosophy of M. L. King, Jr.* (1971); and P. Watters, *Down to Now* (1971).

NEIL R. MCMILLEN
University of Southern Mississippi

SOUTHERN CONFERENCE FOR HUMAN WELFARE (1938–1948) grew out of liberal and radical desires for a general reform organization and was part of Franklin D. Roosevelt's attempt to build an independent southern political base. Its founding convention in Birmingham attracted many political luminaries including Mrs. Roosevelt and Justice HUGO L. BLACK, and it drew favorable comments from both southern and northern observers. The delegates adopted numerous policy recommendations designed to solve the problems described in the National Emergency Council's *Report on the Economic Conditions of the South* (1938) and established a permanent organization.

The SCHW's meager resources limited its activities to a small part of its reform agenda. It advocated greater political and economic opportunities for blacks; it began a hesitant campaign against SEGREGATION, chiefly within the organization itself; and it undertook a campaign for federal abolition of the POLL TAX. Internal schisms further limited its effectiveness and jeopardized its existence. Communists, Socialists, liberals, moderates, radicals, and laborites clashed over various matters, most notably the Russo-Finnish War and American foreign policy, and on occasion tried to turn the SCHW to other purposes. For a time, John L. Lewis schemed to incorporate it into a national third party.

American entry into World Wor II united the organization. New leaders, Clark Foreman and James Dombrowski, fostered cohesion and gave the SCHW dedicated and resourceful direction. They mobilized support for the war effort, worked to spread democratic ideals, and created agencies for continued reform. In 1942 the SCHW began a newspaper, the *Southern Patriot*. Later, state committees were established to get closer to ordinary southerners and to work to register black voters. A CIO endorsement brought in additional sums of money; together with a South-wide tour by MARY MCLEOD BETHUNE in 1946, it helped swell SCHW membership to about 6,000. A dual organization was set up: the Southern Conference for Human Welfare to continue the group's name and political activity; and the Southern Conference Educational Fund, Inc., to conduct a campaign against racial segregation.

The conference's rapid rise was followed by an equally rapid decline. Annoyed at SCHW criticisms of their racial policies in Operation Dixie, CIO leaders publicly denounced the conference. Funds from CIO unions declined, and union activists withdrew from the group. Liberals and conservatives berated it for its Communist connections and for its refusal to support American cold war foreign policy. Moderates and liberals thus withdrawing from the SCHW were joined by persons opposed to its attack on segregation. In the ELECTION OF 1948, its remaining members divided over the candidacies of Harry Truman and Henry Wallace, and after the election the SCHW was formally dissolved. A small group of integrationists, led by Dombrowski and AUBREY WILLIAMS, continued SCEF and the *Southern Patriot* into the 1950s and 1960s.

Long pilloried as a Communist front, the SCHW was in fact a popular front—a mixture of moderate to radical organizations with no one clearly dominant. The SCHW and SCEF directly link the New Deal–World War II era with the CIVIL RIGHTS MOVEMENT of the 1960s. They helped keep alive an unpopular cause whose time had not yet come. As indigenous left-wing integrationist organizations, they illustrate the little-known potential and vitality of twentieth-century southern radicalism.

See important manuscript collections at Tuskegee Institute and Atlanta University; C. H. Foreman, *Phylon* (June, 1951), defense; House Committee on Un-American Activities, *Report* (1947), conservative attack; T. A. Krueger, *Promises to Keep* (1967), SCHW; and I. Klibaner, "Southern Conference Education Fund" (Ph.D. dissertation, University of Wisconsin, 1971).

THOMAS A. KRUEGER
University of Illinois, Urbana

SOUTHERN ECONOMIC JOURNAL (Hanes Hall, University of North Carolina, Chapel Hill, 27514), a quarterly with a circulation of 3,800, was founded in 1933. It is a technical journal of general contemporary economic theory published jointly by the Southern Economic Association and the University of North Carolina. The *Journal* accepts book reviews and articles when the latter are accompanied by a $15 submission fee from SEA members and a $25 submission fee from non-SEA members.

SOUTHERN EDUCATION BOARD was created in 1901 as the executive board of the OGDEN MOVEMENT's annual Conference for Education in the South. Board members included Robert C. Ogden (president), CHARLES D. MCIVER (secretary), George Foster Peabody (treasurer), and J. L. M. CURRY, C. W. DABNEY, EDWIN A. ALDERMAN, Hollis B. Frissell, Wallace Buttrick, William H. Baldwin, Jr., Albert Shaw, WALTER HINES PAGE, and the Honorable H. H. Hanna. By 1914, when it dissolved after Ogden's death, the board had had 26 members, 18 of whom were southerners. Its sole aim was to act as a propaganda agency primarily through "the public press, and more especially public speech . . . for the purpose of stimulating public sentiment in favor of . . . the public schools." Expenditures averaged an estimated $30,000 annually, mostly in the employment of agents who assisted in state educational campaigns. At the midpoint of its existence the board shifted emphasis, on the assumption that the main obstacle to southern educational development was no longer apathy but poverty. Thereafter aid more often took the form of assisting states in the employment of supervisors in specialized areas of education and encouraging the spread of farm demonstration work. Southern educational progress from 1901 to 1914 to a great extent was real due to the activities of the Southern Education Board; but, relatively speaking, Negro school-aged children did not benefit as much as whites, and the southern system of public education remained measurably behind that of the rest of the nation.

See L. R. Harlan, *Separate and Unequal* (1958); C. W. Dabney, *Universal Education in South* (1936); W. E. King, "Growth of Public Schools in North Carolina" (Ph.D. dissertation, Duke, 1970); Robert C. Ogden Papers, Library of Congress; Southern Education Board Papers, University of North Carolina, Chapel Hill; and Charles D. McIver Papers, University of North Carolina, Greensboro.

WILLIAM E. KING
Duke University

SOUTHERN FOLKLORE QUARTERLY (Anderson Hall, University of Florida, Gainesville, 32601), founded in 1937, has a circulation of 900 and is published by the Department of English, University of Florida. The *Journal* accepts book reviews and scholarly articles on the historical and descriptive study of folk material and does not confine its interest to the southern part of the United States.

SOUTHERN GOVERNORS' CONFERENCE. Following a meeting with President Franklin Roosevelt in November, 1934, the governors of eight southeastern states met in December "to perfect a permanent organization designed to bring closer and fuller cooperation" among themselves and between "them collectively and the federal government at Washington." The initial program of the conference was directed at territorial freight rate discrimination (BIRMINGHAM DIFFERENTIAL) but this was expanded (1936) to include efforts to achieve equitable taxation policies, "friendly labor relations," and cooperation with the federal government on industrial development policies. Following World War II, the conference added regional education and other concerns to its agenda. By the 1970s the agenda broadened across virtually all the responsibilities of state government.

Other regional organizations have been created or endorsed by the conference to carry out specific programs: the Southern Regional Education Board (1949), the Southern Interstate Nuclear Board (1961), and the Southern Growth Policies Board (1973). These organizations work closely with the conference on matters of mutual interest, but they do not all contain the same constituent members.

Once characterized as the "most politically boisterous" of the regional governors' conferences, the annual meetings saw the southern Democrats rising up against efforts to remove the poll tax, liberalization of labor and race relations, and encroachment of the federal government on traditional states' roles. Recent history has found the conference considerably more positive and less sectional in outlook. In addition to the old slaveholding states, the conference includes Oklahoma, the territory of the Virgin Islands, and potentially the commonwealth of Puerto Rico.

See G. E. Brooks, *When Governors Convene* (1961); W. R. McDonald, *Southern Governors' Conference* (1949); and E. Black, *Southern Governors and Civil Rights* (1976).

THAD L. BEYLE
University of North Carolina, Chapel Hill

SOUTHERN HISTORICAL ASSOCIATION (History Department, Tulane University, New Orleans, La. 70118), founded in 1934 by 28 prominent southern historians and with a present membership of almost 5,000, meets annually in November. Its membership is drawn from all parts of the United States, and many of the papers read at its annual convention deal with non-American topics; however, the majority of its membership comprises scholars interested in the history of the South itself. The association (since 1935) publishes for its membership the *Journal of Southern History* (Rice University, Houston, Tex. 77001), an outstanding scholarly quarterly. Each issue usually contains four research articles in addition to edited documents or historical notes, book reviews, and news of interest to historians of the South. The *Journal* accepts well-documented material on general American history, but its main interest is in the history of the South, slavery, abolition, the Negro, the Civil War, the Confederacy, and Reconstruction. It offers four awards: in odd-numbered years, the Ramsdell Award of $100 for the best article in the *Journal*; in even-numbered years, the Sydnor Award of $500 for a distinguished book in southern history; in even-numbered years the Graduate Student Award, $50 for the best article published in the *Journal* by a graduate student; and in odd-numbered years, in cooperation with Longwood College, the Simkins Award of $200 for a scholarly first book in the general field of southern history.

SOUTHERN HISTORICAL SOCIETY was first organized in May of 1869 in New Orleans by a group of former Confederates with General BRAXTON BRAGG as chairman. The founders' aim was the collection and preservation of all the unpublished manuscripts and recollections of the Lost Cause before they were gone forever. Affiliates were planned for each of the southern states. The society was not overly successful at first, but it was reorganized at a convention at the Montgomery White Sulphur Springs in Virginia in August, 1873. The headquarters were changed from New Orleans to Richmond, where an archive of Civil War documents was established in the state capitol. General JUBAL A. EARLY was the first president and served with vice-presidents for each state including, among others, leaders such as ZEBULON B. VANCE of North Carolina, Admiral RAPHAEL SEMMES of Alabama, and S. B. BUCKNER of Kentucky. Each vice-president was to serve as ex officio president of an affiliated state society. For well over a year beginning in January, 1874, the society published some of its materials as a regular portion of the *Southern Magazine* of Baltimore. In January, 1876, however, the society launched its own monthly under the title, *Southern Historical Society Papers*. In 1880 the *Papers* were occasionally published only quarterly and finally in 1888 were made annual volumes.

From the first the *Papers*, though limited to the period of the southern Confederacy, were recognized to be of considerable historical value. Memoirs, wartime correspondence, and even unit rosters, which might well have been lost forever, were thus preserved. In all, the *Papers* made up 52 volumes. The Kentucky branch of the society also published for one year (1882–1883) the SOUTHERN BIVOUAC. The society dwindled by the early 1950s to a handful of members in the Richmond area, including DOUGLAS S. FREEMAN. When Freeman died the society ceased to exist. It had been arranged, however, that the last of the contents of its treasury should be used by the VIRGINIA HISTORICAL SOCIETY to complete publication of the proceedings of the Confederate Congress as the last three volumes of the *Papers*. This was done under the editorship of Dr. Frank E. Vandiver in 1952, 1953, and 1959.

See F. L. Mott, *History of American Magazines* (1967), III; A. S. Link and R. W. Patrick (eds.), *Writing Southern History* (1965); *Southern Historical Society Papers* (1876–1959), available in reprints from Kraus Reprint Co.; and E. M. Coulter, *Journal of Southern History* (Feb., 1936).

SOUTHERN HISTORY, PUBLISHERS OF.

Without raising great disagreement perhaps 1873 can be accepted as the earliest date for organized support of the publication of southern history. In that year the SOUTHERN HISTORICAL SOCIETY, composed largely of former Confederates, established headquarters in Richmond and, from 1876 until the society disbanded, published 52 *Papers*; the last appeared in July, 1959. The SOUTHERN HISTORY ASSOCIATION was founded in 1896 and through 1907 sponsored a journal, entitled *Publications*, that ran to 11 volumes.

Major support came also from universities. Johns Hopkins University, responding to the seminar of HERBERT BAXTER ADAMS, began publication in 1883 of *Studies in Historical and Political Science*, many of which dealt with the South. From Columbia University came *Studies in History, Economics, and Public Law*, which reflected the influence of Professor WILLIAM A. DUNNING and his interest in southern topics. Under JOHN SPENCER BASSETT's leadership, Trinity College, now Duke University, published the first of the *Trinity*

College Historical Society Papers in 1897, and three years later the University of North Carolina inaugurated the James Sprunt Studies.

The *South in the Building of the Nation*, a 12-volumed history, was published by the Southern Historical Publication Society in 1909, marking the first attempt to transcend state boundaries and provide a history of the southern regions. The *Journal of Southern History* was founded in 1935; this publication and the various state historical journals now afford historians of the South excellent opportunities for publication of their research. Finally, the influence of the southern university presses and of their directors has been great. A remarkable number of volumes that bear the imprint of these presses represent notable contributions to historical writing. Among the presses that have tended to specialize in works on the history of the South as a whole, in addition to books on their own states, are those of Duke and Louisiana State universities and the Universities of Kentucky, North Carolina, and Tennessee. Especially significant is the 10-volumed *History of the South*, which is being published by Louisiana State University Press under joint sponsorship of Louisiana State University and the Littlefield Fund of the University of Texas.

See W. H. Stephenson, *Southern History in the Making* (1964); W. T. Couch, *Virginia Quarterly Review* (Spring, 1950); T. D. Clark, *Journal of Southern History* (Aug., 1970); L. R. Wilson, *Education and Libraries* (1966); *Southern Historical Society Papers* (July, 1959); and *Southern History Association Publications* (Jan., 1897).

J. ISAAC COPELAND
University of North Carolina, Chapel Hill

SOUTHERN HISTORY, TEACHING OF.

Encouraged by the American Historical Association, the systematic study and teaching of history in institutions of higher education in the South began about 1890. Although the professional organization desired to increase the study of all fields of history in the region, teachers of history there focused their attention on southern history. HERBERT BAXTER ADAMS and his graduate students studied various aspects of southern history in the famous seminars at Johns Hopkins University. In 1896 James C. Ballagh inaugurated a formal lecture course in southern history at Johns Hopkins, and by 1913 six southern colleges and universities were teaching the history of the South. At the same time a number of schools began to teach courses on the history of particular southern states, as well as occasional courses on the Civil War and Reconstruction. Between the First and Second World wars state history courses gave way to or were rivaled by courses on the history of the South. During the interwar period southern universities granted over 100 Ph.D.'s in history, the majority of the recipients having written dissertations on southern topics. As these graduates found teaching positions, usually in southern institutions, they introduced courses on the history of the South. Continuing their research into southern history, these college instructors brought the writing and teaching of the subject closer together, leading a trend in the South to study its own past.

The South's distinct regional history, plus its impact upon American history in general, stimulated the study of the area beyond its boundaries. In 1908 WILLIAM E. DODD introduced a southern history course at the University of Chicago, followed by courses at other northern schools, including Harvard, Yale, and Michigan. By 1940 nearly 100 institutions of higher learning taught courses on the history of the South, and 35 years later nearly one-half of the nation's 3,000 senior colleges and universities included southern history courses in their curricula. Reasons for this rapid growth are not difficult to find. Modern Americans have expressed fascination with both the realities and myths of the antebellum southern civilization. The whole of American history cannot be understood without attention being devoted to southern sectionalism, the Civil War, and Reconstruction. Events after mid-century, not the least of which was the black revolution, have created interest in the roots of the nation's recent dramatic social and political changes. The study and teaching of southern history have a bright future.

See W. H. Stephenson, *Journal of Southern History* (Feb., 1945); M. Billington, *Journal of Southern History* (Aug., 1965); J. J. Mathews, *Journal of Southern History* (Feb., 1965); D. D. Van Tassel, *Journal of Southern History* (Nov., 1957); C. N. Degler, *Journal of Southern History* (Feb., 1964); M. B. Pierson, *Graduate Work in South* (1947); W. Rundell, *In Pursuit of American History* (1970); and D. Perkins and J. L. Snell, *Education of Historians* (1962).

MONROE BILLINGTON
New Mexico State University

SOUTHERN HISTORY ASSOCIATION was officially organized at a meeting on April 24, 1896, at what is now George Washington University. By this date the earlier SOUTHERN HISTORICAL SOCIETY had declined in both membership and influence. Furthermore, a need was felt for a society that would bring together persons whose interest in southern history was not limited to the period of the Confederacy. In early 1896, therefore, an

invitation had gone out from Washington, D.C., bearing almost a hundred signatures of former Confederate generals, college professors, government officials, and others, issuing a call for a new historical society for the South. At its first meeting a modern emphasis was placed on primary research, the reading of carefully prepared papers, and publication, similar to what the recently organized American Historical Association was doing. On June 12, 1896, the Southern History Association held its first annual conference, and in January, 1897, it began issuing its *Publications of the Southern History Association*. The journal published good-quality articles, documents, and book reviews pertaining to all periods of southern history. Unfortunately, the society failed to achieve a broad enough base of either public or academic support. Membership was never much over 200, interest in the meetings soon declined, and the *Publications* ceased to appear after 1907.

See E. M. Coulter, *Journal of Southern History* (Feb., 1936).

SOUTHERN HUMANITIES CONFERENCE (Box 715, Tech Sta., Ruston, La. 71270), a loose association of scholarly societies in the South specializing in different branches of the humanities, publishes two journals: *Southern Humanities Review* (9090 Haley Center, Auburn University, Auburn, Ala. 36830), a quarterly with a circulation of 550 founded in 1967 with financial assistance from Auburn University; and *Humanities in the South*. The latter, published under the aegis of Converse College, is the newsletter of the conference, but it also includes a few brief articles as well. The *Review* publishes poetry, book reviews, scholarly and popular literary and historical articles, and those of other disciplines in the area of general humanities with orientation toward the South. An annual award of $100 is granted for the best piece of fiction or nonfiction published during the year. The conference embraces the following societies: American Academy of Religion, Southern Section; Classical Association of the Middle West and South, Southern Section; North Carolina–Virginia College English Association; Society of Biblical Literature, Southern Section; South Atlantic Modern Language Association; South Atlantic Philosophy of Education Society; South Central College English Association; South Central Modern Language Association; South Central Renaissance Conference; Southeastern College Art Conference; Southeastern American Studies Association; Southeastern Renaissance Conference; Southern Historical Association; Southern Society for Philosophy and Psychology; Southern Society for the Philosophy of Religion; and Southern Speech Communication Association.

SOUTHERN LABOR HISTORY CONFERENCE, first held in 1976, promotes the study and understanding of organized labor in the South, bringing together representatives of both the labor and academic communities. The conference publishes both audiovisual and printed excerpts of the presentations. It is sponsored by the Southern Labor Archives of Georgia State University and the Organized Labor and Workmen's Circle Labor Awards Banquet Committee of Atlanta.

DAVID B. GRACY II
Georgia State University

SOUTHERN LITERARY JOURNAL (English Department, University of North Carolina, Chapel Hill, 27514), begun in 1968, is published semiannually and distributed to approximately 750 subscribers. It accepts reviews and articles on southern literature and culture specifically and pays up to $50.

SOUTHERN LITERARY MESSENGER, a variety magazine that published articles, stories, poems, and reviews, was founded in Richmond, Va., by Thomas W. White in August, 1834. EDGAR ALLAN POE became its editor (1835–1837) and transformed the provincial journal into a nationally known publication through his penetrating and at times scathing book reviews. Early in 1840, MATTHEW FONTAINE MAURY, a naval officer and oceanographer, became associate editor. His well-informed advocacy of naval reform proved effective, and other officers began to contribute. In 1842 Maury became the actual though not the nominal editor, serving until 1843. By 1850 more and more space was devoted to defending the South and its institutions. Finally in 1864, in the midst of Civil War strife, publication was abandoned. The honored name of the *Southern Literary Messenger* was briefly revived (May–July, 1895) in Washington by Mrs. A. Truehart Buck.

See F. L. Mott, *History of American Magazines* (1938), I, brief but informative; R. D. Jacobs, *Poe, Journalist* (1969), detailed footnotes; B. B. Minor, *Southern Literary Messenger* (1905); and D. K. Jackson, *Poe and Messenger* (1934) and *Contributors to Messenger* (1936).

NEIL T. STORCH
University of Minnesota, Duluth

SOUTHERN MANIFESTO (December 14, 1860) was a declaration drawn up by Senator LOUIS T. WIGFALL of Texas and Senator James L. Pugh (1820–1907) of Alabama signifying their belief that compromise negotiations in the Congress had reached an impasse and that the organization of a southern confederacy was the only recourse left to the South. It was signed by six additional senators (including JEFFERSON DAVIS and JOHN SLIDELL) and 23 members of the House from the states of North and South Carolina, Alabama, Georgia, Florida, Louisiana, Texas, Arkansas, and Mississippi. After publication of this manifesto, even most southern moderates came to believe that their efforts to prevent secession would fail.

See A. L. King, *Louis T. Wigfall* (1970); and D. Rowland, *Jefferson Davis* (1923).

SOUTHERN MANIFESTO (1956) was the popular title for the Declaration of Constitutional Principles, a statement attacking the U.S. Supreme Court and its BROWN V. BOARD OF EDUCATION school desegregation decision. The document bore the signatures of 19 senators and 82 House members, all of whom represented states of the former Confederacy. It condemned the Court's "judicial encroachment," pledged a concerted effort to reverse the decision, and commended the efforts of southern state governments "to resist forced integration by any lawful means." Appearing at a time when many of the southern states were enacting legislation to prevent enforcement of the *Brown* decision, the manifesto was part of the general program of "massive resistance" to public school desegregation championed by conservative white southern leaders. Its introduction in Congress on March 12, 1956, marked a high point in the sectional strife over race relations during the period.

See B. Hays, *Southern Moderate Speaks* (1959); D. Shoemaker (ed.), *With All Deliberate Speed* (1957); and N. V. Bartley, *Rise of Massive Resistance* (1969).

NUMAN V. BARTLEY
University of Georgia

SOUTHERN METHODIST UNIVERSITY (Dallas, Tex. 75275) is one of eight Methodist universities in the nation. It was founded in 1911 and first held classes in 1915. After VANDERBILT UNIVERSITY broke the church's control, SMU and EMORY UNIVERSITY became most favored by (and most influenced by) the Methodist College of Bishops. Over 10,000 students are currently enrolled in SMU schools of arts and sciences, business, law, technology, and international studies.

The Methodist Historical Library at SMU houses the papers of several church leaders and institutions, particularly of those from Texas.

See M. M. Thomas, *SMU: First 125 Years* (1973).

SOUTHERN MISSISSIPPI, UNIVERSITY OF

(Hattiesburg, 39401), was founded in 1912 as a state normal school for teachers. The expansion of its programs and enrollments gained university status for the school in 1962, and approximately 8,000 students presently attend. The university library is the repository for the papers of THEODORE G. BILBO, a 1-million-item collection.

SOUTHERN POETRY REVIEW (English De-

partment, North Carolina State University, Raleigh, 27607) is one of the oldest poetry journals with a circulation of over 1,000. It was first published in 1958 at Stetson University in Florida as *Impetus* and is now published biannually or triannually by North Carolina State University with aid from, among others, the North Carolina Arts Council and the National Council of the Arts. The *Review* awards a yearly prize of $100 and attempts to encourage the work of modern southern poets, but only about 35 percent of its contributors are from the South. It pays $3 per poem and publishes a few reviews of books of poetry. The editors make an effort to find new, unknown, and/or young authors. The *Review*, on occasion, also publishes books.

SOUTHERN QUARTERLY (Box 78, Southern

Sta., Hattiesburg, Miss. 39401), sponsored by the University of Southern Mississippi, began in October, 1962, and now has a circulation of approximately 600 (in 1976). It was founded by President William D. McCain of the University of Southern Mississippi. The *Quarterly* is a scholarly journal interested in publishing essays and researched articles from the fields of the humanities and social sciences and does not devote itself exclusively to the South. Since October, 1976, the journal has included a limited number of book reviews. It does not grant awards or pay for articles.

SOUTHERN QUARTERLY REVIEW, a maga-

zine clearly reflecting antebellum thought, lasted from January, 1842, until February, 1857. Started in New Orleans by Daniel Whitaker, who decided after one year to move it to Charleston, S.C., the well-printed magazine claimed a circulation of 2,000. Although it defended slavery and states' rights, when it was sold in 1847 the new owners preferred not to retain the northern-bred Whitaker. After a brief editorship by J. Milton Clapp, WILLIAM GILMORE SIMMS became editor in 1849 at a reported salary of $1,000 a year and made it into an outstanding quarterly. In addition to stressing southern opinions, he also published articles on subjects such as California during the gold rush, the Cuban question, and the Mexican War; the best essays, though, were on literary subjects. When C. Mortimer purchased the magazine in 1854, Simms remained editor for one more year. But when in 1856 the magazine moved to Columbia, S.C., and the Reverend James H. Thornwell took over, it suspended publication after four issues.

See F. L. Mott, *History of American Magazines* (1938); E. R. Rogers, *Four Southern Magazines* (1902); and W. G. Simms, *Letters* (1952–56).

EDWARD L. TUCKER
Virginia Polytechnic Institute and State University

SOUTHERN REGIONAL COUNCIL was char-

tered in Georgia in January, 1944, by five southerners interested in progress and democracy in the South: HOWARD W. ODUM, Charles S. Johnson, RALPH MCGILL, Rufus E. Clement, and Bishop Arthur J. Moore. Two earlier developments culminated in the new organization. First, in October, 1940, the executive committee of the COMMISSION ON INTERRACIAL COOPERATION was instructed by its membership to take steps toward forming an agency concerned with the regional development of the South. Second, three conferences (one of blacks, one of whites, and one interracial) passed resolutions in 1942 and 1943 calling for new blueprints for southern progress. Advocates of the council believed that its functions should include not only race relations but also agricultural, industrial, educational, civic, economic, and social developments of the region.

Members of the SRC come from 13 states: Alabama, Arkansas, Florida, Georgia, Kentucky, Louisiana, Mississippi, North Carolina, Oklahoma, South Carolina, Tennessee, Texas, and Virginia. They represent the South's oldest biracial group of liberal thinkers, and they maintain SRC headquarters in Atlanta. Policies and programs, determined by the entire membership and executed by an executive committee, are primarily educational in nature.

The SRC cooperates with church groups, educational institutions, organized labor, business representatives, and the media so that the reflections of thinking people might focus on major public problems. The operations of the SRC include research and surveys, discussion and information through the media, cooperation with other agencies, consultation services, and wide distribution of proposals for progress. The SRC has published the periodicals *Southern Voices*, *New South*, and *South Today*.

See archives of Southern Regional Council, Atlanta University Center.

A. GILBERT BELLES
Western Illinois University

SOUTHERN REVIEW (Baltimore) was a quarterly established by the historian William Hand Browne and Albert Taylor Bledsoe beginning in January, 1867. Browne retired after a little over a year. This periodical, the second of its name, represented an effort to glorify the Old South and bore an unmistakable antinorthern bias, since editor Bledsoe staunchly stood by the original justifications for slavery and secession. It nevertheless maintained a high degree of literary quality. In 1871 the *Review*'s sponsorship was taken over by the Methodist church of the South (Bledsoe eventually became a Methodist minister), and its pages thereafter were devoted more to religious than to political controversy. Bledsoe died on December 8, 1877, and his capable daughter Sophia Bledsoe Herrick published the *Review* for two years. It ceased publication in 1879.

SOUTHERN REVIEW (Drawer D, University Sta., Baton Rouge, La. 70893). The Old Series (1935–1942) was founded by Robert Penn Warren and Cleanth Brooks. The New Series, begun in 1965 under the editorship of Donald E. Stanford and Lewis P. Simpson, has a circulation of 3,100 and is chiefly a literary quarterly publishing critical essays, poetry, fiction, book reviews, and articles of an intellectual nature on the culture and history of the South and the history of ideas. It pays from three to five cents per word for prose and $20 to $50 per page for poetry.

See A. J. Montesi, "*Southern Review*, 1935–42" (Ph.D. dissertation, Pennsylvania State University, 1955).

SOUTHERN REVIEW (Charleston), a pioneering antebellum literary magazine, was started by Stephen Elliott. Published from February, 1828, to February, 1832, it had eight volumes in all (two numbers to the volume, two volumes to the year). The unsigned articles were devoted to many topics: literature of various countries, as well as con-

temporary concerns such as the tariff, the Bank of the United States, and the treatment of diseases. On Elliott's death, his son Stephen, an attorney and later a bishop of the Protestant Episcopal church, took over. But the man who gave the magazine impetus was HUGH SWINTON LEGARÉ, a lawyer and state representative, who was its editor from 1830 to 1832. A classical scholar, he contributed articles on Athenian and Roman history, Roman literature and orators, and the history and theory of law. His scholarly and pedantic tone, though, proved difficult for many. The magazine suspended publication when he left to assume a political post in Brussels.

See F. L. Mott, *History of American Magazines* (1938); E. W. Parks, *Antebellum Southern Literary Critics* (1962); and J. R. Welsh, *Southern Literary Journal* (Spring, 1971).

EDWARD L. TUCKER
Virginia Polytechnic Institute and State University

SOUTHERN SOCIOLOGICAL CONGRESS was organized in 1912 as an agency through which to discuss southern urban and industrial problems and to promote social reform, professionalism in social work, and religious liberalism. Until 1920 it held annual conventions, which brought northern welfare leaders to various cities in the region and enabled southern social workers and reformers to find mutual support. The congress was sociological in the sense that it addressed problems in a practical rather than a theoretical fashion. It was the regional counterpart of the National Conference of Charities and Correction, with which it held a joint meeting in Memphis in 1914. Instead of being bound to professional organizations, its members gave loyalty to the general purpose: "to study and improve social, civic, and economic conditions in the South."

The congress was convened in Nashville by Ben W. Hooper, a Tennessee governor active in prohibition and penal reform, but it was organized by a group of Nashvillians under the leadership of James E. McCulloch. He had been involved in Methodist education for church and social work and had begun to expand his Social Gospel emphasis on nondenominational lines. The congress provided him with a vehicle for his mission, and as general secretary he exercised a dominant influence in it.

The major activity of the Southern Sociological Congress was the series of annual conventions. Each convention provided the congress with an opportunity to publicize distressing social conditions and the principles of social uplift. The meetings were organized into general sessions, where national and regional leaders gave inspirational addresses, and departmental conferences, which brought together members who shared concerns such as PROHIBITION, courts and prisons, the church and social service, race relations, charities, and public health. State and local welfare organizations were formed in conjunction with the conferences, as were regional agencies such as the Comission of the Southern Universities on Race Relationships, the Conference on Law and Order (on LYNCHING), the Southern District of the Traveler's Aid Society, and the South-wide campaign of the Anti-Saloon League. Between 1914 and 1916 the congress developed a more centralized focus on public health. In addition to publishing literature on the subject, it organized an educational extension service, which carried exhibits and speakers by train to ten southern cities in 1916.

Under the impact of World War I, McCulloch and the congress leadership developed a national orientation, even moving the headquarters from Nashville to Washington, D.C. Increasingly, the congress lost both its regional function and its constituency. Instead of coordinating professional social work in the South, it sought to inspire an amorphous social conscience. With the conclusion of the war, the congress resumed its quest for a regional focus, changing its name to the Southern Cooperative League for Education and Social Service; but its emphasis was narrow, and its reconstitution in 1925 as the Home Betterment League reflected McCulloch's own concerns.

Historically, it had facilitated regional organizations for social justice. Moreover, it had propagated a way of thinking. It imbued the Progressive movement in the South with a crusading and religious emphasis, a rationale for social amelioration based on the conviction that mankind could and should regulate the forces of nature and the conditions of society. Its leaders concluded that societal development should be regulated in the interest of individual worth. In this respect the Southern Sociological Congress was both a reflection of and a catalyst for liberal stirrings in the South.

See D. W. Grantham, *Journal of Southern History* (Feb., 1968); E. C. Chatfield, *Tennessee Historical Quarterly* (Dec., 1960; March, 1961); C. V. Woodward, *Origins of New South* (1951); G. B. Tindall, *Emergence of New South* (1967); and nearly annual volumes edited by J. E. McCulloch and published by the congress under various titles in Nashville (1912–15) and Washington (1918–19).

CHARLES CHATFIELD
Wittenberg University

SOUTHERN SPEECH COMMUNICATION ASSOCIATION

SOUTHERN SPEECH COMMUNICATION ASSOCIATION (P.O. Box 444, University of Richmond, Richmond, Va. 23173) publishes with the aid of a grant from the University of Florida in Gainesville the *Southern Speech Communication Journal* (Department of Speech Communications, Auburn University, Auburn, Ala. 36830), a quarterly founded in 1935 to provide a forum for articles on historical and scientific research in speech communication, drama, radio, and television in the South. It prints only scholarly articles, plus book reviews, news, and notes. The association also circulates to its 2,500 members a mimeographed presidential newsletter. The association maintains an archive in the University of Florida Library and sponsors an annual convention each spring.

SOUTHERN TENANT FARMERS' UNION

SOUTHERN TENANT FARMERS' UNION was founded near Tyronza, Ark., in the summer of 1934 by small businessmen H. L. Mitchell and Clay East. It became the most notable southern response to the role that Franklin D. Roosevelt's AGRICULTURAL ADJUSTMENT ADMINISTRATION crop-reduction scheme played in driving the grandchildren of the slaves—along with many whites—off the land. The STFU is thus significant as part of the worldwide history of URBANIZATION and the "freeing" of the peasant.

Although the biracial STFU's roots are to be found in black southern religious protest and white Populist rhetoric, its leaders were Socialists inspired by Norman Thomas to trade union activity until, in the STFU's most significant phase, they abandoned all but the trappings of unionism to function primarily as a pressure group. Financial support came largely through the New York-based National Sharecroppers' Fund and maverick philanthropist Gardner Jackson in Washington, D.C. Jackson, a liberal New Dealer until dismissed from the Department of Agriculture in the 1935 purge of SHARECROPPER sympathizers, secured contributions from such persons as muckraker Drew Pearson, poet Archibald MacLeish, and Justice LOUIS D. BRANDEIS. Angered by violence against STFU members, Jackson arranged the Cosmos Club dinner that gave birth to the La Follette committee investigating violations of workers' civil rights, the committee that was so instrumental in creating prounion sentiment in the late 1930s. The nation was also becoming "sharecropper-conscious," thanks to the STFU and novelist ERSKINE CALDWELL, long before John Steinbeck created the Joads; this welling sympathy, Jackson's continuing activity, and the establishment of an STFU-inspired Arkansas farm tenancy commission were important in the creation of the FARM SECURITY ADMINISTRATION.

Seeking legitimacy as "a real union," the STFU in 1937 joined the CIO's agricultural union, United Cannery, Agricultural Processing, and Allied Workers of America. Disaster followed because of the sharecroppers' inability to pay dues and the alleged high-handedness of UCAPAWA's Communist leadership. The STFU seceded from UCAPAWA in 1939 and dwindled away from what had once been some 35,000 members centered in Arkansas, Oklahoma, and the Missouri bootheel. Undergoing complete changes of name and locale during and after World War II, the union eventually disbanded in 1960.

See D. H. Grubbs, *Cry from Cotton* (1971); M. D. Naison, in S. Lynd (ed.), *American Labor Radicalism* (1973); STFU Papers, University of North Carolina Library and microfilm; USDA Papers, esp. Solicitor's File, Record Group 16, National Archives; AAA Papers, Record Group 145, National Archives; L. Cantor, *Prologue to Protest Movement* (1969); and Socialist Archives, Duke University Library.

DONALD H. GRUBBS
University of the Pacific

SOUTHWEST ORDINANCE (1790).

When the North Carolina cession of its claim to western lands was accepted by the U.S. government on April 2, 1790, the vast new area bounded by the Ohio River, the Mississippi River, and Spanish Florida was left without any government. As a result, on May 26 the U.S. Congress passed the Southwest Ordinance of 1790, which provided that for purposes of temporary government the territory should be treated as one district and that the inhabitants living therein should enjoy the privileges as set forth in the Northwest Ordinance of 1787. The ordinance further provided that the government of the new territory should be similar to that of the Northwest Territory except for a few conditions specified in the North Carolina Cession Act. A final provision specified that the office of superintendent of Indian affairs be united with that of governor.

See C. E. Carter (ed.), *Territorial Papers of U.S.* (1936), II, IV.

GORDON THOMAS CHAPPELL
Huntingdon College

SOUTHWEST RESEARCH CENTER AND MUSEUM FOR THE STUDY OF NEGRO LIFE AND CULTURE

(Bishop College, Box 566, Dallas, Tex. 75241), founded in 1975, is supported by the National Endowment for the Arts, the Texas commission on arts and humanities, and other grants and publishes book reviews, news, and notes in a quarterly newsletter. The center maintains an archive of material especially oriented to the southwestern Afro-American experience, including private papers as well as the papers of state government officials, works of art, Afro-Americana collection books, magazines, and microfilms. Its purpose is to promote scholarly activities and to develop collections and a bibliographic center all relative to Afro-American culture in the Southwest. One projected specialty is to be a collection of research materials on the black Baptist church.

SOUTHWEST REVIEW

(Southern Methodist University Press, Dallas, Tex. 75275), a quarterly with a circulation of 1,200, was founded in 1915 at the University of Texas as the *Texas Review*, was transferred to SMU in 1924, and was there entitled *Southwest Review*. It now publishes book reviews, historical essays, and both popular and scholarly material having no particular southern emphasis. It pays one-half cent per word, $5 per poem, and $10 per cover photograph. In alternate years it offers the McGinnis Award of $500 for the best fiction and nonfiction.

SOYBEAN

(*Glycine max*) probably originated in eastern Asia, where its only possible wild ancestor, *Glycine ussuriensis*, occurs in China and Korea. Soybean culture had begun in the United States by 1804, possibly earlier. Yields were low until plant breeders early in this century overcame problems associated with photoperiodism, pod shattering, lodging, and others. Eventually ten different groups of varieties were developed for narrow ranges of latitude. The first significant production as an oilseed crop began in the Piedmont region of the Carolinas and Virginia, and the first commercial processing of the domestic crop was done in Elizabeth City, N.C., in a cotton oil mill in 1915. Elsewhere in the South the soybean plant was grown primarily for hay.

Because of the increased demand during and after World War II for vegetable oils and high-protein livestock feeds, soybean plantings for beans increased rapidly. Cultivation spread steadily southward through the fertile floodplain of the lower Mississippi River alluvial valley. Between 1949 and 1969, tenfold increases in soybean acreage were not uncommon in the counties and parishes between southeastern Missouri and northwestern Louisiana. By 1975 a majority of these counties and parishes devoted 60 percent or more of their total harvested cropland to soybeans. In southeastern Missouri the proportion was more than 70 percent. Other southern areas with increasing, but less intensive, soybean culture are parts of the inner Atlantic coastal plain, the Piedmont, the Alabama-Mississippi black belt, and the Texas high plains.

See C. V. Piper and W. J. Morse, *Soybean* (1923); H. W. Johnson and R. L. Bernard, in *Advances in Agronomy* (1962); J. L. Cartter and E. E. Hartwig, in *Advances in Agronomy* (1962); and USDA, *Yearbook of Agriculture* (1948).

L. ARNOLD SINIARD
Memphis State University

SOYBEAN CULTIVATION IN THE SOUTH,
1930–1970
(thousands of acres harvested)

	1930	1940	1950	1960	1970
Ala.	8	11	68	133	609
Ark.	9	63	581	2,409	4,313
Del.	15	25	67	189	162
Fla.			7	30	184
Ga.	10	13	28	75	528
Ky.	9	31	126	199	558
La.	8	2	23	216	1,688
Md.	5	19	71	225	213
Miss.	12	39	358	916	2,336
Mo.	138	109	1,209	2,344	3,150
N.C.	128	190	297	545	876
S.C.	9	11	67	499	997
Tenn.	20	19	182	394	1,229
Tex.		3		75	158
Va.	17	49	152	320	339
W.Va.	2	1	1		

SPANISH-AMERICAN WAR (April–August, 1898).

On April 11, 1898, the United States declared war upon Spain. President William McKinley's decision to ask Congress for a declaration of war was shaped by the long-standing American assumption that the United States had vital interests in Latin America, especially in the Caribbean. The American decision to act upon this assumption when it did was influenced by current cultural assumptions, the imperialist behavior of other great powers, the crisis mentality of the 1890s, and the belief that the American economy had reached a stage where it required more expansion overseas. Less abstract matters complicated the situation: the destruction of American property in Cuba, the disruption of Cuban-American trade, the problems associated with filibustering launched from Florida, the presence of a rebuilt American navy, and humanitarian concerns about war victims.

The war lasted only a short time, but it allowed the United States to take or control Cuba, Puerto Rico, Guam, and the Philippines. A principal defense for these acquisitions was the "white man's burden." Using equally racist assumptions, opponents countered that nonwhites could never be assimilated into the American democracy. Southerners in Congress seized the opportunity to applaud the nation for finally accepting the cornerstone of the color caste system of the South.

In its wake, the war contained other indications that SECTIONALISM was fading. Northern and southern boys alike flocked to the call to arms. The response of the latter reflected the martial spirit of the South and the eagerness of southerners to demonstrate their loyalty, emotions that were echoed in numerous southern newspapers. President McKinley astutely selected JOSEPH WHEELER, Confederate army general and congressman from Alabama, to lead troops in Cuba. Wheeler's march into Cuba accorded with the spirit of the OSTEND MANIFESTO and with those New South boosters who perceived Cuba as a pearl for the commercial empire of the American South.

Most of the American troops embarked for Cuba from Tampa, the largest training center and embarkation point for American forces in the war. Although this assignment severely taxed the limited physical facilities of Tampa, it was an appropriate selection. Tampa, Ibor City, and Key West were principal centers of Cuban refugee settlement and thus of anti-Spanish sentiment and activity in the United States. The Cubans came to Florida to escape Spanish repression and to work as cigar makers. Many were members of the Cuban Revolutionary party and gave from their small wages to support filibusters against Spanish forces in Cuba. There were more than 60 affiliates of the Cuban junta in Tampa, Ibor City, and Key West. On at least one occasion (in 1891) José Martí—until his death in 1895 the leader of the Cuban independence movement—visited Tampa, where he gave a series of speeches to raise money for Cuban independence.

American troops also embarked for the war from New Orleans and Mobile, and Chickamauga served as a troop concentration center. When troop concentrations or troop trains passing through the South included blacks, southern white enthusiasm for the war wavered between fears of masses of armed blacks and calming self-assurances that black armed forces testified to black loyalty.

Such attacks of nerves, however, hardly shook the confidence born of the Spanish-American War. National unity, for whites only, was served by the war. America postured as it took its place among the powers, and blacks (and browns) were in their place at home and abroad. The effect was that of a Victorian set piece with all the appearances of permanence.

See J. C. Appel, *Hispanic-American Historical Review* (Feb., 1956); P. Buck, *Road to Reunion, 1865–1900* (1959); F. Freidel, *Splendid Little War* (1958); W. B. Fowler, *American Diplomatic History Since 1890* (1975); and W. Millis, *Martial Spirit* (1931).

TOM E. TERRILL
University of South Carolina

SPANISH INFLUENCE. Because 11.2 million people (5 percent) in the United States are of Spanish origin, it is essential to eliminate the "black legend" of Spanish incompetence and cruelty in its colonial domination of Florida, Alabama, Mississippi, Louisiana, Tennessee, and Missouri. Writers from Amos Stoddard, who accepted transfer of Spanish Louisiana to the U.S. in 1803–1804, to Theodore Roosevelt have maligned the role of Spain. The present LAND SURVEY SYSTEM and riparian rights in the Spanish borderlands date from Spanish days, as do many of the laws regarding property rights (including those of women) and civil rights (of slaves). In 1769–1770 Alexander O'Reilly instituted Spanish laws based on the Recopilación and Siete Partidas of Spain for Louisiana. The cabildo of New Orleans and Natchez and *ayuntamientos* of St. Augustine and Pensacola were efforts to provide for local self-government. Town meetings throughout the South enabled settlers to suggest laws and adaptations to local needs regarding pollution, livestock, road and levee repairs, and defense. Through the use of Scottish traders, Spain maintained the friendship and support of the southern Indians and developed a system of trade that replaced the mission used in the Southwest.

Spain's interest in the southern portions of the U.S. continued from 1512 to 1821, and its colonial dominion exceeded that of either England or France. Martin de Argüelles, a white child born in St. Augustine in 1566, antedates Virginia Dare as the first of the race born in what is today the United States. Spain's alliance with France during the American Revolution favored the cause of U.S. independence, but after that war Spain checked expansion by frontiersmen through an elaborate system of Indian alliances, frontier forts, and local militia.

With a modified form of free trade for Louisiana, Spain was able to diversify the production to include fishing, livestock, agriculture, and local industries such as cordage, distilleries, and shipbuilding. Trade with the Caribbean flourished.

The cotton gin, introduced in Natchez during 1795, with support for the inventor (John Barcley), began the lucrative cotton industry in Mississippi. Spain modified its traditional religious exclusivism in the Gulf area by allowing Protestants and Jews the right to private worship without requiring anyone to tithe to support the Catholic church. Irish priests in Florida introduced public schools, but in Louisiana the attempt to replace French with Spanish in all legal and educational matters was unsuccessful. Spanish words and phrases do exist in the CAJUN dialect.

See C. M. Fernández-Shaw, *Presencia española* (1972), most comprehensive; C. Gibson, *Spanish Tradition* (1968); H. E. Bolton, *Spanish Borderlands* (1921), early classic, ignores much of Southeast; J. D. L. Holmes, *Guide to Spanish Louisiana* (1970), chronology 1762–1806 plus extensive bibliography, and *Honor and Fidelity* (1965), Spanish troops in Mississippi Valley and Gulf Coast to 1821; R. A. McLemore, *Mississippi* (1973), chap. on Spanish rule by J. D. L. Holmes; J. R. McGovern, *Colonial Pensacola* (1974), chaps. on Spanish rule by I. A. Leonard and J. D. L. Holmes; W. S. Coker *et al.*, *Latin American Research Review* (Summer, 1971), comprehensive, bibliography on Spanish areas of Miss., La., Ala., and Fla.; J. F. McDermott, *Spanish in Mississippi Valley* (1974); A. P. Whitaker, *Spanish-American Frontier* (1927) and *Mississippi Question* (1934); and I. J. Cox, *West Florida Controversy* (1918).

JACK D. L. HOLMES
University of Alabama, Birmingham

SPARKMAN, JOHN JACKSON (1899–), as a U.S. congressman (1937–1947) from a Tennessee Valley district in north Alabama, was a supporter of the NEW DEAL and an internationalist both before and after World War II. Elected to the U.S. Senate over conservative opposition in 1946, he was a leader of forces within the Democratic party in Alabama in efforts to restore loyalty to the national party after the DIXIECRAT victory in Alabama in the ELECTION OF 1948. In the ELECTION OF 1952, he was Adlai E. Stevenson's vice-presidential running mate. In domestic affairs in the post–World War II decades, Sparkman assumed leadership in legislation affecting the home-building industry, small businesses, and banking. Critics charged that his early economic liberalism was significantly moderated as the relative prosperity of the 1950s and 1960s dulled memories of the depression among his constituents. Nonetheless, Sparkman, like his colleague LISTER HILL, refused to base his political career upon appeals to the rising tide of racial sentiment in the postwar decades. In 1973 he became chairman of the Senate Committee on Foreign Relations, succeeding J. WILLIAM FULBRIGHT of Arkansas.

See H. R. Fowler, *Un-Solid South* (1968); and W. D. Barnard, *Dixiecrats and Democrats* (1974).

WILLIAM D. BARNARD
Alabama Commission on Higher Education

SPARTANBURG, S.C. (pop. 46,000), named for the prorevolutionary Spartan Regiment, was incorporated in 1831 and long remained a hamlet dependent on local trade. Nearby were a few small ironworks and pioneer cotton mills. Under Democratic control during Reconstruction, Spartanburg was the focus of violent KU KLUX KLAN activity halted only by federal intervention. Fast population growth (3,253 in 1880; 11,400 in 1900) accompanied the coming of several railroads and the development of several cotton mills. By 1909 ten mills were located near Spartanburg, lured there by abundant waterpower, railroads, and cheap labor. Cotton magnates exercised great influence on the city after the 1880s (Converse College was founded by a cotton manufacturer in 1888; Wofford College had been founded in 1854). During World War I the 27th Division was trained at Camp Wadsworth, and the 40,000 soldiers taxed the city's social, economic, and physical resources. In the twenties the boll weevil depressed the cotton economy; peach orchards were introduced, flourished, and thus continued the city's mixed agricultural and industrial prosperity. The army again stationed troops in the city during World War II (Camp Croft). After the war the growth of textiles lured foreigners to the city, making it cosmopolitan, while the introduction of other industries helped make much of Spartanburg's population prosperous.

See Works Projects Administration, *History of Spartanburg County* (1940); and files of Spartanburg *Journal* (1844–), *Carolina Spartan* (1849–93), and Spartanburg *Herald* (1872–), all on microfilm.

PHILIP N. RACINE
Wofford College

SPAULDING, CHARLES CLINTON (1874–1952), black business executive, was born in Columbus County, N.C. He was appointed general manager of a Durham INSURANCE company in 1900, and his administrative skills, dedication, and shrewd decisions were important factors in the company's rapid growth and success. Spaulding managed the home office, trained new agents, established and supervised agencies in several southern states, and built a tradition of paying claims promptly to gain public confidence. By 1907 the company had over 100,000 policyholders; in 1913 it qualified to become a legal reserve insurance company, and in 1919 the name was changed to the present one: the North Carolina Mutual Life Insurance Company. Throughout most of Spaulding's term as company president (1923–1952), it was the largest black-owned business. Spaulding was trustee of three black universities; president of the National Negro Business League, the National Negro Insurance Association, and the Mechanics and Farmers Bank; and treasurer of the National Negro Bankers Association.

See W. B. Weare, *Black Business* (1973), well researched; R. L. Adams, *Great Negroes* (3rd ed.; 1969); *Who's Who in Colored America* (1950); and E. A. Toppin, *Biographical History of Blacks* (1971).

DE WITT S. DYKES, JR.
Oakland University, Rochester, Mich.

SPEED, JAMES (1812–1887), was born in Jefferson County, Ky., near Louisville. He graduated from Bardstown's St. Joseph's College, studied law at Transylvania University, and in 1833 opened a law office in Louisville. His father and grandfather had long opposed slavery, and the younger Speed also became one of the state's most vocal emancipationists. He sat in the state legislature briefly (1847–1849?), but his antislavery views were not popular with the majority of the people. By 1860–1861, however, when he fought against secession, his prestige had become such that he was credited with being a major influence at Kentucky's convention in preventing the state from joining the southern Confederacy. At Abraham Lincoln's behest he served as mustering officer after Ft. Sumter for the state's first Union volunteers called into service. Speed then served in the Kentucky senate (1861–1863) and in 1864 was appointed by Lincoln to be U.S. attorney general. He remained in this cabinet post until July, 1866, when, in favor of Negro suffrage, he broke with President Andrew Johnson over the latter's Reconstruction policies. Siding in most things with the Radicals, he served as permanent chairman of the "loyalist" convention in Philadelphia in September, 1866, and was a delegate to the Republican National Convention of 1872 and of 1876. In the meantime he resumed his successful legal practice in Kentucky and taught law for several years at the University of Louisville.

See J. Speed, *James Speed* (1914); and *Official Records, Armies*, Ser. 2, Vol. VII.

SPINDLETOP. The spectacular Spindletop oil gusher near Beaumont, Tex., on January 10, 1901, brought a new era to the PETROLEUM industry and the Southwest. In 1892 Pattillo Higgins began exploration and promotional activity that led to the discovery. Anthony F. Lucas, a mining engineer and authority on salt domes, assumed direction of operations in 1899 and drilled through quicksand to bring in the geyser of oil. The discovery set off wild speculations in which fortunes were made and lost. Subsequent development produced oil in unprecedented quantities and restored competition to the industry. Four major companies—Humble, Texaco, Magnolia, and Gulf—had their beginnings in the Spindletop field. Spindletop was followed by the development of other salt-dome oil fields on the Gulf coast of Texas and Louisiana.

See J. A. Clark and M. T. Halbouty, *Spindletop* (1952); C. C. Rister, *Oil! Titan of Southwest* (1949); and B. House, *Southwestern Historical Quarterly* (July, 1946).

MARILYN M. SIBLEY
Houston Baptist University

SPORTS AND PHYSICAL EDUCATION.

Sports and recreational activities were part of the daily lives of people in the southern colonies. With no apology they enjoyed fishing, hunting, riding, horse racing, cockfighting, bowls, ninepins, fencing, fives, quoits, battledore, billiards, and dancing. These immigrants brought their English sporting tradition, which was a fortuitous antidote for their New England cousins, who severely restricted sports and play for religious and economic reasons. In the South, plantation owners and the upper class had the leisure time for sports. The lower classes favored wrestling, boxing, animal baiting, and cockfighting, and the slaves hunted, fished, danced, and attended fairs and horse races.

Southern citizens of the new nation continued their interest in these sports and others up to 1860. In some rural areas colorful ring tournaments exhibited the medieval skills of riding and spearing suspended rings with a lance. Bandy, or shinny, was played by college students in the southeastern states. Boat clubs were organized in coastal cities from Maryland to Texas after 1830, while steamboats raced on the Mississippi River. In the rough frontier areas of Missouri, Arkansas, and Texas, common sports were horse racing, gander pulling, cockfighting, footraces, horseshoe pitching, shooting matches, fist fighting, fishing, and hunting. As the Civil War approached, a growing militaristic spirit was reflected in target-shooting matches. Residents of New Orleans could choose bowling, billiards, pedestrian races, cricket, boxing, or *raquette*, an Indian game similar to lacrosse, played by blacks on Sunday. Slaves throughout the South trained cocks, raced for their owners on horses or in boats, and fought each other in the ring. A Virginia slave, Tom Molyneux, was the best boxer in this country and also fought in England.

Between 1865 and 1920 sports gradually became more democratic and widespread. Sports were allied with a continuing military spirit and benefited from the emerging INDUSTRIALIZATION and URBANIZATION. New sports such as baseball, football, golf, and tennis attracted enthusiasts and challenged religious objections in rural sections. Postwar depression was eased by the proliferation of baseball to almost every community, black and white, although several baseball clubs had existed in Maryland and New Orleans before 1860. Louisville and St. Louis were charter members of the National League in 1876. The Southern League and the Texas League began the Dixie Series in 1888. The New Orleans manager, Abner Powell, originated the rain check, ladies' day, and the Knothole Gang.

College students formed clubs for baseball, track, rowing, gymnastics, fencing, and football. Intercollegiate football competition began at Virginia, Trinity College (later Duke), North Carolina, Vanderbilt, and Missouri by 1890 and then moved rapidly southward to Georgia, Georgia Tech, Alabama, Tulane, Louisiana State, Mississippi, Texas A. & M., Arkansas, and Mississippi State. Seven institutions organized the Southern Intercollegiate Athletic Association in 1894. The first football game between two black colleges—Biddle and Livingston—occurred in 1892, and Howard, Tuskegee, and Atlanta University soon had teams. The Colored Intercollegiate Athletic Association started in 1912 with five members.

Golf and tennis were upper- and middle-class sports until the 1920s. The first courses appeared at Oakhurst, W.Va., in 1884 and at the English settlement of Middlesboro, Ky., in 1889. Tennis received an early start when the New Orleans Lawn Tennis Club was founded by English residents in 1876. However, many southerners viewed tennis and golf as rather effeminate and the affectations of wealthy northerners.

The physical inertia of women was partially overcome in the 1880s, when the national craze for bicycling invaded the South. A courageous pioneer in combating social opposition to women's sports was Clara Baer, who came to Newcomb College of Tulane University in 1891. She taught Swedish gymnastics, introduced basketball, and originated *basquette*, a milder form of basketball. Several of her rule changes for women's basketball were later adopted nationally.

Physical education in schools progressed when

Nashville established a required program in 1869. However, the main impetus came after 1885 from the Turner societies in Kansas City and St. Louis, where Carl Betz and George Wittich introduced German gymnastics. Louisiana in 1894 became the third state (after California and Ohio) to require physical education in its schools.

When Centre College upset Harvard in 1921, it catapulted southern football into national prominence. Between 1926 and 1940 six different southern teams played in the Rose Bowl. Further emphasis and profitable TOURISM resulted from new bowl games—Orange, Sugar, Cotton, and Sun—all beginning in the mid-1930s. New professional football teams in Dallas, Atlanta, and New Orleans in the 1960s lowered segregation barriers. J. F. Rooney found that on a per capita basis the five leading states for producing professional football players were Mississippi, Louisiana, Texas, Alabama, and Georgia. The game itself and its pageantry, such as the Kilgore Rangerettes, have become a way of demonstrating southern chauvinism and sentiments of individualism, religion, militarism, and state-oriented nationalism, regardless of the cost.

The early interest of the South in baseball has continued unabated. Southern states have been the training grounds for thousands of players. Major league expansion has brought new teams to Baltimore, Atlanta, Houston, and Kansas City.

The sensational feats of Atlanta's Robert Jones stimulated interest in golf, and the construction of numerous courses during the Great Depression with federal money provided opportunities for all classes to play. The renowned Masters tournament at Augusta began in 1934, and today nearly half the major professional golf tournaments are held on southern courses.

Although women at white colleges had restricted sports competition, women's track teams from Tuskegee Institute and Tennessee State garnered many national championships. In recent years all southern women have enjoyed increased competition, especially in basketball, volleyball, and tennis. Delta State University won the 1976 women's national basketball championship. Men's basketball is particularly strong in Kentucky and at the Atlantic Coast Conference colleges.

Two prominent twentieth-century leaders in physical education were Edwin Henderson, who worked in the black schools of Washington, D.C., for 50 years, and David Brace, who taught at the University of Texas for over 40 years. Since 1950 many physical education administrators have received their doctorates from George Peabody College.

In the mid-1970s the South has come close to parity with the rest of the country in variety and quality of sports. Professional teams in basketball, hockey, soccer, and tennis have spread into the rapidly growing southern cities. Who would have expected the incomparable Gordie Howe to play hockey for a team in Houston or Kyle Rote, Jr., the son of a Texas football hero, to become a professional soccer star? Houston's Astrodome was a landmark in covered stadium construction only to be followed by the Louisiana Superdome. Yet, even in today's technological age, the southerner still receives as much pleasure from hunting and fishing as did his colonial ancestors.

See D. A. Somers, *Rise of Sports in New Orleans, 1850–1900* (1972), excellent; J. Carson, *Colonial Virginians at Play* (1965), comprehensive; J. F. Rooney, *Geography of American Sport* (1974); E. B. Henderson, *Negro in Sports* (1949); F. Menke, *Encyclopedia of Sports* (1975); J. R. Betts, *America's Sporting Heritage* (1974); J. Durant and O. Bettmann, *Pictorial History of American Sports* (1952); D. B. Van Dalen and B. L. Bennett, *World History of Physical Education* (1971); R. W. Fink, *Research Quarterly* (May, 1952); J. A. Kennard, *Research Quarterly* (Oct., 1970); and James River Country Club golf museum.

BRUCE L. BENNETT
Ohio State University

SPOTSWOOD'S IRON FURNACES. Alexander Spotswood, popular governor of Virginia from 1710 to 1722, was greatly interested in developing new industries in the colony, especially the making of iron (IRON AND STEEL INDUSTRY). In 1714 he planted a colony of Germans at the junction of the Rapidan and Rappahannock, naming the settlement Germanna. There iron was mined, smelted, and cast into pigs the same year. Spotswood erected a second blast furnace at Massaponax, about five miles from Fredericksburg, and a third stone furnace at Fredericksville, about 30 miles southwest of Fredericksburg. In nearby forges artisans made iron tools, andirons, cooking pots, firebacks, and other utilitarian wares. Spotswood's keen interest in Virginia industries was the foundation stone of a great steel-producing nation.

See R. L. Morton, *Colonial Virginia* (1960), II; K. Bruce, *Virginia Iron Manufacture* (1930); and J. B. Pearse, *Concise History of Iron Manufacture of American Colonies* (1876).

J. PAUL HUDSON
Colonial National Historical Park

SPOTSYLVANIA, BATTLE OF (May 9–19, 1864). After the battle of the WILDERNESS, U. S. Grant hoped to destroy R. E. Lee in open country south of the Wilderness, but the Confederates with remarkable speed threw up battleworks and entrenchments against which Grant was forced to hurl his troops. On May 10 the brief success of an attack by 12 Union regiments led by Emory Upton against the Mule Shoe, the northernmost salient of the Confederate fieldworks, caused Grant to decide to repeat Upton's maneuver with the full force of his army. In the early morning hours of May 12, W. S. Hancock's II Corps smashed headlong at the front of the Mule Shoe and quickly overran the Confederates. The VI Corps (H. G. Wright), V Corps (G. K. Warren), and IX Corps (A. E. Burnside) were to follow up with attacks on the immediate and far left and the right of Hancock. Hancock's unexpected ease in overcoming enemy resistance proved to be the Union army's undoing. The huge mass of troops could not move forward and spread out in the narrow confines of the Mule Shoe. JOHN B. GORDON's audacious counterattack threw Hancock back to the outer edge of the fortifications. Other Union troops, especially Wright's VI Corps, met fierce resistance but held on all along the edge of the Confederate trenches and breastworks. At the Bloody Angle, the western side of the salient, the fighting was the most horrible of the war. For 16 hours thousands of Union and Confederate soldiers grappled face to face in a tightly packed area, breaking off combat only after midnight. The exhausted armies rested on May 13, but for the next six days the armies fought in a great arc around Spotsylvania as Grant slowly moved his forces to the east of his enemy. Union losses around Spotsylvania totaled 17,000–18,000; Confederate casualties are estimated at 9,000–10,000.

See S. Foote, *Civil War: Red River to Appomattox* (1974), best recent account; V. J. Esposito (ed.), *West Point Atlas of American Wars* (1959), I; B. Catton, *Stillness at Appomattox* (1953); and *Official Records, Armies*, Ser. 1, Vol. XXXVI, Pts. 1, 2.

MARTIN LICHTERMAN
Union College, Schenectady, N.Y.

SPRINGS OF VIRGINIA lie on both sides of the present Virginia–West Virginia border. The heyday of these medicinal and thermal waters was in the 1830s and 1840s, when hotels and "rows" were frequented every summer by southerners fleeing malaria-ridden lowlands. With westerners and northerners they varied "taking the waters," dancing, hunting, and gaming at White Sulphur by visiting Sweet Chalybeate or the spas of the Blue, Sweet, Salt, and Red and Grey Sulphur. Their popularity resumed after the Civil War, dur

ing the Gay Nineties, and at present especially at the White and the Hot.

See P. Reniers, *Springs of Virginia* (1941); F. Ingalls, *Valley Road* (1949); J. R. Kidd, *West Virginia Historical Magazine Quarterly* (April, 1954); B. R. Kidd, *West Virginia Historical Magazine Quarterly* (July, Oct., 1960); and L. F. Brewster, *Summer Migration* (1947). Contemporary accounts are J. E. Caldwell, *A Tour* (1808, 1951); P. Prolix, *Letters Descriptive* (1837); M. Pencil, *White Sulphur Papers* (1839); W. Burke, *Mineral Springs* (1842); J. J. Moorman, *Virginia Springs* (1846); and L. R. Bishko, *Virginia Magazine of History and Biography* (April, 1972). Hotel registers and records are in West Virginia Collection, West Virginia University Library.

LUCRETIA RAMSEY BISHKO
Charlottesville, Va.

STAMP ACT CRISIS (1765–1766) arose when the Grenville ministry, seeking partial support for the army in America, induced Parliament to levy a tax, effective November 1, 1765, on colonial newspapers, legal documents, and other items. Suspicious of ministerial intentions, alarmed at the threat to provincial legislative assemblies, and fearful of the precedent, Americans resisted. A pamphlet by Daniel Dulany (DULANY FAMILY) of Maryland demolished the notion that virtual representation of the colonists in Parliament empowered it to tax them. Widely reprinted resolutions by the Virginia burgesses affirmed the exclusive right of "Taxation of the People by themselves." Although royal governors prevented delegates from Georgia, North Carolina, and Virginia from attending the Stamp Act Congress at New York in October, 1765, its resolves and petitions, like those of other colonial assemblies, embodied similar statements of principle. Except in Georgia and the Floridas, where a British military presence coincided with relatively weak popular institutions, pressure by the Sons of Liberty, organized to control the use of violence, enabled Americans to continue or resume newspaper publication, vessel clearances, and some court sessions without stamps. Nonimportation movements from Virginia northward also reduced the sale of British goods.

British merchants therefore cooperated with the Rockingham ministry to obtain repeal of the tax in March, 1766. Only a relatively few rejoicing Americans like CHRISTOPHER GADSDEN of South Carolina recognized that the accompanying Declaratory Act (which affirmed the power of Parliament to legislate for the colonies "in all cases whatsoever") was more than a face-saving gesture. But the Stamp Act had produced statements of constitutional principle from which neither side subsequently receded, heightened colonial sus picions of a ministerial conspiracy against liberty, and brought increasingly unified Americans to the brink of rebellion.

See P. Maier, *From Resistance to Revolution* (1972); E. S. and H. M. Morgan, *Stamp Act Crisis* (1962), standard; and J. Shy, *American Revolution* (1973), bibliography.

ROBERT M. WEIR
University of South Carolina

STATES' RIGHTS. The doctrine of states' rights holds that within the federal system of government the states retain certain rights and powers that cannot be taken from them. Historically, the doctrine emerged from the particularism of the colonial experience. Belief in the special virtue of state government was reinforced by the colonies' difficulties with England. After independence, the principle of states' rights underlay the sharp limitations placed upon the powers of Congress under the ARTICLES OF CONFEDERATION.

Although the federal Constitution substantially increased the powers of the national government, it left unclear what the balance between state and national jurisdictions should be, as well as who should mediate between them. The constitutional basis of later states' rights arguments lay in the Twelfth Amendment, which stipulates that "the powers not delegated to the United States by the Constitution, nor prohibited by it to the States, are reserved to the States respectively, or to the people."

In its more extreme forms, the principle of states' rights, building upon notions of state sovereignty and the compact theory of government, has pointed toward NULLIFICATION and SECESSION. In 1798 Thomas Jefferson's Kentucky Resolution argued that the states could collectively declare a federal law unconstitutional and void within their borders (VIRGINIA AND KENTUCKY RESOLUTIONS). In 1832 South Carolina, acting upon the theories of JOHN C. CALHOUN, formally nullified the federal tariff, an act that found little support among other states and drew a vigorous response from President Andrew Jackson. In 1860–1861 the doctrine of states' rights was carried to its fullest extension in the southern states' acts of secession. The military victory of the North signaled the end of these extreme versions of the states' rights argument.

In its milder and more common form, states' rights has meant a policy of strict construction of the Constitution; that is, the argument that the federal government possesses limited and specifically delegated powers. At various times a wide variety of sectional, economic, racial, and other political interests have invoked this Jeffersonian vision of federal limitations. Over time, however, through interpretation of the commerce and other "elastic" clauses of the Constitution by federal courts and via actions of the legislative and executive branches, the powers of the federal government have been expanded and the operational definition of states' rights has been considerably reduced. Still, the principle that the states retain certain distinct powers remains politically and constitutionally alive within the American federal system.

See A. T. Mason, *States Rights Debate* (1972); C. G. Sellers, *States Rights Tradition* (1972), focus on nullification; R. A. Wooster, *Conventions* (1962), studies southern secession conventions; D. Elazan, *Federalism* (1972), as viewed from states; and W. Anderson, *Nation and States* (1955), classic.

JOHN HOWE
University of Minnesota

STAUNTON, VA. (pop. 24,505), is a small industrial city situated approximately 35 miles northwest of Charlottesville. Settled in 1738 as Mill's Place, it was renamed Staunton in 1761. It developed primarily as a trading center and as the seat of Virginia's colonial government in the west. Although it is famous as WOODROW WILSON's birthplace and as the first city to adopt the CITY-MANAGER form of local government, its contemporary importance is as a manufacturer of textiles and furniture and as a shipping center for area quarries, dairy farmers, and wheat and apple growers.

See files of Staunton *Leader* (1904–), *Valley Virginian* (1871–90), and *Spectator* (1869–93), all on microfilm.

STAY LAWS provided for a moratorium or extension of time for paying a debt. During the American Revolution many farmers went into debt to buy new land or equipment, and the postwar depression of the 1780s left them overextended. Taxes and private debts became ruinous for large and small farmers alike; foreclosures were common; and violence occasionally erupted, as in the case of Shays's Rebellion. State legislatures with strong debtor representation—like those in the Carolinas and Georgia—passed stay laws, but creditors mobilized against such agrarian "radicalism," and they eventually won. Presumably most of those who opposed debtor relief lined up with the Federalists in the fight to ratify the new Constitution, which prohibited state legislation "impairing the Obligation of Contracts." After the PANIC OF 1819, the legislatures of Kentucky and

Tennessee enacted stay laws and other forms of debtor relief, but their state courts ruled them unconstitutional.

See M. Jensen, *New Nation* (1950); M. L. Starkey, *Little Rebellion* (1955); F. McDonald, *We the People* (1958); J. T. Main, *Antifederalists* (1961); and W. J. Hamilton, *Missouri Historical Review* (Oct., 1927).

DONALD HOLLEY
University of Arkansas, Monticello

STEEL. See IRON AND STEEL INDUSTRY

STEPHENS, ALEXANDER HAMILTON (1812–1883), lived in the plantation section of east-central Georgia. Shortly after graduating from the University of Georgia in 1832, he became active in the States' Rights party of Georgia. When that party moved into the larger Whig party in 1840, Stephens moved with it and was elected to Congress (1843–1859). As a good Whig he opposed territorial expansion in the 1840s but simultaneously asserted that the South and slavery must have equal rights in the territories. When the Whig president Zachary Taylor supported slavery restriction, Stephens left the party, supported the COMPROMISE OF 1850, and helped create the Constitutional Union party in Georgia. In the 1850s he often acted with the Democrats. Although he never became a Democratic partisan, he remained a partisan of the South. He guided the KANSAS-NEBRASKA ACT through the House and supported the LECOMPTON CONSTITUTION. Even though he doubted that Kansas would become a slave state, he believed that the South needed and deserved Kansas.

In the crisis of 1860 Stephens opposed SECESSION. He acted as a private citizen because he had resigned from Congress in 1859 for reasons still unexplained. Adopting a strict legalism, he insisted that the South wait for the Republicans to commit an illegal act. Even though he fought secession, he helped found the Confederate States of America and accepted its vice-presidency (1861–1865). Because of his narrow legalism and STATES' RIGHTS fanaticism, his role was negative and obstructionist. His political contribution after 1865 did not match his earlier record. Although he became an elder statesman of Georgia politics and served as congressman (1873–1882) and as governor (1882–1883), he had no real impact. He embalmed his principles for posterity in *A Constitutional View of the Late War Between the States*.

See R. Von Abele, *Alexander Stephens* (1946), best, a psychological essay rather than full biography; A. Stephens, *Constitutional View* (2 vols.; 1868–70); M. L.

Avary (ed.), *Recollections of Stephens* (1910), both previous works partly autobiographical; J. Z. Rabun, *American Historical Review* (Jan., 1953); and Stephens Papers, Library of Congress and Manhattanville College, both on microfilm.

WILLIAM J. COOPER, JR.
Louisiana State University

STEPHENSON, WENDELL HOLMES (1899–1970), noted historian and editor, was born in Cartersburg, Ind. After attending Earlham College briefly, he entered Indiana University, earning his bachelor's degree in 1923 and his master's in 1924, whereupon he joined the history faculty of the University of Kentucky. In 1927 he accepted an appointment as associate professor at Louisiana State University while still pursuing a doctorate under ULRICH B. PHILLIPS at the University of Michigan. He received his degree in 1928, and two years later his dissertation was published as *The Political Career of General James H. Lane*. He was the author of four additional books: *Alexander Porter* (1934); *Isaac Franklin* (1938); *The South Lives in History* (his Fleming lectures, 1955); and *Southern History in the Making* (1964), his most acclaimed. A charter member and president (1944) of the SOUTHERN HISTORICAL ASSOCIATION, he was instrumental in establishing the *Journal of Southern History*, which he edited with exacting standards of scholarship and style from its first issue (1935) until 1941. Subsequently at Tulane he edited the *Mississippi Valley Historical Review* (1946–1953) and began coeditorship of the collaborative, multivolumed *A History of the South*. He spent his last years teaching at the University of Oregon.

See T. D. Clark, *Journal of Southern History* (Aug., 1970).

THOMAS A. BELSER, JR.
Auburn University

STEVENSON, ANDREW (1785–1857), was born in Culpeper County, Va. His successful legal practice and ardent support of Jeffersonian principles led to his election to the Virginia house of delegates (1809–1816, 1819–1821), where he also served as Speaker (1812–1816). In 1821 Stevenson was elected to the U.S. House of Representatives and was later chosen Speaker (1827–1834). He vigorously supported Jacksonian policies, such as Indian removal and the bank war. He also condemned the NULLIFICATION movement in South Carolina. His reward was his nomination to be minister to Great Britain (1836–1841). His record—in such complex areas as the right of search at sea, the Maine boundary controversy, and the numerous difficulties stemming from the Canadian rebellions of 1837—was that of a diligent but inflexible worker. For the rest of his life he was a gentleman farmer and also served on the board of visitors and as rector (1856–1857) of the University of Virginia.

See F. F. Wayland, *Andrew Stevenson* (1949), best; Stevenson Papers, Library of Congress; J. Q. Adams, *Memoirs* (1875–77), VI–IX; C. H. Ambler, *Thomas Ritchie* (1913); H. B. Soulsby, *Right of Search* (1933); and B. Willson, *America's Ambassadors to England* (1929).

RICHARD S. CRAMER
San Jose State University

STILES, CHARLES WARDELL (1867–1941), was
born in Spring Valley, N.Y., and studied in Europe. In 1890 he received a Ph.D. degree from the University of Leipzig. After spending time at Robert Koch's laboratory in Berlin and at the Pasteur Institute, Stiles returned to America, where he became zoologist at the U.S. Department of Agriculture's Bureau of Animal Industry. In 1902 he became chief of the Division of Zoology of the U.S. Public Health Service. In that year he demonstrated that HOOKWORM disease was endemic among POOR WHITES in the South, and he declared that the ailment was responsible for the continuing economic depression in the area. He convinced officials of the Rockefeller Foundation to initiate an extensive campaign against hookworm disease, and in 1909 the Rockefeller Sanitary Commission was established, with Stiles as scientific secretary. The campaign emphasized rural sanitation and public HEALTH education, and it was largely successful. In addition to his major role in the campaign to eradicate hookworm disease, Stiles investigated the health problems of cotton mill workers and those of miners.

See Rockefeller Sanitary Commission, *Annual Reports* (1910–14); M. Boccaccio, *Journal of History of Medicine* (Jan., 1972); J. H. Cassedy, *Bulletin of History of Medicine* (March–April, 1971); and C. W. Stiles, *Journal of Parasitology* (Aug., 1939).

MARTIN KAUFMAN
Westfield State College

STITH, WILLIAM (1707–1755), of Charles City
County, Va., attended the College of William and Mary and Queen's College, Oxford (B.A., 1728). On his return to Williamsburg as an ordained clergyman in 1731, he was appointed master of the grammar school and chaplain of the House of Burgesses. He became rector of Henrico Parish in 1736 and president of William and Mary in 1752.

In his correspondence, three published sermons, and scholarly *History of the First Discovery and Settlement of Virginia* (1747), he evinced a highly educated, rational conception of British "liberties," which he transposed to fit the colony's historical development and political disputes. His vocal opposition to Robert Dinwiddie's "pistole fee" (his toast "Liberty and property and no pistole" became the motto of the controversy) cost him a seat on the governor's council and the position of commissary of Virginia's Anglican church. His death almost certainly deprived Virginia of a revolutionary leader.

See W. Stith, *Sermon* (1745–46), *Sinfulness* (1752), and *Nature and Extent* (1753); J. P. Greene, *Quest for Power* (1963); R. L. Morton, *Colonial Virginia* (1960); G. C. Smith, *Virginia Magazine of History and Biography* (July, 1940); T. W. Tate, in L. H. Leder (ed.), *Colonial Legacy* (1971); and T. Tsuruta, "Stith" (Ph.D. dissertation, University of Washington, 1957).

JOHN C. DANN
University of Michigan

STONEMAN'S RAID (March 20–April 23, 1865)
was ordered by U. S. Grant (January 31, 1865) for the purpose of aiding W. T. Sherman's CAROLINAS CAMPAIGN by interrupting communications between Columbia, S.C., and Charlotte, N.C. By the time George Stoneman got under way (March 20) with 4,000 cavalrymen and a battery of artillery, W. T. Sherman had already taken Columbia and had reached Goldsboro, N.C. Therefore, Stoneman entered North Carolina from Jonesboro, Tenn.; following the Watauga and Yadkin valleys to Wilkesboro, N.C., he moved almost due north to raid the Virginia & Tennessee Railroad. He reached Wytheville, Va., where he destroyed a large depot of supplies while detachments burned the railway bridges along 90 miles of road. His approach within 50 miles of Lynchburg caused the evacuation of that city and produced much commotion. Stoneman then struck southeastward into North Carolina against the Danville-to-Charlotte railroad, which was the only line Robert E. Lee could use to effect a junction of forces with JOSEPH E. JOHNSTON. Stoneman headed toward Salisbury, rendering the railroad useless and sending out detachments on both flanks to destroy factories and warehouses. One detachment narrowly missed capturing Jefferson Davis and his cabinet at Greensboro.

On April 12 Stoneman took Salisbury after a brief skirmish against token resistance. His captures here included about 1,300 prisoners, and 14 guns and 10,000 small arms together with vast stores of supplies also fell into his hands. Reaching Hendersonville on April 23, he learned of Johnston's impending surrender, and his expedition came to an end. Had the raid begun earlier, it might have served usefully to protect Sherman's left flank, but the war was practically over before the raid accomplished anything. The only possible benefit from the operation was the closing of Lee's escape routes west and south from Lynchburg.

See J. D. Cox, *March to Sea* (1882), narrative by corps commander; W. T. Sherman, *Memoirs* (1875); and U. S. Grant, *Memoirs* (1886).

CHARLES A. POVLOVICH
California State University, Fullerton

STONE MOUNTAIN, 16 miles east of Atlanta, Ga., is one of the world's largest exposed masses of granite. The monadnock rises 850 feet above the surrounding plain and is seven miles in circumference. The Venable family owned and quarried the mountain until 1958, when they sold it for the purpose of developing a state park, which now comprises 3,200 acres. On Thanksgiving night, 1915, the KU KLUX KLAN was reactivated in a ceremony atop Stone Mountain. Until the site was sold, the Venables permitted the Klan to hold fiery meetings on their "sacred" mountain. In 1916 the UNITED DAUGHTERS OF THE CONFEDERACY commissioned Gutzon Borglum, later of Mount Rushmore fame, to design and carve a Confederate memorial on the mountain. He ultimately began the project in 1923 but was replaced in 1926 by Augustus Lukeman, who labored until funds were depleted in 1928. Under the direction of George Weiblen, the work was completed between 1964 and 1970. The carving (90 feet by 190 feet), which depicts Jefferson Davis, Robert E. Lee, and Stonewall Jackson, all on horseback, is a major southern tourist attraction.

See R. J. Casey and M. Borglum, *Give the Man Room* (1952).

SANFORD H. BEDERMAN
Georgia State University

STONES RIVER, BATTLE OF (December 31, 1862–January 3, 1863), is also called the battle of Murfreesboro. Late in December W. S. Rosecrans marched from Nashville to attack BRAXTON BRAGG, who had concentrated his troops at Murfreesboro, Tenn. On the morning of December 31, the Union army was aligned with Alexander M. McCook on the right, GEORGE H. THOMAS in the center, and THOMAS L. CRITTENDEN on the left. WILLIAM J. HARDEE was on the left of the Confederate line,

LEONIDAS POLK was in the center, and JOHN C. BRECKINRIDGE was on the right. Stones River flowed between Polk and Breckinridge. Rosecrans and Bragg each attacked the other's right wing. The Confederates drove the federal line back to a position where McCook and Thomas were at a right angle with Crittenden. Breckinridge was called across the river to support Hardee. Although vigorously assailed, this Union line held for the remainder of the day. January 1 was quiet except for Confederate cavalry action. On the second, Bragg ordered Breckinridge to recross the river and take the high ground on the Confederate right. Realizing its importance, Rosecrans had moved Crittenden to occupy this position. Late on the second Breckinridge assaulted the federals, but was driven back to his original position of December 31. Both armies held their positions on January 3, and that night Bragg withdrew. Rosecrans did not pursue. Stones River was a tactical victory for Bragg, but he was unable to deliver a killing blow.

See S. Horn, *Army of Tennessee* (1941); T. Connelly, *Autumn of Glory* (1971); and A. Jones, *Confederate Strategy* (1961).

J. H. DEBERRY
Memphis State University

STONO SLAVE CONSPIRACY occurred in 1739 near Charleston, S.C. The insurrection was the most violent in this predominantly black colony's history. Despite rumors of slave unrest and planned revolts, the timing of the outbreak was a surprise, catching white planters at weekend church services. It began at St. Paul's Parish near the Stono River, within 20 miles of Charleston, and its suppression cost the lives of some 20 whites and a larger number of slaves. The insurrection appeared to be timed to the outbreak of war between England and Spain, with St. Augustine, Fla., the ultimate objective of the runaways.

See P. Wood, *Black Majority* (1974), definitive, excellent bibliography; and *South Carolina Commons House Journals*.

ALBERT ABBOTT
Fairfield University

STORYVILLE, the celebrated red-light district of New Orleans, was created in 1897 to limit rather than to glamorize prostitution. Such permissive districts were often established by reformers in the late nineteenth century to try to halt the spread of the urban tenderloin. Much to the dismay of Alderman Sidney Story, author of the New Orleans ordinance, the area took on a life of its own as well as his name. It became the center of the developing JAZZ (MUSIC) and site of some of the most lavish of American brothels, all "in the worst possible taste." The district had its own unofficial mayor, a city hall, and a blue book available for twenty-five cents, which immodestly described the women and the houses in great detail. Story-ville was heir to the city's own tempestuous sex-ual traditions, which dated back to the quadroon balls of the early nineteenth century, and its de-velopment paralleled the Crescent City's own prosperity as a business and convention center. During the First World War, federal officials feared that sailors docking in New Orleans would be-come corrupted, and Mayor Martin Behrman, bowing to considerable federal pressure, closed the district in 1917.

See A. Rose, *Storyville* (1974); A. Rose and E. Souchon, *New Orleans Jazz* (1967), best illustrated history; and S. Longstreet, *Sportin' House* (1965), popular, interpretive, illustrated history. The *Blue Book* has been reprinted privately, but is still scarce.

RICHARD H. COLLIN
University of New Orleans

STRAUDER V. WEST VIRGINIA (100 U.S. 303 [1880]). Strauder, a black man indicted for mur-der, claimed denial of his civil rights under a West Virginia law confining jury service to white male citizens. The U.S. Supreme Court affirmed the purpose of the Fourteenth Amendment as federal protection "to a race recently emancipated" in the enjoyment of all civil rights, including equal pro-tection of the laws. Strauder's trial before a jury "from which the State had expressly excluded every member of his race, because of color alone," however well qualified otherwise, denied him "equal legal protection." This landmark case in-validated express statutory exclusion. *Carter* v. *Texas* (1899), citing the *Strauder* decision, held unconstitutional any racial exclusion by a state, whether through legislative, judicial, executive, or administrative action. *Virginia* v. *Rives* (1880) initiated a contrasting but complementary propo-sition, confirmed by later decisions. The defen-dant has no constitutional right to representation of his race on his jury, only purposeful exclusion being invalid. However, *Norris* v. *Alabama* (1935) held that evidence of long-continued exclusion of blacks, although they composed a substantial part of the county's population and some were quali-fied, established prima facie proof of deliberate exclusion. *Hernandez* v. *Texas* (1954) extended this rule to persons of Mexican extraction.

The *Strauder* and *Rives* cases, therefore, were germinal decisions for the constitutional principle succinctly stated in *Cassell* v. *Texas* (1950): "An accused person is entitled to . . . a jury in the se-lection of which there has been neither inclusion nor exclusion because of race."

See *American Jurisprudence* (1969); *U.S. ex rel. Goldsby* v. *Harpole*, 263 F.2d 71 (1959); *Shepard's U.S. Citations; Shepard's Southern Reporter Citations; Index to Legal Periodicals;* R. Bardolph (ed.), *Civil Rights Record* (1970); R. J. Harris, *Quest for Equality* (1960); and R. L. Stone, *Texas Law Review* (Jan., 1951).

KEMP P. YARBOROUGH
Texas Woman's University

STRIBLING, THOMAS SIGISMUND (1881–1965), with less talent as a writer than some con-temporaries of the southern renaissance, made a significant contribution to the development of the realistic novel about the South. He was among the first to identify certain materials with which any truthful portrayal of southern life must begin. In these materials he recognized the importance for fiction of the middle class and poor whites of the Upper and hill-country South—particularly in the region around Clifton, Tenn., where he was born, and Florence, Ala., where he was partly educated. From 1922 to 1934 Stribling wrote seven novels about life in southern towns and rural areas, which have been thought to be too sociological and too heavily indebted to Sinclair Lewis. The tragic quality of life in the small-town South—with all of its bitterness, suspicion, superstition, and narrow-mindedness—is satirically revealed and often car-icatured in *Birthright* (1922), *Teeftallow* (1926), *Bright Metal* (1928), and *Backwater* (1930). Strib-ling's major work is the trilogy *The Forge* (1931), *The Store* (1932), and *Unfinished Cathedral* (1934), which chronicles the fortunes of the Vaiden fami-ly from shortly before the Civil War to the depres-sion. Full of action and sustained suspense, these novels never lack invention. The characters are not always convincing, though perhaps Miltiades Vaiden and his black half-sister Gracie come most alive. *The Store* is the best of the trilogy and one of the better novels about the period following Reconstruction.

See C. H. Holman, *Roots of Southern Writing* (1972); and W. Eckley, *T. S. Stribling* (1975).

CLAUD B. GREEN
Clemson University

STRIP MINING. Much of the earliest COAL MIN-ING would now be called strip mining. Settlers, noting an outcrop of coal, removed the overburden by hand or with draft animals. Both the amount of coal and damage to the landscape produced by such methods were limited. Strip mining did not become of more than local significance in the United States until the introduction about 1880 of power equipment. The limited capacity and maneuverability of the early power equipment made its use profitable only where land was relatively flat and where coal lay near the surface. In the South, those conditions existed only in Missouri and, to a lesser degree, in western Kentucky. Missouri produced over half a million tons of strip coal as early as 1915 and was by far the largest producer in the South until World War II. The development of a major strip-mining industry in the South can be dated from the outbreak of World War II. Demand for coal was great, and prices were high. Equally important, equipment available was now sufficiently powerful and reliable to make stripping profitable in the mountainous southern Appalachian coalfields. The increase in production was spectacular. In 1940 the South produced 3.7 million tons of strip coal; in 1945 it produced 27.7 million tons. By the close of the war the strip-mining industry was firmly established in the South and, with minor fluctuations, continued to grow. In 1970 the South produced over 118 million tons of surface-mined coal (strip and auger), over 40 percent of the U.S. total. Kentucky and West Virginia accounted for approximately 75 percent of southern production.

See R. F. Munn, *Strip Mining* (1973); and R. H. Sherwood, *Mining Congress Journal* (Nov., 1945).

ROBERT F. MUNN
West Virginia University

STUART, ALEXANDER HUGH HOLMES (1807–1891), represented Virginia's urban and industrial interests as a Whig and Conservative party leader. Born in Staunton, he attended Staunton Academy and the College of William and Mary and graduated from the University of Virginia. A lawyer, Stuart served in the Virginia legislature and U.S. House of Representatives (1841–1843) before becoming secretary of the interior in the FILLMORE ADMINISTRATION (1851–1853). An opponent of secession in the Virginia senate (1857–1861) and an unenthusiastic Confederate, Stuart worked for rapid restoration after the war. After serving as Conservative party leader in the Virginia legislature (1874–1877), he remained active in public life until his death.

See A. F. Robertson, *A. H. H. Stuart* (1925); J. P. Maddes, Jr., *Virginia Conservatives, 1867–1879* (1970); A. C. Cole,

Whig Party in South (1914); and A. H. H. Stuart Papers, University of Virginia Library.

JOHANNA NICOL SHIELDS
University of Alabama, Huntsville

STUART, ARCHIBALD (1757–1832), was a lifelong resident of the Shenandoah Valley and father of ALEXANDER H. H. STUART. As a student at the College of William and Mary, he helped found the Phi Beta Kappa society. He fought under his father, Major Alexander Stuart, against the British at GUILFORD COURTHOUSE (1781). In the Virginia house of delegates (1783–1787), Stuart struggled for religious liberty, legal and judicial reform, and liberalization of the state constitution. He voted to ratify the federal Constitution in 1788. During the 1790s, Stuart helped his friends James Madison and Thomas Jefferson organize the Republican party; and as a state senator (1797–1800) he supported the Virginia Resolutions of 1799 (VIRGINIA AND KENTUCKY RESOLUTIONS). He was a judge of the general court of Virginia (1800–1831) and a presidential elector (1800–1828) for Jefferson, Madison, James Monroe, William Crawford, and John Quincy Adams. Stuart feared unrestricted popular rule.

See A. F. Robertson, *A. H. H. Stuart* (1925), portrait; L. G. Tyler, *William and Mary Quarterly* (April, 1896); *William and Mary Quarterly* (Oct., 1925), papers; R. Beeman, *Old Dominion* (1972); J. R. Pole, *Journal of Southern History* (Feb., 1958); J. Boyd (ed.), *Jefferson Papers* (1950–71); and W. T. Hutchinson and W. M. Rachel, *Madison Papers* (1962–77).

EDWARD K. SPANN
Indiana State University

STUART, JAMES EWELL BROWN (1833–1864), commanded the cavalry division of ROBERT E. LEE's Confederate Army of Northern Virginia during the Civil War. He was born in Patrick County, Va. Jeb Stuart graduated from the U.S. Military Academy in 1854, thirteenth in a class of 46. His early service was mainly with the 1st Cavalry Regiment at Fts. Leavenworth and Riley, Kan. In Kansas he took part in several Indian campaigns, assisted in overcoming the disorder of the BLEEDING KANSAS episode, married Flora Cooke, daughter of Colonel Philip St. George Cooke, and patented a cavalry saber attachment. In October, 1859, Stuart went to Washington to negotiate the sale of his invention to the War Department. Abolitionist John Brown, whom Stuart had encountered in Kansas, seized the arsenal at Harpers Ferry on October 16 (HARPERS FERRY RAID). Stuart assisted Colonel Robert E. Lee in recapturing the arsenal and in taking Brown prisoner.

When Virginia seceded in April, 1861, Stuart resigned his army commission and entered Confederate service as a lieutenant colonel. He established his reputation early in the war by riding completely around G. B. McClellan's Army of the Potomac during the PENINSULAR CAMPAIGN in June, 1862 (STUART'S RIDE). During that ride Stuart and his men captured supplies, disrupted Union communications, and collected important information about enemy troop movements and locations. The following month Stuart was promoted major general.

Stuart's intelligence, audacity, and imagination in conducting cavalry operations were clearly demonstrated in the battles of BULL RUN, ANTIETAM, and CHANCELLORSVILLE, but his reputation has been tarnished by the controversy over another "long ride" around the Army of the Potomac just before the battle of GETTYSBURG. His critics argue that Stuart's ride was an attempt to regain the glory he had lost when surprised by federal cavalry at BRANDY STATION on June 9, 1863. His supporters insist the ride was in keeping with Lee's permissive orders. Nevertheless, as Lee moved north in late June, Stuart was outmaneuvered and was forced into a circuitous ride around the Army of the Potomac. During the ride Stuart was unable to screen Lee's army from the federal cavalry, and, although Lee later commented that Stuart "never brought me a piece of false information," Stuart failed to deliver any information during the disastrous Gettysburg campaign. After Gettysburg, Stuart particularly distinguished himself during the long and arduous WILDERNESS CAMPAIGN of 1864.

In an attempt to counter a federal cavalry raid near Richmond, Stuart was wounded at YELLOW TAVERN on May 11, 1864. He died the next day and was buried in Hollywood Cemetery in Richmond. Jeb Stuart is considered by many to have been one of America's foremost cavalry experts.

See H. B. McClellan, *I Rode with Jeb Stuart* (1885, 1958), best, eyewitness account; *Official Records, Armies*, best primary source; D. S. Freeman, *Lee's Lieutenants* (1942–44); B. Davis, *Jeb Stuart* (1957); and J. W. Thomason, *Jeb Stuart* (1930).

JAMES C. SHEPARD
U.S. Army Military History Research Collection

STUART'S RIDE (June 12–15, 1862). After taking command of the Army of Northern Virginia ROBERT E. LEE needed information on the strength and disposition of the federal Army of the Potomac. JEB STUART was chosen for the task. Liberally interpreting Lee's orders for a reconnaissance

of the federal right wing, Stuart led 1,200 cavalry troopers into enemy territory on June 12, 1862. Within 24 hours he had the intelligence Lee wanted. Stuart could have turned back at this point, but he pressed forward to complete a circuit of G. B. McClellan's army. Despite heat, rugged terrain, and lack of rest, Stuart's cavalry moved so rapidly and unpredictably that the confused Union force was unable to stop them. Late on June 15, 1862, Stuart returned to Confederate territory with 165 prisoners, 260 captured horses and mules, and quantities of arms and equipment. The ride established Stuart's reputation. The military significance of the ride was borne out when the Army of Northern Virginia descended on McClellan's right wing and soundly defeated it at GAINES' MILL on June 27, 1862.

See W. R. Brooksher and D. K. Snider, *Civil War Times Illustrated* (April, 1973); B. Davis, *Jeb Stuart* (1957); H. B. McClellan, *I Rode with Jeb Stuart* (1958); D. S. Freeman, *Lee's Lieutenants* (1942–44); D. Knapp, Jr., *Confederate Horsemen* (1966); and J. E. Cooke, *Wearing of Gray* (1959).

WILLIAM R. BROOKSHER and
DAVID K. SNIDER
U.S. Air Force

STUDENT NONVIOLENT COORDINATING COMMITTEE (later Student National Coordinating Committee), a militant Negro rights organization, was formed in Raleigh, N.C., at a biracial meeting of several hundred student activists in April, 1960. Reflecting the views of Dr. MARTIN LUTHER KING, JR., SNCC's founding statement affirmed the ideal of nonviolence and pledged itself to interracial harmony. Within four years, however, it began openly to question the philosophy of biracialism and the tactic of nonviolence. Although not formally deleting the word *nonviolent* from its name until 1969, it had by 1966 repudiated the CIVIL RIGHTS MOVEMENT's traditional emphasis on interracial brotherhood. Thereafter, the all-Negro SNCC became a virtual synonym for black chauvinism and counterviolence.

Never a membership organization, SNCC employed full-time "field secretaries" to stimulate and coordinate local challenges to SEGREGATION in the South. It was controlled by an executive committee, which elected a chairman (Marion Barry, 1961–1963; John Lewis, 1963–1966; Stokely Carmichael, 1966; H. Rap Brown, 1967–1969). Meager financial support came from student contributors and wealthy donors. A monthly newspaper, the *Student Voice*, was briefly published at the headquarters in Atlanta.

SNCC's earliest efforts were direct-action campaigns to desegregate lunch counters and other segregated facilities in Upper South cities. Encouraged by the Justice Department, it turned after 1961 to voter registration, principally in Mississippi; in 1964 it served as the chief organizer of the Mississippi Summer Project, which brought several hundred northern students into Mississippi to run "freedom schools" and encourage voter registration. SNCC was also the guiding force behind the Mississippi Freedom Democratic party, which sought (and failed) not only to seat delegates at the Democratic National Convention in 1964 but also to unseat Mississippi's congressional delegation in 1965. Following the enactment of the CIVIL RIGHTS ACT OF 1965, SNCC formed the Lowndes County Freedom Organization in an unsuccessful effort to seize control of a black-majority county in Alabama. By this time extremists controlled the organization. When its chairman, H. Rap Brown, was convicted of armed robbery, SNCC collapsed.

See L. Holt, *Summer That Didn't End* (1964); A. J. Matusow, in B. J. Bernstein and A. J. Matusow (eds.), *Twentieth-Century America* (1972); C. Sellers, *River of No Return* (1973); P. Watters, *Encounter with Future* (1965); and P. Watters and R. Cleghorn, *Climbing Jacob's Ladder* (1967).

NEIL R. MCMILLEN
University of Southern Mississippi

STYRON, WILLIAM (1925–), is a native of Newport News, Va. World War II interrupted his education at Davidson College, and he served as a marine lieutenant in the South Pacific. When he returned, he completed his bachelor's degree at Duke (1947) and went to New York to work briefly as an associate editor for McGraw-Hill; he was fired when he was discovered blowing bubbles out the window. His first book, *Lie Down in Darkness* (1951), was generally accepted as the best first novel in a generation. Set in Port Warwick, which very much resembles Newport News, the novel chronicles the sundering of a middle-class family torn by two disparate southern traditions: religiosity and self-indulgence. Styron was recalled for service in the marines in 1951, and his short tour of duty provided the stimulus for *The Long March* (1956), a military allegory that risks comparison to *Billy Budd*. Styron's long-awaited third novel, *Set This House on Fire* (1960), plumbed the contemporary southerner's race guilt, but the narrative is rather flabby and too much of the setting and action is given over to an extraneous evocation of the life-style of rich Americans in innocent postwar Europe. Styron rebounded handsomely, however, with *The Confessions of Nat Turner* (1967). Working with a subject that had intrigued him for 20 years, Styron employed his considerable technical imagination to develop a manner totally appropriate to his matter. Constrained by the paucity of historical detail about Nat Turner (TURNER'S REBELLION), Styron daringly invoked the novelist's right to consider every imaginable cause leading into and every imaginable result leading from the few available facts. The result has been for most readers a rich, enlightening re-creation of the past. At the present time, Styron has as a goal the completion of a fiction growing out of his military experience, *The Way of the Warrior*, though he interrupted himself to write *Sophie's Choice* (1975), a novel dealing with a young writer who came to New York to work for a publisher and got fired for blowing bubbles out. . . .

See J. Baumbach, *Landscape of Nightmare* (1965); E. McNamara, *Western Humanities Review* (Summer, 1961); F. Hoffman, *Art of Southern Fiction* (1967); L. Rubin, *Hollins Critic* (Dec., 1967); and J. Bryer and M. Newman, *Confessions of Nat Turner: A Critical Handbook*, ed. M. Friedman and I. Malin (1970), best available bibliography.

LEWIS A. LAWSON
University of Maryland, College Park

SUBMARINES, CONFEDERATE, or "Davids," included both submersible and partially submersible torpedo gunboats. Although they were mechanically crude, the South viewed them as a new secret weapon with which to break the BLOCKADE of Charleston. One engine-driven David did succeed in damaging—with its spar torpedo—the formidable *New Ironsides* in 1863, but soon afterward, while on a trial run, the David itself became a casualty. The most famous Confederate submersible was *H. L. Hunley*, named after its designer. It was propelled manually by an eight-man crew. Six disastrous trial runs earned it the nickname "Peripatetic Coffin." It did succeed, however, on February 17, 1864, while partially surfaced, in sinking the federal corvette *Housatonic*. Although it was lost with all hands, *Hunley* became the first "submarine" to sink an enemy ship. Eight other Davids were found grounded at Charleston at war's end.

See M. F. Perry, *Infernal Machines* (1965); B. Berry, *Civil War History* (Sept., 1959); R. Walker, *South Atlantic Quarterly* (Oct., 1940); A. L. Kellar, *Virginia Magazine of History and Biography* (July, 1935); H. Von Kolnitz, *U.S. Naval Institute Proceedings* (Oct., 1937); D. W. Thompson, *U.S. Naval Institute Proceedings* (Jan., 1941); C. H. Blair, *U.S. Naval Institute Proceedings* (Oct., 1952); W. M. E. Beard, *U.S. Naval Institute Proceedings* (Sept.–

Oct., 1916); W. A. Alexander, *Southern Historical Society Papers* (1902) and *Munsey* (Aug., 1903); and W. Shugg, *Civil War Times Illustrated* (Feb., 1973), excellent.

NORMAN C. DELANEY
Del Mar College

SUBTREASURY PLAN of the FARMERS' ALLIANCE and the POPULIST PARTY was first proposed by Dr. C. W. MACUNE in 1889. It called for establishing a branch office of the U.S. Treasury Department in every county in the nation producing $500,000 or more of agricultural goods for market. Each branch office or "subtreasury" was to have a warehouse or grain elevator where farmers, for a small storage and handling charge, could store such nonperishable crops as corn, cotton, sugar, tobacco, and wheat. Farmers were to receive in receipt certificates of deposit, which could be converted into 12-month loans at 1 percent interest for an amount up to 80 percent of the market value of stored goods. The loans would be extended by the subtreasury and were to be paid out in federal notes backed by stored commodities.

Both the Alliance and the Populist party hoped that adoption of the subtreasury plan would provide relief for a number of concerns of farmers. The warehouses and grain elevators, constructed and operated by the government, would break the farmers' dependence upon the local monopolies of warehousemen and elevator operators. Low-cost storage facilities and the option of obtaining loans against stored goods would give the farmer some control over the timing of his sale of crops, prevent the sudden collapse of the market price at harvest time, and enable the grower to get the best possible price for his product. Moreover, the loans given by the subtreasury would simultaneously provide relief from the CROP LIEN SYSTEM and inflate the nation's currency by the circulation of the additional federal notes.

Although the subtreasury plan eventually was subordinated to the more popular issue of free and unlimited coinage of silver, various elements of the proposal lived long past the ELECTION OF 1896 and the demise of both the Alliance and the Populist party. The Warehouse Act of 1912, the Federal Farm Loan Act of 1916, the Agricultural Marketing Act of 1929, the Commodity Credit Act of 1933, and the Agricultural Adjustment Act of 1933 all either borrowed elements from the subtreasury plan or used somewhat different measures to relieve the very concerns that originally had led Macune to propose the plan.

See C. V. Woodward, *Origins of New South* (1951); J. C. Malin, *Mississippi Valley Historical Review* (1944–45);

L. Goodwyn, *Democratic Promise* (1976); and R. F. Durden, *Climax of Populism* (1966).

SUFFOLK, VA. (pop. 9,858), approximately 20 miles south of Norfolk, is commonly known as the "Peanut Capital of the World." Besides being an important shipping and processing center for area PEANUT growers, it produces lumber, fertilizers, and ginned cotton. The surrounding area was settled in the 1620s by a group of English Puritans. The Puritans were driven out of the colony in the 1640s, but the area developed the cultivation of tobacco. In 1742 the Virginia legislature established Suffolk as a tobacco inspection station. Although the town was burned in 1779 by the British, it quickly was rebuilt as a market town for area agriculture. It was occupied by federal troops on May 12, 1862, and held throughout the war by Union authorities despite being besieged by General JAMES LONGSTREET in 1863. After an unsuccessful move against New Bern, N.C., Longstreet attacked Suffolk (April 11–May 4, 1863) in the hope of relieving federal pressure against Richmond. Unable to dislodge the city's 25,000 Union defenders, Longstreet broke off the investment having inflicted 260 federal casualties while losing approximately 900 dead, wounded, or missing Confederates.

See *Burton's History of Suffolk* (1907); and files of Suffolk *News-Herald* (1873–), on microfilm.

SUGAR INDUSTRY. There are several hundred different kinds of sugar found in nature. However, sugarcane and sugar beets satisfy virtually all of man's personal and commercial needs at the present time. Although beet sugar comprises approximately 25 percent of the total of sugar refined in the United States, it is not an important southern crop.

Raw sugarcane production added approximately $730 million to the GNP in 1974. Of this total, $458,489,000 was earned from sugarcane grown in Florida, Louisiana, and Texas. In 1974, approximately 1,140,700 acres of sugarcane were harvested in these three southern states. Obviously, the cane sugar industry's economic impact is as important today as it has been in the past.

Sugar was introduced into Louisiana by the French around 1700. However, during the first 80 years of the eighteenth century its production was largely unsuccessful. The British also attempted to grow sugarcane in Florida, Georgia, and South Carolina in the eighteenth century with less success than the French. It waited on Étienne Boré, who is often referred to as the "savior of Louisiana," to prove that the sugarcane industry could become the basis of economic prosperity in Louisiana. Using methods carried from Santo Domingo by Josep Solís and improved upon by Antonio Méndez, Boré in 1795 proved that Louisiana cane sugar would granulate and could be marketed successfully. He then undertook a "propaganda" campaign to convince Louisiana planters to convert to cane sugar production. As was the case in the Caribbean islands, slave labor was used in cane production and resulted in the importation of large numbers of slaves during the early nineteenth century. After emancipation blacks dominated the cane sugar labor force well into the twentieth century. Attempts to introduce nonblack labor in the eighteenth century, especially Henry S. Sanford's experiment with Italian immigrants in the 1880s, were not successful. In the 1960s, as production expanded in Florida, most producers relied on laborers from the Caribbean islands. The average hourly wage paid in 1971 was $2.02, a significant increase from the 92¢ per hour paid in 1962.

Although sugarcane will grow in a variety of soils, the ideal soil is a mixture of sand, silt, clay, and some organic material. Hence, the rich bottomlands of southeastern Louisiana and the mucklands south of Lake Okeechobee in Florida are principal cane areas. Sugarcane needs well-drained soil, as the roots must have access to air. Eighty to 90 inches of rainfall are necessary during the growing season. Cane, which grows rapidly under ideal conditions, resembles a thick forest when fully developed. Cane in Louisiana and Florida is cut by harvesters, but the use of machines is restricted, since they can damage cane roots.

The cane sugar industry has benefited from federal tariff laws. In 1789 a revenue-raising tariff was imposed. The tariff, which produced approximately 20 percent of necessary federal incomes,

was a factor in the expansion of the industry. Except for the brief duty-free period between the McKinley tariff (1890) and the Wilson-Gorman tariff (1894), imported sugar has remained subject to a tariff. Currently the Jones-Costigan Sugar Act of 1934 provides the structure of our present sugar policy. This law was passed so that the United States could keep its domestic sugar industry strong. The act as amended in 1948 and 1971 has had the desired effect.

See J. C. Sitterson, *Sugar Country* (1953); D. G. Johnson, *Sugar Program* (1974); *Sugar Year Book*; R. A. Ballinger, *History of Sugar Marketing* (1971); *Crop Production Annual Summary*; and F. D. Gray, *Sugar and Tropical Products* (n.d.).

RICHARD J. AMUNDSON
Columbus College

SULTANA DISASTER (April 27, 1865). The passenger packet *Sultana* went into service February 4, 1863. Its 260-foot length, 42-foot beam, flat bottom, and 34-inch draft made it an ideal riverboat—one of the best ever constructed. Its coal-burning boilers, however, were as dangerous as bombs. One of many such vessels at the close of the war carrying emaciated Union soldiers recently released from CONFEDERATE PRISONS northward, the *Sultana* took on its human cargo at Vicksburg April 24, 1865. Military officers loaded 2,500 soldiers, passengers, and crewmen aboard a ship licensed to carry 376. At 2:00 A.M. on April 27, just north of Memphis, the overburdened boilers exploded, sending approximately 1,500 to their deaths. The icy Mississippi claimed hundreds who survived the explosion and fire. The highest military authorities eventually whitewashed those responsible for America's greatest marine disaster.

See J. W. Elliott, *Transport to Disaster* (1962); C. D. Berry, *Loss of Sultana* (1892); W. B. Floyd, *Wisconsin Maga-*

SOUTHERN PRODUCTION OF CANE SUGAR, 1850–1970
(in tons[a])

State	1850[b]	1860	1870	1880	1890	1900	1910	1920	1930	1940	1950	1960	1970[c]
Ala.	3,796	79	14	43	177	6							
Ark.			41										
Fla.	1,250	759	432	579	769	129				86,400	77,700	117,600	275,173
Ga.	746	530	292	273	594	103							
La.	102,727	100,785	36,684	78,048	132,774	145,075	325,000	160,200	137,700	213,400	354,460	362,975	402,130
Miss.	176	230	22	30	8								
Mo.		183	22										
N.C.		17	15										
S.C.	304	90	479	104	99	44							
Tenn.	112	1	640										
Tex.	3,341	2,318	918	2,250	2,491	1,267							

[a] One ton is equivalent to 2,200 lbs.
[b] Kentucky produced 129 tons in 1850 only.
[c] Texas resumed production in 1973.

zine of History (Sept., 1927); J. T. Elliott, *Indiana Historical Society Publications* (1913); J. L. Walker, *Cahaba Prison* (1910); and *Official Records, Armies*, Ser. 1, Vols. XLVIII, LII.

GERALD G. HERDMAN
Andrews University

SUMTER, THOMAS (1734–1832), was born near Charlottesville, Va., but in 1765 became a planter in South Carolina. During Lord Cornwallis' southern campaign in 1780, Sumter led a partisan resistance so successfully that the British offered 500 guineas for his betrayal. After a series of scrappy engagements in August and September, 1780, he was commissioned a brigadier general. Despite the nonexistence of state government, he raised a dependable force of state troops by a scheme known as "Sumter's law." He enlisted regulars for ten months' service to be paid in Negroes and plunder captured from Loyalists.

After the war he served in the South Carolina house, founded Stateburg, S.C., and was a member of the South Carolina ratifying convention. Elected to the First Congress (1789), Sumter remained in the House (except 1793–1796) until 1801, when he served in the Senate as a loyal Jeffersonian until 1810.

For the last 22 years (1810–1832), Sumter was besieged with creditors and litigation. It was his daring military schemes that won him fame as "Gamecock of the Revolution" and in whose honor Ft. Sumter was named.

See R. D. Bass, *Gamecock* (1961); J. R. Alden, *South in Revolution, 1763–1789* (1957); A. K. Gregorie, *Thomas Sumter* (1931); and T. P. Abernethy, *South in New Nation, 1789–1819* (1961).

GERALD J. GHELFI
Santa Ana College

SUMTER, S.C. (pop. 23,895), was founded in 1800 and named for General Thomas Sumter, whose home was nearby. It is approximately 40 miles east of Columbia. Development of the city was retarded by the absence of both rail and river transportation. Since its incorporation as a city in 1887, Sumter has developed a diversified economy servicing area cotton, livestock, and truck farmers; manufacturing lumber, textiles, and furniture; and serving as the home of Morris College (1908), a black liberal arts institution.

See files of Sumter *Item* (1894–), on microfilm; and A. K. Gregorie, *History of Sumter County* (1954). Sumter County Library maintains a strong collection of local history materials, including papers prepared by and for Sumter County Historical Society.

SUWANNEE RIVER flows along a meandering 250-mile course through southeastern Georgia and northern Florida. The river rises in Georgia's OKEFENOKEE SWAMP and empties into the Gulf of Mexico approximately 120 miles north of St. Petersburg and 55 miles southwest of Gainesville, Fla. Although it never has been important as an artery of transportation and not a single major city fronts onto the river or its tributaries (the Alapaha and Santa Fe rivers), the Suwannee is famous by virtue of STEPHEN FOSTER's use of its name for his song "Swanee River." Recently, environmental interest has developed in preserving the river area's cypress and hardwood forests.

See C. H. Matschat, *Suwanee River* (1938).

SWAMP RICE NEGROES. Because of the requirements of RICE cultivation in South Carolina, these slaves had of necessity to be among the strongest available to cope with cholera, exposure to malaria and other fevers in the swamplands, and circulatory and respiratory ailments caused by working in water for prolonged periods of time.

See C. D. Rice, *Rise and Fall of Black Slavery* (1975); U. B. Phillips, *American Negro Slavery* (1918); and M. Crum, *Gullah* (1940).

SWAMPS are forested wetlands, in contrast to marshes, which are grass covered. By area, more than three-fourths of U.S. swamps occur in the South, where they extend along the Atlantic and Gulf coastal lowlands from Delaware to Texas. Most occupy inundated bottoms along lower river courses, some extending upstream more than 200 miles from the coast. The largest riverine swamp area covers much of the lower Mississippi Basin as far north as southern Illinois. Other swamps, such as the DISMAL, OKEFENOKEE, and Great Cypress, occupy shallow basins that rise slightly above sea level. Tall trees of bald cypress, tupelo gum, bay, and water oak compose most of the vegetation of southern swamps.

Few people have permanently inhabited these swamps. In the past some have served as temporary refuges for dissident groups, such as oppressed Indians and runaway black slaves (MAROONS), or as inaccessible places where clandestine activities, such as the manufacture of moonshine whiskey, were practiced. Several swamps, however, such as the Atchafalaya Basin in Louisiana, have been the home of generations of "swamp folk," who fish, trap, and occasionally cultivate spots of high ground. Perhaps the most successful use of swamps and adjacent marshes for agriculture was the establishment of tidewater RICE plantations along the coastal lowlands of Georgia and South Carolina from the late 1600s to the Civil War.

Lumbering of cypress has been the most extensive human activity in southern swamps (LUMBER INDUSTRY). This began in Louisiana in the mid-1700s, when cypress lumber was exported to the West Indies and used locally for making sugar casks, ships, and houses. During the late 1800s and early 1900s lumber companies logged most of the swamps on the Atlantic and Gulf coasts and in the lower Mississippi Valley, peak production being reached in 1913. Since then cypress lumbering has declined, and in 1944 the last large virgin stand began to be cut in southeastern Florida. Today, only a few small stands of virgin cypress remain in the South. Many of these have been made wildlife sanctuaries. Southern swamps afford examples of some of the most severe cases of destructive exploitation in the United States.

See M. L. Comeaux, *Atchafalaya Swamp Life* (1972); P. W. Kirk, Jr. (ed.), *Great Dismal Swamp* (1977); S. B. Hilliard, *Geoscience and Man* (June, 1975); J. H. Moore, *Cypress Lumbering* (1967); and C. Carr, *Audubon* (Nov., 1971).

ROBERT C. WEST
Louisiana State University

SWANSON, CLAUDE AUGUSTUS (1862–1939),

born into an established, politically prominent family of populous Pittsylvania County, Va., graduated from Randolph-Macon College and earned a law degree at the University of Virginia in 1886. He practiced law in Chatham. In the Republican- and Populist-inhabited hills of the Fifth Congressional District, he united the warring factions of the Democratic party, which elected him to Congress in 1892. Employing a vivid oratorical style, an attractive personality, and consummate political tactics, he won the lasting loyalty of rural Virginians in the 1890s by his advocacy of free silver, William Jennings Bryan, and rural free delivery of mail.

His ability to deliver the Democratic, and often Republican, votes of his district and of southwestern Virginia earned him entry into a Democratic hierarchy headed by Senator THOMAS S. MARTIN and engineered in part by Swanson's Virginia classmate HENRY FLOOD. Although failing to receive the Democratic convention's gubernatorial nomination in 1901, he triumphed in 1905 in the first Virginia Democratic primary, subsequently being elected governor. Able to cajole the legislature to action, Swanson's governorship, featuring a rebuilt school system, marked the apex of the Virginia Progressive movement. Appointed by his successor to the U.S. Senate, Swanson, a partisan Democrat, supported the Wilson administration, fashioned a regional alliance for naval expansion, led in establishing precedents for federal road funding, and continued his solicitude toward agrarians. As ranking Democrat on the Foreign Relations Committee, Swanson at the Geneva Disarmament Conference of 1932 resisted reductions of naval tonnage allotments. Complementary service as a member and chairman (1917–1919) of the Naval Affairs Committee made Swanson a logical selection by Franklin Roosevelt for secretary of navy, a position he held as a knowledgeable and effective proponent of naval rearmament until his death.

See H. C. Ferrell, Jr., "Claude Swanson" (Ph.D. dissertation, University of Virginia, 1964), *Studies in History of South, 1875–1922* (1966), and "Naval Expansion at Norfolk, Va., and Charleston, S.C." (paper, SHA Convention, Nov., 1971); A. W. Moger, *Virginia* (1968); and R. H. Pulley, *Old Virginia Restored* (1968).

HENRY C. FERRELL, JR.
East Carolina University

SWEATT V. PAINTER (339 U.S. 629 [1950]).

The real battle to overturn legal support for racial segregation in this country was fought and won four years before the famous BROWN V. BOARD OF EDUCATION decision in 1954. The site of that battle was the law school case *Sweatt* v. *Painter*. Refusing to admit black applicants to its university law school, the state of Texas argued that a new law school, provided at the all-black Texas Southern University after the suit was filed, fulfilled its obligation under the "separate but equal" standard. The U.S. Supreme Court disagreed in language that had implications much broader than segregated law schools. The Court noted the serious disparities in faculty and facilities between the established school for whites and the newly opened one for blacks, concluding that it could not find "substantial equality" in the educational opportunities offered in the two schools.

In addition to the disparity in resources, the Court found "the University of Texas Law School possesses to a far greater degree those qualities which are incapable of objective measurement but which make for greatness in a law school." Citing the reputation of faculty, the experience of the administration, the position and influence of alumni, and the school's standing in the community, as well as its traditions and prestige, the Court noted that exclusion of a student from these benefits placed him in an "academic vacuum" and would place him at a serious disadvantage in practice. That whites would not be admitted to the black school was no answer, the Court said, because "equal protection of the laws is not achieved through indiscriminate imposition of inequalities." The Court refused to reexamine whether the separate but equal doctrine met constitutional standards, but the use of intangible assets to measure equality of separate educational facilities made it plain that black schools so long unequal in fact could never be made equal in law.

DERRICK BELL
Harvard University

SYCAMORE SHOALS, TREATY OF (1775), was
an illegal attempt of RICHARD HENDERSON and his associates to purchase lands in Kentucky from the CHEROKEE INDIANS. After DUNMORE'S WAR, Henderson formed the Louisa Company in 1774 to lease instead of purchase a large tract, thereby endeavoring to evade the PROCLAMATION OF 1763. Deciding to disregard the proclamation, he reorganized the company, changing its name to the TRANSYLVANIA COMPANY; the objective was to establish ultimately a proprietary colony. The would-be proprietors proceeded to Sycamore Shoals on the southern bank of the Watauga River (present-day Elizabethton, Tenn.). By March, 1775, over 1,000 Cherokee had assembled for negotiations. Henderson, John Williams, and Thomas and Nathaniel Hart represented the Transylvania Company. On March 17, 1775, for £2,000 and £8,000 worth of goods, the Cherokee sold Kentucky. By that time Henderson had dispatched DANIEL BOONE and 30 axmen to cut a road to the Kentucky River. He also secured for the company additional lands in the Path Deed Treaty so that settlers would not have to travel through Cherokee lands to reach Kentucky.

See W. S. Lester, *Transylvania Colony* (1935); *Virginia Calendar of State Papers*, I, valuable; and J. Haywood, *Tennessee* (1969).

EMMETT M. ESSIN
East Tennessee State University

SYDNOR, CHARLES SACKETT (1898–1954), was
born in Augusta, Ga., and received his doctorate from Johns Hopkins. In 1936, after teaching at Hampden-Sydney and the University of Mississippi, he joined the faculty of Duke, where he remained until his death. Most of Sydnor's writings display a keen interest in Mississippi's past. With Claude Bennett he wrote the school text *Mississippi History* (1930). In *A Gentleman of the Old Natchez Region: Benjamin L. C. Wailes* (1938), he painted a subtle portrait of antebellum society in the Mississippi Valley. His *Slavery in Mississippi* (1933), a work that buttressed the U. B. PHILLIPS view of the institution as benign, paternalistic, and unprofitable, presented one of the first systematic analyses of the profitability of slavery. Elsewhere, in an innovative article, he used demographic techniques, albeit incorrectly, to measure the life expectancy of Mississippi slaves. The scope of Sydnor's last two monographs lies beyond Mississippi: *The Development of Southern Sectionalism* (1948) emphasizes pre–Civil War southern political movements; and *Gentlemen Freeholders* (1952) explores ruling-class politics in colonial Virginia. The first southerner to receive the Harmsworth lectureship at Oxford, Sydnor was elected president of the SOUTHERN HISTORICAL ASSOCIATION in 1939.

See J. K. Bettersworth, *Journal of Mississippi History* (Jan., 1955); and C. Eaton, *Louisiana Historical Quarterly* (April, 1955) and in A. S. Link and R. W. Patrick (eds.), *Writing Southern History* (1965).

ROBERT L. PAQUETTE
University of Rochester

T

TAFT, WILLIAM H., ADMINISTRATION (1909–1913). Taft was not the first or the last Republican president to attempt to strengthen his party with a "southern strategy." He made a number of political overtures to the South, including his precedent-breaking campaign tour of 1908, during which he appealed to southern customs, sentimentality, and interests. He repeatedly emphasized the close affiliation of southern Democrats and northern Republicans on most economic issues. A rapidly developing industrial base in the South guaranteed a more cordial reception to this approach. Taft also struck a responsive chord when he called upon southerners to play again a more active role in national politics. His appointment of numerous southern Democrats to the federal judiciary and other offices was therefore warmly received. Also gratifying to the white South was Taft's policy toward black appointments, which resulted in the wholesale dismissal of black officeholders in the region. His support of LILY-WHITE movements in southern states minimized still further the voice of black Republicans in party affairs. This policy was only temporarily reversed in 1912 because Taft needed the South's "rotten boroughs" to defeat Theodore Roosevelt's challenge to his renomination. His administration also contributed to the discrimination practiced against blacks during this period; for example, JIM CROW flourished in the federal bureaus and offices, a dismal record superseded only during Woodrow Wilson's tenure. Taft's policies and paternalistic attitude toward blacks mirrored both his times and class. Despite Taft's efforts, Republicans made few political gains in the South during his administration. The SOLID SOUTH prevailed.

See Taft Papers, Library of Congress; C. V. Woodward, *Origins of New South* (1951); H. F. Pringle, *Taft* (1939), dated, but not superseded; G. B. Tindall, *Solid South* (1972); D. C. Needham, "Taft" (Ph.D. dissertation, University of Georgia, 1970); and K. W. Dilda, "Taft" (M.A. thesis, East Carolina College, 1970).

DAVID C. NEEDHAM
Presbyterian College

TAIT, CHARLES (1768–1835), was born in Louisa County, Va. He became rector in 1795 of Richmond Academy in Augusta, Ga., where he began a lifelong friendship with WILLIAM H. CRAWFORD.

Leaving after two years, he opened a law practice in Elbert County. In 1799 Tait was elected to the Georgia senate. Between 1803 and 1809 he served as a state circuit court judge and in 1809 was elected to the U.S. Senate. As chairman of the Naval Affairs Committee (1814–1818) and the navy's staunchest supporter, Tait carried out a comprehensive program for expansion of the navy, which included substantial appropriations over an eight-year period, the establishment of the Board of Navy Commissioners, and visions of a naval academy. Tait also helped draw the boundaries for the territory of Alabama and introduced the statehood bill. Leaving the Senate in 1819, he became Alabama's first federal judge. He retired in 1826 to his Alabama plantation and began the study of the geology around Claiborne, which won him membership in the American Philosophical Society and the Academy of Natural Sciences of Philadelphia.

See Tait Papers, Alabama Department of Archives and History, Montgomery; C. H. Moffat, "Charles Tait" (Ph.D. dissertation, Vanderbilt, 1946), comprehensive, complete bibliography; A. C. Tompkins, *Alabama Polytechnic Institute Historical Studies* (4th Ser.; 1910), short but excellent; and J. E. D. Shipp, *Giant Days* (1909).

OSCAR P. FITZGERALD
Naval Historical Center

TALLADEGA, ALA. (pop. 17,662), 40 miles east of Birmingham, is an important trade center for area cotton growers and the manufacturer of textiles, insecticides, and farm machinery. It is near the early boundary of the CREEK and CHEROKEE Indian domains, and the Creeks ceded their rights to the territory during the Jefferson administration. The government gave the site of the present city to John Bruner, a half-breed Indian who had served as an interpreter between whites and Indians. Here, at a fort constructed by Bruner, Andrew Jackson defeated the Creek Indian Confederacy on November 9, 1813, in the first of a series of fights with the Creek Indians.

See G. Jemison, *Historic Tales of Talladega* (1959); W. Wellington, *Talladega County* (2 vols.; 1954); and files of Talladega *Home* (1909–).

TALLAHASSEE, FLA. (pop. 71,897), 160 miles west of Jacksonville near the Georgia state line, was a flourishing APALACHEE INDIAN settlement in 1539, when visited by HERNANDO DE SOTO and his men. A century later Franciscan missionaries came to work among the Indians, and in 1640 the Spanish constructed Ft. San Luis to protect the mission. Lured by the rich, hilly countryside and its many springs and lakes, Spanish colonists quickly settled the surrounding area. In 1824 the Indians were persuaded to leave their village, and Tallahassee ("old town") was made the capital of the Florida Territory. The antebellum town prospered both as the seat of state government and as a market for area cotton growers. Cotton has diminished in its importance to the city's economy, but the community remains the political center of the state as well as the home of FLORIDA STATE UNIVERSITY and Florida Agricultural and Mechanical University (1887).

See B. Groene, *Antebellum Tallahassee* (1971), standard, good bibliography; S. E. Blake, *Tallahassee Yesterday* (1924); H. Dunn, *Yesterday's Tallahassee* (1974), illustrated; C. Paisley, *From Cotton to Quail* (1968), agricultural history; Tallahassee Historical Society, *Annual* (1933–39) and *Apalachee* (1944–); and files of Tallahassee *Democrat* (1914–).

TALMADGE, EUGENE (1884–1946), was a Georgia political firebrand and forerunner of the DIXIECRAT rebellion. His spectacular career was based on an agrarianism that blended the populism of TOM WATSON and the parsimony of Jeffersonianism. Although business interests first saw him as a wild agitator, they soon perceived that his laissez faire business principles worked to their advantage and they quietly supported him. Talmadge, after attending the University of Georgia and practicing law in Atlanta, moved to McRae, where he farmed until 1926, when he was elected commissioner of agriculture. As commissioner he fought the fertilizer "trust," misspent public funds on the Chicago hog market, and built a statewide political base through his weekly agricultural bulletin. Threatened with impeachment, he rode out the storm and in 1932 was elected governor and in 1934 was reelected. His gubernatorial career was marked by dictatorial administration, virulent attacks on NEW DEAL spending, and growing racism. In 1936 and 1938 he was defeated for the U.S. Senate, but the farmers put him back in the governor's chair in 1940 and 1946. In 1942, however, his interference with the university system cost him a four-year term.

His wiry build, keen delight in a political scrap, and "red galluses" indicated a man who kept frenetically active even though he was without ideological direction. He died before being inaugurated for his fourth term, leaving his son Herman Eugene to carry on the dynasty.

See A. L. Henson, *Red Galluses* (1945), campaign biography; V. O. Key, *Southern Politics* (1949); S. M. Lemmon, "Public Career of Talmadge" (Ph.D. dissertation, University of North Carolina, 1952), *Agricultural History* (Jan., 1954), *Georgia Historical Quarterly* (Sept., 1954), and in *Studies in Southern History* (1957); W. Anderson, *Wild Man from Sugar Creek* (1975); and Talmadge Papers, Georgia State Archives, Atlanta.

SARAH MCCULLOH LEMMON
Meredith College

TAMPA, FLA. (pop. 277,767). The Tampa Bay area was visited by several Spanish explorers including HERNANDO DE SOTO, but the first permanent American settlement on this site awaited construction in 1823 of Ft. Brooke. The community around the walled garrison grew throughout the SEMINOLE WARS, partly as the center of Florida's cattle industry. During and after the Civil War the city (which was blockaded and shelled by federal naval forces) suffered severely and actually lost in population. In the 1880s, however, the town began to thrive: two railroad lines established connections, PHOSPHATE deposits were discovered nearby, and Cuban cigar makers made the city the American center of that industry. Tampa was the major port of embarkation for U.S. armed forces leaving for Cuba during the SPANISH-AMERICAN WAR. Modern Tampa, like neighboring Clearwater and St. Petersburg, became a major center for TOURISM during the 1920s. The University of Tampa (1931) and the University of South Florida (1956) are both located here. Besides cigars, phosphates, and tourism, the city draws economic strength as a shipper and canner of citrus fruits and as a manufacturer of construction materials, clothing, prefabricated homes, and dairy and meat products.

See D. Long, *Florida Historical Quarterly* (July, 1966); and files of Tampa *Tribune* (1893–).

TANEY, ROGER BROOKE (1777–1864), was born of prosperous slaveholding parents in Calvert County, Md. He graduated from Dickinson College in 1795 and was admitted to the Maryland bar in 1799. He served two terms in the Maryland legislature as a Federalist before moving in 1823 to Baltimore, where he became a Democrat and supporter of ANDREW JACKSON. In 1827 he was appointed Maryland attorney general and remained there until President Jackson appointed him attorney general of the U.S. in 1831. He served until Jackson appointed him secretary of the treasury in 1833 in order to complete the destruction of the Bank of the United States by depositing public revenues in pet banks, but the Senate rejected the appointment. Jackson appointed him to the U.S. Supreme Court in 1835 but again he was rejected. When JOHN MARSHALL died, Jackson appointed Taney chief justice, and this time he was confirmed (1836).

Taney's major opinions fall into two categories: economic development (primarily banks and transportation) and slavery. Marshall's Court had refused to hear slavery cases, and it had failed to extend effective jurisdiction over business corporations engaged in interstate commerce (*Bank of the U.S.* v. *Deveaux*, 1809). The decisions in the *Charles River Bridge* case and *Briscoe* v. *Commonwealth Bank of Kentucky*, both in 1837, linked economic development with a state's right to encourage its entrepreneurs. The *Charles River Bridge* decision narrowly interpreted corporation charters so that state governments could charter railroad corporations without having to compensate the owners of less efficient forms of transportation. The *Briscoe* decision authorized state-chartered banks to create bank note credit. These decisions aided a laissez faire development policy, which from 1830 to 1860 was highly successful in achieving rapid economic growth. Taney had opposed rechartering the Bank of the United States because it had restrained the credit practices of state banks, which were eager to extend credit to the promoters of local development projects. In the decision of *Bank of Augusta* v. *Earle* (1839), Taney said that comity among the states allowed a corporation to do business in any state unless specifically prohibited; however, states could regulate the activities of these out-of-state corporations.

Two later cases expanded the jurisdiction of the Court over the increasingly large volume of corporate business. In *Louisville, Cincinnati & Charleston Railroad* v. *Lettson* (1844), the *Deveaux* decision was overruled, and it was held that corporations chartered in different states could seek justice in federal courts. Finally, in 1851 (*Genesee Chief* v. *Fitzhugh*) Taney extended admiralty jurisdiction over all inland waterways.

The New York legislature enacted a statute requiring ship captains to list the ages and occupations of incoming passengers in order to prevent New York City's welfare facilities from being overwhelmed by paupers. In *New York* v. *Miln* (1837), the law was sustained as a valid exercise of a state's police power. The implications of the case were not lost on the South, because the New York law was similar to the laws of many slave states that excluded free blacks from settling within their boundaries or expelled them upon manumission. The justices from the slave states also feared that Congress, at some future date, might forbid the interstate slave trade if property in persons (slaves) was considered commerce. The issue surfaced again in the passenger cases (1849), when the Court overturned two tax statutes in northern states that attempted to exclude undesirable emigrants. To the South this action seemed to open the door for congressional regulation of the interstate slave trade. Taney's dissent strongly endorsed the power of the states to exclude persons deemed dangerous to their internal security. Not until 1852 in *Cooley* v. *Board of Wardens* was a compromise reached, when the Court stated that states had concurrent power with Congress to regulate commerce, as long as Congress did not act.

In 1842 in *Prigg* v. *Pennsylvania*, the Court declared unconstitutional Pennsylvania's personal liberty law because it was designed to nullify the federal fugitive slave law; but said states could forbid their law enforcement officers from enforcing federal laws and leave enforcement wholly in the hands of the federal government. A unanimous Court in 1851 in *Strader* v. *Graham* decided that state law governed the status of a black man and that, if a slave voluntarily returned to a slave state after residence in a free state, slavery reattached.

Taney had restrained the Court's entry into politics in *Luther* v. *Borden* (1849) by making a distinction between political and judicial issues, but the famous decision in DRED SCOTT V. SANDFORD (1857) abandoned this policy. Taney attempted to make a settlement of an explosive political issue when he ruled that Congress had no power to exclude slavery from the territories. In the sequel case ABLEMAN V. BOOTH (1859), Taney claimed the Court had exclusive power to interpret the Constitution, a position that guaranteed a collision with the Republican party if it gained national power. The result was that, after the Civil War began, Abraham Lincoln ignored the Court (*e.g.*, *ex parte* MERRYMAN, 1861) while his administration was forging a military-political solution to the problem of preserving national unity.

See A. Bestor, *Illinois State Historical Society Journal* (Summer, 1961) and *American Historical Review* (Jan., 1964); C. G. Haines, *Role of Supreme Court in American Government and Politics* (1957); R. K. Newmyer, *Supreme Court Under Marshall and Taney* (1968); C. W. Smith, *Taney* (1936); C. B. Swisher, *Taney* (1935); C.

Warren, *Supreme Court in U.S. History* (1922), II; and M. L. Winitsky, *Maryland Historical Magazine* (Spring, 1974).

RONALD E. SEAVOY
Bowling Green State University

TARHEEL is a nickname for a North Carolinian. There have been many conflicting explanations for the exact origin of the term, but it is fairly certain that it relates to the fact that a major industry in the state had long been the production of NAVAL STORES: tar, pitch, and turpentine. The usually accepted explanation is that, since the production of tar is dirty, sticky work and since the workers usually went barefoot, a typical citizen of the state had tar stuck to his heels. At first a term of derision, like "rube" or "red-neck," apparently about the time of the Civil War it began to be used with pride by the North Carolinians themselves.

See B. A. Botkin (ed.), *Treasury of Southern Folklore* (1949); and J. Daniels, *Tar Heels* (1941).

TARIFFS. Although the antebellum South accounted for about two-thirds of America's exports and imports, most of the benefit of tonnage and tariff duties went to other sections of the nation. Yet the South had no quarrel with the rest of the nation, for prior to 1816 tariffs had been low and designed primarily for revenue. That year America's first protective tariff, levying duties of 25 percent, was passed. It was designed to protect New England textile mills and ironworks (found chiefly in Pennsylvania) from being hurt by British goods flooding the American market following the end of the War of 1812. Although the South voted 39 to 25 in the U.S. House against the tariff, the extent of southern support was remarkable. President JAMES MADISON proposed the measure to Congress, WILLIAM LOWNDES of South Carolina introduced it in the House, and JOHN C. CALHOUN and HENRY CLAY spoke strongly in favor of it. Frank W. Taussig and others have attributed the South's support to a desire to establish textile manufacturing in its region. Close analysis of votes and speeches does not bear this out. Tariff support was part of the same postwar nationalism that led southerners to back internal improvements and a national bank. The South dominated the government and had been a major supporter of the War of 1812, and many said it was patriotic and wise to aid those industries that had helped save America in the war and might be called upon again. There was also a need to provide revenue for the government. Support was made easier by the great prosperity the South was enjoying and by assurances that the tariff was only a temporary expedient to deal with British "dumping." Four years later when a new tariff bill was introduced, all had changed. The new tariff, with a duty of 33 percent on textiles, was to be permanent and would extend to a long list of additional items. No longer was there a need for revenue, and no longer was there a threat of war with England. Most important, the PANIC OF 1819 had ended the South's prosperity. With only its economic interest to consider, the South from now on would consistently oppose protection. Why, for the benefit of others, should it be taxed in the form of higher prices and face retaliation against its agricultural exports? The 1820 tariff passed despite southern opposition in the House, but was defeated by one vote in the Senate.

A similar bill was successfully passed four years later. It raised duties to a new average high of 37 percent, but exempted coarse wool used to clothe slaves. Protection was granted the SUGAR planters of Louisiana and the HEMP industry of Kentucky. Clay, who grew hemp, argued that the tariff would provide a "home market" for the farmer, but few southerners were convinced, since the market for their staple crops was abroad. Kentucky cast its votes for the tariff, but the rest of the Southwest opposed the bill 14 to three and the South Atlantic states voted 56 to four against it. Earlier, JOHN RANDOLPH had argued for strict construction of the Constitution lest a consolidated nationalism be someday directed against the South and slavery. The South's loss of political power and the rise of abolitionism now made others aware of the danger. During the 1824 debates the legislatures of South Carolina, Georgia, and Alabama passed resolutions denying the constitutionality of protective tariffs.

The tariff of 1828 was the result of election-year politics. Antitariff southerners and Jacksonians raised the rates on raw materials to such levels that it was thought New England would reject the measure and John Quincy Adams would be discredited with protectionists. To the South's consternation the Tariff of Abominations passed. Its duties averaged 41 percent, the highest rates before the Civil War. Of the 12 slave states, only Kentucky and Delaware voted for the tariff. Virginia's legislature joined the ranks of those calling protective tariffs unconstitutional, and some South Carolinians spoke of SECESSION. Calhoun, Andrew Jackson's running mate, urged delay, counseling that Jackson would lower duties after the election. At the same time, Calhoun was the anonymous author of the "South Carolina Exposition and Protest" (1828) issued by the legislature. This declared that South Carolina had a constitutional right to nullify the tariff. In 1832 the tariff was revised, but the duties remained high, averaging 33 percent. Calhoun, who had become alienated from Jackson and had lost the chance to succeed him, now gave his support to NULLIFICATION of the tariff. When Jackson denounced this as treason, a showdown was at hand. The administration introduced, however, the Verplanck bill to reduce tariff duties. Rather than let Jackson gain credit, Clay and Calhoun combined forces to push through the compromise tariff of 1833, which provided for the gradual reduction of duties to a 20 percent level over a ten-year period. No other southern state would challenge Jackson, and, even in South Carolina, a majority of the rice and Sea Island cotton planters in the east and the small subsistence farmers in the northwest were opposed to nullification. Calhoun's support came primarily from growers of short-staple cotton, whose price had fallen sharply as a result of the expansion of the cotton kingdom to fertile new lands in the Southwest. Those on the older, worn-out lands of South Carolina could no longer compete.

Closely fought contests between Democrats and Whigs characterized politics in the years that followed. The Whigs carried most of the South in 1840. But when, in 1842, Clay returned the tariff to the levels of 1832, eight Whig senators from the South deserted party lines. The Democrats won the next election and reversed the situation by passing in 1846 a low tariff, which averaged 26.5 percent. It was pushed through Congress by President James Polk's secretary of the treasury, ROBERT J. WALKER of Mississippi, and it substituted specific for ad valorem duties and dropped the minimum valuation. The bill won in the Senate only through the votes of the two senators from recently annexed Texas. In 1857 HOWELL COBB of Georgia, secretary of the treasury under President James Buchanan, reduced the tariff to the lowest level since 1815. The reductions were made possible because of the prosperity of business and the decision of New England textile manufacturers to prevent competitors from arising by keeping duties low. With Clay dead, Kentucky voted for the low tariff, and only Delaware and Missouri in the South cast majorities against it. The onset of the PANIC OF 1857 led to a revived interest in protection, and the new Republican party made a high tariff one of its principal planks. The South's secession enabled the Republicans to pass the

Morrill tariff in 1861 and to embark upon a long period of protection. HOWARD K. BEALE and Charles A. Beard advanced the thesis that Republicans kept the low-tariff South out of the Union during Reconstruction in order that northeastern businessmen might gain high tariffs. Richard Hofstadter and Stanley Coben have shown, however, that the businessmen were badly divided over the tariff and that neither they nor the Radicals were united in support of any specific economic objective.

Manufacturing existed in the antebellum South on a small scale. E. Stanwood and Taussig thought an inability to use slaves in cotton mills had made the South turn against both manufacturing and the tariff of 1820, but it was not until the agricultural depression of 1828 that manufacturing received its first strong stimulus and a real test was made of black workers. Slaves were used successfully thereafter in cotton mills and factories (it was only after the Civil War that blacks were excluded from the textile industry), but their use was criticized because of fears of insurrection and the belief that working in factories "would make them half-free." On the other hand, the use of whites was opposed because it might produce a class favoring protection. Trying to win acceptance, WILLIAM GREGG and other antebellum textile owners pledged their support to low tariffs. The "cotton mill crusade" of the 1880s revived manufacturing, but through the 1930s the South's chief occupation remained agriculture and southern congressmen wedded themselves firmly to the Democratic party and low tariffs.

The election of WOODROW WILSON enabled the Democrats to lower the tariff in 1913. Working through OSCAR W. UNDERWOOD of Alabama in the House and FURNIFOLD M. SIMMONS of North Carolina in the Senate, they reduced levels to an average of 30 percent, the lowest in half a century. Opposition came from West Virginia and the sugarcane growers of Louisiana, but the remaining 14 southern states lined up behind the administration. The South was also happy to see ratified that year the Sixteenth Amendment authorizing income taxes, for it took away from protectionists their argument that a tariff was needed for revenue. The 1920s saw the return of the Republicans and high tariffs. Southern businessmen through the Southern Tariff Association (organized in 1920) and local chambers of commerce pushed for protection and were joined by some farmers attracted by duties placed on agricultural products. But only 25 percent of southern congressmen supported the Hawley-Smoot Act of 1931, and even smaller percentages voted for the acts of 1921 and 1922. Tariff sentiment was strongest in the border states of Maryland, Kentucky, and Missouri and from the sugarcane and citrus growers of Louisiana and Florida. During the NEW DEAL era the South gave its strong support to the new approach of Secretary of State CORDELL HULL of Tennessee, which was embodied in the Trade Agreement Act of 1934. This act allowed the president to enter into reciprocal trade agreements for the reduction of duties based on the most-favored-nation principle. Working through it and the General Agreement on Tariffs and Trade (GATT) established by the United Nations, the United States by 1951 had made agreements with nations with which it did 80 percent of its trade. These agreements reduced tariffs from the 53 percent rate of 1930–1933 to less than 15 percent. This approach follows David Ricardo's "principle of comparative advantage," which maintains that free trade between nations is always mutually profitable, causing real wages to rise.

A healthy sign since World War II has been the South's lessening dependence on cotton and its greater agricultural diversity and flexibility. Industry has expanded so greatly that since the 1960s only 10 percent of the South's income has come from agriculture. With industry has come renewed support for the Republican party. Although most economists believe a nation's overall growth and living standards are hurt by tariffs, the particular industry involved does benefit from the duties. A natural tendency of weaker industries is to seek help from the government. Part of Richard Nixon's "southern strategy" was to promise the textile industry help against Japanese imports. Although tariff rates have moved downward, spurred by the Kennedy Round of 1962, protection continues through quotas, licensing systems, and other controls. The battle over protection is no longer between Republicans and Democrats or industry and agriculture, but between special interests, who seek or oppose duties depending on whether their particular product is competitive on the world market. Tariffs and quotas are a hidden tax on the consumer, but, with decisions being made by remote bureaucratic specialists, lobbyists are usually better able to influence decisions than the consumer.

See E. Stanwood, *Tariff Controversies* (1903), protectionist bias; F. W. Taussig, *Tariff History* (1923), free-trade bias; C. S. Sydnor, *Southern Sectionalism* (1948); G. R. Taylor, *Transportation Revolution* (1966); G. B. Tindall, *Emergence of New South* (1967); N. W. Preyer, *Journal of Southern History* (Aug., 1959) and *Journal of*

Negro History (April, 1961); and S. Coben, *Mississippi Valley Historical Review* (June, 1959). Best source is original debates and votes of Congress.

NORRIS W. PREYER
Queens College, Charlotte, N.C.

TARPLEY AFFAIR was a result of the letter that JOHN C. CALHOUN wrote to Collin S. Tarpley of Mississippi on July 9, 1849, in the midst of the intense national debate over the WILMOT PROVISO and other sectional issues. In the letter Calhoun urged that Mississippi take the lead in calling for a convention of all the southern states. This convention in turn should issue a pronouncement to all the states of the Union explaining southern grievances, warn the rest of the country of the consequences if these grievances were not remedied, and "take measures preparatory to it, in case they should not be." A state convention held in October, 1849, in Jackson, Miss., did issue a call, which led to the famous NASHVILLE CONVENTION in June, 1850. Calhoun has been falsely accused of desiring the dissolution of the Union because of his influence in these matters.

See P. M. Hamer, *Secession Movement in South Carolina* (1918); C. Hearon, *Mississippi and Compromise of 1850* (1913); and *Congressional Globe* (1846–52).

TATE, JOHN ORLEY ALLEN (1899–1979), was a native of Winchester, Ky., who studied English and classics at Vanderbilt and was graduated *summa cum laude* in 1923. He played an important role in the magazine *Fugitive* (1922–1925), and many of the FUGITIVE group's members were to be his lifelong friends, especially JOHN CROWE RANSOM. In 1924 Allen Tate moved to New York and began a career as writer and editor. In 1928 *Mr. Pope and Other Poems* and *Stonewall Jackson* were published; in 1929, *Jefferson Davis*. After a Guggenheim Fellowship in Europe, Tate returned to the South and started work on I'LL TAKE MY STAND (1930). By 1938 he had edited *Who Owns America?* with Herbert Agar; published two more collections of poetry, *Reactionary Essays*, and *The Fathers* (his only novel); and had become an advisory editor on the *Kenyon Review*. He was writer in residence at Princeton (1939–1942) and consultant in poetry at the Library of Congress (1943–1944). As editor of the SEWANEE REVIEW (1944–1946) he gave that quarterly international stature. After further editorial work and teaching, he was appointed professor of English at the University of Minnesota (1951–1968). Tate's reputation will stand most securely on his criticism and a handful of poems.

See R. Squires (ed.), *Allen Tate and His Work* (1972); and *Southern Review* (Fall, 1976).

GEORGE CORE
Sewanee Review

TATTNALL, JOSIAH (1795–1871), born near Savannah, Ga., was appointed midshipman in 1812. Thus began a distinguished career that covered 53 years in U.S. and Confederate navies. He became a captain in both and flag officer in state (Georgia) service. In 1859, while commanding in the Far East, Tattnall provided assistance to a British fleet defeated by the Chinese. He later received his government's approval for this action. After Georgia seceded, Tattnall resigned from the service despite his opposition to secession. Commanding an improvised "fleet," he failed to defeat a superior federal force in PORT ROYAL SOUND. He briefly commanded the *Merrimack* (*Virginia*), destroying it when Norfolk was lost in May, 1862. After being cleared of charges of improper conduct, Tattnall returned to his state to aid in its defense. After the war, he became an exile in Halifax, Nova Scotia, but returned to Georgia in 1870. He then served as port inspector for Savannah.

See C. C. Jones, *Josiah Tattnall* (1879), partisan but indispensable; *Naval General Court-Martial of Tattnall* (1862); and R. M. Langdon, *U.S. Naval Institute Proceedings* (June, 1959).

NORMAN C. DELANEY
Del Mar College

TAXATION. State and local taxes in the South, though following the general outline of tax history outside the region, have differed from it in important ways. Tax policy has reflected the nature of the economy, the locus of political power, and the demands of social policy in the region. Before the American Revolution, POLL TAXES were typically high, and land was taxed by the acre (rather than by location, quality, or some other index of value). Thus, there was little relationship between ability to pay and the tax levied. Maryland's constitution of 1776 exemplified late eighteenth-century changes; outlawing poll taxes, it required that taxes be levied according to the value of a citizen's real and personal property. Thereafter, southern poll taxes were lighter, and most states levied taxes on land according to value rather than acreage.

In the political economy of the antebellum South, fiscal policy was integrally related to the existence of slavery and the apportionment of legislative representation. In South Carolina, for example, the largest source of public revenue was the tax on slaves. In other southern jurisdictions, as often as not, the tax on slaves was as productive as the other major source of tax revenue, rural real estate. The relationship of these issues can be seen most clearly in Virginia. That state's constitution of 1851, which conceded more legislative power to the predominantly white western counties, also tied the poll tax to the tax on slaves; thus farmers, presumably unwilling to greatly increase their poll taxes, would be less tempted to tax slave property in order to finance internal improvements (*i.e.*, to pass the cost of building railroads in the west to wealthy slaveholders in the east).

The end of slavery forced a transformation of southern tax systems. Slaves constituted such a large share of antebellum property valuation that, even in a border state like Kentucky, the tax base required a generation to recover to 1860 levels. Even to maintain constant tax revenue, therefore, southern state and local governments had generally to levy much higher tax rates on the diminished wealth of their residents. Moreover, emancipation resulted in a redistribution of the tax burden; planters no longer paid property taxes on their laborers, and they and farmers alike paid much higher taxes on rural land, which now produced the bulk of public revenue.

The history of the poll tax mirrors the history of southern society and politics. With the political democratization that accompanied the Revolution, poll taxes were generally much reduced. But it was widely held, both before and after the Civil War, that, though taxation should be geared to the ability to pay, a poll tax should also be levied. Public thought justified property taxation on the grounds that governments served primarily to protect private property, but even men without property should pay something, for they presumably benefited from public spending on schools and the right to vote. Although free blacks were barred from both the suffrage and the schools, they were required to pay poll taxes too, often at much higher rates. For example, in Georgia in the 1850s white men paid $.25, and free black men and women paid $5. After emancipation, when freedmen and whites paid identical poll taxes (higher than the prewar tax on whites—$1 in Georgia), the tax provided much of the support for schools and generally served as a prerequisite for voting. When women were subsequently enfranchised, they too had to pay a poll tax before they could vote. In recent decades, the poll tax has lost its fiscal and political significance.

In the past century, tax systems in the South, like those outside the region, have undergone considerable changes. Beginning in the 1890s, a growing tax base provided additional revenue, much of it used to expand public school systems. After World War I, a tax on motor fuel generated substantial public revenue that was directed to the improvement of highways. Property taxes, particularly on real estate, remain central to the fiscal systems of local jurisdictions, though state governments have sought their income elsewhere. In recent decades, southern state governments typically have derived the bulk of their tax revenue from general and specific sales taxes, with personal and corporate income taxes providing additional income.

See P. Wallenstein, "From Slave South to New South" (Ph.D. dissertation, Johns Hopkins, 1973), discussion of primary sources—revenue laws, tax lists, state financial reports—for Georgia in bibliography, and *Journal of Economic History* (March, 1976); E. Galambos, *Tax Structure of Southern States* (1969); E. J. Ferguson, *William and Mary Quarterly* (April, 1953); R. A. Becker, "Politics of Taxation" (Ph.D. dissertation, University of Wisconsin, 1971) and *William and Mary Quarterly* (July, 1975); J. H. Hollander, *Studies in State Taxation* (1900); G. R. Woolfolk, *Journal of Southern History* (May, 1960); F. D. Ogden, *Poll Tax in South* (1958); J. E. Thorogood, *Financial History of Tennessee Since 1870* (1949); E. Q. Hawk, *Taxation in Alabama* (1931); M. C. Rhodes, *History of Taxation in Mississippi* (1930); N. O. Taff, *Taxation in Kentucky* (1931); and J. M. Kousser, *Shaping of Southern Politics* (1974).

PETER WALLENSTEIN
University of Toronto

TAYLOR, ALFRED ALEXANDER (1848–1931), brother of ROBERT LOVE TAYLOR and leading east Tennessee Republican, was born in Carter County, Tenn. His father, a Civil War Unionist, served in Congress and as Andrew Johnson's commissioner of Indian affairs. Educated in academies in Tennessee and New Jersey, Taylor studied law in Jonesboro and became active in Republican politics, winning a seat in the legislature in 1874. In 1886 he ran unsuccessfully for governor against his brother, a Democrat. The Taylors, both accomplished orators, entertained the state in a joint canvass known as the "war of the roses." Elected to Congress from Tennessee's First District in 1888, 1890, and 1892, Taylor supported the Lodge FORCE BILL, high tariffs, and war claims of southern Unionists. Following his third term he joined his brother on a national lecture tour that was a critical and financial success. Popular with the masses, rather than with Republican bosses, he was thwarted in efforts to secure the gubernatorial nomination again until 1920, when as the sentimental favorite he defeated the Democratic in-

cumbent. Failing to win reelection in 1922, he retired to his home in east Tennessee.

See J. P. Taylor, A. A. Taylor, and H. L. Taylor, *Robert L. Taylor* (1913); P. D. Augsburg, *Bob and Alf Taylor* (1925); L. Hale, "Alf Taylor" (M.A. thesis, Duke, 1940); R. L. Taylor, *Tennessee Historical Quarterly* (Spring, 1969); and G. W. Reichard, *Tennessee Historical Quarterly* (Spring, 1971).

PAUL E. ISAAC
Lamar University

TAYLOR, JOHN (1753–1824), of Caroline, was born in Virginia, probably in Caroline County. He served as a major in the American Revolution, in the Virginia house of delegates (1779–1781, 1783–1785, 1796–1800) and in the U.S. Senate (1792–1794, 1803, 1822–1824). His agricultural experiments and his agricultural and political publications brought him considerable renown. Taylor began publishing pamphlets in 1794. In 1813 he published his famous agricultural work *Arator*, in which he set forth the results of his practical experiments and espoused the virtues of an agrarian society. His political writings were primarily a statement of the political principles of STATES' RIGHTS and agrarian republicanism. His major works include *An Inquiry into the Principles and Policy of the Government of the United States* (1814), *Construction Construed and Constitutions Vindicated* (1820), *Tyranny Unmasked* (1822), and *New Views of the Constitution of the United States* (1823). Taylor argued that the great enemy of agrarian republicanism was a paper and patronage aristocracy that utilized the central government to oppress agriculture.

See H. H. Simms, *Life of J. Taylor* (1932); E. T. Mudge, *Philosophy of J. Taylor* (1939); A. O. Craven, *Soil Exhaustion in Virginia and Maryland* (1925); L. C. Gray, *History of Agriculture in Southern U.S.* (1933); C. Beard, *Economic Origins of Jeffersonian Democracy* (1915); N. E. Cunningham, *Mississippi Valley Historical Review* (Sept., 1963); B. F. Wright, *American Political Science Review* (Nov., 1928); A. O. Craven, *Journal of Southern History* (May, 1938) and *American Historical Review* (Jan., 1928); M. J. Dauer and H. Hammond, *Journal of Politics* (Nov., 1944); D. H. Hagler, "Agrarian Theme in Southern History" (Ph.D. dissertation, University of Missouri, 1968); and J. T. Moore, *Agricultural History* (April, 1976).

D. HARLAND HAGLER
North Texas State University

TAYLOR, RICHARD "DICK" (1826–1879), the only son of ZACHARY TAYLOR, was born near Lexington, Ky. He studied abroad and graduated from Yale in 1845. In 1851 he bought Fashion, a sugar plantation about 20 miles above New Orleans. Originally a Whig, he became a Democrat and served in the state senate, in the 1860 CHARLESTON CONVENTION, and in the Louisiana secession convention. On July 2, 1861, he was appointed colonel of the 9th Louisiana Infantry. In October of that year he became brigadier general of the 8th (Louisiana) Brigade in Virginia and fought under Stonewall Jackson in the SHENANDOAH VALLEY and SEVEN DAYS' battles. In July, 1862, he was appointed major general to command the militarily feeble District of West Louisiana. On April 8, 1864, he defeated the vastly superior force of Nathaniel P. Banks at SABINE CROSSROADS, near Mansfield. As a result of this victory he was promoted lieutenant general, but he also clashed with his superior, EDMUND KIRBY-SMITH. He eventually ended up as commander of the Department of Alabama, Mississippi, and East Louisiana. After the war he traveled, worked to gain lenient treatment for the South, and wrote a highly literate book on his experiences during and after the war. He died in New York City.

See R. Taylor, *Destruction and Reconstruction* (1879), brilliant work; and J. B. Davis, *Louisiana Historical Quarterly* (Jan., 1941), effective biographical sketch.

ALLAN C. ASHCRAFT
Texas A. & M. University

TAYLOR, ROBERT LOVE (1850–1912), politician and humorist, was born in Carter County, in upper east Tennessee. He entered politics as a Democrat and gained recognition in 1878 by winning a congressional election in Tennessee's Republican First District. National fame came in 1886, when he defeated his Republican brother ALFRED TAYLOR for governor in the "war of the roses" campaign. Reelected governor in 1888 and 1896, Taylor practiced the art of country-boy politics and fought the BOURBONS but did not pursue radical agrarian or Populist policies. In 1906 he defeated EDWARD WARD CARMACK and won a term in the U.S. Senate (1907–1912). In a futile effort to unite Tennessee Democrats in 1910, he ran for governor again, but lost to BEN W. HOOPER. Sometimes dismissed as a fiddle-playing buffoon, Taylor, though not a great statesman, was able, intelligent, and humane and a major figure in Tennessee politics. He was one of the most popular lecturers of his time, a great entertainer and superb teller of Tennessee mountain tales. Affectionately known as "Our Bob" and the "Apostle of Sunshine," he became a folk hero in his home state.

See D. M. Robison, *Bob Taylor* (1935); R. L. Hart, *Redeemers, Bourbons, and Populists* (1975); J. P. Taylor, A. A. Taylor, and H. L. Taylor, *Robert L. Taylor* (1913); R. L. Taylor, *Tennessee Historical Quarterly* (Spring, 1969); V. Lindsay, *Collected Poems* (1937); S. B. Smith, *Tennessee History: Bibliography* (1974); and R. L. Taylor Papers, Correspondence of the Governor's Office, Tennessee State Library and Archives, Nashville.

PAUL E. ISAAC
Lamar University

TAYLOR, ZACHARY (1784–1850), was born in Virginia, was reared in Kentucky, and resided in Louisiana. He spent most of his career as a soldier, serving on the frontier and commanding the troops in the SEMINOLE WAR. During the Mexican War his victories at the battles of PALO ALTO, Buena Vista, and Monterrey laid the foundation for massive territorial conquests and made Taylor a national hero. Although Taylor was a political neophyte who had never voted, several leading Whig politicians promoted his presidential candidacy in 1848. They believed his military renown would overcome their party's normal minority status by attracting Democrats to the Whig column. In addition, Taylor, "a Southern man and a slaveholder," could also be run as a sectional candidate in the South, appealing to those concerned by northern resistance to slavery's extension. Both tactics proved effective in 1848.

As president, however, Taylor proved to be much more national than sectional in outlook. Although a supporter of slavery in states where it existed, he was impatient with sectional maneuvering over the territories and particularly refused to champion slavery's expansion. He instigated a move to admit California and New Mexico as states, bypassing the troublesome territorial phase. He refused to countenance the compromise bills pushed by HENRY CLAY and others in 1850, which would have given both North and South partial victories in the dispute. Taylor considered Clay's scheme too encouraging to sectional elements and dangerous to the Union. His intractable stance hamstrung all efforts to pass the compromise in Congress. The situation grew ominous in the summer of 1850, as the southerners, who had once been Taylor's strongest champions, bitterly fought against the president's policies and even threatened secession unless he gave way. Taylor responded even more firmly, determined both to have his way and to hold the Union together. Daniel Webster later reflected that "if General Taylor had lived, we should have had Civil War [in 1850]." But the president became ill at a Fourth of July celebration and died five days later. His successor

Millard Fillmore supported the compromise efforts that finally ended the crisis (COMPROMISE OF 1850).

See H. Hamilton, *Zachary Taylor* (2 vols.; 1941, 1951), definitive biography, *Prologue to Crisis* (1964), and in A. Schlesinger, Jr. (ed.), *History of American Presidential Elections* (1971), II; and D. Potter, *Impending Crisis* (1976). Taylor's few surviving papers are in Library of Congress and on microfilm.

JOEL H. SILBEY
Cornell University

TAZEWELL, HENRY (1753–1799), established a law practice in Brunswick County, Va., the place of his birth. In 1775 he was elected to the general assembly, where he sided with those who favored reconciliation with Great Britain. When conciliatory efforts failed, Tazewell accepted membership in the Virginia constitutional convention of 1776 and vigorously supported the Virginia bill of rights. He served in the general assembly until 1785, when he became a judge, later chief justice, of the Virginia general court. In 1793 he was appointed to the court of appeals, a position he held until his election to the U.S. Senate in 1794. As a senator he upheld the tenets of the Jeffersonians.

See H. B. Grigsby, *Virginia Convention of 1776* (1855) and *Virginia Federal Convention of 1788* (1890); R. B. Tunstall, *Memorial Volume of Virginia Portraiture* (1930); L. W. Tazewell, "Sketches of His Own Family," Virginia State Library; Henry Tazewell Papers, Library of Congress; and Tazewell Family Papers, Virginia State Library.

NORMA LOIS PETERSON
Adams State College

TAZEWELL, LITTLETON WALLER (1774–1860), was a member of the Virginia tidewater planter aristocracy and an eminent attorney and Norfolk businessman. The son of HENRY TAZEWELL and grandson of Benjamin Waller, chief justice of the admiralty court, he was born in Williamsburg. He was a member of the Virginia house of delegates (1804–1806, 1816–1817), congress (1800–1801), and U.S. Senate (1825–1832), and he served as governor (1834–1836). An adherent of Jeffersonianism, Tazewell sought to curb power, whatever its source, but particularly the power of the presidency during the administrations of John Quincy Adams and ANDREW JACKSON. He was a strong proponent of STATES' RIGHTS and equally as ardent an opponent of NULLIFICATION. After TURNER'S REBELLION Tazewell privately advocated a gradual plan of emancipation for Virginia.

See H. B. Grigsby, *L. W. Tazewell* (1860), eulogistic account; N. L. Peterson, *Virginia Cavalcade* (Spring, 1973); R. B. Tunstall, *Memorial Volume of Virginia Portraiture* (1930); L. W. Tazewell, "Sketches of His Own Family," Virginia State Library; and Tazewell Family Papers, Virginia State Library.

NORMA LOIS PETERSON
Adams State College

TEA AND COFFEE never were grown as southern staples, but many experiments were carried out in the eighteenth and nineteenth centuries. Both were introduced without success into the southern colonies during the colonial period. Subsequently, interest in coffee growing was limited to subtropical Florida, where it was planted on Biscayne Bay in the late 1830s and in Manatee County during the 1875–1885 period. When the trees at Bradenton were killed by cold in the mid-1880s, the U.S. Department of Agriculture concluded that coffee could not be grown commercially in the United States.

Tea was reintroduced into the South during the 1840s by Dr. Junius Smith, who cultivated a small tea plantation near Greenville, S.C., during the 1840s and 1850s. In 1850 the agricultural department of the U.S. Patent Office began a campaign to make tea an American crop. The department maintained a nursery in Washington, D.C., for many years and operated a tea farm at Summerville, S.C., from 1881 to 1886. As a result of dissemination of seeds, plants, and literature, tea was widely cultivated in small quantities for domestic use throughout the South between 1850 and 1900. Only one commercial operation, however, survived into the twentieth century. This was a highly publicized 60-acre tea garden on Newington plantation, Pinehurst, S.C., which marketed a crop of 14,000 pounds in 1912, the nation's entire production for that year.

See L. H. Bailey, *American Horticulture* (1906); J. C. Bonner, *Georgia Agriculture* (1964); L. J. Brown, "U. S. Patent Office" (M.A. thesis, Florida State University, 1957); A. P. Chew, *U.S. Department of Agriculture* (1940); L. C. Gray, *History of Agriculture in Southern U.S.* (1958); J. H. Hammond, *Journeys* (1916); H. E. Perrine, *Grandpa's Life* (1885); E. L. R. Pond, *Junius Smith* (1927); E. T. H. Shaffer, *Gardens* (1939); U.S. Department of Agriculture, *Report* (1869–1912); and U.S. Patent Office, *Report* (1849–60).

JOHN HEBRON MOORE
Florida State University

TECHE, BAYOU. See BAYOU TECHE

TELEGRAPHS AND TELEPHONES. Although sweeping generalizations are sometimes made about the impact of distances and relative isolation upon the character of the rural South, little attention has been given by scholars of the region to the development of these communications systems. The nation's first telegraph line was the one from Washington, D.C., to Baltimore constructed by Samuel F. B. Morse in 1844 with a grant of $30,000 from the U.S. government. Despite the success of this pilot demonstration line, the Polk administration failed to exercise its option to purchase Morse's patent rights and turned ownership of the line over to the Magnetic Telegraph Company in 1847. Magnetic, one of several companies using the Morse patent, was headed by AMOS KENDALL, company president and general agent for all members of the Morse patent group. With control of the Washington-to-Baltimore line, Magnetic had a communications system linking the nation's capital to New York City.

Kendall, however, believed on the basis of his experience as postmaster general that the most lucrative telegraph line would be along the South Atlantic seaboard and the Gulf coast. Accordingly, in November, 1846, he organized the Washington & New Orleans Telegraph Company (with himself as treasurer) to construct lines from the District of Columbia through Richmond, Raleigh, Columbia, S.C., and Macon to the Crescent City. Despite the greater construction costs ($200 per mile) and the technological problems involved in operating so lengthy a telegraph line, the Washington–to–New Orleans connection was completed by July, 1848, with spur lines connecting it with Charleston, S.C., and Savannah.

Meanwhile, in the Mississippi River valley, vigorous competition between two separate companies marked construction of two almost parallel telegraph lines from the Ohio River to New Orleans. After considerable maneuvering in the courts and legislatures of area states and a race between the construction crews of the two companies, both lines were fully operational by the summer of 1849. Thus, by the time Congress was debating the provisions of the COMPROMISE OF 1850, virtually all parts of the South enjoyed a line of almost instant communication with the nation's capital and with all major centers of commerce and industry.

The need to transmit messages across the lines of separate companies and the costly duplication of lines seeking to serve the same communities gave telegraphy an inherent drive toward consolidation. The first of the major consolidations occurred in 1852, when the two Mississippi Valley

companies agreed upon a plan of cooperative management. By 1860, the two corporations were thoroughly merged as the Southwestern Telegraph Company headed by Dr. Norvin Green of Kentucky. Two years later several midwestern lines were merged to form what became known as Western Union. And in 1856 Kendall's Magnetic, his Washington & New Orleans, and several northeastern lines were united by purchase or by lease to form what became in 1859 the American Telegraph Company. Under the control of this company, all lines of the old Washington & New Orleans Company were totally rewired. Thus the South began the Civil War with exceptionally efficient telegraphic communications along the trunk line of the Eastern Seaboard.

Secession literally severed the communications network of the American Telegraph Company. Its southern properties were organized as the Confederate Telegraph Company, headed by Dr. William S. Morris, a major southern stockholder in the parent company. Together with the trunk lines of Dr. Green's Southwestern Company, the Confederacy had a U-shaped network of trunk lines running south from Nashville and from Richmond to New Orleans. Although Confederate Postmaster General J. H. REAGAN was given nominal control over all telegraph lines within the South, his deputy was Dr. Morris. Thus operation of telegraphic lines was left largely under private control. Moreover, while the Union army built approximately 15,000 miles of military lines, the Confederate army supplemented private lines with no more than 1,000 miles of military wire. And, despite the destruction of communications systems during the war, all major telegraphic lines in the South were back in operation by the fall of 1865.

The wartime cooperation of the Southwestern and the Confederate Telegraph companies undoubtedly assisted in yet another round of consolidations after the war. In 1865, after Confederate had rejoined its parent American Telegraph Company, the Southwestern and American companies were merged. Meanwhile, Western Union had unified all of the major lines of the Middle and Far West into a single company. The final step toward consolidation was taken in 1866, when the two remaining giants of telegraphy themselves merged, taking the name Western Union. Suspicion of this northern-based company and dissatisfaction with its rates and service caused southern farm groups and Progressives to work for public regulation or government ownership of the telegraph monopoly.

In sharp contrast to the early completion of

southern telegraphic communications, the development of telephonic communications within the South has lagged far behind the pace of the rest of the nation. Telephone systems in the North developed first in the major cities, and the South's slower rate of URBANIZATION early in the twentieth century undoubtedly contributed to a tardier acquisition of telephones. Also, given the South's lower per capita INCOME, the cost of the luxury of a home phone probably slowed the development of telephone systems still more. Indeed, as late as 1969, only four southern states (Delaware, Florida, Maryland, and Missouri) had as many or more phones per 100 persons as the national average (56.7 phones per 100 persons). Alabama, Kentucky, and North Carolina (42 phones per 100 persons); Arkansas, South Carolina, and West Virginia (40 phones per 100 persons); and Mississippi (35 phones per 100 persons) trailed far behind the national average. Surely, the telephone and the telegraph deserve the serious consideration of scholars anxious to explain the economic, cultural, and social development of the South.

See R. L. Thompson, *Wiring a Continent, 1832–1866* (1947); H. Coon, *American Telephone & Telegraph* (1939); N. R. Danielian, *American Telephone & Telegraph* (1939); A. F. Harlow, *Old Wires and New Waves* (1936); and W. J. Harder, *Daniel Drawbaugh* (1960). Pertinent manuscript collections include Henry O'Reilly Papers, New-York Historical Society, very important; Amos Kendall Papers and S. F. B. Morse Papers, Library of Congress, little on southern telegraph. See also U.S. Census Bureau, *Telegraph and Telephone* (1902) and *Telegraphs* (1907).

TELLICO BLOCKHOUSE in Tennessee was the most important of three federal posts established in 1794 for frontier defense in the old Southwest. It was located on the Little Tennessee River, not far from the site of Ft. Loudon and 30 miles southwest of Knoxville. It was sufficiently strong to withstand a siege if the attackers lacked cannon. In 1795 a "factory" for trade with the CHEROKEE Nation was established at Tellico, and four treaties (1798–1805) for Cherokee land cessions were concluded there. In 1797 it was the Tellico post factor who first uncovered and exposed the "Blount conspiracy" (WILLIAM BLOUNT). The blockhouse was closed in 1806, and its troops were moved to Hiwassee Garrison.

See S. J. Folmsbee *et al.*, *Tennessee* (1969); F. P. Prucha, *Guide to Military Posts of U.S.* (1964); and J. G. M. Ramsay, *Annals of Tennessee* (1853).

RICHARD G. STONE, JR.
Western Kentucky University

TEMPERANCE MOVEMENT in the South moved to the same rhythms as its northern counterpart. It made three appearances upon the stage of southern history—in the late 1820s and early 1830s, in the 1840s and 1850s, and again in the 1870s and 1880s—before undergoing a final metamorphosis into prohibitionism. A movement headed by white men, it was accompanied throughout by an unaccustomed performer upon the public stage, the southern woman. It refused, however, to share the spotlight with black performers and because of this never achieved full cooperation with other troupes who did. Like many warm-up acts, it probably contributed to the triumph of its successor PROHIBITION; but the precise extent of its influence has not yet been gauged.

Although temperance societies have been discovered as early as 1813, they first appeared in appreciable numbers in the seaboard states during the late 1820s. By the mid-1830s, these early societies had spread into every state, counted at least 350 local affiliates, and enrolled more than 20,000 people. Often they were formed by Baptist, Methodist, or Presbyterian ministers, at least partly to counteract excessive drinking among their flocks. Administering a pledge that proscribed only distilled spirits, the early societies served for many as an introduction to the merits of total abstinence. Others considered teetotalism too radical a step, however, and by the mid-1830s disputes over this issue, as well as the alleged connection between the northern temperance movement and abolitionism, had sundered or vitiated southern temperance societies.

Revival of the temperance movement on a total abstinence basis began on April 2, 1840, in a Baltimore tavern, when six drinkers initiated a new movement, the Washingtonians. During the next four years, Washingtonian orators pledged thousands in both North and South. It was left to others, however, to consolidate the gains made by the charismatic Washingtonians. The chief among these was the Sons of Temperance, a secret benevolent and fraternal organization, which, by the time it reached its peak in the early 1850s, boasted at least 50,000 members in 1,300 local chapters in eight states of both Upper and Lower South. Other organizations of the antebellum period included the Independent Order of Good Templars, Daughters of Temperance, Cadets of Temperance (for adolescent boys), Templars of Honor and Temperance, Catholic Total Abstinence Union, Cold Water Army (for children), and Friends of Temperance, as well as several smaller orders. Even when supplemented by such organizations, the moral suasionist approach seemed inadequate, and so temperance folk turned to demands for restrictive and prohibitory legislation, both before and after the example of the Maine law of 1851, but with little success. All such efforts were brought to an end by the outbreak of war, and prohibitory legislation under the Confederacy owed more to the needs of wartime production than to the force of temperance sentiment.

Emancipation exposed the paternalism of the southern temperance movement. Southerners began to revive the Sons of Temperance after the war, but gave up the effort after the national body took a stand against segregation in 1871. The IOGT, an international group, then became the South's leading organization, with affiliates in every state by 1876. Northern Good Templars proved amenable to southern demands for segregated chapters, but English Good Templars did not, and the conflict over the South's peculiar system split the order (1876–1887). Nevertheless, in the South in 1880 there were 62,270 white Good Templars of both sexes, in addition to 5,740 segregated black members; together they made up 22 percent of the order's international membership.

After 1874, and especially after organizing tours by the national president Frances E. Willard in 1880–1883, the WOMAN'S CHRISTIAN TEMPERANCE UNION joined the Good Templars in the vanguard of southern temperance forces. Again, temperance folk turned to the state for aid, and the WCTU gained considerable success in securing legislation requiring "scientific" temperance instruction in the public schools. By the time Georgia became the first southern state to adopt prohibition in 1907, this resort to political action had made the temperance movement into a prohibition movement.

See H. A. Scomp, *King Alcohol in Realm of King Cotton* (1888); E. H. Cherrington (ed.), *Standard Encyclopedia of Alcohol Problem* (6 vols.; 1924–30); J. A. Krout, *Origins of Prohibition* (1925), best scholarly study of antebellum period; T. F. Parker, *History of I.O.G.T.* (1882); J. B. Sellers, *Prohibition in Alabama* (1943); D. J. Whitener, *Prohibition in North Carolina* (1945); and C. C. Pearson and J. E. Hendricks, *Liquor in Virginia* (1967).

JACK S. BLOCKER, JR.
Huron College, Ontario

TENANT FARMING became common to southern commercial agriculture after 1865. Farm tenants as a proportion of all farm operators increased to 55 percent in 1930. The absolute number reached a maximum of 1,700,814 in 1935 and thereafter declined. The 124,676 tenants reported in the 1969 census of agriculture composed less than 12 percent of all farm operators.

The first major source of southern tenants was the former slave populace. After the Civil War many large landowners divided their holdings into subunits, which were worked by tenants. The SHARECROPPING system became most common. Landlord and sharecropper each received half the crop and paid half the cost of seed and fertilizer. Various other tenant systems required a specified rent, and the tenant normally provided his own equipment and supplies. The rural white population became the second source of tenants. Rural whites found it increasingly difficult to move into a landowning class in an agrarian economic system where little additional land was available. As a result, by 1930 white tenant families even slightly outnumbered black. The geographic distribution of tenancy evolved in close correspondence with the old southern COTTON- and TOBACCO-producing regions.

Most tenants were landless peasants who accomplished little more than subsistence. CROP LIEN laws and debts owed the landlord assured that minimum cash income was realized, often less than $100 annually. The system inhibited cash flow and indirectly restricted the growth of regional markets, which might have stimulated earlier industrial growth. Social and biologic consequences were equally severe. By 1935 the South contained an excessive rural population with low education levels and poor dietary and health conditions.

The demise of traditional tenancy occurred during the 1940s and 1950s. In varying degrees the BOLL WEEVIL, the attraction of cities, new job opportunities, mechanization, and government controls on agriculture all contributed to the decline. Since World War II a modern tenant variant evolved even as croppers and other tenants were disappearing. Although numerically not great, the modern tenant accounts for a significant part of the southern production of tobacco, cotton, SOYBEANS, PEANUTS, and SUGARCANE. He is typically a landowner with capital, who therefore can expand his agricultural operation by renting additional land. The connotation of the modern tenant is in complete contrast to the traditional tenant varieties who preceded the 1940s.

The single most useful source of data on tenancy is the U.S. census of agriculture. Farms have been enumerated by tenure of operator since 1880; distinctions have been made as to "color and race" since 1900. Numerous items are available relating to a variety of tenant subgroups, such as cash tenants, share cash tenants, crop share tenants, livestock share tenants, and sharecroppers. The modern tenant, though not specifically recognized in census publications, is best analyzed with data on "part owners."

See T. J. Woofter *et al.*, *Landlord and Tenant on Cotton Plantation* (1946); J. S. Fisher, *Southeastern Geographer* (Nov., 1970); and C. S. Aiken, *Southeastern Geographer* (April, 1971).

JAMES S. FISHER
University of Georgia

TENNESSEE consists of 42,244 square miles and ranks thirty-fourth in size among the 50 states. It extends 432 miles from the mountains on the east to the Mississippi River on the west and about one-fifth that distance north to south. The eastern and western borders are natural, but the north and south lines were poorly surveyed and have been subjects of periodic controversy. Within these boundaries Tennesseans have recognized three "Grand Divisions"—east, middle, and west—defined by the general assembly and recognized in the state constitution.

Geography. Topographically, Tennessee is divided into six major and two minor physiographic regions. The major regions are sections of larger ones that extend beyond the borders of the state. The easternmost region is the Unaka Mountain range, part of the APPALACHIANS, covering about 2,600 square miles with several peaks of more than 6,000 feet in elevation. Just west of the Unakas lies the great valley of east Tennessee, a part of the ridge and valley segment of the Appalachians. It covers about 9,200 square miles, gradually slopes from the northeast to the southwest, and includes the Clinch Mountains. The creation of TVA has brought several dams and numerous artificial lakes. Rich in minerals, it includes the cities of Knoxville, Chattanooga, and Oak Ridge, where considerable manufacturing has developed. The CUMBERLAND PLATEAU, called "the Wilderness" by early settlers because of sparse population and limited agricultural opportunities, is the third region. It covers 5,400 square miles and lies west of the great valley. COAL MINING has been a principal activity, and stone from the Crab Orchard Mountains has been a source of income for many years.

The fourth and fifth physiographic regions are the highland rim and the central basin. The rim completely encircles the basin. As Joseph Killebrew, late nineteenth-century writer and public official, observed in 1874, the basin is as "the bottom of an oval dish, of which the Highlands form the broad, flat brim," and was "the center of wealth and political influence and rich in all the elements

of a splendid civilization." The basin covers about 5,500 square miles, and the rim is about twice as large. The basin contains some of the state's richest soil and always has been a productive agricultural area. Before the Civil War, much COTTON was produced, but during the past hundred years that crop has been replaced by grains, TOBACCO, and livestock as the principal money-makers. In the rim, cotton remains a major crop in the southern counties, and tobacco is produced in such abundance in the northern counties that Tennessee is one of the leading producers among the 50 states. The basin, drained by the Cumberland, Elk, and Duck rivers, includes Nashville, Franklin, Clarksville, Murfreesboro, and Columbia among its major cities.

Lying west of the highland rim and across the TENNESSEE RIVER is the sixth region, the Gulf coastal plain of west Tennessee, which covers about 9,000 square miles. A great plain that slopes gradually toward the Mississippi River, it is drained by the Forked Deer, Obion, and Hatchie among other rivers of the area. The southern part of the region has produced cotton in abundance for 150 years and, before the Civil War, made Tennessee the leading cotton producer outside the Deep South. The principal cities are Memphis and Jackson, the former of which for 150 years has been a major cotton center and today is one of the world's leading cottonseed-processing centers.

The two minor regions also are in west Tennessee. The western valley of the Tennessee River lies just to the west of the rim, and the floodplain of the Mississippi River (sometimes called the Mississippi bottoms) lies between the Gulf coastal plain and the Mississippi River.

Early exploration and settlement. Spanish, French, and English explorers and traders were in Tennessee well over 200 years before Europeans established permanent settlements. HERNANDO DE SOTO explored as early as 1540, and he was followed by such Frenchmen as Jacques Marquette, Louis Jolliet, and LA SALLE. Englishmen were not far behind; by the mid-1700s, hundreds had explored the tramontane country west of Virginia and North Carolina. These LONG HUNTERS, who came seeking pelts and furs, were a peculiar breed: fiercely independent, inured to hardship, and unwilling to remain long in any civilized community. Perhaps the best known was DANIEL BOONE, who by 1760 had found his way into present-day Washington County and carved his name and accomplishments on a beech tree. With the conclusion of the FRENCH AND INDIAN WAR in 1763, many people of the Piedmont, intrigued by the

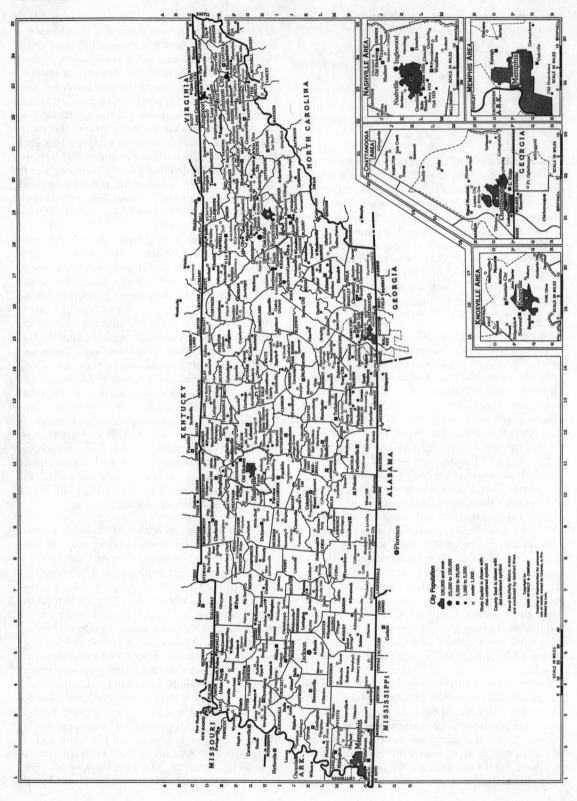

glowing reports of economic potentialities in the West, crossed the Alleghenies. Elisha Walden, for whom a mountain range was named, was among those who led a group of some 20 hunters from Virginia just as the war ended; and a short time later others who left their names on the pages of Tennessee's history—Uriah Stone, Isaac Lindsey, James Harrod, and Michael Stoner, to mention a few—had penetrated the wilderness to the Cumberland Valley.

By the late 1760s people were building one-room log cabins in the secluded valley between the Cumberland Mountains and the Great Smokies. A band of exploring soldiers, who in December, 1768, had traversed the area and found nothing "but a howling wilderness," were amazed early in 1769 to find cabins "on every spot where the range was good." In the two decades that followed, people came in such large numbers that by 1791 more than 35,000 lived on the soil that in five years would become the state of Tennessee.

By the time of the Revolution, two major areas of settlement had developed. The larger of the two was along the Watauga, Nolichucky, and Holston rivers in the northeastern corner of what would become Tennessee. By 1772 its leaders had organized the WATAUGA ASSOCIATION, a "homespun government" born of necessity in the wilderness. The second area—the fertile land of the Cumberland Basin—though explored years earlier, was not settled until the Revolution was well under way. In 1779 James Robertson, in the employ of RICHARD HENDERSON and other investors who composed the TRANSYLVANIA COMPANY, led a group of settlers through CUMBERLAND GAP into Kentucky country along a trail blazed by Daniel Boone and then turned southward to the FRENCH LICK, which he promptly christened Nashborough. Finding a beautiful country well drained by the Cumberland and lesser streams and virgin forests full of wild game, Robertson planted crops and built cabins. In the following spring (1780) he was joined by others, principally wives and children of those who already had reached the Cumberland. These people came by flatboat down the Tennessee River and up the Cumberland under the direction of John Donelson.

Scarcely were guns stacked after the Revolution when tramontane leaders began to talk of separate statehood. They were aware of a provision in the North Carolina constitution of 1776 that provided for eventual statehood for western lands, and they knew of Thomas Jefferson's plan whereby the western country would be divided into 18 states, one of which would comprise the western counties of North Carolina and Virginia. In 1782 some

had listened with interest to another Virginian, Arthur Campbell, whose plan was similar to Jefferson's. Therefore, when in June, 1784, North Carolina ceded to the central government its lands consisting of present-day Tennessee, western leaders moved swiftly. Within a few weeks, they had assembled in Jonesboro, where they selected JOHN SEVIER as chairman, resolved to draft a constitution, and otherwise made preparations for statehood. When the North Carolina legislature in the meantime rescinded the act of cession, frustrated westerners decided to continue their separation movement and therefore proclaimed the "free state of FRANKLIN." Sevier was chosen the governor, a general assembly was convened, and Governor Alexander Martin of North Carolina was informed that the westerners had exercised their "inalienable right" to form "an independent state." When efforts at reconciliation failed, two factions developed in Franklin that ultimately sounded the death knell of the infant state. John Tipton rose in defiance of Sevier, was elected to the North Carolina legislature, and then used his powers to enforce the laws of North Carolina. Border warfare developed, and several men were killed or wounded.

When Governor Sevier's term expired in 1788, the Franklin movement ended for all practical purposes. Sevier was arrested on charges of treason but was never tried. He immediately took an oath of allegiance to North Carolina, was elected to the North Carolina senate, and returned to his former position as brigadier general of the western district. Although unsuccessful, Franklin has continued to be symbolic of a strong spirit of independence by which Tennesseans to this day are characterized. Indeed, historian Eric Lacy has ably pointed to "persistent Franklinism" as being present in Tennessee affairs to this very day.

The new state in the new nation. Franklin failed, but the North Carolina legislature ratified the federal Constitution in November, 1789, and a few weeks later again ceded the western lands to the central government. In May, 1790, George Washington signed into law a measure providing for a government for the new territory and a few weeks later appointed WILLIAM BLOUNT, a frontier speculator he had known in the Constitutional Convention of 1787, as territorial governor. Blount assumed the office with characteristic vigor and soon established his home and territorial capital at White's Fort, which he renamed Knoxville, for Secretary of War Henry Knox.

The Southwest Territory (as the new territory came to be called) consisted of nearly 43,000 square miles. The eastern valley settlements, divided into the counties of Washington, Greene, Sullivan, and Hawkins, had a population of about 28,000. The Cumberland area, consisting of Davidson, Sumner, and Tennessee counties, had about one-fourth that number. More than 100 miles of wilderness separated the two settlements, but Blount kept in touch with political leaders in both, particularly Sevier in the east and James Robertson at Nashville.

Participation in territorial affairs whetted the desires of western leaders for statehood. When Blount called the legislature into special session in 1795 to suggest statehood, he found warm agreement among the lawmakers. The legislators provided for a referendum on the question, which resulted in a strong expression for statehood. A convention was called to meet in Knoxville in January, 1796, and the members drafted a constitution and then appealed to Congress for admission. After several weeks of debate in Congress, with Jeffersonian Republicans successfully countering seaboard Federalist opposition, Tennessee was admitted as the sixteenth state on June 1, 1796. John Sevier was elected governor, William Blount and William Cocke became U.S. senators, and ANDREW JACKSON became the federal representative.

Sevier was a frontier hero well suited, according to western standards, for the governor's office. Elected again in 1797 and in 1799, the Indian fighter, in respect for the constitution, did not run in 1801 but waited until 1803, when he was returned to office by a sound majority in spite of a strong opponent, incumbent Archibald Roane, who boasted the support of Andrew Jackson. He was reelected in 1805 and 1807, then went to Congress, where in 1811 he joined HENRY CLAY, JOHN C. CALHOUN, FELIX GRUNDY, and others in advocating war with England.

The popular Sevier thus dominated Tennessee politics for the first two decades of statehood. Substantial growth and development occurred during that time. The population, about 85,000 in 1796, had tripled when his term expired in 1809. Thousands of people from Virginia and North Carolina entered the state through the Cumberland Gap, but many others came from Pennsylvania and other seaboard states through the gap or directly into the Cumberland territory from Kentucky. The fertile lands around Nashville and the central basin attracted many, so that by 1809 more than 60 percent of the state's population lived in middle Tennessee, as contrasted with only 30 percent ten years earlier. Nashville and Knoxville became thriving frontier towns while Sevier was governor,

each boasting of one or more newspapers, a dozen stores and taverns, sawmills and flour mills, and churches of the BAPTIST, METHODIST, and PRESBYTERIAN denominations. Montgomery Bell purchased from James Robertson the Cumberland Iron Works in Dickson County in 1803 and soon assumed a position as the leading iron producer of the South (IRON AND STEEL INDUSTRY). Land titles were a subject of major controversy, and in 1803, when Andrew Jackson accused Governor Sevier of obtaining thousands of acres for himself by fraud and bribery and referred to him in the Knoxville and Nashville newspapers as "a base coward and poltroon," Sevier was ready to fight him in a duel "outside the neighborhood of Knoxville." While citizens argued over titles, the state government became embroiled in difficulties with North Carolina and the federal government over the right to sell public lands in the state. Finally, in 1806, a "compact" was agreed upon whereby North Carolina's claims made prior to cession would be satisfied and the federal government could dispose of all the ungranted lands west of the Mississippi and in the southwest corner of middle Tennessee, which came to be called the "congressional reservation."

Willie Blount (a half-brother of William Blount) replaced Sevier as governor, and it was during his term that Tennessee became known as the Volunteer State because of its participation in the WAR OF 1812. Tennesseans were not concerned so much about European wars, blockades, orders in council, or sailors' rights, but they became aroused when they heard reports of a giant conspiracy, engineered by the British in Canada and aided by Spaniards in Florida, to unite the northern and southern Indians in a war on the American frontier. The only safe thing to do was to drive the Europeans from the American shores and add their lands to the United States. Congressman Felix Grundy, representing the Nashville district, well expressed this sentiment when he exclaimed in 1811 on the floor of the House: "I therefore feel anxious not only to add the Floridas to the South, but the Canadas to the North of this empire." News of the declaration of war against Great Britain, adopted June 18, 1812, reached Tennessee just in time to make the celebration of Independence Day a riotous occasion.

Thousands of Tennesseans volunteered for military service. General James Winchester led a small contingent to participate in the ineffectual efforts to invade Canada, but most of the fighting by Tennesseans was against the southern Indians until the battle of NEW ORLEANS in January, 1815. Jackson led 2,000 volunteers to Natchez and earned the sobriquet "Old Hickory" in the process. War against the CREEK INDIANS, particularly Jackson's victory at Horseshoe Bend in March, 1814, brought national attention to Tennessee. When peace was agreed upon at Ghent on December 24, 1814, not only Jackson, but other Tennesseans including DAVID CROCKETT, William Carroll, and SAM HOUSTON emerged as military heroes whose newly achieved reputations would pave the way to political success.

Jacksonian domination of Tennessee politics. Perhaps no more controversial figure than Andrew Jackson has appeared on the American scene. Contemporaries seldom were neutral where he was concerned; his friends loved him devotedly, and his enemies hated him with passion. Born in the Waxhaw country along the border of North Carolina and South Carolina, Jackson came to the Tennessee country in 1788 with John McNairy, who had been appointed judge for the Cumberland district. He settled in Nashville, secured a room at the boardinghouse of Mrs. John Donelson, became a successful lawyer and attorney general, and courted Mrs. Donelson's daughter Rachel, who had returned to her mother after separation from her Kentucky husband Lewis Robards. Jackson and Rachel soon were married, even before her divorce decree had been issued, and this act of technical bigamy was to haunt Jackson for the remainder of his political life. The fiery frontier lawyer and soldier soon became embroiled in a variety of quarrels, duels, and brawls, which on occasion almost cost him his life; he was elected to the state court of law and equity, the federal Congress, and the Senate, none of which offices he held for the full elected term. Yet his friends immediately attached political significance to his national prominence as the hero of New Orleans. The seat of political control in the nation remained in the East, but ambitious westerners looked to the time when a president might emerge from one of the tramontane states. General William Carroll, a Nashville merchant who had served under Jackson at New Orleans, personally visited politicians in a half-dozen western states and reported warm support for Jackson. A group of Tennessee politicians, hoping for their own political success as well as that of Jackson, coalesced in Nashville with a plan of pushing Jackson into high elective office and riding into power on the chief's coattails. They considered running him for the presidency in 1820 but retreated after learning of the widespread popularity of President James Monroe. Jackson in the meantime had built a military road from Nashville to New Orleans, which

served to expand Columbia, Lawrenceburg, and other Tennessee communities, suppressed the rogues in Spanish Florida, and facilitated the purchase of Florida. He built a fashionable home outside Nashville called the Hermitage, where he regularly conferred with his friends and supporters.

The Jacksonians determined to push the hero's candidacy for the presidency in 1824; but first they considered whether to offer him for the office of governor or that of U.S. senator, either of which would serve as a stepping-stone to the presidency in 1824. They received considerable encouragement when in July, 1822, the Tennessee legislature nominated him for president. In the following year they agreed, apparently just before the time for election, to offer Jackson's candidacy for the U.S. Senate against incumbent John Williams of Knoxville. Jackson won by a comfortable majority. His abortive race for the presidency in 1824 (ELECTION OF 1824) and his subsequent successes in the ELECTION OF 1828 and the ELECTION OF 1832 are well known.

Jackson's success pushed many Tennesseans into national prominence and for a while rendered Jackson a charismatic hero beloved from Memphis to Bristol. But his success tended to factionalize state politics. When strong national opposition began to crystallize in 1835 in the form of the WHIG PARTY, Tennesseans who had differed with Jackson or who through the years had had little or no admiration for him were in the forefront of the new national party. Jackson's treatment of Calhoun and Clay had alienated Tennesseans who admired the South Carolinian and the Kentuckian; his handling of the Bank of the United States had rebuffed financiers; and his determination to back Martin Van Buren in the ELECTION OF 1836 had chipped away at his foundation of support from the common man in Tennessee. JOHN BELL, a prominent Nashville lawyer and congressman, led the opposition and urged Tennesseans to vote for HUGH LAWSON WHITE for president on the Whig ticket instead of for Van Buren. Although Jackson campaigned in Tennessee for Van Buren and helped to secure his election to the presidency, voters rebuffed the old hero and cast the state's electoral votes for White instead. For the next 16 years, Whigs successfully challenged Jackson's Democrats for control of Tennessee and the reins of national power. The hero did live to see JAMES K. POLK elected to the governorship in 1839 and to the presidency in 1844, even though Polk was defeated in his bid for reelection as governor and failed to win the electoral vote of Tennessee in the presidential election.

The Jackson period was one of substantial development and progress within the state. The population of 422,823 in 1820 had nearly doubled by 1840. The title to west Tennessee had been cleared, Memphis was developing into a leading cotton center on the Mississippi, and cotton and tobacco flourished. Because of the spread of cotton cultivation across the central and southern part of middle and west Tennessee, the slave population, 80,000 in 1820, had more than doubled two decades later. A variety of reforms made life more tolerable for many people—with the exception of the CHEROKEE INDIANS, who were forcibly removed from their holdings in southeastern Tennessee and northern Georgia.

General William Carroll was elected governor in 1821. Except for a two-year period (1827–1829) when Sam Houston served, Carroll conducted an enlightened administration until he was defeated in 1835 for an unprecedented seventh term by an anti-Jacksonian named Newton Cannon. When Carroll was elected, the penal codes needed revision, county jails were inadequate, and a central prison—a "penitentiary house," Carroll said—was needed. Nothing was being done to help the insane. In addition, calls for revision of the constitution of 1796 were increasing.

Legislators quarreled during much of the 1820s over reforms. Why should taxpayers' money be used for "plush surroundings" for criminals, some said; the whipping post, branding iron, and public hangings served as deterrents to crime. Although in 1825 Carroll assembled from Virginia, Pennsylvania, New York, and Maryland considerable information on enlightened attitudes toward criminals and insane people, it was not until 1829 that legislators appropriated the necessary funds for a penitentiary and substituted imprisonment at hard labor for the pillory, stocks, whipping post, branding iron, and other more vicious methods of punishment (PENAL SYSTEMS). By 1831 a penitentiary, located one mile west of Nashville, was in operation where convicts, in addition to hard labor on the prison farm, could learn a trade in hat making, tailoring, carpentry, and other useful skills.

Dorothea Dix, famed crusader for more humane treatment of the mentally ill, visited Tennessee on several occasions and expressed her amazement that so little was being done for the insane (MENTAL HEALTH). It was 1832 before money was appropriated for a state hospital for the insane and several years later before an asylum was completed and placed in operation. TEMPERANCE was a matter to which others gave attention. Governor Carroll condemned excessive drinking and believed that "too free use of ardent spirits" was the main cause of crime. Several temperance societies were organized in the state in the 1820s, and some published newspapers designed (as wrote the editor of the Maryville *Temperance Banner*) to save "husbands and fathers from . . . the horrors of a drunkard's life." Others turned their attention to the abolition of slavery. A strong movement developed in the constitutional convention of 1834 to give the legislature power to emancipate enslaved blacks. Colonization and emancipation societies flourished for a while, principally in east and middle Tennessee. Still other people sought to help the blind, the deaf, the poor, and other unfortunates.

Constitutional reform, accomplished in the convention of 1834, definitely benefited the common man. Henceforth taxes would be apportioned according to the assessed value of land and therefore more equitably than before. Property qualifications were removed as a condition for holding office. County officers would be selected by the qualified voters instead of by the justices of the peace. Divorces henceforth would be granted only by the courts and not by the legislature.

Many Tennesseans turned their attention to lands in Texas in the 1820s and 1830s. The desire for cheap land was not the only reason. The PANIC OF 1819 had bankrupted some who had borrowed too heavily; others like Davy Crockett, who had been defeated politically, or Sam Houston, who had had domestic problems, hoped to make a new start on the frontier. Still others loved adventure and, believing society east of the Mississippi had become static, sought adventure in the Spanish lands of the West. When Mexico gained independence and Texas lands were opened for settlement to Americans in 1821, thousands of Tennesseans rushed there to take up lands. When Texas raised the banner of revolt in 1835, Tennesseans were in the forefront. Leaders included not only Crockett and Houston, but also a Nashville lawyer named George Campbell Childress, who wrote the Texas declaration of independence; Thomas J. Hardeman, a great-uncle of James K. Polk; and William H. Wharton. The annexation of Texas in 1845 was due in no small measure to the efforts of Congressman John Bell and Senator Hugh Lawson White in keeping before Congress many petitions signed by Tennesseans urging annexation.

Partisan fury, 1835–1855. The late state historian and author, Robert H. White, has referred to the two decades 1835–1855 as a period of "partisan fury" in Tennessee politics. It has been the only time in the state's history that a two-party system has functioned so effectively. The Whigs, largely former Democrats who had become disillusioned with Jackson, had elected Newton Cannon governor in 1835 and carried the state for Hugh L. White in the presidential election of 1836. Polk's decision to surrender his congressional seat in 1839 and seek the governorship returned the Jacksonians to temporary control, but Whig James C. Jones twice defeated Polk in close contests in 1841 and 1843. For the next decade the parties alternated control of the governor's office until the Democrats acquired firm control in the election of AN-DREW JOHNSON in 1853. Competition was so intense that in each gubernatorial election only a few hundred votes separated the winner from the loser; indeed, from 1839 to 1855 neither party won as much as 52 percent of the total vote in any gubernatorial election. Governor Aaron V. Brown, for example, won the governorship in 1845 with 50.6 percent of the total vote but lost it two years later when he won only 49.6 percent of the votes. Historian Brian G. Walton has estimated that the level of participation among Tennessee voters reached on some occasions as high as 93 percent, so intense was the political interest within the state.

The center of Democratic control was in middle Tennessee, where Democrats consistently controlled 20 counties to only eight for the Whigs. But east Tennessee and west Tennessee were the Whig strongholds; when Democrats James K. Polk, Andrew Johnson, and others won, they counted on a heavy vote in the middle section to offset that of the east and west. "Parson" WILLIAM G. BROWN-LOW, prominent Elizabethton Whig, in 1841 warmly endorsed a legislative plan to create from the east Tennessee counties a "State of Frankland"; such, wrote the parson, represented the "last hope of freedom from the Nashville yoke."

Both Whigs and Democrats claimed direct descent from Jefferson, professed to have only the best interests of the masses at heart, and accused each other of undermining democratic principles. In the campaigns, both invariably argued national instead of local issues. The bank question, internal improvements at national expense, and the protective tariff were matters of major concern. Democrats, historian J. Milton Henry has written, generally were "dynamic and radical"; Whigs were conservative. Tennessee Whigs, centering in the urban counties, generally were wealthier than Democrats and more identified with commerce and a plantation economy. Although Democrats under Polk hailed expansion as the *summum bonum*, Tennessee Whigs were generally indifferent to expansion and even carried the state for Henry Clay in the presidential election of 1844 over the expansionist from Columbia, Polk. But no single factor explains the political pattern; personalities, as much as anything else, often determined the outcome of an election.

The state at mid-century—social and economic developments. At mid-century most of the people were farmers; indeed, nearly 120,000 families tilled Tennessee soil. Although corn, wheat, and other grains were raised, cotton and tobacco were the chief money crops. The increase in cotton production paralleled that of the Deep South. Tennessee had an annual cotton crop of 2,500 bales in 1810; in 1850 the sale of 194,532 bales was exceeded only by that of the states of Alabama, Georgia, Mississippi, and South Carolina. Tobacco was raised mainly in the northern rim counties, and at mid-century the state's production was exceeded only by that of Kentucky, Maryland, and Virginia. Livestock herds were numbered in the thousands. In 1854 Mark Cockrill, a Davidson County SHEEP raiser, won first premium at the World's Fair in London for the "finest wool in the world." For two decades farmers experimented with SILK, placing more than 1,000 pounds on the market in 1840, but at mid-century interest had declined so that none at all was produced after 1860.

Although most people tilled the soil, some made a living at industry. For more than a half-century Tennesseans produced such quantities of iron that in 1850 the state ranked just behind Pennsylvania and New York in pig iron production. Sawmills and flour mills were operated in every community, and more than a dozen towns supported small textile mills.

The economy was closely geared to transportation. Steamboats were in use by the 1820s, and before that farmers and iron producers would float cargoes down the Tennessee and Cumberland into the Ohio and Mississippi rivers and thence to markets at New Orleans. In the 1830s and 1840s turnpikes were built connecting major towns. It was the decade of the 1850s before locomotives operated successfully, but ultimately the roster of RAILROADS included the Louisville & Nashville and the Memphis & Charlestown, both major lines across the South.

Presbyterians were first to establish churches in Tennessee, but Baptists, Methodists, and other groups were not far behind. The GREAT AWAKEN-ING of 1800 was responsible for considerable denominational growth and, more particularly, the formation of the Cumberland Presbyterian church. This frontier group, having its origins in Dickson County, soon exceeded the regular Presbyterians in churches and members. At mid-century more than a dozen separate Christian groups had been established in all parts of the state, in addition to Jewish congregations (JEWS) in Memphis and Nashville.

Many of the preachers conducted schools during the week. The first educational establishment west of the mountains was a one-room school begun in 1780 by the Reverend Samuel Doak in what is now Washington County. Five years later the North Carolina legislature chartered Davidson Academy in Nashville, a school established by the Reverend Thomas Craighead. In 1794 the territorial legislature chartered Blount College in Knoxville and Greeneville College at Greeneville. Efforts at public education generally were unsuccessful, but academies—male and female—flourished. Several colleges had been established at mid-century. Blount College had blossomed into East Tennessee University and Davidson into the University of Nashville. Cumberland University, established at Lebanon by Cumberland Presbyterians, had a law department as well as a liberal arts program and during the 1850s developed schools of theology and engineering. Bethel College at McLemoresville, Tusculum at Greeneville, Southwestern at Clarksville, and Union at Murfreesboro were among other colleges operating by 1850.

Secession, Civil War, and Reconstruction. Tennesseans did not escape the sectional controversies of the 1850s. The WILMOT PROVISO was denounced by the legislature, and leading politicians were active in the NASHVILLE CONVENTION, which met in 1850 to consider their position with respect to the Union. Legislators denounced William H. Seward as a traitor to the nation for his speech in 1858 in which he predicted ultimate war between the sections, and John Brown's HARPERS FERRY RAID in the following year shocked slaveholders and nonslaveholders alike.

The presidential ELECTION OF 1860 brought forth sectional candidates and paved the way for the formation by the old Whigs of a national party, which they called the CONSTITUTIONAL UNION PARTY. Although Sam Houston, then the governor of Texas, was a leading contender for nomination, Tennessee Senator John Bell became the party's standard-bearer. The campaign was a bitter one. Southern Democrat JOHN BRECKINRIDGE ran well in the state, but Bell won all of the state's electoral votes. ABRAHAM LINCOLN's name did not even appear on the ballot in Tennessee.

South Carolina's secession a few weeks after the election disturbed Tennesseans. In early January,

1861, Governor ISHAM G. HARRIS called the general assembly into special session to consider Tennessee's "federal relations." The members agreed that a referendum should be held on which the people might express an opinion on whether to hold a secession convention. On February 9 the people went to the polls and rejected by a firm majority a convention where secession might be discussed.

A profound change in the sentiment of the people occurred within the next few months. Lincoln, inaugurated in March, 1861, determined to hold the federal forts in the South. His decision to reprovision FT. SUMTER and the subsequent reduction of that fort by southern guns on April 13 aroused people throughout the South. But it was Lincoln's call for 75,000 volunteers to suppress "rebellion" that galvanized the people of Tennessee into action. "Tennessee will not furnish a single man" to fight against the southern states, Governor Harris telegraphed Washington authorities, "but 50,000 if necessary for the defense of our rights and those of our Southern brothers." He promptly called the legislature into a second extra session. Without delay, lawmakers established a referendum for June 8, when the people would vote for or against separation from the Union. By that time some of the state's strongest UNIONISTS— former senator John Bell, former postmaster general CAVE JOHNSON, former governor Neill S. Brown, and others—embraced the Confederacy and urged a vote for separation. The vote to secede was overwhelming except in east Tennessee, where people balloted to remain in the Union and then vainly sought to create a separate Union state. Harris, already having given Confederates permission to erect batteries on the Mississippi River, now ordered 10,000 rifles with bayonets from a New Orleans firm and placed General GIDEON PILLOW temporarily in charge of state troops.

ALBERT SIDNEY JOHNSTON, a Texan who as a professional soldier on duty in the Far West had rushed back to join the Confederacy, was placed in charge of the western theater. He promptly established the "line of the Cumberland" from Columbus, Ky., on the Mississippi across Kentucky's southern border to the Cumberland Gap. Just behind the line, he developed Ft. Henry on the Tennessee River and a few miles to the east Ft. Donelson on the Cumberland River, both in Stewart County in middle Tennessee. Johnston, disgusted with middle Tennesseans for not supplying slaves to help in constructing breastworks, was not ready when Ulysses S. Grant appeared with nearly 20,000 soldiers in early February, 1862. Ft. Henry fell to Captain A. H. Foote's gunboats on February 6, and Donelson was surrendered ten days later (FTS. HENRY AND DONELSON CAMPAIGN). Middle and west Tennessee now were opened to the federals, who rode triumphantly into Nashville on February 24, 1862.

Johnston returned to Corinth, Miss., and Grant established federal headquarters at Savannah, Tenn., not far from the Mississippi line. In early April, Johnston moved to the northwest. On April 6 some of his troops stumbled into a federal outpost, and thus the battle of SHILOH began. After the Confederate troops were repulsed, they returned to Corinth, and middle and west Tennessee were again completely in federal hands.

When President Lincoln received word of Grant's significant victory at Donelson, he determined upon a bold course. He would establish a government for the conquered state and place control in the hands of a military governor. East Tennessean Andrew Johnson, who had been elected to the U.S. Senate in 1858 and who had vigorously opposed secession, was named governor, a position he held until inaugurated vice-president in March, 1865. A controversial figure throughout his time of service in the state, Johnson at least "survived," though he was not effective in developing a loyal government as Lincoln had hoped.

In the summer of 1862, BRAXTON BRAGG replaced P. G. T. BEAUREGARD as commander of the Army of Tennessee. After a brief foray into Kentucky, he established his troops near Murfreesboro in October. When General William S. Rosecrans, federal commander in Nashville, heard of this, he decided to drive the Confederates from middle Tennessee. On December 31 the battle of STONES RIVER near Murfreesboro began. After three days of bitter, indecisive fighting, Bragg withdrew and went into winter quarters in the Shelbyville-Wartrace area, some 30 miles southeast of the battlefield.

When spring came, Bragg continued his retreat, with Rosecrans in pursuit. On September 19–20 the battle of CHICKAMAUGA was fought, in which the federals were hurled back to Chattanooga. Bragg's efforts two months later to take CHATTANOOGA resulted in failure, and his defeated men trudged back into Georgia. Blame for failure and ineptitude continued to be placed upon Bragg, and the hapless commander soon was replaced by General JOHN BELL HOOD of Texas, a bold but injudicious young general who already had lost a leg and the use of one arm in the bloody conflict.

Only east Tennessee remained in the hands of the Confederates, and that section fell with the invasion of Ambrose E. Burnside in September, 1863.

Most of the east Tennesseans had remained loyal to the Union and welcomed the federal troops with exhilaration. The war was over in Tennessee except for Hood's bold attempts in the fall of 1864 to dash quickly across Georgia and Alabama into Tennessee and cut General William T. Sherman's supply lines. Hood's imagination exceeded his judgment. He envisioned taking Nashville, moving on to Louisville and Cincinnati, and perhaps even joining Robert E. Lee in Virginia for an assault on Washington. His efforts met with utter failure as his troops were cut to shreds at FRANKLIN (November 30, 1864) and NASHVILLE (December 15–16, 1864).

Johnson's inauguration as vice-president on March 4, 1865, ended the military governorship in Tennessee. Radical leaders had convened in Nashville in January and provided for elections, in which William G. Brownlow soon was chosen governor. Only a small minority of the people voted in the elections—in west Tennessee, for example, elections were held in only one of the 19 counties—but enough participated to meet the 10 percent requirement established by President Lincoln. After Johnson became president, he sought to restore Tennessee to the Union with all deliberate haste despite opposition from congressional Radicals. After the state legislature ratified the Fourteenth Amendment, Johnson signed a congressional resolution on July 23 restoring the state to its former relationship with the Union. The following year, when the Radicals gained control of Congress and enacted the military Reconstruction Act, Tennessee was the only former Confederate state specifically excluded.

Tennessee did, however, remain in the hands of state Radicals until 1869, and this four-year period was Tennessee's Reconstruction. Brownlow, violently hostile to former Confederates, did little to make the adjustment a smooth one. He offered a $5,000 reward for the arrest of the state's secession governor, called upon unreconstructed rebels to leave the state, and, according to a Memphis newspaper editor, expressed "more vituperativeness and scorching hate than any half a dozen men that ever appeared in American politics." Efforts of state Conservatives to defeat him in the gubernatorial election of 1867 failed dismally. Brownlow's election, together with Negro enfranchisement, accelerated KU KLUX KLAN activity and brought about numerous confrontations between that group and state authorities. Describing the Klan as a "dangerous organization of ex-rebels," Brownlow placed a dozen counties under martial law and signed into law a measure providing for stiff penalties for those who "prowl through the country . . . for the purpose of disturbing the peace." The FREEDMEN'S BUREAU apparently was well received in the state by most people except Klan members; this was due in no small measure to the excellent administration of the bureau's Kentucky-Tennessee division by Clinton B. Fisk.

Conservatives gained control of the state government when Brownlow resigned in 1869 to enter the U.S. Senate. DeWitt C. Senter, Speaker of the Senate, succeeded to the governorship and promptly appointed new county registrars, who proceeded to register former Confederates for voting. In the following year a constitutional convention was held, and in 1871 John C. Brown, a former Confederate general, became governor.

Tennessee thus escaped military Reconstruction. But the Brownlow era was one of confusion for Tennesseans and one in which readjustment between former Confederates and Unionists was rendered difficult. Few gains if any were made by educational reformers or by those who sought peaceful adjustment for freedmen. Radicalism encouraged Ku Kluxism, and respect for law and order came slowly. Very few carpetbaggers came into the state. When the Brownlow period ended, the political sentiment in the state remained very much as it had been before the war. Union sentiment in east Tennessee was translated into support for the Republican party, and former Confederates in middle and west Tennessee embraced the Democratic party more warmly. The state-of-Franklin syndrome again threatened the state's unity.

Recovery and expansion, 1870–1900. The majority of the people returned to agriculture as their chief vocation after the war. The production of cotton and tobacco increased, and the number of farms doubled. Railroad construction and general expansion in the cities created a market for timber. William Hull (father of CORDELL HULL) was one of many loggers who cut and floated thousands of logs downstream to sawmills in Nashville and other towns. Declining agricultural prices resulted in GRANGE and FARMERS' ALLIANCE movements, which soon boasted more than 100,000 members. In 1890 Alliance leaders seized control of the Democratic party, nominated JOHN BUCHANAN for governor, and elected him by a substantial majority.

But the agricultural South had been defeated by the industrial North, and many people believed Tennessee's true economic destiny lay in industry. Extensive iron and coal deposits in east Tennessee brought development to that section and also attracted a fair share of northern businessmen and capital. Soon after the war, a Richmond editor, pointing to the iron and steel industry in Knoxville, where by 1870 nearly 20 percent of the business properties were owned by northerners, thought that "no city of the south except Atlanta" had improved so much since Appomattox. Chattanooga by 1870 had 58 industrial establishments, which employed nearly 2,000 workers. During the next decade, factory workers increased fivefold and the value of manufactured products from $1 million to $3.2 million. By 1900 Chattanooga was a leading steel producer of the South. Memphis, despite tragic YELLOW FEVER epidemics in the 1870s, became the great cotton center of the Upper South and by the turn of the century led the nation in the production of cottonseed oil. Nashvillians by the turn of the century could point to paper mills, sawmills, flour mills, liquor distilleries, an oil refinery, and other manufactories so that by the 1890s manufactured goods exceeded a value of $10 million. Julius E. Raht had opened extensive copper mines with offices at Cleveland, and woolen and flour milling was expanding at Jackson.

The Democratic party, though rent by factions, dominated the political scene after the war. Failure of party leaders to solve the state debt question made possible the election in 1881 of Republican Alvin Hawkins. Indeed the debt question, finally settled in 1883, was one of the thorniest problems the state considered during the three decades after the war, although CONVICT LEASING, not settled until the state purchased 9,000 acres for a new prison in Morgan County in the early 1890s, ranked a close second. What success the Democratic party had in the last decade and a half of the nineteenth century was made possible in no small measure by the charismatic ROBERT L. TAYLOR. The orator from Happy Valley in east Tennessee welded together factions of the Democrats in 1886 and in 1896, when he again was elected governor, and then closed his career as a U.S. senator.

Governor Brownlow discussed public education with legislators soon after his election in 1865. "Thousands of school children," he said, were "about to pass the school age hopelessly illiterate," and therefore a public school system "second to none" should be established at once. Although a public school law was passed in 1867, it was not properly implemented. Governor Brown, succeeding to the statehouse in 1871, turned his attention to the problem. The result was a law enacted in 1873, which became the basis for

Tennessee's modern public school system. Although progress came slowly, most counties had public systems by 1900.

Colleges and universities also made progress during the three decades following Reconstruction. Not only were most of the old ones revived, but new ones were established. In 1879 East Tennessee University became the University of Tennessee and offered four courses of study described in the school bulletin of that year as "agricultural, mechanical, classical, and scientific." Eleven years later a school of law was opened. The University of Nashville was reopened with funds from the PEABODY EDUCATION FUND and soon was changed from a liberal arts to a teacher-training institution. Shortly after the turn of the century, its name was changed to George Peabody College for Teachers, in honor of the eastern merchant and philanthropist. Vanderbilt University, chartered in 1873 with money given by Cornelius Vanderbilt, was hailed by educators at the turn of the century as "the pride of Nashville and of the whole South." Colleges of law, medicine, religion, dentistry, and engineering functioned along with liberal arts. The University of the South at Sewanee was reopened in 1867, and the University of Chattanooga and Fisk at Nashville began at about the same time. More than a dozen other colleges were established or reopened during the period and contributed to the education of Tennesseans.

Tennessee politics to 1930. Few people found Tennessee politics boring in the twentieth century. Republicans, except when occasionally in league with insurgent Democrats, endured lean years and elected only three governors during the three-quarter-century period. New alignments and new issues kept Democratic factionalism alive, and, finding the balm of Bob Taylor no longer effective, old-line Democrats sustained serious tears in the party fabric. Interest in education grew. The New Deal brought TVA and new life to the people. Changing patterns of agriculture also came with the New Deal, and shortly after mid-century cotton was replaced by tobacco as the chief money crop. The cities, industry, and transportation grew along with the population.

PROHIBITION loomed as a major issue at the beginning of the century and became an accomplished fact in 1909 well in advance of the Eighteenth Amendment. Democratic factionalism, with prohibition the chief cause, resulted in Democrats staging a statewide primary for governor in 1908. The incumbent MALCOLM R. PATTERSON (a "wet") was opposed by newspaper editor and former senator EDWARD WARD CARMACK (a "dry"), whom he defeated. Carmack became editor of the Nashville *Tennessean* soon after his race for governor. He promptly embarked upon a type of journalism, repugnant to many, in which he singled out certain friends and supporters of Patterson for special abuse. One who received scathing denunciation was Duncan Cooper, an old-line politician of prominent family, former newspaper publisher, and intimate friend and adviser of Governor Patterson. A gun battle on a Nashville street involving Carmack, Cooper, and Cooper's son Robin resulted, and Carmack was killed. Duncan Cooper was convicted but pardoned immediately by Patterson.

The death of Carmack and the unmitigated haste in which Patterson pardoned Cooper galvanized the drys into action. In the following year (1909), they succeeded in securing the enactment of statewide prohibition and, when Patterson promptly vetoed the measure, passed it over his veto. These "Carmack Democrats" came to be known as independents and united with Republicans in 1910 to elect BEN HOOPER, the second Republican governor since Reconstruction. Although the election of Woodrow Wilson in 1912 helped to reunite the Democrats, the drys continued as a significant force in state politics even though prohibition had been accomplished.

With the Wilson administration came WORLD WAR I, and many Tennesseans volunteered for military service. Nearly 80,000 men served during the war, and about 2,000 were killed in action. Six received the congressional Medal of Honor. Tennessee had its usual share of heroes, but none was honored more extensively and elaborately than Sergeant Alvin C. York, a farm boy from the Cumberland Mountains. Reportedly killing a score of the enemy and capturing many times that number in a single day's action in the Meuse-Argonne sector, he was singled out for special treatment upon his return home. Grateful Tennesseans bought him a farm in his native Fentress County, named an agricultural institute for him, and, four years after his death in 1964, erected a bronze statue in his honor.

The decade of the 1920s was a period of growth and conservatism. ALFRED TAYLOR, colorful brother of former governor Robert L. Taylor, was swept into the statehouse in the Republican landslide of 1920. He was succeeded by Austin Peay, the "road-building governor," remembered for much progressive legislation signed into law, particularly in the field of education. But a measure, not to be classified as progressive—the anti-evolution law—also was placed on the statute books during his administration and brought world attention to Tennessee. When in 1925 a high school teacher in Dayton violated the law, the SCOPES TRIAL resulted, which brought Clarence Darrow and William Jennings Bryan to Dayton, with concomitant publicity not all of which by any means was favorable. Indeed, H. L. Mencken and other journalists of the Northeast made frequent reference to "Tennessee yokels" for many years to come. The law remained on the statute books until 1967.

Twentieth-century agriculture and industry. Phenomenal changes have taken place in the economy of the state during the twentieth century. Tennessee was predominantly an agricultural state at the dawn of the new century, but by 1975 only about 5 percent of the people received their major source of income directly from farming. Urban areas, including a half-dozen counties adjacent to Davidson (Nashville) and Knox (Knoxville), have shown considerable growth in population while predominantly rural counties have declined.

Farmers experienced prosperity in the first two decades of the century, especially when the market was stimulated by European demands. Corn, cotton, and tobacco experienced phenomenal increases in price per unit. By 1933, however, drought and depressed prices had taken their toll, and many Tennesseans left farms never to return; those who remained participated in the various phases of the NEW DEAL farm programs. The large increase in the beef and dairy market after World War II caused many to place their land in permanent pasture for hay and grazing. At mid-century cotton still was king among crops, but corn, tobacco, SOYBEANS, and hay were not far behind. By 1967, however, cotton had been dethroned, with tobacco and soybeans taking first and second place respectively. By 1976, with practically all farms highly mechanized, a point of concern had become the significant decline in the number of small farms. The independent Tennessee farmer rapidly is becoming a "vanishing American."

Industry expanded significantly. At the beginning of the twentieth century, flour and grist milling were the principal industries and accounted for 20 percent of the state's industries. As the century progressed, TEXTILE manufacturing, hardwood products, and iron and steel became increasingly important. World War I brought industry to Tennessee, the most significant of which was the Du Pont Powder Plant at Old Hickory. Costing $80 million, the plant brought more than 20,000 workers to the Nashville suburb, which by spring of 1919 boasted a population of 30,000. When the

war ended, the Du Pont people were able to shift from gunpowder to rayon and cellophane. By the outbreak of World War II, rayon and allied products accounted for a major segment of income from manufacturing; meat-packing and chemical products also were significant. It was chemical and allied products that were most in demand during and immediately following World War II, and by 1947 the CHEMICAL INDUSTRY was the leading one in the state. Food and textile products came a close second and third respectively. Electric power from the TENNESSEE VALLEY AUTHORITY has been a major attraction in drawing industry to the state.

Twentieth-century educational, social, and cultural events. The twentieth century has been a period of considerable progress in the area of education, even though Tennessee has failed to keep pace with other states of the Union in the amount per capita spent on education and teachers' salaries. The first significant breakthrough in providing better public schools came in the general education act of 1909, after a concerted campaign by an "educational lobby" composed of Philander P. Claxton, Robert L. Jones, Semour L. Mynders, and other interested school officials and citizens. The law provided for a substantial increase from the gross revenue of the state to be placed in the general education fund. Three new normal schools, eventually to become Memphis State University, Middle Tennessee State University, and East Tennessee State University, were established respectively at Memphis, Murfreesboro, and Johnson City. A few years later Tennessee Polytechnic Institute at Cookeville (now Tennessee Technological University) was established, the medical and dental units of the University of Tennessee were moved from Knoxville to Memphis, and a two-year branch of the university was established at Martin (now University of Tennessee at Martin). Austin Peay Normal (now Austin Peay State University) was established in 1927, and in 1969 the University of Chattanooga was taken over by the state and became the University of Tennessee at Chattanooga. Major private institutions of higher learning continued to make progress in the twentieth century. Vanderbilt University's total program, particularly its medical and law schools, had attained a national reputation by the beginning of the century. George Peabody for Teachers, Southwestern at Memphis, and University of the South at Sewanee are among other nationally known institutions in the state.

Methodists and Southern Baptists continued to outnumber all other religious groups in Tennessee. Membership in these faiths is well distributed across the state. Some denominations have attempted union, with varying degrees of success. In 1906, for example, the Cumberland Presbyterian church united with the northern Presbyterians—a union that was not entirely successful because many of the Cumberland congregations refused to sanction the move. In 1939 the southern Methodists, northern Methodists, and Methodist Protestants effected a successful union, which with other mergers soon rendered the United Methodist church the largest Protestant body in the world.

Tennessee has produced its share of novelists, poets, journalists, and historians. Among writers of the 1920s and 1930s, none became better known than two Nashville groups, the FUGITIVES and the Agrarians. The former, consisting of 16 poets, published the *Fugitive*, which they devoted almost entirely to poetry. The Agrarians, 12 Vanderbilt University instructors and students, published essays, articles, and books, the best known of which is I'LL TAKE MY STAND (1930). Both groups feared that some of the substantial values of American life were being eroded in the name of material progress, so they emphasized creativity and individuality in contrast to conformity. Although initially dismissed by some critics as harmless visionaries, both Agrarians and Fugitives have been viewed by recent scholars as astute observers of American society in a critical time.

Nashville, once called the "Athens of the South," today also has become known as the country MUSIC center of the world. The GRAND OLE OPRY, begun in 1925 by radio station WSM, has become recognized nationally. Roy Acuff, Hank Williams, and Uncle Dave Macon are but a few of those who have performed on the Nashville stage of country music. In 1967 the Country Music Association Foundation established in Nashville the Country Music Hall of Fame and Museum, which is visited annually by thousands.

Tennessee politics since 1930. The depression brought the expected hard times, with bank and business failures. Coming to the forefront at the same time were a dozen politicians and political bosses as colorful as any who have graced the political stage. LUKE LEA, a newspaper publisher and politician, had teamed with Rogers Caldwell, a successful businessman who with other members of his family had founded Caldwell & Company, to create a financial empire with holdings throughout the South ranging from banks to baseball teams. They allegedly controlled Governor Henry Horton, a rural politician who succeed-

ed Austin Peay upon his death in 1927 and who served until 1933. Under state law, money received from the sale of state bonds could be deposited in approved state banks until it was needed for the projects for which it had been appropriated. Needless to say, most such funds found their way into Caldwell-Lea banks; indeed, funds deposited in the Caldwell-owned Bank of Tennessee increased from $40,000 in 1927, when Horton became governor, to more than $2.2 million by June, 1929. Opposing the Lea-Caldwell group was EDWARD CRUMP, a Memphis businessman-politician who held minor office in Memphis as early as 1905 and who had been elected mayor by 1909. By the time he had finished a term as county trustee (1924), he had established the most powerful local machine in the state and could influence state elections by throwing the enormous vote of Shelby County to his candidates. He seriously competed with Lea's chain of Tennessee newspapers aimed largely at influencing and controlling the rural vote.

On November 8, 1932, the Bank of Tennessee was closed; this triggered other closings across the state, and within a week the enormous Caldwell & Company had been placed in the hands of a receiver. When Tennesseans learned that more than $6.5 million of state funds were on deposit in the Caldwell-Lea banks at the time, a wave of indignation swept the state. Crump led the fight for impeachment of Horton, and a legislative committee charged that he was "fit and capable no longer to hold the office of Governor." Although Horton was not impeached, Lea and others eventually went to prison. More powerful than ever, Crump in 1932 secured the election of Hill McAlister as governor by delivering more than 25,000 votes for the Nashvillian—who needed every one of them to win. Crump garnered more than twice that many in 1936 for Gordon Browning, who soon became his bitter enemy, and then was instrumental in Browning's defeat two years later. In 1948 Browning and ESTES KEFAUVER teamed in a race for governor and U.S. senator and finally defeated the Crump machine. Even so, Crump returned in 1952 with FRANK GOAD CLEMENT to sweep the powerful Browning group again from office. Clement and Buford Ellington controlled state politics by alternating in the governor's office from 1953 to 1971.

The period since WORLD WAR II has been one of considerable growth in Tennessee. A sales tax of 2 percent was levied in 1947 and increased in 1963 and 1976. The funds therefrom have resulted in improved schools and cities. Reapportionment under BAKER V. CARR (1962) and subsequent de-

TENNESSEE POPULATION, 1790–1970

Year	Total	White	Nonwhite Slave	Nonwhite Free	% Growth	Rank U.S.	Rank South
1790	35,691	31,913	3,417	361			
1800	105,602	91,709	13,584	309	195.9	15	7
1810	261,727	215,875	44,535	1,317	147.8	10	6
1820	422,823	339,979	80,107	2,737	61.6	9	5
1830	681,904	535,746	141,603	4,555	61.3	7	4
1840	829,210	640,627	183,059	5,524	21.6	5	2
1850	1,002,717	756,836	239,459	6,422	20.9	5	2
1860	1,109,801	826,722	275,719	7,360	10.7	10	4
1870	1,258,520	936,119		322,401	13.4	9	3
1880	1,542,359	1,138,831		403,528	22.6	12	4
1890	1,767,518	1,336,637		430,881	14.6	13	5
1900	2,020,616	1,540,186		480,430	14.3	14	5
1910	2,184,789	1,711,432		473,357	8.1	17	6
1920	2,337,885	1,885,993		451,892	7.0	19	7
1930	2,616,556	2,138,644		477,912	11.9	16	6
1940	2,915,841	2,406,906		508,935	11.4	15	5
1950	3,291,718	2,760,257		531,461	12.9	16	6
1960	3,567,089	2,977,753		589,336	8.4	17	7
1970	3,923,687	3,293,930		629,757	10.0	17	7

TENNESSEE GOVERNORS

Governor	Party	Term
TERRITORY		
William Blount	Fed.–Rep.	1790–1796
STATE		
John Sevier	Rep.	1796–1801
Archibald Roane	Rep.	1801–1803
John Sevier	Rep.	1803–1809
Willie Blount	Rep.	1809–1815
Joseph McMinn	Rep.	1815–1821
William Carroll	Rep.–Dem.	1821–1827
Sam Houston	Dem.	1827–1829
William Hall	Dem.	1829
William Carroll	Dem.	1829–1835
Newton Cannon	Whig	1835–1839
James K. Polk	Dem.	1839–1841
James C. Jones	Whig	1841–1845
Aaron V. Brown	Dem.	1845–1847
Neill S. Brown	Whig	1847–1849
William Trousdale	Dem.	1849–1851
William B. Campbell	Whig	1851–1853
Andrew Johnson	Dem.	1853–1857
Isham G. Harris	Dem.	1857–1862
Andrew Johnson (military)	Dem.	1862–1865
William G. Brownlow	Rep.	1865–1869
DeWitt C. Senter	Rep.	1869–1871
John C. Brown	Dem.	1871–1875
James D. Porter	Dem.	1875–1879
Albert S. Marks	Dem.	1879–1881
Alvin Hawkins	Rep.	1881–1883
William B. Bate	Dem.	1883–1887
Robert L. Taylor	Dem.	1887–1891
John P. Buchanan	Dem.	1891–1893
Peter Turney	Dem.	1893–1897
Robert L. Taylor	Dem.	1897–1899
Benton McMillin	Dem.	1899–1903
James B. Frazier	Dem.	1903–1905
John I. Cox	Dem.	1905–1907
Malcolm R. Patterson	Dem.	1907–1911
Ben W. Hooper	Rep.	1911–1915
Tom C. Rye	Dem.	1915–1919
A. H. Roberts	Dem.	1919–1921
Alfred A. Taylor	Rep.	1921–1923
Austin Peay	Dem.	1923–1927

Governor	Party	Term
Henry H. Horton	Dem.	1927–1933
Hill McAlister	Dem.	1933–1937
Gordon Browning	Dem.	1937–1939
Prentice Cooper	Dem.	1939–1945
Jim McCord	Dem.	1945–1949
Gordon Browning	Dem.	1949–1953
Frank G. Clement	Dem.	1953–1959
Buford Ellington	Dem.	1959–1963
Frank G. Clement	Dem.	1963–1967
Buford Ellington	Dem.	1967–1971
Winfield Dunn	Rep.	1971–1975
Ray Blanton	Dem.	1975–1979
Lamar Alexander	Rep.	1979–

cisions of the U.S. Supreme Court have resulted in fairer representation. Integration of schools was accomplished, albeit with some difficulty and, in Clinton and Nashville, some attendant violence. Several limited constitutional conventions were held, the most significant one being in 1953, when the governor's term was extended to four years (without the right of succession) and municipalities were given some measure of home rule.

Tennessee since World War II has taken giant steps toward becoming a two-party state. Dwight D. Eisenhower and Richard Nixon carried the state in presidential elections, and in 1966 Howard H. Baker, Jr., became the first popularly elected Republican U.S. senator in Tennessee's history. Four years later Republicans, encouraged by their success, ran Congressman William Brock against the erstwhile popular Albert Gore and defeated him soundly. Then in 1971 Winfield Dunn, a Memphis dentist, became the third Republican governor in the twentieth century. Unwilling to concede the state to the resurgent Republicans, Democrats in 1974 elected west Tennessee contractor and former congressman Ray Blanton to the governorship. In the 1978 gubernatorial campaign, however, Republican Lamar Alexander was the winner.

General guides and histories. Excellent bibliographical guides are S. B. Smith (ed.), *Tennessee History: Bibliography* (1974), most comprehensive; W. T. Alderson and R. H. White, *Guide to Tennessee History* (1959); and R. R. Allen, *Tennessee Books* (1969). Major manuscript guides and resources include H. C. Owsley (ed.), *Guide to Processed Manuscripts of Tennessee Historical Society* (1969) and *Registers of Manuscript Section, Tennessee State Library and Archives* (1959–70); D. C. and R. C. Corbitt (trans. and eds.), *East Tennessee Historical Society Publications* (1937–75), papers from Spanish archives relating to Tennessee, 1783–1900; and J. T. Moore, *Draper Manuscripts Relating to Tennessee* (1919). Single-volumed histories include W. Dykeman, *Tennessee* (1975), most recent; S. J. Folmsbee, R. E. Corlew, and E. Mitchell, *Tennessee* (1969), most comprehensive; and T. P. Abernethy, *From Frontier to Plantation* (1932), good on Civil War period. See also P. M. Hamer, *Tennessee, 1673–1932* (4 vols.; 1932); and Folmsbee, Corlew, and Mitchell, *History of Tennessee* (4 vols.; 1960).

Early and Indian histories. T. M. N. Lewis and M. Kneberg, *Tribes That Slumber* (1958); and J. Mooney, *Myths of Cherokee* (1900), treat prehistory and early Indians. S. C. Williams has five important books on early period: *Dawn of Tennessee, 1541–1776* (1937), *Beginnings of West Tennessee, 1541–1841* (1930), *History of Lost State of Franklin* (1924), *Early Travels in Tennessee Country* (1928), and *Tennessee During Revolutionary War* (1944). Beginnings are well covered also in biographies: W. Masterson, *William Blount* (1954); C. Driver, *John Sevier* (1932); T. E. Matthews, *General James Robertson* (1934); S. C. Williams, *William Tatham* (1947); and J. Bakeless, *Master of Wilderness: Daniel Boone* (1939).

Antebellum era. Abernethy's *Frontier to Plantation*, mentioned above, is best general work. Also see C. Mooney, *Slavery in Tennessee* (1957); B. H. Clark, *Tennessee Yeoman, 1840–1860* (1942); F. L. Owsley, *Plain Folk of Old South* (1949); and R. H. White (ed.), *Messages of Governors of Tennessee* (1942–72), I–VII, illuminating. Numerous biographical studies include R. V. Remini, *Andrew Jackson* (1966), most recent Jackson biography; C. G. Sellers, *James K. Polk, 1795–1843* (1957) and *Polk, 1843–1846* (1966); J. A. Shackford, *David Crockett* (1956) and *The Raven* (1929), Sam Houston; W. N. Chambers, *Old Bullion Benton* (1956), Thomas Hart Benton; and J. H. Parks, *John Bell* (1950) and *Felix Grundy* (1940).

Civil War and Reconstruction. See M. E. R. Campbell, *Attitude of Tennesseans Toward Union, 1847–1861* (n.d.). Military campaigns are ably covered in S. Horn, *Army of Tennessee* (1941); and T. L. Connelly, *Army of Heartland, 1861–1862* (1967) and *Autumn of Glory, 1862–1865* (1971). Biographies of important figures are T. B. Alexander, *Thomas A. R. Nelson* (1956); L. P. Stryker, *Andrew Johnson* (1929); J. H. Parks, *General Leonidas Polk* (1962); and R. S. Henry, *"First with Most" Forrest* (1944). See T. B. Alexander, *Political Reconstruction in Tennessee* (1950); and J. W. Patton, *Unionism and Reconstruction in Tennessee, 1860–1869* (1934), both standard works. See also S. Horn, *Invisible Empire: KKK, 1866–1871* (1939).

Late nineteenth and twentieth centuries. D. M. Robinson, *Bob Taylor and Agrarian Revolt* (1935); and D. Abshire, *South Rejects a Prophet: D. M. Key, 1824–1900* (1967), are both perceptive. See also A. A. Taylor, *Negro in Tennessee, 1865–1880* (1941); P. E. Isaacs, *Prohibition and Politics, 1885–1920* (1965); A. E. Taylor, *Women's Suffrage Movement in Tennessee* (1957); R. Ginger, *Six Days or Forever* (1958), trial of Thomas Scopes; J. Perry, *Democracy Begins at Home* (1944), Tennessee and poll tax; J. B. McFerrin, *Caldwell and Co.* (1939); R. C. Cortner, *Apportionment Cases* (1971); H. D. Graham, *Crisis in Print: Desegregation and Press in Tennessee* (1967); and P. J. Hubbard, *Origins of TVA* (1955), one of best of many works on subject. Able biographies that illumine twentieth century include E. R. Boyce (ed.), *Unwanted Boy* (1963), Ben W. Hooper; C. Hull, *Memoirs* (1948); T. Skeyhill (ed.), *Sergeant York* (1928); J. B. Gorman, *Kefauver* (1971); T. H. Alexander, *Austin Peay* (1929); C. L. Lewis, *Philander Priestly Claxton* (1948); R. Terral, *Newell Sanders* (1935); W. D. Miller, *Mr. Crump of Memphis* (1964); A. G. Gore, *Eye of Storm* (1970); and L. McMillin, *Schoolmaker: Sawner Webb and Bell Buckle Story* (1971).

ROBERT E. CORLEW
Middle Tennessee State University

TENNESSEE, UNIVERSITY OF (Knoxville, 37916), began in 1794 as Blount College, a private and coeducational institution. By 1807, when the school began to receive state aid and was renamed East Tennessee College, it had become a men's institution and remained so until 1892. The offerings were expanded to university size in 1840, but the school was closed and used as a hospital during the Civil War. After the war, an agricultural and mechanical division was added under provisions of the Morrill Land-Grant Act of 1862. Renamed the University of Tennessee in 1879, the school has grown in both size and scope during the twentieth century. In addition to having over 20,000 students on the Knoxville campus, the University of Tennessee system comprises schools at Martin (38238, formerly known as Hall-Moody Junior College), Chattanooga (37403, founded in 1950), and Nashville (37203, founded in 1957). The Knoxville campus libraries maintain a valuable collection of manuscript and documentary materials on Tennessee history since 1783, including the personal and family papers of Philander Priestly Claxton (educator), William A. Dromgoole (journalist), John Eaton (Tennessee Freedmen's Bureau), BEN W. HOOPER, ANDREW JOHNSON, ANDREW JACKSON, WILLIAM CAMPBELL, and JOHN SEVIER. The library also collects materials relating to the Great Smoky Mountains and to businesses of Tennessee and Alabama (leather, livery, hotels, coal mining, merchandising, printing, and public utilities).

See J. R. Montgomery, *University of Tennessee, 1887–1919* (1966).

TENNESSEE COAL & IRON COMPANY started in 1852 as the Sewanee Mining Company to excavate COAL outcroppings on Tennessee's Cumberland Plateau. In 1860 it was reorganized as the Tennessee Coal & Railroad Company. During the war its mine was operated by both the Confederates and the federals. Reconstruction uncertainties, a dwindling coal market, the PANIC OF 1873, and a perennial capital shortage caused instability and frequent postwar reorganizations. JOHN H. INMAN gained control of the concern in 1881, renamed it Tennessee Coal, Iron & Railroad Company, and later acquired coal lands, blast furnaces, coke ovens, and iron ore deposits near Birmingham, Ala. (IRON AND STEEL INDUSTRY). This geographical shift was fortunate, for, when pig iron prices dropped in the early 1890s, the firm was well situated to enter the steel business. Although it produced open-hearth steel by 1899, profits remained elusive. Competition with northern companies was difficult despite the nearby raw materials, because Alabama ore was of low quality, skilled labor was scarce, and the railroads' rate structure was discriminatory. During the 1907 panic, J. P. Morgan convinced President Theodore Roosevelt to suspend the Sherman Antitrust Act to allow United States Steel to purchase a controlling share of the Tennessee company's stock. President William Taft brought suit in 1911 to break up the steel trust, drawing Roosevelt's ire. The suit was decided in the company's favor on March 1, 1920. After the takeover the Tennessee company prospered. With sufficient capital the firm expanded rapidly into finished steel and tin products. In 1952 it was renamed the Tennessee Coal & Iron Division of United States Steel. A decade later the division had about 50 percent of southern steelmaking capacity.

See T. C. & I. Division, United States Steel, *Biography of a Business* (1960); A. Cotter, *United States Steel* (1921); V. S. Clark, *History of Manufactures in U.S.* (1929), II, III; and J. Fuller, "History of Tennessee Coal, Iron, and Railroad Company" (Ph.D. dissertation, University of North Carolina, 1966).

JAMES A. WARD
University of Tennessee, Chattanooga

TENNESSEE HISTORICAL SOCIETY (403 Seventh Ave. N, Nashville, Tenn. 37206), with 3,500 members, has been in almost continuous existence since 1849. The society headquarters are in the Tennessee State Library and Archives Building, which also serves as the repository for the chief collections of the society, including among its many manuscripts the letters and papers of Willie Blount, William Blount, John Donelson, John Coffee, Andrew Jackson, William Trousdale, John Overton, and James Winchester. The organization has provided assistance toward the publication of historical books. It prints a newsletter and since 1942 has published the *Tennessee Historical Quarterly* (circulation 3,200 in 1975), which devotes itself to scholarly articles on Tennessee history, book reviews, and historical news and notices and makes an award of $100 to the author of each year's best article.

See Mrs. J. T. Moore, *Tennessee Historical Quarterly* (Fall, 1944).

TENNESSEE RIVER moves southwest from Knoxville into Alabama, then takes a winding westward course for some 200 miles through north Alabama. Here it turns north and joins the Ohio River at Paducah, Ky. Until recently, the Tennessee was probably more dangerous to navigate and more cantankerous in general than either the Ohio or Mississippi.

Prior to the TENNESSEE VALLEY AUTHORITY, navigation was hampered by unpredictable currents and deadly shoals. The only certain thing about the Tennessee was devastating floods each winter and spring. Steamboating did help the Tennessee Valley, but not as much as it did the regions of many other major rivers. A basic problem was a 30-mile stretch of rapids at Muscle Shoals in northwest Alabama. From Florence, Ala., to Paducah, steamboats did a booming business. However, on the other side of the rapids, from Decatur, Ala., to Knoxville, steamboating was pure speculation and bankrupted many who tried.

Attempts to avoid the rapids by building a canal in the 1830s ended in failure. The first railroad west of the Appalachians was built around the river's breach in 1832 and by 1834 had been expanded to about 40 miles of track. The basic bed of this early road is now part of the Southern Railway system. The track of the 1830s did bypass the danger, but proved to be slow and burdensome. Steamboats had to unload cargo and passengers onto the railroad for the short journey that ended in unloading once again. Frustrating waits were common before another boat was available for yet another loading and the continuation of the long journey, often as far as New Orleans.

The Tennessee River proved to be a disadvantage to the South during the Civil War. With the fall of Ft. Henry (built by the Confederacy near the Kentucky border to prevent Union entry), the federals had control of the river above Decatur (FTS. HENRY AND DONELSON CAMPAIGN). Commercial steamboating began again after the war, but the dangers and problems of navigation were the same as in earlier days. It was not until 1933 that the Tennessee really started to reach its potential.

On April 10, 1933, Franklin Roosevelt asked Congress to establish the TVA to "plan for proper use, conservation, and development of the Tennessee River." The act passed on May 18, 1933. With TVA dams and locks, the river was transformed into well over 600 miles of navigable waterway. Flooding was no longer a problem, and the rapids at Muscle Shoals were safely submerged. TVA has built several dams with hydroelectric-generating plants on the Tennessee. Cries of socialism can be heard even to this day. In the early 1970s TVA opened its first nuclear plant at Brown's Ferry in north Alabama. Other such plants are in the works and can produce many times more energy than the hydroelectric dam.

Even with nuclear plants the Tennessee will not have reached its peak. In recent times, the Tennessee-Tombigbee Waterway Development Authority was created by Congress. The project concerns the joining of navigable streams to connect great southern rivers. It has been estimated that this development would create more than 30 new locks and dams and link over 16,000 miles of inland waterways with the Gulf of Mexico. The great Tennessee River will continue to help shape the destiny of the South.

See University of Alabama Bureau of Public Administration, *Tennessee-Tombigbee Waterway* (1971). Best sources are numerous books and reports published by TVA (1936–). See also J. Goodwin, *Rivers of Alabama* (1968); D. Davidson, *Rivers of America* (1948); and V. Crane, *Mississippi Valley Historical Review* (June, 1916).

JOE E. PETERS
Calhoun Community College

TENNESSEE VALLEY AUTHORITY. The area drained by the Tennessee River system embraces 40,910 square miles and spreads across North Carolina, Virginia, Tennessee, Alabama, Georgia, Mississippi, and Kentucky. From 1821 to 1933, the Tennessee Valley was the subject of considerable national concern. First it was discussed as a major inland transportation channel and later as a source of waterpower. World War I and the shortage of nitrogen for both ammunition and fertilizer made mandatory the development of a major source of power and the perfecting of a process for extract-

ing nitrogen from the air. This resulted in the construction of Wilson Dam and the Muscle Shoals nitrogen plant, neither of which was completed when the war ended. Between 1920 and 1932, there occurred a major debate over the future of the valley, the dam, and the government's nitrogen plant.

Many people favored leasing the valley facilities and relying upon private enterprise—notably Henry Ford and the Alabama Power & Light Company—to develop their potential. Others—notably Senator George Norris of Nebraska—favored government operation of the facilities and public development of the Tennessee River system. At issue, in addition to the question of the disposition of the valley facilities, was the problem of government regulation of privately owned public utilities. Norris and others hoped that federal management of the electricity generated by the Wilson Dam would provide government agencies with a "yardstick" against which to gauge the performance of private utilities. Both Presidents Calvin Coolidge and Herbert Hoover opposed such direct federal involvement in the economy, however, and Hoover in 1931 vetoed one Norris bill, which provided for public operation of the facilities and for the sale of the electricity generated to state and municipal governments.

During the presidential campaign of 1932, Franklin D. Roosevelt in a speech in Portland, Ore., endorsed the principles of public power. Then, early in 1933, the president-elect visited Muscle Shoals and expressed his intention to support the full development of both the river and the valley in keeping with the best principles of public use and conservation. The decade-long debate over the Tennessee Valley facilities came to an end on May 18, 1933, when Congress enacted the Tennessee Valley Authority Act and President Roosevelt immediately signed it into law.

Overall, the TVA Act was an unusual law. It created an independent public agency governed by a three-member board of commissioners. The board, enjoying a maximum amount of autonomy, was considered to be a corporate body. It possessed the force of the writ of eminent domain. It was required to file annually with the president and the Congress a complete financial statement, but it was empowered to engage directly in construction work without having to resort to the use of public contractors and/or competitive bidding. The comptroller general of the United States was given the responsibility for auditing the authority's fiscal affairs, but TVA was given power to conduct its personnel affairs independent of the Civil Service Act, to regulate wages, and to nego-

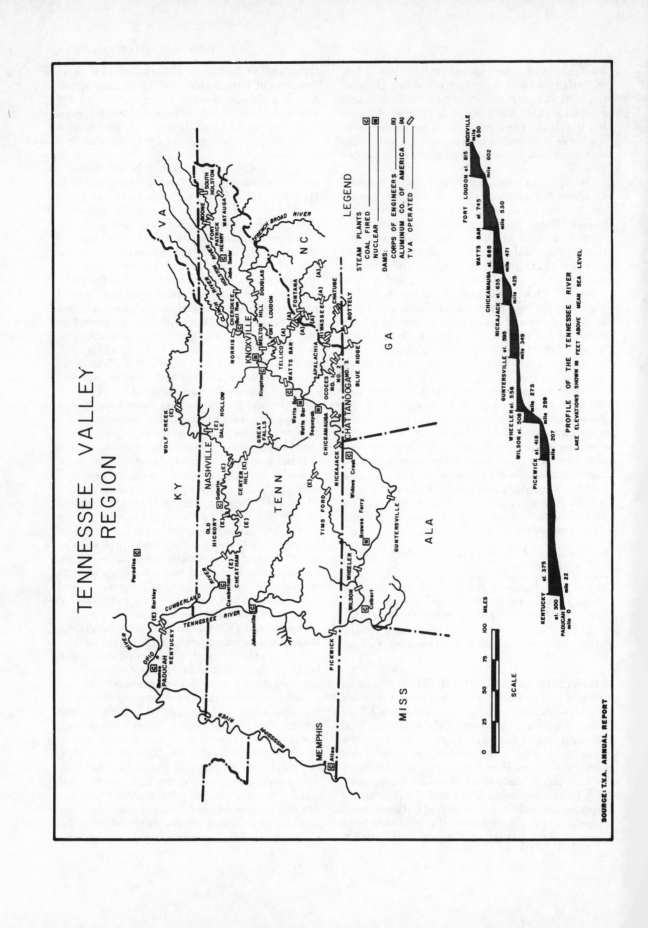

TENNESSEE VALLEY REGION

SOURCE: T.V.A. ANNUAL REPORT

tiate collective agreements with its employees. In addition to receiving control of the Muscle Shoals facilities, the TVA was delegated tremendous powers and broad responsibilities: maximum FLOOD CONTROL, long a problem along the 652-mile course of the Tennessee River; full development of the navigational channel of the river; maximum generation of electric power consistent with flood control and navigational use (ELECTRICITY); proper use and development of marginal lands; instigation of acceptable means of reforestation; and concern for the economic and social well-being of the people of the valley.

The TVA Board of Commissioners, comprising David E. Lilienthal, Harcourt A. Morgan, and Arthur E. Morgan, met for the first time June 16, 1933. An initial and basic decision was to dispense with competitive contractors and, instead, to create TVA's own engineering and construction force. On October 1 construction was begun at Cove Creek (Norris Dam) on the Clinch River north of Knoxville; immediately thereafter construction was begun downstream on Wheeler Dam; and within 18 months preparations were completed for the construction of Pickwick Landing Dam. In every case laborers were largely of valley origin and were trained on the job. In time, 39,000 men were employed on various TVA construction sites.

In the area of human considerations, there were many difficult decisions to be made. The valley was dotted with towns, cemeteries, churches, schools, and other landmarks that soon would disappear beneath the waters of the dammed Tennessee. Graves had to be opened and human remains transferred to new cemeteries above the flood line. Churches had to be removed and rebuilt. Historical landmarks were preserved or noted. To preserve a record of the millions of aboriginal artifacts, TVA employed a small army of archeologists, anthropologists, and workmen to excavate mounds, burial sites, and other places associated with the prehistoric past.

Even before the relocation of the first town or artifact and before the start of construction of the first new dam, TVA's statutory authority was challenged in the federal courts. In August, 1933, the TVA Act was challenged with the contention that Wilson Dam should be used to generate only enough electrical power to supply the needs of the government-owned fertilizer plants (*Ashwander* v. *TVA*, 297 U.S. 288 [1936]). The U.S. Supreme Court, however, upheld the power of the government to construct such dams under the war and commerce clauses of the Constitution and to dispose of its property (including electrical energy) as it saw fit. Subsequently, 18 power companies brought a combined suit against TVA, contending that the United States was creating a vast power conspiracy that worked against the principle of private enterprise under the guise of flood control, navigation, and national defense. Again the Supreme Court upheld the TVA Act, dismissing the suit on the grounds that the utility companies had suffered no legal damage (*Tennessee Electric Company* v. *TVA*, 306 U.S. 118 [1939]).

Although the Supreme Court has upheld the TVA's constitutionality, the project and its operations continue to provoke controversy. The TVA has used its extensive power capacity to encourage the consumption of electricity and the organization of new industrial consumers with the intent of reordering the way of life of valley residents. Moreover, the TVA has been used as a yardstick against which are measured the cost of generating electrical power and the rates charged consumers by privately owned utility companies. These practices have produced thousands of pages of published argument and inspired a persistent advertising campaign directed against the TVA by private utilities.

World War II greatly accelerated the pace of TVA developments. In 1941 the Office of Production Management asked TVA to construct facilities to produce an additional 100,000 kilowatts of power with which to manufacture the ALUMINUM needed for war planes. On February 13, 1943, Douglas Dam on the French Broad River was completed and ready to produce the needed power. During the war, TVA brought older dams and power facilities into production almost on an assembly line basis. Other products of wartime planning and construction were the Shawnee and Kingston steam plants, constructed to supply the insatiable demand for electrical current by the Atomic Energy Commission and the Oak Ridge nuclear project. Although begun during the war, the Shawnee generator did not go into operation until 1953–1954.

Today there are nine dams on the main channel of the Tennessee River between Ft. Loudon (northeast of Knoxville) and Kentucky Dam (near Gilbertsville). There also are five major dams on the headstreams (the Clinch, Holston, French Broad, and Little Tennessee rivers) and 12 smaller impoundments. Aside from the hydroelectric installations, there are the Bull Run, Paradise, Shawnee, Brown's Ferry, Johnsonville, Widow's Creek, and Kingston steam plants. And, in 1975, two of three nuclear units near Athens, Ala., were placed in commercial operation. Collectively, these installations represent over 100 billion kilowatts of generating capacity.

There is now ample evidence of the TVA's success in controlling floodwaters that once rampaged along the Tennessee and Mississippi rivers. The cumulative flood control benefits were reckoned in 1975 to be $1.5 billion—more than six times the amount of capital invested in the construction and maintenance of the flood control reservoirs.

The main stream, with its nine pools and dams, has borne since 1940 an annually growing tonnage of diversified, heavy freight. In 1975 the Tennessee bore an estimated 27.1 million tons of commercial freight ranging from automobiles to sand—this on a river once considered to be unnavigable because of its seasonal fluctuations and its shoals.

Kilowatt production has advanced far beyond the most extravagant predictions of original public power advocates. Moreover, even the mode of production has been altered since Senator Norris urged the public management of Wilson Dam's hydroelectric power. Of the 109.8 billion kilowatts generated by TVA in fiscal 1974, only 23 billion (less than 21 percent) came from hydro-generating stations; 84 billion kilowatts came from coal-burning plants, and in coming years nuclear generators probably will reduce the proportion of hydro-electrical power still further.

Perhaps a better way of understanding the significance of TVA's electrical power production is to consider its impact on the people of the Tennessee Valley. In 1933 the valley was rural, much of it isolated country well beyond the reach of existing electrical transmission lines. Only one farm in 20 had access to electricity, and even the few with electricity used current sparingly as a source of light. Today no one is really without access to electrical power lines. The valley's farmers use electricity not only for illumination, but in recreation, refrigeration, incubation, and mechanization of a hundred different chores.

When Congress turned over to TVA the management of the government's nitrogen-making facilities in 1933, it mandated that the Board of Commissioners experiment with the manufacture of FERTILIZERS and give or sell fertilizers to appropriate educational agencies engaging in further research or experimentation. Accordingly, researchers at TVA's Fertilizer Station (Sheffield, Ala.) have worked closely with state agricultural experiment stations, county demonstration agents, and colleges of agriculture. Their collaboration has resulted in the development of the PHOS-PHATE deposits in eastern Tennessee, in the growth of the commercial fertilizer industry within the valley area, and in improved fertilizers now used around the globe. Tennessee Valley farmland—once ravaged by erosion, floods, and short-sighted patterns of cultivation—has been rebuilt into some of the most productive in the nation. In 1975 TVA area farms produced crops with an average value of $417 per acre (well above the national average of $262 per acre).

In addition to TVA's success in restoring the productivity of farmland, wise management of its shorelines has aided significantly the development of two interrelated industries: recreation and TOURISM. For example, the construction of Barkley Dam on the Cumberland River in the 1950s put two lakes (Kentucky Lake on the Tennessee and Barkley Lake on the Cumberland) on either side of a narrow peninsula or tongue of land containing 170,000 acres. In 1963 Congress appropriated $4 million with which TVA was to develop the "Land Between the Lakes" into a national recreation and conservation area. Today the area entices visitors with three campgrounds, a herd of buffalo, 22 beaches, and over 300 miles of backcountry trails. Nearby, the state of Kentucky maintains three state parks on the shores of one of the two lakes.

In 1935 it was estimated that there were within the valley approximately 14 million acres of existing woodland, an area representing 54 percent of the Tennessee Basin. Yet this woodland was yielding lumber far below the area's capacity, and additional forest was needed for an adequate system of flood control. TVA created a division of forestry relations and instituted a system of forest fire control. By 1954 over 200,000 acres of denuded land had been replanted with 15.6 million seedlings; and by 1975 over 1.5 million acres of land had been reforested. Forest products industries, many of which were new to the region, now produce more than $1 billion worth of products annually and employ some 50,000 workers.

In carrying out its mandate of concern for the economic and social well-being of the population, TVA has wrought a social and economic revolution. There are no simple gauges for measuring change that fully reveal this fact. Per capita income, compared with the average for the nation, was 44 percent in 1933, 61 percent in 1952, and 79 percent in 1976. The TVA also made vital contributions in broad areas of national defense, to the advancement of agriculture through its fertilizer programs, and to southern industrial expansion.

See TVA, *Annual Reports* (1965, 1967, 1974, 1975); G. R. Clapp, *TVA: An Approach* (1955); T. D. Clark, *Emerging*

South (1961); T. D. Clark and A. D. Kirwan, *South Since Appomattox* (1967); J. Dahir, *Region Building* (1955); P. J. Hubbard, *Origins of TVA, 1920–1932* (1961); D. E. Lilienthal, *TVA Democracy* (1944); J. Kyle, *Building TVA* (1958), illustrated; C. H. Pritchett, *TVA* (1943), public administration; and J. S. Ransmeier, *TVA: Economics of Multiple Purpose Stream Planning* (1942).

THOMAS D. CLARK
Indiana University

TENURE OF OFFICE ACT

TENURE OF OFFICE ACT (1867). Determined to frustrate Radical schemes of racial equality in the South, ANDREW JOHNSON sought to interfere with congressional plans for Reconstruction. Although the Republicans had enough votes to override his vetoes, he still retained his prerogatives as commander-in-chief of the army and his control of the patronage. In order to curb these powers, Congress passed the Command of the Army and Tenure of Office acts, the latter over the president's veto (March 2). The law provided that all persons appointed by and with the advice and consent of the Senate could only be removed by and with the advice and consent of the Senate. Cabinet members were to hold office during the term of the president by whom they had been appointed and for one month thereafter, and the president could appoint officers *ad interim* while the Senate was not in session. The measure was passed on the same day as the First Reconstruction Act.

In August, 1867, Johnson removed Secretary of War Edwin M. Stanton and appointed General U. S. Grant secretary *ad interim*. When, upon reassembling, the Senate refused to concur, on February 21, 1868, the president dismissed the secretary again, this time while the Senate was in session. His impeachment for violation of the Tenure of Office Act followed, but for various reasons, including some doubt whether the law actually covered Stanton, who had been appointed by Abraham Lincoln, Johnson was acquitted by one vote. On April 5, 1869, the law was modified so that the president might make removals if he submitted new nominations within 30 days after the commencement of a new session. Not until March 3, 1887, was the act finally repealed.

In *Myers* v. *U.S.* (1926) the U.S. Supreme Court held that presidential removal powers were unlimited. This sweeping decision was somewhat modified in 1935, when the Court in *Humphrey's Executor* v. *U.S.* held that members of independent commissions were not subject to summary removal.

See E. S. Corwin, *Columbia Law Review* (April, 1927) and *President's Removal Power* (1927); H. L. Trefousse, *Impeachment of President* (1975); *Myers* v. *U.S.*, 272 U.S. 52 (1926); and *Humphrey's Executor* v. *U.S.*, 295 U.S. 602 (1935).

HANS L. TREFOUSSE
Brooklyn College, City University of New York

TERRELL, MARY CHURCH

TERRELL, MARY CHURCH (1863–1954), was born in Memphis, attended Oberlin College (A.B., 1884; A.M., 1888), and studied in Europe. She taught at Wilberforce University, in the District of Columbia public schools, and at Howard University. In 1891 she married Robert H. Terrell, who became a judge of the municipal court of the District of Columbia (1902–1925). Service on the District of Columbia board of education (1895–1901, 1906–1911) made her the first black woman member of an American school board. Active in both women's and civil rights organizations, she was a founder and from 1896 to 1901 the first president of the National Association of Colored Women. A charter member of the NATIONAL ASSOCIATION FOR THE ADVANCEMENT OF COLORED PEOPLE (1909), she fought racial discrimination in white organizations and the federal government, campaigned against LYNCHING, and protested the mistreatment of black soldiers. She helped picket the White House in support of women's suffrage in 1917. Terrell was internationally known as a speaker and writer. From 1949 to 1954 she was leader of an interracial group that, through picketing, boycotting, and court action, succeeded in outlawing SEGREGATION in restaurants and stores in the District of Columbia.

See M. C. Terrell, *Colored Woman* (1940), autobiography; E. F. Chittenden, *Negro History Bulletin* (Feb.–March, 1975); E. L. Davis, *Lifting as They Climb* (1937); and E. A. Toppin, *Biographical History of Blacks* (1971).

DE WITT S. DYKES, JR.
Oakland University, Rochester, Mich.

TERTIUM QUIDS.

TERTIUM QUIDS. See QUIDS

TEXARKANA, ARK.

TEXARKANA, ARK. (pop. 21,682), and **TEXARKANA, TEX.** (pop. 10,815), are technically separate civil entities but in reality are one town set astride the state line. Originally it was the site of a CADDO INDIAN village. In 1873 it became a junction of the Cairo & Fulton Railroad and the eastern terminus of the Texas & Pacific. The former railroad sold lots within Arkansas, and the latter developed the land on the Texas side of the line. Nine years later the Texas & St. Louis Railway built a line through the town, and Texarkana has remained an important shipping and transportation center. The city also produces a variety of wood products, refined sulfur, lead, clothing, and textiles and serves as a market for area livestock, dairy, and cotton farmers.

See files of Texarkana *Gazette* (1875–) and *News* (1875–).

TEXAS, popularly known as the Lone Star State for the single star in its flag, is neither a southern nor a western state, but is a southwestern one with a culture and a way of life molded largely by geography, by the influences of the New West and the Old South, and in part by those who came from the American states of the Midwest and North and from many foreign lands. At least 26 racial, national, and ethnic groups have shaped and guided the destiny of Texas for perhaps the past 40,000 years. Thus Texas is not the white, Anglo-Saxon, Protestant state that it is often thought or depicted to be. It is one of the most cosmopolitan states in the Union, and its heritage is more one of ethnic harmony than of racial tensions. Texas is not a simple state and does not yield simple answers. The frontier today still provides the spirit and the willingness to act, and its principal capital goods (oil and gas) provide the capacity to act.

The land and its naming. Some of the cultural relics of earliest man in Texas, and in North America, have been discovered near Lewisville, Denton County, and these push the date of the earliest Paleo-Americans back to more than 37,000 years ago. At the time of the coming of the first known white man, Texas within its modern dimensions is estimated as having had an Indian population of 25,000–30,000 and in 1821 of 20,000.

Modern Texas was settled largely by Spaniards, who approached from the west and south, and by Anglo-Americans, who came from the east. Both had developed pioneering institutions that proved unsatisfactory in certain respects and had to be modified in Texas because of the geography of the country, the nomadic nature of the Indians encountered, and the remoteness of Texas from the main centers of civilization in the New World.

The first Spaniards to found missions among the Indians of the Hasinai Confederacy in the area between the Trinity and Red rivers in 1690 referred to these Indians as the Téjas (meaning "friends" or "allies"). These same Spaniards referred to the area as "the land of the Téjas," hence the derivation of the state's motto (Friendship) and its name Texas. In 1836 the congress of the Republic of Texas arbitrarily set the boundary on the south and west from the mouth of the Rio Grande to its source and thence north to the boundary of the United States at the forty-second parallel. In 1850 Texas sold to the United States approximately one-third of its territory and accepted a boundary substantially as it is today, after a few slight modifications resulting from shifting river channels and a faulty survey.

Modern Texas contains about 7 percent of the total land and water area of the United States and is second only to Alaska in size among the states, for a total of 267,339 square miles. It is as large as the combined area of Connecticut, Maine, Massachusetts, New Hampshire, Rhode Island, New York, Pennsylvania, Ohio, and Illinois. The geographic center of the state is a point a few miles southwest of Mercury in McCulloch County. A glance at a relief map of the United States shows that Texas geologically is a crossroads where four major physiographic subdivisions meet: namely, the Rocky Mountain region, the great western high plains, the great western lower plains, and the Gulf coast forested plains. Texas is divided into a number of natural regions determined by soil and climate. One hundred thirty different soil series, divided into more than 500 soil types, have been identified. The state has in varying quantities almost every mineral resource known to man and since the early 1930s has been first among the states in the value of its mineral production, principally oil, natural gas, and sulfur. More than 540 species of birds—about three-fourths of all the different species found in the United States and more than are to be found in any other state—are to be found in Texas. Texas also has 142 species of wild animals.

In a land of superlatives, Texas has ten climatic subdivisions, with vast differences in elevation, precipitation, wind velocities, humidity, and other conditions affecting both climate and temperature. The mean annual temperature for the period 1941–1970 was 67.11° F., ranging from an average of 59° F. in the northern and western panhandle to an average of 74.1° F. in the extreme south. The average annual rainfall for the same period was 32 inches, ranging from eight inches in the western tip around El Paso to 56 inches along the upper Gulf coast.

Spanish exploration and early settlement. From an established foothold in the West Indies the Spaniards commenced to search the landmass to the west. In 1519 Alonzo Alvarez de Piñeda, while mapping the coast of the Gulf of Mexico, spent 40 days at the mouth of the Rio Grande, which he called Rio de las Palmas. He recommended that a

settlement be made there, but not until more than 200 years later was Matamoros, Mexico, founded as a permanent settlement. Texas again came into history in November, 1528, when the survivors of the Pánfilo de Narváez expedition were wrecked in a storm upon Galveston (Malhado) Island and the adjacent coast. After six years, Alvar Núñez CABEZA DE VACA and three companions, sole survivors, succeeded in crossing Texas to a point near present-day El Paso and in reaching Culiacán in April, 1536, and ultimately Mexico City. They were the first white men to visit and describe the interior of Texas and to see and describe the buffalo. Their reports led to an exploration of west Texas and of the American Southwest by Francisco de Coronado in 1540–1542.

While Coronado explored west Texas, remnants of the HERNANDO DE SOTO expedition under Luis de Moscoso in May, 1542, set out from near the mouth of the Arkansas River to reach Mexico by land, going as far west as the central Brazos River before turning back to the Mississippi. Neither Coronado nor Moscoso had found anything in the interior of Texas to cause Spaniards to return. For the next 150 years the Spaniards gave little thought to Texas, until Spain's control of the Gulf of Mexico was threatened by Frenchmen advancing down the Mississippi River and by LA SALLE's efforts to establish a colony at the mouth of that river. Sailing from France on August 1, 1684, La Salle missed the Mississippi and landed at Matagorda Bay on the Texas coast in February, 1685, where he erected a small, crude wooden fortification named Ft. St. Louis on Garcitas Creek, 30 miles in the interior near present-day Vanderbilt, Tex.

Although the French effort to establish a settlement in the wilds of Texas had failed by 1689, it caused thoughtful and patriotic Spaniards to realize that Spain's claim to the region must be strengthened by occupation. Alonso de León, discoverer of the French fort, found a few Frenchmen living among the Indians, and before returning to Mexico he advanced eastward to the border of the land of the Hasinai (Téjas) Indians, who requested that missionaries be sent among them. Upon his return to Mexico, de León gave a glowing report on the land of the Téjas. He described the land as being very fertile, the climate salubrious, and the people more highly civilized than most aborigines; moreover, he recommended occupation of the country and the dispatching of missionaries to work among the friendly Téjas. As a result, de León and Father Damián Massanet returned to Texas, where on June 1, 1690, the mission of San Francisco de los Téjas was consecrated as the first Spanish mission in east Texas near

present Weches, Houston County. In 1691 the newly appointed governor of the province of Texas and Coahuila, Don Domingo Terán de los Ríos, brought supplies and reinforcements, and a second mission (Santísimo Nombre de María) was located on the Neches, about five miles from the first. Floods, disease, crop failures, a constant shortage of supplies, and Indian fickleness, however, so discouraged the few isolated missionaries that they set fire to the mission of San Francisco (the other having previously been destroyed by flood) on October 25, 1693, and returned to Mexico.

The abandonment of east Texas without authorization from higher authorities did not disturb the officers of government, who concluded that the French threat had never been serious. So far, Spain had used in Texas only the traditional arm of Spanish colonization—the mission. The expense of establishing garrisons (presidios) and permanent civil settlements (villas) would be great and was to be avoided if possible. Yet the first Spanish missions in east Texas, though ending in failure, had been of great importance in establishing Spain's claim to the region, in extending its knowledge of the Indians, geography, and resources of Texas, and in fixing the name Texas to the area. Spain learned, too, that missions at that distance from civilization could not succeed unless sustained by presidios and settlements.

In April, 1699, the French returned to the Gulf of Mexico to establish Biloxi and commenced to extend their Indian trade activities south from their Arkansas post and north and west from Biloxi, founding Mobile in 1702. During the succeeding decade they established a number of trading posts in what is now Alabama, Mississippi, and Louisiana and finally in 1713 erected one at Natchitoches on Red River. The Spaniards were jolted from their lethargy over Texas by the sudden appearance on July 18, 1714, of a French trader by the name of Louis Juchereau de St. Denis, with three French companions, at San Juan Bautista on the Rio Grande. St. Denis had been sent by Governor Antoine de la Mothe Cadillac of Louisiana to develop trade relations with the Spaniards in northern New Spain. Arrested and sent to Mexico City for interrogation, St. Denis was hired as a guide for an expedition fitted out under Domingo Ramón to occupy east Texas not only with missions but also with families and presidios for the protection of both. The expedition reached the land of the Téjas in June, 1716. In time, six missions were strategically located, with the easternmost being that of San Miguel de Linares, established among the Adai Indians at the site of the modern city of Robeline, La., about 15 miles from the French post at Natchitoches.

In 1718 Spain sent Governor Martín de Alarcón of Coahuila to east Texas with reinforcements and orders to establish a halfway station between east Texas and the Rio Grande. Alarcón's expedition established the mission of San Antonio de Valero (later known as the ALAMO) on the San Antonio River and erected a presidio, known as San Antonio de Béxar, across the river. A civil settlement or villa (village) of ten families also was begun, which grew slowly but became the city known today as San Antonio. In 1773 San Antonio became the capital of Spanish Texas and in time the largest and most important Spanish settlement in Texas. Today it has the heaviest concentration of Mexicans and Mexican-Texans (native born and naturalized) in Texas.

In 1719 problems in east Texas were as bad as those that had beset the missionaries in the early 1690s, and now included desertion. The weakness of the Spanish position made the Spaniards the laughingstock of the natives and of the nearby French at Natchitoches. When a short-lived war broke out between France and Spain, a French force from Natchitoches made a raid in the summer of 1719 upon the nearby mission of San Miguel de Linares, captured the place, and instilled such fright that in the course of a few weeks the Spaniards fled from east Texas to San Antonio.

The war ended as suddenly as it had begun, but not before Marqués de San Miguel de Aguayo, a wealthy citizen of Coahuila, was named governor and captain general of the province of Téjas and Coahuila. During 1721 and 1722, Aguayo did much to strengthen Spanish authority in Texas: he reinforced the presidio at San Antonio; witnessed the establishment of a new mission named in his honor (San José de Aguayo); established a strong presidio at Los Adaes; reinforced the presidio on the Angelina; and erected a presidio (Nuestra Señora de Loreto, or simply La Bahía) and a mission (Nuestra Señora del Espíritu Santo de Zuñiga) near the site of La Salle's old fort. Los Adaes was the capital of Texas for the next 50 years (1722–1772). The king also ordered the recruitment of Canary Island families to be sent to east Texas. After many vicissitudes 15 families reached San Antonio on March 9, 1731. The Canary Islanders founded the Villa de San Fernando de Béxar, the first organized town in Texas, and commenced the erection of San Fernando Church, which survives to this day as a cathedral.

As relations between Spain and France continued to improve, the king of Spain ordered an inspection of the northern frontier of New Spain by Pedro de Rivera y Villalón in 1724 for the purpose of curtailing expenditures. As a result, three of the east Texas missions were moved, first to the Colorado in 1730 and then to the San Antonio area the following year. The garrison at Los Adaes was reduced in numbers; the presidio of Dolores was abandoned; and both the mission and the presidio near the Gulf were moved in 1726 to the Guadalupe River (near present-day Victoria) and relocated in 1749 on the San Antonio River at the present site of Goliad.

As French traders from Canada and Louisiana pushed across the Great Plains, up the Red River, and ever deeper into east Texas, crossing the lower Sabine, Spain became more concerned about the security of Texas. At mid-century it began an extensive expansion of its mission program in Texas and established for a brief time between 1745 and 1762 one or more missions, protected by a presidio, near the mouth of the Trinity River, along the San Gabriel in central Texas, and along the San Saba and the upper Nueces rivers. Only in the San Saba project did the principal motive seem to be different. Rumors of rich mineral deposits along the Llano River north of San Antonio and the hope of establishing a line of settlements between Santa Fe and San Antonio seem to have been significant. These new efforts, except at Goliad, survived for only brief periods, and all were abandoned for one reason or another before the American Revolution.

In 1762 western Louisiana passed to the control of Spain, and thus the long conflict between Spain and France for the control of Texas was brought to an end. On its northeast border were the aggressive English, but they were not yet beyond the Appalachians. Spain sought to curtail expenses by carrying out another inspection of Texas and its northern frontier, this time by Marqués de Rubí, who recommended that all missions and presidios in Texas be abandoned except those at San Antonio and La Bahía (Goliad). San Antonio was to be strengthened by the forced removal in 1773 of all settlers from east Texas to that place. East Texas was to be abandoned. At San Antonio the east Texans were quite unhappy and were eventually permitted in 1774 to return eastward as far as the Trinity River; but, this location proving unsatisfactory, they returned in 1779 without authorization to the abandoned buildings of Nuestra Señora de Guadalupe de los Nacogdoches, where they laid out the town of Nacogdoches, the last permanent civil settlement of any consequence founded by the Spaniards in Texas.

In all, Spain had attempted to establish in Texas about 50 missions, most of which lasted for only a short time. The objectives of this missionary activity, all of which was carried out under the leadership of the Franciscans, were to Christianize the Indians, to civilize them, and to hold the country for Spain. Only in the latter objective did it succeed.

Rule in Texas came to an end in 1821 before Spain had to contend with the aggressive westward push of the Anglo-Americans. In several respects Spain's efforts in Texas had been failures. The mission system as it had been developed in New Spain had been designed for communities of sedentary Indians, but in Texas the Indians were nomadic and in most cases had no fixed, permanent settlements. This made the tasks of concentrating, housing, feeding, and developing a system of disciplined labor monumental. Spain's exclusive commercial, monopolistic trade policy destroyed initiative and the development of markets, fostered monopolistic prices, and discouraged settlement. Strict and tyrannical methods of government by underpaid officers led to graft and indifference to the welfare of the settlers, eventually weakened local support of the authorities, and compelled men of enterprise to violate the law. Beyond its control were the vast distances to be covered, floods, droughts, hostile Indians, and the constant pressure of foreigners upon its borders. Spain found no gold or silver of consequence in Texas, and there was plenty of good land for agricultural and grazing purposes closer to home in northern Mexico.

On the positive side, the achievements were many and valuable. Spain successfully held Texas against all contenders until its empire in the New World collapsed. It did a relatively good job in exploring the land, establishing routes of travel (many of which are still used today), and gathering information on the native tribes and on the resources of the land. Spanish names were given to many streams, springs, bays, towns, counties, routes, river crossings, flora, and fauna. Spain's land system is the basis of the Texas land system of today, and many land titles go back to Spanish grants. Spain pacified some of the Indians and civilized a few. It left its imprint upon governmental organization, religion, architecture, law (the property rights of women and community property law), language, custom, dress, and music. Spain introduced cattle to Texas, laying the foundation for that great industry of today, and developed the basic practices, techniques, and terminology used in the industry, such as mustang, rodeo, lariat, sombrero, remuda, vaquero, corral, branding iron, and bandanna.

Farming, ranching, and smuggling were the main occupations. Trade was largely by barter, for coins were extremely scarce. During the late eighteenth century both the missionary and civilian populations of Texas declined. Life was dull, boring, hard, and uncertain. At the end of the Spanish period there were three major centers of population: San Antonio (about 2,500), La Bahía (about 1,200), and Nacogdoches (about 500). The population was more cosmopolitan than is often recognized. In addition to those of Hispanic origin, Criollos and native Spaniards, there were mestizos, Negroes, mulattoes, *indios*, and various combinations of these. There were those who were of Irish and French backgrounds, and soon there would be those before the end of the Spanish period who were English, Dutch, German, and Anglo-Americans.

The Mexican period, 1821–1836. In the late eighteenth and early nineteenth centuries, Anglo-Americans began to enter Spanish Texas as traders and revolutionaries. Even though trading with foreigners was prohibited, many in Texas, even officials, surreptitiously engaged in it. Traders from Louisiana appropriated much of the Indian trade and offered a market for horses, some of which were stolen from the Spanish outposts. Some intruders were opportunists seeking easy gain or adventure; some acted for others, who had political designs, to map and to collect information on the geography, Indians, and resources of the country; others acted in the capacity of double agents, but mainly for gain; and there were military adventurers better known as filibusters. Twice between 1812 and 1821 filibusters entered Texas and proclaimed the establishment of an independent republic. On April 4, 1813, the first "declaration of independence of the state of Texas" was proclaimed at San Antonio by the Republican Army of the North. The army was composed of Anglo-Americans, Frenchmen, Mexican revolutionists, Indian allies, and a sprinkling of outlaws and cutthroats from the neutral ground lying between the Arroyo Hondo and the Sabine River. They issued a constitution that, according to Anglo-American standards, fell far short of providing for free government. A green flag replaced the Mexican flag, but by August, 1813, a strong Spanish force had put the rebels to rout.

The rich lands of Texas also proved attractive to a group of French exiles, who sought to establish on the lower Trinity River in 1818 a settlement (Champ d'Asile) based upon "justice, friendship, and disinterestedness." While claiming it to be the "natural right" of men to seek and establish homes in unsettled lands, they were driven from Texas a few months later by a Spanish force from San Antonio. The French efforts seem to have been directed more to finding a home for Napoleonic exiles than to overthrowing Spanish authority in Texas.

The next year Dr. James Long, a merchant at Natchez and a protégé of General JAMES WILKINSON, posed a serious threat to Spanish authority. Dissatisfied with the U.S. relinquishment of its claim to Texas in the Florida Purchase Treaty of 1819, Long invaded Texas with a force of some 300 men to expel Spanish control and to establish himself as president. On June 21, 1819, he seized Nacogdoches and two days later declared Texas a free and independent republic. A few months later a superior Spanish force drove the filibusters from Texas. In 1820 Long returned from New Orleans with a second and smaller force. He seized Goliad, but was soon besieged, forced to surrender to a Spanish army, and sent to Mexico as a prisoner.

Texas, however, was destined to be settled by peaceful Anglo-Americans, seeking to improve their fortunes by settling and speculating in new, fertile lands that could be had for the asking, except for certain minor fees. On the eve of Mexican independence in December, 1820, MOSES AUSTIN received the endorsement of Governor Antonio Martinez at San Antonio and later the approval of the provincial authorities to settle 300 Anglo-American families in Texas on 200,000 acres of land lying between the Colorado and Brazos rivers. On the way back home Austin became ill and soon died, but not before he had received assurance from his son STEPHEN F. AUSTIN that he would fulfill the commitment to the Spanish authorities. The Spanish concession was later approved by the Mexican government.

Generous land grants, with small fees for surveying, recording, and issuing titles, were available to heads of families and to single men. Grantees must be of good moral character and Catholic in religion, though the latter requirement was soon changed to "followers of the Christian religion." The PANIC OF 1819 upset the fortunes of many in the United States, especially in the West, and the depression that followed, coupled with the U.S. policy of demanding hard money for public lands, caused many persons to become interested in acquiring land in Texas. Furthermore, good land in the United States suitable for growing cotton and corn was becoming scarce and more expensive in Arkansas, Mississippi, Louisiana, Tennessee, Missouri, and other areas as they became more settled.

In November and December, 1821, colonists began to enter Austin's colony, settling along the lower Brazos, Colorado, San Bernardo, Mill Creek, and other streams. The colony's headquarters at San Felipe de Austin, on the Brazos, quickly became the most important Anglo-American settlement in Texas before the Texas revolution in 1836. During the next 15 years more than 25 colonization contracts were received, but only a few contractors (empresarios) were reasonably successful in fulfilling their contracts and many did nothing. The next most successful colonizer to Austin was Green DeWitt of Missouri, who founded the town of Gonzales. The most successful Mexican colonizer was Martín de León, who contracted to settle Mexican families in Texas. He founded the town of Guadalupe-Victoria (now Victoria) on the Guadalupe River. Two Irish colonies were founded with a modest degree of success. John McMullen and James McGloin founded a settlement on the lower Nueces with colony headquarters at San Patricio, and James Power and James Hewetson contracted to settle Irish and Mexican families between the Lavaca and Guadalupe rivers. Their principal settlement was Refugio, near the site of the old mission of Nuestra Señora del Refugio.

The American population increased so rapidly that the Mexican government sought by a law of April 6, 1830, to stop the flow of immigrants into Texas from the United States and to encourage the entrance of Mexican, Swiss, German, English, and other non-American settlers; but Americans continued to come into Texas under various ruses until the restriction was repealed on May 1, 1834. By 1836 there were an estimated 30,000 Anglo-Americans, 5,000 Negro slaves or indentured servants, 4,000–5,000 Mexicans, and 14,200 Indians in Texas. The large American population was increasingly regarded by the Mexicans with suspicion. The colonists were distributed from the Sabine to the Nueces and to a short distance to the west of El Camino Real; but by far the greater numbers were located in the area between the Guadalupe River on the south and east to Nacogdoches and north to El Camino Real (Old San Antonio Road). There had been little mixing of the Americans and Mexicans, since these two groups were seldom in the same area. The Mexicans remained concentrated at San Antonio, La Bahía, Nacogdoches, and Victoria.

Those who immigrated to Texas were in the main farmers and people of some means, though more than a few had left behind unpaid debts and sought a new life in a fresh land. The small amount of crime committed in the colonies indicates that most of the settlers were honest, law-abiding citizens. Most of the colonists came to Texas from

Tennessee, Alabama, Arkansas, Louisiana, and Missouri seeking homes rather than adventure, although there was to be enough of that in the raw environment in which they settled.

The cultural, political, and economic differences between the Mexicans and the Anglo-Americans in Texas became increasingly noticeable, especially as the Americans began to have more contact with the Mexican officials. Differences in language, culture, religion, political systems, and traditions often led to distrust, but there seems to be little support for the contention that the movement for independence was the inevitable result of conflicting cultural backgrounds. Nor can the Texas revolution be regarded as the result of a conspiracy by the Old South slavocracy or of U.S. imperialism. The primary cause of the Texas revolution seems to have been the substitution in Mexico of a dictatorship for the democracy established by the Mexican constitution of 1824. By 1835 the forces of centralism under President Antonio López de Santa Anna had overwhelmed those of federalism; and, when the national leadership sought to subvert the Mexican federal constitution and to tighten governmental control over the colonies, there were bound to be armed encounters. These confrontations led directly to revolution. Although some Mexicans in Texas sided with the Anglo-Americans, most of the Mexican population remained loyal to Mexico. Even the liberals of Mexico, who disliked the centralizing tendencies there, deserted the Texans in their resistance to arbitrary government, believing that the real objective of the Texans was independence.

The opening shots of the Texas revolution—the "Lexington of Texas"—occurred at Gonzales on March 2, 1835, when the Texans refused to surrender a cannon that had been lent them four years earlier for defense against the Indians. The defeat of the Mexican troops sent to retrieve the cannon was quickly followed by the capture of the small Mexican garrisons at Lipantitlán and at Goliad and by the besieging of a larger unit of Mexican troops at San Antonio, culminating in the latter's surrender on December 10, 1835, and their forced withdrawal from Texas.

On March 1, 1836, a convention of delegates from the various municipalities met at WASHINGTON-ON-THE-BRAZOS to determine future action, and there on March 2 they unanimously adopted a declaration of independence allegedly drawn by George C. Childress. The convention then named SAM HOUSTON commander-in-chief of the army and commenced the framing of a constitution to be ratified later by popular vote. Learning on

March 16 that the Alamo and its brave defenders under WILLIAM B. TRAVIS, JAMES BOWIE, and DAVID CROCKETT had fallen on March 6, the convention hastily completed its work. It established an *ad interim* government with DAVID G. BURNET, land speculator and colony contractor, as acting president, and in the early hours of the morning of March 17 it adjourned.

In the meantime, General Houston retreated from Gonzales before the rapidly advancing Mexican forces. At the Brazos River he learned that the Mexican army was divided. The smaller section of it, comparable with the size of his own force, had gone in the direction of Harrisburg and Old Washington (Morgan's Point), hoping to capture the Texas government, which had fled in that direction. Houston, however, crossed the Brazos and turned toward the larger Mexican force under the arrogant and contemptuous Santa Anna. He met and defeated it on the afternoon of April 21 at SAN JACINTO, capturing the president of Mexico, from whom were wrung the treaties of Velasco, calling for the removal of all Mexican troops from Texas and the ending of the war. Although Mexico never recognized the independence of Texas, it made no determined effort after the battle of San Jacinto to subjugate Texas.

The republic and early statehood, 1836–1861. In time, the Republic of Texas was recognized by the United States (1837), France (1839), Great Britain (1840), the Netherlands (1840), and Belgium (1841). For nine years Texas operated as an independent nation, but had more problems than a small, white population of 30,000 to 70,000 could handle. Hostile Indians constituted a serious problem for land-grabbing Texans, although Houston's understanding and tact held the Indians in restraint during the revolution and for two years thereafter; but MIRABEAU B. LAMAR, succeeding Houston as president, not without some provocation carried out an extensive and ruthless campaign designed to expel from Texas all Indians except the Alabama, Coushatta, and Tiwa, leaving the finances of the government, already bad, in an utter shambles. The republic was haunted by problems of taxation and financial instability; inadequate and virtually nonexistent transportation and postal systems; an unruly and, in the end, nonexistent army; and a defiant navy, whose ships before the end of the republic had to be tied up for lack of financial support.

The republic did have some successes, however, and must not be written off as a totally bad experience. The first congress enacted a homestead law, the first anywhere in the United States, and it settled the Sabine boundary issue with the United States. It promoted colonization and settlement, using a modified version of the Spanish-Mexican empresario system, which resulted in many German and French families settling in Texas. Henri Castro introduced 600 French, Swiss, and Alsatian families as a socialist experiment to a grant west of San Antonio. Castroville, which he founded, with its quaint architecture remains an outstanding Texas landmark today. W. S. Peters & Associates (Texas Emigration & Land Company) received a contract to found a colony in north Texas and succeeded in introducing a few Englishmen and French Icarians and many Americans during the short life of the colony. During the days of the republic, German families from central Germany, Bavaria, and Austria poured into Texas in increasing numbers, settling along the frontier at New Braunfels, Boerne, Comfort, Sisterdale, and Fredericksburg, where they maintained an isolated ethnic identity for nearly a century. Many Germans also settled in the coastal plains in the cities of Houston and Galveston and in Austin and Washington counties, where their mixing with other groups promoted increasing cosmopolitanism.

By the time of the Civil War about 10 percent of the white population of Texas was foreign born and included persons from almost every European nation. The growth rate of the state's population between 1846 and 1860 was five times that of the United States during the same period; and the population's unusual heterogeneity made Texas one of the most cosmopolitan states in the Union. The largest town in 1860 was San Antonio with a population of 8,235. In 1850, 96.4 percent of the population was recorded as rural; by 1860 the figure had only dropped to 95.6 percent. Occupations were similar to those found in the South and West of the United States at that time. The census of 1860 listed the occupation of one Dallas man as a "floating trader," and in another county the census enumerator listed one man as the county's "S.O.B." The westward movement of population in Texas had reached the plains country in 1860, where it halted not only because of the Civil War and increased Indian depredations, but also for lack of timber and water. The western third of the state in 1860 had scarcely any white settlers.

A small segment of the population, along with the hostile eastern United States propaganda against anything western and southern, managed to give Texans during the days of the republic and afterward a reputation for sharp dealing, lawlessness, rowdiness, and fraudulence and Texas a reputation as a haven for gamblers, wife deserters, absconding debtors, duelists, drunkards, shiftless characters, and criminals of all sorts far out of proportion to their numbers. Texas was a frontier, and the kinds of people found upon it were little different than those found upon the western frontier of the United States during that time. It is true that the frontier Republic of Texas attracted a number of adventure-craving southern hotheads and quite a number of canny, land-seeking "gentlemen" from the North, as well as from other sections, who were unscrupulous in the methods they used "to get rich quick." Land frauds were numerous. Law enforcement agencies were still weak or nonexistent, and people learned to defend themselves. Texans developed a confidence in their ability to handle any situation themselves. They elected very few demagogues to office and were fortunate in the choice of such leaders as Houston, Stephen Austin, Lamar, THOMAS J. RUSK, John Hemphill, Edward Burleson, ANSON JONES, ASHBEL SMITH, Isaac Van Zandt, William H. and John A. Wharton, J. PINCKNEY HENDERSON, and many others. So there developed in Texas a way of life that persists to this day with its independent spirit, stamina, individualism, "go-ahead" initiative, and pride in everything Texan.

Annexation to the United States on February 19, 1846, ended Texas' brief existence as an independent nation and solved some of the problems of the republic. The financial burden was greatly lessened, for Texas no longer had to make heavy outlays for an army, navy, or diplomatic service. It received a more efficient postal and currency system, but the inadequate protection afforded by U.S. troops on the frontier caused Texas for many years to have to support ranger and "minute men" units to supplement the federal protective measures. Soon after annexation, and in part because of annexation, the state became involved as a part of the United States in the war with Mexico—a war that many in Texas no doubt relished and in which Texans volunteered in numbers far out of proportion to the population of any other state in the Union. Annexation eventually involved it also in the slavery controversy. The transportation problem that had existed before annexation remained one for many years thereafter until the coming of the railroad.

Following annexation, the state's western boundary was finally fixed after a bitter controversy and threatened war with the United States. Texas surrendered approximately one-third of the territory it claimed, for which it received $10 million, thus enabling it to pay off its debt as a republic, to create a permanent school fund, and to finance the construction of a number of badly needed public buildings. Land has always absorbed the interest of Texans. The possibility of acquiring land cheaply had attracted Anglo-Americans to Spanish Texas in 1820, and the availability of free or cheap land was to play a major role in the political, economic, and social development of the state until 1920, when the state disposed of its last remaining public domain. The deep concern that Texans always have had for land is seen in their insistence since 1836 that the commissioner of the general land office be an elected position. Texas has used land, in part, to support the functions of government; to promote settlement through homestead grants and the sale of land cheaply; to reward veterans for military service; to promote railroad development; and to support its public schools, colleges, universities, and eleemosynary institutions through the creation of endowments based upon land.

Civil War and Reconstruction, 1861–1870. It was not difficult for Texas to become associated with the proslavery element of the South. Three-fourths of the state's population in 1860 was born outside Texas, with a majority of the immigrants having come from Arkansas, Missouri, Tennessee, and the Old South. Tennessee contributed 42,265, more than any other American state, a figure that was almost equal to the foreign-born element of 43,422 (including 20,553 Germans and 12,443 Mexicans) in the state's population.

Following the election of Abraham Lincoln, the secession leaders in Texas pushed through SECESSION over the objections of Governor Houston. About 60,000 Texans saw service in the Confederate armies, two-thirds of whom served in the trans-Mississippi West and the others mainly east of the Mississippi River in northern Virginia and elsewhere. Famed Texan units included JOHN BELL HOOD's Texas Brigade and B. F. Terry's Texas Rangers; and individual Texans who will be long remembered for their distinguished military service include John S. Ford, Ben McCulloch, Tom Green, ALBERT SIDNEY JOHNSTON, William C. Young, and Richard W. ("Dick") Dowling. During the war three efforts were made by Union forces to invade Texas: at GALVESTON (October, 1862), at SABINE PASS (September, 1863), and at SABINE CROSSROADS (April, 1864). All ended in failure. The last battle of the war was fought at Palmito Ranch, near Brownsville, on May 13, 1865, resulting in a signal victory for a small Texan unit under Colonel Ford over a much larger federal unit headed for Brownsville. The Texans had not heard of Robert E. Lee's surrender a month before.

Because of its geographic position Texas was fortunate in being removed from the center of military activity; and the Union BLOCKADE of the Texas coast was never an impenetrable one. Having a long land boundary with Mexico, Texans were able to trade with that country and through it with Europe to obtain supplies for the Confederacy and for its civilian population. Trade was probably one of Texas' more important contributions to the war. Texans suffered less than the people in most of the Confederate states. However, before the close of the war, Texans on the home front were beginning to suffer from extreme shortages of sugar, salt, flour, tobacco, cloth, leather goods, plows, wagons, paper, medicines, and medical supplies of various kinds. The burden was increased because of the large influx of refugees from the war to the east and, in the late stages of the conflict, of deserters from the Confederate army, outlaws, and renegades, who prowled the state in increasing numbers. The war forced a readjustment in farming, causing a decline in cotton production and an increase in the growing of food crops. With the collapse of the Confederacy there was a breakdown in state government at all levels, resulting in an increase in lawlessness.

With the commencement of military occupation under General Gordon Granger on June 19, 1865, followed a month later by the arrival of ANDREW JACKSON HAMILTON, a former U.S. congressman from Texas and Unionist who had been named provisional governor of Texas, there was a gradual restoration of law and order. Granger read Lincoln's Emancipation Proclamation on June 19 (called "Juneteenth"), a date that Texas Negroes observe as the date of their liberation. Hamilton called for the election of a convention to frame a new constitution (1866), which recognized national supremacy, declared secession null and void, repudiated all Confederate and state debts incurred during the war, but refused to give the freedmen equal rights with the whites. It did, however, extend to them more privileges and rights than did any other former Confederate state, by providing security for them in person and property and by according to them the same rights before the courts as a white person, except to testify in cases where Negroes were not involved.

JAMES W. THROCKMORTON, a strong opponent of secession but an able Confederate officer, was overwhelmingly elected governor on a platform that barred Negroes from voting. Many Texans now thought that Reconstruction was over and that they would be able to work out their own problems. Throckmorton sought to bring about better law and order and better frontier defense by having the federal occupation troops in the towns, where they were a source of trouble, moved to the frontier. When the Radicals in Congress seized from President ANDREW JOHNSON control over and direction of Reconstruction, however, the whole process of Reconstruction had to be gone through again. A new registration of voters, discriminatory to former Confederates and highly favorable to the freedmen, was carried out; and a new constitution, approved by only 45 of the 90 convention delegates, was ratified by the people in November, 1869. The new constitution (1869) permitted unrestricted Negro suffrage and provided for a great centralization of authority, which proved to be bad under officials who abused their power. The term of office of the governor and other high officials was set at four years, and the governor was given extensive appointive powers. This constitution did more for public education than previous ones by providing for better financial support, equal schooling for all children from six to eighteen years of age, irrespective of race or color, and a centralized state school administration. Later historians of the period say that the constitution was a good one, but under the circumstances it was at the time bitterly criticized. Even the Radicals opposed its adoption on the grounds that it was too conservative and sought to discredit it with President U. S. Grant, but to no avail.

Origins of modern Texas. The heavy hand of the U.S. military authority was seen in the election in 1870 of EDMUND J. DAVIS, a Radical Republican, to the governorship by a narrow vote over Hamilton, a Moderate Republican supported by the Democrats, who had served as provisional governor of Texas (1865–1866). The election was delayed more than six months until the Radical Republicans could make secure their control in Texas. On July 7, 1869, the national executive committee of the Republican party recognized the Davis faction as the regular Republican party in Texas, and a week later President Grant ordered postponement of the election in Texas until November 30, 1869, allowing time for the administration in Washington to conduct a systematic replacement of all Hamilton supporters in federal offices by loyal Davis men. During the interval General J. J. Reynolds, military commander in Texas who had been rebuffed by the Hamilton faction in his aspirations to be a U.S. senator from Texas, was able to put into effect a similar policy for state officeholders. Reynolds also ordered a revision of the list of registrars; a new registration of voters followed under the protection of a detachment of soldiers,

and known Hamilton men were rejected on the slightest excuse. Through the UNION LEAGUE the Negroes were aligned solidly with the Radicals. The election that followed extended over a period of four days (November 30–December 3) with voting taking place only at county seats and under conditions resembling military siege, where voters marched between files of soldiers to cast their ballots. In two counties where the number of Hamilton supporters was definitely in the majority, the military prevented the opening of the polls on the ground that the preservation of public peace demanded it. Reynolds refused to make public the election returns, but certified that Davis had won by a vote of 39,901 to 39,092 for Hamilton. No ballots have come to light.

President Grant on March 30, 1870, signed the congressional act admitting Texas to the Union, and General Reynolds in Texas on April 16 transferred all authority to the civil government. For the next three years Texas was subjected to Radical SCALAWAG (rather than CARPETBAG) rule based on force and corruption. A special state police force of some 200 men was set up directly under control of the governor; men were sometimes arrested and murdered before they were ever placed in jail or brought to trial; the Radical-controlled legislature conferred upon the governor authority to place counties under martial law and to charge the expense thereof to the county; and, to assure a subservient press, state printing contracts were lavishly conferred upon those newspapers favorable to the administration. Finally, in January, 1874, the Democrats under Governor RICHARD COKE regained control of the state administration. The Republican party had been thoroughly discredited by its radical and ruthless leadership, and Texas now became a one-party state; for 105 years, until 1979, no Republican served as governor, and few acknowledged Republicans have held other high office in Texas since 1873.

After the restoration of Democratic rule, it was thought by many that the constitution of 1869 had made it possible for unscrupulous persons to exercise arbitrary and corrupt powers and that the constitution itself would have to go. After the legislature failed to correct the constitution by amendment, a constitutional convention was elected in August, 1875. Among the 90 delegates, 75 Democrats and 15 Republicans, were six Negroes and 41 farmers. Although the GRANGE did not function as a political party, many of the farmers in the convention belonged to the Grange, and the rural delegates exerted a strong influence in the convention for economy, low taxes, debt limitation, a weak, decentralized public school system, regulation of railroads, and restriction of corporate influence in government. The convention was dominated by "old-time" Texans. No delegate had been a member of the convention of 1868–1869. The convention met in a period of depression following the PANIC OF 1873; and retrenchment, economy, and reaction to the times in which the people had lived were of paramount consideration. The result was the longest constitution (1876) in the history of the state, which left little to the discretion of the legislature and administration. There were to be biennial rather than annual legislative sessions as provided by the previous constitution. Regular sessions were limited to 60 days; and, if the legislature stayed in session beyond that time, its members were to be reduced automatically to 40 percent of the regular pay of $5 per day. The legislature was forbidden to incur a debt of more than $200,000, to give or lend the credit of the state to any person or corporation, and to make appropriations for private or individual purposes. The legislature was to create no office with a term greater than two years, and the number of offices to be filled by popular election was increased. A dual system of superior courts was created: a supreme court to handle only civil cases and a court of appeal (court of criminal appeals today) with appellate jurisdiction over all criminal cases.

Railroads were declared to be common carriers; consolidation of competing lines was forbidden; and the legislature was authorized to prohibit unjust discrimination and to set maximum freight and passenger rates. Homestead grants were authorized, but the immigration bureau in the constitution of 1869 was abolished as a waste of money; however, in 1959 a constitutional amendment permitted the Texas state highway department to promote recreational travel in the state and to operate tourist bureaus. The constitution made no effort to discriminate by race or to restrict the right to vote; and no registration of voters was required until the constitution was amended in 1891. Provision was made for segregated but equal public school education. Provisions relative to public school education were not as generous as those under the constitution of 1869, but the public schools were given an enlarged endowment, which ultimately amounted to 42.5 million acres of land. The endowment for the University of Texas, not then established, was changed from 3.2 million acres of good north-central Texas land to 1 million acres to be selected from the unappropriated public domain in west Texas, the sole value of which seemed to be grazing for a few cattle. With the discovery of oil and gas on that land, the University of Texas became one of the most richly endowed institutions in the nation, having a permanent university fund of $669,424,148 in 1974. The permanent school fund for the public schools in 1974 amounted to $1,081,492,087.81.

The constitution of 1876 was a logical product of its era and has endured to the present, although through April, 1975, it had been amended 220 times. In 1974 a state convention, composed of members of the legislature, sought to draft a new one, but could not even approve one to be submitted to the voters. The sixty-fourth legislature later submitted to the voters on November 4, 1975, a series of constitutional amendments similar to the document the convention had failed to approve. Each amendment was soundly defeated.

Although the restoration of law and order and of public credit and the reduction of the public debt seem to have been the state's greatest problems during the period 1874–1887, the formulation of a wise and far-sighted public land policy appears to have been difficult to achieve. Undue speculation, fraud, and the development of large land corporations retarded the economic development of the state and affected state politics for two generations and more.

During the late nineteenth century many public improvements were made. The various state eleemosynary institutions were strengthened and new ones established. Progress was made toward the establishment of institutions of higher learning, beginning with the opening of the Agricultural and Mechanical College of Texas in 1876; the establishment of the first state normal institute (at Huntsville) for the training of teachers; and the creation of the University of Texas (1883) and the University of Texas Medical School (1891). The year 1883 marks the beginning of real public school education in the state.

In the two decades following the Civil War, the federal government began a policy of removing the Plains Indians to reservations. The Indians of western Texas were not always anxious to move or, upon arrival at the reservations in the Indian Territory (Oklahoma), to stay. The peace policies did not work, and the problem of Indian menace was finally solved by an aggressive use of federal military force, by the restoration of autonomy to the state government in 1870, and by the elimination of the buffalo, the chief source of sustenance for the nomadic Plains Indians. By 1879 most of the buffalo were gone from west Texas and so were the Indians, thus opening the way for a rapid spread of the open-range cattle industry across that area and farther west and north, soon to be followed by the small ("nester") farmer staking out his homestead claim. The development of RAILROADS and their extension across west Texas, the discovery of an adequate underground water supply, the development of drilling equipment and windmills to make it available, and the invention and use of barbed wire stimulated settlement. By 1890 the open range ceased to exist, and the big pastures, many of which are in excess of 400,000 acres, came into being. In 1974 livestock and livestock products accounted for 51 percent of the agricultural cash receipts in Texas. The state led nationally in all cattle, beef cattle, cattle feedlots, sheep and lamb, wool, goat, and mohair production. Yet, owing to the introduction of various synthetic fibers and the restoration of foreign competition after World War II, the production of sheep, wool, goats, and mohair was less than half the production of 1970. San Angelo has long been the nation's largest sheep, goat, wool, and mohair market. Over half the world supply (and 97 percent of the U.S. supply) of mohair is produced in Texas. In 1974 Texas ranked ninth in dairy cows, fourth in turkeys, seventh in broilers, tenth in eggs, and fourteenth in hogs in the United States.

The farming frontier gradually extended across the western half of the state after 1870, and railroads and irrigation made settlement of the lower Rio Grande valley possible after 1890. By 1910 approximately one-half the cultivated acreage of the state was devoted to the production of COTTON, and cotton ultimately came to be grown in 238 of the 254 counties of the state. Cotton cultivation in the twentieth century had many almost unsolvable problems, but farmers had persisted in growing it. Although the price declined, cotton almost always returned more income per acre than any other crop; it was the most dependable of crops; and mechanization was more advanced in its production than for any other crops. After 1930 its production shifted from the prairies of central Texas to the south Gulf coastal plain and to the high plains of west Texas, where flatlands and irrigation made it possible to compete more effectively and where long-staple and pima cotton could be grown successfully. On the other hand, CATTLE production in recent years has shifted into the worn-out cotton lands of east Texas.

Until the discovery of significant oil deposits in 1901, cotton and cattle were the principal elements in the state's economy, and even today Texas leads the nation in the production of these two items. Since 1971 grain sorghums have exceeded cotton in acreage and in dollar value produced. Texas vies with Louisiana as the leading rice-producing state, and it has outdistanced Iowa as the leading commercial cattle-feeding state. Texas ranks first among the states in the export of cotton, cottonseed oil, tallow, and lard; second in meats, hides, and skins; fourth in wheat, rice, and fruit; fifth in feed grains, honey, beeswax, and sweet potatoes; sixth in vegetables; and seventh in poultry products.

The number of farms in 1870 was 61,000; by 1900 it was 350,000, and the number of acres in cultivation rose from 3 million to 20 million during the same period, while the percentage of rural population declined from 93.3 to 82.9 percent. In 1940, 33.5 percent of all Texans lived on farms, but by 1970 only 3.5 percent did so. In the period 1870–1930 the size of the average farm increased 20 percent, but by 1975 the number of farms had declined from a high of 495,489 in 1930 to 209,000 in 1975, and the average had increased from 252 acres to 678 acres. Texas continues to lead all states in the number of farms and in total farm acreage (142,566,826 acres in 1970). The total number of farm workers has undergone a steady decline from 491,000 in 1955 to 251,000 in 1974. Since World War II farms have become fewer, larger, more specialized, and more expensive to own and to operate. Irrigation and the use of agricultural chemicals and expensive equipment have become major factors in agricultural production. The average value of land and buildings on Texas farms and ranches increased from $6,196 in 1940 to $151,871 in 1975.

With its great variations in soil, climate, and rainfall, Texas is agriculturally as diversified as the nation as a whole. Texas ranks third among the states, after California and Florida, in the production of truck crops and citrus fruit, which are marketed fresh rather than processed, although processing occurs increasingly in the state. Heaviest production of truck crops is to be found in the lower Rio Grande valley counties, although 124 counties produce commercial crops. Grapefruit accounts for most of the Texas citrus fruit production, with the remainder being largely oranges. More than 98 percent of the Texas citrus fruit production comes from the lower Rio Grande valley, where a wide variety of other fruits is grown in commercial quantity. Texas ruby red grapefruit is famous throughout the nation for its premium quality. The pecan is the only commercial nut crop in the state.

Within two decades after the Civil War, the major railroads in the state had been constructed, and by the close of 1890 the state had 8,710 miles of railroads and by 1975 nearly 10,000 miles of high-quality federal- and state-supported highways. Land grants and low interest rates from the state were great stimuli to rail construction, and the federal interstate highway program and the state gasoline tax have provided the funds to make the state's highway system one of the best in the nation. In the late nineteenth century, the questionable practices of railroads and large business organizations began to create strong demands by farmers through such organizations as the Grange, FARMERS' ALLIANCE, GREENBACKER MOVEMENT, Knights of Labor, and POPULISTS for regulations to ensure fair play in business and the elimination of monopolies. Although there was no objection to big business as such, there came to be much concern for the unfair and ruthless practices used by some businesses. Finally, the Democratic party was forced to support the passage of an antitrust law and to ensure more effective regulation of railroads. JAMES STEPHEN HOGG, first as attorney general and then as governor of Texas, did much to protect the public interest. He assisted in framing the second antitrust law in the nation (March 30, 1889), Kansas having enacted one four weeks before. Hogg secured the establishment of the Texas railroad commission in 1891 and the enactment of a number of other laws designed to protect the public against ruthless exploitation and thus became one of the most popular governors in the history of the state.

Until World War II the leading industries in the state were those engaged in extracting vast quantities of available raw materials to be taken elsewhere to be made into finished products. By 1900 lumbering was the leading industry, having replaced flour and grist milling in 1890. Cottonseed oil and cake had risen to second place, and flour and grist milling had fallen to third position. The manufacture of paper from wood pulp began in Texas in 1911, but expanded rapidly after 1937. Other important Texas industries were railroad car construction and repair, cotton ginning, wood planing, liquor and malt distilling, foundry and machine work, and ceramic production. The value of manufactured products produced in the state rose from $12 million in 1870 to $20 million in 1880 to $70 million during the next decade.

The twentieth century brought confidence and revolutionary changes in Texas. The state had grown in population and wealth, and its natural resources were beginning to be developed on a larger scale. The state's political leaders, though not subservient to big business, certainly, as indicated by Governors Joseph D. Sayers and Samuel W. T. Lanham, did not harbor the suspicions of the agrarian agitators of the 1880s and 1890s. The real industrialization of the state had its beginning with the first major discovery of oil, when the Lucas gusher near Beaumont in 1901 opened the SPINDLETOP oil field (PETROLEUM). In the same year two large, modern meat-packing plants, Armour and Swift, were built at Ft. Worth, and the Kirby Lumber Company, Texas' first multimilliondollar corporation was chartered.

With World War II, Texas began to shift from an extractive economy to an industrial one. The construction of such defense- and war-related industries as aircraft construction, shipbuilding, and petrochemicals gave a great stimulus. Texas was no longer tied primarily to one industry—petroleum—and between 1947 and 1957 manufacturing doubled in Texas while that of the nation increased only 50 percent. The greatest development occurred in aircraft manufacturing, motor vehicle assembly, ship and boat building, basic steel, aluminum, oil field equipment, and tool production. Further stimulus was given in 1961 with the establishment near Houston of the Manned Spacecraft Center (now Lyndon B. Johnson Space Center) of the National Aeronautics and Space Administration.

Today the Gulf coastal area is noted for its huge CHEMICAL and petrochemical industry based upon the utilization of petroleum, natural gas, natural gas liquids, and sulfur in the production of chemicals for plastics, synthetic rubber, carbon black, ethylene, elastomers, styrene, polyethylene, detergents, antifreeze, agricultural chemicals, and many others. Texas City has the only tin smelter in the United States. Thirty percent of all copper refined in the United States is refined at El Paso. At mid-century Houston became the largest city in the South and the third largest port in the nation.

Twentieth-century Texas politics. The early twentieth century witnessed the enactment of laws to protect the health, safety, and welfare of labor and of election reforms to preserve the integrity of the ballot, including the institution of the primary system. On the other hand, the levying of a POLL TAX for voting lessened democracy. Other reforms typical of Texas PROGRESSIVISM include the establishment of a state banking system (1905); the regulation of life insurance companies (1907); laws limiting the hours of work of women, state, and railway employees; and tax reforms designed to equalize the burden of taxation by spreading the tax base, closing loopholes in the laws, and imposing an inheritance tax, but no income tax even to this day (1976). Some advances were made in public school education, but the badly needed equalization of rural to urban schools did not occur until the JAMES E. FERGUSON administration (1915–1917). Rising corporate influence in government caused the enactment of an antilobbying act.

During the closing days of the Progressive administration of Thomas M. Campbell in 1910, the first significant prison reform legislation since the establishment of the penitentiary in 1849 was enacted. Campbell proved to be a friend to both labor and the farmer. In 1917 Ferguson became the first governor to be impeached and removed from office for the improper use of state funds and for receiving questionable loans or gifts from the liquor interests.

The hysteria of the World War I period resulted in several pieces of legislation restricting freedom of speech, promoting loyalty and the teaching of Americanism in the public schools, and restricting voting to citizens. Governor Pat M. Neff (1921–1925), a staunch Baptist, was the first governor to hold a college degree. During the postwar period of lax morality, he stood firmly for moral righteousness in public office, for keeping convicted criminals in the penitentiary, and for strict enforcement of all laws, including the prohibition laws, and he bitterly opposed the antics of the newly formed KU KLUX KLAN, whose capers most Texans seemed to decry.

The post–World War I decade marked a new era for business, but in politics and in political institutions there was much complacency and no strong movement to make changes in state government or in the tax structure. Civil service reform and judicial changes recommended by the governor got nowhere with the legislature, and the voters rejected a constitutional amendment that would have permitted woman suffrage. Public schools and state-supported institutions of higher learning received increased attention and support, however, and public colleges and universities grew both in number and size.

The presidential ELECTION OF 1928 attracted more attention in Texas than did the race for governor. In that year Texas Democrats bolted the party to vote for Herbert Hoover, the Republican presidential candidate, rather than for the Democratic, Catholic, anti-Prohibition candidate Alfred E. Smith.

The panic of 1929 and the GREAT DEPRESSION had no uniqueness for Texas. The Ross Sterling administration (1931–1933) went from one emergency to another, and one crisis had no sooner passed than another was on the horizon. Overproduction and declining oil prices precipitated a crisis in the east Texas oil fields in the summer of 1931. Sterling proclaimed the oil fields under martial law until the Texas railroad commission could work out a system of proration. Publicized as an attempt at conservation, the railroad commission's program established a type of "legal cartel" designed to eliminate competition, set production quotas, and stabilize prices. Today all thought of conservation has gone out the window, and all efforts to limit production have been discarded in the face of an energy shortage and a steady rise in the price of gas and oil.

As the depression deepened, tax payments fell in arrears, and state expenditures for expanded relief programs caused the debt to rise. When he sought reelection in 1932, Sterling found a strong opponent in the old Populist-styled Fergusons. Again MIRIAM A. FERGUSON, wife of James E. Ferguson, ran for election because Pa Ferguson's ineligibility precluded his candidacy, but not his campaigning. Mrs. Ferguson won a close nomination in the second Democratic primary and was elected in November. Her second administration proved to be as clean as her first in 1925–1927 had been tinged with corruption.

Mrs. Ferguson recommended a sales tax as a means of getting badly needed revenue, but the legislature, like its successors, failed to adopt one until 1961, when the state made its first significant change in the tax structure in over 20 years. During the James V. Allred administration, the governor's pardoning power was severely limited and a graduated tax was levied upon chain stores; but the state's finances continued to deteriorate until the coming of World War II, which solved the unemployment problem and stimulated industrial growth. During the war period the legislature reduced expenditures wherever possible, and soon the deficit of $42 million was wiped out. A significant surplus began to accumulate in the state treasury, permitting the legislature to abolish the ad valorem property tax. During the war the rate of industrial activity was the highest ever known up to that time in Texas. Material prosperity prevailed and continued after the war because of further industrial expansion. High prices for farm products continued along with full employment. Per capita personal income rose from $1,935 in 1960 to $4,571 in 1973. Even in 1976 the unemployment rate in Texas was well below the national average, and Texas continued to attract large numbers of newcomers to the state.

In the 1930s and 1940s and thereafter, conservative Democrats showed dissatisfaction with the national party leadership through the formation of such groups as the Democrats for Hoover in the presidential election of 1928 and the Jeffersonian Democrats, vigorous outspoken opponents of Franklin D. Roosevelt in the ELECTION OF 1936. In 1944 conservative Texas Democrats were provoked further by the U.S. Supreme Court's decision in SMITH V. ALLWRIGHT, voiding the state's

WHITE PRIMARY, and formed the Texas Regulars to oppose the Roosevelt-Truman ticket. In 1948 a number of conservative Texas Democrats showed their displeasure with HARRY TRUMAN's policies by supporting the States' Rights or DIXIECRAT ticket. The struggle between the liberal and conservative Democrats in the state intensified after 1948 over the growing issue of desegregation, the disputed senatorial election of LYNDON B. JOHNSON in 1948, and the refusal of the party's presidential nominee in 1952 to support the Texas view of the tidelands oil issue. Middle-of-the-road, conservative Democratic Governor Beauford H. Jester (1947–1949) found that the expanding economy and general prosperity permitted substantial increases in state expenditures without the need to increase taxes. The fifty-first legislature modernized the prison system and reorganized the state's present public school system and its financing. Jester was the first governor of the state of Texas to die in office. In 1972 Dolph Briscoe was elected for a two-year term and, following a constitutional change, was in 1974 elected to a four-year term. The regular session of the legislature in 1951 redrew the state legislative districts for the first time in 30 years, giving more representation to the urban centers; enacted a safety and driver's responsibility law; and created a state building commission to acquire sites for state buildings and to plan and control their construction. In 1955 the legislature created a coordinating board for state colleges and universities, which remains too susceptible to political pressures, even from the members of the legislature, to accomplish the objectives for which it was created.

By an ingenious system of cross-filing, Governor Allan Shivers (1949–1957) led a revolt in 1952 of Texas Democrats against the party's presidential nominee Adlai Stevenson, because Stevenson refused to say that, if elected president, he would sign a quitclaim deed to the tidelands claimed by Texas. The John Connally administration (1963–1969) saw a reorganization and upgrading of the state's system of higher education, the promotion of public libraries, the reorganization and improvement of the state's mental health institutions, the adoption of a new penal code, and the settlement in 1968 of the boundary controversy with Mexico in the Chamizal area, a matter of dispute since 1852.

After World War I the Republicans in Texas enjoyed relative harmony in their ranks, but during the past two decades there has been some growing dissension attributed, in part, to so many conservative Democrats joining the party and forcing it to take a position more to the extreme right.

Even though the Democrats have been divided, the conservative and moderate states' rights elements of the party have dominated the political scene on the state level. Conservative Democrats have crossed over to carry the state for Republican presidential candidates Herbert Hoover, Dwight Eisenhower, Barry Goldwater, and Richard Nixon; since 1961 they have helped elect and sustain one Republican senator and from one to four Republican congressmen from Texas; and, in the 1978 gubernatorial campaign, they helped elect Republican William Clements, Jr., a Dallas oil millionaire. In 1964 the Democrats submerged their internal dissensions sufficiently to support Lyndon Johnson, the native son.

In the last quarter of the twentieth century Texas is still experiencing growing pains. It remains a land of opportunity with a healthy, expanding economy and a population growth rate exceeding the national average. Many of the state's outstanding public, business, and professional men and women have risen to prominence from modest backgrounds to make good through sheer ability and determination. In Texas today there is a strong spirit of independence among its people, as well as a nonconforming pragmatism and dogmatism that stimulate an interest in stability and foster conservatism. Texans are proud of their heritage. In this land of opportunity and contrast there are deep-seated feelings of confidence and self-reliance.

Manuscripts and printed primary sources. Principal depositories of manuscripts are Texas State Archives (S. V. Connor, *Southwestern Historical Quarterly* [Jan., 1956], for guide); University of Texas Archives (C. V. Kielman, *Guide to Manuscript Collection at University of Texas* [1967]); Bexar Archives, at University of Texas, Austin, on microfilm; Rosenberg Library, Galveston; San Jacinto Museum of History; Dallas Historical Society; Spanish Archives, San Antonio (C. E. Castañeda, *Report on Archives of San Antonio* [1937]); Baylor University Library (G. B. Harrison, Jr., *Baylor Bulletin* [Dec., 1940]); and Southwest Collection, Texas Tech University. For fuller listing of depositories, see P. M. Hamer (ed.), *Guide to Archives and Manuscripts* (1961); L. Hanke, *Southwestern Historical Quarterly* (Jan., 1956), materials on Texas history in European archives and libraries; and E. G. Holley and D. D. Hendrick, *Resources of Texas Libraries* (1968).

An invaluable source of information is *Texas Almanac*, published annually 1857–73 (except 1866), 1904, 1910, 1911, 1914, 1925–29 and biennially since 1929. Printed source materials include E. Wallace and D. M. Vigness (eds.), *Documents of Texas History* (1963); C. W. Hackett (ed. and trans.), *Documents Relating to New Mexico, Nueva Vizcaya, and Approaches to 1773* (3 vols.; 1923–27) and *Pichardo's Treatise on Louisiana and Texas* (4 vols.; 1931, 1947), contains documents copied from Spanish and Mexican archives; and M. D. McLean (ed.),

TEXAS POPULATION, 1827–1970

Year	Total	White	Nonwhite Slave	Nonwhite Free	% Growth	Rank U.S.	Rank South
1827	10,000						
1831	20,000				100.0		
1834	24,700				23.5		
1836	53,670 (est.)	34,470		19,200	117.3		
1845	125,000 (est.)				132.9		
1847	135,775	96,775		39,000	7.4		
1848	158,356	115,901		42,455	16.6		
1850	212,592	154,034	58,161	397	34.2	25	12
1860	604,215	420,891	182,566	758	184.2	23	12
1870	818,579	564,700		253,879	35.5	19	9
1880	1,591,749	1,197,237		394,512	94.5	11	3
1890	2,235,527	1,745,935		489,592	40.4	7	2
1900	3,048,710	2,426,669		622,041	36.4	6	2
1910	3,896,542	3,204,848		691,694	27.8	5	1
1920	4,663,228	3,918,165		745,063	19.7	5	1
1930	5,824,715	4,967,172		857,543	24.9	5	1
1940	6,414,824	5,487,545		927,279	10.1	6	1
1950	7,711,194	6,726,534		984,660	20.2	6	1
1960	9,579,677	8,374,831		1,204,846	24.2	6	1
1970	11,196,730	9,717,128		1,479,602	16.9	4	1

TEXAS GOVERNORS

Governor	Party	Term
SPANISH		
Francisco de Garay		1523–1526
Pánfilo de Narváez		1526–1528
Nuño de Guzmán		1528–1530
Hernando de Soto		1538–1543
Domingo Terán de los Ríos		1691–1692
Gregorio de Salinas		1692–1697
Francisco Cuerbo y Valdez		1698–1702
Mathias de Aguirre		1703–1705
Martín de Alarcón		1705–1708
Símon Padilla y Cordova		1708–1712
Pedro Fermin de Echevera y Subisa		1712–1714
Juan Valdez		1714–1716
Martín de Alarcón		1716–1719
Marqués de San Miguel de Aguayo		1719–1722
Fernando Pérez de Almazán		1722–1726
Melchor de Media Villa y Ascona		1727–1730
Juan Antonio Bustillo y Zevallos		1730–1734
Manuel de Sandoval		1734–1736
Carlos Beintes Franquis de Lugo		1736–1737
Fernández de Jáuregui y Urrutia		1737
Prudencio de Orobio y Bazterra		1737–1740
Tomás Felipe Winthuisen		1741–1743
Justo Boneo y Morales		1743–1744
Francisco García Larios		1744–1748
Pedro del Barrio Junco y Espriella		1748–1750

Governor	Party	Term
Jacinto de Barrios y Jáuregui		1751–1759
Angel de Martos y Navarrete		1759–1767
Hugo Oconór		1767–1770
Baron de Ripperdá		1770–1778
Athanase de Mézières		1779
Domingo Cabello y Robles		1778–1786
Bernardo Bonavía		1786
Rafael Martínez Pacheco		1787–1790
Manuel Muñoz		1790–1799
Conde de Manuel de Escandón		1792
Josef Irigoyen		1798 (?)
Juan Bautista de Elguezábal		1799–1805
Antonio Cordero y Bustamante		1805–1808
Manuel Maria de Salcedo		1808–1813
Juan Bautista de las Casas (revolutionary)		1811
Juan Manuel Zambrano		1811
Símon de Herrera		1811
Bernardo Gutiérrez de Lara (revolutionary)		1813
José Antonio Álvarez de Toledo (revolutionary)		1813
Cristóbal Domínguiz		1813
Benito de Armiñan		1813–1815
Mariano Varela		1815–1816
Ignacio Pérez		1816–1817
Manuel Pardo		1817
Antonio María Martinez		1817–1822
MEXICAN		
José Felix Trespalacios		1822–1823
Luciano García		1823

COAHUILA Y TEXAS

Rafael Gonzáles	1824–1826
Victor Blanco	1826–1827
José María Viesca	1827–1831
José María Letona	1831–1832
Juan María de Vera-mendi	1832–1833
Juan José Elguezábal	1834–1835
Augustín Viesca	1835
Ramón Eca y Músquiz	1835

STATE (ANGLO-AMERICAN PROVISIONAL)

Henry Smith	1835–1836
James W. Robinson	1836

PRESIDENTS OF REPUBLIC

David G. Burnet	1836
Sam Houston	1836–1838
Mirabeau B. Lamar	1838–1841
Sam Houston	1841–1844
Anson Jones	1844–1846

STATE

J. Pinckney Henderson		1846–1847
Albert C. Horton (acting)		1846
George T. Wood		1847–1849
P. Hansbrough Bell		1849–1853
James W. Henderson		1853
Elisha M. Pease		1853–1857
Hardin R. Runnels	Dem.	1857–1859
Sam Houston	Ind.	1859–1861
Edward Clark	Dem.	1861
Francis R. Lubbock	Dem.	1861–1863
Pendleton Murrah	Dem.	1863–1865
Fletcher S. Stockdale (acting)	Dem.	1865
Andrew J. Hamilton (provisional)	Rep.	1865–1866
James W. Throckmorton	Dem.	1866–1867
Elisha M. Pease (appointed)	Rep.	1867–1869
Edmund J. Davis	Rep.	1870–1874
Richard Coke	Dem.	1874–1876
Richard B. Hubbard	Dem.	1876–1879
Oran M. Roberts	Dem.	1879–1883
John Ireland	Dem.	1883–1887
Lawrence S. Ross	Dem.	1887–1891
James S. Hogg	Dem.	1891–1895
Charles A. Culberson	Dem.	1895–1899
Joseph D. Sayers	Dem.	1899–1903
Samuel W. T. Lanham	Dem.	1903–1907
Thomas M. Campbell	Dem.	1907–1911
Oscar B. Colquitt	Dem.	1911–1915
James E. Ferguson	Dem.	1915–1917
William P. Hobby	Dem.	1917–1921
Pat M. Neff	Dem.	1921–1925
Miriam A. Ferguson	Dem.	1925–1927
Dan Moody	Dem.	1927–1931
Ross S. Sterling	Dem.	1931–1933
Miriam A. Ferguson	Dem.	1933–1935
James V. Allred	Dem.	1935–1939
W. Lee O'Daniel	Dem.	1939–1941
Coke R. Stevenson	Dem.	1941–1947
Beauford H. Jester	Dem.	1947–1949
Allan Shivers	Dem.	1949–1957
Price Daniel	Dem.	1957–1963
John B. Connally	Dem.	1963–1969
Preston Smith	Dem.	1969–1973
Dolph Briscoe	Dem.	1973–1979
William Clements, Jr.	Rep.	1979–

Robertson's Colony in Texas (3 vols.; 1974–76). See also E. C. Barker (ed.), *Austin Papers* (3 vols.; 1919–24); W. C. Binkley (ed.), *Official Correspondence of Texas Revolution* (2 vols.; 1936); J. H. Jenkins (ed.), *Papers of Texas Revolution* (10 vols.; 1973); G. P. Garrison (ed.), *Diplomatic Correspondence of Republic of Texas* (3 vols.; 1908–11); D. H. Winfrey and J. M. Day (eds.), *Indian Papers of Texas* (5 vols.; 1966); S. V. Connor and V. H. Taylor (eds.), *Texas Treasury Papers* (4 vols.; 1956); C. A. Gulick, Jr., *et al.* (eds.), *Papers of M. B. Lamar* (6 vols.; 1921–27); and A. W. Williams and E. C. Barker (eds.), *Writings of Sam Houston* (8 vols.; 1938–43).

Basic source materials and historical research are published in *Southwestern Historical Quarterly* (1897–); *Yearbook of West Texas Historical Association* (1925–); *Panhandle Plains Historical Review* (1928–); *Mississippi Valley Historical Review* (1914–); *Journal of American History* (1914–); *American West* (1963–); *Journal of Southern History* (1934–); *Southwestern Social Science Quarterly* (1920–); *Texana* (1962–); and *East Texas Historical Journal* (1963–). W. P. Webb and H. B. Carroll (eds.), *Handbook of Texas* (2 vols.; 1952), is a valuable encyclopedia of brief articles on major events, places, and persons.

Bibliographies. Foremost are C. W. Raines, *Bibliography of Texas* (1896, 1955); T. W. Streeter, *Bibliography of Texas, 1795–1845* (5 vols.; 1956); E. W. Winkler, *Texas Imprints, 1846–1860* (1949); E. W. Winkler and L. Friend, *Texas Imprints, 1861–1876* (1963); H. B. Carroll, *Southwestern Historical Quarterly* (July, 1941; April, 1942), county histories; H. B. Carroll and M. R. Gutsch, *Check List of Theses and Dissertations at University of Texas, 1893–1951* (1955); C. Elliott, *Theses on Texas History, 1907–1952* (1955), indexes 51 graduate institutions; J. H. Jenkins, *Bibliography of Texas Town and County Histories* (1965); S. V. Connor, *West Texas County Histories* (1954); R. M. Girard, *Bibliography and Index of Texas Geology, 1933–1950* (1959); J. M. Nance (comp. and ed.), *Check List of Texas Newspapers, 1813–1939* (1941); and T. N. Campbell, *Bibliographical Guide to Archeology of Texas* (1952).

General histories. No definitive history of Texas exists. Satisfactory are J. A. Morfí, *History of Texas, 1673–1779* (2 vols.; 1935); H. Yoakum, *History of Texas* (2 vols.; 1855, 1935); L. J. Wortham, *History of Texas* (5 vols.; 1924); H. H. Bancroft, *History of North Mexican States and Texas* (2 vols.; 1884–89); F. W. Johnson, *History of Texas*, ed. E. C. Barker and E. W. Winkler (5 vols.; 1914–16); C. E. Castañeda, *Our Catholic Heritage, 1519–1936* (7 vols.; 1936–58); R. N. Richardson, *Texas, Lone Star State* (1937, 1943, 1970), best single-volumed history; R. W. Steen, *20th Century Texas* (1942); and F. Goodwyn, *Lone Star Land: 20th Century Texas* (1955).

Specialized studies. See D. A. Suhm and A. D. Krieger, *Introductory Handbook of Texas Archeology* (1954); W. W. Newcomb, Jr., *Indians of Texas* (1961), incl. archeology and extensive bibliography; E. A. H. John, *Storms Brewed in Other Men's Worlds* (1975), excellent on Indians of Texas and Southwest; F. W. Simonds, *Geography of Texas* (1914); W. T. Carter, *Soils of Texas* (1933); E. H. Johnson, *Natural Regions of Texas* (1931); F. W. Gould, *Grasses of Texas* (1975); S. A. Arbingast and L. Kennamer, *Atlas of Texas* (1963); and E. H. Sellards and C. L. Baker, *Geography of Texas* (2 vols.; 1934).

On early exploration and settlement, consult H. E.

Bolton (ed.), *Spanish Exploration in Southwest, 1542–1706* (1925); H. E. Bolton, *Texas in Middle 18th Century* (1915), definitive; T. M. Marshall, *History of Western Boundary of Louisiana Purchase, 1819–1841* (1914); and F. J. Scott, *Historical Heritage of Lower Rio Grande Valley* (1937). Useful works on the revolution and republic include H. G. Warren, *Sword Was Their Passport* (1943); E. H. Spicer, *Cycles of Conquest, 1533–1960* (1962), Indians; S. H. Lowrie, *Culture Conflict, 1821–1835* (1932); J. W. Schmitz, *Texas Culture in Days of Republic* (1960); E. C. Barker, *Mexico and Texas, 1821–1835* (1928, 1965); W. C. Binkley, *Texas Revolution* (1952), definitive; C. E. Castañeda (trans.), *Mexican Side of Texas Revolution* (1928); L. Tinkle, *13 Days to Glory* (1958), Alamo; F. X. Tolbert, *San Jacinto* (1959); S. Siegel, *Political History of Texas Republic* (1956); W. P. Webb, *Texas Rangers* (1935, 1965); E. D. Adams, *British Interests in Texas, 1838–1848* (1963); W. C. Binkley, *Expansionist Movement in Texas, 1836–1850* (1925), definitive; J. D. Hill, *Texas Navy* (1937), scholarly and readable; T. Wells, *Commodore Moore and Texas Navy* (1960), written by naval officer favorable to Moore; W. R. Hogan, *Texas Republic* (1946), scholarly and entertaining social and economic history; J. W. Schmitz, *Texas Statecraft, 1836–1845* (1941); E. Williams, *Animating Pursuits of Speculation* (1949), valuable study of land speculation; and J. H. Smith, *Annexation of Texas* (1911).

On period of statehood, consult M. Tiling, *History of German Element, 1820–1850* (1913); R. L. Biesele, *History of German Settlements, 1831–1861* (1930); T. G. Jordan, *German Seed in Texas Soil* (1966); E. T. Miller, *Financial History of Texas* (1916), scholarly and accurate for period covered; C. W. Ramsdell, *Reconstruction in Texas* (1910); A. S. Lang, *Financial History of Public Lands* (1932); R. McKitrick, *Public Land System of Texas, 1823–1910* (1918); J. A. Williams, *Big Ranch Country* (1954); S. G. Reed, *Texas Railroads* (1941); C. A. Warren, *Texas Oil and Gas Since 1543* (1939); C. C. Rister, *Oil! Titan of Southwest* (1949); J. S. Spratt, *Road to Spindletop: Economic Change, 1875–1901* (1955); W. C. Holden, *Alkali Trails, 1846–1900* (1930); D. K. Green, *Land of Underground Rain: Irrigation, 1919–1970* (1973); F. Eby, *Education in Texas* (1925); C. E. Evans, *Story of Texas Schools* (1955); T. Webb and W. B. Robinson, *Texas Public Buildings of 19th Century* (1974); L. Taylor and D. B. Warren, *Texas Furniture, 1840–1880* (1975); M. Shockley (ed.), *Southwest Anthology* (1967); W. Vann, *Texas Institute of Letters* (1966); P. A. Pinckney, *Painting in Texas* (1967); M. Majors, R. W. Smith, and T. M. Pearce, *Signature of Sun, 1900–1950* (1950), southwestern verse; J. F. Dobie, *Life and Literature of Southwest* (1952); E. F. O'Brien, *Art and Artists of Texas* (1935); L. M. Spell, *Music in Texas* (1938); W. J. McConnell, *Social Cleavages in Texas* (1925); A. Barr, *Black Texans, 1528–1971* (1973); D. Nevin, *Texans* (1968); M. H. Farrow, *Texas Democrats* (1944); P. D. Casdorph, *Republican Party in Texas, 1865–1965* (1965); E. W. Winkler (ed.), *Platforms of Political Parties* (1916); R. C. Martin, *People's Party in Texas* (1933); S. S. McKay, *Texas Politics, 1906–1944* (1952); J. M. Brewer, *Negro Legislators* (1935); H. J. Marburger, *Texas Elections, 1918–1954* (1956); S. S. McKay, *Seven Decades of Constitution of 1876* (1942); C. McCleskey, *Government and Politics of Texas* (1975); A. Barr, *Reconstruction to Reform, 1876–1906* (1971); L. L. Gould, *Progressives and Prohibitionists* (1973); F. Gantt, Jr., *Chief Executives in Texas* (1964); and R. Allen, *Organized Labor in Texas* (1941). See also *Texians and Texans* (1970–), individual booklets on nationalities and ethnic groups, published by Institute of Texas Cultures.

JOSEPH MILTON NANCE
Texas A. & M. University

TEXAS AGRICULTURAL AND MECHANICAL UNIVERSITY (College Station, 77843), founded in 1876, is the state's oldest public institution of higher education. Beginning as a land-grant college for men, it offered instruction in agriculture and engineering to a student body organized as a military school. Its enrollments have nearly doubled since 1960, but its students, "Aggies," retain a closeness and a uniformity that is part of the school's tradition. Current enrollment (including branches at Prairie View and Stephenville) is approximately 25,000 students.

See G. S. Perry, *Story of Texas A. & M.* (1951); D. B. Cofer, *Early History of Texas A. & M.* (1952), *First Five Administrators of Texas A. & M.* (1952), and *Second Five Administrators of Texas A. & M.* (1952); and C. Ousley, *History of A. & M. College of Texas* (1935).

TEXAS CHRISTIAN UNIVERSITY (Ft. Worth, 76129). Addison and Randolph Clark, ministers and teachers, founded Add-Ran Male and Female College at Thorp Spring, Tex., in 1873. The school became affiliated with the DISCIPLES OF CHRIST in 1889 and in 1902 was renamed Texas Christian College. It had been moved to Waco in 1895, but after a fire destroyed its main building it was moved to its present location in 1911. It currently enrolls approximately 5,000 students.

See C. D. Hall, *History of Texas Christian* (1947).

TEXAS QUARTERLY (Box 7517, University Sta., Austin, Tex. 78712), published under the aegis of the University of Texas, was founded in 1958. With a circulation of 2,000, it publishes scholarly articles in every area of the humanities, humor, history, adventure, poetry, and fine arts. Its orientation is national, even international, in scope, but the journal occasionally publishes material on Texas and the South. From time to time the *Quarterly* features articles based on materials from the university's library holdings.

TEXAS STATE GAZETTE began publication in 1849 as the official organ of the state's Democratic party. Undergoing several variations on its original name, the weekly discontinued publication in 1879.

See bound copies at Library of Congress (1853–60); and microfilm from Microfilm Center, Inc., Dallas.

TEXAS STATE HISTORICAL ASSOCIATION

(Sid Richardson Hall, University Sta., Austin, Tex. 78712), founded in 1897, publishes an occasional book, the magazine *Texas Historian* (five times yearly), and the *Southwestern Historical Quarterly*. The *Quarterly* has a circulation of 3,250 (1976). It prefers scholarly articles on the state but accepts a few on other southwestern areas. The association offers three annual awards: for the best article in the *Quarterly*; for the most substantial contribution to Texas history; and for the best paper on local topics among undergraduates in Texas colleges and universities. It also offers a series of prizes for essays written by young people for the junior and senior high school student magazine *Texas Historian*.

See J. B. Frantz, *Southwestern Historical Quarterly* (Jan., 1967).

TEXAS SYSTEM, UNIVERSITY OF, comprises

five major campuses and three medical branches. The oldest and largest part of the system is the university at Austin (78712), founded in 1881. It has an enrollment of approximately 44,000 students in a wide variety of undergraduate and graduate programs of study. The university at Arlington (76019), with an enrollment of 14,000 students, was founded in 1895 as a private junior college. It became a state institution in 1917 and, after being expanded to a senior-level college in 1959, was made a part of the University of Texas System in 1965. The Texas School of Mines and Metallurgy at El Paso (79968) was created in 1913. It was reorganized as Texas Western College in 1949 and was made a part of the university system in 1957. The two newest components are the campuses at Permian Basin (Odessa, 79762) and at San Antonio (78285), both founded in 1973.

The University of Texas System and Texas A. & M. both share the revenues from an endowment of PETROLEUM royalties. Although the endowment is second in value only to that of Harvard University, its provisions restrict expenditures to the support of capital improvements. The university, therefore, traditionally has enjoyed a fine physical plant, but its dependence upon the state legislature for operating funds frequently has made it an issue in and a party to turbulent state politics. Governor JAMES E. FERGUSON, for example, in 1915, 1916, and 1917 demanded the dismissal of several faculty members, objected to the board of regents' selection of a university president at Austin, and vetoed the university's appropriations bill. The conflict led ultimately to a march by the university's student body upon the state capitol and also to the impeachment and conviction of the governor. A second notable war between the university and the state government occurred in the 1940s, when the governor and the legislature sought to curb what they perceived to be the "radicalism" of the faculty. One of the issues was the university's purchase of the "atheistic" and "obscene" papers of such notable English poets as Byron, Browning, Shelley, and Tennyson. Other issues involved the firing of professors, the dismissal in 1944 of President Homer P. Rainey, and the desegregation of the school (SWEATT V. PAINTER).

Despite these periodic problems, the University of Texas System has grown into the largest and one of the finest university programs in the South. In addition to the research materials of the nearby Lyndon Baines Johnson Library, the university library at Austin maintains several collections of special value to scholars of southern history. The Bexar Archives house the civil, religious, and military records of the area of Texas under Spanish and Mexican rule; the Littlefield Collection of maps, books, and newspapers consists of over 30,000 items; the Texas Collection of the Eugene C. Barker Texas History Center is the largest collection of Texana in existence. The library also houses the papers of such notable Texans as MOSES AUSTIN, STEPHEN AUSTIN, JAMES S. HOGG, ANSON JONES, and THOMAS J. RUSK.

See W. E. Long, *For All Time to Come* (1964); W. J. Battle, *Southwestern Historical Quarterly* (April, 1951), surveys 1883–1950; H. Y. Benedict, *Source Book* (1917); T. B. Brewer, *Southwestern Historical Quarterly* (Oct., 1966), history department; G. P. Garrison, *Southwestern Historical Quarterly* (July, 1956), first 25 years; J. J. Lane, *History of University of Texas* (1891); H. P. Rainey, *Tower and Dome* (1971), former president's account of fight with legislature; R. W. Steen, *Southwestern Historical Quarterly* (March, 1955); and O. M. Roberts, *Southwestern Historical Quarterly* (April, 1898), founding of school. Other studies include M. C. Berry, "Student Life, 1883–1938" (Ph.D. dissertation, Columbia, 1965); A. C. Cox, "Rainey Affair" (Ph.D. dissertation, University of Denver, 1970); and C. V. Krelman, "University of Texas Archives" (Ph.D. dissertation, University of Texas, 1960).

TEXIAN is a common spelling (and pronunciation) for Texan that was used especially during the existence of the Republic of Texas (1836–1845) but that apparently continued in use until after the Civil War.

TEXTILE INDUSTRY. The transition of the manufacture of textiles from the household to the factory began in the South with the outbreak of the American Revolution. In Virginia, once the rebellious members of the house of delegates had called for a boycott of British goods, a group of Williamsburg citizens launched the Williamsburg manufactory, where they produced rough woolen and linen goods. At the same time, a planter in the vicinity of Charleston, S.C., gathered together spinning wheels and hand looms upon which he employed a few slaves in making cotton cloth. These simple efforts were undertaken in the face of great difficulties, but they made no significant contribution to the needs of a new nation.

Once the war was at an end and independence had been secured, many European craftsmen saw the United States as a place offering unlimited scope for their training, experience, initiative, and ambition. These men were poor and sought some sort of support from the new national or state governments. A number of these skilled craftsmen reached America and had mills in operation in the vicinity of Nashville, Tenn., in 1789; near Stateburg, S.C., in 1789; and at Danville, Ky., in 1790. This immediate postwar interest in economic experimentation came to an end with the outbreak of the French Revolutionary and subsequent Napoleonic wars, which served as a growing stimulant for agriculture and commerce. The years 1807 and 1808, however, produced a number of textile mills throughout the nation. In 1810 a special census by Albert Gallatin found 330 textile mills and over 10 percent were in the southern states.

In Georgia, John Jacob Schley, a manufacturer from Frederick, Md., and Jacob Gregg, a Pennsylvania jeweler, each built small textile mills. In Virginia, Jabez Smith, sometime mayor of Petersburg, became the chief promoter of textile manufactures, which made that town a leader in manufacturing by 1828. Smith became so well known that he was called on to help establish textile mills in other Virginia towns, in North Carolina, and in distant Alabama in the 1830s and 1840s. Although other mills were established during the WAR OF 1812, the postwar policy of the British government to dump low-priced manufactured goods on the American market stifled a number of these mills despite the protection given by the tariff of 1816.

The PANIC OF 1819 and the continued downward spiral of cotton prices in the 1820s, however, created a renewed interest in the manufacture of cotton into yarn and cloth. The general economic problems led to widespread interest among southern state legislators. The proindustrial report of the Fisher committee of the North Carolina legislature seems to have had a decisive impact throughout the southern states. This "Fisher report," largely the work of Charles Fisher of Salisbury, N.C., was reprinted by *Niles' Register*, the *American Farmer*, and dozens of local papers. It argued that the citizens of North Carolina had to divert a part of their labor and efforts to endeavors other than agriculture or face general ruin. Although North Carolina had all the facilities for manufacturing, its citizens were ignoring these and importing millions of dollars' worth of foreign goods. The annual cotton production of the state, it reported, was 80,000 bales in 1828 with a value of $2.5 million. In the opinion of the committee, the manufacture of the entire crop at home would curtail imports and produce an additional income to the state of $7 million.

John Motley Morehead, landowner, entrepreneur, and politician, became an immediate convert to the proposals in the Fisher report and was soon producing cotton yarns at Leaksville, N.C. That same year saw dozens of groups secure charters from legislatures from Maryland to Mississippi. The growing interest in and profits from manufacturing drew in planters, merchants, politicians, and representatives from every segment of southern society.

After the revival of manufacturing activities in 1828, there was never again a serious decline in southern support for the industry. It was this need for economic diversification that turned most southerners away from John C. Calhoun's NULLIFICATION controversy. The messages of most of the southern governors at the time displayed an open mind on the subject of the tariff and manufacturing. Governor John Murphy of Alabama suggested to his legislators that perhaps the tariff could be beneficial to that state and that if they wished they might register a protest against the "Tariff of Abominations," but he proposed that they make some state money available to encourage industrial entrepreneurs in the state. He repeated some of the ideas of the Fisher report in the promanufacturing part of his message.

There also began an increasing flow of New England immigrants, who saw the South as the land of industrial opportunity. Along the coastal plain from Patapsco Creek, near Baltimore, through Fredericksburg, Richmond, and Petersburg, Va.; Rocky Mount and Fayetteville, N.C.; and farther inland at Greenville, Columbia, and Graniteville, S.C.; Augusta, Athens, Greensboro, Milledgeville, Macon, and Columbus, Ga.; and Prattville, Tuscaloosa, Tallassee, Florence, and Huntsville, Ala., textile mills were in operation and in most instances continue there until the present day.

The PANIC OF 1837 caused the less well financed and managed concerns to fail. By the early forties, however, a new cotton mill campaign was launched, using the basic ideas of the Fisher report, and the expansion of the southern textile industry was redoubled. In this era there were many proindustrial propagandists led by WILLIAM GREGG and Daniel Pratt and a number of lesser-known figures. Throughout the South, editors and manufacturers made every effort to bring the subject before the public. A minority of editors suggested that support for factory building was treason to the agrarian South.

The results were that more factories began to rise on the southern landscape and that other mills were expanded and began to challenge the primacy of the New England textile industry. The Cypress Factory of James Martin near Florence, Ala., was an extensive concern with over 30,000 spindles and hundreds of looms turning out a variety of goods; the Roswell Mills near Atlanta produced both cotton and wool cloth; though the great mills of the Augusta Manufacturing Company languished and suffered from poor management. Nonetheless, by 1850 there were over 200 textile mills in the Southeast, great and small, producing an ever-growing flow of cloth and yarn, generally the rougher and cheaper types, which already were being shipped to the sod-busting frontiersmen. The mill magnates of New England were increasingly turning to the manufacture of finer grades of cottons as the competition from the South began to cut into their markets.

The 1850s brought a period of consolidation of the gains made in the preceding decade and a decline of public attention to the industry. This represented not so much a decline in interest but rather a soft-pedaling of propaganda, as southern spokesmen were defending slavery by attacking the wage slavery of northern mills. The size and number of mills continued to increase as did the efficiency and success of those properly financed and managed. On the eve of the Civil War, 1860, Georgia had 60 cotton mills in operation and other southern states lesser numbers. The southern industry had so challenged New England that southern mills produced 25 percent of the textile products made of cotton.

The war years were a mixed blessing for the southern manufacturer. The division cut off competition from the North and from abroad so that the local mills received greater local patronage. Yet the need to supply both military and civilian markets put an increasing strain on the southern producer. His workers and supervisors were exempt from military service for essential war work, and top officials and owners who wanted to join the army were allowed to do so and then to return to their mills on detached duty. Large numbers of the mills operated 24 hours a day, seven days a week, taxing to both the machinery and the work force. The poor lubricants and overworking of machinery began to cut down productive capacity as the war went on.

The Confederate and state governments exercised increasing control over the sale, and sometimes the price, of the goods produced. The serious inflation made it difficult for management to provide for the purchase of necessary supplies and to set profitable prices. For example, the Holt Mills in Alamance County, N.C., increased its prices steadily, and the price of its yarns, used by local residents to make homespuns, went from ten cents a five-pound hank in 1860 to $5 a hank in 1863. The mill owners engaged in a two-price system for their products, a high price in Confederate notes and a lower price in gold. The pressure for supply was so great that some states imported machinery through the blockade and established factories of their own.

The textile manufacturers as a group came out of the war with greater financial resources than any other group of southerners. They had piled up large reserves of gold from their profiteering, so they were the first southerners to resume their activities after the war. They were soon ordering new machinery from the North and Europe, and often the same families and stockholders were manufacturing cotton goods in the same towns with their prewar labor forces and managers intact.

The war proved to many that manufacturing was a necessity for success in the poverty and ruins of the postwar South, where a new interest was expressed in the long-forgotten POOR WHITE group. The urge to build cotton mills appeared to become a religious experience and way to salvation, economic and otherwise. Every town was told that a cotton mill was all it needed; even through revival meetings this message was put across. The high priests of the new industrial religion were HENRY GRADY of the Atlanta *Constitution*, FRANCIS DAWSON of the Charleston *News and Courier*, and Richard H. Edwards of the *Manufacturers' Record* of Baltimore.

These three men took up the industrial refrain of the NEW SOUTH, using the long-established arguments going back to the Fisher report of 1828 and the writings of Gregg and Pratt and a host of others. Every country editor followed their lead, and soon mills were being financed on stock sold by subscription at ten cents a week or by the exchange of stock for land, building materials, machinery, and anything that would forward the plan. The slow, laborious program went on, and the cotton mill became an ever more familiar sight in southern towns and villages, their towers like the cathedral lanterns of European towns. The growth was steady from that time on until WORLD WAR I, when the southern mills took an even greater share of the textile market. Northern manufacturers were building more new plants in the South as they expanded their production.

The twenties were bad years for the industry in general, but, after the depression began and with the coming of the National Recovery Act and the National Labor Relations Board, there was an acceleration of northern mill companies moving into the South to take advantage of the cheaper labor and to escape unionization and high taxes in New England. By 1976 nearly 75 percent of the textiles manufactured in the United States were made in southern mills.

See J. Blicksilver, *Cotton Manufacturing in Southeast* (1959); R. W. Griffin, *Essays in American Life and Labor* (1974), *North Carolina Historical Review* (Jan., April, 1957), *Alabama Historical Review* (Fall, 1956), *Georgia Historical Quarterly* (Oct., 1958), and *Cotton History Review* (Jan., 1960); E. M. Lander, *Textile Industry in Antebellum South Carolina* (1969); F. Linden, *North Carolina Historical Review* (Oct., 1940); L. Pope, *Millhands and Preachers* (1942); B. Mitchell, *Rise of Cotton Mills* (1921); J. Montgomery, *Cotton Manufacturing of U.S.* (1840, 1970); R. S. Starobin, *Industrial Slavery in Old South* (1970); D. M. Wilhelm, *History of Cotton Textile Industry of Alabama, 1809–1950* (1950); and S. C. Williams, *Tennessee Historical Quarterly* (Sept., 1946).

RICHARD W. GRIFFIN
Northern Virginia Community College

THEATER. English-language theater in America was born in the colonial South and nurtured there through its delicate infancy. Providing relatively a more receptive cultural climate than the Puritan bastions of the Northeast, Virginia and South Carolina have valid claim to several theatrical firsts: the first recorded dramatic production (*Ye Bare and Ye Cubb*, Cowle's Tavern, Accomac County, Va., 1665); the first operating playhouse (in Williamsburg, Va., 1716–1721); the first professional actor to appear in America (Anthony Aston, in Charleston, S.C., 1703); and the first play written in America on an American theme (title unknown, by Aston, also in 1703). Of greater long-range significance were the Virginia appearance and peripatetic activity of two professional touring troupes out of England: the Murray-Kean Company (1751) and Lewis Hallam's London Company of Comedians (1752). Their appearance may be said to mark the beginning of a continuous history of the theater in America.

These pioneering companies blazed the path for other, smaller strolling bands of players, which came to operate in the communities of colonial Virginia, creating an actual "circuit" that soon incorporated the population centers of Georgia and the Carolinas as well. By the late eighteenth century, theaters were to be found in most of the settlements of the Southeast. Built by public subscription, they housed the strolling professionals when they arrived and the local amateur societies. The local playhouse was often one of the first public buildings to be constructed in a given town, as was most notably the case in Washington, D.C., which acquired its first theater in 1800.

The steady development of commercial theater in the South was temporarily arrested in 1811 by the disastrous Richmond, Va., theater fire of December 26, in which 76 persons were killed. The forces of Fundamentalist religiosity, for whom the theater was ever anathema, used the fire to attack both plays and players by representing it as an example of God's wrath against the blasphemers. It was an effective effort, which, coupled with the War of 1812, brought about a theatrical hiatus. But following the war the players returned, reestablished their sway over the southeastern circuit, and began their push into the western hinterland.

Kentucky had seen the advent of commercial theater prior to 1815, but the arrival in that year of the talented company of the English actor-manager Samuel Drake (1768–1854) afforded Kentuckians theater of unprecedented quality. Drake and his troupe, operating out of a Louisville-Lexington-Frankfort nexus, dominated theatrical activity in the western towns for many years. Noah Miller Ludlow (1795–1886), who originally had come west with the Drake company, led a spin-off troupe and was one of the first persons to perform English-language drama in New Orleans (in 1818). Following the establishment of his partnership with yet another notable itinerant player-manager, Solomon Franklin Smith (1801–1869), in 1835, Ludlow was instrumental in developing a major circuit including Mobile, New Orleans, and St. Louis, thus dominating the Southwest until 1853. Another major theatrical entrepreneur, James Henry Caldwell (1793–1863), competed with Ludlow and Smith until 1843. The competition operated to the benefit of all theater lovers and broadened the southwestern circuit to include such emerging urban centers as Natchez, Miss., Nashville, Tenn., and Huntsville, Ala. Caldwell's greatest accomplishments were in New Orleans, where he built a first-rate English-language theater on Camp Street in 1823 and began contracting with the great stars of the period to perform with his excellent repertory company. He culminated his career by opening the magnificent St. Charles Theater in 1835, thus rendering New Orleans one of the theatrical capitals of the Western world.

Between 1820 and 1845, major towns of the Atlantic seaboard continued to attract touring companies and in some cases, most notably Richmond and Charleston, even maintained resident stock companies. Off-season, the members of a local stock company were able to tour the smaller towns of the interior, thus providing drama of remarkably good quality to the smallest of frontier communities. By the eve of the Civil War, the South had become in effect a great regional province of the American theatrical capital, New York. As such, the antebellum South provided the training ground for aspiring actors, actresses, and managers as well as the audiences for the established stars of the day. Theater dominated the commercial entertainment sector, and southern audiences saw drama that in both quantity and quality would never be matched again.

Although the Civil War, surprisingly, did not bring an end to theater in the Confederate South, it did exacerbate certain forces that actually had been present since the mid-nineteenth century. Primary among these was the tendency toward replacement of the resident stock company in all but the largest cities by the touring "combination" companies, which traveled by railroad with a single dramatic show. Moreover, as theater came to face the competition of other forms of commercial entertainment, it became increasingly difficult for the repertory companies to survive. Finally, the quality of the drama selected for performance tended to diminish as despairing managers were forced to cater to the popular taste for escapist fare. Melodrama and the spectacular piece, though not unknown in the earlier years, now came to dominate the stage.

All of these tendencies persisted into the twentieth century. Commercial theater, except in the form of road-show company appearances, virtually disappeared. Vaudeville shows, minstrel shows (MINSTRELSY), and ultimately picture shows forced drama out of the playhouse. The legitimate stage was left to the efforts of the amateurs, in the form of either the age-old "Thespian societies" (now coming to be called Little Theater organizations) or the schools, whose drama departments were able to provide legitimate theater for those who sought it. Since the mid-1950s, however, some important gains have been made. Resident Equity companies have begun to reappear, some of them

excellent. Most are "nonprofit" enterprises endeavoring only to sustain themselves. Some succeed; many do not. Among the successes, the Houston Alley Theatre under the direction of Nina Vance and the Dallas Theater Center under Paul Baker are especially noteworthy. Louisville's Actor's Theatre is a resident Equity company in good health. Atlanta and New Orleans have fared less well despite excellent performance facilities in both cities.

Yet, on a smaller scale, the Springer Theatre Company of Columbus, Ga., founded in 1961 to occupy the lovingly restored old Springer Theater, offers legitimate drama on a seasonal basis and may well provide a model for similar enterprises. Another sign of theatrical health is to be found in the success of a variety of quasi-professional black companies performing ethnic drama, for example, the Dashiki Players and the Free Southern Theater, both operating out of New Orleans. Finally, the concept of the "dinner theater" has caught on in some areas and provides employment for a variety of local Equity actors as well as touring stars. Whether these signs portend a happier future remains to be seen.

See H. F. Rankin, *Theater in Colonial America* (1965); J. H. Dormon, *Theater in Antebellum South* (1967); D. A. Grimsted, *Melodrama Unveiled* (1968); I. Fife, "Theater During Confederacy" (Ph.D. dissertation, Louisiana State University, 1949); C. E. Hamar, *Educational Theatre Journal* (Dec., 1949); E. J. Poggi, *Theater in America* (1968); C. J. Stratman, *Bibliography of American Theatre* (1965); and L. Rachow and K. Hartley, *Guide to Performing Arts* (annual), indispensable index.

JAMES H. DORMON
University of Southwestern Louisiana

THIRTEENTH AMENDMENT (1865). Originating in the antislavery belief that slavery destroyed an inherent right to self-ownership, this brief but revolutionary amendment to the Constitution was proposed in 1864 by the Republican members of Congress: "Neither slavery nor involuntary servitude, except as a punishment for crime . . . shall exist within the United States," and "Congress shall have the power to enforce this article by appropriate legislation." The first amendment designed to accomplish a specific national reform, the first to grant Congress power of execution, and the first during Reconstruction, Article 13 received a strong endorsement from President Abraham Lincoln, as well as the spirited approval of southern blacks.

Such support, however, was far from universal. Northern and then southern Democrats mounted a vigorous campaign to defeat the article, arguing that Section 2 conferred unlimited and unconstitutional powers on the national legislature. Furthermore, as one Kentuckian explained, "With slavery we know the status of the Negro," but what of the liberated slave? Will he remain in the South? Will he enjoy suffrage? One step might lead to another. This and similar opposition arguments were almost successful. Despite an overwhelming Republican majority, an extensive proamendment lobby led by Tennessee secessionist-turned-Unionist W. N. Bilbo, and the political maneuverings of President Lincoln, the article passed the House with only two votes to spare (119 to 56). Even then it passed only with the absence of eight Democrats and the unprecedented attendance of every Republican member.

On the advice of President ANDREW JOHNSON and in the belief that approval by the provisional governments would mean immediate restoration to the Union, southern whites deemed it expedient to ratify the amendment. During the fall of 1865, eight southern and 18 northern states voted the article into law (December 18, 1865). Even then, however, five southern commonwealths (Kentucky, Delaware, Mississippi, Texas, and Florida) either did not act or rejected the amendment. They asked, with some justification: how can the South ratify an amendment abolishing slavery, which can only be done legally by the states, when the southern states have not yet been fully restored to the Union?

Citing authority granted in the article, Congress passed laws in 1866 to protect freedmen, but these statutes as well as the amendment itself soon became inoperative. Through a system of intimidation, violence, and economic coercion, white southerners quickly relegated blacks to a semi-servile condition. Even after the U.S. Supreme Court outlawed PEONAGE in 1910, rural Negroes often remained virtual slaves. It was not until recently that the Court extended the caveat of the amendment to include "the badges of slavery," outlawing, for example, long-standing antimiscegenation laws in the South.

See W. R. Brock, *American Crisis* (1963); E. McKitrick, *Andrew Johnson* (1960); M. Perman, *Reunion Without Compromise* (1973); B. Quarles, *Lincoln and Negro* (1962); and J. G. Randall, *Constitutional Problems Under Lincoln* (1951).

LOREN SCHWENINGER
University of North Carolina, Greensboro

THOMAS, GEORGE HENRY (1816–1870), was born in southeastern Virginia. Following his graduation from West Point in 1840, he served in the SEMINOLE WAR (1840–1841) and on garrison

duty in several southern states. He campaigned throughout the Mexican War in General ZACHARY TAYLOR's army. His service in the 1850s was mainly in the trans-Mississippi West. An imposing, dignified man with a commanding presence, Thomas had a splendid physique, good mind, and strong character. He was honest, direct, and patient and possessed unquestioned physical and moral courage.

As a Civil War battlefield commander, Thomas was distinctly successful. He defeated a Confederate force at Falling Waters, Va., won the battle of MILL SPRINGS, Ky., and was second-in-command in the Union victory at PERRYVILLE, Ky. In the STONES RIVER, middle Tennessee, and CHICKAMAUGA campaigns in Tennessee, he led the XIV Corps, Army of the Cumberland. Replacing William S. Rosecrans as commander of that army, he provided distinguished leadership in successive Union victories—the battle of CHATTANOOGA, battles in the ATLANTA CAMPAIGN, and the battle of NASHVILLE. His greatest triumph in defensive warfare came in the battle of Chickamauga, when, commanding about two-thirds of Rosecrans' broken army, he held his position and earned fame as the "Rock of Chickamauga." In offensive operations his outstanding victory came at Nashville, where he destroyed JOHN B. HOOD's Army of Tennessee.

The cardinal precept of Thomas' command technique was maximum accomplishment with minimum sacrifice. Thus he stressed discipline, training, careful preparation, efficient execution, and high morale. Critics, including William T. Sherman, labeled him slow; but, added Sherman, he was "splendid, victorious, invincible in battle." Most authorities now regard Thomas as one of the best commanders in the Civil War. Few persons contributed more than he to the defeat of the Confederacy.

Unlike fellow Virginian ROBERT E. LEE, Thomas remained faithful to the United States, but promotions and recognition were belated, largely because his loyalty was unjustly suspect and he lacked political support. Nevertheless, he rose to major general in the Regular Army and received the thanks of Congress. Repudiated by Virginia, he was voted state citizenship by the Tennessee legislature. Thomas continued commanding in trans-Appalachia until 1869, when he took charge of the Military Division of the Pacific.

See F. Cleaves, *Rock of Chickamauga* (1948), best biography, good bibliography; E. F. McKinney, *Education in Violence* (1961), biased but useful; *Official Records, Armies*, use "General Index"; R. W. Johnson, *Memoir of Thomas* (1881); T. B. Van Horne, *Army of Cumberland*

(1875) and *Thomas* (1882); S. F. Horn, *Nashville* (1956); G. Tucker, *Chickamauga* (1961); J. A. Garfield, *Works* (1882–83), I; and leading depositories, Library of Congress and National Archives.

FREDERICK D. WILLIAMS
Michigan State University

THOMAS, JAMES P. (1827–1913), born a slave in Nashville, was the son of a famous antebellum judge, John Catron, and a black slave, Sally. He secured a rudimentary education at a Nashville Negro school and in 1846 opened his own barbershop. Securing his freedom in 1851, he left Tennessee, traveled extensively, and finally settled in 1859 in St. Louis, where he began speculating in real estate. Through some spectacular land dealings, large profits from two businesses including a real estate agency, and marriage to the wealthy free mulatto Antoinette Rutgers, Thomas amassed a $250,000 fortune. At the height of his business career (1882), he owned two entire blocks of downtown St. Louis property and lived stylishly with his wife and five children in a large mansion overlooking the Mississippi. But the disastrous tornado of 1896, coupled with the PANIC OF 1893, forced Thomas to mortgage much of his property; he never recovered from the two calamities. In his last years he wrote some reminiscences about life in the antebellum South. His death on December 13, 1913, rated a headline story in the conservative St. Louis *Globe Democrat*.

See L. Schweninger, *Journal of Negro History* (Jan., 1975); and "Reminiscences of James Thomas," manuscript at Howard University Library.

LOREN SCHWENINGER
University of North Carolina, Greensboro

THOMPSON, CLARA MILDRED (1881–), wrote one of the best of the Dunning school state studies of Reconstruction (RECONSTRUCTION, HISTORIOGRAPHY OF). She might have been expected to reflect as much southern white bias as other members of that school, for she was born in Atlanta, but her book *Reconstruction in Georgia: Economic, Social, Political* (1915) is one of the most even-tempered, least prejudiced of the works by W. A. DUNNING's students. Another Dunning scholar, Edwin C. Woolley, had already written on Georgia Reconstruction (1901), but Dunning himself characterized Woolley's book only as a "very useful sketch, dealing with constitutional and political matters." Thompson's book was so much broader in scope and so much more adequate a treatment of the whole subject that it came closer to replacing, rather than merely supplementing, Woolley's work. She also published "Carpet-bag-

gers in the United States Senate," in a book of studies inscribed to Dunning (1914) and an article on the Freedmen's Bureau in Georgia (1921). She was a long-time professor and dean at Vassar and later a professor at the University of Georgia. In 1944 she served as a member of the American delegation to the Conference of Allied Ministers of Education in London, and in 1945 she was a member of the conference to establish UNESCO.

GEORGE R. BENTLEY
University of Florida

THOMPSON, HOLLAND (1873–1940), a noted historian, was born in Randolph County, N.C. He graduated from the University of North Carolina in 1895 and acquired his Ph.D. degree from Columbia in 1906. He taught 40 years at City College of New York. Although a productive scholar and an editor of both *The Book of Knowledge* and *The Book of Lands and People*, Thompson is remembered for his *The New South* (1919), a volume in the Chronicles of America series. It was the first account of the post-Reconstruction South written by an academic historian. It was a laudatory treatment of the REDEEMERS, full of praise for the social and economic progress of the common white man from 1877 to 1918. His book was the standard bibliographical item until the publication of C. VANN WOODWARD's *Origins of the New South* (1951). Thompson also wrote *From Cotton Field to Cotton Mill* (1906), *Prisons of the Civil War* (1911), *The United States* (1915), and *Age of Invention* (1921). At the Philadelphia Sesquicentennial Exposition of 1926, he received a gold medal for "distinguished service to education."

See New York *Times* (Oct. 22, 1940); and A. S. Link and R. W. Patrick (eds.), *Writing Southern History* (1965).

DONALD K. PICKENS
North Texas State University

THOMPSON, JACOB (1810–1885), born in Leesburg, N.C., was graduated from the state university in 1831 and admitted to the bar in 1834. Although unsuccessful as a Democratic candidate for attorney general of Mississippi in 1838, following his move to Pontotoc, Thompson won election to Congress in 1839 and served until 1851. He declined appointments to the U.S. Senate and as consul general in Cuba in 1845 and 1853, respectively. James Buchanan appointed him secretary of the interior in 1857. Resigning in 1861 to serve the Confederacy, Thompson was aide to P. G. T. BEAUREGARD, inspector general under J. C. PEMBERTON, and principal Confederate agent in Canada. Accused of complicity in Abraham Lincoln's assassination, he fled to Europe until 1867. Upon returning, he settled in Memphis and survived charges of embezzlement while in Buchanan's cabinet. Accusations of defalcation of Confederate funds cloud Thompson's reputation.

See O. A. Kinchen, *Confederate Operations* (1970); D. Z. Oldham, "Jacob Thompson" (M.A. thesis, University of Mississippi, 1930); N. O. Forness, "Department of Interior" (Ph.D. dissertation, Pennsylvania State University, 1964); and W. C. Davis, *Civil War Times Illustrated* (May, 1970).

MORTON M. ROSENBERG
Ball State University

THOMPSON'S STATION, BATTLE OF (March 4–5, 1863), was fought in central Tennessee after the battle at STONES RIVER. On March 4 an advance guard of EARL VAN DORN's cavalry corps encountered a federal column under John Coburn proceeding south on the Columbia turnpike to reconnoiter around Spring Hill. Heavily outnumbered, the Confederates retired to Thompson's Station, a hamlet on the Nashville & Decatur Railroad, where they were joined by the main body of their command. Van Dorn's cavalrymen repulsed an assault by the federals the following morning and then forced them back with a spirited counterattack, after which the Union infantry was overwhelmed by superior numbers and compelled to surrender. Total losses were 357 Confederates of nearly 6,000 engaged and 1,588 federals, including prisoners, of a force of 2,837.

See J. A. Wyeth, *That Devil Forrest* (1959); R. G. Hartje, *Van Dorn* (1967); and *Official Records, Armies*, Ser. 1, Vol. XXIII.

JAMES W. MCKEE, JR.
East Tennessee State University

THREE-NOTCHED ROAD, otherwise the Three-Chopped or Three-Chopt Road, was named from the number of "chops" or notches used (according to one account by surveyors honoring George III) to blaze its path. It was an old Indian trail running west from POWHATAN's village below Richmond, Va., to Staunton and beyond; the name was said to recur in Kentucky. More properly, it was that portion of the trail from west of Richmond, via Charlottesville, to Jerman (formerly Woods's) Gap in the Blue Ridge Mountains north of present Waynesboro. It corresponded roughly to the present U.S. Route 250 and Interstate 64. This road left the (James) River Road (Westham Plank Road, Cary Street Road) opposite the present Country Club of Virginia, wound north and west across Henrico County to Short Pump Tavern, and then

followed the watershed between the James and North Anna rivers across Goochland County and along Goochland-Louisa and Fluvanna-Louisa boundaries to Albemarle. It crossed Tuckahoe, Deep Run, and Mechunk creeks and the Rivanna River at Secretary's Ford, passing along Main Street of Charlottesville and subsequently over Ivy Creek and Mechum's River, following the future line of the Chesapeake & Ohio Railroad. It was habitually used by THOMAS JEFFERSON on his journeys to Richmond or Williamsburg.

See M. E. K. Kern, *Trail of Three Notched Road* (2nd ed.; 1929); M. H. Harris, *History of Louisa County, Va.* (1936); and E. Woods, *Albemarle County in Virginia* (1900).

JOSEPH H. HARRISON, JR.
Auburn University

THROCKMORTON, JAMES WEBB (1825–1894), Texas governor and congressman, was born at Sparta, Tenn. In 1836 he moved to Arkansas and in 1841 to Texas. Three years later he left Texas to study medicine with an uncle in Kentucky and later was a surgeon during the Mexican War. He returned to McKinney, Tex., in 1848, and for a short time he practiced medicine. Soon, however, he entered politics and was elected in 1851 as a Whig to the state legislature, where he served for the next ten years. He later became a Union Democrat and, as a member of the secession convention, opposed secession; nonetheless, he served the South as soldier in the trans-Mississippi area and as Confederate commissioner to the Indians. Following the war, he was president of the 1866 constitutional convention and was elected governor on the Conservative ticket. In 1867, however, he was removed by the military. Railroad interests occupied much of his time until 1874, when he was elected to Congress. He served intermittently until 1888, supporting both federal aid to railroads and limited federal regulation of railroads.

See C. Elliott, *Leathercoat* (1938); C. W. Ramsdell, *Reconstruction in Texas* (1910); and R. C. Holbert, "J. W. Throckmorton" (M.A. thesis, University of Texas, 1932).

JAMES ALEX BAGGETT
Union University, Jackson, Tenn.

THURMOND, JAMES STROM (1902–), born in Edgefield, S.C., took a B.S. degree from Clemson in 1923 and studied law at night before being admitted to the bar in 1930. His early career involved service as an educator, city and county attorney, state senator, and circuit judge. Later he was elected governor of South Carolina in 1946 and U.S. senator in 1954, a position he has since held.

While governor he revolted with the DIXIECRAT PARTY against the Harry Truman administration because of Truman's espousal of a civil rights program and headed its 1948 presidential ticket, carrying four southern states in the electoral college. He was first elected to the U.S. Senate as a write-in candidate to fill a vacancy created by the death of Senator Burnet Maybank, who was unopposed in the state primary. Facing an opponent selected by South Carolina's Democratic executive committee in the general election, he promised voters that once elected he would resign in 1956 to permit them to choose a candidate in the party's primary. Keeping his promise, he was unopposed for reelection to finish the term. Subsequently he was victorious again in 1960. Although he switched from the Democrats to the Republican party in 1964, he won three additional terms in 1966, 1972, and 1978.

Thurmond's political actions have earned him a reputation as a "maverick conservative." He has, however, made "liberal" moves that have received less notice. In 1971 he coauthored proposed amendments to the Constitution to extend the franchise to eighteen-year-olds and to assure women equal rights, the first of which has been ratified.

See States' Rights Democrat Papers, Mississippi Department of Archives and History, Jackson; A. Lachicotte, *Strom Thurmond* (1966); and E. M. Lander, *South Carolina* (1960).

RICHARD C. ETHRIDGE
East Central Junior College

TIDELANDS OIL CONTROVERSY, between
the U.S. government and the states of Texas, Louisiana, Alabama, Mississippi, and Florida over ownership of the oil-rich sea bottoms on the Gulf coast, began almost 40 years ago. In brief, the U.S. government maintained that the states owned only the sea bottoms that extended three miles from the shore. The states claimed up to three marine leagues (nine geographic miles) of sea bottom from their respective shores.

Following World War II, when the great value of the oil deposits became apparent, the question became a major political issue. No political resolution materialized, however, and the dispute was finally resolved in a series of court decisions. The major U.S. Supreme Court decision came in 1960, when the Court ruled that Texas and Florida had ownership of the sea bottoms extending a distance of three marine leagues. The Court ruled against

Alabama, Mississippi, and Louisiana; these states' claims were reduced to three miles. Because of the highly irregular and marshy coastline of Louisiana, however, another round of court action ensued to establish firmly its shoreline. The Supreme Court in 1969 appointed a special master to perform this task. At stake were 258,000 acres of oil-rich land. Meanwhile, all revenues collected in the disputed area were held in escrow. In 1974 the special master validated Louisiana's claims to 70,000 acres of the disputed sea bottom, and the Court awarded Louisiana a total of $136 million in escrow funds, bringing to a close almost 30 years of litigation and controversy.

See *LSU Outlook* (Nov., 1974), short but good concerning Louisiana's role; J. Gremillion (attorney general of Louisiana), *Tidelands* (1957), biased but good on historical aspects; and E. Davis, *Louisiana Tidelands Historical Research Project* (1955), good account of early phases of controversy.

ROMAN HELENIAK
Southeastern Louisiana University

TIDEWATER REGION, a low-lying coastal zone,
extends from the DELMARVA PENINSULA to northeastern Florida and from northwestern Florida to the Mississippi delta. The narrow littoral region gradually rises inland 60 to 80 miles with local relief seldom more than ten to 20 feet. Along the Atlantic coast the region is sandy and swampy. Included in the region are the DISMAL SWAMP, the OKEFENOKEE Swamp, and the OUTER BANKS of North Carolina. A narrower stretch of sandy coast lies along the Gulf coast. Plantations and towns tended to locate along the broad estuaries, which served as transportation routes and as protection from the fierce Atlantic storms. The early settlers raised CATTLE, TOBACCO, INDIGO, RICE, and later COTTON, and these were the major exports to Europe. Abundant rainfall and mild climate provide a 200-day growing season highly suitable for agriculture and forest industries of LUMBER, wood pulp, and NAVAL STORES. Commercial fishing always has been important in the region, especially oysters, shrimp, red snapper, and menhaden. In recent years recreational activities have been emphasized through the development of public and private beaches, tourist facilities, retirement centers, and the restoration of historic sites. In addition, some of the marshy areas are being drained, and the local rich muck soils reclaimed. These soils have resulted in high yields, especially in SOYBEANS. The Gulf coast has developed less well agriculturally, and much of the land continues to be held by large PULP AND PAPER compa-

nies. Other activities for which the region is known are shipbuilding, TRUCK FARMING, and large military bases.

See M. E. Austin, *Land Resource Regions and Areas* (1965); and C. B. Hunt, *Natural Regions of U.S. and Canada* (1974).

ROBERT E. CRAMER
East Carolina University

TILLMAN, BENJAMIN RYAN (1847–1918), was born at Chester, the family farm, in Edgefield, S.C. After service in the Confederate army Tillman made a living farming, but failures in cotton from 1883 to 1885 caused him to question both prevailing agricultural practices and the leadership of the state's REDEEMER GOVERNMENT. A speech delivered in 1885 before the state agricultural society and state Grange at Bennettsville projected him into the limelight.

In 1890, garnering support across economic, social, and even family lines, Tillman ran for and won the governorship. Seeking to achieve POPULIST goals within the Democratic party, Tillman-dominated legislatures (1890–1894) enacted numerous measures to found Clemson and Winthrop colleges; to reorganize the University of South Carolina and the state mental institution; to increase assessment of corporate wealth and royalties from the PHOSPHATE deposits; to regulate railroads; to establish a metropolitan police; to revamp congressional districts; and to establish the controversial dispensary. His forces wrote the constitution of 1895, which disfranchised Negroes (DISFRANCHISEMENT).

His U.S. Senate years (1894–1918) witnessed some lessening of his influence at home and the rise of COLE L. BLEASE. Broad national issues aroused little concern among his constituents, but Tillman spoke both on these issues and on time-worn causes identified with the South. He supported free silver and the liberal issue of greenbacks, fought protectionism as "robbery," joined the clamor for the Spanish-American War, and opposed annexation of the Philippines. President Theodore Roosevelt bore the brunt of Tillman's animosity, incurring criticism of his Panamanian and Dominican policies, his early inclinations to uplift the Negro, the Pure Food and Drug Act, the eight-hour day for federal employees, Philippine annexation, and even his reforestation policy. But to his lasting credit, Tillman helped enact the Hepburn Act, thinking it fundamentally good.

See F. B. Simkins, *Tillman Movement* (1962) and *Pitchfork Ben Tillman* (1944); W. J. Cooper, *Conservative Regime* (1968); D. D. Wallace, *History of South Carolina*

(1934); W. W. Ball, *State That Forgot* (1900); Y. Snowden, *South Carolina* (1920), II; and J. C. Hemphill, *Men of Mark* (1908).

ROBERT M. BURTS
Carson-Newman College

TIMROD, HENRY (1829–1867), was after EDGAR A. POE the finest southern poet before the Civil War. He was born in Charleston, S.C., the son of a minor poet, who died when Henry was eight leaving him in poverty. He attended a private school in Charleston and the University of Georgia briefly but withdrew because of poor health. He read law for a short time with JAMES L. PETIGRU. He was a tutor on plantations in the Charleston area between 1850 and 1861. A number of his poems on nature and love were collected and published as *Poems* in 1860. The Civil War fired his imagination, and he celebrated the Confederacy in poems marked by feeling and classical severity, the best being "Ethnogenesis," "The Cotton Boll," "Carolina," "Charleston," and "Ode," commemorating the Confederate dead in Charleston's Magnolia Cemetery. He served briefly in the Confederate army, until poor health forced him to stop. He covered the battle of SHILOH as a war correspondent and worked as a reporter and editor in Charleston and Columbia. The last years of his life are a record of suffering and privation. Timrod had a true lyric voice, and he was a superb occasional poet, but unfortunately for his reputation the cause that called forth his best work lost out in the history of the nation. Hence, he bears the perhaps regrettable title "poet laureate of the Confederacy."

See E. W. Parks, *H. Timrod* (1964); J. B. Hubbell, *Last Years of H. Timrod* (1941); P. H. Hayne, *Poems of H. Timrod* (1873); and J. B. Hubbell, *South in American Literature* (1954).

C. HUGH HOLMAN
University of North Carolina, Chapel Hill

TISHOMINGO CREEK, BATTLE OF. See BRICE'S CROSSROADS, BATTLE OF

TISSUE BALLOTS. In the years after 1876, despite efforts of southerners to gerrymander election districts, there were many areas where Negro voters remained a majority. To prevent Negro control of local affairs, white southerners invented a number of extralegal and illegal devices. One such device was the use by white Democrats of illegal ballots of tissue paper thin enough to permit several to be cast surreptitiously along with the regular ballot printed on a thicker paper. So that the final count would be in accord with the number of voters, an election official or a blindfolded man would withdraw from the boxes the number of ballots in excess of the registrants. Since only ballots of the thicker paper (the legal ballots) were withdrawn, many Republican ballots were discarded while Democratic ballots remained. The tissue ballot remained a feature of elections in many areas of the South until a system of legal DISFRANCHISEMENT emerged after 1890.

See P. Lewison, *Race, Class, and Party* (1963), balanced; W. B. Hesseltine, *South and American History* (1943); and C. V. Woodward, *Origins of New South* (1951).

GLENN M. LINDEN
Southern Methodist University

TOBACCO. When Christopher Columbus visited America, the culture and use of tobacco were common among the Indians. The word *tobacco* originates from the term used by natives of the West Indies for either the rolls of dried leaves or the pipes used in smoking the crushed leaves. Natives used tobacco more for religious ceremonies and for treatment of human diseases than for personal enjoyment.

Within three or four years after the founding of Jamestown in 1607, settlers were shipping small quantities of native tobacco (*Nicotiana rustica*) to England. The *N. rustica*, however, was bitter and harsh compared with the *N. tabacum* grown in the West Indies, Venezuela, and Mexico and shipped to the English by Spanish exporters. John Rolfe imported seeds of *N. tabacum* from Venezuela and Trinidad about 1611. Virginia planters first sun-cured their leaves in heaps on the ground, similar to the way hay is cured. They later learned that hanging the tobacco on lines resulted in a better cure and a milder flavored leaf.

Today's dark air-cured (still called sun-cured) and fire-cured tobaccos of Virginia are similar to the types first grown at Jamestown. A heavier type of air-cured and fire-cured tobacco is grown in Kentucky and middle Tennessee. In fire-curing, open, smoldering sawdust fires in the barns provide some heat and much smoke, resulting in a very dark tobacco rich in gum. Fire-cured tobacco is used mainly for manufacturing snuff. The most important use of dark air-cured leaf is for chewing tobacco.

Maryland is our second oldest type of leaf. Seeds of *oronoko* were introduced to the Maryland-Virginia area around 1610. At first, the leaf was fire-cured, but Maryland is now classified as light air-cured tobacco. It is used to improve the burning properties of the popular American blended cigarettes. More than half the Maryland produced is exported.

In 1839 a method of curing bright tobacco by using charcoal heat was accidentally discovered in Caswell County, N.C. About 1870, flues were constructed to take heat without smoke or gases into the barns. Thus, the bright leaf became known as "flue-cured" tobacco. Methods of flue-curing have evolved to forced-air systems of curing bulk-packed tobacco. Flue-cured tobacco is produced in Virginia, North Carolina, South Carolina, Georgia, Florida, and Alabama. It is the major ingredient of the American blended cigarette and an important export crop.

In the spring of 1864, a plant bed of the little burley variety of tobacco near Higginsport, Ohio, produced some unusual seedlings with cream-colored stalks and midribs and pale green leaves. The result of an apparent mutation, white burley was an immediate success at the marketplace and quickly replaced red burley in Kentucky and surrounding areas. It was first used mostly for chewing and smoking tobacco. With the proliferation of blended cigarettes, however, burley became second to flue-cured in the amount used in domestic cigarettes. It is also exported. The remarkable ability of burley tobacco to absorb flavorings was important in chewing tobacco and is still useful in modern cigarettes. Burley is produced in Kentucky, Tennessee, North Carolina, Virginia, West Virginia, Ohio, Indiana, and Missouri.

Operation of the first practical cigarette-making machine in the Duke factory at Durham, N.C., in 1884 began the modern cigarette era. Then in 1913 R. J. Reynolds introduced the first cigarettes made from a blend of flue-cured, burley, Turkish, and Maryland tobaccos. By 1906, the American Tobacco Company, formed by J. B. Duke, controlled 80 percent of the tobacco industry except cigars. The U.S. Supreme Court ordered dissolution of the American Tobacco Company in 1911 to form today's competitive companies. Major cigarette factories are located in Durham, Winston-Salem, Reidsville, and Greensboro, N.C.; Richmond, Va.; and Louisville, Ky.

The cigar-manufacturing industry originated in the Connecticut Valley, but it was Tampa, Fla., that became the "Clear Havana Cigar Center of the United States." A large amount of shade-grown cigar-wrapper tobacco was once grown in and around Gadsden County, Fla., and Decatur County, Ga. However, production has been drastically reduced in recent years because of increasing costs and the availability of cheaper imports.

SOUTHERN TOBACCO PRODUCTION, 1850–1969
(in thousands of pounds)

	1850	1860	1870	1880	1890	1900	1910	1920	1930	1940	1950	1959	1969	% of U.S. Total
Ala.	165	233	153	452	162	312	91	2,031	357	296	356	492	815	.06
Ark.	219	990	595	970	955	832	316	267	95	82	34	23	2	
Del.		10		1	30	2		2						
Fla.	999	829	157	21	470	1,126	3,506	4,474	9,248	20,322	22,536	23,413	24,142	1.80
Ga.	424	919	289	229	264	1,106	1,486	10,585	82,364	94,409	102,505	98,308	94,625	7.00
Ky.	55,501	108,127	105,306	171,121	221,880	314,288	398,482	504,662	376,649	324,518	404,881	335,099	375,549	28.30
La.	27	40	16	56	47	102	172	221	81	374	257	74	91	
Md.	21,407	38,411	15,785	26,082	12,357	24,589	17,845	17,337	21,624	28,209	35,533	32,568	24,771	1.80
Miss.	50	159	61	415	62	63	19	726	5	17		3	1	
Mo.	17,114	25,086	12,320	12,016	9,425	3,042	5,373	4,075	4,549	5,470	5,237	4,295	4,963	.37
N.C.	11,985	32,853	11,150	26,986	36,375	127,503	138,813	280,163	454,223	715,616	661,982	654,439	674,932	51.00
S.C.	74	104	35	46	223	19,896	25,583	71,193	83,303	118,963	61,263	81,255	129,169	9.70
Tenn.	20,149	43,448	21,465	29,365	36,368	49,158	68,757	112,368	112,237	109,423	127,324	120,653	111,492	8.40
Tex.	67	98	60	221	176	550	162	27	8	3				
Va.	56,803	123,968	37,086	79,989	48,523	122,885	132,979	102,391	115,826	136,754	124,904	127,706	117,548	8.85
W.Va.	Incl. in Va.	Incl. in Va.	2,046	2,296	2,602	3,087	14,356	7,587	5,362	2,166	3,756	2,976	3,109	.20

Perique tobacco, used in small quantities in the manufacture of fancy smoking tobacco, is grown only in St. James Parish, La. Midribs of the tobacco are removed after about eight days of curing, and the leaf strips are made into twists, which are placed in white oak casks. Pressure is applied until the juice oozes out, and the tobacco is then permitted to ferment in its own juice.

See J. C. Robert, *Story of Tobacco* (1967), good bibliography; Tobacco Institute, *Tobacco History Series*; C. E. Gage, *American Tobacco Types, Uses, and Markets* (1942); W. W. Garner, *Production of Tobacco* (1951); and Danville, Va., Tobacco Association, *100 Years of Progress* (1969).

C. L. GUPTON
U.S. Department of Agriculture
and University of Tennessee

TOBACCO MANUFACTURES originated during the seventeenth century in close relation to TOBACCO production, which was centered in Virginia and which extended into Maryland and North Carolina. Much of the tobacco consumed in the colonies was processed by the planters themselves, who cured, twisted, and aged the product before marketing it. The consumer who bought a "twist" of tobacco would then proceed to cut it into small pieces for use in a pipe or into larger sections for chewing or have it dried and grated for snuffing, a habit that sharply increased in popularity during the late eighteenth century. Commercial tobacco factories during the colonial period were centered in northern port cities, where there was no competition from the plantation-based industry and where the demands of domestic and foreign trade could be met.

During the period 1790–1860, commercial tobacco factories became concentrated in the tobacco-growing districts of the South in response to both the supply of raw material and the availability of surplus slave labor. By 1860 Virginia produced 56 percent of the nation's tobacco manufactures with the industry concentrated in Richmond, Petersburg, Lynchburg, and Danville, and the spread of tobacco cultivation westward had created other manufacturing centers in Kentucky, Tennessee, and Missouri. The growth of a rural, frontier society generated a relative decline in pipe smoking and snuff dipping and a marked increase in tobacco chewing. Thus the factories stepped up their production of twist, introduced tobacco compressed into square "plugs," and competed in developing new flavoring formulas to stimulate sales.

During the period 1860–1915, America became a more urban society, and the public taste turned again to smoking tobacco in pipes or in the form of cigars, though a relatively small number of persons preferred it in the milder form of cigarettes. The manufacture of smoking tobacco and cigarettes continued to be southern-based industries. Although the older factory centers in Virginia and Kentucky participated in the general expansion of production, they were surpassed during this period by new manufacturing centers in North Carolina, which were more willing to apply new industrial techniques of tobacco production. Durham, Winston-Salem, and Reidsville became major centers for tobacco manufacturing in North Carolina, and the BULL DURHAM factory in that state became the nation's largest producer of smoking tobacco, after introducing the industry to the importance of trademark symbols and extensive advertising to promote sales. Cigar making remained the only tobacco industry that was not centered in the South, since cigars were made from northern-grown and imported tobaccos, but Tampa, Fla., did become an important southern-based cigar-manufacturing center when political instability in Cuba during the 1880s caused some of the industry there to relocate.

The leading organizer and promoter in the tobacco industry during this period was James Buchanan Duke (DUKE FAMILY). Duke applied new technology and aggressive marketing techniques to building up his family-owned company, and by 1890 he had merged with several competitors into the American Tobacco Company. At its peak this company controlled 80 percent of all tobacco manufacturing in the United States with the exception of cigars, still a small-scale handicraft industry. In the wave of antitrust activities that characterized the Progressive era, Duke's "tobacco trust" was dissolved by the U.S. Supreme Court in 1911.

Since 1915 the tobacco industry in the South has become increasingly dominated by the manufacture of cigarettes, and intensive advertising campaigns by the tobacco companies have played a significant role in increasing cigarette sales. By 1920 cigarettes replaced cigars as the most popular form of smoking in America; by 1938 they composed half of all tobacco sales; by 1960 they composed four-fifths of all such sales. Neither heavy taxation nor attacks by public health officials have had any major effect on reducing cigarette manufactures, but the latter did promote the rise of filter-tipped cigarettes, which in 1952 accounted for only 1.4 percent of total production compared with 83.7 percent by 1973.

See R. K. Heimann, *Tobacco and Americans* (1960), best general survey; J. C. Robert, *Tobacco in America* (1949); S. Wagner, *Tobacco in American History* (1971); N. M. Tilley, *Bright-Tobacco Industry* (1948); R. B. Tennant, *American Cigarette Industry* (1950); C. M. Marin, *Tobacco Literature: Bibliography* (1970), complete; and Arents Tobacco Collection, New York Public Library, best manuscript collection.

GERALD R. POLINSKY
University of South Carolina

TOBACCO RIOTS (1682). In the spring of 1682 many Virginia planters, in desperation at the low market value of TOBACCO, called upon the assembly to institute a scheme of crop reduction in the hope of stimulating prices. But Governor Thomas Culpeper blocked the plan. The frustrated planters took matters into their own hands, and for several weeks mobs destroyed tobacco plants in the fields. The militia was called out to suppress the rioters, and Culpeper had two of the plant cutters executed. This episode, following in the wake of BACON'S REBELLION (1676), illustrates the unsettled character of Virginia in the late seventeenth century.

See T. J. Wertenbaker, *Virginia Under Stuarts* (1958); R. L. Morton, *Colonial Virginia* (1960); T. Saloutos, *Journal of Southern History* (Feb., 1946); and R. M. Brown, in S. G. Kurtz and J. H. Hutson (eds.), *Essays on American Revolution* (1973). Sources include *Journals of House of Burgesses* (1915); W. W. Hening, *Statutes at Large* (1835); *Calendar of British State Papers, Colonial Series* (1860, etc.); and *Virginia Magazine of History and Biography* (1893–94, 1895–96, 1920).

ROBERT DETWEILER
San Diego State University

TOMBIGBEE RIVER is formed in northeastern Mississippi (south of Corinth) and follows a southerly course through western Alabama. At Demopolis, Ala. (in the west-central portion of the state), it receives the waters of the Black Warrior River, a 178-mile-long stream formed in northern Alabama. From Demopolis the Tombigbee flows south to a point approximately 30 miles above Mobile Bay, where it and the ALABAMA RIVER merge to form the MOBILE RIVER. From its origin in Mississippi to its confluence with the Alabama, the Tombigbee follows a 344-mile course and drains an area of almost 20,000 square miles. A system of locks now makes the lower portion of the Tombigbee and the Black Warrior rivers navigable as far as Birmingham. Indeed, this is a heavily traveled inland waterway. In 1950 work was begun to make the Tombigbee navigable above Demopolis and to connect it by way of canals to the TENNESSEE RIVER at Pickwick Dam. The completion of this transportation link would create a direct route between the Tennessee Valley region and Mobile on the Gulf of Mexico, but the enormous costs of the undertaking have forced many delays and may eventually lead to cancellation of the project.

TOMPKINS, DANIEL AUGUSTUS (1851–1914), engineer, manufacturer, and leader in southern industrial development, was born and reared in Edgefield County, S.C. He obtained his education at the University of South Carolina and at Rensselaer Polytechnic Institute at Troy, N.Y., where he was awarded a civil engineer's degree in 1873. After an important apprenticeship and employment in iron and steel businesses in Pennsylvania, Tompkins went to Charlotte, N.C., early in 1883 as a representative of the Westinghouse Machine Company of Pittsburgh. In addition to selling and installing steam engines and electric-generating plants, Tompkins built 500 cottonseed oil mills and 200 cotton-spinning and -weaving mills in an area extending from Texas into Virginia. He was principal owner of cotton mills at Charlotte and High Shoals, N.C., and at Edgefield, S.C. In 1891 Tompkins purchased controlling interest in the Charlotte *Chronicle*. This newspaper was soon called the *Daily Observer*, and in 1903 the *Observer* began publishing the Charlotte *Evening Chronicle*. Two years later Tompkins and the *Observer's* editor, Joseph Pearson Caldwell, acquired controlling interest in the Greenville (S.C.) *News*. Appointed to membership on the U.S. Industrial Commission by President William McKinley in 1899, Tompkins worked diligently in this office until the commission's work was finished.

See B. Mitchell, *Rise of Cotton Mills* (1921); and G. T. Winston, *Builder of New South* (1902).

HOWARD B. CLAY
East Carolina University

TOMPKINS, SALLY LOUISA (1833–1916), born into a distinguished Virginia family, moved to Richmond shortly before the Civil War. She opened a 28-bed hospital in Richmond after the first battle of BULL RUN. Confederate regulations shortly closed such private hospitals, but the proven efficiency of Robertson Hospital convinced Jefferson Davis that it should remain open. To abide by regulations Davis commissioned her a captain in September, 1861, the only woman officer in the Confederate army. Beloved by her patients, Sally Tompkins was dignified, forceful, and tireless. Of the total of 1,350 patients treated at Robertson, only 75 died. Using her own resources, she never accepted any salary. She returned to relative obscurity after Robertson closed in June, 1865, still a spinster, and died in the Home for Confederate Women in Richmond.

See *William and Mary Quarterly* (Jan., 1905; Jan., July, 1930); New York *Times* (July 26, 1916); Richmond *News Leader* and Richmond *Times-Dispatch* (July 26, 1916); E. D. Coleman, *Virginia Cavalcade* (Summer, 1956); R. S. Holzman, *American Mercury* (March, 1959); H. H. Cunningham, *Doctors in Gray* (1958); E. T. James, *Notable American Women* (1971); and manuscripts, Museum of Confederacy, Richmond, Virginia Historical Society, and National Archives.

GERALD G. HERDMAN
Andrews University

TOOMBS, ROBERT AUGUSTUS (1810–1885), was born near Washington, Ga. A product of the plantation aristocracy, he was educated at the University of Georgia (then Franklin College), Union College in Schenectady, N.Y., from which he was graduated in 1828, and the University of Virginia Law School. At an early age he rose to prominence in the state, enjoying a lucrative law practice and leadership in the state legislature. Toombs served as both a Whig congressman (1845–1853) and senator (1853–1861) from Georgia. On the national scene, he was a staunch champion of conservative financing and southern interests. He was also a strong UNIONIST, supporting the controversial COMPROMISE OF 1850 and leading the fight in Georgia for its acceptance and the preservation of the Union. The election of Republican Abraham Lincoln in 1860 and the failure of Congress to resolve sectional differences over slavery, however, convinced him that the interests of the South were no longer safe within the Union. Toombs then helped lead Georgia out of it.

For five months Toombs served the Confederacy as its first secretary of state and then until March, 1863, as a brigadier general (PENINSULAR CAMPAIGN, second BULL RUN, ANTIETAM). His headstrong, independent nature and his constant criticism of Confederate authorities, civil and military, made him a liability rather than an asset to the southern cause. After the war, he fled to Europe to avoid arrest. He returned home in the spring of 1867 and was never troubled again by federal authorities. Yet Toombs was out of step with the changing scene around him. An unreconstructed rebel, he remained uncompromisingly devoted to a shattered image of his state and section. Except for his participation in the constitutional convention of 1877 and his service as legal counsel for the state, he made no significant contributions to postwar Georgia.

See W. Y. Thompson, *Robert Toombs* (1966); papers, University of Georgia Library and Georgia Department of Archives and History; and U. B. Phillips (ed.), *Correspondence of Toombs, Stephens, and Cobb* (1913).

WILLIAM Y. THOMPSON
Louisiana Tech University

TOOMER, JEAN (1894–1967). One book, *Cane* (1923), accounts for Toomer's fame. A new generation of critics, probably following the lead of Robert Bone in *The Negro Novel in America* (1957), tends to label it a novel. Older critics accepted it as a potpourri of short stories, poetry, and one play. Critics generally extol it as a superb exercise in lyricism, a classic of the Harlem renaissance. Toomer (christened Nathan Eugene) was born in Washington, D.C., in the household of his grandfather P. B. S. PINCHBACK. His education after high school, in Wisconsin, Chicago, and New York City, was varied, although he never took a college degree. He was interested in his own physical fitness, as well as in reforming society and learning to write. Three months that he spent in Sparta, Ga., as acting principal of a Negro school had much to do with *Cane*. Toomer, however, not visibly Negro, after *Cane* identified himself almost exclusively with white America. He married twice, and both wives were white. Although Toomer's association with the Harlem renaissance was brief, he continued throughout his life to write, but not as a representative of American blacks. He bombarded publishers, with almost no success.

See H. M. Gloster, *Negro Voices in American Fiction* (1948); R. A. Bone, *Negro Novel in America* (1957); L. Hughes, *Big Sea* (1940); D. T. Turner, *In a Minor Chord* (1971); A. Bontemps' introd. to paperback ed. of *Cane* (1969); and special Toomer issue of *CLA Journal* (June, 1974).

BLYDEN JACKSON
University of North Carolina, Chapel Hill

TORIES. See LOYALISTS

TOURGÉE, ALBION WINEGAR (1838–1905), was born in Williamsfield, Ohio. The son of Methodist farm parents, he attended Kingsville Academy and earned a B.A. degree (1863) and an M.S. degree (1865) at the University of Rochester. A Union infantry volunteer, he spent four months in Confederate prisons and suffered severe battle injuries. In 1865 he migrated to North Carolina, where his hostility to former Confederates and sympathy for blacks and Unionists impelled him into politics. Prior to Radical Reconstruction he was a UNION LEAGUE organizer and newspaper publisher, and in the state constitutional convention of 1868 he was almost solely responsible for a renovation of the state's legal system. He served with distinction as a superior court judge, and as a code commissioner he helped write the state's procedural law and much of its Reconstruction legislation. He was also active in community affairs and invested heavily in local industrial development. As an outspoken yankee and a vigorous opponent of the KU KLUX KLAN, Tourgée provoked constant wrath and denunciation, but his obvious ability, idealism, and courage also won lasting admiration and respect.

Despairing of acceptance in the post-Reconstruction South, Tourgée returned to the North in 1879. Six weeks after his departure his novel *A Fool's Errand by One of the Fools* was published. Based upon his frustrating and exciting experiences in the South, this dramatic and perceptive account was a popular sensation that brought him fame and fortune. It remains a classic account of the realities of southern Reconstruction. Having already published seven volumes of fiction, politics, and law, Tourgée now embarked upon a full-time writing career. His first venture, the magazine *Our Continent*, exhausted his new wealth, but he remained a productive and moderately successful author and public lecturer. His 19 additional volumes of fiction and political analysis included another still significant Reconstruction novel, *Bricks Without Straw* (1880), and *Murvale Eastman: Christian Socialist* (1890). The center of his attention remained the South, the Negro, and reform, and his many publications, lectures, and political activities made him the leading white crusader for racial justice of that time. In 1891 he began a biracial civil rights organization that helped to initiate the PLESSY V. FERGUSON case, which Tourgée unsuccessfully argued before the U.S. Supreme Court. He served the last years of his life as the American consul in Bordeaux, France.

See E. Wilson, *Patriotic Gore* (1962); O. H. Olsen, *Carpetbagger's Crusade* (1965) and *North Carolina Historical Review* (Autumn, 1963); T. L. Gross, *Albion W. Tourgée* (1963); and Tourgée Papers, Chautauqua County Historical Museum, Westfield, N.Y.

OTTO H. OLSEN
Northern Illinois University

TOURISM. As early as the eighteenth century many merchants and planters traveled significant distances for health, socializing, and recreational purposes. As settlement expanded, as the economy changed, and as leisure time was created, health resorts were developed at such sites as Pawley's Island, S.C.; Hot Springs, Ga.; and Hickory, N.C. Over the next 150 years, facilities and opportunities for tourism multiplied as cities grew in size and as improved means of transport between population centers resulted in increased travel for both business and pleasure.

The Civil War brought touring to a halt, and the economic and political environment that followed greatly hampered its recovery. The industrial revolution came slowly to the South, and the potential for extensive touring went unrealized for approximately 50 years except for the intrusion of "yankee" enclaves in such places as Asheville, N.C., and Sea Pines, Ga. By the beginning of the twentieth century, however, the climate of the region, excellent hunting and fishing opportunities, extension of rail service, moderately priced land, low-cost labor, and an aristocratic cultural tradition produced the development of winter resorts along the coasts and summer resorts in the mountains.

World War I marked the beginning of a shift in tourism from a selective activity of the wealthy to a mass recreation opportunity for the rapidly expanding middle class. The war and its military training and travel programs introduced large numbers of northerners to the recreational amenities of the South. The expansion of manufacturing, the Florida land boom, and the modernization of the area were slowed by the Great Depression of 1929, but the dynamic changes wrought by the Second World War so modified the political, social, and economic situation that the region's potential for tourism was finally opened to development.

The growth of the South's tourist industry since 1945 is based on both natural and man-made amenities. Warm and predictably moist winters draw multitudes of tourists, although the peak visitor season is during the hottest summer months. Contrasts between differing landform features— the oceans, beaches, swamps, marshes, plains, mountains, hills, and exotic evergreen broad and needleleaf forests—create attractive vistas for tourists, who enjoy viewing scenery while walking and driving for pleasure.

Relics of important national and regional historic and cultural events, such as colonial settlement, the Revolutionary War, plantation agriculture, and the Civil War, serve as major attractions. The legends and lore of New Orleans, the Fountain of Youth, Charleston, the Swamp Fox, Yorktown, the Alamo, slave auctions, Scarlett O'Hara, the battles of Bull Run, and Richmond make the South the most visited tourist region in the country. Added to these attractions are the modern man-made amenities, which are concentrated in urban areas such as Miami, Houston, and Atlanta or in recreation complexes like Disney World, Six Flags over Texas, and Stone Mountain, Ga.

Since 1900 the significance of tourism to the South's economy has changed dramatically. In the first quarter of this century, tourist facilities were highly concentrated in a few places, and the economic impact was limited. During the past 25 years the tourist industry has become more dispersed, and there has been an incalculable increase in employment, construction, and services related to tourism. Every state in the region attempts to entice the mobile and affluent consumer to visit its area because of the economic benefits that are derived. Today tourism is the second most important generator of basic income in most southern states, far outstripping such famous commodities as peaches in Georgia, tobacco in Kentucky and North Carolina, and cattle in Texas. The importance of tourism is symbolic of the South's transition from an uncomplicated to a highly sophisticated economy.

See F. R. Dulles, *America Learns to Play* (1940), comprehensive; Outdoor Recreation Resources Review Commission, *Participation in Outdoor Recreation* (1962); R. W. Patrick, *Journal of Southern History* (Feb., 1963), twentieth-century bias; M. Clawson and J. L. Knetsch, *Economics of Outdoor Recreation* (1966); U.S. Department of Commerce, *Tourism and Recreation* (1967), latest state-of-the-art study; C. R. Goelder, G. L. Allen, and K. Dicke, *Travel Trends in U.S. and Canada* (1971); C. A. Gunn, *Vacationscape: Designing Tourist Regions* (1972); National Tourism Resources Review Commission, *Destination USA* (1973); U.S. Bureau of Census, *Travel During 1972* (1973); and U.S. Department of Interior, *Outdoor Recreation* (1973).

LISLE S. MITCHELL
University of South Carolina

TRADING POSTS were established for profit and imperial expansion and control. They were a dominant factor in frontier development, and towns grew up in their shadow. Traders bartered cloth, ironware, guns, liquor, and trivia for skins and furs (FUR TRADE). Most important were deer hides, South Carolina exporting 160,000 in 1748. The trade was profitable for both Europeans and Americans, and it drastically modified Indian culture, making the tribes dependent. Policies were frequently fixed by imperial or colonial governments and administered by agents to protect both traders and Indians. Posts were located to command an area or Indian group, usually near a river's mouth, the head of its navigation, or its confluence with another stream or along a trace. They were frequently fortified, providing quarters for troops, clerks, interpreters, and traders and storehouses for trade goods.

Jamestown, Charleston, and Savannah profited as early English posts, while Mobile, Biloxi, and New Orleans similarly served the French. The Spanish presidio and mission were not designed for trade but fostered it, and a line of trading centers stretched from St. Augustine westward to St. Mark's and Pensacola and from Matagorda Bay inland north to Nacogdoches and west to San Antonio and El Paso.

As the English moved westward from the Atlantic coast and the French and Spanish moved northward from the Gulf, posts were established at the FALL LINE (Ft. Henry, Ft. Moore, Ft. Congaree) and beyond on streams flowing to the Atlantic and north of the Gulf along the Chattahoochee (Coweta), Alabama (Ft. Toulouse), Tombigbee (St. Stephen's and Ft. Confederation), Mississippi (Ft. Rosalie, Ft. San Fernando, St. Louis), Arkansas (Arkansas Post), and Red (Natchitoches) rivers. Some Indians were served by traders who packed goods on mules hundreds of miles to Indian villages, bartered all winter, and returned to a post with their furs in the spring.

See V. W. Crane, *Southern Frontier* (1929); P. C. Phillips, *Fur Trade* (1961); J. Adair, *American Indians* (1775); A. P. Whitaker, *Spanish-American Frontier* (1927); H. Bolton and M. Ross, *Debatable Land* (1925); A. J. Morrison, *William and Mary Quarterly* (Oct., 1921); and M. V. Rothrock, *East Tennessee Historical Society Publications* (1929).

WILLIAM A. WALKER, JR.
Northeast Louisiana University

TRANS-OCONEE REPUBLIC (1794) was an episode in the westward settlement of Georgia. Bitter because an earlier pact he had concluded with the Indians had been repudiated, General ELIJAH CLARKE in 1794 marched a band of armed followers south and west of the Oconee River to lay claim to land belonging to the CREEK INDIANS. He erected forts, laid out several towns, created his own military government, and adamantly refused to obey the Georgia governor's orders to move. By September, however, under threat of force from both the federal government and the Georgia militia and faced by desertions among his own followers, he surrendered his settlements and withdrew.

See E. M. Coulter, *Georgia* (1960) and *Mississippi Valley Historical Association Proceedings* (1919–20); and J. E. Callaway, *Early Settlement of Georgia* (1948).

TRANSPORTATION. Water provided the primary means of transportation in the South during the colonial period. The Savannah, Santee, Cape Fear, Altamaha, James, Roanoke, and other rivers served as avenues of trade. Roads were little more than trails. Passenger, freight, and post traffic moved overland slowly and at great expense. Inadequate roads, however, did link all eastern seaboard points by the Revolution.

The new nation's desire for expanded domestic commerce depended upon expanded transport facilities. Albert Gallatin's ambitious plan for roads and canals reflected this need. European conflict and the War of 1812 postponed action. After the Treaty of Ghent, HENRY CLAY included these proposals in his American System. The south faced a serious dilemma. Federal support carried the threat of federal power. Sectional rivalry and constitutional debate forestalled extensive national involvement. The southern states and localities assumed the major governmental burden of transportation development.

The South continued to lag behind in road construction. Federal post and military roads connected towns in the Deep South. By 1830 Maryland had completed about 300 miles of turnpikes. Virginia progressed slowly after adopting a turnpike program in 1817. South Carolina improved the old road between Charleston and Columbia. The antebellum years, however, witnessed few other major improvements.

By 1819 the success of the Erie Canal was apparent. A frenzy of CANAL building gripped the nation in the 1820s and 1830s. The South, however, possessed only 14 percent of the canal mileage in 1850. The James & Kanawha Canal in Virginia and the Chesapeake & Ohio Canal in Maryland required over 70 percent of the total southern canal investment and possessed the same proportion of the region's total canal mileage.

Throughout the antebellum years natural waterways offered the most efficient, least expensive transportation. The rivers of the seaboard continued to serve the TIDEWATER. Flatboats moved the produce of the Ohio Valley and Upper South downriver throughout the period (RIVERCRAFT). The rapid expansion of steamboat traffic on the Ohio and Mississippi-Missouri rivers made New Orleans the most dynamic city in the South. Shipping charges and time requirements fell as nearly 1,000 steamboats plied the Mississippi in 1860. Additionally, the ability to power traffic upriver produced a new and considerable reverse flow.

The application of steam power to river transport presaged the steam railway. By 1835 the locomotive had replaced the horse-drawn car, and the RAILROAD age had begun. The South played a pioneering role in this development. The Baltimore & Ohio Railroad heralded the railroad age. The 136-mile line from Charleston to Hamburg, S.C., completed in 1833, was the second in the nation and at the time the longest in the world under single management. In 1840 the South led the nation in rail mileage, and the Central of Georgia was the longest in the country. Spurred by the investment of state and local governments, the southern states had completed over 9,000 miles of track by the Civil War. The federal government provided the impetus for the Mobile & Ohio. However, local and parochial interests prevailed. Most roads fed individual cities. Developers gave little thought to system. Most of the interior remained without rail service.

The Civil War slowed the pace of railroad construction in the South. Necessary rails and equipment could not be procured. Mobilization strained the equipment and demonstrated the lack of a system. Union troops and excessive use created chaos on the southern lines. Rails in all states suffered damage, and in 1865 half of all lines were inoperable.

Reconstruction and consolidation followed Appomattox. Northern capital flowed south, rebuilding proceeded apace, and new construction began. During the 1870s and 1880s enterprising individuals created regional and national systems out of the local roads. National interests assumed precedence over parochial. Deliberate breaks in lines were eliminated. Rivers were bridged. Standardization of rail gauge became a reality in the mid-1880s. By 1890 the South had 32,000 miles of rail, more than triple that in 1860, though that figure constituted less than 20 percent of the nation's total. The Louisville & Nashville, Missouri Pacific, Texas Pacific, Southern, Atlantic Coast Line, and Seaboard Air Line were major trunk lines by 1916, when total rail mileage peaked. Such cities as Atlanta, Birmingham, Dallas, Ft. Worth, Louisville, and Nashville could correctly portray themselves as rail centers.

A transportation revolution occurred in the 1920s. The automobile, a curiosity at the turn of the century and little more than a toy ten years later, assumed predominance in short-haul passenger traffic. Total rail passengers and passenger miles peaked in 1920. As these figures skidded during the following decade, automobile sales boomed. Between 1920 and 1930 motor vehicle registrations in the South increased by 217 percent and totaled nearly 6,150,000. Other forms of motor transport asserted their importance. Motor bus routes crisscrossed the region. From 1927 to 1935 the total number of buses operating in the country rose from 3,277 to 44,650, an increase of 440 percent. Nearly 5,000 companies operated bus routes. These developments were significant in the South, particularly in the small towns and rural areas. As a massive good-roads campaign began in the 1920s, truck transport became feasible and offered flexibility. Adequate hard-surfaced roads replaced mud and gravel; and the truck, even if more costly in freight charges, provided direct service, freed the shipper from many transfer charges, and provided faster service. By 1940 the highway system represented an investment equivalent to that of the railroads.

AIR TRANSPORT appeared as a reality in the 1930s. Interrupted by World War II it came full scale in the 1950s. Major national air trunk lines such as Braniff and American began in the South and continued to connect that section with the nation. Natural water transport has continued and even grown (INTRACOASTAL WATERWAY). The Tennessee Valley Authority navigation project, begun in 1933, produced 25 million tons of freight in 1970. Barge traffic on the Mississippi is of major proportions. The U.S. Army Corps of Engineers has canalized rivers such as the Arkansas. Mobile, Houston, and New Orleans, among others, are to day major ocean ports. The new supertankers have prompted discussion of superports on the Gulf of Mexico.

Continued URBANIZATION and INDUSTRIALIZATION in the region have produced transportation innovations. Multi- and inter-modal shipping are realities. Computerized traffic control has aided shippers. New modern airports have brought increased safety for passengers and made travel more efficient. Rails, water, highways, and air all provide vital regional, national, and international links.

See C. Goodrich, *Political Science Quarterly* (Sept., 1949); M. Heath, *Journal of Economic History* (1950), Supp. X; M. Klein, *Louisville and Nashville* (1974); J. N. Primm, *Economic Policy and Development of Missouri* (1954); J. Stover, *American Railroads* (1961), brief but incisive; G. R. Taylor, *Transportation Revolution* (1951), most thorough; and G. R. Taylor and I. D. Neu, *American Railroad Network* (1956), most complete on railroad consolidation.

ALLEN L. DICKES
Texas Christian University

TRANSYLVANIA COMPANY, a copartnership organized by RICHARD HENDERSON on January 6, 1775, speculated in western lands and attempted to establish an anachronistic proprietary colony with modified feudal tenure in Kentucky. Richard Henderson & Company (1764) and the Louisa Company (1774) were predecessor ventures. Copartners from these firms—Henderson, John Williams, Thomas Hart, Nathaniel Hart, William Johnston, and John Luttrell—joined Leonard Henley Bullock, David Hart, and James Hogg in the new organization. The company purchased all land between the Kentucky and Cumberland rivers and an access path from the CHEROKEE INDIANS at SYCAMORE SHOALS (March 14–17, 1775). At Boonesborough, Henderson called a convention of Transylvania, consisting of delegates from that settlement, Harrodsburg, Boiling Spring, and St. Asaph. The resultant compact vested most governmental power in the proprietors.

At Oxford, N.C., the proprietors composed a memorial for the CONTINENTAL CONGRESS, to which they sought admission. The Virginia assembly, however, nullified the scheme by creating Kentucky County in December, 1776. Two years later, the assembly granted 200,000 acres on the Green River to the Transylvania associates as compensation. The copartners turned to the Cumberland River area and formulated plans to colonize FRENCH LICK in 1779–1780 with another proprietary arrangement, the Cumberland Compact. In 1783 the North Carolina assembly terminated company control, but granted to the copartners 200,000 acres in Powell's Valley.

See Draper Papers, State Historical Society of Wisconsin, Madison; W. S. Lester, *Transylvania Colony* (1935), definitive; A. Henderson, *Transylvania Company and Founding of Henderson* (1929) and *Filson Club History Quarterly* (Jan., July, Oct., 1947); T. P. Abernethy, *Western Lands and American Revolution* (1937); and S. Livermore, *Early American Land Companies* (1939).

JOHN E. STEALEY III
Shepherd College

TRANSYLVANIA UNIVERSITY (Lexington, Ky. 40508), first institution of higher learning west of the Alleghenies, was chartered in 1780 by the Virginia legislature as a public seminary in Kentucky. After operating briefly in Danville, it was moved to Lexington in 1789. Adding medical and law departments in 1799, the university under the gifted leadership of Horace Holley (1818–1827), a Unitarian minister from Boston, became the center of learning in the Southwest, educating hundreds of doctors, lawyers, and political and business leaders. Among its students were STEPHEN AUSTIN, JEFFERSON DAVIS, JOHN BRECKINRIDGE, RICHARD JOHNSON, CASSIUS CLAY, ALBERT SIDNEY JOHNSTON, and JOHN HARLAN. Barely surviving the Civil War, Transylvania was revived in 1865 by joining Kentucky University, a DISCIPLES OF CHRIST school in Harrodsburg. Under John Bowman's leadership, the university administered the new state Agricultural and Mechanical College (later the University of Kentucky) and the College of the Bible, a Disciples' seminary. Due to widespread criticism, the A. & M. College was detached in 1878 at the same time the College of the Bible became an independent seminary, though for many years closely linked with Transylvania. Now operating primarily as a coeducational liberal arts college, Transylvania has a current enrollment of about 700. Its library has a remarkable old medical collection, as well as some Jefferson Davis papers.

See J. D. Wright, Jr., *Transylvania: Tutor to West* (1975); N. Sonne, *Liberal Kentucky, 1780–1828* (1939); manuscripts, Transylvania University Library Archives; and Shane Collection, Presbyterian Historical Society.

JOHN D. WRIGHT, JR.
Transylvania University

TRAVEL ACCOUNTS. An impressive volume of contemporary source material describing the South in every period is the accounts of travelers to the region. Since 1527, when ALVAR NÚÑEZ CABEZA DE VACA went from Gulf coastal Florida to the Pacific, thousands of literate persons have visited the South. They published essays and books recording experiences and observations. On the heels of Cabeza de Vaca came the Spaniards Pedro de Castañeda de Naxera, the Gentleman of Elvas, and Juan de Oñate. Each described the region around the Gulf of Mexico and the undisturbed state of native culture, manners, economy, and religion.

Frenchmen subsequently came down from Canada following the western waterways. They too described Indian culture, geography, stream flow, and other natural phenomena. They contributed generously to the growing volume of contemporary travel materials and continued to do so into the twentieth century.

John Smith in *A True Relation of Such Occurrences and Noate as Both Happened in Virginia Since the First Planting of That Collony* (1608) was first in a continuous procession of British visitors to America. They swarmed over the land and rushed home to publish essays and books. Scores of them traveled through the colonial South observing all sorts of social and natural phenomena. Among them were John Lawson, HUGH JONES, William Bullock, Ebenezer Cook, and John Fox. Resident officials also observed and described the region, among them William Byrd (BYRD FAMILY), Sir William Berkeley, and John Adair.

Colonial wars brought travelers in fairly large numbers. The French and Indian and the Revolutionary struggles produced both civilian and military travelers. Following 1781 there came a new army of visitors observing the new political experiment, searching for new economic opportunities, and criticizing American departures from British social norms. Below the Potomac they visited GEORGE WASHINGTON, THOMAS JEFFERSON, JAMES MADISON, JOHN MARSHALL, and everybody else of importance. There came political philosophers, settler agents, scientists, artists, religious crusaders, economists, and utopian dreamers. Prior to 1860 most visitors came from the British Isles and western Europe.

By the late nineteenth century, two "grand tours" were defined. One went down Atlantic coastal routes by way of Washington, Baltimore, Richmond, Raleigh, Charleston, and Savannah; the other went by way of Pittsburgh and the Ohio to Kentucky and Tennessee and down the Mississippi to New Orleans. As the old Southwest grew in prominence some travelers reached Montgomery, Jackson, western Louisiana, and Arkansas. Traveling across the South always involved physical ordeal. Visitors advanced on foot and horseback, in stagecoaches, and by flatboats, steamboats, and rail. Later they traveled by automobile.

As slavery became a burning issue, hundreds of observers, domestic and foreign, crossed the South to view the institution. Among them were Alexis de Tocqueville, Frances Wright D'Arusmont, Alexander Mackey, Fredrika Bremer, James Stirling, FREDERICK LAW OLMSTED, Karl Theodore Griesinger, Charles Dickens, and Captain Basil and Margaret Hall. There were, of course, hundreds of others.

The Civil War era brought to the South soldiers, journalists, and civilian visitors. Out of four years of war came an amazing collection of diaries, journals, and other firsthand observations. Few aspects of southern life escaped the visitors' eyes.

The era of Reconstruction saw travelers come to the region to view the ruins of war and slavery and an altered way of southern life. Veterans came to tramp over battlefields where they had fought, family members searched for soldiers' graves, and strategists reviewed battle plans on the ground. Important among the postwar visitors were industrialists and investors, who sought factory and mining sites and general investment opportunities. The last quarter of the nineteenth century produced an unusually large volume of traveler observation.

Visitors came in large numbers throughout the twentieth century. Foreign and native travelers came to investigate racial conditions and political reactions and to savor the romance of a nostalgic South. They wrote of TENANT FARMING, of the scenery, of the CLIMATE, and of social and eco-nomic failures of the region. Even the German Nazis in the 1930s sought support for their doctrine of Aryan supremacy.

Of the scores of travelers who came to the South in the years 1865–1900, few wrote what might be considered major accounts, but collectively the material is significant. Sidney Andrews' *The South Since the War, as Shown by Fourteen Weeks of Travel and Observation in Georgia and the Carolinas* (1866) must be considered of major importance. So must Horace Greeley's *Mr. Greeley's Letters from Texas and the Lower Mississippi* (1871) and Edward King's *The Great South: A Record of Journeys in Louisiana, Texas, the Indian Territory, Missouri, Arkansas, Mississippi, Alabama, Georgia, Florida, South Carolina, Kentucky, Tennessee, Virginia, West Virginia, and Maryland* (1875). SAMUEL L. CLEMENS' *Life on the Mississippi* (1883) rightly or wrongly became a classic.

Visitors to the twentieth-century South left a voluminous body of observation. Two travels characterize this material, Frank Tannebaum's *Darker Phases of the South* (1924) and Andre Siegfried's *America Comes of Age: A French Analysis* (1927). There are many accounts in foreign languages that have never been translated. Among these are Tora Bonnier's *Resa Kring en Resa: I Fredrika Bremers Fotspar* (1950) and Andre Demaison's *Terre d'Amérique* (1939). There are, of course, many other significant accounts, some of which give detailed views of only parts of the South but which collectively present the region in good contemporary perspective.

Again, the body of traveler-related material is voluminous, and it continues to grow. This literature comprises a mixture of objective observation, a monumental amount of utter nonsense, much misunderstanding of facts and regional behavior, careful investigation, a sharp tincture of bigotry and prejudice, and some humor. Historically the values of travel accounts are both positive and negative. Southern historiography would be impoverished without them. Nevertheless, travel accounts must be subjected to the sternest sort of scrutiny. In many instances, however, a traveler's note is almost the only firsthand and contemporary source available to the historian. With all its pluses and minuses notwithstanding, travel literature dealing with the South constitutes an indispensable body of regional Americana.

See T. D. Clark (ed.), *Travels in Old South* (3 vols.; 1956, 1959), *Travels in Confederate States*, comp. E. M. Coulter (1948), and *Travels in New South* (2 vols.; 1962); F. Monoghan, *French Travellers in U.S.* (1932); A. Nevins (ed.), *America Through British Eyes* (1948); and E. L.

Schwab with J. Bull (eds.), *Travels in Old South from Periodicals* (2 vols.; 1973).

THOMAS D. CLARK
Indiana University

TRAVIS, WILLIAM BARRET (1809–1836), was born in Edgefield (now Saluda) County, S.C. After immigrating to Mexican Texas, he was sent by Texas leaders to dismantle the fortifications at the ALAMO. Instead he determined to hold the compound with less than 200 defenders. When Antonio López de Santa Anna, commanding Mexican troops, demanded surrender, Travis replied with a cannon shot. On March 6, 1836, the large army stormed the walls of the compound, and Travis died before the Alamo fell. The heavy casualties Travis inflicted and the time thus dearly bought were factors in the final Texas victory at SAN JACINTO.

See W. B. Travis, *Diary* (1966); M. A. Turner, *W. B. Travis* (1972); A. Williams, *Southwestern Historical Quarterly* (Oct., 1933; Oct., 1934); W. P. Webb (ed.), *Handbook of Texas* (1952); R. Mixon, "W. B. Travis" (M.A. thesis, University of Texas, 1930); W. Lord, *Time to Stand* (1961); L. Tinkle, *13 Days* (1958); A. de Zavala, *Alamo* (1956); F. C. Chabot, *Alamo* (1931); J. S. Ford, *Alamo* (1896); and manuscripts, Texas State Library.

KENNETH FRANKLIN NEIGHBOURS
Midwestern State University

TREES. The southern United States is a unique region with a great variety of trees extending from the high elevation of the southern Appalachian Mountains through the vast pineries of the coastal plain and the subtropical Gulf Coast and Florida regions. Practically the entire region was originally covered with forests. Abundant rainfall, adequate topsoil, and a temperate climate provided environments to support an indigenous growth of over 220 different tree species. The lower slopes of the Appalachians have an especially large variety of trees. This is because the area is a meeting ground for the mountain and southern types. In contrast to Europe and Asia, where the mountain chains lie east-west, the Appalachians generally run from north to south and were not a barrier to plant migration during the past ice ages.

Aesthetically, southern trees include a wide variety of characteristics. The live oak with its massive outstretched limbs is one of the finest trees for use in the large landscape design. Sweet gum, red maple, and the other extensive hardwoods of the Appalachian slopes exhibit fall leaf coloration second to none. Evergreen hardwoods such as magnolia, holly, and gordonia reach the peak of their development in the region. Bald cypress, a close relative of the western redwood, is a characteristic tree of the sluggish river swamps that interlace the lowlands. The southern pines, which grow throughout the coastal plains of the region, provide a major source of the South's wealth through the production of timber and paper. The region's pine forests probably are the world's most extensive. The trees of south Florida, distinct from those of the rest of the South, include tropical species from the West Indies and Central America. Now this region also supports scores of species of exotic trees introduced from the warmer climates.

The early colonists recognized the value of the South's trees, especially the live oak and longleaf pine. The first timber reserves were set aside by Congress in 1799–1817 in the South to assure a supply of live oak for ship timber. The tall, straight pines were also reserved for the British navy by the king, just as was the white pine of New England. Longleaf pine was valuable for the production of NAVAL STORES for the British navy during the colonial period and the American navy after the Revolution.

Extensive southern forests have been set aside for public enjoyment and scientific study. These include the incomparable hardwood forests of the Great Smoky Mountains National Park and the unique tropical forests of the Everglades National Park. Magnificent stands of bald cypress and swamp hardwoods have been reserved in Cork Screw Swamp in Florida and Four-Hole Swamp in South Carolina.

See E. S. Harrar and J. G. Harrar, *Southern Trees* (1962); W. C. Coker, *Southeastern Trees* (1937); Agriculture Yearbook, *Trees* (1949); C. H. Green, *Trees of South* (1939); J. K. Small, *Florida Trees* (1913); D. Sturrock and E. A. Menninger, *South Florida Trees* (1946); and E. L. Little, Jr., *Tree Atlas* (1971).

GURDON L. TARBOX, JR.
Brookgreen Gardens

TRENHOLM, GEORGE ALFRED (1807–1876), born into a tottering Charleston mercantile family and orphaned at seventeen, exemplified the southern self-made man. He began his career as an accountant at John Fraser & Company, a Charleston shipping and commission firm. By 1860 he was head of the company and one of America's richest men, with interests in steamships, railroads, wharves, banks, hotels, cotton presses, plantations, and slaves. Trenholm was successively a Calhounite, nullifier, and fire-eating secessionist. When the war came, he became involved in numerous patriotic and profitable activities for his city, his state, and the Confederacy. His firm's Liverpool branch served as financial agent for Confederate purchases abroad. The company's BLOCKADE-RUNNING ventures were legendary and clearly motivated more by patriotism than profit. Friend and unofficial adviser to Confederate Secretary of the Treasury CHRISTOPHER G. MEMMINGER, Trenholm was a logical choice to succeed Memminger. Inheriting an exhausted treasury on July 18, 1864, Trenholm foundered on the policies of his predecessor. He was pardoned in 1866. Trenholm died beloved but financially beleaguered.

See E. S. Nepveux, *Trenholm* (1973); R. W. Patrick, *Davis and Cabinet* (1944); E. M. Coulter, *Confederate States* (1950); and papers, Library of Congress and South Carolina Historical Society.

PHILIP D. SWENSON
University of Massachusetts, Amherst

TRENT AFFAIR (November–December, 1861). On November 8 Captain Charles Wilkes, USS *San Jacinto*, removed the Confederate commissioners to Britain and France, JAMES MURRAY MASON and JOHN SLIDELL, from the British mail packet *Trent*, en route from Havana to St. Thomas. Wilkes had discussed the seizure with Robert W. Shufeldt, U.S. consul general in Havana, and had consulted his international law volumes. Mason and Slidell were imprisoned in Ft. Warren, Boston. News of the removal reached Britain on November 27, and newspapers vigorously condemned the Lincoln administration. Lord Lyons, British minister in Washington, presented the formal British demand for release to Secretary of State William Seward on December 23, and the commissioners were freed in January, 1862, continuing their interrupted mission on board HMS *Rinaldo*.

The affair demonstrated the possibility of war to the British and Union governments but, despite inflammatory northern and British press comments, also revealed that both governments attached greater importance to the diplomatic status quo expressed in the British proclamation of neutrality (May 13, 1861) and the maintenance of the Atlantic trading community that underpinned it. Given that predilection, Mason and Slidell, captured or freed, were doomed to failure. The southern diplomats never achieved European recognition for the Confederacy. Slidell was the clearer thinker and possibly should have gone to England, but even his abilities would still not have reversed the British adherence to neutrality that was irritated but not overcome by Wilkes's deliberate interruption of the voyage to win recognition.

See G. H. Warren, "Trent Affair" (Ph.D. dissertation, Indiana University, 1969), excellent; F. C. Drake, *Civil War History* (March, 1974); D. P. Crook, *North, South, Powers* (1974), British responses; E. D. Adams, *Great Britain, American Civil War* (1925), still good; and F. Owsley, *King Cotton Diplomacy* (1931).

FREDERICK C. DRAKE
Brock University, Ontario

TRENT'S REACH, BATTLE OF (January 23–24, 1865). During the siege of Petersburg, U. S. Grant was dependent upon supplies brought up the James River to City Point. STEPHEN R. MALLORY ordered Flag Officer John K. Mitchell to block the way with the ironclads *Virginia, Fredericksburg,* and *Richmond,* plus eight minor men-of-war posted at Chaffin's Bluff. Freshets had opened Union obstructions athwart Trent's Reach, and most of the Union naval force was away helping attack FT. FISHER; this left the double-turreted monitor *Onondaga* (Commander William A. Parker) supported by four large-gun shore batteries (Colonel Henry L. Abbot), all, unfortunately for Mitchell, alerted by spies in Richmond. In the night attempt, the most effective Union defense was a powerful Drummond light, whose glare blinded Confederate pilots, forcing them to run vessels aground. At dawn the gunboat *Drewry* was blown up. Mitchell freed his other vessels and retreated, having four men killed or missing and 15 wounded. The Union had three killed and undisclosed wounded.

See *Official Records, Armies,* Ser. 1, Vol. XLVI; and *Official Records, Navies,* Ser. 1, Vol. XI.

R. W. DALY
U.S. Naval Academy

TREVILIAN RAID (June 11–12, 1864). In an effort to disrupt railroad connections in the Shenandoah Valley while he attacked Petersburg, U. S. Grant dispatched Philip Sheridan and two divisions of cavalry to Charlottesville on June 7. There, Sheridan was to join David Hunter, destroy the Virginia Central Railroad all the way to Hanover Junction, and rejoin the Army of the Potomac. Robert E. Lee countered Grant's move by sending WADE HAMPTON's cavalry and FITZHUGH LEE's division to intercept.

On June 11 Sheridan met the two Confederate forces about three miles from Trevilian Station. Since Hampton and Fitz Lee were on two different approaches, Sheridan was able to send a brigade under the command of George Custer around Hampton's right flank. Custer attacked Hampton from the rear while two brigades from Alfred Torbert's division attacked from the front. Hampton was forced to withdraw. In the meantime, David Gregg's division had pushed Fitzhugh Lee back along the Louisa Courthouse Road. Sheridan was frustrated by the Confederate's quick reaction to his raid, and, since Hunter was not in position to reinforce him, he decided to abandon his mission on June 12. After destroying sections of the railroad around Louisa Courthouse, he rejoined Grant on June 28. Hampton, though not the victor, had successfully thwarted Sheridan in his bid to destroy the valley railroads.

See T. Yoseloff, *Campaigns of Civil War* (1963), VI, good account; and Military History Society of Massachusetts, *Shenandoah and Appomattox Campaigns* (1907) and *Wilderness Campaign* (1905).

JOSEPH E. BURLAS, JR.
Military Review

TRIMBLE, ISAAC RIDGEWAY (1802–1888), appointed to West Point from Kentucky shortly after the War of 1812, participated in surveying the CUMBERLAND ROAD. He commanded a Confederate brigade that took part in Stonewall Jackson's SHENANDOAH VALLEY CAMPAIGN and in the SEVEN DAYS' BATTLES. With the assistance of J. E. B. Stuart's cavalry, he captured the Union supply depot at Manassas in August, 1862, but shortly thereafter was severely wounded. In June, 1863, Robert E. Lee gave Trimble command of the troops in the Shenandoah Valley, with whom he advanced as far as Carlisle, Pa. Recalled in haste, he arrived in time to lead William Pender's division in support of George Pickett's left in the famous charge at GETTYSBURG, where he lost a leg and was taken prisoner. After the war he lived in Baltimore.

See G. F. R. Henderson, *Stonewall Jackson and American Civil War* (1898); G. W. Cullum, *Biographies of Regular Officers and Graduates, U.S. Military Academy* (1891); *Annual Reunion, U.S. Military Academy* (1888); *Official Records, Armies*, Ser. 1; *Southern Historical Society Papers* (1898); *Army and Navy Journal* (Jan. 7, 1888); and Baltimore *Sun* (Jan. 3, 1888).

REUBEN ELMORE STIVERS
Bethesda, Md.

TRINITY RIVER is formed in northern Texas by the confluence of three separate streams. West Fork and Clear Fork merge at Ft. Worth. Farther downstream they are joined by Elm Fork at Dallas to form the Trinity. Draining an area of almost 18,000 square miles, the river flows along a 510-mile course from Dallas to Trinity Bay, an arm of Galveston Bay. Although navigable for the first 40 miles above its mouth, the Trinity has never been a major artery of transportation. Yet it flows through the most populous and industrialized part of Tex-

as, and the state's Trinity River Authority, with six major dams and reservoirs, oversees water use for irrigation, conservation, and flood control.

TRINITY UNIVERSITY (San Antonio, Tex. 78212). Three separate Presbyterian colleges (Ewing College, 1848; Chapel Hill College, 1849; and Larissa College, 1855) were all ruined by the Civil War. Accordingly, in 1869 the Presbyterian synod of Texas founded Trinity as a successor institution. Located originally in Tehuacua, the school was moved in 1902 to Waxahachie and in 1942 to San Antonio. Its current coeducational enrollment numbers almost 3,000 students. In addition to preserving the records of the Texas Presbyterian churches and of Trinity and its predecessors, the library maintains the Nixon Texana Collection of books and manuscripts on Texas history.

See D. E. Everett, *Trinity University* (1968).

TRIST, NICHOLAS PHILIP (1800–1874), born in Charlottesville, Va., married Virginia Jefferson Randolph and lived at Monticello. After studying law and serving as confidential secretary to Thomas Jefferson during his last years, Trist after a time moved on to a post in the State Department. He served for a while as confidential secretary to President Andrew Jackson, who eventually appointed him consul to Havana. This post was lucrative, but scandals and a change in administration in 1841 forced his resignation. Because of Trist's knowledge of Spanish, James K. Polk named him peace commissioner to Mexico as the MEXICAN WAR was ending. After initial conflicts, Winfield Scott and Trist worked together to bring about a satisfactory conclusion to the war. While negotiations with the Mexicans were progressing, Polk changed his mind, deciding the terms entrusted to Trist were too lenient, and ordered him home. After soul-searching and with backing from Scott, Trist decided to remain and conclude a treaty on his original terms; the Treaty of Guadalupe Hidalgo (1848) was accepted by a reluctant president and ratified by an even more reluctant Senate. Trist was dismissed from government service. A faithful if not ardent servant of manifest destiny, he has been dismissed by some historians as arrogant and egotistical, but his act of disobedience is honored by Mexico and was probably best for the United States as well.

See R. A. Brent, "Nicholas P. Trist" (Ph.D. dissertation, University of Virginia, 1950); L. M. Sears, *Mississippi Valley Historical Review* (June, 1924); and R. A. Brent, *Southwestern Historical Quarterly* (April, 1954).

ROBERT A. BRENT
University of Southern Mississippi

TRUCK FARMING in the South is the production of vegetables and fruits for sale in a fresh state in urban centers largely outside the region. Representative of these highly perishable crops are tomatoes, beans, peas, cabbages, celery, watermelons, and strawberries. Distribution in distant markets involves a critical dependence upon fast, reliable, refrigerated transportation. The annual nature of these crops requires a short-term investment for their cultivation and harvest. This feature enables the grower to adjust to yearly market demands. Truck crops are therefore distinguished from the more permanent orchard crops such as oranges and peaches, whose production demands a long-range investment and allows less flexibility for producers.

The perishable quality of commercial fruits and vegetables has determined the characteristics of their marketing. Annually the harvesting season moves in a northerly direction, providing each district with a two- to three-week advantage over the next producing region in the seasonal movement. Intense competition as well as perishability has dictated that the produce of a locality be speedily marketed during this brief period. These factors, plus the market's susceptibility to sharp price fluctuations, have prompted the growers' dependence, in the sale of their goods, upon agents having a thorough and current knowledge of the rapidly changing market situation. Moreover, these commission merchants have also been a primary source of financing for producers.

As a viable industry, truck farming in the South was a post–Civil War outgrowth. A harbinger of this development was the sale in New York in 1854 on a small scale of produce grown in the Eastern Shore district of Virginia. Soon after the war, southerners were attracted by the inviting profits made available by the growing demand for fresh produce in the nation's expanding urban centers. This circumstance encouraged an intensive cultivation of specialized crops in well-defined areas. These were scattered throughout a belt of states extending from Delaware to Texas along the Atlantic and Gulf coasts. In the interior, truck cropping was pursued in portions of Arkansas, Kentucky, Missouri, and Tennessee. The availability of cheap land and inexpensive labor increased the southern producers' attraction to this enterprise. Railways such as the Illinois Central and the Atlantic Coast Line provided the vital transportation link with the cities. By 1880 tomatoes were being shipped on a regular basis from the Deep South district surrounding Crystal Springs, Miss., to northern markets by this means. Later development of the motortruck provided an additional method of moving fresh produce to market.

Trucking matured to sizable proportions in the twentieth century. By the late 1930s southern farmers were cultivating well over 40 percent of the nation's truck-farming acreage and were receiving in excess of one-quarter of the industry's total income. Although in 1900 there were no states whose production overshadowed that of the others, at the century's midpoint Florida and Texas were together furnishing over one-half the section's acreage and were accounting for over 60 percent of its return from truck farming. At the close of the third quarter of the twentieth century, these two states remained the region's primary production areas. Far from fostering agricultural self-sufficiency, this complex agricultural industry added only another element to the section's cash-crop economy.

See W. A. Sherman, *Merchandising Fruits and Vegetables* (1928); F. S. Earle, *Yearbook of Agriculture* (1900); R. P. Vance, *Human Geography of South* (1932); A. Oemler, *USDA Annual Report* (1885); Illinois Central Archives, Newberry Library, Chicago; and J. L. McCorkle, Jr., "Mississippi Vegetable Industry" (Ph.D. dissertation, University of Mississippi, 1966).

JAMES L. MCCORKLE, JR.
Northwestern State University of Louisiana

TRUMAN, HARRY S. (1884–1972), was the thirty-third president of the United States. After serving ten years as county judge, he entered national politics in 1934, when he was elected as a Democrat to the U.S. Senate. In 1944 he was elected vice-president, and he assumed the office of president when Franklin D. Roosevelt died in April, 1945. Elected to the presidency in his own right in 1948, he retired from public office in 1953. The grandson of Kentuckians who had migrated westward before the Civil War and who had sympathized with the Confederate cause, Truman was born and reared in Jackson County, Mo., and his political philosophy and career reflected his border-state background. He possessed mild white racist attitudes common in Missouri, but while in the Senate he did not publicly support his conservative southern colleagues in their filibustering efforts, and he did not make speeches about states' rights, the Constitution, or white supremacy. In view of black political power in Missouri, Senator Truman molded a somewhat problack civil rights record.

When the Democrats selected Truman as their vice-presidential candidate, southerners approved, despite his moderate record on civil rights. At the time Truman was thrust into the presidency, southerners considered him "safe" on the subject of civil rights. With black voting strength and demands for more civil rights increasing in the United States during the years immediately following the Second World War (CIVIL RIGHTS MOVEMENT), President Truman faced the difficult political problem of trying to satisfy these demands without alienating white southerners. He hoped to strengthen the Democratic party by appealing to blacks in such a way that they would support the party but without offending white southerners. During the early years of his presidency, Truman tried to satisfy black demands by speaking out for civil rights legislation; but he did not directly pressure Congress to act, thereby hoping not to antagonize the southern bloc. In late 1946 Truman established the President's Committee on Civil Rights, and this committee issued a formal report in 1947 urging action in the civil rights arena. By early 1948 Truman could no longer verbally support civil rights while failing to act; thus, he sent a special message to Congress, in which he demanded action on ten recommendations of the President's Committee on Civil Rights. Many southerners, hostile to any civil rights proposals and any advocate of such proposals, reacted negatively to this speech. Dissident southern politicians soon formed the DIXIECRAT PARTY to oppose Truman's reelection as president. The Dixiecrats hoped to win all the South's electoral votes, which would result in Truman's defeat, after which they planned to restore southern influence in the Democratic party and use that influence to limit the power of the federal government and to protect the "southern way of life."

Aware of the possible consequences of the revolt, Truman worked to conciliate white southerners during the presidential campaign of 1948. He did not have his supporters introduce a new civil rights bill into Congress, and he delayed action to eliminate discrimination in federal employment and SEGREGATION in the armed forces. In his campaign speeches in the South he stressed the region's economic advances resulting from previous Democratic administrations and gave little or no attention to the issue of civil rights. The strategy was successful. Black voters awarded Truman overwhelming support, assuring him the electoral votes of several large northern states. Truman won 50 percent of the popular vote in the South, all but four southern states casting their electoral votes for him. Southerners revealed their continued adherence to the Democratic party, in spite of the explosive racial issue. Truman won the South, but the presidential ELECTION OF 1948 set the stage for dramatic political change in the region in subsequent years.

See R. S. Kirkendall, "Truman and South" (paper, Southern Historical Association Convention, Nov., 1969); W. C. Berman, *Politics of Civil Rights* (1970); H. Sitkoff, *Journal of Southern History* (Nov., 1971); M. Billington, *Journal of Negro History* (April, 1973); B. J. Bernstein (ed.), *Politics and Policies of Truman Administration* (1970); R. A. Garson, *Democratic Party, 1941–1948* (1974); D. R. McCoy and R. T. Ruetten, *Quest and Response* (1973); R. S. Kirkendall, *Truman Period* (1967, 1974); C. Phillips, *Truman Presidency* (1966); and Truman Library, Independence, Mo.

MONROE BILLINGTON
New Mexico State University

TRYON, WILLIAM (1729–1788), was born into a family of lesser nobility at Norbury Park, Surrey. He entered the army in 1751 and rose to the rank of lieutenant colonel. In 1764 he was appointed lieutenant governor of North Carolina under Arthur Dobbs and took over the governorship on Dobbs's death in March, 1765. He was soon faced with the STAMP ACT CRISIS. Tryon resisted protesters' demands but did not attempt force to suppress them. Later, when the REGULATORS emerged, Tryon recognized the justice of some backcountry complaints. Although he initiated some reforms, that policy was diverted by the lowcountry conservatives and corrupt backcountry administrators. In 1768 he led the militia against the Hillsboro demonstrators and again in 1771 headed the low-country gentlemen, who routed the Regulators at the battle of ALAMANCE. Soon after this event Tryon was appointed governor of New York.

In North Carolina, Tryon was disliked in some quarters for his moving of the provincial capital to New Bern and his building of "Tryon's Palace" as the official residence. One of the finest buildings in colonial America, it was too expensive and pretentious for that stage of North Carolina history. Later Tryon gained notoriety for his harsh policies as colonel of a regiment of New York Loyalists. Ill health prompted his retirement to England in 1780.

See W. L. Saunders (ed.), *Colonial Records of North Carolina* (1886–90), VII, VIII; J. S. Bassett, *American Historical Association Annual Report* (1894); and H. T. Lefler and W. S. Powell, *Colonial North Carolina* (1973).

CLARENCE J. ATTIG
Westmar College

TRYON'S LINE. When England issued the PROC-LAMATION OF 1763, it urged that colonial governments delineate boundaries with their Indian neighbors in the hope of stemming future uprisings. On June 1, 1767, Governor WILLIAM TRYON began negotiations with North Carolina's CHERO-KEE to draw such a line. Three days later, three commissioners and a party of Cherokee under Ustenaka began demarcating the boundary. Commencing at Reedy River, they traveled north to Tryon Mountain in present Polk County. From that point they agreed to run the line northeast to Chiswell's Mines (present Austinville, Va.). All white settlers west of the line were to move out before the new year, and no land grants could be issued within one mile east of the border.

See L. De Vorsey, Jr., *Indian Boundary in Southern Colonies* (1966), best; W. L. Saunders (ed.), *Colonial Records of North Carolina* (1886–90), VII; and J. R. Alden, *John Stuart and Southern Colonial Frontier* (1944).

WILLIAM S. PRICE, JR.
North Carolina Division of Archives and History

TUBERCULOSIS. The pathogenic agent of tuberculosis is *Mycobacterium tuberculosis*, a germ that can invade any of the tissues or bones but most commonly attacks the lungs. Paleopathologists have found evidence of this disease in the earliest civilizations, but it was not until the nineteenth century that it was clearly identified as a contagious disorder. Known as consumption, phthisis, and the white plague, it was a major cause of death throughout the Western world until well into the twentieth century. Since it did not sweep dramatically through town and countryside, no systematic records were kept prior to the late nineteenth century. Such records as have survived apply largely to cities, and one can only speculate to what degree they are representative of the country as a whole. They all agree, however, that tuberculosis was the number one killer and that it caused approximately 20 percent of all deaths.

Prior to the Civil War, the disease was probably more serious in the northern states. In part the explanation may lie in the greater number of infants and young people in the South who succumbed to YELLOW FEVER and MALARIA. Dr. Joseph Jones of Louisiana stated in 1882 that pulmonary and mesenteric tuberculosis had caused 30,778 deaths in New Orleans in the years 1844–1882 and that yellow fever had killed another 28,745. Whatever the case, in the later nineteenth century, tuberculosis was at least as severe in the South as in the North, and by the twentieth century the disease occurred primarily in urban centers and impoverished areas in the South.

By 1900 the pathogenic agent had been identified, better diagnostic methods had been developed, and the way was open for a concerted attack on tuberculosis by local, state, and private agencies. The South followed the pattern set by the more progressive health boards and the National Tuberculosis Association (1904) in establishing sanatoriums and promoting large-scale educational programs. However, since poverty and malnutrition are predisposing causes, progress in reducing the incidence of tuberculosis was slower in the more economically backward southern states. Nonetheless, a dramatic reduction was effected. The death rate from tuberculosis in the United States fell from around 200 per 100,000 population in 1900 to less than 46 by 1940. The advent of antibiotics lowered this figure to about three by 1967. Today tuberculosis is primarily a disease of the aged.

See W. D. Postell, *Journal of History of Medicine* (Summer, 1948), one of few on TB in South; J. M. May, *Ecology of Human Disease* (1958); and R. H. Shryock, *Medicine in America* (1966).

JOHN DUFFY
University of Maryland

TUBMAN, HARRIET ROSS (1820?–1913), born into slavery in Dorchester County, Md., became the most celebrated of the "conductors" on the UNDERGROUND RAILROAD. After escaping from slavery in 1849 she is believed to have returned to the South repeatedly and is credited with aiding some 300 slaves to reach freedom. Her activities brought notoriety (a price of $40,000 was put on her head) and an audience of northern abolitionists, among them John Brown. She is thought to have recruited supporters for Brown's abortive HARPERS FERRY RAID in 1859. In 1860 she became active in antislavery circles and was one of the first black women to speak out for women's rights. When the war came Tubman, who had fled briefly to Canada, returned to the United States, where she worked with Union forces around coastal South Carolina as a nurse, soldier, and spy. For these services she was awarded a small pension after the war. Her last years were burdened by financial difficulties, and she died in apparent poverty at Auburn, N.Y.

See S. Bradford, *Scenes in Life of Harriet Tubman* (1869); E. Conrad, *Harriet Tubman* (1943); and A. McGovern, *Runaway Slave* (1965).

ALBERT ABBOTT
Fairfield University

TUCKAHOE was a nickname of Indian origin sometimes applied loosely to all Virginians, but more specifically it was used with reference to the POOR WHITE people living in lower Virginia (or by those living west of the Blue Ridge Mountains to those living to the east of the mountains). It is thought that the term was used because at times these lesser folk were forced to subsist on bulbous roots (like Virginia wake-robin and Indian cucumber root) called tuckahoe. Tuckahoe is also a proper name for several homes, towns, rivers, and regions in the middle states.

See G. E. Shankle, *American Nicknames* (1955); M. M Mathews (ed.), *Dictionary of Americanisms* (1951); and H. D. House, *Wild Flowers* (1942).

TUCKER, GEORGE (1775–1861), born in Bermuda, came to Virginia in 1795. He became active in politics as a Jeffersonian Republican and was elected to the general assembly. After moving to Lynchburg in 1818, he served three terms in Congress (1819–1825). With the opening of the University of Virginia in 1825, Tucker became professor of moral philosophy and chairman of the faculty. He taught a wide spectrum of courses and wrote extensively. Having gained financial independence, he resigned in 1845, freed his slaves, and retired to Philadelphia. He wrote political essays and *belles lettres* for newspapers and magazines, but when *The Valley of Shenandoah* (1824), his novel depicting Virginia life, did not sell, he turned to teaching. He later gained moderate acclaim for *The Laws of Wages, Profits, and Rent, Investigated* (1837); *The Life of Thomas Jefferson* (1837); and *The History of the United States* (1856–1858).

See R. C. McLean, *George Tucker* (1961); and T. R. Snavely, *George Tucker* (1964).

WILLIAM M. E. RACHAL
Virginia Historical Society

TUCKER, HENRY ST. GEORGE (1853–1932), was born in Winchester, Va. (TUCKER FAMILY). He received M.A. (1875) and LL.B. (1876) degrees from Washington and Lee University and practiced law at Staunton, Va., from 1876 to 1889, when he was elected to Congress. During his tenure there (1889–1897) he was outspoken against control of legislative bodies by corporate interests. Defeated for Congress in 1897, he returned to Washington and Lee, where he served as professor of law, dean of the law school, and for a short time acting president. He was president of the American Bar Association in 1904–1905. An antimachine Democrat in a period when Virginia was controlled by the BYRD MACHINE, Tucker was an unsuccessful candidate for governor in 1909 and 1921. He was reelected to Congress, however, in 1922 and served in the House until his death. Basically conservative and a believer in limited government, he espoused STATES' RIGHTS and laissez faire, opposing social legislation including CHILD LABOR and woman suffrage. Tucker wrote two books, *Limitations on the Treaty-Making Power Under the Constitution of the United States* (1915) and *Woman's Suffrage by Constitutional Amendment* (1916), and he edited a work of his father's, *The Constitution of the United States* (1899).

See H. St. George Tucker Papers, University of North Carolina, William and Mary, and Washington and Lee University libraries; V. Dabney, *New Dominion* (1971); A. W. Moger, *Bourbonism to Byrd* (1968); and W. E. Larsen, *Montague of Virginia* (1965).

CATHERINE SILVERMAN
Institute for Research in History

TUCKER FAMILY of Virginia began when St. George Tucker (1752–1827) arrived in the colony in 1772 to attend the College of William and Mary. During the Revolution he chose to support Virginia and attained the rank of colonel. In 1778 he married the widowed Frances Bland Randolph and thereby became the stepfather of her sons, one of whom was JOHN RANDOLPH of Roanoke. Tucker entered the practice of law after the war and was elected a judge of the newly reorganized general court in 1788. In 1790 he succeeded GEORGE WYTHE as law professor at his alma mater but resigned in 1803 just before being elected to the court of appeals. He published his celebrated edition of Blackstone's *Commentaries* in 1803. In 1811 he left the bench but was persuaded to abandon retirement in 1813 to accept James Madison's appointment to be judge of the federal district court in Virginia, which position he held until 1825. Two of Tucker's sons, Henry St. George (1780–1848) and Nathaniel Beverley (1784–1851), became attorneys. The former began practice in Winchester and later entered politics, being elected to Congress in 1815. After two terms he returned to Virginia's general assembly but followed in his father's steps by accepting election to the court of appeals in 1831. He wrote *Commentaries on the Laws of Virginia* (1831) and *Lectures on Constitutional Law* (1843) and taught law at the University of Virginia from 1841 to 1845. Nathaniel Beverley traveled to Missouri after failing to establish a successful law practice. He became circuit court judge in 1818 and held that post until 1826. He returned to Virginia in 1833 and accepted his father's old professorship at William and Mary in 1834. While teaching law Beverley became a prolific writer (*The Partisan Leader* [2 vols.; 1836]) and a staunch states' rights and proslavery advocate.

The family's prominence was maintained by descendants of Henry St. George. One of his sons, Nathaniel Beverley (1820–1890), edited the *Sentinel* in Washington before going to England as U.S. consul. During the Civil War he served as a Confederate purchasing agent in England and Canada. After the war he was implicated in the assassination of Abraham Lincoln, but the charges were never proved. His son and grandsons took part of the family out of law and into the church, but his brother John Randolph Tucker (1823–1897) continued the family's position before the bar. After a successful practice in Virginia, Ran served in Congress from 1875 to 1887 and then returned to teaching law at Washington and Lee University. After an intervening term, his son HENRY ST. GEORGE TUCKER, known as Harry, took his father's seat in Congress. He too left Congress to teach law at Washington and Lee but in 1922 he returned and held his seat until his death. Harry's cousin, the son of Confederate agent Nathaniel Beverley, began the family's role in the priesthood of the Episcopal church. Beverley Dandridge Tucker (1846–1930) became a bishop in Virginia and of his 13 children four became clergymen, two of them becoming bishops. Henry St. George Tucker (1874–1959) became presiding bishop of the church after serving as bishop of Kyoto, Japan, and Virginia; his brother Beverley Dandridge Tucker, Jr. (1882–1969), was bishop of Ohio. Members of the family remain in the law and the church, and one group has moved into the medical profession.

See M. H. Coleman, *St. George Tucker* (1938); S. Hess, *America's Political Dynasties* (1966); J. R. Tucker, *Virginia Law Register* (March, 1896); C. T. Cullen, "St. George Tucker" (Ph.D. dissertation, University of Virginia, 1971); and R. J. Brugger, "Mind and Heart of Beverley Tucker" (Ph.D. dissertation, Johns Hopkins, 1974).

CHARLES T. CULLEN
Institute of Early American History and Culture

TULANE UNIVERSITY (New Orleans, La. 70118) began in 1834 as the Medical College of Louisiana, a school that was absorbed in 1847 by the new University of Louisiana. During the Civil War the university functioned under state control, but it reverted to its status as a private institution after the war and was renamed Tulane after Paul Tulane (merchant), a benefactor, in 1884. The school presently has an enrollment of over 7,000 students and a library of 500,000 manuscripts relating chiefly to the history of Louisiana, New Orleans, and the lower Mississippi Valley. One special collection is the Archive of New Orleans Jazz, featuring books, periodicals, records, sheet music, tapes and piano rolls of the city's unique contribution to American MUSIC. The Tulane library also has personal and family papers of WILLIAM C. C. CLAIBORNE, PIERRE G. T. BEAUREGARD, JEFFERSON DAVIS, ALBERT SIDNEY JOHNSTON, JOHN SLIDELL, and GEORGE W. CABELL, as well as photostats of the dispatches of Spanish governors (1766–1791) with English translations and the records of numerous area business firms and plantations. On permanent deposit with the Tulane library archives is the LOUISIANA HISTORICAL ASSOCIATION Collection of records, diaries, and letters relating chiefly to the battle of New Orleans (1812) and to the Civil War.

See J. P. Dyer, *Tulane, 1825–1950* (1954).

TULLAHOMA CAMPAIGN (June 23–July 4, 1863). This Union advance, directed against BRAXTON BRAGG's Army of Tennessee (30,000 infantrymen and 14,000 cavalrymen), was intended to prevent further reinforcement of the southern armies around Vicksburg, to begin the long-awaited move against Chattanooga, and to exert pro-Union influence in politically ambivalent regions of Tennessee. William Rosecrans, commander of the Union Army of the Cumberland (56,000 infantrymen and 9,000 cavalrymen), ordered David Stanley's cavalry corps and Gordon Granger's reserve corps south from Murfreesboro, Tenn., to threaten Bragg's left. Rosecrans' main advance, by T. L. CRITTENDEN's XXI Corps, GEORGE THOMAS' XIV Corps, and part of Alexander McCook's XX Corps, moved against Bragg's right and rear; the Army of Tennessee, composed of LEONIDAS POLK's corps, WILLIAM HARDEE's corps, NATHAN FORREST's cavalry corps, and JOSEPH WHEELER's cavalry corps, was forced to withdraw to Tullahoma. On June 30, Bragg voluntarily continued the withdrawal to a stronger position south of the Tennessee River. There were 560 Union and 1,634 Confederate casualties. Through skillful maneuver Rosecrans drove Bragg from central Tennessee, prevented the shifting of Confederate troops to Mississippi, and began the Union advance on Chattanooga.

See T. L. Connelly, *Autumn of Glory* (1971); and S. F. Horn, *Army of Tennessee* (1941).

JOHN I. ALGER
U.S. Military Academy

TUPELO, BATTLE OF (July 13–15, 1864), is also called the battle of Harrisburg. It was fought in northeastern Mississippi between A. J. Smith's 14,000-man Union force and NATHAN BEDFORD FORREST's 9,500-man Confederate force temporarily commanded by STEPHEN D. LEE. Smith had been sent from Memphis into Mississippi with orders to prevent Forrest from moving into Tennessee and disrupting the thin supply line of William T. Sherman, then making his advance toward Atlanta (ATLANTA CAMPAIGN). After some excellent tactical maneuvering by his white and black troops, Smith established an entrenched fishhook formation on a low ridge near Tupelo. The Confederates attacked early on the morning of July 14, but the Union lines repulsed the charge and won the battle. On the fifteenth, Smith began to withdraw toward Memphis because of short supplies, was harassed by pursuing Confederates, but on orders from Sherman returned to pursue Forrest. Confederate losses were 1,326; Union losses were 674. Forrest was to worry the Union command again, but Sherman's supply line remained intact.

See B. Stinson, *Civil War Times Illustrated* (July, 1972); E. C. Bearss, *Protecting Sherman's Lifeline* (1971); *Official Records, Armies*, Ser. 1, Vol. XXXIX, Pt. 1; R. S. Henry, *As They Saw Forrest* (1956); and J. A. Wyeth, *That Devil Forrest* (1959).

JOHN F. MARSZALEK
Mississippi State University

TUPELO, MISS. (pop. 20,471), in the northeast section of the state, is located in part of the territory ceded to the United States by the CHICKASAW INDIANS in 1832. The original settlement, Harrisburg, was abandoned in 1859, when the Mobile & Ohio Railway ran its line two miles to the east of the old town. A new settlement, Grim Pond, grew up around the rail line and was later renamed after the many tupelo trees in the area. Tupelo was a Confederate camp for P. G. T. Beauregard's troops after the battle of SHILOH (1862), but the battle of TUPELO actually was fought on the site of the former town of Harrisburg. After the war one of the first of Mississippi's cotton mills was constructed here, and in 1887 tracks of the Memphis & Birmingham Railroad came through the town making it a railroad junction. The modern city is a processing and shipping point for surrounding cotton and dairy farmers. One of the earliest cities to have contracted for electricity from the TENNESSEE VALLEY AUTHORITY, Tupelo manufactures clothing, lighting fixtures, lumber products, and brick.

See Tupelo *Journal* (1870–).

TURNER, HENRY McNEAL (1834–1915), churchman and black nationalist leader, was born free near Newberry, S.C. He became a Methodist lay exhorter in 1854, but joined the all-black AFRICAN METHODIST EPISCOPAL CHURCH in 1858. After training in Baltimore, he was sent in 1862 to a church in Washington, D.C. There he became a popular preacher, helped recruit blacks into the Union army, and was rewarded with appointment as a chaplain in the army. After the war he served for a time in the FREEDMEN'S BUREAU in Georgia. He was a delegate to the Georgia constitutional convention in 1868 and later served in the state legislature until blacks were excluded in 1871. His disillusionment with politics convinced him that blacks could not get true freedom in the United States, and he began a lifelong campaign of agitation for their immigration to Africa. He visited Africa four times in the 1890s. Meanwhile, Turner's influence in his church grew, and in 1880 he was elected a bishop. He wrote frequently for church and general newspapers and founded several journals in Atlanta: *Southern Recorder* (1888), *Voice of Missions* (1892), and *Voice of the People* (1901). In 1893 he convened a national convention of blacks to protest LYNCHING and preach emigration. Throughout the remainder of his long and active life he vigorously denounced white racism, and in 1906 he attracted nationwide attention for proclaiming the American flag "a dirty rag."

See E. S. Redkey, *Black Exodus* (1969) and (ed.), *Respect Black* (1971); M. M. Ponton, *Turner* (1917); J. P. Coan, "AME Church in Africa" (Ph.D. dissertation, Hartford Seminary, 1961); and D. W. Wills, "Social Thought in AME Church" (Ph.D. dissertation, Harvard, 1975).

EDWIN S. REDKEY
State University of New York College, Purchase

TURNER, JOSIAH, JR. (1821–1901), North Carolina politician and newspaper editor, was born in Hillsboro of a wealthy planter family. After graduating from the University of North Carolina, he became a lawyer, editor of the Hillsboro *Recorder*, and manager of his father's plantation. In 1852 he entered politics as a Whig, serving many years as a state legislator. He was a staunch UNIONIST who, in 1860, was one of three members of the general assembly to vote against calling the constitutional convention that passed North Carolina's ordinance of secession. However, once his state seceded, he raised a cavalry company, was elected a captain, and fought until he was wounded in 1862. He then was elected to the Confederate Congress as a peace advocate and a Davis opponent. Elected to the U.S. Congress in 1865, he, along with the other southern members-elect, was not permitted to take his seat. In November, 1868, after being denied his seat in the state legislature because of the requirements of congressional Reconstruction, he purchased the Raleigh *Sentinel* and entered his most influential career.

With a quick, biting wit he ridiculed leading Republicans, especially WILLIAM HOLDEN. In August, 1870, Holden had him arrested illegally. Although Turner was soon released, this incident became one of the charges upon which Holden was later impeached. By 1872, two years after the state had been "redeemed" by the Democrats, Turner began to break with his party. He thought he deserved high office, but his party considered him a liability because of his vituperative nature. Turner became bitter and erratic. In 1876 he was forced to sell the *Sentinel* to pay his debts. In 1880, after he accused several leading Democrats of corruption, he was expelled from the state legislature by his own party for "disorderly conduct." He essentially retired from politics in 1884 after two electoral defeats. He tried a comeback as a POPULIST in 1894, but with no success.

See C. A. Pittman, "Josiah Turner" (M.A. thesis, University of North Carolina, 1968); Raleigh *Sentinel* (1868–76); North Carolina Collection, University of North Carolina Library, good on post-Reconstruction years; and Turner Papers, University of North Carolina Library, sketchy, and Duke University, good on war years.

ROBERTA SUE ALEXANDER
University of Dayton

TURNER'S REBELLION (August 22–23, 1831), the bloodiest SLAVE INSURRECTION in southern history, broke out in a remote backwoods in Southampton County, Va. Nat Turner, the leader, was a thirty-year-old field hand and a slave preacher; he was married, with two and possibly three children. Known as "the Prophet" among Southampton's slaves, Turner had believed all his life that he was marked for a special destiny. From 1825 to 1831, he claimed to have religious visions in which an angry Jehovah appointed him an instrument of divine vengeance, to both free the slaves and punish a guilty white world. Unlike the earlier slave conspirators Denmark Vesey and Gabriel Prosser, Turner concealed his exact plans until the very eve of the rebellion, intending for it to happen spontaneously as he marched from farm to farm.

The holy war began just after midnight on August 22, when Turner's initial recruits murdered his master Joseph Travis and his family. By noon the next day, Turner had from 60 to 70 insurgents,

but they were no match for the white militia, which defeated the force just south of Jerusalem, the county seat. The revolt ended 31 hours after it began, with approximately 60 whites brutally slain and more than 15 homesteads sacked. In retaliation, white volunteers and militiamen savagely murdered at least 120 innocent blacks. At last, Turner and the surviving rebels were arrested and tried in Jerusalem, and 21 blacks, including the Prophet, were hanged. Over the following winter, the Virginia legislature debated whether emancipation and colonization might not be the best way to prevent another rebellion, only to reject the proposal on the grounds that emancipation and colonization were too costly and complicated to carry out. To guard against future insurrections, Virginia and most other southern states enacted stringent new SLAVE CODES and strengthened their militia systems; and southern whites, erroneously blaming the Turner revolt on northern abolitionists, closed ranks behind proslavery propagandists, determined that Negro bondage would remain.

See H. I. Tragle, *Southampton Slave Revolt* (1971), compilation of documents including Turner's "confessions" to Thomas R. Gray, an authentic and reliable source. See also S. B. Oates, *Fires of Jubilee* (1975) and *Nation* (May 31, 1975), for discussion of modern controversy over W. Styron's novel, *Confessions of Nat Turner* (1966).

STEPHEN B. OATES
University of Massachusetts, Amherst

TUSCALOOSA, ALA. (pop. 65,773), is 50 miles southwest of Birmingham near the headwaters of the Black Warrior River. Taking its name from the Creek Indian words for warrior (*tusko*) and black (*loosa*), the town was founded in 1816 after the defeat of the CREEK INDIAN Confederacy. It was named the state's capital in 1826. As the seat of state government and a trading center for area cotton, the town grew and prospered; but, when the capital was moved in 1846 to Montgomery, many of the town's residents and businesses moved with it. The University of Alabama, however, stayed, and the city today remains largely an educational center and a market for cotton and dairy products.

See J. F. Doster, *Alabama Review* (April, 1974); and files of Tuscaloosa *News* (1818–).

TUSCARORA INDIANS. Language, culture, and oral tradition among the Tuscarora, "weavers of shirts" and "gatherers of hemp," support the belief that this Iroquoian tribe migrated to present-day North Carolina from old occupation areas south of the Great Lakes between 1350 and 1600 A.D. Once settled as maize farmers and woodland hunters, the Tuscarora adapted efficiently enough within the TIDEWATER and PIEDMONT ecosystems to become one of the more respected and feared confederacies in the Southeast on the eve of European colonization.

Originally encompassing three cultural tribelets, 24 Tuscarora villages on the Roanoke, Tar, Pamlico, and Neuse rivers housed an estimated 6,000 people when first contacted by Sir Walter Raleigh's Englishmen in the 1580s. Immediate effect of European contact is difficult to assess; however, the census of 1708 taken by John Lawson revealed 15 towns with 2,000 warriors and indicates little demographic or cultural decline.

An intricate component of the southeastern FUR and Indian slave trading nexus (SLAVES, INDIAN) with English settlers, the Tuscarora remained on friendly terms with the colonials until BACON'S REBELLION in 1675. Conflicts ensued thereafter, mostly as a result of white atrocities against Tuscarora women and children, who were taken captive and sold as slaves in the West Indies. This, in addition to perennial westward expansion on Tuscarora lands and legislation designed to restrict Indian civil liberties, led to the Tuscarora War (1711–1713).

This conflict opened western Carolina lands for settlement after the combined forces of Carolinians and Virginians under Colonel John Barnwell decisively defeated the larger part of the Tuscarora Nation. The smaller faction cooperated with the colonials and received an inadequate reservation in Bertie County for their instrumental role in final victory. Cultural decline through disease and white encroachment plagued those who remained in North Carolina. By 1750, traditional lifeways succumbed to the onslaught of western expansion.

Of the defeated survivors, many refugees found friends among the Quakers in Pennsylvania. Most preferred residence with Iroquoian relatives in New York and Canada. In the late colonial wars, these Tuscarora generally sided with the British against the French. During the American Revolution, many of the tribe joined the colonials and aided in American victory. Today the Tuscarora compose an important part of the Iroquois Nation in New York and Ontario. Through revitalization movements, the Tuscarora have maintained old lifeways despite economic dependency on federal funds and local steelworking wages.

See J. Lawson, *History of Carolina* (1718), best primary source to Tuscarora War; J. Barnwell, *Virginia Magazine of History and Biography* (April, 1898); F. R. Johnson,

Tuscaroras (1967), best secondary work; F. W. Hodge, *Tuscaroras* (1906), anthropology; A. Akwens, *Migrations of Tuscarora* (1948), Mohawk Reservation view; E. Johnson, *Legends* (1881), Iroquoian author; and S. H. Witt, *Tuscaroras* (1972), excellent native overview, lacks notes.

WILLIAM R. SWAGERTY
University of California, Santa Barbara

TUSKEGEE INSTITUTE (Tuskegee Institute, Ala. 36088) was founded in 1881 by an act of the Alabama general assembly, which appropriated $2,000 per year for a normal and industrial school. BOOKER T. WASHINGTON became the school's first principal, establishing from the beginning a tradition of black administrative control of the school. He adopted a system of industrial and agricultural education favored by J. L. M. CURRY and managed to make Tuskegee's educational program both palatable to white southerners and attractive to northern philanthropists. By his death in 1915, Washington had increased the school's worth to approximately $2 million and established an influential agricultural extension program. The school had about 1,500 students, two-thirds of them below high school level and none above it.

Washington was succeeded by Robert Russa Moton (1868–1939), a graduate of HAMPTON INSTITUTE. Moton attracted a veterans' hospital for blacks to the campus and withstood racist efforts to control the hospital with an all-white professional staff. He also managed to make peace with Washington's vociferous critics, led an endowment campaign that added $5 million to the school's capital by 1925, and began a college department in 1927. He resigned in 1935 and was replaced by his son-in-law Frederick Douglass Patterson (1901–). Under Patterson's leadership the institute became more of a university, adding a graduate program in 1943, a school of veterinary medicine in 1945, and collegiate nursing in 1953. Patterson also established Tuskegee's leadership among black colleges by leading in the establishment of the United Negro College Fund in 1944. Luther H. Foster (1913–) followed Patterson, and Tuskegee continued its growth. The institute now awards degrees from its schools of applied sciences, arts and sciences, education, engineering, nursing, and veterinary medicine. Current enrollment is approximately 3,500 students.

See esp. L. R. Harlan, *Booker T. Washington* (1972); Tuskegee Archives and catalogs; H. M. Bond, *Negro Education in Alabama* (1939), useful; and H. R. Cayton, *Long Old Road* (1963), social relations in 1930s. Veterans' hospital affair is well treated in P. Daniel, *Journal of Southern History* (Aug., 1970); and in R. Wolters, *New Negro on Campus* (1975). See also W. H. Hughes and

F. D. Patterson, *Robert R. Moton* (1956); and A. W. Jones, *Journal of Negro History* (April, 1975).

CARL S. MATTHEWS
U.S. Department of State

TUTWILER, JULIA STRUDWICK (1841–1916), was an Alabama-born educator, humanitarian, reformer, and author. A spinster with secure family position and support, she first received her early education in Alabama, then traveled and studied extensively in the United States and Europe during the post–Civil War decade. Successful in her career as teacher and administrator in various Alabama institutions, especially as head of Livingston Normal College (1881–1910), she worked unceasingly to increase educational and vocational opportunities for women (particularly the expansion of state-supported teacher-training institutions), self-help and vocational training, and the open admission of women to the University of Alabama. Moved by a religiously inspired humanitarianism, she was active in prison reform, advocating the provision of educational facilities for prisoners and the outlawing of the CONVICT LEASE SYSTEM. Tutwiler was an officer and participant at the national level of the National Education Association and was a program contributor to the international congresses of women held in connection with the 1893 Chicago World's Fair. Of her poems, stories, and articles, best remembered are "Alabama," the state song, and "When the Laurels Bloom," honoring Commodore M. F. MAURY.

See A. G. Pannell and D. E. Wyatt, *Julia S. Tutwiler* (1961); and C. L. Pitts, "Julia S. Tutwiler" (Ed.D. dissertation, George Washington University, 1942).

DOROTHEA E. WYATT
University of Michigan, Flint

TWAIN, MARK. See CLEMENS, SAMUEL LANGHORNE

TWENTY-NEGRO LAW, often called the twenty-nigger law, was one of many CONFEDERATE CONSCRIPTION exemptions that made the smaller farmers claim that the Civil War was "a rich man's war and a poor man's fight" and occasioned a great deal of discontent. The law, enacted October 11, 1862, conferred exemption on any planter or overseer who supervised 20 (a law enacted in March, 1864, changed it to 15) slaves. In spite of the fact that comparatively few persons were so exempt, the law was the focal point of much bitterness and was decried even by some of those in a position to benefit from it. Serious efforts were therefore made in the 1864 version to correct the worst abuses.

See C. Eaton, *History of Southern Confederacy* (1958); and *Official Records, Armies*, Ser. 4, Vol. III.

TWIGGS, DAVID EMANUEL (1790–1862), was born in Richmond County, Ga. From 1812 to 1846 he served in infantry and cavalry units of the U.S. Army. He saw action in the War of 1812, Seminole War, Black Hawk War, and the Mexican War. In 1847 Twiggs served as military governor of Veracruz and directed the vanguard of the Mexico City campaign. After 1848 he commanded the Department of the West; in 1857 he became commander of the Department of Texas. Possessing personal sympathy for the South and facing aggressive secessionist activity in Texas in February, 1861, he surrendered federal property and agreed to remove U.S. troops from the state, bringing about his immediate dismissal from the U.S. Army. Commissioned major general in the Confederate army on May 22, 1861, Twiggs commanded for a short while in New Orleans; but, confronted with the infirmities of old age, he soon resigned and returned to Georgia, where he died.

See C. A. Evans, *Confederate Military History* (1899), VI; and Martin Labor Crimmins Papers, University of Texas Library, Austin.

WILLIAM J. MCNEILL
Lee College

TYDINGS, MILLARD EVELYN (1890–1961), a Maryland Democrat, became nationally prominent during the second of his four Senate terms (1927–1951) as a conservative opponent of the NEW DEAL. One of three main targets in President Franklin Roosevelt's attempted "purge" in the 1938 Democratic primaries, Tydings defeated his New Deal–backed challenger with 58 percent of the vote. Thereafter he remained an outspoken advocate of states' rights and small government and a foe of civil rights measures. With his reputation for conservatism, vigorous independence, and political invulnerability, Tydings was chosen in 1950 to head a Senate inquiry into Senator Joseph McCarthy's charges against the State Department. After the Tydings committee report sharply criticized McCarthy, outside interests for a second time intervened in the Marylander's reelection campaign. Tydings' ensuing defeat in 1950, in part due to an unpopular Democrat-sponsored state sales tax, caused other potential opponents of McCarthyism to fall silent. A cultured gentleman and strong-principled politician, Tydings symbolized the positive side of twentieth-century southern congressional conservatism.

See J. T. Salter, *American Politician* (1938); R. L. Otto, "Maryland Senatorial Election" (M.A. thesis, University of Maryland, 1962); and M. I. Schlonick, "President and Senator" (M.A. thesis, University of Maryland, 1962). By Tydings are *Machine-Gunners* (1930) and *Counter-Attack* (1933). See also Tydings Papers, University of Maryland Library.

GARY W. REICHARD
Ohio State University

TYLER, JAMES HOGE (1846–1925), returned to southwest Virginia after serving in the Confederate army to assume the responsibilities of the family farm. The depressed economic conditions of the region developed in him an early interest in state politics, and he served one term in the state senate (1877–1879) as a friend of the farmer. During the 1880s, while becoming a successful businessman and commercial farmer, he developed the added reputation of a political workhorse attempting to restore Democratic control in the Ninth Congressional District. After two unsuccessful attempts, Tyler was elected governor in 1897. He was a compromise candidate, and his election was a victory for conservatism and the Democratic organization. The last Confederate veteran to occupy the governor's mansion, Tyler represented the passing of an era. Even though he did not significantly change the course of Virginia political history, his unsuccessful race against Senator THOMAS S. MARTIN in 1899 kept alive the issue of the senatorial primary and emphasized the need for election reforms. After leaving the governorship in 1902, Tyler continued to maintain an interest, at times active, in state and national affairs.

See T. E. Gay, "J. Hoge Tyler" (Ph.D. dissertation, University of Virginia, 1969); J. Hoge Tyler Papers, University of Virginia and Virginia Polytechnic Institute libraries; and W. Larsen, *Montague of Virginia* (1965).

THOMAS E. GAY, JR.
Edinboro State College, Edinboro, Pa.

TYLER, JOHN (1790–1862), tenth president of the United States, was born at Greenway, Charles City County, Va. After graduating from the College of William and Mary (1807), he read law and entered politics. As a Jeffersonian Republican, he earned a reputation as an ardent spokesman for southern interests and for strict construction of the Constitution. He disdained the nationalist economic program of John Quincy Adams and HENRY CLAY, supported the 1824 candidacy of WILLIAM H. CRAWFORD, and reluctantly committed himself in 1828 to ANDREW JACKSON's campaign for the presidency. He agreed with Old Hickory's vetoes of the MAYSVILLE ROAD bill and the rechartering of the second Bank of the United States, but broke with him over removal of the deposits and the NULLIFICATION crisis. Tyler in 1832 underscored his commitment to STATES' RIGHTS by casting the lone Senate vote against the FORCE BILL. A year later he joined the emerging Whig party.

On April 4, 1841, Tyler became the first vice-president to achieve the presidency upon the incumbent's death. Tyler vetoed most of Henry Clay's national economic program, signing only grudgingly the moderately protectionist Tariff Act of 1842. The former cost him southern Whig support, and the latter angered southern Democrats. His veto on September 9, 1841, of Clay's cherished national bank prompted congressional Whigs to read him out of the party. Tyler responded by attempting to shape, through the federal patronage, a southern-based states' rights party dedicated to the annexation of Texas. His third secretary of state, JOHN C. CALHOUN, successfully negotiated a treaty of annexation, but it was rejected by the Senate. On May 30, 1844, the Tyler Democrats nominated the president as a proannexation candidate, but he withdrew on August 20 in favor of the regular Democratic nominee JAMES K. POLK.

After leaving office, Tyler retired to his plantation, Sherwood Forest. Although opposed to the slave trade, he owned slaves and believed only time would eliminate the peculiar institution. He voted against the MISSOURI COMPROMISE and consistently espoused the right of slaveholders to take their property into the territories. The former president openly supported SECESSION. He was a delegate to the Confederate Provisional Congress and was subsequently elected to the Confederate House of Representatives, but died before taking his seat.

See O. P. Chitwood, *John Tyler* (1939); R. Seager, *Tyler Too* (1963); and L. G. Tyler, *Letters and Times of Tylers* (3 vols.; 1884–86). Some correspondence is in Library of Congress and Duke University Library. Letters also in *William and Mary Quarterly*, *Virginia Magazine of History and Biography* (July, 1968), and *Tyler's Quarterly Historical and Genealogical Magazine*.

KERMIT L. HALL
Wayne State University

U

UNCLE TOM'S CABIN, Harriet Beecher Stowe's first novel, might be the most influential work of fiction ever published in the United States. Published in 1852, it sold over 300,000 copies the first year. The book crystallized northern sentiment against slavery and confirmed southerners' suspicions that they had little support in the free states. Written in the romantic tradition, the story is a profound indictment of slavery. Stowe examines the inability of people to act in a Christian manner while enmeshed in slavery. Thus Shelby and St. Claire, portrayed as kind and humane masters, send Tom forward to death at the hands of Simon Legree. Slave families are separated because slavery requires economic considerations to overshadow affection for the slave. The system allows loyal, docile, and Christian slaves like Tom to fall into the hands of sadistic monsters such as Legree.

The author's depiction of black people coincided with northern concepts of white supremacy. The slaves never impose themselves on the white population: the militant, near white-skinned George Harris opts for repatriation to Africa; the humble, very black-skinned Tom chooses martyrdom for himself and convinces Cassie, Legree's slave mistress, not to kill her master. The solution to the problems of race, then, lies with the white people. Stowe claimed to model Tom after JOSIAH HENSON, a Christian slave who willingly returned to slavery after a mission for his owner in Ohio and convinced several other slaves to follow his example.

Southern response to the book was intense. Reviewers vilified the author and called the book incendiary. The convincing portrayal of slaveholders expressing doubts about the righteousness of slavery and suggestions of massive amounts of miscegenation created, southerners claimed, a one-sided and false view of the institution. A number of anti-Tom books were published in the South, but none achieved popularity.

See H. B. Stowe, *Key to Uncle Tom's Cabin* (1853), for her explanation of sources for novel; G. F. Holmes, *Southern Literary Messenger* (Oct., 1852), classic southern response; and A. C. Crozier, *Novels of Harriet Beecher Stowe* (1969).

LESTER B. BALTIMORE
Adelphi University

UNDERGROUND RAILROAD was a popular term used to describe the organized system of sympathetic individuals that assisted fugitive slaves in their quest for freedom prior to the Civil War. Unlike the relatively well organized operation of this secretive network in the North, the Underground Railroad in the South developed in a less structured manner. What southern assistance escaping slaves received was generally sporadic and isolated, owing in part to the harsh punishment of the Railroad's agents and conductors.

As early as 1819, Vestal Coffin established an "underground" station near Guilford, N.C. His sons Alfred and Addison carried on his work, as did his cousin LEVI COFFIN, who later moved to Indiana and Ohio, where his continued assistance to fugitives earned him the honorary title of president of the Underground Railroad. Although financially ruined in 1848 because of fines resulting from his failure to obey FUGITIVE SLAVE LAWS, Thomas Garrett of Wilmington, Del., by 1861 had aided over 2,700 escapees. William Chaplin in the District of Columbia, Elisha Tyson in Maryland, John and Ezekial Hunn in Delaware, Laura Haviland in Kentucky, and John Brown in Missouri also engaged in Underground Railroad activities. Despite the aid provided by these and other whites, fugitive slaves relied primarily on fellow slaves and free Negroes for assistance, because blacks rarely betrayed runaways. Several bondmen after successfully escaping from the South returned to conduct other slaves to the free states. Two of the most notable conductors were JOSIAH HENSON and the "Moses" of her people, HARRIET TUBMAN, who ventured south 19 times and led more than 300 slaves to freedom. Whites who conducted fugitives often met fates similar to those of John Fairfield, shot to death in 1860, and Calvin Fairbanks, imprisoned for nearly 17 years.

The border states unquestionably experienced the most severe and constant loss of slave property, primarily due to their geographical propinquity to the North and more developed network of escape routes. Yet the fear generated and suspicion aroused by the Underground Railroad in the South far exceeded the actual effectiveness of the system. Viewed as a blatant attack upon the institution of slavery, the Underground Railroad served to unite the South and strengthen resistance to all such attacks.

See W. H. Siebert, *Underground Railroad* (1898), most complete; L. Gara, *Liberty Line* (1961); K. M. Stampp, *Peculiar Institution* (1956); L. Coffin, *Reminiscences* (1880); and W. Still, *Underground Railroad* (1872).

RALPH LOWELL ECKERT
Louisiana State University

UNDERSTANDING CLAUSE. Mississippi's "understanding clause," enacted in 1890, marked the first successful enactment of racial DISFRANCHISEMENT in the post-Reconstruction South. The spread of political populism in the South helped the enactment of similar voting bars in South Carolina (1895) and Louisiana (1898), with Virginia, Georgia, and Oklahoma following later. Many other states used a poll or property tax, but the POLL TAX often barred both poor white and black voters. A judgment test of a voter's "understanding" of the state constitution, however, permitted the selective enfranchisement of poorer whites.

Black disfranchisement had not been popular in the South, partly because most political factions expected to exploit the new black vote. Although the MISSISSIPPI PLAN of 1875 began the movement, it took a deceptive constitutional convention in 1890 to enact the second Mississippi plan of 1890 with the understanding clause. Ironically, the convention had been called primarily to redress suffrage inequalities in the use of the poll tax in the poor white counties. A political faction representing minority whites from the predominantly black Delta region took over the convention and promulgated the new constitution in the face of almost unanimous newspaper and popular opposition. In effect, the convention delivered political control into the hands of the white minority of the few mainly black counties in Mississippi. The constitution was not put to a state vote because that would be "unnecessary and inexpedient" and because the citizens would not have ratified the constitution.

See C. V. Woodward, *Origins of New South* (1951); V. O. Key, *Southern Politics* (1949) and *Journal of Southern History* (Aug., 1938); and P. Lewison, *Race, Class, and Party* (1932).

RICHARD H. COLLIN
University of New Orleans

UNDERWOOD, OSCAR WILDER (1862–1929), was born in Louisville, attended the University of Virginia (1881–1884), and began the practice of law in Birmingham. Elected to the U.S. House in 1896, he remained a member until 1915. He had entered Congress as a free silverite tainted with Populist ideas, but he became increasingly conservative and an outspoken critic of William Jennings Bryan. His first wife died in 1900, and in 1904 he married Bertha Woodward, daughter of the wealthiest man in Birmingham. Underwood emerged on the national scene in 1911 as chairman of the House Ways and Means Committee and embarrassed the TAFT ADMINISTRATION through the passage of "popgun" tariffs, which were vetoed by the president. By 1912 Underwood was a recognized expert on the tariff, and he unsuccessfully sought the Democratic nomination for president. He piloted through Congress most of the Wilson administration's New Freedom legislation, including the Underwood-Simmons Tariff Act.

Elected to the Senate in 1914, he catapulted to leadership. He secured passage of much of the Wilson war program despite his lack of enthusiasm for many wartime restraints. He was reelected in 1920 and became Senate minority leader. Acknowledged as an able parliamentary leader, Underwood was frustrated by the Senate's archaic rules and favored an effective cloture rule. His fight for private development of Muscle Shoals almost succeeded. He served as a delegate to the Washington Conference and led the successful fight for ratification of the Washington treaties. Cooperation with Warren G. Harding cost Underwood support among Democrats, and in 1923 he resigned as minority leader. Declining Harding's offer to consider him for the U.S. Supreme Court, he ran for the Democratic presidential nomination in 1924. The unsuccessful race saw Underwood supported by railroad interests and opposed by the Ku Klux Klan. The Klan fight weakened Underwood in Alabama, and he retired in 1927 to his Virginia home, Woodlawn.

See O. W. Underwood, *Drifting Sands of Party Politics* (1928); E. C. Johnson, "Oscar W. Underwood" (Ph.D. dissertation, University of North Carolina, 1953); and Underwood Papers, Alabama Archives Department, Montgomery.

EVANS C. JOHNSON
Stetson University

UNIONISTS is the term commonly applied to those southerners who adopted a political position or an emotional commitment favorable to the federal government during the Civil War and the sectional crises that preceded and followed it. These southerners supported the Union for several reasons. One group clung to the intense nationalism that permeated the early national period. Others supported the Union because they were fundamentally opposed to sectionalism or had supported nationalistic economic policies promoted by HENRY CLAY and the WHIG PARTY. Some individuals supported the Union because they believed secession to be either unconstitutional or unsound. Pacifists and some religious groups, particularly the QUAKERS, supported the Union. Finally, those southerners who were opposed to slavery or had reservations about it often supported the Union, though it is impossible to make a binding statement about the relationship between slaveholding and unionism. Some slaveholders were Unionists, but many nonslaveholders were avid in their defense of the South.

Unionism derives its fundamental significance from its role in the sectional crises of 1832–1833, 1850, and 1861–1865. In the first of these, South Carolina attempted to invalidate the tariff legislation of the central government (NULLIFICATION). Even in South Carolina the Unionist element fought the nullificationists; and, when Union men predominated throughout the remainder of the South, South Carolina pulled back from its extreme states' rights position.

From 1833 to 1850 the strength of the Unionists apparently declined, but the Unionist group was still sufficiently strong to win support for the COMPROMISE OF 1850. They managed to control the conventions that were called to determine whether to support a South-wide secession movement. Having averted the immediate threat, the Unionists then campaigned successfully in the early 1850s for leaders who would support the compromise.

After the collapse of the Whig party around 1854, Unionists lost their political base. For this reason they supported the Constitutional Union party in the election of 1860. A few Unionists defected after the election of Abraham Lincoln, but most of them fought for the election of antisecession delegates to the state conventions that met in late 1860 and early 1861 to consider withdrawal from the United States. In the period between Lincoln's election and the firing on Ft. Sumter, Unionists had considerable success in the Upper South, but their strength collapsed when the first shots were fired.

During the war many Unionists reluctantly switched their allegiance to the South, and some continued to hold public office. Others involved themselves with a series of peace movements in 1863 and 1864. The most extreme form of unionism was joining the Union army; at least 50,000 southern men served in the federal forces. An unknown number migrated to the North, and those who stayed at home sheltered deserters and draft dodgers. The area of strongest Union sentiment was the mountain region running from West Virginia through east Tennessee and western North Carolina into northern Alabama.

The presence of Unionists in the South had considerable influence after the war. Continued strife between them and the extreme southern nationalists was a principal factor in the decision to place the South under military rule in 1867. There was a great diversity in their ideas about the method of restoration of the states to the Union. Some supported President Andrew Johnson's mild, rapid approach, but others joined the camp of the Radical Republicans and participated in the governments established under military supervision. Part of the bitterness remained for years after Reconstruction.

See C. N. Degler, *Other South* (1974); F. W. Klingberg, *Southern Claims Commission* (1955); G. L. Tatum, *Disloyalty in Confederacy* (1934); and biographies of individual Unionists.

RICHARD L. ZUBER
Wake Forest University

UNION LEAGUE, sometimes called the Loyal League, was begun in 1862 in Philadelphia as a patriotic society to sustain the spirit of the North. As the war progressed the league began to go south and soon became for all practical purposes an arm of the REPUBLICAN PARTY. Although its membership included many white UNIONISTS and native whites, it was primarily a vehicle for building a following among Negroes. It was originally designed as a secret society to educate Negroes in political matters. New members were introduced to its secret oaths and rituals and then instructed in their rights and duties. The Republican party was usually portrayed as the party of freedom and the Democratic as the party of slavery. Members were urged to vote for Republicans and to exercise their new civil and legal rights. Many parades and public demonstrations were held, and Negroes were taken to the polls on election day. These activities resulted in a number of Republican victories in 1867 and 1868. The league's initial success and rapid growth aroused considerable fear and criticism among many southerners. They accused it of committing violence against former Confederates, of voting freedmen as "cattle," and arousing Negroes with inflammatory remarks. They blamed many of the actions of Negroes upon the league and came to see its very existence as a threat to the South. By late 1868 the league had disbanded across most of the South. It had come under increasing attack by the Klan.

Many of its members had become interested in political and economic activities at the state and national levels. It has continued to exist as a conservative social organization in New York, Philadelphia, and Chicago.

See A. W. Trelease, *White Terror* (1971), best; J. H. Franklin, *Reconstruction* (1961); *KKK Report of Joint Select Committee to Inquire into Condition of Affairs in Late Insurrection States* (13 vols.; 1872); R. S. Henry, *Story of Reconstruction* (1951), somewhat biased; and V. L. Wharton, *Negro in Mississippi* (1947), balanced.

GLENN M. LINDEN
Southern Methodist University

UNITED CONFEDERATE VETERANS, an organization of former Confederate soldiers and sailors, began at New Orleans June 10, 1889. More than 500 of its 1,855 local camps previously existed independently or as constituents of other societies. Its useful organ, CONFEDERATE VETERAN, ran for 40 years (1893–1932). Over the UCV's 62 years, the 28 commanders-in-chief included six C.S.A. generals and several other lower officers, but thereafter none remained except privates. Nevertheless the three who attended the last reunion in 1951 all became UCV "generals." The UCV had an elaborate mock-military structure and "ranks," but the members cared most for local camp activities. Although the organization was decidedly southern, 5 percent of the camps were outside the South. The total number who at any time belonged neared 160,000—25 percent of the southern soldiers who survived the Civil War. Believing that the world misunderstood the South and its people, the UCV sought security and vindication. Fused by common experience, elitism, altruism, mutual benefit, and concern for history, local groups often camped together out-of-doors, and national reunions gathered yearly. The UCV engaged in predictable but impressively ambitious social, relief, and commemorative endeavors. It rationalized efforts to secure state pensions, soldiers' homes, or public financing of Civil War monuments as humanitarian issues transcending politics.

See H. Hattaway, *Louisiana History* (Summer, 1971; Winter, 1975); W. W. White, *Confederate Veteran* (1962), superficial; and UCV Papers, Louisiana State University Archives.

HERMAN HATTAWAY
University of Missouri, Kansas City

UNITED DAUGHTERS OF THE CONFEDERACY (328 North Blvd., Richmond, Va. 23220) was founded in Nashville, Tenn., September 10, 1894.

Various existing groups of women dedicated to perpetuating and honoring the memory of the Confederacy were organized into a single, larger, more effective society. Founders from Savannah and Nashville worked closely with the UNITED CONFEDERATE VETERANS, whose organizational experience proved helpful. Thereafter, the UDC expanded rapidly through state divisions based on local chapters, and today it continues to function actively in most of the United States. Women who were descendants of members of the army, navy, or civil service of the Confederate States of America were eligible for membership. Their official purpose was historical, educational, benevolent, memorial, and social. Activities included erecting monuments, marking Confederate graves, caring for widows and children of veterans, and stimulating the study and the writing of essays and books for a better understanding of the Confederacy. It finished the restoration of the Confederate executive mansion in Richmond and established there and elsewhere museums of the Confederacy. The UDC has furthered the education of southern youth through college scholarships and has founded Confederate book collections in libraries at home and in foreign countries. Current membership is 35,000.

See M. B. Poppenheim *et al., History of UDC* (1956); *Confederate Veteran* (1893–1932); *UDC Bulletin* (1938–44); and *UDC Magazine* (1944–).

JOSEPH B. JAMES
Wesleyan College, Macon, Ga.

UNITED STATES V. CLASSIC (313 U.S. 299 [1941]). In May, 1941, the U.S. Supreme Court decided by a vote of four to three to uphold the right of the federal government to prosecute individuals for having violated the civil rights of citizens in the context of official state action. This decision, which applied specifically to a situation in New Orleans, where a local politician had been charged with voting fraud in a congressional primary, was significant for several reasons. First, the Court made it clear that a congressional primary came under the jurisdiction of the federal government. Second, the Court's decision established a fresh legal basis for using the Federal Criminal Code as an instrument for protecting the rights of citizens deprived of those rights by state action. The Court's minority, consisting of Justices HUGO BLACK, William Douglas, and Frank Murphy, disagreed with this ruling, claiming that the federal statutes used by the majority to justify its position were much too vague and imprecise to warrant such a sweeping new interpretation and that the

decision judicially preempted legislative prerogative. The Court's decision was a solid victory for
the Justice Department's Civil Rights Section,
created by Attorney General Frank Murphy in
1939, which bore the responsibility for bringing
the matter before the high tribunal.

See R. K. Carr, *Federal Protection of Civil Rights* (1947);
J. W. Howard, Jr., *Mr. Justice Murphy* (1968); and P. Murphy, *Constitution in Crisis Times, 1918–1969* (1972).

WILLIAM C. BERMAN
University of Toronto

UNITED STATES V. HIRAM REESE AND MAT-
THEW FOUSHEE (92 U.S. 214 [1875]). Federal
guarantees of Negro suffrage were primary methods by which the northern-based Republican party sought to secure a power base in the South.
Democrats countered with various methods of
Negro DISFRANCHISEMENT. This political struggle
had profound constitutional implications, as this
case demonstrates. The defendants were inspectors of election for the January 30, 1873, municipal
elections in the Third Ward in Lexington, Ky.
They were indicted under the Enforcement Act
of May 31, 1870, for refusing to accept and count
the vote of a black man, William Garner, and
were charged with infringing Garner's Fifteenth
Amendment right to vote. The U.S. Supreme Court
dismissed the indictments on the grounds that the
law went beyond the authority of the Fifteenth
Amendment. The Court reasoned that the amendment did not guarantee the right to vote; it merely
prohibited racial discrimination that infringed
voting rights. This decision signaled the retreat
from federal voting rights enforcement, for it left
to the states the primary responsibility for and
power to secure voting rights.

See Supreme Court Case File No. 6795, Record Group
267, National Archives; W. Gillette, in R. O. Curry (ed.),
Radicalism, Racism, and Party Realignment (1969); E.
Swinney, *Journal of Southern History* (May, 1962); R.
Claude, *Journal of Negro History* (April, 1966); W. W.
Davis, in *Studies in Southern History and Politics* (1914);
J. M. Kousser, *Shaping of Southern Politics* (1974); C. P.
Magrath, *Morrison R. Waite* (1963); C. Warren, *Supreme
Court* (1937), II; and H. Commings and C. McFarland,
Federal Justice (1937).

ROBERT J. KACZOROWSKI
Wagner College

UNITED STATES V. WILLIAM J. CRUIK-
SHANK ET AL. (92 U.S. 542 [1875]). Federal
guarantees of personal safety and fundamental
justice for southern blacks and white Republicans
were basic aims of Reconstruction. The Colfax
riots of April 13, 1873—in which the white sup-

porters of H. C. WARMOTH's appointees to public
offices in Grant Parish, La., massacred black supporters of W. P. KELLOGG's appointees—demonstrated the need for such guarantees. Nine members of the Warmoth faction were convicted in
U.S. circuit court under the Enforcement Act of
May 31, 1870, of intimidating blacks for the purpose of depriving them of certain civil rights. The
Supreme Court, however, overturned the convictions, arguing that the law went beyond the authority of the Fourteenth Amendment to protect
civil rights. This decision sharply curtailed the
amendment's power to protect civil rights by restricting it to correcting state discrimination. This
decision announced the withdrawal of national
protection for persons and property from intimidation and violence in the South. With the UNITED
STATES V. HIRAM REESE decision of the same day,
it foreshadowed the end of Reconstruction.

See Supreme Court Case File No. 7044, Record Group
267, National Archives; Department of Justice Papers,
Source Chronological File for Louisiana, Record Group
60, National Archives, on microfilm; M. W. Johnson,
Louisiana Historical Quarterly (July, 1930); H. O. Les-
tage, *Louisiana Historical Quarterly* (July, 1935); R.
Claude, *Journal of Negro History* (April, 1966); R. J. Kaczorowski, "Civil Rights and Federal Courts During Reconstruction" (Paper, OAH Convention, April, 1975);
C. V. Woodward, *Proceedings of American Philosophical
Society* (Feb., 1966); M. L. Benedict, *Journal of Ameri-
can History* (June, 1974); C. P. Magrath, *Morrison R.
Waite* (1963); C. Warren, *Supreme Court* (1937), II; J. G.
Taylor, *Louisiana Reconstructed* (1974); and H. Com-
mings and C. McFarland, *Federal Justice* (1937).

ROBERT J. KACZOROWSKI
Wagner College

UNIVERSAL NEGRO IMPROVEMENT ASSO-
CIATION was a Negro separatist organization
founded in 1914 by a Jamaica-born black man,
Marcus Garvey. After 1917, from its headquarters
in Harlem, the UNIA taught its members a mixture of racial purity, economic chauvinism, social
separation from white people, and African nationalism. Garvey established the Black Star Steamship Line for trade between the United States and
Africa; he founded the Black Cross Nurses, the
African Legion, and the Negro Factories Corporation; he preached anticolonialism and a black
Christianity. Many hundreds of thousands of
American and West Indian Negroes joined the
UNIA and attended its huge annual conventions,
although in the South its branches, except in New
Orleans and Washington, were weak. Fundamentally the UNIA attracted lower-class blacks who
had left the South for the northern ghettoes dur-
ing and after World War I and who, disillusioned

with the poverty and discrimination there, responded to Garvey's calls for racial pride and a black Zionism. His business ventures failed, as did his back-to-Africa program; the UNIA attracted few upper-class members and came to make its own peace with American white racists. After Garvey was sent to prison for mail fraud in 1925, the association declined, but it was the first black mass movement in the United States.

See E. D. Cronon, *Black Moses* (1955), standard; and T. G. Vincent, *Black Power and Garvey Movement* (1971), sympathetic.

JOHN M. MATTHEWS
Georgia State University

UNIVERSITIES. See COLLEGES AND UNIVERSITIES.

UP-COUNTRY, a colloquial expression used since the early nineteenth century throughout much of the English-speaking world, refers to any interior region removed from the seaboard and its attendant civilization. In the South Atlantic states, the term usually distinguishes the PIEDMONT and the mountain areas from the TIDEWATER. It also may connote the poorer, presumably less literate and less cultured life of yeomen farmers as distinct from coastal planters.

UPSHUR, ABEL PARKER (1790–1844), born in Northampton County, Va., was educated at Princeton and Yale but did not graduate from either. He studied law with WILLIAM WIRT in Richmond and served several terms in the Virginia House of Burgesses. A member of the Virginia constitutional convention of 1829, he opposed many proposed democratic changes. Appointed to the state supreme court in 1826, he served in that capacity until 1841. There was some opposition to his appointment by President John Tyler as secretary of the navy in 1841 and as secretary of state in 1843 because of his extreme views on STATES' RIGHTS and slavery, but he was confirmed in both positions. As secretary of state Upshur was working on the treaty for Texas annexation, which he felt was vital to the security of the South, when in a freak accident he was killed by the explosion of a naval cannon on the battleship *Princeton*. His replacement by JOHN C. CALHOUN undoubtedly delayed the acceptance of Texas into the Union.

See C. H. Hall, *A. P. Upshur* (1963).

ROBERT A. BRENT
University of Southern Mississippi

URBANIZATION. The South possesses the nation's oldest urban center (St. Augustine, Fla., founded in 1565); its urbanization rate in the antebellum period was so rapid that it lagged behind only Great Britain's and that of the rest of the United States in the Western Hemisphere; and, since 1940, the region has been the most rapidly urbanizing section of the country. Despite these achievements, urbanization has been one of the most neglected topics in the South's history. Consequently, the causes for the growth of cities, as well as the comparative lack thereof during various periods, the "uniqueness" of southern urban centers, and the impact of urbanization are all poorly understood themes in southern history.

The causes of scholarly indifference toward southern cities are undoubtedly and understandably rooted in the relatively smaller size of the South's cities and the slower rate of urbanization in the region throughout long stretches of its history. In 1920, for example, the South, with 28.1 percent of its population living in cities, was roughly as urbanized as the entire nation had been in 1880. This 40-year lag in the pace of southern urbanization diminished after 1940. However, the significance of the South's urban growth even after that date was undercut for some observers by the fact that the South in 1970 was still the least urban section of the country.

Why the South failed to keep step with the rest of the nation in urbanization and the growth of large cities is a question that has not been satisfactorily answered. Three factors often mentioned as possible causes of the South's retarded urbanization have been the region's tenacious adherence to the agrarian ideal, the rigidity and backward qualities of its social structure, and its inability to industrialize. Although all of these explanations of the South's deficiencies in urbanization have their merits, they are not completely accepted today by scholars working in the field of southern urban history. Although the agrarian ideal doubtless played a role in hindering urbanization in the region, the strong prourban element of southern culture—manifested in the industrial expositions of the NEW SOUTH era and the urban-promotive ventures of southern "business progressives" during the 1920s—cannot be ignored. Even in the antebellum period, the careers of such diverse individuals as James D. B. De Bow, ANDREW JACKSON, GEORGE FITZHUGH, and JOHN C. CALHOUN involved a surprising amount of urban boosterism. It is useful to remember that Calhoun, a symbol of the antebellum South's resistance to industrialization and protective tariffs, was heavily involved in the 1840s in a trans-Appalachian railroad ven-

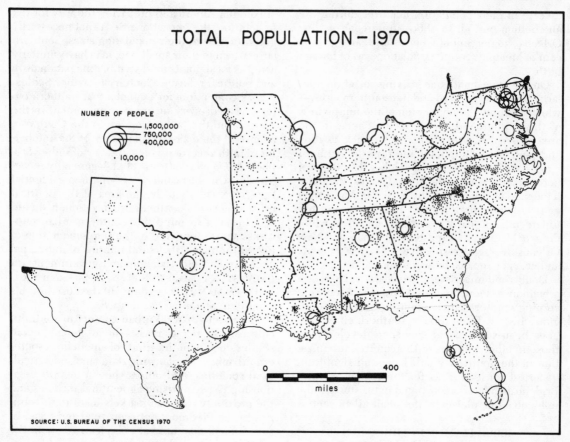

TOTAL POPULATION – 1970

NUMBER OF PEOPLE

1,500,000
750,000
400,000

· 10,000

0   400

miles

SOURCE: U.S. BUREAU OF THE CENSUS 1970

ture designed to promote Charleston's growth. On the basis of fragmentary evidence recently accumulated, there exists now the strong suspicion that the South always has possessed influential elite groups for whom cities and towns were not contrary to the southern way of life. The rigidity of the social structure and the agrarian ideal will thus not explain by themselves the South's difficulties in urbanizing itself. The lack of significant INDUSTRIALIZATION, on the other hand, has a great deal to do with the paucity of large cities in the region; cities with an industrial base are usually larger than those based on COMMERCE and services.

Perhaps less controversial than the causes of the South's tardy urbanization but nonetheless highly debatable is the historical uniqueness of the southern urban environment. The impression persists that southern cities were somehow different. As far as the physical aspects of southern cities are concerned, however, there seems to be little evidence to support this impression. With a few notable and beautiful exceptions like Savan-

nah, Ga., Washington, D.C., and Jackson, Miss., most southern cities, like those in the West, were laid out in accordance with the grid plan. Only in maintaining a preindustrial pattern of central cores of commercial and upper-class housing surrounded by rings of poor and working-class neighborhoods longer than was typical in the United States and also by beginning suburbanization on a grand scale before their centers were as densely populated as those of northern cities have southern cities been significantly different in their spatial arrangements. Even two of the best-known social peculiarities of the southern urban environment—the presence of Negroes and the absence of foreign immigrants—have not always distinguished southern cities from those outside the region. Harlem, New York, and other northern cities began to rival those of the South in acquiring Negro migrants from the countryside as early as the 1890s. Even though southern cities, unlike New York, Chicago, and Boston, failed to capture significant numbers of the "new immigrants" between 1880 and 1920, they were also surprisingly diverse in their population mixtures during the antebellum period. In 1860, 40 percent of New Orleans', 30 percent of Charleston's, and 36 percent of Memphis' white population was of foreign birth.

On the other hand, one striking social dissimilarity between southern and nonsouthern cities—which confirms the impression of the uniqueness of the southern urban world—has been in the area of personal VIOLENCE. As far back as 1890 and perhaps earlier, homicide rates in southern cities have been significantly higher than those of nonsouthern cities in the United States; the homicide rates of Salem and Boston, for example, never rose higher than six per 100,000 during the nineteenth and early twentieth centuries, while those of Memphis, Charleston, Savannah, and New Orleans averaged respectively 41.1, 27.7, 25.6, and 22.2 per 100,000 between 1901 and 1910.

Doubts and uncertainty also characterize scholarly findings about an even thornier problem concerning southern cities—their impact on the region's history. Even though southern cities may have been smaller and slower to develop than those in other sections of the country, urbanization in the South may still have had significant historical consequences for the region. As Carl Bridenbaugh has demonstrated in his study of the influential role played by the small urban centers

URBANIZATION IN THE SOUTH COMPARED WITH OTHER REGIONS OF THE U.S., 1790–1970
(% urbanized of total population)

Date	U.S.	South	Northeast	North Central	West
1790	5.1	2.1	8.1		
1800	6.1	3.0	9.3		
1810	7.3	4.1	10.9	0.9	
1820	7.2	4.6	11.0	1.1	
1830	8.8	5.3	14.2	2.6	
1840	10.8	6.7	18.5	3.9	
1850	15.3	8.3	26.5	9.2	6.4
1860	19.8	9.6	35.7	13.9	16.0
1870	25.7	12.2	44.3	20.8	25.8
1880	28.2	12.2	50.8	24.2	30.2
1890	35.1	16.3	59.0	33.1	37.0
1900	39.7	18.0	61.1	38.6	39.9
1910	45.7	22.5	71.8	45.1	47.9
1920	51.2	28.1	75.5	52.3	51.8
1930	56.2	34.1	77.6	57.9	58.4
1940	56.5	36.7	76.6	58.4	58.5
1950	59.6	44.6	75.4	61.1	59.9
1960	63.1	52.7	72.8	63.9	66.1
1970	73.5	64.6	80.4	71.5	82.9

NOTE: "South" denotes the following states: Del., Md., Va., W.Va., Ky., Tenn., N.C., S.C., Ga., Fla., Ala., Miss., Ark., La., Okla., Tex., and D.C. Definitions of the other regions referred to may be found in U.S. Dept. of Commerce, *General Social and Economic Characteristics of 1970 Census* (1972).

of colonial America in preparing the way for the Revolution, the impact of cities is not necessarily proportionate to their population sizes. Southern cities, despite their small size, may have similarly acted as focal points for disseminating nationalism and political reforms. Contrary to Arthur Schlesinger's contention, for example, that southern cities initiated every disunionist movement in the South from the Jacksonian era to the Civil War, almost all the major urban centers of the antebellum South recorded votes in favor of either Stephen A. Douglas or JOHN BELL—generally recognized as Unionist candidates—in the presidential ELECTION OF 1860. In the area of the political consequences of southern urbanization, it should also be kept in mind that southern urban PROGRESSIVISM pioneered in the implementation of two of the major structural reforms of municipal government: city commission government (or GALVESTON COMMISSION PLAN, first used in 1901) and CITY-MANAGER government (first used in this country in Staunton, Va., in 1908).

The theme of rural-urban conflict in southern culture also needs reassessment. Some recent studies document the efforts of antebellum southern urbanites in organizing state fairs and agricultural societies; and others show a definite relationship between rising agricultural incomes and the proximity to urban markets in 14 rural counties in the Piedmont between 1900 and 1950. In sum, a great deal has yet to be learned about the role of cities and urbanization in southern history.

See B. A. Brownell, *Urban Ethos in South* (1975), best bibliography, *Urban South in Twentieth Century* (1974), and *Mississippi Quarterly* (Spring, 1973). See also A. F. Scott, *Urban Affairs Quarterly* (March, 1966); R. B. Vance and N. J. Demerath, *Urban South* (1954); L. Reissman, in J. C. McKinney and E. T. Thompson (eds.), *South in Continuity and Change* (1965); W. H. Nichols, *Southern Tradition and Regional Progress* (1960); P. C. Stewart, *Virginia Magazine of History and Biography* (Sept., 1973); L. P. Curry, *Journal of Southern History* (Feb., 1974); L. W. Dorsett and A. H. Shaffer, *Journal of Southern History* (Feb., 1972); O. Crenshaw, in E. F. Goldman (ed.), *Historiography and Urbanization* (1941); A. M. Tang, *Economic Development in Southern Piedmont* (1958); D. R. Goldfield, *Journal of Urban History* (Feb., 1976); C. V. Earle and R. Hoffman, *Urban Development in Eighteenth-Century South* (1976); and B. A. Brownell and D. R. Goldfield (eds.), *City in Southern History* (1977).

JAMES M. RUSSELL
University of Tennessee, Chattanooga

URBAN LEAGUE, NATIONAL, was formed in 1911 out of three organizations previously established to help southern black migrants adjust to urban conditions: the National League for the

Protection of Colored Women (1905), the Committee for Improving Industrial Conditions of the Negro in New York City (1905), and the Committee on Urban Conditions Among Negroes in New York (1910). The league started as primarily a New York City organization, but the founder saw the South as a locale for the league's major activity. George E. Haynes, one of the founders, joined the faculty of Fisk University and began a program for training social workers, and efforts were made to promote the teaching of sociology and social work–related courses in other southern black colleges.

Many of the pre–World War I Urban League branches were in southern cities. Richmond, Norfolk, Savannah, Augusta, Atlanta, Birmingham, Memphis, Nashville, and Chattanooga all had Urban League affiliates. The racial climate in southern cities, however, turned out to be hostile to the organization's program of improving the economic conditions of blacks through interracial cooperation. Only in Atlanta, St. Louis, and Louisville were viable branches started during the early years. The league thus turned its attention to serving southern black migrants in northern cities. Later, a few other southern cities, such as New Orleans, organized branches, but these were in a constant struggle for survival. After WHITNEY M. YOUNG, JR., became executive director in 1961, the National Urban League became an active participant in the CIVIL RIGHTS MOVEMENT in the South, especially in the area of voter registration.

See E. K. Jones, *Opportunity* (Jan., 1925); L. H. Wood, *Journal of Negro History* (April, 1924); A. E. Strickland, *History of Chicago Urban League* (1966); N. J. Weiss, *National Urban League* (1974); and G. Parris and L. Brooks, *Blacks in City* (1971).

ARVARH E. STRICKLAND
University of Missouri, Columbia

V

VALDOSTA, GA. (pop. 32,303), 65 miles northeast of Tallahassee, Fla., was founded in 1860 at the junction of three railroads. Originally a center for area lumber and turpentine producers, the modern city produces paper, lumber, textiles, fertilizer, and mobile homes. It is the site of Valdosta State College (1906), and nearby is Moody Air Force Base.

See files of Valdosta *Times* (1867–), on microfilm (1868–69, 1905–15, 1924–), a Democratic daily.

VALENTINE, LILA HARDAWAY MEADE (1865–1921), a Virginia reformer from a prominent Richmond family, combined intellectuality with wit and charm. In 1886 she married Benjamin Batchelder Valentine, a gentleman with a deep sense of public responsibility. On a trip to England in 1892, she was influenced by British liberalism to desire to awaken the social conscience of the South. Believing the paramount need was universal EDUCATION, she organized in 1900 the Richmond Education Association. Her introduction of kindergarten and vocational education into the public schools led her to the executive board of the prestigious Cooperative Educational Association of Virginia. To combat the wretched public HEALTH facilities, she established in 1902 the Instructive Visiting Nurse Association of Richmond, through which in 1904 she initiated the first antituberculosis campaign in Virginia. Converted in 1905 to woman suffrage, she headed the Equal Suffrage League. ELLEN GLASGOW judged her the only woman who combined requisite "intelligence" with "inexhaustible patience." Her support of civil rights and the federal suffrage amendment caused strong conservative opposition.

See Valentine Papers and Woman's Suffrage Manuscripts, Virginia State Library, Richmond; and L. C. Taylor, Jr., *Virginia Magazine of History and Biography* (Oct., 1962).

LLOYD C. TAYLOR, JR.
Texas A. & M. University

VAN BUREN, MARTIN, ADMINISTRATION (1837–1841). Martin Van Buren, as a northerner, knew that he was suspect in the South and hoped that as president he could strengthen relations with southern states. He had long believed in the need for a strong North-South axis for the Democratic party. He believed that a national party committed to states' rights and limited government would be able to avoid sectional rivalries.

During his first few months in office, Van Buren tried to repair some of the damage done by Andrew Jackson during the NULLIFICATION crisis. Believing that the South was underrepresented in the cabinet, Van Buren appointed South Carolina's JOEL R. POINSETT secretary of war in 1837. Van Buren's first choice for this post had been Virginia's influential Senator WILLIAM C. RIVES, but Rives had wanted to be secretary of state instead. With Georgia's JOHN FORSYTH already holding that position, Van Buren saw nothing to gain in removing one southerner to please another. Still, Van Buren refused to become a champion of popular southern causes such as the annexation of Texas. He managed to keep this issue out of the ELECTION OF 1836 and refused to support annexation the following year, fearing that it would touch off a damaging sectional debate in Congress.

Despite these decisions, despite the return to the Democratic party of JOHN C. CALHOUN, Van Buren lost support in the South, primarily because of the PANIC OF 1837. This massive financial collapse forced him to propose an ambitious legislative program. Defections in Virginia and North Carolina robbed him of crucial southern support and were prime factors in the defeat of his legislative proposals and in his unsuccessful bid for reelection.

See J. C. Curtis, *Fox at Bay* (1970); R. A. Brown, *South Atlantic Quarterly* (Winter, 1966); and J. H. Harrison, *Journal of Southern History* (Nov., 1956).

JAMES C. CURTIS
University of Delaware

VANCE, RUPERT BAYLESS (1899–), Kenan Professor of Sociology at the University of North Carolina, is perhaps the best-known and most widely cited sociologist in the South. Born in Plumerville, Ark., he received his A.B. degree in 1920 from Henderson-Brown College, his M.A. degree in economics from Vanderbilt in 1921, and his doctorate from Chapel Hill in 1928. In Vance's first and favorite work, *Human Factors in Cotton Culture* (1929), he characterized cotton tenancy as "our greatest social humiliation," possibly even worse than slavery. His pioneering research into the practice of SHARECROPPING had considerable influence on New Deal land-tenure programs and thus did much to help reduce the scale of this practice. Following the death of his mentor HOWARD W. ODUM, Vance went on to become the nation's foremost advocate of regionalism and exponent of the belief that social planning should be regionally based. The regional school of sociology prevailed among southern sociologists until World War II and is still highly influential. It inspired such organizations as the COMMISSION ON INTERRACIAL COOPERATION, the SOUTHERN REGIONAL COUNCIL, and the SOUTHERN EDUCATION BOARD. Vance supported and expounded the regional theme in numerous articles and monographs and in such scholarly books as *Human Geography of the South* (1932) and *All These People: The Nation's Human Resources in the South* (1945).

EDGAR T. THOMPSON
Duke University

VANCE, ZEBULON BAIRD (1830–1894), lawyer and politician, was born in Buncombe County, N.C. He attended Washington College in Tennessee and studied law at the University of North Carolina. After service in the state house of commons as a Whig, Vance served in the U.S. House of Representatives as a KNOW-NOTHING from 1858 to 1861. He opposed SECESSION but, when Abraham Lincoln mobilized the militia, called for his state to support the Confederacy. He rose from captain to colonel during his year of military service and in 1862 was elected to the first of two terms as governor. When the war ended, Vance was briefly imprisoned but received a pardon and in 1870 was elected to the U.S. Senate though not allowed to sit. From 1876 to 1879 he was again governor but resigned to become U.S. senator, a post he held until his death. Vance is most remembered for his battles with Jefferson Davis over STATES' RIGHTS within the Confederacy and for his later service as senator, when his ability and sense of humor made him popular and influential.

See F. Johnston, *Papers of Z. B. Vance* (1963), I, good, brief biographical synopsis; G. Tucker, *Zeb Vance* (1966); C. Dowd, *Life of Z. B. Vance* (1897); R. Yates, *Confederacy and Vance* (1958); E. Cannon (ed.), *Correspondence of Z. B. Vance* (1971), 1851–53 love letters; and F. Johnston, *North Carolina Historical Review* (April, 1953).

JOHN F. MARSZALEK
Mississippi State University

VANDERBILT UNIVERSITY (Nashville, Tenn. 37240) was founded in 1853 and opened in 1855 as a college of the Methodist Episcopal Church,

South. Its finances ravaged by the Civil War, the school was reorganized, rechartered, and refinanced in 1873 with the help of philanthropist Cornelius Vanderbilt. Growing conflict between the Methodist church leaders and the school was resolved in 1914, when the college became a nonsectarian institution. In addition to substantial gifts from the Vanderbilt family, the school's endowment has been enriched by grants from the Carnegie Foundation and the GENERAL EDUCATION BOARD. The joint university libraries of Vanderbilt and of GEORGE PEABODY and Scarritt colleges maintain numerous collections on the religious, medical, social, and economic history of Tennessee. Notable collections include the Crawford W. Long Papers (medical education), the Tucker W. Clark Papers (family life in Virginia and Kentucky, 1816–1899), the George Pullen Jackson Papers (highland folk music), the Edwin Mims Papers and the John J. Tigert Papers (Vanderbilt University history), the L. C. Glenn Collection (TVA), and the FUGITIVE group's manuscripts and books. Current enrollment is approximately 6,700 students.

See J. O. Gross, *Tennessee Historical Quarterly* (March, 1963); R. A. McGaw, *Brief History of Vanderbilt* (1973); E. Mims, *Chancellor Kirkland of Vanderbilt* (1940) and *History of Vanderbilt* (1946); and J. Wadsworth, "Cornelius Vanderbilt" (Ph.D. dissertation, Brown, 1967).

VAN DORN, EARL (1820–1863), was born in Port Gibson, Miss., graduated from West Point in 1842, and served with distinction in the Mexican War and on the Texas border against the Comanche Indians. During the Civil War, he first commanded the troops of his native state, then moved to Texas as a colonel of Confederate troops. In early 1862 the Confederate War Department dispatched him to Arkansas as the first commander of the trans-Mississippi West. In March he suffered a severe loss at PEA RIDGE against an invading northern army under General Samuel Curtis, a defeat that cost the Confederacy most of its influence across the Mississippi River.

Ordered back to Mississippi, his Pea Ridge veterans arrived too late for the battle of SHILOH. He then joined General BRAXTON BRAGG at Corinth, Miss., and went on to Vicksburg, where he successfully defended that important port city during the second summer of the war. Back in northern Mississippi in early fall, he united with General STERLING PRICE in an ill-prepared attack on Corinth and suffered a severe loss. Called before a court of inquiry for his actions, he escaped censure but not criticism. His next command was a small cavalry unit in northern Mississippi.

At home with mounted infantry, he showed for the first time the mettle expected of him at the war's beginning. On December 20, 1862, he raided General U. S. Grant's supply base at Holly Springs, an action that forced important modifications in the northern commander's invasion plans. Transferred to Tennessee to continue cavalry operations, he fell victim to his own personal problems, being assassinated at Spring Hill by a prominent doctor who claimed that Van Dorn had been involved with his wife. A capable small unit commander, Van Dorn advanced too rapidly in rank for his own good. His military failures coupled with his personal weaknesses leave us with a person we record primarily for the greatness of the war, not his record.

See E. Miller, *Soldier's Honor* (1903), biased defense by his sister; R. Hartje, *Earl Van Dorn* (1967); A. Castel, *Sterling Price* (1968); T. Connelly, *Army of Heartland* (1967); and G. McWhiney, *Braxton Bragg* (1969), I.

ROBERT HARTJE
Wittenberg University

VANN, ROBERT LEE (1887–1940), was born near Ahoskie, N.C., the son of former slaves. After attending Winton Normal School and Virginia Union University, he moved to Pennsylvania and was graduated from the University of Pittsburgh (B.A., 1906; LL.B., 1909). In 1910, while practicing law, he founded and edited the Pittsburgh *Courier*. Despite limited advertising revenue and Vann's initial inexperience, the paper quickly gained a widespread black readership with a circulation of 50,000 by 1920 and over 170,000 by 1936. Vann's editorials reflected his personal association with the Republican party and were frequently quoted or reprinted in other papers throughout the nation. Besides serving as assistant city solicitor for Pittsburgh (1917–1921), Vann was active in national politics as the Republicans' director of Negro publicity in the elections of 1920, 1924, and 1928. In the ELECTION OF 1932, however, he switched his support to Franklin D. Roosevelt. Although he served the Roosevelt administration as an assistant attorney general (the first black ever appointed to that post by a Democrat) and campaigned again for FDR in 1936, he planned to support Wendell Willkie in the election of 1940.

See A. Buni, *Robert L. Vann* (1944); and files of Pittsburgh *Courier* (1910–).

VARDAMAN, JAMES KIMBLE (1861–1930), was born in Jackson County, Tex., and represented Mississippi as a legislator (1890–1894), governor (1904–1908), and U.S. senator (1913–1919). Var-

daman's rise to power was neither easy nor insignificant, for it represented a sharp break in Mississippi politics. During the late nineteenth century, conservative politicians controlled government in Mississippi and catered to the interests of railroads and industry while largely ignoring many demands of small farmers (REDEEMER GOVERNMENTS). At first Vardaman sided with these conservative politicians, who controlled advancement within the Mississippi Democratic party, but twice he failed to secure the gubernatorial nomination at state Democratic conventions. After his second defeat, he began to direct his appeal to the small white farmers. In 1903 in the first election under Mississippi's new primary law, which placed nominations directly in the hands of white voters (most of them small farmers), Vardaman ran for governor and won on a platform calling for agrarian reforms and the abolition of Negro education.

Although Vardaman maintained power as governor and as senator by appealing to white supremacy, he was more than a racist demagogue (DEMAGOGUERY). As governor, for example, he brought railroads under more stringent regulation and abolished the remnants of the CONVICT LEASE SYSTEM. As senator, in addition to supporting all the reforms of Woodrow Wilson's administration, he was one of six senators who voted against American entry into World War I. In the 1918 senatorial primary, one marked by wartime hysteria, PAT HARRISON defeated Vardaman. Voting against entry into the war cost Vardaman his political career.

See W. F. Holmes, *White Chief* (1970); and A. D. Kirwan, *Revolt of Rednecks* (1951).

WILLIAM F. HOLMES
University of Georgia

VELAZQUEZ, LORETA JANETA (1842–?), was the purported author of a romantic autobiography, *The Woman in Battle* (ed. C. J. Worthington, 1876), which described her adventures in the Confederate army disguised as Harry T. Buford. The 606-page narrative explains her love for war, problems of concealing her identity, activities as a spy and blockade-runner, and, after the end of the war, travels in the West, the Caribbean, and South America. Although there is some suspicion that it was a hoax, the account has gained acceptance as evidence of women's participation on the battlefields of the Civil War.

See E. Lonn, *Foreigners in Confederacy* (1940); and M. M. Dowie (ed.), *Women Adventurers* (1893). These secondary accounts are based upon L. J. Velazquez, *Woman in Battle: a Narrative of Loreta Janeta Velaz-*

quez, Otherwise Known as Lieutenant Harry T. Buford, Confederate States Army (1876).

MARY K. BONSTEEL TACHAU
University of Louisville

VENERABLE SOCIETY, officially the Society for the Propagation of the Gospel in Foreign Parts, was a private Anglican missionary organization to develop and support Church of England congregations in England's mainland colonies in North America. The society became the major force in a remarkable growth of Anglicanism in New England and the middle colonies. Virginia and Maryland received no direct aid because the church already had secured public support in the Chesapeake area. Although the society's work in North Carolina and Georgia yielded a meager harvest, it was responsible for the successful implementation of a parish system in tidewater South Carolina. Sporadic efforts to Christianize the Indians failed, but society-supported schools for both whites and blacks constituted a significant element in eighteenth-century education.

See H. P. Thompson, *Into All Lands* (1951); J. Calam, *Parsons and Pedagogues* (1971); C. F. Pascoe, *Two Hundred Years* (1901); and J. K. Nelson, "Anglican Missions" (Ph.D. dissertation, Northwestern University, 1962).

JOHN K. NELSON
University of North Carolina, Chapel Hill

VENEREAL DISEASE. Three major forms of venereal disease are syphilis, gonorrhea, and chancroid (a soft ulcer affecting the genitals). Although these diseases have existed from colonial days to the present, prior to the twentieth century we can only estimate the degree of infection. For most of American history venereal diseases were associated with vice and immorality, and even editors of medical journals were reluctant to discuss the subject. The presence of these disorders is clearly indicated in private diaries and journals and in the many advertisements promising safe and easy cures for "secret diseases." The Louisiana state board of health, reflecting the public attitude, published a 700-page annual report in 1882 in which the only mention of syphilis is to be found in the mortality statistics.

Shortly before World War I, many states established bureaus of venereal disease, but it was not until the mobilization of troops that serious efforts were made to tackle the problem. On the basis of the 3.5 million men examined at induction centers, it was estimated that almost 10 percent of the U.S. population suffered from some form of venereal infection. Stimulated by the army, navy, and Public Health Service, in 1918 and 1919 virtually every state appropriated funds for venereal disease control work. The presence of many army camps in the South gave an added impetus to the drive in this region, and educational campaigns and free clinics uncovered thousands of cases. As interest waned in the postwar years, funds for state and local clinics gradually diminished.

The 1930s saw a renewed assault upon venereal disease. Better case-finding techniques and more conscientious reporting by physicians greatly increased the number of cases reported each year. World War II both intensified the venereal disease problem and brought new weapons to bear on it. The ineffective treatment with mercurials, bismuth, and arsenicals was replaced in the late 1930s with sulfa drugs, and these in turn gave way in 1943–1944 to the much more effective penicillin and subsequent antibiotics.

Selective Service records during World War II showed clearly that the southern population had far more than its share of venereal infections. The incidence of positive serological tests for syphilis ranged from 9 to 17 percent for the southern states compared with an average of between 2 and 3 percent for the rest of the country. The postwar years saw drastic reductions in all forms of venereal disease, but the southern states continued to hold the dubious distinction of having the highest rate of infection.

See W. J. Brown *et al., Syphilis and Other Venereal Diseases* (1970); Louisiana State Board of Health, *Annual Report* (1882); and various state health board reports. No adequate study exists for southern states.

JOHN DUFFY
University of Maryland

VEROT, JEAN MARCEL PIERRE AUGUSTE (1805–1876), was a Roman Catholic bishop and native of France. As titular bishop of Danuba and vicar apostolic of Florida, he condemned the slave trade and detailed a code of rights for owners and slaves in his 1861 sermon *A Tract for the Times: Slavery and Abolitionism.* He was transferred to the Savannah diocese on July 16, 1861, but retained supervision of Florida. During the Civil War he supplied priests to and himself worked among the federals in ANDERSONVILLE PRISON. In his 1866 pastoral letter, he explained the defeat of the Confederacy in terms of the failure of slave owners to fulfill their obligations to the slaves. He welcomed the extinction of slavery and invited the Negroes to share in the benefits of Catholic education. At the Vatican Council of 1870, he insisted that the council should direct attention to condemning the theory that Negroes had no souls. At the final vote he absented himself. When St. Augustine was erected as a diocese in 1870, he chose to return there.

See M. V. Gannon, *Augustin Verot* (1964), extensive use of manuscripts; W. E. Wight, *Catholic Historical Review* (July, 1941); C. Butler, *Vatican Council* (1930); J. G. Shea, *Catholic Church in U.S.* (1892); St. Augustine Diocese Archives; Baltimore Cathedral Archives; and St. Leo's Abbey, Fla.

WILLARD E. WIGHT
Georgia Institute of Technology

VESEY PLOT (1821–1822). The leader of this abortive slave uprising in South Carolina, Denmark Vesey (1767?–1822), spent his early childhood as a slave on the West Indian islands of St. Thomas and Santo Domingo. In 1800, with money he won in a lottery, Vesey purchased his freedom and became a successful carpenter in the city of Charleston. His craftsman status afforded him ample opportunity to travel outside Charleston and contact potential conspirators on the plantations. His character apparently commanded the respect of both blacks and whites, and his literacy and lingual abilities gave him an intellectual control over his associates. He was profoundly influenced by the 1791 slave revolt in Santo Domingo and offered it as an example for his followers. Although plantation slaves and manual laborers constituted the bulk of Vesey's recruits, his chief lieutenants comprised an urban elite of skilled artisans and religious leaders. After being betrayed by a house servant, the conspirators advanced the date of their uprising. Charleston's authorities had taken precautionary steps, however, and the conspiracy collapsed. Vesey and his main followers stood trial and were hanged.

One historian has questioned even the existence of Vesey's plot, attributing it to white paranoia over the overwhelming black population in the Charleston area. He also has shown how both sides in the slavery controversy seized upon the propaganda value of the incident. However, the trial record provides ample proof that a revolt was in the making, although the extent of the plot is unclear. Some testimony placed the total number of conspirators at 9,000 or more, and some as low as 500. The 35 who were hanged and the 43 who were banished may well have represented only the tip of the iceberg. One of the immediate ramifications of the plot was the swift and harsh repression of Charleston's blacks. Black seamen entering the harbor had to either post bond or go to jail. The education of blacks was sharply curbed.

Severe economic sanctions were clamped on free blacks. Moreover, the conspiracy helped to edge South Carolina and the rest of the South toward increasing isolationism, leading to NULLIFICATION and eventually SECESSION.

See J. Lofton, *Insurrection in South Carolina* (1964); R. S. Starobin (ed.), *Denmark Vesey* (1970); J. O. Killens (ed.), *Trial Record* (1970); and R. C. Wade *Journal of Southern History* (May, 1964).

LARRY M. SNAVLEY
Toledo University

VICKSBURG, MISS. (pop. 25,478), at the confluence of the Yazoo and Mississippi rivers, is approximately 40 miles west of Jackson. The site is bounded by high bluffs, and its strategic value was recognized when both the French (early eighteenth century) and the Spanish (1791) constructed forts here. The Spanish Ft. Nogales was named for the area's walnut trees, and flatboatmen on the Mississippi later renamed the spot Walnut Hills. The Reverend Newett Vick constructed a mission church here in 1814, and after his death in 1819 the town was renamed in his honor. As steamboats gradually supplanted flatboats in river traffic, Vicksburg became an important river port soon rivaling Natchez as a cotton market. Its strategic importance on the river was recognized again during the Civil War. It was bombarded by Union riverboats from May 18 to July 26, 1862, and placed under siege by U. S. Grant during the VICKSBURG CAMPAIGN from October, 1862, to July 4, 1863. Badly shattered by the war, the city's economy lay stagnant until 1876, when the Mississippi River changed course, leaving the former river port high and dry. The Yazoo River was diverted, and canals were constructed to reopen the town to river traffic, but not until the 1920s, when the federal government took over these operations, was the city reestablished as a port city. Vicksburg National Military Park (est. 1899) contains over 1,300 acres of fortifications, emplacements, and trenches, and Vicksburg National Cemetery has the graves of over 17,000 Union soldiers slain during the siege.

See H. P. Chapman, *Picturesque Vicksburg* (1895); L. Richardson, *In and About Vicksburg* (1890); and Vicksburg *Post* (1883–).

VICKSBURG CAMPAIGN (October, 1862–July, 1863). The capture of Vicksburg by Ulysses S. Grant crowned one of the most significant military campaigns of the Civil War. By this victory the North divided the Confederacy, thus denying southwestern grain and beef to the South's hungry armies and interdicting the South's trade pipeline to Mexico.

Assuming command of the Army of the Tennessee in late October, 1862, Grant first attempted a two-pronged assault on Vicksburg. He led a part of his army southward through central Mississippi while sending a second force, under William T. Sherman, down the Mississippi River to attack at CHICKASAW BAYOU, north of Vicksburg. Sherman was repulsed with heavy losses, however, and Grant's overland advance was abandoned after Confederate cavalry under EARL VAN DORN and NATHAN BEDFORD FORREST wreaked havoc upon the Union supply lines in northern Mississippi and southwestern Tennessee.

Moving his base of operations to Memphis, Grant now concentrated upon a downriver approach to Vicksburg. Protected on the west by high bluffs and the Mississippi River and on the north by swamps, the heavily fortified Vicksburg presented Grant with a difficult tactical challenge. For about three months, beginning in early 1863, Grant indulged in a number of operations designed to get his army into position to attack Vicksburg. These included the digging of canals west of the Mississippi and efforts to open up navigation of natural waterways east of the river. None of these schemes came close to success, but they occupied the army and enabled Grant to hold the initiative while waiting for a moderation of inclement weather conditions.

By the end of March the weather had improved enough for Grant to build a road from Milliken's Bend to Hard Times, on the west bank of the river several miles below Vicksburg. Massing his army at Hard Times, Grant had Admiral David Porter run his transports past the Vicksburg batteries and get them in position to ferry the army to the east bank of the river. Landing at Bruinsburg on April 30, Grant soon began his advance. In a bold, masterful maneuver, he cut his tenuous supply line and marched rapidly toward Jackson to intercept Confederate General JOSEPH JOHNSTON, who was on the way to reinforce General JOHN C. PEMBERTON, the Confederate commander at Vicksburg. Grant planned first to defeat Johnston, then turn west and strike Pemberton. The plan worked to near-perfection, partly because of brilliant execution by the federal forces and partly because of the indecisiveness of Grant's opponents, particularly Pemberton. Under orders from President Jefferson Davis to defend Vicksburg and from Johnston to join the latter's force, Pemberton cautiously moved eastward. Meanwhile Grant easily defeated a small Confederate force at Raymond (May 12) and proceeded to drive Johnston northward from Jackson (May 14). The Union commander then wheeled westward, defeated Pemberton's army at CHAMPION HILL (May 16), and forced the Confederates back to Vicksburg.

Arriving at Vicksburg on May 19, Grant underestimated the strength of the Confederate defenses and ordered a frontal assault, which failed. After a second effort to carry the city's defenses had a similar result, he decided to lay siege. Subsequently, the Union army received heavy reinforcements, and it was only a matter of time before dwindling food supplies would force the Vicksburg garrison to accede to Grant's demand that it surrender unconditionally. Finally, on July 4, Pemberton gave up the city and his army of 30,000. Five days later, Nathaniel Banks captured PORT HUDSON, giving the Union complete control of the Mississippi River.

See B. Catton, *Grant Moves South* (1960); A. A. Hoehling, *Vicksburg* (1969); E. S. Miers, *Web of Victory* (1955); and P. F. Walker, *Vicksburg* (1960).

DONALD E. REYNOLDS
East Texas State University

VICKSBURG HERALD began publication in 1863 as the successor to the Vicksburg *Daily Citizen* (1859–1863). At the end of the Civil War, it criticized the state's BLACK CODE as a politically foolish insult to northern public opinion. It also urged that blacks be given the right to testify in Mississippi courts. During the course of Reconstruction, however, the *Herald* abandoned moderation. By 1873 it was suggesting that the federal government seize parts of northern Mexico and that southern blacks be relocated there in a separate state. During the hard-fought election campaign of 1875, the *Herald* opined that, when political assassinations proved necessary, white rather than black Republicans should be killed. Although the *Herald* opposed calling the constitutional convention of 1890, which shifted political power from the Delta to the counties of the hills and the piney woods, it probably was the leading journalistic advocate of black DISFRANCHISEMENT and the principal defender of the new constitution's UNDERSTANDING CLAUSE. It was allied with the foes of Senator A. J. McLaurin's Bourbon machine during the 1890s, and in 1903 it was the only daily newspaper in Mississippi to support JAMES K. VARDAMAN's successful bid for the governorship.

See A. D. Kirwan, *Revolt of Rednecks* (1951); and Vicksburg *Herald*, bound copies at Library of Congress (1898–) and microfilm from Bell & Howell (1863–83, 1898–1957) and Library of Congress (1898–1924).

VICKSBURG RIOT (1874) followed the forced resignation and subsequent reinstallation of Peter Crosby, Negro sheriff and tax collector for Warren County, Miss. The black population of Vicksburg and Warren County outnumbered whites better than two to one, and black Republicans dominated the county board of supervisors besides Crosby's office. White conservatives intensely resented this situation and charged that officials had raised taxes inordinately and had managed public funds dishonestly. Black and white militia activity added to the racial tension. Conservatives carried the August, 1874, elections in Vicksburg and then turned to Warren County affairs. A grand jury found malfeasance, but none of the evidence implicated Crosby. Still, a "taxpayers' convention" demanded the resignation of the sheriff and other officers. A rumor that blacks were marching on the town prompted the conservative government of Vicksburg to organize a force to meet them. An agreement to disperse ended when someone fired into the black partisans; before the fighting ended, 35 blacks and two whites had died.

See J. W. Garner, *Reconstruction* (1901), best published account; C. Sallis, "Color Line" (Ph.D. dissertation, University of Kentucky, 1967); V. L. Wharton, *Negro in Mississippi* (1947); and *Congressional Report on Vicksburg Troubles*, 2nd Sess., 43rd Cong., Pt. 1, H.R. 265, Vol. IV, Ser. 1659.

JAMES MURPHY
Southern Illinois University

VINSON, FREDERICK MOORE (1890–1953), was the son of the Louisa, Ky., town jailer. A 1911 Centre College graduate, he practiced law and county politics until elected to Congress in 1924. As a southern Democrat, staunch New Dealer, and House Ways and Means Committee tax expert, Vinson never developed a national following. After 13 years in Congress (1924–1929, 1932–1938) he accepted an appointment to the federal judiciary of the District of Columbia (1937–1943), became economic stabilization director (1943–1945), and served briefly as federal loan administrator and director of war mobilization and reconversion in 1945. In July, 1945, he became secretary of the treasury, floated the last great war bond drive, and pioneered the Bretton Woods Agreements, Marshall Plan, International Monetary Fund, and International Bank for Reconstruction and Development. He was named the thirteenth chief justice (1946–1953) to pull the warring U.S. Supreme Court factions back together. Vinson's last four appointments were unanimously confirmed. He healed the Court's breaches and laid the foundations for later landmark decisions in school desegregation, labor relations, and national security. His last public appearance was to deliver the Court's six-to-three opinion upholding the death penalty of convicted spies Julius and Ethel Rosenberg.

See J. H. Hatcher, "Fred Vinson" (Ph.D. dissertation, University of Cincinnati, 1967); B. Kornitzer, *American Fathers and Sons* (1952); C. H. Pritchett, *Civil Liberties* (1954); and Vinson Papers, University of Kentucky Library and F. Vinson, Jr.

JOHN HENRY HATCHER
National Archives

VIOLENCE has been a pervasive theme in the history of the South. From gentlemen of the Old South meeting with pistols at ten paces to lynch mobs torturing and burning black southerners to attacks against civil rights demonstrators in the mid–twentieth century, violence has continually been an important aspect of southern behavior. In addition to LYNCHING, southerners engaged in such group violence as WHITECAPPING and NIGHT-RIDING as well as FEUDS or vendettas. Furthermore, the region was the home of the terroristic KU KLUX KLAN of the Reconstruction period as well as a stronghold of its twentieth-century successor.

Although DUELING is usually associated with the antebellum South, the practice persisted with some frequency until the late 1880s. The CASH-SHANNON DUEL of 1880 was probably the last fatal duel fought in the South, but it was by no means the last acting out of the code of honor. Increasingly, however, less orderly patterns of personal violence, variously described as "shooting at sight," "street duels," or "personal difficulties," came to replace the formal duel. Often prompted by the same questions of personal honor, reputation, and physical or verbal assault as the duel, these less-structured forms were more spontaneous and therefore usually more lethal. They clearly contributed to the disproportionately high homicide rates long characteristic of the South.

In 1880 journalist Horace V. Redfield found homicide to be from four to 15 times more frequent in the South than elsewhere in the United States. Later studies showed the South's continuing leadership in homicide rates; and, from the early years of the twentieth century to the present, various southern cities have regularly led the nation's cities in homicide. Also, certain parts of the region—such as the Edgefield District in South Carolina, central Texas, and western Kentucky (BLACK PATCH WAR)—developed historical traditions of violence.

One of the more remarkable features of southern violence has been the degree to which "respectable" southerners contributed to high homicide rates. Despite the assertion that blacks and lower-class whites, both of whom have shown high rates of homicide, were primarily responsible for the South's violence, businessmen, doctors, lawyers, editors, and occasionally even ministers engaged in "shooting at sight."

Southern mob violence has been politically, economically, and racially motivated, often precipitated by a combination of these forces. The Ku Klux Klan and other violent groups during Reconstruction attempted to take political power from blacks and their white allies by terrorism. The whitecap movement in Mississippi in the 1890s and again between 1902 and 1906 had both economic and racial objectives. The Kentucky and Tennessee night riders of the early twentieth century had as their target the tobacco trust.

Lynching, which reached its peak in the 1890s and the early years of the twentieth century, has been the most significant form of southern mob violence. Between 1882 and 1951 a total of 4,730 persons were lynched in the United States. Of that total, 3,328 were blacks lynched in the former slave states. Furthermore, the terrorism resulting from the practice of lynching was undoubtedly much more extensive than the number of its victims indicates.

Several factors—including the prevalence of blacks, the rural nature of southern society, climate, poverty, and the widespread ownership of guns—have been suggested to account for the region's propensity for violence. No doubt each of these characteristics contributed to the climate of violence, but both historian Sheldon Hackney and sociologist Raymond D. Gastil found, through the technique of multiple regression analysis, that, even after the cumulative effect of such factors and others is taken into account, there still remains a part of the explanation attributable only to "southernness." That is, both agree that there is something about the world view or culture of the South that has been particularly conducive to violence. Focusing on such a cultural explanation, Frank E. Vandiver suggested a southern "offensive-defense" response to challenges as an explanation for the violent strain in southern history, from the VIRGINIA AND KENTUCKY RESOLUTIONS to modern rejections of black equality.

As important as the fact of southern violence has been the means by which southerners justified it. In 1906 Thomas J. Kernan, an attorney from Louisiana, described a "jurisprudence of lawlessness." Not restricted to the South, his description of the justifications for extralegal violence was most pertinent to that region. According to Kernan, homicidal violence was regularly sanctioned in cases of rape, adultery, seduction, or "traduction of a virtuous woman's character," as well as in the case of a duel fought according to the code of honor or in a fair fight. Clearly, the South's generally more liberal interpretation of the right to self-defense and the related acceptance of violence in defense of personal honor were important factors contributing to the prevalence of violence. As a result, in any list of southern traits, violence must be prominently included.

See H. V. Redfield, *Homicide, North and South* (1880); T. J. Kernan, *American Bar Association Report* (1906); R. M. Brown, *Strain of Violence* (1975); S. Hackney, *American Historical Review* (Feb., 1969); R. D. Gastil, *American Sociological Review* (June, 1971); F. E. Vandiver, *Idea of South* (1964); J. H. Franklin, *Militant South* (1956); W. J. Cash, *Mind of South* (1941); and J. S. Reed, *Political Science Quarterly* (Sept., 1971).

JERRY L. BUTCHER
Shippensburg State College

VIRGINIA. A capsule summary of Virginia's history reveals in sharp focus themes of remarkable continuity. From Jamestown to the present day, the Virginia experience has been generally characterized by social aristocracy, economic agrarianism, political elitism, and cultural homogeneity. As the most ancient of all southern and American commonwealths, Virginia has exhibited those conservative, stable, and possibly stagnant traits that attend seniority. Its antiquity also explains why, for both the nation and for the region, its basic image has been one of maternity.

The seventeenth century. Unlike some other English colonies in America, Virginia was conceived from no radical, zealous, or escapist motive. The English gentlemen who petitioned King James I in 1606 for a charter as the Virginia Company were activated by a variety of purposes, but in brief they can be described as respectable Englishmen in search of respectable profit. The fabulous rewards of the East India Company, founded six years earlier, beckoned. Specifically, it was hoped that Virginia would yield precious metal and naval stores and serve as a trading post for traffic with the natives and, it was hoped, with the Orient. Late in 1606 the company sent out a flotilla of three ships, which reached Virginia the following spring and planted a colony at Jamestown, a quasi-military outpost. From this outpost various reconnaissance expeditions were launched over the next several years, which attempted to locate the supposed Northwest Passage, to discover gold,

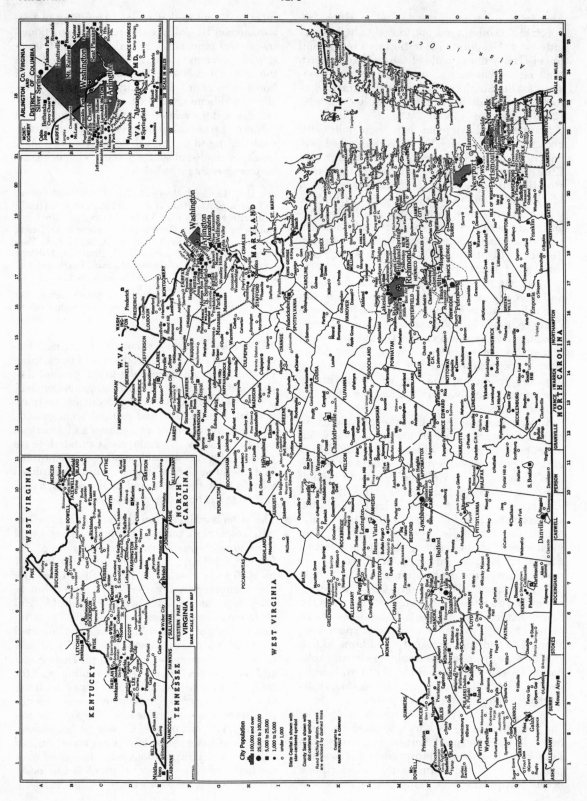

City Population

■ 100,000 and over
● 25,000 to 100,000
● 5,000 to 25,000
• 1,000 to 5,000
∘ under 1,000

State Capital is shown with
star-centered symbol

County Seat is shown with
dot-centered symbol

Rand McNally Metro. areas
are enclosed by dashed lines

Copyright by
RAND M NALLY & COMPANY

and to open trade with the native POWHATAN Indian Confederacy.

The infant colony barely survived its early trials. A clumsy political structure consisting of a governing council of seven discouraged effective leadership, and early efforts to establish a viable economic base for the colony foundered. In 1609 the king granted a new charter giving the company absolute governing rights over the colony to be exercised through a sole governor. The same charter altered the original boundaries, so that Virginia now was to extend "west and northwest" from two locations on the Atlantic coast, one 200 miles south and the other 200 miles north of Old Point Comfort. This established Virginia's later claim to vast areas of interior North America.

A semblance of permanence came to the colony with the administration of Thomas Dale, who became deputy governor in 1611. Dale instituted strict control through the "Lawes Divine, Morall and Martiall." Meanwhile, John Rolfe proved that tobacco could thrive in the Virginia climate, and the colony discovered its future economic mainstay. In 1618 the company introduced the principle of private land ownership, and in 1619 it summoned elective burgesses to sit with the governor and his council in "General Assembly" at Jamestown (HOUSE OF BURGESSES). Both of these latter innovations might best be interpreted not as liberal reforms so much as normal extensions to the New World of English law and custom.

In 1624 the company lost its charter in legal proceedings, and Virginia became the first royal colony, meaning that the king appointed the governor and his council. Without sanction from the king, the royal governors continued to hold elections for burgesses to the general assembly, a testimony to the essential conservatism of the method. King Charles I finally formally approved the practice in 1639. Eventually, the legislature became bicameral, with the council acting as the upper house.

In its first century, Virginia developed almost exclusively within a TIDEWATER context. Approximately 100 miles inland from the CHESAPEAKE BAY, a FALL LINE prevented navigation west thereof on all Virginia's rivers, so settlement expanded instead in maritime fashion along the tidal rivers and estuaries. By 1634, when county government was first introduced, farms and plantations were scattered along the lower James and York rivers and on the Eastern Shore across the bay. Twenty years later, the number of counties totaled 15, distributed northward along the Rappahannock and Potomac rivers as well. By 1700 the counties numbered 23, and the total population reached approximately 70,000, the largest of any colony in North America.

As already mentioned, the economic base for this steady expansion was agrarian, with primary emphasis on the cultivation of tobacco. Typically, in their maritime environment planters were able to export their tobacco from wharves located on their plantations, and this prevented the growth of a major commercial center. Most of the tobacco, especially after passage of the English Navigation Acts of the 1660s, was consigned by individual planters to their FACTORS, or agents, in England. The factors sold the tobacco and in turn forwarded English manufactured goods to Virginia. Throughout most of the colonial period, Virginia traded more with the mother country than did any other mainland colony and therefore fit best into the English mercantilistic ideal (COMMERCE). In 1742, for example, Virginia exported to England tobacco valued at roughly £180,000 sterling, in addition to minor quantities of naval stores, pig iron, and skins; in return it imported English goods valued at £200,000 sterling. The only other significant trade that year consisted of exports of pork, beef, and corn, valued at about £30,000, to the British West Indies.

If Virginia's economy complemented that of the mother country, it also eventually helped create an aristocratic society remarkably similar to its English counterpart. At first, as befitted a pioneer community, the socioeconomic pattern was fluid and unsettled; and some of the indentured servants, who composed the bulk of Virginia's immigrants in the first century, developed upon expiration of their indentures respectable estates and corresponding status. But beginning about 1650 if not sooner, a process of accumulation of lands and stratification of society developed. Middle-class immigrants to Virginia in the 1640s and 1650s included the founders of nearly all those families who achieved aristocratic rank the next century. After 1650, as Virginia expanded geographically, more and more lands were engrossed by the few. By 1658, for example, over 100,000 acres on the Potomac were held by only 30 persons. The HEADRIGHT SYSTEM, whereby each immigrant received 50 acres of land, failed to prevent accumulation of estates simply because they were transferable. The biggest land grab occurred in the 1670s, when Charles II made a gift of the entire Northern Neck peninsula between the Potomac and the Rappahannock rivers to two of his favorites.

Various economic forces encouraged this accumulation process. Chief among them was the vulnerability of the one-crop tobacco economy. Throughout the century, the tobacco trade underwent prolonged periods of depression, during which times the marginal farmers were often forced to sell out to more affluent neighbors. By 1673 one resident Virginian estimated that one-quarter of all white adult males were landless. The foundations for an aristocratic elite were set, and traditional English social distinctions were clearly maintained. In an oft-cited 1673 decision, the York County court convicted a tailor for horse racing, a "sport for gentlemen alone." Seventeenth-century Virginia was no social democracy.

Politically, Virginia likewise developed in orthodox English directions. The governmental system inaugurated in 1619 featured a governor and a mixed legislature of elected and appointed solons that resembled the administrative structure of the Virginia Company itself, which in turn resembled the crown and Parliament model. The later establishment of the county unit of local government was likewise derivative. True, property ownership was not initially a prerequisite for the suffrage (possibly because land titles were sometimes confused), but in 1670 Virginia imitated mother England in this respect as well. Finally, the Church of England was formally supported by the state from the beginning. The parish became another unit of local government, and Anglican vestries thereof taxed all citizens to finance church affairs and also performed the same welfare functions in Virginia as they did in England.

The political forms were orthodox, and the substance was aristocratic. Of all government office-holders, only members of the House of Burgesses were elected. Members of the vestries came to be self-appointed and self-perpetuating. All other officials were appointed by the governor, including the county courts, which were the governing bodies of the counties. This technically put enormous power in the hands of the governor, but in actuality it gave power to those families wealthy enough to influence the governor. Power gravitated especially to members of the governor's council, where appointments were considered to be of lifetime duration.

The system, however oligarchic, functioned smoothly. With the exception of some weird confrontations involving an eccentric Governor John Harvey and his council in the 1630s, Virginia developed tranquilly as a royal colony for half a century. William Berkeley became governor in 1642 and successfully maintained the colony's loyalty to the king during the English civil war of that decade. Even after Parliament's triumph and the execution of Charles I, Virginia proclaimed Charles II its rightful sovereign, thus earning its nickname as the Old Dominion. Some of the king's exiled "Cavaliers" migrated to Virginia after their downfall, contributing a second favorite sobriquet to the colony. Both Berkeley and the colony acquiesced peaceably to parliamentary supremacy in 1652, and for eight years Virginia existed as a little republic. But its satisfaction with the old royalist regime was shown when, in 1660, the general assembly voluntarily elected Berkeley governor, anticipating Charles II's restoration.

In his last years, however, Berkeley evidently lost rapport with segments of the populace. For example, he failed to call new elections for the House of Burgesses for 14 years, producing the "Long Parliament" of Virginia history. In 1676, when he failed to move aggressively enough against Indian threats to satisfy frantic frontiersmen, they turned to Nathaniel Bacon for leadership. BACON'S REBELLION forced Berkeley to flee to the Eastern Shore, but after Bacon's death Berkeley ruthlessly regained control, hanging over 20 of the erstwhile traitors.

What caused Bacon's uprising, the only example of serious political instability in Virginia's colonial history? Some historians have described the rebellion as a revolt by democrats against oligarchs, on both the provincial and local levels. Recent interpretations suggest that the rebellion represented not a democratic uprising but rather a protest by county political elites against a central governing clique.

The eighteenth century. During the seventeenth century there had developed in Virginia a homogeneous Tidewater world that can be described as the most thoroughly Anglo-Saxon transplant in North America. In the eighteenth century, this English enclave would mature economically, socially, politically, and culturally. The total population grew dramatically from 70,000 in 1700 to nearly 700,000 at the time of the first national census 90 years later. As the colony prospered, it also grew slightly less homogeneous. Two important new demographic elements appeared: Negro slaves and Scotch-Irish and German frontiersmen. In fixing the Virginia character, the former proved to be the more important.

Negroes had lived in Virginia since 1619, but as late as 1671 they composed only an estimated 5 percent of the total population. After some early ambiguity about their legal status, the legislature in 1661 established slavery by code. After 1671 numbers of slaves mounted rapidly, and the institution replaced indentured servitude as the main

source of plantation labor. By 1715 slaves constituted a quarter of Virginia's population, and some
Virginians began agitating for laws to discourage
their import. By the time of the Revolution, nearly
half of all Virginia residents were blacks. The
transplanted England had assumed a biracial
complexion.

Slavery, of course, served as the economic base
for the aristocratic society that flowered in tidewater Virginia after 1700. Families such as the
NELSONS, LEES, CARTERS, RANDOLPHS, and Bur-
wells prospered. They built fabulous Georgian
mansions, imported elegant English furniture, and
sent their sons back home for schooling. William
Byrd II (BYRD FAMILY) best illustrates this new
social milieu. A sensitive, erudite, and literary
man, he spent altogether 30 years of his life in
mother England, where he obtained an education, mingled in polite as well as impolite society,
and won selection to the prestigious Royal Society. In Virginia, he served on the council and
helped draw the boundary line between Virginia
and North Carolina. He acquired an immense personal library and inadvertently ensured his modern celebrity by keeping a candid secret diary.

The Tidewater domain of the gentry was exclusively rural (98 percent in 1790) and therefore individualistic. But it possessed a cultural center of
sorts in Williamsburg. Here the College of William and Mary was established in 1693, and here
the political capital was transferred from Jamestown in 1699. In 1728 the first printing press was
set up, and shortly thereafter the VIRGINIA GA-
ZETTE began publication. Richard D. Davis, the
most knowledgeable modern scholar on the subject, maintains that the literary expressions contained in the *Gazette*, in Byrd's writings, and from
many other sources provide evidences of a literary
and intellectual Tidewater society that has been
given short shrift by prejudiced yankee historians.

The colony may have been literary, but it was
not notably literate. A few privately endowed free
schools existed, but rural dispersion and maldistri-
bution of wealth deprived many of even rudimentary education. One study showed that, of the 2,160
men who served on juries in nine Tidewater
counties during the late seventeenth century, 994
could not write. Even more surprising, a survey of
14 counties for the same time period showed that
fully 38 percent of owners of property could not
affix their signatures to their deeds. Probably two-
thirds of adult women were illiterate. Virginia's
Tidewater personality and society were both rustic and polite, elegant and earthy.

In the 1700s political institutions developed
along the lines laid down in the preceding centu-

ry. The council, dominated by the bluebloods,
reached its apex of power at the turn of the century, when its members successfully procured the
recall of Governors Edmund Andros, Francis Nicholson, and Alexander Spotswood. Thereafter,
however, the House of Burgesses rose in stature.

Members of the planter class continued to
dominate all levels of government, but this does
not necessarily imply an oligarchic repression of
the masses. Save for occasional conflicts concerning religious dissenters, political issues with a social class content are notably lacking in eighteenth-century Virginia. Virginia had an informed
and responsible class of gentlemen leaders who
looked upon politics as both a social duty and prerogative. Speaker of the House of Burgesses John
Robinson illustrated the latter syndrome by secretly lending government monies to aristocratic
friends, a fact not discovered until his death in
1766.

Slavery has been described as the most important new demographic element affecting Virginia's overall culture and character. But ironically, by providing a rigidly solid foundation for the
socioeconomic pyramid, its chief effect was to
reinforce the rural, static, and conservative traits
of the dominant race. Furthermore, the slave himself took on the white man's culture, so that tidewater Virginia became biracial but remained homogeneous.

More diversity developed with western expansion. Beginning with the administration of Governor Alexander Spotswood, tidewater Virginia
pushed rapidly into first the northern and then the
southern PIEDMONT. The first Piedmont county
was created in 1721. Only 30 years later, there
were over a dozen. Settlement first advanced up
the river valleys, especially the James. Tobacco
culture spread everywhere, and planters used
shallow boats to float their hogsheads downstream
to the towns that now developed along the fall
line: Richmond, Petersburg, Fredericksburg. The
Piedmont settlers came primarily from the Tidewater, and the economy and culture that grew up
was a roughhewn imitation of that to the east,
though farms were smaller and more self-sufficient.

Beginning in the 1730s, settlement also extended farther west into the great valley of Virginia,
really a succession of valleys lying between the
Blue Ridge on the east and the Alleghenies on the
west. The northern Shenandoah Valley was settled first, and about 20 years later the far Southwest. Germans, Scotch-Irish, and Englishmen all
contributed to this frontier advance, the former
two coming south from Pennsylvania. The Blue

Ridge mountain barrier discouraged bulk exports eastward, and thus a pattern of diversified agriculture developed instead of the tobacco and slavery regime of eastern Virginia.

The valley was heterogeneous ethnically, economically, and especially religiously. The Scotch-Irish brought their Presbyterian faith, and the Germans, a variety of pietistic sects. Although the parish was automatically set up as a substratum of valley counties, no Anglicans could be found to officiate as vestrymen. Parallel to the influx of new religions into the valley, a general religious GREAT AWAKENING developed to the east. As a result of this widespread emotional revival, various dissenting sects organized, especially the Baptists; and, by the time of the Revolution, probably less than half of Virginians belonged to the established church. Even so, the Anglican church was still stronger in Virginia than in any other colony.

The valley had ties to the East, and regional differences can be exaggerated. Indeed, many Tidewater families built their Georgian homes based as much on profits from western LAND SPECULATIONS as from tobacco. George Washington illustrated the tendency for the alert Tidewater man to look westward for his economic future. He eventually became an investor in the OHIO COMPANY, which was organized in 1747 to seek western development beyond the Alleghenies. Other companies were formed with similar intent, the most prominent being the LOYAL COMPANY.

When Robert Dinwiddie became Virginia's governor in 1751, he aggressively supported Virginia's western imperialistic ambitions against the pretensions of the French. Armed clashes between Virginia militia and French troops resulted in 1754, and the FRENCH AND INDIAN WAR was on. The war of course removed the French from North America, but the king's PROCLAMATION OF 1763 temporarily barred Virginia's western advance. Later treaties with Indians opened up more lands, however, and as late as 1775 Washington was planning settlements on the Kanawha River in present-day West Virginia. Virginia's continuing interest in the West was demonstrated during the Revolution, when Governor Patrick Henry sent GEORGE ROGERS CLARK to oust the British from present-day Indiana and Illinois.

Revolution and early national period. During the Revolution and early national periods, Virginia made its great contributions to American development. Equaled only by Massachusetts as a force in the revolutionary struggle, Virginia was second to no other state in leading the young nation afterward. The roster of its statesmen during this half-century—Washington, Jefferson, Madison, Mason, Marshall, Henry, the Randolphs and Lees—reads like a roll call of the greats.

What explains this apparent explosion of political talent? The simplest explanation is neither flattering nor remarkable. During the half-century under discussion, Virginia was the largest colony or state in population and wealth and, as such, automatically carried weight. Second, to the extent that the Revolution represented a defense by Americans of traditional English political liberties or an arrival at political maturity, then Virginia, as the most mature and most Anglicized of the colonies, would naturally be in the forefront. Moreover, Virginia's plantation economy and political system served as breeding grounds for experienced and aristocratic leaders. A traveler once described Virginia's elite as "haughty and jealous of their liberties." Paradoxically, this independent trait may have been underscored by the institution of slavery. Finally, Virginia's huge debts to England (on the eve of the Revolution nearly half of all American debts were owed by Virginians) aggravated imperial relations.

For whatever reasons, Virginians were both effective and nearly united in fighting the Revolution. During the preliminaries, some differences existed between a Piedmont faction led by Patrick Henry, which favored blunt language of protest, and more conservative and possibly polite Tidewater men; but, in broad perspective, Virginians generally agreed that the Stamp Act, the Townshend duties, and the Intolerable Acts were both unconstitutional and dangerous. At one point, in 1768, even the governor's council joined with the burgesses to protest parliamentary claims to the right to levy internal taxes in America. Virginia issued the call for the first Continental Congress in 1774 and sent there one of the most radical of the colonial delegations. In 1775 the incipient rebels extralegally assumed governmental powers in their Virginia localities to enforce the Congress' ordained boycott of British merchandise. The power of crown governor Lord Dunmore simply melted away. In June, 1776, Virginia formally established an independent government under a constitution.

By 1774 and after, then, Virginians were radically for protection of American rights, but were they radicals in the larger sense of wishing to reform the homogeneous Virginia world they knew? The constitution of 1776 made no major alterations in the political structure. The suffrage remained confined to property holders, the lower house of delegates continued to have two delegates per county, and the county courts were made appointive as before.

During and after the Revolution, Thomas Jefferson and James Madison successfully led efforts in the legislature to disestablish the already weakened Anglican church, and Jefferson won repeal of PRIMOGENITURE AND ENTAIL, which he considered a victory against aristocracy. There is also evidence that the size of landed estates declined after the Revolution. On the other hand, talk of establishing public education and of eliminating slavery came to nothing. And six of the first 12 governors of independent Virginia belonged to families that had dominated the colonial council. In the last analysis, the military revolution produced no social revolution within Virginia. The same elites governed, before and after.

If Virginians were basically united in fighting the Revolution, afterward there was more uncertainty as to the proper national course. On the one hand, the new state demonstrated nationalistic inclinations by voluntarily ceding its vast western land claims in the interest of union and by sending the most brilliant as well as nationalistic delegation to the Philadelphia Constitutional Convention of 1787. On the other hand, Virginia nearly refused to ratify the 1787 document, and, though a Virginia native became the first U.S. president, his home state also elected as its two U.S. senators men originally opposed to the new government. This ambivalence toward union continued into the 1790s and, indeed, down to the Civil War and beyond. Virginians took the lead in organizing the DEMOCRATIC-REPUBLICAN PARTY opposition to the centralist Federalists, and Madison, father of the Constitution, wrote the Virginia legislature's resolution of 1798, which strongly espoused states' rights by declaring the Sedition Act of 1798 unconstitutional (VIRGINIA AND KENTUCKY RESOLUTIONS).

That the largest state in the Union, with one of its own as president, should, even more than most states, balk at centralization of national power demands explanations. The most specific explanation is that the dominant force in the new government during the 1790s was northern, not southern. As a rural, farming area, Virginia looked askance at the Hamiltonian federal program, which seemed geared mainly to benefit northern men of commerce and finance. Virginia's congressmen generally united to oppose passage of Alexander Hamilton's legislative program. A more general and therefore satisfying explanation for Virginia's muted nationalism revolves again around the theme of internal cohesion. However weighty in national councils, Virginia, as the oldest state, possessed intense provincial pride, identity, and self-confidence. Even a Virginia-born president,

Thomas Jefferson, would refer to Virginia, not the nation, as "my country." To this day, Virginians possess more local patriotism or parochialism than is true for the natives of most states.

Both of the two national parties had strength in Virginia, but the Republican party always clearly dominated. Its basic constituency lay in those homogeneously rural areas that composed the large part of the state, whereas the FEDERALIST PARTY attracted votes in precisely those areas least typically Virginian: eastern cities, the Northern Neck (which had abandoned tobacco as a staple), the Shenandoah Valley, and the trans-Allegheny area (West Virginia). These nationalistic areas were also roughly those that had favored ratification of the Constitution in 1788, though support for the Constitution was more widespread. This basic geographic alignment continued intact as late as 1812, when several Federalist congressmen from mountain areas voted against "Mr. Madison's War."

After Jefferson and his Virginia heirs assumed the presidency, Virginia's fears of centralization subsided somewhat, and most Virginians supported the moderating, compromising programs of Jefferson and Madison. Yet, even during these climactic years of Virginia's national power, "Old Republicans" such as JOHN TAYLOR of Caroline, JOHN RANDOLPH of Roanoke, and Spencer Roane (1762–1822) preached states' rights and lamented the Jeffersonian apostasy from the true "spirit of '98." Randolph persuaded James Monroe to stand against Madison's inheritance of the presidency in 1808, to no avail. And, as Virginia supreme court justice, Roane later led his assault on centralism against a fellow Virginian, JOHN MARSHALL, sitting on the federal bench, likewise to no avail. Following the WAR OF 1812, however, the nationalism of Virginia's leaders abated, and the sectionalistic doctrines of the Old Republicans became nearly universally accepted in the Old Dominion. Roane was a charter member of the RICHMOND JUNTO, an informal, fluctuating, and shadowy group of Republican politicians who basically dominated state politics the first 40 years of the century. Its chief spokesman, especially in the later years, was Thomas Ritchie (1778–1854), editor of the RICHMOND ENQUIRER. As testimony to its political clout, it need only be observed that the junto always supported that presidential candidate who carried Virginia.

The middle period. From hindsight, the warnings of the Old Republicans proved prophetic, for, even while basking in the golden glory of the VIRGINIA DYNASTY, the Old Dominion was beginning to decline. Since 1820 the nation has elected no resident Virginian to the White House. In the same year, not coincidentally, Virginia slipped from first to second rank in the Union in population. By 1860 it ranked only fifth. From 1820 to 1850, its share of the South's representation in the U.S. House of Representatives declined from one-fourth to one-sixth of the total, and southern leadership passed from Richmond to the cotton South.

The PANIC OF 1819 hit the state hard, and westward migration drained away youthful potential. From 1830 to 1840, Virginia actually lost population. An analysis of the 1850 census shows that a greater percentage of native Virginians had emigrated than was true for any other state. Only the massive sale of surplus slaves to the cotton Southwest averted worse economic disaster. From 1830 to 1860 total numbers of Virginia blacks remained nearly constant, so that their overall percentage in the total population declined from 48 to 34. The tobacco plantation kingdom had passed its heyday. Even before 1800, the Tidewater region had begun to phase out the crop, turning instead to grains. As early as the 1780s, Virginia's exports of wheat and flour approximated three-quarters the value of tobacco exports. Tobacco shifted locus to newer Piedmont soils and ultimately to the southern Piedmont. Overall production after the Revolution stabilized but did not grow. After the panic, many lands in eastern Virginia were simply abandoned.

This economic malaise dampened eastern Virginia's aristocratic serenity and self-assurance. Compounding the economic stagnation of the region was the more rapid growth in the valley and trans-Allegheny areas; and, as the west grew, westerners inevitably demanded a greater voice in affairs of the state. Inevitably too, easterners, already under duress, would resist those demands. The resulting east-west struggle lasted half a century and ultimately produced the formation of West Virginia during the Civil War.

East and west divided over a wide range of issues. Lacking a plantation regime, the west had developed democratic attitudes at odds with the east's traditional elitism. Specifically, the west demanded abolition of property suffrage requirements, direct election of the governor and local county officials, and apportionment of the legislature on the basis of white population only. Easterners stood almost unanimously against these propositions. Economically, the landlocked west considered the maritime east indifferent to its needs for improved transportation. Socially, western Virginians were less bound up with slavery and therefore were more critical of the institution than were their eastern brethren. Culturally,

westerners generally favored a public school system, while easterners clung to less democratic attitudes. Finally, westerners asked that the state capital, transferred during the Revolution from Williamsburg to Richmond, be moved once again to a more geographically central location somewhere in the valley.

Of all the areas of conflict, eastern Virginians were most responsive to western demands for internal improvements. After all, improved access to the west meant expanded trade for the east as well. In 1816, the same year westerners called a convention in Staunton to voice their grievances, the general assembly established a board of public works and laid ambitious plans for the construction of a canal and turnpike system that would eventually connect the James and Kanawha rivers. Construction lagged for decades, but by 1840 the canal had been completed as far upriver as Lynchburg. It was eventually extended in 1851 as far as Buchanan in the central valley, but interconnections with the Kanawha Basin were never finished.

With the advent in the 1820s of RAILROADS, various areas of Virginia competed for economic advantage. In 1824 the legislature gave reluctant consent to extension of the Baltimore & Ohio Railroad across present-day northern West Virginia. In the east, rivalries among Norfolk, Petersburg, and Richmond complicated matters; but, by the eve of the Civil War, interconnecting railways linked Tidewater to Piedmont and Piedmont to the valley, except for its far northern portion. By canal and railway the east had managed to draw the valley into its economic orbit, but not the trans-Allegheny area, part of which was connected instead to Baltimore and part still isolated.

The east was slower to make political concessions to the west. In response to mounting western demands, a constitutional convention was convened in 1829. The new constitution that resulted made some extensions of the suffrage, but demands for popular election of the governor and county courts were rejected. As for apportionment, a compromise was adopted, which arbitrarily allotted seats to designated counties without establishing a formula. The seats allotted roughly corresponded to white population as of 1820 and thus increased the valley's representation, but no provision was made for mandatory reapportionment upon any basis. Inasmuch as eastern whites had outnumbered western whites in 1820 and therefore would still dominate the legislature, trans-Allegheny Virginians rejected the completed document in the state referendum, while all other areas approved it.

Shortly after this referendum, differences between the sections over slavery came to a climax in the legislative debates of 1831 and 1832. In preceding years Virginia had vacillated in its policy toward slavery. During the Revolution it had prohibited slave imports and made voluntary manumission of slaves possible. But in 1806, after GABRIEL'S INSURRECTION in Richmond in 1800, the manumission law had been amended to require expatriation of any slave freed by his master. The bloody TURNER'S REBELLION of 1831 had provoked a serious reexamination of the peculiar institution by the legislature, but a proposal for gradual emancipation had failed to pass the house by a 73 to 58 vote, with only seven delegates east of the Blue Ridge favoring the idea.

To a lesser degree, the regions differed on the issue of public education. In 1817 various legislators, mainly western Virginians, supported a move in the assembly to erect a statewide educational system. But this drive was thwarted by eastern Virginians, who favored instead the establishment of a state university, which was in fact chartered in 1819. In the 1840s another campaign for public schools enlisted wider support and resulted in victory for the principle of local option. By 1850 a few subdivisions, mainly eastern cities and western counties, had set up common school systems attended by an estimated 12 percent of the state's white children, a percentage third lowest among the states.

The census of 1840 had sparked the public school movement by showing that an estimated 8 percent of Virginia whites were illiterate. The same census showed that Virginia whites west of the Blue Ridge outnumbered those to the east for the first time, and this underscored continuing western demands for political concessions. At the constitutional convention of 1850–1851 that resulted, HENRY A. WISE and a few other easterners joined westerners in passing a legislative apportionment arrangement whereby eastern Virginia seemingly lost political control. Representation in the house of delegates was now to be based on white population only. In the senate, the east retained control temporarily, but it was understood that in 1865 it too would be reapportioned on the basis of white population. Western demands for popular elections and manhood suffrage also triumphed, all of which lends credence to the claim that this was a "reform convention." However, in return for apportionment concessions, Wise extracted certain legal protections for slavery. Slaveholdings were to be taxed at an arbitrarily fixed low rate.

The regional struggles within Virginia only imperfectly correlated with the two-party alignments that developed in the Jacksonian age and after. In 1828 and 1832, the national Republican candidates, John Q. Adams and Henry Clay, drew a minority of Virginia votes in some of the same areas formerly carried by the Federalists: the eastern cities, Northern Neck, and mountain counties. Andrew Jackson and the Democrats won large margins in the plantation counties and in the valley. Some western Virginians as well as residents along the Potomac River looked favorably upon schemes of national economic development, but nearly all Virginia congressmen in the 1820s and 1830s opposed national tariffs, internal improvements, and the 1832 bill rechartering the national bank.

After 1832, however, a body of eastern states' rights Democrats, including John Tyler and R. M. T. HUNTER, deserted Jackson because of his nationalistic repression of South Carolina during the nullification crisis and also because of his withdrawal of deposits from the national bank. These Democrats now joined the national Republicans in a new Whig coalition that was schizophrenic but nevertheless formidable. The Whigs, more than the Democrats, controlled state government for the ensuing decade. During the Van Buren years, the Whigs were strengthened by enlisting another body of "conservative" Democrats, led by WILLIAM C. RIVES, who rejected Martin Van Buren's hard money policies. At the same time, some of the eastern Whigs began returning to the Democratic fold, a process accelerated when President Tyler himself was purged from the national party.

The two parties differed more over national than state issues. The Democratic party, still dominated by Ritchie and the Richmond junto, steadfastly supported the national administrations of Jackson, Van Buren, and James K. Polk. During the 1840s, Virginia Democrats supported expansionism and the Mexican War, while Virginia Whigs opposed both, to their electoral advantage in 1847. Concerning state issues, the Whigs answered internal improvement needs by supporting the James River canal, while Democrats pushed more for railroad construction. Otherwise, regional loyalties prevailed over those of party. The leading journalistic organs of both parties favored the reforms advocated mainly by westerners, but among easterners the Whigs were slower to make political concessions.

Throughout all the sectional crises that faced the nation before the Civil War, Virginians of all factions and regions basically coalesced as southerners. In the Missouri controversy of 1820 (MISSOURI COMPROMISE), Virginia's congressmen supported the standard southern arguments that Missouri's state sovereignty would be impugned if conditions were attached to its entry. Of 23 congressmen, 18 even voted against the compromise dividing the remaining Louisiana Territory between slave and free sections. During the NULLIFICATION tension in 1832, Virginia attempted to mediate between the opposing forces, but Governor JOHN FLOYD, a Democrat, warned he would resist movement of federal troops across Virginia to suppress South Carolina. Later, Virginians opposed the WILMOT PROVISO, opposed the COMPROMISE OF 1850 upon passage but haltingly accepted it after the fact, and supported the KANSAS-NEBRASKA ACT of 1854—all acts of regional fidelity. Finally, John Brown's raid at HARPERS FERRY alarmed Virginians as well as southerners generally.

If Virginians were basically united as southerners during these crises, the state was nevertheless more moderate than others farther south. In 1850, for example, Virginia only halfheartedly participated in the NASHVILLE CONVENTION, and in 1851 it declined South Carolina's invitation to another conclave. EDMUND RUFFIN, a southern nationalist, complained that few Virginians responded to his appeals for sectional solidarity. In general, Virginia Whigs were the main moderating influence during the late 1840s and 1850s, but they were also weak and disorganized. Within the Democratic party, the Richmond junto under Ritchie had defended southern rights while conciliating nonsouthern allies, but after 1844 the junto finally lost hold and a more militantly southern posture was assumed by the two major Democratic leaders who came to the fore: first Senator R. M. T. Hunter and then Governor Wise.

General attitudes toward slavery hardened as the relationships between North and South deteriorated. With some minor exceptions, all Virginians—eastern, western, Whig, Democrat—united in either active or passive defense of the institution following the northern abolitionist crusades of the 1830s and 1840s. A few of the intelligentsia, including THOMAS R. DEW, GEORGE FITZHUGH, and Albert T. Bledsoe (1809–1877), aggressively defended slavery on its merits. Virginia Baptists and Methodists, now the dominant religions in Virginia, joined with their southern brethren in seceding from the national churches over the slavery issue in the 1840s, although most Methodists in present-day West Virginia stayed with the northern church. In 1859 JOHN LETCHER, a valley resident and Democratic candidate for governor, was forced to recant his earlier critical remarks about slavery in order to be elected.

Slavery also indirectly permeated the literature produced in or about the commonwealth after 1830. Authors JOHN P. KENNEDY and James K. Paulding wrote novels with Virginia settings that created the plantation myth in southern literature. Native Virginians JOHN ESTEN COOKE, Nathaniel Beverley Tucker, and William Alexander Caruthers wrote works of either sectional romance or sectional defiance. However, EDGAR ALLAN POE, the only major writer among Virginia's authors, managed to avoid work with a regional fixation.

By the 1850s the intensified political and moral assault by the North on slavery, the political compromises, and the improved transportation connections between eastern and western Virginia all combined to lessen internal differences and therefore to strengthen a sense of solidarity with the South at large. But certain economic changes also operated to reduce attachment to the South. Specifically, economic upturn came to eastern Virginia in the 1840s and especially the 1850s. Introduction of fertilizers revived worn-out agricultural lands, and diversification continued as orcharding developed in the valley. Improved transportation facilitated the spread of wheat cultivation, and in 1849 Virginia ranked fourth among American states in that commodity. Tobacco output rose dramatically in the 1850s, preserving Virginia preeminence in the production of that staple.

Diversification also came in the form of industrialization. A variety of factories sprang up in Virginia's growing cities. Richmond and Petersburg had long processed some of Virginia's tobacco; by 1860 the state processed two-thirds of its crop into plug tobacco. The new railroads and the James River canal, by funneling western grains and flour to Richmond, helped produce the rise there of a major flour industry, perhaps the largest concentration in the country. In the 1850s huge quantities of flour were exported around Cape Horn to the California market.

Thus, on the eve of the Civil War, Virginia had developed a modicum of economic diversification, which diminished to a slight degree its economic affiliation with the cotton plantation South. But the state was still less than 10 percent urban in 1860, and Richmond, the metropolis, had only 38,000 residents. No demographic revolution had yet taken place.

In 1860, when the nation verged on collapse, Virginia played a moderating role. In the presidential election of that year, its voters narrowly selected JOHN BELL, a former Whig and the Constitutional Union party candidate, over the more radical southern Democratic nominee. And, when the Lower South precipitously seceded following Abraham Lincoln's election, Virginia's assembly called instead for a national convention of the states in hopes of compromise. Likewise, the Virginia state convention, which met in February to consider the state's proper relation with the Union, marked time for two months hoping for some way out. It should be noted, however, that a strong majority of eastern delegates in the convention favored secession from the start, while valley and trans-Allegheny delegates opposed. After Ft. Sumter and Lincoln's call for militia, most valley and some trans-Allegheny delegates reluctantly joined the vast majority of easterners in the decision to withdraw from the Union. To the end, many trans-Allegheny delegates opposed secession. In the last analysis, the developing rapprochement between eastern and western Virginians came too late to survive the test of fire.

Civil War, Reconstruction, and Redemption. The Civil War was the nation's tragedy and Virginia's calamity. No state suffered more. With the Confederate capital transferred to Richmond, the brunt of the fighting in the East occurred on Virginia's soil, as northern invaders sought to capture and Confederates sought to defend the city. Throughout the war, Confederate troops controlled most of the state, but Union forces early occupied the Norfolk and Alexandria areas, as well as present-day West Virginia. The major fighting began at Manassas in 1861 and ended at Appomattox in 1865. Virginia was the vortex of the slaughter and devastation.

The war served to reinforce in the Old Dominion the age-old traits of conservatism, elitism, and homogeneity. Divested of West Virginia, the reduced commonwealth now possessed a basic community of interest only slightly less cohesive than that of the Tidewater world of 1700. As already shown, before the war the percentage of Negroes in Virginia's population had dropped to 34 in 1860, but with West Virginia eliminated Negroes composed 42 percent of the total in 1870. Although the percentage declined gradually thereafter, it remained as high as 36 as late as 1900. To the extent that white supremacy has been a touchstone of southern identity, Virginia became more southern after the war than before.

Culturally, the war was regressive and reactionary in its impact. With human and economic resources depleted, white illiteracy, already high, increased 30 percent between 1860 and 1870. By 1880 the figure stood at 18.5 percent, and as late as 1900 it was 11 percent, higher than in 1850. In literature the humiliation of defeat fostered in the state as well as in the South at large a cult of the LOST CAUSE. In effective but backward-looking prose, postwar Virginia writers such as THOMAS NELSON PAGE and George W. Bagby portrayed sentimentally and affectionately the golden days before the war. Nostalgia and traditionalism became fetishes.

Economically, the war temporarily retarded Virginia's modest prewar trend toward diversification. In agriculture, five years after Appomattox Virginia produced less tobacco, wheat, and corn and possessed fewer livestock than in 1860. Tobacco production remained sluggish for 30 years, and many tobacco factories folded. The flour industry never recovered its prewar eminence. By the 1880s some recovery came about as Richmond turned to manufacturing the newly fashionable cigarette. In the same decade, newly constructed railroads opened up mountain coal districts, and this indirectly produced the first urban center in the southwest, Roanoke, as well as a new Hampton Roads port for coal export, Newport News. Diversification also developed in agriculture as various parts of the state turned to truck farming, the cultivation of both peanuts and fruit, and horse raising. Nevertheless, prosperity did not return until 1900. From 1870 to 1900 the total population grew at a rate half the national average, so that Virginia ranked only seventeenth among the states by the turn of the century. And its population profile still showed a region predominantly rural (77 percent), with 45 percent of the work force still engaged in farming and only 17 percent occupied in manufacturing or mechanic arts.

Reconstruction in Virginia was a comparatively brief affair, but hardly bland. As in other southern states, President Andrew Johnson attempted speedy restoration of prewar institutions, a task made easier in Virginia by the existence throughout the war of a Union-recognized Virginia government-in-exile, headed by FRANCIS H. PIERPONT. After Appomattox, Pierpont simply transferred headquarters from Alexandria to Richmond, and legislative elections were held on the prewar basis of white suffrage only. The assembly thus elected best represents the postwar spirit of white Virginia in defeat. It accepted the extinction of slavery, but refused to extend the vote to any freedmen, and likewise ignored Pierpont's advice to ratify the FOURTEENTH AMENDMENT. Finally, in an attempt to cope with the new and fearsome element of unowned blacks, stiff vagrancy laws were enacted.

In Virginia and elsewhere, Johnson's brand of Reconstruction gave way in 1867 to Radical Reconstruction. By congressional mandate, Virginia became occupied Military District No. 1, with General John M. Schofield as military commander, supreme over all civil authority. At the constitutional convention that Schofield convened in 1867, Negro and white Republicans outnumbered native white Conservatives by a margin of two to one. The constitution drafted by this convention contained provisions establishing Negro suffrage and a public education system, provisions similar to Reconstruction constitutions throughout the South. Less typically, the constitution also included a clause disfranchising all those whites who had once served the U.S. or Virginia governments and later supported the Confederacy. Even harsher was the provision that any person who had voluntarily supported the Confederacy was to be barred from officeholding of any kind.

Virginia whites who had emphatically rejected the idea of Negro suffrage a few months earlier now offered to accept it and the entire constitution, provided the obnoxious clauses that disqualified whites could be eliminated. President Ulysses S. Grant and Congress agreed that the two clauses should be voted on separately from the main body. Meanwhile, the state Republican party had split into two main factions, and Virginia Conservatives withdrew their candidate from the gubernatorial race of 1869 in order to support the moderate Republican, Gilbert C. Walker, a New Yorker by origin. In the election, voters overwhelmingly approved the new constitution, defeated the disqualifying clauses by fair margins, and narrowly elected Walker. Thus by 1870 white Virginians had effectively regained political control of the commonwealth, and Redemption had seemingly arrived. Most whites naturally shunned the party of Reconstruction and affiliated as Conservatives. Governor Walker, though technically a Republican, also eventually aligned with the new party. Conservatives elected their own as governors in 1873 and 1877, the latter year without Republican opposition. White Virginia was back in the saddle.

But normalcy had not really returned. The apparent Conservative hegemony was fragile for two basic reasons. One was race. Negroes still possessed the suffrage and constituted, especially in the black belt counties of Virginia's southside (south of the James River), a formidable potential opposition or at the least a balance of power. Forty of Virginia's 99 counties had black majorities in 1870. Negroes naturally affiliated en masse with the Republican party of emancipation, so that politics were racially polarized and therefore tense. The second and more important explanation for the fragility of Conservative rule lies within the Civil War's legacy of poverty.

For over a decade after Redemption, the big issue in Virginia politics was how to cope with the prewar debt. In 1871 the general assembly funded with new bonds all of Virginia's prewar debt plus its unpaid interest. The relatively simple act of funding, however, could not assure adequate revenues to pay both the annual interest on the debt and other state expenses. Governor James L. Kemper attempted to persuade bondholders to accept a voluntary downward readjustment of the debt, but this ploy failed and the PANIC OF 1873 further aggravated the state's financial problems. By 1878 the acute shortage of funds forced closure of roughly half of Virginia's barely established public schools. And by 1879 the Conservative white phalanx had divided into two camps: the Funders, who insisted on full payment of the debt, and the Readjusters, who demanded its scaling down.

Led by former General WILLIAM MAHONE, the Readjusters, in cooperation with a group of Negro Republicans, captured control of the legislature in 1879 (READJUSTER MOVEMENT). Within the next two years, the Readjusters and Republicans merged into a single force, and in 1881 the coalition won both the legislative and gubernatorial elections. During their two brief years of power, the Readjusters enacted into law a program consonant with their constituency. Besides scaling down the debt, the new party repealed the POLL TAX enacted in the previous decade by Conservatives, abolished the whipping post, increased funding for public schools, and established a Negro teachers' college. On the national level, Mahone completed the work of the coalition by identifying himself as a Republican in the U.S. Senate.

The rise of the Readjusters represents the only example in Virginia's long history of victory for a class-oriented political movement. Yet, even the Readjuster triumph may be typed as an aberration caused only by extraordinary economic stringency and an externally imposed and internally vulnerable Negro suffrage, both products of war and defeat. White Readjusters never accepted their black allies socially, and, once the financial nightmare had been relieved, they left the coalition and returned to the "white man's party." In 1883 the Conservatives, newly christened Democrats, recaptured control of the assembly, and two years later FITZHUGH LEE, Civil War hero and symbol of the old Virginia mystique, laid successful claim to the governor's mansion.

The Martin and Progressive eras. Viewed in long perspective, Redemption came to Virginia in 1885, not 1870. The Democratic domination established then was destined to last fully 84 years. From 1885 to 1902, it is true, a semblance of two-party competition prevailed. Mahone himself scared the Democrats by running for governor in 1889. And in 1893 distressed farmers fielded a Populist gubernatorial candidate, Edmund Randolph Cocke, who was tacitly endorsed by the declining Republicans. But Virginians, haunted now by the memories associated with the Readjuster coalition, declined to support a new one. Cocke won only 38 percent of the vote, mainly from blacks. The only close political race during these decades, and the last significant example before 1928 of white exodus from the Democratic party, occurred in the presidential election of 1896. Governor CHARLES T. O'FERRALL and other prominent Democratic conservatives bucked the free-silver sentiment that had captured their own party and tacitly supported William McKinley over William Jennings Bryan. Bryan carried the state, but only by a narrow margin.

The emerging Democratic party of these decades was never monolithic. Even on matters racial, white supremacy was the general credo, though differences of opinion existed on how best to maintain it. On other issues, a reasonably durable bifactionalism developed, which pitted a conservative, probusiness wing against a more moderate, socially conscious group. The conservatives dominated the party, and the roots of that control go back to the senatorial election of 1893. In that year, the general assembly rejected the aspirations of the popular Fitzhugh Lee and elected to the Senate THOMAS S. MARTIN, a relatively unknown railroad lobbyist and lawyer. Railroad development had constituted the major new economic development in postwar Virginia, and Martin's election can only be explained on the basis of his railroad connections (or monetary bribes, according to his critics). An unassuming, hardworking man, he forged a political organization that largely controlled Virginia's government for 30 years. His conservatism was of the same cloth as the state he represented.

The anti-Martin or antimachine group, led by WILLIAM A. JONES and ANDREW JACKSON MONTAGUE in the early years, began to coalesce as early as 1897. United at first by moralistic outrage at the devious methods used to win Martin's original election, the "independents" or Progressives proposed popular elections of senators and party nominations by primary as ways to counteract the unhealthy corporate interests that Martin was felt to represent. In a sense, the antimachine people were the real conservatives, unhappy with the corrupt crassness that big business had introduced to Virginia and the nation and longing for a return to older standards. On the other hand, Senator JOHN W. DANIEL, a Martin ally, was the most eloquent Lost Cause orator in Virginia, and the Progressive critics were as likely to be city lawyers, educators, and journalists as blue-blooded farmers or scions thereof.

The factional rivalries came to a head in 1901, when the independents captured temporary control of the Democratic party organization. They adopted the primary mode of nominating senatorial and gubernatorial candidates, and they nominated Montague, who had campaigned hotly against Martin's alleged "ring rule," for governor. In the same year, the same voters who elected Montague also elected a constitutional convention, which drafted a document having two chief effects: better regulation of railroads and DISFRANCHISEMENT of the Negro.

Martin had acquiesced passively in the movement for a new constitution, but members of both factions backed the move to disfranchise the Negro. Some in the Progressive faction had motives more complex than mere maintenance of white supremacy. They argued historically that Negro suffrage had led to rampant vote-buying practices (a reasonably accurate observation), which in turn had placed a premium on money, which in turn had led to machine politics. Remove the purchasable voter, they reasoned, and political morality would be restored. Some Progressives also contended that disfranchisement would encourage development of a vigorous two-party system based on issues other than race. These arguments explain why the Progressives more than the machine conservatives supported disfranchisement.

Through literacy tests and poll taxes, the new constitution of 1902 did eliminate the majority of Negro voters, as well as many white illiterates. By reducing the total electorate to "small and aristocratic proportions," the unintended result was to strengthen, not weaken, the courthouse cadre of Martin's machine. Similarly, the anticipated development of a two-party system failed to materialize. The Virginia Republican party became an impotent group of mountaineer whites plus those few Negroes who managed to qualify to vote. On the other hand, disfranchisement may have had the intended effect of reducing Negrophobia, thus permitting whites to divide on nonracial issues if not into separate parties.

Additional evidences of a Progressive spirit, undoubtedly quickened by the return of economic prosperity, surfaced during the first years of the new century. The most impressive manifestation of this new PROGRESSIVISM came in the realm of public education. Some postwar Virginians had resisted this democratic yankee innovation imposed by the Reconstruction constitution, and this attitude plus the languishing economy kept the educational system skeletal before 1900. But soon after 1900 many Virginians began campaigning for educational renaissance as a main means of producing social and economic uplift. Governor Montague worked vigorously for better schools, and the cause assumed crusade proportions in the "May movement" of 1905. CLAUDE A SWANSON, successful Democratic candidate for governor that year, joined the crusade, and his administration witnessed adoption of several specific advances, including compulsory attendance on a local option basis. Other reforms advanced early in the century included CHILD LABOR regulation, pure food and drug control, penal and eleemosynary improvements, and road construction. The constitution of 1902 had established a state corporation commission, and it proved effective in regulating railroad rates. Later, in 1912, some state Progressives supported the democratic political reforms of the initiative, referendum, and recall.

Although Virginia voters had accepted much of their Progressive program, the antimachine Democrats did not benefit politically. Masterful politician that he was, Martin eventually embraced these reforms as soon as they had proved popular. He had originally opposed the primary reform in 1897 and again in 1899, but by 1904 he accepted the *fait accompli*. He took a dim view of the "hot air" educational crusade of 1905 but nevertheless paid it lip service. And, although he opposed Woodrow Wilson's nomination by the Democrats in 1912, Martin later gave such unswerving loyalty to the administration that Wilson felt obliged to reciprocate on matters of patronage. Thus Virginia's antimachine group, Wilson's original backers in 1911 and 1912, were deprived of political dividends. Martin's timely maneuvers had blurred Democratic bifactionalism by the later Wilson years, and the Martin machine seemed impregnable.

The temperance crusade had contributed to this confusion of factional lines. Beginning in 1901 with the formation of the Anti-Saloon League, temperance forces campaigned first for general tightening of liquor legislation and later, after 1910, for statewide prohibition. JAMES CANNON, JR., later to become a Methodist bishop, spearheaded the agitation and by a policy of relentless pressure finally persuaded the general assembly in 1914 to authorize a prohibition referendum that year. The proposal passed easily, and Virginia became officially dry in 1916. As had been the case with disfranchisement, support for prohibition came from both Democratic factions, from reform-minded Progressives, and from religiously fundamentalist conservatives. But, inasmuch as the Martin machine controlled the legislature, Cannon chose to court its favor by demonstrating massive support. The strategy worked, and in a succession of moves the machine absorbed the movement, profiting both Martin and Cannon politically.

Before Martin's death in 1919, his organization had prevailed through a policy of sagacious compromise and moderation for nearly 30 years. In contrast, his successor as king of Virginia politics, Harry F. Byrd, Sr., would develop a reputation as a rigid conservative, caustically critical of national Democratic leadership. What was there in Martin's Virginia that encouraged his begrudging moderation, and what later provoked Byrd's uncompromising conservatism?

An answer to the former question can be found in early twentieth-century socioeconomic trends. At the turn of the century, there was an atmosphere in Virginia of excitement and expectancy. The Lost Cause cult faded away as veterans died and memories dimmed. Virginians participated in the SPANISH-AMERICAN WAR with patriotic pride. The Civil War's legacy of poverty gave way after 1900 to rising prosperity. In 1905, when Virginia contributed a $50,000 exhibit to the St. Louis world's fair, journalistic commentators rejoiced that the state had at last overcome the degradation of the war. The optimism and calm of early twentieth-century Virginia can also be related to the nation's acceptance of the Virginia and southern racial settlement. When Wilson, a native Virginian, entered the White House, many residents of the Old Dominion felt that spiritual reunion had become fact. A long list of Virginians besides Martin—CARTER GLASS, Jones, Swanson, James Hay, HENRY D. FLOOD, Montague—contributed importantly to the national congressional scene during these years. The state and nation had merged.

Martin's Virginia, in other words, was a Virginia recovered from its Civil War and Reconstruction traumas, once more secure and self-assertive. Furthermore, the state was still basically a homogeneous, rural entity. As late as 1920, its population was over 70 percent rural, and its largest metropolis, Richmond, claimed less than 200,000 residents. Only 29 of the 100 counties had any urban centers at all. In such a tranquil, uncomplex environment, Virginians of Martin's day, much like the Virginia dynasty a century earlier, could afford to be compromising.

The causal factors that produced the Progressive reforms of Martin's day may also explain the development of a minor literary renaissance in the Old Dominion. About the turn of the century, ELLEN GLASGOW began composing her many novels. Eventually labeled a "social history" of Virginia, these works portrayed in realistic fashion the postwar decay of the aristocracy and the rise of a new middle class. Another major Richmond author, JAMES BRANCH CABELL, contributed writings less thematically Virginian but equally modern in form and content. In a sense, both in literature and politics, Virginia had become introspective and flexible.

Modern Virginia. The Virginia world grew more complex after 1920. World War I had brought phenomenal growth in the Hampton Roads naval area, the population there doubling within one year. Industrially, these years also saw the inauguration of major chemical industries in the state. Rayon plants were established in Roanoke, Waynesboro, and other locations; by 1930 Virginia manufactured one-third of the nation's rayon. The decade of the 1920s also witnessed the development of a vastly improved highway system, and this, even more than the earlier railroad revolution, acted to end rural isolation and draw the state into a national economy.

The national depression of the 1930s naturally dampened Virginia's economy, but not as drastically as for the nation as a whole. Unemployment in Virginia was only two-thirds the national average, and the value of industrial products actually rose 22 percent from 1929 to 1936. The state's improved highways began to attract a lucrative tourist business by mid-decade, and the evolution of New Deal bureaucratic largess also launched the spectacular growth of Washington's Virginia suburbs. Thus, the century-long pattern of out-migration of Virginia's whites reversed after 1930. The state gained 11 percent in population from 1930 to 1940, the first time its growth rate had exceeded the national average. Likewise, Virginia's post-1820 decline in ranking among the states was also reversed. In 1930 it ranked twentieth; in 1940, nineteenth.

During the 1940s, the state's demographic profile altered radically. Wartime demands on the federal bureaucracy had the double consequence of producing dramatic population gains for both northern Virginia and the Hampton Roads area.

The state's total population during the decade rose 24 percent, the highest decennial increase since the eighteenth century and high enough to increase Virginia's congressional delegation from nine to ten seats. The extra seat was awarded northern Virginia.

After World War II, the Hampton Roads area continued its rampant growth. The thriving port that colonial Tidewater had never produced finally materialized, with coal as a main export. As early as 1952, total tonnage of trade there ranked second only to New York on the Atlantic coast. In 1960 Norfolk passed Richmond as the state's largest city, and the whole metropolitan area composed roughly one-fifth of Virginia's total population.

The enormous growth of northern Virginia and Hampton Roads, as well as the more modest but still substantial growth of the Richmond area, reversed Virginia's historic westerly flow of population. Nearly all of the population growth now occurred in an "urban corridor" stretching from Washington through Richmond to Hampton Roads, while large sections of rural western Virginia lost population. The state as a whole became more than half urban in 1960, and by the 1970 census the urban percentage reached 63.

While non-Virginian immigrants infiltrated northern Virginia and to a lesser degree Hampton Roads, native Negroes left the state (NEGRO MIGRATION). From 1900 to 1970, the Negro percentage of the total population dwindled from 36 to less than 19. Within the state, Negroes as well as whites also deserted the farm for the city. Even so, changes in the overall Negro percentages reflect migration patterns more than they show change in small-town or rural Virginia. East of the Blue Ridge, the typical county in 1970 could still be described as essentially biracial, and the southside from Danville to Norfolk still maintained a rough popular parity between the races. In 1970 nine of Virginia's 95 counties still had Negro majorities, and 35 still had over 30 percent Negro population.

Economically, Virginia continued to diversify in the 1950s and 1960s. With tobacco and nylon plants, Richmond maintained its position as the largest manufacturing center in the state, but most of the synthetic fiber factories were scattered throughout western Virginia. Except for a major shipbuilding industry at Newport News and a major cotton mill in Danville, the general industrial pattern was one of geographic dispersion and non-specialization. Industrialization and urbanization were not necessarily correlated in Virginia. The typical factory worker was as likely to commute from a family farm as to live in a city apartment. Furthermore, for all its industrial advance, Virginia factories employed a smaller percentage of the work force than did the nation's, while employment in agricultural pursuits continued to be at least slightly higher than national norms. Indeed, because of the northern Virginia suburbs of Washington, more Virginians worked for government than for industry. In 1971 approximately 20 percent of the work force was employed by some agency of state or national government, the highest percentage for any state.

In the postwar years, TOURISM also became big business and contributed to Virginia's economic diversification. John D. Rockefeller, Jr., transformed sleepy Williamsburg into an antiquarian's delight, and thousands of travelers and schoolchildren made pilgrimages there as well as to the shrines of Mount Vernon and Monticello. Other thousands, northerners and southerners alike, visited the somber sites of Civil War deaths. The chief scenic attractions for visitors became the Blue Ridge Parkway and the Skyline Drive.

Based on tourism, industry, agriculture, government, commerce, and mining, Virginia's modern economy thus developed an unusual degree of balance and diversity. And this diversity proved to be a healthy cushion against the type of economic fluctuations that had plagued the earlier tobacco-based colonial economy. Consistently throughout the 1960s and 1970s, Virginia's unemployment rate ranked among the lowest of all the states.

But there were also weaknesses in this newly diversified economy. Indices of per capita income generally showed that Virginia exceeded southern norms but lagged behind all or most non-southern states. In 1950 the typical Virginia industrial worker earned 20 percent less than his national counterpart. After 1950 the gap narrowed markedly; but, even including the affluent Washington suburbs, Virginia's per capita income in 1970 placed it only twenty-eighth among the states, though second only to Florida among southern states.

Somewhat similar statistics describe the educational scene. In 1950 Virginia ranked forty-fifth among the 48 states in the median school years completed by its adult population and last in the percentage of persons aged five to twenty-four enrolled in schools or colleges. In 1961, to cite another dismal statistic, 53 percent of all Virginians could not qualify for induction into the armed forces, 30 percent failing the mental test. This latter figure placed Virginia forty-third among the states.

Thus, despite the educational renaissance after 1900 and the phenomenal economic growth of later decades, the colonial institutions of indentured servitude and slavery and the Civil War aftermath of poverty and regression had left a legacy of illiteracy and economic backwardness difficult to eradicate. Indeed, the problem became, or always had been, cyclical. Because of the lower educational levels among Virginians, industries requiring skilled labor and paying high wages were less attracted to Virginia than were low-skill, low-wage industries such as textiles.

All these changes were in the dimly perceived future when HARRY F. BYRD, SR., assumed chairmanship of the Democratic party in 1922. Virginia was still much the same rural province of preceding centuries, and Byrd, better than Martin, symbolized or evoked the shimmering Virginia mystique drawn from that venerable past. A lineal descendant of the colonial BYRD FAMILY, he showed his affinity for Virginia's rural spirit by developing vast apple orchards in the northern Shenandoah Valley, by acquiring an elegant country estate, and by wearing white suits. More personally likable and more symbolically satisfying than Martin, Byrd was to be Virginia's political boss and godfather for over four decades (BYRD MACHINE).

Byrd first asserted his power and established his conservative image by successfully opposing a road bond issue in a state referendum in 1923. True to the earlier Funder spirit of the 1870s, he honored the maxim "pay-as-you-go," which thereafter became the cardinal financial tenet for the state. Byrd himself was elected governor in 1925 and entered the U.S. Senate in 1933, where he remained for 32 years. The machine he led nearly monopolized state offices. From the 1920s to the early 1960s, every governor elected in Virginia had the Byrd machine's blessing save one, James H. Price, elected in 1937. While governor, however, Price had little success in reducing the machine's hold on the legislature, patronage, or policy. The only other serious breakdown in the smooth functioning of the machine during this period occurred in 1928, when Bishop Cannon rejected Al Smith and campaigned instead for Herbert Hoover. Byrd remained loyal to the Democratic nominee, but Smith—a Catholic, an urbanite, and a "wet"—proved too incompatible with Virginia's Protestant and rural personality. Hoover carried the state.

Throughout the Byrd years, his machine developed a reputation for basically two things: integrity and financial watchfulness or parsimony, depending on the vantage point of the observer. The state developed a good system of highways but consistently ranked among the bottom of the states in per capita expenditures for education, state hospitals, and general social services. This limited government approach was most acceptable to those portions of Virginia most rural or southern in identity. Superficially, Byrd candidates regularly piled up massive majorities in southside Virginia, where Negroes were most numerous. The machine exerted lesser control in the growing cities and in the valley southwest of Roanoke, where a lingering frontier legacy of democracy, poverty, and ignorance proved incompatible with the aristocratic ethos of poll taxes and literacy tests. Finally, it should come as no surprise to discover that the machine had least support in that area of the state that was least Virginian: the Washington suburbs. Here white suits and pillared country mansions seemed anachronistic.

The decline of rural Virginia spelled ultimate doom to the rural style of Byrd politics. By the late 1940s, opposition to Byrd within the Democratic party gathered force. In 1949 Byrd's candidate for governor narrowly bested a pack of four candidates in the Democratic primary, and Byrd himself faced his first serious opposition to senatorial renomination in 1952. In the early 1950s, a "young Turk" group of Democrats in the assembly began to criticize the organization's financial stinginess.

The challenge to the machine also developed outside the Democratic party, and this development had less to do with Virginia's changing demography. The reinvigoration of the Republican party began in 1952, when Dwight Eisenhower carried the state against Adlai Stevenson. It showed more serious dimensions in 1953, when the Republican candidate for governor, Ted Dalton, almost beat the machine candidate, Thomas B. Stanley. The sudden growth of a two-party system can be explained mainly by forces external to the state. Rapport between North and South existing at the opening of the twentieth century began to break down by the 1920s. During New Deal days, Negroes largely shifted their allegiances from the Republican to the Democratic party nationally, and as a result the national party developed more liberal attitudes toward race. This culminated in Harry Truman's espousal of civil rights in 1948. Inevitably, Virginia's segregationists began to desert the national party. Byrd himself adopted a stance of "golden silence" on every presidential race after 1932 save for that of 1952, when he announced he could not vote for Stevenson. Just as inevitably, those Virginians who began voting for national Republican presidential candidates also later began voting Republican in state elections. The Byrd organization thus faced a two-horned challenge of rising liberal strength within the Democratic party, based on demographic change, and desertion of conservatives from the party, based on the logic of national partisan alignments.

The machine met these threats in the same beleaguered, defensive fashion as eastern Virginia had met similar challenges from the west a century earlier. The Byrd machine resisted urban demands for more seats, and not until the 1960s did court decisions give urban Virginia a legislative voice commensurate to numbers (BAKER V. CARR). The Byrd machine also generally opposed demands for poll tax repeal. One of the last Byrd governors, Albertis S. Harrison (1962–1966), defended the poll tax by asserting his preference for an electorate both "small and smart"— surely the most candidly elitist remark by a public figure in recent American history. One last parallel evokes the amazing continuity in Virginia's long history. Before the Civil War, the still-dominant but embattled east achieved greatest statewide consensus in a doomed defense of slavery. In the 1950s the still-dominant but embattled Byrd machine managed its last hurrah in a dramatically popular but doomed defense of SEGREGATION.

Initial official reaction to the U.S. Supreme Court's 1954 desegregation edict was muted and superficially moderate. Governor Stanley appointed an all-white 32-member commission to recommend state policy, and the commission proposed what appeared to be a local option approach, featuring state tuition grants to parents who preferred to boycott integrated public schools. In 1956 Virginia's voters approved by a two-to-one margin the calling of a constitutional convention to make the necessary amendments. Meanwhile, however, the southern forces opposed to integration gained momentum, producing in 1956 a SOUTHERN MANIFESTO signed by nearly all of Dixie's congressmen. Senator Byrd and others now galvanized the organization into a posture of "massive resistance" to integration. As with John C. Calhoun and Henry A. Wise of an earlier day, it was Byrd's logic that only a unified and uncompromising South could turn away the northern threat to southern institutions. In a sense, his position was determined as much by his loyalty to the old Virginia mystique as by a commitment to white supremacy.

How could Virginia massively resist? The basic answer, as recommended by Governor Stanley and adopted by the legislature in 1956, was to close any school integrated and to withhold state funds from any school that attempted to reopen under court order. A tuition grant policy was included as an escape clause. This Draconian and reactionary turn of events marshaled latent liberal voices in the state into opposition, and the whole matter became the main issue in the gubernatorial race of 1957. In that race, Democrat J. LINDSAY ALMOND, staunch defender of massive resistance, sailed to an easy triumph over Republican Ted Dalton, who criticized it. Dalton's percentage of the total vote dropped to 38, seven points less than his record against Stanley four years earlier. He carried only 16 of Virginia's 130 subdivisions, most of them in the mountain southwest.

Denouement came soon after the election. In the fall of 1958, federal courts ordered integration in three Virginia school systems: Warren County, Charlottesville, and Norfolk. Governor Almond dutifully closed the schools affected, but within three months both federal and state courts struck down the closings as unconstitutional. Meanwhile, faced with the reality of locked school buildings and idle children, journalistic and business sentiment in the state swung in favor of a more moderate position. Governor Almond threw in the towel after the court decisions, but to the end Byrd and other organization stalwarts searched for other legal means of resistance. Thus, Almond's program of local option passed the assembly by margins narrower than those that had ordained school closings. Thereafter, Almond became anathema to the organization, which successfully derailed his advocacy of a state sales tax.

Almond's statewide victory in 1957 contradicts the analyses of some historians, who picture massive resistance as a program coerced upon an unwilling state by a minority of extremists from the black belt southside. True, this section gave the most overwhelming support to the program, but native white Virginians in all sections were attracted to the posture of a muscular Virginia once more rising in righteous defiance of the yankee invader. At the height of the tension, the city council of Norfolk, supposedly one of Virginia's most liberal cities, actually voted to close down all its secondary schools, not just those affected by the litigation. And in Warren County, a white county in the Shenandoah, parents became so committed to resistance that many continued to patronize a private segregated academy for several years after the public schools reopened with their handful of Negro students. In the fall of 1959, even when the battle was clearly over, southside Prince Edward County implemented its own brand of local massive resistance by closing county schools. Only after five years of litigation did the U.S. Supreme Court force their reopening. Finally, Byrd himself was overwhelmingly reelected over token opposition in November, 1958, at the very time schools stood closed. If Byrd led Virginia down the path of massive resistance, most

white Virginians were willing, even eager, to follow. In a sense, massive resistance in 1956 was as inevitable as secession in 1860, and equally as tragic.

The courts, not the people, had repudiated massive resistance. For a few more years, the Byrd organization retained power in what may be described as its sunset years. In 1961 Byrd stalwart Albertis S. Harrison easily won the race for governor, and in 1965 an architect of massive resistance, Mills E. Godwin, Jr., triumphed in a closer contest. In 1964 Byrd himself was reelected once again with token opposition. When he later retired in 1965, his son and namesake, Harry F. Byrd, Jr., was appointed to replace him by Governor Harrison.

After 1965, however, the organization quickly disintegrated. The basic forces of realignment, temporarily suspended by the massive resistance interlude, were once again released. In 1964 Byrd had been unable to prevent the state Democratic convention from endorsing President Lyndon Johnson, and in 1966 his son barely won the Democratic primary nomination for the unexpired term. The increasing number of liberal voices within the party hastened the exodus of conservatives therefrom, and in 1969 Linwood Holton won election as Virginia's first Republican governor since Reconstruction. In 1970 Harry Byrd, Jr., left the party of his ancestors to win reelection as an independent. Completing the realignment revolution, erstwhile Democrat Godwin switched to the Republican party in 1973 and won another term as governor.

In his first term, Governor Godwin established a record as a moderate progressive. He brought an end to the pay-as-you-go principle, helped to establish a system of community colleges, and pushed for a sales tax. His successor Holton pushed for an open-housing act, the South's first, and in a meaningful gesture enrolled his children in Richmond's nearly all-black public schools. More emphatically new to Virginia was the astounding rise of Henry Howell of Norfolk. Howell made good races for the governor's chair in 1969, 1973, and 1977. Howell built a deserved reputation as a populist-style orator, excoriating the "big boys" of high finance. His appeal was unabashedly a class pitch to the underdog, and he won support from labor unions, Negroes, miners, and northern and western Virginians: precisely those forces that had clouded Byrd's sunset. Yet Virginia has not yet placed Howell in the governor's mansion. In defeating him in 1973, Godwin campaigned in a more conservative vein than his previously progressive administration would have presaged, and another

Republican, John Dalton, beat Howell in 1977. For that matter, even as the spokesman for a new Virginia, Howell spoke with a down-home southern accent that attracted a good deal of support from some of the same "good old boys" who voted for GEORGE C. WALLACE for president in 1968.

In 1976 it was not clear whether Virginia's demographic revolution had yet wrought a political one. Virginia's delegations to the national Congress were now more Republican than Democratic, but still consistently among the most conservative there. In presidential elections, Virginians had likewise voted for the more conservative Republican candidates in all but one of the contests since 1948. Senator Byrd, Jr., a conservative in his father's mold, ran for reelection as an independent in 1976 and won, and the continuing hold of the Byrd mystique was such that no prominent politician in either party rose to challenge him. From the seventeenth to the twentieth centuries, then, the Byrds and their kind had presided over the social and political scene in Virginia. Perhaps no better illustration than this could be found of the basic continuity of the commonwealth's historical experience.

Manuscripts, printed primary sources, research aids, and journals. The Alderman Library, University of Virginia, has the most impressive collection of Virginiana. The Virginia State Library in Richmond has official and private papers. Other important depositories are Virginia Historical Society in Richmond, University of North Carolina, Duke University, and Library of Congress. Printed primary sources for colonial Virginia are W. W. Hening, *Statutes at Large* (13 vols.; 1809–23), most valuable; W. M. Billings, *Old Dominion, Seventeenth Century* (1975), good one-vol. introduction to miscellaneous sources; and W. P. Palmer *et al.* (eds.), *Calendar of State Papers* (11 vols.; 1875–93). The Virginia State Library has published colonial and early national legislative journals as well as *Virginia State Convention of 1861* (7 vols.; 1965–66). For revolutionary and early national periods, the most important collected papers of major Virginians are J. C. Fitzpatrick (ed.), *Washington* (39 vols.; 1950–74); J. P. Boyd (ed.), *Jefferson* (19 vols.; 1950–74); W. T. Hutchinson *et al.* (eds.), *Madison* (9 vols.; 1962–75); R. A. Rutland (ed.), *George Mason* (3 vols.; 1970); and H. A. Johnson *et al.* (eds.), *John Marshall* (1974). Historical journals are a good source for printed primary documents, and E. G. Swem's *Virginia Historical Index* (2 vols.; 1934–36) indexes the pre-1930 publications of three most important journals: *Virginia Magazine of History and Biography* (1893–); *William and Mary Quarterly* (1893–); and *Tyler's Quarterly* (1919–52). Swem's *Index* covers Hening's *Statutes* and is the single most valuable research aid for early Virginia history. Other research aids are E. G. Swem, *Bibliography* (4 vols.; 1916–32); L. J. Cappon, *Bibliography of Virginia History Since 1865* (1930); E. G. Swem *et al.*, *Bibliography of Virginia, 1607–1689* (1957); L. J. Cappon and S. F. Duff, *Virginia Gazette Index* (2 vols.; 1950); and L. J.

Cappon, *Virginia Newspapers, 1821–1935* (1936). The *Virginia Magazine of History and Biography* has excellent secondary accounts of Virginia history, colonial to modern. The *William and Mary Quarterly* specializes in early American history generally. The *Virginia Cavalcade* (1951–) is a glossy, eye-appealing publication. Occasional articles on Virginia appear in *Journal of Southern History* and *Virginia Social Science Journal*.

Contemporary accounts. Some important works are R. Beverley, *History of Virginia* (1947); H. Jones, *Present State of Virginia* (1956); L. B. Wright (ed.), *Prose Works of William Byrd* (1966); T. Jefferson, *Notes on Virginia* (1955); J. E. Massey, *Autobiography* (1909); J. S. Wise, *End of Era* (1965); J. Cannon, *Own Story* (1955); and J. B. Cabell, *As I Remember It* (1955).

Secondary monographs and articles. See V. Dabney, *New Politics* (1971), best for the last century; M. P. Andrews, *Old Dominion* (1956), poor; M. Fishwick, *New Look at Old Dominion* (1959), collection of imaginative essays; W. E. Hemphill *et al.*, *Cavalier Commonwealth* (1957), readable secondary school text. *History of Virginia* (6 vols.; 1924) includes three volumes by P. A. Bruce, L. G. Tyler, and R. L. Morton on colonial, middle, and modern periods and three volumes of biographical sketches. Also see L. G. Tyler, *Men of Mark* (5 vols.; 1915); R. L. Morton, *Colonial Virginia* (2 vols.; 1960); C. H. Ambler, *Sectionalism in Virginia, 1776–1861* (1910); and A. W. Moger, *Bourbonism to Byrd* (1968), recent period. See W. M. Billings, *Virginia Magazine of History and Biography* (April, 1975), good historiographic introduction to colonial period; C. W. Sydnor, *Gentlemen Freeholders* (1952), colonial politics; D. J. Boorstin, *Colonial Experience* (1958); R. E. Brown and B. K. Brown, *Virginia, 1705–1786* (1964); and T. J. Wertenbaker, *Virginia Under Stuarts* (1914), one of many works by this author.

Specific subjects are developed in L. Griffith, *House of Burgesses* (1963); J. B. Frantz (ed.), *Bacon's Rebellion* (1969); W. F. Washburn, *Governor and Rebel* (1957); J. R. Alden, *R. Dinwiddie* (1973); W. Havighurst, *A. Spotswood* (1967); C. Bridenbaugh, *Seat of Empire* (1950); B. Bailyn, in J. M. Smith (ed.), *Seventeenth-Century America* (1959), politics and society; W. M. Billings, *Virginia Magazine of History and Biography* (Oct., 1970), Bacon's Rebellion; R. Detweiler, *Virginia Magazine of History and Biography* (July, 1972), sectionalism; J. A. Ernst, *Virginia Magazine of History and Biography* (April, 1969), Robinson scandal; J. P. Greene, *William and Mary Quarterly* (Oct., 1959), burgesses; J. C. Rainbolt, *Virginia Magazine of History and Biography* (Oct., 1967), aftermath of Bacon's Rebellion; and J. M. Thornton, *Virginia Magazine of History and Biography* (Jan., 1968), Harvey rebellion. See also P. A. Bruce, *Economic History of Seventeenth Century* (2 vols.; 1935), most detailed introduction to colonial economic history; W. F. Craven, *Seventeenth-Century Virginian* (1971), good demographic analysis; A. P. Middleton, *Tobacco Coast* (1953); J. C. Ballagh, *White Servitude* (1895); J. C. Rainbolt, *Virginia Economy* (1974); C. E. Hatch, *Virginia Magazine of History and Biography* (May, 1957), silk culture; D. C. Klingaman, *Virginia Magazine of History and Biography* (Jan., 1969), coastwise trade; E. S. Morgan, *Virginia Magazine of History and Biography* (July, 1972), headrights; J. Price, *William and Mary Quarterly* (July, 1962), tobacco trade; J. S. Soltow, *Virginia Maga-*

zine of History and Biography (July, 1966), Williamsburg economy; and D. D. Max, *Virginia Magazine of History and Biography* (Jan., 1971), Negro import duties.

The colonial social and cultural milieu is perhaps best pictured in L. B. Wright's *First Gentlemen of Virginia* (1940). Other good general treatments include R. B. Davis, *Literature and Society* (1973); T. P. Abernethy, *Three Virginia Frontiers* (1962); P. A. Bruce, *Institutional History* (2 vols.; 1962) and *Social Life* (1907); C. Bridenbaugh, *Myths and Realities* (1952); and T. J. Wertenbaker, *Planters of Colonial Virginia* (1922). More particular social and cultural topics are developed in J. Carson, *Virginians at Play* (1965); T. W. Tate, *Williamsburg Negro* (1965); W. M. Gewehr, *Great Awakening* (1965); E. Morgan, *Virginians at Home* (1952); E. and D. S. Berkeley, *J. Clayton* (1963); P. Rouse, Jr., *J. Blair* (1971); G. M. Brydon, *Virginia's Mother Church* (2 vols.; 1947, 1952); K. Wurst, *Virginia Germans* (1969); L. Morton, *R. Carter* (1945); J. and N. Ewan, *J. Banister* (1970); G. W. Pilcher, *S. Davies* (1971); P. Marambaud, *William Byrd* (1971); K. L. Carroll, *Virginia Magazine of History and Biography* (April, 1966), Quakers; R. K. MacMaster, *Virginia Magazine of History and Biography* (April, 1972), antislavery; J. C. Rainbolt, *Virginia Magazine of History and Biography* (July, 1971), small planters; B. E. Steiner, *Virginia Magazine of History and Biography* (Oct., 1962), Catholics; and D. R. Rutman (ed.), *Old Dominion* (1964), essays on colonial and revolutionary years.

Revolutionary and early national years are best studied in numerous biographies of leading statesmen: D. Malone, *Jefferson* (5 vols.; 1948–72); D. S. Freeman, *Washington* (6 vols.; 1968); R. R. Beeman, *Henry* (1974); I. Brant, *Madison* (1970); H. Ammon, *Monroe* (1971); R. A. Rutland, *George Mason* (1963); O. P. Chitwood, *R. H. Lee* (1967); D. J. Mays, *E. Pendleton* (2 vols.; 1952); A. Koch, *Jefferson and Madison* (1950); W. C. Bruce, *J. Randolph* (2 vols.; 1922); H. J. Eckenrode, *The Randolphs* (1946); W. R. Gaines, *T. M. Randolph* (1966); J. J. Reardon, *E. Randolph* (1974); A. J. Beveridge, *J. Marshall* (4 vols.; 1916–18); and D. R. Anderson, *W. B. Giles* (1965). General or topical works on revolutionary years include H. J. Eckenrode, *Revolution in Virginia* (1916); A. Williams, *Road to Independence* (1975); T. P. Abernethy, *Western Lands* (1937); I. S. Harrell, *Loyalism in Virginia* (1926); F. H. Hart, *Valley of Virginia* (1942); T. W. Tate, *William and Mary Quarterly* (July, 1962), good summary of prerevolutionary decade; J. L. Anderson, *Virginia Magazine of History and Biography* (Jan., 1974), council; E. M. DelPapa, *Virginia Magazine of History and Biography* (Oct., 1975), Proclamation of 1763; E. G. Evans, *William and Mary Quarterly* (Oct., 1962), planter debts; L. H. Gipson, *Virginia Magazine of History and Biography* (July, 1961), planter debts; and A. R. Riggs, *Virginia Magazine of History and Biography* (July, 1970), A. Lee.

For early national political development, see N. Cunningham, *Jeffersonian Republicans* (1957); R. R. Beeman, *Old Dominion, 1788–1801* (1972); N. K. Risjord, *Old Republicans* (1967) and *Journal of Southern History* (Nov., 1967), Virginia Federalists; H. Ammon, *Journal of Southern History* (Aug., 1953), Republican party origins, and *Virginia Magazine of History and Biography* (July, 1953), Richmond junto; W. E. Dodd, *American Historical Review* (July, 1907), Roane; T. J. Farnham, *Virginia*

Magazine of History and Biography (Jan., 1967), Jay's Treaty; J. H. Harrison, *Virginia Magazine of History and Biography* (April, 1970), Richmond junto; R. L. Ketcham, *Virginia Magazine of History and Biography* (April, 1958), 1798 nullifcation; J. T. Main, *William and Mary Quarterly* (Jan., 1955), 1780s; J. C. Robert, *Virginia Magazine of History and Biography* (Oct., 1972), Wirt; R. E. Thomas, *Journal of Southern History* (Feb., 1953), convention of 1788; and M. F. Wehtje, *Virginia Magazine of History and Biography* (Jan., 1970), War of 1812.

Politics of antebellum Virginia are best unfolded in biographies: C. Hall, *A. P. Upshur* (1964); E. T. Mudge, *J. Taylor* (1939); C. H. Ambler, *T. Ritchie* (1913); O. P. Chitwood, *J. Tyler* (1964); H. H. Simms, *R. M. T. Hunter* (1935); J. P. Frank, *Justice Daniel* (1964); and F. F. Wayland, *A. Stevenson* (1949). Besides C. H. Ambler, *Sectionalism* (1910), the best political survey is H. T. Shanks, *Secession Movement, 1847–1861* (1935). See also H. H. Simms, *Whigs in Virginia* (1929); H. Braverman, *Virginia Magazine of History and Biography* (April, 1952), Conservative revolt; J. E. Fischer, *Virginia Magazine of History and Biography* (Oct., 1973), R. M. T. Hunter; J. S. Knight, *Virginia Magazine of History and Biography* (Oct., 1973), 1840s; C. Simpson, *Virginia Magazine of History and Biography* (Oct., 1975), constitutional convention of 1850; F. L. Williams, *Virginia Magazine of History and Biography* (July, 1967), J. Y. Mason; and J. B. Boles (ed.), *Middle Period* (1973), essays on both political and nonpolitical topics.

Best nonpolitical studies of middle period are R. B. Davis, *Intellectual Life, 1790–1830* (1964); R. McColley, *Slavery and Jeffersonian Virginia* (1964); H. S. Klein, *Slavery, Virginia, and Cuba* (1967); J. C. Robert, *Tobacco Kingdom* (1965); and A. O. Craven, *Soil Exhaustion* (1965). Other detailed studies are A. O. Craven, *E. Ruffin* (1964); L. P. Jackson, *Free Negro* (1942); T. R. Snavely, *George Tucker* (1964); C. B. Dew, *Tredegar Iron Works* (1966); W. K. Bates, *William and Mary Quarterly* (Jan., 1962), 1790 debts; R. S. Berry, *Virginia Magazine of History and Biography* (Oct., 1970), flour industry; A. O. Craven, *Journal of Southern History* (May, 1938), John Taylor; R. B. Davis, *Virginia Magazine of History and Biography* (Jan., 1962), immigrants; E. J. Ferguson, *Journal of Southern History* (Nov., 1962), 1790 debts; R. F. Hunton, *Virginia Magazine of History and Biography* (July, 1961), turnpike movement; W. A. Low, *Virginia Magazine of History and Biography* (July, 1953), merchant-planter relations; D. R. McCoy, *Virginia Magazine of History and Biography* (July, 1975), 1784 port bill; J. T. Main, *Mississippi Valley Historical Review* (Sept., 1954), land distribution; M. L. Rich, *Virginia Magazine of History and Biography* (July, 1968), economics of 1781–89; J. H. Russell, *Journal of Negro History* (July, 1916), Negro slaveholders; J. T. Schelebecker, *Virginia Magazine of History and Biography* (Oct., 1971), valley farming; P. C. Stewart, *Virginia Magazine of History and Biography* (Jan., 1973), railroads; W. K. Wood, *Virginia Magazine of History and Biography* (July, 1975), frontier economy; and W. F. Zornow, *Virginia Magazine of History and Biography* (July, 1954), 1775–89 tariffs.

Particular social and cultural topics are developed in J. C. Robert, *Road from Monticello* (1941); J. D. Allen, *P. P. Cook* (1969); S. B. Oates, *Turner's Rebellion* (1975); D. K. Jackson, *Poe and Literary Messenger* (1934); W. R.

VIRGINIA POPULATION, 1790–1970

Year	Total	White	Nonwhite Slave	Free	% Growth	Rank U.S.	South
1790[a]	747,610	442,117	292,627	12,866		1	1
1800[a]	886,149	514,280	346,968	24,901	18.5	1	1
1810[a]	983,152	551,514	394,357	37,281	10.9	1	1
1820[a]	1,075,069	603,335	427,005	44,729	9.3	2	1
1830[a]	1,220,978	694,300	471,371	55,307	13.6	3	1
1840[a]	1,249,764	740,968	450,361	58,435	2.3	4	1
1850[a]	1,421,661	894,800	472,528	54,333	13.8	4	1
1860[a]	1,596,318	1,047,299	490,865	58,154	12.3	5	1
1870	1,225,163	712,089		513,074	23.3	10	4
1880	1,512,565	880,858		631,707	23.5	14	6
1890	1,655,980	1,020,122		635,858	9.5	15	6
1900	1,854,184	1,192,855		661,329	12.0	17	7
1910	2,061,612	1,389,809		671,803	11.2	20	8
1920	2,309,187	1,617,909		691,278	12.0	20	8
1930	2,421,851	1,770,441		651,410	4.9	20	8
1940	2,677,773	2,015,583		662,190	10.6	19	8
1950	3,318,680	2,581,555		737,125	23.9	15	5
1960	3,966,949	3,142,443		824,506	19.5	14	5
1970	4,648,494	3,761,514		886,980	17.2	14	5

[a] includes present-day West Virginia

VIRGINIA GOVERNORS

Governor	Party	Term
Patrick Henry		1776–1779
Thomas Jefferson		1779–1781
Thomas Nelson, Jr.		1781
Benjamin Harrison		1781–1784
Patrick Henry		1784–1786
Edmund Randolph		1786–1788
Beverley Randolph		1788–1791
Henry Lee	Rep.	1791–1794
Robert Brooke	Rep.	1794–1796
James Wood	Fed.	1796–1799
James Monroe	Rep.	1799–1802
John Page	Rep.	1802–1805
William H. Cabell	Rep.	1805–1808
John Tyler	Rep.	1808–1811
James Monroe	Rep.	1811
George W. Smith	Rep.	1811
James Barbour	Rep.	1812–1814
Wilson C. Nicholas	Rep.	1814–1816
James P. Preston	Rep.	1816–1819
Thomas M. Randolph	Rep.	1819–1822
James Pleasants, Jr.	Rep.	1822–1825
John Tyler	Rep.	1825–1827
William B. Giles	Rep.	1827–1830
John Floyd	Dem.	1830–1834
Littleton W. Tazewell	Whig	1834–1836
Wyndham Robertson	Whig	1836–1837
David Campbell	Whig	1837–1840
Thomas Walker Gilmer	Whig	1840–1841
John Rutherford	Dem.	1841–1842
John M. Gregory	Whig	1842–1843
James McDowell	Dem.	1843–1846
William Smith	Dem.	1846–1849
John B. Floyd	Dem.	1849–1852
Joseph Johnston	Dem.	1852–1856
Henry A. Wise	Dem.	1856–1860
John Letcher	Dem.	1860–1864
William Smith	Dem.	1864–1865
Francis H. Pierpoint	Rep.	1865–1868
Henry H. Wells	Rep.	1868–1869
Gilbert C. Walker	Rep.	1869–1874
James L. Kemper	Con.	1874–1878

Governor	Party	Term
Frederick W. M. Holliday	Con.	1878–1882
William E. Cameron	Readjuster	1882–1886
Fitzhugh Lee	Dem.	1886–1890
Philip W. McKinney	Dem.	1890–1894
Charles T. O'Ferrall	Dem.	1894–1898
James H. Tyler	Dem.	1898–1902
Andrew J. Montague	Dem.	1902–1906
Claude A. Swanson	Dem.	1906–1910
William H. Mann	Dem.	1910–1914
Henry C. Stuart	Dem.	1914–1918
Westmoreland Davis	Dem.	1918–1922
Elbert L. Trinkle	Dem.	1922–1926
Harry F. Byrd, Sr.	Dem.	1926–1930
John G. Pollard	Dem.	1930–1934
George C. Peery	Dem.	1934–1938
James H. Price	Dem.	1938–1942
Colgate W. Darden, Jr.	Dem.	1942–1946
William M. Tuck.	Dem.	1946–1950
John S. Battle	Dem.	1950–1954
Thomas B. Stanley	Dem.	1954–1958
J. Lindsay Almond, Jr.	Dem.	1958–1962
Albertis S. Harrison, Jr.	Dem.	1962–1966
Mills E. Godwin, Jr.	Dem.	1966–1970
A. Linwood Holton	Rep.	1970–1974
Mills E. Godwin, Jr.	Rep.	1974–1978
John Dalton	Rep.	1978–

Taylor, *Cavalier and Yankee* (1963); R. G. Osterweis, *Nationalism and Romanticism* (1967); H. Wish, *George Fitzhugh* (1962); F. L. Williams, *M. F. Maury* (1963); K. M. Bailor, *Virginia Magazine of History and Biography* (July, 1967), John Taylor and slavery; W. H. Daniel, *Virginia Magazine of History and Biography* (Jan., 1972), Baptists and race, and *Virginia Magazine of History and Biography* (April, 1975), Richmond College; P. Hickin, *Virginia Magazine of History and Biography* (April, 1967) and *Journal of Southern History* (May, 1971), antislavery; and R. P. Sutton, *Virginia Magazine of History and Biography* (Jan., 1972), sectionalism and social structure, and *Virginia Magazine of History and Biography* (Jan., 1968), aristocratic social values.

The Civil War years in Virginia are best treated in F. N. Boney, *J. Letcher* (1966), civil politics; and D. S. Freeman, *Lee* (1961), military matters. See also A. H. Bill, *Richmond, 1861–1865* (1946); A. J. Johnston, *Virginia Railroads* (1961); A. A. Fahrner, *Virginia Magazine of History and Biography* (Jan., 1966), Governor Smith; T. M. Priesser, *Virginia Magazine of History and Biography* (Jan., 1975), Negro soldiers; and P. Sowle, *Virginia Magazine of History and Biography* (Jan., 1972), secession.

For postwar years, best political surveys are A. W. Moger, *Bourbonism to Byrd* (1968); J. P. Maddex, *Virginia Conservatives* (1970); C. C. Pearson, *Readjuster Movement* (1969); J. T. Moore, *Virginia Debt Controversy* (1974); and R. R. Jones, *Journal of Southern History* (Aug., 1972), Redeemers and race. Other specialized studies include C. E. Wynes, *Race Relations, 1870–1902* (1961); A. A. Taylor, *Negro in Reconstruction* (1926); R. L. Morton, *Negro in Virginia Politics* (1919); N. M. Blake, *W. Mahone* (1935); W. H. Daniel, *Virginia Magazine of History and Biography* (July, 1968), Baptists and race; W. J. Fraser, *Virginia Magazine of History and Biography* (July, 1971), W. H. Ruffner; R. G. Lowe, *Virginia Magazine of History and Biography* (July, 1972), constitutional convention, 1867; J. P. Maddex, *Virginia Magazine of History and Biography* (Oct., 1975) and *Journal of Southern History* (Nov., 1974), E. A. Pollard; and J. T. Moore, *Journal of Southern History* (May, 1975), *Virginia Magazine of History and Biography* (Jan., 1970), Readjusters, and *Virginia Magazine of History and Biography* (July, 1975), dueling.

General political works for 1885–1920 are R. H. Pulley, *Progressive Impulse* (1968); W. D. Sheldon, *Populism* (1935); W. Larsen, *Montague* (1965); and J. T. Kirby, *W. Davis* (1968). More specific accounts include R. E. Martin, *Negro Disfranchisement* (1938); F. A. Magruder, *Recent Administration* (1912); R. C. McDaniel, *Constitutional Convention, 1901–1902* (1928); A. W. James, *Social Awakening* (1939); R. B. Doss, *Journal of Southern History* (Nov., 1954), 1904 election; R. E. Gay, *Virginia Magazine of History and Biography* (Oct., 1970), corporation commission; D. W. Grantham, *Virginia Magazine of History and Biography* (July, 1958), Wilson era; G. B. Hathorn, *Virginia Magazine of History and Biography* (July, 1958), southwest politics; R. A. Hohner, *Virginia Magazine of History and Biography* (Jan., 1966; Oct., 1967) and *Journal of Southern History* (Feb., 1968), prohibition; W. W. Holt, *Virginia Magazine of History and Biography* (Jan., 1975), Martin, and *Virginia Magazine of History and Biography* (Jan., 1968), constitutional convention; B. I. Kaufman, *Virginia Magazine of History and Biography* (Jan., 1969), Wilson years; A. W. Moger, *Journal of Southern History* (May, 1942), Martin machine, and *Journal of Southern History* (Aug., 1938), 1896 election; R. H. Pulley, *Virginia Magazine of History and Biography* (April, 1967), primary reform; P. Reeves, *Virginia Magazine of History and Biography* (July, 1960), Martin; R. M. Saunders, *Virginia Magazine of History and Biography* (Oct., 1971), populism; W. C. Woolridge, *Virginia Magazine of History and Biography* (Jan., 1967), 1896 election; and C. E. Wynes, *Virginia Magazine of History and Biography* (Oct., 1956), 1893 election.

There are no good political monographs for the 1920s and 1930s, but some good articles are H. C. Ferrell, *East Carolina Publications in History* (1965), on Byrd's early career; J. A. Fry, *Virginia Magazine of History and Biography* (July, 1974), Governor Peery; A. L. Hall, *Virginia Magazine of History and Biography* (July, 1967), 1929 election, and *Virginia Magazine of History and Biography* (July, 1974), 1938 Roosevelt purge; R. T. Hawkens, *Virginia Magazine of History and Biography* (July, 1974), Governor Byrd; R. L. Keinamann, *Virginia Social Science Journal* (Nov., 1973), WPA; M. S. Patterson, *Journal of Southern History* (Nov., 1973), Bishop Cannon; and B. Tarter, *Virginia Magazine of History and Biography* (July, 1974), Byrd's 1932 campaign.

J. H. Wilkinson, *Virginia Politics, 1945–1966* (1968), is an excellent survey of postwar politics. Specialized studes are B. Muse, *Massive Resistance* (1969); R. L. Gates, *Massive Resistance* (1964); B. Smith, *They Closed Their Schools* (1965); S. Cummings and T. Rubel, *Virginia Social Science Journal* (Nov., 1974), Wallace movement; P. R. Henriques, *Virginia Magazine of History and Biography* (July, 1974), 1949 election; and J. R. Sweeney, *Virginia Magazine of History and Biography* (July, 1974), 1948 election. Strangely, no biographies have yet appeared for Martin and Byrd.

Little has been published on nonpolitical aspects of twentieth-century Virginia. J. Gottmann has excellent demographic analysis, *Virginia in Our Century* (1969). See also V. Dabney, *Bishop Cannon* (1949); E. S. Godbold, *Ellen Glasgow* (1972); A. Buni, *Negro in Virginia Politics* (1967); R. D. Hughes and H. D. Leidheiser (eds.), *Virginia Human Resources* (1965); C. C. Pearson and J. E. Hendricks, *Liquor and Anti-Liquor* (1967); R. S. Smith, *Dan River Mills* (1960); W. Gee and W. H. Stauffer, *Living Standards in Virginia* (1929); G. T. Starnes and J. E. Hamm, *Labor Relations* (1934); W. R. Bowie, *Mary Cooke Branch-Mumford* (1942); L. Chambers and J. E. Shank, *Norfolk Newspapers* (1967); W. B. Gatewood, *Virginia Magazine of History and Biography* (April, 1972), Negro troops, 1898; A. Meier and E. Rudwick, *Virginia Magazine of History and Biography* (Oct., 1973), Jim Crow; J. R. Sherman, *Virginia Magazine of History and Biography* (Oct., 1973), black poetry; and L. M. Simms, *Virginia Magazine of History and Biography* (July, 1967), P. A. Bruce.

Theses and dissertations. Recent lists of master's theses and doctoral dissertations on Virginia topics are R. R. Duncan and D. M. Brown, *Virginia Magazine of History and Biography* (Jan., 1971); and R. R. Duncan et al., *Virginia Magazine of History and Biography* (July, 1975).

WILLIAM LARSEN
Radford College

VIRGINIA, UNIVERSITY OF (Charlottesville, 22903). Even while governor of the state during the American Revolution, THOMAS JEFFERSON had suggested establishment of a university as the capstone of a comprehensive system of graded public education. After years of delay by legislatures wary of the costs of his educational scheme, residents of Charlottesville enlisted his aid in building Central College, chartered in 1816. Construction of Central College's campus using Jefferson's designs and under his supervision began the following year. After the legislature in 1818 finally authorized creation of a university (but not the remainder of Jefferson's educational system), it was decided to locate the institution in Charlottesville and to make Central College the base of the new university. A merger of the two institutions' boards of visitors was achieved in 1819.

Jefferson designed not only the original campus and its buildings, but the school's curriculum as well. Unlike many nineteenth-century universities in America, Virginia included neither primary nor preparatory levels of instruction. Somewhat analagous to present-day forms of graduate instruction, the institution was made up of several separate schools: ancient languages, modern languages, mathematics, natural philosophy, natural history, anatomy, moral philosophy, and law. A student enrolled in the university could study in one or in all of these schools, but after graduating from any one school he became a graduate of the university. Although the board of visitors exercised broad authority over the schools and their programs, responsibility for management of the university's affairs was assigned to the faculty and its elected chairman.

The essential structure of Jefferson's university underwent few changes during most of the nineteenth century. Four additional schools, including one of history and literature, were added between 1856 and 1860; and, though the number of schools contracted during the Civil War, it was expanded again after the war. In 1895, however, the campus was gutted by a devastating fire, which forced a major restructuring of the entire institution. The architect Stanford White redesigned the campus. Although he retained and rebuilt the famous Rotunda and Jefferson's original pavilions, he substituted centrally located class buildings for Jefferson's sprawling campus of radiating pavilions. Paralleling this alteration in campus design, the curriculum gave greater emphasis to a common core of undergraduate courses; and in 1905, at the expressed wish of the faculty, administration of the university's affairs was turned over to a president, EDWIN A. ALDERMAN.

Presently the university has a coeducational enrollment of approximately 20,000 students enrolled in a variety of undergraduate and graduate levels of instruction. The library maintains several notable manuscript and archival collections, including the WILLIAM FAULKNER collection of letters, manuscripts, and first editions. The Clifton Waller Barrett Library of American Literature and the papers of such writers as PHILIP A. BRUCE,

JAMES B. CABELL, JOHN ESTEN COOKE, Stephen Crane, ELLEN GLASGOW, Lafcadio Hearn, and William Dean Howells are invaluable to students of southern literature. The library also houses the papers of numerous presidents (Jefferson, Madison, Monroe, Tyler, Wilson) and Virginia political leaders, as well as the records of many eighteenth- and nineteenth-century businesses, several railroads and churches, the city of Alexandria, Va. (1801–1884), and the University of Virginia and its faculty.

See T. P. Abernethy, *Historical Sketch of University of Virginia* (1948); W. B. O'Neal, *Pictorial History of University of Virginia* (1968); P. A. Bruce, *History of University of Virginia, 1819–1919* (1920); N. F. Cabell, *Early History of University of Virginia* (1956); D. M. Culbreth, *University of Virginia* (1908); and J. S. Patton, *Jefferson, Cabell, and University of Virginia* (1906).

VIRGINIA AND KENTUCKY RESOLUTIONS

were the principal Republican protests against the Federalist-inspired Alien and Sedition Acts of June and July, 1798. Republican leaders considered the laws an unconstitutional usurpation of power designed to eliminate criticism of the Adams administration. Because of the political composition of the federal judiciary, Vice-President THOMAS JEFFERSON, the head of the Republican party, sought support from the states. With the cooperation of JAMES MADISON, he secretly drafted a set of resolutions that were given to JOHN BRECKINRIDGE for presentation to the Kentucky legislature. Approved on November 13, 1798, the Kentucky Resolutions asserted that the Union was a compact of the states and that the federal government possessed only limited, delegated powers. Each state retained the right to judge for itself infractions of the compact and the proper means of redress. The resolutions requested the other states to assist in securing the repeal of the "unconstitutional and obnoxious" Alien and Sedition Acts. Madison prepared a similar though milder protest for Virginia. His propositions, passed by the legislature on December 21, maintained that, if the federal government exceeded its constitutional authority, the states could "interpose" to protect their powers and rights. The resolutions invited the other states to join with Virginia in declaring the Alien and Sedition Acts unconstitutional. Contrary to Republican expectations, the other states either condemned or ignored the Virginia and Kentucky Resolutions. In response, the Kentucky legislature adopted on November 14, 1799, additional resolutions, which contained the word *nullification*. The Virginia legislature reaffirmed its position by accepting Madison's "Report of

1800." The Virginia and Kentucky Resolutions were both effective party propaganda and an eloquent defense of civil liberties.

See A. Koch and H. Ammon, *William and Mary Quarterly* (July, 1948), best study; J. M. Smith, *William and Mary Quarterly* (April, 1970); P. Davidson, *American Historical Review* (Jan., 1931); E. Warfield, *Kentucky Resolutions of 1798* (1887); I. Brant, *Madison* (1950); and D. Malone, *Jefferson* (1962).

RAYMOND W. CHAMPAGNE, JR.
University of Scranton

VIRGINIA CAPES, BATTLE OF (Sept. 5, 1781),

doomed the British army of Charles Cornwallis at YORKTOWN. A French fleet, 28 ships under Admiral François de Grasse, arrived in the Chesapeake from the West Indies on August 30. A smaller French squadron carrying heavy siege guns had cleared Newport five days earlier. The British, aware of the danger to Cornwallis, dispatched a 19-ship fleet from New York commanded by Admiral Thomas Graves. On the morning of September 5, Graves, off the Virginia Capes, sighted the French scattered at anchor inside Hampton Roads. Graves could have destroyed the French ships as they straggled out a few at a time. He passed up this opportunity, however, and held back until the French were clear of the bay and formed in line. Only the van ships were closely engaged. The battle was a mere skirmish, but the British ships, driven off, returned to New York. Local naval superiority, which had been consistently British, now belonged to Grasse. Cornwallis was left to his fate.

See H. A. Larrabee, *Decision at Chesapeake* (1964), best; C. L. Lewis, *Admiral De Grasse* (1945); J. B. Scott, *De Grasse à Yorktown* (1931); and W. J. Morgan, *Iron Worker* (Spring, 1958).

WILLIAM JAMES MORGAN
U.S. Department of the Navy

VIRGINIA DECLARATION OF RIGHTS (1776)

ranks with the Declaration of Independence as a statement of the sentiments and aspirations of the revolutionary generation. GEORGE MASON's Virginia declaration set forth the guidelines for a "basis and foundation of government" and then carefully listed the rights of citizens. Human equality, the people as the source of power, and the right of revolution are proclaimed as universal principles, along with other Lockean concepts such as rights to life, liberty, and property. The contemporary and continuing impact of this document cannot be overstated: it is "among the world's most memorable triumphs in applied political theory."

See R. A. Rutland (ed.), *Papers of Mason* (1970); R. A. Rutland, *Bill of Rights* (1955); and E. Dumbauld, *Bill of Rights* (1957).

ALAN S. BROWN
Western Michigan University

VIRGINIA DYNASTY refers to the series of two-

term presidents from Virginia who served from 1801 to 1825: THOMAS JEFFERSON, JAMES MADISON, and JAMES MONROE. The continuation of the dynasty was aided by the emergence of the largely southern-based DEMOCRATIC-REPUBLICAN PARTY and the decline of the predominantly northern-oriented Federalists. Virginia cemented its hold on the presidency by forming an alliance of sorts with New York, whose Republicans generally supported the Virginians for the first office in return for the vice-presidency. Eventual anti-Virginia sentiment was fueled particularly by those New Yorkers, who had grown weary of receiving only second prize. The feeling against Virginia reached a crescendo in 1816, when a strong effort was made to prevent Monroe's nomination in the Republican congressional caucus.

See R. Walters, Jr., *Virginia Dynasty* (1965); G. Dangerfield, *Era of Good Feelings* (1952) and *Awakening of American Nationalism* (1965); M. Smelser, *Democratic Republic* (1968); N. E. Cunningham, Jr., *Jeffersonian Republicans in Power* (1963); and W. G. Morgan, *Virginia Magazine of History and Biography* (Oct., 1972).

WILLIAM G. MORGAN
Tulsa, Okla.

VIRGINIA EXILES, unrepresentative of Virginia

society, were drawn conspicuously from Scottish merchants, royal officials, and Anglican ministers, rather than from the planter classes, and had a TIDEWATER, even urban, tinge. Weak in numbers, Virginia Loyalists were nevertheless active at the beginning of the Revolution and had considerable strength in "transmontane Augusta" county. The few prominent exiles of established Virginia families included Thomas Corbin, Richard Corbin, Jr., Jacob Ellegood, John Grymes, and Attorney General John Randolph. Many of those fleeing to England relocated in Glasgow.

See I. Harrell, *Loyalism in Virginia* (1926); W. Brown, *King's Friends* (1965); and M. B. Norton, *British-Americans* (1972).

PAUL H. SMITH
Library of Congress

VIRGINIA GAZETTE is a journalistic tradition

that embraces several different newspapers. In

addition to those that have been published in Norfolk and Richmond, several Williamsburg newspapers have used this name, including three weeklies. The first weekly *Virginia Gazette* was founded in 1736 by William Parks, previously the founder and editor of the *Maryland Gazette*. This paper continued publication until 1780. A second Williamsburg paper with an extended publication was issued between 1853 and 1926. The present newspaper printed under this revered name began publication in 1930 in Williamsburg.

See composite collection (1736–80), on microfilm from Datamics, Inc., New York; and Williamsburg *Virginia Gazette* (1853–1926, 1930–), on microfilm from Bell & Howell.

VIRGINIA HISTORICAL SOCIETY (P. O. Box 7311, 428 North Blvd., Richmond, Va. 23221),

founded in 1831, has included among its members Henry Clay, Washington Irving, John Marshall, James Madison, John Tyler, and Robert E. Lee. Among the society's library holdings housed in the Battle Abbey are personal papers dating from the seventeenth century of early planters (Philip Ludwell, King Carter, and William Byrd), of royal governors (Alexander Spotswood, William Gooch, and Robert Dinwiddie), of patriots (Peyton Randolph and Arthur and Richard Henry Lee), of presidents (George Washington and Thomas Jefferson) and of Confederate heroes (Robert E. Lee, Stonewall Jackson, and J. E. B. Stuart). The society publishes book reviews and articles of a scholarly nature on Virginia history in the quarterly *Virginia Magazine of History and Biography* (pays a small honorarium for articles), which has a circulation of over 3,000. The society also publishes the semiannual *An Occasional Bulletin* and from time to time volumes of edited historical texts in a documents series.

See *Virginia Magazine of History and Biography* (July, 1931); and W. M. Whitehill, *Independent Historical Societies* (1962).

VIRGINIA MILITARY INSTITUTE (Lexington, Va. 24450) was established in an arsenal in 1839

as Virginia's first state-supported military college. STONEWALL JACKSON, professor of physics (1851–1861), commanded a company of the school's cadets present at the hanging of John Brown. In May, 1864, Colonel Scott Shipp, another VMI professor, led a battalion of 247 cadets at the battle of NEW MARKET. The institute was shelled by Union artillery, but managed to reopen in 1865. It remains a male military academy, partially supported by private donations, with an enrollment of approximately 1,000 cadets. Library collections include the VMI archives (1838–) and the Stonewall Jackson Collection.

See W. Couper, *100 Years at VMI* (4 vols.; 1939); and F. H. Smith, *VMI* (1912).

VIRGINIA POLYTECHNIC INSTITUTE AND STATE UNIVERSITY (Blacksburg, Va. 24061)

started as a land-grant college in 1872, but the first ten years of its existence were quite unsettled. Under the leadership of President John McBryde (1891–1907), however, the university gained stability and underwent considerable growth. Today it is a coeducational institution offering varied programs to approximately 14,000 enrolled students.

See J. P. Cochran, "Virginia Agricultural and Mechanical College, 1872–1919" (Ph.D. dissertation, University of Alabama, 1961).

VIRGINIA QUARTERLY REVIEW (1 W. Range, University of Virginia, Charlottesville, Va. 22903),

founded in 1925 and published under the auspices of the University of Virginia, has a circulation of 4,500. Although it has an interest in southern material and writers, it is not solely a regional publication. It publishes primarily articles on history, philosophy, politics, science, poetry, and literature of a widely general nature (for which it pays $10 per page) and book reviews. The *Review* offers annually the E. C. Balch prizes ranging from $250 to $1,000. Contributors have included Conrad Aiken, T. S. Eliot, Robert Frost, Ezra Pound, Carl Sandburg, Louis Untermeyer, Robert Penn Warren, Thomas Mann, H. L. Mencken, Charles A. Beard, and Jean-Paul Sartre.

VIRGINIA RESOLVES OF 1765 were adopted

in protest of the Stamp Act amid stormy debate on May 30. The text of the four recorded resolves merely repeated former assertions of Virginia's immunity from taxation without consent. The momentous impact of the resolves was due not to the formal words as adopted but to the legends that almost instantaneously surrounded them and their author PATRICK HENRY. In Virginia, word spread of Henry's impassioned "Caesar-Brutus" speech advocating more defiant resolutions that foreshadowed armed resistance unless tyranny were checked. This apparent example of bold intransigence helped precipitate a change throughout America from petitioning to resistance. Tradition credits Henry with a solo part of reckless defiance in this affair; more recent scholarship has discovered signs of diplomatic moderation on his part and of a significant contribution from his associates.

See R. R. Beeman, *Henry* (1974), concise reassessment, further references; E. S. and H. M. Morgan, *Stamp Act* (1963); and E. S. Morgan, *Prologue to Revolution* (1959), documents.

RHYS ISAAC
La Trobe University, Australia

VIRGINIA RESOLVES OF 1769. On May 16 the HOUSE OF BURGESSES unanimously adopted three resolutions asserting Virginian and American rights and a fourth seeking the king's intercession for the colonists. Parliament's imposition of taxes and its proposal to try suspected rebels in England were declared unconstitutional. In asserting the right to collaborate with other colonies, the resolves demonstrated solidarity with the unity proposals embodied in the Massachusetts Circular Letter (February 11, 1768). Governor Botetourt immediately dissolved the Virginia assembly, leaving members free to enter promptly into a nonimportation association (May 18)—an important step toward unit-ing the southern and northern colonies in formal acceptance of this particular resistance strategem. By early 1770 nearly all the colonies were committed to nonimportation, and four southern colonies (Delaware, Maryland, North Carolina, and South Carolina) and two northern (New Jersey and New York) had followed the burgesses in their May 16 resolves.

See W. J. Van Schreeven and R. L. Scribner, *Revolutionary Virginia* (1973), I; and M. Jensen, *Founding of Nation* (1968).

RHYS ISAAC
La Trobe University, Australia

VIRGINIA SUN was the principal journalistic advocate of the state's POPULIST PARTY during the 1890s. Its fortunes paralleled those of the Populists, the paper beginning publication in 1891 and ceasing in 1897.

See L. J. Cappon, *Virginia Newspapers, 1821–1935* (1936); and bound copies (1891–93), at Duke University Library.

VOTING RIGHTS ACT OF 1965. See CIVIL RIGHTS ACT OF 1965

W

WACO, TEX. (pop. 95,326), was originally a village of the Waco Indians called Los Brazos de Dios by the Spanish. Located on the Brazos River approximately 85 miles south of present-day Dallas, the village faced a river crossing used by Spanish soldiers and traders. In 1828 a band of Indians totally destroyed the village and made resettlement unsafe. In 1849, however, a new town was laid out by Jacob de Cordova, a general land agent. Set in the midst of newly cultivated agricultural lands, the city developed primarily as a market town for area cotton growers. A suspension bridge constructed in 1870 to span the Brazos and the advent of rail transportation in 1881 transformed the small market town into a major commercial and distributing center for this part of east-central Texas. Modern Waco continues to be a shipping point for area-grown cotton, grain, and dairy products. It also manufactures tents, glass, mobile homes, furniture, and aviation equipment and serves as the home of BAYLOR UNIVERSITY.

See R. Conger, *Brazos Empire* (1958) and *Highlights of Waco History* (1945); J. Sleeper, *Brief History of Mayors of Waco, 1849–1934* (1934) and *Waco and McLennan County, Texas* (1966); W. H. Curry, *History of Early Waco* (1968); L. J. Barnes, *Early Homes of Waco* (1970); and files of Waco *Tribune-Herald* (1911–).

WADDELL, JAMES IREDELL (1824–1886), born in North Carolina, entered the U.S. Navy as midshipman in 1841. He served 43 months at sea and participated in the Veracruz landing. In 1848 he graduated from the Naval Academy. Waddell tendered his resignation from the U.S. Navy in 1861 while a member of the East India Squadron. He was dismissed from the U.S. Navy in 1862 and joined the Confederate navy. After service at DREWRY'S BLUFF and Charleston, in 1864 he took command of the Confederate privateer *Shenandoah* in the Madeira Islands. Following the cruise of the *Shenandoah*, the only ship to carry the Confederate flag around the world, Waddell surrendered to the British at Liverpool in November, 1865. Eventually returning to the United States, he became a captain of the Pacific Mail Line, then spent his remaining years as commander of the Maryland State Fishery Force.

See manuscript records, U.S. Naval Academy; and Naval Archives, Washington, D.C.

WILLIAM M. DARDEN
U.S. Naval Academy

WAKEFIELD, in Westmoreland County, Va., is the birthplace of GEORGE WASHINGTON. John Washington, the immigrant, purchased land on Bridges Creek in 1664. Seventy-eight years later the property was acquired by George's father Augustine Washington and added to his Pope's Creek plantation, which later became known as Wakefield. The house in which George Washington was born was burned about 1779. The reconstructed memorial house, opened in 1931, is administered by the National Park Service. The exact location of the original house and its appearance have been matters of dispute among authorities.

See D. S. Freeman, *Washington* (1948), I; C. A. Hoppin, *Washington Ancestry* (1932); J. P. Hudson, *Washington Birthplace* (1956); and D. W. Eaton, *Westmoreland Atlas* (1942).

EDWARD M. RILEY
Colonial Williamsburg Foundation

WAKE FOREST UNIVERSITY (Winston-Salem, N.C. 27109) was established in 1834 as a Baptist school based upon a mixed curriculum of academics and manual labor. In 1839, however, the institution was rechartered as a liberal arts college and named Wake Forest College, after the town in which it was located. Traditionally a men's college, it became coeducational during World War II in an effort to boost enrollment. The school moved to a new campus in Winston-Salem in the 1950s and achieved university status in 1967. It presently has approximately 4,000 students enrolled, and its library is the respository of the North Carolina Baptist Historical Society Collection (1870–).

See G. W. Paschal, *History of Wake Forest College* (1935); and C. C. Carpenter, *Medicine at Wake Forest* (1971).

WALKER, DAVID (1785–1830). If any single event may be said to have triggered Nat TURNER'S

REBELLION, it was the publication in Boston of Walker's *Appeal to the Coloured Citizens of the World* (1829). Walker was born in Wilmington, N.C. His mother was a free woman, and his father was a slave. He left North Carolina while in his teens and finally settled in Boston, where he entered the clothing business. Walker was self-taught and read extensively the literature on human slavery, concentrating on the history of resistance to oppression. With the publication of the *Appeal*, a militant antislavery crusade was born. A group of Georgia men bound themselves together by an oath to kill the young author. They also offered a reward of $1,000 for his head and ten times as much for Walker alive. The *Appeal* became one of the most widely read and circulated books written by a black. Following its third edition in 1830, Walker was found dead near the doorway of his shop. The Negro Convention movement, which lasted through the Civil War, began that same year.

See H. Aptheker, *One Continual Cry* (1965), best; C. M. Wiltse (ed.), *David Walker's Appeal* (1965), very interpretative introduction; and H. H. Garnet, *Walker's Appeal* (1848).

GOSSIE H. HUDSON
Lincoln University

WALKER, JOHN WILLIAMS (1783–1823), was born in Amelia County, Va., the son of Jeremiah Walker, a small planter and Baptist preacher who moved to Petersburg, Ga., when John was an infant. After graduating from Princeton in 1810, he moved to Madison County in Mississippi Territory. Here he became a successful planter and, through contact with WILLIAM H. CRAWFORD, CHARLES TAIT, and other Georgians, played a critical role in creation of the Alabama Territory and state. He served as federal territorial judge (1818) and as president of the constitutional convention. When he was U.S. senator (1819–1822), his most significant contribution was adding an amendment to the land law of 1821 permitting purchasers an extension of credit to retain all or part of their lands.

See H. C. Bailey, *J. W. Walker* (1964); and F. L. Owsley, *Alabama Review* (April, 1956).

HUGH C. BAILEY
Francis Marion College

WALKER, LEROY POPE (1817–1884), was elected to the Alabama legislature in 1843 and served as Speaker from 1847 to 1850. He was an early supporter of STATES' RIGHTS and SECESSION. In February, 1861, Jefferson Davis appointed Walker secretary of war, a post for which he was completely unprepared, primarily to represent Alabama in the cabinet. His unfortunate prediction that the Confederate flag would soon fly over the Capitol in Washington and perhaps Boston's Faneuil Hall showed more enthusiasm than understanding of the problems he faced. His lack of administrative and military experience, and the resulting criticism of his handling of the office, caused Davis to accept his resignation in September, 1861. Commissioned a brigadier general, he served in Alabama and west Florida until 1863. Walker resigned his commission in a controversy with BRAXTON BRAGG and sat as presiding judge of a military court until 1865. In 1875 he was president of Alabama's second constitutional convention.

See W. C. Harris, *L. P. Walker* (1962), overlooks important manuscript material; J. B. Jones, *Rebel War Clerk's Diary* (1936); R. W. Patrick, *Jefferson Davis and His Cabinet* (1944); T. M. Owen, *History of Alabama* (1921), IV; and Walker Papers, Alabama Department of Archives and Duke University.

H. NICHOLAS HAMNER
Western Michigan University

WALKER, MARGARET (1915–), was born in Birmingham, Ala., daughter of a Methodist minister, and she saw much of the South as a schoolgirl. Her academic degrees, however, are northern: a B.A. from Northwestern and an M.A. as well as a Ph.D. from the University of Iowa. She has taught at Livingstone College in North Carolina, at West Virginia State College, and since 1949 at Jackson State College. National recognition came to her from the collection of her often Whitmanesque, yet profoundly racial, verse in *For My People* (1942), a winner in the Yale Series of Younger Poets. The currency of her sense of the black experience manifests itself in her *Prophets for a New Day* (1970). *Jubilee* (1966), her only novel, based largely on portraits of her own ancestors, is set in the South from the 1840s to the 1870s.

BLYDEN JACKSON
University of North Carolina, Chapel Hill

WALKER, ROBERT JOHN (1801–1869), was senator from Mississippi (1835–1845), secretary of treasury (1845–1849), and governor of Kansas Territory (1857). Pennsylvania born, he set up a legal practice in Natchez in 1826. Active in both local and state politics, in 1835 he was elected to the U.S. Senate as a Jacksonian and reelected in 1841. Involved in numerous get-rich land schemes, he pushed a preemption law and favored turning over public lands to the states. He advocated annexation of Texas and expansion into Cuba and Mexico.

At the 1844 Democratic convention in Baltimore, he first blocked Martin Van Buren's nomination and then maneuvered JAMES K. POLK's nomination. Appointed secretary of the treasury, he is generally rated among the top holders of the office. He sponsored the free-trade tariff of 1846, the independent treasury, the warehousing system, and the establishment of the Interior Department and financed the Mexican War with minimum economic disruption. He advocated the annexation of all Mexico. His support of James Buchanan in 1856 was rewarded with appointment as governor of the Kansas Territory in 1857. He pledged a free and fair vote on the territory's future. When Buchanan insisted on admitting Kansas under the questionable LECOMPTON CONSTITUTION, Walker resigned and opposed Buchanan's Kansas policy.

Basically antislavery, he supported the Union. In London he undermined Confederate credit. In 1867 he lobbied Alaska's purchase under circumstances that were corrupt. He unsuccessfully argued Georgia and Mississippi cases against Radical Reconstruction and then advised the South to accept its fate. A lifelong expansionist, at his death he was calling for the purchase of Greenland and the Virgin Islands.

See J. P. Shenton, *Robert J. Walker* (1961); and H. D. Jordan, *Mississippi Valley Historical Review* (Dec., 1932).

JAMES P. SHENTON
Columbia University

WALKER, THOMAS (1715–1794), Virginia surgeon and primary agent of the LOYAL COMPANY, led a 1750 expedition into Kentucky through the CUMBERLAND GAP he named. During the French and Indian War, he was a military contractor. As a member of the House of Burgesses, he attempted to legitimate land speculation schemes by encouraging Indian land cessions, serving, for example, as one of Virginia's representatives at the Treaty of Ft. Stanwix (1768). Walker was a business or political associate at various times of George Washington, Benjamin Franklin, Patrick Henry, and Thomas Jefferson, and his patriot sympathies were partly an extension of his opposition to British Indian policy. Before, during, and after the Revolution, Walker worked to extend Virginia's borders at the expense of Indians, European nations, and other states, doing what he could to make his own interests those of Virginia.

See, for manuscripts, British Public Records Office; Clements Library, University of Michigan; Historical So-

ciety of Pennsylvania; Historical Society of Wisconsin; Virginia State Library; and Library of Congress.

ROBERT W. VENABLES
State University of New York, Oswego

WALKER, WILLIAM (1824–1860), was the most successful filibuster of a filibustering age. Born in Nashville, he earned degrees from the University of Nashville and the University of Pennsylvania. European travels and study were followed by stints at medicine, law, and journalism (the New Orleans *Crescent*) and by migration to California (1850). In 1853–1854 he unsuccessfully invaded Lower California and Sonora. Subsequently, the democratic faction in a Nicaraguan civil war invited him to bring military "colonists," and Walker arrived with a small band of men in June, 1855. He rose to power in Nicaragua, capturing the presidency in a controlled election in June, 1856. The "Grey-Eyed Man of Destiny" attracted support throughout the United States in mid-1856 as a symbol of manifest destiny, though the PIERCE ADMINISTRATION turned against him.

Opposition from Franklin Pierce, Cornelius Vanderbilt, Great Britain, Nicaraguan elements, and other Central American countries led Walker to reinstitute slavery in Nicaragua in a desperate bid for southern aid. He was, nevertheless, expelled in 1857 and spent his remaining years organizing expeditions to regain the country. In 1858–1859 he was the focus of a major sectional debate in Congress after a U.S. naval commander stymied an attempt to reconquer Nicaragua. Walker was executed in Honduras in 1860. He had visions of a personal empire over all Central America, with Cuba as a possible appendage. His career left a legacy of anti-Americanism throughout Mexico and Central America.

See W. Walker, *War in Nicaragua* (1860), autobiographical account; W. O. Scroggs, *Filibusters and Financiers* (1916); R. E. May, *Southern Dream of Caribbean Empire* (1973); A. Z. Carr, *World and Walker* (1963), psychological interpretation; L. Greene, *Filibuster* (1937); E. S. Wallace, *Destiny and Glory* (1957); and Walker Papers, Tulane University.

ROBERT E. MAY
Purdue University

WALLACE, GEORGE CORLEY (1919–), began his political career as a progressive state senator supporting Governor JAMES E. FOLSOM. In 1958 Wallace ran for governor as a racial moderate, losing to a segregationist candidate. In 1962, however, Wallace—having gained a reputation as a state circuit judge for his truculence in dealing with the federal courts in civil rights matters—won the gubernatorial contest. His inaugural address was a fiery "Segregation now! Segregation tomorrow! Segregation forever!" In 1963 he sought to block the entry of black students to the University of Alabama. In 1965 he sought to prevent the voting rights march of MARTIN LUTHER KING, JR., from Selma to Montgomery. The resulting violence inflamed national opinion and in large measure contributed to the passage of the CIVIL RIGHTS ACT OF 1965.

Wallace entered several Democratic presidential primaries in 1964 and threatened to revive the Dixiecrat strategy of running as a third-party candidate. In 1966, prevented by law from running for a successive term, he ran his wife Lurleen for governor. With Wallace as her "No. 1 advisor," Mrs. Wallace served until her death in May, 1968. Meanwhile, Wallace was running as a third-party candidate for the presidency. With civil rights strife no longer limited to the South, Wallace's American party had significant appeal. Wallace received almost 10 million popular votes and 46 electoral votes.

Mrs. Wallace had been succeeded by Lieutenant Governor Albert P. Brewer. He ran ahead of Wallace in the first gubernatorial primary of 1970, demonstrating the moderate sentiment that was becoming apparent in southern states. In the runoff, however, Wallace narrowly defeated Brewer.

In 1972 Wallace again sought the Democratic nomination for the presidency, but, the day before sweeping victories in Maryland and Michigan, he was shot while campaigning in Maryland. Gravely wounded, paralyzed from the waist down, and uncertain of recovery, he ended his campaign.

In 1974 Wallace won an unprecedented third term as governor. By 1976 he had built a sophisticated and well-financed political organization for yet another campaign for the presidency. Initially, he seemed to be a formidable contender. But Wallace's losses in southern primaries led to the rapid collapse of his national campaign. Wallace withdrew and returned to Alabama to complete his term as governor.

As governor, Wallace pushed through a program of vastly increased expenditures for highways and for education. Under federal court order, the state also moved to improve the mental health and prison systems. But Wallace had irretrievably linked his political career to the issue of race. His efforts to embody white southern resistance to civil rights in the 1960s overshadowed his accomplishments as governor.

See M. Frady, *Wallace* (1968); N. V. Bartley and H. D. Graham, *Southern Politics and Second Reconstruction* (1975); and N. V. Bartley, *From Thurmond to Wallace* (1970).

WILLIAM D. BARNARD
Alabama Commission on Higher Education

WALLS, JOSIAH THOMAS (1842–1905), although accounts differ, was born in slavery in Winchester, Va., and became the most important black politician in Reconstruction Florida. A member of the state Republican executive committee between 1867 and 1879, he served as assemblyman, state senator, county commissioner, and mayor as well as brigadier general in the Florida militia. He ran for Congress on four occasions, winning three elections. He surrendered his seat following contested cases in 1870 and 1874, serving all but three months of his first term and one month of his third. Walls exemplifies more the itinerant carpetbagger than the illiterate freedman. Discharged from the Union army in Florida, he remained to become owner of 3,000 acres of prime Alachua County farmland, two newspapers, a law firm, and a sawmill. By 1883 he was reported to be the largest truck farmer in Florida. Financially ruined by the freeze of 1894, Walls spent the rest of his life supervising the state agricultural farm for Negroes in Tallahassee.

See C. H. Webber, *Eden of South* (1884); S. D. Smith, *Negro in Congress* (1940); J. M. Richardson, *Negro in Reconstruction Florida* (1965); and P. D. Klingman, *Josiah Walls* (1976) and *Negro History Bulletin* (May, 1974).

PETER D. KLINGMAN
Daytona Beach Community College

WARING, JULIUS WATIES (1880–1968), was a native of Charleston, S.C., who, as judge of the U.S. District Court for Eastern South Carolina (1942–1952), rendered a series of civil rights decisions favorable to blacks. His most historic decision came in 1947 (*Elmore* v. *Rice*), when he upheld the right of blacks to vote in the "private" Democratic primaries in South Carolina (WHITE PRIMARY). The ruling outraged the white citizens of the state and led to the demand by at least one South Carolina congressman that Waring be impeached. In a subsequent decision, Judge Waring voided an attempt by the South Carolina Democratic party to require a "test oath" of black voters. Later, in a 1951 minority opinion, he declared that "segregation is per se inequality." Upon his retirement in 1952, Judge Waring, long since ostracized by Charleston society, moved to New York City, where he became active in civil rights organizations, including the URBAN LEAGUE and AMERICAN CIVIL LIBERTIES UNION.

See V. O. Key, *Southern Politics* (1949); R. Bardolph, *Civil Rights Record* (1970); and New York *Times* (Jan. 12, 1968).

NATHANIEL F. MAGRUDER
Converse College

WARMOTH, HENRY CLAY (1842–1931), was born in Illinois but grew up in Missouri, where he was admitted to the bar at the age of nineteen. He commanded a Union regiment with the rank of lieutenant colonel and served with distinction. He became a member of General J. A. McClernand's staff, fell into disfavor with General U. S. Grant, and was assigned to General Nathaniel Banks's headquarters in New Orleans. Before the end of the Civil War he resigned his commission and became active in Republican politics. In 1868, at age twenty-six, he became Radical Republican governor of Louisiana, and during the next four years he grew wealthy. By 1872 his policies, though not his financial practices, had alienated a large part of the Radical Republican party, and Warmoth supported the Democratic candidate for governor in the election of that year. As a result he was impeached, though never convicted, and replaced by P. B. S. PINCHBACK until WILLIAM PITT KELLOGG could be inaugurated. Warmoth remained in Louisiana for the rest of his life, serving as a delegate to the state constitutional convention of 1879, as a candidate for governor in 1888, and as a delegate to the Republican National Convention in 1896.

See H. C. Warmoth, *War, Politics, and Reconstruction* (1930); Warmoth Papers, University of North Carolina Library and on microfilm; R. N. Current, *Three Carpetbag Governors* (1967); and J. G. Taylor, *Louisiana Reconstructed* (1975).

JOE GRAY TAYLOR
McNeese State University

WARM SPRINGS, GA., is 60 miles southwest of Atlanta. The water of its springs maintains a constant 88° F. and was used for its reputed therapeutic powers by area Indians. By 1832 the site was a popular summer resort for tidewater Georgians, but national renown did not come to the springs until the establishment here in 1927 of the Warm Springs Foundation for the treatment of poliomyelitis. The foundation was created by Franklin D. Roosevelt, who made a gift to it of his 2,600-acre farm and who died here at the "Little White House." Today the foundation provides therapy and rehabilitation to victims of a variety of crippling conditions.

WARNER, WILLARD (1826–1906), born in Granville, Ohio, and educated at Marietta College, had a varied career. He joined the California gold rush in 1849, returned with profits in 1852, then entered the wholesale grocery business in Cincinnati; in 1856 he became general manager of the Newark Machine Works (Ohio). In the Civil War he served with the 76th and 180th Ohio Volunteer Infantry and on General W. T. Sherman's staff during the ATLANTA CAMPAIGN, reaching the brevet rank of major general. He bought a cotton plantation near Prattville, Ala., in 1865. Before moving to Alabama in 1867, he served a two-year term in the Ohio state senate. Elected as a Radical to the Alabama legislature in 1868, he was quickly elected to represent that state in the U.S. Senate to fill a term expiring in 1871. Warner identified himself with the genuine interests of the South and bitterly resented being stigmatized as a CARPETBAGGER. He corresponded with the leading political figures of his day, joined the Liberal Republicans in 1872, and led the opposition to the carpetbagger element in the Republican party in Alabama. Warner pioneered in the development of the postwar iron industry in Cherokee County, Ala., where he built a blast furnace and operated it for the Tecumseh Iron Company from 1874 to 1890. After building two furnaces near Nashville, Warner moved to Chattanooga, where he engaged in various business enterprises and again entered politics as a Republican. He served one term (1897–1898) in the Tennessee house of representatives.

See J. B. Ryan, Jr., *Alabama Review* (Oct., 1971); W. M. Cash, "Alabama Republicans" (Ph.D. dissertation, University of Alabama, 1973); J. H. Woodward II, *Alabama Blast Furnaces* (1940); Warner Papers, Tennessee State Archives; and U.S. Senate, *Report of Committee upon Relations Between Labor and Capital* (1885), IV.

JAMES F. DOSTER
University of Alabama

WAR OF 1812. The southern states gave considerable support to the movement leading to the War of 1812. Southern DEMOCRATIC-REPUBLICANS supported their party leaders on this question as they had earlier supported their policy of economic coercion. Of the 79 votes cast in favor of war in the U.S. House of Representatives on June 4, 1812, the South provided 45, while casting only 12 of the 49 votes against the war. Southerners were determined to protect American national honor and to stop the widespread British interference with American exports. Many of the most prominent war hawks came from the southern states, including HENRY CLAY and RICHARD M.

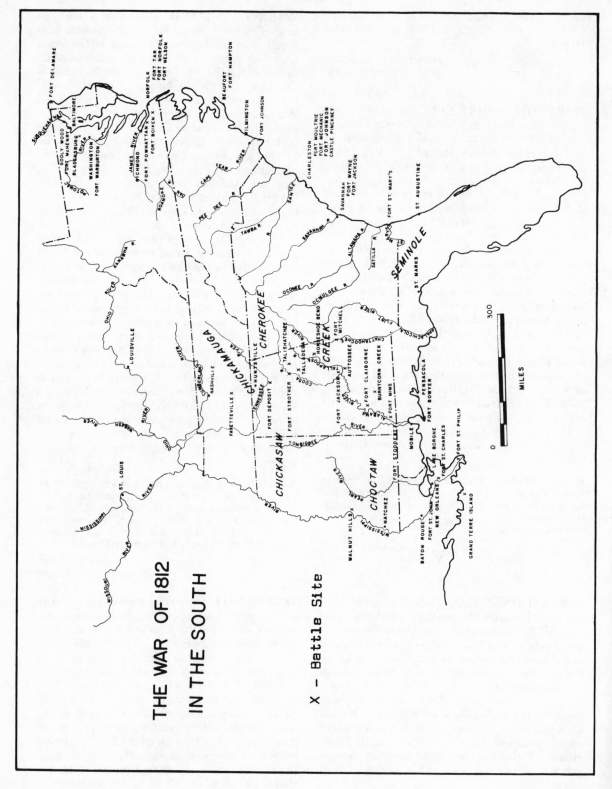

THE WAR OF 1812
IN THE SOUTH

X — Battle Site

JOHNSON of Kentucky, FELIX GRUNDY of Tennessee, and JOHN C. CALHOUN, LANGDON CHEVES, and WILLIAM LOWNDES of South Carolina.

During the actual conflict, though some southern troops participated in fighting along the Canadian frontier, the main military participation by the South resulted from British amphibious operations and from Indian hostilities. In the summer of 1813 part of the CREEK INDIAN Nation took the opportunity presented by the war to launch an attack in the Alabama region of Mississippi Territory. The Creek victory at Ft. Mims in August, 1813, led to American campaigns against the Creeks in the winter of 1813–1814 (CREEK WAR). The main part of the operations was carried out by Tennesseans under ANDREW JACKSON, and their campaign culminated in the defeat of the Creeks at Horseshoe Bend on March 17, 1814, and in extensive Creek land cessions at the Treaty of Ft. Jackson in August of that year.

Throughout the War of 1812, southern coasts were blockaded by the British fleet, leading to severe economic difficulties, and the coastline was also extremely vulnerable to British attacks. The Chesapeake Bay region bore the brunt of the British offensive. In the spring and summer of 1813, the Virginia and Maryland shores were hard hit by British raiding parties, but the most humiliating difficulties were experienced in the summer of 1814. After the defeat of Napoleon, Great Britain hoped to crush the United States by launching major attacks along Lake Champlain and at New Orleans. To facilitate the invasion from Canada, a diversionary operation was launched in Chesapeake Bay in August. American resistance was so weak that the British were able to rout the Americans at the battle of BLADENSBURG on August 24, march into Washington, and burn the public buildings. The British force then turned against Baltimore, but retired without launching a major attack.

Although the British attack along Lake Champlain in the north failed and a peace treaty was signed at Ghent on December 24, 1814, the British attack on New Orleans from Jamaica continued after the official end of hostilities. In an effort to secure the safety of the Gulf coast, American troops had already in 1813 occupied Spanish Mobile, and in 1814 Andrew Jackson acted with vigor to prevent a successful British invasion. The main British assault at NEW ORLEANS did not take place until January 8, 1815, and the battle resulted in a decisive victory for the American defenders. The victory enabled Jackson to achieve a striking national reputation and triggered a burst of national self-confidence in the postwar years.

See R. Horsman, *Causes of War of 1812* (1962) and *War of 1812* (1969); B. Perkins, *Prologue to War* (1961); J. K. Mahon, *War of 1812* (1972); W. Lord, *Dawn's Early Light* (1972); H. Adams, *History* (1889–91); W. S. Brown, *Amphibious Campaign* (1969); G. Byron, *War of 1812 on Chesapeake Bay* (1964); H. S. Halbert and T. H. Ball, *Creek War* (1895); E. Rowland, *Jackson's Campaign* (1926); and C. B. Brooks, *Siege of New Orleans* (1961).

REGINALD HORSMAN
University of Wisconsin, Milwaukee

WARREN, ROBERT PENN (1905–), a native of Guthrie, Ky., was educated at Vanderbilt (*summa cum laude*, 1925), California (M.A., 1927), Yale, and Oxford (as a Rhodes scholar; B.Litt., 1930). The youngest and most talented member of the FUGITIVE group, he is best known as a novelist, but his reputation will come to rest with equal force upon his poetry, criticism, and editing. *John Brown: The Making of a Martyr* (1929) was followed by collections of poetry in 1935, 1942, 1944, and regularly thereafter. *Promises* (1957) is perhaps his best book of verse. He has also written short stories, drama, history, textbooks, and children's books. Among his finest works are *Night Rider* (1939), *All the King's Men* (1946), *Brother to Dragons* (1953), and *The Legacy of the Civil War* (1961). He is the only writer to win Pulitzer prizes for both fiction and poetry. Warren has revolutionized the teaching of English with the textbooks written and edited with Cleanth Brooks, especially *Understanding Poetry* (1938). He had a distinguished career at Louisiana State University, Minnesota, and Yale. With Brooks he was the principal editor of the first series of the Baton Rouge SOUTHERN REVIEW. After WILLIAM FAULKNER and EUDORA WELTY, Warren is the best southern writer of this century, and after Faulkner he is the most influential.

See L. Casper, *Robert Penn Warren* (1960); J. L. Longley, Jr. (ed.), *Robert Penn Warren* (1965); and M. N. Huff, *Robert Penn Warren: Bibliography* (1968).

GEORGE CORE
Sewanee Review

WARRIOR'S PATH, also called Warrior's Trace or Great Warrior's Path, was a well-established Indian trail when explorers entered Kentucky and Tennessee. The path originated on the south bank of the Ohio River opposite the mouth of the Scioto River; led southwest to the Upper Blue Licks; crossed the Red River branch of the Kentucky River east of its mouth; turned southeast and entered the Appalachians from the west through Cumberland Gap; and led generally eastward along the Powell River valley across the Clinch and North Fork of the Holston rivers, where it branched at the Holston. The western branch went southwest across the Nolichucky and French Broad rivers to the Overhill CHEROKEE INDIAN villages on the Little Tennessee and Hiwassee rivers in southeastern Tennessee; the eastern branch led southeast to the CATAWBA villages just southwest of Charlotte, N.C. The Indians used the path to wage war on and maintain alliances with other tribes. Explorers and settlers often avoided the path because of the Indian danger, but THOMAS WALKER, John Finley, DANIEL BOONE, and others used it in the 1750s and 1760s, and Boone followed the path for about 50 miles when his expedition cut the WILDERNESS ROAD in 1775.

See manuscripts, Division of Archives and History, North Carolina Department of Cultural Resources.

BRIT ALLAN STOREY
President's Advisory Council on Historic Preservation

WASHINGTON, BOOKER TALIAFERRO

(1856–1915), educator and race leader, was born in slavery on the James Burroughs plantation near Hale's Ford, Va. His mother Jane was a cook on the plantation, and his father was an unidentified white man. After emancipation Washington moved to Malden, W.Va., where he worked briefly in the coal mines and salt furnaces until he became a house servant for General Lewis Ruffner. He acquired some rudimentary education at a black school in Malden and some training from Viola Ruffner, a former New England schoolteacher, and then entered Hampton Institute, where he studied from 1872 to 1875. At Hampton, Washington came under the influence of General SAMUEL CHAPMAN ARMSTRONG, the school's founder, whose missionary zeal and puritan work ethic profoundly affected Washington. Much of Washington's educational philosophy of industrial education derived from the Hampton experience.

In 1881 Washington founded TUSKEGEE INSTITUTE at Tuskegee, Ala., beginning with three small run-down buildings and a small appropriation from the state of Alabama. He built the school into a model of industrial education and a symbol of black self-help. While his fame as an educator was growing, his role as a race leader was launched with the effect of a single speech at the Atlanta Cotton States and International Exposition in 1895. The speech, often called the ATLANTA COMPROMISE, crystallized Washington's accommodationist racial ideology into the conventional wisdom on race relations of the period. Urging a gradualist approach to racial advancement based on economic striving and self-help, Washington accom-

modated to SEGREGATION but never advocated it as a positive good or the solution of racial strife. "In all things that are purely social," Washington said, "we can be as separate as the fingers, yet one as the hand in all things essential to mutual progress." For the remaining two decades of his life Washington never altered this public position.

Privately, however, he was more complex than his bland public platitudes suggest. From his power base at Tuskegee Institute, Washington developed an elaborate secret life, wherein he privately supported test cases to fight JIM CROW legislation. He was successful in controlling most of the black newspapers through moral suasion, bribery, and secret ownership. With the aid of his secretary and alter ego Emmett Jay Scott (1873–1957), Washington created a complex network of influence and power known as the Tuskegee machine. His secret manipulation of persons and events led his intimate friends to call him "the Wizard."

Washington's influence extended to the national level as he became an adviser to Theodore Roosevelt on political appointments. Few of his contemporaries realized the extent of Washington's patronage, which included not only black political appointments in the South but many white ones as well. Much of Washington's power among blacks came from his direct control of the National Negro Business League, which he founded in 1900, and indirectly through his influence on the leadership of the NATIONAL AFRO-AMERICAN COUNCIL, a civil rights group.

Until his death from overwork, Washington remained the most powerful black American of his time and perhaps the single most powerful black leader in American history. His influence declined, however, especially after 1909 as continuing deterioration of race relations in America led to growing disillusionment among many whites and blacks with Washington's conservative racial strategy. His personal leadership was eventually replaced by such organizations as the NATIONAL ASSOCIATION FOR THE ADVANCEMENT OF COLORED PEOPLE and the National URBAN LEAGUE, and his influence on national politics waned during the Taft administration and was virtually eliminated during Woodrow Wilson's first term.

See A. Meier, *Negro Thought* (1963), best treatment of Washington's racial ideology, and *Journal of Negro History* (Jan., 1953); L. Harlan, *Booker T. Washington* (1972), best biography, *Journal of Southern History* (Aug., 1971), and *American Historical Review* (Oct., 1970); and E. L. Thornbrough, *T. Thomas Fortune* (1972). See also L. Harlan *et al.*, *Booker T. Washington Papers* (1972–), projected 15-vol. series, 4 vols. published to date. Vol. I of the *Washington Papers* contains Washington's two autobiographies, *Story of My Life and Work* (1900) and *Up from Slavery* (1901), plus other autobiographical reminiscences. Two major collections of Washington source materials are in Library of Congress and Tuskegee Institute Archives.

RAYMOND W. SMOCK
University of Maryland

WASHINGTON, BUSHROD (1762–1829), George Washington's nephew, was born in Westmoreland County, Va. Educated at William and Mary, he later served at YORKTOWN. After studying law under the eminent Philadelphia lawyer James Wilson, Washington returned to Westmoreland to practice. A staunch Federalist, he served in both the Virginia house in 1787 and Virginia ratifying convention in 1788. A successful Richmond attorney, he was appointed in 1798 to the U.S. Supreme Court by John Adams and served for 31 years as an able, if not distinguished, associate justice. He wrote the opinions in many of the Marshall Court decisions, most notably the *Dartmouth College* case (1819), and was an authority in matters of maritime law. Washington also led the only successful revolt against the chief justice in *Ogden* v. *Saunders* (1827) and was a founder and first president of the AMERICAN COLONIZATION SOCIETY.

See George Washington Papers, Joseph Story Papers, and American Colonization Society Papers, Library of Congress; Marshall Papers, College of William and Mary; and Bushrod Washington Papers, University of Virginia.

JOSEPH W. COX
Towson State College

WASHINGTON, GEORGE (1732–1799), was born at the Pope's Creek home, in Westmoreland County, Va. Between 1748 and 1751 he was employed by Lord Fairfax in surveying certain properties of the latter beyond the Blue Ridge and at age nineteen was appointed an adjutant general of one of the military districts of Virginia. In 1754 Washington, as lieutenant colonel, fought against the French on the frontiers and afterward accompanied General Edward Braddock as aide-de-camp in an unsuccessful expedition against Ft. Duquesne. The next year he commanded a force that helped take Ft. Duquesne. On January 6, 1759, Washington married Martha Dandridge Custis, a young and wealthy widow, and settled down at Mount Vernon as a planter.

Industrious, acquisitive, and extremely ambitious, Washington soon became one of the largest and richest of Virginia tobacco planters. He was a shrewd land investor and, although he was essentially conservative, so far as scientific discovery was concerned, Washington was by no means old-fashioned. He was greatly concerned with the improvement of agriculture. As early as March of 1760 he designed a plow. Subsequently, he practiced crop rotation, was a marketer of his own brands of flour, diversified his products to raise enough food for his family and help, and, in the process, saved his land while many of his neighbors were losing theirs as a result of following a ruinous one-crop policy.

From 1759 to 1774 he served as a member of the Virginia House of Burgesses. In 1773 he became one of the delegates to the Williamsburg convention, which met to declare the right of the colonists to self-government, and in 1774 was one of the five representatives of Virginia to the General Congress in Philadelphia. On the breaking out of armed resistance to the home country, the CONTINENTAL CONGRESS conferred on him the rank of general and commander-in-chief of the Continental forces. In the face of well-appointed and successful British armies, he had to oppose them with untrained, raw American militia. Washington forced the British to evacuate Boston, but he was defeated in his first battle at Long Island. In 1776–1777 he gained the advantage at Trenton and Princeton, only to be badly defeated again at Brandywine and Germantown. The winning of the battle at Saratoga in October, 1777, by General Horatio Gates secured for the Americans French aid. After Congress approved the ARTICLES OF CONFEDERATION, the war moved south with varying success. Finally, combined French and American operations compelled the surrender of Lord Cornwallis to Washington at YORKTOWN in 1781, which closed the war.

In December, 1783, Washington resigned his commission and retired to private life, from which he was again called forth in 1787 to preside at the convention assembled in Philadelphia to draft the Constitution and place the federal government upon a firm or permanent basis. This accomplished, on February 4, 1789, General Washington was elected president of the newly constituted nation and in 1792 reelected. With no precedent to guide him, he had to depend mainly and often on his innate sense of propriety as to how a president of the United States should act. He was a true southern aristocrat—formal, aloof, and overly sensitive—but his poise, dedication, and strength of character set a worthy example for his successors. His administration can hardly be said to have been "prosouthern" since he more often supported the policies of Alexander Hamilton, which served the interests of the commercial classes more than those of the agriculturalists; but Washington was more concerned with creating a new nation that could hold up its head in the world than he was with furthering the economic aims of any particular section of the country. Washington declined a third nomination to the presidency in 1796, and after his "Farewell Address to the People of the United States," the "Father of His Country" sought his well-won repose, passing the last of his days at Mount Vernon, where he died as he had wished to live, a farmer. He was a giant. His selfless patriotism graced the republic while his gravity and lofty courtesy lent dignity to democratic forms. His self-mastery was a living lesson to democracy with its reputation for turbulence. No more fitting ideal of manhood could have been chosen for a new republic.

Although Washington was characteristically American in his resistance to oppression, his broad humanitarianism, his patriotism, and his ability to conduct a government for eight years in the midst of strife and passions, he was also a southerner for whom Virginia was a homeland. He called it affectionately "an infant woody country" that would in time be considered the "Garden of America," but full of "the Virginia hospitality which is the most agreeable entertainment we can give." A Polish visitor of 1798 to Mount Vernon reported: "I was considered in this home not as a stranger, but rather as a member of the family. They cared about everything which concerned myself." To another observer, Washington in 1798 "spoke . . . like one who looked upon society rather in the mass than in detail, and who regarded the happiness of America but as the first link in a series of universal victories." He was a Virginia gentleman who mirrored the first qualities of the southern aristocracy of his age.

See J. C. Fitzpatrick (ed.), *Writings of Washington* (39 vols.; 1931–44); T. J. Fleming, *First in Their Hearts* (1968); J. T. Flexner, *Washington in American Revolution* (1968) and *Washington and New Nation* (1970); P. L. Ford, *True George Washington* (1896); D. S. Freeman, *George Washington* (7 vols.; 1948–57); T. G. Frothingham, *Washington, Commander in Chief* (1930); and G. Washington, *Diaries, 1748–1799* (4 vols.; 1925) and *Washington: Correspondence avec d'Estaing* (1937).

GEORGE J. SVEJDA
U.S. Department of the Interior

WASHINGTON, MARTHA (1731–1802), was the daughter of John and Frances Jones Dandridge of New Kent County, Va. In 1749 she married Daniel Parke Custis, whose father originally opposed the alliance. Martha so charmed the elder Custis that he willed his estate to the newlyweds. Of their four children, two (Jackie and Patsy) survived. In 1757 Daniel Custis died, leaving Martha a wealthy widow. A second marriage to GEORGE WASHINGTON followed in 1759. Martha's wealth made him a substantial planter. Her two remaining children died, but she and Washington reared two grandchildren left by Martha's son. Preferring domesticity, Martha nevertheless accepted Washington's prominence gracefully. She lent support by her cheerful presence at camp during the Revolution and by her social skills during his presidency. Her joy in their retirement to Mount Vernon was cut short by Washington's death in 1799.

See A. H. Wharton, *Martha Washington* (1897), still best; E. Thane, *Washington's Lady* (1959); and G. Washington biographies, for reference to Martha and complete bibliographies.

JUDITH PULLEY
Appalachian State University

WASHINGTON, D.C., on the Maryland shore of the Potomac River within the ten-mile square ceded to the United States by Virginia and Maryland, became the national capital in 1800, when the government offices moved there from Philadelphia. Southerners had campaigned hard to persuade Congress to place the capital below the Mason-Dixon Line; it was chiefly Virginia statesmen who drafted the terms and secured the passage of the Residence Act in July, 1790. The act specified a site on the Potomac near the head of the tidewater, named Philadelphia the capital for the next ten years, and perpetuated Maryland and Virginia laws within the federal district for that interval, but it empowered the president to make virtually every other decision affecting the future capital.

Washington City was indeed GEORGE WASHINGTON's city. He chose the exact location for the federal district, engaged the French engineer Pierre Charles L'Enfant to prepare a detailed plan of the capital-to-be, and appointed commissioners to oversee building operations. He personally induced the proprietors of the land on which the city was to stand to accept an elaborate financial arrangement that ensured them profits but permitted federal agents to auction off enough high-priced lots to pay for erecting the Capitol, the "President's Palace," and the Treasury. Unhappily, sales of lots lagged so badly that serious financial difficulties and frustrating delays in the building program ensued. By November, 1800, when the Sixth Congress arrived, members found only 372 habitable dwellings, the principal public buildings usable but still unfinished, and large expanses of stump-speckled open space. The one distinctively southern touch on the landscape was the occasional cluster of small ramshackle shanties occupied by hired slaves or free Negroes.

That unpromising beginning notwithstanding, Washingtonians managed to keep the capital on the Potomac even after the British destroyed much of the city in 1814. The great commercial boom southerners had hoped for never materialized, largely because the upper Potomac Valley was infertile, thinly populated, and less accessible to the rich Ohio country than Virginians had supposed. Money invested in the development of the Chesapeake & Ohio Canal brought the city close to bankruptcy until, in 1836, the U.S. Treasury assumed Washington's debt. For years thereafter, local citizens' livelihoods rested mainly on services to the federal government.

Scarcely less important than economic aspirations in shaping the antebellum city's history was the general acceptance of Negro slavery. No president of the VIRGINIA DYNASTY approved of the South's "peculiar institution," but none requested Congress to ban it from the federal district. White residents avoided discussing the matter until northern visitors opened attacks on its persistence in the nation's capital. Although abolitionist sentiment strengthened in Washington in the 1820s, TURNER'S REBELLION and a race riot in the capital in 1835 alienated local white sympathies. City ordinances over the years gradually reduced the dreaded ingress of freedmen and imposed new limitations upon all black activities. Yet, in 1860, 9,200 free Negroes and 1,775 slaves were living peaceably among 50,100 whites, who usually recognized the intelligence and ambition of blacks who built Negro churches and supported Negro schools.

The Civil War brought social revolution in the 1860s: the emancipation of slaves, the city's acquisition of 24,000 former field hands as residents, the obligation a radical Congress foisted upon local taxpayers to supply free schooling for young Negroes, the founding of the biracial Howard University, and the enfranchisement for local elections of all adult males irrespective of race. More astonishing were the election of several Negro councilmen, the passage of two local acts prohibiting racial discrimination in restaurants and other public places, and the publication in 1870 of FREDERICK DOUGLASS' black weekly *New Era*. All these changes shucked off southern mores.

The new order placed some educated blacks in responsible federal jobs and produced an exceptionally good colored school system that maintained its quality into the 1930s. But by 1900 an increasingly rigid racism, heightened by residential segregation and the narrowing of the fields of Negro employment, replaced the nascent biracialism of 1870; two almost completely separate racial communities had emerged before 1916. The relatively slow pace of life, deemed to be a southern quality born of the climate, lingered until World War II, as did southern hospitality among the well-to-do as long as servants were plentiful. But the industrializing and unionizing urban South of the mid–twentieth century had lost most of its regional features; and Washington, 54 percent black in 1960, had become a world capital rather than a southern city.

See C. M. Green, *Washington* (2 vols.; 1962, 1963) and *Secret City* (1967); L. W. Brown, *Free Negroes in D.C., 1790–1846* (1972); E. S. Grier, *Washington's Changing Population* (1961); *Records of Columbia Historical Society of Washington* (1891–1900, 1957–74); and collections at Library of Congress, National Archives, and Howard University Library

CONSTANCE MCLAUGHLIN GREEN
Washington, D.C.

WASHINGTON, D.C., CAPTURE OF (1814).

On August 20, 1814, 4,500 British regulars, marines, and seamen were disembarked near Benedict, Md., from Admiral Alexander Cockrane's ships. Led by General Robert Ross and Admiral George Cockburn, their object was the temporary capture of Washington, D.C. Then, on August 24 at BLADENSBURG—only seven miles from the capital—about 6,000 American militiamen and 1,000 regulars finally tried to offer resistance. Some troops stood their ground, but most militia retreated from the British attack. Pushing on, the British entered Washington that night and proceeded to fire the Capitol, the president's house, public buildings, and public stores. (Despite charges of barbarism, the destruction was not unusual for the time, and Americans had committed similar depredations at York, Upper Canada.) On the night of August 25, they left the city. The administration was shaken. President JAMES MADISON, who had fled the city with other government officials, was embarrassed; Secretary of War John Armstrong was forced to resign; JAMES MONROE took over his office; General William Winder, in command of American forces, was exculpated; and the militia was condemned. The British, to their later regret, were encouraged to attack Baltimore.

See H. Adams, *History of U.S.* (1891), VIII; G. R. Gleig, *Narrative of Campaigns of British Army* (1821); *American State Papers: Military Affairs* (1832), I; J. Armstrong, *Notices* (1840); and H. Ammon, *Monroe* (1971).

JEFFREY KIMBALL
Miami University

WASHINGTON, D.C., GLOBE was founded in 1830 by AMOS KENDALL and Francis P. Blair (BLAIR FAMILY) to serve as the official press organ of the Andrew Jackson administration. The *U.S. Telegraph* had been established earlier to perform a similar function, but DUFF GREEN, its editor, had sided with JOHN C. CALHOUN and the paper lost both the political confidence and printing patronage of the president. With Blair serving both as editor and as a member of Jackson's Kitchen Cabinet, the *Globe's* ties with both the Jackson and VAN BUREN ADMINISTRATIONS were extremely close. After losing its preferred status and all presidential printing contracts during the Harrison and Tyler administrations, the paper was reorganized in 1845 and renamed the Washington *Union* (1845–1859). Thomas Ritchie left his Richmond *Enquirer* to edit this official press organ of the JAMES K. POLK administration. On the eve of the secession crisis, this partisanly Democratic paper adopted yet another name, the Washington *Constitution* (1859–1861), but it ceased publication at the outbreak of the Civil War.

See complete bound copies of *Globe* at Library of Congress, State University of Iowa, University of Chicago, American Antiquities Society, and Historical Society of Pennsylvania.

WASHINGTON, D.C., NATIONAL ERA was published between 1847 and 1860 as an antislavery weekly. Edited by Dr. Gamaliel Bailey, the publication printed among other materials a serialized version of UNCLE TOM'S CABIN.

See complete bound files at Library of Congress, Boston Public Library, Harvard University Library, Waltham, Mass., Public Library, and Cornell University Library; and microfilm from Bell & Howell (1847–60).

WASHINGTON, D.C., NATIONAL INTELLIGENCER, one of the nation's most revered and respected antebellum newspapers, was founded in 1800 and served as the official organ for the Jefferson, Madison, and Monroe administrations. Its first owner and editor, Samuel H. Smith, inaugurated the paper at the expressed wish of Thomas Jefferson. Shunning the personal abuse that characterized much of the period's journalism, Smith strove for at least a degree of objectivity and revealed his biases more through what he failed to print than through what he wrote. When Smith retired from journalism in 1810, the paper became the property of Joseph Gales, Jr. (1786–1860). Gales's editorials encouraged the drift toward war with Great Britain in 1812, regularly promoted aspects of Henry Clay's American System, and loyally defended the policies of his presidential patrons.

The resumption of patisan politics in the 1820s cut the *Intelligencer* adrift both politically and financially. Its endorsement of the candidacy of William H. Crawford in the ELECTION OF 1824 lost for the paper the patronage of the John Quincy Adams administration, and its support of the policies of the Adams administration in turn cost the paper the printing business of the Andrew Jackson administration. Drifting gradually into the WHIG PARTY camp of Henry Clay, the *Intelligencer* denounced the nullification movement, supported a protective tariff, opposed the annexation of Texas, and served as perhaps the best-known journalistic critic of James K. Polk's "offensive war" against Mexico (MEXICAN WAR). Meanwhile Gales and his paper flourished financially as recipients of congressional patronage. In 1825 it began publication of the *Register of Debates in Congress* (4 vols.; 1825–1837), a forerunner of the *Congressional Record*. In 1832 Congress awarded Gales the contract for publication of the *American State Papers* (21 vols.; 1832–1834), and in 1849 it assigned to the *National Intelligencer* the contract for compiling and printing the *Annals of Congress* (42 vols.; 1849–1856).

Although the *Intelligencer* returned to presidential favor during the administration of Millard Fillmore, Gales and his paper clearly were unable to come to grips with the politics of the 1850s. The demise of the Whig party left it without a political affiliation, and Gales never could bring himself to support the Democrats, the Know-Nothings, or the Republicans. Editorials repeatedly called for a return to the basic principal of the MISSOURI COMPROMISE and the COMPROMISE OF 1850. In the ELECTION OF 1860 it endorsed John Bell in the hope that the election would be thrown to the House of Representatives. After resigning itself to the need forcibly to defend the Union, the paper gradually warmed to Abraham Lincoln prior to breaking with his administration over the Emancipation Proclamation.

See W. E. Ames, *History of National Intelligencer* (1971); H. Mahan, "J. Gales and War of 1812" (Ph.D. dissertation, Columbia, 1957); bound copies at Library of Congress (1821–69), Massachusetts Historical Society (1821–61), Western Reserve Historical Society, Cleveland (1821–69), University of Kansas Library (1821–68), and Virginia State Library, Richmond (1821–59); and microfilm from Readex Microprint, New York (1800–20).

WASHINGTON, D.C., POST was founded in 1877 as a Democratic daily and continued its affiliation with that political party until breaking with the Woodrow Wilson administration over the League of Nations. It was edited as a Republican newspaper during the 1920s. Ordered into receivership in 1933, the paper was reorganized, and it has since developed into one of the nation's most respected daily newspapers. Although it is politically independent, it endorsed Republican presidential condidates in the elections of 1948, 1952, and 1956 and Democratic presidential candidates in 1960, 1964, and 1968. The *Post* made as well as reported history during the administration of Richard Nixon with its investigations of the Watergate scandals. One indication of the financial and popular success of the *Post* in recent years was its acquisition in 1954 of the Washington *Times-Herald*. The *Times* (1895–1939) and the *Herald* (1906–1939) merged toward the end of the Great Depression. As the *Times-Herald* (1939–1954) and as separate earlier papers, they had been among the *Post*'s principal competitors for advertising revenues and for readers. The *Post* presently enjoys a daily circulation in excess of 540,000 copies.

See bound files of *Post* at Library of Congress (1877–), Wisconsin Historical Society (1892–), and University of Michigan Library (1878–1913, 1926–); microfilm of *Post* from Bell & Howell (1904–32, 1934–38, 1969–); and microfilm of *Times* (1895–1939), *Herald* (1906–39), and *Times-Herald* (1939–54) from Library of Congress.

WASHINGTON, D.C., STAR-NEWS is an independent daily with a circulation of approximately 420,000 copies. It was formed in 1972 by the merger of the *Evening Star* (1852–1972), long the paper of the Noyes family, and the *Daily News* (1921–1972).

See bound copies of *Star* at Library of Congress (1853–1972), American Antiquities Society (1852–1972), and New York State Library (1914–72); and bound copies of *News* at Library of Congress (1921–72), Duke University Library (1921–72), and State College of Washington, Pullman (1921–72).

WASHINGTON, D.C., U.S. TELEGRAPH began publication in 1826 as an Andrew Jackson administration organ and in competition with the Washington *Intelligencer*. DUFF GREEN, its editor, sided with the John C. Calhoun faction of Jackson's cabinet, however, and the paper lost its presidential patronage to Francis P. Blair's Washington *Globe*. The *Telegraph* ceased publication in 1837.

See bound copies at Library of Congress, University of Georgia Library, Alabama Department of Archives, and Clements Library, University of Michigan.

WASHINGTON AND LEE UNIVERSITY (Lexington, Va. 24450) was founded in 1749 by Scotch-Irish pioneers and named Augusta Academy. Becoming a degree-granting institution in 1782, it was renamed Liberty Hall Academy. GEORGE WASHINGTON made a $50,000 gift to the school causing it to be renamed Washington Academy in 1798 and reorganized as Washington College 15 years later. Upon the end of the Civil War, ROBERT E. LEE became the school's president (1865–1870), and the college added his name upon his death. Traditionally a male, liberal arts college, Washington and Lee has an enrollment of approximately 1,600 students. The library houses the papers of William Fleming, a member of the Continental Congress; Zachariah Johnston, Revolutionary War officer; Robert E. Lee; Governor James H. Price; the Glasgow family; the Reid-White family; and the Tucker family.

See O. Crenshaw, *General Lee's College* (1969); S. S. Brett, Jr., "Henry Ruffner" (Ph.D. dissertation, University of Arizona, 1962); and W. D. Hoyt, *Virginia Historical Magazine* (1940–41).

WASHINGTON-ON-THE-BRAZOS. The history of this town in south-central Texas began in 1821, when land grants offered in the area by STEPHEN F. AUSTIN were accepted by several American colonists. The following year a ferry began operating across the Brazos River near the site. In 1835 it became a Mexican municipality with Joshua Hadley as alcalde. But in 1836, when a convention met here to declare Texas independent of Mexico and to designate Washington-on-the-Brazos the temporary capital of the new Republic of Texas, it was still a backwoods village of about 100 people with tree stumps standing in its only road. It was even difficult for visitors to find a place to stay or anything to eat. Later, in 1842, after repeated moving of the capital, Washington was again the seat of government, and in 1845 President ANSON JONES called a special session of the Texas congress to meet here to accept an American offer of annexation to the United States and to approve a proclamation calling for the election of delegates to a convention to draft a constitution for the future state of Texas. The capital was soon moved again to Austin, however, and later, when the railroads bypassed the little town, its fate was sealed. It remains to this day only a minor farming community of a few hundred people.

See R. N. Richardson, *Texas* (1943); S. V. Connor, *Texas* (1971); W. P. Webb (ed.), *Handbook of Texas* (1952), II; L. W. Newton and H. P. Gambrell, *Social and Political*

History of Texas (1932); G. P. Garrison, *Texas* (1903); and S. Siegel, *Political History of Texas Republic* (1956).

WASHINGTON PEACE CONFERENCE (1861),

called at the suggestion of the general assembly of Virginia, met at Willard's Hotel, February 4–27, 1861. It was a last-ditch effort by moderate leaders of both North and South, particularly the border states, to find a workable compromise to the issue of slavery in the territories, in the states, and in the District of Columbia. Twenty-one states responded by sending 132 representatives. Ominously, the seven states that were about to form the Confederacy sent no representatives, and none were sent by the states of Arkansas, California, Michigan, Minnesota, Oregon, or Wisconsin. Moreover, some representatives came for the express purpose of preventing an acceptable compromise.

Leadership in the conference was exercised by seasoned moderate politicians led by former president JOHN TYLER. JAMES GUTHRIE of Kentucky was chairman of the Committee on Resolutions. The majority report was adopted on February 27 in the form of seven articles for a proposed thirteenth amendment to the U.S. Constitution. Modeled closely on the compromise resolutions previously submitted to the Senate by JOHN J. CRITTENDEN of Kentucky, the new articles called for recognition of the MISSOURI COMPROMISE line; enforcement of the FUGITIVE SLAVE LAW; prohibition of the importation of slaves; protection for slavery in the District of Columbia; compensation for owners of fugitives lost through violence or intimidation; no changes in specified articles of the Constitution without the consent of all the states; and no acquiring of territory without the consent of four-fifths of the Senate. With only five days of its session remaining, the U.S. Senate rejected the proposed amendment by 28 to seven, and the House of Representatives refused to receive the proposal.

See L. E. Chittenden, *Report of Debates and Proceedings of Convention at Washington* (1864), most complete; and R. G. Gunderson, *Old Gentlemen's Convention* (1961), best modern account.

DAVID S. SPARKS
University of Maryland, College Park

WATAUGA ASSOCIATION.

When the Treaty of Lochaber in 1770 left their settlements in territory reserved to the CHEROKEE, settlers on the Watauga River defied an order to leave their homes, and James Robertson and John Bean, two of their leaders, negotiated a long-term lease of their lands from the Cherokee. An assembly of arms-bearing men in May, 1772, formed the Watauga Association. The original document has been lost, but a description exists in a petition to the government of North Carolina in 1776. The Watauga government, which adopted the laws of Virginia, consisted of a council of five members, with both legislative and judicial powers, a sheriff, and a clerk. Its duties included maintenance of order, enlistment of a militia, recording of deeds, issuance of marriage licenses, and trial of offenders against the law. The association was not a great landmark in democracy, but rather a practical expedient to serve only until a permanent government was established with the means of protecting land titles.

See A. V. Goodpasture, *American Historical Magazine* (April, 1898); P. M. Hamer, *Tennessee* (4 vols.; 1933); T. Roosevelt, *Winning of West* (4 vols.; 1904); T. P. Abernethy, *From Frontier to Plantation in Tennessee* (1932, 1967); and S. J. Folmsbee, R. E. Corlew, and E. L. Mitchell, *Tennessee* (1969).

STEPHEN W. BROWN
West Virginia Institute of Technology

WATIE, STAND (1806–1871),

a leader of the CHEROKEE INDIANS, was a member of the tribal faction that advocated removal from Georgia to the West. Watie signed the removal Treaty of New Echota in 1837. During the Civil War, the nontreaty Cherokee adhered to the Union and Watie's followers to the Confederacy. Watie led a brigade in numerous engagements in Indian Territory and at the battle of PEA RIDGE in Arkansas. In 1864 he captured a large federal supply train at Cabin Creek in the Cherokee Nation. The only Indian to rise to the rank of brigadier general in the Civil War, Watie was also the last Confederate general officer to surrender.

See K. A. Franks, "Stand Watie" (Ph.D. dissertation, Oklahoma State University, 1973); E. E. Dale and G. Litton (eds.), *Cherokee Cavaliers* (1939); *Official Records, Armies*, Ser. 1, Vols. III, VIII, XIII, XXII, XXIV, XLI, XLVIII; and papers in Western History Collections, University of Oklahoma and Northeastern Oklahoma State University libraries.

LEROY H. FISCHER
Oklahoma State University

WATSON, THOMAS EDWARD (1856–1922),

was born in Thomson, Ga., to affluent, slave-owning ancestors. His lifelong goals were to revitalize postbellum agriculture, to glorify the farmer and the agrarian ideals of Thomas Jefferson, and to stop the influx of industrial values into the South. He won a seat in 1890 in Congress, where his greatest legislative success was rural free delivery of mail. Impressed with the political progress of FARMERS' ALLIANCE candidates in Georgia in the 1890s, Watson appealed to the self-interest of both whites and blacks, but in doing so he violated strong southern racial traditions. The Democrats, angered and frightened by Watson's apostasy, defeated him in fraudulent congressional races in 1892 and 1894. Embittered by this experience, Watson worked largely outside the party after that. In 1896 Watson was nominated by the POPULIST PARTY to be William Jennings Bryan's running mate. The Democrats also nominated Bryan, but they refused to accept Watson on their ticket. In 1904 and in 1908 Watson was the unsuccessful presidential candidate of the Populists. By 1910, completely frustrated by a lifetime of losing to a hostile industrial economy, Watson became less the objective writer and relied more on sensationalism and scandal to sell his publications. He found a large audience of frustrated people to cater to. He launched an anti-Catholic crusade, inflamed the Leo FRANK CASE into an anti-Jewish crusade, and urged the revival of the KU KLUX KLAN. He opposed the Espionage Act of World War I and wartime conscription so vehemently that the postmaster general denied the U.S. mails to Watson's publications. Watson served in the U.S. Senate until he died a few days after attending the last session of the Sixty-seventh Congress.

See T. E. Watson Papers, University of North Carolina Library; autobiography, *Thomas E. Watson* (1908); A. M. Arnett, *Populist Georgia* (1922); D. W. Grantham, *Hoke Smith* (1958); C. V. Woodward, *Tom Watson* (1938); D. M. Robinson, *Journal of Southern History* (Aug., 1937); T. Carageorge, "Hoke Smith and Tom Watson" (Ph.D. dissertation, University of Georgia, 1963); and S. L. Gray, "T. E. Watson" (M.A. thesis, Emory, 1931).

TED CARAGEORGE
Pensacola Junior College

WATTERSON, HENRY (1840–1921). For a full 50 years, from 1868, when he and fellow newspaperman Walter Haldeman founded the LOUISVILLE COURIER-JOURNAL, until his retirement in 1918, Watterson made his name and the newspaper synonymous with the call for reconciliation between the North and the South. Although born in Tennessee, Watterson grew up in Washington, D.C., hotel rooms, in railroad trains, and on the floor of the U.S. House of Representatives. There, still a child, he watched and listened as his father and the leaders of the era debated the great constitutional issues of the tumultuous 1850s. From this experience he received his real education—he had but four years of formal schooling—and

emerged a confirmed nationalist. Like his father he opposed secession, yet, because he loved the South, he served in the Confederate army and edited the Chattanooga *Rebel*. Immediately following the war, Watterson began championing reconciliation. He was a "reconstructed rebel" who extolled an economic and political alliance between the South and the conservative, capitalistic North.

He was a scrappy fighter who believed wholeheartedly in himself and his causes. He held fast to a handful of uncomplicated ideas. Ever youthful, Watterson played his public role as the feisty Kentuckian to the point of self-dramatization, even though he came in later life to regret his public image as "Marse Henry." He was confidante of presidents, and his life was one long success story. His flamboyant style betrayed him only occasionally, as when he spoke out intemperately for Samuel Tilden during the hotly disputed ELECTION OF 1876 and when he vitriolically condemned the free-silver enthusiasm of the Democratic party in the 1890s. He capped a long and active life by winning the Pulitzer Prize for his ardent prowar editorials in 1917.

See H. Watterson, *"Marse Henry"* (2 vols.; 1919); and J. F. Wall, *Henry Watterson* (1956).

BRUCE CLAYTON
Allegheny College

WATTS, THOMAS HILL (1819–1892), was a prominent Whig in the Alabama legislature during the 1840s and a persistent Unionist spokesman in the 1850s. He campaigned for the CONSTITUTIONAL UNION PARTY in 1860; however, as a STATES' RIGHTS advocate, he voted for secession in the Alabama state convention of 1861. He organized and then led the 17th Alabama Regiment at Pensacola and CORINTH until President Jefferson Davis named him attorney general in April, 1862. Elected governor in the fall of 1863, Watts tried to marshal Alabama's deteriorating resources in the last months of the war while opposing significant military policies of the Richmond government. Pardoned by Andrew Johnson in 1868, he was active in the Democratic party until his death.

See J. H. Lynch, "T. H. Watts" (M.A. thesis, Auburn, 1957); Watts Papers, Alabama Archives; W. L. Fleming, *Civil War Alabama* (1905); and L. Dorman, *Party Politics* (1935).

J. KENT FOLMAR
California State College, California, Pa.

WAXHAWS, BATTLE OF (May 29, 1780). After the British captured Charleston, S.C., during the

American Revolutionary War, Colonel Abraham Buford and over 350 Virginia Continentals, having failed to reinforce the city, withdrew northward. The British dispatched Lieutenant Colonel Banastre Tarleton's corps of 270 dragoons and cavalrymen in pursuit. On May 29, 1780, Tarleton intercepted Buford near the Waxhaws settlement and quickly routed the patriots. Ignoring the Americans' request for quarter, Tarleton's men savagely killed or wounded almost 300 of them. "Tarleton's quarter" thereafter became a synonym for the butchery of surrendered troops. Anti-British southern sentiment intensified, but South Carolina now lay under British control.

See E. McCrady, *South Carolina in Revolution* (1902), best synthesis; R. D. Bass, *Green Dragoon* (1957); N. and S. Hilborn, *Battleground of Freedom* (1970); B. Tarleton, *Campaigns* (1787); and W. D. James, *Marion* (1821).

JOHN C. CAVANAGH
Suffolk University

WAYNE, JAMES MOORE (1790–1867)

WAYNE, JAMES MOORE (1790–1867), a staunch Jacksonian, was the only Georgia congressman (1829–1835) to support the FORCE BILL against NULLIFICATION, and he backed Andrew Jackson during the bank war; he was rewarded with the "southern" vacancy on the U.S. Supreme Court in 1835. He became one of the "most high-toned Federalists on the Bench." He held (passenger cases, 1849) that the commerce power was "exclusively vested in Congress." On corporations he supported Roger B. Taney in the *Charles River Bridge* case (1837) and *Bank of Augusta* v. *Earle* (1839), believing that corporations should be considered citizens. Wayne felt that slavery enjoyed full constitutional protection, concurred with Justice Joseph Story in *Prigg* v. *Pennsylvania* (1842) that federal power over fugitive slaves was exclusive, and pushed the Court to use the DRED SCOTT case (1857) to settle the territorial question. He denied the right of secession and remained on the Court when war came. He upheld Abraham Lincoln's war measures in the prize cases (1863); but he opposed a punitive policy in the South and in 1867 (CUMMINGS V. MISSOURI and *ex parte Garland*) voted to strike down test oaths.

See A. A. Lawrence, *J. M. Wayne* (1943); F. O. Gatell, in L. Friedman and F. L. Israel, *Justices of U.S. Supreme Court* (1969), I; C. B. Swisher, *Taney Period* (1974); and V. C. Hopkins, S.J., *Dred Scott's Case* (1951).

JAMES L. CROUTHAMEL
Hobart and William Smith Colleges

WAYNESBORO, BATTLE OF

WAYNESBORO, BATTLE OF (March 2, 1865), was the last significant engagement in the Shenandoah Valley during the Civil War. Late in February, 1865, Philip H. Sheridan was ordered to march his 10,000-man force from the valley into the Piedmont, where he was to disrupt Confederate supply routes and capture Lynchburg if possible. Only a 1,200-man Confederate unit commanded by JUBAL A. EARLY stood in his way. As Sheridan moved up the valley, Early retired to Waynesboro. On the morning of March 2, 5,000 cavalrymen under George A. Custer completely routed the ragged Confederate line. Except for Early and his immediate staff, the entire Confederate force was captured. The victory placed the Shenandoah Valley under Union control for the first time and gave Sheridan access to Rockfish Gap, the crossing of the Blue Ridge most convenient to fulfilling his orders.

See *Official Records, Armies*, Ser. 1, Vol. XLVI; *Official Atlas of Civil War*; V. D. Golladay, *Virginia Cavalcade* (Summer, 1970); J. A. Early, *Memoir of Last Year* (1867); and P. H. Sheridan, *Memoirs* (1888).

V. DENNIS GOLLADAY
Pensacola Junior College

WAYNESBORO, VA.

WAYNESBORO, VA. (pop. 16,707), in the Shenandoah Valley on the South River, was first settled in 1700. Developing as a market town and a supply center for westward-bound travelers, it was incorporated as a town in 1797. On March 2, 1865, on a ridge just west of town, General George A. Custer met and destroyed the remnants of General Jubal Early's force during Philip Sheridan's Shenandoah campaign (WAYNESBORO, BATTLE OF). Modern Waynesboro manufactures electronic equipment, furniture, and both natural and synthetic textiles. It is the southern terminus of the Skyline Drive.

See files of Waynesboro *News-Virginian* (1892–), on microfilm.

WEAVER, ROBERT CLIFTON

WEAVER, ROBERT CLIFTON (1907–), was born in Washington, D.C. Attending Harvard on a scholarship, he graduated with honors in 1929 with a degree in economics and received a master's degree (1931) and a Ph.D. degree (1934) from the same institution. Weaver entered government service as a race relations officer in the Department of Interior during the New Deal. He was one of the outstanding members of the "black cabinet" during the 1930s. In 1937 he was appointed special assistant to the administrator of the U.S. Housing Authority. From 1940 to 1944, he held administrative positions dealing with employment and training of minorities, serving successively with the National Defense Advisory Commission, Office of Production Management, War Production Board, and War Manpower Commission.

After leaving federal service, he served briefly with the United Nations Relief and Rehabilitation Administration and then as executive director of the Mayor's Committee on Race Relations in Chicago. Between 1947 and 1951 he taught at Northwestern University, Columbia University Teachers College, and New York University School of Education. In 1955 New York Governor Averell Harriman appointed him state rent commissioner. During the 1960 presidential campaign, Weaver served as adviser on civil rights to John F. Kennedy, who later appointed him administrator of the Housing and Home Finance Agency, where he served until 1965. In 1966 President Lyndon B. Johnson nominated him to the newly created cabinet post of secretary of housing and urban development, making Weaver the first black to serve in the cabinet. Leaving HUD on January 1, 1969, on the eve of the return of the Republicans to power, he became president of Bernard M. Baruch College of the City University of New York and remained until 1971. He then became a Distinguished Professor at Hunter College.

See R. C. Weaver, *Negro Labor* (1946), *Negro Ghetto* (1948), *Urban Complex* (1964), and *Dilemmas of Urban America* (1965).

AL-TONY GILMORE
University of Maryland

WEEMS, MASON LOCKE (1759–1825), known as Parson Weems, was born in Anne Arundel County, Md. Ordained in 1784 in England, he served parishes in Maryland to 1792. For 31 years he traveled the southern seaboard as agent for a publisher. His own first volumes were the *Philanthropist* (1799) and *True Patriot* (1802), which espoused a universalist doctrine. *The Life and Memorable Actions of George Washington* (1800), containing the cherry tree story, and the *Life of General Francis Marion* (1809) were fictional biographies. Other moral models he found in *Benjamin Franklin* (1815) and *William Penn* (1822). He is associated with mythmaking and most notably for his life of Washington.

See P. L. Ford and E. E. F. Skeel, *M. L. Weems* (1928–29), supersedes other accounts; C. and E. B. Hurd (eds.), *Treasury of Great American Letters* (1961); W. Meads, *Churches, Ministers, Families of Virginia* (1859); L. C. Wroth, *Parson Weems* (1911); L. A. Everett, *American Heritage* (Dec., 1958); D. D. Van Tassel, *American Heritage* (Feb., 1962); S. G. Fisher, *American Philosophical Society Proceedings* (1912); and B. Henderson, *Publishers Weekly* (Aug. 13, 1973).

MILTON E. FLOWER
Dickinson College

WELDON RAILROAD, BATTLE OF (August 18–21, 1864), was a series of engagements and skirmishes stemming from U. S. Grant's effort to extend his lines west of Petersburg, Va., and to sever R. E. Lee's communications with North Carolina. On August 18, G. K. Warren's V Corps seized a section of the Weldon Railroad near Globe Tavern, then marched on Petersburg three miles to the north. Although the Confederate divisions of HENRY HETH and WILLIAM MAHONE and A. P. HILL's corps halted the drive and scored several tactical victories in the succeeding three days, they failed to break the Union stranglehold on the railroad. In these actions the federals took 4,500 casualties; the Confederates lost 1,600.

See D. S. Freeman, *Lee's Lieutenants* (1946), III, authoritative; J. L. Morrison, Jr. (ed.), *Memoirs of Henry Heth* (1974); S. Foote, *Civil War* (1974), III; and *Official Records, Armies*, Ser. 1, Vol. XLII.

JAMES L. MORRISON, JR.
York College of Pennsylvania

WELFARE, PUBLIC, in the South began when the colonial governments of Virginia and North and South Carolina empowered the church wardens to assess rates for the relief of the poor. The Virginia statute of 1642–1643 was based upon the Elizabethan poor laws, which insisted on local responsibility in the field of public welfare and restriction of aid to those having legal residence in the county or town. Dependent or abandoned children who were not indentured were placed in public or private orphanages. By the end of the eighteenth century, three of the four institutions for dependent children were found in the South. In 1727 the Ursuline Convent of New Orleans was founded as an educational institution; however, by 1734 the Ursulines were ministering to the sick, rearing orphans, and educating black, white, and Indian girls. In 1738 the Bethesda Orphanage was established in Savannah, Ga., by the English minister George Whitefield. The first separate public orphanage was founded in 1790 in Charleston, S.C.

With the separation of church and state after the American Revolution, local civil officials such as overseers of the poor, wardens of the poor, or the Georgia county courts were made responsible for the administration of poor relief. Gradually, almshouses and poor farms became the main resource for not only the impoverished but the insane, the mentally retarded, dependent children, and the disabled. Oftentimes the poor were housed in the local jails along with prostitutes and hardened criminals.

During the 1830s reformers such as Dorothea L. Dix and Samuel G. Howe called for the removal of the physically and mentally handicapped from the almshouses and their placement into institutions designed especially for that particular handicap (MENTAL HEALTH). In 1822 the general assembly of Kentucky provided for the education of the deaf and mute. Beginning in 1834 Georgia and South Carolina, neither having institutions for the education of the deaf, provided funds to send young people to the Kentucky institutions. Other states followed suit for both the deaf and the blind until such time as an institution was established in each state.

The Civil War and its aftermath brought on new and unprecedented relief problems as the Confederate states tried to provide for the dependents of Confederate soldiers. By 1863 it was necessary for the states to come to the aid of local governments with funds for local relief. Furthermore, veterans of the defeated Confederate forces and their dependents were not eligible for federal pensions. Thus this burden had to be borne by the former Confederate states. In 1865 an act of Congress created the FREEDMEN'S BUREAU, which fed and clothed thousands, both black and white, provided medical attention for many, and gave some care and protection for orphaned and abandoned children.

Throughout the nineteenth century, reformers in the North and South rejected in principle public outdoor relief. Typical is the refusal of the committee on public and charitable institutions of the 1870 Louisiana legislature to recommend a bill for outdoor relief because it would "encourage laziness and make the State of Louisiana a receptacle for the poor of other states." Nevertheless, the Louisiana general assembly of 1880 passed a bill urging the parishes (counties) to support all infirm, sick, and disabled paupers residing within their limits except within towns and cities, which were responsible for their own needy.

By the onset of World War I, six of the 11 former Confederate states had boards of charities (later "boards of public welfare") to supervise state agencies. Another welfare reform, mothers' pensions, came as a result of the White House Conference of 1909. This form of outdoor relief was based upon the principle that children should not be taken away from their homes by reason of poverty alone. Illinois enacted a mothers' pension law

in 1911, and by 1934 all of the southern states except Georgia, South Carolina, and the District of Columbia had enacted legislation of this type.

The South was just as unprepared as the other parts of the country when faced with the massive relief problems of the GREAT DEPRESSION, for it too tried to depend solely upon local and private relief. In 1932 New Orleans ranked at the bottom of a list of 31 metropolitan areas in the amount it spent for relief; and, unlike cities such as Atlanta, Memphis, Birmingham, and Charleston, it provided no public relief for black indigents. Moreover, federal relief programs of the NEW DEAL ran afoul of local southern laws and customs. Local authorities administered these programs and allocated funds strictly in accordance with southern law and custom. For example, in allotting Civilian Work Administration jobs, employment offices throughout the South ignored the black skilled worker and, if he worked, he worked at unskilled rates. In Jacksonville, Fla., black families on relief outnumbered white families three to one, but the money was divided according to proportions of the total city population. Thus 15,000 black families received 45 percent of the funds, and 5,000 white families got 55 percent.

After the passage of the Social Security Act of 1935, the federal-state system of giving assistance was changed from an emergency measure to a program of providing grants to states for welfare purposes. This new program called for a central agency of public welfare, which administered assistance given to the aged, dependent children, the needy blind, and the disabled. As each state's program evolved, it became a hodgepodge of separate programs with each state determining its own level of payments, each defining eligibility, each determining whether to accept all of the federal funds available for assistance. For example, in 1968 an average ADC family in Connecticut received $259.95 while a family in Mississippi received $34.15. As of January, 1969, 12 of the 17 states whose expenditures from state and local funds for ADC were insufficient to allow their receipt of the maximum of federal funds were in the South.

Despite large-scale formal and informal exclusion of black and illegitimate children in the South and elsewhere, it was not until Louisiana implemented its "suitable home" policy and simultaneously rejected about 6,000 families and 22,500 children that national and international attention was directed to the discriminatory impact of this type of provision, for blacks represented 90 percent among those affected by this policy. Thus Louisiana had joined six other states—Arkansas,

Georgia, Mississippi, Texas, Virginia, and Michigan, all southern except one—that had made assistance available only to children living with parents in a "suitable home." In 1961 the commissioner of Social Security ruled that no state could impose an eligibility condition that would deny assistance on the basis of home conditions. In 1964 the welfare department of Louisiana began to deny payments to a mother living with a man other than her husband. Nearly 16,000 children, 63 percent black, were barred from ADC payments. The District of Columbia and 19 states, including eight southern ones, had similar "man-in-the-house" regulations. A federal court ruled that Alabama's "substitute father" regulation was unconstitutional. In 1968 the U.S. Supreme Court upheld the lower court.

The welfare rolls continue to mount. Instead of freeing the poor from poverty, today's approach to welfare is actually locking millions into poverty, sometimes for two or three generations. Many relief programs tend to perpetuate the conditions they are designed to alleviate by the built-in incentive against earning income or against family unity. Other criticisms of the present system consist of the indignity of the "means" test and the variations among the states in payments. Finally, three-fifths of the poor at any one time are outside the federal system subsisting in ways we do not understand.

See L. H. Fishel, Jr., *Wisconsin Magazine of History* (Winter, 1964–65); G. R. Bentley, *History of Freedmen's Bureau* (1955); R. E. Moran, *Louisiana History* (Fall, 1973); and E. Wisner, *Social Welfare in South* (1970).

ROBERT E. MORAN, SR.
University of Nebraska, Omaha

WELLS-BARNETT, IDA BELL (1862–1931), was born a slave in Holly Springs, Miss., where she grew up attending Rust College. She became a schoolteacher after an 1878 yellow fever epidemic orphaned her. In the early 1880s she moved to Memphis and soon sued the Chesapeake & Ohio Railroad over its attempt to segregate her into a second-class car. She won $500 in damages, only to see the case reversed by the Tennessee supreme court in 1887. She began writing about her case and soon became editor and part owner of the Memphis *Free Speech*, where her angry editorials led the school board to dismiss her in 1891. A particularly strong editorial against the LYNCHING of three young black businessmen led a mob to wreck her press and try to lynch her the following year. She expanded the editorial for a New York *Age* story and later published a pamphlet on the affair. She became a traveling antilynching speaker in England and the northeastern states, moving to Chicago in 1893, where she damned the segregated World's Columbian Exposition. She married Ferdinand L. Barnett of Chicago, the founder of the weekly *Conservator*, in 1895. Mrs. Wells-Barnett was an active clubwoman and vocal opponent of BOOKER T. WASHINGTON's accommodationist program.

See A. M. Duster (ed.), *Crusade for Justice* (1970), autobiography; and I. B. Wells-Barnett, *On Lynchings* (1969).

CARL S. MATTHEWS
U.S. Department of State

WELTY, EUDORA (1909–), widely honored and praised for her short stories, has lived all her life in Jackson, though her parents were not native Mississippians and she attended college partly in the North. She worked briefly in publicity, until encouragement from the *Southern Review* confirmed her penchant for writing. She worked almost exclusively with Mississippi locales in her earliest stories, *A Curtain of Green* (1941); *The Robber Bridegroom* (1942), a Mississippi adaptation of certain of Grimm's fairy tales, and *The Wide Net* (1943) deal imaginatively with contemporary as well as with such historical and legendary figures of the Natchez Trace as the Harpe brothers, Mike Fink, John J. Audubon, Lorenzo Dow, James Murrell, and Aaron Burr. *Delta Wedding* (1946) and *Losing Battles* (1970) are novels of family life, the latter a raucously funny and deeply moving treatment of the reunion of a poor hill-country farming clan. Her rich sense of southern folk humor pervades *The Ponder Heart* (1954). *The Golden Apples* (1949), one of her finest achievements, successfully combines hints of Celtic folklore and Greek mythology with a closely observed chronicle of a rural small town. The stories of *The Bride of the Innisfallen* (1955) and the novel *The Optimist's Daughter* (1972) range somewhat farther afield. Welty's intense devotion to "place," to the details of Mississippi speech and folkways over a broad social spread, is an essential springboard for her profound artistic exploration of problems of human identity, love, and separateness. Critics have observed a steady broadening of tolerance and sympathy as she has matured; her rich sense of the comic has evolved from acid satire to an ingratiatingly humane understanding. Welty has always considered technical experimentation to be a necessary risk inherent in the act of writing; some of her more recent stories have perplexed casual readers by their indirectness and lack of obvious "point." But her highly sophisticated art richly repays study.

See R. M. V. Kieft, *Eudora Welty* (1962); and A. Appel, Jr., *A Season of Dreams* (1965), both with good bibliographies.

FRANK BALDANZA
Bowling Green State University

WERTENBAKER, THOMAS JEFFERSON (1879–1966), one of the outstanding scholars of early American history, was born in Charlottesville and received his B.A., A.M. (1902), and Ph.D. (1910) degrees from the University of Virginia. He taught briefly at Texas A.&M. and Virginia before he was called to Princeton University in 1910. He remained a member of that faculty until retirement in 1947. In 1947 he was elected president of the American Historical Association. He wrote more than a dozen books and published numerous articles. His books on colonial Virginia—*Patrician and Plebeian* (1910), *Virginia Under the Stuarts* (1914), and *Planters of Colonial Virginia* (1922)—challenged many accepted ideas about the early history of the colony. In his three-volumed *The Old South: The Founding of American Civilization* (1942), he studied the social and cultural history of the colonial period, which gave impetus toward modifying the traditional emphasis on political and economic history. His scholarship attracted many graduate students to his graduate seminars, and his ready wit made him a popular undergraduate teacher. Wertenbaker was indeed a worthy representative of his beloved golden age of Virginia.

See *Directory of American Scholars* (1963), I; and *American Historical Review* (July, 1966).

G. MELVIN HERNDON
University of Georgia

WESLEY, CHARLES HARRIS (1891–), born in Louisville, Ky., pursued a career in education and as a historian. He received the A.B. degree from Fisk (1911), A.M. degree from Yale (1913), and Ph.D. degree from Harvard (1925). He studied at Guild Internationale (Paris, 1915–1916). Wesley rose from instructor to professor and head of the department of history at Howard University (1921–1942). He also served there as dean of the college of arts and sciences (1937–1938) and dean of the graduate school (1938–1942) and was named president of Wilberforce University in Ohio (1942–1947). With the division of Wilberforce and the formation of the state college of mechanical arts and industrial education, Wesley was named president, and in 1951 he had the privilege of naming Central State College, where he served during the formative years to 1965, when he was made president emeritus. A member of numerous educational and historical organizations, he is author of seven books, coauthor of three, and author of more than 100 articles in history and education. From 1952 to 1972 he served as president and director of the Association for the Study of Negro Life and History and in 1976 as executive director of the Afro-American Bicentennial Historical and Cultural Museum in Philadelphia.

See Central State College programs; and *Negro History Bulletin* (Feb., 1963).

J. REUBEN SHEELER
Texas Southern University

WESLEY, JOHN (1703–1791) and **CHARLES** (1707–1788), were reared by Samuel Wesley, an Anglican minister of unbending High Church convictions. Trained at Oxford and ordained, they then searched for some extraordinary challenge. That they found in appointments as missionaries to the Indians in England's newest colony, Georgia. The Georgia mission was a disaster. Charles gave up after six months. When John Wesley found the local tribes unresponsive, he directed his efforts toward the white settlers of Savannah. But his rigid notions of churchmanship enveloped him in controversy, repelled rather than attracted the frontier settlers, and led him to flee in 1737 rather than face civil prosecution stemming from a bungled courtship and the unrealistic demands he had placed upon his parishioners. Shaken by their failures and challenged by their contacts with MORAVIANS in Georgia and in London, the Wesleys discovered through conversion the means for grounding belief and conduct in vital personal experience. In 1739 John began preaching to unchurched thousands throughout the British Isles and founded the powerful METHODIST religious movement. Through the 1750s Charles was his closest associate on the preaching circuits and through prolific hymn writing lent his distinctive feeling to the spiritual life of the English-speaking world.

See N. Curnock (ed.), *Journal of John Wesley* (8 vols.; 1909–16); J. Telford (ed.), *Letters of John Wesley* (8 vols.; 1931); R. McPherson (ed.), *Journal of Earl of Egmont* (1962); B. Semmel, *Methodist Revolution* (1973); and F. Gill, *Charles Wesley* (1964).

JOHN K. NELSON
University of North Carolina, Chapel Hill

WESTERN KENTUCKY UNIVERSITY (Bowling Green, 42101) was opened in 1906 as Western State Normal School. It absorbed Potter College in 1909, Ogden College in 1928 (now the department of science), and Bowling Green Business School in 1963. This coeducational school has been a university since 1966, and it currently has an enrollment of 13,000 students. The library maintains collections of manuscripts relating to Kentucky history, notably the records of the SHAKER settlement at South Union (1807–1922), the Lewis-Starling Papers (late eighteenth-century Virginia and Kentucky), and the manuscripts of several Kentucky authors.

See J. P. Cornette, "History of Western Kentucky State College" (Ph.D. dissertation, George Peabody, 1939); W. F. O'Donnell, *Filson Club History Quarterly* (April, 1956); F. P. Moore, *Filson Club History Quarterly* (Oct., 1954); and J. B. Johnson and L. H. Harrison, *Register of Kentucky Historical Society* (1970), Ogden College.

WEST FLORIDA CONTROVERSY. Spain acquired West Florida during the American Revolution. It extended from the Apalachicola River to the Mississippi and from the 31°31' line to the Gulf of Mexico after 1795 (Treaty of San Lorenzo). Spain kept West Florida when it retroceded Louisiana to France in 1800; but the United States claimed West Florida as part of the LOUISIANA PURCHASE after 1803, thus initiating the controversy. Thomas Jefferson's efforts to obtain it, however, failed. In 1810, as revolution swept Spanish America, the mostly American settlers of the Baton Rouge district of West Florida also revolted. On October 27, 1810, President James Madison claimed American jurisdiction from the Mississippi to the Perdido River, but occupied lands only to the Pearl River. Congress declared the region between the Pearl and Perdido rivers annexed on May 14, 1812, and the occupation took place in 1813–1814. The legality of the American occupation was resolved in the Adams-Onís Treaty (1819), in which Spain ceded East Florida and acknowledged West Florida as American.

See I. J. Cox, *West Florida Controversy* (1918); and P. C. Brooks, *Mississippi Valley Historical Review* (June, 1940).

GILBERT C. DIN
Ft. Lewis College

WEST PALM BEACH, FLA. (pop. 57,375), approximately 70 miles north of Miami, was first settled by a homesteader, Irving R. Henry, in 1880. Thirteen years later, HENRY FLAGLER purchased Henry's farm and developed it as the commercial district of Palm Beach, an island resort. West Palm Beach is now a popular winter resort in its own right, a port of entry, and a producer of data-processing systems, prefabricated homes, and aircraft engines and parts.

See files of Palm Beach *Post* (1908–) and *Times* (1922–).

WESTPORT, BATTLE OF (October 22–23, 1864). The Confederacy's final attempt to secure the allegiance of Missouri failed when STERLING PRICE's cavalry raid into the state was checked near Westport, two miles south of Kansas City. Moving westward from St. Louis, Price's 12,000 horsemen were caught on October 19, 1864, between converging federal columns under Samuel R. Curtis and Alfred Pleasonton. Price attacked westward and on October 22 drove Curtis' men from their positions on the Big Blue River, east-southeast of Westport, back on the town. The lines stiffened, and Price positioned John S. Marmaduke's division at the Big Blue to block Pleasonton's cavalrymen pursuing from the east. Outnumbered three to one, Price attacked early on the twenty-third, planning first to defeat Curtis' predominantly militia army, then to turn back and attack Pleasonton. The western militia rallied, then counterattacked, while Pleasonton charged across the Big Blue and scattered Marmaduke's division. Joseph O. Shelby's desperate rearguard action allowed Price to extricate his army and retreat southward to Texas.

See *Official Records, Armies*, Ser. 1, Vol. XLI; P. B. Jenkins, *Battle of Westport* (1906); H. N. Monett, *Missouri Historical Society Bulletin* (Oct., 1951); and J. Monaghan, *Civil War on Western Border* (1955).

LOUIS D. F. FRASCHÉ
U.S. Army Command and General Staff College

WEST VIRGINIA is in many respects unique among the southern states. It is the only one lying entirely within the Appalachian Highlands and the geocultural APPALACHIA of the twentieth century, and its history has been more typical of that of the mountainous subregion of which it is a part than of the South as a whole. With a mean elevation of more than 1,500 feet, the highest of any state east of the Mississippi River, West Virginia is appropriately known as the Mountain State. It is the youngest of the southern states and the only one born of the tragedy of the Civil War.

Geography and physiography. Despite its predominantly mountainous terrain and its small size—its area of 24,181 square miles ranks it forty-first among the states—West Virginia is a land of contrasts. It spans two great physical subdivisions of the Appalachian Highlands. The valley and ridge province, a bold escarpment known as the Allegheny Front, includes the part of the state lying within the Potomac River watershed. Most of the remainder, comprising about 20,000 square miles, is a part of the Allegheny Plateau, a mountainous or hilly region tilting westward toward the Ohio River, into which most of the streams of the state drain. Historically, the most important resources of West Virginia have been coal, salt, oil, gas, and timber, as well as a variety of fertile soils, particularly along the watercourses.

Within the two major physiographical regions further variations occur. The northern panhandle, resulting from the settlement of a bitter boundary dispute between Virginia and Pennsylvania, has been economically akin to the upper Ohio Valley and to the Pittsburgh-Youngstown-Cleveland industrial area. The eastern panhandle has exhibited close economic and cultural ties with northern Virginia. Prior to the Civil War the tier of counties along the southeastern borders of the state had a distinctly southern flavor, an inclination still evident in many sections. Differences also exist within the mid-Allegheny Plateau, especially between the north-central agricultural and the southern coal regions. Not surprisingly, West Virginia history has sometimes been marked by deep-seated regional antagonisms and particularistic tendencies.

Exploration and early settlement. Until about the end of the third quarter of the seventeenth century, the Virginia backcountry, of which West Virginia was a part, remained almost unknown to Europeans. About that time, however, Virginians began to probe their western frontiers. They were impelled by a sense of curiosity, the urge to adventure, a hope of discovering a water route to the Pacific Ocean, and, above all, a desire to expand an increasingly remunerative fur trade. The most important of the expeditions was that of Thomas Batts and Robert Fallam, who in 1671 chanced upon the westward-flowing New River and followed it to the present Virginia–West Virginia border. Their discovery later became a basis for an English claim to the entire Ohio Valley. In the winter of 1673–1674, young Gabriel Arthur, a member of Captain James Needham's expedition into eastern Tennessee, accompanied an Indian war party, either Cherokee or Yuchi, against the Shawnee in Ohio and became the first Virginian of record to visit present West Virginia.

Although interest in the fur trade remained high, the desire for land for settlement and speculation generally took precedence in Virginia explorations in the early eighteenth century. In 1716 Governor Alexander Spotswood led a party of about 50 gentlemen to the banks of the Shenandoah River with a view to settlement and establishment of a buffer between the French and Indians in the Ohio Valley and Virginia's valuable Piedmont plantations. The real impetus to occupation of the valley of Virginia, of which the extreme eastern panhandle of West Virginia is a part, came with alteration in the Virginia land laws about 1730. Under the new plan, speculators were given 1,000 acres of land for each family that they settled west of the Blue Ridge. They were required, however, to bring in families from outside Virginia and to seat them within a specified time, usually two years.

Thomas, sixth Lord Fairfax, challenged grants made by Virginia within a tract lying between the Potomac and Rappahannock rivers, which had earlier been awarded supporters of Charles II during the interregnum and inherited by Fairfax. After much litigation, the English courts in 1745 upheld the rights of Lord Fairfax, who agreed to recognize grants already made by Virginia. This dispensation of the dispute left most of the eastern panhandle a part of the Fairfax estate, one of the largest private holdings in colonial America. The first settlers of West Virginia, therefore, usually obtained lands from Virginia speculators or became tenants on the semifeudal Fairfax estate.

Tradition credits the first settlement in West Virginia to a Welshman, Morgan Morgan, who arrived at Bunker Hill, in Berkeley County, about 1731, but there is no way of knowing who actually made the initial settlement. Records of the Philadelphia Synod of the Presbyterian church show a settlement at "Potomoke" in Virginia as early as 1719, and there is reason to believe that that unidentified site may have been Shepherdstown. If there were settlements in the state prior to about 1730, however, they were few and tenuous, since it was dangerous for families to venture beyond the mountains without the security of numbers. By the outbreak of the FRENCH AND INDIAN WAR, several thousand persons were living in West Virginia, most of them on the waters of the Potomac, particularly between the Shenandoah and South Branch rivers. About 50 families had by then crossed the mountains from the valley of Virginia to the Greenbrier region, where they acquired lands from the Greenbrier Company.

Most of the early settlers of the eastern panhandle were drawn from the great German and Scotch-Irish migrations to the middle colonies in the first half of the eighteenth century. They began their lives in America as indentured servants. Once their indentures were over, they sought the frontiers, where land was abundant and cheap. Because of legal restrictions upon settlement west of the

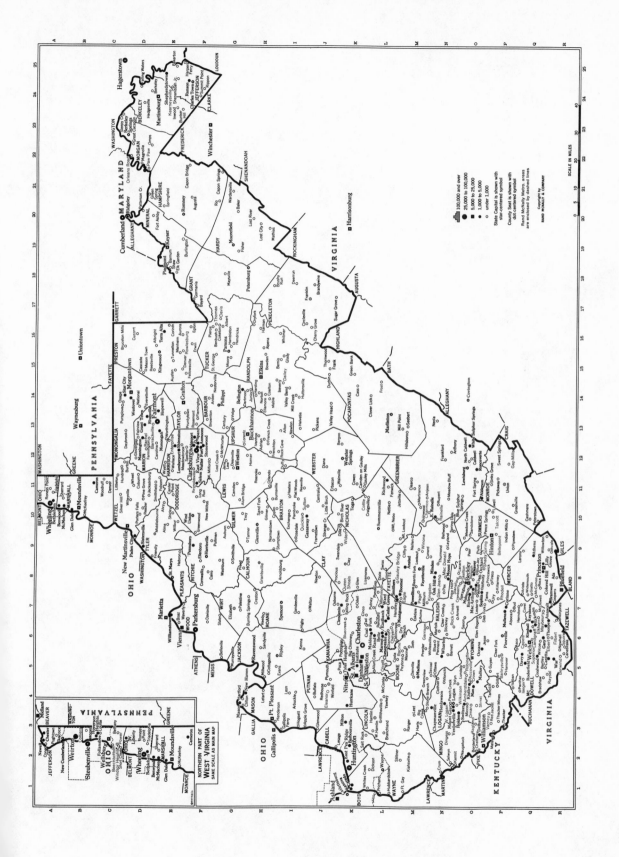

mountains in Pennsylvania, many turned southward into the valley of Virginia and the eastern panhandle of West Virginia. As a result, about one-third of the residents of the Potomac section were Germans, another third were Scotch-Irish, and the remainder English or eastern Virginian, with sprinklings of Dutch, Welsh, and other nationalities. The Greenbrier pioneers, overwhelmingly Scotch-Irish, crossed the Alleghenies from the southern part of the valley of Virginia.

For the first quarter of a century, these pioneers lived in idyllic peace, but the French and Indian War broke up many of their habitations. Indian attacks completely destroyed the Greenbrier settlements in 1755, and hundreds of residents of the upper Potomac fled to the safety of the valley of Virginia. Not until the occupation of the Forks of the Ohio in 1758 by General John Forbes did attacks upon the West Virginia frontiers abate. Settlers on the upper Potomac then began to return to their homes, but those in the Greenbrier Valley made no attempt to repossess their lands until 1761.

The revolutionary era. The elimination of the French from the trans-Appalachian region had a profound effect upon West Virginia history during the years following the Treaty of Paris. In 1763 apprehensive western tribes, led by Pontiac, endeavored to strike a decisive blow at the British before they could recover from the exhaustion of their long struggle with the French. The major assaults were directed against such posts as Ft. Niagara, Detroit, and Ft. Pitt, but West Virginians did not escape. Isolated homesteads in the eastern panhandle were again laid waste, and for a second time the Greenbrier habitations were completely broken up.

Their experiences in the French and Indian War and in Pontiac's uprising affected attitudes of West Virginians toward the PROCLAMATION OF 1763, which closed the trans-Appalachian region to settlement. Prospective settlers and land speculators sullenly submitted to the ban, for they knew only too well the dire consequences of defiance. The treaties of Hard Labour and Ft. Stanwix, concluded in the autumn of 1768 with the Cherokee and the Iroquois, respectively, opened most of West Virginia to settlement. Although the wave of population did not approach those rolling toward the Forks of the Ohio and tributaries of the Tennessee River, it deposited scores of settlers on the waters of the Monongahela, Greenbrier, upper Ohio, and Kanawha, as well as smaller streams.

The Shawnee, whose claims had been ignored in the treaties of Hard Labour and Ft. Stanwix,

offered little resistance to the first advance of settlement into the Allegheny Plateau, but when surveyors and land seekers appeared in Kentucky, their favorite hunting ground, in 1773, they reacted quickly. By the spring of 1774 hostile bands were attacking on a wide front, and West Virginia pioneers again lived in the dreadful shadow of a general Indian war. In the charged atmosphere, atrocities were committed by both Indians and whites. Among them were the unprovoked killing of the family of Logan, a friendly Mingo chief, and a series of attacks upon the Indians led by Michael Cresap (1742–1775). These events culminated in DUNMORE'S WAR, the only battle of which was fought at Point Pleasant, where Virginians led by Andrew Lewis defeated the Indians on October 10, 1774.

Although they were preoccupied with efforts to advance the frontiers and to win their homes from the Indians and a stubborn wilderness, West Virginians were not unconcerned about the troubled relations between England and the American colonies during the years following the French and Indian War. Generally they gave hearty support to the American cause. For most West Virginians the military aspects of the Revolutionary War were but a continuation of hostilities against the Indians northwest of the Ohio River. Despite pledges of neutrality made at Pittsburgh in 1775, these tribes had by 1777 become allies of the British. Among the most significant military actions in West Virginia were the attacks upon Ft. Henry at Wheeling, Ft. Randolph at Point Pleasant, and Ft. Donnally in the Greenbrier region. For six years West Virginia, an exposed frontier, endured a kind of total war. Manifestations of loyalism on the upper Ohio in 1777, however, were quickly suppressed by militia under Zackquill Morgan. An outburst born of war weariness, often termed loyalism, in Hampshire County in 1780 quickly subsided when troops under General Daniel Morgan arrived at the scenes of disorder.

West Virginians gave strong support to the new nation and to the Constitution. Of 14 delegates representing West Virginia counties in the Virginia convention of 1788, 12 voted for ratification of the federal Constitution. Confidence in the new government increased immensely with Anthony Wayne's defeat of the Indians at Fallen Timbers, which eliminated the greatest threat facing tramontane West Virginia, and with the conclusion of Jay's and Pinckney's treaties. Although the Alien and Sedition Acts produced deep divisions among the people, dissension was muffled in the universal approval of the LOUISIANA PURCHASE. In the War of 1812 the nationalism of West Virginians was so intense that they looked with scorn upon any county that could not fill its military quota with volunteers.

The early nineteenth century. In some respects the War of 1812 era marks a watershed in the pre–Civil War history of West Virginia. By then religious, educational, and cultural patterns that were to endure until the separation of West Virginia from Virginia, and even beyond, had been formed. By the end of that conflict trends toward industrial development were discernable, and the shadows of approaching sectional conflict between eastern and western Virginia had fallen over the Old Dominion.

As with most rural folk, religion exerted a profound influence upon the lives of West Virginians. The first two or three generations were predominantly Presbyterian, Quaker, Anglican, Lutheran, German Reformed, and Dunker, a reflection of their national origins. Remote from eastern religious centers, however, they suffered acute neglect by church authorities. With infrequent services and few ministerial visits, old religious ties gradually crumbled.

West Virginians were ripe for the GREAT AWAKENING with its emphasis upon a personal religious experience and the truth of the emotions. Reaping the greatest harvest of souls were the Methodists, who had the advantages of an organization superbly suited to an isolated, mountainous region, the talents of Bishop Francis Asbury, a prestige deriving from their Anglican background, and the rousing effects of their camp-meeting techniques. They were followed by the Baptists, whose democratic organization, use of untrained ministers, and gallant fight for separation of church and state struck responsive chords among the people, not only in West Virginia but throughout the South. The Presbyterians, with their insistence upon a trained ministry, were far behind, as were the Anglicans, whose strength was confined chiefly to parts of the eastern panhandle and a few major towns. Of 548 congregations in West Virginia in 1850, 281 were Methodist, 115 were Baptist, 61 were Presbyterian, and 22 were Episcopalian. Born of evangelistic endeavor and commitment to personal conversion, most churches remained strongly fundamentalist throughout the nineteenth century.

The same conditions that hampered the growth of churches before the arrival of the Methodists and Baptists also proved inhospitable to education. The first schools of West Virginia were of the subscription type, but in 1810 the legislature of Virginia established the literary fund, which pro-

vided tuition for children of impoverished parents. Thousands of children, however, continued to remain out of school, and illiteracy was widespread. In 1829 the legislature, in response to popular appeals, permitted but did not require counties to set up district free school systems. Apparently only four counties in West Virginia took advantage of this opportunity. Despite urgent pleas by civic leaders, such as those expressed in the Clarksburg convention of 1840–1841, there was no statewide system of free public schools until West Virginia became a state in 1863. Academies, few of which were in the southern parts of the state, were available only to the middle classes. Of less than half a dozen colleges in existence on the eve of the Civil War, only Bethany, which was founded by Alexander Campbell, was on a solid footing when the war came.

In an isolated region with limited educational opportunities, newspapers naturally fared poorly. Between 1790, when Nathaniel Willis founded the Jeffersonian *Potomak Guardian* at Shepherdstown, and 1830, no less than 45 newspapers were established in West Virginia, but most were short-lived. Outstanding among pre–Civil War newspapers were the Wheeling *Intelligencer*, an influential organ of the Republican party, and the Charleston *Kanawha Republican*. Two religious journals, the *Christian Baptist* and the *Millenial Harbinger*, both published at Bethany by Alexander Campbell, a founder of the DISCIPLES OF CHRIST church, enjoyed a national circulation. Appropriately, the first book published in West Virginia, *Christian Panoply*, was a vigorous attack upon Deism. The appeal of the pioneer era to later generations of West Virginians appeared in the publication of Joseph Doddridge's famous *Notes on the Settlement and Indian Wars of the Western Parts of Virginia and Pennsylvania* at Wellsburg in 1824 and Alexander Scott Withers' *Chronicles of Border Warfare* at Clarksburg in 1831.

Pre–Civil War industry. Conditions arising from the Napoleonic Wars and the War of 1812 drew attention to the need for domestic manufactures and at the same time afforded advantage to nascent industries by cutting off foreign competition. The series of protective tariffs beginning in 1816 continued wartime benefits. West Virginians, already cognizant of their resources, perceived that their future was tied to the industrial thrust of the nation. Especially stimulated was the salt industry of the Kanawha Valley, which began on a commercial scale in 1797. When the stoppage of salt imports from the British West Indies in the War of 1812 left western markets wide open, Kanawha

Valley salt makers quickly filled the void. Production rose dramatically until 1846, the peak year, when 3,224,786 bushels of salt were produced. The salt business also gave rise to flourishing ancillary industries, particularly the construction of flatboats, coopering, and coal mining.

Aside from the manufacture of salt, industrialization in West Virginia prior to the Civil War was most advanced in the northern panhandle and the Monongahela Valley. Wheeling and Wellsburg were centers of flour, glass, paper, and woolen manufactures. Becoming the western terminus of the National Road in 1818, Wheeling also had a thriving iron industry and was long known as the Nail City. Prominent among the Monongahela Valley industries was the Jackson Iron Works, located at Ice's Ferry on the Cheat River and widely known for the quality of its products.

The coal industry, later to become a pillar of the state's economy, was but slightly developed before the Civil War. Coal mined along the upper Ohio and in the Monongahela Valley was largely consumed by the local iron foundries. Until the 1850s most of that produced in the Kanawha Valley was used at the saltworks. The discovery of cannel coal at Cannelton on the Kanawha River about 1848 and at other nearby places soon afterward seemed to offer an abundant and economical source of much-needed crude oil and led to the opening of about a dozen mines. The success of the Drake oil well in 1859 and the coming of the Civil War, however, quickly put an end to that industry.

These antebellum developments offered a preview of the impact that industrialization would later have upon West Virginia. The salt-manufacturing enterprises completely transformed society in their part of the Kanawha Valley. Previously made up essentially of yeomen farmers, it developed a highly stratified society, with the addition of a wealthy aristocracy of salt makers, a landless laboring class, and hundreds of Negro slaves. By 1830 Wheeling had the beginnings of a labor movement, and William Cooper Howells, the father of the novelist William Dean Howells, was publishing a labor newspaper dedicated to Jacksonian principles.

A sharp distinction must be made, nevertheless, between the industrial potential of West Virginia and actual accomplishment before the Civil War. Industrial growth was severely handicapped by poor transportation, inadequate capital and banking faciliites, and in some areas even a shortage of labor. Although the National Road stimulated the growth of manufacturing at Wheeling, its most beneficial effects were perhaps upon the farms and rural villages along its route. Similarly, the construction by Virginia of the Northwestern Turnpike, connecting Winchester and Parkersburg, the Staunton & Parkersburg Turnpike, and the James River & Kanawha Turnpike contributed more to agricultural growth than to manufacturing. The Baltimore & Ohio Railroad was opened to Wheeling in 1853 and the Northwestern Virginia to Parkersburg in 1857, but otherwise no major lines served the area.

Problems of capital and banking were equally knotty. Resident capital was adequate only to the most modest enterprises, and other difficulties discouraged nonresident investment. Not until 1817 was a state bank established (at Wheeling) and were branch banks authorized at other localities.

Many West Virginians perceived a close relationship between economic retardation and the land policy of Virginia, which under the act of 1779 had given rise to utter confusion of titles and nonresident ownership of much of the state's land. Property belonging to large speculators was generally considered "wild land" and taxed at ridiculously low rates, with the result that eastern legislators could argue with much truth that the taxes raised in West Virginia were insufficient to provide internal improvements and social services desired by the West. Insecure titles also discouraged immigration into West Virginia.

Pre–Civil War political developments. West Virginians' efforts to grapple with some of their problems were thwarted by the planter elements of eastern Virginia who controlled the state government, and by a somewhat antiquated state constitution dating from 1776. Their demands for a new constitutional convention, expressed repeatedly in the press and in legislative halls, as well as in conventions held at Staunton in 1816 and 1825, were rebuffed by an indifferent general assembly. After years of resistance, the legislature finally agreed to a convention, but representation was in accordance with the state's senatorial districts, which had not been reapportioned since 1810. Westerners therefore arrived at the convention under serious disadvantages.

The Virginia constitutional convention of 1829–1830, with its imposing array of stellar political talent, drew national and even international attention. Along with former presidents James Madison and James Monroe, future president John Tyler, Chief Justice John Marshall, and ABEL P. UPSHUR from eastern Virginia were Philip Doddridge, Alexander Campbell, and Lewis Summers from the trans-Allegheny region. But, alas, sectional interests of the Tidewater and Piedmont sections of Virginia prevailed over justice and sound politics. Western demands for suffrage for all white males over twenty-one years old, representation in the general assembly on the basis of white population, and popular election of state and county officials were beaten down. Resentment in the trans-Allegheny parts of the state was so intense that numerous calls were made for separation from Virginia, whose constitution was declared by citizens of Ohio County as "unfit for the government of a free people."

Although bitterness against the eastern establishment slowly subsided and some efforts were made to placate the West through internal improvements and other services, political weaknesses lay heavy upon western hearts. Twenty years later those hearts were lightened when, in the reform convention of 1850–1851, the West won every political concession it had called for in 1829–1830. Jubilant at their long-awaited victories, westerners soon found that they had paid a dear price for their gains. New constitutional provisions included tax exemptions on slaves, thereby shifting the burden of taxation to land, limitations on the use of public credit for internal improvements, and restrictions upon the formation of new counties. All too soon the West realized that it had bargained away future economic possibilities for immediate political benefits. By the time that the Civil War came, unhappiness again reigned in the West.

The Civil War era. The deep antagonisms between eastern and western Virginia came to a climax following the Confederate attack upon Ft. Sumter and President Abraham Lincoln's call for volunteers. An essentially moderate convention, which had assembled at Richmond on February 13, 1861, to consider Virginia's course of action, thereupon became polarized and voted 88 to 55 for secession from the Union. Thirty-two of the 47 delegates from present West Virginia opposed secession. On April 20 they returned home and in numerous mass meetings endeavored to muster popular support against ratification of the secession ordinance.

More significant was the first Wheeling convention, which met May 13–15. Its 426 members, chosen by highly irregular methods, resisted an appeal by John S. Carlile, an early advocate of West Virginia statehood, to declare the trans-Allegheny counties no longer a part of Virginia and deferred action until a referendum had been held on the secession question. When the people of Virginia voted to leave the Union, the second Wheeling convention, meeting from June 11 through June 25, adopted a "declaration of rights," which branded Virginia's secession unconstitutional and declared that its officials had thereby forfeited their offices. The convention then established the "restored," or "reorganized," government of Virginia at Wheeling and filled vacant state offices. It chose FRANCIS H. PIERPONT governor and named Waitman T. Willey and John S. Carlile to the two vacant U.S. Senate seats of Virginia.

The first steps toward the creation of West Virginia were taken at the adjourned session of the second Wheeling convention, which met from August 6 through August 21. After rejecting a proposal by Carlile to include only the counties west of the Alleghenies, the members voted 48 to 27 to form a new state, to be named Kanawha, with boundaries approximating those of present West Virginia. They anticipated no difficulty in obtaining the consent of the restored government of Virginia, which some authorities contend was nothing more than a device to facilitate the new state movement.

Also favoring efforts to create the new state was the military situation in northwestern Virginia. At the outset of the war much of the area to be included in the proposed state was secured to the Union when forces directed by George B. McClellan and William S. Rosecrans drove Confederate troops out of the Monongahela Valley and Jacob D. Cox pushed them out of the Kanawha Valley. Although the Confederates under Thomas J. ("Stonewall") Jackson scored some successes in the eastern panhandle, they never posed a serious military threat to political events at Wheeling.

A constitutional convention, which met at Wheeling from November 26, 1861, until February 18, 1862, changed the name of the proposed state to West Virginia, determined its boundaries, and failed to take any steps toward the elimination of slavery. The fact that West Virginia did not seek to enter the Union as a free state underscores the relative unimportance of slavery per se as a real issue between eastern and western Virginia.

Other hurdles remained to be cleared before statehood could be attained. On May 13, 1862, the pro-Union general assembly of Virginia, in response to a call by Pierpont, met in special session and before the day was over gave its approval for the new state. In Congress, however, the statehood bill ran into difficulties in the Senate Committee on Territories, of which Carlile was a member. Inexplicably Carlile now proposed the addition of 15 counties and a requirement that West Virginia take steps to abolish slavery. A compromise in the form of the Willey amendment to the West Virginia constitution provided that all slaves under twenty-one years old on July 4, 1863, would become free upon reaching that age and that no more slaves might be brought in. After considerable debate the statehood bill passed the Senate 23 to 15 and the House of Representatives 96 to 55. The recalled session of the West Virginia constitutional convention approved the Willey amendment by a vote of 54 to zero, and the people ratified the amended document 27,740 to 572. Obviously, a large number of opponents of statehood did not vote at all. On June 20, 1863, 60 days after Lincoln signed the statehood bill, West Virginia took its place in the Union as the thirty-fifth state.

The new government of West Virginia was installed at Wheeling, whereupon the restored government of Virginia moved to Alexandria. The Republican governor, ARTHUR I. BOREMAN, and the legislature of West Virginia were strongly influenced by wartime hatreds, and one of their early actions was a measure declaring property of enemies of the state forfeited. In 1865 and 1866 they worked together to enact laws requiring voters to take oaths that they had never willingly supported the Confederacy in any way and setting up "loyal" boards in each county to register qualified voters. These patently political moves disfranchised perhaps as many as 20,000 men, most of them Democrats, and gave rise to lasting bitterness.

The proscriptive features of Reconstruction in West Virginia were dealt a heavy blow when federal Judge John J. Jackson ruled that the FIFTEENTH AMENDMENT to the federal Constitution applied to white men as well as to Negroes. The essence of his interpretation was later embodied in the Flick amendment to the state constitution, which conferred the suffrage upon all males over twenty-one years old regardless of color. In the election of 1871 the Democrats turned the Republicans out of office. The following year they replaced the "yankee" constitution of the state with one that has remained the fundamental law to the present time.

Economic developments. Once the tensions of the Reconstruction era were allayed, the dominant theme in the history of West Virginia centered on the development, or exploitation, of the state's abundant natural resources. With the possible exception of Governor Emanuel Willis Wilson (1885–1889), Democratic governors from 1877 to 1897, as in the South generally, were Bourbon in outlook (REDEEMER GOVERNMENTS). The Republicans, who lost the governorship only once between 1897 and 1933, also generally evinced a strong probusiness orientation, although some, notably William E. Glasscock (1909–1913) and Henry D. Hatfield (1913–1917), displayed some Progressive tendencies. Most of the state's chief executives endeavored to provide a climate favorable to industry by seeking improved transportation facilities, an adequate and stable labor supply, and attractive tax legislation. Under these benign conditions, the growth of the coal, oil, gas, and timber industries during the first half-century of statehood was little short of phenomenal.

With 60 of the 117 seams of coal in the state workable, the economy of West Virginia very soon began to revolve around COAL MINING. Coal production rose steadily from 444,648 tons in 1863 to 1,568,000 in 1880 and to 21,153,341 in 1900. Output increased steadily in the twentieth century to reach a record 173,653,816 tons in 1947. Although coal was mined in at least 33 of the state's 55 counties, operations were concentrated south of the Kanawha River and in the upper Monongahela Valley.

The oil industry of West Virginia had its beginnings immediately prior to the Civil War, when the Burning Springs area on the Little Kanawha River experienced an oil boom (PETROLEUM). During the immediate postwar years oil production continued to center in the Little Kanawha Valley. With the more accurate drilling made possible by the anticlinal theory of Israel C. White, West Virginia's world-famous geologist, production in the state rose to 16,195,675 barrels in 1900, the peak year for West Virginia. Similar growth took place in the natural gas industry. In 1906 West Virginia became the leading state in its production and held that position until 1917, its banner year, when 308 million cubic feet were produced.

Concurrent with the rapid expansion of the coal, oil, and gas industries was the growth of timbering and lumbering (LUMBER INDUSTRY). Immensely stimulating the assault upon the native forests was the introduction of the steam-driven band mill and the penetration of the forest lands by railroads. In some areas, however, rafting of logs was important, particularly on the Guyandotte, Elk, and Little Kanawha rivers and Middle Island Creek. The lumber industry reached its zenith in 1909, when 1.5 billion board feet were produced in the state.

The industrial development of West Virginia would have been impossible without completion of a vast network of RAILROADS. At the close of the Civil War the Baltimore & Ohio and the Northwestern Virginia were the only two major lines in the state. Extension of the Chesapeake & Ohio

Railway to Huntington in 1873 led to the opening of the rich Kanawha and New River coalfields. In the 1890s the Norfolk & Western Railway tapped the Pocahontas coalfields and spurred the growth of numerous towns, including Bluefield, Princeton, Bramwell, Williamson, Logan, and Welch. The Western Maryland served the eastern panhandle and the lumber regions of the Alleghenies. Other lines of importance were the Kanawha & Michigan, later a part of the New York Central system, the Virginian, and the Coal & Coke Railroad, the latter in time absorbed by the Baltimore & Ohio. Equally important in many areas were the locks and dams constructed in the Ohio, Kanawha, Monongahela, and other rivers.

During the late nineteenth century, hundreds of industrial communities sprang up in West Virginia. Many, particularly in the coal-mining areas, were under strong paternalistic influences of companies that, often with no other recourse, provided workers' houses, stores at which employees were expected to deal, aid to churches, supplements to schoolteachers' salaries, and even theaters, often pretentiously styled "opera houses." Their benefices, however, never compensated for low wages, long hours of labor, and, in the case of coal mining, the most dangerous of working conditions. Between 1883 and 1915, both dates inclusive, accidents took the lives of 5,613 miners. In the latter year alone 455 miners suffered fatal accidents, while 1,628 were victims of major nonfatal accidents and another 1,541 of minor injuries. Between 1884 and 1915, 36 accidents involved five or more fatalities, the worst being the explosion at Monongah in 1907, which took 361 lives.

Despite unsatisfactory and hazardous working conditions, West Virginia miners were slow to organize, partly because the laws and the courts ordinarily favored the coal companies, which made frequent use of injunctions to restrain picketing and other union activities. By 1902, however, in part with the aid of a remarkable labor leader, "Mother" Mary Jones, the Kanawha coalfields had been organized. Two prolonged and bloody strikes, one on Paint Creek in the Kanawha fields in 1912–1913 and the other in the Logan and Mingo areas in 1920–1921, drew nationwide attention to conditions existing among the state's miners and led to investigations by committees of the U.S. Senate, which found a labor autocracy and a near industrial peonage in some mining areas of the state.

Industrial growth in West Virginia before the First World War wrought significant demographic changes, particularly in the coal-mining regions. In 1915 only 37,918 of the 81,328 coal miners in the state were American whites. A sizable part of the 11,835 Negroes had migrated northward following the Civil War to seek employment in the mines. Of the 31,575 foreign-born miners, over one-third were Italian. Most of the remainder were classified as Hungarian, Polish, Slavic, Austrian, and Russian. Thus, an important new element was superimposed upon communities that had thereto been predominantly northern European in origin and background.

The new industrialism also brought concentrations of wealth that were to have profound effects upon the future of the state. In his inaugural address in 1893 Governor William A. MacCorkle extended a welcoming hand to immigrants seeking opportunities in West Virginia, but he warned that the land and resources of the state were rapidly being acquired by nonresident capitalists and that it faced a future not unlike that of Ireland in its relationship to England. The truth of his prophecy became dishearteningly apparent in the middle of the twentieth century.

More and more the government of West Virginia assumed the character of an industrial plutocracy. Among the opulent and powerful business leaders was Henry Gassaway Davis, a coal, timber, and railroad magnate, who for many years dominated the Democratic party in the state and who in 1904 was his party's nominee for vice-president of the United States. His son-in-law and business associate, STEPHEN B. ELKINS, fell heir to the mantle of Waitman T. Willey and NATHAN GOFF, JR., successively the leading Republican powers in the state. A member of the U.S. Senate and secretary of war in Benjamin Harrison's cabinet, Elkins exerted such influence that the four chief executives of the state from 1897 to 1913 are referred to as the "Elkins governors." The Fairmont coal operator, James Otis Watson, was the father of U.S. Senator Clarence W. Watson and the father-in-law of Governor A. Brooks Fleming, both Democrats. Numerous other industrialists either held or controlled positions of great power at both the state and county levels.

Although industrial development was little short of spectacular during the late nineteenth and early twentieth centuries, West Virginia was still essentially rural at the beginning of the First World War. Agriculture was diversified, with corn, wheat, potatoes, garden vegetables, and apples among its chief crops. Its "pulsating artery," however, was animal husbandry, in which cattle, hogs, and sheep were of special importance. The significance of agriculture in the lives of the people was demonstrated in the rapid growth of the GRANGE from the establishment of the first lodge in Jefferson County in 1873 to 378 lodges in 1876. In 1900

West Virginia had 92,874 farms, and as late as 1950 it still had 81,434, but by the mid-1960s the number had decreased to 34,504.

West Virginians generally cherished the rural character of their state. The Populistic Governor Emanuel Willis Wilson, who waged vigorous campaigns against railroad abuses, corrupt election practices, and other evils, also fought valiantly for laws against stream pollution. Governor Glasscock declared with sincerity that the pen could not describe the "sylvan beauty, rich resources, gracious climate, fields, orchards, rivers, valleys, hills, mountains, and splendid development" of West Virginia. His successor, Henry D. Hatfield, seeking in a Rooseveltian tradition to come to terms with industrialism, nevertheless strove to preserve the quality of life by initiating health programs and promoting other social reforms.

The First World War accelerated the industrial advance of West Virginia. Demands for steel and chemicals, many of which had previously been imported from Germany, made expansion of those industries in the United States imperative. Steel production in West Virginia centered in the northern panhandle at Wheeling and Weirton (IRON AND STEEL INDUSTRY). The CHEMICAL INDUSTRIES were located at Charleston, South Charleston, Belle, and Institute, all in the Kanawha Valley, which quickly became one of the chemical centers of the world. The Second World War further stimulated these industries and extended the manufacture of chemicals into the part of the state along the Ohio River. Other industries experiencing rapid growth during and after the First World War included glassmaking, with more than a dozen centers throughout the state, textile manufacturing, and boatbuilding. Hydroelectric power became increasingly important. Coal production continued to soar. West Virginia became more and more a great industrial workshop, with closer and closer connections to the great corporate enterprises of the nation. The need for skilled workers, technicians, and managerial personnel led to further immigration into the state and gave cities such as Charleston, Huntington, Wheeling, and Weirton an increasingly cosmopolitan character.

Industrial needs forced improvements in the state's highways and rivers. An act of 1891 placed road construction and maintenance in the hands of county courts, which were empowered to require road work of all able-bodied males between the ages of twenty-one and fifty and to raise money through bond issues and special levies. Although the plan was modified by legislation in 1909, 1911, and 1913, it was never adequate for industrial and popular needs. During the administration of Governor John J. Cornwell (1917–1921), roads were classified as state and county highways, a program was designed to provide each county seat with at least one hard-surfaced outlet, membership of the state road commission was increased, and the sale of $5 million in road bonds was authorized. In 1933 the state assumed responsibility for county, or secondary, roads and placed all highways under the jurisdiction of a single road commissioner. Also of significance was the construction in the 1930s of a new series of locks and dams in the Ohio, Kanawha, Monongahela, and other rivers.

Education and culture. The material growth of West Virginia was accompanied by new developments in education. Although funding was perennially inadequate, the state pioneered in several national trends in public school education. In 1876 Alexander Luark Wade introduced a graduating plan into the country schools of Monongalia County. From there it spread to the entire state and ultimately to the nation. In 1933 the legislature, in an effort to remove some of the gross inequities in educational opportunities in various parts of the state, adopted a county unit plan, which became a model for other states.

Almost immediately after the Civil War, West Virginia instituted a system of higher education. In 1867 the legislature established West Virginia University, the state's land-grant college and the capstone of its educational structure. During the 1860s and 1870s it provided normal schools for the education of public schoolteachers. With the growth of the high school movement, these schools expanded their offerings to include additional collegiate work. In the 1920s and 1930s they were authorized to award baccalaureate degrees and were renamed state teachers' colleges. The addition of other curricula led to their redesignation as simply state colleges in the 1930s and 1940s. In 1969 all state-supported institutions of higher learning were placed under the control of a board of regents, which began to emphasize the establishment of a community college system.

Mid-twentieth-century political life. Industrial growth, perhaps the most distinguishing feature of West Virginia during its first half-century of statehood, was interrupted by the GREAT DEPRESSION. Suffering acutely in the depression years, West Virginians sought relief in a change of political leadership. They turned the Republicans, who had dominated state politics since 1897, out of office and entrusted their future to the Democrats. They generally embraced the NEW DEAL philosophy with its concept of social as well as political democracy.

Most of the Democratic governors were attuned to new approaches to the state's problems. With public revenues dwindling, the state's credit in jeopardy, schools closing, and thousands of citizens destitute, Governor Herman Guy Kump (1933–1937) held the forty-first legislature 240 days, the longest session in the history of West Virginia. Compounding the difficulties was an amendment to the constitution, adopted in 1932, which limited tax rates on general property and nearly dried up revenues. The legislature, therefore, drastically revised the tax structure by providing a consumer sales tax earmarked for schools, a personal income tax, and taxes on beer, wine, liquor, and horse racing, while the governor effected rigid economies in government.

Serious factionalism developed in the Democratic party. Kump's successor, Homer A. Holt (1937–1941), represented the relatively conservative "statehouse" wing of the party. The election of Matthew M. Neely (1941–1945) to the governorship represented a victory for the "federal" faction. Strongly backed by organized labor, particularly the United Mine Workers of America, Neely had resigned his seat in the U.S. Senate, where he had considerable seniority. His administration was marked by legislation beneficial to labor and education, the establishment of an interracial commission, the forerunner of the human rights commission, and an unsuccessful attempt to remove President Charles E. Lawall of West Virginia University.

Intraparty strife abated somewhat during the administrations of Clarence W. Meadows (1945–1949) and Okey L. Patteson (1949–1953). Meadows was able to end a vicious fee system provided county sheriffs for feeding prisoners. Perhaps the most conspicuous accomplishments of Patteson were the establishment of the West Virginia University Medical School at Morgantown and the construction of the West Virginia Turnpike, an 88-mile span opened in 1954 and regarded at the time as a marvel of engineering.

Patteson's protégé, young William C. Marland (1953–1957), initiated his administration with a gubernatorial bombshell by proposing a severance tax on natural resources. The tax, which would have struck heavily at the powerful coal industry, was rejected, but the engendered controversy left bitterness within the Democratic party. Although he was idealistic and courageous, Marland was untempered by experience. His mistakes were partly responsible for the election of a Republican, the young and charismatic Cecil Un-

derwood (1957–1961), to the governorship. Underwood had to work with a Democratic legislature, which he did with less than desired success.

In 1960 the Democrats recaptured the governorship with William W. Barron (1961–1965), who in turn was succeeded by Hulett C. Smith (1965–1969), the first commissioner of the new department of commerce. After the expiration of his term as governor, Barron and several of his major appointees were found guilty of accepting bribes and other forms of corruption and were sentenced to prison terms.

Popular indignation at the much-publicized scandals of Barron and his associates and the national swing to the Republicans in 1968 did much to account for the election of Arch A. Moore, Jr. (1969–1977), a Republican, as governor. Although his administrations were marked by conflict with his Democratic legislature and by many problems arising from the interpretation and application of a recently adopted constitutional amendment providing for an executive budget, Moore proved a popular governor. Under a governor's succession amendment to the constitution, adopted in 1970, he ran for reelection in 1972 and defeated John D. ("Jay") Rockefeller IV. In 1976 Rockefeller won the gubernatorial election.

Recent trends. More profoundly affecting the state than the political fluctuations were changes of a social and economic nature. Of utmost importance were those related to coal mining. In 1950 coal mines of the state were mostly of the drift type and employed 119,568 persons. Twenty years later, with production levels about the same, the industry employed only 47,600 men. This change resulted largely from the rapid mechanization of the mines following the Second World War and the increase in surface and auger mining, which in 1970 accounted for about one-fourth of the coal output of the state. Thousands of unemployed miners, many of them young men, left for Cleveland, Akron, Detroit, Chicago, and other industrial centers, and other thousands went on welfare rolls. Between 1950 and 1970 West Virginia suffered a population decline from 2,005,552 to 1,744,237. Its plight drew national attention in 1960, when John F. Kennedy, in his bid for the Democratic presidential nomination, made the resuscitation of Appalachia, epitomized by West Virginia, a cardinal feature of his New Frontier.

Despite numerous federal programs launched during the 15 years following the inauguration of Kennedy, West Virginia remained but little changed. Federal largess could not overcome problems that emanated in part from a vicious absentee ownership of much of the state's land and resources. Twelve million of its 15 million acres of land were in private hands. Two-thirds of the privately held lands were owned or their mineral rights were leased by large corporations, most of them interested in West Virginia's mineral resources. The ten largest landholders in the state, with an aggregate of over 3.2 million acres, were the Continental Oil Company, Chessie System, Inc., Norfolk & Western Railway Company, Georgia-Pacific Corporation, Columbia Gas System, Westvaco Corporation, Eastern Gas & Fuel Associates, Cabot, Inc., Bethlehem Steel Corporation, and Pittston Company, most of which were based in the Northeast. Since much of this corporate property was assessed at minimal value, West Virginia remained a state where in many sections great natural wealth existed side by side with seemingly unconquerable poverty.

As the nation's energy needs assumed an increasing importance in the 1970s, West Virginia seemed destined to play a yet greater role in providing its fossil fuels. Environmentalists viewed this prospect with apprehension, for they saw more scarred hillsides, polluted atmosphere, and dying streams. Indeed, as the state entered the last quarter of the twentieth century, many thoughtful citizens were convinced that the greatest challenge in the foreseeable future would be the reconciliation of West Virginia's responsibilities in meeting the nation's energy requirements with the preservation of its surpassing natural beauty and a quality of life that seemed to be rapidly disappearing.

Manuscripts and printed primary sources. Two major libraries are West Virginia Department of Archives and History, useful for official records; and West Virginia University Library, best collection of public, corporate, and private records relating to the state. Only comprehensive guide, now out of date, to Department of Archives and History is I. C. Davis (comp.), *Bibliography of West Virginia* (1939). Supplement with annual reports of the department. For West Virginia University materials, see J. W. Hess, *Guide to Manuscripts and Archives in West Virginia Collection* (1974). See also Draper Manuscripts, Historical Society of Wisconsin, for pioneer era; Virginia State Library, for official records prior to statehood; Library of Congress; Virginia Historical Society; Duke University Library; and University of North Carolina Library, Chapel Hill. Published documents of special importance are W. P. Palmer *et al.* (eds.), *Calendar of Virginia State Papers* (11 vols.; 1968); W. W. Hening (comp.), *Statutes-at-Large* (13 vols.; 1969), of Virginia; *Proceedings and Debates of Virginia State Convention of 1829–1830* (2 vols.; 1971); C. H. Ambler *et al.* (eds.), *Debates and Proceedings of First Constitutional Convention of West Virginia* (3 vols.; 1942); and *Journal of Constitutional Convention, 1872* (1872). Collections of source material include R. G. Thwaites and L. P. Kellogg (eds.), *Dunmore's War* (1974), *Revolution*

on Upper Ohio (1908), and *Frontier Defense on Upper Ohio* (1912); and L. P. Kellogg (ed.), *Frontier Advance on Upper Ohio* (1916) and *Frontier Retreat on Upper Ohio* (1917), all from Draper Manuscripts; V. A. Lewis, *How West Virginia Was Made* (1909); and E. Cometti and F. P. Summers (eds.), *Thirty-Fifth State* (1966).

General works. Best guide to secondary works is J. W. Hess, *Guide to Study of West Virginia History* (1960). Best general history is C. H. Ambler and F. P. Summers, *West Virginia: Mountain State* (2nd ed.; 1958). Older accounts still useful are J. M. Callahan, *History of West Virginia* (3 vols; 1923) and *Semi-Centennial History of West Virginia* (1913); and T. C. Miller and H. Maxwell, *West Virginia and Its People* (3 vols.; 1913). Geographical conditions are treated in N. M. Fenneman, *Physiography of Eastern U.S.* (1938). Useful factual compendium is *West Virginia* (1941), in WPA American Guide series. Two collections of biographies are G. W. Atkinson and A. F. Gibbens, *Prominent Men of West Virginia* (1890); and G. W. Atkinson (ed.), *Bench and Bar of West Virginia* (1919). Among most reliable county and regional histories are M. K. Bushong, *Jefferson County* (1972); W. T. Doherty, *Berkeley County* (1972); G. W. Atkinson, *Kanawha County* (1876); W. G. Brown, *Nicholas County* (1954); O. F. Morton, *Pendleton County* (1974) and *Monroe County* (1974); W. Haymond, *Harrison County* (1973); D. Davis, *Harrison County* (1970); S. T. Wiley, *Monongalia County* (1883); H. Maxwell, *Randolph County* (1961); H. Maxwell and H. L. Swisher, *Hampshire County* (1972); J. P. Hale, *History of Great Kanawha Valley* (2 vols.; 1891); and J. H. Newton *et al.*, *History of Panhandle* (1879), northern panhandle.

Pioneer era. First-hand accounts of early exploration are C. W. Alvord and L. Bidgood, *First Explorations of Trans-Allegheny Region* (1912); T. Walker, *Journal*, ed. W. C. Rives (1888); and C. Gist, *Journal*, ed. W. M. Darlington (1893). Source materials on pioneer history are J. Doddridge, *Notes on Settlement and Indian Wars* (1960); A. S. Withers, *Chronicles of Border Warfare* (1961); and J. Stuart, *Memoir of Indian Wars* (1971). Also see W. H. Foote, *Sketches of Virginia* (1856); A. Royall, *Sketches of History, Life, and Manners* (1826); and H. Howe, *Historical Collections of Virginia* (1845). Most comprehensive study of pioneer era is O. K. Rice, *Allegheny Frontier* (1970). General works that provide broad perspective include C. W. Alvord, *Mississippi Valley in British Politics* (2 vols.; 1917); R. C. Downes, *Council Fires on Upper Ohio* (1940); J. Sosin, *Whitehall and Wilderness* (1961) and *Revolutionary Frontier* (1967); R. Horsman, *Frontier in Formative Years* (1970); and J. A. Caruso, *Appalachian Frontier* (1959). More restricted in focus are J. P. Hale, *Trans-Allegheny Pioneers* (1971); and R. B. Cook, *Annals of Fort Lee* (1935). For French and Indian War, see O. K. Rice, *West Virginia History* (Jan., 1963). For Dunmore's War, see R. C. Downes, *Mississippi Valley Historical Review* (Dec., 1934); and V. A. Lewis, *Battle of Point Pleasant* (1974). For Revolution, see F. H. Hart, *Valley of Virginia in American Revolution* (1942), which relates in part to West Virginia. For land speculation, see T. P. Abernethy, *Western Lands and American Revolution* (1959); K. P. Bailey, *Ohio Company of Virginia* (1939); A. P. James, *Ohio Company* (1959); G. E. Lewis, *Indiana Company* (1941); C. H. Ambler, *George Washington and West* (1936); and R. B. Cook, *Washington's Western Lands* (1930).

Political history. Role of West Virginia in national affairs is treated in N. K. Risjord, *Journal of Southern History* (Nov., 1967); R. G. Lowe, *Virginia Magazine of History and Biography* (July, 1973); M. F. Wehtje, *West Virginia History* (July, 1968); S. W. Brown, "John George Jackson" (M.A. thesis, Marshall, 1973); and D. P. Jordan, "Virginia Congressmen, 1801–1825" (Ph.D. dissertation, University of Virginia, 1970). For state politics, see C. H. Ambler, *Sectionalism in Virginia* (1910) and *American Historical Review* (July, 1910); H. M. Rice, *Jonathan M. Bennett* (1943); W. D. Barns, *West Virginia History* (April, July, 1973); J. E. Stealey, *West Virginia History* (Oct., 1964); and J. A. Williams, *West Virginia History* (July, 1972), an attempt to find continuity between antebellum and postwar politics. For slavery and its role in political life, see E. M. Steel, *West Virginia History* (July, 1973); O. K. Rice, *Journal of Southern History* (Nov., 1971); and F. Talbott, *West Virginia History* (Oct., 1962; Jan., April, 1963).

For political events surrounding attainment of statehood, see H. T. Shanks, *Secession Movement in Virginia* (1934); G. M. Gray, "Presidential Campaign of 1860 in Virginia" (Ph.D. dissertation, University of Kentucky, 1941); J. C. McGregor, *Disruption of Virginia* (1922); G. D. Hall, *Rending of Virginia* (1902); G. E. Moore, *Banner in Hills* (1963); C. G. Woodson, "Disruption of Virginia" (Ph.D. dissertation, Harvard, 1913); and R. O. Curry, *House Divided* (1964) and *Journal of Southern History* (Nov., 1962), the last two revisionist studies. Important biographical works are C. H. Ambler, *Francis H. Pierpont* (1937) and *Waitman T. Willey* (1954). See also I. A. Woodward on Arthur I. Boreman, *West Virginia History* (July, Oct., 1970); F. G. Ham (ed.), on John J. Davis, *West Virginia History* (Jan., 1963); and D. R. McVeigh, "Charles James Faulkner" (Ph.D. dissertation, University of West Virginia, 1955). Constitutional issues involved in West Virginia statehood are dealt with in J. G. Randall, *Constitutional Problems Under Lincoln* (1951); G. E. Moore, *West Virginia History* (Oct., 1956), considers slavery as factor in formation of state.

Military aspects of Civil War in West Virginia are covered in E. C. Smith, *Borderland in Civil War* (1927); B. B. Stutler, *West Virginia in Civil War* (1963); and, in more limited but more analytical manner, F. P. Summers, *Baltimore and Ohio in Civil War* (1939). Biographical studies on the war include D. S. Freeman, *Lee's Lieutenants* (3 vols.; 1942–44); F. Vandiver, *Mighty Stonewall* (1957); W. W. Hassler, *McClellan* (1957); T. H. Williams, *Hayes of the Twenty-Third* (1965); and articles, including F. L. Klement, *West Virginia History* (April, 1947); F. P. Summers, *West Virginia History* (Oct., 1939); and C. L. Bailes, *West Virginia History* (Oct., 1944).

The nature of Reconstruction in West Virginia may be seen in M. Gerofsky, *West Virginia History* (July, Oct., 1945); C. H. Ambler, *Yale Review* (Aug., 1905); P. D. Casdorph, *West Virginia History* (July, 1968); and portions of revisionist R. O. Curry (ed.), *Radicalism, Racism, and Party Realignment* (1970).

Comprehensive accounts of political affairs since statehood are woefully lacking. Especially perceptive is J. A. Williams, *West Virginia and Captains of Industry* (1976). Useful biographies include F. P. Summers, *Johnson N. Camden* (1937) and *William L. Wilson* (1953); C. M. Pepper, *Henry G. Davis* (1920); G. W. Smith, *Na-*

than Goff, Jr. (1959); and O. D. Lambert, *Stephen B. Elkins* (1955). Useful autobiography is W. A. MacCorkle, *Recollections of Fifty Years* (1928). Articles on political life include L. L. Fisher, *West Virginia History* (April, July, 1963); G. W. Smith, *West Virginia History* (Jan., April, 1962); C. Karr, *West Virginia History* (Oct., 1966; Jan., 1967); P. D. Casdorph, *West Virginia History* (Oct., 1966; Oct., 1973); J. A. Williams, *West Virginia History* (Jan., Oct., 1970); and E. J. Goodall, *West Virginia History* (Oct., 1962; April, July, Oct., 1963; Jan., 1964). Better dissertations are W. D. Barns, "Granger and Populist Movements in West Virginia" (Ph.D. dissertation, University of West Virginia, 1947); W. P. Turner, "John T. McGraw" (Ph.D. dissertation, University of West Virginia, 1960); W. E. Coffey, "Rush Dew Holt" (Ph.D. dissertation, University of West Virginia, 1970); N. S. Penn, "Henry D. Hatfield" (Ph.D. dissertation, Emory, 1973); and N. C. Burckel, "Reform Governors in Missouri, Kentucky, West Virginia, and Maryland, 1900–1918" (Ph.D. dissertation, University of Wisconsin, 1971). A first-rate biography of John W. Davis is W. H. Harbaugh, *Lawyer's Lawyer* (1973). See also J. H. Fenton, *Politics in Border States* (1957); and N. R. Pearce, *Border States South* (1975).

Economic growth. Aspects of agricultural history of West Virginia may be gleaned from L. C. Gray, *History of Agriculture in Southern States* (2 vols.; 1958); but two of best works are W. D. Barns, *West Virginia State Grange* (1973); and, though not dealing specifically with West Virginia, *Ferry Hill Plantation Journal*, ed. F. M. Green (1961).

Only general history of coal mining is P. Conley, *History of West Virginia Coal Industry* (1960), superficial; more useful is J. H. Thompson, *Significant Trends in West Virginia Coal Industry* (1958). For pre–Civil War beginnings, see H. N. Eavenson, *First Century and a Quarter of American Coal Industry* (1941); O. K. Rice, *Journal of Southern History* (Nov., 1965); and J. B. Thomas, "Growth of Coal Industry in Great Kanawha Valley" (M.A. thesis, University of North Carolina, 1967). Strip mining is treated in R. F. Munn, *West Virginia History* (July, 1973), and political power of coal industry in G. F. Massay, *West Virginia History* (April, 1971).

Works on industrial growth include E. D. Thoenen, *History of Oil and Gas Industry in West Virginia* (1964); J. G. Jones, *West Virginia History* (Jan., 1949), natural gas industry; J. E. Stealey, "Salt Industry of Great Kanawha Valley" (Ph.D. dissertation, University of West Virginia, 1970); and R. B. Clarkson, *Tumult on Mountains* (1964), for timbering and lumbering. Other works are L. L. Brown, *West Virginia History* (Oct., 1946), geologist I. C. White; and E. J. Goodall, *West Virginia History* (Oct., 1968), industrial development of Charleston area. Biographies of H. G. Davis, Elkins, Camden, and Goff, already noted, also discuss industrial growth.

Works on transportation are C. H. Ambler, *Transportation in Ohio Valley* (1932); P. Jordan, *National Road* (1966); W. S. Sanderlin, *Great National Project: Chesapeake and Ohio Canal* (1946); W. F. Dunaway, *James River and Kanawha Company* (1922); and J. T. Lambie, *From Mine to Market* (1954), excellent on Norfolk & Western Railway.

Aspects of labor history are treated in E. L. K. Harris and F. J. Krebs, *From Humble Beginnings* (1960); and T. E. Posey, "Labor Movement in West Virginia" (Ph.D.

WEST VIRGINIA POPULATION, 1790–1970

Year	Total	White	Nonwhite Slave	Free	% Growth	Rank U.S.	South
1790[a]	55,873	50,593	4,668	612			
1800[a]	78,592	70,894	7,172	526	40.7		
1810[a]	105,469	93,355	10,836	1,278	34.2		
1820[a]	136,808	120,236	15,119	1,453	29.7		
1830[a]	176,924	157,084	17,673	2,167	29.3		
1840[a]	224,537	203,016	18,488	3,033	26.9		
1850[a]	302,313	278,731	20,500	3,082	34.6		
1860[a]	376,688	355,526	18,371	2,791	24.6		
1870	442,014	42,033		17,981	17.3	27	14
1880	618,457	592,537		25,920	39.9	29	14
1890	762,794	730,077		32,717	23.3	28	14
1900	958,800	915,233		43,567	25.7	28	14
1910	1,221,119	1,156,817		64,302	27.4	28	14
1920	1,463,701	1,377,235		86,466	19.9	27	13
1930	1,729,205	1,614,191		115,014	18.1	27	13
1940	1,901,974	1,784,102		117,872	10.0	25	12
1950	2,005,552	1,890,282		115,270	5.4	29	14
1960	1,860,421	1,770,133		90,288	−7.2	30	14
1970	1,744,237	1,673,480		70,757	−6.2	34	15

[a] All figures also appear within the totals for the population of Virginia.

WEST VIRGINIA GOVERNORS

Governor	Party	Term
Arthur I. Boreman	Rep.	1863–1869
Daniel D. T. Farnsworth	Rep.	1869
William E. Stevenson	Rep.	1869–1871
John J. Jacob	Dem.	1871–1877
Henry M. Mathews	Dem.	1877–1881
Jacob B. Jackson	Dem.	1881–1885
Emanuel W. Wilson	Dem.	1885–1889
Aretas B. Fleming	Dem.	1889–1893
William A. MacCorkle	Dem.	1893–1897
George W. Atkinson	Rep.	1897–1901
Albert B. White	Rep.	1901–1905
William M. O. Dawson	Rep.	1905–1909
William E. Glasscock	Rep.	1909–1913
Henry D. Hatfield	Rep.	1913–1917
John J. Cornwell	Dem.	1917–1921
Ephraim F. Morgan	Rep.	1921–1925
Howard M. Gore	Rep.	1925–1929
William G. Conley	Rep.	1929–1933
Herman G. Kump	Dem.	1933–1937
Homer A. Holt	Dem.	1937–1941
Matthew M. Neely	Dem.	1941–1945
Clarence W. Meadows	Dem.	1945–1949
Okey L. Patteson	Dem.	1949–1953
William C. Marland	Dem.	1953–1957
Cecil H. Underwood	Rep	1957–1961
William W. Barron	Dem.	1961–1965
Hulett C. Smith	Dem.	1965–1969
Arch A. Moore, Jr.	Rep.	1969–1977
John D. Rockefeller IV	Dem.	1977–

dissertation, University of Wisconsin, 1948). See also Mother Mary Jones, *Autobiography* (1971); D. Fetherling, *Mother Jones* (1974); and Fred Mooney's autobiography, *Struggle in Coal Fields*, ed. J. W. Hess (1967).

Cultural developments. For religious history, see W. M. Gewehr, *Great Awakening in Virginia* (1930); F. Asbury, *Journal and Letters*, ed. E. T. Clark (3 vols.; 1958); R. B. Semple, *Baptists in Virginia* (1894); W. B. Posey, *Frontier Mission* (1966); W. W. Sweet, *Religion on American Frontier* (4 vols.; 1931–46) and *Virginia Methodism* (1955); E. T. Thompson, *Presbyterians in South* (1963); J. B. Boles, *Great Revival* (1972); W. Meade, *Old Churches, Ministers, and Families of Virginia* (2 vols.; 1857); G. W. Peterkin, *Protestant Episcopal Church in West Virginia* (1902); W. E. Garrison and A. T. De-Groot, *Disciples of Christ* (1948); and E. A. West, *Search for Ancient Order* (2 vols.; 1957).

Standard work on education is C. H. Ambler, *History of Education in West Virginia* (1951). Negro education is treated in C. G. Woodson, *Early Negro Education in West Virginia* (1921). For collegiate education, see W. K. Woolery, *Bethany Years* (1941); C. C. Regier, *West Liberty* (1939); A. G. Slonaker, *Shepherd College* (1967); K. M. Plummer, *West Virginia Wesleyan College* (1965); J. C. Harlan, *West Virginia State College* (1968); and, for Marshall University, R. G. Toole, *West Virginia History* (Jan., Oct., 1952; Jan., 1953). Useful for beginnings of newspapers, printing, and publishing is O. K. Rice, *West Virginia History* (July, 1953).

Few works of "Appalachianists" can stand the tests of scholarship. Useful is J. C. Campbell, *Southern Highlander and His Home* (1921). Although it does not deal with West Virginia at all, H. M. Caudill, *Night Comes to Cumberlands* (1962), provides more perceptive treatment of the state's culture and problems than does the sociologically oriented J. E. Weller, *Yesterday's People* (1965). Excellent for folk music are J. H. Cox, *Folk-Songs Mainly from West Virginia* (1939), *Folk Songs of South* (1925), and *Journal of American Folk-Lore* (Oct.–Dec., 1934). Best account of famous feud is V. C. Jones, *Hatfields and McCoys* (1948), but definitive treatment remains to be done. Except for the Negro, little has been written on ethnic elements. For the Negro, see, in addition to works previously cited, J. R. Sheeler, "Negro in West Virginia Before 1900" (Ph.D. dissertation, University of West Virginia, 1954); L. R. Harlan, *Booker T. Washington* (1972); and K. R. Bailey, *West Virginia Historical Quarterly* (Jan., 1973).

OTIS K. RICE
West Virginia Institute of Technology

WEST VIRGINIA, UNIVERSITY OF (Morgan-town, 26506),

opened in 1867 as the state-supported Agricultural College of West Virginia. It became a university known by its present name in 1895, and it currently has an enrollment of 17,000 students. Its library houses a rich and varied collection of manuscript materials relating chiefly to West Virginia and the upper Ohio River valley. Included are extensive holdings of county records dating from 1736, the files of numerous businesses, and the personal papers of governors (ARTHUR I. BOREMAN; J. J. Cornwell; A. B. Fleming; William E. Glasscock; Howard M. Gore; Ephraim F. Morgan; FRANCIS HARRISON PIERPONT) and political figures (HENRY G. DAVIS; STEPHEN B. ELKINS; NATHAN GOFF).

See D. Kirby, *West Virginia Historical Quarterly* (Jan., 1952); C. H. Quenzel, *West Virginia Historical Quarterly* (Jan., 1944); and R. C. Woods, *West Virginia Historical Quarterly* (April, 1957).

WEST VIRGINIA CAMPAIGNS (1861–1863).

The strategic importance of western Virginia dictated that both Union and Confederate forces seek its control. Assigned the task of securing the Baltimore & Ohio Railroad, George B. McClellan with 20,000 federal soldiers moved against defending Confederate forces (5,000) under Robert S. Garnett and JOHN PEGRAM in June, 1861. Successive Union victories at PHILIPPI (June 3), RICH MOUNTAIN (July 11), and Carrick's Ford (July 13) slammed Confederate forces into the Alleghenies, where they regrouped under W. W. LORING astride the Staunton-Parkersburg Pike entrance into the Shenandoah Valley. Meanwhile, the Kanawha Valley was penetrated and Charleston occupied on July 25 by the federal brigade of Jacob D. Cox, who drove defending Confederate forces of HENRY WISE back upon Lewisburg. In August, 1861, ROBERT E. LEE assumed control of a Confederate effort to stay the federal advance, but the campaign failed following the defeat of Confederate arms by McClellan's successor William S. Rosecrans at CHEAT MOUNTAIN (September 10–13) and Carnifex Ferry (September 10).

In the spring of 1862, Union forces continued their pressure from the west, Cox driving the Confederate forces of Loring and HENRY HETH back upon the Virginia & Tennessee Railroad and John C. Frémont forcing the small southern army of EDWARD JOHNSON toward Staunton. In September, however, following the transfer of Cox's Kanawha division to reinforce John Pope in northern Virginia, Loring, in the Kanawha campaign, reinvested that valley, retaking Charleston (September 13) and driving federal forces back. Cox returned with his division following the ANTIETAM campaign and in October reoccupied the Kanawha Valley.

Two raids, one by each antagonist, highlighted campaigning in western Virginia in 1863: the Jones-Imboden raid in April, conducted by a small southern force against the Baltimore & Ohio Railroad with limited success; and that executed by Union General W. W. Averell toward the Virginia & Tennessee Railroad via Lewisburg (November 1–8). Averell's move was thwarted after the exhausting defeat of a small Confederate army under General John Echols at Droop Mountain (November 6). Thereafter campaigning was limited to desultory raiding by federal cavalry against the railroad and nearby salt and lead works in southwestern Virginia.

See J. Hotchkiss, *Virginia* (1899); R. White, *West Virginia* (1899); D. S. Freeman, *R. E. Lee* (1935) and *Lee's Lieutenants* (1942); R. U. Johnson and C. C. Buel (eds.), *Battles and Leaders* (1887), I, II; *Official Records, Armies*, Ser. 1, Vols. V, XII, XIX, XX, XXV, XXVII, XXIX, XXXIII, XXXIX, XLIII, XLVI, LI; J. G. Nicolay, *Outbreak of Rebellion* (1882); and R. V. Husley, *West Virginia History* (April, 1972).

F. VAL HUSLEY
West Virginia Institute of Technology

WEST VIRGINIA HISTORICAL SOCIETY

(State Department of Archives and History, Science and Cultural Center, Capitol Complex, Charleston, 25305), founded in 1939, sponsors a museum, library, archives, and manuscript collection. With the Department of Archives and History it publishes *West Virginia History*, a quarterly with a circulation of about 800, which publishes book reviews and scholarly articles on West Virginia history.

WHEAT had a successful beginning in Virginia

two weeks after the founding of Jamestown in 1607, when "English grain" was planted in a small forest opening made by cutting down trees to build a fort. Earlier token efforts in Spanish Florida and other Virginia settlements were failures. Eventually wheat became established throughout the TIDEWATER South as a subsistence crop used as a hedge against starvation while growing the much more valuable tobacco. On occasion, small quantities of surplus wheat were accepted in the colonies as payment of taxes and QUITRENTS.

French cultural preference for wheat bread was behind many unsuccessful attempts to plant this grain along the lower Mississippi. Finally it was recognized that the plant would only grow to straw on rich alluvial floodplains and that other sources of supply had to be found. By 1721 Louisiana plantations were receiving high-quality Illinois wheat shipped down the Mississippi River in deerskin grain sacks. Still some epicures continued to import their favorite flour from France whenever supplies were available.

Many southern farmers were discouraged from growing wheat because of serious disease problems. George Washington is known to have been one who experimented with Siberian varieties in an attempt to avoid losses from rust, smut, and the Hessian fly. Gradually some areas of Maryland and Virginia developed a reputation for high-quality flour and were able to establish an export market supplying the West Indies and Madeira Islands. As demand for grain foods in an increasingly industrialized England became stronger, special qualities of American wheat were finally recognized. London bakers discovered gold in Alabama flour, claiming its low moisture content allowed them to add much water to the dough and thus make a greater profit from sale of heavier bread.

Hearing of the strong market for wheat, farmers in remote areas of North Carolina invented the "rolling hogshead" to skid their grain to mills, where it was prepared for export. Someone in South Carolina began the practice of shipping flour in counterfeit barrels displaying false inspection marks and brand names of well-known northern estates.

Yet, outside of Virginia, wheat in the South usually remained distinctly secondary to CORN, TOBACCO, and COTTON unless abnormally low prices for these crops happened to prevail. Food short-ages caused by the Civil War changed this traditional relationship. Suddenly Georgia farmers were urged to plant wheat everywhere, and it became the patriotic duty of plantation owners to supply Confederate armies. Postwar interest was maintained by wheat-growing societies formed in various parts of Georgia and Alabama. At meetings and conventions, members exchanged information on new cultivation methods and seed varieties.

All southern states, including Florida, produced some wheat until the present century, when an expanding railroad network indirectly caused another cycle of decline to occur. Today cheap transportation threatens completely to overwhelm southern wheat under the enormous yields from highly mechanized farms spread across the vast midwestern wheat belt.

See P. A. Bruce, *Economic History of Virginia in Seventeenth Century* (1935); L. C. Gray, *History of Agriculture in Southern U.S.* (1958); T. P. Kettell, *Southern Wealth and Northern Profits* (1860); C. E. Leighty, *Farm Bulletin* (1917); and W. Range, *Century of Georgia Agriculture* (1954).

ALAN K. CRAIG
Florida Atlantic University

WHEELER, JOSEPH (1836–1906), born in Augusta, Ga., was graduated from West Point in 1859. When Georgia seceded he joined the southern cause. In the first year Wheeler led Alabama infantry with the Army of Tennessee, winning distinction at SHILOH. Given a cavalry command, "Fightin' Joe" never equaled NATHAN B. FORREST's success as an independent raider. In the

SOUTHERN WHEAT PRODUCTION, 1850–1969
(in thousands of bushels)

	1850	1860	1870	1880	1890	1900	1910	1920	1930	1940	1950	1959	1969	% of U.S. Total
Ala.	294	1,218	1,055	1,530	209	629	114	223	15	54	154	1,070	2,333	.18
Ark.	200	958	742	1,270	956	2,450	526	2,051	153	353	289	2,946	6,493	.41
Del.	483	913	895	1,175	1,501	1,871	1,644	1,572	1,975	1,131	1,030	618	716	.05
Fla.	1	3				1						170	923	.07
Ga.	1,089	2,545	2,127	3,160	1,096	1,766	753	1,086	409	1,630	1,415	2,027	2,062	.16
Ky.	2,143	7,395	5,729	11,356	10,707	14,265	8,739	10,375	2,483	3,659	4,491	3,877	5,272	.40
La.		32	10	5		2		6		1		709	564	.04
Md.	4,495	6,103	5,774	8,005	8,348	9,672	9,463	9,621	9,095	6,581	5,719	3,709	3,874	.29
Miss.	138	588	274	219	17	37	5	55	6	39	109	784	1,978	.15
Mo.	2,982	4,228	14,316	24,967	30,114	23,073	29,837	65,210	15,117	30,891	26,000	35,731	26,961	2.00
N.C.	2,130	4,744	2,860	3,397	4,292	4,342	3,827	4,745	3,623	4,969	4,582	8,609	7,327	.55
S.C.	1,066	1,286	784	962	658	1,017	311	631	505	2,122	1,603	3,117	2,165	.16
Tenn.	1,619	5,459	6,189	7,331	8,301	11,924	6,517	6,362	2,481	3,886	3,488	3,469	5,015	.38
Tex.	42	1,478	415	2,568	4,283	12,266	2,561	36,427	44,078	28,096	75,277	50,116	65,088	4.90
Va.	11,213	13,131	7,399	7,826	7,904	8,908	8,007	11,446	8,575	7,212	6,865	5,996	6,478	.49
W.Va.	incl. in Va.	incl. in Va.	2,484	4,002	3,634	4,326	2,576	3,748	1,360	1,782	1,208	512	373	.03

traditional cavalry roles of reconnaissance and flank protection for the army, however, Wheeler was unsurpassed. His boldness and brilliance, such as at PERRYVILLE, where his 1,200 men immobilized 20,000 federals, earned him a major generalship at age twenty-six. He also fought every rearguard action for the army from Shiloh to Atlanta. After the surrender Wheeler fled south but was captured and briefly imprisoned. Paroled, he became a lawyer-planter in north Alabama. Elected to Congress (1881–1882, 1883, 1885–1900), he fought for national reconciliation and Alabama's economic improvement. Wheeler eagerly donned his country's uniform once more to fight in the Spanish-American War and the Philippine insurrection. After retiring, he traveled and spoke widely.

See J. P. Dyer, *Joseph Wheeler* (1941); J. W. Dubose, *General J. Wheeler* (1912), not objective; T. C. Deleon, *Joseph Wheeler* (1899), biased; and E. J. Warner, *Generals in Gray* (1959), brief sketch.

GARY L. R. ANDERSON
U.S. Air Force Academy

WHEELING, W.VA. (pop. 48,188), is on the Ohio River approximately 45 miles southwest of Pittsburgh, Pa. When first settled in 1769 by EBENEZER ZANE and his brothers, the site already was known as Wheeling or Weeling ("place of the skull"), allegedly because of the beheading here of earlier settlers by the Delaware Indians. Ft. Fincastle, constructed in 1774 by order of Virginia's governor Lord Dunmore, was renamed Ft. Henry in 1776 in honor of PATRICK HENRY. The fort was attacked by Indians and British in 1777 and again in 1782. Additional settlers moved to the area after the American Revolution, and in 1793 Zane formally laid out the town of Zanesburg. The town grew rapidly as a commercial center and river port for westward-bound pioneers. The town reclaimed the site's original name in 1806. Although the completion of the CUMBERLAND ROAD to this point in 1819 further expanded the town's commercial importance, the development of area IRON deposits made it equally important as an industrial center. Indeed, antebellum Wheeling rivaled Pittsburgh for the commercial and industrial dominance of the upper Ohio Valley. Strongly Unionist in sentiment, the city hosted the Wheeling conventions of 1861 and 1862, which led directly to the secession from Virginia of that state's western and northern counties. Yet the Civil War, the diminished importance of river transit, and the decline of the Cumberland Road as a commercial artery greatly handicapped the city's hopes for additional growth. Although it lost in its competition with Pittsburgh, Wheeling remains a major commercial and industrial center in the state. It manufactures steel, tin-plated metals, glassware, electrical equipment, plastics, and clothing. Also, both by river and by rail, the city ships lumber, tobacco, limestone and clay.

See files of Wheeling *Gazette* (1826–59), *Intelligencer* (1852–), Republican daily, and *News-Register* (1890–), Democratic daily, all on microfilm.

WHEELING INTELLIGENCER began daily publication in 1852. A Unionist newspaper prior to and during the Civil War, the *Intelligencer* was the leading advocate of separate statehood for the western counties of Virginia. This Republican daily currently has a circulation of approximately 25,000 copies.

See bound volumes at Library of Congress (1852–1916); and microfilm from Bell & Howell (1852–1900, 1911–16, 1928–).

WHIG PARTY was the only powerful, well-organized, and enduring opposition political party the South has known prior to the late twentieth century. Throughout the 1840s, the Whigs persistently contested Democratic party control of the South, winning significant support in the BLACK BELT counties that stretched from the Carolinas to Louisiana. The integrity and harmony of southern Whiggery was increasingly compromised after 1845 by the growing sectional struggle over slavery and the emerging antislavery crusade, which attracted the support of growing numbers of northern Whigs. Following a successful defense of the Unionist cause during the crisis of 1848–1850 (COMPROMISE OF 1850), Whiggery rapidly disintegrated as an effective political organization below the Mason-Dixon Line as southern politicians and citizens united in common defense of the peculiar institution. After 1854, the Whig party in the South for all practical purposes disappeared.

Initial partisans of the Whig cause had been conservative, slavery-oriented defenders of STATES' RIGHTS, outraged at what they considered the unconstitutional, even tyrannical, behavior of Andrew Jackson and his vassal Martin Van Buren during the NULLIFICATION and banking controversies of the early 1830s. However, as HENRY CLAY emerged to dominate the national Whig coalition after the departure of the always uneasy Calhoun faction in 1837 and as the economies of both the North and South continued to expand and diversify during the following decade, southern Whiggery assumed a different cast. Transcending such specific local divisions as state debt repudiation in Mississippi and relief legislation in Kentucky, Louisiana, and Georgia during the hard times of the late thirties and early forties, Whigs embraced the general doctrines of nationalism, sectional harmony based upon mutual trust between slave states and free, and economic advancement along contemporary capitalist-commercial lines of industrial growth and diversification.

What recent scholarship there has been on the topic tends to repudiate ARTHUR C. COLE's early judgment that southern Whigs and Democrats tended to divide along rigid conservative-liberal, slave owner–small farmer, aristocrat-democrat social and economic lines. For a multitude of reasons, Whigs and Democrats attracted the support of all interests, groups, and classes in the antebellum South. The chief distinguishing feature of the parties seems to have been the stress placed by the Whigs after 1840 upon sectional trust and harmony as opposed to the persistent demands of their Democratic opponents that the North acquiesce in the equal rights and interests of slavery. The rapid development of antislavery feeling north and east of the Ohio River after 1845 rendered the Whig position in the South increasingly untenable, and the decline and fall of southern Whiggery in the early 1850s was one of many factors leading inexorably to civil war.

See A. C. Cole, *Whig Party in South* (1913), only full-length study; R. P. McCormick, *Second American Party System* (1966); and C. G. Sellers, *American Historical Review* (Jan., 1954).

LISLE A. ROSE
U.S. Department of State

WHITE, EDWARD DOUGLASS (1845–1921),

ninth chief justice of the U.S. Supreme Court, was born near Thibodeaux, La., the youngest child of a planter family. After service in the Confederate army, he practiced law. He was state senator (1875–1879), associate justice of the Louisiana supreme court (1879–1880), and U.S. senator (1891–1894). In state politics he was a consistent foe of the LOUISIANA STATE LOTTERY. President Grover Cleveland appointed him associate justice of the Supreme Court in 1894, and President William H. Taft elevated him to chief justice in 1910. White's claim to judicial statesmanship rests upon his dissent in 1895 to the Court's invalidating the income tax (*Pollock* v. *Farmers' Loan & Trust Company*), his opinions in the insular cases (1901), and the "rule of reason" in the antitrust cases (1911). His opinions on the Court reflect an innate conservatism that viewed the American constitution-

al system of his day as a model for a well-organized society. His consistency of approach made his theories stand out in the aimless wandering of the Court of his period.

See *Proceedings of Supreme Court of U.S. in Memory of White* (Dec., 1921); R. B. Highsaw, "Chief Justice White" (Ph.D. dissertation, Harvard, 1945); and K. B. Umbreit, *Our Eleven Chief Justices* (1938).

ROBERT B. HIGHSAW
University of Alabama

WHITE, GEORGE HENRY (1852–1918), last

southern congressman of African origin until 1973, was the son of free parents from Bladen County, N.C. A turpentine worker, he attended a succession of schools, including Howard University, from which he was graduated in 1877. White settled in New Bern, N.C., where he taught school, became principal of a black academy, and read law under a native white judge active in Republican politics. In 1880 he won election to the state house, in 1884 to the state senate, and in 1886 and 1890 to the solicitorship of the Second District. After the Democratic legislature detached his home county from the district, he moved to nearby Tarboro and in 1896 swept to victory to the U.S. House of Representatives. Despite mounting white hostility, he won a second term in 1898. While in Washington, he was hailed as one of a new generation of race leaders because of his championing of blacks in the army and efforts to secure passage of an anti-lynching bill. After North Carolina adopted a DIS-FRANCHISEMENT amendment in 1901, White resigned from Congress; with a frustrated curse— "May God damn North Carolina, the state of my birth"—he announced his decision to remain in Washington and practice law. In 1907 he moved to Philadelphia; here he founded a savings bank and oversaw development of a black town, Whitesboro, N.J.

See J. E. Elmore, "North Carolina Negro Congressmen" (M.A. thesis, University of North Carolina, 1964); and H. L. Ingle, "White," unpublished paper.

H. L. INGLE
University of Tennessee, Chattanooga

WHITE, HUGH LAWSON (1773–1840), was

born in Iredell County, N.C. He moved with his family to Tennessee in 1781, trained in the law, and rose to prominence in the frontier gentry. White served on the Tennessee superior court (1801–1807), on the supreme court of appeals, and in the state senate (1807–1809, 1817–1825); from 1812 to 1827, he was president of the Bank of Tennessee. White succeeded Andrew Jackson in the U.S. Senate in 1825. During Jackson's presidency, White drafted the legislation that in 1830 authorized removal of the Indians from the South to west of the Mississippi. White became the rallying point for southerners—Democratic and Whig alike—opposed to Jackson's circumvention of established leaders and to Martin Van Buren's nomination. In 1835 he was nominated as a presidential candidate by the legislatures of Alabama and Tennessee; in 1836 he received over 40 percent of the vote in seven southern states and won majorities in Tennessee and Georgia. White played a crucial role, albeit an unintentional one, in catalyzing the growth of the Whig opposition in the South. He resigned from the Senate in January, 1840.

See L. P. Gresham, "H. L. White" (Ph.D. dissertation, Vanderbilt, 1943), summarized in *Tennessee Historical Quarterly* (Dec., 1944); N. N. Scott, *Memoir of White* (1856); P. Moore, *Journal of Southern History* (Aug., 1936); T. P. Abernethy, *Mississippi Valley Historical Review* (March, 1926); and C. M. Sellers, *James K. Polk* (1957).

SYDNEY NATHANS
Duke University

WHITE, WALTER FRANCIS (1893–1955),

was born in Atlanta, Ga., and earned his B.A. degree at Atlanta University in 1916. The Atlanta of White's youth was a scene of racial unrest. He and his family were threatened during the ATLANTA RACE RIOT in 1906, and he experienced discrimination while working during his school years. After college, he went to work for the black-owned Standard Life Insurance Company. He helped to organize the Atlanta branch of the NAACP and participated in its campaign for better schools for Atlanta's blacks. In 1918 he joined the staff in the national office of the NAACP and became executive secretary in 1931. Under his leadership, the NAACP continued its crusade against lynching and launched a campaign for voting rights. White's light complexion and blond hair allowed him to pose as a white man during his many trips to the South to investigate lynchings and race riots. Numerous articles and several books resulted from his dangerous forays into the South. White joined A. PHILIP RANDOLPH in the March-on-Washington movement in 1941, which led to President Franklin D. Roosevelt's order establishing the Fair Employment Practices Committee. His investigation of discrimination in the armed forces helped pave the way for President Harry Truman's desegregation order in 1948.

See White's autobiography, *Man Called White* (1948); P. Cannon, *Gentle Knight* (1956); and E. R. Embree, *13 Against the Odds* (1944).

ARVARH E. STRICKLAND
University of Missouri, Columbia

WHITECAPPING is a term applied to many forms of group VIOLENCE that erupted in the South. From the KU KLUX KLAN of Reconstruction to REGULATORS of the 1880s, clandestine groups of whites occasionally terrorized Negroes and whites; whitecapping represented a continuation of that tradition. The objectives of the Whitecappers varied from place to place. Sometimes they attempted to uphold moral values by flogging drunkards, wife beaters, and adulterers. In Alabama and Georgia moonshiners organized Whitecap clubs to inflict vengeance upon those they suspected of testifying to federal revenue agents. In Mississippi, Whitecappers consisted of impoverished white farmers who attempted to drive Negro tenants off lands that merchants had acquired through mortgage foreclosures. Whitecapping, in its most common form, was an attempt of whites to terrorize blacks and may be viewed as a connecting link between the Klan of Reconstruction and the Klan of the 1920s.

See H. D. Graham and T. D. Gurr, *Violence in America* (1969); W. F. Holmes, *Journal of Southern History* (May, 1969), *Mid-America* (April, 1973), and *American Jewish Historical Quarterly* (March, 1974); and E. W. Crozier, *White-Caps* (1899).

WILLIAM F. HOLMES
University of Georgia

WHITE CITIZENS' COUNCIL. See CITIZENS' COUNCILS

WHITE OAK SWAMP, BATTLE OF (June 30,

1862), was one of the last of the PENINSULAR CAMPAIGN. As G. B. McClellan was changing his base of operations from White House Landing to HARRISON'S LANDING, R. E. Lee called for simultaneous attacks on his retreating column. A. P. HILL, with J. B. MAGRUDER in support, was to attack the right and center, while T. J. JACKSON was scheduled to close in on the federal rear from the north. To achieve his objective, Jackson first had to cross White Oak Swamp, a ten-mile half-circle of marshy land with a stream running through the center. When he arrived at the swamp, he found the bridge crossing it destroyed and the south side occupied by federal soldiers. He led his troops across the swamp, but federal fire forced him back. It was at this point that Jackson, now exhausted, seemed incapable of any further action. Hill failed to take advantage of a bridge constructed by WADE HAMPTON a short distance away. Jackson also failed to send reinforcements around the swamp to aid JAMES LONGSTREET, then fighting near FRAYSER'S FARM. There was definitely a lack of staff coordination by the Confederates.

See *Official Records, Armies*, Ser. 1, Vol. XI; D. S. Freeman, *Lee's Lieutenants* (1945); B. Catton, *Lincoln's Army* (1951); R. U. Johnson and C. C. Buel (eds.), *Battles and Leaders* (1884–87), II; G. B. McClellan, *Own Story* (1887); T. H. Williams, *Lincoln and His Generals* (1952); and J. P. Cullen, *Peninsular Campaign* (1973).

ALVIN R. SUNSERI
University of Northern Iowa

WHITE PRIMARY was one means by which southern states disfranchised Negroes from 1900 to the 1940s. Custom had excluded blacks during the 1870s and 1880s from county primaries held to select delegates to district conventions. When the POPULIST movement intensified partisan competition for Negro votes in the 1890s, conservative Democrats often resorted to fraud to maintain their supremacy. Ensuing demands for election reform coincided with rising racism; devices designed to restore honesty at the polls also suggested a means of covert DISFRANCHISEMENT. In the statewide primary, state Democratic officials found a way of excluding Negroes from party membership and participation in primary elections.

Until the 1940s state Democratic organizations rather than the states determined voter eligibility in primaries. Texas, following a 1921 U.S. Supreme Court decision that placed primaries outside federal control, barred blacks from primary elecions in 1923. In NIXON V. HERNDON (1927) the Supreme Court ruled that the 1923 law violated the equal protection clause of the Fourteenth Amendment. When Texas subsequently attempted to give the state Democratic executive committee power to define party membership, the Court invalidated that procedure. *Nixon* v. *Condon* (1932) stated that, even if a party was a private association not covered by the Fourteenth Amendment, Texas law, not the party, had given the executive committee its authority. After the state Democratic convention limited party membership to whites, the Supreme Court upheld the convention's action in GROVEY V. TOWNSEND (1935).

The ultimate fate of the white primary depended not on who would determine voter eligibility in the election, but on the primary's place in the state's election apparatus. UNITED STATES V. CLASSIC (1941) found that Louisiana primaries were an integral part of the state's election machinery and within federal jurisdiction; SMITH V. ALLWRIGHT (1944) added to the *Classic* precedent the ruling that Texas primaries could not exclude blacks. In 1948 the federal district court in South Carolina declared the white primary unconstitutional because it was by custom the governing election in the South, and in 1953 the Supreme Court issued a similar decision regarding a Texas county primary.

See V. O. Key, *Southern Politics* (1949); J. M. Kousser, *Shaping Southern Politics* (1974); L. Overacker, *Journal of Negro History* (Jan., 1945); O. D. Weeks, *American Political Science Review* (June, 1948); R. J. Bunche, *Political Status* (1973); J. E. Christensen, "Constitutional Problems" (Ph.D. dissertation, University of Minnesota, 1952); P. Lewinson, *Race, Class, and Party* (1963); D. R. Matthews and J. W. Prothro, *Negroes* (1966); and W. C. Havard, *Changing Politics* (1972).

D. ALAN HARRIS
Old Dominion University

WHITE RIVER, rising in northwest Arkansas, curves slightly into Missouri, forming a watery crescent through the OZARK Mountains along narrow, wooded valleys, some 300 miles of which were impounded during 1913–1966. Leaving the hills near Batesville, Ark., the river turns mainly south through prairies and hardwood flats, vast acreages of which were cleared and drained after 1945 for the cultivation of rice and soybeans. Although known to both French and American trappers, the valley was not described until the naturalist Henry R. Schoolcraft descended it in 1818. Upriver, Schoolcraft saw scattered cabins, one of which belonged to Jacob Wolfe, who settled in 1809 as an Indian agent at present Norfork, Ark. Settlement upriver, though ultimately limited by the scarcity of farmland, actually preceded that downriver. Geographical isolation until the 1940s left the Ozarks culture a living museum of ballads, folklore, and handicrafts. An early habitation on the lower river was at Montgomery's Landing, located at the juncture of the White and the Mississippi and very close to the natural cutoff that directly linked those two with the Arkansas River. Some 50 miles upriver at St. Charles, Ark., in 1862, the Union gunboat *Mound City* exploded with heavy casualties when hit by Confederate land fire.

See J. Fleming, *White River* (1973); V. H. Holder, "Historical Geography" (M.A. thesis, University of Arkansas,

1966); E. C. Bearss *Arkansas Historical Quarterly* (Winter, 1962); D. Huddleston, *Ozark Mountaineer* (Sept., 1972); and H. R. Schoolcraft, *Narrative Journals* (1970).

ROBERT B. WALZ
Southern Arkansas University

WICHITA FALLS, TEX. (pop. 97,564), is on the Wichita River approximately 100 miles northwest of Ft. Worth and 15 miles south of the Oklahoma state line. The area, originally inhabited by Wichita Indians, remained otherwise unsettled until 1861, and not until the 1870s did the present community begin to develop. The city was primarily a cattle town and a market for area agriculture, and its early growth was slow. A line of the Ft. Worth & Denver City Railroad was constructed through the town in 1882, but any significant expansion of the city was hindered by droughts that plagued both farmers and cattlemen alike. Beginning in 1900, a series of dams and irrigation projects was constructed to alleviate the chronic shortage of water. In 1918, just as area agriculture had begun to prosper, the discovery of PETROLEUM further stimulated additional growth. Modern Wichita Falls is the commercial hub of a diversified agricultural area, an oil-refining center, and a manufacturer of electrical equipment, oil rigging, truck bodies, and cotton gins.

See files of Wichita Falls *Times* (1907–).

WICKES, LAMBERT (1742–1777), a Maryland merchant captain, received a commission in the Continental navy and took command of the brig *Reprisal* in April, 1776. That summer he took three prizes and fought off an attack by HMS *Shark*. In the fall he transported Benjamin Franklin to France and became the first American naval officer to cruise in European waters. Raiding in the English Channel during the winter and in the Irish Sea with *Lexington* and *Dolphin* several months later, Wickes terrorized shipping and took numerous prizes. Returning to French ports, he barely escaped HMS *Burford* by boldly jettisoning his guns. Wickes's use of French neutrality angered the British and hastened the outbreak of war between the two European powers. A storm off Newfoundland sank the *Reprisal* and cut short Wickes's colorful career.

See W. B. Clark, *Lambert Wickes* (1932), definitive, complete bibliography and guide to Wickes letters.

OSCAR P. FITZGERALD
Naval Historical Center

WICKHAM, WILLIAMS CARTER (1820–1888), born in Richmond and educated at the University of Virginia, was a Whig planter-lawyer who served in public offices throughout the 1850s and vigorously opposed secession. But when war came he enrolled immediately and fought with the Army of Northern Virginia in the battles of BULL RUN, WILLIAMSBURG, ANTIETAM, FREDERICKSBURG, CHANCELLORSVILLE, GETTYSBURG, WILDERNESS, SPOTSYLVANIA, COLD HARBOR, Rockfish Gap, and WAYNESBORO. In April, 1865, Wickham publicly endorsed the Republican party. Shortly thereafter he became president of the state-controlled Covington & Ohio Railroad. He reorganized it, aligned its interests with Collis P. Huntington of New York, and laid the groundwork for the creation of the Chesapeake & Ohio Railroad. A strong politician as well as businessman and lawyer, Wickham influenced Funder politics in Virginia throughout the Reconstruction decades. He declined to run for governor in 1880 or the U.S. Senate the following year; instead he preferred to remain with his railroad interests, which he did until his death. Uncompromising, strong-willed, committed to industrialization, Wickham was a man of change within the agrarian aristocratic class of Virginia.

See J. P. Maddox, *Virginia Conservatives* (1970), excellent; J. T. Moore, *Two Paths to New South* (1974), excellent; R. U. Johnson and C. C. Buel (eds.), *Battles and Leaders* (1884), III, IV; W. G. Ryckman, *Virginia Magazine of History and Biography* (Oct., 1967); C. W. Turner, *Chessie's Road* (1954); and Bagby and Aylett Papers, Virginia Historical Society.

JOSEPH P. HARAHAN
U.S. Government Historian

WIGFALL, LOUIS TREZEVANT (1816–1874), born in Edgefield, S.C., was controversial in state politics. He and PRESTON BROOKS wounded each other in a duel, and in another quarrel Wigfall killed a man. After bankruptcy, he moved to Texas, where he helped organize the Democratic party and was elected to the Texas legislature and, in 1859, to the U.S. Senate. Wigfall became known as a FIRE-EATER, advocating southern STATES' RIGHTS, slavery, SECESSION, and reopening the African slave trade, wrote the SOUTHERN MANIFESTO (1860), opposed the homestead bill, helped prevent compromises intended to prevent secession, and secretly procured guns and recruits for the South. Typically, Wigfall made his presence felt at FT. SUMTER by rowing under fire to the fort and dictating unauthorized surrender terms to Major Robert Anderson. A hero in the South, Wigfall became a presidential aide, Confederate general, and senator. His conspiracy to impose senatorial hegemony over President Jefferson Davis was disastrous for the Confederacy. He opposed efforts to arm slaves, maintaining that he would rather see the Confederacy defeated. After the war Wigfall fled to England, where he stayed until 1872. He died in Texas.

See L. T. Wigfall Family Papers, Library of Congress; Williams-Chesnut-Manning Collection, University of South Carolina Archives, for Wigfall's early life; L. W. Wright (Wigfall's daughter), *Southern Girl in '61* (1905); and A. L. King, *Louis T. Wigfall* (1970) and *Louisiana Studies* (Spring, 1968).

ALVY L. KING
University of Missouri, St. Louis,

WILCOX, CADMUS MARCELLUS (1824–1890), was born in Wayne County, N.C., but much of his youth was spent in Tennessee, where he attended the University of Tennessee for a time. In 1846 he graduated from West Point, received an appointment as second lieutenant, and was sent to serve in ZACHARY TAYLOR's and later WINFIELD SCOTT's armies in Mexico. He fought with distinction at Monterrey, Veracruz, Cerro Gordo, and Mexico City. After serving for a short time as a first lieutenant in Florida, he taught at the U.S. Military Academy (1842–1857). For a brief period he wrote and translated military textbooks. In June of 1861 he resigned his commission in the U.S. Army and was promptly made a colonel of infantry in the Confederate army. By October, 1861, he had attained the rank of brigadier general. Wilcox fought in virtually every significant battle in the Virginia area including the first and second battles of BULL RUN, the SEVEN DAYS' BATTLES, and the battles of SEVEN PINES, FREDERICKSBURG, CHANCELLORS-VILLE, GETTYSBURG, WILDERNESS, SPOTSYLVAN-IA, PETERSBURG, and APPOMATTOX, rising to the rank of major general dating from August, 1863. He seems to have been both well liked as a man and highly respected as a military commander. Wilcox settled down to a quiet life in Washington, D.C., following the war, declining various offers to serve in foreign armies. Between 1886 and 1890 he served in the federal government as chief of the railroad division of the General Land Office.

See D. S. Freeman, *Lee's Lieutenants* (3 vols.; 1943); letter from C. M. Wilcox, *Southern Historical Society Papers* (Sept., 1877), IV; *Official Records, Armies*, Ser. 1, Vols. XXI, XXV, XXVII; and R. U. Johnson and C. C. Buel (eds.), *Battles and Leaders* (1887), II, IV.

WILDER, JOHN THOMAS (1830–1917), born in rural New York, migrated later to Indiana. When war broke out, he was elected captain in the Union army, and after outstanding performances at SHILOH and CHATTANOOGA he was brevetted a brigadier general. In 1864 he resigned and moved

to Chattanooga, where he helped develop the surrounding region's natural resources. He started the Roane Iron Works, constructed a rail mill in Chattanooga, helped to promote and build the Clinchfield Railroad, speculated in real estate in several southern states, and established an iron furnace in Johnson City, Tenn. Civic-minded, he served variously as Chattanooga's mayor and postmaster.

See M. H. Wilder, *Book of Wilders* (1878); Chattanooga *Times* and Chattanooga *News* (Oct. 21, 1917); G. E. Govan and J. W. Livingood, *Chattanooga Country, 1540–1962* (1963); and S. C. Williams, *General John T. Wilder* (1936).

JAMES A. WARD
University of Tennessee, Chattanooga

WILDERNESS CAMPAIGN (May 5–6, 1864) was the initial clash of the final 11 months of the Civil War in Virginia between the armies of ROBERT E. LEE and Ulysses S. Grant. Fought in a tangled forest of scrub oak and pine located south of the Rapidan River and west of Chancellorsville, the battle was a vicious, confusing struggle. From the outset the opposing forces struggled blindly in the difficult terrain. Commands easily became disorganized as the dense undergrowth and the heavy smoke limited visibility. Coordination between units was haphazard; dangerous gaps, unsupported flanks, and missed opportunities characterized much of the conflict.

The engagement centered along two roads—the Orange Turnpike and the Orange Plank Road. Outnumbered nearly two to one, Lee attacked with two corps on the morning of May 5, striking the federals as they marched southward through the woods. This sudden attack surprised Grant, who ordered his army to regroup immediately. The federals halted the Confederate assault and counterattacked later that day. Lee's thinned ranks were saved from possible disaster by darkness. Early the next morning heavy federal forces broke Lee's line, but the sudden arrival of JAMES LONG-STREET's corps blunted the charge and sent it reeling with a vicious counterattack. Lee lost the initiative, however, when Longstreet was wounded. The battle ended with an abortive Confederate attack on Grant's right. Probably 25,000 men fell in this tactically drawn battle. However, the next day Grant moved out, not in retreat, but southward on the road that led inexorably to Appomattox.

See C. S. Venable, *Southern Historical Society Papers* (1889), excellent; A. A. Humphreys, *Virginia Campaign* (1883); C. W. Battine, *Crisis of Confederacy* (1905); E.

Steere, *Wilderness Campaign* (1960), scholarly and detailed; H. Heth, *Memoirs* (1974); and M. Howard, *Recollections* (1975).

JEFFRY D. WERT
Penn Valley High School, Spring Mills, Pa.

WILDERNESS ROAD was a name for several connecting arteries of the eighteenth-century frontier. One was the GREAT WAGON ROAD (Irish or Pennsylvania Road), from Wadkins Ferry on the Potomac to Ingles Ferry on the New River, which followed the Shenandoah Valley, then crossed the upper James and the headwaters of the Roanoke to the vicinity of present Radford, Va.; this was the main route of Scotch-Irish expansion into the southern Appalachians. Another was a projection of the above road down the middle fork of the Holston River, opened in 1760 by a Virginia regiment under William Byrd in an abortive expedition for the relief of Ft. Loudon. Ft. Chiswell (near present Max Meadows, Va.) rivaled Ft. Pitt as an outpost of western advance. This road ended at Long Island of the Holston (Kingsport, Tenn.).

The Wilderness Road, properly called, marked out by DANIEL BOONE for Colonel RICHARD HENDERSON in March and April, 1775, extended from the Long Island to BOONESBOROUGH on the Kentucky River. It ran north to Moccasin Gap (Gate City, Va.), crossed Clinch and Powell mountains, passed Glade Spring (Jonesville), and thence went through CUMBERLAND GAP. Angling northwest, crossing Pine Mountain and the Cumberland River gorge, it turned due north at the Hazel Patch near present London, Ky., and left the mountains north of Rockcastle River. An alternative route, northwest from Hazel Patch, was opened by BENJAMIN LOGAN in April, 1775, via Crab Orchard to St. Asaph's (Logan's Fort), now Stanford, Lincoln County. It was soon extended to Harrodsburg and the Falls of the Ohio. Danville, Bardstown, and Shepherdsville, Ky., developed on this route. The Wilderness Road was widened to a pack trail under Virginia authority in 1781 from Moccasin Gap to Boonesborough. It and Logan's route were partially relocated by Kentucky and made a wagon road from Cumberland Gap to Crab Orchard in 1796; tolls were instituted in 1797. Boone's trace north of Hazel Patch was abandoned. Wilderness Turnpike was the mountain portion of the State or Kentucky Road to Louisville.

See R. L. Kincaid, *Wilderness Road* (1947); T. Roosevelt, *Winning of West* (1889–96); and P. Rouse, Jr., *Great Wagon Road* (1973).

JOSEPH H. HARRISON, JR.
Auburn University

WILEY, BELL IRVIN (1906–), internationally known American historian whose primary interests are the plain people, the South, and the Civil War, was born in Halls, Tenn. His A.B., M.A., and Ph.D. degrees were earned, respectively, at Asbury, University of Kentucky, and Yale. In 1955 his fellow historians honored him with the presidency of the Southern Historical Association. Wiley has been widely acclaimed as teacher, author, and lecturer. He taught at Asbury, Mississippi Southern, University of Mississippi, Louisiana State, and Emory (1949–1974). He is best known as a publishing historian, and his name is synonymous with the common soldier of the Civil War, his best-known and best-loved books being *The Life of Johnny Reb* (1943) and *The Life of Billy Yank* (1952). *Life* magazine (February 3, 1961) referred to him as "the nation's foremost authority on soldier life in the Civil War." Dr. Wiley, therefore, has been in great demand as a lecturer and speaker the world over.

J. DAVID GRIFFIN
West Georgia College

WILKINS, ROY (1901–), the grandson of a Mississippi slave, was born in St. Louis. After graduating from the University of Minnesota (B.A., 1923), he moved to Kansas City, Mo., where he worked as a reporter for a Negro weekly (Kansas City *Call*) and served as secretary of the local chapter of the NATIONAL ASSOCIATION FOR THE ADVANCEMENT OF COLORED PEOPLE. His vigorous campaign against segregation brought him to the attention of national leaders of the NAACP, and in 1931 he became an assistant secretary of that organization's national office. After the resignation of W. E. B. DU BOIS, Wilkins became editor of the *Crisis* (1934–1949), the official organ of the NAACP. He became executive secretary of the organization after the death of WALTER WHITE in 1955 and served in that position during the CIVIL RIGHTS MOVEMENT of the next ten years. Since 1965 Wilkins has been executive director of the NAACP, its representative at numerous civil rights conferences, and in 1968 served as chairman of the American delegation to the International Conference on Human Rights at Teheran.

See R. Brisbane, *Black Vanguard* (1970); and C. Silberman, *Crisis in Black and White* (1964).

WILKINSON, JAMES (1757–1825), was born in Calvert County, Md. A Revolutionary War veteran who resigned while he was brigadier general for participating in the Conway cabal, Wilkinson became a land speculator in Kentucky. Participating with the Spanish government in a conspiracy to effectuate the secession of the southwestern states from the United States, he became a pensioner of the rival power, a status that continued after he rejoined the U.S. Army (1791). Having been appointed governor of the Louisiana Territory (1805), Wilkinson nevertheless joined with Aaron Burr in a plot that had flexible objectives. Predicated on the probability of war with Spain, the BURR CONSPIRACY envisioned either the separation from the Union of the western states or an invasion of Mexico, or both. Alarmed by the circulation of detailed information, Wilkinson abruptly switched positions. Posing as the savior of New Orleans, he alerted Thomas Jefferson about Burr's plans. The general later became the key witness for the government at Burr's trial in Richmond. After successfully defending himself from a former associate's allegations of treason (1809), Wilkinson failed in a campaign against Montreal during the War of 1812. He retired to a Louisiana plantation and died in Mexico City. If not an actual traitor, the hard-drinking soldier was unquestionably an accomplished intriguer and double-dealer.

See T. R. Hay and M. R. Werner, *Admirable Trumpeter* (1941); T. P. Abernethy, *Burr Conspiracy* (1954); D. Malone, *Jefferson: Second Term* (1974); H. S. Parmet and M. B. Hecht, *Aaron Burr* (1967); D. Clark, *Corruption of Wilkinson* (1809); J. Wilkinson, *Memoirs* (3 vols.; 1816); I. J. Cox, *American Historical Review* (July, 1914); Wilkinson Papers, Historical Society of Chicago; and Letters in Relation to Burr's Conspiracy (1806–08) and Innes Papers, Library of Congress.

HERBERT S. PARMET
Queensborough Community College, City University of New York

WILLIAM AND MARY, COLLEGE OF (Williamsburg, Va. 23185), chartered in 1693, is the second oldest institution of higher learning in the country. In 1781 it became the nation's first true university with colleges of law, medicine, and the arts. The college lost its royal support with the American Revolution and became a private school. The move of the new state's capital from Williamsburg to Richmond in 1779 and the opening of the University of Virginia in 1825 combined to erode gradually the school's premier position among Virginia colleges. Yet William and Mary proudly counted several presidents and Supreme Court justices, as well as numerous governors and legislators, among its graduates. It had been closed temporarily during the Yorktown campaign of the Revolutionary War and again in 1862 during the Civil War when its chief structure, the Wren Building, was burned down. The college failed

fully to recover from the war and was forced by financial difficulties to close again in the 1880s. Reopened in 1888 with limited state assistance, the college became a state-supported institution after the turn of the century. It became coeducational in 1918 and began its renaissance parallel with John D. Rockefeller's restoration of colonial Williamsburg. The library houses collections of numerous persons prominent in Virginia and the South: Presidents THOMAS JEFFERSON, JAMES MADISON, JAMES MONROE, JOHN TYLER, and GEORGE WASHINGTON; Chief Justice JOHN MARSHALL; Governors Lord Dunmore, PATRICK HENRY, and CHARLES T. O'FERRALL; as well as THOMAS R. DEW, GEORGE WYTHE, JOSEPH EGGLESTON JOHNSTON, and Nathaniel Beverley Tucker. Other collections include the CARTER FAMILY Papers, the Thomas Ritchie Papers (1830–1932), the George Washington Southhall Papers (1792–1912), the Peyton Skipworth Papers (1760–1912), and records of several early Virginia mills and the Chesapeake & Ohio Canal.

See G. W. Ewing, *Early Teaching of Science at William and Mary* (1938); H. B. Adams, *College of William and Mary* (1887); and M. Beach, *Bibliographical Guide to American Colleges and Universities* (1975).

WILLIAMS, AUBREY WILLIS (1890–1965), one of the most controversial New Deal figures, was born in Springville, Ala., the son of an itinerant workman. He received little formal education until 1911, when he enrolled in Maryville College in Tennessee. He served in World War I and, on return, qualified as a social worker. After working for ten years as executive director of the Wisconsin Conference of Social Work, he joined the American Public Welfare Association in 1932. In 1933 Harry L. Hopkins, director of the FEDERAL EMERGENCY RELIEF ADMINISTRATION, invited him to come to Washington as his deputy. Williams became deputy director of the WORKS PROGRESS ADMINISTRATION upon its creation in 1935 and was expected to succeed Hopkins when he moved to the Commerce Department in 1939. Williams' outspoken liberalism, however, had offended many, and instead he was appointed full-time director of the NATIONAL YOUTH ADMINISTRATION, an agency he had headed in a part-time capacity since 1935. Upon the demise of the NYA in 1943, Williams joined the FARMERS' UNION as its southern organizer. In 1945, Franklin Roosevelt chose him to head the RURAL ELECTRIFICATION ADMINISTRATION, but the Senate refused to confirm the nomination. Williams then returned to his native Alabama as editor of the periodical *Southern Farm*

and Home. His outspoken support for the civil rights movement, however, led to the failure of the magazine through a consequent loss of circulation and advertising revenue. He returned to Washington, where he died.

See J. Salmond, in *Continuity and Change in Twentieth-Century America* (1975), III; A. Williams Papers, Franklin D. Roosevelt Library; and NYA and WPA Records, National Archives.

JOHN SALMOND
La Trobe University, Australia

WILLIAMS, JOHN SHARP (1854–1932), born in Memphis, was orphaned by his father's death at SHILOH in 1862 and reared by his grandparents on their plantation, Cedar Grove, in Yazoo County, Miss. Educated at the University of Virginia and at the University of Heidelberg in Germany, Williams returned to Yazoo County as a lawyer-planter. He was elected in 1892 to Congress, where he quickly gained a reputation as a skilled debater, and served as Democratic minority leader for three terms (1903–1909). In 1907 he narrowly defeated JAMES K. VARDAMAN for the U.S. Senate. His national reputation and popular appeal enabled him to overcome Vardaman's racist appeals to the electorate. Although an ardent white supremist, Williams represented a more moderate approach than Vardaman to racial questions. In the Senate he favored states' rights, lower tariff, popular election of senators, and regulation of trusts. He was a vigorous supporter of President Woodrow Wilson's policies on preparedness, entrance into World War I, and the League of Nations. An aristocrat and scholar, Williams was known in Washington until his retirement in 1923 as the "Gentleman from Mississippi."

See G. C. Osborn, *Williams* (1943); A. D. Kirwan, *Rednecks* (1951); and W. F. Holmes, *White Chief* (1970).

CHARLES SALLIS
Millsaps College

WILLIAMS, TENNESSEE (1911–). Most important of southern playwrights and a writer of international reputation, Thomas Lanier Williams was born in Mississippi, where he lived until moving to St. Louis in 1923 or 1924. His unhappy youth in St. Louis is depicted with considerable accuracy in *The Glass Menagerie* (1945). *Menagerie* created a reputation that Williams' next successful play, *A Streetcar Named Desire* (1947, Pulitzer Prize) extended and confirmed. *Streetcar*'s Blanche Dubois and Stanley Kowalski, the sensitive, lost southern aristocrat and the dominant, brutal immigrants' son who destroys her, have become established in the American consciousness, vivid archetypal characters, a permanent part of American literature. Others of Williams' important plays include *Summer and Smoke* (1948), *The Rose Tattoo* (1951), *Camino Real* (1953), *Cat on a Hot Tin Roof* (1955, Pulitzer Prize), *Orpheus Descending* (1957), *Suddenly Last Summer* (1958), *Sweet Bird of Youth* (1959), and *The Night of the Iguana* (1961). More recent plays—e.g., *The Milk Train Doesn't Stop Here Any More* (1963) and *Small Craft Warnings* (1972)—have been disappointing. Williams has also written poetry, short stories, one-act plays, a novel (*The Roman Spring of Mrs. Stone*, 1950), and movie scripts (e.g., *Baby Doll*, 1956).

Except for *The Glass Menagerie*, the Mexico of *Night of the Iguana*, and the expressionistic Latin American world of *Camino Real*, the South—small-town, or Gulf Coast, Mississippi or New Orleans—is the locale of all of Williams' major plays. He depicts a far wider variety of life in the South than is usually recognized: among others, the New Orleans slum dweller (*Streetcar*); the poor-white-become-wealthy (*Cat*); the established rich (*Suddenly Last Summer*); the middle class in the professions (*Summer and Smoke*); the foreign born (*Rose Tattoo, Summer and Smoke*); and the corrupt small-time politician (*Sweet Bird*).

At their best, Williams' plays make fine use of Chekhovian techniques: a concatenation of mood against mood, of compassion and objectivity, of comedy and pathos; effective dramatic symbols; evocative dialogue; careful use of setting, light, and sound for the purposes of dramatic impressionism. But much more violent than Chekhov, Williams is also part of the southern Gothic tradition that includes, among others, Edgar Allan Poe and William Faulkner. The accusation of sentimentality and sensationalism is justifiable against Williams at his worst; at his best he incorporates his disturbed and disturbing vision into firm, powerful dramatic structures, which have become part of the standard theatrical repertory in the Western world.

See S. L. Falk, *Tennessee Williams* (1961); E. M. Jackson, *Broken World of Tennessee Williams* (1965); B. Nelson, *Tennessee Williams: Man and His Work* (1961); N. M. Tischler, *Tennessee Williams: Rebellious Puritan* (1961); J. H. Adler, in L. D. Rubin and R. D. Jacobs (eds.), *South: Modern Southern Literature* (1961); W. L. Dusenbury, in *Theme of Loneliness in Modern American Drama* (1960); H. Popkin, *Tulane Drama Review* (March, 1960); G. Weales, *Tennessee Williams* (1965); and E. D.

Williams, *Remember Me to Tom* (1963). Most of his papers are at University of Texas Library.

JACOB H. ADLER
Purdue University

WILLIAMS, THOMAS HARRY (1909–), Boyd

Professor of History at Louisana State University, earned the Ph.D. degree at Wisconsin in 1937. His writings reflect a coveted historical objectivity. He refused to accept either WILLIAM A. DUNNING's racist approach or the Marxist theory of Reconstruction. His appraisal of Civil War campaigns stressed Abraham Lincoln's superior judgment and U. S. Grant's knowledge of overall strategy. He produced moderate evaluations of P. G. T. BEAUREGARD and Rutherford B. Hayes and displayed a thorough grasp of how the military has operated. Williams received the Pulitzer Prize for *Huey Long* (1969), judiciously utilizing oral history of both the elitists and lesser knowns. According to Williams, Long used the wrong means to correct the evils in America; he never overcame the heritage of traditionally corrupt Louisiana politics. In his Organization of American Historians presidential address (1973), Williams asserted that radicalism seldom appeared in the South but manifested itself more intensely than in other sections when occurring, *e.g.*, populism, Long, Lyndon Johnson, and the black civil rights movement. Williams believed that this radicalism now led the South more readily to accept the blacks than the North. But the media, liberal establishment, intellectuals, and eventually the masses failed to accept Johnson. Williams sought a reassessment of Johnson and the South and is currently working on a biography of Johnson.

DONALD R. WHITNAH
University of Northern Iowa

WILLIAMSBURG, BATTLE OF (May 4–5, 1862),

was part of the opening phase of McClellan's PENINSULAR CAMPAIGN of 1862. After stalling the Union advance from Yorktown for over a month through clever ruses, J. B. MAGRUDER moved his Confederate forces to a more defensible position at a line of previously constructed fortifications between Halfway House and Williamsburg, Va. On May 4–5, Joseph Hooker closed to attack but was met with a determined defense. Toward noon of May 5, Confederate forces began a counterattack that drove Hooker's federals from a good portion of the field. Meanwhile, W. S. Hancock's federal brigade began to envelop the Confederate left and eventually forced a Confederate retreat

on the night of May 5. Of 40,768 federal soldiers engaged, 2,239 were killed or missing. The Confederates lost 1,603 of 31,823 engaged.

See D. S. Freeman, *Lee's Lieutenants* (1942); G. F. R. Henderson, *Stonewall Jackson* (1936); and R. U. Johnson and C. C. Buel (eds.), *Battles and Leaders* (1888).

VICTOR HICKEN
Western Illinois University

WILLIAMSBURG, VA. (pop. 9,069), the colonial

and state capital from 1699 to 1779, was first settled in 1632 as Middle Plantation. Located on a peninsula between the York and James rivers, the town was created in 1693 after the burning of Jamestown. Although it was the cultural, educational, and political center of the colony throughout the eighteenth century, it never became particularly large or economically independent of governmental business. After the state's capital was moved to Richmond, the town went into a state of decline. During the PENINSULAR CAMPAIGN of 1862, approximately 40,000 federal soldiers under General George Stoneman engaged 30,000 retreating Confederates there under JAMES LONGSTREET (WILLIAMSBURG, BATTLE OF). The location of the battle was more an accident of timing and logistics than the result of any strategic value of the town. Time had passed by the former colonial capital; in 1912 the town actually forgot to hold local elections. Yet over a hundred original buildings of the old capital survived into the twentieth century, and in 1926 John D. Rockefeller, Jr., set into motion the restoration and reconstruction of the old city. Although the restored city is sometimes ridiculed as "cleaner and more beautiful" than the historic town of the eighteenth century, Williamsburg is often the first stop on the itineraries of visiting foreign dignitaries. Moreover, the educational activities of Colonial Williamsburg, Inc., and the scholarly research sponsored by the Institute for the Study of Early American History have made Williamsburg a model for similar restorations around the country.

See C. Bridenbaugh, *Seat of Empire* (1950); J. H. Soltow, *Virginia Magazine of History and Biography* (July, 1966) and *Economic Role of Williamsburg* (1965); T. B. Lewis, *Window on Williamsburg* (1966), illustrated; M. Whiffen, *Public Buildings of Williamsburg* (1958); E. S. Morgan, *Virginians at Home* (1952); T. W. Tate, *Williamsburg Negro* (1965); and files of ten different papers using the same name, *Virginia Gazette* (1736–80, 1853–55, 1869–71, 1893–1922, 1926–28, 1930–), on microfilm.

WILLIAMS V. MISSISSIPPI (170 U.S. 213 [1898])

is a U.S. Supreme Court case that is often misrepresented as having validated the constitutional DISFRANCHISEMENT of Negroes. Henry Williams was indicted, tried, and convicted by all-white juries and sentenced to be hanged for murder in Washington County, Miss. Cornelius J. Jones, an obscure black lawyer who had been a Republican state legislator from Greenville in 1890, challenged the convictions of Williams and another black client on the grounds that blacks had been unconstitutionally excluded from Mississippi juries. To save his clients' lives, Jones petitioned the U.S. Supreme Court to overturn the decisions of the Mississippi supreme court and the lower state courts by declaring the suffrage clauses of the notorious 1890 Mississippi constitution, and therefore the jury lists drawn from the lists of registered voters, unconstitutional.

Jones had tried to bring the case under the rule of *Yick Wo* v. *Hopkins* (1886), which had said that proven administrative racial discrimination under a law subtly designed to institute such discrimination violated the Fourteenth Amendment to the U.S. Constitution, even though the law did not discriminate on its face. Jones, a small-town lawyer who does not appear to have been assisted in this case by any lawyers with wider experience, showed only the intent on the part of the framers of the Mississippi constitution to discriminate against blacks. Justice Joseph McKenna remarked of the suffrage provisions for a unanimous Supreme Court, "It has not been shown that their actual administration was evil, only that evil was possible under them." On September 19, 1904, the New York *Times* noted that no Negroes had sat on juries in Vicksburg since Henry Williams was hanged.

See *Yick Wo* v. *Hopkins*, 118 U.S. 356 (1886); *Giles* v. *Harris*, 189 U.S. 475 (1901); R. Bardolph, *Civil Rights Record* (1970); and R. Claude, *Supreme Court and Electoral Process* (1970).

J. MORGAN KOUSSER
California Institute of Technology

WILMINGTON, DEL. (pop. 80,386), the principal industrial and commercial city in the state, is approximately 25 miles southwest of Philadelphia, Pa. First settled in 1638 by Swedes as Ft. Christina, the city grew around the point where Brandywine Creek and the Christina River flow into the Delaware River. It was seized by the Dutch in 1655 and the British in 1664 and occupied by George Washington in 1777. The city has always been a coastal port of some significance. Since 1802, however, when the DU PONT FAMILY constructed a powder mill nearby, it has been a major manufacturing center. Still a port of entry and the headquarters of E. I. Du Pont de Nemours & Company, Wilmington also produces leather products, chemicals, textiles, ships, iron products, and automobile parts.

See files of Wilmington *Journal* (1871–) and *News* (1880–) both on microfilm; Library of Historical Society of Delaware and Wilmington Public Library both maintain collections of Delaware historical materials; C. E. Hoffecker, *Wilmington, 1830–1910* (1974); A. T. Lincoln, *Wilmington, 1609–1937* (1937); A. R. O'Brian, *Index to History of Wilmington* (1934), bibliography; and B. Ferris, *History of Original Settlements* (1846).

WILMINGTON, N.C. (pop. 46,169), 30 miles above the mouth of the Cape Fear River, was settled by English colonists in 1730. It was first called New Liverpool, but its name was changed by the royal governor in 1734 to honor the earl of Wilmington. Rapidly developing into a major provincial port and commercial center, it was protected from pirates by construction in 1764 of Ft. Johnston at the mouth of the river (PIRACY). Its defenses against assault by land were less formidable, however, and in 1783 Lord Cornwallis easily occupied the town on his way to Yorktown. During the Civil War the city was a major center for blockade-runners (BLOCKADE-RUNNING); and, prior to its surrender in January, 1865, it was the last remaining port of the Confederacy. Although shifting patterns of commerce prevented the post–Civil War town from regaining its earlier prominence, it remains the state's chief port of entry. Through Wilmington are exported cotton, tobacco, scrap iron, and lumber, while sugar, molasses, and petroleum are imported.

See E. W. MacMillan, *Wilmington's Vanished Homes* (1966); W. L. DeRosset, *Pictorial and Historical New Hanover County* (1938); L. Lee, *Lower Cape Fear* (1965), colonial; H. B. McKoy, *Wilmington* (1967); C. W. Hewlett, *Between the Creeks, 1735–1770* (1971); J. Sprunt, *Tales and Traditions of Lower Cape Fear, 1661–1896* (1896); D. P. Randall, "Economy of Wilmington" (Ph.D. dissertation, University of North Carolina, 1965); and files of Wilmington *Star* (1867–), *Herald* (1851–78), *Journal* (1844–95), *Recorder* (1816–32), *Chronicle* (1839–51), *Gazette* (1799–1816), and *Weekly Post* (1867–84), all on microfilm. Lower Cape Fear Historical Society maintains a local archive.

WILMOT PROVISO (1846) was introduced in the U.S. House by a Pennsylvania Democrat, David Wilmot. It provided that slavery be prohibited in any territory acquired from the Mexican War (1846–1848) and was attached to a $2 million appropriations bill, which President JAMES K. POLK had requested to help negotiate an end to the conflict. The proviso was promoted by a group of Van Buren Democrats, who were anxious to counteract mounting accusations from their constituents that the Van Burenites were continually surrendering to southern interests. After a brief but heated debate (August 8, 1846), the House accepted the bill as amended by an almost solid sectional vote. The Senate adjourned without voting on the measure, but the proviso was expanded in scope and reintroduced frequently in subsequent sessions, causing deep sectional rifts.

A key to the importance of the proviso lay in the extreme position against it taken by JOHN C. CALHOUN. Calhoun emphasized southern honor and rights and urged sectional unity. He contended that the territories were the common property of all the sovereign states and that the federal government, as a mere manager, must therefore permit the movement of all property, including slaves, to all territories and must protect it once it arrived. In this view, the proviso, POPULAR SOVEREIGNTY, and even the MISSOURI COMPROMISE were unconstitutional. Calhoun and others warned that the proviso would be a dangerous precedent, even when applied to territories unconducive to slavery, for it would lead to adverse racial, economic, and political results for the South. So many free states would eventually enter the Union that slavery could be abolished by constitutional amendment. Although the proviso never passed, it helped to arouse intense sectional animosities and was a major cause of the Civil War.

See C. W. Morrison, *Democratic Politics and Sectionalism* (1967); E. Foner, *Journal of American History* (Sept., 1969), excellent; R. A. Lee, *Pacific Northwest Quarterly* (July, 1973), excellent for immediate political results; C. B. Going, *David Wilmot* (1924), dated but useful; A. Bestor, *Journal of Illinois State Historical Society* (Summer, 1961), brilliant; R. R. Russel, *Journal of Southern History* (Nov., 1966); R. R. Stenberg, *Mississippi Valley Historical Review* (March, 1932); and C. E. Persinger, *American Historical Association Annual Report* (1911).

GERALD W. WOLFF
University of South Dakota

WILSON, AUGUSTA JANE EVANS (1835–1909), was born in Augusta, Ga. Her family moved to Texas about 1845 and to Mobile, Ala. in 1849. In 1868 she married Lorenzo Madison Wilson, a successful businessman. An uncompromising supporter of the Confederacy, in 1860 she rejected a suitor because he supported Abraham Lincoln and opposed secession. Her most enthusiastic support of the Confederate cause appeared in the novel *Macaria; or, Altars of Sacrifice* (1863). The avowed purpose of the novel was to espouse the cause of the South and to raise the morale of the

Confederate soldier. *Macaria* was so effective as propaganda that General G. H. THOMAS, commander of yankee troops in Tennessee, banned it among his troops.

In addition to *Macaria*, she published *Inez: A Tale of the Alamo* (1855), written when she was only about fifteen; *Beulah* (1859); *St. Elmo* (1866); *Vashti* (1869); *Infelice* (1875); *At the Mercy of Tiberius* (1887); *A Speckled Bird* (1902); and *Devota* (1907). *St. Elmo*, the novel by which she is best remembered, employs nearly all of the heartwringing devices characteristic of the sentimental novel. The style is erudite; quotations and abstruse references abound. The moral is laid on with a heavy spoon and the pathos so excessive that it invited parody. Soon after the appearance of *St. Elmo*, Charles H. Webb published *St. Twel'mo; or, the Cuneiform Cyclopedist of Chattanooga*, in which he attributes the heroine's turgid erudition to an unabridged dictionary she swallowed as a child.

See W. P. Fidler, *A. E. Wilson* (1951); and Augusta Wilson File, Alabama Department of Archives and History, Montgomery, Ala.

MARION MICHAEL
Texas Tech University

WILSON, WILLIAM LYNE (1843–1900), Confederate soldier, lawyer, politician, author, and educator, won his greatest renown as a Democratic congressional leader during the Cleveland era. Elected in 1882 from a northeastern West Virginia district, Wilson quickly rose to prominence in the U.S. House, becoming chairman of its Ways and Means Committee in 1893. His skillful advocacy of tariff reform earned him a national reputation, but it also antagonized bituminous coal producers in his home district. Consequently, in 1894 Democratic protectionists joined Republicans to deal him a double defeat: first in Congress, where intensive lobbying turned the reformist Wilson bill into the protectionist Wilson-Gorman tariff; then in the fall election, when a bipartisan coalition ousted Wilson from Congress after six terms. Subsequently he served briefly as postmaster general and as president of Washington and Lee University.

See F. P. Summers, *William L. Wilson* (1953); and J. A. Williams, *West Virginia History* (Oct. 1970) and *Maryland Historical Magazine* (Fall, 1973).

JOHN ALEXANDER WILLIAMS
West Virginia University

WILSON, WOODROW (1856–1924). Was Wilson a southerner? The question sounds strange, of course, to anyone who knows that he was born in Staunton, Va., and reared in Augusta, Ga. Wilson absorbed the romantic legends of the South, both at home and at school, the earliest being a preparatory academy in Augusta. He attended Davidson College (1873–1874), took his bachelor's degree from Princeton in 1879, and studied law at the University of Virginia. After practicing law less than two years in Atlanta, he left in 1883 to study history at the Johns Hopkins University, where he earned a doctorate on the strength of his famous book *Congressional Government* (1885). When he accepted a teaching position at Bryn Mawr College in Pennsylvania and left the South for good in 1885, he was almost thirty years old. His biographers, including the distinguished Arthur S. Link, are virtually unanimous in agreeing that Wilson felt a deep attachment to his father (an ardent Confederate), his father's Calvinism, and the traditions of the South. He married Ellen Louise Axson of Rome, Ga., identified himself as a southerner, and defended in books and essays (though not uncritically) the South and its history. The South, he said in an admiring portrait of Robert E. Lee (1896), is "the only place in the country, the only place in the world, where nothing has to be explained to me."

Yet he was, his friends liked to say, one who had put his country above his section. Had he not proved that in his writings (including a multivolumed history of the United States, in which he struck a nationalistic tone), his speeches, and in his fight for quality and liberal reform as president of Princeton University (1902–1910)? He also had proved, to his admirers at least, as governor of New Jersey (1910–1912) that here was no petty politician; he was a leader, a reformer, a conservative liberal. Here obviously was no provincial southerner who could see no further than the Democratic party. As president of the United States (1913–1921), Wilson would impress his moral vision on America, aid the passage of a variety of reform bills, and become, when the situation demanded it, a great leader in a time of war. His vision of international harmony and peace is forever enshrined in his plans for the League of Nations.

But just as surely as Abraham Lincoln's heritage was midwestern, Wilson's was southern. By virtue of his birth, race, class, and education, he stands in a long line of those whom GERALD W. JOHNSON once called the South's "spiritual aristocrats," those men from Thomas Jefferson to Lee to Wilson who have sought to live with honor and idealism. Like them, Wilson was a moralist who held that man has a responsibility to society as well as to himself. His was the gentleman's credo of fair play

and honest competition (hence his fight for tariff reform once he became president); and he revered tradition. A striver himself for outward achievement and inward perfection, Wilson set high standards for behavior. In all of this he was a visionary, an optimist despite his occasional dark moods. He looked confidently upon man because he believed that men were by nature good and moral and capable of intuiting and reasoning their way to moral truths. He was, then, in his views and attitudes of a piece with that spiritual aristocracy of the South that he and his generation called the "real" South. When Wilson's generation lauded him as an "American," they had in mind an ideal type; and that is what Wilson himself was forever striving to become, to live up to. Thus the southerner became the American.

He was both American and southern in his racial assumptions, also, and here his heritage limited his vision and his era's. At heart and in his public pronouncements, he was a paternalist; he believed it his duty *as a white man* and particularly as a leader of men to protect what he considered to be an inferior race. Yet he knew little about southern blacks and, in fact, as it turned out had but token concern for their welfare. He justified the DISFRANCHISEMENT of black voters as a needed "reform" and as president of Princeton worked to discourage blacks from seeking admission. During his presidency, racial segregation in the federal government became the rule, and Wilson, surrounded by his own officials who were less sensitive than he, turned his back on the Negro. He appointed far fewer blacks to offices than his immediate predecessors had. Wilson harbored no conscious ill will toward blacks. His vision, the idealism of his heritage, simply did not include them as full citizens or, it must be said, as human beings as he defined man.

See A. S. Link, *Wilson: Road to White House* (1947), *Journal of Negro History* (Jan., 1947), and *Journal of Southern History* (Feb., 1970); G. C. Osborn, *Woodrow Wilson: Early Years* (1968); H. W. Bragdon, *Woodrow Wilson: Academic Years* (1967); K. L. Wolgemuth, *Journal of Southern History* (Nov., 1958) and *Journal of Negro History* (April, 1959); H. Blumenthal, *Journal of Negro History* (Jan., 1963); N. J. Weiss, *Political Science Quarterly* (March, 1969); and B. Clayton, *Savage Ideal, 1890–1914* (1972).

BRUCE CLAYTON
Allegheny College

WILSON'S CREEK, BATTLE OF (August 10, 1861), developed in southwestern Missouri between Nathaniel Lyon's federal forces and Ben McCulloch's Confederate forces (including

the Missouri State Guard). Lyon had occupied Springfield to facilitate his plan to drive the Confederates from Missouri. Before dawn on August 10, 1861, he led the main column from the north to attack STERLING PRICE's camp near Oak Hill west of Wilson's Creek. Captain Joseph Plummer attacked McCulloch's camp east of the creek, and Colonel Franz Sigel attacked simultaneously from the south. Lyon's surprise attack drove General James Rains's division back over Bloody Hill, but messengers warned McCulloch and Price in time to meet the attack. Plummer's attack at the cornfield was halted by McCulloch's and General H. B. Pearce's forces. McCulloch routed Sigel at Sharps farm and subsequently reinforced Price to halt Lyon by mid-morning. About 10:30 Lyon was struck by a rifle ball and died shortly. Major Samuel Sturgis ordered the withdrawal. McCulloch failed to pursue the federals, but Price occupied Springfield and later Lexington.

Losses on both sides were heavy: of 10,175, the Confederates lost 1,095 killed, wounded, and missing; of 5,400, the federals lost 1,235. Lyon's separation of inferior forces and his death influenced the federal defeat. Wilson's Creek battle was not a major engagement, but a similar Confederate victory at PEA RIDGE, Ark., in March, 1862, might have led to the secession of Missouri and Kentucky, which might have changed the course of the Civil War.

See V. Rose, *Ben McCulloch* (1888); A.Castel, *Sterling Price* (1968); R. U. Johnson and C. C. Buel (eds.), *Battles and Leaders* (1888), I; and *Official Records, Armies,* Ser. 1, Vol. III.

HOMER L. KERR
University of Texas, Arlington

WILSON'S RAID (March 22–April 20, 1865) was a Union cavalry campaign waged by James H. Wilson's corps. With 13,500 men from three divisions (E. M. McCook, Emory Upton, and Eli Long), Wilson left northwestern Alabama and moved toward Selma, a major Confederate manufacturing center. To counter Wilson, Confederate horsemen under NATHAN BEDFORD FORREST moved from Mississippi toward Selma. Wilson took Elyton (now Birmingham) and defeated a portion of Forrest's force near Montevallo on March 31. The next day Wilson routed Forrest at Ebenezer Church, thus opening the road to Selma. While his main force drove on to Selma, Wilson detached J. T. Croxton's brigade to destroy military facilities at Tuscaloosa. On April 2 Upton's and Long's divisions assaulted Selma. Confederate works were lightly held by 5,000 Confederate cavalrymen and con-

scripts under Forrest. After brief resistance, Forrest abandoned the city. Wilson held Selma until April 9, wrecking everything of military value.

Leaving smoldering Selma, Wilson took Montgomery without a fight on the twelfth and moved on toward Columbus, Ga. On the sixteenth, federals struck rebel defenders west of the Chattahoochee, seized bridges into Columbus, and captured another manufacturing center in the last Civil War battle east of the Mississippi. After destroying Columbus' factories, Wilson rode on to Macon, which fell April 20. Here he learned the war had ended. At Macon, Croxton, after wrecking Tuscaloosa and crossing northern Alabama, rejoined the corps.

Wilson reported the loss of 725 men and claimed 8,000 Confederates had been killed, wounded, and captured. The Union cavalry force, which had outfought Forrest, inflicted heavy damage on the Deep South, denying the region to Jefferson Davis as a redoubt from which to continue the war.

See J. H. Wilson, *Under Old Flag* (1912); E. G. Longacre, *Union Stars to Top Hat* (1972); and J. P. Jones, *Yankee Blitzkrieg* (1976).

JAMES P. JONES
Florida State University

WINCHESTER, BATTLES OF (May 25, 1862; June 13–15, 1863; September 19, 1864). The first battle, part of Stonewall Jackson's SHENANDOAH VALLEY CAMPAIGN, followed Jackson's Confederate victories at MCDOWELL, Va., on May 8 and Front Royal, Va., on May 23. Nathaniel P. Banks withdrew 8,000 federals from Strasburg to Winchester May 24–25. Attacking at dawn, RICHARD TAYLOR's Louisiana Brigade broke through, forcing a retreat to the Potomac by 5,000 federals. Jackson took 3,000 prisoners while suffering 400 southern casualties. Victory at Winchester permitted Jackson to advance to Harpers Ferry. This caused two federal corps to be diverted from the PENINSULAR CAMPAIGN. Jackson withdrew to Strasburg May 30–June 1.

Southern victory in the second battle was quickly overshadowed by the loss of the campaign at GETTYSBURG July 1–3. JUBAL A. EARLY's division, led by the 2nd Louisiana Brigade of Harry T. Hays, with Confederate artillery, drove Robert H. Milroy's 8,000 federals from forts near Winchester, taking 3,300 prisoners while suffering 270 southern losses.

The third battle, sometimes called the battle of Opequon, was first of three southern defeats in Philip H. Sheridan's SHENANDOAH VALLEY CAMPAIGN. Early withdrew on August 26 to the west bank of Opequon Creek. A black peddler carried a message from Quaker schoolteacher Rebecca Wright to Sheridan on September 16, saying that South Carolinian JOSEPH B. KERSHAW's division had left on September 14 toward Petersburg. By U. S. Grant's orders, Sheridan attacked at dawn. Virginian ROBERT E. RODES died leading the southern counterattack, finally stopped by the 5th Maine Light Artillery. After David A. Russell's federal counterattack, Early's outnumbered southerners withdrew to Fisher's Hill, leaving 1,800 wounded and 270 killed, to 4,000 wounded and 700 federals killed.

See D. S. Freeman, *Lee's Lieutenants* (1946); G. F. R. Henderson, *Stonewall Jackson* (1898); L. Chambers, *Stonewall Jackson* (1959); P. H. Sheridan, *Personal Memoirs* (1888); R. O'Connor, *Sheridan* (1953); and J. A. Early, in R. U. Johnson and C. C. Buel (eds.), *Battles and Leaders* (1887–88). Less useful are G. E. Pond, *Shenandoah Valley* (1883); S. C. Kellogg, *Shenandoah Valley* (1903); and D. S. Freeman, *R. E. Lee* (1934–35).

JOHN CHARLES BODGER
Whitneyville, Maine

WINCHESTER, VA.

WINCHESTER, VA. (pop. 14,643), is approximately 60 miles west of Washington, D.C., near the northern end of the Shenandoah Valley. The area was settled during the mid–eighteenth century by English and German colonists. In 1756 George Washington constructed Ft. Loudon near here. The town was founded in 1774 and named Fredericktown, but almost immediately was renamed Winchester after the town of the same name in England. The town grew and prospered prior to the Civil War as a market for area agriculture and a supply point for westward-bound pioneers. During Stonewall Jackson's SHENANDOAH VALLEY CAMPAIGN (May 25, 1862), the GETTYSBURG campaign (June 13–15, 1863), the battle of KERNSTOWN (July 23, 24, 1864), and Philip Sheridan's SHENANDOAH VALLEY CAMPAIGN (September 19, 1864), the town and its vicinity were the sites of several minor battles. Although the town has declined in importance as a regional shipping and transportation center, it remains the principal market for area apple growers and hosts the annual Apple Blossom Festival. Also, its factories manufacture automobile parts and textiles.

See F. Morton, *Story of Winchester* (1925); K. G. Greene, *Winchester, 1743–1814* (1926); T. K. Cartmell, *Shenandoah Valley Pioneers, 1738–1908* (1909, 1963); J. E. Norris, *History of Lower Shenandoah Valley* (1890, 1972); and files of Winchester *Gazette* (1788–1825), *Star* (1896–), *News* (1865–1909), *Republican* (1810–62), and *Virginian* (1826–62).

WINDER, JOHN HENRY

WINDER, JOHN HENRY (1800–1865), was born in Somerset County, Md. A graduate of the U.S. Military Academy, he served in the Mexican War. When the Civil War began, he was appointed brigadier general in the Confederate army. During the early years of the war, he was commander of prisons in Richmond. In the summer of 1864 he was placed in charge of all prisons in Alabama and Georgia. Many blamed Winder for the extreme suffering of Union prisoners at ANDERSONVILLE. One prisoner called him a "malign genius"; another referred to him as a "brute." Even Confederate Colonel D. T. Chandler, who inspected Andersonville in August, 1864, recommended that Winder be removed from command. On the other hand, Winder was defended by President Jefferson Davis, Secretary of War J. A. SEDDON, and Adjutant General SAMUEL COOPER as a man of integrity. Winder died in February, 1865, from a heart attack brought on by fatigue and anxiety. Some believe that, had he lived, he rather than HENRY WIRZ would have been tried for the mistreatment of Union prisoners.

See Winder Papers, University of North Carolina Library, mainly pre–Civil War material; O. L. Futch, *Andersonville Prison* (1968); and *Official Records, Armies*, Ser. 2, Vol. VII.

RALPH A. WOOSTER
Lamar University

WINSTON-SALEM, N.C.

WINSTON-SALEM, N.C. (pop. 132, 913). In 1753 a small party of MORAVIANS arrived in the Piedmont from Bethlehem, Pa. Developing a tract of land, which they called "der Wachau" or Wachovia, they established several communities, one of which was founded in 1766 and named Salem. More so than similar Moravian communities, Salem prospered and developed. In 1849 the adjacent town of Winston was founded to serve as the seat of Forsyth County's government. The two towns were ideally situated to become centers for marketing and manufacturing the newly popular bright leaf tobacco after the Civil War. While rapidly developing into one of the major tobacco markets in the world, the towns also became a locus of textile manufactures. In 1913, already a single economic unit, the two cities consolidated to form a single political entity. Since World War II, Winston-Salem also has become an important manufacturer of furniture and communications equipment.

See files of Winston-Salem *Journal* (1897–), *Sentinel* (1885–), *Weekly Chronicle* (1832–51), and *People's Press* (1851–92).

WINTERTHUR PORTFOLIO (H. F. Du Pont Winterthur Museum, Winterthur, Del. 1973S), an annual illustrated journal first issued in 1964, is supported by and is the major publication of Winterthur Museum. *Portfolio* is circulated to approximately 1,800 scholars and institutions and is devoted to scholarly material on the seventeenth to nineteenth centuries, which of a necessity places some emphasis on the South and its craftsmen. In addition to these articles (for which $7–$10 per page is the stipend) and for which it is "actively seeking publishable manuscripts," the museum publishes scholarly books and maintains a library specializing in manuscripts, books, and journals on early American history and culture with special attention to the American decorative arts. The library maintains a rare book, manuscript, and microfilm collection. On the occasion of the annual Winterthur Conference, the lectures delivered there are published in the *Report* and distributed to as many as 4,500 scholars. The museum maintains two M.A. programs for training students interested in museum careers.

WIRT, WILLIAM (1772–1834), was born in Bladensburg, Md. After practicing law in Richmond, Va., he was appointed a government prosecutor in the Burr trial by President Thomas Jefferson in 1807. He was a U.S. attorney and served in the Virginia house of delegates and in the state militia. He was an army contractor during the War of 1812. In 1817 he began 12 years' service as attorney general, the longest tenure ever, under two presidents. He greatly improved the attorney general's office and participated in several historic U.S. Supreme Court cases including *Dartmouth College*. In 1832 Wirt was the Anti-Masonic party's presidential candidate, but ran a poor third. He represented the Indian tribes in the famous Cherokee cases (CHEROKEE NATION V. GEORGIA; WORCESTER V. GEORGIA) and founded an immigrant colony in Florida. He was an editor and wrote popular history, including *The Life of Patrick Henry* (1817).

See J. P. Kennedy, *Memoirs of Wirt* (1856); W. Taylor, *William and Mary Quarterly* (Oct., 1957); M. Cain, *Mid-America* (1965); and manuscripts, Maryland Historical Society and Manuscripts Division, Library of Congress.

MARVIN R. CAIN
University of Missouri, Rolla

WIRZ, HENRY (1822–1865), immigrated to the United States from Switzerland in 1849. In 1854 he settled at Milliken's Bend, La. In 1861 Wirz enlisted as a private and was badly wounded at the battle of SEVEN PINES. He completed several assignments as a prison official and was sent to Europe as a plenipotentiary of the Confederate government. He returned in April, 1864, and assumed command of the interior of the prison camp ANDERSONVILLE. On May 7, 1865, he was arrested by federal authorities and was charged with committing crimes against several prisoners and for conspiring to murder federal prisoners en masse. Despite his plea that the charges were too vague and that he was protected by the surrender terms agreed upon by Generals W. T. Sherman and JOSEPH E. JOHNSTON, he was found guilty by a military court and hanged on November 12, 1865.

See J. M. Page and M. J. Haley, *True Story of Andersonville* (1908); N. P. Chipman, *Tragedy of Andersonville* (1911); W. B. Hesseltine, *Civil War Prisons* (1930); R. R. Stevenson, *Southern Side* (1876); J. H. Stibbs, *Iowa Journal of History and Politics* (1911); L. G. Tyler, *William and Mary Quarterly* (Jan., 1919); H. Wirz, "Last Letter to His Wife," Yale University Library; and D. B. Rutman, *Civil War History* (June, 1960).

ARTHUR V. GRANT
U.S. Military Academy

WISE, HENRY ALEXANDER (1806–1876), governor of Virginia (1856–1860), was born in Accomac County on Chesapeake Bay's Eastern Shore. A member of Congress from 1833 to 1844, he separated from Andrew Jackson during the bank war and joined the Whigs. Although advocating the annexation of Texas and espousing extreme prosouthern positions during the GAG RULE debates, Wise experienced some doubts about slavery's future and fiercely opposed illegal American involvement in the international slave trade while U.S. minister to Brazil (1844–1847). But he was ambitious to join Virginia's TIDEWATER elite, and he gradually enlarged his slaveholdings to 21 hands in 1860. Wise worried about the disloyalty of the nonslaveholders, whom he took particular care to address during his gubernatorial canvass in 1855. Despite his defeat of the illiberal and antislavery Know-Nothings, it proved impossible to protect slavery along Virginia's northern and western borders. It was precisely this region that John Brown chose to attack (HARPERS FERRY RAID), which was why Wise respected him so much and also hanged him, since he believed that Brown's tactics made sense.

As a Confederate brigadier general, Wise attempted in 1861 to preserve southern hegemony in western Virginia. He was miserably defeated and later lost an important engagement at Roanoke Island. His command contributed effectively to the defense of Petersburg in 1864 (RICHMOND-PETERSBURG CAMPAIGN), however, and he later surrendered with it at APPOMATTOX. With his fortunes devastated by war, he returned to Richmond and practiced law. He never sought amnesty.

See B. H. Wise, *A Life* (1899), good, though by grandson; C. Eaton, *Journal of Southern History* (Nov., 1941), believes him too much a liberal; C. Simpson, "Wise, 1850–1861" (Ph.D. dissertation, Stanford, 1973); Wise Papers, University of North Carolina, one microfilm reel; and papers in possession of John Sergeant Wise, Charlottesville, Va., indispensable private collection.

CRAIG SIMPSON
University of Western Ontario

WOFFORD COLLEGE (Spartanburg, S.C. 29301). When the Reverend Benjamin Wofford died in 1850, he willed money for the establishment of a Methodist college. Four years later the school that bears his name was opened. Formerly a men's institution, it is now coeducational and has an enrollment of 1,000 students. The college library is the repository of the papers of the Historical Society of the South Carolina Conference of the Methodist church.

See D. D. Wallace, *History of Wofford College, 1854–1949* (1951).

WOLFE, THOMAS CLAYTON (1900–1938), decided on a writing career while a teenager in Asheville. After attending the University of North Carolina at Chapel Hill (1916–1920) and Harvard (1920–1923), he lived in New York City, intermittently taught English composition at New York University, and traveled in both Europe and the United States. Each of these moves successively widened his horizons and ultimately caused his work to encompass much more than the South of his childhood. He was a garrulous talker who occasionally stammered when excited, and it might fairly be said that he was an instincive writer. Words tumbled out of him onto the page to form huge, undisciplined manuscripts filled with lyric prose. Not until 1928 did Wolfe complete his first novel. Originally called *O Lost*, it was published as *Look Homeward, Angel* (1929). Despite a tremendous accumulation of pages and drafts, his next complete novel did not appear until March, 1935. Entitled *Of Time and the River*, it was quickly followed by *From Death to Morning* (1935), a collection of his short stories.

Although his residence continued to be New York, he did make one trip to Asheville in 1937, his first since the publication of *Look Homeward, Angel*. That novel had featured Asheville, much to the consternation of its citizens, but by 1937 the furor had died down. The spring and summer of 1938 found Wolfe traveling again, this time to the Far West. In Seattle it was discovered that he had a particularly virulent form of tuberculosis. He died at only thirty-eight. From his manuscripts emerged two posthumous novels, *The Web and the Rock* (1939) and *You Can't Go Home Again* (1940), and a final collection of stories, *The Hills Beyond* (1941). To this day, a great quantity of Wolfe's writing remains in manuscript, unpublished.

In assessing Thomas Wolfe's fiction, one can consider only one of his four novels to be "southern." *Look Homeward, Angel* is set in North Carolina (Old Catawba, as he calls it), focusing primarily on Asheville (Altamont), with sections on Chapel Hill (Pulpit Hill). An intensely autobiographical book, it covers roughly the first 20 years of Wolfe's life as he comes to realize an enduring theme in his fiction: all men are essentially alone. Eugene Gant, Wolfe's fictional name in the novel, gradually gets to know himself and to grasp this sense of loneliness. Finally, Eugene determines to flee Old Catawba and its strictures and moves to the larger world beyond. So it was with Wolfe's real life and his subsequent novels. Each contains chapters on Asheville and Wolfe's attitudes toward the South, but each also contains a growing social consciousness, coupled with a search for America instead of just self.

See C. H. Holman, in J. R. Bryer (ed.), *Sixteen Modern American Authors* (1973) and *Loneliness at the Core: Studies in Thomas Wolfe* (1975).

WILLIAM YOUNG
Lynchburg College

WOMAN ORDER was the order General Benjamin Butler issued on May 15, 1862, to end the insulting treatment the women of New Orleans had been meting out to Union soldiers passing by in the streets. Should again any woman show contempt for any Union soldier, she was to be assumed to be "a woman of the town plying her avocation" and would be treated accordingly. The order brought an immediate cessation of this demeaning behavior but it in no way enhanced "Beast" Butler's already ugly reputation throughout the world. Confederate President Jefferson Davis even ordered that if Butler should ever be captured he was to be denied the rights of a prisoner of war and was to be immediately hanged.

See W. B. Hesseltine, *South in American History* (1960); and H. P. Johnson, *Louisiana Historical Quarterly* (April, 1941).

WOMAN'S CHRISTIAN TEMPERANCE UNION,

the largest and one of the most important women's organizations of the nineteenth century, was founded in 1874 at Cleveland, Ohio. It originated in the almost spontaneous crusade of bands of singing, praying women who took to the streets of numerous towns in western New York and Ohio bent on closing saloons and stopping the liquor traffic. The WCTU's greatest era began in 1879, when Frances Willard was elected national president. Under her "do-everything" policy, the WCTU organized 39 different departments of work. In an effort to appeal to and provide activity for the broadest possible range of women, departments were established for peace and arbitration, hygiene, social purity, evangelism, foreign missions, and the franchise among others. Willard saw much of this activity as a first step toward women's broader participation in public and civic life. The franchise department was particularly active, since Willard claimed that the ballot was necessary for "home protection." The WCTU remained the suffragists' best ally through the 1890s.

By the mid-1880s the WCTU, which had established local chapters and state associations throughout the South, claimed over 200,000 members nationally. Most southern suffragists were members of the WCTU, a relationship exploited by LAURA CLAY, Nellie Somerville, Belle Kearney, and other WOMEN'S RIGHTS leaders to advocate suffrage as the means to PROHIBITION. Southern members also lent their support to improving laws relating to women and children and to providing better educational facilities. They were instrumental in establishing industrial homes for girls, securing police matrons, gaining state appropriations to build college dormitories for women, and passing CHILD LABOR laws.

After Frances Willard's death in 1898, the WCTU narrowed the scope of its activities, working primarily for prohibition in close alliance with the Anti-Saloon League. When the Eighteenth Amendment was ratified in 1919, the WCTU turned its efforts toward enforcement of the national law and international prohibition sponsored by the World WCTU established in 1883. Although other women's organizations have now eclipsed it in size and public favor, the WCTU has retained a following and continues its original mission. It maintains national headquarters in Evanston, Ill., publishes the semimonthly *Union Signal*, and claims more than 300,000 members.

See M. Earhart, *Frances Willard* (1944); J. Ansley, *History of Georgia WCTU* (1914); and Willard Memorial Library, National WCTU Headquarters, Evanston, Ill.

PAUL E. FULLER
Wesleyan College, Macon, Ga.

WOMEN. Until recent years the idea of "womanhood" in the South was inextricably linked in both history and fiction with the notion of the "southern lady" or her younger counterpart, the "southern belle." Few southern women actually lived the life of the lady or fully embodied her essential qualities: innocence, modesty, morality, piety, delicacy, self-sacrificial devotion to family, and whiteness. Yet all southern women have been affected by the fusion of sexual imagery with the racial caste system. Southern colonists brought with them the fundamental Western myths about female nature which embodied a polarization between the virgin, pure and untouchable, and the prostitute, dangerously sexual. This dichotomy, associated with images of light and dark, good and evil, gradually took on concrete reality with the emergence of a white planter class based upon a racial slave labor system.

The role of the white lady that emerged in the eighteenth and nineteenth centuries and the dual imagery of the black woman as whore and mammy revealed more about the needs of white planters than about the actual lives of women, white or black. The white lady, revered and sexually repressed, guaranteed the purity of the white race and the future of white civilization. As the symbol of white men's power, she was carefully placed on a moral pedestal within the privacy of the home, well out of the realm of politics and public power. Sexual relations between white women and black men violated the most potent social taboo in southern culture. On the other hand, the white man's guilt-ridden sexual access to black women represented a reenactment of the power relationships of slavery. Yet responsibility for the rape of black women was laid at the feet of the victim, who, it was said, was naturally promiscuous (RAPE COMPLEX). Finally, the black mammy became the nurturant, all-giving mother figure, beloved because she threatened the hierarchy of neither race nor sex. By the middle of the nineteenth century, the myth of the southern lady had become a pillar of the southern defense of slavery. Thus the fusion of race and sex created a southern version of the Victorian cult of true womanhood. Some myths clearly obscured as much as they revealed. The reproductive roles of housewife and mother defined all women, whether they were slaves, wives of YEOMEN FARMERS, industrial workers, or plantation mistresses. Yet such roles did not separate them significantly from the basic work of economic production in an economy that remained primarily rural and agrarian from the earliest colonization to World War II.

As slaves, black women provided much of the field labor that enriched southern society, and they furnished most of the household labor on which the upper-class life-style depended. At the same time they were the central figures in creating and maintaining a unique form of black family structure geared to the exigencies of life under slavery. While they tended the children of the white planter class, they also provided their own children with the emotional support and social skills required for survival and passed on a rich subcultural heritage. Long-term monogamous relationships, highly valued if rare, were characterized by a degree of sexual equality unknown in white society. Southern black women were probably an important source of resistance to the values of white society, and in a few striking cases, such as HARRIET TUBMAN and the UNDERGROUND RAILROAD, they led active resistance to the slave system.

Most adult white women before the Civil War were the wives of yeomen farmers. Their families owned few if any slaves. Like black women their lot was one of constant hard work. "Women's work" included gardening, caring for cows and poultry, spinning, weaving, sewing, baking, preserving, and cheese making as well as the routine duties of meal preparation, housecleaning, and child rearing. Although fieldwork was considered unseemly for a white woman, such social taboos often weakened in the face of grim necessity. In the early colonial period, an acute labor shortage resulted in a wide range of public roles for women, who ran shops, printing presses, and taverns or served their neighbors as lawyers or doctors. Political uprisings such as BACON'S REBELLION involved women not only as passive hostages, but also as talented rebel orators. In seventeenth-century Maryland, Margaret Brent (1600–1671?) wielded considerable political influence and became the first female settler to demand the suffrage. In South Carolina, ELIZA LUCAS PINCKNEY pioneered the growing and processing of INDIGO.

The emergence of the aristocratic lady in the eighteenth and nineteenth centuries rendered such public activity increasingly disreputable. Yet even the ladies of the upper classes had little time for leisure. Most sewed, cooked, cleaned, gardened, tended the sick. On large plantations they administered and supervised the work of an army of household servants. Although they were denied access to a true education (WOMEN'S COLLEGES) and had few legal or political rights, their domestic domain lay at the heart of southern economic life, the plantation. Their administrative duties required the constant exercise of authority in the home while from their pedestals they pretended ignorance of the MISCEGENATION around them. During and after the carnage of the Civil War, women took over and ran farms, shops, and plantations and flocked to cities, where they provided a significant war-industry labor force. With a new sense of competence, many would be reluctant to yield to patriarchal authority at the war's end. During the Reconstruction era, while upper-class white men attempted to regain social and political control of southern society through political pressure and KKK terrorism, women directed much of the actual work of "reconstructing" the ravaged economy. On many plantations and farms, war widows had no choice but to forge ahead alone. On others, women simply continued to act with the assurance and authority gained during the wartime experience.

After the war, black women, with black men, plunged into the backbreaking labor of subsistence farming, but they dreamed of economic independence and education for their children. When paid labor was virtually unavailable to black men, women and girls were able to find employment as domestic servants. Necessity required greater equality between the sexes in both black and white farm families caught in the CROP LIEN SYSTEM than in middle- and upper-class families.

Women also contributed to the development of an industrializing NEW SOUTH. In 1890 the labor force of four leading textile states was 40 percent women and 25 percent children. Such labor represented a continuation of their usual lot of long hours at grueling tasks. On the other hand, it meant a relocation of family from farm to MILL TOWN, separation from children for 10 to 14 hours a day, and no lessening of the basic labor of housework. Such a setting might have entailed a readjustment of marital relations as women and men coped with the fact that women could obtain mill jobs more easily than their husbands. In the sporadic, bloody, and rarely successful labor struggles that erupted in the following decades, women like Ella Mae Wiggins (1900?–1929) of the GASTONIA STRIKE in North Carolina frequently played leading roles in mobilizing revolt. They receded into the background, however, when it came time to elect officers or to hire union organizers. They could stretch the boundaries of their sphere only so far and no farther.

For both white and black women of the growing

middle classes in the late nineteenth and early twentieth centuries, the pathway from domesticity to public political activity lay through the church. In missionary societies beginning in the 1870s and later in the WOMAN'S CHRISTIAN TEMPERANCE UNION, women's clubs, and the YWCA, they began to carve out autonomous arenas in which they developed skills, social concerns, and a new self-image. Direct contact between black and white women's groups was rare, but, as home missionary societies built settlement houses or worked for CHILD LABOR reforms, their constituents inevitably confronted the realities of poverty and racial discrimination.

Southern suffragists drew on the reform activity sparked by such new experiences (WOMEN'S RIGHTS MOVEMENT), but their efforts encountered an immense tide of reaction as repressive racial and sexual imagery accompanied the rise of LYNCHING in the 1890s. The growth of suffragism in the South, led by racial moderates like LAURA CLAY of Kentucky and extremists like KATE GORDON of Mississippi, may have encouraged a trend toward conservatism and racism in the national suffrage movement. No Deep South state passed the Nineteenth Amendment, but many suffragists continued to work in a variety of reform efforts to curb the abuses of child labor and to shorten the hours of working women. Some, like LUCY RANDOLPH MASON, went on to become labor activists.

The emergence of a black middle class after the Civil War created new roles for black women as professionals and church activists as well. These women pursued a separate strand of progressive reform in the South. Beginning in 1895 IDA B. WELLS-BARNETT pioneered in the struggle against lynching. In 1908 the Neighborhood Union in Atlanta initiated among blacks a settlement house movement geared toward generating grass-roots leadership as well as serving the poor. In addition, although black women's role in the struggle for black education has only begun to be unearthed, the leadership of women like Lucy Laney (1854–1933), Charlotte Hawkins Brown (1882–1961), Septima Poinsetta Clark (1898–), and MARY MC-CLOUD BETHUNE indicates their great importance.

By the 1920s the two strands of female reform activity began to come together through the avenues of church societies, the YWCA, and the COMMISSION ON INTERRACIAL COOPERATION. In the 1930s the ASSOCIATION OF SOUTHERN WOMEN FOR THE PREVENTION OF LYNCHING, led by JESSIE DANIEL AMES, reflected the response of a few white women to the prodding of their black sisters.

The second half of the twentieth century marked a turning point in the roles and lives of southern women. Although the FAMILY remained a central institution in southern culture, it was forced to adapt to new needs and circumstances. The twin processes of INDUSTRIALIZATION and URBANIZATION provided a new context within which the older images of the pristine "lady" and her dark sister were rapidly giving way. Mobility from farm to city placed strains on kinship networks and accented the self-sufficiency of the nuclear family unit. Rapidly broadening educational opportunities and an expanding industrial economy, moreover, widened the employment options of both women and blacks. Thus, black and white women met each other less as mistress and servant and more as coworkers in schools, offices, and factories.

In the midst of such changes, traditional southern conservatism on both sexual and racial equality came under sharp attack. The southern CIVIL RIGHTS MOVEMENT drew on the tireless work of women like Ella Baker and Septima Clark and local leaders such as Rosa Parks and Fannie Lou Hamer. Following in the footsteps of pioneers like LILLIAN SMITH and Anne Braden, young white women who joined the challenge to segregation and racial discrimination began to question the whole complex of racial and sexual imagery. Thus they pioneered the feminist revival of the 1960s.

See A. F. Scott, *Southern Lady* (1970); G. Lerner (ed.), *Black Women* (1972); J. C. Spruill, *Women's Life* (1939); J. D. Hall, "Revolt Against Chivalry" (Ph.D. dissertation, Columbia, 1974); E. Morgan, *Virginians at Home* (1952); G. Lerner, *Grimké Sisters* (1967); P. Murray, *Proud Shoes* (1956); W. Jordan, *White over Black* (1968); L. Mac-Donald, *Southern Mill Hills* (1928); M. Haygood, *Mothers of the South* (1972); L. Smith, *Killers of Dream* (1963); H. Gutman, *Journal of Interdisciplinary History* (Autumn, 1975); J. R. Jeffrey, *Feminist Studies* (Fall, 1975); E. M. Carrington, *Women in East Texas* (1975); S. M. Evans, "Personal Politics" (Ph.D. dissertation, University of North Carolina, 1976); and major manuscript collections, Atlanta University and Southern Oral History Program and Southern Historical Collection, University of North Carolina, Chapel Hill. See also *Women's Studies Abstracts*, largely popular and incomplete index.

SARA M. EVANS
University of Minnesota

WOMEN'S COLLEGES. Wesleyan Female College, chartered in 1836 at Macon, Ga., was the first women's college in the United States with the authority to grant degrees. In the same year Mary Lyon established Mount Holyoke Seminary at

South Hadley, Mass. These institutions of higher learning were harbingers of the future, yet in the early nineteenth century, women's education was surrounded by controversy. Critics claimed that women's psychological and physiological natures were unfit for such a venture. Scholars contended that a woman's brain was smaller than a man's and that women could not learn the substance of a classical education. A Georgia legislator announced that "all a lady needs to know is how to weave clothes for her family and how to paint a daisy in water colors." These myths, though harbored by some skeptics well into the twentieth century, subsided as women proved their ability to be educated.

Despite opposition, female seminaries flourished throughout the South before the Civil War. Religious leaders were the main advocates, but many public officials also lent support. Bishop George Pierce told the graduating class of Madison Female Academy (Madison, Ga.) in 1856 that "a female college has come to be the index of progress." By 1860 the legislatures of every southern state except Florida and Arkansas had chartered one or more women's colleges. Many of these institutions were colleges in name only, providing instruction primarily in "ornamental subjects." High on ideals and low on standards, most of these schools were destined for an early demise. Some institutions, however, were of fair quality and offered a classical curriculum. Among these were Wesleyan (1836) and Judson Female Institute in Marion, Ala. (1839).

After the Civil War, women's colleges became firmly established. Educators and philanthropists in the North founded such institutions as Vassar (1865), Smith (1875), Wellesley (1875), Radcliffe (1879), and Barnard (1889). The South followed this lead with Sophie Newcomb (1887), Goucher (1888), Randolph-Macon (1893), and Agnes Scott (1889). These institutions advocated "a sound curriculum, fully abreast of the best institutions of the land." They also expressed a commitment to the ideals of "southern womanhood." Fortunately, these sentiments did not restrict the curriculum. Emphasizing Greek, Latin, and mathematics, these southern colleges compared favorably with their northern counterparts. Goucher, from the beginning, had a progressive curriculum modeled after Johns Hopkins University.

In the twentieth century, southern women's colleges concentrated on developing their curricula, standardizing graduation requirements, and setting up professional programs in music, art, and education. Never as visionary as the northern women's colleges, they nonetheless developed a wide variety of academically sound programs. Thus, by World War I, most of the major women's colleges were fully accredited.

In the 1960s women's colleges underwent much scrutiny. Many critics wondered if they were relevant to the rapidly changing status of women. Some colleges became coeducational or merged with state university systems. Most women's colleges revitalized their curricula, reexamined their aims, and became self-consciously supportive of women. Still a tiny minority on the educational scene, women's colleges are attempting to meet the challenge of the decades to come.

See M. Newcomer, *Century of Higher Education for Women* (1959); T. Woody, *History of Women's Education* (1929), contains long bibliography; and I. M. E. Blandin, *Higher Education of Women in the South* (1909).

DARA DEHAVEN
Emory University

WOMEN'S RIGHTS MOVEMENT

in the South was characterized by irony and paradox. The feminist philosophy of equality for the sexes enjoyed little acceptance in either the Old or the New South. Yet, in certain specific incidents and situations, the South pioneered.

Two South Carolina women, ANGELINA and SARAH GRIMKÉ, were among the nation's first female lecturers. Sarah published a feminist tract, *Letters on the Equality of the Sexes and the Condition of Woman*, a decade before the Women's Rights Convention at Seneca Falls. The Kentucky common school act of 1838, permitting taxpaying widows and spinsters to vote in school elections, made it the first and, until 1861, the only school suffrage state in the nation. In 1839 Mississippi conferred property rights on married women, the first state to do so.

The question of suffrage was raised during Radical Reconstruction. In constitutional conventions in Texas and Arkansas, resolutions to enfranchise women were introduced, but not adopted. Following the Civil War, the legal status of women improved. Wives were given the right to possess and control "separate" property, to have their own bank accounts, to enter into contracts, and to make wills. In general, women were excluded from public office, but in some states they could be state librarians and county school superintendents.

During the 1880s, a few women's rights societies appeared, but most were small and ephemeral. In 1892 the National American Woman Suffrage Association established a southern committee with LAURA CLAY of Kentucky as chairman. The NAWSA sponsored southern speaking tours by such nationally prominent feminists as Susan B. Anthony and held its annual convention in Atlanta in 1895. By the end of the century, agitation for women's rights was being conducted in all of the southern states. The women who embraced this cause were a small but dedicated group. They sought to "advance the industrial, educational and equal rights of women" and to "secure suffrage" by appropriate legislation. They favored better conditions for working women, female physicians and matrons in asylums and prisons, women on school boards, and the removal of legal discriminations. Always, however, their chief concern was enfranchisement.

During the last decade of the nineteenth century, woman suffrage came under consideration as a potential aid to white political supremacy. At the Mississippi constitutional convention of 1890, a resolution was introduced to enfranchise women who owned $300 worth of real estate. Since few Negro women could meet this property qualification, the number of white voters would be increased. A similar proposal was discussed at a constitutional convention in South Carolina in 1895. Neither was adopted. In Louisiana in 1898, however, women made a significant gain when that state's constitution permitted female taxpayers to vote in person or by proxy on questions of taxation.

Bills to enfranchise women were introduced in the legislatures of all southern states. For many years, no concessions were made; but in Arkansas in 1917 the legislature granted women the right to vote in primary elections. Since Arkansas was predominantly Democratic, primary suffrage was almost tantamount to full enfranchisement. At a special session in 1918, the Texas legislature conferred primary suffrage on women. The following year, the Tennessee legislature passed an act enabling women to vote for presidential electors and to participate in municipal elections.

When Congress submitted the federal woman suffrage amendment, the southern states greeted it with hostility. Most refused to ratify, and some adopted resolutions specifically rejecting it. In the opinion of many southerners, the amendment was an infringement of states' rights and a device for increasing the Negro vote. Texas and Arkansas ratified in 1919. Kentucky did likewise in January, 1920. By the summer of that year, the approval of only one more state was needed. In August, Governor A. H. Roberts of Tennessee submitted the question to a special session of the legislature. After a bitter controversy, which attracted nationwide attention, Tennessee ratified, and the Nineteenth Amendment thereby became part of the federal Constitution.

Since 1920 the sphere of southern women has continued to enlarge, and many have held positions of distinction. The South, however, still treasures the traditions of chivalry and femininity. Like the women's rights movement of former generations, contemporary "new" feminism enjoys only limited popularity in the South.

See S. B. Anthony and I. H. Harper, *History of Woman Suffrage* (1902–22), IV, VI; P. E. Fuller, *Laura Clay* (1975); A. F. Scott, *Southern Lady* (1970); A. E. Taylor, *Woman Suffrage in Tennessee* (1957); L. N. Allen, *Alabama Review* (April, 1958); C. Eaton, *Georgia Review* (Summer, 1974); K. R. Johnson, *Journal of Southern History* (Aug., 1972); and A. E. Taylor, *Journal of Southern History* (May, 1951), *Arkansas Historical Quarterly* (Spring, 1956), *Florida Historical Quarterly* (July, 1957), *Journal of Mississippi History* (Feb., 1968), *North Carolina Historical Review* (Jan., April, 1961), *Georgia Historical Quarterly* (June, 1944; Dec., 1958; March, 1959), and *South Carolina Historical Magazine* (April, 1976).

A. ELIZABETH TAYLOR
Texas Woman's University

WOODROW, JAMES (1828–1907), the maternal uncle of WOODROW WILSON and a native of Carlisle, England, moved with his family to Canada and thence to Chillicothe, Ohio, in 1837. He studied at Jefferson College in Pennsylvania; at Harvard University, where he was deeply influenced by Louis Agassiz; and then at Heidelberg, where he earned M.A. and Ph.D. degrees with highest honors. He returned to the United States in 1856 as a professor of natural science at Oglethorpe University. Woodrow was ordained to the Presbyterian ministry in 1859, and in 1861 he accepted a professorship at the theological seminary in Columbia, S.C. Soon thereafter he volunteered as a private in the Confederate army but was transferred to head a medical laboratory engaged in the preparation of medicines. Woodrow taught at South Carolina College (1869–1872, 1880–1897). He was dean of arts and sciences (1888–1891) and president of the college (1891–1897) in the BENJAMIN TILLMAN period, when the continued existence of the college was in doubt. After helping to revive the seminary after the war, Woodrow taught there as well as in South Carolina College, but was deposed from the faculty in 1886 because of his views on evolution. Acquitted of heresy by his own presbytery, he was adjudged guilty by the general assembly of 1888. However, he remained a minister in good standing and was active in church affairs throughout his life.

See J. Woodrow, *Evolution* (1884); C. Eaton, *Journal of Southern History* (Feb., 1962); F. K. Elder, *South Atlantic Quarterly* (Oct., 1947).

LINDA M. MALONEY
University of South Carolina

WOODSON, CARTER GODWIN (1875–1950),
was born in New Canton, Va., the son of former slaves. After attending high school in Huntington, W.Va. (1895–1896), he studied at Berea College (1896–1898) and then served as principal of his old high school in Huntington (1900–1903). He spent the next four years traveling abroad. Following his return to the United States, he earned a B.A. degree (1907) and an M.A. degree (1908) at the University of Chicago and a Ph.D. degree in history (1912) at Harvard. From 1908 to 1918, he spent much of his time teaching in Washington, D.C., high schools. In 1915 he founded the ASSOCIATION FOR THE STUDY OF AFRO-AMERICAN LIFE AND HISTORY to focus attention on the long-neglected history and achievements of American blacks. The association established the *Journal of Negro History* in 1916, with Woodson as editor-director. Woodson was named dean of Howard University's school of liberal arts in 1919; the following year, he accepted a similar post at West Virginia State College. In 1921 he initiated and became president of Associated Publishers, Inc., which specialized in books on black history. Retiring from teaching in 1922, he continued his efforts to increase white awareness of black contributions to American life; for this purpose, he established the *Negro History Bulletin* in 1937. Woodson contributed many books of his own, including *A Century of Negro Migration* (1918) and *The Negro in Our History* (1922).

See K. Miller's introduction to C. G. Woodson, *Negro in Our History* (9th ed.; 1974); C. H. Wesley, *Journal of Negro History* (Jan., 1951); and E. E. Thorpe, *Black Historians* (1971).

L. MOODY SIMMS, JR.
Illinois State University

WOODVILLE REPUBLICAN. Although this
small Mississippi weekly currently has a circulation of only about 2,000 copies, it is a valuable research tool because of the length of its publication and because in the nineteenth century it was regarded as one of the most influential papers in the state. Founded under its present name in 1826, it also has been known as the *Mississippi Democrat* (1831–1832) and the *Southern Planter* (1832).

See bound copies at publisher's (1878–); and microfilm, from University of Pennsylvania (1826–48) and Bell & Howell (1850–1901).

WOODWARD, COMER VANN (1908–), was
born in Vandale, Ark., and educated at Emory University (Ph.B., 1930), Columbia (M.A., 1932), and the University of North Carolina (Ph.D., 1937). He taught at the universities of Florida and Virginia and at Scripps College before going to Johns Hopkins in 1946. He moved to Yale in 1961. Woodward recast modern southern history in three remarkable books: *Tom Watson: Agrarian Rebel* (1938), a brilliant biography of a key Populist leader; *Reunion and Reaction* (1951), a reinterpretation of the Compromise of 1877; and *Origins of the New South, 1877–1913* (1951), a masterful treatment of the post-Reconstruction era. In addition to the crucial struggle between agrarian and industrial forces within the South, Woodward stressed the influential role of the southern Redeemers, the colonial character of the southern economy, the interplay between race and class in the postwar South, the ambivalence of the southern mind, and the central importance of southern populism, which was pictured as indigenous to the region and as stronger and more radical than its western counterpart.

Since the publication of *The Strange Career of Jim Crow* (1955), a pioneering history of racial segregation, Woodward's most significant writings have taken the form of articles and reviews. The essays in *The Burden of Southern History* (1960) were largely concerned with the search for a southern identity, a major theme in Woodward's work. In another collection of essays, *American Counterpoint* (1971), he focused on slavery and racism as a source of dissonance in the North-South dialogue. Deeply attached to progressive values, Woodward has sought to show the relevance of history to contemporary society's understanding of itself. He is a scholar of great originality and subtlety, with a flair for interpretation, a gift for irony, and an elegant literary style.

See D. M. Potter, in M. Cunliffe and R. W. Winks (eds.), *Pastmasters* (1969); J. A. Garraty, *Interpreting American History* (1970); S. Hackney, *Journal of Southern History* (May, 1972); M. O'Brien, *American Historical Review* (June, 1973); and P. M. Gaston, in A. S. Link and R. W. Patrick (eds.), *Writing Southern History* (1965).

DEWEY W. GRANTHAM
Vanderbilt University

WOODWARD, ELLEN SULLIVAN (1887–1971),
a leader of public welfare services in her native Mississippi, became the highest woman federal administrative officer during the NEW DEAL. After serving as Harry L. Hopkins' assistant in the FEDERAL EMERGENCY RELIEF ADMINISTRATION (1933–1935), she became his top assistant in the WORKS PROGRESS ADMINISTRATION as the director of both women's work and the professional "white-collar" projects (1933–1938). She then became a member

of the Social Security Board (1938–1946). In the postwar years she became the director of the Federal Security Administration's Office of International Relations and served as a U.S. delegate to various United Nations rehabilitation and relief sessions and as a consultant to international relief agencies. She retired from the Department of Health, Education, and Welfare in 1954.

See E. L. George, "Woman Appointees of Roosevelt and Truman Administrations," (Ph.D. dissertation, American University, 1972); J. Mangione, *Dream and Deal* (1972); S. Ware, "Women and New Deal" (Ph.D. dissertation, Harvard University, 1978); and Woodward Papers, Mississippi Department of Archives, Jackson, and Elizabeth Schlesinger Library, Radcliffe.

MARTHA H. SWAIN
Texas Woman's University

WOODY, ROBERT HILLIARD (1903–), pioneering revisionist historian of Reconstruction, was born in Haywood County, N.C.. He received his B.Ph. degree (1927) from Emory University and his M.A. (1928) and Ph.D. (1930) degrees from Duke University. In 1929 he began a 40-year career as a member of the faculty of Duke. He was director of the George Washington Flowers Memorial Collection of Southern Americana in the Duke University Library (1937–1948). *South Carolina During Reconstruction* (1932), the first revisionist study of that controversial era, which he wrote with FRANCIS B. SIMKINS, was awarded the William A. Dunning Prize by the American Historical Association in 1931. He edited and wrote a substantial biographical appreciation for *William Preston Few: Papers and Addresses* (1951) and collected a complete set of notes for a biography of Christopher Gadsden. He has contributed 25 articles and more than 200 book reviews to the scholarly literature. "Cataloochee Homecoming," an article in the *South Atlantic Quarterly* (Winter, 1950), is a moving reminiscence of his heritage of the southern mountains and contains his reflections upon the history of some of the people of the South.

See *South Atlantic Quarterly* (Winter, 1974), festschrift.

E. STANLY GODBOLD, JR.
Valdosta State College

WOOL-HAT or woolhatter was a political term of derision used by opponents of Andrew Jackson during the 1820s to describe a member of the working class who supported the Democratic-Republican party. At this time cheap, coarse hats made of wool and hair and stiffened with glue were popular among those who had little money.

Because President Jackson remained popular with many poor, uneducated people in rural and urban areas of the United States, his political opponents, who came to be known as Whigs, continued to label Jackson's Democratic party members the "wool-hat boys." As styles changed and stronger fabrics replaced wool in making cheap head coverings, the term lost its original meaning. Years later, however, it was revived during the Populist era of the 1890s when *Wool Hat* became the title of a Populist newspaper in Georgia.

FRANCES C. ROBERTS
University of Alabama, Huntsville

WORCESTER V. GEORGIA (6 Peters 515 [1832]) had its origins in 1802, when Georgia ceded its western lands (comprising most of the present states of Alabama and Mississippi) to the national government, after the national government had pledged to remove all remaining Indians as soon as possible. The CHEROKEE tried to prevent removal by organizing themselves into a sovereign nation, but Georgia extended its authority over Cherokee lands. The Cherokee sought an injunction from the U.S. Supreme Court to prevent enforcement of state laws but in CHEROKEE NATION V. GEORGIA (1831), tribal sovereignty was denied. Chief Justice John Marshall defined the Cherokee tribe as a "domestic dependent nation . . . in a state of pupilage" that "resembles that of a ward to his guardian," a definition that has subsequently been applied to all Indian tribes. In the meantime (1829) gold had been discovered on Cherokee land, and over 3,000 miners rushed in among the 15,000 Cherokee. In an effort to maintain order, Georgia required a license from all white persons living on Cherokee lands. When 12 missionaries, who were helping the Cherokee to resist, refused to be licensed, they were imprisoned, but one of them, Samuel Worcester, appealed to the Supreme Court. In *Worcester* v. *Georgia* the state licensing statute was declared unconstitutional; however, due to a defect in federal criminal procedure Worcester remained in prison. In any event, President Andrew Jackson would probably have ignored any Court order. Jackson is reported to have said, "Marshall has made his decision, now let him enforce it." In 1835 a treaty of cession was finally concluded, and the Cherokee were removed to Indian Territory (Oklahoma).

See U. B. Phillips, *American Historical Association Annual Report* (1901); and C. Warren, *Supreme Court in U.S. History* (1926).

RONALD SEAVOY
Bowling Green State University

WORKS PROGRESS ADMINISTRATION

(1935–1943), one of the most important agencies established by the NEW DEAL, helped shake the economic, social, and political foundations of the South. Despite working under the lowest wage scales of the WPA's regional differentials, many southerners earned more money through WPA employment than they would have on jobs in agriculture and private industry. The WPA contributed $2.4 billion to the region's economy in the form of wages, while local project sponsors added another $800 million to cover material costs. The WPA built thousands of miles of highways, roads, and streets. Other projects included the distribution of free school lunches, sponsorship of adult education classes, and construction of public buildings, recreational facilities, and airports. WPA research projects compiled valuable data on the South's industrial and agricultural production, natural resources, and population trends.

The WPA probably did more than any other New Deal agency to help southern blacks weather the depression. Appreciating the special problems of blacks, federal WPA administrator Harry Hopkins officially proclaimed that WPA employment was not to be denied to needy workers because of race, and he pressured local WPA administrators to hire blacks. Nonetheless, although the WPA employed northern blacks in numbers exceeding their proportion of the general population, southern blacks were usually underrepresented on WPA rolls. Yet it was because of the general fair-mindedness of the WPA Washington administration that southern blacks received a larger share of relief benefits than ever before.

The WPA was one of the features of the second New Deal that contributed to Bourbon opposition to Franklin Roosevelt. The relief projects raised wages and reduced dependency on the ruling classes, and Hopkins' pronouncements concerning the fair treatment of blacks disturbed the South's racial patterns. Disgruntled southern leaders also believed that the WPA was a factor leading to the "northernization" of the Democratic party. Southern disenchantment in Congress finally culminated in an informal alliance with the Republicans on Capitol Hill, the conservative coalition, which effectively blocked most important New Deal legislation after 1938.

See D. S. Howard, *WPA and Federal Relief Policy* (1943); A. W. Macmahon *et al.*, *Administration of Federal Work Relief* (1941); G. B. Tindall, *Emergence of New South, 1913–1945* (1967); and *Final Report on WPA Program, 1935–1943* (1943).

RONALD E. MARCELLO
North Texas State University

WORLD WAR I

(1914–1918). From the backcountry of Fentress County, Tenn., where Selective Service located Alvin York, to the cotton country of eastern Texas, where black farmers dropped their hoes to go looking for better-paying jobs in the North (NEGRO MIGRATION), World War I had dramatic consequences for southern life. Cotton farmers, watching the bottom drop out of the European market, were the first Americans victimized by the Great War; their anger helped fuel anti-British attitudes that more sophisticated editors and politicians suppressed to join fellow southerner Woodrow Wilson's crusade. Still, ten of the 56 votes in Congress against American entry into the conflict came from the South, and majority leader CLAUDE KITCHIN was credited with swelling the total. Boosters might applaud establishment of military-training camps in communities as disparate as Spartanburg, S.C., Petersburg, Va., and Houston, Tex., but the general populace was unprepared for the influx of conscripts, especially black ones, and violent conflicts sometimes erupted, as at Houston in August, 1917. The changes wrought by installations like the federal nitrate plant at Muscle Shoals, Ala., destined to become the nucleus of the TENNESSEE VALLEY AUTHORITY, were less dramatic but longer lasting.

Southerners exercised power and influence in wartime Washington: from presidential alter ego EDWARD M. HOUSE and cabinet members like ALBERT S. BURLESON, JOSEPHUS DANIELS, and WILLIAM G. MCADOO to House Speaker CHAMP CLARK and War Industries Board head BERNARD BARUCH. They guided the war effort. Some, such as Congressmen Kitchin, with an excess profits tax, and MORRIS SHEPPARD and RICHMOND P. HOBSON, with PROHIBITION, used wartime exigencies to justify enactment of their particular reform measures. All endeavored to benefit their section, most notably in exempting cotton prices from federal regulation; such moves backfired nationally in the congressional elections of 1918, but southerners kept abreast of wartime inflation by producing more commodities and earning the top dollar for their patriotic efforts. Thus, at war's end, southerners supported their president's plan for the League of Nations as much from party loyalty and gratitude for good times as from agreement with abstract principles of internationalism (FOREIGN AFFAIRS).

The war renewed among southerners the notion that theirs was a section that embodied a special kind of patriotism: a "militant and intolerant Americanism," W. J. Cash termed it. Exposure to the world served to lessen provincial attitudes and to give better than 1 million men an appreciation of their role as Americans in the service of a noble cause. Fearful whites were especially concerned that black soldiers had learned too much. With widespread prosperity southerners came to expect increased material comforts as part of their rightful heritage as Americans.

See complete survey in G. B. Tindall, *Emergence of New South, 1913–1945* (1967); A. S. Link, *Wilson* (1947–); A. M. Arnett, *Kitchin* (1937); F. Henri, *Black Migration* (1975); G. Myrdal, *American Dilemma* (1944); R. L. Watson, *Journal of Southern History* (Feb., 1978), southern congressional leadership; S. W. Livermore, *Mississippi Valley Historical Review* (June, 1948); D. W. Grantham, *North Carolina Historical Review* (April, 1949); E. D. Cronon (ed.), *Diaries of Daniels* (1963); and Kitchin Papers, University of North Carolina and National Historical Publications Committee Microfilm.

H. L. INGLE
University of Tennessee, Chattanooga

WORLD WAR II (1939–1945). On the eve of the war the South's economy was heavily weighted with TENANT FARMERS and unskilled laborers. With one-half of the nation's farm population and one-third of its cropland, the South received only one-fourth of the nation's farm income. The low value-adding, low-wage TEXTILE INDUSTRY accounted for more than one-half of all manufacturing workers in seven southern states. With 22 percent of the nation's manufacturing employment in 1939, the South paid 17 percent of the total payroll. Small-scale, low-profit enterprises, which typified southern industry, and low incomes received by most workers and farmers resulted in a serious regional lag in commercial bank assets.

During the war, however, improvement in the structure of the southern economy was facilitated by an accelerated rate of emigration. Between 1940 and 1945 almost 1.6 million persons left the South, four times the number who migrated during the 1935–1940 period. The out-migration, with only Florida and Virginia as notable exceptions, was especially heavy during the first two years of the conflict, when 80 percent of all contracts for war products were let in the non-South. Internal migration also reached record magnitudes during the war years; more than 3 million persons made at least one move within the region. The war gave a great impetus to urban growth, with southern port cities registering especially high gains.

Southerners who remained in agriculture improved their position as the demand for farm products and farm prices rose rapidly. Larger average-sized farms and increased productivity further enhanced net farm income, which grew about threefold between 1940 and 1944. (The rate of change was the same as the rest of the country, but the impact in the South was more significant.) Farm tenancy dropped sharply. In 1945, 41 percent of southern farms were tenant operated compared with 55 percent in 1935. War-generated prosperity provided the region's first major impetus to agricultural mechanization. Between 1940 and 1945 the value of capital equipment per southern farm doubled. Nonetheless, in 1945 only one southern farm in seven had a tractor compared with one in two elsewhere.

The southern manufacturing sector also expanded markedly, stimulated by soaring demand for military hardware and by federal financing of new facilities. During the conflict, 30 percent of all federal expenditures for military and naval installations were made in the South. Between July 1, 1940, and June 30, 1944, $5.2 billion was invested in southern manufacturing facilities; of this amount approximately $1 billion was private capital, the remainder being publicly financed. Half of the $4.2 billion of federal funds went to three states (Texas, Missouri, and Alabama), primarily for explosives and ammunition-loading facilities, aircraft assembly and parts manufacture, and chemical, coal, and petroleum products.

Not until 1943, when the existing industrial system was operating at full capacity, with labor becoming scarce and the virtues of decentralization becoming recognized, were many new plants built in the South. A high proportion of these facilities had a specific purpose and could not readily be converted into peacetime use. When peak production passed, southern plants were the first to be closed.

Due to the timing and special-purpose character of southern war-oriented production, the region failed to enlarge its share of the nation's manufacturing employment and value of output. Nonetheless, during the war years the South's effective manufacturing capacity grew by about 40 percent, and the industrial sector became more diversified, better balanced, and less vulnerable to economic disturbances. Industry groups with the lowest annual wages—TEXTILES, TOBACCO, and LUMBER—declined in relative importance. Industries with higher annual wages—PULP AND PAPER, CHEMICALS, PETROLEUM refining, machinery, and transportation equipment—expanded at a more rapid rate, although employment in these groups was still relatively small.

During the war years the South registered striking advances in personal INCOME. Between 1940 and 1945, per capita income increased 140 percent in the South compared with an approximately 100 percent increase in the non-South. Expanding per capita incomes in the South led to a sharp growth in purchasing power and surging retail sales. Between 1939 and 1947 the Atlanta and Dallas districts of the Federal Reserve Bank increased retail sales 232 percent and 241 percent respectively. No other district posted gains greater than 200 percent; the national average was 158 percent.

Higher incomes of southern farmers and workers also led to a significant regional growth in the level of savings (BANKING), a trend encouraged by shortages of civilian goods during wartime. Assets of southern commercial banks grew by 231 percent between 1939 and 1947 compared with 131 percent in the non-South. Southern-based life INSURANCE companies also increased their premium income, assets, and life insurance in force during the war years, thus mobilizing the resources that were to finance the surge in southern urban real estate construction in the postwar period.

During the war years, the South's black population shared somewhat in the region's prosperity, posting gains in income and employment and accelerating in varied, sometimes subtle ways the movement toward racial equality. Blacks participated fully in the exodus from southern agriculture (NEGRO MIGRATION). Between 1940 and 1950 the number of blacks residing in the South dropped from 77 percent to 68 percent of the national total. The color bar was only slightly bent as most plant managers hired blacks almost exclusively in unskilled and helper categories.

Despite many obstacles, some progress was recorded. Executive Order 8802, issued by President Roosevelt on June 21, 1941, reaffirmed a policy of full participation in the defense program by all persons regardless of race, creed, or color and established the Fair Employment Practices Committee to oversee its enforcement. The committee was ineffective, but a second FEPC, established in May, 1943, had a limited degree of success in integrating southern industry. Very few gains were made by blacks in traditional southern industries, such as textiles and tobacco, where black employment was confined primarily to tasks that white females were unwilling or unable to perform. Progress in black employment took place primarily in larger urban centers during the latter stages of the wartime period and resulted from both a growing tightness of the labor market and more vigorous enforcement of federal antidiscrimination measures.

The tight labor market in various southern industries as well as a favorable attitude by the federal government, through the actions of the War Labor Board, led to significant gains in LABOR UNION membership. It was found that blacks and Mexican-Americans were more easily organized than were white workers. Extensive unionization took place among aluminum, rubber, chemical, and shipyard employees. By 1945 the AFL reported a 100 percent membership increase in southern state federations. The South's mass transportation system became almost completely organized by 1944. The CIO also registered large gains in membership, particularly in petroleum refining, aircraft assembly plants, and packinghouses and among oil and auto workers. Much less success was attained in attempts to organize the more traditional southern industries—textiles, tobacco, lumber, and furniture—and antiunion forces were gaining momentum as the war ended.

The World War II years constituted in many ways a watershed era, moving the South perceptibly closer to the mainstream of national economic and social life. The acquisition by the South of greater amounts of industrial know-how among managers and workers, along with a substantial accumulation of capital and a rise in per capita purchasing power, created a favorable environment for further postwar advances.

See G. B. Tindall, *Emergence of New South* (1967); C. B. Hoover and B. U. Ratchford, *Economic Resources and Policies of South* (1951); U.S. Department of Labor, *Labor in South* (1947); R. C. Weaver, *Negro Labor* (1946); J. B. McFerrin, *Southern Economic Journal* (July, 1947); J. V. Van Sickle, *Southern Economic Journal* (April, 1949); E. C. Griffith, *Southern Economic Journal* (Oct., 1948); and D. Dewey, *Journal of Political Economy* (Aug., 1952).

JACK BLICKSILVER
Georgia State University

WORMLEY HOUSE BARGAIN was envisioned originally as the settlement of the ELECTION OF 1876. Historians interpreted the meeting of February 26–27, 1877, as a compact between southerners E. A. BURKE, E. John Ellis, William M. Levy, and HENRY WATTERSON and Republicans headed by John Sherman and Stanley Matthews. The agreement ensured the election of Rutherford B. Hayes in exchange for the removal of federal troops from the South and presidential recognition of Democratic administrations in Louisiana and South Carolina. Recent historians have stressed that the meeting simply reaffirmed previous agreements: southern Democrats would expedite the electoral count in favor of Hayes in return for home rule, troop removal, and certain economic advantages. The "bargain" should be viewed as but a small part of the overall election settlement.

See P. J. Haworth, *Hayes-Tilden Disputed Election* (1906), old interpretation; C. V. Woodward, *Reunion and Reaction* (1966); and Burke's testimony, *House Miscellaneous Document No. 31*, 45th Cong., 3rd Sess., I, III.

NORBERT A. KUNTZ
St. Michael's College

WORTH, JONATHAN (1802–1869), was born in Guilford County, N.C. He practiced law from 1825 to 1860. After election to the state legislature in 1830, he took a firm stand against NULLIFICATION; thereafter he was a consistent supporter of the idea of union and a devout Whig. In 1840 he served another legislative term, during which he wrote an important act concerning education. Upon its implementation, he served as superintendent of the Randolph County school system for almost 20 years. During those 20 years prior to the Civil War, he also ran several merchandising operations, supervised his farms, practiced law, and served as president of the Fayetteville & Western Plank Road Company. Worth returned to the legislature in the sessions of 1858 and 1860. In the latter he was one of only three members refusing to vote for SECESSION, but he stood by his state. In 1862 he became the treasurer in the administration of Governor ZEBULON B. VANCE, a job he performed conservatively and with considerable skill. When the war ended he remained as treasurer in the provisional government, but resigned in the fall of 1865 to run for governor against WILLIAM W. HOLDEN. Victorious in 1865, he was reelected in the regular election of 1866 and served until his removal in 1868.

See R. L. Zuber, *Jonathan Worth* (1965), only complete biography; papers, in North Carolina Archives, University of North Carolina Library, and Duke University Library; and J. G. deR. Hamilton (ed.), *Correspondence of Jonathan Worth* (1909).

RICHARD L. ZUBER
Wake Forest University

WRIGHT, JONATHAN JASPER (1840–1885), was born in Luzerne County, Pa. After attending Lancasterian University in Ithaca, N.Y., he taught school, studied law privately, and in 1866 became the first black admitted to the bar in Pennsylvania. His career in South Carolina included organizing American Missionary Association schools for blacks (1865), serving as legal adviser for refugees and freedmen (1866–1868), officiating as one of five vice-presidents of the state constitutional convention (1868), and serving as state senator (1868–1870). A well-respected man of considerable ability and a political moderate, Wright was elected by the Republican legislature to fill an unexpired term on the three-man South Carolina state supreme court in February, 1870, and reelected in December, 1870, for a six-year term. Wright wrote 87 of the court's opinions. When the Democrats regained political control, they used false charges to bring impeachment proceedings against Wright. Under pressure, he resigned from the supreme court in 1877, and taught law privately and, for a while, at Claflin College, Orangeburg.

See R. H. Woody, *Journal of Negro History* (April, 1933); A. A. Taylor, *Negro in South Carolina* (1924); E. B. Reynolds and J. R. Faunt, *Biographical Directory of Senate of South Carolina* (1964); W. S. Robinson, *Historical Negro Biographies* (1967); and G. B. Tindall, *South Carolina Negroes* (1952).

DE WITT S. DYKES, JR.
Oakland University, Rochester, Mich.

WRIGHT, RICHARD (1908–1960), son of a sharecropper, was born near Natchez, Miss. The Delta South pervaded his youth. He lived in Mississippi, Tennessee, Arkansas, and again in Mississippi, graduating from the ninth grade of a Jackson school in 1925. Two years later he left Memphis for Chicago. There he worked at low-paying jobs, joined the Communist party—which he was to leave in 1942, though he would always respect Marxism—and became a writer. He was, however, a resident of New York City when the novel *Native Son* made him famous. He died in Paris, France, his home for the last 14 years of his life. Wright is remembered principally for his novels: the naturalistic *Native Son* (1940), with its protagonist Bigger Thomas, one of the epic characters in American fiction; the verbosely existentialist *The Outsider* (1953); the Freudian *Savage Holiday* (1954); his unwitting swan song *The Long Dream* (1958); and the posthumously published but first-written *Lawd Today* (1963). Nevertheless, he was no mean poet. His *Black Power* (1954), a survey of the Gold Coast on the eve of its independence, and *Pagan Spain* (1956) are superior journalism. And in his two collections of short stories, *Uncle Tom's Children* (1938, 1940) and *Eight Men* (1961), the early "Big Boy Leaves Home" may be artistically his finest hour. He told well the story of the move of the southern agrarian Negro into the northern urban ghetto in the documentary *Twelve Million Black Voices* (1941). Of his own formative years in the South he left a moving testament, the autobiographical *Black Boy* (1945).

See J. M. Reilly, *Resources for American Literary Study* (Autumn, 1971), bibliography; C. Webb, *Richard Wright* (1968); M. Fabre, *Unfinished Quest of Richard Wright* (1973); O. Harrington, *Ebony* (Feb. 1961); E. Margolies, *Art of Richard Wright* (1969); D. McCall, *Example of*

Richard Wright (1969); R. A. Bone, *Richard Wright* (1969); N. A. Scott, in A. Gayle (ed.), *Black Expression* (1969); and B. Jackson, *Southern Literary Journal* (Spring, 1971), *CLA Journal* (June, 1969), and *New Letters* (Winter, 1971).

BLYDEN JACKSON
University of North Carolina, Chapel Hill

WYTHE, GEORGE (1726–1806), was born in Elizabeth City County, Va. His only formal education included a brief attendance at the College of William and Mary. After apprenticing with Stephen Dewey, he was admitted to the bar at age twenty. He later removed to Williamsburg, where he became a representative in the House of Burgesses (1754–1755, 1758–1768). He now began studying in earnest the classics, Greek, Latin, and English and Roman law. Admitted to the bar of the general court, Wythe soon was recognized as one of the most learned and skilled practitioners in Virginia. He remained active as a clerk in the house (1769–1775) and became mayor of Williamsburg (1768) and a member of the board of visitors at William and Mary (1769). While in Williamsburg, Wythe, Professor William Small, and Governor Francis Fauquier became inseparable friends. It was Small who brought teacher and student together. In 1762 young THOMAS JEFFERSON began reading law under Wythe's direction, a fruitful arrangement lasting five years.

Wythe opposed the Stamp Act and drafted a bold remonstrance (rejected by his colleagues). He was sent to Congress, where he became a signer of the DECLARATION OF INDEPENDENCE. He returned to Virginia that year to assist in the revision of the laws. In 1779, following his appointment as chancellor, the board of visitors of William and Mary established the premier American "professorship of law and police" and offered Wythe the chair. In 1790 he removed to Richmond, resigned his chair, and in 1801 became one of three district chancellors. His many opinions are marked by erudition, impartiality, and logic. Wythe is remembered foremost as America's first systematic legal educator.

See D. Malone, *Jefferson* (1948–62); W. E. Hemphill, "George Wythe" (Ph.D. dissertation, University of Virginia, 1937); J. P. Boyd, *William and Mary Quarterly* (Oct., 1955); and J. Blackburn, *George Wythe* (1975).

JAMIL SHAHEEN ZAINALDIN
Northwestern University

Y

YADKIN RIVER SETTLEMENTS constituted an important mid-eighteenth-century frontier community in western North Carolina. The Yadkin flows from its headsprings in Watauga County in a grand arc through the North Carolina Piedmont. The first settlements in the Yadkin Valley were made in the southern area when English and Scotch-Irish settlers from South Carolina and the upper Cape Fear River began moving into the region by the mid-1740s. The Yadkin settlements were best known, however, as the southern terminus of the GREAT WAGON ROAD, which ran 435 miles to Philadelphia. Thousands of Scotch-Irish, German, Welsh, and English settlers moved overland from Maryland and Pennsylvania and settled in the Yadkin Valley north of the Granville Line. One group of German MORAVIANS from Pennsylvania settled in the area on the Wachovia tract in 1753. Their villages, especially Salem, became important urban centers in the Carolina backcountry. By far the most important governmental and trading town in the Yadkin area was Salisbury, founded in 1753.

See R. W. Ramsey, *Carolina Cradle* (1964), detailed, but undigested; C. Hammer, *Rhinelanders on Yadkin* (1965); P. Rouse, *Great Wagon Road* (1973); J. S. Brawley, *Rowan Story* (1953); and H. R. Merrens, *Colonial North Carolina* (1964).

HERBERT R. PASCHAL
East Carolina University

YAMASSEE INDIANS were a Muskogean people who lived in eastern Georgia when the Spanish arrived and named the region Guale. The Yamassee lived well inland and, unlike their Indian neighbors who lived closer to the coast, received no Franciscan missionaries until at least 1680. Before the end of the century the Yamassee, offended by the Spanish governor's ill treatment of a chief, moved north to St. Helena and Hilton Head Island, where the English welcomed them. They established at least ten towns northeast of the Savannah River and west from Port Royal, a region long known as "Indian land." Simultaneously, English settlers took up land nearby. Disputes over boundaries and land use followed. Abuses by Carolina traders against the Indians, enslavement, beatings, and theft became intolerable. In 1715 the Yamassee, supported by the CREEK INDIANS, attacked their English neighbors. The South Carolinians quickly organized their defense, soon went on the offensive, and thoroughly thrashed the Yamassee, who fled south to Spanish Florida. From time to time they clashed with the English, but well before the end of the eighteenth century the Yamassee disappeared as an identifiable people.

See J. R. Swanton, *Bureau of American Ethnology Bulletin* (1922); and V. W. Crane, *Southern Frontier* (1929).

RUSSELL S. NELSON, JR.
University of Wisconsin, Stevens Point

YANCEY, WILLIAM LOWNDES (1814–1863). Yancey's father, a South Carolina politician, died when William was three; his mother later married Nathan Beman, a New England preacher who conducted an academy near Sparta, Ga. When Beman became pastor of the Presbyterian Church in Troy, N.Y., Yancey was sent to several northern academies and Williams College, where he perfected his oratorical style, but in 1833 he returned to the South. He edited the Greenville, S.C. *Mountaineer* and vigorously attacked the nullifiers in the struggle against a South Carolina loyalty oath. At the age of twenty-one, he married an heiress and soon thereafter became an Alabama planter.

The panic of 1837, accident, and his own absenteeism and mismanagement dissipated his wife's property, and when he was jailed for killing his wife's uncle in a street brawl he was near financial ruin. Pardoned after three months, he studied law, edited two newspapers, and entered Democratic politics, serving two terms in the Alabama legislature. Elected to Congress in 1844, he resigned in 1846. At the Democratic National Convention of 1848 he introduced the ALABAMA PLATFORM, demanding that neither Congress nor a territorial legislature interfere with slavery in the territories and asking the federal government's protection of the institution in the Mexican Cession. When the platform was rejected, Yancey left the convention. Urging secession in 1850, he acted independently until the ambiguous Democratic platform of 1856 enabled him to rejoin that party. He was one of the fiery spirits in the Montgomery Commercial Convention of 1858 and took counsel with BARNWELL RHETT and EDMUND RUFFIN. When the Democratic convention of 1860 rejected the Alabama Platform, Yancey led a general walkout of the Lower South delegations and left the Democratic party hopelessly disrupted. He was a leader in the Alabama secession convention but was not chosen as a delegate to the Confederate government. Jefferson Davis appointed him commissioner to Great Britain, but after a year's service Yancey resigned in disillusionment and returned to represent Alabama in the Confederate Senate, where he became a leading opponent of Davis. Long in poor health, Yancey died the next year near Montgomery.

See J. W. DuBose, *W. L. Yancey* (1892), biased but useful; C. Eaton, *Mind of Old South* (1967); and R. B. Draughon, Jr., "W. L. Yancey" (Ph.D. dissertation, University of North Carolina, 1968).

RALPH DRAUGHON, JR.
University of Georgia

YAZOO LAND FRAUDS (1789–1814) were a series of schemes designed to engross large parts of the present states of Alabama and Mississippi (the name comes from the Yazoo River) for speculative purposes. In 1789 the Georgia legislature passed an act granting large tracts to three companies for $207,580. The lands covered the new Southwest from the Tombigbee to the Mississippi and around the Great Bend of the Tennessee. The sale did not involve legislative corruption but represented Georgia's attempt to sell lands to which it did not have clear title. Several important southern political figures were associated with these activities, including PATRICK HENRY (Virginia Yazoo Company), JOHN SEVIER and WILLIAM BLOUNT (Tennessee Yazoo Company), and Alexander Moultrie (South Carolina Yazoo Company). Their agents were unable to overcome determined opposition from several quarters, namely the Spanish governor Esteban Miró and southern Indian tribes, especially the CREEKS (led by ALEXANDER MCGILLIVRAY). The companies proposed several settlements, but so vigorous was the opposition that none was ever carried out.

Plans were revived in 1795, when the Georgia legislature granted the same lands and more (some 35 million acres) to four companies, called Georgia, Georgia-Mississippi, Upper Mississippi, and Tennessee, for $500,000. Managers of the bills bribed most of the legislators. The new legislature repealed the act (1796), and JAMES JACKSON resigned from the U.S. Senate and led the fight against the grants. State leaders publicly burned the law, wrote its repudiation into the new state constitution (1798), and repaid the purchase price, but the continuing sale of lands to innocent third parties kept the question before Congress and the courts (FLETCHER V. PECK). Under a final settlement in 1814, Congress paid claimants $4,282,151.

See T. P. Abernethy, *South in New Nation* (1961); C. H. Haskins, *American Historical Association Papers* (1891); J. C. Parish, *Mississippi Valley Historical Review* (Sept., 1930); and manuscripts in Georgia Department of Archives and History, Atlanta.

MALCOLM J. ROHRBOUGH
University of Iowa

YAZOO RIVER BASIN comprises the Yazoo-Mississippi Delta and the tributaries of the Bluff Hills. The Coldwater River merges with the Tallahatchie (Choctaw for "rock river"), then joins the Yalobusha (Choctaw for "tadpole place"). Together they become the Yazoo (Uchee for "leaf") proper. It flows along the loess bluffs bordering the floodplain before merging with the Mississippi. The deferred junction of the parallel-flowing streams gave rise to the term "Yazoo-type stream."

Settlement of the basin has been dependent upon FLOOD CONTROL and water resources management. In the hills, ignorance of conservation practices, overgrazing, and poor timber management have resulted in high runoff and sheet and gully erosion. In the bottomland, silt deposits from hill streams, interior drainage, flooded croplands, and backwater have required improved channel flow, LEVEES, and drainage projects. Initially, however, all flood control rested with the individual landowner.

The major portion of the basin is the Yazoo-MISSISSIPPI DELTA—known simply as the Delta—the triangle-shaped land between the two rivers. Deep loam, clay, and buckshot SOILS make the basin a rich agricultural region. Settled by immigrants from the Southeast and Midwest, it was suited for plantation agriculture. Hill farms, on the other hand, were of the subsistence type. From the basin's initial settlement through 1945, long-staple COTTON was king. Drainage, land clearing, insect infestations, a labor supply, crop failures, and flooding were persistent problems. Today, agriculture is big, mechanized, and diversified business. Although an abundant labor supply attracts industry, out-migration—begun during the 1930s—persists.

See R. L. Brandfon, *Cotton Kingdom* (1967); R. D. Cross, *Atlas of Mississippi* (1974); R. W. Harrison, *Alluvial Empire* (1961); Mississippi Board of Water Commissioners, *Report-Survey of Land and Water Resources of Yazoo-Mississippi River Basin* (1961); *Mississippi Water News*

(Aug., 1969); Mississippi River Commission, *Lower Mississippi Region* (1974); L. L. Seale, "Indian Place-Names in Mississippi" (Ph.D. dissertation, Louisiana State University, 1939); F. E. Smith, *Yazoo River* (1954); and K. G. Williamson, *Magic* (May, 1962).

RANDALL A. DETRO
Nicholls State University

YEADON, RICHARD (1802–1870), was born in Charleston, S.C. Educated at South Carolina College, he was admitted to the bar in 1824. He became a member of the Whig party and was for many years a consistent defender of Unionist principles, opposing NULLIFICATION when JOHN C. CALHOUN advanced it in 1831–1832 and again when ROBERT BARNWELL RHETT tried to revive it in 1844. He served three terms in the South Carolina legislature (1856–1860, 1862–1864). By 1860 Yeadon had modified his position from that of unconditional Unionist to one of "cooperationist." Following Abraham Lincoln's election, he waffled further on his position, and when his state left the Union he approved of its action. He unstintingly supported the Confederate cause until the South's defeat.

See W. L. T. Crocker, "Richard Yeadon" (M.A. thesis, University of South Carolina, 1927); and John C. Ellen, "Public Life of Richard Yeadon" (M.A. thesis, University of South Carolina, 1953).

DONALD E. REYNOLDS
East Texas State University

YELLOW FEVER, an acute infectious virus disease transmitted by the *Aëdes aegypti* mosquito, is characterized by chills, fever, headache, muscular pain, vomiting, jaundice, and a tendency to hemorrhage. Coma or convulsions mark its final stages, with death usually resulting from damage to liver and kidneys. Common synonyms for the disease, especially in nineteenth-century southern writings, were yellow jack, saffron scourge, strangers' disease (newcomers from the North or Europe seemed especially vulnerable), and black vomit (vomitus of partially digested blood from hemorrhaging resembled coffee grounds).

Yellow fever was carried to North American ports by the 1690s on ships from the West Indies. The disease was intermittently reintroduced during the eighteenth and nineteenth centuries by infected persons or mosquitoes on vessels from Latin America, resulting in frequent outbreaks in South Atlantic and Gulf ports during summer and early fall. Each time the virus died out with the coming of frost. Mainly an urban disease carried by a domestic mosquito, yellow fever did not spread easily in rural areas, but its sphere of activity expanded inland from southern ports with the developing transportation network. Major nineteenth-century epidemics occurred in New Orleans, Memphis, Vicksburg, Natchez, Biloxi, Mobile, Galveston, Tampa, Pensacola, Savannah, and Charleston. New Orleans, principal port of entry, was considered the yellow fever capital of the South. Its epidemic of 1853 was probably the worst ever to strike a major American city. Within five months approximately 40 percent of the resident population suffered attacks and 10 percent died of the fever. Extremely widespread in the 1850s, the disease generally diminished in frequency and virulence during the rest of the century. In 1878, however, the Gulf states and the Mississippi Valley suffered the most extensive yellow fever epidemic the country had ever had, with 20,000 deaths among some 120,000 cases and an estimated cost of nearly $200 million. The experience of 1878 stimulated public demand for the national government to enter the quarantine field, led to the establishment of the abortive National Board of Health, influenced the Gulf states to cooperate in quarantine regulations and exchange of information, and intensified scientific investigation of the disease.

Baffled by the erratic spread of the disease, physicians and laymen debated cause, transmission, and prevention. Those who considered yellow fever contagious and imported favored isolation and quarantine; others believed it originated locally in putrefaction and advocated sanitation. Concern over the epidemics brought improved water supply, drainage, and sewerage systems in many communities. Businessmen, physicians, and citizen groups worked for sanitary reform and uniform quarantine and inspection systems. Yellow fever influenced the development of public HEALTH institutions in southern cities and states; it also prompted a greater awareness of regional and national interdependence in matters of health and brought at least some acceptance of federal action in the area. With the discovery in 1900–1901 of the mosquito vector by the U.S. Army Commission in Cuba under WALTER REED, means were available for better control and prevention of the disease. The last epidemic in the country occurred in New Orleans in 1905.

See J. Duffy, *Sword of Pestilence* (1966); J. A. Carrigan, *Louisiana History* (Winter, 1963); J. H. Ellis, *Bulletin of History of Medicine* (1970); G. Augustin, *History of Yellow Fever* (1909); *New Orleans Medical and Surgical Journal* (1844–1906); and *Proceedings of Board of Experts to Investigate Yellow Fever Epidemic* (1878).

JO ANN CARRIGAN
University of Nebraska, Omaha

YELLOW TAVERN, BATTLE OF (May 11, 1864). On May 9, P. H. Sheridan set out to ride around Robert E. Lee, disrupt his communications, and lure J. E. B. STUART's cavalry away from Lee. Sheridan fought several skirmishes with Stuart until, by the eleventh, Stuart had placed himself six miles in front of Richmond at Yellow Tavern. He wished to strike Sheridan's flank rather than meet superior numbers frontally. However, fears for Richmond's safety forced Stuart to place part of his command directly across the enemy's front. At 11 A.M. Sheridan attacked, seizing the road to Richmond. Stuart soon learned that Richmond could hold, and he thereafter took the defensive. By 4 P.M. Sheridan's attack dislodged half the Confederates before being repulsed. Here Stuart was mortally wounded. FITZHUGH LEE took command and was finally forced back, but too late for Sheridan to attempt a raid on Richmond. Sheridan's forces numbered roughly 10,000; Stuart's, 4,500. Federal losses totaled 295; Confederate casualties are indeterminate, but probably somewhat higher. On May 12, Jeb Stuart died.

See D. S. Freeman, *Lee's Lieutenants* (1944), III, full Confederate account; P. H. Sheridan, *Memoirs* (1888), I, self-serving; H. B. McClellan, *J. E. B. Stuart* (1885); and *Official Records, Armies*, Ser. 1, Vol. XXXVI, Pt. 1.

WILLIAM C. DAVIS
Civil War Times Illustrated

YEOMAN FARMER. In the colonial period the word *yeoman* identified a white farmer who owned his own land and distinguished him from both the planter, with his large estate and many slaves, and the poor white of the South. By the time of the American Revolution a majority of southern farmers were in this class, generally owning several hundred acres of land and sometimes a few slaves. The importance of this rural middle class was long obscured by characterizations of southern society, which classified whites as either planters or POOR WHITES. Not until the twentieth century, when FRANK OWSLEY and his students at Vanderbilt University began to study the yeomen of the South, did this group receive adequate recognition.

Owsley estimated that on the eve of the Civil War 80 percent of southern farmers owned their own land, generally farms averaging 100 acres. Most farmed the hill regions and poorer coastal SOILS of the South. Living unostentatiously, they marketed food crops such as corn and wheat or raised livestock. Although in the decade before the Civil War the yeomen were relatively prosperous and as a consequence of political reforms had considerable control over their state governments, the planter class still dominated the section's economy and politics. The yeomen farmers, however, proud and independent in attitude, Protestant and evangelical in religion, and democratic in political views, provided the backbone of southern society.

After the Civil War, pressed by falling crop prices and rising interest rates, more and more farmers slipped into tenancy (TENANT FARMING). In the late nineteenth century, the yeomen organized the GRANGE, FARMERS' ALLIANCE, and POPULIST PARTY to challenge planter and business control of state politics. These efforts were no more successful than later NEW DEAL programs in restoring the yeoman's traditional independence; by 1935, only half of all white farmers owned their own land. Economic dislocations caused by the GREAT DEPRESSION of the 1930s, increased use of farm machinery, and growing URBANIZATION and INDUSTRIALIZATION in the South eventually reversed the increase in farm tenancy; by the mid–twentieth century white tenants had almost disappeared. But an accompanying decline in the South's rural population also reduced the numbers and significance of the yeomanry in southern life.

See F. Owsley, *Plain Folk of Old South* (1949); F. Linden, *Journal of Negro History* (April, 1946); T. Saloutos, *Farmer Movements in South* (1960); and pre–Civil War census materials, Joint University Libraries, Nashville, Tennessee.

RICHARD H. ABBOTT
Eastern Michigan University

YERBY, FRANK GARVIN (1916–), native of Augusta, Ga., studied at Paine College (A.B., 1937) and Fisk University (M.A., 1938). After further graduate studies at the University of Chicago and participation in the FEDERAL WRITERS' PROJECT there, he taught at Florida A. & M. College and Southern University, but he left teaching in 1941 to work in a war plant. In 1944 his story "Health Card," a tale of poor southern blacks, won the O. Henry Award. His first novel, *The Foxes of Harrow* (1946), was an instant success and enabled Yerby to become a full-time writer. A "costume novel" of the Old South, *Foxes* launched a series of more than two dozen such books, as well as short stories, which Yerby produced in the next three decades. These novels were swashbuckling romances designed for popular sales. With *An Odor of Sanctity* (1965) he modified his popular style in a quest for greater substance, and in *The Dahomean* (1971) he began once again to explore his black roots, while remaining in his chosen historical mode. Since 1952 Yerby has lived and worked in France and Spain.

See R. Bardolph, *Negro Vanguard* (1959); R. A. Bone, *Negro Novel in America* (1958); H. Breit, *Writer Observed* (1956); J. M. C. Hughes, *Negro Novelist* (1953); and D. T. Turner, *Massachusetts Review* (Summer, 1968).

LINDA M. MALONEY
University of South Carolina

YORKTOWN, VA. (pop. 311), is a small port town on the York River. Although the area was settled in 1631, the town itself was established in 1691 and designated the county seat in 1698. Located on a high bluff overlooking a narrow beach, the town achieved commercial importance as a tobacco-trading center in the late 1730s, when several trading firms built wharves into the river. Ravaged during the siege of Yorktown in September–October, 1781, the town never recovered as a trading center. The York River is short, and its tributaries do not reach into the Piedmont. Once the adjoining tobacco lands were depleted, Yorktown and the York River area lost out to Richmond and Norfolk in the James River basin. Fire in 1814 destroyed the town's commercial facilities at a time when the town was under pressure from a British fleet. War again ruined the town during the Civil War, when General G. B. McClellan besieged Confederate General JOHN B. MAGRUDER during April–May, 1862 (PENINSULAR CAMPAIGN). The town lay dormant until 1917, when the U.S. Navy built its principal mine depot there. Much of the town, including the Yorktown Battlefield, is now part of the Colonial National Historical Park. The town's population has varied between 250 and 500 persons.

See C. F. Trudell, *Colonial Yorktown* (1971), useful, though no full study exists of postcolonial Yorktown.

D. ALAN WILLIAMS
University of Virginia

YORKTOWN CAMPAIGN (August–October, 1781). General Charles Cornwallis, after campaigning in the Carolinas, invaded Virginia and was at Petersburg May 20. The conquest of Virginia was, in his thinking, demanded if the states to the south were to be firmly held. Cornwallis moved about Virginia shadowed by the marquis de Lafayette's small force. Early in August, Cornwallis was at Yorktown and fortifying, preparatory to establishing a naval station.

Yorktown, an undesirable military location, placed the British army on a narrow peninsula with its back to the water. However, Cornwallis knew that Lafayette did not have the strength to contain him should he elect to move out. And, in the event of dire necessity, he could always be evacuated by the British navy. Naval superiority was the key to Cornwallis' position and security. Unknown to Cornwallis, a French fleet under Admiral François de Grasse had sailed from the West Indies and would arrive in the Chesapeake on August 30. Meanwhile, when intelligence of the French fleet's movement and destination reached Generals George Washington and Rochambeau, the projected assault on New York was abandoned. The American-French armies marched south to converge on Cornwallis.

In the battle off the VIRGINIA CAPES, September 5, Grasse bettered Admiral Thomas Graves's British fleet, which fell back to New York. The troops of Washington and Rochambeau arrived before Yorktown September 28 and opened the siege. Hemmed in by land and cut off from support or rescue by sea, Cornwallis surrendered his army of over 7,000 men on October 19, 1781. The last and most decisive campaign of the Revolution was over.

See H. P. Johnston, *Yorktown Campaign* (1881, 1973); T. J. Fleming, *Beat Last Drum* (1963); H. A. Larrabee, *Decision at Chesapeake* (1964); and W. B. Willcox, *American Historical Review* (Oct., 1946).

WILLIAM JAMES MORGAN
U.S. Department of Navy

YOUNG, STARK (1881–1963). In *The Pavilion* (1951) Stark Young described with loving warmth his family and boyhood in Como, Miss. Family tradition led him to the University of Mississippi for his B.A. degree in 1901, but he pursued his literary studies at Columbia University for the M.A. degree. Young then returned to Mississippi to teach until 1907, when he moved to the University of Texas (1907–1915) and to Amherst (1915–1921). Meanwhile he had begun to publish verse (*The Blind Man at the Window* appeared in 1906), plays, and essays on the theater. In 1921 he joined the editorial staff of the *New Republic* and of *Theatre Arts Monthly*. After a year as drama critic for the New York *Times* (1924–1925) he rejoined the *New Republic*, where he remained until 1947. He continued to publish plays, criticism, and translations from French, Italian, and Russian and added four novels and two volumes of sketches. For the fiction, including his best-known novel *So Red the Rose* (1934), he drew on the family history and legend of his Mississippi boyhood.

See J. M. Bradbury, *Fugitives* (1958); L. B. Cowan, *Fugitive-Agrarian Group* (1959); T. L. Connelly, *Tennessee Historical Quarterly* (March, 1963); A. Martin, *Sewanee*

Review (Jan., 1930); J. Pilkington (ed.), *Stark Young: Letters, 1900–1962* (1975); and papers, Yale, Harvard, Duke, University of Chicago, University of Virginia, and New York Public libraries.

LINDA M. MALONEY
University of South Carolina

YOUNG, WHITNEY MOORE, JR. (1921–1971),

was born in Lincoln Ridge, Ky. His father was president (1935–1966) of Lincoln Institute. Young graduated from Lincoln Institute and Kentucky State College in Frankfort, and he taught high school in Madisonville, Ky., for one year before entering the army. Upon leaving the service, he earned his M.A. degree in social work at the University of Minnesota in 1947. Young began his career with the URBAN LEAGUE as director of industrial relations with the St. Paul, Minn., branch. From 1950 to 1953, he was executive secretary of the Omaha Urban League. In 1954 he left to serve as dean of the Atlanta University School of Social Work. He was an adviser to the Atlanta student activists and to Dr. MARTIN LUTHER KING, JR. He became executive director of the National Urban League in 1961 and made that organization an important part of the CIVIL RIGHTS MOVEMENT. Young was a leader of the march on Washington in 1963, and during his tenure the Urban League became much more active in the South. Young died in Nigeria while attending a conference of American and African leaders.

See E. A. Toppin, *Biographical History of Blacks* (1971); L. E. Lomax, *Negro Revolt* (1963); G. R. Metcalf, *Black Profiles* (1968); and S. L. Wormley and L. H. Henderson (eds.), *Many Shades of Black* (1969).

ARVARH E. STRICKLAND
University of Missouri, Columbia

YULEE, DAVID LEVY (1810–1886), Florida pro-

moter, was born in the West Indies. He was known as David Levy until 1846, when he added the name Yulee, a title given his grandfather by the government of Morocco. He was a delegate to the Florida constitutional convention of 1838, territorial delegate to Congress in 1841, and U.S. senator (1845–1851, 1855–1861). He played a major role in building the Florida Railroad connecting Fernandina on the Atlantic with Cedar Key on the Gulf of Mexico in the late 1850s. During the Civil War he fought successfully to prevent removal of track for use elsewhere by the government. He died in Washington, D.C.

See A. W. Thompson, "David Yulee" (Ph.D. dissertation, Columbia, 1954); C. W. Yulee, *Florida Historical Quarterly* (April, 1909); J. H. Shofner and W. W. Rogers, *Florida Historical Quarterly* (Jan., 1945); and Yulee Papers, University of Florida Library, Gainesville.

RALPH A. WOOSTER
Lamar University

Z

ZANE, EBENEZER (1747–1812), was born in Hardy County, W.Va. (then Virginia). He left the Potomac Valley with two brothers to establish Wheeling on the Ohio River (1770). Zane was instrumental in its defense (Ft. Fincastle) in DUNMORE'S WAR and (renamed Ft. Henry) in the Revolution. This settlement became important to emigrants moving westward on the river or on the CUMBERLAND ROAD. While experimenting to find crops best suited to the region, he originated Zane's Greening, a species of apple that enjoyed long popularity. He held various positions of public trust and represented his county at the Virginia constitutional ratification convention. In 1796 Congress authorized Zane to blaze a road from Wheeling across southeastern Ohio to Limestone (Maysville) on the Kentucky shore of the Ohio River. Zane's Trace not only promoted his own land speculation, but provided an important alternative to the CUMBERLAND GAP and WILDERNESS ROAD in making the Ohio Valley accessible.

See J. G. Patterson, *West Virginia History* (Oct., 1950), best; C. L. Martzolff, *Ohio Archaeological and Historical Society Publications* (1904); and E. Zane Account Books, West Virginia University Library.

DWIGHT L. SMITH
Miami University

ZUBLY, JOHN JOACHIM (1724–1781), born in Switzerland, came to Savannah in 1745 but left for South Carolina in 1747 after serving as assistant to the Anglican minister Bartholomew Zouberbuhler. He returned in 1760 as pastor of a Presbyterian congregation in Savannah, acquiring acclaim by preaching to settlers in German, French, or English and through his published sermons and his correspondence with prominent clergymen such as Ezra Stiles of Yale and John Witherspoon of the College of New Jersey. His forceful writings on colonial rights following the Stamp Act led ultimately to his election to the Georgia provincial convention and to the CONTINENTAL CONGRESS in 1775. Opposing America's drift toward independence, he left Philadelphia under a cloud and subsequently was banished from Georgia as a Loyalist. He returned to British-held Savannah a few months before his death.

See J. J. Zubly, *Revolutionary Tracts* (1972), three pamphlets reprinted with introduction; P. H. Smith (ed.), *Letters of Delegates to Congress* (1976), II; and Zubly Diary, Georgia Historical Society.

PAUL H. SMITH
Library of Congress

ZWAANENDAEL or Swanendael, the "valley of swans," first colony of the Dutch south of the Hudson, was situated within the limits of present-day Lewes, Del., near Cape Henlopen. Settlement in 1631 was directed by Gillis Hossitt as emissary for the Dutch West India Company. It was utterly destroyed by Indians but was followed by a second settlement in 1632 under David de Vries. Lacking further support by the company, its inhabitants gradually dispersed.

See C. A. Weslager, *Dutch Explorers in the Delaware Valley* (1961), includes translations of documents about Zwaanendael; and C. Ward, *Dutch and Swedes on Delaware* (1930).

E. GORDON ALDERFER
Washington, D.C.

INDEX

Fletcher, John Gould, 618
Fletcher, Thomas Clement, 438–39, 852
Fletcher, William A., 230
Fletcher v. Peck, 439, 524, 782
Flood, Henry De La Warr, 439, 166, 1288
Flood control, 439–40, 557, 585; construction for, 289; and dams, 326–27; and levees, 717; and progressivism, 1007; and Public Works Administration, 1012; and TVA, 1205
Florence, Ala., 440–41
Florence, S.C., 441
Florence Prison, 441
Florida, 441–58
Florida (ship), 773
Florida, University of, 458
Florida Agricultural and Mechanical University, 1175
Florida Coast Line Canal & Transportation Company, 59
Florida Company, 181
Florida Division of Archives, History, and Records Management, 59
Florida Historical Confederation, 458
Florida Historical Quarterly, 458
Florida Historical Society, 458
Florida Railroad, 1370
Florida Southern College, 703
Florida State University, 458
Florida Times-Union, 458
Flour. *See* Foods and beverages; Industrialization; Wheat
Flower, George, 876
Flowers and shrubs, 458–60. *See also* Gardens; Plants, wild
Floyd, John, 92, 310
Floyd, John Buchanan, 460, 820, 1284, 1295; at Ft. Donelson, 479
Fluxes, 584
"Fly-up-the-creeks," 251
Fogel, Robert W., 229, 1114
Folch, Juan Vicente, 446, 457
Folk, Joseph Wingate, 460–61, 852
Folklore, 461; Appalachian journals on, 52; in Arkansas, 66; manuscripts on, 77
Folk medicine, 461–63, 139–40, 544
Folsom, James Elisha "Big Jim," 463, 29, 30, 1303
Foner, Eric, 229
Foods and beverages, 463–64, 261, 280, 823
Football, 1158, 1159
"Foot cavalry," 643
Foote, Andrew H., 472, 897; and Fts. Henry and Donelson campaign, 479
Foote, Henry Stuart, 464–65, 830, 835
Foote, Shelby, 727
Forage, 554–55
Foraging, 268
Forbes, John, 494
Forbes, Thomas, 954
Force Bill (1833), **465,** 932
Force Bill (1890), **465**
Ford, Gerald, 402

Ford, John S., 1215
Ford, T. R., 50
Ford, Wendell H., 682
Ford Foundation, 482
Foreign affairs, 466–67
Foreigners, 693; in Civil War, 267. *See also* immigrant groups
Forestry, 467–68. *See also* Trees
Forrest, Nathan Bedford, 468; at battle of Brentwood, 147; at battle of Brice's Crossroads, 147; and battle of Murfreesboro, 865; at Ft. Donelson, 479; and James H. Wilson, 1349; and Ku Klux Klan, 696; and Meridian campaign, 813; raids by, 468–69, 471
Forrest's raids, 468–69
Forstall, Edmond Jean, 752
Forsyth, John, 469, 524, 538, 857
Fort, John Porter, 33
Ft. Beauregard, 994
Ft. Bisland and Irish Bend, battles of, 469, 1043
Ft. Blair, 988
Ft. Brooke, 324
Ft. Caroline, 613, 811, 1073
Ft. Chiswell, 1342
Ft. Christina, 342
Ft. Confederation, 1242
Ft. Congaree, 1242
Ft. Darling, 371
Ft. Delaware, 280, 352
Ft. De Russy, 1043
Ft. Fincastle, 1371
Ft. Fisher, battles of, 469–70, 130
Ft. Gaines, 329
Ft. Gatlin, 944
Ft. George, 1082
Ft. Harrison, 944, 992, 1060
Ft. Henry, 1371, 1242
Fortier, Alcée, 470
Ft. Jackson (La.), 899
Ft. Jackson, Treaty of (1814), 310, 1307
Ft. King, 324
Ft. Lamar, 196
Ft. Lauderdale, Fla., 470
Ft. Lee, 95
Ft. Loudon, 494, 1185, 1352
Ft. McAllister, 1103
Ft. McHenry, 97, 685
Ft. Massac, 494
Ft. Massachusetts, 1103
Ft. Mims, 503, 1307; massacre at, 19, 310
Ft. Monroe, 964
Ft. Moore, 1242
Ft. Morgan, 424, 856, 857
Ft. Motte, 780
Ft. Moultrie, battles of, 470–71, 199
Ft. Pickens, 965
Ft. Pillow massacre, 471, 468
Ft. Prince George, 494
Ft. Pulaski, capture of, 471
Ft. Raleigh National Historic Site, 597
Ft. Randolph, 988
Ft. Rosalie, 316, 828, 1242
Forts, 471–79; table of, 473–78

Ft. St. Philip, 899
Ft. San Carlos, 965
Ft. Sanders, 694
Ft. San Fernando, 1242
Fts. Henry and Donelson campaign, 479, 468
Ft. Smith, Ark., 479–80
Ft. Stanwix, Treaty of (1768), 939, 1323
Ft. Stedman, battle of, 480
Ft. Sumter, 480, 45, 196, 222, 282, 597
Ft. Tombeckbee, 19
Ft. Toulous, 17, 316, 494, 1242
Fortune, Timothy Thomas, 480–81, 880
Ft. Walker, 994
Ft. Watson, 597, 780
Ft. Williams, 985
Ft. Worth, Tex., 481, 870
Forty acres and a mule, 481
Fosdick, Raymond B., 513
Fossils, 192
Foster, Murphy J., 750
Foster, Stephen Collins, 481–82
Foundations for southern history, 482
Four-Hole Swamp, 1246
Fourierism, 493
Fourteenth Amendment, 482–83; and amnesty, 43; and Hugo Black, 123
Fowke, Mary, 803
Fowle, Daniel G., 929
Fowler, C. Lewis, 708
Fox, John, 730, 1244
Foxfire, 52
Fox hunting, 483, 1040. *See also* Recreation
France: and American Indians, 494; colonial wars, 255; and Confederacy, 272; influence of, 492; naval war with, 5
Francis, David Rowland, 484, 852
Frank, Leo, case, 484, 649, 1315
Frankfort, Ky., 484
Frankfort Argus of Western America, 484–85
Frankfort Commonwealth, 485
Frankfort *Western World*, 674
Franklin, Benjamin, 995
Franklin, Jesse, 929
Franklin, John Hope, 485, 48
Franklin, William B., 1078
Franklin, battle of, 485
Franklin, state of, 485–86, 560, 1189
Franklin & Armfield Company, 486, 1117
Franquis de Lugo, Carlos Beintes, 1223
Fraser, Charles, 81
Fraser, J., 607
Frayser's Farm, battle of, 486
Frazier, Edward Franklin, 486, 888
Frazier, James B., 1200
Frederick, Md., 486–87
Fredericksburg, battle of, 487
Fredericksburg, Va., 487–88
Fredicksburg Railroad, 1101
Free blacks, 41. *See also* Negro, free
Freedmen's aid societies, 488
Freedmen's Bank, 489

Q

Quakers, 1015, 173, 1261; in Delaware, 343; and Negro education, 49; in North Carolina, 913; on slavery in Delaware, 345

Quantico, Va., 1015

Quantrill, William Clarke, 1015–1016, 275

Quapaw Indians, 1016, 61

Quarles, Benjamin, 1016, 266

Quatermaster's Department, 284

Quary, Robert, 1140

Quebec Act (1774), 1005

Queen Anne's War, 255, 256, 735

Queens College, 199

Quejos, 417

Quesada, Juan, 457

Quexos, Pedro de, 417

Quids, 1016; and John Randolph of Roanoke, 1027

Quinine, 277

Quiroga y Lozada, Diego de, 457

Quitman, John Anthony, 1017, 830, 835; papers of, 837

Quitrents, 1017

Quoits, 1040, 1158

R

Rabun, William, 538

Racecourses. *See* Horse racing

Radcliffe, Sam, 1003

Radeau, 1061

Rafts. *See* Rivercraft

Raht, Julius E., 1196

Railroads, 1018–22; in Alabama, 20, 26; and Civil War, 222, 224, 273, 284; and commerce, 261; and commercial and political conventions, 293–94; and debts of southern states, 336–38; in Delaware, 346; in Florida, 450; and freight rates, 492; in Georgia, 527; and Hannibal I. Kimball, 687; and labor unions, 701; in North Carolina, 918; and panic of 1873, 953; and panic of 1893, 954; in Tennessee, 1193; in Texas, 1219; and transportation, 1242; in Virginia, 1282; in West Virginia, 1327

Rail splitting, 1040

Rainey, Homer P., 1226

Rainey, Joseph Hayne, 1022–23

Rainey, Ma, 873

Rainfall. *See* Climate; Geology

Rains, Gabriel J., 286

Rains, George Washington, 286

Rains, James, 1349

Raleigh, Sir Walter, 1023, 779, 809, 912, 1064; and Albemarle Sound, 34; and Lost Colony, 314

Raleigh, N.C., 1023

Raleigh News and Observer, 1023–24, 328

Raleigh Register, 1024

Raleigh Standard, 1024

Ramsay, David, 1024, 254

Ramsdell, Charles William, 1024–25, 266; on causes of Civil War, 229

Ramseur, Stephen Dodson, 1025

Ramseur's Mill, battle of, 1025

Randall, James Garfield, 1025, 194, 1037; on causes of Civil War, 229; and slavery, 47

Randolph, Asa Philip, 1025–26

Randolph, Beverley, 1295

Randolph, Edmund, 1026, 36, 47, 1028, 1295

Randolph, Frances Bland, 1252

Randolph, George Wythe, 1026, 268, 284

Randolph, John, of Roanoke, 1026–27, 41, 368, 1281, 1298; and defection from Democratic-Republican party, 357; and duel with Henry Clay, 373; oratory of, 943; and Quids, 1016; and tariffs, 1177

Randolph, Mary Isham, 1027

Randolph, Peyton, 1027, 292, 1028, 1299

Randolph, Sir John, 1028

Randolph, Thomas Mann, 1027, 1295

Randolph, Virginia Jefferson, 1248

Randolph, William, 1027

Randolph family, 1027–28

Randolph-Macon College, 1028; and C. A. Swanson, 1172

Randolph-Macon Women's College, 1356

Rankin, H. F., 1055

Rankin, John, 49

Ransdell, Joseph Eugene, 1028; papers of, 752

Ransom, John Crowe, 1028–29, 497, 618, 727

Ransom, Matt, 985

Rape complex, southern, 1029, 1353

Raper, Arthur, 557

Rapier, James Thomas, 1029–30

Rapier, John H., Sr., 885

Rappahannock River, 1030

Raquette (game), 1158

Rasin, I. Freeman, 793

Raskob, John J., 399

Ravenel, Beatrice, 1138

Rawdon, Lord, 173; and battle of Hobkirk's Hill, 597

Rawick, George, 48

Rawlins (ship), 704

Rayburn, Sam, 1030, 897

Raymond, battle of, 1273

Rayner, Isidor, 794

Rayner, John B., 1030–31

Read, George, 1031, 47, 291, 344, 345, 353

Read, Opie, 1031; and humor, 614

Readjuster movement, 1031–32, 666, 803, 1286; and Arthur administration, 81; and C. T. O'Ferrall, 936–37; and Garfield administration, 509; and James Lawson Kemper, 666; and William Mahone, 774

Reagan, John Henninger, 1032, 267, 278; papers of, 59; and telegraphs and telephones, 1184

Reams Station, battle of, 1032

"Rebel brigadiers," 252

Rebel yell, 1032

Rebolledo, Diego de, 457

Reconstruction, 1032–35; and black codes, 123; and Brooks-Baxter War, 150–51; and carpetbaggers, 182; and debts of southern states, 337; among Indians, 210

Reconstruction, congressional, 1035–36, 1038

Reconstruction, historiography of, 1036–38; and C. M. Thompson, 1232; and F. B. Simkins, 1105; and J. G. Hamilton, 569; and J. H. Franklin, 485; and J. W. Garner, 509; and R. H. Woody, 1359; and W. A. Dunning, 376–77; and W. F. Fleming, 438; and W. W. Davis, 335

Reconstruction Acts, 1038–39, 18

Reconstruction Finance Corporation, 1039–40; and Great Depression, 556

Reconstruction Treaty (1866), 205

Recopilacion de Indias, 750

Recreation, 1040–41; in tidewater region, 1234. *See also* Historic sites and parks; Horse racing

Rector, Henry M., 66, 75, 655; family of, 655

Redeemer governments, 1041–42

Reedeemers, 1042; and William Bloxham, 131

Redemptioners, 620

Red Hawk, 183

Redlegs, 1016

Redpath, James, 256

Red River, 1042

Red River campaigns, 1043; and battles of Ft. Bisland and Irish Bend, 469; and battle of Pleasant Hill, 984; and battle of Sabine Crossroads, 1071

Red River Valley Historical Association, 1043

Redshirts, 510, 1137

Red Sticks War. *See* Creek War

Red Strings, 590

Reece, Byron Herbert, 533

Reed, Harrison, 1043–44, 449, 457, 543

Reed, Joseph, 109

Reed, Walter, 1044, 1367

Reeks, Austin John, 335. *See also* Dawson, Francis W.

Reeve, Tappan, 171

Refugees. *See* Confederate refugees; Expatriates, Confederate

Regency-Hyatt House, 1012

Regionalism, 1044–45, 516, 618–19, 730, 936, 1086, 1269

Regulators, 1045–46, 32, 554, 914

Reid, David S., 919, 929

Reid, Robert R., 448, 457

Reid-White family, 1313

Religion, 1046–47; and African Methodist Episcopal church, 7; and Black Muslims, 125; and blue laws, 132–33; and Calvert family, 172; and camp meetings,